Great Britain

THIS EDITION WRITTEN AND RESEARCHED BY
Neil Wilson,
Oliver Berry, Fionn Davenport, Marc Di Duca, Belinda Dixon, Peter Dragicevich, Damian Harper, Catherine Le Nevez, Hugh McNaughtan, Isabella Noble, Andy Symington

PLAN YOUR TRIP

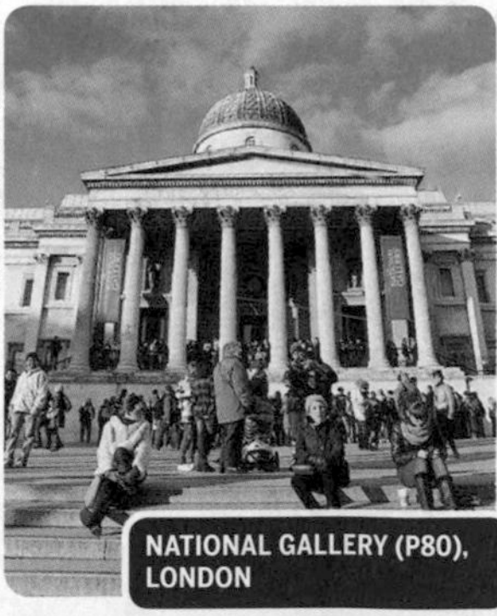

BIKEWORLDTRAVEL / SHUTTERSTOCK ©

NATIONAL GALLERY (P80), LONDON

STENY02 / SHUTTERSTOCK ©

EDINBURGH CASTLE (P763), SCOTLAND

ON THE ROAD

Contents

ON THE ROAD

Contents

Welcome to Great Britain

Buckingham Palace, Stonehenge, Manchester United, The Beatles – Britain does icons like nowhere else, and travel here is a fascinating mix of famous names and hidden gems.

Variety Packed

From the graceful architecture of Canterbury Cathedral to the soaring ramparts of Edinburgh Castle, via the mountains of Wales and the picture-postcard landscape of the Cotswolds, Britain's astounding variety is a major reason to visit. The cities tempt with top-class shops and restaurants, and some of the world's finest museums, while cutting-edge clubs and world-famous theatres provide endless nights to remember. Next day, you're deep in the countryside, high in the hills or enjoying a classic seaside resort. In Britain, there really is something for everyone, whether you're eight or 80, going solo, or travelling with your friends, your kids or your grandma.

Time Travel

A journey through Britain is a journey through history. But not dull and dusty history – this is history you can immerse yourself in. You can lay hands on the megaliths of a 5000-year-old stone circle, or patrol the battlements of a medieval fortress – just as they were patrolled by chain-mail-clad soldiers many centuries ago. Fast-forward to the future and you're admiring 21st-century architecture in Glasgow or exploring the space-age domes of Cornwall's Eden Project.

English Spoken Here

While Britain has a complex culture and esoteric traditions, it feels familiar to many visitors – on the surface, at least – thanks to a vast catalogue of British film and TV exports. And for most visitors, Britain's national language – English – is equally familiar, and one more reason why travel here is a breeze. Of course Wales and Scotland have their own languages, but everyone speaks English too – and all visitors (even Brits) get a little confused by local accents in places such as Devon, Snowdonia and Aberdeen.

Easy Does It

A final thing to remember while you're planning a trip to Britain: getting from place to place is pretty straightforward. Although the locals may grumble (in fact, it's a national pastime), public transport is pretty good and a train ride through the British landscape can be a memorable experience in itself. Whichever way you get around in this compact country, you're never far from the next town, the next pub, the next national park or the next impressive castle on your hit-list of highlights. The choice is endless.

JOE DANIEL PRICE / GETTY IMAGES ©

Why I Love Great Britain

By Neil Wilson, Writer

In a word: variety. Few countries pack so much into a small space. Landscapes that range from the sand dunes of South Wales to the snowfields of the Cairngorms, from the lush, quilted farmland of Kent to the naked limestone scarps of the Yorkshire Dales. Three nationalities, two dozen different dialects, more than 60 proudly individual cities, 1000 breweries, 5000 castles – all in a country you could drive across in a day. Plus weather that can offer four seasons in a single afternoon (but remember the old Scandinavian proverb – there's no such thing as bad weather, only the wrong clothes).

For more about our writers, see p1056

Above: Roman Baths (p317), Bath, England

Great Britain

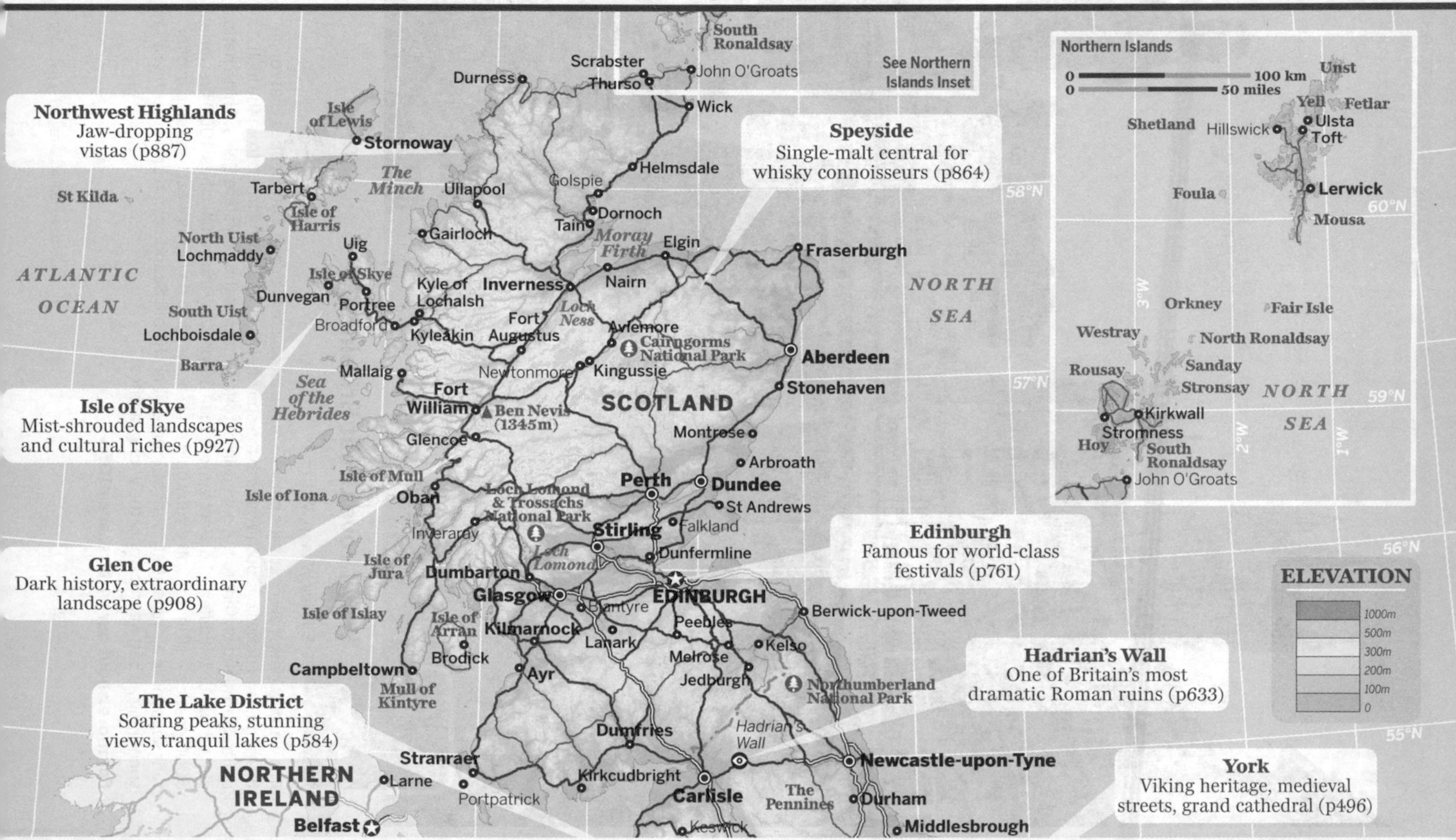

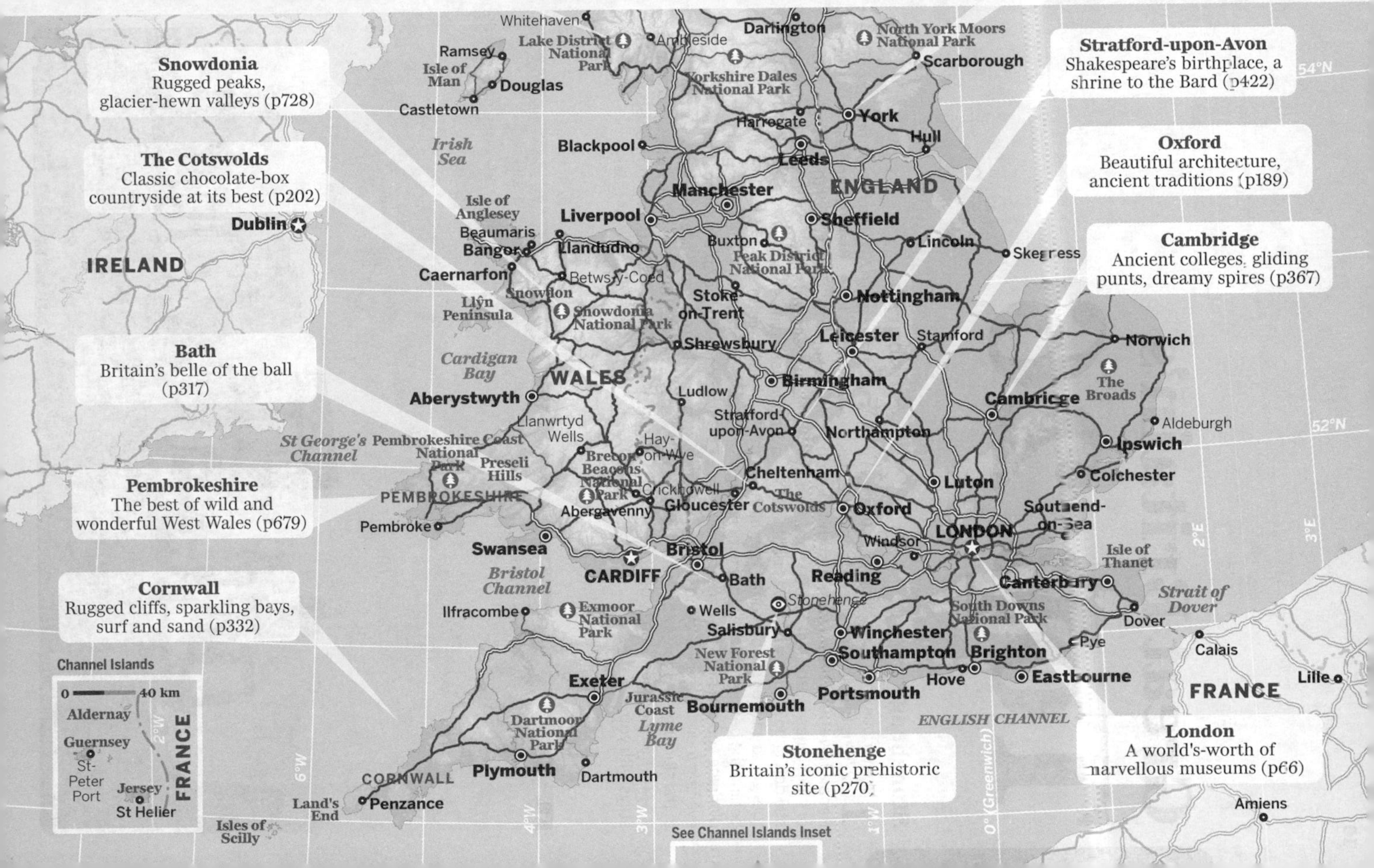
Snowdonia
Rugged peaks, glacier-hewn valleys (p728)
The Cotswolds
Classic chocolate-box countryside at its best (p202)
Bath
Britain's belle of the ball (p317)
Pembrokeshire
The best of wild and wonderful West Wales (p679)
Cornwall
Rugged cliffs, sparkling bays, surf and sand (p332)
Stratford-upon-Avon
Shakespeare's birthplace, a shrine to the Bard (p422)
Oxford
Beautiful architecture, ancient traditions (p189)
Cambridge
Ancient colleges, gliding punts, dreamy spires (p367)
Stonehenge
Britain's iconic prehistoric site (p270)
London
A world's-worth of marvellous museums (p66)
IRELAND
Dublin
ENGLAND
WALES
FRANCE
LONDON
CARDIFF
Irish Sea
Cardigan Bay
St George's Channel
Bristol Channel
ENGLISH CHANNEL
Strait of Dover
Lyme Bay
Channel Islands
Alderney
Guernsey
St-Peter Port
Jersey
St Helier
See Channel Islands Inset
Isles of Scilly
Land's End
Penzance
CORNWALL
Plymouth
Dartmouth
Exeter
Bournemouth
Portsmouth
Southampton
Winchester
Brighton
Hove
Eastbourne
Canterbury
Dover
Calais
Lille
Amiens
Manchester
Liverpool
Leeds
York
Sheffield
Birmingham
Nottingham
Leicester
Bristol
Bath
Oxford
Cambridge
Norwich
Ipswich
Colchester
Swansea
Aberystwyth
Caernarfon
Bangor
Blackpool
Scarborough
Darlington
Hull
Lincoln
Luton
Reading
Salisbury
Stonehenge
Gloucester
Cheltenham
Shrewsbury
Stratford-upon-Avon
Northampton
Pembroke
Ilfracombe
Wells
54°N
52°N

Great Britain's Top 26

Stonehenge

1 Mysterious and compelling, Stonehenge (p270) is Britain's most iconic ancient site. People have been drawn to this myth-laden ring of bluestones for the last 5000 years, and we still don't know quite why it was built. Most visitors get to gaze at the 50-tonne megaliths from behind the perimeter fence, but with enough planning you can book an early-morning or evening tour and walk around the inner ring. In the slanting sunlight, away from the crowds, it's an ethereal place – an experience that stays with you.

Edinburgh

2 Edinburgh (p761) is a city of many moods – famous for its festivals and especially lively in the summer. It's also worth visiting out of season for sights such as the castle silhouetted against a blue spring sky with a yellow haze of daffodils misting the slopes below the esplanade. Or on a chill December morning with the fog snagging the spires of the Old Town, the ancient streets and alleyways more mysterious than ever, rain on the cobblestones and a warm glow beckoning from the window of a pub.
Right: Edinburgh Military Tattoo (p783)

1

WILLIAM TOTI / 500PX ©

MORAG FLEMING / SHUTTERSTOCK ©

IRISPHOTO1 / SHUTTERSTOCK ©

EDDIECLOUD / SHUTTERSTOCK ©

Bath

3 Britain boasts many great cities, but Bath (p317) stands out as the belle of the ball. Thanks to the natural hot springs that bubble to the surface, the Romans built a health resort here. The waters were rediscovered in the 18th century, and Bath became the place to see and be seen by British high society. Today, the stunning Georgian architecture of grand town houses and sweeping crescents (not to mention Roman remains, a beautiful cathedral and a cutting-edge 21st-century spa) means Bath demands your undivided attention.

Isle of Skye

4 Of all Scotland's many islands, Skye (p927) is one of the most famous and best loved by visitors, thanks to a mix of history (the island's link to Bonnie Prince Charlie is forever remembered by 'The Skye Boat Song'), accessibility (the ferry from the mainland has been replaced by a bridge) and sheer beauty. With jagged mountains, velvet moors and towering sea cliffs, Skye's scenery never fails to impress. And for those days when the mist comes in, there are plenty of castles and local museums to explore, and cosy pubs to enjoy.

The Cotswolds

5 The most wonderful thing about the Cotswolds (p202) is that, no matter where you go or how lost you get, you'll always end up in an impossibly picturesque village complete with rose-clad cottages, an ancient church of honey-coloured stone, a pub with sloping floors and fine ales, and a view of the lush green hills. It's easy to leave the crowds behind and find your very own slice of medieval England – and some of the best boutique hotels in the country.

Above right: Bibury village (p203)

ILONGLOVEKING / SHUTTERSTOCK ©

Snowdonia

6 The rugged northwest corner of Wales (p728) has rocky mountain peaks, glacier-hewn valleys, sinuous ridges, sparkling lakes and rivers, and charm-infused villages. The busiest part is around Snowdon itself, where many people hike to the summit, and many more take the jolly rack-and-pinion railway, while to the south and west are rarely trod areas perfect for off-the-beaten-track exploration. And just nearby sit the lovely Llŷn Peninsula and Isle of Anglesey, where the sun often shines, even if it's raining on the mountains.

SEBASTIEN COELL / SHUTTERSTOCK ©

Oxford

7 For centuries, the brilliant minds and august institutions of Oxford University have made Oxford (p189) famous across the globe. You'll get a glimpse of this revered world as you stroll hushed college quads and cobbled lanes roamed by cycling students and dusty academics. The beautiful college buildings, archaic traditions and stunning architecture have changed little over the centuries, coexisiting with a lively, modern, working city.

Football

8 In some parts of the world it's called 'soccer', but here in Britain it's definitely 'football' (p1009). Despite what the fans may say in Italy or Brazil, the English Premier League has some of the world's finest teams. Big names include the globally renowned Arsenal, Liverpool and Chelsea, plus *the* most famous club on the planet: Manchester United. North of the border, Scotland's best-known teams are the Glasgow duo of Rangers and Celtic – their 'old firm' rivalry is legendary – while in Wales the national sport is most definitely rugby.

Bottom: Old Trafford (p555), Manchester

7

CARON BADKIN / SHUTTERSTOCK ©

8

JEAFISH PING / SHUTTERSTOCK ©

JUSTIN FOULKES / GETTY IMAGES ©

TRAVELLIGHT / SHUTTERSTOCK ©

TARGN PLEIADES / SHUTTERSTOCK ©

The Lake District

9 William Wordsworth and his Romantic friends were the first to champion the charms of the Lake District (p584), and it's not hard to see what stirred them. The soaring mountains, whaleback fells, razor-edge valleys and – of course – glistening lakes (as well as England's highest peak), make this craggy corner of the country the spiritual home of English hiking. Strap on the boots, stock up on mint cake and drink in the views: inspiration is sure to follow.

Above: Tarn Hows (p595)

Hadrian's Wall

10 Hadrian's Wall (p633) is one of the country's most revealing and dramatic Roman ruins, its 2000-year-old procession of abandoned forts, garrisons, towers and milecastles marching across the wild and lonely landscape of northern England. This wall was about defence and control, but this edge-of-empire barrier also symbolised the boundary of civilised order – to the north lay the unruly land of the marauding Celts, while to the south was the Roman world of orderly taxpaying, underfloor heating and bathrooms.

Castles & Stately Homes

11 Britain's turbulent history is nowhere more apparent than in the mighty castles that dot the landscape, from romantic clifftop ruins such as Corfe (p256) or sturdy fortresses such as Caernarfon, to formidable Stirling and still-inhabited Windsor. And when the aristocracy no longer needed castles, they built vast mansions known as 'stately homes' at the heart of their country estates. Classics of the genre include Blenheim Palace and Chatsworth House in England, Powis Castle in Wales and Scone Palace (pictured) in Scotland.

HELEN HOTSON / SHUTTERSTOCK ©

PREMIER PHOTO / SHUTTERSTOCK ©

PHB.CZ / SHUTTERSTOCK ©

Cornwall

12 At Britain's far southwestern extremity, the former kingdom of Cornwall (p332) boasts endless miles of coastline with rugged cliffs, sparkling bays, scenic fishing ports and white sandy beaches favoured by everyone from bucket-and-spade families to sun-bronzed surfers. Above the cliffs, the towers of former tin mines now stand like dramatic castles, while inland from the coast is a tranquil landscape of lush farmland and picturesque villages, crowned by the gigantic domes of the Eden Project – a stunning symbol of Cornwall's renaissance.

Above: St Agnes (p362)

Cambridge

13 Abounding with exquisite architecture and steeped in tradition, Cambridge (p367) is a university town extraordinaire. The tightly packed core of ancient colleges, the picturesque riverside 'Backs' (college gardens) and the surrounding green meadows give Cambridge a more tranquil appeal than its historic rival, Oxford. Highlights include the intricate vaulting of King's College Chapel, while no visit is complete without an attempt to steer a punt (flat-bottomed boat) along the river and under the quirky Mathematical Bridge. You'll soon wonder how you could have studied anywhere else.

Stratford-upon-Avon

14 The pretty English Midlands town of Stratford-upon-Avon (p422) is famed around the world as the birthplace of the nation's best-known dramatist, William Shakespeare. Today, the town's tight knot of Tudor streets form a living map of Shakespeare's life and times, while crowds of fans and would-be thespians come to enjoy a play at the theatre or visit the historic houses owned by Shakespeare and his relatives, with a respectful detour to the old stone church where the Bard was laid to rest.

Above: Shakespeare's New Place (p422)

Canterbury Cathedral

15 Few other English cathedrals come close to Canterbury (p156), the top temple of the Anglican Church and a place of worship for over 15 centuries. Its intricate tower dominates the local skyline, its grandeur unsurpassed by later structures. At its heart lies a 12th-century crime scene, the very spot where Archbishop Thomas Becket was put to the sword – an epoch-making event that launched a million pilgrimages and still pulls in the crowds today. A lone candle mourns the gruesome deed, the pink sandstone before it smoothed by 800 years of devout kneeling.

Cardiff

16 The exuberant capital of Wales, compact Cardiff (p653) has emerged as one of Britain's leading urban centres. After a mid-20th-century decline, the city entered the new millennium with vigour and confidence, flexing architectural muscles and revelling in a newfound sense of style. From the historic castle to the ultra-modern waterfront, from lively street cafes to infectious nightlife, from Victorian shopping arcades to the gigantic rugby stadium that is the pulsating heart of the city on match days, Cardiff undoubtedly has buzz.
Bottom: Cardiff Market (p663)

CLAUDIO DIVIZIA / SHUTTERSTOCK ©

JOE DANIEL PRICE / GETTY IMAGES ©

Britain's Pubs

17 Despite the growth of stylish clubs and designer bars, the traditional pub is still the centre of British social life. From the ornate Victorian boozers of London, Edinburgh and Leeds, to the food-focused gastropubs of Yorkshire, Mid-Wales and Devon, and countless rustic country pubs hunkering under thatched roofs and timber beams – Ye Olde Trip to Jerusalem (p456) claims to be the country's oldest – a lunchtime or evening visit to the pub can be one of the best ways to get under the skin of the nation.

Pembrokeshire

18 Perched at the tip of wild and wonderful West Wales, the county of Pembrokeshire (p679) boasts one of Britain's most beautiful and dramatic stretches of coast, with sheer cliffs, natural arches, blowholes, sea stacks, and a wonderful hinterland of tranquil villages and secret waterways. It's a landscape of Norman castles, Iron Age hill forts, holy wells and Celtic saints – including the nation's patron, St David – and intriguing stone monuments left behind by pre-historic inhabitants.

CLAUDIO DIVIZIA / SHUTTERSTOCK ©

MICHAEL THALER / SHUTTERSTOCK ©

JACEK WOJNAROWSKI / SHUTTERSTOCK ©

HELEN HOTSON / SHUTTERSTOCK ©

SILVYANBACHMANN / SHUTTERSTOCK ©

York

19 With its Roman remains and Viking heritage, ancient city walls and maze of medieval streets, York (p496) is a living showcase for the highlights of English history. Join one of the city's many walking tours and plunge into the network of snickleways (narrow alleys), each the focus of a ghost story or historical character. Explore the intricacies of York Minster (pictured), the biggest medieval cathedral in all of northern Europe, or admire the exhibits from more recent times at the National Railway Museum, the world's largest collection of historic locomotives.

Scotland's Northwest Highlands

20 The Highlands abound in breathtaking views, but the far northwest is truly awe-inspiring. The coastal road between Durness and Kyle of Lochalsh offers jaw-dropping scenes at every turn: the rugged mountains of Assynt (p921), the desolate beauty of Torridon and the remote cliffs of Cape Wrath. Add to this Britain's finest whale-watching, and the nooks of warm Highland hospitality found in classic rural pubs and romantic hotels, make this an unforgettable corner of the country.
Above right: Eilean Donan Castle (p927), Dornie

Liverpool

21 For many visitors, Liverpool (p563) will forever be associated with The Beatles, but a visit here proves the city has much more to offer. After a decade of redevelopment, the waterfront is once again the heart of Liverpool, with Albert Dock declared a World Heritage Site of iconic and protected buildings, a batch of top museums ensuring all sides of the city's history are not forgotten, and the Tate Liverpool gallery and Beatles Story museum, celebrating popular culture and the city's most famous musical sons.

22

HARRISON EASTWOOD / GETTY IMAGES ©

23

TARGN PLEIADES / SHUTTERSTOCK ©

24

CHRISTOPH LISCHETZKI / SHUTTERSTOCK ©

British Food

22 Britain offers a groaning table full of traditional eating (p982) experiences. Tuck into national favourites such as fish and chips, Cornish pasties or toad in the hole, followed of course by rhubarb and custard or spotted dick, or indulge yourself in a quintessentially English afternoon tea. And don't miss the chance to sample regional specialities such as jellied eels (London), Scottish haggis, Cumberland sausage, Stilton cheese, Northumberland kippers, Lancashire hotpot, Melton Mowbray pork pies, Welsh lamb, Yorkshire pudding... the list goes on.

Above: Pork pie and mustard

Glen Coe

23 Scotland's most famous glen (p908) combines those two essential qualities of the Highland landscape: dramatic scenery and deep history. The peacefulness and beauty of this valley today belie the fact that it was the scene of a ruthless 17th-century massacre, when the local MacDonalds were murdered by soldiers of the Campbell clan. Some of the glen's finest walks – to the Lost Valley, for example – follow the routes used by the clanspeople trying to flee their attackers, and where many perished in the snow.

Above right: Red deer, Rannoch Moor (p907)

Whisky

24 After tea, Britain's best-known drink is whisky. And while this amber spirit is also made in England and Wales, it is always most associated with Scotland. With more than 2000 whisky brands available, there are distilleries dotted all over Scotland, many open to visitors, with Speyside (p864) one of the main concentrations and a favourite spot for connoisseurs. Before enjoying your tipple, heed these warnings: never spell whisky with an 'e' (that's the Irish variety); and when ordering at the bar, never ask for 'Scotch'. What else would you drink in Scotland?

London's Museums

25 Institutions bright and beautiful, great and small, wise and wonderful – London's got them all. The range of museums (p70) is vast: from generalist exhibitions (British Museum, V&A) to specific themes (Imperial War Museum, London Transport Museum, Natural History Museum); from intriguing private collections (Sir John Soane's Museum, Wallace Collection) to those celebrating people associated with the city (Handel, Dickens, Freud). You could spend weeks without even scratching the surface. And most of them are free!

Below: Natural History Museum (p94)

Golf

26 While some may consider it a good walk spoiled, golf is one of the most popular sports in Britain for participants at all levels and (especially when it comes to major tournaments) for thousands of spectators too. With courses across the country, including some in the most scenic locations, visitors to Britain with a penchant for the little white ball will surely want to try their skill. A highlight for aficionados is a round on the Old Course at St Andrews (p843; pictured), the venerable home of golf.

Need to Know

For more information, see Survival Guide (p1013)

Currency
Pound sterling (£)

Language
English; also Scottish Gaelic and Welsh

Visas
Generally not needed for stays of up to six months. Not a member of the Schengen Zone.

Money
Change bureaux and ATMs widely available, especially in cities and major towns.

Mobile Phones
Most modern mobiles (cells) can function on UK networks, but check before you leave home just in case.

Driving
Traffic drives on the left; steering wheels are on the right side of the car. Most rental cars have manual gears (stick shift).

When to Go

High Season (Jun–Aug)
➡ Weather at its best. Accommodation rates peak – especially for August school holidays.

➡ Roads are busy, especially in seaside areas, national parks, and popular cities such as Oxford, Bath, Edinburgh and York.

Shoulder (Mar–May, Sep & Oct)
➡ Crowds reduce. Prices drop.

➡ Weather often good. March to May is a mix of sunny spells and sudden showers.

➡ September to October can feature balmy summers. For outdoor activities in much of Scotland, May and September are the best months.

Low Season (Nov–Feb)
➡ Wet and cold. Snow falls in mountain areas, especially up north.

➡ Opening hours reduced October to Easter; some places shut for winter. Big-city sights (particularly London's) operate all year.

Useful Websites

BBC (www.bbc.co.uk) News and entertainment from the national broadcaster.

Visit Britain (www.visitbritain.com) Comprehensive official tourism website.

Lonely Planet (www.lonelyplanet.com/great-britain) Destination info, hotel bookings, traveller forum and more.

Traveline (www.traveline.info) Great portal site for public transport in all parts of Britain.

British Arts Festivals (www.artsfestivals.co.uk) Listing hundreds of festivals – art, literature, dance, folk and more.

Important Numbers

Area codes vary in length (eg ☎020 for London, ☎01225 for Bath). Omit the code if you're inside that area. Drop the initial 0 if you're calling from abroad.

Britain (& UK) country code	☎44
International access code	☎00
Emergency (police, fire, ambulance, mountain rescue, coastguard)	☎112 or ☎999

Exchange Rates

Australia	A$1	£0.57
Canada	C$1	£0.58
Europe	€1	£0.85
Japan	¥100	£0.73
New Zealand	NZ$1	£0.56
USA	US$1	£0.75

For current exchange rates, see www.xe.com.

Daily Costs

Budget: Less than £55

➡ Dorm beds: £15–30

➡ Cheap meals in cafes and pubs: £7–11

➡ Long-distance coach: £15–40 (200 miles)

Midrange: £55–120

➡ Double room in midrange hotel or B&B: £65–130 (London £100–200)

➡ Main course in midrange restaurant: £10–20

➡ Long-distance train: £20–80 (200 miles)

Top End: More than £120

➡ Four-star hotel room: from £130 (London from £200)

➡ Three-course meal in a good restaurant: around £40

➡ Car rental per day: from £35

Great Britain on a Shoestring

If you're on a tight budget, there's no getting away from it – Britain isn't cheap. Public transport, admission fees, restaurants and hotel rooms all tend to be expensive compared with their equivalents in many other European countries. But with some careful planning, a trip here doesn't have to break the bank. You can save money by staying in B&Bs instead of hotels, or hostels instead of B&Bs. Motels along motorways and outside large towns are soulless, but who cares? Most of the time you'll be asleep. You can also save by prebooking long-distance coach or train travel – and by avoiding times when everyone else is on the move (like Friday afternoon). Many attractions are free (or offer discounts on quiet days, such as Monday). And don't forget that you won't have to stump up a penny to enjoy Britain's best asset: the wonderful countryside and coastline.

Arriving in Britain

Heathrow Airport (London; p1023) Trains, London Underground (tube) and buses to central London run from just after 5am to before midnight (night buses run later); fares from £5.70 to £21.50. Taxis to central London from Heathrow cost from £45 to £85 (more at peak hours).

Gatwick Airport (London; p1023) Trains to central London run from 4.30am to 1.35am (£10 to £20); hourly buses to central London around the clock from £5. Taxis to central London from Gatwick £100 (more at peak hours).

St Pancras International station (central London) Eurostar trains from Paris or Brussels arrive at this station in central London, connected by many underground lines to other parts of the city.

Victoria Coach Station (central London; p148) Buses from Europe arrive at this central station; frequent underground links to other parts of the city.

Edinburgh Airport (p795) Frequent trams (£5.50) and buses (£4.50) to Edinburgh city centre. Night buses every 30 minutes from 12.30am to 4am (£4). Taxis cost £18 to £28; about 20 to 30 minutes to the city centre.

Manchester Airport (p558) Trains (£5) run to Piccadilly Station every 10 minutes. Buses (£4.10) leave for Manchester Coach Station every 20 minutes.

For much more on **getting around**, see p1024

First Time Great Britain

For more information, see Survival Guide (p1013)

Checklist

- ➡ Check the validity of your passport
- ➡ Check any visa or entry requirements
- ➡ Make any necessary bookings (sights, accommodation, travel)
- ➡ Check airline baggage restrictions
- ➡ Put all restricted items (eg hair gel, pocketknife) in hold baggage
- ➡ Inform your credit-/debit-card company of your trip
- ➡ Organise travel insurance
- ➡ Check mobile (cell) phone compatibility
- ➡ Check rental car requirements

What to Pack

- ➡ Electrical plug adaptor (UK-specific)
- ➡ Umbrella – because the rumours about the weather are true
- ➡ Lightweight waterproof jacket – because sometimes the umbrella is not enough
- ➡ Comfortable walking shoes – Britain's towns and countryside are best explored on foot

Top Tips for Your Trip

- ➡ At major London airports, tickets for express trains into central London are usually available in the baggage arrivals hall; this saves queuing or dealing with machines on the station platform.
- ➡ The best way to get local currency is usually from an ATM, but this term is rarely used in England; the colloquial term 'cash machine' is more common.
- ➡ If staying more than a few days in London, get an OysterCard, the travel card the locals use.
- ➡ Pickpockets and hustlers lurk in the more crowded tourist areas, especially in London. No need to be paranoid, but do be on your guard.
- ➡ Britain's electrical plugs are unlike those in the rest of Europe, so bring (or buy) a UK-specific plug adaptor.

What to Wear

A rain jacket is essential, as is a small backpack to carry it in when the sun comes out. In summer you'll need sunscreen and an umbrella; you're bound to use both.

For sightseeing, comfortable shoes can make or break a trip. If you plan to enjoy Britain's great outdoors, suitable hiking gear is required in higher/wilder areas, but not for casual strolls in the countryside.

Some bars and restaurants have dress codes banning jeans, T-shirts and trainers (sneakers or runners).

Sleeping

Booking your accommodation in advance is recommended, especially in summer, at weekends and on islands (where options are often limited). Book at least two months ahead for July and August.

B&Bs These small, family-run houses generally provide good value. More luxurious versions are more like a boutique hotel.

Hotels British hotels range from half-a-dozen rooms above the pub to restored country houses and castles, with a commensurate range in rates.

Hostels There's a good choice of both institutional and independent hostels, many housed in rustic and/or historic buildings.

Money

ATMs (usually called 'cash machines') are common in cities and towns, but watch out for tampering; a common ruse is to attach a cardreader to the slot. Visa and MasterCard are widely accepted in Britain, except at some smaller B&Bs which take cash or cheque only. Other credit cards, including Amex, are not so widely accepted. Cities and larger towns have banks and exchange bureaux for changing money into pounds, but some bureaux offer poor rates. You can change money at some post offices, which is very handy in country areas; exchange rates are fair.

Bargaining

A bit of mild haggling is acceptable at flea markets and antique shops, but everywhere else you're expected to pay the advertised price.

Tipping

Restaurants Around 10% in restaurants and teashops with table service. Nearer 15% at smarter restaurants. Tips may be added to your bill as a 'service charge'. Paying a tip or a service charge is not obligatory.

Pubs & Bars Not expected unless table service for your meal and drinks is provided, then 10% is usual.

Taxis Around 10%, or rounded up to the nearest pound, especially in London.

Antiques stall, Apple Market, Covent Garden (p81)

Etiquette

Manners The British have a reputation for being polite, and good manners are considered important in most situations. When asking directions, 'Excuse me, can you tell me the way to...' is a better tactic than 'Hey, where's...'

Queues In Britain, queueing ('standing in line' to Americans), whether to board a bus, buy tickets or enter the gates of an attraction, is sacrosanct. Any attempt to 'jump the queue' will result in an outburst of tutting and hard stares.

Escalators If you take an escalator or a moving walkway (especially at tube stations in London), be sure to stand on the right, so folks in a hurry can pass on the left.

Eating

It's wise to book ahead for midrange restaurants, especially at weekends. Top-end restaurants should be booked at least a couple of weeks in advance.

Restaurants Britain's restaurants range from cheap-and-cheerful to Michelin-starred, and cover every cuisine you can imagine.

Cafes Open during daytime (rarely after 6pm), cafes are good for a casual breakfast or lunch, or simply a cup of coffee.

Pubs Most of Britain's pubs serve reasonably priced meals, and many can compete with restaurants on quality.

What's New

The Night Tube
It only took 153 years since its opening day, but London's Underground railway has finally begun operating around the clock (on Friday and Saturday nights). (p151)

Shakespeare's School Room
The Stratford school room where the world's most famous playwright was taught the three Rs from 1571 to 1578 was opened to the public in 2016. (p423)

Lakes Distillery
Watch out, Scotland! The first English whisky distillery for more than a century has opened in Keswick; its first single malt will be available from 2018. (p605)

i360 Tower
Sprouting from the ashes of Brighton's historic West Pier (destroyed by fire in 2003), this futuristic 162m-tall tower with circular glass viewing pod is Brighton's answer to the London Eye. (p179)

Magna Carta
The 800th anniversary of the signing of the Magna Carta in 2015 saw a £22m restoration of Lincoln Castle create a subterranean vault to house one of only four original copies of this iconic document. (p460)

Zip World Blaenau Ffestiniog
Blaenau Ffestiniog's vast Llechwedd Slate Caverns now have the added thrill of zip lines, trampolines, walkways and nets suspended over cathedral-sized voids. (p733)

York City Art Gallery
Yorkshire's reputation as the epicentre of UK sculpture was further enhanced with the opening in 2015 of the revamped York Art Gallery's Centre of Ceramic Arts. (p501)

Sky Garden
One of London's recent landmark skyscrapers, 20 Fenchurch St (nicknamed the Walkie Talkie), now has free access to its spectacular 155m-high rooftop garden and viewing gallery. (p135)

V&A Museum of Design
Dundee's waterfront is graced by a stunning new building that is home to an outpost of London's Victoria & Albert Museum, a showcase for the best of Scottish art and design. (p852)

North Coast 500
This 500-mile circuit (www.northcoast500.com) of northern Scotland's stunning coastline has proved an overnight hit, with thousands of people completing the route by car, campervan, motorbike or bicycle. (p923)

Borders Railway
The longest stretch of new railway line to be built in the UK for more than 100 years opened in September 2015, linking Edinburgh with Tweedbank, near Melrose (www.bordersrailway.co.uk).

For more recommendations and reviews, see lonelyplanet.com/great-britain

If You Like...

Castles & Stately Homes

Tower of London (p83) Landmark of the capital, patrolled by famous Beefeaters and protected by legendary ravens.

Blenheim Palace (p201) A monumental baroque fantasy and one of Britain's greatest stately homes.

Castle Howard (p506) A stunning baroque edifice, best known as the setting for TV series *Brideshead Revisited*.

Warwick Castle (p419) Restored enough to be impressive, ruined enough to be romantic.

Stirling Castle (p836) Classic fortress atop volcanic crag, with stunning views from the battlements.

Beaumaris Castle (p754) Wales is the land of castles; imposing Beaumaris, along with nearby Conwy, Caernarfon and Harlech, is a jointly listed World Heritage Site.

Chatsworth House (p489) The quintessential stately home, a treasure trove of heirlooms and works of art.

Carreg Cennen (p706) The most dramatically positioned fortress in Wales, standing guard over a lonely stretch of Brecon Beacons National Park.

Cathedrals & Ruined Abbeys

St Paul's Cathedral (p85) A symbol of the city for centuries, and still an essential part of the London skyline.

York Minster (p496) One of the largest medieval cathedrals in all of Europe, especially renowned for its windows.

Fountains Abbey (p514) Extensive ruins set in more recently landscaped water gardens – one of the most beautiful sites in Britain.

Canterbury Cathedral (p156) The mother ship of the Anglican Church, still attracting pilgrims and visitors in their thousands.

Melrose Abbey (p822) The finest of all the great Border abbeys; Robert the Bruce's heart is buried here.

Whitby Abbey (p518) Stunning clifftop ruin with an eerie atmosphere that inspired the author of *Dracula*.

St David's Cathedral (p686) An ancient place of worship in Britain's smallest city.

Glastonbury Abbey (p330) The legendary burial place of King Arthur and Queen Guinevere.

Glasgow Cathedral (p801) A shining example of Gothic architecture, and the only mainland Scottish cathedral to have survived the Reformation.

Tintern Abbey (p666) Riverside ruins that inspired generations of poets and artists.

Royal Britain

Buckingham Palace (p73) The Queen's official London residence, best known for its royal-waving balcony and the Changing of the Guard.

Windsor Castle (p225) The largest and oldest occupied fortress in the world, a majestic vision of battlements and towers, and the Queen's weekend retreat.

Westminster Abbey (p70) Where English royalty is crowned and married – most recently William and Kate.

Royal Yacht Britannia (p778) The royal family's onetime floating home during foreign travels, now retired and moored near Edinburgh.

Balmoral Castle (p903) Built for Queen Victoria in 1855 and still a royal Highland hideaway.

Royal Pavilion (p177) Opulent palace built for playboy prince, later King George IV.

Althorp House (p467) Ancestral home and burial place of Diana, Princess of Wales.

Village Idylls

Lavenham (p386) A wonderful collection of exquisitely preserved medieval buildings virtually untouched since the 15th century.

Lacock (p273) Well-preserved medieval village, essentially free of modern development and – unsurprisingly – a frequent set for movies and TV period dramas.

Culross (p851) Scotland's best-preserved 17th-century village, familiar to fans of TV's *Outlander* as Cranesmuir.

Goathland (p523) One of Yorkshire's most attractive villages, complete with village green and traditional steam railway station.

Mousehole (p347) Southwest England overflows with picturesque pint-sized ports, but this is one of the best.

Beddgelert (p738) A conservation village of rough grey stone buildings in the heart of Snowdonia National Park.

Great Outdoors

Lake District (p584) The landscape that inspired William Wordsworth is a feast of mountains, valleys, views and – of course – lakes.

Northumberland National Park (p640) The dramatically empty landscape of England's far north is remote and off the beaten track.

Snowdonia (p728) The best-known slice of nature in Wales, with the grand but surprisingly accessible peak of Snowdon at its heart.

PITSCH22 / SHUTTERSTOCK ©

VISITBRITAIN / BRITAIN ON VIEW / FLOATING HEADS BY SOPHY CAVE, KELVINGROVE ART GALLERY, GLASGOW, SCOTLAND / GETTY IMAGES ©

Top: Culross (p851)

Bottom: Kelvingrove Art Gallery & Museum (p805), Glasgow

Yorkshire Dales (p522) A compact collection of moors, hills, valleys, rivers, cliffs and waterfalls, perfect for easy strolls or hardy treks.

Ben Nevis (p913) Every year thousands of people aim for the summit of Scotland's most famous (and Britain's highest) mountain.

Shopping

Portobello Rd, London (p146) One of London's best-known street markets, surrounded by quirky boutiques and gift stores.

Victoria Quarter, Leeds (p534) Lovely arcades of wrought iron-work and stained glass, home to several top fashion boutiques.

North Laine, Brighton (p183) Narrow streets lined with shops selling books, antiques, collectables, vintage clothing and more.

Cardiff Arcades (p663) Half-a-dozen ornate arcades branch off the city centre main streets, all with speciality shops and cafes.

Isle of Skye (p927) Home to a plethora of workshops and artist's studios, the isle is a great place to find quality handmade arts and crafts.

Hay-on-Wye (p698) The self-proclaimed secondhand-book capital of the world boasts over 30 bookshops and millions of volumes, attracting browsers, collectors and academics from afar.

Industrial Heritage

Ironbridge (p440) The crucible of the Industrial Revolution, where 10 museums for the price of one give fascinating insights.

Blaenavon (p668) A World Heritage Site of well-preserved ironworks and the fascinating Big Pit coal mine.

Kelham Island Museum (p539) A testament to Sheffield's steeltown heritage, anchored by the massive River Don steam engine.

New Lanark (p820) Once the largest cotton-spinning complex in Britain and a testament to enlightened capitalism.

National Railway Museum (p497) A cathedral to Britain's great days of steam; for railway fans of all ages it's the perfect place to go loco.

Roman Remains

Roman Baths (p317) The city of Bath takes its name from these famous Roman remains – a complex of bathhouses around natural thermal waters.

Hadrian's Wall (p633) Snaking coast-to-coast across lonely hills, this 2000-year-old fortified line once marked the northern limit of imperial Roman jurisdiction.

Yorkshire Museum (p499) York's past as the Roman city of Eboracum is chronicled in fascinating detail.

Caerleon (p666) One of three legionary forts in Britain, with impressive remains of barracks, baths and an amphitheatre.

Corinium Museum (p202) Recounts the days when the sleepy Cotswold town of Cirencester was once Corinium, the second-largest Roman city in Britain.

Art Galleries

Tate Britain (p91) One of the best-known galleries in London, full to the brim with the finest local works.

Tate Modern (p90) London's other Tate focuses on modern art in all its wonderful permutations.

BALTIC (p623) Newcastle's very own 'Tate of the North' with work by some of contemporary art's biggest show-stoppers.

National Museum Cardiff (p654) An excellent collection of Welsh artists, plus works by Monet, Renoir, Matisse, Van Gogh, Francis Bacon and David Hockney.

Kelvingrove Art Gallery & Museum (p805) A national landmark in Glasgow – great collection, and a cracking spot to learn about Scottish art.

Yorkshire Sculpture Park (p536) England's biggest outdoor sculpture collection, dominated by the works of Henry Moore and Barbara Hepworth.

Barber Institute of Fine Art (p412) With works by Rubens, Turner and Picasso, this Birmingham gallery is no lightweight.

V&A Museum of Design Dundee (p852) Brand new gallery dedicated to the best of Scottish and international art and design

Arts & Music Festivals

Edinburgh International Festival (p783) The world's biggest festival of art and culture. 'Nuff said.

MS JANE CAMPBELL / SHUTTERSTOCK ©

Notting Hill Carnival (p118)

Glastonbury (p329) Britain's biggest and best-loved music festival.

Hay Festival (p698) A world-class celebration of all things literary at Britain's bookshop capital.

Notting Hill Carnival (p118) London's Caribbean community shows the city how to party.

Pride (p118) Gay and lesbian street parade through London culminating in a concert in Trafalgar Sq.

Grassington Festival (p525) A village in the scenic Yorkshire Dales hosts this amazing two-week cultural extravaganza.

Latitude Festival (p393) An eclectic mix of music, literature, dance, drama and comedy, in a stunning location and of manageable size.

T in the Park (p840) Scotland's biggest music festival takes over the verdant grounds of Strathallan Castle.

Coastal Attractions

Scarborough (p510) The original British beach resort, where 'sea-bathing' first began, way back in the 17th century.

Pembrokeshire (p679) Towering cliffs, rock arches, clean waters and perfect sandy beaches at the tip of west Wales.

Southwold (p393) Genteel old-style seaside town with lovely beach, charming pier and famous rows of colourful beach huts.

Tongue (p919) Sea lochs penetrate the rocky coast in this wild stretch of Scotland's north.

Holkham Bay (p402) A pristine expanse of sand with giant skies stretching overhead.

Llandudno (p750) Beachside Punch-and-Judy shows, a step-back-in-time pier and a classic esplanade.

Gower Peninsula (p675) Family-friendly beaches and surfer hang-outs, backed by sand dunes and tranquil farmland.

Beachy Head & Seven Sisters (p175) Where the South Downs plunge into the sea, these mammoth chalk cliffs provide a dramatic finale.

Month by Month

TOP EVENTS

Glyndebourne, late May–August

Trooping the Colour, mid-June

Glastonbury Festival, late June

Edinburgh International Festival and Fringe, August

Abergavenny Food Festival, September

January

January is mid-winter in Britain. Festivals and events to brighten the mood are thin on the ground, but luckily some include fire – lots of it.

London Parade

A ray of light in the gloom, the New Year's Day Parade in London (to use its official title; www.londonparade.co.uk) is one of the biggest events of its kind in the world, featuring marching bands, street performers, classic cars, floats and displays winding their way through the streets, watched by moe than half a million people.

Up Helly Aa

Half of Shetland dresses up with horned helmets and battleaxes in this spectacular re-enactment of a Viking fire festival, with a torchlit procession leading the burning of a full-size Viking longship. (p959)

Celtic Connections

Glasgow plays host to a celebration of Celtic music, dance and culture (www.celticconnections.com), with participants from all over the globe.

February

Britain can be scenic under snow and sunshine, or more likely grey and gloomy under dark skies. Hang in there...

Jorvik Viking Festival

The ancient Viking capital of York becomes home once again to invaders and horned helmets galore, with the intriguing addition of longship races. (p501)

Fort William Mountain Festival

Britain's capital of the outdoors celebrates the peak of the winter season with ski workshops, mountaineering films and talks by famous climbers (www.mountainfestival.co.uk).

March

Spring finally arrives. There's a hint of better weather, and some classic sporting fixtures grace the calendar. Many locals stay hunkered down at home, though, so hotels offer special rates.

Six Nations Rugby Championship

Highlight of the rugby calendar (www.rbs6nations.com) runs from late January to March, with the home nations playing at London's Twickenham, Edinburgh's Murrayfield and Cardiff's Principality stadiums.

University Boat Race

Annual race down the River Thames in London between the rowing teams from Cambridge and Oxford universities; an institution since 1856 that still enthrals the country. (p115)

April

The weather slowly improves, with warmer and drier days bringing out spring blossoms. Attractions that close for the low season open around the middle of the month or at Easter.

Grand National

Half the country has a flutter on the highlight of the three-day horse race meeting at Aintree on the first Saturday of the month – a steeplechase with a testing course and notoriously high jumps. (p568)

London Marathon

More than 35,000 runners take to the streets; superfit athletes cover the 26.22 miles in just over two hours, while others dress up in daft costumes and take considerably longer.

Beltane

Thousands of revellers climb Edinburgh's Calton Hill for this modern revival of a pagan fire festival (www.beltane.org) marking the end of winter.

Spirit of Speyside

Based in Dufftown, a festival of whisky, food and music, with five days of art, cooking, distillery tours and outdoor activities. (p864)

May

The weather is usually good, with more events to enjoy. There are two public holidays this month (first and last Mondays) so traffic is very busy over the corresponding long weekends.

FA Cup Final

Grand finale of the football (soccer) season for over a century. Teams from across England battle it out over the winter months, culminating in this heady spectacle at Wembley Stadium – the home of English football. (p141)

Chelsea Flower Show

The Royal Horticultural Society flower show at Chelsea is the highlight of the gardener's year. (p115)

Hay Festival

The ever-expanding 'Woodstock of the mind' brings an intellectual influx to booktown Hay-on-Wye. (p698)

Glyndebourne

Famous festival of world-class opera in the pastoral surroundings of East Sussex, running until the end of summer. (p177)

June

Now it's almost summer. You can tell because this month sees the music-festival season kick off properly, while sporting events, from rowing to racing, fill the calendar.

Derby Week

Horse-racing, people-watching and clothes-spotting are on the agenda at this week-long meeting in Epsom, Surrey (www.epsomderby.co.uk).

Cotswolds Olimpicks

Welly-wanging, pole-climbing and shin-kicking are the key disciplines at this traditional Gloucestershire sports day (www.olimpickgames.co.uk), held every year since 1612.

Trooping the Colour

Military bands and bearskinned grenadiers march down London's Whitehall in this martial pageant to mark the monarch's birthday. (p115)

Royal Ascot

It's hard to tell which matters more, the fashion or the fillies, at this highlight of the horse-racing year in Berkshire. (p224)

Wimbledon Tennis

The world's best-known tennis tournament, attracting all the big names, while crowds cheer and eat tons of strawberries and cream. (p118)

Glastonbury

One of Britain's favourite pop and rock gatherings is invariably muddy, and still a rite of passage for every self-respecting British music fan. (p329)

Royal Regatta

Boats of every description take to the water for Henley's upper-crust river jamboree. (p229)

Pride

Highlight of the gay and lesbian calendar, this technicolour street parade heads through London's West End. (p118)

Glasgow's West End Festival

Scotland's second city hosts a major celebration of music and arts. (p808)

Top: London Marathon participants

Bottom: Trooping the Colour (p115) marching band

July

Proper summer. Festivals every week. School summer breaks begin, so there's a holiday tingle in the air, dulled only by busy roads on Fridays, because everyone's going somewhere for the weekend.

Great Yorkshire Show

Harrogate plays host to one of Britain's largest county shows. This is the place for Yorkshire grit, Yorkshire tykes, Yorkshire puddings, Yorkshire beef… (p508)

T in the Park

World-class acts since 1994 ensure this major music festival (www.tinthepark.com) is Scotland's answer to Glastonbury.

Latitude

Relaxed festival in the seaside town of Southwold, with theatre, cabaret, art and literature, plus top names from the alternative music scene. (p393)

International Musical Eisteddfod

Festival of international folk music at Llangollen, with eclectic fringe and big-name evening concerts. (p726)

Royal Welsh Show

Prize bullocks and local produce at this national farm and livestock event in Builth Wells. (p709)

Cowes Week

Britain's biggest yachting spectacular on the choppy seas around the Isle of Wight. (p249)

Womad

Roots and world music take centre stage at this festival (www.womad.org) in a country park in the south Cotswolds.

Port Eliot Festival

Beginning life as a literary festival, now branched out into live music, theatre and outdoor art (www.porteliotfestival.com).

August

Schools and colleges are closed, the sun is shining (hopefully), most people go away for a week or two, and the nation is in holiday mood.

Edinburgh Festivals

Edinburgh's most famous happenings are the International Festival and Fringe, but it also has an event for anything you care to name – books, art, theatre, music, comedy… (www.edinburghfestivals.co.uk).

Notting Hill Carnival

London's famous multicultural Caribbean-style street carnival in the district of Notting Hill. Steel drums, dancers, outrageous costumes. (p118)

National Eisteddfod of Wales

The largest celebration of native Welsh culture, steeped in history, pageantry and pomp; held at venues around the country.

Brecon Fringe Festival

All musical tastes are catered for at this arts festival

Top: Putting the Stone event at the Braemar Gathering (p904)

Bottom: Green Man (p702) festival-goers

in the charming mid-Wales town of Brecon. (p703)

World Bog Snorkelling Championships

Competitors, many in fancy dress, don snorkel and flippers for a swimming race along a muddy ditch in the middle of a peat bog (www.green-events.co.uk).

Green Man Festival

A favourite on the summer music festival circuit, Green Man offers four days of alternative folk and rock music in a verdant Brecon Beacons setting. (p702)

September

The first week of September is still holiday time, but then schools reopen, traffic returns to normal, and the summer party's over for another year. Ironically, the weather's often better than in August.

Bestival

Quirky music festival on the Isle of Wight with a different fancy-dress theme every year. (p251)

Great North Run

Tyneside plays host to the one of the biggest half marathons in the world (www.greatrun.org/great-north-run), with the greatest number of runners in any race at this distance.

Abergavenny Food Festival

The mother of all epicurean festivals and the champion of Wales' burgeoning food scene. (p667)

Ludlow Food & Drink Festival

Great foodie town and a great foodie festival. (p449)

Braemar Gathering

The biggest and most famous Highland Games in the Scottish calendar, traditionally attended by members of the royal family. Highland dancing, caber-tossing and bagpipe-playing. (p904)

October

October means autumn. The leaves on the trees are changing colour, attractions start to shut down for the low season, and accommodation rates drop as hoteliers try to entice a final few guests before winter.

Dylan Thomas Festival

A celebration of the Welsh laureate's work with readings, events and talks in Swansea. (p671)

Falmouth Oyster Festival

The West Country port of Falmouth marks the start of the traditional oyster catching season (www.falmouthoysterfestival.co.uk) with a celebration of local food from the sea and fields of Cornwall.

November

Winter's here, and November is a dull month. The weather is often cold and damp, summer is a distant memory and Christmas is still too far away.

Guy Fawkes Night

Also called Bonfire Night (www.bonfirenight.net); on 5 November fireworks fill Britain's skies in commemoration of a failed attempt to blow up parliament, way back in 1605.

Remembrance Day

Red poppies are worn and wreaths are laid in towns and cities around the country on 11 November in commemoration of fallen military personnel (www.poppy.org.uk).

December

Schools break up earlier, but shops and businesses keep going until Christmas Eve; the last weekend before Christmas Day is busy on the roads as people visit friends and family, or head for the airport.

Stonehaven Fireball Festival

The Scottish fishing town of Stonehaven celebrates Hogmanay with a spectacular procession of fireball-swinging locals (www.stonehavenfireballs.co.uk).

New Year Celebrations

The last night of December sees fireworks and street parties in town squares across the country. London's Trafalgar Sq is where the city's largest crowds gather to welcome the New Year.

Itineraries

2 WEEKS Best of Britain

This circular whistle-stop tour ticks off Britain's greatest hits in an action-packed fortnight.

Start with a full day in Britain's greatest city, **London**, simply walking the streets to admire the world-famous sights: Buckingham Palace, Tower Bridge, Trafalgar Sq and more. Then head southwest to the grand cathedral cities of **Winchester** and **Salisbury**, across to the iconic menhirs of **Stonehenge** and its less well-known counterpart **Avebury Stone Circle**, then onwards to the beautiful historic city of **Bath**.

Loop over to **Chepstow** for its impressive castle, and then continue to **Cardiff**, the Welsh capital. Retrace slightly, then cruise across the classic English countryside of the **Cotswolds** to reach the renowned university city of **Oxford**. Not far away is **Stratford-upon-Avon**, for everything Shakespeare.

Strike out on the long drive north to Scotland's capital, **Edinburgh**, for another great castle, before recrossing the border to **York** for its glorious cathedral and historic city walls. Keep going south to reach **Cambridge**, another landmark university city. Then enjoy the last few days back in London, immersed in galleries, museums, luxury shops, street markets, West End shows, East End cafes – or whatever takes your fancy.

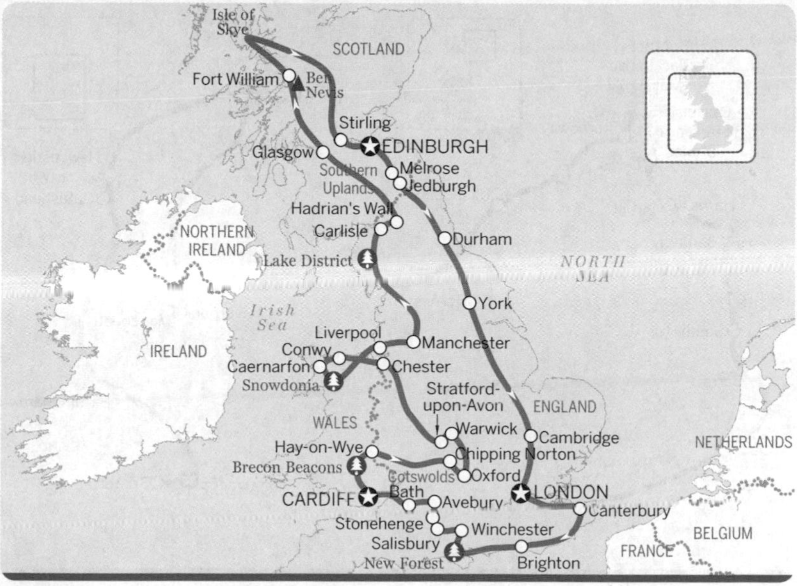

1 MONTH The Full Monty

This is a trip for those with the time, or the urge to see everything.

After a day or two in **London**, head southeast to **Canterbury**, then along the coast to hip and happening **Brighton**. For a change of pace, divert to the **New Forest**, then up to historic **Winchester** and **Salisbury** with their awe-inspiring cathedrals. Next, religion of a different kind: the ancient stone circles at **Stonehenge** and **Avebury**.

Go west to **Bath**, with its grand Georgian architecture, Roman remains and famous spas, and then over the border to reach Wales. Stop off at the energetic little city of **Cardiff**, then head north through to the whaleback hills of the **Brecon Beacons** to reach the quirky book-mad town of **Hay-on-Wye**.

Then it's back to England, and east into the **Cotswolds**, with its rolling hills, quintessential rural scenery and chocolate-box towns like **Chipping Norton**. Not far away is the famous university town of **Oxford**, as well as the ancient town of **Warwick**, with its spectacular castle, and Shakespeare's birthplace **Stratford-upon-Avon**.

Continue north to **Chester**, for its famous city walls, diverting into North Wales for the grand castles at **Conwy** and **Caernarfon**, and the stunning mountains of **Snowdonia**.

Then ferry across the Mersey to **Liverpool**, with its famous musical heritage and revitalised waterfront, or to **Manchester** for a taste of big-city life, followed by a total change of scenery in the **Lake District** mountains. To the north is the sturdy border town of **Carlisle**, and one of Britain's most impressive Roman remains, **Hadrian's Wall**.

Hop across the border to Scotland, via the tranquil Southern Uplands, to reach good-time **Glasgow**. Then trek to **Fort William** (and maybe up **Ben Nevis**, Britain's highest mountain), from where it's easy to reach the beautiful **Isle of Skye**.

Then it's time to head south again, via **Stirling Castle** to **Edinburgh**, and on through the historic abbey towns of **Melrose** and **Jedburgh**.

Back in England, you can marvel at the castle and cathedral of **Durham** and the ancient Viking capital of **York**, before taking in the ancient university city of **Cambridge** and enjoying the last few days of your trip in London.

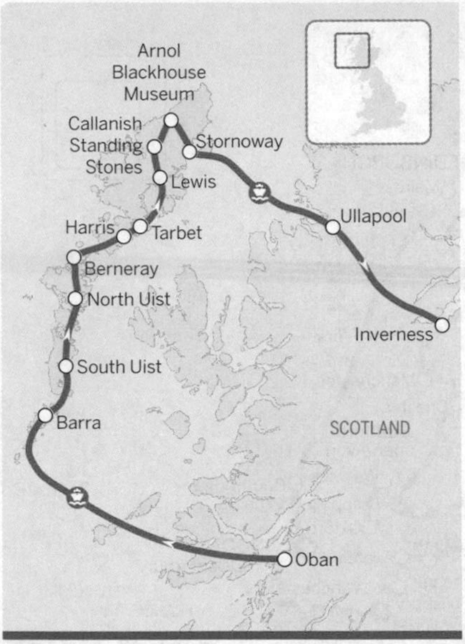

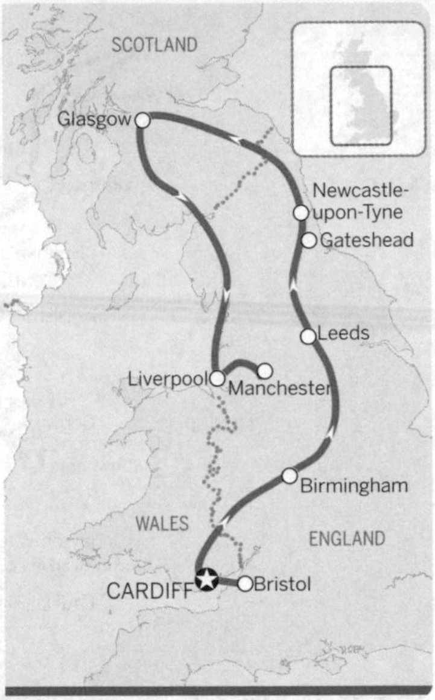

1 WEEK Island Hopscotch

This route is usually done by car, but it also makes a brilliant cycling tour (270 miles, including the 60 miles from Ullapool to Inverness train station, making both start and finish accessible by rail).

From **Oban** it's a five-hour ferry crossing to **Barra**; plan to spend the night here (book ahead). On day two, after a visit to Kisimul Castle and a tour around the island, take the ferry to **South Uist**. Walk the wild beaches of the west coast, sample the local seafood and perhaps go fishing on the island's trout lochs. Continue through Benbecula and **North Uist**, prime birdwatching country.

Overnight at Lochmaddy on North Uist (if you're camping or hostelling, a night at Berneray is a must) before taking the ferry to **Harris**, whose west coast has some of the most spectacular beaches in Scotland. The road continues north from Tarbert (good hotels) through rugged hills to Lewis.

Don't go directly to Stornoway, but loop west via the **Callanish Standing Stones** and **Arnol Blackhouse** museum. Spend your final night in **Stornoway** (eat at Digby Chick), then take the ferry to **Ullapool** for a scenic drive to **Inverness**.

3 WEEKS Urban Odyssey

This route travels through some of Britain's less well-known and revitalised cities.

Kick off in **Bristol**, a city with fierce pride and a rich historic legacy, then cross over to **Cardiff**, once a provincial backwater but now the lively Welsh capital.

Next stop is **Birmingham**, oozing transformation, with a renovated waterside, energised museums and a space-age shopping centre. Onwards to **Leeds**, where rundown factories and warehouses have been turned into loft apartments, ritzy boutiques and stylish department stores.

Shopping not your thing? No problem. Head for **Newcastle-upon-Tyne** and twin-city **Gateshead**; both have given up on heavy industries in favour of art and architecture – and are famous for partying.

Still want more? It's got to be **Glasgow**, Scotland's other great city, boasting fabulous galleries and welcoming pubs. Then it's south to **Liverpool**, which has reinvented itself as a cultural hot spot, with a famous musical heritage and very lively current scene. Finish your tour in **Manchester**, a long-time stage for artistic endeavour, with dramatic new architecture and a rather well-known football club.

Top: St Clement's Church (p938), Harris

Bottom: Kelvingrove Art Gallery (p805), Glasgow

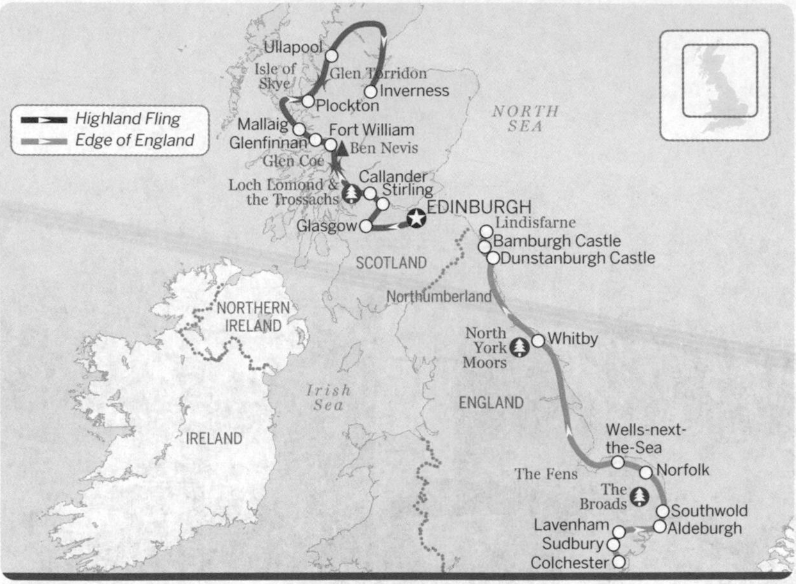

2 WEEKS Highland Fling

This itinerary is a tour of Scotland's finest and most famous sights.

Naturally it starts in **Edinburgh**, where highlights include the renowned castle, as well as the Royal Mile, the new parliament and the haunts of the Old Town. For a change of pace, hop over to **Glasgow** for a day or two as well. Then head northeast to see Scotland's other great castle at **Stirling**. Next stop is **Callander**, a good base for exploring the hills and lochs of the **Trossachs**.

Continue north and the landscape becomes ever more impressive, culminating in the grandeur of **Glen Coe**. Keen hillwalkers will pause for a day at **Fort William** to trek to the top of **Ben Nevis** (plus another day to recover!) before taking the 'Road to the Isles' past glorious **Glenfinnan** to the fishing harbour of **Mallaig**.

Take the ferry to the **Isle of Skye**, then head back to the mainland via the Skye Bridge to reach pretty **Plockton** and magnificent **Glen Torridon**. Onwards, via the outpost of **Ullapool**, takes you into the British mainland's furthest reaches, the remote mountain landscape of Scotland's far northwest, before looping south to finish your tour at the Highland capital, **Inverness**.

2 WEEKS Edge of England

If you like the outdoors, and prefer flocks of birds to crowds of people, try this backwater route along England's eastern fringe.

Start in **Colchester**, then head out into the sleepy county of Suffolk, where quaint villages and market towns such as **Sudbury** and **Lavenham** dot the landscape, while along the coast are wildlife reserves, shingly beaches, fishing ports such as **Aldeburgh**, and the delightfully retro seaside resort of **Southwold**.

Things get even quieter in Norfolk, especially around the misty lakes and windmill-lined rivers of the **Broads**. For beach strolls or historic country pubs, head for the coastal villages near **Wells-next-the-Sea**. Across the border in Lincolnshire lies the eerie, pan-flat landscape of the Fens, now a haven for otters and birdlife.

Continue into the heather-clad **North York Moors,** where humpbacked hills roll all the way to the coast to drop dramatically into the North Sea, and spend some time in the atmospheric seaside town of **Whitby**.

Enjoy a blustery stroll on the wild coast of Northumberland near the castles of **Dunstanburgh** and **Bamburgh**, then end your tour at the holy island of **Lindisfarne**.

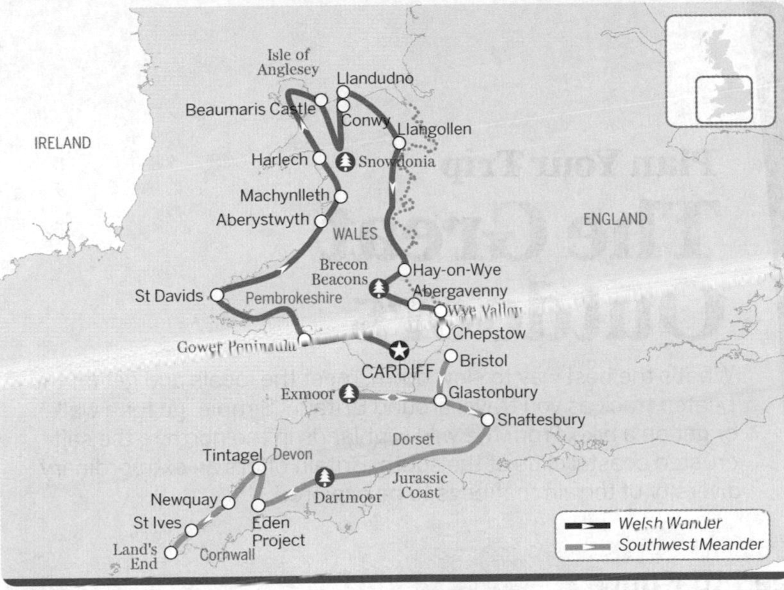

1 WEEK Welsh Wander

The coast and countryside of Wales has long been a favourite with visitors, and this tour includes most of the hot spots. Continue along England's southwest coast for a longer jaunt along Britain's Celtic fringe.

Start in **Cardiff**, with its fantastical castle, gigantic rugby stadium, revitalised waterfront and stunning Millennium Centre. Head west via the beautiful **Gower Peninsula** to reach the clear waters and sandy beaches of Pembrokeshire. Don't miss the ancient cathedral at **St Davids** – Britain's smallest city. Continue up the coast to **Aberystwyth**, then through 'alternative' **Machynlleth** to reach **Harlech** and its ancient castle. Divert to the tranquil Isle of Anglesey and historic **Beaumaris Castle**, then strike through the mountains of Snowdonia to reach **Conwy** (another stunning castle) and the seaside resort of **Llandudno**.

South takes you through **Llangollen**, with its jolly steam trains and vertiginous aqueduct, then along the England–Wales borderlands to book-mad **Hay-on-Wye**. Loop inland to the Welsh foodie capital of **Abergavenny**, then saunter down the Wye Valley to finish at the frontier town of **Chepstow** – and yet another amazing castle.

2 WEEKS Southwest Meander

The southwest of England takes a bit of effort to reach but repays in full with a rich green landscape dotted with hills and moors, surrounded by glistening seas.

Start in **Bristol**, the capital of the West Country, then saunter south to reach **Glastonbury** – famous for its annual music festival and the best place to stock up on candles or crystals at any time of year.

West leads to the walking trails of heathery **Exmoor**, then it's south to Dorset, where highlights include picturesque **Shaftesbury** and the fossil-strewn Jurassic Coast.

Onwards into Devon, and there's a choice of coasts, as well as **Dartmoor**, the highest and wildest hills in southern Britain.

Cross into Cornwall to explore the space-age biodomes of the **Eden Project**. Nearby, but in another era entirely, is **Tintagel Castle**, the legendary birthplace of King Arthur. Depending on your tastes, you can hang-ten in surf-flavoured party-town **Newquay**, or browse the galleries at artistic **St Ives**.

The natural finish to this wild west tour is **Land's End**, where the British mainland comes to a final full stop.

Plan Your Trip

The Great Outdoors

What's the best way to slow down, meet the locals and get off the beaten track as you travel around Britain? Simple: go for a walk, or get on a bike. From the wild Highlands in the north to the salt-crusted coastal cliffs of the south, Britain offers an extraordinary diversity of terrain that begs to be explored.

Need to Know

Best Seasons

Summer (Jun–Aug) Weather usually warm and dry; long evenings with plenty of daylight, too.

Late spring (May) and early autumn (Sep) Fewer crowds; days often mild and sunny. In Scotland, drier weather and fewer midges than high summer.

Best Maps

Ordnance Survey UK's national mapping agency; Explorer series 1:25,000 scale.

Harvey Maps Specially designed for walkers; Superwalker series 1:25,000 scale.

Best Websites

www.walkhighlands.co.uk Superb database of walks of all lengths in Scotland.

www.walkingenglishman.com Short walks in England and Wales.

www.nationaltrail.co.uk Great for specifics on long-distance trails in England and Wales.

www.scotlandsgreattrails.org.uk Long-distance trails in Scotland.

Walking

Walking is the most popular outdoor activity in Britain – for locals and visitors alike. Firstly, because it opens up some beautiful corners of the country, and secondly, because it can be done virtually on a whim. In fact, compared to hiking and trekking in some other parts of the world, it doesn't take much planning at all.

Getting Started

An established infrastructure for walkers already exists in Britain, so everything is easy for visitors or first-timers. Most villages and country towns in areas where walking is popular have shops selling maps and local guidebooks, while the local tourist office can provide leaflets and other information. In the national parks, suggested routes or guided walks are often available. This all means you can arrive in a place for the first time, pick up some info, and within an hour you'll be walking through some of Britain's finest landscapes. No fees. No permits. No worries. It really is almost effortless.

Britain's Footpath Network

Britain is covered in a vast network of footpaths, many of which are centuries old, dating from the time when walking was the only way to get from farm to village, from village to town, from town to coast, or from valley to valley. Any walk you do today will follow these historic paths. Even Britain's longest walks simply link up many shorter paths. You'll also sometimes walk along 'bridleways', originally used for horse transport, and old unsurfaced roads called 'byways'.

Rights of Way

The absolute pleasure of walking in Britain is mostly thanks to the 'right of way' network – public paths and tracks across private property, especially in England and Wales. In Britain, nearly all land (including in national parks) is privately owned, but if there's a right of way you can follow it through fields, pastures, woods, even farmhouse yards, as long as you keep to the route and do no damage. In some mountain and moorland areas, walkers can move freely beyond the rights of way and explore at will. Known as 'freedom to roam', where permitted it's clearly advertised with markers on gates and signposts. For more information see the Access pages on www.naturalengland.org.uk.

Scotland has a different legal system, where the Scottish Outdoor Access Code (www.outdooraccess-scotland.com) allows walkers to cross most private land providing they act responsibly. There are restrictions during lambing time, bird-nesting periods and the grouse- and deer-hunting seasons.

Britain's Best Walking Areas

Although you can walk just about anywhere in Britain, some areas are better than others. Here's a rundown of favourite places, suitable for short walks of a couple of hours, or longer all-day outings.

Southern England

The chalky hills of the South Downs stride across the counties of West Sussex and East Sussex, while the New Forest in Hampshire is great for easy strolls and the nearby Isle of Wight has excellent walking options. The highest and wildest area in southern England is Dartmoor, dotted with Bronze Age remains and granite outcrops called 'tors' – looking for all the world like abstract sculptures. Exmoor has heather-covered hills cut by deep valleys and a lovely stretch of coastline, while the entire coast of the southwest peninsula from Dorset to Somerset offers dramatic walking conditions – especially along the beautiful cliff-lined shore of Cornwall.

Central England

The gem of central England is the Cotswolds, classic English countryside with gentle paths through neat fields, mature woodland and pretty villages of honey-coloured stone. The Marches, where England borders Wales, are similarly bucolic with more good walking options. For something higher, aim for the Peak District, divided into two distinct areas: the White Peak, characterised by limestone, farmland and verdant dales, ideal for gentle strolls; and the Dark Peak, with high peaty moorlands, heather and gritstone outcrops, for more serious hikes.

Northern England

The Lake District is the heart and soul of walking in England, a wonderful area of soaring peaks, endless views, deep valleys and, of course, beautiful lakes. On the other side of the country, the rolling hills of the Yorkshire Dales make it another very popular walking area. Further north, keen walkers love the starkly beautiful hills of

> **WEATHER WATCH**
>
> While enjoying the outdoors, it's always worth remembering the fickle nature of the British weather. The countryside can appear gentle and welcoming, and often is, but sometimes conditions can turn nasty – especially on the higher ground. At any time of year, if you're walking on the hills or open moors, it's vital to be well equipped. You should carry warm and waterproof clothing (even in summer); a map and compass (that you know how to use); and drink and food, including high-energy stuff such as chocolate. If you're really going off the beaten track, leave details of your route with someone.

LONG-DISTANCE TRAILS

Some long-distance walking routes – such as the Pennine Way, the West Highland Way and the Pembrokeshire Coast Path – are well known and well maintained, with signposts and route-markers along the way, as well as being highlighted on Ordnance Survey maps. The most high-profile of these are the national trails, usually very clearly marked on the ground and on the map – ideal for beginners or visitors from overseas (although they're easy to follow, it doesn't mean they're necessarily easy underfoot). A downside of these famous routes is that they can be crowded in holiday times, making accommodation harder to find. An upside is the great feeling of camaraderie with other walkers on the trail.

Northumberland National Park, while the nearby coast is less daunting but just as dramatic – perfect for wild seaside strolls.

South & Mid-Wales

The Brecon Beacons is a large range of gigantic rolling whaleback hills with broad ridges and table-top summits, while out in the west is Pembrokeshire, a wonderful array of beaches, cliffs, islands, coves and harbours, with a hinterland of tranquil farmland and secret waterways, and a relatively mild climate year-round.

North Wales

For walkers, North Wales *is* Snowdonia, where the remains of ancient volcanoes bequeath a striking landscape of jagged peaks, ridges and cliffs. There are challenging walks on Snowdon itself – at 1085m, the highest peak in Wales – and many more on the nearby Glyderau and Carneddau ranges, or further south around Cader Idris.

Southern & Central Scotland

This extensive region embraces several areas just perfect for keen walkers, including Ben Lomond, the best-known peak in the area, and the nearby hills of the Trossachs, lying within the Loch Lomond and The Trossachs National Park. Also here is the splendid Isle of Arran, with a great choice of coastal rambles and high-mountain hikes.

Northern & Western Scotland

For serious walkers, heaven is the northern and western parts of Scotland, where the forces of nature have created a mountainous landscape of utter grandeur, including two of Scotland's most famous place names, Glen Coe and Ben Nevis (Britain's highest mountain at 1345m). Off the west coast lie the dramatic mountains of the Isle of Skye. Keep going north along the western coast, and things just keep getting better: a remote and beautiful area, sparsely populated, with scenic glens and lochs, and some of the largest, wildest and finest mountains in Britain.

Cycling & Mountain Biking

A bike is the perfect mode of transport for exploring back-road Britain. Once you escape the busy main highways, a vast network of quiet country lanes winds through fields and peaceful villages, ideal for cycle-touring. You can cruise through gently rolling landscapes, taking it easy and stopping for cream teas, or you can thrash all day through hilly areas, revelling in steep ascents and swooping downhill sections. You can cycle from place to place, camping or staying in B&Bs (many of which are cyclist-friendly), or you can base yourself in one area for a few days and go out on rides in different directions. All you need is a map and a sense of adventure.

Mountain-bikers can go further into the wilds on the tracks and bridleways that criss-cross Britain's hills and high moors, or head for the many dedicated mountain-bike trail centres where specially built single-track winds through the forests. Options at these centres vary from delightful dirt roads ideal for families to gnarly rock gardens and precipitous dropoffs for hardcore riders, all classified from green to black in ski-resort style.

www.sustrans.org.uk Details of Britain's national network of cycling trails.

www.forestry.gov.uk/england-cycling Guide to forest cycling trails in England.

www.dmbins.com Guide to mountain-biking trails in Scotland.

Fishing

After walking, fishing is Britain's most popular outdoor activity. As well as sea angling, there is excellent fishing for brown trout, grayling, pike, perch, carp and other coarse fish all over the country, while Scotland offers some of the world's best salmon fishing.

Fishing rights to most inland waters are privately owned and you must obtain a permit to fish in them – these are usually readily available from the local fishing-tackle shop or hotel, which are also great sources of advice and local knowledge. Permits cost from around £5 to £20 per day, but salmon fishing on some rivers – notably the Tyne in northeast England, and Scotland's Tweed, Tay and Spey – can be much more expensive (up to £150 a day).

In England and Wales, as well as a permit you will need a rod licence, which can be purchased online (www.postoffice.co.uk/rod-fishing-licence) or from post offices all over the country. This costs £3.75/10/27 for one day/eight days/one year for all freshwater fish except salmon and sea trout, which cost £8/23/72. Rod licences are not required in Scotland.

Fishing in the sea is generally free (except for salmon and sea trout), and neither permit nor rod licence is needed.

www.fishpal.com Information and booking portal for fishing (mostly salmon and trout) all over Britain.

www.fishing.visitwales.com Guide to fishing in Wales.

Surfing & Windsurfing

Britain may not seem an obvious destination for surfing, but conditions are surprisingly good and the large tidal range often means a completely different set of breaks at low and high tides. If you've come from the other side of the world, you'll be delighted to learn that summer water temperatures in southern England are roughly equivalent to winter temperatures in southern Australia (ie you'll still need a wetsuit). At the main spots, it's easy enough to hire boards and wetsuits.

Top of the list are the Atlantic-facing coasts of Cornwall and Devon (Newquay is surf-central, with all the trappings from Kombi vans to bleached hair), and there are smaller surf scenes elsewhere, notably Pembrokeshire and the Gower in Wales, and Norfolk and Yorkshire in eastern England. Hardier souls can head for northern Scotland and the Outer Hebrides, which have some of the best and most consistent surf in Europe.

Windsurfing is hugely popular all around the coast. Top areas include Norfolk, Suffolk, Devon and Cornwall, the Isle of Wight, and the islands of Tiree, Orkney and the Outer Hebrides.

www.surfinggb.com Listings of approved surf schools, courses, competitions and so on.

www.ukwindsurfing.com A good source of info.

Canoeing, Kayaking & Rafting

Britain's west coast, with its sheltered inlets, indented shoreline and countless islands, is ideal for sea kayaking, while its inland lakes and canals are great for Canadian canoeing. In addition, the turbulent spate rivers of Scotland and Wales offers some of Britain's best whitewater kayaking and rafting.

Equipment rental and instruction are readily available in major centres such as Cornwall, Anglesey, the Lake District, Loch Lomond and the Isle of Skye.

www.gocanoeing.org.uk Lists approved canoeing centres in England.

www.canoescotland.org Canoe trails in Scotland.

www.ukrafting.co.uk Whitewater rafting in Wales.

Coasteering

If sometimes a simple clifftop walk just won't cut the mustard, then coasteering might appeal. It's like mountaineering, but instead of going up a mountain, you go sideways along a coast – a steep and rocky coast – with waves breaking around your feet. And if the rock gets too steep, no problem – you jump in and start swimming. Coasteering centres provide wetsuits, helmets and buoyancy aids; you provide an old pair of training shoes and a sense of adventure. The sport is available all around Britain, but the mix of sheer cliffs, sandy beaches and warmer water make Cornwall and Devon prime spots.

www.coasteering.org Info on coasteering in Devon and Cornwall.

Rock Climbing

Britain has a long history of rock climbing and mountaineering, with many of the classic routes having been pioneered in the 19th century. The main rock-climbing areas include the Scottish Highlands, the Lake District, the Peak District and North Wales, plus the sea cliffs of South Wales, Devon and Cornwall, but there are also hundreds of smaller crags situated all over the country.

Comprehensive climbing guidebooks are published by the Scottish Mountaineering Club (www.smc.org.uk), the Fell & Rock Climbing Club (www.frcc.co.uk) and the Climbers Club (www.climbers-club.co.uk).

www.ukclimbing.com Full of useful information.

Horse Riding & Pony Trekking

If you want to explore the hills and moors but walking or cycling is too much of a sweat, seeing the wilder parts of Britain from horseback is highly recommended. In rural areas and national parks like Dartmoor and Northumberland, riding centres cater to all levels of proficiency, with ponies for kids and beginners and horses for the more experienced.

British Horse Society (www.bhs.org.uk) Lists approved riding centres offering day rides or longer holidays on horseback.

Sailing & Boating

Scotland's west coast, with its myriad islands, superb scenery and challenging winds and tides, is widely acknowledged to be one of the finest yachting areas in the world, while the canals of England and Wales offer a classic narrow-boating experience.

Beginners can take a Royal Yachting Association (www.rya.org.uk) training course in yachting or dinghy sailing at many sailing schools around the coast. Narrow-boaters only need a quick introductory lesson at the start of their trip – for more info see www.canalholidays.com.

Skiing & Snowboarding

Britain's ski centres are all in the Scottish Highlands:

Cairngorm Mountain (www.cairngormmountain.org) 1097m; has almost 30 runs spread over an extensive area.

Glencoe (www.glencoemountain.com) 1108m; has five tows and two chairlifts.

Glenshee (www.ski-glenshee.co.uk) 920m; situated on the A93 road between Perth and Braemar; offers the largest network of lifts and the widest range of runs in Britain.

Lecht (www.lecht.co.uk) 793m; the smallest and most remote centre, on the A939 between Ballater and Grantown-on-Spey.

Nevis Range (www.nevisrange.co.uk) 1221m; near Fort William; offers the highest ski runs, the grandest setting and some of the best off-piste potential.

The high season is from January to April, but it's sometimes possible to ski from as early as November to as late as May. It's easy to turn up at the slopes, hire some kit, buy a day pass and off you go.

Weather and snow reports can be obtained from:

Ski Scotland (www.ski-scotland.com)

WinterHighland (www.winterhighland.info)

Lancashire hotpot (p49)

Plan Your Trip

Eat & Drink Like a Local

Britain once had a reputation for bad food, but the nation has enjoyed something of a culinary revolution over the past decade and a half. London is recognised as having one of the best restaurant scenes in the world, while all over the country stylish eateries and gourmet gastropubs are making the most of a newfound passion for quality local produce.

The Year in Food

Best in Spring (Mar–May)

Spring brings fresh asparagus, new potatoes (notably Jersey Royals), pink rhubarb and tender lamb.

Best in Summer (Jun–Aug)

Strawberries, raspberries and other soft fruits are in season along with salad vegetables such as lettuce and radishes, and seafood such as scallops, langoustines, mackerel and cod.

Best in Autumn (Sep–Nov)

Apples and blackberries (often cooked together in a crumble), game including venison and wood pigeon, and shellfish – oysters, mussels and cockles. Also the main season for food festivals.

Best in Winter (Dec–Feb)

Sweet chestnuts (roasted on an open fire), and that classic Christmas combination of goose, root vegetables and Brussels sprouts.

Food Experiences

Meals of a Lifetime

Waterside Inn (p229) Exquisite French food at Alain Roux's classic restaurant, in a romantic setting on the banks of the Thames.

Dinner by Heston Blumenthal (p128) Famous exponent of 'molecular gastronomy' leads you through a tour of Britain's culinary history.

Restaurant Nathan Outlaw (p337) Superb local seafood is the trademark of Cornwall's only Michelin-starred chef.

Three Chimneys (p933) A windswept crofting cottage in a far-flung corner of the Isle of Skye is home to unexpected gastronomic delights.

Hardwick (p667) Set in the heart of mid-Wales gastropub territory, this rustic inn was one of the first on the scene, and still delivers a meal to remember.

St John (p133) A pioneer of 'nose-to-tail' dining (ie eating every part of the animal), St John offers a memorably 'offal' dining experience.

Cheap Treats

Bacon sandwich The breakfast of champions. Debate rages over the choice of sauce – red (tomato ketchup) or brown (spicy pickled fruit sauce).

Beans on toast A comforting childhood classic of tinned baked beans poured over buttered toast, served in many cafes as a breakfast or lunch dish.

Fish and chips The nation's favourite takeaway meal, served in hundreds of chip shops all over the country.

Cockles A classic seaside snack that has been enjoyed by generations of British holidaymakers, sprinkled with vinegar and eaten from a cardboard tub with a wooden fork.

Scotch egg This masterpiece of culinary engineering consists of a hardboiled egg wrapped in sausage meat, coated in breadcrumbs and deep-fried.

Dare to Try

Haggis Scotland's national dish is made from the chopped heart, liver and lungs of a sheep, mixed with oatmeal and onion. Widely available in Scottish restaurants.

Tripe Cow's stomach lining, traditionally poached in milk with onions. A wartime staple, but hard to find in restaurants today – though it's making a comeback.

Stinking Bishop Britain's most pungent cheese, made in Gloucestershire and redolent of old socks. Available from Harrods in London, and many specialist cheese shops.

Jellied eels Traditional London side dish that can still be found in the capital's pie and mash shops.

Local Specialities

Scotland

Scotland may be most famous for haggis, but seafood is where it excels. Fresh lobster, langoustine, salmon and scallops are the favourites of restaurant menus, but look out for traditional dishes such as Arbroath smokies (hot-smoked haddock) and Cullen skink (soup made with smoked haddock, onion, butter and milk). Oats have been a mainstay of the Scottish diet for centuries, appearing in the form of porridge and oatcakes, but also as a coating for fried trout or herring, and in the classic Scottish dessert known as cranachan (whipped cream flavoured with whisky and mixed with raspberries and toasted oatmeal).

Wales

Tender and tasty Welsh lamb is sought after by restaurateurs all over Britain, but it also appears in the rustic local dish known as cawl (pronounced cowl) – a one-pot stew of lamb, bacon, cabbage, potato and swede. Better known is laverbread, which is not bread but seaweed, cooked with oatmeal and often served for breakfast with toast and bacon. Sweet-toothed visitors should look out for Welsh cakes (fruity griddle scones) and bara brith (a dense and spicy fruit cake flavoured with tea and marmalade).

The English Midlands

The Leicestershire town of Melton Mowbray is famed for its pork pies, always eaten cold, ideally with pickle. Only pies handmade in the eponymous town can carry the Melton Mowbray moniker – in the same way that only fizzy wine from the Champagne region of France can carry that name.

Another British speciality from this region that enjoys the same protection is Stilton – a strong white cheese, either plain or blue vein. Only five dairies in all of Britain (four of which are in Derbyshire) are allowed to name the cheese they produce Stilton. Bizarrely, the cheese cannot be made in the village of Stilton in Cambridgeshire, although this is where it was first sold – hence the name.

North of England

The northeast of England is known for its kippers (smoked herring), traditionally grilled with butter and served for breakfast with toast and marmalade on the side, and for pease pudding (a thick stew of yellow split peas cooked in ham stock). The northwest lays claim to Lancashire hotpot (slow-cooked stew of lamb and onion topped with sliced potatoes), Eccles cakes (rounds of flaky pastry filled with currants), and Cumberland sausage (a spiral shaped pork sausage flavoured with herbs). But the most famous of northern specialities is Yorkshire pudding, a light and puffy batter pudding usually served as a side dish with roast beef, that has now been adopted all over Britain.

JUSTIN FOULKES / LONELY PLANET ©

Fish and chips

Southwest England

Cows reared on the rich pastures of Devon and Cornwall create some of Britain's finest dairy produce, notably the famous clotted cream (a very thick cream made by heating full-cream milk) that forms an essential component of Cornish cream teas. Less refined but equally tasty are Cornish pasties (crimped pastry parcels containing cooked vegetables and, less traditionally, minced beef), once the lunchtime staple of miners and farm workers.

London & Southeast England

Ask a Londoner about local food specialities, and you're bound to get the answer: pie and mash, and jellied eels. The staple menu of working-class Londoners since the 19th century, the former consists of a small pie filled with minced beef served with mashed potato and 'liquor' – a parsley-rich gravy made from the stock in which eels have been cooked. The eels are cooled and

VIEW PICTURES / GETTY IMAGES ©

Dinner by Heston Blumenthal (p128), London

set in the jellied stock, and served as a side dish with malt vinegar – try them out at M Manze or Poppies.

Oysters today have an expensive reputation, but in the 19th century they were a cheap and plentiful foodstuff, eaten by all. Whitstable oysters, from Kent – the native British species, unlike the more common, farmed Pacific oysters – have been harvested since Roman times, and still grace the tables of London restaurants and oyster bars.

How to Eat & Drink

In parts of Britain, notably northern England and Scotland, many people use the word 'dinner' for their main midday meal, and 'tea' for a light evening meal. However, this terminology is rarely, if ever, used in restaurants.

When to Eat

Breakfast Served in most hotels and B&Bs between 7am and 9am, or perhaps 8am to 10am on weekends. In cafes, the breakfast menu might extend to 11am through the week. For many visitors, the first meal of the day is what's known as the 'Full English Breakfast' – aka Full Welsh, Scottish, Yorkshire etc – a plateful of fried food that might shock if you're expecting just a bowl of cereal. But it can fuel several hours of energetic sightseeing.

Lunch Generally taken between noon and 2pm, and can range from a sandwich and a bag of crisps to a three-course meal with wine. Many restaurants offer a set menu two-course lunch at competitive prices on weekdays, while cafes often have a daily lunch special, or offer soup and a sandwich.

Afternoon tea A tradition inherited from the British aristocracy and eagerly adopted by the middle classes, a between-meals snack now enjoying a revival in country hotels and upmarket tearooms. It consists of dainty sandwiches, cakes and pastries, plus, of course, a cup of tea, poured from a silver teapot and sipped politely from fine china cups.

Dinner The main meal of the day, usually served in restaurants between 6pm and 9pm, and

NITSAWAN KATERATTANAKUL / SHUTTERSTOCK ©

Afternoon tea

GREAT BRITISH CHEESES

Cheddar Sharp and savoury, Britain's most popular cheese originates in Somerset but is now made all over the country (and, indeed, the world).

Stilton A pungent blue cheese, traditionally eaten after dinner with a glass of port.

Wensleydale Crumbly white cheese from Yorkshire, with a mild, honeyed flavour.

Caerphilly From the Welsh town of the same name, this hard, salty cheese has an annual festival dedicated to it.

Cornish Yarg A rich, creamy cheese characterised by its wrapping of nettle leaves.

Caboc A Highland Scottish cream cheese rolled in oatmeal, whose recipe is more than 500 years old.

consisting of two or three courses – starter, main and dessert. Upmarket restaurants might serve a five-course dinner, with an amuse-bouche to begin, and a fish course between starter and main.

Sunday lunch Another great British tradition. It is the main meal of the day, normally served between noon and 4pm. Many pubs and restaurants offer Sunday lunch, where the main course usually consists of roast beef, lamb or pork, accompanied by roast and mashed potatoes, gravy, and boiled vegetables such as carrots and peas.

Where to Eat

Cafes Traditional cafes are simple eateries serving simple food – sandwiches, pies, sausage and chips. Quality varies enormously: some cafes definitely earn their 'greasy spoon' handle, while others are neat and clean.

Tearooms The tearoom is a British institution, serving cakes, scones and sandwiches accompanied by pots of tea (though coffee is usually available too). Upmarket tearooms may also serve afternoon tea.

Coffee shops In most cities and towns you'll also find coffee shops – both independents and international chains – serving decent lattes, cappuccinos and espressos, and continental-style snacks such as bagels, panini and ciabattas.

Restaurants London has scores of excellent restaurants that could hold their own in major cities worldwide, while eating places in other British cities can give the capital a run for its money (often for rather less money).

Pubs Many British pubs serve a wide range of food, and it's often a good-value option whether you want a toasted sandwich between museum visits in London, or a three-course meal in the evening after touring the castles of Wales.

Gastropubs The quality of food in some pubs is now so high that they have created a whole new genre of eatery – the gastropub. The finest are almost restaurants (a few have been awarded Michelin stars), but others go for a more relaxed atmosphere.

Plan Your Trip

Travel with Children

Britain is ideal for travelling with children because of its compact size, packing a lot of attractions into a small area. So when the kids in the back of the car ask 'Are we there yet?', your answer can often be 'Yes, we are'.

Best Regions for Kids

London

The capital has children's attractions galore; many are free.

Southwest England

Lovely beaches and reliable weather, though crowded in summer.

The Midlands

Caverns and 'show caves', plus former railways now traffic-free cycle routes.

Oxford & the Cotswolds

Oxford has Harry Potter connections; the Cotswolds is ideal for little-leg strolls.

Lake District & Cumbria

Zip wires and kayaks for teenagers; boat rides and Beatrix Potter for youngsters.

Wales

Long coast of beaches and pony-trekking in the hill country. And loads of castles...

Southern Scotland

Edinburgh and Glasgow have kid-friendly museums; the Southern Uplands offer great mountain biking for a range of skill levels.

Scottish Highlands & Islands

Hardy teenagers plunge into outdoor activities; dolphin-spotting boat trips are fun for all the family.

Great Britain for Kids

Many places of interest cater for kids as much as adults. At historic castles, for example, mum and dad can admire the medieval architecture, while the kids will have great fun striding around the battlements. In the same way, many national parks and holiday resorts organise specific activities for children. It goes without saying that everything ramps up in the school holidays.

Bargain Hunting

Most visitor attractions offer family tickets – usually two adults plus two children – for less than the sum of the individual entrance charges. Most offer cheaper rates for solo parents and kids, too. Be sure to ask, as these are not always clearly displayed.

On the Road

If you're going by public transport, trains are great for families: intercity services have plenty of room for luggage and extra stuff like buggies (strollers), and the kids can move about a bit when bored. In contrast, they need to stay in their seats on long-distance coaches.

If you're hiring a car, most (but not all) rental firms can provide child seats – but you'll need to check this in advance. Most will not actually fit the child seats; you need to do that yourself, for insurance reasons.

Dining, not Whining

When it comes to refuelling, most cafes and teashops are child-friendly. Restaurants are mixed: some offer high chairs and kiddy portions; others firmly say 'no children after 6pm'.

Children under 18 are usually not allowed in pubs serving just alcohol. Pubs also serving meals generally allow children of any age (with their parents) in England and Wales, but in Scotland they must be over 14 and must leave by 8pm. If in doubt, simply ask the bar staff.

And finally, a word on another kind of refuelling: Britain is still slightly buttoned up about breastfeeding. Older folks may tut-tut a bit if you give junior a top-up in public, but if done modestly it's usually considered OK.

Children's Highlights

Best Fresh-Air Fun

If the kids tire of castles and museums, you're never far from a place for outdoor activities to blow away the cobwebs.

Wildlife Cruises, Scotland's west coast (p872) What child could resist a boat trip to see seals, porpoises and dolphins, maybe even a whale?

Puzzlewood, Forest of Dean (p220) Wonderful woodland playground with mazy paths, weird rock formations and eerie passageways.

Whinlatter Forest Park, Cumbria (p605) Highlights include a Go Ape adventure park and excellent mountain-bike trails, plus live video feeds from red-squirrel cams.

Bewilderwood, Norfolk (p400) Zip wires, jungle bridges, tree houses, marsh walks, boat trips, mazes and all sorts of old-fashioned outdoor adventure.

Lyme Regis, Dorset (p264) Guided tours to find your very own prehistoric fossil.

Cotswold Farm Park (p210) Child-friendly introduction to the world of farm animals.

Tissington Trail, Derbyshire (p479) Cycling this former railway is fun and almost effortless. You can hire kids' bikes, tandems and trailers. Don't forget to hoot in the tunnels!

7Stanes MTB Centres, Southern Scotland (p829) A network of mountain-biking centres offering everything from easy, family-friendly trails with picnic tables and viewpoints, to more challenging routes for teenagers.

Best Hands-On Action

Please do not touch? No chance. Here are some places where grubby fingers and enquiring minds are positively welcomed.

Science Museum, London (p91) Seven floors of educational exhibits, at the mother of all science museums.

Enginuity, Ironbridge (p443) Endless hands-on displays at the birthplace of the Industrial Revolution.

National Waterfront Museum, Swansea (p671) Great interactive family fun.

Glasgow Science Centre (p805) Bringing science and technology alive through hundreds of engaging exhibits.

Discovery Museum, Newcastle (p621) Tyneside's rich history on display; highlights include a buzzers-and-bells science maze.

At-Bristol, Bristol (p311) One of Britain's best interactive science museums, covering space, technology and the human brain.

Riverside Museum, Glasgow (p804) Top-class interactive museum with a focus on transport.

Jorvik Viking Centre, York (p499) Excellent smells-and-all Viking settlement reconstruction.

Natural History Museum, London (p94) Highlights include the life-size blue whale and animatronic dinosaurs.

BABY-CHANGING FACILITIES

Most museums and other attractions in Britain usually have good baby-changing facilities (cue old joke: I swapped mine for a nice souvenir). Elsewhere, some city-centre public toilets have baby-changing areas, although these can be a bit grimy; your best bet for clean facilities is an upmarket department store. On the road, baby-changing facilities are generally bearable at motorway service stations and OK at out-of-town supermarkets.

ALEX ROBINSON / GETTY IMAGES ©

JOHN CANCALOSI / GETTY IMAGES ©

Top: Japanese spider crab display, Natural History Museum (p94), London

Bottom: Discovering ancient fossils, Lyme Regis (p264), Jurassic Coast

Thinktank, Birmingham (p409) Every display comes with a button or a lever at this 'edutaining' science museum.

National Space Centre, Leicester (p469) Space-suits, zero-gravity toilets and mini-astronaut training – guaranteed to boost little brains.

Centre for Alternative Technology, Machynlleth (p713) Educational, fun and truly green – great for curious kids.

Best Rainy-Day Distractions

For those inevitable gloomy days, head for the indoor attractions; don't forget the nation's great collection of museums. Alternatively, try outdoor stuff like coasteering in Pembrokeshire or canyoning in the Lake District. It's always fun – wet or dry.

Cadbury World, Birmingham (p412) Dentists may cry, but kids love the story of chocolate. And yes, there are free samples.

Underground Edinburgh (p768) Take a guided tour of the haunted vaults beneath the medieval Old Town.

Eden Project, Cornwall (p352) It may be raining outside, but inside these giant domes, it's forever tropical forest or Mediterranean climate.

Cheddar Gorge Caves, Wessex (p328) Finally nail the difference between stalactites and stalagmites in the Westcountry's deep caverns.

Underground Passages, Exeter (p284) Explore medieval catacombs – the only system of its kind open to the public in England.

Best Stealth Learning

Secretly exercise their minds while the little darlings think they are 'just' having fun.

At-Bristol Science Centre (p311) One of the best interactive science museums in England, covering space, technology and the human brain.

Jorvik Viking Centre, York (p499) An excellent smells-and-all Viking settlement reconstruction.

Natural History Museum, London (p94) Animals everywhere! Highlights include the life-size blue whale and the animatronics dinosaurs.

Thinktank, Birmingham (p409) Every display comes with a button or a lever at this edu-taining science museum.

National Space Centre, Leicester (p469) Space-suits, zero-gravity toilets and mini-astronaut training – all guaranteed to fire-up little minds.

Centre for Alternative Technology, Machynlleth (p713) Educational, fun and truly green – great for curious kids.

Planning

When to Go

The best time for families to visit Britain is pretty much the best time for everyone else: from April/May to the end of September. It's worth avoiding August – the heart of school summer holidays – when prices go up and roads are busy, especially near the coast. Other school holidays are two weeks around Easter Sunday, and mid-December to early January, plus three week-long 'half-term' breaks – usually late February (or early March), late May and late October.

Accommodation

Some hotels welcome kids (with their parents) and provide cots, toys and baby-sitting services, while others maintain an adult atmosphere. Many B&Bs offer 'family suites' of two adjoining bedrooms with one bathroom, and an increasing number of hostels (YHA, SYHA and independent) have family rooms with four or six beds – some even with private bathroom attached. If you want to stay in one place for a while, renting a holiday cottage is ideal. Camping is very popular with British families, and there are lots of fantastic campsites, but you'll usually need all your own gear.

Useful Websites

Baby Goes 2 (www.babygoes2.com) Advice, tips and encouragement (and a stack of adverts) for families on holiday.

MumsNet (www.mumsnet.com) No-nonsense advice on travel and more from a vast network of UK mothers.

Regions at a Glance

From the multicultural melting pot of London to the remote islands of the Outer Hebrides, Britain's regions offer a kaleidoscope of classic experiences. Southern England is where you'll find the archetypal English countryside of lush meadows, thatched cottages and games of cricket on the village green. The southwestern counties of Devon and Cornwall are wilder in nature, known for their surf beaches and seafood restaurants. Lovers of mountain scenery will be spoilt for choice in the Scottish Highlands, the Lake District and North Wales, while those who prefer gritty industrial heritage and lively nightlife will enjoy the northern English cities of Manchester, Liverpool and Newcastle. And bang in the middle is Yorkshire, with everything from the gorgeous city of York to the rolling moors of the Yorkshire Dales.

London

History
Entertainment
Museums

Tower of London

The echoes of the footfalls of monarchs, poets, whores and saints can still be detected in places like the Tower of London, Westminster Abbey and St Paul's Cathedral, as well as the pubs and coaching inns that once served Dickens, Shelley, Keats and Byron.

Entertainment

From West End theatres to East End clubs, tennis at Wimbledon to cricket at Lord's or football at Wembley, London's world-famous venues and arenas offer a perpetual clamour of entertainment.

British Museum

While the British Museum is the big crowd-puller, the capital has museums and galleries of every shape and size – and many of the very best are free.

p66

Canterbury & Southeast England

Architecture
History
Food & Drink

Canterbury Cathedral

Canterbury Cathedral is one of the finest cathedrals in Europe, and one of the most holy places in Christendom. Write your own Canterbury tale as you explore its chapels, cloisters and crypts.

Invasion Heritage

The southeast has always been a gateway for Continental arrivals. Castles and fortresses, the 1066 battlefield and Dover's wartime tunnels tell of invasion and defence.

Hops & Grapes

Kent is known as the Garden of England, celebrated for its hops, still used to flavour traditional English beers. Sussex isn't far behind, with England's finest sparkling wine giving the French stuff a run for its euro.

p152

Oxford & the Cotswolds

Architecture
Stately Homes
Villages

Oxford Colleges

Oxford's architecture will never leave you indifferent, whether you gaze across the 'dreaming spires' from the top of Carfax Tower, or explore the medieval streets on foot.

Blenheim Palace

Favoured by the rich and powerful for centuries, this region is scattered with some of the finest country houses in Britain. Top of the pile is the baroque masterpiece of Blenheim Palace, birthplace of Sir Winston Churchill.

The Cotswolds

Littered with picturesque 'chocolate box' scenes of honey-coloured stone cottages, thatched roofs, neat greens and cobbled lanes, the villages of the Cotswolds provide a charming snapshot of rural England.

p187

Bath & Southwest England

Coastline
History
Activities

Cornish Beaches

Britain's southwest peninsula juts determinedly into the Atlantic, fringed by an almost endless chain of sandy beaches, from the picturesque scenery of Kynance Cove to the rolling surf of Newquay.

Roman Remains

The handsome Georgian city of Bath – the whole town is a Unesco World Heritage Site – is home to one of the best preserved Roman bath complexes in the world.

Hiking & Surfing

If you like to take it nice and easy, come to walk the moors or tootle along cycle trails. If you prefer life fast and furious, come to surf the best waves in England or learn to dive or kitesurf.

p232

Cambridge & East Anglia

Architecture
Coastline
Waterways

Historic Churches

From the magnificent cathedrals of Ely, Norwich and Peterborough to Cambridge's King's College Chapel, Trinity's Great Court and the New Court at St John's.

Seaside Resorts

With sandy beaches, seafood, delightful old pubs, globally important bird reserves, historic villages still proud of their nautical heritage and classic seaside resorts such as Southwold and Cromer, the coastline of East Anglia is rich and varied.

The Broads

The Norfolk and Suffolk Broads is a tranquil area of lakes and meandering rivers, and an ideal spot for boating, birding, canoeing, cycling or walking, or just getting back to nature at a leisurely pace.

p363

Birmingham, the Midlands & the Marches

Activities
Stately Homes
Food & Drink

Hiking & Biking

The Peak District National Park, Cannock Chase, the Shropshire Hills, the Roaches, the Malvern Hills, Offa's Dyke Path, the Tissington Trail and the Pennine Cycleway all make this region great.

Chatsworth

Grand houses like Haddon Hall, Burghley House and especially Chatsworth promise sprawling deer-filled grounds and grand interiors.

Curry Capital

Foodies take note: Birmingham is the curry capital of the country (and, increasingly, a magnet for Michelin-starred chefs), while the tiny town of Ludlow is an epicentre of gastronomic exploration.

p405

Yorkshire

Activities
Food & Drink
History

Hiking & Biking

With rolling hills, scenic valleys and moors and a cliff-lined coast all protected by national parks, Yorkshire is a natural adventure playground for hiking, biking, surfing and rock climbing.

Beef, Lamb & Beer

Lush pasture means Yorkshire beef and lamb is sought after, while the famous breweries of Masham turn out excellent real ales, always best sampled in one of Yorkshire's equally excellent traditional pubs.

Ancient Abbeys

From York's Viking heritage and the ancient abbeys of Rievaulx, Fountains and Whitby, to the industrial archaeology of Leeds, Bradford and Sheffield, you can follow several of Britain's most important historical narratives in Yorkshire.

p491

Manchester, Liverpool & Northwest England

History
Sport
Seaside Resorts

Museums

The northwest's collection of heritage sites is testament to the region's rich history and its ability to keep it alive.

Football

Two cities, Liverpool and Manchester, give the world four famous clubs, including the two most successful in English history. The National Football Museum in Manchester is just another reason for fans to visit this region.

Blackpool

The epitome of the classic English seaside resort just keeps on going, thanks to the rides of the Pleasure Beach amusement park, where adrenalin junkies can always find a fix.

p545

The Lake District & Cumbria

Scenery
Activities
Literature

Lakes & Mountains

The Lake District National Park is the most mountainous part of England, home to its highest summit and countless scenic lakes. Some are big and famous, while others are small, hidden and little known.

Walking

If anywhere is the heart and soul of walking in England, it's the Lake District. Casual strollers find gentle routes, while serious hikers can tackle high peaks and fells.

William Wordsworth

The beauty of the Lake District moved William Wordsworth to write his ode to 'a host of golden daffodils', and visiting Wordsworth landmarks is one of the region's big draws.

p580

Newcastle & Northeast England

History
Landscape
Castles

Hadrian's Wall

One of the world's premier Roman sites, this potent symbol of imperial power strides for more than 70 miles across the neck of England. You can travel its length, stopping off at forts along the way.

Northumberland National Park

If it's widescreen vistas you're after, the broad moors, stone villages and expansive views of England's most northerly national park never fail to please.

Alnwick Castle

Northumberland is dotted with some of Britain's finest castles, including the coastal fortresses of Bamburgh and Dunstanburgh, but Alnwick – setting for the Harry Potter movies – is the most famous.

p617

Cardiff, Pembrokeshire & South Wales

Architecture
Coastline
Castles

Victorian Revival

From the whimsical, fairytale structures of Cardiff Castle and Castell Coch to the elegant arcades of the city centre, the Welsh capital has plenty to keep Victorian architectural fans interested.

Pembrokeshire & The Gower

South Wales boasts two of Britain's most beautiful stretches of coast – offering clifftop walks, family-friendly beaches, surfing hot spots and watery adventures such as sea-kayaking and coasteering.

Carreg Cennen

South Wales has some of the country's best castles, but remote Carreg Cennen, in the Brecon Beacons, is the most spectacular of all.

p651

Brecon Beacons & Mid-Wales

Wildlife
Local Culture
Food & Drink

Red Kites

In the mountains and moors of the Brecon Beacons and many other parts of the region you can spot birds of prey – most famously the once-rare red kites, most easily spotted at feeding stations such as Gigrin Farm in Rhayadar.

Market Towns

From book-obsessed Hay-on-Wye to quirky Llanwrtyd Wells and quaint Llandrindod Wells, the market towns of mid-Wales are full of charm.

Abergavenny

Restaurants, inns and gastropubs throughout the region are at the forefront of a new Welsh gastronomy, all focused on the nation's foodie capital at Abergavenny.

p696

Snowdonia & North Wales

Mountains
Industrial Heritage
Coastline

Snowdon

Home to some of Britain's finest mountain scenery outside of the Scottish Highlands, the imposing peaks of Snowdon and its neighbours provide a scenic backdrop for innumerable outdoor pursuits.

Welsh Slate

Welsh slate once roofed much of the world, and the region's quarries and caverns bear witness to the lives of generations of workers, while rejuvenated railways now shunt tourists through spectacular terrain.

Seaside Resorts

From the north coast's popular resort towns to the surf spots and quiet bays of Anglesey and the Llŷn Peninsula, North Wales has plenty of beach to go round.

p722

Edinburgh

Culture
History
Food & Drink

Festival City

Dubbed the Athens of the North, the Scottish capital is a city of art and literature, home to the world's biggest arts festival. Outside festival time, there's plenty to enjoy in the city's many theatres and world-class art galleries and museums.

Edinburgh Castle

Perched on a brooding black crag overlooking the city centre, Edinburgh Castle has played a pivotal role in Scottish history, the focus of the nation's capital city since medieval times.

Eating Out

Edinburgh has more restaurants per head of population than any city in the UK, while Scottish cuisine has been given a makeover by inventive chefs using top-quality local produce.

p761

Glasgow & Southern Scotland

Museums
Historic Buildings
Stately Homes

Kelvingrove Art Gallery & Museum

Glasgow's mercantile and industrial history has left the city with a legacy of wonderful museums and art galleries, dominated by the grand Victorian cathedral of culture, Kelvingrove.

The Great Abbeys

Rolling countryside and ruined abbeys are the big draws along the country's southern border, where you'll find the Gothic ruins of Melrose, Jedburgh and Dryburgh abbeys.

Dumfries House

This region is rich in Adam-designed mansions such as Culzean Castle and Floors Castle, but the almost perfectly preserved Chippendale time-capsule Dumfries House takes top place.

p797

Stirling & Central Scotland

Castles
Islands
Whisky

Stirling Castle

Central and Northeast Scotland are home to the greatest concentration of castles in the country, from the turreted exuberance of Craigievar to the more restrained elegance of Balmoral, but topped by the regal splendour of Stirling.

Island-Hopping

Island-hopping is a great way to explore Scotland's western seaboard, and the islands of this region – wild Jura, scenic Mull and the jewel of Iona – provide a brilliant introduction.

Speyside Distilleries

No trip to Scotland is complete without a visit to a whisky distillery – the Speyside region and the isle of Islay are epicentres of the industry.

p833

Inverness & the Northern Highlands & Islands

Activities
Scenery
History

Hill Walking

The Cairngorm resort of Aviemore, gateway to snow sports in winter and wild hill-walking in summer, and Fort William, self-styled outdoor capital of the UK, offer enough adventure to keep you busy for a year.

Mountain Landscapes

Landscape photographers are spoilt for choice, with classic views ranging from the mountain beauty of Glen Coe and the snow-patched summits of the Cairngorms to the rock pinnacles of the Cuillin Hills.

Prehistoric Sites

This region is rich in prehistoric remains, including the standing stones of Callanish, the neolithic tomb of Maeshowe, and Skara Brae.

p887

On the Road

Inverness & the Northern Highlands & Islands p887
Stirling & Central Scotland p833
Edinburgh p761
Glasgow & Southern Scotland p797
Newcastle & Northeast England p617
The Lake District & Cumbria p580
Yorkshire p491
Manchester, Liverpool & Northwest England p545
Snowdonia & North Wales p722
Birmingham, the Midlands & the Marches p405
Brecon Beacons & Mid-Wales p696
Cambridge & East Anglia p363
London p66
Cardiff, Pembrokeshire & South Wales p651
Canterbury & Southeast England p152
Bath & Southwest England p232
Oxford & the Cotswolds p187

England

DARTMOOR NATIONAL PARK (P298); PAUL NASH / SHUTTERSTOCK ©

England Highlights

❶ **London** (p66) Spending more time than you'd planned in England's (and Britain's) endlessly entertaining capital.

❷ **Bath** (p317) Being a Jane Austen character for a day in this elegant city.

❸ **Lake District** (p584) Wandering lonely as a cloud in the idyllic region.

❹ **York** (p496) Exploring medieval walls, Viking sights and the soaring Gothic minster in these historic settings.

❺ Falling in love with the impossibly quaint villages of the **Cotswolds** (p202).

❻ **Oxford** (p189) Getting some higher education among the dreaming spires.

❼ **Cambridge** (p367) Punting along the river.

❽ **Hadrian's Wall** (p636) Seeing wild scenery and ancient engineering at this historic site.

❾ **Stratford-upon-Avon** (p422) Catching a Shakespeare play or visiting the Bard's grave.

❿ **Canterbury** (p153) Marvelling at one of Europe's greatest cathedrals.

0 100 km
0 50 miles
Berwick-upon-Tweed
Kelso
Melrose
Northumberland National Park
Alnwick
Hadrian's Wall
Newcastle-upon-Tyne
Tynemouth
Durham
Penrith
Darlington
Whitby
North York Moors National Park
Scarborough
Yorkshire Dales National Park
Lancaster
Forest of Bowland
York
Leeds
Grimsby
Manchester
Peak District National Park
Sheffield
Chester
Buxton
Chesterfield
Lincoln
Skegness
Boston
The Wash
Holkam
Stoke-on-Trent
Derby
Nottingham
The Fens
King's Lynn
Norwich
Shrewsbury
Leicester
Stamford
The Broads
Birmingham
Ludlow
Cambridge
Worcester
Stratford-upon-Avon
Hereford
Cheltenham
The Cotswolds
ENGLAND
Colchester
Gloucester
Forest of Dean
Oxford
St Albans
Southend-on-Sea
River Thames
London
Bristol
Windsor
Isle of Thanet
Bath
Newbury
Canterbury
South Downs National Park
Dover
Salisbury
Winchester
Rye
Strait of Dover
New Forest National Park
Worthing
Brighton
Bournemouth
Portsmouth
Eastbourne
Lyme Bay
Weymouth
English Channel
NORTH SEA
Bergen (Norway), Gothenburg (Sweden) & Ijmuiden (Netherlands)
Hamburg (Germany)
Ostend
Veurne
Calais
St-Omer
Boulogne-sur-Mer
FRANCE
Lens
Arras
Mers-les-Bains
Abbeville
Dieppe
Amiens
2°W
1°W
0° (Greenwich)
1°E
2°E
3°E

London

POP 8.7 MILLION / ☎020 / AREA 1 569 SQ KM

Includes ➡

Best Places to Eat

➡ Gymkhana (p125)

➡ Dinner by Heston Blumenthal (p128)

➡ Brasserie Zédel (p125)

➡ Gordon Ramsay (p128)

➡ Ledbury (p129)

Best Places to Sleep

➡ Zetter Hotel & Townhouse (p124)

➡ Citizen M (p120)

➡ Clink78 (p123)

➡ Beaumont (p119)

➡ Hoxton Hotel (p120)

Why Go?

Everyone comes to London with preconceptions shaped by a multitude of books, movies, TV shows and songs. Whatever yours are, prepare to have them exploded by this endlessly fascinating, amorphous city. You could spend a lifetime exploring it and still find that the slippery thing's gone and changed on you. One thing though is constant: that great serpent of a river enfolding the city in its sinuous loops, linking London both to the green heart of England and the world. From Roman times people from around the globe have come to London, put down roots and complained about the weather. This is one of the world's most multicultural cities – any given street yields a rich harvest of languages, and those narrow streets are also steeped in fascinating history, magnificent art, imposing architecture and popular culture. When you add an endless reserve of cool to this mix, it's hard not to conclude that London is one of the world's great cities, if not the greatest.

When to Go

London is a place that you can visit any time of the year. That said, different months and seasons boast different charms.

➡ Spring in the city sees daffodils in bloom and blossom in the trees.

➡ In June, the parks are filled with people, there's Trooping the Colour, summer arts festivals, Field Day in Victoria Park, other music events, gay pride and Wimbledon.

➡ Although the days are getting shorter, autumn in London is alive with festivals celebrating literature, the arts and culture.

➡ London in December is all about Christmas lights on Oxford and Regent Sts, and perhaps a whisper of snow.

History

London first came into being as a Celtic village near a ford across the River Thames, but the city only really took off after the Roman conquest in AD 43. The invaders enclosed their 'Londinium' in walls that still find refrain in the shape of the City (with a capital 'C') of London today.

By the end of the 3rd century AD, Londinium was home to some 30,000 people. Internal strife and relentless barbarian attacks wore the Romans down, however, and they abandoned Britain in the 5th century, reducing the settlement to a sparsely populated backwater.

The Saxons moved in next, their 'Lundenwic' prospering and becoming a large, well-organised town. As the city grew in importance, it caught the eye of Danish Vikings,who launched numerous invasions. In 1016 the Saxons, finally beaten down, were forced to accept the Danish leader Knut (Canute) as King of England, after which London replaced Winchester as capital. In 1042, the throne reverted to the Saxon Edward the Confessor, who built Westminster Abbey.

The Norman Conquest of 1066 saw William the Conqueror march into London, where he was crowned king. He built the White Tower (the core of the Tower of London), negotiated taxes with the merchants, and affirmed the city's right to self-government. From then until the late 15th century, London politics were largely taken up by a three-way power struggle between the monarchy, the Church and city guilds. An uneasy political compromise was reached between the factions, and the city expanded rapidly in the 16th century under the House of Tudor.

In a rerun of the disease that wiped out half of London's population between 1348 and 1350, the Great Plague struck in 1665, and by the time the winter cold arrested the epidemic, 100,000 Londoners had perished. The cataclysm was followed by further devastation when the Great Fire of 1666 sent the city skywards. One upshot of the conflagration was a blank canvas for master architect Sir Christopher Wren to build his magnificent churches.

Despite these setbacks, London continued to grow, and by 1700 it was Europe's largest city, with 600,000 people. An influx of foreign workers brought expansion to the east and south, while those who could afford it headed to the more salubrious environs of the north and west. Georgian London saw a surge in artistic creativity, with the likes of Dr Johnson, Handel, Gainsborough and Reynolds enriching the city's culture, while architects fashioned an elegant new metropolis.

In 1837, 18-year-old Victoria began her epic reign, as London became the fulcrum of the British Empire. The Industrial Revolution saw the building of new docks and railways (including the first underground line in 1863), while the Great Exhibition of 1851 showcased London to the world. During the Victorian era, the city's population mushroomed from just over two million to 6.6 million.

Although London suffered a relatively minor bruising during WWI, it was devastated by the Luftwaffe in WWII, when huge swaths of the centre and East End were flattened and 32,000 people were killed. Ugly housing and low-cost developments followed, and pollutants – both residential and industrial – rose steadily into the air. On 6 December 1952, the Great Smog (a lethal combination of fog, smoke and pollution) descended, killing some 4000 people.

Prosperity gradually returned to the city, and creative energy bottled up in the postwar years was suddenly unleashed. In the 'Swinging Sixties', London became the capital of cool in fashion and music – a party followed morosely by the austere 1970s. Since then the city has surfed up and down the waves of global fortunes, hanging on to its position as the world's leading financial centre.

In 2000, the modern metropolis won its first mayor of London, an elected role covering the City and all 32 urban boroughs. Bicycle-riding Boris Johnson, a Tory (Conservative) with a shock of blond hair and an affable persona, was elected in 2008, and retained his post in the 2012 mayoral election.

Triggered by the shooting of a man by police in Tottenham in August 2011, numerous London boroughs were rocked by riots characterised by looting and arson. Analysts still debate the causes of the disorder, ascribing any number of factors from single-parent families to gang culture, unemployment and criminal opportunism.

Both the Olympics and the Queen's Diamond Jubilee concocted a splendid display of pageantry for London in 2012. New overground train lines opened, a cable car was flung across the Thames and a once rundown and polluted area of East London was regenerated for the Olympic Park. The games themselves were a universally applauded success, kicked off by a stupendous Opening Ceremony orchestrated by Danny Boyle.

London Highlights

1 Regent's Park (p100)
Watching the world pass by in one of London's loveliest parks.

2 British Museum (p102)
Sifting through the booty of an empire at this fine museum.

3 Tower of London (p83)
Exploring the famous castle where several royals met their deaths by guillotine.

4 Westminster Abbey (p70)
Enjoying the awe-inspiring architecture at this holy spot.

5 Lamb & Flag (p134)
Raising a glass while overlooking the Thames from here or another riverside pub.

6 Shoreditch bar hop (p133)

Meeting locals on a cruise around trendy Shoreditch.

❼ **St Paul's Cathedral** (p85) Reaching for the heavens at the top of the dome.

❽ **Tate Modern** (p90) Embarking on a tour of modern and contemporary art.

❾ **Natural History Museum** (p94) Revelling in the astounding displays and gardens set in 5.7 hectares.

❿ **Shakespeare's Globe** (p140) Getting your drama fix at a Shakespearean outdoor theatre.

Sights

The city's main geographical feature is the murky Thames, which snakes around, but roughly divides the city into north and south. The old City of London is the capital's financial district, covering roughly a square mile bordered by the river and the many gates of the ancient (long-gone) city walls: Newgate, Moorgate etc. The areas east of the City are collectively known as the East End. The West End, on the City's other flank, is effectively the centre of London gravity. It actually falls within the City of Westminster, one of London's 32 boroughs and long the centre of government and royalty.

Surrounding these central areas are dozens of former villages (Camden Town, Islington, Clapham etc), each with its own High St, long ago swallowed by London's sprawl.

When the sun shines, make like a Londoner and head to the parks.

Westminster & St James's

Purposefully positioned outside the old City (London's fiercely independent burghers preferred to keep the monarch and parliament at arm's length), Westminster has been the centre of the nation's political power for nearly a millennium. The area's many landmarks combine to form an awesome display of authority, pomp and gravitas. St James's is an aristocratic enclave of palaces, famous hotels, historic shops and elegant edifices, with some 150 historically noteworthy buildings in its 36 hectares.

★Westminster Abbey CHURCH

(Map p72; 020-7222 5152; www.westminster-abbey.org; 20 Dean's Yard, SW1; adult/child £20/9, verger tours £5, cloister & gardens free; 9.30am-4.30pm Mon, Tue, Thu & Fri, to 7pm Wed, to 2.30pm Sat; Westminster) A splendid mixture of architectural styles, Westminster Abbey is considered the finest example of Early English Gothic (1190–1300). It's not merely a beautiful place of worship – the Abbey also serves up the country's history cold on slabs of stone. For centuries, the country's greatest have been interred here, including 17 monarchs from Henry III (died 1272) to George II (1760). Never a cathedral (the seat of a bishop), Westminster Abbey is what is called a 'royal peculiar', administered by the Crown.

Every monarch since William the Conqueror has been crowned here, with the exception of a couple of unlucky Eds who were either murdered (Edward V) or abdicated (Edward VIII) before the magic moment.

At the heart of the Abbey is the beautifully tiled **sanctuary** (or sacrarium), a stage for coronations, royal weddings and funerals. George Gilbert Scott designed the ornate high altar in 1873. In front of the altar is the **Cosmati marble pavement** dating to 1268. It has intricate designs of small pieces of marble inlaid into plain marble, which predicts the end of the world in AD 19,693! At the entrance to the lovely **Chapel of St John the Baptist** is a sublime alabaster Virgin and Child bathed in candlelight.

The most sacred spot in the Abbey, the **shrine of St Edward the Confessor**, lies behind the high altar; access is generally restricted to protect the 13th-century flooring. St Edward was the founder of the Abbey and the original building was consecrated a few weeks before his death. His tomb was slightly altered after the original was destroyed during the Reformation but still contains Edward's remains – the only complete saint's body in Britain. Ninety-minute **verger-led tours** of the Abbey include a visit to the shrine.

The **Quire**, a sublime structure of gold, blue and red Victorian Gothic by Edward Blore, dates back to the mid-19th century. It sits where the original choir for the monks' worship would have been but bears no resemblance to the original. Nowadays, the Quire is still used for singing, but its regular occupants are the Westminster Choir – 22 boys and 12 'lay vicars' (men) who sing the daily services.

Henry III began work on the new building in 1245 but didn't complete it; the Gothic nave was finished under Richard II in 1388. Henry VII's magnificent Perpendicular Gothic-style **Lady Chapel** was consecrated in 1519 after 16 years of construction. The vestibule of the Lady Chapel is the usual place for the rather ordinary-looking **Coronation Chair**, upon which every monarch since the early 14th century has been crowned (apart from joint-monarch Mary II, who had her own chair fashioned for her coronation, which is now in the **Westminster Abbey Museum** (Map p72; 10.30am-4pm).

Apart from the royal graves, keep an eye out for the many famous commoners interred here, especially in **Poets' Corner**, where you'll find the resting places of Chaucer, Dickens, Hardy, Tennyson, Dr Johnson and Kipling, as well as memorials to the other greats (Shakespeare, Jane Austen, Brontë

LONDON IN...

Two Days

Start in **Trafalgar Sq** and see at least the outside of all the big-ticket sights – **London Eye**, **Houses of Parliament**, **Westminster Abbey**, **St James's Park and Palace**, **Buckingham Palace**, **Green Park**, **Hyde Park** and **Kensington Gardens** – and then motor around the **Tate Modern** until you get booted out. In the evening, explore **Soho**. On day two, race around the **British Museum**, then head to the **City**. Start with our **walking tour** and finish in the **Tower of London**. In the evening, head to **Clerkenwell** for international eats, then **Hoxton** and **Shoreditch** for hip bars.

Four Days

Take the two-day itinerary but stretch it to a comfortable pace, spending extra time in the Tate Modern, British Museum and Tower of London. Stop at the **National Gallery** while you're in Trafalgar Sq and explore inside Westminster Abbey and **St Paul's Cathedral**. On your extra evenings, check out **Camden** and **Islington** or enjoy a no-expenses-spared dinner in **Kensington** or **Knightsbridge**.

One Week

Above, and add a day each for **Greenwich**, **Kew Gardens** and **Hampton Court Palace**.

etc). Nearby you'll find the graves of Handel and Sir Isaac Newton.

The octagonal **Chapter House** dates from the 1250s and was where the monks would meet for daily prayer before Henry VIII's suppression of the monasteries some three centuries later. To the right of the entrance to Chapter House is what is claimed to be the oldest door in Britain – it's been there for 950 years. Used as a treasury and 'Royal Wardrobe', the crypt-like **Pyx Chamber** dates from about 1070. Next door in the vaulted undercroft, the museum exhibits the death masks of generations of royalty, wax effigies representing Charles II and William III (who is on a stool to make him as tall as his wife, Mary II), armour and stained glass. Highlights are the graffiti-inscribed Mary Chair (used for the coronation of Mary II) and the Westminster Retable, England's oldest altarpiece, from the 13th century.

Parts of the Abbey complex are free to visitors. This includes the **Cloister** and the 900-year-old **College Garden** (Map p72; ⏲10am-6pm Tue-Thu Apr-Sep, to 4pm Oct-Mar). Adjacent to the abbey is **St Margaret's Church**, the House of Commons' place of worship since 1614, where windows commemorate churchgoers Caxton and Milton, and Sir Walter Raleigh is buried by the altar.

In the works are the **Queen's Diamond Jubilee Galleries**, a new museum and gallery space located in the medieval triforium, and due to open in 2018.

★ **Houses of Parliament** HISTORIC BUILDING

(Map p72; www.parliament.uk; Parliament Sq, SW1; ⊖Westminster) FREE A visit here is a journey to the heart of UK democracy. Officially called the Palace of Westminster, the Houses of Parliament's oldest part is 11th-century **Westminster Hall**, one of only a few sections that survived a catastrophic fire in 1834. Its roof, added between 1394 and 1401, is the earliest-known example of a hammerbeam roof. The rest is mostly a neo-Gothic confection built by Charles Barry and Augustus Pugin (1840–58).

The palace's most famous feature is its clock tower, Elizabeth Tower, aka **Big Ben** (Map p72; ⊖Westminster).

Ben is actually the 13.5-ton bell, named after Benjamin Hall, who was Commissioner of Works when the tower was completed in 1858.

At the business end, parliament is split into two houses. The green-hued **House of Commons** (Map p72; www.parliament.uk/business/commons; ⏲2.30-10pm Mon & Tue, 11.30am-7.30pm Wed, 10.30am-6.30pm Thu, 9.30am-3pm Fri) is the lower house, where the 650 elected Members of Parliament sit. Traditionally the home of hereditary blue bloods, the scarlet-decorated **House of Lords** (Map p72; www.parliament.uk/business/lords; Parliament Sq, SW1; ⏲2.30-10pm Mon & Tue, 3-10pm Wed, 11am-7.30pm Thu, 10am-close of session Fri; ⊖Westminster), with 763 members, now has peers appointed through various means. Both houses debate and vote on legislation, which is then presented to the Queen for her Royal

Westminster & St James's

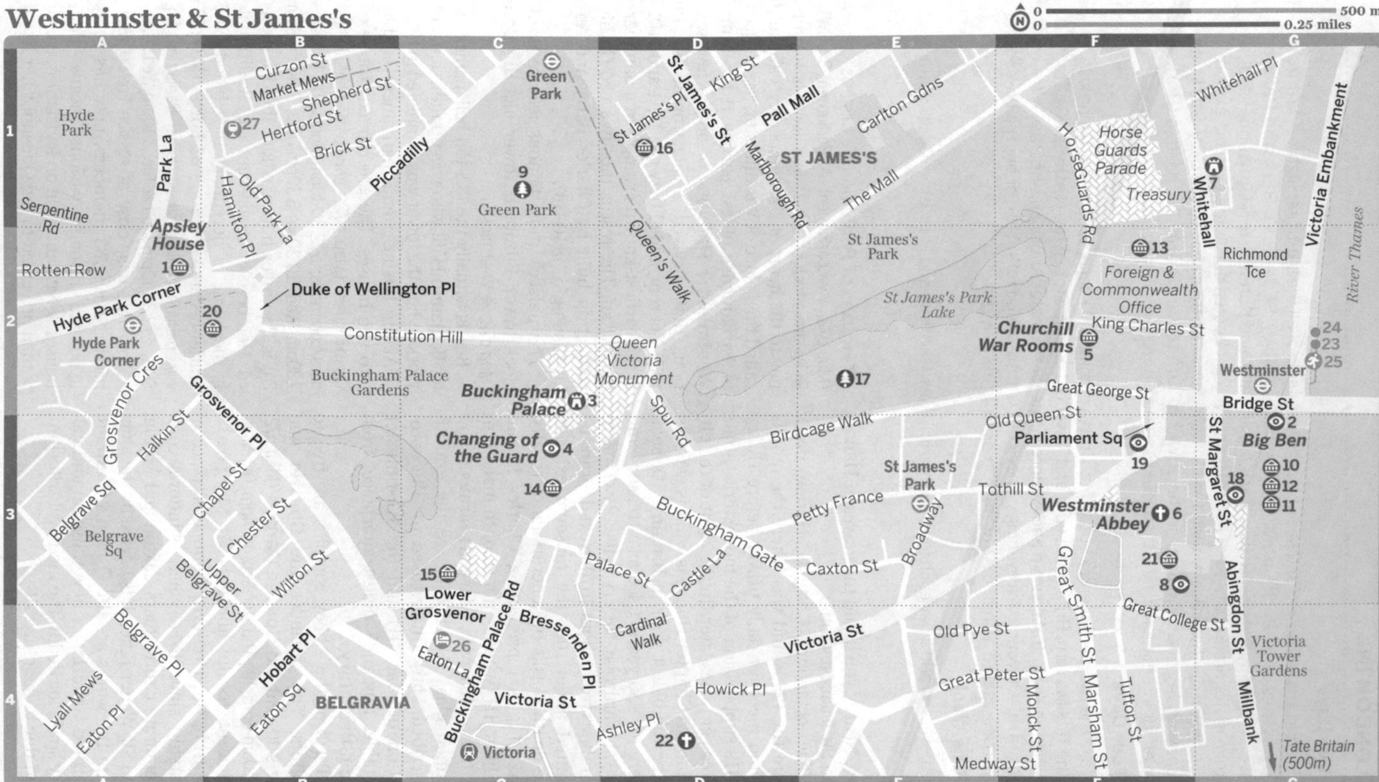

Westminster & St James's

Top Sights

1 Apsley House....A2
2 Big Ben....G3
3 Buckingham Palace....C2
4 Changing of the Guard....C3
5 Churchill War Rooms....F2
6 Westminster Abbey....F3

Sights

7 Banqueting House....G1
8 College Garden....F3
9 Green Park....C1
10 House of Commons....G3
11 House of Lords....G3
12 Houses of Parliament....G3
13 No 10 Downing Street....F2
14 Queen's Gallery....C3
15 Royal Mews....C3
16 Spencer House....D1
17 St James's Park....E2
18 St Stephen's Entrance....G3
19 Supreme Court....F3
20 Wellington Arch....B2
21 Westminster Abbey Museum....F3
22 Westminster Cathedral....D4

Activities, Courses & Tours

23 City Cruises....G2
Houses of Parliament Tours....(see 12)
24 Thames River Boats....G2
25 Westminster Passenger Services Association....G2

Sleeping

26 Goring....C4

Drinking & Nightlife

27 Galvin at Windows....B1

Assent (in practice, this is a formality; the last time Royal Assent was denied was in 1708). At the annual State Opening of Parliament, which takes place in May, the Queen takes her throne in the House of Lords, having arrived in the gold-trimmed Irish State Coach from Buckingham Palace (her crown travels alone in Queen Alexandra's State Coach). It's well worth lining the route for a gawk at the crown jewels sparkling in the sun.

On Saturdays year-round and on most weekdays during parliamentary recesses including Easter, summer and Christmas, visitors can join a 90-minute **guided tour** (Map p72; 020-7219 4114; www.parliament.uk/visiting/visiting-and-tours; adult/child £25.50/11) of both chambers, Westminster Hall and other historic buildings conducted by qualified Blue Badge Tourist Guides in seven languages. Afternoon tea in the Terrace Pavilion overlooking the River Thames is a popular add-on to the tours. Tour schedules change with every recess and are occasionally subject to variation or cancellation due to the State Opening of Parliament and other parliamentary business, so check ahead and book. UK residents can approach their MPs to arrange a free tour and to climb the Elizabeth Tower.

The public entrance to the Houses of Parliament is **St Stephen's Entrance** (Map p72; www.parliament.uk; Parliament Sq, SW1; Westminster), housed within St Stephen's Tower.

★ Buckingham Palace — PALACE

(Map p72; 020-7766 7300; www.royalcollection.org.uk; Buckingham Palace Rd, SW1; adult/child/child under 5 £21.50/12.30/free; 9.30am-7.30pm late Jul–Aug, to 6.30pm Sep; St James's Park, Victoria or Green Park) Built in 1703 for the Duke of Buckingham, Buckingham Palace replaced St James's Palace as the monarch's official London residence in 1837. When she's not delivering her trademark wave to far-flung parts of the Commonwealth, Queen Elizabeth II divides her time between here, Windsor and, in summer, Balmoral. If she's at home, the yellow, red and blue standard is flying. Some 19 lavishly furnished **State Rooms** are open to visitors when Her Royal Highness takes her holidays from late July to September.

Hung with artworks by the likes of Rembrandt, Van Dyck, Canaletto, Poussin and Vermeer, the State Rooms are open for two-hour tours that include the **Throne Room**, with his-and-hers pink chairs initialed 'ER' and 'P'. Access is by timed tickets with admission every 15 minutes (audio guide included).

From 2016, admission included access to *Fashioning a Reign: 90 Years of Style from The Queen's Wardrobe*, an exhibition affording a glimpse at royal couture during the Queen's reign.

Admission also includes access to part of the garden at Buckingham Palace as you exit, although you will have to join the three-hour State Rooms and Garden Highlights Tour (adult/child £27.50/16.40) to see the wisteria-clad Summer House and other famous features, and get an idea of the garden's full 16-hectare size.

Your ticket to Buckingham Palace is good for a return trip if bought direct from the palace ticket office (ask to have it stamped). You can even make your ticket purchase a

WILL RODRIGUES / SHUTTERSTOCK ©

1. Tower of London (p83) 2. Windsor Castle (p225) 3. Hampton Court Palace (p113) 4. Buckingham Palace (p73)

KIRILL 13 / SHUTTERSTOCK ©

KIEV.VICTOR / SHUTTERSTOCK ©

STEPHANIE ROLLOT / SHUTTERSTOCK ©

Royal London

Along with Stonehenge and Big Ben, the current monarch, Queen Elizabeth II, is one of the most potent symbols of England. Pretty much anything connected to the country's royal heritage is a guaranteed attraction – especially the capital's fine collection of palaces and castles.

The Tower of London

The Tower of London has a 1000-year-old history and foundations that date back to Roman times. Over the centuries it's been a royal residence, treasury, mint, prison and arsenal. Today it's home to the spectacular Crown Jewels, as well as red-coated Beefeaters and ravens attributed with mythical power.

Windsor Castle

Although not actually in London, Windsor Castle is near enough to visit on a day-trip. This is the largest and oldest occupied fortress in the world, an astounding edifice of defensive walls, towers and battlements, used for state occasions and as the Queen's weekend retreat.

Hampton Court Palace

Hampton Court Palace is England's largest and grandest Tudor structure, used by King Henry VIII as a riverside hideaway. After admiring the grand interior, you can relax in the extensive gardens, but don't get lost in the 300-year-old maze.

Buckingham Palace

Buckingham Palace has been the monarch's London residence since 1837, and the current Queen divides her time between here, Windsor Castle and Balmoral in Scotland. If she's at home, the 'royal standard' flag flies on the roof. If she's out, you can take a tour to see inside. Either way, don't miss the famous Changing of the Guard.

LOCAL KNOWLEDGE

LONDON: TOP TIPS

➡ London is huge – work by neighbourhood to avoid wasting time (and money) on transport.

➡ An Oyster Card is a cheaper and convenient way to use public transport, but you can also pay by credit or debit card provided it has a contactless function indicated by a symbol of four wavy lines.

➡ Walk – it's cheaper than transport and the best way to discover central London.

➡ For West End performances at bargain prices, opt for standby tickets (which you buy on the day at the venue) or last-minute ticket-booth tickets on Leicester Sq.

➡ To treat yourself to fine dining without breaking the bank, opt for lunch rather than dinner, or try for pre- or post-theatre dinner deals.

donation and gain free access for a whole year (ask at the ticket office).

At 11.30am daily from April to July (on alternate days, weather permitting, for the rest of the year), the old guard (Foot Guards of the Household Regiment) comes off duty to be replaced by the new guard on the forecourt of Buckingham Palace, an event known as the **Changing of the Guard**. Highly popular, the show lasts about 40 minutes (brace for crowds).

Originally designed by John Nash as a conservatory, the **Queen's Gallery** (Map p72; Southern wing, Buckingham Palace, Buckingham Gate, SW1; adult/child £10.30/5.30, with Royal Mews £17.70/9.70; ⏲10am-5.30pm; ⊖St James's Park, Victoria or Green Park) showcases some of the palace's treasures on a rotating basis, through temporary exhibitions. Entrance to the gallery is through Buckingham Gate.

Indulge your Cinderella fantasies while inspecting the exquisite state coaches in the **Royal Mews** (Map p72; www.royalcollection.org.uk; Buckingham Palace Rd, SW1; adult/child £9.30/5.50, with Queen's Gallery £17.70/9.70; ⏲10am-5pm daily Apr-Oct, to 4pm Mon-Sat Nov-March; ⊖Victoria), a working stable looking after the royals' immaculately groomed horses and the opulent vehicles they use for getting from A to B. Highlights include the magnificent Gold State Coach of 1762 and the 1911 Glass Coach.

A Royal Day Out (adult/child £35.60/20) is a combined ticket including the State Rooms, Queen's Gallery and Royal Mews.

Supreme Court — LANDMARK

(Map p72; ☎020-7960 1500, 020-7960 1900; www.supremecourt.uk; Parliament Sq, SW1; ⏲9.30am-4.30pm Mon-Fri; ⊖Westminster) **FREE** The Supreme Court, the highest court in the UK, was the Appellate Committee of the House of Lords until 2009. It is now housed in the neo-Gothic Middlesex Guildhall (1913) on Parliament Sq. There's a permanent exhibition looking at the work and history of the UK's highest court as well as the building's history on the lower-ground floor. The self-guided tour booklet is £1; tours are also available on Fridays (£5; 11am, 2pm and 3pm).

St James's Park — PARK

(Map p72; www.royalparks.org.uk; The Mall, SW1; deckchairs per hr/day £1.50/7; ⏲5am-midnight, deckchairs daylight Mar-Oct; ⊖St James's Park or Green Park) At just 23 hectares, St James's is one of the smallest but best groomed of London's royal parks. It has brilliant views of the London Eye, Westminster, St James's Palace, Carlton Tce and the Horse Guards Parade; the photo-perfect sight of Buckingham Palace from the footbridge spanning the central lake is the best you'll find.

The lake brims with ducks, geese, swans and general fowl, and the rocks on its southern side serve as a rest stop for a half-dozen pelicans (fed at 2.30pm daily).

Green Park — PARK

(Map p72; www.royalparks.org.uk; ⏲24hr; ⊖Green Park) Less manicured than adjoining St James's, 19-hectare Green Park has huge oaks and hilly meadows, and it's never as crowded as its neighbour. It was once a duelling ground and, like Hyde Park, served as a vegetable garden during WWII.

Westminster Cathedral — CHURCH

(Map p72; www.westminstercathedral.org.uk; Victoria St, SW1; tower adult/child/family £6/3/12; ⏲7am-7pm church, 9.30am-5pm Mon-Fri, to 6pm Sat & Sun Bell Tower & exhibition; ⊖Victoria) With its distinctive candy-striped red-brick and white-stone tower features, John Francis Bentley's 19th-century cathedral, the mother church of Roman Catholicism in England and Wales, is a splendid example of neo-

Byzantine architecture. Although construction started here in 1896 and worshippers began attending services seven years later, the church ran out of money and the gaunt interior remains largely unfinished, although some radiant mosaics dazzle from the gloom.

Banqueting House PALACE
(Map p72; ☎020-3166 6000; www.hrp.org.uk/banquetinghouse; Whitehall, SW1; adult/child £6.60/free; ⏰10am-5pm; ⊖Westminster) After the Holbein Gate was demolished in 1759, this is the sole surviving part of the Tudor Whitehall Palace (1532) that once stretched most of the way down Whitehall before going skywards in a 1698 conflagration. Designed by Inigo Jones in 1622 and controversially refaced in Portland stone in the 19th century, Banqueting House was England's first purely Renaissance building and resembled no other structure in the country at the time. The English apparently loathed it for over a century.

No 10 Downing Street HISTORIC BUILDING
(Map p72; www.number10.gov.uk; 10 Downing St, SW1; ⊖Westminster) The official office of British leaders since 1732, when George II presented No 10 to Robert Walpole, this has also been the prime minister's London residence since refurbishment in 1902. For such a famous address, No 10 is a small-looking Georgian building on a plain-looking street, hardly warranting comparison with the White House, for example. Yet it is actually three houses joined into one and boasts roughly 100 rooms plus a 2000-sq-metre garden with a lovely L-shaped lawn.

★**Churchill War Rooms** MUSEUM
(Map p72; www.iwm.org.uk; Clive Steps, King Charles St, SW1; adult/child £17.25/8.60; ⏰9.30am-6pm, last entry 5pm; ⊖Westminster) Winston Churchill coordinated the Allied resistance against Nazi Germany on a Bakelite telephone from this underground military HQ during WWII. The Cabinet War Rooms remain much as they were when the lights were flicked off in 1945, capturing the drama and dogged spirit of the time, while the multimedia **Churchill Museum** affords intriguing insights into the resolute, cigar-smoking wartime leader.

Spencer House HISTORIC BUILDING
(Map p72; ☎020-7514 1958; www.spencerhouse.co.uk; 27 St James's Pl, SW1; adult/child £13/11; ⏰10am-4.45pm Sun Feb-Jul & Sep-Dec; ⊖Green Park) Just outside Green Park is Spencer House, completed in the Palladian style in 1766 for the first Earl Spencer, an ancestor of Princess Diana. The Spencers moved out in 1927 and their grand family home was used as an office, until Lord Rothschild stepped in and returned it to its former glory in 1987 with an £18 million restoration.

★**Apsley House** HISTORIC BUILDING
(Map p72; www.english-heritage.org.uk/visit/places/apsley-house; 149 Piccadilly, Hyde Park Corner, W1; adult/child £8.80/5.20, with Wellington Arch £10.50/6.30; ⏰11am-5pm Wed-Sun Apr-Oct, 10am-5pm Sat & Sun Nov-Mar; ⊖Hyde Park Corner) This stunning house, containing exhibits about the Duke of Wellington, victor of Waterloo against Napoleon Bonaparte, was once the first building to appear when entering London from the west and was therefore known as 'No 1 London'. Wellington memorabilia, including the duke's death mask, fills the basement **gallery**, while an astonishing collection of china and silver, and paintings by Velasquez, Rubens, Van Dyck, Brueghel, Murillo and Goya awaits in the 1st-floor Waterloo Gallery.

Wellington Arch MUSEUM
(Map p72; www.english-heritage.org.uk/visit/places/wellington-arch; Hyde Park Corner, W1; adult/child £4.70/2.80, with Apsley House £10.50/6.30; ⏰10am-6pm Apr-Sep, to 4pm Nov-Mar; ⊖Hyde Park Corner) Dominating the green space throttled by the Hyde Park Corner roundabout, this imposing neoclassical 1826 arch originally faced the Hyde Park Screen, but was shunted here in 1882 for road widening. Once a police station, it is now a gallery with temporary exhibitions and a permanent display about the history of the arch. The open-air balconies (accessible by lift) afford unforgettable views of Hyde Park, Buckingham Palace and the Mall.

West End

A strident mix of culture and consumerism, but more a concept than a fixed geographical area, the West End is synonymous with roof-raising musicals, bright lights, outstanding restaurants and bag-laden shoppers. It casts its net around Piccadilly Circus and Trafalgar Sq to the south, Regent St to the west, Oxford St to the north, Covent Garden to the east and the Strand to the southeast.

Named after the elaborate collars (picadils) that were the sartorial staple of a local 17th-century tailor, Piccadilly became the fashionable haunt of the well-heeled (and collared), and still boasts establishment icons such as the Ritz hotel and the Fortnum &

West End

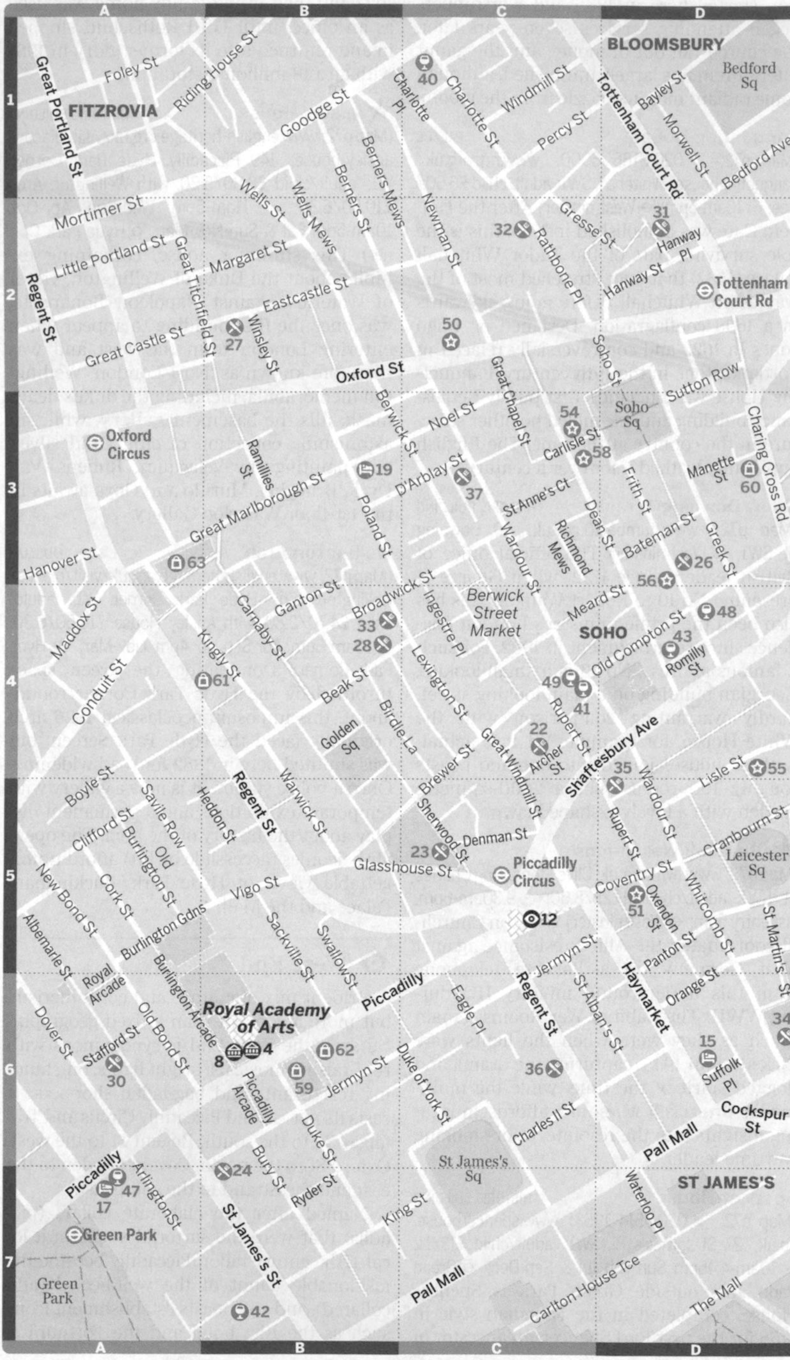
A
B
C
D
1
2
3
4
5
6
7
FITZROVIA
BLOOMSBURY
SOHO
ST JAMES'S
Great Portland St
Foley St
Riding House St
Goodge St
Charlotte Pl
Charlotte St
Windmill St
Tottenham Court Rd
Bayley St
Bedford Sq
Morwell St
Bedford Ave
Percy St
Mortimer St
Wells St
Wells Mews
Berners St
Berners Mews
Newman St
Rathbone Pl
Gresse St
Hanway Pl
Hanway St
Tottenham Court Rd
Little Portland St
Great Titchfield St
Margaret St
Regent St
Eastcastle St
Great Castle St
Winsley St
Oxford St
Great Chapel St
Soho St
Sutton Row
Soho Sq
Charing Cross Rd
Oxford Circus
Ramillies St
Berwick St
Noel St
Carlisle St
D'Arblay St
Great Marlborough St
Poland St
Manette St
St Anne's Ct
Frith St
Dean St
Richmond Mews
Wardour St
Bateman St
Greek St
Hanover St
Broadwick St
Ganton St
Carnaby St
Ingestre Pl
Berwick Street Market
Meard St
Old Compton St
Romilly St
Maddox St
Kingly St
Beak St
Lexington St
Conduit St
Golden Sq
Birdle La
Rupert St
Archer St
Shaftesbury Ave
Great Windmill St
Brewer St
Lisle St
Boyle St
Savile Row
Heddon St
Warwick St
Sherwood St
Clifford St
Old Burlington St
Denman St
Cranbourn St
Leicester Sq
New Bond St
Cork St
Vigo St
Glasshouse St
Piccadilly Circus
Coventry St
Oxendon St
Whitcomb St
St Martin's St
Albemarle St
Burlington Gdns
Sackville St
Swallow St
Jermyn St
Panton St
Royal Arcade
Burlington Arcade
Piccadilly
Eagle Pl
Haymarket
Orange St
Dover St
Stafford St
Old Bond St
Royal Academy of Arts
St Alban's St
Piccadilly Arcade
Duke of York St
Suffolk Pl
Cockspur St
Charles II St
Duke St
Pall Mall
Arlington St
Bury St
St James's Sq
Ryder St
Waterloo Pl
Green Park
St James's St
King St
Green Park
Pall Mall
Carlton House Tce
The Mall
40
31
32
27
50
54
58
19
37
60
63
26
56
48
33
28
43
61
49
41
22
35
55
23
12
51
34
8
4
62
15
30
59
36
24
47
17
42

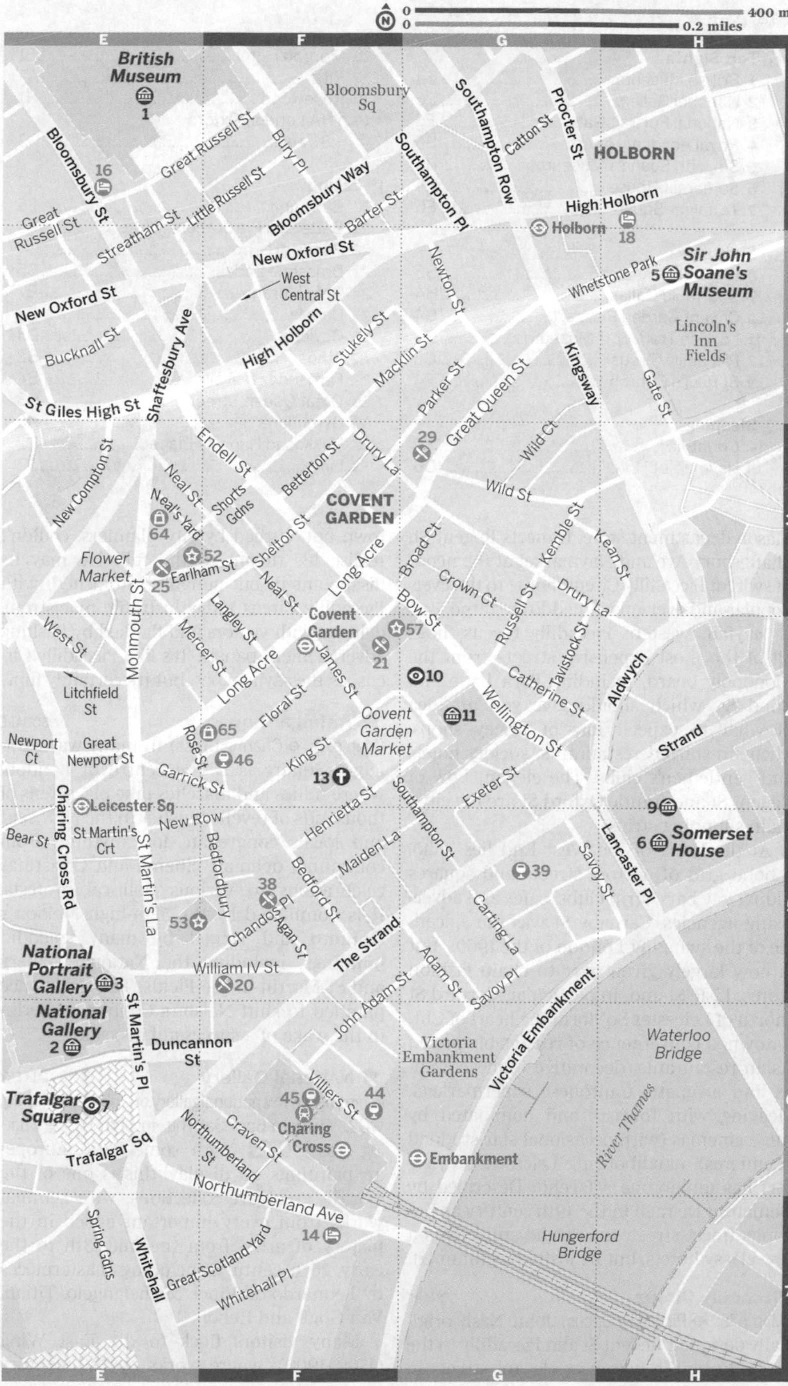

0
400 m
0
0.2 miles
E
F
G
H
1
2
3
4
5
6
7
British Museum
1
Bloomsbury Sq
Southampton Row
Procter St
Catton St
HOLBORN
Great Russell St
Bury Pl
Bloomsbury St
16
Little Russell St
Bloomsbury Way
Southampton Pl
High Holborn
Holborn
18
Great Russell St
Streatham St
Barter St
New Oxford St
Newton St
Sir John Soane's Museum
5
Whetstone Park
West Central St
New Oxford St
Lincoln's Inn Fields
Bucknall St
Shaftesbury Ave
High Holborn
Stukely St
Macklin St
Kingsway
Gate St
St Giles High St
Parker St
Great Queen St
Endell St
Drury La
29
Wild Ct
New Compton St
Neal St
Betterton St
Wild St
Shorts Gdns
Neal's Yard
COVENT GARDEN
Kemble St
64
Shelton St
Kean St
Flower Market
52
Earlham St
Long Acre
Broad Ct
25
Crown Ct
Drury La
Monmouth St
Neal St
Covent Garden
Bow St
57
Russell St
Langley St
Tavistock St
West St
Mercer St
21
James St
Aldwych
Long Acre
10
Catherine St
Litchfield St
Floral St
11
Wellington St
Covent Garden Market
65
Newport Ct
Great Newport St
Rose St
46
King St
Strand
Garrick St
13
Exeter St
Charing Cross Rd
Leicester Sq
Henrietta St
9
Bear St
St Martin's Crt
New Row
Bedfordbury
Southampton St
Lancaster Pl
6
Somerset House
St Martin's La
Maiden La
39
Savoy St
38
Bedford St
Chandos Pl
53
Agar St
Carting La
The Strand
National Portrait Gallery
3
William IV St
Adam St
Savoy Pl
St Martin's Pl
20
John Adam St
Victoria Embankment
National Gallery
2
Duncannon St
Victoria Embankment Gardens
Waterloo Bridge
Trafalgar Square
7
45
Villiers St
44
River Thames
Northumberland St
Craven St
Charing Cross
Embankment
Trafalgar Sq
Northumberland Ave
Spring Gdns
14
Hungerford Bridge
Whitehall
Great Scotland Yard
Whitehall Pl
LONDON

West End

Top Sights
1 British Museum ... E1
2 National Gallery ... E6
3 National Portrait Gallery ... E5
4 Royal Academy of Arts ... B6
5 Sir John Soane's Museum ... H2
6 Somerset House ... H5
7 Trafalgar Square ... E6

Sights
8 Burlington Arcade ... B6
9 Courtauld Gallery ... H4
10 Covent Garden Piazza ... G4
11 London Transport Museum ... G4
12 Piccadilly Circus ... C5
13 St Paul's Church ... F4

Sleeping
14 Corinthia ... F7
15 Haymarket Hotel ... D6
16 Morgan Hotel ... E1
17 Ritz ... A7
18 Rosewood ... H1
19 YHA London Oxford Street ... B3

Eating
20 Barrafina ... F5
21 Battersea Pie Station ... F4
22 Bocca di Lupo ... C4
23 Brasserie Zédel ... C5
24 Cafe Murano ... B7
25 Canela ... E3
26 Ceviche ... D3
27 Ethos ... B2
28 Fernandez & Wells ... B4
29 Great Queen Street ... G3
30 Gymkhana ... A6
31 Hakkasan Hanway Place ... D2
32 Lima ... C2

Mason department store. It meets Regent St, Shaftesbury Ave and Haymarket at the neon-lit swirl of Piccadilly Circus, home to the ever-popular and ever-misnamed Eros statue.

Mayfair, west of Piccadilly Circus, hogs all of the most expensive streets from the Monopoly board, including Park Lane and Bond St, which should give you an idea of what to expect: lots of pricey shops, Michelin-starred restaurants, society hotels and gentlemen's clubs. The elegant bow of Regent St and frantic Oxford St are the city's main shopping strips.

At the heart of the West End lies Soho, a boho grid of narrow streets and squares hiding gay bars, strip clubs, cafes and advertising agencies. Carnaby St was the epicentre of the swinging London of the 1960s, but is now largely given over to chain fashion stores. Lisle St and, in particular, Gerrard St (north of Leicester Sq) form the heart of Chinatown, a convergence of reasonably priced Asian restaurants, decorative Chinese arches and aromatic Cantonese supermarkets. Heaving with tourists and dominated by huge cinemas (with occasional star-studded premieres), neighbouring Leicester Sq (lester) has undergone a facelift. Described by Benjamin Disraeli in the 19th century as Europe's finest street, the Strand still boasts a few classy hotels, but its lustre has dimmed.

Piccadilly Circus SQUARE
(Map p78; Piccadilly Circus) John Nash originally designed Regent St and Piccadilly in the 1820s to be the two most elegant streets in town but, curbed by city planners, couldn't realise his dream to the full. He may be disappointed, but suitably astonished, with Piccadilly Circus today: a traffic maelstrom, deluged with visitors and flanked by flashing advertisement panels. 'It's like Piccadilly Circus', as the saying goes, but it's certainly fun.

★Trafalgar Square SQUARE
(Map p78; Charing Cross) In many ways Trafalgar Square is is the centre of London, where rallies and marches take place, tens of thousands of revellers usher in the New Year and locals congregate for anything from communal open-air cinema and Christmas celebrations to various political protests. It is dominated by the 52m-high **Nelson's Column** and ringed by many splendid buildings, including the National Gallery and St Martin-in-the-Fields. The Nazis once planned to shift Nelson's Column to Berlin in the wake of a successful invasion.

★National Gallery GALLERY
(Map p78; www.nationalgallery.org.uk; Trafalgar Sq, WC2; 10am-6pm Sat-Thu, to 9pm Fri; Charing Cross) FREE With some 2300 European paintings on display, this is one of the world's great art collections, with seminal works from every important epoch in the history of art – from the mid-13th to the early 20th century, including masterpieces by Leonardo da Vinci, Michelangelo, Titian, Van Gogh and Renoir.

Many visitors flock to the East Wing (1700–1900), where works by 18th-century

British artists such as Gainsborough, Constable and Turner, and seminal Impressionist and post-Impressionist masterpieces by Van Gogh, Renoir and Monet await.

★National Portrait Gallery GALLERY

(Map p78; www.npg.org.uk; St Martin's Pl, WC2; 10am-6pm Sat-Wed, to 9pm Thu & Fri; ; Charing Cross or Leicester Sq) FREE What makes the National Portrait Gallery so compelling is its familiarity; in many cases you'll have heard of the subject (royals, scientists, politicians, celebrities) or the artist (Andy Warhol, Annie Leibovitz, Lucian Freud). Highlights include the famous 'Chandos portrait' of William Shakespeare, the first artwork the gallery acquired (in 1856) and believed to be the only likeness made during the playwright's lifetime, and a touching sketch of novelist Jane Austen by her sister.

★Royal Academy of Arts GALLERY

(Map p78; www.royalacademy.org.uk; Burlington House, Piccadilly, W1; adult/child £10/6, prices vary for exhibitions; 10am-6pm Sat-Thu, to 10pm Fri; Green Park) Britain's oldest society devoted to fine arts was founded in 1768, moving to Burlington House exactly a century later. The collection contains drawings, paintings, architectural designs, photographs and sculptures by past and present Academicians such as Joshua Reynolds, John Constable, Thomas Gainsborough, JMW Turner, David Hockney and Norman Foster.

Covent Garden Piazza SQUARE

(Map p78; Covent Garden) London's first planned square is now mostly the preserve of visitors, who flock here to shop among the quaint old arcades, browse through eclectic market stalls and shops, cast coins at street performers pretending to be statues and traipse through the fun London Transport Museum. On the square's west side rises handsome **St Paul's Church** (www.actorschurch.org; Bedford St, WC2; 8.30am-5pm Mon-Fri, varies Sat, 9am-1pm Sun; Covent Garden), built in 1633.

London Transport Museum MUSEUM

(Map p78; www.ltmuseum.co.uk; Covent Garden Piazza, WC2; adult/child £17/free; 10am-6pm Sat-Thu, 11am-6pm Fri; Covent Garden) This entertaining and informative museum looks at how London developed as a result of better transport and contains everything from horse-drawn omnibuses, early taxis, underground trains you can drive yourself, a forward look at Crossrail (a high-frequency rail service linking Reading with east London, southeast London and Essex, due to open in 2018), plus everything in between. Check out the museum shop for imaginative souvenirs, including historical tube posters and 'Mind the Gap' socks.

★Sir John Soane's Museum MUSEUM

(Map p78; www.soane.org; 13 Lincoln's Inn Fields, WC2; 10am-5pm Tue-Sat, plus 6-9pm 1st Tue of month; Holborn) FREE This museum is one of the most atmospheric and fascinating

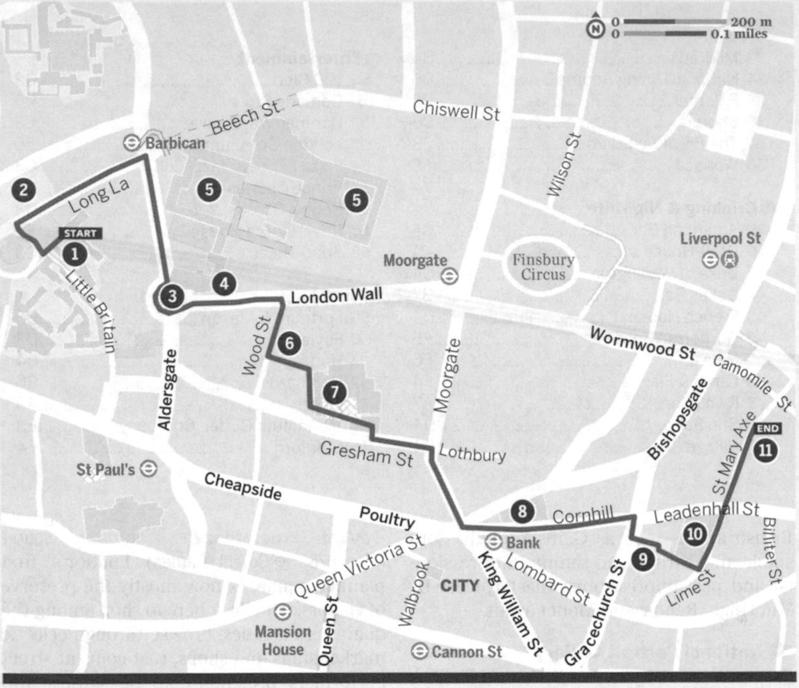

City Walk
A Taste of the City

START ST BARTHOLOMEW-THE-GREAT
END 30 ST MARY AXE (THE GHERKIN)
LENGTH 1.5 MILES; THREE HOURS

The City of London has as much history in its square mile as the rest of London put together; this walk picks out just a few of its highlights.

Start by exploring the wonderful 12th-century **1 St Bartholomew-the-Great** (p87), whose atmospheric interior has been used frequently as a film set. Head through the Tudor gatehouse and turn right towards the colourful Victorian arches of **2 Smithfield Market** (p87), London's last surviving meat market.

Take a right down Long Lane and another at Aldersgate St. Follow the roundabout to the right and nip up the stairs (or take the lift) to the **3 Museum of London** (p86). Explore the museum's excellent galleries or head to the right to the ruins of the **4 Roman city walls** and behind them the distinctive towers of the **5 Barbican** (p142).

Turn right at Wood St to find the remaining **6 tower of St Alban** (1698), all that's left of a Wren-designed church destroyed in WWII bombing in 1940. Turn left into Love Lane and right into Aldermanbury – the impressive 15th-century **7 Guildhall** (p86) is on your left. Crossing its courtyard – note the black outline of the Roman amphitheatre – continue east onto Gresham St, taking a right into Prince's St and emerging onto the busy Bank intersection lined with neoclassical temples to commerce. Behind the Duke of Wellington statue is a metal pyramid detailing the many significant buildings here.

From the **8 Royal Exchange** (p87), follow Cornhill and take a right down Gracechurch St. Turn left into wonderful **9 Leadenhall Market** (p146), roughly where the Roman forum once stood. As you leave the market's far end, **10 Lloyd's of London** (p87) displays its innards for all to see. Once you turn left onto Lime St, **11 30 St Mary Axe** (p87), or 'the Gherkin', looms before you. Built nearly 900 years after St Bartholomew-the-Great, it's tangible testimony to the city's ability to constantly reinvent itself.

in London. The building was the beautiful, bewitching home of architect Sir John Soane (1753–1837), which he left brimming with his vast architectural and archaeological collection, as well as intriguing personal effects and curiosities. The museum represents his exquisite and eccentric tastes, persuasions and proclivities.

★ Somerset House HISTORIC BUILDING
(Map p78; www.somersethouse.org.uk; The Strand, WC2; ⏲ galleries 10am-6pm, Safra Courtyard 7.30am-11pm; ⊖ Charing Cross, Embankment or Temple) Designed by William Chambers in 1775 for royal societies, Somerset House now contains two fabulous galleries. Near the Strand entrance, the **Courtauld Gallery** (Map p78; www.courtauld.ac.uk; Somerset House, The Strand, WC2; adult/child Tue-Sun £7/free, temporary exhibitions an additional £1.50; ⏲ 10am-6pm; ⊖ Charing Cross, Embankment or Temple) displays a wealth of 14th- to 20th-century art, including masterpieces by Rubens, Botticelli, Cézanne, Degas, Renoir, Seurat, Manet, Monet, Leger and others. Downstairs, the Embankment Galleries are devoted to temporary (mostly photographic) exhibitions; prices and hours vary.

Burlington Arcade HISTORIC BUILDING
(Map p78; www.burlington-arcade.co.uk; 51 Piccadilly, W1; ⏲ 9am-7.30pm Mon-Sat, 11am-6pm Sun; ⊖ Green Park) Flanking Burlington House, home to the Royal Academy of Arts, is this delightful arcade, built in 1819. Today it is a shopping precinct for the wealthy, and is most famous for the Burlington Berties, uniformed guards who patrol the area keeping an eye out for such offences as running, chewing gum, whistling, opening umbrellas or anything else that could lower the tone (that the arcade once served as a brothel is kept quiet).

The City

With beguiling churches, hidden gardens and atmospheric lanes stuffed between iconic corporate towers and office blocks, you could spend weeks exploring the City of London, which, for most of its history, *was* London. Its boundaries have changed little since the Romans first founded their gated community here two millennia ago.

It's only in the last 250 years that the City has gone from being the very essence of London and its main population centre to just its central business district. But what a business district it is – the 'square mile' remains at the very heart of world capitalism.

Currently fewer than 10,000 people actually live here, although some 300,000 descend on it each weekday, to generate almost three-quarters of Britain's GDP before squeezing back onto the tube. On Sundays the City (capital 'C') becomes a virtual ghost town; it's nice and quiet, but come with a full stomach – most shops, eateries and pubs are closed.

★ Tower of London CASTLE
(Map p84; ☎ 0844 482 7777; www.hrp.org.uk/toweroflondon; Tower Hill, EC3; adult/child £25/12, audio guide £4/3; ⏲ 9am-5.30pm Tue-Sat, 10am-5.30pm Sun & Mon Mar-Oct, 9am-4.30pm Tue-Sat, 10am-4.30pm Sun & Mon Nov-Feb; ⊖ Tower Hill) The unmissable Tower of London (actually a castle of 22 towers) offers a window into a gruesome and compelling history. This was where two kings and three queens met their deaths and countless others were imprisoned. Come here to see the colourful Yeoman Warders (or Beefeaters), the spectacular Crown Jewels, the soothsaying ravens and armour fit for a *very* large king.

In the 1070s, William the Conqueror started work on the White Tower to replace the castle he'd previously had built here. By 1285, two walls with towers and a moat were built around it and the defences have barely been altered since. A former royal residence, treasury, mint and armoury, it became most famous as a prison when Henry VIII moved to Whitehall Palace in 1529 and started meting out his preferred brand of punishment.

The most striking building is the central **White Tower**, with its solid Norman architecture and four turrets. Today, on the entrance floor it houses a collection from the **Royal Armouries**, including Henry VIII's commodious suit of armour. On the 1st floor is **St John's Chapel**, dating from 1080 and therefore the oldest church in London. To the north stands Waterloo Barracks, which now contains the spectacular **Crown Jewels**, including the platinum crown of the late Queen Mother, set with the 106-carat **Koh-i-Noor (Mountain of Light) diamond**, and the Imperial State Crown, worn by the Queen at the State Opening of Parliament. Slow-moving travelators shunt wide-eyed visitors past the collection. On the far side of the White Tower is the **Bloody Tower**, where the 12-year-old Edward V and his little brother Richard were held 'for their own safety' and later murdered, perhaps by their uncle, the future Richard III. Sir Walter Raleigh

The City

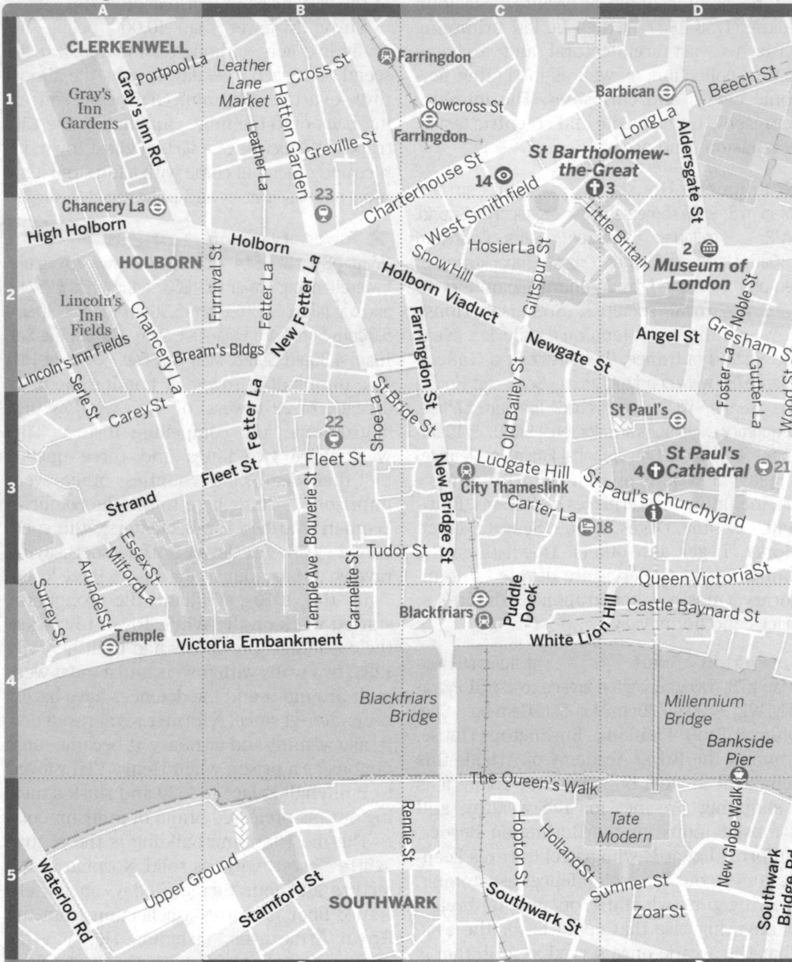

did a 13-year stretch here too under James I, when he wrote his *History of the World*.

In front of the **Chapel Royal of St Peter ad Vincula** stood Henry VIII's scaffold, where nobles such as Anne Boleyn and Catherine Howard (Henry's second and fifth wives) were beheaded. Look out for the latest in the Tower's long line of famous ravens, which legend says could cause the White Tower to collapse should they leave (their wing feathers are clipped in case they get any ideas).

To get your bearings, take the entertaining (and free) guided tour with any of the Beefeaters. Hour-long tours leave every 30 minutes from the bridge near the main entrance; the last tour is an hour before closing.

The red-brick **New Armouries Cafe** in the southeastern corner of the inner courtyard offers hot meals and sandwiches. Book online for cheaper rates for the Tower.

★Tower Bridge BRIDGE

(Map p84; ⊖ Tower Hill) London was a thriving port in 1894 when elegant Tower Bridge was built. Designed to be raised to allow ships to pass, the bridge now functions with electrical engines, replacing the original steam and hydraulic. A lift leads up from the northern

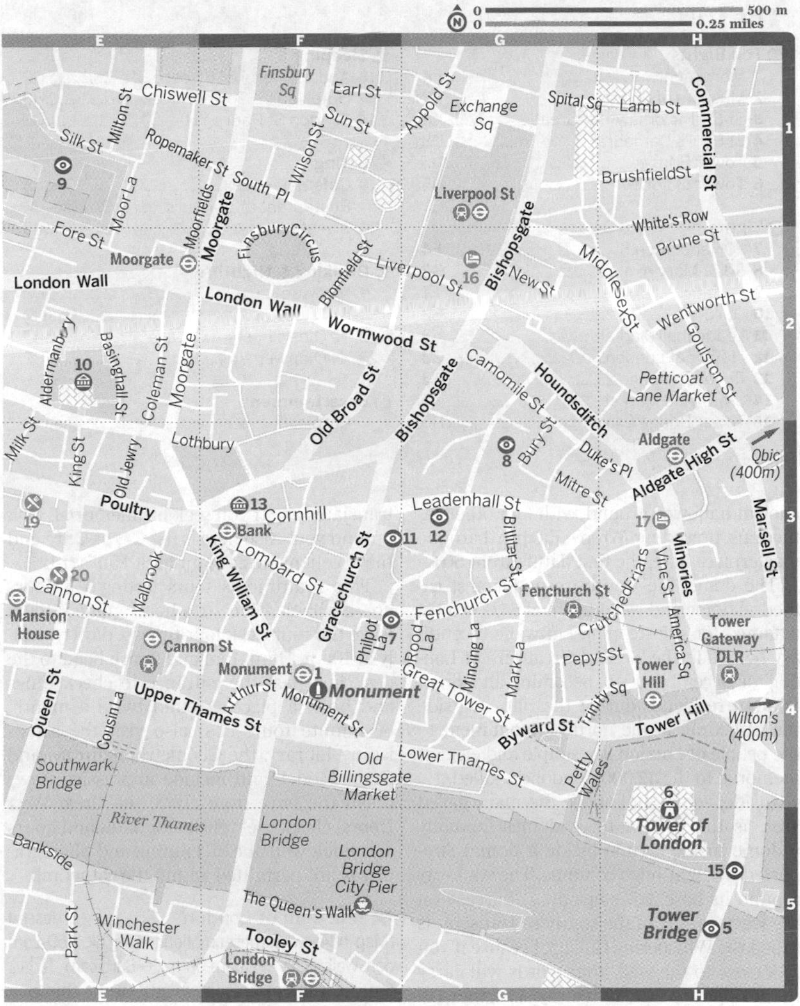

tower to the **Tower Bridge Exhibition** (Map p84; ☎020-7403 3761; www.towerbridge.org.uk; Tower Bridge, SE1; adult/child £9/3.90, incl Monument £11/5; ⏲10am-6pm Apr-Sep, 9.30am-5.30pm Oct-Mar, last admission 30min before closing; ⊖Tower Hill), where the story of its building is recounted within the upper walkway. You then walk down to the fascinating Victorian Engine Rooms, which powered the bridge lifts.

★St Paul's Cathedral CATHEDRAL
(Map p84; ☎020-7246 8350; www.stpauls.co.uk; St Paul's Churchyard, EC4; adult/child £18/8; ⏲8.30am-4.30pm Mon-Sat; ⊖St Paul's) Towering over Ludgate Hill, in a superb position that's been a place of Christian worship for over 1400 years, St Paul's Cathedral is one of London's most majestic and iconic buildings. For Londoners, the vast dome, which still manages to dominate the skyline, is a symbol of resilience and pride, standing tall for more than 300 years. Viewing Sir Christopher Wren's masterpiece from the inside and climbing to the top for sweeping views of the capital is an exhilarating experience.

The cathedral was designed by Wren after the Great Fire and built between 1675 and 1710; it opened the following year. The site is

The City

ancient hallowed ground, with four other cathedrals preceding Wren's English baroque masterpiece here, the first dating from 604.

The dome, the world's second-largest cathedral dome and weighing in at 65,000 tons, is famed for sidestepping Luftwaffe incendiary bombs in the 'Second Great Fire of London' of December 1940, becoming an icon of London resilience during the Blitz. Outside the cathedral, to the north, a monument to the people of London is a simple and elegant memorial to the 32,000 Londoners killed.

Inside, some 30m above the main paved area, is the first of three domes (actually a dome inside a cone inside a dome) supported by eight huge columns. The walkway around its base, 257 steps up a staircase on the western side of the southern transept, is called the Whispering Gallery, because if you talk close to the wall, your words will carry to the opposite side, 32m away. A further 119 steps brings you to the Stone Gallery, 152 iron steps above which is the Golden Gallery at the very top, rewarded with unforgettable views of London. As part of its 300th anniversary celebrations in 2011, St Paul's underwent a £40-million renovation project that gave the church a deep clean. It's not looked this good since they cut the blue ribbon opening the cathedral in 1711.

The crypt has memorials to up to 300 heroes and military demigods, including Wellington and Nelson, whose body lies directly below the dome. But the most poignant memorial is to Wren himself. On a simple slab bearing his name, part of a Latin inscription translates as: 'If you seek his memorial, look around you'. Also here is the **Crypt Café** and the excellent Restaurant at St Paul's (p127).

Free multimedia tours lasting 1½ hours are available. Free 1½-hour guided tours leave the tour desk four times a day (typically at 10am, 11am, 1pm and 2pm); head to the desk just past the entrance to check times and book a place. Around twice a month, 60-minute tours (£8) also visit the astonishing Library, the Geometric Staircase and Great Model, and include impressive views down the nave from above the Great West Doors; check the website for dates and hours and book well ahead. Filming and photography is not permitted within the cathedral.

★Museum of London — MUSEUM

(Map p84; www.museumoflondon.org.uk; 150 London Wall, EC2; 10am-6pm; Barbican) FREE

One of the capital's best museums, this is a fascinating walk through the various incarnations of the city from Roman Londinium and Anglo-Saxon Ludenwic to 21st-century metropolis contained in two-dozen galleries. There are a lot of interactive displays with an emphasis on experience rather than learning.

Guildhall — HISTORIC BUILDING

(Map p84; 020-7332 1313; www.guildhall.cityoflondon.gov.uk; Gresham St, EC2; Bank) FREE

Bang in the centre of the Square Mile, Guildhall has been the City's seat of government for more than 800 years. The present building dates from the early 15th century, making it the only existing secular stone structure to have survived the Great Fire of 1666, although it was severely damaged both then and during the Blitz of 1940.

★ Monument TOWER

(Map p84; www.themonument.info; Junction of Fish Street Hill & Monument St, EC3; adult/child £4/2, incl Tower Bridge Exhibition £10.50/4.70; ⏲9.30am-6pm Apr-Sep, to 5.30pm Oct-Mar; ⊖Monument) Sir Christopher Wren's 1677 column, known simply as the Monument, is a memorial to the Great Fire of London of 1666, whose impact on London's history cannot be overstated. An immense Doric column made of Portland stone, the Monument is 4.5m wide and 60.6m tall – the exact distance it stands from the bakery in Pudding Lane where the fire is thought to have started.

Inns of Court HISTORIC BUILDINGS

All London barristers work from within one of the four atmospheric Inns of Court, positioned between the walls of the old City and Westminster. It would take a lifetime working here to grasp all the intricacies of their arcane protocols, originating in the 13th-century. It's best just to soak up the dreamy ambience of the alleys and open spaces and thank your lucky stars you're not one of the bewigged barristers scurrying about.

★ St Bartholomew-the-Great CHURCH

(Map p84; ☎020-7600 0440; www.greatstbarts.com; West Smithfield, EC1; adult/concession £5/4.50; ⏲8.30am-5pm Mon-Fri, 10.30am-4pm Sat, 8.30am-8pm Sun; ⊖Farringdon or Barbican) Dating to 1123 and adjoining one of London's oldest hospitals, St Bartholomew-the-Great is one of London's most ancient churches. The authentic Norman arches and profound sense of history lend this holy space an ancient calm, while approaching from nearby Smithfield Market through the restored 13th-century half-timbered archway is like walking back in time. The church was originally part of the monastery of Augustinian Canons, but became the parish church of Smithfield in 1539 when King Henry VIII dissolved the monasteries.

Smithfield Market MARKET

(Map p84; www.smithfieldmarket.com; West Smithfield, EC1; ⏲2-10am Mon-Fri; ⊖Farringdon) Smithfield is central London's last surviving meat market. Its name derives from 'smooth field', where animals could graze, although its history is far from pastoral as this was once a place where public executions were held. Visit the market by 7am at the latest to see it in full swing. The Museum of London (p86) is due to move into Smithfield Market by 2021 in a relocation costing £70 million.

Royal Exchange HISTORIC BUILDING

(Map p84; www.theroyalexchange.co.uk; Royal Exchange, EC3; ⏲shops 10am-6pm, restaurants 8am-11pm Mon-Fri; ⊖Bank) The Royal Exchange was founded by Thomas Gresham in 1564, and this imposing, colonnaded building at the juncture of Threadneedle St and Cornhill is the third building on the site – the first was officially opened by Elizabeth I in 1570. It ceased functioning as a financial institution in the 1980s and now houses posh shops, cafes and restaurants.

Lloyd's of London NOTABLE BUILDING

(Map p84; www.lloyds.com/lloyds/about-us/the-lloyds-building; 1 Lime St, EC3; ⊖Aldgate or Monument) While the world's leading insurance brokers are inside underwriting everything from astronauts' lives to Mariah Carey's legs and Tom Jones' chest hair, people outside still stop to gawp at the stainless-steel external ducting, vents and staircases of this 1986 postmodern building designed by Richard Rogers, one of the architects of Paris' Pompidou Centre.

30 St Mary Axe NOTABLE BUILDING

(Gherkin; Map p84; www.30stmaryaxe.info; 30 St Mary Axe, EC3; ⊖Aldgate) Nicknamed 'the Gherkin' for its unusual shape, 30 St Mary Axe is arguably the City's most distinctive skyscraper, dominating the skyline despite actually being slightly smaller than the neighbouring NatWest Tower. Built in 2003 by award-winning Norman Foster, the Gherkin's futuristic exterior has become an emblem of modern London – as recognisable as Big Ben and the London Eye.

South Bank

Londoners once crossed the river to the area controlled by the licentious Bishops of Southwark for all manner of bawdy frolicking frowned upon in the City. It's a much more seemly and temperate area these days, but the frisson of theatre and entertainment survives. While South Bank only technically refers to the area of river bank between Westminster and Blackfriars Bridges (parts of which are actually on the east bank due to the way the river bends), we've used it as a convenient catch-all for those parts of Southwark and Lambeth that sit closest to the river.

Tower of London

TACKLING THE TOWER

Although it's usually less busy in the late afternoon, don't leave your assault on the Tower until too late in the day. You could easily spend hours here and not see it all. Start by getting your bearings on one of the Yeoman Warder (Beefeater) tours; they are included in the cost of admission, entertaining and the easiest way to access the **Chapel Royal of St Peter ad Vincula** ❶, which is where they finish up.

When you leave the chapel, the **Scaffold Site** ❷ is directly in front. The building immediately to your left is Waterloo Barracks, where the **Crown Jewels** ❸ are housed. These are the absolute highlight of a Tower visit, so keep an eye on the entrance and pick a time to visit when it looks relatively quiet. Once inside, take things at your own pace. Slow-moving travelators shunt you past the dozen or so crowns that are the treasury's centrepieces, but feel free to double-back for a second or even third pass.

Allow plenty of time for the **White Tower** ❹, the core of the whole complex, starting with the exhibition of royal armour. As you continue onto the 1st floor, keep an eye out for **St John's Chapel** ❺.

The famous **ravens** ❻ can be seen in the courtyard south of the White Tower. Head next through the towers that formed the **Medieval Palace** ❼, then take the **East Wall Walk** ❽ to get a feel for the castle's mighty battlements. Spend the rest of your time poking around the many other fascinating nooks and crannies of the Tower complex.

BEAT THE QUEUES

» Buy tickets online, avoid weekends and aim to be at the Tower first thing in the morning, when queues are shortest.

» Become a member An annual Historic Royal Palaces membership allows you to jump the queues and visit the Tower (and four other London palaces) as often as you like.

MIKE BOOTH / ALAMY ©

Chapel Royal of St Peter ad Vincula
This chapel serves as the resting place for the royals and other members of the aristocracy who were executed on the small green out front. Several other historical figures are buried here too, including Thomas More.

Scaffold Site
Seven people, including three queens (Anne Boleyn, Catherine Howard and Jane Grey), lost their heads here during Tudor times, saving the monarch the embarrassment of public executions on Tower Hill. The site features a rather odd 'pillow' sculpture by Brian Catling.

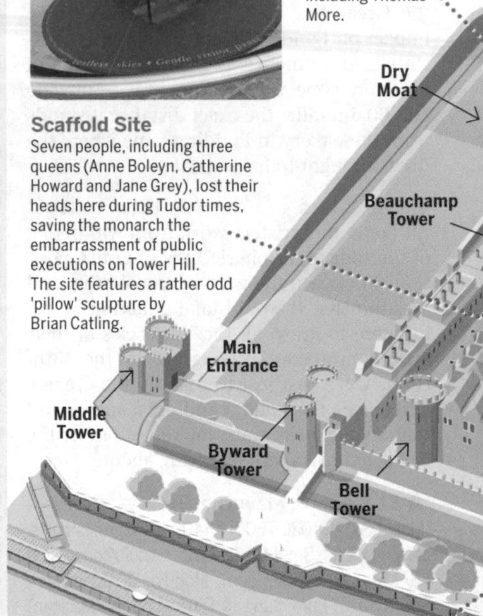

White Tower
Much of the White Tower is taken up with an exhibition on 500 years of royal armour. Look for the virtually cuboid suit made to match Henry VIII's bloated 49-year-old body, complete with an oversized armoured codpiece to protect, ahem, the crown jewels.

CHRISDORNEY / SHUTTERSTOCK ©

St John's Chapel

Kept as plain and unadorned as it would have been in Norman times, the White Tower's 1st-floor chapel is the oldest surviving church from 1080.

TOM HANLEY / ALAMY ©

Crown Jewels

When they're not being worn for ceremonies of state, Her Majesty's bling is kept here. Among the 23,578 gems, look out for the 530-carat 1st Star of Africa diamond at the top of the Sovereign's Sceptre with cross, the largest part of what was then the largest diamond ever found

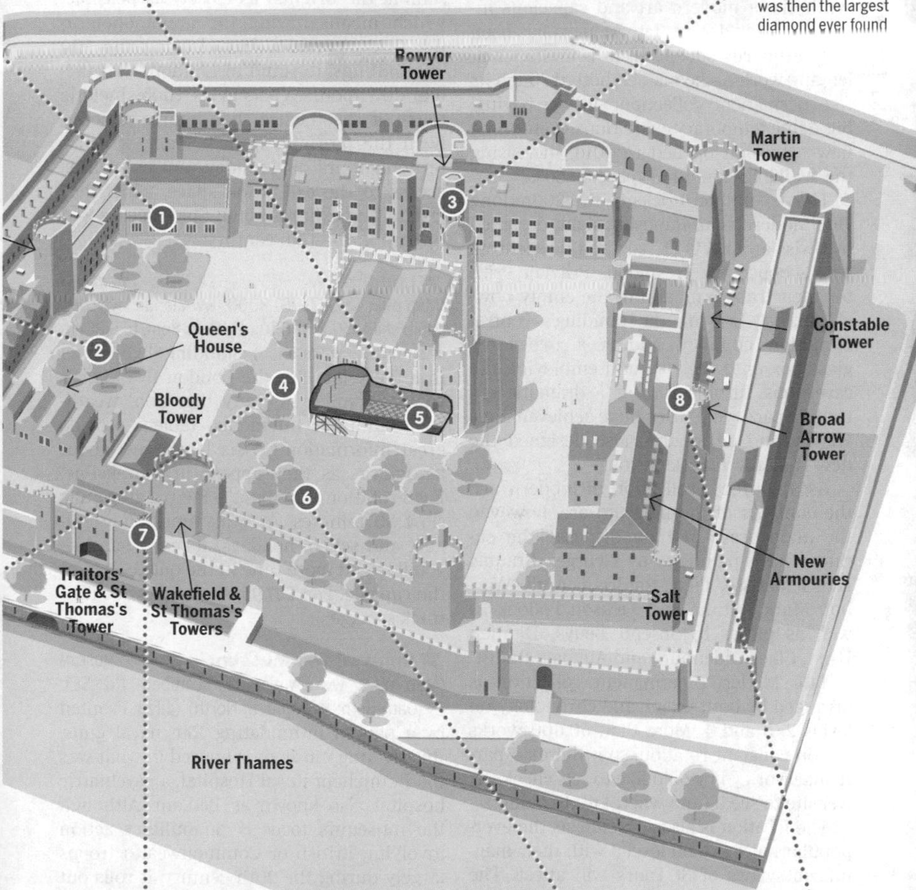

Medieval Palace

This part of the Tower complex was begun around 1220 and was home to England's medieval monarchs. Look for the recreations of the bedchamber of Edward I (1272–1307) in St Thomas's Tower and the throne room of his father, Henry III (1216–72) in the Wakefield Tower.

CRISTIAN SANTINON / SHUTTERSTOCK ©

Ravens

This stretch of green is where the Tower's half-dozen ravens are kept, fed on raw meat and blood-soaked biscuits. According to legend, if the ravens depart the fortress, the Tower will fall.

East Wall Walk

Follow the inner ramparts, starting from the 13th-century Salt Tower, passing through the Broad Arrow and Constable Towers, and ending at the Martin Tower, where the Crown Jewels were stored till the mid-19th century.

★Tate Modern MUSEUM

(Map p92; www.tate.org.uk; Queen's Walk, SE1; ⏲10am-6pm Sun-Thu, to 10pm Fri & Sat; 📶👪; ⊖Blackfriars, Southwark or London Bridge) FREE One of London's most amazing attractions, this outstanding modern- and contemporary-art gallery is housed in the creatively revamped **Bankside Power Station** south of the Millennium Bridge. A spellbinding synthesis of modern art and capacious industrial brick design, Tate Modern has been extraordinarily successful in bringing challenging work to the masses, both through its free permanent collection and fee-paying, big-name temporary exhibitions. A stunning new extension opened in 2016, increasing the available exhibition space by 60%.

The 4.2 million bricks of the 200m-long Tate Modern is an imposing sight, designed by Swiss architects Herzog and de Meuron, who scooped the prestigious Pritzker Prize for their transformation of the empty power station. Leaving the building's central 99m-high chimney, adding a two-storey glass box onto the roof and employing the cavernous Turbine Hall as a dramatic entrance space were three huge achievements. Herzog and de Meuron also designed the new 11-storey Tate extension.

As a supreme collection of modern art, the contents of the museum are, however, the main draw. At their disposal, the curators have paintings by Georges Braque, Henri Matisse, Piet Mondrian, Andy Warhol, Mark Rothko and Jackson Pollock as well as pieces by Joseph Beuys, Damien Hirst, Claes Oldenburg and Auguste Rodin.

Tate Modern's permanent collection is arranged by both theme and chronology on levels 2, 3 and 4. More than 60,000 works are on constant rotation, so if there's a particular work you would like to see, check the website to see if (and where) it's hanging.

The location is also supreme, as the ever-popular balconies on level 3 with their magnificent views of St Paul's will attest. The **Millennium Bridge** (Map p92; ⊖St Paul's or Blackfriars) elegantly conveys views direct from the Tate Modern to St Paul's Cathedral in the City on the far bank of the river. Free guided highlights tours depart at 11am, noon, 2pm and 3pm daily. Audio guides (in five languages) are available for £4 – they contain information about 50 artworks across the gallery and offer suggested tours for adults or children.

To visit the sister-museum Tate Britain, hop on the **Tate Boat** (Map p92; www.tate.org.uk/visit/tate-boat; one-way adult/child £7.50/3.75) from Bankside Pier.

★Shakespeare's Globe HISTORIC BUILDING

(Map p92; www.shakespearesglobe.com; 21 New Globe Walk, SE1; adult/child £14/8; ⏲9am-5pm; 👪; ⊖Blackfriars, Southwark or London Bridge) Unlike other venues for Shakespearean plays, the new Globe was designed to resemble the original as closely as possible, which means having the arena open to the fickle London skies, leaving the 700 'groundlings' to stand in London's spectacular downpours. Visits to the Globe include tours of the theatre (half-hourly, generally in the morning from 9.30am, with afternoon tours on Monday too) as well as access to the exhibition space, which has fascinating exhibits about Shakespeare and theatre in the 17th century.

★London Eye VIEWPOINT

(Map p92; ☎0871 781 3000; www.londoneye.com; adult/child £21.20/16.10; ⏲10am-8pm, to 9.30pm in summer; ⊖Waterloo) Standing 135m high in a fairly flat city, the London Eye affords views 25 miles in every direction, weather permitting. Interactive tablets provide great information (in six languages) about landmarks as they appear in the skyline. Each rotation – or 'flight' – takes a gracefully slow 30 minutes. At peak times (July, August and school holidays) it may seem like you'll spend more time in the queue than in the capsule. For £27.95, showcase your fast-track swagger.

★Imperial War Museum MUSEUM

(Map p92; www.iwm.org.uk; Lambeth Rd, SE1; ⏲10am-6pm; ⊖Lambeth North) FREE Fronted by a pair of intimidating 15in naval guns, this riveting museum is housed in what was the Bethlehem Royal Hospital, a psychiatric hospital also known as Bedlam. Although the museum's focus is on military action involving British or Commonwealth troops largely during the 20th century, it rolls out the carpet to war in the wider sense. Highlights include the state-of-the-art **First World War Galleries** and **Witnesses to War** in the forecourt and atrium above.

Shard NOTABLE BUILDING

(Map p92; www.theviewfromtheshard.com; 32 London Bridge St, SE1; adult/child £30.95/24.95; ⏲10am-10pm; ⊖London Bridge) Puncturing the skies above London, the dramatic splinter-like form of the Shard has rapidly become an icon of London. The viewing platforms

WORTH A TRIP

TATE BRITAIN

Splendidly reopened a few years back with a stunning new art-deco-inspired staircase and a rehung collection, the older and more venerable of the two Tate siblings **Tate Britain** (www.tate.org.uk; Millbank, SW1; ⏰10am-6pm, to 10pm 1st Fri of month; Ⓤ Pimlico) celebrates paintings from 1500 to the present, with works from Blake, Hogarth, Gainsborough, Barbara Hepworth, Whistler, Constable and Turner, as well as vibrant modern and contemporary pieces from Lucian Freud, Francis Bacon and Henry Moore. Join a free 45-minute **thematic tour** (⏰11am) and 15-minute **Art in Focus talks** (Millbank, SW1; ⏰1.15pm Tue, Thu & Sat).

The stars of the show at Tate Britain are, undoubtedly, the light infused visions of JMW Turner in the Clore Gallery. After he died in 1851, his estate was settled by a decree declaring that whatever had been found in his studio – 300 oil paintings and about 30,000 sketches and drawings – would be bequeathed to the nation. The collection at the Tate Britain constitutes a grand and sweeping display of his work, including classics such as *The Scarlet Sunset* and *Norham Castle, Sunrise*.

There are also seminal works from Constable, Gainsborough and Reynolds, as well as the pre-Raphaelites, including William Holman Hunt's *The Awakening Conscience*, John William Waterhouse's *The Lady of Shalott*, *Ophelia* by John Everett Millais and Edward Burne-Jones's *The Golden Stairs*. Look out also for Francis Bacon's *Three Studies for Figures at the Base of a Crucifixion*. Tate Britain hosts the prestigious and often controversial Turner Prize for Contemporary Art from October to early December every year.

The Tate Britain also has a program of ticketed exhibitions which changes every few months; consult the website for details of the latest exhibition. The ticket office closes at 5.15pm.

on floors 68, 69 and 72 are open to the public and the views are, as you'd expect from a 244m vantage point, sweeping, but they come at a hefty price – book online at least a day in advance to save £5.

Old Operating Theatre Museum & Herb Garret — MUSEUM

(Map p92; www.thegarret.org.uk; 9a St Thomas St, SE1; adult/child £6.50/3.50; ⏰10.30am-5pm; Ⓤ London Bridge) This unique museum, 32 steps up a spiral stairway in the tower of **St Thomas Church** (1703), is the unlikely home of Britain's oldest operating theatre. Rediscovered in 1956, the garret was used by the apothecary of St Thomas's Hospital to store medicinal herbs. The museum looks back at the horror of 19th-century medicine – all pre-ether, pre-chloroform and pre-antiseptic.

★ Southwark Cathedral — CHURCH

(Map p92; ☎020-7367 6700; www.cathedral.southwark.anglican.org; Montague Cl, SE1; ⏰8am-6pm Mon-Fri, 9am-6pm Sat & Sun; Ⓤ London Bridge) The earliest surviving parts of this relatively small cathedral are the retrochoir at the eastern end, which contains four chapels and was part of the 13th-century Priory of St Mary Overie, some ancient arcading by the southwest door and an arch that dates to the original Norman church. But most of the cathedral is Victorian. Inside are monuments galore, including a Shakespeare memorial. Catch evensong at 5.30pm on Tuesdays, Thursdays and Fridays, 4pm on Saturdays and 3pm on Sundays.

Design Museum — MUSEUM

(☎020-7940 8790; www.designmuseum.org; 224-238 Kensington High St, W8; ⏰10am-5.45pm; Ⓤ High St Kensington) Dedicated to popularising the importance of good design in everyday life, the Design Museum has a revolving program of special exhibitions. Past shows have ranged from Manolo Blahnik shoes to Formula One racing cars. The annual 'Design of the Year' exhibition showcases the best and latest design innovations – as the museum's tagline has it, 'Someday, the other museums will be showing this stuff'.

HMS Belfast — SHIP

(Map p92; www.iwm.org.uk/visits/hms-belfast; Queen's Walk, SE1; adult/child £14.50/7.25; ⏰10am-6pm Mar-Oct, to 5pm Nov-Feb; Ⓤ London Bridge) HMS *Belfast* is a magnet for naval-gazing kids of all ages. This large, light cruiser – launched in 1938 – served in WWII, helping to sink the German battleship *Scharnhorst*, shelling the Normandy coast on D Day and later participating in the Korean War. Its 6in guns could bombard a target 14 land miles distant. Displays offer a great insight into

South Bank

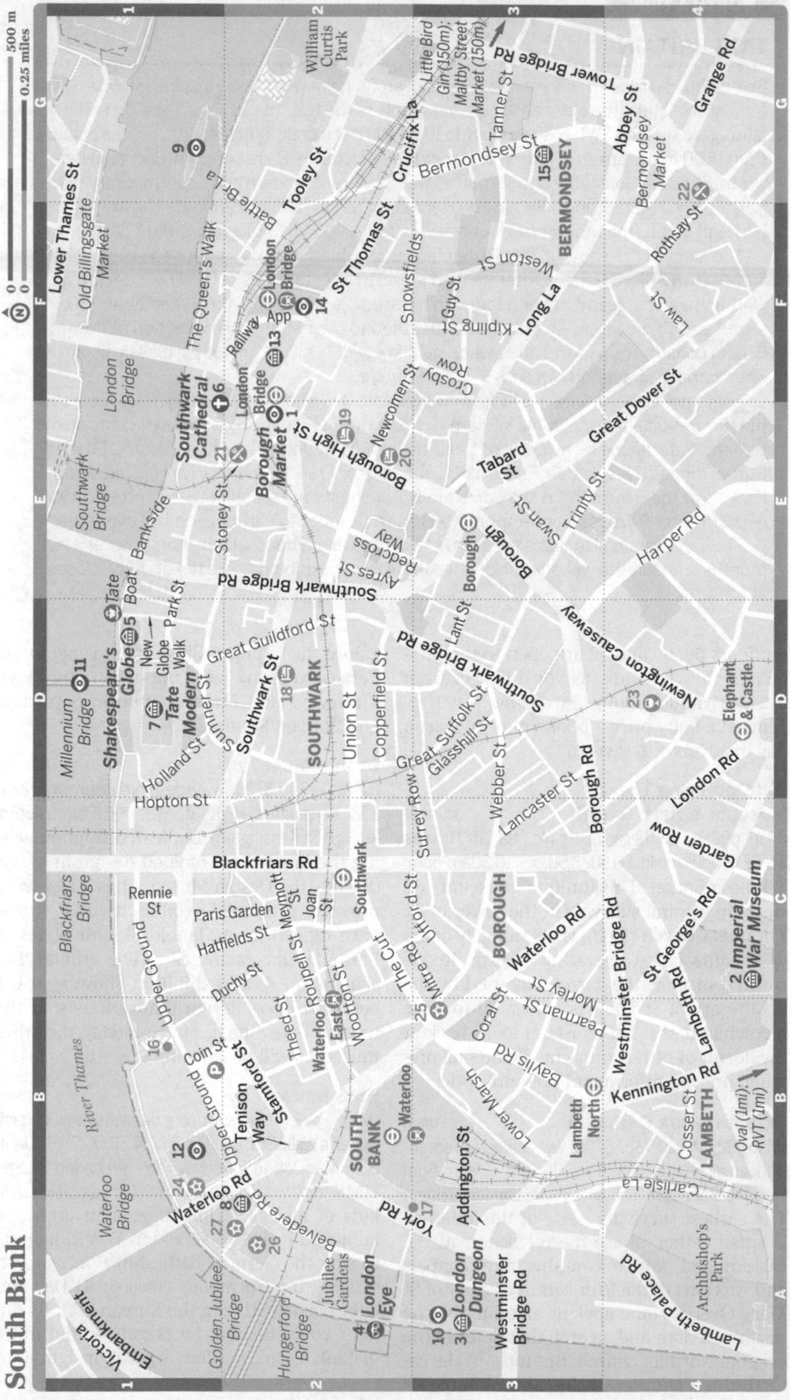
0 500 m
0 0.25 miles
Victoria Embankment
Golden Jubilee Bridge
Hungerford Bridge
Jubilee Gardens
London Eye
London Dungeon
Westminster Bridge Rd
Waterloo Bridge
Waterloo Rd
Belvedere Rd
York Rd
Addington St
Lambeth Palace Rd
Archbishop's Park
River Thames
Upper Ground
Tenison Way
Stamford St
Coin St
SOUTH BANK
Waterloo
Waterloo East
Lower Marsh
Carlisle La
Lambeth North
Kennington Rd
Cosser St
LAMBETH
Oval (1mi); RVT (1mi)
Blackfriars Bridge
Rennie St
Paris Garden
Hatfields St
Duchy St
Theed St
Roupell St
Meymott St
Joan St
Wootton St
The Cut
Mitre Rd
Ufford St
Baylis Rd
Pearman St
Morley St
Coral St
BOROUGH
Waterloo Rd
Westminster Bridge Rd
St George's Rd
Lambeth Rd
Imperial War Museum
Blackfriars Rd
Southwark
Hopton St
Holland St
Millennium Bridge
Shakespeare's Globe
Tate Modern
Sumner St
Southwark St
SOUTHWARK
Union St
Copperfield St
Surrey Row
Great Suffolk St
Glasshill St
Webber St
Lancaster St
Borough Rd
London Rd
Garden Row
Elephant & Castle
New Globe Walk
Tate Boat
Park St
Great Guildford St
Southwark Bridge Rd
Lant St
Newington Causeway
Southwark Bridge
Bankside
Stoney St
Ayres St
Redcross Way
Borough
Swan St
Trinity St
Harper Rd
Borough Market
Southwark Cathedral
Borough High St
Newcomen St
Tabard St
Great Dover St
London Bridge
Railway App
Crosby Row
Kipling St
Guy St
Long La
Law St
Old Billingsgate Market
Lower Thames St
The Queen's Walk
Tooley St
St Thomas St
Snowsfields
Weston St
BERMONDSEY
Rothsay St
Battle Br La
Crucifix La
Bermondsey St
Tanner St
Bermondsey Market
Abbey St
Grange Rd
Tower Bridge Rd
Little Bird Gin (150m); Maltby Street Market (150m)
William Curtis Park
1
2
3
4
A
B
C
D
E
F
G

South Bank

Top Sights
1 Borough Market E2
2 Imperial War Museum C4
3 London Dungeon A3
4 London Eye A2
5 Shakespeare's Globe D1
6 Southwark Cathedral E1
7 Tate Modern D1

Sights
8 Hayward Gallery A2
9 HMS Belfast G1
10 London Sea Life Aquarium A3
11 Millennium Bridge D1
12 National Theatre B1
13 Old Operating Theatre Museum & Herb Garret F2
14 Shard F2
15 White Cube Bermondsey G3

Activities, Courses & Tours
16 London Bicycle Tour B1
17 London Duck Tours A3

Sleeping
18 Citizen M D2
Shangri-La Hotel at the Shard ....(see 14)
19 St Christopher's Inn E2
20 St Christopher's Village E2

Eating
21 Arabica Bar & Kitchen E2
22 M Manze G4
Skylon ....(see 26)

Drinking & Nightlife
23 Ministry of Sound D4
Oblix ....(see 14)
Skylon ....(see 26)

Entertainment
24 BFI Southbank B1
National Theatre ....(see 12)
25 Old Vic B3
26 Royal Festival Hall A2
Shakespeare's Globe ....(see 5)
27 Southbank Centre A2

what life on board was like, in peace times and during military engagements.

★ London Dungeon — HISTORIC BUILDING

(Map p92; www.thedungeons.com/london; County Hall, Westminster Bridge Rd, SE1; adult/child £28.95/24.45; 10am-5pm, to 6pm Sat & Sun; Waterloo or Westminster) Older kids tend to love the London Dungeon, as the terrifying queues during school holidays and weekends testify. It's all spooky music, ghostly boat rides, macabre hangman's drop-rides, fake blood and actors dressed up as torturers and gory criminals (including Jack the Ripper and Sweeney Todd) with interactive scares galore.

London Sea Life Aquarium — AQUARIUM

(Map p92; www.visitsealife.com; County Hall, Westminster Bridge Rd, SE1; adult/child £24.50/18.10; 10am-7pm Mon-Fri, 9am-7pm Sat & Sun; Waterloo or Westminster) Displays look somewhat dated, but there are a couple of stand-out sights, including the shark tunnel, ray lagoon, the Gentoo penguin enclosures (penguins jump and dive at mesmerising speed) and Frozen Planet, with its flickering northern lights. Feeds and talks are scheduled throughout the day so your chances of catching one during your visit are high.

White Cube Bermondsey — GALLERY

(Map p92; www.whitecube.com; 144-152 Bermondsey St, SE1; 10am-6pm Tue-Sat, noon-6pm Sun; London Bridge) FREE The newest and largest of the White Cube galleries – the brainchild of Jay Jopling, dealer to the stars of the Brit Art movement who made his reputation in the 1990s by exhibiting then-unknown artists such as Damien Hirst and Antony Gormley – this gallery impresses with its large exhibition spaces, which lend themselves to monumental pieces or expansive installations using several mediums.

Hayward Gallery — GALLERY

(Map p92; www.southbankcentre.co.uk; Belvedere Rd, SE1; noon-6pm Mon, 11am-7pm Tue-Wed, Sat & Sun, to 8pm Thu & Fri; ; Waterloo) Part of the Southbank Centre, the Hayward hosts a changing roster of contemporary art (video, installations, photography, collage, painting etc) in a 1960s Brutalist building. The gallery was closed for works at the time of research; check the website for details.

★ Borough Market — MARKET

(Map p92; www.boroughmarket.org.uk; 8 Southwark St, SE1; 10am-5pm Wed & Thu, 10am-6pm Fri, 8am-5pm Sat; London Bridge) Located here in some form or another since the 13th century (and possibly since 1014), 'London's Larder' has enjoyed an astonishing renaissance in the past 15 years. Always overflowing with food lovers, inveterate gastronomes, wide-eyed visitors and Londoners in search of inspiration for their dinner party, this fantastic market has become firmly established as a sight in its own right. The market specialises in high-end fresh products; there are also plenty of takeaway stalls and an unreasonable number of cake stalls!

Chelsea & Kensington

Known as the royal borough, Chelsea and Kensington lays claim to the highest income earners in the UK. Kensington High St has a lively mix of chains and boutiques, while even the charity shops along King's Rd resemble fashion outlets. Some of London's most beautiful and fascinating museums, clustered together in South Kensington, are must-sees come rain or shine.

★Victoria & Albert Museum MUSEUM

(V&A; Map p98; www.vam.ac.uk; Cromwell Rd, SW7; 10am-5.45pm Sat-Thu, to 10pm Fri; South Kensington) FREE The Museum of Manufactures, as the V&A was known when it opened in 1852, was part of Prince Albert's legacy to the nation in the aftermath of the successful Great Exhibition of 1851. It houses the world's largest collection of decorative arts, from Asian ceramics to Middle Eastern rugs, Chinese paintings, Western furniture, fashion from all ages and modern-day domestic appliances. The temporary exhibitions are another highlight, covering anything from David Bowie retrospectives to designer Alexander McQueen, special materials and trends.

There are more than 100 galleries in the museum, so pick carefully or join a free one-hour guided tour; there are several a day (they meet close to the information desk in the main hall) on a variety of themes including introductory tours, medieval and Renaissance tours and theatre and performance tours.

★Natural History Museum MUSEUM

(Map p98; www.nhm.ac.uk; Cromwell Rd, SW7; 10am-5.50pm; ; South Kensington) FREE This colossal and magnificent-looking building is infused with the irrepressible Victorian spirit of collecting, cataloguing and interpreting the natural world. The **Dinosaurs Gallery** (Blue Zone) is a must for children, who gawp at the animatronic T-Rex, fossils and excellent displays. Adults for their part will love the intriguing Treasures exhibition in the **Cadogan Gallery** (Green Zone), which houses a host of unrelated objects each telling its own unique story, from a chunk of moon rock to a dodo skeleton.

Also in the Green Zone, the **Mineral Gallery** is a breathtaking display of architectural perspective leading to the **Vault**, where you'll find the **Aurora Collection** of almost 300 coloured diamonds. In the Orange Zone, the vast **Darwin Centre** focuses on taxonomy, showcasing 28 million insects and six million plants in a giant cocoon; glass windows allow you to watch scientists at work.

At the centre of the museum is **Hintze Hall**, which resembles a cathedral nave – quite fitting for a time when the natural sciences were challenging the biblical tenets of Christian orthodoxy. The hall is dominated by the over-arching cast of a Diplodocus skeleton (nicknamed Dippy), which is due to be replaced by the real skeleton of a diving blue whale (*Balaenoptera musculus*), hung from the ceiling, in 2017.

A slice of English countryside in SW7, the beautiful **Wildlife Garden** next to the West Lawn encompasses a range of British lowland habitats, including a meadow with farm gates and a bee tree where a colony of honey bees fills the air.

In 2018, the eastern grounds are also due to be redesigned to feature a geological and palaeontological walk, with a bronze sculpture of Dippy as well as ferns and cycads.

The entire museum and its gardens cover a huge 5.7 hectares and contains 80 million specimens from across the natural world. More than five million visitors come each year, so queues can sometimes get long, especially during the school holidays.

★Science Museum MUSEUM

(Map p98; www.sciencemuseum.org.uk; Exhibition Rd, SW7; 10am-6pm; ; South Kensington) FREE With seven floors of interactive and educational exhibits, this scientifically spellbinding museum will mesmerise adults and children alike, covering everything from early technology to space travel. A perennial favourite is **Exploring Space**, a gallery featuring genuine rockets and satellites and a full-size replica of the 'Eagle', the lander that took Neil Armstrong and Buzz Aldrin to the moon in 1969. The **Making the Modern World Gallery** next door is a visual feast of locomotives, planes, cars and other revolutionary inventions.

The fantastic **Information Age Gallery** on level 2 showcases how information and communication technologies – from the telegraph to smartphones – have transformed our lives since the 19th century. Standout displays include wireless sent by a sinking

Titanic, the first BBC radio broadcast and a Soviet BESM 1965 super-computer. Also on level 2 is **Media Space**, a gallery dedicated to excellent photographic exhibitions from the National Photography Collection (adult/child £8/free).

The 3rd-floor **Flight Gallery** (free tours 1pm most days) is a favourite place for children, with its gliders, hot-air balloons and aircraft, including the Gipsy Moth, which Amy Johnson flew to Australia in 1930. This floor also features a **Red Arrows 3D flight simulation theatre** (adult/children £6/5) and **Fly 360-degree flight-simulator capsules** (£12 per capsule). **Launchpad**, on the same floor, is stuffed with (free) hands-on gadgets exploring physic and the properties of liquids.

Glimpses of Medical History on level 4 isn't as high-tech as the rest of the museum but is highly evocative with models and life-size reconstructions showing how medicine – from childbirth to dentistry – was practised through the ages.

If you've kids under the age of five, pop down to the basement and the **Garden**, where there's a fun-filled play zone, including a water-play area, besieged by tots in orange waterproof smocks.

★Hyde Park — PARK

(Map p98; www.royalparks.org.uk/parks/hyde-park; ⏲5am-midnight; ⊖Marble Arch, Hyde Park Corner or Queensway) At 145 hectares, Hyde Park is central London's largest open space, expropriated from the Church in 1536 by Henry VIII and turned into a hunting ground and later a venue for duels, executions and horse racing. The 1851 Great Exhibition was held here, and during WWII the park became an enormous potato field. These days, there's boating on the **Serpentine**, summer concerts (Bruce Springsteen, Florence + The Machine, Patti Smith), film nights and other warm-weather events.

★Kensington Palace — PALACE

(Map p122; www.hrp.org.uk/kensingtonpalace; Kensington Gardens, W8; adult/child £16.30/free; ⏲10am-6pm Mar-Oct, to 5pm Nov-Feb; ⊖High St Kensington) Built in 1605, the palace became the favourite royal residence under William and Mary of Orange in 1689, and remained so until George III became king and relocated to Buckingham Palace. Today, it is still a royal residence, with the likes of the Duke and Duchess of Cambridge (Prince William and his wife Catherine) and Prince Harry living there. A large part of the palace is open to the public, however, including the King's and Queen's State Apartments.

Kensington Gardens — PARK

(Map p122; www.royalparks.org.uk/parks/kensington-gardens; ⏲6am-dusk; ⊖Queensway or Lancaster Gate) Kensington Gardens is a gorgeous collection of manicured lawns, tree-shaded avenues and basins immediately west of Hyde Park. The picturesque 107-hectare expanse is technically part of Kensington Palace, located in the far west of the gardens. The large **Round Pond** is enjoyable to amble around and also worth a look are the lovely fountains in the **Italian Gardens** (Map p98; Kensington Gardens; ⊖Lancaster Gate), believed to be a gift from Albert to Queen Victoria.

Albert Memorial — MONUMENT

(Map p98; ☎tours 020-8969 0104; Kensington Gardens; tours adult/concession £8/7; ⏲tours 2pm & 3pm 1st Sun of month Mar-Dec; ⊖Knightsbridge or Gloucester Rd) This splendid Victorian confection on the southern edge of Kensington Gardens is as ostentatious as its subject. Purportedly humble, Queen Victoria's German husband Albert (1819–61) insisted he did not want a monument. Ignoring the good prince's wishes, the Lord Mayor instructed George Gilbert Scott to build the 53m-high, gaudy Gothic memorial – the 4.25m-tall gilded statue of the prince, surrounded by 187 figures representing the continents (Asia, Europe, Africa and America), the arts, industry and science, went up in 1876.

Saatchi Gallery — GALLERY

(Map p98; www.saatchigallery.com; Duke of York's HQ, King's Rd, SW3; ⏲10am-6pm; ⊖Sloane Sq) FREE This enticing gallery hosts temporary exhibitions of experimental and thought-provoking work across a variety of media. The white and sanded bare-floorboard galleries are magnificently presented, but save some wonder for Gallery 15, where Richard Wilson's *20:50* is on permanent display. Mesmerising, impassive and ineffable, it's a riveting tour de force. A cool shop chips in on the 1st floor.

Royal Hospital Chelsea — HISTORIC BUILDINGS

(Map p98; www.chelsea-pensioners.co.uk; Royal Hospital Rd, SW3; ⏲grounds 10am-4.30pm Mon-Sat, Great Hall shuts daily noon to 2pm, museum 10am-4pm Mon-Fri; ⊖Sloane Sq) FREE Designed by Christopher Wren, this superb structure was built in 1692 to provide shelter for ex-servicemen. Since the reign of Charles

Victoria & Albert Museum

HALF-DAY HIGHLIGHTS TOUR

The art- and design-packed V&A is vast: we have devised an easy-to-follow tour of the museum highlights to help cover some signature pieces while also allowing you to appreciate some of the grandeur of the museum architecture.

Enter the V&A by the Grand Entrance off Cromwell Rd and immediately turn left to explore the Islamic Middle East Gallery and to discover the sumptuous silk-and-wool **Ardabil Carpet** ❶. Among the pieces from South Asia in the adjacent gallery is the terrifying automated **Tipu's Tiger** ❷. Continue to the outstanding **Fashion Gallery** ❸ with its displays of clothing styles through the ages. The magnificent gallery opposite houses the **Raphael Cartoons** ❹, large paintings by Raphael used to weave tapestries for the Vatican. Take the stairs to Level 2 and the Britain 1500–1760 Gallery; turn left in the

Raphael Cartoons

These seven drawings by Raphael, depicting the acts of St Peter and St Paul, were the full-scale preparatory works for seven tapestries that were woven for the Sistine Chapel in the Vatican.

Fashion Gallery

With clothing from the 18th century to the present day, this circular and chronologically arranged gallery showcases evening wear, undergarments and iconic fashion milestones, such as 1960s dresses designed by Mary Quant.

The Great Bed of Ware

Created during the reign of Queen Elizabeth I, its headboard and bedposts are etched with ancient graffiti; the 16th-century oak Great Bed of Ware is famously name-dropped in Shakespeare's *Twelfth Night*.

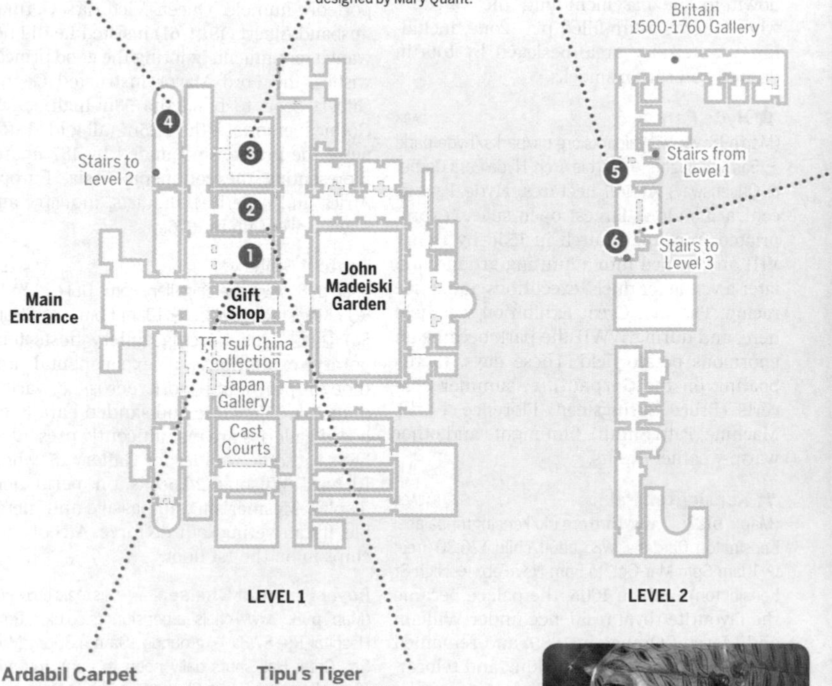

The Ardabil Carpet

One of the world's most beautiful carpets, the Ardabil was completed in 1540, one of a pair commissioned by Shah Tahmasp, ruler of Iran. The piece is most astonishing for the artistry of the detailing and the subtlety of design.

Tipu's Tiger

This disquieting 18th-century wood-and-metal mechanical automaton depicts a European being savaged by a tiger. When a handle is turned, an organ hidden within the feline mimics the cries of the dying man, whose arm also rises.

GREG BALFOUR EVANS / ALAMY ©

gallery to find the **Great Bed of Ware** ❺, beyond which rests the exquisitely crafted artistry of **Henry VIII's Writing Box** ❻. Head up the stairs into the Metalware Gallery on Level 3 for the **Hereford Screen** ❼. Continue through the Ironwork and Sculpture Galleries and through the Leighton Corridor to the glittering **Jewellery Gallery** ❽. Exit through the Stained Glass gallery, at the end of which you'll find stairs back down to level 1.

TOP TIPS

» **More Info** Museum attendants are always at hand along the route.

» **Photography** Allowed in most galleries, except the Jewellery Gallery, the Raphael Cartoons and in exhibitions.

» **Evening Exploration** Avoid daytime crowds: visit the V&A till 10pm on Friday.

MARTIN HESKO / SHUTTERSTOCK ©

Henry VIII's Writing Box
This exquisitely ornate walnut and oak 16th-century writing box has been added to over the centuries, but the original decorative motifs are superb, including Henry's coat of arms, flanked by Venus (holding Cupid) and Mars.

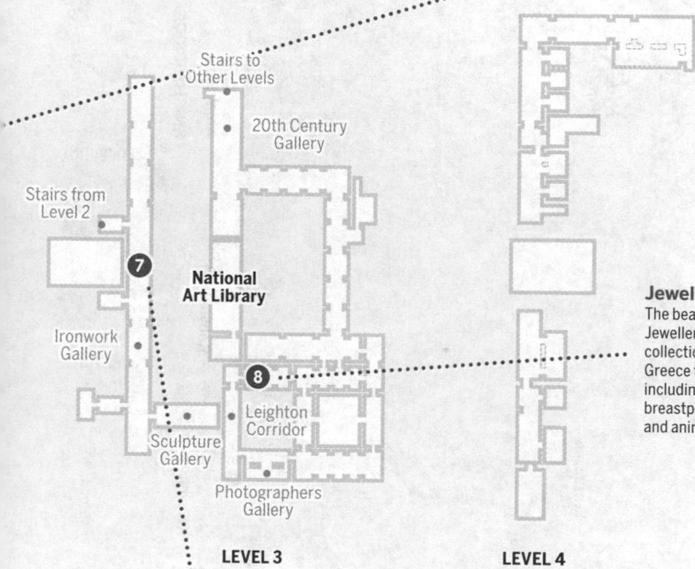

Jewellery Gallery
The beautifully illuminated Jewellery Gallery has a stunning collection of items from ancient Greece to the modern day, including a dazzling gold Celtic breastplate, art-nouveau jewellery and animals fashioned by Fabergé.

The Hereford Screen
Designed by Sir George Gilbert Scott, this awe-inspiring choir screen is a labour of love, originally fashioned for Hereford Cathedral. An almighty conception of wood, iron, copper, brass and hardstone, there were few parts of the V&A that could support its great mass.

Knightsbridge, South Kensington & Chelsea

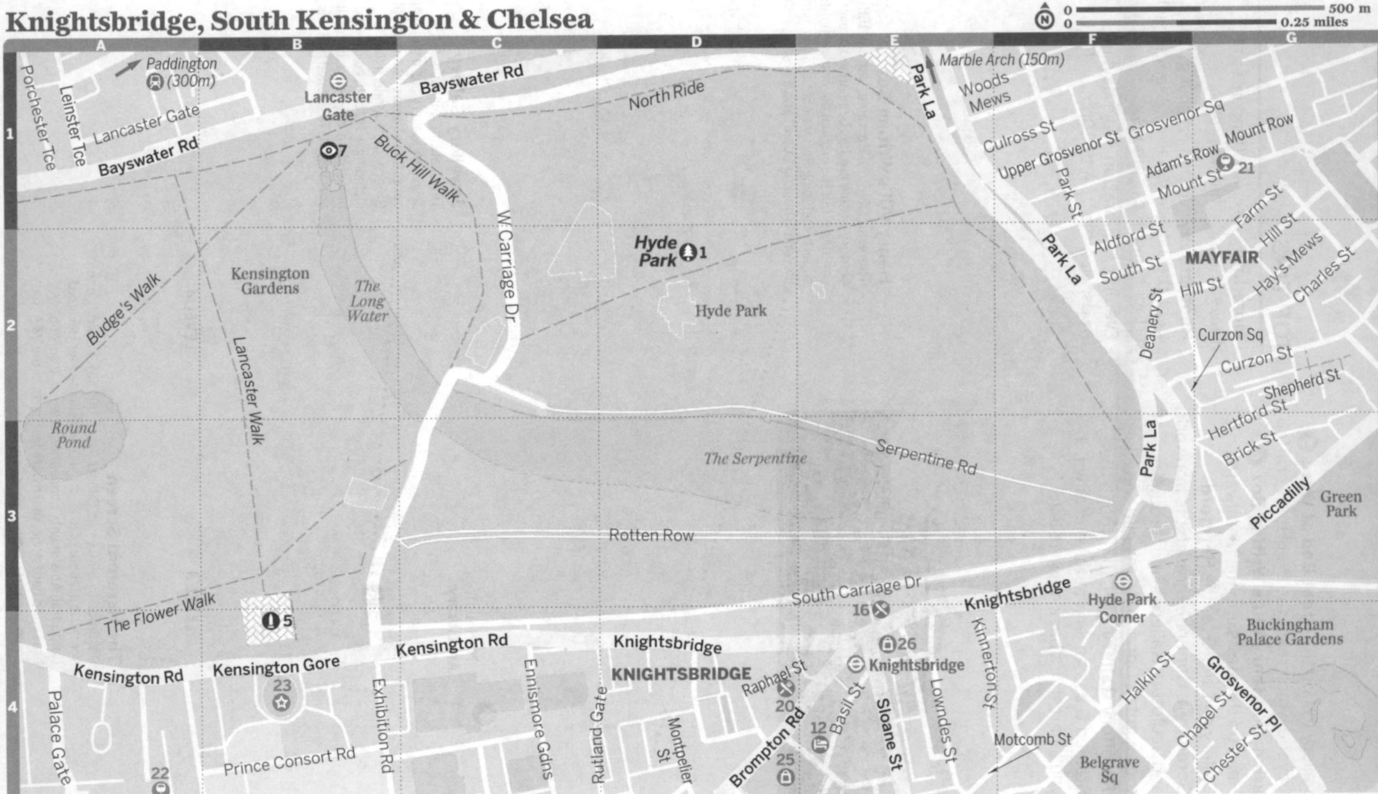

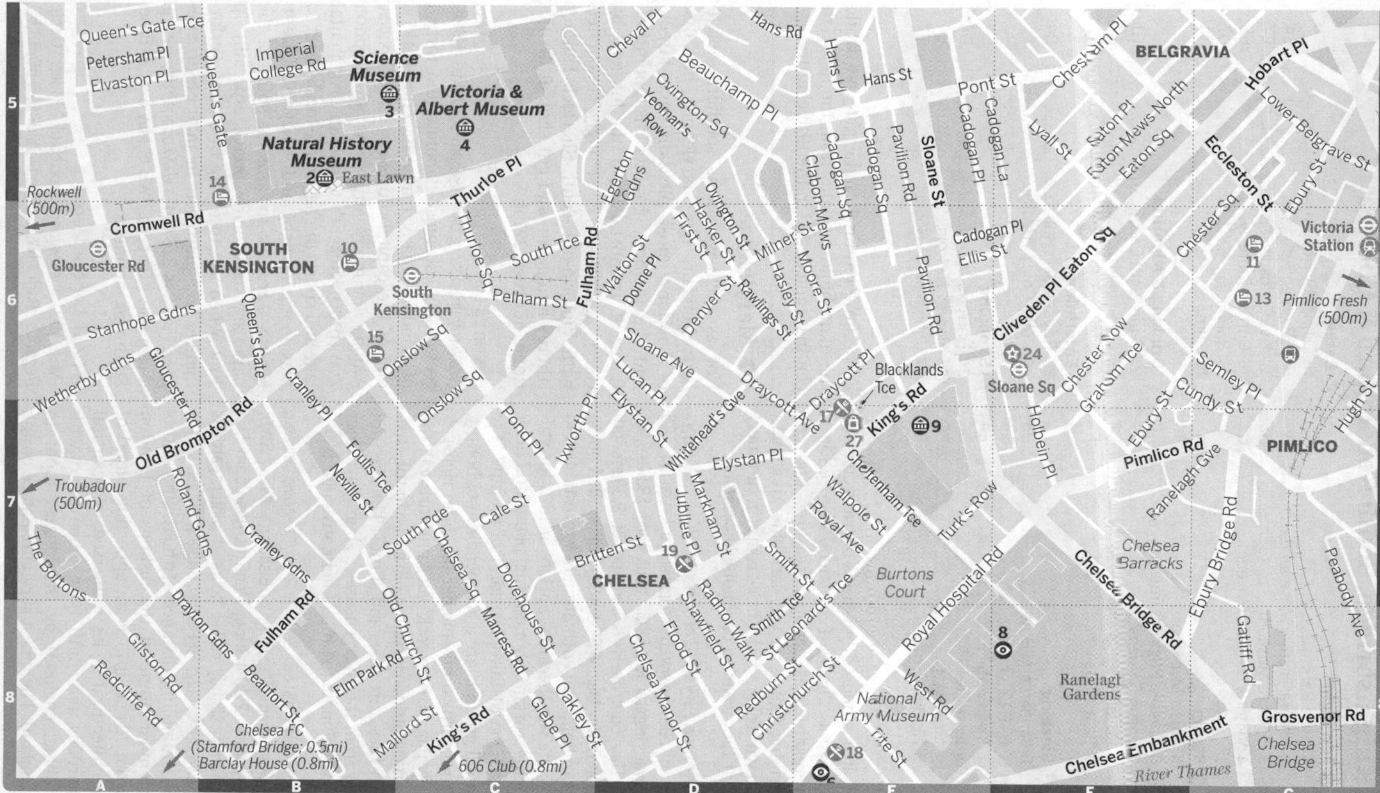
BELGRAVIA
SOUTH KENSINGTON
CHELSEA
PIMLICO
Science Museum
3
Victoria & Albert Museum
4
Natural History Museum
2
East Lawn
Queen's Gate Tce
Petersham Pl
Elvaston Pl
Imperial College Rd
Queen's Gate
Rockwell (500m)
Cromwell Rd
Gloucester Rd
14
10
15
South Kensington
Thurloe Pl
Thurloe Sq
South Tce
Pelham St
Fulham Rd
Stanhope Gdns
Wetherby Gdns
Gloucester Rd
Cranley Pl
Onslow Sq
Old Brompton Rd
Troubadour (500m)
Roland Gdns
The Boltons
Foulis Tce
Neville St
Cranley Gdns
Drayton Gdns
Gilston Rd
Redcliffe Rd
Fulham Rd
Beaufort St
Chelsea FC (Stamford Bridge; 0.5mi) Barclay House (0.8mi)
Elm Park Rd
Old Church St
Mallord St
King's Rd
606 Club (0.8mi)
South Pde
Chelsea Sq
Manresa Rd
Glebe Pl
Oakley St
Dovehouse St
Cale St
Pond Pl
Ixworth Pl
Cheval Pl
Egerton Gdns
Beauchamp Pl
Ovington Sq
Yeoman's Row
Walton St
Donne Pl
Hans Rd
Hans Pl
Hans St
Ovington St
Hasker St
First St
Denyer St
Rawlings St
Hasley St
Milner St
Moore St
Clabon Mews
Cadogan Sq
Pavilion Rd
Sloane St
Cadogan Pl
Cadogan La
Pont St
Chesham Pl
Lyall St
Eaton Pl
Eaton Mews North
Eaton Sq
Hobart Pl
Lower Belgrave St
Eccleston St
Ebury St
Chester Sq
Victoria Station
11
13
Pimlico Fresh (500m)
Cadogan Pl
Ellis St
Cliveden Pl
Eaton Sq
24
Sloane Sq
Chester Row
Graham Tce
Semley Pl
Cundy St
Ebury St
Hugh St
Sloane Ave
Lucan Pl
Elystan St
Whitehead's Gve
Draycott Ave
Draycott Pl
Blacklands Tce
17
27
King's Rd
9
Elystan Pl
Markham St
Jubilee Pl
19
Britten St
Cheltenham Tce
Walpole St
Royal Ave
Smith St
Smith Tce
St Leonard's Tce
Radnor Walk
Shawfield St
Flood St
Chelsea Manor St
Redburn St
Christchurch St
Burtons Court
Turk's Row
Holbein Pl
Pimlico Rd
Ranelagh Gve
Chelsea Barracks
Ebury Bridge Rd
Chelsea Bridge Rd
Royal Hospital Rd
8
Ranelagh Gardens
West Rd
National Army Museum
Tite St
18
Gatliff Rd
Peabody Ave
Grosvenor Rd
Chelsea Embankment
River Thames
Chelsea Bridge
A
B
C
D
E
F
G
5
6
7
8

Knightsbridge, South Kensington & Chelsea

Top Sights
1 Hyde Park D2
2 Natural History Museum B5
3 Science Museum B5
4 Victoria & Albert Museum C5

Sights
5 Albert Memorial B4
6 Chelsea Physic Garden E8
7 Italian Gardens B1
8 Royal Hospital Chelsea F8
9 Saatchi Gallery E7

Sleeping
10 Ampersand Hotel B6
11 B+B Belgravia G6
12 Levin Hotel E4
13 Lime Tree Hotel G6
14 Meininger B5
15 Number Sixteen B6

Eating
16 Dinner by Heston Blumenthal E4
17 Five Fields E7
18 Gordon Ramsay E8
19 Rabbit D7
20 Zuma D4

Drinking & Nightlife
21 Connaught Bar G1
22 Queen's Arms A4

Entertainment
23 Royal Albert Hall B4
24 Royal Court Theatre F6

Shopping
25 Harrods D4
26 Harvey Nichols E4
27 John Sandoe Books E7

II, it has housed hundreds of war veterans, known as Chelsea Pensioners. They're fondly regarded as national treasures, and cut striking figures in the dark-blue greatcoats (in winter) or scarlet frock coats (in summer) that they wear on ceremonial occasions.

Chelsea Physic Garden GARDENS
(Map p98; www.chelseaphysicgarden.co.uk; 66 Royal Hospital Rd, SW3; adult/child £9.50/6.95; 11am-6pm Tue-Fri & Sun Apr-Oct, 9.30am-4pm Mon-Fri Nov-Mar; Sloane Sq) This walled pocket of botanical enchantment was established by the Apothecaries' Society in 1673 for students working on medicinal plants and healing. One of Europe's oldest of its kind, the small grounds are a compendium of botany, from carnivorous pitcher plants to rich yellow flag irises, a cork oak from Portugal, the largest outdoor fruiting olive tree in the British Isles, rare trees and shrubs. The site, not far from the river, ensures a slightly warmer microclimate to protect nonnative plants.

Fulham Palace HISTORIC BUILDING
(www.fulhampalace.org; Bishop's Ave, SW6; palace 12.30-4.30pm Mon-Thu, noon-5pm Sun summer, slightly earlier hours in winter, gardens dawn-dusk daily; Putney Bridge) FREE Within stumbling distance of the Thames, this summer home of the bishops of London from 704 to 1975 is an appealing blend of architectural styles immersed in beautiful gardens and, until 1924, when filled with rubble, enclosed by the longest moat in England. The oldest surviving palace chunk is the little red-brick Tudor gateway, while the main building dates from the mid-17th century, remodelled in the 19th century.

Marylebone

Not as exclusive as its southern neighbour Mayfair, hip Marylebone has one of London's most pleasant high streets and the famous, if rather disappointing, Baker St, immortalised in the hit song by Gerry Rafferty and strongly associated with Victoria-era sleuth Sherlock Holmes (there's a museum and gift shop at his fictional address, 221b).

Regent's Park PARK
(www.royalparks.org.uk; 5am-9.30pm; Regent's Park) The most elaborate and formal of London's many parks, Regent's Park is one of the capital's loveliest green spaces. Among its many attractions are London Zoo (p100), Regent's Canal, an ornamental lake and sports pitches where locals meet to play football, rugby and volleyball. **Queen Mary's Gardens**, towards the south of the park, are particularly pretty, especially in June when the roses are in bloom. Performances take place here in an **open-air theatre** (0844 826 4242; www.openairtheatre.org; Queen Mary's Gardens, NW1; May-Sep; Baker St) during summer.

★**ZSL London Zoo** ZOO
(Map p131; www.londonzoo.co.uk; Outer Circle, Regent's Park, NW1; adult/child £25.50/18.50;

Marylebone

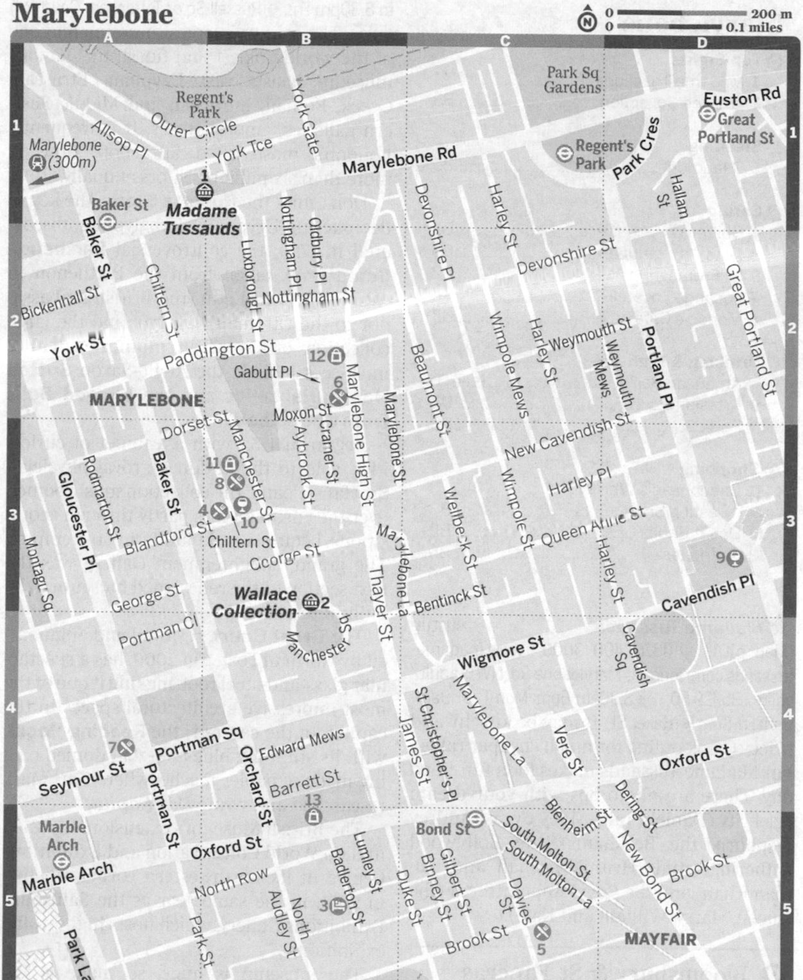

⏲10am-6pm Mar-Sep, to 5pm Oct, to 4pm Nov-Feb; 🚌274) Established in 1828, these 15-hectare zoological gardens are among the oldest in the world. The emphasis nowadays is firmly placed on conservation, education and breeding. Highlights include Penguin Beach, Gorilla Kingdom, Tiger Territory, the walk-through In with the Lemurs, In with the Spiders and Meet the Monkeys. Land of the Lions is a new enclosure to house its Asiatic lions. Feeding sessions and talks take place throughout the day – join in with a spot of afternoon tea (adults/children £19.75/10).

Regent's Canal CANAL

(Map p131) To escape the crowded streets and enjoy a picturesque, waterside angle on North London, take to the canals that once played such a vital role in the transport of goods across the capital. The towpath of the Regent's Canal also makes an excellent shortcut across North London, either on foot or by bike. In full, the ribbon of water runs 9 miles from Little Venice (where it connects with the Grand Union Canal) to the Thames at Limehouse.

Marylebone

★**Madame Tussauds** MUSEUM
(Map p101; ☎0870 400 3000; www.madametussauds.com/london; Marylebone Rd, NW1; adult/child £35/29.50; ⊙8.30am-6pm Mon-Thu, 9am-6pm Fri-Sun; ⊖Baker St) It may be kitschy and pricey (book online for much cheaper rates), but Madame Tussauds makes for a fun-filled day. There are photo ops with your dream celebrity (Daniel Craig, Miley Cyrus, Audrey Hepburn, the Beckhams), the Bollywood gathering (studs Hrithik Roshan and Salman Khan) and the Royal Appointment (the Queen, Harry, William and Kate).

Bloomsbury & St Pancras

With the University of London and British Museum within its genteel environs, it's little wonder that Bloomsbury has attracted a lot of very clever, bookish people over the years. Between the world wars, these pleasant streets were colonised by a group of artists and intellectuals known collectively as the Bloomsbury Group, which included novelists Virginia Woolf and EM Forster and the economist John Maynard Keynes. Russell Sq, its very heart, was laid out in 1800 and is one of London's largest and loveliest.

★**British Museum** MUSEUM
(Map p78; ☎020-7323 8299; www.britishmuseum.org; Great Russell St, WC1; ⊙10am-5.30pm Sat-Thu, to 8.30pm Fri; ⊖Russell Sq or Tottenham Court Rd) FREE The country's largest museum and one of the world's oldest and finest, this famous museum boasts vast Egyptian, Etruscan, Greek, Roman, European and Middle Eastern galleries, among others. It is frequently London's most-visited attraction, drawing more than six million visitors annually.

Don't miss the **Rosetta Stone**, the key to deciphering Egyptian hieroglyphics, discovered in 1799; the controversial **Parthenon Sculptures**, taken from the Parthenon in Athens by Lord Elgin (the British ambassador to the Ottoman Empire); and the large collection of **Egyptian mummies**. Other must-sees include the Anglo-Saxon **Sutton Hoo burial relics** and the **Winged Bulls from Khorsabad**.

Begun in 1753 with a 'cabinet of curiosities' sold to the nation by royal physician Sir Hans Sloane, the collection mushroomed over the ensuing years partly through acquisitions, bequests and plundering the empire. The grand Enlightenment Gallery was the first section of the redesigned museum to be built in the 1820s.

The **Great Court**, restored and augmented by Norman Foster in 2000, has a spectacular glass-and-steel roof, making it one of the most impressive architectural spaces in the capital. In the centre is the **Reading Room**, with its stunning blue-and-gold domed ceiling made of papier mâché, where Karl Marx researched and wrote *Das Kapital*.

The British Museum's extension, the £135 million World Conservation and Exhibitions Centre in its northwestern corner, opened in 2014, in the same year as the Sainsbury Exhibitions Gallery, which hosts high-profile exhibitions.

The museum is huge, so make a few focused visits if you have time, and consider taking one of the free tours. There are 15 free 30- to 40-minute **eye-opener tours** of individual galleries per day. The museum also has free daily gallery talks, a **highlights tour** (adult/child £12/free, 11.30am and 2pm Friday, Saturday and Sunday), free 45-minute **lunchtime gallery talks** (1.15pm Tuesday to Friday) and free 20-minute **spotlight tours** on Friday evenings. Audio guides (£5) can be found at the audio-guide desk in the Great Court.

★**British Library** LIBRARY
(Map p106; www.bl.uk; 96 Euston Rd, NW1; ⊙galleries 9.30am-6pm Mon & Fri, 9.30am-5pm Sat, 9.30am-8pm Tue-Thu, 11am-5pm Sun; 📶; ⊖King's

LOCAL KNOWLEDGE

FREE LONDON

Natural History Museum (p94) Every British child visits this building at least once, and so should you.

Tate Modern (p90) Hosts art designed to perplex and enthral.

Victoria & Albert Museum (p94) It's not overstating it to say that this is the world's greatest art-and-design museum.

National Gallery (p80) One of the world's great art collections, with some 2300 European paintings on display.

Hyde Park (p95) Millions of people come to sunbathe, boat, swim and picnic around the Serpentine, or to hear soapbox oratory at Speaker's Corner.

Science Museum (p94) Seven floors of interactive and educational exhibits.

Wallace Collection (Map p101; www.wallacecollection.org; Hertford House, Manchester Sq, W1; 10am-5pm; Bond St) An enthralling glimpse into 18th-century aristocratic life.

Grant Museum of Zoology (Map p106; www.ucl.ac.uk/museums/zoology; Rockefeller Building, University College London, 21 University St, WC1; 1-5pm Mon-Sat; Euston Sq) Collects 68,000 specimens from around the animal kingdom.

Highgate Cemetery (p112) London's most famous graveyard is also a de facto nature reserve.

Tate Britain (p91) Displays paintings from 1500 to the present; the works of JMW Turner are a particular highlight.

Regent's Park (p100) One of the city's most pleasant green spaces.

Wellcome Collection (p103) Celebrates the intersection of art, science and medicine.

Hampstead Heath (p112) Woodlands and meadows sprawled across 320 hectares.

Cross St Pancras) FREE Consisting of low-slung red-brick terraces and fronted by a large plaza featuring an oversized statue of Sir Isaac Newton, Colin St John Wilson's British Library building is a love-it-or-hate-it affair (Prince Charles likened it to a secret-police academy). Completed in 1997, it's home to some of the greatest treasures of the written word, including the *Codex Sinaiticus* (the first complete text of the New Testament), Leonardo da Vinci's notebooks and a copy of the Magna Carta (1215).

★Wellcome Collection MUSEUM

(Map p106; www.wellcomecollection.org; 183 Euston Rd, NW1; 10am-6pm Tue, Wed & Fri-Sun, to 10pm Thu; Euston Sq) FREE Focusing on the interface of art, science and medicine, this clever and resourceful museum is fascinating. There are interactive displays where you can scan your face and watch it stretched into the statistical average, wacky modern sculptures inspired by various medical conditions, and downright creepy things, such as an actual cross-section of a body and enlargements of parasites (fleas, body lice, scabies) to terrifying proportions.

Charles Dickens Museum MUSEUM

(Map p106; www.dickensmuseum.com; 48 Doughty St, WC1; adult/child £9/4; 10am-5pm, last admission 4pm; ; Chancery Lane or Russell Sq) A £3.5-million renovation made this museum, located in a handsome four-storey house that was the great Victorian novelist's sole surviving residence in London, bigger and better than ever. A period kitchen in the basement and a nursery in the attic were added, and newly acquired 49 Doughty St increased the exhibition space substantially.

Hoxton, Shoreditch & Spitalfields

These revitalised and hip areas northeast of the City have enough sightseeing allure to keep daytime travellers occupied, but things really get going in the evening, when the late-night pubs, clubs and restaurants come into their own. Vibrant Hoxton and Shoreditch form the centre of gravity for nightlife, while Sunday is optimum for strolling leisurely through Spitalfields after a Saturday night out. Over the centuries, waves of immigrants have left their mark here, and it's

The British Museum

A HALF-DAY TOUR

The British Museum, with almost eight million items in its permanent collection, is so vast and comprehensive that it can be daunting for the first-time visitor. To avoid a frustrating trip – and getting lost on the way to the Egyptian mummies – set out on this half-day exploration, which takes in some of the museum's most important sights. If you want to see and learn more, join a tour or grab an audioguide (£5).

A good starting point is the **Rosetta Stone** ❶, the key that cracked the code to ancient Egypt's writing system. Nearby treasures from Assyria – an ancient civilisation centred in Mesopotamia between the Tigris and Euphrates Rivers – including the colossal **Khorsabad Winged Bulls** ❷, give way to the **Parthenon Sculptures** ❸, highpoints of classical Greek art that continue to influence us today. Be sure to see both the sculptures and the monumental frieze celebrating the birth of

Winged Bulls from Khorsabad

This awesome pair of alabaster winged bulls with human heads once guarded the entrance to the palace of Assyrian King Sargon II at Khorsabad in Mesopotamia, a cradle of civilisation in present-day Iraq.

Parthenon Sculptures

The Parthenon, a white marble temple dedicated to Athena, was part of a fortified citadel on the Acropolis in Athens. There are dozens of sculptures and friezes with models and interactive displays explaining how they all once fitted together.

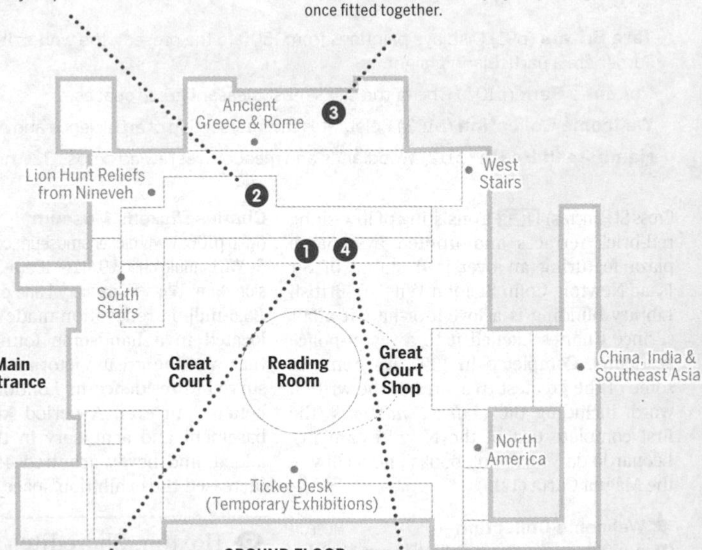

GROUND FLOOR

Rosetta Stone

Written in hieroglyphic, demotic (cursive ancient Egyptian script used for everyday use) and Greek, the 762kg stone contains a decree exempting priests from tax on the first anniversary of young Ptolemy V's coronation.

Bust of Ramesses the Great

The most impressive sculpture in the Egyptian galleries, this 7.5-tonne bust portrays Ramesses II, scourge of the Israelites in the Book of Exodus, as great benefactor.

VISITBRITAIN / JAMES MCCORMICK / GETTY IMAGES ©

FUTURE LIGHT / GETTY IMAGES ©

Athena. En route to the West Stairs is a huge bust of **Pharaoh Ramesses II** (4), just a hint of the large collection of **Egyptian mummies** (5) upstairs. (The earliest, affectionately called Ginger because of wispy reddish hair, was preserved simply by hot sand.) The Romans introduce visitors to the early Britain galleries via the rich **Mildenhall Treasure** (6). The Anglo-Saxon **Sutton Hoo Ship Burial** (7) and the medieval **Lewis Chessmen** (8) follow.

EATING OPTIONS

» **Court Cafes** At the northern end of the Great Court; takeaway counters with salads and sandwiches; communal tables

» **Gallery Cafe** Slightly out of the way near Room 12; quieter; offers hot dishes

» **Court Restaurant** Upstairs overlooking the former Reading Room; sit-down meals

Lewis Chessmen
The much-loved 78 chess pieces portray faceless pawns, worried-looking queens, bishops with their mitres turned sideways and rooks as 'warders', gnawing away at their shields.

FEARGUS COONEY / GETTY IMAGES ©

Egyptian Mummies
Among the rich collection of mummies and funerary objects is 'Ginger', who was buried at the site of Gebelein, in Upper Egypt, more than 5000 years ago, and Katebet, a one-time chantress (ritual performer) at the Amun temple in Karnak.

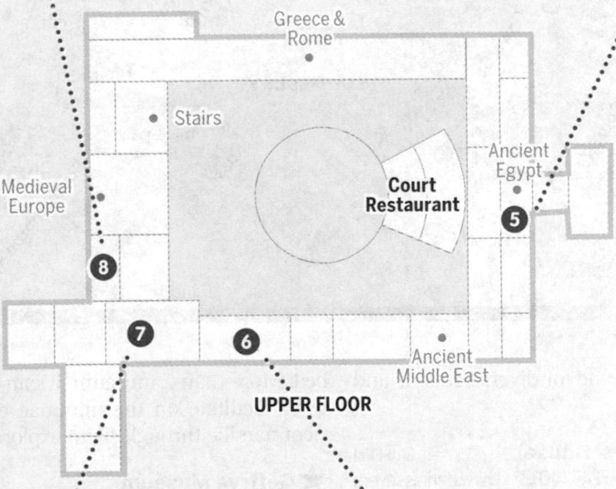

Mildenhall Treasure
Roman gods such as Neptune and Bacchus share space with early Christian symbols like the *chi-rho* (short for 'Christ') on the find's three dozen silver bowls, plates and spoons.

Sutton Hoo Ship Burial
This unique grave of an important (but unidentified) Anglo-Saxon royal has yielded drinking horns, gold buckles and a stunning helmet with face mask.

North Central London

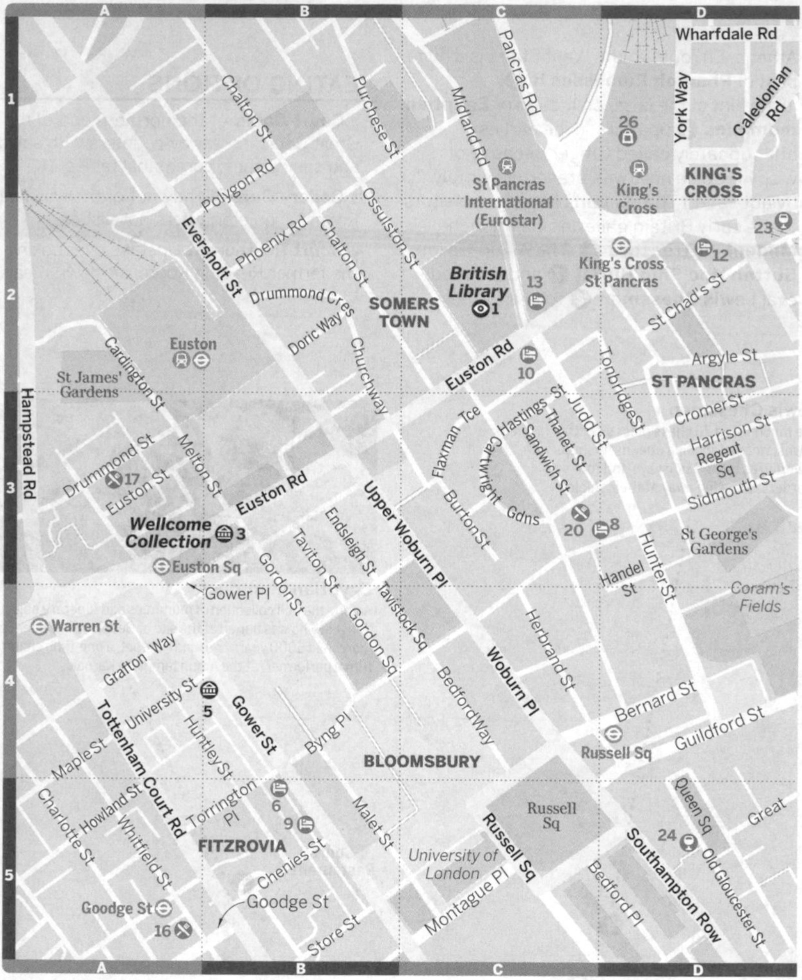

a great place to come for diverse cuisine and vibrant nightlife.

★Dennis Severs' House — MUSEUM

(Map p132; ☎020-7247 4013; www.dennisseverhouse.co.uk; 18 Folgate St, E1; day/night £10/15; ⏲noon-2pm & 5-9pm Mon, 5-9pm Wed & Fri, noon-4pm Sun; ⊖Shoreditch High St) This extraordinary Georgian House is set up as if its occupants – a family of Huguenot silk weavers – had just walked out the door. There are half-drunk cups of tea and partially consumed food, lit candles and, in perhaps unnecessary attention to detail, a full chamber pot by the bed. More than a museum, it's an opportunity to meditate on the minutiae of everyday Georgian life through silent exploration.

★Geffrye Museum — MUSEUM

(Map p132; www.geffrye-museum.org.uk; 136 Kingsland Rd, E2; ⏲10am-5pm Tue-Sun; ⊖Hoxton) FREE If you like nosing around other people's homes, you'll love this museum, entirely devoted to middle-class domestic interiors. Built in 1714 as a home for poor pensioners, these beautiful ivy-clad brick almshouses have been converted into a series of living rooms, dating from 1630 to the

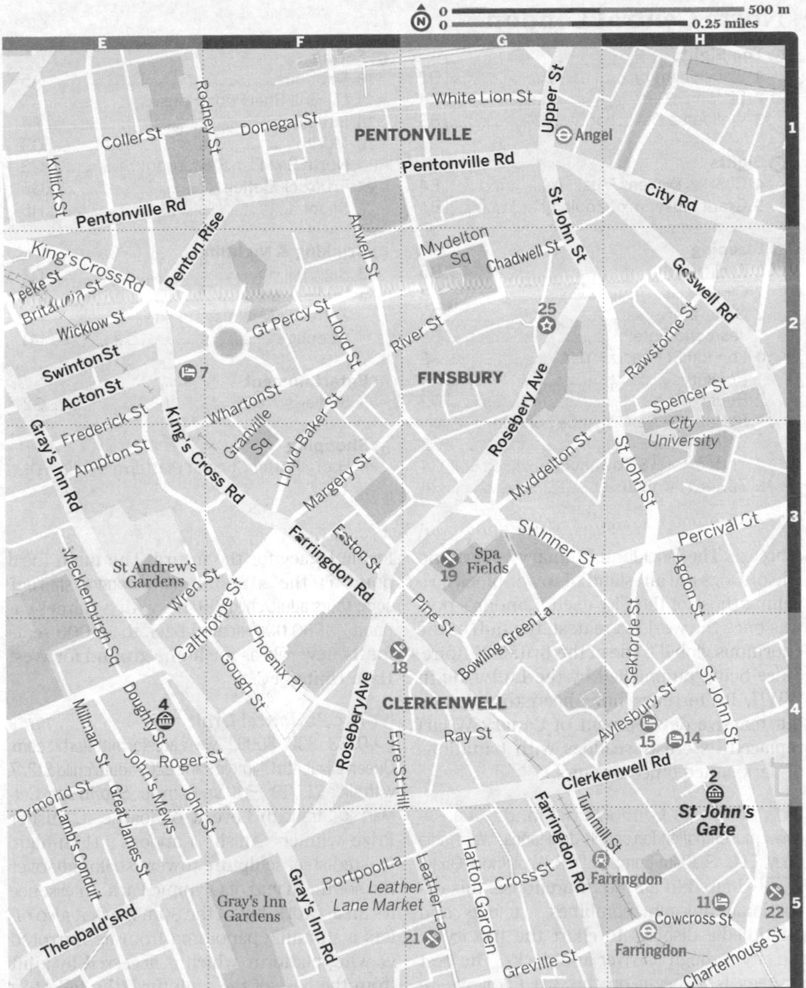

present day. The rear garden is also organised by era, mirroring the museum's exploration of domesticity through the centuries. There's also a very impressive walled herb garden, featuring 170 different plants.

★St John's Gate HISTORIC BUILDING

(Map p106; www.museumstjohn.org.uk; St John's Lane, EC1M; tour suggested donation £5; ⏲10am-5pm Mon-Sat year-round, 10am-5pm Sun July-Aug, tours 11am & 2.30pm Tue, Fri & Sat; ⊖Farringdon) FREE This remarkable Tudor gate dates to 1504. During the 12th century, the Knights Hospitaller (a Christian and military order with a focus on providing care to the sick) established a priory here. Inside is a small museum that covers the history of the order (including rare examples of the knights' armour), as well as its 19th-century revival in Britain as the secular Order of St John and the foundation of St John Ambulance.

The East End & Docklands

A huge area, the East End and Docklands are not rich in sights, but a dramatic new focus has emerged in the Olympic Park, while new Overground lines make transport

North Central London

Top Sights
1 British Library C2
2 St John's Gate H4
3 Wellcome Collection B3

Sights
4 Charles Dickens Museum E4
5 Grant Museum of Zoology B4

Sleeping
6 Arosfa Hotel B5
7 Clink78 ...... E2
8 Generator D3
9 Jesmond Hotel B5
10 London St Pancras YHA C2
11 Rookery H5
12 Rough Luxe D2
13 St Pancras Renaissance London Hotel C2
14 Zetter Hotel & Townhouse H4
15 Zetter Townhouse H4

Eating
16 Dabbous A5
17 Diwana Bhel Poori House A3
18 Little Bay F4
19 Morito G3
20 North Sea Fish Restaurant C3
21 Prufrock Coffee G5
22 St John H5

Drinking & Nightlife
23 Big Chill House D2
24 Queen's Larder D5
Zetter Townhouse Cocktail Lounge ...... (see 14)

Entertainment
25 Sadler's Wells G2

Shopping
26 Harry Potter Shop at Platform 9¾ D1

a breeze. The Docklands' Canary Wharf and Isle of Dogs are an island of tower blocks, rivalling those of the City itself. London's port was once the world's greatest, the hub of the enormous global trade of the British Empire. Since being pummelled by the Luftwaffe in WWII, its fortunes have been topsy-turvy, but massive development of Canary Wharf replaced its crusty seadogs with battalions of dark-suited office workers.

★ **Museum of London Docklands** MUSEUM
(www.museumoflondon.org.uk/docklands; West India Quay, E14; 10am-6pm; DLR West India Quay) FREE Housed in an 1802 warehouse, this educational museum combines artefacts and multimedia displays to chart the history of the city through its river and docks. The best strategy is to begin on the 3rd floor, where displays cover the Roman settlement of Londinium, and work your way down through the ages. Perhaps the most illuminating and certainly the most disturbing gallery is London, Sugar and Slavery, which examines the capital's role in the transatlantic slave trade.

★ **Queen Elizabeth Olympic Park** PARK
(www.queenelizabetholympicpark.co.uk; E20; Stratford) The glittering centrepiece of London's 2012 Olympic Games, this vast 227-hectare expanse includes the main Olympic venues as well as playgrounds, walking and cycling trails, gardens and a diverse mix of wetland, woodland, meadow and other wildlife habitats as an environmentally fertile legacy for the future. The main focal point is the **stadium** (www.london-stadium.com; tours adult/child £19/11), with a Games capacity of 80,000, scaled back to 54,000 seats for its new role as the home ground for West Ham United FC.

★ **ArcelorMittal Orbit** TOWER
(0333 800 8099; www.arcelormittalorbit.com; Queen Elizabeth Olympic Park, E20; adult/child £12/7, with slide £15/10; 10am-6pm Apr-Sep, to 5pm Oct-Mar; Stratford) Love it or loathe it, Turner Prize–winner Anish Kapoor's 115m-high, twisted-steel sculpture towers strikingly over the southern end of Olympic Park. In essence it's an artwork, but at the 80m mark it also offers a stunning panorama from its mirrored viewing platform, which is accessed by a lift from the base of the sculpture (the tallest in the UK). A dramatic tunnel slide running down the tower is the world's highest and longest, coiling 178m down to ground level.

House Mill HISTORIC BUILDING
(www.housemill.org.uk; Three Mill Lane, E3; adult/child £3/free; 11am-4pm Sun May-Oct, 1st Sun only Mar, Apr & Dec; Bromley-by-Bow) One of two remaining mills from a trio that once stood on this small island in the River Lea, House Mill (1776) operated as a sluice tidal mill, grinding grain for a nearby distillery until 1941. Tours, which run according to demand and last about 45 minutes, take visitors to all four floors of the mill and offer a fascinating look at traditional East End industry.

★ **Viktor Wynd Museum of Curiosities, Fine Art & Natural History** MUSEUM

(www.thelasttuesdaysociety.org; 11 Mare St, E8; admission £5; 11am-10pm Wed-Sun; Bethnal Green) Museum? Art project? Cocktail bar? This is not a venue that's easily classifiable. Inspired by Victorian-era cabinets of curiosities (*wunderkabinnet*), Wynd's wilfully eccentric collection includes stuffed birds, pickled genitals, two-headed lambs, shrunken heads, a key to the Garden of Eden, dodo bones, celebrity excrement, ancient Chinese dildos and toys from McDonald's Happy Meals. A self-confessed 'incoherent vision of the world displayed through wonder', make of it what you will. Or stop by for a cocktail (£8) at the tiny bar.

Greenwich

Greenwich (*gren*-itch) straddles the hemispheres and the ages, retaining its own sense of identity based on historic associations with the sea and science and an extraordinary cluster of buildings that have earned 'Maritime Greenwich' a Unesco World Heritage listing.

★ **Old Royal Naval College** HISTORIC BUILDING

(www.ornc.org; 2 Cutty Sark Gardens, SE10; grounds 8am-6pm, to 11pm in summer; DLR Cutty Sark) FREE Designed by Christopher Wren, the Old Royal Naval College is a magnificent example of monumental classical architecture. Parts are now used by the University of Greenwich and Trinity College of Music, but you can still visit the **chapel** and the extraordinary **Painted Hall**, which took artist Sir James Thornhill 19 years to complete. Hour-long, yeomen-led tours (£6) leave at noon daily, taking in areas not otherwise open to the public. Free 45-minute tours take place at least four times daily.

★ **National Maritime Museum** MUSEUM

(www.rmg.co.uk/national-maritime-museum; Romney Rd, SE10; 10am-5pm; DLR Cutty Sark) FREE Narrating the long, briny and eventful history of seafaring Britain, this excellent museum's exhibits are arranged thematically, with highlights including *Miss Britain III* (the first boat to top 100mph on open water) from 1933, the 19m-long golden state barge built in 1732 for Frederick, Prince of Wales, the huge ship's propeller and the colourful figureheads installed on the ground floor. Families will love these, as well as the ship simulator and the 'All Hands' children's gallery on the 2nd floor.

★ **Royal Observatory** HISTORIC BUILDING

(www.rmg.co.uk; Greenwich Park, Blackheath Ave, SE10; adult/child £9.50/5, with Cutty Sark £18.50/8.50; 10am-5pm Sep-Jun, to 6pm Jul & Aug; DLR Cutty Sark, DLR Greenwich, Greenwich) Rising south of Queen's House, idyllic **Greenwich Park** (www.royalparks.org.uk; King George St, SE10; 6am-6pm winter, to 8pm spring & autumn, to 9pm summer; DLR Cutty Sark, Greenwich or Maze Hill) climbs up the hill, affording stunning views of London from the Royal Observatory, which Charles II had built in 1675 to help solve the riddle of longitude. To the north is lovely **Flamsteed House** and the **Meridian Courtyard**, where you can stand with your feet straddling the western and eastern hemispheres; admission is by ticket. The southern half contains the highly informative and free **Weller Astronomy Galleries** and the **Peter Harrison Planetarium** (020-8312 6608; www.rmg.co.uk/whats-on/planetarium-shows; adult/child £7.50/5.50).

Queen's House HISTORIC BUILDING

(www.rmg.co.uk/queens-house; Romney Rd, SE10; 10am-5pm; DLR Cutty Sark) FREE The first Palladian building by architect Inigo Jones after he returned from Italy is as enticing for its form as for its art collection. The Great Hall is a lovely cube shape with an elaborately

EMIRATES AIR LINE CABLE CAR

Capable of ferrying 2400 people per hour across the Thames in either direction, the cable car run by **Emirates Air Line** (www.emiratesairline.co.uk; 27 Western Gateway, E16; one-way adult/child £4.50/2.30, with Oyster Card or Travelcard £3.40/1.70; 7am-9pm Mon-Fri, 8am-9pm Sat, 9am-9pm Sun, closes 8pm Oct-Mar; DLR Royal Victoria, North Greenwich) makes quick work of the journey from the Greenwich Peninsula to the Royal Docks. Although it's mostly patronised by tourists for the views over the river – and the views are ace – it's also listed on the London Underground map as part of the transport network. Oyster Card and Travelcard holders nab discounts for journeys, which are bike-friendly, too.

The River Thames

A FLOATING TOUR

London's history has always been determined by the Thames. The city was founded as a Roman port nearly 2000 years ago and over the centuries since then many of the capital's landmarks have lined the river's banks. A boat trip is a great way to experience the attractions.

There are piers dotted along both banks at regular intervals where you can hop on and hop off the regular services to visit places of interest. The best place to board is Westminster Pier, from where boats head downstream, taking you from the City of Westminster, the seat of government, to the original City of London, now the financial district and dominated by a growing band of skyscrapers. Across the river, the once shabby and neglected South Bank now bristles with as many top attractions as its northern counterpart, including the slender Shard.

In our illustration we've concentrated on the top highlights you'll enjoy from a waterborne

KIEVVICTOR / SHUTTERSTOCK ©

Somerset House

This grand neoclassical palace was once one of many aristocratic houses lining the Thames. The huge arches at river level gave direct access to the Thames until the Embankment was built in the 1860s.

St Paul's Cathedral

Though there's been a church here since AD 604, the current building rose from the ashes of the 1666 Great Fire and is architect Christopher Wren's masterpiece. Famous for surviving the Blitz intact and for the wedding of Charles and Diana, it's looking as good as new after a major clean-up for its 300th anniversary in 2011.

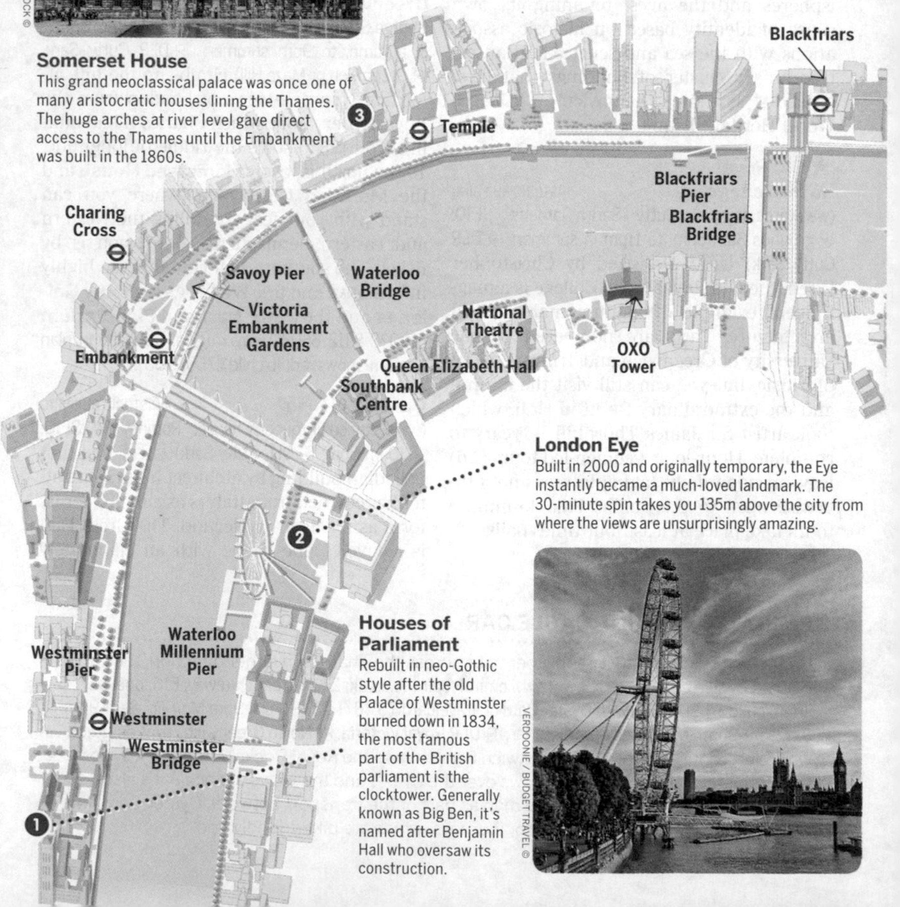

London Eye

Built in 2000 and originally temporary, the Eye instantly became a much-loved landmark. The 30-minute spin takes you 135m above the city from where the views are unsurprisingly amazing.

Houses of Parliament

Rebuilt in neo-Gothic style after the old Palace of Westminster burned down in 1834, the most famous part of the British parliament is the clocktower. Generally known as Big Ben, it's named after Benjamin Hall who oversaw its construction.

VERDOONIE / BUDGET TRAVEL ©

vessel. These are, from west to east, the **Houses of Parliament** ❶, the **London Eye** ❷, **Somerset House** ❸, **St Paul's Cathedral** ❹, **Tate Modern** ❺, **Shakespeare's Globe** ❻, the **Tower of London** ❼ and **Tower Bridge** ❽.

Apart from covering this central section of the river, boats can also be taken upstream as far as Kew Gardens and Hampton Court Palace, and downstream to Greenwich and the Thames Barrier.

BOAT HOPPING

Thames Clippers hop-on/hop-off services are aimed at commuters but are equally useful for visitors, operating every 15 minutes on a loop from piers at Embankment, Waterloo, Blackfriars, Bankside, London Bridge and the Tower. Other services also go from Westminster. Oyster cardholders get a discount off the boat ticket price.

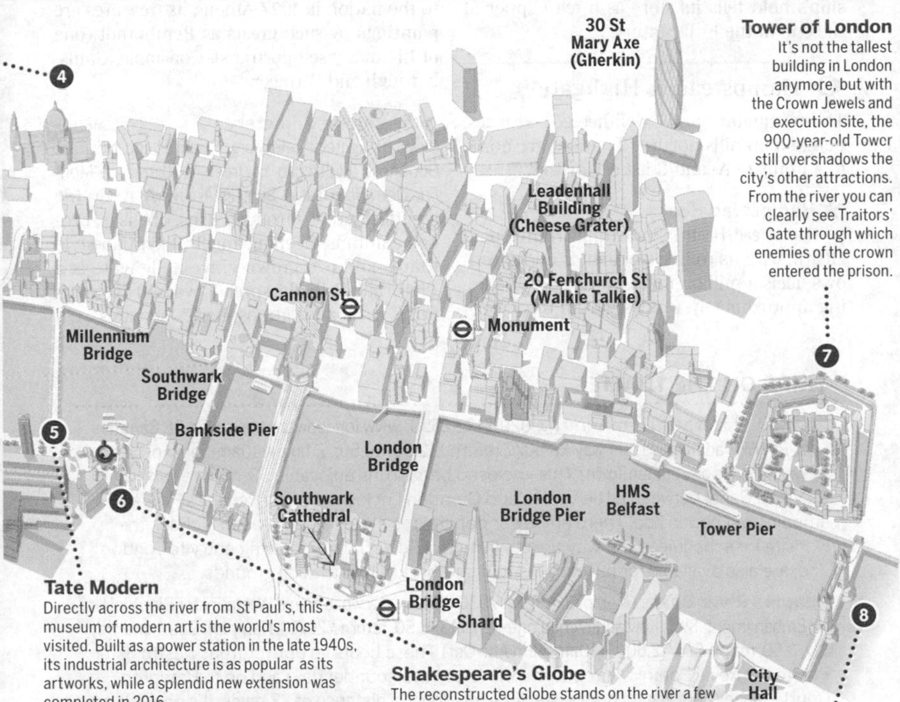

Tower of London

It's not the tallest building in London anymore, but with the Crown Jewels and execution site, the 900-year-old Tower still overshadows the city's other attractions. From the river you can clearly see Traitors' Gate through which enemies of the crown entered the prison.

Tate Modern

Directly across the river from St Paul's, this museum of modern art is the world's most visited. Built as a power station in the late 1940s, its industrial architecture is as popular as its artworks, while a splendid new extension was completed in 2016.

Shakespeare's Globe

The reconstructed Globe stands on the river a few hundred metres from where the original stood (and burnt down in 1613 during a performance). The life's work of American actor Sam Wanamaker, the theatre runs a hugely popular season from April to October each year.

Tower Bridge

It might look as old as its namesake neighbour but one of the world's most iconic bridges was only completed in 1894. Not to be confused with London Bridge upstream, this one's famous raising bascules allowed tall ships to dock at the old wharves to the west and are still lifted up to 1000 times a year.

tiled floor. Climb the beautiful helix-shaped Tulip Stairs up to the 1st floor, where there's a rich collection of paintings and portraits with a sea or seafaring theme from the National Maritime Museum's collection.

★Cutty Sark MUSEUM

(020-8312 6608; www.rmg.co.uk/cuttysark; King William Walk, SE10; adult/child £13.50/7, with Royal Observatory £18.50/8.50; 10am-5pm Sep-Jun, to 6pm Jul & Aug; DLR Cutty Sark) This Greenwich landmark, the last of the great clipper ships to sail between China and England in the 19th century, saw £25 million of extensive renovations largely precipitated by a disastrous fire in 2007. The exhibition in the ship's hold tells its story as a tea clipper at the end of the 19th century.

Hampstead & Highgate

These quaint and well-heeled villages, perched on hills north of London, are home to a litany of A- and B-list celebrities.

★Hampstead Heath PARK

(Hampstead Heath) Sprawling Hampstead Heath, with its rolling woodlands and meadows, feels a million miles away – despite being approximately 4 miles – from the City of London. Covering 320 hectares, most of it woods, hills and meadows, it's home to about 180 bird species, 23 species of butterflies, grass snakes, bats and a rich array of flora.

★Kenwood HISTORIC BUILDING

(EH; www.english-heritage.org.uk; Hampstead Lane, NW3; 10am-5pm; 210) FREE This magnificent neoclassical mansion stands at the northern end of Hampstead Heath in a glorious sweep of landscaped gardens leading down to a picturesque lake. The 17th-century house was substantially remodelled in the 1760s and rescued from developers by Edward Cecil Guinness, 1st Earl of Iveagh, who donated it and the wonderful collection of art it contains to the nation in 1927. Among its treasures are paintings by such greats as Rembrandt (one of his many self-portraits), Constable, Gainsborough and Vermeer.

★Highgate Cemetery CEMETERY

(www.highgatecemetery.org; Swain's Lane, N6; East Cemetery adult/child £4/free; 10am-5pm Mon-Fri, 11am-5pm Sat & Sun; Archway) A Gothic wonderland of shrouded urns, obelisks, broken columns, sleeping angels, Egyptian-style tombs and overgrown graves, Highgate is a Victorian Valhalla spread over 20 wonderfully wild and atmospheric hectares. On

TRIPS ON THE THAMES

London Waterbus Company (020-7482 2550; www.londonwaterbus.co.uk; 58 Camden Lock Pl, NW1; adult/child one-way £8.50/7, return £12.50/10.50; hourly 10am-5pm Apr-Sep; Warwick Ave or Camden Town) This enclosed barge runs enjoyable 50-minute trips on Regent's Canal between Little Venice and Camden Lock, passing by Regent's Park and stopping at London Zoo. There are fewer departures outside high season – check the website for schedules. One-way tickets (adult/child £25/18), including entry to London Zoo, are also available for passengers to disembark within the zoo grounds.

Thames River Boats (Map p72; 020-7930 2062; www.wpsa.co.uk; Westminster Pier, Victoria Embankment, SW1; Kew adult/child one-way £13/6.50, return £20/10, Hampton Court one-way £17/8.50, return £25/12.50; 10am-4pm Apr-Oct) These boats go upriver from Westminster Pier to the Royal Botanic Gardens at Kew (1½ hours, four per day) and on to Hampton Court Palace (another 1½ hours, 11am sailing only), a distance of 22 miles. It's possible to get off the boats at Richmond, but it depends on the tides; check before you sail.

London Duck Tours (Map p92; 020-7928 3132; www.londonducktours.co.uk; County Hall, SE1; adult/child from £26/18; Waterloo) Amphibious craft based on D-Day landing vehicles depart from behind the **London Eye** (p90) near the County Hall and cruise the streets of central London before making a dramatic descent into the Thames at Vauxhall. There's a variety of tours, from the classic sightseeing tour to a James Bond tour and a D Day Duck tour, as well as private tours.

City Cruises (Map p72; 020-7740 0400; www.citycruises.com; single/return from £12.50/16.50, day pass £16.65) Ferry service departing every 30 minutes between Westminster, the London Eye, Bankside, Tower and Greenwich piers, with circular cruises (£11.70) going from Tower and Bankside.

the eastern side, you can pay your respects to the graves of Karl Marx and Mary Ann Evans (better known as novelist George Eliot). The real highlight, however, is the overgrown **West Cemetery**, which can only be visited on a **guided tour** (adult/child £12/6; 1.45pm Mon-Fri, every 30min 11am-3pm Sat & Sun Nov-Mar, to 4pm Apr-Oct); bookings are essential for weekday tours.

Outside Central London

★Kew Gardens — GARDENS

(www.kew.org; Kew Rd; adult/child £15/3.50; 10am-6.30pm Apr-Aug, closes earlier Sep-Mar; Kew Pier, Kew Bridge, Kew Gardens) In 1759 botanists began rummaging around the world for specimens to plant in the 3-hectare Royal Botanic Gardens at Kew. They never stopped collecting, and the gardens, which have bloomed to 120 hectares, provide the most comprehensive botanical collection on earth (including the world's largest collection of orchids). A Unesco World Heritage Site, the gardens can easily devour a day's exploration; for those pressed for time, the **Kew Explorer** (adult/child £5/2) hop-on/hop-off road train takes in the main sights.

Don't worry if you don't know your golden slipper orchid from your fengoky or your quiver tree from your alang-alang; a visit to Kew is a journey of discovery for everyone. Highlights include the enormous early **Victorian Palm House**, a hothouse of metal and curved sheets of glass; the impressive **Princess of Wales Conservatory**; the red-brick, 1631 **Kew Palace** (www.hrp.org.uk/kewpalace; with admission to Kew Gardens; 10.30am-5.30pm Apr-Sep), formerly King George III's country retreat; the celebrated **Chinese Pagoda** designed by William Chambers in 1762 (closed for restoration until 2018); the **Temperate House**, the world's largest ornamental glasshouse (closed for restoration until 2018); and the very enjoyable **Rhizotron & Xstrata Treetop Walkway**, where you can survey the tree canopy from 18m up in the air. A lattice fashioned from thousands of pieces of aluminium illuminated with hundreds of LED lights, the 17m-high **Hive** mimics activity within a real beehive (it's on show till late 2017). Check the website for a full list of activities at Kew from free one-hour walking tours (daily), photography walks, theatre performances, outside cinema as well as a host of seasonal events and things to do.

> **WORTH A TRIP**
>
> **ABBEY ROAD STUDIOS**
>
> Beatles aficionados can't possibly visit London without making a pilgrimage to the famous **Abbey Road Studios** (www.abbeyroad.com; 3 Abbey Rd, NW8; St John's Wood) in St John's Wood. The recording studios themselves are off-limits, so you'll have to content yourself with examining the decades of fans' graffiti on the fence outside. Stop-start local traffic is long accustomed to groups of tourists lining up on the zebra crossing to re-enact the cover of the fab four's 1969 masterpiece *Abbey Road*. In 2010 the crossing was rewarded with Grade II heritage status.

Kew Gardens are easily reached by tube, but you might prefer to take a cruise on a riverboat from the **Westminster Passenger Services Association** (Map p72; 020-7930 2062; www.wpsa.co.uk; return to Hampton Court adult/child £25/12.50; Westminster), which runs several daily boats from April to October, departing from Westminster Pier.

★Hampton Court Palace — PALACE

(www.hrp.org.uk/hamptoncourtpalace; adult/child/family £19/9.50/47; 10am-6pm Apr-Oct, to 4.30pm Nov-Mar; Hampton Court Palace, Hampton Court) Built by Cardinal Thomas Wolsey in 1514 but coaxed from him by Henry VIII just before Wolsey (as chancellor) fell from favour, Hampton Court Palace is England's largest and grandest Tudor structure. It was already one of Europe's most sophisticated palaces when, in the 17th century, Christopher Wren designed an extension. The result is a beautiful blend of Tudor and 'restrained baroque' architecture. You could easily spend a day exploring the palace and its 24 hectares of riverside gardens, including a 300-year-old **maze** (adult/child/family £4.40/2.80/13.20; 10am-5.15pm Apr-Oct, to 3.45pm Nov-Mar).

Take a themed tour led by costumed historians or, if you're in a rush, visit the highlights: **Henry VIII's State Apartments**, including the **Great Hall** with its spectacular hammer-beamed roof; the **Tudor Kitchens**, staffed by 'servants'; the **Wolsey Closet**; the **Chapel Royal**; **William III's & Mary II's Apartments**, the **King's Staircase** and the **Chocolate Kitchens**; Mantegna's **The Triumphs of Caesar**; the restored and recently opened **Cumberland Art Gallery** off Clock

Court; and the magnificent gardens, including the **Kitchen Garden** – and don't miss getting lost in the maze. The **Magic Garden** is a new interactive garden attraction for children and families. Also keep an eye out for the **Real Tennis Court**, dating from the 1620s. Do not overlook exploring the palace's magnificent riverside **gardens**; on a sunny day it reveals London at its very finest and most beautiful. Check the schedule for spectacular shows and **events**, including Tudor jousting, falconry displays, ghost hunts (for children), garden adventures, family trails and more. In summer, fun 15- to 20-minute shire-horse-drawn **charabanc tours** (adult/child £6/3) depart from the East Front Garden between 11am and 5pm.

Ask one of the red-tunic-garbed warders for anecdotes and information. The excellent **audio guides** can be picked up just off Base Court and then dropped off in the bin as you exit the palace to the gardens.

Hampton Court is 13 miles southwest of central London and is easily reached by train from Waterloo. Alternatively, the riverboats that head from Westminster to Kew continue here (adult/child £17/8.50, three hours).

See p112 for more information.

Richmond Park PARK

(⏲7am-dusk; ⊖Richmond) At almost 1000 hectares (the largest urban parkland in Europe), this park offers everything from formal gardens and ancient oaks to unsurpassed views of central London 12 miles away. It's easy to flee the several roads slicing up the rambling wilderness, making the park perfect for a quiet walk or a picnic with the kids, even in summer when Richmond's riverside heaves. Coming from Richmond, it's easiest to enter via Richmond Gate or from Petersham Rd.

Strawberry Hill HISTORIC BUILDING

(www.strawberryhillhouse.org.uk; 268 Waldegrave Rd, TW1; adult/child £12/free; ⏲house 1.40-5.30pm Mon-Wed, noon-5.30pm Sat & Sun Mar-Oct, garden 10am-6pm daily; 🚆Strawberry Hill, ⊖Richmond Station, then bus R68) With its snow-white walls and Gothic turrets, this fantastical and totally restored 18th-century creation in Twickenham is the work of art historian, author and politician Horace Walpole. Studded with elaborate stained glass, the building reaches its astonishing apogee in the gallery, with its magnificent papier-mâché ceiling. For the full magic, join a twilight tour (£20). Last admission to the house is 4pm.

Wimbledon Lawn Tennis Museum MUSEUM

(☎020-8946 6131; www.wimbledon.com/museum; Gate 4, Church Rd, SW19; adult/child £13/8, museum & tour £24/15; ⏲10am-5.30pm, last admission 5pm; 🚆Wimbledon, then bus 93, ⊖Wimbledon) This ace museum details the history of tennis – from its French precursor *jeu de paume* (which employed the open hand) to the supersonic serves of today's champions. It's a state-of-the-art presentation, with plenty of video clips and a projection of John McEnroe in the dressing room at Wimbledon, but the highlight is the chance to see Centre Court from the **360-degree viewing box**. During the championships in June/July, only those with tickets to the tournament can access the museum.

Tours

From erudite to eccentric, tours on offer to see the sights are legion in London. Bus tours, although not particularly cool, are good for those who are short on time. Those with special interests – Jewish London, bird watching, pop music – might consider hiring their own guide.

Original Tour BUS

(www.theoriginaltour.com; adult/child £30/15; ⏲8.30am-8.30pm) A 24-hour hop-on, hop-off bus service with a river cruise thrown in, as well as three themed walks: Changing of the Guard, Rock 'n' Roll and Jack the Ripper. Buses run every five to 20 minutes; you can buy tickets on the bus or online. There's also a 48-hour ticket available (adult/child £40/19), with an extended river cruise.

Big Bus Tours BUS

(www.bigbustours.com; adult/child £26/12.50; ⏲every 20min 8.30am-6pm Apr-Sep, to 5pm Oct & Mar, to 4.30pm Nov-Feb) Informative commentaries in 12 languages. The ticket includes a free river cruise with City Cruises and three thematic walking tours (Royal London, film locations, mysteries). Good online booking discounts available.

London Mystery Walks WALKING

(☎07957 388280; www.tourguides.org.uk; adult/child/family £10/9/20) Tour Jack the Ripper's old haunts at 7pm on Monday, Wednesday, Friday and Sunday. London chocolate tours too (£39) on Sunday at 12.30pm. You must book in advance.

London Beatles Walks WALKING

(☎07958 706329; www.beatlesinlondon.com; adult/child £10/free) Public and private tours following in the footsteps of the fab four. Most tours are just over two hours.

London Bicycle Tour CYCLING
(Map p92; 020-7928 6838; www.londonbicycle.com; 1 Gabriel's Wharf, 56 Upper Ground, SE1; tour incl bike from £23.95, bike hire per day £20; Southwark, Waterloo or Blackfriars) Three-hour tours begin in the South Bank and take in London's highlights on both sides of the river; a night ride is also available. You can also hire traditional or speciality bikes, such as tandems and folding bikes, by the hour or day.

Activities

London Aquatics Centre SWIMMING
(www.londonaquaticscentre.org; Queen Elizabeth Olympic Park, E20; adult/child £4.95/2.50; 6am-10.30pm; Stratford) The sweeping lines and wave-like movement of Zaha Hadid's award-winning Aquatics Centre make it the architectural highlight of Olympic Park (p108). Bathed in natural light, the 50m competition pool beneath the huge undulating roof (which sits on just three supports) is an extraordinary place to swim. There's also a second 50m pool, a diving area, gym, creche and cafe.

Lee Valley VeloPark CYCLING
(0300 0030 610; www.visitleevalley.org.uk/velopark; Abercrombie Rd, E20; 1hr taster adult/child £40/30, pay & ride weekend/weekday £5/4, bike & helmet hire from £8; 9am-10pm; Hackney Wick) An architectural highlight of Olympic Park (p108), the cutting-edge velodrome is open to the public – either to wander through and watch the pros tear around the steep-sloped circuit, or to have a go yourself. Both the velodrome and the attached BMX park offer taster sessions. Mountain bikers and road cyclists can attack the tracks on a pay-and-ride basis.

Up at the O2 ADVENTURE SPORTS
(www.theo2.co.uk/upattheo2; O2, Greenwich Peninsula, SE10; weekdays/weekends from £28/35; hours vary; North Greenwich) London isn't exactly your thrill-seeking destination, but this ascent of the O2 dome is not for the faint-hearted. Equipped with climbing suit and harness, you'll scale the famous white dome to reach a viewing platform perched 52m above the Thames with sweeping views of Canary Wharf, the river, Greenwich and beyond. Hours vary depending on the season (sunset climbs also available).

Festivals & Events

Chinese New Year CULTURAL
(late Jan or early Feb) Chinese New Year sees Chinatown snap, crackle and pop with fireworks, a colourful street parade and eating aplenty.

University Boat Race ROWING
(www.theboatrace.org; late Mar) A posh-boy grudge match held annually since 1829 between the rowing crews of Oxford and Cambridge universities.

Virgin Money London Marathon MARATHON
(www.virginmoneylondonmarathon.com; late Apr) Up to half a million spectators watch the whippet-thin champions and bizarrely clad amateurs take to the streets.

Chelsea Flower Show HORTICULTURE
(www.rhs.org.uk/chelsea; Royal Hospital Chelsea; admission from £23; May) Arguably the world's most renowned horticultural show attracts green fingers from near and far.

Trooping the Colour PARADE
(Jun) Celebrating the Queen's official birthday, this ceremonial procession of troops, marching along the Mall for their monarch's inspection, is a pageantry overload.

Field Day MUSIC
(www.fielddayfestivals.com; Victoria Park, Grove Rd, E3; Jun; Hackney Wick) The annual Field Day music festival has been running in **Victoria Park** (www.towerhamlets.gov.uk/victoriapark; Grove Rd, E3; 7am-dusk; Hackney Wick) since 2007, with performances in recent years from PJ Harvey, Air and James Blake.

Royal Academy Summer Exhibition ART
(www.royalacademy.org.uk; adult/child £9.50/5; mid-Jun–mid-Aug) This is an annual showcase of works submitted by artists from all over Britain, mercifully distilled to 1200 or so pieces.

OUTDOOR CITY SWIMMING

Built in the 1930s but abandoned by the '80s, the **London Fields Lido** (020-7254 9038; www.better.org.uk/leisure/london-fields-lido; London Fields Westside, E8; adult/child £4.80/2.85; 6.30am-9pm; Hackney Central) heated 50m Olympic-size outdoor pool gets packed with swimmers and sunbathers during summer.

Hampton Court Palace

A DAY AT THE PALACE

With so much to explore and seemingly infinite gardens, it can be tricky knowing where to begin. It helps to understand how the palace has grown over the centuries and how successive royal occupants embellished Hampton Court to suit their purposes and to reflect the style of the time.

As soon as he had his royal hands upon the palace from Cardinal Thomas Wolsey, Henry VIII began expanding the **Tudor architecture** ❶, adding the **Great Hall** ❷, the exquisite **Chapel Royal** ❸, the opulent Great Watching Chamber and the gigantic **kitchens** ❹. By 1540 it had become one of the grandest and most sophisticated palaces in Europe. James I kept things ticking over, while Charles I added a new tennis court and did some serious art-collecting, including pieces that can be seen in the recently opened **Cumberland Art Gallery** ❺.

❼ The Maze

Around 150m north of the main bulding

Created from hornbeam and yew and planted in around 1700, the maze covers a third of an acre within the famous palace gardens. A must-see conclusion to Hampton Court, the maze takes the average visitor about 20 minutes to reach the centre.

Tudor Kitchens

These vast kitchens were the engine room of the palace. With a staff of 200 people, there were six spit-rack-equipped fireplaces, with roast meat always on the menu (to the tune of 8200 sheep and 1240 oxen per year).

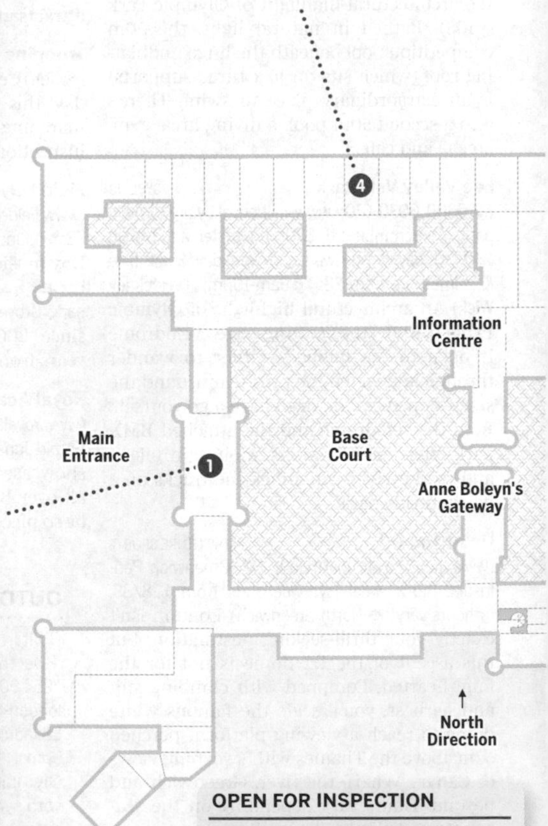

Tudor Architecture

Dating to 1515, the heart of the palace serves as one of the finest examples of Tudor architecture in the nation. Cardinal Thomas Wolsey was responsible for transforming what was originally a grand medieval manor house into a stunning Tudor palace.

OPEN FOR INSPECTION

The palace was opened to the public by Queen Victoria in 1838.

After the Civil War, puritanical Oliver Cromwell warmed to his own regal proclivities, spending weekends in the comfort of the former Queen's bedroom and selling off Charles I's art collection. In the late 17th century, William and Mary employed Sir Christopher Wren for baroque extensions, chiefly the William III Apartments, reached by the **King's Staircase** ❻. William III also commissioned the world-famous **maze** ❼.

TOP TIPS

» Ask one of the red-tunic-garbed warders for anecdotes and information.

» Tag along with a themed tour led by costumed historians or hop on a shire horse-drawn charabanc tour of the east garden in summer

» Grab one of the audio tours from the Information Centre.

PLUSONE / SHUTTERSTOCK ©

The Great Hall
This grand dining hall is the defining room of the palace, displaying what is considered England's finest hammer-beam roof, 16th-century Flemish tapestries telling the story of Abraham, and some exquisite stained-glass windows.

Chapel Royal
The blue-and-gold vaulted ceiling was originally intended for Christ Church, Oxford, but was installed here instead; the 18th-century oak reredos was carved by Grinling Gibbons. Books on display include a 1611 1st edition of the King James Bible, printed by Robert Barker.

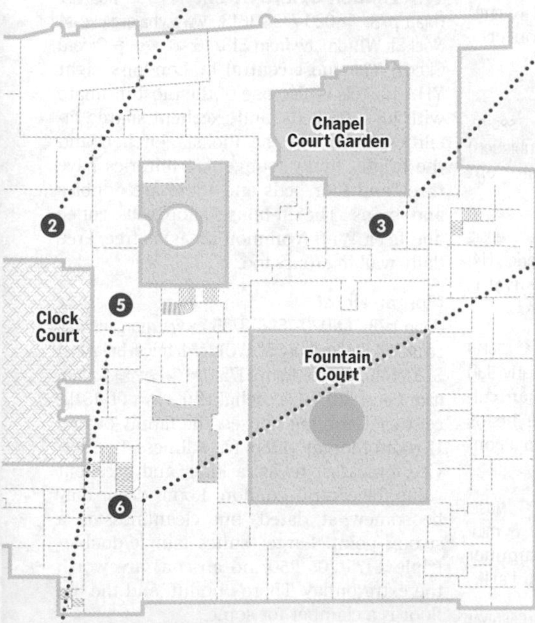

The King's Staircase
One of five rooms at the palace painted by Antonio Verrio and a suitably bombastic prelude to the King's Apartments, the overblown King's Staircase adulates William III by elevating him above a cohort of Roman emperors.

GORDON BELL / SHUTTERSTOCK ©

Cumberland Art Gallery
The former Cumberland Suite, designed by William Kent, has been restored to accommodate a choice selection of some of the finest works from the Royal Collection.

LOCAL KNOWLEDGE

WHY I LOVE LONDON

By Steve Fallon, Writer

Like most Londoners, I revel in all our familiar landmarks – Big Ben, Tower Bridge, the murky Thames, the London Eye. I still thank the former government that made some of the greatest museums and art galleries in the world free to one and all. The choice of restaurants, bars and clubs is legion, and what's not to love about a city with more lush parkland than any other world capital? But the one thing that sets my adopted city apart from any other is its amazing tolerance. 'As long as you don't scare the horses, mate, you'll be all right here,' I was told when I arrived here more than 20 years ago. Guess what...it still hasn't happened.

Meltdown Festival MUSIC
(www.southbankcentre.co.uk; late Jun) The Southbank Centre hands over the curatorial reigns to a legend of contemporary music (Morrissey, Patti Smith or David Byrne) to pull together a full program of concerts, talks and films.

Wimbledon Lawn Tennis Championships SPORTS
(www.wimbledon.com; late Jun; Wimbledon) The world's most splendid tennis event takes place in late June.

Wireless MUSIC
(www.wirelessfestival.co.uk; Finsbury Park, N4; Jul) This popular rock and pop festival is held over three days in July every year.

Pride GAY & LESBIAN
(www.prideinlondon.org; late Jun or early Jul) The big event on the gay and lesbian calendar, a technicolour street parade heads through the West End, culminating in a concert in Trafalgar Sq.

Lovebox MUSIC
(www.loveboxfestival.com; Victoria Park, E9; mid-Jul) London's contribution to the summer music-festival circuit, held in Victoria Park.

Notting Hill Carnival CARNIVAL
(www.thenottinghillcarnival.com; Aug) Every year, for three days during the last weekend of August, Notting Hill echoes to the calypso, ska, reggae and soca sounds of the Notting Hill Carnival. Launched in 1964 by the local Afro-Caribbean community, keen to celebrate its culture and traditions, it has grown to become Europe's largest street festival (up to one million people) and a highlight of London's calendar.

Sleeping

Hanging your hat (and anything else you care to remove) in London can be painfully expensive, and you'll almost always need to book your room well in advance. Decent, central hostels are easy enough to find and also offer reasonably priced double rooms. Bed and breakfasts are a dependable and inexpensive, if rather simple, option. Hotels range from cheap, no-frills chains through boutique choices to luxury five-star historic hotels.

West End

Like in Monopoly, land on a Mayfair hotel and you may have to sell your house, or at least remortgage. This is the heart of the action, and a couple of hostels cater for would be Soho hipsters of more modest means.

YHA London Oxford Street HOSTEL £
(Map p78; 020-7734 1618; www.yha.org.uk; 14 Noel St, W1; dm/tw from £18/46; Oxford Circus) The most central of London's eight YHA hostels is also one of the most intimate with just 104 beds, and excellent shared facilities, including the fuchsia kitchen and the bright, funky lounge. Dormitories have three and four beds and there are doubles and twins. The in-house shop sells coffee and beer. Wi-fi (common areas) is free. Free daily walking tours too.

Morgan Hotel B&B ££
(Map p78; 020-7636 3735; www.morganhotel.co.uk; 24 Bloomsbury St, WC1; s/d/tr incl breakfast £120/145/165, ste from £175; Tottenham Court Rd) In a delightful row of 18th-century Georgian houses, the family-owned 17-room Morgan offers friendliness, fine service, breakfast fit for a king, and excellent value for central London. Room decor may be somewhat dated, but cleanliness is a strong point. Larger suites (single/double/triple £175/205/250, no air-con) are worth the extra outlay. There's no lift, and the top floor is a clamber for some.

Jesmond Hotel B&B ££
(Map p106; 020-7636 3199; www.jesmondhotel.org.uk; 63 Gower St, WC1; s/d/tr/q incl breakfast from £70/90/120/150; Goodge St) The

rooms – cheapest with shared bathroom – at this popular, 15-room family-run Georgian hotel in Bloomsbury are basic but clean and cheerful, there's a small, pretty garden and the price tag is very attractive indeed. There's also laundry service, free wi-fi and good breakfasts for kicking off your London day. Location is highly central.

★Beaumont HOTEL £££
(Map p101; ☎020-7499 1001; www.thebeaumont.com; Brown Hart Gardens, W1; d/studio/ste incl breakfast from £395/625/900; ❄📶; ⊖Bond St) A stylish, handsome and luxurious hotel, the 73-room Beaumont is all deco opulence. Fronted by an arresting chunk of deco-inspired stainless steel and fumed oak sculpture from Antony Gormley called *Room* (part of a £1130-per-night suite), the striking white building dates from 1926. Rooms and suites are swish and elegant, with a 1920s modernist aesthetic. Room prices include local drop-offs in the hotel's vintage Daimler.

★Corinthia HOTEL £££
(Map p78; ☎020-7930 8181; www.corinthia.com; Whitehall Place, SW1; d/ste/penthouse £425/1380/3000; ❄📶🏊; ⊖Embankment) With hotels from Malta to St Petersburg, the Corinthia group's crown jewel is this grand Victorian property in Whitehall. It's as smart as can be, but never overbearing and stuffy. A stay here is a delight, from perfect rooms to flawless service, tempting afternoon tea and a location that ensconces you at the very heart, but just beyond the bustle of London.

★Haymarket Hotel HOTEL £££
(Map p78; ☎020-7470 4000; www.haymarkethotel.com; 1 Suffolk Pl, off Haymarket, SW1; r/ste from £336/504; ❄📶🏊; ⊖Piccadilly Circus) With the trademark colours and lines of hoteliers and designers Tim and Kit Kemp, the Haymarket is beautiful, with hand-painted Gournay wallpaper, signature fuchsia and green designs in the 50 guest rooms, a sensational 18m pool with mood lighting, an exquisite library lounge with honesty bar, and original artwork throughout. Just love the dog silhouettes on the chairs and bar stools.

★Rosewood HOTEL £££
(Map p78; ☎020-7781 8888; www.rosewoodhotels.com/en/london; 252 High Holborn, WC1; d from £380-750, ste £1140-9000; ❄@📶; ⊖Holborn) An £85-million refurb transformed the grand Pearl Assurance building (dating from 1914) into the stunning Rosewood hotel, where an artful marriage of period and modern styles can be found in its 262 rooms and 44 suites. British heritage is carefully woven throughout the bar, restaurant, deli, lobby and even the housekeepers' uniforms.

★Ritz LUXURY HOTEL £££
(Map p78; ☎020-7493 8181; www.theritzlondon.com; 150 Piccadilly, W1; r/ste from £380/770; ❄@📶; ⊖Green Park) What can you say about a hotel that has lent its name to the English lexicon? This 136-room caravanserai has a spectacular position overlooking Green Park and is supposedly the Royal Family's home away from home (it does have a royal warrant from the Prince of Wales and is very close to the palace). All rooms have period interiors and antique furniture.

The City

It bristles with bankers during the week, but you can often net considerable bargains in the City come weekends.

London St Paul's YHA HOSTEL £
(Map p84; ☎020-7236 4965; www.yha.org.uk/hostel/london-st-pauls; 36 Carter Lane, EC4; dm £17-30, d £65-79; @📶; ⊖St Paul's) This 213-bed hostel is housed in the former boarding school for choir boys from St Paul's Cathedral, almost next door. Dorms have between three and 11 beds, and twins and doubles are available. There's a great lounge, licensed cafeteria (breakfast £5.25, dinner from £7 to £10) but no kitchen – and lots and lots of stairs (and no lift). Seven-night maximum stay.

Hotel Indigo Tower Hill BOUTIQUE HOTEL ££
(Map p84; ☎020-7265 1014; www.ihg.com; 142 Minories, EC3; r weekend/weekday from £100/260; ❄📶; ⊖Aldgate) This branch of the US Inter-Continental group's boutique-hotel chain offers 46 differently styled rooms, all with four-poster beds and iPod docking stations. Larger-than-life drawings and photos of the neighbourhood won't let you forget where you are.

Andaz Liverpool Street HOTEL ££
(Map p84; ☎020-7961 1234; www.london.liverpoolstreet.andaz.hyatt.com; 40 Liverpool St, EC2; r weekday/weekend from £180/365; ❄📶; ⊖Liverpool St) This is the London flagship for Hyatt's sophisticated Andaz chain. There's no reception, just black-clad staff who check you in on iPads. The 267 rooms are cool and spacious, with interesting furnishings and lighting scheme. On top of this there are

LOCAL KNOWLEDGE

HOXTON HOTEL

In the heart of hip Shoreditch, the sleek **Hoxton Hotel** (Map p132; ☎020-7550 1000; www.hoxtonhotels.com; 81 Great Eastern St, EC2; r from £49; ❄@📶; ⊖Old St) takes the easyJet approach to selling its rooms – book long enough ahead and you might pay just £49. The 210 renovated rooms are small but stylish, with flat-screen TVs, a desk, fridge with complimentary bottled water and milk, and breakfast (orange juice, granola, yoghurt, banana) in a bag delivered to your door.

five restaurants, two bars, a health club and a subterranean Masonic temple discovered during the hotel's refit in the '90s.

South Bank

Immediately on the south side of the Thames is a fab perch for reaching the central sights, while gauging the personality of South London.

St Christopher's Village HOSTEL £
(Map p92; ☎020-7939 9710; www.st-christophers.co.uk; 163 Borough High St, SE1; dm/r from £15.90/43; @📶; ⊖London Bridge) This 194-bed party-zone hostel has new bathrooms, fresh paint, pod beds with privacy curtains, reading lights, power sockets (British and European) and USB ports, and refurbished common areas. Its two bars, Belushi's and Dugout, are perennially popular. Dorms have four to 22 beds (female-only dorms available); breakfast and linen are included.

The hotel has another branch 100m up the road: **St Christopher's Inn** (Map p92; ☎020-7407 2392; www.st-christophers.co.uk; 121 Borough High St, SE1; dm/r from £13.90/50; @📶; ⊖London Bridge), which sits above a traditional pub. The dorms are smaller and look a little tired, but it's altogether quieter than at the Village.

★Citizen M BOUTIQUE HOTEL ££
(Map p92; ☎020-3519 1680; www.citizenm.com/london-bankside; 20 Lavington St, SE1; r £109-249; ❄@📶; ⊖Southwark) If Citizen M had a motto, it would be 'less fuss, more comfort'. The hotel has done away with things it considers superfluous (room service, reception, bags of space) and instead gone all out on mattresses and bedding (heavenly super-king-size beds), state-of-the-art technology (everything in the room from mood lighting to the TV is controlled through a tablet computer) and superb decor.

Shangri-La Hotel at the Shard HOTEL £££
(Map p92; ☎020-7234 8000; www.shangri-la.com/london/shangrila; 31 St Thomas St, SE1; d/ste from £420/750; ❄@📶🏊; 🚆London Bridge, ⊖London Bridge) The UK's first five-star hotel south of the Thames has breathtaking views from the highest hotel (above ground level) in Western Europe, occupying levels 34 to 52 of the Shard. From the 35th-floor sky lobby to the rooms, the Shangri-La concocts a stylish blend of Chinese aesthetics, Asian hospitality and sharp modernity.

Pimlico & Belgravia

Lime Tree Hotel BOUTIQUE HOTEL ££
(Map p98; ☎020-7730 8191; www.limetreehotel.co.uk; 135-137 Ebury St, SW1; s £120-160, d & tw £180-210, tr £230 incl breakfast; @📶; ⊖Victoria) Family-run for 30 years, this beautiful 25-bedroom Georgian town-house hotel is all comfort, British designs and understated elegance. Rooms are individually decorated, many with open fireplaces and sash windows, but some are smaller than others, so enquire. There is a lovely back garden for late-afternoon rays (picnics encouraged on summer evenings). Rates include a hearty full-English breakfast. No lift.

B+B Belgravia B&B ££
(Map p98; ☎020-7259 8570; www.bb-belgravia.com; 64-66 Ebury St, SW1; d £79-209, studio £130-279; @📶; ⊖Victoria) This spiffing six-floor Georgian B&B, remodelled with contemporary flair, boasts crisp common areas and a chic lounge. The 17 rooms (some with shower, others with bath, half facing the street, half facing the garden) aren't enormous but there's a further batch of studio rooms with compact kitchens at No 82 Ebury St. A pleasant courtyard garden is out back. No lift.

★Goring HOTEL £££
(Map p72; ☎020-7396 9000; www.thegoring.com; Beeston Pl; r/ste from £395/825; ❄📶; ⊖Victoria) Kate Middleton spent her last night as a commoner in the Royal Suite (£8400 per night) before joining the Royal Family, propelling the Goring into an international media glare. Glistening with chandeliers, dotted with trademark fluffy sheep and overseen by highly professional staff, this family-owned hotel is a supremely grand,

albeit highly relaxed, slice of England and Englishness, with a sumptuous garden.

Knightsbridge

Named after a bridge over the River Westbourne, Knightsbridge is where you'll find some of London's best-known department stores and some top hotels.

Levin Hotel HOTEL £££
(Map p98; ☎020-7589 6286; www.thelevinhotel.co.uk; 28 Basil St, SW3; r from £374, ste from £619 incl breakfast; ; Knightsbridge) The luxury 12-room Levin is a bijou boutique gem. Attention to detail (US, EU, UK and Asian sockets in every room, Nespresso coffee machines, fine Egyptian linen, underfloor heating in bathrooms, iPads on request), exquisite design and highly hospitable service create a delightful stay. The gorgeous continental buffet breakfast is complimentary. Room rates start at £274 in low season.

Chelsea & Kensington

Well-turned-out Chelsea and Kensington offer easy access to the museums, natty shopping choices and some of London's best-looking streets.

Meininger HOSTEL £
(Map p98; ☎020-3318 1407; www.meininger-hostels.com; Baden Powell House, 65-67 Queen's Gate, SW7; dm £16-50, s/tw from £60/70; ; Gloucester Rd or South Kensington) Housed in the late-1950s Baden Powell House opposite the Natural History Museum, this 48-room German-run 'city hostel and hotel' has spick-and-span rooms – most are dorms of between four and 12 beds, with pod-like showers. There is also a handful of private rooms. There's good security and nice communal facilities, including a bar and a big roof terrace, plus a fantastic location.

★**Number Sixteen** HOTEL £££
(Map p98; ☎020-7589 5232; www.firmdalehotels.com/hotels/london/number-sixteen; 16 Sumner Pl, SW7; s from £192, d £240-396; ; South Kensington) With uplifting splashes of colour, choice art and a sophisticated-but-fun design ethos, Number Sixteen is simply ravishing. There are 41 individually designed rooms, a cosy drawing room and a fully stocked library. And wait till you see the idyllic, long back garden set around a fountain, or sit down for breakfast in the light-filled conservatory. Great amenities for families.

Ampersand Hotel BOUTIQUE HOTEL £££
(Map p98; ☎020-7589 5895; www.ampersandhotel.com; 10 Harrington Rd, SW7; s £170-192, d £216-360; ; South Kensington) It feels light, fresh and bubbly in the Ampersand, where smiling staff wear denims and waistcoats rather than impersonal dark suits. The common rooms are colourful and airy, and the stylish rooms are decorated with wallpaper designs celebrating the nearby arts and sciences of South Kensington's museums.

Earl's Court & Fulham

West London's Earl's Court is lively, cosmopolitan and so popular with travelling Antipodeans it's nicknamed Kangaroo Valley. There are no real sights, but it has inexpensive digs, an infectious holiday atmosphere and it's a short hop to the action. Further west and abutting the Thames, Fulham is the home of its famous riverside palace.

★**Barclay House** B&B ££
(☎077 6742 0943; www.barclayhouselondon.com; 21 Barclay Rd, SW6; s £110, d £135-168; ; Fulham Broadway) The three dapper, thoroughly modern and comfy bedrooms in this shipshape Victorian house are a dream, from the Phillipe Starck shower rooms, walnut furniture, new double-glazed sash windows and underfloor heating to the small, thoughtful details (fumble-free coat hangers, drawers packed with sewing kits and maps). The cordial, music-loving owners – bursting with tips and handy London knowledge – concoct an inclusive, homely atmosphere.

Rockwell BOUTIQUE HOTEL ££
(☎020-7244 2000; www.therockwell.com; 181-183 Cromwell Rd, SW5; s £120-125, d £145-180, ste from £200; ; Earl's Court) With an understated-cool design ethos and some lovely floor tiling, things are muted, dapper and more than a tad minimalist at the 'budget boutique' 40-room Rockwell. Spruce and stylish, all rooms have showers, the mezzanine suites are peaches and the three rooms looking on to the walled garden (LG1, 2 and 3) are particularly fine.

Notting Hill, Bayswater & Paddington

Don't be fooled by Julia Roberts' and Hugh Grant's shenanigans, Notting Hill and the areas immediately north of Hyde Park are as shabby as they are chic, but they're still cool.

Notting Hill & Bayswater

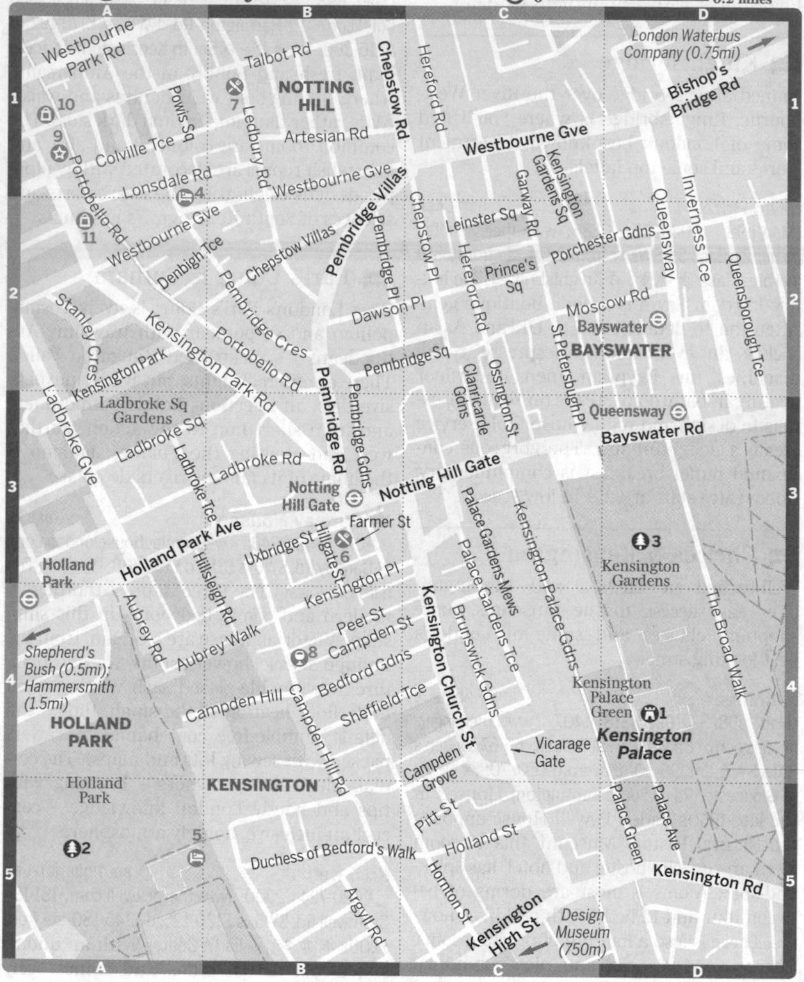

There are some gorgeous gated squares surrounded by Georgian town houses, but the area is better exemplified by the Portobello Road Market and the Notting Hill Carnival. Scruffy Paddington has lots of cheap hotels, with a major strip of unremarkable ones along Sussex Gardens that may be worth checking if you're short on options.

Safestay Holland Park HOSTEL £
(Map p122; ☎020-3326 8471; www.safestay.co.uk; Holland Walk, W8; dm £18, tw from £58, s from £66; wi-fi; ⊖High St Kensington or Holland Park) This new place replaced the long-serving YHA hostel running here since 1958. With a bright and bold colour design, the hostel has four- to eight-bunk dorm rooms, twin-bunk and single-bunk rooms, free wi-fi in the lobby and a fabulous location in the Jacobean east wing of Holland House in **Holland Park** (Map p122; Ilchester Pl; ⏲7.30am-dusk; ⊖High St Kensington or Holland Park).

★**Main House** HOTEL ££
(Map p122; ☎020-7221 9691; www.themainhouse.co.uk; 6 Colville Rd, W11; ste £120-150; wi-fi; ⊖Ladbroke Grove, Notting Hill Gate or Westbourne Park) The four adorable suites at this peach of

Notting Hill & Bayswater

Top Sights
1 Kensington Palace.......D4

Sights
2 Holland Park.......A5
3 Kensington Gardens.......D3

Sleeping
4 Main House.......A1
5 Safestay Holland Park.......A5

Eating
6 Geales.......D3
7 Ledbury.......B1

Drinking & Nightlife
8 Windsor Castle.......B4

Entertainment
9 Electric Cinema.......A1

Shopping
10 Ceramica Blue.......A1
11 Portobello Road Market.......A2

a Victorian midterrace house on Colville Rd make this a superb choice. Bright and spacious, with vast bathrooms, rooms are excellent value and include endless tea and coffee. Cream of the crop is the uppermost suite, occupying the entire top floor. There's no sign, but look for the huge letters 'SIX'. Minimum three-night stay.

Bloomsbury & St Pancras

One step from the West End and crammed with Georgian town-house conversions, these are more affordable neighbourhoods. A stretch of lower-priced hotels runs along Gower St and on the pretty Cartwright Gardens crescent. While hardly a salubrious location, St Pancras is handy with some excellent budget options.

★Clink78 HOSTEL £
(Map p106; 020-7183 9400; www.clinkhostels.com/london/clink78; 78 King's Cross Rd, WC1; dm/r from £16/65 incl breakfast; King's Cross/St Pancras) This fantastic 630-bed hostel is housed in a 19th-century magistrates' courthouse where Dickens once worked as a scribe and members of the Clash stood trial in 1978. Rooms feature pod beds (including overhead storage space) in four- to 16-bed dormitories. There's a top kitchen with a huge dining area and the busy Clash bar in the basement.

Parts of the hostel, including six cells converted to bedrooms and a pair of wood-panelled court rooms used as a cinema and internet room, are heritage-listed. There are all-female dorms too. You'll find an ATM and change machine conveniently in the lobby. Free breakfast included: toast and spreads, cereal, juice, tea and coffee (7am to 10.30am).

Generator HOSTEL £
(Map p106; 020-7388 7666; www.generatorhostels.com/london; 37 Tavistock Pl, WC1; dm/r from £10/08; Russell Sq) With its industrial lines and funky decor, the huge Generator (more than 870 beds) is one of central London's grooviest budget spots. The bar, complete with pool tables, stays open until 2am and there are frequent themed parties. Dorm rooms have between six and 12 beds; backing it up are twins, triples and quad rooms.

London St Pancras YHA HOSTEL £
(Map p106; 020-7388 9998; www.yha.org.uk; 79-81 Euston Rd, NW1; dm/r from £16/60; King's Cross/St Pancras) This hostel with 186 beds spread over eight floors has modern, clean dorms sleeping four to six (nearly all with private facilities) and some private rooms. There's a good bar and cafe, although there are no self-catering facilities. Check out time is 10am.

Arosfa Hotel B&B ££
(Map p106; 020-7636 2115; www.arosfalondon.com; 83 Gower St, WC1; incl breakfast s/tw/tr/f from £82/135/145/178, d £139-175; Goodge St) The Philippe Starck furniture and modern look in the lounge is more lavish than the decor in the hotel's 16 rooms, with cabin-like bathrooms in many of them. About half have been refurbished; they are small but remain good value. There are a couple of family rooms; room 4 looks on to a small but charming garden. Prices rise on Saturdays.

Rough Luxe BOUTIQUE HOTEL £££
(Map p106; 020-7837 5338; www.roughluxe.co.uk; 1 Birkenhead St, WC1; r £209-239; King's Cross/St Pancras) Half-rough, half-luxury is the strapline of this nine-room hotel, and the distressed interior is true to its word. Scraps of old newspaper adorn the walls, along with original artwork, while the vintage 1970s TVs are for show only. Some rooms are admittedly small but service, location and the delightful patio garden at the back more than make up for it.

St Pancras Renaissance London Hotel LUXURY HOTEL £££
(Map p106; 020-7841 3540; www.stpancras-renaissance.co.uk; Euston Rd, NW1; d from £230; ; King's Cross/St Pancras) Housed in the former Midland Grand Hotel (1873), a Gothic, red-brick Victorian marvel designed by Sir George Gilbert Scott, the St Pancras Renaissance counts 245 rooms but only 38 of them are are in the original building; the rest are in an extension at the back and rather bland.

Clerkenwell & Farringdon

★Zetter Hotel & Townhouse BOUTIQUE HOTEL £££
(Map p106; 020-7324 4444; www.thezetter.com; 86-88 Clerkenwell Rd, EC1; d from £222, studio £300-438; ; Farringdon) The Zetter comprises two quite different properties. The original Zetter Hotel is a temple of cool with an overlay of kitsch on Clerkenwell's main thoroughfare. Built using sustainable materials on the site of a derelict office, its 59 rooms are small but perfectly formed. The **Zetter Townhouse** (Map p106; 49-50 St John's Sq; r £222-294, ste £438-480), on a pretty square behind, has just 13 rooms in a lovely Georgian pile.

At the main Zetter, the rooftop studios are the real treat, with terraces commanding superb views across the city. The rooms in the Zetter Townhouse are uniquely decorated in period style but with witty touches such as headboards made from reclaimed fairground carousels. The fantastic cocktail bar is a destination in itself.

Rookery HERITAGE HOTEL £££
(Map p106; 020-7336 0931; www.rookeryhotel.com; 12 Peter's Lane, Cowcross St, EC1; s/d £222/294, ste £474-660; ; Farringdon) This charming warren of 33 rooms has been built in a row of 18th-century Georgian houses and fitted out with period furniture (including a museum-piece collection of Victorian baths, showers and toilets), original wood panelling shipped over from Ireland and artwork selected personally by the owner. Highlights: the small courtyard garden and the two-storey Rook's Nest penthouse suite.

East End & Docklands

★Qbic DESIGN HOTEL ££
(020-3021 3300; www.london.qbichotels.com; 42 Adler St, E1; d £70-250; ; Aldgate East) The 171 rooms of this snappy hotel south of Brick Lane are based around a 'cubi', with each bed and bathroom part of a square-box design. There's a very modern feel throughout, with white tiling, neon signs, and vibrant art and textiles. Rooms are sound-insulated, mattresses excellent and rainforest showers powerful. A great continental buffet breakfast is available for £9.95.

40 Winks BOUTIQUE HOTEL ££
(020-7790 0259; www.40winks.org; 109 Mile End Rd, E1; s/d £120/195 incl breakfast; ; Stepney Green) Short on space but not on style, this two-room boutique guesthouse, housed in an early-18th-century town house in Stepney Green, oozes quirky charm. Owned by a successful designer, the hotel has been used as a location for a number of fashion shoots and the rooms (the single is quite compact) are uniquely decorated with an expert's eye. Book far ahead.

Eating

Dining out in London has become so fashionable that you can hardly open a menu without banging into some celebrity chef or other. The range and quality of eating options has increased exponentially over the last few decades. Waves of immigrant flavours have deeply infused London cuisine and the expectations of modern-day Londoners are demanding. In this section we have sieved out choicer restaurants and cafes noted for their location, value for money, unique character, ambience and, of course, good food. Vegetarians needn't fret: London has a host of dedicated meat-free joints, while most others have veggie offerings.

West End

Mayfair, Soho and Covent Garden are the gastronomic heart of London, with a blinding choice of restaurants and cuisines at budgets to suit booze hounds, theatregoers or determined grazers.

★Shoryu NOODLES £
(Map p78; www.shoryuramen.com; 9 Regent St, SW1; mains £9-15; 11.15am-midnight Mon-Sat, to 10.30pm Sun; Piccadilly Circus) Compact, well-mannered noodle-parlour Shoryu draws in reams of noodle diners to feast at its wooden counters and small tables. It's busy, friendly and efficient, with helpful and informative staff. Fantastic *tonkotsu* pork-broth ramen is the name of the game here, sprinkled with *nori* (dried, pressed sea-

weed), spring onion, *nitamago* (soft-boiled eggs) and sesame seeds. No bookings.

Ceviche SOUTH AMERICAN £
(Map p78; www.cevicheuk.com; 17 Frith St, W1; mains £6-13.50; noon-11.30pm Mon-Sat, to 10.15pm Sun; ; Leicester Sq) This colourfully decorated *bodega* serves some of the most authentic Peruvian food in town. Start with *cancha* (large crunchy corn kernels) and move on to one of the signature dishes of ceviche (fish or shellfish marinated in lime juice with chillies, onion and coriander). Salads made with quinoa and palm hearts are excellent.

The Breakfast Club BREAKFAST £
(Map p78; 020-7434 2571; www.thebreakfastclubcafes.com; 33 D'Arblay St; mains £5-12.50; 8am-10pm Mon-Sat, to 7pm Sun; ; Oxford Circus) This fun and friendly original branch of The Breakfast Club has been successfully frying up for more than a decade and has spawned seven other branches in town. Full or half Monty or All American brekkies are the natural inclination, but chorizo hash browns, pancakes and delights of the El Butty also await (once you reach the front of the queue).

Wahaca MEXICAN $
(Map p78; www.wahaca.com; 66 Chandos Pl, WC2; mains £7-10.50; noon-11pm Mon-Sat, to 10.30pm Sun; ; Covent Garden) This delightful but frequently busy carbon-neutral cantina, part of an ever-expanding and ever-popular chain, styles itself as a 'Mexican-market eating' experience. Choose to share a selection of street snacks (tacos, tostadas, *quesadillas*) or aim for a more traditional main such as chargrilled chicken breast marinated in Yucatecan spices and pineapple juice. Wash it down with one of a dozen tequilas.

Fernandez & Wells CAFE £
(Map p78; www.fernandezandwells.com; 73 Beak St, W1; dishes £4.50-6; 7.30am-6pm Mon-Fri, 9am-6pm Sat & Sun; Piccadilly Circus) A wonderful taste of Spain in Soho, Fernandez serves simple lunches of *jamón* (ham) and cured meats and cheese platters. Grilled chorizo sandwiches are perfect for quick lunchtime bites. The place is usually busy, with a relaxed atmosphere. Excellent coffee.

Mildreds VEGETARIAN £
(Map p78; www.mildreds.co.uk; 45 Lexington St, W1; mains £80-12; noon-11pm Mon-Sat; ; Oxford Circus or Piccadilly Circus) Central London's most inventive vegetarian restaurant, Mildred's heaves at lunchtime so don't be shy about sharing a table in the skylit dining room. Expect the likes of Sri Lankan sweet-potato and cashew-nut curry, pumpkin and ricotta ravioli, Middle Eastern mezze, wonderfully exotic (and filling) salads and delicious stir-fries. There are also vegan and gluten-free options.

Monocle Cafe CAFE £
(Map p101; http://cafe.monocle.com; 18 Chiltern St, W1; mains from £5.50; 7am-7pm Mon-Wed, 7am-8pm Thu & Fri, 8am-8pm Sat, 8am-7pm Sun; ; Baker St) A small and cool ground-floor and basement hideout for the Marylebone hipster set, Monocle Cafe (from the eponymous magazine) is a delightful addition to buzzing Chiltern St. It offers eclectic flavours from Swedish pastries to Japanese and Scandinavian breakfasts, Bircher muesli with strawberries or shrimp *katsu* (breaded shrimp) sandwiches.

Battersea Pie Station BRITISH £
(Map p78; www.batterseapiestation.co.uk; Lower Ground Floor, 28 The Market, Covent Garden, WC2; mains from £7.50; 11am-7pm Sun-Thu, to 8pm Fri-Sat; Covent Garden) Just what Covent Garden needs, this small, white-tiled cafe has a terrific choice of pies (baby or big) to satisfy all levels of hunger, from careful nibblers to voracious teens. Meat is all free-range, flavours are classic and rich (lamb and mint, fish, steak and ale, chicken and mushroom, butternut squash and goat's cheese), each coming with a dollop of mash.

★ **Gymkhana** INDIAN ££
(Map p78; 020-3011 5900; www.gymkhanalondon.com; 42 Albemarle St, W1; mains £8-38, 2/3-course lunch £25/30; noon-2.30pm & 5.30-10.30pm Mon-Sat; ; Green Park) The rather sombre setting is all British Raj: ceiling fans, oak ceiling, period cricket photos and hunting trophies, but the menu is lively, bright and inspiring. For lovers of variety, the seven-course tasting menu (£70; vegetarian menu available £65) or vault menu (£75; vegetarian menu £70) is the way to go, or aim for the seafood menu instead (seven courses £80).

★ **Brasserie Zédel** FRENCH ££
(Map p78; 020-7734 4888; www.brasseriezedel.com; 20 Sherwood St, W1; mains £8.75-30; 11.30am-midnight Mon-Sat, to 11pm Sun; ; Piccadilly Circus) This brasserie in the renovated art-deco ballroom of a former hotel is the Frenchest eatery west of Calais. Favourites include *choucroute Alsacienne*

(sauerkraut with sausages and charcuterie, £14) or a straight-up *steak haché, sauce au poivre et frites* (chopped steak with pepper sauce; £9.75). Set menus (£9.75/12.75 for two/three courses) and *plats du jour* (£14.25) offer excellent value, in a terrific setting. There's a vegetarian menu available, too.

Also here, the **Bar Américain** is a classic deco spot for a pre-dinner libation.

★Barrafina SPANISH ££

(Map p78; www.barrafina.co.uk; 10 Adelaide St, WC2; tapas £6-14.50; noon-3pm & 5-11pm Mon-Sat, 1-3.30pm & 5.30-10pm Sun; Embankment or Leicester Sq) With no reservations, you may need to get in line for an hour or so at this restaurant that does a brisk service in some of the best tapas in town. Divine mouthfuls are served on each plate, from the stuffed courgette flower to the suckling pig and crab on toast, so diners dig their heels in, prepared to wait.

★Palomar JEWISH ££

(Map p78; 020-7439 8777; 34 Rupert St, W1; mains £6.50-19; noon-2.30pm & 5.30-11pm Mon-Sat, noon-3.30pm & 6-9pm Sun; ; Piccadilly Circus) The buzzing vibe at this good-looking celebration of modern-day Jerusalem cuisine (in all its inflections) is infectious, but we could enjoy the dishes cooked up here in a deserted warehouse and still come back for more. The Jerusalem-style polenta and Josperised aubergine are fantastic, but portions are smallish, so sharing is the way to go. Reservations essential.

★Cafe Murano ITALIAN ££

(Map p78; 020-3371 5559; www.cafemurano.co.uk; 33 St James's St, SW1; mains £9-24, 2/3-course set meal £19/23; noon-3pm & 5.30-11pm Mon-Sat; Green Park) The setting may seem somewhat demure at this superb and busy restaurant, but with such a sublime North Italian menu on offer, it sees no need to be flash and of-the-moment. You get what you come for, and the beef carpaccio, crab linguine and lamb ragu are as close to culinary perfection as you can get. Reserve.

Great Queen Street BRITISH ££

(Map p78; 020-7242 0622; www.greatqueenstreetrestaurant.co.uk; 32 Great Queen St, WC2; mains £16.80-18; noon-2.30pm & 5.30-10.30pm Mon-Sat, 1-3.30pm Sun; Holborn) The menu at one of Covent Garden's best places to eat is seasonal (and changes daily), with an emphasis on quality, hearty dishes and fine ingredients – there are always delicious stews, roasts and simple fish dishes. The atmosphere is lively, with a small **cellar bar** (5-12pm Tues-Sat) for cocktails and drinks. Booking is essential (do it online).

National Dining Rooms BRITISH ££

(Map p78; 020-7747 2525; www.peytonandbyrne.co.uk; 1st fl, Sainsbury Wing, National Gallery, Trafalgar Sq, WC2; mains £14.50-21.50; 10am-5.30pm Sat-Thu, to 8.30pm Fri; ; Charing Cross) Right at the very heart of town, chef Oliver Peyton's restaurant at the National Gallery (p80) is a superb choice, its menu featuring an extensive and wonderful selection of British cheeses for a light lunch. For something more filling, go for the monthly changing County Menu, honouring regional specialities from across the British Isles. Set lunch is £19.50 for two courses.

Ethos VEGETARIAN ££

(Map p78; 48 Eastcastle St, W1; lunch/dinner £2.60/2.85 per 100g; 8am-10pm Mon-Fri, 11.30am-10pm Sat, 10am-4pm Sun; ; Oxford Circus) Busy, self-service Ethos sells creative, meat-free food chosen from the buffet and then priced by weight. Doors open for breakfast (smashed avocado on toast, gluten-free porridge with almond milk etc), moving through lunch and dinner (guacamole, chickpea and coconut curry, Japanese-miso aubergine etc) via afternoon tea (£20 per person) and brunch on Sundays.

Bocca di Lupo ITALIAN ££

(Map p78; 020-7734 2223; www.boccadilupo.com; 12 Archer St, W1; mains £8-23; 12.30-3pm & 5.30-11pm Mon-Sat, 12.15-3.15pm & 5.15-9.30pm Sun; Piccadilly Circus) Bocca radiates elegant sophistication from its dark Soho backstreet setting. The menu has dishes from across Italy (with pointers of what region they're from), and every main course can be ordered as a large or small portion, rounded off with a good selection of Italian wines and terrific desserts. It's often full, so make sure to book.

Canela PORTUGUESE ££

(Map p78; www.canelacafe.com; 33 Earlham St, WC2; mains £11-13; 8am-10.30pm Mon-Thu, to 11pm Fri & Sat, to 9pm Sun; ; Covent Garden) This small cafe in Seven Dials at the heart of Covent Garden serves tasty Portuguese and Brazilian dishes. Try the classic dish of the day, opt for the Portuguese national dish *feijoada*, a bean stew with smoked meat, or stop by early for a rustic brekkie. There's a good selection of vegetarian dishes, as well as a strong Portuguese wine list.

★Foyer at Claridge's BRITISH £££

(Map p101; www.claridges.co.uk; 49-53 Brook St, W1; afternoon tea £58, with champagne £68; ⏲tea served 2.45-5.30pm; 📶; ⊖Bond St) Extend that pinkie finger to partake in afternoon tea within the classic art-deco-style foyer of this landmark hotel where the gentle clink of fine porcelain and champagne glasses could be a defining memory of your trip to London. The setting is gorgeous and dress is elegant, smart casual (ripped jeans and baseball caps won't get served).

Chiltern Firehouse MODERN EUROPEAN £££

(Map p101; ☎020-7073 7676; www.chilternfirehouse.com; 1 Chiltern St, W1; mains £24-42; ⏲7-10.30am Mon-Fri, 9-10.30am Sat & Sun, noon-2.30pm Mon-Wed, noon-3pm Thu & Fri, 11am-3pm Sat & Sun, 5.30-10.30pm Mon-Wed, 6-10.30pm Thu-Sun; 📶; ⊖Baker St or Bond St) When they can secure a table, diners come to this splendidly dapper Marylebone Fire Station to celeb-spot and bask in its glorious setting as much as to dine. Chef Nuno Mendes has worked some considerable culinary flair into his menu, but the hype and overarching trendiness guarantee an outlay almost as high as the red-brick chimneys aloft.

The City

You'll be sorely dismayed if you've got an empty belly on a Sunday morning in the City. Even during the busy weekdays, the chain eateries are often your best option.

Café Below CAFE £

(Map p84; ☎020-7329 0789; www.cafebelow.co.uk; St Mary-le-Bow, Cheapside, EC2; mains £8-15.50; ⏲7.30am-2.30pm Mon-Fri, to 9.30pm Wed-Fri; 🖉; ⊖Mansion House or St Paul's) This very atmospheric cafe-restaurant, in the crypt of one of London's most famous churches, offers excellent value and a tasty range of international fare, with as many vegetarian choices as meat choices. Summer sees tables outside in the shady courtyard. Occasional set dinners are available, but check the website or phone in for details.

★Restaurant at St Paul's MODERN BRITISH ££

(Map p84; ☎020-7248 2469; www.harbourandjones.com/restaurant/restaurant-at-st-pauls; Crypt, St Paul's Cathedral, EC4; mains from £14, brunch menu £25; ⏲breakfast 9-11am Thu & Fri, lunch noon-2.15pm, tea 3-4.15pm Mon-Sat; 📶; ⊖St Paul's) The quality of the dishes at this restaurant in the crypt of St Paul's (p85) lives up to the grandeur above. The menu offers two- or three-course lunches, including dishes such as pork-belly confit and goat's-cheese ravioli with spiced tomato.

Sweeting's SEAFOOD £££

(Map p84; ☎020-7248 3062; www.sweetingsrestaurant.co.uk; 39 Queen Victoria St, EC4; mains £15-45; ⏲11.30am-3pm Mon-Fri; ⊖Mansion House) 🍃 A City institution, Sweeting's dates to 1889. It hasn't changed much, with its small sit-down dining area, mosaic floor and narrow counters, behind which stand waiters in white aprons. Dishes include sustainably sourced fish of all kinds (grilled, fried or poached), potted shrimps, eels and Sweeting's famous fish pie (£16). Round it all off with a plate of spotted dick.

South Bank

Popular restaurants feast on iconic riverside views, but cast your net wider and gems crop up everywhere. For a feed with a local feel, head to Borough Market (p93) or Bermondsey St.

M Manze BRITISH £

(Map p92; www.manze.co.uk; 87 Tower Bridge Rd, SE1; mains from £2.95; ⏲11am-2pm Mon, 10.30am-2pm Tue-Thu, 10am-2.30pm Fri, 10am-3pm Sat; ⊖Borough) Dating to 1902, M Manze started off as an ice-cream seller before moving on to selling its legendary staples: pies (minced beef). It's a classic operation, from the ageing tile work to the traditional working-man's menu: pie and mash (£4), pie and liquor (£2.95), and you can take your eels jellied or stewed (£4.65).

★Skylon MODERN EUROPEAN ££

(Map p92; ☎020-7654 7800; www.skylon-restaurant.co.uk; 3rd fl, Royal Festival Hall, Southbank Centre, Belvedere Rd, SE1; grill 3-course menu £25, restaurant 3-course menu £32; ⏲grill noon-11pm Mon-Sat, to 10.30pm Sun, restaurant noon-2.30pm & 5.30-10.30pm Mon-Sat & noon-4pm Sun; 📶; ⊖Waterloo) This excellent restaurant inside the Royal Festival Hall (p142) is divided into grill and fine-dining sections by a large **bar** (⏲noon-1am Mon-Sat, to 10.30pm Sun). The decor is cutting-edge 1950s: muted colours and period chairs (trendy then, trendier now) while floor-to-ceiling windows bathe you in magnificent views of the Thames and the City. The six-course restaurant tasting menu is £59. Booking is advised.

★Arabica Bar & Kitchen MIDDLE EASTERN £££

(Map p92; ☎020-3011 5151; www.arabicabarandkitchen.com; 3 Rochester Walk, Borough Market, SE1; dishes £6-14; ⏰11am-11pm Mon-Wed, 8.30am-11pm Thu, 8.30am-11.30pm Fri & Sat, 11am-4pm Sun; ; ⊖London Bridge) Pan Middle-Eastern cuisine is a well-rehearsed classic these days, but Arabica Bar & Kitchen has managed to bring something fresh to its table: the decor is contemporary and bright, the food delicate and light, with an emphasis on sharing (two to three small dishes per person). The downside of this tapas approach is that the bill adds up quickly.

Belgravia

★Pimlico Fresh CAFE £

(86 Wilton Rd, SW1; mains from £4.50; ⏰7.30am-7.30pm Mon-Fri, 9am-6pm Sat & Sun; ⊖Victoria) This friendly two-room cafe will see you right whether you need breakfast (French toast, bowls of porridge laced with honey or maple syrup), lunch (homemade quiches and soups, 'things' on toast) or just a good old latte and cake.

Knightsbridge

★Dinner by Heston Blumenthal MODERN BRITISH £££

(Map p98; ☎020-7201 3833; www.dinnerbyheston.com; Mandarin Oriental Hyde Park, 66 Knightsbridge, SW1; 3-course set lunch £40, mains £28-42; ⏰noon-2pm & 6-10.15pm; ; ⊖Knightsbridge) Sumptuously presented Dinner is a gastronomic tour de force, taking diners on a journey through British culinary history (with inventive modern inflections). Dishes carry historical dates to convey context, while the restaurant interior is a design triumph, from the glass-walled kitchen and its overhead clock mechanism to the large windows looking onto the park. Book ahead.

Also at hand is a 16th-century Tudor-style private room that seats 12 guests, dining from an extravagant Sapele and Rosewood oval table. Set lunches are available Monday to Friday.

Zuma JAPANESE £££

(Map p98; ☎020-7584 1010; www.zumarestaurant.com; 5 Raphael St, SW7; mains £15-75; ⏰noon-3pm Mon-Fri, noon-3.30pm Sat & Sun, 6-11pm Mon-Sat, 6-10.30pm Sun; ; ⊖Knightsbridge) Zuma oozes style – a modern-day take on the traditional Japanese *izakaya* ('a place to stay and drink sake'), where drinking and eating harmonise. The *robata* (chargrilled) dishes are the stars of the show; wash them down with one of 40 types of sake on offer. Booking is advised, although there are walk-in spaces at the *robata* and sushi counters.

Chelsea & Kensington

These highbrow neighbourhoods harbour some of London's very best (and priciest) restaurants.

★Rabbit MODERN BRITISH ££

(Map p98; ☎020-3750 0172; www.rabbit-restaurant.com; 172 King's Rd, SW3; mains £6-24, set lunch £13.50; ⏰noon-midnight Tue-Sat, 6-11pm Mon, noon-6pm Sun; ; ⊖Sloane Sq) Three brothers grew up on a farm. One became a farmer, another a butcher, while the third worked in hospitality. So they pooled their skills and came up with Rabbit, a breath of fresh air in upmarket Chelsea. The restaurant rocks the agri-chic (yes) look and the creative, seasonal modern British cuisine is fabulous.

★Five Fields MODERN BRITISH £££

(Map p98; ☎020-7838 1082; www.fivefieldsrestaurant.com; 8-9 Blacklands Tce, SW3; 3-course set meal £60; ⏰6.30-10pm Tue-Sat; ; ⊖Sloane Sq) The inventive British cuisine, consummate service and enticingly light and inviting decor of Five Fields are hard to resist, at this triumphant Chelsea restaurant, but you'll need to plan early and book way up front. It's only open five nights a week.

★Gordon Ramsay FRENCH £££

(Map p98; ☎020-7352 4441; www.gordonramsay.com; 68 Royal Hospital Rd, SW3; 3-course lunch/dinner £65/110; ⏰noon-2.30pm & 6.30-11pm Mon-Fri; ⊖Sloane Sq) One of Britain's finest restaurants and London's longest-running with three Michelin stars, this is hallowed turf for those who worship at the altar of the stove. It's true that it's a treat right from the taster to the truffles, but you won't get much time to savour it all. The blowout tasting Menu Prestige (£145) is seven courses of perfection.

Bookings are made in specific sittings and you dare not linger; book as late as you can to avoid that rushed feeling.

Notting Hill, Shepherd's Bush & Hammersmith

Notting Hill teems with good places to eat, from cheap takeaways to atmospheric pubs and restaurants worthy of the fine-dining tag. Shepherd's Bush and Hammersmith to the west pitch in with some fine contenders.

★Potli INDIAN £

(www.potli.co.uk; 319-321 King St, W6; weekday 1-/2-course set lunch £7.95/10.95, mains £7.50-15; noon-2.30pm Mon-Sat, 6-10.15pm Mon-Thu, 5.30-10.30pm Fri-Sat, noon-10pm Sun; ; Stamford Brook or Ravenscourt Park) With its scattered pieces from Mumbai's Thieves Market, Indian-market-kitchen/bazaar cuisine, home-made pickles and spice mixes, plus an accent on genuine flavour, tantalising Potli deftly captures the aromas of its culinary home. Downstairs there's an open kitchen and service is friendly, but it's the alluring menu – where flavours are teased into a rich and authentic India culinary experience – that's the real crowd-pleaser.

★Geales SEAFOOD ££

(Map p122; 020-7727 7528; www.geales.com; 2 Farmer St, W8; 2-course express lunch £9.75, mains £9-39.50; noon-3pm & 6-10.30pm Tue-Fri, noon-10.30pm Sat, noon-4pm Sun; Notting Hill Gate) Frying since 1939 – a bad year for the restaurant trade – Geales has endured with its quiet location on the corner of Farmer St in Hillgate Village. The succulent fish in crispy batter is a fine catch from a menu that also runs to other British faves such as pork belly with apple sauce and crackling, and beef and bacon pie.

★Ledbury FRENCH £££

(Map p122; 020-7792 9090; www.theledbury.com; 127 Ledbury Rd, W11; 4-course set lunch £85, 4-course dinner £95; noon-2pm Wed-Sun & 6.30-9.45pm daily; ; Westbourne Park or Notting Hill Gate) Two Michelin stars and swooningly elegant, Brett Graham's artful French restaurant attracts well-heeled diners in jeans with designer jackets. Dishes – such as hand-dived scallops, ceviche, seaweed and herb oil with frozen English wasabi or Herdwick lamb with salt-baked turnips, celery cream and wild garlic – are triumphant. London gastronomes have the Ledbury on speed-dial, so reservations well in advance are crucial.

Marylebone

You won't go too far wrong planting yourself on a table anywhere along Marylebone's charming High St.

La Fromagerie CAFE ££

(Map p101; www.lafromagerie.co.uk; 2-6 Moxon St, W1; mains £8.50-18; 8am-7.30pm Mon-Fri, 9am-7pm Sat, 10am-6pm Sun; ; Baker St) This deli-cafe has bowls of delectable salads, antipasto, peppers and beans scattered about the long communal table. Huge slabs of bread invite you to tuck in, and all the while the heavenly waft from the cheese room beckons. Cheese boards come in small and large (£9.25 and £16) and breakfast is always a good choice.

Locanda Locatelli ITALIAN ££

(Map p101; 020-7935 9088; www.locandalocatelli.com; 8 Seymour St, W1; mains from £13.50; noon-3pm daily, 6-11pm Mon-Thu, to 11.30pm Fri & Sat, to 10.15pm Sun; ; Marble Arch) This dark but quietly glamorous restaurant in an otherwise unremarkable Marble Arch hotel remains one of London's hottest tables, and you're likely to see some famous faces being greeted by celebrity chef Giorgio Locatelli. The restaurant is renowned for its pasta dishes, and the mains include six fish and five meat dishes. Booking is essential.

Bloomsbury & St Pancras

Diwana Bhel Poori House INDIAN £

(Map p106; 020-7387 5556; www.diwanabph.com; 121-123 Drummond St, NW1; mains £5.10-8.95; noon-11.30pm Mon-Sat, to 10.30pm Sun; ; Euston) One of the best Indian vegetarian restaurants in London, Diwana specialises in Bombay-style *bhel poori* (a tangy, soft and crunchy 'party mix' dish) and *dosas* (filled crispy pancakes made from rice flour). Solo diners should consider a *thali* (a complete meal consisting of lots of small dishes). The all-you-can-eat lunchtime buffet (£7) is legendary while daily specials are £6.60.

North Sea Fish Restaurant FISH & CHIPS ££

(Map p106; www.northseafishrestaurant.co.uk; 7-8 Leigh St, WC1; mains £9.95-23; noon-10.30pm Mon-Sat, 2.30-9.30pm Sun; Russell Sq) The North Sea sets out to cook fresh fish and potatoes – a simple ambition in which it succeeds admirably. Look forward to jumbo-sized plaice or halibut fillets, deep-fried or grilled, and a huge serving of chips. There's takeaway next door if you can't face the rather austere dining room.

Fitzrovia

Tucked away behind busy Tottenham Court Rd, Fitzrovia's Charlotte and Goodge Sts form one of central London's most vibrant eating precincts.

CAMDEN MARKET

Although (or perhaps because) it stopped being cutting-edge several thousand cheap leather jackets ago, **Camden Market** (Map p131; www.camdenmarket.com; Camden High St, NW1; 10am-6pm; Camden Town) gets a whopping 10 million visitors each year and is one of London's most popular attractions. What started out as a collection of attractive craft stalls by Camden Lock on the Regent's Canal now extends most of the way from Camden Town tube station to Chalk Farm tube station.

Dabbous MODERN EUROPEAN ££
(Map p106; 020-7323 1544; www.dabbous.co.uk; 39 Whitfield St, W1; set lunch 3/4 courses £28/35, set dinner 4 courses £59; noon-3pm & 5.30-11.30pm Tue-Sat; ; Goodge St) This award-winning eatery is the creation of Ollie Dabbous, everyone's favourite new chef, so book ahead for dinner or come for lunch. The combination of flavours is inspired – king crab in warm garlic buttermilk, pork with mango, rhubarb with lavender – and at first seems at odds with the industrial, hard-edged decor. But it all works exceedingly well. Reservations essential.

Lima SOUTH AMERICAN £££
(Map p78; 020-3002 2640; www.limalondon.com; 31 Rathbone Pl, W1; mains £22-29; noon-2.30pm Tue-Sun, 5.30-10.45pm Mon-Sat, 5-9pm Sun; ; Tottenham Court Rd) Sublimely zestful and piquant Peruvian flavours percolate at the heart of this fantastic and unassuming Fitzrovia restaurant. The stunningly presented cuisine has pulled a Michelin star, while helpful staff take pride in their work.

Hakkasan Hanway Place CHINESE £££
(Map p78; 020-7927 7000; www.hakkasan.com; 8 Hanway Pl, W1; mains £13.80-100; noon-3pm Mon-Fri, to 4pm Sat & Sun, 5.30-11pm Sun-Wed, to 12.15am Thu-Sat; ; Tottenham Court Rd) This basement Michelin-starred restaurant – hidden down a back alleyway – successfully combines celebrity status, stunning design, persuasive cocktails and sophisticated Chinese food. The low, nightclub-style lighting makes it a good spot for dating or a night out with friends (the bar serves seriously creative cocktails). Book far in advance or come for lunch (three courses £38, also available from 6pm to 7pm).

Camden Town

Camden is great for cheap eats, while neighbouring Chalk Farm and Primrose Hill are salted with gastropubs and upmarket restaurants.

★**Hook Camden Town** FISH & CHIPS £
(Map p131; www.hookrestaurants.com; 65 Parkway Rd, NW1; mains £8-12; noon-3pm & 5-10pm Mon-Thu, noon-10.30pm Fri & Sat, noon-9pm Sun; Camden Town) Working entirely with sustainable small fisheries and local suppliers, Hook also makes all its sauces on-site and wraps its fish in recycled materials, supplying London diners with some extraordinarily fine-tasting morsels. Totally fresh, the fish arrives in panko breadcrumbs or tempura batter, with seaweed salted chips. Craft beers and fine wines are also to hand.

Mango Room CARIBBEAN ££
(Map p131; 020-7482 5065; www.mangoroom.co.uk; 10-12 Kentish Town Rd, NW1; mains £12.50-17; noon-11pm; Camden Town) With its modern, bright decor and excellent service, Mango Room promises a sophisticated Caribbean experience, with food to match: seafood soup, grilled goat's cheese with pesto and mixed-leaf salad, salt fish with ackee (a yellow-skinned Jamaican fruit that has an uncanny resemblance to scrambled eggs), and curried goat with hot pepper and spices, all presented with origami intricacy. Booking recommended.

Islington

Allow at least an evening to explore Islington's Upper St, along with the lanes leading off it.

★**Ottolenghi** BAKERY, MEDITERRANEAN ££
(020-7288 1454; www.ottolenghi.co.uk; 287 Upper St, N1; breakfast £5.50-10.50, lunch mains from £12.90, dinner mains from £11; 8am-10.30pm Mon-Sat, 9am-7pm Sun; ; Highbury & Islington) Mountains of meringues tempt you through the door of this deli-restaurant, where a sumptuous array of baked goods and fresh salads greets you. Meals are as light and bright as the brilliantly white interior design, with a strong influence from the eastern Mediterranean.

Trullo ITALIAN ££
(020-7226 2733; www.trullorestaurant.com; 300-302 St Paul's Rd, N1; mains £15-21; 12.30-2.45pm & 6-10.15pm Mon-Sat, 12.30-3pm Sun; Highbury & Islington) Trullo's homemade pasta is delicious, but the main attraction here is the

Camden Town

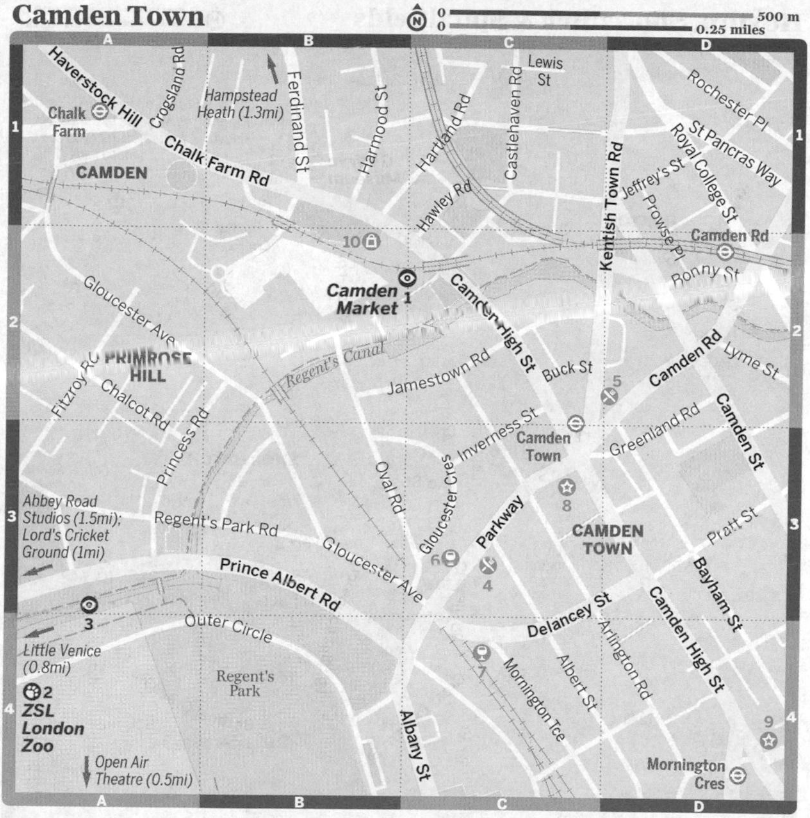

charcoal grill, which churns out the likes of succulent Italian-style pork chops, steaks and fish. The service is excellent, too, although dinner time can get packed.

Le Mercury FRENCH ££
(☎020-7354 4088; www.lemercury.co.uk; 140a Upper St, N1; mains £10.95; ⌚noon-1am Mon-Sat, to 11pm Sun; Ⓤ Highbury & Islington or Angel) An excellent and wildly popular budget French eatery, Le Mercury seems to have all you need in its winning formula: romantic atmosphere with candlelit, petite tables and plants everywhere, combined with superb French food at unbeatable prices. Londoners have long known about this place, so reservations are advised.

Clerkenwell & Farringdon

Clerkenwell's hidden gems are well worth digging for. Pedestrianised Exmouth Market is a good place to start.

Camden Town

Top Sights
1 Camden Market B2
2 ZSL London Zoo A4

Sights
3 Regent's Canal A3

Eating
4 Hook Camden Town C3
5 Mango Room D2

Drinking & Nightlife
6 Dublin Castle C3
7 Edinboro Castle C4

Entertainment
8 Jazz Cafe C3
9 KOKO D4

Shopping
10 Stables Market B2

Hoxton, Shoreditch & Spitalfields

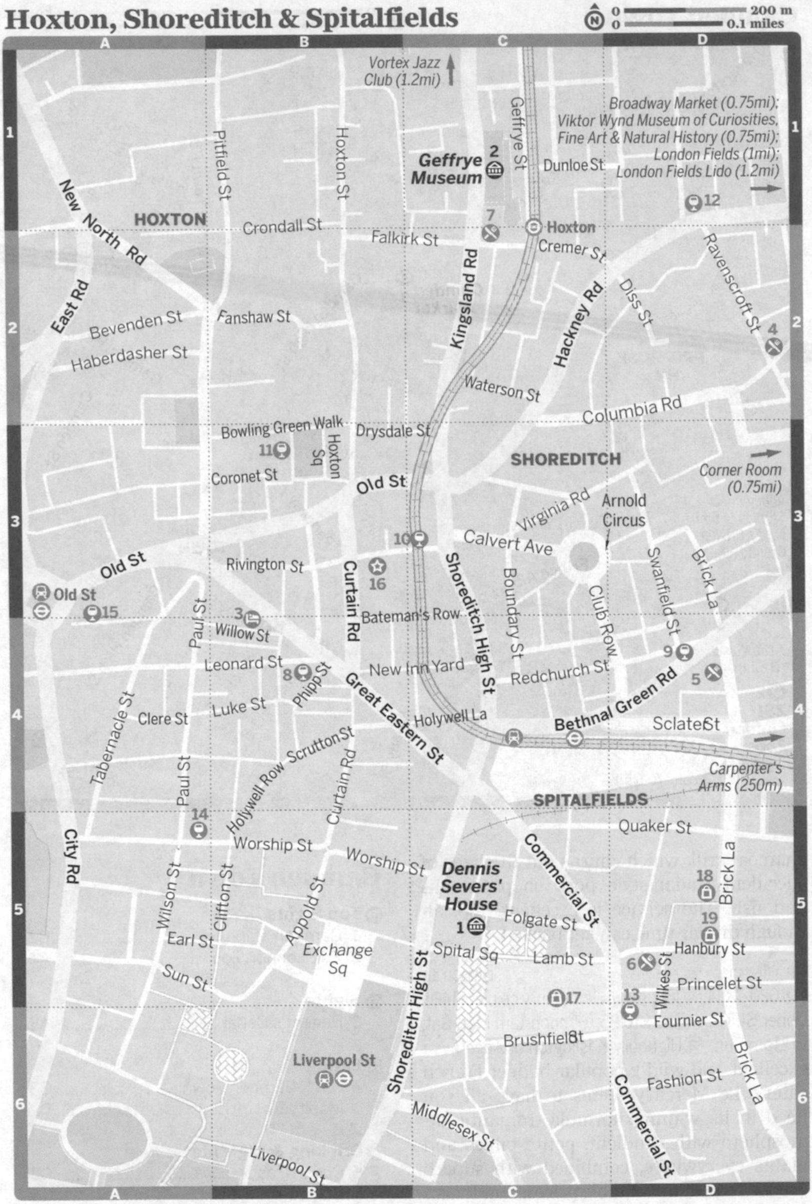

★ **Prufrock Coffee** CAFE £
(Map p106; www.prufrockcoffee.com; 23-25 Leather Lane, EC1N; mains £4-7; 8am-6pm Mon-Fri, 10am-5pm Sat & Sun; ; Farringdon) Not content with being one of the kings of London's coffee-bean scene (it offers barista training and workshops in 'latte art'), Prufrock also dishes up delicious breakfasts, lunches and cuppa-friendly pastries and snacks. Judging by the number of laptops, plenty of customers treat it as their office.

Hoxton, Shoreditch & Spitalfields

★**St John** BRITISH ££
(Map p106; ☎020-7251 0848; www.stjohn restaurant.com; 26 St John St, EC1M; mains £18-21.50; ⊙noon-3pm & 6-11pm Mon-Fri, 6-11pm Sat, 12.30-4pm Sun; ⊖Farringdon) Whitewashed brick walls, high ceilings and simple wooden furniture keep diners free to concentrate on St John's famous nose-to tail dishes. Serves are big, hearty and a celebration of England's culinary past. Don't miss the signature roast bone marrow and parsley salad (£8.90).

★**Morito** TAPAS ££
(Map p106; ☎020-7278 7007; www.morito.co.uk; 32 Exmouth Market, EC1R; tapas £4.50-9.50; ⊙noon-4pm daily, 5-11pm Mon-Sat; 📶; ⊖Farringdon) This diminutive eatery is a wonderfully authentic take on a Spanish tapas bar, with excellent eats. Seats are at the bar, along the window, or on one of the small tables inside or out. It's relaxed, convivial and often completely crammed; reservations are taken for lunch, but dinner is first come, first served, with couples generally going to the bar.

Little Bay EUROPEAN ££
(Map p106; ☎020-7278 1234; www.littlebay farringdon.co.uk; 171 Farringdon Rd, EC1R; mains from £7; ⊙noon-midnight Mon-Sat, to 11pm Sun; ⊖Farringdon) We're talking crushed-velvet ceiling, handmade twisted lamps that improve around the room (as the artist got better) and elaborately painted bar and tables where nymphs frolick. Totally bonkers, but fun. Food is hearty, and good value, with two-course set meals a bargain £10 before 6pm.

Hoxton, Shoreditch & Spitalfields

From the hit-and-miss Bangladeshi restaurants of Brick Lane to the Vietnamese strip on Kingsland Rd, and the Jewish, Spanish, French, Italian and Greek eateries in between, the East End's cuisine is as multicultural as its residents.

Sông Quê VIETNAMESE £
(Map p132; www.songque.co.uk; 134 Kingsland Rd, E2; mains £7.40-9.50; ⊙noon-3pm & 5.30-11pm Mon-Fri, noon-11pm Sat, noon-10.30pm Sun; ⊖Hoxton) With the kind of demand for seats that most London restaurants can only dream of, this no-frills, hospital-green Vietnamese joint often has a line of people waiting. Feeding the denizens of London for almost 15 years, service can be abrupt, but the food is spot-on, with two dozen types of fantastic *pho* (noodle soup) to choose from.

Brick Lane Beigel Bake BAKERY £
(Map p132; 159 Brick Lane, E2; bagels £1-4.20; ⊙24hr; ⊖Shoreditch High St) This relic of the Jewish East End still makes a brisk trade serving dirt-cheap homemade bagels (filled with salmon, cream cheese and/or salt beef) to hungry shoppers and late-night boozers.

Poppies FISH & CHIPS ££
(Map p132; www.poppiesfishandchips.co.uk; 6-8 Hanbury St, E1; mains £5.90-18; ⊙11am-11pm Mon-Thu, to 11.30pm Fri & Sat, to 10.30pm Sun; 📶; ⊖Shoreditch High St) This glorious re-creation of a 1950s East End chippy comes complete with waitresses in pinnies and hairnets, and Blitz memorabilia. As well as the usual fishy suspects, it does those old-time London staples – jellied eels and mushy peas – plus

kid-pleasing, sweet-tooth desserts (sticky toffee pudding or apple pie with ice cream) and a wine list.

The East End

★ Corner Room MODERN BRITISH ££
(☎020-7871 0460; www.townhallhotel.com/cornerroom; Patriot Sq, E2; mains £10-14, 2/3-course lunch £19/23; ⌚7.30-10am Mon-Fri, 7.30-10.30am Sat & Sun, noon-3pm Mon-Thu, noon-4pm Fri-Sun, 6-10pm Mon-Wed & Sun, 6-10.30pm Thu-Sat; ⊖Bethnal Green) Someone put this baby in the corner, but we're certainly not complaining. Tucked away on the 1st floor of the Town Hall Hotel, this relaxed restaurant serves expertly crafted dishes with complex yet delicate flavours, highlighting the best of British seasonal produce. The six-course tasting menu is £45.

★ Brawn BRITISH, FRENCH ££
(Map p132; ☎020-7729 5692; www.brawn.co; 49 Columbia Rd, E2; mains £11.50-28; ⌚noon-3pm Tue-Sat, 6-10.30pm Mon-Sat, noon-4pm Sun; ⊖Hoxton) There's a Parisian bistro feel to this relaxed corner restaurant, yet the menu walks a fine line between British and French traditions. Hence oxtail and veal kidney pie sits alongside plaice Grenobloise, and soufflés are filled with Westcombe cheddar. Try its legendary spicy Scotch-egg starter – a Brit classic delivered with French finesse. The three-course Sunday lunch is £28.

Drinking & Nightlife

You need only glance at William Hogarth's Gin Lane prints from 1751 to realise that Londoners and alcohol have more than a passing acquaintance. The metropolis offers a huge variety of venues to wet your whistle in – from neighbourhood pubs to all-night clubs, and everything in between.

West End

Lamb & Flag PUB
(Map p78; www.lambandflagcoventgarden.co.uk; 33 Rose St, WC2; ⌚11am-11pm Mon-Sat, noon-10.30pm Sun; 📶; ⊖Covent Garden) Pocket-sized Lamb & Flag is brimful of charm and history, squeezed into an alley (where poet John Dryden was mugged in December 1679) on the site of a pub that dates to at least 1772. Rain or shine, you'll have to elbow your way to the bar through the merry crowd drinking outside. Inside are brass fittings and creaky wooden floors.

★ Dukes Bar COCKTAIL BAR
(Map p78; ☎020-7491 4840; www.dukeshotel.com; 35 St James's Pl, SW1; ⌚2-11pm Mon-Sat, 4-10.30pm Sun; 📶; ⊖Green Park) Sip to-die-for martinis like royalty in a gentleman's-club-like ambience at this tidily tucked-away classic bar where white-jacketed masters mix up some awesomely good preparations. Ian Fleming used to drink here, perhaps perfecting his 'shaken, not stirred' Bond maxim. Smokers can ease into the secluded Cognac and Cigar Garden to light up (but cigars must be purchased here).

★ American Bar BAR
(Map p101; www.thebeaumont.com; The Beaumont, Brown Hart Gardens, W1; ⌚11.30am-midnight Mon-Sat, to 11pm Sun; 📶; ⊖Bond St) Sip a bourbon or a classic cocktail in the classic 1930s art-deco striped-walnut ambience of this stylish bar at the hallmark Beaumont hotel (p119). It's central, period and like a gentleman's club, but far from stuffy. Only a few years old, the American Bar feels like its been pouring drinks since the days of the Eton Crop and the Jazz Age.

★ American Bar COCKTAIL BAR
(Map p78; www.fairmont.com/savoy-london/dining/americanbar; The Strand, WC2; ⌚11.30am-midnight Mon-Sat, noon-midnight Sun; ⊖Covent Garden) Home of the Hanky Panky, White Lady and other classic infusions invented here, the seriously dishy and elegant American Bar is an icon of London, with soft cream and blue deco lines and live piano. Cocktails start at £16.50 and peak at a stupefying £5000 (The Original Sazerac, containing Sazerac de Forge from 1857).

Galvin at Windows BAR
(Map p72; www.galvinatwindows.com; London Hilton on Park Lane, 28th fl, 22 Park Lane, W1; ⌚11am-1am Mon-Wed, 11am-2am Thu-Fri, 3pm-2am Sat, 11am-11pm Sun; 📶; ⊖Hyde Park Corner) On the 28th floor of the London Hilton on Park Lane, this swish bar gazes on to awesome views, especially come dusk. Cocktail prices reach similar heights (£12 to £40) but the leather seats are inviting and the marble bar is gorgeous. The one-Michelin-star **restaurant** (same views) offers a giveaway lunch menu (two/three courses £28/33; Monday to Friday).

Connaught Bar COCKTAIL BAR
(Map p98; www.the-connaught.co.uk; Connaught Hotel, Carlos Pl, W1; ⌚4pm-1am Mon-Sat, to midnight Sun; ⊖Bond St) Drinkers who know their stuff

single out the Martini trolley for particular praise, but almost everything at this sumptuous bar at the exclusive and very British Connaught Hotel gets the nod: lavish deco-inspired lines, excruciating attention to detail, faultless service, and some of the best drinks in town. Cocktails, classic and those given a thoroughly contemporary twist, start at £17.

Rivoli Bar COCKTAIL BAR

(Map p78; www.theritzlondon.com/rivoli-bar; Ritz, 150 Piccadilly, W1; ⌚11.30am-11.30pm Mon-Sat, noon-10.30pm Sun; 📶; ⊖Green Park) You may not quite need a diamond as big as the Ritz to drink at this art-deco marvel, but it always helps. All camphor wood, illuminated glass, golden ceiling domes and stunning cocktails, the bar is a lavish art-deco gem. Unlike in some other parts of the Ritz, dress code at the Rivoli is smart casual.

Gordon's Wine Bar BAR

(Map p78; www.gordonswinebar.com; 47 Villiers St, WC2; ⌚11am-11pm Mon-Sat, noon-10pm Sun; ⊖Embankment) Cavernous, dark, candlelit, atmospheric and founded in 1890, Gordon's is a victim of its own success – it's relentlessly busy and unless you arrive before the office crowd does (around 6pm), forget about landing a table. The French and New World wines are heady and reasonably priced. You can nibble on bread, cheese and olives and there's outside garden seating in summer.

French House BAR

(Map p78; www.frenchhousesoho.com; 49 Dean St, W1; ⌚noon-11pm Mon-Sat, to 10.30pm Sun; ⊖Leicester Sq) French House is Soho's legendary boho boozer with a history to match: this was the meeting place of the Free French Forces during WWII, and De Gaulle is said to have drunk here often, while Dylan Thomas, Peter O'Toole and Francis Bacon all ended up on the wooden floor at least once.

The City

★Sky Pod BAR

(Map p84; ☎0333-772 0020; http://skygarden.london/sky-pod-bar; 20 Fenchurch St, EC3; ⌚7am-1am Mon, 7am-2am Tue-Fri, 8am-2am Sat, 9am-midnight Sun; ⊖Monument) One of the best places in the City to get high is the Sky Pod in the Sky Garden on level 35 of the so-called Walkie Talkie. The views are phenomenal – especially from the open-air South Terrace – the gardens are lush and it's the only place where this obstructive and clumsy-looking building won't be in your face.

Madison COCKTAIL BAR

(Map p84; ☎020-3693 5160; www.madisonlondon.net; Rooftop Terrace, One New Change, EC4; ⌚11am-midnight Mon-Wed, to 1am Thu-Sat, to 9pm Sun; ⊖St Paul's) Perched atop One New Change with a drop-dead view of St Paul's and beyond, Madison offers one of the largest public open-air roof terraces you'll ever encounter. There's a full restaurant and bar on one side and a cocktail bar with outdoor seating on the other. We come for the latter. Drinkers must be over 21, dress code is smart casual.

Ye Olde Cheshire Cheese PUB

(Map p84; ☎020-7353 6170; Wine Office Court, 145 Fleet St, EC4; ⌚11.30am-11pm Mon-Fri, noon-11pm Sat; ⊖Chancery Lane) The entrance to this historic pub is via a narrow alley off Fleet St. Over its long history, locals have included Dr Johnson, Thackeray and Dickens. Despite (or possibly because of) this, the Cheshire can feel a bit like a museum. Nevertheless it's one of London's most famous and historic pubs and well worth popping in for a pint.

South Bank

★Little Bird Gin COCKTAIL BAR

(www.littlebirdgin.com; Maltby St, SE1; ⌚10am-4pm Sat, from 11am Sun; ⊖London Bridge) The South London–based distillery opens a pop-up bar in a workshop on **Maltby Street Market** (www.maltby.st; Maltby St, SE1; ⌚9am-4pm Sat, 11am-4pm Sun; ⊖London Bridge) to ply merry punters with devilishly good cocktails (£5 to £7), served in jam jars or apothecary's glass bottles.

★Oblix BAR

(Map p92; www.oblixrestaurant.com; 32nd fl, Shard, 31 St Thomas St, SE1; ⌚noon-11pm; ⊖London Bridge) On the 32nd floor of the Shard (p90), Oblix offers mesmerising vistas of London. You can come for anything from a coffee (£3.50) to a cocktail (from £10) and enjoy virtually the same views as the official viewing galleries of the Shard (but at a reduced cost and with the added bonus of a drink). Live music every night from 7pm.

Ministry of Sound CLUB

(Map p92; www.ministryofsound.com; 103 Gaunt St, SE1; entry £10-22; ⌚10pm-6.30am Fri, 11am-7am Sat; ⊖Elephant & Castle) This legendary club-cum-enormous-global-brand (four bars, three dance floors) lost some 'edge' in the early noughties but, after pumping in top DJs, firmly rejoined the top club ranks. Friday is the Gallery trance night, while

GAY & LESBIAN LONDON

The West End, particularly Soho, is the visible centre of gay and lesbian London, with venues clustered around Old Compton St and its surrounds. However, Soho doesn't hold a monopoly on gay life. Generally, London is a safe place for lesbians and gays. It's rare to encounter any problem with sharing rooms or holding hands in the inner city, although it would pay to keep your wits about you at night and be conscious of your surroundings.

Some venues to get you started include the following:

Village (Map p78; www.village-soho.co.uk; 81 Wardour St, W1; ⏲5pm-1am Mon-Tue, to 2am Wed-Sat, to 11.30pm Sun; ⊖Piccadilly Circus) The Village is always up for a party, whatever the night of the week. There are karaoke nights, 'discolicious' nights, go-go-dancer nights – take your pick. And if you can't wait until the clubs open to strut your stuff, there is a dance floor downstairs, complete with pole, of course. Open till 3am on the last weekend of the month.

She Soho (Map p78; ☎020-7287 5041; www.she-soho.com; 23a Old Compton St, W1D; ⏲4-11.30pm Mon-Thu, to 12.30am Fri & Sat, to 10.30pm Sun; ⊖Leicester Sq) Soho lost a lesbian bar (Candy Bar) but gained another with this intimate and dimly lit basement place with DJs at weekends, comedy, cabaret, live music and party nights. Open till 3am on the last Friday and Saturday of the month.

Heaven (Map p78; www.heavennightclub-london.com; Villiers St, WC2; ⏲11pm-5am Mon, Thu & Fri, 10pm-5am Sat; ⊖Embankment or Charing Cross) This 37-year-old, perennially popular gay club under the arches beneath Charing Cross station is host to excellent live gigs and club nights. Monday's Popcorn (mixed dance party, all-welcome door policy) offers one of the best weeknight's clubbing in the capital. The celebrated G-A-Y takes place here on Thursday (G-A-Y Porn Idol), Friday (G-A-Y Camp Attack) and Saturday (plain ol' G-A-Y).

Duke of Wellington (Map p78; 77 Wardour St, W1; ⏲noon-midnight Mon-Fri, 11am-midnight Sat, noon-11.30pm Sun; ⊖Leicester Sq) This seasoned pub off Old Compton St is often busy but has few pretensions, attracting a more beardy, fun-loving gay crowd, many of whom gather outside in warmer months.

RVT (Royal Vauxhall Tavern; www.rvt.org.uk; 372 Kennington Lane, SE11; entry £4-8; ⏲7pm-midnight Mon-Thu, 9pm-3am Fri, 9pm-2am Sat, 3pm-midnight Sun; ⊖Vauxhall) Rough around the edges to say the least, the Royal Vauxhall Tavern is the perfect antidote to the gleaming new wave of uppity gay venues now crowding Vauxhall's gay village. Saturday's Duckie, tagged 'London's Authentic Honky Tonk', is the club's signature queer performance night, while Sunday Social is cabaret and dance, till midnight.

Two Brewers (www.the2brewers.com; 114 Clapham High St, SW4; admission after 10pm £3-6; ⏲4pm-2am Sun-Thu, to 4am Fri & Sat; ⊖Clapham Common) Clapham exudes an inner suburban feel, the High St in particular, but the long-standing Two Brewers endures as one of the best London gay bars outside the gay villages of Soho, Shoreditch and Vauxhall. Here there's a friendly, laid-back, local crowd who come for a quiet drink during the week and some madcap cabaret and dancing at weekends.

Saturday sessions offer the crème de la crème of house, electro and techno DJs.

Chelsea & Kensington

Queen's Arms PUB

(Map p98; www.thequeensarmskensington.co.uk; 30 Queen's Gate Mews, SW7; ⏲noon-11pm Mon-Sat, to 10.30pm Sun; ⊖Gloucester Rd) Just around the corner from the Royal Albert Hall, this godsend of a blue-grey painted pub in an adorable cobbled mews setting off bustling Queen's Gate beckons with a cosy interior and a right royal selection of ales – including selections from small, local cask brewers – and ciders on tap.

The fine pub menu can sew up din-dins, with burger-and-a-beer offers on Mondays for a tenner.

Bloomsbury & St Pancras

Big Chill House PUB

(Map p106; www.wearebigchill.com; 257-259 Pentonville Rd, N1; ⏲11am-midnight Sun-Wed, to 1am Thu, to 3am Fri & Sat; 📶; ⊖King's Cross St Pancras) Come the weekend, the only remotely chilled-out space in this large, buzzy Victorian pub is its first-rate and generously proportioned rooftop terrace. It's run by the people behind the Big Chill record label, so it can be counted on for a varied roster of live music and DJs. The sound system is fantastic and entry is free most nights.

Queen's Larder PUB

(Map p106; www.queenslarder.co.uk; 1 Queen Sq, WC1; ⌚11.30am-11pm Mon-Sat, noon-10.30pm Sun; ⊖Russell Sq) In a lovely square southeast of Russell Sq is this pub, so called because Queen Charlotte, wife of 'Mad' King George III, rented part of the pub's cellar to store special foods for her husband while he was being treated nearby. It's a tiny but wonderfully cosy pub; there are benches outside for fair-weather fans and a dining room upstairs.

69 Colebrooke Row COCKTAIL BAR

(www.69colebrookerow.com; 69 Colebrooke Row, N1; ⌚5pm-midnight Sun-Thu, to 2am Fri & Sat; ⊖Angel) Also known as 'the bar with no name', this tiny establishment may be nothing much to look at, but it has a stellar reputation for its cocktails (£10.50). The seasonal drinks menu is steeped in ambitious flavours and blends, with classic drinks for more conservative palates. Hard to find a seat at the best of times, so make sure you book ahead.

Draft House BAR

(Map p78; www.drafthouse.co.uk; 43 Goodge St, W1; ⌚noon-11pm Mon-Thu, to midnight Fri & Sat; 📶; ⊖Goodge St) Although you can line your tummy with good nosh, Draft House is largely about the beer choice it crams into its pea-sized premises. This is a public house for ale aficionados, where you can happily corner a Flying Dog Gonzo Imperial Porter or a head-spinning Samichlaus 14%.

Notting Hill, Bayswater & Paddington

★Troubadour BAR

(www.troubadour.co.uk; 263-267 Old Brompton Rd, SW5; ⌚8.30am-midnight; 📶; ⊖Earl's Court) On a compatible spiritual plane to Paris' Shakespeare and Company Bookshop, this eccentric, time-warped and convivial boho bar-cafe has been serenading drinkers since the 1950s. (Deep breath) Adele, Paolo Nutini, Joni Mitchell and (deeper breath) Jimi Hendrix and Bob Dylan have performed here, and there's still live music (folk, blues) and a large, pleasant garden open in summer.

Windsor Castle PUB

(Map p122; www.thewindsorcastlekensington.co.uk; 114 Campden Hill Rd, W11; ⌚noon-11pm Mon-Sat, to 10.30pm Sun; 📶; ⊖Notting Hill Gate) A classic tavern on the brow of Campden Hill Rd, this place has history, nooks and charm on tap. It's worth the search for its historic compartmentalised interior, roaring fire (in winter), delightful beer garden (in summer) and affable regulars (most always). According to legend, the bones of Thomas Paine (author of *Rights of Man*) are in the cellar.

Dove PUB

(☎020-8748 9474; www.dovehammersmith.co.uk; 19 Upper Mall, W6; ⌚11am-11pm Mon-Sat, noon-10.30pm Sun; 📶; ⊖Hammersmith or Ravenscourt Park) Severely inundated by the epic floodwaters of 1928, this gem of a 17th-century Fuller's pub revels in historic charm and superb Thames views. Scottish poet James Thompson was reputedly inspired to write the lyrics to 'Rule Britannia' here in the 18th century. It was Graham Greene's local, Hemingway and Dylan Thomas drank here, too, and William Morris lived nearby.

Marylebone

Purl COCKTAIL BAR

(Map p101; ☎020-7935 0835; www.purl-london.com; 50-54 Blandford St, W1; ⌚5-11.30pm Mon-Thu, to midnight Fri & Sat; ⊖Baker St or Bond St) Purl is a fabulous underground drinking den. Decked out in vintage furniture, it serves original and intriguingly named cocktails (What's Your Poison? or Mr Hyde's No 2) and a punch of the day. It's all subdued lighting and hushed-tone conversations, which only adds to the mysterious air. Booking recommended.

Artesian BAR

(Map p101; ☎020-7636 1000; www.artesian-bar.co.uk; Langham Hotel, 1c Portland Pl, W1; ⌚11am-2am Mon-Sat, to midnight Sun; 📶; ⊖Oxford Circus) For a dose of colonial glamour with a touch of Oriental elegance, the sumptuous bar at the Langham hits the mark, though it's often packed. With the largest collection in town, rum is the speciality here and award-winning cocktails (£17) are concocted from the 60 varieties on offer.

Camden Town

★Dublin Castle PUB

(Map p131; www.thedublincastle.com; 94 Parkway, NW1; ⌚1pm-2am; ⊖Camden Town) There's live punk or alternative bands most nights in this comfortingly grungy pub's back room (cover charges are usually between £4.50 and £7). DJs take over after the bands on Friday, Saturday and Sunday nights.

★**Edinboro Castle** PUB
(Map p131; www.edinborocastlepub.co.uk; 57 Mornington Tce, NW1; noon-11.30pm Mon-Fri, 10am-11.30pm Sat, noon-10.30pm Sun; ; Camden Town) Large and relaxed Edinboro enjoys a refined atmosphere, gorgeous furniture perfect for slumping, a fine bar and a full menu. The highlight, however, is the huge beer garden, complete with warm-weather BBQs and foosball table and adorned with coloured lights on long summer evenings.

Clerkenwell & Farringdon

★**Zetter Townhouse Cocktail Lounge** COCKTAIL BAR
(Map p106; 020-7324 4545; www.thezettertownhouse.com; 49-50 St John's Sq, EC1V; 7.30am-12.45am; Farringdon) Tucked away behind an unassuming door on St John's Sq, this ground-floor bar is quirkily decorated with plush armchairs, stuffed animal heads and a legion of lamps. The cocktail list takes its theme from the area's distilling history – recipes of yesteryear and homemade tinctures and cordials are used to create interesting and unusual tipples. House cocktails are all £10.50.

★**Ye Olde Mitre** PUB
(Map p84; www.yeoldemitreholborn.co.uk; 1 Ely Ct, EC1N; 11am-11pm Mon-Fri; ; Farringdon) A delightfully cosy historic pub with an extensive beer selection, tucked away in a backstreet off Hatton Garden, Ye Olde Mitre was built in 1546 for the servants of Ely Palace. There's no music, so the rooms only echo with amiable chit-chat. Queen Elizabeth I danced around the cherry tree by the bar, they say. Closed Saturday and Sunday.

Hoxton, Shoreditch & Spitalfields

★**XOYO** CLUB
(Map p132; www.xoyo.co.uk; 32-37 Cowper St, EC2A; hours vary; Old St) This fantastic Shoreditch warehouse club throws together a pulsingly popular mix of gigs, club nights and art events. Always buzzing, the varied line-up – expect indie bands, hip hop, electro, dubstep and much in between – attracts a mix of clubbers, from skinny-jeaned hipsters to more mature hedonists (but no suits).

★**Worship St Whistling Shop** COCKTAIL BAR
(Map p132; 020-7247 0015; www.whistlingshop.com; 63 Worship St, EC2A; 5pm-midnight Mon & Tue, to 1am Wed & Thu, to 2am Fri & Sat; Old St) While the name is Victorian slang for a place selling illicit booze, this subterranean drinking den's master mixologists explore the experimental outer limits of cocktail chemistry and aromatic science, as well as concocting the classics. Many ingredients are made with the rotary evaporators in the on-site lab. Cocktail masterclasses also run.

Happiness Forgets COCKTAIL BAR
(Map p132; www.happinessforgets.com; 8-9 Hoxton Sq, N1; 5-11pm; ; Old St) This low-lit, basement bar with good-value cocktails is relaxed and intimate, overseen by considerate and professional staff. You won't want to leave: look for the signs for Ruby cafe and take the stairs heading down. It's worth reserving.

BrewDog BAR
(Map p132; www.brewdog.com; 51-55 Bethnal Green Rd, E1; noon-midnight; ; Shoreditch High St) BrewDog is an ale aficionado's paradise, with 18 different brews on tap, hundreds by the bottle and Dirty Burgers to soak it all up with. Its own crowd-funded ecobrewery sits up in Scotland, near Aberdeen, but it stocks plenty of other microbrewery beers, too.

Book Club BAR
(Map p132; 020-7684 8618; www.wearetbc.com; 100-106 Leonard St, EC2A; 8am-midnight Mon-Wed, to 2am Thu & Fri, 10am-2am Sat, 10am-midnight Sun; ; Old St) A creative vibe animates this fantastic one-time Victorian warehouse, which hosts DJs and oddball events (life drawing, workshops, twerking lessons, the Crap Film Club) to complement the drinking and enthusiastic ping-pong and pool playing. Food is served throughout the day and there's a scruffy basement bar below.

Sager + Wilde WINE BAR
(Map p132; www.sagerandwilde.com; 193 Hackney Rd, E2; 5pm-midnight Mon-Fri, 2pm-midnight Sat & Sun; ; Hoxton) A handsome addition to the East End drinking scene, this quietly stylish wine bar offers a modish bar-

bites menu, an eye-catching glass-brick bar counter and excellent wines by the bottle and glass. There are a few outdoor tables for street-side supping.

Ten Bells PUB
(Map p132; www.tenbells.com; 84 Commercial St, E1; noon-midnight Sun-Wed, to 1am Thu-Sat; ; Shoreditch High St) With its large windows and beautiful tiles, this landmark Victorian pub is perfectly positioned for a pint after a wander around Spitalfields Market. The most famous Jack the Ripper pub, it was patronised by his last victim before her grisly end – and possibly by the serial killer himself. Gin menu and homemade pork scratchings offered.

Cargo BAR, CLUB
(Map p132; www.cargo-london.com; 83 Rivington St, EC2A; noon-1am Sun-Thu, to 3am Fri & Sat; Shoreditch High St) Cargo is one of London's most eclectic clubs. Under its brick railway arches you'll find a dance floor, bar and outside terrace adorned with two original Banksy images. The music policy (hip hop, pop, R&B, club classics) is varied, with plenty of up-and-coming bands also in the line-up. Food is available throughout the day.

The East End

★Prospect of Whitby PUB
(57 Wapping Wall, E1; noon-11pm; ; Wapping) Once known as the Devil's Tavern, the Whitby is said to date from 1520, making it the oldest riverside pub in London. Famous patrons have included Charles Dickens and Samuel Pepys. It's firmly on the tourist trail, but there's a smallish terrace overlooking the Thames, a restaurant upstairs, open fires in winter and a pewter-topped bar.

★Carpenter's Arms PUB
(www.carpentersarmsfreehouse.com; 73 Cheshire St, E2; 4-11.30pm Mon-Wed, noon-11.30pm Thu & Sun, noon-12.30pm Fri & Sat; ; Shoreditch High St) Once owned by infamous gangsters the Kray brothers (who bought it for their old ma to run), this chic yet cosy pub has been beautifully restored and its many wooden surfaces positively gleam. A back room and small yard provide a little more space for the convivial drinkers. There's a huge range of draught and bottled beers and ciders.

Greenwich

★Cutty Sark Tavern PUB
(www.cuttysarktavern.co.uk; 4-6 Ballast Quay, SE10; 11am-11pm Mon-Sat, noon-10.30pm Sun; DLR Cutty Sark) Housed in a delightful bow-windowed, wood-beamed Georgian building directly on the Thames, the Cutty Sark is one of the few independent pubs left in Greenwich. Half a dozen cask-conditioned ales on tap line the bar, there's an inviting riverside seating area opposite and an upstairs dining room looking out on to glorious views. It's a 10-minute walk from the DLR station.

Trafalgar Tavern PUB
(020-8858 2909; www.trafalgartavern.co.uk; 6 Park Row, SE10; noon-11pm Mon-Thu, noon-midnight Fri, 10am-midnight Sat, 10am-11pm Sun; DLR Cutty Sark) This elegant tavern with big windows overlooking the Thames is steeped in history. Dickens apparently knocked back a few here – and used it as the setting for the wedding breakfast scene in *Our Mutual Friend* – and prime ministers Gladstone and Disraeli used to dine on the pub's celebrated whitebait.

Hampstead & Highgate

★Holly Bush PUB
(www.hollybushhampstead.co.uk; 22 Holly Mount, NW3; noon-11pm Mon-Sat, to 10.30pm Sun; ; Hampstead) This beautiful Grade II–listed Georgian pub opens to an antique interior, with a secluded hilltop location, open fires in winter and a knack for making you stay longer than you planned. Set above Heath St, it's reached via the Holly Bush Steps.

Outside Central London

★White Cross PUB
(www.thewhitecrossrichmond.com; Water Lane, TW9; 10am-11pm Mon-Sat, to 10.30pm; ; Richmond) The riverside location and fine food and ales make this bay-windowed pub on the site of a former friary a winner. There are entrances for low and high tides, but when the river is at its highest, Cholmondeley Walk running along the Thames floods and the pub is out of bounds to those not willing to wade. Wellies are provided.

★City Barge PUB
(www.metropolitanpubcompany.com/our-pubs/the-city-barge; 27 Strand on the Green, W4;

(noon-11pm Mon-Thu, noon-midnight Fri, 10am-midnight Sat, 10am-10.30pm Sun; ; Gunnersbury) In a line of small riverside cottages facing wooded Oliver's Island (where Cromwell is alleged to have taken refuge), this excellent pub looks straight onto the muddy Thames. Once known as the Navigators Arms, there has been a pub here since the Middle Ages (1484, to be exact), although the Luftwaffe gave it a dramatic facelift (as has a recent, attractive refurb).

☆ Entertainment

From West End luvvies to East End geezers, Londoners have always loved a spectacle. With bear-baiting and public executions long on the no-no list, they've fallen back on what London does well: some of the world's best theatre and live-music choices. For a comprehensive list of what to do on any given night, check out *Time Out*, the *Evening Standard* and *Metro*.

☆ Theatre

From West End luvvies to East End geezers, Londoners have always loved a spectacle. With bear-baiting and public executions long on the no-no list, they've fallen back on what London does well: some of the world's best theatre and live-music choices. The term 'West End' – as with Broadway – generally refers to the big-money productions such as musicals, but also includes other heavyweights. Off West End – including venues such as the Almeida and Donmar Warehouse – is where you'll generally find the most original works.

★ Shakespeare's Globe THEATRE

(Map p92; 020-7401 9919; www.shakespearesglobe.com; 21 New Globe Walk, SE1; seats £10-43, standing £5; Blackfriars or London Bridge) If you love Shakespeare and the theatre, the Globe will knock your theatrical socks off. This authentic Shakespearean theatre is a wooden 'O' without a roof over the central stage area, and although there are covered wooden bench seats in tiers around the stage, many people (there's room for 700) do as 17th-century 'groundlings' did, standing in front of the stage.

Because the building is quite open to the elements, you may have to wrap up. Groundlings note: umbrellas are not allowed, but cheap raincoats are on sale. A warning: two pillars holding up the stage canopy (the so-called Heavens) obscure much of the view in section D; you'd almost do better to stand. Unexpected aircraft noise features in some plays.

The theatre season runs from late April to mid-October and includes works by Shakespeare and his contemporaries such as Christopher Marlowe.

If you don't like the idea of standing in the rain or sitting in the cold, opt for an indoor candlelit play in the **Sam Wanamaker Playhouse**, a Jacobean theatre similar to the one Shakespeare would have used in winter. The programming also includes opera.

★ Wilton's THEATRE

(020-7702 2789; www.wiltons.org.uk; 1 Graces Alley, E1; tour £6; tours 6pm most Mon, bar 5-11pm Mon-Sat; Tower Hill) A gloriously atmospheric example of one of London's Victorian public-house music halls, Wilton's hosts a variety of shows, from comedy and classical music to theatre and opera. One-hour guided tours offer an insight into its fascinating history. The Mahogany Bar is a great way to get a taste of the place if you're not attending a performance.

National Theatre THEATRE

(Map p92; 020-7452 3000; www.nationaltheatre.org.uk; South Bank, SE1; 9.30am-11pm Mon-Sat, noon-6pm Sun; Waterloo) England's flagship theatre (its full name is the Royal National Theatre) showcases a mix of classic and contemporary plays performed by excellent casts in three theatres (Olivier, Lyttelton and Dorfman). Outstanding artistic director Nicholas Hytner oversaw a golden decade at the theatre, with landmark productions such as *War Horse*. His replacement, Rufus Norris, started in April 2015.

Travelex tickets costing just £15 are available to certain performances during the peak period; same-day tickets also cost £15. Under-18s pay half price. Likened by Prince Charles to a nuclear power station, the theatre's purpose-designed architecture is considered an icon of the Brutalist school.

Almeida THEATRE

(020-7359 4404; www.almeida.co.uk; Almeida St, N1; £10-38; Highbury or Islington) Housed in a Grade II–listed Victorian building, this plush 325-seat theatre can be relied on for imaginative programming.

Donmar Warehouse THEATRE

(Map p78; 0844 871 7624; www.donmarwarehouse.com; 41 Earlham St, WC2; Covent Garden) The cosy Donmar Warehouse is London's

FOOTBALL IN LONDON

As the capital of a football-mad nation, expect half of London to be watching the beautiful game during the cooler months.

Wembley Stadium (☎0800 169 9933; www.wembleystadium.com; tours adult/child £19/11; ⊖Wembley Park) The city's landmark national stadium where England traditionally plays its international matches and where the FA Cup final is contested. Tours visit the England changing rooms, the players' tunnel, the Royal Box and you can get your hands on (a replica of) the FA Cup.

Chelsea (☎0871 984 1955; www.chelseafc.com; Stamford Bridge, Fulham Rd SW6; stadium tours & museum adult/child £20/13; ⏱museum 9am-5pm, 10am-4pm Sun; ⊖Fulham Broadway) Tours of Stamford Bridge, Chelsea FC's football ground and access to the museum.

West Ham United (www.whufc.com; Boleyn Ground, Green St, Upton Park, E13; tours adult/child £19/11; ⊖Upton Park) From the start of the new season in 2016, the Olympics Stadium became West Ham United's new ground. See the website for details of tours.

Tottenham Hotspur (www.tottenhamhotspur.com; White Hart Lane, 748 High Rd, N17; tour adult/child £20/9; 🚆White Hart Lane) The 90-minute to two-hour tour takes Spurs supporters to all key areas of White Hart Lane, including the players' dressing room.

'thinking person's theatre'. Current artistic director Josie Rourke has staged some intriguing and successful productions, including the well-received comedy *My Night with Reg*.

Royal Court Theatre — THEATRE

(Map p98; ☎020-7565 5000; www.royalcourttheatre.com; Sloane Sq, SW1; tickets £12-38; ⊖Sloane Sq) Equally renowned for staging innovative new plays and old classics, the Royal Court is among London's most progressive theatres and has continued to foster major writing talent across the UK. There are two auditoriums: the main Jerwood Theatre Downstairs, and the much smaller studio Jerwood Theatre Upstairs. Tickets for Monday performances are £10.

Old Vic — THEATRE

(Map p92; ☎0844 871 7628; www.oldvictheatre.com; The Cut, SE1; ⊖Waterloo) American actor Kevin Spacey took the theatrical helm of this stalwart of the London theatre scene in 2003, giving it a new lease of life. He was succeeded in April 2015 by Matthew Warchus (who directed *Matilda the Musical* and the film *Pride*). In 2016, Warchus was directing the musical *Groundhog Day*, which was set to start at the Old Vic.

☆ Live Music

It goes without saying that London is a crucible of musical talent, with young bands gigging around venues citywide.

★Jazz Cafe — LIVE MUSIC

(Map p131; ☎020-7485 6834; www.thejazzcafelondon.com; 5 Parkway, NW1; ⊖Camden Town) The name would have you think jazz is the main staple, but it's only a small slice of what's on offer. The intimate club-like space also serves up funk, hip hop, R&B, soul and rare groove, with big-name acts regularly dropping in. Saturday club night is soul night.

★Pizza Express Jazz Club — JAZZ

(Map p78; ☎020-7439 4962; www.pizzaexpresslive.com; 10 Dean St, W1; admission £10-35; ⏱live music 7-10.30pm Mon-Thu, 7-11pm Fri & Sat, midday-3.30pm & 6.30-10pm Sun; ⊖Tottenham Court Rd) Pizza Express has been one of the best jazz venues in London since opening in 1969. It may be a strange arrangement, in a basement beneath the main chain restaurant, but it's highly popular. Lots of big names perform here and promising artists such as Norah Jones, Jamie Cullum and the late Amy Winehouse played here in their early days.

★606 Club — BLUES, JAZZ

(☎020-7352 5953; www.606club.co.uk; 90 Lots Rd, SW10; ⏱7-11.15pm Sun-Thu, 8pm-12.30am Fri & Sat; 🚆Imperial Wharf) Named after its old address on King's Rd, which cast a spell over jazz lovers London-wide back in the '80s, this fantastic, tucked-away basement jazz club and restaurant gives centre stage to contemporary British-based jazz musicians nightly. The club can only serve alcohol to people who are dining and it is highly advisable to book to get a table.

★ Vortex Jazz Club JAZZ

(020-7254 4097; www.vortexjazz.co.uk; 11 Gillet Sq, N16; 8pm-midnight; Dalston Kingsland) With a fantastically varied menu of jazz, the Vortex hosts an outstanding line-up of musicians, singers and songwriters from the UK, US, Europe, Africa and beyond. It's a small venue so make sure you book if there's an act you particularly fancy.

★ O2 Academy Brixton LIVE MUSIC

(www.o2academybrixton.co.uk; 211 Stockwell Rd, SW9; doors open 7pm most nights; Brixton) It's hard to have a bad night at the Brixton Academy, even if you leave with your soles sticky with beer, as this cavernous former-5000-capacity art-deco theatre always thrums with bonhomie. There's a properly raked floor for good views, as well as plenty of bars and an excellent mixed bill of established and emerging talent. Most shows are 14-plus.

★ KOKO LIVE MUSIC

(Map p131; 020-7388 3222; www.koko.uk.com; 1a Camden High St, NW1; 7-11pm Sun-Thu, 6.30pm-4am Fri, from midnight Sat; Mornington Cres) Once the legendary Camden Palace, where Charlie Chaplin, the Goons and the Sex Pistols performed, KOKO is maintaining its reputation as one of London's better gig venues. The theatre has a dance floor and decadent balconies and attracts an indie crowd with Club NME on Friday. There are live bands most nights and it has a great roof terrace.

O2 Arena LIVE MUSIC

(www.theo2.co.uk; Peninsula Sq, SE10; North Greenwich) One of the city's major concert venues, hosting all the biggies – the Rolling Stones, Paul Simon and Sting, One Direction, Ed Sheeran and many others – inside the 20,000-capacity arena. It's also a popular venue for sporting events. The smaller Indigo at the O2 seats 2350.

Ronnie Scott's JAZZ

(Map p78; 020-7439 0747; www.ronniescotts.co.uk; 47 Frith St, W1; 7pm-3am Mon-Sat, to midnight Sun; Leicester Sq or Tottenham Court Rd) Ronnie Scott originally opened his jazz club on Gerrard St in 1959 under a Chinese gambling den. It moved here six years later and became widely known as Britain's best jazz club. Gigs are at 8.15pm (8pm Sunday) with a second sitting at 11.15pm Friday and Saturday (check though), followed by the more informal Late, Late Show until 3am.

100 Club LIVE MUSIC

(Map p78; 020-7636 0933; www.the100club.co.uk; 100 Oxford St, W1; admission £8-20; check website for gig times; Oxford Circus or Tottenham Court Rd) This legendary London venue has always concentrated on jazz, but also features swing and rock. It's showcased Chris Barber, BB King and the Stones, and was at the centre of the punk revolution and the '90s indie scene. It hosts dancing swing gigs and local jazz musicians, the occasional big name, where-are-they-now bands and top-league tributes.

☆ Classical Music

With a raft of world-class symphony orchestras, a batch of opera companies, various smaller ensembles, brilliant venues, reasonable prices and high standards of performance, London is a classical capital. Keep an eye out for the free (or nearly so) lunchtime concerts held in many of the city's churches.

Royal Albert Hall CONCERT VENUE

(Map p98; 0845 401 5034; www.royalalberthall.com; Kensington Gore, SW7; South Kensington) This splendid Victorian concert hall hosts classical-music, rock and other performances, but is famously the venue for the BBC-sponsored Proms. Booking is possible, but from mid-July to mid-September Proms punters queue for £5 standing (or 'promenading') tickets that go on sale one hour before curtain-up. Otherwise, the box office and prepaid-ticket collection counter are through door 12 (south side of the hall).

Royal Festival Hall CONCERT VENUE

(Map p92; 0844 875 0073; www.southbankcentre.co.uk; Southbank Centre, Belvedere Rd, SE1; admission £6-60; ; Waterloo) The hall's amphitheatre seats 3000 and is one of the best places for catching world- and classical-music artists. The sound is fantastic, the programming impeccable and there are frequent free gigs in the wonderfully expansive foyer.

Barbican PERFORMING ARTS

(Map p84; box office 020-7638 8891; www.barbican.org.uk; Silk St, EC2; box office 10am-8pm Mon-Sat, from 11am Sun; Barbican) Home to the wonderful London Symphony

Orchestra and its associate orchestra, the lesser-known BBC Symphony Orchestra, the arts centre also hosts scores of other leading musicians, focusing in particular on jazz, folk, world and soul artists. Dance is another strong point here, while film covers recent releases as well as film festivals and seasons.

☆ Opera & Dance

Royal Opera House OPERA
(Map p78; ☎020-7304 4000; www.roh.org.uk; Bow St, WC2; tickets £7-250; ⊖Covent Garden) The £210-million redevelopment for the millennium gave classic opera a fantastic setting in London, and coming here for a night is a sumptuous – if pricey – affair. Although the program has been fluffed up by modern influences, the main attractions are still the opera and classical ballet – all are wonderful productions and feature world-class performers.

Midweek matinees are usually cheaper than evening performances and restricted-view seats cost as little as £7. There are same-day tickets (one per customer available to the first 67 people in the queue) from 10am for £8 to £44 and student standby tickets for £10. Half-price standby tickets four hours before the performance are only occasionally available. Free lunchtime recitals are held on Mondays, when possible, in the Crush Room or Paul Hamlyn Hall, depending on the program.

Sadler's Wells DANCE
(Map p106; ☎020-7863 8000, 0844 412 4319; www.sadlerswells.com; Rosebery Ave, EC1R; ⊖Angel) A glittering modern venue that was, in fact, first established in 1683, Sadler's Wells is the most eclectic modern-dance and ballet venue in town, with experimental dance shows of all genres and from all corners of the globe. The Lilian Baylis Studio stages smaller productions.

London Coliseum OPERA
(Map p78; ☎020-7845 9300; www.eno.org; St Martin's Lane, WC2; ⊖Leicester Sq) The London Coliseum is home to the English National Opera (ENO), celebrated for making opera modern and more relevant, as all productions are sung in English. The building, built in 1904 and lovingly restored 100 years later, is very impressive. The English National Ballet also does regular performances at the Coliseum. Tickets range from £12 to £99.

☆ Comedy

Comedy Store COMEDY
(Map p78; ☎0844 871 7699; www.thecomedystore.co.uk; 1a Oxendon St, SW1; admission £8-23.50; ⊖Piccadilly Circus) One of the first (and still one of the best) comedy clubs in London. Wednesday and Sunday night's Comedy Store Players is the most famous improvisation outfit in town, with the wonderful Josie Lawrence; on Thursdays, Fridays and Saturdays' Best in Stand Up features the best on London's comedy circuit.

Comedy Cafe Theatre COMEDY
(Map p132; ☎020-7739 5706; www.comedycafetheatre.co.uk; 68 Rivington St, EC2A; admission free-£12; ⊖Shoreditch High St) This purpose-built comedy venue offers comedy and dinner, with two-hour shows starting at 8pm most Friday and Saturday nights. The free New Act Night on Wednesdays is a good option for some wincing entertainment. The attached **Bedroom Bar** (www.bedroom-bar.co.uk) has live music most nights.

Soho Theatre COMEDY
(Map p78; ☎020-7478 0100; www.sohotheatre.com; 21 Dean St, W1; admission £10-25; ⊖Tottenham Court Rd) The Soho Theatre has developed a superb reputation for showcasing new comedy-writing talent and comedians. It's also hosted some top-notch stand-up or sketch-based comedians including Alexei Sayle and Doctor Brown, plus cabaret.

☆ Cinemas

Glitzy premieres usually take place in one of the mega multiplexes in Leicester Sq.

Electric Cinema CINEMA
(Map p122; ☎020-7908 9696; www.electriccinema.co.uk; 191 Portobello Rd, W11; tickets £8-22.50; ⊖Ladbroke Grove) Having notched up its first centenary a few years back, the Electric is one of the UK's oldest cinemas, updated. Avail yourself of the luxurious leather armchairs, sofas, footstools and tables for food and drink in the auditorium, or select one of the six front-row double beds! Tickets are cheapest on Mondays.

Prince Charles CINEMA
(Map p78; www.princecharlescinema.com; 7 Leicester Pl, WC2; tickets £8-16; ⊖Leicester Sq) Leicester Sq cinema-ticket prices are brutal, so wait until the first-runs have moved to the Prince Charles, central London's cheapest

WORTH A TRIP

HARRY POTTER SHOP

With Pottermania refusing to die down and Diagon Alley impossible to find, if your junior witches and wizards are seeking a wand of their own, take the family directly to King's Cross Station to **Harry Potter Shop at Platform 9¾** (Map p106; www.harrypotterplatform934.com; King's Cross Station, N1; ⌚8am-10pm Mon-Sat, 9am-9pm Sun; ⊖King's Cross St Pancras). This little wood-panelled store also stocks jumpers sporting the colours of Hogwarts' four houses (Gryffindor having pride of place) and assorted merchandise, including, of course, the books.

cinema, where nonmembers pay only £8 to £10 for new releases. Also on the cards are minifestivals, Q&As with film directors, classics, sleepover movie marathons and exuberant sing-along screenings of *Frozen, The Sound of Music* and *Rocky Horror Picture Show.*

BFI Southbank CINEMA
(Map p92; ☎020-7928 3232; www.bfi.org.uk; Belvedere Rd, SE1; tickets £8-12; ⌚11am-11pm; ⊖Waterloo) Tucked almost out of sight under the arches of Waterloo Bridge is the British Film Institute, containing four cinemas that screen thousands of films each year (mostly art house), a gallery devoted to the moving image and the mediatheque, where you watch film and TV highlights from the BFI National Archive.

☆ Rugby

World Rugby Museum MUSEUM
(☎020-8892 8877; www.rfu.com; adult/child £8/6, with tour £20/12; ⌚10am-5pm Tue-Sat, 11am-5pm Sun) In the east stand of Twickenham Stadium, this museum exhibits the world's largest and most comprehensive collection of rugby memorabilia. Tours are an extra feature.

☆ Cricket & Tennis

Wimbledon Championships SPECTATOR SPORT
(☎020-8944 1066; www.wimbledon.com/championships/tickets) For a few weeks each June and July, the sporting world's attention is fixed on the quiet southern suburb of Wimbledon, as it has been since 1877. Most show-court tickets for the Wimbledon Championships are allocated through public ballot, applications for which usually begin in early August of the preceding year and close at the end of December.

Entry into the ballot does not mean entrants will get a ticket. A quantity of show-court, outer-court, ground tickets and late-entry tickets are also available if you queue on the day of play, but if you want a show-court ticket it is recommended you camp the night before in the queue. See www.wimbledon.com for details.

Lord's STADIUM
(☎tour info 020-7616 8595; www.lords.org; St John's Wood Rd, NW8; tours adult/child £20/12; ⌚tours hourly 10am-3pm; ⊖St John's Wood) The 'home of cricket' is a must for any devotee of this particularly English game. Book early for the Test matches here, but cricket buffs should also take the absorbing and anecdote-filled 100-minute tour of the ground and facilities. Tours take in the famous Long Room, where members watch the games surrounded by portraits of cricket's great and good, and a museum featuring evocative memorabilia that will appeal to fans old and new.

Oval SPECTATOR SPORT
(☎0844 375 1845; www.kiaoval.com; Kennington, SE11; international match £20-350, county £20-35; ⊖Oval) Home to the Surrey County Cricket Club, the Oval is London's second cricketing venue after Lord's. As well as Surrey matches, it also regularly hosts international test matches. Getting tickets for county games is relatively straightforward, but it's much harder for international fixtures. The season runs from April to September.

Shopping

From charity-shop finds to designer bags, there are thousands of ways to spend your hard-earned cash in London. Many of the big-name shopping attractions, such as Harrods, Hamleys, Camden Market and Old Spitalfields Market, have become must-sees in their own right. Chances are that with so many temptations, you'll give your wallet a full workout.

West End

Oxford St is the place for high-street fashion, while Regent St cranks it up a notch. Bond St has designers galore, Savile Row is all about bespoke tailoring and Jermyn St is the place for smart clobber (particularly shirts).

★ Fortnum & Mason DEPARTMENT STORE

(Map p78; www.fortnumandmason.com; 181 Piccadilly, W1; 10am-9pm Mon-Sat, 11.30am-6pm Sun; Piccadilly Circus) With its classic *eau de nil* colour scheme, London's oldest grocery store (established 1707), refuses to yield to modern times. Its staff still clad in old-fashioned tailcoats, its glamorous food hall supplied with hampers, cut marmalade, speciality teas and so forth, Fortnum and Mason is *the* quintessential London shopping experience.

Hatchards BOOKS

(Map p78; www.hatchards.co.uk; 187 Piccadilly, W1; 9.30am-8pm Mon-Sat, noon-6.30pm Sun; Green Park or Piccadilly Circus) London's oldest bookshop dates to 1797. Holding three royal warrants (hence the portrait of the Queen), it's a stupendous independent bookstore, with a solid supply of signed editions and bursting at its smart seams with very browsable stock. There's a strong selection of first editions on the ground floor as well as regular literary events.

Selfridges DEPARTMENT STORE

(Map p101; www.selfridges.com; 400 Oxford St, W1; 9.30am-10pm Mon-Sat, 11.30am-6pm Sun; Bond St) Selfridges loves innovation – it's famed for its inventive window displays by international artists, gala shows and, above all, its amazing range of products. It's the trendiest of London's one-stop shops, with labels such as Boudicca, Luella Bartley, Emma Cook, Chloé and Missoni; an unparalleled food hall; and Europe's largest cosmetics department.

Liberty DEPARTMENT STORE

(Map p78; www.liberty.co.uk; Great Marlborough St, W1; 10am-8pm Mon-Sat, noon-6pm Sun; Oxford Circus) An irresistible blend of contemporary styles in an old-fashioned mock-Tudor atmosphere, Liberty has a huge cosmetics department and an accessories floor, along with a breathtaking lingerie section, all at very inflated prices. A classic London souvenir is a Liberty fabric print, especially in the form of a scarf.

Stanford's BOOKS, MAPS

(Map p78; www.stanfords.co.uk; 12-14 Long Acre, WC2; 9am-8pm Mon-Sat, 11.30am-6pm Sun; Leicester Sq or Covent Garden) Trading from this address for more than 100 years, this granddaddy of travel bookshops and seasoned seller of maps, guides and literature is a destination in its own right. Ernest Shackleton and David Livingstone and, more recently, Michael Palin and Brad Pitt have all popped in here.

Hamleys TOYS

(Map p78; www.hamleys.com; 188-196 Regent St, W1; 10am-9pm Mon-Fri, 9.30am-9pm Sat, noon-6pm Sun; Oxford Circus) Claiming to be the world's oldest (and some say, the largest) toy store, Hamleys moved to its address on Regent St in 1881. From the ground floor – where staff glide UFOs and foam boomerangs through the air with practised nonchalance – to Lego World and a cafe on the 5th floor, it's a layer cake of playthings.

Foyles BOOKS

(Map p78; www.foyles.co.uk; 107 Charing Cross Rd, WC2; 9.30am-9pm Mon-Sat, 11.30am-6pm Sun; Tottenham Court Rd) With four miles of shelving, you can bet on finding even the most obscure of titles in London's most legendary bookshop. Once synonymous with chaos, Foyles long ago got its act together and in 2014 moved just down the road into the spacious former home of Central St Martins. Thoroughly redesigned, its stunning new home is a joy to explore.

Cadenhead's Whisky & Tasting Shop DRINK

(Map p101; www.whiskytastingroom.com; 26 Chiltern St, W1; Baker St) Scotland's oldest independent bottler of pure, nonblended whisky from local distilleries, this excellent shop is a joy for anyone with a passion for *uisge* (the gaelic word for 'water'). All bottled whiskies derive from individually selected casks, without any filtrations, additions or colouring, guaranteeing purity. Regular whisky tastings are held downstairs (maximum 12 people).

Monmouth Coffee Company FOOD & DRINKS

(Map p78; www.monmouthcoffee.co.uk; 27 Monmouth St, WC2; pastry & cakes from £2.50; 8am-6.30pm Mon-Sat; Tottenham Court Rd or Leicester Sq) Essentially a shop selling beans from just about every coffee-growing country, Monmouth, here since 1978, has a few wooden alcoves at the back where you can squeeze in and savour blends from around the world as well as cakes from local patisseries.

Knightsbridge, Kensington & Chelsea

Knightsbridge draws the hordes with quintessentially English department stores.

LOCAL KNOWLEDGE

LONDON'S MARKETS

Perhaps the biggest draw for visitors are the capital's famed markets. A treasure trove of small designers, unique jewellery pieces, original framed photographs and posters, colourful vintage pieces and bric-a-brac, they are the antidote to impersonal, carbon-copy shopping centres.

The most popular markets are Camden, Old Spitalfields and Portobello Road, which operate most days, but there are dozens of others, such as Brick Lane's excellent Sunday Upmarket, which only pop up on the weekend. Camden and Old Spitalfields are both mainly covered, but even the outdoor markets are busy, rain or shine.

Portobello Road Market (Map p122; www.portobellomarket.org; Portobello Rd, W10; ⌚8am-6.30pm Mon-Wed, Fri & Sat, to 1pm Thu; ⊖Notting Hill Gate or Ladbroke Grove) Lovely on a warm summer's day, Portobello Road Market is an iconic London attraction with an eclectic mix of street food, fruit and veg, antiques, curios, collectables, vibrant fashion and trinkets. Although the shops along Portobello Rd open daily and the fruit and veg stalls (from Elgin Cres to Talbot Rd) only close on Sunday, the busiest day by far is Saturday, when antique dealers set up shop (from Chepstow Villas to Elgin Cres).

Sunday UpMarket (Map p132; www.sundayupmarket.co.uk; Old Truman Brewery, 91 Brick Lane, E1; ⌚10am-5pm Sun; ⊖Shoreditch High St) The best of all the Sunday markets, this workaday covered car park fills up with young designers selling their wares, quirky crafts and a drool-inducing array of food stalls.

Stables Market (Map p131; Chalk Farm Rd, NW1; ⌚10am-6pm; ⊖Chalk Farm) Connected to the Lock Market, the Stables is the best part of the Camden Market complex, with antiques, Asian artefacts, rugs, retro furniture and clothing.

Camden Passage Market (www.camdenpassageislington.co.uk; Camden Passage, N1; ⌚8am-6pm Wed & Sat, 11am-6pm Sun-Tue, Thu & Fri; ⊖Angel) Not to be confused with Camden Market, Camden Passage is a pretty cobbled lane in Islington lined with antique stores, vintage-clothing boutiques and cafes. Scattered along the lane are four separate market areas devoted to antique curios and whatnots. The main market days are Wednesday and Sunday. Stallholders know their stuff, so bargains are rare.

Old Spitalfields Market (Map p132; www.oldspitalfieldsmarket.com; Commercial St, E1; ⌚10am-5pm Mon-Fri, 11am-5pm Sat, 10am-5pm Sun; ⊖Shoreditch High St) Traders have been hawking their wares here since 1638 and it's still one of London's best markets. Today's covered market was built in the late 19th century, with the more modern development added in 2006. Sundays are the biggest and best days, but Thursdays are good for antiques and Fridays for independent fashion. There are plenty of food stalls, too.

Broadway Market (www.broadwaymarket.co.uk; Broadway Market, E8; ⌚9am-5pm Sat; 🚌394) There's been a market down this pretty street since the late 19th century. The focus these days is artisan food, arty knick-knacks, books, records and vintage clothing. Stock up on edible treats then head to London Fields (Richmond Rd, E8; ⊖Hackney Central) for a picnic.

Leadenhall Market (Map p84; www.cityoflondon.gov.uk/things-to-do/leadenhall-market; Whittington Ave, EC3; ⌚10am-6pm Mon-Fri; ⊖Bank or Monument) A visit to this covered mall off Gracechurch St is a step back in time. There's been a market on this site since the Roman era, but the architecture that survives is all cobblestones and late-19th-century Victorian ironwork. Leadenhall Market appears as Diagon Alley in *Harry Potter and the Philosopher's Stone* and an optician's shop was used for the entrance to the Leaky Cauldron wizarding pub in *Harry Potter and the Goblet of Fire*.

Greenwich Market (www.greenwichmarketlondon.com; College Approach, SE10; ⌚10am-5.30pm; 🚇DLR Cutty Sark) One of the smallest of London's ubiquitous markets, but Greenwich Market holds its own in quality. On Tuesdays, Wednesdays, Fridays and weekends, stallholders tend to be small, independent artists, offering original prints, wholesome beauty products, funky jewellery and accessories, cool fashion pieces and so on. On Tuesdays, Thursdays and Fridays, you'll find vintage, antiques and collectables. Loads of street food too.

★ John Sandoe Books BOOKS

(Map p98; www.johnsandoe.com; 10 Blacklands Tce, SW3; ⌚9.30am-6.30pm Mon-Sat, 11am-5pm Sun; ⊖Sloane Sq) The perfect antidote to impersonal book superstores, this atmospheric three-storey bookshop in 18th-century premises is a treasure trove of literary gems and hidden surprises. It's been in business for almost 60 years and loyal customers swear by it, while knowledgeable booksellers spill forth with well-read pointers and helpful advice.

Harrods DEPARTMENT STORE

(Map p98; www.harrods.com; 87-135 Brompton Rd, SW1; ⌚10am-9pm Mon-Sat, 11.30am-6pm Sun; ⊖Knightsbridge) Garish and stylish in equal measures, perennially crowded Harrods is an obligatory stop for visitors, from the cash-strapped to the big spenders. The stock is astonishing, as are many of the price tags. High on kitsch, the 'Egyptian Elevator' resembles something out of an Indiana Jones epic, while the memorial fountain to Dodi and Di (lower ground floor) merely adds surrealism.

Harvey Nichols DEPARTMENT STORE

(Map p98; www.harveynichols.com; 109-125 Knightsbridge, SW1; ⌚10am-8pm Mon-Sat, 11.30am-6pm Sun; ⊖Knightsbridge) At London's temple of high fashion, you'll find Chloé and Balenciaga bags, the city's best denim range, a massive make-up hall with exclusive lines and great jewellery. The food hall and in-house restaurant, **Fifth Floor**, are, you guessed it, on the 5th floor. From 11.30am to midday, it's browsing time only.

Notting Hill, Bayswater & Paddington

Ceramica Blue HOMEWARES

(Map p122; www.ceramicablue.co.uk; 10 Blenheim Cres, W11; ⌚10am-6.30pm Mon-Sat, noon-5pm Sun; ⊖Ladbroke Grove) A lovely spot for colourful, eclectic and handsome crockery, imported from more than a dozen countries. There are Japanese eggshell-glaze teacups, serving plates with tribal South African designs, candelabra from Italy, gorgeous table cloths from Provence, Turkish hand-decorated glass and much more.

Marylebone

Daunt Books BOOKS

(Map p101; www.dauntbooks.co.uk; 83 Marylebone High St, W1; ⌚9am-7.30pm Mon-Sat, 11am-6pm Sun; ⊖Baker St) An original Edwardian bookshop, with oak panels and gorgeous skylights, Daunt is one of London's loveliest travel bookshops. It has two floors and stocks general fiction and nonfiction titles as well.

Hoxton, Shoreditch & Spitalfields

★ Rough Trade East MUSIC

(Map p102; www.roughtrade.com; Old Truman Brewery, 91 Brick Lane, E1; ⌚9am-9pm Mon-Thu, 9am-8pm Fri, 10am-8pm Sat, 11am-7pm Sun; ⊖Shoreditch High St) No longer directly associated with the legendary record label (home to The Smiths, The Libertines and The Strokes, among many others), but this huge record store is still the best place to come for music of an indie, soul, electronica and alternative bent. Apart from the impressive selection of CDs and vinyl, it also dispenses coffee and stages promotional gigs.

The East End & Docklands

Westfield Stratford City MALL

(http://uk.westfield.com; Westfield Ave, E20; ⌚10am-9pm Mon-Fri, 9am-9pm Sat, noon-6pm Sun; ⊖Stratford) Right by Queen Elizabeth Olympic Park (p108), this is Britain's third-largest mall – a behemoth containing more than 250 shops, 70 places to eat and drink, a 17-screen Vue cinema, a bowling alley, a 24-hour casino and a Premier Inn hotel. In its first week of trading in 2011, it raked in £20 million from shoppers.

ℹ Information

DANGERS & ANNOYANCES

London is a fairly safe city for its size, so exercising common sense should keep you secure.

If you're getting a cab after a night's clubbing, make sure you go for a black taxi or a licensed minicab firm. Many of the touts operating outside clubs and bars are unlicensed and can therefore be unsafe.

Pickpocketing does happen in London, so keep an eye on your handbag and wallet, especially in bars and nightclubs, and in crowded areas such as the Underground.

EMERGENCY

Police/Fire/Ambulance (☎999)

Rape & Sexual Abuse Support Centre (☎0808 802 9999; www.rasasc.org.uk; ⌚noon-2.30pm & 7-9.30pm)

Samaritans (☎ toll-free 116 123; www.samaritans.org) For anyone in emotional distress.

INTERNET ACCESS

Virtually every hotel in London now provides wi-fi free of charge (only a couple of budget places have it as an add-on).

A huge number of cafes, and an increasing number of restaurants, offer free wi-fi to customers, including chains such as Starbucks, Costa and Pret a Manger.

MEDICAL SERVICES

St Thomas' Hospital (☎ 020-7188 7188; www.guysandstthomas.nhs.uk; Westminster Bridge Rd, SE1; ⊖ Waterloo or Westminster) Large hospital across the Thames from Westminster.

University College London Hospital (☎ 0845 155 5000, 020-3456 7890; www.uclh.nhs.uk; 235 Euston Rd, NW1; ⊖ Warren St or Euston) One of central London's busiest hospitals.

TOURIST INFORMATION

Visit London (www.visitlondon.com) can fill you in on everything from attractions and events to tours and accommodation.

City of London Information Centre (Map p84; www.visitthecity.co.uk; St Paul's Churchyard, EC4; 9.30am-5.30pm Mon-Sat, 10am-4pm Sun; wi-fi; ⊖ St Paul's) Multilingual tourist information, fast-track tickets to City attractions and guided walks (adult/child £7/6).

Greenwich Tourist Office (☎ 0870 608 2000; www.visitgreenwich.org.uk; Pepys House, 2 Cutty Sark Gardens, SE10; 10am-5pm; DLR Cutty Sark) Has a wealth of information about Greenwich and the surrounding areas. Free daily guided walks leave at 12.15pm and 2.15pm.

PLAN YOUR TRIP

Three months before Book weekend performances of top shows; make dinner reservations for renowned restaurants with celebrity chefs; snap up tickets for must-see temporary exhibitions; book accommodation at boutique properties.

One month before Check listings on entertainment sites such as **Time Out** (www.timeout.com/london) for fringe theatre, live music and festivals, and book tickets.

A few days before Check the weather with the **Met Office** (www.metoffice.gov.uk) .

Getting There & Away

AIR

There are a number of London Airports. For more information, see p684.

BUS

Victoria Coach Station (Map p98; 164 Buckingham Palace Rd, SW1; ⊖ Victoria) Long-distance and international buses arrive and depart fromVictoria coach station, close to the Victoria tube and rail stations.

TRAIN

Main national rail routes are served by a variety of private train-operating companies. Tickets are not cheap, but trains between cities are usually quite punctual. Check **National Rail** (www.nationalrail.co.uk) for timetables and fares.

Eurostar (www.eurostar.com) is the high-speed passenger rail service that links St Pancras International Station with Gare du Nord in Paris (or Bruxelles Midi in Brussels), with between 14 and 16 daily departures. Fares vary enormously, from £69 for the cheapest return to upwards of £300 for a fully flexible return at busy periods.

Getting Around

TO/FROM THE AIRPORTS

Gatwick

Gatwick Express (www.gatwickexpress.com; one-way/return adult £19.90/34.90, one-way/return child £9.95/17.45) This dedicated train service links the station near the South Terminal with Victoria station in central London every 15 minutes. From the airport, there are services between 4.35am and 12.50am. From Victoria, they leave between 3.30am and at 12.32am. The journey takes 30 minutes.

National Rail (www.nationalrail.co.uk) Regular train services to/from London Bridge (30 minutes, every 15 to 30 minutes), London King's Cross (55 minutes, every 15 to 30 minutes) and London Victoria (30 minutes, every 10 to 15 minutes). Fares vary depending on the time of travel and the train company, but allow £10 to £20 for a single.

National Express (www.nationalexpress.com) Coaches (one-way from £6, 80 minutes to two hours) run throughout the day from Gatwick to Victoria Coach station. Services leave hourly around the clock.

EasyBus (www.easybus.co.uk) Runs 19-seater minibuses to Gatwick every 15 to 20 minutes on two routes: one from Earl's Court/West Brompton and from Waterloo (one-way from £5.95). The service runs round the clock. Journey time averages 75 minutes.

Heathrow

Heathrow Express (www.heathrowexpress.com; one-way/return £22/36) This high-speed train whisks passengers from Heathrow Central station (serving Terminals 2 and 3) and Terminal 5 to Paddington in 15 minutes. Terminal 4 passengers should take the free interterminal shuttle train to Heathrow Central and board there. Trains run every 15 minutes from just after 5am in both directions to between 11.25pm (from Paddington) and 11.40pm (from the airport). Three Underground stations on the Piccadilly line serve Heathrow: one for Terminals 2 and 3, another for Terminal 4, and the terminus for Terminal 5. The Underground, commonly referred to as 'the tube' (one-way £5.10, from central London one hour, every three to nine minutes) is the cheapest way of getting to Heathrow. Leaving from the airport, it runs from just after 5am to 11.45pm, and heading to the airport it runs from 5.45am to 12.30am (and all night Friday and Saturday, with reduced frequency). Buy tickets at the station.

National Express (www.nationalexpress.com) Coaches (one-way from £6, 35 to 90 minutes, every 30 minutes to one hour) link the Heathrow Central bus station with Victoria coach station. The first bus leaves the Heathrow Central bus station (at Terminals 2 and 3) at 4.40am, with the last departure just before 11pm. The first bus leaves Victoria at 3am, the last just before midnight.

At night, the **N9 bus** (£1.50, 1¼ hours, every 20 minutes) connects Heathrow with central London, terminating at Aldwych.

London City

Docklands Light Railway (DLR; www.tfl.gov.uk/dlr) Stops at London City Airport station (one-way £2.80 to £3.30). The journey to Bank takes just over 20 minutes, and trains go every eight to 10 minutes from just after 5.30am to 12.15am Monday to Saturday, and 7am to 11.15pm Sunday.

Luton

National Rail (www.nationalrail.co.uk) Services (one-way from £10, 35 to 50 minutes, every six to 30 minutes, from 7am to 10pm) run from London Bridge and London King's Cross stations to Luton Airport Parkway station, from where an airport shuttle bus (one-way £1.60) will take you to the airport in 10 minutes.

Stansted

Stansted Express (☎ 0845 8500150; www.stanstedexpress.com; one-way/return £19/32) This rail service (45 minutes, every 15 to 30 minutes) links the airport and Liverpool St station. From the airport the first train leaves at 5.30am, the last about 12.30pm. Trains depart Liverpool St station from 3.40am to 11.25pm.

> **INTERNET RESOURCES**
>
> **Lonely Planet** (www.lonelyplanet.com/london) Bookings, traveller forum and more.
>
> **Londonist** (www.londonist.com) A website about London and everything that happens in it.
>
> **Transport for London** (www.tfl.gov.uk) Essential tool for staying mobile in the capital.
>
> **BBC London** (www.bbc.co.uk/news/england/london) The latest news about London.

National Express (www.nationalexpress.com) Coaches run around the clock, offering well over 100 services per day. The A6 runs to Victoria coach station (one-way from £12, 85 minutes to more than two hours, every 20 minutes) via North London. The A9 runs to Liverpool St station (one-way from £10, 60 to 80 minutes, every 30 minutes).

EasyBus (www.easybus.co.uk) Services to Baker St and Old St tube stations every 15 minutes. The journey (one-way from £4.95) takes one hour from Old St, 1¼ hour from Baker St.

Terravision (www.terravision.eu) Coaches link Stansted to both Liverpool St train station (bus A51, one-way/return from £8/14, 55 minutes) and Victoria coach station (bus A50, one-way/return from £9/15, 75 minutes) every 20 to 40 minutes between 6am and 1am.

BICYCLE

Like Paris and other European cities, London has its own cycle-hire scheme called **Santander Cycles** (☎ 0343 222 6666; www.tfl.gov.uk/modes/cycling/santander-cycles), also variously referred to as 'Barclays Bikes' after their former sponsor, or 'Boris bikes' after the city's mayor, Boris Johnson (2008–16), who launched the initiative. The bikes have proved as popular with visitors as with Londoners.

The idea is simple: pick up a bike from one of the 700 docking stations dotted around the capital. Cycle. Drop it off at another docking station.

The access fee is £2 for 24 hours. All you need is a credit or debit card. The first 30 minutes are free. It's then £2 for any additional period of 30 minutes.

You can take as many bikes as you like during your access period (24 hours), leaving five minutes between each trip.

The pricing structure is designed to encourage short journeys rather than longer rentals; for those, go to a hire company. You'll also find that although easy to ride, the bikes only have three

OYSTER CARD

The Oyster Card is a smart card on which you can store credit towards 'prepay' fares, as well as Travelcards valid for periods from a day to a year. Oyster Cards are valid across the entire public transport network in London. All you need to do when entering a station is touch your card on a reader (which has a yellow circle with the image of an Oyster Card on it) and then touch again on your way out. The system will then deduct the appropriate amount of credit from your card, as necessary. For bus journeys, you only need to touch once upon boarding.

The benefit lies in the fact that fares for Oyster Card users are lower than standard ones. If you are making many journeys during the day, you will never pay more than the appropriate Travelcard (peak or off-peak) once the daily 'price cap' has been reached.

Oyster Cards can be bought (£5 refundable deposit required) and topped up at any Underground station, travel information centre or shop displaying the Oyster logo.

To get your deposit back along with any remaining credit, simply return your Oyster Card at a ticket booth.

Contactless cards (which do not require chip and pin or a signature) can now be used directly on Oyster Card readers and are subject to the same Oyster fares. The advantage is that you don't have to bother with buying, topping up and then returning an Oyster Card, but foreign visitors should bear in mind the cost of card transactions.

gears and are quite heavy. You must be 18 to buy access and at least 14 to ride a bike.

CAR

London has a congestion charge in place to reduce the flow of traffic into its centre. For full details, log on to www.tfl.gov.uk/roadusers/congestioncharging.

The congestion-charge zone encompasses Euston Rd and Pentonville Rd to the north, Park Lane to the west, Tower Bridge to the east and Elephant and Castle and Vauxhall Bridge Rd to the south. As you enter the zone, you will see a large white 'C' in a red circle.

If you enter the zone between 7am and 6pm Monday to Friday (excluding public holidays), you must pay the £11.50 charge (payable in advance or on the day) or £14 on the first charging day after travel to avoid receiving a fine (£130, or £65 if paid within 14 days).

You can pay online, at newsagents, petrol stations or any shop displaying the 'C' sign.

PUBLIC TRANSPORT

Boat

There are a number of companies operating along the River Thames. Only **Thames Clippers** (www.thamesclippers.com) really offers commuter services, however. It's fast, pleasant and you're almost always guaranteed a seat and a view.

Thames Clipper boats run regular services between Embankment, Waterloo (London Eye), Blackfriars, Bankside (Shakespeare's Globe), London Bridge, Tower Bridge, Canary Wharf, Greenwich, North Greenwich and Woolwich piers (adult/child £7.50/3.75), from 6.55am to around midnight (from 9.29am weekends).

Thames Clipper River Roamer tickets (adult/child £17.35/8.65) give freedom to hop on and hop off boats on most routes all day.

You can get a discount of one-third off the standard fare and off the price of River Roamer tickets if you're a pay-as-you-go Oyster Card holder or Travelcard holder (paper ticket or on Oyster Card). Children under five go free on most boats.

Bus

London's ubiquitous red double-decker buses afford great views of the city, but be aware that the going can be slow, thanks to traffic jams and dozens of commuters getting on and off at every stop.

There are excellent bus maps at every stop detailing all routes and destinations served from that particular area (generally a few bus stops within a two- to three-minute walk, shown on a local map).

Bus services normally operate from 5am to 11.30pm.

- More than 50 night-bus routes (prefixed with the letter 'N') run from around 11.30pm to 5am.
- There are also another 60 bus routes operating 24 hours; the frequency decreases between 11pm and 5am.
- Oxford Circus, Tottenham Court Rd and Trafalgar Sq are the main hubs for night routes.
- Night buses can be infrequent and stop only on request, so remember to ring for your stop.
- Don't forget the Night Tube which runs along five lines for 24 hours on Fridays and Saturdays, and can either be used as an alternative or in concert with night buses.

Underground, DLR & Overground

The London Underground ('the tube'; 11 colour-coded lines) is part of an integrated-transport system that also includes the **Docklands Light Railway** (DLR; www.tfl.gov.uk/dlr; a driverless overhead train operating in the eastern part of the city) and Overground network (mostly outside of Zone 1 and sometimes underground). Despite the never-ending upgrades and 'engineering works' requiring weekend closures, it is overall the quickest and easiest way of getting around the city, if not the cheapest.

The first trains operate from around 5.30am Monday to Saturday and 6.45am Sunday. The last trains leave around 12.30am Monday to Saturday and 11.30pm Sunday.

Additionally, selected lines (the Victoria and Jubilee lines, plus most of the Piccadilly, Central and Northern lines) run all night on Fridays and Saturdays to get revellers home, with trains every 10 minutes or so.

During weekend closures, schedules, maps and alternative route suggestions are posted in every station, and staff are at hand to help redirect you.

Some stations, most famously Leicester Sq and Covent Garden, are much closer in reality than they appear on the map.

MINICABS

- Minicabs, which are licensed, are cheaper (usually) competitors of black cabs.
- Unlike black cabs, minicabs cannot legally be hailed on the street; they must be hired by phone or directly from one of the minicab offices (every high street has at least one and most clubs work with a minicab firm to send revellers home safely).
- Don't accept unsolicited offers from individuals claiming to be minicab drivers – they are just guys with cars.
- Minicabs don't have meters; there's usually a fare set by the dispatcher. Make sure you ask before setting off.
- Your hotel or host will be able to recommend a reputable minicab company in the neighbourhood; every Londoner has the number of at least one company. Or phone a large 24-hour operator such as **Addison Lee** (☎020-7387 8888; www.addisonlee.com).
- Apps such as **Uber** (www.uber.com) or **Kabbee** (www.kabbee.com) allow you to book a minicab in double-quick time.

TAXI

The black cab is as much a feature of the London cityscape as the red double-decker bus. Licensed black-cab drivers have the 'Knowledge', acquired after rigorous training and a series of exams. They are supposed to know 25,000 streets within a six-mile radius of Charing Cross/Trafalgar Sq and the 100 most-visited spots of the moment, including clubs and restaurants.

- Cabs are available for hire when the yellow sign above the windscreen is lit; just stick your arm out to signal one.
- Fares are metered, with the flagfall charge of £2.60 (covering the first 248m during a weekday), rising by increments of 20p for each subsequent 124m.
- Fares are more expensive in the evenings and overnight.
- You can tip taxi drivers up to 10%, but most Londoners simply round up to the nearest pound.
- Apps such as **Hailo** (www.hailocab.com) use your smartphone's GPS to locate the nearest black cab. You only pay the metered fare.

Canterbury & Southeast England

Includes ➡

Best Places to Eat

- ➡ Deeson's (p159)
- ➡ Allotment (p169)
- ➡ Iydea (p180)
- ➡ Terre à Terre (p181)
- ➡ Town House (p184)

Best Places to Sleep

- ➡ Bleak House (p164)
- ➡ Jeake's House (p172)
- ➡ Wallett's Court (p168)
- ➡ Reading Rooms (p163)
- ➡ Hotel Una (p180)

Why Go?

Rolling chalk hills, venerable Victorian resorts, fields of hops and grapes sweetening in the sun: welcome to England's southeast, four soothing counties' worth of country houses, fairy-tale castles and the country's finest food and drink. That fruit-ripening sun shines brightest and longest on the coast, warming a string of seaside towns wedged between formidable chalk cliffs. There's something for everyone here, from the medieval quaintness of Sandwich to the bohemian spirit of hedonistic Brighton and the more genteel grandeur of Eastbourne.

The southeast is also pock-marked with reminders of darker days. The region's position as the front line against Continental invaders has left a wealth of turbulent history, including the 1066 battlefield, Dover Castle's secret war tunnels and scattered Roman ruins.

England's spiritual heart is Canterbury; its cathedral and ancient Unesco-listed attractions are essential viewing for any 21st-century pilgrim.

When to Go

➡ May is a good time to get creative in Brighton at Great Britain's second-largest arts festival.

➡ During June, don your top hat and breeches to revel in frilly Victoriana at the Dickens festival in Broadstairs.

➡ Any time between May and October is ideal for a hike along the South Downs Way, which runs the length of England's newest national park.

➡ In summer, head to Thanet's glorious beaches for some proper seaside fun.

Activities

The southeast of England may be Britain's most densely populated corner, but there are still plenty of off-the-beaten-track walking and cycling routes to enjoy.

Cycling

Finding quiet roads for cycle touring takes a little extra perseverance in the southeast of England, but the effort is richly rewarded. Long-distance routes that form part of the **National Cycle Network** (NCN; www.sustrans.org.uk) include the **Downs & Weald Cycle Route** (110 miles; NCN Routes 2, 20 and 21) from London to Brighton and on to Hastings, and the **Garden of England Cycle Route** (165 miles; NCN Routes 1 & 2) from London to Dover and then Hastings.

You'll also find less demanding routes on the NCN website. Meanwhile, there are plenty of uppers and downers to challenge mountain bikers on walking trails, such as the **South Downs Way National Trail** (100 miles), which takes between two and four days to complete.

Walking

Two long-distance trails meander steadily westward through the region, and there are plenty of shorter ambles to match your schedule, stamina and scenery wish-list.

The **South Downs Way National Trail** (www.nationaltrail.co.uk/south-downs-way) is a 100-mile National Trail through England's newest national park. It's a beautiful roller-coaster walk along prehistoric drove roads between Winchester and Eastbourne.

The 153-mile **North Downs Way National Trail** (www.nationaltrail.co.uk/north-downs-way) walk begins near Farnham in Surrey, but one of its most beautiful sections runs from near Ashford to Dover; a loop takes in Canterbury near its end.

Heading from Pevensey Castle to Rye (32 miles), the **1066 Country Walk** serves as a continuation of the South Downs Way.

Information

Kent Attractions (www.kentattractions.co.uk)

Tourism South East (www.visitsoutheastengland.com) The official website for south and southeast England.

Visit Kent (www.visitkent.co.uk)

Visit Surrey (www.visitsurrey.com)

Visit Sussex (www.visitsussex.org)

Getting There & Around

The southeast is easily explored by train or bus, and many attractions can be visited as a day trip from London. Contact the **National Traveline** (www.travelinesoutheast.org.uk) for comprehensive information about public transport in the region.

BUS

Explorer tickets (adult/child £7.20/5.10) provide unlimited day-long travel on most buses throughout the region. Buy them on the first bus you board.

TRAIN

Secure 33% discounts on most rail fares in the southeast by purchasing a **Network Railcard** (per year £30). Three adults can travel with you for the same discounted fare, and you save 60% on fares for children under 15.

KENT

Kent isn't described as the garden of England for nothing. Within its sea-lined borders you'll find a landscape of gentle hills, fertile farmland, cultivated country estates and fruit-laden orchards. It could also be described as the beer garden of England as it produces the world-renowned Kent hops and some of the country's finest ales and wines from its numerous vineyards. At its heart is spellbinding Canterbury, crowned by its enthralling cathedral. You'll also find beautiful coastal stretches dotted with beach towns and villages, from old-school Broadstairs to gentrified Whitstable and the aesthetically challenged port town of Dover.

Canterbury

POP 55,240

Canterbury tops the charts for English cathedral cities and is one of southern England's top attractions. Many consider the World Heritage–listed cathedral that dominates its centre to be one of Europe's finest, and the town's narrow medieval alleyways, riverside gardens and ancient city walls are a joy to explore. But Canterbury isn't just a showpiece for the past – it's a bustling, busy place with an energetic student population and a wide choice of contemporary bars, restaurants, venues and independent shops. Book ahead for the best hotels and eateries: pilgrims may no longer flock here in their thousands, but tourists certainly do.

Canterbury & the Southeast Highlights

❶ **Brighton & Hove** (p177) Shopping, tanning and partying in the hedonist capital of the southeast.

❷ **Canterbury** (p153) Making a pilgrimage to one of England's most important religious sites.

❸ **Dover Castle** (p167) Exploring the atmospheric WWII tunnels beneath this sprawling castle.

❹ **Rye** (p170) Wandering the cobbled lanes of one of England's prettiest towns.

❺ **Leeds Castle** (p160) Kicking back at this moated marvel.

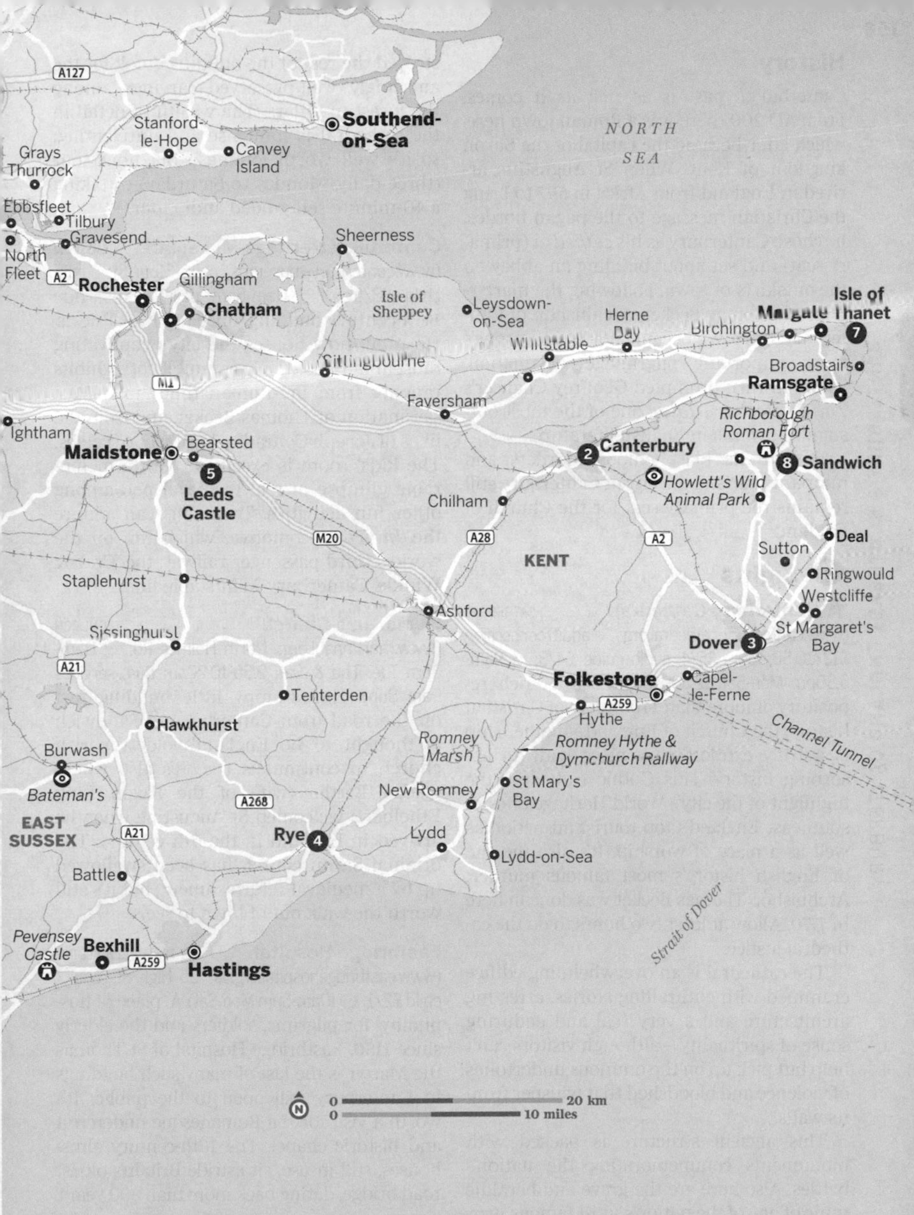

6 Beachy Head (p175) Scrambling up this spectacular headland in snow-white chalk.

7 Isle of Thanet (p163) Shaking out your beach towel for some seaside fun.

8 Sandwich (p165) Getting hopelessly lost in crooked medieval streets.

History

Canterbury's past is as rich as it comes. From AD 200 there was a Roman town here, which later became the capital of the Saxon kingdom of Kent. When St Augustine arrived in England from Africa in 597 to bring the Christian message to the pagan hordes, he chose Canterbury as his *cathedra* (primary seat) and set about building an abbey on the outskirts of town. Following the martyrdom of Thomas Becket, Archbishop of Canterbury, the town became northern Europe's most important pilgrimage destination, which in turn prompted Geoffrey Chaucer's *The Canterbury Tales,* one of the most outstanding works in English literature.

Despite its blasphemous murders and rampant tourism, the city of Canterbury still remains the primary seat for the Church of England.

Sights

★Canterbury Cathedral CATHEDRAL
(www.canterbury-cathedral.org; adult/concession £12/10.50, tours £5/4, audio guide £4/3; 9am-5.30pm Mon-Sat, 12.30-2.30pm Sun) A rich repository of more than 1400 years of Christian history, the Church of England's mother ship is a truly extraordinary place with an absorbing history. This Gothic cathedral, the highlight of the city's World Heritage Sites, is southeast England's top tourist attraction as well as a place of worship. It's also the site of English history's most famous murder: Archbishop Thomas Becket was done in here in 1170. Allow at least two hours to do the cathedral justice.

The cathedral is an overwhelming edifice crammed with enthralling stories, arresting architecture and a very real and enduring sense of spirituality – although visitors can't help but pick up on the ominous undertones of violence and bloodshed that whisper from its walls.

This ancient structure is packed with monuments commemorating the nation's battles. Also here are the grave and heraldic tunic of one of the nation's most famous warmongers, Edward the Black Prince (1330–76). The spot in the northwest transept where Becket met his grisly end has drawn pilgrims for more than 800 years and is marked by a flickering candle and a striking modern altar.

The doorway to the crypt is beside the altar. This cavernous space is the cathedral's highlight, the only survivor from the cathedral's last devastating fire in 1174, which destroyed the rest of the building. Look for the amazingly well-preserved carvings among the forest of pillars. The wealth of detail in the cathedral is immense and unrelenting, so it's well worth joining a one-hour tour (three daily, Monday to Saturday) or taking a 40-minute self-guided audio tour.

Canterbury Heritage Museum MUSEUM
(www.canterbury-museums.co.uk; Stour St; adult/child £8/free; 11am-5pm daily) This fine 14th-century building, once the Poor Priests' Hospital, now houses the city's captivating museum. It contains a jumble of exhibits ranging from pre-Roman times to the assassination of Thomas Becket, and from the likes of Joseph Conrad to locally born celebs. The kids' room is excellent, with a memorable glimpse of real medieval poo among other fun activities. Train fans can admire the *Invicta* locomotive, which ran on the world's third passenger railway, the 'Crab & Winkle' Canterbury–Whitstable line.

St Martin's Church CHURCH
(www.martinpaul.org; North Holmes Rd; 11am-3pm Tue, Thu & Sat, 9.50-10.20am Sun, services 9am Sun) This stumpy little building just off the road from Canterbury to Sandwich is thought to be England's oldest parish church in continuous use. It's also where Queen Bertha (wife of the Saxon King Ethelbert) welcomed St Augustine when he arrived in England in the 6th century. The original Saxon church has been swallowed up by a medieval refurbishment, but it's still worth the walk out of town to see.

Eastbridge Hospital HISTORIC BUILDING
(www.eastbridgehospital.org.uk; 25 High St; adult/child £2/1; 10am-5pm Mon-Sat) A 'place of hospitality' for pilgrims, soldiers and the elderly since 1180, Eastbridge Hospital of St Thomas the Martyr is the last of many such buildings in Canterbury still open to the public. It's worth a visit for the Romanesque undercroft and historic chapel. The 16th-century almshouses, still in use, sit astride Britain's oldest road bridge, dating back more than 800 years.

Roman Museum MUSEUM
(www.canterburymuseums.co.uk; Butchery Lane; adult/child £8/free; 10am-5pm) This fascinating subterranean archaeological site gives an insight into Canterbury's everyday life almost two millennia ago. Visitors can stroll a reconstructed Roman marketplace and rooms, including a kitchen, as well as view Roman mosaic floors. Everything you see

Canterbury

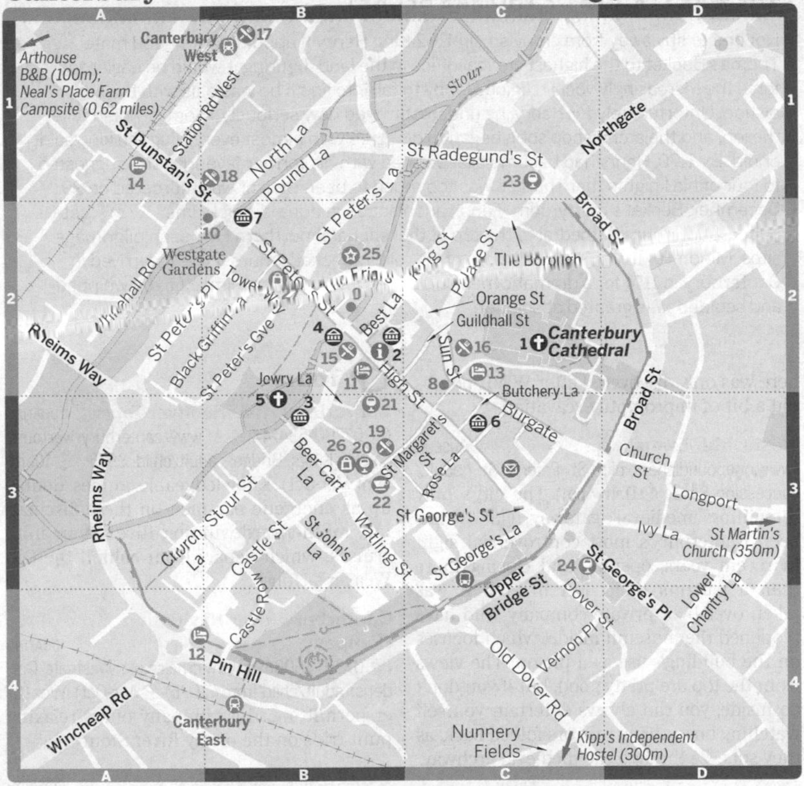

Canterbury

Top Sights
1 Canterbury Cathedral C2

Sights
2 Beaney House of Art & Knowledge B2
3 Canterbury Heritage Museum B3
4 Eastbridge Hospital B2
5 Greyfriars Chapel B3
6 Roman Museum C3
7 West Gate Towers B2

Activities, Courses & Tours
8 Canterbury Guided Tours C2
9 Canterbury Historic River Tours B2
10 Canterbury River Navigation Company B2

Sleeping
11 ABode Canterbury B2
12 Castle House A4
13 Cathedral Gate Hotel C2
14 House of Agnes A1

Eating
15 Boho B2
16 Deeson's C2
17 Goods Shed B1
18 Refectory Kitchen B1
19 Tiny Tim's Tearoom B3

Drinking & Nightlife
20 Alberry's Wine Bar B3
21 Foundry Brewpub B3
22 Micro Roastery B3
23 Parrot C1
24 Steinbeck & Shaw C3

Entertainment
25 New Marlowe Theatre B2

Shopping
26 Chaucer Bookshop B3
27 Revivals B2

THE MARTYRDOM OF THOMAS BECKET

Not one to shy away from cronyism, in 1162 King Henry II appointed his good mate Thomas Becket to the highest clerical office in the land, figuring it would be easier to force the increasingly vocal religious lobby to fall into line if he was pals with the archbishop. Unfortunately for Henry, he underestimated how seriously Thomas would take the job, and the archbishop soon began to disagree with almost everything the king said or did. By 1170, Henry had become exasperated with his former favourite and suggested to four of his knights that Thomas was too much to bear. Becket was murdered on 29 December. Becket's martyrdom – and canonisation in double-quick time (1173) – catapulted Canterbury Cathedral to the top of the league of northern European pilgrimage sites. Mindful of the growing criticism of his role in Becket's murder, Henry arrived in Canterbury in 1174 for a dramatic *mea culpa* and, after allowing himself to be whipped and scolded, was granted absolution.

here was only discovered after WWII bombs did a bit of impromptu excavation.

West Gate Towers MUSEUM
(www.onepoundlane.co.uk; St Peter's St; adult/concession £4/3; ⏲11am-4pm) The city's only remaining medieval gateway (1380) has been Canterbury's most controversial sight in recent years, opening and closing more than a parson's Bible. But in 2015 it was taken over by a private company who have reopened the museum inside, which focuses on the building's use as a prison. The views from the top are pretty good, but if you don't go inside, you can always entertain yourself watching buses, wing mirrors folded back, as they squeeze through the medieval archway.

Greyfriars Chapel CHURCH
(⏲2-4pm Mon-Sat Easter-Sep) You'll find Greyfriars Chapel in serene riverside gardens behind Eastbridge Hospital. The first monastery built in England by Franciscan monks in 1267, its grounds are a tranquil city-centre spot to unfurl the picnic blanket.

Beaney House of Art & Knowledge MUSEUM
(18 High St; ⏲9am-5pm Mon-Wed, Fri & Sat, 9am-7pm Thu, 10am-5pm Sun) FREE This mock-Tudor edifice is the grandest on the main shopping thoroughfare, if not the most authentic. Formerly called the Royal Museum & Art Gallery, it has housed Canterbury's main library, a museum and an art gallery since 1899 – it's current name is in honour of the 19th-century benefactor who funded the original building. In addition to the city's main library and the tourist office, the mixed bag of museum exhibitions is worth half an hour between the main sights.

Tours

Canterbury Historic River Tours BOATING
(☎07790-534744; www.canterburyrivertours.co.uk; Kings Bridge; adult/child £9/5; ⏲10am-5pm Mar-Oct) Knowledgeable guides double up as energetic oarsmen on these fascinating, multi-award-winning River Stour mini cruises, which depart from behind the Old Weaver's House.

Canterbury River Navigation Company BOATING
(☎07816-760869; www.crnc.co.uk; Westgate Gardens; adult/child from £10/6; ⏲Apr-Oct) Weather permitting, this company offers relaxing punt trips on the pretty River Stour.

Canterbury Guided Tours WALKING
(☎01227-459779; www.canterburyguidedtours.com; adult/child/concession £7.50/5.50/7; ⏲11am Feb-Oct, plus 2pm Jul-Sep) Guided walking tours leave from opposite the Canturbury Cathedral entrance. Tickets can be purchased from the tourist office.

Festivals & Events

Canterbury Festival PERFORMING ARTS
(☎box office 01227-787787; www.canterburyfestival.co.uk; ⏲mid-Oct–early Nov) Myriad musicians, comedians, theatre groups and other artists from around the world come to party during this festival, which runs for almost three weeks.

Sleeping

Kipp's Independent Hostel HOSTEL £
(☎01227-786121; www.kipps-hostel.com; 40 Nunnery Fields; dm £16.50-24.50, s £25-35, d £50-70; @📶) Occupying a red-brick town house in a quietish residential area less than a mile from the city centre, these superb back-

packer digs enjoy a homey atmosphere, clean (though cramped) dorms and rave reviews.

House of Agnes HOTEL ££
(☎01227-472185; www.houseofagnes.co.uk; 71 St Dunstan's St; r from £89-125; @📶) This rather wonky 13th-century beamed inn, mentioned in Dickens' *David Copperfield,* has eight themed rooms bearing names such as 'Marrakesh' (Moorish), 'Venice' (carnival masks), 'Boston' (light and airy) and 'Canterbury' (antiques and heavy fabrics). If you prefer your room to have straight lines and right angles, there are eight less exciting, but no less comfortable, 'stable' rooms in the garden annexe.

Cathedral Gate Hotel HOTEL ££
(☎01227-464381; www.cathgate.co.uk; 36 Burgate; s/d £50/112, without bathroom £50/81.50; 📶) Predating the spectacular cathedral gate it adjoins, this quaint 15th-century hotel is a medieval warren of steep staircases and narrow passageways leading to 27 pleasingly old-fashioned rooms with angled floors, low doors and cockeyed walls. Some have cathedral views, while others overlook pretty Buttermarket. There's no lift.

Arthouse B&B B&B ££
(☎07976-725457; www.arthousebandb.com; 24 London Rd; r from £65; P📶) A night at Canterbury's most laid-back digs, housed in a 19th-century fire station, is a bit like sleeping at a really cool art student's pad. The theme is funky and eclectic, with furniture by local designers and artwork by the instantly likeable artist owners, who have a house-studio out back.

Castle House B&B ££
(☎01227-761897; www.castlehouse hotel.co.uk; 28 Castle St; r from £90; P📶) This historic guesthouse sits opposite the ruins of Canterbury's Norman castle, and incorporates part of the old city walls. The spacious, tasteful, high-ceilinged Georgian-style rooms have pretty views and bags of space and there's a secluded garden out back.

★ABode Canterbury HOTEL £££
(☎01227-766266; www.abodecanterbury.co.uk; 30-33 High St; r from £98; 📶) The 72 rooms at this supercentral hotel, the only boutique hotel in town, are graded from 'comfortable' to 'fabulous', and for the most part live up to their names. They come with features such as handmade beds, chesterfield sofas, tweed cushions and beautiful modern bathrooms. There's a splendid champagne bar, restaurant and tavern, too.

Eating

★Tiny Tim's Tearoom CAFE £
(www.tinytimstearoom.com; 34 St Margaret's St; mains £6-10.50; ⏲9.30am-5pm Tue-Sat, 10.30am-4pm Sun) It's no mean feat to be declared 'Kent Tearoom of the Year', but this swish 1930s cafe was awarded the accolade in 2015. It offers hungry shoppers big breakfasts bursting with Kentish ingredients, and tiers of cakes, crumpets, cucumber sandwiches and scones plastered in clotted cream. On busy shopping days you are guaranteed to queue for a table.

Refectory Kitchen BRITISH £
(☎01227-638766; www.refectorykitchen.com; 16 St Dunstan's St; mains around £8; ⏲8am-5pm Mon-Wed, 8am-4pm & 6-9.30pm Thu & Fri, 9am-4pm & 6-9.30pm Sat, 9am-3pm Sun) This tiny, wood-beamed cafe serves all-day breakfasts and a short menu of light lunch and dinner mains containing Kentish ingredients as far as possible. The welcome is friendly, the atmosphere welcoming, but things get very busy at mealtimes

Boho INTERNATIONAL £
(43 St Peter's St; snacks £4-14; ⏲9am-6pm Mon-Thu, to 10pm Fri & Sat, 10am-5pm Sun) This hip eatery in a prime spot on the main drag is extraordinarily popular and you'll be lucky to get a table on busy shopping days. Cool tunes lilt through the chic retro dining space while chilled diners chow down on humongous burgers, full-monty breakfasts and imaginative, owner-cooked international mains. Boho doesn't do bookings, so be prepared to queue.

★Deeson's BRITISH ££
(☎01227-767854; www.deesonsrestaurant.co.uk; 25-26 Sun St; mains £15-24; ⏲noon-3pm & 5-10pm) Put the words 'local', 'seasonal' and 'tasty' together and you have this superb British eatery. Local fruit and veg; award-winning wines, beers and ciders; fish from Kent's coastal waters; and the odd ingredient from the proprietor's own allotment are all served in a straightforward, contemporary setting just a Kentish apple's throw from the Canterbury Cathedral gates.

Goods Shed MARKET ££
(☎01227-459153; www.thegoodsshed.co.uk; Station Rd West; mains £17-20; ⏲market 9am-7pm Tue-Sat, 10am-4pm Sun, restaurant 8am-9.30pm Tue-Sat, 9am-3pm Sun) Farmers market, food hall and fabulous restaurant rolled into one, this converted warehouse by the Canterbury West train station is a hit with everyone

WORTH A TRIP

LEEDS CASTLE

The immense moated pile **Leeds Castle** (www.leeds-castle.com; adult/child £24.50/16.50; ⏲10am-6pm Apr-Sep, to 5pm Oct-Mar), just east of Maidstone is, for many, the world's most romantic castle, and it's certainly one of the most visited in Britain. The formidable, hefty structure balancing on two islands is known as something of a 'ladies castle'. This stems from the fact that in its more than 1000 years of history, it has been home to a who's who of medieval queens, most famously Henry VIII's first wife, Catherine of Aragon.

The castle was transformed from fortress to lavish palace over the centuries, and its last owner, the high-society hostess Lady Baillie, used it as a princely family home and party pad to entertain the likes of Errol Flynn, Douglas Fairbanks and John F Kennedy.

The castle's vast estate offers enough attractions of its own to justify a day trip: peaceful walks, a duckery, aviary and falconry demonstrations. You'll also find possibly the world's sole dog-collar museum, plenty of kids' attractions and a hedge maze, overseen by a grassy bank from where fellow travellers can shout encouragement or misdirections.

Since Lady Baillie's death in 1974, a private trust has managed the property. This means that some parts of the castle are periodically closed for private events.

Trains run from London Victoria to Bearsted, where you catch a special shuttle coach to the castle.

from self-caterers to sit-down gourmets. The chunky wooden tables sit slightly above the market hubbub but in full view of its appetite-whetting stalls. Daily specials exploit the freshest farm goodies the Garden of England has to offer.

Drinking & Nightlife

Steinbeck & Shaw CLUB
(www.steinbeckandshaw.co.uk; 41 St George's Pl; ⏲6pm-2am Mon-Thu, to 3am Fri & Sat) Canterbury's newest nightclub has a super-cool, 21st-century interior with urban and retro elements. The weekly program is a mixed bag of rock and house and is as popular with students as with tourists and Kentish trendoids.

Foundry Brewpub BREWERY
(www.thefoundrycanterbury.co.uk; White Horse Lane; ⏲noon-midnight Mon-Thu, noon-late Fri & Sat, noon-11pm Sun) Canterbury's brewpub pumps out award-winning craft beers in the industrial setting of a former foundry. It also stocks a wide range of local and national ales and ciders and serves light snacks and meals.

Micro Roastery COFFEE
(www.microroastery.co.uk; 4 St Margaret's St; ⏲8am-6pm Mon-Fri, 9am-6pm Sat, 10am-5pm Sun; Wi-Fi) Owned by an Anglo-Peruvian couple, this new cafe imports, roasts, grinds and sells its unsurpassed beans and blends. There's local art on the walls; the furniture is upholstered in coffee-bean sacks; and a La Marzocco espresso machine pumps out strong brews.

Parrot PUB
(www.theparrotonline.com; 1-9 Church Lane; ⏲noon-10pm Mon-Sat, to 9.30pm Sun) Built in 1370 on Roman foundations, Canterbury's oldest boozer has a snug, beam-rich pub downstairs and a much-lauded dining room upstairs under yet more ageing oak. Many a local microbrewed ale is pulled in both venues.

Alberry's Wine Bar CLUB
(www.alberrys.co.uk; 38 St Margaret's St; ⏲11am-3am) An after-hours music bar that puts on everything from smooth live jazz to DJ-led drum and bass to commercial pop. It's a two-level place where you can relax over a cocktail upstairs before heading down to the basement bar.

Entertainment

New Marlowe Theatre THEATRE
(☎01227-787787; www.marlowetheatre.com; The Friars) Canterbury's main theatre attracts popular, fast-selling productions on national tour. Check out that bizarre auditorium, with its dark faux veneers contrasting sharply with the lifejacket-orange seating. The Studio in the same complex is a more intimate performance venue.

Shopping

Chaucer Bookshop BOOKS
(6-7 Beer Cart Lane; ⏲10am-5pm Mon-Sat, 11am-4pm Sun) Antiquarian and used books plus interesting prints and drawings.

Revivals CLOTHING
(42 St Peter's St; 10am-5pm Mon-Sat, to 4pm Sun) The city's best vintage-clothing emporium.

Information

Post Office (19 St George's St; 9am-5.30pm Mon-Sat, 10.30am-2.30pm Sun) On the 1st floor of WH Smiths.

Tourist Office (01227-862162; www.canterbury.co.uk; 18 High St; 9am-5pm Mon-Wed, Fri & Sat, to 7pm Thu, 10am-5pm Sun) Located in the Beaney House of Art & Knowledge. Staff can help book accommodation, excursions and theatre tickets.

Getting There & Away

BUS

The city's **bus station** (St George's Lane) is just within the city walls. Canterbury connections:

Dover (National Express; £5.80, 40 minutes, hourly)

London Victoria (National Express; £15.50, two hours, hourly)

Margate (£5.30, 50 minutes, four hourly)

Ramsgate (£5.30 45 minutes, hourly)

Sandwich (£3.70, 40 minutes, three hourly)

Whitstable (£4.70, 30 minutes, every 10 minutes)

TRAIN

There are two train stations, Canterbury East for London Victoria and Canterbury West for London's Charing Cross/St Pancras stations. Canterbury connections:

Dover Priory (£8.20, 25 minutes, half-hourly) Runs from Canterbury East train station.

London St Pancras (£34.80, one hour, hourly) High-speed service.

London Victoria/Charing Cross (£29.30, 1¾ hours, two hourly)

Getting Around

Canterbury's centre is mostly set up for pedestrians. Car parks are dotted along and just inside the walls, but to avoid heavy traffic, day trippers may prefer to use one of three Park & Ride sites, which cost £3 per day and connect to the centre by bus every eight minutes (7am to 7.30pm Monday to Saturday, 10am to 6pm Sun).

Whitstable

POP 30,195

Perhaps it's the oysters, harvested since Roman times? Maybe it's the weatherboard houses and shingle beach? Or perhaps it's the pleasingly old-fashioned main street with galleries, been-there-forever outfitters and emporia of vintage clothing? Most likely it's for all of these reasons that Whitstable has become a bit of a weekend mecca for metropolitan types looking for refuge from the city hassle. It's also a simple day trip from Canterbury, to which it is linked by regular local bus.

Sights

Whitstable Museum & Gallery MUSEUM
(www.canterburymuseums.co.uk; 5 Oxford St; adult/concession £3/2; 11am-4.30pm) This modest museum has glass cases examining Whitstable's oyster industry, the Crab & Winkle Railway which once ran from Canterbury, and the local fishing fleet, as well as a corner dedicated to actor Peter Cushing, star of several Hammer Horror films and the town's most famous resident, who died in 1994.

Festivals & Events

Whitstable Oyster Festival FOOD & DRINK
(www.whitstableoysterfestival.co.uk; late Jul) For a week in late July, the town hosts a seafood, arts and music extravaganza offering a packed schedule of events, from history walks, crab catching and oyster-eating competitions to a beer festival and traditional 'blessing of the waters'.

Sleeping

Hotel Continental HOTEL ££
(01227 280280; www.hotelcontinental.co.uk; 29 Beach Walk; r from £75;) The rooms at this elegant seaside art-deco building have undergone a complete refit and are now bright and breezy quarters with light-painted wood cladding, brilliant white beds and sparkling bathrooms. There's a decent restaurant and bar on the premises.

Whitstable Bay B&B ££
(01227-779362; www.whitstablebay.com; 74 Joy Lane; s/d from £65/70; P) This much-lauded B&B is a short stroll southwest of High St and offers three very well-appointed and stylishly decorated doubles in a quiet residential area. Continental breakfast is free, but a full English is £6.50 extra.

Eating

Samphire MODERN BRITISH ££
(01227-770075; www.samphirewhitstable.co.uk; 4 High St; mains £10-19; 10am-10pm) The shabby-chic jumble of tables and chairs, big-print wallpaper and blackboard menus create the perfect stage for meticulously crafted mains containing East Kent's most flavour-packed

ingredients. An interesting side dish is its namesake samphire, an asparagus-like plant that grows on sea-sprayed rocks and cliffs, often found on menus in these parts.

★**Sportsman Pub** BRITISH £££
(www.thesportsmanseasalter.co.uk; Faversham Rd; mains around £20; ⌚restaurant noon-2pm & 7-9pm Tue-Sat, 12.30-2.45pm Sun, bar noon-3pm & 6-11pm Tue-Sat, noon-10pm Sun) The anonymous and oddly named village of Seasalter, 4 miles east of Whitstable, would hardly receive a trickle of visitors wereit not for the deceivingly ramshackle Sportsman Pub, East Kent's only eatery adorned with a Michelin star. Local ingredients from sea, marsh and woods are crafted by Whitstable-born chef Stephen Harris into taste-packed Kentish creations that have food critics drooling.

Wheeler's Oyster Bar SEAFOOD £££
(☎01227-273311; www.wheelersoysterbar.com; 8 High St; mains £18.50-22.50; ⌚10.30am-9pm Mon, Tue & Thu, 10.15am-9.30pm Fri, 10am-10pm Sat, 11.30am-9pm Sun) Squeeze onto a stool by the bar or into the four-table Victorian dining room of this baby-blue and pink restaurant, choose from the seasonal menu and enjoy the best seafood in Whitstable. This place knows its stuff, as it's been serving oysters since 1856. Bookings are highly recommended unless you're travelling solo. Cash only.

Drinking & Nightlife

Old Neptune PUB
(www.neppy.co.uk; Marine Tce; ⌚noon-10.30pm) A ramshackle pub about as far onto the beach as it's possible to get (it's been washed away several times by high tides) with cosy winter window seats and wonky floorboards. Summer sees drinkers tumble out onto the shingle and there's regular live music.

Getting There & Away

BUS

Whitstable has connections to Canterbury (£4.70, 30 minutes, every 10 minutes) and London Victoria (£15.50, 2¼ hours, three daily).

TRAIN

Whitstable has the following connections:

London St Pancras (£28, one hour 20 minutes, hourly)

London Victoria (£22, one hour 20 minutes, hourly)

Margate (£7.20, 20 minutes, twice hourly)

Ramsgate (£9.30, 36 minutes, twice hourly)

Margate

POP 49,700

A popular resort for more than two centuries, Margate's late-20th-century slump was long and bleak as British holidaymakers ditched Victorian frump for the carefree *costas* of Spain. But this grand old seaside, with fine-sand beaches and artistic associations, has bounced off the bottom. Major cultural regeneration projects – including the spectacular Turner Contemporary art gallery – are slowly reversing the town's fortunes, and on busy days even the odd non-English speaker can be overheard in the newly minted cafes and rejuvenated old town.

Sights

★**Turner Contemporary** GALLERY
(www.turnercontemporary.org; Rendezvous; ⌚10am-6pm Tue-Sun) FREE This blockbuster contemporary art gallery, bolted together on the site of the seafront guesthouse where master painter JMW Turner used to stay, is one of East Kent's top attractions. Within the strikingly featureless shell the only thing distracting the eye, apart from the artwork on display, is the sea view from the floor-to-ceiling windows. These allow you to appreciate the very thing Turner loved so much about Margate – the sea, sky and refracted light of the north Kent coast.

The gallery is attracting top-notch contemporary installations by high-calibre artists such as Tracey Emin (who grew up in Margate) and Alex Katz. When you're finished with the art, culinary creations await in the cafe and the gift shop is excellent.

Shell Grotto GROTTO, CAVE
(www.shellgrotto.co.uk; Grotto Hill; adult/child £3.50/1.50; ⌚10am-5pm Apr-Oct, 11am-4pm Sat & Sun Nov-Mar) Margate's unique attraction is a mysterious subterranean grotto, discovered in 1835. It's a claustrophobic collection of rooms and passageways embedded with 4.6 million shells arranged in symbol-rich mosaics. It has inspired feverish speculation over the years; some think it a 2000-year-old pagan temple, others an elaborate 19th-century hoax. Either way, it's an exquisite place worth seeing.

Dreamland AMUSEMENT PARK
(www.dreamland.co.uk; Marine Terrace; adult/child £18/15; ⌚11am-9pm May-Oct) Given the kiss of life using lottery and council funds, Margate's famous amusement park is slowly coming back to life after a decade of lying

derelict. The main attraction here is the so-called Scenic Railway, a 1920s heritage-listed wooden roller coaster that was rebuilt after an arson attack in 2008. But there are plenty of other period rides and attractions to keep adults and kiddies thrilled, some shipped in from other defunct, 20th-century amusement parks across the country.

Sleeping & Eating

★Reading Rooms B&B £££
(☎01843-225166; www.thereadingroomsmargate.co.uk; 31 Hawley Sq; r £100, 📶) Occupying an unmarked 18th-century Georgian town house on a tranquil square just five minutes' walk from the sea, this luxury boutique B&B is stylish. Generously cut rooms with waxed wooden floors and beautiful French antique reproduction furniture contrast with the 21st-century bathrooms fragrant with Ren cosmetics. Breakfast is served in your room. Bookings essential; no children or pets.

Sands Hotel BOUTIQUE HOTEL £££
(☎01843-228228; www.sandshotelmargate.co.uk; 16 Marine Dr; r £120-200; ❄📶) This beautifully styled boutique hotel sits right on Margate's seafront. It features an understated sand-hued theme throughout, the southeast's best bathrooms, and a restaurant with spectacular bay views, which around half of the rooms also share. The entrance is hidden under the arches on the seafront next to the hotel's very own summertime ice-cream parlour.

★Mad Hatter CAFE £
(www.facebook.com/TheMadHatterMargate; 9 Lombard St; snacks & light meals £3.50-11; ⏱11am-5.30pm Sat, other days occasionally Jul & Aug) This unmissable, completely cuckoo eatery run by a top-hatted proprietor packs two rooms of a 1690s house with regalia and knick-knackery from down the ages. Christmas decorations stay up all year and the toilets are original Victorian porcelain. The yummy cakes and snacks are all homemade. Just a shame it isn't open more often.

Great British Pizza Company PIZZA £
(www.greatbritishpizza.com; 14 Marine Dr; pizzas £4-9.50; ⏱noon-9pm Tue-Sat, to 3pm Sun; 📶) A world away from your normal 'British pizza', the delicious cheese-topped wheels at this cool hang-out are made from the best local and Italian ingredients. On the seafront, this popular spot has a funkily eclectic but simple dining space, heart-pumping coffees and gelato containing nothing that it shouldn't.

ISLE OF THANET

You won't need a wetsuit or a ferry to reach the Isle of Thanet and its towns of Margate, Ramsgate and Broadstairs: the 2-mile-wide Wantsum Channel, which divides the island from the mainland, silted up in the 16th century, transforming the East Kent landscape forever. In its island days, Thanet was the springboard for several epoch-making episodes in English history. It was here that the Romans kicked off their invasion in the 1st century AD and where St Augustine landed in AD 597 to launch his conversion of the pagans. If global warming forecasts are right, Thanet could once again be an island by the end of the century.

Information

Tourist Office (☎01843-577577; www.visitthanet.co.uk; Droit House, Stone Pier; ⏱10am-5pm daily Easter-Oct, 10am-5pm Tue-Sat Nov-Easter) Next to the Turner Contemporary art gallery, the tourist office serves all of the Isle of Thanet. It hands out *The Isle*, a glossy magazine crammed with Thanet listings.

Getting There & Away

BUS

Departure and arrival points for local buses are Queen St and adjacent Cecil St.

Broadstairs (Thanet Loop Bus; £1.90, up to every 10 minutes)

Canterbury (£5.20, 50 minutes, three hourly)

London Victoria (National Express; £14.50, three hours, seven daily)

Ramsgate (Thanet Loop Bus; £2.30, up to every 10 minutes)

TRAIN

The train station is just a few steps from the beach. There are twice-hourly services to London Victoria (£35.50, one hour 50 minutes) and a high-speed service to London St Pancras (£41.40, 1½ hours) every hour.

Broadstairs

POP 25,000

While its bigger, brasher neighbours seek to revive and regenerate themselves, quaint little Broadstairs quietly gets on with what it's done best for the past 150 years – wowing visitors with its tight sickle of reddish sand (Viking Bay) and sun-warmed lapping sea.

Charles Dickens certainly thought it a pretty spot, spending most summers here between 1837 and 1859. The resort now plays the Victorian nostalgia card at every opportunity and names every second business after the works of its most famous holidaymaker.

Sights

Dickens House Museum MUSEUM
(www.dickensfellowship.org; 2 Victoria Pde; adult/child £3.75/2.10; ⊙1-4.30pm Easter–mid-Jun & mid-Sep–Oct, 10am-4.30pm mid-Jun–mid-Sep, 1-4.30pm Sat & Sun Nov) This quaint museum is Broadstairs' top attraction and the former home of Mary Pearson Strong – Dickens' inspiration for the character of Betsey Trotwood in *David Copperfield*. Diverse Dickensiana on display includes letters from the author.

Festivals & Events

Dickens Festival CULTURAL
(www.broadstairsdickensfestival.co.uk; ⊙late Jun) Broadstairs' biggest bash, this annual, week-long festival held in mid-June culminates in a banquet and ball in Victorian fancy dress.

Sleeping & Eating

Copperfields Guest House B&B ££
(☎01843-601247; www.copperfieldsbb.co.uk; 11 Queen's Rd; s/d £65/85; 📶) 🌿 This vegetarian B&B offers three homely rooms with en suite, and a warm welcome from the owners and pet Yorkie. It also caters for vegans, and all products in the bathrooms are cruelty-free.

★**Bleak House** HISTORIC HOTEL £££
(☎01843-865338; www.bleakhousebroadstairs.co.uk; Fort Rd; r £155-250, apt £300; 📶) This former Napoleonic-era fortress overlooking the beach was converted into an opulent Victorian residence just in time for one Charles Dickens to rent it for 22 summers (1837–59). From the lounge bar to the Copperfield suite with its Viking Bay views and five-star bathroom, the whole caboodle oozes unique period character. Building tours run from 10am to 6pm.

★**Wyatt & Jones** BRITISH ££
(www.wyattandjones.co.uk; 23-27 Harbour St; mains £6-19; ⊙9-11am, noon-3pm & 6.30-9pm Wed & Thu, to 10pm Fri & Sat, 9am-5pm Sun) Broadstairs' best offering is this contemporary British restaurant just a few steps off the beach. Savour unashamedly local dishes such as Whitstable oysters, local bream, mussels and chips, or a day-launching breakfast in the uncluttered interior of gun-metal blue and scratched timber floors. Then admire your expanding waistline in the retro mirror wall.

Tartar Frigate BRITISH ££
(www.tartarfrigate.co.uk; 42 Harbour St; mains £16.50-24.50; ⊙11am-11pm) Dating back to the 18th century, this seafront pub is a great place to be in summer when tourists and locals alike spill out onto the beach. The seafood restaurant upstairs serves up excellent fare and there are great views of the bay. The pub also puts on regular live folk music.

Getting There & Away

BUS

Broadstairs connections include the following:

Canterbury (£5.20, 1½ hours, twice hourly)

London Victoria (National Express, £14.50, 3¼ hours, seven daily)

Margate (Thanet Loop Bus; £1.90, 21 minutes, up to every 10 minutes)

Ramsgate (Thanet Loop Bus; £1.50, 14 minutes, up to every 10 minutes)

TRAIN

Broadstairs is connected to London Victoria (£22.50, two hours, hourly) and by high-speed service to London St Pancras (£39.30, one hour 20 minutes, twice hourly).

Ramsgate

POP 39,600

The most varied of Thanet's towns, Ramsgate has a friendlier feel than rival Margate and is more vibrant than its quaint little neighbour Broadstairs. A forest of masts whistles serenely in the breeze below the handsomely curved walls of Britain's only royal harbour, and the seafront is surrounded by bars and cosmopolitan street cafes. Just one celebrity chef away from being described as 'up and coming', Ramsgate retains a shabbily undiscovered charm, its sweeping, environmentally sanctioned Blue Flag beaches and some spectacular Victorian architecture making it well worth the visit.

Sights

Spitfire Memorial Museum MUSEUM
(www.spitfiremuseum.org.uk; Manston Rd; ⊙10am-5pm Apr-Oct, to 4pm Nov-Mar) FREE Around 4 miles northwest of Ramsgate's town centre at Manston Airport, this purpose-built museum stores two WWII planes: one a Spitfire, the other a Hurricane. Both look factory-fresh but are surprisingly delicate so, sadly, there's

no clambering on board. Gathered around the planes are myriad flight-associated exhibits, many relating to Manston's role as an airfield during the Battle of Britain. Take bus 38 or 11 from King St and ask the driver to drop you off as near as possible.

Ramsgate Maritime Museum MUSEUM
(www.ramsgatemaritimemuseum.org; The Clock House, Royal Harbour; adult/child £2/1; ⏲10am-5pm Tue-Sun Easter-Sep) Interesting but erratically opening museum displaying loot from the more than 600 ships that have been wrecked on the notorious Goodwin Sands off this stretch of coast.

Sleeping & Eating

Royal Harbour Hotel HOTEL ££
(☎01843-591514; www.royalharbourhotel.co.uk; Nelson Crescent 10/11; s/d from £79/100) Occupying two regency town houses on a seafront crescent, this boutique hotel feels enveloped in warmth and quirkiness – an eclectic collection of books, magazines, games and art line the hotel. Rooms range from tiny nautical-esque 'cabins' to country-house style, four-poster doubles, most with postcard views over the forest of masts below and all are perfectly appointed with bags of character.

Glendevon Guesthouse B&B ££
(☎01843-570909; www.glendevonguesthouse.co.uk; 8 Truro Rd; s/d from £52.50/70; P 📶) Run by energetic and very knowledgeable hosts, this comfy guesthouse takes the whole ecofriendly thing very seriously, with guest recycling facilities, eco-showers and even energy-saving hairdryers. The hallways of this grand Victorian house, a block back from the Ramsgate seafront, are decorated with work by local artists. All rooms have kitchenettes, and breakfast is a convivial affair taken around a communal table.

Vinyl Head Cafe CAFE £
(2-3 Addington Street; snacks £1-5; ⏲9am-3pm Tue-Sun) Located off the beaten track on a quiet road running up from the western end of the harbour, this groovy community cafe offers great coffee and homemade cakes, locals to chat with and retro sounds on vinyl.

Bon Appetit FRENCH ££
(www.bonappetitramsgate.co.uk; 4 Westcliff Arcade; mains £7-21; ⏲noon-2.30pm & 7pm-late Tue-Sat) The best eatery on Westcliff, this first-rate bistro serves up French-inspired dishes in a simple dining room or with alfresco harbour views. Ingredients on the menu are of the seasonal and locally sourced ilk, with finely crafted mains including delights such as pan-fried Kentish pheasant and Dover sole.

Information

Tourist Office (☎01843-598750; www.ramsgatetown.org; Customs House, Harbour Pde; ⏲10am-4pm Mon-Sun) A small, staffed visitor centre with out-of-hours brochure stands.

Getting There & Away

BUS

Ramsgate has the following bus connections:

Broadstairs (Thanet Loop Bus; £1.50, up to every 10 minutes)

London Victoria (National Express; £14.50, three hours, six daily)

Margate (Thanet Loop Bus; £2.30, up to every 10 minutes)

Sandwich (£3, 25 minutes, hourly)

TRAIN

Ramsgate has train services to London Victoria (£22.50, two hours, twice hourly) and a high-speed service to London St Pancras (£39.70, 1¼ hours, twice hourly).

Sandwich

POP 5000

As close as you'll get to a living museum, Sandwich was once England's fourth city (after London, Norwich and Ipswich). It's a fact hard to grasp as you wander its drowsy medieval lanes, ancient churches, Dutch gables, crooked peg-tiled roofs and overhanging timber-framed houses. Once a port to rival London, Sandwich began its decline when the entrance to the harbour silted up in the 16th century, and this once-vital gateway to and from the Continent spent the next 400 years retreating into quaint rural obscurity. Preservation is big here, with huge local interest in period authenticity. The tiny 100-seat cinema is preserved as an art-deco museum piece and the 1920s garage deals more in classic cars than modern vehicles. Within the town's historical core, unlisted buildings are the exception.

Sights

Sandwich's web of medieval and Elizabethan streets is perfect for ambling through and getting pleasantly lost (as many do). Strand Street in particular has one of the country's highest concentrations of half-timbered buildings. Ornate brickwork on some houses betrays the strong influence of 350 Protestant Flemish refugees (referred to as 'the Strangers'), who settled in the town in the 16th century at the invitation of Elizabeth I.

Sandwich Quay WATERFRONT

Several attractions line the River Stour. First up is a cute little flint-chequered Barbican tollgate built by Henry VIII, which controls traffic flow over the river's only road bridge. Nearby rises Fishergate, built in 1384 and once the main entrance to the town, through which goods from the Continent and beyond once passed. On fair-weather days, hop aboard the **Sandwich River Bus** (☎07958 376183; www.sandwichrb.uk; adult/child 30min trip £7/5, 1hr £12/8; ⊙every 30-60min 11am-6pm Thu-Sun Apr-Sep) beside the toll bridge for seal-spotting trips along the River Stour and in Pegwell Bay, or for an interesting way to reach the **Richborough Roman Fort** (Richborough Rd; h10am-6pm Apr-Sep, to 5pm Wed-Sun Oct, to 4pm Sat & Sun Nov-Mar; adult/child £5.80/3.40).

Salutation Gardens GARDENS

(www.the-salutation.com; The Salutation, Knightrider St; admission £7; ⊙10am-5pm) Just along from Fishergate, this set of exquisite gardens was laid out behind a 1912 mansion by leading early-20th-century garden designers Jekyll and Lutyens. In the mid-noughties the exquisite site was brought back to life by Dom and Steph Parker, nationally known as minor celebrities from British TV's *Gogglebox* show. The gardens suffered major flooding in 2013 but have largely recovered. There's a superb tearoom in the grounds and you can stay with Dom and Steph in their multi-million-pound mansion.

St Peter's CHURCH

(King St; ⊙10am-5pm) The oldest church in Sandwich is now no longer used for worship. It's a real mixture of styles and years: its tower collapsed in dramatic fashion in 1661 and it was rebuilt with a bulbous cupola by the Flemish 'Strangers'. At the time of research, work was underway to make this accessible to visitors for unsurpassed views of Sandwich.

Guildhall Museum MUSEUM

(www.sandwichtowncouncil.gov.uk; Guildhall; adult/child £1/50p; ⊙10.30am-12.30pm & 2-4pm Tue, Wed, Fri & Sat, 2-4pm Thu & Sun Apr-Nov) Sandwich's small but thorough museum is a good place to start exploring the town. Exhibitions examine the town's rich past as a Cinque Port, its role in various wars, and the gruesome punishments meted out to felons, fornicators and phoney fishers.

Sleeping & Eating

★Bell Hotel HOTEL ££

(☎01304-613388; www.bellhotelsandwich.co.uk; Sandwich Quay; s/d from £100/105; 📶) Today the haunt of celebrity golfers, the Bell Hotel has been sitting on the town's quay since Tudor times, though much of the remaining building is from the 19th century. A splendid sweeping staircase leads to luxurious rooms, some with pretty quay views. The Old Dining Room restaurant is one of East Kent's poshest nosh spots.

No Name Shop DELI, BISTRO ££

(www.nonameshop.co.uk; No Name St; snacks £1.90-6.25, meals £6.95-13.50; ⊙8am-5pm Mon-Sat, 9am-4pm Sun) This far-from-anonymous French-owned deli (downstairs) and bistro (upstairs) near the bus stop is a pleasantly aromatic spot for a quick sandwich in Sandwich or an 'oozylicious' *croque monsieur*, as well as more sophisticated dishes, followed by a relaxing glass of something Gallic. Very popular among locals, some of whom seem to regularly prefer it over their own kitchens.

King's Arms BRITISH ££

(☎01304-617330; www.kingsarms-sandwich.co.uk; cnr Church & Strand Sts; light meals £4-11, mains £11-17; ⊙noon-3pm & 6-10pm; 📶) This cosy 15th-century inn opposite St Mary's church serves quality English food and very popular Sunday lunches in a beamed dining room heated by large fireplaces. There are six B&B rooms upstairs.

Information

Tourist Office (☎01304-613565; www.open-sandwich.co.uk; Guildhall, Cattle Market; ⊙10am-4pm Mon-Sat Apr-Oct) Located in the historic Guildhall.

Getting There & Away

BUS

Buses go to Ramsgate (£3, 22 minutes, hourly), Dover (£7.90, 45 minutes, hourly) and Canterbury (£5.20, 40 minutes, three hourly).

TRAIN

Trains run from Dover Priory train station (£6.90, 22 minutes, hourly), Ramsgate (£5, 12 minutes, hourly) and London St Pancras (£30.20, two hours, hourly).

Dover

POP 37,400

Down-in-the-dumps Dover has certainly seen better days. Its derelict postwar architecture and shabby town centre is a sad introduction to England for travellers arriving on cross-Channel ferries and cruise ships, most of whom pass through quickly. Lucky, then, that the town has a couple of stellar attractions to redeem it. The port's vital strategic position so close to mainland Europe gave rise to a sprawling hilltop castle, which has some 2000 years of history to its credit. The spectacular white cliffs, as much a symbol of English wartime resilience as Winston Churchill or the Battle of Britain, rear in chalky magnificence to the east and west.

Sights

★Dover Castle CASTLE

(EH; adult/child £18.30/11; ⌚10am-6pm Apr-Jul & Sep, 9.30am-6pm Aug, to 5pm Oct, 10am-4pm Sat & Sun Nov-Mar; P) Occupying top spot, literally and figuratively, in Dover's townscape, this most impressive of castles was built to bolster the country's weakest point at the shortest sea crossing to mainland Europe. The highlights here are the unmissable **secret wartime tunnels** (Dover Castle; adult/child £18.30/11; ⌚10am-6pm Apr-Jul & Sep, 9.30am-6pm Aug, to 5pm Oct, 10am-4pm Sat & Sun Nov-Mar) and the **Great Tower**, but the huge area it sprawls across has a lot of other bits, so allow at least three hours for your visit, more if you stand to admire the views across the Channel to France.

The site has been in use for as many as 2000 years. On the vast grounds are the remains of a **Roman lighthouse**, which dates from AD 50 and may be the oldest standing building in Britain. Beside it lies the restored Saxon **Church of St Mary** in Castro.

The robust 12th-century Great Tower, with walls up to 7m thick, is a medieval warren filled with interactive exhibits and light-and-sound shows that take visitors back to the times of Henry II.

However the biggest draw of all is the network of secret wartime tunnels. The claustrophobic chalk-hewn passageways were first excavated during the Napoleonic Wars and then expanded to house a command post and hospital in WWII. The highly enjoyable 50-minute guided tour (every 20 minutes, included in the ticket price) tells the story of one of Britain's most famous wartime operations, code-named Dynamo, which was directed from here in 1940 and saw hundreds of thousands of men evacuated from the beaches at Dunkirk. The story is told in a very effective way, with video projected sharply onto the tunnel walls and sounds rumbling through the rock. At one point, the entire passageway is consumed in flames and at others visitors are plunged into complete darkness.

Roman Painted House RUINS

(www.theromanpaintedhouse.co.uk; New St; adult/child £3/2; ⌚10am-5pm Tue-Sun Jun-Sep; P) A crumbling 1960s bunker is the unlikely setting for some of the most extensive, if stunted, Roman wall paintings north of the Alps. Several scenes depict Bacchus (Roman god

A SWIG OF KENT & SUSSEX

With booze cruises over to Calais almost a thing of the past, many Kent and Sussex drinkers are rediscovering their counties' superb home-grown beverages. Both counties produce some of the most delicious ales in the country and the southeast's wines are even outgunning some traditional Continental vintners.

Kent's **Shepherd Neame Brewery** (☎01795-542016; www.shepherdneame.co.uk; 10 Court St, Faversham; tours £11.50) is Britain's oldest and cooks up aromatic ales brewed from Kent-grown premium hops. Sussex's reply is **Harveys Brewery** (p176), which perfumes Lewes town centre with a hop-laden scent. Book in advance for tours of either brewery.

Mention 'English wine' not too long ago and you'd likely hear a snort of derision. Not any more. Thanks to warmer temperatures and determined winemakers, English wine, particularly of the sparkling variety, is developing a fan base all of its own.

Award-winning vineyards can be found in both Sussex and Kent, whose chalky soils are likened to France's Champagne region. Many vineyards now offer tours and wine tastings. Some of the most popular are **Biddenden Vineyards** (☎01580-291726; www.biddendenvineyards.com; tours free; ⌚tours 10am Wed & Sat), 1.2 miles from Wealden, and **Chapel Down Vinery** (☎01580-766111; www.englishwinesgroup.com; Tenterden; tours £10; ⌚tours daily Apr-Nov), located 2.5 miles south of Tenterden on the B2082.

Dover

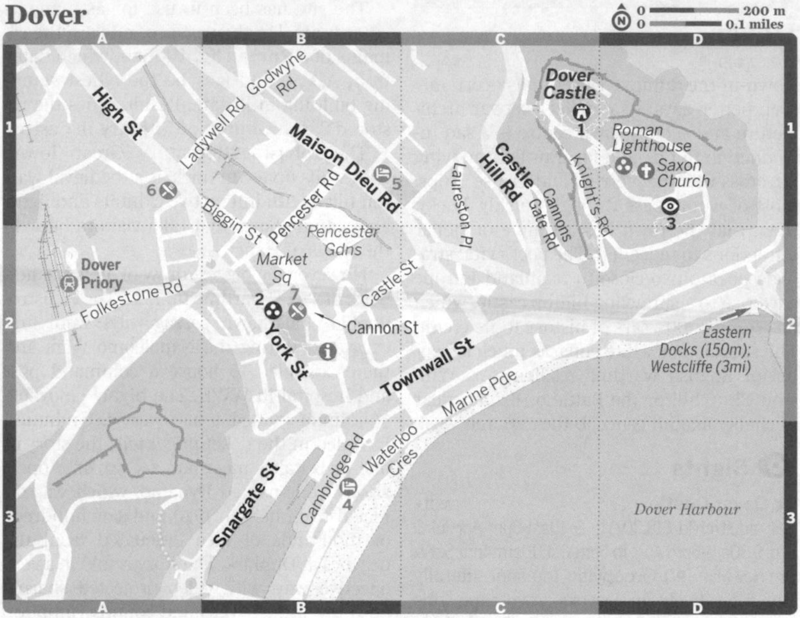

Dover

Top Sights

1 Dover Castle C1

Sights

2 Roman Painted House B2
3 Secret Wartime Tunnels D1

Sleeping

4 Dover Marina Hotel B3
5 East Lee Guest House B1

Eating

6 Allotment A1
7 La Salle Verte B2

of wine and revelry), which makes perfect sense as this large villa was built around AD 200 as a *mansio* (hotel) for travellers needing a little lubrication to unwind.

Sleeping

Dover Marina Hotel HOTEL ££
(☎01304-203633; www.dovermarinahotel.co.uk; Waterloo Cres; r £97-164; wi-fi) Just a few steps from Dover's beach, this seafront hotel crams 81 rooms of varying dimensions into a gently curving 1870s edifice. The undulating corridors show the building's age, but there's nothing wonky about the rooms with their trendy ethnic fabrics, big-print wallpaper and contemporary artwork. Half the rooms have unrivalled sea views and 10 boast much-sought-after balconies.

East Lee Guest House B&B ££
(☎01304-210176; www.eastlee.co.uk; 108 Maison Dieu Rd; d £65-80; P wi-fi) This lovely terracotta-shingled town house impresses with its grand, elegantly decorated communal areas, scrupulously maintained rooms, energetic hosts and excellent, varied breakfasts.

★ **Wallett's Court** HOTEL £££
(☎01304-852424; www.wallettscourt.com; Westcliffe, St Margaret's-at-Cliffe; d from £135; P wi-fi pool) With its soothing spa, first-rate restaurant and perky service, this is one relaxing country house. Digs at this place, set in rolling farmland, range from spacious Jacobean guest rooms to beamed converted barns to a canvas wigwam (for a night of 'glamping'). Heading towards Deal, turn right off the A258 after almost 2 miles for Westcliffe.

Eating

La Salle Verte CAFE £
(14-15 Cannon St; snacks £2-6; ⊙9am-5pm Mon-Sat) A much-loved coffee or lunch halt with fascinating black-and-white images of old

Dover lining the walls, an intimate cellar and friendly staff. Fills up at lunch, even on winter Wednesdays.

★ Allotment BRITISH ££
(www.theallotmentdover.com; 9 High St; mains £8.50-16; ⏲8.30am-10pm Tue-Sat) Dover's best dining spot plates up local fish and meat from around Canterbury, seasoned with herbs from the tranquil garden out back, for breakfast, lunch and dinner. Cleanse your palette with a Kentish wine in a relaxed, understated setting as you admire the view of the Maison Dieu (13th-century pilgrims' hospital) directly opposite through the exquisite stained-glass frontage.

Information

Tourist Office (☎01304-201066; www.whitecliffscountry.org.uk; Market Sq; ⏲9.30am-5pm Mon-Sat year-round, 10am-3pm Sun Apr-Sep) Located in the Dover Museum.

Getting There & Away

BOAT

Ferries depart for France from the Eastern Docks below the castle. Fares vary according to season and advance purchase. Services seem to be in a constant state of flux with companies rising and falling as often as the Channel's swell.

DFDS (☎0871-5747235; www.dfdsseaways.co.uk) Services to Dunkirk (two hours, every two hours) and Calais (1½ hours, at least hourly).

P&O Ferries (☎0871-6642020; www.poferries.com) Runs to Calais (1½ hours, every 40 to 60 minutes).

BUS

Dover has bus connections to the following:

Canterbury (£5.10, 40 minutes, four hourly)

London Victoria (coach 007; £15.50, 2½ to 3½ hours, 12 daily)

Sandwich (£5.70, 50 minutes, hourly)

TRAIN

Dover is connected by train to Ramsgate (£9.60, 35 minutes, hourly) via Sandwich and by high-speed service to London St Pancras (£40, one hour, hourly).

Getting Around

It's quite a long walk between the Eastern Docks and the train station, especially with luggage. The special bus was discontinued a couple of years ago so you'll have to take a **taxi** (☎01304-201915; www.dovertaxis.com). It's also quite an uphill slog to the castle.

The White Cliffs of Dover

Immortalised in song, film and literature, the iconic white cliffs of Dover are embedded in the national consciousness, and are a big 'Welcome Home' sign to generations of travellers and soldiers. The cliffs rise to 100m high and extend on either side of Dover, but the best bit is the 6-mile stretch that starts about 2 miles east of town, properly known as the Langdon Cliffs. A trail runs along the cliffs as far as St Margaret's Bay, a popular spot among locals.

Sights & Activities

South Foreland Lighthouse HISTORIC BUILDING
(NT; adult/child £6/3; ⏲guided tours 11am-5.30pm Fri-Mon mid-Mar–Oct) From the Langdon Cliffs tourist office, follow the stony path east along the clifftops for a bracing 2-mile walk to the stout Victorian South Foreland Lighthouse. This was the first lighthouse to be powered by electricity and is the site of the first international radio transmissions, in 1898.

St Margaret's Bay VILLAGE
A mile further along the clifftop trail from the South Foreland Lighthouse, you will reach the delightful village of St Margaret's Bay, a gap in the chalk with a sun-trapping shingle beach. This is the closest point to France and many a cross-Channel swimmer has stepped into the briny here.

Dover Sea Safari BOATING
(☎01304-212880; www.doverseasafari.co.uk; Dover Sea Sports Centre, Esplanade; adult/child £35/20; ⏲year-round) This company offers exciting, fast-moving rigid inflatable tours of the White Cliffs plus seal-spotting trips to Pegwell Bay.

Dover White Cliffs Tours BOATING
(☎07971-301379; www.doverwhiteclifftours.com; adult/child £10/5; ⏲daily Jul & Aug, Sat & Sun Apr-Jun, Sep & Oct) This company runs 40-minute sightseeing trips at least three times daily from Dover's Western Docks.

Eating

Coastguard Pub PUB FOOD ££
(www.thecoastguard.co.uk; St Margaret's Bay; mains £10-16; ⏲10am-11pm Mon-Sat, to 10pm Sun; P 📶) This welcoming seafront pub at St Margaret's Bay is the closest tavern to France in England. Recently refurbished, the bar and dining room are a cosy spot on winter evenings, heated by a real fire. In

summer, retreat to the terrace with lovely beach and Channel views. The British pub-food menu features superb fish and chips.

Getting There & Away

At the end of the trail along the cliffs at St Margaret's Bay, bus 15 shuttles back to Dover or onto Deal every hour.

EAST SUSSEX

Home to rolling countryside, medieval villages and gorgeous coastline, this inspiring corner of England is besieged by weekending Londoners whenever the sun pops out. And it's not hard to see why as you explore the cobbled medieval streets of Rye; wander around historic Battle, where William the Conqueror first engaged the Saxons in 1066; and peer over the edge of the breathtaking Seven Sisters chalk cliffs and Beachy Head near the genteel seaside town of Eastbourne. Brighton, a highlight of any visit, offers some kicking nightlife, offbeat shopping and British seaside fun. Off the beaten track, you can stretch your legs on the South Downs Way, which traverses England's newest national park, the South Downs National Park.

Rye

POP 4770

Possibly the south of England's quaintest town, Rye is a little nugget of the past, a medieval settlement that looks like someone hit the pause button on time. Even the most hard-boiled cynic can't fail to be softened by Rye's cobbled lanes, mysterious passageways and crooked half-timbered Tudor buildings. Tales of resident smugglers, ghosts, writers and artists abound.

Rye was once one of the Cinque Ports, occupying a high promontory above the sea. Today the town rises 2 miles from the briny; sheep graze where the Channel's strong tides once swelled.

Sights

Mermaid Street AREA

Most start their exploration of Rye on famous Mermaid St, a short walk from the Rye Heritage Centre. It bristles with 15th-century timber-framed houses with quirky house names such as 'The House with Two Front Doors' and 'The House Opposite'.

Driving Tour
Dover to Rye

START DOVER EASTERN DOCKS
END RYE
LENGTH 35.5 MILES; AT LEAST FOUR HOURS (WITHOUT DUNGENESS PENINSULA DETOUR)

If you've just rolled off a cross-Channel ferry or have a day away from a cruise ship docked in Dover, instead of heading north to London, why not take this fascinating route along the white cliffs and across the flat marshes of the Kent–Sussex border to discover some of the southeast's hidden corners. Buses 100, 101 and 102 follow this route between Dover, Lydd and Hastings.

Starting at the exit to Dover's frantic **1 Eastern Docks**, where all cross-Channel ferries tie up, take the A20 along the seafront. After a few minutes, this dual carriageway begins to climb onto the famous white cliffs west of Dover. Your first stop is just outside town – take the turning for **2 Samphire Hoe** nature park, a ledge of parkland created between the white cliffs and the sea using 5 million cu metres of chalk excavated during the construction of the Channel tunnel. It's a fine spot for a picnic as you watch the 30 local species of butterfly flutter by.

Back on the A20, it's a mere 1¾ miles to the exit for the village of Capel-Le-Ferne (on the B2011). Well signposted at the end of the village is the **3 Battle of Britain Memorial**, a striking monument to the airmen who took part in the decisive struggle with the Luftwaffe in the skies above Kent and Sussex. An airman seated at the centre of a huge Spitfire propeller looks out serenely across the Channel and there's a new multimedia visitors centre and museum experience to enjoy. Returning to the B2011, a few gear changes will have you on the outskirts of **4 Folkestone**. Take a left at the first roundabout then the sixth right onto Dover Rd. This will take you into the centre of this formerly grand old resort, once a favourite stomping ground of royal *bon viveur* King Edward VII and a forgotten piece of England's seaside past. Take a stroll through the seafront Leas Coastal Park with its subtropical flora, then halt for fish and chips at the old fish market before ambling up through the Creative Quarter,

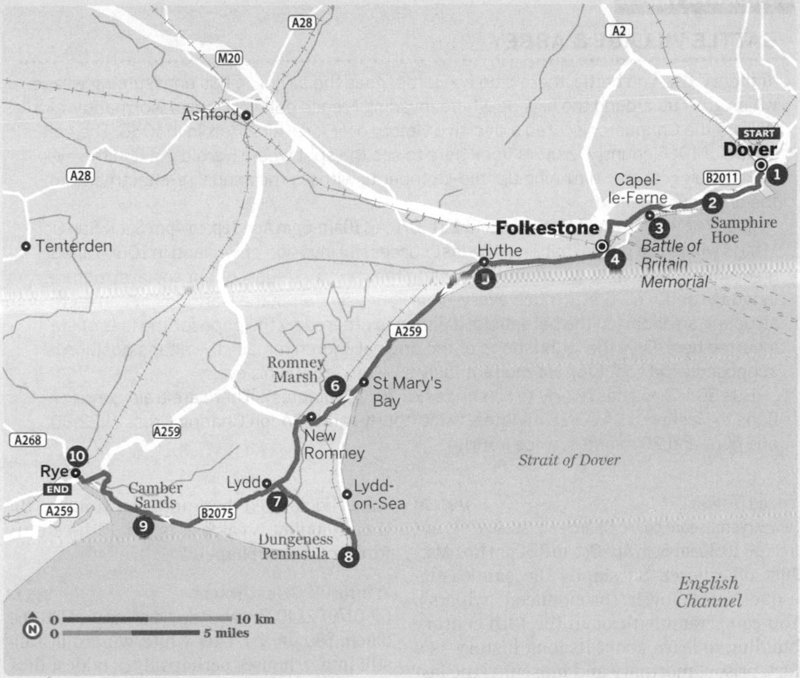

Folkestone's old town now occupied by artists studios and craft shops.

Heading out of Folkestone to the west on the A259 Sandgate Rd, you pass through Sandgate with its antique shops and shingle beach. From there it's another 2.5 miles to fascinating little **5 Hythe**. You could spend a full day in this original Cinque Port. Not only is it the eastern terminus of the fascinating narrow-gauge Romney, Hythe and Dymchurch Railway (RH&D Railway), but the Royal Military Canal also flows through the town and there's a quaint high street and beach to explore.

Heading ever west, a series of not-so-attractive shingle resorts such as Dymchurch and St Mary's are strung along the A259, cowering below their huge dykes, which keep the high tides from turning this stretch of the coast into sea bottom. You've now left the white cliffs behind and are entering the **6 Romney Marsh**, a flat, sparsely populated landscape of reed beds and sheep-dotted fields. There's a visitor centre (www.kentwildlifetrust.org.uk) between St Mary's Bay and New Romney (on the A259) for those with time.

Having negotiated New Romney, another of the original five Cinque Ports, just outside the town take the turning to the left onto the B2075, which leads to **7 Lydd**, a quaint former corporate member of the Cinque Ports. From here, detour along the lonely Dungeness Rd, which heads across the flats of the eerie **8 Dungeness Peninsula**, a low shingle spit dominated by a brooding nuclear power station. As well as boasting the southeast's largest seabird colony, it's also the western terminus of the RH&D Railway.

Back in Lydd, stick with the B2075 heading west for 6 miles until you reach Camber. Thought the entire south coast had just shingle beaches? Well, the main attraction here is **9 Camber Sands**, a wide expanse of golden grains and dunes, ideal for picnicking and strolling.

The B2075 winds through shingly, scrubby wetlands until it rejoins the A259 at the hamlet of East Guldeford, where you should turn left towards Rye. Along the roads around here you will see the main source of revenue from the Romney Marsh – thousands of sheep grazing on the verdant flats. The A259 barrels across the marshes, eventually depositing you in **10 Rye**, one of the southeast's quaintest towns.

WORTH A TRIP

BATTLE VILLAGE & ABBEY

'If there'd been no battle, there'd be no Battle,' goes the saying in this unassuming village, which grew up around the hillside where invading French duke William of Normandy, aka William the Conqueror, scored a decisive victory over local king Harold in 1066. The epicentre of 1066 country, visitors flock here to see the spot where Harold got it in the eye, with the biggest crowd turning up mid-October to witness the annual re-enactment on the original battlefield.

The **Battle Abbey** (EH; adult/child £10.10/6; ⏲10am-6pm Apr-Sep, to 4pm Sat & Sun Oct-Mar) is where the pivotal battle in the last successful invasion of England in 1066 raged: an event that had an unparalleled impact on the country's subsequent social structure, language and, well, pretty much everything. Four years after, the Normans began constructing an abbey on the battlefield, a penance ordered by the pope for the loss of life incurred here. Only the foundations of the original church remain; the altar's position is supposedly the spot King Harold famously took an arrow in his eye.

Bus 304/305 goes hourly to Hastings (£2.70, 28 minutes). There are train connections to Hastings (£4.20, 15 minutes, twice hourly) and London Charing Cross (£22.30, one hour and 20 minutes, twice hourly).

Ypres Tower MUSEUM
(www.ryemuseum.co.uk; Church Sq; adult/child £4/free; ⏲10.30am-5pm Apr-Oct, to 3.30pm Nov-Mar) Just off Church Sq stands the sandcastle-esque Ypres Tower (pronounced 'wipers'). You can scramble through the 13th-century building to learn about its long history as a fort, prison, mortuary and museum (the last two at overlapping times), and an annexe contains one of the last surviving Victorian women's prisons in the country. From here, there are widescreen views of Rye Bay, Dungeness nuclear power station and even France on very clear days.

Church of St Mary the Virgin CHURCH
(Church Sq; tower adult/child £3.50/1; ⏲9am-5.30pm Apr-Sep, to 4.30pm Nov-Mar) Rye's church is a hotchpotch of medieval and later styles. Its turret clock is the oldest in England (1561) still working with its original pendulum, which swings above your head as you enter. Climb the tower for pretty views of the town and surroundings, then inspect the small exhibition of interesting old objects found in and around Rye.

Sleeping

★ **Jeake's House** HOTEL ££
(☎01797-222828; www.jeakeshouse.com; Mermaid St; s/d from £75/95; P 📶) Situated on Mermaid St, this 17th-century town house once belonged to US poet Conrad Aitken. The 11 rooms are named after writers who stayed here. The decor was probably slightly less bold then, minus the beeswaxed antiques and lavish drapery. Take a pew in the snug book-lined bar and, continuing the theme, enjoy breakfast in an 18th-century former Quaker chapel.

Windmill Guesthouse B&B ££
(☎01797-224027; www.ryewindmill.co.uk; Mill Lane; d from £80; P 📶) This white windmill, sails still intact, houses perhaps Rye's oddest digs. The shape of the building means room sizes vary, as do standards. The two-storey much sought-after 'Windmill Suite' is located almost at the top, enjoying 360-degree views. Breakfast is served in the former granary and the octagonal guest lounge occupies the mill's base. Book ahead.

George in Rye HOTEL £££
(☎01797-222114; www.thegeorgeinrye.com; 98 High St; d from £135; @ 📶) This old coaching inn has managed to reinvent itself as a contemporary boutique hotel while staying true to its roots. Downstairs, an old-fashioned wood-panelled lounge is warmed by roaring log fires, while the guest rooms in the main building, created by the set designer from the film *Pride & Prejudice,* are chic and understated.

Mermaid Inn HOTEL £££
(☎01797-223065; www.mermaidinn.com; Mermaid St; s/d from £90/150; P) Few inns can claim to be as atmospheric as this ancient hostelry, dating from 1420. Each of the 31 rooms is different, but all are thick with dark beams and lit by leaded windows, and some are graced by secret passageways that now act as fire escapes. It also has one of Rye's best restaurants.

Eating

Simon the Pieman CAFE £

(3 Lion St; snacks £2.50-9; ⌚9.30am-4.45pm Mon-Fri, to 5.30pm Sat, 12.30-5.30pm Sun) Many local cream-tea cognoscenti assert this traditional tearoom, Rye's oldest, does the best scone-cream-jam combo this side of Romney Marsh. Further foes of tooth and waistline tempt from the shop's window.

Haydens CAFE £

(www.haydensinrye.co.uk; 108 High St; snacks/meals £4.50-9; ⌚10am-5pm) Long-time believers in organic and fair-trade produce, Haydens dishes up delicious omelettes, ploughman's lunches, salads and bagels in a light, breezy cafe. There's a wonderful elevated terrace at the back with great views over town and country. Also runs an excellent seven-room ecofriendly guesthouse upstairs.

Landgate Bistro BRITISH ££

(www.landgatebistro.co.uk; 5-6 Landgate; mains £14-20; ⌚noon-3.30pm Sat & Sun, 7-11pm Wed-Sat) Escape the medieval excesses of Rye's central eateries to this fresh bistro, slightly off the tourist trail near the impressive 14th-century Landgate. The focus here is on competently crafted dishes using local lamb and fish. The dining space is understated with tables gathered around an ancient fireplace.

Information

Rye Heritage Centre (☎01797-226696; www.ryeheritage.co.uk; Strand Quay; ⌚10am-5pm Apr-Oct, shorter hours Nov-Mar) See a town-model audiovisual history (£3.50) and, upstairs, a freaky collection of still-functional penny-in-the-slot novelty machines. Also runs themed walking tours of the town; see the website for details.

Getting There & Away

There are twice-hourly buses to Dover (bus 100; £6.40, two hours) and Hastings (bus 100/101; £5.60, 40 minutes).

Change in Ashford for services to London St Pancras (£31.70, 1½ hours, hourly).

Hastings

POP 90,300

Forever associated with the Norman invasion of 1066 (even though the crucial events took place 6 miles away), Hastings thrived as one of the Cinque Ports and, in its Victorian heyday, was one of the country's most fashionable resorts. After a period of steady decline, the town is enjoying a mini-renaissance, and these days is an intriguing mix of tacky resort, fishing port and arty New Age hang-out.

Sights

Stade AREA

(Rock-A-Nore Rd) The seafront area known as the Stade (below East Hill) is home to distinctive black clapboard structures known as Net Shops. These were built to store fishing gear back in the 17th century, but some now house fishmongers who sell off the catch of Europe's largest beach-launched fishing fleet, usually hauled up on the shingle behind. All these fishy goings-on keep the Stade very much a working place, with the combined pong of diesel and guts scenting the air.

Hastings Museum & Art Gallery MUSEUM

(www.hmag.org.uk; Johns Place, Bohemia Rd; ⌚10am-5pm Tue-Sat, noon-5pm Sun Apr-Sep, shorter hours Oct-Mar) FREE A short walk west of the train station, this marvellous little museum is housed in a red-brick mansion. Highlights inside include the intricately Moorish Durbar Hall and a section on John Logie Baird, who invented television while recuperating from an illness in Hastings between February 1923 and November 1924.

Jerwood Gallery GALLERY

(www.jerwoodgallery.org; Rock-A-Nore Rd; adult/child £9/3.50; ⌚11am-5pm Tue-Sun) Large, purpose-built exhibition venue at the end of the Stade used for temporary shows of contemporary British art as well as themed installations from the Jerwood collection. The building has a great cafe with sunny Channel views.

Hastings Castle RUINS

(www.discoverhastings.co.uk; Castle Hill Rd; adult/child £7/5; ⌚10am-4pm Easter-Sep) This fortress was built by William the Conquerer, and an exhibition in the grounds tells the story of the castle and the Battle of Hastings in 1066.

Sleeping & Eating

Swan House B&B ££

(☎01424-430014; www.swanhousehastings.co.uk; 1 Hill St; s/d from £90/120; @🛜) Inside its 15th-century timbered shell, this place blends contemporary and vintage chic to perfection. The four rooms feature organic toiletries, fresh flowers, hand-painted walls and huge beds. The guest lounge, where pale sofas, painted floorboards and striking modern sculpture rub shoulders with beams and a huge stone fireplace, is a stunner.

The Laindons B&B ££
(☎01424-437710; www.thelaindons.com; 23 High St; s/d from £105/120; 📶) Occupying a Georgian grade II–listed former coaching inn, this cosy B&B is just five minutes' amble from the seafront at the quieter end of High St. The five beautifully appointed rooms flood with sea-refracted light from the huge Georgian windows, illuminating the blend of breezy contemporary design and antique furnishings. Owner-cooked breakfasts are taken around a communal table.

Dragon Bar INTERNATIONAL ££
(www.dragon-bar.uk; 71 George St; mains £10-17.50, weekday lunch menu £7; ⏲noon-11pm; 📶) The younger end of the alternative old-town crowd is attracted to this atmospheric, hip bar-restaurant hang-out. It's full of dark walls, mismatched furniture and beaten leather sofas, and the eclectic menu features everything from Madras curry to Winchelsea lamb and pizzas.

Drinking & Nightlife

Hanushka Coffee House CAFE
(28 George St; ⏲9.30am-6pm) Hastings' best caffeine stop resembles a very well-stocked secondhand bookshop with every inch of wall space packed with browsable titles. The low-lit and tightly packed space in between provokes inter-table interaction, or you can seek sanctuary on the sofas and perches in the window.

Information

Tourist Office (☎01424-451111; www.visit1066country.com; Aquila House, Breeds Pl; ⏲9am-5pm Mon-Fri, 9.30am-5.30pm Sat, 10.30am-4pm Sun Apr-Sep, slightly shorter hours Oct-Mar)

Getting There & Away

BUS

Hastings has the following bus connections:

Eastbourne (bus 98/99; £4.60, 75 minutes, four hourly)

London Victoria (National Express; £14.40, three hours, daily)

Rye (buses 100/101; £5.60, 40 minutes, twice hourly)

TRAIN

Hastings has connections with Brighton (£13.30, one hour to 80 minutes, three hourly), via Eastbourne, and London Victoria (£17.80, two hours, hourly).

Getting Around

Hastings has two delightful old Victorian funiculars, the East Hill Cliff and West Hill Cliff Railways, useful if you need to get up onto the cliffs and don't fancy the walk. The **East Hill Cliff Railway** (Rock-A-Nore Rd; adult/child return £2.50/1.50; ⏲10am-5.30pm Apr-Sep, 11am-4pm Sat & Sun Oct-Mar) funicular ascends from the Stade to Hastings Country Park, while the **West Hill Cliff Railway** (George St; adult/child return £2.50/1.50; ⏲10am-5.30pm Mar-Sep, 11am-4pm Oct-Mar) funicular saves visitors' legs when climbing up to Hastings Castle. Otherwise the town can be easily tackled on foot.

Eastbourne

POP 99,400

Despite its official title as 'Britain's sunniest town', Eastbourne has been slow to throw off its unattractive image as death's waiting room by the chilly Channel, all snoozing octogenarians in deckchairs and fusty guesthouses populated by vitamin D–deprived bank-holidaying Scots. But while much of this is still to be found here, in the last decade or so an influx of students and the arrival of the southeast's largest Polish community have given the town a sprightlier feel.

Eastbourne's 3.5-mile sweeping, palm-tree-lined seafront is one of the UK's grandest. Add to this a fresh modern art gallery and the recently created South Downs National Park that nudges its western suburbs and Eastbourne certainly makes an enjoyable day trip from London or Brighton. It's also the start and end point for a hike along the 100-mile South Downs Way.

Sights

Towner Art Gallery GALLERY
(☎01323-434670; www.townereastbourne.org.uk; Devonshire Park, College Rd; ⏲10am-5pm Tue-Sun) FREE One of the southeast's most exciting exhibition spaces, this purpose-built structure has temporary shows of contemporary work on the ground and 2nd floors, while the 1st floor is given over to rotating themed shows created from the gallery's 5000-piece collection. Building tours include a peek inside the climate-controlled art store; see the website for times.

Eastbourne Pier LANDMARK
(⏲24hr) Mercifully saved by some clever firefighting when a huge blaze broke out in the amusement arcade at the land end of the structure on 30 July 2014, it took just over a year for this ramshackle piece of rusty Victoriana jutting into the Channel to come back from the dead. The amusement arcade wasn't rebuilt, a pleasant open decking space replacing the slot machines. This is part of a long-overdue clean-up of the town's most lovable sight.

Tours

Sussex Voyages BOATING
(☎01293-888780; www.sussexvoyages.co.uk; Lower Quayside, The Waterfront, Sovereign Harbour Marina; adult/child £25/14) Hour-long Beachy Head and Seven Sisters boat tours leaving from Sovereign Harbour (take hourly bus 51) on rigid-hulled inflatables. Reservations essential.

Sleeping & Eating

Albert & Victoria B&B ££
(☎01323-730948; www.albertandvictoria.com; 19 St Aubyns Rd; s/d from £35/70; 📶) Book ahead to stay at this delightful Victorian terraced house, whose fragrant rooms, canopied beds, crystal chandeliers and secluded walled garden for summer breakfasts are mere paces from the seafront promenade. The four rooms are named after four of Queen Victoria's offspring.

Big Sleep HOTEL ££
(☎01323-722676; www.thebigsleephotel.com; King Edward's Pde; s/d from £44/59; 📶) Hip, fresh and friendly, this seafront hotel has 50 gob-smacking rooms with big-print wallpaper, retro furnishings, and curtains that resemble sheep that might have been grazing on Beachy Head just a few hours prior. A trendy bar, big basement games room and Channel views make this Eastbourne's coolest kip.

Lamb Inn PUB FOOD ££
(www.thelambeastbourne.co.uk; 36 High St; mains £10-17; ⏲11am-11pm Sun-Thu, to midnight Fri & Sat) This ancient Eastbourne institution located less than a mile northwest of the train station in the under-visited Old Town has been plonking Sussex ales on the bar for eight centuries, and now also serves gourmet British pub grub. A holidaying Charles Dickens also left a few smudged napkins here when he stayed across the road. Buses 1, 1A and 12 stop nearby.

Belgian Cafe BELGIAN ££
(www.thebelgiancafe.co.uk; 11-23 Grand Pde; mains £10-18.50; ⏲11am-11pm) If you didn't know that Belgian beer can taste of fruit; the national dish is mussels and chips; and Tintin hails from its capital, Brussels, you will once you've experienced this popular cafe near the pier. Fifty types of mussel dishes and the same number of Belgian ales are available.

Information

Tourist Office (☎01323-415 415; www.visiteastbourne.com; Cornfield Rd; ⏲9am-5.30pm Mon-Fri, to 5pm Sat, 10am-1pm Sun May-Sep, closed Sun & shorter hours Oct-Apr)

Getting There & Away

There are buses to Brighton (bus 12; £4, 75 minutes, up to every 10 minutes) and Hastings (bus 98/99; £4.50, one hour and 10 minutes, three hourly). Twice-hourly trains service Brighton (£10.60, 30 to 40 minutes) and London Victoria (£17.80, 1½ hours).

South Downs National Park

The South Downs National Park, more than 600 sq miles of rolling chalk downs, stretches west from Eastbourne for about 100 miles. The South Downs Way extends its entire length.

Sights

Beachy Head LANDMARK
(www.beachyhead.org.uk) The famous cliffs of Beachy Head are the highest point of the chalky rock faces that slice across the rugged coastline at the southern end of the South Downs. It's off the B2103, from the A259 between Eastbourne and Newhaven. From here the stunning **Seven Sisters Cliffs** undulate their way west. A clifftop path (a branch of the South Downs Way) rides the waves of chalk as far as picturesque Cuckmere Haven.

Pevensey Castle RUINS
(EH; Castle Rd, Pevensey; adult/child £5.80/3.40; ⏲10am-6pm Apr-Sep) The ruins of William the Conqueror's first stronghold sit 5 miles east of Eastbourne, just off the A259. Regular train services between London Victoria and Hastings via Eastbourne stop at

Westham, half a mile from Pevensey. Picturesquely dissolving into its own moat, the castle marks the point where William the Conqueror landed in 1066, just two weeks before the Battle of Hastings.

Sleeping

★Belle Tout Lighthouse B&B £££
(☎01323 423-185; www.belletout.co.uk; South Downs Way, Beachy Head, Eastbourne; d from £165) Perched precariously close to the edge of the white cliffs, this decommissioned lighthouse is a truly wonderful place to stay. The building has had an incredible past, almost destroyed in WWII, used by the BBC to film *The Life and Loves of a She-Devil* and famously moved back from the cliff edge in 1999 before becoming a quirky guesthouse.

Lewes

POP 17,300

Strung out along an undulating High St flanked by elegant Georgian buildings, a part-ruined castle and a traditional brewery, Lewes (pronounced 'Lewis') is a charmingly affluent hillside town with a turbulent past and fiery traditions. Off the main drag, however, there's a more intimate atmosphere as you descend into twisting narrow streets called twittens – the remainder of the town's original medieval street plan.

One of Lewes' claims to fame is that it straddles the 0 degrees line of longitude. An inconspicuous plaque on Western Rd marks the meridian, though modern measuring methods have actually placed the line around 100m to the east.

Sights & Activities

Lewes Castle & Barbican House Museum CASTLE
(www.sussexpast.co.uk; 169 High St; adult/child £7.40/4; ⏲10am-5.30pm Tue-Sat, 11am-5.30pm Sun & Mon; P) Now little more than a set of ruins, this castle was built shortly after the 1066 Norman invasion. It never saw warfare, but there were riotous celebrations following the navy's victory over the Spanish Armada in 1588, when happy citizens blew great chunks out of the castle's walls. They left enough standing for it to remain an impressive sight though, and its windy keep, visible for miles around, affords panoramic views across the town and beyond.

The attached Barbican House Museum has a good collection of Lewesiana, but the star attraction is the incredibly accurate town model, glued together by an army of volunteers in the mid-1980s and showing how the town looked a century earlier. Viewing is accompanied by a 12-minute film relating the homo-Sussexicus' historical advancement from cavemen to Victorians.

Harveys Brewery TOURS
(☎01273-480217; www.harveys.org.uk; Bridge Wharf; per person £3; ⏲three evenings a week Jun, Jul & Sep-Nov) Sussex's Harveys Brewery perfumes Lewes town centre with a hop-laden scent. Book several months in advance for tours.

Festivals & Events

★Lewes Bonfire Celebrations FIREWORKS
(www.lewesbonfirecelebrations.com; ⏲5 Nov) Lewes holds what it claims is the biggest Bonfire Night bash in the world with tens of thousands of people descending on the town to watch a carnival, fireworks display and effigies of villains of the day going up in flames.

Sleeping & Eating

Castle Banks Cottage B&B ££
(☎01273-476291; www.castlebankscottage.co.uk; 4 Castle Banks; s/d £42.50/85; 📶) Tucked away in a quiet lane near the castle, this tiny guesthouse has just two rooms. The easy-going travel-writer proprietor is a mine of information about the area's local history. Breakfast is served in the secluded garden in summer.

Shelleys HOTEL £££
(☎01273-472361; www.the-shelleys.co.uk; 135-136 High St; r from £130; 📶) Full of old-fashioned charm, this 16th-century manor house was once home to the earl of Dorset and was owned by the Shelley family (of Percy Bysshe fame). It has cosy, country rooms and an above standard restaurant overlooking a lovely walled garden.

Bill's CAFE £
(www.bills-website.co.uk; 56 Cliffe High St; mains & snacks £3.50-12; ⏲8am-11pm) Part grocers, part delicatessen, part rustic-styled cafe, this insanely popular place envelopes customers in its colours and smells then dishes up melt-in-the-mouth tartlets, gourmet pizzas, salads, desserts and other artisanal snacks. Get here early at meal times, and even in-between times, as it's normally chock-a-block.

Real Eating Company BRITISH ££
(18 Cliffe High St; mains £10-19; ⏲8.30am-9pm Mon-Sat, 10am-5pm Sun) This large, airy cafe-brasserie stretches back to a lovely outside terrace and serves kick-starting breakfasts, gourmet fish and chips, and substantial British meat-and-two-veg combos, all made with Sussex ingredients as much as possible.

Shopping

Fifteenth Century Bookshop BOOKS
(www.oldenyoungbooks.co.uk; 99 High St; ⏲10am-5.30pm Mon-Sat) Rummage through antiquarian treasures and new editions at the fabulous, half-timbered bookshop housed in a former candle factory.

Information

Tourist Office (☎01273-483448; www.lewes.gov.uk; 187 High Street; ⏲9.30am-4.30pm Mon-Fri, to 4pm Sat, 10am-2pm Sun Apr-Sep, closed Sunday & shorter hours Sat Oct-Mar)

Getting There & Away

Lewes' only useful bus connection goes to Brighton (£3.50, 30 minutes, four hourly).

Lewes has the following rail connections:

Brighton (£4.30, 15 minutes, four hourly)
Eastbourne (£7.70, 20 minutes, three hourly)
London Victoria (£17.80, one hour to 1½ hours, four hourly)

Brighton & Hove

POP 275,800

Raves on the beach, Graham Greene novels, mods and rockers in bank-holiday fisticuffs, naughty weekends for Mr and Mrs Smith, the UK's biggest gay scene and the Channel's best clubbing – this coastal city evokes many images for the British. But one thing is certain: with its bohemian, hedonistic vibe, Brighton is where England's seaside experience goes from cold to cool.

Brighton is without doubt Britain's most colourful and outrageous city. Here burlesque meets contemporary design; grotty hostels share thin walls with kinky boutique hotels; microbrewed ales share bar space with 'sex on the beach'; and stags watch drag. The city returned the UK's first Green Party MP, Valentine's Day is celebrated with unusual gusto, and according to the 2001 census, it has the UK's highest Jedi population.

The highlight for the sightseeing visitor is the Royal Pavilion, a 19th-century party palace built by the Prince Regent, who kicked off Brighton's love of the outlandish.

LOCAL KNOWLEDGE

GLYNDEBOURNE THEATRE

In 1934, science teacher John Christie and his opera-singer wife Audrey Mildmay decided to build a 1200-seat opera house in the middle of nowhere. It seemed a magnificent folly at the time, but now **Glyndebourne** (☎01273-812321; www.glyndebourne.com; Glyndebourne) is one of England's best venues for the lyric arts, from late May to the end of August. Tickets can be like gold dust, so book well ahead. Glyndebourne is 4 miles east of Lewes off the B2192.

Sights

★**Royal Pavilion** PALACE
(☎03000-290901; http://brightonmuseums.org.uk/royalpavilion; Royal Pavilion Gardens; adult/child £12.30/6.90; ⏲9.30am-5.45pm Apr-Sep, 10am-5.15pm Oct-Mar) The city's must-see attraction is the Royal Pavilion, the glittering party pad and palace of Prince George, later Prince Regent and then King George IV. It's one of the most opulent buildings in England, and certainly the finest example of early-19th-century chinoiserie anywhere in Europe. It's an apt symbol of Brighton's reputation for decadence. An unimpressed Queen Victoria called the Royal Pavilion 'a strange, odd Chinese place', but for visitors to Brighton it's an unmissable chunk of Sussex history.

The entire palace is an eye-popping spectacle, but some interiors stand out even amid the riot of decoration. The dragon-themed banqueting hall must be the most incredible in all of England. More dragons and snakes writhe in the music room, with its ceiling of 26,000 gold scales, and the then-state-of-the-art kitchen must have wowed Georgians with its automatic spits and hot tables. Prince Albert carted away all of the furniture, some of which has been loaned back by the present queen.

Brighton Museum & Art Gallery MUSEUM, GALLERY
(www.brighton-hove-museums.org.uk; Royal Pavilion Gardens; adult/child £5.20/3; ⏲10am-5pm Tue-Sun) Set in the Royal Pavilion's renovated stable block, this museum and art gallery has a glittering collection of 20th-century art and design, including a crimson

Brighton & Hove

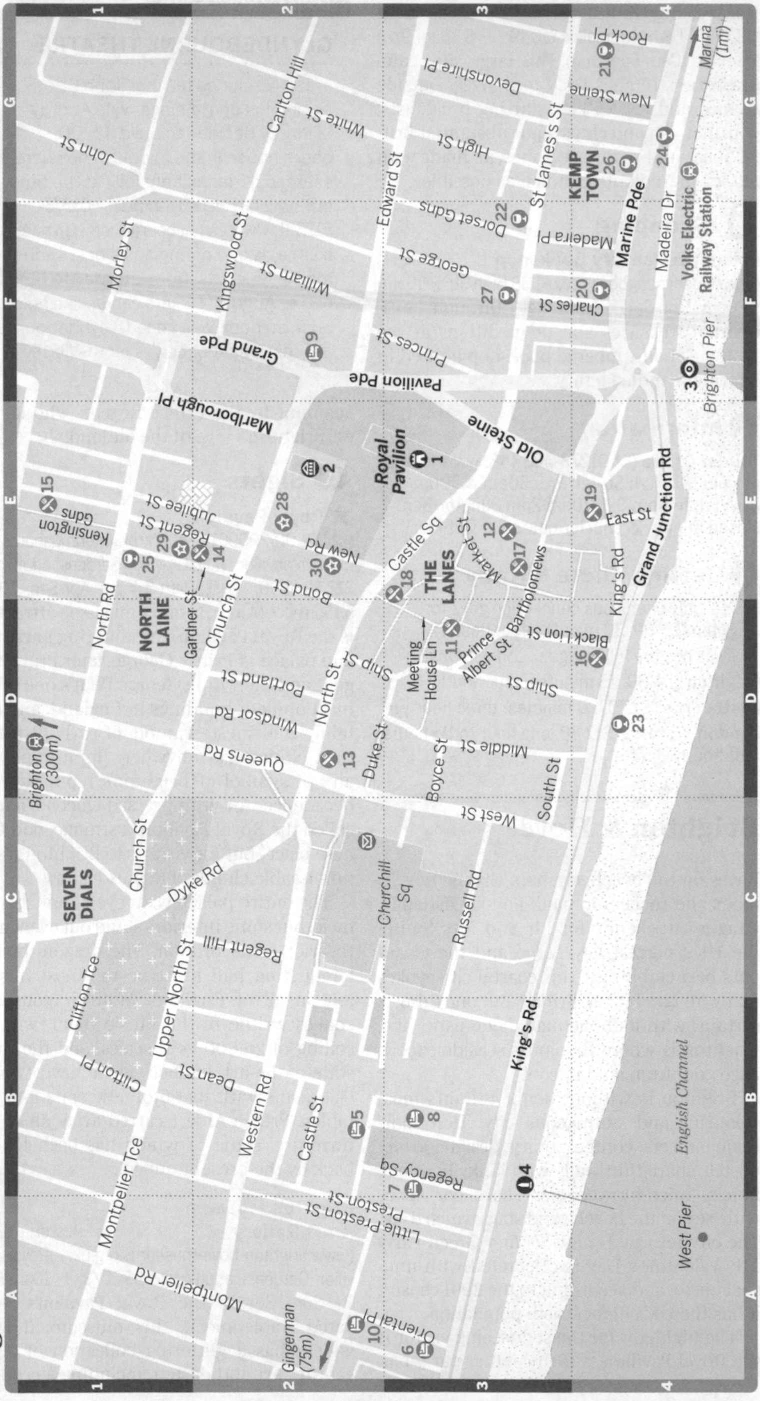

Brighton & Hove

Top Sights

1 Royal Pavilion ... E3

Sights

2 Brighton Museum & Art Gallery ... E2
3 Brighton Pier ... F4
4 i360 Tower ... B3

Sleeping

5 Artist Residence ... B2
6 Baggies Backpackers ... A3
7 Hotel Pelirocco ... B3
8 Hotel Una ... B3
9 Kipps Brighton ... F2
10 Neo Hotel ... A2

Eating

11 Choccywoccydoodah ... D3
12 English's of Brighton ... E3
13 Foodilic ... D2
14 Infinity Foods Kitchen ... E2
15 Iydea ... E1
16 JB's American Diner ... D4
17 Plateau ... E3
18 Riddle & Finns ... E3
19 Terre à Terre ... E4

Drinking & Nightlife

20 A Bar ... F4
21 Brighton Rocks ... G4
22 Bulldog ... F3
23 Coalition ... D4
24 Concorde 2 ... G4
25 Dorset ... E1
26 Legends Club ... G4
Patterns ... (see 20)
27 Queen's Arms ... F3

Entertainment

28 Brighton Dome ... E2
29 Komedia Theatre ... E1
30 Theatre Royal ... E2

Salvador Dalí sofa modelled on Mae West's lips. There's also an enthralling gallery of world art, an impressive collection of Egyptian artefacts, and an 'Images of Brighton' multimedia exhibit containing a series of oral histories and a model of the defunct West Pier.

i360 Tower TOWER

(☎ 03337-720 360; www.britishairwaysi360.com; Lower King's Rd; adult/child £15/7.50; ⏰10am-7.30pm Sun-Thu, to 9.30pm Fri & Sat) Brighton's newest attraction opened in 2016, at the point the now defunct West Pier used to make landfall. The world's most slender tower is a brutal, 162m-tall column of reinforced steel and concrete rising rudely in space-age spectacle from the seafront, a huge, impaled, glass doughnut taking 'passengers' 138m above the city for some gob-smacking vistas of the Sussex coast. The idea is that profits from the i360, a 21st-century 'vertical pier', will one day be used to rebuild the West Pier.

Brighton Pier LANDMARK

(www.brightonpier.co.uk; Madeira Dr) This grand century-old pier is the place to experience Brighton's tackier side. There are plenty of stomach-churning fairground rides and dingy amusement arcades to keep you entertained, and candy floss and Brighton rock to chomp on while you're doing so. Just west are the sad remains of the **West Pier** (www.westpier.co.uk), a skeletal iron hulk that attracts flocks of starlings at sunset.

Festivals & Events

Brighton Festival PERFORMING ARTS

(☎ 01273-709709; www.brightonfestival.org; ⏰May) After Edinburgh, this is the UK's biggest arts festival. It draws star performers from around the globe for three weeks by the sea.

Brighton Pride LGBT

(www.brighton-pride.org; ⏰early Aug) One of the UK's biggest gay bashes, with a rainbow-hued parade and concerts in Preston Park.

Sleeping

Kipps Brighton HOSTEL £

(☎ 01273-604182; www.kipps-brighton.com; 76 Grand Pde; dm £14-35, d £42-90; @ 📶) The owners of Canterbury's award-winning hostel have created equally commendable budget digs here in Brighton. There's a real cafe vibe around reception, and facilities include a communal kitchen. Free movie, pizza and pub nights successfully separate guests from their wi-fi-enabled devices.

Baggies Backpackers HOSTEL £

(☎ 01273-733740; www.baggiesbackpackers.com; 33 Oriental Pl; dm/d £16/40; 📶) With a warm, familial atmosphere, worn-in charm, attentive service and clean, snug dorms, this long-established hostel is a Brighton institution.There's a cosy basement music and chill-out room, and a TV lounge piled high with video cassettes that have somehow survived the digital revolution. The hostel has sister establishments in Bath and Bournemouth.

★No 27 Brighton B&B ££

(☎01273-694951; www.brighton-bed-and-breakfast.co.uk; 27 Upper Rock Gardens; s £61.50-72.50, d £84-110) Brighton's top B&B has five sumptuous rooms, perfectly done out with antique flourish. All the fabrics, furniture and decoration has been painstakingly selected to fit an understated theme, the overarching topic being people related to King George IV. Some rooms have sea views, but the superb decor may have you looking around more than out. Breakfast (£7.50) is served on crisp linen and fine English china.

Hotel Pelirocco HOTEL ££

(☎01273-327055; www.hotelpelirocco.co.uk; 10 Regency Sq; s £65-125, d £95-125; wi-fi) One of Brighton's sexiest and nuttiest places to stay, the Pelirocco has become the ultimate venue for a flirty rock-and-roll weekend. Flamboyant rooms, some designed by artists, include the 'Dollywould' room paying homage to Dolly Parton, the 'Modrophenia' room on a Mod and pop art theme, and the 'Pretty Vacant' double, a shrine to the Sex Pistols.

The room everyone wants, or wishes they could have, is the 'Kraken's lair' suite with 3m circular bed, mirrored ceiling and pole-dancing area.

Snooze HOTEL ££

(☎01273-605797; www.snoozebrighton.com; 25 St George's Tce; s/d from £75/95; wi-fi) The retro styling at this eccentric Kemptown pad features everything from vintage posters and bright '60s and '70s wallpaper to Bollywood film posters, floral sinks and mad clashes of colour. It's more than just a gimmick – the rooms are comfortable and spotless, and there are great meat-free breakfasts. You'll find it just off St James' St, about 500m east of New Steine.

Blanch House BOUTIQUE HOTEL ££

(☎01273-603504; www.blanchhouse.co.uk; 17 Atlingworth St; r from £109; @ wi-fi) Themed rooms are the name of the game at this boutique hotel, but there's nothing tacky about them – swish art-deco styling rules in the Legacia Room, while the Snowstorm is a frosty vision in white and tinkling ice. The magnificently stylish fine-dining restaurant is all white leather banquettes and space-age swivel chairs and there's a fine cocktail bar. From New Steine, walk for 150m east along St James' St then turn right into Atlingworth St.

Neo Hotel BOUTIQUE HOTEL ££

(☎01273-711104; www.neohotel.com; 19 Oriental Pl; r £90-200; wi-fi) You won't be surprised to learn the owner of this gorgeous hotel is an interior stylist. The nine rooms could have dropped straight from the pages of a design magazine, each finished in rich colours and tactile fabrics, with bold floral and Asian motifs, and black-tiled bathrooms. Wonderful breakfasts include homemade smoothies and pancakes.

★Hotel Una BOUTIQUE HOTEL £££

(☎01273-820464; www.hotel-una.co.uk; 55-56 Regency Sq; s £55-75, d £115-200, all incl breakfast; ❄ wi-fi) All of the 19 generous rooms here wow guests with their bold-patterned fabrics, supersized leather sofas, in-room freestanding baths and vegan, veggie or carnivorous breakfast in bed. Some, such as the two-level suite with its own mini-cinema, and the under-pavement chambers with their own spa and Jacuzzi, are truly show-stopping and not as expensive as you might expect.

All this plus a cool cocktail bar and lots of time-warp period features make the Una our numero uno.

★Artist Residence BOUTIQUE HOTEL £££

(☎01273-324 302; www.artistresidencebrighton.co.uk; 33 Regency Sq; d £129-260; wi-fi) Eclectic doesn't quite describe the rooms at this wonderful 23-room town-house hotel, set amid the splendour of Regency Sq. As befits the name, every bedroom is a work of funky art with bold wall murals, bespoke and vintage furniture, rough wood cladding and in-room roll-top baths. The Set Restaurant downstairs already has a glowing reputation. Book direct and breakfast is free.

Eating

★Iydea VEGETARIAN £

(www.iydea.co.uk; 17 Kensington Gardens; mains £6-8; ⏲9.30am-5.30pm; wi-fi ✎) Even by Brighton's lofty standards, the food at this multi-award-winning vegetarian cafe is a treat. The daily-changing choices of curries, lasagnes, felafel, enchiladas and quiches are full of flavour and can be washed down with a selection of vegan wines, organic ales and homemade lemonades. If you're on the hop, you can get any dish to takeaway in environmentally-friendly packaging.

Choccywoccydoodah CAFE £

(www.choccywoccydoodah.com; 3 Meeting House Lane; cakes & snacks £2-5; ⏲10am-6pm Mon-Sat, 11am-5pm Sun) Even if you're not hungry or thirsty, this incredible chocolate emporium, painted blood red inside and out, is a must-see. The downstairs is packed with outrageous Belgian chocolate creations, fake rococo mirrors, sprays of artificial flowers and tassled lampshades. Head upstairs to the small cafe where every single item on sale contains chocolate. Madly popular so be prepared to queue.

Foodilic BUFFET £

(www.foodilic.com; 60 North St; takeaway box £5, buffet £7; ⏲8am-9.30pm Mon-Sat, to 6pm Sun) It's as good for breakfast (£4.50) as for a late dinner, but it's the eat-till-you-burst buffet of scrumptious healthy fare that packs out this funky place all day long. Slightly a victim of its own success, it could do with bigger premises – you'll queue at lunchtime and inside things get cramped.

Infinity Foods Kitchen VEGETARIAN £

(www.infinityfoodskitchen.co.uk; 50 Gardner St; mains £3.50-8; ⏲9am-5pm Mon-Sat, 10am-4pm Sun; 📶📝) The sister establishment of Infinity Foods wholefoods shop (health food co-operative and Brighton institution) serves a wide variety of vegetarian and organic food, with many vegan and wheat- or gluten-free options including tofu burgers, mezze platters and veggie sausage sandwiches. There's seating upstairs with views of the passing hipster mob.

★Terre à Terre VEGETARIAN ££

(☎01273-729051; www.terreaterre.co.uk; 71 East St; mains £15; ⏲noon-10.30pm Mon-Fri, 10am-11pm Sat, 10am-10pm Sun; 📝) Even staunch meat eaters will rave about this legendary vegetarian restaurant. A sublime dining experience, from the vibrant modern space to the menus and inventive dishes stuffed with excitingly zingy ingredients. There's also plenty for vegans. Desserts are on the steep side.

Gingerman MODERN EUROPEAN ££

(☎01273-326688; www.gingermanrestaurants.com; 21a Norfolk Sq; 2-/3-course menu £17/20; ⏲12.30-2pm & 7-10pm Tue-Sun) Hastings seafood, Sussex beef, Romney Marsh lamb, local sparkling wines and countless other seasonal, local and British treats go into the adroitly flash-fried and slow-cooked dishes served at this snug 32-cover eatery. Reservations are advised. Norfolk Sq is a short walk west along Western Rd from the Churchill Square shopping centre.

Riddle & Finns SEAFOOD ££

(www.riddleandfinns.co.uk; 12 Meeting House Lane; mains £14-36; ⏲noon-late Sun-Fri, 11.30am-11pm Sat) Regarded as the town's most refined seafood spot, R&F is light on gimmicky interiors (think white butcher's shop tiles, marble tables and candles) but heavy on taste. With the kitchen open to the street outside, chefs put on a public cooking class with every dish as they prepare your smoked haddock in champagne sauce or wild sea bass.

English's of Brighton SEAFOOD ££

(☎01273-327980; www.englishs.co.uk; 29-31 East St; mains £15-30; ⏲noon-10pm) A 70-year-old institution and celebrity haunt, this local seafood paradise dishes up everything from Essex oysters to locally caught lobster and Dover sole. It's converted from fishers' cottages, with shades of the elegant Edwardian era inside and alfresco dining on the pedestrian square outside.

Plateau INTERNATIONAL ££

(☎01273-733085; www.plateaubrighton.co.uk; 1 Bartholowmews; tapas £6-16, mains around £30; ⏲noon-4pm & 6-10pm) This relative newcomer to the Brighton feeding scene serves up superb tapas such as Sussex chorizo, roast bone marrow and mozzarella with peas, mint and lemon as well as pricey mains. The shabby-retro interior includes scuffed floorboards and stained glass that belonged to a previous incarnation of the building. At night the place morphs into a wine and cocktail bar.

JB's American Diner FAST FOOD ££

(http://jbsdiner.co.uk; 31 King's Rd; burgers £7-10, mains £6.50-15; ⏲10am-10pm Mon-Sat, 9am-10pm Sun) The waft of hot dogs as you push open the door, the shiny red-leather booths, the stars and stripes draped across the wall, the 1950s soundtrack twanging in the background and the colossal portions of burgers, fries and milkshakes – in short, this is a hefty slab of authentic Americana teleported to the Brighton seafront.

🍷 Drinking & Nightlife

Concorde 2 CLUB

(www.concorde2.co.uk; Madeira Dr) Brighton's best-known and best-loved club is a disarmingly unpretentious den, where DJ Fatboy Slim pioneered the Big Beat Boutique and still occasionally graces the decks. Each month there's a huge variety of club nights, live bands and concerts by international names.

Coalition BAR

(www.coalitionbrighton.com; 171-181 Kings Rd Arches; ⏲10am-5am Mon-Fri, to 7am Sat) On a

GAY & LESBIAN BRIGHTON

Brighton has the most vibrant gay community in the country outside London and Kemptown (aka Camptown). On and off St James's St is where it's all at. The old Brunswick Town area of Hove is a quieter alternative to the traditionally cruisy (and sometimes seedy) scene in Kemptown. For up-to-date information on the gay scene in Brighton, check out www.gay.brighton.co.uk and www.realbrighton.com, or pick up the free monthly magazine *Gscene* (www.gscene.com) from gay venues.

Legends Club (www.legendsbrighton.com; 31-34 Marine Pde; ⏲ bar 11am-5am, club 10pm-5am Wed & Fri-Sun) Located beneath the Legends Hotel this is arguably the best gay bar and club in town.

A Bar (www.amsterdam.uk.com; 11-12 Marine Pde; ⏲ noon-2am; 📶) Extremely hip bar and sauna in the Amsterdam hotel; its sun terrace is a particular hit.

Brighton Rocks (www.brightonrocksbar.co.uk; 6 Rock Pl; ⏲ 4-11pm Mon-Thu, to 1am Sat, noon-11pm Sun; 📶) Incongruously located in an alley of garages and used-car lots, this cocktail bar is firmly established on the Kemptown gay scene, but welcomes all-comers with Sussex Martinis, well-executed plates of food and theme parties.

Queen's Arms (www.queensarmsbrighton.com; 7 George St; ⏲ 3pm-late) And they ain't talking Victoria or Elizabeth! Plenty of camp cabaret and karaoke at this pub.

Bulldog (www.bulldogbrighton.com; 31 St James's St; ⏲ 11am-late) Longest-running gay bar in Brighton; mostly frequented by men.

summer's day, there's nowhere finer to sit and watch the world go by than at this popular beach bar, diner and club. All sorts of events happen here, from comedy to live music and club nights.

Black Dove PUB
(www.blackdovebrighton.com; 74 St James's St; ⏲ 4pm-late) Eclectic hangout with shabby-chic furnishings, huge antique ceiling fans, a bar stocked with unusual tipples and a quirky basement snug. Live acoustic music and local DJs provide the soundtrack for evening quaffing that spills out onto the pavements when the mercury is high.

Patterns CLUB
(www.patternsbrighton.com; 10 Marine Pde; ⏲ Wed-Sat, hours vary) Some of the city's top club nights are held at this ear-numbing venue. The music is top priority here, attracting a young, up-for-it crowd.

Dorset PUB
(www.thedorset.co.uk; 28 North Rd; ⏲ 9am-late; 📶) In fine weather this laid-back Brighton institution throws open its doors and windows, and tables spill out onto the pavement. You'll be just as welcome for a morning coffee as for an evening pint here, and should you not leave between the two, there's a decent gastropub menu.

☆ Entertainment

Brighton Dome THEATRE
(☎ 01273-709709; www.brightondome.org; Church St) Once the stables for King George IV's horses, this art-deco complex houses three theatre venues within the Royal Pavilion estate. ABBA famously won the 1974 Eurovision Song Contest here.

Theatre Royal THEATRE
(☎ 0844 871 7650; New Rd) Built by decree of the Prince of Wales in 1806, this grand venue hosts musicals, plays and operas.

Komedia Theatre COMEDY
(☎ 0845 293 8480; www.komedia.co.uk; 44-47 Gardner St) A stylish comedy, theatre and cabaret venue attracting the best stand-up acts from the English-speaking world.

🛍 Shopping

In the market for a pair of vegan shoes, a gauche portrait of a Lego man or a letter opener in the shape of something naughty? Whatever item you yearn for, old or new, you'll probably find it in Brighton. The tightly packed **Lanes** is the most popular shopping district, its every twist and turn jam-packed with jewellers and gift shops, coffee shops and boutiques selling everything from antique firearms to hard-to-find vinyls.

There's another, less-claustrophobic shopping district in **North Laine**, a series of partially pedestrian thoroughfares north of the Lanes, including Bond, Gardner, Kensington and Sydney Sts, lined with retro-cool boutiques and bohemian cafes. Mainstream chains gather within the Churchill Square shopping centre and along Western Rd.

Information

Incredibly, Brighton closed its busy tourist office in 2013, replacing it with 15 information points across the city, mostly racks of brochures in hotels, shops and museums. Contact **Visit Brighton** (01273-290337; www.visitbrighton.com) for information.

Jubilee Library (Jubilee St; 10am-7pm Mon, Tue & Thu, to 5pm Wed, Fri & Sat, 11am-5pm Sun) Bring ID to sign up for free internet sessions.

Post Office (2-3 Churchill Sq; 9am-5.30pm Mon-Sat, 11am-3pm Sun) Located within WH Smiths.

Getting There & Away

BUS

Standard bus connections:

Arundel (bus 700; two hours, twice hourly)

Chichester (bus 700; three hours, twice hourly)

Eastbourne (bus 12; 70 minutes, up to every 10 minutes)

London Victoria (National Express; from £10, 2½ hours, hourly)

TRAIN

London-bound services pass through Gatwick Airport (£9.80, 25 to 40 minutes, up to five hourly).

Chichester (£13, 50 minutes, half-hourly)

Eastbourne (£10.60, 30 to 40 minutes, half-hourly)

Hastings (£13.30, one hour 20 minutes, half-hourly)

London St Pancras (£17.20, 1¼ hours, half-hourly)

London Victoria (£17.80, one hour, three-hourly)

Portsmouth (£15.30, 1½ hours, hourly)

Getting Around

Day bus tickets (£5) are available from the drivers of all Brighton and Hove buses. Alternatively, a £3.60 PlusBus ticket on top of your rail fare gives unlimited bus travel for the day.

The city operates a pricey pay-and-display parking scheme. In the town centre, it costs between £1 and £3.60 per hour for a maximum stay of two hours. Alternatively, there's a Park & Ride 2.5 miles northwest of the centre at Withdean, from where bus 27 zips into town.

Cab companies include **Brighton Streamline Taxis** (01273-202020) and **City Cabs** (01273-205205), and there's a taxi rank at the junction of East and Market Sts.

WEST SUSSEX

West Sussex offers a welcome respite from fast-paced adventures. The serene hills and valleys of the South Downs ripple across the county, fringed by sheltered coastline. Beautiful Arundel and cultured Chichester make good bases from which to explore the county's winding country lanes and remarkable Roman ruins.

Arundel

POP 3500

Arguably the prettiest town in West Sussex, Arundel is clustered around a vast fairy-tale castle, and its hillside streets overflow with antique emporiums, teashops and a host of eateries. While much of the town appears medieval – the whimsical castle has been home to the Dukes of Norfolk for centuries – most of it dates back to Victorian times.

Sights

Arundel Castle CASTLE

(www.arundelcastle.org; adult/child £18/9; 10am-5pm Tue-Sun Easter-Oct) Arundel Castle was first built in the 11th century but all that's left of the early structure are the modest remains of the keep. It was ransacked during the English Civil War, and most of what you see today is the result of reconstruction by the eighth, 11th and 15th dukes of Norfolk between 1718 and 1900. The current duke still lives in part of the castle, whose highlights include the atmospheric keep, the massive Great Hall and the library.

Arundel Cathedral CATHEDRAL

(www.arundelcathedral.org; London Rd; 9am-6pm Apr-Oct, to dusk Nov-Mar) FREE Arundel's ostentatious 19th-century Catholic cathedral is the other dominating feature of the town's impressive skyline. Commissioned by the 15th duke of Norfolk in 1868, the impressive structure was designed by Joseph Aloysius Hansom (inventor of the Hansom cab) in the French Gothic style, but shows much

Victorian economy and restraint. Although small for a cathedral – it holds just 500 worshippers – Hansom's clever layout makes the building seem a lot bigger.

Sleeping & Eating

Arundel House B&B ££
(01903-882136; www.arundelhouseonline.com; 11 High St; d/ste from £90/125;) The contemporary chambers at this lovely 'restaurant with rooms' may be slightly low-ceilinged, but they're clean-cut and very comfortable, with showers big enough for two. The restaurant downstairs serves some of the best food in Arundel, which, happily, extends to breakfast.

Arden Guest House B&B ££
(01903-884184; www.ardenguesthouse.net; 4 Queens Lane; d £99, without bathroom £89; P) For the classic British B&B experience, head to this seven-room guesthouse just over the river from the historical centre. Rooms are kept fresh and tick all the boxes; the hosts are amiable; and the breakfasts are cooked. No pets or children under 14 and only 10% off if you're travelling solo.

Bay Tree MODERN EUROPEAN ££
(www.thebaytreearundel.com; 21 Tarrant St; mains £11-18; 11.30am-3pm & 6.30pm-late Mon-Fri, 10.30am-4.30pm & 6.30pm-late Sat & Sun) The ideal lunch stop after a spot of antique hunting on Tarrant St, the Bay Tree serves up expertly prepared dishes in a pleasingly simple setting with just varnished oak tables and the odd objet d'art to distract you from your food. Pastas, panini, risottos and dishes large and small inhabit the menu, as does a highly recommended full English breakfast.

★ **Town House** BRITISH £££
(01903-883847; www.thetownhouse.co.uk; 65 High St; set lunch/dinner from £17.50/25.50; noon-2.30pm & 7-9.30pm Tue-Sat) The only thing that rivals the 16th-century Florentine gilded-walnut ceiling in this compact and very elegant eatery is the sparkling atmosphere and acclaimed British cuisine with a European twist. Book ahead. Town House also has well-appointed rooms to let.

Getting There & Away

Bus 700 runs to Brighton (two hours, twice hourly).

Arundel has the following train connections:

Brighton (£10.70, 1¼ hours, twice hourly) Change at Ford or Barnham.

Chichester (£4.60, 25 minutes, twice hourly) Change at Ford or Barnham.

London Victoria (£17.80, 1½ hours, twice hourly)

Chichester

POP 28,700

A lively Georgian market town still almost encircled by its medieval town walls, the administrative capital of West Sussex keeps watch over the plains between the South Downs and the sea. Visitors flock to Chichester's splendid cathedral, streets of handsome 18th-century town houses and its famous theatre, and of course to its pedestrianised shopping streets packed with big-name and independent shops. A Roman port garrison in its early days, the town is also a launch pad to other fascinating Roman remains, as well as to Arundel and the coast.

Sights

Chichester Cathedral CATHEDRAL
(www.chichestercathedral.org.uk; West St; 7.15am-7pm, free tours 11.15am & 2.30pm Mon-Sat) This understated cathedral was begun in 1075 and largely rebuilt in the 13th century. The freestanding church tower went up in the 15th century; the spire dates from the 19th century, when its predecessor famously toppled over. Inside, three storeys of beautiful arches sweep upwards and Romanesque carvings are dotted around. Interesting features to track down include a smudgy stained-glass window added by artist Marc Chagall in 1978 and a glassed-over section of Roman mosaic flooring.

On the left as you enter there's a small exhibition on the history of the building, and little further on the treasury displays heaps of church plates and an interesting collection of 13th-century oak chests. The peaceful cloisters are home to an excellent cafe, all the profits from which go to the upkeep of the cathedral.

Pallant House Gallery GALLERY
(www.pallant.org.uk; 9 North Pallant; adult/child £9/free; 10am-5pm Tue, Wed, Fri & Sat, to 8pm Thu, 11am-5pm Sun) A Queen Anne mansion built by a local wine merchant, handsome Pallant House and a 21st-century wing host this superb gallery. The focus is on mostly British, 20th-century art. Show-stoppers Patrick Caulfield, Lucian Freud, Graham Sutherland, Frank Auerbach and Henry Moore are interspersed with international

names such as Emil Filla, Le Corbusier and RB Kitaj. Most of these older works are in the mansion, while the newer wing is packed with pop art and temporary shows of modern and contemporary work.

Novium Museum MUSEUM
(www.thenovium.org; Tower St; ⌚10am-5pm Mon-Sat, to 4pm Sun Apr-Oct, 10am-5pm Mon-Sat Nov-Mar) FREE Chichester's purpose-built museum provides a home for the eclectic collections of the erstwhile District Museum, as well as some artefacts from Fishbourne Palace and a huge mosaic from Chilgrove Roman villa. The highlight is the set of Roman *thermae* (baths) discovered in the 1970s, around which this six-million-pound wedge of architecture was designed.

Sleeping & Eating

Trents B&B ££
(☎01243-773714; www.trentschichester.co.uk; 50 South St; d from £75; 📶) Just about the only place to sleep in the thick of the city centre action, the five snazzy rooms above this trendy bar-cum-restaurant are understandably popular.

Ship Hotel BOUTIQUE HOTEL £££
(☎01243-778000; www.theshiphotel.net; North St; s/d from £103/145; 📶) The grand central staircase in this former Georgian town house climbs to 36 fairly spacious rooms of commanding period chic. It's the most enticing option in town and it also boasts a snazzily styled restaurant. Book well ahead.

Duke & Rye AMERICAN £
(14 West St; mains £4-11; ⌚11am-11pm Mon-Sat, noon-8pm Sun; 📶) Occupying a large deconsecrated church opposite Chichester Cathedral, this temple of food and ale allows you to refuel and kick back in an incongruously ecclesiastical setting, recently updated to include shabby-chic areas of funky wallpaper, frilly standard lamps and Persian carpets. The US diner-style menu of burgers and sundaes is sure to bust your belt and invoke a holy thirst.

Amelie & Friends INTERNATIONAL ££
(☎01243-771444; www.amelieandfriends.com; 31 North St; mains £12.50-18; ⌚noon-2.30pm & 5.30-9pm Mon-Fri, noon-3pm & 5-9pm Sat, noon-2.30pm Sun) This award-winning, vaguely Gallic-feeling restaurant serves up finely crafted seasonal dishes with a slight bias towards seafood in a stylishly simple dining room and a peaceful garden out back.

WORTH A TRIP

ROMAN FISHBOURNE PALACE

Fishbourne Palace (www.sussexpast.co.uk; Roman Way; adult/child £8.90/4.70; ⌚10am-5pm Mar-Oct, reduced hours & days rest of the year) is the largest-known Roman residence in Britain. The palace lies 1.5 miles west of Chichester, just off the A259 (take bus 700 from outside Chichester Cathedral). Happened upon by labourers in the 1960s, it's thought that this once-luxurious mansion was built around AD 75 for a romanised local king. Housed in a modern pavilion are its foundations, hypocaust and painstakingly re-laid mosaics.

The centrepiece is a spectacular floor depicting Cupid riding a dolphin, flanked by sea horses and panthers. There's also a fascinating little museum and replanted Roman gardens.

Service is the best in the city and the menu is a mix of the familiar (gourmet fish and chips, banoffee pie) and less oft encountered (chicory-stuffed crêpes, Bermuda Seafood Chowder).

Entertainment

Chichester Festival Theatre THEATRE
(☎01243-781312; www.cft.org.uk; Oakland's Park) Built in 1962, this somewhat Soviet-looking playhouse has a long and distinguished history. Sir Laurence Olivier was the theatre's first director, and Ingrid Bergman, Sir John Gielgud and Sir Anthony Hopkins have all played here. Today it hosts a mix of entertainment from musicals to opera, stand-up comedy to Shakespeare.

Information

Tourist Office (☎01243-775888; www.visitchichester.org; Novium Museum, Tower St; ⌚10am-5pm Mon-Sat, to 4pm Sun) Located in the Novium Museum.

Getting There & Away

BUS

Chichester has bus connections to the following:

Brighton (bus 700; £4.80, three hours, up to three hourly)

London Victoria (National Express; £16, three hours 40 minutes, eight daily) Change at Gatwick Airport.

Portsmouth (bus 700, £4.50, one hour 10 minutes, up to three hourly)

TRAIN

Chichester has train connections to the following:

Arundel (£4.60, 20 minutes, twice hourly) Change at Ford or Barnham.

Brighton (£13, 50 minutes, twice hourly)

London Victoria (£17.50, 1½ hours, half-hourly)

Portsmouth (£7.60, 30 to 40 minutes, twice hourly)

SURREY

Surrey is popular with affluent London commuters who've had kids, moved out of the city and bought a country pad. For the most part, though, it's made up of uninspiring towns and dull, sprawling suburbs. Further away from the roaring motorways and packed rush-hour trains, the county reveals some inspiring landscapes made famous by authors Sir Arthur Conan Doyle, Sir Walter Scott and Jane Austen.

Farnham

POP 39,500

Nudging the border with Hampshire and joined at the hip with the garrison settlement of Aldershot, affluent Farnham is Surrey's prettiest town and its most worthwhile destination. Blessed with lively shopping streets of Georgian symmetry, a 12th-century castle and some soothing river walks, this easygoing market town makes for an undemanding day trip from London, just an hour away.

Sights

Museum of Farnham MUSEUM

(www.farnhammaltings.com; 38 West St; 10am-5pm Tue-Sat) FREE This engaging little museum is located in the splendid Willmer House, a Georgian mansion built in 1718 for the wealthy hop merchant and maltster John Thorne. Themed rooms trace Farnham's history from flint-tool days to Bakelite nostalgia. A corner is dedicated to William Cobbett, the town's most famous son, a 19th-century reformer, radical member of parliament, writer and journalist who established Hansard (the official record of what is said in parliament).

Cobbett's bust takes pride of place in the peaceful garden out the back, where you'll also find a timber gallery housing temporary exhibitions.

Farnham Castle CASTLE

(EH; 01252-721194; www.farnhamcastle.com; Castle St; palace adult/child £3.50/2.50, keep free; palace 2-4pm Wed, keep 9am-5pm Mon-Fri, 10am-4pm Sat & Sun, closed Jan) Farnham Castle was constructed in 1138 by Henry de Blois, the grandson of William the Conqueror. There's not much left of the castle keep today except the beautiful old ramparts. Even if the keep is closed, it's worth walking around the outside for the picturesque views.

Open only one afternoon a week, the residential palace was built in the 13th century as a stopover for the bishops of Winchester on London journeys. From 1926 to the 1950s, it was used by the bishops of Guildford.

Sleeping & Eating

Bush Hotel HOTEL ££

(01252-234800; www.mercure-uk.com; The Borough; r from £89; P) Farnham's top address is this finely appointed 17th-century inn right in the heart of the action. Rolling renovations keep things fresh, and there's a snug beamed bar and highly recommended restaurant that spills into the pretty courtyard.

Brasserie Blanc FRENCH ££

(www.brasserieblanc.com; 5 Castle St; mains £13.50-20; 8am-10pm Mon-Thu, to 10.30pm Fri & Sat, 8.30am-9pm Sun) For a bit of Gallic class, head to this understated eatery near Farnham Castle, one of French chef Raymond Blanc's 18 UK restaurants. The simply laid tables, low-watt art-deco lighting and art-covered walls create a modestly stylish atmosphere, and there's a walled garden out the back. The menu is a mostly seasonal list of finely crafted dishes cooked using choice ingredients shipped in from France.

Getting There & Away

There is a daily bus to London Victoria (National Express; £9.90, 1½ hours) and half-hourly services to Hindland (30 minutes to one hour).

There are twice-hourly train services to both London Waterloo (£15.70, one hour) and Winchester (£19.90, 60 to 80 minutes); you will need to change at Woking for the latter.

Oxford & the Cotswolds

Best Places to Eat

- ➡ Hind's Head (p229)
- ➡ Edamamé (p197)
- ➡ Le Champignon Sauvage (p219)
- ➡ Waterside Inn (p229)
- ➡ Wheatsheaf (p209)

Best Places to Sleep

- ➡ Star Cottage (p205)
- ➡ Barnsley House (p204)
- ➡ Glove House (p201)
- ➡ Bradley (p217)

Why Go?

Sprinkled with gorgeous little villages, this part of the country is as close to the old world English idyll as you'll get. It's a haven of rolling green-cloaked hills, rose-clad cottages, graceful stone churches and thatched roofs. Add to this alluring mix the legendary university city of Oxford, with its majestic architecture, historic air and lively student scene, and it's obvious why the region is a magnet for visitors.

Although the roads and most popular villages are busy in summer, it's easy to get off the tourist trail. The golden-hued Cotswolds work their finest magic when you find your very own romantic hideaway. Buckinghamshire, Bedforshire and Hertfordshire conceal splendid country houses, while Windsor delights with regal character. In the far west, the Forest of Dean beckons with outdoor-adventure appeal.

Much of the area is an easy day trip from London, but Oxford and the Cotswolds deserve at least several leisurely days.

When to Go

- ➡ Welcome the dawn with Oxford's Magdalen College Choir, which sings hymns from atop the college tower, on May Morning (1 May).
- ➡ In July, sip champagne and watch the rowers whizz by at Henley Royal Regatta.
- ➡ Walking in the Cotswolds is ideal from April to June and in September, when the weather is (mostly) in your favour, without the July and August crowds.
- ➡ In early October, Cheltenham kicks into bookish action for its famous 10-day Literature Festival.
- ➡ Gather among glamorous crowds in June for the country's greatest annual racing meet, Royal Ascot.

Oxford & the Cotswolds Highlights

1 **Oxford** (p189) Following in the footsteps of JRR Tolkien, CS Lewis and Oscar Wilde as you explore magical colleges.

2 **The Cotswolds** (p202) Wandering between perfect gold-tinged Cotswolds villages, such as Chipping Campden.

3 **Windsor** (p225) Catching a glimpse of regal life at the Queen's weekend hideaway.

4 **Blenheim Palace** (p201) Lording it up at one of Britain's greatest stately homes in Woodstock.

5 **Stowe** (p222) Getting lost in a serene world of spectacular 18th-century landscaped gardens.

6 **Gloucester Cathedral** (p220) Strolling the elegant cloisters of this exquisite Perpendicular Gothic creation.

7 **Painswick** (p215) Exploring a beautiful and unspoilt town in the Cotswolds.

8 **Making of Harry Potter** (p223) Unleashing your inner wizard at this studio tour.

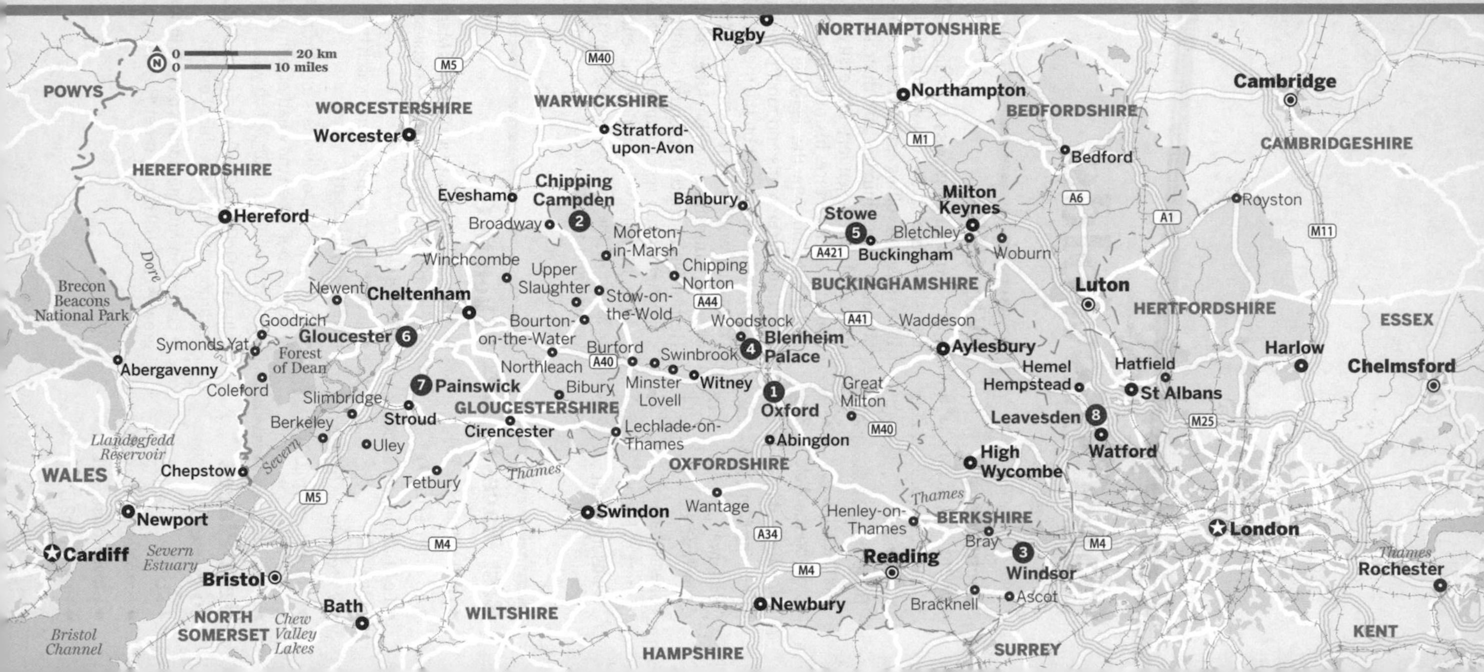

Activities

Cycling

Gentle gradients and wonderfully scenic panoramas make the Cotswolds ideal for cycling, with only the steep western escarpment offering a challenge to the legs. Plenty of quiet country lanes and byways criss-cross the region. You can also follow the signposted **Thames Valley Cycle Way** (NCN Routes 4 and 5) between Oxford and Windsor (and on to London).

Mountain bikers can use a variety of bridleways in the Cotswolds and Chilterns. In the west of the region, the Forest of Dean has many dirt-track options and some dedicated mountain-bike trails.

Walking

The Cotswolds offer endless opportunities for day hikes as well as something for the more ambitious.

Cotswold Way (www.nationaltrail.co.uk/cotswold-way) The 102-mile path between Bath and Chipping Campden takes about a week to walk; it's easily accessed from many points en route if you'd like to hike a smaller section.

Thames Path (www.nationaltrail.co.uk/thamespath) This 184-mile path follows the river downstream from its source near Cirencester to London.

Gloucestershire Way This 100-mile path links Chepstow to Tewkesbury via Stow-on-the-Wold.

Oxfordshire Way (www.oxfordshire.gov.uk/countryside) In Oxfordshire, this 65-mile signposted trail tracks from Bourton-on-the-Water to Henley-on-Thames.

Wychwood Way (www.oxfordshire.gov.uk/countryside) The 37-mile loop from Woodstock runs through an ancient royal forest.

Ridgeway (www.nationaltrail.co.uk/ridgeway) This picturesque 87-mile walk meanders along the chalky grassland of the Wiltshire Downs near Avebury, down into the Thames Valley and then along the spine of the Chilterns to Ivinghoe Beacon near Aylesbury in Buckinghamshire.

Getting There & Around

A car will give you the most freedom, especially for exploring the small villages of the Cotswolds. Oxford, Moreton-in-Marsh, Stroud, Cheltenham, Gloucester, Bletchley, Hatfield, St Albans, Henley-on-Thames and Windsor are plugged into the train network; all have services to London, in most cases direct. Other direct trains go as far afield as Birmingham, Manchester and Newcastle (from Oxford), and Cardiff, Edinburgh and Exeter (from Cheltenham).

Local buses link larger towns to each other and to their surrounding villages. Services are run by various operators. For timetables, use the journey planner tool on **Traveline** (www.traveline.info).

OXFORD

POP 159,994

One of the world's most famous university cities, Oxford is a beautiful, privileged place. It is steeped in history and studded with august buildings, yet maintains the feel of a young city, thanks to its large student population. The elegant honey-toned buildings of the university's colleges, scattered throughout the city, wrap around tranquil courtyards along narrow cobbled lanes, and, inside their grounds, a studious calm reigns. The city's famed spires twirl into the sky above.

Oxford is a wonderful place to wander: the oldest colleges date back to the 13th century, and little has changed inside the hallowed walls since. But along with the rich history, tradition and energetic academic life, there is a busy, lively world beyond the college walls, and the city's non-university majority far outnumber the academic elite. Just as in Cambridge, the existence of 'town' beside 'gown' makes Oxford more than simply a bookish place of learning.

History

Strategically placed at the confluence of the Rivers Cherwell and Thames (called the Isis here, from the Latin *Tamesis*), Oxford was a key Saxon town, heavily fortified by Alfred the Great during the war against the Danes. It continued to grow under the Normans, who founded its castle in 1071.

By the 11th century, the Augustinian abbey in Oxford had begun training clerics, and when Anglo-Norman clerical scholars were expelled from the Sorbonne in 1167, the abbey began to attract students in droves. The first three colleges – University, Balliol and Merton – were founded in the mid-13th century. Alongside Oxford's growing prosperity grew the enmity between local townspeople and new students ('town and gown'), culminating in the St Scholastica's Day Massacre in 1355, which started as an argument over beer but resulted in 90 deaths.

Thereafter, the king ordered that the university be broken up into colleges, each of which developed its own traditions.

The university, largely a religious entity at the time, was rocked in the 16th century by the Reformation; the public trials and burning at the stake of Protestant heretics under Mary I; and by the subsequent hanging, drawing and quartering of Catholics under her successor Elizabeth I. As the Royalist headquarters, Oxford backed the losing side during the Civil War, but flourished after the restoration of the monarchy, with some of its most notable buildings constructed in the late 17th and early 18th centuries.

The arrival of the canal system in 1790 had a profound effect on Oxford. By creating a link with the Midlands' industrial centres, work and trade suddenly expanded beyond the academic core. This was further strengthened by the construction of the railways.

The city's real industrial boom came, however, when William Morris began producing cars here in 1913. With the success of his Bullnose Morris and Morris Minor, his Cowley factory went on to become one of the largest motor plants in the world. Although works have been scaled down since, Minis still run off BMW's Cowley production line today.

Sights

University of Oxford

For those wondering where exactly to find the University of Oxford, the usual answer is: everywhere. Much of Oxford's centre is taken up by graceful university buildings and elegant colleges, each one individual in its appearance and academic specialities. The most visited strip, flanked by colleges and the Bodleian Library, is Catte St.

The first colleges (Balliol, Merton and University) were built in the 13th century, with at least three more being added in each of the following three centuries. Newer colleges, such as Keble, were added in the 19th and 20th centuries to accommodate an ever-expanding student population. Tradition dies hard at Oxford, however: it wasn't until 1877 that lecturers were allowed to marry, and female students were only finally admitted in 1878. It took another 42 years before women were granted degrees. To date, 26 British prime ministers have been educated at the University of Oxford.

Today, there are 38 colleges catering to 22,600 students. Not all are open to the public. For those that are, visiting hours change with term and exam schedules, and there's usually an admission fee. Check www.ox.ac.uk for full visiting details.

★Pitt Rivers Museum MUSEUM
(01865-270927; www.prm.ox.ac.uk; South Parks Rd; noon-4.30pm Mon, 10am-4.30pm Tue-Sun) FREE Hidden away through a door at the back of the Oxford University Museum of Natural History, this wonderfully creepy anthropological museum houses a treasure trove of half a million objects from around the world – more than enough to satisfy any armchair adventurer. One of the reasons it's so brilliant is the fact there are no computers, interactive displays or shiny modern gimmicks. Dim lighting lends an air of mystery to glass cases stuffed with the prized booty of Victorian explorers.

Trinity College COLLEGE
(01865-279900; www.trinity.ox.ac.uk; Broad St; adult/child £2/1; 10am-12.15pm & 1.30-4pm Mon-Fri, 1.30-4pm Sat & Sun) Founded in 1555, this small college is worth a visit to see the lovely 17th-century garden quad, designed by Christopher Wren. Its exquisitely carved chapel is one of the city's most beautiful and a masterpiece of English baroque. Famous students have included Cardinal Newman, William Pitt the Elder and two other British prime ministers.

Exeter College COLLEGE
(01865-279600; www.exeter.ox.ac.uk; Turl St; 2-5pm) FREE Founded in 1314, Exeter is known for its elaborate 17th-century dining hall and ornate Victorian Gothic chapel housing *The Adoration of the Magi*, a William Morris tapestry (Morris was an undergraduate here), and a psychedelic bombast of gold mosaic and stained glass. The college inspired the fictional Jordan College in the *His Dark Materials* trilogy by Philip Pullman, who also studied at Exeter.

Sheldonian Theatre THEATRE
(01865-277299; www.admin.ox.ac.uk/sheldonian; Broad St; adult/child £3.50/2.50, tours £8/6; 10am-4pm daily Mar-Nov, to 3pm Mon-Sat Dec-Feb) Begun in 1663, this monumental building was the first major work of Christopher Wren, then a professor of astronomy. Inspired by the classical Theatre of Marcellus in Rome, it has a rectangular front end, a semicircular back and railings decorated with classical busts. The ceiling in the main hall is blanketed by a fine 17th-century painting of the triumph of truth over ignorance; the ceil-

ing's remarkable length was made possible by ingenious braces made of shorter timbers.

New College COLLEGE
(01865-279500; www.new.ox.ac.uk; Holywell St; adult/child £4/3; 11am-5pm Easter-Oct, 2-4pm Nov-Feb) Established in 1379, New College was the first in Oxford for undergraduates and is a fine example of the glorious Perpendicular Gothic style. The chapel is full of treasures, including superb medieval stained glass (much of it original) and Sir Jacob Epstein's disturbing statue of Lazarus. The 15th-century cloisters and 19th-century evergreen oak featured in *Harry Potter and the Goblet of Fire*. During term time, visitors can attend the beautiful Evensong, a choral church service held nightly at 6.15pm.

Bridge of Sighs BRIDGE
(Hertford Bridge; New College Lane) As you stroll along New College Lane, look up at the steeped Bridge of Sighs linking the two halves of Hertford College. Completed in 1914, it's sometimes erroneously referred to as a copy of the famous bridge in Venice, but it bears a much closer resemblance to that city's Rialto Bridge.

★ **Bodleian Library** LIBRARY
(01865-287400; www.bodleian.ox.ac.uk/bodley; Catte St; tours £6-14; 9am-5pm Mon-Sat, 11am-5pm Sun) Oxford's Bodleian Library is one of the oldest public libraries in the world and quite possibly the most impressive one you'll ever see. Visitors are welcome to wander around the central quad and the foyer exhibition space. For £1 you can visit the Divinity School, but the rest of the complex is only accessible on guided tours. Check timings online or at the information desk. Advance tickets are only available for extended tours; others must be purchased on the day.

Radcliffe Camera LIBRARY
(www.bodleian.ox.ac.uk; Radcliffe Sq) The sandy-gold Radcliffe Camera is the quintessential Oxford landmark and undoubtedly one of the city's most photographed buildings. This beautiful circular, columned library and reading room, filled with natural light and focused on the humanities, was built between 1737 and 1749 in grand Palladian style, and has Britain's third-largest dome. The only way to see the interior is to join an extended 1½-hour tour (£14) of the Bodleian Library.

University Church of St Mary the Virgin CHURCH
(01865-279111; www.university-church.ox.ac.uk; High St; 9.30am-5pm Mon-Sat, 11.30am-5pm Sun Sep-Jun, 9am-6pm daily Jul & Aug) FREE With a tower dating from 1280 and a Perpendicular Gothic nave, this relatively unadorned church is most famous as the site of the 1556 trial of three Anglican bishops during the reign of Mary I. All three were later burned at the stake for heresy on Broad St. Inside, there's a memorial to the victims of the Reformation – both Protestant and Catholic.

All Souls College COLLEGE
(01865-279379; www.asc.ox.ac.uk; High St; 2-4pm Mon-Fri, closed Aug) FREE One of the wealthiest and most peaceful Oxford colleges, All Souls was founded in 1438 as a centre of prayer and learning. It's one of several graduate colleges, though it doesn't accept just any old Oxford graduate. Each year, the university's top finalists sit a fellowship exam, with an average of only two achieving the grade. It's said to be the hardest entrance exam in the world, and fellowship of the college is one of the country's highest academic honours.

St Edmund Hall COLLEGE
(01865-279000; www.seh.ox.ac.uk; Queen's Lane; 10am-4pm) FREE St Edmund Hall ('Teddy Hall' to residents) was founded sometime before 1317 and is the sole survivor of the original medieval halls, the teaching institutions that preceded colleges in Oxford. It's best known for its small late-17th-century chapel, later decorated by William Morris and Edward Burne-Jones. Mohawk chief Oronhyatekha studied here in 1862 (and eloped with the principal's daughter).

Magdalen College COLLEGE
(01865-276000; www.magd.ox.ac.uk; High St; adult/child £5/4, 45min tours £6; 1-6pm Oct-Jun, noon-7pm Jul-Sep, tours 6pm daily Jul-Sep) Set amid 40 hectares of private lawns, woodlands, river walks and deer park, Magdalen (*mawd*-lin), founded in 1458, is one of the wealthiest and most beautiful of Oxford's colleges. It has a reputation as an artistic college. Some of its notable students have included writers Julian Barnes, Alan Hollinghurst, CS Lewis, John Betjeman, Seamus Heaney and Oscar Wilde, not to mention Edward VIII, TE Lawrence 'of Arabia', Dudley Moore and Cardinal Thomas Wolsey.

Beyond the elegant Victorian gateway, you'll find the medieval chapel (with its

Oxford

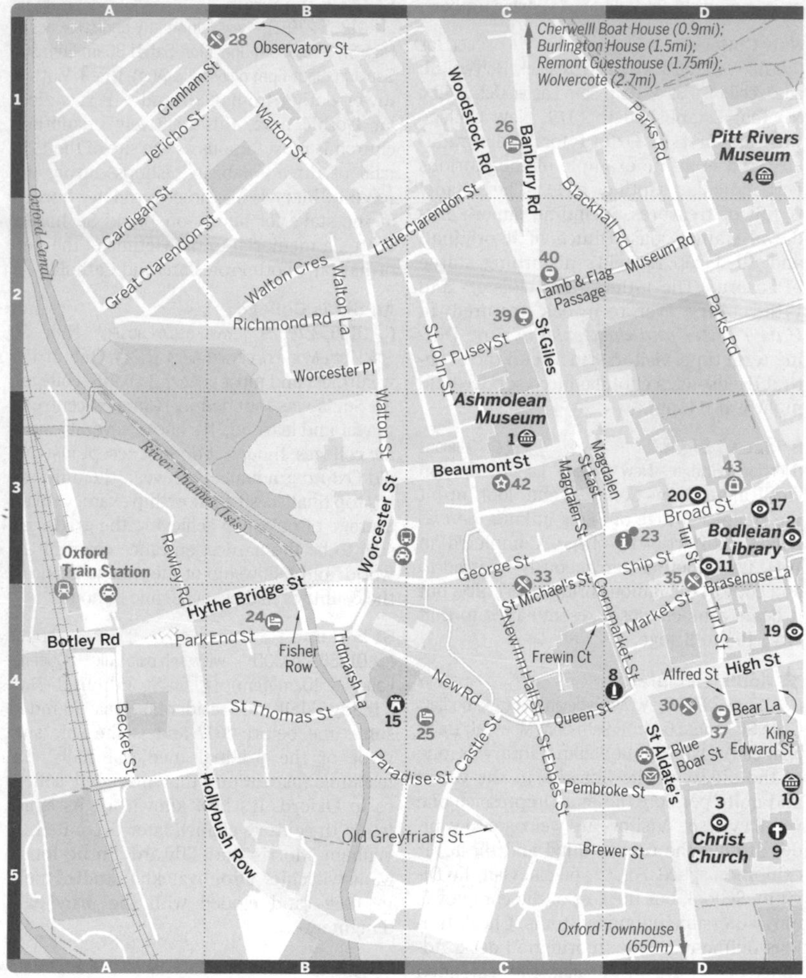

glorious 15th-century tower). From here, move on to the remarkable, now-restored 15th-century cloisters, some of Oxford's finest and with strange animals perched on the buttresses. The fantastic gargoyles and grotesques along the frontage here are thought to have inspired CS Lewis' stone statues in *The Chronicles of Narnia*. Behind the cloisters, lovely Addison's Walk leads through the grounds and along the banks of the River Cherwell for just under a mile. In the mid-1870s, you might have encountered Oscar Wilde taking his pet lobster for a stroll.

The college also has a fine choir that sings Hymnus Eucharisticus at 6am on May Day (1 May) from the top of the 44m bell tower.

Botanic Garden GARDENS

(☎01865-286690; www.botanic-garden.ox.ac.uk; High St; adult/child £5/free; ⏲9am-6pm May-Aug, to 5pm Mar, Apr, Sep & Oct, to 4pm Nov-Feb) Sweeping along the banks of the River Cherwell, Oxford's peaceful botanic garden was founded in 1621 for the study of medicinal plants; it's the oldest of its kind in England and remains a department of the university. Inside, you'll find a lily house, a rock gar-

den and the bench that Lyra and her extra-universal lover Will vow to visit once a year in Phillip Pullman's *His Dark Materials*.

Merton College COLLEGE

(☎01865-276310; www.merton.ox.ac.uk; Merton St; adult/child £3/free; ⊙2-5pm Mon-Fri, 10am-5pm Sat & Sun) Founded in 1264, Merton is the oldest of Oxford's colleges and the first to adopt collegiate planning, bringing scholars and tutors together into a formal community and providing a planned residence for them. Its distinguishing architectural features include large gargoyles, whose expressions suggest that they're about to throw up, and the charming 14th-century **Mob Quad** – the first of the college quads.

Just off the quad is a 13th-century **chapel** and the **Old Library** (admission on guided tour only), the oldest medieval library in use (look for the chained books). It is said that Tolkien, a Merton English professor, spent many hours here writing *The Lord of the Rings* and that the trees in the Fellows' Garden inspired the ents of Middle Earth. Other literary giants associated with Merton include TS Eliot and Louis MacNeice;

Oxford

Top Sights

1	Ashmolean Museum	C3
2	Bodleian Library	D3
3	Christ Church	D5
4	Pitt Rivers Museum	D1

Sights

5	All Souls College	E4
6	Botanic Garden	F4
7	Bridge of Sighs	E3
8	Carfax Tower	D4
9	Christ Church Cathedral	D5
10	Christ Church Picture Gallery	D5
11	Exeter College	D3
12	Magdalen College	F4
13	Merton College	E4
14	New College	E3
15	Oxford Castle Unlocked	B4
16	Radcliffe Camera	E3
17	Sheldonian Theatre	D3
18	St Edmund Hall	E4
19	St Mary's Passage	D4
20	Trinity College	D3
21	University Church of St Mary the Virgin	E4

Activities, Courses & Tours

	Bill Spectre's Ghost Trails	(see 15)
	Blackwell's Walking Tours	(see 43)
22	Magdalen Bridge Boathouse	F4
23	Oxford Official Guided Walking Tours	D3

Sleeping

24	Central Backpackers	B4
25	Malmaison	C4
26	Old Parsonage Hotel	C1
27	Oxford Coach & Horses	H4

Eating

28	Branca	B1
29	Café Coco	G5
30	Chiang Mai Kitchen	D4
31	Door 74	H5
32	Edamamé	E3
33	Handle Bar Cafe & Kitchen	C3
34	Kazbar	G5
35	Turl St Kitchen	D3
36	Vaults & Garden	E4

Drinking & Nightlife

37	Bear Inn	D4
38	Café Tarifa	G5
39	Eagle & Child	C2
40	Lamb & Flag	C2
41	Turf Tavern	E3

Entertainment

42	Oxford Playhouse	C3

Shopping

43	Blackwell's	D3

Thomas Bodley, founder of Oxford's Bodleian Library, was a fellow here.

From July to September, you can join 40-minute guided tours of the college grounds (£5). Also in summer, keep an eye out for posters advertising candlelit concerts in the chapel.

Behind Merton College is the ominously named **Dead Man's Walk**, so called because the medieval Jewish community, who were not allowed to bury their dead within the city, would take bodies along this route to the Jewish cemetery (now the Botanic Garden).

★Christ Church COLLEGE

(☎01865-276492; www.chch.ox.ac.uk; St Aldate's; adult/child £8/7; ⏲10am-4.15pm Mon-Sat, 2-4.15pm Sun) The largest of all of Oxford's colleges, with 650 students, and the one with the grandest quad, Christ Church is also its most popular. Its magnificent buildings, illustrious history and latter-day fame as a location for the *Harry Potter* films have tourists visiting in droves. The college was founded in 1524 by Cardinal Thomas Wolsey, who suppressed the 9th-century monastery existing on the site to acquire the funds for his lavish building project.

Over the years, numerous luminaries have been educated at Christ Church, including Albert Einstein, philosopher John Locke, poet WH Auden, Charles Dodgson (Lewis Carroll; who immortalised the then-dean's daughter in his *Alice in Wonderland* tales), and no fewer than 13 British prime ministers. The main entrance is below the imposing 17th-century **Tom Tower**, the upper part of which was designed by former student Sir Christopher Wren. Great Tom, the 6-tonne tower bell, still chimes 101 times each evening at 9.05pm (Oxford is five minutes west of Greenwich) to sound the curfew imposed on the original 100 students – plus the one added in 1663.

Visitors must head further south down St Aldate's to the visitors' entrance (where there may be queues). From here, you go up to the **Great Hall**, the college's spectacular dining room, with its hammer-beam roof and imposing portraits of past scholars. It was replicated in film studios as the Hogwarts dining hall for the *Harry Potter* films. The hall often closes between noon and 2pm.

Coming down the grand fan-vaulted staircase (where Professor McGonagall welcomed Harry in *Harry Potter and the Philosopher's Stone*), you'll enter **Tom Quad**, Oxford's largest and arguably most impressive quadrangle, with a statue of Mercury in its pond.

From the quad, you access 12th-century **Christ Church Cathedral** (01865-276150; www.chch.ox.ac.uk/cathedral; St Aldate's; admission free; 10am-4.15pm Mon-Sat, 2-4.15pm Sun). It was originally the abbey church and then the college chapel, but was declared a cathedral by Henry VIII when he broke from the Catholic Church, suppressed more monasteries and convents, and gave the college its current name in 1546. It was formerly known as Cardinal's College.

Inside, brawny Norman columns are topped by elegant vaulting, and beautiful stained-glass windows illuminate the walls. Keep an eye out for the 13th-century reliquary of St Frideswide, Oxford's patron saint, whose Anglo-Saxon shrine was a focus of pilgrimage prior to the college being built. Other notable features include the stained-glass depiction of the murder of Thomas Becket, dating from 1320, above the side altar on the right. As this is a working Anglican cathedral, there's no charge to visit it for private prayer or to attend a service – talk to the porters at the main gate. Evensong is held at 6pm most days.

Finally, you'll pass through the 15th-century **cloister**, a relic of the ancient Priory of St Frideswide.

To the south of the college is **Christ Church Meadow**, a leafy expanse bordered by the Rivers Cherwell and Isis, ideal for leisurely walking.

Christ Church Picture Gallery GALLERY
(01865-276172; www.chch.ox.ac.uk/gallery; Oriel Sq; adult/child £4/2; 10.30am-4.15pm Mon-Sat, 2-4.15pm Sun, closed Tue Oct-Jun) Christ Church's impressive stash of precious masterpieces dates from 1300 to 1750, and has a particular focus on the Italian Renaissance. Paintings by such greats as Tintoretto, Veronese and van Dyck take pride of place, and there's an exalted collection of drawings by Michelangelo, Leonardo da Vinci, Rubens and Raphael. Admission is half-price with a valid Christ Church ticket. Free guided tours at 2.30pm on Monday.

Other Sights

★ Ashmolean Museum MUSEUM
(01865-278000; www.ashmolean.org; Beaumont St; 10am-5pm Tue-Sun) FREE Britain's oldest public museum, second in repute only to London's British Museum, was established in 1683 when Elias Ashmole presented the university with the collection of curiosities amassed by the well-travelled John Tradescant, gardener to Charles I. Today its four floors feature interactive displays, a giant atrium, glass walls revealing galleries on different levels and a beautifully sited rooftop restaurant.

Collections, displayed in bright, spacious, attractive galleries within one of Britain's best examples of neoclassical architecture, span the world.

Historical treasures include Egyptian mummies, Islamic art, Indian textiles, ancient documents, rare porcelain, tapestries, silverware, priceless musical instruments, extensive displays of European art and, famously, the Anglo-Saxon Alfred Jewel.

Carfax Tower TOWER
(Queen St; adult/child £2.50/1.50; 10am-5pm) This central landmark, towering over what has been a crossroads for 1000 years, is the sole reminder of Oxford's medieval St Martin's Church and affords good views over the city centre.

St Mary's Passage STREET
With a doorway sporting a lion's head knocker, flanked by two golden fawns, this tiny alley is often said to have inspired CS Lewis' magical world in *The Chronicles of Narnia*. While this may or may not be true, it's nonetheless a pretty little corner, tucked between High St and the much-photographed Radcliffe Camera.

Activities

A quintessential Oxford experience, punting is all about sitting back in a flat-bottomed boat and sipping Pimms (the typical English summer drink) as you watch the city's glorious architecture float by. This, of course, requires someone else to do the hard work – punting is far more difficult than it appears. If you decide to give it a go alone, a deposit for the punt is usually charged. Most punts hold five people including the punter. Punt rental typically costs £16 to £24 per hour.

Magdalen Bridge Boathouse BOATING
(01865-202643; www.oxfordpunting.co.uk; High St; chauffeured 4-person punt per 30min £30,

WORTH A TRIP

TOLKIEN'S RESTING PLACE

Lord of the Rings author JRR Tolkien is buried with his wife Edith at **Wolvercote Cemetery** (Banbury Rd, Wolvercote; admission free; 7am-8pm Mon-Fri, 8am-8pm Sat & Sun Apr-Sep, to 5pm Oct-Mar), 2 miles north of Oxford city centre. The names Beren and Lúthien are carved on their gravestone, a reference to the love between a mortal man and an elf maiden who gave up her immortality to be with him.

punt rental per hour £24; 9.30am-dusk Feb-Nov) Right beside Magdalen Bridge, this is the most central location to hire a punt, chauffeured or otherwise. From here, you can head downstream around the Botanic Garden and Christ Church Meadow or upstream around Magdalen Deer Park. You can also hire row boats and pedaloes.

Cherwell Boat House BOATING
(01865-515978; www.cherwellboathouse.co.uk; 50 Bardwell Rd; punt rental per hour £16-18; 10am-dusk mid-Mar–mid-Oct) Head a mile north of central Oxford (along Banbury Rd then right onto Bardwell Rd) for a countryside punt on the River Cherwell, where the most popular destination is the busy Victoria Arms pub. Row boats and canoes are also available.

Tours

Bill Spectre's Ghost Trails WALKING
(07941 041811; www.ghosttrail.org; Oxford Castle Unlocked; adult/child £8/6; 6.30pm Fri & Sat) For a highly entertaining, theatrical and informative look at Oxford's dark underbelly, join Victorian undertaker Bill Spectre on a 1¾-hour tour of the city's most haunted sites. It departs from **Oxford Castle Unlocked** (www.oxfordcastleunlocked.co.uk; 44-46 Oxford Castle); no bookings needed. Audience participation likely.

Oxford Official Guided Walking Tours WALKING
(01865-686441; www.experienceoxfordshire.org/official-tours; 15-16 Broad St; adult/child from £12/7.50) Tours of Oxford city and colleges (10.45am and 1pm year-round, plus 11am and 2pm at busy times), along with a bewildering array of themed tours, from *Inspector Morse, Alice in Wonderland* and *Harry Potter* to medieval Oxford, William Morris and stained-glass itineraries. Check online for details or book at the tourist office (p200).

Blackwell's Walking Tours WALKING
(01865-333602; www.blackwells.co.uk/oxford; 48-53 Broad St; tours £9; mid-Apr–Oct) From spring to autumn, Oxford's most renowned bookshop runs a variety of literary-themed walking tours. Choices include the Inklings Walking Tour, which leads you to favourite haunts of JRR Tolkien, CS Lewis and other Inklings-group members.

Sleeping

Book ahead between May and September and on weekends. If you're stuck, you'll find plenty of B&Bs along Iffley, Abingdon, Banbury and Headington Rds. There's a cluster of budget accommodation near the train station.

Central Backpackers HOSTEL £
(01865-242288; www.centralbackpackers.co.uk; 13 Park End St; dm £20-25;) A welcoming budget option between the train station and town centre, above a bar. This small hostel has basic, bright and cheerful dorms, with lockers, for four to 12 people, a rooftop terrace and a small TV lounge. There's a six-bed women-only dorm.

★ **Oxford Coach & Horses** B&B ££
(01865-200017; www.oxfordcoachandhorses.co.uk; 62 St Clement's St; s/d/tr £125/135/165;) Once an 18th-century coaching inn, this fabulous English-Mexican-owned boutique B&B hides behind a fresh powder-blue exterior, just a few metres from the Cowley Rd action. The eight light-filled rooms are cosy, spacious and individually styled in soothing pastels with the odd splash of purple, turquoise or exposed wood. The converted ground floor houses an airy, attractive breakfast room.

Burlington House B&B ££
(01865-513513; www.burlington-hotel-oxford.co.uk; 374 Banbury Rd, Summertown; s/d from £70/96;) Twelve elegantly contemporary rooms with patterned wallpaper, immaculate bathrooms, dashes of colour and luxury touches are available at this beautifully refreshed Victorian merchant's house. Personal service is as sensational as the delicious breakfast, complete with organic eggs, fresh orange juice and homemade bread, yoghurt and granola. It's 2 miles north of central Oxford, with good public transport links.

Remont B&B ££
(☎ 01865-311020; www.remont-oxford.co.uk; 367 Banbury Rd, Summertown; r £127-147; P @) All modern style, subtle lighting and colourful furnishings, this 25-room guesthouse has a range of rooms decked out in cool neutrals with silky bedspreads, abstract art, vibrant bedheads, writing desks and plasma-screen TVs. There's a sunny garden and roomy breakfast hall out the back, plus good public transport into the centre (it's 2.5 miles north).

University Rooms Oxford UNIVERSITY ACCOMMODATION ££
(www.universityrooms.com; s £37-70, d £75-110, q 138-195;) During university holidays (Christmas, Easter and summer), you can sleep inside Oxford's hallowed colleges and breakfast in a grand hall by staying in student rooms. Most are functional singles with basic furnishings and shared bathrooms, though there are also a few en suites, twins and small flats available. Some rooms have views over college quads.

Oxford Townhouse BOUTIQUE HOTEL £££
(☎ 01865-722500; www.theoxfordtownhouse.co.uk; 90 Abingdon Rd; s £120, d £145-175, all incl breakfast; P) Just two months old at research time, this gorgeously restyled duo of Victorian town houses combines subtly chic rooms, good breakfasts and a warm welcome, half a mile south of the centre. Rooms are comfy, grey-toned and minimalist-modern in style, with white-and-navy stripy blankets, varnished-wood desks and blue flourishes, though mostly quite small (considering prices). Colourful paintings of Oxford adorn the walls.

Malmaison HISTORIC HOTEL £££
(☎ 01865-689944; www.malmaison.com; Oxford Castle, 3 New Rd; d/ste from £190/325; P) This converted former Victorian prison is one place you might just wish to be locked up in. Attached to Oxford's castle, it's now a sophisticated, thoroughly contemporary hotel with plush interiors, sultry lighting and polished service. Each of the 95 slick rooms has a giant bed and is made from three cells.

Old Parsonage Hotel BOUTIQUE HOTEL £££
(☎ 01865-310210; www.oldparsonage-hotel.co.uk; 1-3 Banbury Rd; r from £229; P) Tucked into a 17th-century stone house cloaked in wisteria, this 35-room boutique property achieves the perfect blend of period charm and modern luxury. Oscar Wilde once made it his home. The atmospheric interior has an impressive contemporary art collection, artfully mismatched furniture and tastefully styled rooms in reds, purples and greys, with handmade beds and marble bathrooms.

Eating

★ Edamamé JAPANESE £
(☎ 01865-246916; www.edamame.co.uk; 15 Holywell St; mains £6-9.50; ◷ 11.30am-2.30pm Wed, 11.30am-2.30pm & 5-8.30pm Thu-Sat, noon-3.30pm Sun;) The queue out the door speaks volumes about the food quality at this tiny, deliciously authentic place. All light wood, dainty trays and friendly bustle, this is Oxford's top spot for gracefully simple, flavour-packed Japanese cuisine. Dishes include fragrant chicken-miso ramen, tofu stir-fry and, on Thursday night, sushi. No bookings; arrive early and be prepared to wait. Cash only at lunch.

★ Vaults & Garden CAFE £
(☎ 01865-279112; www.thevaultsandgarden.com; University Church of St Mary the Virgin, Radcliffe Sq; mains £7-10; ◷ 8.30am-6pm;) Hidden away in the vaulted 14th-century Old Congregation House of the University Church, this buzzy local favourite serves a wholesome seasonal selection of soups, salads, pastas, curries, sandwiches and cakes, including plenty of vegetarian and gluten-free options. It's one of Oxford's most beautiful lunch venues, with additional tables in a pretty garden overlooking Radcliffe Sq.

Handle Bar Cafe & Kitchen CAFE £
(Bike Zone, 28-32 St Michael's Street; dishes £5-7; ◷ 8am-10pm Mon-Sat, 10am-7pm Sun;) Hot on Oxford's simmering coffee-culture scene, this bubbly bike-themed cafe gets packed with students, professionals and a few lucky tourists. They're here for luscious, health-focused bites, such as spiced avocado-and-feta toast, kale-wrapped halloumi and fresh-fruit smoothie 'pots', plus tasty cakes, teas and coffees. A raised penny-farthing serves as centrepiece and bikes dangle from the ceiling.

Oli's Thai THAI £
(☎ 01865-790223; www.olisthai.com; 38 Magdalen Rd; mains £6-12; ◷ noon-3pm Tue, noon-2pm & 5-10pm Wed-Sat) With a sunny front terrace and a tiny interior, family-run Oli's is well off the tourist track but absolutely worth seeking out. A Thai chef lends authenticity to the short but delicate, dynamic menu. It's a mile southeast of Magdalen Bridge, along Iffley Rd then Magdalen Rd. Tables get booked up months in advance, so reserve well ahead.

Fishes PUB FOOD ££

(01865-249796; www.fishesoxford.co.uk; North Hinksey Village; mains £13-20; 9.30am-11pm Mon-Thu, to midnight Fri & Sat, to 10.30pm Sun; P) In a delightful country setting, 1.5 miles west of central Oxford, this buzzy gastropub draws a regular local crowd with its excellent menu of classy modern-British offerings like crunchy ricotta-filled pastry, dry-aged steaks, enormous deli boards and chalkboard specials. Dine in the bright, cosy-smart interior or grab a deck chair or picnic rug in the chilled-out garden. Bookings recommended.

Turl St Kitchen MODERN BRITISH ££

(01865-264171; www.turlstreetkitchen.co.uk; 16-17 Turl St; mains £11-19; 8-10am, noon-2.30pm & 6.30-10pm;) A twice-daily-changing menu transforms meals into exquisite surprises at this lively, super-central multilevel cafe-restaurant. Fresh, organic, sustainable and locally sourced produce is thrown into creative contemporary combinations, perhaps starring veggie tajines, roast beef, hake-and-chorizo skewers or fennel-infused salads. Proceeds support a local charity. The interior is a rustic-chic mix of blue-tiled floors, faded-wood tables and fairy lights. Good cakes and coffee.

Kazbar TAPAS ££

(01865-202920; www.kazbar.co.uk; 25-27 Cowley Rd; tapas £3.50-6; 5pm-midnight Mon-Fri, noon-12.30am Sat, noon-11pm Sun;) Both sultry and stylish, this energetic Moroccan-inspired bar-restaurant has hanging lanterns, draped fabrics, low lighting, warm colours and a fun, fresh vibe. It's usually filled with a fashionable crowd sipping cocktails and tucking into superb Spanish and North African tapas, perhaps hummus dips, chilli-prawns or cheese platters.

Chiang Mai Kitchen THAI ££

(01865-202233; www.chiangmaikitchen.co.uk; 130a High St; mains £7-15; noon-10.30pm Mon-Sat, noon-10pm Sun;) Real-deal Thai cuisine in a little heart-of-Oxford alley, complete with tear-jerkingly hot *sôm·đam* (spicy papaya salad), a range of curries, plenty of seafood, rice and noodle favourites, and standout classics such as stir-fried chicken with cashew nuts. There's an excellent vegetarian menu.

Café Coco MEDITERRANEAN ££

(01865-200232; www.cafecoco.co.uk; 23 Cowley Rd; breakfast £4.50-9, mains £7-12; 10am-10pm Mon-Thu, to midnight Fri, 9am-midnight Sat, 9am-10pm Sun;) This Cowley Rd institution is a hugely popular brunching destination, decorated with classic posters, warm yellow walls, chunky mirrors and a plaster-cast clown in an ice bath. The global menu ranges from cooked and 'healthy' breakfasts to pizzas, salads, burgers, pastas, mezze platters, Mediterranean mains and zingy fresh juices. Or just swing by for cocktails (happy hour 5pm to 7.30pm).

Door 74 MODERN BRITISH ££

(01865-203374; www.door74.co.uk; 74 Cowley Rd; mains £10-14; 11am-2.30pm & 5-9.30pm Tue-Sat, 11am-2.30pm Sun;) This cosy little place woos fans with its rich mix of British and Mediterranean flavours, friendly service and intimate setting. The menu is limited and tables are tightly packed, but the cooking is consistently good (pastas, risottos, burgers) and weekend brunches (full English, French toast, salmon with scrambled eggs etc) are supremely filling. Book ahead.

Branca ITALIAN ££

(01865-556111; www.branca.co.uk; 110-111 Walton St, Jericho; mains £8-17; 10am-10pm) Big, bright and bustling, glitzy Jericho favourite Branca serves cool cocktails and savoury focaccia to complement elegant, well-prepped pizzas, pastas, risottos, and Italian meat and seafood grills. It fills up fast and also runs the deli next door. There's a decent-value, two-course lunch deal (£14) from Monday to Saturday.

Drinking & Nightlife

Bear Inn PUB

(01865-728164; www.bearoxford.co.uk; 6 Alfred St; 11am-11pm Sun-Thu, to midnight Fri & Sat) Arguably Oxford's oldest pub (there's been a pub on this site since 1242), the atmospherically creaky Bear requires all but the most vertically challenged to duck their heads when passing through doorways. A curious tie collection covers the walls and ceilings, and there are usually a couple of worthy guest ales and artisan beers.

Eagle & Child PUB

(01865-302925; www.nicholsonspubs.co.uk/theeagleandchildoxford; 49 St Giles; noon-11pm) Affectionately known as the 'Bird & Baby', this quirky pub dates from 1650 and was once a favourite haunt of authors JRR Tolkien and CS Lewis and a few other Inklings. Its narrow wood-panelled rooms and selection of real ales, craft beers and gins still attract a mellow crowd.

Turf Tavern PUB
(☎01865-243235; www.turftavern-oxford.co.uk; 4-5 Bath Pl; ⏰11am-11pm) Squeezed down a narrow alleyway, this tiny medieval pub (from at least 1381) is one of Oxford's best loved. It's where US president Bill Clinton famously 'did not inhale'; other patrons have included Oscar Wilde, Stephen Hawking and Margaret Thatcher. Home to 11 real ales, it's always crammed with students, professionals and the odd tourist. Plenty of outdoor seating.

Café Tarifa BAR
(☎01865-256091; www.cafe-tarifa.co.uk; 56-60 Cowley Rd; ⏰5pm-midnight Mon-Fri, to 1am Sat, to 11pm Sun) Themed around a Spanish kitesurfing town, this low-key lounge spot is big on neo-Moorish style, with cushioned booths, low-slung tables, tile-patterned sinks and cushy beanbags. There's a wide selection of cocktails, plus movie nights and live music.

Lamb & Flag PUB
(cnr St Giles & Lamb & Flag Passage; ⏰noon-11pm Mon-Sat, to 10.30pm Sun) Born as a 17th-century tavern, this relaxed wood-walled hideaway is still a good bet for a sturdy pint or glass of wine. It's said that Thomas Hardy wrote part of his novel *Jude the Obscure* within its walls, while authors CS Lewis and JRR Tolkien were once regulars. Pint purchases help fund PhD scholarships at St John's College (which manages the pub).

☆ Entertainment

If you're a fan of classical music you'll be spoilt for choice in Oxford, which has a host of excellent venues and regular concerts throughout the year. There's also a lively theatre scene. See www.dailyinfo.co.uk or www.musicatoxford.com for listings.

★Creation Theatre THEATRE
(☎01865-766266; www.creationtheatre.co.uk) Performing in a variety of nontraditional venues, including city parks, Blackwell's bookshop, Oxford Castle and various colleges, this ambitious theatre company produces highly original, mostly Shakespearean shows featuring plenty of magic, quirk and special effects.

Oxford Playhouse THEATRE
(☎01865-305305; www.oxfordplayhouse.com; Beaumont St) The city's main stage for quality drama also hosts an impressive selection of touring music, dance and theatre performances. The Burton Taylor Studio often features quirky student productions and other innovative pieces.

WORTH A TRIP

LE MANOIR AUX QUAT'SAISONS

As Oxford itself has no Michelin-starred restaurants, local food lovers make the 10-mile pilgrimage east to the impressive stone manor house **Le Manoir aux Quat'Saisons** (☎01844-278881; www.belmond.com/le-manoir-aux-quat-saisons-oxfordshire; Church Rd, Great Milton; 5-course lunch/dinner £82/138; ⏰7.30-10am, 11.45am-2.15pm & 6.45-9.30pm; ✎). Chef Raymond Blanc has been working his magic here for more than 30 years, presenting imaginative, complex and exquisitely presented dishes. Book well ahead and dress smartly.

Catweazle Club LIVE MUSIC
(www.catweazleclub.com; East Oxford Social Club, 44 Princes St; admission £6; ⏰8pm Thu) Legendary open-mic night, featuring musicians, poets, writers and all sorts of bohemian performers.

O2 Academy LIVE MUSIC
(☎01865-813500; www.academymusicgroup.com/o2academyoxford; 190 Cowley Rd) Oxford's busiest club and live-music venue hosts everything from big-name DJs and international touring artists to indie bands and hard rock.

Shopping

★Blackwell's BOOKS
(☎01865-792792; www.blackwell.co.uk; 48-51 Broad St; ⏰9am-6.30pm Mon-Sat, 11am-5pm Sun) The most famous bookshop in the most studenty of cities, Blackwell's is a book-lover's dream with its vast range of literature, academic treatises and guilty pleasures. Make sure you visit the Norrington Room in the basement – an immense inverted step pyramid lined with 3 miles of shelves, constructed in 1966. From April to October, Blackwell's runs literary-themed walking tours (p196).

ℹ Information

John Radcliffe Hospital (☎01865-741166; www.ouh.nhs.uk; Headley Way, Headington; ⏰24hr) Located 2.5 miles east of Oxford city centre.

Post Office (102 St Aldate's; ⏲9am-5.30pm Mon-Sat)

Tourist Office (☎01865-686430; www.experienceoxfordshire.com; 15-16 Broad St; ⏲9.30am-5pm Mon-Sat, 10am-3.30pm Sun) Covers the whole of Oxfordshire, stocks printed Oxford walking guides, and books official walking tours.

Getting There & Away

BUS

Oxford's **bus station** (Gloucester Green) is in the centre, near the corner of Worcester and George Sts. The main bus companies are **Oxford Bus Company** (☎01865-785400; www.oxfordbus.co.uk), **Stagecoach** (☎01865-772250; www.stagecoachbus.com) and **Swanbrook** (☎01452-712386; www.swanbrook.co.uk).

Destinations include the following:

Burford (route 853; £3.80, 45 minutes)
Cambridge (X5; £13, 3¾ hours)
Chipping Norton (S3; £4.60, one hour)
Cheltenham (route 853; £8, 1½ hours)
London Victoria (Oxford Tube/X90; £15, 1¾ hours)
Woodstock (S3; £3.70, 30 minutes)

National Express (☎0871-7818181; www.nationalexpress.com) coach destinations service the following:

Bath (£7, two hours)
Birmingham (£13.50, two hours)
Bristol (£7, three hours)
London Victoria (£16, two hours)

Oxford Bus Company runs 'The Airline' service to/from Heathrow (£23, 1½ hours) and Gatwick (£28, two hours) airports.

CAR

Driving and parking in central Oxford is a nightmare. There are five Park & Ride car parks on major routes leading into town. Parking costs £2 to £4 per day; buses run to/from the centre every 15 to 30 minutes (return £2.80, 12 to 25 minutes).

TRAIN

Oxford's main train station (Botley Rd) is conveniently placed on the western side of the city centre. Destinations include the following:

Birmingham (£18, 1¼ hours)
London Paddington (£25, 1¼ hours)
Manchester (£50, three hours)
Moreton-in-Marsh (£9.90, 35 minutes)
Newcastle (£111, 4½ hours)
Winchester (£17, 1¼ hours)

Oxford Parkway station (Banbury Rd), 4 miles north of the centre, has trains to London Marylebone (£25, one hour). It's convenient if you're staying in Summertown and has bus links to central Oxford.

Getting Around

BICYCLE

Cycling is a popular way to get around Oxford. **Cyclo Analysts** (☎01865-424444; www.cycloanalysts.com; 150 Cowley Rd; per day/week from £10/36; ⏲9am-6pm Mon-Sat) and **Summertown Cycles** (☎01865-316885; www.summertowncycles.co.uk; 200-202 Banbury Rd, Summertown; per day/week £18/35; ⏲9am-5.30pm Mon-Sat, 10am-4pm Sun) sell, repair and rent out bikes, including hybrids.

BUS

Oxford Bus Company and Stagecoach serve an extensive local network with regular buses on major routes. A short journey costs £2.10 (return £3.50); consider a day pass (£4). Tickets are purchased on the bus (cash only).

TAXI

There are taxi ranks at the train station and bus station, as well as on St Giles and at Carfax. Alternatively, contact **001 Taxis** (☎01865-240000; www.001taxis.com; New Inn Yard, 108 St Aldate's) or **Oxford Minicab Service** (☎01865-987749; www.oxfordminicab.co.uk; 25 Croft Rd).

AROUND OXFORD

Rustic charm is in abundant supply in the villages and towns surrounding Oxford. They make excellent day-trip options or stop-off destinations if you're heading west into the Cotswolds. To the northwest, Witney has a pretty town centre, but the major highlight is Woodstock's magnificent Blenheim Palace, birthplace of Sir Winston Churchill. Southwest of Oxford, the Vale of the White Horse offers some intriguing prehistoric attractions.

Woodstock

POP 2521

Old pubs, antique stores and fine stone houses dominate the well-heeled centre of beautiful Woodstock, 8 miles northwest of Oxford, which has long been linked to royal history. But what really draws the crowds here is Blenheim Palace, the extravagant baroque pile that was the birthplace of Sir Winston Churchill.

Sights

★Blenheim Palace PALACE

(☎01993-810530; www.blenheimpalace.com; Woodstock; adult/child £24.90/13.90, park & gardens only £14.90/6.90; ⏲palace 10.30am-5.30pm, park & gardens 9am-6pm; P) One of Britain's greatest stately homes, Blenheim Palace is a monumental baroque fantasy designed by Sir John Vanbrugh and Nicholas Hawksmoor, and built between 1705 and 1722. The land and funds to build the house were granted to John Churchill, Duke of Marlborough, by a grateful Queen Anne, after his victory over the French at the 1704 Battle of Blenheim. Sir Winston Churchill was born here in 1874. Now a Unesco World Heritage Site, Blenheim (*blen*-num) is home to the 12th duke.

Inside, beyond majestic oak doors, the house is stuffed with statues, tapestries, ostentatious furniture, priceless china and giant oil paintings in elaborate gilt frames. Visits start in the **Great Hall**, a soaring space topped by a 20m-high ceiling adorned with images of the first duke. To the right upon entering is the **Churchill Exhibition**, dedicated to the life, work, paintings and writings of Winston Churchill. The British prime minister was a descendant of the Dukes of Marlborough, as was Princess Diana, and is buried nearby in Bladon graveyard.

From here, you can wander through the various grand **state rooms** independently or join one of the free 45-minute guided tours, which depart every 30 minutes throughout the day (except Sunday, when there are guides in all rooms). Highlights include the famous Blenheim Tapestries, a set of 10 large wall hangings commemorating the first duke's triumphs; the State Dining Room, with its painted walls and *trompe l'oeil* ceilings; and the magnificent Long Library, overlooked by an elaborate 1738 statue of Queen Anne.

Afterwards, head upstairs to the 'Untold Story', where a ghostly chambermaid leads you through a series of tableaux recreating important scenes from the palace's history. From February to September, you can also join additional tours (adult/child £6/5) of the Duke's private apartments, the palace's bedrooms or the household staff areas.

If the crowds in the house become too oppressive, escape into the vast, lavish **gardens and parklands**, parts of which were landscaped by the great Lancelot 'Capability' Brown. A minitrain (50p) takes visitors to the Pleasure Gardens, which feature a yew maze, adventure playground, lavender garden and butterfly house. For quieter and longer strolls, there are glorious walks of up to 4.5 miles, leading past lakes to an arboretum, rose garden, cascade and temple, and Vanbrugh's Grand Bridge.

Tickets can be purchased on arrival or online up to 24 hours in advance.

WORTH A TRIP

KELMSCOTT MANOR

Tucked away in the countryside 20 miles west of Oxford, **Kelmscott Manor** (☎01367-252486; www.sal.org.uk/kelmscott-manor; Kelmscott; adult/child £9.50/5; ⏲11am-5pm Wed & Sat Apr-Oct) is a gorgeous garden-fringed Tudor pile that was once the summer home of 19th-century poet and artist William Morris, founder of the Arts and Crafts movement. The interior is true to his philosophy that one should not own anything that is neither beautiful nor useful, and the house contains many of Morris' personal effects, as well as fabrics and furniture designed by him and his associates.

Sleeping & Eating

★Glove House B&B £££

(☎01993-813475; www.theglovehouse.co.uk; 24 Oxford St; s £155-165, d £170-180, ste £200-220; wi-fi) Luxuriously renovated but proudly displaying evidence of its venerable age, this elegant 400-year-old town house conceals three sumptuous rooms with the added bonus of a glorious rear garden. The Charlbury suite has a free-standing copper bath-tub in its wonderful lounge-equipped bathroom.

La Galleria ITALIAN ££

(☎01993-813381; www.lagalleriawoodstock.com; 2 Market Pl; mains £11-23; ⏲noon-2pm & 7-10pm Tue-Sun; ✎) Big windows bathe the simple interior of this much-loved Italian restaurant in light. It's an old-fashioned kind of place, with heavy swag curtains, pink tablecloths and flowers on every table. Primarily Sardinian, the menu ranges from silky pastas and light salads to smartly cooked veal and fish. There's a decent-value three-course lunch menu (£14.95) Tuesday to Saturday.

Vale of the White Horse

Lying around 20 miles southwest of Oxford, this verdant valley is notable for the historic market town of Wantage, birthplace of

Alfred the Great (AD 849–899). But it's most interesting attractions are far older. Clustered together 8 miles west of Wantage on White Horse Hill, you'll find the Uffington White Horse (Britain's most ancient chalk figure), 700 BC Uffington Castle and Wayland's Smithy (a neolithic long barrow).

Sights

Uffington White Horse LANDMARK
(NT; www.nationaltrust.org.uk; White Horse Hill; dawn-dusk) FREE Just below Oxfordshire's highest point, this highly stylised horse image is the oldest chalk figure in Britain, dating from the Bronze Age. It was created around 3000 years ago by cutting trenches out of the hill and filling them with blocks of chalk; local inhabitants have maintained the figure for centuries. Perhaps it was planned for the gods: it's best seen from the air above. It's a half-mile walk east through fields from the hillside car park, signposted off the B4507.

Dragon Hill LANDMARK
(NT; www.nationaltrust.org.uk; White Horse Hill; dawn-dusk) FREE A 10m-high, flat-topped mound, Dragon Hill was believed by locals to be the site where St George slew the dragon, although it's possibly an Iron Age ritual site. It sits just below the Uffington White Horse, signposted off the B4507.

THE COTSWOLDS

Rolling gracefully across six counties, the Cotswolds are a delightful tangle of gloriously golden villages, thatch-roofed cottages, evocative churches, rickety almshouses and ancient mansions of honey-coloured stone. If you've ever lusted after exposed beams, cream teas or cuisine crammed full of local produce, look no further.

The booming medieval wool trade brought wealth to the Cotswolds, leaving behind a proliferation of exquisite buildings. In 1966, the region was declared an Area of Outstanding Natural Beauty (AONB). At 790 sq miles, it's England's second-largest protected area after the Lake District. Though it extends from north of Chipping Campden to south of Bath, the bulk of it lies in Gloucestershire. More than 83% is farmland but, even so, around 139,000 people live within the AONB itself.

These gentle yet dramatic hills are perfect for walking, cycling and horse riding, crisscrossed by a network of long-distance tracks, most notably the 102-mile Cotswold Way.

Cirencester

POP 16,325

Charming Cirencester (siren-sester) is the most significant town in the southern Cotswolds, just 15 miles south of Cheltenham. Refreshingly unpretentious, it's nonetheless an elegant and affluent town. It's difficult to believe that under the Romans (who called the town Corinium), Cirencester was second only to London in terms of size and importance (though little of this period remains). The medieval wool trade brought more success, with wealthy merchants funding the building of a superb church.

Today, Cirencester's lively Monday and Friday markets and warren-like antique shops remain as important as the upmarket boutiques and fashionable delis that line its narrow streets. Beautiful Victorian architecture flanks the busy Market Sq (the heart of the town) and the surrounding streets showcase a harmonious medley of buildings from various eras.

Sights

★Corinium Museum MUSEUM
(01285-655611; www.coriniummuseum.org; Park St; adult/child £5.20/2.50; 10am-5pm Mon-Sat, 2-5pm Sun Apr-Oct, to 4pm Nov-Mar;) Most of this wonderful modern, well-presented museum is, of course, dedicated to Cirencester's Roman past, with reconstructed rooms, videos and interactive displays that bring the era to life. Among an array of highlights, you'll see a beautiful set of floor mosaics (including a 4th-century mosaic showing mythical musician Orpheus charming animals) and the 2nd-century 'Jupiter column', a carved capital depicting Bacchus and his drunken mates. There's also an excellent Anglo-Saxon section, plus exhibits on medieval Cirencester and the town's prosperous wool trade.

St John the Baptist's Church CHURCH
(01285-659317; www.cirenparish.co.uk; Market Sq; 10am-4pm) Commenced in 1100, the cathedral-like St John's is one of England's largest parish churches. It boasts an outstanding Perpendicular Gothic tower with flying buttresses (c 1400) and a majestic three-storey south porch, which was built as an office by late-15th-century abbots but subsequently became the medieval town hall. Soaring arches, magnificent fan vaulting and a Tudor nave adorn the light-filled

interior, where, in a wall safe, you'll find the **Boleyn Cup**, made for Anne Boleyn in 1535.

Sleeping

★No 12 B&B ££
(☎01285-640232; www.no12cirencester.co.uk; 12 Park St; d/ste £130/150; P) A welcoming Georgian town house right in the centre of Cirencester, No 12 offers four gloriously unfussy, very private rooms kitted out with a tasteful mix of antiques and modern furnishings. Romantic room 1 has an in-room bath, the suite overlooks the lovely garden, and there are piles of feather pillows, extra-long beds, splashes of red and slick modern bathrooms throughout.

Kings Head LUXURY HOTEL £££
(☎01285-700900; www.kingsheadhotel.co.uk; 24 Market Pl; d/ste from £125/300;) At this plush spot opposite Cirencester's church, a glam refurb means super-polished service and slick boudoirs behind a 19th-century facade. Original exposed beams, red-brick walls and wood panelling pop up between Nespresso machines and Apple TVs. Standard rooms are wonderfully contemporary and comfy; suite 103 is a stunner with an in-room copper bath. Enjoy the tucked-away spa, cosy bar and smart **restaurant** (mains £11-17; 7.30am-10am, noon-2.30pm & 6.30-9.30pm Mon-Sat, 7.30-10.30am, noon-4pm & 6-9pm Sun).

Eating

Jack's CAFE £
(☎01285-640888; vwww.facebook.com/jackscoffeecirencester; 44 Black Jack St; dishes £4-8; 9am-5pm Mon-Sat, 11am-5pm Sun) Raid the stunning display of home-baked cakes, brownies, scones and flapjacks and snuggle into a cosy corner at this lively, locally popular cafe, right next to Cirencester's museum. There's also good coffee, along with tasty soups, salads, sandwiches and other light lunches.

Made by Bob MODERN BRITISH ££
(☎01285-641818; www.foodmadebybob.com; Corn Hall, 26 Market Pl; mains £10-20; 7.30-10am & noon-5.30pm Mon-Thu, 7.30-10am, noon-5pm & 7-9pm Fri, 8-10am & noon-5.30pm Sat) Part deli, part fashionable brasserie, Bob's is a huge hit for its casual atmosphere and sophisticated, inventive modern British fare featuring locally sourced products and cooked in an enormous open-plan kitchen. The breakfast selection is excellent (granola, smashed avocado, full English), while lunch bites include salads, soups, pastas, risottos and charcuterie platters. No bookings taken.

Jesse's Bistro MODERN BRITISH £££
(☎01285-641497; www.jessesbistro.co.uk; The Stableyard, 14 Black Jack St; mains £14.50-24; 11.45am-2.45pm Mon, 11.45am-2.45pm & 6.45-9.30pm Tue-Sat, 11.45am-5pm Sun) Hidden away in a cobbled stable yard, Jesse's is a wonderful little place, filled with flagstone floors, wood-beamed ceilings and mosaic tables. Delectable dishes come fresh from the semi-open-plan kitchen and feature local, seasonal produce, such as Cornish fish and Cotswolds meat from the adjacent butcher.

Information

Tourist Office (☎01285-654180; www.cotswolds.com; Corinium Museum, Park St; 10am-5pm Mon-Sat, 2-5pm Sun Apr-Oct, to 4pm Nov-Mar) Stocks a leaflet detailing a self-guided walk around the town (50p).

Getting There & Away

Trains run between London Paddington (£25, 1¾ hours) and Kemble, 4.5 miles south of Cirencester.

Stagecoach, Pulhams and Cotswold Green serve Cirencester. Most buses stop outside the Corn Hall on Market Pl. Buses run to/from the following:

Cheltenham (route 51; £3.60, 40 minutes)
Gloucester (route 852; £2.60, 1¼ hours)
Northleach (route 855; £2.70, 20 minutes)
Stroud (route 54/54A; £3.50, 40 minutes)
Tetbury (route 881; £2.50, 30 minutes)

National Express (www.nationalexpress.com) coach destinations:

Birmingham (£15, 2½ hours)
Leeds (£53, 6¾ hours)
London Victoria (£13, 2½ hours)
Newcastle-upon-Tyne (£60, 11 hours)
Nottingham (£28, 5¼ hours)

Bibury

POP 627

Once described by William Morris as England's most beautiful village, Bibury is the Cotswolds at its most picturesque (and popular), with a cluster of perfect riverside cottages and a tangle of narrow streets flanked by attractive stone buildings. It's 8 miles northeast of Cirencester.

The Cotswolds

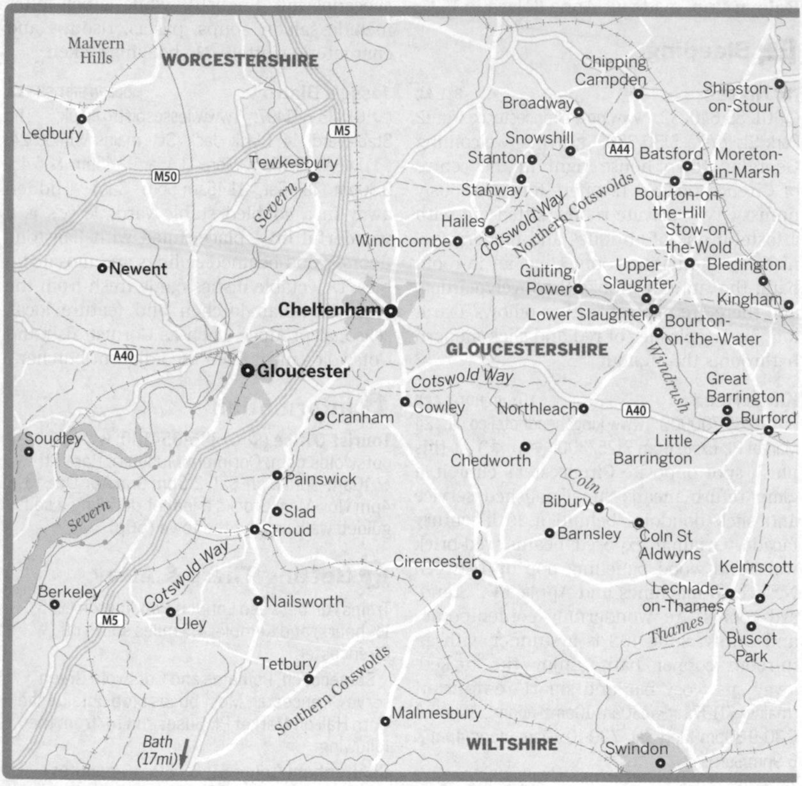

Sights

★Arlington Row STREET

This perfectly rustic sweep of cottages (originally a 14th-century wool store, converted in the 17th century) is Bibury's most famous attraction and overlooks Rack Isle, a riverside wildlife refuge once used as a cloth-drying and cattle-grazing area. It has served as a backdrop for many films (most notably *Stardust*) and is thought to be a contender for Britain's most photographed street.

Church of St Mary the Virgin CHURCH

(Church Rd; 10am-dusk) Bibury's Saxon-built church has been much altered since its original construction, but many 8th-century features are still visible among the 12th-, 13th- and 15th-century additions. It's just off the B4425 as you enter the village from the northeast.

Sleeping

New Inn PUB ££

(01285-750651; www.new-inn.co.uk; Main St, Coln St Aldwyns; r incl breakfast £79-169;) The popular jasmine-clad New Inn offers quirky contemporary comfort in 16th-century surroundings, both in the main pub building and a neighbouring cottage. The 15 bedrooms are spacious and atmospheric, with bold colours, fluffy throws, smart furnishings, the odd free-standing bath-tub and a few wood beams. It's 2 miles southeast of Bibury.

★Barnsley House LUXURY HOTEL £££

(01285-740000; www.barnsleyhouse.com; B4425, Barnsley; r incl breakfast from £249;) For pure Cotswolds indulgence and romance, this 1697 country house and its famously beautiful garden take some beating. Each of the 18 rooms is individually styled, and while some have lavish oriental touches

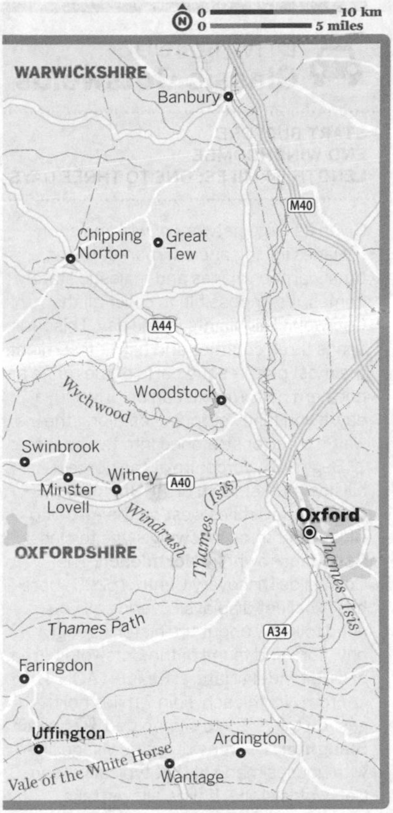

or in-room baths overlooking private gardens, most are elegantly understated in their decor. Facilities include a soothing spa, heated pool, private cinema, restaurant and pub. Service is superb.

Getting There & Away

Pulhams bus 855 heads to/from Cirencester (£2.20, 15 minutes), Barnsley (£1.50, 10 minutes) and Northleach (£2.20, 20 minutes); there is no Sunday service.

Burford

POP 1410

Slithering down a steep hill to a medieval crossing point on the River Windrush, the remarkable village of Burford, 20 miles west of Oxford, is little changed since its glory days at the height of the wool trade. It's a particularly picturesque place with a striking mix of stone cottages, fine gold-tinged Cotswold town houses and the odd Elizabethan or Georgian treasure. Throw in a wonderfully well-preserved, centuries-old church and an array of delightful hotels and restaurants, and Burford makes an attractive stop. Antique shops, chintzy tearooms and specialist boutiques peddle nostalgia to the many visitors who make it here in summer, but, despite the crowds, it's easy to get off the main drag and wander along quiet side streets seemingly lost in time.

Sights

St John the Baptist's Church CHURCH

(www.burfordchurch.org; Church Lane; 9am-5pm) Commenced in 1175 and added to over the years, Burford's sturdy stone church has managed to survive reformers and Roundheads (supporters of parliament against the king in the English Civil War) with its fan-vaulted ceiling, Norman west doorway, 15th-century spire and several grand tombs intact. The finest of these is the macabre 1625 Tanfield tomb, with colourful effigies of a noble couple in all their finery on top and as skeletons below.

Cotswold Wildlife Park ZOO

(01993-823006; www.cotswoldwildlifepark.co.uk; Bradwell Grove; adult/child £15/10; 10am-6pm Apr-Oct, to 5pm Nov-Mar, last admission 90 minutes before closing;) Younger visitors in particular will enjoy this hugely popular 64-hectare wildlife centre, 3 miles south of Burford. Among its vast 250-specie menagerie, there are penguins, zebras, lions, reindeer, otters, endangered white rhinos and much more. A miniature train takes the excitement up a notch.

Sleeping & Eating

★ **Star Cottage** B&B ££

(01993-822032; www.burfordbedandbreakfast.co.uk; Meadow Lane, Fulbrook; r £110-125, apt £115-140;) A mile northeast of Burford, this wonderful old Cotswold cottage has two brilliantly comfortable and character-filled en-`suite rooms done up in tastefully creative blues, whites and greys, with gorgeous quilted curtains. The smaller room has a grand canopied bed; the bigger one includes a beautiful bathroom; and the back barn hosts an independent four-person apartment. Home-cooked, locally sourced breakfasts are fantastic.

Swan Inn PUB ££

(☎01993-823339; www.theswanswinbrook.co.uk; Swinbrook; s £90-100, d £125-150, ste £195, all incl breakfast; P 📶 👪) All soft pastels, country comfort and dashes of colour, The Swan sits right by the River Windrush in tiny Swinbrook, 3 miles east of Burford. The six cosy, elegant stable-building rooms overlook orchards, including a plush top-floor suite with sloping ceilings (perfect for families). The newer riverside cottage has five delightful rooms in slightly more contemporary style. There's an excellent **restaurant** (mains £15-20; ⊙noon-2pm & 7-9pm; P) also.

Bull HOTEL ££

(☎01993-822220; www.bullatburford.co.uk; 105 High St; s £70-120, d £75-180, all incl breakfast; P 📶) Stay at this refurbished 15th-century coaching inn and you'll be following in the footsteps of guests as illustrious as Charles II and Horatio Nelson. Plusher rooms feature four-poster beds, floral fabrics and antique furniture, but all rooms have old-world charm. The **restaurant** (mains £12-18; ⊙noon-2.30pm & 6.30-9pm) delivers beautifully executed dishes that make the most of local ingredients.

Angel PUB FOOD ££

(☎01993-822714; www.theangelatburford.co.uk; 14 Witney St; mains £14-17; ⊙noon-10pm; 📶 🌱 👪) Set in a stylishly revamped 16th-century coaching inn, this buzzy pub turns out a tasty modern British menu with a choice between refined flavour-packed mains and 'pub classics'. Enjoy roaring fires and cosy cushioned booths in winter, or eat alfresco in the lovely walled garden in warmer weather. There are three homey rooms upstairs (£110 to £130, including breakfast).

Information

Tourist Office (☎01993-823558; www.oxfordshirecotswolds.org; 33a High St; ⊙9.30am-5pm Mon-Sat, 10am-4pm Sun) Advises on local walks.

Getting There & Away

Stagecoach and Swanbrook buses run to/from Burford. Most buses stop on High or Sheep St. Bus destinations include the following:

Cheltenham (route 853; £4.20, 45 minutes)
Gloucester (route 853; £5.50, 1¼ hours)
Oxford (route 853; £3.80, 45 minutes)
Minster Lovell (route 233/853; £1.80, 10 to 20 minutes)
Witney (route 233/853; £3.20, 19 minutes)
Woodstock (route 233; £4, one hour)

Driving Tour
Classic Cotswolds

START BURFORD
END WINCHCOMBE
LENGTH 54 MILES; ONE TO THREE DAYS

Given its large network of winding country lanes linking ancient market towns, time-warped villages and majestic stately homes, it's impossible to cover all the Cotswolds' highlights in one day. This tour spans three counties and ticks off some of the most picturesque parts of the range's northern half. While it can be driven in a day, if you fancy stopping off along the way, it's better stretched into two or three.

Begin in Oxfordshire at the gorgeous hillside market town of **1 Burford**, then head 10 miles west on the A40 into Gloucestershire, following signs to classic Cotswolds town **2 Northleach**. The Cotswolds Discovery Centre (p209) here has excellent displays covering all you need to know about the history, geography, flora and fauna of the Cotswolds Area of Outstanding Natural Beauty (AONB).

From Northleach, spin 7 miles northeast on the A429 to signposted **3 Lower Slaughter**, a serene riverside village lined with houses made of that typical golden Cotswolds stone. If time allows, take the 1-mile walk northwest to **4 Upper Slaughter**, less visited than its sibling but no less attractive, thanks to its idyllic setting between a small ford and the hills. If you've booked ahead, stop for lunch at Michelin-starred Lords of the Manor (p209), housed in an exquisite Jacobean mansion.

Continue 3 miles north on the A429 to **5 Stow-on-the-Wold**, the highest of the Cotswold villages at 244m and a market town since the 12th century. Peruse the market square, then take the A429 north. After 4.5 miles you'll reach busy **6 Moreton-in-Marsh**, known for its weekly Tuesday market and excellent local food shops.

Next, zip 3 miles west on the A44 to tiny **7 Bourton-on-the-Hill**, filled with attractive 17th- and 18th-century cottages. It's famous for two things: the gibbeting cage in which the bodies of dead highwaymen were hung in the 19th century, and horse training – there are several stud farms in the vicinity of the village. Horse & Groom

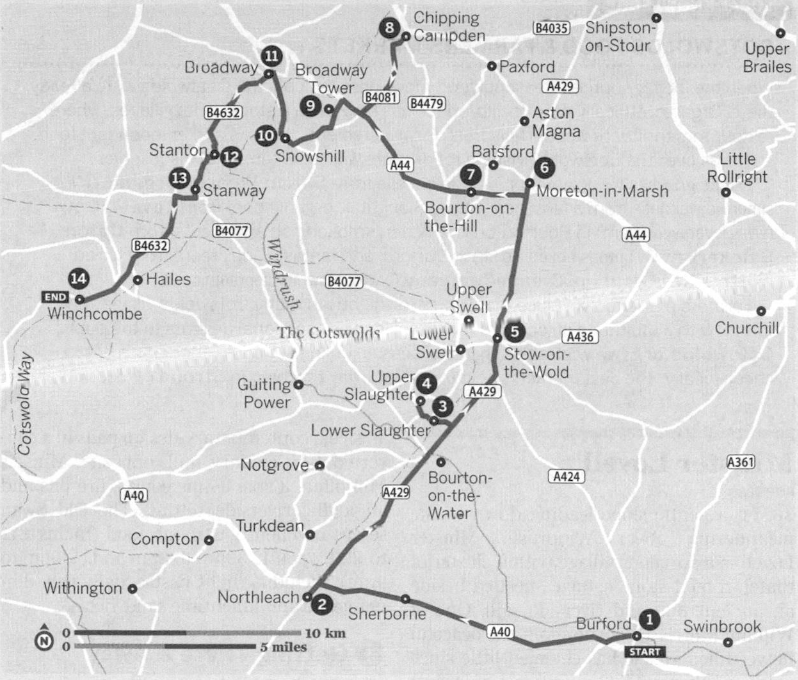

(p211) here is a good alternative spot to pause for lunch.

Head 3 miles west on the A44, then turn right (northeast) onto the B4081 to **8 Chipping Campden**, one of the Cotswold's most bucolic towns. After admiring 15th-century **St James' Church** (p212) and the honey-toned buildings along High St backtrack to the A44. Drive a mile northwest, crossing into the Worcestershire corner of the Cotswolds, and turn off at signposted **9 Broadway Tower** (www.broadwaytower.co.uk), an 18th-century Gothic folly perched spectacularly atop the escarpment.

Leaving Broadway Tower, continue 1 mile south and turn right (southwest) at the crossing. You'll soon see signs to pretty little **10 Snowshill**, a mile further on and one-time film set for *Bridget Jones's Diary*. If you're visiting in June or July, you'll swing by spectacularly purple fields of flowering lavender. From Snowshill, whizz 2.5 miles north to **11 Broadway**. After cruising along broad High St, hop on the B4632 southwest towards Cheltenham.

After 3 miles, take the left (east) turn-off to **12 Stanton**, a tiny stunner of a village. Its houses are crafted out of gold-tinged Cotswolds stone, with not a shop or quaint tearoom in sight. The buildings most likely to catch your eye are Jacobean **Stanton Court** and **St Michael & All Angels' Church**, with its fine Perpendicular tower and beguiling medieval interior.

You'll undoubtedly see walkers passing through Stanton, heading along the Cotswold Way to **13 Stanway**, a mile south; follow the narrow road that runs parallel to the trail. There is little more to idyllic Stanway than a few thatched-roofed cottages, a church and Stanway House (www.stanwayfountain.co.uk), a magnificent Jacobean mansion hidden behind a triple-gabled gatehouse. Its beautiful baroque water gardens feature Britain's tallest fountain. The manor has been the private home of the Earls of Wemyss for 500 years and has a delightful, lived-in charm.

Traverse Stanway, turn right (west) onto the B4077 and then left (southwest) back onto the B4632. After 3.5 miles, you'll reach **14 Winchcombe**, an ancient Anglo-Saxon town and walkers' favourite with good sleeping and eating options, including 5 North St (p215). You'll probably want to stay overnight to explore wonderful Sudeley Castle (p214) in the morning. Otherwise, continue 8 miles southwest on the B4632 to Cheltenham.

LOCAL KNOWLEDGE

COTSWOLDS FOOD & FARMERS MARKETS

When the locally sourced, seasonal food movement took off, the Cotswolds were already there. Organic, ethically produced produce has long been a staple in its villages, where restaurants thrill with wonderfully fresh local ingredients. In delis and independent food shops all over the Cotswolds, visiting food-lovers will make tempting discoveries.

Edible goodies to look out for include cheese from **Simon Weaver Organic** (www.simonweaver.net), from a farm near Upper Slaughter; organic beef from **LoveMyCow** (www.lovemycow.com) in Bourton-on-the-Water; smoked fish and meats from **Upton Smokery** (www.uptonsmokery.co.uk) in Burford; and fantastic ice cream from **Chedworth's Cotswold Ice Cream Company** (www.cotswold-icecream.co.uk).

Farmers markets take place monthly or fortnightly in many Cotswolds villages and towns, with a multitude of local producers selling their seasonal delights to the public. **Cotswolds.org** (www.cotswolds.org) publishes an online schedule, though it's best to check locally. The best market is held every Saturday morning in **Stroud** (⌚Sat).

Minster Lovell

POP 1236

Set on a gentle slope leading down to the meandering River Windrush, Minster Lovell is a gorgeous village with a cluster of thatch-roofed stone cottages nestled beside an ancient pub and riverside mill. One of William Morris' favourite spots, the peaceful flower-filled village has changed little since medieval times. It's 18 miles west of Oxford and divided into two halves: Old Minster, recorded in the Domesday Book (1086), and the rather newer (less charming) Minster Lovell, across the river and up the hill.

Sights

Minster Lovell Hall HISTORIC BUILDING

(EH; www.english-heritage.org.uk; Old Minster; ⌚24hr) FREE Old Minster's main sight is Minster Lovell Hall, the 15th-century riverside manor house that was originally home to Viscount Francis Lovell. Abandoned in 1747, the manor is now in ruins. You can pass through the vaulted porch to peek past blackened walls into the roofless great hall, the interior courtyard and the crumbling tower, while the wind whistles eerily through the gaping windows. To get here, walk through the church gardens at the eastern end of Old Minster.

Sleeping & Eating

Old Swan & Minster Mill LUXURY HOTEL £££

(☎01993-774441; www.oldswanandminstermill.com; Old Minster; r/ste incl breakfast from £125/295; P 📶 ✈ ⚶ 🐾) This luxurious, mostly hydro-powered complex has 14 charming period-style rooms in a 600-year-old pub and 39 sleek, contemporary-design pads in a converted 19th-century mill, opposite. Minster Mill offers a spa, tennis courts, fire pits and an idyllic riverside setting. The Old Swan serves excellent gastropub food (mains £12 to £20, open 12.30pm to 3pm and 6.30pm to 9pm), including light pastas, daily fish, dinner game and lunchtime sandwiches.

Getting There & Away

Stagecoach and/or Swanbrook buses serve the following:

Burford (route 233/853; £1.70, 10 to 20 minutes)

Cheltenham (route 853; £5.10, 50 minutes)

Gloucester (route 853; £6.20, 1¼ hours)

Oxford (route S2/853; £4, one hour)

Witney (route 233/S2/853; £2.70, seven to 30 minutes)

Northleach

POP 1923

Little visited and underappreciated, Northleach has been a small market town since 1227 and comprises late-medieval cottages, imposing merchants' stores and half-timbered Tudor houses. A wonderful mix of architectural styles clusters around Market Sq and the narrow laneways leading off it. Northleach is 14 miles southeast of Cheltenham.

Sights

Chedworth Roman Villa ARCHAEOLOGICAL SITE

(NT; ☎01242-890256; www.nationaltrust.org.uk; Yanworth; adult/child £9/4.50; ⌚10am-5pm Mar-Oct, to 4pm Feb & Nov; P) Rediscovered by a gamekeeper in 1864, Chedworth's extensive ruins represent one of the largest, most luxurious Roman villas in England. Though the earliest section dates to around AD 175, it's thought to have been at its most magnificent around AD 362, with two sets of bathhouses, a water shrine and a formal dining room with underfloor heating. The stars are the exquisite, well-preserved mosaics. Free guided 45-minute tours offer a good introduction. It's 4.5 miles west of Northleach, signposted from the A429.

Church of St Peter & St Paul CHURCH
(www.northleach.org; Church Walk; 9am-5pm) The grandeur and complexity of this masterpiece of the Cotswold Perpendicular style is testimony to its wool-era wealth. Although the chancel and 30m tower date to the 14th century, the building was extensively reworked during the 15th-century wool boom. A modern highlight is the 1964 stained-glass window behind the altar (depicting Christ in Glory), while earlier treasures include an unusual 14th-century font.

Cotswolds Discovery Centre INTERPRETATION CENTRE
(Escape to the Cotswolds; www.cotswoldsaonb.org.uk; A429; 9.30am-4.30pm; P) FREE Housed in Northleach's Old Prison, this is the official visitors centre for the Cotswolds Area of Outstanding Natural Beauty (AONB), with displays outlining the area's history, ecology, traditions and attractions. There's also a cosy cafe and a collection of agricultural wagons in the rear courtyard.

Sleeping & Eating

★**Wheatsheaf** BOUTIQUE HOTEL £££
(01451-860244; www.cotswoldswheatsheaf.com; West End; r incl breakfast £123-255; P) The 14 different rooms at this former coaching inn blend atmospheric period touches, such as free-standing bath-tubs, with modern comforts that include power showers, organic toiletries and country-chic decor. Downstairs, there's an outrageously popular **restaurant** (mains £14-27; 8-10am, noon-3pm & 6-9pm Mon-Thu & Sun, to 10pm Fri & Sat; P) dishing up delightful seasonal British dishes with a contemporary twist.

Getting There & Away

Swanbrook or Pulhams buses head to/from the following destinations:

Burford (route 853; £2.20, 15 minutes)
Cheltenham (route 801/853; £2.70, 30 minutes)
Cirencester (route 855; £2.70; 20 minutes)
Gloucester (route 853; £3.30, one hour)
Moreton-in-Marsh (route 801; £2.20, 45 minutes)
Oxford (route 853; £6.60, one hour)

The Slaughters

POP 400

The picture-postcard villages of Upper and Lower Slaughter, 3.5 miles southwest of Stow-on-the-Wold, manage to maintain their unhurried medieval charm despite receiving a multitude of visitors. The village names have nothing to do with abattoirs; they are derived from the Old English 'sloughtre', meaning slough or muddy place. Today the River Eye is contained within limestone banks and meanders peacefully through the two villages past classic gold-tinged Cotswolds houses and the 17th-century Slaughters Manor House (now an upmarket hotel).

Sleeping & Eating

Lords of the Manor MODERN BRITISH £££
(01451-820243; www.lordsofthemanor.com; Upper Slaughter; 3-course dinner £72.50; noon-1.30pm Sat & Sun, 6.45-9pm daily; P) Set inside a dazzling countryside manor, this romantic Michelin-starred restaurant concocts imaginative, beautifully presented dishes with French touches and plenty of quality local produce. It also serves popular afternoon teas and has 26 plush, comfy **rooms** (r incl breakfast £150-465; P). Book ahead.

Getting There & Away

Buses are not permitted through the Slaughters, so a car is your best option (unless you're hiking).

Stow-on-the-Wold

POP 2042

The highest town in the Cotswolds (244m), 4.5 miles south of Moreton-in-Marsh, Stow is anchored by a large market square surrounded by handsome buildings and steep-walled alleyways, originally used to funnel sheep into the fair. It's still an important market town and has long held a strategic place in Cotswold history, standing on the Roman Fosse Way (now the A429 here) and at the junction of six roads. Today it's famous for its twice-yearly Stow Horse Fair, and at other times, it attracts plenty of visitors with its scenic hilltop market-town appeal.

WORTH A TRIP

DAYLESFORD ORGANIC

A country-chic temple to the Cotswolds' organic movement, **Daylesford Organic** (01608-731700; www.daylesford.com; Daylesford; 8am-5pm Mon-Wed, 8am-8pm Thu-Sat, 10am-4pm Sun) is a sprawling, award-winning agricultural operation that grew from turning a family farm sustainable over 35 years ago. The gleaming food hall is crammed with Daylesford-brand produce. The excellent (though pricey) cafe-restaurant dishes up daily-changing menus of organic-fuelled treats (£7 to £17). There's also a luxury spa, plus an upmarket boutique. It's 4 miles east of Stow-on-the-Wold.

Sights

Cotswold Farm Park ZOO

(01451-850307; www.cotswoldfarmpark.co.uk; Guiting Power; adult/child £10.50/9.50; 10.30am-5pm mid-Feb–Oct, to 4.30pm Nov–mid-Dec; P) Owned by TV presenter Adam Henson, Cotswold Farm Park is designed to introduce little ones to the world of farm animals while also preserving rare breeds, such as Exmoor ponies and Cotswold Lion sheep. There are milking demonstrations, lamb-feeding sessions, an adventure playground, a 2-mile wildlife walk and pedal tractors to ride on. It's 6 miles west of Stow-on-the-Wold, signposted from the B4077 and B4068.

Sleeping & Eating

King's Head Inn PUB ££

(01608-658365; www.thekingsheadinn.net; The Green, Bledington; s £75-100, d £100-130, all incl breakfast; P) Overlooking a peaceful green 4.5 miles southeast of Stow, this stylishly revamped 15th-century cider house blends old and new to perfection, with 12 subtly luxurious, individually styled rooms and a good **restaurant** (mains £12-18; noon-2pm & 6.30-9pm Mon-Sat, noon-3pm & 6.30-9pm Sun; P). Cosy rooms in the original building burst with old-world character (exposed beams, check-print rugs). The six quieter, contemporary-design courtyard rooms are more sumptuous, featuring power showers and Nespresso machines.

Old Stocks Inn BOUTIQUE HOTEL £££

(01451-830666; www.oldstocksinn.com; Market Sq; r £139-279;) Right on Stow's square, this 17th-century inn is looking fantastically fresh after a bold, contemporary makeover that beautifully mixes period charm (exposed beams, slender staircases) with modern comforts (capsule-coffee kits, retro phones). Decor features bright whites, hot turquoises and patterned pillows. The most affordable rooms are snug attic-style affairs with sloping ceilings, while more lavish 'Great' rooms have claw-foot baths.

Getting There & Away

Pulhams buses serve the following destinations, Monday to Saturday:

Cheltenham (route 801; £3, 1¼ hours)

Moreton-in-Marsh (route 801; £1.70, 10 minutes)

Northleach (route 801; £2.10, 30 minutes)

Chipping Norton

POP 6300

Often overlooked, the hilly, pretty town of Chipping Norton ('Chippy') has plenty of quiet side streets to wander, a fine wool-era church and none of the classic Cotswolds crowds. Handsome Georgian buildings, old coaching inns and the pillared 19th-century town hall cluster around the market square, while on Church St you'll find a row of beautiful honey-tinged almshouses built in the 17th century.

Sights

St Mary's Church CHURCH

(01608-646202; www.stmarysc norton.com; Church St; 10am-dusk) Chipping Norton's secluded church is a classic example of the Cotswold wool churches, with a magnificent Perpendicular nave and clerestory, several alabaster tombs and fluted, diamond-shaped pillars. While it was mostly built in 1448, two of the arches in the chancel date to around 1200. In the hexagonal porch, carved 15th-century ceiling bosses include a sheep overpowering a wolf and the possibly pagan but common visitor to British churches, the Green Man.

Eating

Wild Thyme MODERN BRITISH ££

(01608-645060; www.wildthymerestaurant.co.uk; 10 New St; mains £18-20, 2-/3-course set menu from £20/25; 7-9pm Tue & Wed, noon-2pm & 7-9pm Thu, noon-2pm & 6.30-9.30pm Fri & Sat) A little 'restaurant with rooms', Wild Thyme thrills palates with top-notch creative dishes packed with flavour, such as asparagus and goat's cheese risotto or steamed brill with shellfish ravioli. The desserts – from apple crumble to chocolate sharing platters – are nothing short of sublime. Hidden upstairs are three brilliantly cosy pastel-painted **rooms** (s £65-75, d £75-85;).

Shopping

★Jaffé & Neale Bookshop Cafe BOOKS

(01608-641033; www.jaffeandneale.co.uk; 1 Middle Row; 9.30am-5.30pm Mon Sat, 11am-5pm Sun;) This brilliant independent bookshop serves delicious cakes and coffees to tables squeezed between the bookshelves or in the cosy upstairs reading lounge with sofas.

Getting There & Away

Stagecoach and/or Pulhams buses head to/from the following destinations:

Oxford (route S3; £4.60, one hour)

Stratford-upon-Avon (route 50; £5.85, 50 minutes)

Witney (route X9; £3.90, 40 minutes)

Woodstock (route S3; £4, 20 minutes)

Moreton-in-Marsh

POP 3493

Home to some beautiful 17th- and 18th-century buildings but plagued by the heavy traffic that clogs up its broad High St (A429; built on top of the Roman Fosse Way), Moreton-in-Marsh is a major transport hub known for its excellent food shops stocking local Cotswold produce. On Tuesday, the town bursts into life for its weekly market. It's 4.5 miles north of Stow-on-the-Wold.

Sights

★Cotswold Falconry Centre AVIARY

(01386-701043; www.cotswold-falconry.co.uk; Batsford Park; adult/child £10/5; 10.30am-5pm mid-Feb–mid-Nov; P) Home to over 150 birds of prey (owl, vulture, eagle and, of course, falcon), this exciting spot offers displays of the ancient practice of falconry at 11.30am, 1.30pm and 3pm daily (plus 4.30pm April to October). The birds fly at their best on windy days. Various hands-on experiences (from £40) include a one-hour 'Flying Start' during which visitors get to fly hawks.

Batsford Arboretum PARK

(01386-701441; www.batsarb.co.uk; Batsford Park; adult/child £7.20/3.15; 9am-5pm Mon-Sat, 10am-5pm Sun; P) Created by Bertie Mitford (Lord Redesdale) in 1880, these exotic 22-hectare woodlands feature around 1600 species of labelled trees, bamboos and shrubs from Nepal, China, Japan and North America. Many of these are rare or endangared, or were planted pre-WWI. Highlights include vast American redwoods, flowering Japanese cherries (at their best in spring), an enormous davidia and the strangely churchlike 'cathedral' lime.

WORTH A TRIP

COTSWOLDS DISTILLERY

Launched in 2014, the ambitious, ecofriendly gin and whisky distillery **Cotswolds Distillery** (01608-238533; www.cotswoldsdistillery.com; Phillip's Field, Whichford Road, Stourton; tours without/with tasting £6/10; tours 11am & 2pm, shop 9am-5pm Mon-Sat, 11am-4pm Sun) sits tucked into the northern Cotswolds, 7 miles north of Chipping Norton. You can tour the facilities and learn all about how its delicious Cotswolds-flavoured liquors are produced, before wrapping up with a tasting session. Book ahead.

Sleeping & Eating

White Hart Royal Hotel HOTEL ££

(01608-650731; www.whitehartroyal.co.uk; High St; s/d incl breakfast from £75/95; P) 'Royal' relates to the fact that Charles I once stayed here during the Civil War, and while he probably didn't use the iPod docks, flat-screen TVs and en-suite rooms, he certainly walked down the atmospheric half-timbered corridors. Standard rooms aren't particularly characterful, though they're comfy and well equipped. The downstairs **restaurant** (mains £12-20, 6-9pm Mon-Sat, noon-2pm & 6-9pm Sun) has plenty of charm.

★Horse & Groom PUB FOOD ££

(01386-700413; www.horseandgroom.info; Bourton-on-the-Hill; mains £12.50-21.50; noon-2pm daily, 7-9pm Mon-Sat; P) The bubbly, laid-back Horse & Groom, 2 miles west of Moreton-in-Marsh, excels at upmarket country cooking showcasing local lamb, beef and vegetables, alongside flavour-filled fish dishes, all colourfully chalked up on a board in the bar. It's a firm favourite with well-heeled horsey types. It also has five swish **rooms** (s £80, d £120-170) upstairs.

Getting There & Away

BUS

From Monday to Saturday, Pulhams, Stagecoach and/or Johnsons Excelbus buses head to/from the following:

Broadway (route 21/22; £3.20, 30 minutes)
Cheltenham (route 801; £3.30, 1½ hours)
Chipping Campden (route 21/22; £3.20, 50 minutes)
Cirencester (route 855; £2.70, one hour)
Northleach (route 855; £2.20, 40 minutes)
Stow-on-the-Wold (route 801; £1.70, 10 minutes)
Stratford-upon-Avon (route 21/22/23/50; £5.85, one hour)

TRAIN

The train station is towards the northern end of town, just off High St. Trains head to/from the following:

Hereford (£18, 1¾ hours)
Ledbury (£17, 1½ hours)
London Paddington (£35, 1½ hours)
Oxford (£9.90, 35 minutes)
Worcester (£12.40, 40 minutes)

Chipping Campden

POP 2037

An absolute gem in an area full of pretty towns, Chipping Campden is a glorious reminder of Cotswolds life in medieval times. The graceful curving main street is flanked by a perfectly picturesque array of stone cottages, fine terraced houses, ancient inns and historic homes, most made of that beautiful honey-coloured Cotswolds stone. There are particularly striking thatch-roofed cottages along Westington, at the southwestern end of town. Despite its obvious allure, Chipping Campden remains relatively unspoiled by visiting crowds. It is, however, popular with walkers rambling along the Cotswold Way, which tracks 102 miles northeast from Bath to Chipping Campden.

While the village's name derives from the Old English 'ceapen', meaning 'market', 'Chippy's' visible prosperity derives from its past as a successful wool town.

Sights

St James' Church CHURCH
(☎01386-841927; www.stjameschurchcampden.co.uk; Church St; admission by donation; ⌚10am-4.30pm Mon-Sat, noon-4pm Sun Apr-Oct, 11am-3pm Mon-Sat, 2-4pm Sun Nov-Mar) Built in the late 15th century in Perpendicular Gothic style, on wool-trade riches, imposing St James' has a splendid tower and some graceful 17th-century monuments. Inside, you can see one of the earliest priest vestments on record, dating back to 1400. On Church St, just outside, stands a remarkable row of almshouses constructed in 1612.

Grevel House HISTORIC BUILDING
(High St; ⌚closed to the public) One of the grandest residences on High St, 14th-century Grevel House was once home to highly successful wool merchant William Grevel and is Chipping Campden's oldest building. Admire the splendid Perpendicular Gothic–style gabled window and sundial from the street.

Hidcote GARDENS
(NT; www.nationaltrust.org.uk; Hidcote Bartrim; adult/child £10.90/5.45; ⌚10am-6pm, to 5pm Oct, shorter hours Nov, Dec & mid-Feb–Mar, closed Jan; P) About 4 miles northeast of Chipping Campden, Hidcote is one of the finest examples of Arts and Crafts landscaping in Britain, with a series of outdoor 'rooms' filled with flowers and rare plants from across the globe. It owes its unique beauty to 20th-century avid garden designer Lawrence Johnston.

Sleeping & Eating

Eight Bells Inn PUB ££
(☎01386-840371; www.eightbellsinn.co.uk; Church St; s £60-95, d £95-140, all incl breakfast; wi-fi) This refurbished 14th-century inn is a particularly friendly and atmospheric place to stay, featuring six bright, modern rooms with iron bedsteads, soothing neutral decor, flowery wallpaper and warm accents. Room 7, with its chunky old-world beams, is especially striking. The cosy **pub** (mains £13-16; ⌚noon-2pm & 6.30-9pm Mon-Thu, noon-2.30pm & 6.30-9.30pm Fri & Sat, 12.15-9pm Sun; family-friendly, pet-friendly) downstairs serves good modern British country cooking.

Chef's Dozen MODERN BRITISH ££
(☎01386-840598; www.thechefsdozen.co.uk; High St; 3-/4-course set menu £28/45; ⌚6.30-9pm Tue-Thu, noon-1.30pm & 6.30-9pm Fri & Sat) Superb organic, field-to-fork cooking powered by local produce and delivered by changing seasonal menus is the draw at this fresh, friendly culinary star. Settle into the tastefully understated cream-coloured dining room for skilfully concocted, beautifully

creative dishes, such as wild-rabbit ravioli or risotto filled with Cotswolds cheeses. Outside, tables dot a sweet, discreet courtyard.

Information

Tourist Office (☎ 01386-841206; www.campdenonline.org; Old Police Station, High St; ⊙ 9.30am-5pm daily mid-Mar–mid-Nov, 9.30am-1pm Mon-Thu, to 4pm Fri-Sun mid-Nov–mid-Mar) Pick up a town guide (£1.50) for a self-guided walk around Chipping Campden's most significant buildings. Guided tours are run by the Cotswold Voluntary Wardens from May to September (suggested donation £3).

Getting There & Away

From Monday to Saturday, Johnsons Excelbus services head to/from Moreton-in-Marsh (route 21/22; £3.20, 50 minutes), Broadway (route 21/22/24; £2.70, 20 minutes) and Stratford-upon-Avon (route 21/22/24; £4.20, 50 minutes).

Marchants bus 606S (Sunday only) runs to/from Broadway (£4.50, 20 minutes), Cheltenham (£8, one hour), Stratford-upon-Avon (£4.50, 25 minutes) and Winchcombe (£8, 35 minutes). Marchants bus 606 runs to the same destinations Monday to Saturday.

Broadway

POP 2540

A quintessentially English village with a smattering of antique shops, tearooms and art galleries, Broadway has inspired writers, artists and composers in times past with its graceful, golden-hued cottages set at the foot of a steep escarpment. Unsurprisingly, it's one of the more popular Cotswolds spots, just 5 miles west of Chipping Campden.

If the village of **Snowshill**, 2.5 miles south, looks familiar, that's because it featured in hit film *Bridget Jones's Diary*. A local house was used as Bridget's parents' home.

Sights

Ashmolean Museum Broadway MUSEUM
(☎ 01386-859047; www.ashmoleanbroadway.org; Tudor House, 65 High St; adult/child £5/2; ⊙ 10am-5pm Tue-Sun) Partnered with Oxford's famous Ashmolean Museum, this grand converted 17th-century coaching inn has fascinating displays of local crafts, antiques and historical detail spanning from the 17th-century to the present day. Collections include Winchcombe pottery, vintage furniture, elaborate tapestries and paintings by 18th-century artists Joshua Reynolds and Thomas Gainsborough.

Snowshill Manor & Garden HOUSE
(NT; www.nationaltrust.org.uk; Snowshill; adult/child £10.40/5.40; ⊙ noon-5pm mid-Mar–Oct) About 3 miles south of Broadway lies this wonderful Cotswold mansion, once home to marvellously eccentric poet and architect Charles Paget Wade (1883–1956). The house contains Wade's extraordinary collection of crafts and design, taking in everything from musical instruments to Southeast Asian masks and Japanese samurai armour. The impressive gardens were designed as an extension of the house, with pools, terraces and wonderful views.

Sleeping & Eating

Russell's HOTEL ££
(☎ 01386-853555; www.russellsofbroadway.co.uk; The Green, 20 High St; r incl breakfast from £120; ⊙ restaurant noon-2.15pm & 6-9.15pm Mon-Sat, noon-2.30pm Sun; P 📶 🐾) Sleek and stylish Russell's has seven spacious, individually designed rooms, some with exposed beams, four-poster beds and armchairs, and all with modern luxuries such as contemporary bathrooms and fresh white styling. It's known for its beautifully executed modern-British fare (mains £16 to £26), including Sunday roasts.

Foxhill Manor DESIGN HOTEL £££
(☎ 01386-852711; www.foxhillmanor.com; Farmcombe Estate; r incl breakfast from £375; P 📶 🐾) Occupying a 1904 mansion on 160 hectares of hillside estate, 2.5 miles northeast of Broadway, ultra-luxurious Foxhill is all Cotswolds chic with stripped-back Scandi-influenced style. From dazzlingly bold decor (leopard-print cushions, a hot-pink bathroom, twin window-facing baths) to period stucco-work, the eight sleek all-different suites sparkle with character. The in-house chef cooks according to personal requests.

Mount Inn PUB FOOD ££
(☎ 01386-584316; www.themountinn.co.uk; Stanton; mains £13-22; ⊙ noon-1pm & 6-9pm; P) Perched above pretty honey-washed Stanton, 3 miles southwest of Broadway, the Mount Inn is one of the Cotswolds' most idyllically positioned pubs. The food's fantastic too: hearty country fare carefully prepared with contemporary flair. Menus range over breaded local St Eadburgha cheese, beer-battered haddock, gammon steaks, mushroom-halloumi burgers and daily-changing seasonal specials. Outdoor benches revel in those glorious hilltop views.

Information

Tourist Office (01386-852937; www.visit-broadway.co.uk; Russell Sq; 10am-5pm Mon-Sat, 11am-3pm Sun Apr-Oct, 10am-4pm Mon-Sat Nov-Mar) Sells maps of local walks.

Getting There & Away

Marchants and Johnsons Excelbus buses head to the following destinations:

Cheltenham (route 606/606S; £3.10, 35 minutes)

Chipping Campden (route 21/22/24/606S; £2.70 to £4.50, 20 minutes)

Moreton-in-Marsh (route 21/22; £3.20, 30 minutes)

Stratford-upon-Avon (route 21/22/24/606S; £4.20, one hour)

Winchcombe (route 606/606S; £2.80, 30 minutes)

Winchcombe

POP 4538

Winchcombe, 8 miles northeast of Cheltenham, is very much a working, living town, where butchers, bakers and independent shops line the main streets. It was capital of the Anglo-Saxon kingdom of Mercia and one of the major towns in the Cotswolds until the Middle Ages, as well as an important tobacco producer. Today, the remnants of this illustrious past can still be seen in Winchcombe's dramatic stone and half-timbered buildings. Keep an eye out for the picturesque cottages on Vineyard St and Dents Tce.

Winchcombe is particularly popular with and ideally situated for walkers.

Sights

Sudeley Castle CASTLE

(01242-604244; www.sudeleycastle.co.uk; adult/child £14.50/5.50; 10am-5pm mid-Mar–Oct; P) Winchcombe's main attraction, this magnificent castle has welcomed many a monarch over its thousand-year history, including Richard III, Henry VIII and Charles I. It's most famous as the home and final resting place of Catherine Parr (Henry VIII's widow), who lived here with her fourth husband, Thomas Seymour. You'll find **Catherine's tomb** in the castle's Perpendicular Gothic St Mary's Church, making this the only private house in England where a queen is buried. There are also 10 splendid gardens here.

Henry VIII and Anne Boleyn visited Sudeley together in 1535. Princess Elizabeth (before becoming Elizabeth I) was part of the household until Seymour's inappropriate displays of affection towards her prompted Catherine to banish her from the premises. Lady Jane Grey (the ill-fated 'Nine Days Queen') was also sent here to live with the Seymours, and was the chief mourner at Catherine's funeral (1548).

The house is still a family home and some of the interior may be off-limits to visitors, but you can get a good sense of its grand proportions while visiting the exhibitions of costumes, memorabilia and paintings, and the gorgeous surrounding grounds. The gardens include spectacular avenues of sculpted yews, an intricate knot garden (inspired by the pattern of one of Elizabeth I's gowns) and aviaries containing magnificently coloured pheasants. The rose-filled **Queen's Garden**, based on its original Tudor parterre, gets its name from having been strolled in by four English queens (Anne Boleyn, Catherine Parr, Lady Jane Grey and Elizabeth I).

Hailes Abbey RUINS

(EH; www.english-heritage.org.uk; Hailes; adult/child £5/3; 10am-6pm Jul & Aug, to 5pm Easter-Jun, Sep & Oct; P) Three miles northeast of Winchcombe lie the meagre ruins of this 13th-century Cistercian abbey, once one of England's main pilgrimage centres, due to a long-running medieval scam. The abbey was said to possess a vial of Christ's blood, which turned out to be merely coloured water; before the deception came to light, thousands of pilgrims contributed to the abbey's wealth. Free audio guides lead you around.

Belas Knap Long Barrow ARCHAEOLOGICAL SITE

(EH; www.english-heritage.org.uk; near Charlton Abbots; dawn-dusk) FREE Dating from around 3000 BC, Belas Knap is one of the country's best-preserved neolithic burial chambers, with a 'false' portal leading to nowhere. The remains of 31 people were found when its four chambers were excavated. At 290m, views across Sudeley Castle and the surrounding countryside are breathtaking. The barrow can be accessed from Winchcombe by a 2½-mile hike south along the Cotswold Way. Alternatively, park on Corndean Lane and take a steep half-mile walk up across fields.

Sleeping & Eating

Wesley House B&B ££

(01242-602366; www.wesleyhouse.co.uk; High St; s £70-95, d £85-110; restaurant noon-2pm & 7-9pm Tue-Sat, noon-2pm Sun;) Methodist founder John Wesley once stayed in this wonderful 15th-century half-timbered town house with five pleasantly styled rooms and a warm welcome. 'Mumble Meadow', splashed with reds, overlooks the street, while 'Almsbury' has its own terrace gazing out across the countryside. Downstairs is split between a relaxed bar and grill, and a more formal restaurant serving fabulous modern-British cuisine (mains £16 to £24).

★5 North St MODERN EUROPEAN **£££**
(☎01242-604566; www.5northstreetrestaurant.co.uk; 5 North St; 2-/3-course lunch £26/30, 3- to 7-course dinner £47-70; ⏲7-9pm Tue, noon-1.30pm & 7-9pm Wed-Sat, noon-1.30pm Sun; ✎) This long-standing Michelin-starred restaurant is a treat from start to finish, from its splendid 400-year-old timbered exterior to the elegant, inventive creations you eventually find on your plate. Marcus Ashenford's cooking is rooted in traditional seasonal ingredients, but the odd playful experiment (such as duck-egg pasta or malt ice cream) adds that extra magic. Vegetarians will enjoy their own dedicated menu.

Information

Tourist Office (☎01242-602925; www.winchcombe.co.uk; Town Hall, High St; ⏲10am-4pm daily Apr-Oct, to 3pm Sat & Sun Nov-Mar) Has maps of local walks and runs free guided town tours at 11am and 2.30pm on Sunday, Easter to October.

Getting There & Away

The **Gloucestershire Warwickshire Railway** (GWR; ☎01242-621405; www.gwsr.com; day pass adult/child £16/7; ⏲Mar-Dec; 👪) runs between Winchcombe and Cheltenham (£12, 25 minutes).

Marchants buses travel to/from Broadway (route 606/606S; £2.80, 30 minutes) and Cheltenham (route 606/606S/W1/W2; £2.50, 20 to 45 minutes).

Painswick

POP 1762

One of the most beautiful and unspoilt towns in the Cotswolds, hilltop Painswick sits 10 miles southwest of Cheltenham, but it sees only a trickle of visitors. You can wander the narrow winding streets and admire the picture-perfect cottages, handsome stone town houses and medieval inns at your own leisure. Keep an eye out for Bisley St, the original main drag, which was superseded by the now ancient-looking New St in medieval times.

WORTH A TRIP

PRINCE CHARLES' HIGHGROVE

The private residence of Prince Charles and the Duchess of Cornwall, **Highgrove** (☎0303 123 7310; www.highgrovegardens.com; Doughton; tours £25; ⏲Apr-mid-Oct) is famous for its exquisite, sustainable, organic gardens, which include rows of shape-clipped yews and a 'carpet garden' modelled on an oriental rug. Two-hour garden tours run on select days. Tickets (prebooked) sell out far in advance, though last-minute tickets are sometimes available through **Highgrove Shop** (www.highgroveshop.com; 10 Long St; ⏲9.30am-5pm Mon-Sat, 10.30am-4pm Sun). Highgrove is a mile southwest of Tetbury.

The bucolic little village of Slad, 2 miles south of Painswick in the Slad Valley, was once the much-loved home of writer Laurie Lee, who immortalised its beauty in *Cider with Rosie*.

Sights

Painswick Rococo Garden GARDENS
(☎01452-813204; www.rococogarden.org.uk; off B4073; adult/child £7/3.30; ⏲10.30am-5pm mid-Jan–Oct; P 👪) Just north of Painswick, this stunner is the only garden of its type in England, designed by Benjamin Hyett in the 1740s as a vast 'outdoor room' and now restored to its former glory. Winding paths soften the otherwise strict geometrical precision, leading visitors around the central vegetable garden, plunge pool and pond to the many Gothic follies dotted across the grounds. Among these is the eccentric Red House, with Latin quotes from the Song of Solomon etched into its stained-glass windows.

St Mary's Church CHURCH
(www.stmaryspainswick.org.uk; New St; ⏲9.30am-dusk) Painswick centres on this fine 14th-century, Perpendicular Gothic wool church, surrounded by 18th-century table-top tombs and clipped yew trees that resemble giant lollipops. Legend has it that only 99 trees could ever grow here, as the devil would shrivel the 100th tree. They planted it anyway, to celebrate the millennium and – lo and behold! – one of the trees toppled several years later. In the street, at the foot of the churchyard, stands a rare set of iron stocks.

Sleeping & Eating

Troy House B&B ££
(☎01452-812339; www.troyguesthouse.co.uk; Gloucester St; s/d £75/85;) This great little B&B sleeps guests in four sweet, spacious rooms, two of which occupy their own separate rear cottage accessed from a pretty courtyard. They're prettily decked out with soothing cream decor, comfy beds and baskets of toiletries, and freshly cooked breakfasts are excellent.

★ **The Painswick** LUXURY HOTEL £££
(☎01452-813688; www.thepainswick.co.uk; Kemps Lane; r/ste from £119/344; restaurant noon-2.30pm & 7-9.30pm;) Relaunched in 2016 after a seriously chic makeover, The Painswick blends 18th-century architecture with boldly contemporary decor, a laid-back feel and 16 individually decorated, pastel-painted rooms. All come with luxury comforts, including Nespresso machines; some have claw-foot bath-tubs, others four-poster beds or tile-floored bathrooms. There are massage/treatment rooms, plus a futuristic bar, colour-popping lounge and good modern restaurant (mains £15 to £24).

Woolpack PUB FOOD ££
(☎01452-813429; www.thewoolpackslad.com; Slad; mains £11-16; noon-midnight;) A wonderfully authentic old-world village pub with a lively local buzz, the Woolpack was a favourite watering hole of Slad-based writer Laurie Lee, whose portrait and books adorn the walls. It's perfect for a pint, stocking excellent locally brewed beers including Uley Bitter. The tempting daily-changing seasonal menu delivers classic gammon or fish and chips alongside pastas, burgers, curries and pizzas (Monday). Slad is 2 miles south of Painswick.

WORTH A TRIP

SLIMBRIDGE WETLAND CENTRE

A pioneer in wetlands conservation, the 325-hectare reserve **Slimbridge Wetland Centre** (WWT; ☎01453-891900; www.wwt.org.uk/slimbridge; Bowditch, Slimbridge; adult/child £11.90/6.55; 9.30am-5.30pm Apr-Oct, to 5pm Nov-Mar;) has provided a haven for thousands of migratory and resident birds since 1946. The observation tower affords spectacular 360-degree views for spotting some of the 200-plus feathered species, which range from visiting swallows, peregrine falcons, white-fronted geese and Bewick's swans to hot-pink resident flamingos. Migratory birds visit in winter, while spring brings plenty of chicks. There's an array of activities, including self-led canoeing (£5). The reserve is 5 miles northeast of Berkeley, off the A38.

Information

Tourist Office (☎01452-812278; www.painswicktouristinfo.co.uk; Gravedigger's Hut, St Mary's Church, New St; 10am-4pm Mon & Wed-Fri, to 1pm Tue & Sat Mar-Oct) In the church grounds.

Getting There & Away

Stagecoach bus 61 heads to/from Cheltenham (£3.40, 32 minutes) and Stroud (£2, 15 minutes).

Uley

POP 998

This lovely little hamlet, with its quaint village green and jumble of pretty houses, sits below the overgrown remains of the largest Iron Age hill fort in England, Uley Bury. There are some fascinating sights nearby, including two prehistoric long barrows. Uley is 7.5 miles southwest of Stroud.

Sights

Uley Bury ARCHAEOLOGICAL SITE
(24hr) FREE England's largest Iron Age hill fort dates from about 300 BC and sprawls across 13 (overgrown) hectares above Uley. You can follow the 1.1-mile perimeter track around its ramparts, which afford fabulous views over Uley and the Severn Vale. If you're driving, an unsignposted 100m track leads to a corner of the bury from a small car park, 1 mile north of Uley on the B4066. For walkers, a steep path climbs up to the bury from Uley's village church.

From the car park, you can also follow part of the Cotswold Way a short distance north to Uley Long Barrow, a 3500 BC burial mound.

Woodchester Mansion HOUSE
(☎01453-861541; www.woodchestermansion.org.uk; Woodchester Park, Nympsfield; adult/child £7.50/free; 11am-5pm Tue-Sat late Mar-Oct) Untouched since the mid-1870s, grand, graceful Woodchester Mansion was abandoned before it was finished. Doors open to nowhere, fireplaces are stuck halfway up walls, and corridors end at ledges with views of the ground

below. The house also features some impressive gruesome gargoyles and is home to one of England's most important colonies of horseshoe bats and several resident ghosts. Marked trails lead through the surrounding parkland. It's 3 miles north of Uley, off the B4066.

Getting There & Away

Stagecoach bus 35 heads to/from Stroud (£2.80, 35 minutes), though you're better off with your own car.

WESTERN GLOUCESTERSHIRE

West of the Cotswolds, Gloucestershire's greatest asset is the elegant Regency town of Cheltenham, home to tree-lined terraces, upmarket boutiques and a tempting collection of hotels and restaurants. The county capital, Gloucester, is well worth a visit for its magnificent Perpendicular Gothic cathedral. Just southwest lies Berkeley, with its historic Norman castle. Further west, the Forest of Dean is a leafy backwater perfect for walking, cycling, kayaking and other adventure activities.

WORTH A TRIP

BERKELEY CASTLE

The fine red-stone **Berkeley Castle** (☎01453-810303; www.berkeley-castle.com; adult/child £11/6; 11am-5pm Sun-Wed Apr-Oct; P) has been the home of the Berkeleys for nearly 900 years, and little has changed since it was built as a sturdy Norman fortress. Edward II was imprisoned and then allegedly murdered here in 1327 on the order of his wife and her lover. Visits include the 12th-century keep, the King's Gallery (with cell and dungeon) and the spectacular medieval Great Hall (lined with tapestries). Free 45-minute guided tours run every 30 minutes.

Cheltenham

POP 115,700

Cheltenham, on the western edge of the Cotswolds, is the region's major town, and retains an air of gracious refinement left over from its heyday as a spa resort in the 18th century. At the time, it rivalled Bath as the place for sick rich people to go, and today it still has many graceful Regency buildings and manicured squares. These days, however, it's best known for its racecourse and mid-March horse races.

Cheltenham's excellent hotel and restaurant offerings make it a much more appealing base to the region than the county town of Gloucester (12 miles west), but it's unlikely to be the highlight of your trip.

Central Cheltenham extends around the grand tree-lined Promenade, at the southern end of which lies the fashionable Montpellier area.

Sights

Montpellier AREA

As well as its handsome architecture, Montpellier hosts a lively collection of bars, restaurants, hotels and independent shops and boutiques. Along **Montpellier Walk**, 32 caryatids (draped female figures based on those of Athens' Acropolis) act as structural supports between the 1840s shops, each balancing an elaborately carved cornice on her head. Directly opposite are the pretty Montpellier Gardens, established in 1809.

The Wilson MUSEUM, GALLERY

(☎01242-237431; www.thewilson.org.uk; Clarence St; 9.30am-5.15pm) FREE Cheltenham's excellent museum depicts local life through the ages and has wonderful displays on William Morris and the Arts and Crafts movement, including a painted pine table designed by Morris. It also contains exhibits on British ceramics, fine art and jewellery, and the Roman era. A section on Captain Scott's ill-fated expedition to Antarctica highlights the important role of local lad Edward Wilson, for whom the museum is named.

Sleeping

★**Bradley** B&B ££

(☎01242-519077; www.thebradleyhotel.co.uk; 19 Royal Pde, Bayshill Rd; s/d from £94/99; P) This brilliantly preserved Regency house in Montpellier has lost none of its original flair in its transition into a fabulous, wonderfully comfortable B&B. Each of the six rooms has its own individual style, combining antique furniture, vintage trinkets and original artwork with modern amenities.

Wyastone Townhouse B&B ££

(☎01242-245549; www.wyastonehotel.co.uk; Parabola Rd; s/d from £75/125; P) A keen young couple heads up this lovely white

Cheltenham

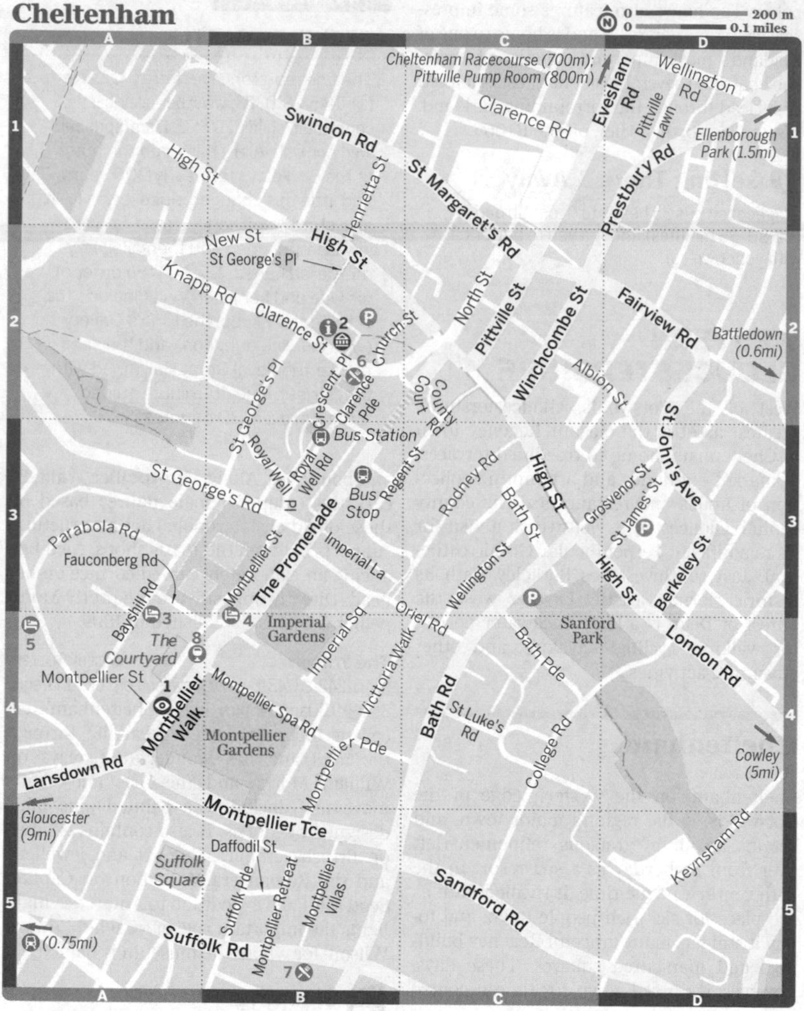

Cheltenham

Sights

1 Montpellier A4
2 The Wilson B2

Sleeping

3 Bradley A4
4 No 131 .... B4
5 Wyastone Townhouse A4

Eating

6 L'Artisan B2
7 Le Champignon Sauvage B5

Drinking & Nightlife

8 John Gordons A4

Victorian house in Montpellier. Rooms in the main house are grander than those surrounding the pretty back courtyard, but all 16 are comfortable and well equipped. Decor is bright and fresh, with paintings by local artists. There are plenty of tips on Cheltenham and the Cotswolds, plus wonderful homemade breakfasts. Excellent value.

No 131 BOUTIQUE HOTEL **£££**

(☎01242-822939; www.no131.com; 131 The Promenade; r incl breakfast £145-335; wi-fi) Housed in a stunning Georgian building, No 131 is an exquisite luxury addition to Cheltenham's hotel scene. The 11 supremely comfortable, country-chic rooms combine original artwork, antique touches (such as 19th-century claw-foot baths) and contemporary comforts (Nespresso machines, iPod docks). Some have in-room baths, others step-down walk-in showers. Scented candles dot the corridors, the bar buzzes and there's a luxe, laid-back vibe.

Eating & Drinking

L'Artisan FRENCH ££
(☎01242 571257; www.lartisan-restaurant.com; 30 Clarence St; mains £12-20; ⊙noon-2pm & 6-9pm Tue-Sat;) Decked with ornate mirrors, red-striped velvet chairs and mini-chandeliers, yellow-walled L'Artisan delights with its bubbly atmosphere and smartly prepared, thoroughly French food. Meals begin with homemade breads and spreads, followed by fluffy risotto, stuffed chicken breast, a choice of omelettes or a 'fish-duo' dish. Service from the efficient staff is superb.

★**Le Champignon Sauvage** FRENCH £££
(☎01242-573449; www.lechampignonsauvage.co.uk; 24-28 Suffolk Rd; 2-/3-/4-course menu £50/63/73; ⊙12.30-1.30pm & 7.30-8.45pm Tue-Sat) For nearly 30 years, this two-Michelin-starred Cheltenham institution has been delighting visitors and locals alike with chef David Everitt-Matthias' finely executed dishes and imaginative flavour combinations. We're not alone in thinking it's Gloucestershire's best restaurant. The set lunch and dinner menus are good value.

John Gordons WINE BAR
(☎01242-245985; www.johngordons.co.uk; 11 Montpellier Arcade; ⊙10.30am-10pm Mon-Wed, to 11pm Thu, to 1am Fri & Sat, noon-9pm Sun) This elegantly low-key wine-and-spirits bar delivers a wonderful globetrotting selection of whiskies, gins, wines, beers and ciders, accompanied by local cheese boards, charcuterie platters and other light bites (£3 to £14). Perfect for sampling enormous glass goblets of highly popular Cotwolds-distilled gin (with tonic, of course).

Festivals

Cheltenham Literature Festival LITERATURE
(www.cheltenhamfestivals.com; ⊙early Oct) One of the world's oldest book-focused festivals kicks off over 10 days in autumn, hosting an astounding array of talks, workshops, interviews and debates by 600 top writers, actors, scholars and other literary figures.

Information

Tourist Office (☎01242-237431; www.visitcheltenham.com; The Wilson, Clarence St; ⊙9.30am-5.15pm) Inside the town museum.

Transport

BUS

Stagecoach, Pulhams, Marchants and Swanbrook operate local buses from Cheltenham. Most buses depart from the **bus station** (Royal Well Rd); some use stops along the Promenade. Bus destinations include the following:

Broadway (route 606/606S; £3.10, 35 minutes)
Cirencester (route 51; £3.60, 40 minutes)
Gloucester (route 10/94/97/98/99; £3.20, 45 minutes)
Oxford (route 853; £8, 1½ hours)
Stow-on-the-Wold (route 801; £3, 1¼ hours)
Stratford-upon-Avon (route 606S, Sunday only; £8, 1½ hours)
Stroud (route 61; £3.60, 45 minutes)
Winchcombe (route 606/606S; £2.50, 20 minutes)

National Express coach destinations:

Birmingham (£12, 1½ hours)
Bristol (£9, 1½ hours)
Leeds (£42, 5½ hours)
London Victoria (£7, three hours)
Newcastle-upon-Tyne (£56, eight hours)
Nottingham (£25, four hours)

TRAIN

Cheltenham Spa train station is a mile west of the centre. Buses (£2) run to/from the station every 10 minutes. Services include the following:

Bath (£14.30, 1½ hours)
Bristol (£9, 40 minutes)
Cardiff (£18, 1½ hours)
Edinburgh (£130, six hours)
Exeter (£23, 1¾ hours)
Gloucester (£4.60, 10 minutes)
London Paddington (£33, 2¼ hours)

Forest of Dean

The Forest of Dean is the oldest oak forest in England and a wonderfully scenic place for outdoor adventure activities. The 42-sq-mile woodland, designated England's first National Forest Park in 1938, was formerly a royal hunting ground and a centre of iron and coal mining. Its mysterious depths supposedly inspired the forests of JRR Tolkien's Middle Earth books, and key scenes in *Harry Potter & the Deathly Hallows* were filmed here.

WORTH A TRIP

GLOUCESTER CATHEDRAL

The spectacular **Gloucester Cathedral** (☎01452-528095; www.gloucestercathedral.org.uk; 12 College Green; admission free, tower tours adult/child £7/1; ⏲7.30am-6pm) is among the first and finest examples of the English Perpendicular Gothic style. A Norman church was built here by a group of Benedictine monks in the 12th century, on the site of a Saxon abbey, and further elements (including the present-day tower) were added in the 15th century. When Edward II died in 1327 under suspicious circumstances at nearby Berkeley Castle, the church became his burial place.

Inside, the best of Norman Romanesque and Gothic design are skilfully combined with sturdy columns, creating a sense of gracious solidity. From the 14th-century wooden choir stalls, you'll get a good view of the imposing 22m-high **Great East Window**, the largest in Europe when it was installed in the 1350s. Beneath the window in the northern ambulatory is **Edward II's tomb**, a magnificently elaborate work in alabaster that turned the place into a important pilgrimage spot for 70 years after his death. Right behind the altar is the late-15th-century **Lady Chapel**, a glorious patchwork of carved stone and stained glass.

One of the cathedral's most resplendent treasures is the exquisite **Great Cloister**, which featured in the first, second and sixth *Harry Potter* films. Completed in 1367, it contains the earliest example of fan vaulting in England and is matched in beauty only by Henry VII's chapel at Westminster Abbey. When the sun shines through, stained-glass windows tinge the cloister pink.

The Forest of Dean also gives its name to one of Gloucestershire's districts, which includes the towns of Newent and Coleford, north and west (respectively) of the forest itself. To the northwest, the forest spills over into Herefordshire. The River Wye skirts its west edge, offering glorious views to canoeists paddling out from the village of Symonds Yat.

A good place to begin exploring the forest proper is the **Dean Heritage Centre** (☎01594-822170; www.deanheritagecentre.com; Camp Mill, Soudley; adult/child £7.20/5.40; ⏲10am-5pm Apr-Oct, to 4pm Nov-Mar; P 🚻), just outside Soudley, within the forest's eastern fringe.

Sights

★International Centre for Birds of Prey AVIARY

(☎01531-820286; www.icbp.org; Boulsdon House, Newent; adult/child £10.90/7; ⏲10.30am-4.30pm Feb-Nov; P) Watch raptors swoop and dive at this large, long-standing countryside complex, 2 miles southwest of Newent (follow the signs). There are three flyings per day (11.30am, 2pm and 4.15pm), along with aviaries housing 70 species of owls, falcons, kestrels, eagles, buzzards, hawks, kites and other birds of prey from all over the world. For the hands-on feel, choose from a range of 'experience days', such as Hunting or Owls (from £70).

Clearwell Caves CAVE

(☎01594-832535; www.clearwellcaves.com; Clearwell; adult/child £6.50/4.50; ⏲10am-5pm mid-Feb–Dec; P 🚻) Descend into the damp subterranean world of a 4500-year-old iron and ochre mine, comprising a warren of dimly lit passageways, caverns and pools, and home to several species of bats. 'Deep Level Caving' sessions (adult/child £25/18) take you even further in. From November, the caves are transformed into a hugely popular Christmas grotto. They're signposted off the B4228, a mile south of Coleford.

Puzzlewood FOREST, FARM

(☎01594-833187; www.puzzlewood.net; Perrygrove Rd, Coleford; adult/child £6.50/5; ⏲10am-5pm Apr-Sep, to 3.30pm Wed, Sat & Sun Mar, Nov & Dec; P 🚻) A pre-Roman open-cast ore mine, overgrown with eerie moss-covered trees, Puzzlewood is a 6-hectare woodland web of paths, weird rock formations, tangled vines, rickety bridges, 200 uneven steps and dark passageways seemingly designed to leave you disorientated. Parts of hit TV shows *Doctor Who* and *Merlin*, as well as *Star Wars: The Force Awakens*, were shot here. There's a mile of pathways to explore and kids will love the farm animals. Find it a mile south of Coleford on the B4228.

WORTH A TRIP

SYMONDS YAT VILLAGE & ROCK

Symonds Yat Right on the northwest edge of the Forest of Dean, squeezed between the River Wye and the towering limestone outcrop Symonds Yat Rock, Symonds Yat is a tiny, endearing tangle of pubs, guesthouses and campsites, with great walks and a couple of canoeing centres. It's split into two halves by the river, which are connected by an ancient hand-hauled ferry (adult/child/bicycle £1.20/60p/60p; dawn to dusk).

Symonds Yat Rock (Symonds Yat East; admission free; 24hr; P) Soaring 504m high above Symonds Yat East, this limestone outcrop has outstanding wraparound views of the River Wye and the surrounding countryside. It's a favourite spot for birdwatchers; you may be lucky enough to spot the resident pair of peregrine falcons whooshing by the drop-off. You can walk up from Symonds Yat East. A kiosk atop the rock sells drinks and snacks, and peaceful walking trails continue east through the forest.

Wyedean Canoe & Adventure Centre (01600-890238; www.wyedean.co.uk; Symonds Yat East; half-day hire from £23) Hires out canoes and kayaks, and organises white-water trips, archery, high ropes, abseiling, caving, rock climbing and stand-up paddle-boarding (SUP). Opening hours depend on the conditions.

Activities

Way2Go Adventures ADVENTURE SPORTS
(01594-800908; www.way2goadventures.co.uk; 20 Forest Rd, Milkwall) Offers a range of canoeing, kayaking, raft-building, stand-up paddle-boarding (SUP) and Nordic-walking expeditions. Opening hours depend on the conditions. Milkwall is 1 mile southeast of Coleford.

Sleeping

Wye Valley YHA HOSTEL £
(0845 371 9666; www.yha.org.uk; Welsh Bicknor; dm £15-25, d £30, summer bell tents from £49; Mar-Oct; P) This austere former Victorian rectory overlooks the countryside from lovely riverside grounds, 2 miles southeast of Goodrich. It offers neat shared-bathroom doubles and dorms for four to 10 people, plus breakfast, dinner, riverside barbecues and walking tips. It's well signposted, but drivers should expect a long, steep, difficult access road; follow signs near Goodrich Castle and fork right where the road splits.

Garth Cottage B&B ££
(01600-890364; www.garthcottage-symondsyat.com; Symonds Yat East; s/d £50/85; mid-Mar–Oct; P) Garth Cottage is an exceedingly friendly and efficiently run family-owned B&B, right by the River Wye, next to the ferry crossing. Comfy, chintzy, spotlessly maintained rooms have floral fabrics, tea and coffee kits and gorgeous river views. Home-cooked breakfasts are excellent. Discounted rates available for longer stays.

★ **Tudor Farmhouse** BOUTIQUE HOTEL £££
(01594-833046; www.tudorfarmhousehotel.co.uk; High St, Clearwell; d £100-200, ste £200-230, all incl breakfast; P) Sleep in a chic, contemporary world of whites, creams and spiralling Tudor-era staircases, inside a beautifully updated farmhouse. A range of stylish rooms, most with exposed beams, check-print blankets and Nespresso machines, rambles across the main house. The spacious 'Roost' suite, with its claw-foot bath, is particularly romantic. More rooms sit in adjacent buildings. There's also an exceptional modern British **restaurant** (mains £13-25, 2-/3-course set lunch £22/25; 8am-10pm, noon-5pm & 6.30-9pm; P).

★ **Saracens Head Inn** MODERN BRITISH ££
(01600-890435; www.saracensheadinn.co.uk; Symonds Yat East; mains £11-18; noon-2.30pm & 6.30-9pm; P) Creatively prepared modern British dishes crammed with local ingredients tick all boxes at this welcoming riverside gastropub, right beside the ferry crossing. Menus range from garlic-grilled chicken, brioche burgers and veggie risottos to baked Camembert platters, featuring plenty of seasonal specials. Delicious desserts might include sensational smashed cheesecake. Dine in the warm pub-restaurant or at river-view benches outside. Bookings recommended.

BUCKINGHAMSHIRE, BEDFORDSHIRE & HERTFORDSHIRE

Now on the edge of London's commuter belt, these three green-clad counties once served as rural boltholes for the city's rich and titled, especially when the stench and grime of the industrial age was at its peak. The sweeping valleys and forested hills are still scattered with majestic stately homes and splendid gardens, many of which are open to the public.

The 324-sq-mile **Chilterns Area of Outstanding Natural Beauty** (AONB; www.visitchilterns.co.uk) extends southwest from Hitchin (Hertfordshire), through Bedfordshire and Buckinghamshire, to Oxfordshire.

Woburn

POP 933

Blissfully set within the Bedfordshire countryside, 6 miles southeast of Milton Keynes, this peaceful village has existed since the 10th century. Despite hosting a couple of big attractions, the county's only Michelin-starred restaurant and a busy main road, it's still charmingly sleepy.

OFF THE BEATEN TRACK

STOWE GARDENS

Covering 160 hectares, the glorious **Stowe Gardens** (NT; 01280-817156; www.nationaltrust.org.uk; New Inn Farm; adult/child £11.20/5.60; 10am-6pm Mar-Oct, to 4pm Nov-Feb; P) were shaped in the 18th century by Britain's greatest landscape gardeners. Among them was master landscape architect Lancelot 'Capability' Brown, who kickstarted his career at Stowe. The gardens are best known for their many temples and follies, commissioned by the super-wealthy Richard Temple (1st Viscount Cobham), whose family motto was *Templa Quam Dilecta* (How Delightful are Your Temples). Paths meander past lakes, bridges, temples, fountains and cascades, and through Capability Brown's Grecian Valley.

Sights

Woburn Abbey HOUSE

(01525-290333; www.woburnabbey.co.uk; Park St; adult/child £16/7.25; house 11am-5pm mid-Mar–Oct, gardens 10am-5pm mid-Mar–Oct; P) Originally a Cistercian abbey but dissolved by Henry VIII and awarded to the Earl of Bedford (the current Duke of Bedford still calls it home), Woburn Abbey is a wonderful country pile set within a 1200-hectare deer park. The opulent house displays paintings by Gainsborough, Reynolds and van Dyck, and an impressive 21 views of Venice by Canaletto. Highlights include Queen Victoria's bedroom, beautiful wall hangings and cabinets in the Chinese Room, plus the mysterious story of the Flying Duchess.

Woburn Safari Park ZOO

(www.woburnsafari.co.uk; Woburn Park; adult/child £23/16; 10am-5pm mid-Feb–Oct) Sprawling across 150 hectares, this is the country's largest drive-through animal reserve. Rhinos, lions, zebras, bison, monkeys, elephants, giraffes, wolves and wallabies roam the grounds, while in the 'foot safari' area, you can see sea lions, penguins, meerkats and lemurs.

Eating

★**Paris House** MODERN BRITISH £££

(01525-290692; www.parishouse.co.uk; Woburn Park, London Rd; lunch £43, dinner £91-109; noon-1.30pm & 7-8.30pm Wed & Thu, to 9pm Fri & Sat, noon-2pm Sun) On the Woburn Estate, Paris House is a handsome black-and-white structure that the 9th duke of Bedford took a shine to on a visit to the French capital and had shipped back here. During WWII, the Queen often stayed here. Now it's Bedfordshire's top and only Michelin-starred restaurant, serving exquisite, six- to 10-course set tasting menus of beautifully presented contemporary cuisine.

Information

The Woburn Passport ticket (adult/child £29.99/18.99), valid April to November, can be used on two separate days within any 12-month period and gives access to both Woburn Abbey and Woburn Safari Park.

Waddesdon

POP 1797

Straddling the A41, 5 miles northwest of Aylesbury, sleepy little Waddesdon is well worth a visit for its splendid 19th-century manor.

WORTH A TRIP

WARNER BROS STUDIO TOUR: THE MAKING OF HARRY POTTER

Whether you're a fair-weather fan or a full-on Potterhead, the magical **Warner Bros Studio Tour: The Making of Harry Potter** (☎0345 084 0900; www.wbstudiotour.co.uk; Studio Tour Dr, Leavesden, WD25; adult/child £35/27; ⏰10am-8pm, hours vary; P; Watford Junction, then shuttle bus) is well worth the admittedly hefty admission price. You'll need to book your visit for an allocated time slot, arrive 20 minutes beforehand and allow two to three hours to do the complex full justice. It starts with a short film before you're ushered through giant doors into the actual set of Hogwarts' Great Hall – just the first of many 'wow' moments.

From here, you're free to explore the rest of the complex at your own pace, including a large hangar featuring all the most familiar interior sets (Dumbledore's office, the Gryffindor common room, Hagrid's hut), another starring Platform 9¾ and the Hogwarts Express, and an outdoor section with the exterior of Privet Dr, the purple triple-decker Knight Bus, Sirius Black's motorbike and a shop selling snacks and butterbeer (sickly sweet). Along the way, video screens burst into life to discuss elements of the production.

Other highlights include the animatronic workshop (say 'Hi' to the Hippogriff) and a stroll down Diagon Alley. All your favourite *Harry Potter* creatures are on display, from an enormous Aragog to Dobby the House-Elf. But the most magical treat is saved for last – a shimmering, gasp-inducing 1:24 scale model of Hogwarts, used for the exterior shots.

Then comes the biggest challenge for true fans and parents: a quite extraordinary gift shop stocked with all your wizardry accessories, including uniforms for each of the Hogwarts houses and replicas of the individually designed wands used by pretty much any character you can think of.

If you're driving, there's a large free car park, plus extensive directions on the website. Otherwise, catch a train to Watford Junction from London Euston (£9.80, 20 minutes), then take the shuttle bus (return £2.50, 10 minutes).

Sights

Waddesdon Manor HOUSE

(NT; ☎01296-653226; www.waddesdon.org.uk; off A41; adult/child £18/9, gardens only £9/4.50; ⏰house noon-4pm Wed-Fri, 11am-4pm Sat & Sun, gardens 10am-5pm Wed-Sun late Mar-Dec; P) A remarkable French Renaissance chateau-style fairy-tale palace, Waddesdon Manor was completed in 1889 for the Baron Ferdinand de Rothschild so that he could showcase his collection of French decorative arts and throw glamorous parties. Taking in its ostentatious gold-stone magnificence, it's easy to imagine the greats of Victorian society living it up in the palatial rooms. Admission to the house is by guided tours (book ahead); guests are free to wander the exquisite gardens.

Very little indoors space is left unadorned; only the Bachelors' Wing stands out as being noticeably more restrained. On display is an outstanding collection of Dutch Old Masters paintings, English portraits (by the likes of Reynolds and Gainsborough), Sèvres porcelain and ornate furniture, and the extensive wine cellars.

The beautiful gardens boast a superb formal parterre, adorned with colour-bursting flowers and a Pluto and Proserpine fountain, as well as contemporary sculptures, a rose garden and a rococo-revival aviary filled with rare, exotic birds.

From April to October, the manor operates a free daily shuttle bus to/from Aylesbury (check times online).

Sleeping & Eating

Five Arrows Hotel HOTEL £££

(☎01296-651727; www.thefivearrows.co.uk; High St; s/d incl breakfast from £85/210; P) Five Arrows is an elaborate half-timbered inn that was originally built to house the artisans working on nearby Waddesdon Manor. The 16 rooms have been stylishly renovated, and guests are entitled to free access to the manor gardens. The bright, elegant **restaurant** (mains £17-23; ⏰noon-2.15 & 6.30-9.15pm; P) serves excellent refined modern British fare in a plush setting.

Getting There & Away

Waddesdon is on the A41, 5 miles northwest of Aylesbury, which has two train stations with regular links to London Marylebone (£16, one hour). **Red Rose Travel** (www.redrosetravel.com)

ROYAL ASCOT

Join the glitterati in your finest outfit for **Royal Ascot** (☎0844 346 3000; www.ascot.co.uk; Ascot; Windsor Enclosure per day from £34, Queen Anne Enclosure per day from £75; ⏲mid-Jun), the biggest racing meet of the year, going strong since 1711. The royal family, A-list celebrities and other rich and famous gather here to show off their Jimmy Choos and place the odd bet. It's essential to book tickets well in advance for this five-day festival.

You can soak up the atmosphere from the Windsor Enclosure or head for the Queen Anne Enclosure to rub shoulders with the ladies in fancy hats.

buses 16 and 17 run between Waddesdon and Aylesbury (£3, 15 minutes) Monday to Saturday.

St Albans

POP 82,146

Under the name Verulamium, St Albans was the third-biggest city in Roman Britain. Its current name derives from Alban, a Christian Roman soldier who was martyred here in about AD 250, becoming the first English martyr. These days, it's a bustling and prosperous market town bordering London's northwestern fringes, with a host of crooked Tudor buildings, elegant Georgian town houses and a fantastic multi-era cathedral.

Sights

★St Albans Cathedral CATHEDRAL

(☎01727-890200; www.stalbanscathedral.org; off High St & Holywell Hill; admission free; ⏲8.30am-5.45pm, free tours 11.30am & 2.30pm Mon-Fri, 11.30am & 2pm Sat, 2.30pm Sun) Built by King Offa of Mercia in 793 around the tomb of St Alban, who was martyred here in approximately AD 250, this massive cathedral is a magnificent melange of Norman Romanesque and Gothic architecture. The longest medieval nave in the country gives way to ornate ceilings, semi-lost 13th-century wall paintings, rounded Norman arches built with reused brick from Roman Verulamium and, of course, the shrine of St Alban, hidden behind a stone reredos.

Verulamium Museum MUSEUM

(☎01727-751810; www.stalbansmuseums.org.uk; St Michael's St; adult/child £5/2.50; ⏲10am-5.30pm Mon-Sat, 2-5.30pm Sun) This fantastic multimedia exposé of everyday life in Roman Verulamium includes household objects, farming utensils, legionnaires' armour, statuary, jewellery, glassware, coins, pottery and grave goods. The big highlight, however, is the Mosaic Room, where five superb mosaic floors, uncovered between 1930 and 1955, are laid out, including a beautiful shell-shaped mosaic dating to around AD 130. The adjacent Verulamium Park contains the remains of a basilica, bathhouse, mosaic and parts of the city wall.

Sleeping & Eating

St Michael's Manor Hotel HOTEL £££

(☎01727-864444; www.stmichaelsmanor.com; Fishpool St; d incl breakfast £145-200; [P] [wifi]) In a lovely lakeside position, this 500-year-old manor offers 30 opulent, individually styled rooms hidden down hushed carpeted corridors. The eight contemporary-design 'luxury garden' rooms are sumptuously sleek, with deep purples, rich reds, patterned wallpaper and, for 'Mulberry', a four-poster bed and mirrored bathroom door. Rooms in the manor itself are less sparkly, but win fans with comfortably updated historical charm.

Lussmanns Fish & Grill MODERN BRITISH ££

(☎01727-851941; www.lussmans.com; Waxhouse Gate, off High St; mains £13-20; ⏲noon-9.30pm Sun-Thu, to 10.30pm Fri & Sat; [menu]) A bright, modern restaurant just steps from the cathedral, Lussmanns serves a changing, season-focused, ethically sourced menu of creative British dishes with Mediterranean touches and mostly local ingredients, such as pomegranate-infused salad or chicken with pancetta. There's a good-value set lunch with a glass of wine (two/three courses £12.50/17.95).

Information

Tourist Office (☎01727-864511; www.enjoystalbans.com; Alban Arena, off St Peter's St; ⏲10am-4.30pm Mon-Sat)

Getting There & Away

Regular trains run between St Albans City, a mile east of the centre, and London King's Cross/St Pancras (£11.60, 20 minutes) and London Blackfriars (£11.60, 30 minutes).

THE THAMES VALLEY

This prosperous part of the world, spreading west from London, acts as a country getaway for some of England's most influential figures. Within easy reach of the capital and yet entirely different in character, its pastoral landscape features handsome villages, historic houses and some of the top attractions in the country. Windsor Castle draws crowds to Windsor and Eton in search of royal pomp, while Henley-on-Thames is famous for its July rowing regatta. Meanwhile, the little village of Bray stakes its claim as the country's gastronomic capital with a string of Michelin-starred restaurants.

Windsor & Eton

POP 31,225

Dominated by the massive bulk of Windsor Castle, the twin Thames-side towns of Windsor and Eton have a rather surreal atmosphere, with the morning pomp and ceremony of the changing of the guards in Windsor, and the sight of schoolboys dressed in formal tailcoats wandering the streets of tiny Eton. Windsor town centre is full of expensive boutiques, grand cafes and buzzing restaurants. Eton, immediately north across the river, is far quieter, its one-street centre flanked by antique shops and art galleries. Both are easily accessible as a day trip from London.

Sights

★Windsor Castle CASTLE, PALACE

(☎0303 123 7304; www.royalcollection.org.uk; Castle Hill; adult/child £20/11.70; ⏲9.30am-5.15pm Mar-Oct, 9.45am-4.15pm Nov-Feb; ♿; 🚌702 from London Victoria, 🚆London Waterloo to Windsor & Eton Riverside, 🚆London Paddington to Windsor & Eton Central via Slough) The world's largest and oldest continuously occupied fortress, Windsor Castle is a majestic vision of battlements and towers. It's used for state occasions and is one of the Queen's principal residences; if she's at home, the Royal Standard flies from the Round Tower. Join a free guided tour (every half-hour) of the wards or take a handheld multimedia tour of the lavish State Apartments and beautiful chapels. Some sections may be off-limits if in use. Book tickets online to avoid queues.

William the Conqueror first established a royal residence in Windsor in 1080. Since then successive monarchs have rebuilt, remodelled and refurbished the castle complex to create the massive, sumptuous palace that stands here today. Henry II replaced the original wooden stockade in 1170 with a stone round tower and built the outer walls to the north, east and south; Elizabeth I carried out major palace-wide renovations; Charles II gave the State Apartments a glorious baroque makeover; George IV swept in with his team of artisans; and Queen Victoria refurbished an ornate chapel in memory of her beloved Albert.

➡ Queen Mary's Dolls' House

Your first stop is likely to be the incredible dolls' house designed by Sir Edwin Lutyens for Queen Mary between 1921 and 1924, on a scale of 1:12. The attention to detail is spellbinding: there's running water, electricity and lighting, tiny Crown Jewels, vintage wine in the cellar and mini-books by literary greats in the library. You may have to queue.

➡ State Apartments

The Grand Staircase, flanked by armour, weapons and a statue of Queen Victoria, sets the tone for a collection of absolutely spectacular rooms, dripping in gilt and screaming 'royal' from every painted surface and sparkling chandelier. Highlights include St George's Hall, used for state banquets of up to 162 people; its soaring ceilings are covered in the painted shields of the Knights of the Garter. For more intimate gatherings (just 60 people), the Queen entertains in the Waterloo Chamber, commemorating the 1815 victory over Napoleon, with portraits of

WORTH A TRIP

BLETCHLEY PARK

Once England's best-kept secret **Bletchley Park** (☎01908-640404; www.bletchleypark.org.uk; Bletchley; adult/child £17.25/10.25; ⏲9.30am-5pm; 🅿) was the scene of an enormous code-breaking operation during WWII, dramatised in the 2014 film *The Imitation Game*. At its peak, almost 8500 people worked here in total secrecy, intercepting up to 20,000 enemy messages a day, then decrypting, translating and interpreting the correspondence. Inside Block B, you can see the Bombe machine itself, crucial to the breaking of the code; volunteers will happily explain its inner workings.

Windsor & Eton

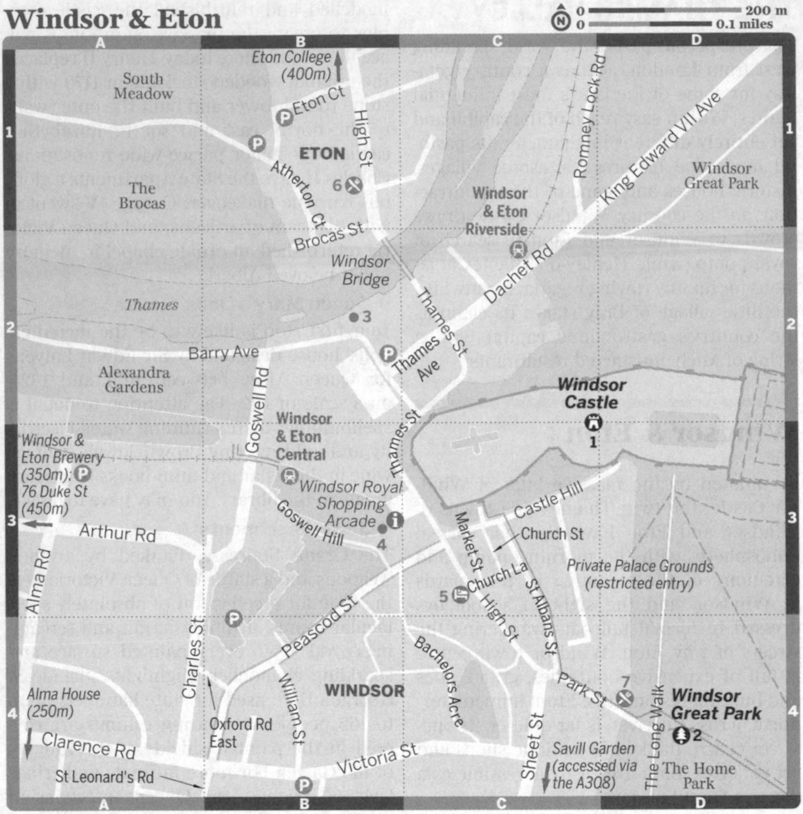

Windsor & Eton

Top Sights
1 Windsor Castle C3
2 Windsor Great Park D4

Activities, Courses & Tours
3 French Brothers B2
4 Royal Windsor Town Walks B3

Sleeping
5 Macdonald Windsor Hotel C3

Eating
6 Gilbey's B1
7 Two Brewers D4

statesmen including the Duke of Wellington and George IV.

The State Apartments house some exquisite pieces of art, among them works by Rubens, Canaletto and Anthony van Dyck.

➡ St George's Chapel

This elegant chapel, commissioned for the Order of the Garter by Edward IV in 1475, is one of England's finest examples of Perpendicular Gothic architecture. The nave and beautiful fan-vaulted roof were completed under Henry VII, but the final nail was driven under Henry VIII in 1528.

Along with Westminster Abbey, it serves as a royal mausoleum, housing the remains of 10 monarchs, including Henry VIII, Jane Seymour, Charles I and the present queen's father (King George VI), mother (Queen Elizabeth) and sister (Princess Margaret).

St George's Chapel closes on Sunday, but time your visit well and you can attend a morning service or Evensong at 5.15pm.

➡ Albert Memorial Chapel

Built in 1240 and dedicated to St Edward the Confessor, the small Albert Memorial Chapel was the place of worship for the Order of the Garter until St George's Chapel snatched away that honour. After the death of Prince Albert at Windsor Castle in 1861, Queen Victoria ordered its elaborate redecoration as a tribute to her husband and consort. A major feature of the restoration is the magnificent vaulted roof, whose gold mosaic pieces were crafted in Venice.

There's a monument to the prince, although he's actually buried with Queen Victoria in the Royal Mausoleum at Frogmore House in Windsor Great Park. Their youngest son, Prince Leopold (Duke of Albany), is, however, buried in the Albert Memorial Chapel.

➡ Changing of the Guard

A fabulous spectacle, with triumphant tunes from a military band and plenty of foot stamping from smartly attired lads in red uniforms and bear-skin caps, the changing of the guard draws crowds to Windsor Castle each day. It takes place at 11am Monday to Saturday from April to July, and on alternate days from August to March.

★ Windsor Great Park PARK

(☎01753-860222; www.windsorgreatpark.co.uk; Windsor; ⌚dawn-dusk) FREE Stretching from Windsor Castle almost all the way southwest to Ascot, Windsor Great Park covers just under 8 sq miles and features a lake, walking tracks, a bridleway, gardens and a deer park with 500 free-roaming red deer. Its popular Long Walk is a 2.7-mile jaunt south from King George IV Gate, south of the castle, to the 1831 Copper Horse statue of George III on Snow Hill, the park's highest point. From Windsor, public access is via Park St.

Eton College NOTABLE BUILDING

(☎01753-370100; www.etoncollege.com; High St, Eton; ⌚closed to the public) Eton College is the largest and most famous public (meaning private and fee-paying) boys' school in England, and arguably the most enduring symbol of England's class system. High-profile alumni include 19 British prime ministers, countless princes, kings and maharajas, famous explorers, authors, actors and economists – among them Princes William and Harry, George Orwell, Ian Fleming, John Maynard Keynes, Bear Grylls and Eddie Redmayne.

Eton was founded by Henry VI in 1440 with a view towards educating 70 highly qualified boys awarded a scholarship from a fund endowed by the king. Every year since then, 70 King's Scholars have been chosen based on the results of a highly competitive exam; these pupils are housed in separate quarters from the 1300 or so other students. All pupils are boarders and must wear formal tailcoats, waistcoats and white collars to lessons (though the top hats went out in 1948).

At the time of writing, no public visits or tours of Eton College were available. Small-group tours may begin in early 2017; check the website.

Runnymede HISTORIC SITE

(NT; www.nationaltrust.org.uk; Windsor Rd, Old Windsor; parking per hr £1.50; ⌚site dawn-dusk, car park 8.30am-7pm Apr-Sep, to 5pm Oct, Nov, Feb & Mar, to 4pm Dec & Jan; P) FREE In June 1215, King John met his barons in this field, 3 miles southeast of Windsor; over the following days they hammered out an agreement on a basic charter of rights guaranteeing the liberties of the king's subjects and restricting the monarch's absolute power. The document they signed was the Magna Carta, the world's first constitution. Today, the field remains much as it was, yet adorned with several modern-day memorials and two 1929 lodges, designed by Edwin Lutyens.

The Magna Carta formed the basis for statutes and charters throughout the world's democracies. Both the national and state constitutions of the USA, drawn up more than 500 years later, paraphrase it. To recognise its importance, the American Bar Association erected the **Memorial to Magna Carta** here in 1957 in the style of a Greek temple, across the field from the car park. A short uphill path nearby leads to the 1965 **President John F Kennedy Memorial**, which sits between trees on an acre of land gifted to the US. In the middle of the main field stands **The Jurors**, a 12-bronze-chair memorial honouring the Magna Carta's 800th anniversary (2015).

After stomping through the muddy field to these three memorials, it's possible to continue uphill on a 1.5-mile loop track to the moving **Commonwealth Airforces Memorial**, where the names of 20,000 WWII airmen without graves from the UK, Canada, New Zealand, Australia, India and South Africa are inscribed.

Bus 71 from Windsor (£4.20, 10 minutes) stops half a mile northwest of Runnymede, on Windsor Rd (A308).

READING FESTIVAL

Each August Bank Holiday weekend, up to 87,000 revellers descend on the industrial town of Reading for one of the country's biggest rock-music events. The **Reading Festival** (☎020-70093001; www.readingfestival.com; Reading; tickets day/weekend £66.50/213; ⊙Aug). is a three-day extravaganza featuring a top line of rock, indie, punk, metal and alternative artists. Set up camp for the weekend or just book a day ticket.

Tours

French Brothers BOATING

(☎01753-851900; www.frenchbrothers.co.uk; Windsor Promenade, Barry Ave, Windsor; ⊙10am-5pm mid-Feb–Oct) Offers a variety of boat trips along the Thames to/from Runnymede (return adult/child £14.40/9.60) and around Windsor (adult/child from £7.40/4.95).

Royal Windsor Town Walks WALKING

(☎01753-743900; www.windsor.gov.uk; Tourist Office, Old Booking Hall, Windsor Royal Shopping Arcade, Thames St; adult/child £7.50/6.50; ⊙11.45am Sat & 2.30pm Sun Easter-Aug) Detailed one-hour tours depart from the tourist office; you can also book online.

Sleeping

Alma House B&B ££

(☎01753-862983; www.almahouse.co.uk; 56 Alma Rd, Windsor; s/d from £65/75;) Within this pretty Victorian town house, half a mile southwest of the castle, the four smartly revamped rooms feature comfy beds, plenty of light and tasteful cream or purple decor. Two rooms accommodate families, as does the equally homey annexe room out the back. Breakfast is a minimal self-service continental spread.

Macdonald Windsor Hotel HOTEL £££

(☎0344 879 9101; www.macdonaldhotels.co.uk/Windsor; 23 High St, Windsor; r from £158;) Looking small and quaint from the road but magically transforming into 120 elegant rooms beyond its revolving door, the floral-scented Windsor is the slickest choice in town. Dark browns, creams, reds and purples add a plush, rich feel to the resolutely modern decor and facilities (such as capsule-coffee kits), and service hits that perfect friendly and professional note. Some rooms have castle glimpses.

Eating & Drinking

Two Brewers PUB FOOD ££

(☎01753-855426; www.twobrewerswindsor.co.uk; 34 Park St, Windsor; mains £12.50-17; ⊙11.30am-11pm Mon-Thu, 11.30am-11.30pm Fri & Sat, noon-10.30pm Sun) Pack into this atmospheric 18th-century inn perched on the edge of Windsor Great Park for tasty, well-prepped pub meals that are a cut above the usual pub grub. Menus range from soups, salads and tapas to steaks, fishcakes and cheese boards. Outdoor sunny benches front the flower-covered exterior; inside, think low-beamed ceilings, dim lighting and a roaring winter fire.

Gilbey's MODERN BRITISH £££

(☎01753-854921; www.gilbeygroup.com; 82-83 High St, Eton; mains £17-23, 2-/3-course menu £22.50/28.50; ⊙6-10pm Mon, noon-3pm & 6-10pm Tue-Sun) Small but perfectly formed, this bistro-restaurant in the heart of Eton is one of the area's best. Terracotta tiling, deep-green decor and a sunny courtyard garden and conservatory give Gilbey's the feel of a European cafe, complemented by an extensive wine list and a superb modern-British menu of soups, steaks, pies, artisan cheeses and Sunday lunches.

Windsor & Eton Brewery BREWERY

(☎01753-854075; www.webrew.co.uk; 1 Vansittart Estate, Windsor; ⊙8am-6pm Mon-Fri, 10am-3pm Sat) Call into this boutique brewery, just west of Windsor's centre, to sample and stock up on hoppy delights such as the award-winning Knight of the Garter pale ale, Eton Rifles or the royal-wedding special, the Windsor Knot. It's worth enquiring about the occasional two-hour tours, which take you behind the scenes.

Information

Tourist Office (☎01753-743900; www.windsor.gov.uk; Old Booking Hall, Windsor Royal Shopping Arcade, Thames St; ⊙10am-5pm Apr-Sep, to 4pm Oct-Mar) Pick up a heritage walk map (£2.20).

Getting There & Away

BUS

From Windsor, Courtney buses head to/from Bray (route 16/16A; £3.30, 30 minutes). First buses connect Windsor and Eton with Heathrow terminal 5 (route 60/61/71/77; £5, 30 to 50 minutes). Green Line (www.greenline.co.uk) coaches head to/from London Victoria (£6, two hours).

TRAIN

Trains from Windsor & Eton Riverside (Dachet Rd) go directly to London Waterloo (£10, one hour). Trains from Windsor & Eton Central (Thames St), changing at Slough for London Paddington (£10, 28 to 46 minutes), are quicker.

Bray

POP 8425 (PARISH)

It's strange to think that this tiny village of flint, brick and half-timbered cottages strung along the Thames, 4.5 miles northwest of Windsor, could be Britain's gastronomic capital. Yet Bray is home to one of only three restaurants in the UK to be rated three-star (the highest possible honour) in 2016 by foodie bible, the Michelin guide. On top of that, two of the local pubs also sport a Michelin star, while Heston Blumenthal's much-garlanded Fat Duck restaurant reopened in Bray in late 2015.

There's little more to do here than to dine fabulously.

Eating

★ Waterside Inn FRENCH £££

(☎01628-620691; www.waterside-inn.co.uk; Ferry Rd; mains £53-59, 2-/3-course lunch £49.50/62; ⏲noon-2pm & 7-10pm Wed-Sun, closed end Dec-end Jan) From the moment the uniformed valet opens your car door, until the last tray of petit fours is served, you know this three-Michelin-starred restaurant is something special. For more than 40 years, chef Alain Roux has been working his magic, constructing exceptional dishes for a small army of staff to serve, in a room looking out on the Thames. It also has rooms (from £260).

★ Hind's Head GASTROPUB £££

(☎01628-626151; www.hindsheadbray.com; High St; mains £18-30; ⏲noon-2.30pm & 6.15-9.15pm Mon-Sat, noon-3.30pm Sun; Ⓟ) Oozing atmosphere, this 15th-century pub offers the chance to experience Heston Blumenthal's highly creative cuisine in a relatively affordable, informal setting. The food's less zany than his signature cooking style, but there are still plenty of whimsical touches. Try the chicken, ham and leek pie with wholegrain mustard cream or the onion-wrapped bread-and-cheese royale with Marmite emulsion.

Fat Duck MODERN BRITISH £££

(☎01628-580333; www.thefatduck.co.uk; High St; degustation menu per person £255; ⏲noon-2pm & 7-9pm Tue-Sat) Arguably the most famous restaurant in the country, the Fat Duck – whizz-bang chef Heston Blumenthal's signature eatery – is exceedingly difficult to get into at the best of times. Following a 2015 sojourn in Melbourne, Australia, it's now back with a hungrily awaited, eye-poppingly priced journey-themed menu for those lucky enough to score a reservation (available three months in advance).

Henley-on-Thames

POP 11,494

The attractive commuter town of Henley, 15 miles northwest of Windsor, is synonymous with the world-famous Henley Royal Regatta rowing tournament. At other times of year, it remains a pretty riverside town that's a delight to stroll around, particularly along the Thames, and has a couple of minor attractions.

Sights

River & Rowing Museum MUSEUM

(☎01491-415600; www.rrm.co.uk; Mill Meadows; adult/child £11/9; ⏲10am-5pm; Ⓟ) For the lowdown on Henley's rowing tradition, visit this excellent, modern museum, half a mile south of the train station. The airy 1st-floor galleries tell the story of rowing as an Olympic sport, alongside striking boat displays that include the early-19th-century Royal Oak, Britain's oldest racing boat. Downstairs, a sweet 3D exhibition pays homage to Kenneth Grahame's *The Wind in the Willows,* whose river is thought to have been inspired by this area's section of the Thames.

Festivals & Events

Henley Royal Regatta SPORTS

(www.hrr.co.uk; tickets £27-30; ⏲Jul) This world-renowned, five-day rowing tournament sees Henley burst into action. Although rowers of the highest calibre compete, it has grown into a major social fixture for the upwardly mobile and the main event can be overshadowed by their champagne-fuelled antics. Still, picnicking in the public enclosure and watching the rowers' boats whizz by makes for a good, sunny day out.

Literary Britain

Britain's literary heritage is astoundingly rich and globally renowned. As the English language spread around the world in the colonial era, so too did its literature, with novelists such as Charles Dickens and George Eliot and poets including Samuel Taylor Coleridge being read far from home in the late 18th and 19th centuries.

BASPHOTO / SHUTTERSTOCK ©

EQROY / SHUTTERSTOCK ©

1. Canterbury (p153), England
The town forever linked to Geoffrey Chaucer's *The Canterbury Tales*, stories told by fictional pilgrims as they headed to Canterbury to visit Thomas Becket's shrine.

2. Laugharne, Wales
Dylan Thomas spent his final four years at this Boathouse overlooking the Taf Estuary.

3. Haworth (p538), England
The Brontë sisters lived most of their lives in this pretty Yorkshire village.

4. Stratford-upon-Avon (p422), England
William Shakespeare, arguably the most important writer in the English language, was born here.

NATALIA SIDOROVA / SHUTTERSTOCK ©

Bath & Southwest England

Includes ➡

Best Places to Eat

- ➡ Paul Ainsworth at No 6 (p338)
- ➡ Riverford Field Kitchen (p293)
- ➡ Menu Gordon Jones (p325)
- ➡ Boathouse (p251)

Best Places to Sleep

- ➡ Vintage Vacations (p250)
- ➡ Scarlet (p340)
- ➡ Queensberry Hotel (p322)
- ➡ Hotel du Vin Exeter (p285)

Why Go?

England's southwest is simply spectacular. Here the past is ever present – prepare for close encounters with iconic stone circles, Iron Age hill forts and Roman baths. Blockbuster stately homes border romantic castles; serene cathedrals frame sumptuous Georgian cityscapes. The landscape immerses you in the myths of kings Arthur and Alfred the Great, and the writings of Thomas Hardy, Jane Austen and Daphne du Maurier.

But the southwest also has an eye to the future. Here you can tour alternative eco-towns, pioneering restaurants and cool surfer hang-outs, and sleep in campsites peppered with chic yurts and retro campervans. Then there are three wildlife-rich national parks, fossil-studded shores, England's best surf spots and a coastline flecked with exquisite bays, towering rock formations and tranquil sweeps of sandy beach. It all gives you a bit of a dilemma – with England's West Country you won't know what to do first.

When to Go

- ➡ Cliffs, hillsides and formal gardens burst into fragrance and blooms in April and May, when seasonal attractions also reopen and boat trips start.
- ➡ Music festival fever takes hold in June at ultracool Glastonbury, and on the funky Isle of Wight.
- ➡ The peak holiday season and the best weather (in theory) is in July and August.
- ➡ The end of school summer holidays in September brings cheaper sleep spots, quieter beaches and warmer seas. The Isle of Wight goes all groovy at bohemian Bestival.
- ➡ Bigger waves draw surfers to Cornwall and north Devon in October; meanwhile Exmoor's deer rut sees huge stags battle for supremacy, and the winter storm-watching season begins.

Activities

Cycling

Cycling the southwest is a superb, if strenuous, way to experience England's great outdoors. The region's National Cycle Network (NCN) routes include the **West Country Way** (NCN Route 3), a 240-mile jaunt from Bristol to Padstow via Glastonbury, Taunton and Barnstaple, and the 103-mile **Devon Coast to Coast Cycle Route** between Ilfracombe and Plymouth.

The 160-mile, circular **Wiltshire Cycleway** skirts the county's borders. In Hampshire, the New Forest's hundreds of miles of cycle paths snake through a wildlife-rich environment, while the Isle of Wight boasts 62 miles of bike-friendly routes and its very own cycling festival (p247).

Off-road mountain-biking highlights include the North Wessex Downs, Exmoor National Park and Dartmoor National Park. Many cycle trails trace the routes of old railway lines, including Devon's 11-mile **Granite Way** between Okehampton and Lydford, and Cornwall's popular 18-mile **Camel Trail** linking Padstow with Bodmin Moor.

For more information contact **Sustrans** (www.sustrans.org.uk) and local tourist offices.

Walking

Often called the 630-mile adventure, the **South West Coast Path** is Britain's longest national walking trail, stretching from Minehead in Somerset via Land's End to Poole in Dorset. You can pick it up along the coast for short and spectacular day hikes or tackle longer stretches. The **South West Coast Path Association** (www.southwestcoastpath.org.uk) has a detailed website and publishes an annual guide.

For wilderness hikes, the national parks of **Dartmoor** and **Exmoor** are hard to beat. Dartmoor is bigger and more remote; Exmoor's ace in the pack is a cracking 34 miles of precipitous coast. The region's third national park, the **New Forest**, is an altogether gentler affair, offering hundreds of miles of heritage trails.

Other hiking highlights are Exmoor's 51-mile **Coleridge Way** (www.coleridgeway.co.uk), the Isle of Wight and Bodmin Moor, while Wiltshire's 87-mile **Ridgeway National Trail** (www.nationaltrail.co.uk/ridgeway) starts near Avebury and winds through chalk downland and the wooded Chiltern hills.

Surfing & Boating

North Cornwall, and to a lesser extent north Devon, serves up the best surf in England. Party town Newquay is the epicentre; other top spots are Bude in Cornwall and Croyde in Devon. Region-wide surf conditions can be found at www.magicseaweed.com.

For sailing, highlights includes Britain's 2012 Olympic sailing venues at Weymouth and Portland, and the yachting havens of the Isle of Wight, Falmouth, Dartmouth and Poole.

Other Activities

The southwest is prime territory for kitesurfing, windsurfing, diving, sea kayaking, white-water kayaking and wakeboarding. The sport of stand-up paddleboarding (SUP) continues to grow in popularity, especially in calm water spots.

Plenty of firms also offer caving, coasteering, mountainboarding, climbing and kite-buggying. Check out www.visitsouthwest.co.uk for links to the region's counties and activity operators.

Getting Around

BUS

The region's bus network is fairly comprehensive, but becomes patchy away from main towns. **National Express** (www.nationalexpress.com) often provides the quickest bus link between cities and larger towns. **PlusBus** (www.plusbus.info) adds local bus travel to your train ticket (from £2 per day). Participating cities include Bath, Bournemouth, Bristol, Exeter, Plymouth, Salisbury, Truro and Weymouth. Buy tickets at train stations.

First (www.firstgroup.com) One of the region's largest bus companies, operating in Bath, Bristol, Cornwall, Dorset, Portsmouth and Somerset. It offers subregional tickets, such as the Freedom Travelpass, covering Bath, Bristol and northeast Somerset (one day/week £13.50/59).

More (www.wdbus.co.uk) Useful service across Wiltshire and Dorset and into the New Forest. Does day tickets (adult/child £8.50/5.50) and seven-day network tickets (£25) for south-coast routes.

Stagecoach (www.stagecoachbus.com) A key provider in Cornwall, Devon, Hampshire and Somerset. Offers a range of one-day tickets (adult/child from £4/3) and weekly Megarider fares from £8 (no child fare).

CAR

The main car-hire firms have offices at the region's airports and main-line train stations; rates reflect those elsewhere in the UK.

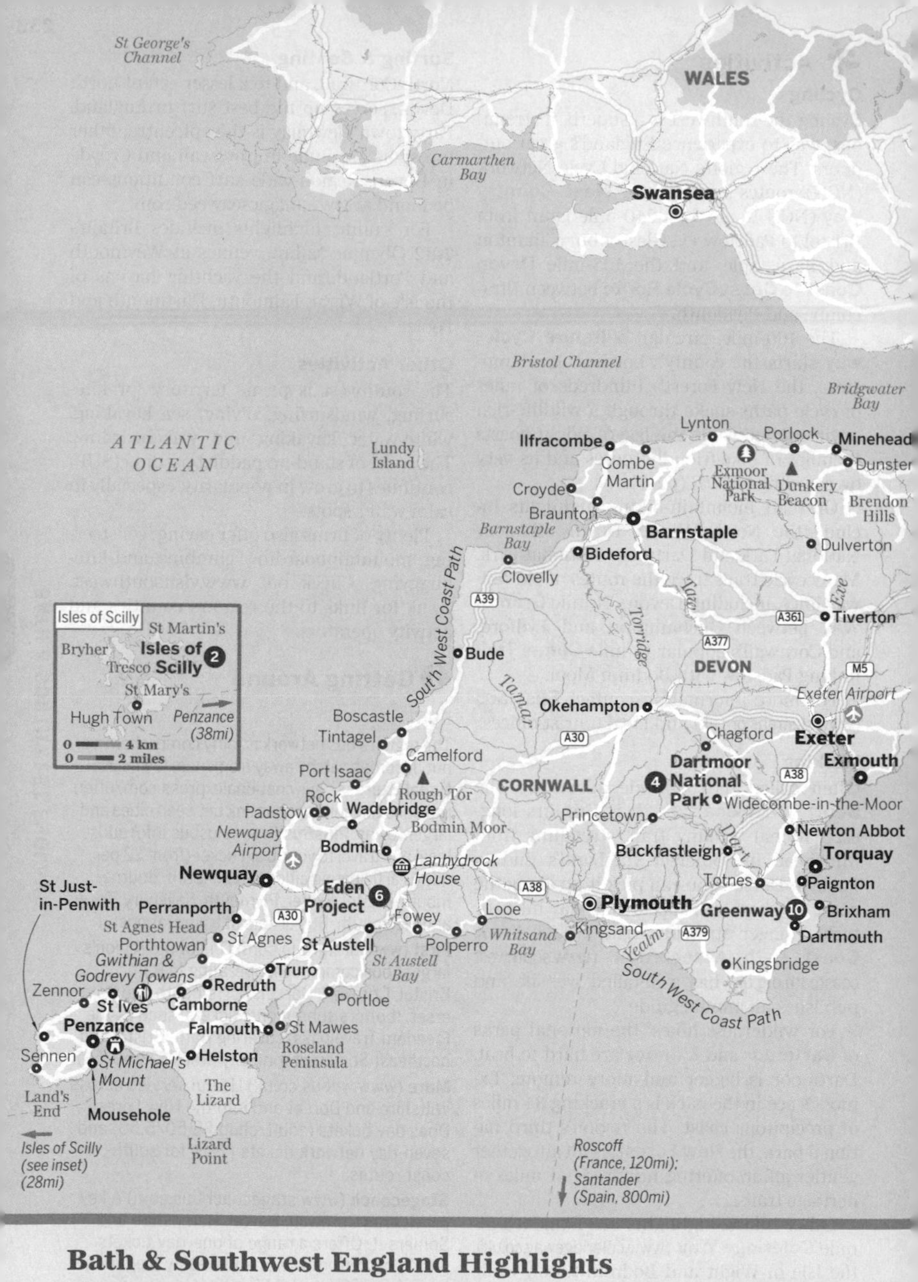

Bath & Southwest England Highlights

1 Stonehenge (p270) Taking a magical dawn walk inside the massive sarsen ring.

2 Isles of Scilly (p359) Ferry-hopping around the UK's most idyllic archipelago.

3 Royal Crescent (p320) Strolling England's most glorious Georgian street.

4 Dartmoor National Park (p298) Striding the park's remote, high hills.

5 Portsmouth (p240) Staring at the vast, ancient timbers of Henry VIII's warship.

6 Eden Project (p352) Marvelling at space-age biomes.

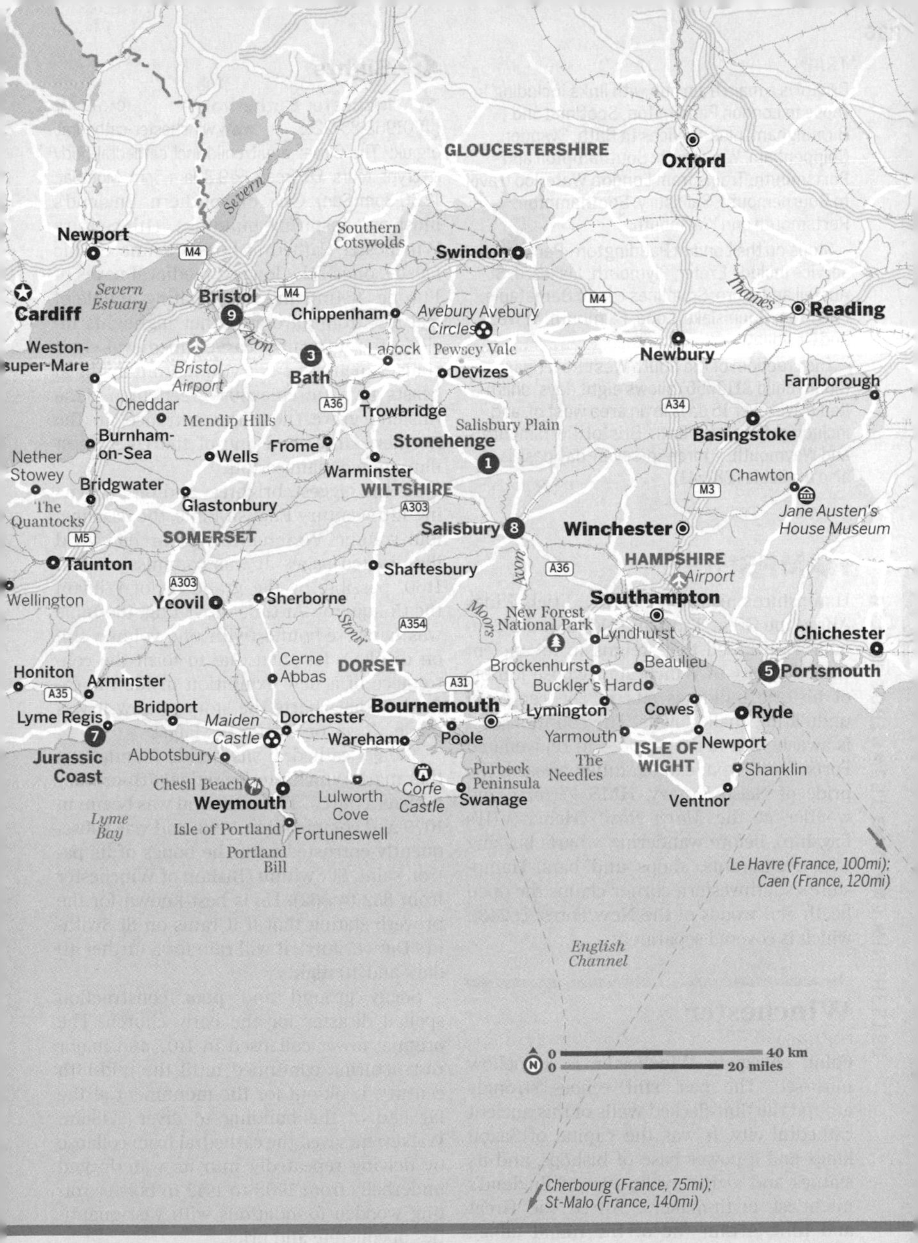

7 Jurassic Coast (p264)
Foraging for 200-million-year-old fossils on Dorset's shore.

8 Salisbury (p267)
Savouring the city's soaring, serene cathedral.

9 SS Great Britain (p309)
Stepping on the deck of Brunel's groundbreaking steamship in Bristol.

10 Greenway (p291)
Discovering the locations behind the murder plots at Agatha Christie's enchanting home.

TRAIN

Bristol is a main train hub with links including those to London Paddington, Scotland and Birmingham, plus services to Bath, Swindon, Chippenham, Weymouth, Southampton and Portsmouth. Trains from London Waterloo travel to Bournemouth, Salisbury, Southampton, Portsmouth and Weymouth.

Stops on the London Paddington–Penzance service include Exeter, Plymouth, Liskeard, St Austell and Truro. Spur lines run to Barnstaple, Paignton, Gunnislake, Looe, Falmouth, St Ives and Newquay.

The Freedom of the South West Rover pass (adult/child £112/56) allows eight days' unlimited travel over 15 days in an area west of, and including, Salisbury, Bath, Bristol, Portsmouth and Weymouth. A three-in-seven-day pass is also available (£81/41).

HAMPSHIRE

Hampshire's history is regal and rich. Kings Alfred the Great, Knut and William the Conqueror all based their reigns in its ancient cathedral city of Winchester, whose jumble of historic buildings sits in the centre of undulating chalk downs. The county's coast is awash with heritage too – in rejuvenated Portsmouth you can clamber aboard the pride of Nelson's navy, HMS *Victory*, and wonder at the *Mary Rose* (Henry VIII's flagship), before wandering wharfs buzzing with restaurants, shops and bars. Hampshire's southwestern corner claims the open heath and woods of the New Forest (p243), which is covered separately.

Winchester

POP 116,600

Calm, collegiate Winchester is a mellow must-see. The past still echoes strongly around the flint-flecked walls of this ancient cathedral city. It was the capital of Saxon kings and a power base of bishops, and its statues and sights evoke two of England's mightiest myth-makers: Alfred the Great and King Arthur (he of the round table). Winchester's architecture is exquisite, from the handsome Elizabethan and Regency buildings in the narrow streets to the wondrous cathedral at its core, while its river valley location means there are charming waterside trails to explore.

Sights

★ Winchester Cathedral CATHEDRAL
(☎01962-857225; www.winchester-cathedral.org.uk; The Close; adult/child incl cathedral body & crypt tours £8/free; ⊙9.30am-5pm Mon-Sat, 12.30-3pm Sun) One of southern England's most awe-inspiring buildings, 11th-century Winchester Cathedral boasts a fine Gothic facade, one of the longest medieval naves in Europe (164m), and a fascinating jumble of features from all eras. Other highlights include the intricately carved medieval choir stalls, which sport everything from mythical beasts to a mischievous green man, Jane Austen's grave (near the entrance, in the northern aisle) and one of the UK's finest illuminated manuscripts.

As the biggest, brightest and best surviving 12th-century English Bible, the dazzling, four-volume **Winchester Bible** has vivid illuminated pages. It was commissioned in 1160, possibly by the grandson of William the Conqueror. At time of writing, the Bible was being re-bound (with one volume still on display). It's then due to form the centrepiece of a new exhibition inside the cathedral that charts the story of how it was made. Check online for the latest.

Today's cathedral sits beside foundations that mark Winchester's original 7th-century minster church. The cathedral was begun in 1070 and completed in 1093, and was subsequently entrusted with the bones of its patron saint, St Swithin (Bishop of Winchester from 852 to 862). He is best known for the proverb stating that if it rains on St Swithin's Day (15 July), it will rain for a further 40 days and 40 nights.

Soggy ground and poor construction spelled disaster for the early church. The original tower collapsed in 1107 and major restructuring continued until the mid-15th century. Look out for the monument at the far end of the building to diver William Walker; he saved the cathedral from collapse by delving repeatedly into its waterlogged underbelly from 1906 to 1912 to bolster rotting wooden foundations with vast quantities of concrete and brick.

Choral **evensong** (5.30pm Mon-Sat, 3.30pm Sun) is atmospheric; other Sunday services take place at 8am, 9.45am and 11am.

The highly informative, one-hour **Cathedral Body Tours** (10am-3pm Mon-Sat) and atmospheric **Crypt Tours** (10.30am, 12.30pm & 2.30pm Mon-Sat) are included in the admission price for Winchester

Winchester

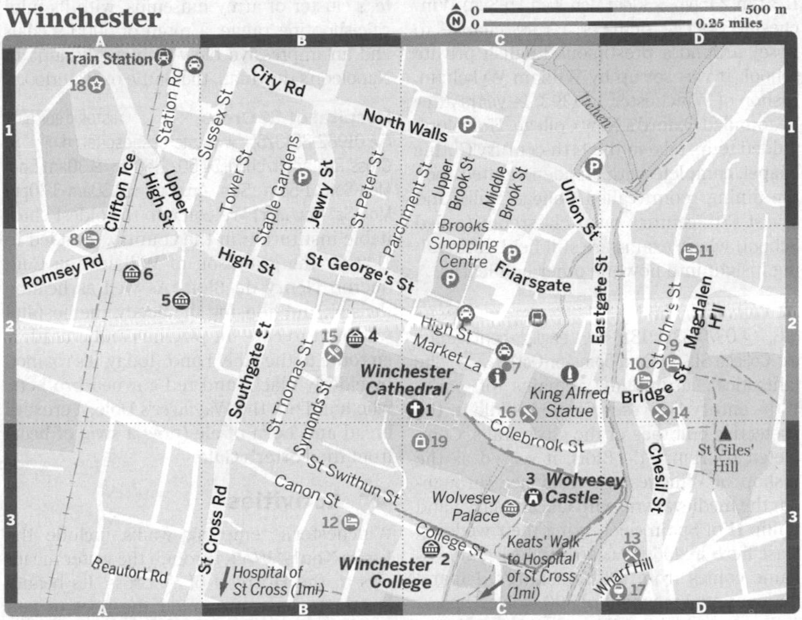

Winchester

Top Sights

- 1 Winchester Cathedral ... C2
- 2 Winchester College ... C3
- 3 Wolvesey Castle ... C3

Sights

- 4 City Museum ... B2
- 5 Round Table & Great Hall ... A2
- 6 Royal Green Jackets Museum ... A2

Activities, Courses & Tours

- 7 Guided Walks ... C2

Sleeping

- 8 5 Clifton Terrace ... A2
- 9 Magdalen House ... D2
- 10 No 5 ... D2
- 11 St John's Croft ... D2
- 12 Wykeham Arms ... B3

Eating

- 13 Black Rat ... D3
- 14 Chesil Rectory ... D2
- 15 Old Vine ... B2
- 16 River Cottage Canteen ... C2

Drinking & Nightlife

- 17 Black Boy ... D3

Entertainment

- 18 Railway Inn ... A1

Shopping

- 19 Deanery Porch ... C3

Cathedral. **Tower and Roof Tours** (2.15pm Monday, Wednesday, Friday and Saturday, plus 11.30am Saturday, May to September) cost £6 and take you on to the roof for views as far as the Isle of Wight. These tours are popular – book well in advance.

On the Crypt Tour look out for Sound II, an enigmatic life-size depiction of a contemplative man by Anthony Gormley. The Tower and Roof Tour will see you clambering 213 steps up narrow stairwells, navigating an interior gallery high above the nave and visiting the bell chamber.

The cathedral's **tree-fringed lawns** make for tranquil spots to take time out, especially on the quieter south side beyond the cloisters; the permanent secondhand book stall in the **Deanery Porch** (The Close; ⏲10am-4pm Sat & Sun) provides great bargain hunting.

★ **Winchester College** HISTORIC BUILDING
(☎01962-621209; www.winchestercollege.org; College St; adult/child £7/free; ⏲tours 10.15am,

11.30am, 2.15pm, 3.30pm Mon, Wed, Fri-Sun) Winchester College delivers a rare chance to nosey around a prestigious English private school. It was set up by William Wykeham, Bishop of Winchester, in 1393, 14 years after he founded Oxford's New College. Hour-long guided tours take in the 14th-century Gothic chapel, complete with wooden vaulted roof, the dining room (called College Hall), and a vast 17th-century open classroom (called School) where exams are still held. A revealing insight into how the other half learns.

★ **Wolvesey Castle** CASTLE
(EH; ☎ 0370-333 1181; www.english-heritage.org.uk; College St; ⏲ 10am-5pm Apr-Oct) FREE The fantastical, crumbling remains of early-12th-century Wolvesey Castle huddle in the protective embrace of the city's walls. Completed by Henry de Blois, it served as the Bishop of Winchester's residence throughout the medieval era, with Queen Mary I and Philip II of Spain celebrating their wedding feast here in 1554. According to legend, its name comes from a Saxon king's demand for an annual payment of 300 wolves' heads. Today, the bishop lives in the (private) **Wolvesey Palace**, next door.

City Museum MUSEUM
(www.hampshireculturaltrust.org.uk; The Square; ⏲ 10am-4pm Mon-Sat, noon-4pm Sun, closed Mon Nov-Mar) FREE A people-centred canter through Winchester's past with jewellery, mosaics, sculpture, coins and tobacco tins charting a narrative from the Iron Age, via the Romans and Anglo-Saxons, to the present day.

Round Table & Great Hall HISTORIC BUILDING
(☎ 01962-846476; www.hants.gov.uk/greathall; Castle Ave; suggested donation £3; ⏲ 10am-5pm) FREE Winchester's cavernous Great Hall is the only part of 11th-century Winchester Castle that Oliver Cromwell spared from destruction. Crowning the wall like a giant-sized dartboard of green and cream spokes is what centuries of mythology have dubbed King Arthur's Round Table. It's actually a 700-year-old copy, but is fascinating nonetheless. It's thought to have been constructed in the late 13th century and then painted in the reign of Henry VIII (King Arthur's image is unsurprisingly reminiscent of Henry's youthful face).

Royal Green Jackets Museum MUSEUM
(The Rifles; ☎ 01962-877826; www.winchestermilitarymuseums.co.uk; Peninsula Barracks, Romsey Rd; adult/child £4/free; ⏲ 10am-5pm Tue-Sat year-round, plus Mon & Sun Jul-Sep) The pick of Winchester's cluster of army museums, with its mini rifle-shooting range, a room of 6000 medals and an impressive blow-by-blow diorama of Napoleon's downfall, the Battle of Waterloo.

Hospital of St Cross HISTORIC BUILDING
(☎ 01962-851375; www.stcrosshospital.co.uk; St Cross Rd; adult/child £4.50/2.50; ⏲ 9.30am-5pm Mon-Sat, 1-5pm Sun Apr-Oct, 10.30am-3.30pm Mon-Sat Nov-Mar) Welcome to the oldest charitable institution in the country, founded in 1132 by the grandson of William the Conqueror, Henry de Blois. As well as healing the sick and housing the needy, the hospital was built to care for pilgrims and crusaders en route to the Holy Land. Today, it's roamed by elderly black- and red-gowned brothers, who hand out the Wayfarer's Dole; a crust of bread and horn of ale (now a swig of beer) from the Porter's Gate.

Activities

Winchester's tempting walks include the 1-mile **Keats' Walk** through the water meadows to the Hospital of St Cross. Its beauty is said to have prompted the poet to pen the ode *To Autumn*; pick up the trail near Wolvesey Castle. Alternatively, head down Wharf Hill, through the water meadows to St Catherine's Hill (1 mile), or take the tranquil **Riverside Walk** from Wolvesey Castle along the River Itchen's banks to High St.

Tours

Guided Walks WALKING
(☎ 01962-840500; www.winchestertouristguides.com; adult/child £5/free; ⏲ Mon-Sat Apr-Oct, weekly Nov-Mar) These 90-minute walks include City Highlights and Upper and Lower Winchester. In peak season, up to four leave daily from the tourist office (p240).

Sleeping

★ **St John's Croft** B&B ££
(☎ 01962-859976; www.st-johns-croft.co.uk; St John's St; s/d/f £55/90/120; P 📶) You may well fall in love with this oh-so-casually stylish, rambling Queen Anne town house, where rattan carpets are teamed with bulging bookcases, and Indian art with shabby-chic antiques. The rooms are vast, the garden is tranquil and breakfast is served beside the Aga in the country-house kitchen.

5 Clifton Terrace B&B ££
(☎ 01962-890053; cliftonterrace@hotmail.co.uk; 5 Clifton Tce; s £75-85, d £80-90, f from £110; 📶)

There's a captivating air of easygoing elegance about this tall Georgian town house. Family heirlooms sit beside candy-striped rugs and peppermint-green, claw-foot baths – it's great value too.

Magdalen House B&B ££
(☎01962-869634; www.magdalen-house.co.uk; 5 Magdalen Hill; s/d/f £60/70/112; P 📶) Pastel-themed bedrooms are arranged over three floors in this peaceful, modern hillside house. The family room opens out directly on to a sunny terrace – the doubles trump that though, with views over rooftops to Winchester Cathedral.

No 5 B&B ££
(☎01962-863838; www.no5bridgestreet.co.uk; 5 Bridge St; d £121-146; 📶) Subtle tweedy-meets-tartan motifs are used to good effect here, with soft, checked throws bookending beds draped in gentle grey. Spacious bathrooms, feature fireplaces and a downstairs bistro add to the appeal. Choosing not to have breakfast knocks £22 off the price of a double room.

★ **Wykeham Arms** INN £££
(☎01962-853834; www.wykehamarmswinchester.co.uk; 75 Kingsgate St; s/d/ste £85/150/200; P 📶) At 250-odd years old, the Wykeham bursts with history – it used to be a brothel and also put Nelson up for a night (some say the events coincided). Creaking stairs lead to plush bedrooms that manage to be both deeply established but also on-trend; brass bedsteads meet jazzy throws, oak dressers sport stylish lights. Simply smashing.

The eccentric bar is a bit of a mustn't-miss experience. Tankards and school canes hang from the ceiling; worn school desks lend pint-supping an illicit air and sizzling sausages (75p each) are served nightly at 6pm.

There's also a wide-ranging food menu, from juicy burgers and fish and chips to satisfying creations adorned with cheffy flourishes.

Eating

River Cottage Canteen BRITISH ££
(☎01962-457747; www.rivercottage.net; Abbey Mill, Abbey Mill Gardens; mains £9-17; ⏰noon-3pm & 6-9.15pm Tue-Sat; 🖉) The setting is pretty idyllic – beside a rushing river in an imaginatively converted Georgian mill. And the food is memorable too: plump for vegetable or meat sharing platters, sole with seaweed butter, or a spicy white bean and leek soup.

Chesil Rectory BRITISH ££
(☎01962-851555; www.chesilrectory.co.uk; 1 Chesil St; mains £14-21; ⏰noon-2.20pm & 6-9.30pm) It's almost as if they created a checklist for a great date: hushed tones, flickering candles, dark beams. They get the food right too, from lighter offerings such as white onion risotto, to sticky, glossy beef ribs, and pork made fragrant by apple and vanilla.

Old Vine PUB FOOD ££
(☎01962-854616; www.oldvinewinchester.com; 8 Great Minster St; mains £10-20; ⏰noon-2.30pm & 6.30-9pm) Ask for table with a view of Winchester's captivating Cathedral Green, soak up the mellow, old-inn atmosphere, then choose between comfort food (beef, mushroom and ale pie) and fancier fare: perhaps a melting lamb shank braised in red wine.

★ **Black Rat** MODERN BRITISH £££
(☎01962-844465; www.theblackrat.co.uk; 88 Chesil St; mains £20-24, 2/3 course lunch £26/29; ⏰7-9.15pm daily, noon-2.15pm Sat & Sun) The aromas are irresistible, the food frankly fabulous, the cooking highly technical and the ingredients dare to surprise – expect lamb neck to be joined by beer-and-onion purée, black pudding by scallops, and charred octopus by chorizo. That'll be why the Black Rat deserves its Michelin star.

Drinking & Nightlife

Black Boy PUB
(www.theblackboypub.com; 1 Wharf Hill; ⏰noon-11pm Mon-Thu, to midnight Fri & Sat, to 10.30pm Sun) Two open fires, a battered foosball table, a random array of dented antiques, a clutch of draught ciders and five real ales make this a legendary local. Any time after noon, check to see if they still have any Black Boy Bangers (£2.50) – a sausage in a crispy roll – the fried onions and mustard are optional.

Railway Inn LIVE MUSIC
(www.railwayinn.pub; 3 St Paul's Hill; ⏰5pm-midnight Sun-Thu, to 2am Fri, to 1am Sat) Easily the area's best live-music and DJ space, the two-venue Railway's offer of local and touring bands showcases everything from rock and blues to folk and jazz.

Information

Discovery Centre (www3.hants.gov.uk/wdc; Jewry St; ⏰9am-6.45pm Mon-Fri, to 4.45pm Sat, 11am-2.45pm Sun; 📶) Free internet access.

Tourist Office (☎01962-840500; www.visitwinchester.co.uk; High St; ⏰10am-5pm Mon-Sat, plus 11am-4pm Sun May-Sep)

ℹ Getting There & Away

Winchester is 65 miles west of London. Direct National Express **buses** shuttle to London Victoria every two hours (£14, 1¾ hours). Trains leave half-hourly to hourly for London Waterloo (£32, 1¼ hours) and hourly for Portsmouth (£11, 1¼ hours). There are also fast links to the Midlands.

ℹ Getting Around

Bikes can be hired from the tourist office, per half-/full day £7/10 (a £50 deposit is needed).

Park & Ride car parks (per day £3) are signed off junctions 10 and 11 of the M3. There are taxi ranks on the High St, and outside the train station and tourist office, or call **Wintax** (☎01962-878727; www.wintaxcars.com).

Portsmouth

POP 205,100

The world-class collection of maritime heritage at Portsmouth more than demands a day trip. Here you can roam around three stunning historic ships, a submarine and an impressive cluster of museums. Nauticalia done, the city's Point district tempts with cobbled streets and ancient pubs, the Spinnaker Tower delivers jaw-dropping views, and the port makes a prime launch pad for the Isle of Wight.

Sights

★Portsmouth Historic Dockyard HISTORIC SHIPS

(☎02392-839766; www.historicdockyard.co.uk; Victory Gate; All Attractions ticket adult/child £33/23; ⏰10am-5.30pm Apr-Oct, to 5pm Nov-Mar) Portsmouth's blockbuster draw sees you gazing at the evocative hulk of Henry VIII's flagship, the Mary Rose, and jumping aboard HMS Victory – the warship Nelson captained at the Battle of Trafalgar. Then there's the Victorian HMS Warrior, the WWII-era submarine HMS Alliance (p242) and a wealth of imaginative, maritime-themed museums, along with waterborne harbour tours. Visiting more than one exhibit makes the All Attractions ticket (rather than single attraction tickets) the best value. There's a 20% discount for buying online.

Harbour tours (p242) are also included in the All Attractions ticket. Last admission to the dockyard is one hour before closing.

★Mary Rose Museum MUSEUM

(www.maryrose.org; Portsmouth Historic Dockyard; adult/child £18/13; ⏰10am-5.30pm Apr-Oct, to 5pm Nov-Mar) The raising of the 16th-century warship the *Mary Rose* in 1982 was an extraordinary feat of marine archaeology. The £35-million, boat-shaped museum that's been built around her gives uninterrupted views of the preserved timbers of her massive hull. The ship can also be seen from tiered galleries that reconstruct life on each deck, using some of the 19,000 artefacts that were raised with her. Items on display range from the military, including scores of cannons and hundreds of longbows, to the touchingly prosaic: water jugs, hair combs, leather shoes and even the skeleton of Hatch, the ship's dog. This 700-tonne floating fortress was Henry VIII's favourite vessel, but she sank suddenly off Portsmouth while fighting the French in 1545. Of a crew of 400, it's thought 360 died.

★HMS Victory HISTORIC SHIP

(www.hms-victory.com; Portsmouth Historic Dockyard; adult/child £18/13; ⏰10am-5.30pm Apr-Oct, to 5pm Nov-Mar) As resplendent as she is venerable, HMS *Victory* was Lord Nelson's flagship at the Battle of Trafalgar (1805) and the site of his famous dying words 'Kiss me, Hardy', after victory over the French had been secured. This remarkable ship is topped by a forest of ropes and masts, and weighted by a swollen belly filled with cannons and paraphernalia for an 850-strong crew. Clambering through the low-beamed decks and crew's quarters is an evocative experience.

In the summer, tours are self-guided. But between November and March, hugely popular 50-minute guided tours are held. Arrive early to bag a place – you can't book in advance.

★HMS Warrior HISTORIC SHIP

(www.hmswarrior.org; Portsmouth Historic Dockyard; adult/child £18/13; ⏰10am-5.30pm Apr-Oct, to 5pm Nov-Mar) Anywhere else, the magnificent warship HMS *Warrior* would grab centre stage. This stately dame was at the cutting edge of technology when she was built in 1860, riding the transition from wood to iron and sail to steam. The gleaming upper deck, vast gun deck and dimly lit cable lockers conjure up vivid pictures of life in the Victorian navy.

Portsmouth

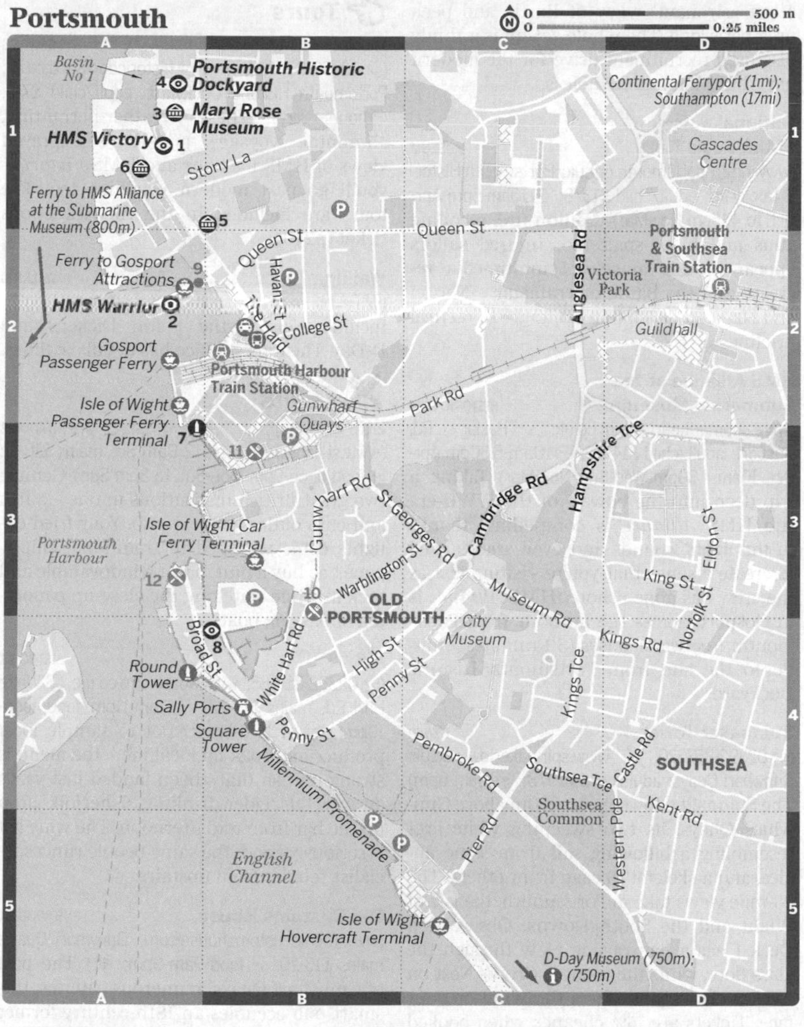

Portsmouth

Top Sights
1 HMS Victory ... A1
2 HMS Warrior ... A2
3 Mary Rose Museum ... A1
4 Portsmouth Historic Dockyard ... A1

Sights
5 Action Stations! ... B1
6 National Museum of the Royal Navy ... A1
7 Spinnaker Tower ... A3
8 The Point ... B4

Activities, Courses & Tours
9 Harbour Tours ... A2

Eating
10 A Bar ... B3
11 Old Customs House ... B3
12 Still & West ... A3

Action Stations! MUSEUM
(www.actionstations.org; Portsmouth Historic Dockyard; adult/child £18/13; ⌚10am-5.30pm Apr-Oct, to 5pm Nov-Mar) Stroll into Action Stations!, a warehouse full of child-friendly interactive gadgets, to command a warship, gaze

at an astronaut's view of Earth, and peek up a periscope. The whole set-up is a thinly disguised recruitment drive for the modern navy, but it's fun nonetheless.

National Museum of the Royal Navy MUSEUM
(www.nmrn-portsmouth.org.uk; Portsmouth Historic Dockyard; adult/child £13/8; ⏲10am-5pm Apr-Oct, to 4.15pm Nov-Mar) Cannon-fire, recoiling guns and blood-spattered, injured sailors appear in this museum's multimedia re-creation of the Battle of Trafalgar – Nelson and Napoleon even pop up to give a tactical briefing.

HMS Alliance at the Submarine Museum HISTORIC SHIP
(www.submarine-museum.co.uk; Haslar Rd, Gosport; adult/child £14/10; ⏲10am-5.30pm Apr-Oct, 10am-4.30pm Wed-Sun Nov-Mar) Taking a trip deep into the bowels of the WWII-era sub HMS *Alliance* is compelling, thanks to the lights, sounds and even smells used to create a sense that you're visiting just as the crew has gone ashore. HMS *Alliance* is in Gosport, across the harbour from Portsmouth; free water buses (30 minutes) shuttle to the site from Portsmouth Historic Dockyard.

Spinnaker Tower TOWER
(☎02392-857520; www.spinnakertower.co.uk; Gunwharf Quays; adult/child £10/8; ⏲10am-6pm) The Spinnaker Tower soars 170m above Gunwharf Quays, its two sweeping white arcs resembling a billowing sail from some angles, and a skeletal ribcage from others. The 23-mile views take in Portsmouth, the Isle of Wight and the South Downs. Observation Deck 1 has a hair-raising view through the glass floor, while the roofless Crow's Nest on Deck 3 allows you to feel the wind on your face. Tickets are 15% cheaper when booked online.

The Point HISTORIC SITE
The Point's characterful cobbled streets are dotted with higgledy-piggledy houses and salty sea-dog pubs, their terraces prime places to watch streams of ferries and naval ships. Here you can climb Henry V's **Round Tower** and stroll along the fort's walls to the 15th-century **Square Tower**. Underneath, cavernous vaults frame **Sally Ports**: openings in the defences that used to give captains access to the sea, and now lead sun worshippers on to a tiny shingle beach.

Tours

Harbour Tours BOATING
(☎02392-839766; www.historicdockyard.co.uk; Portsmouth Historic Dockyard; adult/child £7/5; ⏲hours vary) These weather-permitting, 45-minute voyages provide salt-sprayed views of HMS *Warrior* and HMS *Victory* – you'll go past modern warships too. The tours are included in the All Attractions ticket (p240).

Walking Tours WALKING
(☎02392-826722; adult/child £3/free) Themes include Nelson, the Point, Dickens and D-Day. The tourist office has details of times.

Eating

Still & West PUB FOOD £
(www.stillandwest.co.uk; 2 Bath Sq; mains £10-17; ⏲food noon-9pm Mon-Sat, to 8pm Sun) Genius: two great British institutions in one – a fish and chip outlet inside a pub. Your fried delights come wrapped in traditional chippy paper, so buy a pint, bag a window table and tuck in while watching the close-up panorama of passing boats.

A Bar BISTRO ££
(☎02392-811585; www.abarbistro.co.uk; 58 White Hart Rd; mains £13-22; ⏲11am-11pm, food noon-10pm; 📶) A laid-back spot to sample local produce and soak up local life – the menu is strong on fish that's been landed just yards away, while cider-drinking fisherfolk prop up the bar from midafternoon. The wine list is seriously good; the same people run a specialist retailer from upstairs.

Old Customs House PUB FOOD ££
(www.theoldcustomshouse.com; Gunwharf Quays; mains £13-20; ⏲food 9am-9pm; 📶) The best of Gunwharf Quays' numerous eateries, this smart pub occupies an 18th-century former Royal Marine hospital. Now better-than-average bar food (think confit rabbit leg, goats cheese and quinoa salad, and sea trout with pickled samphire) is served up alongside its raspberry-red walls and gilt-framed mirrors.

Information

Portsea Library (www.johnpoundscentre.co.uk; John Pounds Centre, 23 Queen St; ⏲10.30am-4.30pm Mon-Fri) Free internet access.

Tourist Office (☎02392-826722; www.visitportsmouth.co.uk; Clarence Esplanade;

⏲10am-5.30pm Apr-Sep, to 5pm Oct-Mar) In the D-Day Museum in Southsea.

Getting There & Away

Portsmouth is 100 miles southwest of London.

BOAT

Car and passenger ferries and hovercraft link Portsmouth to the Isle of Wight (p247).

Several routes run from Portsmouth to France. Prices vary wildly depending on times and dates of travel – an example one-way fare is £130 for a car and two adults on the Portsmouth–Cherbourg route. Book in advance, be prepared to travel off-peak and look out for special deals.

Brittany Ferries (www.brittanyferries.co.uk) Runs regular services from Portsmouth to St Malo (10¾ hours), Caen (seven hours), Cherbourg (three hours) and Le Havre (eight hours) in France, and twice weekly services to Santander (24 hours) and Bilbao (24 hours) in Spain.

Condor Ferries (www.condorferries.co.uk) Runs a weekly car-and-passenger service from Portsmouth to Cherbourg (6½ hours) between June and September.

BUS

From Monday to Saturday, there are hourly, direct National Express buses from London Victoria (£14, two hours). Bus 700 runs to Chichester (£4.50, one hour).

TRAIN

Direct trains run hourly from London Victoria (£33, two hours) and half-hourly from London Waterloo (£33, 2½ hours). For the Historic Dockyard, get off at the final stop, Portsmouth Harbour.

Other departures:

Brighton £16, two hours, hourly

Chichester £8, 40 minutes, two per hour

Southampton £10, one hour, three trains per hour

Winchester £11, 1¼ hours, hourly

Getting Around

Bus 1 runs every 20 minutes between Portsmouth Harbour bus station and South Parade Pier in Southsea, via Old Portsmouth. An all-day ticket is £4.20.

Every 15 minutes the **Gosport Passenger Ferry** (www.gosportferry.co.uk; The Hard; adult/child/bicycle return £3.30/2.10/1.20; ⏲5.30am-midnight) shuttles from **Portsmouth Harbour** train station to Gosport.

Taxi ranks are near the Portsmouth Harbour bus and train stations. Or call **Aquacars** (☎02392-654321; www.aquacars.co.uk; ⏲24hr).

New Forest

With typical, accidental, English irony the New Forest is anything but new – it was first proclaimed a royal hunting preserve in 1079. It's also not much of a forest, being mostly heathland ('forest' is from the Old French for 'hunting ground'). Designated a national park in 2005, the forest's combined charms make it a joy to explore. Wild ponies mooch around pretty scrubland, deer flicker in the distance and rare birds flit among the foliage. Genteel villages dot the landscape, connected by a web of walking and cycling trails.

Activities

New Forest Activities ADVENTURE SPORTS
(☎01590-612377; www.newforestactivities.co.uk; High St, Beaulieu) Runs sessions in canoeing (adult/child per two hours £32/17), kayaking (per two hours £32) and archery (adult/child per 1½ hours £22/17).

Walking

The forest is prime hiking territory. Ordnance Survey (OS) produces a detailed, 1:25,000 Explorer map (New Forest; No 22, £9); Crimson's *New Forest Short Walks* (£8) features 20 day hikes of 2 to 6 miles.

Lyndhurst tourist office (p244) stocks maps and guides; they're also available from its website.

Ranger Walks WALKING
(☎0300 068 0400; www.forestry.gov.uk/newforestevents; from £5.50) Day walks including those themed around photography, ponies and the unique way the New Forest is managed.

Cycling

- The New Forest makes for superb cycling country, with 100 miles of routes linking the main villages and the key railway station at Brockenhurst.
- *The New Forest By Bike* map (£3.50) features 22 routes ranging from 8 to 32 miles. The *New Forest Cycling Guide* (£4) features six day-cycle routes of between 4 and 22 miles on a 1:25,000 OS map.
- Maps and guides can be bought from Lyndhurst tourist office (p244) or via its website.
- To rent bikes, you'll need to pay a deposit (usually £20) and provide identification.

CAMPING IN THE NEW FOREST

The New Forest is a haven for campers. The **Forestry Commission** (www.campingintheforest.co.uk) runs 10 relatively rural sites. Lyndhurst's **tourist office** has a leaflet (50p) detailing other designated areas; see also www.thenewforest.co.uk.

AA Bike Hire CYCLING
(☎02380-283349; www.aabikehirenewforest.co.uk; Fern Glen, Gosport Lane, Lyndhurst; adult/child per day £10/5) Based in Lyndhurst's main car park.

Cyclexperience CYCLING
(New Forest Cycle Hire; ☎01590-624808; www.newforestcyclehire.co.uk; 2 Brookley Rd, Brockenhurst; adult/child per day £17.50/9) Based at Brockenhurst train station.

Country Lanes CYCLING
(☎01590-622627; www.countrylanes.co.uk; train station, Brockenhurst; adult/child per day £18/9) Based in a vintage railway carriage.

Forest Leisure Cycling CYCLING
(☎01425-403584; www.forestleisurecycling.co.uk; The Cross, Burley; adult/child per day £17/9) Has easy links on to nine cycle routes.

Horse Riding

A number of stables welcome beginners.

Arniss Equestrian Centre HORSE RIDING
(☎01425-654114; www.arnissequestrian.co.uk; Godshill, Fordingbridge; per hr £27) Caters for all skill levels.

Burley Manor HORSE RIDING
(☎01425-403489; www.burleymanorridingstables.com; Ringwood Rd, Burley; per 1/2 hr £33/60) Also does pub rides.

Burley Villa HORSE RIDING
(Western Riding; ☎01425-610278; www.burleyvilla.co.uk; near New Milton; per hr from £35) Runs rides using traditional English and also Western saddle styles (per 90 minutes £48).

Information

Tourist Office (☎02380-282269; www.thenewforest.co.uk; main car park, Lyndhurst; ⏰10am-5pm Easter-Oct, to 4pm Nov-Easter) The national park's main tourist office, set in the New Forest Centre, has a wealth of information including walking and cycling maps, and camping guides.

Getting There & Around

BUS

- National Express buses stop at Lyndhurst, Lymington and Ringwood.
- Regular local services run between the park's main towns, Bournemouth (£8.50) and Southampton (£7.40).
- The **New Forest Tour** (www.thenewforesttour.info; adult per 1/2/5 days £15/20/30, child £8/10/15; ⏰hourly 10am-6pm mid-Jun–mid-Sep) has three connecting routes of hop-on/hop-off buses, passing through Lyndhurst's main car park, Brockenhurst train station, Lymington, Beaulieu and Exbury.

TRAIN

- Two trains an hour run to Brockenhurst from London Waterloo (£18, two hours) via Winchester (£12, 30 minutes) and on to Bournemouth (£8, 20 minutes).
- Local trains also shuttle twice an hour between Brockenhurst and Lymington (£4, 10 minutes).

Lyndhurst, Brockenhurst & Around

The quaint country villages of Lyndhurst and Brockenhurst are separated by just 4 miles. Their picturesque accommodation options and superb eateries ensure they're atmospheric bases from which to explore the New Forest.

Sights

New Forest Museum MUSEUM
(www.newforestcentre.org.uk; main car park, Lyndhurst; ⏰10am-5pm Apr-Oct, to 4pm Nov-Mar) FREE Features a local labourer's cottage (complete with socks drying beside the fire), potato dibbles and a cider press. The mini-film makes for an accessible introduction to the park – listen too for recordings of the autumn pony sales, which take place after the annual drifts (round-ups).

Beaulieu HISTORIC BUILDING
(☎01590-612345; www.beaulieu.co.uk; adult/child £24/12; ⏰10am-6pm Apr-Sep, to 5pm Oct-Mar) Petrolheads, historians and ghost-hunters gravitate to Beaulieu (*bew*-lee) – a vintage car museum, stately home and tourist complex centred on a 13th-century Cistercian monastery. Motor-maniacs will be in raptures at Lord Montague's **National Motor Museum**. Tickets are valid for a year; it's up to £5 cheaper to buy in advance, online. Beaulieu is served by the New Forest Tour.

The abbey at the heart of modern-day Beaulieu was a key one. After Henry VIII's monastic land-grab of 1536, it fell to the ancestors of the current proprietors, the Montague family. Today the motor museum presents a splendid collection that spans early classics, F1 cars and jet-powered land-speed record-breakers including *Bluebird*, which broke the 403mph (649km/h) limit in 1964. Celebrity wheels include those driven by James Bond and Mr Bean.

Beaulieu's grand but homely palace began life as a 14th-century Gothic abbey gatehouse, and received a 19th-century Scottish baronial makeover from Baron Montague in the 1860s. Listen out for eerie Gregorian chanting – the abbey is supposedly one of England's most haunted buildings.

Sleeping

Daisybank Cottage B&B ££

(☎01590-622086; www.bedandbreakfast-newforest.co.uk; Sway Rd, Brockenhurst; s £90, d £110-130; P 📶) The five gorgeous themed suites here are mini pamper palaces. Expect aromatic smellies in gleaming bathrooms, stylish luxurious furnishings and lots of little extras: breakfasts laden with New Forest goodies, handmade chocolates, smartphone docks, DAB radios and range-baked cakes on arrival.

Little Hayes B&B ££

(☎02380-283816; www.littlehayesguesthouse.co.uk; 43 Romsey Rd, Lyndhurst; s £70-80, d £100-110) Pine mini-four-poster beds, smart bathrooms and bright colour schemes, ranging from raspberry to aquamarine, lift this friendly B&B above the crowd. Bedroom 5, with its slanting ceiling and roomy bathroom, is particularly appealing.

★**The Pig** BOUTIQUE HOTEL £££

(☎0345 225 9494; www.thepighotel.co.uk; Beaulieu Rd, Brockenhurst; r £175-265; P 📶) One of the New Forest's classiest hotels remains an utter delight: log baskets, croquet mallets and ranks of guest gumboots give things a country-house air; espresso machines and minilarders lend bedrooms a luxury touch. In fact, all this effortless elegance makes it feel like you've just dropped by a friend's (very stylish) rural retreat.

Eating

★**The Pig** MODERN BRITISH ££

(☎0345 225 9494; www.thepighotel.co.uk; Beaulieu Rd, Brockenhurst; mains £10-17; ⊙noon-2.30pm & 6.30-9.30pm; 📶) Add this to your must-eat-here list. The Pig's creative chefs devise menus by the 'micro-season'; they change hourly depending on what's been found when foraging or in the hotel's kitchen garden. This results in imaginative combos, which might feature pungent wild garlic, punchy, house-smoked ham or a creamy risotto of just-picked mushrooms.

Oak Inn PUB FOOD ££

(☎02380-282350; www.oakinnlyndhurst.co.uk; Pinkney Lane, Bank; mains £12-24; ⊙noon-2.00pm & 6-9pm Mon-Fri, noon-9pm Sat & Sun) The essence of old England has been poured into this convivial, flower-framed inn. Horse brasses and dried hops hang over diners tucking into charcuterie platters, succulent pan-seared New Forest venison, roasted Hampshire pheasant and Lymington crab.

Getting There & Away

Bus 6 shuttles between Lyndhurst, Brockenhurst and Lymington (£3.70, hourly Monday to Saturday, five on Sunday); so does the New Forest Tour (p244).

Trains run twice an hour between Brockenhurst and Lymington (£4, 10 minutes).

Buckler's Hard

For such a tiny place, this picturesque huddle of 18th-century cottages, near the mouth of the River Beaulieu, has a big history. It started in 1722, when a duke of Montague built a port to finance a Caribbean expedition. His dream faltered, but when war with France came, this embryonic village and sheltered gravel waterfront became a secret boatyard where several of Nelson's triumphant Battle of Trafalgar warships were built. In the 20th century it played its part in the preparations for the D-Day landings.

Sights

Buckler's Hard Story MUSEUM

(☎01590-616203; www.bucklershard.co.uk; adult/child £6.50/4.50; ⊙10am-5pm Apr-Sep, to 4pm Oct-Mar) The hamlet's fascinating Maritime Museum and heritage centre chart the inlet's shipbuilding history and role in WWII, and feature immaculately preserved 18th-century labourers' cottages.

Sleeping & Eating

Master Builder's House Hotel HOTEL ££

(☎01590-616253; www.hillbrookehotels.co.uk; d £105-170; ⊙food noon-3pm & 7-9pm; P) In this beautifully restored 18th-century hotel, 25 stately but stylish rooms feature soft lighting, burnished trunks and plush fabrics.

The atmospheric river-view **restaurant** (mains £12-23) delivers classy, classic dishes, while the wood-panelled **Yachtsman's Bar** serves quality pub grub (mains £7-16).

Lymington

POP 15,400

Yachting haven, New Forest base and jumping-off point to the Isle of Wight – the appealing Georgian harbour town of Lymington has several strings to its tourism bow. This former smuggler's port offers nautical shops, prime eating and sleeping spots and, in Quay St, an utterly quaint cobbled lane.

Sights & Activities

St Barbe Museum MUSEUM

(☎01590-676969; www.stbarbe-museum.org.uk; New St; adult/child £5.45/2.70; ⊙10am-4pm Mon-Sat) Explores tales of boatbuilders, sailors, smugglers, salt-makers and farmers through a mix of models, hands-on displays and artefacts. The museum was closed at the time of writing for a £2-million revamp but due to reopen soon.

Puffin Cruises BOATING

(☎07850-947618; www.puffincruiseslymington.com; Town Quay) The best trip is an exhilarating, three-hour sunset surge across the Solent to the Isle of Wight (adult/child £20/9, 6pm Monday, Wednesday, Friday and Saturday, May to October), where the Needles lighthouse and towering chalk stacks loom from the water.

Sleeping

Auplands B&B ££

(☎01590-675944; www.auplands.com; 22 Southampton Rd; s £55-65, d £75-85; P 📶) Your genial hosts have been running this B&B for more than 30 years, and it shows in their supremely efficient systems and easy charm. Snug rooms feature pine, bottled water and big plants, while the eateries of Lymington are only a 10-minute stroll away.

★**Mill at Gordleton** BOUTIQUE HOTEL £££

(☎01590-682219; www.themillatgordleton.co.uk; Silver St, Hordle; d £195-175, ste £175-295; P 📶) Step inside here and know, instantly, you're going to be looked after, beautifully. Wicker, velvet and gingham dot exquisite rooms (each one comes with a sweet soft toy duck), while the garden is a magical mix of rushing water, fairy lights and modern sculpture. The Mill is 4 miles west of Lymington.

Stanwell House BOUTIQUE HOTEL £££

(☎01590-677123; www.stanwellhouse.com; 14 High St; d £145-205, ste £256; @ 📶) There are boutique tweaks everywhere at Stanwell. Swish Georgian rooms manage to be both period and modern: the four-poster ones feature dark woods and zingy colours, while the high-tech suites are simply irresistible – two even have their own roof terrace for sunny days and moonlit nights.

Eating

Fish & Chips FISH & CHIPS £

(130 High St; mains £8; ⊙noon-2.30pm & 4.30-8.30pm Mon-Fri, noon-9pm Sat, noon-7.30pm Sun) They're often queuing out the door at this classic British chippy, which boasts great fish, laminate tables and pickled eggs. Eat in or take away.

Ship Inn PUB FOOD ££

(☎01590-676903; www.theshiplymington.co.uk; The Quay; mains £9-17; ⊙food noon-10pm; 🖉) A pub for all seasons: knock back summertime drinks on the waterside terrace; in winter, a toasty log burner gets you warm. Hearty food ranges from sticky, marinated chicken to homemade beetroot and truffle ravioli; drinks totter from tangy real ales to vintage champagne.

★**Elderflower** MODERN BRITISH £££

(☎01590-676908; www.elderflowerrestaurant.co.uk; 5 Quay St; mains £19-24; ⊙noon-2.30pm & 6.30-9.30pm Tue-Sat, noon-2.30pm Sun) An Anglo-French feel infuses Elderflower – from the truffle-scented braised New Forest venison, to the apple and vanilla soufflé, which comes with custard laced with Calvados. Or opt for the tapas-style *petites assiettes* (£2 to £10); perhaps pine-smoked mussels, wild mushroom *bordaliase* or beef rib that's been slow-cooked for 72 hours.

Information

Library (☎0300 555 1387; North Close; ⊙9am-5pm Mon, Wed, Thu & Sat, to 7pm Tue & Fri; 📶) Free internet access.

Getting There & Away

Lymington has two train stations: Lymington Town and Lymington Pier. Isle of Wight ferries connect with Lymington Pier. Trains run to

Southampton (£11, 40 minutes), with a change at Brockenhurst, twice an hour.

Wightlink Ferries (☎ 0333 999 7333; www.wightlink.co.uk) has car and passenger ferries that run hourly to Yarmouth on the Isle of Wight (30 minutes). An adult/child foot-passenger day-return costs £14.60/7.30. Car fares start at around £60 for a short-break return.

ISLE OF WIGHT

On the Isle of Wight these days there's something groovy in the air. For decades this slab of rock anchored off Portsmouth has been a magnet for family holidays, and it still has seaside kitsch by the bucket and spade. But now the proms and amusement arcades are framed by pockets of pure funkiness. A brace of music festivals draws party-goers, just-caught seafood is served in kooky fishers' cafes, and cool camping rules – here sites are dotted with ecoyurts and vintage campervans. Yet still the isle's principal appeal remains: a mild climate, myriad outdoorsy activities and a 25-mile shore lined with beaches, dramatic white cliffs and tranquil sand dunes.

Activities

Cycling

With 200 miles of cycle routes, the Isle of Wight makes pedal pushers smile. The island's official visitor website (www.visitisleofwight.co.uk) lists suggested trips (complete with maps), ranging from family-friendly tootles along former railway routes to the 50-mile, cliff-climbing **Chalk Ridge Extreme**. A **Cycling Festival** (☎ 01983-821000; www.sunseaandcycling.com) is held every September.

Bike rentals start at around £13/45 per day/week. Many firms deliver and collect on orders over £30.

Tavcycles CYCLING
(☎ 01983-812989; www.tavcycles.co.uk; 140 High St, Ryde) Offers rates ranging from half-day (£7) and 24 hours (£15) to one week (£45).

Top Gear CYCLING
(☎ 01983-299056; www.top-gearhire.com; 1 Terminus Rd, Cowes; adult per day/week £15/70, child per day/week £13/70) Delivers bikes island-wide.

Wight Cycle Hire CYCLING
(☎ 01983-761800; www.wightcyclehire.co.uk; Station Rd, Yarmouth; adult day/week £16/70, child day/week £10/40) Also rents electric bikes (per day £35) and tandems (per day £32).

Walking

This is one of the best spots in southern England for rambling with 500 miles of well-marked walking paths, including 67 miles of coastal routes. The island's two-week **walking festival** (www.isleofwightwalkingfestival.co.uk; ⏲ May) is billed as the UK's largest.

Water Sports

Water sports are serious business on the Isle of Wight. Cowes is the sailing centre, surfers and wind- and kitesurfers flock to the southwest, especially around Compton Bay, while powerboats run trips out to the Needles rocks.

Isle of Wight Adventure Activities ADVENTURE SPORTS
(☎ 01983-755838; www.isleofwightadventureactivities.co.uk; Freshwater) Runs activities ranging from surfing, stand-up paddle-boarding and kayaking (per two hours adult/child £40/25) to archery (per hour £12).

Information

The Isle of Wight's main **tourist office** (☎ 01983-813813; www.visitisleofwight.co.uk; High St, Newport; ⏲ 10.30am-3.30pm Mon-Fri, to 2.30pm Sat) is in Newport; small-scale information points include those at the main ferry ports.

Getting There & Away

Hovertravel (☎ 01983-717700; www.hovertravel.co.uk; day-return adult/child £19/9.60) Shuttles foot passengers between Southsea (a Portsmouth suburb) and Ryde, half-hourly to hourly.

Red Funnel (☎ 02380-019192; www.redfunnel.co.uk) Runs car-and-passenger ferries between Southampton and East Cowes (same-day return adult/child £16.80/8.40, from £45 with car, 60 minutes, hourly) and high-speed passenger ferries between Southampton and West

> **CAR FERRY COSTS**
>
> The cost of car ferries to the Isle of Wight can vary enormously. Save by booking ahead, asking about special offers and travelling off-peak (midweek and later in the day). Long stays are cheaper and some deals include admission to island attractions. Booking online can mean paying £20 less.

Isle of Wight

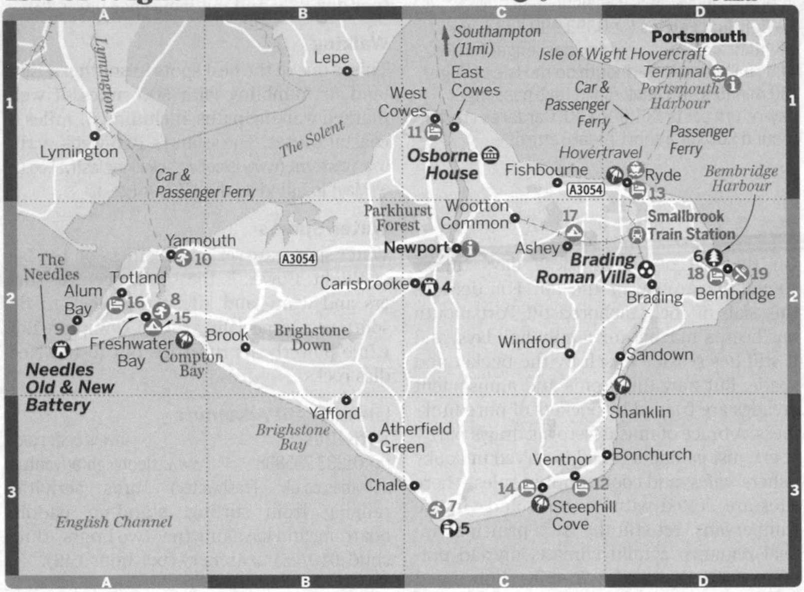

Isle of Wight

Top Sights
1 Brading Roman Villa D2
2 Needles Old & New Battery A2
3 Osborne House C1

Sights
4 Carisbrooke Castle C2
5 St Catherine's Lighthouse C3
St Catherine's Oratory .... (see 5)
6 St Helens Duver D2

Activities, Courses & Tours
7 Blackgang Chine C3
8 Isle of Wight Adventure Activities A2
9 Needles Pleasure Cruises A2
Tavcycles .... (see 13)
Top Gear .... (see 11)
10 Wight Cycle Hire A2

Sleeping
11 Fountain C1
Hambrough .... (see 12)
12 Harbour View C3
13 Kasbah D1
14 Lighthouse C3
onefiftycowes .... (see 11)
15 Really Green A2
16 Totland Bay YHA A2
17 Vintage Vacations C2
18 Xoron Floatel D2

Eating
Ale & Oyster .... (see 12)
Black Sheep .... (see 13)
Boathouse .... (see 14)
Crab Shed .... (see 14)
Floating Cafe & Shop .... (see 18)
19 Pilot Boat D2
Spyglass Inn .... (see 12)

Cowes (same-day return adult/child £24/12, 25 minutes, one to two per hour).

Wightlink Ferries (☎ 0333 999 7333; www.wightlink.co.uk) Operates passenger ferries every half-hour from Portsmouth to Ryde (day-return adult/child £18.40/9.20, 22 minutes). It also runs hourly car-and-passenger ferries from Portsmouth to Fishbourne (45 minutes) and from Lymington to Yarmouth (30 minutes). For both, an adult/child foot passenger day-return costs £14.60/7.30. Car fares start at around £60 for a short-break return.

Getting Around

BUS

Southern Vectis (www.islandbuses.info) runs buses between the eastern towns roughly every 30 minutes. Regular services to the remoter southwest, especially between Blackgang Chine and Brook, are less frequent, but between April and September, the **Island Coaster** (www.islandbuses.info; per day adult/child £10/5, per 2 days adult/child £15/7.30) makes four return circuits a day along the southern shore from Ryde around to Yarmouth, in the west.

Rover Tickets cover all Southern Vectis routes: one day (adult/child £10/5) or two days (adult/child £15/7.30).

CAR

1st Call (☎01983-400055; www.1stcallcar-sales.com; 15 College Close, Sandown; per day/week from £30/150) Collects and delivers island wide

TRAIN

Island Line trains (www.southwesttrains.co.uk) run twice hourly from Ryde to Shanklin (same-day return £4.40, 25 minutes), via Smallbrook Junction, Brading and Sandown.

Cowes & Around

Pack your yachting cap – the hilly Georgian harbour town of Cowes is famous for Cowes Week in early August; first held in 1826, it's one of the biggest and longest-running sailing regattas in the world. Fibreglass playthings and vintage sailing boats line Cowes' waterfronts, which are lopped into East and West Cowes by the picturesque River Medina. The island's capital, Newport, is 5 miles south.

Sights

★Osborne House HISTORIC BUILDING

(EH; ☎01983-200022; www.english-heritage.org.uk; York Ave, East Cowes; adult/child £15/9; ⏲10am-6pm Apr-Sep, to 5pm Oct; P) Lemon-frosted and Italianate, Osborne House is pure Victorian pomp. Built in the 1840s at the behest of Queen Victoria, the monarch grieved here for many years after her husband's death. Extravagant rooms include the opulent Royal Apartments and Durbar Room; other highlights are horse and carriage rides, the Swiss Cottage – where the royal ankle-biters would play – and the stroll down Rhododendron Walk to Her Majesty's private beach.

Carisbrooke Castle CASTLE

(EH; ☎01983-522107; www.english-heritage.org.uk; Castle Hill, Newport; adult/child £9/5; ⏲10am-6pm Apr-Sep, to 5pm Oct, to 4pm Sat & Sun Nov-Mar; P) Charles I was imprisoned here before his execution in 1649. Today you can clamber the sturdy ramparts and play bowls on the very green the doomed monarch used.

Festivals & Events

Cowes Week SPORTS

(www.aamcowesweek.co.uk; ⏲Aug) One of the biggest and longest-running sailing regattas in the world.

Sleeping

★onefiftycowes B&B ££

(☎07795 296399; www.onefiftycowes.co.uk; 150 Park Rd, West Cowes; s £60-75, d £85-90; P 📶) All the trappings of a luxury hotel, all the individuality of a B&B – at onefiftycowes, wicker chairs sit beside stand-alone sinks; feature fireplaces are stacked with sea-smoothed pebbles. The best room is Solent, where a pair of binoculars is waiting to help you gaze at the partial sea views.

Fountain HOTEL ££

(☎0845 608 6040; www.fountaininn-cowes.co.uk; High St, West Cowes; s £60-100, d £75-110; 📶) Georgian-repro style rules at this appealing harbourside inn, where mock-flock wallpaper and old, wooden furniture define comfy rooms; number 21 has slanting ceilings and prime views of the bustling quay. The snug bar and sunny terrace are good places to sample pints and pub-grub classics (mains £9; open 11am to 10pm).

Ryde & Around

The nippiest foot-passenger ferries between Wight and Portsmouth alight in **Ryde**, a workaday but appealing Victorian town rich in the trappings of the British seaside. Next come the cutesy village of **Brading**, with its fine Roman villa, and photogenic **Bembridge Harbour**, which is fringed by sandy beaches.

Further south lie the twin resort towns of **Sandown** and **Shanklin**, boasting promenades and hordes of families wielding buckets and spades.

Sights

★Brading Roman Villa RUINS

(☎01983-406223; www.bradingromanvilla.org.uk; Morton Old Rd, Brading; adult/child £9.50/4.75; ⏲10am-5pm) The exquisitely preserved mosaics here (including a famous cockerel-headed man) make this one of the finest Romano-British sites in the UK. Wooden walkways lead over rubble walls and brightly painted tiles, allowing you to gaze right down on to the ruins below.

St Helens Duver NATURE RESERVE
(NT; www.nationaltrust.org.uk; ⌚24hr; P) At this idyllic sand-and-shingle spit bordering the mouth of the River Yar, trails snake past swathes of sea pink, marram grass and rare clovers. It's signed from the village of St Helens, near Bembridge Harbour.

Isle of Wight Steam Railway HERITAGE RAILWAY
(☎01983-882204; www.iwsteamrailway.co.uk; return adult/child £12/6, 1st class £17/11; ⌚mid-Apr–Sep) Regularly chugs the one-hour journey from Smallbrook Junction to Wootton Common.

Sleeping

★Vintage Vacations CAMPGROUND £
(☎07802 758113; www.vintagevacations.co.uk; Ashey, near Ryde; 4-person caravans per week £475-710; ⌚Apr-Oct; P) The bevy of 1960s Airstream trailers on this farm are vintage chic personified. The gleaming aluminium shells shelter lovingly selected furnishings ranging from cheerful patchwork blankets to vivid tea cosies. Alternatively, opt for a beach-shack retreat, a 1930s scout hut, or the Mission: a late-Victorian tin chapel.

Xoron Floatel B&B ££
(☎01983-874596; www.xoronfloatel.co.uk; Bembridge Harbour; d £70; P) A truly unique spot to drop off – this former WWII gunboat is now a cheery, bunting-draped houseboat. Tiny, comfy cabins come complete with pocket-sized bathrooms, while the harbour views from the flower-framed sun deck are simply superb.

Kasbah B&B ££
(☎01983-810088; www.kasbahiw.com; 76 Union St, Ryde; d £70; 📶) Kasbah brings a burst of North Africa to the streets of East Wight. Chunky wooden furniture and vibrant furnishings give bedrooms a Moroccan feel; some also have water views. The downstairs bar is lively – if you're not a night owl, avoid weekends or ask for a room on the top floor.

Eating

Pilot Boat PUB FOOD £
(☎01983-872077; www.thepilotboatinn.com; Station Rd, Bembridge; mains £9; ⌚noon-2pm & 6-8pm; P📶) It's a good sign when customers can just sit down and play the pub's piano and guitars – a convivial atmosphere that's enhanced by a log-burner, ships' flags and quality homemade grub (think local crab salad and big bowls of chilli). Meanwhile, the spick-and-span bedrooms (doubles £90) are attractively nautically themed.

Black Sheep CAFE £
(☎01983-811006; www.theblacksheepbar.co.uk; 53 Union St, Ryde; mains £8-10; ⌚noon-3pm Mon-Thu, to 8pm Fri & Sat) Chilled tunes on the music system, piles of newspapers and a palm-dotted terrace draw the locals to this laid-back Ryde venue – as do the regular live music sessions and a menu that spans home-made burgers, steaming bowls of mussels, and honey, fig and black pudding focaccia.

Floating Cafe & Shop SEAFOOD ££
(☎01983-874758; www.thebestdressedcrabintown.co.uk; Fisherman's Wharf, Bembridge Harbour; mains £6-22; ⌚10am-4pm daily Easter-Dec, 10am-4pm Sat & Sun Jan-Easter) Welcome to an idyllic spot to munch your lunch. At this bijou cafe tacked on to a pontoon, the day's crab and lobster harvest is turned into supremely tasty sandwiches, salads and soups. Best eaten at one of the tables perched beside the water as local fishing boats unload their catch. It's deservedly popular – book. From mid-July to late August the cafe is open until 8.30pm.

Ventnor & Around

The Victorian town of Ventnor slaloms so steeply down the island's southern coast that it feels more like the south of France. The shops in the town's winding streets are worth browsing and the seafront is well worth a stroll.

Sights & Activities

St Catherine's Lighthouse LIGHTHOUSE
(☎01983-730435; www.trinityhouse.co.uk; near Niton; adult/child £4/3; ⌚1-4.30pm Jul & Aug, hours vary Apr-Jun & Sep) A crenellated 19th-century navigational aid that marks the island's southernmost point. Tours climb the 90-odd steps up to the lantern room, revealing sweeping sea views.

St Catherine's Oratory LIGHTHOUSE
(near Niton) FREE Known locally as the Pepperpot, this 10.5m, octagonal, 14th-century tower constitutes England's only surviving medieval lighthouse.

Blackgang Chine AMUSEMENT PARK
(☎01983-730330; www.blackgangchine.com; Blackgang; admission £91.50; ⌚10am-5pm Apr-Jul, to 6pm Aug, to 4pm Sep-Mar) A kid-friendly

ISLE OF WIGHT MUSIC FESTIVALS

The isle's festival tradition kicked off in 1968, when an estimated 200,000 hippies came to see the Doors, the Who, Joni Mitchell and rock icon Jimi Hendrix' last performance. A generation on, its gatherings are still some of England's top musical events.

Isle of Wight Festival (www.isleofwightfestival.com) Held in mid-June, past headline acts include Stereophonics, Muse, the Red Hot Chili Peppers, the Kings of Leon and the Rolling Stones.

Bestival (www.bestival.net) Held in early September, Bestival delights in an eclectic, alternative feel, drawing the Super Furry Animals, Scissor Sisters, Candi Staton and more.

attraction themed around dinosaurs, pirates and dragons, which features water gardens, animated shows and a hedge maze.

Sleeping & Eating

Harbour View B&B ££
(St Augustine Villa; 01983-852285; www.harbourviewhotel.co.uk; The Esplanade, Ventnor; s £80-96, d £89-105; P) Country-house collectables dot this Italianate Victorian villa, where wing-backed chairs sit in stately bedrooms and rich red fabrics frame sea views. And what views! Watch the sun set from your sofa or the waves roll from your four-poster bed.

Hambrough B&B £££
(01983-856333; www.thehambrough.com; Hambrough Rd, Ventnor; d £120-230; P) It's the little touches that make a big difference at this boutique B&B. Subtle, sleek furnishings, espresso machines (which even froth the milk) and Isle of Wight smoked salmon for breakfast. Two bedrooms have balconies directly overlooking the sea – in some top-floor rooms you can even watch the waves from your bath-tub.

Spyglass Inn PUB FOOD ££
(01983-855338; The Esplanade, Ventnor; mains £10-25; noon-9.30pm) When a beachfront pub is this bedecked with pirate paraphernalia, ships' lanterns and lifebelts, you tend to be wary of the meals. No need. The seafood platters and salads here are superb, especially the grilled, garlic-butter-laced lobster – book these, they tend to sell out.

Ale & Oyster BISTRO ££
(01983-857025; www.thealeandoyster.co.uk; The Esplanade, Ventnor; mains £9-20; noon-2pm & 6-9pm Wed-Sun) Modern takes on Isle of Wight produce include wild mushroom and smoked garlic risotto, crab mornay, and hazelnut-dusted pan-seared scallops. Best enjoyed on the terrace set right beside Ventnor's esplanade.

Steephill Cove

Steephill Cove's tiny, sandy beach is fringed by buildings that range from stone cottages to rickety-looking shacks. Beach finds festoon porches dotted with driftwood furniture and draped with fishing nets; a tiny clapboard **lighthouse** presides over the scene. It's all studiedly nautical, but still very nice.

Sleeping & Eating

★**Lighthouse** APARTMENT £
(07903-689984; www.steephill-cove.co.uk; Steephill Cove; 6 people per week £990-1950) This is the sea-view sleep spot of your dreams. A white, two-storey, clapboard lighthouse where the style is pure New England beach chic and the setting is right beside the shore. Lie in bed watching the waves, take a few steps to the beach to swim in the sea, stroll out to dine on your private deck. Heavenly.

The same people run a boathouse (sleeping six people, per week £950 to £1490) and the romantic, two-person Crow's Nest (£390 to £600) nearby.

Crab Shed CAFE £
(Steephill Cove; snacks £5; noon-3pm Apr-Sep) Lobster pots and fishing boats line the slipway outside a shack that's a riot of sea-smoothed spas, cork floats and faded buoys. Irresistible treats include meaty crab salads, mackerel ciabatta and crumbly crab pasties.

★**Boathouse** SEAFOOD £££
(01983-852747; www.steephill-cove.co.uk; Steephill Cove; mains £19-41; noon-3pm Thu-Tue late May–early Sep) Arrive early enough, and you'll see Steephill Cove's fishers (Jimmy and Mark) landing your lunch – the sanded wooden tables here are just steps from the sea. It makes a spellbinding spot to sip chilled wine, sample succulent lobster and revel in Wight's new-found driftwood chic. Booking essential.

Getting There & Away

Steephill Cove is 1 mile west of Ventnor and is off-limits to cars. Walk from the nearby Botanical Gardens (parking £5), or hike from the hillside car park 200m west of Ventnor Esplanade, then follow the (sometimes steep) coast path until you arrive.

West Wight

Rural and remote, Wight's westerly corner is where the island really comes into its own. Sheer white cliffs rear from a surging sea as the stunning coastline peels west to Alum Bay and the most famous chunks of chalk in the region: the **Needles**. These jagged rocks rise, shardlike, out of the sea, like the backbone of a prehistoric sea monster. West Wight is also home to arguably the isle's best beach: sandy, windswept **Compton Bay**.

Sights & Activities

★Needles Old & New Battery FORT
(NT; 01983-754772; www.nationaltrust.org.uk; The Needles; adult/child £6.30/3.10; 11am-4pm mid-Mar–Oct) The Victorian fort complex at Wight's western tip is home to two gun emplacements where engrossing displays reveal how the site was established in 1862, served in two world wars and then became a secret Cold War rocket-testing base. Walk to the battery along the cliffs from Alum Bay (1 mile) or hop on the **tourist bus** (www.islandbuses.info; per 24hr adult/child £10/5; 10am-5pm mid-Mar–Sep) that runs twice hourly between battery and bay.

Needles Pleasure Cruises BOATING
(01983-761587; www.needlespleasurecruises.co.uk; Alum Bay; adult/child £5.50/3.50; 10.30am-4.30pm Easter-Oct) Twenty-minute voyages run half-hourly from Alum Bay beach to the towering Needles chalk stacks, providing cracking views of those soaring white cliffs.

Sleeping

★Really Green CAMPGROUND £
(07802 678591; www.thereallygreenholidaycompany.com; Blackbridge Rd, Freshwater Bay; yurt per week £375-705; Easter-Oct; P) Roughing it has never been so smooth. The two- to five-person, fully furnished yurts on this tree-shaded site feature four-poster beds, futons, wood-burning stoves and time-worn antiques. It's set amid secluded fields with river views. A local farm shop-deli is just a few minutes' walk away.

Totland Bay YHA HOSTEL £
(0845 371 9348; www.yha.org.uk; Hirst Hill, Totland Bay; dm/d £18/25; P) Creaking, cheerfully run Victorian house with a maximum of eight beds per room and staff happy to share local info.

DORSET

Holiday hot spot Dorset offers a checklist of charms. Its shoreline is one of Britain's best and boasts the Jurassic Coast – a World Heritage Site flecked with sea-carved bays, crumbly cliffs and beaches loaded with fossilised souvenirs. Swimming, kayaking and hiking here are memorable indeed. Inland, Thomas Hardy's lyrical landscape serves up vast Iron Age hill forts, rude chalk figures, fairy-tale castles and must-see stately homes. Then there are resorts alive with party animals, golden beaches flanked by millionaires' mansions, and sailing waters that have hosted Olympic events. Time then to add Dorset to your holiday list.

Information

Visit Dorset (www.visit-dorset.com) The county's official tourism website.

Getting There & Around

TRAIN

One train route runs from Bristol through Bath and Dorchester West to Weymouth (£20, three hours, at least six daily).

Another hourly service connects London Waterloo with Weymouth (£20, three hours), via Southampton, Bournemouth, Poole and Dorchester South.

BUS

First (www.firstgroup.com) runs bus routes linking the main towns.

More (www.morebus.co.uk) is the key bus operator in Bournemouth, Poole and surrounding rural areas.

Bournemouth

POP 183,491

If one thing has shaped Bournemouth, it's the beach. This glorious, 7-mile strip of soft sand first drew holidaymakers in the Victorian days. Today the resort attracts both elderly coach parties and youthful stag parties – on Saturday nights fancy-dress is everywhere; angels in L-plates meet men in mankinis. But

Bournemouth is more than just a full-on party town. It also boasts some hip hideaways, great restaurants, tempting water sports, and in Boscombe, 2 miles east of the centre, a suburb with a cool urban-surfer vibe.

Sights & Activities

Bournemouth Beach BEACH

Bournemouth's sandy shoreline regularly clocks up seaside awards. It stretches from Southbourne in the far east to Alum Chine in the west – an immense promenade backed by some 3000 deckchairs, ornamental gardens, kids' playgrounds and cafes. The resort also has two piers. Around **Bournemouth Pier** you can hire brightly painted **beach huts** (☎01202-451781; www.bournemouthbeachhuts.co.uk; per day/week £40/158), deckchairs (per day £3), windbreaks (£5.50) and parasols (£6). **Boscombe Pier** is a focus for water sports.

Russell-Cotes MUSEUM

(☎01202-451858; www.russellcotes.com; Russell-Cotes Rd; adult/child £6/4; ⏲10am-5pm Tue-Sun) Ostentation oozes from almost every inch of this arresting structure – a mash-up of Italianate villa and Scottish baronial pile. It was built at the end of the 1800s for Merton and Annie Russell-Cotes as somewhere to showcase the remarkable range of souvenirs gathered on their world travels.

Alum Chine GARDENS

(Mountbatten Rd; ⏲24hr) Bournemouth's 1920s heyday is beautifully evoked at a subtropical enclave containing plants from the Canary Islands, New Zealand, Mexico and the Himalayas; their bright-red bracts, silver thistles and purple flowers are set against a glittering sea. It's 1.5 miles west of Bournemouth Pier.

Sorted Watersports WATER SPORTS

(☎01202-300668; www.sortedsurfschool.co.uk; Overstrand Bldg, Undercliff Dr) From its base on Boscombe promenade, Sorted runs lessons in surfing and stand-up paddleboarding (per two hours £30). It also hires out wetsuits (two/eight hours £10/30), surfboards (two/eight hours £10/30), stand-up paddleboards (one/two hours £15/25), and kayaks (one/two hours £15/25).

Sleeping

Bournemouth Backpackers HOSTEL £

(☎01202-299491; www.bournemouthbackpackers.co.uk; 3 Frances Rd; dm/d £15/34; P 📶) Three- to six-bed dorms in a suburban house dotted with travellers' totems – one wall is lined with chocolate-bar wrappers from around the world. It's for non-UK citizens only, and reservations are only accepted via the booking form on the website.

★**B&B by the Beach** B&B ££

(☎01202-433632; www.bedandbreakfastbythebeach.co.uk; 7 Burtley Rd, Southbourne; d £110; P 📶) Prepare for a winning combo: charming owners and delightful rooms. Themes and colours encompass yachting, deep aquamarine and ruby red. Relaxation comes courtesy of the flower-framed terrace, posh chocs and homemade cake – best sampled with the complimentary glass of wine.

★**Urban Beach** BOUTIQUE HOTEL ££

(☎01202-301509; www.urbanbeach.co.uk; 23 Argyll Rd; s £72, d £99-180; P @ 📶) Still slumber spot of choice for Bournemouth's hip visitors, Urban Beach revels in a 'no-worries' air that sees free loans of wellingtons, umbrellas and DVDs. Bold black, dark grey and vivid lime define stylish bedrooms, while the decked terrace is full of fashionistas tucking into fare from the upscale bistro (open noon to 10pm).

Mory House B&B ££

(☎01202-433553; www.moryhouse.co.uk; 31 Grand Ave, Southbourne; s £55-70, d £75-97, f from £117; P 📶) In this serene, pristine B&B, stained glass and an elegant stairwell hint at the house's Edwardian age. Contemporary bedrooms are styled in muted colours; the pick is number 3, where a pint-sized balcony is an ideal spot to nibble one of the cookies or sweets you'll find scattered around. There's also a family room (sleeps four).

Amarillo B&B ££

(☎01202-553884; www.amarillohotel.co.uk; 52 Frances Rd; s £35-45, d £70-90; P 📶) Amarillo's smart, stylish bedrooms are great value; expect jazzy wallpaper, snazzy throws and subtle lighting.

Eating

★**Urban Reef** BISTRO ££

(☎01202-443960; www.urbanreef.com; Undercliff Dr, Boscombe; mains £8-22; ⏲9am-10pm, winter times vary; 📶) On sunny weekends a cool crowd queues out the door at funky Urban Reef. No wonder: a waterfront deck and balcony, punchy coffee, top-notch snacks and quality, sustainable restaurant fare. On stormy days snuggle down beside the log burner and listen to the sound of sea.

Reef Encounter BISTRO ££

(www.reef-encounter.com; 42 Sea Rd, Boscombe; mains £7-15; ⏲11am-10pm Mon-Fri, 9am-10pm Sat & Sun, shorter hours winter; 📶) Big squishy sofas, a mellow soundtrack and a sea-view terrace give this chilled-out eatery a surf bar vibe. Imaginative takes on brunch include smoked salmon, egg and avocado, or opt for tasty burgers, ribs and wings – perhaps while sipping a cool beer, watching the waves.

West Beach SEAFOOD ££

(☎01202-587785; www.west-beach.co.uk; Pier Approach; mains £15-35; ⏲noon-3pm & 6-10pm) The seafood and setting are hard to beat – bag a chair on the decking beside the sand, watch the waves lap Bournemouth Pier and tuck into perfectly cooked, perfectly fresh fish; perhaps grey mullet with chorizo and saffron oil, or a shellfish platter piled high with oysters, langoustines, cockles and clams.

Drinking & Nightlife

Sixty Million Postcards PUB

(www.sixtymillionpostcards.com; 19 Exeter Rd; ⏲noon-midnight Sun-Thu, to 2am Fri & Sat) An oasis of hipster grunginess amid pound-a-pint Bournemouth, Sixty Million draws a decidedly beatnik crowd. Worn wooden floors and fringed lampshades frame events encompassing retro DJ sets, live bands, discos, movie and comedy nights, Sunday pub quizzes and jazz 'n' jumble sales.

Old Firestation CLUB

(www.oldfirestation.co.uk; 36 Holdenhurst Rd; ⏲Thu-Sat 10pm-3am) Mixes touring gigs, club nights and student parties; music takes in indie, punk, rock 'n' roll and old skool.

Information

Rio Internet Cafe (☎01202-312021; 130 Commercial Rd; per hr £1.80; ⏲10am-7pm Mon-Fri, to 5pm Sat & Sun)

Tourist Office (☎01202-451734; www.bournemouth.co.uk; Pier Approach; ⏲10am-5pm Apr-Oct, to 4pm Nov-Mar) Set right beside Bournemouth Pier.

Getting There & Around

BUS

Direct National Express routes include the following:

Bristol £20, four hours, daily Monday to Saturday

London £15, 2½ hours, hourly

Oxford £18, 3½ hours, three daily

Southampton £8, 50 minutes, hourly

Useful local buses:

Poole bus M1/M2; £2.30, 25 minutes, every 15 minutes

Salisbury bus X3; £8.50, 1¼ hours, at least hourly

A **Morebus Zone A Dayrider** (adult/child £4.10/3.60) gives a day's unlimited travel in much of Poole, Bournemouth and neighbouring Christchurch.

TRAIN

Destinations include the following:

Dorchester South £12, 45 minutes, hourly

London Waterloo £24, 2¾ hours, hourly

Poole £4.10, 12 minutes, half-hourly

Weymouth £14.60, one hour, hourly

Poole

POP 147,645

In the quaint old port of Poole there's a whiff of money in the air: the town borders Sandbanks, a gorgeous beach backed by some of the world's most expensive chunks of real estate. Big bucks aside, Poole also boasts excellent eateries and is the springboard for a raft of water sports and some irresistible boat trips.

Sights

Brownsea Island ISLAND

(NT; ☎01202-707744; www.nationaltrust.org.uk; adult/child £6.30/3.15; ⏲10am-5pm late Mar–Oct) On this small, wooded island in the middle of Poole Harbour, trails weave through heath and woods, past peacocks, red squirrels, red deer and a wealth of bird life – the water-framed views on to the Isle of Purbeck are stunning. Free guided walks focus on the wartime island, smugglers and pirates. Boats, run by **Brownsea Island Ferries** (☎01929-462383; www.brownseaislandferries.com; ⏲10am-5pm late Mar-Oct), leave from Poole Quay (adult/child return £10.75/6.75) and Sandbanks (adult/child return £6.50/5) at least hourly.

Waterfront Museum MUSEUM

(☎01202-262600; www.boroughofpoole.com/museums; 4 High St; ⏲10am-5pm Mon-Sat, noon-5pm Sun) FREE The building alone is worth seeing – a beautifully restored 15th-century warehouse. The star exhibit is a 2300-year-old **Iron Age logboat** dredged up from Poole Harbour. At 10m long and 14 tonnes, it's the largest to be found in southern Britain and probably carried 18 people.

Sandbanks BEACH

A 2-mile, wafer-thin peninsula of land that curls around the expanse of Poole Harbour, Sandbanks is studded with some of the most expensive houses in the world. But the white-sand beaches that border them are free, have some of the best UK water-quality standards and are home to a host of water-sports operators.

Sleeping

Old Townhouse B&B ££

(☎01202-670950; www.theoldtownhouse.co.uk; 7 High St; s/d £65/95; 📶) A delightful air of old England settles cosily over this quayside B&B. It's largely down to the gleaming wood, big burnished brass taps and furnishings that aren't afraid to echo heritage styles. A central setting and tiny patio add to the appeal.

Quayside B&B ££

(☎01202-683733; www.poolequayside.co.uk; 9 High St; s/d/f £45/75/85; 📶) Snug rooms in pine and bright, blocky prints in the heart of the old harbour.

Merchant House B&B £££

(☎01202-661474; www.themerchanthouse.org.uk; 10 Strand St; s £110, d £140-160) Tucked just one street back from the water's edge, tall, red-brick Merchant House is boutiquery at its best. Hefty wood sculptures, wicker rocking chairs and crisp linen ensure it's stylish; the odd teddy bear keeps it cheery too.

Eating

Storm SEAFOOD ££

(☎01202-674970; www.stormfish.co.uk; 16 High St; mains £16-20; ⌚6-10pm Mon-Sat) How rare is this: the dish you're eating could well have been caught by the chef? At chilled-out Storm, fisher Pete also rattles the pots 'n' pans, delighting in dishing up intense Goan fish curry, local pollack with Welsh rarebit crust, and spicy Dorset clams.

Poole Arms PUB FOOD ££

(www.poolearms.co.uk; Poole Quay; mains £9-16; ⌚noon-9pm Sun-Thu, to 9.30pm Fri & Sat) The grub at this ancient pub is strong on locally landed seafood – try the homemade fish pie, local crab or pan-fried herring roe. Order some New Forest beer, then settle down in the snug, wood-lined bar with the locals, or on the terrace overlooking the quay.

★ **Guildhall Tavern** FRENCH £££

(☎01202-671717; www.guildhalltavern.co.uk; 15 Market St; mains £18-20; ⌚noon-4pm & 6pm-midnight Tue-Sat) Poole's top table consistently delights as it combines local ingredients with lashings of French flair. Predictably, fish features strongly – the vanilla-infused confit salmon is superb; succulent skate wing comes *à la Provençale* – but *boeuf bourguignon* and rosemary-scented Dorset lamb also make carnivores smile. Book.

Information

Tourist Office (☎01202-262600; www.pooletourism.com; 4 High St; ⌚10am-5pm Sep-Jun, to 6pm Jul & Aug) Now set inside the Waterfront Museum.

Getting There & Around

BOAT

Brittany Ferries (☎0330 159 7000; www.brittany-ferries.com) sails between Poole and Cherbourg in France (4½ hours, one daily). Summer return prices start at around £85 for foot passengers and £310 for a car and two adults.

Sandbanks Ferry (☎01929-450203; www.sandbanksferry.co.uk; per pedestrian/car £1/4.10; ⌚7am-11pm) makes the four-minute trip from Sandbanks to Studland every 20 minutes. It's a shortcut from Poole to Swanage, Wareham and the Isle of Purbeck, but the summer queues can be a pain.

WATER SPORTS – POOLE HARBOUR

Poole Harbour's sheltered coasts may inspire you to get on the water. Operators cluster near the Sandbanks peninsula.

Poole Harbour Watersports (☎01202-700503; www.pooleharbour.co.uk; 284 Sandbanks Rd) Does lessons in stand-up paddleboarding (SUP; per 1½ hours £20), windsurfing (per three hours £45) and kitesurfing (per day £99), plus memorable kayak and SUP tours (per three hours £30 to £40).

Watersports Academy (☎01202-708283; www.thewatersportsacademy.com; 15 Banks Rd) Offers kitesurfing lessons (per day £100), windsurfer sessions (per two hours/days £25/110), sailing courses (per two hours/days £65/165) and wakeboarding and water-skiing lessons (per hour £60).

WORTH A TRIP

KINGSTON LACY

Dorset's must-see stately home **Kingston Lacy** (NT; ☎01202-883402; www.nationaltrust.org.uk; Wimborne Minster; adult/child £13.50/6.70; ⏲house 11am-5pm Mar-Oct, to 4pm Nov-Dec, grounds 10am-6pm Mar-Oct, to 4pm Nov-Feb; P) looks every inch the setting for a period drama. It overflows with rich decor, most famously in the Spanish Room, which is smothered with gold and gilt. Other highlights are the hieroglyphics in the Egyptian Room and the elegant marble staircase and loggia. Artworks include the overwhelming ceiling fresco *The Separation of Night and Day*, by Guido Reni, and paintings by Rubens, Titian and Van Dyck. Kingston Lacy is 2.5 miles west of Wimborne.

BUS

Bournemouth bus M1/M2; £2.30, 25 minutes, every 15 minutes

London Victoria National Express; £25, 3½ hours, every two hours

Sandbanks bus 52; £3.50, 25 minutes, hourly Monday to Saturday

A Morebus Zone A Dayrider (adult/child £4.10/3.60) gives a day's unlimited travel in much of Poole and Bournemouth.

TAXI

Dial-a-Cab (☎01202-666822; www.pooletaxis.co.uk)

TRAIN

Bournemouth £4.10, 12 minutes, half-hourly

Dorchester South £10.20, 30 minutes, at least hourly

London Waterloo £17, 2¼ hours, half-hourly

Weymouth £14, 45 minutes, hourly

Corfe Castle

The massive, shattered ruins of Corfe Castle loom so dramatically from the landscape it's like blundering into a film set. The defensive fragments tower over an equally photogenic village, which bears the castle's name and makes for a romantic spot for a meal or an overnight stay.

Sights

★Corfe Castle CASTLE
(NT; ☎01929-481294; www.nationaltrust.org.uk; The Square; adult/child £8.50/4.25; ⏲10am-6pm Apr-Sep, to 4pm Oct-Mar) The startling, fractured battlements of one of Dorset's most famous landmarks were once home to Sir John Bankes, Charles I's right-hand man. The Civil War saw the castle besieged by Cromwellian forces; in 1646 the plucky Lady Bankes directed a six-week defence and the castle fell only after being betrayed from within. The Roundheads then gunpowdered Corfe Castle apart; turrets and soaring walls still sheer off at precarious angles – the splayed-out gatehouse looks like it's just been blown up.

Swanage Steam Railway HERITAGE RAILWAY
(☎01929-425800; www.swanagerailway.co.uk; adult/child return £12.50/7.60; ⏲daily Apr-Oct, Sat & Sun Nov-Mar) Vintage steam trains puff at least hourly between Swanage and Norden (25 minutes), stopping at Corfe Castle.

Sleeping & Eating

Ammonite B&B £
(☎01929-480188; www.ammonite-corfecastle.co.uk; 88 West St; s £55, d £65-85; P📶) The pleasing bedrooms at this tranquil edge-of-village B&B feature pastels and pine, while the Aga-cooked breakfast includes local eggs, homemade jams and crusty bread from Corfe Castle's bakery.

Olivers B&B ££
(☎01929-477111; www.oliverscorfecastle.com; 5 West St; s/d/f £80/95/105) Tucked away in the heart of the old village in a charismatic street, Olivers combines honey-coloured beams with country-cottage chic: reproheritage armchairs, mock-flock wallpaper and chunky wood furniture. Stylish, restful, great-value rooms.

Castle Inn PUB FOOD ££
(☎01929-480208; www.castleinncorfe.co.uk; 63 East St; mains £12-20; ⏲noon-3pm & 6-9pm Mon-Sat, noon-9pm Sun; 🖉) The locals' choice. Prepare to dine, beside flagstone floors and ancient beams festooned with fairy lights, on tasty pub classics, plus some specials-board surprises: perhaps sea bass given a kick by smoked paprika, or a gutsy chickpea stew.

Getting There & Away

Bus 40 shuttles hourly between Poole, Wareham, Corfe Castle and Swanage. The 15-minute trip to Wareham costs £4.40.

Lulworth Cove & Around

POP 740

In this stretch of southeast Dorset the coast steals the show. For millions of years the elements have been creating an intricate shoreline of curved bays, caves, stacks and weirdly wonderful rock formations – most notably the massive natural arch at Durdle Door.

The charismatic hamlet of Lulworth Cove is a pleasing jumble of thatched cottages and fishing gear, which winds down to a perfect crescent of white cliffs.

Sights & Activities

Lulworth Cove Heritage Centre INTERPRETATION CENTRE
(☎01929-400587; www.lulworth.com; main car park, Lulworth Cove; ⊙10am-5pm) Excellent displays outline how geology and erosion have combined to shape the area's remarkable shoreline. Staff can advise about walks too.

Stair Hole Bay BAY
(Lulworth Cove) Stair Hole Bay sits just a few hundred yards west of Lulworth Cove. This diminutive semicircle is almost enclosed by cliffs that feature tiny rock arches – a route in that's popular with kayakers. On the landward side is the delightfully named **Lulworth Crumple**, where layers of rock form dramatically zigzagging folds.

★**Durdle Door** LANDMARK
The poster child of Dorset's Jurassic Coast, this immense, sea-fringed, 150-million-year-old Portland stone arch was created by a combination of massive earth movements and erosion. Today it's framed by shimmering bays; bring a swimsuit and head down the hundreds of steps for an unforgettable dip. You can park at the top of the cliffs (two hours £3, four hours £4), but it's best to hike the coast path from Lulworth Cove (1 mile).

Lulworth Castle CASTLE
(EH; ☎01929-400352; www.lulworth.com; East Lulworth; adult/child £5/3; ⊙10.30am-5pm Sun-Fri Apr-Dec) A confection in creamy, dreamy white, this baronial pile looks more like a French chateau than a traditional English castle. Built in 1608 as a hunting lodge, it's survived extravagant owners, extensive remodelling and a disastrous fire in 1929. It has been extensively restored – check out the reconstructed kitchen and cellars, then climb the tower for sweeping coastal views. It costs £3 to park.

★**Jurassic Coast Activities** ADVENTURE SPORTS
(☎01305-835301; www.jurassiccoastactivities.co.uk; Lulworth Cove; per person £60; ⊙up to 3 tours daily) This unmissable, three-hour paddle offers jaw-dropping views of Dorset's heavily eroded coast. Starting at Lulworth Cove, you glide through Stair Hole's caves and stacks, across Man O'War Bay, then under the stone arch at Durdle Door, stopping for swims and picnics along the way.

Sleeping

Lulworth YHA HOSTEL £
(☎0845 371 9331; www.yha.org.uk; School Lane, West Lulworth; dm £13-23, d £40; P) Hills stretch out alongside, and sheep bleat outside, this cosy, chalet-style, edge-of-village hostel.

Durdle Door Holiday Park CAMPGROUND £
(☎01929-400200; www.lulworth.com; sites £26-43; ⊙Mar-Oct; P) Attractive, spacious site, just minutes from the creamy cliffs, and 1.5 miles west of the hamlet of Lulworth Cove.

★**Lulworth Cove** INN ££
(☎01929-400333; www.lulworth-coveinn.co.uk; Main Rd, Lulworth Cove; d £110-150; P 🛜) What do you get for a £1.4-million refurbishment? A veritable vision of driftwood chic – whitewashed floorboards, aquamarine panels, painted wicker chairs and roll-top baths. Add cracking sea views, a mini roof terrace

LAWRENCE OF ARABIA

The tiny cottage **Clouds Hill** (NT; ☎01929-405616; www.nationaltrust.org.uk; near Bovington; adult/child £6/3; ⊙11am-5pm Mar–Oct; P) that was home to TE Lawrence (1888–1935), provides a compelling insight into a complex man. The British soldier became legendary after working with Arab tribes against Turkish forces in WWI. Look out for Lawrence's evocative desert-campaign photos, his French crusader castle sketches and the desk where he abridged *Seven Pillars of Wisdom*.

The four idiosyncratic rooms include a surprisingly comfortable cork-lined bathroom, an aluminium foil–lined bunk room and a heavily beamed music room. The house is much as Lawrence left it – he died at the age of 46 after a motorbike accident on a nearby road.

and top-quality gastropub grub (mains £9 to £15; food served from noon to 9pm) and you have an irresistible inn.

Bishops INN £££
(01929-400552; www.bishopslulworth.co.uk; Main Rd, Lulworth Cove; d £160-180;) An idyllic setting, pared-down designs, top-notch linen and pamper-yourself toiletries combine to make this a memorable place to stay – especially if you opt for a room with Lulworth Cove views. Or just lounge beside the pool, which also overlooks that circle of bay. Tasty food (mains £15 to £20; served from noon to 2.30pm and 7pm to 9pm) spans lobster, risotto and *moules*.

Eating & Drinking

Cove Fish SEAFOOD £
(01929-400807; Lulworth Cove; fish from £3, crab £3-4; 10am-4pm Tue-Sun Easter-Sep, plus some winter weekends) The seafood piled high in this shed by the path to the beach has been caught by ninth- and 10th-generation fishermen Joe and Levi. Bag some fish for the barbecue, or settle at the wobbly table and tuck into Lulworth Cove crab (£3 to £4) or lobster – a meal that's travelled food yards not miles.

★Castle PUB
(www.thecastleinn-lulworthcove.co.uk; West Lulworth; noon-10pm;) A head-spinning array of 40-plus ciders make this thatched pub a magnet for fans of the golden elixir. From quaffable Bumble Berry (4%) to epic Old Rosie (7.3%), this 'permanent cider festival' thoughtfully offers sampler trays (three different thirds of a pint) to help you get through a few.

Getting There & Away

Bus 104 links Lulworth with Wareham (£5, 35 minutes, two daily, Monday to Saturday).

Dorchester & Around

POP 19,143

With Dorchester, you get two towns in one: a real-life, bustling county town and Thomas Hardy's fictional Casterbridge. The Victorian writer was born nearby and his literary locations can still be found among Dorchester's white- and red-brick Georgian terraces. Here you can also visit Hardy's former homes and see his original manuscripts. Add cracking archaeological sites and attractive places to eat and sleep and you have an appealing base for a night or two.

Sights

★Dorset County Museum MUSEUM
(01305-262735; www.dorsetcountymuseum.org; High West St; adult/child £5.35/3.50; 10am-5pm Mon-Sat Apr-Oct, to 4pm Nov-Mar) The Thomas Hardy collection here is the world's largest, offering extraordinary insights into his creative process. You can see from text in Hardy's cramped handwriting where he's crossed out one word and substituted another. There's also an atmospheric reconstruction of his study at Max Gate and a letter in which Siegfried Sassoon requests permission to dedicate his first book of poems to Hardy.

Jurassic Coast fossil exhibits include a huge ichthyosaur and 1.8m plesiosaur fore paddle. Bronze and Iron Age finds from Maiden Castle include a treasure trove of coins and neck rings, while Roman artefacts include 70 gold coins, nail cleaners and (toe-curlingly) ear-picks.

Roman Town House HISTORIC BUILDING
(www.romantownhouse.co.uk; Northern Hay; 24hr) FREE The knee-high flint walls and beautifully preserved mosaics here powerfully conjure up the Roman occupation of Dorchester (then Durnovaria). Peek into the summer dining room to see the underfloor heating system (hypocaust), where charcoal-warmed air circulated around pillars to produce a toasty 18°C (64°F).

Maiden Castle ARCHAEOLOGICAL SITE
(EH; www.english-heritage.org.uk; dawn-dusk; P) FREE Occupying a massive slab of horizon on the southern fringes of Dorchester, Maiden Castle is the largest and most complex Iron Age hill fort in Britain. The first defences were built on the site around 500 BC – in its heyday it was densely populated with clusters of roundhouses and a network of roads. The Romans besieged and captured Maiden Castle in AD 43 – an ancient Briton skeleton with a Roman crossbow bolt in the spine was found at the fort.

Sleeping

★Beggars Knap B&B ££
(01305-268191; www.beggarsknap.co.uk; 2 Weymouth Ave; s £60-80, d £80-100, f from £115; P) Despite the name, this altogether fabulous, vaguely decadent guesthouse is far from impoverished. Opulent rooms drip with chandeliers and gold brocades; beds draped in fine cottons range from French sleigh

LOCAL KNOWLEDGE

THOMAS HARDY'S DORCHESTER

Thomas Hardy fans can hunt down the *Mayor of Casterbridge* locations hidden among modern Dorchester. They include **Lucetta's House** (Trinity St), a grand Georgian affair with ornate doorposts in Trinity St, while in parallel South St, a red-brick, mid-18th-century building (now a bank) is named as the inspiration for the **house of the mayor** (South St) himself. The **tourist office** (p259) sells book location guides.

Max Gate (NT; ☎01305-262538; www.nationaltrust.org.uk; Alington Ave; adult/child £6/3; ⊙11am-5pm Wed-Sun mid-Mar–Oct; P) Novelist Thomas Hardy was a trained architect and designed this attractive house, where he lived from 1885 until his death in 1928. *Tess of the D'Urbervilles* and *Jude the Obscure* were both written here, and the house contains several pieces of original furniture. It's a mile east of Dorchester, on the A352.

Hardy's Cottage (NT; ☎01305-262366; www.nationaltrust.org.uk; Higher Bockhampton; adult/child £6/3; ⊙11am-5pm Wed-Sun mid-Mar–Oct; P) This picturesque cob-and-thatch house is the birthplace of writer Thomas Hardy. It features evocative, sparsely furnished rooms and a lush garden. It's in Higher Bockhampton, 3 miles northeast of Dorchester.

to four-poster. You could pay much, much more and get something half as nice.

Westwood B&B ££
(☎01305-268018; www.westwoodhouse.co.uk; 29 High West St; s/d/f £75/95/130; 📶) A skilled designer has been at work in this 18th-century town house, producing a contemporary-meets-Georgian style: muted greens, brass lamps, subtle checks and minisofas. The modern bathrooms glint, while tiny fridges harbour fresh milk for your tea.

Yalbury Cottage HOTEL ££
(☎01305-262382; www.yalburycottage.com; Lower Bockhampton; s/d £85/120; P📶) It's almost your archetypal English cottage: framed by flowers and crowned by moss-studded thatch. Inside fresh, simple, gently rustic bedrooms overlook the garden or fields. The restaurant (two/three courses £33/38) serves up top-notch takes on British classics in convivial, clublike rooms; it's open 6.30pm to 8.30pm daily and noon to 2pm Sunday; bookings required.

It's in Lower Bockhampton, 3 miles east of Dorchester.

Eating

★No 6 FRENCH ££
(☎01305-267679; www.no6-restaurant.co.uk; 6 North Sq; mains £20; ⊙noon-2pm & 6.30-9pm Tue-Fri, 6-10pm Sat) The local goodies here are dished up with more than a soupçon of French finesse. Expect oven-roasted duck with a Normandy cider sauce; net-fresh, simply cooked fish, and a corker of a West Country–themed cheese board, showcasing caved-aged Cheddar, Somerset Brie and smoked Dorset Red.

Trinity SEAFOOD ££
(☎01305-757428; Trinity St; mains from £11-20; ⊙noon-3pm & 7-10pm Wed Sat) Trinity's open-plan kitchen-dining room means mouth-watering aromas waft around you. A menu that spans continents means those aromas might involve anything from smoked haddock chowder and hake linguine to jerk fish. It's no frills but great fun and the seafood is super fresh. Cash only.

Sienna MODERN BRITISH ££
(☎01305-250022; www.siennadorchester.co.uk; 36 High West St; mains £16-19; ⊙noon-2pm & 7-9pm Tue-Sat) The menu at Sienna is peppered with rarities; expect to find barbecue broccoli, jerk carrot or squid ink arranged on your plate. The puddings are imaginative too – perhaps try the chocolate mousse with hints of prune, orange and earl grey.

Entertainment

Plaza Cinema CINEMA
(☎01305-262488; www.plazadorchester.com; Trinity St) A four-screen art-deco gem, resplendent in red, black and gold, where the glamorous setting upstages the movies.

Information

Tourist Office (☎01305-267992; www.visit-dorset.com; Antelope Walk; ⊙9am-5pm Mon-Sat Apr-Oct, to 4pm Nov-Mar)

Getting There & Away

BUS

London Victoria National Express; £23, four hours, one daily

JURASSIC COAST

The kind of massive, hands-on geology lesson you wish you had had at school, the Jurassic Coast is England's first natural World Heritage Site, putting it on a par with the Great Barrier Reef and the Grand Canyon. This striking shoreline stretches from Exmouth in East Devon to Swanage in Dorset, encompassing 185 million years of the Earth's history in just 95 miles. It means you can walk, in just a few hours, many millions of years in geological time.

It began when layers of rocks formed, their varying compositions determined by different climates: desertlike conditions gave way to higher then lower sea levels. Massive earth movements then tilted all the rock layers, forcing most of the oldest formations to the west, and the youngest to the east. Next, erosion exposed the different strata.

The differences are very tangible. Devon's rusty-red Triassic rocks are 200–250 million years old. Lyme Regis' fossil-rich, dark-clay Jurassic cliffs are 190 million years old. Pockets of much younger, creamy-coloured Cretaceous rocks (a mere 65–140 million years old) pop up, notably around Lulworth Cove, where erosion has sculpted a stunning display of bays, stacks and rock arches.

The coast's website (www.jurassiccoast.com) is a great information source; also look out locally for the highly readable *Official Guide to the Jurassic Coast* (£4.95), or buy it at www.jurassiccoasttrust.org.

Lyme Regis Bus X51; £4.60, 1¼ hours, hourly Monday to Saturday
Sherborne Bus 216 via Cerne Abbas; £4.50, one hour, four to six daily Monday to Saturday
Weymouth Bus 10; £1.80, 30 minutes, half-hourly

TRAIN

Dorchester has two train stations.

Trains leave Dorchester West for Bath and Bristol (£20, three hours, at least six daily).

Services from Dorchester South, running at least hourly, include the following:
Bournemouth £12, 45 minutes
London Waterloo £32, 2¾ hours
Southampton £25, 1½ hours
Weymouth £5, 10 minutes

Cerne Abbas & the Cerne Giant

If you had to describe an archetypal sleepy Dorset village, you'd come up with something a lot like Cerne Abbas: houses run the gamut of English architectural styles, roses climb countless doorways and half-timbered houses frame a honey-coloured, 12th-century church. But this village also packs one heck of a surprise: the Cerne Giant; a vast chalk figure of a naked man.

Sights

★Cerne Giant LANDMARK
(24hr; P) FREE Rarely do you find such a nudge-nudge, wink-wink tourist attraction. Nude, full frontal and notoriously well endowed, this hillside chalk figure is revealed in all his glory. And he's in a stage of excitement that wouldn't be allowed in most magazines. The giant is around 60m high and 51m wide and his age remains a mystery; some claim he's Roman but the first historical reference comes in 1694, when three shillings were set aside for his repair. These days a car park provides grandstand views.

The Victorians found it all deeply embarrassing and allowed grass to grow over his most outstanding feature. Today the hill is grazed by sheep and cattle, though only the sheep are allowed to do their nibbling over the giant – the cows would do too much damage to his lines.

Sleeping & Eating

★New Inn INN ££
(01300-341274; www.thenewinncerneabbas.co.uk; 14 Long St; d £95-140, ste £170; P) Only in England could the New Inn actually be more than 400 years old. Rooms are crammed with heritage character; expect dark panelling, vast gilt mirrors and beams in the bathrooms. Or opt for the modern annex where painted wood and blue-and-white furnishings rule. The suites (especially Cerne) are gorgeous, boasting stand-alone baths in the bedrooms.

Abbots B&B ££
(01300-341349; www.abbotsbedandbreakfast.co.uk; 7 Long St; s/f £60/130, d £75-85;) The top-floor rooms here are big on atmosphere and small on head space, with duck-or-

regret-it lintels for those over 6ft. It's charming throughout though, with rooms decked-out in light grey, lemon and blue. The cakes in the cafe (open 10am to 4pm) are real diet busters.

Getting There & Away

Dorchester is 8 miles south. Bus X11 (four to six daily Monday to Saturday) goes to Dorchester (£2.60, 30 minutes) and Sherborne (£3, 30 minutes).

Weymouth

POP 52,168

At just over 225 years old, Weymouth is a grand dame of a resort with a couple of tricks up her faded sleeve. Candy-striped kiosks and deckchairs line a golden, 3-mile beach; chuck in cockles and chippies and prepare to promenade down seaside memory lane. But Weymouth is about more than just that sandy shore; the town boasts a bustling harbour, some superb seafood restaurants and easy access to the water sports centres of the neighbouring Isle of Portland.

Sights & Activities

Weymouth Beach BEACH

The nostalgia-inducing offerings along Weymouth's sandy shore could see you marvelling at highly skilled sand sculptors, renting a deckchair or pedalo, descending a helter-skelter, trampoline-bouncing, watching Punch and Judy shows, or riding a donkey.

Nothe Fort FORT

(☎01305-766626; www.nothefort.org.uk; Barrack Rd; adult/child £8/1; ⏰10.30am-5.30pm Apr-Sep) Weymouth's photogenic 19th-century defences are studded with cannons, searchlights and 30cm coastal guns. Exhibits detail Dorset's Roman invasion, a Victorian soldier's drill and Weymouth in WWII.

Sea Life AQUARIUM

(☎0871 423 2110; www.sealifeweymouth.com; Lodmoor Country Park; £23; ⏰10am-5pm Apr-Oct, to 4pm Nov-Mar; P) Highlights include sharks, penguins and seahorses. Tickets fall to £16.50 if bought in advance.

Coastline Cruises BOATING

(☎01305-785000; www.coastlinecruises.com; Brewers Quay; adult/child return £10/6; ⏰10.30am daily Apr-Oct) This wind-blown 90-minute jaunt passes Weymouth's historic fortifications and crosses Portland Harbour's vast 2012 Olympic sailing waters before sailing into Portland Harbour. Boats leave from Weymouth Harbour's west side.

Sleeping

★Roundhouse B&B ££

(☎01305-761010; www.roundhouse-weymouth.com; 1 The Esplanade; d £85-145; 📶) The decor here is as gently eccentric as the owner – vivid interiors combine sky blue, purple and shocking pink with fluffy cushions and snazzy modern art. But the best bit is the views; you can see both the beach out front and the harbour behind from all bedrooms.

B+B B&B ££

(☎01305-761190; www.bb-weymouth.com; 68 The Esplanade; s £60-80, d £70-100; P📶) As far a cry from chintz and pine as you can imagine, this style-conscious B&B opts for minimalist rooms (some have sea views) and a host of freebies – mineral water, biscuits and espressos that are best enjoyed in the hip 1st-floor lounge overlooking the bay.

Old Harbour View B&B ££

(☎01305-774633; www.oldharbourviewweymouth.co.uk; 12 Trinity Rd; s/d £70/98; P📶) In this pristine Georgian terrace, you get boating themes in the fresh, white bedrooms, and boats right outside the front door. One room overlooks the busy quay, the other faces the back.

Eating

★Marlboro FISH & CHIPS £

(www.marlbororestaurant.co.uk; 46 St Thomas St; mains from £7.50; ⏰noon-9.45pm) A sustainable slant and a 40-year history help lift this traditional chippy, just yards from Weymouth's quay, above its rivals – mackerel features among the long list of super-fresh fish. Take it away and duck the seagulls or get munching in the bay-windowed, licensed cafe (open till 8pm).

Dining Room Steakhouse MODERN BRITISH ££

(☎01305-783008; www.thediningroomweymouth.co.uk; 67 St Mary St; mains £10-25; ⏰6-9pm Wed-Sat) Despite the name, it's not all steaks here; you could also plump for grilled lobster, marinated lamb or slow-braised barbecue ribs. But it's the sirloin, fillet, rib-eye and T-bone most folks comes for. That or a Tomahawk – a whopping 46oz slab of meat that feeds two to three.

Dorset Burger Co BURGERS ££

(DBC; ☎01305-780888; www.thedorsetburgercompany.co.uk; 6 King St; burgers £9-13; ⏰6-8pm

WATER SPORTS – PORTLAND HARBOUR

At 890-hectare Portland Harbour, just south of Weymouth, you can glide in 2012 Olympic sailing waters. Local waters also offer superb diving, with a huge variety of depths, seascapes and wrecks. In addition to local operators, Weymouth's **Old Harbour Dive Centre** (01305-760888; www.oldharbourdivecentre.co.uk; 11 Nothe Pde) runs a range of PADI courses (90 minutes/four days £45/430), hires equipment and charters RIBs.

OTC (07817 717904; http://uk.otc-windsurf.com; Osprey Quay, Portland Harbour) Offers lessons in stand-up paddleboarding (SUP; one/two hours £25/40) and windsurfing (£45/95/185 per two hours/one day/two days). It also rents out SUP boards (per hour £10) and windsurfing boards and sails (per hour £15).

Andrew Simpson Sailing Centre (01305-457400; www.andrewsimpsonsailing.org; Osprey Quay, Portland Harbour) Runs RYA lessons (adult/child per two days £175/199).

Dive Beyond (01305-861441; www.divebeyond.co.uk; Castletown, Portland) Runs a five-day PADI open-water course (£475), rents equipment (full kit per day £45) and runs RIB trips to dive sites (from £15).

Mon-Fri, noon-8.30pm Sat & Sun) Hand-patted, juicy, chargrilled burgers, made mostly from Dorset produce.

No 4 SEAFOOD ££
(01305-780010; www.no4.restaurant; 4 Trinity Rd; mains £13-20; noon-2pm Tue-Sun, 6.30-9pm Tue-Sat) Fittingly, given the many fishing boats moored right outside, at driftwood-dotted No 4 the seafood is as fresh as it comes. Feast on a simply grilled catch of the day that's dotted with capers or laced with lemon butter. Or plump for some flavour-packed fish soup.

Information

Tourist Office (01305-561983; www.visit-dorset.com; 7 Coburg Place, St Thomas St; 10am-5pm Mon-Sat year-round, plus 10am-4pm Sun Apr-Oct)

Getting There & Away

BUS

The Jurassic Coaster bus X53 (four daily to hourly, no service winter Sundays) travels from Weymouth to Wareham (50 minutes), Poole (1½ hours), Abbotsbury (35 minutes), Lyme Regis (1¾ hours), Axminster (two hours) and Exeter (three hours). A Day Rider ticket costs adult/child £10/5; shorter fares are available.

Dorchester Bus 10; £1.80, 30 minutes, half-hourly

Fortuneswell, Isle of Portland Bus 1; £1.80, 20 minutes, four per hour

London National Express; £23, 4¼ hours, one direct daily

Portland Bill, Isle of Portland Bus 501; £1.80, 45 minutes, five daily June to September only

TRAIN

At least hourly services include the following:

Bournemouth £15, one hour

Dorchester South £5, 10 minutes

London Waterloo £25, three hours

Services every two hours:

Bath £26, two hours

Bristol £18, 2¾ hours

Isle of Portland

The 'Isle' of Portland is a hard, high comma of rock fused to the rest of Dorset by the ridge of Chesil Beach. On its 150m central plateau, a quarrying past still holds sway, evidenced by huge craters and large slabs of limestone. Portland offers jaw-dropping views down on to 18-mile Chesil Beach and the neighbouring Fleet – Britain's biggest tidal lagoon.

Proud, and at times bleak and rough around the edges, Portland is decidedly different from the rest of Dorset, and is all the more compelling because of it. The Isle's industrial heritage, water-sport facilities, rich bird life and starkly beautiful cliffs make it worth at least a day trip.

Sights

★Tout Quarry OUTDOORS
(near Fortuneswell; 24hr; P) FREE Portland's white limestone has been quarried for centuries and has been used in some of the world's finest buildings, such as the British Museum and St Paul's Cathedral. Tout Quarry's disused workings now house 53 sculptures that have been carved into the rock in situ, resulting in a fascinating combination

of the raw material, the detritus of the quarrying process and the beauty of chiselled works.

Portland Castle CASTLE
(EH; ☎01305-820539; www.english-heritage.org.uk; Liberty Rd, Chiswell; adult/child £5.30/3.10; ⏲10am-6pm Apr-Sep, to 5pm Oct) A particularly fine product of Henry VIII's castle-building spree, with expansive views over Portland harbour.

Portland Lighthouse LIGHTHOUSE
(☎01305-821050; www.trinityhouse.co.uk; Portland Bill; adult/child £7/5; ⏲10am-5pm Jun-Sep; P) For a real sense of Portland's remote nature, head to its southern tip, Portland Billt, to climb the 41m-high, candy-striped lighthouse. It offers breathtaking views of rugged cliffs and the Race, a surging vortex of conflicting tides. The interactive displays in the former lighthousekeepers' cottages include Into the Dark; a re-creation of sailing into stormy seas.

The lighthouse is also open some weekends outside the main season – call for the latest times.

Sleeping & Eating

Portland YHA HOSTEL £
(☎0845-3719339; www.yha.org.uk; Castle Rd, Castletown; dm £19, q £39-60; P 📶) Comfy, rambling Edwardian house with sea views from most dorms.

★ **Queen Anne House** B&B ££
(☎01305-820028; www.queenannehouse.co.uk; 2 Fortuneswell; s £55-60, d £80-95; 📶) It's impossible to know which room to pick: White, with skylight, beams and a hobbit-esque door; Lotus, with its grand furniture; ornate Oyster with its half-tester bed; or the suite with a French bath and miniconservatory. It doesn't matter though – they're all great value and gorgeous.

★ **Crab House Cafe** SEAFOOD ££
(☎01305-788867; www.crabhousecafe.co.uk; Portland Rd, Wyke Regis; mains £11-22; ⏲noon-2pm & 6-8.30pm Wed-Sat, noon-3.30pm Sun) This is where the locals make for on hot summer days, to sit beside the Fleet Lagoon amid beach-shack-chic tucking into fresh-as-it-gets seafood. Fish is enlivened by chilli, curry, lemon and herbs; crab comes spicy Chinese-style or whole for you to crack; and the oysters come with either pesto and Parmesan or bacon and cream.

Cove House PUB FOOD ££
(☎01305-820895; www.thecovehouseinn.co.uk; Chiswell Seafront; mains £10-18; ⏲noon-2.30pm & 6-9pm Mon-Fri, noon-9pm Sat & Sun) Extraordinary Chesil Beach views, memorable sunsets and great grub (try the Lyme Bay scallops) in a history-rich fishers' inn.

Getting There & Away

Bus 1 runs from Weymouth to Fortuneswell (£1.80, 20 minutes, four per hour).

Between June and September only bus 501 goes from Weymouth to Portland Bill (£1.80, 45 minutes, five daily).

Chesil Beach

One of the most breathtaking beaches in Britain, Chesil is 18 miles long, 15m high and moving inland at the rate of 5m a century. This mind-boggling, 100-million-tonne pebble ridge is the baby of the Jurassic Coast. A mere 6000 years old, its stones range from pea-sized in the west to hand-sized in the east.

Sights & Activities

Chesil Beach Centre INTERPRETATION CENTRE
(Fine Foundation; ☎01305-206191; www.dorsetwildlifetrust.org.uk; Ferrybridge; ⏲10am-5pm Easter-Sep, to 4pm Oct-Easter) FREE This centre, at the start of the bridge to Portland, is a great gateway to the beach. The pebble ridge is at its highest here – 15m compared to 7m at Abbotsbury. From the car park an energy-sapping hike up sliding pebbles leads to the constant surge and rattle of waves on stones and dazzling views of the sea, with the thin pebble line and the expanse of the Fleet Lagoon behind.

★ **Abbotsbury Swannery** WILDLIFE RESERVE
(☎01305-871130; www.abbotsbury-tourism.co.uk; New Barn Rd, Abbotsbury; adult/child £12/9; ⏲10am-5pm late Mar–Oct) Every May some 600 free-flying swans choose to nest at this swannery, which shelters in the Fleet Lagoon, protected by the ridge of Chesil Beach. Wandering the network of trails that winds between the swans' nests is an awe-inspiring experience that's punctuated by occasional territorial displays (think snuffling coughs and stand-up flapping), ensuring that even the liveliest children are stilled.

The swannery is at the picturesque village of Abbotsbury, 10 miles from Weymouth off the B3157.

Lyme Regis

POP 3637

Fantastically fossiliferous Lyme Regis packs a heavyweight historical punch. Rock-hard relics of the past pop out repeatedly from the surrounding cliffs – exposed by the landslides of a retreating shoreline. Lyme is now a pivot point of the Unesco-listed Jurassic Coast: fossil fever is definitely in the air and everyone, from proper palaeontologists to those out for a bit of fun, can engage in a spot of coastal rummaging. Add sandy beaches and some delightful places to sleep and eat, and you get a charming base for explorations.

Sights

Lyme Regis Museum MUSEUM
(☎01297-443370; www.lymeregismuseum.co.uk; Bridge St; adult/child £4/free; ⏲10am-5pm Easter-Oct, 11am-4pm Wed-Sun Nov-Easter) In 1814 local teenager Mary Anning found the first full ichthyosaur skeleton near Lyme Regis, propelling the town on to the world stage. A famous fossilist in her day, Miss Anning did much to pioneer the science of modern-day palaeontology. This museum, on the site of her former home, tells her story and exhibits spectacular fossils and prehistoric finds.

Cobb LANDMARK
First built in the 13th century, Lyme's iconic, curling sea defences have been strengthened and extended over the years, and so don't present the elegant line they once did, but it's still hard to resist wandering their length to the tip.

Dinosaurland MUSEUM
(☎01297-443541; www.dinosaurland.co.uk; Coombe St; adult/child £5/4; ⏲10am-5pm mid-Feb–mid-Oct) This joyful, mini, indoor Jurassic Park overflows with fossilised remains; look out for belemnites, a plesiosaurus and an impressive locally found ichthyosaur. Lifelike dinosaur models will thrill youngsters – the rock-hard tyrannosaur eggs and 73kg dinosaur dung will have them in raptures.

Town Mill HISTORIC BUILDING
(☎01297-444042; www.townmill.org.uk; Mill Lane; requested donation £2.50; ⏲11am-2pm Mon-Fri, to 4pm Sat & Sun Apr-Oct) FREE An atmospheric, creaking, grinding, 14th-century working watermill. Cafes, art galleries, a jewellery workshop and microbrewery sit alongside. Winter hours vary; call to check.

Activities

Undercliff WALKING
This wildly undulating, 304-hectare nature reserve just west of Lyme was formed by massive landslides. They've left a challenging hiking landscape of slipped cliffs, fissures and ridges, where paths snake between dense vegetation, exposed tree roots and tangles of brambles. The Undercliff starts a mile west of central Lyme Regis; follow footpath signs from Holmbush Car Park.

Sleeping

Sanctuary B&B £
(☎01297-445815; www.lyme-regis.demon.co.uk; 65 Broad St; s/d £45/56) A B&B for bibliophiles: the charming, chintzy, volume-filled bedrooms here sit inside a four-floor, 18-room bookshop. Ancient tomes that just beg to be perused are everywhere – they can delay you en route to (the excellent) breakfast, but handily there's a wonderfully relaxed vibe. And yes – that price *is* right.

FOSSIL HUNTING

Fossil fever is catching. Lyme Regis sits in one of the most unstable sections of Britain's coast, and regular landslips mean nuggets of prehistory keep tumbling from the cliffs.

Joining a guided walk aids explorations. Three miles east of Lyme, the **Charmouth Heritage Coast Centre** (☎01297-560772; www.charmouth.org; Lower Sea Lane, Charmouth; ⏲10.30am-4.30pm daily Easter-Oct, Thu-Sun Nov-Easter) FREE runs one to seven trips a week (adult/child £7.50/3). Or, in Lyme itself, Lyme Regis Museum holds three to seven walks a week (adult/child £11/6); local expert **Brandon Lennon** (☎07854 377519; www.lymeregisfossilwalks.com; adult/child £8/6; ⏲Sat-Mon) also leads expeditions. All walks are popular, so book early.

For the best chances of a find, visit within two hours of low water. If you do hunt by yourself, official advice is to check tide times and collect on a falling tide, observe warning signs, keep away from cliffs, only pick up from the beach and always leave some behind for others. Oh, and tell the experts if you find a stunner.

Coombe House B&B ££
(☎ 01297-443849; www.coombe-house.co.uk; 41 Coombe St; d £64-72, 5-person apt per week £360-630; P) The airy, easygoing, stylish bedrooms in this fabulous-value guesthouse are full of bay windows, wicker and white wood. Breakfast is delivered to your room on a trolley, complete with homemade bread and a toaster – perfect for a lazy lie-in in Lyme.

★ **Hix Townhouse** B&B £££
(☎ 01297-442499; www.hixtownhouse.co.uk; 1 Pound St; d £120-150, ste £165;) With its witty designer decor, luxury flourishes and in-town location, this 18th-century terrace is hard to resist. Each room playfully conjures a leisure theme (think gardening, fishing, reading etc); the pick is Sailing with its mock portholes, artfully arranged ropes, mini roof terrace and gorgeous sea views.

Eating

★ **Alexandra** BRITISH £
(☎ 01297-442010; www.hotelalexandra.co.uk; Pound St; afternoon tea £7.50-29; ⊙ 3-5.30pm; P) It's like the setting for an Agatha Christie, minus the murder. Wicker chairs dot manicured lawns, glittering Lyme Bay sweeps out behind. The perfect spot for a proper English afternoon tea, complete with scones, jam and dainty sandwiches.

Harbour Inn PUB FOOD ££
(☎ 01297-442299; www.harbourinnlymeregis.co.uk; Marine Pde; mains £9-25; ⊙ noon-2.30pm & 6-9pm) A flower-framed, beachside verandah, smart but snug interior and some of the best bistro-pub grub in town – the bouillabaisse is suitably intense.

Millside MODERN BRITISH ££
(☎ 01297-445999; www.themillside.co.uk; 1 Mill Lane; mains £13-18; ⊙ noon-2.30pm Tue-Sun, 6.30-9pm Tue-Sat) West Country foodstuffs pack the menu in this stylish eatery, from juicy burgers topped with Cheddar from Cheddar, to fish freshly caught on the local day boats. Millside's compact terrace makes a tempting spot for lunch on a sunny day.

★ **Hix Oyster & Fish House** SEAFOOD £££
(☎ 01297-446910; www.hixoysterandfishhouse.co.uk; Cobb Rd; mains £13-23; ⊙ noon-10pm) Expect sweeping views of the Cobb and dazzling food at this super-stylish, open-plan cabin. Lyme Bay shellfish soup comes with Cornish pastis liqueur; Newlyn hake head comes with Poole cockles. Perhaps start by slurping oysters: Brownsea Island or Portland molluscs come at £2.75 a pop.

> **WORTH A TRIP**
>
> ### FORDE ABBEY
>
> Built in the 12th century as a Cistercian monastery, **Forde Abbey** (☎ 01460-220231; www.fordeabbey.co.uk; Chard; house adult/child £12.50/free, gardens £10/free; ⊙ house noon-5pm Tue-Fri & Sun May-Oct, gardens 10am-5.30pm daily year-round) has been a private home since 1649. The building boasts magnificent plasterwork ceilings and fine tapestries but the gardens steal the show: 12 hectares of lawns, ponds, shrubberies and flower beds with hundreds of rare and beautiful species. Forde Abbey is 10 miles north of Lyme Regis; public transport is a nonstarter.

Information

Tourist Office (☎ 01297-442138; www.visit-dorset.com; Church St; ⊙ 10am-5pm Mon-Sat Apr-Oct, to 3pm Nov-Mar)

Getting There & Away

Bus X51 (£4.60, 1¼ hours, hourly Monday to Saturday) shuttles to Dorchester.

Bus X53 (four daily to hourly, no service winter Sundays) goes west to Exeter (£7.20) and east to Weymouth (£7.40) via Chesil Beach.

Sherborne

POP 9581

Sherborne gleams with a mellow, orangey-yellow stone - it's been used to build a cluster of 15th-century buildings and the impressive abbey church at their core. This serene town exudes wealth.

Sights

Sherborne Abbey CHURCH
(☎ 01935-812452; www.sherborneabbey.com; Abbey Cl; suggested donation £4; ⊙ 8am-6pm Apr-Sep, to 4pm Oct-Mar) At the height of its influence, the magnificent Abbey Church of St Mary the Virgin was the central cathedral of 26 succeeding Saxon bishops. Established early in the 8th century, it became a Benedictine abbey in 998 and functioned as a cathedral until 1075. The church has mesmerising fan vaulting that's the oldest in the country, a central tower supported by Saxon Norman piers and an 1180 Norman porch.

Sherborne Old Castle CASTLE

(EH; ☎01935-812730; www.english-heritage.org.uk; Castleton; adult/child £4/2.40; ⏰10am-5pm Apr-Jun, Sep & Oct, to 6pm Jul & Aug) These days the epitome of a picturesque ruin, Sherborne's Old Castle was built by Roger, Bishop of Salisbury, in 1120 – Elizabeth I gave it to her one-time favourite Sir Walter Raleigh in the late 16th century. It became a Royalist stronghold during the English Civil War, but Cromwell reduced it to rubble after a 16-day siege in 1645, leaving just the fractured southwest gatehouse, great tower and north range.

Sherborne New Castle CASTLE

(☎01935-812072; www.sherbornecastle.com; New Rd; house & gardens adult/child £11/free, gardens only £6/free; ⏰11am-5pm Tue-Thu, Sat & Sun Apr-Oct) Sir Walter Raleigh began building the impressive Sherborne New Castle in 1594, but only got as far as the central block before being imprisoned by James I. James promptly sold the castle to Sir John Digby who added the splendid wings you see today. In 1753 the grounds received a mega-makeover at the hands of landscape-gardener extraordinaire Capability Brown who added a massive lake and the 12-hectare waterside gardens.

Tours

Walking Tours WALKING

(www.sherbornewalks.co.uk; tours £5; ⏰10.30am Tue & Thu Jul-Sep) Ninety-minute trips exploring the photogenic old town, leaving from the tourist office.

Sleeping & Eating

★**Cumberland House** B&B ££

(☎01935-817554; www.bandbdorset.co.uk; Green Hill; d £75-80; P) Artistry oozes from these history-rich rooms – bright scatter rugs sit on flagstone floors; lemon and oatmeal walls undulate between wonderfully wonky beams. Gourmet breakfasts include freshly squeezed orange juice; arrive around 4pm and expect an offer of tea, taken in the garden or beside the fire.

Stoneleigh Barn B&B ££

(☎01935-389288; www.stoneleighbarn.co.uk; North Wootton; s £60-75, d £80-95, f from £160; P) Warm, weathered stone and extensive gardens ensure this 18th-century barn delights on the outside. Inside, exposed trusses frame spacious rooms that are decorated in line with the colours of their namesake flowers; choose from orchid, lilac or rose. Stoneleigh is 3 miles southeast of Sherborne.

George PUB FOOD ££

(www.thegeorgesherborne.co.uk; 4 Higher Cheap St; mains £9-13; ⏰noon-2.30pm & 6-9pm;) It's five centuries since Sherborne's oldest, cosiest inn pulled its first pint; today it signals its age with wooden settles polished smooth by countless behinds. The food is enduring pub grub fare: robust steaks, ham and egg, homemade puds and a 'roast of the day'.

★**Green** MODERN BRITISH £££

(☎01935-813821; www.greenrestaurant.co.uk; 3 The Green; mains £20-25; ⏰noon-2.30pm & 6.30-9.30pm Tue-Sat) In this affable, elegant eatery, the furniture is more chic than shabby and the food is pure West Country élan. Dorset goodies might include steamed Lyme Bay brill made fragrant with wild garlic, or saddle of local rabbit studded with wild mushrooms. For a great-value feed, plump for the cracking *menu du jour* (three courses £20).

Information

Tourist Office (☎01935-815341; www.visit-dorset.com; Digby Rd; ⏰9.30am-4pm Mon-Sat Apr-Nov, to 3pm Dec-Mar)

Getting There & Away

BUS

Dorchester (Bus X1; £4.50, one hour, four to six daily Monday to Saturday) Via Cerne Abbas (30 minutes)

Yeovil Bus 57/58; £4.50, 15 minutes, 10 daily Monday to Saturday

TRAIN

Hourly services:

Exeter £18, 1¼ hours

London Waterloo £20, 2½ hours

Salisbury £14, 45 minutes

WILTSHIRE

Wiltshire is rich in the reminders of ritual and packed with not-to-be-missed sights. Its verdant landscape is littered with more mysterious stone circles, processional avenues and ancient barrows than anywhere else in Britain. It's a place that teases and tantalises the imagination – here you'll experience the prehistoric majesty of Stonehenge and the atmospheric stone ring at Avebury. Add the serene 800-year-old cathedral at Salisbury, the supremely stately homes at Stourhead and Longleat and the impossibly pretty village of Lacock, and you have a county crammed full of English charm waiting to be explored.

Information

There's a large tourist office in Salisbury (p270).

Visit Wiltshire (www.visitwiltshire.co.uk) also has tourist information.

Getting There & Around

BUS

Wiltshire's bus coverage can be patchy, especially in the northwest.

First (www.firstgroup.com) Serves west Wiltshire.

Salisbury Reds (www.salisburyreds.co.uk) Covers Salisbury and many rural areas; offers one-day Rover Tickets (£8.50) and seven-day passes (Salisbury area £13.50, network-wide £24).

Stagecoach (www.stagecoachbus.com) Provides services around Swindon and Salisbury.

TRAIN

Rail lines run from London Waterloo to Salisbury (£25, 1½ hours, half-hourly), and beyond to Exeter and Plymouth, branching off north to Bradford-on-Avon, Bath and Bristol.

Salisbury

POP 40,300

Centred on a majestic cathedral that's topped by the tallest spire in England, Salisbury makes an appealing Wiltshire base. It's been an important provincial city for more than a thousand years, and its streets form an architectural timeline ranging from medieval walls and half-timbered Tudor town houses to Georgian mansions and Victorian villas. Salisbury is also a lively, modern town, boasting plenty of bars and restaurants, plus a concentrated cluster of excellent museums.

Sights

★Salisbury Cathedral CATHEDRAL

(01722-555120; www.salisburycathedral.org.uk; Cathedral Close; requested donation adult/child £7.50/free; 9am-5pm Mon-Sat, noon-4pm Sun) England is endowed with countless stunning churches, but few can hold a candle to the grandeur and sheer spectacle of 13th-century Salisbury Cathedral. This early English Gothic–style structure has an elaborate exterior decorated with pointed arches and flying buttresses, and a sombre, austere interior designed to keep its congregation suitably pious. Its statuary and tombs are outstanding; don't miss the daily tower tours and the cathedral's original, 13th-century copy of the **Magna Carta** (9.30am-4.30pm Mon-Sat, noon-3.45pm Sun).

The cathedral was built between 1220 and 1258. Beyond its highly decorative **West Front**, a small passageway leads into the 70m-long **nave**, lined with handsome pillars of Purbeck stone. In the north aisle look out for a fascinating **medieval clock** dating from 1386, probably the oldest working timepiece in the world. At the eastern end of the ambulatory the glorious **Prisoners of Conscience** stained-glass window (1980) hovers above the ornate **tomb** of Edward Seymour (1539–1621) and Lady Catherine Grey. Other monuments and tombs line the sides of the nave, including that of William Longespée, son of Henry II and half-brother of King John. When the tomb was excavated a well-preserved rat was found inside Longespée's skull.

Salisbury's 123m crowning glory, its **spire**, was added in the mid-14th century, and is the tallest in Britain. It represented an enormous technical challenge for its medieval builders; it weighs around 6500 tons and required an elaborate system of cross-bracing, scissor arches and supporting buttresses to keep it upright. Look closely and you'll see the additional weight has buckled the four central piers of the nave.

Sir Christopher Wren surveyed the cathedral in 1668 and calculated that the spire was leaning by 75cm. A brass plate in the floor of the nave is used to measure any shift, but no further lean was recorded in 1951 or 1970. Despite this, reinforcement of the notoriously 'wonky spire' continues to this day.

The cathedral really comes into its own during **evensong**, which takes place at 5.30pm Monday to Saturday and 4.30pm on Sunday, during term time only.

The best way to experience the cathedral is on a 90-minute tower tour (there are one to five daily), which sees you climbing 332 vertigo-inducing steps to the base of the spire for jaw-dropping views across the city and the surrounding countryside. They only take 12 people on each tour; booking is essential. Adults £12.50, children £8.

Cathedral Close HISTORIC SITE

Salisbury's medieval cathedral close, a hushed enclave surrounded by beautiful houses, has an other-worldly feel. Many of the buildings date from the 13th century, although the area was heavily restored during an 18th-century clean-up by James Wyatt. The close is encircled by a sturdy outer wall,

Salisbury

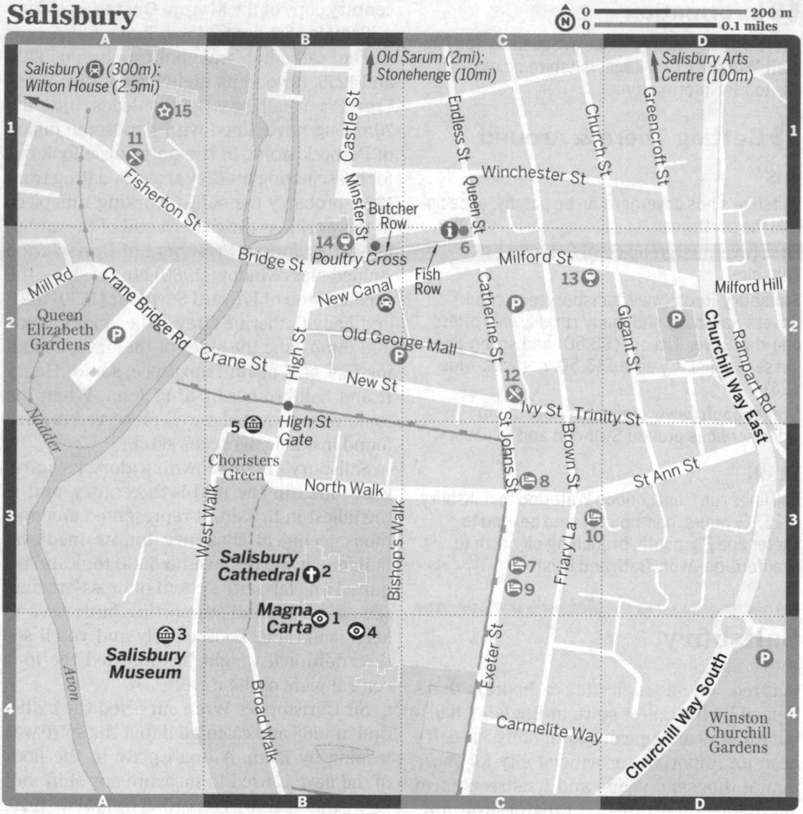

Salisbury

Top Sights
1 Magna Carta B4
2 Salisbury Cathedral B3
3 Salisbury Museum A4

Sights
4 Cathedral Close B4
5 Mompesson House B3

Activities, Courses & Tours
6 Salisbury Guides C2

Sleeping
7 Cathedral View C3
8 Chapter House C3
9 Spire House C3
10 St Ann's House C3

Eating
11 Anokaa A1
12 Cloisters C2

Drinking & Nightlife
13 Chapel C2
14 Haunch of Venison B2

Entertainment
15 Salisbury Playhouse A1

constructed in 1333; the stout gates leading into the complex are still locked every night.

★ **Salisbury Museum** MUSEUM
(☎01722-332151; www.salisburymuseum.org.uk; 65 Cathedral Close; adult/child £8/4; ⏰10am-5pm Mon-Sat year-round, plus noon-5pm Sun Jun-Sep) The hugely important archaeological finds here include the Stonehenge Archer, the bones of a man found in the ditch surrounding the stone circle – one of the arrows found alongside probably killed him. With gold coins dating from 100 BC and a Bronze

Age gold necklace, it's a powerful introduction to Wiltshire's prehistory.

Mompesson House HISTORIC BUILDING
(NT; ☎01722-335659; www.nationaltrust.org.uk; Cathedral Close; adult/child £6.30/3; ⏰11am-5pm Sat-Wed mid-Mar–Oct) Magnificent plasterwork ceilings, exceptional period furnishings and a sweeping carved staircase grace this fine Queen Anne (1701) building. All that made it the perfect location for the 1995 film *Sense and Sensibility*.

Old Sarum ARCHAEOLOGICAL SITE
(EH; ☎01722-335398; www.english-heritage.org.uk; Castle Rd; adult/child £4.50/2.70; ⏰10am-6pm Apr-Sep, to 5pm Oct, to 4pm Nov-Mar; P) The huge ramparts of Old Sarum sit on a grass-covered hill 2 miles north of Salisbury. You can wander the grassy ramparts, see the original cathedral's stone foundations, and look across the Wiltshire countryside to the spire of the present Salisbury Cathedral. Medieval tournaments, open-air plays and mock battles are held on selected days. Bus X5 runs twice an hour from Salisbury to Old Sarum (£2.30, hourly on Sundays). It's also a stop on the Stonehenge Tour bus (p270).

★**Wilton House** HISTORIC BUILDING
(☎01722-746714; www.wiltonhouse.com; Wilton; house & grounds adult/child £15/8; ⏰11.30am-5pm Sun-Thu May-Aug; P) Stately Wilton House provides an insight into the rarefied world of the British aristocracy. One of England's finest stately homes, it's been the house of the earls of Pembroke since 1542, and has been expanded, improved and embellished by successive generations. Highlights are the **Single** and **Double Cube Rooms**, designed by the pioneering 17th-century architect Inigo Jones.

Wilton House is 2.5 miles west of Salisbury; bus R3 runs from Salisbury (£2.70, 10 minutes, one to three hourly Monday to Saturday).

Tours

Salisbury Guides WALKING
(☎07873-212941; www.salisburycityguides.co.uk; adult/child £6/3; ⏰11am daily Apr-Oct, 11am Sat & Sun Nov-Mar) These 90-minute trips leave from the tourist office.

Sleeping

★**Chapter House** INN ££
(☎01722-412028; www.thechapterhouseuk.com; 9 St Johns St; r £100-140) In this 800-year-old boutique beauty, wood panels and wildly wonky stairs sit beside duck-your-head beams. The cheaper bedrooms are swish but the posher ones are stunning, starring slipper baths and the odd heraldic crest. The pick is room 6, where King Charles is reputed to have stayed. Lucky him.

St Ann's House B&B ££
(☎01722-335657; www.stannshouse.co.uk; 32 St Ann St; s £64, d £89-110; wifi) The aromas wafting from breakfast may well spur you from your room: powerful coffee; cinnamon-and-lemon banana bread; chilli and beef sausages; poached eggs and Parma ham. Utter elegance reigns upstairs where well-chosen antiques, warm colours and Turkish linen ensure a supremely comfortable stay.

Cathedral View B&B ££
(☎01722-502254; www.cathedral-viewbandb.co.uk; 83 Exeter St; s £75-85, d £80-100; P wifi) Admirable attention to detail defines this Georgian town house, where miniature flower displays and home-baked biscuits sit in quietly elegant rooms. Breakfasts include prime Wiltshire sausages and the B&B's own bread and jam, while homemade lemon drizzle cake will be waiting for your afternoon tea.

Spire House B&B ££
(☎01722-339213; www.salisbury-bedandbreakfast.com; 84 Exeter St; s/d/f £60/75/90; P wifi) In this B&B of beautifully kept, sweet rooms, the easygoing vibe extends to breakfast (add £5): chalk up your choice on a blackboard the night before. Options include slow-cooked blueberry-studded porridge, croissants and pastries, and local bacon and eggs.

Eating & Drinking

Anokaa INDIAN ££
(☎01722-414142; www.anokaa.com; 60 Fisherton St; mains £12-18; ⏰noon-2pm & 5.30-11pm; vegetarian) The pink-neon and multicoloured bubble displays signal what's in store here: a supremely modern version of Indian cuisine. The spice and flavour combos make the ingredients sing; the meat-free menu makes vegetarians gleeful, and the lunchtime buffet (£9) makes everyone smile.

Cloisters PUB FOOD ££
(www.cloisterspubsalisbury.co.uk; 83 Catherine St; mains £9-19; ⏰noon-9pm) The building dates from 1350, it's been a pub since the 1600s and, today, improbably warped beams reinforce an age-old vibe. It's a convivial spot for beefy burgers and homemade pies, or classier

evening fare such as pesto-dusted salmon fillet, and lamb steaks with redcurrant sauce.

Haunch of Venison PUB
(www.haunchpub.co.uk; 1 Minster St; ⏲11am-11pm Mon-Sat, to 6pm Sun) Featuring wood-panelled snugs, spiral staircases and crooked ceilings, this 14th-century drinking den is packed with atmosphere – and ghosts. One is a cheating whist player whose hand was severed in a game – look out for his mummified bones on display inside.

Chapel CLUB
(www.chapelnightclub.co.uk; 34 Milford St; ⏲9.30pm-3am Thu-Sat) Buzzing three-room club with adjoining bar where the DJ sets range from funk to '90s hip hop and chart 'n' cheese.

☆ Entertainment

Salisbury Playhouse THEATRE
(☎01722-320333; www.salisburyplayhouse.com; Malthouse Lane) A producing theatre that also hosts top touring shows and musicals.

Salisbury Arts Centre ARTS CENTRE
(☎01722-321744; www.salisburyartscentre.co.uk; Bedwin St) An innovative venue showcasing cutting-edge theatre, indie films, dance and live gigs.

Information

Library (www.wiltshire.gov.uk; Market Walk; internet per 30min £1; ⏲10am-7pm Mon, Tue, Fri, 9am-5pm Wed, Thu & Sat; ☎)
Tourist Office (☎01722-342860; www.visitsalisbury.co.uk; Fish Row; ⏲9am-5pm Mon-Fri, 10am-4pm Sat, 10am-2pm Sun)

Getting There & Away

BUS

Direct National Express services:
Bath £11, 1¼ hours, one daily
Bristol £11, 2¼ hours, one daily
London (£17, three hours, three daily) Via Heathrow.

Local services include the following:
Devizes Bus 2; £5.50, one hour, hourly Monday to Saturday
Shaftesbury Bus 29; £4.80, 1¼ hours, five daily Monday to Saturday

Tour buses leave to **Stonehenge** (☎01202-338420; www.thestonehengetour.info; adult/child £27/17) regularly.

TRAIN

Half-hourly connections include the following:
Bath £10, one hour
Bradford-on-Avon £13, 40 minutes
Bristol £15, 1¼ hours
London Waterloo £25, 1½ hours
Southampton £10, 30 minutes

Hourly connections:
Exeter £20, two hours
Portsmouth £20, 1¼ hours

Stonehenge

Welcome to Britain's most iconic archaeological site. This compelling ring of monolithic stones has been attracting a steady stream of pilgrims, poets and philosophers for the last 5000 years and is still a mystical, ethereal place – a haunting echo from Britain's forgotten past, and a reminder of those who once walked the ceremonial avenues across Salisbury Plain.

Sights

★**Stonehenge** ARCHAEOLOGICAL SITE
(EH; ☎0370 333 1181; www.english-heritage.org.uk; adult/child same-day tickets £18/11, advance booking £15.50/9.30; ⏲9am-8pm Jun-Aug, 9.30am-7pm Apr, May & Sep, 9.30am-5pm Oct-Mar; Ⓟ) An ultramodern makeover at ancient Stonehenge has brought an impressive visitor centre and the closure of an intrusive road (now restored to grassland). The result is a far stronger sense of historical context; dignity and mystery returned to an archaeological gem.

A pathway frames the ring of massive stones. Although you can't walk in the circle, unless on a recommended Stone Circle Access Visit (p272), you can get close-up views. Admission is through timed tickets – secure a place well in advance.

Stonehenge is one of Britain's great archaeological mysteries: despite countless theories about the site's purpose, ranging from a sacrificial centre to a celestial timepiece, in truth, no one knows for sure what drove prehistoric Britons to expend so much time and effort on its construction.

The first phase of building started around 3000 BC, when the outer circular bank and ditch were erected. A thousand years later, an inner circle of granite stones, known as bluestones, was added. It's thought that these mammoth 4-tonne blocks were hauled from the Preseli Mountains in South Wales, some 250 miles away – an almost inexplicable feat for Stone Age builders equipped with only the simplest of tools. Although no

Stonehenge

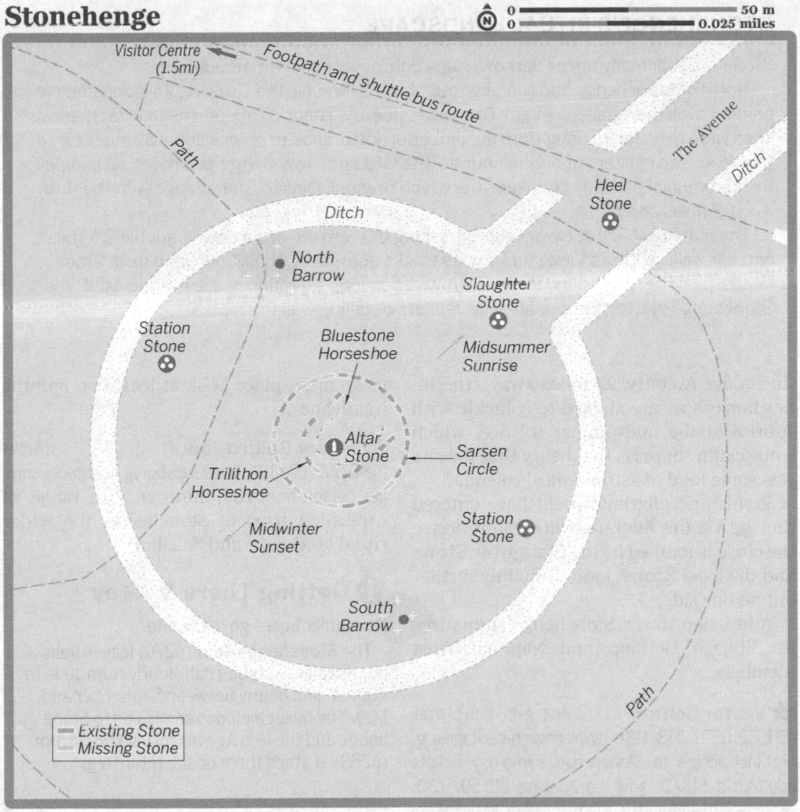

one is entirely sure how the builders transported the stones so far, it's thought they probably used a system of ropes, sledges and rollers fashioned from tree trunks – Salisbury Plain was still covered by forest during Stonehenge's construction.

Around 1500 BC, Stonehenge's main stones were dragged to the site, erected in a circle and crowned by massive lintels to make the trilithons (two vertical stones topped by a horizontal one). The sarsen (sandstone) stones were cut from an extremely hard rock found on the Marlborough Downs, 20 miles from the site. It's estimated dragging one of these 50-tonne stones across the countryside would require about 600 people.

Also around this time, the bluestones from 500 years earlier were rearranged as an inner **bluestone horseshoe** with an **altar stone** at the centre. Outside this the **trilithon horseshoe** of five massive sets of stones was erected. Three of these are intact; the other two have just a single upright. Then came the major **sarsen circle** of 30 massive vertical stones, of which 17 uprights and six lintels remain.

Much further out, another circle was delineated by the 58 Aubrey Holes, named after John Aubrey, who discovered them in the 1600s. Just inside this circle are the **South** and **North Barrows**, each originally topped by a stone. Like many stone circles in Britain

TICKETS FOR STONEHENGE

Stonehenge operates by timed tickets, meaning if you want to guarantee your entry you have to book in advance – even English Heritage and National Trust members entitled to free admission. If you're planning a peak-season visit, it's best to secure your ticket well in advance.

STONEHENGE'S RITUAL LANDSCAPE

Stonehenge actually forms part of a huge complex of ancient monuments.

North of Stonehenge and running roughly east–west is the **Cursus**, an elongated embanked oval; the smaller **Lesser Cursus** is nearby. Theories abound as to what these sites were used for, ranging from ancient sporting arenas to processional avenues for the dead. Two clusters of burial mounds, the **Old** and **New Kings Barrows**, sit beside the ceremonial pathway **the Avenue**, which originally linked Stonehenge with the River Avon, 2 miles away.

The **National Trust** (www.nationaltrust.org.uk) website has a downloadable 3.5-mile circular walk (A King's View) that traces tracks across the chalk downland from Stonehenge, past the Cursus and Kings Barrows and along a section of the Avenue itself. The Stonehenge **visitor centre** also has leaflets detailing walking routes.

(including Avebury, 22 miles away), the inner horseshoes are aligned to coincide with sunrise at the midsummer solstice, which some claim supports the theory that the site was some kind of astronomical calendar.

Prehistoric pilgrims would have entered the site via the **Avenue**, whose entrance to the circle is marked by the **Slaughter Stone** and the **Heel Stone**, located slightly further out on one side.

Admission to the Stonehenge site is free for English Heritage and National Trust members.

★ **Visitor Centre** INTERPRETATION CENTRE
(EH; ☎0370 333 1181; www.english-heritage.org.uk; incl access to Stonehenge, same-day tickets adult/child £18/11, advance booking £15.50/9.30; ⏲9am-8pm Jun-Aug, 9.30am-7pm Apr, May & Sep, 9.30am-5pm Oct-Mar) Stonehenge's swish new visitor centre sees you standing in the middle of an atmospheric 360-degree projection of the stone circle through the ages and seasons – complete with midsummer sunrise and swirling star-scape. Engaging audiovisual displays detail the transportation of the stones and the building stages, while 300 finds from the wider site include flint chippings, bone pins and arrowheads, there's also a striking re-creation of the face of a Neolithic man whose body was found nearby.

☞ Tours

★ **Stone Circle Access Visits** WALKING
(☎0370 333 0605; www.english-heritage.org.uk; adult/child £32/19) Circle-access visits are an unforgettable experience. Visitors normally have to stay outside the stone circle itself, but on these self-guided walks, you get to wander around the core of the site, getting up-close views of the iconic bluestones and trilithons. Each visit only takes 26 people; to secure a place book at least two months in advance.

Salisbury Guided Tours HISTORY
(☎07775 674816; www.salisburyguidedtours.com; per person from £80) Runs a wide range of expert-led trips to Stonehenge, the wider ritual landscape and Salisbury.

ℹ Getting There & Away

No regular buses go to the site.

The **Stonehenge Tour** (p270) leaves Salisbury's railway station half-hourly from June to August, and hourly between September and May. The ticket includes admission to Stonehenge and the Iron Age hill fort at **Old Sarum** (p269); it stops there on the return leg.

Stourhead

★ **Stourhead** HISTORIC BUILDING
(NT; ☎01747-841152; www.nationaltrust.org.uk; Mere; adult/child £14.10/7.10; ⏲11am-4.30pm mid-Feb–late Oct, to 3.30pm late Oct–late Dec; P) Overflowing with vistas, temples and follies, Stourhead is landscape gardening at its finest. The Palladian house has some fine Chippendale furniture and paintings by Claude and Gaspard Poussin, but it's a sideshow to the magnificent 18th-century gardens (open 9am to 5pm, November to March, to 6pm April to October), which spread out across the valley. Stourhead is off the B3092, 8 miles south of Frome.

A picturesque 2-mile garden circuit takes you past the most ornate follies, around the lake and to the Temple of Apollo; a 3.5-mile side trip can be made from near the Pantheon to **King Alfred's Tower** (NT; ☎01747-841152; www.nationaltrust.org.uk; near Mere; adult/child £4/2; ⏲noon-4pm Sat & Sun Mar-Oct), a 50m-high folly with wonderful views.

Longleat

★Longleat ZOO

(☎01985-844400; www.longleat.co.uk; all-inclusive ticket adult/child £34/24, house & grounds £18.50/13.50; ⏲10am-5pm Feb–mid-Oct, to 7pm late Jul & Aug; P) Half ancestral mansion, half wildlife park, Longleat was transformed into Britain's first safari park in 1966, turning Capability Brown's landscaped grounds into an amazing drive-through zoo populated by a menagerie of animals more at home in the African wilderness than the fields of Wiltshire. Longleat also has a throng of attractions, including a historic house, narrow-gauge railway, Doctor Who exhibit, Postman Pat village, pets' corner and butterfly garden.

Longleat was the first English stately home to open its doors to the public. That decision was prompted by finance: heavy taxes and mounting post-WWII bills meant the house had to earn its keep.

The house itself contains fine tapestries, furniture and decorated ceilings, as well as seven libraries containing around 40,000 tomes. The highlight, though, is an extraordinary series of paintings and psychedelic murals by the present-day marquess, who was an art student in the '60s and upholds the long-standing tradition of eccentricity among the English aristocracy – check out his website (www.lordbath.co.uk).

Longleat is just off the A362, 3 miles from Frome. It's open until 6pm on many summer weekends.

Lacock

POP 1159

With its geranium-covered cottages and higgledy-piggledy rooftops, pockets of the medieval village of Lacock seem to have been preserved in mid-19th-century aspic. The village has been in the hands of the National Trust since 1944, and in many places is remarkably free of modern development – there are no telephone poles or electric street lights and the main car park on the outskirts keeps it largely traffic-free. Unsurprisingly, it's a popular location for costume dramas and feature films – the village and its abbey pop up in the Harry Potter films, *Downton Abbey, The Other Boleyn Girl* and BBC adaptations of *Wolf Hall, Moll Flanders* and *Pride and Prejudice*.

Sights

Lacock Abbey ABBEY

(NT; ☎01249-730459; www.nationaltrust.org.uk; Hither Way; adult/child £12/6; ⏲10.30am-5.30pm Mar-Oct, 11am-4pm Nov-Feb) Lacock Abbey is a window into a medieval world. Founded as an Augustinian nunnery in the 13th century, its deeply atmospheric rooms and stunning Gothic entrance hall are lined with bizarre terracotta figures; spot the scapegoat with a lump of sugar on its nose. Some of the original structure is evident in the cloisters and there are traces of medieval wall paintings too.

Fox Talbot Museum MUSEUM

(NT; ☎01249-730459; www.nationaltrust.org.uk; Hither Way; incl Lacock Abbey adult/child £12/6; ⏲10.30am-5.30pm Mar-Oct, 11am-4pm Nov-Feb) William Henry Fox Talbot (1800–77) pioneered the photographic negative. A prolific inventor, he began developing the system in 1834 while working at Lacock Abbey. The museum details his groundbreaking work and displays a superb collection of his images.

Sleeping & Eating

★Sign of the Angel INN ££

(☎01249-730230; www.signoftheangel.co.uk; 6 Church St; r £120-140; P 📶) Every inch of this gorgeous, 15th-century restaurant-with-rooms is rich in heritage pizzazz. Burnished beams, slanting floors and open fires meet duck-down duvets, upcycled furniture and neutral tones, delivering a fresh provincial rustic feel. Treats include luxury toiletries, chef-baked cookies and a free glass of prosecco (if you book one of the swisher rooms).

Red Lion INN ££

(☎01249-730456; www.redlionlacock.co.uk; 1 High St; d £120; P 📶) In atmospheric Lacock, where better to sleep than a Georgian coaching inn that oozes ambience. Step on flagstone floors past open fires, up a grand staircase to sweet rooms where padded cushions line mullioned windows with picture-postcard views of ancient streets. The food's notable too (mains £13, served noon to 8pm).

King John's Hunting Lodge CAFE £

(☎01249-730313; www.kingjohnslodge.2day.ws; 21 Church St; snacks from £5; ⏲10.30am-4pm Wed-Sun Feb–mid-Dec; P) Afternoon tea is a must at Lacock's oldest building, where a cosy, beam-lined room and a peaceful garden set the scene for dainty china, light lunches and tasty cakes.

George Inn PUB FOOD ££
(www.georgeinnlacock.co.uk; 4 West St; mains £10-16; ⏲food noon-2.30pm & 6-9pm Mon-Sat, 6-8pm Sun) Sample well-executed, classic pub grub and some of the six local ales at this 14th-century, horse brass–hung pub.

Avebury & Around

POP 530

While the tour buses head straight for Stonehenge, prehistoric purists make for the massive stone circle at Avebury. Though it lacks the dramatic trilithons of its sister site across Salisbury Plain, Avebury is just as rewarding to visit. It's bigger and older, and a large section of the village is actually inside the stones – footpaths wind around them, allowing you to really soak up the extraordinary atmosphere. Avebury also boasts an encircling landscape that's rich in prehistoric sites and a manor house where restored rooms span five completely different eras.

Sights

★Avebury Stone Circle ARCHAEOLOGICAL SITE
(NT; ☎01672-539250; www.nationaltrust.org.uk; ⏲24hr; P) FREE With a diameter of 348m, Avebury is the largest stone circle in the world. It's also one of the oldest, dating from 2500 to 2200 BC. Today, more than 30 stones are in place; pillars show where missing stones would have been. Wandering between them emphasises the site's sheer scale, evidenced also by the massive bank and ditch that line the circle; the quieter northwest sector is particularly atmospheric. National Trust–run guided walks (£3) are held on most days.

Avebury henge originally consisted of an outer circle of 98 standing stones of up to 6m in length, many weighing 20 tonnes. The stones were surrounded by another circle delineated by a 5m-high earth bank and a ditch up to 9m deep. Inside were smaller stone circles to the north (27 stones) and south (29 stones).

In the Middle Ages, when Britain's pagan past was an embarrassment to the Church, many of the stones were buried, removed or broken up. In 1934 wealthy businessman and archaeologist Alexander Keiller supervised the re-erection of the stones; he later bought the site for posterity using funds from his family's marmalade fortune.

Modern roads into Avebury neatly dissect the circle into four sectors. Starting at High St, near the Henge Shop (p276), and walking round the circle in an anticlockwise direction, you'll encounter 11 standing stones in the southwest sector. They include the **Barber Surgeon Stone**, named after the skeleton of a man found under it – the equipment buried with him suggests he was a barber-cum-surgeon.

The southeast sector starts with huge **portal stones** marking the entry to the circle from **West Kennet Ave**. The **southern inner circle** stood in this sector and within this ring was the obelisk and a group of stones known as the Z Feature. Just outside this smaller circle, only the base of the Ring Stone survives.

In the **northern inner circle** in the northeast sector, three sarsens remain of what would have been a rectangular **cove**. The northwest sector has the most complete collection of standing stones, including the massive 65-tonne **Swindon Stone**, one of the few never to have been toppled.

★Avebury Manor HISTORIC BUILDING
(NT; ☎01672-539250; www.nationaltrust.org.uk; adult/child £6.75/3.35; ⏲11am-5pm Apr-Oct, to 4pm mid-Feb–Mar, 11am-4pm Thu-Sun Nov & Dec) The mother of all makeovers at this 16th-century manor house used original techniques and materials to recreate interiors spanning five periods. Being hands-on is encouraged here, so now you can sit on beds, play billiards and listen to the gramophone in rooms that range from Tudor, through Georgian to the 1930s. Visits are by timed ticket only; arrive early to bag a slot.

Silbury Hill ARCHAEOLOGICAL SITE
(EH; www.english-heritage.org.uk; P) FREE Rising abruptly from the fields just south of Avebury, 40m-high Silbury Hill is the largest artificial earthwork in Europe, comparable in height and volume to the Egyptian pyramids. It was built in stages from around 2500 BC, but the precise reason for its construction remains unclear. Direct access to the hill isn't allowed, but you can view it from a lay-by on the A4.

West Kennet Long Barrow ARCHAEOLOGICAL SITE
(EH; ☎0370 333 1181; www.english-heritage.org.uk; ⏲dawn-dusk) FREE England's finest burial mound dates from around 3500 BC. Its entrance is guarded by huge sarsens and its roof is made out of gigantic overlapping capstones. About 50 skeletons were found when it was excavated; finds are on display at the Wiltshire Heritage Museum in Deviz-

Avebury

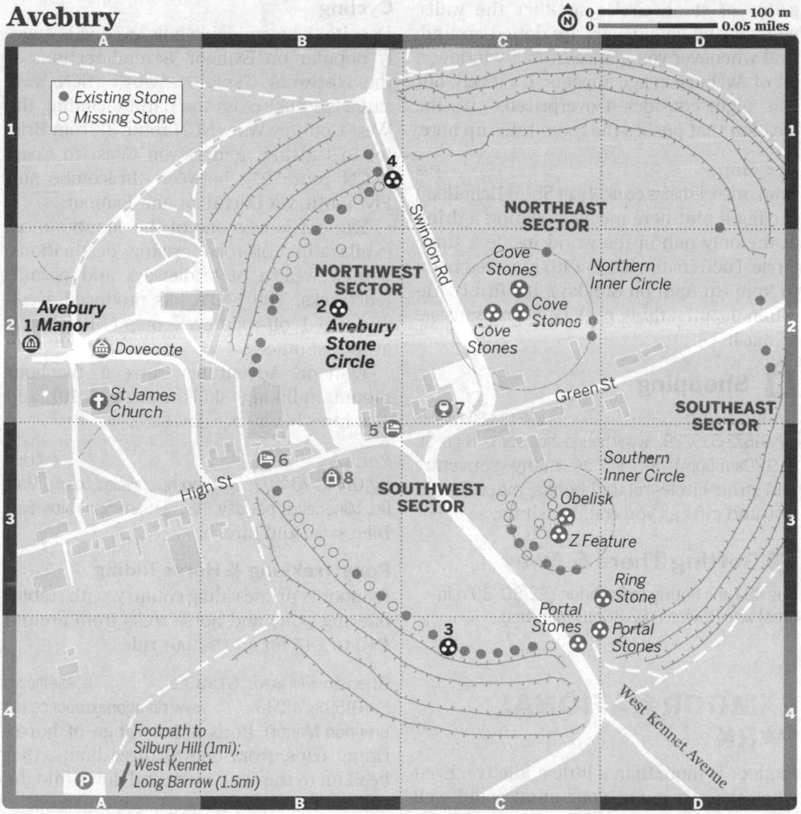

es. The barrow is a half-mile walk across fields from the parking lay-by.

A footpath also leads from Avebury Stone Circle to West Kennet (2 miles), passing the vast earthwork of Silbury Hill en route.

Sleeping & Eating

★Manor Farm B&B **££**
(☎01672-539294; www.manorfarmavebury.com; High St; s £70-80, d £90-100; P 📶) A rare chance to sleep in style inside a stone circle – this red-brick farmhouse snuggles just inside Avebury henge. The elegant, comfy rooms blend old woods with bright furnishings, while the windows provide spine-tingling views of those 4000-year-old standing stones.

Avebury Lodge B&B **£££**
(☎01672-539023; www.aveburylodge.co.uk; High St; s/d £140/175; P 📶) It's as if gentlemanly archaeologists are still in situ: antiquarian

Avebury

Top Sights
1 Avebury Manor A2
2 Avebury Stone Circle B2

Sights
3 Barber Surgeon Stone C4
4 Swindon Stone B1

Sleeping
5 Avebury Lodge B3
6 Manor Farm B3

Drinking & Nightlife
7 Red Lion C2

Shopping
8 Henge Shop B3

prints of stone circles smother the walls, pelmets and chandeliers are dotted around. And whenever you glance from a window, a bit of Avebury henge appears. It's lovely, but you might consider it overpriced – it's the location that pushes the room rates up here.

Red Lion PUB
(www.oldenglishinns.co.uk; High St; ⏲11am-11pm) Having a pint here means downing a drink at the only pub in the world inside a stone circle. Food (mains £8 to £16) is served noon to 9pm (to 8pm on Sunday). It's firmly traditional stuff – think pork belly and sausage 'n' mash.

Shopping

Henge Shop GIFTS & SOUVENIRS
(☎01672-539229; www.hengeshop.com; High St; ⏲9.30am-5pm) Stocks as many souvenirs and stone circle–related books, maps, jewellery and gifts as you could wish for.

Getting There & Away

Bus 49 runs hourly to Swindon (£2.80, 30 minutes) and Devizes (£2.80, 10 minutes).

EXMOOR NATIONAL PARK

Exmoor is more than a little addictive. Even when you get home, your mind could well return to its broad, russet views. In the middle sits the higher moor, an empty, expansive, other-worldly landscape of tawny grasses and huge skies. Here picturesque Exford makes an ideal village base. In the north, sheer, rock-strewn river valleys cut into the plateau and coal-black cliffs lurch towards the sea. Amid these towering headlands, charismatic Porlock and the twin villages of Lynton and Lynmouth are atmospheric places to stay. Relaxed Dulverton delivers a country-town vibe, while appealing Dunster boasts cobbled streets and a russet-red castle. And everywhere on Exmoor, life is attuned to the rhythm of the seasons; it's a glimpse into another world. Visit – but you're likely to be planning to return before you leave.

Activities

Exmoor Adventures OUTDOORS
(☎07976-208279; www.exmooradventures.co.uk) Runs kayaking, canoeing, mountain-biking, coasteering and rock-climbing sessions.

Cycling

Despite the formidable hills, cycling is hugely popular on Exmoor. Several sections of the **National Cycle Network** (NCN; www.sustrans.org.uk) cross the park, including the West Country Way (NCN route 3) from Bristol to Padstow, and Devon Coast to Coast (NCN route 27), between Ilfracombe and Plymouth, via Dartmoor and Exmoor.

Exmoor is also one of the county's most exhilarating off-road cycling destinations, with a wealth of bridleways and permitted tracks. The ENPA has produced a colour-coded, off-road cycle map (£10); buy it at tourist offices.

Exmoor Adventures runs a five-hour mountain-biking skills course (£50) and also hires bikes (per day £25).

Pompys CYCLING
(☎01643-704077; www.pompyscycles.co.uk; Mart Rd, Minehead; per day £18; ⏲9am-5pm Mon-Sat) Bike sales and hire.

Pony Trekking & Horse Riding

Exmoor is prime riding country, with stables offering pony and horse treks from around £40 to £45 for a two-hour ride.

Brendan Manor Stables HORSE RIDING
(☎01598-741246; www.ridingonexmoor.co.uk; Brendon Manor) Runs a full range of horse-riding trips, from one to three hours, that head on to the open moor and down into the valleys. Prices start at £30. Lynton-based.

Burrowhayes Farm HORSE RIDING
(☎01643-862463; www.burrowhayes.co.uk; West Luccombe; per 1/2 hr £22/42) Based near Porlock, Burrowhayes runs a wide range of treks that go into the Horner Valley and on to the moor. Plus special half-hour pony rides for children (£12).

Outovercott Stables HORSE RIDING
(☎01598-753341; www.outovercott.co.uk; near Lynton; per hr £30) Outovercott's treks on to Exmoor's exposed moorland range from one-hour trips for novices to excursions for more experienced riders, which take in views of the Valley of Rocks and the coastline.

Walking

The open moors and a profusion of marked bridleways make Exmoor an excellent area for hiking. The best-known routes are the **Somerset & North Devon Coast Path**, which is part of the **South West Coast Path** (www.southwestcoastpath.org.uk), and the Exmoor section of the **Two Moors Way**,

Exmoor National Park

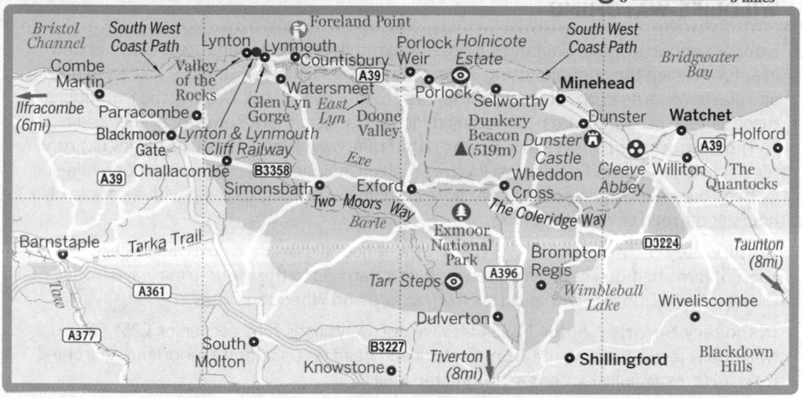

which starts in Lynmouth and travels south to Dartmoor and beyond.

Another superb route is the **Coleridge Way** (www.coleridgeway.co.uk), which winds for 51 miles through Exmoor, the Brendon Hills and the Quantocks. Part of the 180-mile **Tarka Trail** cuts through the park; join it at Combe Martin, hike along the cliffs to Lynton/Lynmouth, then head across the moor towards Barnstaple.

Organised walks run by the ENPA are held throughout the year and include deer safaris, nightjar walks and dark-sky strolls.

Information

Active Exmoor www.activeexmoor.com
Snowdrop Valley www.wheddoncross.org.uk/snowdropvalley.htm
Visit Exmoor www.visit-exmoor.co.uk
What's On Exmoor www.whatsonexmoor.com

There are three Exmoor National Park Authority tourist offices, in **Dulverton** (☎ 01398-323841; www.exmoor-nationalpark.gov.uk; 7-9 Fore St; ⏰10am-5pm Apr-Oct, limited winter hours), **Dunster** (☎ 01643-821835; www.exmoor-nationalpark.gov.uk; The Steep; ⏰10am-5pm Apr-Oct, limited winter hours) and Lynmouth (p282).

Getting Around

The **MoorRover** (☎ 01643-709701) is an on-demand minibus that can take you anywhere on Exmoor. Prices range from £10 to £30, depending on distances involved. It'll also carry bikes and provide a luggage transfer service. Book at least a day ahead.

Exmoor's bus routes are listed at the **ExploreMoor** (www.exploremoor.co.uk) website. Be aware: some services are seasonal, and the more remote ones are particularly prone to change. Services include the following:

28 (at least hourly) Shuttles from Taunton to the resort of Minehead (1¼ hours).
300 (two services a day from Monday to Saturday in July and August only) Heads along the coast from Minehead to Lynmouth, via Porlock.
309/310 (13 services daily, Monday to Saturday) Runs from Barnstaple via Parracombe to Lynton or Lynmouth, year-round.
467 (one daily, Monday to Friday) Runs from Minehead to Dulverton (one hour), via Dunster and Wheddon Cross.

Dulverton

POP 1500

The southern gateway to Exmoor National Park, Dulverton sits at the base of the Barle Valley near the confluence of two key rivers: the Exe and Barle. A traditional country town, it's home to a collection of gun sellers, fishing-tackle stores and gift shops, and makes an attractive edge-of-moor base.

Sights

★Tarr Steps LANDMARK

(⏰24hr) FREE Exmoor's most famous landmark is an ancient stone clapper bridge shaded by gnarled old trees. Its huge slabs are propped up on stone columns embedded in the River Barle. Local folklore aside (which declares it was used by the devil for sunbathing), it first pops into the historical record in the 1600s, and has had to be rebuilt after 21st-century floods. The steps are signed off the B3223 Dulverton-to-Simonsbath road, 5 miles northwest of Dulverton.

LOCAL KNOWLEDGE

WILDLIFE-WATCHING

Exmoor supports one of England's largest wild red deer populations, best experienced in autumn when the annual 'rutting' season sees stags bellowing, charging at each other and clashing horns in an attempt to impress prospective mates. Despite their numbers, these skittish creatures are notoriously difficult to spot without some local knowledge.

The **Exmoor National Park Authority** (ENPA; www.exmoor-nationalpark.gov.uk) runs regular wildlife-themed guided walks (free), which include evening deer-spotting hikes. Or head out on an organised jeep safari to combine scenic sightseeing with a couple of hours of off-road wildlife-watching.

Barle Valley Safaris (01643-841326; www.exmoorwildlifesafaris.co.uk; adult/child £35/25) Runs half-day 4WD wildlife-watching safaris on to the moor. Trips leave from Dulverton and Dunster, with pickups from Exford and Wheddon Cross.

Discovery Safaris (01643-863444; www.discoverysafaris.com; per person £25) These twice-daily jeep safaris set off from Porlock and head up on to open moorland searching for wildlife, especially Exmoor's famous red deer.

Exmoor Safari (01643-831229; www.exmoorsafari.co.uk; Exford; adult/child £35/16) Long-running wildlife-watching operator that uses 4WD vehicles and local knowledge to search out red deer. Also does special photography-themed trips.

Sleeping

★Streamcombe Farm B&B ££
(01398-323775; www.streamcombefarm.co.uk; Streamcombe Lane, near Dulverton; s £65-75, d £80-100; P) In this enchanting, 18th-century farmhouse, stylish, rustic-chic bedrooms feature chimney breasts and reclaimed joists, and the only sounds are the sheep, deer and pheasants outside. There's woodland camping (per person £9) and a two-person shepherd's hut (£85) too.

Town Mills B&B ££
(01398-323124; www.townmillsdulverton.co.uk; High St; s/d £85/95; P) The top choice if you want to stay in Dulverton itself is a thoroughly contemporary riverside mill with creamy carpets, magnolia walls and bursts of floral art.

Tarr Farm HOTEL £££
(01643-851507; www.tarrfarm.co.uk; Tarr Steps; s/d £90/150; P) This is the place to really lose yourself: a charming farmhouse nested among the woods near Tarr Steps, 7 miles from Dulverton. The nine rooms are spacious and luxurious, with spoil-yourself extras such as organic bath goodies and homemade biscuits.

Eating

Exclusive Cake Co BAKERY £
(www.exclusivecakecompany.co.uk; 19 High St; snacks from £3; 9am-4pm Mon-Fri, to 2pm Sat) Real rarities stack the shelves here: Exmoor ale, cheese and wholegrain-mustard bread; Somerset cider cake; venison and port pie. Note the typically Exmoor warning: 'Game pies may contain lead shot.'

★Woods BISTRO ££
(01398-324007; www.woodsdulverton.co.uk; 4 Bank Sq; mains £15-20; noon-2pm & 7-9.30pm) With its deer antlers, hunting prints and big wood-burning stove, Woods is Exmoor to its core. No surprise then to find menus full of full-bodied flavours: expect venison confit, belly pork with black pudding, and wild mushrooms with truffle and white wine.

The bar menu (£10 to £12, served between 6pm and 9.30pm) is simpler stuff – think steak, omelette Arnold Bennett and lamb rogan josh.

Tarr Farm Inn RESTAURANT ££
(01643-851507; www.tarrfarm.co.uk; Tarr Steps; snacks from £5, dinner mains £13-27; 11am-2.30pm & 6.30-9.30pm) All comers are welcome here: walkers and families come for cream teas (served from 11am to 5pm) and hearty lunches, while after-dark diners sample more formal country fare. It's all deservedly a hit with the waxed-jacket-wearing regulars.

The inn is set beside the Tarr Steps stone bridge; it's signed off the B3223 Dulverton–Simonsbath road, 5 miles northwest of Dulverton.

Exford

Tucked into the banks of the River Exe at the heart of Exmoor, Exford is a delightful medley of cottages and slate-roofed houses clustered around a village green.

Sleeping

Exford YHA HOSTEL £
(☎01643-831229; www.yha.org.uk; Exe Mead, Exford; dm/d £20/50; P) An imaginative revamp has given the lounge and kitchen of this hikers' favourite a glamorous edge. A cracking cooked breakfast (£8) is served in the White Horse inn, opposite, while the hostel's woodland setting, beside the babbling River Exe (campsites per adult £10), is divine.

Exmoor White Horse INN £££
(☎01643-831229; www.exmoor-whitehorse.co.uk; Exford; d £180-205; P ᯤ) Step through the door here to find everything you want from an Exmoor coaching inn: a friendly bar with a real fire, a local-produce packed restaurant (mains £14 to £22) and smoothly comfy rooms. On summer afternoons, the riverside beer terrace is a firm favourite with the locals – an idyllic spot to watch the horse riders trot by.

Dunster

POP 850

Centred on a scarlet-walled castle and a medieval yarn market, Dunster is one of Exmoor's oldest villages, a tempting tangle of cobbled streets, bubbling brooks and packhorse bridges.

Sights

★**Dunster Castle** CASTLE
(NT; ☎01643-821314; www.nationaltrust.org.uk; Castle Hill; adult/child £10.30/5.15; ⏲11am-5pm Mar-Oct; P) Rosy-hued Dunster Castle crowns a densely wooded hill. Built by the Luttrell family, who once owned much of northern Exmoor, the oldest sections are 13th century, although the turrets and exterior walls are 19th-century additions. Look out for Tudor furnishings, 17th-century plasterwork and a ridiculously grand staircase. Leave time to explore the colourful terraced gardens, with their riverside walks and views across Exmoor's shores.

Watermill HISTORIC BUILDING
(NT; ☎01643-821759; www.nationaltrust.org.uk; Mill Lane; ⏲10am-5pm Mar-Oct) Most of the original cogs, wheels and grinding stones still rotate away in this working 18th-century mill; there's a picturesque riverside tearoom alongside.

Admission to the mill is included in tickets to Dunster Castle.

Sleeping & Eating

Spears Cross B&B ££
(☎01643-821439; www.spearscross.co.uk; 1 West St; d £97-107; P ᯤ) 'We simply like to make breakfasts more fun', says the owner of this 15th-century B&B. That explains tummy-tempting options such as scrambled egg with watercress, tomatoes and Cheddar, and muffins topped with asparagus and poached egg. The just-as-delicious decor sees age-old beams frame wood panels, floral furnishings and raspberry-red walls.

Mill Stream Cottage B&B ££
(☎01643-821966; www.millstreamcottagedunster.co.uk; 2 Mill Lane; s £60, d £74-84) In the 1600s this was Dunster's workhouse; now it's a sweet-as-pie guesthouse with country cottage–style rooms. There are homemade cakes on arrival and home-baked biscuits on the tea tray, plus an oh-so-comfy guest lounge where you can snooze in front of the wood burner.

Luttrell Arms INN £££
(☎01643-821555; www.luttrellarms.co.uk; High St; r £140-195; P ᯤ) You almost need a ladder to climb up to the high four-poster bed in the feature room at this exquisite old coaching inn. In medieval times, this was the guesthouse of the Abbots of Cleeve. Even the more standard rooms are gorgeous; expect a plethora of brass plates, beams and a plaster fireplace or two.

Reeve's BRITISH ££
(☎01643-821414; www.reevesrestaurantdunster.co.uk; 20 High St; mains £18; ⏲7-9pm Tue-Sat, noon-2pm Sun) The eponymous chef at seriously stylish Reeve's is an award winner. No wonder: the complex creations here truly showcase Exmoor produce. Perhaps opt for slow-roast pig's cheek with veal and cider jus, or tender lamb roasted with rosemary and garlic.

Getting There & Away

Bus 467 (one daily, Monday to Friday) runs north to Minehead and south to Dulverton (one hour), via Wheddon Cross.

The 22-mile **West Somerset Railway** (☎01643-704996; www.west-somerset-railway.

co.uk; 24hr rover tickets adult/child £19/9.50) stops at Dunster during the summer, with four to seven trains daily from May to October.

Porlock & Around

The coastal village of Porlock is one of the prettiest on the Exmoor coast; the huddle of thatched cottages lining its main street is framed on one side by the sea, and on the other by houses clinging to the steeply sloping hills behind. Winding lanes lead to the charismatic breakwater of Porlock Weir, 2 miles to the west, with its arching pebble beach and striking coastal views.

Sights

Porlock Weir HARBOUR
(24hr; P) FREE Porlock Weir's stout granite quay curves around a shingly beach, which is backed by pubs, fishers' storehouses and a scattering of seasonal shops. The weir has been around for almost a thousand years (it's named in the Domesday Book as 'Portloc') and makes a glorious place for a pub lunch and a stroll, with stirring views across the Vale of Porlock and easy access to the coast path.

Holnicote Estate HISTORIC BUILDINGS
(NT; 01643-862452; www.nationaltrust.org.uk; near Porlock; 24hr; P) FREE The 50-sq-km Holnicote Estate sweeps southeast out of Porlock, taking in a string of impossibly pretty villages. Picturesque **Bossington** leads to charming **Allerford**, with its 15th-century packhorse bridge. The biggest, **Selworthy**, offers eye-catching Exmoor views, a cafe, a shop, and cob-and-thatch cottages clustering around the village green.

Sleeping & Eating

★**Millers at the Anchor** BOUTIQUE HOTEL ££
(01643-862753; www.millersuk.com/anchor; Porlock Weir; s £85-105, d £85-155; P) Stuffed with antiques, overflowing with piled-up books, and scattered with exotic rugs, Millers delivers an enjoyably overwhelming dose of English eccentricity. Gilt-framed mirrors jostle with marble busts, vast beds and captivating views of Porlock Weir. But the chess set in the lounge and the quirky home cinema may tempt you from your room.

Sea View B&B ££
(01643-863456; www.seaviewporlock.co.uk; High Bank, Porlock; d £65-70;) If somewhere is this cheap it really shouldn't be this nice. But Sea View actually is. Tiny rooms are pleasantly packed with painted furniture, trinkets and oil paintings plus thoughtful extras – blister plasters and muscle soak for hikers tackling Porlock's precipitous hills.

Ship Inn PUB FOOD ££
(Top Ship; 01643-862507; www.shipinnporlock.co.uk; High St, Porlock; mains £8-16; noon-2.30pm & 6-8.30pm; P) Poet Coleridge and pal Robert Southey both downed pints in this 13th-century thatched Porlock inn – you can even sit in a snug still dubbed 'Southey's Corner'. Substantial pub food – mainly steaks, roasts and stews – is served in the bar.

Culbone BRITISH ££
(01643-862259; www.theculbone.com; near Porlock; mains £9-25; noon-2.30pm & 6-9pm Mon-Sat, noon-3pm Sun; P) This smart restaurant-with-rooms is a carnivore's delight. Plump for the 28-day aged Devon Red steaks and choose from three different cuts, and sauces including horseradish and rosemary, garlic and shallot, or creamy Devon Blue cheese.

Cafe Porlock Weir BRITISH ££
(01643-863300; www.thecafeporlockweir.co.uk; Porlock Weir; mains £10-20; noon-8pm Wed-Sun) The food here regularly notches up awards; shore views and an assured, country-house ambience add to the appeal. Ingredients from moor and shore pack the menu, making a window table an atmospheric spot to tuck into crab risotto, nutty butter-doused skate or chargrilled rib-eye steak.

Information

Porlock Tourist Office (01643-863150; www.porlock.co.uk; West End, Porlock; 10am-5pm Mon-Sat Easter-Oct, to 12.30pm Tue-Sat Nov-Easter)

Getting There & Away

Bus 300 (two services a day from Monday to Saturday in July and August only) heads from Porlock east along the coast to Minehead, and west to Lynmouth.

Drivers can choose from two picturesque routes into Porlock village. The New Road Toll Road sweeps through pine forests and round U-bends, while Porlock Hill (A39) is a brake-burning 1:4 descent. Another toll road, the Porlock Scenic (Worthy) Toll Road, provides an alternative, bouncing, route up out of Porlock Weir.

Lynton & Lynmouth

Tucked in amid precipitous cliffs and steep, tree-lined slopes, these twin coastal towns are a landscape painter's dream. Bustling Lynmouth sits beside the shore, a busy harbour lined with pubs and souvenir shops. On the clifftop, Lynton feels much more genteel and well-to-do. A cliffside railway links the two: it's powered by the rushing West Lyn river, which feeds numerous cascades and waterfalls nearby.

Sights

★ Cliff Railway HERITAGE RAILWAY

(☎01598-753486; www.cliffrailwaylynton.co.uk; adult single/return £2.70/3.70, child £1.60/2.20; ⏰10am-5pm Feb-May, Sep & Oct, to 7pm Jun-Aug) This extraordinary piece of Victorian engineering sees two cars, linked by a steel cable, descend and ascend the sloping cliff face according to the weight of water in the cars' tanks. All burnished wood and polished brass, it's been running since 1890 and makes for an unmissable ride.

Flood Memorial Hall INTERPRETATION CENTRE

(The Esplanade, Lynmouth; ⏰9am-5pm Easter-Oct) FREE On 16 August 1952 a huge wave of water swept through Lynmouth after torrential rain. The devastation was immense: 34 people lost their lives; four bridges and countless houses were washed away. This exhibition features photos of the destroyed buildings and the personal testimonies of those involved.

Activities

Popular hiking trails among Lynton and Lynmouth's spectacular scenery include ones to the lighthouse at **Foreland Point**; to **Watersmeet**, 2 miles east of Lynmouth (reached via the gorgeous East Lyn river glade); and along the scenic **Glen Lyn Gorge**.

Valley of the Rocks WALKING

The dramatic geology in this valley was described by poet Robert Southey as 'rock reeling upon rock, stone piled upon stone, a huge terrifying reeling mass'. Look out for the formations dubbed the Devil's Cheesewring and Ragged Jack – and also the feral goats that wander the tracks. Its a mile's walk west of Lynton along a cracking coast path.

Sleeping

★ Rock House B&B ££

(☎01598-753508; www.rock-house.co.uk; Manor Green, Lynmouth; s £45-88, d £110-125) The setting is simply superb: right on Lynmouth's pocket-sized harbour, steep hills sloping up on three sides. Contemporary rooms sport leather headboards, lilac scatter cushions and mini-armchairs. All have extraordinary views; the best is number 4, where the window is right next to the beach.

Bath Hotel HOTEL ££

(☎01598-752238; www.bathhotellynmouth.co.uk; The Esplanade, Lynmouth; d £78-130; P 📶) A pair of third-generation hoteliers are breathing fresh life into the Bath Hotel, a feature of the town since Victorian days. To a stylish new cocktail bar add rooms teaming lime fabrics with dark leather and cracking harbour and headland views.

North Walk House B&B ££

(☎01598-753372; www.northwalkhouse.co.uk; North Walk, Lynton; d £66-71; P 📶) Stripped wooden floors, stripy bedspreads and colourful rugs give North Walk House a gently funky feel. The views over the sea and rugged cliffs are fantastic, while the all-organic breakfasts feature Exmoor bacon and sausages, and Aga-baked eggs.

Rising Sun INN £££

(☎01598-753223; www.risingsunlynmouth.co.uk; Harbourside, Lynmouth; d £160-190) At the Rising Sun a 14th-century smugglers' haunt has been transformed into a romantic hideaway with a sleek designer feel. Elegant flourishes are everywhere, from the anglepoise lamps and local art to the soft, tasteful throws. Ask for a sea-view room to watch the tide rise and fall in the harbour just outside.

STARGAZING ON EXMOOR

Exmoor holds the distinction of being named Europe's first International Dark Sky Reserve. The ENPA runs free night-time stargazing strolls; eerie hilltop hikes where the inky blackness is punctuated by mesmerising constellations. The authority's (free) *Dark Sky Discovery* leaflets feature star charts and maps. For optimum views, central, higher Exmoor is best; try the hills around Dunkery Beacon.

Eating

Charlie Friday's CAFE £
(www.charliefridays.co.uk; Church Hill, Lynton; snacks from £4; ⏲10am-5pm Tue-Sun Feb-Nov) A funky, friendly hang-out serving melting pastries, thick sarnies and fair-trade, two-shot espresso that really packs a punch.

Bath Bar PUB FOOD ££
(☎01598-752238; www.bathhotellynmouth.co.uk; The Esplanade, Lynmouth; mains £14; ⏲noon-9pm, winter hours vary) The Bath brings a burst of shipwreck chic to Lynmouth, thanks to a copper bar top, curved ship's decking and a figurehead who isn't entirely clothed. Best surveyed while tucking into a stacked-high Bath Burger, complete with Exmoor ale and black treacle–braised brisket, onion jam and blue-cheese mousse.

Rising Sun MODERN BRITISH ££
(☎01598-753223; www.risingsunlynmouth.co.uk; Harbourside, Lynmouth; mains £14-26; ⏲noon-2.30pm & 6-9pm) At the harbourside Rising Sun, head chef Matthew Terrett delights in showcasing not only Exmoor meat and vegetables, but also the fresh seafood landed along this rugged shore. Seasonal treats might include succulent lobster, fresh sea bass and local mussels, all served up with confidence and more than a dash of élan.

Information

Lynmouth Tourist Office (☎01598-752509; www.exmoor-nationalpark.gov.uk; The Esplanade, Lynmouth; ⏲10am-5pm) An Exmoor National Park Authority Tourist Office.

Lynton Tourist Office (☎01598-752225; www.lynton-lynmouth-tourism.co.uk; Lynton Town Hall, Lee Rd; ⏲10am-5pm Mon-Sat, to 2pm Sun)

DEVON

Devon offers freedom. Its rippling, beach-fringed landscape is studded with historic homes, vibrant cities and wild, wild moors. So here you can ditch schedules and to-do lists and hike a rugged coast path, take a scenic boat trip, or get lost in hedge-lined lanes that aren't even on your map.

Discover collegiate Exeter, touristy Torquay, yachting-haven Dartmouth and alternative Totnes. Or escape to wilderness Dartmoor and the remote, surf-dashed north coast. Sample wine made from the vines beside you and food that's fresh from field, furrow or sea. Go surfing, cycling, kayaking, horse riding, sea swimming and barefoot beachcombing.

Information

Visit Devon (www.visitdevon.co.uk) The first port of call for all things Devonian.

Getting Around

BUS

Most bus services between larger towns and villages are now run by Stagecoach, with a number of smaller coach companies offering infrequent services to other areas. Dartmoor is poorly served by buses, so you'll need a car or bike to explore here.

There are several bus passes available: the **Devon Day Ticket** (adult/child/family £8.50/5.70/17) covers all companies, while the **Stagecoach Explorer** (adult/child/family £7.70/5.10/15.40) and **Megarider Gold** (1/4 weeks £27/97) tickets only cover Stagecoach buses.

Traveline South West (www.travelinesw.com) is a great online tool for travel planning, while the Devon interactive bus map (https://new.devon.gov.uk/travel) provides a useful visual map of bus routes.

TRAIN

Devon's main line skirts southern Dartmoor, running from Exeter to Plymouth and on to Cornwall. Branch lines include the 39-mile Exeter–Barnstaple Tarka Line; the 15-mile Plymouth–Gunnislake Tamar Valley Line and the scenic Exeter–Torquay Paignton line. There are also several lovely steam railways.

The **Freedom of Devon & Cornwall Rover** (3 days adult/child £46.45/23.30, 8 days £71.20/35.60) ticket is good value if you're doing a lot of travel by train, offering three days travel out of seven days, or eight days of travel out of 15 days.

Exeter

POP 117,800

Well heeled and comfortable, Exeter exudes evidence of its centuries-old role as the spiritual and administrative heart of Devon. The city's Gothic cathedral presides over pockets of cobbled streets; medieval and Georgian buildings, and fragments of the Roman city stretch out all around. A snazzy new shopping centre brings bursts of the modern, thousands of university students ensure a buzzing nightlife, and the vibrant quayside acts as a launch pad for cycling or kayaking trips. Throw in some stylish places

Exeter

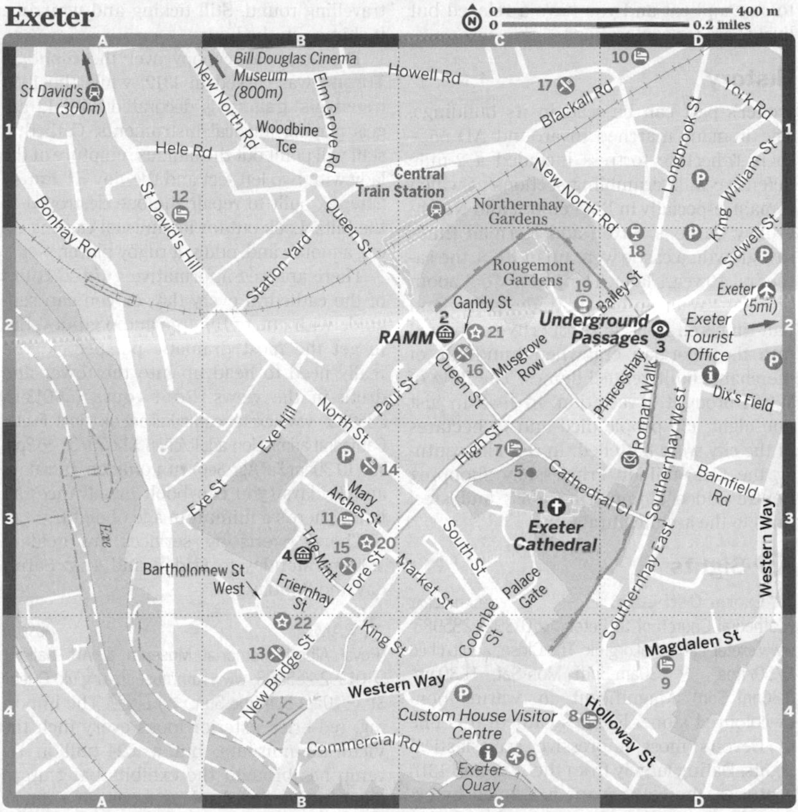

Exeter

Top Sights
1 Exeter Cathedral C3
2 RAMM C2
3 Underground Passages D2

Sights
4 St Nicholas Priory B3

Activities, Courses & Tours
Exeter Cathedral Guided Tours .... (see 1)
Exeter Cathedral Roof Tours .... (see 1)
5 Redcoat Tours C3
6 Saddles & Paddles C4

Sleeping
7 ABode Exeter C3
8 Globe Backpackers C4
9 Hotel du Vin Exeter D4
10 Raffles D1
11 St Olaves B3
12 Townhouse A1

Eating
13 @Angela's B4
14 Herbies B3
15 Jasmine Thai B3
16 Ruby C2
17 Rusty Bike C1

Drinking & Nightlife
18 Old Firehouse D2
19 Timepiece C2

Entertainment
20 Bike Shed B3
21 Exeter Phoenix C2
22 Exeter Picturehouse B4

to stay and eat and you have a relaxed but lively base for explorations.

History

Exeter's past can be read in its buildings. The Romans marched in around AD 55 – their 17-hectare fortress included a 2-mile defensive wall, crumbling sections of which remain, especially in Rougemont and Northernhay Gardens. Saxon and Norman times saw growth: a castle went up in 1068, the cathedral 40 years later. The Tudor wool boom brought Exeter an export trade, riches and half-timbered houses; prosperity continued into the Georgian era when hundreds of merchants built genteel homes. The Blitz of WWII brought devastation. In 1942 in just one night, 156 people died and 12 hectares of the city were flattened. In the 21st century, the £220-million Princesshay Shopping Centre added shimmering glass and steel lines to the architectural mix.

Sights

★Exeter Cathedral CATHEDRAL

(Cathedral Church of St Peter; ☎01392- 285983; www.exeter-cathedral.org.uk; The Close; adult/child £7.50/free; ⏲9.30am-5pm Mon-Sat, 11.30am-3.30pm Sun) Magnificent in warm, honey-coloured stone, Exeter's cathedral is one of Devon's most impressive ecclesiastical sights. Dating largely from the 12th and 13th centuries, the **west front** is framed by extraordinary medieval statuary, while inside the ceiling soars upwards to the longest span of unbroken Gothic vaulting in the world, dotted with ornate ceiling bosses in gilt and vibrant colours. Look out for the scale Lego model that's being built beside the main entrance; for £1 you can add a brick.

The site has been a religious one since at least the 5th century, but the Normans started the current building in 1114; the towers of today's cathedral date from that period. In 1270 a 90-year remodelling process began, introducing a mix of Early English and Decorated Gothic styles.

Above the **Great West Front** scores of weather-worn figures line a once brightly painted screen that now forms England's largest collection of 14th-century sculpture. Inside, the exquisitely symmetrical ceiling soars up and along, towards the north transept and the 15th-century **Exeter Clock**: in keeping with medieval astronomy it shows the earth as a golden ball at the centre of the universe with the sun, a fleur-de-lys, travelling round. Still ticking and whirring, it chimes on the hour.

The huge oak canopy over the **Bishop's Throne** was carved in 1312, while the 1350 **minstrels' gallery** is decorated with 12 angels playing musical instruments. Cathedral staff will point out the famous sculpture of the lady with two left feet and the tiny **St James Chapel**, built to repair the one destroyed in the Blitz. Look out for its unusual carvings: a cat, a mouse and, oddly, a rugby player.

There are free informative **guided tours** of the cathedral every day, or you can self-guide with one of the free audio guides. But to get the most dramatic perspective you really need to head up into the tower and drink in the views. **Roof tours** (☎01392-285983; www.exeter-cathedral.org.uk; incl Exeter Cathedral admission adult/child £12.50/5; ⏲2pm Tue, 10.30am Sat Apr-Sep) run only on Tuesdays and Fridays (you can book in advance online). There's a minimum age of eight.

Choral **evensong** services are held at 5.30pm Monday to Friday, and 4pm Saturday and Sunday.

★RAMM MUSEUM

(Royal Albert Memorial Museum & Art Gallery; ☎01392-265858; www.rammuseum.org.uk; Queen St; ⏲10am-5pm Tue-Sun; 📶) FREE The imposing, red-brick exterior looks every inch the Victorian museum, but a £24-million revamp has brought the exhibits bang up to date. Interactive displays focus on Exeter's heritage from prehistory to the present, as well as global exploration and the concept of collecting. Look out for Exeter's Roman-era artefacts, local Tudor carvings and the striking ethnographic displays, which include African masks, samurai armour and the mummy of Shep en-Mut.

★Underground Passages UNDERGROUND

(☎01392-665887; www.exeter.gov.uk/passages; Paris St; adult/child £6/4; ⏲9.30am-5.30pm Mon-Sat, 10am-4pm Sun Jun-Sep, 10.30am-4.30pm Tue-Fri, 9.30am-5.30pm Sat, 11am-4.30pm Sun Oct-May) Prepare to crouch down, don a hard hat and possibly get spooked in what is the only publicly accessible system of its kind in England. These medieval vaulted passages were built to house pipes bringing fresh water to the city. Guides lead you on a scramble through the network telling tales of ghosts, escape routes and cholera. The last tour is an hour before closing; they're popular – book ahead.

Bill Douglas Cinema Museum MUSEUM
(☎01392-724321; www.bdcmuseum.org.uk; Old Library, Prince of Wales Rd; ⏰10am-5pm; P) FREE This eccentric museum is a must for cinephiles, containing a vast hoard of film-themed memorabilia amassed by Scottish filmmaker Bill Douglas, best known for his semi-autobiographical trilogy about his childhood. Douglas was also an avid collector, amassing more than 50,000 cinematic collectibles, encompassing magic lanterns, peep shows, original cels from Disney films, Charlie Chaplin bottle stoppers, James Bond board games, vintage film posters, *Star Wars* toys and more. It's on the Exeter University campus, a mile northwest of the city centre.

St Nicholas Priory HISTORIC BUILDING
(☎01392-265858; www.exeter.gov.uk/priory; The Mint) Originally part of a medieval Benedictine monastery, and later a lavish Elizabethan manor house, this 900-year-old building is currently closed for renovations – check the website for updates.

Powderham Castle HISTORIC BUILDING
(☎01626-890243; www.powderham.co.uk; adult/child £11.50/9.50; ⏰11am-4.30pm Sun-Fri Apr-Jun, Sep & Oct, to 5.30pm Jul & Aug; P) The historic, and current, home of the Earl of Devon, Powderham is a stately but still friendly place that was built in 1391 and remodelled in the Victorian era. A visit takes in a fine wood-panelled Great Hall, parkland with 650 deer and glimpses of life 'below stairs' in the kitchen. Powderham is on the River Exe near Kenton, 8 miles south of Exeter.

Activities

Saddles & Paddles OUTDOORS
(☎01392-424241; www.sadpad.com; Exeter Quay; ⏰9am-6pm) Rents out bikes (adult per hour/day £6/15), kayaks (£10/35) and Canadian canoes (£15/50); the tourist office stocks maps.

Tours

★**Redcoat Tours** WALKING
(☎01392-265203; www.exeter.gov.uk/visiting; ⏰3-6pm daily Apr-Oct, 2 daily Nov-Mar) FREE For an informed and entertaining introduction to Exeter's history, tag along on one of these 1½-hour tours. Themes range from murder and trade to the Tudors and religion – there are even torchlight prowls through the catacombs and evening ghost walks. Tours leave from Cathedral Yard or the Quay; there's no need to book.

LOCAL KNOWLEDGE

CATHEDRAL ROOF TOURS

For a sensational view of Exeter Cathedral , book one of these high-rise guided roof tours. Climb 251 steps up spiral staircases, head out onto the sweeping roof, then gaze down on the city from the edge of the North Tower. They're popular so book two weeks ahead.

Sleeping

Globe Backpackers HOSTEL £
(☎01392-215521; www.exeterbackpackers.co.uk; 71 Holloway St; dm/d £17.50/45; ⏰reception 8.30am-noon & 3.30-11pm; P 📶) Rightly a firm favourite among budget travellers, this spotlessly clean, relaxed, rambling former town house boasts three doubles, roomy dorms and six shared wet-room showers. There's a pleasant lounge, a rather undersized kitchen, free wi-fi and lockers for storage.

Townhouse B&B ££
(☎01392-494 994; www.townhouseexeter.co.uk; 54 St David's Hill; s £52-72, d £80-100; P 📶) One of the better B&B options in Exeter – built from red brick, clad in ivy, and with nine smart rooms with wood floors, grey-and-crimson colour schemes and plenty of original features, such as fireplaces and sash windows.

St Olaves HOTEL ££
(☎01392-217736; www.olaves.co.uk; Mary Arches St; s £75-90, d £90-109; P 📶) Whitewashed and Georgian, this smart house was built for a wealthy merchant and later served as a vicarage. These days it's a stylish if rather staid hotel, with 15 spacious rooms featuring brass bedsteads and plush furnishings; some overlook the garden. The central staircase is seriously grand.

Raffles B&B ££
(☎01392-270200; www.raffles-exeter.co.uk; 11 Blackall Rd; s £48-55, d/f from £78/88; P 📶) The antique dealer owner has peppered each room of this late-Victorian town house with heritage features – look out for Bakelite radios, wooden plant stands and polished trunks. Largely organic breakfasts and a walled garden add to the appeal.

★**Hotel du Vin Exeter** BOUTIQUE HOTEL £££
(☎01392-790120; www.hotelduvin.com/locations/exeter; Magdalen St; d £119-169, ste £189; @ 📶 🏊) This impressive red-brick edifice (once

Exeter's eye hospital) has recently been acquired by the plush Hotel du Vin chain. Quietly stylish, the rooms incorporate aspects of the building's Victorian architecture (bay windows, cornicing, wood floors) into their palette of muted colours, offbeat wallpapers and Scandi-style sofas. Elsewhere, there's a stylish octagon-shaped restaurant, an excellent bar and design touches aplenty.

ABode Exeter HOTEL £££
(01392-319955; www.abodehotels.co.uk/exeter; Cathedral Yard; r £100-350;) Of all the city's hotels, this one surely boasts the best location – it's smack bang on the cathedral green, and you'll be able to see the towers from your window if you bag one of the top-drawer 'Fabulous' rooms. The building is Georgian, but the style is contemporary: off-kilter floors and stained glass meet muted colours and minimalist furnishings.

Eating

★Rusty Bike MODERN BRITISH ££
(01392-214440; www.rustybike-exeter.co.uk; 67 Howell Rd; mains £13-20; 5-10pm Mon-Sat, noon-10.30pm Sun) It's in the city, but Rusty's soul is rooted deep in the countryside. It's all about farm-to-plate dining here (or 'welly to belly', as they put it), with as much as possible coming from local suppliers – game from local estates, wild veg foraged by hand, Aberdeen Angus beef reared at nearby farms.

Jasmine Thai BISTRO ££
(01392-689988; www.jasmine-thai.co.uk; 153 Fore St; mains £11-19; noon-2.30pm Mon-Sat, 6-10pm daily) A spicy new addition to Exeter, this Thai restaurant has proved very popular. You can play safe with the classics – red, green, Penang or jungle curries – or go for something special, like whole sea bass with Thai herbs or 'weeping tiger' steak. Thai-style decor – Buddhas, pagodas and the like – complete the Far Eastern feel.

Ruby BURGERS ££
(01392-436168; www.rubyburgers.com; 74 Queen St; mains £6-11; 10am-10pm) Exeter's boutique burger joint, beloved by hipsters, students and local diners of all ages. It's all studiously trendy: retro in style, fast and furious in service, with a menu that takes in classic burgers plus sliders, panko-crusted chicken fillets and 'falloumi' burgers for veggies. Extra marks for the puns on the specials board – fancy a 'Mother Ducka' or 'Notorious P.I.G', anyone?

Herbies VEGETARIAN ££
(01392-258473; 15 North St; mains £7-12; 11am-2.30pm Mon-Sat, 6.30-9.30pm Tue-Sat;) Cosy and gently groovy, Herbies has been cheerfully feeding Exeter's veggies and vegans for more than 20 years. Tuck into delicious Tuscan mushrooms, Moroccan tagine, or butter bean, thyme and squash risotto.

@Angela's MODERN BRITISH £££
(01392-499038; www.angelasrestaurant.co.uk; 38 New Bridge St; mains £19.50-28.50; 6-9.30pm Mon-Sat) A slightly old-fashioned fine-dining restaurant, big on rich, filling dishes such as rosemary-garlic lamb loin and roast monkfish in a creamy sauce. The feel is rather formal, with starched white tablecloths and napkins shaped like shells – lovely, if you like that sort of thing.

Drinking & Nightlife

★Old Firehouse PUB
(01392-277279; www.oldfirehouseexeter.co.uk; 50 New North Rd; noon-2am Mon-Wed, to 3am Thu-Sat, to 1am Sun) Step into the snug, candlelit interior of this Exeter institution and feel instantly at home. Here, dried hops hang from rafters above flagstone floors and walls of exposed stone. The range of draught ciders and cask ales is truly impressive, while the pizzas, served after 9pm, have kept countless students fed.

Timepiece CLUB
(www.timepiecenightclub.co.uk; Little Castle St; 9.30pm-1.30am Mon-Wed, 10pm-2am Fri & Sat) A student's late-night favourite, with nights devoted to indie, electro, house and cheesy club classics.

Entertainment

Bike Shed THEATRE
(01392-434169; www.bikeshedtheatre.co.uk; 162 Fore St; noon-midnight Mon-Thu, to 2am Fri & Sat, 5-11pm Sun) Emerging writers are profiled in the Bike Shed's rough 'n' ready subterranean, brick-lined performance space. Its vintage cocktail bar makes a hip setting for live music and DJ sets on Friday and Saturday nights.

Exeter Phoenix ARTS CENTRE
(01392-667080; www.exeterphoenix.org.uk; Bradninch Pl, Gandy St; 10am-11pm Mon-Sat,;) Exeter's art and soul, the Phoenix is a buzzing blend of indie cinema, performance space, galleries and a cool cafe-bar (snacks to 9pm).

WORTH A TRIP

RIVER COTTAGE CANTEEN

Known for his media campaigns on sustainability and organic food, TV chef Hugh Fearnley-Whittingstall has broadcast most of his TV shows from his home base at **River Cottage HQ** (☎01297-630300; www.rivercottage.net; Trinity Hill Rd, Axminster; 2-course lunch £55, 4-course dinner £70-90), near Axminster, 30 miles from Exeter. Though the house suffered a serious fire in 2012, it's since been rebuilt and is very much back in business. If you fancy seeing where the magic happens, you can book in for a sumptuous four-course meal, made with produce from Hugh's own garden, or attend one of the regular cooking courses. A cheaper option is to dine at his **canteen** (☎01297-631715; www.rivercottage.net; Trinity Sq, Axminster; mains £8-16; ⏲9am-5pm daily, 6.30-9pm Tue-Sat;) in Axminster village nearby.

Exeter Picturehouse CINEMA
(☎0871 902 5730; www.picturehouses.co.uk; 51 Bartholomew St West) An intimate, independent cinema, screening mainstream and art-house movies.

Information

Custom House Visitor Centre (☎01392-271611; customhouse@exeter.gov.uk; 46 The Quay; ⏲10am-5pm daily Apr-Oct, 11am-4pm Nov-Mar) is a small tourist office near the quay.

Exeter Library (Castle St; per 30min £3; ⏲9am-6pm Mon, Tue, Thu & Fri, 10am-5pm Wed, 9am-4pm Sat;) has internet access and free wi-fi.

Exeter Tourist Office (☎01392-665700; www.heartofdevon.com; Dix's Field; ⏲9am-5pm Mon-Sat Apr-Sep, 9.30am-4pm Mon-Sat Oct-Mar) is efficient and well run, with plenty of info on Exeter and the rest of Devon.

Police Station (☎08452-777444; Heavitree Rd; ⏲24hr)

Royal Devon & Exeter Hospital (Barrack Rd) caters for accident and emergency.

Getting There & Away

AIR

Exeter International Airport (www.exeter-airport.co.uk) is 6 miles east of the city. Flights connect with several UK cities, including Manchester, Newcastle, Edinburgh and Glasgow, as well as to the Isles of Scilly and the Channel Islands. Flights also travel to European cities, including Paris, Amsterdam and Dublin.

Bus 56 runs from Exeter St David's train station and Exeter bus station to Exeter International Airport (£3, 30 minutes, hourly 7am to 6pm).

BUS

Services include the following:

Lyme Regis (£7.70, six daily Monday to Friday, five on Saturday and Sunday) Bus X52 runs via Beer; four services continue to Bridport.

Plymouth bus X38; £9.70, 1¼ hours, every other hour Monday to Saturday, two on Sunday

Totnes bus X64; £9.70, 50 minutes, eight daily Monday to Friday, seven on Saturday, three on Sunday

Transmoor Link/Bus 82 runs on summer Saturdays and Sundays only (mid-May to mid-September), making one trip each way from Exeter to Tavistock (£5.80) via Moretonhampstead, Postbridge, Princetown and Yelverton.

TRAIN

Main-line trains stopping at St David's train station include the following:

Bristol £27.50, 1¼ hours, half-hourly

London Paddington £47.50, 2½ hours, half-hourly

Paignton £6.60, 50 minutes, half-hourly

Penzance £20.40, three hours, half-hourly to hourly

Plymouth £9.10, one hour, half-hourly

Torquay £6.60, 45 minutes, half-hourly to hourly

Totnes £11, 35 minutes, half-hourly

Some branch-line services also go through Central train station.

Getting Around

BICYCLE

Saddles & Paddles (p285) rents out bikes.

BUS

Bus H (two to four per hour) links St David's train station with Central train station and the High St, passing near the bus station.

CAR

Most of the major car-hire firms have desks at the airport, and a few have concessions at the train station too.

There are plenty of car parks in the city centre, but there can be heavy traffic during rush hour and on weekends. Park & Ride buses (adult/child return £2.50/1.60) operate every 20 minutes, running from Sowton (near M5, junction 30) and Matford (near M5, junction 31) Monday to Saturday, and from Honiton Rd (near M5, junction 29) daily.

TAXI

There are taxi ranks at St David's train station and on High and Sidwell Sts.

Capital Taxis (☎01392-434343)

Club Cars (☎01392-213030)

Gemini (☎01392-666666)

Torquay & Around

POP 114, 266

It may face the English Channel, rather than the Med, but the coast around Torquay has long been dubbed the English Riviera; famous for palm trees, piers and russet-red cliffs. At first glance, Torquay itself is the quintessential English seaside resort in flux, beloved by both the coach-tour crowd and stag- and hen-party animals. But a mild microclimate and an azure circle of bay have also drawn a smarter set and Torquay now competes with foodie-hub Dartmouth for fine eateries. The area also boasts unique attractions that range from an immense aviary to a surreal model village. Add an Agatha Christie connection, fishing boats and steam trains, and it all adds up to some grand days out beside the sea.

Torquay's neighbouring resort, Paignton, and its Victorian pier, sits 3 miles south. The fishing port of Brixham is 5 miles further south again.

Sights & Activities

Torquay boasts no fewer than 20 beaches and an impressive 22 miles of coast. Holidaymakers flock to the central (but tidal) **Torre Abbey Sands**; locals head for the sand-and-shingle beaches beside the 73m red-clay cliffs around **Babbacombe**.

Train buffs won't want to miss a trip from Paignton aboard the Dartmouth Steam Railway (p291).

Living Coasts ZOO
(☎0844-474 3366; www.livingcoasts.org.uk; Beacon Quay; adult/child £12.20/9.15; ⊙10am-5pm) An enormous open-plan aviary bringing you up close to free-roaming penguins, punk-rocker-style tufted puffins and irresistibly cute otters. Booking online saves money and queues.

Babbacombe Model Village EXHIBITION
(☎01803-315315; www.model-village.co.uk; Hampton Ave; adult/child £10.95/8.95; ⊙10am-4pm, until 9pm some summer evenings) Prepare for a fabulously eccentric, 1.6-hectare world in miniature, complete with small-scale Stonehenge, football stadium, beach, castle (under attack from a fire-breathing dragon) and thatched village where firefighters are tackling a blaze. Visit in the evening for illuminations; think pocket-sized Piccadilly Circus, complete with flashing signs. The height of kitsch, but improbably good fun.

Babbacombe Cliff Railway RAIL
(☎01803-328750; www.babbacombecliffrailway.co.uk; adult/child return £2.20/1.50; ⊙9.30am-4.55pm Feb-Oct) At Babbacombe, a glorious 1920s funicular railway sees you climbing into a tiny wooden carriage and rattling up and down rails set into the cliff.

Paignton Zoo ZOO
(☎0844-474 2222; www.paigntonzoo.org.uk; Totnes Rd, Paignton; adult/child £16.95/12.75; ⊙10am-5pm; P) A conservation charity runs this innovative, 32-hectare zoo, where spacious enclosures recreate habitats as varied as savannah, wetland, tropical forest and desert. High spots include the orangutan island, a vast glass-walled lion enclosure and a lemur wood, where you walk over a plank suspension bridge as the primates leap around in the surrounding trees. Then there's the steamy crocodile swamp with pathways winding over and beside Nile, Cuban and saltwater crocs, some up to 6m long.

Sleeping

Torquay Backpackers HOSTEL £
(☎01803-299924; www.torquaybackpackers.co.uk; 119 Abbey Rd; dm/d £17/38; @ 📶) Photos of grinning past guests plaster noticeboards; flags of all nations drape the walls at this budget stalwart. There are luxuries too: a DVD den and a decked, alfresco pool-table terrace, but dorms can be a bit noisy as it's popular with stag and hen dos. There's a £1 surcharge for Friday and Saturday stays.

Hillcroft B&B ££
(☎01803-297247; www.thehillcroft.co.uk; 9 St Lukes Rd; r £79, d £105-120; P @ 📶) One of the better B&B options in Torquay town, with rooms styled after Morocco, Bali, Lombok and Tuscany. The pick of the rooms are the spacious suites: Provençal, with ormolu bed and sitting room, or India with Indian art and four-poster bed.

AGATHA CHRISTIE

Torquay is the birthplace of the 'Queen of Crime', Agatha Christie (1890–1976), author of 75 novels and 33 plays, and creator of Hercule Poirot, the moustachioed, immodest Belgian detective, and Miss Marple, the surprisingly perceptive busybody spinster. Born Agatha Miller, she grew up, courted and honeymooned in Torquay, and also worked as a hospital dispenser here during WWI, thus acquiring her famous knowledge of poisons.

The tourist office stocks the free Agatha Christie Mile leaflet, which guides you around significant local sites, while **Torquay Museum** (☎01803-293975; www.torquaymuseum.org; 529 Babbacombe Rd; adult/child £6.45/3.95; ⊙10am-4pm) has a collection of photos, handwritten notes and displays devoted to her famous detectives. The highlight, though, is Greenway (p291), her summer home near Dartmouth. The Greenway Ferry (p292) sails there from Torquay's Princess Pier – it's best to book. Boats also go from Dartmouth and Totnes; a steam train runs from Paignton.

★**Cary Arms** BOUTIQUE HOTEL £££
(☎01803-327110; www.caryarms.co.uk; Babbacombe Beach; d £195-295, ste £375-450; P 🛜 👪) In a dreamy spot beside Babbacombe's sands, this heritage hotel has more than a hint of a New England beach retreat. Bright, light-filled rooms with candy-stripe throws and white furniture shimmer with style, and the best have sea-view balconies. There's a divine spa, too.

Orestone HOTEL £££
(☎01803-328098; www.orestonemanor.com; Rock House Lane; r £150-275, ste £350; P 🛜) A refined hideaway, in a wooded valley 3 miles north of Torquay. With its gabled facade and plush public areas, there's a dash of period elegance here, and the rooms vary widely in terms of space and comfort: classic doubles are a bit small and floral, so it's worth spending for extra style and roominess. The terrace is gorgeous, overlooking subtropical gardens to the sea.

Eating

★**The Elephant** MODERN BRITISH ££
(☎01803-200044; www.elephantrestaurant.co.uk; 3 Beacon Tce; 2-course lunch menu £14.50, mains £15.50-24; ⊙noon-2pm & 6.30-9pm Tue-Sat) This fine-dining beauty remains Torquay's premier foodie destination, although it's slimmed down operations by combining two restaurants into one. It's run by chef Simon Hulstone, who still has a taste for seasonal food and elaborate presentation, but these days it's a more relaxed affair. Expect quality bistro dishes like scallop ceviche and sticky-braised pig's cheeks, made with top Devonian ingredients.

Number 7 SEAFOOD ££
(☎01803-295055; www.no7-fish.com; 7 Beacon Tce; mains £13.75; ⊙noon-1.45pm Wed-Sat year-round, 7-9pm daily Jul-Sep, Tue-Sat Oct-Jun) No-fuss fish is the order of the day at this small family-run bistro. The decor's a bit dated, but the food is as fresh as ever: crab, lobster, scallops and cod steaks, laced with garlic butter or dusted with Moroccan spices.

Rockfish SEAFOOD ££
(☎01803-212175; 20 Victoria Pde; mains £11.95-18.95; ⊙noon-9.30pm) Mitch Tonks' rapidly expanding mini-chain of seafood restaurants has opened a new branch on the Torquay seafront, and its taste for relaxed catch-of-the-day dining has unsurprisingly proved popular. Whitewashed wood and nautical knick-knacks give it a shipshape ambience, and the food takes in everything from classic fish and chips to a take on Italian *fritto misto* (mixed fried fish).

Information

Post Office (7-13 Union St)

Torquay Tourist Office (☎01803-211211; www.theenglishriviera.co.uk; Vaughan Pde; ⊙9.30am-2pm Mon-Sat) Torquay's main tourist office covers Torquay, Paignton and Brixham.

Getting There & Away

BUS

Brixham (Bus 12; £4.10, 50 minutes, half-hourly) Via Paignton.

Dartmouth (£4.50, 1¼ hours, hourly Mon-Sat) Stagecoach Gold.

Totnes (£3.50, 45 minutes, half-hourly Mon-Sat, seven on Sunday) Stagecoach Gold.

FERRY

Regular ferries (p293) shuttle between Torquay and Brixham (one way/return £2/3).

TRAIN

Trains run from Exeter via Torquay (£6, 45 minutes, half-hourly to hourly) to Paignton (£6, 52 minutes).

Brixham

POP 17,457

An appealing, pastel-painted tumbling of fishermen's cottages leads down to Brixham's horseshoe harbour where arcades and gift shops coexist with winding streets, brightly coloured boats and one of England's busiest fishing ports. Although picturesque, Brixham is far from a neatly packaged resort, and its brand of gritty charm offers an insight into work-a-day life along Devon's coast.

Sights

Golden Hind HISTORIC SHIP

(☎01803-856223; www.goldenhind.co.uk; The Quay; adult/child £7/5; ⏲10.30am-4pm Mar-Oct) Devon explorer Sir Francis Drake carried out a treasure-seeking circumnavigation of the globe aboard the *Golden Hind*, in the late 1500s. This full-sized replica sees you crossing the gangplank, clambering below decks, peering into the captain's cabin and prowling around the poop deck.

Brixham Heritage Museum MUSEUM

(☎01803-856267; www.torbaymuseums.com; Bolton Cross; adult/child £2/free; ⏲10am-4pm Tue-Fri, 10am-1pm Sat) An eclectic collection of exhibits explores the town's salty history, majoring on sailboats, smuggling, shipbuilding and sea rescues. There are reconstructions of a fisherman's cottage and police cell, but it's the sepia-tinted photos of the town's past that steal the imagination.

Tours

★Fish Market FOOD & DRINK

(☎07973 297620; bfmt2014@gmail.com; The Quay; tours incl breakfast £12.50) Life in Brixham revolves around the fish market, and it's possible to book a guided tour during summer months. You'll see ice-lined fish trays, white-coated buyers and a bustling auction, then have breakfast at the Fishermen's Mission – but you'll need to be an early riser, as the action kicks off at 6am. Bookings essential.

Eating & Drinking

David Walker & Son SEAFOOD £

(www.davidwalkerandson.com; Unit B, Fish Market; ⏲9am-3pm Mon-Fri, 8am-3pm Sat) Fish doesn't get any fresher than at Mr Walker's fish stall, where all the catches of the day are piled high on beds of ice. Crab, lobster, skate, hake and sea bass – there's no telling which little fishy you'll find for your dishy.

Beamers SEAFOOD ££

(☎01803-854777; www.beamersrestaurant.co.uk; 19 The Quay; mains £16.95-29.95; ⏲6.30-9pm Wed-Mon; 🖉) A superior seafood choice, where all the fish is sourced on a daily basis straight from the quayside market. Samphire, saffron and Pernod spring some menu surprises; bagging a window table secures an absorbing harbour view.

Maritime PUB

(www.themaritime.co.uk; 79 King St; ⏲7-11pm) Eccentric old boozer smothered in thousands of key rings, stone jugs and chamber pots, presided over by a chatty parrot called Mr Tibbs.

Getting There & Away

Regular ferries (p293) shuttle between Brixham and Torquay (one way/return £2/3).

Kingswear (bus 22; £3.20, 15 minutes, half-hourly to hourly) Ferry connections (p292) continue to Dartmouth.

Torquay (bus 12; £4.10, 50 minutes, half-hourly) Via Paignton.

Dartmouth & Around

POP 10,716

Home to the nation's most prestigious naval college, the riverside town of Dartmouth is surely one of Devon's prettiest, awash with pastel-coloured, punch-drunk 17th- and 18th-century buildings leaning at crazy angles, and a picturesque harbour stacked with yachts and clanking boat masts. It's distinctly chic these days, but it's still a working port, and the triple draw of regular riverboat cruises, the art-deco house of Coleton Fishacre and Agatha Christie's former home at Greenway make Dartmouth all but irresistible.

Dartmouth is on the west side of the Dart estuary. It's linked to the village of Kingswear on the east bank by fleets of car and foot ferries, providing a key transport link to Torquay.

Sights

★ Greenway HISTORIC BUILDING
(NT; ☎01803-842382; www.nationaltrust.org.uk; Greenway Rd, Galmpton; adult/child £10.30/5.10; ⏰10.30am-5pm) High on Devon's must-see list, the captivating summer home of crime writer Agatha Christie sits beside the placid River Dart. Part-guided tours allow you to wander between rooms where the furnishings and knick-knacks are much as she left them. The bewitching waterside gardens include features that pop up in her mysteries, so you get to spot locations made notorious by fictional murders. Car parking needs to be prebooked; the best way to arrive is by Greenway Ferry (p292) or on foot.

Christie owned Greenway between 1938 and 1959, and the house feels frozen in time: check out the piles of hats in the lobby, the books in her library, the clothes in her wardrobe, and listen to her speak (via a replica radio) in the drawing room. In the gardens, woods are speckled with splashes of magnolias, daffodils and hydrangeas frame the water, while the planting creates intimate, secret spaces – the boathouse and views over the river are sublime. In Christie's book *Dead Man's Folly,* Greenway doubles as Nasse House, with the boathouse making an appearance as a murder scene.

The Greenway Ferry runs to the house year-round, or you can take the Dartmouth Steam Railway from Paignton to Greenway Halt and walk half a mile through the woods. The last way to arrive is to hike along the picturesque **Dart Valley Trail** from Kingswear (4 miles).

★ Coleton Fishacre HISTORIC BUILDING
(NT; ☎01803-842382; www.nationaltrust.org.uk; Brownstone Rd, near Kingswear; adult/child £10.30/5.10; ⏰10.30am-5pm; Ⓟ) For an evocative glimpse of Jazz Age glamour, drop by the former home of the D'Oyly Carte family of theatre impresarios. Built in the 1920s, its faultless art-deco embellishments include original Lalique tulip uplighters, comic bathroom tiles and a stunning saloon – complete with tinkling piano. The croquet terrace leads to deeply shelved subtropical gardens and vistas of the sea. Hike the 4 miles along the cliffs from Kingswear, or drive.

Dartmouth Castle CASTLE
(EH; ☎01803-833588; www.english-heritage.org.uk/visit/places/dartmouth-castle; adult/child £6.10/3.70; ⏰10am-6pm Apr-Sep, to 5pm Oct, to 4pm Sat & Sun Nov-Mar) Encounter mazy passages, atmospheric guardrooms and great views from the battlements. Get there via the tiny, open-top Castle Ferry (p292).

★ Dartmouth Steam Railway RAIL
(☎01803-555872; www.dartmouthrailriver.co.uk; Torbay Rd, Paignton; adult/child/family return £16/9.50/43.25; ⏰4-9 trains daily Mar-Nov) Chugging from seaside Paignton to the beautiful banks of the River Dart, these vintage trains roll back the years to the age of steam. The 7-mile, 30-minute journey puffs past Goodrington Sands stopping at Greenway Halt (near Agatha Christie's former home), then the village of Kingswear, where ferries shuttle across to picturesque Dartmouth.

There are various other trips available, involving coastal cruises and excursions on a paddle steamer; see the website for the full round-up.

Sleeping

★ Bayard's Cove B&B ££
(☎01803-839278; www.bayardscoveinn.co.uk; 27 Lower St; d £125-155, f £185; 📶) Crammed with character and bursting with beams, Bayard's Cove sees you sleeping amid whitewashed stone walls and huge church candles. The lavish family suites feature grand double beds and kids' cabins, complete with bunk beds and tiny TVs; there are even estuary glimpses from the rooms.

Alf Resco B&B ££
(☎01803-835880; www.cafealfresco.co.uk; Lower St; d from £70-90, apt £100) Ahoy, me hearties – not content with providing some of the town's yummiest food, Alf's also offers a couple of cosy rooms, bunk beds in the 'Crew's Quarters' and a 'Captain's Cabin', squeezed in under the rafters with all the atmosphere of a ship's cabin (lanterns, panelled walls, watery views and all).

Just B GUESTHOUSE ££
(☎01803-834311; www.justbdartmouth.com; reception 17 Fosse St; r £75-110) The nine chi-chi options here range from bedrooms with bathrooms to mini-apartments, all featuring snazzy furnishings, crisp cottons and comfy beds. They're scattered over three central properties, and the 'just B' policy (no '&B' means no breakfast) keeps prices down.

Eating

★ Alf Resco CAFE £
(☎01803-835880; www.cafealfresco.co.uk; Lower St; mains from £6; ⏰7am-2pm; 📶) An eclectic

crowd hangs out at Alf's – you'll be eating among hipsters, families, tourists and river-boat crews. The same menu spans breakfast through to lunch; expect piled-high fry-ups, irresistible pastries and eye-opening espressos. The gorgeous B&B rooms (p291) are pure shabby chic.

Rockfish FISH & CHIPS ££

(☎01803-832800; www.rockfishdevon.co.uk; 8 South Embankment; mains £10-18; ⊙noon-9.30pm) The Dartmouth outpost of Mitch Tonks' four-strong bistro chain. Seafood is the speciality, and the weathered boarding and maritime decor fit right in along Dartmouth's streets. The fish and chips are delicious.

★**Seahorse** SEAFOOD £££

(☎01803-835147; www.seahorserestaurant.co.uk; 5 South Embankment; mains £19-28; ⊙noon-3pm Tue-Sun, 6-10pm Tue-Sat) What Rick Stein is to Cornwall, Mitch Tonks is to Devon – a seafood supremo, with a clutch of restaurants across the county. The Seahorse is the Tonks original, and still the best: a classic fish restaurant where the just-landed produce is roasted over open charcoals. Leather banquettes, wood floors and a wine wall give it a French bistro feel.

Information

Tourist Office (☎01803-834224; www.discoverdartmouth.com; Mayor's Ave; ⊙10am-4pm Mon, Tue & Thu-Sat)

Getting There & Away

BUS

Plymouth (£7.20, 2½ hours, hourly Monday to Saturday) Stagecoach bus 3. Two buses run as far as Kingsbridge on Sunday.

Totnes (£3.70, 50 minutes, hourly Monday to Saturday) Stagecoach bus X64 continues to Exeter.

FERRY

Several ferries run from Dartmouth's quay:

Castle Ferry (www.dartmouthcastleferry.co.uk; adult/child return £5/3; ⊙10am-4.45pm Apr-Oct) Runs to Dartmouth Castle.

Dartsmouth–Kingswear Higher Ferry (☎07866 531687; www.dartmouthhigherferry.com; car/pedestrian one way £5.60/60p; ⊙6.30am-10.45pm) Carries cars and pedestrians across the estuary every six minutes, and enables you to avoid the town's narrow streets.

Dartmouth–Kingswear Lower Ferry (www.southhams.gov.uk/DartmouthLowerFerry; car/pedestrian £4.50/1.50; ⊙7.10am-10.55pm) The town's oldest ferry service, in business since the 1300s. It's a float boat that's pulled by a tug moored alongside.

Greenway Ferry (☎01803-882811; www.greenwayferry.co.uk; adult/child return £8.50/6.50) Boats to Greenway and Dittisham, plus scenic river cruises.

TRAIN

The Dartmouth Steam Railway (p291) links Kingswear and Paignton.

Totnes & Around

POP 8041

Totnes has such a reputation for being alternative that local jokers wrote 'twinned with Narnia' under the town sign. For decades famous as Devon's hippie haven, ecoconscious Totnes also became Britain's first 'transition town' in 2005, when it began trying to wean itself off a dependence on oil. Sustainability aside, Totnes boasts a tempting vineyard, a gracious Norman castle and a mass of fine Tudor buildings, and is the springboard for a range of adrenaline sports.

Sights & Activities

★**Sharpham Wine & Cheese** WINERY

(☎01803-732203; www.sharpham.com; ⊙10am-6pm May-Sep, 10am-5pm Mar & Apr, 10am-3pm Oct-Dec, booking required for some tours; P) This is one of Devon's most prestigious vineyards, particularly known for its crisp, sparkling whites. You can explore the steep vine-covered hills on your own (£8.95), and then head for the shop for a taste or a sit-down meal in the excellent **Anchorstone Café** (☎01803-732178; www.anchorstoneatsharphamvineyard.co.uk; Sharpham Vineyard; mains £7-15; ⊙10am-4.30pm, lunch served noon-2.30pm Apr-Sep; ✎). Longer tours including tutored tastings are available by reservation.

The vineyard is 3 miles south of Totnes, off the A381.

Totnes Castle CASTLE

(EH; ☎01803-864406; www.english-heritage.org.uk; Castle St; adult/child £4/2.40; ⊙10am-6pm Apr-Sep, to 5pm Oct, to 4pm Sat & Sun Nov-Mar) The outer keep of Totnes' Norman motte-and-bailey fortress crowns a hill at the top of town, providing engrossing views over higgledy-piggledy rooftops and the river valley. Look for the medieval toilet, too (but maybe don't use it).

Dartington Estate HISTORIC SITE

(☎01803-847000; www.dartington.org; ⊙gardens dawn-dusk, visitor centre 9am-5pm) Henry VIII gave this pastoral 324-hectare estate to two of his wives (Catherines Howard and Parr). For many years it was home to the town's art college; now the 14th-century manor house hosts events, including the renowned classical music and literature festivals. There's also a great art-house cinema, a decent pub and you can even stay here if you like – but the gorgeous grounds are definitely worth a wander even if not. It's about 2 miles northwest of Totnes.

★**Dynamic Adventures** ADVENTURE SPORTS
(☎01803-862725; www.dynamicadventurescic.co.uk; The Shops at Dartington, Dartington) The superb activities on offer here include canoeing and kayaking (per half-/full day £35/70) and sea kayaking (from £75), as well as rock climbing and archery (both per hour £15). It also rents bikes (half-/full day £12/16). It's based 2 miles northwest of Totnes.

Totnes Kayaks KAYAKING
(☎07799 403788; www.totneskayaks.co.uk; The Quay, Stoke Gabriel; 1/3/6hr £20/25/40) On these self-guided paddles beside unspoilt hills, it's best to go with the tide (owner Tom will advise); so either upriver past Sharpham Vineyard, or downriver to the charming village of Dittisham. You set off from sleepy Stoke Gabriel, 5 miles southeast of Totnes.

Sleeping & Eating

★**Dartington Hall** B&B ££
(☎01803-847147; www.dartington.org; Dartington, near Totnes; s/d from £59/99; P) The wings of this idyllic, ancient manor house have been carefully converted into rooms that range from heritage themed to deluxe modern. Ask for one overlooking the grassy, cobble-fringed courtyard and settle back for a truly tranquil night's sleep. The estate is about 1.5 miles from Totnes.

Willow VEGETARIAN £
(☎01803-862605; 87 High St; mains £5-10; 11am-8pm Sun-Tue, 11am-9pm or 10pm Wed-Sat;) Totnes' alternative crowd makes a beeline for this long-standing veggie and wholefood cafe, as homely as an old tie-dyed T-shirt. Quiches, hotpots, salads, moussaka, gluten-free cakes – you'll find them all here. There's a weekly curry night.

★**Riverford Field Kitchen** MODERN BRITISH ££
(☎01803-762074; www.riverford.co.uk; Wash Barn; 3-course lunch/dinner £23.50/27; noon-2.30pm daily, 6-10pm most evenings;) This ecofriendly, organic, plough-to-plate farm is where everyone wants to eat when they come to Totnes (booking essential). It began as a food-box scheme, and has now branched out with a delightful barn bistro, where diners sit communally at long wooden tables and hand round dishes of the day. Rustic flavours rule: delicious salads, roast meats, imaginative veggie options.

Rumour PUB FOOD ££
(☎01803-864682; www.rumourtotnes.com; 30 High St, Totnes; mains £9-18; noon-3pm Mon-Sat, 6-9pm daily) Rumour is a local institution – a narrow, cosy pub-restaurant with low lighting, funky local art and newspapers to read. It's legendary for its pizzas (£9), but there's lots more choice too – risottos, steaks, stews and fish of the day.

Information

Tourist Office (☎01803-863168; www.totnesinformation.co.uk; Coronation Rd; 10am-4pm Mon-Sat Apr-Oct, 10am-4pm Mon-Fri, 10am-1pm Sat Nov-Mar) Small but well-stocked tourist office with lots of good links to local accommodation and activity providers.

Getting There & Around

BOAT

Boats shuttle downriver to Dartmouth with the **Dartmouth Steam Railway and Riverboat Company** (☎01803-555872; www.dartmouthrailriver.co.uk).

BUS

Totnes has a good bus service, although some buses and coaches run a rather Byzantine timetable. Useful options:

Exeter (£9.70, every two hours Monday to Saturday, three on Sunday) Stagecoach Bus X64; continues to Dartmouth in the opposite direction.

Plymouth (£3.40, one hour, half-hourly Monday to Friday, hourly at weekends) Stagecoach Gold.

Torquay (£3.70, 45 minutes, half-hourly Monday to Friday, hourly at weekends) Stagecoach Gold.

TRAIN

Trains go at least hourly to Exeter (£11, 35 minutes) and Plymouth (£8, 30 minutes).

The quaint **South Devon Steam Railway** (www.southdevonrailway.co.uk; adult/child return £14/8.40; 3-9 trains daily Apr-Oct) chuffs to Buckfastleigh, on the edge of Dartmoor.

Plymouth & Around

POP 258,000

For decades, some have dismissed Plymouth as sprawling and ugly, pointing to architectural eyesores and sometimes palpable poverty. But the arrival of high-profile chefs Hugh Fearnley-Whittingstall and Mitch Tonks, and ongoing waterfront regeneration begs a rethink. Yes, the city, an important Royal Naval port, suffered WWII bomb damage, and today it is still sometimes more gritty than pretty, but Plymouth is also packed with possibilities: swim in an art-deco lido; tour a gin distillery; learn to kayak; roam an aquarium; take a boat trip across the bay; then see a top-class theatre show and party till dawn. And the ace in the pack? Plymouth Hoe – a cafe-dotted, wide grassy headland offering captivating views of a boat-studded bay.

History

Plymouth's history is dominated by the sea. The first recorded cargo left in 1211 and by the late 16th century it was the port of choice for explorers and adventurers. It's waved off Sir Francis Drake, Sir Walter Raleigh, the fleet that defeated the Spanish Armada, the pilgrims who founded America, Charles Darwin, Captain Cook and countless boats carrying emigrants to Australia and New Zealand.

During WWII Plymouth suffered horrendously at the hands of the Luftwaffe – more than 1000 civilians died in the Blitz, which reduced the city centre to rubble. The 21st century has brought regeneration to waterfront areas, a £200-million Drake Circus shopping centre and a growing university, bringing a burst of new buildings and 30,000 students to the heart of town.

Sights

★Plymouth Hoe LANDMARK

Francis Drake supposedly spied the Spanish fleet from this grassy headland overlooking Plymouth Sound (the city's wide bay); the bowling green on which he finished his game was probably where his **statue** now stands. The wide villa-backed promenade features scores of war memorials, including the immense **Plymouth Naval Memorial**, which commemorates Commonwealth WWI and WWII sailors who have no grave but the sea.

Smeaton's Tower LIGHTHOUSE

(☎01752-304774; www.plymouth.gov.uk/museumsmeatonstower; The Hoe; adult/child £3/1.50; ⏲10am-5pm Tue-Sun) The red-and-white stripes of Smeaton's Tower rise from the middle of the Plymouth Hoe headland. The whole 21m structure used to stand on the Eddystone Reef, 14 miles offshore, and was transferred here, brick by brick, in the 1880s. For an insight into past lighthouse keepers' lives, head up 93 stone steps and through the circular rooms to emerge onto an open-air platform with stunning views of the city, Dartmoor and the sea.

★Barbican AREA

(www.plymouthbarbican.com) For a glimpse of what Plymouth might have looked like before the bombers of the Luftwaffe had their way, head down to this historic harbour area, where the part-cobbled streets are lined with Tudor and Jacobean buildings, and old dockside warehouses have been turned into bars, restaurants and art galleries. It's also famous as the point from which the Pilgrim Fathers set sail for the New World in 1620: the **Mayflower Steps** mark the spot.

The original passenger list can be seen on the side of **Island House** nearby. The steps also commemorate Captain James Cook's 1768 voyage of discovery and the first emigrant ships to Australia and New Zealand.

These days the Barbican is one of the city's liveliest, funkiest areas – not to mention one of its prettiest. Drink it all in, me hearties.

★Plymouth Gin Distillery DISTILLERY

(☎01752-665292; www.plymouthdistillery.com; 60 Southside St; tours £7; ⏲6 tours daily) This heavily beamed distillery has been concocting gin since 1793, making it the oldest producer of the spirit in the world. The Royal Navy ferried it round the world in countless officers' messes and the brand was specified in the first recorded recipe for a dry martini in the 1930s. Tours thread past the stills and take in a tutored tasting before retiring to the beautiful, Grade II-listed cocktail bar for a complimentary G&T. You can book places online.

Plymouth Fish Market MARKET

(☎01752-204738; www.plymouthfisheries.co.uk; Sutton Harbour) Around 60,000 tonnes of fish pass through this fish market on Sutton Harbour, making it the second biggest by volume in England after Billingsgate. It's an amazing sight when it's in full flow, and it's possible to arrange a guided tour with the harbour-

Plymouth

0 500 m
0 0.25 miles

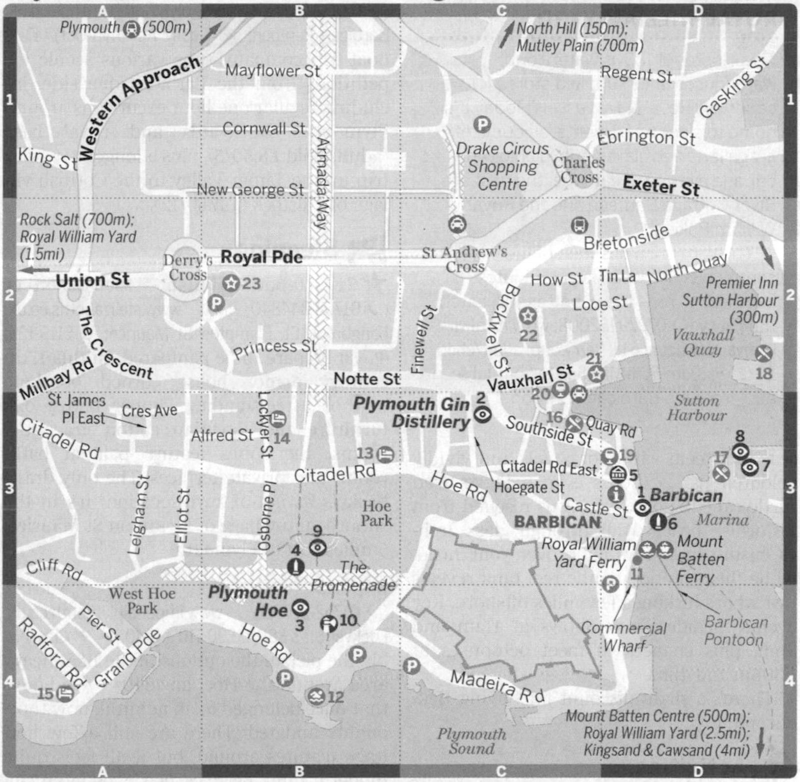

Plymouth

Top Sights

1 Barbican D3
2 Plymouth Gin Distillery C3
3 Plymouth Hoe B4

Sights

4 Drake Statue B3
5 Island House D3
6 Mayflower Steps D3
7 National Marine Aquarium D3
8 Plymouth Fish Market D3
9 Plymouth Naval Memorial B3
10 Smeaton's Tower B4

Activities, Courses & Tours

11 Plymouth Boat Trips D3
12 Tinside Lido B4

Sleeping

13 Acorns & Lawns B3
14 Imperial B3
15 Sea Breezes A4

Eating

16 Catch 22 .... C3
17 Rockfish D3
18 Supha's Street Emporium D2

Drinking & Nightlife

19 Dolphin D3
20 Live Lounge C2

Entertainment

21 Annabel's C2
22 Plymouth Arts Centre C2
23 Theatre Royal B2

master (p.bromley@sutton-harbour.co.uk). There are also regular Fish In Sutton Harbour (FISH) guided tours with a local fisherman; check its Facebook page for the latest.

National Marine Aquarium AQUARIUM
(☎0844 893 7938; www.national-aquarium.co.uk; Rope Walk; adult/child £14.95/10.95; ⏲10am-5pm, to 6pm Apr-Sep) The sharks here swim in coral

LOCAL KNOWLEDGE

ROYAL WILLIAM YARD

This cluster of 1830s waterfront warehouses once supplied stores for countless Royal Navy vessels. Today it's home to sleek apartments, a couple of art galleries, a relaxed pub, a chic wine bar and a string of eateries; the best are River Cottage Canteen and the Royal William Bakery.

The yard is 2 miles west of the city centre; bus 34 (£1.20, eight minutes, half-hourly) runs there; better still, catch the **ferry** (☎07979 152008; www.royalwilliamyardharbour.co.uk/ferry.php; adult/child £3/2; ⏰10am-5pm May-Sep to 6pm Jul & Aug) from the Barbican Pontoon.

seas that teem with moray eels and vividly coloured fish – there's even a loggerhead turtle called Snorkel who was rescued from a Cornish beach. Walk-through glass arches ensure huge rays glide over your head, while the gigantic Atlantic reef tank reveals just what's lurking a few miles offshore. Key events include Shark Shows at 11am and 3pm, plus chances to meet octopuses at 1.30pm and 4pm.

There's a slight discount for buying tickets online.

Activities

★Tinside Lido SWIMMING
(☎01752-261915; www.everyoneactive.com; Hoe Rd; adult/child/family £4/3/11.60; ⏰noon-6pm daily Mon-Fri Oct-May, 10am-6pm Jun-Sep, evening swim 6-7.30pm Wed) This glorious outdoor swimming pool is one of Plymouth's great surprises. Nestled beneath the Hoe with views over Plymouth Sound, it's a gem of the Jazz Age: built in 1935 with a blend of sleek white curves and chequerboard blue tiles, it's like something straight out of an F Scott Fitzgerald novel (only in Plymouth).

Mount Batten Centre WATER SPORTS
(☎01752-404567; www.mount-batten-centre.com; 70 Lawrence Rd) A great way to explore Plymouth from a different angle is to get onto the water. This water sports and activity centre is out on the Mount Batten peninsula, linked to the Barbican by a passenger ferry (www.mountbattenferry.com; adult/child return £3/2). Two-hour taster sessions in a sit-on-top kayak cost £18.50, or you can try out sailing or stand-up paddleboarding for £19.95.

Plymouth Boat Trips BOAT TOUR
(☎01752-253153; www.plymouthboattrips.co.uk; Barbican Pontoon; ⏰4 daily Apr–mid-Oct) This boat-trip company runs various scenic expeditions from the Barbican quayside, including regular one-hour excursions around Plymouth's Dockyards and naval base (adult/child £8.50/5), plus a longer 4½-hour trip up the Tamar Valley to the Cornish village of Calstock (£17.50/12).

Sleeping

★St Elizabeth's House BOUTIQUE HOTEL ££
(☎01752-344840; www.stelizabeths.co.uk; Longbrook St, Plympton St Maurice; d £119-129; P 📶) Prepare to be pampered. In this 17th-century manor house turned boutique bolthole, free-standing slipper baths, oak furniture and Egyptian cotton grace the rooms; the suites feature palatial bathrooms and private terraces. The only drawback is its out-of-town location: it's in the suburb-cum-village of Plympton St Maurice, 5 miles east of Plymouth.

Imperial HOTEL ££
(☎01752-227311; www.imperialplymouth.co.uk; Lockyer St; s £80, d £90-110, f £140; P 📶) Probably the pick of the options in the B&B-heavy area around the Hoe: an 1840s town house that once belonged to an admiral, now thoroughly updated. There are still a few heritage features around, but it all feels quite modern: think beige carpets, wooden furniture and the odd bit of Orla Kiely wallpaper. There's a 12-space car park.

Acorns & Lawns B&B ££
(☎01752-229474; www.acornsandlawnsguesthouse.com; 171 Citadel Rd; d £60-75; 📶) A small, modern B&B set back a little from the Hoe, with views to grassy lawns from the front-facing rooms. It concentrates on getting the basics right: there's a touch of Ikea-chic to the rooms, with minimal clutter and fresh, modern decor, and a pleasant lounge-breakfast room with varnished laminate floors and colourful art. On-street parking costs £2 per day.

Sea Breezes B&B ££
(☎01752-667205; www.plymouth-bedandbreakfast.co.uk; 28 Grand Pde; s/d/f £55/85/105; P) 'Luxury to rival the finest 5* hotels' trumpets the blurb – well let's not get carried away, but this six-roomer is still a good option, with tasteful rooms in whites and sea blues, complete with plush cushions, cast-iron bedsteads, old-fashioned alarm

clocks and other thoughtful touches. Sea views abound, and owner Anne Anderson is a fine hostess.

Premier Inn Sutton Harbour HOTEL ££
(☎0871 527 8882; www.premierinn.com; 28 Sutton Rd; r £69-99; ❄ 📶 👪) Yes, yes, it's part of a national chain, and it might be corporate and functional, but it's still an eminently practical sleep. The decor is inoffensive bordering on bland – cream walls, MDF furniture, plain bathrooms – but you're in a prime spot here overlooking Sutton Harbour. It won't be your most memorable night's sleep, but practicality trumps posh sometimes.

Eating

★ **Supha's Street Emporium** ASIAN £
(☎01752-228513; www.suphas.co.uk; Unit 1, East Quay House; dishes £6.95-14.95; ⏲noon-9pm Tue & Sun, noon-10pm Wed-Sat; 🖉) An exotic new addition to the up-and-coming area around Sutton Harbour, this joint specialises in spicy, flavourful Thai-style street food: classic massaman curry, steamed sea bass, larb and papaya salads, and much more. There's a choice of ways to dine: small street plates, platters to share, mix-and-match curries. All are authentic and delicious, and there are plenty of veggie options, too.

Royal William Bakery CAFE, BAKERY £
(www.royalwilliambakery.com; Royal William Yard; mains £3-6; ⏲8.30am-4.30pm; 🖉) Piles of huge, just-cooked loaves, tureens full of soup, crumbly pastries and irresistible cakes – this is a bakery like few others. The serve-yourself style is so laid-back you don't get a bill – just tell them what you've eaten and they'll tot it up at the end. The Royal William Yard is 2 miles west of the city centre, on bus route 34.

★ **Rock Salt** MODERN BRITISH ££
(☎01752-225522; www.rocksaltcafe.co.uk; 31 Stonehouse St; mains lunch £12.95-14.95, dinner £14.95-19.95; ⏲noon-3pm & 5-9.30pm; 📶) Local boy Dave Jenkins has worked wonders at his little brasserie, which has deservedly built up a loyal local following and scooped foodie awards, too. It suits all times of day: tuck into fluffy eggs royale for breakfast, enjoy a light butternut squash risotto for lunch, and savour slow-braised ox cheek for dinner. A local diner par excellence.

Catch 22 SEAFOOD
(☎07557 476530; @Catch22; Quay Rd; mains £10-14; ⏲noon-8pm) 🍃 This fishy pop-up has taken the harbour by storm since it opened. Run by Mark Tam and Sam Johnson, it began as a hole-in-the-wall, serving simple, no-nonsense seafood such as fresh mussels, tempura squid and garlic king prawns. It's proved a huge hit, so they've teamed up with neighbours at the Live Lounge to offer seating, evening barbecues and feast nights.

River Cottage Canteen MODERN BRITISH ££
(☎01752-252702; www.rivercottage.net; Royal William Yard; mains £10-18; ⏲10am-11pm Mon-Sat, to 4pm Sun; 🖉) Hugh Fearnley-Whittingstall's gaff focuses firmly on local, sustainable, seasonal, organic goodies. Expect meats to be roasted beside an open fire, fish to be simply grilled and familiar veg to be given a revelatory makeover. It's in the Royal William Yard, 2 miles west of the city centre; catch bus 34.

Rockfish SEAFOOD ££
(☎01752-255974; www.therockfish.co.uk; 3 Rope Walk; mains £9.95-14.95; ⏲noon-9.30pm) In renowned southwest chef Mitch Tonks' cheery bistro (handily set right beside the fish market), perfectly cooked cod comes with as many chips as you can eat; roasted scallops, steamed prawns and sweet Devon crab feature on the imaginative menu, too.

Drinking & Nightlife

Like any Royal Navy city, Plymouth has a more-than-lively nightlife. Union St is clubland, Mutley Plain and North Hill have a studenty vibe, while the Barbican has more restaurants amid the bars. All three areas can get rowdy, especially at weekends.

Dolphin PUB
(☎01752-660876; 14 The Barbican; ⏲10am-11pm) This gloriously unreconstructed Barbican boozer is all scuffed tables, padded bench seats and an authentic, no-nonsense atmosphere. Feeling peckish? Get a fish-and-chip takeaway from two doors down, then settle down with your pint.

Live Lounge BAR
(☎07714 001991; 11 The Parade; ⏲10am-4am) One of many bars and clubs dotted around the Barbican, this night spot is worth a look for its vaulted interior and decent cocktails.

Vignoble WINE BAR
(www.levignoble.co.uk; Royal William Yard; ⏲noon-11.30pm) A bijou hang-out where you can sample taster-sized glasses of your chosen vintages. It's at the Royal William Yard, 2 miles west of the city centre.

Entertainment

★ Annabel's CABARET

(www.annabelscabaret.co.uk; 88 Vauxhall St; ⏲9pm-2am Thu, 8.30pm-3am Fri & Sat) Saucy showmanship comes to the Barbican at Annabel's, a late-night cabaret club where you never quite know what the night's entertainment might be – be it burlesque or blues, comedy or country. It's great fun, and the lounge-bar vibe is spot on.

Plymouth Arts Centre CINEMA

(☎01752-206114; www.plymouthartscentre.org; 38 Looe St; ⏲10am-8.30pm Tue-Sat, from 4pm Sun) Combines a cracking independent cinema, modern-art exhibitions, and a licensed, vegetarian-friendly bistro (closed Sunday).

Theatre Royal THEATRE

(TRP; ☎01752-267222; www.theatreroyal.com; Royal Pde) Plymouth's main theatre stages large-scale touring and home-grown productions; its studio space, the Drum, is renowned for featuring new writing.

Information

Plymouth Library (Drake Circus; per 30min £2; ⏲9am-6pm Mon-Fri, to 5pm Sat; wi-fi) Internet access and free wi-fi.

Police Station (Charles Cross; ⏲24hr)

Tourist Office (☎01752-306330; www.visitplymouth.co.uk; 3 The Barbican; ⏲9am-5pm Mon-Sat, 10am-4pm Sun Apr-Oct, 10am-4pm Mon-Sat Nov-Mar) Local literature aplenty, plus advance tickets for many attractions.

Getting There & Away

BUS

National Express services include the following:

Bristol £16 to £21, three hours, four to six daily

Exeter £5, one to 1½ hours, four daily

London £27.80, five to six hours, six daily

Penzance £6.20, 3¼ hours, five daily

Local services:

Exeter Bus X38; £9.70, 1¼ hours, twice hourly Monday to Saturday, three on Sunday

Totnes Stagecoach Gold; £3.40, one hour, half-hourly Monday to Friday, hourly at weekends

TRAIN

Services include the following:

Bristol £18.50 to £27.90, two hours, two or three hourly

Exeter £8.60, one hour, half-hourly

London Paddington £54, 3¼ hours, half-hourly

Penzance £10, two hours, half-hourly

Totnes £8, 30 minutes, half-hourly to hourly

Dartmoor National Park

Dartmoor is Devon's wild heart. Covering 368 sq miles, this vast national park feels like it's tumbled straight out of a Tolkien tome, with its honey-coloured heaths, moss-smothered boulders, tinkling streams and eerie granite hills (known locally as tors).

On sunny days, Dartmoor is idyllic: ponies wander at will and sheep graze beside the road, making for a cinematic location used to memorable effect in Steven Spielberg's WWI epic *War Horse*. But Dartmoor is also the setting for Sir Arthur Conan Doyle's *The Hound of the Baskervilles*, and in sleeting rain and swirling mists you'll understand why; the moor morphs into a bleak wilderness where tales of a phantom hound can seem very real indeed.

It's a haven for outdoor activities, including hiking, cycling, riding, climbing and white-water kayaking, and there are plenty of rustic pubs and country-house hotels to hunker down in when the fog rolls in.

Activities

Dartmoor is a fantastic place to get out and active, whether that means an afternoon hike or a horseback hack. For a broad-based overview, multi-activity providers such as **CRS Adventures** (☎01364-653444; www.crsadventures.co.uk; Holne Park, Ashburton) and Adventure Okehampton (p300) offer a range of ways to get your pulse racing.

Walking

Some 730 miles of public footpaths snake across Dartmoor's open heaths and rocky tors. The Pathfinder *Dartmoor Walks* (£12) guide has 28 hikes of up to 9 miles, while its *Dartmoor Short Walks* (£8) focuses on family-friendly treks.

The 18-mile **Templer Way** is a two- to three-day stretch from Haytor to Teignmouth, while the **West Devon Way** forms a 36-mile trek linking Okehampton and Plymouth. The 95-mile **Dartmoor Way** circles from Buckfastleigh in the south, through Moretonhampstead, northwest to Okehampton and south through Lydford to Tavistock. The 117-mile **Two Moors Way** runs from Wembury on the south Devon coast, across Dartmoor and Exmoor to Lynmouth, on the north coast.

Be prepared for Dartmoor's notoriously fickle weather and carry a map and compass – many trails are not way-marked. The Ord-

Dartmoor National Park

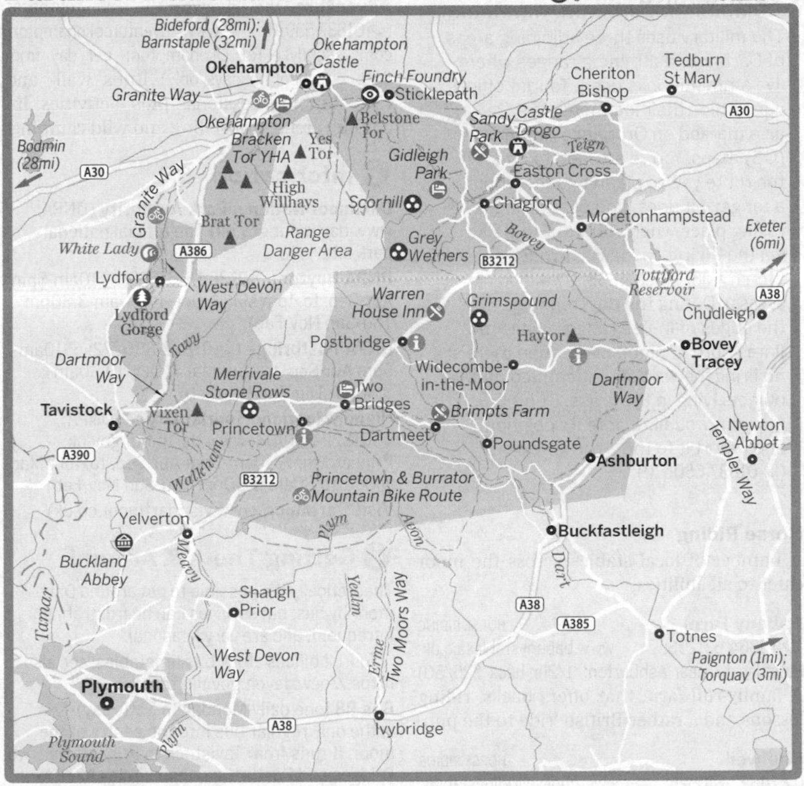

nance Survey (OS) Explorer 1:25,000 map No 28, *Dartmoor* (£8), is the most comprehensive and shows park boundaries and Ministry of Defence firing-range areas.

★Moorland Guides HIKING
(www.moorlandguides.co.uk; adult £5-10, child free) Wide range of walks, from one-hour rambles to strenuous all-day hikes, on themes spanning heritage, geology, wildlife, myths and navigation.

DNPA Guided Walks HIKING
(www.dartmoor.gov.uk/visiting; adult/child £5/free) Led by national park rangers, these organised hikes cover a variety of aspects of the moor (geology, natural history and so on), and cater for various fitness levels. They range from one to six hours.

Cycling

Routes include the 11-mile **Granite Way**, which runs, now entirely off-road, along a former railway line between Okehampton and Lydford. The 13-mile **Princetown & Burrator Mountain Bike Route** is a challenging moorland circuit along tracks and bridleways taking in Princetown, Sheepstor village and Burrator Reservoir. Tourist offices also sell the *Dartmoor Cycling Map* (£13).

Devon Cycle Hire CYCLING
(☎01837-861141; www.devoncyclehire.co.uk; Sourton Down, near Okehampton; per day adult/child £16/12; ⏰9am-5pm Thu-Tue Apr-Sep) On the Granite Way. It will deliver bikes for a small charge.

Princetown Cycle Hire CYCLING
(☎01822-890238; www.princetowncyclehire.co.uk; Fox Tor Cafe, Two Bridges Rd, Princetown; per day adult/child £18.50/10; ⏰9am-5pm) Based at the Fox Tor Cafe, this is handy for the Princetown & Burrator Mountain Bike Route.

WARNING

The military uses three adjoining areas of Dartmoor as training ranges where live ammunition is used. Tourist offices can outline their locations; they're also marked on Ordnance Survey (OS) maps. You're advised to check if the route you're planning falls within a range; if it does, find out if firing is taking place when you want to walk via the **Firing Information Service** (0800 458 4868; www.mod.uk/access). During the day, red flags fly at the edges of in-use ranges, while red flares burn at night. Even when there's no firing, beware of unidentified metal objects lying in the grass. Don't touch anything you find: note its position and report it to the **Commandant** (01837-650010).

Horse Riding

A number of local stables across the moor cater to all abilities.

Babeny Farm HORSE RIDING
(01364-631296; www.babenystables.co.uk; Poundsgate, near Ashburton; 1/2hr hack £25/50) A family-run farm that offers hacks, riding lessons and a rather British 'ride to the pub'.

Cholwell HORSE RIDING
(01822-810526; www.cholwellridingstables.co.uk; near Mary Tavy; 1/2hr £22/40) A family-run stables that caters for novices and experts. It's near an old silver mine on the edge of the moor near the village of Mary Tavy, about halfway between Okehampton and Tavistock.

Shilstone Rocks HORSE RIDING
(01364-621281; www.dartmoorstables.com; Widecombe-in-the-Moor; per 1/2hr £40/55) This experienced riding centre offers one- and two-hour hacks from its base near Widecombe (advance bookings are required). It also breeds Dartmoor ponies.

White-Water Sports

The raging River Dart makes Dartmoor a top spot for thrill seekers. Experienced kayakers can get permits from the Dartmoor National Park Authority. For white-water kayaking, go for Dynamic Adventures (p293), near Totnes. Rivers are only open from October to mid-March.

Climbing

Adventure Okehampton OUTDOORS
(01837-53916; www.adventureokehampton.com; Klondyke Rd, Okehampton; per day from £60; school holidays only) Runs wall- and rock-climbing sessions, plus activities including archery, abseiling and wild camping.

Information

Dartmoor National Park Authority (DNPA; www.dartmoor.gov.uk) The official national park site.

DNPA Haytor (01364-661520; 10am-5pm Apr-Sep, to 4pm Mar & Oct, 10.30am-3.30pm Thu-Sun Nov-Feb)

DNPA Postbridge (01822-880272; 10am-5pm Apr-Sep, to 4pm Mar & Oct, 10.30am-3.30pm Thu-Sun Nov-Feb)

Higher Moorland Tourist Office (DNPA; 01822-890414; www.dartmoor.gov.uk; Princetown; 10am-5pm Apr-Sep, to 4pm Mar & Oct, 10.30am-3.30pm Thu-Sun Nov-Feb)

Visit Dartmoor (www.visitdartmoor.co.uk)

Getting There & Around

Theoretically it's possible to get around Dartmoor by bus, but services can be frustratingly infrequent, and are very seasonal.

Tourist offices stock bus timetables; see also https://new.devon.gov.uk/travel.

Bus 98 (one daily Monday to Saturday) This is the only regular bus into the centre of the moor. It runs from Tavistock to Princetown, Two Bridges and Postbridge, then circles back to Yelverton. A couple of afternoon buses repeat the run as far as Princetown and back.

Bus 23 (first Saturday every month) Travels from Tavistock to Exeter via Princetown, Postbridge, Two Bridges and Moretonhampstead, but it only runs once a month.

Bus 6A (hourly Monday to Saturday, three Sunday) Skirts the northern edge of the moor en route from Bude to Exeter, stopping in Okehampton.

Bus 178 (two daily Monday to Saturday) Travels from Newton Abbot to Okehampton, via Bovey Tracey, Chagford and Morteonhampstead.

Haytor Hoppa Runs on Saturdays between June and September only, providing four buses between Newton Abbot, Bovey Tracey, Haytor and Widecombe-in-the-Moor (daily fare £5).

Princetown

POP 1767

Set in the heart of the remote, higher moor, Princetown is dominated by the grey, foreboding bulk of Dartmoor Prison and on bad weather days the town can have a bleak feel.

But it's also a useful insight into the harsh realities of moorland life and makes an atmospheric base for some excellent walks.

Sights

Higher Moorland Tourist Office INTERPRETATION CENTRE
(DNPA; ☎01822-890414; Tavistock Road, Princetown; ⌚10am-5pm daily Apr-Sep, to 4pm Mar & Oct, 10.30am-3.30pm Thu-Sun Nov-Feb) Heritage displays include those on tin workings, gunpowder factories and legends, and there's a stunning time-lapse video. The office used to be the Duchy Hotel; one former guest was Sir Arthur Conan Doyle, who went on to write *The Hound of the Baskervilles*. Dartmoor lore recounts local man Henry Baskerville took the novelist on a carriage tour, and the brooding landscape he encountered, coupled with legends of huge phantom dogs, inspired the thriller.

Dartmoor Prison Museum MUSEUM
(☎01822-322130; www.dartmoor-prison.co.uk; Princetown; adult/child £3.50/2.50; ⌚9.30am-4.30pm Mon-Thu & Sat, 9.30am-4pm Fri & Sun; P) In the early 1800s Princetown's jail was home to French and American prisoners of war, becoming a convict jail in 1850. Just up from the looming gates, this museum provides a chilling glimpse of life inside. Look out for straitjackets, manacles, escape stories and the makeshift knives made by modern prisoners. You can also book a guided walk (adult/child £6.50/5.50) that skirts the prison perimeter and heads into otherwise out-of-bounds French and American cemeteries.

The prison itself is still in use: it's currently home to around 640 inmates.

Sleeping & Eating

Prince of Wales PUB, HOSTEL £
(☎01822-890219; www.theprinceofwalesprincetown.co.uk; Tavistock Rd; dm/s/d £10/45/65; P) Roaring fires, low ceilings, a friendly landlord – the Prince is the place where everyone pops in for a pint of home-brewed Jail Ale and a plate of something hot and filling. But there's another reason to stop in. There are simple B&B rooms, and a bargain bunkhouse out the back, with unexpected luxuries including central heating and a drying room.

Tor Royal Farm B&B ££
(☎01822-890189; www.torroyal.co.uk; Tor Royal Lane, near Princetown; s £60, d £80-100; P 📶) An easygoing, country cottage–styled farmhouse packed with lived-in charm. The rooms are rather old-fashioned – cream-and-white furniture, puffy bedspreads, easy chairs – but they're very cosy, and the sumptuous afternoon tea (£14) is reason to stay here alone, with Victoria sponges, cupcakes and fancies galore.

Two Bridges HOTEL £££
(☎01822-892300; www.twobridges.co.uk; Two Bridges; r £120-230; P 📶) Perhaps the definitive historic moorland hotel: polished wood panels, huge inglenook fireplaces, and a guest list that includes Wallis Simpson, Winston Churchill and Vivien Leigh. The Premier and Historic rooms look positively museum worthy, with massive wooden four-poster beds and antique furniture aplenty; cheaper rooms are heavy on the florals. It's 1.5 miles northeast of Princetown.

Fox Tor Cafe CAFE £
(☎01822-890238; www.foxtorcafe.com; Two Bridges Rd; mains £3-12; ⌚9am-5pm Mon-Fri, 7.30am-5pm Sat, 7.30am-5pm Sun) Known as FTC to locals, this friendly little cafe is a favourite for hearty breakfasts, doorstep sandwiches and massive chunks of cake, but it does more filling fare too, such as spicy chillis and mushroom stroganoff. There's a basic bunkhouse (dorm £11) out the back where hikers and bikers stay.

Postbridge & Around

POP 170

The quaint hamlet of Postbridge owes its popularity, and its name, to its medieval stone slab or clapper bridge; a 13th-century structure with four, 3m-long slabs propped up on sturdy columns of stacked stones. Walking over takes you across the rushing East Dart River; a picturesque spot to whip off your boots and plunge your feet into water that's quite possibly never felt so cold.

Sleeping & Eating

Brimpts Farm B&B £
(☎0845 034 5968; www.brimptsfarm.co.uk; sites per person £5, s/d/f £42.50/65/97.50; P) A beauty of a Dartmoor farm, as traditional as afternoon tea, and all the better for it. There's a choice of sleeps: quaint, frilly B&B rooms, two camping fields or five timber-and-aluminium camping pods, all with bewitching moorland views. It does lovely grub, too: hearty breakfasts, packed lunches and cracking cream teas. It's off the B3357, Two Bridges–Dartmeet road.

DRIVING ON DARTMOOR

Dartmoor's roads are exciting to drive, but large stretches have unfenced grazing so you'll come across Dartmoor ponies, sheep and even cows in the middle of the road. Many sections have a 40mph speed limit. Car parks on the moor can be little more than lay-bys; their surface can be rough to very rough.

Dartmoor YHA HOSTEL £
(Bellever; ☎0845 371 9622; www.yha.org.uk; dm £19-23, q £59-89; P) A characterful former farm on the edge of a conifer plantation, with a huge kitchen, lots of rustic stone walls and cosy dorms. It also rents out bikes. It's a mile south of Postbridge.

Runnage Farm Camping Barns HUT £
(☎01822-880222; www.runnagecampingbarns.co.uk; dm £10; P) A couple of old barns on this handsome farm have been turned into bunkhouses, with basic raised beds, simple cooking facilities, and toilets and showers in a separate building. They can be centrally heated for £13 a night. There's another barn reserved for groups. It's 1.5 miles east of Postbridge: take the 'Widecombe' turning off the B3212 Moretonhampstead road.

★**Warren House Inn** PUB FOOD £
(www.warrenhouseinn.co.uk; mains £8.75-12.75; ⊙kitchen noon-8.30pm, shorter hours winter) Marooned amid miles of moorland, this Dartmoor institution exudes a hospitality only found in pubs in the middle of nowhere. A fire that's been burning (apparently) since 1845 warms stone floors, trestle tables and hikers munching robust food; the Warreners' Pie (local rabbit) is legendary. It's on the B3212, some 2 miles northeast of Postbridge. The bar's open 11am to 11pm.

Widecombe-in-the-Moor

POP 566

With its honey-grey buildings and imposing church tower, this is archetypal Dartmoor, down to the ponies grazing on the village green. The village is commemorated in the traditional English folk song of Widecombe Fair, a traditional country pageant that takes place on the second Tuesday of September.

Sights

St Pancras Church CHURCH
St Pancras' immense 40m tower has seen it dubbed the Cathedral of the Moor. Inside search out the boards telling the fire-and-brimstone tale of the violent storm of 1638 – it knocked a pinnacle from the roof, killing several parishioners. As ever on Dartmoor, the devil was blamed, said to be in search of souls.

Sleeping & Eating

Manor Cottage B&B £
(☎01364-621218; www.manorcottagedartmoor.co.uk; d £50-65; P 📶) Roses climb around the doorway of this quaint, ancient, village-centre cottage. The best billet is a bedroom-bathroom suite at the top of its own spiral staircase. Breakfasts feature berry compote, local sausages and eggs freshly laid by the hens clucking around outside.

★**Rugglestone Inn** PUB FOOD ££
(☎01364-621327; www.rugglestoneinn.co.uk; mains £11; ⊙meals served noon-2pm & 6.30-9pm) Just one pint at this wisteria-clad pub is enough to make you want to drop everything and move to Dartmoor. It's a classic wood-beamed, low-ceilinged, old-fashioned village boozer, full of local characters and packed with history. There are lots of real ales on tap, and the menu features pies, lasagne, quiches and potted crab.

Getting There & Away

Widecombe's bus service is woeful – bus 672 stops once a week (Wednesday) en route to Buckfastleigh and Newton Abbot. On summer Saturdays Widecombe is served by the Haytor Hoppa (p300).

Chagford & Moretonhampstead

With its wonky thatches and cream- and white-fronted buildings, Chagford clusters on the edge of Dartmoor around a picturesque square. But this apparently timeless moorland scene is also now home to some supremely stylish places to eat and sleep.

The bustling market town of Moretonhampstead sits 5 miles east.

Sights

★**Castle Drogo** HISTORIC BUILDING
(NT; ☎01647-433306; www.nationaltrust.org.uk; near Drewsteignton; adult/child £9/4.45; ⊙11am-5pm mid-Mar–Oct; P) Three miles northeast

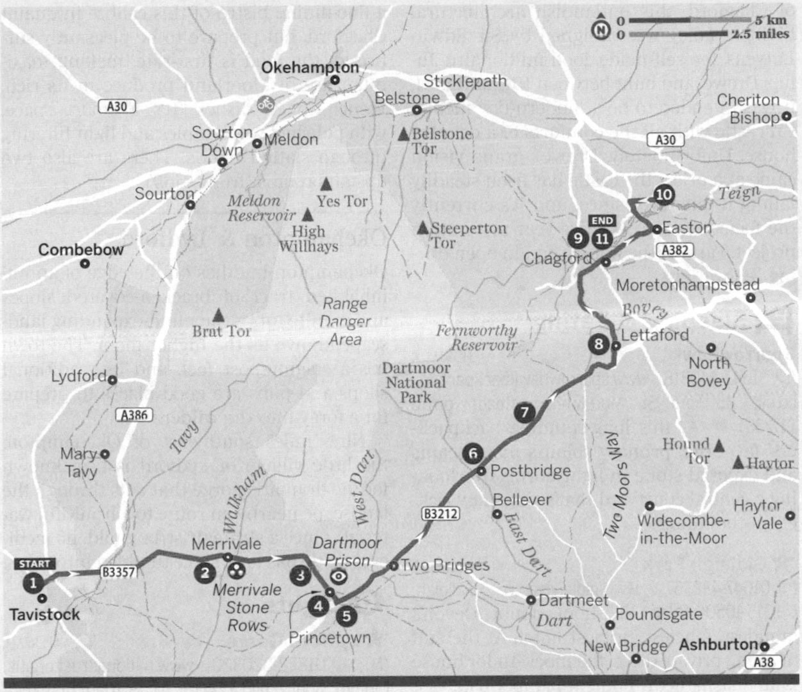

Driving Tour
A Dartmoor Road Trip

START TAVISTOCK
END CHAGFORD
LENGTH 20 MILES; ONE DAY

Driving on Dartmoor is like being inside a feature film: compelling 360-degree views are screened all around. This scenic, west-to-east transmoor traverse sweeps up and through this wilderness, taking in a bleak prison, prehistoric remains, a rustic pub and a unique castle.

Start by strolling among the fine 19th-century architecture of ❶ **Tavistock**, perhaps dropping by its Pannier Market to rummage for antiques. Next take the B3357 towards Princetown. It climbs steeply (expect ears to pop), crosses a cattle grid (a sign you're on the moor 'proper') and crests a hill to reveal swaths of honey-coloured tors. Soon you're at ❷ **Merrivale**. Park up on the right, just after the Dartmoor Inn, and stroll over the rise (due south) to discover a snaking stone row; a tiny stone circle and a standing stone are just 100m further on.

Back in the car, after a short climb, turn right towards Princetown, glimpsing the brooding bulk of Dartmoor Prison (you can't stop here; there's a better vantage point later). Call in at the ❸ **Dartmoor Prison Museum** (p301) to explore the jail's grim story. Cut through rugged ❹ **Princetown**, before picking up the B3212 towards Two Bridges; the ❺ **lay-by** immediately after you leave Princetown provides prime Dartmoor Prison views. As you follow signs for Moretonhampstead, an expansive landscape unfurls. At ❻ **Postbridge**, park and stroll over the 700-year-old bridge, then dangle hot feet in the cold River Dart. A few miles further on, the ❼ **Warren House Inn** (p302) makes an atmospheric spot for lunch. Around ❽ **Lettaford** take one of the signed, plunging lanes to ❾ **Chagford** to visit its quaint, thatch-dotted square. Scour some of its wonderfully old-fashioned shops, then head to ❿ **Castle Drogo** (p302) to explore a unique 1920s stately home. Finish the day back at Chagford at ⓫ **22 Mill Street** (p304); a truly classy spot to eat and sleep.

of Chagford, this outlandish architectural flight of fancy was designed by Sir Edwin Lutyens for self-made food-millionaire Julius Drewe, and built between 1911 and 1931, it was intended to be a modern-day medieval castle with all the comforts of a country house. Unfortunately, Drewe's grand vision came at a price: the castle has been steadily falling to bits ever since, and it's currently the focus of a massive five-year restoration project. Parts of the house remain open during renovations.

Sleeping & Eating

Sparrowhawk HOSTEL £
(☎01647-440318; www.sparrowhawkbackpackers.co.uk; 45 Ford St, Moretonhampstead; dm/d £17/38) At this long-standing backpackers' favourite, primary colours meet beams and exposed stone in light dorms overlooking a central courtyard that's ringed by rickety outbuildings.

★Gidleigh Park HOTEL £££
(☎01647-432367; www.gidleigh.com; Gidleigh; r £315-1050; P) Without doubt Devon's grandest, fanciest, priciest hotel. At the end of a long private drive, the mock-Tudor house is an unashamedly opulent pamper pad: vast suites with wet-room showers, luxurious lounges with crackling fires, and a stellar restaurant (lunch/dinner menu from £30/118) overseen by multiple-Michelin-starred Michael Wignall. It's 2 miles west of Chagford.

Horse GASTROPUB ££
(☎01647-440242; www.thehorsedartmoor.co.uk; 7 George St, Moretonhampstead; mains £5-19; food served 12.30-2.30pm Tue-Sat, 6.30-10pm daily) You've got to love a place that bills itself as a 'pub and nosebag'. Despite the village location, this is a hip gastropub that wouldn't feel out of place in the big city: it serves simple, well-done food including mussels, antipasti, chargrilled rib-eye and lots of pizzas.

Sandy Park INN ££
(☎01647-433267; www.sandyparkinn.co.uk; Sandy Park, Chagford; mains £8-12; 4-11pm Tue, noon-11pm Wed-Sat; P) This thatched pub is a good bet for no-nonsense, back-to-basics nosh that won't break the bank – battered haddock, beef lasagne and korma curry.

22 Mill Street RESTAURANT £££
(☎01647-432244; www.22millst.com; 22 Mill St, Chagford; 2-/3-course lunch menu £19/24, 2-/3-course dinner menu £36/42; noon-2.30pm & 7-9pm Wed-Sat) You might not be expecting a fine-dining bistro of this calibre in quaint Chagford, but prepare to be pleasantly surprised: the food is first-rate, making maximum use of Moorland produce in its rich, French-tinged dishes. It's a smart space, with polished wood tables and light filtering through slatted blinds. There are also two upstairs rooms (from £169).

Okehampton & Lydford

Okehampton huddles on the edge of an uninhabited tract of bracken-covered slopes and granite tors – the mind-expanding landscape known as the higher moor. The town has a staging-post feel, and its traditional shops and pubs are good places to prepare for a foray into the wilderness.

Nine miles southwest of Okehampton, the little village of Lydford is best known for the dramatic gorge that cuts through the landscape nearby en route to a beautiful waterfall. Once a strategic stronghold, its medieval castle has long since tumbled into ruins.

Sights

★Lydford Gorge WATERFALL
(NT; ☎01822-820320; www.nationaltrust.org.uk; Lydford; adult/child £7.40/3.70; 10am-5pm mid-Mar–Oct) This plunging gorge is the deepest in the southwest, and can be reached via a 1.5-mile rugged riverside hike past a series of bubbling whirlpools (including the fearsome Devil's Cauldron) to the thundering, 30m-high White Lady waterfall.

Okehampton Castle CASTLE
(EH; ☎01837-52844; www.english-heritage.org.uk; Castle Lodge, Okehampton; adult/child £5/3; 10am-5pm Apr-Oct, to 6pm Jul & Aug) The town's castle dates back to Norman times, strategically sited on top of a rocky escarpment. Once Devon's largest castle, it's now a picturesque ruin; little remains of the interior, but several of the stout exterior walls still stand.

Finch Foundry HISTORIC SITE
(NT; ☎01837-840046; www.nationaltrust.org.uk; Sticklepath; adult/child £5.60/2.80; 11am-5pm mid-Mar–Oct; P) A century ago, this dramatic building would have thundered to the sound of clanging hammers and grinding metal. It was one of the busiest tool factories in the southwest, turning out hundreds of chisels, knives, shears and scythes a day. Though it's not quite the industrial powerhouse of yesteryear, it's still a working forge, powered by three working watermills. You can drive

or cycle there, or follow a 4-mile (3½-hour) walk east along the Tarka Trail from Okehampton.

Sleeping & Eating

Okehampton Bracken Tor YHA HOSTEL £
(☎0844 293 0555; www.yha.org.uk/hostel/okehampton-bracken-tor; Saxongate; dm £24; reception 8-10am & 4-8pm; P @ wifi) Budget-conscious outdoors types love this one: a 100-year-old country house, set in 1.6-hectare grounds on the fringe of the higher moor – it also offers climbing, canoeing and bike hire. It's a mile south of Okehampton; be aware, there's another YHA hostel in Okehampton itself.

★**Dartmoor Inn** INN ££
(☎01822-820221; www.dartmoorinn.com; Moorside, Lydford; d £115; P) It might look venerable, but don't be fooled; behind the whitewashed exterior, this coaching inn is a thoroughly modern affair, light, bright and bang up to date. Most people stop in for the superb food, such as confit duck leg and butterflied lamb rump (mains £11.95 to £19.95), but it's worth spending the night: rooms sparkle with Roberts radios, sleigh beds and posh linens.

Castle INN ££
(☎01822-820241; www.castleinnlydford.com; Lydford; d £70-95; P wifi) With nearly five centuries of pint-pulling behind it (parts of the building date from the 16th century), this village inn has views of Lydford's castle to match its beamed, olde-worlde interior. The grub is hardly haute cuisine – steaks, beef-and-ale pies, beer-battered fish – but it's enough to stave off hunger after a long hike along the gorge. Chintzy rooms are also available.

Information

Tourist Office (☎01837-53020; www.everythingokehampton.co.uk; Museum Courtyard, 3 West St, Okehampton; 10am-5pm Mon-Sat Apr-Oct, to 4pm Mon, Fri & Sat Nov-Mar)

Croyde & Braunton

POP 8131

While surfers in Cornwall head for Newquay, bros and bro-ettes in Devon make a beeline for Croyde. Devon's north coast receives essentially the same swell as Cornwall's, but the scene is a lot less brash than around Newquay: here, the thatched cottages and pubs of the old village sit happily alongside the surf shops and wetsuit-hire firms. It's a fun, friendly mix, and ideal for some seaside fun.

The more run-of-the-mill market town of Braunton is 4 miles inland.

Sights & Activities

The water's hard to resist in Croyde. **Ralph's** (☎01271-890147; Hobbs Hill, Croyde; surfboard & wetsuit per 4/24hr £12/18, bodyboard & wetsuit £10/15; 9am-dusk mid-Mar–Dec) is among those hiring equipment. Lessons are provided by **Surf South West** (☎01271-890400; www.surfsouthwest.com; Croyde Burrows, Croyde; per half-/full day £34/64; Mar-Nov) and **Surfing Croyde Bay** (☎01271-891200; www.surfingcroydebay.co.uk; 8 Hobbs Hill, Croyde; per half-/full day £35/70).

★**Museum of British Surfing** MUSEUM
(☎01271-815155; www.museumofbritishsurfing.org.uk; Caen St, Braunton; adult/child £2/free; 11am-3pm Wed-Mon Easter-Dec) Few museums are this cool. Vibrant surfboards and vintage wetsuits line the walls, sepia images catch your eye. The stories are compelling: 18th-century British sailors riding Hawaiian waves; England's 1920s home-grown surf pioneers – here heritage meets hanging ten.

Braunton Burrows WILDLIFE RESERVE
(www.brauntonburrows.org; 24hr) FREE The vast network of dunes here is the UK's largest. Paths wind past sandy hummocks, salt marshes, purple thyme, yellow hawkweed and pyramidal orchids. The burrows were also the main training area for American troops before D-Day. Mock landing craft are still hidden in the tufted dunes near the car park at its southern tip.

Sleeping & Eating

★**Baggy** HOSTEL, B&B £
(www.baggys.co.uk; Baggy Point; dm/d from £35/110; wifi) It doesn't get much sleeker than this surf lodge–cum-cafe set right on the coast path beside Croyde Bay. The dorms are supersmart, the sea-view doubles positively boutiquey, and breakfast (served till 11am) can be eaten on decking watching the waves.

Ocean Pitch CAMPGROUND £
(☎07581 024348; www.oceanpitch.co.uk; Moor Lane, Croyde; sites per 2 adults £26-30; mid-Jun–Sep; P wifi) A surfers' favourite, set at the northern end of Croyde Bay with brilliant views of the breakers. If you don't feel like pitching, you can rent a pre-erected bell tent

(£85 per night, two-night minimum) or even a classic VW camper (£99 per night, two-night minimum).

Thatch INN ££
(☎01271-890349; www.thethatchcroyde.com; 14 Hobbs Hill, Croyde; d £60-110, f £130) A legendary venue among surfers, this cavernous, thatched pub's trendy bedrooms feature subtle creams, stripes and checks; the owners offer extra rooms above another pub and in the cottage opposite. The pick, though, are at their nearby (quieter) Priory, where elegant beams frame exposed stone. Decent pub grub, too (mains £9.95 to £14.95).

Devonia Cottage B&B ££
(☎01271-891434; www.devoniacottage.com; 32 St Marys Rd, Braunton; d £95-105;) Far and away the best B&B in Braunton, this bewitching place is run by a husband-and-wife team who've previously run a chalet in the Alps, so they know how to look after guests. The two rooms feel up to date but still have country touches such as hefty beams and pine doors – we liked Mavericks for its Velux skylights and cosy spot under the eaves.

Information

Tourist Office (☎01271-816688; www.visitbraunton.co.uk; Caen St, Braunton; 10am-3pm Mon-Fri, to 1pm Sat) Inside Braunton's museum.

Ilfracombe & Around

POP 11,509

If there's anywhere that sums up the faded grandeur of the British seaside, it's surely Ilfracombe. Framed by precipitous cliffs, elegant town houses, crazy golf greens and a promenade strung with twinkling lights, it's a place that sometimes seems pickled in a bygone age. But look beneath the surface and you'll find there's another side to Ilfracombe – it's a favourite hang-out for the artist Damien Hirst, who's donated a controversial statue to the seafront, and is now home to some intriguing eateries. St-Tropez it may not be, but Ilfracombe deserves a look.

Sights & Activities

★Verity LANDMARK
(The Pier) FREE Pregnant, naked and holding aloft a huge spear, Damien Hirst's 20m statue, *Verity*, towers above Ilfracombe's harbour mouth. On the seaward side her skin is peeled back, revealing sinew, fat and foetus. Critics say she detracts from the scenery, the artist says she's an allegory for truth and justice. Either way, she's drawing the crowds.

Ilfracombe Aquarium AQUARIUM
(☎01271-864533; www.ilfracombeaquarium.co.uk; The Pier; adult/child £4.50/3.50; 10am-4.30pm, to 5.45pm late Jul & Aug) Recreates aquatic environments from Exmoor to the Atlantic, via estuary, rock pool and harbour.

★Tunnelsbeaches SWIMMING
(☎01271-879882; www.tunnelsbeaches.co.uk; Granville Rd; adult/child £2.50/1.95; 10am-5pm Apr-Jun, Sep & Oct, to 7pm Jul & Aug) It was a remarkable feat – in 1823 hundreds of Welsh miners hacked, by hand, the four tunnels here out of solid rock. They lead to a strip of beach where you can still plunge into the sea from Victorian tidal bathing pools.

Sleeping & Eating

Ocean Backpackers HOSTEL £
(☎01271-867835; www.oceanbackpackers.co.uk; 29 St James Pl; dm £16-19, d £42-48, f £68-75; P@) Brightly painted en-suite dorms, a convivial kitchen and free coffee lend this long-established indie hostel a laid-back vibe; the giant world map in the lounge has kick-started countless travellers' tales. The doubles and family rooms are great value.

★Norbury House B&B ££
(☎01271-863888; www.norburyhouse.co.uk; Torrs Park; d £85-110, f £120-145; P) Each of the rooms in this gorgeous guesthouse is done up in a different style: choose from pop art, art deco or contemporary chic. Fabulous soft furnishings, a light-filled sitting room (complete with baby grand piano), charming hosts and cracking sea-and-town views seal the deal.

Olive Branch & Room BISTRO ££
(☎01271-879005; www.olivebranchguesthouse.co.uk; 56 Fore St; mains £21-23; 6.30-9pm Tue-Sat;) Up-and-coming chef Thomas Carr (a protégé of Nathan Outlaw) has recently taken over the reigns of this smart bistro-B&B, so you can expect top-class seafood and other refined dishes served in an intimate Georgian town-house setting. The upstairs rooms are lovely too (doubles £85 to £105), spacious and stylish, with grandstand bay views.

The Quay EUROPEAN ££
(☎01271-868090; www.11thequay.co.uk; 11 The Quay; mains £15-25; 10am-10pm) Ilfracombe's hippest harbourside hang-out by far is owned

by artist Damien Hirst (he of the cut-in-half cows and pickled sharks). His creations line the walls, so you get to tuck into lobster macaroni or Exmoor Angus steaks while studying models of his statue *Verity* and, with delicious irony, fish in formaldehyde.

Information

Tourist Office (☎01271-863001; www.visit-ilfracombe.co.uk; The Seafront; ⏲9.30am-4.30pm Mon-Fri, from 10.30am Sat & Sun) Inside the Landmark Theatre.

Getting There & Away

Services include the following:

Bus 21/21A (half-hourly Monday to Saturday, hourly Sunday) Runs to Barnstaple (£2.40, 40 minutes) via Braunton (£1.80).

Bus 300 Heads to Lynton and Lynmouth (£3.80, 45 minutes) twice on Saturday and once on Sunday.

Clovelly

POP 440

Clovelly is the quintessential, picture-postcard Devon village. Its cottages cascade down cliffs to meet a curving crab claw of a harbour that is lined with lobster pots and set against a deep-blue sea. A clutch of impossibly picturesque inns and B&Bs makes it even harder to leave.

Sights & Activities

Clovelly Historic Village HISTORIC SITE
(www.clovelly.co.uk; adult/child £7/4.40; ⏲9am-6.30pm Jun-Sep, 9.30am-5pm Apr, May & Oct, 10am-4pm Nov-Mar; P) Clovelly is privately owned, and admission is charged at the hilltop visitor centre. The village's cobbled streets are so steep that cars can't cope, so supplies are still brought in by sledge; you'll see these big bread baskets on runners leaning outside homes. Charles Kingsley, author of the children's classic *The Water Babies,* spent much of his early life in Clovelly – don't miss his former **house**, or the highly atmospheric **fisherman's cottage** and the village's twin **chapels**.

Sleeping & Eating

Donkey Shoe Cottage B&B £
(☎01237-431601; www.donkeyshoecottage.co.uk; 21 High St; s/d £30/60) A country-style B&B plumb on Clovelly's crazily steep hill, with wooden floors, raspberry-red walls and sea views – the best is from room 3, under the eaves.

★**Berridon Farm** CAMPGROUND ££
(☎01409-241552; www.berridonfarm.co.uk; near Bradworthy; 3 nights £400-680, 7 nights £500-1060; ⏲Easter–mid-Oct; P) At Berridon, camping goes seriously comfy. Here five- or six-person, insulated safari-style tents sport a leather sofa and wood-burner oven, plus proper beds and a flushing toilet. If it's wet, head for the shabby-chic sitting-eating-playing space in a converted barn. It's all tucked away 11 miles south of Clovelly.

Red Lion INN £££
(☎01237-431237; www.stayatclovelly.co.uk/red-lion; d £156-190) The best of the village's brace of inns, in a super waterside position with quaint, low-ceilinged rooms offering a choice of aspects: big, blue sea views, or an equally sweet outlook across the harbour front. It's plush and rather old-fashioned, and there's a choice of settings for dinner: the atmospheric bar for pub grub, or a smarter dining room for formal food.

Information

Clovelly Visitor Centre (☎01237-431781; www.clovelly.co.uk; ⏲9am-6.30pm Jun-Sep, 9.30am-5pm Apr, May & Oct, 10am-4pm Nov-Mar) The visitor centre and ticket office is at the entrance to the village.

Getting There & Away

Bus 319 (five daily Monday to Saturday) runs between Clovelly, Hartland Village, Bideford (£2.20, 40 minutes) and Barnstaple (£3, one hour). This bus goes to Bude (£3.80, one daily Monday to Saturday) in the opposite direction.

BRISTOL

POP 442,500

If ever there was a British city on the rise, it's Bristol. Once a centre for heavy industry, over the last few decades the southwest's largest city has reinvented itself as a hub of culture and creativity. From Clifton's iconic suspension bridge to Brunel's groundbreaking steamship, the SS *Great Britain,* it's a city that's awash with historical interest. But Bristol is also known for its offbeat, alternative character, and you'll find a wealth of art collectives, community-run cafes and music venues dotted around – not to mention murals left behind by the city's most notorious son, the mischievous street artist Banksy.

Throw in the revamped harbourside, the landmark new M Shed history museum and

Bristol

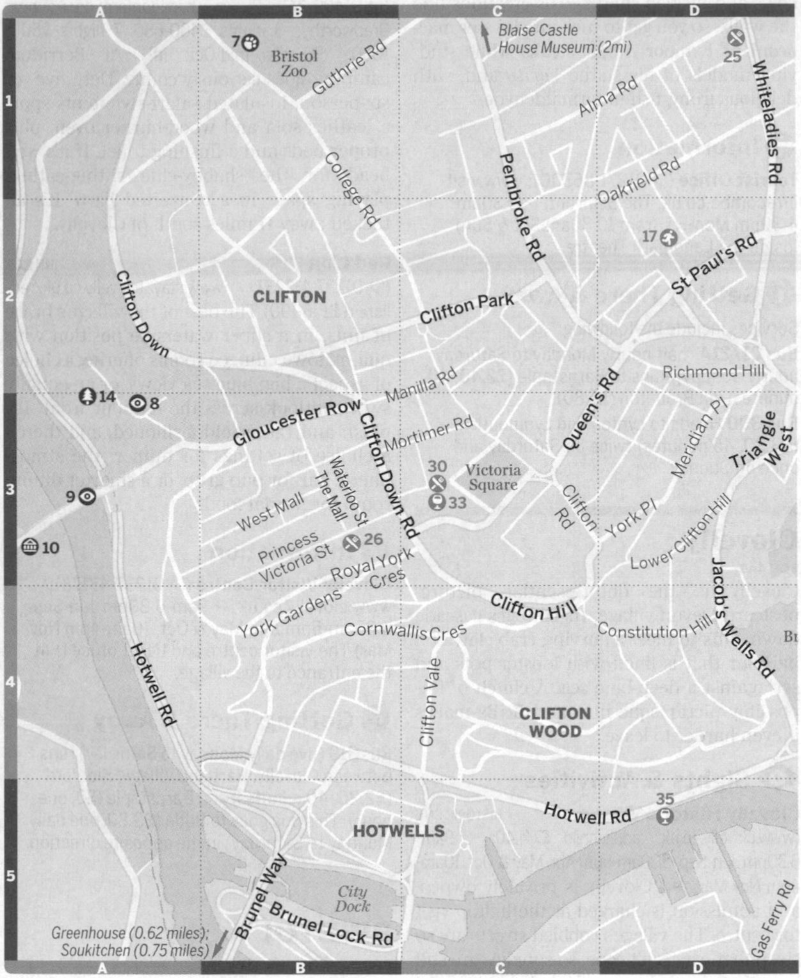

a fast-growing foodie reputation, and it's little wonder that Bristol was recently named Britain's most liveable city. Gert lush, as they might say round these parts.

History

The city began as a Saxon village and developed into the medieval river port of Brigstow, an important trading centre for cloth and wine.

In 1497 'local hero' John Cabot (actually a Genoese sailor called Giovanni Caboto) sailed from Bristol to discover Newfoundland in 1497. The city subsequently become one of Britain's major ports, growing rich on the 'Triangular Trade', in which African slaves were shipped across the Atlantic to New World colonies, where they were bartered for luxury goods such as sugar, rum, tobacco and cotton that fetched a healthy profit back home. Much of Bristol's 18th-century splendour – including Clifton's terraces and the Old Vic theatre – were partly financed on profits from the trade.

After being usurped by rival ports in London and Liverpool, Bristol repositioned itself as an industrial and shipbuilding centre, and in 1840 became the western terminus

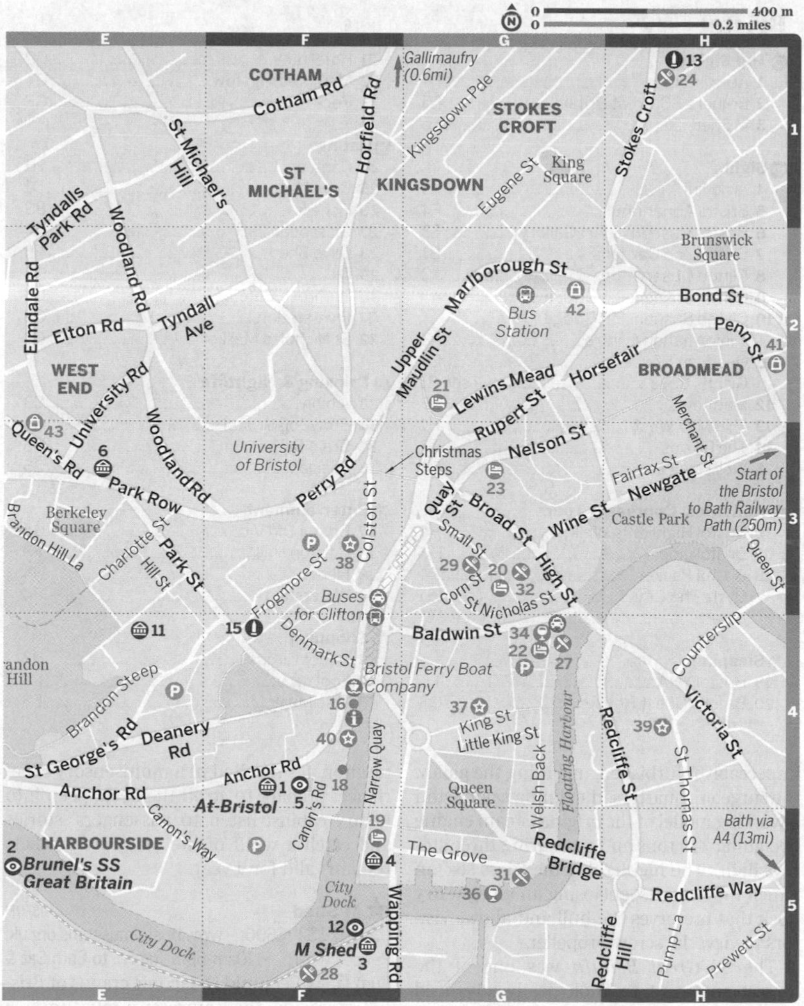

for the newly built Great Western Railway line from London.

In the early 20th century, local engineers pioneered the development of a groundbreaking aeroplane design known as the Bristol Boxkite, and the city became a hub for aeronautics; many parts for Concorde were made in nearby Filton. Unfortunately, Bristol's industrial importance made it a target for German bombing during WWII, and much of the city centre and harbourside was reduced to rubble.

In 2006, the city celebrated the bicentenary of the birth of Isambard Kingdom Brunel, the pioneering Victorian engineer responsible for (among many other things) the Great Western Railway, the Clifton Suspension Bridge and SS *Great Britain*.

Sights

★Brunel's SS Great Britain HISTORIC SITE
(☎0117-926 0680; www.ssgreatbritain.org; Great Western Dock, Gas Ferry Rd; adult/child £14/8; ⏲10am-5.30pm Apr-Oct, to 4.30pm Nov-Mar) Bristol's pride and joy is the mighty, innovative steamship, the SS *Great Britain,* designed by engineering genius Isambard Kingdom Brunel in 1843. The ship's interior has been

Bristol

Top Sights
1 At-Bristol F4
2 Brunel's SS Great Britain E5
3 M Shed F5

Sights
4 Arnolfini F5
5 Bristol Aquarium F4
6 Bristol Museum & Art Gallery E3
7 Bristol Zoo Gardens B1
8 Clifton Observatory A3
9 Clifton Suspension Bridge A3
10 Clifton Suspension Bridge Information Centre A3
11 Georgian House E4
Giant's Cave .... (see 8)
12 Matthew F5
13 Mild Mild West H1
14 The Downs A3
15 Well Hung Lover F4

Activities, Courses & Tours
16 Bristol Highlights Walk F4
17 Bristol Lido D2
18 Bristol Packet F4
Cycle The City .... (see 16)
Lanes .... (see 23)

Sleeping
19 Bristol YHA F5
20 Brooks Guest House G3
21 Hotel du Vin G2
22 Mercure Brigstow G4
23 Rock n' Bowl G3

Eating
24 Canteen H1
25 Cowshed D1
26 Fishers B3
27 Glassboat G4
28 Olive Shed F5
29 Ox G3
30 Primrose Café C3
31 Riverstation G5
32 St Nicholas Market G3

Drinking & Nightlife
33 Albion C3
34 BrewDog Bristol G4
35 Grain Barge D5
36 Thekla G5

Entertainment
37 Bristol Old Vic G4
38 Colston Hall F3
39 Fleece H4
40 Watershed F4

Shopping
41 Cabot Circus H2
42 Loot G2
43 Rise Music E3

impeccably refurbished, including the galley, the surgeon's quarters, the dining saloon and a working model of the original steam engine (weighing 340 tons and measuring three storeys high). The highlight is the 'glass sea' on which the ship sits, enclosing an airtight dry dock that preserves the hull and allows visitors to view the screw propeller.

The SS *Great Britain* was one of the largest and most technologically advanced steamships ever built, measuring 98m from stern to tip. The ship has had a chequered history. Between 1843 and 1886, she served her intended duty as a passenger liner, completing the transatlantic crossing between Bristol and New York in just 14 days. Unfortunately, enormous running costs and mounting debts led her towards an ignominious fate: she was eventually sold off and subsequently served as a troop vessel, quarantine ship, emigration transport and coal hulk, before finally being scuttled near Port Stanley in the Falklands in 1937.

Happily, that wasn't the end. The ship was towed back to Bristol in 1970, and has since undergone an impressive 30-year restoration. It's resulted in a multisensory experience: prepare to stroll the deck, peep into luxury cabins, listen to passengers' stories and catch a whiff of life on board. Tickets remain valid for a year.

★M Shed MUSEUM
(☎0117-352 6600; www.bristolmuseums.org.uk; Princes Wharf; ⏰10am-5pm Tue-Fri, to 6pm Sat & Sun) **FREE** Set amid the iconic cranes of Bristol's dockside, this impressive museum is a treasure trove of memorabilia. The exhibits are divided into three sections (People, Place and Life), and provide a panoramic overview of Bristol's history – from slaves' possessions and vintage buses to Wallace and Gromit figurines and a set of decks once used by Massive Attack.

Banksy's unsettling *Grim Reaper* stencil was right on the waterline of the party boat *Thekla*, but it was removed amid much controversy and now sits on the 1st floor.

It's all highly interactive and child-friendly. In summer, look out for special weekend activities including the chance to ride on the dock cranes, watch the old Pyronaut fireboat in action or catch a lift aboard one of the world's oldest steam tugs (see the website for times). The museum also runs guided tours exploring the harbour's history.

Matthew HISTORIC SITE
(☎0117-927 6868; www.matthew.co.uk; Princes Wharf; ⏰10am-4pm Tue-Sun Mar-Oct, Sat & Sun Nov-Feb) FREE The most striking thing about this replica of the vessel in which John Cabot made his landmark voyage from Bristol to Newfoundland in 1497 is its size. At 24m it seems far too small, but it would have carried a crew of around 18. Step aboard to climb below into their quarters, walk the deck and gaze up at the rigging.

Arnolfini GALLERY
(☎0117-917 2300; www.arnolfini.org.uk; 16 Narrow Quay; ⏰10am-6pm Tue-Sun) FREE The city's avant-garde art gallery occupies a hulking warehouse by the river, and remains the top venue in town for modern art, as well as occasional exhibitions of dance, film and photography.

Bristol Aquarium AQUARIUM
(☎0117-929 8929; www.bristolaquarium.co.uk; Harbourside; adult/child £14.50/10; ⏰10am-5pm) The underwater habitats you'll encounter here include a Bay of Rays, a Coral Sea, a Shark Tank and an Amazon River Zone. The underwater viewing tunnel adds extra appeal. There's a £2 discount per ticket for buying online.

★ At-Bristol MUSEUM
(☎0845 345 1235; www.at-bristol.org.uk; Anchor Rd; adult/child £14.60/9.40; ⏰10am-5pm Mon-Fri, to 6pm Sat & Sun) Bristol's interactive science museum has zones featuring space, technology, sport, the sea and the human brain. In the Curiosity Zone you get to walk through a tornado, spin on a human gyroscope and strum the strings of a virtual harp. There's also a 3D planetarium with evening stargazing shows. It's fun, interactive, and should keep you and the kids entertained for hours.

Georgian House HISTORIC BUILDING
(www.bristolmuseums.org.uk; 7 Great George St; ⏰11am-4pm Sat-Tue Apr-Oct) FREE Once the home of the wealthy West India merchant John Pinney, this 18th-century house provides an evocative insight into aristocratic life in Bristol during the Georgian era. It's decorated in period style, typified by the huge kitchen (complete with cast-iron roasting spit), book-lined library and grand drawing rooms, as well as Pinney's cold-water plunge-pool in the basement.

Bristol Museum & Art Gallery MUSEUM
(☎0117-922 3571; www.bristolmuseums.org.uk; Queen's Rd; ⏰10am-5pm Mon-Fri, to 6pm Sat & Sun) FREE You're in for a few surprises at this classic old Edwardian museum. Look out for the *Paint-Pot Angel* by world-famous street artist Banksy in the entrance hall; a funerary statue with an upturned pink paint pot on her head, she's designed to challenge our expectations of museum exhibits and the value of art. It's also a reminder of the artist's hugely popular 2009 exhibition here. Just above sits the Bristol Boxkite, a prototype propeller-powered biplane, which dangles from the ceiling.

Clifton Suspension Bridge BRIDGE
(www.cliftonbridge.org.uk) Clifton's most famous (and photographed) landmark is the 76m-high Clifton Suspension Bridge, which spans the Avon Gorge. It was designed by master engineer Isambard Kingdom Brunel with construction beginning in 1836, although Brunel died before its completion in 1864. It's free to walk or cycle across; car drivers pay a £1 toll.

There's an **information centre** (www.cliftonbridge.org.uk; ⏰10am-5pm) near the tower on the Leigh Woods side. Free bridge tours take place at 3pm on Saturday and Sunday from Easter to October.

The Downs PARK
(👪🐾) The grassy parks of Clifton Down and Durdham Down (often referred to as just the Downs) fan out from the Clifton Suspension Bridge and make a fine spot for a picnic. Nearby, the **Clifton Observatory** (☎0117-974 1242; www.cliftonobservatory.com; Litfield Rd, Clifton Down; adult/child £2.50/1.50; ⏰10am-5pm Feb-Oct, to 4pm Nov-Jan) houses a **camera obscura** and a tunnel leading down to the **Giant's Cave**, a natural cavern that emerges halfway down the cliff with dizzying views across the Avon Gorge.

Bristol Zoo Gardens ZOO
(☎0117-974 7399; www.bristolzoo.org.uk; Cecil Rd; adult/child £17/11; ⏰9am-5.30pm; P) Highlights at the city's award-winning zoo include a family of eight western lowland gorillas (bossed by silverback Jock) and the Seal and Penguin Coast, where African penguins, eider ducks and South American fur seals lounge around. There's also a reptile and bug zone, a butterfly forest, a lion

enclosure, a monkey jungle and the **Zooropia** (adult/child £8/7) treetop adventure park. Online tickets are 15% cheaper. To get here from the city centre, catch bus 8/9.

Activities

Lanes BOWLING

(☎ 0117-325 1979; www.thelanesbristol.co.uk; Nelson St; games £4-6; ⏰ noon-11pm Sun-Thu, to 2am Fri & Sat) The five vintage Brunswick lanes at this boutique bowling alley are all gleaming metal and polished wood. You'll also find a craft-beer bar and huge, crispy New York–style pizzas.

Bristol Packet BOATING

(☎ 0117-926 8157; www.bristolpacket.co.uk; Wapping Wharf, Gas Ferry Rd) This boat company cruises around the harbour area (adult/child £6/4, six sailings daily April to October, and on winter weekends). There are also weekly cruises to the spectacular Avon Gorge from April to September (adult/child £17/13) and a Sunday afternoon trip to Beese's Tea Gardens (£13/8, runs April to September). Cruises to Bath (£28.50/21) run once a month from May to September.

Cycle the City CYCLING

(☎ 07873-387167; www.cyclethecity.org; 1 Harbourside; tours £15) These 1½-hour bike tours of Bristol's expansive harbourside are an ideal way to take in the city's main waterfront sights. The fee includes bike, helmet and an expert guide. The same firm also rents out bikes (per day £16). They don't have a shop, so bike hire and tours need to be prebooked. The bike collection point, and starting point for the tours, is No 1 Harbourside.

Bristol Highlights Walk WALKING

(www.bristolwalks.co.uk; adult/child £6/3; ⏰ 11am Sat Mar-Nov) Tours the old town, city centre and harbourside, leaving from the tour-

BANKSY – STREET ARTIST

If there's one Bristolian nearly everyone has heard of, it's **Banksy** (www.banksy.co.uk) – the guerrilla street artist whose distinctive stencilled style and provocative artworks have earned him worldwide notoriety.

Though his true identity is a secret, it's believed Banksy was born in 1974 in Yate, 12 miles from Bristol, and honed his artistic skills in a local graffiti outfit. His works take a wry view of 21st-century culture – especially capitalism, consumerism and the cult of celebrity. Among his best-known pieces are the production of spoof banknotes (featuring Princess Diana's head instead of the Queen's), a series of murals on Israel's West Bank barrier (depicting people digging holes under and climbing ladders over the wall) and a painting of a caveman pushing a shopping trolley at the British Museum (which the museum promptly claimed for its permanent collection). His documentary *Exit Through the Gift Shop,* about an LA street artist, was nominated for an Oscar in 2011.

Long despised by the authorities, Banksy has become an unlikely tourist magnet. Though many of his works are short-lived, a good few still survive around the city. The **Well Hung Lover** (Frogmore St) depicts an angry husband, a two-timing wife, and a naked man dangling from a window. The startling **Paint-Pot Angel** (think pink paint meets funerary monument) resides in the foyer of the **Bristol Museum & Art Gallery** (p311) and is a reminder of the artist's hugely popular 2009 exhibition there. **Mild Mild West** (80 Stokes Croft) features a Molotov cocktail–wielding teddy bear facing three riot police and is thought to be a wry comment on Bristol's edgy-yet-comfy vibe. A stencil of the **Grim Reaper** rowing a boat, which used to sit right on the waterline of the party boat the *Thekla*, is now on the 1st floor of the city's **M Shed Museum** (p310). There are other artworks further out from the city centre; the **tourist office** (p316) sells an excellent Banksy info sheet (50p) and can advise on locations.

Banksy hit the headlines once more in 2014 when one of his murals unexpectedly appeared on a wooden panel outside the Broad Plain Boys' Club. Known as **Mobile Lovers**, the mural depicted a young couple who appear to be embracing but are actually staring into their phones. Predictably enough, a furore over ownership ensued, but the artist made it clear that he had painted the mural as a gift to the boys' club (which he's thought to have attended as a young man). After a few months on display at the Bristol City Museum, the work was sold for £400,000 to a private collector in August 2014, with all the proceeds going to fund the boys' club's ongoing projects. Good on ya, Banksy.

ist office (p316) – there's no need to book. Themed tours exploring Clifton, medieval Bristol and the history of Bristol's slave and wine trades run on request.

Festivals & Events

Bristol Shakespeare Festival THEATRE
(www.bristolshakespeare.org.uk; Jul) One of Britain's biggest outdoor festivals devoted to the Bard runs throughout July.

Encounters FILM
(www.encounters-festival.org.uk; Sep) Bristol's largest film fest.

Sleeping

Bristol YHA HOSTEL £
(0845 371 9726; www.yha.org.uk; 14 Narrow Quay; dm £13-22, d £30-70; @) Few hostels can boast a position as good as this one, beside the river in a red-brick warehouse. Facilities include kitchens, a cycle store, a games room and the excellent Grainshed coffee lounge. As ever, the dorms are fairly functional, while the doubles can be expensive.

Rock n' Bowl HOSTEL £
(0117-325 1980; www.thelanesbristol.co.uk/hostel; 22 Nelson St; dm £13-18, d £45;) A cheery, well-run backpackers' favourite set in a rambling 1930s building, with street art covering the walls, a table-tennis table in the huge chill-out room, and free breakfast.

Brooks Guest House B&B ££
(0117-930 0066; www.brooksguesthousebristol.com; Exchange Ave; d £90-130, trailers £100-105;) Improbable as it seems, three vintage Airstream trailers sit on the AstroTurf of the bijou roof garden at this central Bristol B&B. They're predictably tiny but still feature seating areas and pocket-sized bathrooms. In the guesthouse, bedrooms are compact but pleasing, with olive colour schemes and tartan throws.

Greenhouse B&B ££
(0117-902 9166; www.thegreenhousebristol.co.uk; 61 Greenbank Rd; s/d £85/115; P) No bells and whistles here – just a lovely, friendly, quiet B&B in Southville, a few minutes' stride to the river and the centre. Cream rooms, white sheets and an excellent organic breakfast make it well worth considering. The free parking is a real bonus.

Mercure Brigstow HOTEL ££
(0117-929 1030; www.mercure.com; Welsh Back; d £90-200;) A harbourside location and attractive modern design make the Mercure a good, central option. All rooms boast 'floating' beds, curved panel walls and tiny TVs set into bathroom tiles (gimmicky, yes, but fun). The cheaper rooms face the back, the pricier ones look out over the water; some have balconies and pod coffee machines.

★ **Number 38** B&B £££
(01179-466 905; www.number38clifton.com; 38 Upper Belgrave Rd, Clifton; s/ste £115/180, d £130-165; P) Perched on the edge of the Downs, this upmarket B&B is *the* choice for style-conscious travellers. The rooms are huge and contemporary – sombre greys and smooth blues dictate the palette, luxury is provided by waffle bathrobes and designer bath goodies, and city views unfold from the roof terrace. The two suites have gleaming, old-fashioned metal baths.

Hotel du Vin HOTEL £££
(0117-403 2979; www.hotelduvin.com; Narrow Lewins Mead; d £145-170, ste £194-260; P) This luxury British hotel brand is a fave with well-heeled city-breakers. Their Bristol outpost occupies an old sugar warehouse, and mixes industrial chic and sleek minimalism: exposed brick and iron pillars meet futon beds and claw-foot baths. The rooms are named after vintage champagnes; the best are the split-level mezzanine suites.

The stylish bistro is great, too.

Eating

Canteen CAFE £
(0117-923 2017; www.canteenbristol.co.uk; 80 Stokes Croft; mains £4-10; 10am-midnight Mon-Thu, to 1am Fri & Sat, to 11pm Sun;) Occupying the ground floor of an old office block, this community-run cafe sums up Bristol's alternative character: it's all about slow food, local suppliers and fair prices, whether you pop in for a bacon butty, veggie chilli or sit-down supper. It's not signed on the outside – look out for the hipsters on the terrace and the lettering: Hamilton House.

St Nicholas Market MARKET £
(www.stnicholasmarketbristol.co.uk; Corn St; 9.30am-5pm Mon-Sat) The city's lively street market has a bevy of food stalls selling everything from mezze platters to pulled-pork rolls from barbecue specialists **Grillstock**. Lines can be long at lunchtime, but it's worth the wait. Look out too for the Wednesday **farmers markets**.

Olive Shed BISTRO £
(☎0117-929 1960; www.theoliveshed.com; Princes Wharf; mains £4-8; ⏰11am-10pm Tue-Sat, to 4pm Sun) With tables right beside Bristol's Floating Harbour, this rustic eatery is a top spot for a waterfront lunch. It serves tapas and twists on Mediterranean food; think cured and torched mackerel, mushrooms made pungent by smoked garlic, and smoked chicken made spicy by harissa.

★**Riverstation** BRITISH ££
(☎0117-914 4434; www.riverstation.co.uk; The Grove; lunch 2/3 courses £14/17, dinner mains £15-18; ⏰noon-2.30pm & 6-10.30pm) Riverstation is one of Bristol's original dining-out destinations, and still leads the pack. The waterside location is hard to beat, with a view over the Floating Harbour, but it's the food that keeps the punters coming back: classic in style with a strong European flavour, from French fish soup to steak *à la béarnaise*.

Fishers SEAFOOD ££
(☎0117-974 7044; www.fishers-restaurant.com; 35 Princess Victoria St; mains £14-25; ⏰noon-3pm & 5.30-10pm daily, closed Mon lunch) Bristol's top choice for fish dishes rustles up everything from pan-fried sea bass with chorizo to succulent grilled whole lobster. The hot shellfish platter (£46 for two people) is made for sharing. The simple setting, with its white-washed walls, ships' lanterns and nautical knick-knacks, adds to the maritime vibe.

Cowshed BRITISH ££
(☎0117-973 3550; www.thecowshedbristol.com; 46 Whiteladies Rd; 2/3-course lunch £11/13, dinner mains £14-26; ⏰noon-2.45pm & 6-10pm Mon-Sat, noon-4pm & 6.30-9.15pm Sun) Country food with a modern twist is served at the Cowshed. The focus is on quality, locally sourced meat – aged beef, wild rabbit, pork belly, plus the *pièce de résistance*, 'steak on stone', served sizzling on a hot lava rock. The three-course lunch is excellent value.

Primrose Café BISTRO ££
(☎0117-946 6577; www.primrosecafe.co.uk; 1 Boyce's Ave; lunch mains £7-9, dinner mains £14-20; ⏰9am-5pm & 6-10pm Tue-Sat, 9.30am-3pm Sun, 9am-5pm Mon) A Clifton classic, as perfect for morning coffee as for a proper sit-down dinner. With its pavement tables and wooden interior, it feels like a Bristolian version of a Parisian street cafe. It's particularly choice for breakfast: the eggs Benedict and Belgian waffles are legendary.

Ox BRITISH ££
(☎0117-922 1001; www.theoxbristol.com; The Basement, 43 Corn St; mains £13-29; ⏰noon-2.30pm Mon-Fri, 5-10.30pm Mon-Sat, noon-4pm Sun) Gorgeous, highly polished wood, glinting brass, low lighting and cool jazz ensure this sleek eatery resembles a posh Pullman dining car that's somehow been bestowed with some Pre-Raphaelite murals. The food is aimed firmly at the carnivores; expect charcuterie platters, gourmet burgers and five choices of steak cut.

It's very easy to miss – look for the marble stairs winding down beneath the Wetherspoon pub.

Soukitchen MIDDLE EASTERN ££
(☎0117-966 6880; www.soukitchen.co.uk; 277 North St; mains £8-14; ⏰noon-2.30pm Wed-Sun, 5.30-9pm Tue-Sun) Middle Eastern market food is the stock-in-trade at this friendly diner in Southville, with characteristic dishes such as borek (filo pies stuffed with meat or vegetables), mix-and-match mezze platters and flame-grilled kebabs. Honest food with heart.

Glassboat FRENCH ££
(☎0117-332 3971; www.glassboat.co.uk; Welsh Back; lunch 2/3 courses £10/12, dinner mains £17-21; ⏰8-11.30am, noon-3pm & 5.30-10pm daily,

WORTH A TRIP

TYNTESFIELD HOUSE

Formerly the aristocratic home of the Gibbs family, **Tyntesfield** (NT; ☎01275-461900; www.nationaltrust.org.uk; Wraxall; adult/child £14/7, gardens only £9/4.50; ⏰house 10am-6pm Mar-Oct, 11am-3pm Nov-Feb, gardens 10am-5pm year-round) is one of the National Trust's most important acquisitions of recent years. A fairy-tale mansion bristling with pinnacles and turrets, brimful of sweeping staircases and cavernous, antique-filled rooms, the house gives an insight into the lavish lives once enjoyed by England's aristocratic families. Entry is via timed ticket and includes a guided tour. The house is 7 miles southwest of Bristol, off the B3128.

LOCAL KNOWLEDGE

BRISTOL LIDO

Bath isn't the only southwestern city with its own outdoor hot tub. It's a little-known fact that Bristol sits on its own system of geothermal springs, which bubble up through the rocks beneath the Avon Gorge. During the 19th century, these naturally heated waters turned the area around Hotwells into a popular spa resort, where Georgian bathers flocked to try the curative waters (which were believed to alleviate a variety of conditions including consumption, asthma, dropsy and venereal diseases). The area even had its own funicular railway between Hotwells and Clifton, which served as a bomb shelter during WWII.

Though Bristol's days as a spa town may be over, you can still experience a flavour of its hot-water heyday thanks to the wonderful **Bristol Lido** (☎0117-933 9530; www.lidobristol.com; Oakfield Pl; nonmembers £20; ⏰nonmembers 1-4pm Mon-Fri). Originally opened as the Clifton Lido in 1849, the baths fell into disrepair and were closed in 1990, but have been carefully restored over the last few years. They're now a real local secret, with a beautiful 24m outdoor swimming pool that's kept at a constant temperature of around 24°C. Spa treatments and massage sessions are also available, and there's even an excellent bistro.

The only drawback for nonlocals is that priority is given to members. On weekends and busy days, the lido is closed for day visitors, so phone ahead to make sure there's space.

closed Sun evening) This converted river barge is great for a romantic dinner, with candle-lit tables and harbour views through a glass extension. The stylish food revolves around French and Italian flavours.

Drinking & Nightlife

BrewDog Bristol PUB
(www.brewdog.com; 58 Baldwin St; ⏰noon-midnight Sun-Wed, to 1am Thu-Sat) The Bristol outlet of Britain's punk brewery draws both the just-finished work crowd and those who want to linger – the cluster of tables out front prove popular on warm nights. Expect to find ales such as Libertine Black, Vagabond Pale and Hardcore on tap.

Thekla CLUB
(www.theklabristol.co.uk; The Grove, East Mud Dock; ⏰Thu-Sat 9.30pm-3am or 4am) Bristol's clubboat has nights for all moods: electro-punk, indie, disco and new wave, plus regular live gigs during the week. Check the website for the latest.

Albion PUB
(www.thealbionclifton.co.uk; Boyce's Ave; ⏰9am-midnight Mon-Sat, to 11pm Sun) The well-heeled drinkers of Clifton make a beeline for this smart pub for a postwork pint. It also dishes up top-notch food, the likes of which range from classy bar-menu classics to treacle-marinated pork chops (mains £9 to £14).

Grain Barge PUB
(www.grainbarge.com; Mardyke Wharf, Hotwell Rd; ⏰noon-11pm Sun-Thu, to 11.30pm Fri & Sat) This lovingly converted 1930s cargo vessel used to transport barley and wheat. Fittingly it's now used by the Bristol Beer Factory to showcase its craft ales. There's live music on Thursday nights (from 8pm).

Entertainment

Watershed CINEMA
(www.watershed.co.uk; 1 Canon's Rd) Bristol's digital-media centre hosts regular art-house programs and film-related events, including the Encounters Festival (p313) in September.

Bristol Old Vic THEATRE
(☎0117-987 7877; www.bristololdvic.org.uk; 103 The Cut) Bristol's much-respected, stately theatre (one of England's oldest) hosts big touring productions in its ornate auditorium, plus more experimental work in its smaller studio.

Fleece LIVE MUSIC
(www.thefleece.co.uk; 12 St Thomas St) A gig-pub favoured by indie artists.

Colston Hall LIVE MUSIC
(☎0844 887 1500; www.colstonhall.org; Colston St) Bristol's historic concert hall now has a new gleaming five-floor annex. It tends to attract the best bands and big-name comedy acts.

Shopping

Bristol is good for shopping, but you'll need to get out of the centre if you want to avoid the high-street chains, which cluster around **Cabot Circus** (www.cabotcircus.com; Glass

House; ⏲10am-8pm Mon-Sat, 11am-5pm Sun) and **Broadmead**.

Stokes Croft and Gloucester Rd are the best areas for independent shops, especially vintage clothing, crafts and secondhand music. Clifton is more upmarket, with high-end designer, homeware and antiques shops.

Rise Music MUSIC
(☎0117-929 7511; www.rise-music.co.uk; 70 Queen's Rd; ⏲10am-7pm Mon-Sat, noon-6pm Sun) Bristol's top independent record shop has racks of CDs and vinyl, regular events and a coffee bar downstairs.

Loot CLOTHING
(☎0117-922 0633; www.gimmetheloot.co.uk; 9 Haymarket Walk; ⏲10am-5.30pm Mon-Sat, 11am-5pm Sun) The city's largest vintage clothing shop is lodged, incongruously, at the base of the Premier Inn.

ℹ Information

Bristol Royal Infirmary (www.uhbristol.nhs.uk; Marlborough St; ⏲24hr)

Bristol Tourist Office (☎0906 711 2191; www.visitbristol.co.uk; E-Shed, 1 Canons Rd; ⏲10am-4pm Mon-Sat, 11am-4pm Sun) Calling the phone number costs the premium rate of 50p per minute.

ℹ Getting There & Away

AIR

Bristol International Airport (☎0871-3344344; www.bristolairport.co.uk) Bristol's airport is 8 miles southwest of the city. Destinations in the UK and Ireland include Aberdeen, Edinburgh, Cork, Glasgow and Newcastle (mainly handled by easyJet). Direct flights to cities in mainland Europe include those to Barcelona, Berlin, Milan and Paris. On-the-day parking at the airport is expensive; booking online in advance is much cheaper.

Bristol Airport Flyer (http://flyer.bristolairport.co.uk; ⏲24hr) Runs shuttle buses (one way/return £7/11, 30 minutes, every 10 minutes at peak times) from the bus station and Temple Meads.

Checker Cars (☎01446-711747; www.checkercars.com) Bristol Airport's official taxi service. Prices start from around £27 from the city centre.

BUS

National Express coaches go to Birmingham (£22, two hours, six to eight daily), London (£21, 2½ hours, hourly), Cardiff (£10, 1¼ hours, every two hours) and Exeter (£15, two hours, five daily).

Useful local buses include:

Bath (£5.50, 50 minutes, four per hour Monday to Saturday, half-hourly on Sunday) Bus 38/39/X39.

Wells (£5.50, one hour, half-hourly to hourly) Bus 376, which then goes on to Glastonbury (£5.50, 1¼ hours).

TRAIN

Bristol is an important rail hub, with regular services to London Paddington provided by the **Great Western Railway** (www.gwr.com) and services to northern England and Scotland mainly covered by **CrossCountry** (www.crosscountrytrains.co.uk). Book ahead for the best deals.

DESTINATION	COST (£)	TIME (HR)	FREQUENCY
Birmingham	26	1½	hourly
Edinburgh	80	6½	hourly
Exeter	14	1	half-hourly
Glasgow	85	6½	hourly
London	32	1¾	half-hourly
Penzance	35	5½	hourly
Truro	40	4	hourly

ℹ Getting Around

Traveline South West (www.travelinesw.com) provides comprehensive details of both travel around the region, and in and around Bristol city.

BICYCLE

Bristol Bike Project (☎0117-942 1794; www.thebristolbikeproject.org; City Rd; per day Mon-Fri £12, per weekend £25; ⏲9am-6pm Mon-Fri, 10.30am-5.30pm Sat) A community-run bike shop and rental outlet in Stokes Croft.

Roll for the Soul (☎07856-544471; www.rollforthesoul.org; 2 Quay St; ⏲8am-6pm Mon & Tue, to 9pm Wed-Fri, 10am-9pm Sat) Not-for-profit bike cafe and bike workshop – great for meeting like-minded cycling buddies.

BOAT

Bristol Ferry Boat Company (☎0117-927 3416; www.bristolferry.com) Ferry services feature two, hourly routes: Hotwells runs west, with stops including Millennium Sq and the SS *Great Britain*. Temple Meads runs east, with stops including Welsh Back, Castle Park (for Cabot Circus) and Temple Meads (for the train station). Boats leave from the dock near the tourist office. Fares depend on distance travelled; an all-day pass is adult/child £6.50/5.50.

BUS

Bus journeys in Bristol's city centre cost £1 for up to three stops; longer trips cost £1.50. A Day-Rider pass (£4.50) provides unlimited travel.

Bus 8/9 To Clifton (10 minutes), Whiteladies Rd and Bristol Zoo Gardens every 15 minutes from St Augustine's Pde. Add 10 minutes from Temple Meads.

Bus 73/X73 Runs every 20 minutes from Bristol Parkway Station to the centre (£3.50, 30 minutes).

CAR & MOTORCYCLE

Heavy traffic and pricey parking make driving in Bristol a headache. **Park & Ride Buses** (☎0117-9020 157; www.ctplusbristol.org; peak/off-peak return £4/3; ⏲6am-9.30pm Mon-Fri, 7am-8pm Sat) run every 20 minutes from Portway, Bath Rd and Long Ashton. Note that overnight parking is not permitted at the Park & Ride car parks.

TAXI

You can usually find a cab at the taxi rank on **St Augustine's Pde** (St Augustine's Pde), and there are plenty of dial-a-fares: try **Streamline Taxis** (☎0117-926 4001; www.bristolstreamlinetaxis.com) or **1st Call Taxi** (☎0117-955 5111; www.1stcalltaxis.net). If you're taking a nonmetered cab, agree on the fare in advance.

BATH

POP 88,900

Britain's littered with beautiful cities, but precious few compare to Bath. Home to some of the nation's grandest Georgian architecture – not to mention one of the world's best-preserved Roman bathhouses – this slinky, sophisticated, snooty city, founded on top of natural hot springs, has been a tourist draw for nigh on 2000 years.

Bath's heyday really began during the 18th century, when local entrepreneur Ralph Allen and his team of father-and-son architects, John Wood the Elder and Younger, turned this sleepy backwater into the toast of Georgian society, and constructed fabulous landmarks such as the Circus and Royal Crescent.

History

Legend has it King Bladud, a Trojan refugee and father of King Lear, founded Bath some 2800 years ago when his pigs were cured of leprosy by a dip in the muddy swamps. The Romans established the town of Aquae Sulis in AD 44 and built the extensive baths complex and a temple to the goddess Sulis-Minerva.

Long after the Romans decamped, the Anglo-Saxons arrived, and in 944 a monastery was founded on the site of the present abbey. Throughout the Middle Ages, Bath was an ecclesiastical centre and a wool-trading town, but it wasn't until the early 18th century that Ralph Allen and the celebrated dandy Richard 'Beau' Nash made Bath the centre of fashionable society. Allen developed the quarries at Coombe Down, constructed Prior Park and employed the two John Woods (father and son) to create Bath's signature buildings.

During WWII, Bath was hit by the Luftwaffe during the so-called Baedeker raids, which targeted historic cities in an effort to sap British morale. Several houses on the Royal Crescent and the Circus were badly damaged, and the city's Assembly Rooms were gutted by fire, although all have since been restored.

In 1987, Bath became the only city in Britain to be declared a Unesco World Heritage Site in its entirety, leading to many subsequent wrangles over construction and development, most recently concerning the design of the redeveloped Thermae Bath Spa and SouthGate shopping centre.

Sights

★Roman Baths HISTORIC BUILDING

(☎01225-477785; www.romanbaths.co.uk; Abbey Churchyard; adult/child £15/9.50; ⏲9am-9pm Jul & Aug, to 5pm Sep-Jun) In typically ostentatious style, the Romans constructed a complex of bathhouses above Bath's three natural hot springs, which emerge at a steady 46°C (115°F). Situated alongside a temple dedicated to the healing goddess Sulis-Minerva, the baths now form one of the best-preserved ancient Roman spas in the world, and are encircled by 18th- and 19th-century buildings. Bath's premier attraction can get very busy. To dodge the worst crowds, avoid weekends, July and August.

The heart of the complex is the **Great Bath**, a lead-lined pool filled with steaming, geothermally heated water from the so-called 'Sacred Spring' to a depth of 1.6m. Though now open-air, the bath would

> **MUSEUM DISCOUNTS**
>
> Saver tickets covering the Roman Baths and the Fashion Museum cost adult/child/family £21/11/53. There's also a joint ticket covering No 1 Royal Crescent and the Museum of Bath Architecture for £13/5/28.

Bath

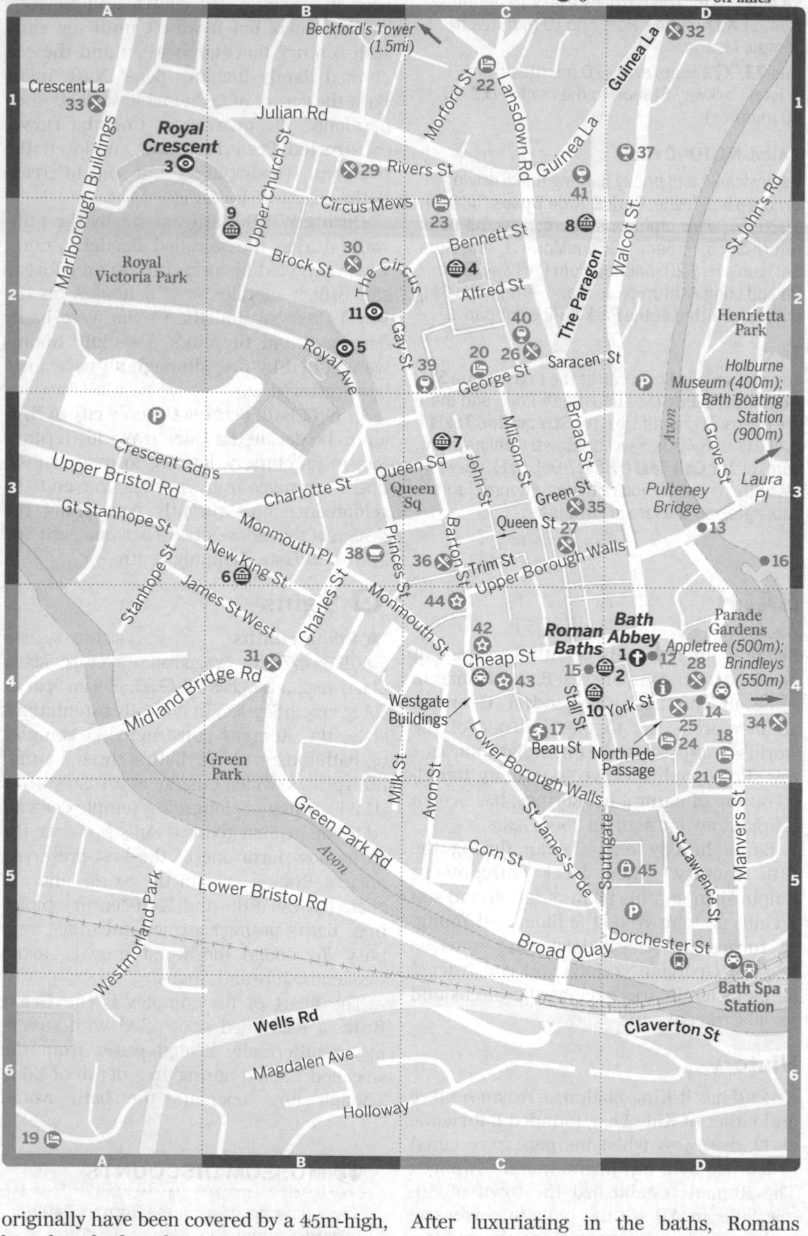

originally have been covered by a 45m-high, barrel-vaulted roof.

More bathing pools and changing rooms are situated to the east and west, with excavated sections revealing the **hypocaust system** that heated the bathing rooms. After luxuriating in the baths, Romans would have reinvigorated themselves with a dip in the circular **cold-water pool**, which now has life-size films of bathers projected on to the walls.

Bath

Top Sights

1	Bath Abbey	D4
2	Roman Baths	D4
3	Royal Crescent	A1

Sights

4	Bath Assembly Rooms	C2
	Fashion Museum	(see 4)
5	Georgian Garden	B2
6	Herschel Museum of Astronomy	B3
7	Jane Austen Centre	C3
8	Museum of Bath Architecture	C2
9	No 1 Royal Crescent	B2
10	Pump Room	C4
11	The Circus	B2

Activities, Courses & Tours

12	Bath Abbey Tower Tours	D4
13	Bath City Boat Trips	D3
14	Bizarre Bath Comedy Walk	D4
15	Mayor's Guide Tours	C4
16	Pulteney Cruisers	D3
17	Thermae Bath Spa	C4

Sleeping

18	Bath Backpackers	D4
19	Grays Bath	A6
20	Halcyon Apartments	C2
21	Henry	D4
22	Hill House Bath	C1
23	Queensberry Hotel	C2
24	Three Abbey Green	D4

Eating

25	Acorn	D4
26	Adventure Cafe Bar	C2
27	Bertinet Bakery	C3
28	Café Retro	D4
29	Chequers	B1
30	Circus	B2
31	Green Park Station	B4
32	Hudson Steakhouse	D1
33	Marlborough Tavern	A1
	Pump Room Restaurant	(see 10)
	Sally Lunn's	(see 25)
34	Sotto Sotto	D4
35	Tasting Room	C3
36	Thoughtful Bread Company	C3

Drinking & Nightlife

37	Bell Inn	D1
38	Colonna & Smalls	B3
39	Moles	C2
40	Same Same But Different	C2
41	Star Inn	C1

Entertainment

42	Komedia	C4
43	Little Theatre Cinema	C4
44	Theatre Royal	C4

Shopping

45	SouthGate	D5

The **King's Bath** was added sometime during the 12th century around the site of the original Sacred Spring. Every day, 1.5 million litres of hot water still pour into the pool. Beneath the Pump Room are the remains of the **Temple of Sulis-Minerva**.

There is also a fascinating **museum** displaying artefacts discovered on the site. Look out for the famous gilded bronze head of Minerva and a striking carved Gorgon's Head, as well as some of the 12,000-odd Roman coins thrown into the spring as votive offerings to the goddess.

The complex of buildings around the baths were built in stages during the 18th and 19th centuries. The two John Woods designed the buildings around the Sacred Spring, while the famous **Pump Room** (www.romanbaths.co.uk; Stall St; ⏲10am-5pm) FREE was built by their contemporaries, Thomas Baldwin and John Palmer, in neoclassical style, complete with soaring Ionic and Corinthian columns. The building now houses a restaurant (p324) which serves a magnificent afternoon tea (£22, or £31 with champagne). You can also sample the spring waters, which were believed in Victorian times to have curative properties. If you're lucky, you might even have music provided by the Pump Room's string trio.

Admission to the Roman Baths includes an audioguide, featuring a commentary in eight languages. One of the English guides is read by bestselling author Bill Bryson. Free hourly guided tours start at the Great Bath. Saver tickets covering the Roman Baths and the Fashion Museum cost adult/child/family £21/11/53.

★Bath Abbey CHURCH

(www.bathabbey.org; Abbey Churchyard; requested donation adult/student £2.50/1.50; ⏲9.30am-5.30pm Mon, 9am-5.30pm Tue-Fri, 9am-6pm Sat, 1-2.30pm & 4.30-5.30pm Sun) Looming above the city centre, Bath's huge abbey church was built between 1499 and 1616, making it the last great medieval church raised in England. Its most striking feature is the west facade, where angels climb up and down

WORTH A TRIP

PRIOR PARK ESTATE

Partly designed by the landscape architect Capability Brown, the grounds of **Prior Park** (NT; ☎01225-833977; www.nationaltrust.org.uk; Ralph Allen Dr; adult/child £6.50/3.40; ⏲10am-5.30pm Feb-Oct daily, to 4pm Sat & Sun Nov-Jan), an 18th-century estate on Bath's southern fringe, feature cascading lakes and a graceful **Palladian bridge**. It's one of only four such structures in the world (look out for the period graffiti, some of which dates back to the 1800s).

The park is a mile south of Bath's centre. Bus 1 (every 45 minutes) stops nearby, as does Bath City Sightseeing's 'City Skyline' tour (p321).

stone ladders, commemorating a dream of the founder, Bishop Oliver King.

Tower tours (www.bathabbey.org; adult/child £6/3; ⏲10am-5pm Apr-Aug, 11am-3pm Sep-Mar, no tours Sun) leave on the hour from Monday to Friday, and every half-hour on Saturday.

Jane Austen Centre MUSEUM
(☎01225-443000; www.janeausten.co.uk; 40 Gay St; adult/child £11/5.50; ⏲9.45am-5.30pm Apr-Oct, 10am-4pm Nov-Mar) Bath is known to many as a location in Jane Austen's novels, including *Persuasion* and *Northanger Abbey*. Although Austen lived in Bath for only five years, from 1801 to 1806, she remained a regular visitor and a keen student of the city's social scene. Here, guides in Regency costumes regale you with Austen-esque tales as you tour memorabilia relating to the writer's life in Bath.

Herschel Museum of Astronomy MUSEUM
(☎01225-446865; www.herschelmuseum.org.uk; 19 New King St; adult/child £6.50/3; ⏲1-5pm Mon-Fri, 11am-5pm Sat & Sun Mar-Sep) In 1781 astronomer William Herschel discovered Uranus from the garden of his home, now converted into a museum. The house is little changed since the 18th century; an astrolabe in the garden marks the position of Herschel's telescope.

★**Royal Crescent** ARCHITECTURE
(Royal Cres) Bath is famous for its glorious Georgian architecture, and it doesn't get any grander than this semicircular terrace of majestic town houses overlooking the green sweep of Royal Victoria Park. Designed by John Wood the Younger (1728–82) and built between 1767 and 1775, the houses appear perfectly symmetrical from the outside, but the owners were allowed to tweak the interiors, so no two houses are quite the same. **No 1 Royal Crescent** offers you an intriguing insight into life inside.

A walk east along Brock St from the Royal Crescent leads to **the Circus** (The Circus), a ring of 33 houses divided into three semicircular terraces. Plaques on the houses commemorate famous residents such as Thomas Gainsborough, Clive of India and David Livingstone. The terrace was designed by John Wood the Elder, but he died in 1754, and the terrace was completed by his son in 1768.

To the south along Gravel Walk is the **Georgian Garden** (off Royal Ave; ⏲9am-5pm) FREE, restored to resemble a typical 18th-century town-house garden.

Bath Assembly Rooms HISTORIC BUILDING
(NT; www.nationaltrust.org.uk; 19 Bennett St; ⏲10.30am-5pm Mar-Oct, to 4pm Nov-Feb) FREE When they opened in 1771, the city's glorious Assembly Rooms were where fashionable Bath socialites gathered to waltz, play cards and listen to the latest chamber music. Rooms open to the public include the card room, tearoom and ballroom – all lit by their original 18th-century chandeliers.

Fashion Museum MUSEUM
(☎01225-477789; www.fashionmuseum.co.uk; Assembly Rooms, 19 Bennett St; adult/child £8.75/6.75; ⏲10.30am-5pm Mar-Oct, to 4pm Nov-Feb) The collections on display in the basement of the Assembly Rooms include costumes from the 17th to late 20th centuries. Some exhibits change annually; check the website for the latest.

Museum of Bath Architecture MUSEUM
(☎01225-333895; www.museumofbatharchitecture.org.uk; The Vineyards, The Paragon; adult/child £5.50/2.50; ⏲2-5pm Tue-Fri, 10.30am-5pm Sat & Sun mid-Feb–Nov) The stories behind the building of Bath's most striking structures are explored here, using antique tools, displays on Georgian construction methods and a 1:500 scale model of the city.

A joint ticket covering the Museum of Bath Architecture and No 1 Royal Crescent costs adult/child/family £13/5/28.

Holburne Museum GALLERY
(☎01225-388569; www.holburne.org; Great Pulteney St; ⏲10am-5pm Mon-Sat, 11am-5pm Sun) FREE Sir William Holburne, the 18th-century aristocrat and art fanatic, amassed a huge collection, which now forms the core of the Holburne Museum, in a lavish mansion at the end of Great Pulteney St. The museum houses a roll call of works by artists including Turner, Stubbs, William Hoare and Thomas Gainsborough, as well as 18th-century majolica and porcelain.

American Museum in Britain MUSEUM
(☎01225-460503; www.americanmuseum.org; Claverton Manor; adult/child £11/6.50; ⏲noon-5pm Tue-Sun late Mar-Oct, to 4.30pm late Nov–mid-Dec) Britain's largest collection of American folk art, including First Nations textiles, patchwork quilts and historic maps, is housed in a fine mansion a couple of miles from the city centre. Several rooms have been decorated to resemble a 17th-century Puritan house, an 18th-century tavern and a New Orleans boudoir c 1860. A free shuttle bus (11.40am to 5pm) leaves from Terrace Walk, beside Parade Gardens.

Activities

Various cruise operators offer boat trips up and down the River Avon from the Pulteney Bridge area, including **Pulteney Cruisers** (☎01225-863600; www.bathboating.com; Pulteney Bridge; adult/child £9/4; ⏲mid-Mar–Nov) and **Bath City Boat Trips** (☎07974 560197; www.bathcityboattrips.com; Pulteney Sluice Gate; adult/child £10/8). There's not much difference between the tours; most last around an hour. Between mid-March and November there are at least five sailings a day.

★**Thermae Bath Spa** SPA
(☎01225-331234; www.thermaebathspa.com; Hot Bath St; Mon-Fri £34, Sat & Sun £37; ⏲9am-9.30pm, last entry 7pm) Taking a dip in the Roman Baths might be off-limits, but you can still sample the city's curative waters at this fantastic modern spa complex, housed in a shell of local stone and plate glass. The showpiece is the open-air rooftop pool, where you can bathe in naturally heated, mineral-rich waters with a backdrop of Bath's cityscape – a mustn't-miss experience, best enjoyed at dusk.

Tickets includes steam rooms, waterfall showers and a choice of two swimming pools.

Bath Boating Station BOATING
(☎01225-312900; www.bathboating.co.uk; Forester Rd; 1st hr adult/child £7/3.50, additional hrs £4/2; ⏲10am-6pm Easter-Sep) You can pilot your own vessel down the Avon from this Victorian-era boathouse, which rents out traditional skiffs, rowing boats and Canadian canoes. It's in the suburb of Bathwick, a 20-minute walk northeast from the city centre.

Tours

★**Bizarre Bath Comedy Walk** WALKING
(☎01225-335124; www.bizarrebath.co.uk; adult/student £8/5; ⏲8pm Mar-Oct) Fabulously daft city tour mixing street theatre and live performance. Leaves nightly from outside the Huntsman Inn on North Pde Passage. Most of the walk is wheelchair-accessible.

Mayor's Guide Tours WALKING
(☎01225-477411; www.bathguides.org.uk; ⏲10.30am & 2pm Sun-Fri, 10.30am Sat) FREE Excellent historical tours provided free by the Mayor's Corp of Honorary Guides; tours cover about 2 miles and are wheelchair-accessible. They leave from within the Abbey Churchyard, outside the Pump Room. There are extra tours at 7pm on Tuesdays and Thursdays May to September.

Bath City Sightseeing BUS
(Bath Bus Company; ☎01225-444102; www.bathbuscompany.com; adult/child £14.50/9; ⏲10am-5pm, reduced services Jan-Mar) Two hop-on/hop-off city tours on open-topped buses, with commentary in seven languages. Tickets last 24 hours, or two consecutive days.

Festivals & Events

Bath has a busy program of festivals. All bookings are handled by **Bath Festivals** (☎01225-462231; www.bathfestivals.org.uk).

Bath Literature Festival LITERATURE
(www.bathlitfest.org.uk; ⏲Feb & Mar) Major book festival in late February or early March.

Bath International Music Festival MUSIC
(www.bathmusicfest.org.uk; ⏲May) Mainly classical and opera, plus smaller gigs of jazz, folk and world. Events run mid- to late May.

Bath Fringe Festival THEATRE
(www.bathfringe.co.uk; ⌚May-Jun) Major theatre festival around mid-May to early June.

Sleeping

Bath has a wide range of hotels and B&Bs, and gets extremely busy in the height of summer when prices peak. Be aware, they also rise by anything from £10 to £50 a room at weekends year-round. Few hotels have on-site parking, although some offer discounted rates at municipal car parks.

Bath Backpackers HOSTEL £
(☎01225-446787; www.hostels.co.uk/bath; 13 Pierrepont St; dm £12-17) The showers are scarce, and it's a bit grimy and battered, but this hostel is still beloved by budget travellers for bargain rates, a prime location, a friendly vibe and a 24-hour 'dungeon' (in truth a sound-proofed basement where you don't have to 'keep the noise down').

Bath YHA HOSTEL £
(☎0845 371 9303; www.yha.org.uk; Bathwick Hill; dm £13-22, d from £39; ⌚reception 7am-11pm; P @) Split across an Italianate mansion and a modern annex, this impressive hostel is a steep climb (or a short hop on bus U1 or U18) from the city. The listed building means the rooms are huge, and some have period features such as cornicing and bay windows.

★**Three Abbey Green** B&B ££
(☎01225-428558; www.threeabbeygreen.com; 3 Abbey Green; d £90-200, apt £160;) Rarely in Bath do you get somewhere as central as this Georgian town house with such spacious rooms. Elegant, 18th-century-style furnishings are teamed with swish wet-room bathrooms, and the opulent Lord Nelson suite features a vast four-poster bed. There's also a two-person, self-catering apartment nearby (two-night minimum stay).

Henry B&B ££
(☎01225-424052; www.thehenry.com; 6 Henry St; s £80-95, d £100-145, f from £175;) This tall town house has one of the best positions in Bath, literally steps from the centre. The seven rooms and a self-catering apartment are jazzed up by modern floral motifs, striped cushions and mints on the pillows. The family room and free cot may also suit.

Appletree B&B ££
(☎01225-337642; www.appletreebath.com; 7 Pulteney Gardens; s £80-150, d £90-160; P) Owner, Ling, ran a city-centre hotel for 15 years, and those skills shine throughout this classy B&B. Bedrooms are named after the eponymous fruit. The best is Royal Gala, which features a sleigh bed and sofa, but even the cheaper rooms are bright and fresh and dotted with Asian art.

★**Queensberry Hotel** HOTEL £££
(☎01225-447928; www.thequeensberry.co.uk; 4 Russell St; r £125-185, ste £225-275;) Award-winning, quirky Queensberry is Bath's best boutique spoil. Four Georgian town houses have been combined into one seamlessly stylish whole, where heritage roots meet snazzy designs; expect everything from gingham checks and country creams to bright upholstery, original fireplaces and free-standing tubs. Rates exclude breakfast; parking is £7.

The hotel's Olive Tree Restaurant is excellent, too.

Grays Bath B&B £££
(☎01225-403020; www.graysbath.co.uk; Upper Oldfield Park; d £90-205;) Boutique treat Grays is a beautiful blend of modern, pared-down design and family treasures, many picked up from the owners' travels. All the rooms are individual: choose from floral, polka dot or maritime stripes. Perhaps the pick is the six-sided, curling room 12 in the attic, with partial city views.

The owners also run a smaller but equally smart B&B on the east side of town, **Brindleys** (☎01225-310444; www.brindleysbath.co.uk; 14 Pulteney Gardens; d £135-200; P).

Halcyon Apartments RENTAL HOUSE £££
(☎01225-585100; www.thehalcyon.com/apartments; 15a George St; apt £150-300;) The spacious, two- to four-people apartments set in this Georgian building blend heritage features (sash windows and high ceilings) with modern fixtures and furnishings. Quite the stylish pied-à-terre.

Hill House Bath B&B £££
(☎01225-920520; www.hillhousebath.co.uk; 25 Belvedere; r £150-170; P) When you walk through the door here it almost feels like you're staying with friends. The decor showcases the owners' quirky tastes – dog-print cushions, retro pictures and objets d'art abound. Breakfasts are packed with local ingredients and include homemade marmalade and jam.

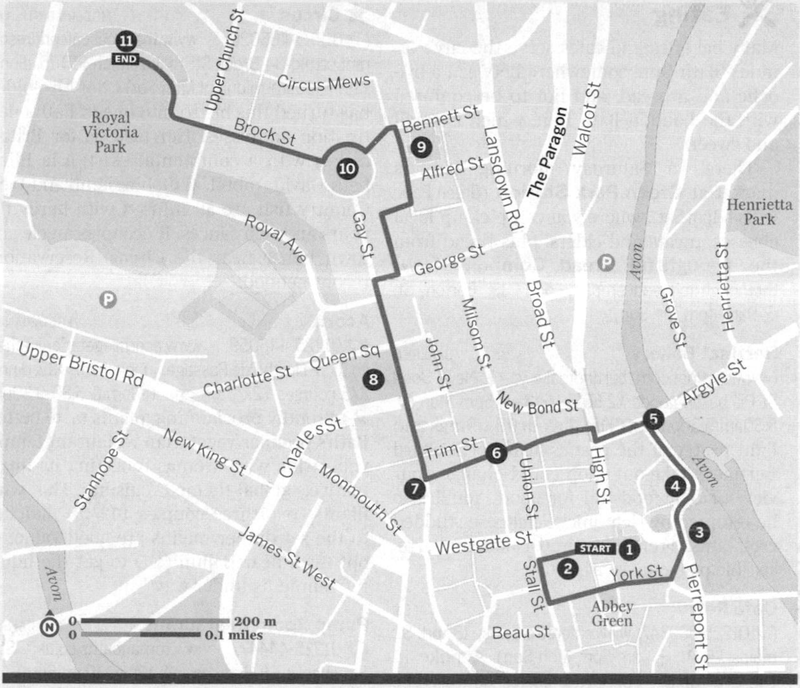

Walking Tour Bath

START BATH ABBEY
FINISH ROYAL CRESCENT
LENGTH 1.5 MILES; TWO HOURS

Start this architectural amble at **1 Bath Abbey** (p319), the city's iconic ecclesiastical edifice, built on the site of an 8th-century chapel. From the abbey square, head south along Stall St for a view of the 19th-century **2 Pump Room** (p319). Turn left onto York St, and follow it east to **3 Parade Gardens**, a Victorian park framed by the River Avon.

From here, the Grand Parade leads north; look out for the building on the corner, **4 The Empire**, built as a luxurious hotel in 1901. At the northern end of the Grand Parade is **5 Pulteney Bridge**, designed by Robert Adams in 1773, one of only a handful in the world to be lined with shops. West of the bridge, **6 Upper Borough Walls** marks the northern extent of medieval Bath; if you look closely, you might spot some sections of the medieval wall that remain.

At Sawclose, you'll see the elaborate facade of Bath's **7 Theatre Royal** (p325), which has been staging productions since 1805. From here, follow Barton St on to **8 Queen Square**, the oldest of Bath's Georgian squares, built as a showpiece development between 1728 and 1736 to demonstrate the talents of its architect, John Wood the Elder.

Head north on to Gay St, and right on to George St. Next to the Porter pub, an alley leads north, emerging next to the **9 Assembly Rooms** (p320), the heart of Georgian Bath's social life. Continue to Bennett St and turn left until you reach **10 the Circus** (p320), designed to echo the Colosseum in Rome. The three-tiered pillars exhibit the key styles of classical architecture (Doric, Ionic and Corinthian) and the facades are supposedly studded with masonic symbols.

From here, Brock St leads west to Bath's Georgian glory, the **11 Royal Crescent** (p320). Constructed by John Wood the Younger in 1774, the terrace is now Grade I listed, making it as architecturally significant as Buckingham Palace. The elegant Royal Crescent Hotel is at number 16.

Eating

Many bakeries and cafes serve the city's famous 'Bath Bun', somewhere between a brioche and a bread, and not to be confused with the London Bath Bun, which is small and sweet.

There's a Saturday morning farmers market at **Green Park Station** (Green Park; 8am-1pm Sat), where you can pick up local cheeses, meats and ciders, plus bread from the **Thoughtful Bread Company** (www.thethoughtfulbreadcompany.com; 19 Barton St; 9am-4pm Tue-Sun).

Bertinet Bakery BAKERY £
(www.bertinet.com/bertinetbakery; 1 New Bond St Pl; baked goods £2.50-5; 8am-5pm Mon-Fri, 8.30am-5.30pm Sat) The flavourful fillings and light pastry of the pasties at baker Richard Bertinet's take-out shop could change your view of that foodstuff for good. You'll also be tempted by rich quiches, cheese-studded croissants, French-inspired cakes and irresistible pistachio swirls.

Café Retro CAFE £
(01225-339347; www.caferetro.co.uk; 18 York St; mains £5-11; 9am-5pm Mon-Sun) A poke in the eye for the corporate coffee chains. The paint job's scruffy, the crockery's ancient and none of the furniture matches, but that's all part of the charm: this is a cafe from the old school, and there are few places better for burgers, butties or cake. Takeaways (in biodegradable containers) are available from Retro-to-Go next door.

Adventure Cafe Bar CAFE £
(www.adventurecafebar.co.uk; 5 Princes Bldgs, George St; mains £5-10; 8.30am-3am Mon-Fri, 9am-3am Sat & Sun) This cool cafe-bar, just a slipper's throw from the Assembly Rooms, offers something to everyone at most times of the day: morning cappuccino, lunchtime ciabatta and late-night beer and cocktails. There's great outdoor seating in the back.

Sally Lunn's CAFE £
(01225-461634; www.sallylunns.co.uk; 4 North Pde Passage; mains £6-17; 10am-9.30pm Sun-Thu, to 10pm Fri & Sat) Eating a bun at Sally Lunn's is just one of those things you have to do in Bath. It's all about proper English tea here, brewed in bone-china teapots, with finger sandwiches and dainty cakes served by waitresses in frilly aprons.

★**Circus** MODERN BRITISH ££
(01225-466020; www.thecircuscafeandrestaurant.co.uk; 34 Brock St; mains lunch £10-15, dinner £19; 10am-midnight Mon-Sat) Chef Ali Golden has turned this bistro into one of Bath's destination addresses. Her taste is for British dishes with a continental twist, à la Elizabeth David: rabbit, Wiltshire lamb and West Country fish are all infused with herby flavours and rich sauces. It occupies an elegant town house near the Circus. Reservations recommended.

Acorn VEGETARIAN ££
(01225-446059; www.acornvegetariankitchen.co.uk; 2 North Pde Passage; lunch mains £12, dinner 2/3 courses £27/33; noon-3pm & 5.30-9.30pm;) Proudly proclaiming 'plants taste better', Bath's premier vegetarian restaurant tempts you inside with aromas reflecting its imaginative, global-themed cuisine. The wine flights (two/three courses £12/18) matched to the set dinner menus are good value; or opt for a pear Bellini (£7) to get the liquid refreshments under way.

Pump Room Restaurant CAFE ££
(01225-444477; www.romanbaths.co.uk; Stall St; snacks £6-8, dishes £8-12; 10am-5pm) Elegance is everywhere in this tall, Georgian room, from the string trio and Corinthian columns to the oil paintings and glinting chandeliers. It sets the scene perfectly for morning coffee, classic lunches and the dainty sandwiches and cakes of their famous afternoon tea (£22 to £40 per person).

Chequers GASTROPUB ££
(01225-360017; www.thechequersbar.com; 50 Rivers St; mains £10-25; bar noon-11pm daily, food 6-9pm daily, noon-2.30pm Sat & Sun) A discerning crowd inhabits Chequers, a pub that's been in business since 1776, but which has a menu that's bang up to date thanks to head chef Tony Casey. Forget bar-food staples, here it's hake with octopus and wild rice.

Sotto Sotto ITALIAN ££
(01225-330236; www.sottosotto.co.uk; 10 North Pde; mains £10-20; noon-2pm & 5-10pm) The setting is superb – an artfully lit vaulted brick chamber – and the food matches it for style. Authentic Italian dishes are likely to include Parma ham–wrapped sea bass sautéed in white wine, and a spicy seafood and Tuscan bean pasta. A top tip: don't forgo the garlicky sautéed spinach side.

Tasting Room TAPAS ££

(☎ 01225-483070; www.tastingroom.co.uk; 6 Green St; mains £6-13; ⏲ 10.30am-11pm Wed-Sat, to 4.30pm Mon & Tue) High-class vintages, tapas and piled-high platters of meats and cheese are the *modi operandi* of this slinky cafe-bar, located above Bath's premier wine merchant.

Marlborough Tavern GASTROPUB ££

(☎ 01225-423731; www.marlborough-tavern.com; 35 Marlborough Bldgs; mains £13-25; ⏲ bar noon-11pm, food noon-2pm & 6-9.30pm) The queen of Bath's gastropubs has food that's closer to that of a fine-dining restaurant – think duo of venison and pork tenderloin rather than bog-standard meat-and-two-veg. Chunky wooden tables and racks of wine behind the bar give it an exclusive, classy feel.

★**Menu Gordon Jones** MODERN BRITISH £££

(☎ 01225-480871; www.menugordonjones.co.uk; 2 Wellsway; 5-course lunch £40, 6-course dinner £55; ⏲ 12.30-2pm & 7-9pm Tue-Sat) If you enjoy dining with an element of surprise, then Gordon Jones' restaurant will be right up your culinary boulevard. Menus are dreamt up daily and showcase the chef's taste for experimental ingredients (eel, haggis and smoked milk foam) and madcap presentation (test tubes, edible cups, slate plates). It's superb value given the skill on show. Reservations essential.

Hudson Steakhouse STEAK £££

(☎ 01225-332323; www.hudsonsteakhouse.co.uk; 14 London St; mains £22-34; ⏲ 5-10.30pm) Steak, steak and more steak is this acclaimed eatery's raison d'être. Tuck into top-quality cuts from porterhouse to prime fillet, all sourced from a Staffordshire farmers' co-op.

Their early-evening special of a steak and a glass of wine (£15) is a bargain.

Drinking & Nightlife

★**Colonna & Smalls** CAFE

(www.colonnaandsmalls.co.uk; 6 Chapel Row; ⏲ 8.30am-5.30pm Mon-Sat, 10am-4pm Sun; 📶) If you're keen on caffeinated beans, this is a cafe not to miss. A mission to explore coffee ensures that there are three guest espresso varieties and smiley staff happy to share their expertise. They'll even tell you that black filter coffee – yes, filter coffee – is actually the best way to judge high-grade beans.

★**Star Inn** PUB

(www.abbeyales.co.uk; 23 The Vineyards, off the Paragon; ⏲ noon-2.30pm & 5.30-11pm Mon-Fri, noon-11pm Sat, noon-10.30pm Sun) Not many pubs are registered relics, but the Star is – it still has many of its 19th-century bar fittings. It's the brewery tap for Bath-based Abbey Ales; some ales are served in traditional jugs, and you can even ask for a pinch of snuff in the 'smaller bar'.

Bell Inn PUB

(www.thebellinnbath.co.uk; 103 Walcot St; ⏲ 11.30am-11pm Mon-Sat, noon-10.30pm Sun) To join Bath's bohemian muso crowd, head to this welcoming, laid-back locals' favourite. You'll find a real fire, swathes of draped hops and a bar billiards table (£1 a go). Plus live music (Monday and Wednesday at 9pm, Sunday at 1pm) that ranges from acoustic, country and folk to echoes of the blues.

Same Same But Different BAR

(www.same-same.co.uk; 7a Prince's Bldgs, Bartlett St; ⏲ 8am-11pm Tue-Fri, 9am-11pm Sat, 10am-5pm Sun) Boho hang-out for the town's trendies, tucked down an alley off George St. Savour wine by the glass, snack on tapas or sip a cappuccino with the Sunday papers.

Moles CLUB

(www.moles.co.uk; 14 George St) Bath's main music venue keeps the crowds happy with a musical diet of indie, electro pop, club classics and cheese.

Entertainment

Komedia COMEDY

(☎ 0845 293 8480; www.komedia.co.uk; 22-23 Westgate St) Renowned comedy venue featuring touring shows and the sell-out Krater Saturday Comedy Club. Also live music and films.

Little Theatre Cinema CINEMA

(www.picturehouses.com; St Michael's Pl) Bath's excellent art-house cinema screens fringe films and foreign-language flicks.

Theatre Royal THEATRE

(☎ 01225-448844; www.theatreroyal.org.uk; Sawclose) Bath's historic theatre dates back 200 years. Major touring productions go in the main auditorium and smaller shows appear in the Ustinov Studio.

Shopping

Bath's main shopping centre is **SouthGate** (www.southgatebath.com), where you'll find all the major chain stores.

Smaller shops tend to be a little north of the centre. Milsom St is good for upmarket fashion, while Walcot St is lined by quirky independent food shops, design stores and vintage-clothing retailers.

ℹ Information

Bath Tourist Office (☎ 0844 847 5256; www.visitbath.co.uk; Abbey Chambers, Abbey Churchyard; ⏰ 9.30am-5.30pm Mon-Sat, 10am-4pm Sun) Calls are charged at the premium rate of 50p per minute.

Royal United Hospital (☎ 01225-428331; www.ruh.nhs.uk; Combe Park)

ℹ Getting There & Away

BUS

Bath's **bus and coach station** (Dorchester St) is near the train station.

National Express coaches run direct to London (£33, 3½ hours, eight to 10 daily). Two-hourly services also run to London Heathrow (£27, three hours). Services to many other destinations change at Bristol.

Local buses include the following:

Bristol bus 38/39/X39; £5.50, 50 minutes, four per hour Monday to Saturday, half-hourly on Sunday

Wells bus 173; £5.50, one hour 15 minutes, two per hour Monday to Saturday, hourly Sunday)

TRAIN

Bath Spa station is at the south end of Manvers St. Many services connect through Bristol, including those to the southwest and north of England.

Direct services include:

Bristol £7.30, 15 minutes, three per hour

Cardiff Central £20, one hour, hourly

London Paddington £38, 1½ hours, half-hourly

Salisbury £18, one hour, hourly

ℹ Getting Around

BICYCLE

Bath is hilly, but the canal paths along the Kennet and Avon Canal and the 13-mile **Bristol & Bath Railway Path** (www.bristolbath railwaypath.org.uk) are great to explore by bike.

Bath Bike Hire (☎ 01225-447276; www.bath-narrowboats.co.uk; Sydney Wharf; per day £15; ⏰ 9am-5pm, shorter hours in winter) Ten-minute walk from the centre. Handy for the canal and railway paths.

Take Charge Bikes (☎ 01225-789568; www.takechargebikes.co.uk; 1 Victoria Bldgs, Lower Bristol Rd; per day £17; ⏰ 9am-5.30pm Mon-Fri, to 4.30pm Sat) Rents electric bikes.

BUS

Bus U18 runs from the bus station, High St and Great Pulteney St up Bathwick Hill past the YHA to the university every 20 minutes (£1.20).

Bus 4 runs to Bathampton (£1.50, 30 minutes, one to two per hour).

CAR & MOTORCYCLE

Bath has serious traffic problems, especially at rush hour. **Park & Ride services** (☎ 0871-2002233; return Mon-Fri £3.30, Sat & Sun £2.60; ⏰ 6.15am-8.30pm Mon-Sat, 9.30am-6pm Sun) operate from Lansdown to the north, Newbridge to the west and Odd Down to the south. It takes about 10 minutes to the centre; buses leave every 10 to 15 minutes.

There's a good, central car park underneath the SouthGate shopping centre (two/eight hours £3.50/14, after 6pm £2 to £5).

SOMERSET

With its pastoral landscape of hedgerows, fields and hummocked hills, sleepy Somerset is the very picture of the rural English countryside, and makes the perfect escape from the bustle of Bath and the hustle of Bristol. Things certainly move at a drowsier pace around these parts – it's a place to wander, ponder and drink in the sights at your own pace.

The cathedral city of Wells is an atmospheric base for exploring the limestone caves and gorges around Cheddar, while the hippie haven of Glastonbury is handy for venturing on to the wetlands of the Somerset Levels and the high hills of the Quantocks.

ℹ Information

➡ The Taunton **tourist office** (☎ 01823-340470; www.visitsomerset.co.uk/taunton; Fore St; ⏰ 9.30am-4.30pm Mon-Sat) is the best source of information about Somerset as a whole.

➡ www.visitsouthsomerset.co.uk is another useful source of information.

ℹ Getting There & Around

➡ The M5 heads south past Bristol to Bridgwater and Taunton, while the A39 leads west across the Quantocks to Exmoor.

➡ Key train services link Bath, Bristol, Bridgwater, Taunton and Weston-super-Mare.

➡ **First** (www.firstgroup.com) is a key local bus operator. For timetables and general information, contact **Traveline South West** (www.travelinesw.com).

Wells & Around

POP 11,340

In Wells, small is beautiful. This is England's smallest city, and only qualifies for the title thanks to a magnificent medieval cathedral, which sits beside the grand Bishop's Palace – the official residence of the Bishop of Bath and Wells since the 12th century.

Medieval buildings and cobbled streets radiate out from the cathedral green to a marketplace that has been the bustling heart of Wells for some nine centuries (Wednesday and Saturday are market days). Film buffs might also recognise it from the hit British comedy *Hot Fuzz* – the film's final shoot-out was filmed here.

Sights

★Wells Cathedral CATHEDRAL

(Cathedral Church of St Andrew; www.wellscathedral.org.uk; Cathedral Green; requested donation adult/child £6/3; ⏲7am-7pm Apr-Sep, to 6pm Oct-Mar) Wells' gargantuan Gothic cathedral sits plumb in the centre of the city, surrounded by one of the largest cathedral closes anywhere in England. It was built in stages between 1180 and 1508, and consequently showcases several Gothic styles. Among its notable features are the **West Front**, decorated with more than 300 carved figures, and the famous **scissor arches** – an ingenious architectural solution to counter the subsidence of the central tower.

In the north transept is a **mechanical clock** dating from 1392 – the second-oldest in England after the one at Salisbury Cathedral – which shows the position of the planets and the phases of the moon.

Other highlights include the elegant **Lady Chapel** (1326), the fan-vaulted **Chapter House** (1306) and the celebrated **chained library**, which contains books and manuscripts dating back to 1472. Outside, the covered cloister known as the **Chain Bridge** enabled clerics to reach the cathedral without getting their robes wet.

Free guided tours run regularly from Monday to Saturday. You'll need a photography permit (£3) to take pictures.

Cathedral Close HISTORIC SITE

Wells Cathedral forms the centrepiece of a cluster of ecclesiastical buildings dating back to the Middle Ages. Facing the west front, on the left are the 15th-century **Old Deanery** and the **Wells Museum** (www.wellsmuseum.org.uk; 8 Cathedral Green; adult/child £3/1; ⏲10am-5pm Mon-Sat Easter-Oct, to 4pm Nov-Easter).

Further north, **Vicars' Close** is a stunning 14th-century cobbled street, with a chapel at the end; members of the cathedral choir still live here. It is thought to be the oldest complete medieval street in Europe.

Bishop's Palace HISTORIC BUILDING

(www.bishopspalacewells.co.uk; Market Place; adult/child £7/3; ⏲10am-6pm Apr-Oct, to 4pm Nov-Mar) Built for the bishop in the 13th century, this moat-ringed palace is purportedly the oldest inhabited building in England. Inside, the palace's state rooms and ruined great hall are worth a look, but it's the shady gardens that are the real draw. The natural springs after which Wells is named bubble up in the palace's grounds.

Wookey Hole CAVE

(www.wookey.co.uk; adult/child £18.50/14; ⏲10am-5pm Apr-Oct, to 4pm Nov-Mar) The River Axe has gouged out this network of deep limestone caverns, which are famous for striking stalagmites and stalactites, one of which is the legendary Witch of Wookey Hole, who was turned to stone by a local priest. Admission to the caves is by guided tour; up on top you'll find beyond-kitsch tourist attractions ranging from a penny arcade to a mirror maze. Wookey Hole is 3 miles northwest of Wells; look out for brown signs on the A371.

Sleeping

Stoberry House B&B **££**

(☎01749-672906; www.stoberryhouse.co.uk; Stoberry Park; s £85, d £95-155; P 📶) It's hard to know which is more beautiful: the lush, 2.5-hectare garden, or the house that overflows with rich fabrics, plush cushions and boutique flourishes. Expect pod coffee machines, luxury teas, books to browse and the use of a well-stocked pantry. It's all tucked away in a private estate.

Ancient Gate House Hotel HOTEL **££**

(☎01749-672029; www.ancientgatehouse.co.uk; 20 Sadler Street,; s £90-95, d £110-125; 📶) This old hostelry is partly built right into the cathedral's west gate. Rooms are decorated in regal reds and duck-egg blues; the best have four-poster beds and knockout cathedral views through latticed windows. They're £15 extra, and worth it.

WORTH A TRIP

CHEDDAR GORGE

Carved out by glacial meltwater during the last ice age, these limestone cliffs form England's deepest natural canyon, in places towering 138m above the twisting B3135. Beneath the cliffs, **Cheddar Gorge** (www.cheddargorge.co.uk; Explorer Ticket adult/child £20/14; ⏲10.30am-5.30pm) is riddled with miles of subterranean caves. Cox's Cave and Gough's Cave are the easiest to reach, decorated with impressive displays of stalactites and stalagmites. Admission covers parking in the gorge and entry to the caves. Cheddar Gorge is about 20 miles northwest of Wells on the A371.

X-Treme (☎01934-742343; www.cheddargorge.co.uk/x-treme; 1½-hr trips adult/child £22/20) Cheddar Gorge's main outdoors company offers guided caving trips lasting around 1½ hours. Crawling, climbing ladders and squeezing through small spaces inevitably means you'll get wet and dirty. But that photo featuring mud-caked dungarees, helmet and head torch is worth it. X-Treme runs rock-climbing sessions too (adult/child £22/20).

Cheddar Gorge Cheese Company (☎01934-742810; www.cheddargorgecheeseco.co.uk; The Cliffs, Cheddar; adult/child £2/free; ⏲10am-5pm Easter-Oct, winter hours vary) Along with its caves, Cheddar is also famous as the home of the nation's favourite cheese, produced here since the 12th century (Henry II considered it 'the best cheese in Britain', and the king's accounts from 1170 record that he purchased around 4644kg of the stuff). At this cheesemaker you can watch the whole creamy, gooey transformation process from a viewing gallery, then buy some tangy, whiffy souvenirs at the shop.

Beryl B&B ££
(☎01749-678738; www.beryl-wells.co.uk; Hawkers Lane; s £75-95, d £110-160; P 📶 🏊) This grand gabled mansion offers a taste of English eccentricity. Every inch of the house is crammed with antique atmosphere, and the rooms boast grandfather clocks, chaises longues and four-posters galore. It's about a mile from Wells.

★**Babington House** LUXURY HOTEL £££
(☎01373-812266; www.babingtonhouse.co.uk; near Frome; r £270-410; P 📶 🏊) It's eye-poppingly pricey, but this lauded design hotel is one of Britain's most luxurious. It's a mash-up of *Homes & Gardens* and *Wallpaper:* heritage beds, antique dressers and period fireplaces meet minimalist furniture, sanded wood floors and retro lamps. There's a cool library, 45-seat private cinema and spa in the old cowshed. It's 14 miles east of Wells.

Eating

Strangers with Coffee CAFE £
(☎07728 047233; 31 St Cuthbert St; cakes £2-5; ⏲7.30am-4pm Tue-Sat) 'Life is too short to drink bad coffee' says the sign – something they've taken to heart here as they work caffeinated magic with some of the best beans in town. There's a tempting selection of cakes to match.

★**Goodfellows Cafe & Seafood Restaurant** CAFE ££
(☎01749-673866; www.goodfellowswells.co.uk; 5 Sadler St; mains £11-24; ⏲11am-3pm daily, 6-9.30pm Wed-Sat) There's a choice of eating options in Goodfellows' three vibrant rooms: the continental cafe menu offers cakes, pastries and light lunches (opt to pay either £10 or £19 for two courses and a drink). Or book for an evening fine-dining experience; £29 gets you three classy courses, while the five-course seafood tasting menu (£49) is an absolute treat.

Square Edge BISTRO ££
(☎01749-671166; www.square-edgecafe.co.uk; 2 Town Halls Bldgs; mains £8-18; ⏲9am-5pm Mon-Wed, to 8.30pm Thu-Sat, 10am-3pm Sun) There's an easygoing charm to Square Edge, a retro eatery where 1950s movie posters frame old jukeboxes and vintage radios. Treats range from garlicky portobello mushrooms on soda bread toast, to steak with Stilton sauce. Hard-to-resist puddings might include blueberry Bakewell slice or a supremely sticky Eton mess.

Information

Tourist Office (☎01749-671770; www.wellssomerset.com; 8 Cathedral Green; ⏲10am-5pm Mon-Sat Easter-Oct, to 4pm Nov-Easter)

Getting There & Away

The bus station is south of Cuthbert St, on Princes Rd. Useful services include the following:

Bath bus 173; £5.50, 1¼ hours, half-hourly Monday to Saturday, hourly Sunday

Bristol bus 376; £5.50, one hour, half-hourly

Cheddar Bus 26 (£4.50, 25 minutes, hourly Monday to Saturday) continues to Weston-super-Mare (£5.50, 1¼ hours).

Glastonbury bus 37/375/376; £3.50, 15 minutes, several times an hour

Glastonbury

POP 8900

Ley lines converge, white witches convene and every shop is filled with the aroma of smouldering joss sticks in good old Glastonbury, the southwest's undisputed capital of alternative culture. Now famous for its annual musical mudfest, held on Michael Eavis' farm in nearby Pilton, Glastonbury has a much more ancient past: the town's iconic tor was an important pagan site, and is rumoured by some to be the mythical Isle of Avalon, King Arthur's last resting place. It's also allegedly one of the world's great spiritual nodes, marking the meeting point of many mystical lines of power – so if you feel the need to get your chakras realigned, this is definitely the place. Whatever the truth of the various legends swirling round Glastonbury, one thing's for certain – watching the sunrise from the top of the tor is an experience you won't forget in a hurry.

Sights

★**Glastonbury Tor** LANDMARK

(NT; www.nationaltrust.org.uk) FREE Topped by the ruined, medieval **Chapel of St Michael**, the iconic hump of Glastonbury Tor is visible for miles around, and provides Somerset with one of its most unmistakable landmarks. It takes half an hour to walk up from the start of the trail on Well House Lane; the steepest sections are stepped. Between April and Septembe,r a regular Tor Bus (adult/child £3/1.50) shuttles from St Dunstan's car park near Glastonbury Abbey to the trailhead on Well House Lane; alternatively, it's a 20-minute walk.

The tor is the focal point for a wealth of local lore. According to Celtic legend, the tor is the home of Arawn or Gwyn ap Nudd, king of the underworld and lord of the faeries. A more famous legend identifies the tor as the mythic Isle of Avalon, where King Arthur was taken after being mortally wounded in battle, and where Britain's 'once and

GLASTONBURY FESTIVAL

To many people, Glastonbury is synonymous with the **Glastonbury Festival of Contemporary Performing Arts** (www.glastonburyfestivals.co.uk; tickets from £228; Jun or Jul), a majestic (and frequently mud-soaked) extravaganza of music, theatre, dance, cabaret, carnival, spirituality and general all-round weirdness that's been held on and off on farmland in Pilton, just outside Glastonbury, for the last 40-plus years (bar the occasional off-year to let the farm recover).

The first event was held in 1970, when young dairy farmer Michael Eavis decided to stage his own British version of Woodstock on his land at Worthy Farm. Eavis borrowed £15,000 and invited some bands to play on a couple of makeshift stages in a field. Entry was £1, which included a pint of milk from Eavis' dairy herd; among the performers was Marc Bolan of T-Rex, who arrived in typically flamboyant style in his own velvet-covered Buick.

Forty-something years later, the festival has become the world's longest-running pop-music festival, attracting crowds of more than 120,000. It's even had a feature-length film made about it, directed by Julien Temple. Eavis' daughter Emily has since taken over the day-to-day running of the festival, and her decision to give headline slots to artists such as Dolly Parton, Jay-Z and U2 has led many people to grumble that Glastonbury's gone mainstream – but with acts such as the Rolling Stones and the Arctic Monkeys still lining up to play, Glastonbury's status as the UK's premier outdoor party looks safe for years to come.

More importantly, even the local councillors seem to have come around; after years of wrangling, in 2014 the festival was granted an unprecedented 10-year licence, a sign that the powers-that-be have recognised the festival's status as a national treasure. Tickets usually go on sale in the autumn, and always sell out within a matter of minutes, so you need to get in lightning-quick if you want to go.

Glastonbury

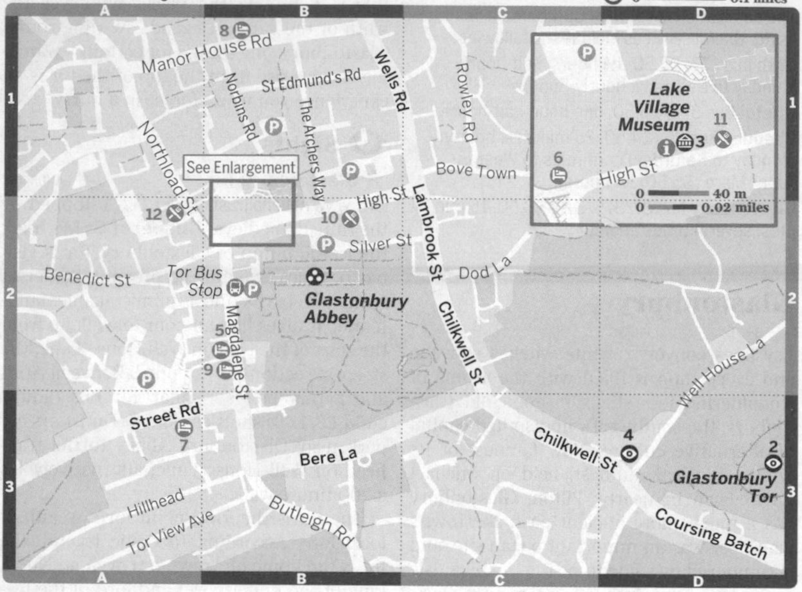

Glastonbury

Top Sights
1 Glastonbury Abbey B2
2 Glastonbury Tor D3
3 Lake Village Museum D1

Sights
4 Chalice Well & Gardens D3

Sleeping
5 Covenstead B2
6 Crown Glastonbury Backpackers C1
7 Glastonbury Townhouse A3
8 Glastonbury White House B1
9 Magdalene House B2

Eating
10 Hundred Monkeys Cafe B2
11 Rainbow's End D1
12 Who'd a Thought It Inn A2

future king' sleeps until his country calls again. Others believe that the tor marks an ancient mystical node where invisible lines of energy, known as ley lines, converge.

It's easy to see why the tor has inspired so many myths. It's a strange presence in an otherwise pan-flat landscape, and in ancient times (when the area around Glastonbury was covered by water for much of the year), the tor would indeed have appeared as an island, wreathed in mists and cut off by rivers, marshes and bogs.

Chalice Well & Gardens GARDENS
(☎01458-835528; www.chalicewell.org.uk; Chilkwell St; adult/child £4.20/2.10; ⏰10am-6pm Apr-Oct, to 4.30pm Nov-Mar) Shaded by yew trees and criss-crossed by quiet paths, the Chalice Well & Gardens have been sites of pilgrimage since the days of the Celts. The iron-red waters from the 800-year-old well are rumoured to have healing properties, good for everything from eczema to smelly feet; some legends also identify the well as the hiding place of the Holy Grail.

★Glastonbury Abbey RUINS
(☎01458-832267; www.glastonburyabbey.com; Magdalene St; adult/child £7.60/4.70; ⏰9am-8pm Jun-Aug, to 6pm Mar-May, Sep & Oct, to 4pm Nov-Feb) The scattered ruins of Glastonbury Abbey give little hint that this was once one of England's great seats of ecclesiastical power. It was torn down following Henry VIII's dissolution of the monasteries in 1539, and the last abbot, Richard Whiting, was hung, drawn and quartered on the tor. Today's striking ruins include some of the nave walls, the remains of **St Mary's chapel**, and

the crossing arches, which may have been scissor-shaped like those in Wells Cathedral.

The grounds also contain a **museum**, **cider orchard** and **herb garden**. According to legend, the abbey's famous holy thorn tree sprang from the staff of Joseph of Arimathea, Jesus' great-uncle, who supposedly visited the abbey following Christ's death. It blooms at Christmas and Easter.

The abbey even has an Arthurian connection. In the 12th century, monks supposedly uncovered a tomb in the abbey grounds inscribed *Hic iacet sepultus inclitus rex arturius in insula avalonia*, or 'Here lies buried the renowned King Arthur in the Isle of Avalon'. Inside the tomb were two entwined skeletons, purportedly those of Arthur and his wife Guinevere. The bones were reburied beneath the altar in 1278, but were lost following the abbey's destruction.

★Lake Village Museum MUSEUM
(The Tribunal, 9 High St; adult/child £3.50/2; ⏲10am-3pm Mon-Sat) The Lake Village Museum displays finds from a prehistoric bog village discovered in nearby Godney. The houses were clustered in about six groups and built from reeds, hazel and willow. It's thought they were occupied by summer traders who lived the rest of the year around Glastonbury Tor.

Sleeping

Crown Glastonbury Backpackers HOSTEL £
(☎01458-833353; 4 Market Pl; dm £25, d £35-50; @🛜) Well worn, grungy and set above a proper boozers bar, this friendly, erstwhile backpackers' favourite still draws in the travellers thanks to the big kitchen, comfy lounge, heart-off-the-action location and cheap beds.

Covenstead B&B ££
(☎01458-830278; www.covenstead.co.uk; Magdalene St; s £60, d £70-90; P🛜) It's as if they've distilled the wacky essence of Glastonbury and poured it all over this weirdly wonderful B&B. The downstairs is a riot of oddities: mock skeletons, witches hats, upcycled antlers and draped python skins. Bedroom themes range from fairy via green man and Gothic to Halloween honeymoon. A tad crazy, yes, but also delightfully done.

Magdalene House B&B ££
(☎01458-830202; www.magdalenehouseglastonbury.co.uk; Magdalene St; s £70-95, d £90-105, f £130-140; P🛜) Artfully decorated Magdalene used to be a school run by Glastonbury's nuns, and one room still overlooks the abbey grounds. Each of the tall, light rooms is an array of olive, oatmeal and other soft tones, while tasteful knick-knacks give it all a homely feel.

Glastonbury Townhouse B&B ££
(☎01458-831040; www.glastonburytownhouse.co.uk; Street Rd; r £75-120; P🛜) Nothing too outlandish about this place – just a solid, red-brick, Edwardian town house, with a clutch of quiet rooms, lots of painted furniture and a contemporary vibe. Breakfast, served overlooking the garden, can be vegetarian, vegan, or dairy- or gluten-free.

Glastonbury White House B&B ££
(☎01458-830886; www.theglastonburywhitehouse.com; 21 Manor House Rd; s/d £60/80; P🛜) There's a serene feel to this two-room guesthouse with its subtle, natural tones, clawfoot baths, cast-iron fireplaces and polished wooden floors. Organic elements feature strongly, from handmade cotton fabrics and fair-trade soap to optional vegetarian breakfasts (£10 extra each) served till 10.30am. Checkout is also delightfully relaxed: noon.

Eating

Rainbow's End VEGETARIAN £
(☎01458-833896; www.rainbowsendcafe.com; 17b High St; mains £5-9; ⏲10am-4pm; 🌿) This psychedelic cafe sums up the Glastonbury spirit, with its all-veggie food, potted plants and mix-and-match furniture. Tuck into homity pie or a hot quiche, followed by scrumptious homemade cake. There's a small patio out back.

WORTH A TRIP

LORD POULETT ARMS

Hinton St George's deliciously olde-worlde village pub **Lord Poulett Arms** (☎01460-73149; www.lordpoulettarms.com; Hinton St George; mains £14-20; ⏲noon-2pm & 6-9pm; P) has been named Somerset Dining Pub of the Year numerous times. No wonder: the hearty food is fantastic and the building oozes country atmosphere, with beams, roaring fires and stacks of ale barrels behind the bar. Hard to fault.

It even has quirky rooms (singles £60 to £65, doubles £85 to £95) upstairs. It's roughly 15 miles from Yeovil and Taunton.

OFF THE BEATEN TRACK

SOMERSET LEVELS

Flat as a pancake, sub-sea-level and criss-crossed with canals (known locally as rhynes), the Somerset Levels are one of England's largest native wetlands. Covering almost 250 sq miles between the Quantock and Mendip Hills, they're brilliant for bird-spotters – particularly in October and November, when huge flocks of starlings (properly known as murmurations) descend on the area. Nature reserves have been established at Ham Wall, Shapwick Heath, Sedgemoor and Westhay.

The flat landscape of the Levels also makes it ideal for cycling. Several trails pass through the village of Langport, including the long-distance River Parrett Trail.

Bocabar BRITISH ££
(☎01458-440558; htpp://glastonbury.bocabar.co.uk; Morland Rd; lunch £5-10, dinner £13.50-19.95; ⏲9.30am-11pm Tue-Thu, to 1am Fri & Sat, 10am-5pm Sun & Mon) There's been quite a transformation at this cavernous red-brick building: from old sheepskin factory to hip hang-out. It's now home to live bands and events several times a week, and features a pan-global menu that takes in Thai curries, classic steaks, gourmet burgers and adventurous crêpes. The industrial-chic vibe adds appeal.

It's about 1.5 miles southwest of the town centre along Morland Rd.

Hundred Monkeys Cafe BISTRO ££
(www.hundredmonkeyscafe.com; 52 High St; mains £8-15; ⏲8am-6pm Sun-Wed, to 10pm Thu, to 9pm Fri & Sat; 🖉) A buzzy bistro featuring pine furniture, handwritten blackboards and a fair-trade, seasonal ethos that infuses the mezze platters, pasta dishes, curries and risottos – with plenty of gluten-free and vegan options. The tea selection is enormous and the wines are biodynamic; best enjoyed on Thursday, acoustic music night.

Who'd a Thought It Inn PUB FOOD ££
(www.whodathoughtit.co.uk; 17 Northload St; mains £11-21; ⏲noon-9pm) In this pleasantly peculiar locals' pub, antique bottles and vintage advertising signs sit beside swathes of dried hops and an old red telephone box, while an upside-down bike dangles from the ceiling. The food is solid pub fare – think sausages, pies and steaks – but there are usually specials chalked above the bar.

ℹ Information

Glastonbury Tourist Office (☎01458-832954; www.glastonburytic.co.uk; The Tribunal, 9 High St; ⏲10am-3.30pm Mon-Fri, to 4.30pm Sat)

ℹ Getting There & Away

There is no train station in Glastonbury.

Useful bus routes include:

Taunton bus 29; £5.50, 1½ hours, four daily Monday to Saturday

Wells bus 37/375/376; £3.50, 15 minutes, several times an hour

CORNWALL

You can't get further west than the ancient Celtic kingdom of Cornwall (or Kernow, as it's known to Cornish speakers). Blessed with the southwest's wildest coastline and most breathtakingly beautiful beaches, this proudly independent peninsula has always marched to its own tune.

While the staple industries of old – mining, fishing and farming – have all but disappeared, Cornwall has since reinvented itself as one of the nation's creative corners. Whether it's exploring the space-age domes of the Eden Project, sampling the culinary creations of a celebrity chef or basking on a deserted beach, you're guaranteed to feel the itch of inspiration. Time to let a little Kernow into your soul.

Since 2006, Cornwall's historic mining areas have formed part of the UK's newest Unesco World Heritage Site, the Cornwall & West Devon Mining Landscape (www.cornish-mining.org.uk).

ℹ Getting There & Away

It's pretty easy to get to Cornwall these days, although its far westerly location means travel times from most locations in the UK are long.

The county's main airport is located just outside Newquay, with links to London Gatwick and other major cities.

The main train line from London Paddington runs through the centre of the county before terminating at Penzance.

The major road into Cornwall, the A30, is prone to traffic jams in summer. The A38 from

Plymouth over the Tamar Bridge into Cornwall is an alternative, but it's a more circuitous route.

Five miles from Newquay, Cornwall's main airport **Newquay Cornwall Airport** (☎01637-860600; www.newquaycornwallairport.com) currently offers direct daily flights to Manchester and London Gatwick with **Flybe** (www.flybe.com) and the Isles of Scilly with IoS Skybus (p359).

First Kernow bus 56 (26 minutes, hourly Monday to Saturday, five on Sunday) runs from Newquay's bus station to Padstow. A taxi will cost £15 to £25 from the town centre.

Various seasonal destinations around the UK and Europe are also offered during the summer.

Getting Around

Bus, train and ferry timetables can be found on the **Traveline South West** (☎0871 200 2233; www.travelinesw.com) website.

The useful **Great Scenic Railways** (www.greatscenicrailways.com) website features online booking and timetables for Cornwall's regional railways.

BUS

Cornwall's main bus provider is **First Kernow** (☎customer service 0845 600 1420, timetables 0871 200 2233; www.firstgroup.com/cornwall), which operates the majority of services between major towns. The county's other big bus company, Western Greyhound, went into administration in 2015, and although some of its routes are now operated by smaller coach companies, many were axed, leaving some rural communities stranded without a regular bus service.

TRAIN

Cornwall's main railway line follows the coast as far as Penzance, with branch lines to Gunnislake, Looe, Falmouth, St Ives and Newquay.

Most trains are provided by **Great Western Railway** (☎0345 7000 125; www.gwr.com), although **Crosscountry Trains** (☎0844 811 0124; www.crosscountrytrains.co.uk) also run through major stations.

TRANSPORT PASSES

Several passes cover public transport in Cornwall.

Ride Cornwall Ranger (adult/child/family £10/7.50/20) is the best all-round value covering bus and train travel across Cornwall.

There are also Day Ranger tickets for all of Cornwall's branch railway lines, as well as 'Two Together' and 'Groupsave' tickets for two and four adults travelling together.

Freedom of Devon & Cornwall Rover (3-day adult/child £46.45/23.20, 8-day adult/child £71.20/35.60) provides three days' train travel in seven, or eight days' travel in 14. Valid after 9am and anytime weekends.

Bude

POP 9242

Just a scant few miles across the Devon border, Bude is a breezy seaside town with a bevy of impressive beaches, as well as a lovely seawater lido built in the 1930s. The town itself isn't much to look at, but the stunning coastline on its doorstep makes it worthy of a stop.

Sights & Activities

Bude's beaches are definitely its main asset. Closest is **Summerleaze**, a bucket-and-spade affair with lots of space at low tide, and the beautiful **Bude Sea Pool** (www.budeseapool.net) FREE. North across Summerleaze Down is **Crooklets**, offering golden sand and rock pools at low tide.

To reach Bude's other beaches requires either a car or a hike along the coast path. Three miles south of town is **Widemouth Bay** (*wid*-mouth), a broad, sandy beach good for both families and surfers. Two miles further is the shingly beach of **Millook**, followed by the dramatic cliffs around **Crackington Haven**.

Three miles north of town are the National Trust–owned **Northcott Mouth** and **Sandymouth**.

A mile further on is pebbly **Duckpool**, often quiet even in summer.

Bude Castle MUSEUM

(www.thecastlebude.org.uk; The Castle; ⏲10am-5pm Easter-Oct, 10am-4pm Nov-Easter; 📶) FREE Housed in a peculiar folly behind

WORTH A TRIP

MONTACUTE HOUSE

Built in the 1590s for Sir Edward Phelips, a speaker of the House of Commons, **Montacute House** (NT; ☎01935-823289; www.nationaltrust.org.uk; Montacute; adult/child £11.40/5.70; ⏲house 11am-4.30pm Mar-Oct, noon-3pm Sat & Sun Nov-Feb, gardens 10am-5pm daily Mar-Oct, 11am-4pm Wed-Sat Nov-Feb) contains some of the finest 16th- and 17th-century interiors in the country. It's plasterwork, chimney pieces and tapestries are renowned, but the highlight is the **Long Gallery** – the longest such hall in England, it's rich in Elizabethan portraits.

Montacute is 5 miles west of Yeovil on the A3088.

WORTH A TRIP

CAMEL VALLEY VINEYARD

Cornwall might not seem like an obvious place for wine-making, but local entrepreneur Bob Lindo has been producing award-winning vintages at his **Camel Valley Vineyard** (01208-77959; www.camelvalley.com; shop 10am-5pm Mon-Sat, tours 2.30pm Mon-Fri & 5pm Wed) since 1989. The range includes award-winning whites and rosés, and a bubbly that's Champagne in all but name. Aficionados say the wines have a fresh, light quality that comes from the mild climate and pure sea air. Vineyard tours run regularly and you can taste and buy the goods in the on-site shop.

Summerleaze beach, Bude Castle was built by local inventor Sir Goldsworthy Gurney, whose creations included theatrical limelight and steam carriages. The building now houses a small **heritage centre**, which roves through Bude's maritime, geological and social history. There's also a cafe on the top floor.

Raven Surf School SURFING
(07860-465499; www.ravensurf.co.uk; per lesson £35) A reliable school run by Mike Raven, a former surfing champion. It also offers surf life-saving and instructor courses, as well as accommodation in 'surf pods' (ecofriendly wooden cabins) and a campsite nearby.

Big Blue Surf School SURFING
(01288-331764; www.bigbluesurfschool.co.uk; per lesson £30) A recommended school that offers lessons mainly to beginner and intermediate surfers. Special lessons for disabled surfers and a 'women's club' on Tuesday evenings and Saturday mornings are some of its main attractions.

Sleeping & Eating

Bangor's Organic B&B ££
(01288-361297; www.bangorsorganic.co.uk; Poundstock; d £100; P) This ecofriendly B&B sits near Poundstock, 7 miles from Bude. The house is elegantly Victorian and the two rooms are fairly frilly, but the draw is the rural setting; it's set among 2 hectares, and you'll find fresh-picked veg and just-laid eggs on the breakfast table. Gill and Neil are your friendly hosts, and also run an excellent farm shop.

Elements Hotel HOTEL ££
(01288-275066; www.elements-life.co.uk; Marine Dr; s £60, d £79-120; P) Smart clifftop hotel with 11 rooms in whites and creams, big coastal views from the outdoor deck, a gym and Finholme sauna, and surf packages courtesy of nearby Raven Surf School. The downstairs bar does decent food, too.

Beach at Bude HOTEL £££
(01288-389800; www.thebeachatbude.co.uk; Summerleaze Cres; r £135-237.50; P) For a proper hotel stay, complete with all the pampering, this is definitely the choice in Bude. The main sell is the fine position behind Summerleaze beach, but the rooms are attractive too: spacious and smart, with neutral tones, pine headboards and Lloyd Loom chairs, conjuring the feel of a New England beach cabin.

The Bank TAPAS £
(01288-352070; www.thebankatbude.co.uk; Pethericks Mill; tapas £4.25-8.95; 3-10pm Tue-Sat) It's a little way from the town centre, but this relaxed joint is a popular weekend haunt for locals, serving authentic Spanish tapas in a sweet setting inside a former mill. It also serves paella and more substantial fish and shellfish dishes. Follow the road south from the tourist office towards the A39 and look out for signs.

Life's a Beach CAFE ££
(01288-355222; www.lifesabeach.info; Summerleaze; mains lunch £8-12, dinner £16.50-22.50; 10.30am-3pm & 7-10pm Mon-Sat year-round, 10.30am-3pm Sun) This beachside bistro overlooking Summerleaze has a split personality: by day it's a beach cafe serving coffees, panini and ice creams; by night it's a smart seafood restaurant. It's the most popular place to eat in town, so book ahead.

Information

Bude Tourist Office (01288-354240; www.visitbude.info; The Crescent; 10am-5pm Mon-Sat, plus 10am-4pm Sun summer) Beside the main car park near Bude Castle.

Getting There & Away

First Kernow bus 95/96 (six daily Monday to Saturday, four on Sunday) stops in Bude en route from Camelford (one hour 10 minutes) via Tintagel (50 minutes), Boscastle (40 minutes) and the beaches south of Bude.

Most buses also connect onwards to Wadebridge via Port Isaac, Polzeath, Rock and nearby beaches.

Boscastle

POP 641

Nestled in the crook of a steep coombe (valley) at the confluence of three rivers, Boscastle's seagoing heritage stretches back to Elizabethan times. With its quaint cottages, flower-clad cliffs, tinkling streams and sturdy quay, it's almost impossibly photogenic.

But the peaceful setting belies some turbulent history: in 2004 Boscastle was devastated by one of Britain's largest-ever flash floods, which carried away cars, bridges and buildings. The village has since been rebuilt, but look closely and you'll still spot reminders of the floods dotted around.

Sights

Museum of Witchcraft MUSEUM

(01840-250111; www.museumofwitchcraftandmagic.co.uk; The Harbour; adult/child £5/4; 10.30am-6pm Mon-Sat, 11.30am-6pm Sun Mar-Nov) This oddball museum claims to house the world's largest collection of witchy memorabilia, from haunted skulls to hags' bridles and voodoo dolls. It's half-tacky, half-spooky, and some of the more 'controversial' exhibits might perturb kids of a sensitive disposition (or adults, for that matter).

Sleeping & Eating

Boscastle YHA HOSTEL £

(0845 371 9006; boscastle@yha.org.uk; Palace Stables, The Harbour; dm £19-25; Apr-Nov) Boscastle's shoebox-sized hostel was all but washed away by the floods, but it's been completely renovated. It's in one of the village's oldest buildings beside the harbour, but be prepared for small dorms, especially considering the price.

Orchard Lodge B&B ££

(01840-250418; www.orchardlodgeboscastle.co.uk; Gunpool Lane; d £95-110; P) Uphill from the harbour, Geoff and Shirley Barratt have turned their whitewashed house into a charming B&B bolthole, with each room boasting its own mix-and-match furnishings and fabrics, and hallways plastered with Thomas Hardy quotes. There's a two-night minimum stay in summer, and rates get cheaper the longer you stay.

Boscastle House B&B ££

(01840-250654; www.boscastlehouse.co.uk; Tintagel Rd; s/d from £60/110; P) The fanciest of Boscastle's B&Bs, in a Victorian house overlooking the valley, with five classy rooms with a bright, contemporary feel, mixing neutral colours with bold print wallpapers. Charlotte has bay-window views, Nine Windows has his-and-hers sinks and a free-standing bath, and Trelawney has ample space and its own sofa.

Boscastle Farm Shop CAFE £

(01840-250827; www.boscastlefarmshop.co.uk; cakes & teas £3-5; 10am-5pm; P) Half a mile from the harbour on the B3263, this excellent farm shop sells its own produce, including ruby-red beef and possibly the best sausages on the north coast. In the cafe, tall windows look onto fields and coast – the perfect setting for a cream tea.

Waterloo Restaurant BRITISH £££

(01840-250202; www.wellingtonhotelboscastle.com; The Harbour; 2-/3-course menu £30/37.50; dinner 6.30-9.30pm Tue-Sat) This turreted coaching inn dates back to the 16th century (previous guests include King Edward VII and Guy Gibson of Dambusters fame). It's an old-fashioned place – flock carpets, burnished furniture, upholstered chairs – and the restaurant continues the trad theme. It's now run by Kit Davis, who previously ran his own restaurant in Bude.

Information

Boscastle Tourist Office (01840-250010; www.visitboscastleandtintagel.com; The Harbour; 10am-5pm Mar-Oct, 10.30am-4pm Nov-Feb) Not far from the quay, and with some useful leaflets on local history and walks.

Getting There & Away

The coastal 95/96 bus (six daily Monday to Saturday, four on Sunday) stops in Tintagel as it trundles from Camelford to Bude.

Tintagel

POP 1822

The spectre of King Arthur looms large over Tintagel and its clifftop castle. Though the present-day ruins mostly date from the 13th century, archaeological digs have revealed the foundations of a much earlier fortress, fuelling speculation that Arthur may indeed have been born at the castle as locals like to claim.

The village itself isn't terribly exciting, but if you're looking for a cheesy King Arthur souvenir, you'll find them in ample supply.

Sights

★Tintagel Castle CASTLE
(EH; ☎01840-770328; adult/child £7.90/4.70; ⏲10am-6pm Apr-Sep, to 5pm Oct, to 4pm Nov-Mar) Famous as the supposed birthplace of King Arthur, Tintagel's stunning clifftop castle has been occupied since Roman times and once served as a residence for Cornwall's Celtic kings, but the present castle is largely the work of Richard, Earl of Cornwall, who built a castle here during the 1230s. Though the Arthurian links may be tenuous, it's certainly a fine spot for a fortress: clinging to black granite cliffs, surrounded by booming surf and wheeling gulls, it's the classic fairy-tale castle.

Though much of the structure has crumbled away, it's still possible to make out several walls and much of the original layout. Part of the castle stands on a rocky outcrop cut off from the mainland, and is accessed via a wooden bridge and a very steep staircase (vertigo sufferers beware).

Trails lead along the headland to the atmospheric medieval chapel of **St Glebe's**, and down on the beach below the castle, the rocky mouth of **Merlin's Cave** is exposed at low tide – local legend claims it's where the wizard once wove his spells.

It's a steep walk down to the castle from the village car parks; in summer, Land Rover taxis shuttle up and down throughout the day.

Old Post Office HISTORIC BUILDING
(NT; ☎01840-770024; Fore St; adult/child £4/2; ⏲10.30am-5.30pm mid-Mar–Sep, 11am-4pm Oct) One of the National Trust's oldest properties, this is one of the best-preserved examples of a traditional 16th-century Cornish longhouse, topped by pepper-pot chimneys and riddled with tiny rooms. As its name suggests, it was used as a post office during the 19th century.

Getting There & Away

First Kernow bus 95/96 (six daily Monday to Saturday, four on Sunday) stops in Tintagel en route from Camelford (15 minutes) to Bude (50 minutes).

Port Isaac

POP 721

A few miles southwest of Tintagel is the classic Cornish fishing harbour of Port Isaac, a cluster of cobbled alleyways, slender opes (lanes) and cobwalled cottages collected around a medieval harbour and slipway.

Though still a working harbour, Port Isaac is best known as a filming location: the Brit film *Saving Grace* and the TV series *Doc Martin* have both used the village as a ready-made backdrop. A short walk west leads to the neighbouring harbour of **Port Gaverne**, while a couple of miles west is **Port Quin**, now owned by the National Trust.

Cornwall's chef *du jour*, Nathan Outlaw, has made the village his culinary centre of operations.

Sleeping & Eating

Old School Hotel HOTEL ££
(☎01208-880721; www.theoldschoolhotel.co.uk; Fore St; d £115-165; P 🛜) A small hotel that was originally Port Isaac's schoolhouse (*Doc Martin* fans might recognise it as the village school in the TV show). Appropriately, rooms are named after school subjects: top of the class are Latin, with its sleigh bed and cupboard bathroom; Biology, with its sofa and church-style windows; and split-level Mathematics, with shared terrace and bunk-beds for the kids.

Outlaw's Fish Kitchen SEAFOOD £
(☎01208-881183; www.outlaws.co.uk/fishkitchen; 1 Middle St; mains £6-10; ⏲noon-3pm & 6-9pm Tue-Sun Jun-Sep, Mon-Sat Oct-May) Nathan Outlaw's newest venture is this tiny fish restaurant, which specialises in small seafood tasting plates made to share. The exact menu is dictated by whatever's brought in on the day by Port Isaac's fishermen, and the restaurant is tiny, so bookings are essential.

Fresh from the Sea SEAFOOD ££
(☎01208-880849; www.freshfromthesea.co.uk; 18 New Rd; sandwiches £5.50-9.50, mains £10.50-20) Local man Callum Greehalgh takes out his boat daily in search of crab and lobster, then brings it back to sell at his dinky Port Isaac shop. Seafood doesn't get any fresher – a crab salad with glass of wine costs £12.50, and a whole lobster is £20. Depending on the season, oysters from nearby Porthilly cost £1.50 each.

★Restaurant Nathan Outlaw SEAFOOD £££
(☎01208-862737; www.nathan-outlaw.com; 6 New Rd; tasting menu £119; ⏲7-9pm Wed-Sat, plus noon-2pm Fri & Sat) Port Isaac's prestige has skyrocketed since Cornwall's top chef, Nathan Outlaw, moved his main operation here from Rock. This is the place to experience Outlaw's passion for Cornish fish and seafood. His style is surprisingly classic, relying on top-notch ingredients rather than cheffy tricks. As you'd expect of a twice Michelin-starred restaurant, it's expensive, but very much a tell-your-friends experience.

Getting There & Away

First Kernow bus 95/96 stops in Port Isaac at least four times daily en route between Camelford and Bude.

Padstow & Rock

POP 3162

If anywhere symbolises Cornwall's changing character, it's Padstow. This once-sleepy fishing port has been transformed into one of the county's most cosmopolitan corners thanks to celebrity chef Rick Stein, whose property portfolio encompasses several restaurants, shops and hotels, as well as a seafood school and fish-and-chip bar.

The 'Stein Effect' has certainly changed the place: Padstow feels more Kensington chic than Cornish quaint these days, with fancy restaurants and boutiques sitting alongside the old pubs and pasty shops. Whether the town's managed to hold on to its soul in the process is debatable, but it's still hard not to be charmed by the setting.

Across the Camel Estuary from Padstow is Rock, a once-quiet village that's been reinvented as an über-exclusive holiday destination. Nearby lies the long sweep of Daymer Bay, and between the two resorts is the treacherous sandbank known as the Doom Bar.

Sights & Activities

Padstow is surrounded by fine beaches, including the so-called Seven Bays: Trevone, Harlyn, Mother Ivey's, Booby's, Constantine, Treyarnon and Porthcothan.

National Lobster Hatchery NATURE DISPLAY
(☎01841-533877; www.nationallobsterhatchery.co.uk; South Quay; adult/child £3.75/1.75; ⏲10am-7.30pm Jul & Aug, to 4pm or 5pm Sep-Jun) In an effort to combat falling lobster stocks, this harbourside hatchery rears baby lobsters in tanks before returning them to the wild. Displays detail the crustaceans' life cycle, and there are viewing tanks where you can watch the residents in action. You can also book 30-minute 'Meet the Expert' tours (adult/child £12/6), which allow you a glimpse into work behind the scenes.

Prideaux Place HISTORIC BUILDING
(☎01841-532411; www.prideauxplace.co.uk; Prideaux Pl; house & grounds adult £8.50, grounds only £3; ⏲house 1.30-4pm Sun-Thu, grounds & tearoom 12.30-5.30pm Apr-Oct) Much favoured by directors of costume dramas, the stately Grade I-listed manor was built by the Prideaux-Brune family, purportedly descendants of William the Conqueror. Guided tours last around an hour and take in state rooms, staircases and Prideaux-Brune heirlooms, as well as the house's extensive collection of teddy bears.

Camel Trail CYCLING
(www.cornwall.gov.uk/cameltrail) The old Padstow–Bodmin railway was closed in the 1950s, and has now been turned into Cornwall's most popular bike trail. The main section starts in Padstow and runs east through Wadebridge (5.75 miles), but the trail runs on all the way to Poley Bridge on Bodmin Moor (18.3 miles). Bikes can be hired from **Padstow Cycle Hire** (☎01841-533533; www.padstowcyclehire.com; South Quay; per day adult/child £15/7; ⏲9am-5pm, to 9pm summer) or **Trail Bike Hire** (☎01841-532594; www.trailbikehire.co.uk; Unit 6, South Quay; adult £14, child £5-8; ⏲9am-6pm) at the Padstow end, or from **Bridge Bike Hire** (☎01208-813050; www.bridgebikehire.co.uk; adult £12-14, child £6-9; ⏲10am-5pm) at the Wadebridge end.

Pumps and helmets are usually included, but tandems and kids' trailers cost extra.

Most people do the route from Padstow and back, so it's often quieter (and much easier to find parking) if you start from the Wadebridge side.

Padstow Boat Trips BOATING
(www.padstowboattrips.com; South Quay) Between Easter and October, the **Jubilee Queen** (☎07836-798457; www.padstowboattrips.co.uk; South Quay; adult/child £12/7) runs scenic trips along the coastline, while **Padstow Sealife Safaris** (☎01841-521613; www.padstowsealifesafaris.co.uk; 2hr cruise adult/child £39/25) visits local seal and seabird colonies.

For something racier, 15-minute **speedboat trips** (£7) zip past the treacherous sandbank of Doom Bar and the beaches of Daymer Bay, Polzeath, Hawkers Cove and

Tregirls. The main Padstow Boat Trips website keeps listings of all the local operators.

Sleeping

Treyarnon Bay YHA HOSTEL £
(☎0845 371 9664; treyarnon@yha.org.uk; Treyarnon Bay; dm £22-25; ⊙reception 8-10am & 2-10pm; P ☁) A super 1930s-built beach hostel on the bluffs above Treyarnon Bay. Rooms are big and there's a good cafe, plus barbecues in summer – and the sunsets are spectacular. It's 4.5 miles east of Padstow: there's parking on-site, but the nearest bus stop is at Constantine, about a 20-minute walk away.

Althea Library B&B ££
(☎01841-532579; www.altheahouse-padstow.co.uk; 64 Church St, Padstow; d £90-120; P ☁) If you want to be in Padstow proper, this charming ivy-clad house is hard to better. There are two stylish self-catering suites: Rafters is accessed via a private staircase, while Driftwood has a pine four-poster bed. It's luxurious – both suites have sofas, Nespresso coffee machines, baths and small studio kitchens. There's also a nearby cottage for longer stays.

Woodlands B&B ££
(☎01841-532426; www.woodlands-padstow.co.uk; Treator; d £118-138; P ☁) A mile or so from Padstow's harbourside on the A389, offering green fields and distant flashes of sea, this is a great B&B base for Padstow, run by larger-than-life Hugo Woolley, who masterminds the legendary breakfasts and also sells his own boutique brand of granolas and mueslis. Rooms are a bit heavy on the creams and frills, but cosy nonetheless.

St Enodoc Hotel HOTEL £££
(☎01208-863394; www.enodoc-hotel.co.uk; Rock Rd; r £195-495; P ☁) Supremely sophisticated this place most certainly is, but cheap it certainly isn't (hardly a surprise in uber-chic Rock). Rooms are elegant, with muted tones offset by bright scatter cushions, cappuccino-coloured carpets, distressed dressers and artwork by Penzance painter Jessica Cooper. There's a very smart spa, too.

Eating

Chough Bakery BAKERY £
(☎01841-533361; www.thechoughbakery.co.uk; 1-3 The Strand, Padstow; pasties £3-5) Padstow's finest pasties, bar none – they've scooped top honours in the World Pasty Championships several times.

Cornish Arms GASTROPUB ££
(☎01841-520288; www.rickstein.com/the-cornish-arms.html; St Merryn; mains £7-18; ⊙11.30am-11pm) This country pub near the village of St Merryn is now owned by the Stein empire, and offers updated pub classics such as scampi-and-chips and pint-of-prawns, with a characteristically creative spin. The Sunday roast is phenomenally popular, so arrive early. It's a 3-mile drive from Padstow.

Rojano's in the Square ITALIAN ££
(☎01841-532796; www.rojanos.co.uk; 9 Mill Sq, Padstow; pizzas & pastas £8.50-17) Now under the stewardship of Paul Ainsworth, this excellent little Italian bistro turns out fantastic wood-fired pizzas, spicy pastas and antipasti.

Rick Stein's Cafe EUROPEAN ££
(☎01841-532700; Middle St, Padstow; mains £10.95-19.95; ⊙8am-9.30pm) Stein's backstreet bistro takes its inspiration from the chef's globetrotting travels, with dishes ranging all the way from the Far East to the Mediterranean: classic mussels with saffron, or Thai-spiced seafood broth. The vibe is relaxed, but you'll still need to book.

★ **Paul Ainsworth at No 6** BRITISH £££
(☎01841-532093; www.paul-ainsworth.co.uk/number6; 6 Middle St, Padstow; 2-/3-course lunch £19/26, dinner mains £28-40; ⊙noon-2.30pm & 6-10pm Tue-Sat) Rick Stein might be the household name, but Paul Ainsworth is touted by those in the know as Padstow's top chef. His food combines surprising flavours and impeccable presentation with a refreshingly unpretentious approach, and the town-house setting along one of Padstow's backstreets makes a relaxed, unfussy place to dine. Now Michelin-starred, this is Padstow's prime table.

TV fans might recognise his signature dessert, 'A Fairground Tale', from BBC2's *Great British Menu*.

Seafood Restaurant SEAFOOD £££
(☎01841-532700; www.rickstein.com; Riverside, Padstow; 3-course lunch £40, mains £19.50-65.50; ⊙noon-2pm & 6.30-10pm) Rick Stein's flagship seafooderie needs no introduction – it's one of Britain's foremost fish addresses, with an expensive menu offering treats such as fresh Padstow lobster and sumptuous *fruits de mer*. The setting is lovely, with a light-filled dining room and a conservatory overlooking the harbour. You'll generally need to book months in advance, although last-minute lunch tables sometimes crop up.

Information

Padstow Tourist Information Centre (☎01841-533449; www.padstowlive.com; North Quay; ⏲10am-5pm Mon-Sat, 10am-4pm Apr-Sep, 10am-4pm Mon-Sat Oct-Mar) In a red-brick building on the quayside.

Getting There & Away

There are a couple of car parks beside the harbour in Padstow, but they fill up quickly, so it's usually a better idea to park at one of the large car parks at the top of town and walk down.

The only useful bus is First Kernow bus 56 (hourly Monday to Saturday, five on Sunday, one hour 25 minutes) which runs along the coast via Harlyn Bay, Constantine Bay, Porthcothan, Mawgan Porth, Newquay Cornwall Airport, Porth Beach and Newquay.

Newquay

POP 19,423

If Padstow is Cornwall's Cannes, then Newquay is its Costa del Sol. Perched on the cliffs above a cluster of white-sand beaches, and packed with enough pubs, bars and dodgy clubs to give Ibiza a run for its money, it's become the summer venue of choice for beer boys, beach bums and surf addicts alike, all of whom descend on the town in their droves in summer. Newquay is also the capital of Cornish surfing, and if you're looking to learn how to brave the waves, this is the place to do it.

Sights

Newquay has a truly stunning location among some of North Cornwall's finest beaches. The best known is **Fistral**, England's most famous surfing beach. It's nestled on the west side of Towan Head, a 10-minute walk from the town centre.

To the east of Towan Head are Newquay's other main beaches. Just below town are **Towan**, **Great Western** and **Tolcarne**, followed by nearby **Lusty Glaze**. All offer good swimming and lifeguard supervision throughout summer.

You'll need transport to reach Newquay's other beaches. North of Lusty Glaze is **Porth**, a long, narrow beach that's popular with families, followed a couple of miles further by the massive curve of **Watergate Bay**, home to Jamie Oliver's much-vaunted restaurant, Fifteen Cornwall. Two miles north brings you to **Mawgan Porth**, a horseshoe-shaped bay that often stays quieter than its neighbours.

LOCAL KNOWLEDGE

BEDRUTHAN STEPS

Roughly halfway between Newquay and Padstow loom the stately rock stacks **Bedruthan Steps** (Carnewas; NT; www.nationaltrust.org.uk/carnewas-and-bedruthan-steps). These mighty granite pillars have been carved out by the relentless action of thousands of years of wind and waves, and now provide a stirring spot for a stroll. The area is owned by the National Trust, who also runs the car park and cafe. There's no admission fee, but if you're not a NT member you will have to pay for parking.

You'll find even more beaches to the southwest of Newquay, including the large, sandy, family-friendly beaches of **Crantock** (about 3 miles from town) and **Holywell Bay** (6 miles from town).

Blue Reef Aquarium AQUARIUM
(☎01637-878134; www.bluereefaquarium.co.uk/newquay; Towan Promenade; adult/child/family £10.50/8.25/35.50; ⏲10am-6pm; 👪) Small aquarium on Towan beach, with touch pools and various deep-sea denizens, including reef sharks, loggerhead turtles and a giant Pacific octopus. There's a discount for online bookings.

Newquay Zoo ZOO
(☎01637-873342; www.newquayzoo.org.uk; Trenance Gardens; adult/child/family £13.60/10.20/42.60; ⏲10am-5pm; 👪) Newquay's miniature zoo isn't a world-beater, but its population of penguins, lemurs, parrots and snakes will keep the kids happy. The Tropical House and Toad Hall are particularly good fun, and key events include penguin feeding at noon and lion feeding at 2.30pm.

Trerice HISTORIC BUILDING
(NT; ☎01637-875404; www.nationaltrust.org.uk/trerice; adult/child £7.65/3.80; ⏲house 11am-5pm, gardens 10.30am-5pm) Built in 1751, this National Trust–owned Elizabethan manor is most famous for the elaborate barrel-roofed ceiling of the Great Chamber, and some fantastic original 16th-century stained glass among the 576 panes that make up the great window. It's 3.3 miles southeast of Newquay.

Activities

Newquay's brimming with surf schools, but the quality is variable. Choose one that offers small-group sessions, and ideally has a no-stag-party policy. Ask about teachers' accreditation and experience, and whether they travel to beaches other than Fistral – good schools follow the best waves.

English Surfing Federation Surf School SURFING
(01637-879571; www.englishsurfschool.com; lessons from £35) One of the most experienced and efficient large schools, linked with Rip Curl and staffed by fully English Surfing Federation–approved instructors (including the British team coach). It also offers coasteering and bodyboarding.

Kingsurf Surf School SURFING
(01637-860091; www.kingsurf.co.uk; lessons from £30) A good option if you prefer to avoid the Fistral hustle, this school at Mawgan Porth has five young instructors and gets a tick for personal attention and small class sizes.

Extreme Academy ADVENTURE SPORTS
(01637-860840; www.extremeacademy.co.uk; Watergate Bay) Owned by the Watergate Bay Hotel, this is a large and efficient operation that offers the full gamut of water sports: surfing, of course, as well as more unusual options such as stand-up paddleboarding and handplaning (which involves catching a wave with a miniature surfboard attached to your wrist).

EboAdventure OUTDOORS
(0800 781 6861; www.eboadventure.co.uk) Surfing's not the only sport in Newquay – you could also try kitebuggying, kayaking, stand-up paddleboarding and coasteering (a mix of rock climbing, scrambling and wild swimming). This multi-activity centre is based at the Penhale Training Camp, at the northern end of Holywell Bay.

Sleeping

Newquay Townhouse B&B £
(01637-620009; www.newquaytownhouse.co.uk; 6 Tower Rd; d £50-70; P) A decent B&B near Newquay's town centre, with bright rooms livened up with stripy cushions and wicker furniture.

★Scarlet HOTEL £££
(01637-861600; www.scarlethotel.co.uk; Mawgan Porth; r from £240; P) For out-and-out luxury, Cornwall's fabulously chic, adults-only ecohotel takes the crown. In a regal location above Mawgan Porth, 5 miles from Newquay, it screams designer style, from the huge sea-view rooms with their funky furniture and minimalist decor to the luxurious spa, complete with meditation lounge, outdoor hot tubs and wild swimming pool. The restaurant's a beauty, too.

Watergate Bay Hotel HOTEL £££
(01637-860543; www.watergatebay.co.uk; Watergate Bay; d £265-410, ste £365-490; P) Originally built for Victorian tourists arriving on the (long-disappeared) railway line from Newquay, this old hotel has had a totally 21st-century transformation: its rooms shine in slinky pinks, candy stripes and sea blues, the style is sleek and minimal, and there's a choice of restaurants. It's big on activities, too, provided by the attached Extreme Academy.

Eating

Zacry's MODERN BRITISH ££
(01637-861231; www.watergatebay.co.uk/food-and-drink/zacrys; Watergate Bay; 2-/3-course menu £29.50/36.50; 6.30-9.30pm) The newest offering at the Watergate Bay Hotel is a faintly American affair: a smart bistro with wooden booths arranged in a gentle curve, overlooking a semi-open-plan kitchen. Head chef Neil Haydock has a taste for Stateside flavours, so expect things like chargrilled sirloin and seafood succotash on the menu. The food is great, but kids aren't encouraged.

Boathouse BISTRO ££
(01637-874062; www.the-boathouse-newquay.co.uk; South Quay Hill; mains £12.35-18.40, seafood platters £42-64; 10am-11pm) The pick of the places to eat in downtown Newquay, hidden away from the hustle at the bottom of the hill beside the fishing quay. Appropriately enough, it's a seafood specialist, taking its catch straight from the day boats – lemon sole, pollock, crawfish, spider crab and lobster, plus sumptuous *fruits de mer* platters. A lovely surprise.

Beach Hut BISTRO ££
(01637-860877; Watergate Bay; mains £10-18; 9am-9pm) Lodged beneath Jamie Oliver's Fifteen Cornwall, this beachside bistro is a great bet for simple surf 'n' turf: sticky pork ribs, 'extreme' burgers and a different fish every day.

Lewinnick Lodge BISTRO ££
(01637-878117; www.lewinnicklodge.co.uk; Pentire Head, Newquay; mains £12.50-20; 8am-10pm) For lunch with a view, this smart cafe-bistro is the choice. It's perched right

on the cliffs of Pentire Head, giving a knockout perspective on the coastline around Newquay. The style is modern, all bleached wood and plate glass, and the food is decent too: gourmet burgers, mussels and Thai-style salads are on the menu. Rooms (from £170) are extremely pleasant.

Fifteen Cornwall ITALIAN £££
(☎01637-861000; www.fifteencornwall.com; Watergate Bay; 2-/3-course lunch menu £26/32, 5-course dinner menu £65; ⏲8.30am-10am, noon-2.30pm & 6.15-9.15pm) Owned by celeb chef Jamie Oliver, this restaurant on Watergate Bay serves Jamie's trademark Italian food while simultaneously training young apprentices. The vibe is relaxed (white walls, street-art murals, retro furniture) and the beach view is stunning through the floor-to-ceiling windows, but the prices are on the high side.

Drinking & Nightlife

Newquay's drinking spots aren't sophisticated: cheesy clubs and brash bars abound, and the town centre gets notoriously rowdy on Friday and Saturday nights, especially in summer.

Chy BAR
(http://chybarandkitchen-newquay.co.uk; 12 Beach Rd; ⏲9am-11pm) Chrome, wood and leather dominate this cafe-bar overlooking Towan beach. The action continues till late at the Koola nightclub downstairs.

Central PUB
(11 Central Sq; ⏲11am-midnight Sun-Thu, to 1am Fri & Sat) As its name suggests, this pre-club pub is in the heart of town, and is usually packed at weekends.

Information

Newquay Tourist Office (☎01637-854020; www.visitnewquay.org; Marcus Hill; ⏲9.15am-5.30pm Mon-Fri, 10am-4pm Sat & Sun) Small but well-stocked office, which can help you arrange everything from accommodation to surf lessons.

Getting There & Away

AIR

Five miles from town, **Newquay Cornwall Airport** (p333) currently offers direct daily flights to Manchester and London Gatwick with **Flybe** (www.flybe.com) and the Isles of Scilly with **Isles of Scilly Skybus** (p359). Various seasonal destinations around the UK and Europe are also offered during summer.

BUS

Newquay's bus station is on Manor Rd. Useful destinations:

Newquay Cornwall Airport Bus 56; 26 minutes, hourly Monday to Saturday, five on Sunday

Padstow Bus 56; 26 minutes, hourly Monday to Saturday, five on Sunday

St Agnes (bus 87; 50 minutes, hourly) Also stops at Crantock, Holywell Bay and Perranporth before continuing to Truro.

Truro (bus 90/92/93; 70 minutes, half-hourly Monday to Saturday) The fastest bus to Truro; the various routes travel via different villages but all terminate in Truro.

Wadebridge Bus 95; 50 minutes, five daily Monday to Saturday

TRAIN

Newquay is on the branch line between Newquay and Par (Atlantic Coast Line; £4.70, 45 minutes), from where you can hop aboard the main London–Penzance line.

Perranporth to Porthtowan

Southwest of Newquay, Cornwall's craggy northern coastline dips and curves through a stunning panorama of wild, sea-smacked cliffs and golden bays, including the family-friendly beach of Perranporth, the old mining town of St Agnes and the surfy hangout of Porthtowan.

Sights & Acitivities

Perranporth Beach BEACH
(P 👪) Perranporth's huge, flat, sandy beach is popular with bucket-and-spading families and surfers alike. It's over a mile long, backed by dunes and rocky cliffs, and usually has space even on the busiest days, and it's home to the Watering Hole (p342).

★**Chapel Porth** COVE
(P) Two miles from St Agnes is one of Cornwall's most beautiful coves, Chapel Porth, a wild, rocky beach framed by steep, gorse-covered cliffs, owned by the National Trust. Above the cove is the ruined engine stack of **Wheal Coates**, which still boasts its chimney and winding house, from where the coast path winds all the way to the blustery outcrop of **St Agnes Head**.

Blue Hills Tin Streams EXHIBITION
(☎01872-553341; www.bluehillstin.com; adult/child £6.50/3; ⏲10am-2pm Tue-Sat mid-Apr–mid-Oct) A

mile east of St Agnes (signed to Wheal Kitty) is the rocky valley of **Trevellas**, home to one of Cornwall's last tin manufacturers where you can watch the whole tinning process, from mining and smelting through to casting and finishing. Handmade jewellery is sold in the shop.

Eating & Drinking

Chapel Porth Cafe CAFE £
(Chapel Porth; sandwiches & cakes £2-4; ⏲10am-5pm) The Chapel Porth Cafe is a local institution, serving hot chocolate, cheesy baguettes and the house speciality: hedgehog ice cream (vanilla ice cream topped with clotted cream and hazelnuts).

Blue Bar BISTRO ££
(☎01209-890329; www.blue-bar.co.uk; Porthtowan; mains £8-16; ⏲10am-11pm) For a seaside sundowner or a lunchtime snack by the sand, this Porthtowan cafe is tough to beat (unfortunately everyone knows about it, so arrive early).

Bolingey Inn PUB FOOD ££
(☎01872-571626; Penwartha Rd, Bolingey; mains £10-16; ⏲noon-11pm) The ivy-covered Bolingey Inn is the best pub around Perranporth for food, and has a valley location about 2 miles drive inland.

Watering Hole BAR
(www.the-wateringhole.co.uk; Perranporth Beach; ⏲10am-11pm) One of Cornwall's oldest beach bars, the Watering Hole was nearly washed away during heavy storms in 2014. It's a nice spot for a sundowner, and has regular bands.

Getting There & Away

First Kernow buses:

Bus 57 (two daily) To Perranporth and St Agnes in one direction, to Porthtowan, Gwithian and St Ives in the other direction.

Bus 87 (hourly Monday to Saturday, slightly fewer on Sunday) Stops in St Agnes on its way from Newquay via Crantock, Holywell and Perranporth to Truro.

St Ives

POP 9870

Even if you've seen St Ives many times before, it's still hard not to be dazzled as you gaze across its improbably pretty jumble of slate roofs, church towers and turquoise bays. Once a busy pilchard harbour, St Ives later became the centre of Cornwall's arts scene in the 1920s and '30s, and the town is still an artistic centre, with numerous galleries and craft shops lining its winding cobbled streets, as well as the southwestern outpost of the renowned Tate Museum.

Unfortunately, change has come at a price – St Ives is packed throughout summer, and prices here are substantially higher than other parts of Cornwall. To see it at its best, avoid school holidays an July and August.

Sights & Activities

The largest town beaches are Porthmeor and Porthminster, both of which have sand and space aplenty. Between them juts the grassy promontory known as the Island, topped by the tiny pre-14th-century Chapel of St Nicholas. On the peninsula's east side is the little cove of Porthgwidden, often a good place to escape the crowds.

★ **Tate St Ives** GALLERY
(☎01736-796226; www.tate.org.uk/stives; Porthmeor Beach) Hovering like a concrete curl above Porthmeor Beach, St Ives' celebrated art museum has been closed for a huge renovation project, which will include the addition of an entire new wing. Work was scheduled for completion in spring 2017 – check the website for the latest news.

Barbara Hepworth Museum MUSEUM
(☎01736-796226; Barnoon Hill; adult/child £6.60/5.50; ⏲10am-5pm Mar-Oct, to 4pm Nov-Feb) Barbara Hepworth (1903–75) was one of the leading abstract sculptors of the 20th century and a key figure in the St Ives art scene. Her studio on Barnoon Hill has remained almost untouched since her death and the adjoining garden contains several of her most notable sculptures, many of which were inspired by the elemental forces she discovered in her adopted Cornish home: rock, sea, sand, wind, sky. Free private tours are also available to provide extra context.

St Ives Boats BOATING
(☎0777 300 8000; www.stivesboats.co.uk; adult/child £10/8) From the harbour front, several operators including St Ives Boats offer fishing trips and scenic cruises, including to the grey seal colony on Seal Island. If you're really lucky, you might even spot a porpoise or a basking shark in summer.

Leach Pottery GALLERY
(☎01736-796398; www.leachpottery.com; Higher Stennack; adult/child £4.50/free; ⏲10am-5pm

West Cornwall

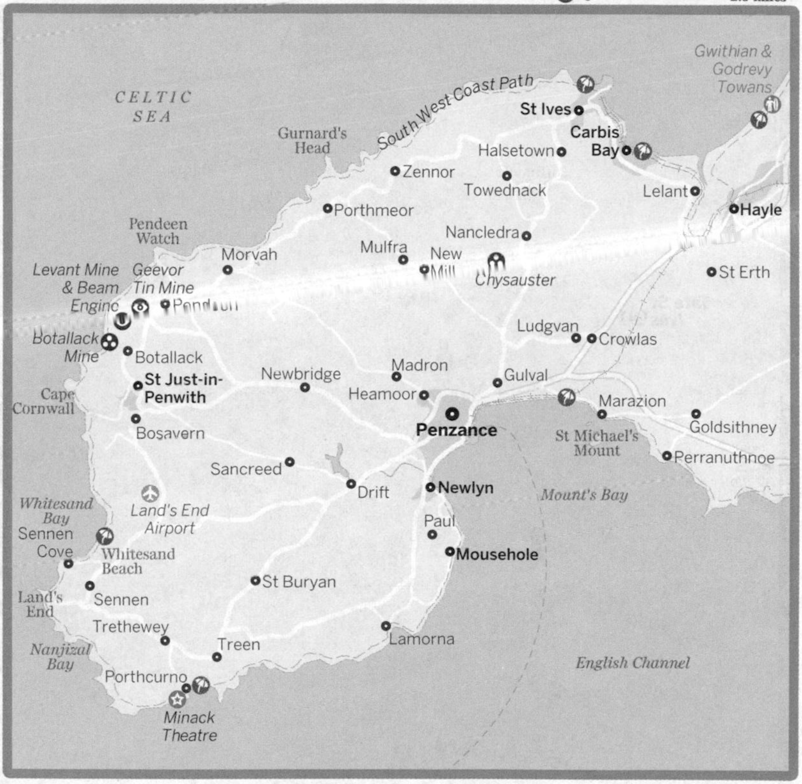

Mon-Sat, 11am-4pm Sun) While other St Ives artists broke new ground in sculpture and abstract art, the potter Bernard Leach was hard at work reinventing British ceramics in his studio in Higher Stennack. Drawing inspiration from Japanese and oriental sculpture, and using a unique hand-built 'climbing' kiln based on ones he had seen in Japan, Leach's pottery created a unique fusion of Western and Eastern ideas.

Sleeping

Primrose Valley Hotel HOTEL ££

(☎01736-794939; www.primroseonline.co.uk; Primrose Valley; r £135-180; P 🛜) Reopened after comprehensive refurbishment, this chic hotel has one massive selling point – it's a minute's walk from Porthminster's sands. But there are plenty more pluses too – such as its light, attractive rooms in taupes, greys, checks and sea blues, and quirky design touches including wicker lamps, Scandi-style dressers and model ships. It feels very modern and impeccably designed throughout.

11 Sea View Terrace B&B ££

(☎01736-798440; www.11stives.co.uk; 11 Sea View Tce; d £120-140; P 🛜) Occupying one of the classic Edwardian villas lining the upper part of St Ives, this three-suite B&B is a chic place to stay. The two front 'suites' have lovely town and sea views, while the rear one overlooks a garden patio; for more space, there's a smart holiday flat (£350 to £975 per week).

Treliska B&B ££

(☎01736-797678; www.treliska.com; 3 Bedford Rd; d £70-90; 🛜) This B&B is a bargain in pricey St Ives, especially given the location, just steps from the town centre. The trade-off is the room size: most are on the small side (ask for room 5 if it's space you're after).

St Ives

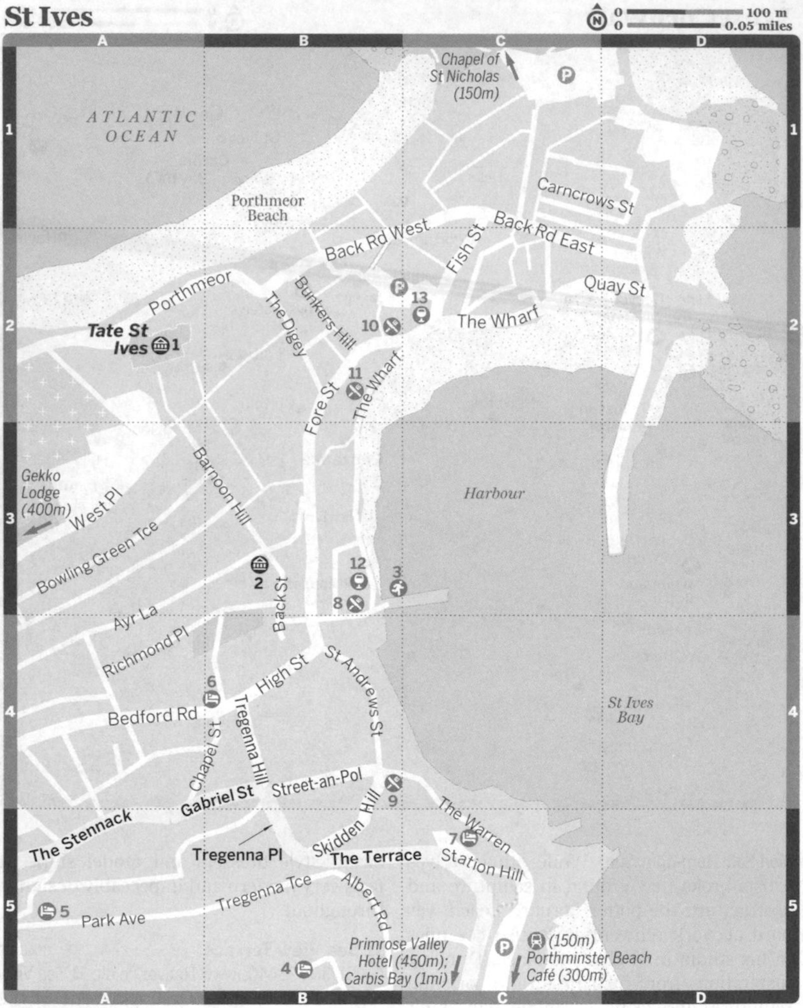

St Ives

Top Sights
1 Tate St Ives A2

Sights
2 Barbara Hepworth Museum B3

Activities, Courses & Tours
3 St Ives Boats B3

Sleeping
4 11 Sea View Terrace.............................. B5
5 Little Leaf Guest House......................... A5
6 Treliska.. B4
7 Trevose Harbour House C5

Eating
8 Alba B3
9 Blas Burgerworks................................... B4
10 Moomaid of Zennor B2
11 Porthminster Kitchen B2

Drinking & Nightlife
12 Hub B3
13 Sloop Inn C2

Little Leaf Guest House B&B ££
(01736-795427; www.littleleafguesthouse.co.uk; Park Ave; r £85-125;) A reliable, ecofriendly B&B in the upper part of town, which offers excellent rates, especially in the low season. It's on a terrace overlooking the town's rooftops. Rooms are sweet and simple, finished in creamy colours and pine furniture. Ask for rooms 2 or 5 if you're after a sea view. Parking is the only problem.

Trevose Harbour House B&B £££
(01736-793267; www.trevosehouse.co.uk; 22 The Warren; d £185-275;) A stylish six-room town house on the winding Warren, restored with a sea-themed combo of fresh whites and stripy blues. It's been beautifully finished – Neal's Yard bathstuffs, iPod docks and retro design pieces in the rooms, plus a book-lined lounge and minimalist courtyard patio. It's boutique through and through.

Boskerris HOTEL £££
(01736-795295; www.boskerrishotel.co.uk; Boskerris Rd, Carbis Bay; d £170-280; P) Just along the coast from St Ives in the suburb of Carbis Bay, this upmarket mini-hotel offers plenty of reasons to stay: smart rooms in cool monotones, an elegantly uncluttered design aesthetic, lovely bathrooms with free-standing bath-tubs and swish ceramic sinks, and a cracking patio overlooking the bay. It's great value in the low season.

Blue Hayes HOTEL £££
(01736-797129; www.bluehayes.co.uk; Trelyon Ave; r £150-270; P) Riviera luxury in a St Ives hotel, with manicured grounds, a balustraded breakfast terrace and five suite-sized rooms. The Trelyon Suite even has its own private roof terrace.

Eating

Moomaid of Zennor ICE CREAM £
(www.moomaidofzennor.com; Wharf; from £2; 9am-5pm) This ice-cream maker is a local legend, and makes all of its 30 flavours on the home farm just outside Zennor, using only its own milk and Rodda's clotted cream. Exotic concoctions include fig and mascarpone and pear cider sorbet.

★ **Porthminster Beach Café** BISTRO ££
(01736-795352; www.porthminstercafe.co.uk; Porthminster Beach; mains £15-22; 9am-10pm) This is no ordinary beach cafe: it's a full-blown bistro with a gorgeous sun-trap terrace and a superb Mediterranean-influenced menu, specialising in seafood. Tuck into rich bouillabaisse, seafood curry or Provençal fish soup, and settle back to enjoy the breezy beach vistas. It's published its own cookbook, too, if you fancy taking the recipes home.

Porthminster Kitchen BISTRO ££
(01736-799874; www.porthminster.kitchen; Wharf; mains lunch £7.50-15, dinner £11-17; 9am-10pm) Run by the same team as Porthminster Beach Café, this is a welcome new addition to the harbourside in St Ives. It showcases fresh, zingy, fusion food, from tuna sashimi and sea trout with Asian mushrooms to Malay veggie curry – there's an emphasis on minimising gluten and dairy too. The quayview dining room is lovely.

Blas Burgerworks CAFE ££
(01736-797272; The Warren; burgers £10-12.50; noon-9.30pm Jul & Aug, 5.30-9.30pm rest of year) St Ives' boutique burger joint, with an ecofriendly manifesto and an imaginative menu. Go for a 6oz Classic Blasburger, or branch out with a guacamole and corn salsa-topped Rancheros, or a Smokey with beetroot, aged cheddar and homemade piccalilli (plenty of veggie options, too). The owners also run the excellent Halsetown Inn, just outside St Ives.

Halsetown Inn PUB FOOD ££
(01736-795583; www.halsetowninn.co.uk; Halsetown; mains £13-22.50; noon-2pm & 6-9pm) Prime pub grub a mile from St Ives in tiny Halsetown. It's still the village boozer – local ales, first-name bar staff, cosy crannies to hunker down in – but the food is a notch above the norm thanks to the owners, who also run Blas Burgerworks. Expect posh mains such as chicken pithivier and cider-baked ham, plus a cracking Sunday roast.

Alba MODERN BRITISH £££
(01736-797222; www.thealbarestaurant.com; Old Lifeboat House; 2-/3-course dinner menu £21.95/25.95, mains £16-28.95; noon-2pm & 6-10pm) Other restaurants have come and gone in St Ives, but this harbourside bistro next to the old lifeboat station continues to excel. It's in a converted boathouse, with a split-level layout: diner-style downstairs, more formal upstairs (book well ahead for the prime window tables). First-class fish and seafood are the mainstays. The set dinner menu is only available from 5.30pm to 7pm.

Drinking & Entertainment

Sloop Inn INN
(☎01736-796584; www.sloop-inn.co.uk; Wharf; ⊙11am-11pm) This beam-ceilinged boozer is as comfy as an old pair of slippers, with a few tables on the harbour and lots of local ales.

Hub BAR
(www.hub-stives.co.uk; Wharf; ⊙9am-11pm) The open-plan Hub is the heart of St Ives' (limited) nightlife: coffee and burgers by day, cocktails after dark.

Getting There & Away

BUS

Bus 17/17A/17B (£5, 30 minutes, half-hourly Monday to Saturday, hourly Sunday) The quickest route to Penzance, via Lelant and Marazion.

Bus 16/16A (£5, hourly Monday to Saturday) An alternative route to Penzance; bus 16A travels via Zennor and the Gurnard's Head pub, while bus 16 goes via Halsetown, Ludgvan and Gulval.

TRAIN

The branch train line from St Ives is worth taking just for the coastal views.

Trains shuttle between St Ives train station and St Erth (£3, 14 minutes, half-hourly), where you can catch connections along the Penzance–London Paddington main line.

Zennor & St Just

The twisting B3306 from St Ives is a roller coaster of a road, winding through a stark landscape of ancient drystone walls, barren moorland, tiny villages and rocky bluffs. The landscape here feels wild and ancient, a world away from some of Cornwall's more gentrified corners.

Sights

Church of St Senara CHURCH
(Zennor) This little church in the hamlet of Zennor dates from at least 1150. Inside, a famous carved chair depicts the legendary Mermaid of Zennor, who is said to have fallen in love with the singing voice of local Matthew Trewhella. Locals say you can still sometimes hear them singing down at nearby Pendour Cove – and even if you don't, the views along the coast path are reward enough.

★**Geevor Tin Mine** MINE
(☎01736-788662; www.geevor.com; adult/child £12.95/7.50; ⊙9am-5pm Sun-Fri Mar-Oct, to 4pm Nov-Feb) Just north of St Just near Pendeen, this historic mine closed in 1990 and now provides a powerful insight into the dark, dingy and dangerous conditions in which Cornwall's miners worked. Above ground, you can view the dressing floors and the original machinery used to sort the minerals and ores, before taking a guided tour into some of the underground shafts. Claustrophobes need not apply.

Botallack Mine RUINS
Clinging to the cliffs near Levant, this dramatic engine house has abandoned mine shafts extending right out beneath the raging Atlantic waves. It's a treacherous climb down, so it's best viewed from a distance from nearby **Botallack Head**.

Levant Mine & Beam Engine HISTORIC SITE
(www.nationaltrust.org.uk/levant-mine-and-beam-engine; adult/child £7.20/3.60; ⊙10.30am-5pm Sun-Fri) At this clifftop site, one of the world's only working beam engines is still in thunderous action. Built in 1840, these great engines were the powerhouses behind the Cornish mining boom, powering mineral trains and pumping water from the shafts. Lovingly restored by a team of enthusiasts, it's a sight to behold when it's in full steam.

Cape Cornwall LANDMARK
Jutting out from the cliffs near St Just is Cornwall's only 'official' cape, a craggy finger of land topped by an abandoned minestack. Below the cape is the rocky beach of **Priest's Cove**, while nearby are the ruins of **St Helen's Oratory**, supposedly one of the first Christian chapels built in West Cornwall.

Sleeping & Eating

Zennor Chapel Guesthouse B&B
(☎01736-798307; www.zennorchapelguesthouse.com; r from £80; Ⓟ) As its name hints, this attractive B&B (previously a hostel) occupies a former church on the edge of the village. There are five rooms, most of which still boast original ecclesiastical features, including beautiful arched windows. There's a range of sleeping configurations – doubles, twins and family with bunkbeds. There's also a cafe and gift shop downstairs.

★**Gurnard's Head** BRITISH ££
(☎01736-796928; www.gurnardshead.co.uk; near Zennor; mains £12-19.95, r £115-180; Ⓟ) On the wonderful coast road between Zennor and St Just, you can't miss the Gurnard's – its name is emblazoned on the roof. Run by

WORTH A TRIP

MINACK THEATRE & PORTHCURNO

In terms of theatrical settings, the **Minack** (☎01736-810181; www.minack.com; tickets from £10) takes top billing. Carved into the crags overlooking Porthcurno and the azure-blue Atlantic, this amazing clifftop amphitheatre was the lifelong passion of theatre-lover Rowena Cade, who dreamt up the idea in the 1930s. It's now a hugely popular place for alfresco theatre, with plays staged from mid-May to mid-September.

Just up the valley from the Minack Theatre, the redeveloped **Porthcurno Telegraph Museum** (☎01736-810966; www.telegraphmuseum.org; adult/child £8.50/5; ⏲10am-5pm) recounts the area's role as Britain's first hub for transatlantic telecommunications – until 1970, sub-sea cables carried messages here from all over the world. There's an intriguing museum containing a communications kit – vintage radios, transistor valves and so on – and you can explore a network of underground tunnels built here during WWII.

the Inkin brothers (who also own Mousehole's Old Coastguard Hotel) this is the quintessential Cornish country pub, with wooden furniture, book-lined shelves and sepia prints conjuring a cosy, lived-in feel. It's renowned for its food.

Sennen & Land's End

Beyond St Ives, the coastline gets wilder and emptier as you near Cornwall's tip at Land's End, the westernmost point of mainland England, where the coal-black cliffs plunge into the pounding surf, and the views stretch all the way to the Isles of Scilly on a clear day.

Unfortunately, the decision to build the **Legendary Land's End** (☎0871 720 0044; www.landsend-landmark.co.uk; day ticket adult/child £12/9; ⏲9am-5pm Mar-Oct; 👪) theme park on the headland in the 1980s hasn't done much to enhance the view. Take our advice: just pay for the car park, skip the tacky multimedia shows and opt for an exhilarating clifftop stroll instead. Look for the historic **Longships Lighthouse**, on a reef 1.25 miles out to sea.

From Land's End, follow the coast path west to the secluded cove of **Nanjizal Bay**, or east to the old harbour of Sennen, which overlooks the glorious beach of **Whitesand Bay**, the area's most impressive stretch of sand.

Mousehole

POP 697

With a tight tangle of cottages and alleyways gathered behind the granite breakwater, Mousehole (*mow*zle) looks like something from a children's storybook (a fact not unnoticed by author Antonia Barber, who set her much-loved fairy tale *The Mousehole Cat* here). In centuries past, this was Cornwall's busiest pilchard port, but the fish dried up at the turn of the century, and the village now survives mostly on tourist traffic.

Packed in summer and deserted in winter, it's ripe for a wander, with a maze of slips, net-lofts and courtyards. It's also well known for its Christmas lights, and as the home of 'stargazey pie', a pilchard pie in which the fish heads are left poking through the pie's crust.

Sleeping & Eating

Old Coastguard Hotel HOTEL £££

(☎01736-731222; www.oldcoastguardhotel.co.uk; The Parade; d £187.50-277.50; P 📶 🐾) Now run by the owners of the Gurnard's Head, this coastal beauty has a much more relaxed atmosphere than it used to. Rooms are still classic – restrained colour schemes, stately beds – and the best ones obviously have a sea view. Seafood takes prominence in the smart sea-view restaurant (mains £13.50 to £18.50), and there's a cliff garden for soaking up the rays.

★ **2 Fore St** FRENCH ££

(☎01736-731164; www.2forestreet.co.uk; Fore St; mains £11-20; ⏲noon-2pm & 7-9pm) Culinary sophistication on the Mousehole seafront. It's young but has already gained plenty of admirers, including *Harden's* and the *Good Food Guide*. Inside, stripped wood, cool colours and harbour views; outside, a sweet garden shaded by palms and canvas umbrellas. The menu wears its French influences on its sleeve, as you might expect from a head chef who trained under Raymond Blanc.

Penzance

POP 21,168

Overlooking the majestic sweep of Mount's Bay, the old harbour of Penzance has a salty, sea-blown charm that feels altogether more authentic than many of Cornwall's polished-up ports. Its streets and shopping arcades still feel real and a touch ramshackle, and there's nowhere better for a windy-day walk than the town's seafront Victorian promenade. Along the way look out for the elegant sight of Jubilee Pool, the town's lovely outdoor lido, recently restored.

The nearby harbour of **Newlyn** is still home to Cornwall's largest fishing fleet, and the harbour is filled with bobbing boats of every shape and description.

Sights & Activities

Penlee House Gallery & Museum GALLERY
(www.penleehouse.org.uk; Morrab Rd; adult/child £4.50/3; 10am-5pm Mon-Sat Easter-Sep, 10.30am-4.30pm Oct-Easter) Penzance's historic art gallery displays paintings by artists of the Newlyn School (including Stanhope Forbes and Lamorna Birch) and hosts regular exhibitions. The nearby Penlee Gardens are well worth a stroll.

Tremenheere Sculpture Garden GARDENS
(01736-448089; www.tremenheere.co.uk; adult/child £8/4.50; 10am-4pm Mon-Thu, 10am-5pm Fri-Sun;) This inventive garden opened just outside Penzance in 2012. The landscaped gardens sit in a sheltered valley awash with artworks and installations: look out for a 'sky-view' chamber by James Turrell, a 'black mound' of tree stumps by David Nash and a 'Camera Obscura' by Billy Wynter, offering a unique panorama of the gardens and Mount's Bay.

There's also a super cafe, Tremenheere Kitchen (lunches £8 to £14), and there are family events such as den-building and art workshops during school holidays.

★ **Jubilee Pool** SWIMMING
(www.jubileepool.co.uk; Western Promendade Rd; adult/child £4.75/3.80; 10.30am-6pm Wed-Mon, to 8pm Tue late-May-early-Sep) After being thoroughly battered during recent winter storms, Penzance's glorious seawater lido has reopened and regained its place as the town's pride and joy. Built in 1935, it's a bold statement of art-deco styling, sleek, sharp and whitewashed – the perfect backdrop for sea bathing in style. There's discounted entry after 3.30pm (adult/child £3.10/2.50).

Sleeping

Penzance YHA HOSTEL £
(0845 371 9653; penzance@yha.org.uk; Castle Horneck, Alverton; dm £19-25;) Penzance's YHA is inside an 18th-century house on the edge of town. It's a rambling place, with a cafe, laundry and four- to 10-bed dorms. It's a 15-minute walk from the harbour front.

★ **Venton Vean** B&B ££
(01736-351294; www.ventonvean.co.uk; Trewithen Rd; r £86-97;) The picture of a modern B&B, finished in stylish greys and blues, with stripped wood floors, bay windows and a keen eye for design. Rooms 1 and 2 are the most spacious; the former overlooks Penlee Memorial Park. The sumptuous breakfast choice includes pancakes, smoked Newlyn fish, avocado on sourdough toast, and a Mexican-style feast of tortillas and refried beans.

★ **Artist Residence Penzance** B&B ££
(01736-365664; www.arthotelcornwall.co.uk; 20 Chapel St; d £115-145, 2-bed apt from £255;) Hands down the most entertaining place to stay in Penzance, this B&B on Chapel St is like sleeping inside an art gallery. All rooms are designed by a local artist, and all are bright, colourful and brimming with imagination (we particularly liked the Attic Lofts). There are apartments for longer stays, and food is available in the Cornish Barn.

Chapel House Penzance B&B ££
(01736-362024; www.chapelhousepz.co.uk; Chapel St; r from £150;) In one of Chapel St's most historic buildings – a sea-captain's house that was for many years an arts centre – this beautiful B&B has become a favourite of travel supplements, and it's not hard to see why. The six rooms ooze design credentials: retro furniture, waterfall baths, oak beds, sleek bathrooms, all carefully blended with the house's Georgian architecture.

Eating

★ **Shore** MODERN BRITISH ££
(01736-362444; www.theshorerestaurant.uk; 13/14 Alverton St; 2-/3-course lunch £18/24, dinner mains £17.50-20; noon-2pm & 6.30-9pm Tue-Sat) Penzance's hottest new table (and one of the hottest in Cornwall, come to think of it) is this barn-storming bistro overseen

Penzance

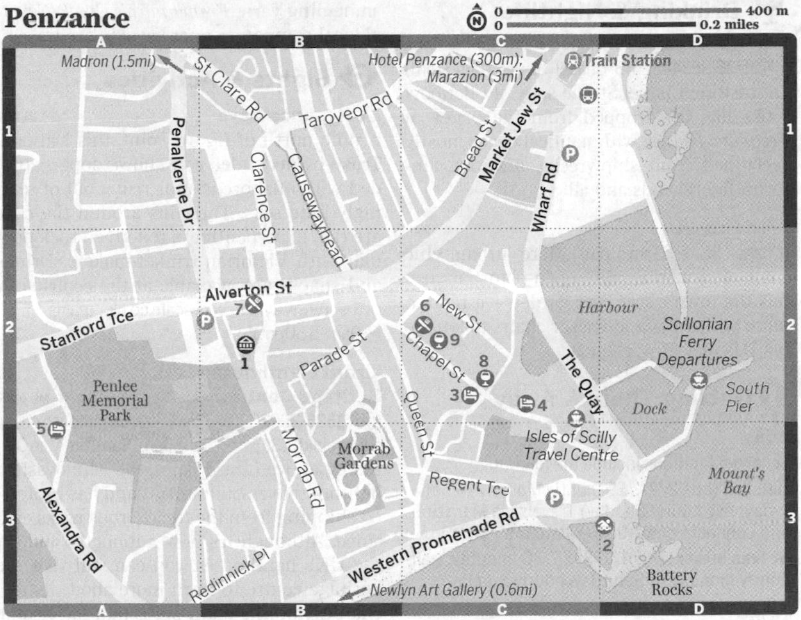

by chef Bruce Rennie, a veteran of many a Michelin-starred kitchen. It's all about seafood here, sourced from the Newlyn day boats and served with a strong French-Italian influence.

★Ben's Cornish Kitchen BRITISH ££
(☎01736-719200; www.benscornishkitchen.com; Marazion; 2-/3-course dinner £24/29; ⏰noon-1.30pm & 7-8.30pm Tue-Sat; 🖉) Blink and you'll miss Ben Prior's unassuming restaurant as you zip along Marazion's main street, but diners travel from far and wide to taste his classical cooking, which majors in meaty Cornish flavours with a French influence. It's won national awards from Waitrose, *The Good Food Guide* and the Trencherman's guide, and tables are getting scarce – book well ahead.

★Tolcarne Inn PUB FOOD ££
(☎01736-363074; www.tolcarneinn.co.uk; Tolcarne Pl, Newlyn; mains £15-22; ⏰noon-2.15pm & 7-9pm Tue-Sat, noon-2.15pm Sun) This old Newlyn inn is run by talented local chef Ben Tunnicliffe, who's fast turned it into the area's primo gastropub. The ethos is refreshingly honest – top-quality fish, seafood and locally sourced meat, served with minimal fuss. Bookings advisable, especially for Sunday lunch.

Penzance

Sights
1 Penlee House Gallery & Museum B2

Activities, Courses & Tours
2 Jubilee Pool D3

Sleeping
3 Artist Residence Penzance C2
4 Chapel House Penzance C2
5 Venton Vean A3

Eating
6 Bakehouse C2
7 Shore B2

Drinking & Nightlife
8 Admiral Benbow C2
9 Zero Lounge C2

Bakehouse MEDITERRANEAN ££
(☎01736-331331; www.bakehouserestaurant.co.uk; Chapel St; mains £10.95-19.95; ⏰6-10pm Mon-Sat) Down an alley off Chapel St, this no-nonsense bistro serves unpretentious food such as fish served with Med-style marinades, and steaks with spicy rubs.

Drinking & Nightlife

Admiral Benbow PUB

(☎01736-363448; 46 Chapel St; ⊙11am-11pm) On historic Chapel St, the salty old Benbow looks like it's dropped from the pages of *Treasure Island*, with nautical decor mostly reclaimed from shipwrecks: anchors, lanterns, figureheads and all.

Zero Lounge BAR

(Chapel St; ⊙11am-11pm) More urban chic than olde worlde, this open-plan bar also has the town's best beer garden – a hidden patio with sofas and wicker chairs to lounge on. DJs play at weekends.

Getting There & Away

BUS

Local destinations include the following:

Helston (bus 2/2A; £5, hourly Monday to Saturday, two hourly Sunday) Travels via Marazion and connects onwards to Falmouth.

St Ives buses 17/17A/17B; £5, 30 minutes, half-hourly Monday to Saturday, hourly Sunday

TRAIN

Penzance is the last stop on the line from London Paddington.

Truro £6.60, 30 minutes

St Ives £4.20, 50 minutes) Change at St Erth.

Exeter £20.40, three hours

London Paddington £62.60, 5½ hours

The Lizard

Once notorious as a smugglers' haven and an ill-famed graveyard for ships, the rugged Lizard Peninsula offers Cornwall's wildest coastal panoramas. Wind-lashed in winter, in summer its heaths and cliffs blaze with wild flowers, and its beaches and coves are perfect for a bracing swim.

The main town is **Helston**, famous for its annual street party, **Flora Day**, held on 8 May. Pretty villages are dotted along the peninsula's coastline: the old harbour of **Coverack**, the beaches of **Mullion** and the idyllic thatched-cottage cove of **Cadgwith** are well worth a visit.

Towards Lizard Point lie the dramatic satellite dishes of **Goonhilly Downs** and the beautiful National Trust beach of **Kynance Cove**, which has to be one of Cornwall's most photogenic beaches.

Along the peninsula's northern edge runs **Helford River**, lined by creeks and inlets that famously inspired Daphne du Maurier's smuggling yarn, *Frenchman's Creek*. Several local companies offer kayaking tours.

Sights & Activities

★ **Kynance Cove** BEACH

A mile north of Lizard Point, this National Trust–owned inlet is a showstopper, studded with offshore islands rising out of searingly blue seas. The cliffs around the cove are rich in serpentine, a red-green rock popular with Victorian trinket-makers. Drinks and snacks are available at the ecofriendly **cafe** (www.kynancecovecafe.co.uk; mains £5-14; ⊙9am-5.30pm).

Lizard Lighthouse Heritage Centre MUSEUM

(☎01326-290202; www.lizardlighthouse.co.uk; adult/child £3/2; ⊙11am-5pm Sun-Thu Mar-Oct) Rising above Lizard Point, the whitewashed lighthouse was built in 1751 and has protected shipping from the treacherous rocks ever since. Although it's now automated like all the UK's lighthouses, you can still visit the heritage centre to learn more about its mechanics and the many ships that have come to grief nearby. You can also take informative guided tours (adult/child £7.50/4.50) into the tower to see the lamp room and foghorn.

Cornish Seal Sanctuary WILDLIFE RESERVE

(☎01326-221361; www.visitsealife.com/gweek; adult/child £14.95/12.50; ⊙10am-5pm; 🚹) Towards the northwest of the Lizard Peninsula, this sanctuary cares for sick and orphaned seals washed up along the Cornish coastline before returning them to the wild. There are also resident populations of otters, penguins and Californian sea lions.

Aberfal Outdoor Pursuits KAYAKING

(☎07968 770756; www.aberfaloutdoorpursuits.co.uk; half-/full day £35/50) Half- and full-day guided kayaking trips along the Helford on sit-on-top kayaks.

Sleeping & Eating

Lizard YHA HOSTEL £

(☎0845 371 9550; www.yha.org.uk; Lizard Point; dm £19-25; ⊙Apr-Oct) Once a Victorian hotel next to the lighthouse, now a YHA hostel, this has to rank pretty high in the 'UK's best budget beds' list. It's in a spectacular situation, overlooking miles of wild cliffs and coast, and it's typically well run: a range of dorms, a self-catering kitchen, a spacious lounge, but no cafe.

WORTH A TRIP

ST MICHAEL'S MOUNT

Looming in the middle of Mount's Bay and connected to the mainland via a cobbled causeway, the abbey-crowned island **St Michael's Mount** (NT; 01736-710507; www.stmichaelsmount.co.uk; house & gardens adult/child £12.50/6; house 10.30am-5.30pm Sun-Fri Jul-Sep, 10.30am-5pm Mar-Jun & Oct) is an unforgettable sight – and one of Cornwall's most iconic images. Initially a Benedictine monastery, and later the seat of the St Aubyn family, it's a must-visit. You can catch the ferry (adult/child £2/1) from nearby Marazion at high tide, but it's worth arriving at low tide so you can walk across the causeway, as pilgrims did centuries ago.

There's been a monastery here since at least the 5th century, but the present abbey was mostly built by Benedictine monks during the 12th century. Highlights include the rococo drawing room, the armoury, the 14th-century church and the amazing clifftop gardens.

Recent excavations including a Bronze Age axe head, dagger and metal clasp have proved the island has been inhabited since ancient times.

Though it's still owned by the St Aubyn family, the abbey is run by the National Trust. The hourly 17B bus shuttles between Marazion and Penzance (£2).

★Kota INTERNATIONAL ££

(01326-562407; www.kotarestaurant.co.uk; 2-/3-course menu £20/25, mains £13.95-21.95; 6-9pm Tue-Sat) Half-Maori, half Chinese-Malay, chef Jude Kereama takes his culinary inspiration from his globetrotting travels, and his menu is spiced with exotic flavours, from Szechuan to Thai and Malaysian. His main restaurant is in a converted mill in Porthleven, 3 miles south of Helston. He also has another cafe-bistro, Kota Kai, along the quay.

Kota Kai Bar & Kitchen CAFE ££

(01326-574411; www.kotakai.co.uk; mains £7.95-18.95; noon-2pm & 5.30-9.30pm Mon, Tue & Thu-Sat, noon-2.30pm Sun;) On the 1st floor of a waterfront building overlooking Porthleven's harbour, this zingy cafe is run by chef Jude Kereama, and showcases his taste for spicy, exotic dishes: laksa curry, tom yum soup, five-spiced squid. The views over the quay are super.

Halzephron Inn PUB FOOD ££

(01326-240406; www.halzephron-inn.co.uk; mains £10.25-21.95; 11am-11pm) On the cliffs above the cove of Gunwalloe, 5 miles south of Helston, this is a historic Cornish local, whitewashed and slate-topped, with brassy trinkets above the bar, stout beams and a menu of beer-battered fish, grilled gammon steak, duck breast and the like. It's cosy and stone-walled, with lots of nooks and crannies, and a small patio outside.

Falmouth & Around

POP 20,775

Few seaside towns in Cornwall boast such an arresting location as Falmouth, overlooking the broad Fal River as it empties into the English Channel. Backed by green hills and blue water, Falmouth is criss-crossed by cobbled lanes, salty old pubs and trendy cafes. It makes an ideal base for exploring Cornwall's south coast, and has a wealth of bars and bistros, a trio of beaches and the nation's foremost maritime museum.

Though it's now mainly supported by students at Falmouth University in nearby Penryn, the town made its fortune during the 18th and 19th centuries thanks to lucrative maritime trade – the deep water offshore is the third-deepest natural harbour in the world, and the town grew rich when tea clippers, trading vessels and mail packets stopped here to unload their cargoes. Falmouth is still an important centre for ship repairs – you can look over the dockyard cranes as you head to Pendennis Point.

Sights & Activities

Falmouth's bucket-and-spade beaches aren't quite up to north coast standards, but they're nice enough for paddling and sun lounging. All the beaches have car parks, but they fill up quickly in summer. The 367 bus (hourly Monday to Friday, four times on Saturday) runs from the Moor bus station to Gyllyngvase and Swanpool.

National Maritime Museum MUSEUM
(☎01326-313388; www.nmmc.co.uk; Discovery Quay; adult/child £12.50/5; ⏰10am-5pm) Falmouth's most high-profile museum is located on the much revamped area around Discovery Quay. It's the sister outpost of the National Maritime Museum in Greenwich, London, and focuses on Falmouth's history as a seafaring port, supplemented by regular nautically themed exhibitions. The centrepiece is the impressive **Flotilla Gallery**, where an array of small boats is suspended from the ceiling on steel wires.

Pendennis Castle CASTLE
(EH; ☎01326-316594; www.english-heritage.org.uk; adult/child £7.90/4.70; ⏰10am-6pm daily Mar-Sep, 10am-5pm Oct, 10am-4pm Sat & Sun Nov-Feb) Designed to work in tandem with its sister castle in St Mawes across the estuary, this Tudor castle sits proudly on Pendennis Point, and was built as part of Henry VIII's massive castle-building program to reinforce England's coastline. You can wander around several of the castle floors and the Tudor gun deck, as well as the governor's bedroom, a WWI guardhouse and the WWII-era Half-Moon Battery. Listen out for the Noonday Gun blasting out at midday.

Fal River Boat Trips BOATING
Falmouth's main pier is the departure point for boat trips along the Fal River and ferries to Flushing and St Mawes. There are several operators, all offering similar routes: Enterprise Boats (p355) is the best known, and runs regular trips to Truro and St Mawes via Trelissick Gardens.

CORNWALL'S GREAT GARDENS

Eden Project (☎01726-811911; www.edenproject.com; adult/child/family £25/15/69, joint ticket with Lost Gardens of Heligan £34.65/18/93.50; ⏰9.30am-6pm, last admission 4.30pm) Lodged at the bottom of a disused clay pit, the giant biomes of the Eden Project – the largest greenhouses in the world – have become Cornwall's most celebrated landmark and an essential visit. Looking like a Bond villain's lair, Eden's bubble-shaped biomes maintain miniature ecosystems that enable all kinds of weird and wonderful plants to flourish – from stinking rafflesia flowers and banana trees in the rainforest biome to cacti and soaring palms in the Mediterranean biome.

Lost Gardens of Heligan (☎01726-845100; www.heligan.com; adult/child £13.50/6; ⏰10am-6pm Mar-Oct, to 5pm Nov-Feb) This is Cornwall's real-life secret garden. Formerly the family estate of the Tremaynes, Heligan's magnificent 19th-century gardens fell into disrepair following WWI, and have since been restored to their former splendour by the brains behind the Eden Project, Tim Smit, and a huge army of gardeners, horticulturalists and volunteers.

Trebah Garden (☎01326-252200; www.trebahgarden.co.uk; adult/child £9/3; ⏰10.30am-5.30pm, last entry 4.30pm) Trebah Garden was planted in 1840 by Charles Fox, younger brother of Alfred, who established nearby Glendurgan Garden. It's less formal, with gigantic rhododendrons, gunnera and jungle ferns lining the sides of a steep ravine leading down to the quay and shingle beach. There's a pleasant cafe and souvenir shop beside the ticket office. Admission to the gardens is half-price from November to February.

Glendurgan Garden (NT; ☎01326-250906; www.nationaltrust.org.uk/glendurgan-garden; adult/child £8.10/4.05; ⏰10.30am-5.30pm Tue-Sun) Glendurgan was established by Alfred Fox in the 1820s to show off the many weird and wonderful plants being brought back from the far corners of the empire, from Himalayan rhododendrons to Canadian maples and New Zealand tree ferns. Tumbling down a stunning subtropical valley, the garden offers breathtaking views of the Helford, as well as a lovely ornamental maze and a secluded beach near Durgan village. The gardens are now owned by the National Trust.

Potager Garden (☎01326-341258; www.potagergarden.org; suggested donation £3; ⏰10am-5pm Thu-Sun) It's a considerable drive from Falmouth but this gorgeous kitchen garden near Constantine is well worth the detour. Rescued from dilapidation by its current owners, it's been renovated by volunteers into a delightful working garden modelled on the French 'potager'. Highlights include the 30m greenhouse and super cafe, and there are outdoor games to play and hammocks to lounge around on. The garden also hosts craft workshops from time to time. Check the website for directions.

Sleeping

Falmouth Lodge Backpackers HOSTEL £
(☎01326-319996; www.falmouthbackpackers.co.uk; 9 Gyllyngvase Tce; dm/s £19/28, d per person from £28) In a mock-Tudor house at the top of town, this friendly hostel makes a fun budget stay. Rooms are small but clean and cosy, there's an Aga in the kitchen and a DVD lounge, and owner Judi often holds impromptu barbecues for guests.

Highcliffe Contemporary B&B B&B ££
(☎01326-314466; www.highcliffefalmouth.com; 22 Melvill Rd; s £68, d £99-150; 📶) Vintage furniture and upcycled design pieces give each of the rooms here its own individual feel. The pick of the bunch is the light-filled Attic Penthouse, with skylight windows overlooking Falmouth Bay. Room service breakfasts are served in picnic baskets, or you can tuck into pancakes and Hog's pudding in the dining room.

Bosanneth B&B ££
(☎01326-314649; www.bosanneth.co.uk; Gyllyngvase Hill; d from £90; 📶) There's a mix-and-match decorative vibe running through this eight-room B&B. Some of the rooms feel vintage, with old mirrors, reclaimed furniture and classic colours, while others go for a more up-to-date look. The 'oasis' garden is a particular delight.

Greenbank HOTEL £££
(☎01326-312440; www.greenbank-hotel.co.uk; Harbourside; r £129-259; P📶) The queen of Falmouth's hotels, with a knockout position overlooking the boat-filled estuary towards Flushing. It feels rather like the setting for an Agatha Christie novel – nautical knick-knacks and ships in cabinets dot the public areas, and tall windows look out onto the water. The rooms are more modern, decorated in inoffensive beiges and creams. Sea views command premium prices.

Eating

Good Vibes Café CAFE £
(☎01326-211870; 28 Killigrew St; sandwiches and salads £5.95-7.45; ⏰8.30am-5.30pm Mon-Sat) Look no further for lunch than this lovely, contemporary cafe on the Moor, which does a brisk trade from breakfast through to teatime. It's popular for its copious breakfasts, creative sandwiches (which range from pulled spiced chicken to peanut-and-mackerel bagel), crunchy salads and irresistible cakes. There's free cucumber water on tap, plus smoothies and juices galore.

★**Oliver's** BISTRO ££
(☎01326-218138; www.oliversfalmouth.com; 33 High St; mains £16.50-23.50; ⏰noon-2pm & 7-9pm Tue-Sat) Run by chef Ken Oliver, this little bistro is the place everyone wants to dine in Falmouth, but the tiny dining room means you'll have to book well ahead. White walls and pine tables provide a stripped-back match for Ken's imaginative, Mediterranean-inspired food. Local foragers provide many ingredients.

★**Wildebeest** VEGAN ££
(☎01326-210602; 13 Arwenack St; mains £8.25-10.25; ⏰10am-4pm & 5.30-11pm Mon & Wed-Sat) Veggies rejoice: this superb bistro serves up some of the most delicious food of any of Falmouth's restaurants, all 100% vegan. From fiery Malaysian laksa to raw pad Thai, every dish here sparkles with exotic flavours – and the icecream (made with coconut oil and cashew nuts) has to be tasted to be believed. The only drawback? It's tiny.

★**Wheelhouse** SEAFOOD ££
(☎01326-318050; Upton Slip; mains £8-15; ⏰6-10pm Wed-Sat) Hidden down a narrow alley off Church St, this backstreet shellfish bar is all about the hands-on dining experience: crab, scallops, mussels and lobsters are served in their shells, complete with cracking tools. There are two sittings, but both are always packed out – you will need to book well ahead, ideally a week or two in advance.

Star & Garter GASTROPUB ££
(☎01326-316663; http://starandgarter.squarespace.com; 52 High St; mains £15-20; ⏰noon-3pm & 6-9pm) At the top of the old High Street among antique shops and health-food stores, this ancient old boozer has been slaking the town's thirst for several centuries. Its most recent reincarnation is as a gourmet gastropub focusing on nose-to-tail dining, so the menu is meat-heavy (think ox tongue and chargrilled pork leg). Ask for one of the harbour-view tables.

Courtyard Deli DELI, CAFE ££
(☎01326 319526; www.courtyarddeli.co.uk; 2 Bells Court; mains £8-12; ⏰8.30am-5.30pm Mon-Sat, 10.30am-4pm Sun) Small is beautiful, as this cosy deli-diner ably demonstrates. Charcuterie, tarts, salads and quiches fill the counter cabinets, and there are regular evening dinner sessions. It's up an easy-to-miss alley, next to Beerwolf Books.

Drinking & Nightlife

★ Beerwolf Books PUB
(☎01326-618474; www.beerwolfbooks.com; 3 Bells Court; ⏲noon-midnight) Quite possibly the greatest idea ever, anytime, anywhere: a pub and bookshop rolled into one, meaning you can browse for reading material before settling down for a pint of real ale.

Hand Bar BAR
(☎01326-319888; 3 Old Brewery Yard; ⏲noon-1am) Pete Walker's craft-beer bar showcases his knowledge, gained while running Leeds' North Bar: esoteric choices such as New York's Brooklyn Brewery and Bodmin's Harbour Brewing Co are among the regulars on tap – although esoterica equals expensiveness. It's fittingly situated in a former brewery, with a few courtyard tables outside, but space is limited inside.

The Front PUB
(☎01326-212168; Custom House Quay; ⏲11am-11.30pm) The beer-buffs' choice: a cosy spit-and-sawdust pub, with scuffed wood floors and a copious choice of real ales served straight from wooden casks. The entrance is down a small hill off Arwenack St.

Boathouse PUB
(☎01326-315425; Trevethan Hill) Lively split-level pub offering great views across the river to Flushing, and decent food.

Festivals

Falmouth Oyster Festival FOOD & DRINK
(www.falmouthoysterfestival.co.uk; ⏲Oct) Feast on fresh oysters, mussels and other crustaceans during this October festival, which also hosts cookery classes and culinary demos.

Information

Fal River Information Centre (☎01326-741194; www.falriver.co.uk; 11 Market Strand, Prince of Wales Pier; ⏲9.30am-5.30pm Mon-Sat, 10am-4pm Sun)

Getting There & Away

Falmouth is at the end of the branch train line from Truro (£4.20, 24 minutes), where you can catch connections with the mainline service from Penzance to stations including Plymouth, Exeter and London Paddington.

Falmouth's **Moor Bus Station** (The Moor) is central. **First Kernow** (www.firstgroup.com/cornwall) has the following bus routes:

U1 (£5, half-hourly Monday to Saturday, hourly Sunday) To Truro via Penryn.

U2 (£5, hourly) To Redruth via Penryn.

2 (every two hours Monday to Saturday) To Penzance via Helston.

35/35A (£5, hourly Monday to Saturday) Stops at Glendurgan and Trebah Gardens en route to Helston.

LOCAL KNOWLEDGE

FERRYBOAT INN

The lovely riverside pub **Ferryboat Inn** (☎01326-250625; www.thewright-brothers.co.uk/ferryboat-inn.html; Helford Passage; mains £8-20; ⏲11am-11pm) is now owned by the Wright Brothers, Britain's premier oyster entrepreneurs, who also run the oyster farm at nearby Porth Navas. Outside, there are wooden picnic tables with dreamy views over the Helford River; inside, it's all wood, slate and open plan. It's great for food – oysters, shellfish and the Sunday roast are strong points. Bus 35 passes hourly from Falmouth.

Truro

POP 17,431

Centred on its three-spired 19th-century cathedral, Truro is Cornwall's capital city. Once a busy river port and one of Cornwall's five Stannary towns (where tin was assayed and stamped for export), these days it's a busy commercial city, with a lively centre dominated by the usual coffee shops and chain stores.

Remnants of the city's elegant Georgian past can be seen on **Lemon St** and **Walsingham Place**.

Sights & Activities

Truro Cathedral CHURCH
(www.trurocathedral.org.uk; High Cross; suggested donation £5; ⏲7.30am-6pm Mon-Sat, 9am-7pm Sun) Built on the site of a 16th-century parish church in soaring Gothic Revival style, Truro Cathedral was completed in 1910, making it the first cathedral built in England since St Paul's. Inside, the vast nave contains some fine Victorian stained glass and the impressive Father Willis Organ.

Royal Cornwall Museum MUSEUM
(☎01872-272205; www.royalcornwallmuseum.org.uk; River St; ⏲10am-5pm Mon-Sat) FREE Collections at the county's main museum encompass everything from geological specimens

to Celtic torques and a ceremonial carriage. Upstairs there's an Egyptian section and a little gallery with some surprising finds: a Turner here, a van Dyck there, and several works by the Newlyn artist Stanhope Forbes.

★Enterprise Boats BOATING
(☎01326-374241; www.falriver.co.uk; return adult/child £15/7.50) Two miles downriver from Truro's city centre, past the green expanse of Boscawen Park, is the riverside hamlet of Malpas, from where ferries chug out along the River Fal all the way to Falmouth. It's a wonderfully scenic trip that putters past wooded riverbanks and hidden inlets; some boats also stop at Trelissick en route. Free double-deckers run from the Truro harbour-master's office to the pontoon at Malpas, although depending on the tides you can often ride the boat right back to Truro.

Sleeping

Mannings Hotel HOTEL ££
(☎01872-270345; www.manningshotels.co.uk; Lemon St; r £105-115, apt £135; P, wi-fi) The best place to stay in the city centre. The part-Georgian building has been tastefully modernised, with bright colours and functional furniture, even if the general vibe feels a tad corporate. There are 'aparthotels' for longer stays, and the private car park is useful.

Merchant House Hotel HOTEL ££
(☎01872-272450; www.merchant-house.co.uk; 49 Falmouth Rd; s/d/f £79/99/119; P) This Victorian house is handy for town, and refurbishment has brightened up the rooms. Some have skylights, others overlook the garden. It's popular with business travellers and organised coach tours, however, so it's worth reserving well ahead.

Eating & Drinking

★Falmouth Bay Seafood Café SEAFOOD ££
(☎01872-278884; www.falmouthbayseafoodcafe.com; Castle Villa, 53 Castle St; mains £11.95-22.95; ⌚noon-3.30pm, 5.30-10pm Mon-Sat) Rightly touted as Truro's top restaurant, this smart seafooderie focuses on the fruits of the sea – tuck into fresh Fal oysters or Falmouth Bay scallops, then go for the seafood platter (£38). The pre-theatre menu is good value: £14.50/17.50 for two/three courses, served from 5.30pm to 7pm.

Sam's in the City BISTRO ££
(☎01872-859819; www.samscornwall.co.uk; 1-2 New Bridge St; mains £11.95-21.95; ⌚9am-10pm) Fowey's long-standing restaurant has come to the city, in a former jeweller's on one of Truro's oldest streets. The menu is split between seafood classics, steaks, city salads and sharing platters – plus bouillabaisse and seafood feasts for the very hungry.

★108 Coffee CAFE
(☎07582 339636; www.108coffee.co.uk; 108c Kenwyn St; ⌚7am-6pm Mon-Fri, 8am-6pm Sat) Set up in 2011 by unapologetic coffee nuts Paul and Michelle, this is the premier place for a caffeine fix in Truro. The beans come courtesy of Cornwall's renowned coffee roasters Origin Coffee, and the flat whites and espressos are as good as any the county has to offer (you can even text your order ahead to save waiting).

Old Ale House PUB
(☎01872-271122; 7 Quay St; ⌚noon-11pm) A proper ale-drinker's pub, with sawdust on the floor, beer mats on the ceiling and a menu of guest ales. Ask at the bar for a handful of peanuts to snack on.

Information

Tourist Office (☎01872-274555; www.visittruro.org.uk; Boscawen St; ⌚9am-5.30pm Mon-Fri, to 5pm Sat) In a small office beside the Hall for Cornwall's rear entrance.

Getting There & Away

BUS

Truro's bus station is beside Lemon Quay.

Bus U1 (£5, half-hourly Monday to Saturday, hourly Sunday) To Truro via Penryn.

Bus 14/14A (£5, 1½ hours, hourly Monday to Saturday) To St Ives.

Bus 18 (£5, half-hourly Monday to Saturday, hourly Sunday) To Penzance.

TRAIN

Truro is on the main London Paddington–Penzance line and the branch line to Falmouth.

Bristol £46.50, 3½ hours
Exeter £18.40, 2¼ hours
Falmouth £4.20, 30 minutes
London Paddington £62.60, 4½ hours
Penzance £6.60, 30 minutes

Fowey

POP 2273

In many ways, Fowey feels like Padstow's south-coast sister; a workaday port turned well-heeled holiday town, with a tumble of pastel-coloured houses, portside pubs and tiered terraces overlooking the wooded banks of the Fowey River. The town's wealth was founded on the export of china clay from the St Austell pits, but it's been an important port since Elizabethan times, and later became the adopted home of the thriller writer Daphne du Maurier, who used the nearby house at Menabilly Barton as the inspiration for *Rebecca*.

Today it's an attractive and increasingly upmarket town, handy for exploring Cornwall's southeastern corner.

Sights & Activities

Readymoney Cove BEACH

From the town centre, the Esplanade leads down to this little cove and the remains of the small Tudor fort of **St Catherine's Castle** FREE.

Polkerris Beach BEACH

(www.polkerrisbeach.com) A couple of miles west of Fowey is the area's largest and busiest beach. Sailing lessons, windsurfing and stand-up paddleboarding are all available.

Hall Walk HIKING

(www.nationaltrust.org.uk/fowey-estuary/trails/fowey-hall-walk) This 3.5-mile circular walk starts across the river from Fowey in Bodinnick, winding along the wooded shores of Pont Pill Creek before following the coastline to the harbour of Polruan, from where you can catch a ferry back to Fowey. You can download a route guide from the National Trust website.

Encounter Cornwall KAYAKING

(☎07976 466123; www.encountercornwall.com; Golant; adult/child £25/15) Three-hour trips from Golant, just north of Fowey, with a choice of exploring creek or coastline. It also offers two-hour 'sundowner' expeditions and stand-up paddleboarding trips.

Sleeping

★**Coriander Cottages** B&B ££

(☎01726-834998; www.foweyaccommodation.co.uk; Penventinue Lane; r £100-135; P 📶) A delightfully rural cottage complex on the outskirts of Fowey, with ecofriendly accommodation in a choice of open-plan, self-catering barns, all with quiet country views. The stone barns have been beautifully modernised, and use a combination of solar panels, ground-source heating and rainwater harvesting to reduce environmental impact. A lovely retreat.

Cormorant Hotel HOTEL ££

(☎01726-833426; www.cormoranthotel.co.uk; Golant; d £135-235) Up the creek in Golant (about 5 miles by road), this small hotel has a superb riverside location, and many of its rooms have water-view balconies. They're split into three comfort levels: go for a Superior with view for the premium price-comfort ratio.

Old Quay House HOTEL £££

(☎01726-833302; www.theoldquayhouse.com; 28 Fore St; d £160-340; 📶) The epitome of Fowey's upmarket trend, this exclusive quayside hotel is all natural fabrics, rattan chairs and tasteful tones, and the rooms are a mix of estuary-view suites and attic penthouses. Very Kensington, not very Cornish.

WORTH A TRIP

POLPERRO

Even in a county where picturesque fishing harbours seem to fill every cove, it's hard not to fall for Polperro – a warren of cottages, boat stores and alleyways, all set around a stout granite harbour. Unsurprisingly, this was once a smugglers' hideout, and it's still a place with a salty, sea-dog atmosphere, despite the inevitable summer crowds. The coast path between Polperro and Looe is particularly scenic, especially around **Talland Bay**.

The main car park is 750m uphill from the village, from where it's a 15-minute stroll down to the quayside. Apart from simply wandering and soaking up the scenery, it's worth popping into the ramshackle **Heritage Museum** (☎01503-272423; The Warren; adult/child £2/0.50; ⏲10am-4.30pm or 5pm Mar-Oct), which explores the town's maritime history.

Eating & Drinking

Lifebuoy Cafe CAFE £

(☎07715 075869; www.thelifebuoycafe.co.uk; 8 Lostwithiel St; mains £5-10; ⏰8am-5pm) Everyone's favourite brekkie stop in Fowey, this friendly cafe is a riot of character, from the brightly coloured furniture and polka-dot bunting to the vintage Action Men on the shelves. Wolf down a Fat Buoy brekkie or a classic fish-finger butty, washed down with a mug of good old English tea.

Dwelling House CAFE £

(☎01726-833662; 6 Fore St; tea £3-6; ⏰10am-6.30pm May-Sep, to 5.30pm Wed-Sun Oct-Apr) Top spot for tea (20-plus varieties) and dainty cakes (decorated with sprinkles and icing swirls, and served on a proper cake stand).

Sam's BISTRO ££

(☎01726-832273; http://samscornwall.co.uk/fowey; 20 Fore St; mains £7.95-15.95; ⏰noon-9pm) Sam's has been a stalwart in Fowey for years. Booth seats, day-glo menus and a lively local vibe keep the feel laid-back, and the menu of burgers, fish, salads and steaks proves perenially popular. No bookings.

King of Prussia PUB

(www.kingofprussia.co.uk; Town Quay; ⏰11am-11pm) Fowey has lots of pubs, but you might as well go for the one with the best harbour view, named after notorious 'free trader' (otherwise known as smuggler) John Carter.

Information

Fowey Tourist Information Centre (☎01726-833616; www.fowey.co.uk; 5 South St; ⏰9.30am-5pm Mon-Sat, 10am-4pm Sun) Lots of information on Fowey and southeast Cornwall.

Getting There & Away

Bus services are limited: the only really useful service is bus 24 (hourly Monday to Saturday, six on Sunday), which runs to St Austell, Heligan and Mevagissey. It also stops at Par train station, where you can catch trains on the main London–Penzance line.

Polruan Ferry (www.ctomsandson.co.uk/polruan-ferry; adult/child/bicycle £1.80/0.80/1; ⏰last ferry 11pm May-Sep, 7pm Oct-Apr) Passenger ferry to Polruan. In winter and on summer evenings, it runs from Town Quay; during the day, it runs from Whitehouse Slipway on the Esplanade.

Bodinnick Ferry (www.ctomsandson.co.uk/bodinnick-ferry; car & 2 passengers/pedestrian/bicycle £4.60/1.80/free; ⏰last ferry 8.45pm Apr-Oct, 7pm Nov-Mar) Car ferry crossing the river to Bodinnick.

Looe

POP 5280

Tucked into the long curve of coast between the Fowey River and Plymouth Sound, Looe is half historic fishing port, half bucket-and-spade resort. Split into East and West Looe and linked by a historic arched bridge, it's a pleasant base for exploring Cornwall's southeastern reaches, and has some lovely beaches nearby.

Sights

Looe Island ISLAND

A mile offshore from Hannafore Point is the densely wooded Looe Island (officially known as St George's Island), a 9-hectare nature reserve and a haven for marine wildlife. Between May and September, trips are offered by the **Islander** (☎07814 139223; return adult/child £7/5, plus landing fee £3/1) from the quayside near the lifeboat station, but they're dependent on the weather and tides.

Wild Futures Monkey Sanctuary WILDLIFE RESERVE

(☎01503-262532; www.monkeysanctuary.org; St Martins; adult/child £8.50/5; ⏰11am-4.30pm Sat-Thu; 👪) Half a mile west of town, this wildlife centre is guaranteed to raise 'aaahhhs' over its woolly and capuchin monkeys, many of which were rescued from captivity.

Sleeping

Penvith Barns B&B ££

(☎01503-240772; www.penvithbarns.co.uk; St-Martin-by-Looe; r £75-80; P📶🐾) Escape the Looe crowds at this rural barn conversion in the nearby hamlet of St-Martin-by-Looe, run by friendly owners Graham and Jules. Rooms range from small to spacious: the Piggery is tiny and tucked under the eaves, while the Dairy has enough space for a spare bed and sofa. A bit of a bargain.

Commonwood Manor B&B £££

(☎01503-262929; www.commonwoodmanor.com; St Martins Rd; d £75-95; P📶🏊) In a prime position on the hillside of East Looe, this elegant manor house is a cut above the bargain-basement B&Bs you'll find around the rest of Looe. Rooms are a touch frilly and pastel heavy, but if you can bag one of the bay-window bedrooms you'll be rewarded with the best sea views in town.

Information

Looe Tourist Office (☎01503-262072; www.visit-southeastcornwall.co.uk; Guildhall, Fore St; ⏲10am-5pm Easter-Oct)

Getting There & Away

Plymouth Citybus provides the only buses to Looe. Bus 71A/72 (hourly Monday to Saturday, five on Sunday) runs from Plymouth via Looe and Polperro.

Bodmin Moor

It can't quite boast the wild majesty of Dartmoor, but Bodmin Moor has a bleak beauty all of its own. Pockmarked with heaths and granite hills, including **Rough Tor** (row-tor; 400m) and Cornwall's highest point, **Brown Willy** (419m), it's a desolate place that works on the imagination; for years there have been reported sightings of the Beast of Bodmin, a large, black catlike creature, although no one's ever managed to snap a decent picture.

Apart from the hills, the moor's main landmark is **Jamaica Inn**, made famous by Daphne du Maurier's novel of the same name – although it's disappointingly been modernised since the author's day.

Sights & Activities

Golitha Falls — WATERFALL

Around 1.25 miles west of St Cleer, these crashing waterfalls are one of the most renowned beauty spots on the moor. Around the falls are the remains of the ancient oak woodland that once covered much of the moor. There is a car park half a mile's walk from the reserve near Draynes Bridge.

Carnglaze Caverns — CAVE

(☎01579-320251; www.carnglaze.com; adult/child £6/4; ⏲10am-5pm) Slate was once extensively mined on the moor, leaving behind a network of deep caverns such as these ones outside St Neot. Several of the caves are open to the public and can be visited on an underground tour.

Bodmin & Wenford Railway — RAIL

(☎01208-73555; www.bodminandwenfordrailway.co.uk; rover pass adult/child £13/6; ⏲3-5 daily trains May-Sep, fewer at other times) Run by enthusiasts, this steam railway – the only 'standard gauge' line of its type left in Cornwall – chuffs and clatters for 6.5 miles between Bodmin and Boscarne Junction. Many trains are still decked out in their original 1950s livery. At the Boscarne end, the line links up with the Camel Trail (p337); bikes can be taken on the trains if there's space.

Look out for special trips in summer, including Pullman-style dining trains with a silver-service supper, plus murder mystery and pub quiz trains.

Eating

★St Tudy Inn — MODERN BRITISH ££

(☎01208-850656; www.sttudyinn.com; St Tudy; mains £14-25; ⏲meals served noon-2.30pm & 6.30-9pm Mon-Sat, noon-2.30pm Sun) Run by the locally lauded chef Emily Scott, whose previous restaurant in Port Isaac received rave reviews, this village pub has fast become one of east Cornwall's top dining destinations. The old pub has been stripped down and sleekened, and Scott's trademark light, fresh, imaginative food takes centre stage. It's a gastropub of the first order – bookings essential.

★Woods Cafe — CAFE ££

(☎01208-78111; www.woodscafecornwall.co.uk; Cardinham Woods; mains £6-12; ⏲10.30am-4.30pm) In an old woodsman's cottage lost among the trees of Cardinham, this cracking cafe has become a dining destination in its own right – it's locally famous for its home-baked cakes, cockle-warming soups and sausage sarnies.

WORTH A TRIP

COTEHELE HOUSE

At the head of the Tamar Valley sits the Tudor manor of **Cotehele** (NT; ☎01579-351346; St Dominick; adult/child £10/5, grounds only £6.50/3.25; ⏲house 11am-4pm, gardens dawn-dusk daily), one of the Edgcumbe dynasty's modest country retreats. The cavernous great hall is the centrepiece, and the house has an unparalleled collection of Tudor tapestries, armour and furniture.

Outside, the gardens sweep down past the 18th-century Prospect Folly to Cotehele Quay, where there's a discovery centre exploring the history of the Tamar Valley and a vintage sailing barge, the **Shamrock**.

ISLES OF SCILLY

While only 28 miles west of the mainland, in many ways the Isles of Scilly feel like a different world. Life on this archipelago of around 140 tiny islands seems hardly to have changed in decades: there are no traffic jams, no supermarkets, no multinational hotels, and the only noise pollution comes from breaking waves and cawing gulls. That's not to say that Scilly is behind the times – you'll find a mobile signal and broadband on the main islands – but life ticks along at its own island pace. Renowned for glorious beaches, there are few places better to escape the outside world.

Only five islands are inhabited: St Mary's is the largest, followed by Tresco, while only a few hardy souls remain on Bryher, St Martin's and St Agnes. Regular ferry boats run between all five islands.

Unsurprisingly, summer is by far the busiest time. Many businesses shut down completely in winter.

Information

Isles of Scilly Tourist Information Centre (☎01720-424031; www.visitislesofscilly.com; Porthcressa Beach, St Mary's; ⏱9am-5.30pm Mon-Sat, 9am-2pm Sun Mar-Oct, 10am-2pm Mon-Fri Nov-Feb)

Scilly Online (www.scillyonline.co.uk)

Simply Scilly (www.simplyscilly.co.uk)

Getting There & Away

Bookings for flights and ferries are handled by the **Isles of Scilly Travel Centre** (☎0845 710 5555; www.islesofscilly-travel.co.uk; Quay St; ⏱8am-6.30pm Mon-Sat) in Penzance. There's also a small enquiries office in High Town on St Mary's.

Bad weather and fog often play havoc with the islands' travel schedules, so it's worth checking on the latest status before you set out – the Ios Travel Twitter account is very useful (@IoSTravel).

Isles of Scilly Skybus (☎01736-334220; www.islesofscilly-travel.co.uk) Since the closure of the helicopter service in 2013, planes provide the only air link to the islands. There are several flights daily from Land's End Airport, near Zennor, and Newquay Airport. Adult fares start at £70 one way. Summer flights also run from Exeter, Bristol and Southampton.

Scillonian III (☎0845 710 5555; www.islesofscilly-travel.co.uk; ⏱Apr-Oct) Scilly's ferry plies the notoriously choppy waters between Penzance and St Mary's (one-way adult £49.50). There's at least one daily crossing in summer, but there are no ferries in winter. Seasickness is a distinct possibility: be prepared

Getting Around

Inter-island ferries between St Mary's and the other islands are provided by the **St Mary's Boatmen's Association** (p360). If you're staying at one of the hotels on Tresco, there's also a separate transfer service.

The only bus and taxi services are on St Mary's. All flights are met by **Paulgers Transport** (☎01720-423701; adult/child return £7.50/3.50), who will run you to wherever you're staying, or straight to the quayside if you're travelling to other islands.

St Mary's

POP 2200

St Mary's is the largest and busiest island in Scilly, and the main point of arrival for flights and ferries. About a mile west of the airport is the main settlement of **Hugh Town**, home to most of the island's hotels, shops and guesthouses, as well as the main harbour.

Most people never get much further than **Porthcressa**, Hugh Town's narrow sandy beach, but there are plenty of other coves that can be reached on foot or by bike, including **Porth Hellick**, **Watermill Cove** and the remote **Pelistry Bay**.

Sights

Isles of Scilly Museum MUSEUM

(Church St, Hugh Town; adult/child £3.50/1; ⏱10am-4.30pm Mon-Fri, 10am-noon Sat Easter-Sep, 10am-noon Mon-Sat Oct-Easter) The small Isles of Scilly Museum explores the islands' history, with an eclectic mix of archaeological finds and shipwreck artefacts. Among the collection are Neolithic remains such as tools and jewellery, clay pipes left behind by generations of sailors, a couple of sailing boats and a small exhibition on Ted Heath, the English prime minister who loved Scilly so much he was buried here.

Tours

Scilly Walks WALKING

(☎01720-423326; www.scillywalks.co.uk; adult/child £6/3) Three-hour archaeological and historical tours, plus guided walking trips to other islands, conducted by local historian and archaeologist Katherine Sawyer.

Island Wildlife Tours WALKING
(☎01720-422212; www.islandwildlifetours.co.uk; half-/full day £6/12) Regular birdwatching and wildlife walks with local character and resident twitcher Will Wagstaff, the undisputed authority on Scilly's natural history. Most tours start at 9.45am or 10am on St Mary's, but there are regular tours on other islands too; you need to add on the cost of the boat transfer.

Island Sea Safaris BOATING
(☎01720-422732; www.islandseasafaris.co.uk) Trips to see local seabird and seal colonies (adult/child £33/25), plus one-hour 'island taster' tours (£24 per person). Also rents wetsuits and snorkelling gear.

Sleeping

Garrison Campsite CAMPGROUND £
(☎01720-422670; tedmoulson@aol.com; Tower Cottage, Garrison; sites £9.20-11.45;) Three and a half hectares of sea-view camping above Hugh Town, with electrical hook-ups, wi-fi and a laundry-cum-shower block. It'll even pitch a tent for you.

Mincarlo B&B ££
(☎01720-422513; www.mincarlo.info; s £42-50, d £85-112;) You couldn't ask for a better location on St Mary's than this little guesthouse: it's in a prime spot with views all the way to Hugh Town from the western end of Town Beach. Rooms are plain and cosy (the attic's a bargain), there's a lounge with local books to browse, breakfast is great, and owners Nick and Bryony are full of local info.

Isles of Scilly Country Guesthouse B&B ££
(☎01720-422440; www.scillyguesthouse.co.uk; High Lanes; d £94-114;) Run by Bavarian expat Sabine Schraudolph, this guesthouse is one of the comfiest on St Mary's. The large rooms are chintz-free and look out across St Mary's fields, and Sabine serves Bavarian goodies such as *apfelstrudel* in her conservatory-cum-coffee house.

Star Castle Hotel HOTEL £££
(☎01720-422317; www.star-castle.co.uk; The Garrison; r incl dinner £127-324;) Shaped like an eight-pointed star, this former fort on Garrison Point is one of Scilly's star hotels, with heritage-style castle rooms and more modern garden suites. It's stuffy and expensive, but the views are the best on the island, and at least prices include dinner. It gets a lot cheaper outside the peak months between May and September.

Eating

Juliet's Garden Restaurant RESTAURANT ££
(☎01720-422228; www.julietsgardenrestaurant.co.uk; lunch mains £7-12, dinner mains £14-24.95; noon-4pm & 6-9pm) St Mary's long-standing bistro, in business for three decades, is still the best place to eat. It's in a converted barn 15 minutes' walk from town: expect gourmet salads and sandwiches by day, plus classier plates of pan-roasted bream, slow-roast lamb and whole lobster after dark, served by candlelight. The garden is glorious on a sunny day.

Dibble & Grub CAFE ££
(☎01720-423719; www.dibbleandgrub.com; lunch £6-12, dinner £10-16; 10am-10pm Apr-Sep) Smart beachside cafe beside Porthcressa, housed in the island's old fire station. The menu dabbles in tapas and Mediterranean-style classics.

Getting Around

The airport bus (£3) departs from Hugh Town 40 minutes before each flight, while the **Island Rover** (☎01720-422131; www.islandrover.co.uk; tickets £8) offers a twice-daily sightseeing trip in a vintage bus in summer.

For taxis on St Mary's, try **Island Taxis** (☎01720-422126), **Scilly Cabs** (☎01720-422901) or **St Mary's Taxis** (☎01720-422142) or airport taxi **Paulgers Transport** (p359).

St Mary's Boatmen's Association (☎01720-423999; www.scillyboating.co.uk) provides regular ferry services from St Mary's to Scilly's other islands. Returns to/from one island cost adult/child £9.50/4.50, or you can take a 'circular' return via another island for £15/7.50.

Tresco

POP 175

A short boat hop across the channel from St Mary's brings you to Tresco, the second-largest island, once owned by the monks of Tavistock Abbey and now leased by locals from the Duchy of Cornwall. It's a proper old-fashioned island getaway – for decades there was just one pub and one hotel on the island. The main attraction here is the island's fabulous subtropical garden, but it's a lovely place just to wander.

Sights

★Tresco Abbey Garden GARDENS

(☎01720-424105; www.tresco.co.uk/stay/abbey-garden; adult/child £15/free; ⊙10am-4pm) One of Scilly's great attractions is this subtropical estate, laid out in 1834 on the site of a 12th-century Benedictine priory by the horticultural visionary Augustus Smith. The gardens are now home to more than 20,000 exotic species, from towering palms to desert cacti and crimson flame trees, all nurtured by the temperate gusts of the Gulf Stream. Admission also covers the **Valhalla collection**, made up of figureheads and nameplates salvaged from the many ships that have foundered off Tresco's shores.

Sleeping & Eating

New Inn PUB, HOTEL £££

(☎01720-422849; contactus@tresco.co.uk; r £120-320) Compared with Tresco's two wallet-shreddingly expensive hotels, the New Inn is a comparative bargain. The rooms are soothingly finished in buttery yellows and pale blues, although inevitably you'll have to fork out for a view. The inn itself serves good food (mains £10 to £18), mainly standards such as pollock and chips, steaks and the like.

Bryher

Only around 70 people live on Bryher, Scilly's smallest and wildest inhabited island. Covered by rough bracken and heather, and fringed by white sand, this slender chunk of rock takes a fearsome battering from the Atlantic – Hell Bay hasn't earned its name for nothing. But on a bright sunny day, it's an island idyll par excellence, ideal for exploring on foot. Several small sandy beaches can be reached along the coast path, including the impressive sweep of **Rushy Bay**. For the best views, hike up to the top of **Watch Hill**, from where you can drink in a panorama right across Scilly.

Sleeping & Eating

Bryher Campsite CAMPGROUND £

(☎01720-422886; www.bryhercampsite.co.uk; sites £10.25; 🐾) Bare-bones camping, in a secluded spot surround by drystone walls and just steps from the sea. Hot showers and tractor transport are included in the nightly rates.

Hell Bay Hotel HOTEL £££

(☎01720-422947; www.hellbay.co.uk; d £205-350) Pretty much the poshest place to stay in Scilly – a true island getaway blending New England–style furnishings with sunny golds, sea blues and pale wood beams. It has the feel of a luxurious beach villa, with lovingly tended gardens and an excellent restaurant (three-course menu £45). Garden-view suites are the cheapest.

Bryher Shop DELI £

(☎01720-423601; www.brryhershop.co.uk; ⊙9am-5.30pm Mon-Sat, 10am-1pm Sun) Pick up all your essential supplies at the island's charming general store.

Fraggle Rock CAFE ££

(☎01720-422222; www.bryher.co; mains £8-15; ⊙9am-9pm; 📶) This relaxed cafe also doubles as Bryher's pub. The menu's mainly quiches, salads and burgers, ideally served in the front garden, where chickens scratch around and there are views out to Hangman's Rock. It's a lively evening hang-out in season. There are a few timber-clad cabins (£620 to £1090 per week) if you feel like staying.

St Martin's

POP 136

The northernmost of the main islands, little St Martin's is rightly renowned for its beaches. Worth hunting out are **Lawrence's Bay** on the south coast, which becomes a broad sweep of sand at low tide; the secluded cove of Perpitch in the southeast; and **Great Bay** on the north, arguably Scilly's finest beach.

Sights & Activities

St Martin's Vineyard WINERY

(☎01720-423418; www.stmartinsvineyard.co.uk; ⊙tours 10.45am-4pm Tue-Thu) The UK's smallest and most southwesterly vineyard produces its own range of white wines. Tours are conducted by owners Val and Graham Thomas.

Scilly Diving DIVING

(☎01720-422848; www.scillydiving.com) Situated in Higher Town, this dive outfit offers diving courses and single dives.

Sleeping

Accommodation is limited apart from one super-expensive hotel, **St Martin's on the Isle** (☎01720-422090; www.stmartinshotel.co.uk; d £300-560), and a handful of B&Bs.

St Martin's Campsite CAMPGROUND £
(☎01720-422888; www.stmartinscampsite.co.uk; sites £10-11.50; ⏲Mar-Oct) The second-largest campsite in Scilly at the western end of Lawrence's Bay, with 50 pitches spread across three fields. There are coin-operated washing machines and showers, and eggs and veg are available for your morning fry-up.

Polreath B&B ££
(☎01720-422046; www.polreath.com; Higher Town; d £110-120) This friendly granite cottage has small rooms and a sunny conservatory serving cream teas, homemade lemonade and evening meals. Weekly stays required May to September.

Eating & Drinking

Little Arthur Farm CAFE £
(☎01720-422457; www.littlearthur.co.uk; ⏲10.30am-4pm daily) A little slice of the good life on St Martin's, this small-scale farm has diversified in all kinds of imaginative directions. There's a cafe-bistro, it grows its own produce and even makes shoes – and there's an ecocabin to stay in too (£380 per week).

Adam's Fish & Chips SEAFOOD £
(☎01720-422457; takeaway fish & chips £8; ⏲6-8.30pm Tue-Thu, noon-2.30pm Sat Jul & Aug, 6-8.30pm Tue & Thu Sep-Jun) The fish here is as fresh as it gets – whatever's caught on the day is what ends up in your batter. It's run by Adam and Emma, who live and work on Little Arthur Farm nearby.

Island Bakery BAKERY £
(☎01720-42211; www.theislandbakery-stmartins.com; ⏲9am-5pm Mon-Sat) This homespun bakery run by Barney and Ella McLachlan turns out fresh bread, pizzas and, of course, homemade pasties.

Seven Stones PUB
(☎01720-423777; sevenstonesinn@gmail.com; mains £8-12; ⏲10am-11pm) Gorgeous pub and the island's only boozer, so it's the heart of the action every night of the week. Decent grub, Cornish ales and super views of the other islands from the terrace.

St Agnes

POP 170

Scilly's southernmost island feels really remote, with a string of empty coves and a scattering of prehistoric sites. Visitors disembark at Porth Conger, near the old lighthouse, from where you wander along the coast path around the whole island.

At low tide, a narrow sand bar appears to the neighbouring island of **Gugh**, where many ancient burial sites and a few chamber tombs can be found. The **Troy Town Maze** is slightly more recent, thought to have been fashioned from stones around 200 years ago.

Sleeping & Eating

Troytown Farm CAMPGROUND £
(☎01720-422360; www.troytown.co.uk; adult £9.50, tents £2-8) Once a flower farm, St Martin's minuscule campsite offers meadow camping with superb sea views, and also rents three self-catering cottages (from £550 per week). Transport by tractor from the quay costs £3.50.

Covean Cottage COTTAGE ££
(☎01720-422620; http://st-agnes-scilly.org/covean.htm; d £88-104) Pretty much the only B&B on the island, this little stone-walled cottage has three pretty sea-view rooms. There's also a small cafe, which serves brekkies and light meals cooked up by the owner.

★**Turk's Head** PUB FOOD ££
(☎01720-422434; mains £8-14; ⏲11am-11pm Mon-Sat, noon-10.30pm Sun) You can almost smell the history at Britain's most southerly alehouse. It's covered in maritime memorabilia – model ships in glass cabinets, vintage maps of the islands, black-and-white photos of seafarers – and there are few finer places to sup a pint. You might even be treated to a sea shanty if the local lads are in the mood.

Cambridge & East Anglia

Includes ➡

Best Places to Eat

➡ Midsummer House (p377)

➡ Roger Hickman's (p397)

➡ Butley Orford Oysterage (p392)

➡ Great House (p387)

➡ Picnic Fayre (p399)

Best Places to Sleep

➡ Varsity (p376)

➡ Sutherland House (p391)

➡ Swan (p387)

➡ Dedham Hall (p382)

➡ Cley Windmill (p399)

Why Go?

Unfurling gently eastwards to the sea, the vast flatlands of East Anglia are a rich web of lush farmland, melancholy Fens and sparkling rivers. The area is justly famous for its sweeping sandy beaches, big skies and the bucolic landscape that once inspired Constable and Gainsborough.

It's not all rural idyll though: rising out of the Fens is the world-famous university town of Cambridge, with its stunning classical architecture and earnest attitude, and to the east is the cosmopolitan city of Norwich. Around them, magnificent cathedral cities, pretty market towns and implausibly picturesque villages are testament to the enormous wealth amassed here during medieval times, when the wool and weaving industries flourished.

Meanwhile, the meandering coastline is peppered with pretty fishing villages and traditional bucket-and-spade resorts, while inland is the languid, hypnotic charm of the Norfolk Broads, an ideal location for serious relaxation.

When to Go

➡ To best explore the Cambridge colleges, avoid Spring (early April to mid-June), when they close to visitors as students prepare for exams.

➡ June and August show the Norfolk and Suffolk beaches and the Norfolk Broads at their best. But in school holidays (late July to August) it gets busy and accommodation prices rise.

➡ World-class classical music comes to Suffolk in the Aldeburgh Festival in June. In July, Southwold's eclectic Latitude Festival offers alternative rock, comedy and theatre.

➡ November's Ways With Words literature festival draws big-name authors to Southwold.

➡ Exquisite music fills Cambridge's King's College Chapel in December, culminating in the Festival of Nine Lessons and Carols on Christmas Eve.

Cambridge & East Anglia Highlights

❶ **Cambridge** (p367) Punting past historic colleges then enjoying the heavenly evensong at King's College Chapel.

❷ **Lavenham** (p386) Soaking up the medieval architecture in this atmospheric market town.

❸ **Norwich** (p394) Marvelling at the exquisite rib vaulting in the city's fine cathedral.

❹ **Aldeburgh** (p392) Dining on sublime seafood and walking the prom in a laid-back resort.

❺ **Sandringham** (p403) Nosying around the drawing room of the Queen's country estate.

❻ **Norfolk Broads** (p401) Canoeing your way through unique tranquil waterways.

❼ **Imperial War Museum** (p378) Discovering the history of the British and American air forces.

❽ **Holkham Beach** (p402) Wandering barefoot along immense, pine-backed golden sands.

❾ **Audley End** (p383) Delighting in one of Britain's grandest stately homes.

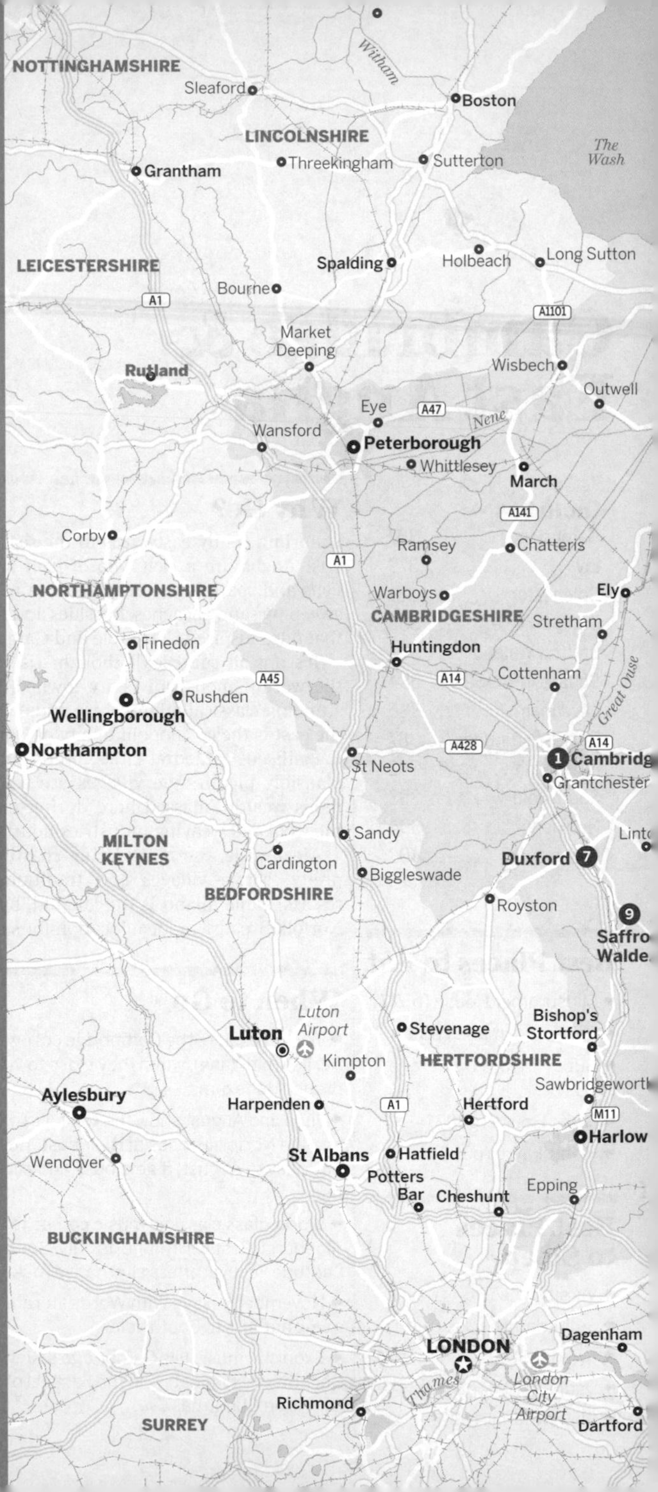

Titchwell Marsh RSPB Nature Reserve
Burnham Deepdale
Holkham
8
Wells-next-the-Sea
Cley-next-the-Sea
Sheringham
Cromer
20 km
10 miles
Hunstanton
Peddars Way and North Coast Path
Holkham Hall
Blakeney
Sustead
Mundesley
NORTH SEA
Little Walsingham
Baconsthorpe
A149
Sandringham
5
Houghton Hall
Fakenham
Blickling Hall
Weavers' Way
Palling
Castle Rising
Harpley
A1067
Aylsham
How Hill
Potter Heigham
King's Lynn
Peddars Way
NORFOLK
Wroxham
Winterton
Ranworth
6
Norfolk Broads
Dereham
Norwich
3
Acle
Great Yarmouth
A47
Swaffham
Norfolk Broads National Park
Stradsett
Wymondham
Swainsthorpe
Reedham
A1065
A134
A11
Loddon
Attleborough
Lowestoft
Mundford
Military Camp
Thetford Forest
Bungay
Kessingland
Thetford
Rushford
Diss
A143
Suffolk Coast National Nature Reserve
Southwold
A143
Dunwich
Ixworth
RSPB Minsmere
Bury St Edmunds
A1120
A14
Saxmundham
Newmarket
Thorpeness
Stowmarket
A14
SUFFOLK
A12
Aldeburgh
4
Suffolk Coast Path
A143
Butley
Lavenham
2
Woodbridge
Sutton Hoo
Orford
Ipswich
Long Melford
Kersey
Hadleigh
Alderton
Sudbury
Finchingfield
Dedham Vale
Felixstowe
Halstead
Wormingford
Harwich
Baintree
Colchester
Frinton-on-Sea
Walton-on-the-Naze
Blackwater
Layer de la Haye
Tiptree
Brightlingsea
Clacton-on-Sea
Witham
Mersea Island
A12
Chelmsford
ESSEX
NORTH SEA
Brentwood
Southend-on-Sea
Canvey Island
KENT
Leysdown-on-Sea
Rochester
Chatham
Margate

History

East Anglia was a major Saxon kingdom; the dazzling treasures unearthed in the ship burial at Sutton Hoo in Suffolk have revealed how complex a society it was.

The region's heyday came during the wool boom of the Middle Ages when Flemish weavers settled in the area; many of the grand local churches date from this time – Cambridge University was founded in this period, too.

By the 17th century, much of the region's marshland and bog had been drained and converted into arable land.

It was in East Anglia's emergent, Puritan bourgeoisie that the seeds of the English Civil War were sown. Oliver Cromwell, the uncrowned king of the parliamentarians, was a small-time merchant residing in Ely when he answered God's call to take up arms against what he saw as the fattened and corrupt monarchy of Charles I.

East Anglia's fortunes waned in the 18th century, when the Industrial Revolution flourished in northern England. During WWII the region became an ideal base for the Royal Air Force and the United States Air Force in the fight against Nazi Germany, thanks to its flat, open landscape and close proximity to mainland Europe.

Activities

East Anglia is an appealing destination for walkers, cyclists and kayakers. Here you can discover miles of coastline, take time touring vast expanses of level land and glide along snaking inland waterways.

The coast and Norfolk Broads are also beloved by sailors – those without their own craft can easily hire boats and arrange lessons. Alternatively putt-putt your way gently around the Broads in a motor boat or paddle a kayak or canoe along the slow-moving rivers. Then there are the wide and frequently empty beaches of the Norfolk coast, which make great spots for land yachting and kitesurfing.

Cycling

Famously one of England's flattest regions, East Anglia offers gorgeous cycling along the Suffolk and Norfolk coastlines and in the Fens. Meanwhile, the Tour de France snaked its way through East Anglia in 2014. Mountain bikers should head for Norfolk's **Thetford Forest** (www.forestry.gov.uk/thetfordforestpark), while much of the popular on- and off-road, 93-mile Peddars Way is also open to cyclists.

Walking

The **Peddars Way and Norfolk Coast Path** (www.nationaltrail.co.uk/peddarsway) is a seven-day, 93-mile national trail from Knettishall Heath, near Thetford, to Cromer. The first half takes in an ancient Roman road. The trail then meanders along the beaches, sea walls, salt marshes (great for birdwatching) and fishing villages of the coast.

Curving further south, the 50-mile **Suffolk Coast Path** links Felixstowe and Lowestoft, via Snape Maltings, Aldeburgh, Dunwich and Southwold.

Information

Visit East of England (www.visiteastofengland.com) has more info.

Getting There & Around

Public transport links between London, the Midlands and East Anglia are excellent. Services within the region are generally good; as ever there are fewer connections to smaller towns and villages.

BUS

- A host of smaller firms, plus two main companies, **First** (www.firstgroup.com) and **Stagecoach** (www.stagecoachbus.com), run the region's bus networks.
- **Traveline East Anglia** (www.travelineeastanglia.org.uk) has timetables.

TRAIN

- Regional rail provider **Abellio Greater Anglia** (www.abelliogreateranglia.co.uk) offers the Anglia Plus Pass (one/three days travel out of seven costs £18/36.)

CAMBRIDGESHIRE

Many visitors to Cambridgeshire never make it past the captivating university city of Cambridge, where august old buildings, student cyclists in academic gowns and glorious chapels await. But beyond this breathtaking seat of learning, the flat reclaimed Fens, lush farmland and myriad waterways make perfect walking and cycling territory, while the extraordinary cathedral at Ely and the rip-roaring Imperial War Museum at Duxford would be headline attractions anywhere else.

Getting Around

Public transport radiates from Cambridge, a mere hour's train ride from London King's Cross (£23, two to four per hour). This line continues north through Ely to King's Lynn in Norfolk. Branch lines run east to Norwich and into Suffolk.

Cambridge

POP 123,900

Abounding with exquisite architecture, exuding history and tradition and renowned for its quirky rituals, Cambridge is a university town extraordinaire. The tightly packed core of ancient colleges, the picturesque riverside 'Backs' (college gardens) and the leafy green meadows surrounding the city give it a more tranquil appeal than its historic rival Oxford.

Like 'the Other Place', as Oxford is known locally, the buildings here seem unchanged for centuries, and it's possible to wander the college buildings and experience them as countless prime ministers, poets, writers and scientists have done. Sheer academic achievement seems to permeate the very walls: cyclists loaded down with books negotiate cobbled passageways, students relax on manicured lawns and great minds debate life-changing research in historic pubs. First-time punters zigzag erratically across the river and those long past their student days wonder what it would have been like to study in such splendid surroundings.

History

Despite roots stretching back to the Iron Age, Cambridge was little more than a rural backwater until the 11th century, when an Augustinian order of monks set up shop here – the first of the religious institutions that eventually became the colleges. When the university town of Oxford exploded in a riot between town and gown in 1209, a group of scholars, fed up with the constant brawling between locals and students, upped and joined what was to become the University of Cambridge. Cambridge wasn't spared by the riots, and brawls between town and gown took place with disturbing regularity here as well.

The first Cambridge college, Peterhouse (never Peterhouse *College*), was founded in 1284, and in 1318 Pope John XXII's papal bull declared Cambridge to be an official university.

By the 14th century, royalty, nobility, churches, trade guilds and anyone rich enough could court prestige by founding their own colleges, though the system was shaken up during the Reformation with the dissolution of the monasteries. It was 500 years before female students were allowed into the hallowed grounds, though, and even then they were only allowed into the women-only colleges Girton and Newnham, founded in 1869 and 1871 respectively. By 1948, Cambridge minds had broadened sufficiently to allow women to actually graduate.

The honour roll of famous Cambridge students and affiliates reads like an international who's who of high achievers: 92 Nobel Prize winners (more than any other institution in the world), 13 British prime ministers, nine archbishops of Canterbury, an immense number of scientists, and a healthy host of poets and authors. This is the town where Newton refined his theory of gravity, Whipple invented the jet engine and Crick and Watson (relying heavily on the work of Rosalind Franklin, also a scientist at Cambridge) discovered DNA. William Wordsworth, Lord Byron, Vladimir Nabokov, Stephen Hawking and Stephen Fry all studied here too.

Today the university remains one of the best for research worldwide. Thanks to some of the earth-shaking discoveries made here, Cambridge is inextricably linked to the history of learning.

Sights

Cambridge University comprises 31 colleges, though not all are open to the public.

★**King's College Chapel** CHURCH

(☎01223-331212; www.kings.cam.ac.uk/chapel; King's Pde; adult/child £9/6; ⏲9.30am-3.15pm Mon-Sat & 1.15-2.30pm Sun term time, 9.30am-4.30pm daily, to 3.30pm Dec, Jan & university holidays) In a city crammed with showstopping buildings, this is the scene-stealer. Grandiose, 16th-century King's College Chapel is one of England's most extraordinary examples of Gothic architecture. Its inspirational, intricate 80m-long, fan-vaulted ceiling is the world's largest and soars upwards before exploding into a series of stone fireworks. This hugely atmospheric space is a fitting stage for the chapel's world-famous choir; hear it during the magnificent, free, **evensong** (term time only; 5.30pm Monday to Saturday, 10.30am and 3.30pm Sunday).

King's **steeples** have long been a magnet for student night climbers (p377) and today images of the chapel adorn thousands of postcards, tea towels and choral CDs. But it was begun in 1446 as an act of piety by Henry VI and was only finished by Henry VIII around 1516.

The lofty **stained-glass windows** that flank the chapel's sides ensure it's remarkably light. The glass is original, rare survivors of the excesses of the Civil War in this

Cambridge

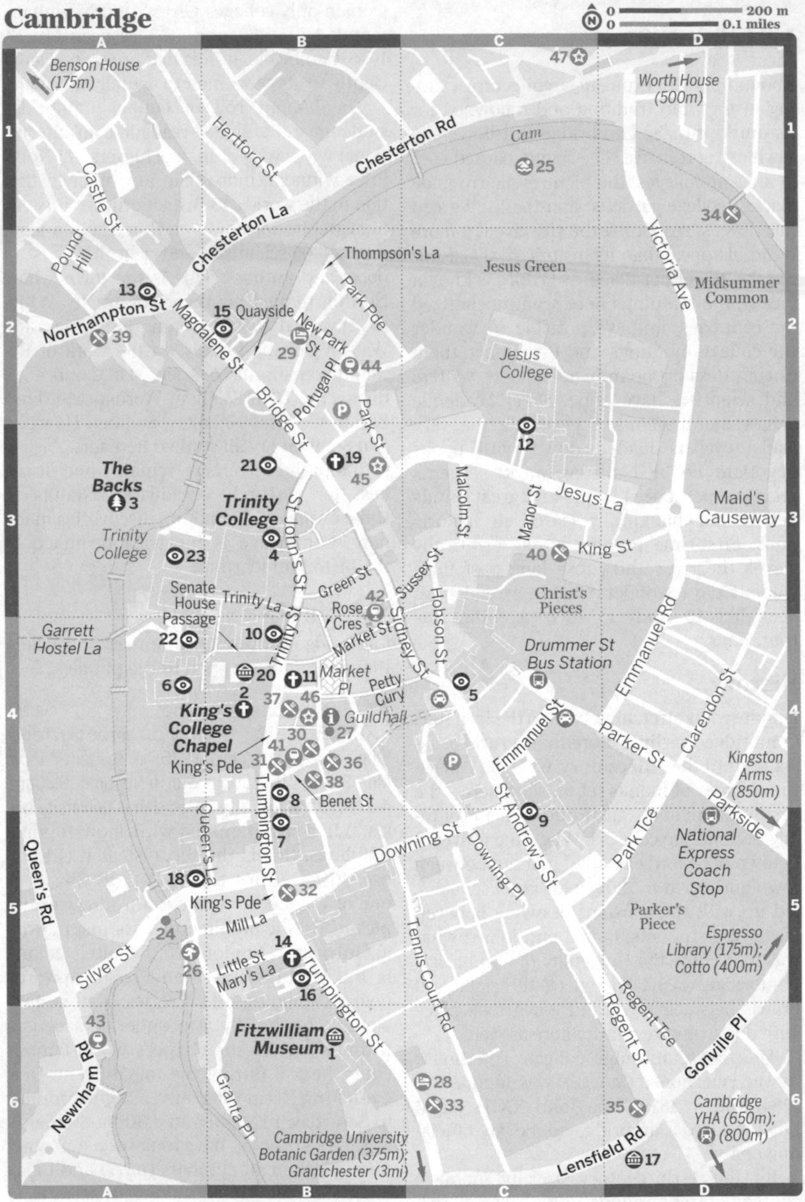

region. It's said that these windows were ordered to be spared by Cromwell himself, who knew of their beauty from his own studies in Cambridge.

The antechapel and the choir are divided by a superbly carved **wooden screen**, designed and executed by Peter Stockton for Henry VIII. The screen bears his master's initials entwined with those of Anne Boleyn. Look closely and you may find an angry human face (possibly Stockton's) amid the elaborate jungle of mythical beasts and

Cambridge

Top Sights
1 Fitzwilliam Museum ... B6
2 King's College Chapel ... B4
3 The Backs ... A3
4 Trinity College ... B3

Sights
5 Christ's College ... C4
6 Clare College ... A4
7 Corpus Christi College ... B5
8 Corpus Clock ... B4
9 Emmanuel College ... C5
10 Gonville & Caius College ... B4
11 Great St Mary's Church ... B4
12 Jesus College ... C3
13 Kettle's Yard ... A2
14 Little St Mary's Church ... B5
15 Magdalene College ... B2
Pepys Library ... (see 15)
16 Peterhouse ... B5
17 Polar Museum ... D6
18 Queens' College ... A5
19 Round Church ... B3
20 Senate House ... B4
21 St John's College ... B3
22 Trinity Hall College ... A4
23 Wren Library ... A3

Activities, Courses & Tours
24 Cambridge Chauffeur Punts ... A5
Granta Moorings ... (see 43)
25 Jesus Green Pool ... C1
26 Scudamore's Punting ... A5
27 Walking Tours ... B4

Sleeping
28 Hotel du Vin ... C6
29 Varsity ... B2

Eating
30 Aromi ... B4
31 Chop House ... B4
32 Fitzbillies ... B5
33 Hot Numbers ... C6
34 Midsummer House ... D1
35 Oak Bistro ... D6
36 Pint Shop ... B4
37 Rainbow ... B4
38 Smokeworks ... B4
39 St John's Chop House ... A2
40 Urban Shed ... C3

Drinking & Nightlife
41 Eagle ... B4
42 Fez ... B3
43 Granta ... A6
44 Maypole ... B2

Entertainment
45 ADC ... B3
46 Cambridge Arts Theatre ... B4
47 Portland Arms ... C1

symbolic flowers. Above is the magnificent bat-wing **organ**, originally constructed in 1686, though much altered since.

Beyond the thickly carved, dark-wood choir stalls, light suffuses the high **altar**, which is framed by Rubens' masterpiece *Adoration of the Magi* (1634) and the magnificent east window. To the left of the altar in the side chapels, an **exhibition** charts the construction stages and methods.

Note the chapel itself (but not the grounds) *is* open during the exam period (April to June).

Each Christmas Eve, King's College Chapel stages the **Festival of Nine Lessons & Carols**. It's broadcast globally by the BBC, and to around 300 American radio stations. You can also queue for a place – if you start early enough (often by around 9am), you could well get in.

Senate House HISTORIC BUILDING
(Senate House Passage) This beautiful classical structure (not open to the public), tucked in beside King's College, was designed in 1730 by James Gibbs. Graduations are held here in summer, when gowned and mortar-boarded students parade the streets. Look out for the degree class lists that are posted outside at the end of the academic year.

Great St Mary's Church CHURCH
(www.gsm.cam.ac.uk; Senate House Hill; 10am-4pm Mon-Sat, 1-4pm Sun) FREE The foundations of Cambridge's sublime university church date from 1010. It was burnt to the ground in the 1290s and rebuilt in 1351. The major expansion of 1478–1519 resulted in the late-Gothic Perpendicular style you see today. Striking features include the mid-Victorian stained-glass windows, seating galleries and two organs – unusual in a church. The **tower** (adult/child £3.90/2.50) was added in 1690; climb it for superb vistas of Cambridge's dreamy spires.

Gonville & Caius College COLLEGE
(www.cai.cam.ac.uk; Trinity St; 9am-2pm, closed late Apr–mid-Jun) FREE Known locally as Caius (pronounced 'keys'), Gonville and Caius boasts three fascinating **gates**: Virtue, Humility and Honour. They symbolise the progress of the good student, since the third

gate (the Porta Honoris, a fabulous domed and sundial-sided confection) leads to the Senate House (p369) and thus graduation. Former students include Francis Crick (of DNA-discoverers Crick and Watson) and Edward Wilson, of Scott's tragic Antarctic expedition. The megastar of astrophysics, Stephen Hawking, is currently a fellow here.

The college was actually founded twice, first by a priest called Gonville, in 1348, and then again in 1557 by Dr Caius (his given name was Keys – it was common for academics to use the Latin form of their names), a brilliant physician who supposedly spoiled his legacy by insisting in the statutes that the college admit no 'deaf, dumb, deformed, lame, chronic invalids, or Welshmen'.

Trinity Hall College COLLEGE

(01223-332500; www.trinhall.cam.ac.uk; Trinity Lane; admission by donation; 9.15am-noon & 2pm-dusk, closed early Apr-Jun) Wedged cosily among the great and famous colleges (but unconnected to better-known Trinity), diminutive Trinity Hall was founded in 1350 as a refuge for lawyers and clerics escaping the ravages of the Black Death. The college's **chapel** is one of the most beautiful in Cambridge; you can visit for evensong during some terms; check with the college for details.

Graduates include writer JB Priestley, astrophysicist Stephen Hawking and actor Rachel Weisz. The college's 16th-century **library** (not normally open to the public) has original Jacobean reading desks and books chained to shelves.

★Trinity College COLLEGE

(www.trin.cam.ac.uk; Trinity St; adult/child £3/1; 10am-4.30pm, closed early Apr–mid-Jun) The largest of Cambridge's colleges, Trinity offers an extraordinary Tudor gateway, an air of supreme elegance and a sweeping Great Court – the largest of its kind in the world. It also boasts the renowned and suitably musty **Wren Library** (www.trin.cam.ac.uk; noon-2pm Mon-Fri, plus 10.30am-12.30pm Sat term time only) FREE, containing 55,000 books dated before 1820 and more than 2500 manuscripts. Works include those by Shakespeare, St Jerome, Newton and Swift – and AA Milne's original *Winnie the Pooh;* both Milne and his son, Christopher Robin, were graduates.

As you enter Trinity through the part-gilded gate, have a look at the **statue** of the college's founder, Henry VIII, that adorns it. His left hand holds a golden orb, while his right grips not the original sceptre but a table leg, put there by student pranksters and never replaced. It's a wonderful introduction to one of Cambridge's most venerable colleges, and a reminder of who really rules the roost.

In the **Great Court** beyond, scholastic humour gives way to wonderment, thanks to its imposing architecture and sheer size. To the right of the entrance is a small tree, planted in the 1950s and reputed to be a descendant of the apple tree made famous by Trinity alumnus Sir Isaac Newton. Other alumni include Francis Bacon, Lord Byron, Tennyson, HRH Prince Charles (legend has it his bodyguard scored higher in exams than he did), at least nine prime ministers (British and international) and more than 30 Nobel Prize winners.

The college's vast **hall** has a dramatic hammer-beam roof and lantern; beyond lie the dignified cloisters of **Nevile's Court**. Henry VIII would have been proud to note, too, that his college would eventually come to throw the best party in town, the lavish May Ball (p375) in June, though you will need a fat purse, and a friend on the inside, to get an invitation.

St John's College COLLEGE

(www.joh.cam.ac.uk; St John's St; adult/child £8/5; 10am-5pm Mar-Oct, to 3.30pm Nov-Feb, closed mid-Jun) Alma mater of six prime ministers, three saints and Douglas Adams (author of *The Hitchhiker's Guide to the Galaxy*), St John's is superbly photogenic. It's also the second-biggest college after Trinity. Founded in 1511 by Henry VII's mother, Margaret Beaufort, it sprawls along both riverbanks, joined by the Bridge of Sighs, a masterpiece of stone tracery and focus for student pranks. Going into St John's or taking a punting tour are the only ways to get a clear view of the structure.

Over the bridge is the 19th-century **New Court**, an extravagant neo-Gothic creation, and out to the left are impressive views of the Backs (p371). Parts of the college are much older and the chapel, though smaller than King's, is one of Cambridge's hidden gems.

Round Church CHURCH

(www.christianheritage.org.uk; Bridge St; admission £2.50; 10am-5pm Mon-Fri, 1.30-5pm Sat, 1.30-4pm Sun) Cambridge's atmospheric Round Church is one of only four such structures in England. It was built by the mysterious Knights Templar in 1130 and shelters an unusual circular nave ringed by chunky Norman pillars – the carved stone faces that crown them bring the 12th century vividly to life.

Jesus College COLLEGE
(www.jesus.cam.ac.uk; Jesus Lane; ⏰9am-5pm, closed early Apr–mid-Jun) FREE This tranquil 15th-century college was once a nunnery of St Radegund before the Bishop of Ely, John Alcock, expelled the nuns for 'improvidence, extravagance and incontinence'. Highlights include a Norman arched **gallery**, a 13th-century **chancel** and art-nouveau features by Pugin, Ford Madox Brown, William Morris (ceilings) and Burne-Jones (stained glass). Illustrious alumni include Thomas Cranmer, burnt in Oxford for his faith during the Reformation, and long-running BBC and PBS radio journalist and presenter Alistair Cooke.

Magdalene College COLLEGE
(www.magd.cam.ac.uk; Magdalene St; ⏰8am-6pm, closed early Apr–mid-Jun) FREE Riverside Magdalene often catches people out – the college name is properly pronounced 'Maud-lyn'. This former Benedictine hostel's greatest asset is the **Pepys Library** (www.magd.cam.ac.uk; Magdalene St; ⏰2-4pm Mon-Fri year-round, 11.30am-12.30pm & 1.30-2.30pm Sat May-Aug, 2-4pm Mon-Sat Oct-Apr, closed Sep) FREE housing 3000 books bequeathed by the mid-17th-century diarist to his old college. This idiosyncratic collection of beautifully bound tomes is ordered by height. Treasures include vivid medieval manuscripts and the *Anthony Roll*, a 1540s depiction of the Royal Navy's ships. Magdalene was the last college to let women study there; when they were finally admitted in 1988, some male students wore black armbands and flew the college flag at half mast.

Kettle's Yard HOUSE
(www.kettlesyard.co.uk; Castle St) FREE Closed at time of writing but due to reopen in late 2017, Kettle's Yard offers a very personal glimpse into the incredible home of HS 'Jim' Ede, a former curator at the Tate Gallery in London. In his deceptively roomy cottage, all the furniture, ceramics and art – such as the collection of 20th-century works by Miró, Henry Moore and others – is arranged just so, allowing you a real sense of the man's intriguing personality.

★The Backs PARK
Behind the Cambridge colleges' grandiose facades and stately courts, a series of gardens and parks line up beside the river. Collectively known as the Backs, the tranquil green spaces and shimmering waters offer unparalleled views of the colleges and are often the most enduring image of Cambridge for visitors. The picture-postcard snapshots of student life and graceful bridges can be seen from the riverside pathways and pedestrian bridges – or the comfort of a chauffeur-driven punt.

For the best views of the fanciful **Bridge of Sighs** head into St John's College (p370). Built in 1831, it's best observed from the stylish bridge designed by Wren just to the south, also on St John's grounds. The oldest river crossing is at **Clare College** (www.clare.cam.ac.uk; Trinity Lane; £3.50; ⏰dawn-dusk, closed early Apr–mid-Jun), built in 1639 and ornamented with decorative balls. Its architect was paid a grand total of 15p for his design and, feeling aggrieved at such a measly fee, it's said he cut a chunk out of one of the balls adorning the balustrade so the bridge would never be complete.

Most curious of all is the flimsy-looking wooden construction (visible from Silver St) which joins the two halves of Queens' College. Known as the **Mathematical Bridge**, it was first built in 1749. Despite what unscrupulous guides may tell you, it wasn't the handiwork of Sir Isaac Newton (he died in 1727), originally built without nails, or taken apart by academics who then couldn't figure how to put it back together.

Queens' College COLLEGE
(www.queens.cam.ac.uk; Queen's Lane; £3; ⏰10am-4pm, closed early Apr–mid-Jun) Gorgeous 15th-century Queens' College sits elegantly astride the river, connected by the unscientific-looking Mathematical Bridge. Highlights include: two enchanting medieval courtyards, **Old Court** and **Cloister Court**; the beautiful half-timbered **President's Lodge**; and the tower in which Dutch scholar and reformer Desiderius Erasmus lodged from 1510 to 1514.

Corpus Christi College COLLEGE
(www.corpus.cam.ac.uk; King's Pde; £2.50; ⏰10.30am-4.30pm mid-Jun–Sep, 2-4pm Oct–early Apr) Corpus Christi was founded in 1352, a heritage reflected in its exquisite buildings and a monastic atmosphere that radiates from the medieval **Old Court**. Look out for the fascinating sundial and plaque to playwright and past student Christopher Marlowe (1564–93), who penned *Doctor Faustus* and *Tamburlaine*. New Court (a mere 200 years old) leads to the **Parker Library**, which holds the world's finest collection of Anglo-Saxon manuscripts (open Monday and Thursday afternoons to tourist office–run tours).

VISITING THE COLLEGES

Colleges close to visitors over the two-week Christmas break, and while students are preparing for and sitting exams – between early April and mid-June. Be aware, too, that opening hours can vary from day to day, so if you have your heart set on visiting a particular college, contact it in advance to avoid disappointment.

Corpus Clock LANDMARK

(Benet St) Made from 24-carat gold, the Corpus Clock displays the time through a series of concentric LED lights. A hideous-looking insect 'time-eater' crawls across the top. The clock is only accurate once every five minutes. At other times it slows or stops and then speeds up, which, according to its creator, JC Taylor, reflects life's irregularity.

Christ's College COLLEGE

(www.christs.cam.ac.uk; St Andrew's St; 9am-4pm, closed early May–mid-Jun) FREE Christ's College is a venerable institution at more than 500 years old. It's gleaming **Great Gate** is emblazoned with heraldic carvings of Tudor roses, a portcullis and spotted Beaufort yale (antelope-like creatures). Its founder, Lady Margaret Beaufort, hovers above like a guiding spirit. A stout oak door leads into **First Court**, one of Cambridge's more picturesque front courts and the only circular one. Hunt out the **gardens** dedicated to alumnus Charles Darwin; they feature species brought back from his famous Galapagos voyage.

Emmanuel College COLLEGE

(www.emma.cam.ac.uk; St Andrew's St; 9am-6pm, closed early Apr–mid-Jun) FREE The 16th-century Emmanuel College ('Emma' to students) is famous for its exquisite **chapel** designed by Sir Christopher Wren. Seek out the plaque commemorating John Harvard (who graduated with a BA in 1632), a scholar here who later settled in New England and left his money to a certain Cambridge College in Massachusetts – now Harvard University.

Little St Mary's Church CHURCH

(www.lsm.org.uk; Trumpington St; 9am-6pm) FREE The church's unwieldy original name was St Peter's-without-Trumpington-Gate, which gave St Peter's College itself its name. Inside is a memorial to student Godfrey Washington, great-uncle of George. His family coat of arms was the stars and stripes, the inspiration for the US flag. Henry Cavendish, the first person to measure the density of water, also studied here. He also calculated the planet's weight: about 6 billion trillion metric tons, by the way.

Peterhouse COLLEGE

(www.pet.cam.ac.uk; Trumpington St; 9am-5pm, closed early Apr–mid-Jun) FREE The oldest and smallest college, charming Peterhouse was founded in 1284. Much of the college was rebuilt or added to over the years, including the exceptional little **chapel** built in 1632, but the beautifully restored **main hall** is bona-fide 13th century.

★Fitzwilliam Museum MUSEUM

(www.fitzmuseum.cam.ac.uk; Trumpington St; donation requested; 10am-5pm Tue-Sat, noon-5pm Sun) FREE Fondly dubbed 'the Fitz' by locals, this colossal neoclassical pile was one of the first public art museums in Britain, built to house the fabulous treasures that the seventh Viscount Fitzwilliam bequeathed to his old university. Expect Roman and Egyptian grave goods, artworks by many of the great masters and some quirkier collections: banknotes, literary autographs, watches and armour.

The building's unabashedly over-the-top appearance sets out to mirror its contents; this ostentatious jumble of styles mixes mosaic with marble, and Greek with Egyptian. The **lower galleries** are filled with priceless treasures spanning the ancient world; look out for a Roman funerary couch, an inscribed copper votive plaque from Yemen (c AD 100–200), a figurine of Egyptian cat goddess Bastet, splendid Egyptian sarcophagi and mummified animals, plus dazzling illuminated manuscripts. The **upper galleries** showcase works by Leonardo da Vinci, Titian, Rubens, the impressionists, Gainsborough and Constable, right through to Rembrandt and Picasso; standout works include the tender *Pietà* by Giovanni del Ponte and Salvator Rosa's dark and intensely personal *L'Umana Fragilita*.

The Fitz has a tragic footnote: although begun by George Basevi in 1837, he didn't live to see its completion. While working on Ely Cathedral he stepped back to admire his handiwork, slipped and fell to his death.

One-hour guided tours (£6) of the museum are held at 2.30pm Saturday.

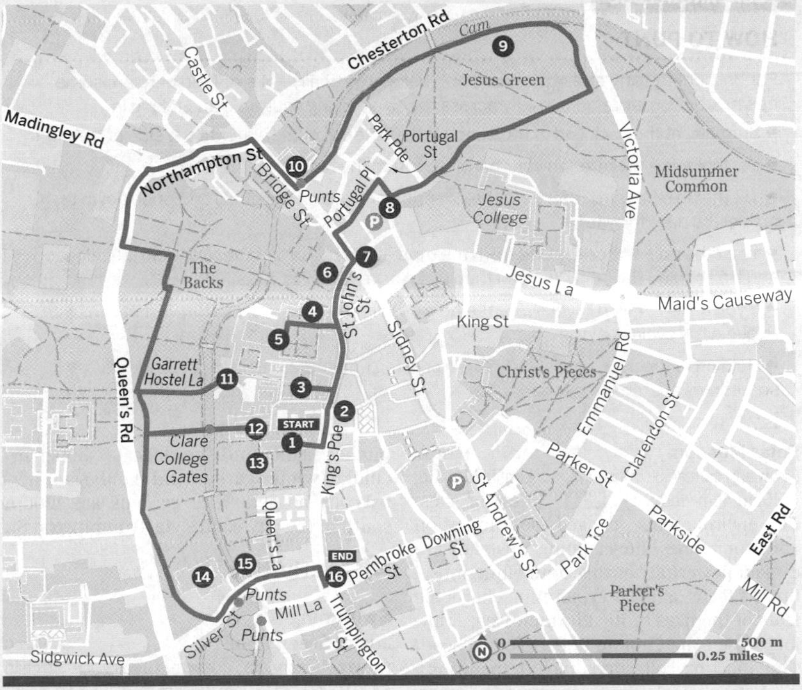

City Walk
The Colleges and the Backs

START KING'S COLLEGE CHAPEL
END FITZBILLIES
LENGTH 3 MILES; FOUR HOURS

From divine 1 **King's** (p367), stroll north, diverting into 2 **Great St Mary's** (p369) and climbing the tower for fine Cambridge views. Next, dodge the cyclists and touting tour guides before ducking into atmospheric 3 **Gonville & Caius** (p369) to marvel at its ornate gates. 4 **Trinity's** (p370) elaborate entranceway towers up on the left; head through it into the college's Great Court; marvel at the architecture, then make for the absorbing 5 **Wren Library** (p370), with its extraordinary historic books. Next, pause to admire the gorgeous 6 **St John's** (p370) before dropping into the captivating, 12th-century 7 **Round Church** (p370). Cut right between the sweet terraces of narrow Portugal Pl – at the end, the 8 **Maypole** (p378) pub is a friendly place to eat or drink.

Next head diagonally across Jesus Green, to consider a dip in the bijou open-air 9 **pool** (p374). Then stroll southwest beside the river, passing locks and houseboats. Cross at the bridge beside 10 **Magdalene College** (p371), where the unique Pepys Library is well worth a detour.

Northampton St reminds you the 21st century does exist, then it's on to the path through the Backs, where the stately sweep of St John's College shelters amid the trees, Trinity sits next door. Next play zigzag with college paths and the river: nip up 11 **Garret Hostel Lane** for a closer view of punts, bridges and college facades. Then it's back to the path, before another detour left leads to the gates of 12 **Clare College** (p371), where the Fellow's Garden is a real must-see.

Back on the Backs, next comes the impressive west end of King's; the Palladian 13 **Fellows' Building** is just to the right. After curving beside 14 **Queens'** (p371), cut left. On Silver St's bridge spy the chunky 15 **Mathematical Bridge** (p371) on the left, and the fleets of punts on the right. Time to rest. Where better than 16 **Fitzbillies** (p376) for a Chelsea bun and a steaming cup of tea.

LOCAL KNOWLEDGE

HOW TO PUNT

Punting looks pretty straightforward but, believe us, really – it's not. So here are some tips to stop you zigzagging wildly across the river, losing your pole and falling in.

➡ Standing at the back end of the punt, lift the pole out of the water at the side of the punt.

➡ Let the pole slide through your hands to touch the bottom of the river.

➡ Tilt the pole forward (that is, in the direction of travel of the punt) and push down to propel the punt forward.

➡ Twist the pole to free the end from the mud at the bottom of the river, and let it float up and trail behind the punt. You can then use it as a rudder to steer.

➡ If you haven't fallen in yet, raise the pole out of the water and into the vertical position to begin the cycle again.

➡ Hold on to the pole, particularly when passing under Clare Bridge, as students sometimes snatch them for a giggle.

Polar Museum MUSEUM

(www.spri.cam.ac.uk/museum; Lensfield Rd; ⏲10am-4pm Tue-Sat) FREE Tales of hostile environments, dogged determination and, sometimes, life-claiming mistakes are evoked powerfully at this compelling museum. Its focus on polar exploration charts the feats of the likes of Roald Amundsen, Fridtjof Nansen and Captain Robert Falcon Scott. The affecting collections include paintings, photographs, clothing, equipment, maps, journals and last messages left for loved ones by Scott's polar crew.

Other exhibits include models of ships that ventured into sub-zero Arctic and Antarctic waters, innovative equipment such as the 'Nansen cooker' and interactive displays on ice and climate change. The section devoted to the people of the Arctic includes Inuit carvings and scrimshaw (etched bones), a Sami knife with a carved reindeer-horn sheath, a walrus tusk with walrus hunt scenes etched on it, and particularly fine examples of *tupilak* (carved caribou-horn figures with ancestor souls captured inside) from Greenland. The museum is run by the Scott Polar Institute, founded with part of the relief fund set up in the wake of the explorer's ill-fated South Pole expedition – these days it takes a lead role in climate-change research.

Cambridge University Botanic Garden GARDENS

(www.botanic.cam.ac.uk; 1 Brookside; adult/child £5/free; ⏲10am-6pm Apr-Sep, to 5pm Feb, Mar & Oct, to 4pm Nov-Jan) Founded by Charles Darwin's mentor, Professor John Henslow, the beautiful Botanic Garden is home to 8000 plant species, a wonderful arboretum, glasshouses (containing both fierce carnivorous pitcher plants and the delicate slipper orchid), a winter garden and flamboyant herbaceous borders. The gardens are 1200m south of the city centre via Trumpington St.

Activities

Swimming

Jesus Green Pool SWIMMING

(www.better.org.uk; Jesus Green; adult/child £4.50/2.40; ⏲7.30am-7.30pm Mon, Tue & Fri, noon-7.30pm Wed, Thu, Sat & Sun May-Sep) A slender, 100-yard, 1920s open-air swim spot; popular with poolside sunbathers too.

Punting

Gliding a self-propelled punt along the Backs is a blissful experience – once you've got the hang of it. It can also be a manic challenge to begin. If you wimp out, you can always opt for a relaxing chauffeured punt. Punt hire costs around £20 to £28 per hour; 45-minute chauffeured trips of the Backs cost about £15 to £19 per person. One-way trips to Grantchester (1½ hours) start at around £18 per person.

Scudamore's Punting BOATING

(☎01223-359750; www.scudamores.com; Granta Place; chauffeured punt per 45min per person £16-19, 6-person self-punt per hr £22-28; ⏲9am-dusk) Hires punts, rowing boats, kayaks and canoes. Offers up to £5 discount if you book online.

Cambridge Chauffeur Punts BOATING

(www.punting-in-cambridge.co.uk; Silver St Bridge) Runs regular chauffeured punting tours (per hour adult/child £16/7) and also self-hire (six-person punt per hour £22).

Granta Moorings BOATING
(www.puntingincambridge.com; Newnham Rd; chauffeured punt per 50min per person £15, 6-person self-punt per hr £24; ⏲9.30am-dusk Mar-Oct) Handily sited punt-rental company if you're heading towards Grantchester. Runs reduced services in winter.

Tours

★Walking Tours WALKING
(☎01223-791501; www.visitcambridge.org; Peas Hill) The tourist office runs **guided two-hour tours** (adult/child £19/9) taking in two of the most memorable colleges; they might include King's College Chapel, Queens', Pembroke or St John's. The price includes admission to the colleges. Tours leave from the tourist office. They're popular: book.

Year-round, tours run at 11am and 1pm Monday to Friday, at 11am, noon, 1pm and 2pm Saturday, and at 1pm Sunday. In July and August, there are extra daily tours at noon and 2pm.

Colourful, one-hour **Ghost Tours** (adult/child £7/5) take place on Friday and Saturday; start times vary from 6pm to 8pm. The Ghost Tours leave from the Guildhall.

Festivals & Events

Cambridge has a jam-packed cultural schedule. For one-off events, check out the notices tied to railings all over the city centre, especially around St Mary's Church.

Bumps SPORTS
(www.cucbc.org/bumps; ⏲Feb & Jun) Traditional rowing races along the Cam (or the Granta, as the Cambridge stretch is called), in which college boat clubs compete to 'bump' the crew in front.

Beer Festival BEER
(www.cambridgebeerfestival.com; ⏲May) Hugely popular five-day beer and cider extravaganza on Jesus Green, featuring brews from all over the country as well as a great range of British cheeses.

May Balls CULTURAL
(⏲early Jun) The biggest student events of the year, the name of these formal balls don't match the month they're held in (June) because college authorities decided that May's traditional booze-fuelled revelry – just before the exams – wasn't such a great idea. Now they take place after the exams, but in a typically Cambridge quirk, they keep their old name.

Folk Festival MUSIC
(www.cambridgefolkfestival.co.uk; ⏲late Jul–early Aug) Acclaimed four-day music fest in Cherry Hinton Hall, 4 miles southeast of the city centre. It's hosted the likes of Van Morrison, Ladysmith Black Mambazo, Christy Moore, Imelda May, Paul Simon and KT Tunstall.

Cambridge Shakespeare Festival THEATRE
(www.cambridgeshakespeare.com; ⏲Jul & Aug) The bard's best-loved works performed in outdoor settings.

Sleeping

Cambridge YHA HOSTEL £
(☎0845-371 9728; www.yha.org.uk; 97 Tenison Rd; dm £18-26, d £39-59; @📶) Smart, friendly, recently renovated, deservedly popular hostel with compact dorms and good facilities. Handily, it's near the railway station.

University Rooms Cambridge B&B ££
(www.universityrooms.com/en/city/cambridge/home; s/d from £46/80) For an authentic taste of university life, check into a student room in one of a range of colleges. Accommodation varies from functional singles (with shared bathroom) overlooking college courts to more modern, en-suite rooms in nearby annexes. Breakfast is often in hall (the students' dining room). Rooms are largely available during university holidays (June to August, Christmas, and March to April).

Worth House B&B ££
(☎01223-316074; www.worth-house.co.uk; 152 Chesterton Rd; s £75-85, d £95-145; P📶) The welcome is wonderfully warm, the great-value rooms utterly delightful. Soft grey and cream meets candy-stripe reds, fancy bathrooms boast claw-foot baths and tea trays are full of treats. There's also a three-person, self-catering apartment (per week £550) two doors down.

Benson House B&B ££
(☎01223-311594; www.bensonhouse.co.uk; 24 Huntingdon Rd; s £75-115, d £110-115; P📶) Lots of little things lift Benson a cut above – sleep among feather pillows and Egyptian cotton linen, sip tea from Royal Doulton bone china, then tuck into award-winning breakfasts featuring kippers, croissants and fresh fruit.

Tudor Cottage B&B ££
(☎01223-565212; www.tudorcottageguesthouse.co.uk; 292 Histon Rd; s/d £50/80; P📶) Sweet features help make this neat-as-a-pin guesthouse feel like a home from home, from

bedrooms boasting gleaming bathrooms to the ranks of speciality teas, cereals, cakes and muffins at the breakfast table. It's just under 2 miles north of the city centre; bus 8 stops just outside.

Rosa's B&B ££
(01223-512596; www.rosasbedandbreakfast.co.uk; 53 Roseford Rd; s £55-70;) One for solo travellers: a friendly, family-run B&B where the two bright, snug, singles have accents of chocolate-brown and lime. It's 2 miles north of the city centre; there's free on-road parking outside and bus 8 runs nearby.

★Varsity BOUTIQUE HOTEL £££
(01223-306030; www.thevarsityhotel.co.uk; Thompson's Lane; d £190-350;) In the 44 individually styled rooms of riverside Varsity, wondrous furnishings and witty features (Union Jack footstools, mock-flock wallpaper) sit beside floor-to-ceiling glass windows, espresso machines and smartphone docks. The views out over the colleges from the roof terrace are, frankly, gorgeous.

★Hotel du Vin BOUTIQUE HOTEL £££
(01223-928991; www.hotelduvin.com; 15 Trumpington St; d £159-259, ste £250-425;) One of the country's swishest, coolest chains delivers again here. Achingly beautiful rooms sport roll-top baths, monsoon showers and custom-made beds, the cosy cellar bar is vaulted, the bistro (two/three courses £17/20) is chic, and the luxuriously appointed suites (expect rotating TVs, mini-cinemas and surround sound) are simply divine.

Felix BOUTIQUE HOTEL £££
(01223-277977; www.hotelfelix.co.uk; Whitehouse Lane, Huntingdon Rd; s £205, d £220-285, ste £325-345;) It's the bold modern art and imaginative design (fuchsia-pink chairs amid stately polished wood) that nudge Felix into the boutique sleep spots. That and the silk curtains, luxurious linens and stone-and-slate bathrooms. Felix is 1.5 miles northwest of the city. The Penthouse suite, up in the eaves, is an utterly romantic retreat.

Eating

★Urban Shed SANDWICHES £
(www.theurbanshed.com; 62 King St; sandwiches from £4.25; 8.30am-5pm Mon-Thu, 8.30am-4.30pm Fri, 9am-6pm Sat, 10am-4pm Sun) Somewhere between a retro goods shop and a sandwich bar, unorthodox Urban Shed has a personal service ethos so strong that regular customers have a locker for their own mug. Decor teams old aeroplane seats with cable-drum tables, their own-blend coffee is mellow and the sandwiches range is superb.

Hot Numbers CAFE £
(www.hotnumberscoffee.co.uk; 4 Trumpington St; snacks from £5; 7am-7pm Mon-Fri, 8am-6pm Sat & Sun;) Hipster hang-out with maple-smoked bacon for breakfast, single-origin bean coffee, craft beers, cool tunes and a laid-back vibe.

Espresso Library CAFE £
(www.espressolibrary.co.uk; 210 East Rd; mains £5-9; 7am-7pm Mon & Tue, to 9pm Wed & Thu, to 11pm Fri & Sat, 9am-6pm Sun;) A chilled soundtrack and a customer laptop on almost every table signal that this industrial-chic cafe is a student favourite. That'll be partly down to the wholesome food – think frittata with sweet potatoes and spinach, or juicy portobello mushrooms in brioche buns – and partly down to some cracking coffee.

Aromi ITALIAN £
(www.aromi.co.uk; 1 Benet St; mains £4.50; 9am-7pm Sun-Thu, to 8pm Fri & Sat;) Sometimes you should yield to temptation. So be drawn in by a window full of stunning Sicilian pizza and feast on light, crisp bases piled high with fresh spinach and Parma ham. Then succumb to the indecently thick hot chocolate; may as well make it a large.

Aromi also has another cafe a few doors down on Peas Hill.

Fitzbillies CAFE £
(www.fitzbillies.com; 52 Trumpington St; mains £6-12; 8am-6pm Mon-Fri, 9am-7pm Sat, 10am-6pm Sun) Cambridge's oldest bakery has a soft, doughy place in the hearts of generations of students, thanks to its ultrasticky Chelsea buns and other sweet treats. Pick up a bagful to take away or munch in comfort in the quaint cafe.

Rainbow VEGETARIAN £
(www.rainbowcafe.co.uk; 9a King's Pde; mains £7-11; 10am-10pm Tue-Sat, to 3pm Sun;) Quite a treat for non-meat-eaters: a cheery basement bistro, tucked away at the end of an alley off King's Parade. In this warren of cosy rooms, rickety tables set the scene for an eclectic range of veg that's been transformed into a variety of bakes, roasts, pastas and pies.

There are also tasty gluten-free options.

Pint Shop MODERN BRITISH ££
(01223-352293; www.pintshop.co.uk; 10 Peas Hill; mains £12-21; noon-10pm) Popular Pint

LOCAL KNOWLEDGE

PRANKSTERS, NIGHT CLIMBERS & CUBES

In a city with so much concentrated mental prowess, it is perhaps inevitable that the student community would excel at all kinds of mischief. The most impressive prank ever to take place in Cambridge – lifting an Austin Seven van on to the roof of the landmark Senate House (p369) in 1958 – involved a great deal of planning from four mechanical sciences students and spawned a number of copycat pranks, including suspending another Austin Seven from the ornate Bridge of Sighs (p370).

King's College has long been a target of night climbers – students who get their thrills by scaling the lofty heights of out-of-bounds buildings at night. The sport is taken very seriously – to the point where a Trinity College student, Geoffrey Winthrop Young, wrote the *Roof Climber's Guide to Trinity* in 1900. If you're in Cambridge after a particularly spectacular climber excursion, you may find some out-of-place objects atop the pinnacles of King's College Chapel (p367) – anything from a traffic cone to a Santa hat.

Finally, there's the Cubes (Cambridge University Breaking and Entering Society): its objective is to access places members shouldn't be and leave distinctive calling cards – the most famous being the wooden mallard in the rafters of Trinity's Great Hall.

Shop's vision is to embrace eating and drinking equally. So it's created both a busy bar specialising in craft beer (10 on keg and six on draft) and a stylish dining room serving classy versions of traditional grub (dry aged steaks, gin-cured sea trout, charcoal-grilled plaice). All in all, hard to resist.

Smokeworks BARBECUE ££
(www.smokeworks.co.uk; 2 Free School Lane; mains £9-17; 11.45am-10.30pm Mon-Thu, to 11pm Fri & Sat, to 9.30pm Sun;) This dark, industrial-themed dining spot draws discerning carnivores and local hipsters with its melt-in-your-mouth ribs, wings and wonderfully smoky pulled pork. The service is friendly and prompt and their salted caramel milkshakes come in a glass the size of your head.

Kingston Arms PUB FOOD ££
(www.kingston-arms.co.uk; 33 Kingston St; mains £5-16; noon-2pm & 6-10pm Mon-Fri, noon-10pm Sat & Sun;) Great gastropub grub – from roasts to homemade risotto and recession-busting mains (held at £5) – keeps stomachs satisfied at the award-winning Kingston. More than 10 real ales, stacked board games and a students-meet-locals clientele deliver a contemporary Cambridge vibe.

It's 1 mile southeast of the centre.

Chop House BRITISH ££
(www.cambscuisine.com/cambridge-chop-house; 1 King's Pde; mains £15-22; noon-10.30pm Mon-Sat, to 9.30pm Sun) The window seats here deliver some of the best views in town – on to King's College's hallowed walls. The food is pure English establishment too: hearty steaks and chops and chips, plus a scattering of fish dishes and suet puddings. It's also open from 10am to noon for coffee and cakes.

Sister restaurant **St John's Chop House** (www.cambscuisine.com/st-johns-chop-house; 21 Northampton St; mains £11-27; noon-3pm & 6-10.30pm Mon-Fri, noon-11pm Sat, noon-9.30pm Sun) sits near the rear entrance to St John's College.

Oak Bistro BISTRO ££
(01223-323361; www.theoakbistro.co.uk; 6 Lensfield Rd; mains £14-24, set lunch 2/3 courses £14/17; noon-2.30pm & 6-9.30pm Mon-Sat) Truffle oil, salsa verde and rosemary jus are the kind of flavour intensifiers you'll find at this friendly but classy neighbourhood eatery where locally sourced duck, lamb and beef come cooked just so. The set lunch remains a bargain.

★**Midsummer House** MODERN BRITISH £££
(01223-369299; www.midsummerhouse.co.uk; Midsummer Common; 5/8 courses £48/105; noon-1.30pm Wed-Sat, 7-9.30pm Tue-Sat;) At the region's top table, chef Daniel Clifford's double-Michelin-starred creations are distinguished by depth of flavour and immense technical skill. Sample transformations of coal-baked celeriac, Cornish crab, and roast pigeon with wild garlic before a pear, blueberry and white chocolate delight.

Wine flights start at £45. Unusually, there are vegetarian versions of both the set menus.

Cotto INTERNATIONAL £££
(01223-302010; www.cottocambridge.co.uk; 183 East Rd; 3 courses £65-70; 6.30-9pm Wed-Sat;) An irresistible blend of

WORTH A TRIP

IMPERIAL WAR MUSEUM

At Europe's biggest aviation museum, **Imperial War Museum** (www.iwm.org.uk; Duxford; adult/child £16.35/8.15; ⏲10am-6pm Easter-Oct, to 4pm Nov-Easter; P 🚸), some 200 lovingly preserved vintage aircraft are housed in several enormous hangars. The vast airfield showcases everything from dive bombers to biplanes, Spitfire and Concorde. The awe-inspiring **American Air Museum** hangar pays homage to US WWII servicemen, hosting the largest collection of American civil and military aircraft outside the USA.

Duxford is 9 miles south of Cambridge at Junction 10 of the M11. Buses only run to the museum on Sunday (bus 132; £3.90, 50 minutes).

artistry and precision ensure chef Hans Schweitzer's creations look gorgeous and taste fabulous. Delights might include seafood velouté or the signature dish Cotto venison Wellington, followed perhaps by 'Hans-made chocolates' or coconut brûlée.

🍷 Drinking & Nightlife

★Eagle PUB
(www.eagle-cambridge.co.uk; Benet St; ⏲8am-11pm Mon-Sat, to 10.30pm Sun) Cambridge's most famous pub has loosened the tongues and pickled the grey cells of many an illustrious academic; among them Nobel Prize–winning scientists Crick and Watson, who discussed their research into DNA here (note the blue plaque by the door). Fifteenth-century, wood-panelled and rambling, its cosy rooms include one with WWII airmen's signatures on the ceiling. The food, served all day, is good too.

Fez CLUB
(www.cambridgefez.com; 15 Market Passage; ⏲10.30pm-3am Tue-Sat) Hip hop, dancehall, R&B, techno, funk, indie, house and garage; top-name DJs and club nights – you'll find it all at Cambridge's most popular club, the Moroccan-themed Fez.

Maypole PUB
(www.maypolefreehouse.co.uk; 20a Portugal Pl; ⏲11.30am-midnight Sun-Thu, to 1am Fri & Sat) A dozen pumps dispensing real ale, a roomy beer garden and a friendly, unreconstructed vibe make this red-brick pub popular with the locals. That and hearty, homemade Italian food and festivals championing regional and microbrewery beers.

Granta PUB
(www.granta-cambridge.co.uk; 14 Newnham Rd; ⏲11am-11pm) If the exterior of this picturesque waterside pub, overhanging a pretty mill pond, looks strangely familiar, it could be because it is the darling of many a TV director. No wonder: with its snug deck, riverside terrace and punts moored up alongside, it's a highly atmospheric spot to sup and watch the world drift by.

☆ Entertainment

ADC THEATRE
(☎01223-300085; www.adctheatre.com; Park St) This famous student-run theatre is home to the university's Footlights comedy troupe whose past members include Emma Thompson, Hugh Laurie and Stephen Fry.

Cambridge Arts Theatre THEATRE
(☎01223-503333; www.cambridgeartstheatre.com; 6 St Edward's Passage) Cambridge's biggest bona-fide theatre puts on everything from highbrow drama and dance, to panto and shows fresh from London's West End.

Junction PERFORMING ARTS
(☎01223-511511; www.junction.co.uk; Clifton Way) Theatre, dance, comedy, live bands and club nights at a contemporary performance venue near the railway station. It's 1.5 miles southeast of the city centre, down Regent St (later Hills Rd).

Portland Arms LIVE MUSIC
(www.theportlandarms.co.uk; 129 Chesterton Rd; ⏲noon-11.30pm Mon-Thu, to 12.30am Fri & Sat, to 11pm Sun) A popular student haunt, the 200-capacity Portland is the best spot in town to catch a gig and see the pick of up-and-coming bands. It has a wood-panelled saloon bar, a spacious terrace and monthly comedy nights too.

ℹ Information

Addenbrooke's (www.cuh.org.uk; Hills Rd; ⏲24hr emergency room) Four miles southeast of the centre.

Cantab Millenium Services (☎01223-322306; 95 Mill Rd; per hour £1.50; ⏲9.30am-6.30pm) Internet cafe.

Tourist Office (☎01223-791500; www.visitcambridge.org; Peas Hill; ⏰10am-5pm Mon-Sat, 11am-3pm Sun Apr-Oct, 10am-5pm Mon-Sat Nov-Mar)

Getting There & Away

BUS

Buses run by **National Express** (☎0871 781 8181; www.nationalexpress.com; Parkside) leave from Parkside. Direct services include the following:

Gatwick £37, 3¾ hours, nine daily
Heathrow £25, 2¾ hours, hourly
London Victoria £5, 2½ hours, two-hourly
Oxford £12, 3½ hours, every 30 minutes
Stansted £10, 45 minutes, two-hourly

CAR

Cambridge's centre is largely pedestrianised. The city's multistorey car parks charge between £3 and £4.60 for two hours.

Five free Park & Ride car parks (parking per day £1) circle the city on the major routes, with buses (return tickets £2.70) shuttling into the city centre every 10 to 15 minutes between around 7am and 8pm Monday to Saturday, 9am to 5.45pm Sunday.

TRAIN

The train station is 1.5 miles southeast of the centre. Direct services:

Birmingham New Street £55, three hours, hourly
Bury St Edmunds £10, 40 minutes, hourly
Ely £5,15 minutes, three per hour
King's Lynn £10, 50 minutes, hourly
London King's Cross £23, one hour, two to four per hour
Stansted Airport £10, 35 minutes, hourly

Getting Around

BICYCLE

Cambridge is incredibly bike-friendly, with two wheels providing an ideal, and atmospheric, way to get around town.

Recommended bicycle hire outfits:

City Cycle Hire (www.citycyclehire.com; 61 Newnham Rd; per half-day/day/week £7/10/25; ⏰9am-5.30pm Mon-Fri, plus 9am-5pm Sat Apr-Oct) A mile southwest of the city centre.

Rutland Cycling (☎01223-307655; www.rutlandcycling.com; Corn Exchange St; per 4hr/day £7/10; ⏰9am-6pm Mon-Fri, 10am-5pm Sun) In the heart of town, underneath the Grand Arcade shopping centre. There's another branch on Station Rd at the train station.

BUS

- Bus routes run around town from the **main bus station** (Drummer St).
- Many operate until around 11pm.
- C1, C3 and C7 stop at the train station.
- A Dayrider ticket (£4.10) provides 24 hours, unlimited, citywide bus travel.

Grantchester

POP 540

Old thatched cottages with gardens covered in flowers, breezy meadows and classic cream teas aren't the only reason to make the pilgrimage along the Cam to the picture-postcard village of Grantchester. You'll also be following in the footsteps of some of the world's greatest minds on a 3-mile walk, cycle or punt that has changed little since Edwardian times.

Eating

★**Orchard Tea Garden** CAFE £
(☎01223-551125; http://mlsb.org/orchard-teagarden; Mill Way; lunch mains £4-10, cakes £3; ⏰9.30am-7.30pm Jun-Aug, to 5.30pm Mar-May & Sep-Nov, to 4.30pm Dec-Feb) After an idyllic punt, walk or cycle to Grantchester from Cambridge beside the Cam, flop into a deckchair under a leafy apple tree and wolf down calorific cakes or light lunches at this quintessentially English spot. This was the favourite haunt of the Bloomsbury Group who came to camp, picnic, swim and discuss their work.

Getting There & Away

- Grantchester is 3 miles from Cambridge; you can punt, walk or cycle beside the Cam.
- Bus 18 runs from Cambridge to Grantchester (£2.50, 15 minutes, hourly Monday to Saturday).

Ely

POP 20,256

A small but charming city dominated by a jaw-dropping cathedral, Ely makes an excellent day trip from Cambridge. It takes its name (*ee*-lee) from the eels that once inhabited the surrounding undrained Fens. From the Middle Ages onward, Ely was one of the biggest opium-producing centres in Britain, with high-class ladies holding 'poppy parties' and local mothers sedating their children with 'poppy tea'. Today, beyond the dizzying heights of the cathedral towers, Ely is a cluster of medieval streets lined with traditional tearooms and pretty Georgian houses; a quaint quayside adds extra appeal.

Sights

★Ely Cathedral CATHEDRAL

(www.elycathedral.org; The Gallery; adult/child £8/free, incl tower tour £15/free; 7am-6.30pm) Ely Cathedral's stunning silhouette dominates the whole area; it's dubbed the 'Ship of the Fens' because it's so visible across the vast, flat sweeps of land. The early-12th-century **nave** dazzles with clean, uncluttered lines and a lofty sense of space. Look out for the entrancing ceiling, the masterly 14th-century **Octagon**, and **towers** that soar upwards in shimmering colours. Standard admission includes a ground-floor **guided tour**. The **tower tours** (three to five daily) deliver behind-the-scenes glimpses, 165 steps and remarkable views.

Ely has been a place of worship and pilgrimage since at least 673, when Etheldreda, daughter of the king of East Anglia, founded a nunnery here (shrugging off the fact that she had been twice married in her determination to become a nun). She was canonised shortly after her death. The nunnery was sacked by the Danes, rebuilt as a monastery, demolished and then resurrected as a church after the Norman Conquest. In 1109, Ely became a cathedral. Gothic arches were added later to support the weight of the mighty walls.

The vast 14th-century **Lady Chapel** is filled with eerily empty niches that once held statues of saints and martyrs. They were hacked out unceremoniously by iconoclasts during the English Civil War. But the delicate tracery remains, overseen by a rather controversial statue of *Holy Mary* by David Wynne, unveiled in 2000 to mixed reviews. The cathedral's beauty has made it a popular film location: you may recognise some of its fine details from scenes in *Elizabeth: The Golden Age* and *The Other Boleyn Girl*. For optimum atmosphere, visit during evensong (5.30pm Monday to Saturday, 4pm Sunday) or a choral service (10.30am Sunday).

Oliver Cromwell's House MUSEUM

(www.olivercromwellshouse.co.uk; 29 St Mary's St; adult/child £4.90/3.40; 10am-5pm Apr-Oct, 11am-4pm Nov-Mar) England's premier Puritan (p642) lived in this attractive, half-timbered house with his family from 1636 to 1647, when he was the local tithe collector. The interior has been restored to reflect the fixtures and fittings that would have been part of their daily lives – expect flickering candles, floppy hats and writing quills.

Ely Museum MUSEUM

(www.elymuseum.org.uk; Market St; adult/child £4.50/1; 10.30am-5pm Mon-Sat, 1-5pm Sun Apr-Oct, 10.30am-4pm Wed-Sat, 1-4pm Sun Nov-Mar) Housed in the Old Gaol House, this quirky little museum appropriately features gruesome prison tableaux inside prisoners' cells, plus displays on the Romans, the Anglo-Saxons, the Long Barrow burial ground at nearby Haddlington, and the formation of the Fens. You are also initiated into the mysteries of old Ely trades such as leatherwork and eel-catching.

Sleeping & Eating

★Peacocks B&B **££**

(01353-661100; www.peacockstearoom.co.uk; 65 Waterside; d £125-150) Walk into the roomy suites here and feel instantly at home. In Cottage, floral Laura Ashley wallpaper graces a sweet sitting area and bedroom; in Brewery, the vintage books, gilt mirrors and burnished antiques are reminiscent of a grand gentlemen's club.

Riverside Inn B&B **££**

(01353-661677; www.riversideinn-ely.co.uk; 8 Annesdale; s £59-69, d £89-120; P) In this Georgian guesthouse on Ely's quay, rooms are enriched by dull golds, deep reds, brocade bedspreads, dark furniture and sparkling bathrooms. Just the place to gaze at the houseboats and rowers bobbing about on the River Great Ouse.

★Peacocks CAFE **£**

(www.peacockstearoom.co.uk; 65 Waterside; snacks from £7; 10.30am-4.30pm Wed-Sun, plus Tue Jun-Sep) An award-winning cafe serving a vast selection of teas and cream teas, luscious homemade soups, salads, cakes and scones. Eat inside surrounded by fun knick-knacks and bone china, or in the bijou garden framed by drooping wisteria.

Old Fire Engine House BRITISH **££**

(01353-662582; www.theoldfireenginehouse.co.uk; 25 St Mary's St; lunch 2/3 courses £17/22, mains £16; noon-2pm & 7-9pm Mon-Sat, noon-2pm Sun) Eating here is like sampling the dishes cooked up in a (decidedly classy) classic East Anglian farmhouse kitchen. Seasonal and local produce rule, so treats might include locally smoked eel or roast guinea fowl with wild mushrooms, rounded off with some custard-smothered, steamed treacle and ginger pudding.

Information

Tourist Office (☎01353-662062; www.visitely.org.uk; 29 St Mary's St; ⏰10am-5pm Apr-Oct, 11am-4pm Nov-Mar) Stocks leaflets on the picturesque Eel Trail (50p) and Fen Rivers Way (£2) circular walks.

Getting There & Away

You can walk to Ely from Cambridge, along the 17-mile, riverside Fen Rivers Way. Rail connections include the following:

Cambridge £3, 20 minutes, three per hour

King's Lynn £7, 30 minutes, every 30 minutes

Norwich £17, one hour, every 30 minutes

ESSEX

The county's inhabitants have been the butt of snobbery and some of England's cruellest jokes for years, thanks to pop-culture stereotypes. But beyond the fake tans and slots 'n' bumper car resorts, the county's still-idyllic medieval villages and rolling countryside provided inspiration for Constable, one of England's best-loved painters. Here, too, is the historic town of Colchester, while even Southend-on-Sea, the area's most popular resort, has a softer side in the traditional cockle-sellers and cobbled lanes of the sleepy suburb Old Leigh.

Colchester

POP 180,420

Dominated by its sturdy castle and extensive Roman walls, Colchester is Britain's oldest recorded city, dating from the 5th century BC. In AD 43 the Romans came, saw, conquered and constructed their northern capital Camulodunum. It was razed by Boudica just 17 years later. In the 11th century, the invading Normans built a mighty castle; today it's set amid narrow streets that are home to a striking new arts space and some half-timbered gems.

Sights

★Colchester Castle CASTLE

(www.cimuseums.org.uk; Castle Park; adult/child £7.60/4.75; ⏰10am-5pm Mon-Sat, 11am-5pm Sun) Built in 1076 on the foundations of the Roman Temple of Claudius, England's largest surviving Norman keep is bigger than that of the Tower of London. Over the centuries it's been a royal residence, a prison and home to a Witchfinder General. Now a £4-million restoration has brought 21st-century technology to its 11th-century walls. Look out for mobile phone apps and tablet hire, and a cracking *son et lumiere* recreating lost internal structures and bringing the building's history to life.

firstsite ARTS CENTRE

(www.firstsite.uk.net; Lewis Gardens; ⏰10am-5pm; 👪) FREE Colchester's shiny, curved, glass-and-copper arts centre brings the town bang up to date. It's as striking inside as out: installations flow seamlessly into one another amid a wealth of space and light. Temporary visual art displays are cunningly juxtaposed with historical works; the one permanent exhibition is the magnificent Berryfield Mosaic – a Roman artefact found on firstsite's location in 1923, and now under glass in the centre of the gallery space.

Hollytrees Museum MUSEUM

(www.cimuseums.org.uk; Castle Park; ⏰10am-5pm Mon-Sat) FREE It's like walking into a period drama: a Georgian town house dating from 1718, filled with toys and costumes, watches and clocks. Reminders of the domestic life of the wealthy owners and their servants are everywhere, with quirky exhibits that include a shipwright's baby carriage in the shape of a boat, a make-your-own Victorian silhouette feature and an intricate, envy-inducing doll's house.

Sleeping & Eating

North Hill HOTEL ££

(☎01206-574001; www.northhillhotel.com; 51 North Hill; s/d/ste £90/100/120; 📶) Ask for a room in the characterful, cottage-style back building of this sleek sleep spot and you'll be rewarded with wonky beams, exposed red brick and plush modern furnishings. Stylish, more contemporary rooms sit in the former solicitor's chambers next door – it comes complete with ranks of law books on the shelves.

★Company Shed SEAFOOD ££

(☎01206-382700; http://thecompanyshed.co; 129 Coast Rd, West Mersea; mains £5-16; ⏰9am-4pm Tue-Sat, 10am-4pm Sun) Bring your own bread and wine to this seaside shack to tuck into mussels, oysters, prawns, lobster, jellied eels, smoked fish or their signature seafood platter. It's all courtesy of the Howard family, eighth-generation oyster-harvesters. The shed is on Mersea Island, 9 miles south of Colchester. Check the times of high water – it's not accessible on particularly high tides.

You can't book; arrive early (by 11.30am in the summer) to be sure of a meal.

Green Room MODERN BRITISH ££
(☎01206-574001; www.northhillhotel.com; 51 North Hill; mains £12-18; ⊙noon-2.30pm & 6-9.30pm Mon-Sat, noon-8pm Sun) Local, seasonal comfort-food classics are given a contemporary twist at this smart, friendly restaurant, where dishes range from fish and chips or venison with wilted spinach to a gorgeously garlicky grilled lobster. Their working lunch (mains £6 to £8) is a snip.

Information

Tourist Office (☎01206-282920; www.visitcolchester.com; Castle Park; ⊙10am-5pm Mon-Sat) Inside the Hollytrees Museum.

Getting There & Away

➡ National Express buses run to London Victoria roughly every two hours (£10, 2½ hours).

➡ Trains shuttle to London Liverpool St (£15, one hour, every 15 minutes).

Dedham Vale

John Constable's romantic visions of country lanes, springtime fields and babbling creeks were inspired by and painted in this serene vale. The artist was born and bred in East Bergholt in 1776 and, although you may not see the rickety old cart pictured in his renowned painting *The Hay Wain*, the picturesque cottages, rolling countryside and languid charm remain.

Now known as Constable Country, Dedham Vale centres on the villages of Dedham, East Bergholt and Flatford. With leafy lanes, arresting pastoral views and graceful old churches, it's a glorious area to explore on foot or by bike.

Sights

Flatford Mill HISTORIC BUILDING
(Flatford, near East Bergholt; P) Constable fans will recognise red-brick Flatford Mill immediately, as it appears in many of his canvases and remains as idyllic a setting today. It was once owned by the artist's family and is now used as an education centre, so although you can take in picture-perfect views from front and back, you can't go in.

Flatford HISTORIC BUILDING
(Bridge Cottage, NT; ☎01206-298260; www.nationaltrust.org.uk; Bridge Cottage, near East Bergholt; parking £4; ⊙10.30am-5.30pm Apr-Oct, to 3.30pm Sat & Sun Nov-Mar; P) FREE Set right beside Flatford Mill – a feature of several Constable paintings – thatched Bridge Cottage has an exhibition that provides a fine introduction to the artist's life and works. Daily guided tours (£3, noon and 2pm, April to October) take in views of Flatford Mill, Willy Lott's House (which features in *The Hay Wain*) and other sites that pop up in Constable's paintings. There are also self-guided routes.

Courses

Painting Courses COURSE
(☎01206-323027; www.dedhamhall.co.uk; Brook St, Dedham; nonresidents per 3/7 days £325/380) For those inspired by Dedham Vale's bucolic landscapes, atmospheric Dedham Hall (p382) runs acclaimed painting courses in a converted, 14th-century barn. You can just visit each day for lessons, but it's more fun to stay, when the fee (double per three/seven nights from £450/740) includes dinner, bed and breakfast.

Sleeping & Eating

★**Dedham Hall** B&B ££
(☎01206-323027; www.dedhamhall.co.uk; Brook St, Dedham; s/d £75/120; P) An air of authentic old England infuses Dedham Hall, a delightfully relaxed 15th-century farmhouse where overstuffed armchairs sit beside ancient beams, candlesticks perch above red-brick fireplaces and plump pillows rest on cosy beds. Add a dappled garden dotted with chairs and it's really rather hard to leave.

Residents can also tuck into elegant, imaginative dinners (dinner and B&B for two costs £190).

Sun INN ££
(☎01206-323351; www.thesuninndedham.com; High St, Dedham; d £145; P 🛜) The centuries-old Sun is the epitome of heritage-chic: creaking floors and wonky walls surround upcycled mirrors, brass bedsteads and subtle colour schemes that team terracotta with a gentle yellow and olive with green. The pick of the rooms is church-view Elsa, where an immense bed is framed by armchairs and a bathroom is tucked in behind a wood-panelled door.

Milsoms HOTEL ££

(☎01206-322795; www.milsomhotels.com; Stratford Rd, Dedham; d £100-210; P 📶) Sure-footed design gives the rooms here a real sense of fun: red-leather armchairs, angle-poise lamps and retro phones meet vast leaning mirrors and jazzy modern art. Their bicycle and canoe hire service opens up tranquil explorations of Dedham Vale.

Or drop by the hip, buzzy restaurant (open noon to 9.30pm, mains £9 to £28) for local steaks, mezze boards, duck tacos and lush ice cream.

Maison Talbooth BOUTIQUE HOTEL £££

(☎01206-322367; www.milsomhotels.com; Stratford Rd, Dedham; ste £150-450; P 📶 🏊) In secluded grounds overlooking Constable's Dedham Vale, this fabulous retreat sees guests luxuriating in swish suites with goose-feather duvets and don't-want-to-get-up beds, and destressing in its hot tub, spa and heated outdoor pool, complete with pool house with a blazing log fire.

Sun PUB FOOD ££

(www.thesuninndedham.com; High St, Dedham; mains £13-20; ⌚noon-2.30pm & 6-9.30pm) Surprisingly, dishes infused with flavours of the Med appear on the scrubbed wooden tables of this old English inn. It's wood-panelled walls and beams provide a fine setting for risotto enriched with wild garlic, pasta stuffed with nettle and chard, and creamy vanilla-scented panna cotta.

Getting There & Away

Flatford Mill is a lovely 2-mile walk from Manningtree train station.

Bus links from Colchester:

Dedham Buses 80, 81 and 102 (£2.40, 30 minutes, two to seven daily).

East Bergholt Buses 93 and 94 (£2.80, 40 minutes, hourly Monday to Saturday).

Saffron Walden

POP 15,210

The 12th-century market town of Saffron Walden is a delightful knot of half-timbered houses, narrow lanes, crooked roofs and ancient buildings. It gets its name from the purple saffron crocus (source of the world's most expensive spice), which was cultivated in the surrounding fields between the 15th and 18th centuries. If you can, time a visit to Tuesday or Saturday morning when markets stalls fill the centre of town.

Sights

Saffron Walden Museum MUSEUM

(www.saffronwaldenmuseum.org; Museum St; adult/child £2.50/free; ⌚10am-4.30pm Tue-Sat, 2-4.30pm Sun) In the excellent museum, itself dating from 1835, you'll find an eclectic collection of artefacts covering everything from local history and 18th- and 19th-century costumes to geology, a partially interactive natural-history exhibit, Victorian toys and ancient Egyptian items. There's a sandpit for young archaeologists and a fascinating 'Worlds of Man' collection, ranging from West African carvings and weaponry to Inuit bone harpoons. The bramble-covered ruins of Walden Castle Keep, built about 1125, lie in the grounds.

St Mary the Virgin CHURCH

(www.stmaryssaffronwalden.org; Church St; ⌚9am-5pm) FREE St Mary's oldest parts date back to 1250. A symbol of the town's saffron-inspired golden age, it is one of the largest churches in the county and features some impressive Gothic arches and local landowner Lord Audley's tomb.

Bridge End Gardens GARDENS

(Bridge End; ⌚gardens 24hr, maze & kitchen garden 9am-3pm Mon-Thu, to 1pm Fri, 10am-4pm Sat & Sun) FREE Careful restoration of these seven interlinked gardens has brought them back

WORTH A TRIP

AUDLEY END HOUSE & GARDENS

Positively palatial in its scale, style and the all-too-apparent ambition of its creator, the first Earl of Suffolk, the fabulous early-Jacobean **Audley End House & Gardens** (EH; ☎01799-522842; www.english-heritage.org.uk; off London Rd; adult/child £16.60/10; ⌚house noon-5pm Apr-Sep, to 4pm Oct, gardens 10am-6pm Apr-Sep, to 5pm Oct) eventually did become a royal palace when it was bought by Charles II in 1668. Lavishly decorated rooms glitter with silverware, priceless furniture and paintings, making it one of England's grandest country homes. The fine landscaped park was designed by Lancelot 'Capability' Brown. Audley End House is 1 mile west of Saffron Walden off the B1383.

to their former Victorian glory. Try to visit when the maze and produce-packed kitchen garden are open too.

Eating

Eight Bells PUB FOOD ££

(www.8bells-pub.co.uk; 18 Bridge St; mains £12-18; noon-9.30pm;) A warm mix of medieval character and contemporary style, this 16th-century gastropub serves up the likes of roast Suffolk lamb, lavender-cured duck and – fittingly – a vivid pea and courgette risotto, with saffron for extra spice.

Scrubbed wooden floors, half-timbered walls, abstract art, deep leather sofas and roaring fires make it an attractive place to sip on a pint, too.

Cafe Coucou CAFE ££

(www.cafecoucou.co.uk; 17 George St; mains £8-11; 9am-5pm Mon-Sat) Delicious homemade quiches, huge scones, chunky doorstep sandwiches and salads sell like hot cakes at this cheerful family-run cafe.

Information

Tourist Office (01799-524002; www.visitsaffronwalden.gov.uk; 1 Market Pl; 9.30am-5pm Mon-Sat) Stocks a good leaflet (free) outlining a trail around the town's historic buildings.

Getting There & Away

Bus 7 runs between Saffron Walden and Cambridge (£4.40, 1¼ hours, seven daily Monday to Saturday).

The nearest train station is 2 miles west of Saffron Walden at Audley End. Bus 301 links Audley End train station with Saffron Walden (£1.90, 15 minutes, hourly Monday to Saturday). Train services from there include the following:

Cambridge £7, 15 minutes, every 20 minutes

London Liverpool St £10, one hour, twice hourly

Southend-on-Sea & Around

POP 177,900

Full of flashing lights and fairground rides, Southend is London's weekend playground, replete with gaudy amusements and packed-out nightclubs. But as well as all that, there's a glorious stretch of sandy beach, an absurdly long pier and, in the suburb of Old Leigh, echoes of a traditional fishing village.

Sights

Southend Pier LANDMARK

(www.southend.gov.uk/pier; Western Esplanade; adult/child £2/1; 8am-6pm Mon-Fri, to 8pm Sat & Sun Apr-Sep, 9am-5pm Wed-Sun Oct-Mar) Welcome to the world's longest pier – a staggering 1.341 miles long, to be precise – built in 1830 and a magnet for boat crashes, storms and fires, the last of which ravaged its tip in 2005. Today, a peaceful if windy stroll to the restored Pier Head reveals a cafe, sun deck, gift shop, exhibition space and active lifeboat station. Hopping on the **Pier Railway** (one-way adult/child £4/2.20) saves the long slog back.

Pier Museum MUSEUM

(01702-611214; www.southendpiermuseum.co.uk; Western Esplanade; adult/child £1.50/50p; 11am-5pm Sat, Sun, Tue & Wed May-Oct) Southend's seaside heyday springs to life in this charming museum, where a Victorian toast-rack tram from the pier sits beside a functioning signal box, sepia photos and period costumes. The best bits though are the still-working antique penny-slot machines.

Old Leigh AREA

Cobbled streets, cockle sheds, art galleries and craft shops define atmospheric Old Leigh. It's a long stroll west along Southend's seafront, or a short hop on the local train.

Sleeping & Eating

Roslin Beach HOTEL ££

(01702-586375; www.roslinhotel.com; Thorpe Esplanade; s £71-130, d £109-159, ste £154-245; food noon-3pm & 6-9.30pm Mon-Sat, noon-5pm & 7-9pm Sun;) Seafront Roslin is all New England beach-house chic: sculptural driftwood features, seashell-framed mirrors and sand drifting up the steps. De-knot in the sauna, soak in the spa then sample locally caught whitebait (mains £10 to £22) on the water-view terrace, framed by swaying palms.

Osborne Bros SEAFOOD £

(www.osbornebros.co.uk; High St, Leigh-on-Sea; snacks/mains £2.50/8; 8am-5pm) Part fish stall, part bare-bones cafe, Osbourne's is set right on Old Leigh's waterfront and serves up expansive Thames Estuary views. Best observed while tucking into crab, jellied eels or a seafood platter (cockles, mussels, prawns and crayfish; £8) and downing a pint from the pub next door.

They often stay open later in the summer and on fine weekends.

★ Simply Seafood SEAFOOD £££
(☎01702-716645; www.simply-seafood.com; 1 The Cockle Sheds, Leigh-on-Sea; mains £18-35; ⌚noon-3.30pm & 5-10pm Tue-Sat, noon-4.30pm Sun) Tucked under the flyover just west of Old Leigh, this bright little eatery lets locally sourced seafood shine. The oysters are from the River Chelmer, the crab is from Cromer and the fish is from the boats just outside. Scallops come perfectly seared and the *fruits de mer* platter is superb. Despite the name, there's a trio of steak options too.

ℹ Information

Tourist Office (☎01702-215620; www.visitsouthend.co.uk; Southend Pier, Western Esplanade; ⌚8.30am-9pm Jun-Sep, 10am-6pm Wed-Sun Oct-May) At the entrance to the pier.

ℹ Getting There & Away

The easiest way to arrive is by train. The town's most useful train stations are Central (10 minutes' walk from the sea) and Victoria (15 minutes from the shore). Services include the following:

Leigh-on-Sea (from Central) £3, seven minutes, every 15 minutes.

London Fenchurch St (from Central) £12, 1¼ hours, three per hour.

London Liverpool St (from Victoria) £17, one hour, three per hour.

SUFFOLK

Suffolk is dotted with picturesque villages seemingly lost in time. The county made its money on the back of the medieval wool trade, and magnificent churches and lavish Tudor homes attest to the area's wealthy past. To the west are the picture-postcard villages of Lavenham and Long Melford. Further north, Bury St Edmunds ushers in historic buildings and a market-town vibe, while the appealing seaside resorts of Aldeburgh and Southwold overflow with genteel charm.

ℹ Getting Around

Ipswich is the county's main transport hub. **Traveline** (www.travelineeastanglia.org.uk) details bus routes.

Train connections from Ipswich include the following:

Bury St Edmunds £9, 30 minutes, one to two per hour

London Liverpool St £20, 1¼ hours, two per hour

Norwich £15, 40 minutes, two per hour

Long Melford

POP 2800

Two Elizabethan manors and some fine eateries make Long Melford deserving of a detour. Its expansive village green, antiques shops and string of independent stores provide other excellent reasons to meander on through.

Sights

Kentwell Hall HISTORIC BUILDING
(☎01787-310207; www.kentwell.co.uk; adult/child £12.20/9.20; ⌚hours vary; P) Gorgeous, turreted Kentwell Hall may date from the 1500s and be full of Tudor grandeur, but it's still used as a private home, resulting in a wonderfully lived-in feel. Kentwell is framed by a rectangular moat, glorious gardens and an irresistible rare-breeds farm. Tudor re-enactment events see the whole estate bristle with bodices, codpieces and hose. Opening hours are erratic, it tends to be open 11am to 5pm during school summer holidays, plus other weekends; call to check.

Melford Hall HISTORIC BUILDING
(NT; www.nationaltrust.org.uk; Hall St; adult/child £7.50/3.75; ⌚noon-5pm Wed-Sun Apr-Oct; P) From outside, the romantic Elizabethan mansion of Melford Hall seems little changed since it entertained Queen Elizabeth I in 1578. Inside, there's a panelled banqueting hall, masses of Regency and Victorian finery, and a display on Beatrix Potter, a cousin of the Hyde Parkers, who owned the house from 1786 to 1960.

Holy Trinity CHURCH
(www.longmelfordchurch.com; Church Walk; ⌚10am-6pm Apr-Oct, to 4pm Nov-Mar) FREE Magnificent Holy Trinity is more cathedral-sized than church-sized, a spectacular example of a 15th-century wool church. The stained-glass windows and flint-and-stone flushwork are outstanding.

Sleeping & Eating

Black Lion HOTEL ££
(☎01787-312356; www.blacklionhotel.net; The Green; s/d/ste £100/125/175; P 📶) There's more than a hint of the Scottish Highlands at the smashing Black Lion, thanks to tartan carpets, open fires and ancient-looking oil paintings. Flamboyant bedrooms, all swag curtains and feature beds, are named after classy wines – Yquem is, fittingly, floor-to-ceiling rich red.

GAINSBOROUGH'S HOUSE

Most visitors to Sudbury come to see Thomas Gainsborough's atmospheric birthplace **Gainsborough's House** (www.gainsborough.org; 46 Gainsborough St; adult/child £6.50/2; ⏲10am-5pm Mon-Sat, 11am-5pm Sun), now home to the world's largest collection of his work. The 16th-century house and gardens feature a Georgian facade built by the artist's father. Inside, look out for *Pitminster Boy* in the entrance hall; the exquisite *Portrait of Harriett; Viscountess Tracy*, celebrated for its delicate portrayal of drapery; and the landscapes that were his passion.

Bull INN ££

(☎01787-378494; www.oldenglishinns.co.uk; Hall St; s £60, d £80-120; P 📶) Built, probably, for a wool merchant in 1450, this cavernous pub has been pulling pints since around 1580. The carved ceilings and heraldic crests in its bars attest to that grand age. Check into a front-facing bedroom for maximum atmosphere enhanced by aged beams and dark wood.

Decent pub grub (think slow-cooked lamb shank, and beef and ale pie) is served between noon and 9.30pm (mains £9 to £12).

★Scutcher's MODERN BRITISH £££

(☎01787-310200; www.scutchers.com; Westgate St; mains £19-29; ⏲noon-2pm & 7-9.30pm Thu-Sat) Beautiful reinventions of traditional ingredients ensure this unpretentious place is renowned throughout the Stour Valley. Local Gressingham duck is given an Asian twist; fish ragout comes with a vermouth sauce; the hot, grilled cheese is paired with quince. It's modern, classy and assured.

Getting There & Away

Bus links include the following:

Bury St Edmunds £4.10, 50 minutes, hourly Monday to Saturday

Sudbury £1.50, 10 minutes, hourly Monday to Saturday

Lavenham

POP 1413

One of East Anglia's most beautiful and rewarding towns, the former wool-trade centre of Lavenham is home to a collection of exquisitely preserved medieval buildings that lean and lurch to dramatic effect. Lavenham's 300 half-timbered, pargeted and thatched houses have been left virtually untouched since the 15th century; many are now superb places to eat and stay.

Sights & Activities

Lavenham Guildhall HISTORIC BUILDING

(NT; www.nationaltrust.org.uk; Market Pl; adult/child £6.20/3.10; ⏲11am-5pm daily Mar-Oct, to 4pm Sat & Sun Nov-Feb) Lavenham's most enchanting buildings are clustered along High St, Water St and around the unusually triangular Market Pl. They're dominated by this early-16th-century whitewashed guildhall – a superb example of a close-studded, timber-framed building. It is now a local-history museum with displays on the wool trade and medieval guilds; in its tranquil garden you can see dye plants that produced the typical medieval colours.

Little Hall HISTORIC BUILDING

(www.littlehall.org.uk; Market Pl; adult/child £4/free; ⏲10am-1pm Mon, 1-4pm Tue-Sun Easter-Oct) Caramel-coloured, 14th-century Little Hall was once home to a successful wool merchant. Inside, the rooms of this medieval gem were restored to period splendour through the efforts of the Gayer-Anderson twins who made it their home in the 1920s and 1930s.

St Peter & St Paul CHURCH

(www.lavenhamchurch.wordpress.com; Church St; ⏲8.30am-5.30pm) This late-Perpendicular structure seems to lift into the sky, with its beautifully proportioned windows, soaring flint tower and gargoyle waterspouts. Built between 1485 and 1530, it was one of Suffolk's last great wool churches, completed on the eve of the Reformation, and is now a lofty testament to Lavenham's past prosperity.

Guided Walks WALKING

(☎01787-248207; adult/child £4.50/free; ⏲2.30pm Sat & 11am Sun Easter-Oct) Delve deep into the stories behind Lavenham's beautiful buildings on these guided strolls. They leave from the tourist office; there's no need to book.

Sleeping & Eating

Angel HOTEL ££

(☎01787-247388; www.cozypubs.co.uk; Market Pl; s £80-109, d £99-119; ⏲food noon-3pm & 6-10pm Mon-Fri, noon-10pm Sat, noon-8pm Sun; P 📶) In Lavenham's oldest building, dark-green corridors lead to gorgeously renovated, large, bright, beam-scored rooms. The eclectic decor in the bar (think theatrical spotlights and battered travelling trunks) echoes a menu that ranges confidently from English inn standards to superfood salads and hefty *a la carte* dishes (mains £12 to £24).

Brett Farm B&B ££

(☎ 01787-248533; www.brettfarm.com; The Common; d £80) Totally tranquil Brett Farm is on the far fringe of Lavenham, a modern bungalow decked out in blue gingham and pine. But it's the setting that sells it – in its 11 hectares of fields and paddocks, alive with birdsong, tables and chairs sit in the shade beside a stream.

★ **Swan** HOTEL £££

(☎ 01787-247477; www.theswanatlavenham.co.uk; High St; s/d/ste £100/140/315; P 📶) Marvellously medieval and utterly indulgent, the Swan might just spoil you in terms of other places to stay. Tasteful furnishings team oatmeal with olive and gentle reds, latticework of ancient wood climbs all around. The service is smooth, while the suites are simply stunning: expect soaring arched ceilings criss-crossed with beams.

The spa boasts a sauna, steam room and heated outdoor jacuzzi plunge-pool. Perhaps relax there before heading to the hotel's Airmen's Bar, so called because of the wall bearing the signatures of the US pilots based nearby during WWII.

Lavenham Priory APARTMENT £££

(☎ 01787-247404; www.lavenhampriory.co.uk; Water St; 2-person apt per 2 nights/week £325/900; P 📶) A rare treat – sumptuously restored, two- to six-person, 13th-century cottages that steal your heart as soon as you walk in. The history-rich rooms feature crooked beams, carved oak staircases, wood-burning stoves and antique furniture. And a complimentary hamper full of local food.

★ **Great House** MODERN BRITISH ££

(☎ 01787-247431; www.greathouse.co.uk; Market Pl; 3-course lunch/dinner £25/37; ⏲ noon-2.30pm Wed-Sun, 7-9.30pm Tue-Sat) Contrasting cultures combine so well here: traditional meets modern, East Anglian ingredients meet French cuisine. Which could see you eating roasted Norfolk (Gressingham) duck or braised Suffolk pork, then dispatching coffee and praline *millefeuille* or tangy morsels of French and Suffolk cheese.

They also do a great-value, two-course lunch (£20).

ℹ Information

Tourist Office (☎ 01787-248207; www.heartofsuffolk.co.uk; Lady St; ⏲ 10am-4.45pm Mar-Oct, 11am-3pm Sat & Sun Nov-Feb) Tucked in beside central Market Pl.

ℹ Getting There & Away

Bus 753 runs to Bury St Edmunds (£4, 30 minutes) hourly, Monday to Saturday.

Bury St Edmunds

POP 41,113

In Bury, the past is ever present. A centre of pilgrimage for centuries, its history-rich features include an atmospheric ruined abbey, handsome Georgian architecture and tranquil gardens. The chance to visit two breweries proves pretty tempting too.

Sights

Abbey Gardens RUINS

(Mustow St; ⏲ dawn-dusk) FREE Now a picturesque ruin in parkland behind the cathedral, Bury's once-mighty abbey still impresses despite the townspeople having made off with much of the stone after the dissolution of the monasteries. The walls are striking (especially on the west side), having crumbled and eroded into a series of fantastical shapes. Other highlights are the decorative Great Gate, the diminutive dovecote and the flower-filled gardens.

You enter the Abbey Gardens via one of two well-preserved old gates: the staunch mid-14th-century **Great Gate** is intricately decorated and ominously defensive, with battlements, a portcullis and arrow slits. The other entrance sits further up Angel Hill, where a gargoyle-studded early-12th-century **Norman Tower** looms.

Just beyond the Great Gate is a peaceful garden where the **Great Court** was once a hive of activity; further on a **dovecote** marks the only remains of the Abbot's Palace. Most impressive, however, are the remains of the western front, where the original abbey walls were burrowed into in the 18th century to make way for homes. The houses are still in use and look as if they've been carved out of the stone like caves. Nearby is **Samson Tower** and in front of it is a beautiful statue of St Edmund by Dame Elisabeth Frink (1976). The rest of the abbey spreads eastward like a ragged skeleton, with various lumps and pillars hinting at its immense size.

WORTH A TRIP

SUTTON HOO

Somehow missed by plundering grave robbers and left undisturbed for 1300 years, the hull of an enormous Anglo-Saxon ship was discovered at **Sutton Hoo** (NT; ☎01394-389700; www.nationaltrust.org.uk; Sutton Hoo, near Woodbridge; adult/child £8.20/4.10; ⊙10.30am-5pm Easter-Oct, 10.30am-4pm Sat & Sun Nov-Easter; P ♿) in 1939, buried under a mound of earth. The vessel was the final resting place of Raedwald, king of East Anglia until AD 625, and was stuffed with Saxon riches, reflecting a sophisticated culture that's conveyed beautifully in on-site displays.

The massive effort that went into Raedwald's burial gives some idea of just how important a man he was, while the elaborate nature of the treasures transformed perceptions of the era. Many of the original finds and a full-scale reconstruction of his ship and burial chamber can be seen in the visitor centre. The finest treasures, including the king's exquisitely crafted helmet, shields, gold ornaments and Byzantine silver, are displayed in London's British Museum, but replicas are on show here, along with an original prince's sword.

Paths encircle the 18 burial mounds (which look like bumps in the ground) that make up the 'royal cemetery'. You can only walk on to them as part of one-hour **guided tours** (adult/child £2.50/1.25), which provide a fascinating insight into the site. There's normally at least one tour a day; call to check for times. Sutton Hoo is 3 miles east of Woodbridge and 11 miles northeast of Ipswich off the B1083.

St Edmundsbury Cathedral CATHEDRAL
(www.stedscathedral.co.uk; Angel Hill; requested donation adult/child £3/50p; ⊙8.30am-6pm) The 45m-high tower of this cathedral was only completed in 2005 and is a vision in Lincolnshire limestone – its traditional Gothic-style construction conveys how many English cathedrals must have looked fresh from the stonemason's chisel. Most of the building is early 16th century, though the eastern end is post-1945. The overall effect is light and lofty, with a gorgeous hammer-beam roof and a striking sculpture of the crucified Christ by Dame Elisabeth Frink in the north transept. Free, 30-minute guided **tours** (11am Mon-Sat, May-Sep) provide an in-depth insight into the cathedral's heritage.

St Mary's Church CHURCH
(www.wearechurch.net; Honey Hill; donation requested; ⊙10am-4pm Mon-Sat, to 3pm Nov-Mar) St Mary's is one of the largest parish churches in England, and it contains the tomb of Mary Tudor – Henry VIII's sister and a onetime queen of France. Built around 1430, it's famous for its hammer-beam roof, which features a host of vampirelike angels swooping from the ceiling. A bell is still rung to mark curfew, as it was in the Middle Ages.

Greene King Brewery BREWERY
(☎01284-714297; www.greeneking.co.uk; Westgate St; visitor centre free, tours £12; ⊙10.30am-4.30pm Mon-Sat) They've been crafting some of England's favourite booze in this working brewery since 1799. Explore the town's 900-year-old brewing heritage in the visitor centre, then take a **tour** (2pm Mon-Fri, & 11am Wed-Sun, 12.30pm & 3.30pm Sat) that winds past the vats and pipes of the historic brewhouse, takes in sweeping town views from the roof, and heads to the Brewery Tap for tipples from the casks. The tours are popular – book.

Moyse's Hall MUSEUM
(www.stedmundsbury.gov.uk/moyseshall; Cornhill; adult/child £4/2; ⊙10am-5pm Mon-Sat, noon-4pm Sun) Set in an impressive 12th-century undercroft, Moyse's Hall's rarities include a locket containing some of Mary Tudor's hair and finds from Bury's ruined abbey. Displays chart the key episodes in the town's past, including the chilling Bury witch trials.

Theatre Royal HISTORIC BUILDING
(NT; ☎01284-769505; www.theatreroyal.org; Westgate St) A real treat, Britain's only working Regency playhouse features ornate gilding, sweeps of boxes and a *trompe l'oeil* ceiling, all revealed on self-led (free) and guided (£6.50) front-of-house and backstage **tours**. These tend to be held between February and November; times vary – call to check.

Sleeping

★Chantry HOTEL ££
(☎01284-767427; www.chantryhotel.com; 8 Sparhawk St; s/ste £75/145, d £115-130; P @ 📶) Pretty much everything feels right about the Chantry – a family-run town house that's

somewhere between a hotel and a B&B. Sash windows and cast-iron fireplaces signal its Georgian origins; French beds and walk-in showers add contemporary comfort; the convivial lounge and tiny bar help you feel at home.

Old Cannon B&B ££
(01284-768769; www.oldcannonbrewery.co.uk; 86 Cannon St; s/d £96/130) In these rooms run by a hip microbrewery, converted outhouses feature smart bedrooms with gentle checks and terracotta walls. Each room is named after one of their beers – you get a free bottle on arrival. If you like it, pop into the pub just next door.

Fox INN ££
(01284-705562; www.oldenglishinns.co.uk; 1 Eastgate St; d £119-150; P) Slumber in these converted animal barns and be surrounded by carefully kept original features: bleached beams, weathered brick walls and even the livestock tethering rings. Painted wicker chairs and the odd chandelier add another layer of class. Cheap Sunday night deals mean prices can go as low as £85 for a double room.

Angel HOTEL ££
(01284-714000; www.theangel.co.uk; 3 Angel Hill; d £115-180, ste £330; P) The more expensive rooms at this ivy-clad Georgian coaching inn are pretty special: expect luxury bathrooms, quirky mock-1700s furnishings (the odd bright-pink plastic chair) and suites with stand-alone copper baths. The cheaper rooms, although perfectly comfortable, have much less pizzazz.

Eating & Drinking

★**Pea Porridge** MODERN BRITISH ££
(01284-700200; www.peaporridge.co.uk; 29 Cannon St; mains £13-18; noon-1.45pm Thu-Sat, 6.30-9pm Tue-Sat) Warmth, happy chatter and great aromas greet you at this intimate neighbourhood eatery. Imaginative dishes borrow from the cuisines of Italy and France – choose from salt cod, risotto, Normandy black sausage or Breckland muntjac loin – you're on to a winner any which way.

Their *menus du jour* (two/three courses £14.50/18.50) are a bargain.

Maison Bleue FRENCH £££
(01284-760623; www.maisonbleue.co.uk; 31 Churchgate St; mains £29-40; noon-2pm & 7-9.30pm Tue-Sat) Settle into this elegant eatery for modern French cuisine that's supremely stylish and bursting with flavour. Creations might include roasted Norfolk black chicken, seared scallops, or caramelised Dingley Dell pork. The set menus (three-course lunch/dinner £25/37) are great value.

★**Old Cannon** PUB
(01284-768769; www.oldcannonbrewery.co.uk; 86 Cannon St; 11am-11pm) In this microbrewery, gleaming mash tuns sit alongside the funky bar – try the Rusty Gun (ABV 4%) or the more feisty St Edmund's Head (5%). A fair bit of the ale goes into the food (served 8.30am to 9pm Monday to Saturday, to 3pm Sunday); perhaps sample some Gunner's Daughter sausages and bacon cured in stout.

Nutshell PUB
(www.thenutshellpub.co.uk; The Traverse; 11am-11pm Mon-Thu, to midnight Fri & Sat, noon-10.30pm Sun) Tiny benches, tiny tables, a ceiling smothered in international banknotes and a suspended pufferfish: it's amazing what they've squeezed into this thimble-sized, memorabilia-packed, timber-framed pub, recognised by the *Guinness Book of Records* as Britain's smallest.

If you're not squeamish, look out for the almost-mummified 400-year-old cat.

Information

Tourist Office (01284-764667; www.visit-burystedmunds.co.uk; The Apex Centre, Charter Sq; 10am-5pm Mon-Sat)

Getting There & Away

BUS

The main bus station is on St Andrew's St North.

Cambridge (£5, one hour, hourly Monday to Saturday) Stagecoach bus 11.

London Victoria (£12, 3½ hours, three daily) National Express.

TRAIN

The train station is a 10-minute walk north of the centre of town.

Cambridge £10, 40 minutes, hourly

Ely £10, 30 minutes, every two hours

Orford

POP 713

Secluded and seductive, the gorgeous village of Orford, 6 miles south of Snape Maltings, is worth a detour. It's a laid-back spot dotted with pretty houses and dominated by a rarity: curiously polygonal Orford Castle.

PIYA SUKCHIT / SHUTTERSTOCK ©

1. Alnwick Castle (p642), Northumberland Coast
Favoured as a film set, the castle starred as Hogwarts for the early *Harry Potter* movies.

2. Eastgate clock (p559), Chester
Built for Queen Victoria's Diamond Jubillee in 1897.

3. Windmill, Norfolk Broads (p400)
Water-lovers can boat down 125 miles of lock-free waterways in this protected wetland area.

4. Library of Birmingham (p408), Birmingham
Architecture resembling an elaborately wrapped present.

DAVIDELLIOTTPHOTOS / SHUTTERSTOCK ©

Sights

Orford Castle CASTLE
(EH; www.english-heritage.org.uk; Orford; adult/child £6.90/4.10; 10am-6pm Apr-Sep, to 5pm Oct, to 4pm Sat & Sun Nov-Mar; P) This 12th-century structure has an innovative, 18-sided drum design with three square turrets. From the roof there are glorious views of the nature reserve of Orford Ness.

Orford Ness NATURE RESERVE
(NT; www.nationaltrust.org.uk; adult/child incl ferry crossing £4/2; 10am-5pm Tue-Sat Jul-Sep, 10am-5pm Sat late Mar–Jun & Oct) Wind-whipped, remote Orford Ness is the largest vegetated shingle spit in Europe and was once used as a secret military testing ground; now it's a nature reserve and is home to rare wading birds, animals and plants. Ferries run from Orford Quay: the last leaves at 2pm and returns from the reserve at 5pm. Spaces can be limited – arrive early to reserve a seat.

Eating

Pinney's SEAFOOD £
(www.pinneysoforford.co.uk; The Quay; from £3.50; 10am-4.30pm, to 4pm Sun) Sells own-smoked seafood treats, including eel, prawns and sardines, plus meats and just-caught fish.

★ **Butley Orford Oysterage** SEAFOOD ££
(01394-450277; www.pinneysoforford.co.uk; Market Hill; mains £8-18; noon-2.15pm daily, plus 6.30-9pm daily Aug, Wed-Sat Apr-Jul, Sep & Oct, Fri & Sat Nov-Mar) They catch and smoke much of the superb seafood they serve here themselves; treats include Butley oysters and garlic-laced griddled prawns. Expect metal chairs, chalked-up menus, fabulous food and bags of charm.

Getting There & Away

Buses run to Melton (£2.20, 30 minutes, two buses daily Monday to Saturday), with regular connections from there to Aldeburgh and Ipswich.

Aldeburgh

POP 3225

The time-warped coastal town of Aldeburgh (*orld*-bruh) is one of the region's most charming. Its picturesque streets and sweeping shingle beach are lined with pastel-coloured houses, independent shops, art galleries and ramshackle fresh-fish kiosks. Its connections with composer Benjamin Britten and two festivals might also draw you to the town.

Sights

Moot Hall MUSEUM
(www.aldeburghmuseum.org.uk; Market Cross Pl; adult/child £2/free; noon-5pm Jun-Aug, 2.30pm-5pm Apr, May, Sep & Oct) Displays on fishing, shipbuilding, coastal defences and Regency-era tourism set in an intricately carved, timber-framed, 16th-century house.

Scallop SCULPTURE
(near Thorpe Rd car park) Maggi Hambling's sculpture commemorates Aldeburgh's links with 20th-century composer Benjamin Britten, who spent much of his life in the town. With 4m of inscribed, scallop shell–shaped steel, its beachside setting has proved controversial locally. It's a short stroll north of town along the seafront.

Festivals & Events

Aldeburgh Festival MUSIC
(www.aldeburgh.co.uk; Jun) Founded by local composer Benjamin Britten in 1948, this exploration of classical music is one of East Anglia's biggest, taking in new, reinterpreted and rediscovered pieces, and visual arts.

Aldeburgh Food & Drink Festival FOOD & DRINK
(www.aldeburghfoodanddrink.co.uk; late Sep) A two-day celebration of Suffolk produce and top-class cooking.

Sleeping & Eating

★ **Ocean House** B&B ££
(01728-452094; www.oceanhousealdeburgh.co.uk; 25 Crag Path; s £50, d £100-120, apt per week £1050) You are just seven paces (count them) from the beach at Ocean House, and many of the rustic-chic bedrooms directly overlook the surging sea. The five-person self-catering apartment comes with homely kitchen and pint-sized balcony, while the top-floor double is a true delight: water views on three sides and a sitting room with a baby grand.

Dunan House B&B ££
(01728-452486; www.dunanhouse.co.uk; 41 Park Rd; d £90-100, f £105-115; P) Evidence of the artist owners' efforts are everywhere: bright abstracts, self-portraits and pottery galore. Vivid walls alternate between red, orange and lemon. Vintage books and battered travelling chests lie around, while the top-floor family suite even has binoculars for zoomed-in estuary views.

Fish & Chip Shop FISH & CHIPS £
(www.aldeburghfishandchips.co.uk; 226 High St; mains £5-6; ⌚noon-2pm Tue-Sun, 5-9pm Thu-Sat) Aldeburgh has a reputation for the finest fish and chips in the area; this is the best place to find out why.

★**Lighthouse** MODERN BRITISH ££
(☎01728-453377; www.lighthouserestaurant.co.uk; 77 High St; mains £11-19; ⌚noon-2pm & 6.30-10pm; 👪) The new owner of this bright bistro was a waiter here for years and a sense of enthusiastic friendliness pervades the place. The food is special too; fish is a real strength, although meat-lovers might prefer guinea-fowl confit or a nice juicy steak. Be aware though, the local cod and seafood risotto is pretty hard to beat.

Regatta Restaurant SEAFOOD ££
(☎01728-452011; www.regattaaldeburgh.com; 171 High St; mains from £10, 2/3 courses £15/18; ⌚noon-2pm & 6-10pm) At Regatta, the fish is simple but good; from crispy salt and pepper squid, via their own-smoked salmon, to classic combinations such as halibut, samphire, new potatoes and salad.

Information

Tourist Office (☎01728-453637; www.thesuffolkcoast.co.uk; 48 High St; ⌚10am-3pm Mon-Sat, noon-4pm Sun)

Getting There & Away

Bus 64/65 runs hourly Monday to Saturday to Ipswich (£7, 1½ hours), where you can make connections to the rest of the region.

Southwold

POP 1090

Southwold's reputation as a well-heeled holiday getaway has earned it the nickname 'Kensington-on-Sea', after the upmarket London borough, and its lovely sandy beach, pebble-walled cottages, cannon-dotted clifftop and rows of beachfront bathing huts are undeniably picturesque. It's all attracted many artists, including JMW Turner, Charles Rennie Mackintosh, Lucian Freud and Damien Hirst.

Sights & Activities

Adnams BREWERY
(☎01502-727225; www.adnams.co.uk; Adnams Pl; tours £12; ⌚2-4 tours daily Mar-Sep) Spend an hour touring the high-tech kit inside this Victorian brewery, indulge in a 30-minute tutored tasting, then select a free bottle of beer to take home. Book.

You can also now be shown around the Adnams gin distillery. Those under 18 can't go on the tours.

Seafront & Pier AREA
(www.southwoldpier.co.uk; ⌚pier 9am-5pm, to 8pm Fri-Sun) FREE Southwold's shore-front is its main attraction. Amble along the promenade, admire the squat 19th-century **lighthouse** then drop by the 190m **pier**, first built in 1899 and recently reconstructed. Its **Under the Pier Show** (⌚10am-6pm, to 8pm Fri-Sun) sports a kooky collection of handmade amusement machines combining daft fun with political satire.

Coastal Voyager BOATING
(☎07887 525082; www.coastalvoyager.co.uk; Blackshore, Southwold Harbour) Trips include a 30-minute high-speed blast around the bay (adult/child £26/13), a leisurely 3½-hour cruise up the Blyth Estuary (£30/15) and a three-hour voyage to Scroby Sands (£40/20) to see a seal colony and wind farm.

Festivals & Events

Latitude Festival ART
(www.latitudefestival.co.uk; Henham Park; ⌚Jul) An eclectic mix of music, literature, dance, drama and comedy set in a country estate.

Ways with Words LITERATURE
(www.wayswithwords.co.uk; ⌚Nov) Talks and readings by big-name authors in venues around town.

Sleeping & Eating

Home@21 B&B ££
(☎01502-722573; www.homeat21.co.uk; 21 North Pde; d £99-125; 📶) The sea-view bedrooms here are splendid: plenty of space, cosy furnishings and big windows overlooking Southwold's pier and shore. The back-facing rooms are less striking but still perfectly sweet. The life-size plaster 'dancing girl' in the sunny guest lounge tends to prompt a smile.

★**Sutherland House** HOTEL £££
(☎01502-724544; www.sutherlandhouse.co.uk; 56 High St; d £90-199; P📶) Past guests at this former mayor's residence include a future James II and the Earl of Sandwich. They'd probably approve of the present appearance; pargeted ceilings, exposed beams and freestanding baths – it's top-quality, luxurious heritage-chic.

Supper time (mains £16 to £20; noon to 2pm and 7pm to 9pm, closed Monday) sees prime local ingredients transformed by flourishes such as bouillabaisse sauce, dill crackers and microherbs.

Swan HOTEL **£££**
(01502-722186; www.adnams.co.uk; Market Sq; s £115-125, d £185-255; P) It's a boon for beer lovers – an entire hotel owned by Southwold brewery giant Adnams. A £4-million refurbishment is bringing this venerable inn bang up to date. Expect vivid colours and contemporary bathrooms alongside plenty of 17th-century elegance. In the bar, staff are just itching to serve you a beer brewed right next door.

Coasters MODERN BRITISH **££**
(01502-724734; www.coastersofsouthwold.co.uk; 12 Queen St; mains £10-22; noon-2.30pm & 6-9pm) Punchy flavours and rich ingredients are the mainstay of this intimate bistro, where a wide-ranging menu skips nimbly from whole crab and Stilton glazed beef to Dingley Dell Suffolk pork sausages with mustard mash.

Information

Tourist Information (01502-523442; www.eastsuffolk.gov.uk/visitors; North Green; 10am-1pm & 2-5pm Mon-Sat, 11am-4pm Sun) Southwold's tourist office has closed; this information point is inside the town library.

Getting There & Away

Services are limited. Bus 146 runs to Norwich (£4, 1½ hours, hourly Monday to Saturday). For services south, including to Aldeburgh, catch bus 88A to Halesworth (£2.70, 30 minutes, hourly Monday to Saturday) and continue from there.

NORFOLK

Big skies, sweeping beaches, windswept marshes, meandering inland waterways and pretty flint houses combine to great effect in Norfolk. They say the locals have 'one foot on the land, and one in the sea' and you're never far from water here, whether it's beside the windmill-framed rivers of the tranquil Norfolk Broads or the wide, birdlife-rich sands of the shore. Inland, the bustling city of Norwich offers a fine castle and cathedral, a lively market and some truly excellent places to sleep and eat.

Getting Around

Norwich is the transport hub. Train connections include those to London Liverpool St (£20, two hours, two per hour).

Traveline (www.travelineeastanglia.org.uk) details bus routes. One of the most useful is the frequent **Coasthopper Bus** (www.coasthopper.co.uk), which hugs the shore on its route between Cromer and King's Lynn.

Norwich

POP 132,512

The affluent and easygoing city of Norwich (*norr*-ich) is a rich tapestry of meandering alleys liberally sprinkled with architectural jewels – spoils of the city's medieval wool boom. A magnificent cathedral and impressive Norman castle bookend the city centre; in between, crooked half-timbered buildings line quiet lanes. Thriving markets and a large student population enhance the city's relaxed vibe. Add quick access to the Broads and Norfolk's beaches, and you have an excellent base from which to explore.

Sights

★**Norwich Cathedral** CATHEDRAL
(www.cathedral.org.uk; The Close; donations requested; 7.30am-6pm) Norwich's most impressive landmark is a magnificent Anglican cathedral. Its barbed spire soars higher than any in England except Salisbury's, while the size of its cloisters is second to none. Highlights include the mesmerising ceiling and striking modern features of the **Hostry**, where high-tech displays explore the cathedral's past. The one-hour **guided tours** (donation requested, hourly Monday to Saturday, 11am to 3pm) are an engaging way to find out more.

Work started on the cathedral in 1096 and it remains one of the finest Anglo-Norman abbey churches in the country. The sheer size of its nave is striking, but its most renowned feature is the superb Gothic rib vaulting added in 1463. Among the spidery stonework are 1200 sculpted roof bosses depicting Bible stories. Together they represent one of the finest achievements of English medieval masonry.

Similar bosses can be seen in closer detail in the cathedral's remarkable, two-storey **cloisters**. Built between 1297 and 1430, they are unique in England and were originally built to house a community of about 100 monks.

Norwich

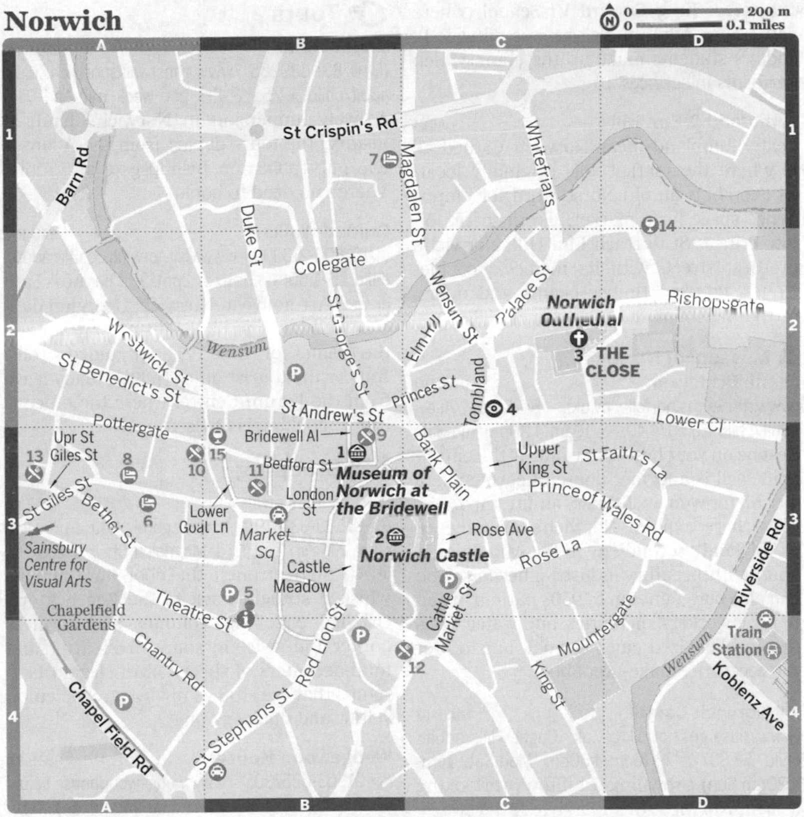

Norwich

Top Sights

1 Museum of Norwich at the Bridewell ... B3
2 Norwich Castle ... B3
3 Norwich Cathedral ... C2

Sights

4 Tombland & Elm Hill ... C2

Activities, Courses & Tours

Ghost Walks ... (see 14)
5 Guided Walks ... B3

Sleeping

6 38 St Giles ... A3
7 Gothic House ... B1
8 St Giles House ... A3

Eating

9 Bishops ... B3
10 Grosvenor Fish Bar ... A3
11 Library ... B3
Mustard ... (see 1)
12 No 12 ... C4
13 Roger Hickman's ... A3

Drinking & Nightlife

14 Adam & Eve ... D1
15 Birdcage ... B3

Above the bronze font (which came from a nearby chocolate factory), look out for *Censing Angel* (2012) – a suspended celestial figure woven out of willow branches by sculptor Joy Whiddett, trailing the words 'peace', 'hope' and 'love'.

Outside the cathedral's eastern end is the grave of the WWI heroine Edith Cavell, a Norfolk-born nurse who was executed for helping hundreds of Allied soldiers escape from German-occupied Belgium. The handsome cathedral close also contains the old

chapel of King Edward VI School (where naval hero Admiral Nelson was educated). Today's students make up the choir, which performs in services.

Tombland & Elm Hill AREA

Leafy Tombland, near Norwich Cathedral, is where the market was originally located ('tomb' is an old Norse word for empty, hence space for a market). From there, follow Princes St to reach Elm Hill, Norwich's prettiest street, with its medieval cobblestones, crooked timber beams and doors, intriguing shops and tucked-away cafes.

★ Museum of Norwich at the Bridewell MUSEUM

(www.museums.norfolk.gov.uk; Bridewell Alley; adult/child £5.50/4.40; ⌚10am-4.30pm Tue-Sat) Best be on your best behaviour: 14th-century Bridewell is a former house of correction, a 'prison for women, beggars and tramps'. Displays here explore Norwich's prominence as England's second city in the Middle Ages and its 19th-century industrial heritage. You can also play games in a 1950s parlour, listen to shoe workers' memories, and watch films in a pocket-sized cinema. Look out too for the eccentric, snake-proof boot.

★ Norwich Castle MUSEUM

(www.museums.norfolk.gov.uk; Castle Hill; adult/child £8.80/7; ⌚10am-4.30pm Mon-Sat, 1pm-4.30pm Sun) Crowning a hilltop overlooking central Norwich, this massive, 12th-century castle is one of England's best-preserved examples of Anglo-Norman military architecture. Its superb **interactive museum** crams in lively exhibits on Boudica, the Iceni, the Anglo-Saxons and the Vikings. Perhaps the best bit though is the atmospheric keep itself with its graphic displays on grisly punishments meted out in its days as a medieval prison. Twice-daily **guided tours** (adult/child £3.50/2.80) run around the battlements and creepy dungeons.

Sainsbury Centre for Visual Arts GALLERY

(www.scva.ac.uk; University of East Anglia; ⌚10am-6pm Tue-Fri, to 5pm Sat & Sun) FREE The region's most important centre for the arts is housed in the first major public building by renowned architect Norman Foster. Its eclectic collections include works by Picasso, Moore, Degas and Bacon, and are displayed beside curios from Africa, the Pacific and the Americas.

The gallery is in the University of East Anglia's grounds, 2 miles west of the city centre. To get there take bus 25, 22 or 26.

Tours

Ghost Walks WALKING

(☎07831 189985; www.ghostwalksnorwich.co.uk; adult/child £7/5; ⌚2-3 per week mid-Apr–Dec) A lively immersion in Norwich's haunted history; the tours depart from the Adam & Eve pub (p398) on Bishopsgate at 7.30pm. There's no need to book.

Guided Walks WALKING

(☎01603-213999; www.visitnorwich.co.uk; adult/child £5/1.50; ⌚11am or 2pm, 2-12 per week Easter-Oct) Art-nouveau Norwich, Georgian dandies and 1000 years of history are among the themes for these 1½-hour guided strolls. Run by the tourist office (p398), many leave from the Forum Centre, where the office is based; booking is advised.

Sleeping

Gothic House B&B ££

(☎01603-631879; www.gothic-house-norwich.com; King's Head Yard, Magdalen St; s/d £65/95; P 📶) Step through the door here and be whisked straight back to the Regency era. Original panelling, columns and cornices border the swirling stairs; fresh fruit and mini-decanters of sherry sit in elegant bedrooms that are studies in olive green, lemon yellow and duck-egg blue.

Wedgewood House B&B ££

(☎01603-625730; www.wedgewoodhouse.co.uk; 42 St Stephens Road; d £80-90; P 📶) The vibrant throws, contemporary prints, central location and parking all appeal at this homely B&B. But it's the breakfasts that really shine: home-baked bread, homemade yoghurt and no fewer than 10 jams and marmalades concocted by the owner – the rhubarb and ginger and the pink grapefruit and lemon are particularly zingy.

No 15 B&B ££

(☎01603-250283; www.number15bedandbreakfast.co.uk; 15 Grange Rd; s/d £55/75; 📶) The breakfasts at this vegetarian B&B are packed with treats: organic eggs, veggie sausages, artisan-baked walnut bread and grilled halloumi cheese. The furnishings are low allergy, but high on style – expect sanded wooden furniture, soft lights and bright fabrics. It's a mile west of the centre; bus 25 runs nearby.

★ 38 St Giles B&B £££

(☎01603-662944; www.38stgiles.co.uk; 38 St Giles St; s/ste £95/245, d £130-160; P 📶) At boutique 38 St Giles it seems everything gleams –

CAMBRIDGE & EAST ANGLIA NORWICH

WORTH A TRIP

HAUNTED BLICKLING HALL

Largely remodelled in the 17th century for Sir Henry Hobart, James I's chief justice, **Blickling Hall** (NT; www.nationaltrust.org.uk; Blickling; adult/child £12.65/6.80; ⌚house noon-5pm Wed-Mon Easter-Oct, grounds 11am-4pm Wed-Sun; P) began life in the 11th century as a manor house and bishop's palace. The grand Jacobean state rooms are stuffed with fine Georgian furniture, pictures and tapestries; the plaster ceiling in the Long Gallery is spectacular. The estate's vast parklands are criss-crossed with cycling and walking routes.

In 1437 the isolated house was claimed by the Boleyn family and passed through the generations to Thomas, father of Anne Boleyn. Anne was executed by her husband Henry VIII in 1533, who opted to have her beheaded. It's said that on the anniversary of her death a coach drives up to the house, drawn by headless horses, driven by headless coachmen and containing the queen with her head on her lap.

Blickling Hall is 15 miles north of Norwich off the A140.

from the highly polished floorboards to the aged cherry-red sofas. Mustard yellow and rich rugs add another layer of charm, while breakfast time brings local and organic meats and eggs, plus home-baked bread.

St Giles House HOTEL £££
(☎01603-275180; www.stgileshousehotel.com; 41 St Giles St; d/ste £130/220; P 📶) There's more than a whiff of art nouveau about luxurious St Giles House; built in 1919, it teams a grand entrance hall with an ornate facade. Period flourishes echo on into bedrooms that are full of bold patterns and fluid curves – the spa, bistro and cocktail terrace are rather splendid too.

Eating

Grosvenor Fish Bar FISH & CHIPS £
(www.fshshop.com; 28 Lower Goat Lane; mains from £5; ⌚11am-7.30pm Mon-Sat) At this groovy chippy-with-a-difference, chips come with fresh cod goujons, sea-bass wraps come with spicy mango salsa and a 'Big Mack' is crispy mackerel fillet tucked into a bread roll. Take away or chow down on the benches inside.

Mustard CAFE £
(www.mustardcoffeebar.co.uk; 3 Bridewell Alley; snacks/mains £2/7; ⌚8am-5pm Mon-Sat; 📶) You'll find a suitably bright-yellow colour scheme at this funky, student-friendly cafe set on the site of the original Colman's Mustard shop. Quality dishes delight in being homemade (think warm pitta stuffed full of halloumi and roasted peppers) and include rarities such as chorizo Scotch eggs. They even roast their own coffee beans.

Bishops MODERN BRITISH ££
(☎01603-767321; www.bishopsrestaurant.co.uk; 8 St Andrew's Hill; lunch/dinner 2 courses £15/29; ⌚noon-2.30pm & 6-9.45pm Tue-Sat) Unusual, unexpected and Norfolk ingredients are the mainstays of menus at Bishops. Sample smoked eel with horseradish, pigeon Wellington or slow-braised Suffolk pork belly. Then satisfy your sweet tooth with a mocha fondant and salted-caramel ice cream.

Library BRASSERIE ££
(☎01603-616606; www.thelibraryrestaurant.co.uk; 4a Guildhall Hill; mains £12-20; ⌚noon-2.30pm & 6-10pm Mon-Sat, noon-4pm Sun) The chef here has a penchant for grilling over woodsmoke; those flavours infuse everything from chicken, lamb and beef to fennel seeds. It's a hit, as is the setting – with Victorian bookcases lining the walls of what was once a library, dining here has a clublike feel.

No 12 BISTRO ££
(www.number12norwich.org; 12 Farmers Ave; mains £7-15; ⌚noon-3pm & 5-8.30pm Mon-Sat, noon-3pm Sun) Lounge music plays, heather-hued tartan covers the walls, beams sit above beige-leather bar stools: it sounds weird but it works. Food ranges from light lunch standards to truffle-infused risotto and beef *bourguignon*.

★**Roger Hickman's** MODERN BRITISH £££
(☎01603-633522; www.rogerhickmansrestaurant.com; 79 Upper St Giles St; dinner 2/3/7 courses £36/45/60; ⌚noon-2.30pm & 7-10pm Tue-Sat) Understated elegance is everywhere here: pale floorboards, white linen and unobtrusive service. Dishes might include venison with figs, monkfish with octopus, or pork-cheek terrine –

flair, imagination and a simple dedication to quality run right through. The lunches (two/three courses £20/25) are a cracking deal.

Drinking & Nightlife

★Birdcage PUB
(www.thebirdcagenorwich.co.uk; 23 Pottergate; 11am-midnight;) Formica tables, chilled tunes, cupcakes and cocktails make this beatnik drinking den a one-of-a-kind delight. Drop by for a Bums Life Drawing session (yes, really) and classy nibbles; or ferry in fish and chips from the shop over the lane.

Adam & Eve PUB
(Bishopsgate; 11am-11pm Mon-Sat, noon-10.30pm Sun) Norwich's oldest-surviving pub has been slaking thirst since 1249, when the cathedral builders used to drop by. Tiny, with a sunken floor and part-panelled walls, it attracts a mixed band of regulars, choristers and ghost hunters, drawn by the fine malt whiskies and real ales.

Information

Tourist Office (01603-213999; www.visitnorwich.co.uk; Millennium Plain; 9.30am-5.30pm Mon-Sat, plus 10.30am-3.30pm Sun mid-Jul–mid-Sep) Inside the Forum Centre.

Getting There & Away

AIR

Norwich International Airport (www.norwichinternational.com) is 4 miles north of town. Connections go to Amsterdam, Aberdeen, Edinburgh, Exeter and Manchester year-round; there are also summer flights to Spain and the Channel Islands.

BUS

The **bus station** (Queen's Rd) is 400m south of the castle. Follow Red Lion St into St Stephen's St and then turn left on to Surrey St. **National Express** (www.nationalexpress.com) and **First** (www.firstgroup.com) are among the operators:

Cromer Bus X44; £3.60, one hour, hourly
King's Lynn Bus X1; £9, 1½ hours, hourly
London Victoria £10, three hours, every two hours

CAR

Norwich has free parking at six Park & Ride locations. Buses (£3.50) run to the city centre up to every 15 minutes from around 7am to 7pm, Monday to Saturday.

TRAIN

The train station is off Thorpe Rd, 600m east of the castle.

Cambridge £17, 1¼ hours, hourly
Ely £12, one hour, twice hourly
London Liverpool St £20, two hours, two per hour

COASTHOPPER BUS

- The **Coasthopper Bus** (www.coasthopper.co.uk) runs from Cromer to King's Lynn; stops include Cley, Blakeney, Wells, Holkham and Burnham Deepdale.
- Services are frequent from April to September; less so the rest of the year.
- Single fares start at £1.40; passes are also available (one/three/seven days £9.50/20/33).

Cromer

POP 7949

The once-fashionable Victorian resort of Cromer is a relaxed mix of old-school English seaside resort and appealing fishing port. Here, brightly painted houses line narrow lanes dotted with nonchain shops. Its main attractions remain sweet-tasting Cromer crab, the atmospheric pier and an appealing stretch of pebbly shore.

Sights

Henry Blogg Museum MUSEUM
(Lifeboat Museum; www.rnlicromer.org.uk; The Gangway; 10am-5pm Tue-Sun Apr-Sep, to 4pm Oct-Mar) FREE Tap out a message in Morse and spell your name in semaphore flags – hands-on gizmos add to the appeal of this excellent museum, as do the well-told tales of brave sea rescues and the WWII lifeboat sitting proudly inside.

Felbrigg Hall HISTORIC BUILDING
(NT; www.nationaltrust.org.uk; Felbrigg; adult/child £9.90/4.70; 11am-5pm Sat-Wed Mar-Sep, to 4pm Oct; P) An elegant Jacobean mansion boasting a fine Georgian interior and splendid facade, as well as gorgeous walled gardens and an orangery. It's 2 miles southwest of Cromer, off the B1436

Sleeping & Eating

★Red Lion INN ££
(01263-514964; www.redlioncromer.co.uk; Brook St; s £63-95, d £115-140, ste £150-180;

P) Coloured floor tiles, wooden banisters and stained glass signal this seafront inn's 18th-century heritage; stylish, sea-themed rooms bring it right up to date. All bedrooms come with baths, cafetière coffee and fresh milk – the pick is the suite (room 7), where you can see the sea from both the balcony and the tub. The cosy, flint-walled, sea-view bar is the ideal spot to down a pint.

★ Davies SEAFOOD **£**

(7 Garden St; crab £3.50-6; 8.30am-5pm Mon-Sat, 10am-4pm Sun Apr-Oct, 8.30am-4pm Tue-Sat Nov-Mar) Less a fish shop, more a local institution – at Davies the crab is caught by its own day boat (the *Richard William*) and is boiled, cracked and dressed on-site. Other treats include cockles, mussels and homemade pâté; the mackerel and horseradish one has quite a kick.

Rocket House CAFE **£**

(www.rockethousecafe.co.uk; The Gangway; mains £5-10; 9am-4pm Mon-Fri, 10am-5pm Sat & Sun) Set right on the seafront, Rocket House delivers an airy interior and a balcony that almost overhangs the waves. Light dishes include ploughman's with Norfolk Dapple and Binham Blue cheese, locally smoked mackerel salad, and their renowned Cromer crab platter.

They're also open on summer Saturday evenings (6pm to 9.30pm from mid-May to September); it's best to book.

Getting There & Away

Trains run to Norwich (£7, 45 minutes, hourly). The **Coasthopper Bus** (www.coasthopper.co.uk) shuttles west along the coast to King's Lynn, roughly every half-hour in summer.

Cley-next-the-Sea

POP 450

As the name suggests, the sleepy village of Cley (pronounced 'cly') huddles beside the shore. Here, a cluster of pretty cottages surrounds a photogenic windmill, and bird-rich marshes fan out all around.

Sights

Cley Marshes NATURE RESERVE

(www.norfolkwildlifetrust.org.uk; near Cley-next-the-Sea; adult/child £5/free; dawn-dusk; P) One of England's premier birdwatching sites, Cley Marshes has more than 300 resident bird species, plentiful migrants and a network of walking trails and bird hides amid its golden reeds.

Even if you're not into birdwatching, don't miss the (free) cafe-cum-visitor centre where seats and telescopes line up beside vast picture windows with panoramic reserve views. This is birdwatching for softies; sip a latte while enjoying zoomed-in images of marsh harriers.

Sleeping & Eating

★ Cley Windmill B&B **£££**

(01263 740209; www.cleymill.co.uk; High St; d £160-200, apt per week £570; P) With the kind of wonky walls you'd expect from a circular, 18th-century agricultural building, Cley Windmill is packed with character. Rooms are named after their former functions (the crazy-shaped Barley Bin is gorgeous), and many look out directly over reed-filled salt marshes. A sweet, four-person self-catering cottage sits just next door.

George INN **£££**

(01263-740652; www.thegeorgehotelatcley.co.uk; High St; d £120-345) The George may be an age-old English inn, but the style is all contemporary north-Norfolk chic. Sure-footed design sees bare floorboards and feature fireplaces teamed with upcycled armchairs and quirky chests of drawers. Opt for a room overlooking the marshes for mesmerising views of wind-ruffled reeds.

★ Picnic Fayre DELI **£**

(www.picnic-fayre.co.uk; High St; 9am-5pm Mon-Sat, 10am-4pm Sun) A deli to ditch the diet for, crammed full of imaginative versions of English picnic classics – pork pies with chorizo, sausages smothered with sweet chill sauce, and home-baked lavender bread. Plus gooey homemade fudge and Portuguese custard tarts. Yum.

Cley Smokehouse DELI **£**

(www.cleysmokehouse.com; High St; 9.30am-4.30pm) Flavour-packed, home-smoked fish, shellfish and cured meats.

Information

Visitor Centre (www.norfolkwildlifetrust.org.uk; Cley Marshes; 10am-5pm Apr-Oct, to 4pm Nov-Mar) Here, seats and telescopes line up beside vast picture windows with panoramic views of the bird reserve. There's a cafe too.

EXPLORING THE NORFOLK BROADS

Why Should I Wish to Visit a Swamp?

These vast wetlands were formed when the rivers Wensum, Bure, Waveney and Yare flooded the big gaping holes inland, which had been dug by 12th-century crofters looking for peat. They comprise fragile ecosystems and, protected as a national park, are home to some of the UK's rarest plants and birds – the appeal to birdwatchers and naturalists is obvious. Apart from that, if you've ever envisioned yourself captaining your own boat and living afloat, there are 125 miles of lock-free waterways to explore. Or if paddling a canoe and losing yourself in the hypnotic lapping of water away from the rest of humanity appeals, there's plenty of scope for that, too.

What Is There to See and Do that Doesn't Involve Water?

Museum of the Broads (☎01692-581681; www.museumofthebroads.org.uk; The Staithe, Stalham; adult/child £5/2.50; ⊙10am-4pm Easter-Oct) Five miles north of Potter Heigham off the A149, this museum features fine boats and colourful displays on the local marshmen, their traditional lifestyles, peat extraction and modern conservation. You can ride on a steam launch too.

Toad Hole Cottage (How Hill; ⊙10.30am-5pm Mon-Sat Apr-Oct) FREE The life of Fen dwellers is revealed at this tiny cottage, which shows how an eel-catcher's family lived and the tools they used to work surrounding marshes.

Bewilderwood (www.bewilderwood.co.uk; Hornig Rd, Hoveton; adult/child £15.50/13.50; ⊙10am-5.30pm Easter-Oct) A forest playground for children and adults alike, with zip wires, jungle bridges, tree houses and old-fashioned outdoor adventure involving plenty of mud, mazes and marsh walks.

St Helen's Church (Ranworth; ⊙9am-5pm) The Broads' most impressive ecclesiastical attraction is this 14th-century church, known locally as the 'Cathedral of the Broads'. It features a magnificent painted medieval rood screen and a 15th-century *antiphoner* – a rare illustrated book of prayers.

Bure Valley Steam Railway (www.bvrw.co.uk; Aylsham; adult/child return £13/6.50; ⊙2-6 trains daily Apr-Oct; P) Steam buffs will love this train, which puffs along 9 miles of narrow-gauge tracks between Aylsham and Wroxham. You can make the return trip by boat.

Blakeney

POP 801

The pretty village of Blakeney was once a busy fishing and trading port before its harbour silted up. These days it offers an inviting seafront walk lined with yachts, and boat trips out to a 500-strong colony of common and grey seals that live, bask and breed on nearby Blakeney Point.

Tours

Bishop's Boats BOATING

(☎01263-740753; www.bishopsboats.com; Blakeney Quay; adult/child £12/6; ⊙1-4 daily Apr-Oct) Hour-long trips to see the seals at Blakeney Point; the best time to come is between June and August when the common seals pup.

Beans Seal Trips BOATING

(☎01263-740505; www.beansboattrips.co.uk; Morston Quay; adult/child £12/6; ⊙1-4 daily Apr-Oct) Boat journeys out to the hundreds-strong Blakeney Point seal colony. The departure point is Morston Quay, 1½ miles east of Blakeney.

Sleeping & Eating

Kings Arms INN ££

(☎01263-740341; www.blakeneykingsarms.co.uk; Westgate St; s/d £60/80; P) Sweet, simple, old-style rooms (expect bright colours and pine) in a pub that's so welcoming you might not want to leave. Order some substantial pub grub (its fish and chips are famous; mains from £8 to £15; meals served noon to 9pm) then, for some great theatre gossip, ask landlady Marjorie about her career on the stage.

How Do I Get Around?

Driving around the Broads is missing the point and pretty useless. The key centres of Wroxham, on the A1151 from Norwich, and Potter Heigham, on the A1062 from Wroxham, are reachable by bus from Norwich and Great Yarmouth, respectively. From there, you can either take to the water or to the trails.

Exploring by Boat

Launches range from large cabin cruisers to little craft with outboards; they can be hired for anything from a couple of hours' gentle messing about on the water to week-long trips. Tuition is given. Depending on boat size, facilities and season, an eight-person boat costs from around £18 per hour, from £68 for four hours and from £114 for one day. Week-long rental ranges from around £660 to £1330, including fuel and insurance. **Broadland Day Boats** (☎01692-667659; www.dayboathire.com; Ludham) hires boats and canoes. **Barnes Brinkcraft** (☎01603-782625; www.barnesbrinkcraft.co.uk; Wroxham) does short- and long-term rental, while **Broads Tours** (☎01603-782207; www.broads.co.uk; Wroxham) lets out boats by the day and week, and runs boat trips. **Blakes** (☎0345-498 6184; www.blakes.co.uk) arranges all manner of boating holidays.

Exploring by Canoe

Paddlers can find canoes for hire for £27 to £35 per day; **Rowan Craft** (www.rowancraft.com; Geldeston) and **Waveney River Centre** (www.waveneyrivercentre.co.uk; Burgh St Peter) are recommended. **Mark the Canoe Man** (www.thecanoeman.com; half-day trips £25) knows the secrets of the Broads and arranges guided trips to areas the cruisers can't reach (from £25), as well as offering canoe and kayak hire, weekend camping canoe trails (two nights £65) and two-day canoe and bushcraft trips (adult/child £175/125).

Exploring by Foot & Bike

A web of walking trails stretches across the region, including the 61-mile **Weavers' Way**, which stretches from Cromer to Great Yarmouth, taking in some choice landscapes along the way. The Broads' highest point, How Hill, is just 12m above sea level, so superhero levels of fitness are not required. The section between Aylsham and Stalham is open to bicycles.

Broadland Cycle Hire (www.norfolkbroadscycling.co.uk) and **Martha's Cottage** (www.marthascottagecyclehire.co.uk; Barnby) are among the bicycle-rental firms. Expect to pay between £12 and £18 per day; child seats and tandems are also available.

Moorings MODERN BRITISH ££

(☎01263-740054; www.blakeney-moorings.co.uk; High St; mains £7-22; ⌚10.30am-9pm Tue-Sat, to 5pm Sun) Perfectly pitched fish dishes have won this bistro a loyal following – try the roast monkfish with squid and tangy harissa, or keep it simple with avocado-dotted sweet local crab; the classic meat and veg dishes are tempting too. Mustn't-miss puddings include plum crumble with custard, and a gooey treacle sponge.

Wells-next-the-Sea

POP 2165

Charming Wells excels at both land and sea. Rows of attractive Georgian houses and flint cottages snake down to a boat-lined quay; to the north sits a vast golden beach, backed by pine-covered dunes.

Sights

Wells Beach BEACH

(Ⓟ) Fringed by dense pine forests and undulating dunes, Wells' sandy shore stretches for miles to the west, with brightly coloured beach huts clustering beside the water and wooden steps leading up into the woods. It's all tucked away at the end of a mile-long road; you can walk, drive or hop on a miniature train. Parking is available.

Wells & Walsingham Railway HERITAGE RAILWAY

(www.wellswalsinghamrailway.co.uk; Stiffkey Rd; adult/child return £9/7; ⌚4-5 trains daily Apr-Oct; Ⓟ) The longest 10.25in narrow-gauge railway in the world puffs for 5 picturesque miles from Wells to the village of Little Walsingham, the site of religious shrines and the ruined but still impressive Walsingham Abbey.

Sleeping & Eating

Wells YHA HOSTEL £
(☎0845-371 9544; www.yha.org.uk; Church Plains; dm £20-26, d £49-65; P) Set in the heart of town in an ornately gabled early-20th-century church hall.

★Old Customs House B&B ££
(☎01328-711463; www.eastquay.co.uk; East Quay; s £80-90, d £100-110; P ☎) The stately but comfy feel here comes courtesy of worn wood panels, alcoves full of books and gorgeous creek views. Choose from the snug Captain's Quarters or a grand four-poster room. Breakfasts see you discussing what you'd like with the owner – perhaps goats-cheese omelette or smoked haddock.

Wells Beach Cafe CAFE £
(Wells Beach; mains £4; ⏲10am-5pm Easter-Oct, to 4pm Nov-Easter; ☎) This locals' favourite rustles up bacon baps, homemade chilli and decadent hot chocolates. Outside sits a corral of picnic tables; inside there's a wood-burning stove for when the wind whips in.

Crown BRITISH ££
(☎01328-710209; www.crownhotelnorfolk.co.uk; The Buttlands; mains £7-20; ⏲noon-2.30pm & 6-9pm) Renowned for robust dishes made from locally sourced ingredients.

Information

Tourist Office (☎01328-710885; www.visitnorthnorfolk.com; Staithe St; ⏲10am-4pm Mon-Sat, to 1pm Sun Apr-Oct)

Holkham

Little Holkham may have only two big assets, but both are highly impressive: a grand country-house estate and a spectacular stretch of sandy shore.

Sights

★Holkham National Nature Reserve WILDLIFE RESERVE
(www.holkham.co.uk; parking per 2hr/day £3/6.50) Beach, dunes, salt marsh, grazing marsh, pinewoods and scrub – a high number of habitats pack into 37-sq-km Holkham Reserve. It's easily accessed from the car park at Lady Anne's Dr in Holkham village. From there, ribboning pathways lead through forests, via bird hides and on to an expansive, pristine shore.

Holkham Hall & Estate HISTORIC BUILDING
(www.holkham.co.uk; Holkham; adult/child £15/7.50, parking £3; ⏲noon-4pm Sun, Mon & Thu Apr-Oct; P) Holkham Hall is the ancestral seat of the original Earl of Leicester and still belongs to his descendants. A severe Palladian mansion, it's largely unadorned on the outside but the interior is sumptuous, with a red velvet–lined saloon, copies of Greek and Roman statues, the luxurious Green State Bedroom, and fluted columns in the Marble Hall. It's set in a vast deer park (open 9.30am to 5pm daily), which was designed by William Kent.

Burnham Deepdale

POP 800

Walkers flock to this lovely coastal spot, with the tiny village of Burnham Deepdale (which merges seamlessly into Brancaster Staithe) strung along a rural road. Edged by the beautiful Norfolk Coast Path, surrounded by beaches and reedy marshes, alive with bird life and criss-crossed by cycling routes, Burnham Deepdale is also the base for a whole host of water sports.

Sights

Titchwell Marsh NATURE RESERVE
(RSPB; www.rspb.org.uk; Titchwell; parking £5; ⏲dawn-dusk; P) Tiny Titchwell has a big asset: the Titchwell Marsh Nature Reserve, where marshland, sandbars and lagoons attract vast numbers of birds. Summer brings marsh harriers, avocets, terns and nesting bearded tits; in winter you'll see more than 20 species of wading birds and countless ducks and geese.

Titchwell Marsh is some 2 miles west of Burnham Deepdale.

Sleeping & Eating

Deepdale Farm HOSTEL £
(☎01485-210256; www.deepdalefarm.co.uk; Burnham Deepdale; dm £25-30, d £30-60, camping £10-20; P @ ☎) For backpackers it really doesn't get much better than Deepdale Farm: spick-and-span en-suite dorms and doubles in converted stables, a homely well-equipped kitchen, a barbecue area,

WORTH A TRIP

THE QUEEN'S SANDRINGHAM ESTATE

Both monarchists and those bemused by the English system will have plenty to mull over at **Sandringham** (www.sandringhamestate.co.uk; Sandringham; adult/child £14/7; 11am-4.45pm Easter-Sep, to 3.45pm Oct; P), the Queen's country estate. It's set in 25 hectares of beautifully landscaped gardens, and wandering around sumptuous reception rooms regularly used by the royals reveals a wealth of objets d'art and glinting gifts from European and Russian royal families.

Sandringham was built in 1870 by the then Prince and Princess of Wales (who later became King Edward VII and Queen Alexandra) and the house's features and furnishings remain much as they were in Edwardian days. The stables, meanwhile, now house a flag-waving museum filled with diverse royal memorabilia. The superb vintage-car collection includes the very first royal motor from 1900, and the buggy in which the Queen Mother would bounce around race tracks.

There are **guided tours** (£3.50, 11am & 2pm Wed & Sat) of the gardens. The shop stocks organic goodies produced on the vast estate. Sandringham is 6 miles northeast of King's Lynn off the A149. Bus 11 runs from King's Lynn (£4.70, 30 minutes, hourly).

and a cosy lounge warmed by a wood-burning stove. Campers get to go glam in a tepee or yurt, or casual in a good old tent.

★**Titchwell Manor** HOTEL £££
(01485-210221; www.titchwellmanor.com; Titchwell; d £125-235; P@) Dreamy Titchwell Manor is a swish, oh-so-contemporary hotel set in a grand Victorian house; expect lovingly upcycled furniture and bold colours in chic rooms ranging from those beside the herb-garden courtyard to ones with corking sea views. The stylish restaurant and terrace set the scene for modern tapas and acclaimed à la carte dishes (mains £12 to £31; food served from noon to 2pm and 6pm to 9pm).

★**White Horse** MODERN BRITISH ££
(01485-210262; www.whitehorsebrancaster.co.uk; Main Rd, Brancaster Staithe; mains £13-22; 11am-9pm; P) The White Horse gastropub's imaginative menu more than sets it apart from its competitors. Choose from seafood and tapas-style dishes including brown crab custard, cod and dill, scorched bass or tempura Brancaster oysters. The bedrooms (doubles £140 to £230) embody the seaside with their subtle colour schemes.

Information

Tourist Office (01485-210256; www.deepdalefarm.co.uk; Burnham Deepdale; 8am-11am & 2-8pm Mon-Sat, to 7pm Sun)

King's Lynn & Around

POP 12,200

Once one of England's most important ports, King's Lynn was long known as 'the Warehouse on the Wash'. In its heyday, it was said you could cross from one side of the River Great Ouse to the other by simply stepping from boat to boat. Something of the salty port-town tang can still be felt in old King's Lynn, with its cobbled lanes, vibrant weekly markets, and narrow streets flanked by old merchants' houses.

Sights

King's Lynn Minster CHURCH
(St Margaret's Church; www.stmargaretskingslynn.org.uk; St Margaret's Pl; 8am-6pm) The patchwork of styles here includes Flemish brasses and a remarkable 17th-century moon dial, which tells the tide, not the time. You'll find historic flood-level markings by the west door.

Opposite, the 1421 Trinity Guildhall has an attractive stone facade.

Stories of Lynn MUSEUM
(www.kingslynntownhall.com; Saturday Market Pl; adult/child £5/3.50; 10am-4.30pm) A £2-million revamp has seen archive sources converted into multimedia exhibits, so you'll experience the stories of local seafarers, explorers, mayors and ne'er-do-wells. It's all set in the 15th-century Guildhall and parts of the town's Georgian jail, where you get to roam around the cells.

Lynn Museum MUSEUM
(www.museums.norfolk.gov.uk; Market St; adult/child £4.20/3.20; ⏲10am-5pm Tue-Sat, noon-4pm Sun) High points here include a large hoard of Iceni gold coins and the Seahenge Gallery, which tells the story behind the construction and preservation of the early Bronze Age timber circle, which survived for 4000 years, despite being submerged on the Norfolk shoreline – it was only discovered in 1998. The exhibits include a life-size replica of the monument, which you can stand inside.

True's Yard MUSEUM
(www.truesyard.co.uk; North St; adult/child £3/1.50; ⏲10am-4pm Tue-Sat) Housed in two restored fishers' cottages – the only remainder of the district's once bustling, fiercely independent fishing community – this museum explores the lives and traditions of the fisherfolk, who were packed like sardines into cottages such as these.

Castle Rising CASTLE
(www.castlerising.co.uk; Castle Rising; adult/child £4.50/3; ⏲10am-6pm Apr-Oct, to 4pm Wed-Sun Nov-Mar; P) There's something bordering on ecclesiastical about the beautifully embellished keep of this castle, built in 1138 and set in the middle of a massive earthwork – unsurprisingly it shares stonemasons with some of East Anglia's finest cathedrals. Castle Rising was also once the home of Queen Isabella, who (allegedly) arranged the gruesome murder of her husband, Edward II. It's 4 miles northeast of King's Lynn. Bus 11 runs here (£2, 15 minutes, hourly).

Houghton Hall HISTORIC BUILDING
(www.houghtonhall.com; near King's Lynn; adult/child £15/5; ⏲11am-4.30pm Wed, Thu & Sun May-late Sep; P) Built for Britain's first de-facto prime minister, Sir Robert Walpole, in 1730, the grand Palladian-style Houghton Hall is worth seeing for the ornate staterooms alone, where stunning interiors overflow with gilt, tapestries, velvets and period furniture. The surrounding grounds, home to 600 deer, and the 2-hectare walled garden are dotted with contemporary sculptures, making for grand but pleasant rambling. Houghton Hall is just off the A148, 13 miles east of King's Lynn.

Festivals & Events

King's Lynn Festival CULTURAL
(www.kingslynnfestival.org.uk; ⏲Jul) East Anglia's most important cultural gathering, with a diverse mix of music, from medieval ballads to opera, as well as literary talks.

Sleeping & Eating

★ **Bank House** BOUTIQUE HOTEL ££
(☎01553-660492; www.thebankhouse.co.uk; King's Staithe Sq; s £85-129, d £115-220; P 📶) There's so much to love here: a quayside setting, gently funky decor and luxury bathrooms all make this stylish Georgian town house pretty hard to turn down. The best bedroom (the expansive Captain's Room) is gorgeous; but even cheaper, river-view 'Cosy' is still charming.

Downstairs, the hip purple and pink themed brasserie (dishes £5 to £14; served noon to 8.30pm) serves seriously good modern British food.

Market Bistro MODERN BRITISH ££
(☎01553-771483; www.marketbistro.co.uk; 11 Saturday Market Pl; mains £14-22; ⏲noon-2pm & 6-8.30pm Tue-Sat) A commitment to Norfolk ingredients has won this friendly, family-run eatery heaps of fans. Seasonal specials might include succulent local asparagus with quail egg or pan-fried haddock with pickled cockles and seaweed sauce. A combo of their small dishes (£3 to £4) is ideal for a light lunch.

Information

Tourist Office (☎01553-763044; www.visitwestnorfolk.com; Purfleet Quay; ⏲10am-5pm Mon-Sat, noon-5pm Sun Apr-Sep, to 4pm Oct-Mar) Arranges guided heritage walks (adult/child £5/1) at 2pm Tuesdays, Fridays and Saturdays between May and October.

Getting There & Away

Bus The **Coasthopper** (www.coasthopper.co.uk) bus runs from King's Lynn along the shore all the way to Cromer (£8.60, 2½ hours).

Train There are hourly trains from Cambridge (£8, 50 minutes) via Ely, and also from London King's Cross (£24, 1¾ hours).

Birmingham, the Midlands & the Marches

Includes ➡

Best Places to Eat

- ➡ The Cross (p422)
- ➡ Hammer & Pincers (p473)
- ➡ Hercules Revived (p472)
- ➡ Chatsworth Estate Farm Shop Cafe (p490)

Best Places to Sleep

- ➡ Warwick Castle Accommodation (p421)
- ➡ George Hotel (p465)
- ➡ Brownsover Hall (p427)
- ➡ Hotel Maiyango (p470)

Why Go?

If you're searching for quintessential English landscapes – green valleys, chocolate-box villages of wonky black-and-white timbered houses, woodlands steeped in legend such as Nottinghamshire's Sherwood Forest, and stately homes that look like the last lord of the manor just clip-clopped out of the stables – you'll find it here in the country's heart.

You'll also find the relics of centuries of industrial history, exemplified by the World Heritage–listed mills of Ironbridge and the Derwent Valley, and by today's dynamic cities, including Britain's second-largest, Birmingham: a canal-woven industrial crucible reinvented as a cultural melting pot and creative hub, with striking 21st-century architecture and red-hot restaurant, bar and nightlife scenes. Beyond them are tumbling hills where the air is so clean you can taste it. Walkers and cyclists flock to these areas, particularly the Peak District National Park and the Shropshire Hills, to vanish into the vastness of the landscape.

When to Go

- ➡ February or March (depending when Lent falls) sees the wonderful chaos of Shrovetide football in Ashbourne.
- ➡ Shakespeare takes a back seat to contemporary wordsmiths at Stratford's Literary Festival in April/May.
- ➡ Foodies will want to head to Ludlow's famous Food and Drink Festival in September.
- ➡ From May to September, the Long Mynd and Stiperstones Shuttle runs from the Carding Mill Valley near Church Stretton to the villages atop the Long Mynd heath and moorland plateau in the glorious Shropshire Hills.
- ➡ June to September is the best season for walking and cycling in the Peak District.

Birmingham, the Midlands & the Marches Highlights

1 Library of Birmingham (p408) Surveying the buzzing city of Birmingham from its library's rooftop 'secret garden'.

2 Peak District (p479) Hiking, cycling or driving through England's inaugural national park.

3 Woolsthorpe Manor (p463) Contemplating the apple tree that inspired Isaac Newton's theories on gravity at his former home.

4 Ironbridge Gorge (p440) Museum-hopping in the birthplace of the Industrial Revolution.

5 King Richard III: Dynasty, Death & Discovery (p467) Learning about King Richard III's life, death and the extraordinary discovery of his remains in Leicester.

6 Stratford-upon-Avon (p422) Visiting the Bard's schoolroom and reimagined town house before catching a Royal Shakespeare Company performance in his Tudor home town.

7 Morgan Motor Company (p432) Touring Great Malvern's venerable car factory and taking a car for a spin through the surrounding hills.

8 Burghley House (p464) Wandering the opulent halls and grand gardens of this stately Stamford home.

North Sea
Humber
Scunthorpe
M180
Grimsby
Doncaster
M1
Rotherham
Gainsborough
Market Rasen
Louth
Sheffield
A57
Worksop
Trent
Eyam
Chatsworth House
Sherwood Forest National Nature Reserve
Tuxford
Lincoln
Horncastle
Skegness
Chesterfield
Bakewell
A1(M1)
Waddington
Spilsby
Hardwick Hall
Matlock Bath
Newstead Abbey
Edwinstowe
Clipstone
A16
Cromford
Newark-on-Trent
Coningsby
Southwell
Witham
A17
Belper
M1
A46
Sleaford
Boston
The Wash
Ashbourne
Nottingham
Derby
Grantham
East Midlands Airport
A38
Woolsthorpe Manor
Wymeswold
Spalding
A17
Burton-upon-Trent
National Forest
Loughborough
Melton Mowbray
A1
The Fens
Packington
A16
Whitwell
Oakham
Stamford
Sutton Cheney
M1
Tamworth
Leicester
Rutland Water
Edith Weston
Burghley House
Peterborough
Drayton Manor
Bosworth Battlefield
A47
Lyddington
A5
Market Harborough
Birmingham Airport
Kettering
Coventry
Rugby
Kenilworth
Stoneleigh Abbey
Althorp House
M40
Warwick
Northampton
Cambridge
Charlecote Park
Sulgrave Manor
Stratford-upon-Avon
Stoke Bruerne
Towcester
M1
Silverstone
Banbury
Milton Keynes
Luton
3
5
6
8

Activities

Famous walking trails such as the **Pennine Way** and **Limestone Way** struggle across the Peak District's hills, while challenging cycling routes include the **Pennine Cycleway**. The Marches, tracing the English–Welsh border, are also wonderful walking territory.

Watersports abound at Rutland Water; Hereford and Ironbridge Gorge offer canoeing and kayaking.

Getting There & Around

Birmingham Airport (BHX; ☎0871 222 0072; www.birminghamairport.co.uk) and **East Midlands Airport** (EMA; ☎0871 271 0711; www.eastmidlandsairport.com), near Derby, are the main air hubs.

There are excellent rail connections to towns across the Midlands. **National Express** (☎08717 818181; www.nationalexpress.com), at Birmingham Coach Station, and local bus companies connect larger towns and villages, though services are reduced in the low season. For general route information, consult **Traveline** (☎0871 200 2233; www.travelinemidlands.co.uk). Ask locally about discounted all-day tickets.

BIRMINGHAM

POP 1,073,045

Regeneration, renewal and grand-scale construction continue at a breathless pace in Britain's second-largest city. A state-of-the-art library, gleaming shopping centre atop revitalised New St Station, beautifully restored Victorian buildings and a tram-line extension through the city's heart are just some of the recently completed initiatives of its Big City Plan. These come hot on the heels of the striking Mailbox and Bullring shopping malls and iconic Selfridges building's 'bubblewrapped' facade. Work has started on the first phase of the centrepiece Paradise development's new hotels, public spaces, and glitzy residential and commercial buildings, due to open in 2018.

Alongside Birmingham's picturesque canals, waterside attractions, outstanding museums and galleries is an explosion of gastronomic restaurants, cool and/or secret cocktail bars and craft breweries. Thriving legacies of the city's industrial heritage include its Jewellery Quarter, Cadbury manufacturing plant and former custard factory turned cutting-edge creative hub. 'Brum', as it's dubbed by locals, is buzzing.

History

Birmingham was first mentioned in the Domesday Book of 1086, where it was described as a small village, home to a handful of villagers and two ploughs, with a total value of £1. From these humble beginnings, Brum exploded into an industrial and mercantile hub, building its fortunes first on the wool trade and then on metalworking from the 16th century.

The Lunar Society brought together the leading geologists, chemists, scientists, engineers and theorists of the mid-18th century and Birmingham became the world's first industrialised town, attracting a tide of workers from across the nation.

In the mid-1800s enlightened mayors such as Joseph Chamberlain (1836–1914) cleaned out the slums and filled the centre with grand civic buildings. Later, WWII bombers and overzealous town planners took their toll, and swaths of the centre were demolished in a bid to transform Birmingham into 'Britain's Motor City'.

Recent years have seen an explosion of regeneration projects, with 21st-century landmarks appearing all over the city.

Sights

City Centre

Birmingham's grandest civic buildings are clustered around pedestrianised **Victoria Square**, at the western end of New St, dominated by the stately facade of **Council House** (Victoria Sq), built between 1874 and 1879. The square was given a facelift in 1993, with modernist sphinxes and a **fountain** topped by a naked female figure, nicknamed 'the floozy in the jacuzzi' by locals, overlooked by a disapproving **statue of Queen Victoria**.

To the west, **Centenary Square** is bookended by the art-deco Hall of Memory War Memorial, the **International Convention Centre** (ICC; Broad St) and Symphony Hall. There's a gleaming golden **statue** of Birmingham's Industrial Revolution leading lights Matthew Boulton, James Watt and William Murdoch. Centenary Sq's showpiece is the spiffing Library of Birmingham.

★**Library of Birmingham** LIBRARY
(www.libraryofbirmingham.com; Centenary Sq; ground fl 9am-9pm Mon & Tue, 11am-9pm Wed-Fri, 11am-5pm Sat, rest of bldg 11am-7pm Mon & Tue, to 5pm Wed-Sat;) Resembling a glittering

BIRMINGHAM IN TWO DAYS

Start off in the centre, dropping into the eclectic **Birmingham Museum & Art Gallery** (below). Walk west through Centenary Sq, stopping to check out the **Library of Birmingham** (p408) before reaching the Birmingham Canals. From here you can take a **canal cruise** (p413) or while away an afternoon at the **National Sea Life Centre** (p410) or **Ikon Gallery** (below). Dine that night at one of Birmingham's cutting-edge restaurants such as **adam's** (p415). On day two, indulge your inner shopaholic at the gleaming shopping malls of the **Bullring** (p417) and **Mailbox** (p417), which both have good options for lunch. In the afternoon, catch up on some social history at the museum **Birmingham Back to Backs** (below). After dark, kick off a pub crawl at the **Lost & Found** (p415).

stack of gift-wrapped presents, the Francine Houben–designed Library of Birmingham is an architectural triumph. Opened in 2013, it features a subterranean amphitheatre, spiralling interior, viewing decks and glass elevator to the 7th-floor 'secret garden' with panoramic views over the city. In addition to its archives, photography and rare-book collections (including Britain's most important Shakespeare collection), there are gallery spaces, 160-plus computers and a cafe. The British Film Institute Mediatheque provides free access to the National Film Archive.

Birmingham Museum & Art Gallery MUSEUM

(☎0121-348 8038; www.birminghammuseums.org.uk; Chamberlain Sq; ⊙10am-5pm Sat-Thu, 10.30am-5pm Fri;) FREE Major Pre-Raphaelite works by Rossetti, Edward Burne-Jones and others are among the highlights of the delightful Birmingham Museum and Art Gallery's impressive collection of ancient treasures and Victorian art.

Birmingham Back to Backs HISTORIC BUILDING

(NT; ☎0121-666 7671; www.nationaltrust.org.uk; 55-63 Hurst St; tours adult/child £7.85/4.55; ⊙1-5pm Tue-Thu, 10am-5pm Fri-Sun) Quirky tours of this cluster of restored back-to-back terraced houses take you through four working-class homes, telling the stories of those who lived here between the 1840s and the 1970s. Book ahead by phone for the compulsory guided tour.

For an even more vivid impression of what life was like here, you can book to stay in basic three-storey period cottages at 52 and 54 Inge St (doubles with wi-fi from £119). Guests receive a free Back to Backs tour.

Town Hall HISTORIC BUILDING

(☎0121-780 3333; www.thsh.co.uk; Victoria Sq) Constructed in 1834 and styled after the Temple of Castor and Pollux in Rome, Birmingham's neoclassical Town Hall is now used as a venue for classical concerts and stage performances.

Birmingham Cathedral CATHEDRAL

(☎0121-262 1840; www.birminghamcathedral.com; Colmore Row; entry by donation; ⊙8am-6.30pm Mon-Fri, 9am-5pm Sat & Sun) Dedicated to St Philip, this small but perfectly formed cathedral was constructed in a neoclassical style between 1709 and 1715. Pre-Raphaelite artist Edward Burne-Jones was responsible for the magnificent stained-glass windows.

Thinktank MUSEUM

(☎0121-348 0000; www.birminghammuseums.org.uk; Millennium Point, Curzon St; adult/child £13/9.50; ⊙10am-5pm) A 10-minute walk northeast of the centre, surrounded by the footprints of vanished factories, the Millennium Point development incorporates this entertaining and ambitious attempt to make science accessible to children. Highlights include galleries on the past (Birmingham's industrial breakthroughs), present (how stuff works) and future, as well as an outdoor science garden and digital planetarium (included in the admission price).

Birmingham Canals

During the industrial age, Birmingham was a major hub on the English canal network and today the city has more miles of canals than Venice. Narrow boats still float through the heart of the city, passing a string of glitzy wharfside developments.

Ikon Gallery GALLERY

(☎0121-248 0708; www.ikon-gallery.org; 1 Oozells Sq; ⊙11am-5pm Tue-Sun) FREE Within the glitzy Brindley Pl development of banking offices and designer restaurants, a converted Gothic schoolhouse contains the

Birmingham

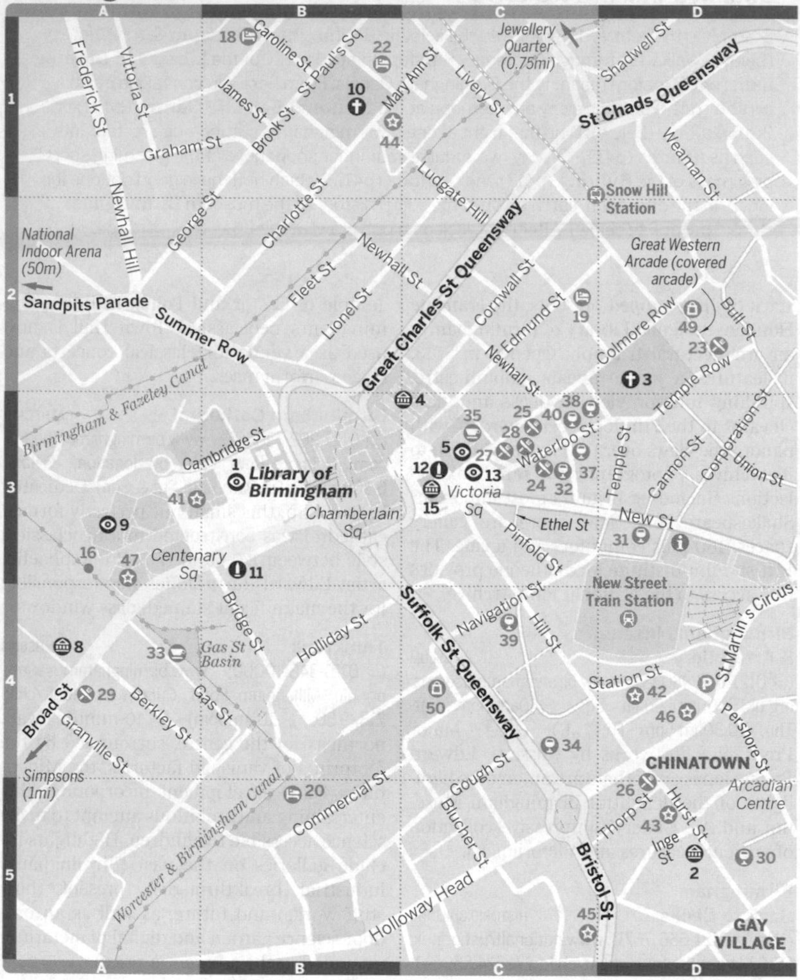

cutting-edge Ikon Gallery. Prepare to be thrilled, bemused or outraged, depending on your take on conceptual art.

National Sea Life Centre AQUARIUM
(☎0121-643 6777; www.visitsealife.com; 3a Brindley Pl; £17.50; ⏰10am-5pm Mon-Fri, to 6pm Sat & Sun) The Sir Norman Foster–designed National Sea Life Centre is England's largest inland aquarium. Its tanks teem with exotic marine life including razor-jawed hammerhead sharks, turtles and otters. Prepurchase tickets online for fast-track entry and get discounts of up to 40% off walk-in rates. Book online too for 15-minute behind-the-scenes tours (£1.50) offering access to otherwise out-of-bounds areas, and for one-hour feeding tours (£65 to £105; minimum age 12), feeding turtles, penguins or (if you're game) sharks.

Jewellery Quarter

Birmingham has been a major jewellery player since Charles II acquired a taste for it in 17th-century France. The gentrifying Jewellery Quarter, three-quarters of a mile northwest of the centre, still produces 40% of UK-manufactured jewellery. Dozens of work-

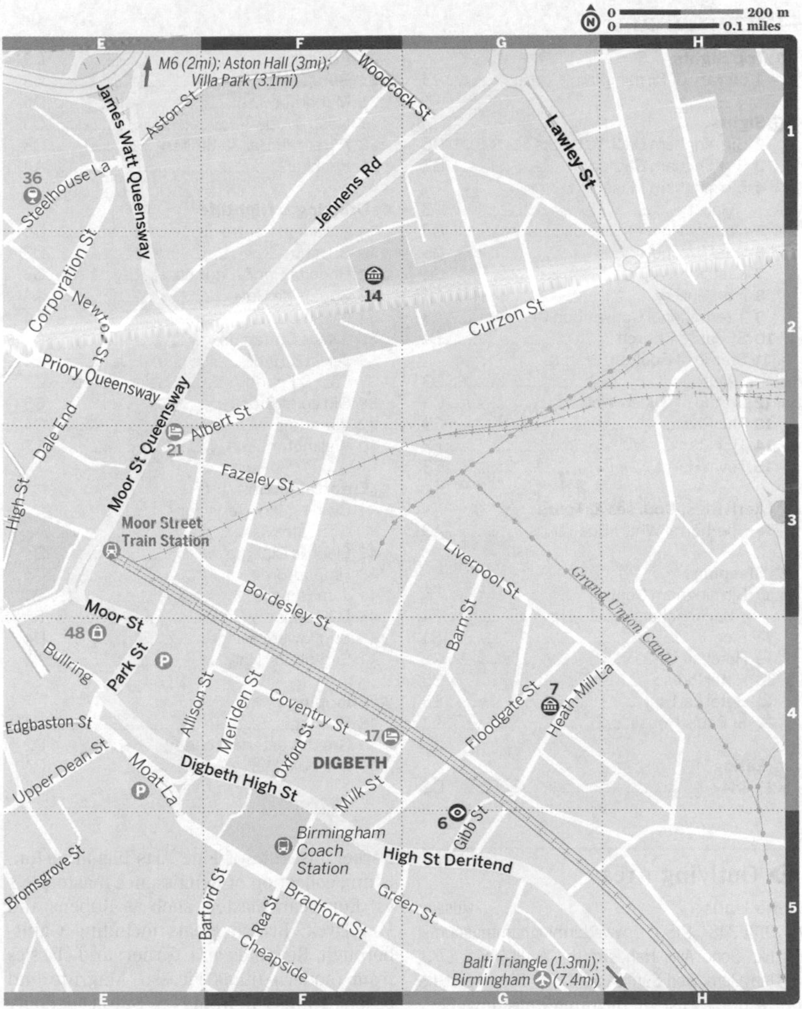

shops open to the public are listed in the free booklet *Jewellery Quarter: the Essential Guide,* available from tourist offices and local businesses, or visit www.jewelleryquarter.net.

Take the metro from Snow Hill or the train from Moor St to Jewellery Quarter station.

Museum of the Jewellery Quarter MUSEUM

(☎0121-348 8140; www.birminghammuseums.org.uk; 75 Vyse St; adult/child £7/3; ⏲10.30am-5pm Tue-Sat) The Smith & Pepper jewellery factory is preserved as it was on its closing day in 1981 after 80 years of operation. Guided tours lasting around one hour explain the long history of the trade in Birmingham and let you watch master jewellers at work. Entry to the temporary exhibition space and shop is free.

St Paul's Church CHURCH

(www.stpaulsjq.church; St Paul's Sq; ⏲10am-4pm Tue-Sat) St Paul's Sq is dominated by this beautiful 18th-century Georgian church, where 'Birmingham Brains' Matthew Boulton and James Watt came to pray. Free organ recitals take place on the first Thursday of the month from 1.15pm to 1.45pm (no reservations necessary).

Birmingham

Outlying Areas

Soho House MUSEUM

(☎0121-348 8150; www.birminghammuseums.org.uk; Soho Ave, Handsworth; adult/child £7/3; ⊙11am-3pm Wed-Sun Easter-Oct) Situated 1.5 miles northwest of Birmingham's Jewellery Quarter, Soho House is where industrialist Matthew Boulton lived from 1766 to 1809. Among the restored 18th-century chambers is the dining room where Boulton and members of the esteemed Lunar Society met to discuss their world-changing ideas during the greatest technological leap forward since the invention of the wheel. From Priory Queensway, take bus 74 or 75 to the Lozells stop, from where it's a five-minute walk.

★**Barber Institute of Fine Arts** GALLERY

(☎0121-414 7333; http://barber.org.uk; University of Birmingham, Edgbaston; ⊙10am-5pm Mon-Fri, 11am-5pm Sat & Sun) FREE At the University of Birmingham, 3 miles south of the centre, the Barber Institute of Fine Arts has an astonishing collection of Renaissance masterpieces; European masters such as Rubens and Van Dyck; British greats including Gainsborough, Reynolds and Turner; and classics from modern titans Picasso, Magritte and others. Trains run from New St to University station, from where it's a 10-minute walk.

Cadbury World MUSEUM

(☎0844 880 7667; www.cadburyworld.co.uk; Linden Rd, Bournville; adult/child £16.75/12.30; ⊙11am-4.30pm, hours vary) The next best thing to Willy Wonka's chocolate factory is Cadbury World, 4 miles south of Birmingham. It aims to educate visitors about the history of cocoa and the Cadbury family, but sweetens the deal with free samples, displays of chocolate-making machines, and chocolate-themed rides. Opening hours vary; bookings are essential at peak times. Last entry is 90 minutes before closing. Frequent trains run from Birmingham New St Station to Bournville, from where it's a signposted 10-minute walk.

Aston Hall HISTORIC BUILDING
(☎0121-348 8100; www.birminghammuseums.org.uk; Trinity Rd, Aston; house adult/child £8/3, grounds free; ⊙11am-4pm Tue-Sun Easter-Oct) Set in lush grounds 3 miles north of the centre, this well-preserved hall was built in extravagant Jacobean style between 1618 and 1635. The sumptuous interiors are full of friezes, moulded ceilings and tapestries. Trains run from New St to Aston station, then it's a 10-minute walk.

Tours

Big Brum Buz BUS TOUR
(☎0121-427 2555; www.birmingham-tours.co.uk; day ticket adult/child £12/5; ⊙10.30am, 12.30pm & 2.30pm Sat & Sun May-Sep) Hop-on/hop-off bus tour visiting the Jewellery Quarter, Golden Mile, Edgbaston and Digbeth.

Sherborne Wharf Boat Trips BOAT TOUR
(☎0121-455 6163; http://sherbornewharf.co.uk; Sherborne St; adult/child £8/6; ⊙11.30am, 1pm, 2.30pm & 4pm Easter-Nov, Sat & Sun Dec-Easter) Nostalgic narrow-boat cruises from the quayside by the International Convention Centre.

Festivals & Events

Frankfurt Christmas Market & Craft Fair CHRISTMAS MARKET
(www.birmingham.gov.uk/frankfurtmarket; ⊙mid-Nov–mid-Dec) Some 200 food, drink and craft stalls from Birmingham's twin city in Germany and from local purveyors fill the centre during the UK's largest Christmas market from mid-November to mid-December.

Sleeping

Chains dominate Birmingham's hotel scene, which is aimed at business travellers, ensuring high weekday prices. Look out for cheap deals at weekends or for longer stays. Accommodation is often tight but 14 new hotels are now in the pipeline and due for completion over the coming years.

B&Bs are concentrated outside the centre in Acocks Green (to the southeast) or Edgbaston and Selly Oak (to the southwest).

Birmingham Central Backpackers HOSTEL £
(☎0121-643 0033; www.birminghambackpackers.com; 58 Coventry St; dm/d/tr/q incl breakfast from £14/36/57/72; @ 📶) Despite the railway-bridge-right-next-door setting, Birmingham's purple and turquoise backpacker hostel is recommended for its convenience to the bus station and choice of clean, multicoloured dorms or Japanese-capsule-style pods. Excellent facilities include a lounge with DVDs and regular movie nights, a bar (note you can't BYO alcohol) and a self-catering kitchen.

★**Hotel La Tour** HOTEL ££
(☎0121-718 8000; http://hotel-latour.co.uk; Albert St; d from £119; ❄ 📶) Sunlight streams through floor-to-ceiling windows into the public areas and spacious rooms of this state-of-the-art independent hotel, purpose built in 2012. Tech-savvy room features include digitally controlled 'do not disturb' signs and media hubs. There's a 24-hour gym and a swish Modern British restaurant, **Mr White's English Chophouse**, run by star chef Marco Pierre White.

St Pauls House BOUTIQUE HOTEL ££
(☎0121-272 0999; www.saintpaulshouse.com; 15-20 St Paul's Sq; d from £119; P ❄ 📶) Opened in 2016, this independent addition to Birmingham's accommodation scene has 34 fresh, contemporary rooms with welcoming touches such as hot-water bottles in woollen covers. Upcycled decor in its hip bar and restaurant includes industrial-style ropes referencing the building's original use as a rope factory. The park-facing Jewellery Quarter location is a winner.

Hotel du Vin BOUTIQUE HOTEL ££
(☎0121-794 3605; www.hotelduvin.com; 25 Church St; d from £124; ❄ @ 📶) Housed in the handsome Victorian precincts of the former Birmingham Eye Hospital, this red-brick beauty has real class, with wrought-iron balustrades, classical murals and seasoned charms. Art deco-inspired rooms have spectacular bathrooms; there's a spa and gym, a bistro with shabby-chic worn floorboards and a stellar wine list, plus a pub and lounge bar with comfy, duffed-up leather furniture.

Hotel Indigo BOUTIQUE HOTEL ££
(☎0121-643 2010; www.hotelindigobirmingham.co.uk; The Cube, Wharfside St; d from £90; 📶 🏊) A stylish operation on the 23rd and 24th floors of the Mailbox's annex, The Cube, Hotel Indigo marries a handy location with snazzy amenities including a small swimming pool and great views from its 52 rooms (some with balconies). Panoramic vistas continue on the 25th floor from the **Marco Pierre White Steakhouse Bar & Grill** and **Laurent Perrier Champagne Bar**.

Bloc HOTEL ££
(☎0121-212 1223; www.blochotels.com; St Paul's, Caroline St; d from £75; ❄📶) Located in the Jewellery Quarter, Bloc excels in sharp, contemporary pod design. Rooms are tiny but space is cleverly stretched: flatscreen TVs are built into walls; there's under-bed storage; and bathrooms are compact but with luxe shower heads. Book carefully: rooms come with window or without. Good online specials.

Eating

Dining options span cool cafes and cosy pubs to gastronomic extravaganzas, with dozens of innovative new openings every year. Inexpensive restaurants are scattered throughout Chinatown, on the south-western side of the Bullring shopping mall.

Praza INDIAN ££
(☎0121-456 4500; http://praza.co.uk; 94-96 Hagley Rd, Edgbaston; mains £11-12, banquet menus £29-39; ⊙5-11.30pm Mon-Sat) The runaway success of Indian restaurant/cocktail bar Pushkar led the owners to open this sister restaurant in Edgbaston, with its own signature dishes (*nilgiri* – slow-cooked chicken in fragrant herb curry) and cocktails (Red Carpet, with Midori, cucumber, vodka, strawberries and cranberry juice). The monumental Grade II–listed Georgian mansion has *Great Gatsby*–style art-deco styling and two levels of dining.

Bureau GASTROPUB ££
(☎0121-236 1110; www.thebureaubar.co.uk; 110 Colmore Row; mains £7-19.50, platters £12; ⊙kitchen 10am-10pm Tue-Sat, to 8pm Sun & Mon, bar 10am-10.30pm Mon, to midnight Tue-Thu, to 1am Fri & Sat, to 8pm Sun) While this gleaming marble ex-office building dating from 1902 serves stupendous cocktails (such as hickory-smoked Bloody Marys), it's above all worth visiting for its food. Winning dishes include a duck Scotch egg (soft-boiled duck egg encased in confit of duck and a deep-fried breadcrumb shell, served in a nest of watercress with red-onion jam). Its roof terrace is a suntrap.

Purecraft Bar & Kitchen GASTROPUB ££
(☎0121-237 5666; www.purecraftbars.com; 30 Waterloo St; mains £11-18; ⊙kitchen noon-10pm Mon-Sat, to 5pm Sun, bar 11am-11pm Mon-Thu, 11am-midnight Fri & Sat, noon-10pm Sun) Fabulous dishes created in the open kitchen of this craft-beer-lover's paradise come with suggested beer pairings. The menu changes monthly but might include Lawless Lager-battered fish and chips (with Veltins Pilsner); Brewer's Grain asparagus and broad-bean risotto (with Odell St Lupulin American Pale Ale); grilled plaice with beer-and-parsley butter and Jersey Royal new potatoes (with Purity Mad Goose).

Nosh & Quaff AMERICAN ££
(☎0121-236 4246; http://noshandquaff.co.uk; 130 Colmore Row; mains £10-18, whole lobster £25; ⊙11am-11pm) North American fare at this cavernous, uberhip venue spans gourmet burgers, hot dogs and slow-cooked, hickory-glazed ribs, plus sides such as charred corn on the cob and sweet-potato wedges with sour cream, but the star is the whole lobster flown in live from Canada and dressed with garlic and lemon-butter sauce. The rockin' bar serves great craft beers.

Pushkar INDIAN ££
(☎0121-643 7978; http://pushkardining.com; 245 Broad St; 2-/3-course lunch menus £11/14, mains £8-19; ⊙noon-2.30pm & 5-11.30pm Mon-Fri, 5-11.30pm Sat, 5-11pm Sun) Classy north Indian and Punjabi cuisine is served up in this glass-fronted, white tableclothed, gold-trimmed dining room. The elegant presentation extends to boxed menus and serviette-wrapped naan bread as well as stunning cocktails. Lunch menus are an excellent deal. Its swanky spin-off, Praza, in Edgbaston, is also superb.

1847 VEGETARIAN ££
(☎0121-236 2313; www.by1847.com; 26 Great Western Arcade, Colmore Row; 2-/3-course menus £19.75/25.50; ⊙noon-3pm & 5-10pm Mon-Fri, noon-10.30pm Sat, noon-8pm Sun; ✍👪) 🌿 Occupying two levels in a gorgeous, heritage-listed Victorian shopping arcade, this chic spot proves that vegetarian and vegan food can be cutting-edge, from starters such as mushroom and liquorice pâté, wild-mushroom cappuccino and pear and fennel confit to mains including cider-battered halloumi, and lush desserts such as passionfruit and chia crème brûlée, and spiced clotted cream. Kids' menus available.

Maharaja INDIAN ££
(☎0121-622 2641; www.maharajarestaurant.co.uk; 25 Hurst St; mains £6.75-11.25; ⊙noon-2pm & 5.30-11pm Mon-Sat; ✍) Impeccable service sets this intimate north Indian restaurant apart from its neighbours, as does the superior food. Creative starters, naan breads and a dish of the day keep the menu fresh; the

homemade paneer (pillowy Indian cottage cheese) is exceptional.

★ Simpsons MODERN BRITISH £££
(☎0121-454 3434; www.simpsonsrestaurant.co.uk; 20 Highfield Rd; menus lunch £35, dinner £55-85; ⏰noon-2pm & 7-9pm Mon-Thu, noon-2pm & 7-9.30pm Fri & Sat, noon-4.30pm Sun;) It's worth the 2.5-mile journey southwest of the centre to this gorgeous Georgian mansion in leafy Edgbaston for sensational Michelin-starred menus (kids and vegetarians catered for). You can also stay in one of four luxurious bedrooms upstairs (from £110; Monday to Saturday only) or take an all-day cookery class (from £135 including three-course lunch, Saturdays). Reservations recommended.

Adam's MODERN BRITISH £££
(☎0121-643 3745; www.adamsrestaurant.co.uk; New Oxford House, 16 Waterloo St; 3-course lunch menu £35, dinner menus £60-85; ⏰noon-2pm & 7-9.30pm Tue-Sat) Michelin-starred restaurant Adam's has proved such a success story that it recently located to larger, ritzier premises and still wows with intricately prepared and presented flavour combinations such as venison with banana, shallots and red cabbage, purple broccoli with brown shrimp and Béarnaise sauce, or sea trout with morels, broad beans and oregano. Book well ahead.

Drinking & Nightlife

Like all British cities, Birmingham has plenty of chain pubs, but fantastic independents continue to spring up all over the city.

Nightlife hubs in Birmingham include Broad St (aka the 'golden mile' – some say for the prevalence of fake tan here) and Chinatown's **Arcadian Centre** (www.thearcadian.co.uk; Hurst St). Postindustrial Digbeth has alternative clubs and club events in and around the Custard Factory (p416).

★ Jake's Coffee Box COFFEE
(off Colmore Row; ⏰7am-4pm Mon-Thu, 7am-3pm Fri, 8am-2pm Sat) A classic red British telephone box on a pedestrian laneway has been ingeniously repurposed as a tiny coffee bar, where Jake brews espressos, flat whites, Americanos, cappuccinos and lattes using Birmingham-roasted Quarterhorse beans. He also serves snacks including gourmet sausage rolls (pork, asparagus and black pepper; pork and wild boar), brownies, choc-chip cookies and carrot cake, plus occasional BBQs.

GAY & LESBIAN BIRMINGHAM

Birmingham's lively gay scene is centred on the **Gay Village** south of the Bullring around Hurst St. The area throngs with the bold, bright and beautiful on weekend nights and peaks during May's **Birmingham Pride** (www.birminghampride.com; ⏰May) festivities. For up-to-the-minute information on the Brummie scene, check www.visitgaybrum.com

★ Jekyll & Hyde PUB
(☎0121-236 0345; www.thejekyllandhyde.co.uk; 28 Steelhouse Lane; ⏰noon-11pm Mon-Thu, to midnight Fri, to 1am Sat) Potent cocktails (or rather 'elixirs, concoctions and potions') at this trippy spot are served in sweets jars, watering cans, teapots and miniature bath-tubs – even a washbag (with rum-mint toothpaste and kaffir lime). Downstairs, Mr Hyde's emporium has a cosy drawing room and *Alice in Wonderland*–themed courtyard; upstairs is Dr Jekyll's Gin Parlour with more than 90 different gins.

Lost & Found BAR
(http://the-lostandfound.co.uk; 8 Bennett's Hill; ⏰11am-11pm Mon-Thu, to 1am Fri & Sat, to 10pm Sun) Fictitious Victorian-era explorer/professor Hettie G Watson is the inspiration for the botanical-library theme of this bar in an 1869-built former bank. Inside the domed entrance, elevated seating is surrounded by plants, birdcages, books and maps, while a bookcase conceals the entrance to Hettie's 'secret emporium' bar (try your luck around 7.30pm on a Friday or Saturday).

Wellington PUB
(www.thewellingtonrealale.co.uk; 37 Bennett's Hill; ⏰10am-midnight) The pastel wallpaper, timber bar and polished brass give the impression the Welly is frozen in time, but this specialist real ale pub has been recently spruced up and shelters a timber-decked roof terrace. Its 15 hand-pulled beers (and three ciders) include favourites from Black Country and Wye Valley as well as rare brews.

Bacchus BAR
(☎0121-632 5445; www.nicholsonspubs.co.uk; Burlington Arcade, New St; ⏰11am-11pm Sun-Thu, to 1am Fri & Sat) Buried beneath the Burlington Arcade, this darkened drinking den has the ambience of a decadent underworld. Down a faux-marble-encased staircase, crumbling

LOCAL KNOWLEDGE

DIGBETH'S CREATIVE QUARTER

Just over a mile southeast of the centre, Digbeth's creative quarter centres on the **Custard Factory** (☎0121-224 7777; www.custardfactory.co.uk; Gibb St) , a hip art and design enclave set in the converted buildings of the factory that once churned out British favourite Bird's Custard. The open-plan space is now full of small galleries, quirky design boutiques, vintage-clothing outlets, skateboard shops and affordable, offbeat cafes. There's also a mini skate ramp and free ping-pong tables.

Check out the artist-run experimental gallery **Eastside Projects** (www.eastsideprojects.org; 86 Heath Mill Lane; ⏲noon-5pm Wed-Sat) nearby.

pillars and giant Grecian murals give way to soaring medieval-style stone arches, swords, suits of armour and candelabras.

Old Joint Stock PUB
(☎0121-200 1892; www.oldjointstocktheatre.co.uk; 4 Temple Row West; ⏲8am-11pm Mon-Fri, 9am-11pm Sat, 10am-5pm Sun; 📶) A vast high-ceilinged temple of a pub, housed in a former bank and beloved by a high-spirited after-work crowd. Upstairs, an 80-seat theatre puts on plays and comedy shows.

Canalside Cafe CAFE
(☎0121-643 3170; 35 Worcester Bar, Gas St; ⏲9am-11pm Mon-Sat, to 10.30pm Sun) Narrow boats glide past the terrace of this 18th-century lock-keeper's cottage, where the low-ceilinged interior is strung with nautical paraphernalia and warmed by an open fire. Drop by for a cuppa, real ale or cider (or warming mulled cider in winter).

☆ Entertainment

Tickets for most Birmingham events can be purchased through entertainment mega-corp **TicketWeb** (☎0333 321 9990; www.ticketweb.co.uk; ⏲phone lines open 9am-8pm Mon-Fri, 10am-4pm Sat & Sun). Free publications listing gigs and events include the excellent *Brum Notes* (www.brumnotes.com).

Live Music

The **Barclaycard Arena** (☎0121-780 4141; www.barclaycardarena.co.uk; King Edwards Rd), north of Brindley Pl, and the **National Exhibition Centre Arena** (☎0121-780 4141; www.thenec.co.uk; North Ave; 📶), near Birmingham Airport, host stadium-fillers from the world of rock and pop.

Sunflower Lounge LIVE MUSIC
(☎0121-632 6756; http://thesunflowerlounge.com; 76 Smallbrook Queensway; ⏲bar noon-1am Mon-Thu, to 2am Fri & Sat, to 11pm Sun) This quirky little indie bar matches a magnificent alternative soundtrack with a regular program of live gigs and DJ nights.

Jam House LIVE MUSIC
(☎0121-200 3030; www.thejamhouse.com; 3-5 St Paul's Sq; ⏲6pm-midnight Tue & Wed, to 1am Thu, to 2am Fri & Sat) Pianist Jools Holland was the brains behind this moody, smart-casual music venue (dress accordingly). Acts range from jazz big bands to famous soul crooners. Over 21s only.

O2 Academy LIVE MUSIC
(☎box office 0844 477 2000; www.academymusicgroup.com/o2academybirmingham; 16-18 Horsefair, Bristol St; ⏲box office noon-4pm Mon-Sat) Birmingham's leading venue for big-name rockers and tribute bands as well as up-and-coming talent.

Symphony Hall CLASSICAL MUSIC
(☎0121-345 0600; www.thsh.co.uk; Broad St) The City of Birmingham Symphony Orchestra's official home is the ultramodern Symphony Hall. Shows also take place in the handsome auditorium at the Town Hall (p409).

Theatre & Cinema

Electric Cinema CINEMA
(www.theelectric.co.uk; 47-49 Station St; standard/deluxe seats £7.80/13.50) Topped by its art deco sign, this is the UK's oldest working cinema, operating since 1909. It screens mainly art-house films. Be waited upon in plush two-seater sofas or have a drink in the small bar (complete with an absinthe fountain).

Birmingham Repertory Theatre THEATRE
(☎0121-236 4455; www.birmingham-rep.co.uk; Centenary Sq) Founded more than a century ago, today 'the Rep' has three performance spaces: the Main House; the more experimental Door; and a 300-seat studio theatre presenting edgy drama and musicals, with an emphasis on contemporary work.

Hippodrome THEATRE
(☎0844 338 5000; www.birminghamhippodrome.com; Hurst St) Hosts the Birmingham Royal Ballet.

Sport

Birmingham has three football (soccer) clubs within striking distance: Birmingham City Football Club, West Bromwich Albion ('West Brom') and, most famously, Aston Villa Football Club, who play at **Villa Park** (☎0333 323 5353; www.avfc.co.uk; Trinity Rd, Witton; tours adult/child £15/10).

Shopping

Bustling markets sell fresh food and cheap imported clothes in the pedestrian precincts surrounding the Bullring.

Great Western Arcade SHOPPING ARCADE
(www.greatwesternarcade.co.uk; btwn Colmore Row & Temple Row; ⏰arcade 6.30am-10pm Mon-Sat, 10.50am-5.30pm Sun, shop hours vary) This glass-roofed, tiled-floored Victorian-era arcade is a jewel filled with mostly independent shops.

Mailbox MALL
(www.mailboxlife.com; 61 Wharfside St; ⏰mall 10am-7pm Mon-Sat, 11am-5pm Sun, shop hours vary) Birmingham's stylish canalside shopping experience, the redevelopment of the former Royal Mail sorting office, comes complete with designer hotels, a fleet of upmarket restaurants, the luxury department store Harvey Nichols and designer boutiques. Its super-snazzy metallic extension, The Cube, houses Marco Pierre White's **Steakhouse Bar & Grill** on the 25th floor.

Bullring MALL
(www.bullring.co.uk; St Martin's Circus; ⏰10am-8pm Mon-Fri, 9am-8pm Sat, 11am-5pm Sun) Split into two vast retail spaces – the East Mall and West Mall – the Bullring has all the international brands and chain cafes you could ask for, plus the standout architectural wonder of Selfridges, which looks out over the city like the compound eye of a giant robot insect.

Information

As in most large cities, it's wise to avoid walking alone late at night in unlit areas. And as in most British cities, the centre, especially south of the Bullring and on and around Broad St, can be rowdy with revellers on weekend nights.

Digbeth bus station and its surrounds can be quite rough after dark.

Birmingham Children's Hospital (☎0121-333 9999; www.bch.nhs.uk; Steelhouse Lane) Has an accident and emergency department.

Heartlands Hospital (☎0121-424 2000; www.heartofengland.nhs.uk; Bordesley Green East) Located 4 miles east of the centre; has an accident and emergency department.

Heart of England Tourist Board (☎01905-887690; www.visitheartofengland.com)

Police Station (☎emergency 999, non-emergency 101; www.west-midlands.police.uk; Steelhouse Lane)

Tourist Office (☎0844 888 3883; www.visitbirmingham.com; cnr Corporation & New Sts; ⏰9am-5pm Mon-Sat, 10am-4pm Sun) Kiosk with racks of info on activities, transport and sights.

Getting There & Away

AIR

Birmingham Airport (p408), 8 miles east of the centre, has direct flights to destinations around the UK and Europe as well as direct long-haul routes to Dubai, India, the USA and Canada.

Fast and convenient trains run regularly between New St and Birmingham International station (£3.60, 20 minutes, every 10 minutes). The station is linked to the terminal by the Air-Rail Link monorail (free; two minutes; frequent), which runs from 5.15am to 2am.

Alternatively, take bus 97 or 900 (£2.30, 30 minutes, up to two hourly) from Moor St Queensway, which run 24 hours.

A taxi from the airport to the centre costs about £30.

BUS

Most intercity buses run from **Birmingham Coach Station** (☎0871 781 8181; Mill Lane, Digbeth), but the X20 to Stratford-upon-Avon (£5.20, 1½ hours, up to 14 daily) also leaves from a more convenient stop on Carr's Lane, opposite Moor St Station.

National Express coaches link Birmingham with major cities across the country, including the following.

London Victoria £5 to £12.50, 2¾ hours, every 30 minutes

Manchester £4, three hours, 12 daily

Oxford £5, 2¼ hours, six daily

TRAIN

Most long-distance trains leave from New St Station, but Chiltern Railways runs to London Marylebone (£48, two hours, half-hourly) from Birmingham Snow Hill, and London Midland runs to Stratford-upon-Avon (£7.70, one hour, half-hourly) from Snow Hill and Moor St stations.

Construction on the High Speed Rail (HS2) line – connecting London with Birmingham in just 40 minutes – is set to commence in 2017 and be completed by 2026.

Useful services from New St:

Derby £16.60, 40 minutes, four per hour

Leicester £13.40, one hour, two per hour

London Euston £51.20, 1½ hours, every 15 minutes
Manchester £35.50, 1¾ hours, half-hourly
Nottingham £18.10, 1¼ hours, three per hour
Shrewsbury £14.30, one hour, two per hour

Getting Around

CAR

During central Birmingham's ongoing construction, traffic into and around the city is severely disrupted and parking is limited. Check with your accommodation about access (don't rely on your satnav). Most roadworks are expected to be completed by late 2018. All the big car-hire companies have town and airport offices.

PUBLIC TRANSPORT

Local buses run from a convenient hub on Corporation St, just north of the New St junction. For routes, pick up a free copy of the *Network Birmingham Map and Guide* from the tourist office. Single-trip tickets start from £1.90.

Commuter trains to destinations in the north of Birmingham (including Aston) operate from Moor St train station, close to Selfridges.

Birmingham's single tram line, the **Metro** (http://nxbus.co.uk), links New St Station with Wolverhampton via the Jewellery Quarter, West Bromwich and Dudley. Tickets start from £1. An extension from New St to Birmingham Town Hall and Centenary Sq should be open by the time you read this.

Various saver tickets covering buses and trains are available from **Network West Midlands** (☎0121-2147 7550; www.networkwestmidlands.com; New St station; ⊙8.30am-5.30pm Mon-Sat) at New St Station. **TOA Taxis** (☎0121-427 8888; www.toataxis.co.uk) is a reliable black-cab taxi firm.

WARWICKSHIRE

Warwickshire could have been just another picturesque English county of rolling hills and market towns were it not for the birth of a rather well-known wordsmith. William Shakespeare was born and died in Stratford-upon-Avon, and the sights linked to his life are a magnet for tourists from around the globe. Famous Warwick Castle attracts similar crowds. Elsewhere visitor numbers dwindle but Kenilworth has atmospheric castle ruins, Rugby celebrates the sport that takes its name at its World Rugby Hall of Fame, and Coventry claims two extraordinary cathedrals and an unmissable motoring museum.

Getting There & Around

Coventry is the main transport hub, with frequent rail connections to London Euston and Birmingham New St.

Coventry

POP 337,428

Coventry was once a bustling hub for the production of cloth, clocks, bicycles, automobiles and munitions. It was this last industry that drew the German Luftwaffe in WWII: on the night of 14 November 1940, the city was so badly blitzed that the Nazis coined a new verb, *coventrieren,* meaning 'to flatten'. The city faced a further setback with the collapse of the British motor industry in the 1980s, but is undergoing a resurgence today thanks to its redeveloped and expanded university, and its proximity to London. A handful of medieval streets that escaped the bombers offer a glimpse of old Coventry.

Sights

★ Coventry Transport Museum MUSEUM
(☎024-7623 4270; www.transport-museum.com; Hales St; ⊙10am-5pm) FREE This stupendous museum has hundreds of 'cars', from horseless carriages to jet-powered, land-speed record breakers. There's a brushed-stainless-steel DeLorean DMC-12 (of *Back to the Future* fame) with gull-wing doors, alongside a gorgeous Jaguar E-type, a Daimler armoured car and, for 1970s British-design-oddity enthusiasts, a Triumph TR7 and an Austin Allegro 'Special'. View the Thrust SCC, the current holder of the World Land Speed Record and the Thrust 2, the previous record holder.

Coventry Cathedral CATHEDRAL
(☎024-7652 1210; www.coventrycathedral.org.uk; Priory Row; adult/child £6/free; ⊙cathedral 10am-4pm Mon-Sat, noon-3pm Sun, ruins 9am-5pm daily) The evocative ruins of **St Michael's Cathedral**, built around 1300 but destroyed by Nazi incendiary bombs in the Blitz, stand as a permanent memorial to Coventry's darkest hour and as a symbol of peace and reconciliation. Climb the 180 steps of the **Gothic spire** (adult/child £2.50/free) for panoramic views.

Symbolically adjoining St Michael's Cathedral's sandstone walls is the Sir Basil Spence–designed modernist architectural masterpiece **Coventry Cathedral**, with a futuristic organ, stained glass and Jacob Epstein statue of the devil and St Michael.

Herbert Art Gallery & Museum GALLERY
(☎024-7623 7521; www.theherbert.org; Jordan Well; 10am-4pm Mon-Sat, noon-4pm Sun) FREE Behind Coventry's twin cathedrals, the Herbert has an eclectic collection of paintings and sculptures (including work by TS Lowry and Stanley Spencer), a delightful cafe and lots of activities aimed at kids. The history gallery and thought-provoking gallery on peace and reconciliation are worth a look-in.

St Mary's Guildhall HISTORIC BUILDING
(☎024-7683 3328; www.stmarysguildhall.co.uk; Bayley Lane; 10am-4pm Sun-Thu mid-Mar–Sep) FREE One of the most evocative insights into pre-WWII Coventry is this half-timbered and brick hall where the town's trades came together in the Middle Ages to discuss town affairs. As one of England's finest guildhalls, it was chosen to be a jail for Mary Queen of Scots. Stained-glass windows glorify the kings of England; further down the hall stands WC Marshall's statue of Lady Godiva. Look out for the medieval tapestry depicting Henry VI.

Sleeping & Eating

Coventry makes an easy day trip from Birmingham but if you want to stay, the tourist office can help find accommodation.

Blue Bistro BISTRO ££
(☎024-7622 9274; www.blue-bistro.com; 21 Spon St; mains £12-17.50; 5-9pm Wed-Sat, 1-6pm Sun) A half-timbered building dating from 1450 with exposed beams and wooden furniture is the setting for beautifully cooked and presented bistro fare (braised lamb shanks, BBQ pork ribs, pan-fried sea bass...).

Playwrights CAFE ££
(☎024-7623 1441; www.playwrightsrestaurant.co.uk; 4-6 Hay Lane; mains lunch £5-8.50, dinner £10-19.50; 10am-9pm Mon-Thu, 9am-10.30pm Fri & Sat, 10am-8pm Sun;) On the lovely cobbled lane leading from Earl St to the cathedral, this bright, inviting cafe, bar and bistro is as good for breakfast as it is for lunch or an intimate dinner. Vegetarians and vegans are catered for with separate menus, as are kids. Tables are set up on the cobbles in warmer weather.

Information

The **tourist office** (☎024-7622 5616; www.visitcoventryandwarwickshire.co.uk; Bayley Lane; 9.30am-12.30pm & 1-4.30pm Mon-Fri, from 10am Sat & Sun) is housed in the restored tower of St Michael's Cathedral.

Getting There & Away

National Express buses serve most parts of the country.

Buses X17 and X19 (every 15 minutes) go to Kenilworth (£2.70, 25 minutes) and Warwick (£2.90, 35 minutes).

Regular services include the following:

Birmingham (£4.50, 30 minutes, every 10 minutes)

London Euston (£49, 1¼ hours, every 10 to 20 minutes)

Rugby (£5.70, 10 minutes, up to four per hour)

Warwick

POP 58,679

Regularly name-checked by Shakespeare, Warwick was the ancestral seat of the Earls of Warwick, who played a pivotal role in the Wars of the Roses. Despite a devastating fire in 1694, Warwick remains a treasure-house of medieval architecture with rich veins of history and charming streets, dominated by the soaring turrets of Warwick Castle.

Sights

★ **Warwick Castle** CASTLE
(☎0871 265 2000; www.warwick-castle.com; Castle Lane; castle adult/child £25.20/22.20, castle & dungeon £30.20/27.20; 10am-6pm Apr-Sep, to 5pm Oct-Mar; P) Founded in 1068 by William the Conqueror, stunningly preserved Warwick Castle is the biggest show in town. The ancestral home of the earls of Warwick remains impressively intact, and the Tussauds Group has filled the interior with flamboyant, family-friendly attractions that bring the castle's rich history to life. Waxworks populate the private apartments; there are also jousting tournaments, daily trebuchet firings, themed evenings and a dungeon. Discounted online tickets provide fast-track entry. A fabulous range of accommodation options (p421) opened in 2016.

Collegiate Church of St Mary CHURCH
(☎01926-403940; www.stmaryswarwick.org.uk; Old Sq; church entry by £2 donation, tower adult/child £2.50/1; 10am-6pm Apr-Sep, to 4.30pm Oct-Mar) This magnificent 1123-founded Norman church was badly damaged in the Great Fire of Warwick in 1694 but is packed with 16th- and 17th-century tombs. Highlights include the Norman crypt with a 14th-century extension; the impressive Beauchamp Chapel, built between 1442 and 1464 to enshrine the mortal remains of the earls of Warwick;

Warwick

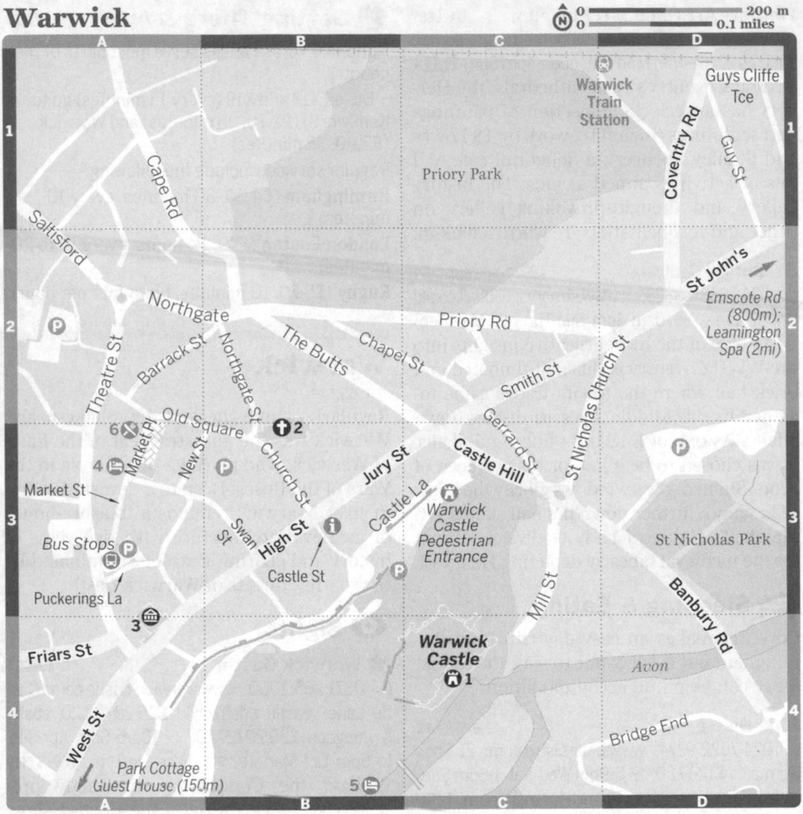

Warwick

Top Sights
1 Warwick Castle C4

Sights
2 Collegiate Church of St Mary B3
3 Lord Leycester Hospital A4

Sleeping
4 Rose & Crown A3
5 Warwick Castle Accommodation B4

Eating
6 Tailors A3

and, up 134 steps, the **tower**, which provides supreme views over town (kids must be aged over eight).

Lord Leycester Hospital HISTORIC BUILDING

(☎01926-491422; www.lordleycester.com; 60 High St; adult/child £5.90/4.90, garden only £2; ⏰10am-5pm Tue-Sun Apr-Sep, to 4pm Oct-Mar) A survivor of the 1694 fire, the wonderfully wonky Lord Leycester Hospital has been used as a retirement home for soldiers (but never as a hospital) since 1571. Visitors can wander around the chapel, guildhall, regimental museum and restored walled garden, which includes a knot garden and a Norman arch.

Sleeping & Eating

Park Cottage Guest House B&B **££**

(☎01926-410319; www.parkcottagewarwick.co.uk; 113 West St; s £59-80, d £80-99, f £92.50-115; P 📶 👪) Southwest of the centre, this stand-alone 16th-century wattle-and-daub building once served as the dairy for Warwick Castle. There are seven pretty rooms, each with a teddy bear, original floors and a courtyard garden. Two of its rooms can accommodate up to two adults and two children.

Rose & Crown PUB ££
(☎01926-411117; www.roseandcrownwarwick.co.uk; 30 Market Pl; s/d/f incl breakfast from £80/100/105;) Dating from the 17th century, this inn on the town square has five lovely, spacious and tastefully decorated rooms upstairs from the pub and another eight in the building across the lane, as well as great ales and bottled beers and superior food (mains £12.50 to £27). Four of its rooms are set up for families.

★ **Warwick Castle Accommodation** RESORT £££
(☎01926-406660; www.warwick-castle.com; Warwick Castle; tower ste/lodge/glamping tent per night from £550/203/149;) Accommodation offerings at Warwick Castle cater for all budgets, and include two days' castle admission. The castle itself now contains two four-poster-bed Tower Suites (including a private tour, champagne and breakfast). The riverside **Knight's Village** has woodland and knight-themed lodges (all with terraces and some with kitchenettes) and medieval entertainment. Themed tents (with shared bathrooms) make up the **Glamping** ground.

Tailors MODERN BRITISH £££
(☎01926-410590; www.tailorsrestaurant.co.uk; 22 Market Pl; 2-/3-course lunch menus £18/23, 2-/3-/6-course dinner menus £29.50/39.50/62.50; ⊙noon-1.30pm & 6.30-8.45pm Tue-Sat) Set in a former tailor's shop, this elegant restaurant, owned and run by two young-gun chefs, serves prime ingredients – guinea fowl, pork belly and lamb from named farms – complemented by the likes of beetroot meringue, black truffle and fennel candy, and black-pudding crumble. One to watch.

Information

Warwick's **tourist office** (☎01926-492212; www.visitwarwick.co.uk; Court House, Jury St; ⊙9.30am-4.30pm Mon-Fri, 10am-4.30pm Sat, 10am-4pm Sun) is within the flagstone-floored Court House (1725).

Getting There & Away

BUS

Buses depart from outside **Westgate House** (Market St).

National Express coaches serve London Victoria (£12.50, 3½ hours, up to four daily).

Stagecoach X16, X17 and X18 run to Coventry (£5.20, 1¼ hours, every 15 minutes Monday to Saturday) via Kenilworth (£3.75, 35 minutes).

Stagecoach bus 18A goes to Stratford-upon-Avon (£4.30, 45 minutes, half-hourly Monday to Saturday, hourly Sunday).

TRAIN

The train station is half a mile northeast of the centre on Station Rd.

Trains run to Birmingham (£6.80, 40 minutes, half-hourly), Stratford-upon-Avon (£6.60, 30 minutes, hourly) and London Marylebone (£31.80, 1½ hours, every 20 minutes).

Kenilworth

POP 23,480

An easy deviation off the A46 between Warwick and Coventry, the atmospheric ruin of Kenilworth Castle was the inspiration for Walter Scott's *Kenilworth,* and it still feels pretty inspiring today. The town is essentially split into two by Finham Brook: the historic village-like area, of most interest to visitors, is on the northern side, while the southern side is the commercial centre.

Sights

Kenilworth Castle CASTLE
(EH; ☎01926-852078; www.english-heritage.org.uk; Castle Green; adult/child £10.10/6; ⊙10am-6pm mid-Mar–Sep, shorter hours Oct–mid-Mar;) This spine-tingling ruin sprawls among fields and hedges on Kenilworth's outskirts. Built in the 1120s, the castle survived the longest siege in English history in 1266, when the forces of Lord Edward (later Edward I) threw themselves at the moat and battlements for six solid months. The fortress was dramatically extended in Tudor times, but it fell in the English Civil War and its walls were breached and water defences drained. Don't miss the magnificent restored Elizabethan gardens.

Stoneleigh Abbey HISTORIC BUILDING
(☎01926-858535; www.stoneleighabbey.org; adult/child £9.50/4.50, garden only £4.50/free; ⊙tours 11.30am, 1pm & 2.30pm Sun-Thu Easter-Oct, garden 11am-5pm Sun-Thu Easter-Oct;) The kind of stately home that makes movie directors go weak at the knees, this 850-year-old country house 2 miles east of Kenilworth, off the B4115 by the River Avon, name-drops Charles I and Jane Austen among its roll-call of visitors. Completed in 1726 and only viewable on tours (included in admission), the abbey's splendid Palladian west wing contains richly detailed plasterwork ceilings and wood-panelled rooms. The landscaped grounds are fine picnic territory.

Sleeping & Eating

The Old Bakery B&B ££
(☎01926-864111; www.theoldbakery.eu; 12 High St; s/d/tr from £75/95/115; bar 5.30-11pm Mon-Sat, to 10.30pm Sun; P) Located down High St east of the castle, this appealing B&B has attractively attired modern rooms and a cosy, welcoming bar serving real ales on the ground floor.

Harringtons on the Hill MODERN BRITISH ££
(☎01926-852074; www.harringtonsonthehill.com; 42 Castle Hill; mains £10-19; noon-3pm & 6-11pm Mon-Sat, noon-4pm Sun) In an adorable bow-fronted cottage festooned with flower boxes opposite Kenilworth Castle, chef Ryan New re-creates his success at some of London's top tables. Dishes include pan-fried sea bass in garlic butter, bacon-wrapped pork medallions, and venison with horseradish mash and redcurrant jus – at impressively reasonable prices.

★**The Cross** GASTROPUB £££
(☎01926-853840; www.thecrosskenilworth.co.uk; 16 New St; 2-/3-course lunch menus £25/30, 5-course dinner tasting menu £65, with wines extra £35, mains £25-32; noon-2pm & 6.30-10pm Mon-Thu, noon-2pm & 6-10pm Fri, noon-2.30pm & 6-10pm Sat, noon-4pm Sun) One of England's culinary jewels, this Michelin-starred gastropub occupies a romantic 19th-century inn. Prepare to be dazzled by exquisite creations such as seared scallops with smoked butter and roast cauliflower, squab pigeon with cracked wheat and yoghurt, and a Black Forest sphere with toasted-almond ice cream.

SHAKESPEARE HISTORIC HOMES

Five of the most important buildings associated with Shakespeare contain museums that form the core of the visitor experience at Stratford. All are run by the Shakespeare Birthplace Trust (www.shakespeare.org.uk).

Tickets for the three houses in town – Shakespeare's Birthplace, Shakespeare's New Place and Hall's Croft – cost adult/child £17.50/11.50. If you also visit Anne Hathaway's Cottage and Mary Arden's Farm, you can buy a combination ticket covering all five properties (£26.25/17).

Vegetarian menus are available; junior gourmands have their own three-course children's menu (£12).

Getting There & Away

From Monday to Saturday, buses X17 and X19 run every 15 minutes between Coventry (£2.70, 25 minutes) and Kenilworth and on to Warwick (£3.75, 20 minutes). There are no buses on Sunday.

Stratford-upon-Avon

POP 27,455

The author of some of the most quoted lines ever written in the English language, William Shakespeare was born in Stratford in 1564 and died here in 1616. Experiences linked to his life in this unmistakably Tudor town range from the touristy (medieval re-creations and Bard-themed tearooms) to the humbling (Shakespeare's modest grave in Holy Trinity Church) and the sublime (taking in a play by the world-famous Royal Shakespeare Company).

Sights

★**Shakespeare's Birthplace** HISTORIC BUILDING
(☎01789-204016; www.shakespeare.org.uk; Henley St; incl Shakespeare's New Place & Halls Croft adult/child £17.50/11.50; 9am-5.30pm Jul & Aug, to 5pm Sep-Jun) Start your Shakespeare quest at the house where the world's most popular playwright supposedly spent his childhood days. In fact, the jury is still out on whether this really was Shakespeare's birthplace, but devotees of the Bard have been dropping in since at least the 19th century, leaving their signatures scratched on to the windows. Set behind a modern facade, the house has restored Tudor rooms, live presentations from famous Shakespearean characters, and an engaging exhibition on Stratford's favourite son.

★**Shakespeare's New Place** HISTORIC SITE
(☎01789-204016; www.shakespeare.org.uk; cnr Chapel St & Chapel Lane; incl Shakespeare's Birthplace & Hall's Croft adult/child £17.50/11.50; 9am-5.30pm Jul & Aug, 9am-5pm mid-Mar–Jun, Sep & Oct, 10am-4pm Nov–mid-Mar) When Shakespeare retired, he swapped the bright lights of London for a comfortable town house at New Place, where he died of unknown causes in April 1616. The house was demolished in 1759, but an attractive Elizabethan knot garden occupies part of the grounds.

A major restoration project has uncovered Shakespeare's kitchen and incorporated new exhibits in a reimagining of the house as it would have been. You can also explore the adjacent Nash's House, where Shakespeare's granddaughter Elizabeth lived.

Hall's Croft HISTORIC BUILDING
(☎01789-204016; www.shakespeare.org.uk; Old Town; incl Shakespeare's Birthplace & Shakespeare's New Place adult/child £17.50/11.50; ⏲10am-5pm mid-Mar–Oct) The handsome Jacobean town house belonging to Shakespeare's daughter Susanna and her husband, respected doctor John Hall, stands south of the centre. The exhibition offers fascinating insights into medicine in the 16th and 17th centuries, and the lovely walled garden sprouts with aromatic herbs employed in medicinal preparations.

Holy Trinity Church CHURCH
(☎01789-266316; www.stratford-upon-avon.org; Old Town; Shakespeare's grave adult/child £2/1; ⏲8.30am-6pm Mon-Sat, 12.30-5pm Sun Apr-Sep, shorter hours Oct-Mar) The final resting place of the Bard is said to be the most visited parish church in all of England. Inside are handsome 16th- and 17th-century tombs (particularly in the Clopton Chapel), some fabulous carvings on the choir stalls and, of course, the grave of William Shakespeare, with its ominous epitaph: 'cvrst be he yt moves my bones'.

Anne Hathaway's Cottage HISTORIC BUILDING
(☎01789-204016; www.shakespeare.org.uk; Cottage Lane, Shottery; adult/child £10.25/6.50; ⏲9am-5pm mid-Mar–Oct, closed Nov–mid-Mar) Before tying the knot with Shakespeare, Anne Hathaway lived in Shottery, 1 mile west of the centre of Stratford, in this delightful thatched farmhouse. As well as period furniture, it has gorgeous gardens and an orchard and arboretum, with examples of all the trees mentioned in Shakespeare's plays. A footpath (no bikes allowed) leads to Shottery from Evesham Pl. The **City Sightseeing** (☎01789-299123; www.city-sightseeing.com; adult/child £13.90/6.95; ⏲every 30min Apr-Sep, less frequently Oct-Mar) bus stops here.

Mary Arden's Farm HISTORIC SITE, FARM
(☎01789-204016; www.shakespeare.org.uk; Station Rd, Wilmcote; adult/child £13.25/8.50; ⏲10am-5pm mid-Mar–Oct, closed Nov–mid-Mar) Shakespeare genealogists can trace the family tree to the childhood home of the Bard's mother at Wilmcote, 3 miles west of Stratford. Aimed squarely at families, the working farm traces country life over the centuries, with nature trails, falconry displays and a collection of rare-breed farm animals. You can get here on the City Sightseeing bus, or cycle via Anne Hathaway's Cottage, following the Stratford-upon-Avon Canal towpath.

Shakespeare's School Room HISTORIC SITE
(www.shakespearesschoolroom.org; King Edward VI School, Church St; adult/child £8.90/5.50; ⏲11am-5pm Mon-Fri during school term, 10am-5pm Sat, Sun & school holidays) Shakespeare's alma mater, King Edward VI School (still a prestigious grammar school today), incorporates a vast black-and-white timbered building, dating from 1420, that was once the town's guildhall. Upstairs, in the Bard's former classroom, you can sit in on mock-Tudor lessons, watch a short film and test yourself on Tudor-style homework.

It's adjacent to the 1269-built **Guild Chapel** (cnr Chapel Lane & Church St; ⏲services 10am Wed, noon 1st Sat of month Apr-Sep).

Tours

Guided Town Walks WALKING
(☎07855-760377; www.stratfordtownwalk.co.uk; adult/child £6/3; ⏲11am Mon & Fri, 11am & 2pm Sat & Sun) Popular and informative, these two-hour guided town walks depart from Waterside, opposite Sheep St.

Avon Boating BOATING
(☎01789-267073; www.avon-boating.co.uk; The Boathouse, Swan's Nest Lane; river cruises adult/child £6/4; ⏲9am-dusk Easter-Oct) Avon Boating runs 40-minute river cruises that depart every 20 minutes from either side of the main bridge. It also rents rowboats, canoes and punts (per hour £6) and motorboats (per hour £33).

Stratford Town Ghost Walk WALKING
(☎07855-760377; www.stratfordtownwalk.co.uk; adult/child £6/4; ⏲7.30pm Fri & Sat) Chill-seekers can take the two-hour Stratford Town Ghost Walk departing from Waterside, opposite Sheep St.

Festivals & Events

Stratford Literary Festival LITERATURE
(☎01789-470185; www.stratfordliteraryfestival.co.uk; ⏲Apr or May) A highlight of Stratford's cultural calendar is the week-long annual Stratford Literary Festival, which attracts literary big-hitters of the calibre of John Simpson and Jonathan Miller.

Stratford-upon-Avon

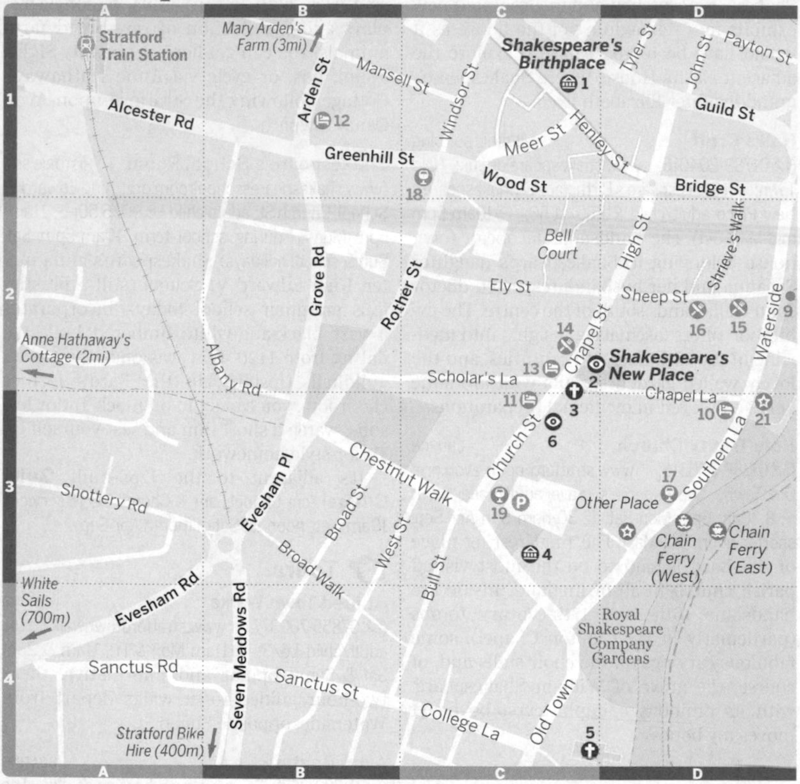

Sleeping

B&Bs are plentiful, particularly along Grove Rd and Evesham Pl, but vacancies can be hard to find during the high season; check listings on www.shakespeare-country.co.uk. The tourist office can help with bookings for a £5 fee.

Stratford-upon-Avon YHA HOSTEL £
(☎0845 371 9661; www.yha.org.uk; Hemmingford House, Wellesbourne, Alveston; dm/d/camping pod from £19/90/89; P @ ☎ ♿) Set in a large 200-year-old mansion 1.5 miles east of the town centre, this superior hostel attracts travellers of all ages. Of its 32 rooms and dorms, 16 are en suite, as are four-person camping pods with kitchenettes. There's a canteen, bar and kitchen. Buses X15, X18 and 18A run here from Bridge St. Wi-fi is available in common areas.

Falcon Hotel HOTEL ££
(☎01789-279953; www.sjhotels.co.uk; Chapel St; d/f from £85/145; P ☎ ♿) Definitely request a room in the original 15th-century building, not the soulless modern annex or dingy 17th-century garden house of this epicentral hotel. This way you'll get the full Tudor experience – creaky floorboards, wonky timbered walls and all. Open fires blaze in the public areas but the best asset is the bargain-priced-for-Stratford car park (£5). Family rooms sleep three people.

Emsley Guesthouse B&B ££
(☎01789-299557; www.theemsley.co.uk; 4 Arden St; d £65-90, f £105-130; P ☎) This lovely five-bedroom Victorian property has a personable owner, very clean and attractive accommodation, and a large, pretty family room at the top with an exposed-beam ceiling. Weekends require a two-night minimum stay.

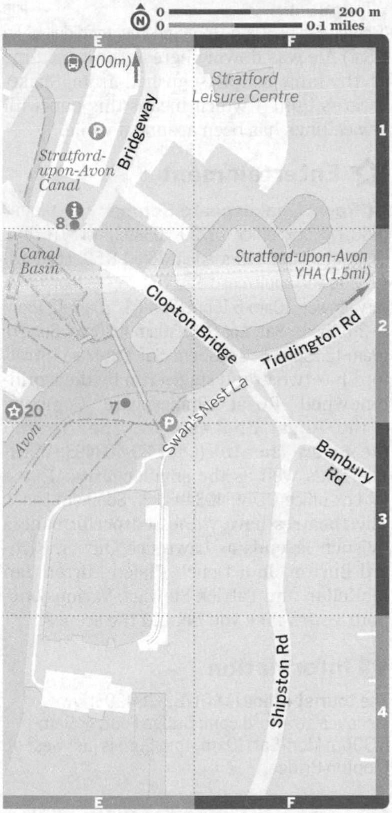

Stratford-upon-Avon

Top Sights
1 Shakespeare's Birthplace C1
2 Shakespeare's New Place C2

Sights
3 Guild Chapel C2
4 Hall's Croft C3
5 Holy Trinity Church C4
6 Shakespeare's School Room C3

Activities, Courses & Tours
7 Avon Boating E2
8 City Sightseeing E1
9 Guided Town Walks D2
Stratford Town Ghost Walk .... (see 9)

Sleeping
10 Arden Hotel D3
11 Church Street Townhouse C3
12 Emsley Guesthouse B1
13 Falcon Hotel C2

Eating
Church Street Townhouse .... (see 11)
14 Edward Moon's C2
15 Fourteas D2
16 Lambs D2

Drinking & Nightlife
17 Dirty Duck D3
18 Old Thatch Tavern C1
19 Windmill Inn C3

Entertainment
20 Royal Shakespeare Company E2
21 Swan Theatre D3

White Sails B&B ££
(01789-550469; www.white-sails.co.uk; 85 Evesham Rd; s £75-100, d £105-130;) Plush fabrics, framed prints, brass bedsteads and shabby-chic tables and lamps set the scene at this intimate property on the town's western edge. The four individually furnished rooms come with flatscreen TVs, climate control and glamorous bathrooms.

Church Street Townhouse BOUTIQUE HOTEL £££
(01789-262222; www.churchstreet-th.co.uk; 16 Church St; d from £110;) Some of the dozen rooms at this exquisite hotel have free-standing claw-foot bathtubs, and all have iPod docks, flatscreen TVs and luxurious furnishings. Light sleepers should avoid room 1, nearest the bar. The building itself is a centrally located 400-year-old gem with a first-rate restaurant and bar. There's a minimum two-night stay on weekends.

Arden Hotel HOTEL £££
(01789-298682; www.theardenhotelstratford.com; Waterside; d incl breakfast from £129; P @) Facing the Swan Theatre, this elegant property has a sleek brasserie and champagne bar. Its 45 rooms feature designer fabrics and its bathrooms are full of polished stone.

Eating

Fourteas TEAROOM £
(01789-293908; www.thefourteas.co.uk; 24 Sheep St; dishes £4-7, afternoon tea with/without Prosecco £18.50/14; 9.30am-5pm Mon-Sat, 11am-4pm Sun) Breaking with Stratford's Shakespearean theme, this tearoom takes the 1940s as its inspiration with beautiful old teapots, framed posters and staff in period costume. As well as premium loose-leaf teas and homemade cakes, there are hearty breakfasts, delicious sandwiches (fresh poached salmon, brie and grape), a hot dish

of the day and indulgent afternoon teas (gluten-free options available).

Church Street Townhouse BISTRO ££
(☎01789-262222; www.churchstreettownhouse.com; 16 Church St; mains £11-24; ⏰kitchen noon-3pm & 5-9.45pm, bar 8am-midnight Mon-Sat, to 10.30pm Sun; 📶) This lovely restaurant is a fantastic place for immersing yourself in Stratford's historic charms. The food is delightful and the ambience impeccably congenial and well presented. Music students from Shakespeare's old grammar school across the way tinkle the piano ivories daily at 5.30pm, though it can be hard to hear over the bar noise.

Lambs MODERN EUROPEAN ££
(☎01789-292554; www.lambsrestaurant.co.uk; 12 Sheep St; mains £13-19; ⏰5-9pm Mon, noon-2pm & 5-9pm Tue-Sat, noon-2pm & 6-9pm Sun) Lambs swaps Shakespeare chintz in favour of Venetian blinds and modern elegance but throws in authentic 16th-century ceiling beams for good measure. The menu embraces Gressingham duck, deep-fried goats cheese and slow-roasted lamb shank, backed up by a strong wine list.

Edward Moon's MODERN BRITISH ££
(☎01789-267069; www.edwardmoon.com; 9 Chapel St; mains £10-17; ⏰11am-2.30pm & 5-9.30pm Mon-Fri, 11am-3pm & 5-10pm Sat, 11am-3pm & 5-9pm Sun) Named after a famous travelling chef who cooked up the flavours of home for the British colonial service, this snug eatery serves delicious, hearty English dishes, many livened up with herbs and spices from the East. Kids get pared-down versions of adult dishes.

Drinking & Nightlife

★Old Thatch Tavern PUB
(www.oldthatchtavernstratford.co.uk; Greenhill St; ⏰11.30am-11pm Mon-Sat, noon-6pm Sun; 📶) To truly appreciate Stratford's olde-worlde atmosphere, join the locals for a pint at the town's oldest pub. Built in 1470, this thatched-roofed, low-ceilinged treasure has great real ales and a gorgeous summertime courtyard.

Dirty Duck PUB
(Black Swan; Waterside; ⏰11am-11pm Mon-Sat, to 10.30pm Sun) Also called the 'Black Swan', this enchanting riverside alehouse is the only pub in England to be licensed under two names. It's a favourite thespian watering hole, with a roll-call of former regulars (Olivier, Attenborough et al) that reads like a who's who of actors.

Windmill Inn PUB
(Church St; ⏰10am-11pm Sun-Thu, to midnight Fri & Sat) Ale was flowing here at the same time as rhyming couplets gushed from Shakespeare's quill – which means this pub with low ceilings has been around a while.

Entertainment

★Royal Shakespeare Company THEATRE
(RSC; ☎box office 01789-403493; www.rsc.org.uk; Waterside; tours adult £6.50-8.50, child £3-4.50, tower adult/child £2.50/1.25; ⏰tour times vary, tower 10am-6.15pm Sun-Fri, 10am-12.15pm & 2-6.15pm Sat Apr-Sep, 10am-4.30pm Sun-Fri, 10am-12.15pm & 2-4.30pm Sat Oct-Mar) Stratford has two grand stages run by the world-renowned Royal Shakespeare Company – the **Royal Shakespeare Theatre** and the **Swan Theatre** (☎01789-403493; Waterside) – as well as the smaller **Other Place** (☎box office 01789-403493; 22 Southern Lane). The theatres have witnessed performances by such legends as Lawrence Olivier, Richard Burton, Judi Dench, Helen Mirren, Ian McKellan and Patrick Stewart. Various one-hour **tours** take you behind the scenes.

Information

The **tourist office** (☎01789-264293; www.discover-stratford.com; Bridge Foot; ⏰9am-5.30pm Mon-Sat, 10am-4pm Sun) is just west of Clopton Bridge.

Getting There & Away

BUS

National Express coaches and other bus companies run from Stratford's Riverside bus station (behind the Stratford Leisure Centre on Bridgeway). Services include the following:

Birmingham National Express; £8.50, one hour, two per day

London Victoria National Express; £7, three hours, three per day

Oxford National Express; £10.80, one hour, two per day

CAR

If you're driving, be warned that town car parks charge high fees, 24 hours a day.

TRAIN

From Stratford-upon-Avon train station, London Midland runs to Birmingham (£7.70, 50 minutes, half-hourly), Chiltern Railways serves London Marylebone (£28.90, two hours, up to two per hour) and East Midlands runs to Warwick (£6.60, 30 minutes, hourly).

The nostalgic **Shakespeare Express Steam Train** (☎0121-708 4960; www.shakespeare express.com; adult/child £20/15) chugs twice every Sunday in July and August between Stratford and Birmingham Snow Hill; journey time is one hour.

Getting Around

From 10am to 6pm April to October, a 1937-built, hand-wound **chain ferry** (one-way 50p) yo-yos across the Avon (one way 50p).

A bicycle is handy for getting out to the outlying Shakespeare properties. **Stratford Bike Hire** (☎07711-776340; www.stratford bikehire.com; The Stratford Greenway, 7 Seven Meadows Rd; bike rental per half-/full day from £10/15; ⏲9.30am-5pm) will deliver to your accommodation for free within a 6-mile radius of Stratford.

Rugby

POP 101,373

Warwickshire's second-largest hub, Rugby is an attractive market town whose history dates back to the Iron Age. But it's most famous for the sport that was invented here and now takes its name, and is a place of pilgrimage for fans.

The game was invented at prestigious Rugby School in 1823 when William Webb Ellis is said to have caught the ball during a football match and broken the rules by running with it. Situated just across from the **Webb Ellis Rugby Football Museum** (☎01788-567777; 5-6 Matthews St; ⏲9.30am-5pm Mon-Sat) FREE, the school itself is closed to the public, but you can peek at the hallowed ground through the gates on Barby Rd. A gleaming golden **statue of William Webb Ellis** (Lawrence Sheriff St) stands outside the main Rugby School gates on Lawrence Sheriff St.

A whizz-bang new interactive World Rugby Hall of Fame has opened in the **Rugby Art Gallery, Museum & Library** (☎01788-533201; www.ragm.co.uk; Little Elborow St; ⏲10am-5pm Tue-Fri, to 4pm Sat; 📶) FREE.

Sleeping & Eating

★**Brownsover Hall** HISTORIC HOTEL ££
(☎01788-546100; www.brownsoverhall.co.uk; Brownsover Lane, Old Brownsover; d from £82; P📶) Set in 2.8 hectares of woodland and manicured gardens 2.7 miles north of Rugby, this Grade II–listed Gothic Revival manor (where Frank Whittle designed the turbo jet engine) has 47 rooms, split between the creaking old house with monumental central timber staircase and the more modern converted stables. Friendly staff are ultraefficient. Ask about dinner, bed and breakfast packages.

Manor Farm Shop & Cafe CAFE, DELI £
(☎01788-869002; www.manorfarmcatthorpe.co.uk; Main St, Catthorpe; dishes £4-11; ⏲cafe & shop 9am-6pm Mon-Sat, 10am-5pm Sun;) On this working farm 4.5 miles northeast of Rugby, you can pet rare-breed animals, pick your own fruit (priced by weight) and browse the deli. Blackboard specials at the barn-like cafe might include pies (cottage; steak and ale), liver and bacon casserole, and rabbit stew, along with vegetarian options such as cheesy leek and potato bake, and full English breakfasts.

Café Vin Cinq FRENCH, INTERNATIONAL ££
(☎01788-541304; www.cafevincinq.com; 25 High St; mains £14-20; ⏲6-10pm Mon-Fri, 11am-2.30pm & 6-10pm Sat) French fare mostly figures on the menu (coq au vin, bouillabaisse, top-tier steak), but successful forays elsewhere span Thailand (fiery red curry) to British home turf (puddings include Eton-mess cheesecake and warm treacle tart with clotted cream). The space is beautiful, both inside (vintage furniture, patterned wallpaper, chandeliers) and out (look for the aqua facade and red-and-white-checked pavement tables).

WORTH A TRIP

ALTON TOWERS

Phenomenally popular **Alton Towers** (☎0871 222 3330; www.altontowers.com; Farley Lane, Alton; adult/child £51.60/45.60, water park £17.50/12.75; ⏲amusement park 10am-6pm mid-Jul–Aug, to 5pm Easter–mid-Jul, Sep & Oct, closed Nov-Easter, water park 10am-8pm mid-Jul–Aug, to 4pm Sep–mid-Jul) , 4 miles east of Cheadle off the B5032, offers maximum G-force for your buck. Wild rides include the Th13teen, Nemesis, Oblivion and 2016-opened Galactica coasters. Gentler thrills span carousels and stage shows to a pirate-themed aquarium and splashtastic **water park** (check ahead for seasonal closures). Book online to skip ticket queues and take advantage of discounted entry deals. The on-site **hotel** (d from £192) offers themed rooms plus perks such as an hour's early park entry.

Drinking

★William Webb Ellis PUB

(22 Warwick St; ⊙11am-11pm Mon-Thu, to 1am Fri & Sat, to 10pm Sun) Rugby's passion for its home-grown sport reaches fever pitch here. Memorabilia covers the walls, staff wear jerseys, cocktails are all rugby-themed (whisky-based 'Half Time'; Kahlúa- and vodka-laced 'Full Time'; Baileys and sambuca 'Scrum Shot'...), as is the food (provenance-inspired 'Six Nations Sausages'), and TVs not only screen live matches but also reruns of vintage fixtures. Unmissable.

Information

Rugby's **tourist office** (☎01788-533217; www.enjoyrugby.co.uk; Little Elborow St; ⊙10am-4pm Mon-Sat) is inside the Rugby Art Gallery, Museum and Library.

Getting There & Away

Rugby is 13 miles east of Coventry, served by regular trains (£5.70, 10 minutes, up to four hourly). Trains also serve Birmingham (£9.50, 40 minutes, two to four per hour) and Leicester (£14, one hour, hourly).

STAFFORDSHIRE

Despite being wedged between the ever-expanding conurbations of Birmingham and Manchester, Staffordshire is surprisingly green, with the northern half of the county rising to meet the rugged hills of the Peak District.

Getting There & Around

Regular trains and National Express buses serve Stafford and other major towns. The main local bus operator is **First Group** (☎08456 020 121; www.firstgroup.com). The public-transport pages at www.staffordshire.gov.uk and Traveline (p408) have details of services.

Lichfield

POP 32,219

Even without its magnificent Gothic cathedral – one of the most spectacular in the country – this charming cobbled market town would be worth a visit to tread in the footsteps of lexicographer and wit Samuel Johnson, and natural philosopher Erasmus Darwin, grandfather of Charles. Johnson once described Lichfield folk as 'the most sober, decent people in England', which was rather generous considering that this was the last place in the country to stop burning people at the stake.

Sights

★Lichfield Cathedral CATHEDRAL

(☎01543-306100; www.lichfield-cathedral.org; 19 Cathedral Close; admission by donation; ⊙7am-6.15pm Mon-Fri, 8am-6.15pm Sat, 7.30am-4.30pm Sun) Crowned by three dramatic towers, Lichfield Cathedral is a Gothic fantasy, constructed in stages from 1200 to 1350. The enormous vaulted nave is set slightly off line from the choir, creating a bizarre perspective when viewed from the west door, and carvings inside the cathedral still bear signs of damage caused by Civil War soldiers sharpening their swords.

Erasmus Darwin House HISTORIC BUILDING

(☎01543-306260; www.erasmusdarwin.org; Beacon St; ⊙11am-5pm Apr-Oct, to 4pm Thu-Sun Nov-Mar) FREE After turning down the job of royal physician to King George III – perhaps a lucky escape, considering the monarch's descent into madness – Erasmus Darwin became a leading light in the Lunar Society, debating the origins of life with luminaries including Wedgwood, Boulton and Watt decades before his grandson Charles came up with the theory of evolution. The former house of the 'Grandfather of Evolution' contains some intriguing personal effects. At the back, a fragrant herb garden leads to Cathedral Close.

Samuel Johnson Birthplace Museum MUSEUM

(☎01543-264972; www.samueljohnsonbirthplace.org.uk; Breadmarket St; ⊙10.30am-4.30pm Apr-Sep, 11am-3.30pm Oct-Mar) FREE This absorbing museum charts the life of the pioneering lexicographer, poet and critic Samuel Johnson, who moved to London from his native Lichfield and devoted nine years to producing the first major dictionary of the English language. Johnson's first dictionary helped define the word 'dull' with this example: 'to make dictionaries is dull work'. On the 1st floor, a short dramatised film narrates Johnson's life story. It's a lovely property to explore.

Lichfield Museum MUSEUM

(☎01543-256611; www.stmaryslichfield.co.uk; Market Sq; museum free, tower adult/child £3/1.50; ⊙9.30am-3.30pm daily late Mar–mid-Sep, Mon-Sat mid-Sep–late Mar) Exhibits cover 1300 years of Lichfield history at this museum inside the old St Mary's Church. Climb the tower's 120 steps for sweeping city views.

Sleeping & Eating

George Hotel HOTEL ££
(☎01543-414822; www.thegeorgelichfield.co.uk; 12-14 Bird St; s/d from £90/105; P 📶) Part of the Best Western group, this old Georgian pub has been upgraded into a comfortable midrange hotel with 44 rooms that scores points for location rather than atmosphere.

Damn Fine Cafe CAFE £
(www.damnfinecafelichfield.co.uk; 16 Bird St; dishes £4-10; ⊙9am-4pm Tue, Thu & Fri, to 3.30pm Wed, to 5pm Sat, 10am-4pm Sun; 👪) Teeming with locals, this cafe is a handy spot for sandwiches, soup, filling bacon-and-sausage breakfasts (served all day) or vegetarian toad-in-the-hole. Order and pay at the counter.

Chapters Cathedral Coffee Shop CAFE £
(☎01543-306125; 19 Cathedral Close; dishes £3.50-8; ⊙9am-5pm Mon-Sat, 10am-4pm Sun Jul & Aug, 9am-4pm Mon-Sat, 10am-4pm Sun Sep-Jun) Ensconced in a fine 18th-century house overlooking its 13th-century walled garden on one side and the cathedral on the other, Chapters serves morning and afternoon tea and Sunday lunches.

★ **Trooper** GASTROPUB ££
(☎01543-480413; www.thetrooperwall.co.uk; Watling St, Wall; mains £9.50-23; ⊙kitchen noon-9.15pm Mon-Wed, to 9.45pm Thu-Sat, to 8pm Sun, bar noon-midnight Mon-Sat, to 10pm Sun; 👪) 🍃 Situated 3 miles southwest of Lichfield in the tiny village of Wall, this idyllic gastropub prides itself on ingredients such as 28-day aged steak (served with hand-cut, beef-dripping-fried chips and sweet tomato chutney) and pork belly (with apple and quince jus) plus vegetarian options using herbs from its gardens. It has fabulous real ales and a sunny beer garden too.

Wine House MODERN BRITISH ££
(☎01543-419999; www.thewinehouselichfield.co.uk; 27 Bird St; mains £10-40; ⊙noon-10pm Mon-Sat, to 6pm Sun) Astutely selected whites, reds, champagnes and rosés, including many by-the-glass options, complement the seriously good cooking at these smart, red-brick premises. Choices range from pancetta-wrapped, fig-stuffed pork fillet to steamed Scottish mussels with tail-on tiger prawns and squid-ink risotto.

WORTH A TRIP

LORD LICHFIELD'S SHUGBOROUGH

The regal, neoclassical mansion **Shugborough** (☎0845 459 8900; www.shugborough.org.uk; Great Haywood; adult/child £15/9, garden only £3.50; ⊙11am-5pm Wed-Mon mid-Mar–mid-Oct, garden 11am-5pm daily year-round) is the ancestral home of royal photographer Lord Lichfield. A good proportion of the wall space is devoted to his work; the highlight is the staterooms' collection of exquisite Louis XV and XVI furniture. One-hour guided tours (included in admission) run between 11am and 1pm. Shugborough is 6 miles east of Stafford on the A513; bus 825 linking Stafford and Lichfield stops 1 mile from the manor (£3.10, 20 minutes, half-hourly Monday to Saturday, hourly Sunday).

Drinking & Nightlife

★ **Whippet Inn** PUB
(www.whippetinnmicro.co.uk; 21 Tamworth St; ⊙noon-2.30pm & 4.30-10pm Wed & Thu, noon-10pm Fri & Sat, noon-5pm Sun) 🍃 All of the ales at this adorable little one-room micropub are sourced within a 50-mile radius of Lichfield and there's also a wonderful selection of handcrafted cloudy and clear West Country, Welsh and Scottish ciders, along with British wines, but it resolutely doesn't serve lager, keg beer or spirits. Artisan bar snacks include pork pies, Scotch eggs and sausage rolls.

Information

The **tourist office** (☎01543-256611; www.stmaryslichfield.co.uk; Market Sq; ⊙9.30am-4pm Mon-Sat year-round plus 10am-4pm Sun Easter-Sep) is in the Lichfield Museum.

Getting There & Away

The bus station is opposite the main Lichfield City train station on Birmingham Rd. Bus 825 serves Stafford (£3.60, 1½ hours, half-hourly Monday to Saturday, hourly on Sunday).

Lichfield has two train stations:

Lichfield City Trains to Birmingham (£5, 35 minutes, every 20 minutes) leave from Lichfield City station in the centre.

Lichfield Trent Valley Trains to London Euston (£37, 1¾ hours, up to two per hour) run from Lichfield Trent Valley station on the eastern side of town 1.5 miles east of the centre.

WORTH A TRIP

THE POTTERIES - STOKE-ON-TRENT

Situated at the heart of the Potteries (the famous pottery-producing region of Staffordshire) Stoke-on-Trent is famed for its ceramics. Don't expect cute little artisanal producers: this was where pottery shifted to mass production during the Industrial Revolution, and Stoke today is a sprawl of industrial townships tied together by flyovers and bypasses. There are dozens of active potteries that you can visit in the greater area, including the famous Wedgwood factory.

The **tourist office** (☎01782-236000; www.visitstoke.co.uk; Bethesda St, Hanley; ⏰10am-5pm Mon-Sat, 11am-4pm Sun) has information on all the potteries that are open to the public.

Potteries Museum & Art Gallery (☎01782-236000; www.stokemuseums.org.uk; Bethesda St, Hanley; ⏰10am-5pm Mon-Sat, 11am-4pm Sun) For a thorough overview of the Potteries area's history, this museum/gallery houses an extensive ceramics display, from Toby jugs and jasperware to outrageous ornamental pieces. Other highlights include treasures from the 2009-discovered Staffordshire Hoard (the largest hoard of Anglo-Saxon gold and silver metalwork ever found, incorporating 5.1kg of gold, 1.4kg of silver and some 3500 pieces of jewellery); displays on the WWII Spitfire, created by the Stoke-born aviator Reginald Mitchell; and artworks by TS Lowry and Sir Henry Moore.

Wedgwood Visitor Centre (☎01782-282986; www.worldofwedgwood.com; Wedgwood Dr, Barlaston; factory tour & museum adult/child £15/7.50, factory tour only £10/5, museum only £7.50/3.75; ⏰10am-5pm Mon-Fri, to 4pm Sat & Sun) Set in attractive parkland 8 miles south of Hanley, the modern production centre for Josiah Wedgwood's porcelain empire displays an extensive collection of historic pieces, including plenty of Wedgwood's delicate, neoclassical blue-and-white jasperware. The fascinating industrial process is revealed, and there's an interesting film on Josiah's life and work, including his involvement in canal-building and opposition to slavery.

WORCESTERSHIRE

Famed for its eponymous condiment, invented by two Worcester chemists in 1837, Worcestershire marks the transition from the industrial heart of the Midlands to the peaceful countryside of the Welsh Marches. The southern and western fringes of the county burst with lush countryside and sleepy market towns, while the capital is a classic English county town, whose magnificent cathedral inspired the composer Elgar to write some of his greatest works.

Activities

The 210-mile riverside **Severn Way** winds through Worcestershire en route from Plynlimon in Wales to the sea at Bristol. A shorter challenge is the 100-mile **Three Choirs Way**, linking Worcester to Hereford and Gloucester. The Malvern Hills (p433) are also prime country for walking and cycling; information is available at www.malvernhillsaonb.org.uk.

Getting There & Away

Worcester is a convenient rail hub. Kidderminster is the southern railhead of the quaint Severn Valley Railway (p445).

Buses and trains connect larger towns, but bus services to rural areas can be frustratingly infrequent; search the transport pages at www.worcestershire.gov.uk or Traveline (p408) for bus companies and timetables.

Worcester

POP 99,600

Worcester (pronounced *woos*-ter) has enough historic treasures to forgive the architectural eyesores from the postwar love affair with all things concrete. The home of the famous Worcestershire sauce (an unlikely combination of fermented tamarinds and anchovies), this ancient cathedral city was the site of the last battle of the Civil War, the Battle of Worcester, which took place on 3 September 1651. The defeated Charles II only narrowly escaped the pursuing Roundheads by hiding in an oak tree, an event still celebrated in Worcester every 29 May, when government buildings are decked out with oak sprigs.

Sights

★ **Worcester Cathedral** CATHEDRAL
(☎01905-732900; www.worcestercathedral.co.uk; 8 College Yard; cathedral free, tower adult/child £4/2,

tours £4/free; ⌚7.30am-6pm, tower 11am-5pm Sat Apr-Oct, tours 11am & 2.30pm Mon-Sat Apr-Nov, Sat Dec-Mar) Rising above the River Severn, Worcester's majestic cathedral is best known as the final resting place of Magna Carta signatory King John. The strong-legged can tackle the 249 steps to the top of the **tower**, from where Charles II surveyed his troops during the disastrous Battle of Worcester. Hour-long **tours** run from the gift shop. Several works by local composer Edward Elgar had their first public outings here – to appreciate the acoustics, come for **evensong** (5.30pm Monday to Saturday, 4pm Sunday).

Commandery MUSEUM
(☎01905-361821; www.worcester.gov.uk; College St; adult/child £5.50/2.50; ⌚10am-5pm Tue-Sat, 1.30-5pm Sun) The town's history museum is housed in a splendid Tudor building that served as King Charles II's headquarters during the Battle of Worcester. Engaging audio guides and interactive exhibits tell the story of Worcester during key periods in its history. A highlight is the 'painted chamber', covered with intriguing 15th-century religious frescos.

Royal Worcester Porcelain Works MUSEUM
(☎01905-21247; www.museumofroyalworcester.org; Severn St; adult/child £6/free; ⌚10am-5pm Mon-Sat Mar-Oct, to 4pm Nov-Feb) Up there with the country's most famous potteries, the Royal Worcester porcelain factory gained an edge over its rivals by picking up the contract to provide fine crockery to the English monarchy. An entertaining audio tour reveals some quirkier sides to the Royal Worcester story, including its brief foray into porcelain dentures and 'portable fonts' designed for cholera outbreaks. The shop has some splendid pieces, from monk-shaped candle-snuffers to decorated thimbles and pill boxes.

Sleeping & Eating

Diglis House Hotel HOTEL ££
(☎01905-353518; www.diglishousehotel.co.uk; Severn St; d £78-153; P 📶) Next to the boathouse in a gorgeous waterside setting, this rambling yet cosy 28-room Georgian house is a short stroll from the cathedral. The best rooms have four-poster beds, luxe bathrooms and river views. Guests can work out at the nearby gym for free.

Lenchford Inn INN ££
(☎01905-620229; www.thelenchfordinn.co.uk; Shrawley; d/tr/f from £75/90/95; P 📶 👪) An easy 8-mile drive north of Worcester, this sprawling inn on the banks of the Severn is a haven of tranquillity. Its nine en suite rooms (including family rooms) are old-fashioned but spacious and squeaky clean, and all open onto a communal balcony or terrace with river views. There's a cavernous restaurant (kids' menu available) and sociable bar.

Mac & Jac's DELI, CAFE £
(www.macandjacs.co.uk; 44 Friar St; dishes £4.50-14; ⌚9am-5pm Mon-Sat) This Friar St outfit has a lovely deli downstairs and a relaxing cafe upstairs for caffeine, sandwiches with fillings such as brie and grape, and a wholesome menu of hot dishes such as crispy pork belly with toasted almonds and coriander. Look out for gourmet supper evenings (two-/three-course menus £27/33). There's a second location in Great Malvern (p433).

★**Old Rectifying House** MODERN BRITISH ££
(☎01905-619622; www.theoldrec.co.uk; North Parade; mains £13-24.50; ⌚kitchen noon-3pm & 6-9pm Tue-Thu, noon-9.30pm Fri & Sat, noon-6pm Sun, bar noon-11pm Tue-Thu, to 12.30am Fri & Sat, to 11pm Sun) Worcester's hippest dining space has a candlelit, painted-brick interior and umbrella-shaded courtyard tables. Its switched-on menu features dishes such as roast pigeon breast with black pudding and watercress or dry-aged rib-eye with duck egg and red-wine jus. DJs often hit the decks in the lounge bar, which mixes mighty cocktails including 'Walnut of Wall St'.

Drinking & Entertainment

★**Cardinal's Hat** PUB
(☎01905-724006; www.the-cardinals-hat.co.uk; 31 Friar St; ⌚noon-11pm Mon-Sat, to 10.30pm Sun; 📶) Dating from the 14th century, and claiming a resident ghost, Worcester's oldest pub has had a grand makeover that highlights its original features including log-burning stoves. English craft beers and ciders dominate the taps; its menu concentrates on locally sourced British classics (Scotch eggs, pies, kippers, artisan cheese platters). Upstairs are four Georgian-style boutique guest rooms (doubles £80 to £125).

Marr's Bar LIVE MUSIC
(☎01905-613336; www.marrsbar.co.uk; 12 Pierpoint St; ⌚8pm-late) The best live-music venue for miles around, Marr's still has its original sprung dance floors from its days as a dance studio. There's a lively schedule of gigs, acts, comedy shows, acoustic and jamming evenings most nights.

Information

Located inside the Grade I–listed Guildhall, dating from 1721, the **tourist office** (☎01905-726311; www.visitworcestershire.org/worcester; Guildhall, High St; ⊙9.30am-5pm Mon-Sat) has details of history-focused town walks.

Getting There & Away

BUS

The **bus station** is inside the Crowngate Centre on Friary Walk. National Express has services to London Victoria (£19.20, 3½ hours, two daily).

TRAIN

Worcester Foregate is the main rail hub, but services also run from Worcester Shrub Hill. Regular trains:

Birmingham £8.10, one hour, every 20 minutes
Great Malvern £5.20, 15 minutes, up to four per hour
Hereford £9.40, 50 minutes, hourly
Ledbury £6.80, 25 minutes, hourly
London Paddington £18, 2½ hours, hourly

Great Malvern

POP 32,900

Tumbling down the side of a forested ridge about 7 miles southwest of Worcester, the picturesque spa town of Great Malvern is the gateway to the Malverns, a soaring 9-mile-long range of volcanic hills that rise unexpectedly from the surrounding meadows. In Victorian times, the medicinal waters were prescribed as a panacea for everything from gout to 'sore eyes' – you can test the theory by sampling Malvern water at public wells dotted around the town.

WORTH A TRIP

ELGAR BIRTHPLACE MUSEUM

England's most popular classical composer is celebrated with appropriate pomp and circumstance at **Elgar Birthplace Museum** (☎01905-333224; www.elgarmuseum.org; Crown East Lane, Lower Broadheath; adult/child £7.50/3.50; ⊙11am-5pm Fri-Thu Easter–mid-Sep), housed in the humble country cottage where Edward Elgar was born in 1857. Admission includes an audio guide with musical interludes so that you can appreciate what all the fuss is about.

The cottage is 4 miles west of Worcester; you'll need your own transport.

Sights

★ **Morgan Motor Company** MUSEUM
(☎01684-584580; www.morgan-motor.co.uk; Pickersleigh Rd; museum free, tours adult/child £20/10; ⊙museum 8.30am-5pm Mon-Thu, to 3pm Fri, tours 10am, 12.30pm & 2.30pm Mon-Fri) FREE Morgan has been handcrafting elegant sports cars since 1909, and you can still see the mechanics at work on two-hour guided tours of the unassuming shed-like buildings comprising the factory (prebooking essential), and view a fleet of vintage classics adjacent to the museum. If buying one of these beautiful machines is beyond your budget, you can rent one per day/week from £200/975, including insurance, for a spin through the Malvern Hills.

Great Malvern Priory MONASTERY
(☎01684-561020; www.greatmalvernpriory.org.uk; Church St; ⊙9am-5pm) FREE The 11th-century Great Malvern Priory is packed with remarkable features, from original Norman pillars to surreal modernist stained glass. The choir is enclosed by a screen of 15th-century tiles and the monks' stalls are decorated with delightfully irreverent 14th-century misericords, depicting everything from three rats hanging a cat to the mythological reptile, the basilisk. Charles Darwin's daughter Annie is buried here.

Malvern Museum of Local History MUSEUM
(☎01684-567811; www.malvernmuseum.co.uk; Priory Gatehouse, Abbey Rd; adult/child £2/50p; ⊙10.30am-5pm Mar-Oct) Straddling Abbey Rd in the grand Priory Gatehouse (c 1470), the town museum offers a thorough exploration of Great Malvern's claims to fame, including spring waters, medieval monasteries, the Malvern Hills and Morgan Motors.

Tours

Great Malvern Walking Tours WALKING
(adult/child £3/50p; ⊙tours 10.30am Sat & Sun Apr-Sep) Walking tours departing from the tourist office explore the town's medieval and Victorian history over 1½ hours (no reservations needed).

Sleeping & Eating

Como House B&B ££
(☎01684-561486; www.comohouse.co.uk; Como Rd; s/d £45/70; P ❄ 🛜) This handsome stone house benefits from a quiet location away from the central bustle. Rooms are snug, the garden is a delight and the mood is restoratively calm. Vegetarian and gluten-free

breakfasts are available on request, and the friendly owners will pick you up from the station and drop you off by the walking trails.

Abbey Hotel HOTEL £££

(☎01684-892332; www.sarova-abbeyhotel.com; Abbey Rd; d £149-205; P @) Tangled in vines like a Brothers Grimm fairy-tale castle, this stately property has 103 elegant rooms in a prime location by the museum and priory.

Mac & Jac's CAFE £

(www.macandjacs.co.uk; 23 Abbey Rd; dishes £4.50-14; 9am-7pm Tue-Sat, 10am-4pm Sun) Creative salads, flatbreads, sharing plates, spelt risotto and a savoury tart of the day are served up at this fresh addition to the town's dining scene. It's the sister branch of the popular Worcester (p431) cafe, set in a chic white-painted shopfront near the Great Malvern Priory.

St Ann's Well Cafe CAFE, VEGETARIAN £

(☎01684-560285; www.stannswell.co.uk; St Ann's Rd; dishes £2-4.50; 11.30am-3.30pm Tue-Fri, 10am-4pm Sat & Sun Easter-Sep;) A s-t-e-e-p climb above St Ann's Rd (so best to check opening times beforehand), this quaint cafe is set in an early-19th-century villa, with mountain-fresh spring water bubbling into a carved basin by the door. All-vegetarian food (including vegan options) spans soups to pies, filled baguettes, cakes, pastries and puddings.

Fig Tree MODERN BRITISH ££

(☎01684-569909; www.thefigtreemalvern.co.uk; 99b Church St; mains £8-17.50; noon-2pm & 5.30-9.30pm Tue-Sat) Tucked down an alleyway off Church St, this 19th-century former stable serves Mediterranean-inspired fare such as marinated pork chops with caramelised apple, red onion and rosemary potatoes, and chargrilled chicken with minted yoghurt and saffron rice.

☆ Entertainment

Theatre of Small Convenience THEATRE

(☎01684-568933; www.wctheatre.co.uk; Edith Walk; shows adult/child £2.50/1.50; Easter-Sep) Set in a converted Victorian public lavatory decked out with theatrical Italianate flourishes, this quirky place has just 12 seats and a program running from puppet shows to poetry and opera. Shows usually last five to 10 minutes.

Malvern Theatres THEATRE

(☎01684-892277; www.malvern-theatres.co.uk; Grange Rd) One of the country's best provincial theatres, this long-established cultural hub packs in a lively program of classical music, dance, comedy, drama and cinema.

WALKING IN THE MALVERN HILLS

The jack-in-the-box Malvern Hills, which dramatically pop up out of the Severn plains on the boundary between Worcestershire and Herefordshire, rise to the lofty peak of the Worcester Beacon (419m), reached by a steep 3-mile climb above Great Malvern. More than 100 miles of trails traipse over the various summits, which are mostly capped by exposed grassland, offering the kind of views that inspire orchestral movements.

The Great Malvern tourist office (below) has racks of pamphlets covering popular hikes, including a map of the mineral-water springs, wells and fountains of the town and surrounding hills. The enthusiast-run website www.malverntrail.co.uk is also a goldmine of useful walking information.

A single £4 parking ticket per day is valid at locations throughout the hills.

ℹ Information

The **tourist office** (☎01684-892289; www.visitthemalverns.org; 21 Church St; 10am-5pm Apr-Oct, 10am-5pm Mon-Sat, to 4pm Sun Nov-Mar) is a mine of walking and cycling information.

ℹ Getting There & Away

Buses are limited, making trains your best bet. The train station is east of the centre, off Ave Rd.

Services include the following:

Hereford £7.90, 35 minutes, hourly

Ledbury £5, 10 minutes, hourly

Worcester £5.20, 15 minutes, up to four hourly

HEREFORDSHIRE

Adjoining the Welsh border, Herefordshire is a patchwork of fields, hills and cute little black-and-white villages, many dating back to the Tudor era and beyond.

Activities

As well as the famous **Offa's Dyke Path**, walkers can follow the **Herefordshire Trail**

SUPPING CIDER - HEREFORDSHIRE STYLE

The **Herefordshire Cider Route** (www.ciderroute.co.uk) drops in on numerous local cider producers, where you can try before you buy, and then totter off to the next cidery. Mindful of road safety, tourist offices have maps and guide booklets to help you explore by bus or bicycle.

Westons Cider Mills (01531-660108; www.westons-cider.co.uk; The Bounds, Much Marcle; tours adult/child £10/4; 9am-5pm Mon-Fri, 10am-5pm Sat & Sun) If you only have time to visit one Herefordshire cider-maker, make it Westons Cider Mills, just under a mile west of the tiny village of Much Marcle, its house brew is even served in the Houses of Parliament. Informative tours (1½ hours) start at 11am, 12.30pm, 2pm and 3.30pm, with free cider and perry tastings for the grown-ups. There's also a fascinating bottle museum.

Walwyn Arms (01531-660601; www.bucaneer.co.uk; Much Marcle; mains £9.50-17; kitchen noon-2.30pm & 6-9.30pm Mon-Sat, noon-4pm & 6-9pm Sun, bar 11am-11pm Mon-Sat, to 10pm Sun) Westons ciders are served at this welcoming country pub, just across from Westons Cider Mills. Cider is also used in many dishes, such as the scrumptious twice-baked, mature cheddar and Old Rosie scrumpy soufflé, and cider-battered haddock fillet, with chips and mushy peas. It also has great lunchtime sandwiches (eg prawn and Bloody Mary mayonnaise) on hand-cut bread.

(www.herefordshiretrail.com) on a 150-mile circular loop through Leominster, Ledbury, Ross-on-Wye and Kington. Only slightly less ambitious is the 136-mile **Wye Valley Walk** (www.wyevalleywalk.org), which runs from Chepstow in Wales through Herefordshire and back out again to Plynlimon. Then there's the **Three Choirs Way**, a 100-mile route connecting the cathedrals of Hereford, Worcester and Gloucester.

Cyclists can trace the **Six Castles Cycleway** (NCN Route 44) from Hereford to Leominster and Shrewsbury, or NCN Route 68 to Great Malvern and Worcester.

Getting Around

Trains run frequently to destinations including Hereford and Ledbury, with bus connections on to the rest of the county. For bus timetables, contact Traveline (p408).

Hereford

POP 60,000

Surrounded by apple orchards and rolling pastures at the heart of the Marches, straddling the River Wye, Hereford is best known for prime steaks, cider and the Pretenders (three of the original band members – guitarist James Honeyman-Scott, bassist Pete Farndon and drummer Martin Chamers – were locals). Its key draw for visitors is its magnificent cathedral.

Sights & Activities

★Hereford Cathedral CATHEDRAL
(01432-374202; www.herefordcathedral.org; 5 College Cloisters; cathedral entry by £5 donation, Mappa Mundi £6; cathedral 9.15am-5.30pm Mon-Sat, to 3.30pm Sun, Mappa Mundi 10am-5pm Mon-Sat mid-Mar–Oct, to 4pm Nov–mid-Mar) After Welsh marauders torched the original Saxon cathedral, the Norman rulers of Hereford erected a larger, grander cathedral on the same site, which was subsequently remodelled in a succession of medieval architectural styles.

The signature highlight is the magnificent **Mappa Mundi**, a single piece of calfskin vellum intricately painted with some rather fantastical assumptions about the layout of the globe in around 1290. The same wing contains the world's largest surviving chained library of rare manuscripts manacled to the shelves.

Cider Museum & King Offa Distillery BREWERY
(01432-354207; www.cidermuseum.co.uk; Pomona Pl; adult/child £5.50/3; 10am-5pm Mon-Sat Apr-Oct, 11am-3pm Mon-Sat Nov-Mar) Displays at this brewery and museum cover cider-making history and you can sample the delicious modern brews. Look for the fine *costrels* (minibarrels) used by agricultural workers to carry their wages, which were partially paid in cider. It's half a mile west of the centre; follow Eign St and turn south along Ryelands St.

Ultimate Left Bank CANOEING
(☎01432-264807; www.leftbankcanoehire.co.uk; 15 Bridge St; canoe hire half-day/day £20/25) Rents open canoes to paddle along the River Wye.

Sleeping

Charades B&B £
(☎01432-269444; www.charadeshereford.co.uk; 32 Southbank Rd; s/d from £55/61; P@☎) Handy for the bus station, this imposing Victorian house has six inviting rooms with high ceilings, big and bright windows, and some with soothing countryside views. The house itself has character in spades – look for old service bells in the hall and the plentiful *Titanic* memorabilia.

Kidwells Guest House B&B £
(☎01432-270315; www.kidwellshouse.com; 9 Newtown Rd; s/d £55/65, without bathroom £35/55; P☎) The 20 comfortable rooms at this welcoming B&B in the north of town come in varying categories, including two with big balconies and one with its own courtyard. A sunlit conservatory opens onto a large garden.

★**Castle House** BOUTIQUE HOTEL £££
(☎01432-356321; www.castlehse.co.uk; Castle St; s/d/ste from £130/150/190; P☎) Set in a regal Georgian town house that was once the luxurious digs of the Bishop of Hereford, this tranquil 16-room hotel has a sophisticated restaurant, sunny garden spilling down to the river, and magnificent rooms and suites. Another eight newer rooms (some wheelchair accessible) are a short walk away at 25 Castle St.

Eating & Drinking

★**A Rule of Tum** BURGERS £
(☎01432-351764; www.aruleoftum.com; 32 Aubrey St; burgers £7-9.50; ⊙noon-10pm Mon-Sat, to 8pm Sun) Exposed brick, elongated wooden benches and a courtyard garden are the backdrop for brioche-bun burgers that justify the trip to Hereford alone. Standouts include the Hereford Hop (pulled beef shin, Hereford Hop cheese, dill pickles and mustard mayo), Welsh lamb with celeriac slaw, and portobello mushroom with tangy Shropshire blue cheese (veggie burgers are cooked on a separate grill).

La Madeleine FRENCH ££
(☎01432-265233; www.church-street-cafe-restaurant-hereford.co.uk; 17 Church St; mains £7.50-17, 2-course dinner menu £15; ⊙9.30am-4pm Mon, Tue & Thu, to 10pm Wed, to 10.30pm Fri, to 4.30pm Sat; 👪) La Madeleine's pretty, bare-boards interior, outdoor tables in the vine-draped garden and stylish French menu – breakfast croissants, lunchtime tarts and dinner dishes such as fillet steak with horseradish crème fraiche, fries and green-bean salad – are enough to make any Parisian homesick. Shakes in vintage milk bottles are a kid favourite. During evening services, last orders are at 8pm.

★**Beer in Hand** PUB
(www.beerinhand.co.uk; 136 Eign St; ⊙5-10pm Mon-Thu, 4-11pm Fri & Sat, noon-11pm Sun) Ciders at this independent pub are sublime and most are locally sourced. It's also the tap room for its own Odyssey beers (such as Black Out, a dark-malt, full-bodied American Black Ale brewed with fresh oranges, which it brews on the nearby National Trust Brockhampton Estate). There are board games but no TVs.

Lichfield Vaults PUB
(www.lichfieldvaultshereford.co.uk; 11 Church St; ⊙10.30am-midnight Sun-Thu, to 2am Fri & Sat; ☎) On a cobbled lane near the cathedral, sociable 18th-century pub 'The Lich' opens to a decked beer garden out back. Regular live-music events include a monthly blues Sunday lunch. Jovial Greek Cypriot host Andy serves up superior Greek food including meatballs, meze plates and more.

Venue CLUB
(www.venuehereford.co.uk; Gaol St; ⊙10pm-3am Fri & Sat) Edgy, underground DJs and alternative sounds are constantly on the billing at Hereford's leading club (formerly known as the Jailhouse). Look out for secret sets by big-name spinners.

Information

Hereford's **tourist office** (☎01432-268430; www.visitherefordshire.co.uk; St Owen St; ⊙9.30am-4pm Wed-Fri) is inside the town hall.

Getting There & Away

BUS

The bus station is on Commercial Rd, 500m northeast of the town centre. National Express goes to London Victoria (£21.10, 4½ hours, up to four daily) and Gloucester (£5.60, one hour, four daily).

Local services to destinations including Ross-on-Wye (Bus 44; £3.90, 50 minutes, five daily Monday to Friday, four Saturday) depart from St Owen St in the town centre.

TRAIN

The train station is 950m northeast of the centre.

Regular services:

Birmingham (£16, 1½ hours, hourly)

Ledbury (£6.20, 15 minutes, hourly)

London Paddington (£39.70, three hours, hourly – either direct or with a change in Newport, South Wales)

Ludlow (£9.80, 25 minutes, half-hourly)

Worcester (£9.40, 50 minutes, half-hourly)

Ross-on-Wye

POP 10,582

Set on a red sandstone bluff over a kink in the River Wye, hilly Ross-on-Wye was propelled to fame in the 18th century by Alexander Pope and Samuel Taylor Coleridge, who penned tributes to philanthropist John Kyrle, Man of Ross, who dedicated his life and fortune to the poor of the parish.

Sights

Market House GALLERY

(01989-260675; www.madeinross.co.uk; Market Pl; 10am-4pm) FREE The 17th-century Market House sits atop weathered sandstone columns in Market Pl. The salmon-pink building is now home to artist collective Made in Ross, whose members live and work in a 20-mile radius, and exhibit and sell their arts and crafts here. Regular markets take place on the square out front.

Sleeping & Eating

White House Guest House B&B ££

(01989-763572; www.whitehouseross.com; 13 Wye St; s/d/tr/f £50/70/90/100; P) This 18th-century stone house has a scenic location across the road from the River Wye. Vivid window boxes give it a splash of colour, and the seven quiet and comfortable rooms (some with river views) are decorated in shades of burgundy and crisp white. Family rooms sleep up to four people.

Truffles Delicatessen DELI £

(www.trufflesdeli.co.uk; 46 High St; dishes £2.50-5.50; 8am-5pm Mon-Sat, 11am-5pm Sun) Packed to the rafters with local artisan products (cheeses, breads, chutneys et al), Truffles also has stellar sandwiches, soups and salad boxes to takeaway for a riverside picnic.

Pots & Pieces CAFE £

(www.potsandpieces.com; 40 High St; dishes £3-6; 9am-4.45pm Mon-Fri, 10am-4.45pm Sat year-round plus 11am-3.45pm Sun Jun-Sep) Browse ceramics and crafts at this tearoom by the market place, and choosing from cakes such as lemon drizzle, coffee, and walnut and carrot. Savoury options includes quiches, sandwiches and a soup of the day.

King's Head MODERN BRITISH ££

(01989-763174; www.kingshead.co.uk; 8 High St; mains £12-19; kitchen noon-2.15pm & 6.30-9pm, bar noon-11pm;) Dating from the 14th century, this unassuming inn is a charmer, with a low-lit front dining room and glass conservatory. Menu favourites include beer-battered haddock, pan-seared salmon with basil mash and Welsh lamb loin with red cabbage. Some of its 15 chocolate- or oyster-toned rooms (double £65 to £105) have four-poster beds; there's limited guest parking.

Ledbury

POP 9636

Creaking with history and dotted with antique shops, Ledbury's crooked black-and-white streets zero in on a delightfully leggy medieval **Market House**. The timber-framed structure is precariously balanced atop a series of wooden posts supposedly taken from the wrecked ships of the Spanish Armada.

Almost impossibly cute Church Lane, crowded with tilting timber-framed buildings, runs its cobbled way from High St to the town church. At the top of the lane lies the 12th-century church of **St Michael & All Angels** (www.ledburyparishchurch.org.uk; Church St; 9am-5.30pm Easter-Oct, to 4pm Nov-Mar), with a splendid 18th-century spire and tower divided from its medieval nave.

Sleeping & Eating

Verzon House Hotel HOTEL £££

(01531-670381; www.verzonhouse.com; Hereford Rd, Trumpet; s/d/ste from £80/110/180; P) The ultimate country-chic retreat, this lovely Georgian farmhouse 3.8 miles northwest of Ledbury on the A438 has eight luxuriously appointed rooms with tactile fabrics, free-standing baths, goose-down pillows, and deep-pile carpets. Locally sourced produce underpins the menu at its smart brasserie (two-/three-course lunch menus £23/27, dinner mains £14 to £32).

Feathers Hotel HOTEL £££

(01531-635266; www.feathers-ledbury.co.uk; 25 High St; d from £110; P) A Ledbury landmark, this black-and-white Tudor hotel looms over the main road. Of its 22 rooms, those in the oldest part of the building come with sloping floorboards, painted beams and much more character than rooms in the modern extension. There's an atmospheric wood-panelled restaurant, **Quills** (mains £10-26), and an indoor heated swimming pool.

Chez Pascal FRENCH ££

(01531-634443; www.chezpascal.co.uk; Church Lane; mains £14-16; 9.30am-5.30pm Mon-Thu, to 11pm Fri & Sat) Set in a delightful courtyard with garden tables, this place is the locals' go-to address for fine dining. French owner/chef/*patissier* Pascal's mains include classics such as pan-fried pheasant in red wine, seafood ragout and fish gratin, but it's his desserts such as ginger and lemon torte and raspberry tarts that are the stars of the show.

Shopping

★Three Counties Cider Shop DRINKS

(www.onceuponatree.co.uk; 5a The Homend; 10am-5.30pm Tue-Thu, to 6pm Fri & Sat) The aroma of apples pervades this charming little shop filled with artisan cider, perry and juices from producers in three counties (Herefordshire, Worcestershire and Gloucestershire). A dozen ciders and perries are on tap to try; you can also buy locally produced gourmet goods including cider chocolates, chutneys and jams.

Getting There & Away

Buses are limited but regular train services include the following:

Great Malvern £5, 10 minutes, hourly

Hereford £6.20, 15 minutes, hourly

Worcester £6.80, 25 minutes, hourly

SHROPSHIRE

Sleepy Shropshire is a glorious scattering of hills, castles and timber-framed villages tucked against the Welsh border. Highlights include castle-crowned Ludlow, industrial Ironbridge and the beautiful Shropshire Hills, which offer the best walking and cycling in the Marches.

Activities

Walking

The rolling Shropshire Hills call out to walkers like a siren. Between Shrewsbury and Ludlow, the landscape rucks up into dramatic folds, with spectacular trails climbing the flanks of **Wenlock Edge** and the **Long Mynd** near Church Stretton. The county is also crossed by long-distance trails, including the famous **Offa's Dyke Path** and the popular **Shropshire Way**, which meanders around Ludlow and Church Stretton.

Cycling

Mountain bikers head for the muddy tracks that traverse the **Long Mynd** near Church Stretton, while road riders aim for the **Six Castles Cycleway** (NCN 44), which runs for 58 miles from Shrewsbury to Leominster.

Tourist offices sell copies of *Cycling for Pleasure in the Marches,* a pack of five maps and guides covering the entire county. You can also download free cycling guides from www.travelshropshire.co.uk.

Getting There & Around

Shrewsbury is the local transport hub, with good bus and rail connections. Church Stretton and Ludlow also have handy rail services.

From May to September, Shropshire Hills Shuttles (www.shropshirehillsshuttles.co.uk) runs useful bus services along popular hiking routes on weekends and bank holidays.

Shrewsbury

POP 71,715

A delightful jumble of winding medieval streets and timbered Tudor houses leaning at precarious angles, Shrewsbury was a crucial front in the conflict between the English and the Welsh in medieval days. Even today, the road bridge running east towards London is known as the English Bridge to mark it out from the Welsh Bridge leading northwest towards Holyhead. Shrewsbury is also the birthplace of Charles Darwin (1809–82).

The pronunciation of the town's name has long been a hot topic. In 2015, a charity debate hosted by University Centre Shrewsbury declared '*shroos*-bree' (rhyming with 'grew') the winner over the posher '*shrows*-bree' (rhyming with 'grow'), as did a survey by the *Shropshire Star,* though you'll still hear both pronunciations in the town and across British media.

Sights

St Mary's Church CHURCH

(www.visitchurches.org.uk; St Mary's St; 10am-5pm Mon-Sat May–early Dec, to 4pm Mon-Sat early Dec–Apr) The fabulous interior of this tall-spired medieval church contains an impressive collection of stained glass, including a 1340 window depicting the Tree of Jesse

Shrewsbury

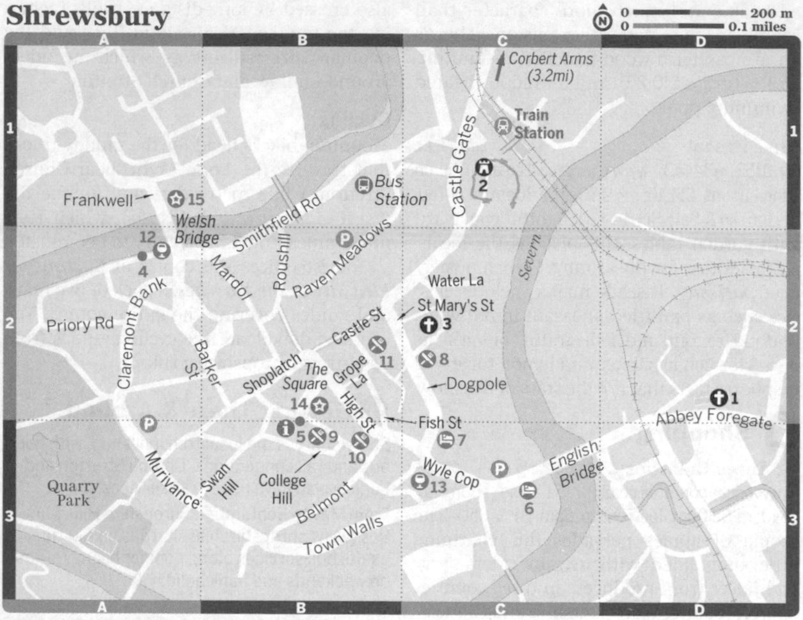

Shrewsbury

Sights

1 Shrewsbury Abbey ... D2
2 Shrewsbury Castle ... C1
3 St Mary's Church ... C2

Activities, Courses & Tours

4 Sabrina ... A2
5 Shrewsbury Walking Tours ... B3

Sleeping

6 Lion & Pheasant ... C3
7 Old House Suites ... C3

Eating

8 Drapers Hall ... C2
9 Ginger & Co ... B3
10 Golden Cross ... B3
11 No 4 Butcher Row ... B2

Drinking & Nightlife

12 Armoury ... A2
13 Henry Tudor House ... C3

Entertainment

14 Old Market Hall Film & Digital Media ... B2
15 Theatre Severn ... A1

(a biblical representation of the lineage of Jesus) and a magnificent oak ceiling in the nave, which largely collapsed in a huge gale in 1894 when the top of the spire blew off. Much of the glass in the church is sourced from Europe, including some outstanding Dutch glass from 1500.

Shrewsbury Abbey CHURCH

(☎01743-232723; www.shrewsburyabbey.com; Abbey Foregate; admission by donation; ⏰10am-4pm Apr-Oct, 10.30am-3pm Nov-Mar) All that remains of a vast, cruciform Benedictine monastery founded in 1083 is the lovely red-sandstone Shrewsbury Abbey. Twice used for meetings of the English Parliament, the Abbey church lost its spire and two wings when the monastery was dissolved in 1540. It sustained further damage in 1826 when engineer Thomas Telford ran the London–Holyhead road right through the grounds. Nevertheless, you can still see some impressive Norman, Early English and Victorian features, including an exceptional 14th-century west window.

Shrewsbury Castle CASTLE

(☎01743-358516; www.shropshireregimentalmuseum.co.uk; Castle St; adult/child £4/1; ⏰10.30am-5pm Mon-Wed, Fri & Sat, to 4pm Sun Jun–mid-Sep, to 4pm Mon-Wed, Fri & Sat mid-Feb–

May & mid-Sep–mid-Dec) Hewn from flaking red Shropshire sandstone, the town castle contains the **Shropshire Regimental Museum**. There are fine views from **Laura's Tower** and the battlements. The lower level of the **Great Hall** dates from 1150.

Tours

Sabrina BOATING
(☎01743-369741; www.sabrinaboat.co.uk; Victoria Quay; adult/child £8/4; ⏰hourly 11am-4pm Mar-Oct) Enjoy Shrewsbury from the water on board the Sabrina, which cruises the River Severn. Ghost cruises run from 7pm to 10.30pm on Monday evenings. There are music nights from 7.30pm to 10.30pm on Tuesdays. All trips last 45 minutes and leave from Victoria Quay near the Welsh Bridge.

Shrewsbury Walking Tours WALKING
(☎01743-258888; adult/child £7.50/2.50; ⏰2pm Mon-Sat, 11am Sun May-Sep, 2pm Tue-Sat, 11am Sun Oct, 2pm Sat Nov-Mar) Guided 1½-hour circuits of the historic centre depart from the tourist office (p440).

Sleeping

Old House Suites B&B ££
(☎07813-610904; www.theoldhousesuites.com; The Old House, 20 Dogpole; ste £85-100; P 📶) Shrewsbury's most historic place to hang your tricorn, the Old House has three lavish suites, all with views of the garden from a gloriously crooked timbered Tudor town house that was once owned by one of Catherine of Aragon's courtiers. The owner conducts hour-long history tours of the property for guests. It's up the steps from the Dogpole bus stop.

Lion & Pheasant BOUTIQUE HOTEL ££
(☎01743-770345; www.lionandpheasant.co.uk; 50 Wyle Cop; s/d incl breakfast from £99/119) This former coaching inn is now a stylish town house offering 22 individually styled rooms with comfy goose- and duck-down pillows. Original features throughout the property include magnificent exposed timber beams. Classy modern British fare is served in the white-washed restaurant (mains £14 to £23).

Corbet Arms PUB ££
(☎01743-709232; www.thecorbetarms.com; Church Rd, Uffington; d £65-105; P 📶 👪) Peacefully situated 4 miles east of Shrewsbury in the pint-sized village of Uffington, this family-friendly pub has nine beautifully appointed en suite rooms reached by a staircase. Try for top-floor room 10, which has exposed beams, a spacious sitting area and panoramic views of the surrounding countryside. High-quality pub food includes outstanding Sunday roasts.

Eating & Drinking

Ginger & Co CAFE £
(30-31 Princess St; dishes £4-9.50; ⏰8.30am-5pm Mon-Sat, 10am-4pm Sun; 📶) 🌿 A successful crowd-funding campaign propelled the opening of this airy, L-shaped cafe filled with upcycled furniture. It's a great option for a light brunch or lunch (smashed avocado on artisan toast with oak-smoked streaky bacon), snacks (lemon and Earl Grey scones with homemade raspberry jam), good coffee and vitamin-packed smoothies. Gluten-free, dairy-free and vegan options abound.

★**Golden Cross** MODERN BRITISH ££
(☎01743-362507; www.goldencrosshotel.co.uk; 14 Princess St; mains £10.50-19.50; ⏰noon-2.30pm & 5.30-9.30pm Tue-Sat, noon-2.30pm Sun) Overwhelmingly romantic, this candlelit inn dating from 1428 has an impeccably executed menu spanning mains such as roast pumpkin and chestnut gnocchi or garlic- and rosemary-marinated lamb with creamed leek to lush desserts like rose *panna cotta* with poached rhubarb. Upstairs, five exquisite guest rooms (doubles £75 to £150) have luxurious touches including freestanding bathtubs and chaise longues.

No 4 Butcher Row CAFE ££
(☎01743-366691; www.number-four.com; 4 Butcher Row; lunch mains £7-12, 2-/3-course dinner menus £18/22; ⏰9am-4pm Mon-Wed, to 11pm Thu-Sat; 👪) Tucked away near St Alkmond's Church, this hip, bare-boards split-level cafe is best known for its fantastic breakfasts, from eggs Benedict to bacon baguettes or a full English with freshly squeezed juices. Light lunches include burgers and gourmet salads (eg black pudding, spinach, mozzarella and potato); dinner is a more upmarket affair (slow-roast pork belly with apple and potato mash).

Drapers Hall FRENCH £££
(☎01743-344679; www.drapershallrestaurant.co.uk; 10 St Mary's Pl; mains £18-24; ⏰noon-2.30pm & 6.30-9pm; P 📶) The sense of history is palpable in this beautifully preserved 16th-century hall, fronted by an elegant Elizabethan facade. Award-winning Anglo-French haute cuisine is served in rooms adorned with wood panelling and artwork, and upstairs there are spectacular heirloom-filled bedrooms (doubles £90 to £155).

WORTH A TRIP

ATTINGHAM PARK

Built in imposing neoclassical style in 1785, **Attingham Park** (NT; ☎01743-708123; www.nationaltrust.org.uk; Atcham; house & grounds adult/child £11.25/5.60, grounds only £6.75/3.35; ⊙house 10.30am-5.30pm mid-Mar–early Nov, grounds 8am-7pm May-Sep, 9am-6pm Mar-Apr & Oct, 9am-5pm Nov-Feb) looks like something straight out of a period drama with its grand columned facade, manicured lawns, and stagecoach turning circle in the courtyard. The landscaped grounds swirl around an ornamental lake and are home to some 300 fallow deer. The restored walled garden is a picture.

Attingham Park is 4 miles southeast of Shrewsbury; take bus 81 or 96 (£2.10, 20 minutes, six per day Monday to Saturday).

Henry Tudor House PUB

(www.henrytudorhouse.com; Barracks Passage; ⊙noon-11pm Mon-Thu, 11am-1am Fri & Sat, noon-10pm Sun) Tucked off Wyle Cop, this seriously overhanging black-and-white beauty was built in the early 15th century and is where Henry VII stayed before the Battle of Bosworth. Today it melds old and new with a zinc bar, light-filled conservatory and birdcage-encased chandeliers. Live gigs regularly take to the stage. Superb food too.

Armoury PUB

(www.armoury-shrewsbury.co.uk; Victoria Quay; ⊙noon-11pm Mon-Sat, to 10.30pm Sun) Despite being a modern creation, this cavernous brick space with long wooden tables, floor-to-ceiling bookshelves, assorted collectables and the aromas of fine cooking feels like it has been here for generations.

☆ Entertainment

Old Market Hall Film & Digital Media CINEMA

(☎01743-281281; www.oldmarkethall.co.uk; The Square; tickets adult/child £8/6.50; ⊙10am-9pm Mon-Sat, noon-6pm Sun;) Catch mainstream and art-house movies in a charming Elizabethan setting.

Theatre Severn THEATRE

(☎01743-281281; www.theatresevern.co.uk; Frankwell Quay) This much-acclaimed riverside theatre and music venue hosts everything from pop gigs and comedy nights to plays and classical concerts.

ℹ Information

The **tourist office** (☎01743-258888; www.visitshrewsbury.com; The Square; ⊙10am-5pm daily Apr-Oct, Tue-Sun Nov-Mar) shares space with the Shrewsbury Museum and Art Gallery.

ℹ Getting There & Away

BUS

The **bus station** (Smithfield Rd) is beside the river.

Regular services:

Birmingham National Express; £6.70, 1½ hours, three daily

Church Stretton Bus 435; £3, 45 minutes, hourly Monday to Friday, every two hours Saturday

Ironbridge Bus 96; £3, 50 minutes, every two hours Monday to Saturday

London Victoria National Express; £20.70, 5½ hours, three daily

Ludlow Bus 435; £3.85, 1½ hours, hourly Monday to Friday, every two hours Saturday

TRAIN

The train station is on the northeastern edge of the centre at the bottom of Castle Foregate.

Trains to destinations in England and Wales include the following:

Birmingham £14.60, one hour, every two hours

Holyhead £45.60, 2½ hours, up to two per hour

London Euston £70.40, 2¾ hours, every 20 minutes

Ludlow £12.70, 30 minutes, half-hourly

Swansea £26.50, three hours, hourly

ℹ Getting Around

Dave Mellor Cycles (☎01743-366662; www.davemellorcycles.com; 9a New St, Frankwell; per half/full day £7.50/15; ⊙9am-6pm Mon-Sat) Rents bikes for adults (no kids' bikes available).

Ironbridge Gorge

POP 2582

Strolling or cycling through the woods, hills and villages of this peaceful river gorge, it's hard to believe such a sleepy enclave could really have been the birthplace of the Industrial Revolution. Nevertheless, it was here that Abraham Darby perfected the art of smelting iron ore with coke in 1709, making it possible to mass-produce cast iron for the first time.

Abraham Darby's son, Abraham Darby II, invented a new forging process for producing single beams of iron, allowing Abraham Darby III to astound the world with the first-ever iron bridge, constructed in 1779. The bridge remains the focal point of this World Heritage Site, and 10 very different museums tell the story of the Industrial Revolution in the buildings where it took place.

Sights & Activities

★Iron Bridge BRIDGE

FREE The flamboyant, arching and gravel-strewn Iron Bridge, which gives the area its name, was built to flaunt the new technology invented by the pioneering Darby family. At the time of its construction in 1779, nobody could believe that anything so large – it weighs 384 tonnes – could be built from cast iron without collapsing under its own weight. There's a small exhibition on the bridge's history at the former **toll house** (www.ironbridge.org.uk; 10am-5pm Sat & Sun Mar–early Nov, to 4pm Sat & Sun early Nov–Feb, daily during school holidays) FREE.

★Museum of the Gorge MUSEUM

(01952-433424; www.ironbridge.org.uk; The Wharfage; adult/child £4.50/3.15; 10am-5pm) An ideal place to kick off your Ironbridge Gorge visit is the Museum of the Gorge. Occupying a Gothic riverside warehouse, it offers an overview of the World Heritage Site using film, photos and exhibits, including a 12m-long 3D model of the town in 1796.

Blists Hill Victorian Town MUSEUM

(01952-433424; www.ironbridge.org.uk; Legges Way; adult/child £16.25/10.75; 10am-5pm early Mar–early Nov, to 4pm early Nov–early Mar) Set at the top of the Hay Inclined Plane (a cable lift that once transported coal barges uphill from the Shropshire Canal), Blists Hill is a lovingly restored Victorian village repopulated with townsfolk in period costume, busy with day-to-day chores. There's even a bank, where you can exchange your modern pounds for shillings to use at the village shops. In summer, a Victorian fair is an added attraction for young ones.

Museum of Iron MUSEUM

(www.ironbridge.org.uk; Wellington Rd; adult/child, £8.85/5.65, incl Darby Houses £9.25/6.35; 10am-5pm) Set in the brooding buildings of Abraham Darby's original iron foundry, the Museum of Iron contains some excellent interactive exhibits. As well as producing the girders for the Iron Bridge, the factory became famous for heavy machinery and extravagant ornamental castings, including the gates for London's Hyde Park.

Darby Houses MUSEUM

(01952-433424; www.ironbridge.org.uk; Darby Rd; adult/child £5.30/3.75, incl Museum of Iron Darby Houses £9.25/6.35; 10am-5pm early Mar–early Nov) Just uphill from the Museum of Iron, these beautifully restored 18th-century homes housed generations of the Darby family in gracious but modest Quaker comfort. In the Rosehill house, kids and adults can try on Victorian dress and view china displays. The highlight of the Darby family house is the study where Abraham Darby III designed the Iron Bridge. Admission includes access to the family's Quaker cemetery.

Coalport China Museum & Tar Tunnel MUSEUM

(www.ironbridge.org.uk; Coalport High St; museum adult/child £8.85/5.65, Tar Tunnel £3.40/2.50; 10am-5pm early Mar–early Nov) As ironmaking fell into decline, Ironbridge diversified into manufacturing china pots, using the fine clay mined around Blists Hill. Dominated by a pair of towering bottle kilns, the atmospheric old china-works now contains an absorbing museum tracing the history of the industry, with demonstrations of traditional pottery techniques. A short stroll along the canal brings you to the 200-year-old **Tar Tunnel**, an artificial watercourse that was abandoned when natural bitumen started trickling from its walls.

Jackfield Tile Museum MUSEUM

(01952-433424; www.ironbridge.org.uk; adult/child £8.85/5.65; 10am-5pm) Once the largest tile factory in the world, Jackfield was famous for its encaustic tiles, with ornate designs produced using layers of different coloured clay. Tiles are still produced here today for period restorations. Gas-lit galleries re-create ornately tiled rooms from past centuries, including Victorian public

IRONBRIDGE GORGE PASSPORT

The 10 Ironbridge museums are administered by the Ironbridge Gorge Museum Trust (p444). You'll save considerably by buying a passport ticket (adult/child £25/15) at any of the museums or the tourist office. Valid for 12 months, it allows unlimited entry to all of Ironbridge Gorge's sites.

Ironbridge Gorge

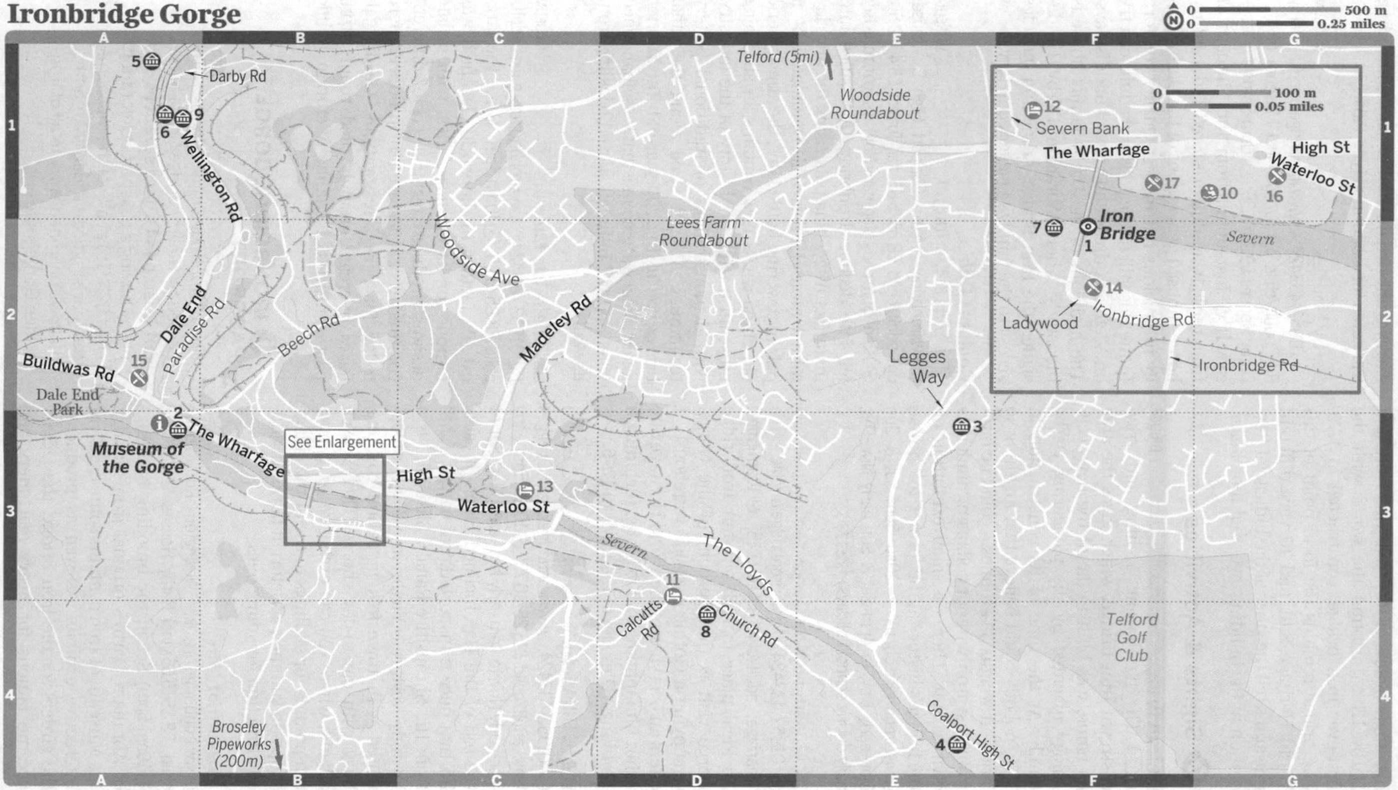

Ironbridge Gorge

Top Sights

1 Iron Bridge F2
2 Museum of the Gorge A3

Sights

3 Blists Hill Victorian Town E3
4 Coalport China Museum & Tar Tunnel E4
5 Darby Houses A1
6 Enginuity A1
7 Iron Bridge Tollhouse F2
8 Jackfield Tile Museum D4
9 Museum of Iron A1

Activities, Courses & Tours

10 Ironbridge Leisure G1
Shropshire Raft Tours .... (see 2)

Sleeping

11 Calcutts House D3
12 Library House F1
13 Ye Olde Robin Hood C3

Eating

14 D'arcys at the Station F2
15 Deli-Dale A2
16 Pondicherry G1
17 Restaurant Severn F1

conveniences. The museum is on the south bank of the Severn – cross the footbridge at the bottom of the Hay Inclined Plane. Tile-decorating **workshops** take place on Tuesdays (from 10am; £5).

Enginuity MUSEUM
(www.ironbridge.org.uk; Wellington Rd; adult/child £8.85/6.95; 10am-5pm) Kids will love this levers-and-pulleys science centre where they can control robots, move a steam locomotive with their bare hands (and a little engineering know-how) and power up a vacuum cleaner with self-generated electricity.

Shropshire Raft Tours RAFTING
(01592-426100; www.shropshirerafttours.co.uk; The Wharfage; rafting trips adult/child £14.95/6.95; by reservation 9am, 11.30am, 2pm & 4.30pm Easter-Oct, plus 7pm Jul & Aug) Ironbridge Gorge might not have any rapids but you can take a gentle, highly enjoyable 90-minute trip along a 1.2-mile stretch of the River Severn floating past stunning gorge scenery with this eco-conscious outfit. Life jackets are provided.

Ironbridge Leisure CANOEING, KAYAKING
(01952-426111; 31 High St; kayak/canoe rental from £30; 9am-8pm Sat & Sun Easter-Oct) In summer, when the river is at a safe level, you can rent canoes and kayaks to explore the gorge and surrounding areas on 5-mile excursions (around three hours) or multiday camping trips.

Sleeping

Ye Olde Robin Hood PUB £
(01952-433071; www.holdensyeolderobinhoodinnironbridge.co.uk; 33 Waterloo St; s/d from £50/70; P) The three spotless rooms at this quaint, white-washed, traditional inn on the banks of the River Severn come with king-size mattresses. The bar is a sociable spot where you're treated like a regular from the moment you walk in the door.

★ **Library House** B&B ££
(01952-432299; www.libraryhouse.com; 11 Severn Bank; s/d from £75/95; P) Up an alley off the main street, this lovingly restored Georgian library building is hugged by vines, backed by a beautiful garden and decked out with stacks of vintage books, curios, prints and lithographs. There are four charmingly well-preserved, individually decorated rooms, named Milton, Chaucer, Eliot and Hardy. The affable dog whipping around is Millie.

Calcutts House B&B ££
(01952-882631; www.calcuttshouse.co.uk; Calcutts Rd; s/d from £50/65; P) This former ironmaster's pad dates from the 18th century. It's tucked away on the south bank around the corner from the Jackfield Tile Museum (p441), about a mile east of the bridge. Its traditionally decorated rooms have heaps of character, and one is furnished with an outsized 200-year-old four-poster bed.

Eating

Deli-Dale DELI £
(01952-432508; www.deli-dale.com; Dale End, Coalbrookdale; dishes £3.50-6; 8.30am-4.30pm Mon-Wed & Fri, 9am-4pm Sat, 10-4pm Sun;) This wonderful deli is far and away the best place in the area for a light meal. Steaming-hot soups, salads, cakes and sandwiches are all freshly made; take them away or else dine in the cosy shop or at umbrella-shaded picnic tables in the courtyard. Call 48 hours ahead to order bountiful picnic baskets (£12 to £21.50).

WORTH A TRIP

COSFORD ROYAL AIR FORCE MUSEUM

The famous **Cosford Royal Air Force Museum** (☎01902-376200; www.rafmuseum.org.uk; Shifnal; ⏰10am-5pm), 13 miles east of Ironbridge, is run by the Royal Air Force, whose pilots steered many of these winged wonders across the skies. Among the 70 aircraft displayed are the Vulcan bomber (which carried Britain's nuclear deterrent) and the tiny helicopter-like FA330 Bachstelze glider that was towed behind German U-boats to warn them of enemy ships. You can also try out a Black Hawk simulator. It's a half-mile walk from Cosford train station, on the Birmingham–Shrewsbury line.

Pondicherry INDIAN ££
(☎01952-433055; www.pondicherryrestaurant.co.uk; 52 Waterloo St; mains £11-16; ⏰6-11pm Mon-Thu, to midnight Fri & Sat, to 10.30pm Sun) Original features of this 1862-built former police station and courtroom include four lock-up cells (one's now the takeaway waiting area), the magistrate's bench, and blue-painted bars on the windows. Above-average contemporary Indian cuisine includes crowd-pleasers such as tandoori platters and chicken tikka masala along with chef specialities such as lamb *saag mamyam* (braised Staffordshire lamb with spinach and spices).

D'arcys at the Station MEDITERRANEAN ££
(☎01952-884499; www.darcysironbridge.co.uk; Ladywood; mains £11.50-15; ⏰6-9.30pm Tue-Sat) Just over the bridge by the river, the handsome old station building is the backdrop for flavoursome Mediterranean dishes, from Moroccan chicken to Cypriot kebabs and Tuscan bean casserole.

Restaurant Severn BRITISH, FRENCH £££
(☎01952-432233; www.restaurantsevern.co.uk; 33 High St; 2-/3-course lunch £18.95/20.95, dinner from £25.95/27.95; ⏰6.30-8.30pm Wed-Sat, noon-1.30pm Sun) The highly praised fare at this small, unadorned riverside restaurant is a winning English–French hybrid. The locally sourced menu changes weekly but incorporates creations such as Shropshire venison medallions with cognac and sundried cranberry sauce. Menu prices rise slightly on Fridays and Saturdays.

ℹ Information

The **tourist office** (☎01952-433424; www.visitironbridge.co.uk; The Wharfage; ⏰10am-5pm) is located at the Museum of the Gorge.

Ironbridge Gorge Museum Trust (☎01952-433424; www.ironbridge.org.uk)

ℹ Getting There & Away

The nearest train station is 6 miles away at Telford, from where you can travel to Ironbridge on bus 96 (£2.10, 15 minutes, six per day Monday to Saturday). The same bus continues from Ironbridge's tourist office to Shrewsbury (£3, 50 minutes). Bus 99 runs from Bridgnorth (£3.20, 45 minutes, nine per day Monday to Saturday) and bus 88 runs to Much Wenlock (£3.60, 25 minutes, every two hours Monday to Saturday).

ℹ Getting Around

At weekends and on bank holidays from Easter to mid-September, the Gorge Connect bus (£2.20; Museum Passport holders £1) runs from Telford bus station to all the museums on the north bank of the Severn.

Much Wenlock & Around

POP 3041

With one of those quirky names that abound in England, Much Wenlock is as charming as it sounds. Surrounding the time-worn ruins of Wenlock Priory, the streets are studded with Tudor, Jacobean and Georgian houses, and locals say hello to everyone.

Sights

Guildhall HISTORIC BUILDING
(☎01952-727509; Wilmore St; ⏰11am-4pm Fri-Mon Apr-Oct) FREE Built in classic Tudor style in 1540, the wonky Guildhall features some splendidly ornate woodcarving. One of the pillars supporting it was used for public floggings in medieval times.

Wenlock Priory RUINS
(EH; ☎01952-727466; www.english-heritage.org.uk; 5 Sheinton St; adult/child incl audio guide £4.70/2.80; ⏰10am-6pm Apr-Sep, to 5pm Oct, to 4pm Sat & Sun Nov-Mar; P) The maudlin Cluniac ruins of Wenlock Priory rise up from vivid green lawns, sprinkled with animal-shaped topiary. Raised by Norman monks over the ruins of a Saxon monastery from AD 680, the hallowed remains include a finely decorated chapterhouse and an unusual carved lavabo, where monks came to ceremonially wash before eating.

Sleeping & Eating

Wilderhope Manor YHA HOSTEL £

(☎0845 371 9149; www.yha.org.uk; Longville-in-the-Dale; dm/d/f from £16/65/99; P) A gloriously atmospheric gabled greystone Elizabethan manor, with spiral staircases, wood-panelled walls, an impressive stone-floored dining hall and spacious, oak-beamed rooms – this is hostelling for royalty. It's 7.5 miles southwest of Much Wenlock, best reached by your own wheels.

Raven Hotel HOTEL ££

(☎01952-727251; www.ravenhotel.com; Barrow St; d £120-130, ste £150; P 📶) Much Wenlock's finest place to stay is this 17th-century coaching inn and converted stables with oodles of historical charm and rich country-chic styling. Overlooking a flower-filled courtyard, the excellent **restaurant** (lunch mains £12.50-18, dinner two-/three-/five-/seven-course menus £29/39/45/59) serves classic Mediterranean and British fare.

Fox PUB FOOD ££

(☎01952-727292; 46 High St; mains £10-23; ⏲5-9pm Mon-Fri, noon-9pm Sat, noon-8pm Sun; 📶) Warm yourself by the massive fireplace, then settle down in the dining room to savour locally sourced venison, pheasant and beef, swished down with a pint of Shropshire ale. Candlelit dinners here are lovely. It also has five contemporary **rooms** (s/d/f from £65/85/115).

Information

The **tourist office** (☎01952-727679; www.shropshire.gov.uk; The Square; ⏲10.30am-1pm & 1.30-5pm Apr-Oct, 10.30am-1pm & 1.30-4pm Fri-Sun Nov-Mar) has a modest museum of local history (admission free).

Getting There & Away

Bus 436 links Shrewsbury with Much Wenlock (£3.10, 35 minutes, hourly Monday to Saturday) and continues on to Bridgnorth (£3, 20 minutes). Bus 18 runs to Ironbridge (£2.90, 30 minutes, every two hours Monday to Saturday).

Bridgnorth & Around

POP 12,212

Cleaved into two by a dramatic sandstone bluff that tumbles down to the River Severn, Bridgnorth is one of Shropshire's finest-looking historic towns, with a wealth of architectural charm despite much of the High Town succumbing to fire in 1646 during the Civil War.

Around its namesake church, the High Town's adorable **St Leonard's Close** contains some of the most attractive buildings and almshouses in town, including a splendid six-gabled house, once part of the grammar school.

A 19th-century cliff railway – Britain's steepest – and several narrow lanes drop down from the High Town to the Low Town, including the vertiginous pedestrian Cartway, at the bottom of which is **Bishop Percy's House**, dating from 1580.

Sights & Activities

Daniels Mill MILL

(☎01746-762753; www.danielsmill.co.uk; The Cankhorn, Eardington; adult/child £5/4; ⏲11am-4pm Thu-Sun Easter-Oct) England's largest working water-powered mill still produces flour for local bakers. Visitors get a personal tour of the working machinery from the resident miller. It's located 1 mile south of the centre, reached on foot or with your own wheels.

Severn Valley Railway RAIL

(☎01299-403816; www.svr.co.uk; Hollybush Rd; adult one-way/return £13.50/19, child £9.50/13; ⏲daily May-Sep, Sat & Sun Oct-Apr) Bridgnorth is the northern terminus of the Severn Valley Railway; its historic steam or diesel locomotives chug down the valley to Kidderminster (one hour), starting from the station on Hollybush Rd. Check the calendar for additional event dates.

Cyclists can follow a beautiful 20-mile section of the Mercian Way (NCN Route 45) beside the railway line towards the Wyre Forest.

Bridgnorth Cliff Railway RAIL

(☎01746-762052; www.bridgnorthcliffrailway.co.uk; entrances 6a Castle Tce & Underhill St; return £1.60; ⏲8am-8pm Mon-Sat & noon-8pm Sun May-Sep, to 6.30pm Oct-Apr) Britain's steepest inland railway has trundled 50m up the cliff since 1892. At the top, a pedestrian walkway (affording astonishing night-time panoramas) curves around the bluff to a pretty park dotted with scattered masonry, some leaning at an incredible angle (all that remains of **Bridgnorth Castle**), and passes the grand and imposing Thomas Telford–designed and cupola-topped **St Mary's Church**.

Sleeping & Eating

Severn Arms Hotel HOTEL ££

(☎01746-764616; www.thesevernarms.co.uk; 3 Underhill St; s with/without en suite from £32/46, d £66, f £75;) At the bottom of the bluff conveniently positioned right next to the cliff railway, this comfortable riverside Georgian property has fabulous bridge views. The helpful owners can direct you to parking a few minutes' walk away over the bridge. Family rooms can sleep up to two adults and two children.

Cinnamon Cafe CAFE £

(☎01746-762944; Waterloo House, Cartway; dishes £5-8; ⊙9am-6pm Mon-Fri, 10am-4pm Sat;) Sweeping views extend from the dining room and terrace of this licensed cafe near the top of the Cartway. It serves up savoury bakes (many vegetarian and vegan), plus quiches, homemade muesli and cakes.

Information

Bridgnorth's **tourist office** (☎01746-763257; www.visitbridgnorth.co.uk; Listley St; ⊙9.30am-5pm Mon-Fri, 9am-5pm Sat) is inside the town library.

Getting There & Away

Bus 436 runs from Shrewsbury to Bridgnorth (£3.40, one hour, hourly Monday to Saturday), via Much Wenlock (£3.40, 25 minutes). Bus 99 runs to Ironbridge (£3.40, 30 minutes, every two hours Monday to Saturday).

Church Stretton & Around

POP 2789

Tucked in a deep valley formed by the Long Mynd and the Caradoc Hills, Church Stretton is an ideal base for walks or cycle tours through the Shropshire Hills. Although black-and-white timbers are heavily in evidence, most of the buildings in town are 19th-century fakes, built by the Victorians who flocked here to take the country air.

Sights & Activities

Walking is the big draw here. The tourist office has maps and details of local mountain-biking circuits and horse-riding stables (riding info is also available at www.shropshireriding.co.uk).

Church Stretton clings to the steeply sloping sides of the **Long Mynd**, Shropshire's most famous hill, which rises to 517m. Dubbed 'Little Switzerland' by the Victorians, this desolate but dramatic bluff is girdled by walking trails that offer soaring views over the surrounding countryside. Most people start walking from the National Trust car park (per day £3.60) at the end of the **Carding Mill Valley** (www.cardingmillvalley.org.uk), half a mile west of Shrewsbury Rd. A small **tearoom** (Carding Mill Valley; dishes £3.50-7.50; ⊙10am-5pm Apr-Oct, to 4pm Nov-Mar) here provides refreshments.

A maze of single-track roads climbs over the Long Mynd to the adjacent ridge of **Stiperstones**, crowned by a line of spooky-looking crags. You can continue right over the ridge, passing the Bog tourist office and cafe in a Victorian-era school next to the ruins of an abandoned mining village, heading to the village of Snailbeach, with its intriguing mining relics.

Snailbeach MINE

(☎01952-405105; www.shropshiremines.org.uk) The former lead- and silver-mining village of Snailbeach is littered with intriguing, rusting machinery relics. The **Bog Centre** (☎01743-792484; www.bogcentre.co.uk; The Bog, Stiperstones; ⊙noon-5pm Mon, 10am-5pm Tue-Sun Easter-Sep, noon-4pm Mon, 10am-4pm Tue-Sun Oct–early Nov;) sells self-guided trail leaflets (50p) to explore the site, or you can join one of two guided tours. The 30-minute **Day Level & Surface Tour** (every 30 minutes 11am to 4pm Sunday June to September; adult/child £7.50/3) covers the mine's exterior and entrance. The 2½-hour **Roberts/Perkins Level Tour** (by reservation Sunday June to September; adult/child £5/3) takes you deep into the mine.

Plush Hill Cycles CYCLING

(☎01694-720133; www.plushhillcycles.co.uk; 8 The Square; per half/full day from £17/22; ⊙9am-5.30pm Mon, Tue, Thu & Fri, 9am-5pm Sat, 10am-4pm Sun) Plush Hill Cycles rents a range of mountain bikes and electric bikes. Rates include helmets, maps and child seats; a £50 cash deposit is required. Handily, it offers free delivery within a 10-mile radius if you spend £40 or more.

Sleeping & Eating

Bridges Long Mynd YHA HOSTEL £

(☎01588-650656; www.yha.org.uk; Bridges; dm from £19, camping per person from £8; P) On the far side of the Long Mynd, this wonderfully isolated hiker favourite is housed in a former school in the tiny hamlet of Bridges. No wi-fi, no mobile-phone reception, no credit cards, no online bookings. Cross the

Mynd to Ratlinghope, from where it's 1.1 miles southwest, or take the Long Mynd & Stiperstones Shuttle bus.

Mynd Guest House B&B ££

(☎01694-722212; www.myndhouse.co.uk; Ludlow Rd, Little Stretton; s/d from £55/80; P) Just under 2 miles south of Church Stretton, this inviting guesthouse has splendid views across the valley and backs directly onto the Mynd. The four rooms are named after local hills; there's a small bar and lounge stocked with local books, and a room for drying your boots.

Berry's Coffee House CAFE £

(☎01694-724452; www.berryscoffeehouse.co.uk; 17 High St; dishes £3.50-8; 9am-5pm;) A particularly cosy cafe with loads of rooms in an 18th-century house, Berry's offers an organic, free-range, fair-trade, home-cooked menu, including Shropshire breakfasts and locally produced Shropshire white wines, ales and ciders. No credit cards.

Bridges PUB FOOD ££

(☎01588-650260; www.thebridgespub.co.uk; Ratlinghope; mains lunch £5.50-9.50, dinner £10-18; kitchen 11.30am-9pm Mon-Sat, 12.30-8.30pm Sun, bar 11am-11pm;) Some 5 miles northeast of Church Stretton, at the base of Long Mynd by the river, this is one of those secret country pubs revered for its live music, riverside terrace, relaxed accommodation (dorm/double from £27/55) and impressive food (lamb shank and mint sauce; beef lasagne...). Mini burgers, battered fish and sausages are among the choices on the kids' menu.

Information

Adjoining the library, Church Stretton's **tourist office** (☎01694-723133; www.churchstretton.co.uk; Church St; 9.30am-1pm & 1.30-5pm Mon-Sat Apr-Sep, 9.30am-1pm & 1.30-3pm Mon-Sat Oct-Mar) has abundant walking information and free internet terminals.

Getting There & Away

BUS

Bus 553 runs from Shrewsbury to Bishop's Castle via Stiperstones and Snailbeach (£3.70, one hour, five daily Monday to Saturday).

From May to September, the **Long Mynd & Stiperstones Shuttle** (www.shropshirehillsaonb.co.uk; Day Rover ticket £7; May-Sep) runs from the Carding Mill Valley near Church Stretton to the villages atop the Long Mynd, passing the YHA at Bridges, and Stiperstones near the Snailbeach mine.

TRAIN

Trains between Ludlow (£7.10) and Shrewsbury (£6.20) stop in Church Stretton hourly, taking 15 minutes from either end. Alternatively, take bus 435 from Shrewsbury or Ludlow (£2.95, 40 minutes, hourly Monday to Friday, every two hours Saturday).

Bishop's Castle

POP 1630

Set amid blissfully peaceful Shropshire countryside, Bishop's Castle is a higgledy-piggledy tangle of timbered town houses and Old Mother Hubbard cottages. The High St climbs from the town church to the refurbished Georgian **town hall** (1765) abutting the crooked 16th-century **House on Crutches** (☎01588-630556; www.hocmuseum.org.uk; High St; 2-5pm Sat & Sun Apr-Sep) FREE, which also houses the small town **museum**.

Local artists' work is exhibited in the gallery upstairs from the **tourist office** (☎01588-630023; www.bishopscastletownhall.co.uk; High St; 10am-4pm Mon-Sat).

Sights & Activities

Walkers can hike from north Bishop's Castle along the **Shropshire Way** (www.shropshirewalking.co.uk), which joins up with the long-distance **Offa's Dyke Path** and **Kerry Ridgeway** to the west. The northern sections of the Shropshire Way climb to the high country of the Stiperstones and the Long Mynd near Church Stretton. Bishop's Castle also lies on the popular **Six Castles Cycleway** (NCN Route 44) between Shrewsbury and Leominster.

★**Kerry Vale Vineyard** WINERY

(☎01588-620627; www.kerryvalevineyard.co.uk; Pentreheyling; tours £10-25; tours noon Wed, Sat, Sun & bank holidays Apr-Oct, shop & cafe 10am-4pm Tue-Sun mid-Mar–Dec) More than 6000 vines are now planted over 2.4 hectares of the former Pentreheyling Roman Fort, where pottery and metalwork have been uncovered and are displayed at the winery shop. Tours range from a 90-minute guided walk through the vines, with a talk on the site's Roman history and three tastings, to three-hour guided visits with five tastings, a tutorial and afternoon tea including the vineyard's own sparkling wine. Or pop by the cafe for a tasting flight (from £2).

Sleeping & Eating

Poppy House B&B ££
(☎01588-638443; www.poppyhouse.co.uk; 20 Market Sq; s/d from £40/60, cafe dishes £2.50-9.50; ⏲cafe 10am-4pm Wed-Mon;) Attached to a friendly **cafe**, this sweet guesthouse has lovely, individual rooms with latch-doors and loads of old beams. Doubles cost £80 on Saturday nights. Children aged five to 16 are charged £20 per night when staying in their parents' rooms; under fives stay free.

Castle Hotel HOTEL ££
(☎01588-638403; www.thecastlehotelbishopscastle.co.uk; Market Sq; s/d/f incl breakfast from £75/95/140;) This solid-looking 18th-century coaching inn was built with stones from the now-vanished Bishop's Castle, which also contributed the gorgeous wood panelling in the dining room (mains £11 to £22). All 12 en suite rooms are lovely, with modern fabrics meeting old antique furniture; three-bed family rooms and cots are available. Doubles start at £115 on weekends.

New Deli DELI £
(35 High St; dishes £2.50-8.50; ⏲9.30am-4.30pm Tue-Sat) Locally made English and Welsh cheeses and breads, along with hams, salamis and sausages, premade salads, preserves, chutneys and pickles, cakes and biscuits, and ales, wines and liqueurs at this enticing deli mean you're spoiled for choice for picnic fare while walking in the surrounding hills.

Drinking

Three Tuns PUB
(www.thethreetunsinn.co.uk; Salop St; ⏲noon-11pm Mon-Sat, to 10pm Sun;) Bishop's Castle's finest watering hole is attached to the tiny Three Tuns Brewery, which has been rolling barrels of nut-brown ale across the courtyard since 1642. It's a lively local, and the ales are delicious. Jazz, blues and brass bands perform regularly in summer.

Getting There & Away

Bus 553 runs to and from Shrewsbury (£3.60, 1¼ hours, four per day Monday to Saturday).

Ludlow

POP 11,003

On the northern bank of the swirling River Teme, this genteel market town fans out from the rambling ruins of its fine Norman castle, with some superb black-and-white Tudor buildings lining its cobbled streets.

Sights & Activities

Ludlow is ringed by wonderful landscapes. Starting just outside Ludlow Castle's entrance, the waymarked **Mortimer Trail** walking route runs for 30 miles through idyllic English countryside to Kington in Herefordshire. The tourist office has leaflets describing the trail, or visit www.exploremortimercountry.com.

Hire bikes from **Wheely Wonderful** (☎01568-770755; www.wheelywonderfulcycling.co.uk; Petchfield Farm, Elton; adult/child bikes per day from £20/15; ⏲9am-5pm Mon-Sat, by reservation Sun Apr-Oct), 5 miles west of Ludlow.

Ludlow Castle CASTLE
(☎01584-873355; www.ludlowcastle.com; Castle Sq; adult/child £5/2.50; ⏲10am-6pm daily Aug, to 5pm Apr-Jul & Sep, to 4pm Oct, Nov, Feb & Mar, to 4pm Sat & Sun Dec & Jan) Perched in an ideal defensive location atop a cliff above a crook in the river, the town castle was built to ward off the marauding Welsh – or to enforce the English expansion into Wales, perspective depending. Founded after the Norman conquest, the castle was dramatically expanded in the 14th century.

The Norman chapel in the inner bailey is one of the few surviving round chapels in England, and the sturdy keep (built around 1090) offers wonderful views over the hills.

Church of St Laurence CHURCH
(www.stlaurences.org.uk; 2 College St; admission by £3 donation; ⏲10am-5pm) One of Britain's largest parish churches, the church of St Laurence contains grand Elizabethan alabaster tombs and delightfully cheeky medieval misericords carved into its medieval choir stalls, including a beer-swilling chap raiding his barrel. The Lady Chapel contains a marvellous **Jesse Window** originally dating from 1330 (although the glass is mostly Victorian). Four windows in St John's Chapel date from the mid-15th century, including the honey-coloured **Golden Window**. Climb 200 steps up the **tower** (included in donation) for stunning views.

Ludlow Brewing Company BREWERY
(☎01584-873291; www.theludlowbrewingcompany.co.uk; The Railway Shed, Station Dr; tours £6; ⏲tours 3pm Mon-Fri, 2pm Sat, pub 10am-5pm Mon-Thu, to 6pm Fri, to 4pm Sat) Up an inconspicuous laneway, the Ludlow Brewing Company

produces award-winning all-natural brews and sells directly from the brewery and its airy, post-industrial-style bar. Hour-long tours include one pint and six samples.

Ghost Walk WALKING
(www.shropshireghostwalks.co.uk; adult/child £5/4; 8pm Fri Easter-Dec) Search for spooks on this 90-minute ghost walk from outside the Church Inn on the Buttercross.

Festivals & Events

Ludlow Spring Festival CULTURAL
(www.ludlowspringestival.co.uk; mid-May) The three-day Ludlow Spring Festival uses the castle as its dramatic backdrop for more than 100 beer, cider and food stalls, a vintage car show and live concerts.

Ludlow Food & Drink Festival FOOD & DRINK
(www.foodfestival.co.uk; Sep) Established in 1995, the Ludlow Food and Drink Festival spans a long weekend in September.

Sleeping

Feathers Hotel HISTORIC HOTEL ££
(01584-875261; www.feathersatludlow.co.uk; 21 Bull Ring; s/d/f from £95/145/180;) Behind the ornate timbered Jacobean facade, this 1619-built treasure is all tapestries, creaky wood furniture, timber beams and stained glass: you can almost hear the cavaliers toasting the health of King Charles. The best rooms are in the old building; rooms in the newer wing lack the character and romance. The **restaurant** (2-/3-course menus £34.50/42) is highly recommended.

Clive BOUTIQUE HOTEL ££
(01584-856565; www.theclive.co.uk; Bromfield Rd, Bromfield; d/f incl breakfast from £89/137.50;) For foodies, this is Ludlow's ultimate place to stay. Located 4 miles northwest of town adjoining the Ludlow Food Centre (p452), it has its own top-end restaurant; breakfast is served at the Ludlow Kitchen. Many of its 15 spacious rooms are on ground level; family rooms have two sleeping areas separated by a bathroom, giving parents and kids their own space.

Charlton Arms INN ££
(01584-872813; www.charltonarms.co.uk; Ludford Bridge; d £100-160;) The pick of the rooms at this landmark inn overlook the River Teme, and the pick of those have terraces (one with an outdoor hot tub as well as a four-poster bed). A family room sleeps three people. Its restaurant, also opening to a terrace, serves top-quality Modern British cuisine, and there's a large free car park and superb service.

Dinham Hall Hotel HOTEL £££
(01584-876464; www.dinhamhall.com; Dinham Rd; s/d/ste from £120/135/235;) A resplendent 18th-century country manor, Dinham Hall has views of the castle and the river from gorgeous rooms full of heirloom furniture. Its superb fine-dining restaurant, **Elliots**, is renowned for its afternoon teas (from 3pm; per person from £18).

Eating & Drinking

Green Cafe CAFE £
(01584-879872; www.thegreencafe.co.uk; Mill on the Green, Linney; dishes £5-11; 10am-4pm Tue-Sun Feb-Dec;) The Slow Food–accredited Green Cafe takes full advantage of its riverside position overlooking the weir with 25 alfresco seats (plus another 30 inside). Outstanding food spans warm salt brisket-beef baps (soft bread rolls) to ox tongue with hazelnut pesto and lemon polenta cake. Wines, beers and ciders are from small-scale producers. Kids' menus include hot chocolates or smoothies.

Ludlow Kitchen CAFE £
(01584-856020; www.ludlowkitchen.co.uk; Bromfield Rd, Bromfield; breakfast £3.50-8.50, lunch mains £7-12.50; 7am-5.30pm Mon-Sat, 8am-4pm Sun;) Produce from the Ludlow Food Centre (p452) artisanal farm shop is served at this sunlit cafe 4 miles northwest of Ludlow off Bromfield Rd (the A49). Fantastic breakfasts (homemade toasted muesli; full English fry-ups with farmhouse eggs, organic bacon and black pudding; eggs royale) are the precursor to lunch dishes such as Ludlow Brewing Company beer-battered cod with zingy tartar.

Fish House SEAFOOD £
(01584-879790; www.thefishhouseludlow.co.uk; 50 Bull Ring; taster plates £4-10, shellfish platter £68; noon-3pm Wed-Sat) Except on Saturdays when it's first-come, first-served, bookings are recommended for the barrel tables at this stylish fish and oyster bar. It sources Britain's best seafood: Whitby dressed crab, Arbroath smokies and Bigbury Bay oysters. Taster plates come with organic bread, lemon and mayo. The house shellfish platter, available Fridays and Saturdays only, is best washed down with champagne.

1

4

CORNFIELD / SHUTTERSTOCK ©

3

1. Conwy Castle (p750), North Wales
Head to the battlements for panoramic views from this World Heritage–listed site.

2. Ffestiniog Railway (p744), Llŷn Peninsula
The world's oldest surviving narrow-gauge railway links Blaenau Ffestiniog with Porthmadog.

3. St Giles Cathedral (p767), Edinburgh
The 15th-century High Kirk of Edinburgh was named after the patron saint of cripples and beggars.

4. Murder & Mayhem bookshop (p701), Hay-on-Wye
Secondhand-bookshop capital Hay-on-Wye hosts the famous Hay Festival, a leading festival of literature and the arts.

Wheatsheaf Inn PUB
(www.wheatsheafludlow.co.uk; Lower Broad St; ⏲noon-11pm) Under the medieval Broadgate, the quiet little Wheatsheaf Inn has stone walls, exposed wooden beams, two toasty fireplaces and a good choice of local ales.

Church Inn PUB
(www.thechurchinncom; Buttercross, King St; ⏲10am-midnight Mon-Thu, to 1am Fri & Sat, to 11pm Sun) The hop-strewn Church Inn is a cosy little escape with a pulpit at the bar. It's tucked away on the narrow lane beside the old butter market.

☆ Entertainment

Ludlow Assembly Rooms CINEMA
(☎01584-878141; www.ludlowassemblyrooms.co.uk; adult standard/balcony £7/8, child £6.50/7.50) Overlooking the market square, the Ludlow Assembly Rooms double as the town cinema.

Shopping

★**Ludlow Food Centre** FOOD & DRINKS
(☎01584-856000; www.ludlowfoodcentre.co.uk; Bromfield Rd, Bromfield; ⏲9am-5.30pm Mon-Sat, to 4.30pm Sun) More than 80% of the cheeses, meats, breads, fruit and vegetables are sourced from the surrounding region and tantalisingly displayed at this enormous farm shop stocking over 4000 products in all. Watch through viewing windows to see traditional preserves, pies, ice cream and more being made. It's signposted 4 miles northwest of Ludlow off Bromfield Rd (the A49).

Ludlow Market MARKET
(www.ludlowmarket.co.uk; Castle Sq; ⏲9.30am-2pm Mon, Wed, Fri & Sat) Ludlow Market takes place on the market square on the site of the old Victorian town hall, demolished overnight in 1986. Various spin-off markets (farmers markets, flea markets, book markets and craft markets) take place on Thursdays and Sundays.

Information

Ludlow's **tourist office** (☎01584-875053; www.visitshropshirehills.co.uk; Castle Sq; ⏲10am-5pm daily Apr-Sep, to 4pm Mon-Sat Oct-Mar) contains a small local-history exhibit (adult/child £1/free).

Getting There & Away

Bus 435 runs to Shrewsbury (£3.85, 1½ hours, hourly Monday to Friday, every two hours Saturday) via Church Stretton (£2.95, 40 minutes).

Trains run frequently from the station on the north edge of town to Hereford (£9.80, 25 minutes, half-hourly) and Shrewsbury (£12.70, 30 minutes, half-hourly), some via Church Stretton (£7.10, 15 minutes, hourly).

NOTTINGHAMSHIRE

Say Nottinghamshire and people think of one thing – Robin Hood. Whether the hero woodsman existed is hotly debated, but the county plays up its connections to the outlaw. Storytelling seems to be in Nottinghamshire's blood – local wordsmiths include provocative writer DH Lawrence, of *Lady Chatterley's Lover* fame, and hedonistic poet Lord Byron. The city of Nottingham is the bustling hub, but venture into the surrounding countryside and you'll discover historic towns and stately homes surrounding the green bower of Sherwood Forest.

Getting There & Around

National Express and **Trent Barton** (☎01773-712265; www.trentbarton.co.uk) buses provide the majority of bus services. See **Traveline** (☎0871 200 2233; www.travelineeastmidlands.co.uk) for timetables. Trains run frequently to most large towns, and to many smaller villages in the Peak District.

Nottingham & Around

POP 310,800

Forever associated with men in tights and a sheriff with anger-management issues (aka the Robin Hood legend) Nottingham is a dynamic county capital with big-city aspirations, atmospheric historical sights, and a buzzing music and club scene thanks to its spirited student population.

Sights

★**Nottingham Castle** CASTLE, GALLERY
(☎0115-876 1400; www.nottinghamcastle.org.uk; Lenton Rd; adult/child £6/5, cave tours £5/free; ⏲10am-5pm daily mid-Feb–Oct, to 4pm Wed-Sun Nov–mid-Feb, cave tours hourly noon-3pm) Nottingham's castle crowns a sandstone outcrop worm-holed with caves and tunnels. Founded by William the Conqueror, the original castle was held by a succession of English kings before falling in the English Civil War. Its 17th-century manor-house-like replacement contains a local-history **museum** and **art gallery**. Various cave tours include one through underground

passageway **Mortimer's Hole**, emerging alongside five 17th-century cottages comprising the **Museum of Nottingham Life at Brewhouse Yard** (☎0115-876 1400; www.nottinghamcity.gov.uk; Castle Blvd; adult/child £2.50/free; ⊙noon-4pm Sat & Sun year-round). The much-photographed **statue of Robin Hood** (Castle Rd) stands in the former moat.

City of Caves CAVE
(☎0115-988 1955; www.cityofcaves.com; Drury Walk, Upper Level, Broadmarsh Shopping Centre; adult/child £7.95/5.95, incl Galleries of Justice £15/11.75; ⊙10.30am-4pm) Over the centuries, the sandstone underneath Nottingham has been carved into a honeycomb of caverns and passageways. Audio tours (Monday to Friday) and performance tours (weekends and school holidays) lead you from the top level of the Broadmarsh shopping centre through a WWII air-raid shelter, a medieval underground tannery, several pub cellars and a mock-up of a Victorian slum dwelling. Book ahead.

Galleries of Justice MUSEUM
(☎0115-952 0555; www.galleriesofjustice.org.uk; High Pavement; adult/child £9.95/7.95, incl City of Caves £15/11.75; ⊙9am-6pm Mon-Fri, 10am-5.30pm Sat & Sun, tours 10am-4pm Mon-Fri, 10.30am-4pm Sat & Sun) In the grand Georgian Shire Hall, the Galleries of Justice offers a ghoulish stroll through centuries of British justice, including medieval trials by fire and water. Audio tours run on Mondays and Tuesdays; live-action tours with 'gaolers' run from Wednesday to Sunday (daily during school holidays).

Nottingham Contemporary GALLERY
(☎0115-948 9750; www.nottinghamcontemporary.org; Weekday Cross; ⊙10am-6pm Tue-Sat, 11am-5pm Sun) FREE Behind its lace-patterned concrete facade, Nottingham Contemporary holds edgy, design-driven exhibitions of paintings, prints, photography and sculpture.

St Mary's Church CHURCH
(www.nottinghamchurches.org; High Pavement; ⊙8am-6.30pm) The most atmospheric time to visit this historic church dating from Saxon times is during evensong (6.15pm Wednesday, 6.30pm Sunday).

Wollaton Hall HISTORIC BUILDING
(☎0115-876 3100; www.wollatonhall.co.uk; Wollaton Park, Derby Rd; tours adult/child £5/3, grounds free; ⊙tours 11am, 2pm & 3pm, grounds 8am-8pm Mon-Fri, 9am-8pm Sat & Sun mid-Feb–Oct, 9am-7pm Mon-Fri, 10am-7pm Sat & Sun Nov–mid-Feb) Built in 1588 for land owner and coal mogul Sir Francis Willoughby by avant-garde architect Robert Smythson, Wollaton Hall sits within 200 hectares of grounds roamed by fallow and red deer. Along with extravagant rooms from the Tudor, Regency and Victorian periods, there's a natural-history museum and industrial museum.

Wollaton Hall is 2.5 miles west of Nottingham city centre; take bus 30 or 2 from Victoria bus station (£2.20, 15 minutes, every 15 minutes Monday to Saturday, half-hourly Sunday).

Newstead Abbey HISTORIC BUILDING
(☎01623-455900; www.newsteadabbey.org.uk; adult/child house £7/5, garden only £1; ⊙house noon-5pm Sat & Sun, garden 10am-5pm daily) The evocative lakeside ruins of Newstead Abbey are inextricably associated with the original tortured romantic, Lord Byron (1788–1824), who owned the house until 1817. Founded as an Augustinian priory in around 1170, it was converted into a residence in 1539.

Newstead Abbey is 12 miles north of Nottingham, off the A60. Pronto buses (£3.20, 25 minutes, every 10 minutes Monday to Saturday, half-hourly Sunday) from Victoria bus station stop at the gates, a mile from the house and gardens.

Activities & Tours

★ **Ezekial Bone Tours** WALKING
(☎07941 210986; www.ezekialbone.com; Robin Hood Town Tours adult/child £12/7; ⊙Robin Hood Town Tours by reservation 2pm Sat Mar-Oct) Hugely entertaining, history-focused **Robin Hood town tours** are led by 'modern-day Robin Hood' Ezekial Bone (aka historian/actor/writer Ade Andrews). Tours last 2½ hours, departing from the Cross Keys pub. Check Bone/Andrews' website for 90-minute **Lace Market tours** and 80-minute **Guts & Gore ghost tours**, plus **Robin Hood Sherwood Forest tours** by request.

National Ice Centre SKATING
(☎0843 373 3000; www.national-ice-centre.com; Bolero Sq; skating £6.50, skate hire £2) The UK's first ice centre with twin Olympic-sized (60m x 30m) rinks sits on Bolero Sq, named for Nottingham skaters Jayne Torvill and Christopher Dean's historic 1984 gold-medal-winning routine. The complex incorporates the East Midland's premier entertainment venue, the **Motorpoint Arena**, which hosts sporting fixtures, competitions and performances. Daily skating session times (including weekend disco sessions) are posted online.

Nottingham

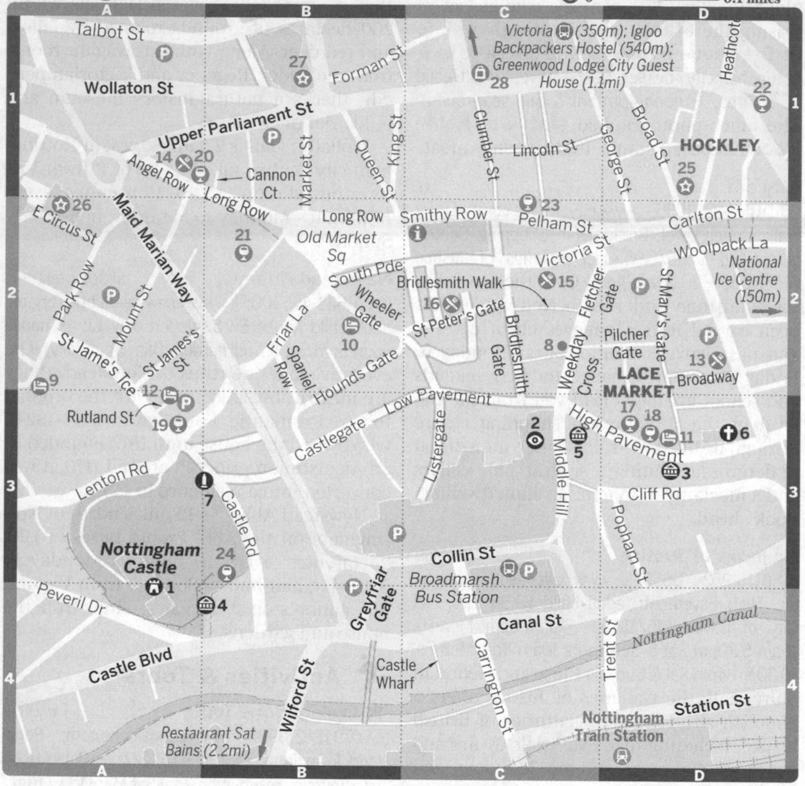

Festivals & Events

Goose Fair CULTURAL
(www.nottinghamcity.gov.uk; early Oct) The five-day Goose Fair has evolved from a medieval travelling market to a modern funfair.

Robin Hood Beer & Cider Festival DRINK
(www.beerfestival.nottinghamcamra.org; mid-Oct) In the castle grounds, this four-day tasting festival features more than 1000 beers and 200 ciders.

Robin Hood Pageant CULTURAL
(www.nottinghamcastle.org.uk; late Oct) This family-friendly pageant takes place over two days in late October.

Sleeping

Igloo Hybrid Hostel HOSTEL £
(0115-948 3822; www.igloohostel.co.uk; 4-6 Eldon Chambers, Wheeler Gate; dm from £19, s/d sleep box from £29/64, s without/with en suite from £34/48, d without/with en suite £72/98;) Opened in 2015, the sister property of the much-loved **Igloo Backpackers Hostel** (0115-947 5250; www.igloohostel.co.uk; 110 Mansfield Rd; dm/d from £19/44;) has an epicentral location footsteps from the Old Market Sq. Its Japanese capsule-style 'Sleep Boxes' incorporate USB ports and reading lights; there's a well-equipped self-catering kitchen and a sociable courtyard garden.

★ **Lace Market Hotel** BOUTIQUE HOTEL ££
(0115-948 4414; www.lacemarkethotel.co.uk; 29-31 High Pavement; s/d incl breakfast from £85/135;) In the heart of the trendy Lace Market, this elegant Georgian town house's sleek rooms have state-of-the-art furnishings and amenities; some come with air-conditioning. Its fine-dining restaurant, Merchants (p456), and adjoining genteel pub, the **Cock & Hoop** (www.lacemarkethotel.

Nottingham

Top Sights

1 Nottingham Castle A4

Sights

2 City of Caves C3
3 Galleries of Justice D3
4 Museum of Nottingham Life at Brewhouse Yard B4
5 Nottingham Contemporary C3
6 St Mary's Church D3
7 Statue of Robin Hood B3

Activities, Courses & Tours

8 Ezekial Bone Tours C2

Sleeping

9 Hart's A2
10 Igloo Hybrid Hostel B2
11 Lace Market Hotel D3
12 St James Hotel A3

Eating

13 Annie's Burger Shack D2
14 Aubrey's Traditional Crêperie A1
15 Delilah Fine Foods C2
Hart's Restaurant (see 9)
Merchants (see 11)
16 Purecraft Bar & Kitchen C2

Drinking & Nightlife

17 Brass Monkey D3
18 Cock & Hoop D3
19 Crafty Crow A3
20 Dragon A1
21 Malt Cross B2
22 NG1 D1
23 Tilt C2
24 Ye Olde Trip to Jerusalem B3

Entertainment

25 Broadway Cinema D1
26 Nottingham Playhouse A2
27 Theatre Royal & Royal Concert Hall B1

Shopping

28 Victoria Shopping Centre C1

co.uk; 25 High Pavement; 11am-11pm Mon-Thu, to midnight Fri, to 1am Sat, to 10.30pm Sun), are both superb.

St James Hotel BOUTIQUE HOTEL ££
(0115-941 1114; www.stjames-hotel.com; St James's Tce; s/d/ste £74.50/89.50/204.50;) Stunning patterned wallpaper, richly coloured textured fabrics and designer elements such as stag heads made from stainless steel set the striking St James apart. It's in an increasingly vibrant area right by Nottingham Castle and historic pubs plus hip new bars and restaurants. More than 500 books line its library shelves; parking is available next door (per 24 hours £11).

Hart's BOUTIQUE HOTEL £££
(0115-988 1900; www.hartsnottingham.co.uk; Standard Hill, Park Row; incl breakfast d £93-212, ste £127-302; P) Within the former Nottingham General Hospital compound, the city's swishest hotel has ultracontemporary rooms in a striking modernist building; its renowned **restaurant** (mains £16-30; noon-2.30pm & 6-10pm;) is housed in a historic red-brick wing. Work out in the small gym or unwind in the private garden.

Eating

★Delilah Fine Foods DELI, CAFE £
(www.delilahfinefoods.co.uk; 12 Victoria St; dishes £4-16, platters £15-35; 8am-7pm Mon-Fri, 9am-7pm Sat, 11am-5pm Sun;) Impeccably selected cheeses (more than 150 varieties), pâtés, meats and more from artisan producers are available to take away or eat on-site at this gourmand's dream, housed in a grand former bank with mezzanine seating.

Annie's Burger Shack BURGERS, AMERICAN £
(www.anniesburgershack.com; 5 Broadway; burgers £8.90-13.20, breakfast £6-10; 8-10.15am & noon-11.30pm Mon-Thu, 8-10.15am & noon-12.30am Sat, noon-11.30pm Sun;) More than 30 different burgers (available in vegan, veggie or meat versions) are on the menu at Annie's, a wildly popular joint in the Lace Market that stays true to its owner's US roots (and adds real ales to its offerings). Midweek breakfast menus feature American classics (blueberry pancakes with maple syrup and bacon; Boston franks 'n' beans). Book ahead.

Aubrey's Traditional Crêperie CREPERIE £
(www.aubreystraditionalcreperie.com; 14-16 West End Arcade; dishes £2.75-8; 10am-6pm Wed-Sat;) Traditional down to its savoury galettes made with buckwheat flour, its sweet crêpes including salted caramel and its Breton ciders, this little hole-in-the-wall is a charming spot for an inexpensive lunch. Alongside the classics, there are galettes you'll never see in Brittany, such as black olives, caramelised onions, sun-dried tomatoes and balsamic, or ginger, chilli relish, rucola and chorizo, too.

Purecraft Bar & Kitchen GASTROPUB ££

(☎0115-934 9040; www.purecraftbars.com; 13 St Peter's Gate; mains £9-16, platters £8.50-9.50; ⊙kitchen noon-10pm Mon-Sat, to 6pm Sun, bar 11am-11pm Mon-Thu, 11am-midnight Fri & Sat, noon-10pm Sun) Purecraft matches artisan beers from around the world with well-crafted fare, including platters (Wyre Forest–reared pig board; British cheese board), light bites (such as a Scotch egg with Purity-beer ketchup, stout-cured ham and Old Winchester cheese rarebit), Wagyu burgers, and traditional pork pies with homemade piccalilli pickle relish. The original of its two locations is in Birmingham (p414).

Merchants GASTRONOMY £££

(☎0115-948 4414; www.lacemarkethotel.co.uk; 29-31 High Pavement; mains £19-30, 2-/3-course lunch menus £14.50/18.50, 3-course dinner menu £45; ⊙7-10am, noon-2pm & 5-10pm Mon-Sat, 7-10.30am & noon-2pm Sun) A stunning, coffered-ceilinged dining room sets the stage for some of Nottingham's finest dining. Knock-out combinations include Texel lamb with pistachio and courgette; Irish sea trout with samphire and radish; and morrels, broad beans and goats curd. Follow up with equally adventurous desserts such as poached-rhubarb panna cotta with black-pepper crumble and basil ice cream.

Restaurant Sat Bains GASTRONOMY £££

(☎0115-986 6566; www.restaurantsatbains.com; Lenton Lane; 7-/10-course tasting menus £85/95; ⊙6-9pm Wed & Thu, 6-9.45pm Fri & Sat; ✎) Chef Sat Bains has been awarded two Michelin stars for his wildly inventive Modern European cooking. Book well in advance and beware of hefty cancellation charges. It also has eight chic **guest rooms** (d £140-190, ste £285). It's 2 miles southwest of the centre off the A52.

Drinking & Nightlife

★Ye Olde Trip to Jerusalem PUB

(☎0115-947 3171; www.triptojerusalem.com; Brewhouse Yard, Castle Rd; ⊙11am-11pm Sun-Thu, to midnight Fri & Sat) Carved into the cliff below the castle, this atmospheric alehouse claims to be England's oldest pub. Founded in 1189, it supposedly slaked the thirst of departing crusaders, and its rooms and cobbled courtyards are still the most ambient place in Nottingham for a pint. Book ahead for informal tours (£2.50) of its cellars and caves.

★Crafty Crow PUB

(www.craftycrownotts.co.uk; 102 Friar Lane; ⊙noon-11pm Sun-Thu, 11am-midnight Fri & Sat; 📶) Rotating brews at this beer specialist include several from its own Nottingham-based Magpie Brewery, made from British hops and malts, plus hand-pulls from local microbreweries and more than a dozen craft beers and ciders on tap. Timber-planked walls line the TV-free split-level space; don't miss the bathrooms with sinks and taps made out of kegs. Gastropub food is locally sourced.

Dragon PUB

(www.the-dragon.co.uk; 67 Long Row; ⊙noon-midnight Mon-Thu, noon-2am Fri & Sat, 11am-10pm Sun; 📶) The Dragon has a fabulous atmosphere at any time, thanks to homemade food, a good beer garden and funky music on weekends. But it peaks from 7.30pm on Tuesdays when it hosts the Racing Room (race entry £5) – an awesome Scalextric slot-car race around a scale model of Nottingham along 180ft of track.

Brass Monkey BAR

(www.brassmonkeybar.co.uk; 11 High Pavement; ⊙5pm-3am Mon-Sat, 8pm-3am Sun) Nottingham's original cocktail bar rocks the Lace Market with DJ sets and quirky takes on favourites such as elderflower mojitos. The roof terrace gets packed on summer evenings.

Tilt COCKTAIL BAR

(www.tiltbar.co.uk; 9 Pelham St; ⊙5pm-midnight Tue-Thu, to 1.30am Fri & Sat) This tiny 1st-floor cocktail bar serves up a brilliant array of live blues offerings as well as cocktails that are giving their competition (in Nottingham, that's a lot!) a run for their money. House specialities include a Blues Blazer (cognac and Drambuie flamed with vanilla sugar and orange peel).

NG1 CLUB

(☎0115-958 8440; www.ng1club.co.uk; 76-80 Lower Parliament St; ⊙11pm-6am Fri, to 6.30am Sat) A fixture on Notthingham's late-night scene, NG1 is unpretentious, hedonistic fun, with four bars and two dance floors belting out house, electro, pop and more. It's gay-friendly and all-welcoming.

Malt Cross PUB

(www.maltcross.com; 16 St James's St; ⊙11am-11pm Mon-Fri, 10am-midnight Sat, 10am-10pm Sun) A fine place for a pint, the Malt Cross occupies a stately old Victorian music hall,

SHERWOOD FOREST NATIONAL NATURE RESERVE

If Robin Hood wanted to hide out in Sherwood Forest today, he'd have to disguise himself and the Merry Men as day trippers on mountain bikes. Now covering just 182 hectares of old growth forest, it's nevertheless a major destination for Nottingham city dwellers.

Until a proposed new visitor centre opens, the **Sherwood Forest Visitor Centre** (www.nottinghamshire.gov.uk; Swinecote Rd, Edwinstowe; ⏲10am-5.30pm Easter-Oct, to 4.30pm Nov-Mar), on the B6034, is an uninspiring collection of faded late-20th-century buildings housing cafes, gift shops et al. It's the departure point for walking trails passing Sherwood Forest landmarks such as the **Major Oak** (1 mile return), a broad-boughed oak tree (propped up by supporting rods) alleged to have sheltered Robin of Locksley.

For informative guided walks through forest, contact Ezekial Bone Tours (p453).

Sherwood Pines Cycles (☎01623-822855; www.sherwoodpinescycles.co.uk; Sherwood Pines Forest Park, Clipstone; bike hire adult/child per hour £9/8, per day £28/20; ⏲9am-5pm Thu-Tue, to 7pm Wed) rents bikes. From Nottingham, take the Sherwood Arrow bus (£5, 55 minutes, four per day Monday to Saturday, two on Sunday).

Robin Hood Festival (www.nottinghamshire.gov.uk; ⏲early Aug) The week-long Robin Hood Festival is a massive medieval reenactment that takes place in the forest in early August.

where past performers included Charlie Chaplin. It's now a community space run by the Christian Charity Trust hosting art exhibitions and live music. Top-notch bar food includes towering burgers.

☆ Entertainment

Nottingham Playhouse THEATRE
(☎0115-941 9419; www.nottinghamplayhouse.co.uk; Wellington Circus) Beside Anish Kapoor's enormous *Sky Mirror* dish, the Playhouse puts on serious theatre, from stage classics to the avant-garde. Nottingham's artistic community congregates at its attached restaurant and bar.

Theatre Royal & Royal Concert Hall THEATRE, LIVE MUSIC
(☎0115-989 5555; www.trch.co.uk; Theatre Sq; ⏲booking office 9.30am-8.30pm Mon-Sat) Sharing the same building and booking office, the Theatre Royal and Royal Concert Hall host musicals, touring theatre shows and veteran music acts. Backstage tours can be arranged (£6.50, 90 minutes).

Broadway Cinema CINEMA, GALLERY
(www.broadway.org.uk; 14-18 Broad St; cinema tickets adult/child £8.20/4) Along with an independent cinema, this artistic hub has a media-arts gallery and a cafe-bar where you can actually hear yourself talk.

ℹ Information

Nottingham's friendly **tourist office** (☎0844 477 5678; www.experiencenottinghamshire.com; The Exchange, 1-4 Smithy Row; ⏲9.30am-5.30pm Mon-Sat year-round, plus 11am-5pm Sun late Jul–Aug & mid–late Dec) has racks of info and Robin Hood merchandise.

ℹ Getting There & Away

AIR

East Midlands Airport (p408) is 13.5 miles southwest of central Nottingham; Skylink buses pass the airport (one way/return £5/9.90, one hour, at least hourly, 24 hours).

BUS

Local services run from the Victoria bus station, behind the **Victoria Shopping Centre** (Lower Parliament St) on Milton St. Bus 100 runs to Southwell (£4.15, 55 minutes, every 30 minutes Monday to Saturday, hourly Sunday) and bus 90 to Newark (£5, 50 minutes, every 30 minutes Monday to Friday, hourly Saturday, every two hours Sunday).

Long-distance buses operate from the **Broadmarsh bus station** (Collin St).

Frequent National Express services:

Birmingham £10.90, 2¼ hours, eight daily

Derby £7.80, 40 minutes, six Monday to Saturday, four Sunday

Leicester £5.50, 55 minutes, hourly or better

London Victoria £14, 3½ hours, hourly or better

TRAIN

The train station is on the southern edge of the town centre.

Derby £7.30, 30 minutes, four hourly

Lincoln £11.30, one hour, hourly

London King's Cross/St Pancras £29.50, two hours, at least two per hour Monday to Saturday, at least hourly Sunday

Manchester £23.50, two hours, up to two per hour

Getting Around

For information on buses within Nottingham, call **Nottingham City Transport** (0115-950 6070; www.nctx.co.uk). A Robin Hood Day Ticket gives you unlimited travel on buses and trams within the city for £4.50.

Trams are operated by **Nottingham Express Transit** (www.thetram.net; single/day ticket from £2.20/4). A single-stage bus ticket costs £1.10.

Nottingham City Council's bike-share scheme, **City Card Cycles** (www.citycardcycles.co.uk; per day £1), has rental bikes available from Nottingham's tourist office and Broadmarsh bus station. Register using a credit card, then use the code sent to your phone to unlock the bikes.

Southwell

POP 6900

A graceful scattering of grand, wisteria-draped country houses, pretty little Southwell is straight out of the pages of a novel from the English Romantic period.

Sights

★Southwell Minster CHURCH

(www.southwellminster.org; Church St; suggested donation £5; 8am-7pm Mar-Oct, to 6.30pm Nov-Feb) Rising from the village centre, the awe-inspiring Southwell Minster, built over Saxon and Roman foundations, blends 12th- and 13th-century features including zigzag door frames and curved arches. Its chapterhouse features some unusual stained glass and detailed carvings of faces, animals and leaves of forest trees.

Southwell Workhouse MUSEUM

(NT; www.nationaltrust.org.uk; Upton Rd; adult/child £8/4; noon-5pm daily Aug, Wed-Sun mid-Feb–Jul & Sep-Nov) On the road to Newark, 1 mile east of the village centre, the Southwell Workhouse is a sobering reminder of the tough life faced by paupers in the 19th century. You can explore the factory floors and workers' chambers accompanied by an audio guide narrated by 'inmates' and 'officials'. Free one-hour guided tours of the exteriors take place at 11am.

Sleeping & Eating

Saracen's Head Hotel HISTORIC HOTEL ££

(01636-812701; www.saracensheadhotel.com; Market Pl; s/d/f/ste incl breakfast from £90/100/130/150; P) Set around a flower-filled courtyard in the village heart, this rambling, black-and-white timbered coaching inn has 27 beautifully refurbished rooms (some with four-poster beds and claw-foot baths) across its old and new wings. Illustrious past guests included Charles I, Lord Byron and Dickens. Its oak-panelled restaurant serves traditional British fare (two-/three-course menus £15.95/19.95).

Mosedales Bakery BAKERY £

(7 King St; dishes £3-8; 9am-4pm Mon-Fri, 8.30am-4pm Sat, 9.30am-3pm Sun) Queues at this central village bakery regularly extend out the door.

Getting There & Away

Bus 100 runs from Nottingham (£4.15, 55 minutes, half-hourly Monday to Saturday, hourly on Sunday). For Newark-on-Trent, take bus 28 or 29 (£4, 20 minutes, half-hourly).

Newark-on-Trent

POP 37,457

Newark-on-Trent paid the price for backing the wrong side in the English Civil War. After surviving four sieges by Oliver Cromwell's men, the town was ransacked by Roundheads when Charles I surrendered in 1646. Today, the riverside town is a peaceful place worth a stop to wander its castle ruins.

Sights

Newark Castle CASTLE

(www.newark-sherwooddc.gov.uk/newarkcastle; Castle Gate; grounds admission free, tours adult/child £5/2.50; grounds 9am-6pm, tours 11am, 1pm & 3pm Wed & Fri-Sun) In a pretty park overlooking the River Trent, the ruins of Newark Castle include an impressive Norman gate and a series of underground passages and chambers. The real King John, portrayed as a villain in the Robin Hood legend, died here in 1216. Book tour tickets online at www.palacenewarktickets.com. Concerts, festivals and various cultural events regularly take place in the grounds.

Newark Air Museum MUSEUM
(☎01636-707170; www.newarkairmuseum.org; Drove Lane, Winthorpe; adult/child £8.50/4.50; ⊙10am-5pm Mar-Oct, to 4pm Nov-Feb) Situated 2 miles east of Newark by the Winthorpe Showground, this air museum has an impressive collection of aircraft, including a fearsome Vulcan bomber.

Eating & Drinking

Old Bakery Tea Rooms TEAROOM £
(☎01636-611501; www.oldbakerytearooms.co.uk; 4 Queens Head Ct; mains £6-12; ⊙9.30am-5pm Mon-Sat; ✎) Everything, including to-die-for scones, is baked fresh on the premises at the Old Bakery Tea Rooms, housed in an enchanting *Hansel and Gretel*-like 15th-century Tudor building. Lunch specials include soups, frittata, bruschetta and smoked-salmon brioche. Cash only.

Castle Barge BAR
(www.castlebarge.co.uk; The Wharf; ⊙10.30am-11pm) Moored on the River Trent overlooking Newark Castle, this former grain barge, which once plied the waters between Hull and Gainsborough, is an idyllic spot for a local ale. It serves decent food; there's additional picnic seating on the riverbanks.

Information

The **tourist office** (☎01636-655765; www.newark-sherwooddc.gov.uk/tourism; 14 Appleton Gate; ⊙10am-5pm) is on the northeastern edge of the historic centre.

Getting There & Away

Buses 28 and 29 serve Southwell (£4, 25 minutes, up to four per hour).

Newark has two train stations:

Newark North Gate Trains on the East Coast Main Line serve London King's Cross (£20, 1½ hours, two per hour) and the north.

Newark Castle East Midlands trains serve Leicester (£12.80, 1¼ hours, hourly), Nottingham (£6.10, 30 minutes, two per hour) and Lincoln (£5.10, 30 minutes, up to two hourly).

LINCOLNSHIRE

Lincolnshire unfolds over low hills and the sparsely populated, pancake-flat Fens where the farmland is strewn with windmills and, more recently, wind turbines. Surrounding the history-steeped county town of Lincoln you'll find seaside resorts, scenic waterways, serene nature reserves and stone-built towns tailor-made for English period dramas.

Two of the county's most famous 'yellow-bellies' (as Lincolnshire locals call themselves) were Sir Isaac Newton, whose home, Woolsthorpe Manor, can be visited, and the late former prime minister Margaret Thatcher, the daughter of a humble greengrocer from the market town of Grantham.

Activities

Traversing the area occupied by Norse invaders in the 9th century, the 147-mile **Viking Way** walking trail snakes across the gentle hills of the Lincolnshire Wolds from the banks of the River Humber to Oakham in Rutland.

Cyclists can find information on routes across the county in any of the local tourist offices. The 33-mile **Water Rail Way** is a flat, sculpture-lined on-road cycling route that follows the River Witham through classic Fens countryside along the former railway line between Lincoln and Boston.

Detailed information on activities is available at www.visitlincolnshire.com.

Getting There & Around

East Midlands trains connect Lincoln, Newark Castle and Nottingham. Newark North Gate and Grantham lie on the East Coast Main Line between London King's Cross and Edinburgh.

Local buses link Lincolnshire's towns but services are slow and infrequent. Check the transport pages at www.lincolnshire.gov.uk, which also has cycling route info.

Comprehensive transport information is available from Traveline (p452).

Lincoln

POP 96,200

Ringed by historic city gates – including the Newport Arch on Bailgate, a relic from the original Roman settlement – this beautiful city's old centre is a tangle of cobbled medieval streets surrounding a colossal 12th-century cathedral. The lanes that topple over the edge of Lincoln Cliff are lined with Tudor town houses, ancient pubs and quirky independent stores.

Flanking the River Witham at the base of the hill, the new town is less absorbing, but the revitalised Brayford Waterfront development by the university is a popular spot to watch the boats go by.

Sights

★Lincoln Cathedral CATHEDRAL
(☎01522-561600; www.lincolncathedral.com; Minster Yard; adult/child joint ticket with castle £16/10, cathedral £8/4.80 Mon-Sat, by donation Sun; ⏲7.15am-8pm Mon-Fri, to 6pm Sat & Sun Jul & Aug, 7.15am-6pm Mon-Sat, to 5pm Sun Sep-Jun, evensong 5.30pm Mon-Sat, 3.45pm Sun) Towering over the city like a medieval skyscraper, Lincoln's magnificent cathedral is a breathtaking representation of divine power on earth. The great tower rising above the crossing is the third-highest in England at 83m, but in medieval times, a lead-encased wooden spire added a further 79m, topping even the great pyramids of Giza. One-hour **guided tours** (included in admission) take place at least twice daily; there are also tours of the roof and tower (£4, book in advance).

★Lincoln Castle CASTLE
(☎01522-554559; www.lincolncastle.com; Castle Hill; adult/child joint ticket with cathedral £16/10, castle, Magna Carta exhibition & walls £12/7.20, walls only £5/3; ⏲10am-5pm Apr-Sep, to 4pm Oct-Mar) One of the first castles erected by the victorious William the Conqueror to keep his new kingdom in line, Lincoln Castle offers awesome views over the city and miles of surrounding countryside. A major restoration program, completed in 2015, has opened up the entire castle walls and given the 1215 **Magna Carta** (one of only four copies) a swanky, subterranean new home. One-hour guided tours, included in castle admission, depart from the eastern gate; check the blackboard for times.

Bishops' Palace HISTORIC SITE
(EH; ☎01522-527468; www.english-heritage.org.uk; Minster Yard; adult/child £5.70/3.40; ⏲10am-6pm Wed-Sun Easter-Sep, to 5pm Wed-Sun Oct, to 4pm Sat & Sun Nov-Easter) Beside Lincoln Cathedral lie the time-ravaged but still imposing ruins of the 12th-century Bishops' Palace, gutted by parliamentary forces during the Civil War. From here, the local bishops once controlled a diocese stretching from the Humber to the Thames. Entertaining audio guides are included in admission. Free 30-minute guided tours take place at noon, 2pm and 4pm on Fridays from Easter to October.

Collection MUSEUM
(www.thecollectionmuseum.com; Danes Tce; ⏲10am-4pm, from 10.45am 1st Mon of month) FREE Archaeology bursts into life with loads of hands-on displays. Kids can handle artefacts and dress up in period costume. Check out the crushed skull of a 4000-year-old 'yellowbelly' (the local term for, well, the locals), pulled from a Neolithic burial site near Sleaford. Free one-hour tours run at 2pm on Saturdays. Look out for various evening events.

Usher Gallery GALLERY
(www.thecollectionmuseum.com; Danes Tce; ⏲10am-4pm, from 10.45am 1st Mon of month) FREE A handsome Edwardian building decorated with carvings of cow skulls houses an impressive collection of works by greats such as Turner, Lowry and English watercolourist Peter de Wint (1784–1849).

Museum of Lincolnshire Life MUSEUM
(www.lincolnshire.gov.uk; Old Barracks, Burton Rd; ⏲10am-4.30pm) FREE Displays at this charming community museum housed in an old Victorian barracks span everything from Victorian farm implements to the tin-can tank built in Lincoln for WWI. Around the corner from the museum is the cute little **Ellis Mill** (www.lincolnshire.gov.uk; Mill Rd; ⏲2-5pm Sat & Sun Apr-Sep, 2-4pm Sun Oct-Mar) FREE, which ground the town's flour in the 18th century and is still in use today.

Tours

Ghost Walks WALKING
(☎01522-874056; adult/child £5/3; ⏲7pm Wed-Sat year-round) Genuinely spooky 75-minute ghost walks depart adjacent to the tourist office in Castle Sq.

Brayford Belle BOATING
(☎01522-881200; www.lincolnboattrips.co.uk; Brayford Wharf North; adult/child £7/4; ⏲tours 11am, 12.15pm, 1.30pm, 2.45pm & 3.45pm Easter–mid-Oct) Boat trips aboard the *Brayford Belle* travel along the River Witham and Fossdyke Navigation, a canal system dating back to Roman times. No credit cards.

Walking Tours WALKING
(☎01522-521256; www.lincolnguidedtours.co.uk; adult/child £4/free; ⏲tours 11am daily Jul & Aug, Sat & Sun Jun, Sep & Oct) History-focused 90-minute guided walking tours run from outside the tourist office.

Sleeping

★Castle Hotel BOUTIQUE HOTEL ££
(☎01522-538801; www.castlehotel.net; Westgate; incl breakfast s £90-130, d £110-150, coach house £250-270; P 🛜 👪) Each of the Castle Hotel's 18 rooms have been exquisitely refurbished

Lincoln

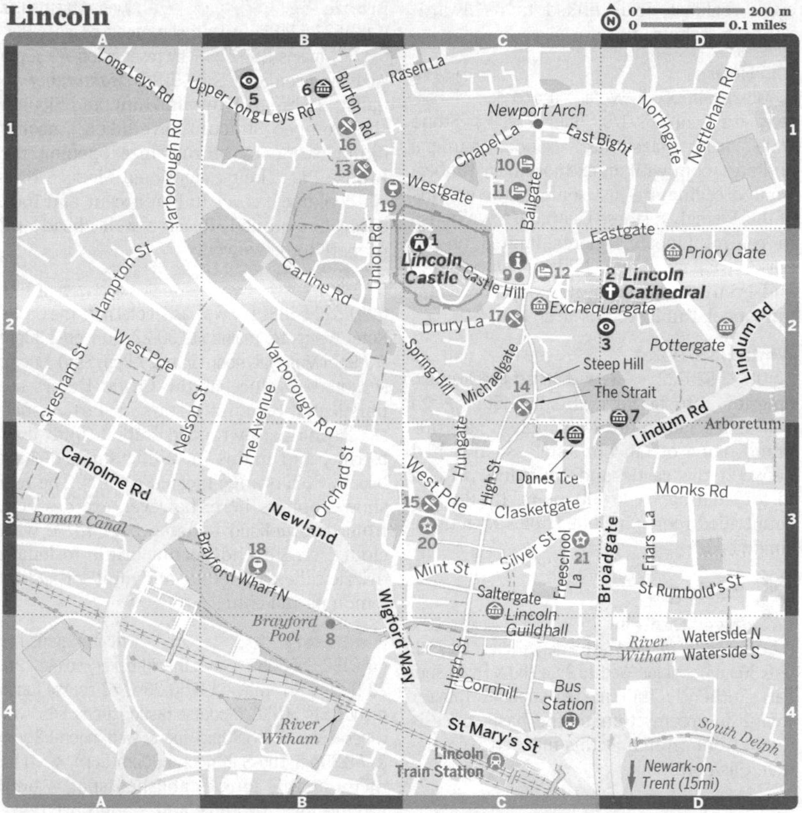

Lincoln

Top Sights
1 Lincoln Castle C2
2 Lincoln Cathedral D2

Sights
3 Bishops' Palace.................................... D2
4 Collection C3
5 Ellis Mill... B1
6 Museum of Lincolnshire Life B1
7 Usher Gallery D2

Activities, Courses & Tours
8 Brayford Belle B4
9 Ghost Walks C2
Walking Tours .... (see 9)

Sleeping
10 Bail House C1
11 Castle Hotel C1
12 White Hart Hotel.................................. C2

Eating
13 Bronze Pig B1
14 Jew's House.. C2
15 La Bottega Delitalia.............................. C3
16 Old Bakery B1
Reform .... (see 11)
17 Wig & Mitre C2

Drinking & Nightlife
18 Electric Bar & Restaurant..................... B3
19 Strugglers Inn....................................... B1

Entertainment
20 Home Nightclub C3
21 Lincoln Drill Hall.................................... C3

in olive, truffle and oyster tones, as has its four-person coach house. Built on the site of Lincoln's Roman forum in 1852, the red-brick building's incarnations variously included a school and WWII lookout station. Take advantage of great-value dinner, bed and breakfast deals linked to its award-winning restaurant Reform.

Bail House B&B ££
(01522-541000; www.bailhouse.co.uk; 34 Bailgate; d/f from £69/179;) Stone walls, worn flagstones, secluded gardens and one room with an extraordinary timber-vaulted ceiling are just some of the charms of this lovingly restored Georgian town house in central Lincoln. There's limited on-site parking, a garden and children's playground, and even a seasonal heated outdoor swimming pool. Family rooms sleep four.

White Hart Hotel HOTEL ££
(01522-526222; www.whitehart-lincoln.co.uk; Bailgate; d/tr/ste from £110/150/160;) You can't get more venerable than this grand dame of Lincoln hotels, sandwiched between the castle and cathedral, with a history dating back 600 years. Its flowing countrified rooms include triples with three single beds.

Eating

La Bottega Delitalia CAFE, DELI £
(01522-537775; 9 West Pde; dishes £3-7.50; 8.30am-4pm Mon-Wed, to 9pm Thu & Fri, to 3pm Sat) Authentic Italian fare such as lobster ravioli in creamy tomato and basil sauce is made from scratch at this inexpensive cafe-deli. Cash only.

MINIMISING LINCOLN'S HILLS

Walking between Lincoln's old and new towns can feel like an Everest expedition, but fortunately there are alternatives.

The **Steep Hill Shuttle** (wwww, visit lincoln.com; single ticket adult/child £1.50/70p, all-day pass £3/1.60; 9.10am-2.45pm & 4.10-5.20pm Mon-Sat) runs every 20 minutes, making 13 stops including the castle, cathedral, Newport Arch, Brayford Waterfront and the train and bus stations. To tour the city in comfort, hop aboard the open-topped **Tour Lincoln** (www.visitlincoln.com; adult/child £10/4; 10.30am-4.30pm Jun-Sep, 10.30am-4.30pm Sat & Sun Mar-May & Oct) bus, which stops at nine key sights. Tickets are sold at the tourist office and on board. Tours last one hour; tickets are valid all day. One child under 16 travels free per paying adult.

Bronze Pig MODERN BRITISH ££
(01522-524817; www.thebronzepig.co.uk; 4 Burton Rd; mains £16-27; by reservation 7-9.30pm Wed-Sat, noon-3pm Sun) BBC *Masterchef* finalist, Irishman Eamonn Hunt, and Sicilian chef Pompeo Siracusa have taken Lincoln's dining scene by storm since opening the Bronze Pig. Their exceptional Modern British cooking has an Italian accent and food is locally sourced. Reserve well ahead and prepare to be wowed.

Reform MODERN BRITISH ££
(01522-538801; www.castlehotel.net; The Castle Hotel, Westgate; mains £12.50-22; noon-2.30pm & 7-9pm Mon-Sat, noon-3pm & 7-9pm Sun) Local, seasonal produce at the Castle Hotel's sophisticated restaurant stars in starters such as Parma-ham-wrapped rabbit and liver terrine, and mains including smoked duck breast with orange-pickled carrots. The real show-stoppers here, however, are desserts, from caramelised banana *tarte Tatin* with clotted cream and peanut brittle to lemon drizzle cake with lemon and mint sorbet and lemon panna cotta.

Old Bakery MODERN BRITISH ££
(01522-576057; www.theold-bakery.co.uk; 26-28 Burton Rd; mains £17.50-26, 2-/3-course lunch menus £14.50/18, 5-course tasting menu £48, with wines £65; 7-8.30pm Tue & Wed, noon-1.30pm & 7-8.30pm Thu-Sat, noon-1.30pm Sun) The menu at this long-established spot is built around local produce and – appropriately – freshly baked bread. It also offers regular half-day cookery lessons (from £95) and has three quaint guest rooms upstairs (doubles £75 to £80; two are en suite and the third has a private but separate bathroom).

Wig & Mitre PUB FOOD ££
(01522-535190; www.wigandmitre.com; 30 Steep Hill; mains £12.50-19.50; kitchen 8.30am-10.30pm Mon-Sat, to 10pm Sun, bar 8.30am-midnight Mon-Sat, to 11pm Sun;) Civilised pub-restaurant the Wig & Mitre has an excellent menu yet retains the ambience of a friendly local. Food is served throughout the day, from morning fry-ups to lunchtime sandwiches and filling evening roasts. Look out for wine tastings and gourmet evenings.

Jew's House MODERN EUROPEAN ££
(01522-524851; www.jewshouserestaurant.co.uk; 15 The Strait (Steep Hill); 2-/3-course lunch menu £16.50/19.95, mains £16-24.50; 7-9.30pm Tue, noon-2pm & 7-9.30pm Wed-Sat) This local favourite serves up gourmet fare in atmos-

WORTH A TRIP

AROUND GRANTHAM

Grantham, around 40kms from Lincoln, has few sights itself but there are some fascinating properties in the surrounding countryside.

Woolsthorpe Manor (NT; www.nationaltrust.org.uk; Water Lane; house & grounds adult/child £6.45/3.27, grounds only £3.50/2.27; ⏲11am-5pm Wed-Mon Mar-Oct, Fri-Sun Nov-Feb) Sir Isaac Newton fans may feel the gravitational pull of the great man's birthplace, about 8 miles south of Grantham. The humble 17th-century house contains reconstructions of Newton's rooms; the apple that inspired his theory of gravity allegedly fell from the tree in the garden. There's a nifty kids' science room and a cafe. Take Centrebus 28 from Grantham (£2.60, 25 minutes, four per day Monday to Saturday).

Belton House (NT; ☎01476-566116; www.nationaltrust.org.uk; Belton; house & grounds adult/child £13.10/8.40, grounds only £10.30/7; ⏲house 12.30-5pm Wed-Sun Mar-Oct, closed Nov-Feb, grounds 9.30am-5.30pm Mar-Oct, to 4pm Nov-Feb) Amid 14.2 hectares of elegant formal gardens, Belton House is a dream location for English period dramas, *Jane Eyre*, *Tom Jones* and the Colin Firth version of *Pride and Prejudice* among them. Built in 1688 in classic Restoration style, the house retains stunning original features including ornate woodcarvings by master Dutch carver Grinling Gibbons. It's off the A607 2.5 miles northeast of Grantham, served by Stagecoach bus 1 (£2.20, 15 minutes, hourly Monday to Saturday, every two hours Sunday).

Belvoir Castle (☎01476 871001; www.belvoircastle.com; Belvoir; castle tours adult/child £15/8, gardens only £8/5; ⏲castle tours by reservation, gardens 11am-5pm Mar-Sep, hours can vary) The Duke and Duchess of Rutland's ancestral home, Belvoir (pronounced 'beaver') is a 19th-century baroque and Gothic fantasy built over the ruins of three previous castles. Still inhabited by the Manners family, it overflows with tapestries, priceless furniture and ancient oil paintings. Although the castle is in Leicestershire, Grantham (6 miles east in Lincolnshire) is the nearest town. Bus 9 (£2.60, 20 minutes, four per day Monday to Saturday) stops at Chequers Inn, from where it's a 20 minute walk.

Chequers Inn (☎01476-870701; www.chequersinn.net; Main St, Woolsthorpe by Belvoir; mains £11-20; ⏲kitchen noon-2.30pm & 6-9.30pm Mon-Sat, noon-4pm & 6-8.30pm Sun, bar 10am-11pm Mon-Sat, noon-9pm Sun; 🐾) Dine on some of the finest food in the Midlands in the rambling garden bordering a sheep-filled paddock or inside by the open fire of this charming inn, 7 miles southwest of Grantham. There's a fabulous range of ciders and real ales on tap and, across the lane, the former stables house four simple but stylish guest rooms (single/double/loft £50/70/120).

pheric surrounds in one of England's oldest houses; the Romanesque Jew's House was constructed around 1160. For the ultimate indulgence, go for the six-course tasting menu (by reservation, £70).

Drinking & Nightlife

Strugglers Inn PUB
(83 Westgate; ⏲noon-midnight Tue & Wed, to 1am Thu-Sat, to 11pm Sun & Mon) A sunny walled-courtyard beer garden out back, a cosy interior and a superb selection of real ales on tap make this the pick of Lincoln's independent pubs.

Electric Bar & Restaurant BAR
(☎01522-565182; www.electricbarandrestaurant.co.uk; 5th fl, DoubleTree by Hilton Lincoln, Brayford Wharf North; ⏲11am-11pm Sun-Thu, to midnight Fri & Sat; 📶) On the top floor of Lincoln's snazzy four-star DoubleTree Hilton Hotel, this swish spot with glittering river views has a great cocktail list with more than 40 choices, including pineapple and black-pepper daiquiris, and 'Lincoln Aphrodisia' with limoncello, passionfruit and Prosecco. Live jazz plays regularly; the restaurant serves sophisticated British dishes with a retro twist.

Entertainment

Home Nightclub LIVE MUSIC
(www.homelincoln.co.uk; Park St; ⏲11.30am-11pm Mon & Wed, to 3am Tue & Thu-Sat, 7pm-3am Sun) Spread over six rooms with live music and dance tunes and a total of eight bars, this cavernous venue is a home from home for Lincoln's students.

LINCOLNSHIRE: BOMBER COUNTY

Following WWI the Royal Air Force (RAF) was formed in 1918 and two years later its college was established in Lincolnshire. During WWII, England's 'Bomber County' was home to numerous squadrons and by 1945 had more airfields (49) than any other in the country. US Navy flying boats flew antisubmarine patrols and B-29 bombers were based here.

Lincoln's tourist office has details of the county's aviation legacies.

Battle of Britain Memorial Flight Visitor Centre (☎01522-552222; www.lincolnshire.gov.uk/bbmf; Dogdyke Rd, Coningsby; hangar tours adult/child £6.50/4.50; ⏲10am-5pm Mon-Fri) See spitfires and the four-engined *Lancaster City of Lincoln* at the Battle of Britain Memorial Flight Visitor Centre on 90-minute hangar tours. Interconnect bus 5 (£4.10, 50 minutes, hourly Monday to Saturday) runs here from Lincoln.

Lincolnshire Aviation Heritage Centre (☎01790-763207; www.lincsaviation.co.uk; East Kirkby, near Spilsby; adult/child £7/3; ⏲9.30am-5pm Mon-Sat Easter-Oct, 10am-4pm Mon-Sat Nov-Easter) An original WWII Bomber Command airfield complete with its original wartime control tower is now home to the Lincolnshire Aviation Heritage Centre. It's 30 miles southeast of Lincoln via the A153; there's no public transport.

Waddington Air Show (www.waddingtonairshow.co.uk; ⏲Jul) The RAF's Waddington Air Show takes place in Waddington, 3 miles south of Lincoln, on the first weekend in July. Book tickets and accommodation well ahead.

Lincoln Drill Hall ARTS CENTRE
(☎01522-873894; www.lincolndrillhall.com; Freeschool Lane) Downhill near the train station, this late 19th-century former drill hall hosts bands, orchestras, stage shows, comedy and daytime festivals.

Information

Lincoln's friendly **tourist office** (☎01522-545458; www.visitlincoln.com; 9 Castle Hill; ⏲10am-5pm Mon-Sat, 10.30am-4pm Sun, hours can vary) is located in a 16th-century black-and-white building.

Getting There & Away

BUS

The **bus station** (Melville St) is just northeast of the train station in the new town.

National Express runs direct bus services from Lincoln to London Victoria (£20.20, 5¼ hours, up to two daily) and Birmingham (£17, 3¼ hours, one daily).

Local Stagecoach buses include bus 1 to Grantham (£5, 1¼ hours, hourly Monday to Saturday, five on Sunday).

TRAIN

The train station is 250m east of the Brayford Waterfront development in the new town.

Boston £13.60, 1¼ hours, hourly, change at Sleaford

Newark-on-Trent (Newark Castle) £5.10, 25 minutes, half-hourly Monday to Saturday, fewer on Sunday

Nottingham £11.30, one hour, hourly

Sheffield £14.50, 80 minutes, hourly

York £37.10, two hours, up to two per hour

Stamford

POP 19,704

One of England's prettiest towns, Stamford seems frozen in time, with elegant streets lined with honey-coloured limestone buildings and hidden alleyways dotted with alehouses, interesting eateries and small independent boutiques. A forest of historic church spires rises overhead and the gently gurgling River Welland meanders through the town centre. It's a favourite with filmmakers seeking the postcard vision of England, and appears in everything from *Pride and Prejudice* to the *Da Vinci Code*.

Sights

★**Burghley House** HISTORIC BUILDING
(www.burghley.co.uk; house & garden adult/child £14/7, garden only £8.50/5.50; ⏲house 11am-5pm Sat-Thu mid-Mar–Oct, park & garden 8am-6pm Jun-Sep, to 5pm mid-Mar–May & Oct) Set in more than 810 hectares of grounds, landscaped by Lancelot 'Capability' Brown, opulent Burghley House (pronounced 'bur-lee') was built by Queen Elizabeth's chief adviser William Cecil, whose descendants still live here. It bristles with cupolas, pavilions, belvederes and chimneys; the lavish staterooms are a particular

highlight. In early September, the renowned Burghley Horse Trials take place here. The estate is 1.3 miles southeast of Stamford; follow the marked path for 15 minutes through the park by Stamford train station.

St Mary's Church CHURCH

(www.stamfordstmary.com; St Mary's St; ⏲8am-6pm, hours can vary) A charmingly wonky broach spire tops the 12th-century St Mary's Church. Classical concerts are held here in summer; tickets (from £14) are sold at Stamford's tourist office

Sleeping & Eating

Stamford Lodge B&B ££

(☎01780-482932; www.stamfordlodge.co.uk; 66 Scotgate; s/d £75/95; 📶) Centrally situated, this 18th-century former bakehouse has four fresh, modern rooms and excellent breakfasts made from ingredients sourced from local farmers markets.

★ **George Hotel** HISTORIC HOTEL £££

(☎01780-750750; www.georgehotelofstamford.com; 71 St Martin's; s/d/4-poster from £120/195/260; P📶🐾) Stamford's luxurious landmark inn opened its doors in 1597. Today its 45 individually sized and decorated rooms impeccably blend period charm and modern elegance. Superior modern British cuisine is served at its oak-panelled restaurant, while its more informal garden-room restaurant hosts afternoon teas in its courtyard. Its two bars include a champagne bar.

William Cecil at Stamford HISTORIC HOTEL £££

(☎01780-750070; www.hillbrookehotels.co.uk; High St, St Martins; s/d/tr/f from £100/135/185/215; P📶) Within the Burghley Estate, this stunningly renovated hotel has 27 rooms inspired by Burghley House, with period furnishings and luxuries such as Egyptian cotton linens and complimentary organic vodka. Family rooms sleep two adults and two kids. The smart restaurant creates stylish British classics and opens to a wicker-chair-furnished patio.

No 3 The Yard MODERN BRITISH ££

(☎01780-756080; www.no3theyard.co.uk; 3 Ironmonger St; mains £14.50-21.50; ⏲11.30am-2.30pm & 6-9.30pm Tue-Thu, 11.30am-2.30pm & 6-10pm Fri & Sat, noon-3pm Sun) Tucked away in a courtyard off a narrow laneway, No 3 The Yard serves upmarket fare such as pan-fried sea trout with minted Jersey Royal new potatoes, Norfolk samphire and lemon hollandaise. Try a multicourse menu (two-/three-course lunch menus £16/19.50, three-course dinner menu £22) for an excellent deal.

Tobie Norris PUB

(www.kneadpubs.co.uk; 12 St Pauls St; ⏲11am-11pm Mon-Thu, to midnight Fri & Sat, noon-10.30pm Sun) A wonderful stone-walled, flagstone-floored pub, the Tobie Norris has a warren of rooms with open fireplaces, a sunny, flower-filled courtyard and wholesome local ales. Wood-fired pizzas (more than 40 different kinds) are a speciality.

Information

The **tourist office** (☎01780-763203; www.southwestlincs.com; 27 St Mary's St; ⏲9.30am-5pm Mon-Sat; 📶) is inside the Stamford Arts Centre.

Getting There & Away

Centrebus 4 runs to Grantham (£4.10, one hour, three per day Monday to Friday, two Saturday) and National Express to London Victoria (£15.50, four hours, one daily).

Trains run to Birmingham (£22.80, 1½ hours, hourly), Nottingham (£24.30, 1½ hours, hourly) via Leicester (£13.40, 40 minutes), and Stansted Airport (£32.70, 1¾ hours, hourly) via Cambridge (£23.70, 1¼ hours) and Peterborough (£8, 15 minutes).

Boston

POP 66,500

It's hard to believe that sleepy Boston was the inspiration for its larger and more famous American cousin. Although no Boston citizens sailed on the *Mayflower*, the port became a conduit for persecuted Puritans fleeing Nottinghamshire for religious freedom in the Netherlands and America. In the 1630s, the fiery sermons of Boston vicar John Cotton inspired many locals to follow their lead, among them the ancestors of John Quincy-Adams, the sixth American president. These pioneers founded a namesake town in the new colony of Massachusetts and the rest, as they say, is history.

Sights

St Botolph's Church CHURCH

(www.parish-of-boston.org.uk; Church St; tower adult/child £3/1; ⏲church visiting hours 8.30am-4pm Mon-Sat, 7.30am-4pm Sun, tower 10am-3.30pm Mon-Sat, 1-3.30pm Sun, last climb 3pm) Built in the early 14th century, St Botolph's Church (the name Boston is a corruption of 'St Botolph's Stone') is known locally as the

Stump, in reference to the truncated appearance of its 88m-high tower. Puff your way up the 365 steps on a clear day and you'll see out to Lincoln, 32 miles away.

Guildhall MUSEUM
(☎01205-365954; www.bostonguildhall.co.uk; South St; ⏲10.30am-3.30pm Wed-Sat) FREE Before escaping to the New World, the Pilgrim Fathers were briefly imprisoned in the 14th-century Guildhall. It's one of Lincolnshire's oldest brick buildings, dating from the 1390s and situated close to the River Witham. Inside are fun interactive exhibits, as well as a restored 16th-century courtroom and a re-created Georgian kitchen. Regular temporary exhibitions are also free.

Maud Foster Windmill MILL
(☎01205-352188; www.maudfoster.co.uk; 16 Willoughby Rd; adult/child £4/2; ⏲10am-5pm Wed & Sat; 📶) About 800m northeast of Market Pl, England's tallest working windmill has seven floors that creak and tremble with every turn of the sails; it sells bags of flour milled on-site. Self-caterers can stay in the granary next door (double from £430 for three nights including a windmill tour and parking; children not permitted).

ℹ Information

The **tourist office** (☎01205-365954; www.bostonguildhall.co.uk; South St; ⏲10.30am-3.30pm Wed-Sat) is inside the Guildhall.

WORTH A TRIP

SULGRAVE MANOR

The impressively preserved Tudor mansion **Sulgrave Manor** (☎01295-760205; www.sulgravemanor.org.uk; Manor Rd, Sulgrave; adult/child £7.90/3.60, garden only £3.60/free; ⏲10am-5pm Sat-Thu Aug, Sat & Sun late Mar–Jul, Sep & Oct) was built by Lawrence Washington in 1539. The Washington family lived here for almost 120 years before Colonel John Washington, the great-grandfather of America's first president George Washington, sailed to Virginia in 1656.

Sulgrave Manor is 20 miles southwest of Northampton, just off the B4525 near Banbury; you'll need your own wheels to get here.

ℹ Getting There & Away

Trains connect Boston with Leicester (£22.80, 2½ hours, hourly) and Lincoln (£13.60, 1¼ hours, hourly) via a change at Sleaford.

NORTHAMPTONSHIRE

Dotted with villages full of pincushion cottages with thatched roofs and Tudor timbers, Northamptonshire also has a string of stately manors, including the ancestral homes of George Washington and Diana, Princess of Wales.

ℹ Getting Around

Northampton is the county's hub for transport; Traveline (p452) has timetable information for buses and trains. Trains run by London Midland are useful for getting to/from Northampton.

Stoke Bruerne

POP 373

About 8 miles south of Northampton, brightly painted barges frequent this charming little village nestled against the Grand Union Canal, the main drag of England's canal network. From here, you can follow the waterways all the way to Leicester, Birmingham or London.

Sights & Activities

Canal Museum MUSEUM
(www.canalrivertrust.org.uk/the-canal-museum/stoke-bruerne; 3 Bridge Rd; adult/child £4.75/2.75; ⏲10am-5pm Apr-Oct, shorter hours Nov-Mar) A converted corn mill houses the entertaining Canal Museum, which charts the history of the canal network and its bargemen, lock-keepers and pit workers. Scale models abound; outside you can see the historic narrowboat *Sculptor*, listed on the National Historic Boat Register.

Indian Chief CRUISE
(☎01604-862428; www.boatinn.co.uk; cruises adult/child £3.50/2.50; ⏲11.30am-3pm Sun & bank-holiday weekends) One-hour canal trips aboard the *Indian Chief* narrowboat depart year-round from the Boat Inn.

Sleeping

Waterways Cottage B&B ££
(☎01604-863865; www.waterwayscottage.co.uk; Bridge Rd; d £55-80; P📶) Right on the canal, Waterways Cottage is an adorable thatched

cottage right off the front of a biscuit box. There's a two-night minimum stay.

Boat Inn PUB FOOD ££
(☎01604-862428; www.boatinn.co.uk; mains £6.50-24; ⏰kitchen noon-3pm & 6-9pm Mon-Fri, noon-9pm Sat, noon-8.30pm Sun, bar 9am-11pm Mon-Sat, to 10.30pm Sun) A canalside landmark, this sociable local pub has a relaxed bistro and more formal restaurant and a great range of ales.

Getting There & Away

If you're not travelling by canal boat, then your own wheels are the next-best mode of transport.

Bus 86 runs between Stoke Bruerne and Northampton (£4.50, 45 minutes, four per day Monday to Saturday) as does bus X4 (£4.50, 25 minutes, four per day Sunday).

WORTH A TRIP

ALTHORP HOUSE

The ancestral home of the Spencer family, **Althorp House** (☎01604-770107; www.spencerofalthorp.com; adult/child £18.50/11; ⏰11am-3pm early Jul–early Sep, hours vary May–early Jul & early–late Sep, closed late Sep–Apr) is the final resting place of Diana, Princess of Wales, commemorated by a memorial. The outstanding art collection features works by Rubens, Gainsborough and Van Dyck. Tickets are limited; prebook by phone or online.

Althorp – pronounced 'altrup' – is off the A428, 5.5 miles northwest of Northampton; a taxi costs around £20. Stagecoach Northampton–Rugby bus 96 (£2.35, hourly, Monday to Saturday) passes the estate gates, from where it's a 1-mile walk. Profits go to charities supported by the Princess Diana Memorial Fund.

LEICESTERSHIRE

Leicestershire was a vital creative hub during the Industrial Revolution, but its factories were a major target for German air raids in WWII and most towns in the county still bear the scars of war-time bombing. Nevertheless, there are some impressive remains, from Elizabethan castles to Roman ruins. The busy, multicultural capital Leicester is enjoying new-found fame due to the recent discovery and reburial of King Richard III's remains and its football team's against-all-odds 2016 Premier League win – one of the greatest upsets in British sporting history.

Getting There & Around

Leicester is well served by buses and trains. For bus routes and timetables, visit the 'Roads and Transport' pages at www.leicestershire.gov.uk.

Regular buses connect Rutland to Leicester, Stamford and other surrounding towns.

Leicester

POP 337,653

Built over the buried ruins of two millennia of history, Leicester (*les*-ter) suffered at the hands of the Luftwaffe and postwar planners but an influx of textile workers from India and Pakistan from the 1960s transformed the city into a bustling global melting pot.

The astonishing 2012 discovery and 2013 identification of the remains of King Richard III in a Leicester car park sparked a flurry of developments, including a spiffing visitor centre on the site, and the restoration of the cathedral, where the king was reburied in 2015. And sporting history was made in 2016, when Leicester City Football Club won the Premier League against 5000:1 odds at the beginning of the season, having never won a top-division championship in the club's 132-year existence.

Sights & Activities

★**King Richard III: Dynasty, Death & Discovery** HERITAGE CENTRE
(www.kriii.com; 4a St Martin's Pl; adult/child £7.95/4.75; ⏰10am-4pm Sun-Fri, to 5pm Sat) Built following the incredible 2012 discovery and 2013 DNA testing of King Richard III's remains, Leicester's high-tech King Richard III visitor centre encompasses three fascinating sections. Dynasty explores his rise to become the final Plantagenet king. Death delves into the Battle of Bosworth, when Richard became the last English king to be killed in battle. Discovery details the University of Leicester's archaeological dig and identification, and lets you view the site of the grave in which he was found.

★**Leicester Cathedral** CATHEDRAL
(www.leicestercathedral.org; Peacock Lane; ⏰10am-5pm Mon-Sat, 12.30-2.30pm Sun) FREE Pride of place at this substantial medieval cathedral goes to the contemporary

Leicester

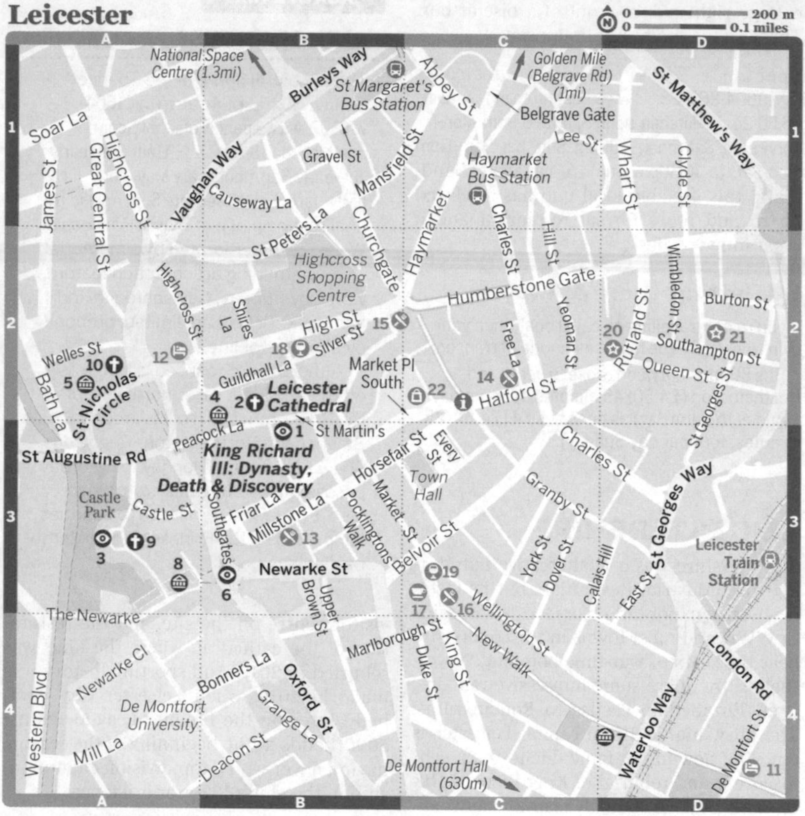

Leicester

Top Sights
1 King Richard III: Dynasty, Death & Discovery B3
2 Leicester Cathedral B2

Sights
3 Great Hall A3
4 Guildhall B2
5 Jewry Wall Museum A2
Leicester Castle .... (see 3)
6 Magazine B3
7 New Walk Museum & Art Gallery D4
8 Newarke Houses Museum A3
9 St Mary de Castro A3
10 St Nicholas Church A2

Sleeping
11 Belmont Hotel D4
12 Hotel Maiyango A2

Eating
13 Boot Room B3
14 Good Earth C2
15 Walkers B2
16 White Peacock C3

Drinking & Nightlife
17 Bread & Honey C3
18 Globe B2
19 XY Club C3

Entertainment
20 Curve Theatre D2
21 Phoenix Square D2

Shopping
22 Leicester Market C2

FINDING KING RICHARD III

It's an amazing story. Philippa Langley, a member of the Richard III Society, spent four-and-a-half years researching the whereabouts of King Richard's remains after his demise at Bosworth (p470). The 1924-founded society's aim is to research the king's life and to achieve a more balanced characterisation of him than that of a cruel and calculating figure, as portrayed by Shakespeare and various authors and historians. Langley narrowed it down to a Leicester car park, built over the site of the long-since-demolished Greyfriars church. But it took her another three years to persuade the city council to excavate.

Archaeologists from the University of Leicester carried out the dig in August 2012, unearthing a skeleton just three weeks later. In February 2013, the bones were confirmed by DNA analysis as those of the late king.

The university was also able to undertake a facial reconstruction using the king's skull, giving the modern world its first true image of Richard III. The reconstruction is on permanent display at Leicester's state-of-the-art King Richard III: Dynasty, Death & Discovery (p467) visitor centre along with the site where he'd been buried for more than 500 years.

Richard's remains were reburied in Leicester Cathedral (p467) in 2015 following a procession from Bosworth.

A free Richard III Audio Tour, downloadable from Leicester's tourist office (p472), covers key Richard sites in the city and county.

limestone tomb atop the vault where the remains of King Richard III were reburied in 2015, following the discovery of his skeleton nearby. Look too for the striking carvings on the cathedral's roof supports.

Guildhall HISTORIC BUILDING
(www.leicester.gov.uk/leisure-and-culture; Guildhall Lane; ⏲11am-4.30pm) **FREE** Leicester's perfectly preserved 14th-century guildhall, one of England's finest, is reputed to be the most haunted building in Leicester. You can search for spooks in the magnificent Great Hall, the wood-panelled 'Mayor's Parlour' and the old police cells, which contain a reconstruction of a 19th-century gibbet.

New Walk Museum & Art Gallery MUSEUM, GALLERY
(www.leicester.gov.uk/leisure-and-culture; 53 New Walk; ⏲10am-5pm Mon-Sat, 11am-5pm Sun; 📶) **FREE** Highlights of this grand Victorian museum include the dinosaur galleries, the painting collection (with works by Turner and Degas) and the Egyptian gallery, where real mummies rub shoulders with displays about Boris Karloff's *The Mummy* film. Littlies under five can let loose in the interactive Den.

National Space Centre MUSEUM
(www.spacecentre.co.uk; Exploration Drive; adult/child £14/11; ⏲10am-4pm Mon-Fri, to 5pm Sat & Sun) Although British space missions usually launch from French Guiana or Kazakhstan, Leicester's space museum is a fascinating introduction to the mysteries of the spheres. The ill-fated *Beagle 2* mission to Mars was controlled from here. Fun, kid-friendly displays cover everything from astronomy to the status of current space missions. The centre is off the A6 about 1.5 miles north of the city centre. Take bus 54 (15 minutes, every 20 minutes) from Charles St.

Newarke Houses Museum MUSEUM
(www.leicester.gov.uk/leisure-and-culture; The Newarke; ⏲10am-5pm Mon-Sat, 11am-5pm Sun) **FREE** Sprawling over two 16th-century mansions, this entertaining museum details the lifestyle of locals through the centuries. Don't miss the walk-through re-creation of a WWI trench, and the trophies of the Royal Leicestershire Regiment, including an outrageous snuff box made from a tiger's head.

Leicester Castle RUINS
(Castle View) Scattered around the Newarke Houses Museum are the ruins of Leicester's medieval castle, where Richard III spent his final days before the Battle of Bosworth. The most impressive chunk of masonry is the monumental gateway known as the **Magazine** (Newarke St), once a storehouse for cannonballs and gunpowder. Clad in Georgian brickwork, the 12th-century **Great Hall** (Castle Yard) stands behind a 15th-century gate near the church of **St Mary de Castro** (www.stmarydecastro.org.uk; 15 Castle View; ⏲noon-2pm Mon-Fri, 2-4pm Sat), where Geoffrey Chaucer was married in 1366.

WORTH A TRIP

BOSWORTH BATTLEFIELD

Given a few hundred years, every battlefield ends up simply a field, but the site of the Battle of Bosworth – where Richard III met his maker in 1485 – is enlivened by the entertaining **Bosworth Battlefield Heritage Centre** (☎01455-290429; www.bosworthbattlefield.org.uk; Ambion Lane, Sutton Cheney; adult/child £7.95/4.75; ⏲heritage centre 10am-5pm, last admission 4pm, grounds 7am-dusk) full of skeletons and musket balls. Enthusiasts in period costume reenact the battle each August. The battlefield is 16 miles southwest of Leicester at Sutton Cheney, off the A447. A taxi from Leicester costs around £25.

Jewry Wall Museum MUSEUM
(www.visitleicester.info; St Nicholas Circle; ⏲11am-4.30pm Feb-Oct) FREE You can see fine Roman mosaics and frescoes in this museum exploring the history of Leicester from Roman times to the modern day. In front of the museum is the **Jewry Wall**, part of Leicester's Roman baths. Tiles and masonry from the baths were incorporated in the walls of neighbouring **St Nicholas Church** (www.stnicholasleicester.com; St Nicholas Circle; admission by donation; ⏲2-4pm Sat, 5.30-6.30pm Sun). A free audio tour is downloadable from the tourist office (p472) website.

Great Central Railway RAIL
(☎01509-632323; www.gcrailway.co.uk; return adult/child £16/9) Steam locomotives chug from Leicester North station on Redhill Circle to Loughborough Central, following the 8-mile route along which Thomas Cook ran the original package tour in 1841. The locos operate most weekends year-round and some summer weekdays; check timetables online.

For Leicester North station, take bus 127 (£4.20, 20 minutes, every 10 minutes) from Haymarket bus station (p472) on Charles St.

Festivals & Events

Leicester Caribbean Carnival CULTURAL
(www.leicestercarnival.com; ⏲Aug) Colourful costumes galore fill Leicester on the first Saturday in August during the biggest Caribbean celebration in the country after London's Notting Hill Carnival. Musicians perform on two stages; there's a fun fair, a supervised play area for kids, and a slew of food and drink stalls.

Leicester Comedy Festival COMEDY
(www.comedy-festival.co.uk; ⏲Feb) England's longest-running comedy festival draws big names as well as fresh talent for eight days in February, when more than 700 shows take place in more than 60 different venues.

Sleeping

★**Hotel Maiyango** BOUTIQUE HOTEL ££
(☎0116-251 8898; www.maiyango.com; 13-21 St Nicholas Pl; d from £79; ❄📶) At the end of the pedestrian High St, this sophisticated pad has 14 spacious rooms, decorated with handmade Asian furniture, contemporary art and massive plasma TVs. In addition to its candlelit **Maiyango Restaurant & Bar**, serving the city's best cocktails, it also has a fabulous **Kitchen Deli** gourmet cafe and store.

Belmont Hotel HOTEL ££
(☎0116-254 4773; www.belmonthotel.co.uk; 20 De Montfort St; s/d/f from £60/75/89; P❄@📶👪) Owned and run by the same family for four generations, the 19th-century Belmont has stylish contemporary, individually designed rooms and a fantastic location overlooking leafy New Walk. Family rooms have a double bed and bunks. Its restaurant is highly regarded; the two bars, Jamie's and Bowie's, open to a terrace and a conservatory respectively.

Eating

Walkers BAKERY £
(Walker & Son; www.walkerspies.co.uk; 4-6 Cheapside; dishes 90p-£5; ⏲8.30am-5.30pm Mon-Sat) For lunch on the run, you can't beat Walkers' towering pork pies. These are the original premises where Walkers was founded in 1824; it's since sold its famous crisp brand but the pies remain a family business today. Other pie varieties include chicken, bacon and mushroom, farmhouse steak, game and pulled pork. There's a handful of pavement tables out front.

Good Earth VEGETARIAN £
(☎0116-262 6260; 19 Free Lane; mains £3.50-6.50; ⏲10am-3pm Mon-Fri, to 4pm Sat; ✍) 🍃 This venerable vegetarian cafe is justifiably popular for its daily changing wholesome veggie bakes; huge, fresh salads; and homemade cakes.

Boot Room BISTRO ££
(☎0116-262 2555; www.thebootroomeaterie.co.uk; 29 Millstone Lane; mains £13-19.50; ⏲noon-2pm &

5.30-9.30pm Tue-Fri, noon-2.30pm & 5.30-10pm Sat; 📶) A former shoe factory now houses this contemporary independent bistro. Premium ingredients are used in dishes from roast Cornish cod with smoked tomato risotto to duck leg with Clonakilty black pudding. Save room for the soufflé of the day for dessert.

White Peacock MODERN BRITISH £££
(☎0116-254 7663; www.the-white-peacock.co.uk; 14-16 King St; 2-/3-course lunch menus £15/18, 2-/3-course dinner menus £26.50/28.50; ⏰noon-3pm & 5.30-9.15pm Tue-Fri, noon-3pm & 6-9.45pm Sat) The beautiful Grade II–listed building housing this fine-dining restaurant overlooks pedestrianised New Walk. Chef Phillip Sharpe's ambitious menus might start with goats-cheese panna cotta with balsamic jelly and move on to roast pork belly with black pudding and smoked-celeriac purée, ending with Turkish-delight crème brûlée with dark chocolate and pistachio sorbet.

Drinking & Nightlife

Bread & Honey COFFEE
(15 King St; ⏰7.30am-2.30pm Mon-Sat; 📶) Beans from single farm estates and co-ops sourced and roasted by London-based Monmouth are brewed up at this little bare-boards hole-in-the-wall; the flat whites here are the best for miles. It also whips up smoothies in summer, steaming soups in winter, and fantastic cakes (chocolate fudge cake with white-chocolate icing; honey-glazed banana loaf) all year.

XY Club CLUB
(www.xyclub.co.uk; 2 King St; ⏰10.30pm-6am Fri & Sat) Behind a towering mock-Tudor facade, XY's resident and visiting DJs serve up diverse beats. Special weeknight events are listed on the website.

Globe PUB
(www.everards.co.uk; 43 Silver St; ⏰11am-11pm Sun-Thu, to 1am Fri & Sat) In the atmospheric Lanes – a tangle of alleys south of the High St – this old-fashioned pub has fine draught ales and a crowd that rates its drinks by quality rather than quantity.

Entertainment

Curve Theatre THEATRE
(☎0116-242 3595; www.curveonline.co.uk; 60 Rutland St; backstage tours adult/child £3/2) This sleek artistic space hosts big-name shows and some innovative modern theatre, and has good accessibility for theatre-goers who are aurally or visually impaired. Call the ticket office to book backstage tours. The bar is a sophisticated place for a sundowner.

Phoenix Square CINEMA
(☎0116-242 2800; www.phoenix.org.uk; 4 Midland St; tickets adult/child from £7.50/5.50) Phoenix is Leicester's premier venue for art-house films and digital media.

De Montfort Hall LIVE MUSIC
(☎0116-233 3111; www.demontforthall.co.uk; Granville Rd) Big orchestras, ballets, musicals and other big song-and-dance performances are on the bill at this huge venue.

Shopping

Leicester Market MARKET
(www.leicestermarket.co.uk; Market Pl; ⏰outdoor market 7am-6pm Mon-Sat, indoor market 9am-5pm Mon-Sat) More than 300 stalls at Leicester's indoor and outdoor markets sell everything from organic vegetables to aromatic spices, fish and shellfish, new and secondhand clothes, and homewares, electronic goods, cosmetics, jewellery, flowers and fabrics.

LOCAL KNOWLEDGE

THE GOLDEN MILE

Lined with sari stores, jewellery emporiums and curry houses, Belgrave Rd – aka the Golden Mile – is an essential stop for authentic Indian vegetarian food.

There are more top-notch eateries than you can shake a chapatti at. Top pick is **Bobby's** (☎0116-266 0106; www.eatatbobbys.com; 154-156 Belgrave Rd; dishes £3.75-6; ⏰11am-10pm Mon-Fri, 10am-10pm Sat & Sun; 🌱), famed for its *namkeen* – lentil-flour snacks that come in myriad shapes and sizes. Shops along the strip sell *mithai* (Indian sweets), which involve sugary combinations of nuts, fruit and milk curds.

Belgrave Rd is about 1 mile northeast of the Leicester's centre – follow Belgrave Gate and cross Burleys Flyover, or take bus 2 or 127 (seven minutes, every five minutes) from St Margaret's bus station (p472) or bus 5 from Haymarket bus station (p472).

Information

Leicester's helpful **tourist office** (☎0116-299 4444; www.visitleicester.info; 51 Gallowtree Gate; ⊙9.30am-5.30pm Mon-Sat, 10am-4pm Sun) has reams of city and countywide info. Ask about guided walking tours (£5; times vary).

Getting There & Away

BUS

Intercity buses operate from **St Margaret's bus station** (Gravel St), north of the centre. The useful Skylink bus runs to East Midlands Airport (£7, 50 minutes, at least hourly, 24 hours) and continues on to Derby (one hour).

National Express services:

Coventry £6.70, 45 minutes, four daily
London Victoria £14, 2¾ hours, four daily
Nottingham £5, 45 minutes, four daily

TRAIN

East Midlands trains:

Birmingham £13.40, one hour, two per hour
London St Pancras £79.50, 1¼ hours, two to four hourly

Getting Around

The centre is cut off from the suburbs by a tangle of underpasses and flyovers, but downtown Leicester is easy to get around on foot.

Local buses depart from **Haymarket bus station** (Charles St) and nearby St Margaret's bus station. For unlimited transport on local buses, buy a Flexi Day Ticket (£5).

WORTH A TRIP

GASTROPUB: HERCULES REVIVED

One of the joys of travelling through the Midlands is chancing upon a picture-perfect country pub serving food that could hold its own in the world's gastronomic capitals. And **Hercules Revived** (☎01455-699336; www.herculesrevived.co.uk; Sutton Cheney; mains £10.50-21.50; ⊙noon-2.30pm & 6-9.30pm Mon-Sat, noon-2.30pm & 6-8pm Sun), in a 17th-century coaching inn, is just 1.2 miles east of Bosworth Battlefield (p470). Inspired starters (Stilton brûlée!) precede amazing mains such as seared duck breast in wild-blackberry sauce.

RUTLAND

Tiny Rutland was merged with Leicestershire in 1974, but in 1997 regained its 'independence' as England's smallest county.

Rutland Water

Rutland centres on Rutland Water, a vast artificial reservoir created by the damming of the Gwash Valley in 1976. Covering 4.19 sq miles, the reservoir attracts some 20,000 birds, including ospreys.

Sights & Activities

Rutland Water Nature Reserve NATURE RESERVE
(www.rutlandwater.org.uk; Egleton; adult/child incl parking £5.70/3.30; ⊙9am-5pm Mar-Oct, to 4pm Nov-Feb) Near Oakham, the Rutland Water Nature Reserve has hides where you can view the abundant birdlife.

Normanton Church CHURCH
(☎01780-686800; www.anglianwater.co.uk; Normanton; ⊙hours vary Apr-Oct, closed Nov-Mar) FREE This quaint church is saved from inundation by a limestone barrier wall. Inside are displays on the history of the Rutland reservoir. Many concerts and private events such as weddings take place here, so check ahead to make sure it's open.

Rutland Belle CRUISE
(☎01572-787630; www.rutlandwatercruises.com; Whitwell; adult/child £8.50/5.50; ⊙hourly noon-3pm Mon-Sat, 11am-3pm Sun mid-Jul–Aug, shorter hours Apr–mid-Jul, Sep & Oct) Take a 45-minute cruise from Whitwell to Normanton on the southern shore of the Rutland reservoir, returning to Whitwell.

Rutland Watersports WATER SPORTS
(☎01780-460154; www.anglianwater.co.uk/leisure; Whitwell Leisure Park, Bull Brigg Lane, Whitwell; windsurf/kayak/SUP rental per hour from £7; ⊙9am-7pm Fri-Tue, to 8pm Wed & Thu Apr-Oct, shorter hours Nov-Mar) Aquatic activities with Rutland Watersports include windsurfing, kayaking and SUP (stand-up paddleboarding). You can rent gear or take lessons.

Rutland Sailing School BOATING
(☎01780-721999; www.rutlandsailingschool.co.uk; Gibbet Lane, Edith Weston; sailboat hire per hour from £20, half-day sailing courses adult/child from £125/105; ⊙7.30am-dusk Apr-Oct) Rents boats and runs sailing courses.

Rockblok CLIMBING
(☎01780-460060; www.rockblok.com; Whitwell Leisure Park, Bull Brigg Lane, Whitwell; climbing/high ropes £4/10, bike hire adult/child £23/10; ⏲9am-7pm mid-Mar–mid-Sep, to 4pm mid-Sep–mid-Mar) Tackle a vertigo-inducing high-ropes course, an outdoor climbing wall or rent bikes for a gentle pedal around the Rutland lake shore.

Giant-Bike CYCLING
(☎01780-720888; www.giant-rutland.co.uk; Normanton; bike rental per day adult/child £20/10, ⏲9am-6pm) Close to the Normanton boat jetty, Giant-Bike rents road bicycles, along with tandems, electric bikes and trailers.

Sleeping & Eating

Hambleton Hall HISTORIC HOTEL £££
(☎01572-756991; www.hambletonhall.com; Hambleton; s/d incl breakfast from £220/295; P 📶) One of England's finest country hotels, rambling former hunting lodge Hambleton Hall, built in 1881, sits on a peninsula jutting out into Rutland Water, 3 miles east of Oakham. Its luxuriant floral rooms and Michelin-starred restaurant (two-/three-course lunch menus £29/37.50, three-course dinner menus £69) are surrounded by gorgeous gardens.

Information

Situated near Empingham, the **Rutland Water Visitor Centre** (☎01780-686800; www.rutlandwater.org.uk; Skyes Lane, Empingham; ⏲9am-5pm mid-Mar–mid-Sep) has a snack kiosk, walking and cycling trails, and information on the area.

Getting There & Away

Bus 9 links Oakham with Stamford (£3.10, 45 minutes, hourly Monday to Saturday) via Rutland Water's north shore.

Trains link Oakham with Leicester (£12.20, 30 minutes, hourly or better).

DERBYSHIRE

The Derbyshire countryside is painted in two distinct tones: the lush green of rolling valleys criss-crossed by dry stone walls, and the barren mottled brown hilltops of the high, wild moorlands. The biggest draw here is the Peak District National Park, which preserves some of England's most evocative scenery, attracting legions of hikers, climbers, cyclists and cave enthusiasts.

WORTH A TRIP

GASTROPUB: HAMMER & PINCERS

For a mind-blowing meal, head to the idyllic gastropub **Hammer & Pincers** (☎01509-880735; www.hammerandpincers.co.uk; 5 East Rd, Wymeswold; mains £14.50-24.50, 8-course menu £45, with wine £65; ⏲noon-2pm & 6-9.30pm Tue-Sat, to 4pm Sun; 🖉), set in bucolic gardens at the edge of the cute village of Wymeswold. Everything is homemade, down to the breads and condiments; seasonal specialities might include cider-cured sea trout, gin-marinated pheasant and rosemary rhubarb sorbet. Don't miss its signature twice-baked cheese soufflé. It's 16 miles north of Leicester via the A46.

Getting There & Away

East Midlands Airport (p408) is the nearest air hub, and Derby is well served by trains, but connecting services to smaller towns are few. In the Peak District, the Derwent Valley Line runs from Derby to Matlock. Edale and Hope lie on the Hope Valley Line from Sheffield to Manchester.

For a comprehensive list of Derbyshire bus routes, visit the 'Transport and Roads' pages at www.derbyshire.gov.uk.

Derby

POP 252,500

Gloriously sited at the southeastern edge of the Derbyshire hills that roll towards the Peak District, Derby is one of the Midlands' most energetic, creative cities. This was one of the crucibles of the Industrial Revolution: almost overnight, a sleepy market town was transformed into a major manufacturing centre, producing everything from silk to bone china, and later locomotives and Rolls-Royce aircraft engines. The city suffered the ravages of industrial decline in the 1980s, but bounced back with impressive cultural developments and a rejuvenated riverfront.

Sights

Derby Cathedral CATHEDRAL
(www.derbycathedral.org; 18 Irongate; ⏲8.30am-5.15pm Mon-Sat, 8am-6pm Sun) Founded in AD 943 and reconstructed in the 18th century. Derby Cathedral's vaulted ceiling towers above a fine collection of medieval tombs, including the opulent grave of the oft-married

LOCAL KNOWLEDGE

CONKERS & THE NATIONAL FOREST

The **National Forest** (www.nationalforest.org) is an ambitious project to generate new areas of sustainable woodland by planting 30 million trees in Leicestershire, Derbyshire and Staffordshire, covering a total area of 128,000 acres or 200 sq miles. More than eight million saplings have already taken root, and all sorts of visitor attractions are springing up in the forest.

Conkers (☎01283-216633; www.visitconkers.com; Rawdon Rd, Moira; adult/child £9.05/7.95; ⊙10am-6pm Easter–mid-Sep, to 5pm mid-Sep–Easter) A family-oriented nature centre, Conkers has interactive displays, indoor and outdoor playgrounds (the latter includes high and low ropes courses), a viewing tower and boardwalks through the woodlands. It's 20 miles northwest of Leicester off the A444.

Hicks Lodge (☎01530-274533; Willesley Wood Side, Moira; bike rental per day adult/child £30/15; ⊙trails 8am-dusk, bike hire & cafe 9am-5pm Fri-Wed, 9am-9pm Thu mid-Feb–Oct, 10am-4pm Mon-Wed & Fri, 9am-9pm Thu, 9am-5pm Sat & Sun Nov–mid-Feb) Bike trails through the National Forest include a flat 2km path around the lake from this cycle centre, which rents wheels and organises guided tours and night rides. The attached cafe serves coffee, cakes and sandwiches.

National Forest YHA (☎0845 371 9672; www.yha.org.uk; 48 Bath Lane, Moira; dm/d/f from £15/49/65; P) Situated 300m west of Conkers along Bath Lane, this hostel has impressive ecofriendly features (such as greywater and solar biomass boiler usage), spotless en suite rooms, and a restaurant serving local produce and organic wines. Family rooms sleep up to five people.

Bess of Hardwick, who at various times held court at Hardwick Hall, Chatsworth House and Bolsover Castle. Peregrine falcons nest in the tower; follow their progress at www.derbyperegrines.blogspot.com.

Derby Museum & Art Gallery MUSEUM
(www.derbymuseums.org; The Strand; ⊙10am-5pm Tue-Sat, noon-4pm Sun) FREE Local history and industry displays include fine ceramics produced by Royal Crown Derby and an archaeology gallery.

Quad GALLERY, CINEMA
(☎01332-290606; www.derbyquad.co.uk; Market Pl; gallery free, cinema tickets £5-17; ⊙gallery 11am-6pm Mon-Sat, noon-6pm Sun, cinema 11am-9pm) A striking modernist cube on Market Pl, Quad contains a futuristic art gallery and an art-house cinema.

Royal Crown Derby Factory MUSEUM
(☎01332-712800; www.royalcrownderby.co.uk; Osmaston Rd; museum & factory tour adult/child £5/2.50, museum only £2/1; ⊙museum 10am-4pm Mon-Sat, factory tours 1.30pm Tue-Thu, shop 10am-5pm Mon-Sat, tearoom 10am-4pm Tue-Fri) Derby's historic potteries still turn out some of the finest bone china in England, from edgy Asian-inspired designs to the kind of stuff your grandma collects. Reservations are essential for factory tours lasting 90 minutes, including a visit to the museum. Royal Crown Derby's china (including seconds and discontinued items) is sold at its on-site shop, and is used as tableware at its elegant tearoom.

Sleeping

Cathedral Quarter Hotel HOTEL ££
(☎01332-546080; www.cathedralquarterhotel.com; 16 St Mary's Gate; s/d incl breakfast from £60/80;) A bell's peal from the cathedral, this grand Georgian edifice houses Derby's finest digs. The service is as polished as the grand marble staircase and there's an on-site spa and fine-dining restaurant.

Farmhouse at Mackworth INN ££
(☎01332-824324; www.thefarmhouseatmackworth.com; 60 Ashbourne Rd; d/f incl breakfast from £70/90; P) Overhauled by pub conglomerate Marston's, designer inn the Farmhouse at Mackworth is just 2.5 miles northwest of Derby in undulating countryside, with the bonus of plentiful free parking. Its 10 boutique rooms have checked fabrics, rustic timber cladding and chrome fittings, plus amenities including Nespresso machines and fluffy robes. There's a fabulous bar and restaurant with a Josper charcoal oven. Family rooms sleep three.

Eating

Forge BURGERS £

(☎01332-987030; www.forgederby.com; 1-6 Blacksmiths Yard, Sadler Gate; burgers £7.50-13; ⏰kitchen noon-9pm Mon-Sat, noon-5pm Sun) Creative twists on burgers made from local ingredients (English flour, Derbyshire beef) include the Fire Starter (jalapeños, red chillies and hot-pepper sauce) and the love-it-or-hate-it PJ (with peanut butter and raspberry jam), with more than two dozen choices in all. Its terrace opens onto the paved Blacksmiths Yard, home to more great restaurants and bars.

Wonky Table BISTRO ££

(☎01332-295000; www.wonkytable.co.uk; 32 Sadler Gate; mains lunch £5.50-12, dinner £15-18; ⏰5-10pm Mon, noon-2pm & 5-10pm Tue-Sat) Inside an inviting retro-vintage dining room with exposed-brick walls, Wonky Table features a slimmed-down daytime menu plus sandwiches such as warm goats cheese with caramelised onion and walnuts. But it really comes into its own at dinner with dishes including honey and balsamic goose breast, rosemary-crusted lamb rump, and beetroot and goats-cheese risotto balls with watercress cream.

Darleys MODERN BRITISH £££

(☎01332-364987; www.darleys.com; Waterfront, Darley Abbey Mill; mains £21.50-25, 2-/3-course lunch menus £20/25; ⏰noon-2pm & 7-9pm Mon-Sat, noon-2.30pm Sun) Two miles north of the centre, this upmarket restaurant has a gorgeous setting in a bright, converted mill overlooking the river. Classy fare spans semolina-coated lamb belly with mint jelly to guinea-fowl Kiev with wilted spinach, and raspberry and rhubarb soufflé.

Drinking & Nightliife

★**Brooklyn Social** BAR

(34-35 Sadler Gate; ⏰noon-midnight Mon-Thu, noon-1am Fri & Sat, 11am-11pm Sun) Opened by Derby local Tom Warner following stints in East London and the US, this triple-decker Grade II–listed space is styled after a neon-lit American dive bar, with retro, vintage and industrial decor. Cocktails (such as Stewed, Screwed and Tattooed, with Sailor Jerry spiced rum with ginger beer, honey and fiery Tabasco) and craft beers complement its awesome burgers.

★**Old Bell Hotel** PUB

(www.bellhotelderby.co.uk; 51 Sadler Gate; ⏰11.30am-11.30pm Sun-Thu, to 1.30am Fri & Sat) Dating from 1650 and hosting Bonnie Prince Charlie's soldiers in 1745, this history-steeped black-and-white inn languished from late last century until its recent restoration by valiant local entrepreneur Paul Hurst. There's a crackling open fire and a central courtyard (and, allegedly, more than a few ghosts). Top-notch food here includes fine dining restaurant Zest.

Silk Mill PUB

(www.silkmillderby.co.uk; 19 Full St; ⏰noon-11pm Mon-Thu, to midnight Fri & Sat, to 10.30pm Sun; 📶) Live music plays at this real-ale pub several times a week including Sunday jazz.

Ye Olde Dolphin PUB

(☎01332-267711; www.yeoldedolphin.co.uk; 5a Queen St; ⏰11.30am-11pm Mon-Thu, 11.30am-midnight Fri, 11am-midnight Sat, noon-11pm Sun) Dating from 1530, Derby's oldest pub has a hearty menu and live music in the beer garden from Thursday to Saturday. Ask about its ghost tours.

Shopping

Bennetts DEPARTMENT STORE

(www.bennettsirongate.co.uk; 8 Irongate; ⏰9am-5pm Mon-Sat, 11am-4pm Sun) Founded as an ironmongers in 1734 and still retaining an ironmongery, Derby's historic department store has evolved over the centuries to sell beautiful clothes, homewares, gifts and more. On the 1st-floor interior balcony, the excellent **Lisa Jean at Bennetts Brasserie** (☎01332-344621; www.lisajean-bennetts.co.uk; mains £8.50-12.50, 5-course champagne breakfast £24; ⏰9am-3pm Mon-Sat, 11am-2pm Sun) specialises in five-course champagne breakfasts (served until 2pm).

Information

Derby's **tourist office** (☎01332-643411; www.visitderby.co.uk; Market Pl; ⏰9.30am-4.30pm Mon-Sat Apr-Sep, 10am-3.30pm Mon-Sat Oct-Mar) is situated under the Assembly Rooms in the main square.

Getting There & Around

AIR

East Midlands Airport (p408), 11.5 miles southeast of Derby, is served by regular Skylink buses (£4.30, 30 minutes, at least hourly, 24 hours).

WORTH A TRIP

KEDLESTON HALL

Sitting pretty in vast landscaped grounds, the neoclassical mansion **Kedleston Hall** (NT; Kedleston; house & gardens adult/child £12/6, garden only £5/2.50; house noon-5pm Sat-Thu Feb-Oct, garden 10am-6pm Feb-Oct, to 4pm Nov-Jan) is a must for fans of stately homes. Entering the house through a grand portico, you'll reach the breathtaking Marble Hall with massive alabaster columns and statues of Greek deities.

Kedleston Hall is 5 miles northwest of Derby, off the A52. Bus 114 between Derby and Ashbourne (£3.20, 30 minutes, up to six per day Monday to Saturday) passes the Smithy, 1 mile northwest of Kedleston.

BUS

Local and long-distance buses run from Derby's bus station, immediately east of the Westfield shopping mall. Highpeak has hourly buses between Derby and Buxton (£5.90, 1¾ hours), via Matlock (£4.30, 35 minutes) and Bakewell (£4.80, 1¼ hours). Five buses continue to Manchester (£8, 2¼ hours).

Other services:

Leicester Skylink; £7, 1½ hours, one to two per hour

Nottingham Red Arrow; £5, 35 minutes, every 10 minutes Monday to Saturday, three per hour Sunday

TRAIN

The train station is about half a mile southeast of the centre on Railway Tce.

Birmingham £18.40, 40 minutes, four hourly

Leeds £33.60, 1½ hours, two hourly

London St Pancras £72, 1¾ hours, up to four hourly

Ashbourne

POP 7800

Perched at the southern edge of the Peak District National Park, Ashbourne is a pretty patchwork of steeply slanting stone streets lined with cafes, pubs and antique shops.

Sleeping & Eating

Compton House B&B ££

(01335-343100; www.comptonhouse.co.uk; 27-31 Compton St; d £70; P) Fresh, clean, frilly rooms, a warm welcome and a central location make this the pick of Ashbourne's B&Bs.

Flower Cafe CAFE £

(5 Market Pl; mains £5.50-12.50; 8.30am-5pm;) Soups such as parsnip, chorizo and chestnut, broccoli and Stilton, and spicy bean and lentil are a year-round speciality at this cute-as-a-button cafe where everything is homemade. In summer it also cooks delicious quiches (cheesy leek and mushroom; bacon, brie and cranberry...). Gluten-free and dairy-free dishes are plentiful.

Bramhalls DELI, CAFE £

(01335-342631; www.bramhallsdeli.co.uk; 22 Market Pl; dishes £4-8; 8am-5pm Mon-Sat, 9am-5pm Sun) A great little deli and cafe, Bramhalls serves stylish light meals and sandwiches, and excellent homemade pastries, breads, cold meats as well as more than 60 varieties of cheese.

Drinking

Smith's Tavern PUB

(36 St John's St; 11am-3pm & 5-11pm Sun-Fri, noon-10.30pm Sat) On the main shopping street, this tiny pub has a big selection of real ales and an old piano at the back.

Information

The **tourist office** (01335-343666; www.visitashbourne.co.uk; Market Pl; 10am-5pm Jun-Aug, shorter hours Mar-May & Sep-Dec, closed Jan & Feb) is inside Ashbourne's town hall.

Getting There & Around

Bus services include the following:

Buxton Highpeak routes 441 and 442; £4.30, 1¼ hours, eight daily Monday to Saturday, five Sunday.

Derby Trent Barton Swift; £4, 40 minutes, hourly Monday to Saturday, five Sunday.

Cycle Hire Centre (01335-343156; www.peakdistrict.gov.uk/visiting/cycle; Mapleton Lane; half-day/day from £14/17; 9.30am-5.30pm Mar-Nov, shorter hours Dec-Feb)

Matlock Bath

POP 753

Unashamedly tacky, Matlock Bath (not to be confused with the larger, work-a-day town of Matlock 2 miles north) looks like a seaside resort that somehow lost its way and ended up at the foot of the Peak District National Park. Following the River Derwent through a sheer-walled gorge, the main promenade is lined with amusement arcades, tearooms, fish-and-chip shops, pubs and shops catering to the bikers who congregate here on summer weekends. Outside summer, the town is considerably quieter.

Sights & Activities

Steep paths climb the eastern side of the gorge, reached by pedestrian bridges from the A6. The tourist office has details of longer, more challenging walks in the hills.

Beware: many of the lanes up the side of the valley are too narrow for cars, with no space for turning (or parking).

Peak District Lead Mining Museum MUSEUM
(☎01629-583834; www.peakdistrictleadmining-museum.co.uk; The Grand Pavilion, South Pde; museum adult/child £4/3, mine £4.50/3.50, combined ticket £7/5; ⏲10am-5pm Apr-Oct, 11am-3pm Wed-Fri, to 4pm Sat & Sun Nov-Mar) An educational introduction to the mining history of Matlock is provided by this enthusiast-run museum set in an old Victorian dance hall. Kids can wriggle through its maze of tunnels and shafts while adults browse historical displays. At noon and 2pm daily from April to October (at weekends only from November to March) you can go into the workings of the **Temple Mine** and pan for 'gold' (well, shiny minerals). Reservations for mine tours are recommended.

Heights of Abraham AMUSEMENT PARK
(☎01629-582365; www.heightsofabraham.com; Dale Rd; adult/child £15/10.50; ⏲10am-4.30pm daily mid-Mar–Oct, Sat & Sun mid-Feb–mid-Mar, closed Nov–mid-Feb) A spectacular **cable-car ride** (accessible with admission ticket only) from the bottom of the gorge brings you to this hilltop leisure park, its cave and mine tours and fossil exhibitions are a winner with kids.

Peak Rail RAIL
(☎01629-580381; www.peakrail.co.uk; adult/child £8.50/4.50; ⏲Mar-Nov, hours vary) From a tiny platform by Sainsbury's supermarket on the outskirts of the town of Matlock (not Matlock Bath), nostalgic steam trains trundle along a 4-mile length of track to the nearby village of Rowsley, home to Caudwell's Mill. Tickets include unlimited travel on the day of purchase.

Sleeping

Hodgkinson's Hotel & Restaurant HOTEL ££
(☎01629-582170; www.hodgkinsons-hotel.co.uk; 150 South Pde; d/f incl breakfast from £95/145; P 📶 👪) The eight rooms at this central Grade II–listed Victorian beauty conjure up Matlock's golden age with antique furnishings, flowery wallpaper and cast-iron fireplaces. Arrive early to nab one of its five parking spaces. The **restaurant** (2-/3-course menus £26/29) has just 18 seats so bookings are advised. Service is superb.

DERWENT VALLEY MILLS

Unlikely as it may sound, the industrial mills that line the Derwent Valley are ranked up there with the Taj Mahal on the Unesco World Heritage list.

Cromford Mill (☎01629-823256; www.cromfordmills.org.uk; Mill Lane, Cromford; tour adult/child £3/2.50; ⏲9am-5pm, tours 11am, 1pm & 2.30pm Sat-Thu, by reservation 11am Fri) Founded in the 1770s by Richard Arkwright, the Cromford Mill was the first modern factory, producing cotton on automated machines, powered by a series of waterwheels along the River Derwent. This prototype inspired a succession of mills, ushering in the industrial age. The Arkwright Society runs fascinating tours. It's 1 mile south of Matlock Bath (a 20-minute walk), or you can take the train one stop to Cromford (70p, three minutes, hourly).

Caudwell's Mill (☎01629-734374; www.caudwellsmill.co.uk; Rowsley; mill tours adult/child £4.50/2; ⏲mill tours 9.30am-4.30pm, shop 9am-5pm) This chugging, grinding, water-powered mill still produces flour the old-fashioned way – 25 different types are for sale, along with eight different oat products, and yeast and biscuits. The mill has various craft workshops and a tearoom. You can get to Rowsley direct from Matlock Bath by Highpeak bus (£2.80, 15 minutes, hourly) on the route to Bakewell, or take the Peak Rail steam train and follow the riverside path from the station.

Grouse & Claret INN ££
(01629-733233; www.grouseclaretpub.co.uk; Station Rd, Rowsley; d/f incl breakfast from £75/90; P) In the village of Rowsley, 6.2 miles northwest of Matlock Bath, this 18th-century stone inn has been revamped by pub operator Marston's and now has eight comfy, country-style wallpapered rooms (some sleeping up to three people), a restaurant and a huge, sunny beer garden with umbrella-shaded tables.

Ashdale Guest House B&B ££
(01629-57826; www.ashdaleguesthouse.co.uk; 92 North Pde; s/d from £50/70; P) Just beyond the bling of the amusement-arcade-lined main promenade framed by towering monkey-puzzle trees, this tall 1840s-built stone house has four spacious, tastefully decorated rooms and organic breakfasts.

Shopping

Scarthin Books BOOKS
(www.scarthinbooks.com; The Promenade, Cromford; 9am-6pm Mon-Sat, noon-6pm Sun) More than 100,000 new and secondhand books cram 12 rooms in this biblio-paradise, which hosts regular literary events and has a vegetarian cafe (dishes £3.50 to £6.50) serving organic pizza, wraps, pies and burritos.

Information

The **tourist office** (01629-583834; www.visitpeakdistrict.com; The Grand Pavilion, South Pde; 10am-5pm Apr-Oct, 11am-3pm Wed-Fri, to 4pm Sat & Sun Nov-Mar) is located at the Peak District Lead Mining Museum.

Getting There & Away

Matlock is a hub for buses around the Peak District.

Bakewell Highpeak; £3.30, 30 minutes, hourly

Derby Transpeak; £4.30, 35 minutes, hourly

Trains run hourly between Matlock Bath and Derby (£5.60, 30 minutes, hourly).

Chesterfield & Around

POP 104,300

The eastern gateway to the Peaks, Chesterfield is worth a stop to see the astonishing crooked spire rising atop St Mary & All Saints Church and the magnificent Elizabethan mansion Hardwick Hall nearby.

Sights

St Mary & All Saints Church CHURCH
(01246-206506; www.chesterfieldparishchurch.org.uk; Church Walk; spire tours adult/child £5/3; church 9am-5pm Mon-Sat, 8am-6.30pm Sun, spire tours Mon-Sat) FREE. Dating from 1360, the 68m-high spire is twisted in a right-handed corkscrew and leans several metres south-west. It's the result of the lead casing on the south-facing side having buckled in the sun. Learn more at the engaging **Chesterfield Museum & Art Gallery** (01246-345727; www.chesterfield.gov.uk/museum; St Mary's Gate; 10am-4pm Mon & Thu-Sat; FREE).

Hardwick Hall HISTORIC BUILDING
(NT; www.nationaltrust.org.uk; house & garden adult/child £13.10/6.55, garden only £6.55/3.30, incl Hardwick Old Hall £19.10/10.15; house 11am-5pm Wed-Sun late Feb–Oct, to 3pm Wed-Sun Nov-late Feb, garden 9am-6pm daily year-round) One of the most complete Elizabethan mansions in the country, Hardwick Hall was designed by eminent architect Robert Smythson. The hall featured all the latest mod-cons of the time, including fully glazed windows. The atmospheric interiors are decked out with magnificent tapestries and oil paintings of forgotten dignitaries.

The hall was home to the 16th-century's second-most powerful woman, Elizabeth, Countess of Shrewsbury (known to all as Bess of Hardwick) who amassed a staggering fortune by marrying wealthy noblemen with one foot in the grave. Hardwick Hall was constructed using her inheritance from hubby number four, who shuffled off this mortal coil in 1590.

Set aside time to explore the formal gardens or the longer walking trails of Hardwick Park.

Next door to the manor is Bess' first house, **Hardwick Old Hall** (EH; www.english-heritage.org.uk; adult/child £6.60/4, incl Hardwick Hall £19.10/10.15; 10am-6pm Wed-Sun Easter-Sep, to 5pm Oct, shorter hours Nov-Easter), now a romantic ruin administered by English Heritage.

Hardwick Hall is 10 miles southeast of Chesterfield, just off the M1; it's best reached by your own wheels.

Information

The **tourist office** (012246-345777; www.visitchesterfield.info; Rykneld Sq; 9am-6pm Mon-Sat) is directly opposite St Mary and All Saints Church.

Getting There & Away

BUS

From Chesterfield coach station on Beetwell St, bus 170 serves Bakewell (£3.30, 50 minutes, hourly).

TRAIN

Chesterfield lies on the main rail line between Nottingham (£12.50, 45 minutes, up to three per hour) and Derby (£11.10, 25 minutes, up to three per hour), which continues to Sheffield (£5.10, 15 minutes, up to three per hour). The station is just east of the centre.

PEAK DISTRICT

Rolling across the Pennines' southernmost hills is the glorious Peak District National Park. Ancient stone villages are folded into creases in the landscape, and the hillsides are littered with stately homes and rocky outcrops. The Dark Peak is dominated by exposed moorland and gritstone 'edges', while to the south, the White Peak is made up of the limestone dales.

No one knows how the Peak District got its name – certainly not from the landscape, which has hills and valleys, gorges and lakes, wild moorland and gritstone escarpments, but no peaks. The most popular theory is that the region was named for the Pecsaetan, the Anglo-Saxon tribe who once populated this part of England.

Founded in 1951, the Peak District was England's first national park and is Europe's busiest. But even at peak times, there are 555 sq miles of open English countryside in which to soak up the scenery.

Activities

Climbing & Caving

The limestone sections of the Peak District are riddled with caves and caverns, including a series of 'showcaves' in Castleton, Buxton and Matlock Bath. For serious caving (or potholing) trips, the first port of call should be the website www.peakdistrictcaving.info, run by caving store **Hitch n Hike** (☎01433-651013; www.hitchnhike.co.uk; Hope Rd, Bamford; ⏲9am-5.30pm), near Castleton, which has gear and advice for climbing.

England's top mountaineers train in this area, which offers rigorous technical climbing on a series of limestone gorges, exposed tors (crags) and gritstone 'edges' that extend south into the Staffordshire Moorlands. Gritstone climbing in the Peak District is predominantly on old-school trad routes, requiring a decent rack of friends, nuts and hexes. Bolted sport routes are found on several limestone crags in the Peak District, but many use ancient pieces of gear and most require additional protection. The crags are best reached with your own transport; check seasonal bus services with tourist offices.

Cycling

Plunging dales and soaring scarps provide a perfect testing ground for cyclists, and local tourist offices are piled high with cycling maps and trail guides. For easy traffic-free riding, head for the 17.5-mile **High Peak Trail**, which follows the old railway line from Cromford, near Matlock Bath, to Dowlow near Buxton. The trail winds through beautiful hills and farmland to Parsley Hay, where the **Tissington Trail**, part of NCN Route 68, heads south for 13 miles to Ashbourne. Trails are off-road on dedicated cycle paths, suitable for road bikes.

Mirroring the Pennine Way, the **Pennine Bridleway** is another top spot to put your calves through their paces. Around 120 miles of trails have been created between Middleton Top and the South Pennines, and the route is suitable for horse riders, cyclists and walkers. You could also follow the **Pennine Cycleway** (NCN Route 68) from Derby to Buxton and beyond. Other popular routes include the **Limestone Way**, running south from Castleton to Staffordshire, and the **Monsal Trail & Tunnels** between Bakewall and Wyedale, near Buxton.

PEAK DISTRICT TRANSPORT PASSES

Handy bus passes cover travel in the Peak District.

The **Peaks Plus ticket** (Peaks Plus adult/child £7.50/5, Peaks Plus Xtra £12.50/7) offers all-day travel on Trent Barton buses, including the Transpeak between Ashbourne, Matlock Bath and Buxton. Its Peaks Plus Xtra ticket includes all transport on Transpeak and TM buses between Derby, Sheffield and Buxton.

The **Derbyshire Wayfarer ticket** (adult/child £12.40/6.20) covers buses and trains throughout the county and as far afield as Sheffield. One child under 16 travels free per paying adult.

Peak District National Park

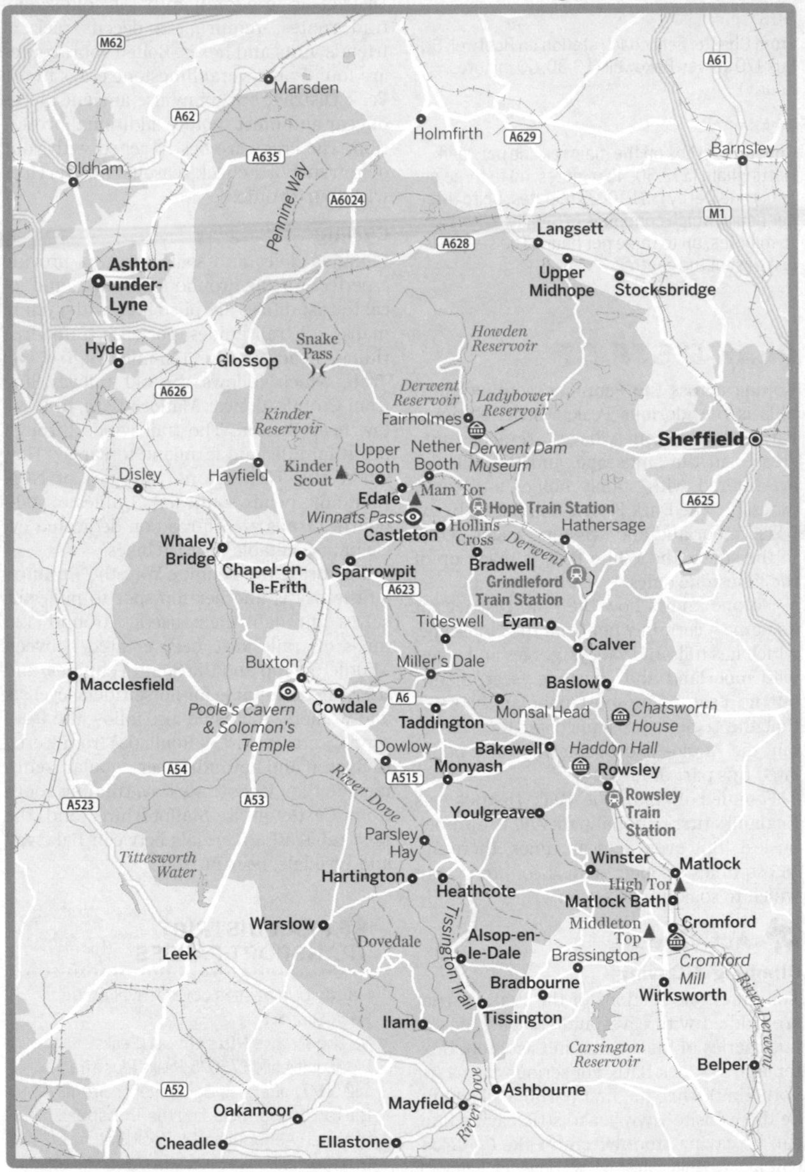

Peak Tours (01457-851462; www.peak-tours.com; mountain-bike rental per day £20) delivers rental bikes anywhere in the Peak District, and offers guided cycling tours. The Peak District National Park Authority (p481) operates several cycle-hire centres renting road, mountain, tandem and electric bikes as well as kids' bikes.

Walking

The Peak District is one of the most popular walking areas in England, with awe-inspiring vistas of hills, dales and sky that attract legions of hikers in summer. The White Peak is perfect for leisurely strolls, which can start from pretty much anywhere. Be sure to close gates behind you as you go. When exploring the rugged territory of the Dark Peak, make sure your boots are waterproof and beware of slipping into rivulets and marshes.

The Peak's most famous walking trail is the **Pennine Way**, which runs north from Edale for more than 250 miles, finishing in the Scottish Borders. If you don't have three weeks to spare, you can reach the pretty town of Hebden Bridge in Yorkshire comfortably in three days.

The 46-mile **Limestone Way** winds through the Derbyshire countryside from Castleton to Rocester in Staffordshire, following footpaths, tracks and quiet lanes. Many people walk the 26-mile section between Castleton and Matlock in one long, tiring day, but two days is better. Tourist offices have a detailed leaflet.

Other popular routes include the **High Peak Trail**, **Tissington Trail**, and **Monsal Trail & Tunnels**. Numerous short walks are available.

Information

Tourist offices or national-park visitor centres include Buxton, Bakewell, Castleton and Edale. The **Peak District National Park Authority** (www.peakdistrict.gov.uk) website has reams of information on transport, activities and local events.

Getting There & Away

Buses run from regional centres such as Sheffield and Derby to destinations across the Peak District. Be aware that buses are much more frequent at weekends, and many services close down completely in winter. Bakewell and Matlock (not Matlock Bath) are the two main hubs – from here you can get anywhere in the Peak District. Timetables are available from all tourist offices as well as Traveline (p452). Trains run to Matlock Bath, Buxton, Edale and several other towns and villages.

Buxton

POP 24,001

The 'capital' of the Peak District National Park, albeit just outside the park boundary, Buxton is a confection of Georgian terraces, Victorian amusements and parks in the rolling hills of the Derbyshire dales. The town built its fortunes on its natural warm-water springs, which attracted health tourists in Buxton's turn-of-the-century heyday.

Today, visitors are drawn here by the flamboyant Regency architecture and the natural wonders of the surrounding countryside. Tuesdays and Saturdays are market days, bringing colour to the grey limestone marketplace.

Sights

Buxton's historic centre overflows with Victorian pavilions, concert halls and glasshouse domes. Its most famous building is the turreted Opera House (p484).

★ Pavilion Gardens GARDENS

(www.paviliongardens.co.uk; 9.30am-5pm) FREE Adjoining Buxton's opulent Opera House (p484) is the equally flamboyant Pavilion Gardens. These 9.3 hectares are dotted with domed pavilions; concerts take place in the bandstand throughout the year. The main building contains a tropical greenhouse, a nostalgic cafe and the tourist office (p484).

Devonshire Dome HISTORIC BUILDING

(Devonshire Rd) A glorious piece of Victoriana, the Devonshire Dome forms part of the campus of the University of Derby. It is also home to **Devonshire Spa** (01298-330334; www.devonshiredome.co.uk; 1 Devonshire Rd; 2hr body spa £20, ocean or frangipani wrap £50, day package from £95; 9am-6pm Tue, Wed, Sat & Sun, to 9pm Thu & Fri), which offers a full range of pampering treatments.

Buxton Baths HISTORIC BUILDING

(The Crescent) In Victorian times, spa activities centred on the extravagant Buxton Baths complex, built in grand Regency style in 1854. The various bath buildings are fronted by a grand, curving facade, known as the **Crescent**, inspired by the Royal Crescent in Bath. It's expected to reopen in 2019 as a five-star hotel and spa.

Slopes PARK

(24hr) Opposite the Crescent, aptly named park the Slopes rises steeply in a series of grassy terraces. Climbing them provides the definitive view over Buxton's Victorian rooftops.

Buxton Museum & Art Gallery MUSEUM, GALLERY

(www.derbyshire.gov.uk/leisure/buxton_museum; Terrace Rd; 9.30am-5.30pm Tue-Fri, to 5pm Sat year-round, plus 10.30am-5pm Sun Easter-Sep) FREE In a handsome Victorian building,

Buxton

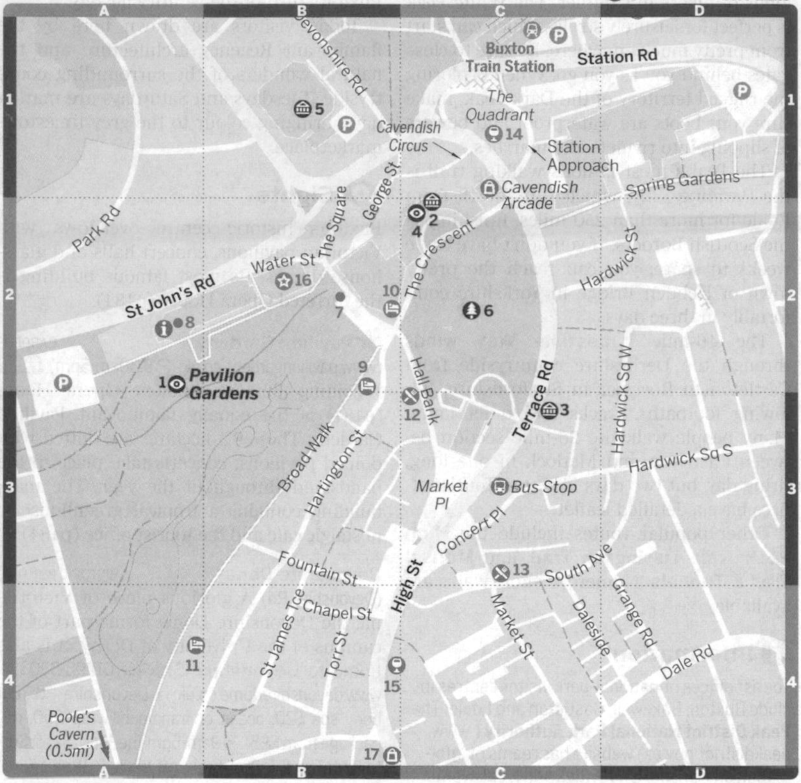

Buxton

Top Sights

1 Pavilion Gardens A2

Sights

2 Buxton Baths C2
3 Buxton Museum & Art Gallery C3
4 Crescent C2
5 Devonshire Dome B1
6 Slopes C2

Activities, Courses & Tours

7 Buxton Tram B2
Devonshire Spa .... (see 5)
8 Roman Buxton Town Walks A2

Sleeping

9 Grosvenor House B2
10 Old Hall Hotel B2
11 Roseleigh Hotel A4

Eating

12 Columbine Restaurant C3
13 Number 13 .... C3

Drinking & Nightlife

14 Barbarella's C1
15 Old Sun Inn B4

Entertainment

16 Opera House B2

Shopping

17 Scrivener's Books & Bookbinding B4

the town museum displays local historical bric-a-brac and curiosities from Castleton's Victorian-era 'House of Wonders', including Harry Houdini's handcuffs.

Poole's Cavern CAVE

(☎01298-26978; www.poolescavern.co.uk; adult/child £9.75/5.25; ⊙9.30am-5pm Mar-Oct, 10am-4pm Sat & Sun Nov-Feb) A pleasant mile-long stroll southwest from the centre brings you to Poole's Cavern. This magnificent natural limestone cavern is reached by descending 28 steps; the temperature is a cool 7°C. Tours lasting 50 minutes run every 20 minutes from March to October and at 10.30am, 12.30pm and 2.30pm from November to February.

From the cavern's car park, a 20-minute walk leads up through Grin Low Wood to **Solomon's Temple**, a ruined tower with fine views over the town.

Activities

★ Buxton Tram BUS
(☎ 01298-79648; adult/child £6/4; ⏲ hourly 10am-5pm Easter-Oct, 11am-4pm Nov-Easter) From the Pavilion Gardens (p481), this vintage milk float takes you on a 12mph, hour-or-so circuit of the centre on its entertaining 'Wonder of the Peak' tour. There are only eight seats, so booking ahead is recommended. The same company also offers hour-long walking tours at 2pm daily (adult/child £6/4) from the same departure point.

Roman Buxton Town Walks WALKING
(walking tours by donation; ⏲ 11am daily Jun-Aug, Sat Sep-May) Hour-long Roman Buxton town walks depart from the tourist office (p484).

Parsley Hay Cycle Hire CYCLING
(☎ 01298-84493; www.peakdistrict.gov.uk/visiting/cycle; bike hire per half/full day adult from £14/17, child from £9/12; ⏲ 9.30am-5pm Mar-Oct, 10am-4pm Nov-Feb) Rent mountain bikes, tandems and electric bikes from the Peak District National Park Authority's Parsley Hay Cycle Hire, 8 miles south of Buxton on the A515 at the junction of the High Peak and Tissington Trails.

Sleeping

Old Hall Hotel HISTORIC HOTEL ££
(☎ 01298-22841; www.oldhallhotelbuxton.co.uk; The Square; s/d incl breakfast from £69/79; 📶 🐾) There's a tale to go with every creak of the floorboards at this history-soaked establishment, supposedly the oldest hotel in England. Among other esteemed residents, Mary, Queen of Scots, stayed here from 1576 to 1578, albeit against her will. The rooms are still the grandest in town, and there are several bars, lounges and dining options.

Roseleigh Hotel B&B ££
(☎ 01298-24904; www.roseleighhotel.co.uk; 19 Broad Walk; s/d from £44/55; P @ 📶) This gorgeous family-run B&B in a roomy old Victorian house has lovingly decorated rooms, many with fine views over the Pavilion Gardens. The owners are a welcoming couple, both seasoned travellers, with plenty of interesting stories. There's a minimum two-night stay on summer weekends.

Grosvenor House B&B ££
(☎ 01298-72439; www.grosvenorbuxton.co.uk; 1 Broad Walk; s/d/f from £55/70/100; P 📶 👪) Overlooking the Pavilion Gardens, the Grosvenor is an old-school Victorian guesthouse with a huge parlour overlooking the park. Its eight rooms (including one family room sleeping three people) have floral upholstery, floral drapes and, well, floral everything else, really. There's a minimum two-night stay at peak times, when singles aren't available.

Eating & Drinking

Columbine Restaurant MODERN BRITISH ££
(☎ 01298-78752; www.columbinerestaurant.co.uk; 7 Hall Bank; mains £13.50-20; ⏲ 7-10pm Mon & Wed-Sat) 🌿 On the lane leading down beside the town hall, this understated restaurant is the top choice among in-the-know Buxtonites. The chef conjures up imaginative dishes primarily made from local produce. Bookings recommended. Two of its three dining areas are in the atmospheric stone cellar.

Number 13 MODERN BRITISH ££
(☎ 01298-25397; www.number13.co.uk; cnr Market St & South Ave; mains £9-17; ⏲ 4.30-10.30pm Mon-Fri, noon-10.30pm Sat & Sun) 🌿 Burgers, pies, steaks and fish dishes are the stock-in-trade of this busy town-centre restaurant. Live jazz swings in the bar on Sunday afternoons. Upstairs, basic double **rooms** cost £50 per night.

Barbarella's WINE BAR
(www.barbarellaswinebar.co.uk; 7 The Quadrant; ⏲ noon-11pm Sun-Thu, to midnight Fri & Sat; 📶 🐾) Black-and-white paisley wallpaper, chandeliers and glossy timber tables make this sleek retro wine bar the hottest drinking den in Buxton. Stellar food too.

Old Sun Inn PUB
(www.theoldsuninnbuxton.com; 33 High St; ⏲ noon-11pm Mon & Wed, to 11.30pm Tue, Thu & Sun, to midnight Fri & Sat) The cosiest of Buxton's pubs, with a warren of rooms full of original features, a dozen ales on tap, and a lively crowd that spans the generations.

WORTH A TRIP

CATHEDRAL OF THE PEAK

Cathedral of the Peak (☎01298-871317; www.tideswellchurch.org; Commercial Rd, Tideswell; ⊙9am-6pm) dominates the former lead-mining village of Tideswell, 10km east of Buxton. The massive parish church of St John the Baptist – aka the Cathedral of the Peak – has stood here virtually unchanged since the 14th century. Look out for the wooden panels inscribed with the Ten Commandments and grand 14th-century tomb of local landowner Thurston de Bower, depicted in full medieval armour. It's 8 miles east of Buxton, linked by buses 65 and 68 (£2.40, 30 minutes, hourly Monday to Saturday, every two hours Sunday).

☆ Entertainment

Opera House OPERA
(☎0845 127 2190; www.buxtonoperahouse.org.uk; Water St; tours £2.50; ⊙tours usually 11am Sat) Buxton's gorgeously restored Opera House hosts a full program of drama, dance, concerts and comedy. It's the focal point for festivities including the **Buxton Festival** (www.buxtonfestival.co.uk; ⊙Jul).

Shopping

Scrivener's Books & Bookbinding BOOKS
(☎01298-73100; www.scrivenersbooks.co.uk; 42 High St; ⊙9.30am-5pm Mon-Sat, noon-4pm Sun) At this delightfully chaotic bookshop, sprawling over five floors, books are filed in piles and the Dewey system has yet to be discovered.

Cavendish Arcade ARCADE
(www.cavendisharcade.co.uk; Cavendish Circus; ⊙9am-6pm Mon-Sat, 10am-5pm Sun, shop hours vary) Retaining its original eggshell-blue tiles, Cavendish Arcade houses boutiques selling upmarket gifts.

Information

Buxton's helpful, well-organised **tourist office** (☎01298-25106; www.visitpeakdistrict.com; Pavilion Gardens; ⊙9.30am-5pm; 📶) has useful leaflets on walks in the area.

Getting There & Away

Buses stop on both sides of the road at **Market Pl** (Market Pl). The hourly Highpeak runs to Derby (£5.90, 1¾ hours), via Bakewell (£3.80, 30 minutes) and Matlock Bath (£3.30, one hour). Five Highpeak services run to Manchester (£5.30, 1¼ hours).

To reach Sheffield take bus 65 (£5.80, 1¼ hours, every two hours Monday to Saturday, three services Sunday).

Northern Rail has trains to/from Manchester (£10.10, one hour, hourly).

Castleton & Around

POP 706

Guarding the entrance to the forbidding Winnats Pass gorge, charming Castleton is a magnet on summer weekends for Midlands visitors – come midweek if you want to enjoy the sights in relative peace and quiet. The village's streets are lined with leaning stone houses, with walking trails criss-crossing the surrounding hills. A wonderfully atmospheric castle crowns the ridge above, and the bedrock below is riddled with fascinating caves.

Sights & Activities

Situated at the base of 517m-high Mam Tor, Castleton is the northern terminus of the **Limestone Way**, which follows narrow, rocky Cave Dale, far below the east wall of the castle. The tourist office has maps and leaflets, including details of numerous easier walks.

Peveril Castle CASTLE
(EH; www.english-heritage.org.uk; adult/child £5.10/3; ⊙10am-6pm Easter-Sep, to 5pm Oct, to 4pm Sat & Sun Nov-Easter) Topping the ridge to the south of Castleton, a 350m walk from the town centre, this evocative castle has been so ravaged by the centuries that it almost looks like a crag itself. Constructed by William Peveril, son of William the Conqueror, the castle was used as a hunting lodge by Henry II, King John and Henry III, and the crumbling ruins offer swooping views over the Hope Valley.

Castleton Museum MUSEUM
(☎01629-816572; www.peakdistrict.gov.uk; Buxton Rd; ⊙10am-5.30pm late Jul–early Sep, to 5pm Apr–late Jul & early Sep–Oct, shorter hours early Nov–Mar) FREE Attached to the tourist office (p486), the cute town museum has displays on everything from mining and geology to rock climbing, hang-gliding and the curious **Garland Festival** (⊙29 May).

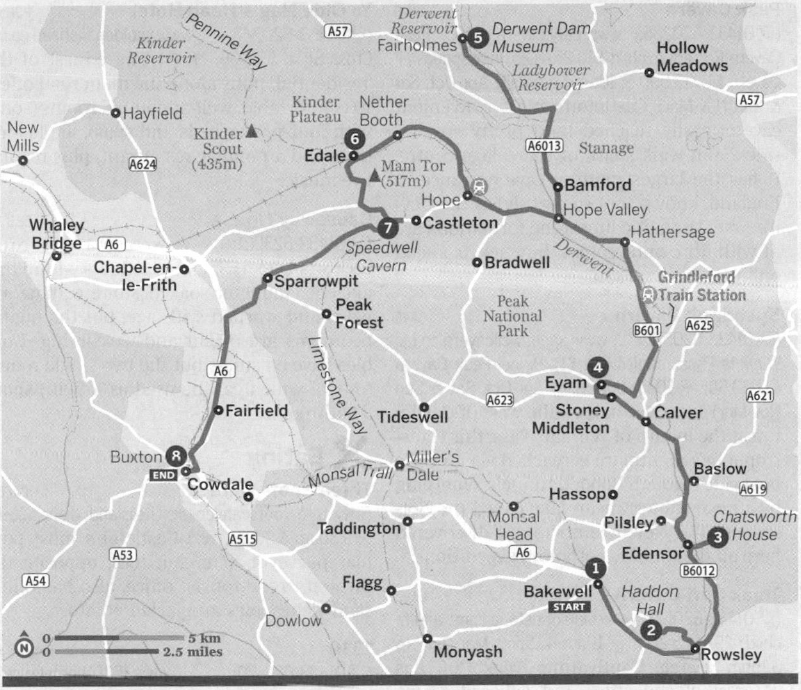

Driving Tour
Peak District

START BAKEWELL
END BUXTON
LENGTH 52 MILES; ONE TO TWO DAYS

Although you can drive this route in a few hours, there's a lot to see, so pack your hiking boots and consider breaking your journey overnight. Fuel your car at the pretty town of **1 Bakewell** (p488), famed for its distinctive Bakewell Pudding. Head south on the A6 for 3.5 miles to Rowsley and turn left on winding Church Lane for 2 miles to visit the atmospheric medieval manor **2 Haddon Hall** (p489).

Return to Rowsley, turn left on the A6 and left on the B6012 – follow it for 2.9 miles before turning right to reach the 'Palace of the Peak', **3 Chatsworth House** (p489).

Back on the B6012, turn right to join the A619. At Baslow, home to the country hotel and Michelin-starred restaurant Fischer's Baslow Hall, turn left at the roundabout and travel along the A623 for 3.4 miles to the turn-off for **4 Eyam** (p488). Drive up the hill to reach its quaint museum, where you can learn about the town's poignant plague history. There's fantastic walking here.

Continue up the hill and turn right on Edge Rd, then right on Sir William Hill Rd and left on the B601 at Grindleford. Continue to Hathersage and turn left on the A6187 to Hope Valley. From here, turn right on the A6013, passing Ladybower Reservoir, to reach the **5 Derwent Dam Museum** (p487). Pop in to learn about the Dambusters squadron's 'bouncing bombs' tests here during WWII.

It's 5.8 miles back to the Hope Valley turn-off. Then turn right onto Hathersage Rd, right again on Edale Rd and follow the valley to stretch your legs at another prime walking destination, **6 Edale** (p487). Scenery peaks when you travel southwest towards Castleton, climbing the steep hill near 517m-high Mam Tor, to Winnats Rd, then following the spectacular former coral-reef canyon Winnats Pass to explore **7 Speedwell Cavern** (p486).

From Speedwell Cavern, head west along Arthurs Way on to Winnats Rd. Turning right on the A623 brings you to the riot of Victoriana in the former spa town of **8 Buxton** (p481).

Peak Cavern CAVE

(☎01433-620285; www.peakcavern.co.uk; Peak Cavern Rd; adult/child £10.25/8.25, incl Speedwell Cavern £17/13.50; ⏰10am-5pm daily Apr-Oct, Sat & Sun Nov-Mar) Castleton's most convenient cave is easily reached by a pretty streamside 250m walk south of the village centre. It has the largest natural cave entrance in England, known (not so prettily) as the Devil's Arse. Dramatic limestone formations are lit with fibre-optic cables. Buy tickets ahead online in peak season.

Speedwell Cavern CAVE

(☎01433-620512; www.speedwellcavern.co.uk; Winnats Pass; adult/child £11/9, incl Peak Cavern £17/13.50; ⏰10am-5pm daily Apr-Oct, Sat & Sun Nov-Mar) Just over half a mile west of Castleton at the mouth of Winnats Pass, this claustrophobe's nightmare is reached via an eerie boat ride through flooded tunnels, emerging by a huge subterranean lake called the Bottomless Pit. New chambers are discovered here all the time by potholing expeditions.

Treak Cliff Cavern CAVE

(☎01433-620571; www.bluejohnstone.com; adult/child £9.50/5.20; ⏰10am-4.15pm Mar-Oct, to 3.15pm Nov-Feb) Captivating Treak Cliff has a forest of stalactites and exposed seams of colourful Blue John Stone, which is still mined to supply the jewellery trade. Tours focus on the history of mining; kids can polish their own Blue John Stone during school holidays. It's just under a mile west of Castleton's village centre.

Blue John Cavern CAVE

(☎01433-620638; www.bluejohn-cavern.co.uk; adult/child £11/6; ⏰9.30am-5.30pm Apr-Oct, to dusk Nov-Mar) Up the southeastern side of Mam Tor, 2 miles west of Castleton, Blue John is a maze of natural caverns with rich seams of Blue John Stone that are still mined every winter. You can get here on foot up the closed section of the Mam Tor road.

Sleeping

Rowter Farm CAMPGROUND £

(☎01433-620271; 2-person sites £10; ⏰Easter-Oct; P 🐾) About 2 miles west of central Castleton, this simple camping field (no lounge area or shop) has a stunning location up in the hills. Showers cost 50p. Drivers should approach via Winnats Pass (take the left fork at the top, and the first left immediately after); on foot, follow the Cave Dale path.

Ye Olde Nag's Head Hotel PUB ££

(☎01433-620248; www.yeoldenagshead.co.uk; Cross St; d £50-95; 📶🐾) The cosiest of the 'residential' pubs along the main road offers 10 comfortable, well-appointed rooms (some with four-poster beds and spas), ale tasting trays and a popular restaurant, plus regular live music.

Causeway House B&B ££

(☎01433-623921; www.causewayhouse.co.uk; Back St; s/d from £35/75) The floors within this ancient character-soaked stone cottage are worn and warped with age, but the quaint bedrooms are bright and welcoming. Doubles have en suites but the two single rooms (one of which can be used as a twin) share a bathroom.

Eating

Three Roofs Cafe CAFE £

(www.threeroofscafe.co.uk; The Island; dishes £6-11; ⏰9.30am-4.30pm; 📶) Castleton's most popular purveyor of cream teas, opposite the turn-off to the tourist office, also has filling sandwiches, pies and jacket potatoes.

1530 ITALIAN ££

(☎01433-621870; www.1530therestaurant.co.uk; Cross St; mains lunch £5-7.50, dinner £8-17; ⏰noon-2pm & 6-8.30pm Wed & Thu, noon-2pm & 6-9.30pm Fri & Sat, noon-2pm & 6-8pm Sun & Mon; 🖉) Crispy thin-crust pizzas and fresh pastas such as king prawn, crab, crayfish and calamari linguine are the speciality of Castleton's swish Italian flag-bearer.

★**Samuel Fox** MODERN BRITISH £££

(☎01433-621562; www.samuelfox.co.uk; Stretfield Rd, Bradwell; mains lunch £12.50-14, dinner £13.50-21; ⏰kitchen 6-9pm Wed & Thu, noon-2pm & 6-9pm Fri & Sat, 1-8pm Sun Feb-Dec; P 📶) In the Hope Valley village of Bradwell, 2.5 miles southeast of Castleton, this enchanting inn owned by pedigreed chef James Duckett serves exceptional Modern British cuisine: rare roasted venison with pickled red cabbage and roast pheasant with braised sprouts, bacon and parsnips. Rates for the gorgeous pastel-shaded **guest rooms** upstairs (s/d £95/130) include a sumptuous breakfast plus sherry, grapes and chocolates.

Information

The **tourist office** (☎01629-816572; www.peakdistrict.gov.uk; Buxton Rd; ⏰10am-5.30pm late Jul–early Sep, to 5pm Apr–late Jul & early

Sep–Oct, shorter hours early Nov–Mar) is in the Castleton Museum.

Getting There & Away

Bus services include the following:

Bakewell Bus 173; £3.10, 50 minutes, four daily via Hope (five minutes) and Tideswell (20 minutes)

Buxton Bus 68; £3.90, one hour (departs Castleton in the morning and returns in the afternoon Monday to Saturday)

The nearest train station is at Hope, an easy 2-mile walk east of Castleton, on the line between Sheffield (£5.50, 30 minutes, every two hours) and Manchester (£11.10, 55 minutes, hourly).

Derwent Reservoirs

North of the Hope Valley, the upper reaches of the Derwent Valley were flooded between 1916 and 1935 to create three huge reservoirs to supply Sheffield, Leicester, Nottingham and Derby with water. These constructed lakes soon proved their worth – the **Dambusters** squadron carried out practice runs over Derwent Reservoir before unleashing their 'bouncing bombs' on the Ruhr Valley in Germany in WWII. Their exploits are detailed in the **Derwent Dam Museum** (www.dambusters.org.uk; Fairholmes; 10am-4pm Sun) FREE in the western tower atop the dam.

These days, the Ladybower, Derwent and Howden Reservoirs are popular destinations for walkers, cyclists and mountain bikers – and lots of ducks, so drive slowly!

Fairholmes is a good base for walking and cycling, with a **cycle-hire centre** (01433-651261; www.peakdistrict.gov.uk; Fairholmes; per half/full day adult £14/17, child £10/12; 10am-4.30pm Mon-Fri, to 5.30pm Sat & Sun Apr-Oct, 10am-3.30pm Sat & Sun Nov-Mar).

Fairholmes' **tourist office** (01433-650953; www.peakdistrict.gov.uk; Fairholmes; 10am-4.30pm Mon-Fri, to 5.30pm Sat & Sun Apr-Oct, 10am-3.30pm Sat & Sun Nov-Mar) dispenses walking and cycling advice. It's 2 miles north of the A57 linking Sheffield and Manchester. Buses are limited at best, so you really need your own wheels.

Edale

POP 316

Surrounded by majestic Peak District countryside, this cluster of stone houses centred on a pretty parish church is an enchanting place to pass the time. Edale lies between the White and Dark Peak areas, and is the southern terminus of the Pennine Way. Despite the remote location, the Manchester–Sheffield train line passes through the village, bringing throngs of weekend visitors.

Activities

Walking is the number-one drawcard here, with plenty of diverting strolls for less committed hill walkers.

As well as trips to Hollins Cross and Mam Tor, on the ridge dividing Edale from Castleton, you can walk north onto the **Kinder Plateau**, dark and brooding in the mist, gloriously high and open when the sun's out. This was the setting for a famous act of civil disobedience by ramblers in 1932 that paved the way for the legal 'right to roam' and the creation of England's national parks.

Weather permitting, a fine circular walk starts by following the **Pennine Way** through fields to **Upper Booth**, then up a path called Jacobs Ladder and along the southern edge of Kinder, before dropping down to Edale via the steep rocky valley of Grindsbrook Clough, or the ridge of Ringing Roger.

Sleeping & Eating

Upper Booth Farm CAMPGROUND £

(01433-670250; www.upperboothcamping.co.uk; Upper Booth; sites per person/car £6/4, camping barn per person £8; Easter–early Nov; P) Located along the Pennine Way 1.8 miles west of Edale, this peaceful campsite is set on a working farm and is surrounded by spectacular scenery. For hikers, there's a camping barn and small shop. Customised hampers (from £20; preorder when booking) can be filled with locally baked cakes, breads, biscuits, flapjacks, eggs, honey, BBQ meats and preserves, and more.

Fieldhead Campsite CAMPGROUND £

(01433-670386; www.fieldhead-campsite.co.uk; sites per person/car from £6/3.50; Apr-Sep; P) Right next to the Moorland Tourist Office (p488), this pretty and well-equipped campsite spreads over six fields, with some pitches right by the river. Showers cost 20p.

Edale YHA HOSTEL £

(0845 371 9514; www.yha.org.uk; Rowland Cote, Nether Booth; dm/d/f from £11.50/65/69; P@) Spectacular views across to Back Tor unfold from this country-house hostel

1.5 miles east of Edale, signposted from the Hope road. Check availability ahead as it's often busy with school groups.

Stonecroft B&B ££
(☎01433-670262; www.stonecroftguesthouse.co.uk; Grindsbrook; s/d from £55/99; P 📶) This handsomely fitted-out stone house, built in the 1900s, has two comfortable bedrooms. Vegetarians and vegans are well catered for – host Julia is an award-winning chef and the organic breakfast (with gluten-free options) is excellent. Packed lunches (£7.50) are available by request when booking. Bike rental costs £30 per day. Free pick-up from the train station can be arranged.

Rambler Inn PUB FOOD ££
(☎01433-670268; www.theramblerinn.com; Grindsbrook; mains £9-20; ⏱kitchen noon-9.30pm Mon-Sat, to 8pm Sun, bar noon-11pm Mon-Fri, to midnight Sat, to 9pm Sun; P 📶) Edale's heart and soul, this cosy stone pub serves real ales, and filling fare such as steaks, pork pies and local lamb casseroles. There's a kids' menu, B&B **rooms** (d/tr/f from £85/105/125) and occasional live music.

Information

Topped by a sedum turf 'living roof' with a waterfall splashing across its glass panels, the eco-conscious **Moorland Tourist Office** (☎01433-670207; www.peakdistrict.gov.uk; Fieldhead; ⏱9.30am-5pm Apr-Sep) has maps and displays on the moors.

Getting There & Away

Trains run from Edale to Manchester (£11, every hour, 45 minutes) and Sheffield (£7.10, every two hours, 40 minutes).

Eyam

POP 926

Quaint little Eyam (ee-em), a former lead-mining village, has a poignant history. In 1665 the town was infected by the dreaded Black Death plague, carried here by fleas on a consignment of cloth from London, and the village rector, William Mompesson, convinced villagers to quarantine themselves. Some 270 of the village's 800 inhabitants succumbed, while surrounding villages remained relatively unscathed. Today, Eyam's sloping streets of old cottages backed by rows of green hills are delightful to wander.

Sights & Activities

Eyam Parish Church CHURCH
(www.eyam-church.org; Church St; ⏱9am-6pm Easter-Sep, to 4pm Oct-Easter) Many victims of the village's 1665 Black Death plague outbreak were buried at Eyam's church. You can view stained-glass panels and moving displays telling the story of the outbreak. The churchyard contains a Celtic cross carved in the 8th century.

Eyam Museum MUSEUM
(www.eyam.museum.org.uk; Hawkhill Rd; adult/child £2.50/2; ⏱10am-4.30pm Tue-Sun Easter-Oct) Vivid displays on the Eyam plague are the centrepiece of the engaging town museum, alongside exhibits on the village's history of lead-mining and silk-weaving.

Sleeping

Crown Cottage B&B ££
(☎01433-630858; http://crown-cottage.co.uk; Main Rd; s/d from £50/70; P 📶) Opposite the post office, this walker- and cyclist-friendly stone house full of pottery ornaments is crammed to the rafters most weekends, when there's a minimum two-night stay. There's secure bike storage and a piano for guests to play.

Miner's Arms PUB ££
(☎01433-630853; www.theminersarmseyam.co.uk; Water Lane; s/d £45/70; 📶) Although its age isn't immediately obvious, this traditional village inn was built shortly before the Black Death hit Eyam in 1665. Inside you'll find beamed ceilings, affable staff, a blazing open fireplace, comfy en suite rooms and good-value pub food (mains £8 to £12.50).

Getting There & Away

Bus services include the following:

Bakewell Bus 275; £3.60, 20 minutes, three per day Monday to Saturday

Buxton Buses 65 and 66; £3.60, 40 minutes, five per day Monday to Saturday, three Sunday

Sheffield Bus 65; £5.70, 40 minutes, five per day Monday to Saturday, three Sunday

Bakewell & Around

POP 3950

The second-largest town in the Peak District, charming Bakewell is a great base for exploring the limestone dales of the White Peak. Filled with storybook stone buildings, the town is ringed by famous walking trails

WORTH A TRIP

CHATSWORTH HOUSE

Known as the 'Palace of the Peak', the vast edifice **Chatsworth House** (☎01246-565300; www.chatsworth.org; house & gardens adult/child £20/12, gardens only £12/7, playground £6, park admission free; ⊙10.30am-5pm late May–early Sep, shorter hours mid-Mar–late May & early Sep–early Jan), 3 miles northeast of Bakewell, has been occupied by the earls and dukes of Devonshire for centuries. Inside, the lavish apartments and mural-painted staterooms are packed with priceless paintings and period furniture. The house sits in 25 sq miles of grounds and ornamental gardens, some landscaped by Lancelot 'Capability' Brown. Kids will love the farmyard adventure playground.

From Bakewell, take bus 218 (£2.40, 15 minutes, half-hourly).

and stately homes, but it's probably best known for its famous Bakewell Pudding, a pastry shell filled with jam and frangipane invented here in 1820.

Sights

All Saints Church CHURCH

(www.bakewellchurch.co.uk; South Church St; £2 donation requested; ⊙9am-5pm Apr-Oct, to 4pm Nov-Mar) Up on the hill above Rutland Sq, All Saints Church is packed with ancient features, including a 14th-century font, a pair of Norman arches, some fine heraldic tombs, and a collection of crude stone gravestones and crosses dating from the 12th century.

Old House Museum MUSEUM

(www.oldhousemuseum.org.uk; Cunningham Pl; adult/child £4/2; ⊙11am-4pm) Set in a time-worn stone house near All Saints Church, the Old House Museum explores local history. Check out the Tudor loo and the displays on wattle and daub, a traditional technique for building walls using woven twigs and cow dung.

Thornbridge Brewery BREWERY

(☎01629-815999; www.thornbridgebrewery.com; Buxton Rd; tours adult/child £7.50/3; ⊙tours 3pm Wed & Fri, shop 9am-4.30pm Mon-Fri, 10am-2pm last Sun of month) Vibrant brews from this riverside brewery include a fruity strawberry-blonde ale, I Love You Will You Marry Me; a Rhubarbe De Saison; Bamberg smoked-bock beer; and Vienna-style lager Kill Your Darlings; as well as collaborations with international independents. Tours lasting 1½ hours take you behind the scenes and include tastings in Thornbridge glasses, which you get to keep afterwards. Under-fives aren't permitted on tours. It's half a mile from the centre on the northwestern edge of town.

Haddon Hall HISTORIC SITE

(www.haddonhall.co.uk; Haddon Rd; adult/child £13.50/7; ⊙10.30am-5pm daily May-Sep, Sat-Mon Apr & Oct, to 4pm early–mid Dec) With stone turrets, time-worn timbers and walled gardens, Haddon Hall, 2 miles south of Bakewell on the A6, looks exactly like a medieval manor house should. Founded in the 12th century, it was expanded and remodelled throughout medieval times. The 'modernisation' stopped when the house was abandoned in the 18th century. Take the Highpeak bus from Bakewell (£2.30, 10 minutes, hourly) or walk along the footpath through the fields, mostly on the east side of the river.

Activities

Walking and cycling are, of course, the main activities in the area. The scenic **Monsal Trail** follows the path of a disused railway line from Combs Viaduct on the outskirts of Bakewell to Topley Pike in Wye Dale (about 3 miles east of Buxton) including a number of reopened old railway tunnels, covering 8.5 miles in all.

For a rewarding shorter walk, follow the Monsal Trail for 3 miles to the dramatic viewpoint at **Monsal Head**, where you can pause for refreshment at the **Monsal Head Hotel** (☎01629-640250; www.monsalhead.com; Monsal Trail; mains £11.50-16; ⊙kitchen noon-8pm Sun-Thu, to 9pm Fri & Sat; P 🐾), which serves real ales and excellent Modern British cuisine. With more time to kill, continue to **Miller's Dale**, where viaducts give a spectacular vista across the steep-sided valley. The tourist offices at Bakewell and Buxton have full details.

Other walking routes go to the stately homes Haddon Hall and Chatsworth House.

Sleeping

Melbourne House & Easthorpe B&B ££
(☎01629-815357; www.bakewell-accommodation.co.uk; Buxton Rd; d from £70; P) Occupying a picturesque, creeper-covered building (Melbourne House) dating back more than three centuries and a new annex (Easthorpe), with uncluttered, neutral-toned rooms, this inviting B&B is handily situated on the main road leading to Buxton.

Rutland Arms Hotel HOTEL £££
(☎01629-812812; www.rutlandarmsbakewell.co.uk; The Square; s £64-76, d £92-165; P) Jane Austen is said to have stayed in room 2 of this aristocratic, recently refurbished stone coaching inn while working on *Pride and Prejudice*. The more expensive of its 33 rooms have lots of Victorian flourishes.

Eating & Drinking

Bakewell's streets are lined with sweet tearooms and bakeries selling Bakewell Pudding.

★**Chatsworth Estate Farm Shop Cafe** CAFE, DELI £
(www.chatsworth.org; Pilsley; dishes £4.50-10; cafe & shop 9am-5pm Mon-Sat, 10am-5pm Sun;) One of the finest places to eat in the Peak District, this bucolic cafe serves hearty breakfasts (eggs Benedict with Chatsworth-cured bacon or salmon; strawberry-and-honey Chatsworth yoghurt with muesli) until 11.30am before turning out lunches (steak-and-kidney suet pudding; traditional roasts) until 3pm, and an afternoon menu. Over half the products at its adjacent farm shop are produced on the estate.

Old Original Bakewell Pudding Shop BAKERY, TEAROOM £
(www.bakewellpuddingshop.co.uk; The Square; dishes £7-12; 8.30am-6pm Mon-Sat, 9am-6pm Sun) One of those that claims to have invented the Bakewell Pudding, this place has a lovely 1st-floor tearoom with exposed beams. It serves light meals and afternoon teas on tiered trays.

Piedaniel's FRENCH ££
(☎01629-812687; www.piedaniels-restaurant.com; Bath St; mains lunch £12, dinner £15-25; noon-2pm & 7-9pm Tue-Sat) Chefs Eric and Christiana Piedaniel's Modern French cuisine is the toast of the in-town restaurants. A white-washed dining room is the exquisite setting for the likes of prawn and fennel bisque with *quenelles* (feather-light flour, egg and cream dumplings) followed by lobster and salmon thermidor or lemon sole stuffed with scallop mousse.

★**Fischer's Baslow Hall** GASTRONOMY £££
(☎01246-583259; www.fischers-baslowhall.co.uk; 259 Calver Rd, Baslow; 2-/3-/7-course lunch menus £20/27/60, 2-/3-/9-course dinner menus £55/72/80; noon-2pm & 7-9pm;) Some 4 miles northeast of Bakewell, this 1907-built manor house has a magnificent Michelin-starred dining room showcasing British produce (Derbyshire lamb, Yorkshire game, Cornish crab...) along with vegetables from its kitchen garden.

Six sumptuous floral bedrooms are in the main house, with another five in the adjacent garden house (doubles from £200); weekend-night stays (from £344) include a three-course meal.

Castle Inn PUB
(☎01629-812103; www.oldenglishinns.co.uk; Bridge St; 8am-10pm Sun-Thu, to midnight Fri & Sat;) The ivy-draped Castle Inn is one of the better pubs in Bakewell, with four centuries of practice in rejuvenating hamstrung hikers (and their dogs – pets are warmly welcomed here). Gourmet burgers are a menu highlight (mains from £8 to £19). It also has four comfortable rooms (double/family from £85/95). Enter via Castle St.

Information

Bakewell's **tourist office** (☎01629-816558; www.visitpeakdistrict.com; Bridge St; 9.30am-5pm Apr-Oct, 10.30am-4.30pm Nov-Mar) is inside the old Market Hall; helpful staff can book accommodation.

Getting There & Away

Bakewell lies on the Highpeak bus route. Buses run hourly to Buxton (£3.30, 30 minutes), Derby (£4.80, 1¼ hours) and Matlock Bath (£3.30, 30 minutes). Five services a day continue to Manchester (£6, 1¾ hours).

Other services:

Castleton Bus 173; £3.10, 50 minutes, four per day

Chesterfield Bus 170; £3.30, 50 minutes, hourly

Yorkshire

Includes ➡

Best Places to Eat

➡ Pipe and Glass Inn (p544)

➡ Norse (p509)

➡ Hare Inn (p516)

➡ Crafthouse (p533)

➡ Cochon Aveugle (p504)

Best Places to Sleep

➡ Millgate House (p529)

➡ Windmill (p511)

➡ West Park (p508)

➡ Art Hostel (p532)

Why Go?

With a population as big as Scotland's and an area half the size of Belgium, Yorkshire is almost a country in itself. It has its own flag, its own dialect and its own celebration, Yorkshire Day (1 August). While local folk are proud to be English, they're even prouder to be natives of 'God's Own County'.

What makes Yorkshire so special? First, there's the landscape – with its brooding moors and green dales rolling down to a dramatic coastline, Yorkshire has some of Britain's finest scenery. Second, there's the sheer breadth of history – every facet of the British experience is represented here, from Roman times to the 21st century.

But Yorkshire's greatest appeal lies in its people. Industrious and opinionated, they have a wry wit and shrewd friendliness. Stay here for a while and you'll come away believing, like the locals, that God is indeed a Yorkshirewoman.

When to Go

➡ The weeklong Jorvik Festival in February sees York taken over by a Viking invasion.

➡ Spring brings drifts of yellow daffodils to brighten the roadsides in the Dales and North York Moors; the Three Peaks Race takes place in Horton-in-Ribblesdale.

➡ Agriculture is celebrated at the Great Yorkshire Show in Harrogate in July. At the same time of year Yorkshire's coastal sea cliffs become a frenzy of nesting seabirds.

➡ September is the ideal time for hiking in the Yorkshire Dales; the Walking Festival in Richmond also takes place in this month. York goes all gourmet with its annual 10-day food festival, while Harrogate gets green-fingered during its Autumn Flower Show.

Yorkshire Highlights

❶ **York** (p496) Exploring the medieval streets of the city and its awe-inspiring cathedral.

❷ **Yorkshire Dales National Park** (p522) Getting off the beaten track and exploring the lesser-known corners.

❸ **Fountains Abbey** (p514) Wandering among the atmospheric medieval ruins.

❹ **Scarborough** (p510) Being beside the seaside, and enjoying this town's traditional bucket-and-spade atmosphere.

❺ **North Yorkshire Moors Railway** (p517) Riding on one of England's most scenic train lines.

❻ **Whitby** (p518) Sitting on the pier and tucking into the world's best fish and chips.

❼ **Castle Howard** (p506) Reliving the story of *Brideshead Revisited* amid the aristocratic splendour.

❽ **Malham Cove** (p525) Pulling on your hiking boots and tackling the steep paths around this scenic cove.

❾ **National Coal Mining Museum for England** (p537) Discovering mining's dark side.

❿ **National Media Museum** (p535) Enjoying the high-tech, hands-on exhibits.

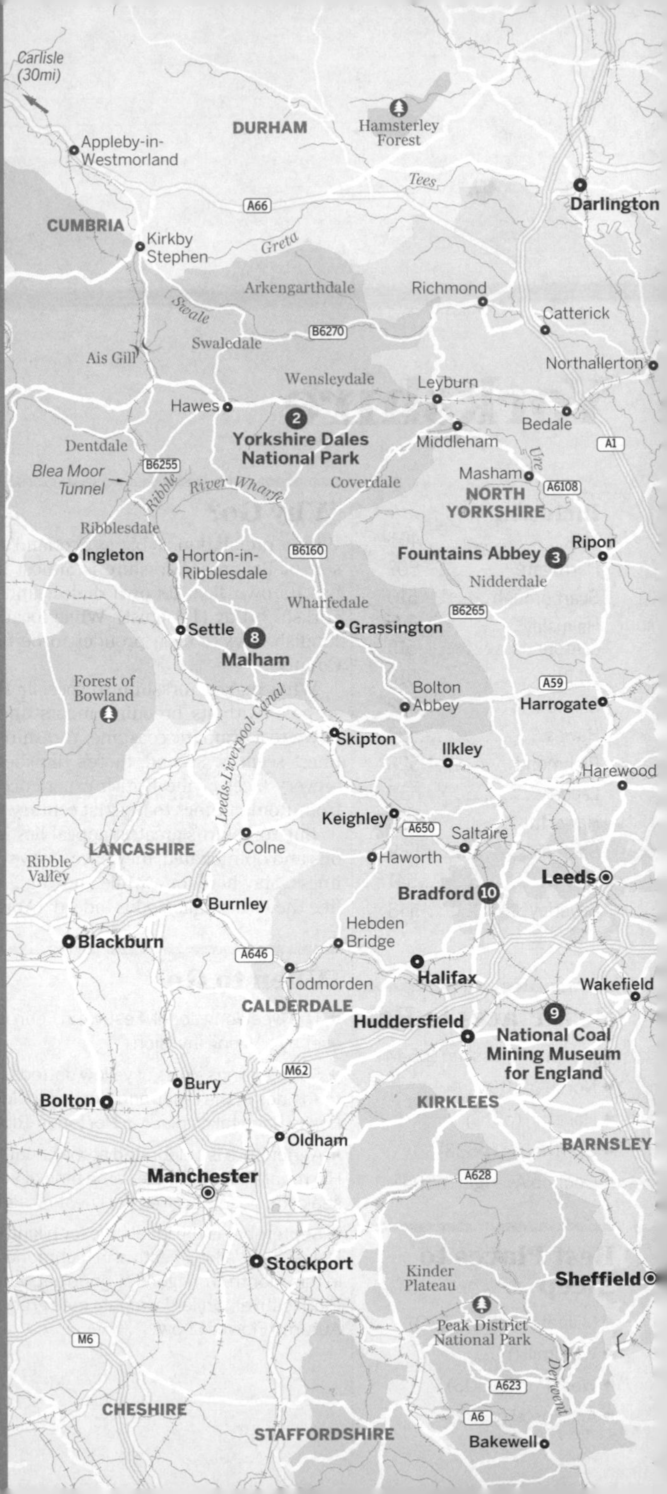

0 20 km
0 10 miles
Billingham
Middlesbrough
Stockton-on-Tees
A174
A171
Whitby
6
Stokesley
Danby
Esk
Hawsker
NORTH SEA
Grosmont
Robin Hood's Bay
Leven
A171
A19
North York Moors National Park
5
North Yorkshire Moors Railway
The Hambleton Hills
Seph
Hutton-le-Hole
Lastingham
4
Scarborough
Helmsley
Pickering
Thirsk
Seven
Derwent
Hertford
Filey
Bempton Cliffs Nature Reserve
Rye
A19
Cleveland Hills
Malton
Flamborough Head
Castle Howard
7
Boroughbridge
B1363
Kirkham Priory
Bridlington
A64
Great Driffield
A166
A59
1
York
Hull
Wetherby
A1079
EAST RIDING OF YORKSHIRE
Hornsea
South Dalton
A1
A19
Beverley
A164
Selby
Barlby
Hull
Hull Ferry Terminal
Monk Fryston
Howden
Ouse
To Rotterdam & Zeebrugge
Humber
Patrington
Trent
Easington
NORTH LINCOLNSHIRE
Kilnsea
A15
High Ackworth
Thorne
Grimsby
Spurn Head
Scunthorpe
Cleethorpes
Doncaster
NORTHEAST LINCOLNSHIRE
A15
Rotherham
Gainsborough
Market Rasen
Worksop
LINCOLNSHIRE
A158
NOTTINGHAMSHIRE
A57
esterfield
Lincoln
DERBYSHIRE

History

As you drive through Yorkshire on the main A1 road, you're following in the footsteps of the Roman legions who conquered northern Britain in the 1st century AD. In fact, many Yorkshire towns – including York, Catterick and Malton – were founded by the Romans, and many modern roads (including the A1, A59, A166 and A1079) follow the alignment of Roman roads.

When the Romans departed in the 5th century, native Britons battled for supremacy with invading Teutonic tribe the Angles and, for a while, Yorkshire was part of the Kingdom of Northumbria. In the 9th century the Vikings arrived and conquered most of northern Britain, an area that became known as the Danelaw. They divided the territory that is now Yorkshire into *thridings* (thirds), which met at Jorvik (York), their thriving commercial capital.

In 1066 Yorkshire was the scene of a pivotal showdown in the struggle for the English crown, when the Anglo-Saxon king, Harold II, rode north to defeat the forces of the Norwegian king, Harold Hardrada, in the Battle of Stamford Bridge, before returning south for his appointment with William the Conqueror – and a fatal arrow – in the Battle of Hastings.

The inhabitants of northern England did not take the subsequent Norman invasion lying down. In order to subdue them, the Norman nobles built a chain of formidable castles throughout Yorkshire, including those at York, Richmond, Scarborough, Pickering and Helmsley. The Norman land grab formed the basis of the great estates that supported England's medieval aristocrats.

By the 15th century, the duchies of York and Lancaster had become so wealthy and powerful that they ended up battling for the English throne in the Wars of the Roses (1455–87). The dissolution of the monasteries by Henry VIII from 1536 to 1540 saw the wealth of the great abbeys of Rievaulx, Fountains and Whitby fall into the hands of noble families, and Yorkshire quietly prospered for 200 years, with fertile farms in the north and the Sheffield cutlery business in the south, until the big bang of the Industrial Revolution transformed the landscape.

South Yorkshire became a centre of coal mining and steel-making while West Yorkshire nurtured a massive textile industry, and the cities of Leeds, Bradford, Sheffield and Rotherham flourished. By the late 20th century another revolution was taking place. The heavy industries had died out, and the cities of Yorkshire were reinventing themselves as shiny, high-tech centres of finance, higher education and tourism.

Activities

Yorkshire's varied landscape of wild hills, tranquil valleys, high moors and spectacular coastline offers plenty of opportunities for outdoor activities. See www.outdooryorkshire.com for more details.

Cycling

Yorkshire's hosting of the start of the 2014 Tour de France saw a huge upsurge in interest in cycling, and resulted in the establishment of the **Tour de Yorkshire** (www.letour.yorkshire.com) annual cycle race from 2015. The county has a vast network of country lanes that are perfect for road cyclists, although the national parks also attract lots of motorists so even minor roads can be busy at weekends.

North York Moors MOUNTAIN BIKING
(www.mtb-routes.co.uk/northyorkmoors) Off-road bikers can avail themselves of the network of bridleways, former railways and disused mining tracks now converted for two-wheel use. Dalby Forest (www.forestry.gov.uk/dalbyforest), near Pickering, sports purpose-built mountain-biking trails of all grades from green to black, and there are newly waymarked trails at the Sutton Bank visitor centre.

Moor to Sea Cycle Route CYCLING
(www.moortoseacycle.net) A network of routes between Pickering, Danby and the coast includes a 20-mile traffic-free route that follows a disused railway line between Whitby and Scarborough.

White Rose Cycle Route CYCLING
(www.sustrans.org.uk; NCN Rte 65) A 131-mile road cruise from Middlesborough to York and on to Hull and Hornsea, via the dramatic western scarp of the North York Moors and the rolling Yorkshire Wolds, with a traffic-free section on the old railway between Selby and York.

Yorkshire Dales Cycleway CYCLING, MOUNTAIN BIKING
(www.cyclethedales.org.uk) An exhilarating 130-mile loop, taking in the best of the national park; the website also details the route followed by Stage 1 of the 2014 Tour de France. There's lots of scope for off-road riding, with about 500 miles of bridleways and trails – for inspiration, go to www.mtbthedales.org.uk.

Walking

For shorter walks and rambles, the best area is the **Yorkshire Dales**, with a great selection of walks through scenic valleys or over wild hilltops, with a few higher summits thrown in for good measure. The East Riding's **Yorkshire Wolds** hold hidden delights, while the quiet valleys and dramatic coast of the **North York Moors** also offer many opportunities.

Cleveland Way WALKING
(www.nationaltrail.co.uk/clevelandway) A venerable moor-and-coast classic that circles the North York Moors National Park on its 109-mile, nine-day route from Helmsley to Filey.

Coast to Coast Walk WALKING
(www.wainwright.org.uk/coasttocoast.html) One of England's most popular walks: 190 miles across northern England from the Lake District through the Yorkshire Dales and North York Moors National Parks. The Yorkshire section takes a week to 10 days and offers some of the finest walking of its kind in England.

Dales Way WALKING
(www.dalesway.org.uk) A charming and not-too-strenuous 80-mile amble from the Yorkshire Dales to the Lake District, following the River Wharfe through the heart of the Dales and finishing at Bowness-on-Windermere.

Pennine Way WALKING
(www.nationaltrail.co.uk/pennineway) The Yorkshire section of England's most famous walk runs for more than 100 miles via Hebden Bridge, Malham, Horton-in-Ribblesdale and Hawes, passing near Haworth and Skipton.

White Rose Way WALKING
(www.whiteroseway.co.uk) A long-distance trail covering the 104 miles from Leeds' city centre to Scarborough, taking in remote and picturesque Yorkshire villages along the way.

Wolds Way WALKING
(www.nationaltrail.co.uk/yorkshirewoldsway) A beautiful but oft-overlooked walk that winds through the most scenic part of Yorkshire's East Riding district.

ℹ Information

The **Yorkshire Tourist Board** (www.yorkshire.com) has plenty of general leaflets and brochures, for postal and email enquiries only. For more detailed information, contact local tourist offices.

ℹ Getting There & Around

The major north–south road transport routes – the M1 and A1 motorways – run through the middle of Yorkshire, serving the key cities of Sheffield, Leeds and York. If you're arriving by sea from northern Europe, Hull in the East Riding district is the region's main port.

Traveline Yorkshire (☎ 0871 200 2233; www.yorkshiretravel.net) provides public-transport information for all of Yorkshire.

BUS

Long-distance coaches operated by **National Express** (☎ 08717 818181; www.nationalexpress.com) serve most cities and large towns in Yorkshire from London, the south of England, the Midlands and Scotland.

Bus transport around Yorkshire is frequent and efficient, especially between major towns. Services are more sporadic in the national parks, but are still adequate for reaching most places, particularly in summer months (June to September).

TRAIN

The main rail line between London and Edinburgh runs through Yorkshire, with at least 10 trains calling each day at York and Doncaster, where you can change trains for other Yorkshire destinations. There are also direct links to northern cities such as Manchester and Newcastle. For timetable information, contact **National Rail Enquiries** (☎ 08457 48 49 50; www.nationalrail.co.uk). There are direct services between the major towns and cities of Yorkshire.

NORTH YORKSHIRE

This, the largest of Yorkshire's four counties – and the largest county in England – is also the most beautiful. Unlike the rest of northern England, it has survived almost unscathed by the Industrial Revolution. Since the Middle Ages, North Yorkshire has been almost exclusively about sheep and the woolly wealth they produce.

Rather than closed-down factories, mills and mines, the human-made monuments dotting the landscape in these parts are of the stately variety – the great houses and wealthy abbeys that sit, ruined or restored, as a reminder that there was plenty of money to be made off the sheep's back.

All the same, North Yorkshire's biggest attraction is an urban one. While the genteel spa town of Harrogate and the bright and breezy seaside resorts of Scarborough and Whitby have many fans, nothing compares to the unparalleled splendour of York, England's most-visited city outside London.

York

POP 198,000

Nowhere in northern England says 'medieval' quite like York, a city of extraordinary cultural and historical wealth that has lost little of its pre-industrial lustre. A magnificent circuit of 13th-century walls encloses a medieval spider's web of narrow streets. At its heart lies the immense, awe-inspiring York Minster, one of the most beautiful Gothic cathedrals in the world. York's long history and rich heritage is woven into virtually every brick and beam, and the modern, tourist-oriented city – with its myriad museums, restaurants, cafes and traditional pubs – is a carefully maintained heir to that heritage.

Try to avoid the inevitable confusion by remembering that around these parts, *gate* means street and *bar* means gate.

History

In AD 71 the Romans built a garrison called Eboracum, which in time became a large fort with a civilian settlement around it. Hadrian used it as the base for his northern campaign, while Constantine the Great was proclaimed emperor here in AD 306. When the Roman Empire collapsed, the town was taken by the Anglo-Saxons, who renamed it Eoforwic and made it the capital of the independent kingdom of Northumbria.

In 625 a Roman priest, Paulinus, arrived and converted King Edwin and his nobles to Christianity; two years later they built the first wooden church here. For most of the next century, the city was a major centre of learning, attracting students from all over Europe. In 866 the next wave of invaders arrived, this time the Vikings, who gave the town a more tongue-friendly name, Jorvik. It was their capital for the next 100 years, and during that time they turned the city into an important trading port.

King Eadred of Wessex drove out the last Viking ruler in 954 and reunited Danelaw with the south, but trouble quickly followed. In 1066 King Harold II fended off a Norwegian invasion at Stamford Bridge, east of York, but was defeated by William the Conqueror a few months later in the Battle of Hastings.

After William's two wooden castles were captured by an Anglo-Scandinavian army, he torched the entire city (and Durham) and the surrounding countryside. The Normans then set about rebuilding it, adding a grand new minster. Over the next 300 years York (a contraction of the Viking name Jorvik) prospered through royal patronage, textiles, trade and the Church.

Throughout the 18th century the city was a fashionable social centre dominated by the aristocracy, who were drawn by its culture and new racecourse. When the railway arrived in 1839, thousands of people were employed in new industries that sprang up around it, such as confectionery (the Terry's and Rowntree's brands were founded here). These industries went into decline in the latter half of the 20th century, but by then a new invader was asking for directions at the city gates, armed only with a guidebook.

Sights

★York Minster CATHEDRAL

(www.yorkminster.org; Deangate; adult/child £10/free, incl tower £15/5; ⌚9am-5.30pm Mon-Sat, 12.45-5pm Sun, last admission 30min before closing) The remarkable York Minster is the largest medieval cathedral in all of northern Europe, and one of the world's most beautiful Gothic buildings. Seat of the archbishop of York, primate of England, it is second in importance only to Canterbury, seat of the primate of *all* England – the separate titles were created to settle a debate over the true centre of the English church. If this is the only cathedral you visit in England, you'll still walk away satisfied.

The first church on this site was a wooden chapel built for the baptism of King Edwin of Northumbria on Easter Day 627, whose location is marked in the crypt. It was replaced with a stone church built on the site of a Roman basilica, parts of which can be seen in the foundations. The first Norman minster was built in the 11th century and, again, you can see surviving fragments in the foundations and crypt.

The present minster, built mainly between 1220 and 1480, manages to encompass all the major stages of Gothic architectural development. The transepts (1220–55) were built in Early English style; the octagonal chapter house (1260–90) and nave (1291–1340) in the Decorated style; and the west towers, west front and central (or lantern) tower (1470–72) in Perpendicular style.

➡ Nave

Entrance to the minster is via the west door, which leads into the unusually tall and wide nave. The aisles (to the sides) are roofed in stone, in contrast to the central roof, which is wood painted to look like stone. On both sides of the nave are painted stone shields of the nobles who met with Edward II at a parliament in York. Also note the dragon's head projecting from the gallery – it's a crane believed to have been used to lift a font cover. There are several fine windows dating from the early 14th century, but the most impressive is the **Great West Window** (1338) above the entrance, with its beautiful heart-shaped stone tracery.

➡ Transepts & Chapter House

The south transept was badly damaged by fire in 1984, but has been fully restored. It is dominated by the exquisite **Rose Window** commemorating the union of the royal houses of Lancaster and York, through the marriage of Henry VII and Elizabeth of York, which ended the Wars of the Roses and began the Tudor dynasty

Opposite, in the north transept, is the magnificent **Five Sisters Window**, with five lancets over 15m high. This is the minster's oldest complete window; most of its tangle of coloured glass dates from around 1250. Just beyond it to the right is the 13th-century **chapter house**, a fine example of the Decorated style. Sinuous and intricately carved stonework – there are more than 200 expressive carved heads and figures – surrounds an airy, uninterrupted space.

➡ Choir Screen & East Window

Separating the choir from the nave is a superb 15th-century choir screen with 15 statues depicting the kings of England from William I to Henry VI. Beyond the screen and the carved wooden stalls of the choir is the lady chapel and, behind it, the high altar, which is dominated by the huge **Great East Window** (1405). At 23.7m by 9.4m – roughly the size of a tennis court – it is the world's largest medieval stained-glass window and the cathedral's single most important treasure. Needless to say, its epic size matches the epic theme depicted within: the beginning and end of the world as described in Genesis and the Book of Revelations.

➡ Undercroft

A set of stairs in the south transept leads down to the undercroft (open 10am to 5pm Monday to Saturday, 1pm to 5pm Sunday), the very bowels of the building. In 1967 the minster foundations were shored up when the central tower threatened to collapse; while engineers worked frantically to save the building, archaeologists uncovered Roman and Norman remains that attest to the site's ancient history – one of the most extraordinary finds was a Roman culvert, still carrying water to the Ouse. An interactive exhibition here, **York Minster Revealed**, leads visitors through 2000 years of history on the site of the cathedral. The nearby **treasury** houses 11th-century artefacts including relics from the graves of medieval archbishops.

➡ Crypt

The crypt, entered from the choir close to the altar, contains fragments from the Norman cathedral, including the font showing King Edwin's baptism, which also marks the site of the original wooden chapel. Look out for the **Doomstone**, a 12th-century carved stone showing a scene from the Last Judgement with demons casting doomed souls into Hell.

➡ Tower

At the heart of York's cathedral is the massive tower, which is well worth climbing for the unparalleled views of York. You'll have to tackle a fairly claustrophobic climb of 275 steps and, most probably, a queue of people with cameras in hand. Access to the tower is from the south transept.

★ National Railway Museum MUSEUM

(www.nrm.org.uk; Leeman Rd; ⏲10am-6pm; P 🚻) FREE While many railway museums are the sole preserve of lone men in anoraks comparing dog-eared notebooks and getting high on the smell of machine oil, coal smoke and nostalgia, this place is different. York's National Railway Museum – the biggest in the world, with more than 100 locomotives – is so well presented and crammed with fascinating stuff that it's interesting even to folk whose eyes don't mist over at the thought of a 4-6-2 A1 Pacific class thundering into a tunnel.

Highlights for the trainspotters among us include a replica of George Stephenson's **Rocket** (1829), the world's first 'modern' steam locomotive; the sleek and streamlined **Mallard**, which set the world speed record for a steam locomotive in 1938 (126mph); a

THE YORK PASS

If you plan on visiting a number of sights, you can save yourself some money by using a **YorkPass** (www.yorkpass.com). It gives you free access to more than 30 pay-to-visit sights in and around York, including York Minster, Jorvik and Castle Howard. You can buy it at York tourist office or online; prices for one/two/three days are adult £38/50/60, child £20/26/30.

York

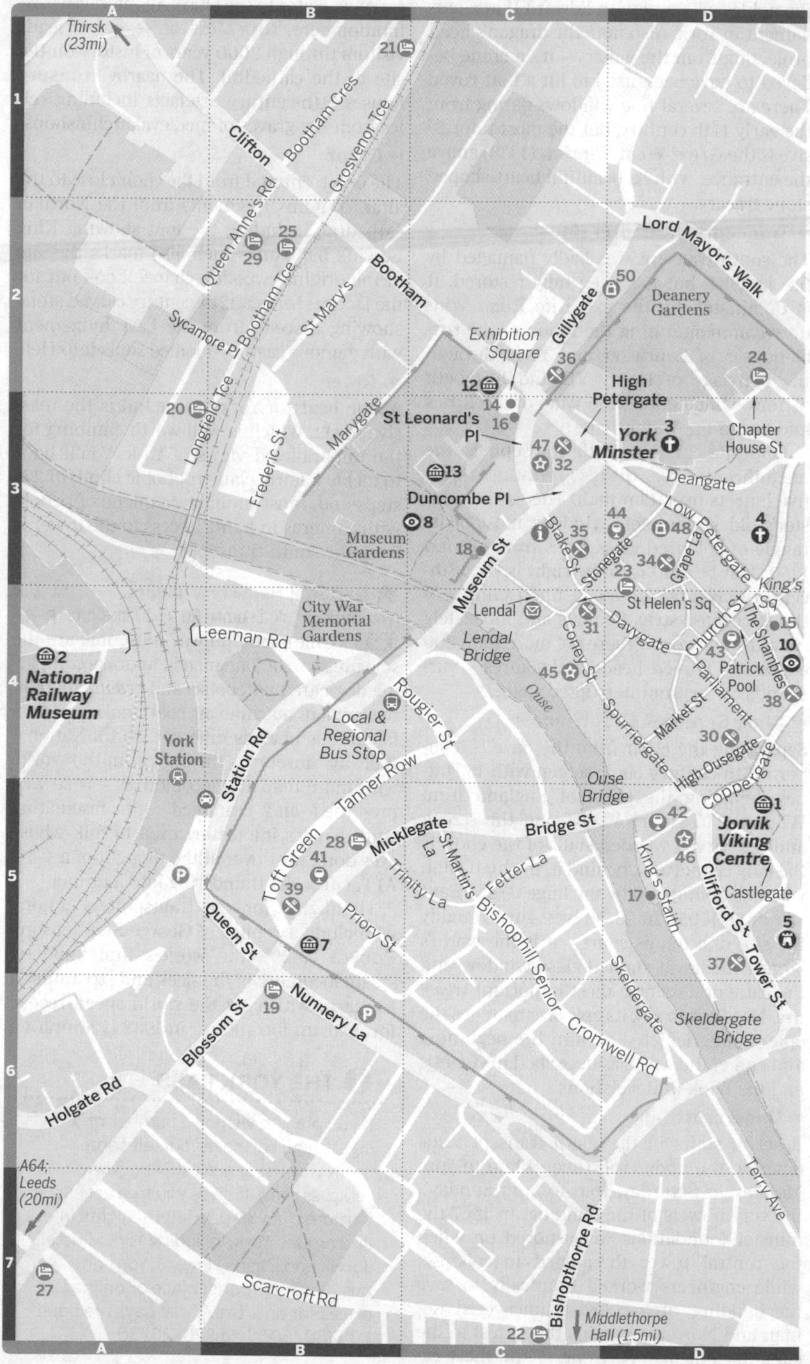

A
B
C
D
1
2
3
4
5
6
7
Thirsk (23mi)
21
Clifton
Bootham Cres
Grosvenor Tce
Queen Anne's Rd
25
29
Bootham
Bootham Tce
St Mary's
Sycamore Pl
Lord Mayor's Walk
Deanery Gardens
50
Gillygate
Exhibition Square
36
24
12
14
16
St Leonard's Pl
High Petergate
York Minster
3
Chapter House St
20
Longfield Tce
Frederic St
Marygate
47
32
13
Duncombe Pl
Deangate
8
Museum Gardens
44
48
4
Low Petergate
Grape La
35
Blake St
Stonegate
34
18
Museum St
23
King's Sq
St Helen's Sq
City War Memorial Gardens
Lendal
31
Davygate
Church St
The Shambles
15
10
Leeman Rd
Lendal Bridge
43
Patrick Pool
2
National Railway Museum
Coney St
45
Ouse
Parliament
38
Rougier St
Local & Regional Bus Stop
Spurriergate
Market St
York Station
Station Rd
Tanner Row
30
High Ousegate
Ouse Bridge
Coppergate
1
Jorvik Viking Centre
42
Bridge St
Micklegate
28
St Martin's La
46
Toft Green
41
Trinity La
Fetter La
King's Staith
Castlegate
Clifford St
39
17
Bishophill Senior
Queen St
Priory St
5
7
Tower St
37
Skeldergate
19
Blossom St
Nunnery La
Skeldergate Bridge
Cromwell Rd
Holgate Rd
A64; Leeds (20mi)
Terry Ave
Bishopthorpe Rd
27
Scarcroft Rd
22
Middlethorpe Hall (1.5mi)

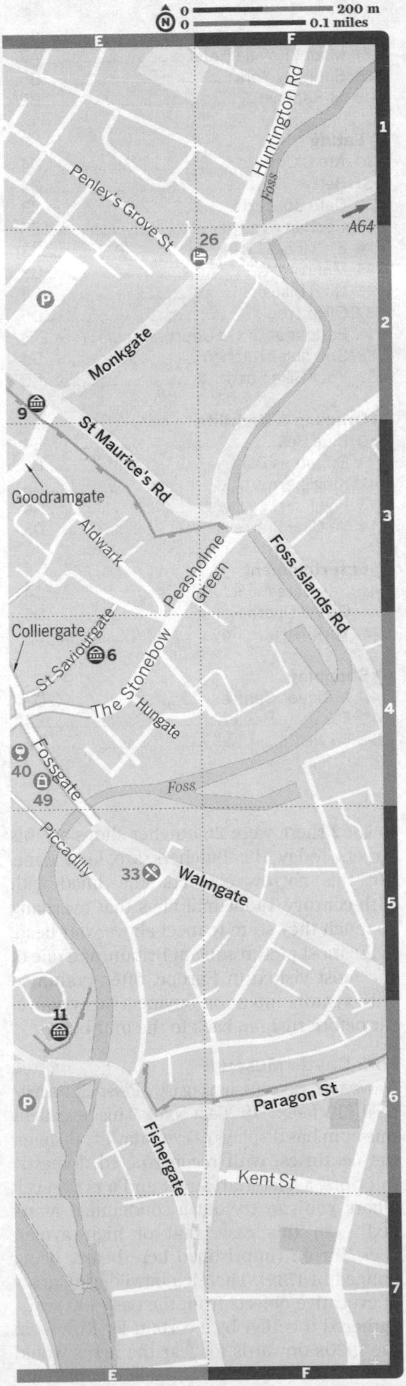

1960s Japanese **Shinkansen bullet train**; and the world-famous **Flying Scotsman**, the first steam engine to break the 100mph barrier (now restored to full working order). There's also a massive 4-6-2 loco from 1949 that's been cut in half to demonstrate how it works (daily talk at 4pm).

Even if you're not a rail nerd, you'll enjoy looking through the gleaming, silk-lined carriages of the **royal trains** used by Queens Mary, Adelaide and Victoria and King Edward VII, or having a *Brief Encounter* moment over tea and scones at the museum's station platform cafe. Allow at least two hours to do it all justice.

The museum is about 400m west of the train station and if you don't fancy walking you can ride the roadtrain (adult/child £2/1, April to October) that runs between the minster and museum every 30 minutes from 11am to 4pm.

★ Jorvik Viking Centre MUSEUM

(www.jorvik-viking-centre.co.uk; Coppergate; adult/child £10.25/7.25; ⌚10am-5pm Apr-Oct, to 4pm Nov-Mar) Interactive multimedia exhibits aimed at bringing history to life often achieve exactly the opposite, but the much-hyped Jorvik manages to pull it off with aplomb. Thoroughly restored and reimagined following flood damage in 2015, it's a smells-and-all reconstruction of the Viking settlement unearthed here during excavations in the late 1970s, experienced via a 'time-car' monorail that transports you through 9th-century Jorvik (the Viking name for York). You can reduce time waiting in the queue by booking your tickets online.

While some of the 'you will now travel back in time' malarkey is a bit naff, it's all done with a sense of humour tied to historical authenticity that will give you a pretty good idea of what life must have been like in Viking-era York. In the museum exhibition at the end of the monorail, look out for the Lloyds Bank coprolite, a fossilised human stool that measures an eye-watering 9in long and half a pound in weight, and must be the only turd in the world to have its own Wikipedia entry.

Yorkshire Museum MUSEUM

(www.yorkshiremuseum.org.uk; Museum St; adult/child £7.50/free; ⌚10am-5pm) Most of York's Roman archaeology is hidden beneath the medieval city, so the superb displays in the Yorkshire Museum are invaluable if you want to get an idea of what Eboracum was

York

like. There are maps and models of Roman York, funerary monuments, mosaic floors and wall paintings, and a 4th-century bust of Emperor Constantine. Kids will enjoy the dinosaur exhibit, centred around giant ichthyosaur fossils from Yorkshire's Jurassic coast.

Museum Gardens GARDENS

(entrances on Museum St & Marygate; ⏲dawn-dusk) FREE In the grounds of the peaceful Museum Gardens, you can see the **Multangular Tower**, a part of the City Walls that was once the western tower of the Roman garrison's defensive ramparts. The Roman stonework at the base has been built over with 13th-century additions. On the other side of the gardens are the ruins of **St Mary's Abbey**, dating from 1270 to 1294. The ruined **Gatehall** was its main entrance, providing access from the abbey to the river.

The Shambles STREET

The Shambles takes its name from the Saxon word *shamel*, meaning 'slaughterhouse' – in 1862 there were 26 butcher shops on this street. Today the butchers are long gone, but this narrow cobbled lane, lined with 15th-century Tudor buildings that overhang so much they seem to meet above your head, is the most picturesque in Britain, and one of the most visited in Europe, often crammed with visitors intent on buying a tacky souvenir before rushing back to the tour bus.

York Castle Museum MUSEUM

(www.yorkcastlemuseum.org.uk; Tower St; adult/child £10/free; ⏲9.30am-5pm) This excellent museum has displays of everyday life through the centuries, with reconstructed domestic interiors, a Victorian street and a prison cell where you can try out a condemned man's bed – in this case, that of highwayman Dick Turpin (imprisoned here before being hanged in 1739). There's a bewildering array of evocative objects from the past 400 years, gathered together by a certain Dr Kirk from the 1920s onwards for fear the items would become obsolete and disappear completely.

Dig MUSEUM
(www.digyork.com; St Saviour's Church, St Saviourgate; adult/child £6.50/6; 10am-5pm, last admission 4pm;) Under the same management as Jorvik (p499), Dig cashes in on the popularity of archaeology programs on TV by giving you the chance to be an 'archaeological detective', unearthing the secrets of York's distant past as well as learning something of the archaeologist's world – what they do, how they do it and so on. Aimed mainly at kids, it's much more hands-on than Jorvik and a lot of its merit depends on how good – and entertaining – your guide is.

Clifford's Tower CASTLE
(EH; www.english-heritage.org.uk; Tower St; adult/child £5.20/3.10; 10am-6pm Apr-Sep, to 5pm Oct) There's precious little left of York Castle except for this evocative stone tower, a highly unusual four-lobed design built into the castle's keep after the original one was destroyed in 1190 during anti-Jewish riots. An angry mob forced 150 Jews to be locked inside the tower and the hapless victims took their own lives rather than be killed. There's not much to see inside, but the views over the city are excellent.

Church of the Holy Trinity CHURCH
(www.holytrinityyork.org; Goodramgate; 10am-5pm Tue-Sat May-Sep, to 4pm Oct-Apr) FREE Tucked away behind an inconspicuous gate and seemingly cut off from the rest of the town, the Church of the Holy Trinity is a fantastically atmospheric old building, having survived almost unchanged for the past 200 years (it has no electricity or running water). Inside are rare 17th- to 18th-century box pews, 15th-century stained glass and wonky walls that seem to have been built without plumb line or spirit level.

York City Art Gallery GALLERY
(www.yorkartgallery.org.uk; Exhibition Sq; adult/child £7.50/free; 10am-5pm Mon-Fri, to 6pm Sat, 11am-4pm Sun) After a major restoration, York Art Gallery reopened in 2015 with a new art garden and an exhibition dedicated to British ceramics (www.centreofceramicart.org.uk) – the **Wall of Pots** houses more than 1000 pieces dating from Roman times to the present day. As well as an impressive collection of Old Masters, there are works by LS Lowry, Picasso, Grayson Perry, David Hockney, and the controversial York artist William Etty who, in the 1820s, was the first major British painter to specialise in nudes.

Tours

Ghost Hunt of York WALKING
(www.ghosthunt.co.uk; adult/child £6/4; tours 7.30pm) The kids will just love this award-winning and highly entertaining 75-minute tour laced with authentic ghost stories. It begins at the top end of The Shambles, whatever the weather (it's never cancelled) and there's no need to book, just turn up and wait till you hear the handbell ringing…

Yorkwalk WALKING
(www.yorkwalk.co.uk; adult/child £6/5; tours 10.30am & 2.15pm Feb-Nov) Offers a series of two-hour walks on a range of themes, from the classics – Roman York, the snickelways (narrow alleys) and City Walls – to walks focused on chocolates and sweets, women in York, and the inevitable graveyard, coffin and plague tour. Walks depart from Museum Gardens Gate on Museum St; there's no need to book.

YorkBoat BOATING
(www.yorkboat.co.uk; King's Staith; adult/child from £8/4; tours 10.30am, noon, 1.30pm & 3pm Feb-Nov) Hour-long cruises on the River Ouse, departing from King's Staith and, 10 minutes later, Lendal Bridge. Special lunch, dinner and evening cruises are also offered.

York Citysightseeing BUS
(www.city-sightseeing.com; day ticket adult/child £13/5; 9am-5.30pm Easter-Nov) Hop-on, hop-off route with 20 stops, calling at all the main sights. Buses leave every 10 to 30 minutes from Exhibition Sq near York Minster.

Association of Voluntary Guides WALKING
(www.avgyork.co.uk; tours 10.15am year-round, 2.15pm Apr-Oct, 6.15pm Jun-Aug, 1.15pm Nov-Mar) FREE Free two-hour walking tours of the city, setting out from Exhibition Sq in front of York Art Gallery.

Festivals & Events

Jorvik Viking Festival CULTURAL
(www.jorvik-viking-festival.co.uk) For a week in mid-February, York is invaded by Vikings as part of this festival, which features battle re-enactments, themed walks, markets and other bits of Viking-related fun.

York Food Festival FOOD & DRINK
(www.yorkfoodfestival.com) For 10 days in September/October, discover all that's good to eat and drink in Yorkshire, with stalls, tastings, cookery demonstrations and more.

LOCAL KNOWLEDGE

YORK CITY WALLS

If the weather's good, don't miss the chance to walk York's **City Walls** (www.yorkwalls.org.uk), which follow the line of the original Roman walls and give a whole new perspective on the city. Allow 1½ to two hours for the full circuit of 4.5 miles or, if you're pushed for time, the short stretch from Bootham Bar to Monk Bar is worth doing for the views of the minster.

Start and finish in the Museum Gardens or at **Bootham Bar** (on the site of a Roman gate), where a multimedia exhibit provides some historical context, and travel clockwise. Highlights include **Monk Bar**, which is the best-preserved medieval gate and still has a working portcullis, and **Walmgate Bar**, England's only city gate with an intact barbican.

At Monk Bar you'll find the **Richard III Experience** (www.richardiiiexperience.com; Monk Bar; adult/child incl Henry VII Experience £5/3; ⏲10am-5pm Apr-Oct, to 4pm Nov-Mar), a museum which sets out the case of the murdered 'Princes in the Tower' and invites visitors to judge whether their uncle, Richard III, killed them. The **Henry VII Experience** (www.richardiiiexperience.com; Micklegate Bar; adult/child incl Richard III Experience £5/3; ⏲10am-4pm) at Micklegate Bar charts the history of the city walls and the reign of England's first Tudor king.

York Christmas CHRISTMAS

(www.visityork.org/christmas) Kicking off with St Nicholas Fayre market in late November, the run-up to Christmas is an extravaganza of street decorations, market stalls, carol singers and mulled wine.

Sleeping

Beds can be hard to find in midsummer, even with inflated high-season rates. The tourist office's accommodation booking service charges £4, which might be the best four quid you spend if you arrive without a reservation.

Prices get higher the closer you are to the city centre. However, there are plenty of decent B&Bs on the streets north and south of Bootham. Southwest of the centre, B&Bs are clustered around Scarcroft, Southlands and Bishopthorpe Rds.

★Fort HOSTEL £

(☎01904-620222; www.thefortyork.co.uk; 1 Little Stonegate; dm/d from £18/74; wifi) This boutique hostel showcases the work of young British designers, creating affordable accommodation with a dash of character and flair. There are six- and eight-bed dorms, along with six doubles, but don't expect a peaceful retreat – the central location is in the middle of York's nightlife, and there's a lively club downstairs (earplugs are provided!).

Safestay York HOSTEL £

(☎01904-627720; www.safestayyork.co.uk; 88-90 Micklegate; dm/tw from £18/75; @ wifi family) Housed in a Grade I Georgian building that was once home to the High Sheriff of Yorkshire, this is a large and well-equipped boutique hostel with cool decor and good facilities. It's popular with school groups and stag and hen parties – don't come here looking for peace and quiet!

York YHA HOSTEL £

(☎0845 371 9051; www.yha.org.uk; 42 Water End, Clifton; dm/q from £15/79; P @ wifi family) Originally the Rowntree (Quaker confectioners) mansion, this handsome Victorian house makes a spacious and child-friendly youth hostel, with most of its rooms four-bed dorms. Often busy, so book early. It's about a mile northwest of the city centre; there's a riverside footpath from Lendal Bridge (poorly lit, so avoid after dark). Alternatively, take bus 2 from the train station or Museum St.

★Hedley House Hotel HOTEL ££

(☎01904-637404; www.hedleyhouse.com; 3 Bootham Tce; d/f from £105/115; P wifi family) This redbrick terrace-house hotel sports a variety of smartly refurbished, family-friendly accommodation, including rooms that sleep up to five, and some self-catering apartments – plus it has a sauna and spa bath on the outdoor terrace at the back, and is barely five minutes' walk from the city centre through the Museum Gardens.

Bar Convent B&B ££

(☎01904-643238; www.bar-convent.org.uk; 17 Blossom St; s/d £67/96; wifi) This elegant Georgian redbrick mansion just outside Micklegate Bar, less than 10 minutes' walk from the train station, houses a working convent, a cafe, a conference centre and exhibition, and also offers excellent B&B accommodation. Open to visitors of all faiths and none. Charming bedrooms are modern and well equipped, breakfasts are superb, and there's a garden and hidden chapel to enjoy.

Beech House B&B ££
(☎01904-634581; www.beechhouse-york.co.uk; 6-7 Longfield Tce; s/d from £50/80; 📶) Smart, businesslike bedrooms and a warm welcome from the friendly owners promise a comfortable stay at this redbrick terrace house. It enjoys an excellent location, both quiet and central, with the city centre a 10-minute walk away through the Museum Gardens.

Monkgate Guesthouse B&B ££
(☎01904-655947; www.monkgateguesthouse.com; 65 Monkgate; s/d/f from £50/78/117; P📶) This attractive guesthouse lies just outside the city walls. It has seven brightly decorated bedrooms including a special family suite that has a separate bedroom for two kids.

St Raphael B&B ££
(☎01904-645028; www.straphaelguesthouse.co.uk; 44 Queen Anne's Rd; d/tr £94/125; P📶) Set in a historic house with that distinctively English half-timbered look, this B&B has a great central location, bright and airy bedrooms, and the smell of home-baked bread wafting up from the breakfast room.

Dairy Guesthouse B&B ££
(☎01904-639367; www.dairyguesthouse.co.uk; 3 Scarcroft Rd; d/f from £80/100; 📶) A lovely Victorian home that has retained many of its original features, including pine doors, stained glass and cast-iron fireplaces. But the real treat here is the flower- and plant-filled courtyard leading to the cottage-style rooms. Minimum two-night stay at all times.

Brontë House B&B ££
(☎01904-621066; www.bronte-guesthouse.com; 22 Grosvenor Tce; s/d/f from £45/85/115; 📶) The Brontë has five homely en suite rooms, each individually decorated; top of the range is the romantic double bedroom with a carved 19th-century headboard and velvet canopy. Breakfasts are served in a period dining room with magnificent carved oak sideboard, and include Yorkshire black pudding and local farm eggs.

★ **Middlethorpe Hall** HOTEL £££
(☎01904-641241; www.middlethorpe.com; Bishopthorpe Rd; s/d from £118/126; P📶) This breathtaking 17th-century country house is set in 8 hectares of parkland, once the home of diarist Lady Mary Wortley Montagu. The rooms are divided between the main house, restored courtyard buildings and three cottage suites. All are beautifully decorated with original antiques and oil paintings that have been carefully selected to reflect the period.

Grays Court HISTORIC HOTEL £££
(☎01904-612613; www.grayscourtyork.com; Chapter House St; d from £170; P📶) Although it's practically in the shadow of York Minster, this medieval mansion feels more like a country-house hotel, set in lovely gardens ringed by the old city walls, with bedrooms that combine antique furniture with modern comfort and design. The oldest part of the building is 11th century, and King James I once dined in the Long Gallery, now an excellent restaurant, Parlour at Grays Court (p504).

Mount Royale Hotel & Spa HOTEL £££
(☎01904-628856; www.mountroyale.co.uk; The Mount; s/d/ste from £95/125/225; P📶) A grand, early-19th-century heritage-listed building converted into a superb luxury hotel, complete with a solarium, beauty spa and outdoor heated tub and swimming pool. The rooms in the main house are gorgeous, but best of all are the open-plan garden suites, reached via an arcade of tropical fruit trees and bougainvillea.

Eating

★ **Mannion's** CAFE, BISTRO £
(☎01904-631030; www.mannionandco.co.uk; 1 Blake St; mains £6-11; ⏰9am-5.30pm Mon-Fri, to 6pm Sat, 10am-5pm Sun) Expect to queue for a table at this busy bistro (no reservations), with its maze of rustic, wood-panelled rooms and selection of daily specials. Regulars on the menu include eggs Benedict for breakfast, a chunky Yorkshire rarebit made with home-baked bread, and lunch platters of cheese and charcuterie from the attached deli. Oh, and pavlova for pudding.

Shambles Kitchen FAST FOOD £
(☎01904-674684; www.shambleskitchen.co.uk; 28 The Shambles; mains £6; ⏰9am-4pm Mon-Fri, to 5pm Sat, 10am-4pm Sun) Fast food doesn't mean unhealthy at this hugely popular little takeaway (there are only three tables inside). The place is best known for its pulled-pork sandwiches on sourdough bread, but there are also yummy vegetarian wraps, daily specials such as Goan curry and Korean chicken, and a choice of freshly made juices and smoothies.

Your Bike Shed CAFE £
(☎01904-633777; www.yourbikeshed.co.uk; 148-150 Micklegate; mains £4-7; ⏰9am-5pm Mon-Sat,

10am-5pm Sun;) Reinvigorated by the 2014 Tour de France (which began in Yorkshire) and the annual Tour de Yorkshire (from 2015), York's cycling scene has latched onto this cool cafe and bike workshop. Fitted out with recycled furniture and classic bikes, it serves reviving portions of halloumi burger, pie and peas, and carrot cake to hungry cyclists, washed down with excellent coffee.

★No 8 Bistro BISTRO ££
(01904-653074; www.no8york.co.uk/bistro; 8 Gillygate; 3-course lunch/dinner £16/25; noon-10pm Mon-Thu, 9am-10pm Fri-Sun;) A cool little place with modern artwork mimicking the Edwardian stained glass at the front, No 8 offers a daylong menu of classic bistro dishes using fresh local produce, including Jerusalem artichoke risotto with fresh herbs, and Yorkshire lamb slow-cooked in hay and lavender. It also does breakfast (mains £6 to £9) and Sunday lunch (two courses £18). Booking recommended.

★Parlour at Grays Court CAFE, BRITISH ££
(www.grayscourtyork.com; Chapter House St; mains £9-20; 10am-5pm & 6-9pm;) An unexpected pleasure in the heart of York, this 16th-century mansion (now a hotel) has more of a country-house atmosphere. Relax with coffee and cake in the sunny garden, enjoy a light lunch of Yorkshire rarebit, or indulge in a dinner of scallops and sea bass in the oak-panelled Jacobean gallery. The daytime menu includes traditional afternoon tea (£18.50).

Café Concerto CAFE, MEDITERRANEAN ££
(01904-610478; www.cafeconcerto.biz; 21 High Petergate; mains lunch £6-9, dinner £13-19; 9am-9pm) Walls papered with sheet music, chilled jazz on the stereo, and battered, mismatched tables and chairs set the bohemian tone in this comforting coffee shop-cum-bistro. Expect breakfasts, bagels and cappuccinos big enough to float a boat in during the day, and a sophisticated Mediterranean-style menu in the evening.

Ate O'Clock BISTRO ££
(01904-644080; www.ateoclock.co.uk; 13a High Ousegate; mains £8-18; noon-2pm & 6-9.30pm Tue-Fri, noon-2.30pm & 5.30-9.30pm Sat;) A tempting menu of classic bistro dishes (sirloin steak, slow-roasted pork belly, pan-fried duck breast) made with fresh Yorkshire produce has made this place hugely popular with locals – book a table to avoid disappointment. A three-course dinner costs £19.50 from 6pm to 7.55pm Tuesday to Thursday.

Olive Tree MEDITERRANEAN ££
(01904-624433; www.theolivetreeyork.co.uk; 10 Tower St; mains £9-21; noon-2pm & 5.30-10pm) Local produce gets a Mediterranean makeover at this bright and breezy bistro. Classic pizza and pasta dishes are complemented by more ambitious recipes such as crayfish and chorizo risotto, and Moroccan lamb stew. The set menu (lunch and dinner, pre-6.30pm Friday and Saturday) offers two courses for £15.

Bettys TEAHOUSE ££
(www.bettys.co.uk; St Helen's Sq; mains £6-14, afternoon tea £18.95; 9am-9pm Sun-Fri, 8.30am-9pm Sat;) Old-school afternoon tea, with white-aproned waiters, linen tablecloths and a teapot collection ranged along the walls. The house speciality is the Yorkshire Fat Rascal, a huge fruit scone smothered in melted butter, but the smoked haddock with poached egg and hollandaise sauce (seasonal) is our favourite lunch dish. No bookings – queue for a table at busy times.

El Piano VEGAN ££
(01904-610676; www.el-piano.com; 15 Grape Lane; lunch £12, 2-course dinner £15; 11am-10pm Mon-Sat, noon-9pm Sun;) With a menu that's 100% vegan, nut-free and gluten-free, this colourful, Hispanic-style spot is a vegetarian haven. Downstairs there's a lovely cafe, and upstairs, three themed rooms. The menu offers dishes such as felafel, onion bhaji, corn fritters and mushroom-and-basil salad, either in tapas-size portions or as mixed platters. There's also a takeaway counter.

★Cochon Aveugle FRENCH £££
(01904-640222; www.lecochonaveugle.uk; 37 Walmgate; 6-/9-course tasting menu £40/60; 6-9pm Tue-Sat) Black-pudding macaroon? Strawberry and elderflower sandwich? Blowtorched mackerel with melon gazpacho? Fussy eaters beware – this small restaurant with huge ambition serves an ever-changing tasting menu (no à la carte) of infinite imagination and invention. You never know what will come next, except that it will be delicious. Bookings essential.

Drinking & Nightlife

★Blue Bell PUB
(01904-654904; bluebellyork@gmail.com; 53 Fossgate; 11am-11pm Mon-Thu, to midnight Fri & Sat, noon-10.30pm Sun) This is what a proper English pub looks like – a tiny, 200-year-old wood-panelled room with a smouldering fireplace, decor untouched since 1903, a pile of ancient board games in the corner, friendly

and efficient bar staff, and Timothy Taylor and Black Sheep ales on tap. Bliss, with froth on top – if you can get in (it's often full).

Ye Olde Starre PUB
(www.taylor-walker.co.uk; 40 Stonegate; 11am-11pm Sun-Wed, to midnight Thu-Sat;) Licenced since 1644, this is York's oldest pub – a warren of small rooms and a small beer garden, with a half-dozen real ales on tap. It was used as a morgue by the Roundheads (supporters of parliament) during the Civil War, but the atmosphere has improved considerably since then.

Pivní CRAFT BEER
(www.pivni.co.uk; 6 Patrick Pool; noon-11.30pm Sun-Thu, 11am-11.30pm Fri & Sat;) A slick, modern pub set in an ancient half-timbered house, Pivní provides an atmospheric setting for sampling its range of more than 80 draught and bottled craft beers from all over the world.

Brigantes Bar CRAFT BEER
(01904-675355; www.brigantesyork.co.uk; 114 Micklegate; noon-11pm) On a street that is notorious for its Saturday-night drunken revelry, Brigantes is a wood-panelled haven of peace and sophistication, with 10 hand-pulled ales (mostly from Yorkshire) on tap and a dining room that serves classic comfort food such as nachos, burgers and fish and chips.

King's Arms PUB
(01904-659435; King's Staith; 11am-11pm Mon-Sat, noon-10.30pm Sun) York's best-known pub enjoys a fabulous riverside location, with tables spilling out onto the quayside. It's the perfect spot on a summer evening, but be prepared to share it with a few hundred other people.

Entertainment

York Theatre Royal THEATRE
(01904-623568; www.yorktheatreroyal.co.uk; St Leonard's Pl) Well-regarded productions of theatre, opera and dance are staged here.

Grand Opera House LIVE MUSIC, COMEDY
(0844 871 3024; www.facebook.com/GrandOperaHouseYork; Clifford St) Despite the name, there are no operas staged here; instead, there's a wide range of entertainment, from live bands and popular musicals to stand-up comics and pantomime.

City Screen Picturehouse CINEMA
(0871 902 5726; www.picturehouses.co.uk; 13-17 Coney St;) An appealing modern building in a converted printing works, screening both mainstream and art-house films. There's also a nice cafe-bar on the terrace overlooking the river.

Shopping

Coney St, Davygate and the adjoining streets are the hub of York's city-centre shopping scene, but the real treats are the secondhand bookshops, and antique, bric-a-brac and independent shops to be found along Gillygate, Colliergate, Fossgate and Micklegate.

Fossgate Books BOOKS
(01904-641389; fossgatebooks@hotmail.co.uk; 36 Fossgate; 10am-5.30pm Mon-Sat) A classic, old-school secondhand bookshop, with a maze of floor-to-ceiling shelves crammed with titles covering every subject under the sun, from crime fiction and popular paperbacks to arcane academic tomes and 1st editions.

Inkwell MUSIC
(07846 610777; www.ink-well.co.uk; 10 Gillygate; 10am-5.30pm Mon-Sat, 11am-4pm Sun) Laid out like an old schoolroom, complete with desks and blackboard, this place is a welcoming haven for anyone interested in vinyl records: as well as new and reissued vinyl, there are wooden crates filled with secondhand LPs, and you can even buy record players to play them on. There's also a good selection of secondhand books and comics.

Antiques Centre ANTIQUES
(www.theantiquescentreyork.co.uk; 41 Stonegate; 9am-5.30pm Mon-Sat, to 4pm Sun) A Georgian townhouse with a veritable maze of rooms and corridors, showcasing the wares of about 120 dealers selling everything from lapel pins and snuffboxes to oil paintings and longcase clocks. And the house is haunted as well...

Information

Post Office (22 Lendal; 8.30am-5.30pm Mon-Fri, to 4pm Sat)

York Hospital (01904-631313; www.yorkhospitals.nhs.uk; Wiggington Rd) Has an emergency department; located a mile north of the centre.

York Tourist Office (01904-550099; www.visityork.org; 1 Museum St; 9am-5pm Mon-Sat, 10am-4pm Sun) Visitor and transport info for all of Yorkshire, plus accommodation bookings, ticket sales and internet access.

Getting There & Away

BUS

York does not have a bus station; intercity buses stop outside the train station, while local and regional buses stop here and also on **Rougier St**, about 200m northeast of the train station.

For timetable information, call **Traveline Yorkshire** (☎ 0871 200 2233; www.yorkshiretravel.net) or check the computerised 24-hour information points at the train station and Rougier St. There's a bus information point in the train station's Travel Centre.

Birmingham £29, 3½ hours, one daily
Edinburgh £40, 6¼ hours, one daily
London from £25, 5½ hours, three daily
Newcastle £15.40, 2¼ hours, two daily

CAR

A car is more hindrance than help in the city centre, so use one of the Park & Ride car parks at the edge of the city. If you want to explore the surrounding area, rental options include **Europcar** (☎ 0844 846 0872; www.europcar.co.uk; Queen St; ⊙ 8am-6pm Mon-Fri, to 3pm Sat), located next to the long-stay car park at the train station.

TRAIN

York is a major railway hub, with frequent direct services to many British cities.

Birmingham £45, 2¼ hours, two per hour
Cambridge (change at Peterborough) £71, 2¾ hours, hourly
Edinburgh £60, 2½ hours, every 30 minutes
Leeds £13.90, 25 minutes, every 15 minutes
London Kings Cross £80, two hours, every 30 minutes
Manchester £25, 1½ hours, every 15 minutes
Newcastle £25, one hour, every 30 minutes
Scarborough £14, 50 minutes, hourly

Getting Around

Central York is easy to get around on foot – you're never more than 20 minutes' walk from any of the major sights.

BICYCLE

The tourist office has a useful free map showing York's cycle routes, or visit iTravel-York (www.itravelyork.info/cycling). Castle Howard (15 miles northeast of York via Haxby and Strensall) is an interesting destination, and there's also a section of the **Trans-Pennine Trail cycle path** (www.transpenninetrail.org.uk) from Bishopthorpe in York to Selby (15 miles) along the old railway line.

You can rent bikes from **Cycle Heaven** (☎ 01904-622701; www.cycle-heaven.co.uk; York Railway Station, Station Rd; ⊙ 8.30am-5.30pm Mon-Fri, 9am-5pm Sat year-round, 11am-4pm Sun May-Aug) at the train station for £20 per day.

BUS

Local bus services are operated by First York (www.firstgroup.com/york). Single fares range from £1 to £3, and a day pass valid for all local buses is £4 (available on the bus or at Park & Ride car parks).

TAXI

Station Taxis (☎ 01904-623332; www.yorkstationtaxis.co.uk; Train Station, Station Rd) has a kiosk outside the train station.

Castle Howard

Stately homes may be two a penny in England, but you'll have to try pretty damn hard to find one as breathtaking as **Castle Howard** (www.castlehoward.co.uk; adult/child house & grounds £17.50/9, grounds only £9.95/7; ⊙ house 10.30am-4pm, last admission 4pm, grounds 10am-5pm; P), a work of theatrical grandeur and audacity set in the rolling Howardian Hills. This is one of the world's most beautiful buildings, instantly recognisable from its starring role in the 1980s TV series *Brideshead Revisited* and in the 2008 film of the same name (both based on Evelyn Waugh's 1945 novel).

When the Earl of Carlisle hired his pal Sir John Vanbrugh to design his new home in 1699, he was hiring a man who had no formal training and was best known as a playwright. Luckily, Vanbrugh hired Nicholas Hawksmoor, who had worked as Christopher Wren's clerk of works – not only would Hawksmoor have a big part to play in the house's design, but he and Vanbrugh would later work wonders with Blenheim Palace. Today the house is still home to the Hon Simon Howard and his family and he can often be seen around the place.

If you can, try to visit on a weekday when it's easier to find the space to appreciate this hedonistic marriage of art, architecture, landscaping and natural beauty. As you wander about the peacock-haunted grounds, views open up over Vanbrugh's playful Temple of the Four Winds, Hawksmoor's stately mausoleum and the distant hills, but the great baroque house with its magnificent central cupola is an irresistible visual magnet. Inside, the house is full of treasures – the breathtaking Great Hall with its soaring Corinthian pilasters, Pre-Raphaelite stained glass in the chapel, and corridors lined with classical antiquities.

The entrance courtyard has a good cafe, a gift shop and a farm shop filled with foodie delights from local producers.

Castle Howard is 15 miles northeast of York, off the A64. There are several organised tours from York; check with the tourist office for up-to-date schedules. Stephenson's of Easingwold (www.stephensonsofeasingwold.co.uk) bus 181 links York with Castle Howard (£10 return, 40 minutes, four times daily Monday to Saturday year-round, three on Sunday May to September).

Harrogate

POP 73,580

The quintessential Victorian spa town, prim and pretty Harrogate has long been associated with a certain kind of old-fashioned Englishness – the kind that seems the preserve of retired army majors and formidable dowagers who take the *Daily Telegraph* and always vote Tory. They come to Harrogate to enjoy the flower shows and gardens that fill the town with magnificent displays of colour, especially in spring and autumn. It is fitting that the town's most famous visitor was Agatha Christie, who fled here incognito in 1926 to escape her broken marriage.

And yet, this picture of Victoriana redux is not quite complete. While it's undoubtedly true that Harrogate remains a firm favourite of visitors in their golden years, the town has plenty of smart hotels and trendy eateries catering to the boom in Harrogate's newest trade – conferences. All those dynamic young sales-and-marketing guns have to eat and sleep somewhere.

Sights & Activities

Royal Pump Room Museum MUSEUM
(www.harrogate.gov.uk; Crown Pl; adult/child £4/2.35; 10.30am-5pm Mon-Sat, 2-5pm Sun Apr-Oct, to 4pm Nov-Mar) You can learn all about Harrogate's history as a spa town in the ornate Royal Pump Room, built in 1842 over the most famous of the town's sulphurous springs. It gives an insight into how the phenomenon of visiting spas to 'take the waters' shaped the town and records the illustrious visitors it attracted. At the end, you get the chance to sample the spa water, if you dare.

The ritual of visiting spa towns as a health cure became fashionable in the 19th century and peaked during the Edwardian era in the years before WWI. Charles Dickens visited Harrogate in 1858 and described it as 'the queerest place, with the strangest people in it, leading the oddest lives of dancing, newspaper-reading and dining' – sounds quite pleasant, really.

Montpellier Quarter AREA
(www.montpellierharrogate.com) The most attractive part of town is the Montpellier Quarter, overlooking Prospect Gardens between Crescent Rd and Montpellier Hill. It's an area of pedestrianised streets lined with restored 19th-century buildings that are now home to art galleries, antique shops, fashion boutiques, cafes and restaurants – an upmarket annex to the main shopping area around Oxford and Cambridge Sts.

Turkish Baths SPA
(01423-556746; www.turkishbathsharrogate.co.uk; Parliament St; £15.50-29.50, guided tours per person £3.75; guided tours 9-10am Wed) Plunge into Harrogate's past at the town's fabulously tiled Turkish Baths. This mock-Moorish facility is gloriously Victorian and offers a range of watery delights: hot rooms, steam rooms, plunge pools and so on. A visit is likely to last about 1½ hours. There's a complicated schedule of opening hours that are by turns single sex or mixed, so call or check online

WORTH A TRIP

KIRKHAM PRIORY & STONE TROUGH INN

The picturesque ruins of **Kirkham Priory** (EH; www.english-heritage.org.uk; adult/child £4.50/2.70; 10am-6pm Wed-Sun Apr-Sep, daily Aug, 10am-5pm Wed-Sun Oct; P) rise gracefully above the banks of the River Derwent, sporting medieval floor tiles and an impressive 13th-century gatehouse encrusted with heraldic symbols.

The traditional country inn **Stone Trough Inn** (01653-618713; Kirkham; mains £11-18; food served noon-9pm Mon-Sat, to 8pm Sun; P) is full of cosy nooks, with exposed stone walls, timber beams and open fires, and serves gourmet-style pub classics (eg fish and chips, steak pie with peas and gravy). An added attraction is the outdoor terrace with great views over the Derwent valley and the ruins of Kirkham Priory. Three-course Sunday lunch is £17.

for details. If you prefer to remain dry, there are also guided tours of the building.

Festivals & Events

Spring Flower Show HORTICULTURE
(www.flowershow.org.uk; £16-17.50) The year's main event, held in late April. A colourful three-day extravaganza of blooms and blossoms, flower competitions, gardening demonstrations, market stalls, crafts and gardening shops.

Great Yorkshire Show AGRICULTURE
(www.greatyorkshireshow.co.uk; adult/child £27/13) Staged over three days in mid-July by the Yorkshire Agricultural Society. Expect all manner of primped and prettified farm animals competing for prizes, and entertainment ranging from showjumping and falconry to cookery demonstrations and hot-air-balloon rides.

Sleeping

★**Bijou** B&B ££
(01423-567974; www.thebijou.co.uk; 17 Ripon Rd; s/d from £59/94; P wi-fi) Bijou by name and bijou by nature, this jewel of a Victorian villa sits firmly at the boutique end of the B&B spectrum – you can tell that a lot of thought and care has gone into its design. The husband-and-wife team who own the place make fantastic hosts, warm and helpful but unobtrusive.

Hotel du Vin BOUTIQUE HOTEL ££
(01423-856800; www.hotelduvin.com/locations/harrogate; Prospect Pl; r/ste from £95/255; P wi-fi) An extremely stylish boutique hotel – the loft suites with exposed oak beams, hardwood floors and designer bathrooms are among the nicest rooms in town, but even the standard bedrooms are spacious and very comfortable (though they can be noisy), each with a huge bed draped in soft Egyptian cotton.

Acorn Lodge B&B ££
(01423-525630; www.acornlodgeharrogate.co.uk; 1 Studley Rd; s/d from £49/89; P wi-fi) Attention to detail makes the difference between an average and an excellent B&B, and the details at Acorn Lodge are spot on: stylish decor, crisp cotton sheets, powerful showers and perfect poached eggs for breakfast. The location is good too, just 10 minutes' walk from the town centre.

Arden House B&B ££
(01423-509224; www.ardenhousehotel.co.uk; 69-71 Franklin Rd; s/d from £58/80; P wi-fi) This grand old Edwardian house has been given a modern makeover with stylish contemporary furniture, Egyptian-cotton bed linen and posh toiletries, but still retains some lovely period details, including tiled cast-iron fireplaces. Attentive service, good breakfasts and a central location are the icing on the cake.

★**West Park** BOUTIQUE HOTEL £££
(01423-524471; www.thewestparkhotel.com; 19 West Park; r/ste from £140/200; wi-fi) Overlooking the grassy expanse of the Stray just five minutes' walk south of the town centre, this classy hotel combines tastefully designed modern bedrooms with a popular restaurant and cocktail bar. Treat yourself to one of the two penthouse suites and you can watch TV while soaking in the bath-tub, or sip champagne on the private roof terrace.

Eating

Fat Badger PUB FOOD ££
(01423-505681; www.thefatbadgerharrogate.com; Cold Bath Rd; mains £10-16; food served noon-9.30pm Mon-Thu, to 10pm Fri & Sat, to 9pm Sun; wi-fi, family) This is a Harrogate (ie posh) interpretation of a typical English pub, all polished wood, gilt-framed mirrors, wing-back armchairs and leather-bench booths, with the occasional stuffed animal for decoration. It's a convivial spot to enjoy a pub lunch of mussels with bacon and cider, or steak and chips, followed by a pint of Yorkshire ale at one of the outdoor tables.

Bettys TEAROOM ££
(01423-814070; www.bettys.co.uk; 1 Parliament St; mains £6-14, afternoon tea £18.95; 9am-9pm; family) A classic tearoom in a classic location

HARLOW CARR BOTANICAL GARDENS

A huge green thumbs-up to Harrogate's gardeners: the town has some of the most beautiful public gardens in England. Flower fanatics should make for the **Harlow Carr Botanical Gardens** (www.rhs.org.uk/gardens/harlow-carr; Crag Lane, Beckwithshaw; adult/child £11/5.50; 9.30am-6pm Mar-Oct, to 4pm Nov-Feb), the northern showpiece of the Royal Horticultural Society, which are 1.5 miles southwest of town; take the B6162 Otley Rd, or walk through the Pine Woods southwest of the Valley Gardens. Last admission is one hour before closing time.

LOCAL KNOWLEDGE

EAT & DRINK LIKE A LOCAL

Yorkshire pudding The classic local dish, these puffy batter puddings are traditionally served with roast beef, but Yorkshire tearooms often serve them as a dish in themselves, with gravy. Try them at Ye Olde Naked Man (p526) in Settle.

Theakston's ale Theakston's was turning out best bitter long before the term 'craft beer' had been thought of. Try it at pubs all over Britain, or at Theakston's Brewery (p511) in Masham.

Wensleydale cheese Famous as the favourite snack of animated characters Wallace and Gromit, this crumbly white cheese is made in the heart of the Yorkshire Dales. Try it at the source, at Wensleydale Creamery (p527) in Hawes.

Yorkshire rhubarb Traditionally grown in the 'rhubarb triangle' near Wakefield, Yorkshire forced rhubarb (early-season rhubarb grown in darkness) has achieved Protected Designation of Origin status. Try the Michelin-starred rhubarb trifle at the Pipe and Glass (p544) near Beverley.

Curd tart A very old Yorkshire dish, a bit like cheesecake, traditionally baked for the Whitsun holiday. Try it at Bettys (p508) in Harrogate.

Parkin A rich and sticky cake made with oatmeal and flavoured with ginger and treacle. Try it at Thomas of Helmsley (p517).

with views across the park, Bettys is a local institution. It was established in 1919 by a Swiss immigrant confectioner who took the wrong train, ended up in Yorkshire and decided to stay. There are exquisite home-baked breads, scones and cakes, quality tea and coffee, and a gallery hung with art nouveau marquetry.

Le Jardin BISTRO ££

(01423-507323; www.lejardin-harrogate.com; 7 Montpellier Pde; mains £9-15; 11.30am-2.30pm & 6-11.30pm Mon-Sat, noon-3pm Sun;) This cool little bistro has a snug atmosphere, especially in the evening when candlelight adds a romantic glow; the food is basic bistro fare – grilled chicken, gammon steak, sausage and mash. During the day, locals throng to the tables to enjoy great salads, sandwiches and homemade ice cream. The early-bird menu offers two/three courses for £9.95/12.95 from 6pm to 7pm.

★ **Norse** SCANDINAVIAN £££

(01423-202363; www.norserestaurant.co.uk; 22 Oxford St; 4-/8-course tasting menu £40/60; 6-9pm Tue-Sat) Norse injects some fun into fine dining, with a choice of tasting menus that blends the best of British produce with Scandinavian inspiration to produce unusual flavour combinations such as beetroot, cocoa and horseradish; pork, oyster and peas; and yoghurt, gooseberry and orange blossom. The drinks list includes carefuly chosen craft beers and cocktails plus wine. Bookings essential.

Drinking & Nightlife

★ **Bean & Bud** COFFEE

(01423-508200; www.beanandbud.co.uk; 14 Commercial St; 8am-5pm Mon-Sat;) Small and unpretentious, this place has been around since 2010 and serves what might be the finest cup of coffee in town, if not Yorkshire. There's a choice of two freshly ground blends every day, plus a selection of top-quality white, green, oolong and black teas.

Harrogate Tap CRAFT BEER

(01423-501644; www.harrogatetap.co.uk; Station Pde; 11am-11pm Sun-Thu, 11am-midnight Fri, 10am-midnight Sat;) Set in a restored red-brick railway-station building dating from 1862, the Tap does a grand job of conjuring up the ambience of a bustling Victorian pub, but with the added attractions of a dozen hand-pulled cask ales, another dozen keg taps, and a menu of around 130 bottled craft beers from all over the world.

North Bar CRAFT BEER

(01423-520772; www.northbar.com/harrogate; Cheltenham Pde; 8am-11pm Mon-Thu, 8am-midnight Fri, 9am-midnight Sat, 10am-11pm Sun;) Spread over three floors, this new branch of Leeds' famous North Bar not only brings a bit of big-city chic to Harrogate's rather staid pub scene, but also a refreshingly international beer menu and all-day service that kick-starts the morning with quality coffee and croissants.

Entertainment

Royal Hall LIVE MUSIC
(01423-500500; www.royalhall.co.uk; Ripon Rd) A gorgeous Edwardian theatre that is now part of the conference-and-events venue Harrogate International Centre. The musical program covers orchestral and choral performances, piano recitals, jazz and more.

Harrogate Theatre THEATRE
(01423-502116; www.harrogatetheatre.co.uk; Oxford St) A historic Victorian theatre that dates from 1900, staging variety, comedy, musicals and dancing.

Information

Harrogate Tourist Office (01423-537300; www.visitharrogate.co.uk; Crescent Rd; 9am-5.30pm Mon-Sat, 10am-1pm Sun Apr-Oct, 9.30am-5pm Mon-Sat Nov-Mar)

Post Office (11 Cambridge Rd; 9.30am-5.30pm Mon-Sat)

Getting There & Away

Bus Harrogate & District (www.harrogatebus.co.uk) bus 36 connects Harrogate with Leeds (£6.50, 45 minutes, every 10 to 20 minutes) and Ripon (£6.20, 30 minutes, every 15 minutes).

Train There are trains to Harrogate from Leeds (£8.20, 35 minutes, every 30 minutes) and York (£8.50, 40 minutes, hourly).

Scarborough

POP 61,750

Scarborough retains all the trappings of the classic seaside resort, but is in the process of reinventing itself as a centre for the creative arts and digital industries. The Victorian spa has been redeveloped as a conference and entertainment centre, a former museum has been converted into studio space for artists, a vast new water park opened in 2016, and there's free, open-access wi-fi along the promenade beside the harbour – an area being promoted as the town's bar, cafe and restaurant quarter.

As well as the usual seaside attractions, Scarborough offers excellent coastal walking, a geology museum, one of Yorkshire's most impressively sited castles, and a renowned theatre that is the home base for popular playwright Alan Ayckbourn, whose plays always premiere here.

Sights

★**Scarborough Castle** CASTLE
(EH; www.english-heritage.org.uk; Castle Rd; adult/child £6.10/3.70; 10am-6pm Apr-Sep, to 5pm Oct, to 4pm Sat & Sun Nov-Mar) The massive medieval keep of Scarborough Castle occupies a commanding position atop its headland. Legend has it that Richard I loved the views from here so much that his ghost just keeps coming back. Take a walk out to the edge of the cliffs, where you can see the 2000-year-old remains of a **Roman signal station**; clearly the Romans appreciated this viewpoint too.

★**Rotunda Museum** MUSEUM
(www.rotundamuseum.co.uk; Vernon Rd; adult/child £3/free; 10am-5pm Tue-Sun;) The Rotunda Museum is dedicated to the coastal geology of northeast Yorkshire, which has yielded many of Britain's most important dinosaur fossils. The strata in the local cliffs were also important in deciphering England's geological history. Founded by William Smith, 'the father of English geology', who lived in Scarborough in the 1820s, the museum has original Victorian exhibits as well as a hands-on gallery for kids.

Sea Life Sanctuary AQUARIUM
(www.sealife.co.uk; Scalby Mills; adult/child 2yr & under £18/free; 10am-6pm, last admission 5pm; P) At this family-oriented attraction (tickets are much cheaper if you buy online) you can see coral reefs, turtles, octopuses, seahorses, otters and many other fascinating creatures, though the biggest draw is the **Seal Pool** (feeding times 11.30am and 2.30pm). The centre is at the far north end of North Beach; the miniature North Bay Railway (p514) runs the three-quarter-mile route. A lot of the attractions are outdoors, so it's not an ideal rainy-day refuge.

Peasholm Park PARK
(www.peasholmpark.com; Columbus Ravine; 24hr) FREE Set back from North Bay, Scarborough's beautiful Edwardian pleasure gardens are famous for their summer sessions of **Naval Warfare** (adult/child £4.10/2.30; 3pm Mon, Thu & Sat Jul & Aug), when large model ships reenact famous naval battles on the boating lake (check the website for dates).

St Mary's Church CHURCH
(Castle Rd; 10am-4pm Mon-Fri, 1-4pm Sun May-Sep) FREE This church dates from the 12th to the 15th centuries (boards inside explain its history), but it is most notable for the little

WORTH A TRIP

BREWERIES IN MASHAM VILLAGE

Masham is 9 miles northwest of Ripon on the AG108 to Leyburn. Bus 159 from Richmond to Ripon stops at Masham.

Theakston's Brewery (☎01765-680000; www.theakstons.co.uk; The Brewery, Masham; tour adult/child £7.50/4.75; ⊙10.30am-5.30pm Jul & Aug, to 4.30pm Sep-Jun) Founded in 1827, and still run by the Theakston family (despite a spell in the ownership of global brewer Scottish & Newcastle), Theakston's has long been one of Yorkshire's most famous breweries. Old Peculier, its best-known ale, takes its name from the Peculier of Masham, a parish court established in medieval times to deal with offences such as drunkenness and brawling. There's a visitor centre which doubles as a bar, and four tours a day (six in August) of the brewery works.

Black Sheep Brewery (☎01765-680101; www.blacksheepbrewery.com; Wellgarth, Masham; tours adult/child £8.50/4.95; ⊙10am-5pm Sun-Wed, to 11pm Thu-Sat; P 👪) Founded in 1992 by the 'black sheep' of the Theakston family, who refused to work for the multinational company that took over Yorkshire's highly regarded Theakston's brewery in 1987, this place has grown to be just as famous as its near neighbour. There are four tours a day, plus an excellent restaurant where you can wash down your lunch with a pint of the brewery's own ale.

cemetery across the lane that contains the **grave of Anne Brontë**, sister of Charlotte and author of *The Tenant of Wildfell Hall*.

Activities

There are some decent waves on England's northeast coast, supporting a growing surf scene. A top spot is **Cayton Bay**, 4 miles south of town, where you'll find **Scarborough Surf School** (☎01723-585585; www.scarboroughsurfschool.co.uk; Cayton Bay). The best time for waves is September to May.

Back in town, you can get information and advice from the **Secretspot Surf Shop** (☎01723-500467; www.secretspot.co.uk; 4 Pavilion Tce; ⊙9am-5pm Mon-Fri) near the train station.

Sleeping

YHA Scarborough HOSTEL £
(☎01723-361176; www.yha.org.uk; Burniston Rd; dm/q from £18/70; P 👪) An idyllic hostel set in a converted 17th-century water mill, 2 miles north of town along the A166 to Whitby. Take bus 3 or 3A from York Place to the Ivanhoe pub; it's a five-minute walk from there.

★**Waves** B&B ££
(☎01723-373658; www.scarboroughwaves.co.uk; 39 Esplanade Rd, South Cliff; s/d from £54/79; P 📶) 🍃 Crisp cotton sheets and powerful showers make for comfortable accommodation at this retro-styled B&B, but it's the second B that's the real star – the breakfasts range from vegan-friendly fruit salads and smoothies to fry-ups, kippers and kedgeree. A unique selling point is the jukebox in the lounge, loaded with 1960s and '70s hits. It's 0.75 miles south of the centre, off the A165 (Ramshill Rd).

★**Windmill** B&B ££
(☎01723-372735; www.scarborough-windmill.co.uk; Mill St; d from £85; P 📶) Quirky doesn't begin to describe this place, a beautifully converted 18th-century windmill in the middle of town. There are two self-catering cottages and three four-poster doubles around a cobbled courtyard, but try to secure the balcony suite (from £110 a night) in the upper floors of the windmill itself, with great views from the wraparound balcony.

Helaina B&B ££
(☎01723-375191; www.hotelhelaina.co.uk; 14 Blenheim Tce; r from £90; ⊙daily Apr-Nov, Fri & Sat only Feb & Mar; 📶) Location, location, location – you'd be hard-pressed to find a place with a better sea view than this elegant guesthouse perched on the clifftop overlooking North Beach. And the view inside is pretty good too, with sharply styled contemporary furniture and cool colours. The cheaper rooms are on the small side; it's worth paying extra for a sea-view room (from £100).

Interludes B&B ££
(☎01723-360513; www.interludeshotel.co.uk; 32 Princess St; s/d £45/70; 📶) Established in 1991 by owners with a flair for the theatrical, this lovely, gay-friendly Georgian guesthouse is plastered with old theatre posters, prints and other thespian mementoes. The individually decorated rooms feature flights of fancy that will put a smile on your face. No children.

Scarborough

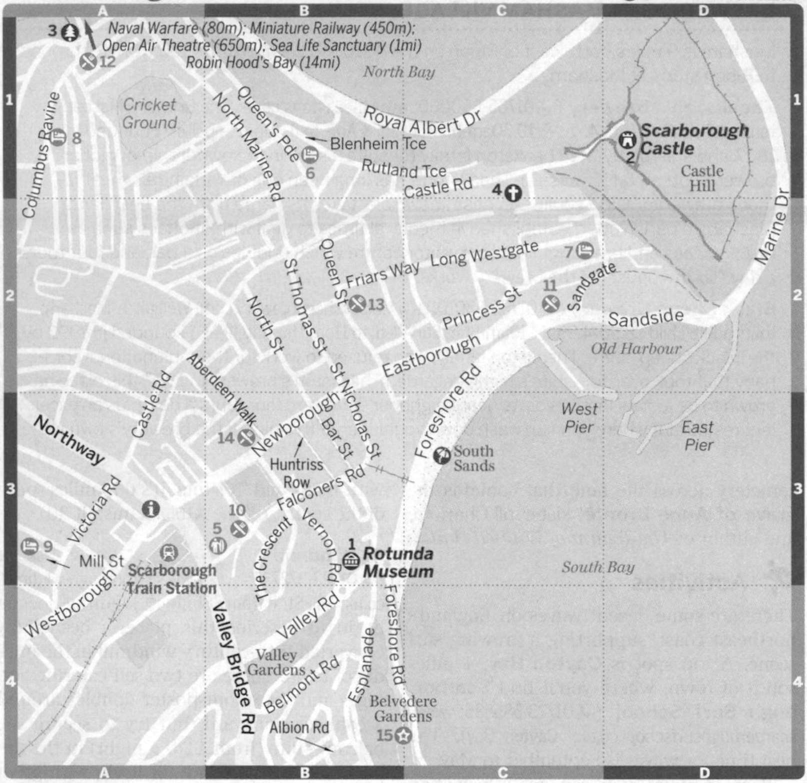

Scarborough

Top Sights
1 Rotunda Museum B3
2 Scarborough Castle D1

Sights
3 Peasholm Park A1
4 St Mary's Church C1

Activities, Courses & Tours
5 Secretspot Surf Shop B3

Sleeping
6 Helaina B1
7 Interludes C2
8 North Bay Guest House A1
9 Windmill A3

Eating
10 Cafe Fish B3
11 Golden Grid C2
12 Jeremy's A1
13 Lanterna B2
14 Roasters B3

Entertainment
15 Scarborough Spa B4

North Bay Guest House B&B ££
(☎01723-374406; therussells1@btinternet.com; 137 Columbus Ravine; s/d from £34/79;) Cosy and colourful bedrooms, big breakfasts and wonderfully welcoming owners create exceptional value at this excellent B&B, within easy walking distance of Peasholm Park, North Bay Railway and the beach at North Bay.

Eating

Roasters CAFE £
(www.roasterscoffee.co.uk; 8 Aberdeen Walk; mains £4-7; 9am-5pm) A funky coffee shop with chunky pine tables, bentwood chairs and an excellent range of freshly ground coffees. There's a juice and smoothie bar too, and the

lunch menu includes ciabatta sandwiches, salads and jacket potatoes.

★Cafe Fish SEAFOOD ££

(☎01723-500301; www.cafefish.co.uk; 19 York Pl; mains £11-26; ⏰5.30-10pm) This is the place to come for top-quality local seafood without the fuss: freshly landed Scarborough lobster and crab, Scottish oysters, mussels and scallops, and North Sea cod, haddock and hake all simply prepared and reasonably priced. For those who don't want fish, there's a decent choice of meat and vegetarian dishes too.

★Jeremy's BRITISH, FRENCH ££

(☎01723-363871; www.jeremys.co; 33 Victoria Park Ave; mains £16-25, 3-course lunch Sun £25; ⏰6-9.30pm Thu-Sat, noon-3pm Sun, plus 6-9.30pm Tue & Wed Jul & Aug;) A fantastic neighbourhood bistro run by a chef who won his Michelin credentials with Marco Pierre White, this off-the-beaten-track gem sports an art deco ambience and a menu that blends the best of Yorkshire and British produce with French inventiveness and flair. Best to book at weekends.

Golden Grid FISH & CHIPS ££

(☎01723-360922; www.goldengrid.co.uk; 4 Sandside; mains £9-20; ⏰11.30am-11pm;) The Golden Grid is a sit-down fish restaurant that has been serving the best cod in Scarborough since 1883. Its starched white tablecloths and starched white aprons are staunchly traditional, as is the menu: as well as cod and chips, oysters, and freshly landed crab and lobster, there's sausage and mash, roast beef and Yorkshire pudding, and steak and chips.

★Lanterna ITALIAN £££

(☎01723-363616; www.lanterna-ristorante.co.uk; 33 Queen St; mains £15-24; ⏰7-9.30pm Tue-Sat) A snug, old-fashioned Italian trattoria that specialises in fresh local seafood (including lobster, from £32) and classic dishes from the old country such as *stufato de ceci* (chickpea stew with oxtail) and white-truffle dishes in season (October to December, £30 to £45). As well as sourcing Yorkshire produce, the chef imports delicacies direct from Italy.

☆ Entertainment

Open Air Theatre CONCERT VENUE

(☎01723-818111; www.scarboroughopenairtheatre.com; Burniston Rd) Europe's largest open-air theatre, with its stage on an island in a lake, stages big-name concerts throughout the summer season.

Scarborough Spa MUSIC, DANCE

(☎01723-821888; www.scarboroughspa.co.uk; Foreshore Rd;) The revitalised spa complex stages a varied program of entertainment, especially in the summer months: orchestral performances, variety shows, popular musicals and old-fashioned afternoon-tea dances.

ℹ Information

There's free wi-fi internet access along the harbour front from West Pier to East Pier.

There's a small **information point** (☎01723-383636; www.discoveryorkshirecoast.com; Stephen Joseph Theatre, Westborough; ⏰9am-5pm) in the lobby of the theatre; a second kiosk operates in summer at the Open-Air Theatre box office, opposite the entrance to Peasholm Park.

ℹ Getting There & Away

BUS

Bus 128 (www.eyms.co.uk) travels along the A170 from Helmsley to Scarborough via Pickering, while Arriva (www.arrivabus.co.uk) buses 93 and X93 come from Middlesborough and Whitby via Robin Hood's Bay. Coastliner (www.coastliner.co.uk) bus 843 runs to Scarborough from Leeds and York.

Helmsley £7.60, 1¾ hours, hourly Monday to Saturday, four times on Sunday

Leeds £12.30, 2¾ hours, hourly

Whitby £5.70, one hour, every 30 minutes

York £11.30, 1¾ hours, hourly

TRAIN

Hull £12, 1½ hours, hourly

Leeds £20, 1¼ hours, hourly

York £14, 50 minutes, hourly

ℹ Getting Around

Tiny Victorian-era funicular railways rattle up and down Scarborough's steep cliffs between town and beach. The **Central Tramway** (www.centraltramway.co.uk; Marine Pde; per person 90p; ⏰9.30am-5.45pm Feb-Jun, Sep & Oct, to 9.30pm Jul & Aug) connects the Grand Hotel with the promenade, while the **Spa Cliff Lift** (www.scarboroughspa.co.uk/cliff_lift; Esplanade; per person £1; ⏰at least 10am-5pm, hours vary, check website) runs between Scarborough Spa and the Esplanade.

Open-top bus 109 shuttles back and forth along the seafront between Scarborough Spa and the Sands complex on North Bay (£2, every 20 minutes 9.30am to 3pm). The service runs daily from Easter to September, weekends only in October. An all-day, hop on-hop off ticket costs £3.

WORTH A TRIP

FOUNTAINS ABBEY & STUDLEY ROYAL

The alluring and strangely obsessive **water gardens** of the Studley Royal estate were built in the 18th century to enhance the picturesque ruins of 12th-century **Fountains Abbey** (NT; www.fountainsabbey.org.uk; adult/child £13/6.50; ⏲10am-6pm Apr-Sep, to 5pm Sat-Thu Oct-Mar; P). Together, they present a breathtaking picture of pastoral elegance and tranquillity that have made them a Unesco World Heritage site and the most visited of all the National Trust's pay-to-enter properties.

After falling out with the Benedictines of York in 1132, a band of rebel monks came here to establish their own monastery. Struggling to make it alone, they were formally adopted by the Cistercians in 1135. By the middle of the 13th century, the new abbey had become the most successful Cistercian venture in the country. After the Dissolution, when Henry III confiscated church property, the abbey's estate was sold into private hands, and between 1598 and 1611 **Fountains Hall** was built using stone from the abbey ruins. The hall and ruins were united with the Studley Royal estate in 1768.

Studley Royal was owned by John Aislabie, once Chancellor of the Exchequer, who dedicated his life to creating the park after a financial scandal saw him expelled from parliament. The main house of Studley Royal burnt down in 1946, but the superb landscaping, with its serene artificial lakes, survives almost unchanged from the 18th century.

The remains of the abbey are impressively grandiose, gathered around the sunny Romanesque **cloister**, with a huge vaulted **cellarium** leading off the west end of the church. Here, the abbey's 200 lay brothers lived, and food and wool from the abbey's farms were stored. At the east end is the soaring **Chapel of Nine Altars** and on the outside of its northeast window is a Green Man carving (a pre-Christian fertility symbol).

A choice of scenic walking trails leads for a mile from the abbey ruins to the famous water gardens, designed to enhance the romantic views of the ruined abbey. Don't miss **St Mary's Church** (⏲noon-4pm Apr-Sep) above the gardens.

Fountains Abbey is 4 miles west of Ripon off the B6265. Bus 139 travels from Ripon to Fountains Abbey visitor centre year-round (£2.60 return, 15 minutes, four times daily Monday to Saturday, seven on Sundays in summer).

The miniature **North Bay Railway** (www.nbr.org.uk; return adult/child £3.50/2.70; ⏲10.30am-3pm daily Apr-Sep, Sat & Sun year-round) also runs to North Beach.

For a taxi, call **Station Taxis** (☎01723-366366; www.taxisinscarborough.co.uk); £5 should get you to most places in town.

NORTH YORK MOORS NATIONAL PARK

Inland from the north Yorkshire coast, the wild and windswept North York Moors rise in desolate splendour. Three-quarters of all the world's heather moorland is found in Britain, and this is the largest expanse in England. Ridge-top roads climb up from lush green valleys to the bleak open moors, where weather-beaten stone crosses mark the lines of ancient roadways. In summer, heather blooms in billowing drifts of purple haze.

This is classic walking country. The moors are criss-crossed with footpaths old and new, and dotted with pretty, flower-bedecked villages. The national park is also home to one of England's most picturesque steam railways. The park produces the useful *Out & About* visitor guide, available from tourist offices and hotels. See also www.northyorkmoors.org.uk.

ℹ Information

There are two national park visitor centres, providing information on walking, cycling, wildlife and public transport.

Moors National Park Centre (☎01439-772737; www.northyorkmoors.org.uk; Lodge Lane, Danby; ⏲10am-5pm Apr-Oct, 10.30am-4pm Nov-Mar, Sat & Sun only Jan & Feb; 👪)

Sutton Bank National Park Centre (☎01845-597426; www.northyorkmoors.org.uk; Sutton Bank, by Thirsk; ⏲10am-5pm Apr-Oct, 10.30am-4pm Nov-Mar, Sat & Sun only Jan & Feb; 📶)

ℹ Getting Around

On Sundays and bank holiday Mondays from late May to September, a number of minibus services aimed at hikers shuttle around various locations within the national park; all are detailed on the Moorsbus (www.moorsbus.org) website.

For example, the **Moors Explorer** (☎ 01482-592929; www.eyms.co.uk) service runs from Hull to the Moors National Park Centre in Danby, via Beverley, Pickering, Hutton-le-Hole and the Lion Inn at Blakey, with a shuttle between Danby and Pickering. An all-day hop-on, hop-off ticket costs £12.50.

The North Yorkshire Moors Railway (www.nymr.co.uk), running between Pickering and Whitby, is an excellent way of exploring the central moors in summer. If you're planning to drive on the minor roads over the moors, beware of wandering sheep and lambs – hundreds are killed by careless drivers every year.

Helmsley & Around

POP 1515

Helmsley is a classic North Yorkshire market town, a handsome huddle of old stone houses, historic coaching inns and – inevitably – a cobbled market square (market day is Friday), all basking under the watchful gaze of a sturdy Norman castle. Nearby are the romantic ruins of Rievaulx Abbey, several excellent restaurants and a fistful of country walks.

Sights

Helmsley Castle CASTLE
(EH; www.english-heritage.org.uk; Castlegate; adult/child £6.40/3.80; 10am-6pm Apr-Sep, to 5pm Oct, to 4pm Sat & Sun Nov-Mar; P) The impressive ruins of 12th-century Helmsley Castle are defended by a striking series of deep ditches and banks, to which later rulers added the thick stone walls and defensive towers. Only one tooth-shaped tower survives today, following the dismantling of the fortress by Sir Thomas Fairfax after the Civil War. The castle's tumultuous history is well explained in the visitor centre.

Helmsley Walled Garden GARDENS
(www.helmsleywalledgarden.org.uk; adult/child £7.50/free; 10am-5pm Apr-Oct) Helmsley Walled Garden would be just another plant-and-produce centre were it not for its dramatic setting next to Helmsley Castle and its fabulous selection of flowers, fruits and vegetables (some of them rare), not to mention the herbs, which include 40 varieties of mint. If you're into horticulture with a historical twist, this is Eden.

Duncombe Park Gardens GARDENS
(www.duncombepark.com; adult/child £5/3; 10.30am-5pm Sun-Fri Apr-Aug; P) South of Helmsley lies the superb ornamental landscape of Duncombe Park estate, laid out in 1718 for Thomas Duncombe (whose son would later build Rievaulx Terrace) with the stately Georgian mansion of Duncombe Park House at its heart. From the house (not open to the public) and formal gardens, wide grassy walkways and terraces lead through woodland to mock-classical temples, while longer walking trails are set out in the landscaped parkland, now protected as a nature reserve.

★ **Rievaulx Abbey** RUINS
(www.english-heritage.org.uk; adult/child £8/4.80; 10am-6pm Apr-Sep, to 5pm Oct, to 4pm Sat & Sun Nov-Mar; P) In the secluded valley of the River Rye about 3 miles west of Helmsley, amid fields and woods loud with birdsong, stand the magnificent ruins of Rievaulx Abbey (*ree*-voh). The extensive remains give a wonderful sense of the size and complexity of the community that once lived here, and their story is fleshed out in a series of fascinating exhibits in a new museum and visitor centre.

This idyllic spot was chosen by Cistercian monks in 1132 as a base for their missionary activity in northern Britain. St Aelred, the third abbot, famously described the abbey's setting as 'everywhere peace, everywhere serenity, and a marvellous freedom from the tumult of the world'. But the monks of Rievaulx were far from unworldly and soon created a network of commercial interests ranging from sheep farms to lead mines.

There's an excellent 3½-mile **walking trail** from Helmsley to Rievaulx Abbey; Helmsley tourist information point can provide route leaflets and advise on buses if you don't want to walk both ways. This route is also the opening section of the Cleveland Way.

On the hillside above the abbey is **Rievaulx Terrace** (www.nationaltrust.org.uk; adult/child £5.95/3; 11am-5pm May-Aug, to 4pm Mar, Apr, Sep & Oct; P), built in the 18th century by Thomas Duncombe II as a place to admire views of the abbey. Note that there's no direct access between the abbey and the terrace, and the two sites have separate admission fees. Their entrance gates are about a mile apart along a narrow road (steeply uphill if you're heading from the abbey to the terrace).

Sleeping

Canadian Fields CAMPGROUND ££
(☎ 01439-772409; www.canadianfields.co.uk; Gale Lane; safari tents £60-90; Feb–mid-Nov; P) This luxury campsite 3 miles east of Helmsley offers comfortable and unusual accommodation in 'safari tents': spacious canvas-walled cabins with kitchens, electricity

North York Moors National Park

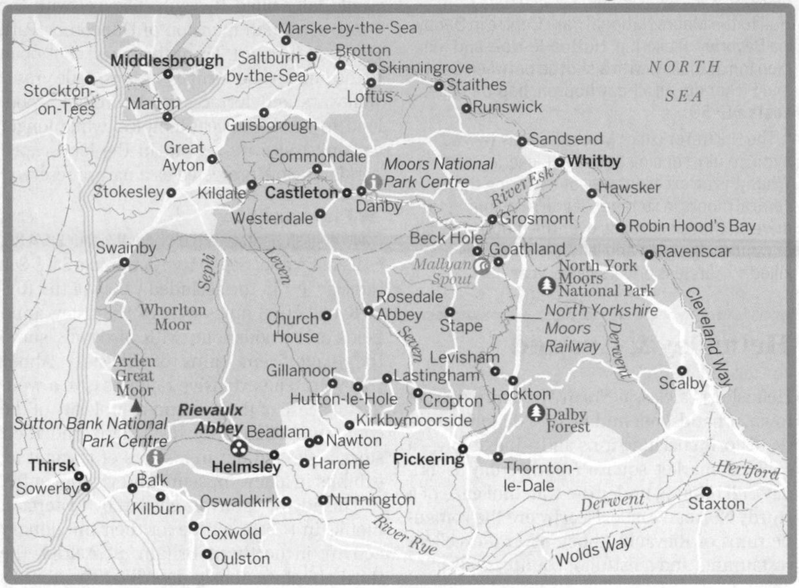

and wood-burning stoves. There are also sites where you can pitch your own tent (from £15 a night), and a bar-restaurant housed in a giant tepee provides a convivial social hub.

Helmsley YHA HOSTEL £
(☎0845 371 9638; www.yha.org.uk; Carlton Lane; dm/q from £15/49; P wi-fi family) This hostel's location, just 400m east of the market square at the start of the Cleveland Way, means it's often busy, so book in advance.

Feathers Hotel INN ££
(☎01439-770275; www.feathershotelhelmsley.co.uk; Market Pl; s/d from £90/100; P wi-fi family pets) One of a number of old coaching inns on the market square that offer B&B, decent grub and a pint of hand-pumped real ale. There are four-poster beds in some bedrooms and historical trimmings throughout.

Feversham Arms HOTEL £££
(☎01439-770766; www.fevershamarms.com; High St; r from £200; P wi-fi pool) A rustic hotel given a designer makeover, the Feversham Arms has a snug and sophisticated atmosphere where country charm meets boutique chic. Individually decorated bedrooms are complemented by an excellent restaurant, spa treatments and a heated outdoor pool in the central courtyard.

Eating

★Hare Inn MODERN BRITISH £££
(☎01845-597769; www.thehare-inn.com; Scawton; per person £30-60; ⊙noon-2.30pm & 6-9pm Wed-Sat, noon-4pm Sun; P) The phrase 'hidden gem' is overused, but here it is entirely appropriate – drowsing in a secluded hamlet 4 miles west of Helmsley, the Hare is a 21st-century restaurant in a 13th-century inn, where gourmet dining is relaxed, informal and even fun. There's no á la carte, just a choice of three tasting menus that change continually to take advantage of seasonal produce.

★Star Inn MODERN BRITISH £££
(☎01439-770397; www.thestaratharome.co.uk; Harome; mains £16-29; ⊙11.30am-2pm Tue-Sat, 6.15-9.30pm Mon-Sat, noon-6pm Sun; P family) This thatch-roofed country pub is home to a Michelin-starred restaurant, with a menu specialising in top-quality produce from the surrounding countryside: Whitby crab with pickled cockles and avocado 'ice', or roast English quail with braised salsify and bergamot preserve. There's also a set three-course menu for £25 (Monday to Saturday). Harome is about 2 miles southeast of Helmsley off the A170.

The Star is the sort of place you won't want to leave, and the good news is you don't have to – the adjacent lodge has nine magnificent bedrooms (£170 to £260), each decorated in classic but luxurious country style.

Shopping

Hunters of Helmsley FOOD & DRINKS
(01439-771307; www.huntersofhelmsley.com; 13 Market Pl; 9am-4.30pm Sun-Thu, 8am-5.30pm Fri & Sat) Offers a cornucopia of locally made chutneys, jams, beers, cheeses, bacon, gourmet pies and sausage rolls, jams, sweets and ice cream – a great place to stock up for a posh picnic.

Thomas of Helmsley FOOD & DRINKS
(01439-770249; 18 Market Pl; 7.30am-5.30pm Mon-Sat, 10am-4pm Sun) A butcher and deli specialising in local produce, including delicious homemade sausages.

Information

There's a **tourist office** (www.visitryedale.co.uk; Cut-Price Bookstore, 11 Market Pl; 9.30am-5.30pm Mon-Sat, 11am-4.30pm Sun) in a local bookshop, providing leaflets, maps and public-transport advice.

Getting There & Away

All buses stop in the main square. Bus 31X runs from York to Helmsley (£7.60, 1¼ hours, four daily Monday to Saturday). From Scarborough, take bus 128 (£7.60, 1¾ hours, hourly Monday to Saturday, four times on Sunday) via Pickering.

Pickering

POP 6590

Pickering is a lively market town with an imposing Norman castle that advertises itself as the 'gateway to the North York Moors'. That gateway is the terminus of the wonderful North Yorkshire Moors Railway, a picturesque survivor from the great days of steam.

Two scenic drives head north across the moors: the A169 to Whitby leads past the **Hole of Horcum** beauty spot and the hiking trails of **Goathland**; and the Blakey Ridge road (beginning 6 miles west of town) passes through the pretty village of **Hutton-le-Hole** and the famous **Lion Inn** on the way to Danby.

Sights

North Yorkshire Moors Railway HERITAGE RAILWAY
(NYMR; www.nymr.co.uk; Pickering-Whitby day-rover ticket adult/child £30/13.50; Apr-Oct) This privately owned railway runs for 18 miles through beautiful countryside from Pickering to Whitby. Lovingly restored steam locos pull period carriages resplendent with polished brass and bright paintwork, appealing to railway buffs and day trippers alike. For visitors without wheels, it's excellent for reaching out-of-the-way spots and devising walks between stations.

Pickering Castle CASTLE
(EH; www.english-heritage.org.uk; Castlegate; adult/child £5.10/3.10; 10am-6pm Apr-Sep, to 5pm Oct) Pickering Castle is a lot like the castles we drew as kids: thick stone outer walls circle the keep, and the whole lot is perched atop a high motte (mound) with great views of the surrounding countryside. Founded by William the Conqueror, it was added to and altered by later kings.

Sleeping & Eating

★**Eleven Westgate** B&B ££
(01751-475111; www.elevenwestgate.co.uk; 11 Westgate; s/d £65/89;) Just a few minutes' walk west of the town centre, Eleven Westgate is a pretty house with patio and garden offering top-value accommodation in cosy bedrooms. Cyclists are well catered for, with a bike wash, drying room and secure storage. Breakfast choices include the full Yorkshire fry-up or a vegetarian version.

17 Burgate B&B ££
(01751-473463; www.17burgate.co.uk; 17 Burgate; s/d £95/110;) Tea and cake on arrival set the mood at this elegant Georgian town house; its quiet and luxurious bedrooms exude a period atmosphere. Breakfast (cooked on an Aga stove, of course) makes the most of locally sourced produce, along with homemade marmalade and muesli.

★**White Swan Hotel** HOTEL £££
(01751-472288; www.white-swan.co.uk; Market Pl; r from £149;) The top spot in town successfully combines a smart pub, a superb restaurant serving local produce cooked with a Continental twist (mains £14 to £25), and a luxurious boutique hotel. Nine modern rooms in the converted coach house up the ante, with flatscreen TVs and other stylish paraphernalia adding to the luxury found throughout the hotel.

Pickering Station Tearoom CAFE £
(Park St; mains £4-6; ⌚8.30am-4pm) The tearoom at Pickering station serves excellent home-baked goodies and tasty lunch specials such as Yorkshire pudding with roast beef and gravy.

Information

The **tourist office** (Morlands Newsagent, 7 Market Pl; ⌚5am-5.30pm Mon-Sat, to 12.30pm Sun) has the usual details, as well as plenty of railway-related info.

Getting There & Away

Bus 128 between Helmsley (£4.50, 40 minutes) and Scarborough (£5.50, 50 minutes) runs hourly via Pickering. Bus 840 between Leeds and Whitby links Pickering with York (£8.80, 70 minutes, hourly).

Whitby

POP 13,215

Whitby is a town of two parts, split down the middle by the River Esk. It's also a town with two personalities – on the one hand, a busy commercial and fishing port (once home to 18th-century explorer Captain James Cook) with a bustling quayside fish market; on the other, a traditional seaside resort, complete with sandy beach, amusement arcades and promenading holidaymakers. Keeping a watchful eye over the town is an atmospheric ruined abbey atop the East Cliff, the inspiration and setting for part of Bram Stoker's Gothic horror story *Dracula*.

Whitby is also famous for the jet (fossilised wood) that has been mined from its sea cliffs for centuries. This smooth black substance was popularised in the 19th century when Queen Victoria took to wearing mourning jewellery made from Whitby jet. In recent years these morbid associations have seen the rise of a series of hugely popular Goth festivals.

Sights

★**Whitby Abbey** RUINS
(EH; www.english-heritage.org.uk; adult/child £7.90/4.70; ⌚10am-6pm Apr-Sep, to 5pm Oct, to 4pm Tue-Sat Nov, to 4pm Sat & Sun Dec-Mar; P) There are ruined abbeys; and there are picturesque ruined abbeys. And then there's Whitby Abbey, dominating the skyline above the East Cliff like a great Gothic tombstone silhouetted against the sky. Looking as though it was built as an atmospheric film set rather than a monastic establishment, it is hardly surprising that this medieval hulk inspired the Victorian novelist Bram Stoker (who holidayed in Whitby) to make it the setting for Count Dracula's dramatic landfall.

From the end of Church St, the 199 steps of **Church Stairs** will lead you steeply up to Whitby Abbey. By car, you have to approach from the A171 Scarborough road to the east side of the bridge over the River Esk.

★**Captain Cook Memorial Museum** MUSEUM
(www.cookmuseumwhitby.co.uk; Grape Lane; adult/child £5.40/3.50; ⌚9.45am-5pm Apr-Oct, 11am-3pm Mar) This fascinating museum occupies the house of the ship owner with whom Cook began his seafaring career. Highlights include the attic where Cook lodged as a young apprentice, Cook's own maps and letters, etchings from the South Seas, and a wonderful model of the *Endeavour*, with the crew and stores all laid out for inspection.

Whitby Sands BEACH
Whitby Sands, stretching west from the harbour mouth, offers donkey rides, ice-cream vendors and bucket-and-spade escapades, though the sand is mostly covered at high tide. The beach can be reached on a path from Whitby Pavilion, or from West Cliff via the **cliff lift** (per person 60p; ⌚10am-5.30pm May-Sep), an elevator that has been in service since 1931.

Whitby Museum MUSEUM
(www.whitbymuseum.org.uk; Pannett Park; adult/child £5/free; ⌚9am-5pm Mon-Sat, 9.30am-4.30pm Sun; 👪) Set in a park to the west of the town centre is the wonderfully eclectic Whitby Museum, with displays of fossil plesiosaurs and dinosaur footprints, Captain Cook memorabilia, ships in bottles, jet jewellery and the gruesome 'Hand of Glory', a preserved human hand reputedly cut from the corpse of an executed criminal.

Activities

Whitby Whale Watching WILDLIFE
(☎07941 450381; www.whitbywhalewatching.net; Brewery Steps; per person £40) Join a four-hour cruise offshore to spot marine wildlife. Sightings of seals, porpoises and dolphins are almost guaranteed year-round, but August and September offer the best chances of seeing whales (usually Minke whales, more rarely humpback, sei and fin).

Trailways CYCLING
(☎01947-820207; www.trailways.info; Old Railway Station, Hawsker; per day from £17; ⏰9.30am-6pm) Bike-rental place in an old railway station on the Whitby to Scarborough cycle path, 2.5 miles southeast of Whitby.

Festivals & Events

Whitby Goth Weekends CULTURAL
(www.whitbygothweekend.co.uk; tickets 1/2 days £34/65) Goth and steampunk heaven, with live-music gigs, events and the Bizarre Bazaar – dozens of traders selling Goth gear, jewellery, art and music. Held twice yearly in late April or early May and late October or early November.

Whitby Spring Session MUSIC, ART
(www.moorandcoast.co.uk; tickets from £40) Beards, sandals and real ale abound at this traditional festival of folk music, dance and dubious Celtic art on the May Bank Holiday weekend.

Sleeping

YHA Whitby HOSTEL £
(☎0845 371 9049; www.yha.org.uk; Church Lane; dm/tw £23/59; P @ 📶 👪) With an unbeatable setting in an old mansion next to the abbey, this hostel is incredibly popular – you'll have to book well in advance to get your body into one of the bunks here. Hike up the 199 steps from the town, or take bus 97 from the train station to Whitby Abbey (twice hourly Monday to Saturday).

Harbour Grange HOSTEL £
(☎01947-600817; www.whitbybackpackers.co.uk; Spital Bridge; dm from £18; P) Less than 10 minutes' walk from the train station, this clean and basic hostel is conveniently located and has great views – it has picnic tables right beside the harbour. There's an 11.30pm curfew – just the ticket for a night when you don't want to paint the town red.

★**La Rosa Hotel** HOTEL ££
(☎01947-606981; www.larosa.co.uk/hotel; 5 East Tce; d £86-135; 📶) 🍃 Weird, but wonderful. Lewis Carroll, author of *Alice in Wonderland,* once stayed in this house while holidaying in Whitby. And entering today is like stepping through the looking glass into an antique world of love-it-or-hate-it Victorian bric-a-brac and kitsch. Eight quirky and atmospheric bedrooms (one with a wooden bath!), great sea views, no TVs, and breakfast served in a basket in your room.

Trailways APARTMENT ££
(☎01947-820207; www.trailways.info; Hawsker; per week high season £699; P) If travelling on the North Yorkshire Moors Railway has given you a taste for trains, how about sleeping in one? Trailways has a beautifully converted InterCity 125 coach parked at the old Hawsker train station on the Whitby–Scarborough cycle route, offering luxurious self-catering accommodation with all mod cons for two to six people.

Langley Hotel B&B ££
(☎01947-604250; www.langleyhotel.com; 16 Royal Cres; s/d from £70/105; 📶) With its cream-and-crimson colour scheme, and a gilt four-poster bed in one room, this grand old guesthouse exudes a whiff of Victorian splendour. Go for room 1, 2 or 6, if possible, to make the most of the panoramic views – the same as those enjoyed in 1897 by Bram Stoker, author of *Dracula,* who holidayed a few doors along at No 6.

Shepherd's Purse GUESTHOUSE ££
(☎01947-820228; www.theshepherdspurse.com; Sanders Yard, Church St; d £65-85; 📶) This place offers a romantic hideaway clustered around a hidden courtyard off busy Church St. The en suite bedrooms are charmingly rustic and, while the four-poster beds can feel a bit as though they've been shoehorned in, the atmosphere is cute rather than cramped. Two-night minimum stay April to October; breakfast is not provided.

CAPTAIN COOK – WHITBY'S ADOPTED SON

Although he was born in Marton (now a suburb of Middlesborough), the renowned explorer Captain James Cook has been adopted by Whitby. Ever since the first tourists got off the train in Victorian times, local entrepreneurs have mercilessly cashed in on Cook's memory, as endless Endeavour Cafes and Captain Cook Chip Shops testify.

Still, Whitby played a key role in Cook's eventual success as a world-famous explorer. It was here that he first went to sea, serving his apprenticeship with local ship owners, and the design of the ships used for his voyages of discovery – including the *Endeavour* – were based on the design of Whitby 'cats', flat-bottomed ships that carried coal from Newcastle to London.

Whitby

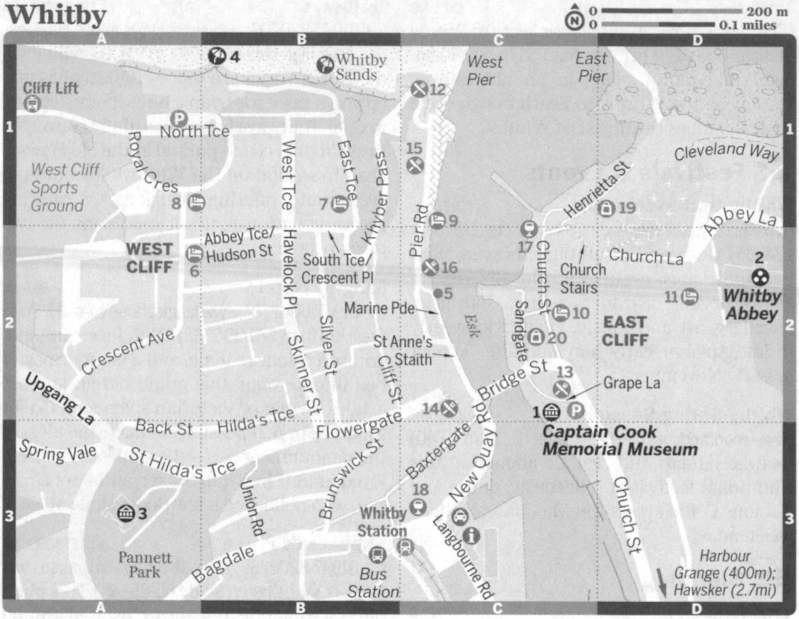

Whitby

Top Sights
1 Captain Cook Memorial Museum......... C2
2 Whitby Abbey......... D2

Sights
3 Whitby Museum......... A3
4 Whitby Sands......... B1

Activities, Courses & Tours
5 Whitby Whale Watching......... C2

Sleeping
6 Argyle House......... A2
7 La Rosa Hotel......... B1
8 Langley Hotel......... A1
9 Marine Hotel......... C1
10 Shepherd's Purse......... C2
11 YHA Whitby......... D2

Eating
12 Fisherman's Wife......... C1
13 Humble Pie 'n' Mash......... C2
14 Java Cafe-Bar......... C2
15 Magpie Cafe......... C1
16 Moon & Sixpence......... C2

Drinking & Nightlife
17 Duke of York......... C2
18 Station Inn......... C3

Shopping
19 Fortune's Kippers......... D1
20 Hildoceras......... C2

Argyle House B&B ££
(01947-821877; www.argyle-house.co.uk; 18 Hudson St; per person £37-43; wi-fi) Lovely Victorian guesthouse near the West Sands, comfortable as old slippers, with kippers for breakfast. Discount available for multinight stays.

★**Marine Hotel** INN £££
(01947-605022; www.the-marine-hotel.co.uk; 13 Marine Pde; r £100-195; wi-fi) Feeling more like minisuites than ordinary hotel accommodation, the four bedrooms at the Marine are quirky, stylish and comfortable; it's the sort of place that makes you want to stay in rather than go out. Ask for one of the two rooms with a balcony – they have great views across the harbour.

Eating

Humble Pie 'n' Mash BRITISH £
(www.humblepie.tccdev.com; 163 Church St; mains £6; noon-8pm Mon-Sat, to 4pm Sun) Superb homemade pies with fillings ranging

from lamb, leek and rosemary to roast veg and goats cheese, served in a cosy timber-framed cottage.

Java Cafe-Bar CAFE £
(01947-821973; 2 Flowergate; mains £5-8; 8am-6pm;) A cool little diner with stainless-steel counters and retro decor, music videos on the flatscreen and a menu of healthy salads, sandwiches and wraps washed down with excellent coffee.

★**Fisherman's Wife** SEAFOOD ££
(01947-603500; thefishermanswife.co.uk; Khyber Pass; mains £8-15; noon-8.30pm Mon-Thu, to 8.45pm Fri & Sat, to 8pm Sun;) With a prime location overlooking the beach and harbour entrance and smart staff dressed in navy-blue aprons, this is the place to enjoy local seafood in style. Whitby lobster (half/whole around £20/36 depending on market prices) is served as a salad, grilled with garlic, or thermidor style, while local crab comes with smoked salmon, avocado, apple and fennel.

★**Moon & Sixpence** BRASSERIE ££
(01947-604416; www.moon-and-sixpence.co.uk; 5 Marine Pde; mains £9-18; 9am-midnight;) This brasserie and cocktail bar has a prime position, with views across the harbour to the abbey ruins. The seafood-dominated menu concentrates on hearty, straightforward dishes such as chunky vegetable soup, seafood chowder, fish pie, homemade burgers, and mussels and chips. Excellent breakfasts too, including local Fortune's kippers with brown bread and butter.

Magpie Cafe SEAFOOD ££
(www.magpiecafe.co.uk; 14 Pier Rd; mains £8-23; 11.30am-9pm;) The Magpie flaunts its reputation for serving the 'World's Best Fish and Chips'. Damn fine they are too, but the world and his dog knows about it and summertime queues can stretch along the street. Takeaway fish and chips cost £4.95; the sit-down restaurant is more expensive, but offers a wide range of seafood dishes, from grilled sea bass to paella.

Drinking & Nightlife

Station Inn PUB
(www.stationinnwhitby.co.uk; New Quay Rd; 10am-midnight Mon-Sat, to 11.30pm Sun;) The best place in town for atmosphere and real ale, with its impressive range of cask-conditioned beers including Timothy Taylor's Golden Best and Ossett Silver King. Live music Wednesday, Friday, Saturday and Sunday.

Duke of York PUB
(www.dukeofyork.co.uk; Church St; 11am-11pm Sun-Thu, to 11.30pm Fri, to midnight Sat;) A popular watering hole at the bottom of the Church Stairs, serving Timothy Taylor ales, fish and chips, and great views over the harbour.

Shopping

Fortune's Kippers FOOD
(01947-601659; www.fortuneskippers.co.uk; 22 Henrietta St; 9am-3pm Mon-Sat, 10am-1pm Sun) Fortune's has been making kippers (smoked herring) at this little smokehouse since 1872, and still turns out some of Britain's best; they're on the breakfast menu in many of Whitby's hotels and B&Bs. How to cook them? Either smear with butter and grill until bubbling, or poach in boiling water for five minutes.

Hildoceras GIFTS & SOUVENIRS
(01947-604188; 12 Sandgate; 10am-6pm) Fascinating gift shop selling all kinds of stuff, including fossils, minerals, crystals, insects preserved in amber, jewellery and leather goods.

Information

Whitby Tourist Office (01947-602674; www.visitwhitby.com; Langbourne Rd; 9.30am-6pm Apr-Oct, to 4.30pm Nov-Mar)

Getting There & Away

Bus Two buses, 93 and X93, run south to Scarborough (£5.70, one hour, every 30 minutes), with every second bus going via Robin Hood's Bay (£4, 15 minutes, hourly); and north to Middlesborough (£5.70, one hour, hourly), with fewer services on Sunday.

DRACULA IN WHITBY

The famous story of *Dracula*, inspiration for a thousand lurid horror movies, was written by Bram Stoker while holidaying in Whitby in 1897 (a blue plaque at 6 Royal Cres marks the house where he stayed). Although most Hollywood versions of the tale concentrate on deepest, darkest Transylvania, a large part of the original book was set in Whitby, and many of the sites can still be seen today.

Get hold of a *Dracula Trail* leaflet (£1) from the tourist office, which will lead you around all the places in town linked to Bram Stoker and Dracula.

The Coastliner service 840 runs from Leeds to Whitby (£13.50, 3¼ hours, six times daily Monday to Saturday) via York and Pickering.

Train Coming from the north, you can get to Whitby by train along the Esk Valley Railway from Middlesborough (£6.80, 1½ hours, four per day), with connections from Durham and Newcastle. From the south, it's easier to get a train from York to Scarborough, and then a bus from Scarborough to Whitby.

Robin Hood's Bay

Picturesque Robin Hood's Bay has nothing to do with the hero of Sherwood Forest – the origin of its name is a mystery, and the locals call it Bay Town or just Bay. But there's no denying that this fishing village is one of the prettiest spots on the Yorkshire coast.

Leave your car at the parking area in the upper village (£3.50 for four hours), where 19th-century ships' captains built comfortable Victorian villas, and walk downhill to Old Bay, the oldest part of the village (don't even think about driving down). This maze of narrow lanes and passages is dotted with tearooms, pubs, craft shops and artists' studios (there's even a tiny cinema) and at low tide you can go down onto the beach and fossick around in the rock pools.

Sights

Old Coastguard Station INTERPRETATION CENTRE
(www.nationaltrust.org.uk; The Dock; 10am-5pm Apr-Nov, to 4pm Sat & Sun Dec-Mar) FREE National Trust visitor centre housing an exhibition about local geology and natural history.

Eating & Drinking

Swell Cafe CAFE £
(www.swell.org.uk; Chapel St; mains £3-8; 9.30am-3.30pm Mon-Fri, to 4pm Sat & Sun;) Great coffee, soup, salads and sandwiches, and a terrace with a view over the beach.

Ye Dolphin PUB
(01947-880337; King St; 11.30am-11pm Mon-Sat, noon-11pm Sun;) The Bay's best pub for ambience and real ale; the local folk-music club meets here on Friday evenings.

Getting There & Away

Robin Hood's Bay is 6 miles southeast of Whitby. Bus 93 runs hourly between Whitby and Scarborough via Robin Hood's Bay; the bus stop is at the top of the hill, in the new part of town.

YORKSHIRE DALES NATIONAL PARK

The Yorkshire Dales – named from the old Norse word *dalr*, meaning 'valleys', and protected as a national park since the 1950s – is the central jewel in the necklace of three national parks strung across the throat of northern England, with the dramatic fells of the Lake District to the west and the brooding heaths of the North York Moors to the east.

From well-known names such as Wensleydale and Ribblesdale to the obscure and evocative Langstrothdale and Arkengarthdale, the park's glacial valleys are characterised by a distinctive landscape of high heather moorland, stepped skylines and flat-topped hills. Down in the green valleys, patchworked with drystone dykes and little barns, are picture-postcard villages where sheep and cattle still graze on village greens. And in the limestone country of the southern Dales you'll find England's best examples of karst scenery (created by rainwater dissolving the underlying limestone bedrock).

Getting There & Around

About 90% of visitors to the park arrive by car, and the narrow roads can become extremely crowded in summer. Parking can also be a serious problem. If you can, try to use public transport as much as possible.

Bus services are limited, and many run in summer only, some on Sundays and bank holidays only; pick up a DalesBus timetable from tourist offices, or consult the Dalesbus (www.dalesbus.org) website. The main routes run from Richmond to Ribblehead via Reeth, Keld and Hawes; from Richmond to Leyburn; and from Skipton to Kettlewell via Grassington.

By train, the best and most interesting access to the Dales is via the famous **Settle–Carlisle Line** (p528). Trains run between Leeds and Carlisle, stopping at Skipton, Settle and numerous small villages, offering unrivalled access to the hills straight from the station platform.

Skipton

POP 14,625

This busy market town on the southern edge of the Dales takes its name from the Anglo-Saxon *sceape ton* (sheep town). There are no prizes for guessing how it made its money. Market days bring crowds from all over and giving the town something of a festive atmosphere.

WORTH A TRIP

GOATHLAND

This picture-postcard halt on the North Yorkshire Moors Railway stars as Hogsmeade train station in the Harry Potter films, and the village appears as Aidensfield in the British TV series *Heartbeat*. It's also the starting point for lots of easy and enjoyable walks, often with the chuff-chuff-chuff of passing steam engines in the background.

One of the most popular hikes is to head northwest from the train station (via a gate on the platform on the far side from the village) to the hamlet of Beck Hole, where you can stop for a pork pie and a pint of Black Sheep at the wonderfully atmospheric **Birch Hall Inn** (www.beckhole.info; Beck Hole; ⏲11am-11pm May-Sep, shorter hours & closed Tue Oct-Apr; 👪🐾), where it's like stepping into the past. Return to Goathland via the waterfall at Mallyan Spout (total 4 miles).

An alternative to the hike is to walk or cycle from Goathland along Beck Hole Rd (just over 1 mile); best not to drive, as the road is narrow and twisty and there's nowhere to park.

Sights & Activities

High St STREET

Skipton's pride and joy is the broad and bustling High St, one of the most attractive shopping streets in Yorkshire. There's a **general market** on High St four days a week (Monday, Wednesday, Friday and Saturday), and on the first Sunday of the month the nearby canal basin hosts a **farmers market** (⏲9am-3pm).

Skipton Castle CASTLE

(www.skiptoncastle.co.uk; High St; adult/child £7.80/4.90; ⏲10am-6pm Mon-Sat, noon-6pm Sun Apr-Sep, to 5pm Oct-Mar) A gate to the side of the church at the north end of High St leads to Skipton Castle, one of the best-preserved medieval castles in England, a fascinating contrast to the ruins you'll see elsewhere.

Pennine Cruisers BOATING

(www.penninecruisers.com; The Wharf, Coach St; per person £4; ⏲10.30am-dusk Mar-Oct) No trip to Skipton is complete without a cruise along the Leeds–Liverpool Canal, which runs through the middle of town. Pennine Cruisers runs half-hour trips to Skipton Castle and back.

Sleeping

Park Hill B&B ££

(☎01756-792772; www.parkhillskipton.co.uk; 17 Grassington Rd; d £85; P@🛜) 🍃 From the complimentary glass of sherry on arrival to the hearty breakfasts based on local produce, farm-fresh eggs and home-grown tomatoes, this B&B provides a real Yorkshire welcome. It enjoys an attractive rural location half a mile north of the town centre, on the B6265 road towards Grassington.

Carlton House B&B ££

(☎01756-700921; www.carltonhouseskipton.co.uk; 46 Keighley Rd; s/d from £40/60) A handsome house with five pretty and comfortable rooms (there are no frills, but lots of floral prints) this B&B is deservedly popular on account of its friendly welcome, and is just a short walk south of the town centre.

Eating & Drinking

Bizzie Lizzies FISH & CHIPS £

(☎01756-701131; www.bizzielizzies.co.uk; 36 Swadford St; mains £6-10; ⏲11am-9pm; 👪🐾) An award-winning sit-down fish-and-chip restaurant overlooking the canal. There's also a takeaway counter offering fish and chips for £5, open to 11.30pm.

★**Le Caveau** BRITISH ££

(☎01756-794274; www.lecaveau.co.uk; 86 High St; mains £17-20; ⏲noon-2.30pm & 7-9.30pm Tue-Fri, 5-9.30pm Sat) 🍃 Set in a stylishly decorated 16th-century cellar with barrel-vaulted ceilings, this friendly bistro offers a seasonal menu built lovingly around fresh local produce. Daily specials include dishes such as home-cured sea trout with mustard aioli, and cider-marinated pork fillet with crispy black pudding. On weekdays you can get a two-course lunch for £12.

Filmore & Union HEALTH FOOD ££

(☎01756-700738; www.filmoreandunion.com; 66 High St; mains £8-16; ⏲8am-6pm Mon-Wed, to 10pm Thu-Sat, 9am-5pm Sun; 🛜🌶🐾) This San Francisco–inspired, Yorkshire-based chain of restaurants (there are branches in York, Leeds, Beverley and Harrogate) specialises in fresh salads, smoothies and juices. There are lots of vegetarian, vegan, low-sugar and gluten-free options alongside healthy meat dishes including burgers, steaks and chicken *shawarma* (skewers).

Narrow Boat PUB
(www.narrowboatskipton.co.uk; 38 Victoria St; noon-11pm;) A traditionally styled pub with a great selection of local ales and foreign beers, friendly service and bar meals.

Information

The **tourist office** (01756-792809; www.welcometoskipton.com; High St; 9.30am-4pm Mon-Sat & 10am-4pm 1st Sun of month) is in the town hall.

Getting There & Away

Skipton is the last stop on the Metro rail network from Leeds (£9.40, 45 minutes, half-hourly, hourly on Sunday). Three buses a day (weekdays only) link Skipton with Settle (£6.20, 40 minutes)

Grassington

The perfect base for jaunts around the south Dales, Grassington's handsome Georgian centre teems with walkers and visitors throughout the summer months, soaking up an atmosphere that – despite the odd touch of faux rusticity – is as attractive and traditional as you'll find in these parts.

Highlight of the year is June's Grassington Festival, a two-week celebration of the arts.

Sleeping & Eating

Ashfield House B&B ££
(01756-752584; www.ashfieldhouse.co.uk; Summers Fold; r from £105;) A secluded 17th-century country house behind a walled garden, with exposed stone walls, open fireplaces and an all-round cosy feel. It's just off the main square.

Yorkshire Dales National Park

0 10 km
0 5 miles

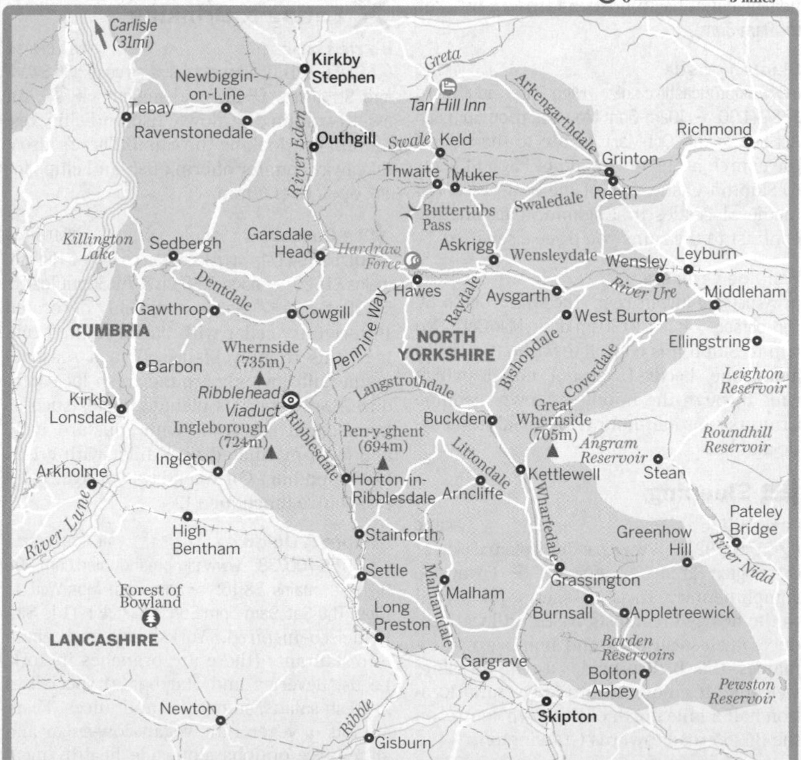

★Devonshire Fell
HOTEL £££

(01756-718111; www.devonshirefell.co.uk; Burnsall; r from £129;) This former gentleman's club for mill owners has a very contemporary feel, with beautiful modern furnishings crafted by local experts. The conservatory (used as a restaurant and breakfast room) has a stunning view over the valley. It's 3 miles southeast of Grassington on the B6160.

Corner House Cafe
CAFE £

(01756-752414; www.cornerhousegrassington.co.uk; 1 Garr's Lane; mains £6-9; 10am-4pm;) This cute little white cottage, just uphill from the village square, serves good coffee and unusual homemade cakes (citrus and lavender syrup sponge is unexpectedly delicious), as well as tasty lunch specials such as *croque monsieur* (gourmet toasted ham-and-cheese sandwich) or chicken and chorizo gratin. Breakfast, served till 11.30am, ranges from cinnamon toast to the full English fry-up.

Festivals & Events

Grassington Festival
ART

(www.grassington-festival.org.uk) Highlight of the cultural year in the Yorkshire Dales is the Grassington Festival, a two-week arts extravaganza held in June that attracts many big names in music, theatre and comedy, and also includes offbeat events like drystone-walling workshops.

Information

The **tourist office** (01756-751690; Hebden Rd; 10am-5pm Apr-Oct, to 4pm Sat & Sun Nov, Dec, Feb & Mar) is beside the big car park on the edge of town.

Getting There & Away

Grassington is 6 miles north of Skipton; take bus 72 from Skipton bus or train station (£3.90, 30 minutes, hourly Monday to Saturday), or X43 (hourly, Sunday) from the bus station only. For onward travel, bus 72 continues up the valley to the villages of Kettlewell and Buckden.

Malham

POP 120

Stretching west from Grassington to Ingleton is the largest area of limestone country in England, a distinctive landscape pockmarked with potholes, dry valleys, limestone pavements and gorges. Two of the most spectacular features – Malham Cove and Gordale Scar – lie near the pretty village of Malham.

Activities

★Malham Cove
AMPITHEATRE

A 0.75-mile walk north from Malham village lies Malham Cove, a huge rock amphitheatre lined with 80m-high vertical cliffs. Peregrine falcons nest here in spring, when the Royal Society for the Protection of Birds (RSPB) sets up a birdwatching lookout. You can hike up the steep steps on the left-hand side of the cove (on the Pennine Way footpath) to see the extensive limestone pavement above the cliffs. Another 1.5 miles further north is **Malham Tarn**, a glacial lake and nature reserve.

A mile east of Malham is spectacular **Gordale Scar**, a deep limestone canyon with scenic cascades and remains of an Iron Age settlement.

Sleeping

YHA Malham
HOSTEL £

(0845 371 9529; www.yha.org.uk; dm/tw £25/55;) You will find this recently refurbished, purpose-built hostel across the bridge from the village centre. The facilities are top-notch, including a shop, a bar and a cafe, and young children are well catered for.

★Beck Hall
HOTEL ££

(01729-830332; www.beckhallmalham.com; d £90-110;) Ideally located for walks to Malham Cove, this rambling 17th-century country house has a gurgling beck (stream) flowing through the garden, 18 individually decorated rooms, all chunkily rustic with old-style furnishings and some with antique four-poster beds, and a lovely oak-panelled lounge with an open fire in winter.

Information

The **national park centre** (01969-652380; www.yorkshiredales.org.uk; 10am-5pm Apr-Oct, to 4pm Sat & Sun Nov-Mar) in the car park at the southern edge of the village has the usual information. See also www.malhamdale.com.

Getting There & Away

There are between two and five buses a day (except Tuesday and Thursday) from Skipton to Malham (£4, 45 minutes), and the Malham Tarn Shuttle bus links Settle and Malham (£3.50, 25 minutes) four times daily on Sundays only, Easter to October. Check the Dalesbus website (www.dalesbus.org) or ask at Skipton tourist office for details. Note that Malham is reached via narrow roads that can get very congested in summer, so leave your car at the national park centre and walk into the village.

Ribblesdale & the Three Peaks

Scenic Ribblesdale cuts through the south-western corner of the Yorkshire Dales National Park, where the skyline is dominated by a trio of distinctive hills known as the Three Peaks: Whernside (735m), Ingleborough (724m) and Pen-y-ghent (694m). Easily accessible via the Settle–Carlisle railway line, this is one of England's most popular areas for outdoor activities, attracting thousands of hikers, cyclists and cavers each weekend.

At the head of the valley, 5 miles north of Horton, is the spectacular 30m-high Ribblehead Viaduct, built in 1874 and, at 400m, the longest on the Settle–Carlisle Line. You can hike there along the Pennine Way and travel back by train from Ribblehead station.

Settle

POP 3660

The busy market town of Settle, dominated by its grand neo-Gothic town hall, is the gateway to Ribblesdale and marks the beginning of the scenic part of the famous Settle–Carlisle railway line. Narrow cobbled streets lined with shops and pubs lead out from the central market square (Tuesday is market day), and the town offers plenty of accommodation options.

OFF THE BEATEN TRACK

EXPLORING THE DALES

Whether on two wheels or four, one of the joys of the Yorkshire Dales is exploring the hidden corners of the lesser-known valleys. From Swaledale, climb up to the moors above Arkengarthdale in search of the **Tan Hill Inn** (01833-628246; www.tanhillinn.com; Tan Hill, Reeth; 8am-11.30pm Jul & Aug, noon-9.30pm Sep-Jun;), Britain's highest pub, or seek out the picture-postcard village green at **West Burton**, at the entrance to Bishopdale. From Grassington, make your way north along lovely Littondale and stop for a pint at the **Falcon Inn** (www.thefalconinn.com; Arncliffe; noon-3pm & 7-11pm Mon-Thu, noon-11pm Fri & Sat, noon-10.30pm Sun), where beer is still served from a jug on the counter.

Eating

Ye Olde Naked Man CAFE £

(Market Pl; mains £4-8; 9am-5pm Thu-Tue, to 4pm Wed;) Formerly an undertaker's (look for the 'naked man' on the outside wall, dated 1663), Ye Olde Naked Man serves superb Yorkshire pudding with a choice of fillings.

Information

The **tourist office** (01729-825192; Town Hall, Cheapside; 9.30am-4pm Mon-Sat year-round, to 4pm Sun Apr-Oct, 10am-2pm Sun Nov-Mar) has maps and guidebooks.

Getting There & Away

Trains from Leeds heading to Carlisle stop at Settle station near the town centre (£12.40, one hour, every two hours).

Horton-in-Ribblesdale

POP 560

A favourite with outdoor enthusiasts, the little village of Horton-in-Ribblesdale and its railway station is 5 miles north of Settle. Everything centres on the Pen-y-Ghent Cafe, which acts as the village tourist office, wet-weather retreat and hikers' information centre.

Horton is the starting point for climbing Pen-y-ghent and doing the Three Peaks Walk; it's also a stop on the Pennine Way.

Sleeping & Eating

Holme Farm Campsite CAMPGROUND £

(01729-860281; tent sites £4 plus per person £3, shower £1) A basic, no-frills campsite next door to the Golden Lion pub, much used by Pennine Way hikers.

Golden Lion INN £

(01729-860206; www.goldenlionhotel.co.uk; s/d from £45/70, bunkhouse per person £12;) The Golden Lion is a lively pub that offers comfortable B&B rooms, a 15-bed bunkhouse, and three public bars where you can tuck into a bit of grub washed down with a pint of hand-pulled ale.

Pen-y-Ghent Cafe CAFE £

(mains £3-6; 9am-5.30pm Mon & Wed-Fri, 8am-5.30pm Sat & Sun;) A traditional cafe run by the same family since 1965, the Pen-y-Ghent fills walkers' fuel tanks with fried eggs and chips, homemade scones and pint-sized mugs of tea. It also sells maps, guidebooks and walking gear.

Hawes

POP 885

Hawes is the beating heart of Wensleydale, a thriving and picturesque market town (market day is Tuesday) with several antique, art and craft shops that has the added attraction of its own waterfall in the village centre. On busy summer weekends, however, Hawes' narrow arteries can get seriously clogged with traffic. Leave the car in the parking area beside the national park centre at the eastern entrance to the village.

Sights

Dales Countryside Museum MUSEUM
(☎01969-666210; www.dalescountrysidemuseum.org.uk; Station Yard; adult/child £4.50/free; ⊙10am-5pm, closed Jan; P) Sharing a building with the national park centre, the Dales Countryside Museum is a beautifully presented social history of the area that explains the forces shaping the landscape, from geology to lead mining to land enclosure.

Wensleydale Creamery MUSEUM
(www.wensleydale.co.uk; adult/child £2.50/1.50; ⊙10am-4pm; P) Wensleydale Creamery is devoted to the production of a crumbly white cheese that's the favourite of animation characters Wallace and Gromit. You can visit the cheese museum, watch cheesemakers in action in the viewing gallery, and then try-before-you-buy in the shop (which is free to enter). A new interactive exhibit for kids explains the process from grass to cow to cheese.

Hardraw Force WATERFALL
(www.hardrawforce.com; Hardraw; per person £2.50; P) About 1.5 miles north of Hawes is 30m-high Hardraw Force, the highest unbroken waterfall in England, but by international standards not that impressive (except after heavy rain). Access is via a lovely landscaped walk (400m) from the car park behind the Green Dragon Inn, which levies an admission fee.

Sheepdog Demonstrations FARM
(www.sheepdogdemo.co.uk; Hardraw; adult/child £5/1; ⊙6.30pm Thu May-Aug, 2.30pm Thu Sep & Oct; P) On Thursdays from May to October, a local farmer gives demonstrations of working sheepdogs, held in a field 800m north of Hawes on the minor road towards Hardraw.

Sleeping & Eating

Bainbridge Ings Caravan & Camp Site CAMPGROUND £
(☎01969-667354; www.bainbridge-ings.co.uk; hikers & cyclists per person £6, site, car & 2 adults £16;) An attractive site set around a spacious farmhouse in stone-walled fields about half a mile east of Hawes. Fresh-laid eggs are sold on-site.

YHA Hawes HOSTEL £
(☎0845 371 9120; www.yha.org.uk; Lancaster Tce; dm/tw £25/55;) A modern place on the western edge of town, at the junction of the main A684 (Aysgarth Rd) and B6255, this is a family-friendly hostel with great views of Wensleydale. Cheaper rates (dorm bed from £13) on weekdays.

Herriot's Guest House B&B ££
(☎01969-667536; www.herriotsinhawes.co.uk; Main St; s/d from £48/80;) A delightful guesthouse set in an old stone building close to the bridge by the waterfall, Herriot's has seven comfy en suite bedrooms set above an art gallery and coffee shop.

Green Dragon Inn INN ££
(☎01969-667392; www.greendragonhardraw.co.uk; Hardraw; B&B per person £35-50; P) A fine old pub with flagstone floors, low timber beams, ancient oak furniture and Theakston's on draught. The Dragon serves up a tasty steak-and-ale pie and offers bunkhouse accommodation (per person £17.50), camping (per person £8) or B&B in plain but adequate rooms, as well as a pair of larger, more comfortable suites. One mile northwest of Hawes.

Cart House TEAROOM £
(☎01969-667691; Hardraw; mains £4-7; ⊙10am-5pm mid-Mar–Oct) This craft shop and tearoom offers a healthy diet of homemade soup, organic bread and a 'Fellman's Lunch' of Wensleydale cheese, pickle and salad. There's a basic campsite at the back (£8 per person, including tent and car). One mile northwest of Hawes.

Information

Hawes National Park Centre (☎01969-666210; Station Yard; ⊙10am-5pm Apr-Oct, limited hours Nov, Dec, Feb & Mar, closed Jan)

Getting There & Away

Buses 156 and 157 run from Hawes to Leyburn (£5.50, 50 minutes, four daily), where you can connect with buses to or from Richmond.

From Garsdale station on the Settle–Carlisle Line, bus 113 runs to Hawes (20 minutes, two to four daily Monday to Friday). On Sundays and bank holidays from April to September, bus 831 goes from Richmond to Hawes (£4, one hour and 20 minutes, twice daily) via Reeth and Keld, and on to Ribblehead station (£3.50, 25 minutes). Confirm bus times with Traveline Yorkshire or a tourist office before using these routes.

Richmond

POP 8415

The handsome market town of Richmond is one of England's best-kept secrets, perched on a rocky outcrop overlooking the River Swale and guarded by the ruins of a massive castle. A maze of cobbled streets radiates from the broad, sloping market square (market day is Saturday), lined with elegant Georgian buildings and photogenic stone cottages, with glimpses of the surrounding hills and dales peeking through the gaps.

Sights & Activities

Richmond Castle CASTLE

(EH; www.english-heritage.org.uk; Tower St; adult/child £5.90/3.50; 10am-6pm Apr-Sep, to 5pm Oct, to 4pm Sat & Sun Nov-Mar) The impressive heap that is Richmond Castle, founded in 1070, was one of the first castles in England since Roman times to be built of stone. It's had many uses through the years, including a stint as a prison for conscientious objectors during WWI (there's a small and sobering exhibition about their part in the castle's history). The best part of a visit is the view from the top of the remarkably well-preserved 30m-high keep, which towers over the town.

Richmondshire Museum MUSEUM

(www.richmondshiremuseum.org.uk; Ryder's Wynd; adult/child £3/free; 10.30am-4.30pm Easter-Oct) The Richmondshire Museum is a delight, with local history exhibits including an early Yorkshire cave-dweller and displays about lead mining, which forever altered the Swaledale landscape a century ago. You can also see the original set that served as James Herriot's surgery in the TV series *All Creatures Great and Small.*

Green Howards Museum MUSEUM

(www.greenhowards.org.uk; Trinity Church Sq; adult/child £4.50/free; 10am-4.30pm Feb-Dec) Military buffs will enjoy the three floors of this museum, which pays tribute to the famous Yorkshire regiment.

Georgian Theatre Royal TOURS

(www.georgiantheatreroyal.co.uk; Victoria Rd; adult/child £5/2; tours hourly 10am-4pm Mon-Sat mid-Feb–mid-Nov) The Georgian Theatre Royal, built in 1788, is the most complete Georgian playhouse in Britain. Tours include a look at the country's oldest surviving stage scenery, painted between 1818 and 1836.

SETTLE–CARLISLE LINE

The 72-mile **Settle–Carlisle Line** (SCL; www.settle-carlisle.co.uk), built between 1869 and 1875, offers one of England's most scenic railway journeys. The line's construction was one of the great engineering achievements of the Victorian era: 5000 labourers armed with picks and shovels built 325 bridges and 21 viaducts and blasted 14 tunnels in horrific conditions – nearly 200 of them died in the process. Trains run between Leeds and Carlisle via Settle about eight times per day. (The section between Appleby and Armathwaite is closed for repairs until March 2017.)

The first section of the journey from Leeds is along the Aire Valley, stopping at Keighley, where the Keighley & Worth Valley Railway (p538) branches off to Haworth, Skipton (gateway to the southern Dales) and Settle. The train then labours up the valley beside the River Ribble, through Horton-in-Ribblesdale, across the spectacular **Ribblehead Viaduct** and then through Blea Moor Tunnel to reach remote **Dent station**, at 350m the highest main-line station in the country.

The line reaches its highest point (356m) at Ais Gill, where it leaves the Dales behind before easing down to Kirkby Stephen. The last halts are Appleby and Langwathby, just northeast of Penrith (a jumping-off point for the Lake District), before the train finally pulls into Carlisle.

The entire journey from Leeds to Carlisle takes two hours and 40 minutes. Various hop-on, hop-off passes are also available for one or three days. You can pick up a free SCL timetable – which includes a colour map of the line and brief details about places of interest – from most Yorkshire stations.

Festivals & Events

Richmond Walking & Book Festival LITERATURE
(www.booksandboots.org) In September/October Richmond hosts 10 days of guided walks, talks, films and other events.

Sleeping

★Old Dairy B&B ££
(01748-886057; www.olddairylowrow.wordpress.com; Low Row, Swaledale; r £65-75;) Near Reeth, 15 miles west of Richmond, the Old Dairy is a lovingly restored 200-year-old house in the very heart of the Dales with two homely guest bedrooms enjoying lovely views across the dale. The owners are a fount of knowledge on local walking, cycling and mountain biking, and can provide stargazing and astrophotography guidance from their 'dark sky' garden.

Frenchgate Hotel HOTEL ££
(01748-822087; www.thefrenchgate.co.uk; 59-61 Frenchgate; s/d from £88/118;) Nine elegant bedrooms occupy the upper floors of this converted Georgian town house, now a boutique hotel decorated with local art. The rooms have cool designer fittings that set off a period fireplace here, a Victorian roll-top bath there. Downstairs there's an excellent restaurant (three-course dinner £39) and a hospitable lounge with oak beams and an open fire.

Frenchgate Guest House B&B ££
(01748-823421; www.66frenchgate.co.uk; 66 Frenchgate; s/d from £70/100;) A gorgeous guesthouse perched at the top of a cobbled lane and decorated in period style. Two of the eight luxurious bedrooms have superb views across the valley of the River Swale, as does the breakfast room.

★Millgate House B&B £££
(01748-823571; www.millgatehouse.com; Market Pl; r £125-165;) Behind an unassuming grey door lies the unexpected pleasure of one of the most attractive guesthouses in England. While the house itself is a Georgian gem crammed with period details, it is overshadowed by the multi-award-winning garden at the back, which offers superb views over the River Swale and the Cleveland Hills. If possible, book the Garden Suite.

MOUNTAIN-BIKING YORKSHIRE'S DALES

The epicentre of mountain-biking in the Yorkshire Dales, the **Dales Bike Centre** (01748-884908; www.dalesbikecentre.co.uk; Fremington; bike hire per day £35; 9am-5pm;), 12 miles west of Richmond, provides bike hire (both mountain and road bikes), a bike shop and repair service, advice and trail maps, guided rides (£100 per day for up to eight people), a brilliant cafe (best coffee in the Dales) and comfortable bunkhouse accommodation for up to 14 people (four-bunk room £116 a night).

Eating & Drinking

Cross View Tearooms TEAROOM £
(www.crossviewtearooms.co.uk; 38 Market Pl; mains £5-10; 9am-5.30pm;) So popular with locals that you might have to queue for a table at lunchtime, the Cross View is the place to go for a hearty breakfast, homemade cakes, a hot lunch, or just a nice cup of tea.

★George & Dragon PUB FOOD ££
(01748-518373; www.georgeanddragonhudswell.co.uk; Hudswell; mains £8-10; food served noon-2pm & 6-9pm Mon-Sat, noon-4pm Sun;) A mile and a half west of Richmond, on a minor road south of the river, the George & Dragon is a genuine local pub, owned and managed by the community. It serves a small menu of freshly prepared pub grub, including sausage and mash, rabbit pie, and roast beef and Yorkshire pudding. The terrace at the back offers outdoor drinking and dining with gorgeous views across the dale.

Rustique FRENCH ££
(01748-821565; www.rustiquerichmond.co.uk; Chantry Wynd, Finkle St; mains £12-22; noon-9pm) Tucked away in an arcade, this cosy bistro has consistently impressed with its mastery of French country cooking, from *confit de canard* (duck slow roasted in its own fat) to *moules marinière* (mussels with white wine, garlic and cream). Booking is recommended.

Black Lion Hotel PUB
(www.blacklionhotelrichmond.co.uk; Finkle St; 11am-11pm;) Cosy bars, low beams and good beer and food.

Information

There's a **tourist office** (☎01609-532980; www.richmond.org; Richmond Library, Queens Rd; ⏰10am-6pm Mon & Thu, to 5pm Tue & Fri, to noon Wed, to 1pm Sat) in the local library with the usual maps and guides, plus several leaflets showing walks in town and the surrounding countryside.

Getting There & Away

From Darlington (on the railway between London and Edinburgh) it's easy to reach Richmond on bus X26 or X27 (£4.70, 30 minutes, every half-hour, hourly on Sunday). All buses stop in Market Pl.

On Sundays and bank-holiday Mondays only, from May to September, the Northern Dalesman bus 830 runs from Richmond to Hawes (£4, 1½ hours, one daily) via Reeth, and continues to Ribblehead (£6.50, two hours, one daily).

WEST YORKSHIRE

It was the tough and unforgiving textile industry that drove West Yorkshire's economy from the 18th century onward. The woollen mills, factories and canals built to transport raw materials and finished products defined much of the county's landscape. But that's all in the past, and recent years have seen the transformation of this once hard-bitten area into quite the picture postcard.

Leeds and Bradford, two adjoining cities so big they've virtually become one, are undergoing radical redevelopment and reinvention, prettifying their town centres and tempting more adventurous tourists with new museums, galleries and restaurants. Beyond the cities lies a landscape of wild moorland dissected by deep valleys dotted with old mill towns and villages, scenes that were so vividly described by the Brontë sisters, West Yorkshire's most renowned literary export and biggest tourist draw.

Getting Around

The Metro is West Yorkshire's highly efficient train and bus network, centred on Leeds and Bradford, which are also the main gateways to the county. For transport information, contact **West Yorkshire Metro** (☎0113-245 7676; www.wymetro.com).

Day Rover tickets (£8) are good for one day's unlimited travel on Metro buses and trains after 9.30am on weekdays and all day at weekends. A range of additional Rover tickets covering buses and/or trains, plus heaps of useful Metro maps and timetables, are available from bus and train stations and tourist offices in West Yorkshire.

Leeds

POP 751,500

One of the fastest-growing cities in the UK, Leeds is the glitzy embodiment of rediscovered northern self-confidence. A decade and a half of redevelopment has seen the city centre transform from near-derelict mill town into a vision of 21st-century urban chic, with sky-scraping office blocks, glass-and-steel waterfront apartment complexes and renovated Victorian shopping arcades. The financial crisis of 2008–10 saw many flagship development projects grind to a halt, but tower cranes have sprouted on the skyline again.

The openings of the Leeds Arena entertainment venue and Leeds Trinity shopping centre in 2013 have been followed by a new southern entrance to the train station, a new Hilton Hotel near Leeds Arena, and yet another retail mall, Victoria Gate, to the east of Vicar Lane. Now something of a shopping mecca, it's little wonder the city has garnered the nickname 'Knightsbridge of the North'.

Sights

★Royal Armouries MUSEUM

(www.royalarmouries.org; Armouries Dr; ⏰10am-5pm; P 🚻) FREE Leeds' most interesting museum was originally built in 1996 to house armour and weapons from the Tower of London, but subsequently expanded to cover 3000 years' worth of combat and self-defence. It all sounds a bit macho, but the exhibits are as varied as they are fascinating, covering subjects as varied as jousting, fencing and Indian elephant armour. To get here, walk east along the river from Centenary Footbridge (10 minutes), or take bus 70 from Infirmary St (50p, 10 minutes, four per hour).

Leeds Industrial Museum MUSEUM

(www.leeds.gov.uk/armleymills; Canal Rd, Armley; adult/child £3.80/1.90; ⏰10am-5pm Tue-Sat, 1-5pm Sun; P 🚻) One of the world's largest textile mills has been transformed into a museum telling the story of Leeds' industrial past, both glorious and ignominious. The city grew rich from the textile industry, but at some cost in human terms – working conditions were Dickensian. As well as a selection of mill machinery, there's a particularly informative display about how cloth is made. The museum is 2 miles west of the city centre; take bus 15 from the train station.

Leeds

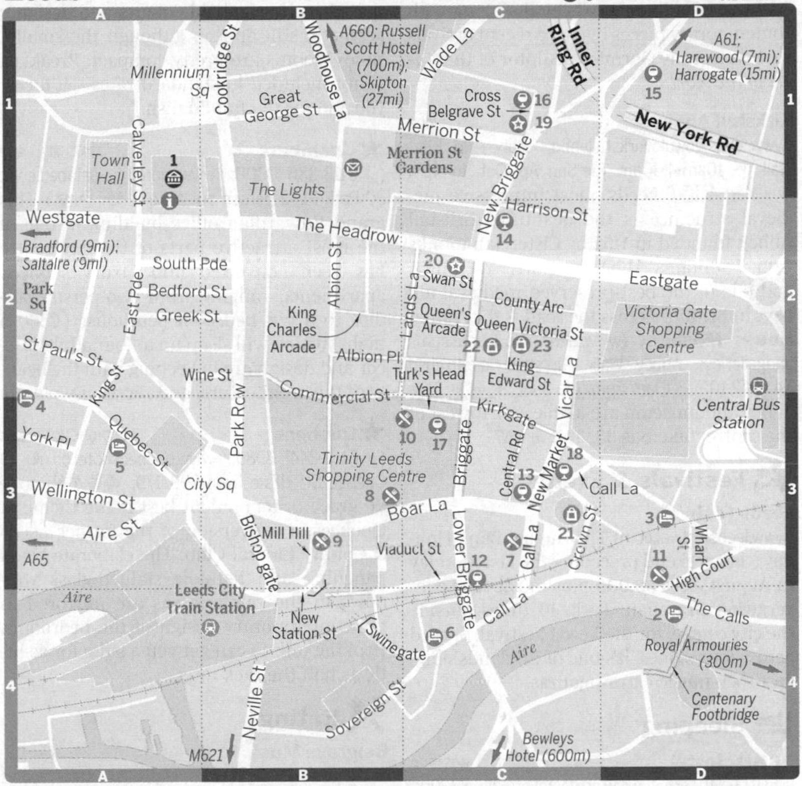

Leeds

Sights

1 Leeds Art Gallery A1

Sleeping

2 42 The Calls D4
3 Art Hostel D3
4 Chambers A3
5 Quebecs A3
6 Roomzzz Leeds City C4

Eating

7 Art's Cafe Bar & Restaurant C3
Belgrave Music Hall & Canteen .... (see 19)
8 Crafthouse B3
9 Friends of Ham B3
10 Pintura C3
11 Shears Yard D3

Drinking & Nightlife

12 Bar Fibre C3
13 HiFi Club C3
14 North Bar C2
15 Reliance D1
16 Sandinista C1
17 Whitelocks C3
18 Wire C3

Entertainment

19 Belgrave Music Hall & Canteen C1
20 City Varieties C2

Shopping

21 Corn Exchange C3
22 Harvey Nichols C2
23 Victoria Quarter C2

Leeds Art Gallery GALLERY
(www.leeds.gov.uk/artgallery; The Headrow; 10am-5pm Mon, Tue & Thu-Sat, noon-5pm Wed, 1-5pm Sun;) FREE The municipal gallery – closed for roof repairs until 2017 – is packed with 19th- and 20th-century British

heavyweights – Turner, Constable, Stanley Spencer, Wyndham Lewis et al – along with contemporary pieces by more recent arrivals such as Antony Gormley, sculptor of the *Angel of the North*.

Kirkstall Abbey CHURCH
(www.leeds.gov.uk/kirkstallabbey; Abbey Rd, Kirkstall; ⏲10am-4.30pm Tue-Sun Apr-Oct, to 4pm Nov-Mar) FREE Leeds' most impressive medieval structure is the beautiful Kirkstall Abbey, founded in 1152 by Cistercian monks from Fountains Abbey in North Yorkshire, and one of the best-preserved medieval abbeys in Britain. Across the road is the **Abbey House Museum** (www.leeds.gov.uk/museumsandgalleries; Abbey Walk, Kirkstall; adult/child £4.20/2.10; ⏲10am-5pm Tue-Sun; P) The abbey and museum are 3 miles northwest of the centre; take bus 33, 33A or 757.

Festivals & Events

Leeds Festival MUSIC
(www.leedsfestival.com) The August Bank Holiday (the weekend preceding the last Monday in August) sees 50,000-plus music fans converge on Bramham Park, 10 miles outside the city centre, for the Leeds Festival. Spread across four stages, it's one of Englands's biggest rock-music extravaganzas.

Sleeping

★**Art Hostel** HOSTEL £
(☎0113-345 3363; www.arthostel.org.uk; 83 Kirkgate; dm/tw £22.50/55;) Set in an appealingly grungy 200-year-old brick building in the middle of Leeds' nightlife zone, this brand-new hostel is a great advert for the revitalisation of the city centre. Each room has been individually designed by a local artist, and the hostel is full of recycled furniture and innovative ideas.

Roomzzz Leeds City APARTMENT ££
(☎0203 504 5555; www.roomzzz.co.uk; 10 Swinegate; 2-person apt from £79; @) This outfit offers bright and modern luxury apartments complete with fitted kitchen, with the added advantage of 24-hour hotel reception, and a great city-centre location; a second branch, Roomzzz Leeds City West, is half a mile west on Burley Rd.

42 The Calls BOUTIQUE HOTEL ££
(☎0113-244 0099; www.42thecalls.co.uk; 42 The Calls; r from £89; @) This pioneer of the boutique-hotel scene (it opened in 1991), set in a 19th-century grain mill overlooking the river, is looking a little frayed around the edges but its bold colours and designer aesthetic still appeal, although the smaller 'study' rooms are pretty compact. Breakfast is not included in standard rates – it'll cost you £15 for the full English.

★**Chambers** APARTMENT £££
(☎0113-386 3300; www.morethanjustabed.com; 30 Park Pl; 2-person apt from £145; P) This grand Edwardian office building in one of the most attractive parts of the city centre has been converted into luxury serviced apartments, ranging from two-person studios to a two-bedroom penthouse (£360 a night) which will sleep up to four adults. Decor and design are in keeping with the beauty of the architecture, and service is spot on.

★**Quebecs** BOUTIQUE HOTEL £££
(☎0113-244 8989; www.quebecshotel.co.uk; 9 Quebec St; d/ste from £99/179; @) Victorian grace at its opulent best is the theme of Quebecs, a conversion of the former Leeds & County Liberal Club. The elaborate wood panelling and heraldic stained-glass windows in the public areas are mirrored in the contemporary design of the bedrooms. Booking online can get you a suite for as little as half the rack rate.

Eating

Belgrave Music Hall & Canteen STREET FOOD £
(www.belgravemusichall.com; 1 Cross Belgrave St; mains £4-8; ⏲food served 11am-10pm) The Belgrave is a bar and music venue that also has a great kitchen – make that two kitchens. One serves artisan pizza (watch out for the napalm chilli sauce), the other probably the best burgers in Yorkshire, all at great-value prices. And every 2nd Saturday of the month the place hosts the **Belgrave Feast** (⏲11am-8pm), an art market and street food festival.

★**Friends of Ham** DELI ££
(☎0113-242 0275; www.friendsofham.co.uk; 4-8 New Station St; mains £7-20; ⏲11am-11pm Mon-Thu, to 1am Fri & Sat, to 10pm Sun;) We're not sure how to describe this place, other than that it's a stylish bar that serves the finest charcuterie and cheeses – Spanish, French, British – accompanied by fine wines and craft beers. The food is carefully selected and prepared, and utterly delicious; you can order individual tapas-like portions, or huge sharing platters with olive-oil-drizzled bread. Also, brunch (11am till noon).

Pintura BASQUE ££

(☎ 0113-430 0915; www.pinturakitchen.co.uk; Unit 3.26, Trinity Leeds; tapas £4-8; ⏲ noon-10pm Mon-Fri, 10am-10pm Sat & Sun) Set beside the northern entrance to the Trinity shopping mall (from Lands Lane), this tapas bar is huge (spread over three floors) but always packed, so it must be doing something right. Seek out the more authentically Basque dishes – *bacalao* (salt cod) and *morcilla* (black pudding) – among the classic Spanish crowd-pleasers like *albondigas* (meatballs) and *gambas a la plancha* (prawns in garlic and chilli).

Shears Yard MODERN BRITISH ££

(☎ 0113-244 4144; www.shearsyard.com; 11-15 Wharf St; mains £11-25; ⏲ 5.30-10pm Tue-Sat, 11am-3pm Sat, noon-5pm Sun;) Acres of exposed brick, concrete floors and a soaring roof provide an industrial-chic setting (it's a former rope-making yard) for painterly presentations of imaginative (and intriguingly described) dishes such as ox-cheek fritter with roast-onion consommé, or squid with puffed potato and coriander emulsion. A two-/three-course dinner menu is available for £16.50/19.50 Tuesday, Wednesday and Thursday evenings, and before 7pm on Friday.

Art's Cafe Bar & Restaurant INTERNATIONAL ££

(www.artscafebar.co.uk; 42 Call Lane; mains £7-17; ⏲ noon-11pm;) Local art on the walls and a bohemian vibe throughout make this a popular place for quiet reflection, a chat and a really good cup of coffee. The dinner menu offers six classic dishes, while the early-bird menu (pre-7pm, except Saturday) offers three courses for £15.

★ Crafthouse MODERN BRITISH £££

(☎ 0113-897 0444; www.crafthouse-restaurant.com; Level 5, Trinity Leeds, 70 Boar Lane; mains £22-37; ⏲ noon-2.45pm & 5-10pm Mon-Sat, noon-10pm Sun;) This rooftop restaurant makes a big impression, with cool grey and black decor and huge picture windows overlooking the neighbouring church tower. The food is similarly striking, with bold flavour combinations such as charcoal salmon with nasturtium leaves, or quail with sour green strawberry. A two-/three-course set menu (£20/25) is available on Sundays.

Drinking & Nightlife

Reliance CRAFT BEER

(☎ 0113-295 6060; www.the-reliance.co.uk; 76-78 North St; ⏲ noon-11pm Mon-Thu, to midnight Fri & Sat, to 10.30pm Sun;) Despite being relatively new, the Reliance is one of those comfortable-as-old-slippers bars where you can happily while away an afternoon reading or chatting, pausing only to order another pint of Roosters pale ale (brewed in Yorkshire, of course) or snack on a platter of homemade charcuterie (yes, they make it themselves).

Bar Fibre CLUB

(www.barfibre.com; 168 Lower Briggate; ⏲ noon-1am Sun-Thu, to 3am Fri, to 4am Sat) Leeds' most popular gay bar, which spills out onto the cheekily named Queen's Court, is where the beautiful people congregate; dress code is...dressy, so look your best or you won't get in. There's another cluster of gay bars downhill at the junction of Lower Briggate and The Calls.

Sandinista COCKTAIL BAR

(www.sandinista.co.uk; 5/5a Cross Belgrave St; ⏲ 3pm-3am Mon-Thu, noon-3am Fri-Sun;) This laid-back bar has a Latin look and a unifying theme (it's named after the Clash's fourth album), attracting an eclectic clientele with its independent taste in music and unpretentious atmosphere. If you enjoy a well-mixed cocktail, but aren't too fussed about looking glam, this is the spot for you.

Whitelocks PUB

(www.whitelocksleeds.com; 6-8 Turk's Head Yard; ⏲ 11am-midnight Mon-Thu, to 1am Fri & Sat, to 11pm Sun;) There's lots of polished wood, gleaming brass and colourful stained glass in this popular traditional pub, which dates from 1715. Theakston's, Deuchars IPA and several other real ales are on tap, there's a log fire in winter, and in summer the crowds spill out into the courtyard.

North Bar CRAFT BEER

(www.northbar.com; 24 New Briggate; ⏲ 11am-1am Mon & Tue, to 2am Wed-Sat, noon-midnight Sun;) There's a Continental feel to this long and narrow, minimalist bar, enhanced by the unfamiliar beer labels, from Dortmunder and Duvel to Schneider and Snake Dog. In fact, North is dedicated to the best of world beers, with more than a dozen ales on tap and scores more in bottles. Good selection of malt whisky too.

HiFi Club CLUB

(www.thehificlub.co.uk; 2 Central Rd; ⏲ 11pm-3am Wed & Fri-Sun) This intimate club makes a good break from the hard-core sound of electronic dance: if it's Tamla Motown or the percussive beats of dance-floor jazz that shake your

WORTH A TRIP

HISTORIC SALTAIRE VILLAGE

Saltaire, a Victorian-era landmark and Unesco World Heritage Site, was an industrial village purpose-built in 1851 by philanthropic wool baron and teetotaller Titus Salt. The village's huge factory is now **Salts Mill** (www.saltsmill.org.uk; Victoria Rd; ⌚10am-5.30pm Mon-Fri, to 6pm Sat & Sun; P), a splendidly bright and airy cathedral-like building where the main draw is a permanent exhibition of works by Bradford-born artist David Hockney.

In a fitting metaphor for the shift in the British economy from making things to selling them, this former engine of industry is now a shrine to retail therapy, with shops selling books, crafts and outdoor equipment, and a cafe and restaurant. Saltaire's **tourist office** (☎01274-437942; www.saltairevillage.info; Salts Mill, Victoria Rd; ⌚10am-5pm Apr-Sep, to 4pm Oct-Mar) has maps of the village and provides information on local walks.

Saltaire is easily reached by train from Leeds (£3.70, 15 minutes, every 30 minutes).

booty, this is the spot for you. Also has stand-up comedy sessions on Saturday evenings.

Wire CLUB

(www.wireclub.co.uk; 2-8 Call Lane; ⌚11pm-3am) This small, atmospheric basement club, set in a forest of Victorian cast-iron pillars with brick-vaulted ceilings, throbs to a different beat every night, from rock and roll to drum and bass; the only rule is: no mainstream music. Popular with local students.

☆ Entertainment

★Belgrave Music Hall & Canteen LIVE MUSIC

(☎0113-234 6160; www.belgravemusichall.com; 1 Cross Belgrave St; ⌚11am-midnight Sun-Wed, to 1am Thu, to 3am Fri & Sat) The Belgrave has it all – as well as being the city's best live-music venue, its three floors encompass a huge bar bristling with craft-beer taps, two kitchens (p532) serving the best street food in town, loads of shared tables and sofa space for socialising, and a fantastic roof terrace with views across the city. Why would you ever leave?

City Varieties LIVE MUSIC, COMEDY

(www.cityvarieties.co.uk; Swan St) Founded in 1865, City Varieties is the world's longest-running music hall, where the likes of Harry Houdini, Charlie Chaplin and Lily Langtry once trod the boards. Reopened after a major revamp in 2011, the program now features stand-up comedy, live music, pantomime and old-fashioned variety shows.

Shopping

Victoria Quarter MALL

(www.victoria-quarter.co.uk; Vicar Lane) The mosaic-paved, stained-glass-roofed Victorian arcades of Victoria Quarter, between Briggate and Vicar Lane, are well worth visiting for aesthetic reasons alone. Dedicated shoppers can join the footballers' wives browsing boutiques by Louis Vuitton, Vivienne Westwood and Swarovski. The flagship store here, of course, is **Harvey Nichols** (www.harveynichols.com; 107-111 Briggate; ⌚10am-7pm Mon-Sat, 11am-5pm Sun).

Corn Exchange SHOPPING CENTRE

(www.leedscornexchange.co.uk; Call Lane; ⌚10am-6pm Mon-Sat, 10.30am-4.30pm Sun; Wi-Fi) The dramatic Corn Exchange, built in 1865 to house grain-trade merchants, has a wonderful wrought-iron roof that today shelters a fine collection of independent shops and boutiques selling everything from art and fashion to jewellery and beauty products.

Information

Leeds Tourist Office (☎0113-242 5242; www.visitleeds.co.uk; Leeds Art Gallery, Headrow; ⌚10am-5pm Mon-Sat, 11am-3pm Sun; Wi-Fi) is in the basement of the city art gallery, next to the gallery shop.

Post Office (St John's Centre, 116 Albion St; ⌚9am-5.30pm Mon-Sat)

Getting There & Away

AIR

Leeds Bradford International Airport (www.leedsbradfordairport.co.uk) is 11 miles northwest of the city via the A65, and has flights to a range of domestic and international destinations. The Flying Tiger (www.flyingtigerbus.co.uk) 757 bus runs between Leeds bus station and the airport (£3.60, 40 minutes, every 20 to 30 minutes, hourly on Sunday). A taxi costs about £20.

BUS

National Express (www.nationalexpress.com) serves most major cities, while Yorkshire Coastliner (www.coastliner.co.uk) buses run to York,

Scarborough and Whitby. A Day Tripper Plus (£15) gives unlimited travel on all Coastliner buses for a day.

London £10 to £20, five hours, hourly

Manchester £3 to £6, 1¼ hours, every 30 minutes

Scarborough £12.30, three hours

Whitby £13.50, 3¾ hours

York £6.50, 1¼ hours

TRAIN

Leeds City station has good rail connections with the rest of the country, and is also the starting point for trains on the famous Settle–Carlisle railway line (p528).

London King's Cross £85, 2¼ hours, hourly

Manchester £20, one hour, hourly

Sheffield £13, one hour, twice hourly

York £13.90, 25 minutes, every 15 minutes

GETTING AROUND

Leeds City Bus (www.wymetro.com) runs every few minutes from 6.30am to 7.30pm Monday to Saturday, linking the bus and train stations with all the main shopping areas in the city centre (£1 flat fare); CityBus 70 South Bank (50p flat fare) links the train station and Infirmary St with Leeds Dock (for the Royal Armouries).

Various WY Metro Day Rover passes covering trains and/or buses are good for reaching Bradford, Haworth and Hebden Bridge.

Bradford

POP 522,452

Their suburbs may have merged into one sprawling urban conurbation, but Bradford remains far removed from its much more glamorous neighbour, Leeds. Thanks to its role as a major player in the wool trade, Bradford attracted large numbers of immigrants from Bangladesh and Pakistan during the 20th century. Despite occasional racial tensions, these new arrivals have helped reinvigorate the city and give it new energy (plus a reputation for superb curry restaurants). A high point of the year is the colourful Bradford Festival, a multicultural celebration of music, dance, arts, crafts and food.

Sights

★National Media Museum MUSEUM

(www.nationalmediamuseum.org.uk; off Little Horton Lane; 10am-6pm) FREE Bradford's top attraction is the National Media Museum, an impressive glass-fronted building that chronicles the story of photography, film, TV, radio and the web from 19th-century cameras and early animation to digital technology and the psychology of advertising. There's lots of hands-on stuff too – you can film yourself in a bedroom scene, pretend to be a TV newsreader, or play 1970s and 80s video games. There's also an **IMAX cinema** (www.picturehouses.com; National Media Museum; adult/child £12/9.50) here.

The museum looks out over **City Park**, Bradford's award-winning central square, which is home to the Mirror Pool, the country's largest urban water feature.

Festivals & Events

Bradford Festival CULTURAL

(www.bradfordfestival.org.uk) This colourful Bradford Festival in July is a high point of the year: a multicultural celebration of music, dance, arts, crafts and food, with most events happening around City Park in the town centre.

Eating

Bradford is famous for its curries – it was voted the Curry Capital of Britain for five years running from 2011 to 2015 – so don't miss out on trying one of the city's hundred or so restaurants. A great help is the Bradford Curry Guide (www.visitbradford.com/explore/Bradford_Curry_Guide.aspx), which helps sort the rogan josh from the rubbish nosh.

Kashmir INDIAN £

(01274-726513; 27 Morley St; mains £4-6; 11am-2am Sun-Thu, to 4am Fri & Sat;) Bradford's oldest curry house has top tucker, served with no frills and no booze (although it is BYO). Whatever you do, go for a table upstairs, as the soul-destroying, windowless basement has all the character of a 1950s factory canteen. It's just around the corner from the National Media Museum.

Zouk Tea Bar INDIAN ££

(01274-258025; www.zoukteabar.co.uk; 1312 Leeds Rd; mains £8-12; noon-midnight;) This modern and stylish cafe-restaurant staffed by chefs from Lahore serves everything from *chana puri* (curried chickpeas) for lunch to legendary lamb Nihari (slow-cooked lamb with a thick and spicy sauce) for dinner.

Getting There & Away

Bradford is on the Metro train line from Leeds (£3.80, 20 minutes, three or four per hour).

Hebden Bridge

POP 4235

Tucked tightly into a fold of a steep-sided valley, Yorkshire's funkiest little village is a former mill town that refused to go gently with the dying of industry's light. Instead, it raged a bit and then morphed into an attractive little tourist trap with a distinctly bohemian atmosphere. The town is home to university academics, artists, diehard hippies and a substantial gay community. All of this explains the abundance of craft shops, organic cafes and secondhand bookstores.

The town centre was badly hit by flooding at Christmas 2015, but most businesses were quickly back on their feet. There are many cultural events on the calendar, culminating in late June/early July with the annual Hebden Bridge Arts Festival (hebdenbridgeartsfestival.co.uk).

Sights & Activities

Heptonstall VILLAGE

(www.heptonstall.org) Above Hebden Bridge lies the much older village of Heptonstall, its narrow cobbled street lined with 500-year-old cottages and the ruins of a beautiful 13th-century church. But it's the churchyard of the newer **St Thomas' Church** (1854) that draws literary pilgrims, for here is buried the poet Sylvia Plath (1932–63), wife of another famous poet, Ted Hughes (1930–98), who was born in nearby Mytholmroyd.

Gibson Mill HISTORIC BUILDING

(NT; www.nationaltrust.org.uk; adult/child £4.50/2.20; ⏲11am-4pm Sat-Thu Mar-Oct, to 3pm Sat & Sun Nov-Feb; P) This renovated 19th-century cotton mill houses a visitor centre with exhibitions covering the industrial and social history of the mill and its former workers. It is set amid the woods and waterfalls of local beauty spot **Hardcastle Crags** (open dawn to dusk, admission free), 1.5 miles north of town, reachable via a 30-minute riverside walk.

Hebden Bridge Cruises CRUISE

(☎07966 808717; http://hebdenbridgecruises.com; Stubbing Wharf, King St; per person £15; ⏲1pm & 2.15pm Sat) Join a colourful canal boat for a guided cruise along the Rochdale Canal, with tea and scones included in the price. Departs from the Stubbing Wharf pub, half a mile west of the town centre.

Sleeping & Eating

Hebden Bridge Hostel HOSTEL £

(☎01422-843183; www.hebdenbridgehostel.co.uk; Birchcliffe Centre, Birchcliffe Rd; dm/tw/q £20/55/75; ⏲Easter-early Nov; P@📶) Just 10 minutes' walk uphill from the town centre, this hostel is set in a peaceful stone building, complete with sunny patio, tucked behind a former Baptist chapel (look for the green hostel signs). There's a cosy library, comfy and clean en suite rooms, and a vegetarian-food-only kitchen. The hostel is closed from 10.30am to 5pm daily.

★**Thorncliffe B&B** B&B ££

(☎01422-842163; www.thorncliffe.uk.net; Alexandra Rd; s/d £55/75; 📶) This delightful Victorian house is perched on the hill above town, and the guest accommodation is perched at the top of the house – a spacious and peace-

YORKSHIRE'S WORLD-CLASS ART

Yorkshire Sculpture Park (www.ysp.co.uk; Bretton Park, near Wakefield; parking 2hr/all day £5/8; ⏲10am-5pm; P) One of England's most impressive collections of sculpture is scattered across the formidable 18th-century estate of Bretton Park, 200-odd hectares of lawns, fields and trees. A bit like the art world's equivalent of a safari park, the Yorkshire Sculpture Park showcases the work of dozens of sculptors both national and international. But the main focus of this outdoor gallery is the work of local heroes Barbara Hepworth (1903–75), who was born in nearby Wakefield, and Henry Moore (1898–1986).

Hepworth Wakefield (☎01924-247360; www.hepworthwakefield.org; Gallery Walk, Wakefield; parking £5; ⏲10am-5pm Tue-Sun; P) West Yorkshire's standing in the international arts scene got a boost in 2011 when the Yorkshire Sculpture Park was joined by this award-winning gallery of modern art, housed in a stunningly angular building on the banks of the River Calder. The gallery has been built around the works of Wakefield-born sculptor Barbara Hepworth, perhaps best known for her work *Single Form*, which graces the UN Headquarters in New York.

WORTH A TRIP

HISTORY OF COAL

For close to three centuries, West and South Yorkshire were synonymous with coal production. The collieries shaped and scarred the landscape and entire villages grew up around the pits. The industry came to a shuddering halt in the 1980s, but the imprint of coal is still very much in evidence, even if there's only a handful of collieries left. One of these, the former Caphouse Colliery, **National Coal Mining Museum for England** (www.ncm.org.uk; Overton, near Wakefield; 10am-5pm, last tour 3.15pm; P) FREE is now this fascinating museum, a superb testament to the inner workings of a coal mine.

The highlight of a visit is the underground tour (departing every 10 minutes): equipped with helmet and head-torch, you descend almost 140m in the 'cage', then follow subterranean passages to the coal seam where massive drilling machines now stand idle. Former miners work as guides and explain the detail – sometimes with a suitably authentic and almost impenetrable mix of local dialect (known in Yorkshire as 'Tyke') and technical terminology.

At ground level there are audiovisual displays, some fascinating memorabilia (including sketches by Henry Moore), and exhibits about trade unions, strikes and the wider mining communities – only a bit over-romanticised in parts. You can also stroll round the pit-pony stables (their equine inhabitants also now retired) or the slightly eerie bathhouse, unchanged since the miners scrubbed off the coal dust for the last time and emptied their lockers.

The museum is 10 miles south of Leeds on the A642 between Wakefield and Huddersfield, reached via Junction 40 on the M1. By public transport, take a train from Leeds to Wakefield (£3.50, 15 to 30 minutes, at least hourly), and then bus 232 towards Huddersfield (£3.10, 25 minutes, hourly)

ful attic double with private bathroom and lovely views across the valley, and a 1st-floor en suite double room, but without the views. A continental, vegetarian breakfast is served in your room.

Mooch CAFE £
(01422-846954; 24 Market St; mains £4-9; 9am-8pm Wed-Mon;) This chilled-out little cafe-bar exemplifies Hebden's alternative atmosphere, with a menu that includes a full-vegan breakfast, brie-and-grape ciabatta, and Mediterranean lunch platters of olives, hummus, stuffed vine leaves, tabouli and more. There's also Krombacher beer on draught, excellent espresso, and outdoor tables through the back.

★ **Green's Vegetarian Café** VEGETARIAN ££
(01422-843587; www.greensvegetariancafe.co.uk; Old Oxford House, Albert St; mains lunch £5-9, dinner £11; 11am-3pm Wed-Sun, 6.30-10pm Fri & Sat;) One of Yorkshire's best vegetarian restaurants, Green's adopts a gourmet attitude towards veggie and vegan cuisine, serving dishes such as Sicilian *caponata* (aubergines, red pepper, celery, olives and capers) with spaghetti, and Thai green curry with chickpeas, squash and tofu. Breakfast (11am to noon) includes superb scrambled free-range eggs on toasted focaccia. Book a table to avoid disappointment, especially for dinner.

☆ Entertainment

Trades Club LIVE MUSIC
(01422-845265; www.thetradesclub.com; Holme St) Built in 1923 as a social club by the local trades unions, this place was revived in the 1980s and has since gone on to become one of the UK's coolest live-music venues, hosting names as big and diverse as the Buzzcocks, Patti Smith, the Fall and Martha Wainwright in recent years, as well as a host of up-and-coming indie talent.

Information

Hebden Bridge Visitor & Canal Centre
(01422-843831; www.hebdenbridge.co.uk; Butlers Wharf, New Rd; 10am-5pm mid-Mar–mid-Oct, shorter hours rest of year) has a good stock of maps and leaflets on local walks and bicycle routes, and information on the weekly flea market and farmers market.

Getting There & Away

Hebden Bridge is on the train line from Leeds (£5.40, 50 minutes, every 20 minutes Monday to Saturday, hourly on Sunday) to Manchester (£9.50, 30 minutes, three or four per hour).

Haworth

POP 6380

It seems that only Shakespeare himself is held in higher esteem than the beloved Brontë sisters – Emily, Anne and Charlotte – judging by the eight million visitors a year who trudge up the hill from the train station to pay their respects at the handsome parsonage where the literary classics *Jane Eyre* and *Wuthering Heights* were penned.

Not surprisingly, the whole village is given over to Brontë-linked tourism, but even without the literary associations Haworth is still worth a visit, though you'll be hard-pressed not to be overwhelmed by the cottage industry that has grown up around the Brontës and their wonderful creations.

Sights

Haworth Parish Church CHURCH

(Church St; 9am-5.30pm Mon-Sat) Your first stop in Haworth should be the parish church, a lovely old place of worship built in the late 19th century on the site of the older church that the Brontë sisters knew, which was demolished in 1879. The Brontë family vault lies beneath a pillar in the southeast corner, and a polished brass plaque on the floor commemorates Charlotte and Emily; Anne is buried at St Mary's Church in Scarborough.

Brontë Parsonage Museum MUSEUM

(www.bronte.org.uk; Church St; adult/child £7.50/3.75; 10am-5.30pm Apr-Oct, to 5pm Nov-Mar) Set in a pretty garden overlooking Haworth parish church and graveyard, the house where the Brontë family lived from 1820 to 1861 is now a museum. The rooms are meticulously furnished and decorated exactly as they were in the Brontë era, including Charlotte's bedroom, her clothes and her writing paraphernalia. There's also an informative exhibition, which includes the fascinating miniature books the Brontës wrote as children.

STEAM ENGINES & RAILWAY CHILDREN

The **Keighley & Worth Valley Railway** (www.kwvr.co.uk; adult/child return £11/5.50, Day Rover £16/8) runs steam and classic diesel engines between Keighley and Oxenhope via Haworth. It was here, in 1969, that the classic 1970 movie *The Railway Children* was shot: Mr Perks was stationmaster at Oakworth, where the Edwardian look has been meticulously maintained. Trains operate about hourly at weekends all year, and in holiday periods they run hourly every day.

Activities

Above Haworth stretch the bleak moors of the South Pennines – immediately familiar to Brontë fans. The tourist office has leaflets on local walks to endless Brontë-related places. A 6.5-mile favourite leads to **Top Withins**, a ruined farm thought to have inspired *Wuthering Heights,* even though a plaque clearly states that the farmhouse bore no resemblance to the one Emily wrote about.

Other walks can be taken around the **Brontë Way**, a longer route linking Bradford and Colne via Haworth. Alternatively, you can walk or cycle the 8 miles south to Hebden Bridge via the scenic valley of Hardcastle Crags.

Sleeping

Apothecary Guest House B&B £

(01535-643642; www.theapothecaryguesthouse.co.uk; 86 Main St; s/d £40/60;) A quaint and ancient building at the top end of the main street with oak beams and narrow, slanted passageways that lead to smallish rooms with cheerful decor; excellent value.

YHA Haworth HOSTEL £

(0845 371 9520; www.yha.org.uk; Longlands Dr; dm/tw £13/29;) In keeping with Haworth's Brontë heritage, the YHA hostel is set in a brooding Victorian Gothic mansion complete with games room, lounge, cycle store and laundry. It's on the northeastern edge of town, off Lees Lane.

★ **Old Registry** B&B ££

(01535-646503; www.theoldregistryhaworth.co.uk; 2-4 Main St; r £80-125;) This place is a bit special. It's an elegantly rustic guest-house where each of the carefully themed rooms has either a four-poster bed, a whirlpool bath or valley views. The Secret Garden room sports floral textiles and a glorious view across parkland to the lower village with, if you're lucky, a steam train chuffing sedately by.

Ye Sleeping House B&B ££

(01535-546992; www.yesleepinghouse.co.uk; 8 Main St; s/d from £58/64;) This welcoming B&B has a cosy, country-cottage atmosphere, with just three small rooms and a friendly resident cat. Try to get the one ensuite room, which can sleep a family of four and has great views over the valley.

Eating

Cookhouse CAFE, BISTRO £
(☎01535-958904; www.thecookhousehaworth.co.uk; Main St; mains £4-9; ⏲10am-5.30pm; 📶👪) A bright and breezy cafe that serves a bracing breakfast menu (till 11.45am) that includes eggs Benedict and bacon, cheese and onion hash, and mouth-watering lunch dishes such as bangers and mash with onion gravy, pulled pork sandwiches with barbecue sauce or toasted crumpets with Wensleydale cheese and chutney.

Cobbles & Clay CAFE £
(www.cobblesandclay.co.uk; 60 Main St; mains £5-8; ⏲8.45am-5pm; 🌿👪) This attractive, child-friendly cafe not only offers fair-trade coffee and healthy salads and snacks – Tuscan bean stew, or hummus with pita bread and raw veggie sticks – but also provides the opportunity to indulge in a bit of pottery painting.

Haworth Old Hall PUB FOOD ££
(☎01535-642709; www.hawortholdhall.co.uk; Sun St; mains £10-15) A 16th-century pub serving real ale and decent food, with a glorious beer garden for alfresco drinking and dining. If you want to linger longer, two comfortable doubles cost from £60 each.

Information

The **Haworth Tourist Office** (☎01535-642329; www.visitbradford.com/discover/Haworth.aspx; 2-4 West Lane; ⏲10am-5pm Apr-Sep, to 4pm Oct-Mar) has an excellent supply of information on the village, the surrounding area and, of course, the Brontës.

Getting There & Away

From Leeds, the easiest approach is via Keighley, which is on the Metro rail network. Bus 500 (www.keighleybus.co.uk) runs from Keighley bus station to Haworth (£2.20, 20 minutes, hourly) and continues to Todmorden and Hebden Bridge. However, the most interesting way to get from Keighley to Haworth is via the Keighley & Worth Valley Railway (p538).

SOUTH YORKSHIRE

What wool was to West Yorkshire, so steel was to South Yorkshire. A confluence of natural resources – coal, iron ore and ample water – made this part of the country a crucible of the British iron and steel industries. From the 18th to the 20th centuries, the region was the industrial powerhouse of northern England.

Sheffield's and Rotherham's blast furnaces and the coal pits of Barnsley and Doncaster may have closed long ago, but the hulking reminders of that irrepressible Victorian dynamism remain, not only in the old steelworks and pit heads (some of which have been converted into museums and exhibition spaces), but also in the grand civic buildings that grace Sheffield's city centre, fitting testaments to the untrammelled ambitions of their 19th-century patrons.

Sheffield

POP 551,800

Steel is everywhere in Sheffield. Today, however, it's not the steel of the foundries, mills and forges that made the city's fortune, nor the canteens of cutlery that made 'Sheffield Steel' a household name, but the steel of scaffolding and cranes, of modern sculptures and supertrams, and of new steel-framed buildings rising against the skyline.

The steel industry that made the city famous is long since gone, but after many years of decline Sheffield is on the up again – like many of northern England's cities, it has grabbed the opportunities presented by urban renewal with both hands and is working hard to reinvent itself. The new economy is based on services, shopping and the 'knowledge industry' that flows from the city's universities.

Since 2000 the city centre has been in the throes of a massive redevelopment that will continue into 2020 and beyond, so expect building sites and roadworks for several years to come.

Sights

★**Kelham Island Museum** MUSEUM
(www.simt.co.uk; Alma St; adult/child £6/free; ⏲10am-4pm Mon-Thu, 11am-4.45pm Sun; 🅿👪) Sheffield's prodigious industrial heritage is the subject of this excellent museum, set on a human-made island in the city's oldest industrial district. Exhibits cover all

WORTH A TRIP

MAGNA

At its peak, the Templeborough steelworks was the world's most productive steel smelter, with six 3000°C, electric-arc furnaces producing 1.8 million tonnes of metal a year. The mile-long **Magna** (☎01709-720002; www.visitmagna.co.uk; Sheffield Rd, Templeborough, Rotherham; adult/child £11.95/9.95; ⏲10am-5pm, last entry 4pm; P 👪), which once had a 10,000-strong workforce, is now an unashamed celebration of heavy industry, and a hands-on paradise for kids of all ages, with a huge range of science and technology exhibits. Magna is 4 miles northeast of Sheffield, just off the M1 motorway near Rotherham; phone in advance to check opening times.

A vast, dimly lit building, smelling vaguely of machine oil, hot metal and past glory, houses a series of displays based on the themes of earth, air, water and fire. The latter section is especially impressive, with a towering tornado of flame as a centrepiece and the chance to use a real electric arc to create your own tiny puddle of molten steel (if only for a moment or two). The hourly 'Big Melt' – a massive sound, light and fireworks show – memorably reenacts the firing up of one of the original arc furnaces.

aspects of industry, from steel-making to knife-sharpening – don't miss Little Mesters Lane, where the city's last remaining cutler (knife-maker) continues his trade. The most impressive display is the thundering 12,000-horsepower River Don steam engine (the size of a house) that gets powered up twice a day – don't miss it. The museum is 800m north of the city centre.

Winter Gardens GARDENS
(Surrey St; ⏲8am-6pm; 📶) Pride of place in Sheffield's city centre goes to this wonderfully ambitious public space with a soaring glass roof supported by graceful arches of laminated timber. The 21st-century architecture contrasts sharply with the nearby Victorian **town hall** and the **Peace Gardens** – complete with fountains, sculptures, and lawns full of lunching office workers whenever there's a bit of sun.

Graves Gallery GALLERY
(www.museums-sheffield.org.uk; Surrey St; ⏲11am-4pm Tue-Sat) FREE This gallery has a neat and accessible display of British and European art from the 16th century to the present day; the big names represented include Turner, Sisley, Cézanne, Gaugin, Miró, Klee, Picasso and Damien Hirst.

Abbeydale Industrial Hamlet MUSEUM
(www.simt.co.uk; Abbeydale Rd S; adult/child £4/free; ⏲10am-4pm Mon-Thu, 11am-4.45pm Sun; P 👪) In the days before steel mills, metalworking was a cottage industry (just like wool and cotton). For a glimpse of that earlier, more innocent era, you can explore the restored 18th-century forges, workshops and machines at this industrial museum, 4 miles southwest of the centre on the A621 (towards the Peak District).

Sleeping & Eating

Leopold Hotel BOUTIQUE HOTEL ££
(☎0845 078 0067; www.leopoldhotel.co.uk; 2 Leopold St; r from £70; 📶) Housed in a former grammar-school building, Sheffield's first boutique hotel brings some much-needed style and sophistication to the city's accommodation scene (but without a London-sized price tag). Rooms can suffer late-night noise from the bars on Leopold Sq – ask for a quiet room at the back.

Houseboat Hotels HOUSEBOAT ££
(☎01909 569393; www.houseboathotels.com; Victoria Quays, Wharfe St; s/d/q from £79/99/159; P 👪) Here's something a bit different: kick off your shoes and relax on board your very own permanently moored houseboat, complete with self-catering kitchen and patio area. Guests are entitled to discounts on the gym and pool facilities at the Hilton across the road.

Marmaduke's CAFE £
(www.marmadukescafedeli.co.uk; 22a Norfolk Row; mains £6-11; ⏲9am-5pm Mon-Sat, 10am-4pm Sun; 📶 ✍) 🍃 This appealingly cramped and chaotic cafe, crammed with recycled furniture and fittings and run by a young and enthusiastic crew, serves a breakfast menu (until 11.30am) that highlights local and organic produce, and lunch dishes that range from deli sandwiches and quiche to vegetarian specials such as the halloumi and herb burger.

Street Food Chef TEX-MEX £
(☎0114-275 2390; www.streetfoodchef.co.uk; 90 Arundel St; mains £3-6; ⏰10am-10pm Mon-Sat, to 9pm Sun) Local students flock to this down-to-earth Mexican canteen for its freshly prepared, great-value meals, including nachos, burritos, tacos and quesadillas with a choice of chilli-laced meat or veggie fillings, available to sit in or take away.

★ **Vero Gusto** ITALIAN ££
(☎0114-276 0004; www.verogusto.com; 12 Norfolk Row; mains £9-27; ⏰11am-11pm Tue-Sat; 📶) Gusto is a *real* Italian restaurant, from the Italian owners serving homemade Italian food to the genuine Italian coffee enjoyed by Italian customers reading Italian newspapers…you get the idea. Coffee and home-baked Italian cakes and pastries are served in the afternoon, plus lunch and dinner menus of exquisite Italian cuisine. It's best to book for dinner.

Drinking & Entertainment

Fat Cat CRAFT BEER
(☎0114-249 4801; www.thefatcat.co.uk; 23 Alma St; ⏰noon-11pm Sun-Thu, to midnight Fri & Sat) One of Sheffield's finest pubs, the Fat Cat serves a wide range of real ales (some brewed on the premises) in a wonderfully unreconstructed interior. There are three bars (one nonsmoking), good pub grub, and a roaring fire in winter. It's north of the city centre, and handy for Kelham Island Museum.

Showroom CINEMA
(☎0114-275 7727; www.showroomworkstation.org.uk; 15 Paternoster Row) This is the largest independent cinema in England, set in a grand art deco complex and screening a great mix of art-house, offbeat and not-quite-mainstream films.

Information

Post Office (Norfolk St; ⏰8.30am-5.30pm Mon-Fri, to 3pm Sat)

Sheffield Tourist Office (☎0114-275 7754; www.welcometosheffield.co.uk; Surrey St; ⏰9.30am-5pm Mon-Fri, to 4pm Sat, closed 1-1.30pm)

Getting There & Away

For all travel-related info for Sheffield and South Yorkshire, contact **Travel South Yorkshire** (☎01709-515151; www.travelsouthyorkshire.com).

BUS

The bus station, called the Interchange, is just east of the centre, about 250m north of the train station.

Leeds £4.70, one hour, hourly
Manchester £8.70, 1½ hours, four daily
London £14, four hours, four daily

TRAIN

Leeds £13, one hour, twice hourly
London St Pancras £75, 2½ hours, hourly
Manchester £15, one hour, twice hourly
York £16, 1¼ hours, twice hourly

EAST RIDING OF YORKSHIRE

The rolling farmland of the East Riding of Yorkshire meets the sea at Hull, a no-nonsense port that looks to the broad horizons of the Humber estuary and the North Sea for its livelihood. Just to its north, and in complete contrast to Hull's salt and grit, is Beverley, the East Riding's most attractive town, with lots of Georgian character and one of England's finest churches.

Hull

POP 284,320

Properly known as Kingston-upon-Hull (the ancient harbour on the River Hull was granted a royal charter in 1299 and became King's Town), Hull has long been the principal port of England's east coast, with an economy that grew up around wool and wine trading, whaling and fishing.

Named as UK City of Culture 2017 (www.hull2017.co.uk), the town has set about redeveloping its waterfront and Old Town; a minor cultural renaissance has taken place in the Fruitmarket district around Humber St, where derelict buildings have been reclaimed as artists' studios and performance spaces.

Though it's not going to win any prizes for prettiness, Hull has a gritty appeal for those who appreciate Britain's industrial past and enjoy getting away from the beaten tourist path. Famous as the home of poet Philip Larkin, the city harbours some fine Victorian civic architecture, a clutch of fascinating museums and one of Britain's best aquariums.

Sights & Activities

★ The Deep AQUARIUM

(☎01482-381000; www.thedeep.co.uk; Tower St; adult/child £12/10; ⏰10am-6pm, last entry 5pm; P 👪) Hull's biggest tourist attraction is The Deep, Britain's most spectacular aquarium, housed in a colossal angular building that appears to lunge above the muddy waters of the Humber like a giant shark's head. Inside, it's just as dramatic, with echoing commentaries and computer-generated interactive displays that guide you through the formation of the oceans and the evolution of sea life.

The largest aquarium tank is 10m deep, filled with sharks, stingrays and colourful coral fishes, with moray eels draped over rocks like scarves of iridescent slime. A glass elevator plies up and down inside the tank, though you'll get a better view by taking the stairs. Don't miss the cafe on the top floor, which has a great view of the Humber estuary.

Ferens Art Gallery GALLERY

(☎01482-300300; www.hullcc.gov.uk/ferens; Queen Victoria Sq; ⏰10am-5pm Mon-Sat, 1.30-4.30pm Sun) FREE Following extensive renovations, the Ferens Art Gallery reopened in 2017 as part of Hull's City of Culture celebrations, with an exhibition of Spencer Tunick's **Sea of Hull** (a photographic installation where more than 3000 naked volunteers, covered in blue body paint, filled the city streets). The permanent art collection ranges from old masters like Frans Hals to modern works by Stanley Spencer, Peter Blake, David Hockney and Gillian Wearing.

Arctic Corsair HISTORIC SITE

(www.hullcc.gov.uk/museums; ⏰10am-4.30pm Wed & Sat, 1.30-4.30pm Sun Apr-Oct) FREE Marooned in the mud of the River Hull around the back of the Streetlife Museum, this Atlantic trawler is a veteran of the 1970s so-called 'Cod Wars' when the UK and Iceland clashed over fishing rights. Free guided tours – request at **Hull & East Riding Museum** (www.hullcc.gov.uk/museums; High St; ⏰10am-5pm Mon-Sat, 1.30-4.30pm Sun) FREE reception desk – reveal the hardships of fishing north of the Arctic Circle.

LOCAL KNOWLEDGE

HULL PIER TOILETS

There are not too many places where a public toilet counts as a tourist attraction, but coach parties regularly stop to take photos of the **Hull Pier Toilets** (Nelson St). These gorgeous Edwardian temples of lavatorial luxury, resplendent with gleaming white tile, polished copper piping, varnished mahogany and a minor jungle of potted plants.

Spurn Lightship MUSEUM

(www.hullcc.gov.uk/museums; Castle St; ⏰1.30-4pm Sun late Jun–mid-Sep) FREE Built in 1927, this lighthouse-ship once served as a navigation mark for ships entering the notorious Humber estuary. Now safely retired in the marina, it houses an engaging exhibition about its own history, and offers an interesting contrast between the former living quarters of captain and crew.

Old Town AREA

Hull's Old Town, whose grand public buildings retain a sense of the prosperity the town once knew, occupies the thumb of land between the River Hull to the east and Princes Quay to the west. The most impressive legacy is the **Guildhall** (Low Gate; ⏰8.30am-4.30pm Mon-Thu, to 3.30pm Fri) FREE, a huge neoclassical building that dates from 1916.

Sleeping & Eating

Garden Mews B&B £

(☎01482-215574; http://the-garden-mews-gb.book.direct; 13-14 John St; s/d/f from £30/45/60; 📶 👪) Overlooking leafy Kingston Sq, and close to the New Theatre, this is one of the best-value B&B options in the city centre; the rooms are nothing fancy, but are tidy and comfortable, and the owners are friendly and helpful.

Kingston Theatre Hotel HOTEL ££

(☎01482-225828; www.kingstontheatrehotel.com; 1-2 Kingston Sq; s/d/ste £75/110/190; 📶 👪) One of Hull's most pleasant places to stay, this hotel has elegant bedrooms, friendly service and an excellent breakfast, and enjoys a quiet location on a park-like square opposite the New Theatre. Good discounts available via website.

Bait SEAFOOD ££

(☎01482-343088; www.baithull.co.uk; 13-15 Princes Ave; mains £11-18; ⏰noon-2.30pm & 5-9pm Tue-Thu, noon-9.30pm Fri-Sun) 🌿 Hull's seafaring tradition is reflected in a menu dominated by the best of British seafood, including Lindisfarne oysters au naturel, lobster bisque, grey mullet with cider and onion chutney, smoked haddock risotto and good old-fashioned fish pie. There are meat and vegetarian dishes too, and the rustic, chunky-timber decor engenders a lively and informal atmosphere.

Fudge AMERICAN ££
(01482-441019; www.fudgefood.com; 93 Princes Ave; mains £8-17; 10.30am-3pm Tue-Thu & Sun, 9am-3pm Fri & Sat, 6-9pm Tue-Sun;) This funky cafe decked out in pink and peppermint colours serves hearty brunches, cakes and coffee all day, but also offers a tempting USA-style menu of dishes that include juicy burgers (beef or veggie), creole chicken, po' boys and deli sandwiches.

★**1884 Dock Street Kitchen** MODERN BRITISH £££
(01482-222260; www.1884dockstreetkitchen.co.uk; Humber Dock St; mains £17-33; noon-2pm Tue-Sat, 6-9.30pm Mon-Sat, noon-3pm Sun;) Poster boy for the city's redeveloping waterfront, this big and bold enterprise tries to blend British cuisine with a sepia-tinted, late-19th-century New York-steakhouse look, and just about pulls it off. As well as the steaks, the menu is strong on Scottish seafood, Yorkshire pork and Lancashire lamb, and dishes dotted with wild garlic and duck egg. Three-course lunch menu £21.

Drinking & Entertainment

Olde Black Boy PUB
(01482-215040; 150 High St; 5.30-11.30pm Mon-Tue, 12.30-11.30pm Wed-Sun) A favourite watering hole of poet Philip Larkin, Hull's oldest pub has been serving ale since 1726. Oak floors and roof beams, dark-wood panelling and a snug log fire in winter make for a great atmosphere, and there's live folk music on Wednesdays.

Fuel CLUB
(www.fuel-hull.co.uk; 6 Baker St; 11pm-3am Wed, 8pm-6am Fri & Sat;) A nondescript facade conceals what is currently Hull's hottest club, proudly but not exclusively gay, with camp comedy and drag shows as well as DJs and dancers.

Fruitspace LIVE MUSIC, COMEDY
(01482-221113; www.fruitspace.co.uk; 62-63 Humber St;) A focus for the cultural revival of Hull's Fruitmarket district, this former industrial space is now a multipurpose venue incorporating a bar, cinema and stage. There are regular live gigs by local bands (and occasional big names), a monthly comedy club and, on the third Sunday of the month, the Humber Street Market.

Information

Hull Tourist Office (01482-300300; www.visithullandeastyorkshire.com; 1 Paragon St; 10am-5pm Mon-Sat, 11am-3pm Sun)

Beverley

POP 30,590

Handsome, unspoilt Beverley is one of the most attractive towns in Yorkshire, largely on account of its magnificent minster – a rival to any cathedral in England – and the tangle of streets that lie beneath it, each brimming with exquisite Georgian and Victorian buildings.

All the sights are a short walk from either the train or bus station. There's a large market on Saturdays in the square called Saturday Market, and a smaller one on Wednesdays in the square called...Wednesday Market.

Sights

★**Beverley Minster** CHURCH
(www.beverleyminster.org; St John St; 9am-5pm Mon-Sat, noon-5pm Sun Mar-Oct, to 4pm Nov-Mar;) FREE One of the great glories of English religious architecture, Beverley Minster is the most impressive church in the country that is not a cathedral. The soaring lines of the exterior are imposing, but it is inside that the charm and beauty lie. The 14th-century north aisle is lined with original stone carvings, mostly of musicians; much of our knowledge of early musical instruments comes from these images. You'll also see goblins, devils and grotesque figures. Look out for the bagpipe player.

Construction began in 1220 – the third church to be built on this site, with the first dating from the 7th century – and continued for two centuries, spanning the Early English, Decorated and Perpendicular periods of the Gothic style.

Close to the altar, the elaborate and intricate **Percy Canopy** (1340), a decorative frill above the tomb of local aristocrat Lady Eleanor Percy, is a testament to the skill of the sculptor and the finest example of Gothic stone carving in England. In complete

WORTH A TRIP

PIPE & GLASS INN

Set in a picturesque hamlet 4 miles northwest of Beverley, the **Pipe and Glass Inn** (01430-810246; www.pipeandglass.co.uk; West End, South Dalton; mains £11-30; noon-2pm & 6.30-9.30pm Tue-Sat, noon-4pm Sun;) is a charming country pub which has held a Michelin star since 2010. The setting may be delightfully informal, with weathered timber tables, stone hearths and leather sofas, but a great deal of care is lavished on the food – even seemingly simple dishes such as fish pie are unforgettable.

If you want to stay the night, there are five luxurious bedrooms to choose from (£180 to £225 per night, including breakfast).

contrast, in the nearby chancel is the 10th-century Saxon **frith stool**, a plain and polished stone chair that once gave sanctuary to anyone escaping the law.

In the roof of the tower is a restored treadwheel crane, where workers ground around like hapless hamsters to lift the huge loads necessary to build a medieval church. Access to the roof is by guided tour only (per person £5).

Beverley Westwood PARK

(Walkington Rd) The western edge of Beverley is bounded by this large area of common pasture studded with mature trees, which has been used as grazing for local livestock for centuries. The land, owned 'in common' by the community since 1380, is overseen by the Pasture Masters, a group of men elected from the Freemen of Beverley each March. Contented cows amble across the unfenced road, while walkers stroll and enjoy the gorgeous views of Beverley Minster.

Sleeping & Eating

★YHA Beverley Friary HOSTEL £

(0845 371 9004; www.yha.org.uk; Friar's Lane; dm/d from £15/49;) In Beverley, the cheapest accommodation also has the best setting and location. This hostel is housed in a beautifully restored 14th-century Dominican friary mentioned in Chaucer's *The Canterbury Tales*, and is only 100m from the minster and a short walk from the train station.

Kings Head INN ££

(01482-868103; www.kingsheadpubbeverley.co.uk; 38 Saturday Market; r from £90;) A Georgian coaching inn given a modern makeover, the Kings Head is a lively pub with 10 bright and stylish rooms above the bar. The pub opens late on weekend nights, but earplugs are supplied for those who don't want to join the revelry!

Vanessa Delicafe CAFE ££

(01482-868190; www.vanessadelicafe.co.uk; 21-22 Saturday Market; mains £7-15; 9am-4.30pm Mon-Sat, 10am-3.30pm Sun;) This popular cafe sits above a delicatessen, with sofas and bookshelves scattered among the tables, and window seats overlooking the market square. Settle down for cappuccino and cake with the Sunday papers, or tuck into hearty lunch specials such as venison burger or a Yorkshire platter of pork pie, roast ham, cheese and chutney.

Grant's Bistro 22 MODERN BRITISH £££

(01482-887624; www.grantsbistro.co.uk; 22 North Bar Within; mains £14-25; noon-2pm Fri & Sat, 6-9.30pm Mon-Sat;) A great place for a romantic dinner à deux, with darkwood tables, fresh flowers and candlelight. The menu makes the most of fresh local beef, game and especially seafood, with dishes such as pan-fried scallops with black pudding, and a decent choice of vegetarian options. A two-/three-course lunch is £15/20.

Information

Beverley Tourist Office (01482-391672; www.visithullandeastyorkshire.com/beverley; 34 Butcher Row; 9.30am-5pm Mon-Sat)

Getting There & Away

There are frequent bus services from Hull, including numbers 121, 122, 246 and X46/X47 (£4.05, 30 minutes, every 20 minutes). Bus X46/X47 links Beverley with York (£6.45, 1¼ hours, hourly).

Trains run regularly to Scarborough (£13.70, 1¼ hours, every two hours) and Hull (£6.80, 15 minutes, twice hourly).

Manchester, Liverpool & Northwest England

Includes ➡

Best Places to Eat

- ➡ Northcote Hotel (p576)
- ➡ Manchester House (p556)
- ➡ Little Fish Cafe (p577)
- ➡ Simon Radley at the Grosvenor (p562)
- ➡ Salt House (p570)

Best Places to Sleep

- ➡ Inn at Whitewell (p576)
- ➡ 2 Blackburne Terrace (p569)
- ➡ King Street Townhouse (p554)
- ➡ Stone Villa (p561)
- ➡ Richmond Hotel (p568)

Why Go?

Two rival cities with rich traditions, a medieval masterpiece, an island unto itself and some of the finest countryside in England...this is just a flavour of what the northwest has to offer. Dominating the region is Manchester, arguably England's most exciting city and the unofficial capital of the north. Just across the Pennines is Liverpool, fiercely proud of its own heritage and well able to put it up to its bigger neighbour in all matters from food to football. Near to both is Chester, a historic Tudor postcard with a legacy dating back to Roman times. And, just to prove that the northwest isn't all about humankind's concrete footprint, you can get away from it all in some of Britain's most beautiful – and walkable – countryside, in northern Lancashire and on the Isle of Man.

When to Go

➡ The world's most famous steeplechase – the Aintree Grand National – is run just outside Liverpool over the first weekend in April.

➡ May and June are Tourist Trophy (TT) Festival season on the Isle of Man – beloved of motor enthusiasts the world over.

➡ In the arts, the highlight is the Manchester International Festival, a biennial showstopper held in July.

➡ Music buffs should visit Liverpool in the last week of August for madness at Creamfields dance-fest and for the Mathew St Festival, an ode to all things Beatles.

➡ The football (soccer) season runs from late August until May.

Manchester, Liverpool & Northwest England Highlights

1 International Slavery Museum (p566) Learning a history lesson at Liverpool's most emotionally charged museum.

2 Beatles' Childhood Homes (p567) Visiting the Liverpool houses where John and Paul grew up – and wrote their earliest hits.

3 HOME (p557) Catching a show at Manchester's exciting and provocative arts centre.

4 City Walls (p559) Tramping Chester's fortifications like the Romans did 2000 years ago.

5 Lady Isabella Laxey Wheel (p578) Visiting the world's largest working waterwheel.

6 Pleasure Beach (p572) Letting your adrenalin flow on a roller-coaster in Blackpool.

7 People's History Museum (p549) Learning about social justice in Manchester.

8 Philharmonic (p570) Enjoying a drink in this Liverpool pub, one of Britain's most beautiful.

Activities

Walking & Cycling

In between the urban bits, the northwest is surprisingly good for walking and cycling options, notably in northern Lancashire's Ribble Valley, home to plenty of good walks including the 70-mile Ribble Way (p574). The historic village of Whalley, in the heart of the Ribble Valley, is the meeting point of the two circular routes that make up the 260-mile Lancashire Cycle Way (p574).

The Isle of Man has top-notch walking and cycling opportunities. Regional tourism websites contain walking and cycling information, and tourist offices stock free leaflets as well as maps and guides (usually £1 to £5) that cover walking, cycling and other activities.

Boating

The waterways of the northwest have been crucial to the region's development. You can explore some of its more important canals with **Wandering Duck** (www.wanderingduck.co.uk; 2-night trip per person incl meals from £145) in Manchester, while a boat trip across the Mersey is a Liverpool must-do.

Information

Visit north west (www.visitnorthwest.com) is the centralised tourist authority; for the Isle of Man check out **Isle of Man** (www.visitisleofman.com).

Getting Around

The towns and cities covered are all within easy reach of each other, and are well linked by public transport. The two main cities, Manchester and Liverpool, are only 34 miles apart and are linked by hourly bus and train services. Chester is 18 miles south of Liverpool, but is also easily accessible from Manchester by train or via the M56. Blackpool is 50 miles to the north of Manchester and Liverpool, and is also well connected on the M6.

MANCHESTER

POP 527,240

The weather tagline on Manchester radio station Key 103FM introduces the forecast for 'the greatest city in the world'. It's a ridiculous bit of local hyperbole, but behind the bluster Mancunians both native-born and imported are convinced they live in a pretty fabulous city. A rich blend of history and culture is on show in its museums, galleries and art centres, but what makes Manchester really fun is the swirl of hedonism that lets you dine, drink and dance yourself into happy oblivion.

The uncrowned capital of the north is also the driving force of the Northern Powerhouse, a government programme of investment and development that looks to corral northern England's 15 million people into a collective force to rival London and the southeast. As a result, the city centre looks like a construction site, with a host of new buildings rising up from streets that are being dug up so as to lay down miles of new tram line. The city of the future is being built today.

History

Canals and steam-powered cotton mills were what transformed Manchester from a small, disease-infested provincial town into a big, disease-infested industrial city. It all happened in the 1760s, with the opening of the Bridgewater Canal between Manchester and the coal mines at Worsley in 1763, and with Richard Arkwright patenting his super cotton mill in 1769. Thereafter Manchester and the world would never be the same again. When the canal was extended to Liverpool and the open sea in 1776, Manchester – dubbed 'Cottonopolis' – kicked into high gear and took off on the coal-fuelled, steam-powered gravy train.

There was plenty of gravy to go around, but the good burghers of 19th-century Manchester made sure that the vast majority of the city's swollen citizenry (with a population of 90,000 in 1801, and two million 100 years later) who produced most of it never got their hands on any of it. Their reward was life in a new kind of urban settlement: the industrial slum. Working conditions were dire, with impossibly long hours, child labour, work-related accidents and fatalities commonplace. Mark Twain commented that he would like to live here because the 'transition between Manchester and Death would be unnoticeable'. So much for Victorian values.

The wheels started to come off towards the end of the 19th century. The USA had begun to flex its own industrial muscles and was taking over a sizeable chunk of the textile trade; production in Manchester's mills began to slow, and then it stopped altogether. By WWII there was hardly enough cotton produced in the city to make a tablecloth. The postwar years weren't much better: 150,000 manufacturing jobs were lost between 1961 and 1983, and the port – still the UK's third largest in 1963 – finally closed

MANCHESTER IN ONE DAY

Start your exploration in the light-filled galleries of the **Manchester Art Gallery** (below), home to one of the most important collections in the north. The **Museum of Science & Industry** (below) will take up at least a couple of hours – more if you've got kids or you're a science geek. Alternatively, the **People's History Museum** (below) is a fascinating exploration of social history. Lunch on Chinese food at **Tattu** (p555) or take your pick at **The Kitchens** (p554) Hop on the tram to Salford Quays, where you can explore the **Imperial War Museum North** (p553) or take a guided tour of the norther headquarters of the **BBC** (p553); fans of Manchester United should take the tour of **Old Trafford** (p555), where they'll get to stand in the tunnel and pretend they're players. Make dinner reservations for **Manchester House** (p556).

After dinner, head to the Northern Quarter and have your choice of ale at the **Port Street Beer House** (p556) or a more musical pint at **The Castle Hotel** (p556); there's often a gig on at the attached venue, or you can head south towards Castlefield and take in a film or a play at the superb **HOME** (p557) arts centre.

in 1982 due to declining traffic. The nadir came on 15 June 1996, when an IRA bomb wrecked a chunk of the city centre, but the subsequent reconstruction proved to be the beginning of the glass-and-chrome revolution so much in evidence today.

Sights

City Centre

★People's History Museum MUSEUM

(☎0161-838 9190; www.phm.org.uk; Left Bank, Bridge St; ⏲10am-5pm) FREE The story of Britain's 200-year march to democracy is told in all its pain and pathos at this superb museum, housed in a refurbished Edwardian pumping station. You clock in on the 1st floor (literally: punch your card in an old mill clock, which managers would infamously fiddle with so as to make employees work longer) and plunge into the heart of Britain's struggle for basic democratic rights, labour reform and fair pay.

Amid displays like the (tiny) desk at which Thomas Paine (1737–1809) wrote *Rights of Man* (1791), and an array of beautifully made and colourful union banners, are compelling interactive displays, including a screen where you can trace the effects of all the events covered in the museum on five generations of the same family. The 2nd floor takes up the struggle for equal rights from WWII to the current day, touching on gay rights, antiracism initiatives and the defining British sociopolitical landmarks of the last 50 years, including the founding of the National Health Service (NHS), the Miners' Strike and the widespread protests against the Poll Tax.

★Museum of Science & Industry MUSEUM

(MOSI; ☎0161-832 2244; www.msimanchester.org.uk; Liverpool Rd; special exhibits £2.50-4; ⏲10am-5pm) FREE Manchester's rich industrial legacy is explored in this excellent museum set within the enormous grounds of the old Liverpool St Station, the oldest rail terminus in the world. The large collection of steam engines, locomotives and original factory machinery tell the story of the city from the sewers up, while a host of new technology (flight simulator, 4D cinema) look to the future. Take Metrolink to Deansgate-Castlefield or Metroshuttle No 2.

It's an all-ages kind of museum, but the emphasis is on making sure the young 'uns don't get bored – they could easily spend a whole day poking about, testing an early electric-shock machine here and trying out a printing press there. You can get up close and personal with fighter jets and get to grips with all kinds of space-age technology. In the Revolution Manchester Gallery a unique barcode activates a series of games and challenges that you can follow up on at home. A unifying theme is that Manchester and Mancunians had a key role to play: this is the place to discover that Manchester was home to the world's first stored-program computer (a giant contraption nicknamed 'baby') in 1948 and that the world's first submarine was built to the designs of local curate Reverend George Garrett in 1880.

★Manchester Art Gallery ART MUSEUM

(☎0161-235 8888; http://manchesterartgallery.org; Mosley St; tours 20min/1hr free/£80; ⏲10am-5pm

Manchester

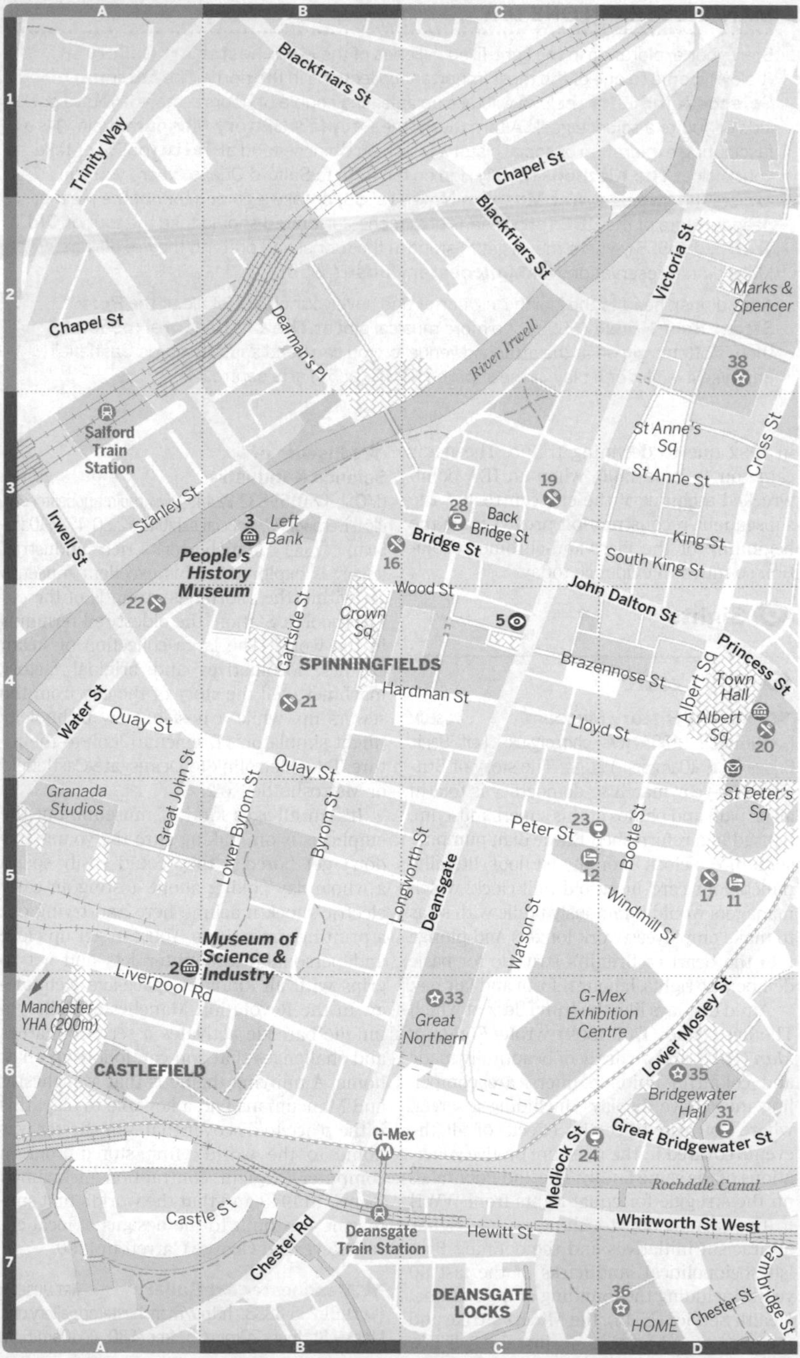
A
B
C
D
1
2
3
4
5
6
7
Blackfriars St
Trinity Way
Chapel St
Victoria St
Marks & Spencer
Dearman's Pl
River Irwell
38
Salford Train Station
St Anne's Sq
Cross St
St Anne St
19
28
Back Bridge St
Stanley St
Irwell St
3 Left Bank
King St
Bridge St
16
South King St
People's History Museum
Wood St
John Dalton St
22
Crown Sq
5
Gartside St
Princess St
SPINNINGFIELDS
Brazennose St
Albert Sq
Town Hall
Hardman St
21
Water St
Albert Sq
Lloyd St
Quay St
20
Great John St
Lower Byrom St
Byrom St
St Peter's Sq
Granada Studios
23
Peter St
Bootle St
12
Longworth St
Deansgate
17
11
Watson St
Windmill St
Museum of Science & Industry
2
Liverpool Rd
Lower Mosley St
Manchester YHA (200m)
33
Great Northern
G-Mex Exhibition Centre
CASTLEFIELD
35
Bridgewater Hall
31
G-Mex
Medlock St
24
Great Bridgewater St
Rochdale Canal
Castle St
Chester Rd
Deansgate Train Station
Hewitt St
Whitworth St West
Cambridge St
DEANSGATE LOCKS
36
HOME
Chester St

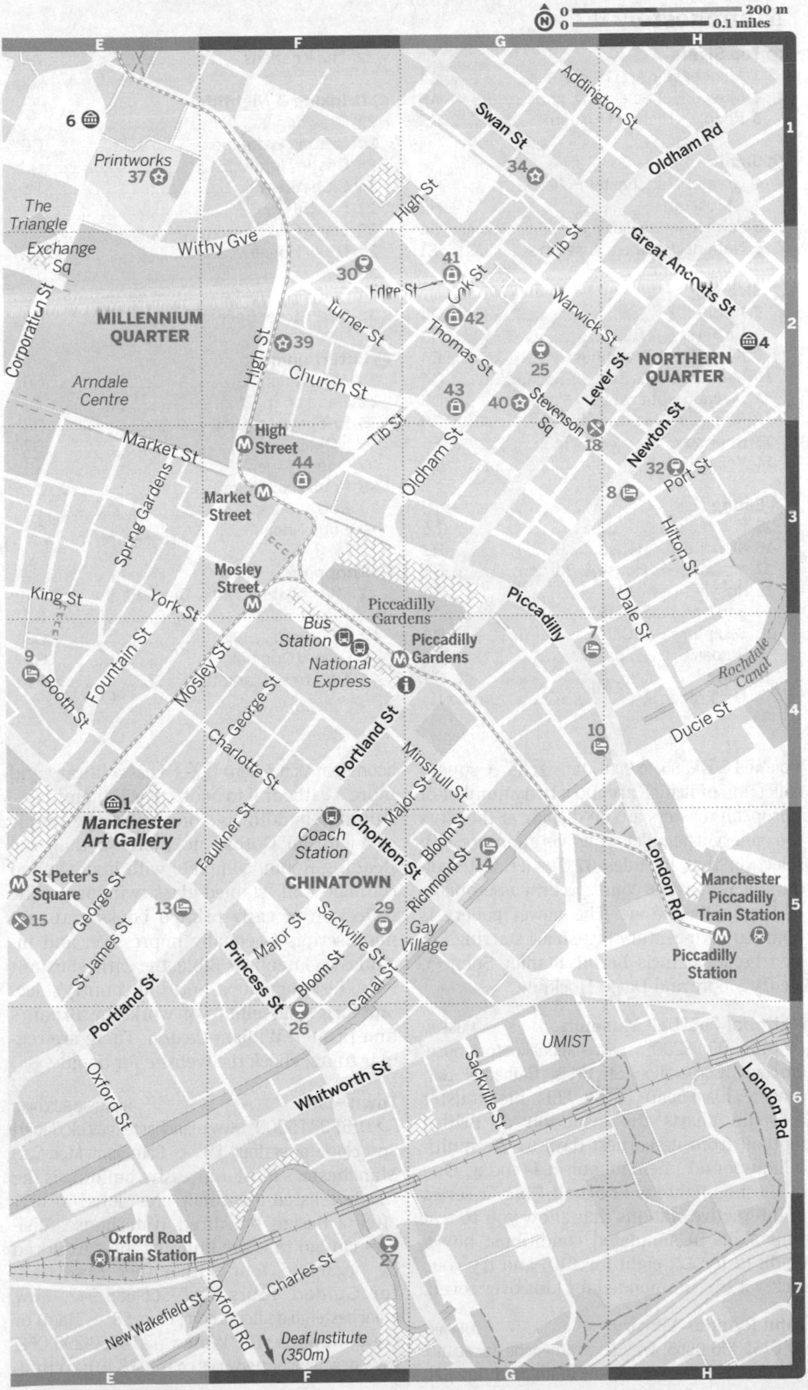

0 200 m
0 0.1 miles
E
F
G
H
1
2
3
4
5
6
7
6
Printworks
37
The Triangle
Exchange Sq
Corporation St
MILLENNIUM QUARTER
Arndale Centre
Withy Gve
High St
39
Church St
Turner St
30
Edge St
41
Oak St
42
Thomas St
43
Swan St
Addington St
34
Oldham Rd
High St
Tib St
Great Ancoats St
Warwick St
25
40
Stevenson Sq
Lever St
NORTHERN QUARTER
4
Newton St
18
32
Port St
8
Hilton St
Tib St
Oldham St
High Street
Market St
44
Market Street
Spring Gardens
King St
York St
Mosley Street
Piccadilly Gardens
Bus Station
National Express
Piccadilly Gardens
Piccadilly
7
Dale St
Rochdale Canal
Ducie St
10
9
Booth St
Fountain St
Mosley St
George St
Charlotte St
Portland St
Minshull St
Major St
1
Manchester Art Gallery
Faulkner St
Coach Station
Chorlton St
Bloom St
Richmond St
14
London Rd
Manchester Piccadilly Train Station
Piccadilly Station
St Peter's Square
15
George St
13
CHINATOWN
29
Gay Village
St James St
Major St
Sackville St
Princess St
Bloom St
Canal St
Portland St
26
UMIST
Oxford St
Whitworth St
Sackville St
London Rd
Oxford Road Train Station
27
Charles St
New Wakefield St
Oxford Rd
Deaf Institute (350m)
MANCHESTER, LIVERPOOL & NORTHWEST ENGLAND

Manchester

Top Sights
1 Manchester Art Gallery E4
2 Museum of Science & Industry A5
3 People's History Museum B3

Sights
4 Greater Manchester Police Museum H2
5 John Rylands Library C4
6 National Football Museum E1

Sleeping
7 ABode G4
8 Hatters H3
9 King Street Townhouse E4
10 Malmaison G4
11 Midland Hotel D5
12 Radisson Blu Edwardian C5
13 Roomzzz E5
14 Velvet Hotel G5

Eating
15 Fumo E5
16 Manchester House B3
17 Mr Cooper's House & Garden D5
18 Rosylee Tearooms G3
19 San Carlo Cicchetti C3
20 Sculpture Hall Cafe D4
Smoak Grill .... (see 10)
21 Tattu B4
The French .... (see 11)
22 The Kitchens A4

Drinking & Nightlife
23 Brewdog C5
24 Britons Protection C6
25 Castle Hotel G2
26 Club Alter Ego F6
27 Fac251 .... F7
28 Liar's Club C3
29 Molly House F5
30 Odd F2
31 Peveril of the Peak D6
32 Port Street Beer House H3

Entertainment
33 AMC Cinemas C6
34 Band on the Wall G1
35 Bridgewater Hall D6
36 HOME D7
37 Odeon Cinema E1
38 Royal Exchange D2
39 Ruby Lounge F2
40 Soup Kitchen G2

Shopping
41 Manchester Craft & Design Centre G2
42 Oi Polloi G2
43 Oxfam Originals G2
44 Tib Street Market F3

Mon-Wed & Fri-Sun, to 9pm Thu) FREE A superb collection of British art and a hefty number of European masters are on display at the city's top gallery. The older wing has an impressive selection that includes 37 Turner watercolours, as well as the country's best assemblage of Pre-Raphaelite art. The newer gallery is home to 20th-century British art starring Lucien Freud, Francis Bacon, Stanley Spencer, Henry Moore and David Hockney.

National Football Museum MUSEUM
(☎0161-605 8200; www.nationalfootballmuseum.com; Corporation St, Urbis, Cathedral Gardens; ⏰10am-5pm) FREE This blockbuster museum charts the evolution of British football from its earliest days to the multi-billion-pound phenomenon it is today. One of the highlights is **Football Plus**, a series of interactive stations that allow you to test your skills in simulated conditions; buy a credit (2 for £5, eight for £10) and try your luck – it's recommended for kids over seven.

John Rylands Library LIBRARY
(☎0161-306 0555; www.library.manchester.ac.uk/rylands; 150 Deansgate; ⏰10am-5pm Tue-Sat, noon-5pm Mon & Sun) FREE Less a library and more a cathedral to books, Basil Champneys' stunning building is a breathtaking example of Victorian Gothic, no more so than the Reading Room, complete with high-vaulted ceilings and stained-glass windows. The collection of early printed books and rare manuscripts is equally impressive, and includes a Gutenberg Bible, the earliest extant New Testament text and the country's second-largest assembly of works by Britain's first printer, William Caxton. There are regular tours; check the website for details.

Town Hall HISTORIC BUILDING
(☎0161-234 5000; www.manchester.gov.uk; Albert Sq; clock-tower tour £9; ⏰9am-5pm Mon-Sat) Manchester's most impressive building is the Grade I–listed town hall, completed in 1877 after a design by Alfred Waterhouse. Visitors can go into the building, best explored by organised tour with either **Manchester Guided Tours** (☎07505-685 942; www.manchesterguidedtours.com; tours £8; ⏰11am) or **New Manchester Walks** (☎07769-298 068; www.newmanchesterwalks.com; £8-10); climb

the 85m-high tower and grab a bite in the beautiful Sculpture Hall cafe. Unfortunately, the grandest room of all, the Great Hall (decorated with murals by Ford Madox Ford) is open only for official business.

Salford Quays

Just west of the city centre lies Salford Quays, home to some of Manchester's big-ticket attractions and MediaCityUK, the northern hub of both the BBC and ITV. It is easily reached via Metrolink (£2.80). Check out www.mediacityuk.co.uk for more info.

Imperial War Museum North MUSEUM
(0161-836 4000; www.iwm.org.uk/north; Trafford Wharf Rd; 10am-5pm) FREE Inside Daniel Libeskind's aluminum-clad architectural stunner is a war museum with a difference, exploring the effects of conflict on society rather than fetishising the instruments of destruction. Six mini exhibitions within the main hall examine war since the beginning of the 20th century from a variety of perspectives, including the role of women and the influence of science and technology. Catch the Metrolink to Harbour City or MediaCityUK.

MediaCityUK MEDIA CENTRE
(0161-886 5300; www.mediacityuk.co.uk; Salford Quays; adult/child £11/7.25; tours 10.30am, 12.30pm & 3pm Mon-Wed, Sat & Sun) The BBC's northern home is but one significant element of this vast, 81-hectare site. Besides hosting six departments of the national broadcaster (BBC Breakfast, Children's, Sport, Radio 5 Live, Learning, and Future Media & Technology), it is also home to the set of the world's longest-running soap opera, the perennially popular *Coronation Street* (which broadcasts on ITV). To get here take the Metrolink to MediaCityUK.

There are no plans as yet to offer tours of the Corrie set, but you can visit the BBC's impressive set-up and see the sets of some of TV's most iconic programs on a guided 90-minute tour that also includes a chance for kids to 'make' a program in an interactive studio; see www.bbc.co.uk/showsandtours. For refuelling, there are plenty of cafes and restaurants in the area.

Lowry ARTS CENTRE
(0161-876 2020; www.thelowry.com; Pier 8, Salford Quays; 11am-6pm Sun-Fri, 10am-8pm Sat) With multiple performance spaces, bars, restaurants and shops, this contemporary arts centre attracts more than a million visitors a year to its myriad functions, which include everthing from big-name theatrical productions to comedy, kids' theatre and even weddings. The centre is also home to 300 beautifully humanistic depictions of urban landscapes by LS Lowry (1887–1976), who was born in nearby Stretford, and after whom the complex is named. Get here by Metrolink to Harbour City or MediaCity UK.

Festivals & Events

Screenings at the Garden Leftbank FILM
(www.spinningfieldsonline.com; The Garden, Irwell Sq, Spinningfields; 5.30pm Thu May-Jul) FREE Summer season of outdoor films, complete with deckchairs, beginning in May. Grab some food from The Kitchens and enjoy the show.

Manchester International Festival ART
(0161-238 7300; www.mif.co.uk) A three-week-long biennial arts festival of artist-led new work across visual arts, performance and popular culture. The next festival is scheduled for July 2017.

Manchester Food & Drink Festival FOOD & DRINK
(www.foodanddrinkfestival.com; mid-Oct) Manchester's superb foodie scene shows off its wares over 10 days in mid-October. Farmers markets, pop-up restaurants and gourmet events are just part of the UK's biggest urban food fest.

Sleeping

★ **Manchester YHA** HOSTEL $
(0845 371 9647; www.yha.org.uk; Potato Wharf; dm/d from £10/80; P @) This purpose-built canalside hostel in the Castlefield area is one of the best in the country. It's a top-class option with four- and six-bed dorms, all with bathroom, as well as three doubles and a host of good facilities. Potato Wharf is just left off Liverpool Rd.

Hatters HOSTEL $
(0161-236 9500; http://hattershostels.com; 50 Newton St; dm/s/d from £16/35/50; P @) The old-style lift and porcelain sinks are the only leftovers of this former milliner's factory, now one of the best hostels in town. The location is a boon: smack in the heart of the Northern Quarter, you won't have to go far to get the best of alternative Manchester.

ABode HOTEL $$
(☎0161-247 7744; www.abodemanchester.co.uk; 107 Piccadilly St; r from £100; ❄@📶) The original fittings at this converted textile factory have been combined successfully with 61 bedrooms divided into four categories of ever-increasing luxury: Comfortable, Desirable, Enviable and Fabulous on Fifth, the latter being five seriously swanky top-floor suites.

Midland Hotel HOTEL $$
(☎0161-236 3333; www.qhotels.co.uk; 16 Peter St; r from £100; ❄@📶) This newly refurbished Grade II–listed Edwardian hotel is back to its elegant best. Its 312 rooms are all elegantly appointed: the junior suites have a separate lounge while the seven Midland suites once entertained royalty. Downstairs, Simon Rogan's The French (p556) and **Mr Cooper's House & Garden** (www.mrcoopershouseandgarden.co.uk; mains £15-25; ⏲noon-2pm & 5-10pm Mon-Thu, noon-2.30pm & 5-10pm Fri-Sat, 1-8pm Sun) restaurants are among the best in the city.

Roomzzz APARTMENT $$
(☎0161-236 2121; www.roomzzz.co.uk; 36 Princess St; r from £99; ❄@📶) The inelegant name belies the designer digs inside this beautifully restored Grade II building, which features serviced apartments equipped with a kitchen and the latest connectivity gadgetry, including sleek iMac computers and free wi-fi throughout. There's a small pantry, with food for sale downstairs. Highly recommended if you're planning a longer stay.

Malmaison HOTEL $$
(☎0161-278 1000; www.malmaison.com; Piccadilly St; r from £105; ❄@📶) Drop-dead trendy and full of red crushed velvet, deep purples, art deco ironwork and signature black-and-white tiles, Malmaison Manchester follows the chain's quirky design style and passion for cool, although rarely at the expense of comfort: the rooms are terrific. The **Smoak Grill** (☎0161-278 1000; Piccadilly St; mains £14-26, steaks £25-45) downstairs is hugely popular.

Radisson Blu Edwardian HOTEL $$
(☎0161-835 9929; www.radissonblu-edwardian.com/manchester; Peter St; r from £100; P@📶) Gladstone, Dickens and Fitzgerald…just some of the names associated with the historic Free Trade Hall, now an elegant business hotel with high-end trimmings and decor. It has done its best to preserve the memories of the building's most famous visitors: suites are named after Bob Dylan and Shirley Bassey, while meeting rooms carry the names of Disraeli, Thackeray and Pankhurst.

★**King Street Townhouse** BOUTIQUE HOTEL $$$
(☎0161-667 0707; www.eclectichotels.co.uk; 10 Booth St; r/ste from £210/£350; ❄@📶🏊) Arguably the city centre's finest lodgings is in this beautiful 1872 Italian Renaissance-style former bank, now an exquisite boutique hotel with 40 bedrooms ranging from snug to suite. Furnishings are the perfect combination of period elegance and contemporary style. On the top floor is a small spa with an infinity pool overlooking the town hall; downstairs is a nice bar and restaurant.

Velvet Hotel BOUTIQUE HOTEL $$$
(☎0161-236 9003; www.velvetmanchester.com; 2 Canal St; r from £115; 📶) Nineteen beautiful bespoke rooms each oozing style: there's the sleigh bed in room 24, the double bath of room 34, the saucy framed photographs of a stripped-down David Beckham (this is Gay Village, after all!). Despite the tantalising decor and location, this is not an exclusive hotel and is as popular with straight visitors as it is with the same-sex crowd.

Eating

Manchester's choice of restaurants is second only to London. Spinningfields, just off Deansgate, has some of the most interesting spots in the centre while the Northern Quarter is great for offbeat cafes and organic eats.

Sculpture Hall Cafe CAFE $
(Town Hall, Albert Sq; mains £3.95-6.95, afternoon tea £12.50; ⏲8am-4pm Mon-Fri, 10am-4pm Sat & Sun) The lovely cafe in the town hall has sandwiches, salads, traditional Lancashire hotpots (a kind of stew topped with sliced potatoes) as well as afternoon tea, which comes with savoury and sweet treats like potted Yorkshire ham rillette and Manchester sponge cake. The champagne version costs £19.95.

The Kitchens INTERNATIONAL $
(http://thekitchensleftbank.com; Irwell Sq; mains £4-12; ⏲noon-3pm Mon-Wed, to 9pm Thu-Sun, Bangers & Bacon 7am-midnight Mon-Fri, from 9.30am Sat & Sun) Gathered under the one roof are a number of 'street food' producers including Bangers and Bacon (@bangersandbacon), Chaat Cart (Indian street food; @chaatcart), the Hip Hop Chip Shop (@thehiphopchippy), Dim Sum Su (@dimsumsu) and Well Hung (@wellhungkitchen), which serves 28-day aged steaks and sandwiches. They're all terrific: check the Twitter handles for updates.

MANCHESTER'S FOOTBALL SIDES

If modern football is made up of equal parts spectacle, soap opera and sporting drama, then Manchester has the ingredients to offer the greatest show on earth. Home to two of the world's best-known clubs, in 2016 the city welcomed the world's most famous managers: the 'Chosen One', José Mourinho has taken over at United, while Josep 'Pep' Guardiola has lent his stylish and successful brand of football to City. They're both enormously successful, and their very presence will draw some of the best talent in the world, but what will really attract the world's attention is the intensity of their rivalry, which became acrimonious when Mourinho was in charge of Real Madrid and Guardiola of Barcelona. Let the show begin…

Old Trafford (Manchester United Museum & Tour; ☎0161-868 8000; www.manutd.com; Sir Matt Busby Way; tours adult/child £18/12; ⏲museum 9.30am-5pm, tours every 10min 9.40am-4.30pm except match days) You don't have to be a fan of the world's most famous football club to enjoy a visit to their impressive 75,000-plus capacity stadium, but it helps. The museum tour includes a walk down the tunnel onto the edge of the playing surface of the 'Theatre of Dreams', where Manchester United's superstar footballers exercised their Premier League supremacy for 20 years, guided by the peerless Sir Alex Ferguson. To reach here take the Metrolink to Old Trafford.

Other highlights of the excellent tour include a seat in the stands, a stop in the changing rooms and a peek at the players' lounge (from which the manager is banned unless invited by the players) – all ecstatic experiences for a Man United devotee. The museum has a comprehensive history of the club and a state-of-the-art call-up system that means you can view your favourite goals.

Etihad Stadium Tour (Manchester City; ☎0161-444 1894; www.mcfc.co.uk; Etihad Campus; tours adult/child £17/11; ⏲9am-5pm Mon-Sat, 10am-4pm Sun except match days) On this 70-minute tour of Manchester City's home ground you'll visit the players' dressing room, lounge and warm-up room; sit in the manager's seat in the dugout; get a bird's-eye view from the directors' box; and stand in the tunnel with the (recorded) roar of 55,000 fans in your ears. There's also a small museum and the inevitable steer into the kit shop. To reach here catch Metrolink to Etihad Campus.

★Rosylee Tearooms CAFE **$$**
(www.rosylee.com; 11 Stevenson Sq; mains £10-12, 2-/3-course menu £11.95/14.95; ⏲noon-9pm Mon-Thu, 10am-10pm Fri-Sat, 10am-6pm Sun) A touch of Edwardian and Georgian elegance in the heart of the Northern Quarter, this gorgeous tearooms has expanded its menu to offer a range of British classics like beer-battered haddock and chips and steak suet pudding. The afternoon tea (£18.25 or £25.25 if you want a glass of bubbles) is superb.

San Carlo Cicchetti ITALIAN **$$**
(www.sancarlocicchetti.co.uk; King St W, House of Fraser; small plates £6.95-8.95; ⏲8am-11pm Mon-Fri, from 9am Sat, 9am-10pm Sun) Celebrity chef Aldo Zilli has designed the superlative menu at this ornate Italian restaurant on the ground floor of House of Fraser. Instead of big plates of carb overload, though, you get smaller dishes known as *cicchetti*. The truffle and pecorino ravioli are divine. It also serves more standard egg dishes for breakfast.

Tattu CHINESE **$$**
(☎0161-819 2060; www.tattu.co.uk; Gartside St, 3 Hardman Sq, Spinningfields; mains £14-27; ⏲noon-3pm & 5-10.45pm Mon-Thu, noon-10.45pm Fri-Sun) One of the most beautiful restaurants in town is this newish and supremely elegant Chinese spot in Spinningfields. From the nautical-themed downstairs bar (dark-wood booths, hanging anchors) to the upstairs deck, where you can dine beneath a cherry tree, the decor is as stylish as the food is tasty; we loved the saffron miso black cod.

Fumo ITALIAN **$$**
(www.sancarlofumo.co.uk; 1 St Peter's Sq; dishes £4.50-7.95; ⏲noon-11pm Mon-Sat, to 10pm Sun) This glass-fronted restaurant specialises in Venetian-style tapas known as *cicchetti* – you can take your pick from a broad-ranging menu that includes a variety of carpaccios, pasta, meats and even minipizzas. It's part of the same group that run the equally good San Carlo Cicchetti on the ground floor of House of Fraser.

LOCAL KNOWLEDGE

GREATER MANCHESTER POLICE MUSEUM

One of the city's best-kept secrets is the superb **Greater Manchester Police Museum** (www.gmpmuseum.co.uk; 57a Newton St; 10.30am-3.30pm Tue) housed within a former Victorian police station. The original building has been magnificently – if a little creepily – brought back to life, and you can wander in and out of 19th-century cells where prisoners rested their heads on wooden pillows; visit a restored magistrates' court from 1895 and examine the case histories (complete with mugshots and photos of weapons) of some of the more notorious names to have passed through its doors.

★ Manchester House MODERN BRITISH $$$
(www.manchesterhouse.uk.com; Tower 12, 18-22 Bridge St; mains £37, 10-/14-course tasting menu £70/95;) This much-praised restaurant atop a nondescript '60s-era tower serves molecular cuisine, but with a Manchester twist. Chef Aiden Byrne offers a simplified version of Blumenthal and Adriá, but without sacrificing any of the taste: the constantly changing menu (including exclusively veggie) is simply exceptional and this is one of the best places to eat in the northwest. Reservations are essential.

The French MODERN BRITISH $$$
(0161-932 4198; www.the-french.co.uk; Midland Hotel, 16 Peter St; 6-/10-course menu £65/85; noon-1.30pm & 6.30-9.30pm) The revamped restaurant of the Midland Hotel (where Rolls met Royce to make motoring history) is now home to Simon Rogan's exquisite Modern British cuisine, which uses exclusively local produce grown on his farm in Cartmel, Cumbria, home to his Michelin-starred L'Enclume restaurant. The 10-course tasting menu (not available lunchtime Wednesday to Friday) is a feast you won't soon forget.

Drinking & Nightlife

★ Port Street Beer House CRAFT BEER
(39-41 Port St; 4pm-midnight) Fans of real ale love this Northern Quarter boozer with its seven hand pulls, 18 draught lines and more than 100 beers from around the world, including gluten-free ales and some heavy hitters: Brewdog's Tactical Nuclear Penguin is a 32% stout but at £45 a bottle you won't need more than one. It hosts regular tastings and tap takeovers.

★ Sankey's CLUB
(0161-950 4201; www.sankeys.info; Radium St, Ancoats; admission free-£6; 10.30pm-5am Fri & Sat) If you're a fan of techno, electro or any kind of nonmainstream house music, then a pilgrimage to Sankeys – where The Chemical Brothers, Daft Punk and others got their start – should on no account be missed. Its commitment to top-class music is unwavering, with world-renowned DJs mixing it up with residents. One of the best clubs in Britain.

Castle Hotel PUB
(66 Oldham St; noon-1am Sun-Thu, to 2am Fri-Sat) Old-fashioned boozer founded in 1776 with a strong musical heritage: John Peel interviewed Joy Division's Ian Curtis here in 1979 and some of its fine selection of ales – Build a Rocket Boys, Trooper – are named after songs by local band Elbow. There's a small music venue attached that hosts regular gigs.

Brewdog BAR
(35 Peter St; noon-1am Mon-Sat, to midnight Sun) The Manchester branch of this bolshie Scottish brewery ('we brew hardcore beer for punks' is their tagline) has all of the beers that have made it such a huge hit across the country – 5am Red Ale, Brixton Porter and Dead Pony Pale Ale – as well as some stronger IPAs from its Amplified range.

Britons Protection PUB
(0161-236 5895; 50 Great Bridgewater St; noon-midnight Mon-Thu, to 1am Fri & Sat, to 11pm Sun) Whisky – over 300 different kinds of it (the Cu Dhub 'black whisky' is a particular treat with its touch of coffee and honey) – is the beverage of choice at this liver-threatening, proper English pub that also does homestyle meals (gammon, pies etc). An old-fashioned boozer with open fires in the back rooms and a cosy atmosphere…perfect on a cold evening.

Liar's Club BAR
(www.theliarsclub.co.uk; 19a Back Bridge St; 5pm-4am Mon-Sat, to 3am Sun;) A basement bar designed in the style of a speakeasy/tiki lounge, the Liar's Club serves strong cocktails to an assorted clientele of revellers, students and off-duty bar staff. A great atmosphere any night of the week.

Odd BAR

(☎0161-833 0070; www.oddbar.co.uk; 30-32 Thomas St; ⊙11am-midnight Sun-Wed, to 1am Thu, to 2am Fri & Sat) This eclectic little bar – with its oddball furnishings, wacky tunes and anti-establishment crew of customers – is the perfect antidote to the increasingly similar look of so many modern bars. A slice of Mancuniana to be treasured.

Fac251 CLUB

(☎0161 272 7251; www.factorymanchester.com; 112-118 Princess St; admission £1-6; ⊙11pm-4am Mon-Sat) Located in Tony Wilson's former Factory Records HQ, Fac251 is one of the most popular venues in town. There are three rooms, all with a broad musical appeal, from drum and bass to Motown and indie rock. Something for everybody, from Monday's Quids In (for students) to the Big Weekender on Saturday (commercial R & B).

☆ Entertainment

★**HOME** ARTS CENTRE

(☎0161-200 1500; http://homemcr.org; 2 Tony Wilson Pl, First St; tickets £5-20; ⊙box office noon-8pm; bar 10am-11pm Mon-Thu & Sun, to midnight Fri-Sat) One of Britain's best new arts centres, Home has two theatre spaces that host provocative new work in a variety of contexts, from proscenium sets to promenade pieces. The five cinema screens show the latest indie releases as well as classics. There's also a ground-floor bar and a cafe on the first floor.

Cinemas

AMC Cinemas CINEMA

(www.amccinemas.co.uk; The Great Northern, 235 Deansgate; ⊙noon-11pm) A 16-screen multiplex in a retail centre that was formerly a goods warehouse for the Northern Railway Company.

Odeon Cinema CINEMA

(www.odeon.co.uk; The Printworks, Exchange Sq; ⊙noon-11pm) A 20-screen complex in the middle of the Printworks centre.

Classical Music

Bridgewater Hall CONCERT VENUE

(☎0161-907 9000; www.bridgewater-hall.co.uk; Lower Mosley St) The world-renowned Hallé Orchestra has its home at this enormous and impressive concert hall, which hosts up to 250 concerts and events a year. It has a widespread program that includes opera, folk music, children's shows, comedy and contemporary music.

Cricket

Lancashire County Cricket Club CRICKET

(☎0161-282 4000; www.lccc.co.uk; Warwick Rd; tickets £15, test matches £40; 🚊Old Trafford) The genteel game of cricket is a big deal here and the biggest game of Lancashire's season is the Roses match against Yorkshire. They – and their limited overs team, the Lancashire Lightning – play their matches at Old Trafford (same name, different but adjacent ground to the football stadium), where international test matches are also played occasionally.

GAY & LESBIAN MANCHESTER

The city's gay scene is unrivalled outside London and caters to every taste. Its healthy heart beats loudest in the Gay Village, centred on handsome Canal St. Here you'll find bars, clubs, restaurants and – crucially – karaoke joints that cater almost exclusively to the pink pound.

Big Weekend (☎0161-831 7700; www.manchesterpride.com; ⊙Aug) One of the UK's biggest Pride festivals, attracting in excess of 500,000 people over the August Bank Holiday at the end of the month.

Molly House (www.themollyhouse.com; 26 Richmond St; ⊙noon-midnight Mon & Tue, to 1am Wed, Thu & Sun, to 2am Fri & Sat) You won't go far wrong in this bar, which has terrific ales, a fine tapas menu and a door policy that encourages relaxed contemplation over adrenalin-charged debauchery.

Club Alter Ego (105-107 Princess St; ⊙11pm-5am Thu-Sat) Look no further for your clubbing needs.

For more information, check with the **Lesbian & Gay Foundation** (☎0161-235 8035; http://lgbt.foundation; 5 Richmond St; ⊙4-10pm). Up-to-date information is also available at www.visitmanchester.com under LGBT.

Live Music

Soup Kitchen LIVE MUSIC
(http://soup-kitchen.co.uk; 31-33 Spear St; £3-5; ⏲noon-11pm Mon-Wed & Sun, to 1am Thu, to 4am Fri & Sat) By day a typical Northern Quarter canteen-style cafe, but at night this is one of the city's best places to catch live music, with a full schedule of gigs by all kinds of indie acts passing through town. When the bands are done, the excellent DJs kick in and it often goes until 6am.

Deaf Institute LIVE MUSIC
(www.thedeafinstitute.co.uk; 135 Grosvenor St; ⏲10am-midnight) Excellent midsized venue in a former institute for the deaf; also includes a smaller venue in the basement and a cafe on the ground floor. It's where you'll hear alt rock and pop by dozens of local bands we guarantee you've never heard of (as well as some visiting bands you may have).

Ruby Lounge LIVE MUSIC
(☎0161-834 1392; www.therubylounge.com; 28-34 High St; tickets around £8; ⏲noon-midnight, clubs 11pm-3am) Terrific live-music venue in the Northern Quarter that features mostly rock bands. It gets very loud. After the bands there's usually a club night that runs until late.

Band on the Wall LIVE MUSIC
(☎0161-834 1786; www.bandonthewall.org; 25 Swan St; ⏲5-11pm) A top-notch venue that hosts everything from rock to world music, with splashes of jazz, blues and folk thrown in.

Theatre

Royal Exchange THEATRE
(☎0161-833 9833; www.royalexchange.co.uk; St Anne's Sq) Interesting contemporary plays are standard at this magnificent, modern theatre-in-the-round.

Shopping

King St, with its 14 listed buildings, is Manchester's most elegant shopping street, lined with high-end boutiques and independent retailers. The Northern Quarter is all about boho indie styles, while Spinningfields has a handful of swanky shops. Market St and the Arndale Centre are where you'll find the mainstay of the city's high-street shopping.

Manchester Craft & Design Centre ARTS & CRAFTS
(www.craftanddesign.com; 17 Oak St; ⏲10am-5.30pm Mon-Sat, 11am-5pm Sun) This award-winning centre (in a building dating from 1873) stocks jewellery, ceramics, bags and furnishings all handmade by local designers. There's also a cafe on the premises.

Oi Polloi CLOTHING
(www.oipolloi.com; 63 Thomas St; ⏲10am-6pm Mon-Sat) Besides the impressive range of casual footwear, this hip boutique also stocks a range of designers including A Kind of Guise, LA Panoplie, Nudie Jeans Co and Fjällräven.

Oxfam Originals VINTAGE
(Unit 8, Smithfield Bldg, Oldham St; ⏲10am-6pm Mon-Sat, noon-5pm Sun) If you're into retro, this terrific store has high-quality gear from the 1960s and '70s. Shop in the knowledge that it's for a good cause.

Tib Street Market MARKET
(☎0161-234 7357; Tib St; ⏲10am-5pm Sat) Up-and-coming local designers get a chance to display their wares at this weekly market where you can pick up everything from purses to lingerie and hats to jewellery.

Information

Cameolord Chemist (St Peter's Sq; ⏲8am-midnight)

Manchester Royal Infirmary (Oxford Rd; ⏲24hr)

Post Office (Town Hall Annexe, Albert Sq; ⏲9am-6pm Mon-Fri)

Visitor Information Centre (www.visitmanchester.com; 1 Piccadilly Gardens; guided tours daily £8; ⏲10am-5.15pm Mon-Sat, to 4.30pm Sun)

Getting There & Away

AIR

Manchester Airport (☎0161-489 3000; www.manchesterairport.co.uk) The airport is 12 miles south of the city.

Bus (30 minutes, £4.10) Every 20 minutes to Manchester Coach Station (Chorlton St)

Metrolink (40 minutes, £4.20) Every 12 minutes; change at Cornbrook or Firswood for city centre.

Taxi (25 to 40 minutes, £20 to £30)

Train (20 minutes, £5) Every 10 minutes to Piccadilly Station.

BUS

National Express (☎08717 81 81 81; www.nationalexpress.com) serves most major cities from the coach station (Chorlton St):

Leeds (£4, one hour, hourly)

Liverpool (£6.50, 1½ hours, hourly)

London (£20.70, 4¼ hours, hourly)

TRAIN

Manchester Piccadilly (east of Piccadilly Gardens) is the main station for most mainline train services across Britain; Victoria Station (north of the National Football Museum) serves destinations in the northwest including Blackburn, Halifax and Huddersfield but also Leeds and Liverpool. The two stations are linked by Metrolink. Off-peak fares are considerably cheaper. Destinations include the following:

Blackpool (£16.90, 1¼ hours, half-hourly)
Liverpool Lime St (£9.20, 45 minutes, half-hourly)
London Euston (£110, three hours, seven daily)
Newcastle (£64.90, three hours, six daily)

Getting Around

The excellent public transport system can be used with a variety of Day Saver tickets. For enquiries about local transport, including night buses, contact**Travelshop** (0161-228 7811; www.tfgm.com; 1 Piccadilly Gardens; 7am-6pm Mon-Sat, 10am-6pm Sun).

BUS

The Metroshuttle is a free service with three separate routes around the heart of Manchester every 10 minutes. Pick up a map from the tourist office. Most local buses start from **Piccadilly Gardens**.

METROLINK

The Metrolink (www.metrolink.co.uk) light-rail network is the best way to get between Victoria and Piccadilly train stations (and the G-Mex for Castlefield), as well as further afield to Salford Quays, Didsbury and other suburbs. It also serves the airport, but you need to change at either Cornbrook or Firswood. Trams run every few minutes throughout the day from 6am to 11pm. Buy your tickets from the platform machine.

TRAIN

Castlefield is served by Deansgate station with suburban rail links to Piccadilly, Oxford Rd and Salford stations.

CHESTER

POP 79,645

With a red-sandstone, Roman-era wall wrapped around a tidy collection of Tudor- and Victorian-era buildings, Chester is one of English history's greatest gifts to the contemporary visitor. The walls were built when this was Castra Devana, the largest Roman fortress in Britain.

Beyond the cruciform-shaped historic centre, Chester is an ordinary, residential town; it's hard to believe today, but throughout the Middle Ages Chester made its money as the most important port in the northwest. However, the River Dee silted up over time and Chester fell behind Liverpool in importance.

Sights

★City Walls LANDMARK

A good way to get a sense of Chester's unique character is to walk the 2-mile circuit along the walls that surround the historic centre. Originally built by the Romans around AD 70, the walls were altered substantially over the following centuries but have retained their current position since around 1200. The tourist office's *Walk Around Chester Walls* leaflet is an excellent guide and you can also take a 90-minute guided walk.

Of the many features along the walls, the most eye-catching is the prominent **Eastgate**, where you can see the most famous clock in England after London's Big Ben, built for Queen Victoria's Diamond Jubilee in 1897.

At the southeastern corner of the walls are the **wishing steps**, added in 1785. Local legend claims that if you can run up and down these uneven steps while holding your breath your wish will come true.

Just inside Southgate, known here as **Bridgegate** (as it's located at the northern end of the Old Dee Bridge), is the **Bear & Billet** (www.bearandbillet.com; 94 Lower Bridge St; noon-11.30pm) pub, Chester's oldest timber-framed building, built in 1664, and once a toll gate into the city.

★Rows ARCHITECTURE

Besides the City Walls, Chester's other great draw is the Rows, a series of two-level galleried arcades along the four streets that fan out in each direction from the **Central Cross**. The architecture is a handsome mix of Victorian and Tudor (original and mock) buildings that house a fantastic collection of individually owned shops.

Chester Cathedral CATHEDRAL

(01244-324756; www.chestercathedral.com; 12 Abbey Sq; 9am-6pm Mon-Sat, 11am-4pm Sun) FREE Originally a Benedictine abbey built on the remains of an earlier Saxon church dedicated to St Werburgh (the city's patron saint), it was shut down in 1540 as part of Henry VIII's dissolution frenzy, but reconsecrated as a cathedral the following year. Despite a substantial Victorian facelift,

Chester

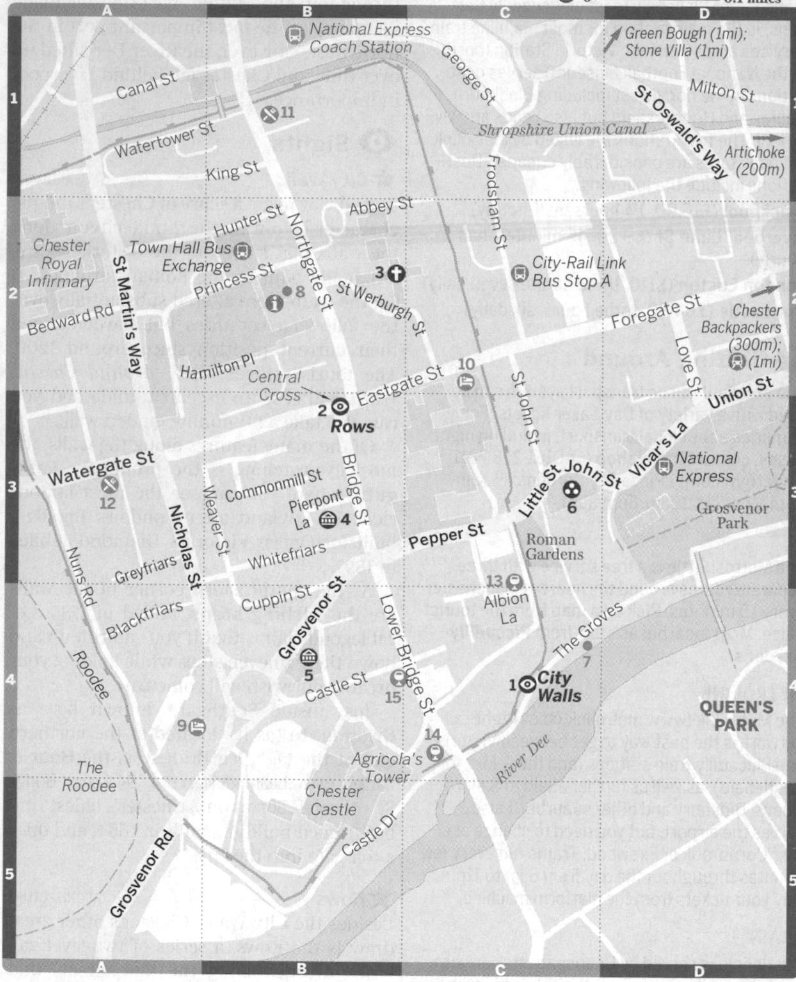

Chester

Top Sights
1 City Walls C4
2 Rows B3

Sights
3 Chester Cathedral B2
4 Dewa Roman Experience B3
5 Grosvenor Museum B4
6 Roman Amphitheatre C3

Activities, Courses & Tours
Cathedral Tours .... (see 3)
7 Chester Boat C4
8 Chester Tour B2

Sleeping
9 ABode Chester A4
10 Chester Grosvenor Hotel & Spa C2

Eating
11 Joseph Benjamin B1
12 Mockingbird Taproom A3
Simon Radley at the Grosvenor .... (see 10)

Drinking & Nightlife
13 Albion C3
14 Bear & Billet C4
15 Brewery Tap B4

the cathedral retains much of its original 12th-century structure. You can amble about freely, but the **tours** (adult/child 1hr tour £8/6, 30min tour £6; ⏲1hr tour 11am & 3pm daily, 30min tour 12.30pm & 1.15pm Mon-Tue, also 2pm & 4pm Wed-Sat) are excellent, as they bring you to to the top of the panoramic bell tower.

Grosvenor Museum MUSEUM
(☎01244-972197; www.grosvenormuseum.co.uk; 27 Grosvenor St; ⏲10.30am-5pm Mon-Sat, 1-4pm Sun) FREE Excellent museum with the country's most comprehensive collection of Roman tombstones. At the back of the museum is a preserved Georgian house, complete with kitchen, drawing room, bedroom and bathroom.

Dewa Roman Experience MUSEUM
(☎01244-343407; www.dewaromanexperience.co.uk; Pierpoint Lane; adult/child £5.50/3.95; ⏲9am-5pm Mon-Sat, 10am-5pm Sun Feb-Nov, 10am-4pm Dec-Jan) What was life like in Roman times? Begin your journey in the hold of a galley ship, where Grapus the Oars Master talks about the dangers of life at the edge of the known world. You then walk down a reconstructed Roman street lined with a granary, barracks, bathhouse and tavern – all built to serve the needs of the 20th Legion.

Roman Amphitheatre ARCHAEOLOGICAL SITE
(Little St John St) FREE Just outside the city walls is what was once an arena that seated 7000 spectators (making it the country's largest); some historians have suggested that it may have also been the site of King Arthur's Camelot and that his knights' 'round table' was really just this circular construction. Excavations continue; during summer months there are occasional shows held here.

Blue Planet Aquarium AQUARIUM
(www.blueplanetaquarium.com; adult/child £17/12.25; ⏲10am-5pm Mon-Fri, to 6pm Sat & Sun) Things aren't done by halves around Chester, where you'll find the country's largest aquarium, Blue Planet. It's home to 10 different kinds of shark, which can be viewed from a 70m-long moving walkway that lets you eye them up close. The aquarium is 9 miles north of Chester at junction 10 of the M53 to Liverpool. Buses 1 and 4 run there every half-hour from Chester Town Hall Bus Exchange.

Tours

Chester Tour WALKING TOUR
(www.chestertours.org.uk; Northgate St, Town Hall Visitor Information Centre; adult/concession £7/6) Ninety-minute guided walking tours covering various aspects of the city's history, including the Chester Tour (10.30am and 2pm daily), and a handful of seasonal walks that run from Easter to the end of October. Recommended are the Walls Walk (11.30am Wednesday and Saturday) and the Rows Revealed (11.00am Monday and Thursday), which includes finding a 16th-century priest hole hidden behind a fireplace. The tours depart from the town hall.

Chester Boat BOAT TOUR
(☎01244-325394; www.chesterboat.co.uk; Boating Station, Souters La, The Groves; tours £6.50-20) Runs 30-minute and two hour-long cruises up and down the Dee, including a foray into the gorgeous Eaton Estate, home of the duke and duchess of Westminster. All departures are from the riverside along the promenade known as the Groves.

Sleeping

Chester Backpackers HOSTEL $
(☎01244-400185; www.chesterbackpackers.co.uk; 67 Boughton; dm/s/d from £16/22/34; 📶) Comfortable dorm rooms with nice pine beds in a typically Tudor white-and-black building. It's just a short walk from the city walls and there's also a pleasant garden.

★**Stone Villa** B&B $$
(☎01244-345014; www.stonevillachester.co.uk; 3 Stone Pl, Hoole Rd; s/d from £60/85; P 📶; 🚌9) This award-winning, beautiful 1850 villa has everything you need for a memorable stay. Elegant bedrooms, a fabulous breakfast and welcoming, friendly owners all add up to one of the best lodgings in town. The property is about a mile from the city centre.

ABode Chester HOTEL $$
(☎01244-347000; www.abodechester.co.uk; Grosvenor Rd; r from £100; P ❄ 📶) Contemporary hotel with 84 rooms all equipped with handcrafted Vispring beds and handsome bathrooms complete with monsoon showers. Good toiletries, flatscreen TVs and cashmere throws on the bed give it a touch of elegance. The 5th-floor restaurant bore TV chef Michael Caines' name until December 2015, but though he's no longer involved it is still an excellent dining choice.

★**Chester Grosvenor Hotel & Spa** HOTEL $$$
(☎01244-324024; www.chestergrosvenor.com; 58 Eastgate St; r from £195; P@) The black-and-white timbered Grosvenor is the city's top hotel by location – right next to the Eastgate Clock – and quality, offering a five-star experience throughout. The lobby's main feature is the chandelier, with 28,000 pieces of crystal; move on from there to the huge rooms with exquisite period furniture. There's also a top spa (open to nonguests) and a Michelin-starred restaurant, Simon Radley at the Grosvenor.

Eating

Mockingbird Taproom CAJUN $$
(www.mockingbirdtaproom.co.uk; 85 Watergate St; mains £10-15; ⏰noon-10pm Mon-Wed, to 1am Thu-Fri, 10am-1am Sat, to 11pm Sun) If you like your food with a kick, then the menu at this Cajun-inspired place is for you. Burgers, crawfish, oysters, ribs and a selection of burritos, nachos and fajitas all come with a choose-your-own level of spiciness, but we went for a mean-lookin' gumbo, Lucifer Licked: chicken, sweet potato and spicy sausage – finished with the Taproom's own 'Howling at the Moon' sauce. Hot.

Artichoke MODERN BRITISH $$
(www.artichokechester.co.uk; The Steam Mill, Steam Mill St; mains £13-17; ⏰10am-3.30pm & 5-10pm Mon-Sat, 10am-8pm Sun) One of a number of warehouse conversions along the Shropshire Union Canal (now known as the Canal Quarter), this cafe-bar serves sandwiches and smaller bites as well as tasty main courses like sea trout in a sweet pea wasabi velvet cream, and confit of duck legs with Jersey potatoes, pancetta and red cabbage. It's a popular drinking spot too.

Joseph Benjamin MODERN BRITISH $$
(☎01244-344295; www.josephbenjamin.co.uk; 140 Northgate St; mains £13-17; ⏰noon-3pm Tue-Sat, also 6-9.30pm Thu-Sat & noon-4pm Sun) A bright star in Chester's culinary firmament is this combo restaurant, bar and deli that delivers carefully prepared local produce to take out or eat in. Excellent sandwiches and gorgeous salads are the mainstay of the takeaway menu, while the more formal dinner menu features fine examples of modern British cuisine.

★**Simon Radley at the Grosvenor** MODERN BRITISH $$$
(☎01244-324024; www.chestergrosvenor.com; 58 Eastgate St, Chester Grosvenor Hotel; tasting menu £99, à la carte menu £75; ⏰6.30-9pm Tue-Sat) Simon Radley's formal restaurant (you're instructed to arrive 30 minutes early for drinks and canapés) has served near-perfect Modern British cuisine since 1990, when it was first awarded the Michelin star that it has kept ever since. The food is divine and the wine list extensive. One of Britain's best, but why no second star? Smart attire, no children under 12.

Drinking & Nightlife

Brewery Tap PUB
(www.the-tap.co.uk; 52-54 Lower Bridge St; ⏰noon-11pm, to 10.30pm Sun) If you're looking for the best pint in the city, the aficionados at the Campaign for Real Ale (CAMRA) reckon you'll get it at this boozer in a Grade II–listed Jacobean banqueting hall; its seven taps offer a rotating range of quality brews from all over England.

Albion PUB
(www.albioninnchester.co.uk; Park St; ⏰noon-11pm) No children, no music and no machines or big screens (but plenty of Union Jacks). This 'family hostile' Edwardian classic pub is a throwback to a time when ale-drinking still had its own rituals. Still, this is one of the finest pubs in northwest England precisely because it doggedly refuses to modernise.

Information

Tourist Office (☎01244-402111; www.visitchester.com; Town Hall, Northgate St; ⏰9am-5.30pm Mon-Sat, 10am-5pm Sun Mar-Oct, 9.30am-4.30pm Mon-Fri, 9am-4pm Sat, 10am-4pm Sun Nov-Feb)

Getting There & Around

BUS

Local buses leave from the **Town Hall Bus Exchange** (Princess St). **National Express** (☎08717 81 81 81; www.nationalexpress.com) coaches stop on Vicar's Lane, just opposite the tourist office by the Roman amphitheatre. Destinations include the following:

Birmingham £13.90, two hours, four daily
Liverpool £8, one hour, four daily
London £27.60, 5½ hours, three daily
Manchester £7.60, 1¼ hours, three daily

TRAIN

The train station is about a mile from the city centre via Foregate St and City Rd, or Brook St. City-Rail Link buses are free for people with rail tickets, and operate between the station and **Bus Stop A** (Frodsham St). Destinations include the following:

Liverpool (£6.90, 45 minutes, hourly)
London Euston £69, 2½ hours, hourly
Manchester £12.60, one hour, hourly

LIVERPOOL

POP 467,500

Few English cities are as shackled by reputation as Liverpool, and none has worked so hard to outgrow the clichés that for so long have been used to define it.

A hardscrabble town with a reputation for wit and an obsessive love of football, Liverpool also has an impressive cultural heritage: it has more listed buildings than any other city outside London, its galleries and museums are among the best in the country, and its ongoing program of urban regeneration is slowly transforming the city centre into one of the most pleasant cities in northern England to have a wander in. And then there are the Beatles: Liverpool cherishes them not because they're wedded to the past but because the Beatles are such a central part of the tourist experience that it would be crazy *not* to do so.

The main attractions are Albert Dock (west of the city centre) and the trendy Ropewalks area (south of Hanover St and west of the two cathedrals). Lime St station, the bus station and the Cavern Quarter – a mecca for Beatles fans – lie just to the north.

History

Liverpool grew wealthy on the back of the triangular trading of slaves, raw materials and finished goods. From 1700 ships carried cotton goods and hardware from Liverpool to West Africa, where they were exchanged for slaves, who in turn were carried to the West Indies and Virginia, where they were exchanged for sugar, rum, tobacco and raw cotton.

As a great port, the city drew thousands of Irish and Scottish immigrants, and its Celtic influences are still apparent. Between 1830 and 1930, however, nine million emigrants – mainly English, Scots and Irish, but also Swedes, Norwegians and Russian Jews – sailed from here to the New World.

The start of WWII led to a resurgence of Liverpool's importance. More than one million American GIs disembarked here before D-Day and the port was, once again, hugely important as the western gateway for transatlantic supplies. The GIs brought with them the latest American records, and Liverpool was thus the first European port of call for the new rhythm and blues that would eventually become rock and roll. Within 20 years, the Mersey Beat was *the* sound of British pop, and four mop-topped Scousers had formed a skiffle band…

Sights

The wonderful Albert Dock is the city's biggest tourist attraction and key to understanding the city's history, but the city

LIVERPOOL IN ONE DAY

Start your day at the **Beatles Story** (p566) on the Albert Dock: it's an excellent intro to the Fab Four but fans should make sure to have booked a **morning tour** (p567) to Mendips and 20 Forthlin Road, the childhood homes of John Lennon and Paul McCartney respectively, which leaves from Albert Dock. If you're not a die-hard Beatles fan, then visit the **Museum of Liverpool** (p567) and, just south, the **International Slavery Museum** (p566). Lunch at **Salt House** or **Etsu** (p570).

If you've still got a cultural hunger, you can head to the city centre to explore the **Walker Art Gallery** (p565) or the wonderful natural science exhibits of the **World Museum** (p565). Football fans should make the trip to **Anfield** (p566) and take the tour of Liverpool Football Club. For dinner you could make a reservation for **London Carriage Works** or **The Art School** (p570).

After dinner, be sure to get a drink at the **Philharmonic** (p570), after which you can take in a gig across the street at the **Philharmonic Hall** (p571). If you're into something a little more adrenalised, the clubs of the Baltic Triangle are worth a punt: our favourite is **Constellations** (p570), which always has something interesting going on.

Liverpool

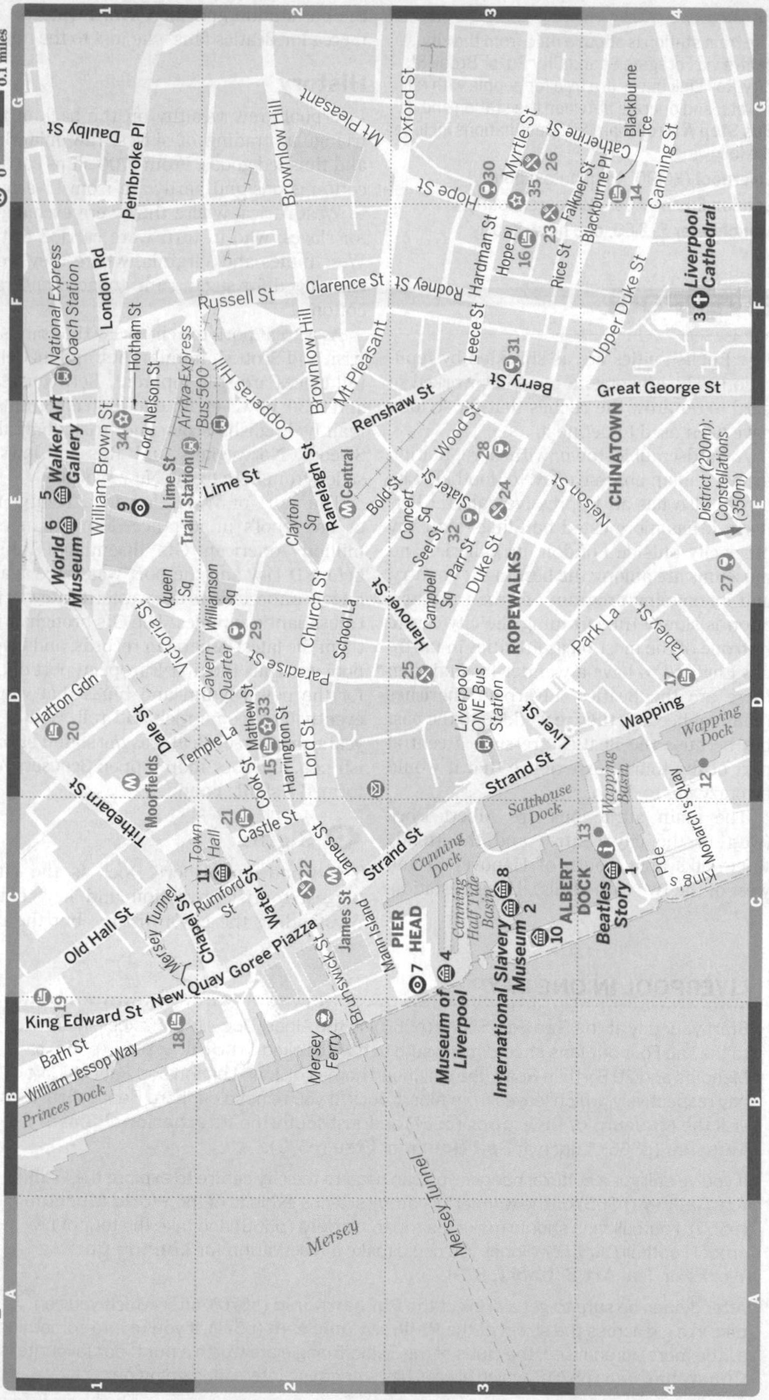

200 m
0.1 miles
Walker Art Gallery
World Museum
National Express Coach Station
Lime St Train Station
Arriva Express Bus 500
Central
Moorfields
Cavern Quarter
Town Hall
Liverpool ONE Bus Station
ROPEWALKS
CHINATOWN
PIER HEAD
Museum of Liverpool
International Slavery Museum
ALBERT DOCK
Beatles Story
Liverpool Cathedral
District (200m); Constellations (350m)
Mersey Ferry
Princes Dock
Canning Dock
Canning Half Tide Basin
Salthouse Dock
Wapping Basin
Wapping Dock
Mersey
Mersey Tunnel
Dauby St
Pembroke Pl
London Rd
Hotham St
Lord Nelson St
William Brown St
Lime St
Russell St
Mt Pleasant
Brownlow Hill
Oxford St
Clarence St
Rodney St
Hope St
Hardman St
Hope Pl
Myrtle St
Catherine St
Blackburne Tce
Blackburne Pl
Falkner St
Rice St
Canning St
Upper Duke St
Leece St
Berry St
Renshaw St
Great George St
Copperas Hill
Ranelagh St
Clayton Sq
Bold St
Wood St
Concert Sq
Slater St
Seel St
Parr St
Duke St
Nelson St
Campbell Sq
Hanover St
Church St
School La
Queen Sq
Williamson Sq
Victoria St
Paradise St
Hatton Gdn
Dale St
Temple La
Mathew St
Harrington St
Lord St
Cook St
Castle St
Tithebarn St
Old Hall St
Chapel St
Rumford St
Water St
James St
Strand St
Liver St
Wapping
Park La
Tabley St
Monarch's Quay
King's Pde
Mann Island
Brunswick St
New Quay
Goree Piazza
King Edward St
Bath St
William Jessop Way

Liverpool

Top Sights
1 Beatles Story C4
2 International Slavery Museum C3
3 Liverpool Cathedral F4
4 Museum of Liverpool C3
5 Walker Art Gallery E1
6 World Museum E1

Sights
7 Beatles Story Pier Head C3
8 Merseyside Maritime Museum C3
9 St George's Hall E1
10 Tate Liverpool C3
11 Western Approaches Museum C2

Activities, Courses & Tours
12 Beatles' Childhood Homes Tour D4
13 Magical Mystery Tour C4

Sleeping
14 2 Blackburne Terrace G4
15 Hard Days Night Hotel D2
16 Hope Street Hotel F3
17 Liverpool YHA D4
18 Malmaison B1
19 Radisson Blu B1
20 Richmond Hotel D1
21 Tune Hotel C2

Eating
22 Etsu C2
23 HOST F3
London Carriage Works .... (see 16)
24 Monro E3
25 Salt House D3
26 The Art School G3

Drinking & Nightlife
27 24 Kitchen Street E4
28 Arts Club E3
29 Everyman Bistro D2
30 Philharmonic G3
31 Red Door F3
32 The Merchant E3

Entertainment
33 Cavern Club D2
34 O2 Academy E1
35 Philharmonic Hall G3

centre is where you'll find most of Liverpool's real day-to-day life.

City Centre

★World Museum MUSEUM

(0151-478 4399; www.liverpoolmuseums.org.uk/wml; William Brown St; 10am-5pm) FREE Natural history, science and technology are the themes of the oldest museum in town, which opened in 1853. Its exhibits range from live bugs to human anthropology. This vastly entertaining and educational museum is spread across five themed floors, from the live fish aquarium on the 1st floor to the planetarium on the 5th, where you'll also find exhibits dedicated to space (moon rocks, telescopes etc) and time (clocks and timepieces from the 1500s to 1960). Highly recommended.

★Liverpool Cathedral CHURCH

(0151-709 6271; www.liverpoolcathedral.org.uk; Upper Duke St; visitor centre & tower admission £5.50; 8am-6pm) Liverpool's Anglican cathedral is a building of superlatives. Not only is it Britain's largest church, it's also the world's largest Anglican cathedral. It is the work of Sir Gilbert Scott, who also gave us the red telephone box and the Southwark Power Station in London, now the Tate Modern. The central bell is the world's third largest (with the world's highest and heaviest peal), while the organ, with its 9765 pipes, is likely the world's largest operational model.

The visitor centre features *Great Space;* this 10-minute, panoramic high-definition movie about the history of the cathedral is followed by your own audiovisual tour, courtesy of a headset. Your ticket also gives you access to the cathedral's 101m tower, from which there are terrific views of the city and beyond – on a clear day you can see Blackpool Tower. The cathedral is also home to a collection of artworks, including a piece over the West Doors called *For You* by Tracey Emin: a pink neon sign that says 'I felt you and I knew you loved me'.

★Walker Art Gallery GALLERY

(0151-478 4199; www.liverpoolmuseums.org.uk/walker; William Brown St; 10am-5pm) FREE The city's foremost art gallery is the national gallery for northern England, housing an outstanding collection of art from the 14th to the 21st centuries. Its strong suits are Pre-Raphaelite art, modern British art and sculpture – not to mention the rotating exhibits of contemporary expression. It's a family-friendly place too: the ground-floor Big Art for Little People gallery is designed for under-eights and features interactive

LIVERPOOL'S FOOTBALL SIDES

Anfield Stadium Tour (www.liverpoolfc.com; stadium tour adult/child £19.50/13.50) Fans of Liverpool FC will relish the Anfield Stadium Tour as it grants them entry to the home dressing room and down the tunnel past the famous 'This is Anfield' sign into the pitchside dugout. The tour is currently an abridged version, however, while the Main Stand is being redeveloped: from January 2017 a bigger and better tour will be launched.

The ground is 2.5 miles northeast of the city centre. Take bus 26 or 27 from Liverpool ONE bus station or bus 17 from Queen St Bus Station.

Goodison Park Tours (☎0151-530 5212; www.evertonfc.com; adult/child £12/6; ⏰11am & 1pm Mon, Wed & Fri, 10am, noon, 2pm & 4pm Sun) Tours (75 minutes) of Everton FC's Goodison Park stadium, including the ubiquitous visit to the dressing room and the pitchside dugout. Compared to other more modern stadiums, Goodison is almost quaintly antiquated. There are no tours on match day or the afternoon before a home match.

exhibits and games that will (hopefully) result in a lifelong love affair with art.

St George's Hall CULTURAL CENTRE
(☎0151-707 2391; http://liverpoolcityhalls.co.uk; William Brown St; ⏰10am-5pm) FREE Liverpool's most impressive building is the Grade I–listed St George's Hall, a magnificent example of neoclassical architecture that is as imposing today as it was when it was completed in 1854. Curiously, it was built as law courts and a concert hall – presumably a judge could pass sentence and then relax to a string quartet.

Inside, you can visit the recently refurbished courtroom and robing room, stop by the cells below, and get a nice vantage point on the Great Hall, home to Britain's third-largest organ (its 7737 pipes were pipped by the organ in London's Albert Hall, and then both were topped by the gargantuan organ built for Liverpool Cathedral). The building also hosts concerts, corporate gigs and a host of other civic get-togethers; it is also the focal point of any citywide celebration.

Western Approaches Museum MUSEUM
(www.liverpoolwarmuseum.co.uk; 1-3 Rumford St; adult/child £6/4; ⏰10.30am-4.30pm Mon-Thu & Sat Mar-Oct, last admission 1hr before closing) The secret command centre for the Battle of the Atlantic, the Western Approaches, was abandoned at the end of the war with virtually everything left intact. You can get a good glimpse of the labyrinthine nerve centre of Allied operations, including the all-important map room, where you can imagine playing a real-life, full-scale version of Risk.

Albert Dock

Liverpool's biggest tourist attraction is Albert Dock, 2.75 hectares of water ringed by enormous cast-iron columns and impressive five-storey warehouses that make up the country's largest collection of protected buildings and are a World Heritage Site. A fabulous development program has really brought the dock to life – here you'll find several outstanding museums and an extension of the Tate Gallery, as well as a couple of top-class restaurants and bars.

★ **Beatles Story** MUSEUM
(☎0151-709 1963; www.beatlesstory.com; adult/child £14.95/9; ⏰9am-7pm, last admission 5pm) Liverpool's most popular museum won't illuminate any dark, juicy corners in the turbulent history of the world's most famous foursome – there's ne'er a mention of internal discord, drugs or Yoko Ono – but there's plenty of genuine memorabilia to keep a Beatles fan happy. Your ticket also gets you entry to the exhibit (p567) at the Beatles Story extension on Pier Head.

Particularly impressive is the full-size replica Cavern Club (which was actually tiny) and the Abbey Rd studio where the lads recorded their first singles, while George Harrison's crappy first guitar (now worth half a million quid) should inspire budding, penniless musicians to keep the faith.

★ **International Slavery Museum** MUSEUM
(☎0151-478 4499; www.liverpoolmuseums.org.uk/ism; ⏰10am-5pm) FREE Museums are, by their very nature, like a still of the past, but the extraordinary International Slavery Museum resonates very much in the present. It reveals slavery's unimaginable horrors – including Liverpool's own role in the triangular slave trade – in a clear and uncompromising manner. It does this through a remarkable series of multimedia and other

displays, and it doesn't baulk at confronting racism, slavery's shadowy ideological justification for this inhumane practice.

The history of slavery is made real through a series of personal experiences, including a carefully kept ship's log and captain's diary. These tell the story of one slaver's experience on a typical trip, departing Liverpool for West Africa. The ship then purchased or captured as many slaves as it could carry before embarking on the gruesome 'middle passage' across the Atlantic to the West Indies. The slaves that survived the torturous journey were sold for sugar, rum, tobacco and raw cotton, which were then brought back to England for profit. Exhibits include original shackles, chains and instruments used to punish rebellious slaves – each piece of metal is more horrendous than the next.

It's heady, disturbing stuff, but as well as providing an insightful history lesson, we are reminded of our own obligations to humanity and justice throughout the museum, not least in the Legacies of Slavery exhibit, which explores the continuing fight for freedom and equality.

Merseyside Maritime Museum MUSEUM

(☎0151-478 4499; www.liverpoolmuseums.org.uk/maritime; ⏰10am-5pm) **FREE** The story of one of the world's great ports is the theme of this excellent museum and, believe us, it's a graphic and compelling page-turner. One of the many great exhibits is Emigration to a New World (in the basement), which tells the story of nine million emigrants and their efforts to get to North America and Australia; the walk-through model of a typical ship shows just how tough conditions on board really were.

Tate Liverpool GALLERY

(☎0151-702 7400; www.tate.org.uk/liverpool; special exhibitions adult/child from £5/4; ⏰10am-5.50pm) **FREE** Touted as the home of modern art in the north, this gallery features a substantial checklist of 20th-century artists across its four floors, as well as touring exhibitions from the mother ship on London's Bankside. But it's all a little sparse, with none of the energy we'd expect from the world-famous Tate. The **Clore Learning Centre** lets kids (and adults) take a break from the serious business of viewing art to make their own.

North of Albert Dock

The area to the north of Albert Dock is known as **Pier Head**, after a stone pier built in the 1760s. This is still the departure point for ferries across the River Mersey, and was for millions of migrants their final contact with European soil.

The Museum of Liverpool is an impressive architectural interloper, but pride of place in this part of the dock still goes to the trio of Edwardian buildings known as the 'Three Graces', dating from the days when Liverpool's star was still ascending: the Port of Liverpool Building, the Cunard Building and the Royal Liver Building, which is topped by Liverpool's symbol, the famous 5.5m copper Liver Bird.

★ **Museum of Liverpool** MUSEUM

(☎0151-478 4545; www.liverpoolmuseums.org.uk/mol; Pier Head; ⏰10am-5pm) **FREE** Liverpool's storied past is explored through an interactive exploration of the city's cultural and historical milestones: the railroad, poverty, wealth, *Brookside* (a popular '80s TV soap opera set in the city), the Beatles and football (the film on the meaning of the game to the city is worth the 15 minutes). The desire to tell all of the city's rich story means there isn't a huge amount of depth, but the kids will love it.

The museum is constantly introducing new elements and temporary exhibitions, with a view towards ensuring that all visits are connected with a contemporary experience of the city. Recent exhibits include Liverpool and War (the collection of photographs taken during the Blitz in WWII is especially poignant) and Pride and Prejudice, an exploration of the city's LGBT identity.

Beatles Story Pier Head EXHIBITION

(☎0151-709 1963; www.beatlesstory.com; Mersey Ferries Terminal, Pier Head; adult/child £14.95/9; ⏰10am-6pm) If you haven't had enough Beatles at the main Beatles Story museum, your ticket also gains you entry to the annexe on Pier Head, with its rotating Fab Four–related photo exhibitions, a 4D cinema and a shop with a huge collection of Beatles merchandise.

☞ Tours

★ **Beatles' Childhood Homes Tour** TOUR

(☎0151-427 7231; www.nationaltrust.org.uk; Jury's Inn, 31 Keel Wharf, Wapping Dock; adult/child £23/7.25; ⏰10am, 11am, 2.15pm & 3.15pm Wed-Sun Mar-Nov) The most intimate portrait of John and Paul comes courtesy of the National Trust–organised tour of their childhood homes. John lived at Mendips with his Aunt Mimi from 1945 to 1963 (which is also the time period covered by Sam Taylor-Wood's superb 2009 biopic of the young Lennon, *Nowhere Boy*), while Paul lived at a plain terraced home at 20 Forthlin Rd. All tours depart from Jury's Inn on Wapping Dock bar the 3.15pm tour, which goes from Speke Hall (www.nationaltrust.org.uk).

A particular highlight of 20 Forthlin Rd is the lounge room where John and Paul wrote early songs like 'Love Me Do' and 'I Saw Her Standing There'.

Magical Mystery Tour TOUR
(☎0151-703 9100; www.cavernclub.org; per person £16.95; ⏲tours hourly 11am-4pm) Two-hour tour that takes in all Beatles-related landmarks – their birthplaces, childhood homes, schools and places such as Penny Lane and Strawberry Field – before finishing up in the Cavern Club (which isn't the original). Departs from opposite the tourist office on Albert Dock.

Beatles Fab Four Taxi Tour DRIVING TOUR
(☎0151-601 2111; www.thebeatlesfabfourtaxitour.co.uk; 2/3hr tour £50/60) Themed tours of the city's mop-top landmarks: there's the three-hour original Lennon tour or the two-hour Epstein express tour. Pick-ups arranged when booking. Up to five people per tour.

Festivals & Events

Gin Festival Liverpool FOOD & DRINK
(www.ginfestival.com; Lutyens Crypt, Metropolitan Cathedral of Christ the King; admission £7.50; ⏲late Jul) One hundred different kinds of gin, including 40 new varieties and bespoke blends, are available for consumption at the UK's largest festival devoted to the drink. The festival takes place in the crypt of the Catholic cathedral – buy your drinks token (£5 per drink) and off you go! Over 18s only.

Liverpool International Music Festival MUSIC
(☎0151-239 9091; www.limfestival.com; ⏲late Jul) A festival showcasing local bands and international acts across five different venues spread throughout the city during the last weekend of July

International Beatleweek MUSIC
(www.cavernclub.org; ⏲late Aug) Tribute bands keep the crowds entertained across a week in late August of Beatles-inspired music and talks organised by the Cavern Club.

Creamfields MUSIC, DANCE
(www.creamfields.com; ⏲Aug Bank Holiday) An alfresco dance-fest that brings together some of the world's best DJs and dance acts during the last weekend in August. It takes place at the Daresbury Estate near Halton, Cheshire.

THE GRAND NATIONAL

The world's most famous steeplechase, and one of England's most cherished events, the **Grand National** (☎0151-522 2929; www.aintree.co.uk; Aintree Racecourse, Ormskirk Rd; 🚌300, 311, 345, 350 & 351 from Liverpool ONE bus station, 🚆Aintree from Liverpool Central) takes place on the first Saturday in April across 4.5 miles and over the most difficult fences in world racing. Its protagonists are 40-odd veteran stalwarts of the jumps, ageing bruisers full of the oh-so-English qualities of grit and derring-do. Book tickets well in advance. Aintree is 6 miles north of the city centre.

Sleeping

Tune Hotel HOTEL $
(☎0151-239 5070; www.tunehotels.com; 3-19 Queen Bldgs, Castle St; r from £40; ❄@📶) A slightly upscale version of a pod hotel, Tune offers a comfortable night's sleep (courtesy of a superb mattress and good-quality linen) in a range of en suite rooms. The cheapest of them have no windows and are quite small, but at this price and in this location, it's an easy sacrifice to make. Bathrooms have power showers.

Liverpool YHA HOSTEL $
(☎0845-371 9527; www.yha.org.uk; 25 Tabley St; dm from £11; P📶) It may have the look of an Eastern European apartment complex, but this award-winning hostel, adorned with plenty of Beatles memorabilia, is one of the most comfortable you'll find anywhere in the country. The dorms with en suite bathrooms even have heated towel rails.

★**Richmond Hotel** HOTEL $$
(www.richmondliverpool.com; 24 Hatton Garden; d from £80, 2-bedroom apt from £199) Centrally located and fully renovated, the Richmond offers a convenient choice of accommodation, from classic doubles and suites to fully equipped, self-catering one-, two- and three-bedroom apartments. All of the rooms have high-spec decor, including 50in flatscreen TVs and fancy toiletries. Guests also have access to the hotel spa.

(NEVER) LET IT BE

They broke up more than 40 years ago and two of their members are dead, but the Beatles are bigger business than ever in Liverpool.

Most of it centres around tiny Mathew St, site of the original Cavern Club, which is now the main thoroughfare of the 'Cavern Quarter'. Here you can shuck oysters in the Rubber Soul Oyster Bar, buy a George pillowcase in the From Me to You shop and put it on the pillows of the Hard Day's Night Hotel. Ringo may have disparaged the city in 2008 by declaring that he missed nothing about it, but the city's tourist authorities continue to exploit Liverpool's ties to the world's most famous group and have done so with enormous success – the original, Beatles-oriented Mathew St Festival was enormously popular, attracting over 350,000 fans; it's now the Liverpool International Music Festival (p568) and explores music beyond the Fab Four.

Wandering around Mathew St is plenty of fun – and the Beatles Shop is best for memorabilia – but if you really want a bit of Beatles lore, you'll have to visit the National Trust–owned **Mendips**, the home where John lived with his aunt from 1945 to 1963, and **20 Forthlin Road**, the plain terraced home where Paul grew up; you can only do so by prebooked Beatle's Childhood Home Tour (p567). The 3.15pm tour leaves from Speke Hall.

If you'd rather do it yourself, the tourist offices stock the *Discover Lennon's Liverpool* guide and map, and Ron Jones' *The Beatles' Liverpool*.

Hope Street Hotel BOUTIQUE HOTEL **$$**
(☎0151-709 3000; www.hopestreethotel.co.uk; 40 Hope St; r/ste from £90/120; @📶) One of the classiest digs in town is this handsome boutique hotel on the city's most elegant street. King-sized beds draped in Egyptian cotton, oak floors with underfloor heating, LCD TVs and sleek modern bathrooms are but the most obvious touches of sophistication at this supremely cool address. Breakfast, taken in the marvellous London Carriage Works, is £16.50.

Radisson Blu HOTEL **$$**
(☎0151-966 1500; www.radissonblu.co.uk; 107 Old Hall St; r from £90; @📶) The rooms at this funky Scandinavian design hotel are divided into 'Ocean', with regal blues and views of the docks and the Mersey, and 'Urban', with luscious reds and purples and city views. Each comes with all the designer gadgetry you'd expect: flatscreen TVs, free high-speed wi-fi and superhip bathrooms. They're not especially huge, but they're very cool, baby.

Malmaison HOTEL **$$**
(☎0151-229 5000; www.malmaison.com; 7 William Jessop Way, Princes Dock; r/ste from £80/125; P@📶) Malmaison's preferred colour scheme of plum and black is everywhere in this purpose-built hotel, which gives it an air of contemporary sophistication. Everything about the Liverpool Mal is plush, from the huge beds and the deep baths to the heavy velvet curtains and the excellent buffet breakfast. After a while, you'll ignore the constantly piped music of the Beatles.

Hard Days Night Hotel HOTEL **$$**
(☎0151-236 1964; www.harddaysnighthotel.com; Central Bldgs, North John St; r £70-115, ste from £500; @📶) You don't have to be a fan to stay here, but it helps: unquestionably luxurious, the 110 ultramodern rooms are decorated with specially commissioned drawings of the Beatles. And if you opt for one of the suites, named after Lennon and McCartney, you'll get a white baby grand in the style of 'Imagine' and a bottle of fancy bubbly.

★ **2 Blackburne Terrace** B&B **$$$**
(www.2blackburneterrace.com; 2 Blackburne Tce; r £160-180; ❄@📶) This exquisite B&B is in a converted Grade II–listed Georgian town house built in 1826. The four rooms are all beautifully appointed with gorgeous period furniture and the attention to detail is superb, from the birdseye maple French secretaire in Room 2 to the freestanding bath in Room 3. All have great views of the cathedral.

Eating

The foodie revolution has completely overhauled the local dining scene, resulting in a host of trendy new spots, the establishment of some exceptional gastropubs and the emergence of a handful of fine-dining restaurants as good as any you'll find anywhere

LOCAL KNOWLEDGE

NIGHTLIFE: THE BALTIC TRIANGLE

Forget Ropewalks – most of Liverpool's best nightlife is in the Baltic Triangle, a once-run-down area of warehouses roughly between the city centre and the docks just north of Toxteth that is now the city's self-styled creative hub. Best spots to check out include **24 Kitchen Street** (www.facebook.com/24kitchenstreet; 24 Kitchen St; tickets £8-12; ⏲9pm-4am Fri & Sat), the-recycling-yard-turned-multipurpose-venue **Constellations** (☎051-345 6302; www.constellations-liv.com; 37-39 Greenland St; ⏲9am-midnight Mon-Thu, to 2am Fri & Sat, 10am-midnight Sun) and **District** (☎07812-141 936; www.facebook.com/District-473098799400626; 61 Jordan St; ⏲7pm-4am Fri-Sat), the first venue to open in the area.

in Britain. You'll find the widest choice in Ropewalks, along Hardman and Hope Sts, and in the streets around Dale St.

★Salt House SPANISH $$
(www.salthousetapas.co.uk; Hanover Sq; tapas £5-8; ⏲noon-10.30pm) Liverpool has grown fond of its Spanish tapas bars, and this gorgeous spot – half deli, half restaurant – is the best of them. The cooking is authentic, varied and delicious, from the choice of charcuterie to the wonderful fish dishes. The takeaway counter at the deli does fab sandwiches too.

The Art School MODERN BRITISH $$
(☎0151-230 8600; www.theartschoolrestaurant.co.uk; 1 Sugnall St; 2-/3-course prix fixe £23.50/29, tasting menu £89;) The old lantern room of a Victorian 'home for destitute children' is now one of the top spots in town for contemporary British cuisine, courtesy of chef Paul Askew (ex–London Carriage Works). Choose from expertly presented British classics from a series of menus, including two vegetarian and one vegan. The wine list is superb.

Etsu JAPANESE $$
(☎0151-236 7530; www.etsu-restaurant.co.uk; 25 The Strand, off Brunswick St; mains £12.95-16.95, 15-piece sashimi £14; ⏲noon-2.30pm & 5-9pm Tue, Thu & Fri, 5-9pm Wed & Sat, 4-9pm Sun) The best Japanese food in town is to be had in this contemporary spot on the ground floor of an office building. The speciality of the house is its fresh sushi and sashimi, but you'll find the usual selection of Japanese classics, from chicken *kara-age* (crispy fried chicken pieces marinated in soy, ginger and garlic) to *unagi don* (grilled eel over rice).

HOST ASIAN, FUSION $$
(www.ho-st.co.uk; 31 Hope St; mains £10-14; ⏲11am-11pm Mon-Sat, noon-10pm Sun;) A bright, airy room with the look of a chic, contemporary New York brasserie serves up excellent pan-Asian dishes like Indonesian braised lamb with fried rice, and red duck coconut curry with lychees. The starter nibbles are pretty delicious too.

Monro GASTROPUB $$
(☎0151-707 9933; www.themonro.com; 92 Duke St; 2-course lunch £12.50, dinner mains £11.50-18; ⏲11am-11pm) The Monro has become one of the city's favourite spots for lunch, dinner and, especially, weekend brunch. The changing menu of classic British dishes made with ingredients sourced as locally as possible has transformed this handsome old pub into a superb dining experience. It's tough to find pub grub this good elsewhere.

London Carriage Works MODERN BRITISH $$$
(☎0151-705 2222; www.thelondoncarriageworks.co.uk; 40 Hope St; 2-/3-course meal £19.50/25.50, mains £15-30; ⏲7-10am, noon-3pm & 5-10pm Mon-Fri, 8-11am & noon-10pm Sat, to 9pm Sun) Head chef Dave Critchley has picked up where Paul Askew left off and continues to set the culinary tone for the city. This award-winning restaurant successfully blends ethnic influences from around the globe with staunch British favourites and serves up the result in a beautiful dining room – actually more of a bright glass box divided only by a series of sculpted glass shards. Reservations are recommended.

Drinking & Nightlife

★Philharmonic PUB
(36 Hope St; ⏲10am-midnight) This extraordinary bar, designed by the shipwrights who built the *Lusitania,* is one of the most beautiful bars in all of England. The interior is resplendent with etched and stained glass, wrought iron, mosaics and ceramic tiling – and if you think that's good, just wait until you see inside the marble men's toilets, the only heritage-listed lav in the country.

Red Door COCKTAIL BAR
(21-23 Berry St; ⏲7pm-2am Mon-Wed, 6pm-4am Thu, 5pm-4am Fri & Sat, 5pm-1am Sun) The cock-

tail fad is given full expression at this lovely bar, where the bartenders take an almost annoying pride in the theatrical quality of their creations – the 'Rise and Shine' (Southern Comfort, orange juice, grenadine and banana liqueur) comes topped with smoking dry ice for effect. It also has a big selection of gins.

The Merchant BAR
(40 Slater St; noon-midnight Mon-Thu & Sun, to 2am Fri, to 3am Sat) This new bar is in a converted merchant's house and has something of a Scandi feel to it – stripped-back walls, wooden bar tables – which made it the 'in' spot at the time of writing. The bar serves 50 different craft beers, gin by the goblet and – wait for it – Prosecco on tap. Good DJs provide the soundtrack.

Everyman Bistro BAR
(www.everymanplayhouse.com; Williamson Sq; 8.30am-11pm Mon-Thu, to midnight Fri & Sat;) This Liverpool institution reopened in 2014 in a new location and is better than ever. The downstairs bar and bistro are packed most evenings, making this one of the best places in town for a drink and a bite. The wifi is stronger than in most other bars.

Arts Club CLUB
(0151-707 6171; www.academymusicgroup.com/artsclubliverpool; 90 Seel St; £4-11; Mon-Sat) This converted theatre is home to one of Liverpool's most beloved clubs, despite going through several name and management changes. It still hosts some fabulous nights, with a mix of live music and DJs keeping everyone entertained with some of the best music in town.

Entertainment

Philharmonic Hall CLASSICAL MUSIC
(0151-709 3789; www.liverpoolphil.com; Hope St) One of Liverpool's most beautiful buildings, the art deco Phil is home to the city's main classical orchestra, but it also stages the work of avant-garde musicians such as John Cage and Nick Cave.

Cavern Club LIVE MUSIC
(0151-236 1965; www.cavernclub.org; 8-10 Mathew St; admission before/after 2pm free/£4; 10am-midnight Mon-Wed & Sun, to 1.30am Thu, to 2am Fri & Sat) It's a faithful reconstruction of the club where the Beatles played their early gigs, and not even on the same spot (the original club was a few doors away), but the 'world's most famous club' is still a great spot to see local bands, including (invariably) Beatles cover bands.

O2 Academy LIVE MUSIC
(0151-794 6868; www.academymusicgroup.com/o2academyliverpool; Liverpool University, 11-13 Hotham St; 7-11pm) This midsize venue fits about 1200 people and is the place to see those bands that are on the rise (or on the fall).

Information

Merseyside Police Headquarters (0151 709 6010; Canning Pl)
Royal Liverpool University Hospital (0151-706 2000; Prescot St)
Post Office (Liverpool ONE; 9am-5.30pm Mon-Sat)
Tourist Office (0151-707 0729; www.visitliverpool.com; Anchor Courtyard; 10am-6pm) Small office in Albert Dock.

Getting There & Away

AIR

Liverpool John Lennon Airport (0870-750 8484; www.liverpoolairport.com; Speke Hall Ave) serves a variety of international destinations as well as destinations in the UK (Belfast, London and the Isle of Man). The airport is 8 miles south of the centre.
Arriva Express (www.arriva.co.uk; £4.30; 4.45-12.15am) bus 500 runs every 30 minutes to Liverpool ONE bus station. The journey is about 30 minutes. A taxi to the city centre should cost no more than £20.

BUS

The **National Express Coach Station** (www.nationalexpress.com; Norton St) is 300m north of Lime St train station. There are services to/from most major towns including the following:
Birmingham £13.20, 2½ hours, five daily
London £25.80, five to six hours, six daily
Manchester £2, one hour, hourly
Newcastle £12, 5½ hours, three daily

DON'T MISS

BEST PUBS FOR A PINT IN THE NORTHWEST

Philharmonic (p570), Liverpool

Port Street Beer House (p556), Manchester

Albion (p562), Chester

Peveril of the Peak (0161-236 6364; 127 Great Bridgewater St; 11am-11pm), Manchester

TRAIN

Liverpool's main station is Lime St. It has hourly services to almost everywhere, including the following:

Chester £6.90, 45 minutes

London Euston £31, 3¼ hours

Manchester £8.20, 45 minutes

Getting Around

BOAT

The famous **Mersey ferry** (www.merseyferries.co.uk; 1 way/return £2.60/3.20) crossing for Woodside and Seacombe departs from Pier Head Ferry Terminal, next to the Royal Liver Building (to the north of Albert Dock).

CAR & MOTORCYCLE

You won't really have much use for a car in Liverpool, but if you have a car the good news is that parking in most sheltered and open car parks is relatively cheap – usually between £2.50 and £3.50 *per day*. The only exception is the huge car park at Liverpool ONE, which costs £2.50 an hour and £16 for a day. Car break-ins are a significant problem, so leave absolutely nothing of value in the car.

PUBLIC TRANSPORT

Liverpool ONE Bus Station (www.merseytravel.gov.uk; Canning Pl) is in the city centre. Local public transport is coordinated by Merseytravel (www.merseytravel.gov.uk). The Saveaway ticket (adult/child £5.20/2.70) allows for one day's off-peak (after 9.30am) travel on all bus, train and ferry services throughout Liverpool and the Wirral (on the far side of the Mersey). Tickets are available at shops throughout the city.

Merseyrail (www.merseyrail.org) is an extensive suburban rail service linking Liverpool with the Greater Merseyside area. There are four stops in the city centre: Lime St, Central (handy for Ropewalks), James St (close to Albert Dock) and Moorfields (for the Liverpool War Museum).

TAXI

ComCab (☎0151-298 2222)

LANCASHIRE

As you travel north, past the concrete blanket that covers much of the southern half of the county, Lancashire's undulating landscape begins to reveal itself in all its bucolic glory. East of Blackpool – the faded queen of beachside holidays – the Ribble Valley is a gentle and beautiful appetiser for the Lake District that lies beyond the county's northern border. Lancaster is the county's handsome, Georgian capital.

Blackpool

POP 142,065

Blackpool's enduring appeal – in the face of low-cost airlines transporting its natural constituents to sunnier coasts – is down to its defiant embrace of a more traditional kind of holiday, coupled with the high-tech adrenalin hit of its famed Pleasure Beach amusement park.

The town is also famous for its tower and its three piers. A successful ploy to extend the brief summer holiday season is the Illuminations, when, from early September to early November, 5 miles of the Promenade are illuminated with thousands of electric and neon lights.

Sights

Blackpool Pleasure Beach AMUSEMENT PARK

(☎box office 0871-222 9090, enquiries 0871-222 1234; www.blackpoolpleasurebeach.com; Ocean Beach; Pleasure Beach Pass £6, 1-day Unlimited Ride wristband adult/child £30/27; ⏲hours vary, usually 10am-8pm in summer) The main reason for Blackpool's immense popularity is the Blackpool Pleasure Beach, a 16-hectare collection of more than 145 rides that attracts some seven million visitors annually. As amusement parks go, it's easily the best in Britain.

Rides are divided into categories, and once you've gained entry to the park with your Pleasure Beach Pass you can buy tickets for individual categories or for a mixture of them all. Alternatively, an Unlimited Ride wristband includes the £6 entrance fee; there are great discounts if you book your tickets online in advance. There's also the option of a Speedy Pass (£15), which saves you the hassle of queuing for rides by allocating you a specific ride time – rent it and add as many people to it as you want. You can go one better with the VIP Speedy Pass (£25), which cuts queuing time by 50%; or with the VIP Plus Speedy Pass (£45), which reduces wait time to almost nothing. There are no set times for closing; it depends how busy it is.

Blackpool Tower ENTERTAINMENT COMPLEX

(☎0844-856 1000; www.theblackpooltower.com; Tower Pass door price adult/child £53.45/41;

(⌚ from 10am, closing hours vary) Built in 1894, this 154m-high tower is Blackpool's most recognisable landmark. Watch a 4D film on the town's history in the **Blackpool Tower Eye** (a 2011 addition), before taking the elevator up to the observation deck, which has splendid views and only a (thick) glass floor between you and the ant-sized people below. Visitors are strongly urged to buy their tickets online as buying them at the door can be up to 50% more expensive.

Down at ground level, the **dungeon** exhibit sits alongside the old Moorish circus and the magnificent rococo ballroom, with its extraordinary sculptured and gilded plasterwork, murals, chandeliers and couples gliding across the beautifully polished wooden floor to the melodramatic tones of a huge Wurlitzer organ. There's also **Jungle Jim's** adventure playground for kids.

Sleeping

Number One BOUTIQUE HOTEL **$$**
(☎ 01253-343901; www.numberoneblackpool.com; 1 St Lukes Rd; s/d from £85/125; P 📶) Far fancier than anything else around, this stunning boutique guesthouse is all luxury and contemporary style. Everything exudes a discreet elegance, from the dark-wood furniture and high-end mod cons to the top-notch breakfast. It's on a quiet road just set back from the South Promenade near the Pleasure Beach amusement park.

Big Blue Hotel HOTEL **$$**
(☎ 01253-400045; www.bigbluehotel.com; Blackpool Pleasure Beach; r from £90; P @ 📶 👪) A handsome family hotel with smartly kitted-out rooms. Kids are looked after with DVD players and computer games, while its location at the southern entrance to Blackpool Pleasure Beach should ensure that everyone has something to do.

Information

Tourist office (☎ 01253-478222; www.visitblackpool.com; Festival House, Promenade; ⌚ 9am-6pm Mon-Tue, to 5pm Wed-Sat, 10am-4pm Sun)

Getting There & Away

BUS

The central coach station is on Talbot Rd, near the town centre. Services include the following:

London £38.10, seven hours, four daily

Manchester £8.60, 1¾ hours, four daily

TRAIN

The main train station is Blackpool North, about five blocks east of the North Pier on Talbot Rd. Most arrivals change in Preston, but there's a direct service from the following:

Manchester £16.90, 1¼ hours, half-hourly

Liverpool £18.10, 1½ hours, seven daily

Preston £7.80, 30 minutes, half-hourly

Getting Around

With more than 14,000 car-parking spaces in Blackpool, you'll have no problem parking. A host of travel-card options for trams and buses ranging from one day to a week are available at the tourist office and most newsagents. The tramway (one stop £1.60, up to 16 stops £2.60; ⌚ from 10.30am Apr-Oct) shuttles funsters for 11 miles, including along the pier as far as the Fylde Coast (also serving the central-corridor carparks), every eight minutes or so throughout the day.

Lancaster

POP 140,000

Lancashire's handsome Georgian county town is a quiet enough burg these days, but all around is evidence of the wealth it accrued in its 18th-century heyday, when it was an important trading port and a key player in the slave trade.

Sights

Lancaster Castle CASTLE
(☎ 01524-64998; www.lancastercastle.com; Castle Park; adult/child £8/6.50; ⌚ 10am-5pm, guided tours hourly 10am-3pm Mon-Fri, every 30min Sat & Sun) Lancaster's most imposing building is the castle, built in 1150 but added to over the centuries: the **Well Tower** dates from 1325 and is also known as the Witches' Tower because its basement dungeon was used to imprison the accused in the infamous Pendle Witches Trial of 1612. Also dating from the early 14th century is the impressive twin-towered **gatehouse**. Visits are by guided tour only as the castle is used as a Crown Court.

Also imprisoned here was George Fox (1624–91), founder of the Quaker movement. The castle was heavily restored in the 18th and 19th centuries to suit a new function as a prison, and it continued to house Category C prisoners until 2011 – the A wing of the prison is now part of the guided tour.

Priory Church CHURCH

(Priory Cl; ⏲9.30am-5pm) Immediately next to Lancaster Castle is the equally fine priory church, founded in 1094 but extensively remodelled in the Middle Ages.

Judges' Lodgings MUSEUM

(Church St; adult/child £3/2; ⏲11am-4pm Mon-Fri, from noon Sat & Sun Jun & Jul, 1-4pm Mon-Sat Easter-May & Aug-Oct) The former home of witch-hunter Thomas Covell (who 'caught' the poor Pendle women), Lancaster's oldest town house, a Grade I–listed Georgian building, is now home to a **Museum of Furnishings** by master builders Gillows of Lancaster, whose work graces the Houses of Parliament. It also houses a **Museum of Childhood**, which has memorabilia from the turn of the 20th century.

Williamson Park & Tropical Butterfly House GARDENS

(Tropical Butterfly House adult/child £3.20/2.60; ⏲10am-5pm Apr-Sep, to 4pm Oct-Mar; 🚌25 or 25A from train station) Lancaster's highest point is the 22-hectare spread of this elegant park, the highlights of which are (besides the views) the **Tropical Butterfly House**, full of exotic and stunning species, and the **Ashton Memorial**, a 67m-high baroque folly built by Lord Ashton (the son of the park's founder, James Williamson) for his wife. The memorial stands on what was once Lancaster Moor, the spot where until 1800 those sentenced to death at the castle were brought to meet the hangman.

Sleeping & Eating

Borough BOUTIQUE HOTEL $$

(☎01524-64170; www.theboroughlancaster.co.uk; 3 Dalton Sq; r £100; P@📶) The Borough has nine beautifully appointed rooms – each with an Italian marble wet-room bathroom for added luxury – spread over two floors of this elegant Georgian building. The downstairs bar has a microbrewery attached, so you don't have to go far to get your fill of locally made cask ales.

Sun Hotel & Bar HOTEL $$

(☎01524-66006; www.thesunhotelandbar.co.uk; 63-65 Church St; r from £90; P📶) A fine hotel in a 300-year-old building with a rustic, old-world look that stops at the bedroom doors – beyond them are 16 stylish and contemporary rooms. The pub downstairs is one of the best in town and a top spot for a bit of grub; mains cost between £10 and £12.

Whale Tail Cafe VEGETARIAN $

(www.whaletailcafe.co.uk; 78a Penny St; mains £6-8; ⏲9am-4.30pm Mon-Sat, 10am-3pm Sun; 🖉) 🍃 This gorgeous 1st-floor veggie restaurant has an elegant dining room and a more informal plant-filled courtyard for lunch on a sunny day. The spicy bean burger is particularly good. Food here is locally produced and, where possible, organic.

RIBBLE VALLEY

Known locally as 'Little Switzerland', Lancashire's most attractive landscapes lie east of the brash tackiness of Blackpool and north of the sprawling urban areas of Preston and Blackburn.

The northern half of the valley is dominated by the sparsely populated moorland of the Forest of Bowland, which is a fantastic place for walks, while the southern half features rolling hills, attractive market towns and ruins, with the River Ribble flowing between them.

Ribble Valley Food Trail (www.ribblevalleyfoodtrail.com) An award-winning food trail highlighting the produce of more than 30 local growers, chefs and restaurateurs, showcasing the rich gourmet bounty available in the region. Download the brochure from the website.

Ribble Way One of the most popular long-distance paths in northern England is the Ribble Way, a 70-mile footpath that follows the River Ribble from its source at Ribblehead (in the Yorkshire Dales), passing through Clitheroe to the estuary at Preston.

Lancashire Cycle Way (www.visitlancashire.com) The Ribble Valley is well covered by the northern loop of the Lancashire Cycle Way; for more information about routes, safety and so on, contact **Blazing Saddles** (☎01442-844435; www.blazingsaddles.co.uk; 35 West End, Hebden Bridge, West Yorkshire), a Yorkshire-based bike shop.

Information

Tourist Office (☎01524-582394; www.visitlancashire.com; The Storey, Meeting House Lane; ⏲9am-5pm Mon-Sat)

Getting There & Away

Lancaster Bus Station is the main hub for transport throughout Lancashire, with regular buses to all the main towns and villages.

Lancaster is on the main west-coast railway line and on the Cumbrian coast line. Destinations include the following:

Carlisle £21.80, one hour, hourly
Manchester £17.40, one hour, hourly
Morecambe £3.20, 15 minutes, half-hourly

Clitheroe

POP 14,765

The Ribble Valley's largest market town is best known for its impressive Norman keep, built in the 12th century and now, sadly, standing empty; from it there are great views of the river valley below.

Sights

Norman Keep & Castle Museum HISTORIC BUILDING
(Castle Hill; museum adult/child £4.20/3.10; ⏲keep dawn-dusk, museum 11am-4pm Mar-Oct, noon-4pm Mon, Tue & Fri-Sun Nov-Feb) Dominating the skyline for the last 800 years is this Norman keep, England's smallest and the only remaining castle in the country to have kept a royal garrison during the Civil War. It was built in 1186 and captured by royalist troops in 1644, but managed to avoid destruction afterwards. The extensive grounds are home to a museum that explores 350 million years of local history.

Festivals & Events

Clitheroe Food Festival FOOD & DRINK
(http://clitheroefoodfestival.com; ⏲mid-Aug) A food festival showcasing local producers that attracts in excess of 20,000 people during the second Saturday of August. One of the highlights is the Pudding Feast, where locals compete for the best homemade dessert.

Sleeping & Eating

Old Post House Hotel HOTEL $$
(☎01200-422025; www.posthousehotel.co.uk; 44-48 King St; s/d from £65/95; P Wi-Fi) A former post office is now Clitheroe's most handsome hotel, with 11 superbly decorated rooms.

Emporium BRITISH
(Moor La; mains £14-19; ⏲noon-2.30pm & 6.30-9.30pm Mon-Sat, noon-4.30pm Sun) This combination craft shop, bar, cafe and restaurant is one of the most popular spots in town. The excellent menu in the brasserie keeps the focus firmly on local dishes, with a particular emphasis on meat dishes (Goosnargh chicken and duck, locally sourced lamb and beef). On Sundays there's live jazz.

Information

Tourist Office (☎01200-425566; www.visitribblevalley.co.uk; Church Walk; ⏲9am-5pm Mon-Sat)

Getting There & Away

Clitheroe has direct bus services to all the small towns and villages in northern Lancashire as well as bigger towns like Blackburn (bus 22, 40 minutes, every half-hour).

There are direct trains to Manchester from Clitheroe (£10.80, 1½ hours, 10 daily).

Forest of Bowland

This vast grouse-ridden moorland is somewhat of a misnomer. The use of 'forest' is a throwback to an earlier definition, when it served as a royal hunting ground. Today it is an Area of Outstanding Natural Beauty (AONB), which makes for good walking and cycling. The **Pendle Witch Way**, a 45-mile walk from Pendle Hill to northeast of Lancaster, cuts right through the area, and the Lancashire Cycle Way runs along the eastern border. The forest's main town is **Slaidburn**, about 9 miles north of Clitheroe on the B6478.

Other villages worth exploring are **Newton**, **Whitewell** and **Dunsop Bridge**.

Sleeping & Eating

Slaidburn YHA HOSTEL $
(☎0845-371 9343; www.yha.org.uk; King's House; dm £13; ⏲Apr-Oct) A converted 17th-century village inn that is especially popular with walkers and cyclists.

Hark to Bounty Inn INN $$
(☎01200-446246; www.harktobounty.co.uk; Slaidburn; s/d from £45/90) This marvellous 13th-century inn has atmospheric rooms with exposed oak beams. An excellent restaurant downstairs specialises in homemade herb breads (mains £10 to £17).

★Inn at Whitewell INN $$$
(☎01200-448222; www.innatwhitewell.com; s/d from £95/132) Once the home of Bowland's forest keeper, this superb guesthouse with antique furniture, peat fires and Victorian claw-foot baths is one of the finest accommodations in northern England. Everything is top-notch, including the views: it's like being in the French countryside. Its restaurant (mains £19-26) is top-notch too.

★Northcote Hotel MODERN BRITISH $$$
(☎01254-240555; www.northcote.com; Northcote Rd, Langho; mains £45-55; ⏲noon-2pm & 7-9.30pm) One of the finest restaurants in northern England, Northcote's Michelin-starred menu is the unpretentious, delicious creation of chef Nigel Haworth and sommelier Craig Bancroft. Duck, lamb, beef and chicken are given the Modern British treatment and the result is fantastic. Upstairs are 26 beautifully styled bedrooms (from £265), making this one of the northwest's top gourmet getaways. Bookings recommended.

ISLE OF MAN

Forget what you may have heard on the mainland: there's nothing odd about the Isle of Man (Ellan Vannin in Manx, the local lingo) and even its famous tail-less cat isn't that strange. No, the island's reputation for oddity is entirely down to its persistent insistence that it do its own thing, rejecting England's warm embrace in favour of a semiautonomous status (it is home to the world's oldest continuous parliament, the Tynwald), which really just lets it continue operating as a popular tax haven.

What you'll find here is beautiful scenery in the lush valleys, barren hills and rugged coastlines. In 2016 Unesco designated the Isle of Man a Biosphere Reserve (one of five in the UK) marking it out as one of the most beautiful spots in Britain to enjoy nature. That bucolic charm is shattered during the world-famous summer season of Tourist Trophy (TT) motorbike racing, which attracts around 50,000 punters and bike freaks every May and June. Needless to say, if you want a slice of silence, be sure to avoid the high-rev bike fest.

Activities

With plenty of great marked trails, the Isle of Man is a firm favourite with walkers and is regularly voted one of the best walking destinations in Britain. Ordnance Survey (OS) Landranger Map 95 (£8.99) covers the whole island, while the free *Walks on the Isle of Man* is available from the tourist office in Douglas. There are four waymarked long-distance paths on the island:

Bayr Ny Skeddan (14 miles) The 'Herring Road' is a coastal path between Castletown and Peel; the route was the traditional path taken by Manx fishermen.

Heritage Trail (26 miles) A coastal footpath along the old Douglas-to-Peel railway line, waymarked with a blue sign showing a gull in flight.

Millennium Way (26 miles) Runs the length of the island between Sky Hill and Castle Rushen amid spectacular scenery.

Raad ny Foillan (95 miles) The most demanding of all the island's walks is the 'Road of the Gull,' a well-marked path that makes a complete circuit of the island and normally takes about five days to complete.

The island has six designated off-road mountain-biking trails, each with varying ranges of difficulty. See www.visitisleofman.com for details.

Festivals & Events

Isle of Man Food & Drink Festival FOOD & DRINK
(www.gov.im; Villa Marina Gardens, Douglas; £3; ⏲mid-Sep) Over two days in mid-September more than 50 of the island's producers gather to showcase their wares. There's plenty of street food, baked goods, beer and cider, as well as music.

Isle of Man Walking Festival WALKING
(www.iomevents.com; ⏲mid-May) Takes place over five days in May.

Information

Most of the island's historic sites are operated by Manx Heritage (www.manxnationalheritage.im). You can also check out www.iomevents.com for listings of what's on in the Isle of Man, along with accommodation and other tourist information.

Tourist Office (☎01624-686766; www.visitisleofman.com; Sea Terminal Bldg, Douglas; ⏲9.15am-7pm May-Sep, closed Sun Oct-Apr)

Getting There & Away

AIR

Ronaldsway Airport (www.iom-airport.com) is 10 miles south of Douglas near Castletown. The following airlines have services to the island:

Aer Lingus Regional (www.aerlingus.com; from £30)
Citywing (www.citywing.com; from £40)
Easyjet (www.easyjet.com; from £20)
Flybe (www.flybe.com; from £21)

BOAT

Isle of Man Steam Packet (www.steam-packet.com; foot passenger single/return from £18/33, car & 2 passengers return from £150) offers a car ferry and high-speed catamaran service from Liverpool and Heysham to Douglas. From mid-April to mid-September there's also a service to Dublin and Belfast.

Getting Around

Buses link the airport with Douglas every 30 minutes between 7am and 11pm. Taxis have fixed fares to destinations throughout the island; a cab to Douglas costs £20, to Peel £25.

The island has a comprehensive bus service (www.gov.im); the tourist office in Douglas has timetables and sells tickets. It also sells the Go Explore ticket (one day adult/child £16/8, 3 day £32/16), which gives you unlimited public-transport use, including the tram to Snaefell and Douglas' horse-trams.

Bikes can be hired from **Simpsons Ltd** (01624-842472; www.cyclehire.im; 15-17 Michael St, Peel; per day/week £15/90; 9am-5pm Mon-Sat) in Peel.

Petrolheads will love the scenic, sweeping bends that make for some exciting driving – and the fact that outside of Douglas town there's no speed limit. Naturally, the most popular drive is along the Tourist Trophy (TT) route. Car-hire operators have desks at the airport, and charge from around £38 per day.

The 19th-century electric and steam **rail services** (01624-663366; www.iombusandrail.info; Mar-Oct) are a thoroughly satisfying way of getting from A to B:

Douglas–Castletown–Port Erin Steam Train Return £12.40
Douglas–Laxey–Ramsey Electric Tramway Return £12.40
Laxey–Summit Snaefell Mountain Railway Return £12

Douglas

POP 27,000

The island's largest town and most important commercial centre is a little faded around the edges and a far cry from its Victorian heyday when it was, like Blackpool across the water, a favourite with British holidaymakers. The bulk of the island's hotels and restaurants are still here – as well as most of the finance houses that are frequented so regularly by tax-allergic Brits.

Sights

Manx Museum & National Art Gallery MUSEUM
(MH; www.manxnationalheritage.im; Kingswood Grove; 10am-5pm Mon-Sat) FREE This modern museum begins with an introductory film to the island's 10,000-year history and then races through it, making various stops including Viking gold and silver, the history of the Tynwald, the island's internment camps during WWII and famous TT races. Also part of the museum is the National Art Gallery, which has works by the island's best-known artists including Archibald Knox and John Miller Nicholson.

Sleeping

Saba's Glen Yurt YURT $$
(www.sabasglenyurt.com; Close Ny Howin, Main Rd, Union Mills; 2-person yurt £110) In the conservation area of Union Mills you can bed down in a solar-powered eco-yurt that comes equipped with a king-sized bed and a wood burner. Outside are hot tubs filled with steaming water that you can sink in to up to your shoulders. It's 2.5 miles northeast of town on the road to Peel.

Inglewood BOUTIQUE HOTEL $$
(01624-674734; www.inglewoodhotel-isleofman.com; 26 Palace Tce, Queens Promenade; s/d incl breakfast from £42.50/85; P@) Sea-view suites in this beautifully refurbished, friendly hotel have big wooden beds and leather sofas. The homemade breakfasts are superb, and the residents' bar specialises in whisky from all over the world.

Claremont Hotel HOTEL $$$
(01624-617068; www.claremonthoteldouglas.com; 18-22 Loch Promenade; r from £200; P@) The island's fanciest hotel is this newly refurbished classic hotel on the promenade, with huge rooms kitted out with handsome wooden floors and comfortable beds with crisp linen.

Eating

★**Little Fish Cafe** SEAFOOD $$
(www.littlefishcafe.com; 31 North Quay; mains £11.50-14.50; 9am-9pm) Superb seafood presented in a variety of ways, from hake with mustard and lemon butter to a Kerala-style fish curry. For brunch, the Queenie Po'Boy –

battered Manx queenies (queen scallops), paprika mayo and avocado on sourdough brioche – is divine. It also does meat dishes, but the real focus is on the sea.

14North MODERN BRITISH $$

(☎01624-664414; www.14north.im; 14 North Quay; mains £18-22; ⏰noon-2.30pm & 6-9.30pm Mon-Sat) An old timber merchant's house is now home to this smart restaurant specialising in local dishes including pickled herring, lamb rump and, of course, queenies.

Tanroagan SEAFOOD $$

(☎01624-472411; www.tanroagan.co.uk; 9 Ridgeway St; mains £17-20; ⏰noon-2pm & 6-9.30pm Mon-Sat) The place for all things from the sea, this elegant restaurant serves fresh fish straight off the boats, giving them the merest of Continental twists or just a spell on the hot grill. Reservations are recommended.

Drinking & Nightlife

Bath & Bottle COCKTAIL BAR

(6 Victoria St; ⏰noon-2.30pm & 5-11pm Tue-Wed, to 1am Thu, noon-2am Fri-Sat) A cocktail bar styled like a gin joint from the roaring twenties – it does excellent cocktails and on Wednesdays at 8pm there are classic films in the Speakeasy Cinema.

Bar George BAR

(www.bargeorge.im; St George's Chambers, 3 Hill St; ⏰11am-midnight) An elegant option for a glass of wine.

Around Douglas

North of the capital, the dominant feature is Snaefell (621m), the island's tallest mountain. You can follow the Tourist Trophy (TT) circuit up and over the mountain towards Ramsey, or take the alternate route along the coast, going through Laxey, where you can also take the electric tram to near the top of Snaefell, from which it's an easy walk to the summit.

Sights

Grove Museum of Victorian Life MUSEUM

(MH; www.manxnationalheritage.im; Andreas Rd, Ramsey; adult/child £5/2.50; ⏰10am-5pm Jun-Aug, to 4pm Sep) On the edge of Ramsey, on the north of the island, is this imposing house, built in the mid-19th century by Liverpool shipping merchant Duncan Gibb as a summer retreat for himself and his family. The house has been maintained pretty much as it was in its Victorian heyday, and you can wander through its period rooms – and even learn what it was like to be a scullery maid! The house was occupied by the Gibb family until the 1970s.

Maughold Church & Stone Crosses CHRISTIAN

(MH; www.manxnationalheritage.im; Maughold) The church in the small village of Maughold is on the site of an ancient Celtic monastery founded in AD 600; a small shelter houses quite a good selection of stone crosses and ancient inscriptions dating from the 6th to the 13th centuries.

★**Great Laxey Wheel** WATER WHEEL

(MH; www.manxnationalheritage.im; Mines Rd, Laxey; adult/child £5/2.50; ⏰9.30am-5pm Apr-Oct) It's no exaggeration to describe the Lady Isabella Laxey Wheel, built in 1854 to pump water from a mine, as a 'great' wheel: it measures 22m across and can draw 1140L of water per minute from a depth of 550m. The largest wheel of its kind in the world, it's named after the wife of the then lieutenant-governor.

Lonan Old Church CHURCH

The wheel-headed cross at Lonan Old Church, just north of Douglas, is the island's most impressive early Christian cross.

Castletown & Around

At the southern end of the island is Castletown, a quiet harbour town that was originally the capital of the Isle of Man. The town is home to the old parliament and one of the finest castles on the island.

Sights

Castle Rushen CASTLE

(MH; www.manxnationalheritage.im; Castletown Sq, Castletown; adult/child £6/3; ⏰10am-5pm Apr-Aug, to 4pm Sep-Oct) Castletown is dominated by the impressive 13th-century Castle Rushen. You can visit the gatehouse, medieval kitchens, dungeons and the Great Hall. The flag tower affords fine views of the town and coast.

Nautical Museum MUSEUM

(MH; www.manxnationalheritage.im; Bridge St, Castletown; adult/child £5/2.50; ⏰10am-4pm Easter-Oct) This small museum displays, among other things, its pride and joy, *Peggy*, a boat built in 1791 and still housed in its original boathouse.

Balladoole Iron Age Fort ARCHAEOLOGICAL SITE
FREE This collection of ancient monuments between Castletown and Cregneash includes a Bronze Age grave dating to 10,000 BC, a Christian chapel from around 900 AD and the remains of a 36ft-long Viking ship used to bury a man and a woman. The buried ship was uncovered in 1945 by a German refugee and a team from the local WWII internment camp.

Cregneash Village Folk Museum MUSEUM
(MH; www.manxnationalheritage.im; adult/child £5/2.50; 10am-5pm Apr-Aug, to 4pm Sep) On the southern tip of the island, the Cregneash Village Folk Museum recalls traditional Manx rural life.

Eating

Castle Deli @ Radcliffe Butchers DELI $
(4 Malew St, Castletown; 8am-5pm Mon-Sat) Decent sandwiches with meats from the butcher next door. The selection of cheeses and fish is pretty good too.

Port Erin & Port St Mary

Port Erin is a smallish Victorian seaside resort that plays host to the small **Railway Museum** (Station Rd; adult/child £2/1; 9.30am-4.30pm Apr-Oct, guided tours also 7.30pm & 9.30pm Thu, 11am-1pm Sun mid-Jul–mid-Sep). Port St Mary lies across the headland and is linked to by steam train.

Sights

Calf of Man BIRD SANCTUARY
(www.manxnationalheritage.im; Apr-Sep) This small island just off Cregneash is on one of western Britain's major bird migration routes, and 33 species breed annually here, including Manx shearwaters, kittiwakes, razorbills and shags. Other species normally observed on the island include peregrines, hen harriers, choughs and ravens. It's been an official bird sanctuary since 1939. **Gemini Charter** (01624-832761; www.geminicharter.co.uk; trips £25-30 per person) runs birdwatching trips to the island from Port St Mary.

Sleeping

Aaron House B&B $$
(01624-835702; www.aaronhouse.co.uk; The Promenade, Port St Mary; r from £70) Victorian-style Aaron House is a B&B that has fussed over every detail, from the gorgeous brass beds and claw-foot baths to the old-fashioned photographs on the walls. The sea views are also sensational.

Falcon's Nest Hotel HOTEL
(01624-834077; www.falconsnesthotel.co.uk; Station Rd, Port Erin; s/d from £55/90;) The Victorian Falcon's Nest Hotel, once supremely elegant, is now just handsome in a nostalgic sort of way. The rooms aren't noteworthy, but the views over the water are superb.

Peel

POP 4280

Peel is the west coast's most appealing town, with a fine sandy beach.

Sights

Peel Castle CASTLE
(MH; www.manxnationalheritage.im; adult/child £5/2.50; 10am-5pm Jun-Aug, to 4pm Sep-Oct) Peel's big attraction is the ruin of the 11th-century Peel Castle, stunningly positioned atop St Patrick's Island and joined to Peel by a causeway.

House of Manannan MUSEUM
(MH; www.manxnationalheritage.im; adult/child £6/3; 10am-5pm) The House of Manannan museum uses interactive displays to explain Manx history and its seafaring traditions. It includes reconstructions of a Viking longship and longhouse and a Celtic roundhouse.

Sleeping & Eating

Fernleigh Hotel B&B $$
(01624-842435; www.isleofman-bedandbreakfast.com; Marine Pde; d from £75; Feb-Nov;) Comfortable and family-run B&B with 12 decent bedrooms.

Creek Inn PUB FOOD $
(01624-842216; www.thecreekinn.co.uk; East Quay; mains around £8; 10am-11pm) For a better-than-average bite, head to this sea-dog kind of pub on the waterfront. It has a decent bar menu, including Manx queenies (scallops served with white cheese sauce).

The Lake District & Cumbria

Best Places to Eat

- ➡ Lake Road Kitchen (p593)
- ➡ L'Enclume (p613)
- ➡ Old Stamp House (p593)
- ➡ Rogan & Company (p613)
- ➡ Drunken Duck (p596)

Best Places to Sleep

- ➡ Forest Side (p594)
- ➡ Brimstone Hotel (p599)
- ➡ Daffodil Hotel (p594)
- ➡ Augill Castle (p616)
- ➡ Wasdale Head Inn (p603)

Why Go?

'No part of the country is more distinguished by its sublimity', mused the grand old bard of the lakes, William Wordsworth, and a couple of centuries on his words still ring true. In terms of natural splendour, nowhere in England can compare to the Lake District. For centuries, poets, painters and perambulators alike have been flocking here in search of inspiration and escape, and it's still the nation's favourite place to revel in the majesty of the English landscape.

The main draw here is undoubtedly the Lake District National Park – England's largest, at 885 sq miles. Every bend in the road reveals more eye-popping views: deep valleys, plunging passes, glittering lakes, whitewashed inns, barren hills. But it's worth exploring beyond the national park's boundaries too: the old towns of Carlisle, Kendal and Penrith are full of historical interest and Cumbria's coast has a windswept charm all of its own.

When to Go

- ➡ The Lake District is the UK's most popular national park; visit in early spring and late autumn for the smallest crowds.
- ➡ The weather is also notoriously fickle – showers can strike at any time of year, so bring wet-weather gear just in case.
- ➡ Cumbria's largest mountain festival is held in Keswick in mid-May, while the Beer Festival in June welcomes ale aficionados from across the globe.
- ➡ Ambleside's traditional sports day on the last Saturday in July features events such as hound trailing and Cumbrian wrestling; Grasmere's annual sports day takes place on the August Bank Holiday.
- ➡ In November the world's greatest liars congregate on Santon Bridge for their annual fibbing contest.

History

Neolithic settlers arrived in the Lake District around 5000 BC. The region was subsequently occupied by Celts, Angles, Vikings and Romans. During the Dark Ages it marked the centre of the ancient kingdom of Rheged.

During the Middle Ages, Cumbria marked the start of the 'Debatable Lands', the wild frontier between England and Scotland. Bands of raiders known as Border Reivers regularly plundered the area, prompting the construction of defensive *pele* towers and castles at Carlisle, Penrith and Kendal.

The area became a centre for the Romantic movement during the 19th century, largely thanks to the Cumbrian-born poet William Wordsworth, who also championed the need to protect the Lake District's landscape from overdevelopment – a dream that was achieved in 1951 when the Lake District National Park was formed.

The present-day county of Cumbria was formed from the neighbouring districts of Cumberland and Westmorland in 1974.

Activities

Cycling

Cycling is a great way to explore the Lake District and Cumbria, as long as you don't mind the hills. For short mountain-bike rides, the trails of Grizedale Forest (p597) and Whinlatter Forest Park (p605) are very popular.

Long-distance touring routes include the 70-mile **Cumbria Way** between Ulverston, Keswick and Carlisle; the 140-mile **Sea to Sea Cycle Route** (C2C, NCN 7; www.c2c-guide.co.uk), which begins in Whitehaven and cuts east across the northern Pennines to Newcastle; and the 173-mile **Reivers Route** (NCN 10; www.reivers-route.co.uk) from the River Tyne to Whitehaven.

Several local buses (including bus 599 from Bowness to Grasmere, bus X33 from Ambleside to Ravenglass and the Cross Lakes Experience) have space for bikes. There's also the new summer-only bus 800 along Windermere's eastern shore, which can carry 12 bikes. It runs several times a day in July and August, plus on weekends in May and June. You pay the standard bus fare plus £1.50 for each bike. For more information see www.golakes.co.uk/travel/by-bus.aspx.

Walking

For many people, hiking is the main reason for a visit to the Lake District. All tourist offices and bookshops sell maps and guidebooks, such as Collins' *Lakeland Fellranger* and Ordnance Survey's *Pathfinder Guides*. Purists prefer Alfred Wainwright's seven-volume *Pictorial Guides to the Lakeland Fells* (1955–66) – part walking guides, part illustrated artworks, part philosophical memoirs – with painstakingly hand-penned maps and text.

Maps are essential: the Ordnance Survey's 1:25,000 *Landranger* maps are used by most official bodies, while some hikers prefer the Harvey *Superwalker* 1:25,000 maps.

Long-distance trails that pass through Cumbria include the 54-mile **Allerdale Ramble** from Seathwaite to the Solway Firth, the 70-mile **Cumbria Way** from Ulverston to Carlisle and the 191-mile **Coast to Coast** from St Bees to Robin Hood's Bay in Yorkshire. Door-to-door baggage services such as **Coast to Coast Packhorse** (☎017683-71777; www.c2cpackhorse.co.uk) or **Sherpa Van** (☎0871-520 0124; www.sherpavan.com) transport luggage from one destination to the next.

Other Activities

Cumbria is a haven for outdoor activities, including rock climbing, orienteering, horse riding, archery, fell (mountain) running and *ghyll* (waterfall) scrambling. Contact the Outdoor Adventure Company (p611), Rookin House (p590) or Keswick Adventure Centre (p605).

Getting There & Away

National Express coaches run direct from London Victoria and Glasgow to Windermere, Carlisle and Kendal.

Carlisle is on the main West Coast train line from London Euston to Manchester and Glasgow. To get to the Lake District, you need to change at Oxenholme for Kendal and Windermere. The lines around the Cumbrian Coast and between Settle and Carlisle are particularly scenic.

Getting Around

Traveline (☎0871-200 2233; www.traveline northeast.info) provides comprehensive travel information.

There are round-the-lake ferry services on Windermere, Coniston Water, Ullswater and Derwentwater. Windermere also has a ferry service (p589).

Traffic can be heavy during peak season and holiday weekends. Many Cumbrian towns use timed parking permits for on-street parking, which you can pick up free from local shops and tourist offices.

Cumbria & the Lake District Highlights

❶ **Scafell Pike** (p603) Climbing to the summit of England's highest mountain.

❷ **Hill Top** (p595) Spotting the inspirations for Beatrix Potter's tales.

❸ **Steam Yacht Gondola** (p597) Cruising Coniston Water in stately 19th-century style.

❹ **Grizedale Forest** (p597) Cycling woodland trails surrounded by outdoor art.

❺ **Honister Pass** (p606) Delving into the depths of the Lake District's last slate mine.

❻ **La'al Ratty** (p614) Catching the miniature steam trains into Eskdale.

❼ **Dove Cottage** (p593) Exploring Wordsworth's much-loved Lakeland cottage.

❽ **Carlisle Castle** (p614) Patrolling the battlements of Carlisle's mighty medieval fortress.

❾ **Sarah Nelson's Shop** (p595) Sampling world-famous gingerbread in Grasmere.

❿ **Helvellyn** (p610) Braving the ridge walk via Striding Edge to the summit.

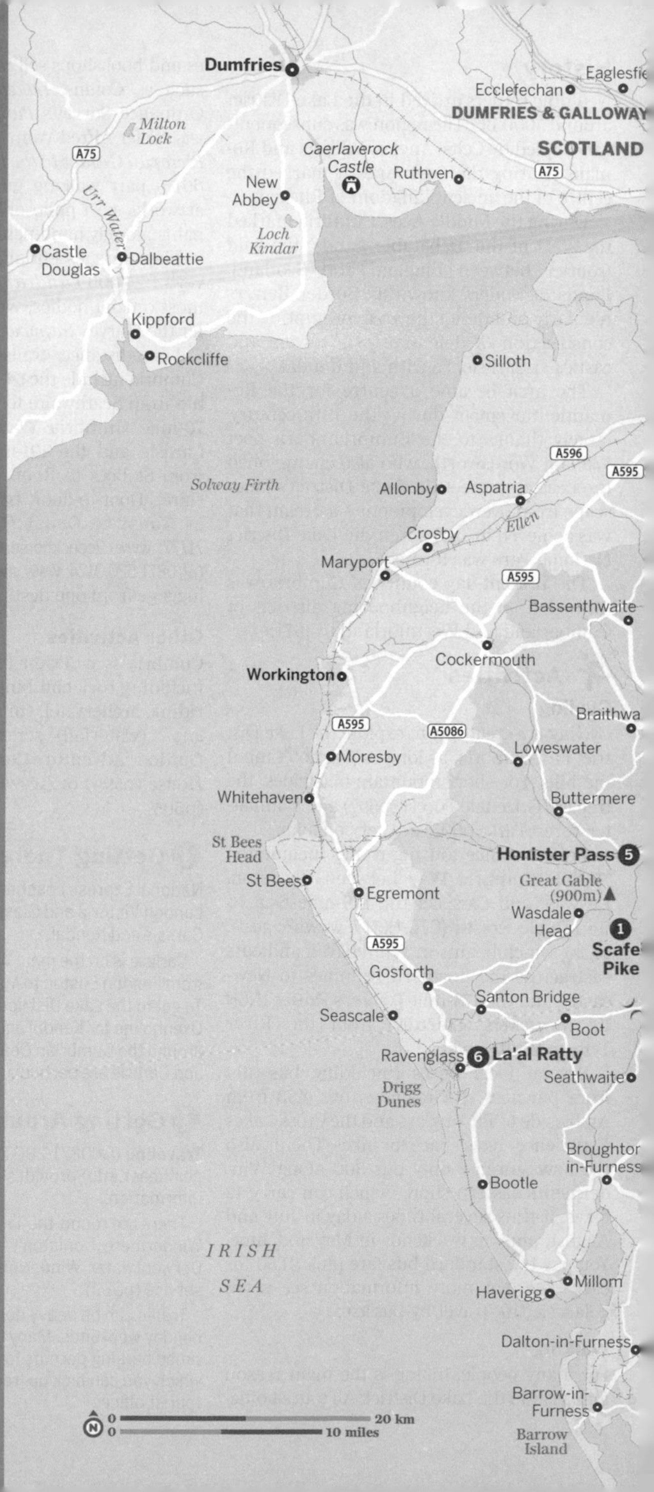

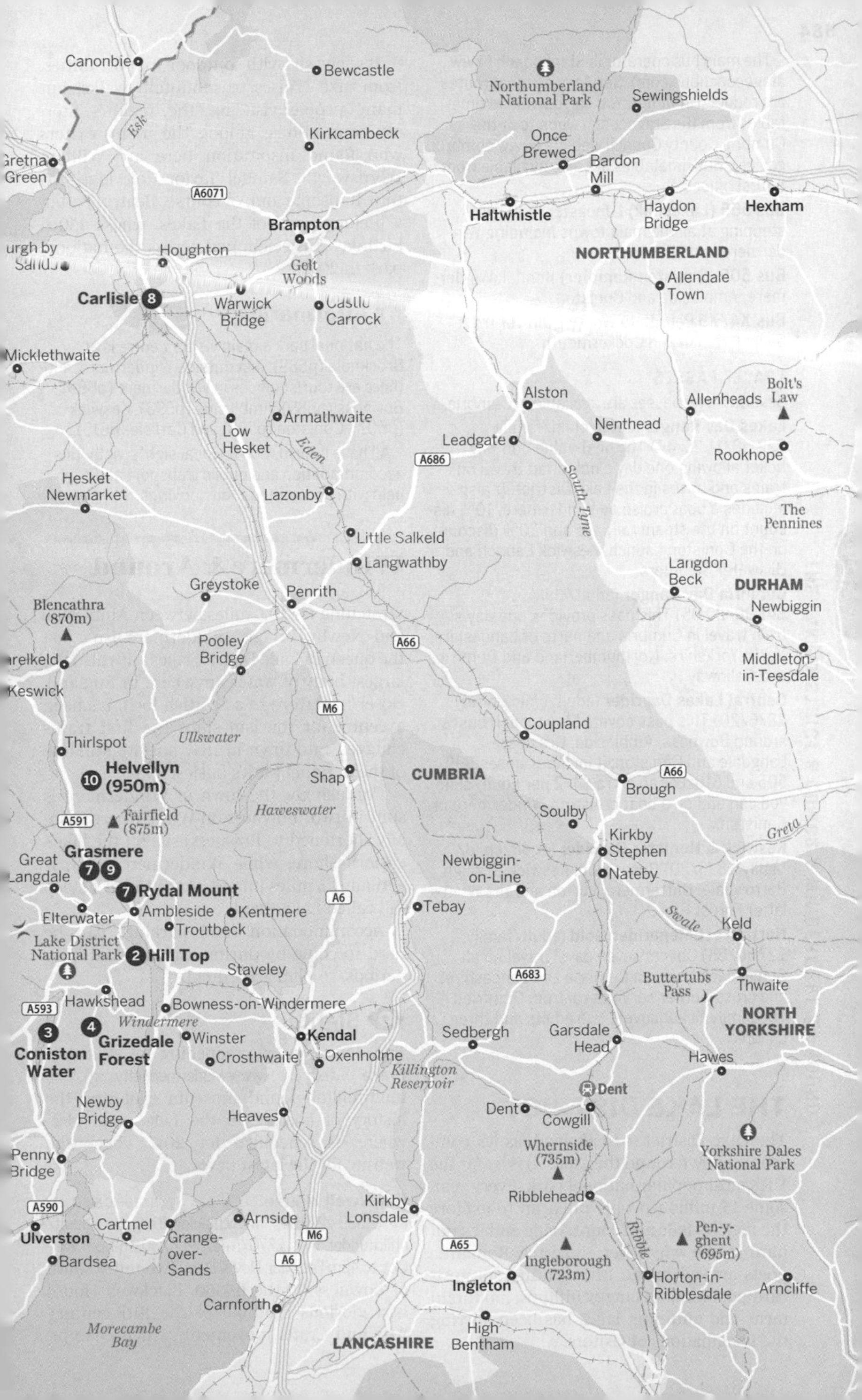

Canonbie
Bewcastle
Esk
Gretna Green
Kirkcambeck
A6071
Brampton
urgh by Sands
Houghton
Gelt Woods
Carlisle 8
Warwick Bridge
Castle Carrock
Micklethwaite
Low Hesket
Armathwaite
Eden
Hesket Newmarket
Lazonby
Little Salkeld
Langwathby
Greystoke
Penrith
Blencathra (870m)
Pooley Bridge
relkeld
Keswick
M6
Thirlspot
Ullswater
10 Helvellyn (950m)
Shap
Haweswater
A591
Fairfield (875m)
Grasmere
Great Langdale
7 9
7 Rydal Mount
Ambleside
Kentmere
Elterwater
Troutbeck
Lake District National Park
2 Hill Top
Staveley
Hawkshead
Bowness-on-Windermere
A593
Windermere
3 Coniston Water
4 Grizedale Forest
Winster
Crosthwaite
Kendal
Oxenholme
Newby Bridge
Heaves
Penny Bridge
A590
Ulverston
Cartmel
Grange-over-Sands
Arnside
Bardsea
M6
A6
Carnforth
Morecambe Bay
Northumberland National Park
Sewingshields
Once Brewed
Bardon Mill
Haltwhistle
Haydon Bridge
Hexham
NORTHUMBERLAND
Allendale Town
Alston
Bolt's Law
Allenheads
Nenthead
Leadgate
A686
Rookhope
South Tyne
The Pennines
Langdon Beck
DURHAM
Newbiggin
A66
Middleton-in-Teesdale
Coupland
CUMBRIA
A66
Brough
Soulby
Greta
Kirkby Stephen
Newbiggin-on-Line
Nateby
A6
Tebay
Swale
Keld
A683
Buttertubs Pass
Thwaite
NORTH YORKSHIRE
Sedbergh
Garsdale Head
Hawes
Killington Reservoir
Dent
Dent
Cowgill
Whernside (735m)
Yorkshire Dales National Park
Ribblehead
Kirkby Lonsdale
Ribble
Pen-y-ghent (695m)
A65
Ingleborough (723m)
Ingleton
Horton-in-Ribblesdale
Arncliffe
High Bentham
LANCASHIRE

The main bus operator is Stagecoach (www.stagecoachbus.com). Services on most routes are reduced in winter. You can download timetables from the Stagecoach website or the Cumbria County Council website (www.cumbria.gov.uk). Bus timetables are also available from tourist offices.

Bus 555 (Lakeslink) Lancaster to Keswick, stopping at all the main towns including Windermere and Ambleside.

Bus 505 (Coniston Rambler) Kendal, Windermere, Ambleside and Coniston.

Bus X4/X5 Penrith to Workington via Troutbeck, Keswick and Cockermouth.

TRAVEL PASSES

Several travel passes are available in Cumbria.

Lakes Day Ranger (adult/child/family £22.50/11.25/44) The best-value one-day ticket allowing one day's unlimited travel on trains and buses in the Lake District. It also includes a boat cruise on Windermere, 10% discount on the steam railways and 20% discount on the Coniston Launch, Keswick Launch and Ullswater Steamers.

Cumbria Day Ranger (adult/child £41.90/20.95) This pass provides one day's train travel in Cumbria and parts of Lancashire, North Yorkshire, Northumberland and Dumfries and Galloway.

Central Lakes Dayrider (adult/child/family £8/6/20) This pass covers Stagecoach buses around Bowness, Ambleside, Grasmere, Langdale and Coniston; it includes buses 599, 505 and 516. For an extra £4/2 per adult/child you can add on a boat cruise on Windermere or Coniston.

Keswick & Honister Dayrider (adult/child/family £8/6/20) Buses from Keswick through Borrowdale, Buttermere, Lorton and the Whinlatter Forest Park.

North West Megarider Gold (adult/family £27.30/55) Covers seven days' travel on all Stagecoach buses in Cumbria and Lancashire, and cross-border services to/from Dumfries. The family ticket covers two adults and three children.

THE LAKE DISTRICT

The Lake District (or Lakeland, as it's commonly known round these parts) is by far the UK's most popular national park. Every year, some 15 million people pitch up to explore the region's fells and countryside and it's not hard to see why. Ever since the Romantic poets arrived in the 19th century, its postcard panorama of craggy hilltops, mountain tarns and glittering lakes has been stirring the imaginations of visitors.

It's awash with outdoor opportunities, from lake cruises to mountain walks, but many people visit for the region's literary connections: among the many writers who found inspiration here are William Wordsworth, Samuel Taylor Coleridge, Arthur Ransome and, of course, Beatrix Potter, a lifelong lover of the Lakes, whose 150th birthday was celebrated across the national park in 2016.

Information

The national park's main visitor centre is at Brockhole (p589), just outside Windermere, and there are tourist offices in Windermere (p589), Bowness (p589), Ambleside (p593), Keswick (p607), Coniston (p598) and Carlisle (p615).

All have information on local sights, activities, accommodation and public transport and can help with accommodation bookings.

Windermere & Around

POP 5423

Stretching for 10.5 miles between Ambleside and Newby Bridge, Windermere isn't just the queen of Lake District lakes – it's also the largest body of water anywhere in England, closer in stature to a Scottish loch. It's been a centre for tourism since the first trains chugged into town in 1847 and it's still one of the national park's busiest spots.

Confusingly, the town of Windermere is split in two: Bowness-on-Windermere (usually shortened to Bowness) sits on the lake's eastern shore, while Windermere Town is actually 1.5 miles inland, at the top of a steep hill called Lake Road.

Accommodation (and parking) can be hard to come by during holidays and busy periods, so plan accordingly.

Sights

The long-awaited reopening of **Windermere Jetty** (www.windermerejetty.org), a multimillion-pound museum exploring the history of boating in the Lakes and elsewhere, is scheduled for 2017; check the website for the latest news.

Blackwell House HISTORIC BUILDING
(01539-722464; www.blackwell.org.uk; adult/child under 16yr £7.70/free; 10.30am-5pm Apr-Oct, to 4pm Feb, Mar, Nov & Dec) Two miles south of Bowness on the B5360, Blackwell House is a glorious example of the 19th-century Arts and Crafts movement, which champi-

Lake District

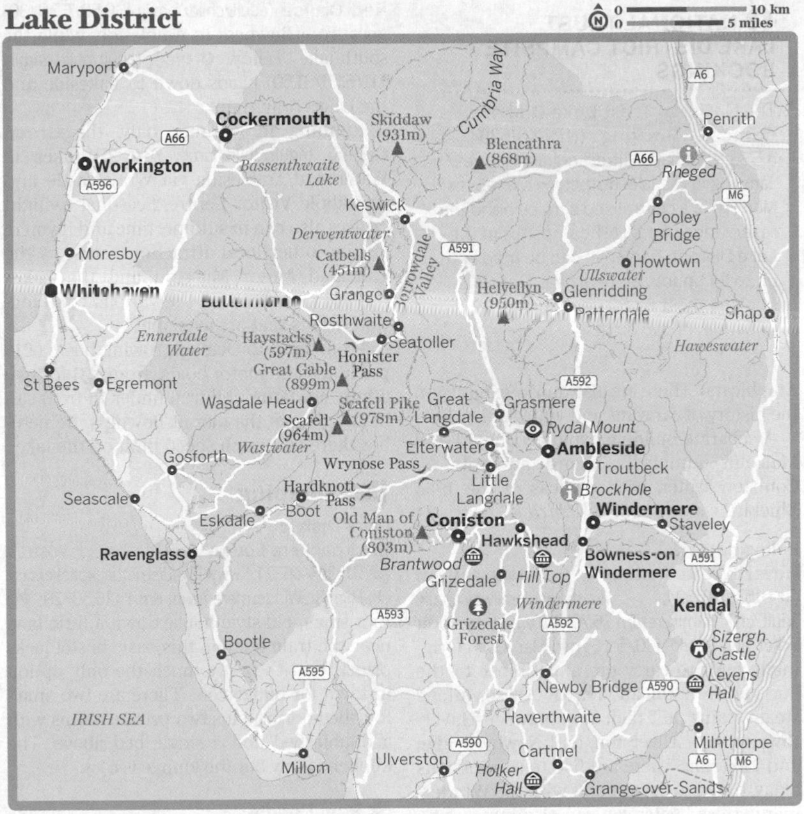

oned handmade goods and craftsmanship over the mass-produced mentality of the Industrial Revolution.

Designed by Mackay Hugh Baillie Scott for Sir Edward Holt, a wealthy brewer, the house shimmers with Arts and Crafts details: light, airy rooms, bespoke craftwork, wood panelling, stained glass and Delft tiles. The mock-medieval Great Hall and serene White Drawing Room are particularly fine. The cafe has brilliant views over Windermere.

Fell Foot Park GARDENS

(NT; www.nationaltrust.org.uk/fell-foot-park; ⏲8am-8pm Apr-Sep, 9am-5pm Oct-Mar, cafe 10am-5pm) FREE Located at the southern end of Windermere, 7 miles south of Bowness, this 7-hectare lakeside estate originally belonged to a manor house. It's now owned by the National Trust and its shoreline paths and grassy lawns are ideal for a sunny day picnic. There's a small cafe and rowing boats are available for hire.

Lakes Aquarium AQUARIUM

(☎015395-30153; www.lakesaquarium.co.uk; Lakeside; adult/child £6.95/4.95; ⏲9am-6pm Apr-Oct) At the southern end of the lake near Newby Bridge, this aquarium explores a range of underwater habitats from tropical Africa through to Morecambe Bay. Windermere Lake Cruises (p586) and the Lakeside & Haverthwaite Railway (p586) stop right beside the aquarium or you could catch bus 6/X6 from Bowness. There's a £1 discount per ticket for online bookings.

Lakeland Motor Museum MUSEUM

(☎015395-30400; www.lakelandmotormuseum.co.uk; Backbarrow; adult/child £8.50/5; ⏲9.30am-5.30pm Apr-Sep, to 4.30pm Oct-Mar) Two miles south of Newby Bridge on the A590, this car museum houses a wonderful collection of antique cars: classic (Minis, Austin Healeys, MGs), sporty (DeLoreans, Audi Quattros, Aston Martins) and downright odd (Scootacars,

NATIONAL TRUST LAKE DISTRICT CAMPSITE BOOKINGS

The **National Trust Lake District Campsite Bookings** (NT; 015394-32733; www.nationaltrust.org.uk/features/camping-in-the-lake-district; 10am-5pm Mon-Fri) is a centralised service handling reservations for all NT campsites in the Lake District. Bookings can be made up to 24 hours before arrival. Online bookings cost £2.50 and must be for a minimum of two nights.

Amphicars). There are also quirky exhibits on the history of caravans and vintage bicycles.

A separate building explores Donald and Malcolm Campbell's record attempts on Coniston Water, with replicas of the 1935 Bluebird car and 1967 *Bluebird K7* boat.

Lakeside & Haverthwaite Railway HERITAGE RAILWAY
(015395-31594; www.lakesiderailway.co.uk; adult/child/family return £6.70/4.10/19, 1-day rover ticket adult/child £10/5; mid-Mar–Oct) Originally built to carry ore and timber to the ports at Ulverston and Barrow, these vintage steam trains puff their way between Haverthwaite, near Ulverston, and Newby Bridge and Lakeside. There are five to seven trains a day, timed to correspond with the Windermere cruise boats; you can also buy combo tickets that include a lake cruise to Bowness or Ambleside.

Activities

Windermere Lake Cruises BOATING
(015394-43360; www.windermere-lakecruises.co.uk; tickets from £2.70) Since the launch of the first passenger ferry in 1845, cruising has been an essential part of every Windermere itinerary. Some vessels are modern, but there are some period beauties dating back to the 1930s.

There are various colour-coded cruise options exploring different areas of the lake. All boats allow you to disembark and catch a later ferry back.

The **Freedom of the Lake ticket** (adult/child/family £19.50/9.75/52.50) allows a day's unlimited travel on all routes.

The most popular route is the **Islands Cruise** (adult/child/family £8/4/21), a 45-minute circular cruise around Windermere's shoreline and islands. The north-lake **Red Cruise** (adult/child/family £10.50/6.30/30) goes from Bowness to Ambleside, while the south-lake **Yellow Cruise** (adult/child/family £11/6.50/31.50) heads down to Lakeside and the Lakes Aquarium.

Running in summer only, the **Green Cruise** (adult/child/family £8/4/21) takes in Waterhead/Ambleside via Wray Castle and Brockhole Visitor Centre. Seasonal twilight cruises also run in summertime and if you're visiting other local attractions, such as the Lakeland Motor Museum and the Lakes Aquarium, ask about the various combination tickets that are available.

From April to October, rowing boats (£15 per hour) and motor boats (from £31 for two adults per hour; children under 16 free) can be hired from the pier at Bowness. Remember there's a 10mph speed limit on the lake.

Sleeping

Lake District Backpackers Lodge HOSTEL £
(015394-46374; www.lakedistrictbackpackers.co.uk; High St, Windermere Town; dm/r £16.50/39; @) In a small, old-style house down a little lane near the train station, this basic hostel lacks pizazz, but it's pretty much the only option in town for budgeteers. There are two small four-bed dorms, plus two private rooms with a double bed and a single bed above. The kitchen is tiny but the lounge is cosy.

★**Rum Doodle** B&B ££
(015394-45967; www.rumdoodlewindermere.com; Sunny Bank Rd, Windermere Town; d £85-119; P) Named after a classic travel novel about a fictional mountain in the Himalayas, this B&B zings with imagination. Its rooms are themed after places and characters in the book, with details like book-effect wallpaper, vintage maps and old suitcases. Top of the heap is The Summit, snug under the eaves with a separate sitting room. Two-night minimum in summer.

★**Boundary** B&B ££
(015394-48978; www.boundaryonline.com; Lake Rd, Windermere Town; d £99-210; P) A refined choice, sleek and chic, with neutral-toned rooms all named after great English cricketers: top picks are Hobbs, with bay window and vast bathroom, and Ranji, with cute flamingo wallpaper and a free-standing in-room bathtub. The downstairs lounge has a trendy wood burner and copies of *Wisden's Almanac* to browse.

Windermere Town

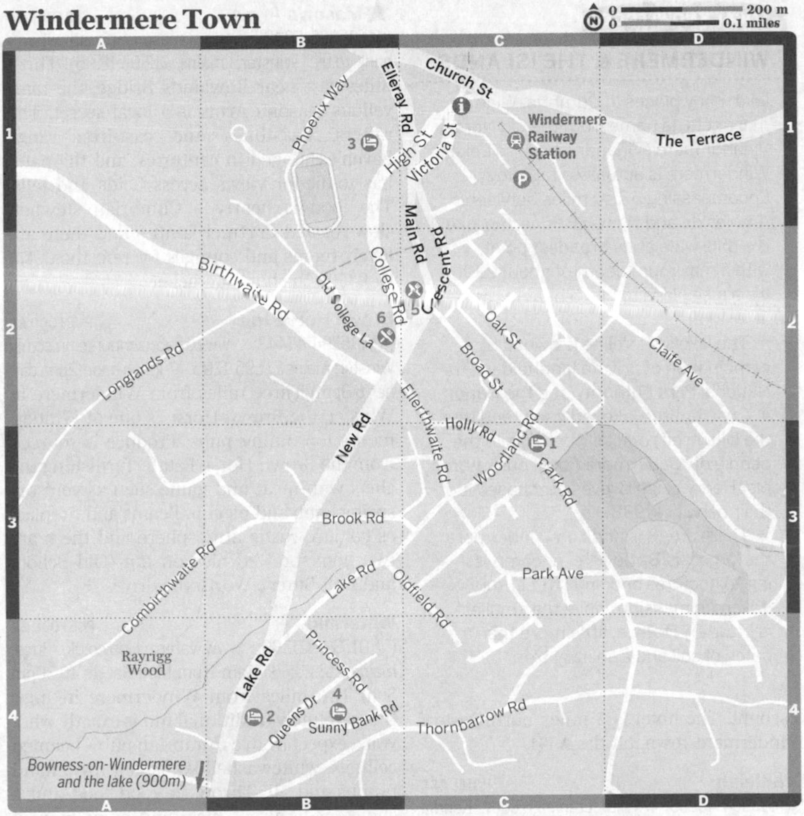

1 Park Road B&B **££**
(☎015394-42107; www.1parkroad.com; 1 Park Rd, Windermere Town; d £82-112; P 📶) It's the little treats that keep this cosy guesthouse a cut above: bath goodies from Pure Lakes and The White Company, iPod docks in every room and homemade baked beans and marmalade for breakfast. Rooms are comfortable and the rates stay reasonable year-round – a rarity in Windermere.

Gilpin Lodge HOTEL **£££**
(☎015394-88818; www.gilpinlodge.co.uk; Crook Rd; r £335-615; P) Windermere's B&Bs might be pushing up their rates to silly levels, but this famously posh country-house retreat shows them how it should be done. The fabulously fancy rooms are named after fells; garden suites even have their own decks and outdoor hot tubs; and the new Lake House comes with its own chauffeur. A superb restaurant, spa and hectares of grounds complete the package.

Windermere Town

Sleeping

1	1 Park Road	C3
2	Boundary	B4
3	Lake District Backpackers Lodge	B1
4	Rum Doodle	B4

Eating

5	Homeground	C2
6	Hooked	B2

Samling HOTEL **£££**
(☎015394-31922; www.thesamlinghotel.co.uk; Ambleside Rd; r £220-670) If money's no object, this deluxe country house is the choice. The chic rooms and cottages are classically styled and feature luxury touches such as split-level mezzanines, rain showers and private lounges. Its restaurant has a Michelin star too. Early bookings score a substantial

LOCAL KNOWLEDGE

WINDERMERE & THE ISLANDS

Like many places in Cumbria, Windermere gets its name from the old Norse, Vinandr mere (Vinandr's lake; so Lake Windermere is actually a tautology). Encompassing 5.7 sq miles between Ambleside and Newby Bridge, the lake is a mile wide at its broadest point, with a maximum depth of about 220m. It's a nice place to hire a boat for the afternoon.

The lake's shoreline is owned by a combination of private landholders, the National Park Authority and the National Trust, but the lakebed itself (and thus the lake itself) officially belongs to the people of Windermere (local philanthropist Henry Leigh Groves purchased it on their behalf in 1938).

There are 18 islands on Windermere: the largest is **Belle Isle**, encompassing 16 hectares and an 18th-century Italianate mansion, while the smallest is **Maiden Holme**, little more than a patch of soil and a solitary tree.

discount. The hotel is 3 miles northwest of Windermere Town, off the A591.

Cranleigh HOTEL £££
(015394-43293; www.thecranleigh.com; Kendal Rd, Bowness-on-Windermere; d £119-189, ste £305-515; P) This guesthouse has gone all out on the decor, but strip away the snazziness and it's still just a B&B. It's worth bumping up to the superior for the spacious bathrooms or maybe blowing the budget on one of the two over-the-top suites (check out the Sanctuary, complete with Bose stereo, glass bath and picture-fireplace).

Eating

Homeground CAFE £
(015394-44863; www.homegroundcafe.co.uk; 56 Main Rd, Windermere Town; coffees £2-4, mains £7-10; 9am-5pm) Windermere gets its own boutique coffee house, serving excellent flat whites, pour overs and ristrettos, accompanied by a fine display of milk art. It's super for brunch too, with bang-on-trend options like a lavish eggs Benedict and maple-bacon waffles. All in all, a thoroughly welcome new addition to town.

★ **Mason's Arms** PUB FOOD ££
(015395-68486; www.masonsarmsstrawberrybank.co.uk; Winster; mains £12.95-18.95) Three miles east near Bowlands Bridge, the marvellous Mason's Arms is a local secret. The rafters, flagstones and cast-iron range haven't changed in centuries, and the patio has to-die-for views across fields and fells. The food is hearty – Cumbrian stewpot, slow-roasted Cartmel lamb – and there are lovely rooms and cottages for rent too (£175 to £350). In short, a cracker.

Brown Horse Inn PUB FOOD ££
(015394-43443; www.thebrownhorseinn.co.uk; Winster; mains £11.95-17.95; lunch noon-2pm, dinner 6-9pm) Three miles from Windermere in Winster, the Brown Horse is one of Windermere's top dining pubs. Produce is sourced from the Brown Horse Estate, furnishing the chefs with meat and game such as venison, spring lamb and pigeon. Beams and fireplaces conjure rustic atmosphere and there are two home-brewed ales on tap (Old School and Best Bitter). Worth the drive.

Watermill PUB FOOD ££
(01539-821309; www.watermillinn.co.uk; Ings; mains £12-20; 11am-11pm Mon-Sat, to 10.30pm Sun) Two miles from Windermere in Ings, this resolutely traditional inn is exactly what you'd expect from a Cumbrian pub – beamed ceilings, whitewashed walls, log fires, hand pumps and all. Throw in good food and a choice of 16 ales – including home-brewed Collie Wobbles – and it's no wonder it's scooped lots of local awards.

Porto BISTRO ££
(015394-48242; www.porto-restaurant.co.uk; 3 Ash St, Bowness-on-Windermere; mains £14.95-24.45, set menu £18.95; noon-4pm & 6-10pm Wed-Mon) The classiest address in Bowness, tucked away in a whitewashed building on Ash St, and serving adventurous British bistro food (slate plates and sparse presentation present and correct). Head chef David Bewick previously worked with Gordon Ramsay and Nigel Haworth so he knows what's what. The afternoon tea is a cracker too.

Hooked SEAFOOD ££
(015394-48443; www.hookedwindermere.co.uk; Ellerthwaite Sq, Windermere Town; mains £19.95-21.95; 5.30-10.30pm Tue-Sun) Seafood might not be something you immediately think of when deciding what to eat in

Windermere, but Paul White's first-class fish restaurant is well worth considering. He likes to keep things classic: hake with Mediterranean veg and pesto, sea trout with peas and pancetta or lemon sole with capers and parsley butter. It's small, so bookings are essential.

Angel Inn PUB FOOD ££
(☎015394-44080; www.the-angelinn.com; Helm Rd, Bowness-on-Windermere; mains £10.95-16.50; ⏲11.30am-4pm & 5-9pm) This smart gastropub sits atop a grassy knoll near the Bowness shoreline and offers superior pub grub: think deli boards and Thai chicken supreme. Arrive early if you want to bag a table on the lawn – the lake views are great, so they go fast. A recent refurb has brightened up its rooms (£90 to £150) with natural fabrics and checked accents.

Drinking & Nightlife

Hawkshead Brewery BREWERY
(☎01539-822644; www.hawksheadbrewery.co.uk; Mill Yard, Staveley) This craft brewery has its own beer hall in Staveley, 3 miles east of Windermere. Core beers include Hawkshead Bitter, dark Brodie's Prime and fruity Red. Guided tours can be arranged in advance.

Hole in T' Wall PUB
(☎015394-43488; Fallbarrow Rd, Bowness-on-Windermere; ⏲11am-11pm) Bowness' oldest boozer, dating back to 1612 and offering lashings of rough-beamed, low-ceilinged atmosphere.

Information

Bowness Tourist Office (☎0845 901 0845; bownesstic@lake-district.gov.uk; Glebe Rd, Bowness-on-Windermere; ⏲9.30am-5.30pm) Bowness' tourist office is beside the lake jetties.

Brockhole National Park Visitor Centre (☎015394-46601; www.lake-district.gov.uk; ⏲10am-5pm Easter-Oct, to 4pm Nov-Easter) In a 19th-century mansion 3 miles north of Windermere on the A591, this is the Lake District's flagship visitor centre. It also has a teashop, an adventure playground and gardens.

Windermere Tourist Office (☎015394-46499; www.windermereinfo.co.uk; Victoria St, Windermere Town; ⏲8.30am-5pm) Windermere's tourist office is now run by the outdoor-activity provider **Mountain Goat** (☎015394-45161; www.mountain-goat.com; Victoria St, Windermere).

Getting There & Away

BOAT

To cross Windermere by car, bike or on foot, head south of Bowness to the **Windermere Ferry** (www.cumbria.gov.uk/roads-transport/highways-pavements/windermereferry.asp; car/bicycle/pedestrian £4.40/1/50p; ⏲every 20 minutes 6.50am-9.50pm Mon-Fri, 9.10am-9.50pm Sat & Sun Mar-Oct, to 8.50pm Nov-Feb), which shuttles between Ferry Nab on the east bank to Ferry House on the west bank.

BUS

There's one daily National Express coach from London (£31.50, eight hours) via Lancaster and Kendal.

Bus 555/556 Lakeslink (£5.20 to £10.80, at least hourly including Sundays) Starts at the train station, stopping at Troutbeck Bridge (five minutes), Brockhole Visitor Centre (seven minutes), Ambleside (£5.20, 15 minutes), Grasmere (£6.50, 30 minutes) and Keswick (£10.80, one hour). In the opposite direction it continues to Kendal (£6.70, 25 minutes).

Bus 505 Coniston Rambler (£3.50 to £4.50, hourly including Sundays) Travels from Bowness to Coniston (£4.50, 50 minutes) via Troutbeck, Brockhole, Ambleside, Skelwith Fold, Hawkshead and Hawkshead Hill. Two buses a day serve Kendal.

Bus 599 Lakes Rider (£4 to £6.50, three times hourly including weekends) Open-top bus between Bowness, Troutbeck, Brockhole, Rydal Church (for Rydal Mount), Dove Cottage and Grasmere. Some buses stop at Windermere train station.

OFF THE BEATEN TRACK

WRAY CASTLE & CLAIFE HEIGHTS

Windermere's quieter west side is a good place to escape the crowds. North of the ferry landings at Ferry House, a network of woodland paths winds across **Claife Heights**, while the nearby National Trust–owned estate of **Wray Castle** (NT; www.nationaltrust.org.uk/wray-castle; adult/child £8.50/4.25; ⏲10am-5pm) encompasses 25 hectares of lakeside grounds and a turreted 19th-century mansion, once used as a holiday home by Beatrix Potter's family.

TRAIN

Windermere is the only town inside the national park accessible by train. It's on the branch line to Kendal and Oxenholme.

DESTINATION	ONE-WAY FARE (£)	DURATION (HR)
Edinburgh	61.20	2½
Glasgow	53.50	2¼-2¾
Kendal	4.70	15min
Lancaster	13.90	45min
London Euston	102.50	3½
Manchester Piccadilly	36.20	1½

Troutbeck

Nestled among the fells to the north of Windermere, on the road towards Kirkstone Pass, this rural hamlet feels a world away from the Bowness bustle, with wonderful views over Windermere.

Sights & Activities

Townend HISTORIC BUILDING

(NT; ☎01539-432628; www.nationaltrust.org.uk/townend; adult/child £5.90/3.25; ⏰1-5pm Wed-Sun Mar-Oct, daily school holidays) Reopened after major renovations, the historic farmhouse at Townend contains a collection of vintage farming tools, possessions and furniture that belonged to the Browne family, who owned the house until 1943. Hourly guided tours run from 11am to 1pm.

Rookin House OUTDOORS

(☎017684-83561; www.rookinhouse.co.uk; Troutbeck) This activities centre between Penrith and Keswick offers a huge range of outdoor fun, from the usual horse riding, clay-pigeon shooting and archery to the weird and wonderful (ever fancied driving a JCB or an Argo cat? Now's your chance).

Sleeping & Eating

Queen's Head INN ££

(☎015394-32174; www.queensheadhotel.com; d £99-110; P) This 17th-century coaching inn and pub in Troutbeck is a winning blend of old and new. The bedrooms are surprisingly fancy, with bright bedspreads, flatscreen TVs and teddy bears, but it's the solid food and ale that keeps the place busy (mains £12.95 to £16.95). There's a three-course menu (£20) chalked up over the fireplace.

★**Mortal Man** PUB FOOD ££

(☎015394-33193; www.themortalman.co.uk; Troutbeck; mains £8.95-15.95; P 🐾) Troutbeck's oldest pub, dating from 1689, with a gabled facade, traditional rooms (£89 to £105) and a cracking fell-view beer garden. The food mainly centres on 'pub classics' such as bangers and mash and shepherd's pie. In case you're wondering about the curious name, have a look at the pub sign on your way in – it's taken from an old Lakeland rhyme.

Getting There & Away

Bus 508 from Windermere costs £3.20. It travels every two hours Monday to Friday, with four daily on Saturday and Sunday.

Ambleside

POP 2529

Once a busy mill and textile centre at Windermere's northern tip, Ambleside is an attractive little town, built from the same slate and stern grey stone that's so characteristic of the rest of Lakeland. Ringed by fells, it's a favourite base for hikers, with a cluster of outdoors shops and plenty of cosy pubs and cafes providing fuel for adventures.

Sights & Activities

Armitt Museum MUSEUM

(☎015394-31212; www.armitt.com; Rydal Rd; adult/child £3.50/free; ⏰10am-5pm) Despite some damage incurred during the 2015 floods, Ambleside's excellent little museum is back up and running. It hosts some intriguing seasonal exhibitions alongside its core collection, populated with artefacts relating to important Lakeland characters such as Beatrix Potter, National Trust founder Canon Hardwicke Rawnsley and photographers Herbert Bell and the Abraham Brothers. There are also original canvases by the modernist artist Kurt Schwitters, a German refugee who settled in Ambleside after WWII.

★**Rydal Mount** HISTORIC BUILDING

(☎015394-33002; www.rydalmount.co.uk; adult/child £7.50/3.50, grounds only £4.50; ⏰9.30am-5pm Mar-Oct, 11am-4pm Wed-Mon Nov, Dec & Feb) The poet William Wordsworth's most famous residence in the Lake District is undoubtedly Dove Cottage (p593), but he actually spent a great deal more time at Rydal Mount, 1.5 miles northwest of Ambleside, off the A591. This was the Wordsworth family's home from 1813 until the poet's death in 1850 and the house contains a treasure trove of Wordsworth memorabilia. Bus 555 (and bus 599 from April to October) stops at the end of the drive.

Downstairs you can wander around the library, dining room and drawing room (look out for William's pen, inkstand and picnic box in the cabinets as well as a famous portrait of the poet by the American painter Henry Inman hanging above the fireplace). Upstairs are the family bedrooms and Wordsworth's attic study, containing his encyclopedia and a sword belonging to his brother John, who was lost in a shipwreck in 1805.

The gardens are lovely too; Wordsworth fancied himself as a landscape gardener and much of the grounds were laid out according to his designs. Below the house is Dora's Field, a peaceful meadow in which Wordsworth planted daffodils in memory of his eldest daughter, who died from tuberculosis in 1847.

Stock Ghyll Force WALKING
Ambleside's most popular walk is the half-hour stroll up to the 18m waterfall of Stock Ghyll Force; the trail is signposted behind the old Market Hall at the bottom of Stock Ghyll Lane. If you feel energetic, you can follow the trail beyond the falls up **Wansfell Pike** (482m), a reasonably steep walk of about two hours.

Low Wood Watersports BOATING
(015394-39441; www.englishlakes.co.uk/watersports; Low Bay Marina) This centre offers waterskiing, sailing and kayaking and has row boats and motor boats for hire. Kayaks cost from £15 per hour, canoes £18 per hour.

Sleeping

★Ambleside YHA HOSTEL £
(0845 371 9620; www.yha.org.uk; Lake Rd; dm £21-30; P) One of the YHA's flagship Lake District hostels, this huge lakeside house is a fave for activity holidays (everything from kayaking to ghyll scrambling). Great facilities (kitchen, bike rental, boat jetty and bar) mean it's heavily subscribed, so book well ahead. Families can book out dorms as private rooms. The hostel is halfway between Ambleside and Windermere on Lake Rd (the A591).

Low Wray CAMPSITE £
(NT; bookings 015394-63862; www.ntlakescampsites.org.uk; campsites £13-35.50, eco pods £45-55; campsite arrivals 3-7pm Sat-Thu, to 9pm Fri Mar-Oct) One of the most popular of the National Trust's four Lakeland campsites, in a fine spot along Windermere's shores, 3 miles from Ambleside along the B5286. There are 120 tent pitches, nine hard pitches for caravans, plus a handful of camping pods and two safari tents. Choose from lake view, woodland, field or water's edge. Bus 505 stops nearby.

Regent Hotel HOTEL ££
(015394-32254; www.regentlakes.co.uk; Waterhead Bay; d £99-195; P) This small lakeside hotel is a bit of a bargain. The rooms offer different settings: some have balconies overlooking the garden, others have bunks for the kids or walk-in wet rooms and a few sneak in views over Windermere. The top-floor Sail Loft has romantic skylights and its own private deck terrace.

Gables B&B ££
(015394-33272; www.thegables-ambleside.co.uk; Church Walk; d £102-122; P) One of Ambleside's best-value B&Bs in a double-gabled house (hence the name) in a quiet spot overlooking the recreation ground. Spotty cushions and colourful prints keep things cheery, but room sizes are variable (in this instance, bigger is definitely better). Guests receive discounts at the owner's restaurant, **Sheila's Cottage** (015394-33079; The Slack; mains £12.50-18; noon-2.30pm & 6.30-10pm).

Riverside B&B ££
(015394-32395; www.riverside-at-ambleside.co.uk; Under Loughrigg; d £112-122; P) Lodged beside the River Rothay half a mile from town, this detached Victorian villa is distinguished by its luxuries: walking guides, ethical bath products and fresh chutneys from the Hawkshead Relish Company. Two rooms have spa baths, one a pine four-poster.

Lakes Lodge B&B ££
(015394-33240; www.lakeslodge.co.uk; Lake Rd; r £106-129; P) This modish mini hotel offers a touch more luxury than Ambleside's other guesthouses. The rooms are all about clean lines, stark walls and zero clutter and most have a full-size wall mural featuring

LAKE GLAMPING

Wild in Style (yurts 4 nights from £290, vardo wagons 3 nights £285) constructs yurts and gypsy 'vardo' caravans, and is currently located at two campsites in the Lake District: Low Wray near Ambleside and Hoathwaite near Coniston.

DON'T MISS

TOP FIVE CLASSIC LAKELAND HIKES

The Lake District's most famous fell-walker, the accountant-turned-author Alfred Wainwright, recorded 214 official fells in his seven-volume *Pictorial Guides* (as if that weren't enough, he usually outlines at least two possible routes to the top or in the case of Scafell Pike, five). If you only have limited time, here are five hikes that offer a flavour of what makes fell walking in the Lake District so special.

Scafell Pike (978m) The daddy of Lakeland hikes, a six- to seven-hour slog to the top of England's highest peak. The classic route is from Wasdale Head.

Helvellyn (950m) Not for the faint hearted; a vertiginous scramble along the knife-edge ridge of Striding Edge. It takes at least six hours starting from Glenridding or Patterdale.

Blencathra (868m) A mountain on its own, Blencathra offers a panoramic outlook on Keswick and the northern fells. Count on four hours from Threlkeld.

Haystacks (597m) Wainwright's favourite mountain and the place where his ashes were scattered. It's a steep, three-hour return hike from Buttermere village.

Catbells (451m) The fell for everyone, accessible to six-year-olds and septuagenarians. It's on the west side of Derwentwater and takes a couple of hours to climb.

a local beauty spot. Some are in the main building while others are in an attached annexe. Breakfast is served in a puce-and-lime-coloured dining room.

Randy Pike B&B £££

(015394-36088; www.randypike.co.uk; r Mon-Fri £200, Sat & Sun £225) Managed by the owners of Grasmere's Jumble Room restaurant, Andy & Chrissy Hill, this former hunting lodge feels more like a stay in the country with friends than a night in a B&B. The three rooms ooze bohemian style: distressed wood floors, quirky furniture and mix-and-match fabrics, plus iPods loaded up with music. There's even a Tardis in the garden.

The house is about 2.5 miles from Ambleside, off the B5286 to Hawkshead.

Waterhead Hotel HOTEL £££

(08458-504503; www.englishlakes.co.uk; Lake Rd; r £140-350;) Ambleside's main hotel has a super position beside the lake shore. The exterior is classic Lakeland, all solid stone and bay windows, but inside it's very much a modern hotel with spacious rooms stocked with heritage furniture and designer fabrics, and a sophisticated restaurant, the Mountain View. It's very family friendly and there are good online discounts.

Eating

Apple Pie CAFE £

(015394-33679; www.applepieambleside.co.uk; Rydal Rd; lunches £4-10; 9am-5.30pm) For a quick lunch stop, you won't go far wrong at this friendly little caff, which serves stuffed sandwiches, hot pies, baked spuds and yummy cakes (the apple pie is a local legend). It also has some great-value rooms (doubles £60 to £80) in the house next door.

Zeffirelli's ITALIAN £

(015394-33845; www.zeffirellis.com; Compston Rd; pizzas & mains £8-14; 11am-10pm) A beloved local landmark, Zeff's is often packed out for its quality pizza and pasta. The £20.75 Double Feature deal includes two courses and a ticket to the cinema (p593) next door.

Fellini's VEGETARIAN ££

(015394-32487; www.fellinisambleside.com; Church St; mains £12.95; 5.30-10pm;) Fear not, veggies: even in the land of the Cumberland sausage and the tattie hotpot (lamb, vegetable and potato stew), you won't go hungry thanks to Fellini's sophisticated 'vegeterranean' food. The dishes are creative – think brazil nut, hazelnut and almond roast or onion, leek and feta filo pie.

Lucy's on a Plate CAFE, BISTRO ££

(015394-31191; www.lucysofambleside.co.uk; Church St; mains £12.95-20.95; 9am-5pm Mon-Fri, to 10pm Sat & Sun) This long-standing boho bistro has been an Ambleside feature for years – and it's still popular. The decor's eclectic – mix-and-match furniture, knick-knacks – and the dishes are similarly quirky (for Rumpy Pumpy, Wild About Bambi and Bobbing Bobotie, read roast lamb, venison and South African stew).

★Lake Road Kitchen BISTRO £££

(☎015394-22012; www.lakeroadkitchen.co.uk; Lake Rd; 5-/8-course tasting menu £50/80; ⏰6-9.30pm Wed-Sun) This much-lauded new bistro has brought some dazzle to Ambleside's dining scene. Its Noma-trained head chef James Cross explores the 'food of the north', and his multicourse tasting menus are chock-full of locally sourced, seasonal and foraged ingredients, from shore-sourced seaweed to forest-picked mushrooms. Presentation is impeccable, flavours are experimental and the Scandi-inspired decor is just so. A meal not to miss.

★Old Stamp House BISTRO £££

(☎015394-32775; www.oldstamphouse.com; Church St; dinner mains £19-26; ⏰12.30-2pm Wed-Sat, 6.30-10pm Tue-Sat) An Ambleside treat: classy food with impeccable Cumbrian provenance. The dishes feel simultaneously familiar and fresh – Herdwick hogget (lamb) freshened with peas, beans and barley stew or roast duck with salsify, chicory and orange. It's in the cellar of the building where Wordsworth once worked as Distributor of Stamps: beams, whitewashed walls, scuffed wood and monochrome photos set a stylish scene.

Drinking & Entertainment

Ambleside has plenty of pubs: locals favour the **Golden Rule** (☎015394-32257; www.robinsonsbrewery.com/goldenrule; Smithy Brow) for its ale selection, while the **Royal Oak** (☎015394-33382; www.johnbarras.com/pub/royal-oak-ambleside/s6627/; Market Pl) packs in the post hike punters.

Zeffirelli's Cinema CINEMA

(☎015394-33100; Compston Rd; tickets before/after 6.45pm £7/8.50) Ambleside's two-screen Zeffirelli's Cinema is next to Zeffirelli's restaurant (p592), with extra screens in a converted church down the road.

Information

Hub (☎015394-32582; tic@thehubofambleside.com; Central Bldgs, Market Cross; ⏰9am-5pm) The tourist office and the post office are both here.

Getting There & Around

BICYCLE

Biketreks (☎015394-31505; www.biketreks.net; Rydal Rd; per day £20)

Ghyllside Cycles (☎015394-33592; www.ghyllside.co.uk; The Slack; per day £18)

BUS

Bus 555 Runs at least hourly (including Sundays) to Grasmere and Keswick (£8.20), Bowness and Windermere (£5.20) and Kendal (£6.70) in the opposite direction.

Bus 599 Open-top service that leaves at least hourly (including weekends) to Grasmere (£8.20), Bowness (£5.20), Windermere (£5.20) and Brockhole Visitor Centre; four buses daily continue to Kendal (£6.70). Prices similar to bus 555.

Bus 505 To Hawkshead and Coniston (£4.20, hourly including Sundays).

Bus 516 To Elterwater and Langdale (£3.70, seven daily).

Grasmere

POP 1458

Even without its connections to the Romantic poets, gorgeous Grasmere would still be one of the Lakes' biggest draws. It's one of the prettiest of the Lakeland hamlets, huddled at the edge of an island-studded lake surrounded by woods, pastures and slate-coloured hills, but most of the thousands of trippers come in search of its famous former resident, the poet William Wordsworth, who set up home at nearby Dove Cottage in 1799. With such a rich literary heritage, Grasmere, unsurprisingly, gets busy.

Sights

★Dove Cottage HISTORIC BUILDING

(☎015394-35544; www.wordsworth.org.uk; adult/child £7.50/4.50; ⏰9.30am-5.30pm) On the edge of Grasmere, this tiny, creeper-clad cottage (formerly a pub called the Dove & Olive Bough) was famously inhabited by William Wordsworth between 1799 and 1808. The cottage's cramped rooms are full of artefacts: try to spot the poet's passport, a pair of his spectacles and a portrait (given to him by Sir Walter Scott) of his favourite dog Pepper. Entry is by timed ticket to avoid overcrowding and includes an informative guided tour.

Wordsworth lived here happily with his sister Dorothy, wife Mary and three children John, Dora and Thomas until 1808 when the family moved to another nearby house at Allen Bank and the cottage was rented by Thomas de Quincey (author of *Confessions of an English Opium Eater*).

Tickets also include admission to the **Wordsworth Museum & Art Gallery** next door, which houses one of the nation's main collections relating to the Romantic movement, including many original manuscripts and some creepy death masks of some famous Romantic figures.

St Oswald's Church CHURCH
(Church Stile) In the churchyard of this tiny chapel in the centre of Grasmere are the Wordsworth's family graves: look out for tombstones belonging to William, Mary, Dorothy and all three children. Samuel Taylor Coleridge's son Hartley is also buried here.

Grasmere Lake & Rydal Water LAKE
Quiet paths lead along the shorelines of Grasmere's twin-set lakes. Rowing boats can be hired at the northern end of Grasmere Lake from the **Grasmere Tea Gardens** (☎015394-35590; Stock Lane; ⌚9.30am-5pm), which is a five-minute walk from the village centre.

Sleeping

Grasmere Hostel HOSTEL £
(☎015394-35055; www.grasmerehostel.co.uk; Broadrayne Farm; dm £20-23; P @) This stylish indie hostel has a vaguely Scandi feel, with unexpected luxuries like a Nordic sauna, skylights, two kitchens and en suite bathrooms for each dorm. Porthole windows provide impressive views over the fells. It's in a converted farmhouse on the A591 about 1.5 miles north of the village, near the Traveller's Rest pub.

TOP LAKE DISTRICT CAMPSITES

In addition to the four excellent campsites run by the National Trust (near Ambleside, Great Langdale, Wasdale and Coniston), there are more great places to sleep under the stars:

Bowkerstead Farm (p597)

Fisherground Farm (p602)

Syke Farm (☎01768-770222; www.sykefarmcampsite.com; adult/child £8/4; ⌚Easter-Oct)

Quiet Site (☎07768-727016; www.thequietsite.co.uk; campsites £15-37, pods £35-60, hobbit holes £65-90; ⌚year-round; P wifi)

Seatoller Farm (☎017687-77232; www.seatollerfarm.co.uk; adult/child £7/3.50; ⌚Easter-Oct)

Heidi's Grasmere Lodge B&B ££
(☎0774-382 7252; www.heidisgrasmerelodge.co.uk; Red Lion Sq; d £99-130; wifi) This plush B&B plonked above Heidi's cafe in the centre of the village offers six superfeminine rooms full of frilly cushions and Cath Kidston–style patterns. They're quite small but very comfy: room 6 has its own sun patio, reached via a spiral staircase.

How Foot Lodge B&B ££
(☎015394-35366; www.howfootlodge.co.uk; Town End; d £76-85; P) Just a stroll from Dove Cottage, this stone house has six rooms finished in fawns and beiges; the nicest are the deluxe doubles, one with a sun terrace and the other with a private sitting room. Rates are an absolute bargain considering the location.

★**Forest Side** BOUTIQUE HOTEL £££
(☎015394-35250; www.theforestside.com; r incl full board £279-399; P wifi) For out-and-out luxury, this boutique beauty is the place. Run by renowned hotelier Andrew Wildsmith, it's a design palace: chic interiors decorated with crushed-velvet sofas, bird-of-paradise wallpaper, stag heads and 20 swish rooms classed from 'Cosy' to 'Jolly Good', 'Superb', 'Grand' and 'Master'. Chef Kevin Tickle previously worked at L'Enclume, and now runs the stellar restaurant here using produce from the kitchen garden.

★**Daffodil Hotel** BOUTIQUE HOTEL £££
(☎015394-63550; www.daffodilhotel.co.uk; d £99-159, ste £179-259; P wifi family) Opened in 2012, this upscale hotel occupies a Victorian building but the 78 rooms zing with modern style: swirly carpets, art prints and bold shades of lime, purple and turquoise. There's a choice of lake or valley views and lovely bathrooms with pan-head showers and Molton Brown bath products. A fine restaurant and luxurious spa complete the package. Rather good.

It's just off the A591 heading north towards Grasmere from Ambleside; if you pass Dove Cottage, you've missed it.

Eating & Drinking

Baldry's Tea Room CAFE £
(☎015394-35301; Red Lion Sq; lunch £5-9; ⌚10am-5pm) As traditionally English as a Sunday roast, this old-school tearoom is the spot for a classic cream tea served in a bone-china pot and accompanied by buttery scones, flapjacks or a slice of Victo-

ria sponge. There are rarebits, salads and corned beef sandwiches for lunch too.

★Jumble Room MODERN BRITISH ££

(☎015394-35188; www.thejumbleroom.co.uk; Langdale Rd; dinner mains £14.50-21; ⏲5.30-9.30pm Wed-Mon) Husband-and-wife team Andy and Crissy Hill have turned this village bistro into a much-loved dining landmark. It's a really fun and friendly place to dine. Spotty crockery, cow murals and primary colours set the boho tone, matched by a magpie menu taking in everything from lentil dhal and Japanese-spiced steak to pinatubo chicken (cooked in Asian spices and coconut milk).

Lewis's BISTRO ££

(☎015394-35266; Broadgate; mains £12.50-18.95; ⏲noon-2pm & 6-9pm) Formerly Sara's Bistro, this small restaurant turns out hearty dishes ranging from roast lamb with red wine jus to Morecambe Bay sea bass with samphire. It's enthusiastically run by its eponymous owner. This is homespun rather than haute cuisine and a little overpriced, but worth a try.

Traveller's Rest PUB

(☎015394-35604; www.lakedistrictinns.co.uk/travellers-rest; A591, near Grasmere; mains £8-16; ⏲10am-11pm) With its sputtering fires and inglenook bar, this 16th-century coaching inn on the A591 makes a fine place for a pint and a simple pie supper.

Shopping

★Sarah Nelson's Gingerbread Shop FOOD

(☎015394-35428; www.grasmeregingerbread.co.uk; Church Cottage; ⏲9.15am-5.30pm Mon-Sat, 12.30-5pm Sun) In business since 1854, this famous sweetshop next to the village church makes Grasmere's essential souvenir: traditional gingerbread with a half-biscuity, half-cakey texture (six/12 pieces for £3.50/5.95) cooked using the original top-secret recipe. Friendly service by ladies dressed in frilly pinafores and starched bonnets is an added bonus.

Getting There & Away

The regular 555 bus runs from Windermere to Grasmere (15 minutes) via Ambleside, Rydal Church and Dove Cottage. The open-top 599 (two or three per hour in summer) runs from Grasmere via Ambleside, Troutbeck Bridge, Windermere and Bowness. Both buses charge the same fares: Grasmere to Ambleside is £5.80, to Windermere it's £6.50.

Hawkshead

POP 1640

Lakeland villages don't come much more perfect than pint-sized Hawkshead, a jumble of whitewashed cottages, cobbled lanes and old pubs lost among bottle-green countryside between Ambleside and Coniston. The village has literary cachet too – Wordsworth went to school here and Beatrix Potter's husband, William Heelis, worked here as a solicitor for many years (his old office is now an art gallery).

Cars are banned in the village centre.

Sights

Beatrix Potter Gallery GALLERY

(NT; www.nationaltrust.org.uk/beatrix-potter-gallery; Red Lion Sq; adult/child £6/3; ⏲10.30am-5pm Sat-Thu mid-Mar–Oct) As well as being a children's author, Beatrix Potter was also a talented botanical painter and amateur naturalist. This small gallery (housed in what were once the offices of Potter's husband, solicitor William Heelis) contains a collection of her watercolours depicting local flora and fauna. She was particularly fascinated by mushrooms. The gallery celebrated Beatrix Potter's 150th birthday in 2016 with a special exhibition featuring extracts from the author's coded journal.

★Tarn Hows LAKE

(NT; www.nationaltrust.org.uk/coniston-and-tarn-hows) FREE Two miles off the B5285 from Hawkshead, a winding country lane wends its way to this famously photogenic artificial lake, now owned by the National Trust. Trails wind their way around the lake shore and surrounding woodland – keep your eyes peeled for red squirrels in the treetops.

There's a small National Trust car park, but it fills quickly. Several buses, including the 505, stop nearby.

★Hill Top HISTORIC BUILDING

(NT; ☎015394-36269; www.nationaltrust.org.uk/hill-top; adult/child £10/5, admission to garden & shop free; ⏲house 10am-5.30pm Mon-Thu, 10am-4.30pm Fri-Sun, garden to 5.45pm Mon-Thu, to 5pm Fri-Sun) Two miles south of Hawkshead in the tiny village of Near Sawrey, this idyllic farmhouse was purchased in 1905 by Beatrix Potter and was used as inspiration for many of her tales: the house features directly in *Samuel Whiskers, Tom Kitten, Pigling Bland* and *Jemima Puddleduck,* among others, and you might recognise the kitchen

THE CROSS LAKES EXPERIENCE

If you're not driving, the **Cross Lakes Experience** (www.mountain-goat.co.uk/Cross-Lakes-Experience; adult/child return £12.45/7.15; Apr-Nov) is a handy way to travel from Bowness to Hawkshead, including travel on the Windermere Ferry (p589) and a minibus on to Hill Top and Hawkshead. It's operated by Mountain Goat (p589).

garden from *Peter Rabbit*. Entry is by timed ticket; it's very, very popular, so try visiting in the late afternoon or on weekdays to avoid the worst crowds.

Clad in climbing ivy and stocked with memorabilia, the house looks like something out of a storybook, but Beatrix only actually lived here until her marriage to William Heelis. In 1913 the newly wed couple moved to a larger farm at Castle Cottage nearby, where the author wrote many more tales and lived until her death in 1943.

She bequeathed Hill Top (along with Castle Cottage and more than 1600 hectares of land) to the National Trust with the proviso that the house should be left with her belongings and decor in situ. The house formed the centrepiece for celebrations to mark the author's 150th birthday in 2016.

Sleeping & Eating

Hawkshead YHA HOSTEL £
(0845-371 9321; www.yha.org.uk; dm £10-21; P @) This impressive YHA is lodged in a Grade II–listed Regency house overlooking Esthwaite Water, a mile from Hawkshead along the Newby Bridge road. It's a fancy spot considering the bargain prices: the dorms and kitchen are large and there are camping pods outside as well as bike rentals. The 505 stops at the end of the lane.

Yewfield B&B ££
(015394-36765; www.yewfield.co.uk; Hawkshead Hill; s £49, d £106-140; P) This rambling Victorian mansion is one of the best options around Hawkshead, although it's out of the way on the road to Coniston, near Tarn Hows. It's run by the owners of Zeffirelli's in Ambleside and offers a range of comfortable rooms and antique-stocked lounges, plus ecofriendly touches like a wood-mass boiler and all-veggie breakfasts. Discounts available for three nights.

Summer Hill Country House HOTEL ££
(015394-36180; www.summerhillcountryhouse.com; Hawkshead Hill; d £102-122; P @) On Hawkshead Hill, this 1700s house has a wonderfully out-of-the-way setting, 3 miles from both Coniston and Hawkshead. The five rooms vary in shape and size, but all feature posh bath products and net-connected Mac Minis for getting online or watching DVDs. The garden boasts sculptures and a summer house that belonged to John Ruskin.

Love Shack COTTAGE £££
(015394-41242; www.lakedistrictloveshack.com; Cunsey; 3 days £500-850, r per week £700-1250) Built on the site of a 1960s love shack (hence the name), this supercool, ecofriendly cabin is the brainchild of artists Karen Guthrie and Adam Sutherland. It's a mix of modern and retro – reclaimed timber, organic paints and oak floors meet funky furnishings and shagadelic love seats, all in a secluded woodland location not far from Near Sawrey.

Queen's Head PUB FOOD ££
(015394-36271; www.queensheadhawkshead.co.uk; Main St; mains £12-15; noon-3pm & 6-10pm) The best choice of several pubs in Hawkshead, with the requisite head-knockingly low ceilings and oak-panelled walls. Decent food plus pleasant four-poster rooms (£98–£158) above and more in a modern annexe.

★ **Drunken Duck** PUB FOOD £££
(015394-36347; www.drunkenduckinn.co.uk; Barngates; lunch mains £7-12, dinner mains £22; noon-2pm & 6-10pm; P) Long one of the Lakes' premier dining destinations, the Drunken Duck blends historic pub and fine-dining restaurant. On a wooded crossroads on the top of Hawkshead Hill, it's renowned for its luxurious food and home-brewed ales, and the flagstones and sporting prints conjure a convincing country atmosphere. Book well ahead for dinner or take your chances at lunchtime.

If you fancy staying, you'll find the rooms (£105 to £325) are just as fancy as the food. The pub's tricky to find: drive along the B5286 from Hawkshead towards Ambleside and look out for the brown signs.

Getting There & Away

Hawkshead is linked with Windermere, Ambleside and Coniston by bus 505 (£3.50 to £4.50; hourly including Sundays).

Coniston

POP 641

Hunkered beneath the pock-marked peak known as the **Old Man of Coniston** (803m), this lakeside village was originally established to support the local mining industry and the surrounding hilltops are littered with the remains of old copper workings. These days most people visit with two things in mind: to cruise on the lovely old Coniston Launch or to tramp to the top of the Old Man, a steep but rewarding return hike of around 7 miles.

Coniston's other claim to fame is as the location for a string of world-record speed attempts made by Sir Malcolm Campbell and his son, Donald, between the 1930s and 1960s. Tragically, after beating the record several times, Donald was killed during an attempt in 1967 when his futuristic jetboat *Bluebird* flipped at around 320mph. The boat and its pilot were recovered in 2001, and Campbell was buried in the cemetery of St Andrew's church.

Sights

Brantwood HISTORIC BUILDING

(015394-41396; www.brantwood.org.uk; adult/child £7.50/free, gardens only £4.95/free; 10.30am-5pm mid-Mar–mid-Nov, to 4pm Wed-Sun mid-Nov–mid-Mar) John Ruskin (1819–1900) was one of the great thinkers of 19th-century society. A polymath, philosopher, painter and critic, he expounded views on everything from Venetian architecture to lace-making. In 1871 Ruskin purchased this lakeside house and spent the next 20 years modifying it, championing handmade crafts (he even designed the wallpaper). Look out for his vast hoard of shells and several works by JMW Turner.

Boats run regularly from Coniston. Alternatively, look out for signs on the B5285.

Coniston Water LAKE

Coniston's gleaming 5-mile lake – the third largest in the Lake District after Windermere and Ullswater – is a half-mile walk from town along Lake Rd. The best way to explore the lake is on one of the two cruise services or, better still, by paddle. Dinghies, rowing boats, canoes, kayaks and motor boats can be hired from the **Coniston Boating Centre** (015394-41366; www.conistonboatingcentre.co.uk; Coniston Jetty).

Activities

Coniston Water famously inspired Arthur Ransome's classic children's tale *Swallows and Amazons*. Peel Island, towards the southern end of the lake, doubles in the book as Wild Cat Island, while the *Gondola* steam yacht allegedly gave Ransome the idea for Captain Flint's houseboat.

★ **Steam Yacht Gondola** BOATING

(NT; 015394-63850; www.nationaltrust.org.uk/steam-yacht-gondola; Coniston Jetty; half lake adult/child return £11/5.50, full lake adult/child/family £21.50/10/51) Built in 1859 and restored in the 1980s by the National Trust, this wonderful steam yacht looks like a cross between a Venetian *vaporetto* and an English houseboat, complete with cushioned saloons and polished wood seats. It's a stately way of seeing the lake, especially if you're visiting Brantwood, and it's even ecofriendly: since 2008 it's been powered by waste wood.

GRIZEDALE FOREST

Grizedale Forest (www.forestry.gov.uk/grizedale), stretching for 2428 hectares across the hilltops between Coniston Water and Esthwaite Water, has nine walking trails and seven cycling trails to explore – some are easy and designed for families while others are geared towards hardcore hikers and bikers. Along the way you'll spot more than 40 outdoor sculptures hidden in the undergrowth, created by artists since 1977 (there's a useful online guide at (www.grizedalesculpture.org). Visit the tourist office (0300 067 4495; grizedale@forestry.gsi.gov.uk; 10am-5pm summer, 10am-4pm winter) for more information.

Velo Bikes (01229-860335; www.velobikes.co.uk; adult/child per half-day from £20/12; 9am-5pm) Rents out mountain bikes and supplies trail maps. Last hire at 3pm.

Bowkerstead Farm (01229-860208; www.grizedale-camping.co.uk; Satterthwaite; adult/child £7/3, camping pods £30; Apr-Sep) Pitch beside the trees of Grizedale Forest, either in your own tent, a luxury yurt or a timber eco pod. There's also a bunk-barn for hikers and a farm shop for supplies.

There are several 45-minute half-lake trips per day from mid-March to October. Longer 105-minute full-lake cruises run a few times per week and cover the history of Ransome, the Campbells and Ruskin. There's also a Walkers' Cruise and special picnic and Sunday-afternoon-tea cruises in summer. There's a 10% discount for National Trust members.

Coniston Launch BOATING

(015394-36216; www.conistonlaunch.co.uk; Coniston Jetty; northern service adult/child return £11/5.50, southern £16.50/8.25) Coniston's two modern launches have been solar powered since 2005. The regular 45-minute **northern service** calls at the Waterhead Hotel, Torver and Brantwood, while the 105-minute **southern service** sails from Monday to Thursday with a different theme depending on the day; it's Swallows and Amazons on Monday and Wednesday, and the Campbells on Coniston on Tuesday and Thursday.

Sleeping

Coppermines YHA HOSTEL £

(0845-371 9630; www.yha.org.uk; dm from £16; reception 7-11am & 5-10pm Easter-Oct) Up a steep rock road 1.5km from the village, this rustic hostel once provided accommodation for local copper miners. It's now a walkers' favourite, allowing guests to get an early start on the Old Man; dorms are small but there's a kitchen, showers and even a licensed bar.

Lakeland House B&B ££

(015394-41303; www.lakelandhouse.co.uk; Tilberthwaite Ave; s £30-60, d £65-99, ste £90-160) You're smack-bang in the centre of Coniston at this good-value, basic B&B above Hollands cafe. The rooms have been recently renovated with fresh colours and updated bathrooms; some have dormer windows, others views of the Old Man. The Lookout Suite has its own sitting room and in-room bathtub.

Bank Ground Farm B&B ££

(015394-41264; www.bankground.com; East of the Lake; d from £90; P) This lakeside farmhouse has literary cachet: Arthur Ransome used it as the model for Holly Howe Farm in *Swallows and Amazons*. Parts of the house date back to the 15th century, so the rooms are snug. Some have sleigh beds, others exposed beams. The tearoom is a beauty too, and there are cottages for longer stays. Two-night minimum.

Eating & Drinking

Steam Bistro BISTRO ££

(01539-441928; www.steambistro.co.uk; Tilberthwaite Ave; 2-/3-course menu £18.95/22.95; 6-11pm Wed-Sun) This swish new bistro has become the go-to address for Coniston dining. Its magpie menu borrows lots of global flavours – you'll find everything from crispy chilli beef with pak choi to Greek-style *kleftiko* (slow-cooked lamb) with minted pesto on the specials board. Even better, they're all *prix fixe* (fixed-price menus).

Sun Hotel PUB

(015394-41248; www.thesunconiston.com; 10am-11pm) Famously used as an HQ by Donald Campbell during his fateful campaign, this trad boozer is a good place for a pint, with a fell-view beer garden and cosy crannies to hunker down in – look out for Campbell memorabilia. Food (mains £12 to £20) is hit-and-miss at busy times. It's up a small hill beside the bridge over Church Beck.

Black Bull PUB

(015394-41335; www.conistonbrewery.com/black-bull-coniston.htm; Yewdale Rd; 10am-11pm) Coniston's main meeting spot, the old Black Bull offers a warren of rooms and a popular outside terrace. The pub grub's good (mains £8 to £18) but it's mainly known for its home-brewed ales: Bluebird Bitter and Old Man Ale are always on tap and there are seasonal ones too.

Information

Coniston Tourist Office (015394-41533; www.conistontic.org; Ruskin Ave; 9.30am-5.30pm Easter-Oct, to 4pm Nov-Easter) This privately run tourist office has stacks of info on the Coniston area, including a schedule of guided walks.

Getting There & Away

Bus 505 runs to Windermere (£4.50, hourly including Sundays) via Ambleside, with a couple of daily connections to Kendal (£9.50, 1¼ hours).

The Coniston Bus-and-Boat ticket (adult/child £18/8) includes return bus travel on the 505, plus a trip on the launch and entry to Brantwood.

Elterwater & Great Langdale

Travelling north from Coniston, the road passes into the wild, empty landscape of Great Langdale, one of Lakeland's iconic hiking valleys. As you pass the pretty village of Elterwater, imposing fells stack up like dominoes along the horizon, looming over a pastoral patchwork of tumbledown barns and lime-green fields.

Activities

Langdale's best-known hike is the multipeak route up and over the **Langdale Pikes**: Pike O' Stickle (709m), Loft Crag (682m), Harrison Stickle (736m) and Pavey Ark (700m). Across the valley are the rippled summits of **Bowfell** (902m) and the **Crinkle Crags**, which represent a serious challenge even for experienced walkers.

Sleeping

Great Langdale Campsite CAMPSITE £
(NT; ☎015394-63862; www.nationaltrust.org.uk/features/great-langdale-campsite; Great Langdale; sites £13-23, extra adult £6, pods £35-57.50; ⊙arrivals 3-7pm Sat-Thu, to 9pm Fri; P) Quite possibly the most spectacularly positioned campsite in the Lake District, spread out over grassy meadows overlooked by Langdale's fells. It gets crowded in high season, but 140 sites can be booked in advance; another 30 are on a first-come, first-served basis. Camping pods and yurts are also available.

Langdale YHA HOSTEL £
(☎0845-371 9748; www.yha.org.uk; High Close, Loughrigg; dm £13-25; ⊙reception 7-10am & 5-10.15pm Mar-Oct; P @) If you didn't know this was a hostel, you'd think it was a grand country hotel: vast, Victorian, set in private grounds with its own arboretum. Big dorms with sash windows overlook the fells and there's a cavernous kitchen and lounge (with original ornate fireplace). The cafe serves breakfast, packed lunches and a two-course 'supper club'.

★**Old Dungeon Ghyll** HOTEL ££
(☎015394-37272; www.odg.co.uk; Great Langdale; s £58, d £116-132; P 🛜 🐾) Affectionately known as the ODG, this inn is awash with Lakeland heritage: many famous walkers have stayed here, including Prince Charles and mountaineer Chris Bonington. It's endearingly olde worlde (well-worn furniture, four-poster beds) and even if you're not staying, the slate-floored, fire-warmed Hiker's Bar is a must for a posthike pint – it's been the hub of Langdale's social life for decades.

★**Brimstone Hotel** HOTEL £££
(☎015394-38062; www.brimstonehotel.co.uk; Langdale Estate, Great Langdale; r £220-350; P) This lavish cottage complex on the Langdale Estate takes luxury to another level. The huge suites are more London-chic than Lakeland-cosy; mezzanine floors, sleek tiles, private patios and futuristic log-burners are standard, and then of course there's a reading room, spa, restaurant and private woodland. A new spa is being built, which should be open by the time you read this.

★**Eltermere Inn** HOTEL £££
(☎015394-37207; www.eltermere.co.uk; Elterwater; r £145-295; P 🛜) This charming inn is one of Lakeland's loveliest backwater boltholes. Rooms are simple and classic, tastefully decorated in fawns and taupes with quirky features such as window seats and free-standing baths. The food's excellent too, served in the inn's snug bar; afternoon tea is served on the lawn on sunny days.

Eating

Stickle Barn PUB FOOD £
(☎015394-37356; Great Langdale; mains £6-12) A walkers' fave, this lively pub near the Old Dungeon Ghyll serves filling food such as curries, chillis and hotpots.

Chesters by the River CAFE ££
(☎015394-32553; www.chestersbytheriver.co.uk; Skelwith Bridge; lunch mains £8-15; ⊙9am-5pm) Beside a rattling brook at Skelwith Bridge, halfway between Ambleside and Elterwater, this smart cafe is definitely more gourmet than greasy spoon: delicious salads, specials and cakes make it well worth a stop. There's a chic gift shop too; items include slate souvenirs from the workshop around the corner.

Getting There & Away

Bus 516 (six daily Monday to Friday, seven on weekends) is the only bus, with stops at Ambleside, Skelwith Bridge, Elterwater and the Old Dungeon Ghyll Hotel in Great Langdale. The fare from Ambleside all the way into Great Langdale is £4.80.

1

2

England's Great Outdoors

JOE DUNCKLEY / SHUTTERSTOCK ©

The English love the great outdoors, and every weekend sees a mass exodus from the towns and cities to the hills, moors and coastline. Hiking and biking are the most popular pursuits but there's a huge range of activities available – and getting wet and muddy can actually be a highlight of your trip!

Walking

England can seem crowded, but away from the cities there are many beautiful areas, perfect for walking. You can go for a short riverside stroll or a major hike over mountain ranges – or anything in between. The best places include the Cotswolds, the Lake District and the Yorkshire Dales.

Cycling

A bike is ideal for getting to know England's countryside. Areas such as Suffolk, Yorkshire and Wiltshire offer a vast network of quiet country roads ideal for cycle touring. For off-road fun, mountain bikers can go further into the wilds in places such as the Peak District, the North Yorkshire Moors and the South Downs.

. Riding along the North Pennines (p620) **2.** Surfers at Newquay 339), Cornwall **3.** Hadrian's Wall (p633) has a range of easy walks

Horse Riding

If you want to explore the hills and moors at a more leisurely place, seeing the wilder parts of England from horseback is the way to go. In rural areas and national parks such as Dartmoor and Northumberland, there are riding centres catering to all levels of proficiency.

Surfing

England may not be an obvious destination for surfers, but conditions can be surprisingly good at key locations. Top of the list are the west-facing coasts of Cornwall and Devon, while there are smaller scenes on the east coast, notably in Norfolk and Yorkshire.

Eskdale

POP 304

Historically the valley of Eskdale was known for its many mines, which extracted rich reserves of iron, copper and other minerals from the surrounding fells. These days it's hikers' country and a pocket-sized steam railway that formerly served the mines has now been turned into a much-loved tourist attraction.

The village of Eskdale Green holds a traditional country fair over the August Bank Holiday, when local shepherds and breeders show off their prize Herdwicks and there are displays of hound trailing, fell running and local craftwork.

Sleeping & Eating

Fisherground Farm CAMPSITE £
(019467-23349; www.fishergroundcampsite.co.uk; adult/child £6.50/3.50, car £2.50; Mar-Oct;) Family-friendly camping in idyllic Eskdale, handy for the Ravenglass & Eskdale Railway. It gets very busy in summer so it's better reserved for the shoulder months.

Stanley House B&B ££
(019467-23327; www.stanleyghyll-eskdale.co.uk; Eskdale; s £64, d £110-120, f £140-170; P) This turn-of-the-century house is halfway down the Eskdale valley, near Beckfoot station. It's a real home away from home: guests are given the run of the place with cosy lounges, rhododendron-filled gardens and an 'open larder' stocked with help-yourself beans, bread and spaghetti hoops. First-floor rooms are dog friendly and the house's hot water and heating comes from an eco-friendly biomass boiler.

Woolpack Inn PUB FOOD ££
(019467-23230; www.woolpack.co.uk; Boot; mains £8.50-14.95; P) This old Eskdale inn has a split personality: half contemporary cafe, half trad pub. Each has its own corresponding menu: salads, cakes and light bites in the cafe, filling tatie hotpot and Cumberland bangers in the inn. Rooms are plain but decent value (singles £60, doubles £80 to £110) and most have views of the Eskdale fells.

Getting There & Away

The trains of the Ravenglass & Eskdale Railway (p614) run up the valley as far as the village of Dalegarth, a short walk from Boot.

Wasdale

Carving its way for 5 miles from the Cumbrian coast, the craggy, wind-lashed valley of Wasdale is where the Lake District scenery takes a turn for the wild. Ground out by a long-extinct glacier, the valley is home to the Lake District's highest and wildest peaks, as well as the steely grey expanse of Wastwater, England's deepest and coldest lake. Wasdale's fells are an irresistible draw for hikers, especially those looking to conquer England's tallest mountain, **Scafell Pike** (978m).

THE STEEPEST ROAD IN ENGLAND?

Zigzagging over fells between the valleys of **Little Langdale** and **Eskdale** is one of the Lake District's most infamous mountain roads. Used since ancient times and later substantially improved by the Romans, this old packhorse route provided a vital trading link between the central valleys of Lakeland and the ports dotted along the Cumbrian Coast. En route it traverses both of England's highest road passes, **Wrynose** and **Hardknott**, and in places the road reaches forbidding gradients of 1 in 3. At the top of Hardknott Pass, there's a ruined Roman fort where you can still see the remains of the walls, parade ground and commandant's house. The views from here to the coast are stunning.

It's perfectly drivable if you take things slow and steady, but probably best avoided if you're a hesitant reverser or don't like driving next to steep drops (caravans and buses should definitely steer clear). Things to note: it's single-carriage most of the way, and passing places are few and far between, so be prepared for vehicles going the opposite way. Also make sure your brakes are in good order and top up the water in your radiator – you'll do most of the road in first or second gear.

To get to the passes from Ambleside, follow road signs on the A593 to Skelwith Bridge, then turn off to Little Langdale. When you reach the Three Shires Inn, the road gets really steep. Alternatively, you can approach from the west: drive along the A595 coast road and turn off towards Eskdale, then follow the road past Boot to the passes.

Sights & Activities

Wastwater LAKE

In his 1810 *Guide to the Lakes,* William Wordsworth described Wastwater as 'long, narrow, stern and desolate', and it's a description that still seems apt. The lake itself is owned by the National Trust and is the deepest body of water in the national park (around 79m at its deepest point). It's also one of the coldest and clearest; very little life can survive in its inhospitable waters, apart from the hardy Arctic char.

★Scafell Pike HIKING

The roof of England at 978m, England's highest mountain features on every self-respecting hiker's bucket list. The classic route starts from Wasdale Head; it's hard going but within the reach of most moderately fit walkers, although it's steep and hard to navigate in bad weather. It's a return trip of around six to seven hours and proper gear is essential: raincoat, rucksack (backpack), map, food and water, and decent hiking boots. A favourable weather forecast is preferable to make the most of the views.

Sleeping

Wasdale Hall YHA HOSTEL £

(☎0845-371 9350; www.yha.org.uk; Wasdale Hall, Nether Wasdale; dm £18-30; ⊙reception 8-10am & 5-10.30pm; P) This lakeside hostel on the shores of Wastwater has the kind of location you'd normally pay through the nose for. It's in a 19th-century mock-Tudor mansion that still boasts most of its period architecture, including original roof trusses and latticed windows. It has the usual self-catering facilities plus a very decent restaurant.

Wasdale Head Campsite CAMPSITE £

(NT; ☎bookings 015394-63862; www.ntlakes-campsites.org.uk; sites £13-23, extra adult £6, pods £35-57.50; ⊙reception 8-10.30am Mon-Fri, 8-10.30am & 5-6.30pm Sat & Sun) This National Trust campsite is in a fantastically wild spot, nestled beneath the Scafell range. Facilities are basic (laundry room, showers), but the views are out of this world. Camping pods and tipis provide a bit more shelter in case Wasdale's notorious weather decides to make an appearance.

★Wasdale Head Inn B&B ££

(☎019467-26229; www.wasdale.com; s £59, d £118-130, tr £177; P 📶) Hunkering beneath the brooding bulk of Scafell Pike, this 19th-century hostelry is full of hill-walking heritage. It's wonderfully old-fashioned and covered in vintage photos and climbing memorabilia. The rooms are cosy, with roomier suites in a converted stable. The wood-panelled dining room serves fine food, with humbler grub and ales from the Great Gable Brewing Co available in Ritson's Bar.

Getting There & Away

There are no longer any scheduled bus services to Wasdale Head.

Gosforth Taxis (☎01946-734800)

Cockermouth

POP 9146

Set at the confluence of the River Cocker and River Derwent, the Georgian town of Cockermouth is best known as the birthplace of William Wordsworth and the home base of the renowned Jenning's Brewery. Unfortunately, its position beside two major rivers means it has suffered serious flooding – most recently in 2009 and 2015, when much of the town centre was swamped.

Sights

★Wordsworth House HISTORIC BUILDING

(NT; ☎01900-824805; Main St; adult/child £7.20/3.60; ⊙11am-5pm Sat-Thu Mar-Oct) The Romantic poet William Wordsworth was born on 7 April 1770 at this handsome Georgian house at the end of Main St. Built around 1745, the house has been meticulously restored based on accounts from the Wordsworth archive: the kitchen, drawing room, study and bedrooms all look much as they would have to a young William. Costumed guides help bring things to life. Unfortunately the ground floor and kitchen garden were inundated in the 2015 floods; restoration work is ongoing.

Jennings Brewery BREWERY

(☎01900-821011; www.jenningsbrewery.co.uk; adult/child £9/4.50; ⊙guided tours 1.30pm Wed-Sat) Real-ale aficionados will be familiar with the Jennings name – it has been brewing beers since 1874 and its pints are pulled at pubs all over the Lake District. Guided tours trace the brewing process, followed by a tasting session of Cocker Hoop and Sneck Lifter in the Old Cooperage Bar. Children must be over 12.

OFF THE BEATEN TRACK

ENNERDALE

If you really want to leave the outside world behind, the remote valley of Ennerdale is definitely the place. Just to the north of Wasdale, this valley and its namesake lake were once home to slate mines and large timber plantations, but these are slowly being removed and the valley is being returned to nature as part of the Wild Ennerdale project (www.wildennerdale.co.uk).

Needless to say, the valley is paradise if you prefer your trails quiet. Several popular routes head over the fells to Wasdale, while walking towards Buttermere takes you past the **Black Sail YHA** (0845-371 9680; www.yha.org.uk; dm £25-30; reception 8am-10am & 5-10pm, hostel open mid-Mar–Oct), a marvellously remote hostel inside a shepherd's bothy. Much loved by mountaineers and hikers, it's become a YHA landmark. Space is very limited, so make sure you book ahead.

Sleeping & Eating

Six Castlegate B&B ££
(01900-826749; www.sixcastlegate.co.uk; 6 Castlegate; s £60-80, d £80-90; P) Georgian and Grade II–listed, this elegant B&B has a hint of grandeur. All the rooms are named after fells: go for Blencathra, Melbreak or Latrigg if you're after maximum space.

Old Homestead B&B ££
(01900-822223; www.byresteads.co.uk; Byresteads Farm; s £40-50, d £60-80; P) Byre is an old English dialect word meaning 'cowshed', but you certainly won't be roughing it with the animals at this lovely farm conversion. The rooms are sweet and traditional, blending classic pine, flagstones and rendered walls with modern luxuries like power showers and underfloor heating. The Cruck Rooms and Master's Loft are the pick of the bunch. It's 2 miles from Cockermouth.

★**Merienda** CAFE £
(017687-72024; www.merienda.co.uk; 7a Station St; mains £4-8; 8am-9pm Mon-Thu, 8am-10pm Fri & Sat, 9am-9pm Sun) This Cockermouth fave is now open daily and has recently opened a second branch in Keswick. The interior is light and airy and the Med-tinged food is packed with flavour, with a good balance between meat and veggie-friendly dishes. Carnivores might enjoy a generous slow-cooked BBQ brisket burger, while herbivores should try the excellent baked eggs with feta and aubergine.

Information

Tourist Office (01900-822634; www.cockermouth.org.uk; 4 Old Kings Arms Lane; 10am-4pm Mon-Fri, to 2pm Sat) In a new location just off the main street, next to Boots Chemists.

Getting There & Away

Bus X4/X5 (half-hourly Monday to Saturday, hourly Sunday) travels from Cockermouth to Keswick (£5.30) and Penrith (£7.10).

Keswick

POP 4821

The most northerly of the Lake District's major towns, Keswick has perhaps the most beautiful location of all: encircled by cloud-capped fells and nestled alongside the idyllic, island-studded lake of Derwentwater, a silvery curve criss-crossed by puttering cruise boats. It's also brilliantly positioned for further adventures into the nearby valleys of Borrowdale and Buttermere.

Sadly, the town suffered heavy damage during the 2015 floods when the rivers Greta and Derwent burst their banks; the lake level rose by roughly a metre and the A591 between Keswick and Grasmere was partially washed away, effectively cutting off the north and south halves of the national park. Many businesses found themselves under metres of water and two bridges on the popular Keswick to Threlkeld Railway Path vanished. The town is slowly getting back to business, but you can still expect some disruption and ongoing renovations when you visit.

Sights

★**Keswick Museum** MUSEUM
(017687-73263; www.keswickmuseum.org.uk; Station Rd; adult/child £4/2.50; 10am-4pm) Finally reopened after a long program of refurbishment, Keswick's quirky town museum explores the area's history, from ancient archaeology through to the arrival of industry in the Lakes. It's a diverse collection, taking in everything from neolithic axe-heads

mined in the Langdale valley to a huge collection of taxidermied butterflies. Its best-known exhibits are a 700-year-old mummified cat and the Musical Stones of Skiddaw, a weird instrument made from hornsfel rock that was once played for Queen Victoria.

Castlerigg Stone Circle MONUMENT
FREE Set on a hilltop a mile east of town, this jaw-dropping stone circle consists of 48 stones that are between 3000 and 4000 years old, surrounded by a dramatic ring of mountain peaks.

Lakes Distillery DISTILLERY
(☎017687-88850; www.lakesdistillery.com; tours £12.50; ⏲11am-6pm) The first and only distillery in the Lake District, this spirit-maker has made a big splash since opening in 2014. It's located on a 'model farm' built during the 1850s and was founded by a team of master distillers; so far its range includes a gin, a vodka and a flagship whisky. Guided tours take you through the process and include a tasting of the three spirits, plus a £5 voucher for use in the shop.

Activities

Hiking opportunities abound around Keswick. The most popular is Catbells (451m), a mini mountain on the west shore of Derwentwater, which is easily reached via the Keswick Launch. More challenging options include the imposing bulk of Skiddaw (931m), which looms north of town, and Blencathra (868m), another classic fell to the northeast.

The 2015 floods damaged parts of the paths on all three fells, but they were navigable at the time of writing – check with the tourist office to make sure.

★**Keswick Launch** BOATING
(☎017687-72263; www.keswick-launch.co.uk; round-the-lake adult/child/family £10.25/5.15/24) Shimmering to the south of Keswick, studded with islands and ringed by craggy fells, Derwentwater is undoubtedly one of the prettiest of the Lakeland lakes.

As always, getting out on the water is the best way to explore. The Keswick Launch runs regular cross-lake excursions, and rowboats and motor boats (£12/27 per hour) can be hired next to the jetties.

Keswick Adventure Centre OUTDOORS
(☎017687-75687; www.keswickadventurecentre.co.uk; Newlands) This activity centre in Keswick organises hikes and has a climbing wall.

Whinlatter Forest Park OUTDOORS
(www.forestry.gov.uk/whinlatter) FREE Encompassing 4.6 sq miles of pine, larch and spruce, Whinlatter is England's only true mountain forest, rising sharply to 790m about 5 miles from Keswick. The forest is a designated red squirrel reserve; you can check out live video feeds from squirrel cams at the visitor centre (☎01768-778469; ⏲10am-4pm). It's also home to two exciting mountain-bike trails and the **Go Ape** (www.goape.co.uk/days-out/whinlatter; adult/child £33/25; ⏲9am-5pm mid-Mar-Oct) treetop assault course. You can hire bikes from **Cyclewise** (☎017687-78711; www.cyclewise.co.uk; Whinlatter Forest Park; 3hr hire adult/child £19/15; ⏲10am-5pm), next to the visitor centre.

Keswick Mountain Bikes CYCLING
(☎017687-75202; www.keswickbikes.co.uk; 133 Main St; adult bikes per day £15-40; ⏲9.30am-5.30pm) Mountain bikes can be hired from Keswick Mountain Bikes. The road-specific shop is above the Lakeland Pedlar Cafe.

Festivals & Events

Keswick Mountain Festival OUTDOORS
(www.keswickmountainfestival.co.uk) This May festival celebrates all things mountainous.

Keswick Beer Festival BEER
(www.keswickbeerfestival.co.uk) Lots and lots of beer is drunk during Keswick's real-ale fest in June.

Sleeping

★**Howe Keld** B&B ££
(☎017687-72417; www.howekeld.co.uk; 5-7 The Heads; s £60-85, d £112-130; P 📶) This gold-standard B&B pulls out all the stops: goose-down duvets, slate-floored bathrooms, chic colours and locally made furniture. The best rooms have views across Crow Park and the golf course, and the breakfast is a pick-and-mix delight. Free parking is available on The Heads if there's space.

★**Lookout** B&B ££
(☎017687-80407; www.thelookoutkeswick.co.uk; Chestnut Hill; d £95-120; P 📶) The clue's in the name: this fine B&B is all about the views – there's a stunning panorama of fells filling every window. It's in a gabled 1920s house but feels modern with cappuccino-and-cream colour schemes, wooden beds and minimalist glass showers. Take Penrith Rd west and turn right onto Chestnut Hill; the B&B is on the left.

WORTH A TRIP

HONISTER PASS & MINE

From Borrowdale, a narrow, perilously steep road snakes up the fellside to Honister Pass, home to the last working slate mine left in the UK.

Honister Slate Mine (017687-77230; www.honister-slate-mine.co.uk; mine tour adult/child £12.50/7.50; tours 10.30am, 12.30pm & 3.30pm Mar-Oct) Underground tours venture deep into the bowels of Honister's old 'Edge' and 'Kimberley' mines (a tour into the 'Cathedral' mine runs on Friday by request, but you'll need eight people and it costs £19.75).

Via Ferrata (classic route adult/child £35/25, Xtreme £39.50/29.50) Part of the Honister Slate Mine, the UK's first 'iron way' is a vertiginous system of clifftop ropes and ladders once used by slate miners. It's exhilarating, but unsurprisingly you'll need a head for heights. There's also an extreme version that involves traversing a single rope 'Infinity Bridge' – not for the faint-hearted. All-day pass including mine tour costs adult/child £56.50/43.50.

Linnett Hill B&B ££
(017687-44518; www.linnetthillkeswick.co.uk; 4 Penrith Rd; s £48, d £85-95;) Much recommended by travellers, this lovingly run B&B has lots going for it: crisp white rooms, a great location near Fitz Park and keen prices that stay the same year-round. Breakfast is good too: there's a blackboard of specials to choose from and the dining room has gingham-check tablecloths and a crackling wood burner.

Powe House B&B ££
(017687-73611; www.powehouse.com; Portinscale; s £48-65, d £84-92; P) Pleasantly removed from the Keswick crush about a mile from town in Portinscale, this smart detached house has six great-value bedrooms. Ask for room 3 or room 5 if you're after maximum space or room 2 if you'd like a view of Skiddaw from your bed.

★**Cottage in the Wood** HOTEL £££
(017687-78409; www.thecottageinthewood.co.uk; Braithwaite; d Sun-Thu £110-190, Fri & Sat £120-205; restaurant 6.30-9pm Tue-Sat; P) For a secluded spoil, head for this out-of-the-way bolthole, on the road to Whinlatter Forest, in a completely modernised coaching inn. Elegant rooms survey woods and countryside: the Mountain View rooms overlook the Skiddaw Range, but we liked the superprivate Attic Suite and the Garden Room, with its wood floors and wet-room. The restaurant's fantastic too (set dinner menu £55).

Eating & Drinking

Pumpkin Cafe CAFE £
(017687-75973; 19 Lake Rd; lunches £4-8; 8.30am-5pm Mon-Sat) An ever-popular lunch stop, this cafe-bakery-deli is under new owners but the menu remains the same. Order a deli sandwich or a mix-and-match Mediterranean salad and chase it down with a flat white and a slice of heavenly carrot cake. There's seating upstairs or you can order to go.

Morrel's BRITISH ££
(017687-72666; www.morrels.co.uk; Lake Rd; 3-course menu £21.95, mains £12-19.50; 5.30-9pm Tue-Sun) Probably the best option for dinner in town, Morrel's is a modern bistro serving fusion dishes like Cajun salmon, Asian-style pork belly and summer risotto. Glossy wood, spotlights and pop-art prints of Steve McQueen and Marilyn Monroe give it character.

Pheasant Inn PUB FOOD ££
(017687-76234; www.the-pheasant.co.uk; Bassenthwaite Lake; mains £13.50-21; restaurant 7-9pm Tue-Sat, noon-2pm Sun, bistro noon-4.30pm & 6-9pm) A short drive along Bassenthwaite Lake is this fine-dining pub. Hunting prints and pewter tankards cover the old bar, stocked with vintage whiskies and Lakeland ales, and the two restaurants (informal bistro and smart restaurant) serve superior country food. The afternoon tea's done in the proper English fashion too, served on a tiered cakestand with scones and cucumber sandwiches.

Square Orange CAFE, BAR
(017687-73888; www.thesquareorange.co.uk; 20 St John's St; 10am-11pm Sun-Thu, 10am-midnight Fri & Sat) This lively little hang-out has become a real draw for Keswick's hipsters, shakers and drinkers, with regular live music, a tapas and pizza menu, an impressive range of wines and ales and the best coffee in town. There are even board games to keep you entertained.

Dog & Gun PUB
(☎017687-73463; 2 Lake Rd; ⏰11am-11pm) Benches, beams, hearths, rugs: the old Dog is the picture of a Lakeland pub. Look out for Thirst Rescue ale, which donates part of its proceeds to the Keswick Mountain Rescue Team.

Shopping

★**George Fisher** SPORTS & OUTDOORS
(☎017687-72178; www.georgefisher.co.uk; 2 Borrowdale Rd; ⏰9am-5.30pm Mon-Sat, 10am-4pm Sun) Quite possibly the most famous outdoors shop in the Lake District, founded in 1967 and still the place where discerning hikers go to buy their gear (even if it is a bit more expensive than the chains). There are three floors of boots, tents and gear, and the boot-fitting service is legendarily thorough.

Information

Post Office (48 Main St; ⏰9am-5.30pm Mon-Fri, to 12.30pm Sat)

Tourist Office (☎017687-72645; keswicktic@lake-district.gov.uk; Moot Hall, Market Pl; ⏰9.30am-5.30pm Apr-Oct, to 4.30pm Nov-Mar) The town's tourist office is well run and the staff are very informed; it also sells discounted tickets for the Keswick Launch.

Getting There & Away

The Keswick & Honister Dayrider (p584) buys unlimited travel on buses in the Keswick area, including to Borrowdale and Buttermere. Useful buses from Keswick:

Bus 555/556 Lakeslink Hourly to Grasmere (£7.70, 40 minutes), Ambleside (£8.20, 45 minutes), Windermere (£8.90, one hour) and Kendal (£9.60, 1½ hours).

Bus 77/77A Circular route (five to seven daily) from Keswick via Portinscale, Catbells, Grange, Seatoller, Honister Pass, Buttermere, Lorton and Whinlatter.

Bus 78 (at least hourly Monday to Friday, half-hourly weekends) The main Borrowdale bus, with stops at Lodore, Grange, Rosthwaite and Seatoller.

Borrowdale

POP 417

With their patchwork of craggy hills, broad fields, tinkling streams and drystone walls, the side-by-side valleys of Borrowdale and Buttermere are many people's idea of the quintessential Lakeland landscape. Once a centre for mineral mining (especially for slate, coal and graphite), this is walkers' country these days and, apart from the odd rickety barn or puttering tractor, there's precious little to spoil the view.

South of Keswick, the B5289 tracks Derwentwater into the heart of Borrowdale, winding past the small farming villages of Grange-in-Borrowdale, Rosthwaite and Stonethwaite.

Sights & Activities

Lodore Falls WATERFALL
At the southern end of Derwentwater, this famous waterfall featured in a poem by Robert Southey, but it's only worth visiting after a good spell of rain. It's in the grounds of the Lodore Hotel; there's an honesty box for donations.

Bowder Stone OUTDOORS
A mile south from Grange, a turn-off leads up to the geological curiosity known as the Bowder Stone, a 1870-ton lump of rock left behind by a retreating glacier. A small step-ladder leads to the top of the rock.

Watendlath Tarn LAKE
This National Trust–owned tarn is reached via a turn-off on the B5285 south of Keswick. On the way the road passes over one of the Lake District's most photographed pack-horse crossings at **Ashness Bridge**. Parking at the tarn is free for NT members, but the road is narrow and has few passing places so it's more pleasant to walk up in summer.

Platty+ BOATING
(☎017687-76572; www.plattyplus.co.uk; kayaks & canoes per hour £8-15) Based at the Lodore Boat Landings at the southern end of Derwentwater, this company hires out kayaks, canoes, rowing boats and sailing dinghies. It also runs instruction courses.

Sleeping & Eating

Derwentwater Independent Hostel HOSTEL £
(☎017687-77246; www.derwentwater.org; Barrow House; dm £20.50-22.50, d £49-54, tr £72-77, q £93-104; P @) Built as a 19th-century mansion, this grand Grade II–listed house is one of Britain's most architecturally ostentatious hostels. Previously YHA-owned, now private, it's a thing of beauty: many rooms have original features like plasterwork and fireplaces. The 88 beds are split across 11 bedrooms; smaller dorms can be booked by groups and families.

★Langstrath Inn B&B ££
(☎017687-77239; www.thelangstrath.com; Stonethwaite; d £106-136; ⊙restaurant noon-2-30pm & 6-8.30pm Tue-Sun; P 📶) This simple country inn makes one of the best little bases in Borrowdale, we reckon. Its eight rooms are snug and simple, with crimson throws and the occasional roof beam to add character – but it's the views that really sell the place. Hearty, unpretentious food (dinner mains £13.95) and ales from Hawkshead Brewery are served in the restaurant.

Yew Tree Farm B&B ££
(☎017687-77675; www.borrowdaleherdwick.co.uk; Rosthwaite; d £85; P) There are floral patterns galore at this sturdy Cumbrian farmhouse in rural Rosthwaite, with three rooms snuggled among cob walls and tiny windows (no wi-fi or TV!). It's run by working sheep farmers and you'll be able to spot Herdwicks in the nearby fields. Breakfast is huge and the **Flock In Tea-Room** over the road serves delicious cakes and puddings.

ℹ Getting There & Away

Bus 77/77A (£2.30 to £7.70, five to seven daily) makes a circular route from Keswick via all of Borrowdale's villages, over Honister Pass and through Buttermere. Bus 78 (£2.30 to £4, at least hourly) shuttles through Borrowdale as far as Seatoller. If you're planning on making a return journey the same day, it's cheaper to buy the Keswick & Honister Dayrider (p584) than a return fare.

Buttermere

POP 121

Up and over Honister Pass, the road drops sharply into the deep bowl of Buttermere, gouged out by a steamroller glacier and backed by a string of impressive peaks and emerald-green hills. The valley's twin lakes, **Buttermere** and **Crummock Water**, were once joined but became separated by glacial silt and rockfall. The little village of Buttermere sits halfway between the two and provides a wonderfully cosy base for exploring the rest of the valley and the many nearby fells, including **Haystacks** (597m), the favourite mountain and the last resting place of the patron saint of Lakeland walkers, the author Alfred Wainwright.

From here the B5289 exits the valley's northern edge and heads back towards Keswick.

Sleeping & Eating

Buttermere YHA HOSTEL £
(☎0845-371 9508; www.yha.org.uk; dm £10-30; ⊙reception 8.30-10am & 5-10.30pm, hostel mid-Mar–Oct; P 📶 👪) Perched in a perfect position on the Honister–Buttermere road, this excellent hostel has rooms looking out across the lake. The decor is smart, colourful and surprisingly modern. There's a great cafe-kitchen and plenty of quads and six-bed dorms – but note that the hostel is open to individual travellers at weekends and during summer holidays.

★Kirkstile Inn PUB FOOD ££
(☎01900-85219; www.kirkstile.com; mains £11.50-15.95) A finer country pub you could not hope to find. Hidden away near the little lake of Loweswater, a mile or so north of Buttermere, the Kirkstile is a joy: crackling fires, oak beams, worn carpets, wooden bar and all. Rooms (singles £64, doubles £98 to £115) are quaint; some have views across Lorton Vale. It's particularly known for its award-winning ales (try the Loweswater Gold).

Bridge Hotel PUB FOOD ££
(☎017687-70252; www.bridge-hotel.com; mains £10-16; P 📶) As the name suggests, it's right beside Buttermere's village bridge. There's standard pub food in the bar or more upmarket fare in the smart-casual restaurant. Frilly rooms (singles £74.50, doubles £159 to £169) and an antique ambience define the old Bridge.

ℹ Getting There & Away

Bus 77/77A (£5.60, five to seven daily) serves Buttermere and Honister Pass from Keswick. For return journeys the same day, save a bit of cash by buying the Keswick & Honister Dayrider (p584).

Ullswater & Around

After Windermere, the second-largest lake in the Lake District is **Ullswater**, stretching for 7.5 miles between **Pooley Bridge** and **Glenridding** and **Patterdale** in the south. Carved out by a long-extinct glacier, the deep valley in which the lake sits is flanked by an impressive string of fells, most notably the razor ridge of **Helvellyn**, Cumbria's third-highest mountain at 950m. The area is also famous as the place where William Wordsworth was inspired to write his best-known poem, 'Daffodils'.

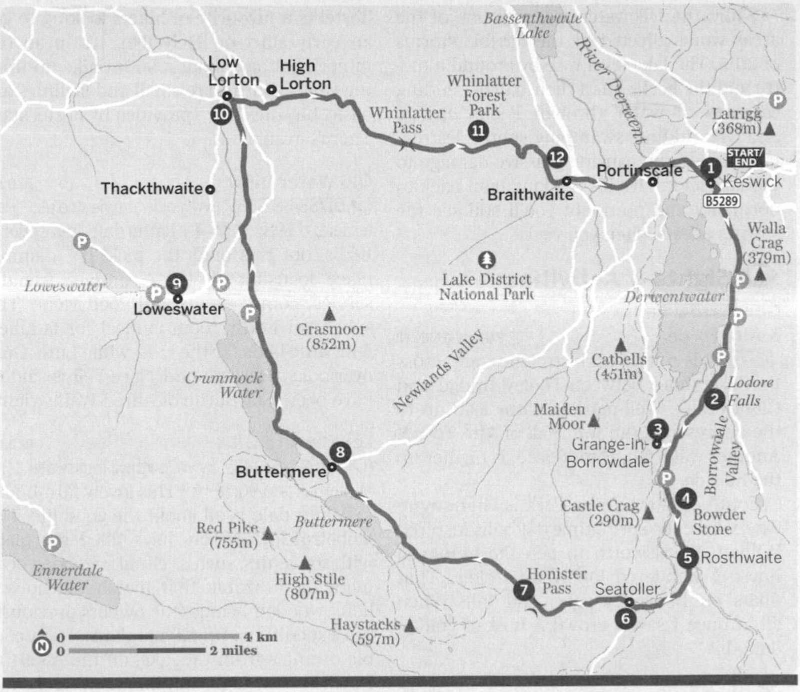

Driving Tour Borrowdale & Buttermere

START KESWICK
END KESWICK
LENGTH 28 MILES; THREE TO FOUR HOURS

This is one of the Lakes' most beautiful road trips, taking in the unspoilt scenery of the Borrowdale, Buttermere and Lorton Valleys. It's a perfect day trip out of Keswick.

Begin with breakfast in **1 Keswick**, then head along the B5289 into Borrowdale. First stop is **2 Lodore Falls** (p607), a pretty cascade at the southern end of Derwentwater. Next, detour to the little hamlet of **3 Grange-in-Borrowdale**, where a trail leads up the slate-strewn sides of Castle Crag, a small fell with great views over Borrowdale.

From Grange, carry on to the huge boulder known as the **4 Bowder Stone** (p607), shifted into position by the long-gone glacier that carved out the Borrowdale Valley. Pootle on to **5 Rosthwaite** for cake at the Flock In TeaRoom or to **6 Seatoller** for lunch.

In the afternoon tackle the steep crawl up to **7 Honister Pass** (p606), where you can pick up some slate souvenirs, take a tour down into the depths of the old slate mine or tackle the hair-raising *via ferrata*.

From here the road drops down into the beautiful valley of **8 Buttermere**. Spot the zigzag peaks of High Stile, Haystacks and Red Pike looming over the lake, stop off for a drink at the Fish Inn and remember to pay your respects to hiker and author Alfred Wainwright inside St James' Church.

Continue along the shore of Crummock Water past **9 Loweswater**, where you could make an optional but very worthwhile detour via the excellent Kirkstile Inn. When you reach **10 Low Lorton**, a right-hand turn carries you over Whinlatter Pass to **11 Whinlatter Forest** (p605). The forest park makes a good spot for a late-afternoon stop; there's a pleasant cafe at the visitor centre, as well as informative displays on the local wildlife.

There are a couple of great options for dinner on your way back to Keswick: Cottage in the Wood (p606) just before **12 Braithwaite** or the traditional Pheasant Inn (p606) on the shores of Bassenthwaite Lake.

Sadly, the Ullswater area was one of the areas worst affected by the terrible storms of 2015. The lake level rose by around a metre and the becks burst their banks, sending cascades of water through Pooley Bridge and Glenridding, swamping shops, destroying bridges and causing massive damage to the lake shore. It's been a long haul back to normality and no doubt you'll still see the storm's effects when you visit.

Sights & Activities

Gowbarrow Park & Aira Force PARK, WATERFALL

FREE This rolling park stretches out across the lake shore between Pooley Bridge and Glenridding. Well-marked paths lead up to the impressive 20m waterfall of **Aira Force**. Another waterfall, **High Force**, is further up the hillside.

South of Gowbarrow Park is **Glencoyne Bay**, where the springtime daffodils inspired William Wordsworth to pen the immortal lines: 'I wandered lonely as a cloud/That floats on high o'er vales and hills/When all at once I saw a crowd/A host of golden daffodils.'

★ Helvellyn HIKING

Along with Scafell Pike, this challenging hike is the one everyone wants to do. The classic ascent takes in the twin ridges of Striding and Swirral Edge, which are spectacular but very exposed and involve some scrambling and dizzyingly steep drops on either side – if you're at all nervous of heights, Helvellyn is probably not the fell for you. The usual routes climb up through Glenridding or Patterdale. Always check the weather forecast and take all the necessary supplies.

Ullswater 'Steamers' BOATING

(017684-82229; www.ullswater-steamers.co.uk; round-the-lake adult/child £13.90/6.95) Back in service after 2015's damaging storms, Ullswater's historic steamers are a memorable way to explore the lake. The various vessels include the stately *Lady of the Lake,* launched in 1877, supposedly the world's oldest working passenger boat. The boats run east–west from Pooley Bridge to Glenridding via Howtown; there are nine daily sailings in summer, three in winter.

Sleeping & Eating

Helvellyn YHA HOSTEL £

(0845-371 9742; www.yha.org.uk; Greenside; dm £13-25; Easter-Oct) This back-of-beyond hostel is a favourite of hikers looking to get an early start on Helvellyn. It's in an old miner's cottage about a 900m hike up from the valley. Dorms are small and facilities are basic, but meals are provided by hostel staff. There's even a bar.

Old Water View B&B ££

(017684-82175; www.oldwaterview.co.uk; Patterdale; d £98; P) Patterdale has several B&Bs, but this one's the pick. It's a simple place focusing on the essentials: friendly service, comfy rooms and good value. The split-level Bothy room is ideal for families, with attic beds for the kids, while Little Gem overlooks a stream and Place Fell is said to have been a favourite of Alfred Wainwright.

Lowthwaite B&B B&B ££

(017684-82343; www.lowthwaiteullswater.com; Matterdale; d £96; P) This lovely farmhouse in Matterdale is all about the good life. The globetrotting owners have filled the place with souvenirs, such as chunky wooden beds made in Tanzania that match the house's hefty wooden beams (the owners previously ran expeditions up Kilimanjaro). It's a couple of miles from the lake, off the A5091 to Dockray. Two-night minimum on weekends.

Fellbites CAFE ££

(01768-482781; Glenridding; lunch mains £3.95-9.95, dinner mains £12.50-18; 9am-8.30pm Thu-Tue, to 5.30pm Wed) This cafe beside the main car park in Glenridding has something to fill you up at any time of day: generous fry-ups for breakfast; soups, pulled-pork burgers and rarebits for lunch; lamb shanks and duck breast for dinner. It's honest, no-fuss grub.

Traveller's Rest PUB FOOD ££

(017684-82298; Glenridding; mains £5.50-15; 10am-11pm) Down a pint with a view of the fells at Traveller's Rest, a Glenridding stalwart. The food might be plain (steaks, pies, mixed grills) but the portions are huge.

Information

Ullswater Tourist Office (017684-82414; ullswatertic@lake-district.gov.uk; Glenridding; 9am-5pm Apr-Oct) has comprehensive advice on hikes and activities around Ullswater.

Getting There & Away

The Ullswater Bus-and-Boat Combo ticket (adult/child/family £15.50/8.50/33) includes a day's travel on bus 108 with a return trip on an Ullswater Steamer; buy the ticket on the bus.

Bus 108/508 travels from Penrith to Patterdale via Pooley Bridge and Glenridding (£5.20, nine daily Monday to Friday, four on weekends).

Kendal

POP 28,586

Technically Kendal isn't in the Lake District, but it's a major gateway town. Often known as the 'Auld Grey Town' thanks to the sombre grey stone used for many of its buildings, Kendal is a bustling shopping centre with some good restaurants, a funky arts centre and intriguing museums. But it'll forever be synonymous in many people's minds with its famous mint cake, a staple item in the nation's hiking packs ever since Edmund Hillary and Tenzing Norgay munched it during their ascent of Everest in 1953.

Kendal is a bit low on quality sleeping options and it's easily visited from Windermere.

Sights & Activities

Abbot Hall Art Gallery GALLERY
(☎01539-722464; www.abbothall.org.uk; adult/child £7/free, joint ticket with Museum of Lakeland Life & Industry £8.60; ⏲10.30am-5pm Mon-Sat Apr-Oct, to 4pm Nov-Mar) Kendal's fine art gallery houses one of the northwest's best collections of 18th- and 19th-century art. It's especially strong on portraiture and Lakeland landscapes: look out for works by Constable, John Ruskin and local boy George Romney, a key figure in the Kendal School. Look out for signposts as you head south along Kirkland Rd.

Museum of Lakeland Life & Industry MUSEUM
(☎01539-722464; www.lakelandmuseum.org.uk; adult/child £5/free, joint ticket with Abbot Hall Art Gallery £8.60; ⏲10.30am-5pm Mon-Sat Mar-Oct, to 4pm Nov-Feb) Directly opposite Abbot Hall, this museum re-creates various scenes from Lakeland life during the 18th and 19th centuries, including a farmhouse parlour, a Lakeland kitchen, an apothecary and the study of Arthur Ransome, author of *Swallows and Amazons* – look out for some of his original sketchbooks.

Levens Hall HISTORIC BUILDING
(☎015395-60321; www.levenshall.co.uk; house & gardens adult/child £12.80/5, garden only £9.50/4; ⏲house noon-4.30pm, gardens 10am-5pm Sun-Thu Mar-Oct) This Elizabethan manor is built around a mid-13th-century *pele* tower and fine Jacobean furniture litters the house, although the real draw is the 17th-century topiary garden: a surreal riot of pyramids, swirls, curls, pompoms and peacocks straight out of *Alice in Wonderland*.

A major project to reface the West Elevation with lime mortar should be completed by the time you read this.

Outdoor Adventure Company OUTDOORS
(☎01539-722147; www.theoutdooradventurecompany.co.uk; Old Hutton) An experienced outdoors centre near Kendal offering lots of activities from archery to tank-driving.

Festivals & Events

Kendal Calling MUSIC
(www.kendalcalling.co.uk) The Lake District's largest outdoor music festival is held in July and welcomes around 12,000 people to the Lowther Deer Park near Kendal. Recent headliners include Madness, The Charlatans, Elbow and Kaiser Chiefs.

Kendal Mountain Festival OUTDOORS
(www.mountainfest.co.uk) Annual mountain-themed celebration encompassing films, books and talks in November.

Eating

Brew Brothers CAFE £
(☎01539-722237; www.brew-brothers.co.uk; 69 Highgate; mains £8.50-10; ⏲8.30am-5.30pm Mon-Sat) The hipster cafe comes to Kendal at this new number on Highgate. With its scruffy wood furniture and black-aproned baristas, it's got the aesthetic down, but its owners are Lakeland through and through – they previously ran a cafe in Windermere. Go for smashed avocado and poached eggs for brekkie, then for lunch wolf down a hot smoked-salmon sandwich. Yum.

1657 Chocolate House CAFE £
(☎01539-740702; 54 Branthwaite Brow; lunches £3-8) A chocaholic's delight: handmade chocolates and Kendal mint cake in the basement, plus umpteen varieties of hot chocolate in the upstairs cafe.

★ **Punch Bowl Inn** PUB FOOD ££
(☎015395-68237; www.the-punchbowl.co.uk; Crosthwaite; mains £13.95-19.95; ⏲noon-4pm & 5.30-8.30pm; Ⓟ) If you don't mind a drive, there's no doubt – this renowned gastropub in the village of Crosthwaite is the best place to eat around Kendal. Whitewashed outside, carefully modernised inside, it's a cosy,

inviting space to dine. Chef Scott Fairweather's superb food blends classic dishes with cheffy ingredients (oyster mousse, potato croquettes, pea fricassée, salsify).

The rooms (£105 to £305) are lovely too: they're all different, but the nicest ones have reclaimed beams, sloping eaves, slate-floored bathrooms and his-and-hers claw-foot tubs.

New Moon BISTRO ££

(☎01539-729254; www.newmoonrestaurant.co.uk; 129 Highgate; mains £12.95-17.50; ⊙11.30am-2.15pm & 5.30-9pm Tue-Sat) For bistro dining in Kendal, this long-standing address is the place, with a varied menu encompassing almond-crusted cod, veggie tarts, Moroccan-style chicken, Cumbrian rump steak and plenty more besides – so you're pretty much guaranteed to find a taste to tickle your fancy. The two-course pre-7pm menu is great value at £13.95.

☆ Entertainment

Brewery Arts Centre THEATRE, CINEMA

(☎01539-725133; www.breweryarts.co.uk; Highgate) A cracking arts centre with a gallery, cafe, theatre and two cinemas, hosting the latest films as well as music, theatre, dance and much more.

Shopping

★**Low Sizergh Barn** FOOD

(☎015395-60426; www.lowsizerghbarn.co.uk; ⊙9am-5.30pm) A prodigious selection of Lakeland goodies are available at this farm shop, just outside Kendal on the A590. Breads from Grange Bakery, meats from Mansergh Hall, cheeses from Thornby Moor Dairy and beers from the Coniston Brewery Co are just some of the treats in store. There's also a farm trail and woodland walk to follow if the weather's nice.

ℹ Getting There & Away

The train line from Windermere runs to Kendal (£4.70, 15 minutes, hourly) en route to Oxenholme.

Bus 555/556 Regular bus (half-hourly Monday to Saturday, hourly at weekends) to Windermere (£6.70, 30 minutes), Ambleside (£6.90, 40 minutes) and Grasmere (£8.90, 1¼ hours).

Bus 106 To Penrith (£10.80, 80 minutes, one or two daily Monday to Friday).

CUMBRIAN COAST

While the central lakes and fells pull in a never-ending stream of visitors, surprisingly few ever make the trek west to explore Cumbria's coastline. And that's a shame: while it might not compare to the wild grandeur of Northumberland or the rugged splendour of Scotland's shores, Cumbria's coast is well worth exploring – a bleakly beautiful landscape of long sandy bays, grassy headlands, salt marshes and seaside villages stretching all the way from Morecambe Bay to the shores of the Solway Coast. There's an important seabird reserve at St Bees Head and the majestic grounds of Holker Hall are well worth a wander.

Historically, Cumbria's coast served the local mining, quarrying and shipping industries and Barrow-in-Furness remains a major shipbuilding centre. More controver sial is the nuclear plant of Sellafield, a major employer but still dividing opinion half-a-century on from its inception.

Sights

★**Holker Hall** HISTORIC BUILDING

(☎015395-58328; www.holker.co.uk; adult/child £12/free; ⊙house 11am-4pm, grounds 10.30am-5pm Wed-Sun Mar-Oct) Three miles east of Cartmel on the B5278, Holker Hall has been the family seat of the Cavendish family for nigh on four centuries. Though parts of the house date from the 16th century, the house was almost entirely rebuilt following a devastating fire in 1871. It's a typically ostentatious Victorian affair, covered with mullioned windows, gables and copper-topped turrets outside and filled with a warren of lavishly over-the-top rooms inside.

Muncaster Castle CASTLE

(☎01229-717614; www.muncaster.co.uk; adult/child £13.50/6.75; ⊙gardens & owl centre 10.30am-5pm, castle noon-4pm Sun-Fri) This crenellated castle, 1.5 miles east of Ravenglass, was originally built around a 14th-century *pele* tower, constructed to resist Reiver raids. Home to the Pennington family for seven centuries, the castle's architectural highlights are its great hall and octagonal library, and outside you'll find an ornamental maze and splendid grounds. The castle is also home to a hawk and owl centre, which stages several flying displays a day.

Muncaster is also known for its numerous ghosts: keep your eyes peeled for the Mun-

WORTH A TRIP

CARTMEL

Tiny Cartmel is known for three things: its 12th-century **Cartmel Priory** (9am-5.30pm May-Oct, to 3.30pm Nov-Apr), one of only a handful to have survived the ravages of the dissolution of the monasteries largely unscathed, its **miniature racecourse** and its world-famous sticky toffee pudding, sold at the **Cartmel Village Shop** (015395-36280; www.cartmelvillageshop.co.uk; 9am-5pm Mon-Sat, 10am-4.30pm Sun).

More recently it's become known as the home of chef Simon Rogan (dubbed Cumbria's answer to Heston Blumenthal). His flagship restaurant, **L'Enclume** (015395-36362; www.lenclume.co.uk; Cavendish St; set lunch £49, lunch & dinner menu £130; noon-1.30pm & 6.30-8.30pm Tue-Sun), showcases his boundary-pushing cuisine and madcap presentation as well as his passion for foraged ingredients.

He also runs a less formal bistro, **Rogan & Company** (015395-35917; www.roganandcompany.co.uk; The Square; 2-/3-course set lunch £18/24, mains £18.95-26.95; noon-2pm Tue-Sat, 6.30-9pm Mon-Sat, 12.30-5pm Sun), across the village. This village bistro focuses on classic British dishes like pork belly, butter-poached cod and roasted plaice, perfected and perfectly presented. It's cosy and welcoming, with fires and wooden interiors, and the Sunday roast is an utter feast. Bookings are essential for both.

Also worth a visit is the **Cavendish Arms** (015395-36240; www.thecavendisharms.co.uk; Cavendish St; mains £16-21; 11am-11pm), where you'll be treated to seriously upmarket food. Exposed beams, worn wood and a sunflower-yellow facade conjure an olde-worlde vibe, and there's a sunny beer garden too.

caster Boggle and a malevolent jester known as Tom Fool (hence 'tomfoolery').

Laurel & Hardy Museum MUSEUM

(01229-582292; www.laurel-and-hardy.co.uk; Brogden St, Ulverston; adult/child £5/2.50; 10am-5pm Easter-Oct, closed Mon & Wed rest of year) Founded by avid Laurel and Hardy collector Bill Cubin back in 1983, this madcap museum in Ulverston (the birthplace of Stan Laurel) has new premises inside the town's old Roxy cinema. It's crammed floor-to-ceiling with cinematic memorabilia, from original posters to film props, and there's a shoebox-sized cinema showing back-to-back Laurel and Hardy classics. Now run by Bill's grandson, it's a must for movie buffs.

South Lakes Safari Zoo ZOO

(www.southlakessafarizoo.com; Melton Tce, Lindal-inFurness, Ulverston; adult/child £16.50/9; 10am-5pm) This zoo has recently reinvented itself as the UK's first pedestrian safari, in which visitors can wander up close to the animals, hand-feed giraffes and lemurs and see vultures, macaws and condors flying past (thankfully the keepers still take charge of the big cats). There are regular feeding opportunities throughout the day – £3 buys a pass for one feeding session. Though it's still essentially a zoo, the lack of cages makes for an intriguing and different experience.

St Bees Head WILDLIFE RESERVE

(RSPB; stbees.head@rspb.org.uk) Five-and-a-half miles south of Whitehaven and 1½ miles north of the tiny town of St Bees, this wind-battered headland is one of Cumbria's most important reserves for nesting seabirds. Depending on the season, species nesting here include fulmars, kittiwakes and razorbills as well as Britain's only population of resident black guillemots. There are over 2 miles of cliff paths to explore.

Getting There & Around

The Furness and Cumbrian Coast railway lines loop 120 miles from Lancaster to Carlisle, stopping at the coastal resorts of Grange, Ulverston, Ravenglass, Whitehaven and Workington. The **Cumbria Coast Day Ranger** (adult/child £19.50/9.75) covers a day's unlimited travel on the line and works out cheaper than a return journey from Carlisle or Lancaster.

Northern & Eastern Cumbria

Many visitors speed through the northern and eastern reaches of Cumbria in a headlong dash for the Lake District, but it's worth taking the time to venture inland from the national park. It might not have the big-name fells and chocolate-box villages, but it's full of interest: traditional towns, crumbling

LOCAL KNOWLEDGE

RAVENGLASS & ESKDALE RAILWAY

Affectionately known as La'al Ratty, the pocket-sized **Ravenglass & Eskdale Railway** (☎01229-717171; www.ravenglass-railway.co.uk; adult/child/family return £13.50/6.75/38;) was originally built to ferry iron ore from the Eskdale mines to the coast. These days it's one of Cumbria's most beloved family attractions, with miniature steam trains that chug for 7 miles along the Eskdale valley between the coastal town of Ravenglass and the village of Dalegarth. There are seven to 14 trains a day depending on the season. A five-day Ratty Rover pass costs £40/20/110 per adult/child/family.

castles, abandoned abbeys and sweeping moors, all set alongside the magnificent Roman engineering project of Hadrian's Wall.

Carlisle

POP 75,306

Carlisle isn't Britain's prettiest city, but it has history and heritage aplenty. Precariously perched on the frontier between England and Scotland, in the area once ominously dubbed the 'Debatable Lands', Cumbria's capital is a city with a notoriously stormy past: sacked by the Vikings, pillaged by the Scots and plundered by the Border Reivers, the city has been on the front line of England's defences for more than 1000 years.

Reminders of the past are evident in its great crimson castle and cathedral, built from the same rosy-red sandstone as most of the city's houses. On English St, you can also see two massive circular **towers** that once flanked the city's gateway.

The closest section of Hadrian's Wall begins at nearby Brampton.

Sights

★Carlisle Castle CASTLE

(EH; ☎01228-591922; www.english-heritage.org.uk/visit/places/carlisle-castle/; Castle Way; adult/child £6.40/3.80, joint ticket with Cumbria's Museum of Military Life £9.20/5.15; 10am-5pm Apr-Sep, to 4pm Oct-Mar) Carlisle's brooding, rust-red castle lurks on the north side of the city. Founded around a Celtic and Roman stronghold, the castle's Norman keep was added in 1092 by William Rufus, and later refortified by Henry II, Edward I and Henry VIII (who added the supposedly cannon-proof towers). From the battlements, the stirring views stretch as far as the Scottish borders.

The castle also houses **Cumbria's Museum of Military Life** (☎01228-532774; adult/child £4/2, joint ticket with Carlisle Castle £9.20/5.15; 10am-6pm Apr-Oct, to 5pm Sat-Thu Nov-Mar), which houses collections of military memorabilia associated with the region's regiments.

The castle has witnessed some dramatic events over the centuries: Mary, Queen of Scots, was imprisoned here in 1568, and the castle was the site of a notorious eight-month siege during the English Civil War, when the Royalist garrison survived by eating rats, mice and the castle dogs before finally surrendering in 1645. Look out for some medieval graffiti and the 'licking stones' in the dungeon, which Jacobite prisoners supposedly lapped for moisture.

Carlisle Cathedral CHURCH

(☎01228-548151; www.carlislecathedral.org.uk; 7 The Abbey; suggested donation £5, photography £1; 7.30am-6.15pm Mon-Sat, to 5pm Sun) Built from the same red sandstone as Carlisle castle, Carlisle's cathedral began life as a priory church in 1122 and became a cathedral when its first abbot, Athelwold, became the first bishop of Carlisle. Among its notable features are the 15th-century choir stalls, the barrel-vaulted roof and the 14th-century East Window, one of the largest Gothic windows in England. Surrounding the cathedral are other priory relics, including the 16th-century Fratry and the Prior's Tower.

Tullie House Museum MUSEUM

(☎01228-618718; www.tulliehouse.co.uk; Castle St; adult/child £7.70/free; 10am-5pm Mon-Sat, 11am-5pm Sun) Carlisle's flagship museum covers 2000 years of the city's past. The Roman Frontier Gallery explores Carlisle's Roman foundations, while the Border Galleries cover the Bronze Age through to the Industrial Revolution. Two new galleries flesh out the story: the Border Reivers covers the marauding bandits who once terrorised the area, while the Vikings Revealed exhibition displays finds from the Cumwhitton Viking cemetery, including helmets, swords and grave goods. The top-floor Lookout has cracking views of the castle.

Settle to Carlisle Railway HERITAGE RAILWAY
(www.settle-carlisle.co.uk; day-ranger ticket adult/child £15/7.50) This historic railway route travels from Carlisle to Settle in North Yorkshire and is famous for its views across the Yorkshire Dales.

Sleeping

★ **Willowbeck Lodge** B&B ££
(01228-513607; www.willowbeck-lodge.com; Lambley Bank, Scotby; d £100-130;) If staying in the city centre isn't important, then this palatial B&B is the top choice in the city. The four rooms are huge, contemporary and plush, with luxuries like underfloor heating, Egyptian-cotton bedding and tasteful shades of beige and taupe. Some rooms have balconies overlooking the gardens and pond. There's also a restaurant, **Fini's Kitchen** (mains £14 to £22).

Crown & Mitre HISTORIC HOTEL ££
(01228-525491; www.peelhotels.co.uk/hotels/crown-and-mitre-hotel-carlisle-cumbria-england; English St; d £72.50-118.50;) You will not find a grander edifice in Carlisle than this imposing Edwardian pile, built as the city's poshest hotel following the arrival of the railway. It still has a hint of its original splendour in the lobby and staircase, but the rooms feel pretty corporate these days. It's worth upgrading to King for more up-to-date decor.

Warwick Hall B&B £££
(01228-561546; www.warwickhall.org; Warwick-on-Eden; s £88-130, d £128-164) This fine country house 2 miles from the centre along Warwick Rd is a real country retreat. With its huge rooms, high ceilings and old-fashioned decor, it feels a bit like staying on an aristocratic friend's estate. There are hectares of grounds and even a stretch of river for fishing.

Eating

Hell Below & Co FUSION £
(01228-548481; www.hellbelowandco.co.uk; 14 Devonshire St; mains £8-9.50; 11am-midnight Mon-Sat) A new menu has given this trendy brick-walled, bare-wood bar-bistro a fresh lease of life: it spans the gamut from cheese and charcuterie sharing boards to steaks, fajitas and flat-iron chicken. If you're not hungry, inventive cocktails like bubblegum sours and starburst cosmos are served.

Foxes Cafe Lounge CAFE £
(01228-491836; www.foxescafelounge.co.uk; 18 Abbey St; mains £4-8; 8am-4.30pm) Swing by this cool cafe for a pastry and cappuccino or an apple-and-elderflower smoothie – or better still, settle in for a hearty brunch (available in carnivorous and veggie versions).

David's BRITISH ££
(01228-523578; www.davidsrestaurant.co.uk; 62 Warwick Rd; 2-course lunch £16.95, dinner mains £15.95-25.50; noon-3.30pm & 6.30-11pm Tue-Sat) For many years this town-house restaurant has been the address for formal dining in Carlisle and there's no sign that's going to change. It majors in rich, traditional dishes with a strong French flavour: lamb with a pistachio crust and port gravy, roast chicken with leek and tarragon mash. The house is full of period architecture too.

Drinking & Entertainment

Botchergate is the centre of Carlisle's nightlife. It gets rowdy at closing time.

Fats PUB
(01228-511774; 48 Abbey St; 11am-11pm) A less hectic alternative to Botchergate's pubs. DJs and comedy nights are held regularly.

Brickyard CONCERT VENUE
(01228-512220; www.thebrickyardonline.com; 14 Fisher St) Carlisle's grungy gig venue, housed in the former Memorial Hall.

Information

Tourist Office (01228-625600; www.historic-carlisle.org.uk; Greenmarket; 9.30am-5pm Mon-Sat, 10.30am-4pm Sun)

Getting There & Away

BUS

National Express coaches depart from the bus station on Lonsdale St for destinations including London (£29.60 to £34.50, 7½ hours, two or three direct daily), Manchester (£27.70, three to 3½ hours, three daily) and Glasgow (£19.70, two hours, four to six daily).

Keswick bus 554; £12.10, 70 minutes, four daily Monday to Saturday, three on Sunday

Penrith bus 104; £6.50, 40 minutes, half-hourly Monday to Saturday, nine on Sunday

TRAIN

Carlisle is on the west-coast line from London to Glasgow. It's also the terminus for the scenic Cumbrian Coast and Tyne Valley Lines, as well as the historic Settle to Carlisle Railway across the Yorkshire Dales. The following are the main destinations:

Glasgow £28, 1¼ hours

SOUTH TYNEDALE RAILWAY

The heritage narrow-gauge **South Tynedale Railway** (☎01434-381696, timetable 01434-382828; www.south-tynedale-railway.org.uk; adult/child return to Lintley £10/4; ⊙Apr-Oct), the highest such in England, puffs for 3.5 miles of scenic track between Alston in Cumbria and Lintley in Northumberland. En route you pass over three landmark viaducts at South Tyne, Gilderdale and Whitley.

Lancaster £30, 45 minutes
London Euston £113.50, 3½ hours
Manchester £56, 2 hours, 10 minutes
Newcastle-upon-Tyne £15.90, 1½ hours

Getting Around

To book a taxi, call **Radio Taxis** (☎01228-527575) or **Cumbria Cabs** (☎01228-899599).

Penrith

POP 15,181

Just outside the borders of the national park, red-brick Penrith perhaps has more in common with the stout market towns of the Yorkshire Dales. It's a solid, traditional place with plenty of cosy pubs and quaint teashops and a lively market on Tuesdays. It's also the main gateway for exploring the picturesque Eden Valley.

Sights

Rheged VISITOR CENTRE
(☎01768-868000; www.rheged.com; ⊙10am-6pm) Cunningly disguised as a Lakeland hill 2 miles west of Penrith, this visitor centre houses an Imax cinema and temporary exhibitions. There's also a large retail hall selling Cumbrian foodstuffs and souvenirs. Local chef Peter Sidwell runs cooking classes and is also responsible for the cafe menu.

Penrith Castle RUIN
(⊙7.30am-9pm Easter-Oct, to 4.30pm Nov-Easter) The ruins of Penrith Castle loom on the edge of town opposite the train station. Built in the 14th century by William Strickland (later Bishop of Carlisle and Archbishop of Canterbury), it was later expanded by Richard III to resist Scottish raids, one of which razed the town in 1345.

Sleeping & Eating

Brooklands B&B ££
(☎01768-863395; www.brooklandsguesthouse.com; 2 Portland Pl; s £40-60, d £85-95;) The town's top B&B by some considerable margin, lodged in a terrace of red-brick houses on Portland Pl. It's Victorian outside, but inside it has fancy furnishings and posh extras such as White Company toiletries, in-room fridges and chocolates on the tea tray. There's a four-poster room too.

★ **Augill Castle** HOTEL £££
(☎01768-341967; www.stayinacastle.com; Kirkby Stephen; r £180-240;) If you've always dreamt of staying in a bona fide British castle, then this stately pile in Kirkby Stephen is definitely the place. All the trappings are here – crenellated turrets, stained-glass windows, cavernous rooms – and inside the design vibe is rather groovy, with a mix of antique furniture and contemporary furnishings. There's even a minicinema. It's 25 miles southeast of Penrith.

★ **Four & Twenty** BISTRO ££
(☎01768-210231; www.fourandtwentypenrith.co.uk; 14 King St; lunch mains £10, dinner mains £14-18; ⊙noon-2.30pm & 6.30-9.30pm Tue-Sat) Proper fine dining with a reasonable price tag is the modus operandi at this fine bistro, which blends sleek decor with rustic wood, banquette seats and mix-and-match furniture. Expect sophisticated dishes such as twice-baked Stilton soufflé and braised blade of beef with caramelised onion rösti. If you're going to eat out in Penrith, this is the place to do it.

Information

The Tourist Office (☎01768-867466; pen.tic@eden.gov.uk; Middlegate; ⊙9.30am-5pm Mon-Sat, 1-4.45pm Sun) also houses Penrith's tiny museum.

Getting There & Away

There are frequent train connections to Carlisle (£10.50, 15 minutes) and Lancaster (£18.50, one hour).

The bus station is northeast of the centre, off Sandgate.

Carlisle bus 104; £6.50, 40 minutes, half-hourly Monday to Saturday, nine on Sunday
Cumbrian coast (bus X4/X5; £6.50 to £10.20, half-hourly Monday to Saturday, hourly Sunday) Via Rheged, Keswick and Cockermouth.

Newcastle & Northeast England

Includes ➡

Best Places to Eat

- ➡ Jolly Fisherman (p643)
- ➡ Cross Lanes Organic Farm Shop (p633)
- ➡ Bouchon Bistrot (p638)
- ➡ Broad Chare (p625)
- ➡ House of Tides (p626)

Best Places to Sleep

- ➡ Langley Castle Hotel (p638)
- ➡ Marshall Meadows Country House Hotel (p648)
- ➡ Otterburn Castle Country House Hotel (p641)
- ➡ Jesmond Dene House (p625)

Why Go?

The irrepressible city of Newcastle-upon-Tyne anchors England's northeast. Set on the mighty River Tyne, this former industrial powerhouse's steep hills are lined with handsome Victorian buildings, and many of its one-time factories and warehouses have been transformed into galleries, museums, bars and entertainment venues. Newcastle's nightlife is legendary, and revelling in an evening on the tiles here is a quintessential experience.

Newcastle is also an ideal gateway for escaping into the northeast's utterly wild, starkly beautiful countryside – from the rounded Cheviot Hills to brooding Northumberland National Park and the remote North Pennines. Spectacular Hadrian's Wall cuts a lonely path through the landscape, dotted with dramatic fortress ruins that are haunting reminders of the bloody struggle with the Scots to the north, while the region's unspoilt coastline takes in long, desolate beaches, wind-worn castles and tiny, magical islands offshore.

When to Go

- ➡ Costumed re-enactments and Roman celebrations take place throughout the year at Hadrian's Wall.
- ➡ The best time to discover the region's miles of wide sandy beaches is during the summer season (June to August), although for surfers, Tynemouth's world-class waves are best (if chilliest) in winter and spring.
- ➡ September and October are great for losing yourself in the autumnal landscapes of Northumberland National Park.
- ➡ September is also the month to grab a Newkie Brown ale, or your running shoes, and join the party along the route of Tyneside's Great North Run, one of the world's biggest half-marathons.

Newcastle & Northeast England Highlights

1 Victoria Tunnel (p623) Exploring a coal-wagon tunnel and WWII air-raid shelter beneath Newcastle's streets.

2 Kielder Observatory (p640) Stargazing from this observatory in the Northumberland International Dark Sky Park.

3 Holy Island (Lindisfarne) (p646) Negotiating the tidal causeway to reach this other-worldly pilgrimage site.

4 Bowes Museum (p633) Viewing extraordinary objets d'art in this château-housed museum at Barnard Castle.

5 Berwick Walls (p647) Circumnavigating

the Elizabethan walls of England's northernmost city, Berwick-upon-Tweed.

6 Durham River Cruises (p631) Cruising on the tranquil River Wear, taking in Durham's city, castle and wondrous cathedral.

7 Hadrian's Wall (p633) Hiking along the remains of this Roman wall.

8 Hartlepool (p628) Learning about the fascinating maritime and wartime history of this coastal town.

9 Beamish Open-Air Museum (p632) Reliving the northeast's industrial age at this working museum.

10 Alnwick Castle (p642) Wandering the halls of Harry Potter's Hogwarts, aka Alnwick Castle.

History

Violent history has shaped this region more than any other in England, primarily because of its frontier position. Although Hadrian's Wall didn't serve as a defensive barrier, it marked the northern limit of Roman Britain and was the Empire's most heavily fortified line. Following the Romans' departure, the region became part of the Anglian kingdom of Bernicia, which united with the kingdom of Deira (encompassing much of modern-day Yorkshire) to form Northumbria in 604.

The kingdom changed hands and borders shifted several times over the next 500 years as Anglo-Saxons and Danes struggled to seize it. The land north of the River Tweed was finally ceded to Scotland in 1018, while the nascent kingdom of England kept everything below it.

The arrival of the Normans in 1066 saw William I eager to secure his northern borders against the Scots. He commissioned most of the castles you see along the coast, and cut deals with the prince bishops of Durham to ensure their loyalty. The new lords of Northumberland became very powerful because, as Marcher Lords (from the use of 'march' as a synonym of 'border'), they kept the Scots at bay.

Northumberland's reputation as a hotbed of rebellion intensified during the Tudor years, when the largely Catholic north, led by the seventh duke of Northumberland, Thomas Percy, rose up against Elizabeth I in the defeated Rising of the North in 1569. The Border Reivers, raiders from both sides of the border in the 16th century, kept the region in a perpetual state of lawlessness that only subsided after the Act of Union between England and Scotland in 1707.

Coal mines were the key to the 19th-century industrialisation of the northeast, powering steelworks, shipyards and armament works that grew up along the Tyne and Tees. In 1825 the mines also spawned the world's first steam railway, the Stockton & Darlington, built by local engineer George Stephenson. Social strife emerged in the 20th century, however, with mines, shipbuilding, steel production and the railway industry all winding down during the Great Depression and postwar years. Reinventing the northeast has been a mammoth task but continues apace.

Activities

Walking and cycling opportunities abound in this region. But be prepared for wind and rain at any time of year and for very harsh conditions in winter. Regional tourism websites contain walking and cycling information, and tourist offices stock maps and guides covering walking, cycling and other activities.

Cycling

The northeast has some of England's most inspiring cycle routes.

Part of the National Cycle Network (NCN), a long-time favourite is the 200-mile **Coast & Castles Cycle Route** (www.coast-and-castles.co.uk), which runs south–north along the glorious Northumberland coast between Newcastle-upon-Tyne and Berwick-upon-Tweed and Edinburgh, Scotland.

The 140-mile **Sea to Sea Cycle Route** (www.c2c-guide.co.uk) runs across northern England between the Cumbrian coast (Whitehaven or Workington) and Tynemouth or Sunderland via the northern Lake District and wild North Pennines' hills.

The other coast-to-coast option is the **Hadrian's Cycleway** (www.hadrian-guide.co.uk), a 175-mile route between South Shields or Tynemouth and Ravenglass in Cumbria along Hadrian's Wall.

Walking

The North Pennines – along with the Cheviots further north – are considered 'England's last wilderness'. Long routes through the hills include the famous **Pennine Way National Trail**, which keeps mainly to the high ground between the Yorkshire Dales and the Scottish border, but also crosses sections of river valley and some tedious patches of plantation. The whole route is around 270 miles, but the 70-mile section between Bowes and Hadrian's Wall is a fine four-day taster.

Hadrian's Wall has a huge range of easy loop walks taking in forts and other historical highlights.

One of the finest walks along the windswept **Northumberland coast**, between the villages of Craster and Bamburgh via Dunstanburgh, includes two of the region's most spectacular castles. Another superb coastal trail is the 30-mile **Berwickshire Coastal Path** (www.walkhighlands.co.uk/borders/berwickshire-coastal-path.shtml) from Berwick-upon-Tweed to the village of Cockburnspath in Scotland.

Getting There & Around

BUS

Bus transport around the region can be difficult, particularly around the more remote reaches of western Northumberland. Contact **Traveline** (☎ 0871-200 2233; www.travelinenortheast.info) for information on connections, timetables and prices.

TRAIN

The East Coast Main Line runs north from London King's Cross to Edinburgh via Durham, Newcastle and Berwick; Northern Rail operates local and interurban services in the north, including west to Carlisle.

There are numerous Rover tickets for single-day travel and longer periods; check www.networkonetickets.co.uk.

Newcastle-upon-Tyne

POP 280,200

Against its dramatic backdrop of Victorian elegance and industrial grit, this fiercely independent city harbours a spirited mix of heritage and urban sophistication, with excellent art galleries and a magnificent concert hall, along with boutique hotels, some exceptional restaurants and, of course, interesting bars: Newcastle is renowned throughout Britain for its thumping nightlife, bolstered by an energetic, 42,000-strong student population. The city retains deep-rooted traditions, embodied by the no-nonsense, likeable locals.

Allow at least a few days to explore the Victorian city centre and quayside areas along the Tyne and across the river in Gateshead, as well as the rejuvenated Ouseburn Valley to the east, shabby-chic Jesmond to the north, and, on the coast, the surf beaches of Tynemouth.

Sights

City Centre

Newcastle's grand Victorian centre, a compact area bordered roughly by Grainger St to the west and Pilgrim St to the east, is one of the most compelling examples of urban rejuvenation in England. Down by the quays are the city's most recognisable attractions – the iconic bridges that span the Tyne and the striking buildings that flank it.

Newcastle Castle CASTLE
(☎ 0191-230 6300; www.newcastlecastle.co.uk; Castle Garth; adult/child £6.50/3.90; ⏲ 10am-5pm) The stronghold that put both the 'new' and 'castle' into Newcastle has been largely swallowed up by the train station, leaving only a few remaining fragments including the square Norman keep and the Black Gate, both fresh from a £1.67-million restoration. Exhibits inside the two buildings cover the history of the city, its castle and its residents from Roman times onwards. The 360-degree city views from the keep's rooftop are the best in town.

★**Discovery Museum** MUSEUM
(https://discoverymuseum.org.uk; Blandford Sq; ⏲ 10am-4pm) FREE Tyneside's rich history is explored at this unmissable museum. Exhibitions spread across three floors of the former Co-operative Wholesale Society building around the mightily impressive 30m-long *Turbinia*, the fastest ship in the world in 1897 and the first to be powered by steam turbine. Other highlights are a section on shipbuilding on the Tyne, with a scale model of the river in 1929, and the 'Story of Newcastle', spanning the city's history from Pons Aelius (Roman Newcastle) to Cheryl Cole.

★**Great North Museum** MUSEUM
(☎ 0191-208 6765; https://greatnorthmuseum.org.uk; Barras Bridge; general admission free, planetarium adult/child £2.50/1.50; ⏲ 10am-5pm Mon-Fri, to 4pm Sat, 11am-4pm Sun) The contents of Newcastle University's museums and the prestigious Hancock Museum's natural-history exhibits come together in the latter's neoclassical building. The result is a fascinating jumble of dinosaurs, Roman altar stones, Egyptian mummies, Samurai warriors and impressive taxidermy. Standout exhibits include a life-size *Tyrannosaurus rex* recreation and an interactive model of Hadrian's Wall showing every milecastle and fortress. There's also lots of hands-on stuff

BRIDGING THE TYNE

The most famous view in Newcastle is the cluster of Tyne bridges, the most famous of these being the **Tyne Bridge** (1925–28). Its resemblance to Australia's Sydney Harbour Bridge (1923–32) is no coincidence, as both were built by the same company, Dorman Long of Middlesbrough. The quaint little **Swing Bridge** (1876) pivots in the middle to let ships through. Nearby, the **High Level Bridge** (1849), designed by Robert Stephenson, was the world's first combined road and railway bridge. The most recent addition is the multiple-award-winning **Millennium Bridge** (aka Blinking Bridge; 2002), which opens like an eyelid to let ships pass.

Newcastle-upon-Tyne

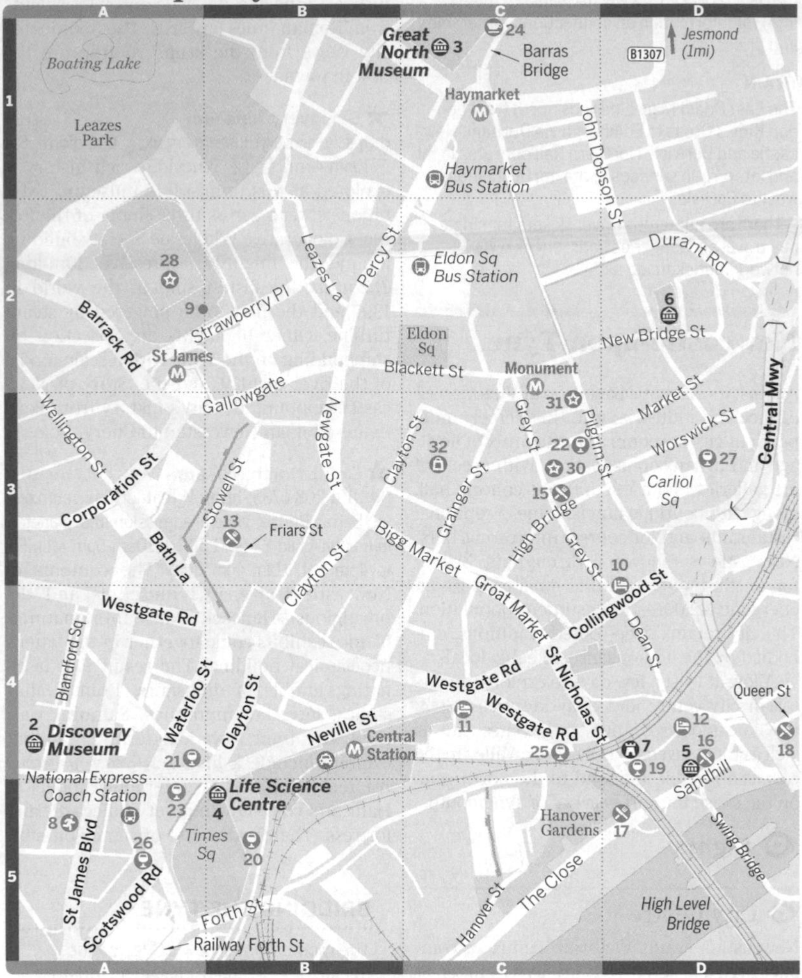

for kids and a planetarium with screenings throughout the day.

Laing Art Gallery GALLERY

(www.laingartgallery.org.uk; New Bridge St; ⏲10am-5pm Tue-Sat, 2-5pm Sun) FREE The exceptional collection at the Laing includes works by Gainsborough, Gauguin and Henry Moore, and an important collection of paintings by Northumberland-born artist John Martin (1789–1854). Check the 'What's On' section of the website for free events including talks and tours. Temporary exhibitions often incur an extra charge.

★Life Science Centre MUSEUM

(☎0191-243 8210; www.life.org.uk; Times Sq; adult/child £14/8; ⏲10am-6pm Mon-Sat, 11am-6pm Sun) Part of a sober-minded institute devoted to the study of genetic science, this centre lets you discover the secrets of life through a fascinating series of hands-on exhibits. The highlight is the Motion Ride, a simulator that lets you 'experience' bungee jumping and the like (the 4D film changes every year). There are lots of thought-provoking arcade-style games, and if the information sometimes gets lost on the way, never mind, kids will love it. Book ahead at busy times.

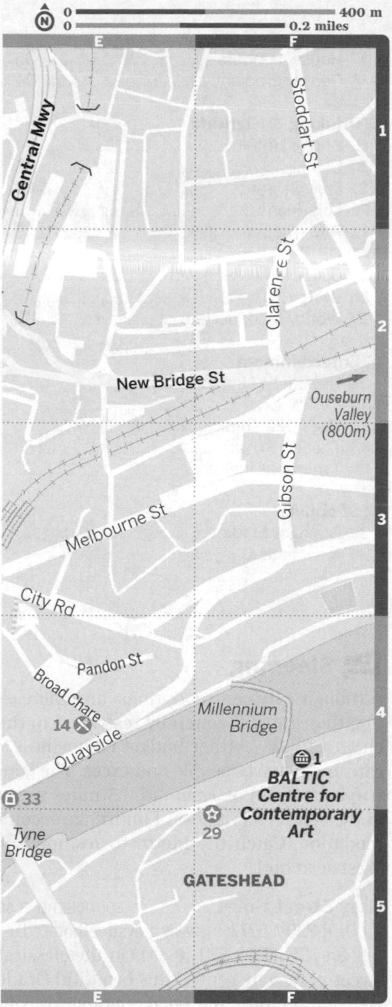

Mornings on school days see it filled with groups; visit after 2pm to avoid the crowds.

Ouseburn Valley

Now semiregenerated, Newcastle's 19th-century industrial heartland, Ouseburn Valley, 1 mile east of the city centre, has potteries, glass-blowing studios and other creative workspaces, along with pubs, bars and entertainment venues.

★Victoria Tunnel HISTORIC SITE
(☎0191-261 6596; www.ouseburntrust.org.uk; Arch 6, Stepney Bank; tours adult/child £6/4; ⏲by reservation) Walking Newcastle's streets, you'd never know this extraordinary tunnel runs for 2.5 miles beneath your feet. Built between 1839 and 1842 as a coal-wagon thoroughfare, it was used as an air-raid shelter during WWII. Volunteer-led, two-hour tours take you through an atmospheric 700m-long level section of the tunnel. Book ahead as numbers are limited to 12 participants, and wear good shoes and a washable jacket for the limewashed walls. Tours finish at Ouse St, near the Quayside.

Ouseburn Farm FARM
(☎0191-232 3698; www.bykerbridge.org.uk/farm; Ouseburn Rd, adjacent Lime St; ⏲9.30am-4.30pm Mon-Fri, 10.30am-4.30pm Sat & Sun) FREE Shetland ponies, sheep, goats, pigs, chickens and agricultural crops are the last thing you'd expect to find in Newcastle, but you can see them all at this community farm. Eggs, dairy products and more are sold at its farm shop and used in dishes served at its tearoom.

Seven Stories – The Centre for Children's Books MUSEUM
(www.sevenstories.org.uk; 30 Lime St; adult/child £7.70/6.60; ⏲10am-5pm Mon-Sat, to 4pm Sun) A marvellous conversion of a handsome Victorian mill has resulted in Seven Stories, a very hands-on museum dedicated to the wondrous world of children's literature. Across the seven floors you'll find original manuscripts and artwork from the 1930s onwards, and a constantly changing program of kid-oriented exhibitions, activities and events designed to encourage the AA Milnes of the new millennium.

Gateshead

The area of Newcastle south of the Tyne is the 'town' (neighbourhood, really) of Gateshead. Local authorities are now promoting the whole kit-and-caboodle–on-Tyne as 'NewcastleGateshead'.

★BALTIC – Centre for Contemporary Art GALLERY
(www.balticmill.com; Gateshead Quays; ⏲10am-6pm) FREE Once a huge mustard-coloured grain store, BALTIC is now a huge mustard-coloured art gallery rivalling London's Tate Modern. There are no permanent exhibitions; instead, rotating shows feature the work and installations of some of contemporary art's biggest show-stoppers. The complex has artists in residence, a performance space, a cinema, a bar, a spectacular

Newcastle-upon-Tyne

Top Sights
1 BALTIC – Centre for Contemporary Art ... F4
2 Discovery Museum ... A4
3 Great North Museum ... C1
4 Life Science Centre ... B5

Sights
5 Bessie Surtees House ... D4
6 Laing Art Gallery ... D2
7 Newcastle Castle ... D4

Activities, Courses & Tours
8 Lane 7 ... A5
9 St James Park Tours ... A2

Sleeping
10 Grey Street Hotel ... D4
11 Royal Station Hotel ... C4
12 Vermont Hotel ... D4

Eating
13 Blackfriars ... B3
14 Broad Chare ... E4
15 Fat Hippo Underground ... C3
16 Hop & Cleaver ... D4
17 House of Tides ... D5
18 Quay Ingredient ... D4

Drinking & Nightlife
19 Bridge Hotel ... D4
20 Digital ... B5
21 Eazy Street ... A4
22 Lola Jeans ... C3
23 Powerhouse ... A5
24 QB Tea House ... C1
25 Split Chimp ... C4
26 Switch ... A5
27 World Headquarters ... D3

Entertainment
28 Newcastle United Football Club ... A2
29 Sage Gateshead ... F5
30 Theatre Royal ... C3
31 Tyneside Cinema ... C3

Shopping
32 Grainger Market ... C3
33 Newcastle Quayside Market ... E4

rooftop restaurant (bookings essential) and a ground-floor restaurant with riverside tables. A 4th-floor outdoor platform and 5th-floor viewing box offer fabulous panoramas of the Tyne.

Activities

★ Lane 7 BOWLING
(☎0191-261 6161; http://lane7.co.uk; 80-90 St James's Blvd; bowling from £6; ⏰4pm-midnight Mon-Thu, 11am-2am Fri & Sat, 11am-midnight Sun) Not only does this supercool bowling alley have 10 walnut lanes, it also has a slot-car Racing Ring, ping-pong tables, Donkey Kong arcade games, pool tables and a karaoke room, as well as a gastropub menu (pulled-pork buns; gourmet hot dogs) and a craft-beer bar. Kids are welcome until 7pm.

Festivals & Events

Great North Run SPORTS
(www.greatrun.org) Newcastle's 13.1-mile half-marathon takes place in mid-September. Entry is by ballot, otherwise join the locals cheering on the entrants along the route, which goes from the city centre across the Tyne Bridge and through Gateshead to South Shields.

Sleeping

Although city-centre options are increasing, they are still generally restricted to the chain variety – either budget or business – catering to party people and execs. The gentrifying suburb of Jesmond, 1.5 miles north of the centre, has a host of midrange accommodation. Catch the Metro to Jesmond or West Jesmond.

Grey Street Hotel BOUTIQUE HOTEL $$
(☎0191-230 6777; www.greystreethotel.co.uk; 2-12 Grey St; d from £70; ❄📶) On the classiest street in the city centre, this beautiful Grade II–listed building has been adapted for contemporary needs, including triple glazing on the sash windows. Individually designed rooms have big beds and handsome modern furnishings.

Newcastle Jesmond Hotel HOTEL $$
(☎0191-239 9943; www.newcastlejesmondhotel.co.uk; 105 Osborne Rd; s/d/f from £55/75/105; P📶👪) Rooms aren't huge at this freshly refurbished red-brick property footsteps from the bars and restaurants of Osborne Rd, but they're cosy, comfy and come with the bonus of free parking (though spaces are limited, so get in quick). Family rooms sleep three people. Wi-fi can be patchy.

Royal Station Hotel HOTEL $$
(☎0191-232 0781; www.royalstationhotel.com; Neville St; s/d from £58/63; P 📶 🏊) Newcastle's hotels don't come better located than this Grade I- and II-listed Victorian beauty attached to Central Station. Above the chandeliered lobby, the 144 streamlined, unfussy rooms include cheaper, broom-cupboard-size 'small doubles' (from £60); there's a small indoor pool. Staff couldn't be friendlier or more helpful. Arrive early – the 20 free on-street car spaces are first-come, first-served.

Avenue B&B $$
(☎0191-281 1396; 2 Manor House Rd; s/d/f from £45/70/85; 📶 👪) In a peaceful residential area, this basic but well-run, family-friendly B&B has good breakfasts and friendly hosts.

★ **Jesmond Dene House** HOTEL $$$
(☎0191-212 3000; http://jesmonddenehouse.co.uk; Jesmond Dene Rd; s/d/ste from £109/119/169; P ❄ @ 📶) Large, gorgeous bedrooms at this exquisite property are furnished in a modern interpretation of the Arts and Crafts style and have stunning bathrooms complete with underfloor heating, as well as the latest tech. The fine-dining restaurant (p626) is sublime.

Vermont Hotel HERITAGE HOTEL $$$
(☎0191-233 1010; www.vermont-hotel.com; Castle Garth; d/ste from £119/179; P 📶 👪) Early 20th-century elegance reigns at this magnificent stone building (the former County Hall), which has an art deco ballroom, 101 rooms with marble bathrooms and glossy timber (including interconnecting rooms for families and sumptuous suites), two bars and a fine-dining restaurant. Limited on-site parking is first-come, first-served but free. Its 11 luxury self-catering apartments (two-/four-person apartments from £169/229) are located nearby.

Eating

City Centre

Quay Ingredient CAFE $
(☎0191-447 2327; http://quayingredient.co.uk; 4 Queen St; dishes £3-17; ⏲8am-5pm; 📶) Beneath the Tyne Bridge's soaring steel girders, this chic little hole in the wall has a devoted following for its eggs Benedict (and Florentine, and Montreal), but don't discount the rest of the menu: Craster kippers with pickled beetroot, scampi with homemade tartar sauce, pulled beef with bourbon....

WORTH A TRIP

SEGEDUNUM FORT

The last strong post of Hadrian's Wall was the fort of **Segedunum** (☎0191-278 4217; htttp://segedunumromanfort.org.uk; Buddle St, Wallsend; adult/child £5.95/free; ⏲10am-5pm Jun–mid-Sep, to 4pm Easter-May & mid-Sep–early Nov, to 2.30pm Mon-Fri early Nov-Easter) , 5 miles east of Newcastle at the 'wall's end', now the Newcastle suburb of Wallsend. Beneath the 35m-high tower, which you can climb for terrific views, is an absorbing site that includes a reconstructed Roman bathhouse (with steaming pools and frescos) and a museum offering a fascinating insight into life during Roman times.

Segedeunum is a three minute walk from the Wallsend Metro station (from Newcastle £3.20, 20 minutes).

★ **Broad Chare** GASTROPUB $$
(☎0191-211 2144; www.thebroadchare.co.uk; 25 Broad Chare; mains £10-19.50; ⏲kitchen noon-2.30pm & 5.30-10pm Mon-Sat, noon-5pm Sun) Spiffing English classics and splendid cask ales are served in the dark-wood bar and mezzanine of this perfect gastropub. Starters such as crispy pig ears, pork pies and venison terrine are followed by mains including a divine grilled pork chop with black pudding and cider sauce and desserts such as treacle tart with walnut brittle to finish.

Fat Hippo Underground BURGERS $$
(☎0191-447 1161; www.fathippo.co.uk; 2-6 Shakespeare St; burgers £8-14; ⏲noon-10pm Mon-Thu, 11am-10.30pm Fri & Sat, 11am-10pm Sun) An arched brick basement houses this city-centre offshoot of Jesmond favourite the Fat Hippo (p626). Its namesake Fat Hippo burger comes with double beef patties, bacon, chorizo, cheese, onion rings and secret house sauce; there are some great chicken and veggie burgers as well as triple-cooked fries. Kids' burgers cost £5.

Hop & Cleaver GASTROPUB $$
(☎0191-261 1037; www.hopandcleaver.com; 44 Sandhill; mains £9-18; ⏲kitchen noon-9pm Sun-Thu, to 10pm Fri & Sat, bar 11am-1am) Inside the magnificent Jacobean **Bessie Surtees House** (http://historicengland.org.uk; 41-44 Sandhill; ⏲10am-4pm Mon-Fri) FREE, this hip spot is great for a drink (it brews its own small-batch craft beers) but the food (including house-smoked meats) is equally brilliant:

WORTH A TRIP

ANGEL OF THE NORTH

Nicknamed the Gateshead Flasher, this extraordinary 200-tonne, rust-coloured, winged human frame **Angel of the North** (Durham Rd, Low Eighton) has loomed over the A1 (M) some 6 miles south of Newcastle since 1998. Sir Antony Gormley's iconic work (which saw him knighted in 2014) stands 20m high, with a wingspan wider than a Boeing 767. Bus 21 from Newcastle's Eldon Sq (£2.10, 20 minutes) stops here. There's a free car park by the base.

smoky brisket with apple-and-onion fritters; 12-hour cooked pulled pork with homemade slaw and BBQ sauce; charred, Bourbon-marinated ribs; beer-steamed and roasted chicken. Veggie options exist but are limited.

★House of Tides GASTRONOMY **$$$**
(☎0191-230 3720; http://houseoftides.co.uk; 28-30 The Close; 7-/8-course lunch menus £35/60, with wine £65/110, 8-course dinner menu £68, with wine £118; ⏲noon-2pm & 6-9.30pm Tue-Fri, noon-2pm & 5-10pm Sat) A 16th-century merchant's house is now home to Newcastle's most celebrated restaurant. Michelin-starred chef Kenny Atkinson (a past two-time winner of the BBC's Great British Menu) works with premium ingredients – Orkney scallops, Norfolk quail, wild blackberries, black truffles and nasturtiums – on regularly changing menus. Vegetarians and other dietary requirements can be catered by prior arrangement.

★Blackfriars BRITISH **$$$**
(☎0191-261 5945; www.blackfriarsrestaurant.co.uk; Friars St; mains £12-25; ⏲noon-2.30pm & 5.30-11pm Mon-Sat, noon-4pm Sun) A 12th-century friary is the atmospheric setting for 'modern medieval' cuisine. Check the table-mat map for the provenance of your cod, woodpigeon or rare-breed pork. Everything else is made from scratch on site, including breads, pastries, ice creams and sausages. Bookings recommended.

Jesmond

Fat Hippo BURGERS **$$**
(☎0191-340 8949; www.fat-hippo.co.uk; 35a St Georges Tce, West Jesmond; burgers £8-14; ⏲noon-9.30pm Mon-Thu, noon-10pm Fri, 11am-10pm Sat, 11am-9.30pm Sun) Humongous burgers arrive on wooden planks with steel buckets of triple-fried, hand-cut chips at this local success story. Stinky Pete comes with blue cheese, jalapeño peppers and red-onion jam; 4x4 has a whopping four patties. Veggie options include Mac the Ripper (mac 'n cheese balls with lettuce and white BBQ sauce). Sides span deep-fried gherkins to house-made slaw.

Pizzeria Francesca PIZZERIA **$$**
(134 Manor House Rd; pizza & pasta £5-8.40, mains £9-17; ⏲noon-2.30pm & 5-9.30pm Mon-Sat) Excitable waiters and huge portions of pizza and pasta keep locals queuing at the door of this chaotic, cheerful neighbourhood restaurant – get in line and wait because you can't book in advance.

Jesmond Dene House MODERN BRITISH **$$$**
(☎0191-212 5555; http://jesmonddenehouse.co.uk; Jesmond Dene Rd; mains £16-36, 2-/3-course lunch menus £19.50/22; ⏲7-10am, noon-5pm & 7-9pm Mon-Thu, 7-10am, noon-5pm & 7-9.30pm Fri, 7.30-10.30am, noon-5pm & 7-9.30pm Sat, 7.30-10.30am & noon-9pm Sun) Head chef Michael Penaluna is the architect of an exquisite regional menu – venison from County Durham, oysters from Lindisfarne and herbs plucked straight from the garden. The result is a gourmet extravaganza.

Drinking & Nightlife

Newcastle can get seriously rowdy on Friday and Saturday nights, especially the areas around Bigg Market (just south of Newgate St) and Newcastle Central Station. Less raucous alternatives include Jesmond's bars and the Ouseburn Valley, which attracts a mellower, arty crowd.

City Centre

★Bridge Hotel PUB
(http://sjf.co.uk/our-pubs/bridge-hotel; Castle Sq; ⏲11.30am-11pm Mon-Thu, to midnight Fri & Sat, noon-10.30pm Sun) Dating from 1901, this jewel of a traditional pub retains original features including Victorian snugs, carved woodwork, stained-glass windows and mosaic tiles. At least 11 hand-pulled ales are on tap; mellow live music (folk; singer-songwriters) plays almost every night. Its panoramic beer garden overlooking the High Level and Tyne bridges incorporates part of Newcastle's medieval city walls.

Lola Jeans COCKTAIL BAR
(www.lolajeans.co.uk; 1-3 Market St; ⏲noon-midnight Mon-Thu, to 1am Fri-Sun) At this Jazz

Age-styled bar, dazzling cocktails – Fog on the Tyne (Bols Genever, Newcastle Brown Ale reduction, rose lemonade and nettle cordial); Garden of Babylon (white rum, passionfruit, lime, sugar snap peas, brown sugar and mango); Hot Buttered Horchata (dark rum, condensed almond milk and chai spices) – come in vintage glassware and are accompanied by a classy BBQ menu.

World Headquarters CLUB
(www.welovewhq.com; Curtis Mayfield House, Carliol Sq; ⏲11pm-4am, days vary) Dedicated to the genius of black music – funk, rare groove, dance-floor jazz, northern soul, genuine R&B, lush disco, proper house, reggae and more – this brilliant club is a world away from commercial blandness.

Split Chimp PUB
(www.splitchimp.pub; Arch 7, Westgate Rd; ⏲4-9pm Tue, 4-10pm Wed, 3-10pm Thu, 1-11pm Fri & Sat) Covered in retro chimp montages but actually named for the wood that's wedged behind ale casks to tip them, this tiny, two-level micropub inside a railway viaduct has a 31ft-long skittle alley and hosts occasional live music. Hand-pulled local ales rotate on the taps; it also has craft beers, ciders and wine.

QB Tea House TEAHOUSE
(☎0191-261 4861; www.quilliambrothers.com; Claremont Buildings, 1 Eldon Pl; ⏲10am-midnight Mon-Fri, 9am-midnight Sat) Set up by a trio of brothers as 'an alternative to Newcastle's boozy scene', this hip Hungarian-style teahouse with postindustrial decor has over 100 types of tea as well as a tiny cinema screening cult films (dates vary), plus various gigs and art events.

Digital CLUB
(http://yourfutureisdigital.com; Times Sq; ⏲11pm-3am Mon & Thu-Sat) A two-floored cathedral to dance music, this megaclub was voted one of the top 20 clubs in the world by *DJ Magazine* thanks to one of the best sound systems you're ever likely to hear. Live acts rock the house too.

Ouseburn Valley

★Tyne Bar PUB
(☎0191-265 2550; www.thetyne.com; 1 Maling St; ⏲noon-11pm Mon-Thu, to midnight Fri & Sat, to 10.30pm Sun; 📶) An outdoor stage hosting free gigs, a free jukebox, beer-garden-style seating under one of the brick arches of the Glasshouse Bridge and a sprawling expanse of grass with knockout river views make this tucked-away waterfront pub a magnet for in-the-know locals. Free bar food is laid on between 7pm and 9pm on Tuesdays.

Ship Inn PUB
(☎0191-222 1322; Stepney Bank; ⏲noon-10pm Mon-Thu, to midnight Fri & Sat, to 11pm Sun) Maritime memorabilia and historic photos of the Ouseburn Valley fill this red-brick charmer, which has been pouring pints since the early 1800s. On busy days the elbow-bending spills out onto the small green in front.

☆ Entertainment

The Crack (www.thecrackmagazine.com) has comprehensive theatre, music, cinema and club listings for the entire northeast.

Sage Gateshead LIVE MUSIC
(☎0191-443 4661; www.sagegateshead.com; Gateshead Quays) Norman Foster's magnificent chrome-and-glass horizontal bottle is a stunner in itself but, as the home of the Northern Sinfonia and Folkworks, also presents outstanding live music.

GAY & LESBIAN NEWCASTLE

Newcastle's dynamic gay scene centres on the 'Pink Triangle', formed by Waterloo, Neville and Collingwood Sts, though venues stretch south to Scotswood Rd. Check www.gaynewcastle.co.uk for venues, parties and events.

Eazy Street (www.eazy-street.co.uk; 8-10 Westmorland Rd; ⏲noon-3am) Called Camp David in a previous life, this gay and all-welcoming bar draws a crowd for its nightly feast of DJs and cabaret drag shows.

Powerhouse (9-19 Westmorland Rd; ⏲11pm-4am Mon, 10pm-4am Tue-Thu, 10pm-5am Fri & Sat) Mixed but mainly gay, this massive four-floor club has flashing lights, a pumping sound system and lots of suggestive posing.

Switch (10a Scotswood Rd; ⏲9pm-1.30am Mon, 9pm-2am Thu, 6pm-2.30am Fri, 5pm-3am Sat, 5pm-2am Sun) This small late-night bar, formerly known as Loft, remains supremely popular.

WORTH A TRIP

HARTLEPOOL

Steelworks and shipyards made this North Sea coastal town's fortunes in the 19th century, but also made it a WWI target. On 16 December 1914 it was hit by 1150 shells, killing 117 people including 29-year-old Durham Light Infantry Private Theophilus Jones, the war's first soldier killed on British soil. Hartlepool's defence batteries returned fire, damaging three enemy ships and becoming England's only coastal battery to fire its guns in the conflict.

After WWII the collapse of both the steel and ship-building industries saw Hartlepool languish until the revitalisation of its marina around the turn of the millennium, and it makes a fascinating stop to explore its wartime and maritime heritage.

Hartlepool's Maritime Experience (☎01429-860077; www.hartlepoolsmaritime experience.com; Jackson Dock, Maritime Ave; adult/child £9.25/7; ⏲10am-5pm Easter-Oct, 11am-4pm Nov-Easter) This superb family attraction incorporates both the Museum of Hartlepool, with exhibits from the Bronze Age to today, and the 1817-built HMS *Trincomalee*, the oldest British warship still afloat, as well as re-created businesses – gunsmith, swordsmith and so on – along its historic quayside. Costumed staff and audio guides do a great job of bringing it to life.

Heugh Gun Battery Museum (☎01429-270746; www.heughbattery.com; Moor Tce; adult/child £5/3; ⏲10am-4pm Thu-Sun) Atop the windswept Hartlepool Headland, about 2 miles west of the centre, you can visit the underground magazines, parade ground, museum and panoramic observation tower at the 19th-century Heugh (pronounced 'yuff') Gun Battery – one of Hartlepool's two defence batteries to return WWI fire.

Bus 22 to/from Durham (£6.10, 1¼ hours, hourly) stops at the train station. Trains link Hartlepool with Newcastle (£9.20, 45 minutes, hourly).

Tyneside Cinema CINEMA

(☎0191-227 5500; www.tynesidecinema.co.uk; 10 Pilgrim St) Opened in 1937 as Newcastle's first newsreel cinema, this art deco picture house with plush red-velvet seats still screens newsreels (11.15am daily) as well as mainstream and offbeat movies, and archive British Pathé films. Free one-hour guided tours of the building run at 11am on Monday, Tuesday, Friday and Saturday.

Theatre Royal PERFORMING ARTS

(☎08448 112121; www.theatreroyal.co.uk; 100 Grey St) The winter home of the Royal Shakespeare Company is full of Victorian splendour and has an excellent program of drama, along with major musicals, pantomimes, opera, ballet, comedy and contemporary dance.

Head of Steam @ The Cluny LIVE MUSIC

(www.headofsteam.co.uk; 36 Lime St; ⏲noon-11pm Mon-Thu, to midnight Fri & Sat, to 10.30pm Sun) Based at the artist cooperative 36 Lime St, touring acts and local talent – from experimental prog-rock heads to up-and-coming pop goddesses – fill the bill every night of the week. This is the original of several other venues in Newcastle and throughout Britain.

Shopping

Newcastle Quayside Market MARKET

(under the Tyne Bridge; ⏲9am-4pm Sun) Stalls displaying jewellery, photographic prints, art, clothing, homewares and more set up along the quays around the Tyne Bridge every Sunday. Buskers and food stalls add to the street-party atmosphere.

Grainger Market MARKET

(www.graingermarket.org.uk; btwn Grainger & Clayton Sts; ⏲9am-5.30pm Mon-Sat) Trading since 1835, Newcastle's gorgeous, heritage-listed covered market has over 100 stalls selling everything from fish, farm produce, meat and vegetables to clothes, accessories and homewares. Between alleys 1 and 2, look out for the historic Weigh House, where goods were once weighed. There are some fantastic food stalls to pick up lunch on the run.

Information

Newcastle currently doesn't have a physical tourist office, but information is available at www.newcastlegateshead.com.

Newcastle City Centre Police Station (☎emergency 999, non-emergency 101; www.northumbria.police.uk; Forth Banks; ⏲24hr)

Getting There & Away

AIR

Newcastle International Airport (0871 882 1121; www.newcastleairport.com), 7 miles north of the city off the A696, has direct services to many UK and European cities as well as long-haul flights to Dubai. Tour operators fly charters to the USA, Middle East and Africa.

The airport is linked to town by the Metro (£3.30, 25 minutes, every 12 minutes).

BUS

Local and regional buses leave from Haymarket or Eldon Sq bus stations. National Express buses arrive and depart from the **coach station** (St James Blvd) on St James Blvd. For local buses around the northeast, the excellent-value Explorer North East ticket (adult/child £9.70/8.60) is valid on most services.

Buses X15 and X18 run north to Berwick-upon-Tweed (£6.80, two hours, every two hours). National Express offers services to Edinburgh (£13.40, three hours, three daily), London (£22, seven hours, three daily) and Manchester (£22.50, 4½ hours, four daily).

TRAIN

Newcastle is on the main rail line between London and Edinburgh and is the starting point of the scenic Tyne Valley Line west to Carlisle.

Alnmouth (for bus connections to Alnwick) £10.30, 25 minutes, hourly

Berwick-upon-Tweed £7.50, 45 minutes, up to two per hour

Carlisle £15.90, 1½ hours, hourly

Durham £6.80, 10 minutes, every 20 minutes

Edinburgh £49, 1½ hours, every 30 minutes

Hartlepool £9.20, 45 minutes, hourly

London King's Cross £138, three hours, every 30 minutes

York £40, one hour, at least two per hour

Getting Around

CAR

Two tollway **vehicle tunnels** (TT2; www.tt2.co.uk; 1 way £1.70, notes & copper coins not accepted) travel beneath the Tyne.

PUBLIC TRANSPORT

There's a large bus network, but the best means of getting around is the excellent Metro (www.nexus.org.uk), with single fares from £1.70. Several saver passes are also available.

The DaySaver (£2.80 to £4.80) gives unlimited Metro travel for one day for travel after 9am, and the DayRover (adult/child £7/3.90) gives unlimited travel on all modes of transport in the Tyne and Wear county for one day for travel any time.

TAXI

On weekend nights taxis can be rare; try **Noda Taxis** (0191-222 1888; www.noda-taxis.co.uk), which has a kiosk outside the entrance to Central Station.

Tynemouth

POP 67,520

The mouth of the Tyne, 9 miles east of Newcastle, is one of the best surf spots in England, with great all-year breaks off the immense, crescent-shaped Blue Flag beach, which occasionally hosts the National Surfing Championships.

Sights & Activities

Tynemouth Priory RUINS

(EH; www.english-heritage.org.uk; Pier Rd; adult/child £5.20/3.10; 10am-6pm Apr-Sep, to 5pm Oct, 10am-4pm Sat & Sun Nov-Mar) Built by Benedictine monks on a strategic bluff above the mouth of the Tyne in the 11th-century ruins, Tynemouth Priory was ransacked during the Dissolution in 1539. The military took over for four centuries, only leaving in 1960, and today the skeletal remains of the priory church sit alongside old military installations, their guns aimed out to sea at an enemy that never came.

Tynemouth Surf Company SURFING

(0191-258 2496; www.tynemouthsurf.co.uk; Grand Pde; 10am-5.30pm) For all your surfing needs, call into this friendly surf company, which also provides two-hour group lessons for £25 per person at 2pm daily (when the surf's up) from March to October. The

NEWCASTLE UNITED FOOTBALL CLUB TOUR

Newcastle United Football Club (NUFC; 0844 372 1892; www.nufc.co.uk; St James Park, Strawberry Pl) is more than just a football team – it's the collective expression of Geordie hope and pride. The club's hallowed ground, St James Park, is always packed, but you can take a **stadium tour** (adult/child £15/8, rooftop tours £20/15; stadium tours 11.30am, 12.30pm & 2.30pm non-match days, 10.30am match days, rooftop tours noon & 2pm Sat non-match days) that includes the dugout and changing rooms, as well as rooftop tours. Match tickets go on public sale about two weeks before a game.

adjoining chilled surf cafe morphs into a cool bar and live-music venue at night.

Sleeping & Eating

Grand Hotel HERITAGE HOTEL **$$$**

(☎0191-293 6666; www.grandhotel-uk.com; Grand Pde; incl breakfast d £96-199, f £156-196) Many of the 46 rooms at this landmark 1872-built hotel (the one-time summer residence of the duke and duchess of Northumberland) and neighbouring town house overlook the beach, and some have four-poster beds and spa baths, though wi-fi's only reliable in public areas. Its Victorian-style bar, drawing room serving high tea, and fine-dining restaurant (mains £12 to £22) are excellent.

Barca Art Cafe CAFE **$$**

(☎0191-257 7959; www.barcaart.co.uk; 68 Front St; mains £12-17; ⏲kitchen 5-10pm Mon-Sat, noon-6pm Sun, bar noon-1am daily) This funky hybrid restaurant, bar and art gallery (the works by local artists are all for sale) has an ambitious, contemporary menu, although vegetarian options, aside from some of its tapas dishes, are few. DJs spin on Saturday nights from 10pm.

Getting There & Away

From Newcastle, the easiest way to reach Tynemouth is by Metro (£3.20, 25 min, every 12 min).

Durham

POP 48,069

England's most beautiful Romanesque cathedral, a huge castle, and, surrounding them both, a cobweb of hilly, cobbled streets usually full of upper-crust students attending England's third university of choice (after Oxford and Cambridge) make Durham an ideal day trip from Newcastle or overnight stop.

Sights

★Durham Cathedral CATHEDRAL

(www.durhamcathedral.co.uk; Palace Green; cathedral by donation, tower adult/child £5/2.50, cathedral guided tours adult/child £5/4.50; ⏲cathedral 7.30am-6pm Mon-Sat, to 5.30pm Sun, tower noon-2pm Wed & Sat, cathedral tours 10.30am, 11am & 2pm Jun-Aug, 11am & 2pm Sep-May) This monumental cathedral is the definitive structure of the Anglo-Norman Romanesque style, a resplendent monument to the country's ecclesiastical history and, since 1986, a Unesco World Heritage Site. Beyond the main door – and the famous **Sanctuary Knocker**, which medieval felons would strike to gain 37 days asylum within the cathedral before standing trial or leaving the country – the interior is spectacular. Climbing the tower's 325 steps rewards you with show-stopping vistas.

Durham was the first European cathedral to be roofed with stone-ribbed vaulting, which upheld the heavy stone roof and made it possible to build pointed transverse arches – the first in England, and a great architectural achievement. The central tower dates from 1262, but was damaged in a fire caused by lightning in 1429 and unsatisfactorily patched up until it was entirely rebuilt in 1470. The western towers were added in 1217–26.

The northern side of the beautiful, 1175-built **Galilee Chapel** features rare surviving examples of 12th-century wall painting (thought to feature portraits of Sts Cuthbert and Oswald). Galilee Chapel also contains the **tomb of the Venerable Bede**, the 8th-century Northumbrian monk turned historian: his *Ecclesiastical History of the English People* is still the prime source of information on the development of early Christian Britain. Among other things, Bede introduced the numbering of years from the birth of Jesus. He was first buried at Jarrow, but in 1022 a miscreant monk stole his remains and brought them here.

Other highlights include the 14th-century **Bishop's Throne**; the beautiful stone **Neville Screen** (1372–80), which separates the high altar from **St Cuthbert's tomb**; and the mostly 19th-century **Cloisters** where you'll find the **Monk's Dormitory**, now a library of 30,000 books. There are audiovisual displays on the building of the cathedral and St Cuthbert, and a rolling program of exhibitions.

★Durham Castle CASTLE

(☎0191-334 2932; www.dur.ac.uk/durham.castle; Palace Green; admission by guided tour only, adult/child £5/3.50; ⏲by reservation) Built as a standard motte-and-bailey fort in 1072, Durham Castle was the prince bishops' home until 1837, when it became the University of Durham's first college. It remains a university hall today. Highlights of the 45-minute tour include the 17th-century **Black Staircase** and the beautifully preserved **Norman chapel** (1080).

Each successive prince bishop sought to put his particular imprint on the place, but restoration and reconstruction were necessary in any case as the castle is built of soft stone on soft ground.

Durham

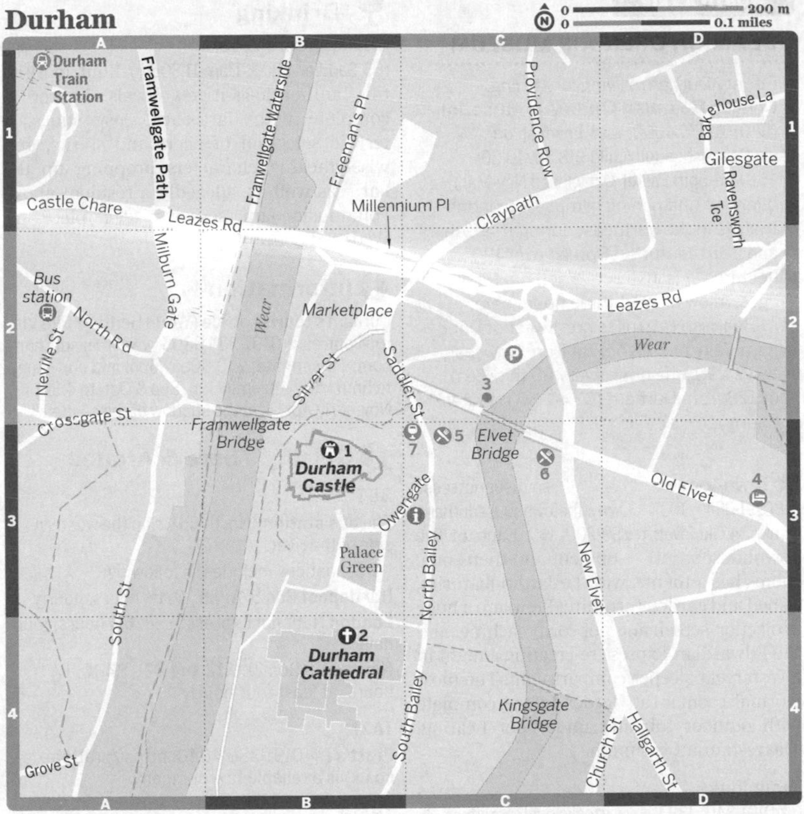

Activities

Browns Boathouse BOATING

(☎0191-386 3779; Elvet Bridge; per hour adult/child £6/4; ⏰10am-6pm Easter-late Sep) Rent a row boat for a romantic river excursion.

Prince Bishop River Cruiser BOATING

(☎0191-386 9525; www.princebishoprc.co.uk; Browns Boathouse, Elvet Bridge; adult/child £8/5; ⏰cruises 12.30pm, 2pm & 3pm Jun-Sep, call for times Oct-May) Wonderfully scenic one-hour cruises take you out on the Wear.

Sleeping & Eating

Honest Lawyer INN $$

(☎0191-378 3780; www.strhotels.co.uk; Croxdale Bridge, Croxdale; d £58-83, f £89-110; P 🛜 👪 🐾) An easy 3-mile drive south of Durham on the A167, this handy spot has mostly motel-style rooms with countrified chequered fabrics and parking outside the door. Family rooms sleep up to four people. The main building has a timber bar and restaurant serving good pub grub in generous portions.

Durham

Top Sights
1 Durham Castle....B3
2 Durham Cathedral....B4

Activities, Courses & Tours
Browns Boathouse....(see 3)
3 Prince Bishop River Cruiser....C2

Sleeping
4 The Townhouse....D3

Eating
5 Cellar Door Durham....C3
6 Tealicious....C3

Drinking & Nightlife
7 Shakespeare Tavern....C3

WORTH A TRIP

BEAMISH OPEN-AIR MUSEUM

County Durham's living, breathing, working **Beamish Open-Air Museum** (☎0191-370 4000; www.beamish.org.uk; Beamish; adult/child £18.50/10.50; ⊙10am-5pm Easter-Oct, closed Nov-Mar) offers an unflinching glimpse into industrial life in the northeast during the 19th and 20th centuries. Spread over 120 hectares, it is instructive and fun for all ages. Allow at least three hours here.

Beamish is 9 miles northwest of Durham. Take bus 28 or 28A from Newcastle (£4.90, one hour, every 30 minutes) or 128 from Durham (£3.40, 30 minutes, hourly).

★**Townhouse** BOUTIQUE HOTEL $$$
(☎0191-384 1037; www.thetownhousedurham.co.uk; 34 Old Elvet; d £99-200; 📶) Each of the Townhouse's 11 opulent-and-then-some rooms has a theme, with Le Jardin featuring a shed and garden furniture; Premiere a huge projection screen and popcorn machine; and the Edwardian Express re-creating a night in a yesteryear sleeper compartment. The most 'normal' room is the Garden Lodge, complete with outdoor tub and underfloor heating. The restaurant is superb.

Tealicious CAFE $
(☎0191-340 1393; www.tealicioustearoom.co.uk; 88 Elvet Bridge; dishes £2-5.50, high tea adult/child £12.50/6.95; ⊙10am-4pm Tue-Sat, noon-4pm Sun) Inside this quaint pastel-blue and white building, amid vintage decor, treats include homemade cakes (such as white-chocolate cheesecake or ginger and lime), sandwiches, and over a dozen blends of tea served from individual pots on fine bone china. High tea here is a treat. It's tiny so book ahead.

Cellar Door Durham MODERN BRITISH $$
(☎0191-383 1856; www.thecellardoordurham.co.uk; 41 Saddler St; mains £11-22, 2-/3-course lunch menus £14/17; ⊙10.30am-10.30pm) Accessed from an inconspicuous door on Saddler St, this 12th-century building has glorious river views, including from the alfresco terrace. The Mediterranean-meets-Britain menu features starters such as twice-baked Camembert soufflé, mains including beef ribs with smoked mash and beer-pickled onions, and desserts such as chocolate and brown butter terrine with pistachio ice cream. Service is spot on.

Drinking

Shakespeare Tavern PUB
(63 Saddler St; ⊙11am-11.30pm) Built in 1190, this authentic-as-it-gets locals' boozer is complete with dartboard, cosy snugs, a terrific selection of beers and spirits, and wise-cracking characters propping up the bar – as well as, allegedly, a resident ghost. Folk-music jam sessions take place on Wednesday evenings.

Information

Durham's **tourist office** (World Heritage Site Visitor Centre; ☎0191-334 3805; www.thisisdurham.com; 7 Owengate; ⊙9.30am-6pm mid-Jun–Aug, to 5pm early Apr–mid-Jun, Sep & Oct, to 4.30pm Nov-early Apr) is in the shadow of the castle.

Getting There & Around

BUS

The **bus station** (North Rd) is on the western side of the river.

Destinations include the following:

Hartlepool Bus 57A; £6.10, 1¼ hours, hourly

London National Express; £28, 6½ hours, four daily

Newcastle Bus 21, X12 and X21; £4.10, 1¼ hours, at least four hourly

TAXI

Pratt's (☎0191-386 4040; http://prattstaxis.co.uk) is a reliable taxi company.

TRAIN

The East Coast Main Line provides speedy connections to destinations including the following:

Edinburgh £61, 1½ hours, hourly

London King's Cross £138, three hours, every 30 minutes

Newcastle £6.80, 10 minutes, three hourly

York £33.90, 50 minutes, four hourly

Barnard Castle

POP 5694

The charming market town of Barnard Castle, better known as 'Barney', is a traditionalist's dream, full of antiquarian shops and atmospheric old pubs. It's a wonderful setting for the town's twin draws: a daunting ruined castle and an extraordinary French chateau.

Sights

Barnard Castle CASTLE
(EH; www.english-heritage.org.uk; Scar Top; adult/child £5/3; ⊙10am-6pm Easter-Sep, to 5pm Oct, 10am-4pm Sat & Sun Nov-Easter) Built on a cliff

above the River Tees by Guy de Bailleul and rebuilt around 1150, Barnard Castle was partly dismantled some four centuries later, but its ruins still manage to cover two very impressive hectares with wonderful river views. Also here is a sensory garden.

★ Bowes Museum MUSEUM
(www.thebowesmuseum.org.uk; Newgate; adult/child £10.50/free; ⏲10am-5pm) A monumental chateau half a mile east of the centre contains the lavishly furnished Bowes Museum. Funded by 19th-century industrialist John Bowes, and opened in 1892, this brainchild of his Parisian actress wife, Josephine, was built by French architect Jules Pellechet to display a collection the Bowes had travelled the world to assemble. The star attraction is the marvellous 18th-century mechanical swan, which performs every day at 2pm. If you miss it, a film shows it in action.

Look for works by Canaletto, El Greco and Goya as well as 55 paintings by Josephine herself. Among the 15,000 other objets d'art are incredible dresses from the 17th century through to the 1970s as part of an exhibit on textiles through the ages, and clocks, watches and tableware in gold and silver in the precious-metals section. It also houses finds unearthed from the nearby Binchester Roman Fort.

Sleeping & Eating

Old Well Inn INN $$
(☎01833-690130; http://theoldwellinn.co.uk; 21 The Bank; s/d incl breakfast from £60/83;) Built over a huge well (not visible), this old coaching inn has 10 enormous rooms. No 9 is the most impressive with its own private entrance, flagstone floors and a bath. The pub has regional ales on tap that you can sip in the leafy beer garden in fine weather.

Jersey Farm Country Hotel HOTEL $$
(☎01833-638223; www.jerseyfarmhotel.co.uk; Darlington Rd; s/d from £72/99; P) Another genteel farmhouse conversion, right? Wrong. The 22 rooms here sport cool retro colour schemes and gadgets galore. The restaurant is a clean-cut affair (mains £7.50 to £16). It's 1.3 miles east of the town centre signposted just off Darlington Rd (the A67).

★ Cross Lanes Organic Farm Shop DELI, CAFE
(☎01833-630619; www.crosslanesorganics.co.uk; Cross Lanes; dishes £4.50-11; ⏲cafe 8.30am-4pm, shop 8.30am-5pm Mon-Sat, 10am-5pm Sun;) Sheep graze on the grass-covered roof of this award-winning farm shop and cafe 1.5 miles south of Barnard Castle. The cavernous interior brims with all-organic produce; breakfasts (home-cured bacon, homemade sausages and eggs from the farm's chickens) segue into lunches including gourmet sandwiches, steak or veggie burgers and wood-fired pizzas, and 'rustic afternoon tea' with organic cream and wild-fruit jams.

> WORTH A TRIP
>
> ### KNITSLEY FARM SHOP & CAFE
>
> It's worth stopping off at **Knitsley Farm Shop & Cafe** (☎01207-592059; www.knitselyfarmshop.co.uk; East Knitsley Grange Farm, Knitsley; dishes £3.50-9.50; ⏲shop 10am-5pm Tue-Sat, to 4pm Sun, cafe 10am-5pm Tue-Fri, 9.30am-5pm Sat, 9.30am-4pm Sun), 12 miles northwest of Durham en route to Northumberland National Park and Hadrian's Wall, to stock up on its incredible cheeses, meats, homemade sweets, cakes and breads. It's even better if you can make time to dine at its wonderful cafe on fresh-as-it-gets soups, farmyard sausages, and pulled-pork and crackling baps.

Information

Tourist Office (☎01833-631107; www.thisisdurham.com; 3 Horsemarket; ⏲10am-4pm Mon & Wed-Sat) In the Witham building's arts and community centre.

Getting There & Away

Barnard Castle is poorly served by public transport so you really need your own wheels.

Hadrian's Wall

Named in honour of the emperor who ordered it built, Hadrian's Wall was one of Rome's greatest engineering projects. This enormous 73-mile-long wall was built between AD 122 and 128 to separate Romans and Scottish Picts. Today, the awe-inspiring sections that remain are testament to Roman ambition and tenacity.

When completed, the mammoth structure ran across the island's narrow neck, from the Solway Firth in the west almost to the mouth of the Tyne in the east. Every Roman mile (0.95 miles) there was a gateway guarded by a small fort (milecastle) and

OFF THE BEATEN TRACK

RABY CASTLE

Sprawling **Raby Castle** (www.rabycastle.com; Staindrop; castle, gardens & park adult/child £10/4.50, gardens & park only £6/2.50; ⏲1-4.30pm Sun-Fri Jul & Aug, 1-4.30pm Sun-Wed May, Jun & Sep) was a stronghold of the Catholic Neville family until it engaged in some ill-judged plotting (the 'Rising of the North') against the oh-so Protestant Queen Elizabeth in 1569. Most of the interior dates from the 18th and 19th centuries, but the exterior remains true to the original design, built around a courtyard and surrounded by a moat. It's 6.8 miles northeast of Barnard Castle; take bus 85A (£3, 15 minutes, every two hours Monday to Saturday).

between each milecastle were two observation turrets. Milecastles are numbered right across the country, starting with Milecastle 0 at Wallsend – where you can visit the wall's last stronghold, Segedunum (p625) – and ending with Milecastle 80 at Bowness-on-Solway.

A series of forts were developed as bases some distance south (and may predate the wall), and 16 lie astride it.

Activities

The **Hadrian's Wall Path** (www.nationaltrail.co.uk/hadrians-wall-path) is an 84-mile national trail that runs the length of the wall from Wallsend in the east to Bowness-on-Solway in the west. The entire route should take about seven days on foot, giving plenty of time to explore the rich archaeological heritage along the way.

Information

There are tourist offices in Hexham, Haltwhistle and Corbridge. The Walltown Visitor Centre (p640), aka the Northumberland National Park Visitor Centre, is located at Greenhead.

Hadrian's Wall Country (http://hadrianswallcountry.co.uk) is the official portal for the area.

Getting There & Around

BUS

The AD122 Hadrian's Wall bus (five daily, Easter to late September) is a hail-and-ride service that runs between Hexham and Carlisle, with one bus a day starting and ending at Newcastle's Central Station and not all services covering the entire route. Bikes can be taken aboard AD122 buses, but space is limited. Bus 185 zips between Birdoswald Roman Fort and Carlisle via Haltwhistle the rest of the year (three daily, Monday to Saturday only).

Bus 10 links Newcastle with Hexham (1½ hours, every 30 minutes).

West of Hexham the wall runs parallel to the A69, which connects Carlisle and Newcastle. Buses 85 and 685 run along the A69 hourly, passing 2 miles to 3 miles south of the main sites throughout the year.

All these services can be used with the Hadrian's Wall Rover Ticket (adult/child 1 day £12.50/6.50, 3 days £25/13, 7 days £50/26), available from bus drivers and tourist offices. Show your Rover Ticket to get 10% off admission to all museums and attractions.

CAR & MOTORCYCLE

Your own wheels are the easiest way to get around, with one fort or garrison usually just a short hop from the next. Parking costs £4/15 per day/week; tickets are valid at all sites along the wall.

The B6318 follows the course of the wall from the outskirts of Newcastle to Birdoswald. The main A69 road and the railway line follow 3 or 4 miles to the south.

TRAIN

The railway line between Newcastle and Carlisle (Tyne Valley Line; £15.90, 1½ hours, hourly) has stations at Corbridge, Hexham, Haydon Bridge, Bardon Mill, Haltwhistle and Brampton. Not all services stop at all stations.

Corbridge

POP 3011

Above a curve in the Tyne, Corbridge's shady, cobbled streets are lined with old-fashioned shops and pubs. Inhabited since Saxon times when there was a substantial monastery, many of its charming buildings feature stones from nearby Corstopitum.

Sights

Corbridge Roman Site & Museum HISTORIC SITE
(EH; www.english-heritage.org.uk; Corchester Lane; adult/child £6.10/3.70; ⏲10am-6pm Easter-Sep, to 5pm Oct, 10am-4pm Sat & Sun Nov-Easter) What's left of the Roman garrison town of Corstopitum lies about half a mile west of Market Pl on Dere St, once the main road from York to Scotland. It's the oldest fortified site in the area, predating the wall itself by some 40 years. Most of what you see here, though, dates from around AD 200, when the fort had developed into a civilian settlement and was the main base along the wall.

You get a sense of the domestic heart of the town from the visible remains. The Corbridge Museum displays Roman sculpture and carvings, including the amazing 3rd-century **Corbridge Lion**.

Sleeping & Eating

2 The Crofts B&B $$
(☎01434-633046; www.2thecrofts.co.uk; Newcastle Rd; s/d from £55/75; P 📶) By far the best place in town to drop your pack, this secluded B&B occupies a beautiful period home half a mile east of the town centre. The two high-ceilinged, spacious rooms are en suite and the energetic owner cooks a mean breakfast (packed lunches can also be organised). Guests are welcome to play the piano.

★**Corbridge Larder** DELI, CAFE $
(☎01434-632 948; www.corbridgelarder.co.uk; 18 Hill St; dishes £4-7, dinner mains £10; ⏱9am-5pm Mon-Fri, 9am-5pm & 6.30-10.30pm Sat, 10am-4pm Sun) Gourmet picnic fare at this fabulous deli includes bread, more than 100 varieties of cheese, chutneys, cakes, chocolates and wine (you can get hampers made up) as well as made-to-order sandwiches, pies, quiches, tarts, and antipasti and meze delicacies. Upstairs from the wonderland of provisions there's a small sit-down cafe. On Saturday evenings it hosts dinners accompanied by live music.

Black Bull BRITISH $$
(www.oldenglishinns.co.uk; Middle St; mains £8-17; ⏱kitchen noon-9pm, bar noon-midnight; 📶 👪) A menu of British comfort food, such as beef burgers, fish in beer batter and slow-cooked lamb, and a series of low ceilinged, atmospheric dining rooms, make this tavern dating from 1755 a cosy spot to hole up. Sundays offer a choice of five different roasts.

Hadrian's Wall & Northumberland National Park

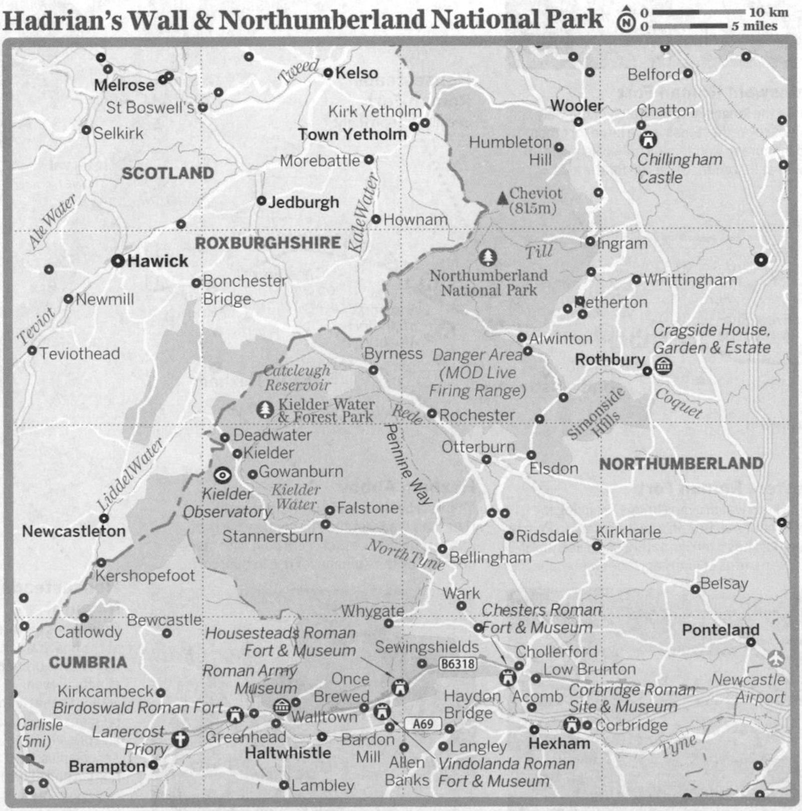

Hadrian's Wall

ROME'S FINAL FRONTIER

Of all Britain's Roman ruins, Emperor Hadrian's 2nd-century wall, cutting across northern England from the Irish Sea to the North Sea, is by far the most spectacular; Unesco awarded it world cultural heritage status in 1987.

We've picked out the highlights, one of which is the prime remaining Roman fort on the wall, Housesteads, which we've reconstructed here.

GANNET77 / GETTY IMAGES ©

Housesteads' granaries

Nothing like the clever underground ventilation system, which kept vital supplies of grain dry in Northumberland's damp and drizzly climate, would be seen again in these parts for 1500 years.

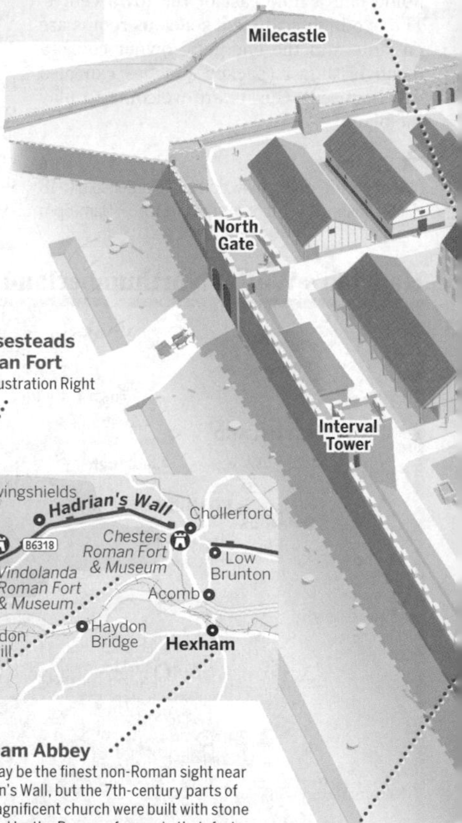

STEPHEN DOREY / GETTY IMAGES ©

Birdoswald Roman Fort

Explore the longest intact stretch of the wall, scramble over the remains of a large fort then head indoors to wonder at a full-scale model of the wall at its zenith. Great fun for the kids.

Housesteads Roman Fort

See Illustration Right

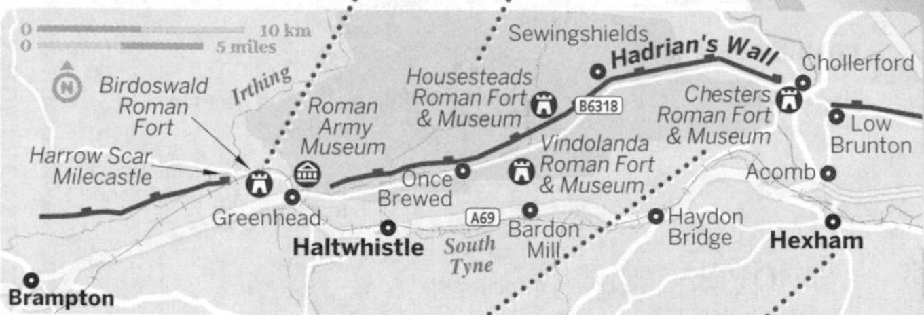

Chesters Roman Fort

Built to keep watch over a bridge spanning the River North Tyne, Britain's best-preserved Roman cavalry fort has a terrific bathhouse, essential if you have months of nippy northern winter ahead.

NEIL HOLMES / GETTY IMAGES ©

Hexham Abbey

This may be the finest non-Roman sight near Hadrian's Wall, but the 7th-century parts of this magnificent church were built with stone quarried by the Romans for use in their forts.

VISITBRITAIN/BRITAIN ON VIEW / GETTY IMAGES ©

Housesteads' hospital

Operations performed at the hospital would have been surprisingly effective, even without anaesthetics; religious rituals and prayers to Aesculapius, the Roman god of healing, were possibly less helpful for a hernia or appendicitis.

Housesteads' latrines
Communal toilets were the norm in Roman times and Housesteads' are remarkably well preserved – fortunately no traces remain of the vinegar-soaked sponges that were used instead of toilet paper.

QUICK WALL FACTS & FIGURES

» **Latin name** Vallum Aelium

» **Length** 73.5 miles (80 Roman miles)

» **Construction date** AD 122–128

» **Manpower for construction** Three legions (around 16,000 men)

» **Features** At least 16 forts, 80 milecastles, 160 turrets

» **Did you know** Hadrian's wasn't the only Roman wall in Britain – the Antonine Wall was built across what is now central Scotland in the AD 140s, but it was abandoned soon after

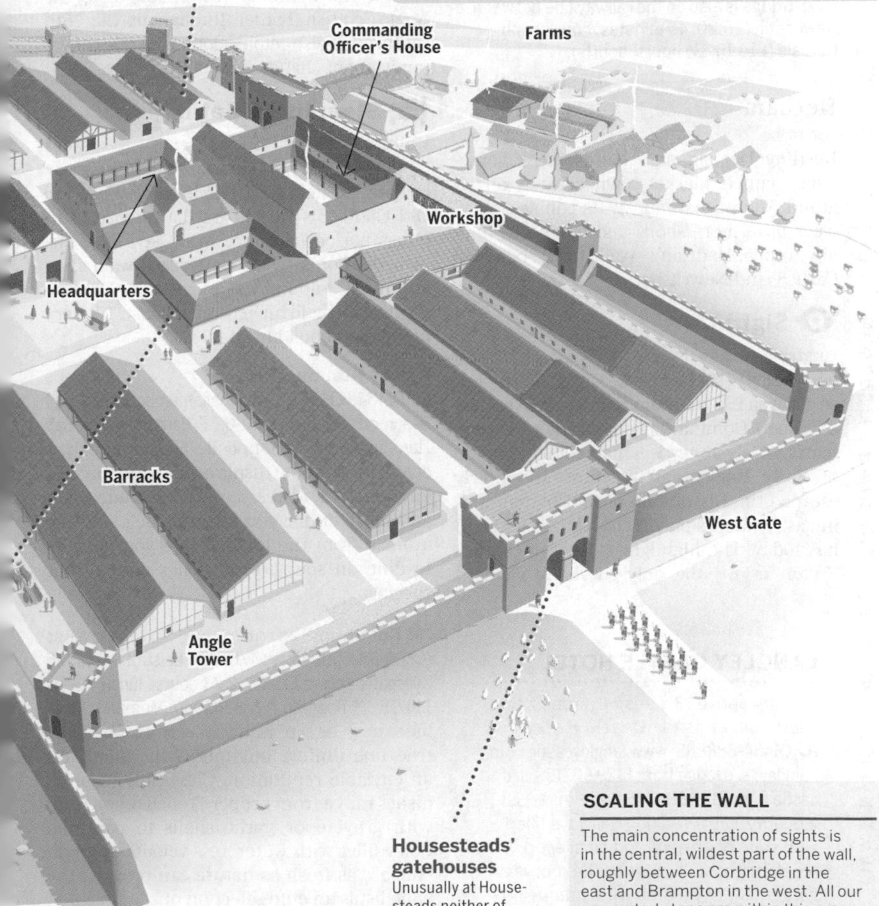

Housesteads' gatehouses
Unusually at Housesteads neither of the gates faces the enemy, as was the norm at a Roman fort – builders aligned them east-west. Ruts worn by cart wheels are still visible in the stone.

FREE GUIDES

At some sites knowledgeable volunteer heritage guides are on hand to answer questions and put meat on the wall's stony bones.

SCALING THE WALL

The main concentration of sights is in the central, wildest part of the wall, roughly between Corbridge in the east and Brampton in the west. All our suggested stops are within this area and follow an east–west route. The easiest way to travel is by car, scooting along the B6318, but special bus AD122 will also get you there. Hiking along the designated Hadrian's Wall Path (84 miles) allows you to appreciate the achievement up close.

Information

Corbridge's **tourist office** (☎01434-632815; www.visitnorthumberland.com; Hill St; ⏲10am-4.30pm Mon-Sat Easter-Oct, closed Nov-Mar) occupies a corner of the library.

Getting There & Away

Buses 85, 685 and X85 between Newcastle (£4.80, 45 minutes, hourly) and Carlisle (£7.10, 2¼ hours, hourly) come through Corbridge, as does bus 10 from Newcastle (£5.10, one hour, every 30 minutes) to Hexham (£3, 20 minutes, every 30 minutes), where you can connect with the Hadrian's Wall bus AD122.

Corbridge is also on the railway line between Newcastle (£6.20, 45 minutes, hourly) and Carlisle (£14.10, 1½ hours, hourly).

Hexham

POP 13,100

Bustling Hexham is a handsome if somewhat scuffed market town centred on its grand Augustinian abbey. Its cobbled alleyways have more shops and amenities than any other Hadrian's Wall town between Carlisle and Newcastle.

Sights

Hexham Abbey CHURCH

(www.hexhamabbey.org.uk; Beaumont St; suggested donation £3; ⏲9.30am-5pm, Saxon crypt 11am & 3.30pm) Dominating tiny Market Pl, Hexham's stately abbey is a marvellous example of Early English architecture. It cleverly escaped the Dissolution of 1537 by rebranding as Hexham's parish church, a role it still has today. The highlight is the 7th-century **Saxon crypt**, the only surviving element of St Wilifrid's Church, built with inscribed stones from Corstopitum in 674.

Old Gaol HISTORIC BUILDING

(www.hexhamoldgaol.org.uk; Hallgate; adult/child £3.95/2.50; ⏲11am-4.30pm Mon-Sat Aug, 11am-4.30pm Tue-Sat Apr-Jul & Sep, 11am-4.30pm Tue & Sat Oct, Nov, Feb & Mar, closed Dec) Completed in 1333 as England's first purpose-built prison, today this strapping stone structure's four floors tell the history of the jail in all its gruesome glory. The history of the Border Reivers – a group of clans who fought, kidnapped, blackmailed and killed each other in an effort to exercise control over a lawless tract of land along the Anglo-Scottish border throughout the 16th century – is also retold, along with tales of the punishments handed out in the prison.

LANGLEY CASTLE HOTEL

Soaring above 12 acres of gardens, the 1350-built **Langley Castle Hotel** (☎01434-688888; www.langleycastle.com; Langley; s/d lodge from £129.50/159, s/d castle from £199.50/245,; P 📶 👪 🐾) is a beauty, with creaking hallways filled with suits of armour and an alleged resident ghost. Its nine castle rooms are gorgeously appointed with antique furnishings (most have four-poster beds); there are splendid views of the castle from its adjacent, recently converted lodge. Check for dinner, bed and breakfast packages.

Sleeping & Eating

Hallbank Guest House B&B $$

(☎01434-605567; www.hallbankguesthouse.com; Hallgate; d/f from £120/130; P 📶) Behind the Old Gaol, this fine Edwardian house combines period elegance with stylishly furnished rooms with patterned wallpaper, autumnal colours and huge beds. Evening meals can be arranged on request. It's very popular so book ahead.

Deli at Number 4 DELI, CAFE $

(☎01434-608091; www.deliatnumber4.co.uk; 4 Beaumont St; dishes £2-6; ⏲9am-5pm Mon-Sat, 11am-5pm Sun) 🍃 Opposite Hexham's abbey, colourful window displays of artisan breads, local cheeses, olives, jams, homemade cakes and more entice you into this deli, and the aromas from the kitchen lure you upstairs to dine on soups, sandwiches and various specials.

★**Bouchon Bistrot** FRENCH $$

(☎01434-609943; www.bouchonbistrot.co.uk; 4-6 Gilesgate; mains £12-20, 2-/3-course lunch menus £14/15; ⏲noon-2pm & 6-9.30pm Mon-Sat) Hexham may be an unlikely setting for some true fine dining, but this Gallic affair has an enviable reputation. Classically inspired dishes range from proper French onion soup with gruyère or garlic snails to pan-fried Coley fillet with watercress velouté. Ingredients are as fresh as nature can provide; the wine list is an elite selection of champagnes, reds and whites.

Information

Hexham's **tourist office** (☎01670-620450; www.visitnorthumberland.com/hexham;

Queen's Hall, Beaumont St; ⏲10am 5pm Mon-Fri, to 4pm Sat) is inside the library.

Getting There & Away

Buses 85, 685 and X85 between Newcastle (£4.80, 1¼ hours, every 30 minutes) and Carlisle (£6.60, 1½ hours, every 30 minutes) come through Hexham; the AD122 Hadrian's Wall bus connects with other towns along the wall. Bus 10 (£5.50, 1½ hours, every 30 minutes) also links Hexham with Newcastle.

Hexham is on the scenic railway line between Newcastle (£6.90, 40 minutes, hourly) and Carlisle (£13, one hour, hourly).

Haltwhistle & Around

POP 3811

The village of Haltwhistle, little more than two intersecting streets, has more key Hadrian's Wall sights in its surrounds than anywhere else along the wall, but tourist infrastructure here is surprisingly underdeveloped.

Haltwhistle is one of the places that claims to be the geographic centre of the British mainland, although the jury is still out.

Sights

★Housesteads Roman Fort & Museum HISTORIC SITE

(EH; www.english-heritage.org.uk; Haydon Bridge; adult/child £7/4.10; ⏲10am-6pm Easter-Sep, to 5pm Oct, to 4pm Nov-Easter) The most dramatic site of Hadrian's Wall – and the best-preserved Roman fort in the whole country – is at Housesteads, 4 miles north of Bardon Mill on the B6318, and 6.5 miles northeast of Haltwhistle. From here, high on a ridge and covering 2 hectares, you can survey the moors of Northumberland National Park, and the snaking wall, with a sense of awe at the landscape and the aura of the Roman lookouts.

Up to 800 troops were based at Housesteads at any one time. Its remains include an impressive hospital, granaries with a carefully worked out ventilation system and barrack blocks. Most memorable are the spectacularly situated communal flushable latrines. Information boards show what the individual buildings would have looked like in their heyday. There's a scale model of the entire fort in the small museum at the ticket office.

Vindolanda Roman Fort & Museum HISTORIC SITE

(www.vindolanda.com; Bardon Mill; adult/child £6.07/3.86, with Roman Army Museum £9.55/5.50; ⏲10am-6pm Apr-Sep, to 5pm Oct, to 4pm Nov-Mar) The extensive site of Vindolanda offers a fascinating glimpse into the daily life of a Roman garrison town. The time-capsule museum is just one part of this large, extensively excavated site, which includes impressive parts of the fort and town (excavations continue) and reconstructed turrets and temple.

It's 1.5 miles north of Bardon Mill between the A69 and B6318, and 5.8 miles northeast of Haltwhistle.

Roman Army Museum MUSEUM

(www.vindolanda.com; Greenhead; adult/child £5/2.95, with Vindolanda £9.55/5.50; ⏲10am-6pm Apr-Sep, to 5pm Oct, 10am-4pm Sat & Sun Nov-Mar) On the site of the Carvoran Roman Fort a mile northeast of Greenhead, near Walltown Crags, this revamped museum has three new galleries covering the Roman army and expanding and contracting Empire; the wall (with a 3D film illustrating what the wall was like nearly 2000 years ago and today); and colourful background detail to Hadrian's Wall life (such as how the soldiers spent their R&R time in this lonely outpost of the Empire).

Birdoswald Roman Fort HISTORIC SITE

(EH; ☎01697-747602; www.english-heritage.org.uk; Gilsland, Greenhead; adult/child £6.10/3.70; ⏲10am-6pm Apr-Sep, to 5pm Oct, 10am-4pm Sat & Sun Nov-Mar) Technically in Cumbria, the remains of this once-formidable fort on an escarpment overlooking the beautiful Irthing Gorge are on a minor road off the B6318, about 3 miles west of Greenhead. The longest intact stretch of wall extends from here to Harrow's Scar Milecastle.

Sleeping

Greenhead HOSTEL, B&B $

(☎01697-747411; www.greenheadhotelandhostel.co.uk; Greenhead; dm/d incl breakfast from £15/85; ⏲Apr-Sep; P 📶) A converted 1866-built Methodist chapel by a trickling stream houses this independent hostel 3 miles west of Haltwhistle near the Roman Army Museum. There's a laundry and roomy kitchen, but if you don't feel like cooking, Greenhead's hotel across the road has a restaurant and bar with wi-fi. It's served by the Hadrian's Wall bus AD122.

★Ashcroft B&B $$

(☎01434-320213; www.ashcroftguesthouse.co.uk; Lanty's Lonnen, Haltwhistle; s/d/apt from £72/94/140; P 📶 👪) British B&Bs don't get better than this elegant Edwardian vicarage surrounded by nearly a hectare of beautifully

CHESTERS ROMAN FORT & MUSEUM

The superbly preserved Roman cavalry remains at **Chesters Roman Fort & Museum** (EH; ☎01434-681379; www.english-heritage.org.uk; Chollerford; adult/child £6.20/3.70; ⏰10am-6pm Easter-Sep, to 5pm Oct, 10am-4pm Sat & Sun Nov-Easter) are set among idyllic green woods and meadows near the village of Chollerford. Originally constructed to house up to 500 troops from Asturias in northern Spain, they include part of a bridge (best appreciated from the eastern bank), four gatehouses, a bathhouse and an underfloor heating system. The museum has a large Roman sculpture collection; there's a simple tearoom on site. It's served by Hadrian's Wall bus AD122.

manicured, terraced lawns and gardens. Inside, the nine rooms – some with private balconies and terraces – have soaring ceilings and every 21st-century gadget imaginable. Breakfast is served in a grand dining room; there's also a self-catering apartment on the grounds sleeping up to five people.

Holmhead Guest House B&B $$

(☎01697-747402; http://bandb-hadrianswall.co.uk; Greenhead; campsites per person £7, dm/s/d from £13.50/55/70; P 📶 👪) Built using recycled bits of the wall on whose foundations it stands, this superb farmhouse half a mile north of Greenhead offers comfy rooms, a basic bunk barn and five unpowered campsites. The Pennine Way and the Hadrian's Wall Path pass through the grounds and Thirwall Castle's jagged ruins loom above. Ask to see the 3rd-century Roman graffiti.

ℹ Information

On the main street, Haltwhistle's small **tourist office** (☎01434-321863; www.visitnorthumberland.com; Mechanics Institute, Westgate; ⏰10am-4.30pm Mon-Fri, to 1pm Sat Apr-Oct, 10am-1pm & 1.30-4.30pm Mon-Fri, 10am-1pm Sat Nov-Mar) has information on the wall's attractions.

The Northumberland National Park's visitor centre, **Walltown Visitor Centre** (☎01697-747151; www.northumberlandnationalpark.org.uk; Greenhead; ⏰10am-6pm Apr-Sep, to 5pm Oct, 10am-4pm Sat & Sun Nov-Mar) is located at Greenhead.

ℹ Getting There & Away

Bus 685 runs to Hexham (£3.40, 25 minutes, hourly) and Newcastle (£6.50, 1½ hours, hourly).

Haltwhistle is also linked by train to Hexham (£6.40, 20 minutes, hourly) and Newcastle (£12.60, one hour, hourly).

Northumberland National Park

England's last great wilderness is the 405 sq miles of natural wonderland that make up the country's least populated national park. The finest sections of Hadrian's Wall run along its southern edge and the landscape is dotted with prehistoric remains and fortified houses – the thick-walled *peles* were the only solid buildings built here until the mid-18th century.

Adjacent to the national park, the Kielder Water & Forest Park is home to the vast artificial lake Kielder Water, holding 200,000 million litres. Surrounding its 27-mile-long shoreline is England's largest plantation forest, with 150 million spruce and pine trees.

The lack of population here helped see the area awarded dark-sky status by the International Dark Skies Association in late 2013 (the largest such designation in Europe), with controls to prevent light pollution.

👁 Sights

★**Kielder Observatory** OBSERVATORY

(☎0191-265 5510; www.kielderobservatory.org; Black Fell, off Shilling Pot; public observing session adult/child £16.50/15; ⏰by reservation) For the best views of the Northumberland International Dark Sky Park, attend a stargazing session at this state-of-the-art, 2008-built observatory. In addition to public observing there are a host of events, including family astronomy, astrophotography and star camps. Book well ahead for all events, which sell out quickly, and dress as you would for the ski slopes (it's seriously chilly here at night). At the signs towards Kielder Observatory and Skyspace, turn left; it's a 2-mile drive up the track.

Cragside House, Garden & Estate HISTORIC BUILDING, GARDENS

(NT; ☎01669-620333; www.nationaltrust.org.uk; adult/child £15.80/7.90, gardens & estate only £10.20/5.10; ⏰house 11am-5pm Tue-Sun mid-Mar–Oct, gardens 10am-6pm Tue-Sun mid-Mar–Oct) Situated 1 mile northeast of Rothbury is the astonishing country retreat of the first

Lord Armstrong. In the 1880s the house had hot and cold running water, a telephone and alarm system, and was the first in the world to be lit by electricity, generated through hydropower. The sprawling Victorian gardens feature lakes, moors and one of Europe's largest rock gardens. Visit late May to mid-June to see Cragside's famous rhododendrons in bloom. It's just off the B6341.

Chillingham Castle CASTLE
(☎ 01668-215359; www.chillingham-castle.com; Chillingham; castle adult/child £9.50/5.50, Chillingham Wild Cattle £8/3, castle & Chillingham Wild Cattle £16/6; ⏲ castle noon-5pm Sun-Fri Apr-Oct, Chillingham Wild Cattle tours 10am, 11am, noon, 2pm, 3pm & 4pm Mon-Fri, 10am, 11am & noon Sun Easter to Oct, by reservation Nov-Easter) Steeped in history, warfare, torture and ghosts, 12th-century Chillingham is said to be one of the country's most haunted places, with spectres from a phantom funeral to Lady Mary Berkeley seeking her errant husband. Owner Sir Humphrey Wakefield has passionately restored the castle's extravagant medieval staterooms, stone-flagged banquet halls and grisly torture chambers. Chillingham is 6 miles southeast of Wooler.

Bus 470 (three daily Monday to Saturday) between Alnwick (£3.70, 30 minutes) and Wooler (£3.10, 20 minutes) stops at Chillingham.

Activities

The most spectacular stretch of the **Hadrian's Wall Path** is between Sewingshields and Greenhead in the south of the park.

There are many fine walks through the Cheviots (including a clamber to the top of the 815m-high Cheviot, the highest peak in the range), frequently passing by prehistoric remnants; local tourist offices can provide maps, guides and route information.

Though at times strenuous, cycling is a pleasure here; roads are good and traffic is light.

Kielder Water is a watersports playground (and midge magnet; bring insect repellent), and also has walking and cycling as well as great birdwatching. Visit www.visitkielder.com for more information.

Sleeping

Wooler YHA HOSTEL $
(☎ 0845 371 9668; www.yha.org.uk; 30 Cheviot St, Wooler; dm/d/hut from £15.50/35/42; ⏲ Mar-Nov; P 📶) In a low, red-brick building above Wooler, this handy hostel contains 57 beds in a variety of rooms (including four handcrafted 'shepherds' huts' sleeping two to three people on bunk beds), a modern lounge and a small restaurant, as well as a self-catering kitchen, drying room and bike storage.

★**Otterburn Castle Country House Hotel** HISTORIC HOTEL $$
(☎ 01830-520620; www.otterburncastle.com; Main St, Otterburn; incl breakfast d £90-140, f £110-170; P 📶 👪) Founded by William the Conqueror's cousin Robert Umfraville in 1086 and set in almost 13 hectares of grounds, this story-book castle has 17 recently refurbished, astonishing-value rooms, some with four-poster beds. Exceptional modern British fare is served in its wood-panelled **Oak Room Restaurant** (2- /3-course menus £29.50/35.50). Cheaper meals are available in the **Stable Bar & Bistro** (mains £8.50 to £16.50).

Katerina's Guest House B&B $$
(☎ 01669-620691; www.katerinasguesthouse.co.uk; High St, Rothbury; d £80; 📶) Beamed ceilings, stone fireplaces and en-suite rooms with fridges and canopied four-poster beds make Katerina's one of Rothbury's best choices. Bakeries, cafes and pubs abound along the street.

Information

For information, contact the **National Park** (☎ 01434-605555; www.northumberlandnationalpark.org.uk). As well as tourist offices in towns including **Wooler** (☎ 01668-282123; www.wooler.org.uk; Cheviot Centre, 12 Padgepool Pl, Wooler; ⏲ 10am-4.30pm Apr-Oct, 10am-4.30pm Mon-Sat Nov-Mar) and **Rothbury** (☎ 01669-620887; www.visitkielder.com; Coquetdale Centre, Church St, Rothbury; ⏲ 10am-4.30pm Mon-Sat, 10.30am-4pm Sun Apr-Oct, closed Nov-Mar), there's a national park office, the Walltown Visitor Centre (p640), near Haltwhistle. All offices can help find accommodation.

Getting There & Around

Public transport options are limited at best – to explore properly you really need your own wheels.

Bus 808 (£3.70, 55 minutes, one daily Monday to Saturday) runs between Otterburn and Newcastle.

Bus 15 serves Alnwick from Rothbury (£4, 25 minutes, four daily Monday to Saturday).

Buses 470 and **473** link Wooler and Alnwick (£3.90, 50 minutes, hourly). Buses 267 and 464 run between Wooler and Berwick-up-on-Tweed (£3.90, 50 minutes, hourly)

LOCAL KNOWLEDGE

AMBLE PUFFIN FESTIVAL

For eight days from late May to early June, the town of Amble celebrates the hatching of puffin chicks on Coquet Island (just offshore) with **Amble Puffin Festival** (http://amblepuffinfest.co.uk). Events include local history talks, guided birdwatching walks, exhibitions, watersports, a craft fair, a food festival and live music. There's also a kayak fishing competition and a daily teddy bear parachute drop.

Northumberland Coast

Northumberland's coast, like its wild and remote interior, is sparsely populated. You won't find any hurdy-gurdy seaside resorts, but instead charming, castle-crowned villages strung along miles of wide, sandy beaches that you might just have to yourself.

Alnwick

POP 8116

Northumberland's historic ducal town, Alnwick (pronounced 'annick') is an elegant maze of narrow cobbled streets beneath its colossal medieval castle. Alnwick is also home to an enchanting bookshop and spectacular Alnwick Garden.

Sights

★**Alnwick Castle** CASTLE
(www.alnwickcastle.com; The Peth; adult/child £14.95/7.75, with Alnwick Garden £25.60/10.90; ⏲10am-5.30pm Easter-Oct) Set in parklands designed by Lancelot 'Capability' Brown, the imposing ancestral home of the duke of Northumberland has changed little since the 14th century. It's a favourite set for film-makers and starred as Hogwarts for the first couple of Harry Potter films. The interior is sumptuous and extravagant; the six rooms open to the public – staterooms, dining room, guard chamber and library – have an incredible display of Italian paintings, including Titian's *Ecce Homo* and many Canalettos. Various free tours include several focusing on Harry Potter and other productions that have used the castle as a backdrop, including British comedy series *Blackadder*.

For the best views of the castle's exterior, take The Peth to the River Aln's northern bank and follow the woodland trail east.

Alnwick Garden GARDENS
(www.alnwickgarden.com; Denwick Lane; adult/child £12.10/4.40, with Alnwick Castle £25.60/10.90; ⏲10am-6pm Easter-Oct, to 4pm Nov-Easter) This 4.8-hectare walled garden incorporates a series of magnificent spaces surrounding the breathtaking Grand Cascade – 120 separate jets spurting some 30,000L of water down 21 weirs. Half a dozen other gardens include a Franco-Italian-influenced Ornamental Garden (with over 15,000 plants), a Rose Garden and a fascinating Poison Garden, home to some of the deadliest – and most illegal – plants in the world, including cannabis, magic mushrooms, belladonna and tobacco.

Sleeping

★**Alnwick Lodge** B&B, CAMPGROUND $$
(☎01665-604363; www.alnwicklodge.com; West Cawledge Park, A1; tent sites from £12, B&B s/d/f from £55/72/100; P 🛜 👪 🐾) Situated 2 miles south off the A1, this gorgeous Victorian farmstead has 15 antique-filled rooms with quirky touches like free-standing, lidded baths. Cooked breakfasts are served around a huge circular banqueting table. You can also go 'glamping' in restored gypsy caravans, wagons and shepherds' huts (from £45, linen per bed £15; shared bathrooms), or pitch up on the sheltered meadow.

White Swan Hotel HOTEL $$
(☎01665-602109; www.classiclodges.co.uk; Bondgate Within; d/f from £115/135; P 🛜 👪 🐾) Alnwick's top address is a 300-year-old coaching inn in the heart of town. Rooms are all superbly appointed (including family rooms that sleep up to four). Its architectural showpiece is the fine-dining **Olympic Restaurant** (mains £11-18, 2-/3-course lunch menus £12/15, 3-course dinner menu £31.50; ⏲noon-3pm & 5-9pm).

Drinking

Bari Tea CAFE
(www.baritea.co.uk; 28 Narrowgate; ⏲11am-4pm Easter-Sep, 11am-4pm Thu-Mon Oct-Easter; 🛜) Some 30 different varieties of loose-leaf tea are on offer at this tearoom, accompanied by scones, cakes and slices. High tea costs £10 for two people.

Shopping

★**Barter Books** BOOKS
(☎01665-604888; www.barterbooks.co.uk; Alnwick Station, Wagon Way Rd; ⏲9am-7pm) If you're familiar with the renaissance of the

WWII 'Keep Calm and Carry On' slogan, it's thanks to this wonderfully atmospheric secondhand bookshop in Alnwick's Victorian former railway station. While converting the station, the owner came across a set of posters – the framed original is above the till – and turned it into a successful industry.

Coal fires, velvet ottomans, reading rooms and a cafe make this a place you could spend days in, the silence interrupted only by the tiny rumble of the toy train that runs along the track above your head.

Taste of Northumberland FOOD, DRINK

(4-6 Market Pl; 10am-3pm Mon-Sat) Alnwick-distilled rum and Lindisfarne-made mead along with a range of boutique English gins and Scottish whiskies are sold at this locavore shop in the town centre. Alnwick rum is also used in seasonal Christmas puddings sold here.

Information

Alnwick's **tourist office** (01670-622152; www.visitalnwick.org.uk; 2 The Shambles; 9.30am-5pm Mon-Sat, 10am-4pm Sun Easter-Oct, 10am-4pm Mon-Sat Nov-Easter) is by Market Pl.

Getting There & Away

Buses X15 and X18 run to Berwick-upon-Tweed (£6.10, 50 minutes, every two hours) and Newcastle (£6.30, one hour, every two hours).

Alnwick's nearest train station is at Alnmouth, connected to Alnwick by bus X18 (£2.70, 10 minutes, hourly). Alnmouth's train services include Berwick-upon-Tweed (£13.60, 20 minutes, up to two per hour), Edinburgh (£38.90, one hour, up to two per hour) and Newcastle (£10.30, 30 minutes, up to two per hour).

Craster

POP 305

Sandy, salty Craster is a small, sheltered fishing village about 6 miles northeast of Alnwick, and is famous for its kippers. In the early 20th century, 2500 herring were smoked here daily. The kippers still produced today often grace the Queen's breakfast table.

Sights

Dunstanburgh Castle CASTLE

(EH; www.english-heritage.org.uk; Dunstanburgh Rd; adult/child £5.20/3.10; 10am-6pm Easter-Sep, to 4pm Oct, 10am-4pm Sat & Sun Nov-Easter) The dramatic 1.5-mile walk along the coast from Craster (not accessible by car) is the most scenic path to this moody, weather-beaten castle. Its construction began in 1314 and it was strengthened during the Wars of the Roses, but left to crumble, becoming ruined by 1550. Parts of the original wall and gatehouse keep are still standing and it's a tribute to its builders that so much remains. You can also reach the castle on foot from Embleton (1.5 miles), but access can be cut off at high tide.

Eating

★ **Jolly Fisherman** GASTROPUB $$

(01665-576461; www.thejollyfishermancraster.co.uk; Haven Hill; mains lunch £7-10, dinner £15-22; kitchen 11am-3pm & 5-8.30pm Mon-Sat, noon-7pm Sun, bar 11am-11pm Mon-Thu, to midnight Sat, to 9pm Sun;) Crab (in sensational soup, sandwiches, fish platters and more) is the speciality of this superb gastropub, but Paul Bocuse–trained chef John Blackmore's other amazing creations include roast pheasant with tarragon mustard, and game pie with Northumbrian venison and wood pigeon. Great wine list, wonderful real ales, a roaring fire in the bar and stunning beer garden overlooking Dunstanburgh Castle too.

Shopping

★ **Robson & Sons** FOOD

(01665-576223; www.kipper.co.uk; Haven Hill; kippers per kilo from £9; 9am-4.30pm Mon-Sat, 10am-4pm Sun) Four generations have operated this traditional fish smokers; loyal customers include the Royal Family. It's best known for its kippers, but also smokes salmon and other fish.

Information

Craster's **tourist office** (01665-576007; www.visitnorthumberland.com; Quarry Car Park; 10am-4.30pm Easter-Oct) opens in the warmer months.

Getting There & Away

Bus X18 runs to Berwick-upon-Tweed (£6.10, 1½ hours, every two hours) and Newcastle (£5.60, 1½ hours, every two hours). Bus 418 links Craster to Alnwick (£5.10, 30 minutes, hourly).

Embleton Bay

Beautiful Embleton Bay, a pale wide arc of sand, stretches from Dunstanburgh past the endearing, sloping village of Embleton and curves in a broad vanilla-coloured strand around to end at Low Newton-by-the-Sea, a tiny whitewashed, National Trust–preserved village.

Sights & Activities

Behind the bay is a path leading to the **Newton Pool Nature Reserve**, an important spot for breeding and migrating birds such as black-headed gulls and grasshopper warblers. There are a couple of hides where you can peer out at them. You can continue walking along the headland beyond Low Newton, where you'll find **Football Hole**, a delightful hidden beach between headlands. The easiest access to Dunstanburgh Castle (p643) is from Craster; the walk to the castle from Embleton Bay can be cut off at high tide.

Sleeping & Eating

Joiners Arms PUB **$$$**

(01665-576112; http://joiners-arms.com; High Newton-by-the-Sea; d £140-155; P) Locals love this gastropub and for good reason: ingredients are sourced nearby, the seafood and steaks are excellent (mains £13 to £20) and families are warmly welcomed. But for visitors, it's also a fantastic place to stay: five contemporary guest rooms are individually and exquisitely decorated with details like exposed brick, freestanding baths and four-poster beds.

Ship Inn PUB FOOD **$$**

(01665-576262; www.shipinnnewton.co.uk; Low Newton-by-the-Sea; mains £8.50-18; kitchen noon-2.30pm & 7-8pm Wed-Sat, noon-2.30pm Sun-Tue, bar 11am-11pm Mon-Sat, 11am-10pm Sun Apr-Oct, reduced hours Nov-Mar) Set around a village green, this wonderful pub brews 26 different beers – blond, wheat, rye, bitter, stout and seasonal – using local River Coquet water. The food is first-rate, too, from local crab to slow-cooked Peelham Farm lamb shanks with lemon and parsley couscous. No credit cards. Live music often plays at weekends.

Getting There & Away

Bus X18 to Newcastle (£5.60, 1¾ hours, every two hours) and Berwick-upon-Tweed (£5.50, 1¼ hours, every two hours) stops outside the Joiners Arms. Bus 418 (£5.10, 40 minutes, hourly) links the village of Embleton with Alnwick.

Bamburgh

POP 300

High up on a basalt crag, Bamburgh's mighty castle looms over the quaint village – a clutch of houses around a pleasant green – which continues to commemorate the valiant achievements of local heroine Grace Darling.

Sights

Bamburgh Castle CASTLE

(www.bamburghcastle.com; Links Rd; adult/child £10.75/5; 10am-5pm mid-Feb–Oct, 11am-4.30pm Sat & Sun Nov–mid-Feb) Northumberland's most dramatic castle was built around a powerful 11th-century Norman keep by Henry II. The castle played a key role in the border wars of the 13th and 14th centuries, and in 1464 was the first English castle to fall during the Wars of the Roses. It was restored in the 19th century by the great industrialist Lord Armstrong, and is still home to the Armstrong family.

Its name is a derivative of Bebbanburgh, after the wife of Anglo-Saxon ruler Aedelfrip, whose fortified home occupied this basalt outcrop 500 years earlier. Antique furniture, suits of armour, priceless ceramics and artworks cram the castle's rooms and chambers, but top billing goes to the neo-Gothic **King's Hall** with wood panelling, leaded windows and hefty beams supporting the roof.

RNLI Grace Darling Museum MUSEUM

(www.rnli.org; 1 Radcliffe Rd; 10am-5pm Easter-Sep, 10am-4pm Tue-Sun Oct-Easter) FREE Born in Bamburgh, Grace Darling was the lighthouse keeper's daughter on Outer Farne who rowed out to the grounded, flailing SS *Forfarshire* in 1838 and saved its crew in the middle of a dreadful storm. This refurbished museum even has her actual coble (row boat) as well as a film on the events of that stormy night. Grace was born just three houses down from the museum and is buried in the churchyard opposite. Her ornate wrought-iron and sandstone tomb was built tall so as to be visible to passing ships.

Eating

★**Mizen Head** MODERN BRITISH **$$**

(01668-214254; www.mizen-head.co.uk; Lucker Rd; mains £10-32.50; 6-9pm Mon-Wed, noon-1.45pm & 6-9pm Thu-Sun; P) Bamburgh's best place to eat and/or stay is this stunning restaurant with rooms. Local seafood – lobster thermidor, roast turbot with asparagus, tarragon and lemon butter – is the kitchen's speciality, along with chargrilled steaks. Its six rooms with chequered fabrics and black-and-white coastal prints are light, bright and spacious (doubles from £100 to £140). Switched-on staff know their stuff.

Driving Tour Northumberland Coast

START NEWBIGGIN-BY-THE-SEA
END BERWICK-UPON-TWEED
LENGTH 78 MILES; ONE DAY

It's possible to shadow the coast to the Scottish border from Tynemouth, but the scenery really picks up at **1 Newbiggin-by-the-Sea**. Newbiggin's beach was restored in 2007, when over 500,000 tonnes of Skegness' sand was relocated here to counteract erosion, and Sean Henry's gigantic bronze sculpture *The Couple* was installed offshore.

Continuing north along the A1068 coast road for 13 miles brings you to the fishing port of **2 Amble**, with a boardwalk along the seafront and puffin cruises. Less than 2 miles north, biscuit-coloured **3 Warkworth** is a cluster of houses around a loop in the River Coquet, dominated by the craggy ruin of 14th-century Warkworth Castle. The castle features in Shakespeare's *Henry IV* Parts I and II, and the 1998 film *Elizabeth* was shot here. A few hundred metres upriver, the tiny 14th-century Warkworth Hermitage is carved into the rock.

Some 5 miles north of Warkworth is **4 Alnmouth**, with brightly painted houses and pretty beaches. It's another 5 miles inland to the bustling town of **5 Alnwick** to see its imposing castle – which starred as Harry Potter's Hogwarts – and glorious Alnwick Garden. Turn back towards the coast and follow the B1339 for 4.7 miles before turning east on Windside Hill to **6 Craster**, famed for its smoked kippers, which you can buy direct from the smokery. Don't miss a meal at the Jolly Fisherman, which has spectacular views of brooding Dunstanburgh Castle. Around 5 miles north at **7 Low Newton-by-the-Sea**, in Embleton Bay, pause for a pint brewed at the Ship Inn.

Past the village of Seahouses (the departure point for the Farne Islands), quaint **8 Bamburgh** is home to the most dramatic castle yet. Another 17 miles on, via a tidal causeway (check tide times!), the sacred priory ruins of isolated, otherworldly **9 Holy Island (Lindisfarne)** still attract spiritual pilgrims. Return to the mainland where, 14 miles north, you can walk almost the entire length of the Elizabethan walls encircling England's northernmost city, beautiful **10 Berwick-upon-Tweed**.

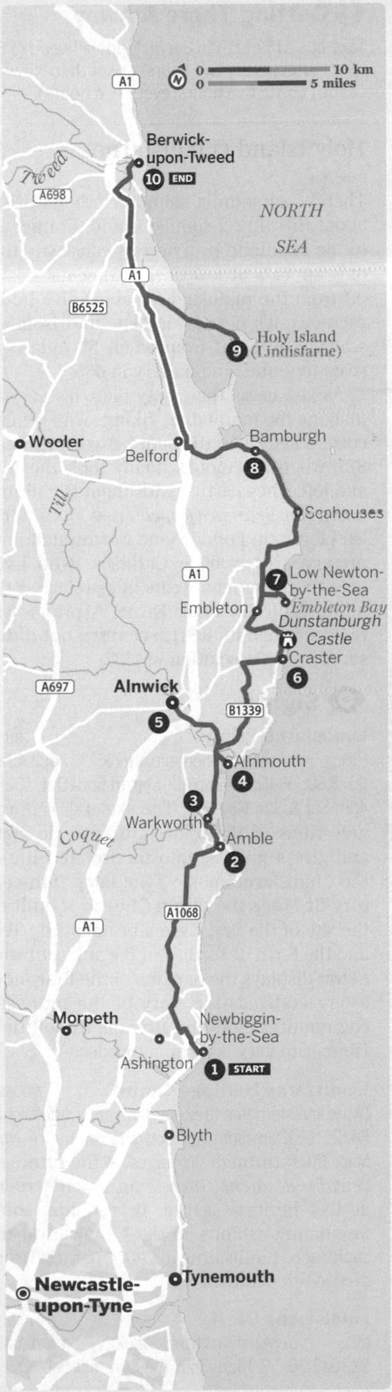

Getting There & Away

Take bus X18 north to Berwick-upon-Tweed (£6, 35 minutes, every two hours) or south to Newcastle (£6.10, two hours, every two hours).

Holy Island (Lindisfarne)

POP 160

There's something almost other-worldly about this tiny, 2-sq-mile island. Connected to the mainland by a narrow causeway that only appears at low tide, cutting the island off from the mainland for about five hours each day, it's fiercely desolate and isolated, scarcely different from when St Aidan arrived to found a monastery in 635.

As you cross the empty flats, it's easy to imagine the marauding Vikings who repeatedly sacked the settlement between 793 and 875, when the monks finally took the hint and left. They carried with them the illuminated *Lindisfarne Gospels* (now in the British Library in London) and the miraculously preserved body of St Cuthbert, who lived here for a couple of years but preferred the hermit's life on Inner Farne. A priory was re-established in the 11th century, but didn't survive the Dissolution in 1537.

Sights

Lindisfarne Priory RUINS

(EH; www.english-heritage.org.uk; adult/child £6/3.60; 10am-6pm Apr-Sep, to 5pm Oct, 10am-4pm Sat & Sun Nov-Mar) The skeletal, red and grey ruins of the priory are an eerie sight and give a glimpse into the isolated life of the Lindisfarne monks. The later 13th-century **St Mary the Virgin Church** is built on the site of the first church between the Tees and the Firth of Forth, and the adjacent **museum** displays the remains of the first monastery and tells the story of the monastic community before and after the Dissolution. Hours can vary according to tides.

Lindisfarne Heritage Centre MUSEUM

(www.lindisfarne-centre.com; Marygate; adult/child £4/2; 10am-5pm Apr-Oct, shorter hours Nov-Mar) Flick through 20 pages of the luminescent *Lindisfarne Gospels* on touch screens at this heritage centre. It also has some fascinating exhibits on the Vikings and the sacking of Lindisfarne in 793. Opening times are tide-dependent.

Lindisfarne Castle CASTLE

(NT; www.nationaltrust.org.uk; adult/child £7.30/3.60; 10am-3pm Tue-Sun mid-Feb–Oct & some weekends Nov–mid-Feb) Built atop a rocky bluff in 1550, this tiny, storybook castle was extended and converted by Sir Edwin Lutyens from 1902 to 1910 for Mr Hudson, the owner of *Country Life* magazine – you can imagine some of the decadent Gatsby-style parties to have graced its alluring rooms. It's half a mile east of the village. Opening times can vary due to tide times.

Sleeping & Eating

Crown & Anchor INN $$

(01289-389215; http://holyislandcrown.co.uk; Market Pl; s £55-80, d £70-100;) The only locally run inn on the island is a relaxed, down-to-earth spot with brightly coloured guest rooms and solid pub grub (steak-and-ale pie, rib-eye steak with onion rings; mains £6.50 to £18), but the biggest winner is the beer garden with a postcard panorama of the castle, priory and harbour.

Manor House Hotel HOTEL $$

(01289-389207; http://manorhouseholyisland.com; Market Sq; s/d/f incl breakfast from £60/95/180; P) Wake up to views of the harbour, priory and castle from some of the 10 modern rooms at this 1870s manor. Rates fall outside summer; be sure to book ahead. Its **Priory Restaurant** (mains £9 to £14), on the ground floor, opens to a large beer garden and utilises seasonal, local produce. Bike storage is available.

Lindisfarne Inn INN $$

(01289-381223; www.lindisfarneinn.co.uk; Beal; s/d/f from £70/76/125; P) Although on the mainland (on the A1 next to the turn-off to the causeway), this is a handy alternative to island accommodation and/or dining if you're cutting it fine with crossing times. Its 21 spotless, modern rooms are set far back enough that road noise isn't a problem. Well-above-average bar food includes a catch-of-the-day fisherman's pie (mains £10 to £20). There's wi-fi in the bar only.

Pilgrim's Coffee House COFFEE, CAFE $

(www.pilgrimscoffee.com; Marygate; 9.30am-5pm Sun-Fri, to 9pm Sat Mar-Nov, closed Dec-Feb, hours can vary;) Fairtrade organic beans and compostable packaging are used by this fabulous independent coffee roastery. The living-room-like dining space with Chesterfield armchairs and a blazing open fire is a cosy spot for sandwiches, jacket potatoes, and homemade cakes, slices and shortbread, plus pizzas and cocktails on Saturday

WORTH A TRIP

FARNE ISLANDS

During breeding season (roughly May to July), you can see feeding chicks of 20 seabird species (including puffin, kittiwake, Arctic tern and eider duck), and some 6000 grey seals, on the **Farne Islands** (NT; www.nationaltrust.org.uk; adult/child excl boat transport £5.75/2.90; by reservation, season & conditions permitting Apr-Oct), a rocky archipelago three miles offshore from the fishing village of Seahouses. Four boat operators, contactable through Seahouses' **tourist office** (01670-625593; http://visitnorthumberland.com; Seafield car park, Seahouses; 10am-4.30pm Easter-Oct), depart from Seahouses' dock, including **Billy Shiel** (01665-720308; www.farne-islands.com; adult/child 2.5hr tour £15/10, 6hr tour £35/20).

Crossings can be rough (impossible in bad weather); wear warm, waterproof clothing and an old hat to guard against the birds!

Bus X18 links Seahouses with Berwick-upon-Tweed (£5.70, 45 minutes, every two hours) and Newcastle (£6.60, two hours, every two hours). Bus 418 runs to Alnwick (£5.30, 55 minutes, hourly).

nights. On sunny days the courtyard garden is a treat.

Shopping

St Aidan's Winery FOOD, DRINK

(Lindisfarne Mead; www.lindisfarne-mead.co.uk; Prior Lane; 9am-6pm Easter-Oct, 10am-5pm Nov-Easter depending on tides) Mead made on Lindisfarne by St Aidan's Winery to a traditional Roman recipe using locally drawn water and honey. Free tastings let you try its three varieties – original, blood orange and spiced – as well as some of its fortified wines (ginger, wild strawberry, elderberry, blackberry, cherry and more). Other products include mead-based chocolate truffles and jams.

Getting There & Around

The island can sometimes be reached by bus 477 from Berwick-upon-Tweed (£4.50, 40 minutes, depends on tides); check with Berwick's tourist offices for updated information.

Drivers need to pay close attention to crossing-time information posted at tourist offices and on notice boards throughout the area, and at www.holy-island.info. Every year drivers are caught midway by the incoming tide and have to abandon their cars.

Park in the signposted car park (£4.60 per day). A shuttle bus (£2 return) runs from the car park to the castle every 20 minutes from Easter to September; alternatively it's a level 300m walk to the village centre and 1 mile to the castle.

Berwick-upon-Tweed

POP 11,500

England's northernmost city is a picturesque fortress town, cleaved by the River Tweed, which is spanned by the Grade I-listed Berwick Bridge (aka Old Bridge), built from sandstone between 1611 and 1624, and the Royal Tweed (1925–28).

Berwick is the stubborn holder of two unique honours: it is the most fought-over settlement in European history (between 1174 and 1482 it changed hands 14 times between the Scots and the English); and its football team, Berwick Rangers, are the only English team to play in the Scottish League (albeit in lowly Scottish League Two). Although firmly English since the 15th century, Berwick retains its own identity, with locals south of the border speaking with a noticeable Scottish whirr.

Sights

★**Berwick Walls** HISTORIC SITE

(EH; www.english-heritage.org.uk; dawn-dusk) FREE You can walk almost the entire length of Berwick's hefty Elizabethan walls, begun in 1558 to reinforce an earlier set built during the reign of Edward II. The mile-long walk is a must, with wonderful, wide-open views. Only a small fragment remains of the once mighty **border castle**, most of the building having been replaced by the train station.

Berwick Barracks MUSEUM, GALLERY

(EH; www.english-heritage.org.uk; The Parade; adult/child £4.60/2.80; 10am-6pm Easter-Sep, to 4pm Oct, closed Nov-Easter) Designed by Nicholas Hawksmoor, Britain's oldest purpose-built barracks (1717) now house an assortment of museums and art galleries, covering a history of the town and British soldiery since the 17th century. The **Gymnasium Gallery** hosts big-name contemporary art exhibitions.

Cell Block Museum MUSEUM
(Marygate; adult/child £2/50p; ⏲tours 10am & 2pm Mon-Fri Easter-Sep) The original jail cells in the upper floor of the town hall (1750–61) have been preserved as a chilling museum devoted to crime and punishment. Tours take in the public rooms, museum, jail and belfry.

Tours

Time to Explore Guided Tours WALKING
(☎01289-330218; www.visitberwick.com; 106 Marygate; Town & Walls adult/child £7/free; ⏲by reservation 11am Mon-Fri Easter-Oct) Passionate local Derek Sharman leads 1¼-hour Town & Walls tours taking in Berwick's highlights. Tours depart from the tourist office.

Sleeping

Berwick YHA HOSTEL $
(☎0845 371 9676; www.yha.org.uk; Dewars Lane; dm/d from £10/58; P@☎) A 240-year-old granary has been converted into a state-of-the-art hostel with 55 beds in all-en-suite dorms and private rooms. Contemporary facilities include a TV room, a laundry and wi-fi in common areas. Staff are terrifically friendly and helpful.

★**Marshall Meadows Country House Hotel** HERITAGE HOTEL $$
(☎01289-331133; http://marshallmeadowshotel.co.uk; Marshall Meadows; incl breakfast s £70-90, d £89-139, f £99-149; P☎🐾) England's most northerly hotel, just 600m from the Scottish border, is a treasure. Set in 6 hectares of woodland and ornamental gardens, the Georgian manor has 19 rooms (including a ground-floor family room) with countrified checked and floral fabrics, two cosy bars with open fireplaces and a conservatory. Breakfast (including kippers) is served in the oak-panelled restaurant (two-/three-course dinner menus £21.95/29.95).

The Berwickshire Coastal Path walking trail runs alongside the property.

Granary Guesthouse B&B $$
(☎01289-304403; www.granaryguesthouse.co.uk; 11 Bridge St; s/d from £80/96; P☎) 🍃 In a charming town-centre location, Berwick's most romantic B&B has three fresh, elegant and contemporary guest rooms, locally sourced and/or organic breakfasts (gluten-free options available) and an on-site beauty treatment room offering massages.

Eating & Drinking

Audela MODERN BRITISH $$
(☎01289-308827; www.audela.co.uk; 41-47 Bridge St; breakfast dishes £5.50-9.50, mains lunch £5.50-11.50, dinner £8-19; ⏲9am-9pm; 👪) 🍃 Named for the last vessel to be built at Berwick Shipyard (in 1979), Audela is the town's top table. Local suppliers provide the ingredients for dishes like twice-backed Northumberland cheese soufflé, halibut with lemon butter sauce and herb-crusted rack of lamb, served in a striking sage-green dining room. Lunchtime gourmet sandwiches include Berwick crab and lime mayo.

Barrels Alehouse PUB
(59-61 Bridge St; ⏲noon-midnight Sun-Thu, to 1am Fri & Sat; ☎) Berwick's best watering hole attracts a mixed, laid-back crowd who can be found sipping real ales and micro-distilled gins and whiskies at all hours. On Friday nights, live music plays in the atmospherically dingy basement bar.

Information

The **tourist office** (☎01670-622155; www.visitberwick.com; 106 Marygate; ⏲10am-5pm Mon-Sat, 11am-4pm Sun Easter-Sep, 10am-4pm Mon-Sat Oct-Easter) is in the centre of town.

Getting There & Away

BUS

Buses stop on Golden Sq (where it meets Marygate). National Express coaches between Edinburgh (£11.60, 1¼ hours, twice daily) and London (£33, eight hours, twice daily) stop here.

Other options include buses X15 (via Alnwick) and X18 to Newcastle (£6.80, 2½ hours, every two hours) and bus 477 to Holy Island, aka Lindisfarne (£4.50, 40 minutes, depends on tides; check with Berwick's tourist offices for updated information).

TRAIN

On the East Coast Main Line linking London and Edinburgh, Berwick-upon-Tweed is almost exactly halfway between Edinburgh (£25.10, 40 minutes, two per hour) and Newcastle (£26.10, 45 minutes, two per hour).

Wales

PEMBROKESHIRE COAST PATH (P682); MICHAEL THALER / SHUTTERSTOCK ©

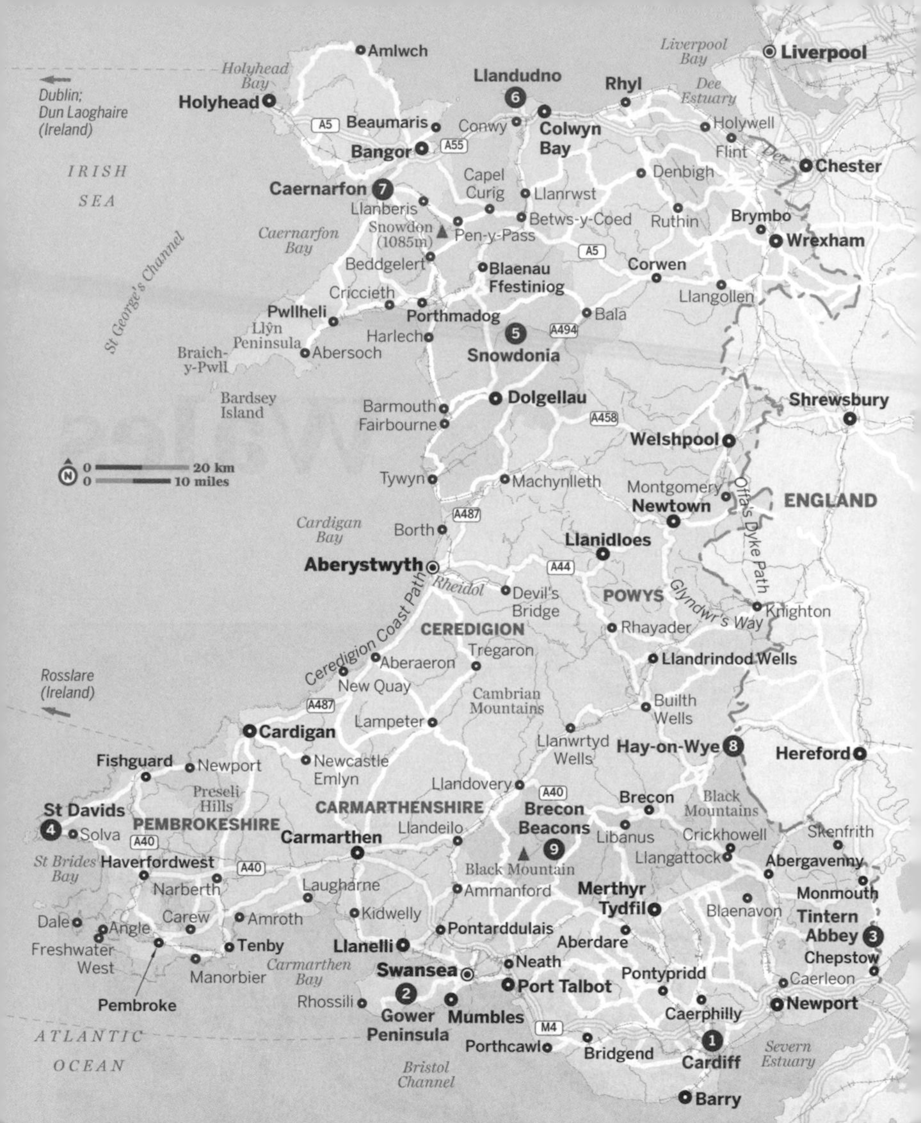

Wales Highlights

❶ **Cardiff** (p653) Exploring the Welsh capital, with its castle, shopping arcades and nightlife.

❷ **Gower Peninsula** (p675) Catching some breaks or enjoying the coastal views.

❸ **Tintern Abbey** (p666) Marvelling at the picture-perfect ruins in the beautiful Wye Valley.

❹ **St Davids** (p686) Enjoying this tiny town with its beautiful cathedral and idyllic setting.

❺ **Snowdonia** (p728) Climbing Wales' highest peak, Snowdon, or enjoying more gentle exercise.

❻ **Llandudno** (p750) Buying fish and chips and strolling along the pier.

❼ **Caernarfon Castle** (p745) Seeing one of the most impressive of Wales' forts.

❽ **Hay-on-Wye** (p698) Wandering through a book-lover's heaven.

❾ Walking in the mountains, then eating in the gastropubs of the **Brecon Beacons** (p698).

Cardiff, Pembrokeshire & South Wales

Includes ➡

Best Places to Eat

- The Whitebrook (p666)
- Restaurant James Sommerin (p662)
- Grove (p685)
- Purple Poppadom (p661)
- Mosaic (p672)

Best Places to Sleep

- Number 62 (p660)
- Larkhill Tipis (p674)
- Pentower (p692)
- Tŵr y Felin (p689)
- Old School Hostel (p690)

Why Go?

Stretching from historic border town Chepstow through to the jagged Pembrokeshire Coast in the west, South Wales really packs in the sights.

Hugging the border, the Wye Valley is the birthplace of British tourism. For more than 200 years people have come to explore this tranquil waterway and its winding, wooded vale, where the majestic ruins of Tintern Abbey have inspired generations of poets and artists.

The nation's capital, Cardiff, flies the flag for big-city sophistication in the land of the red dragon. Just out of Swansea, Wales' second city, the Gower Peninsula revels in its coastal beauty. To the north, the fecund heartland of rural Carmarthenshire offers country comfort in abundance.

Beyond Cardiff, the biggest draw in South Wales remains Pembrokeshire, where almost 200 miles of magical shoreline has been declared a national park, delineated by craggy cliffs, golden sands, chocolate-box villages and seaside resorts.

When to Go

- Wales' home matches in the Six Nations Rugby Championship warm the spirits of locals and visitors alike during chilly February and March. Early daffodils pop out to celebrate St David's Day on 1 March – spend it in the saint's city, St Davids.
- If you're planning some coastal walking, April to July are the driest months.
- Many of Cardiff's big festivals hold out until July, including the Cardiff International Food & Drink Festival, the Everyman Open Air Theatre Festival and the Welsh Proms. In August, the warmest month, knights storm the castle, classic motor boats converge and gay pride takes over the streets.

Cardiff, Pembrokeshire & South Wales Highlights

1. **Cardiff** (p653) Diving into the attractions and nightlife of Wales' dynamic capital city.
2. **Rhossili** (p677) Watching the surf break over the long sandy bay at the tip of spectacular Gower Peninsula.
3. **St Davids** (p686) Exploring the laid-back little city with the spectacular cathedral and gnarly surf beach.
4. **Tintern Abbey** (p666) Strolling riverside ruins in the glorious Wye Valley.
5. **National Botanic Garden of Wales** (p678) Marvelling at Norman Foster's greenhouse dome.
6. **Tenby** (p681) Building sandcastles at this colourful seaside resort.
7. **Pembrokeshire Coast Path** (p682) A breathtaking collision of rock and sea.
8. **Caerphilly Castle** (p669) Crossing the moat and wandering into a fairytale.
9. **Blaenavon** (p668) Feasting on World Heritage sites and world-class cheese.

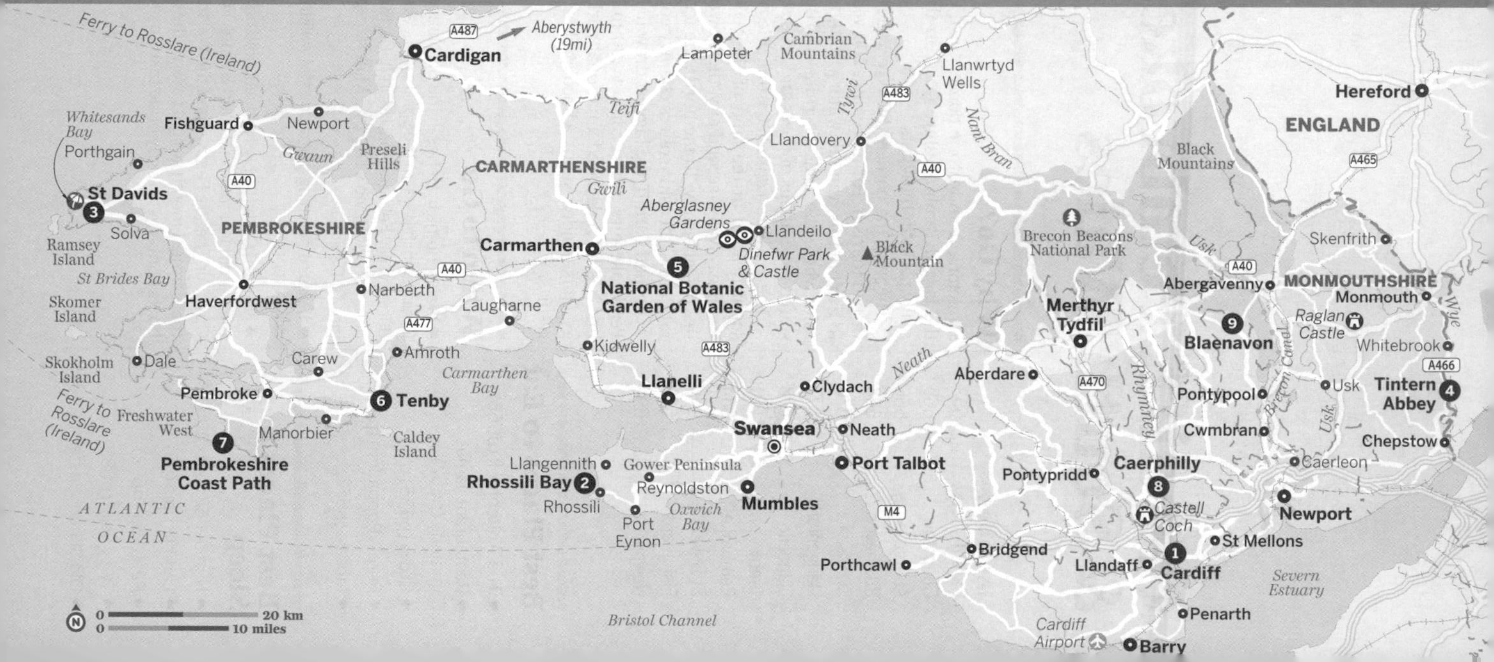

CARDIFF

POP 346,000

The capital of Wales since only 1955, Cardiff has embraced the role with vigour, emerging in the new millennium as one of Britain's leading urban centres. Caught between an ancient fort and an ultramodern waterfront, compact Cardiff seems to have surprised even itself with how interesting it has become.

The city has entered the 21st century pumped up on steroids, flexing its recently acquired architectural muscles as if it's still astonished to have them. This newfound confidence is infectious, and these days it's not just the rugby that draws crowds into the city. Come the weekend, a buzz reverberates through the streets as swarms of shoppers hit the Hayes, followed by waves of revellers descending on the capital's thriving pubs, bars and live-music venues.

Cardiff makes an excellent base for day trips to the surrounding valleys and coast, where you'll find castles, beaches, interesting industrial sites and ancient monuments.

History

In AD 75 the Romans built a fort where Cardiff Castle now stands. The name Cardiff probably derives from Caer Tâf (Fort on the River Taff) or Caer Didi (Didius' Fort), referring to Roman general Aulus Didius. After the Romans left Britain the site remained unoccupied until the Norman Conquest. In 1093 a Norman knight named Robert Fitzhamon (conqueror of Glamorgan and later earl of Gloucester) built himself a castle within the Roman walls and a small town grew up around it. Both were damaged in a Welsh revolt in 1183 and the town was sacked in 1404 by Owain Glyndŵr during his ill-fated rebellion against English domination.

The first of the Tudor Acts of Union in 1536 put the English stamp on Cardiff and brought some stability. But despite its importance as a port, market town and bishopric, only 1000 people were living here in 1801.

The city owes its present stature to iron and coal mining in the valleys to the north. Coal was first exported from Cardiff on a small scale as early as 1600. In 1794 the Bute family – which owned much of the land from which Welsh coal was mined – built the Glamorganshire Canal for the shipment of iron from Merthyr Tydfil down to Cardiff. In 1840 this was supplanted by the new Taff Vale Railway.

A year earlier the second marquess of Bute had completed the first docks at Butetown, just south of Cardiff, getting the jump on other South Wales ports. By the time it dawned on everyone what immense reserves of coal there were in the valleys – setting off a kind of black gold rush – the Butes were in a position to insist that it be shipped from Butetown. Cardiff was off and running.

The docklands expanded rapidly, the Butes grew staggeringly rich and the city boomed, its population mushrooming to 170,000 by the end of the 19th century and to 227,000 by 1931. A large, multiracial workers' community known as Tiger Bay grew up in the harbourside area of Butetown. In 1905

CARDIFF IN...

Two Days

Start with a stroll around the historic city centre, stopping to explore the **National Museum Cardiff** (p654) and **Cardiff Castle** (p654) along the way. Lunch could be a picnic in **Bute Park** (p655) with treats acquired at **Cardiff Market** (p663) or, if the weather's not cooperating, a meal at any of the reasonably priced central-city eateries. Spend your second day heading back to the future at Cardiff Bay (p655), where you can immerse yourself in forward-thinking architecture and have a **Doctor Who Experience** (p656).

Four Days

Spend your third morning strolling through the past at **St Fagans National History Museum** (p657), then take a day trip to Penarth (p662). On your last day, head north to explore **Llandaff Cathedral** (p658), then continue on to **Castell Coch** (p660) and **Caerphilly Castle** (p669). For your last night in the Welsh capital, blast away the cobwebs in one of the city's live-music venues (p663).

Cardiff

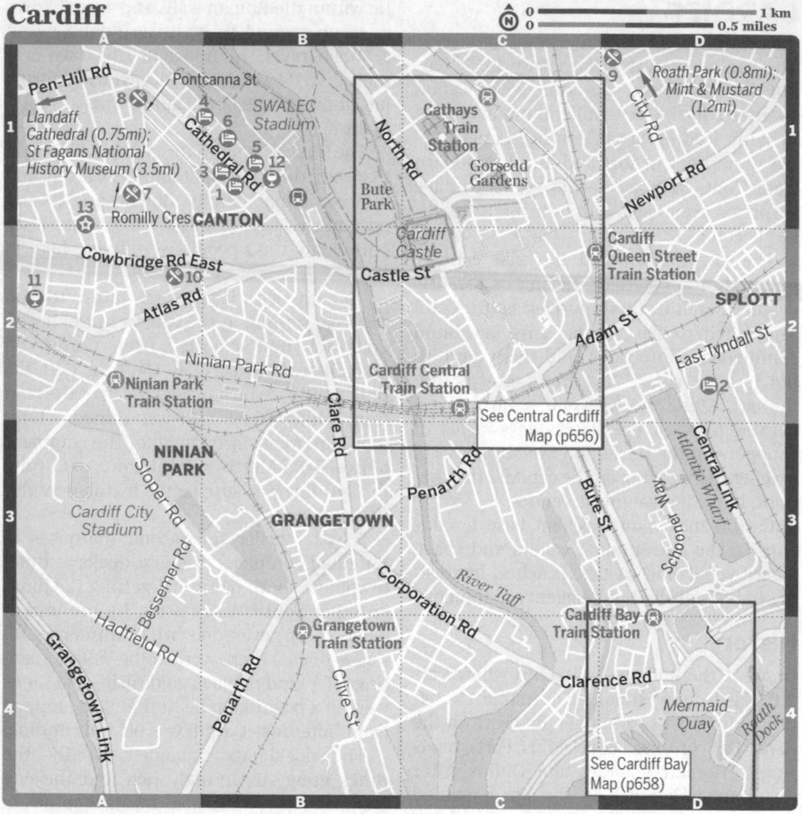

Cardiff was officially designated a city, and a year later its elegant Civic Centre was inaugurated. In 1913 Cardiff became the world's top coal port, exporting some 13 million tonnes of the stuff.

The post-WWI slump in the coal trade and the Great Depression of the 1930s slowed this expansion. The city was badly damaged by WWII bombing, which claimed over 350 lives. Shortly afterwards the coal industry was nationalised, which led to the Butes packing their bags and leaving town in 1947, donating the castle and a large chunk of land to the city.

Wales had no official capital and the need for one was seen as an important focus for Welsh nationhood. Cardiff had the advantage of being Wales' biggest city and boasting the architectural riches of the Civic Centre. It was proclaimed the first ever capital of Wales in 1955, chosen via a ballot of the members of the Welsh authorities. Cardiff received 36 votes to Caernarfon's 11 and Aberystwyth's four.

Sights

City Centre

★National Museum Cardiff MUSEUM

(Map p656; ☎0300 111 2 333; www.museumwales.ac.uk; Gorsedd Gardens Rd; ⏱10am-4pm Tue-Sun) **FREE** Devoted mainly to natural history and art, this grand neoclassical building is the centrepiece of the seven institutions dotted around the country that together form the Welsh National Museum. It's one of Britain's best museums; you'll need at least three hours to do it justice, but it could easily consume the best part of a rainy day.

★Cardiff Castle CASTLE

(Map p656; ☎029-2087 8100; www.cardiffcastle.com; Castle St; adult/child £12/9, incl guided tour

Cardiff

Sleeping
1 Beaufort Guest House B1
2 Cardiff Central YHA D2
3 Cathedral 73 .... B1
4 Lincoln House B1
5 Number 62 .... B1
6 Saco Cardiff B1

Eating
7 Bully's A1
8 Fish at 85 .... A1
9 Oz Urfa D1
10 Purple Poppadom A2

Drinking & Nightlife
11 The Lansdowne A2
12 Y Mochyn Du B1

Entertainment
13 Chapter A1

£15/11; ⏲9am-5pm) There's a medieval keep at its heart, but it's the later additions to Cardiff Castle that really capture the imagination. During the Victorian era, extravagant mock-Gothic features were grafted onto this relic, including a clock tower and a lavish banqueting hall. Some but not all of this flamboyant fantasy world can be accessed with a regular castle entry; the rest can be visited as part of a guided tour.

★**Bute Park** PARK
(Map p656; www.cardiff.gov.uk/parks; ⏲7.30am-sunset) Flanked by the castle and the River Taff, Bute Park was donated to the city along with the castle in 1947. Together with Sophia Gardens, Pontcanna Fields and Llandaff Fields the park forms a green corridor that stretches northwest for 1½ miles to Llandaff. All were once part of the Bute's vast holdings.

★**Principality Stadium** STADIUM
(Millennium Stadium; Map p656; ☎029-2082 2432; www.principalitystadium.wales; Westgate St; tours adult/child £13/9) This spectacular stadium squats like a stranded spaceship on the River Taff's east bank. Originally christened Millennium Stadium (the new name's a nod to sponsors, not the monarchy), this 74,500-seat, £168-million, three-tiered, retractable-roofed arena was completed in time to host the 1999 Rugby World Cup. If you can't get tickets to a match, it's well worth taking a tour. Book online or at the **WRU Store** (Map p656; www.wru.co.uk; 8 Westgate St; ⏲9.30am-5.30pm Mon-Sat, 10am-4pm Sun).

Yr Hen Lyfrgell CULTURAL CENTRE
(The Old Library; Map p656; www.yrhenlyfrgell.wales; The Hayes) *Croeso* (welcome) to a bastion of the Welsh language in the overwhelmingly English-speaking capital. Cardiff's beautiful old library has been converted into a showcase for all things Cymraeg, with an excellent **gift shop** (www.bodlon.com; Yr Hen Lyfrgell, The Hayes; ⏲9am-5pm), a stylish cafe/bar, and rooms where Welsh language lessons are held. Everyone's welcome, even if the only Welsh you can muster is a timid *bore da* (good morning). While you're here, check out the gorgeous Victorian tiles lining the library's original entrance and call into the **Cardiff Story museum** (☎029-2034 6214; www.cardiffstory.com; Yr Hen Lyfrgell, The Hayes; ⏲10am-4pm Mon-Sat) FREE.

Cardiff Bay

Lined with important national institutions, Cardiff Bay is where the modern Welsh nation is put on display in an architect's playground of interesting buildings, large open spaces and public art. The bay's main commercial centre is Mermaid Quay, packed with bars, restaurants and shops.

It wasn't always this way. By 1913 more than 13 million tonnes of coal were being shipped from Cardiff's docks. Following the post-WWII slump the docklands deteriorated into a wasteland of empty basins, cut off from the city by the railway embankment. The bay outside the docks, which has one of the highest tidal ranges in the world (more than 12m between high and low water), was ringed for up to 14 hours a day by smelly, sewage-contaminated mudflats. The nearby residential area of Butetown became a neglected slum.

Since 1987 the area has been radically redeveloped. The turning point came with the completion of a state-of-the-art tidal barrage in 1999.

★**Wales Millennium Centre** ARTS CENTRE
(Map p658; ☎029-2063 6464; www.wmc.org.uk; Bute Pl, Cardiff Bay; tours adult/child £6/free; ⏲9am-7pm) The centrepiece and symbol of Cardiff Bay's regeneration is the superb Wales Millennium Centre, an architectural masterpiece of stacked Welsh slate in shades of purple, green and grey topped with an overarching bronzed steel shell. Designed

Central Cardiff

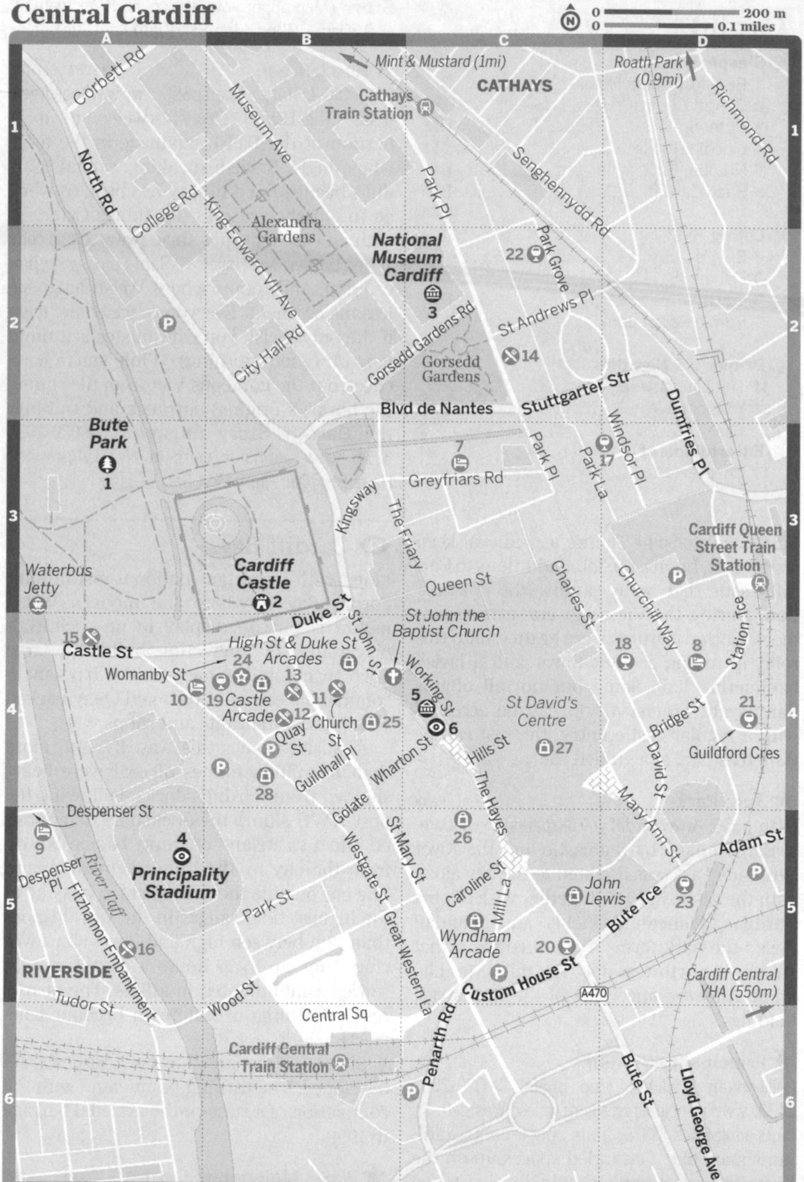

by Welsh architect Jonathan Adams, it opened in 2004 as Wales' premier arts complex, housing major cultural organisations such as the Welsh National Opera, National Dance Company, BBC National Orchestra of Wales, Literature Wales, HiJinx Theatre and Tŷ Cerdd (Music Centre Wales).

Doctor Who Experience GALLERY

(Map p658; ☎0844 801 2279; www.doctorwhoexperience.com; Porth Teigr; adult/child £15/11;

Central Cardiff

Top Sights
1 Bute Park A3
2 Cardiff Castle B3
3 National Museum Cardiff C2
4 Principality Stadium A5

Sights
5 Cardiff Story C4
6 Yr Hen Lyfrgell C4

Sleeping
7 Park Plaza C3
8 Premier Inn Cardiff City Centre D4
9 River House A5
10 Safehouse A4

Eating
11 Cafe Cittá B4
12 Casanova B4
13 Coffee Barker B4
14 Park House C2
15 Pettigrew Tea Rooms A4
16 Riverside Market A5

Drinking & Nightlife
17 Buffalo Bar D3
18 Eagle D4
19 Full Moon B4
20 Golden Cross C5
21 Gwdihŵ D4
22 Pen & Wig C2
23 Porter's D5

Entertainment
24 Clwb Ifor Bach B4

Shopping
Bodlon ..... (see 6)
25 Cardiff Market B4
26 Morgan Quarter C5
27 St David's C4
28 WRU Store B4

10am-5pm (last admission 3.30pm) daily Jul & Aug, Tue-Sun Mar-Jun, Sep & Oct, Wed-Sun Nov-Feb) The huge success of the reinvented classic TV series *Doctor Who,* produced by BBC Wales, has brought Cardiff to the attention of sci-fi fans worldwide. City locations have featured in many episodes; and the first two series of the spin-off *Torchwood* were also set in Cardiff Bay. Capitalising on Timelord tourism, this interactive exhibition is located right next to the BBC studios where the series is filmed – look out for the Tardis hovering outside.

Visitors find themselves sucked through a crack in time and thrown into the role of the Doctor's companion. It's great fun – especially when you come face to face with full-size Daleks in full 'ex-ter-min-ate' mode. But don't blink – there are weeping angels about. The 'experience' only takes about 20 minutes but afterwards you're transported into a large two-level warehouse, where you can wander at your leisure around the displays of sets, costumes and props spanning the show's 50-year run.

Cathays & Roath

The bohemian heart of Cardiff lies in the suburbs immediately to the east of the city centre. Proximity to the university makes Cathays' tightly packed Victorian terrace houses popular with students, and while parts of Roath are more well-heeled, the City Rd strip is a little gritty and fabulously multicultural. Few tourists make their way here, but if you want to get a broader taste of Cardiff life, take a stroll along the narrow thoroughfare that starts as City Rd and then morphs into Crwys Rd and then Whitchurch Rd.

Roath Park PARK
(www.cardiff.gov.uk/parks; Lake Rd, Roath; 7.30am-sunset) Long and narrow Roath Park rivals Bute Park as Cardiff's favourite green space. The third marquess of Bute gifted the land in 1887, and the boggy marsh

DON'T MISS

ST FAGANS

At **St Fagans National History Museum** (0300 111 2 333; www.museumwales.ac.uk; St Fagans; parking £5; 10am-5pm), historic buildings from all over the country have been dismantled and re-erected in the semirural surrounds of St Fagans village, five miles west of central Cardiff. More than 40 buildings are on show, including thatched farmhouses, barns, a watermill, a school, an 18th-century Unitarian chapel and shops selling period-appropriate goods. Buses 32, 32A and 320 (£1.80, 26 minutes) head here from Cardiff. By car it's reached from the continuation of Cathedral Rd.

Cardiff Bay

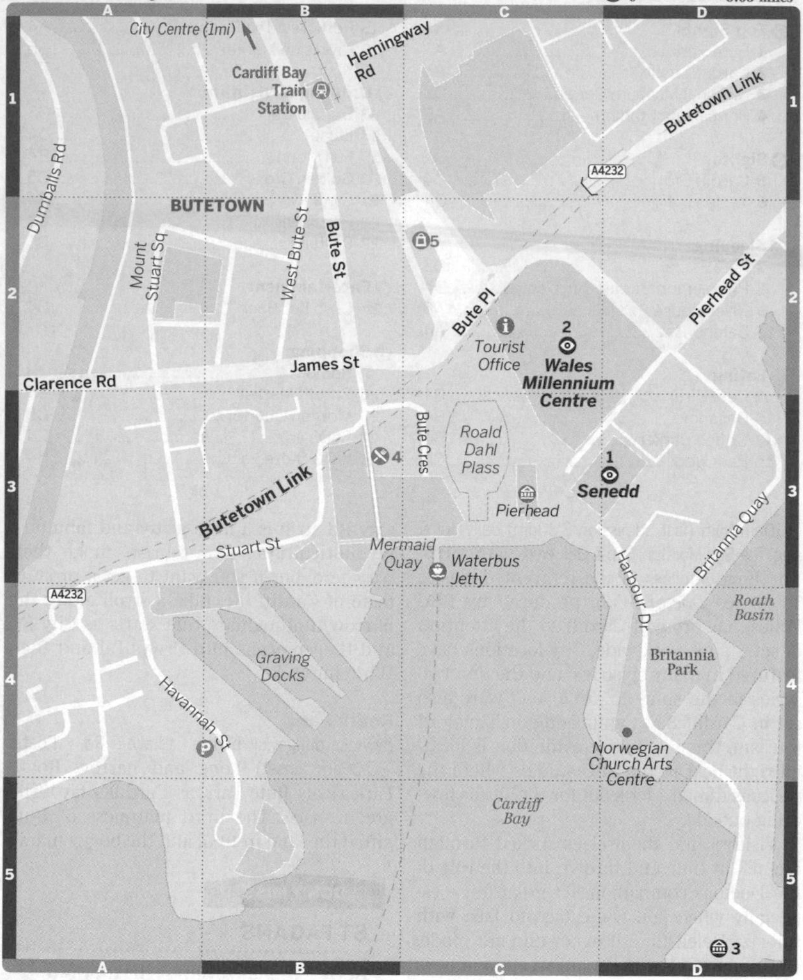

at its northern end was transformed into a large lake by the erection of a dam. The rest was laid out in the Victorian style, with rose gardens, tree-lined paths, lawns and wild nooks. A cutesy lighthouse was added to the lake in 1915 as a memorial to Captain Robert Falcon Scott.

Llandaff

Llandaff is a peaceful suburb 2 miles northwest of the castle – a former village clustered around a green that has been swallowed up by the expanding city. Buses 25, 62 and 63 run along Cathedral Rd to Llandaff every 10 minutes (twice hourly on Sunday and in the evening).

Llandaff Cathedral CATHEDRAL
(029-2056 4554; www.llandaffcathedral.org.uk; Cathedral Green, Llandaff; 7am-6.30pm Sun, 9am-6.30pm Mon-Sat) This venerable cathedral is set in a hollow near the River Taff, on the site of a 6th-century monastery founded by St Teilo. The present building was begun in 1120, but it crumbled throughout the Middle Ages, and during the Reformation and Civil War it was used as an alehouse and

Cardiff Bay

then an animal shelter. Derelict by the 18th century, it was largely rebuilt in the 19th, and then repaired again following a German bombing raid in 1941.

Festivals & Events

Six Nations SPORTS
(www.rbs6nations.com; Feb & Mar) The premier European rugby championship, with Wales taking on England, Scotland, Ireland, Italy and France. Cardiff normally hosts two home games – the atmosphere is supercharged. Book accommodation well in advance.

Festival of Voice MUSIC
(www.festivalofvoice.wales; early Jun) New in 2016, this 10-day festival held in even-numbered years celebrates the human voice across a variety of genres. The stellar starting lineup included gospel choirs, the Welsh National Opera and the likes of Van Morrison, John Cale, Rufus Wainwright, Bryn Terfel, Anna Calvi, Femi Kuti and Ronnie Spector.

Sleeping

Cardiff has Wales' broadest range of accommodation, including luxury hotels, personable guesthouses and some great hostels.

Most places have higher rates on Friday and Saturday nights. It can be almost impossible to find a bed anywhere near the city on big sporting weekends, especially rugby internationals, so keep an eye on the fixtures and choose another date or book well ahead. It's sometimes so bad that hotels as far away as Swansea get swamped with the overflow.

City Centre

★ **River House** HOSTEL $
(Map p656; 029-2039 9810; www.riverhousebackpackers.com; 59 Fitzhamon Embankment, Riverside; dm/s/d incl breakfast from £17/40/42;) Professionally run by a helpful young brother-and-sister team, the River House has a well-equipped kitchen, small garden and cosy TV lounge. The private rooms are basically small dorm rooms and share the same bathrooms. A free breakfast of cereal, toast, pastries and fruit is provided.

★ **Safehouse** HOSTEL $
(Map p656; 029-2037 2833; www.safehousehostel.com; 3 Westgate St; dm/s/d without bathroom from £14/35/37;) There aren't too many hostels with a grand Victorian sitting room to rival Safehouse's. Built in 1889, this lovely red-brick office building has been thoughtfully converted into a boutique hostel with private rooms and four- to 12-bed dorms. Each bunk bed has its own built-in locker and electrical socket. It's on a busy road, so earplugs are a sensible precaution.

Cardiff Central YHA HOSTEL $
(Map p654; 0800 0191 700; www.yha.org.uk; 1 East Tyndall St; dm/r from £15/39;) Until recently this slick establishment was a Mercure hotel, and aside from converting some of the bedrooms into dorms and adding a guest kitchen, the YHA have had the good sense to leave it substantially unchanged. All rooms have modern hotel-style bathrooms and there's plenty of parking. It's flanked by busy roads, but not far from the city centre.

Premier Inn Cardiff City Centre HOTEL $
(Map p656; 029-2034 9910; www.premierinn.com; 10 Churchill Way; r from £40;) The Cardiff branch of Britain's biggest chain has 200 beds in a squat mirror-clad former office tower, right in the city centre. It's not flash, but it's comfortable, clean and terrific value – although you'll need to book early and pay in advance to secure the cheapest rates. Request a higher floor for a quieter room.

★ **Park Plaza** HOTEL $$$
(Map p656; 029-2011 1111; www.parkplazacardiff.com; Greyfriars Rd; r £119-189;) Luxurious without being remotely stuffy, the Plaza has all the five-star facilities you'd expect from an upmarket business-orientated hotel. The snug reception sets the scene, with a gas fire blazing along one wall and comfy wingback

WORTH A TRIP

Castell Coch (Cadw; www.cadw.gov.wales; Castle Rd, Tongwynlais; adult/child £6/4.20; ⌚9.30am-5pm Mar-Oct, 10am-4pm Nov-Feb), Cardiff Castle's fanciful little brother, sits perched atop a thickly wooded crag on the northern fringes of the city. It was the summer retreat of the third marquess of Bute and, like Cardiff Castle, was designed by William Burges in gaudy Victorian Gothic style. Raised on the ruins of Gilbert de Clare's 13th-century Castell Coch (Red Castle), the Butes' Disneyesque holiday home is a monument to high camp. An excellent audioguide is included in the admission price.

chairs. The rear rooms have leafy views over the Civic Centre.

Pontcanna & Canton

Long, leafy Cathedral Rd is lined with B&Bs and small hotels, nearly all of them in restored Victorian town houses. It's only a 15- to 20-minute walk from the city centre, or a £10 taxi ride from the train or bus stations. Street parking is unrestricted but can be tricky to find during working hours.

★Number 62 GUESTHOUSE $$
(Map p654; ☎07974 571348; www.number62.com; 62 Cathedral Rd, Pontcanna; s/d from £68/77; 📶) The only thing stopping us calling Number 62 a B&B is that breakfast is only offered as an add-on. The cosy, comfortable rooms come with thoughtful extras such as body lotion, make-up wipes and cotton buds. It also has one of the most lovingly tended front gardens of all of the converted town houses on this strip.

★Lincoln House HOTEL $$
(Map p654; ☎029-2039 5558; www.lincolnhotel.co.uk; 118 Cathedral Rd, Pontcanna; r £90-150; P📶) Walking a middle line between a large B&B and a small hotel, Lincoln House is a generously proportioned Victorian property with heraldic emblems in the stained-glass windows of its sitting room, and a separate bar. For added romance, book a four-poster room.

Saco Cardiff APARTMENT $$
(Map p654; ☎08451 220405; www.sacoapartments.co.uk; 76 Cathedral Rd, Pontcanna; apt from £117; P📶) This large town house has been given a contemporary makeover and converted into serviced apartments, complete with comfortable lounges and fitted kitchens. They're set up for longer visits but one-night stays are possible midweek. The two-bedroom apartments are good value for families with kids; there's an extra sofa bed in the lounge.

Beaufort Guest House B&B $$
(Map p654; ☎029-2023 7003; www.beauforthousecardiff.co.uk; 65 Cathedral Rd, Pontcanna; s/d from £57/82; P📶) Despite a thorough refurbishment, the Beaufort retains an old-fashioned Victorian atmosphere, with period-style furniture, gilt mirrors, heavy drapes and even a portrait of the old Queen herself. The breakfast room is ready for royalty, with candlesticks and blue-and-white china adding a touch of grandeur.

Cathedral 73 B&B $$$
(Map p654; ☎029-2023 5005; www.cathedral73.com; 73 Cathedral Rd; r/ste from £150/225; P📶) This upmarket boutique B&B has nine rooms, suites and apartments in a beautifully restored Victorian town house occupying a prominent corner on the Cathedral Rd strip. Downstairs there's a chichi tea room and piano bar, and there's a pretty garden terrace at the rear.

Eating

City Centre

★Riverside Market MARKET $
(Map p656; www.riversidemarket.org.uk; Fitzhamon Embankment, Riverside; ⌚10am-2pm Sun; 🌿) What it lacks in size, Riverside Market makes up for in sheer yumminess, its stalls heaving with cooked meals, cakes, cheese, organic meat, charcuterie and bread. There are lots of options for vegetarians and an excellent coffee stall.

Pettigrew Tea Rooms CAFE $
(Map p656; ☎029-2023 5486; www.pettigrew-tearooms.com; West Lodge, Castle St; mains £5-8; ⌚8.30am-5.30pm) Cuppas and cakes are served on delicate china at this perfectly dahling little tea room within the crenellated confines of Bute Park's 1863 gatehouse. Cucumber sandwiches and cream scones are the customary accompaniment to the extensive range of tea on offer – or try the

ploughman's platter if you're after something more hearty.

Coffee Barker CAFE $
(Map p656; Castle Arcade; mains £5.50-8.50; 8.30am-5.30pm Mon-Sat, 10.30am-4.30pm Sun;) Slink into an armchair, sip on a silky coffee and snack on salmon scrambled eggs or a sandwich in what is Cardiff's coolest cafe. There are plenty of magazines and toys to keep everyone amused.

Cafe Cittá ITALIAN $$
(Map p656; 029-2022 4040; www.cafecitta.com; 4 Church St; mains £7.50-13; noon-9pm Tue-Sat;) Once you're lured through the door by the delicious scents wafting out of the wood-fired oven, you won't want to escape this little slice of *la dolce vita*. The authentic *linguine alla puttanesca* is proof that some traditions shouldn't be messed with. There are only a handful of tables, so book ahead.

Casanova ITALIAN $$$
(Map p656; 029-2034 4044; www.casanovacardiff.co.uk; 13 Quay St; 2-/3 course lunch £14/18, dinner £25/30, vegetarian £20/25; noon-2.30pm & 5.30-10pm Mon-Sat;) Rather than offering generic Italian dishes or the specialities of just one region, this little charmer offers a selection of authentic regional dishes from all over Italy. The result is a varied menu with half-a-dozen options for each course, including more unusual dishes such as ox-tongue terrine and truffled goats cheese with honey.

Park House MODERN EUROPEAN $$$
(Map p656; 029-2022 4343; www.parkhouserestaurant.co.uk; 20 Park Pl; mains £26-28, 2-/3-course lunch £21/26; 11am-4pm & 5.30-10pm Tue-Sat, noon-4pm Sun;) The ambience is rather stuffy, but the menu at this private members' club is anything but conservative, adding subtle Asian flavours to classic European dishes. Dress up and push the buzzer for admittance.

Pontcanna & Canton

★ Purple Poppadom INDIAN $$
(Map p654; 029-2022 0026; www.purplepoppadom.com; 185a Cowbridge Rd East, Canton; mains £13-18, 2-course lunch £11; noon-2pm & 5.30-11pm Tue-Sat, 1-9pm Sun) Trailblazing a path for 'Nouvelle Indian' cuisine, chef Anand George's kitchen offers its own unique take on regional dishes from all over the subcontinent – from Kashmir to Kerala. Meals are thoughtfully constructed and artfully presented.

Bully's FRENCH $$
(Map p654; 029-2022 1905; www.bullysrestaurant.co.uk; 5 Romilly Cres, Pontcanna; mains £19-22; noon-2pm & 6.30-9pm Mon-Sat, noon-3.30pm Sun;) An assortment of odd things (bank notes, receipts from famous restaurants etc) cover the walls of this cosy neighbourhood bistro, giving little indication of the high-quality French-style dishes served here. The set three-course lunches for two are great value (£35 all up, including half a bottle of wine).

★ Fish at 85 SEAFOOD $$$
(Map p654; 029-2023 5666; www.fishat85.co.uk; 85 Pontcanna Rd, Pontcanna; mains £19-24; noon-2.30pm & 6-9pm Tue-Sat) By day a fishmongers (hence the lingering smell), by night an elegant restaurant with Cape Cod-ish decor and candles floating in water-filled

GAY & LESBIAN CARDIFF

Cardiff's small gay and lesbian scene is focused on a cluster of venues on Churchill Way and Charles St. The big event is the annual **Pride Cymru** (www.pridecymru.co.uk; mid-Aug), held in mid-August.

Golden Cross (Map p656; 282 Hayes Bridge Rd; noon-11pm Mon & Tue, to 2am Wed-Sun;) One of the oldest pubs in the city and a long-standing gay venue, this Victorian bar retains its handsome stained glass, polished wood and ceramic tiles. It hosts drag, cabaret, games and karaoke nights, and there's a little dance floor.

Eagle (Map p656; 029-2114 0000; www.eaglecardiff.com; 39 Charles St; 5pm-3am Mon-Fri, to 5am Sat, to midnight Sun) A bastion for blokiness, the Eagle has a gay-men-only policy after 9pm on weekends, enabled by a membership system (£3 annually). There's no DJ, drag or back room, just a friendly little basement bar open until the wee smalls. Special events cover the spectrum from kink to karaoke. They also operate the Eagle 50 sauna across the road.

WORTH A TRIP

PENARTH

Well-heeled Penarth has transformed from an old-fashioned seaside resort to a virtual suburb of Cardiff, despite it being in the neighbouring county. It's connected to Cardiff Bay by the freshwater lake formed by the construction of the barrage and it now sports a busy marina on the lakefront.

One of the draws to Penarth is **Restaurant James Sommerin** (☎029-2070 6559; www.jamessommerinrestaurant.co.uk; The Esplanade; mains £20-25, 6/9 courses £60/80; ⏲noon-10.30pm Tue-Sun). The chef with his name on the window earned a Michelin star for his previous Monmouthshire restaurant and is surely on track for another one here. Everything that proceeds from the kitchen is as exquisite looking as it is tasting, incorporating multiple textures, well-balanced flavours and tricksy molecular-gastronomy techniques.

jars, Fish at 85 is Cardiff's premier spot for a seafood dinner. The menu cherry-picks the best of the day's catch, offering half-a-dozen varieties, exquisitely cooked and in huge portions.

Cardiff Bay

Moksh INDIAN $$
(Map p658; ☎029-2049 8120; www.moksh.co.uk; Ocean Bldg, Bute Cres, Cardiff Bay; mains £6-18; ⏲noon-2.30pm & 6-11pm; ☑) Moksh's tangerine walls and Buddhist imagery provide ample warning that this is not your typical Indian restaurant. A Goan influence pervades but an adventurous approach incorporates snatches of Chinese, Tibetan, Indonesian and even Moroccan cuisine.

Cathays & Roath

★**Oz Urfa** MIDDLE EASTERN $
(Map p654; ☎029-2048 8739; 156 City Rd, Roath; mains £8-12; ⏲10am-11pm) Brightly lit, cheap and exceedingly cheerful, this humble eatery specialises in the food of 'Turkey, Mesopotamia and the Mediterranean'. This translates as delicious mezze, whole roast lamb, fish dishes and shish kebabs cooked over a charcoal grill. Serves are enormous: if you're not too hungry, consider sharing one main between two.

★**Mint & Mustard** INDIAN $$
(☎029-2062 0333; www.mintandmustard.com; 134 Whitchurch Rd, Cathays; mains £8.25-15; ⏲noon-2pm & 5-11pm; ☑) Specialising in seafood dishes from India's southern state of Kerala, this excellent restaurant combines an upmarket ambience with attentive service and delicious, beautifully presented food. If you're not enticed by the lobster, prawn and fish dishes, there are plenty of vegetarian options and an excellent crusted lamb biryani.

Drinking & Nightlife

City Centre

Gwdihŵ BAR
(Map p656; ☎029-2039 7933; www.gwdihw.co.uk; 6 Guildford Cres; ⏲3pm-midnight Sun-Wed, noon-2am Thu-Sat) The last word in Cardiff hipsterdom, this cute little bar has an eclectic line-up of entertainment (comedy, DJs and lots of live music, including microfestivals that spill over into the car park) but it's a completely charming place to stop for a drink at any time. If you're wondering about the name, it's the Welsh take on an owl's call.

Buffalo Bar BAR
(Map p656; ☎029-2031 0312; www.buffalocardiff.co.uk; 11 Windsor Pl; ⏲noon-3am) A haven for cool kids about town, the laid-back Buffalo features retro furniture, tasty food, life-affirming cocktails and alternative tunes. There's a small beer garden at the rear, while upstairs a roster of cutting-edge indie bands takes to the stage.

Full Moon BAR
(Map p656; ☎029-2037 3022; www.thefullmooncardiff.com; 1/3 Womanby St; ⏲7pm-midnight Sun-Wed, to 3am Thu, 5pm-4am Fri & Sat) There are no pretences at this friendly, grungy rock bar. Sample from the large selection of rum, whisky and vodka, or try the 'jar of green shit' if you dare. On weekends DJs spin a kooky but highly danceable blend of ska, funk, Motown, soul, punk and indie pop while, upstairs, the Moon Club thrums to live bands.

Pen & Wig PUB
(Map p656; ☎029-2037 1217; www.penandwigcardiff.co.uk; 1 Park Grove; ⏲11.30am-midnight) Latin legal phrases are printed on the walls

of this solidly traditional pub, but there's nothing stuffy about the large beer garden or the entertainment roster (open-mic Mondays, quiz Tuesdays, live-music Saturdays). *Caveat emptor:* the impressive range of ales may induce *mens rea* the morning after.

Porter's BAR
(Map p656; ☎029-2125 0666; www.porterscardiff.com; Bute Tce; ⏰5pm-12.30am Mon-Thu, to 3am Fri, noon-3am Sat, to midnight Sun) There's something on most nights at this friendly attitude-free bar, whether it's a quiz, live music, comedy, theatre or a movie screening (there's a little cinema attached). There's a surprisingly wonderful urban beer garden out the back, under the shadow of the railway tracks.

Pontcanna & Canton

The Lansdowne PUB
(Map p654; ☎029-2022 1312; www.thelansdownecardiff.co.uk; cnr Lansdowne & Beda Rds, Canton; ⏰noon-11pm) With charmingly scruffy rooms sprawling around a central bar, the Lansdowne has an esteemed reputation for its food and for its range of craft beer and cider. They even run their own mini beer festival every June.

Y Mochyn Du PUB
(Map p654; ☎029-2037 1599; www.ymochyndu.com; Sophia Close; ⏰noon-11pm) Right by SWALEC Stadium, the 'Black Pig' is both the de facto cricketer's pub and one of the few places in Cardiff where you might hear Welsh spoken. There's a big variety of beer on tap, including a range of craft ales. Once you've checked out the cricketing memorabilia, head outside to the city's best beer garden.

☆ Entertainment

Pick up a copy of **Buzz** (www.buzzmag.co.uk), a free monthly magazine with up-to-date entertainment listings, available from the tourist office, bars, theatres and the like. The staff at tourist offices can also help out with recommendations.

★**Clwb Ifor Bach** LIVE MUSIC
(Map p656; ☎029-2023 2199; www.clwb.net; 11 Womanby St) The legendary Clwb has broken many a Welsh band since it first opened its doors as a Welsh-language social club in 1983, building a reputation as Cardiff's most important indie music venue. It now hosts bands performing in many tongues – from young upstarts to more established acts – along with regular club nights.

Chapter THEATRE, CINEMA
(Map p654; ☎029-2030 4400; www.chapter.org; Market Rd, Canton) The city's edgiest arts venue, Chapter has a varied rota of contemporary drama, as well as art exhibitions, arthouse cinema, workshops, alternative theatre and dance performances. There's also a very popular cafe-bar, with a big range of European beers and real ale on tap.

Shopping

If you thought Cardiff's 21st-century makeover was all about political edifices, arts centres and sports stadiums, think again. One of the most dramatic developments in the central city is the transformation of the Hayes shopping strip, with the giant, glitzy extension of the St David's shopping centre now eating up its entire eastern side. Balancing this modern mall is a historic network of Victorian and Edwardian shopping arcades spreading their dainty tentacles either side of St Mary St.

Cardiff Market MARKET
(Map p656; btwn St Mary & Trinity Sts; ⏰8.30am-5.30pm Mon-Sat) For an age-old shopping experience, head to this Victorian covered market, which is packed with stalls selling everything from fresh fish to mobile-phone covers. Stock up here for a picnic in Bute Park with goodies such as fresh bread, cheese, cold meats, barbecued chicken and Welsh cakes. Music fans should head upstairs to Kelly's Records.

Craft in the Bay CRAFTS
(Map p658; ☎029-2048 4611; www.makersguildinwales.org.uk; Lloyd George Ave, Butetown; ⏰10.30am-5.30pm) This retail showcase for the Welsh Makers Guild cooperative sells work by its members, including a wide range of ceramics, textiles, jewellery, glassware and ironwork.

St David's MALL
(Map p656; www.stdavidscardiff.com; The Hayes; ⏰9.30am-8pm Mon-Sat, 11am-5pm Sun; 📶) Immense is the best way to describe this shiny shopping centre. All of the famous chains you could name have a home here, along with a smorgasbord of eateries, a cinema multiplex and a large branch of the John Lewis department store, which dominates its south end.

Morgan Quarter SHOPPING ARCADE
(Map p656; www.morganquarter.co.uk; btwn St Mary St & The Hayes) Cardiff's oldest arcade (1858), the Royal, connects up with the Morgan Arcade via a series of covered lanes, forming a ritzy shopping precinct called the Morgan Quarter. Along with name-brand fashion, there are shops selling skateboards, vintage books and antiques. Look out for Spillers Records, the excellent Wally's Delicatessen, The Plan cafe and Liam Gallagher's pricey menswear boutique Pretty Green.

Information

Tourist Office (Map p658; ☎029-2087 3573; www.visitcardiff.com; Wales Millennium Centre, Bute Pl, Cardiff Bay; ⏰10am-6pm Mon-Sat, to 4pm Sun) Information, advice and souvenirs.

University Hospital of Wales (☎029-2074 7747; www.cardiffandvaleuhb.wales.nhs.uk; The Gateway, Heath Park) Cardiff's main accident and emergency department, located 2 miles north of the Civic Centre.

Getting There & Away

AIR

Cardiff Airport (☎01446-711111; www.cardiff-airport.com) is 12 miles southwest of Cardiff, past Barry. Aside from summer-only services and charters, these are the airlines flying into Cardiff and the destinations they serve:

Aer Lingus (www.aerlingus.com) Dublin.

Citywing (www.citywing.com) Anglesey.

Eastern Airways (www.easternairways.com) Aberdeen, Newcastle.

Flybe (www.flybe.com) London City, Glasgow, Edinburgh, Belfast, Cork, Dublin, Jersey, Paris, Berlin, Munich, Milan, Faro.

KLM (www.klm.com) Amsterdam.

Ryanair (www.ryanair.com) Tenerife-South.

Thomson Airways (www.thomson.co.uk) Málaga, Alicante, Gran Canaria, Tenerife-South, Lanzarote.

Vueling (www.vueling.com) Málaga, Alicante.

BUS

Cardiff's central bus station has closed for a major redevelopment and is due to reopen near the train station in a revitalised Central Square in 2018. In the meantime there are temporary bus stops scattered all around the inner city. See www.traveline.cymru for details.

Bus destinations include Newport (£2.10, 38 minutes, frequent), Abergavenny (£9.10, 2½ hours, 12 daily), Brecon (£8.30, 1¾ hours, eight daily), Swansea (£4.50, 1¼ hours, at least hourly) and Aberystwyth (£17, four hours, two daily).

Megabus (http://uk.megabus.com) offers one-way coach journeys from London to Cardiff (via Newport) from as little as £5.

National Express (www.nationalexpress.com) coaches depart from **Cardiff Coach Station** (Map p654; Sophia Gardens), with destinations including Tenby (£18, 2¾ hours, daily), Swansea (£3.50, one hour, four daily), Chepstow (from £4.80, one hour, four daily), Bristol (£6.10, one hour, four daily) and London (from £5, 3½ hours, four daily).

TRAIN

Trains from major British cities arrive at Cardiff Central station, on the southern edge of the city centre. Direct services to/from Cardiff include London Paddington (from £40, two hours, two per hour), Abergavenny (£14, 45 minutes, frequent), Swansea (£9.20, one hour, two per hour), Fishguard Harbour (from £10, three hours, two daily) and Holyhead (from £24, five hours, six daily). For the latest timetables and bookings, see www.thetrainline.com.

Getting Around

TO/FROM THE AIRPORT

The T9 Cardiff Airport Express bus (£5, 40 minutes, every 20 minutes) heads between the airport and the city centre via Cardiff Bay.

The 905 shuttle bus (£1, 10 minutes) links the airport terminal to nearby Rhoose Cardiff Airport train station. Trains to Cardiff Central station (£4.40, 33 minutes) run hourly Monday to Saturday and twice-hourly on Sunday.

FlightLink Wales (☎029-2025 3555) has the airport taxi concession, providing minibus shuttles to the city, either on a shared basis (£35) or for exclusive use (£60).

PUBLIC TRANSPORT

Boat

Two boats run alternating waterbus services along the River Taff from Bute Park (Map p656) to Mermaid Quay (Map p658), departing every half-hour from 10.30am to 5pm. The journey takes about 25 minutes and costs £4 each way.

Bus

Local buses are operated by **Cardiff Bus** (☎029-2066 6444; www.cardiffbus.com; s trip/day pass £1.80/3.60); buy your ticket from the driver (no change given). Useful routes from stops scattered around the city centre include the Baycar to Cardiff Bay; 13 and 28 to Roath Park; 38 to the City/Crwys/Whitchurch Rd strip through Cathays and Roath; 25, 62 and 63 via Cathedral Rd to Llandaff; and 32 to St Fagans.

Train

Generally the buses are more convenient for short trips than the trains, although there are a handful of stations scattered around the city including Cardiff Central, Cardiff Queen St, Cardiff Bay, Cathays and Grangetown. Expect to pay around £2.

MONMOUTHSHIRE (SIR FYNWY)

You need only ponder the preponderance of castles to realise that this pleasantly rural county was once a wild frontier. The Norman marcher lords kept stonemasons extremely busy, erecting mighty fortifications to keep the unruly Welsh at bay. Despite this stone line marking out a very clear border along the Rivers Monnow and Wye, the 1543 second Act of Union left Monmouthshire in a kind of jurisdictional limbo between England and Wales. This legal ambiguity wasn't put to rest until 1974 when Monmouthshire was definitively confirmed as part of Wales.

The River Wye, Britain's fifth-longest, flows from the mountains of Mid-Wales, tootles its way into England and then returns to the middle ground – forming the border of the two countries – before emptying into the River Severn below Chepstow. Much of it is designated an area of outstanding natural beauty (www.wyevalleyaonb.org.uk), famous for its limestone gorges and dense broadleaved woodland.

Chepstow (Cas-gwent)

POP 14,200

Chepstow is an attractive market town nestled in a great S-bend in the River Wye, with a magnificent Norman castle and one of Britain's best-known racecourses. It was first developed as a base for the Norman conquest of southeast Wales, later prospering as a port for the timber and wine trades. As river-borne commerce gave way to the railways, Chepstow's importance diminished to reflect its name, which means 'market place' in Old English.

Sights

★Chepstow Castle CASTLE

(Cadw; www.cadw.gov.wales; Bridge St; adult/child £4.50/3.40; 9.30am-5pm Mar-Oct, 10am-4pm Nov-Feb) Imposing Chepstow Castle perches atop a limestone cliff overhanging the river, guarding the main river crossing from England into South Wales. It is one of the oldest castles in Britain – building started in 1067, less than a year after William the Conqueror invaded England. The impressive Great Tower dates from this time and includes bricks plundered from the nearby Roman town of Caerwent. It was extended over the centuries, resulting in a long, narrow complex snaking along the hill.

Sleeping & Eating

Three Tuns PUB $$

(01291-645797; www.threetunschepstow.co.uk; 32 Bridge St; s/d from £50/75) This early 17th-century pub by the castle has had an artful makeover, with rugs and antique furniture complementing the more rugged features of the ancient building. There's often live music downstairs on weekends, but the noise winds down at 11pm.

Riverside Wine Bar TAPAS $$

(01291-628300; www.theriversidewinebar.co.uk; 18a The Back; mains £8-14; 5-11pm Wed, noon-11pm Thu-Sun) Sink into a leather couch and quaff on a wine while grazing through antipasto and cheese platters, skewers, tortillas, pizza and tapas. Heavy gilt-framed mirrors and feature wallpaper set the tone, while in summer the action spills outside.

Getting There & Away

BUS

From Chepstow's **bus station** (Thomas St), buses head to/from Newport (£3.80, 40 minutes, frequent), Tintern (£3, 13 minutes, 11 daily), Monmouth (£3.80, 40 minutes, hourly) and Bristol (£5.50, 55 minutes, hourly). Sunday services are limited.

National Express (www.nationalexpress.com) has up to four coaches a day to/from London (from £12, three hours), Cardiff (from £4.80, one hour) and Swansea (from £11, two hours).

TRAIN

There are direct trains to/from Gloucester (£9.80, 30 minutes, frequent), Newport (£7.30, 23 minutes, 14 daily), Cardiff (£9.60, 40 minutes, 16 daily), Swansea (from £11, 1¾ hours, daily) and Fishguard Harbour (from £18, 3¾ hours, daily).

Lower Wye Valley

The A466 road follows the snaking, steep-sided valley of the River Wye from Chepstow to Monmouth, passing through

WORTH A TRIP

ROMAN CAERLEON

Hidden in plain view beneath the small, genteel town of Caerleon is one of the largest and most important Roman settlements in Britain. After the Romans invaded in AD 43, they controlled their new territory through a network of forts and military garrisons. The top tier of military organisation was the legionary fort, of which there were only three in Britain – at Eboracum (York), Deva (Chester) and Isca (Caerleon).

Caerleon ('Fort of the Legion') was the headquarters of the elite 2nd Augustan Legion for more than 200 years, from AD 75 until the end of the 3rd century. It wasn't just a military camp but a purpose-built township some 9 miles in circumference, complete with a large amphitheatre and a state-of-the-art Roman baths complex.

National Roman Legion Museum (www.museumwales.ac.uk/en/roman; High St; ⏲10am-5pm Mon-Sat, 2-5pm Sun) Put your Caerleon explorations into context at this excellent museum, which paints a vivid picture of what life was like for soldiers in one of the most remote corners of the Empire. It displays a host of intriguing Roman artefacts uncovered locally, from jewellery to armour, including a section of mosaic floor found in the neighbouring churchyard.

Caerleon Roman Fortress Baths (Cadw; www.cadw.gov.wales; High St; ⏲9.30am-5pm daily Apr-Oct, 9.30am-5pm Mon-Sat & 11am-4pm Sun Nov-Mar) Like any good Roman town, Caerleon had a grand public bath complex. Parts of the outdoor swimming pool, *apodyterium* (changing room) and *frigidarium* (cold room) remain under a protective roof, and give some idea of the scale of the place. Projections of bathers splashing through shimmering water help bring it to life.

the straggling village of Tintern with its famous abbey. This is a beautiful drive, rendered particularly mysterious when a twilight mist rises from the river and shrouds the illuminated ruins.

Sights

★Tintern Abbey HISTORIC BUILDING

(Cadw; www.cadw.gov.wales; Tintern; adult/child £5.50/4.10; ⏲9am-5pm Mar-Oct, 10am-4pm Nov-Feb; Ⓟ) The haunting riverside ruins of this sprawling monastic complex have inspired poets and artists through the centuries, including William Wordsworth, who penned *Lines Composed a Few Miles Above Tintern Abbey* during a visit in 1798, and JMW Turner, who made many paintings and drawings of the site. It was founded in 1131 by the Cistercian order and left to fall into picturesque ruin after the monks were booted out by Henry VIII in 1536.

Sleeping & Eating

Tŷ Bryn B&B $$

(☎01594-531330; www.wyevalleystay.co.uk; Monmouth Rd, Llandogo; r £75-90; Ⓟ📶) Perched on a hillside overlooking a pretty stretch of the river in the village of Llandogo, this old stone house has friendly young owners and three comfortable en suite rooms, two of which have river views.

★The Whitebrook MODERN BRITISH $$$

(☎01600-860254; www.thewhitebrook.co.uk; Whitebrook; 2-/3-/7-course lunch £25/29/47, 3-/7-course dinner £54/67, r incl dinner from £214; ⏲noon-2pm Wed-Sun, 7-9pm Tue-Sun; Ⓟ📶) Hidden down narrow country lanes in a remote part of the Wye Valley, this wonderful Michelin-starred restaurant-with-rooms is well worth the effort it takes to reach it. Every plate that proceeds from the kitchen is a little work of art, packed with interesting flavours. If a sober driver is an unlikely prospect, book one of the eight elegant rooms upstairs.

Getting There & Away

Eleven buses a day (fewer on Saturday, none on Sunday) stop here on their journey between Chepstow (13 minutes) and Monmouth (30 minutes).

Abergavenny

POP 10,100

Bustling, workaday Abergavenny has played many roles on history's stage: Roman fort,

Norman stronghold, tanning and weaving centre, and prison for Hitler's deputy. Its enviable location between three shapely hills – the Blorenge, Ysgyryd Fawr (Skirrid), and Sugar Loaf – makes it a superb base for walkers, while its annual food festival and its acclaimed restaurants (the best of which are actually just out of town) attract lovers of fresh, organic, seasonal Welsh cuisine.

Its ancient name, Y Fenni (Welsh for 'place of the smiths'), was given to a stream that empties into the River Usk here, and later anglicised to Gavenny (Abergavenny means 'mouth of the Gavenny'). The Romans established Gobannium Fort here, exactly a day's march from their garrison at Caerleon, which they maintained from AD 57 to 400. Not long after the Norman conquest, a marcher lord, Hamelin de Ballon, built the castle and the town's regional importance grew.

Sights

★ St Mary's Priory Church CHURCH

(☎01873-858787; www.stmarys-priory.org; Monk St; ⏲9am-4pm Mon-Sat) Although you wouldn't guess it from the outside, this large stone church has been described as the 'Westminster Abbey of South Wales' because of the remarkable treasury of aristocratic tombs that lies within. It was founded at the same time as the castle (1087) as part of a Benedictine priory, but the present building dates mainly from the 14th century, with 15th- and 19th-century additions and alterations.

Festivals & Events

Abergavenny Festival of Cycling SPORTS

(www.abergavennyfestivalofcycling.co.uk; ⏲Jul) A mid-July lycra-enthusiasts' meet incorporating the Iron Mountain Sportives, participatory events with 20-mile, 40-mile, 70-mile and 100-mile courses.

Abergavenny Food Festival FOOD & DRINK

(www.abergavennyfoodfestival.co.uk; ⏲Sep) The most important gastronomic event in Wales, held on the third weekend in September, with demonstrations, debates, competitions, courses, stalls and the odd celebrity. But the real drawcard is that this is an enthusiastically local festival, run by volunteers, and not some big-budget food producer's showcase. Kooky things can and do happen.

Sleeping & Eating

Angel Hotel HOTEL $$

(☎01873-857121; www.angelabergavenny.com; 15 Cross St; r/cottage from £89/177; P 📶) Abergavenny's top hotel is a fine Georgian building that was once a famous coaching inn. Choose between sleek, sophisticated rooms in the hotel itself, in an adjoining mews, in a Victorian lodge near the castle or in the 17th-century Castle Cottage (sleeping four). There's also a good **restaurant** (mains restaurant £14-18, bar £6-14; ⏲noon-11pm) and bar.

Cwtch Cafe CAFE $

(☎01873-855466; 58 Cross St; mains £4-6; ⏲9am-5pm Mon-Sat; 📶) Stylish and wonderfully friendly, Cwtch (Welsh for 'hug') entices a scrum of regulars through the doors with its home-made cakes, coffee and lunchtime dishes such as rarebit, pancakes with crispy bacon, quiche and veggie lasagne.

The Hardwick MODERN BRITISH $$

(☎01873-854220; www.thehardwick.co.uk; Old Raglan Rd; mains £15-23, s/d from £115/135; ⏲noon-3pm & 6.30-10pm; P) This traditional inn with an old stone fireplace and low ceiling beams has become, under the direction of chef Stephen Terry, a showcase for the best of unpretentious country cooking. Save room for the home-made ice cream. The Hardwick is 2 miles south of Abergavenny on the B4598. Attached are eight elegant rooms.

★ Walnut Tree MODERN BRITISH $$$

(☎01873-852797; www.thewalnuttreeinn.com; Old Ross Rd, Llanddewi Skirrid; mains £21-29, 2-/3-course lunch £25/30; ⏲noon-2.30pm & 6.30-10pm Tue-Sat) Established in 1963, the Michelin-starred Walnut Tree serves the cuisine-hopping meat and seafood creations of chef Shaun Hill, with a focus on fresh, local produce. If you're too full to move far after dinner, elegant cottage accommodation is available. The Walnut Tree is 3 miles northeast of Abergavenny on the B4521.

Information

Nevill Hall Hospital (☎01873-732732; www.wales.nhs.uk; Brecon Rd; ⏲24hr) Emergency service.

Tourist Office (☎01873-853254; www.visitabergavenny.co.uk; Tithe Barn, Monk St; ⏲10am-2pm Tue-Sat)

WORTH A TRIP

RAGLAN

The last great medieval castle to be built in Wales, **Raglan Castle** (Cadw; www.cadw.wales.gov.uk; adult/child £4.50/3.40; 9.30am-5pm Mar-Oct, 10am-4pm Nov-Feb; P) was designed more as a swaggering declaration of wealth and power than a defensive fortress. A magnificent, sprawling complex built of dusky pink and grey sandstone, it was constructed in the 15th and 16th centuries by Sir William ap Thomas and his son William Herbert, the first earl of Pembroke.

Its centrepiece, the lavish Great Tower, a hexagonal keep ringed by a moat, bears a savage wound from the civil wars of the 1640s, when it was besieged by Cromwell's soldiers. After the castle's surrender the tower was undermined, until eventually two of the six walls collapsed. The impressive courtyards beyond the Great Tower display the transition from fortress to grandiose palace, with ornate windows and fireplaces, gargoyle-studded crenelations and heraldic carvings.

Raglan Castle is on the busy A40, 8 miles southwest of Monmouth and 9 miles southeast of Abergavenny. Buses heading between the two stop at Raglan village, which is a five-minute walk from the castle.

Getting There & Away

BUS

Direct bus services to/from Abergavenny's **station** include Cardiff (£9.10, 2½ hours, 12 daily), Merthyr Tydfil (£6.40, 1½ hours, 13 daily), Monmouth (£3.40, 45 minutes, seven daily), Brecon (£3.40, 45 minutes, 12 daily) and Hereford (£5.30, 50 minutes, six daily).

TRAIN

There are direct trains to/from Cardiff (£14, 45 minutes, frequent), Swansea (£25, 1½ hours, 15 daily), Tenby (from £18, 3¾ hours, daily), Holyhead (from £30, four hours, seven daily) and Manchester (from £25, three hours, 15 daily).

SOUTH WALES VALLEYS

The valleys fanning northwards from Cardiff and Newport were once the heart of industrial Wales. Although the coal, iron and steel industries have withered, the valley names – Rhondda, Cynon, Rhymney, Ebbw – still evoke a world of tight-knit working-class communities, male voice choirs and rows of neat terraced houses set amid a scarred, coal-blackened landscape. Today the region is fighting back against its decline by creating a tourist industry based on industrial heritage – places such as the Rhondda Heritage Park, Big Pit and Blaenavon Ironworks are among Wales' most impressive tourist attractions.

History

The valleys' industrial economy emerged in the 18th century, based on the exploitation of the region's rich deposits of coal, limestone and iron ore. At first the iron trade dictated the need for coal, but by the 1830s coal was finding its own worldwide markets and people poured in from the countryside looking for work. The harsh and dangerous working conditions provided fertile ground for political radicalism – Merthyr Tydfil elected Britain's first ever Labour Party MP in 1900, and many locals went to fight in the Spanish Civil War in the 1930s.

Blaenavon (Blaenafon)

POP 6060

Of all the valley settlements that were decimated by the demise of heavy industry, the one-time coal and iron town of Blaenavon shows the greenest shoots of regrowth, helped in large part by the awarding of Unesco World Heritage status in 2000 to its unique conglomeration of industrial sites. Its proximity to Brecon Beacons National Park and Abergavenny doesn't do it any harm either.

Sights

Blaenavon World Heritage Centre MUSEUM
(01495-742333; www.visitblaenavon.co.uk; Church Rd; 10am-5pm Tue-Sun) FREE Housed in an artfully converted old school, this centre contains a cafe, tourist office, gallery, gift shop and, more importantly, excellent interactive, audiovisual displays that explore the industrial heritage of the region.

Blaenavon Ironworks HISTORIC SITE
(Cadw; www.cadw.gov.wales; North St; 10am-5pm Easter-Oct, to 4pm Tue-Thu Nov-Easter) FREE

When it was completed in 1789, this ironworks was among the most advanced in the world. Today the site is one of the best-preserved of all its Industrial Revolution contemporaries, with a motion-activated audiovisual display within the hulking remains of one of the blast furnaces serving to rattle the ravens that now call it home. Also on display are the ironworkers' tiny terraced cottages, furnished as they would have been at different points in history.

Pontypool & Blaenavon Railway HERITAGE RAILWAY
(☎01495-792263; www.pontypool-and-blaenavon.co.uk; day pass adult/child £10/5) Built to haul coal and passengers, this railway has been restored by local volunteers, allowing you to catch a steam train from the town centre to Furnace Sidings (near Big Pit) and on to Whistle Halt, which at 396m is one of the highest stations in Britain. Check online for timetables.

★Big Pit National Coal Museum MINE
(☎0300 111 2333; www.museumwales.ac.uk; car park £3; ⏲9.30am-5pm, guided tours 10am-3.30pm; P) FREE Fascinating Big Pit provides an opportunity to explore a real coal mine and get a taste of what life was like for the miners who worked here up until 1980. Tours descend 90m into the mine and explore the tunnels and coalfaces in the company of an ex-miner guide. Above ground, you can visit various colliery buildings including the 1939 pithead baths, filled with displays on the industry and the evocative reminiscences of ex-miners.

Sleeping & Eating

Oakfield B&B $$
(☎01495-792829; www.oakfieldbnb.com; 1 Oakfield Tce, Varteg Rd; s/d £42/69; P 📶) The clued-up owners of this spick-and-span B&B are a fount of local knowledge. Their three well-appointed rooms have a fresh, modern feel to them. Two have en suite bathrooms, while the third is an interconnected family suite with a bathroom on the landing.

Coffi 1860 CAFE $
(☎01495-790127; 76 Broad St; mains £6; ⏲8am-3pm; 📶) With leadlight windows, art deco fixtures and shamrock tiling on the walls, this lovely old converted shop is a great place to soak up local life. The food stretches to cooked breakfasts, sandwiches, jacket potatoes, stews, curries, quiches, cakes and proper Sunday lunches.

Butterflies PUB FOOD $$
(☎01495-791044; www.butterfliesblaenavon.co.uk; 31 Old Queen St; mains £11-23; ⏲6-10pm Tue, Wed & Sat, noon-2.30pm & 6-10pm Thu & Fri, 1-4pm Sun; 🖉) Serving surprisingly sophisticated food for a small-town pub in a former mining town, cosy Butterflies has meaty offerings that stretch to an excellent *boeuf en croute* (beef in a mushroom-lined pastry crust) and chateaubriand. If that all sounds a bit too fancy, there are pub favourites to fall back on (lasagne, burgers, steak-and-ale pie), along with fish and vegetarian options.

Shopping

Blaenavon Cheddar Company FOOD & DRINKS
(☎01495-793123; www.chunkofcheese.co.uk; 80 Broad St; ⏲10am-5pm Mon-Sat) Showcasing the company's range of award-winning handmade cheese, some of which is matured down in the Big Pit mine shaft, this little store also stocks a range of Welsh specialty ale, chutney, mustard and other local produce.

Getting There & Away

Bus X24 heads to/from Newport (£7.10, one hour) several times per hour.

Caerphilly (Caerffili)

POP 30,400

The town of Caerphilly, with its fairy-tale castle, guards the entrance to the Rhymney Valley to the north of Cardiff. Its name is synonymous with a popular variety of mild, slightly crumbly, hard white cheese that was once made in farmhouses all over South Wales.

Its other claim to fame was as the birthplace of Tommy Cooper, a much-loved British comedian who died while performing a live TV show in 1984. A statue of Cooper in his trademark fez and with a rabbit at his feet overlooks the castle from near the tourist office.

Sights

★Caerphilly Castle CASTLE
(Cadw; www.cadw.gov.wales; adult/child £6/4.20; ⏲9.30am-5pm Mar-Oct, 10am-4pm Nov-Feb) You could be forgiven for thinking that

WORTH A TRIP

RHONDDA VALLEY

Until its last pit closed in 1990, the Rhondda Valley was synonymous with coal mining. That industrial heritage is celebrated within the buildings of the Lewis Merthyr coal mine, which was closed in 1983. The highlight of **Rhondda Heritage Park** (☎01443-682036; www.rhonddaheritagepark.com; Trehafod; tour adult/child £3.75/2.65; ⏰10.30am-4.30pm Tue-Sat, tours 11.30am & 1.30pm) is the 40-minute Underground Experience (bookings advised), where you don a miner's helmet and lamp and, accompanied by an ex-miner, descend to the coalface. The compelling commentary vividly re-creates the experience of mine workers, and hammers home the social impact of the coal industry.

Other displays include recreated domestic interiors and shops, and a sobering section on the Tynewydd Colliery disaster of 1877. Upstairs there's a cafe and an art space.

The mine is located just off the A4058 in Trehafod, between Pontypridd and Porth. There are trains every half hour from Cardiff Central station to Trehafod (£6.90, 35 minutes), from where it's a 10-minute walk to the heritage park.

Caerphilly Castle – with its profusion of towers and crenellations reflected in a duck-filled lake – was a film set rather than an ancient monument. While it is often used as a film set, it is also one of Britain's finest examples of a 13th-century fortress with water defences.

Festivals & Events

Big Cheese FOOD, FAIR
(www.caerphilly.gov.uk; Caerphilly; ⏰Jul) Any festival that includes a Cheese Olympics and a Tommy Cooper Tent has got to be worth a look. On the last weekend of July, Caerphilly welcomes more than 80,000 people to three days of family-oriented fun and games that offer everything from fireworks to falconry, comedy acts to cheese tasting, and a traditional fun fair.

Information

Caerphilly Tourist Office (☎029-2088 0011; www.visitcaerphilly.com; The Twyn; ⏰10am-5pm) Not only is this friendly office a good place to stock up on information, it's also the only place in town selling Caerphilly cheese – along with Penderyn spirits and locally made chocolates. There's a small cafe attached.

Getting There & Away

The easiest way to reach Caerphilly from Cardiff is by train (single/return £4.40/6.90, 19 minutes, at least two per hour).

Frequent buses head to/from Cardiff (£3.80, 39 minutes) and Newport (£3.80, 40 minutes). Bus 26 from Cardiff stops near Castell Coch en route, making it possible to visit both castles in one day. Sunday services are less frequent.

Swansea (Abertawe)

POP 239,000

Dylan Thomas called Swansea an 'ugly, lovely town', and that remains a fair description of Wales' second-largest city today. It's currently in the grip of a Cardiff-esque bout of regeneration that's slowly transforming the drab, postwar city centre into something more worthy of its setting on the glorious 5-mile sweep of Swansea Bay.

The city's Welsh name, Abertawe, describes its location at the mouth of the Tawe, where the river empties into the bay. The Vikings named the area Sveins Ey (Swein's Island), probably referring to the sandbank in the river mouth.

Swansea makes up for some visual shortcomings with a visceral charm. A hefty student population takes to the city's bars with enthusiasm, and pockets of hipness have emerged in inner suburbs such as Sketty and Uplands, which is, conveniently, where all the best B&Bs are located.

History

The Normans built a castle here, but Swansea didn't hit its stride until the Industrial Revolution, when it developed into an important copper-smelting centre. Ore was first shipped in from Cornwall, across the Bristol Channel, but by the 19th century it was arriving from Chile, Cuba and the USA in return for Welsh coal.

By the 20th century the city's industrial base had declined, although Swansea's oil refinery and smaller factories were still judged a worthy target by the Luftwaffe, which devastated the city centre in 1941. It was rebuilt as a rather drab retail development in the 1960s, '70s and '80s, but gradual regeneration is slowly imbuing it with more soul.

Sights & Activities

National Waterfront Museum MUSEUM
(☎0300 111 2333; www.museumwales.ac.uk; South Dock Marina, Oystermouth Rd; ⏰10am-5pm) FREE Housed in a 1901 dockside warehouse with a striking glass and slate extension, this museum's 15 hands on galleries explore Wales' industrial history and the impact of industrialisation on its people, making much use of interactive computer screens and audiovisual presentations. The effect can be a bit overwhelming but there is a lot of interesting stuff here, including displays on the Welsh music industry (artefacts include Bonnie Tyler's gold and Duffy's platinum discs) and a section on 'women's work'.

Dylan Thomas Centre MUSEUM
(☎01792-463980; www.dylanthomas.com; Somerset Pl; ⏰10am-4.30pm) FREE Housed in the former guildhall, this unassuming museum contains absorbing displays on the Swansea-born poet's life and work. It pulls no punches in examining the propensity of Dylan Thomas for puffing up his own myth; he was eventually trapped in the legend of his excessive drinking. Aside from the collection of memorabilia, what really brings his work to life are the recordings of performances of his work.

★**Egypt Centre** MUSEUM
(www.egypt.swan.ac.uk; Mumbles Rd, Sketty; ⏰10am-4pm Tue-Sat) FREE Swansea University's collection of ancient Egyptian antiquities includes a fascinating array of everyday artefacts, ranging from a 4000-year-old razor to a mummified crocodile. Kids can try their hand at Muppet mummification. It's located in the suburb of Sketty, halfway between the city centre and the Mumbles.

LC2 SWIMMING
(☎01792-484672; www.thelcswansea.com; Oystermouth Rd; water park adult/child £7/4; ⏰4-8pm Mon-Fri, 9am-8pm Sat, Sun & school holidays; 👪) The Marine Quarter's flash £32-million leisure centre includes a gym, a toddler's play centre and a 10m indoor climbing wall, but best of all is the water park, complete with a wave pool, water slides and the world's first indoor surfing ride.

Festivals & Events

Dylan Thomas Festival LITERATURE
(www.dylanthomas.com; ⏰Oct-Nov) This festival celebrates Swansea's most famous son with poetry readings, talks, films and performances from 27 October (his birthday) to 9 November (the date he died).

Sleeping

Premier Inn Swansea Waterfront HOTEL $
(☎0871-527 9212; www.premierinn.com; Langdon Rd; r from £35; 📶) It's hard to beat the value offered by this shiny new waterfront hotel, just across the river from the town centre. The rooms are generically smart, comfortable and well-equipped. Book early to take advantage of the cheapest rates and request a room with a view. If you're driving, be aware that the parking lot next door is relatively pricey.

★**Christmas Pie B&B** B&B $$
(☎01792-480266; www.christmaspie.co.uk; 2 Mirador Cres, Uplands; s/d £53/82; P📶) The name suggests something warm and comforting, and this suburban villa does not disappoint. The three en suite bedrooms are all individually decorated. Plus there's fresh fruit and an out-of-the-ordinary, vegetarian-friendly breakfast selection.

Mirador Town House B&B $$
(☎01792-466976; www.themirador.co.uk; 14 Mirador Cres, Uplands; s/d from £60/80; 📶) Kooky and kitsch in the extreme, all seven B&B rooms here are well kitted out and elaborately themed – Roman, Mediterranean, African, Venetian, Egyptian, Asian and French – with murals on the walls and sometimes the ceilings as well. The exuberant hosts are enthusiastic cheerleaders for the area.

Eating

★**Square Peg** CAFE $
(☎01792-206593; www.squarepeg.org.uk; 29b Gower Rd, Sketty; mains £5; ⏰8am-7pm Mon-Fri, to 5pm Sat) With mismatched stools reupholstered in recycled denim and kooky local photography blanketing the walls, this is exactly the hip kind of place you'd expect to deliver seriously good coffee. With two blends on the go at any given time, it doesn't disappoint. The menu includes tasty light breakfasts, wraps, salads, soups, sandwiches and home baking.

Swansea

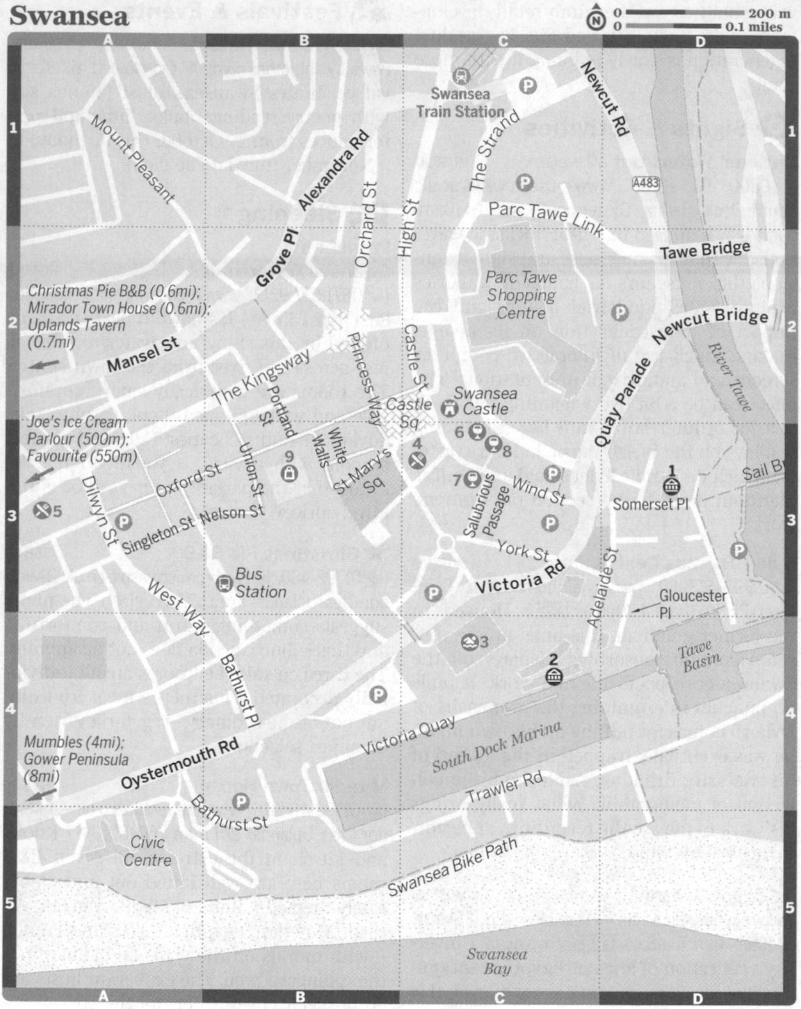

Joe's Ice Cream Parlour ICE CREAM **$**
(www.joes-icecream.com; 85 St Helen's Rd; cones/sundaes from £1.45/4.10; ⏲11am-9pm) For an ice-cream sundae or a cone, locals love Joe's, a Swansea institution founded in 1922 by Joe Cascarini, son of immigrants from Italy's Abruzzi mountains.

★Mosaic TAPAS **$$**
(☎01792-655225; www.mosaicswansea.com; 11 St Helen's Rd; tapas £3.50-8.50, platters £15-20; ⏲noon-2.30pm Fri & Sat, 6-11pm Wed-Sat; 🌱) Set back from the road in an old brick warehouse, and with a menu as eclectic as its decor, this chic eatery specialises in 'world fusion tapas'. This translates to small plates and tasty platters designed to be shared, including a deliciously smoky red-capsicum hummus and juicy garlic king prawns. The attached cocktail bar is very cool indeed.

★Favourite CHINESE **$$**
(☎01792-515230; www.favouritechinese.co.uk; 87 Bryn-y-Mor Rd; mains £7-14; ⏲noon-3pm & 5-10pm Tue-Fri, noon-10pm Sat & Sun; 📶🌱) Opened by expats frustrated by what passed for their national cuisine in these parts, this characterful, intimate restaurant focuses on au-

Swansea

Sights

1 Dylan Thomas Centre....D3
2 National Waterfront Museum....C4

Activities, Courses & Tours

3 LC2....C4

Eating

4 Hanson at the Chelsea....C3
5 Mosaic....A3

Drinking & Nightlife

6 Kon-Tiki....C3
7 No Sign Bar....C3
8 Prohibition....C3

Shopping

9 Swansea Market....B3

thentic, MSG-free Chinese dishes, including a wide range of seafood, vegetable and tofu concoctions. The staff are absolutely delightful and more than willing to guide you down unfamiliar menu paths.

Hanson at the Chelsea SEAFOOD $$
(01792-464068; www.hansonatthechelsea.co.uk; 17 St Mary's St; mains £14-22, 2-/3-course lunch £15/18; noon-2pm daily, 7-9pm Mon-Sat) Perfect for a romantic liaison, this elegant little dining room is discreetly tucked away behind the frenzy of Wind St. Seafood's the speciality, although the menu also contains plenty of meaty dishes, and blackboard specials are chalked up daily.

Slice MODERN BRITISH $$$
(01792-290929; www.sliceswansea.co.uk; 73-75 Eversley Rd, Sketty; 3 courses £39; noon-2pm Fri-Sun, 6.30-9pm Wed-Sun) The simple decor – wooden floors and furniture, and pale walls – stands in contrast to the elaborate dishes emanating from Slice's kitchen. Its elegantly presented food is terrific: locally sourced meat, fish, cheese and beer, plus home-made bread and home-grown herbs.

Drinking & Nightlife

In a city synonymous with Dylan Thomas you'd expect some hard drinking to take place…and you'd be right. Swansea's main boozing strip is Wind St (rhymes with 'blind', as in drunk), and on weekends it can be a bit of a zoo, full of generally good-natured alcopop-fuelled teens teetering around on high heels. *Buzz* magazine (free from cafes and bars around town) has its finger on the local scene's pulse.

Prohibition COCKTAIL BAR
(www.prohibition-bar.co.uk; Green Dragon Lane; 9pm-late Wed-Sat) Slink down a side lane from Wind St, give a knowing nod to the bouncer lurking in the shadows, enter the corridor, push back the bookcase and enter an illicit world where attractive mixologists dispense charm and first-rate cocktails in equal serves to an appreciative in-the-know clientele. There's no sign: look for it two doors up from Kon-Tiki bar.

Kon-Tiki COCKTAIL BAR
(01792-462896; 10 The Strand; 6pm-midnight Sun-Thu, to 1.30am Fri & Sat) Hidden down the hill from Wind St, cool Kon-Tiki offers all the requisite elements for a tropical beach fantasy: faux Polynesian statues, cocktails served in tiki cups, flax matting on the walls and Bob Marley on the stereo. On the weekends it adopts a clubby vibe and a £1 cover charge.

No Sign Bar BAR
(01792-465300; www.nosignwinebar.com; 56 Wind St; 11am-midnight) Once frequented by Dylan Thomas (it appears as the Wine Vaults in his story *The Followers*), the No Sign stands out as the only vaguely traditional bar left on Wind St. It's a long, narrow haven of dark-wood panelling, friendly staff, good pub grub and a seasonal beer selection. On weekends there's live music downstairs in the Vault.

Uplands Tavern PUB
(01792-458242; www.facebook.com/theuplandstavern; 42 Uplands Cres, Uplands; 11am-11pm) A former Thomas hang-out, Uplands still serves a quiet daytime pint in the Dylan Thomas snug. Come nightfall, it turns into a different beast altogether as the hub of the city's live-music scene, attracting a mixed crowd of students and local regulars.

Shopping

★ **Swansea Market** MARKET
(www.swanseaindoormarket.co.uk; Oxford St; 8am-5.30pm Mon-Sat) There's been a covered market in Swansea since 1652 and at this site since 1830. Rebuilt in 1961 after being bombed in WWII, the current version is a buzzing place to sample local specialities, like cockles, laver bread and Welsh cakes hot from the griddle.

Information

Morriston Hospital (☎01792-702222; www.wales.nhs.uk; Heol Maes Eglwys, Morriston) Accident and emergency department, 5 miles north of the city centre.

Police Station (☎101; www.south-wales.police.uk; Grove Pl)

Getting There & Away

BUS

Swansea's **bus station** (Plymouth St) is on the western edge of the city centre, by the Quadrant shopping centre.

National Express (☎0871 781 8181; www.nationalexpress.com) coaches head to/from Tenby (from £5, 1½ hours, two daily), Cardiff (£3.50, one hour, four daily), Chepstow (from £11, two hours, four daily), Bristol (£11, 2½ hours, six daily) and London (from £7, five hours, five daily).

Other direct bus services head to/from Cardiff (£4.50, 1¼ hours, at least hourly), Llanelli (£5.70, 40 minutes, half-hourly), Carmarthen (£9.20, 50 minutes, hourly), Llandeilo (£5.70, 1½ hours, seven daily) and Aberystwyth (£12, 2¾ hours, two daily).

TRAIN

The train station is 600m north of Castle Sq along Castle St and High St. Direct train services to/from Swansea include London Paddington (from £47, three hours, hourly), Abergavenny (£25, 1½ hours, hourly), Cardiff (£9.20, one hour, half-hourly), Tenby (£15, 1½ hours, seven daily) and Llandrindod Wells (£13, 2½ hours, four daily).

Getting Around

First Cymru (www.firstgroup.com) runs most of the local services, including buses to the Mumbles and as far as the Pennard Cliffs car park in Southgate on the Gower Peninsula. Drivers take cash for single fares, or you can pay via a mobile-phone app (see website for details).

OFF THE BEATEN TRACK

Puffed-up American turkeys escort guests around the fairy-lit grounds of this off-the-grid glamping site, **Larkhill Tipis** (☎01559-3715881; www.larkhilltipisandyurts.co.uk; Cwmduad; tents from £70). Five different styles of tent are available, each from a different part of the world, and all are comfortably furnished with their own beds, gas cookers and wood fires. It's in a remote spot, 7 miles southeast of Newcastle Emlyn.

The Mumbles (Y Mwmbwls)

POP 16,600

Strung out along the shoreline at the southern end of Swansea Bay, the Mumbles has been Swansea's seaside retreat since 1807, when the Oystermouth Railway was opened. Built for transporting coal, the horse-drawn carriages were soon converted for paying customers, and the now defunct Mumbles train became the first passenger railway service in the world.

Once again fashionable, with bars and restaurants vying for trade along the promenade, the Mumbles received a boost to its reputation when its most famous daughter, Hollywood actor Catherine Zeta-Jones, built a £2-million luxury mansion at Limeslade, on the south side of the peninsula. Singer Bonnie Tyler also has a home here.

The origin of the Mumbles' unusual name is uncertain, although one theory is that it's a legacy of French seamen who nicknamed the twin rounded rocks at the tip of the headland *Les Mamelles* – 'the breasts'.

Sights

Going west from Mumbles Head there are two small bays, **Langland Bay** and **Caswell Bay**, which are shingly at high tide but expose hectares of golden sand at low water. Both are popular with families and surfers. About 500m west of Caswell, along the coast path, is beautiful **Brandy Cove**, a tiny secluded beach away from the crowds.

★Clyne Gardens GARDENS

FREE Spanning 20 hectares, these magnificent gardens are particularly impressive in spring when the azaleas and rhododendrons are at their most spectacular. Plus there are bluebell woods, wildflower meadows and a bog garden to explore. The entrance is by the Woodman Pub at the Swansea end of the Mumbles Rd strip.

Oystermouth Castle CASTLE

(☎01792-635478; www.swansea.gov.uk/oystermouthcastle; Castle Ave; adult/child £3/1.50; ⏲11am-5pm Easter-Sep) It wouldn't be Wales without a castle, hence the trendy shops and bars of Newton Rd are guarded by a majestic ruin. Once the stronghold of the Norman lords of Gower, it's now the focus of summer Shakespeare performances. There's a fine view over Swansea Bay from the battlements.

Sleeping

Tides Reach Guest House B&B $$
(01792-404877; www.tidesreachguesthouse.com; 388 Mumbles Rd; s/d from £65/79;) Our favourite Mumbles B&B, Tides Reach was for sale when we visited, so we're hoping the new owners maintain the same friendly service and delicious breakfasts. Some rooms have sea views; the best is suite-like room 9, where the dormer windows open out to create a virtual deck from within the sloping roof.

Patricks with Rooms BOUTIQUE HOTEL $$$
(01792-360199; www.patrickswithrooms.com; 638 Mumbles Rd; r £120-175;) Patricks has 16 individually styled bedrooms in bold contemporary colours, with art on the walls, fluffy robes and, in some of the rooms, roll-top baths and sea views. Downstairs there's an upmarket restaurant and bar.

Eating & Drinking

Front Room CAFE $
(01792-362140; 618 Mumbles Rd; mains £5-8; 10am-4pm Tue-Sun;) With seashell chandeliers and local art on the walls, this convivial little cafe is a pleasant place to tuck into a cooked breakfast, Welsh rarebit, ploughman's lunch, sandwich (of the toasted or doorstop variety) or traditional high tea (£15 for two people).

Munch of Mumbles MODERN BRITISH $$
(01792-362244; www.munchofmumbles.com; 650 Mumbles Rd; 2-/3-course lunch £16/20, dinner £25/30; noon-2.30pm Wed-Sun, 6.30-9.30pm Wed-Sat;) Small, cosy and romantic, with flowers and candles on the tables, Munch offers a top-notch bistro menu, with half a dozen choices for each course. You can bring your own wine for a small corkage charge.

Jones WINE BAR
(01792-361764; www.jonesbar.co.uk; 61 Newton Rd; 4.30-11pm Tue-Thu & Sun, to 12.30am Fri & Sat) The best of the Newton Rd wine bars, Jones buzzes with 40-somethings giving the chandeliers a run for their money in the bling stakes. There's no chance Dylan Thomas ever did hang out here, or would if he still could, but there's a good wine list and a friendly vibe.

Getting There & Away

Buses 2, 3 and 37 head between Swansea and the Mumbles (20 minutes). Bus 2C continues on to Caswell Bay.

Gower Peninsula (Y Gŵyr)

With its broad butterscotch beaches, pounding surf, precipitous clifftop walks and rugged, untamed uplands, the Gower Peninsula feels a million miles from Swansea's urban bustle – yet it's just on the doorstep. This 15-mile-long thumb of land stretching west from the Mumbles was designated the UK's first official Area of Outstanding Natural Beauty in 1956. The National Trust owns about three-quarters of the coast and you can hike the entire length of the coastline on the Wales Coast Path. The peninsula also has the best surfing in Wales outside Pembrokeshire.

The main family beaches, patrolled by lifeguards during the summer, are Langland Bay, Caswell Bay and Port Eynon. The most impressive, and most popular with surfers, is the magnificent 3-mile sweep of Rhossili Bay at the far end of the peninsula. Much of Gower's northern coast is salt marsh, which provides an important habitat for wading birds and wildfowl.

DUDE LOOKS LIKE A LADY

In 1823, the Reverend William Buckland discovered a human skeleton dyed with red ochre in a cave on the Gower coast. As he also found jewellery buried along with the bones, the good vicar assumed the deceased must be a woman. Being a devout Christian, he believed she must date from the Roman era, as she could not be older than the biblical flood. The 'Red Lady', as the skeleton became known, was therefore a Roman prostitute or witch, according to Buckland.

Modern analysis shows that the Red Lady was actually a man – possibly a tribal chief – who died, aged around 21, some 33,000 years ago. Dating from before Britain was abandoned during the last Ice Age, his are the oldest human remains found in the UK, and one of the oldest known ritual burials in Western Europe. The Red Lady's peaceful seaside slumber is no more – he's now residing at Oxford University.

Parkmill & Around

Some of the Gower's best and most secluded beaches are on the stretch between the Mumbles and Oxwich Bay, particularly in the area around the small tourist village of Parkmill.

Sights

Three Cliffs Bay BEACH

Three Cliffs Bay is named for the pyramid-like, triple-pointed crag pierced by a natural arch that juts out into the water at its eastern point. It's regularly voted one of the most beautiful beaches in Britain, and it's particularly impressive when viewed from the impossibly picturesque ruins of 13th-century **Pennard Castle**. Glinting below, the Pennard Pill stream empties into the bay, creating dangerous currents for swimmers at high tide. The craggy headland is a popular rock-climbing site.

Sleeping

Nicholaston Farm CAMPGROUND $

(01792-371209; www.nicholastonfarm.co.uk; Penmaen; site from £16; Easter-Sep) This working farm overlooking Oxwich Bay offers field camping with a view. There's also an attractive little farm shop/cafe and an excellent ablutions block.

★Llethryd Barns B&B $$

(01792-391327; www.llethrydbarns.co.uk; Llethryd; ste £80-100; P) Set in a U-shape around a central courtyard, this venerable set of stone farm buildings has been converted into seven guest suites, each with a mezzanine bedroom. They all have their own courtyard entrance, so there's no sense that you're intruding in someone else's house. It's located 2 miles north of Parkmill on the B4271.

Parc-le-Breos House HOTEL $$

(01792-371636; www.parc-le-breos.co.uk; Parkmill; r from £98; P) Set in its own private estate north of the main road, Parc-le-Breos offers en suite B&B accommodation in a Victorian hunting lodge. The majestic lounge, games room and dining room downstairs have grand fireplaces that crackle into action in winter.

Getting There & Away

Buses head to/from Swansea (36 minutes, 10 daily), Oxwich (15 minutes, seven daily), Reynoldston (14 minutes, eight daily), Port Eynon (27 minutes, four daily) and Rhossili (31 minutes, eight daily).

WORTH A TRIP

Wandering the formal walled gardens at **Aberglasney Gardens** (01558-668998; www.aberglasney.org; Llangathen; adult/child £7.30/3.70; 10am-6pm Apr-Oct, 10.30am-4pm Nov-Mar) feels a bit like walking into a Jane Austen novel. They date from the 17th century and contain a unique cloister built solely as a garden decoration. There's also a pool garden, a 250-year-old yew tunnel and a 'wild' garden in the bluebell woods to the west.

At its heart stands a semi-restored Elizabethan manor house, where you can watch a video on the estate's history and view temporary art exhibitions. The derelict kitchens have been converted into a glass-roofed atrium garden full of subtropical plants such as orchids, palms and cycads. Out on the terrace, a whitewashed and flagstoned tearoom sells cakes and snacks.

Aberglasney is in the village of Llangathen, just off the A40, 4 miles west of Llandeilo.

Port Eynon

The three-quarter-mile stretch of rock-strewn beach at Port Eynon is Gower's busiest – in summer, at least.

Around the bay's southern point is **Culver Hole**, a curious stone structure built into the cliff. Legend has it that it was a smugglers' hiding place, but the mundane truth is that it served as a dovecote (pigeons were a valuable food source in medieval times; the name comes from Old English *culufre*, meaning 'dove'). It's quite tricky to find – the easiest route is signposted from the YHA – and is only accessible for three hours either side of low tide; make sure you don't get caught out by the rising waters.

The coastal walk between Port Eynon and Rhossili (7 miles) is along the wildest and most dramatic part of the Gower coast, and is fairly rough going. Halfway along is a cave called Goats Hole, where the Red Lady of Paviland (p675) was found.

Sleeping

★Port Eynon YHA HOSTEL $

(☎0800 019 1700; www.yha.org.uk; Port Eynon; dm/r from £18/39; ⊙Easter-Oct; 📶) Worth special mention for its spectacular location, this former lifeboat station is as close as you get to the sea without sleeping on the beach itself. It's cosier than your average hostel, with sea views from the lounge and friendly owners. There are washbasins in the rooms but most share bathrooms.

Culver House APARTMENT $$

(☎01792-720300; www.culverhousehotel.co.uk; Port Eynon; apt £90-125; 📶) This renovated 19th-century house offers eight self-contained apartments with all the mod cons. The upper apartments have balconies, while most of those on the ground floor open onto cute little gardens.

Getting There & Away

Buses head to/from Swansea (one hour, four daily), Parkmill (27 minutes, four daily), Reynoldston (15 minutes, five daily), Rhossili (13 minutes, daily) and Llangennith (one hour, three daily).

Rhossili

Saving the best for last, the Gower Peninsula ends spectacularly with the 3 miles of golden sand that edges Rhossili Bay. Facing nearly due west towards the very bottom of Ireland, this is one of Britain's best and most popular surfing beaches. When the surf's up, swimming can be dangerous. At low tide the stark, ghostly ribs of the *Helvetica,* a Norwegian barque wrecked in a storm in 1887, protrude from the sand in the middle of the beach. South of the village is the Viel (pronounced 'vile'), a rare surviving example of a patchwork of strip-fields first laid out in medieval times.

Sights

★Worms Head ISLAND

The southern extremity of Rhossili Bay is guarded by a promontory, which turns into an island at high tide. Worms Head takes its name from the Old English *wurm*, meaning 'dragon' – a reference to its snaking, Loch Ness monster profile. Seals bask around its rocks, and the cliffs are thick with razorbills, guillemots, kittiwakes, fulmars and puffins during nesting season (April to July).

Information

Rhossili Visitor Centre (☎01792-390707; www.nationaltrust.org.uk/gower; Coastguard Cottages, Rhossili; ⊙10.30am-4pm) The National Trust's centre has information on local walks and wildlife, and an audiovisual display upstairs.

Getting There & Away

Buses head to/from Swansea (one hour, 10 daily), Parkmill (31 minutes, eight daily), Port Eynon (13 minutes, one daily) and Reynoldston (17 minutes, six daily).

Llangennith

Surfers flock to this pretty village at the northern end of Rhossili Bay where there's a good local pub and a large campsite right by the beach.

Activities

PJ's Surf Shop SURFING

(☎01792-386669; www.pjsurfshop.co.uk; Llangennith; wetsuits/surfboards/body boards per day £11/11/6; ⊙9am-5pm) Run by former surf champion Peter Jones, this is a centre of activity for local surfers. It also operates a 24-hour surfline (0901 603 1603; calls per minute 60p).

Progress Surf SURFING

(☎01792-550019; www.swanseasurfing.com; lessons 2hr/day £25/50) Offers introductory surf lessons at either Caswell Bay or Llangennith, depending on conditions.

Sleeping

King's Head HOTEL $$

(☎01792-386212; www.kingsheadgower.co.uk; Llangennith; r £99-150; P📶🐾) Up the hill behind the **pub** (mains £5-11; ⊙11am-10pm) of the same name, these two stone blocks have been simply but stylishly fitted out with modern bathrooms and pale stone tiles. As well as the 20 rooms here, there are a further seven in a nearby house.

Getting There & Away

There are direct buses to/from Swansea (1½ hours, three daily), Port Eynon (one hour, three daily), Reynoldston (30 minutes, three daily) and Llanmadoc (10 minutes, five daily).

CARMARTHENSHIRE (SIR GAERFYRDDIN)

Castle-dotted Carmarthenshire has gentle valleys, deep-green woods and a small, partly sandy coast. Caught between dramatic neighbours – Pembrokeshire to the west and the Brecon Beacons to the east – it remains much quieter and less explored. If your interests stretch to gardens, stately homes and all things green, add this quiet county to your itinerary.

Llanarthne

POP 765

Little Llanarthne is as pleasantly rural and slow-paced as dozens of other Carmarthenshire villages, and would have remained indistinguishable from the pack if it wasn't for the opening of the National Botanic Garden of Wales nearby. Fancy accommodation and a celebrity-helmed eatery have followed in the garden's wake.

Sights

★National Botanic Garden of Wales GARDENS

(☎01558-667149; www.botanicgarden.wales; Llanarthne; adult/child £8.90/4.50; ⏲10am-6pm Apr-Sep, to 4.30pm Oct-Mar) Concealed in the rolling Tywi valley countryside, this lavish complex opened in 2000 and is still maturing. Formerly an aristocratic estate, the garden has a broad range of plant habitats, from lakes and bogs to woodland and heath, with lots of decorative areas and educational exhibits. The centrepiece is the Norman Foster–designed **Great Glasshouse**, a spectacular glass dome sunken into the earth.

The garden is 2 miles southwest of Llanarthne village, signposted from the main roads.

Sleeping & Eating

Llwyn Helyg Country House B&B $$$

(☎01558-668778; www.llwynhelygcountryhouse.co.uk; r £119-145; P 📶) Although there's a Georgian look to this huge stone house on the edge of the village, it's actually a modern build. The three guest bedrooms are luxuriously decked out with dark wooden furniture, white Italian marble en suites and spa baths, and to preserve the rarefied atmosphere, it doesn't take bookings for children under 16.

★Wright's Food Emporium DELI, CAFE $$

(☎01558-668929; www.wrightsfood.co.uk; B4300; mains £6.50-13; ⏲11am-5pm Sun, 11am-7pm Mon, 9am-7pm Wed & Thu, 9am-late Fri & Sat; P 📶 🐾) Sprawling through the rooms of an old village pub, this hugely popular deli-cafe serves sandwiches, salads and massive antipasto platters packed full of top-notch local and imported ingredients. Wash it all down with a craft beer or something from its range of small-estate, organic wine.

Getting There & Away

Up to two buses a day stop here en route between Carmarthen (30 minutes) and Llandeilo (20 minutes). Some also stop at the botanic garden.

Llandeilo

POP 1800

Set on a hill encircled by the greenest of fields, Llandeilo is little more than a handful of narrow streets lined with grand Georgian and Victorian buildings and centred on a picturesque church and graveyard. The surrounding region was once dominated by large country estates, and though they have long gone, the deer, parkland, trees and agricultural character of the landscape are their legacy. Used by many travellers as a springboard for the wilder terrain of Brecon Beacon National Park, it's within a short drive of magical Carreg Cennen (p706) castle.

Sights

★Dinefwr HISTORIC BUILDING

(NT, Cadw; ☎01558-824512; www.nationaltrust.org.uk; adult/child £6.50/3.50, parking £6; ⏲house 11am-6pm daily Easter-Oct, 11am-4pm Fri-Sun Nov-Easter; P) This idyllic, 324-hectare, beautifully landscaped estate, immediately west of Llandeilo, incorporates a deer park, pasture, woods, an Iron Age fort, the hidden remains of a Roman fort, a 12th-century castle and Newton House, a wonderful 17th-century manor with a Victorian facade. The house is presented as it was in Edwardian times, focusing particularly on the experience of servants in their downstairs domain. Other rooms recall Newton's WWII incarnation as a hospital, and the former Billiard Room is now a tearoom.

Dinefwr Castle is set on a hilltop in the southern corner of the estate and offers fantastic views from its walls and towers across the Tywi to the foothills of the Black

Mountain. In the 17th century it suffered the indignity of being converted into a picturesque garden feature.

There are several marked walking routes around the grounds, some of which are accessible to visitors with disabilities. Keep an eye out for fallow deer and the rare herd of White Park cattle.

Sleeping & Eating

Cawdor HOTEL $$
(01558-823500; www.thecawdor.com; Rhosmaen St; r £65-150, ste/apt £200/210; P) Grey-and-pink-striped carpet leads to well-appointed rooms with marble-clad bathrooms in this grand Georgian inn. The downstairs bar serves tasty meals, or you can opt for a more formal feed in the restaurant.

★Ginhaus Deli DELI $
(01558-823030; www.ginhaus.co.uk; Market St; mains £6.50-9; 8am-6pm Mon-Thu, to 8pm Fri & Sat;) Specialising in the very finest things in life, namely gin and cheese, this hip deli-cafe also serves cooked breakfasts, filled baguettes, quiches, tarts, fresh juices and delicious oddities such as laver bread and cockle crostini. On Friday and Saturday nights it branches out to pizza.

Getting There & Away

Buses head to/from Swansea (£5.70, 1½ hours, seven daily), Carmarthen (42 minutes, 10 daily), Llanarthne (20 minutes, two daily), Llangathen (six minutes, eight daily) and Llandovery (40 minutes, eight daily).

Llandeilo is on the Heart of Wales line, with direct trains to/from Cardiff (from £20, 2¼ hours, two daily), Swansea (£7.30, one hour, five daily), Llandovery (£3.50, 20 minutes, five daily), Llandrindod Wells (£7.90, 1½ hours, four daily) and Shrewsbury (£14, three hours, four daily).

Pumsaint

A cluster of stone houses on the surprisingly busy A482 between Lampeter and Llanwrda, Pumsaint is an obscure kind of place distinguished largely by one important historical site and a truly excellent pub. The name means 'five saints', which is a reference to five mysterious hollows on a standing stone positioned near its famous goldmines. The reality is far less saintly: the stone was simply an anvil used by the Romans.

Sights

Dolaucothi Gold Mines MUSEUM
(NT; 01558-650177; www.nationaltrust.org.uk; Pumsaint; adult/child £8/3.95; 11am-5pm Easter-Oct) Set in a beautiful wooded estate, this is the only known Roman goldmine in the UK. The exhibition and the mining machinery above ground are interesting, but the main attraction is the chance to go underground on a guided tour of the old mine workings. Back at the surface, there's a sediment-filled water trough where you can try your hand at panning for gold.

Eating

★Dolaucothi Arms PUB FOOD $$
(01558-650237; www.thedolaucothiarms.co.uk; A482; mains £8-15; 5-11pm Tue-Thu, noon-11pm Fri & Sat, noon-8pm Sun; P) Even hardened city slickers might be tempted to village life if a local pub this good could be guaranteed. This 16th-century drovers' inn has a friendly front bar, complete with board games and open fire, and upstairs are three comfortable bedrooms. However it's the restaurant that draws the crowds, serving country cuisine with a contemporary twist.

Getting There & Away

The 289 bus between Lampeter and Llandovery stops here at least once a day on weekdays.

PEMBROKESHIRE

The Pembrokeshire coast is what you imagine the world would look like if God were a geology teacher. There are knobbly hills of volcanic rock, long thin inlets scoured by glaciers, and stratified limestone pushed up vertically and then eroded into arches, blowholes and sea stacks. All along the shoreline towering red and grey cliffs play leapfrog with perfect sandy beaches.

This wild and incredibly beautiful landscape is the county's greatest asset and in summer people flock here from all over Britain to enjoy the spectacular walking, surfing, coasteering and sea kayaking, as well as the glorious beaches and abundant marine life. On top of its natural assets, Pembrokeshire offers a wealth of Celtic and pre-Celtic sites, forbidding castles, fascinating islands and little St Davids – the magical mini-city with its chilled vibe, spectacular cathedral and abiding association with Wales' patron saint.

Saundersfoot

POP 2630

Cute-as-a-button Saundersfoot has a long, lovely beach with a sweet little harbour at one end, built in 1829 for the shipment of coal. Nowadays the only mining activity hereabouts is carried out by the toddlers digging in the golden sand. Well-kept old houses cling to the hilly streets radiating up from the town centre, where there are some interesting shops to peruse.

It makes for a quieter base than neighbouring Tenby, which is only an hour's walk away along the coast path.

Sights

The Reptile Experience ZOO

(07940 793845; www.reptile-experience.co.uk; Brewery Tce; adult/child £8/5; 10am-5pm Apr-Oct, call ahead Nov-Mar) Come face to face with huge snakes, hairy spiders and all sorts of other slippery, creepy and crawly critters during an hour-long hands-on experience.

DON'T MISS

PEMBROKESHIRE COAST NATIONAL PARK

Established in 1952, Pembrokeshire Coast National Park (Parc Cenedlaethol Arfordir Sir Benfro) takes in almost the entire coast and its offshore islands, as well as the moorland hills of Mynydd Preseli in the north. Pembrokeshire's sea cliffs and islands support huge breeding populations of sea birds, while seals, dolphins, porpoises and whales are frequently spotted in coastal waters.

There are three national-park information centres (in Tenby, St Davids and Newport) and the local tourist offices scattered across Pembrokeshire are well stocked with park paraphernalia. The free annual publication *Coast to Coast* (online at www.pembrokeshire-coast.org.uk) has lots of information on park attractions, a calendar of events and details of park-organised activities, including guided walks, themed tours, cycling trips, pony treks, island cruises, canoe trips and minibus tours. It's worth getting it for the tide tables alone – they're a necessity for many legs of the coast path.

Folly Farm ZOO

(01834-812731; www.folly-farm.co.uk; Begelly; adult/child £11/9.25; 10am-5pm;) If your toddler's tolerance for castles and churches is waning, this combination zoo/petting farm/fun fair/amusement park could be the antidote. Once they've tired of the pirate ship, dragon playground and ride-on diggers, there's a large menagerie to explore, including lemurs, meerkats, monkeys, giraffes, zebras and an excellent penguin enclosure. It's located on the A478, 3 miles north of Saundersfoot.

Sleeping

Trevayne Farm CAMPGROUND $

(01834-813402; www.trevaynefarm.co.uk; Monkstone; sites from £11; Easter-Oct;) Based on a working 40-hectare permaculture farm, this large clifftop site has beautiful sea views and two separate fields so back-to-basics tenters can avoid the looming motorhomes. The campsite is a mile south of the town centre via the coast path, or 2 miles by road.

★**Cliff House** B&B $$

(01834-813931; www.cliffhousebbsaundersfoot.co.uk; Wogan Tce; s/d from £57/75;) It's well worth lugging your bags up the short but steep road from the town centre to this wonderful little Victorian-era B&B. There are only five rooms, and the two on the top have glorious sea views. A guest lounge encourages fraternisation, and there's an extremely handy communal fridge, DVD library and book exchange.

St Brides Spa Hotel HOTEL $$$

(01834-812304; www.stbridesspahotel.com; St Brides Hill; s/d from £130/160;) Pembrokeshire's premier spa hotel offers the chance to relax after a massage in a small hydrotherapy pool overlooking the beach, before dining in the candlelit Cliff restaurant. The bedrooms are stylish and modern, in colours that evoke the seaside.

Eating

★**Coast** MODERN BRITISH $$

(01834-810800; www.coastsaundersfoot.co.uk; Coppet Hall Beach; mains £12-26; noon-2.30pm & 6.30-9.30pm daily Mar-Oct, Wed-Sun Nov-Feb;) The spectacular beachfront setting is more than matched by the culinary wizardry emanating from chef Will Holland's kitchen at this award-winning restaurant. Whether you choose from the more adventurous 'Will's menu' or opt for something

Pembrokeshire

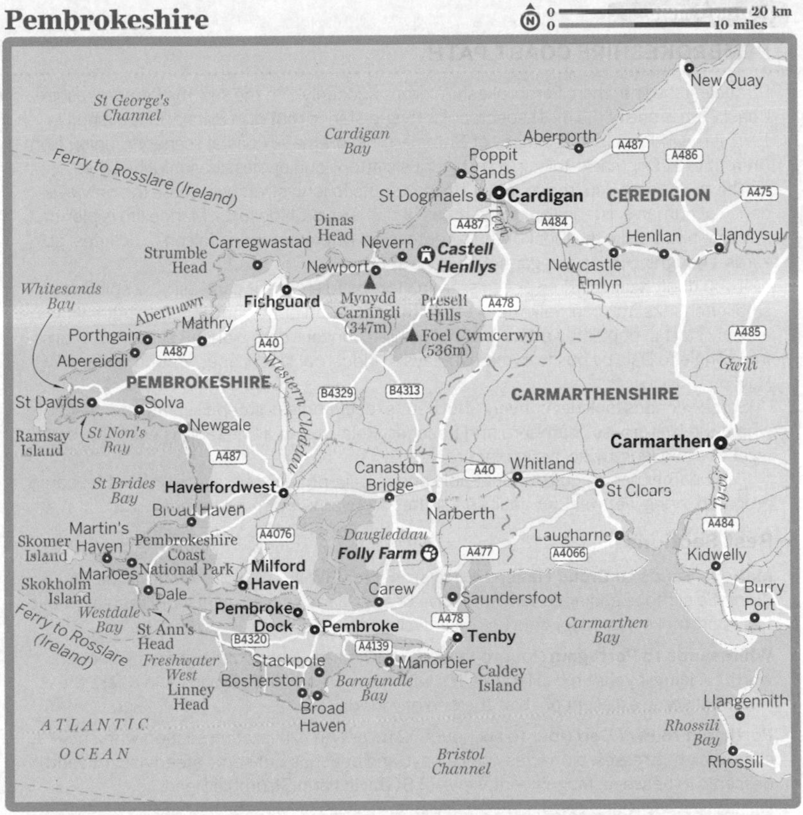

simpler and slightly cheaper from the 'market menu', prepare to be wowed. Local seafood and game feature prominently. The service is great too.

★Cliff MODERN BRITISH **$$**
(☎01834-812304; www.stbridesspahotel.com; St Brides Hill; mains £16-21; ⏲6-9pm) Candles flicker and the views stretch out for miles from the dining room of this upmarket restaurant, attached to the St Brides Spa Hotel (p680). Welsh produce mixes with Asian and Middle Eastern flavours on a menu that includes several fish dishes, local lamb and beef, and a couple of vegetarian options.

ℹ Information

Tourist Office (☎01834-842402; www.visitpembrokeshire.com; Saundersfoot Library, Regency Hall; ⏲10am-4pm Mon-Wed & Sat, to 6pm Thu & Fri Apr-Oct, 10am-1pm Wed & Sat, 2.30-5pm Thu & Fri Nov-Mar)

ℹ Getting There & Away

Saundersfoot's train station is a mile from the centre of town. Direct services head to/from Newport Gwent (from £12, three hours, daily), Cardiff (from £10, 2¾ hours, daily), Swansea (£15, 1½ hours, seven daily), Tenby (£3.40, seven minutes, nine daily) and Pembroke (£7.40, 37 minutes, nine daily).

Direct buses head to/from Tenby (10 minutes, hourly), Narberth (34 minutes, 10 daily) and Haverfordwest (one hour, 10 daily).

Tenby (Dinbych Y Pysgod)

POP 4700

Perched on a headland with sandy beaches either side, Tenby is a postcard-maker's dream. Houses are painted from the pastel palette of a classic fishing village, interspersed with the white elegance of Georgian mansions. The main part of town is still constrained by its Norman-built walls,

DON'T MISS

PEMBROKESHIRE COAST PATH

Straddling the line where Pembrokeshire drops suddenly into the sea, the Pembrokeshire Coast Path is one of the most spectacular long-distance routes in Britain. Established in 1970, it meanders along 186 miles of Britain's most dramatic coastal scenery running from Amroth to St Dogmaels, taking in vertiginous clifftops and endless beautiful beaches.

The route takes you from popular holiday spots to long stretches where the only evidence of human existence are the ditches of numerous Celtic forts. Marine life is plentiful, and rare birds make the most of the remote cliffs, where peregrine falcons, red kites, buzzards, choughs, puffins and gannets can be spotted.

If you don't have the time or the stamina for the full route, it can easily be split into smaller chunks. You can walk the trail in either direction but a south–north route allows an easy start in populated areas and builds up to longer, more isolated stretches. Skip from Angle to Dale by bus to avoid two days of industrial landscapes around Milford Haven.

Some sections look deceptively short but expect endless steep ascents and descents where the trail crosses harbours and beaches. Referring to a tide table is essential if you want to avoid lengthy delays in places.

The weather can be quite changeable and mobile-phone coverage is unreliable; come prepared, bring wet-weather gear and something warm, even in summer.

Best Sections

Marloes Sands to Broad Haven (4½ to six hours, 13 miles) A wonderful walk along dramatic clifftops ending at an impressive beach. Many access points and regular public transport make it good for short circular walks too.

Whitesands to Porthgain (four to five hours, 10 miles) A beautiful but taxing section worth tackling if your time is limited. It's within easy reach of St Davids and offers the reward of some excellent nosh at the end of your day.

Porthgain to Pwll Deri (four to six hours, 12 miles) An exhilarating section with sheer cliffs, rock buttresses, pinnacles, islets, bays and beaches but some steep ascents and descents in between. Magnificent views of St Davids and Strumble Head.

Newport to St Dogmaels (six to eight hours, 15.5 miles) A tough, roller-coaster section with frequent steep hills but spectacular views of the wild and rugged coast and its numerous rock formations, sheer cliffs and caves.

funnelling holidaymakers through medieval streets lined with pubs, ice-cream parlours and gift shops.

Without the tackiness of the promenade-and-pier beach towns, it tastefully returns to being a sleepy little place in the low season. In summer it has a boisterous, boozy, holiday-resort feel.

History

Tenby flourished in the 15th century as a centre for the textile trade, exporting cloth in exchange for salt and wine. Cloth making declined in the 18th century, but the town soon reinvented itself as a fashionable watering place. The arrival of the railway in the 19th century sealed its future as a resort, and William Paxton (owner of the Middleton estate in Carmarthenshire, now home to the National Botanic Garden of Wales; p678) developed a saltwater spa here. Anxiety over a possible French invasion of the Milford Haven waterway led to the construction in 1869 of a fort on **St Catherine's Island**.

Among those who have taken inspiration or rest here are Horatio Nelson, Jane Austen, George Eliot, JMW Turner, Beatrix Potter and Roald Dahl. The artist Augustus John was born here, and he and his sister Gwen lived here during their early life.

Sights

Tudor Merchant's House HISTORIC BUILDING
(NT; ✆01834-842279; www.nationaltrust.org.uk; Quay Hill; adult/child £5/2.50; ⏲11am-5pm Wed-Mon Easter-Jul, Sep & Oct, daily Aug, Sat & Sun Nov-Easter) This handsomely restored 15th-century town house is set up as it would

have been in its heyday, with colourful wall hangings, period-style beds and kitchen implements. The curators have drawn the line at recreating the scent of the open cesspit next to the kitchen though.

Caldey Island ISLAND
(☎01834-844453; www.caldey-island.co.uk; adult/child £12/6; ⊙Mon-Sat May-Sep, Mon-Thu Apr & Oct) Connected to Tenby by a seasonal boat service, Caldey Island is home to grey seals, sea birds and a red-topped, whitewashed monastery that houses a community of around a dozen Cistercian monks. Join a free guided tour or wander around at your own pace. Make sure you visit sandy **Priory Bay**, the **lighthouse**, the village **museum**, the **old priory** and **St Illtyd's Church**, with its oddly shaped steeple. Inside is a stone with inscriptions in Ogham (an ancient Celtic script).

Sleeping

Southside HOTEL $$
(☎01834-844355; www.southsidetenby.co.uk; Picton Rd; s/d £45/80; 📶) Rooms are spacious, comfortable and not at all chintzy at this friendly little private hotel just outside the town walls. Three of the four rooms have en suites, while the other has a private bathroom accessed from the corridor.

Myrtle House HOTEL $$
(☎01834-842508; www.myrtlehousehoteltenby.com; St Mary's St; r £70; 📶) There's an old-fashioned feel to this friendly, family-run hotel in a Georgian town house in the old part of town. Don't expect anything in the way of views, but it's well located not far from the steps leading down to Castle Beach.

Penally Abbey HOTEL $$$
(☎01834-843033; www.penally-abbey.com; Penally; r from £145; P📶🐾) Set on a hillside overlooking Carmarthen Bay, this country-house hotel is built on the site of an ancient monastery in the village of Penally, 2 miles southwest of Tenby along the A4139. The 11 bright and comfortable rooms are spread between the main house and the neighbouring coach house, and there's an impressive restaurant attached.

Eating

Mooring CAFE $$
(☎01834-842502; www.themooringtenby.com; 15 High St; mains breakfast £3.50-6.50, lunch £6.50-9.25, dinner £13-19; ⊙8.30am-9pm; 📶🐾) Although it's anchored to the High St, this fresh, modern eatery drifts breezily from a daytime cafe serving comfort food (cooked breakfasts, sandwiches, bangers and mash, mac cheese) into a sophisticated bistro after dark. The coffee's good too.

Blue Ball Restaurant INTERNATIONAL $$
(☎01834-843038; www.theblueballrestaurant.co.uk; Upper Frog St; mains £15-20; ⊙6-9pm Wed-Sat, 12.30-2.30pm Sun) Polished wood, old timber beams and exposed brickwork create a rustic atmosphere in this cosy restaurant. The menu makes good use of local produce, veering from Asian-influenced dishes to traditional Welsh faggots (offal-filled meatballs).

Plantagenet House MODERN BRITISH $$$
(☎01834-842350; www.plantagenettenby.co.uk; Quay Hill; lunch £10-12, dinner £20-38; ⊙noon-2.30pm & 5.30-9.30pm, reduced hours winter; ✎) Atmosphere-wise, this place instantly impresses; it's perfect for a romantic, candle-lit dinner. Tucked down an alley in Tenby's oldest house, it's dominated by an immense 12th-century Flemish chimney hearth. The menu ranges from acclaimed seafood to organic beef.

Information

National Park Centre (☎01834-845040; www.pembrokeshirecoast.org.uk; South Pde; ⊙9.30am-5pm daily Apr-Sep, 10.30am-3.30pm Mon-Sat Oct-Mar) Information and interesting displays about Pembrokeshire Coast National Park.

Police Station (☎101; www.dyfed-powys.police.uk; Warren St)

Tourist Office (☎01437-775603; www.visitpembrokeshire.com; Upper Park Rd; ⊙9am-5pm Mon-Sat Sep-May, daily Jun-Aug)

Getting There & Away

BUS

The **bus station** (Upper Park Rd) is next to the tourist office on Upper Park Rd.

There are direct buses to/from Narberth (47 minutes, 11 daily), Saundersfoot (10 minutes, hourly), Manorbier (20 minutes, hourly), Pembroke (45 minutes, hourly) and Haverfordwest (1¼ hours, hourly).

National Express (p674) coaches head to/from London (from £18, 6¾ hours, daily), Birmingham (£40, 5¾ hours, daily), Cardiff (£18, 2¾ hours, daily), Swansea (from £5, 1½ hours, two daily) and Pembroke (£2, 20 minutes, daily).

TRAIN

There are direct trains to/from Newport Gwent (from £12, three hours, daily), Cardiff (from £10, 2¾ hours, daily), Swansea (£15, 1½ hours, seven daily), Narberth (£4.90, 19 minutes, nine daily) and Pembroke (£5.50, 20 minutes, nine daily).

Pembroke (Penfro)

POP 7550

Pembroke is not much more than a single street of neat Georgian and Victorian houses guarded by a whopping great castle. This mighty fortress fell only once – in 1648, following a 48-day siege by Cromwell during the English Civil War. After this, the town was stripped of its encircling walls.

Nowadays more people live in Pembroke Dock, a sprawling expanse of grim housing abutting a commercial port, just down the hill from the historic town. In 1154 local traders scored a coup when a Royal Act of Incorporation made it illegal to land goods anywhere in the Milford Haven waterway except at Pembroke Dock. Between 1814 and 1926 more than 260 Royal Navy ships were built here, and the dock served as a Royal Air Force base for flying boats during WWII. Aside from a 19th-century Martello tower in the harbour, there's nothing to see down here.

Sights

★Pembroke Castle CASTLE

(☎01646-684585; www.pembroke-castle.co.uk; Main St; adult/child £6/5; ⏲10am-5pm; 👪) This spectacular and forbidding castle was the home of the earls of Pembroke for over 300 years and the birthplace of Henry VII, the first Tudor king. A fort was established here in 1093 by Arnulph de Montgomery, but most of the present buildings date from the 13th century. It's a great place for both kids and adults to explore – wall walks and passages run from tower to tower, and there are vivid exhibitions detailing the castle's history.

Sleeping

Woodbine B&B $$

(☎01646-686338; www.pembrokebedandbreakfast.co.uk; 84 Main St; s/d from £50/65; 📶) This well-kept, forest-green Georgian town house presents a smart face to Pembroke's main drag. The three pretty guest rooms are tastefully furnished, with original fireplaces and contemporary wallpaper. Two have en suites, while the family room has its bathroom out on the corridor.

Tregenna B&B $$

(☎01646-621525; www.tregennapembroke.co.uk; 7 Upper Lamphey Rd; s/d £50/65; P📶) If your image of B&Bs is tainted by creaky-floored, chintz-filled cottages run by cranky empty-nesters, prepare to have it challenged by this large, friendly, modern establishment on the eastern edge of Pembroke. Each of the five guest rooms has its own bathroom and there's a large sun-filled breakfast room at the rear.

PEMBROKESHIRE COASTAL BUS SERVICES

The hiker's best friend, Pembrokeshire's coastal buses operate on four main routes three times a day in each direction from May to September. For the remainder of the year the Puffin Shuttle, Strumble Shuttle and Poppit Rocket operate two services a day on Thursdays and Saturdays only. For timetables, see www.pembrokeshiregreenways.co.uk or pick up a copy of the national park's *Coast to Coast* magazine.

Coastal Cruiser (364/388/387) Loops around Pembroke Dock, Pembroke, Freshwater East, Stackpole Quay, Bosherston, Broad Haven, St Govan's Head, Freshwater West and Angle.

Puffin Shuttle (400) Heads between St Davids and Martin's Haven, stopping in Solva, Newgale, Broad Haven, Little Haven and Marloes.

Strumble Shuttle (404) Heads between Fishguard and St Davids, calling at Goodwick, Strumble Head, Tregwynt Woollen Mill, Trefin, Porthgain and Abereiddi. The first bus of the day starts from Newport and the last terminates there.

Poppit Rocket (405) Heads between Fishguard and Cardigan. Stops include Pwllgwaelod, Newport, Moylgrove, Poppit Sands and St Dogmaels. From October to April it only covers the stops between Newport and Cardigan.

Eating

★Food at Williams CAFE $
(☎01646-689990; www.foodatwilliams.co.uk; 18 Main St; mains £5-8.50; ⏲9am-4.30pm Mon-Sat, 10am-3pm Sun; 📶) Pop into this bright and cheerful cafe in the morning for a cooked breakfast or in the afternoon for a glass of wine and Welsh cheese platter on the terrace.

Waterman's Arms PUB FOOD $$
(☎01646-682718; www.watermansarmspembroke.co.uk; 2 The Green; mains £8-18; ⏲noon-11pm; ✎) The Waterman's crowd-pleasing menu includes the likes of lamb shanks, burgers, steaks, curries and giant Yorkshire puddings laden with meat and gravy. The outdoor terrace is a suntrap on a summer afternoon, with fine views across the Mill Pond to the castle. There's often live music on the weekends.

Information

Tourist Office (☎01437-776454; www.visitpembrokeshire.com; Library, Commons Rd; ⏲10am-5pm Mon-Wed, Fri & Sat, to 7pm Thu Apr-Oct, 11am-5pm Tue, Thu & Fri, to 1pm Sat Nov-Mar)

Getting There & Away

BOAT

Irish Ferries (☎08717 300 500; www.irishferries.com; car & driver from £74) has two sailings a day on the four-hour route between Pembroke Dock and Rosslare in the southeast of Ireland.

BUS

There are direct buses to/from Tenby (45 minutes, hourly), Manorbier (27 minutes, hourly), Pembroke Dock (10 minutes, half-hourly) and Haverfordwest (29 minutes, half-hourly). The seasonal Coastal Cruiser (p684) loops in both directions between Pembroke, Angle, Freshwater West, Bosherston and Stackpole, terminating at Pembroke Dock.

National Express (p674) coaches head to/from London (from £26, seven hours, daily), Birmingham (£40, six hours, daily), Cardiff (£18, 3½ hours, daily), Swansea (£8, two hours, two daily) and Tenby (£2, 20 minutes, daily).

TRAIN

Trains stop in both Pembroke and Pembroke Dock. There are direct services to/from Newport Gwent (from £12, 3½ hours, daily), Cardiff (from £10, 3¼ hours, daily), Swansea (£15, two hours, seven daily), Narberth (£8.40, 48 minutes, eight daily) and Tenby (£5.50, 20 minutes, nine daily).

Narberth (Arberth)

POP 1930

An arty little town full of independent shops, cafes, restaurants and galleries, Narberth is a gem. Despite being light on specific sights, it's well worth a stop en route west for its lively vibe, passion for food and thriving retail scene. Somehow managing to beat the economic odds, butchers, delis, antique shops and boutiques line the streets. There's also a friendly food festival in September, a ruined Norman castle and an interesting town hall with a double stairway.

Sights

Narberth Museum MUSEUM
(☎01834-860500; www.narberthmuseum.co.uk; Church St; adult/child £3.50/2; ⏲10am-5pm Wed-Sat) Housed in a wonderfully atmospheric restored bonded-stores building, this whiz-bang museum celebrates the rich history of Narberth and the surrounding area. You can learn about medieval siege warfare and Narberth Castle through models and interactive games; walk historic streets and visit the shops; or listen to Welsh folk stories in the story-telling chair.

Sleeping

★Max & Caroline's GUESTHOUSE $
(☎01834-861835; www.maxandcarolines.com; 2a St James St; s/d £40/60; 📶) Why bother serving breakfast when you're situated directly above Narberth's best cafe? That's the philosophy at this excellent family-run guesthouse, and it means that its two handsomely furnished guest rooms can be rented a little more cheaply than you'd otherwise expect for the high standards on offer.

Canaston Oaks HOTEL $$
(☎01437-541254; www.canastonoaks.co.uk; Canaston Bridge; r/ste from £113/122; P📶) Set alongside a working farm 3 miles west of Narberth (near the intersection of the A40 and A4075), this mini-hotel has eight en suite rooms positioned around a Celtic-cross-shaped garden. The larger rooms have spa baths. Expect hearty breakfasts and charming Welsh hospitality.

★Grove HOTEL $$$
(☎01834-860915; www.thegrove-narberth.co.uk; Molleston; r from £189, 3-course lunch/dinner £29/59; ⏲restaurant noon-2.30pm & 6-9.30pm;

P) A truly magical place to stay, this luxurious country house hotel is secluded south of Narberth, surrounded by manicured lawns, mature trees and wildflower meadows. The sumptuous rooms blend period character with contemporary style, while the renowned restaurant is Pembrokeshire's finest, serving a creative menu of modern Welsh cuisine.

Eating

Narberth's town centre offers an excellent array of eateries, and nearby hotel Grove houses our favourite Pembrokeshire restaurant.

Plum Vanilla CAFE $
(01834-862762; www.plumvanilla.com; 2a St James' St; mains £6-12; 9am-5pm Mon-Sat) Adorned with technicolor chandeliers and vividly painted walls, this friendly little bohemian cafe has a loyal local clientele who flock here for the cooked breakfasts, homemade soups, interesting salads, luscious desserts and daily specials. Be prepared to wait for a table at lunchtime.

Dragon Inn PUB FOOD $$
(01834-860257; www.thedragonnarberth.com; Water St; mains £8-12; 11am-11pm) Stone walls, slab floors and low ceilings all hint at the venerable age of this old village pub. While seafood is the chef's speciality, it's hard to go past the slow-roasted beef with all the trimmings for Sunday lunch.

Getting There & Around

Bus destinations include Carmarthen (37 minutes, three daily), Saundersfoot (34 minutes, 10 daily), Tenby (47 minutes, 11 daily), Haverfordwest (24 minutes, hourly) and Cardigan (£4.05, one hour, three daily).

There are direct trains to/from Newport Gwent (from £12, 2¾ hours, daily), Cardiff (from £10, 2½ hours, two daily), Swansea (from £15, 1¼ hours, eight daily), Tenby (£4.90, 19 minutes, nine daily) and Pembroke (£8.40, 48 minutes, eight daily).

St Davids (Tyddewi)

POP 1840

Charismatic St Davids (yes, it has dropped the apostrophe from its name) is Britain's smallest city, its status ensured by the magnificent 12th-century cathedral that marks Wales' holiest site. The birth and burial place of the nation's patron saint, St Davids has been a place of pilgrimage for 1500 years.

The setting itself has a mystical presence. The sea is just beyond the horizon on three sides, so you're constantly surprised by glimpses of it at the ends of streets. Then there are those strangely shaped hills in the distance, sprouting from an ancient landscape.

Today St Davids attracts hordes of non-religious pilgrims too, drawn by the town's laid-back vibe and the excellent hiking, surfing and wildlife-watching in the surrounding area.

History

Dewi Sant (St David) founded a monastic community here in the 6th century, only a short walk from where he was born at St Non's Bay. In 1124 Pope Callistus II declared that two pilgrimages to St Davids were the equivalent of one to Rome, and three were equal to one to Jerusalem. The cathedral has seen a constant stream of visitors ever since.

Sights

Centre

★St David's Cathedral CATHEDRAL
(www.stdavidscathedral.org.uk; suggested donation £3, tours £4; 8.30am-6pm Mon-Sat, 12.45-5.30pm Sun) Hidden in a hollow and behind high walls, St David's Cathedral is intentionally unassuming. The valley site was chosen in the vain hope that the church would be overlooked by Viking raiders, but it was ransacked at least seven times. Yet once you pass through the gatehouse separating it from the town and its stone walls come into view, it's as imposing as any of its contemporaries.

Built on the site of a 6th-century chapel, the building dates mainly from the 12th to the 14th centuries. Extensive works were carried out in the 19th century by Sir George Gilbert Scott (architect of London's Albert Memorial and St Pancras) to stabilise the building. The distinctive **west front**, with its four pointed towers of purple stone, dates from this period.

The atmosphere inside is one of great antiquity. As you enter the **nave**, the oldest surviving part of the cathedral, the first things you'll notice are the sloping floor and the outward lean of the massive, purplish-grey pillars linked by semicircular Norman Ro-

St Davids

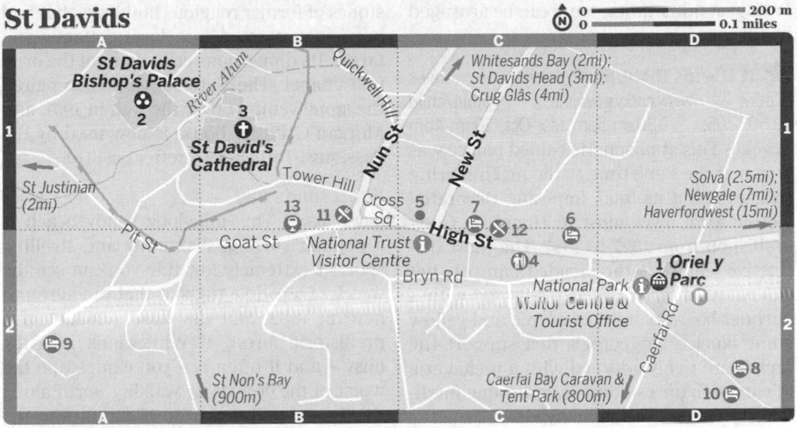

St Davids

Top Sights
1 Oriel y Parc D2
2 St Davids Bishop's Palace A1
3 St David's Cathedral B1

Activities, Courses & Tours
4 Ma Sime's Surf Hut C2
5 TYF Adventure C1

Sleeping
6 Bryn Awel C2
7 Coach House C1
8 Moorings D2
9 Ramsey House A2
10 Tŵr y Felin D2

Eating
11 Bishops B1
12 St Davids Food & Wine C2

Drinking & Nightlife
13 Farmer's Arms B1

manesque arches, a result of subsidence. Above is a richly carved 16th-century oak ceiling, adorned with pendants.

At the far end of the nave is a delicately carved 14th-century Gothic **pulpitum** (screen), which bears a statue of St David dressed as a medieval bishop, and contains the tomb of Bishop Henry de Gower (died 1347), for whom the Bishop's Palace was built.

Beyond the pulpitum is the magnificent **choir**. Check out the mischievous carved figures on the 16th-century misericords (under the seats), one of which depicts pilgrims being seasick over the side of a boat. Don't forget to look up at the colourfully painted lantern tower above (those steel tie rods around the walls were installed in the 19th century to hold the structure together).

Between the choir and the high altar is the object of all those religious pilgrimages – a **shrine** containing the bones of St David and St Justinian. Destroyed during the Reformation, it was restored and rededicated in 2012, adorned with five new Byzantine-style icons by artist Sara Crisp.

Accessed from the north wall of the nave, the **Treasury** displays vestments and religious paraphernalia crafted from precious metals and stones. Just as valuable are the treasures in the neighbouring **library** (entry £1), the oldest of which dates to 1505.

Towards the rear of the cathedral is the low-lit **Holy Trinity Chapel**, distinguished by a superb fan-vaulted ceiling dating from the early 16th century, and the light-filled **Lady Chapel**.

Lord Rhys ap Gruffydd, the greatest of the princes of South Wales, and his son Rhys Gryg are known to be buried in the cathedral, although their effigies in the south choir aisle date only from the 14th century. Gerald of Wales, an early rector of the cathedral, has a gravestone here, but scholars suggest he is actually buried at Lincoln Cathedral.

In August there are hour-long guided tours at 11.30am Monday and 2.30pm

Friday; at other times, tours can be arranged in advance.

★St Davids Bishop's Palace RUINS

(Cadw; www.cadw.gov.wales; adult/child £3.50/2.65; ⏲9.30am-5pm Mar-Oct, 10am-4pm Nov-Feb) This atmospheric ruined palace was begun at the same time as the neighbouring cathedral, but its final, imposing Decorated Gothic form owes most to Henry de Gower, bishop from 1327 to 1347. The most distinctive feature is the arcaded parapet that runs around the courtyard, adorned with a chequer-board pattern of purple and yellow stone blocks. The corbels that support the arches are richly adorned with a menagerie of carved figures – animals, grotesque mythical creatures and human heads.

★Oriel y Parc GALLERY

(Landscape Gallery; ☎01437-720392; www.orielyparc.co.uk; cnr High St & Caerfai Rd; ⏲10am-4pm) Occupying a bold, semicircular, environmentally friendly building on the edge of town, Oriel y Parc is a winning collaboration between the Pembrokeshire Coast National Park Authority and the National Museum Wales. Not only does it function as a tourist office and national-park visitor centre, it houses changing exhibitions from the museum's art collection. The focus is on landscapes, particularly Pembrokeshire scenes.

Surrounds

St Non's Bay RUINS, CHURCH

Immediately south of St Davids, this ruggedly beautiful spot is named after St David's mother and traditionally accepted as his birthplace. A path leads to the 13th-century **ruins of St Non's Chapel**. Only the base of the walls remains, along with a stone marked with a cross within a circle, believed to date from the 7th century. Standing stones in the surrounding field suggest that the chapel may have been built within an ancient pagan stone circle.

On the approach to the ruins is a pretty little **holy well**. The sacred spring is said to have emerged at the moment of the saint's birth and the water is believed to have curative powers. Although pilgrimages were officially banned following the suppression of Catholicism in the 16th century, the faithful continued to make furtive visits.

The site has now come full circle. In 1935 a local Catholic, Cecil Morgan-Griffiths, built the **Chapel of Our Lady & St Non** out of the stones of former religious buildings that had been incorporated into local cottages and farms. Its dimensions echo those of the original chapel. The Catholic Church repaired the stone vaulting over the well in 1951, and Morgan-Griffiths' house is now used by the Passionist Fathers as a retreat centre.

Whitesands Bay BEACH

(Porth Mawr) This mile-long sandy beach is a popular surfing, swimming and strolling spot. At extremely low tide you can see the wreck of a paddle tugboat that ran aground here in 1882, and the fossil remains of a prehistoric forest. If Whitesands is really busy – and it often is – you can escape the worst of the crowds by walking north along the coastal path for 10 to 15 minutes to the smaller, more secluded beach at **Porthmelgan**. Whitesands is 2 miles northwest of St Davids. If you drive, expect to pay an extortionate amount for parking (£5 even for a short stop in winter!). Otherwise catch the Celtic Coaster bus or walk, but you're well advised to stop in at the tourist office for directions.

St Davids Head AREA

This atmospheric heather-wreathed promontory was fortified by the ancient Celts. The jumbled stones and ditch of an Iron Age rampart are still visible, as are rock circles, which once formed the foundations of huts. The tip of the headland is a series of rock and turf ledges, a great place for a picnic or wildlife-spotting – in summer you can see gannets diving and choughs soaring. Adding to the ancient ambience, wild ponies can often be spotted.

Ramsey Island BIRD SANCTUARY

Ramsey Island (Ynys Dewi) lies off the headland to the west of St Davids, ringed by dramatic sea cliffs and an offshore armada of rocky islets and reefs. The island is a Royal Society for the Protection of Birds (RSPB) reserve famous for its large breeding population of choughs – members of the crow family with glossy black feathers and distinctive red bills and legs – and for its grey seals.

You can reach the island by boat from the tiny harbour at St Justinian, 2 miles west of St Davids. Longer boat trips run up to 20 miles offshore, to the edge of the Celtic Deep, to spot whales, porpoises and dolphins. What you'll see depends on the weather and the time of year: July to September are the best months. Porpoises are seen on most trips, dolphins on four out of five, and there's a 40% chance of seeing whales. The most common species is the minke, but pilot whales, fin whales and orcas have also been spotted.

Thousand Islands Expeditions is the only operator permitted to land day trippers on the island. Voyages of Discovery, Aquaphobia and Venture Jet head out to the island but don't land there.

Activities

Ma Sime's Surf Hut SURFING

(01437-720433; www.masimes.co.uk; 28 High St; 2hr group lesson £35; 10am-5pm Easter-Oct) Rents wetsuits (£8), surfboards (£15) and body boards (£8) from both its shop in St Davids and, in the summer holidays, from the beach at Whitesands (p688). Also runs a surf school at Whitesands from May to October.

TYF Adventure ADVENTURE

(01437-721611; www.tyf.com; 1 High St) Organises coasteering, surfing, sea-kayaking and rock-climbing trips from its St Davids base.

Sleeping

Centre

Ramsey House B&B $$

(01437-720321; www.ramseyhouse.co.uk; Lower Moor; tw/d £110/120; P) The young owners have created a fashionable boutique-style B&B from their house on the outskirts of the little city. The six rooms are all different but feature bold wallpapers, matching chandeliers, silky throws, goose-down duvets and stylish bathrooms.

Moorings B&B $$

(01437-720876; www.waterings.co.uk; Anchor Dr; s/d from £70/90; P) Offering more privacy than your typical B&B, the Moorings has only two rooms in the main house but a further five in an attached outbuilding opening on to the garden. The garden rooms are large and suite-like, with a semi-separated sitting area and their own external entrances. Breakfasts are excellent.

Coach House B&B $$

(01437-720632; www.thecoachhouse.biz; 15 High St; s/d from £70/95;) The bright, simple rooms at the Coach House are just part of its appeal. Friendly and helpful hosts, great breakfasts and the central location all conspire to make it one of St Davids' better options.

Bryn Awel B&B $$

(01437-720082; www.brynawel-bb.co.uk; 45 High St; s/d £85/90;) A pretty little terraced house on the main street, Bryn Awel has small but cosy rooms (all en suite). The owners are keen outdoors enthusiasts, and can advise on the best local spots for walking and birdwatching.

★ **Tŵr y Felin** HOTEL $$$

(01437-725555; www.twryfelinhotel.com; Caerfai Rd; r/ste from £160/240) Incorporating an odd circular tower that was once a windmill, this chic boutique hotel is St Davids' most upmarket option. The entire building is lathered with contemporary art, with dozens of pieces in the lounge-bar and restaurant alone. The 21 bedrooms are all luxurious, but the most spectacular is the three-level circular suite in the tower itself.

Surrounds

St Davids YHA HOSTEL $

(0800 019 1700; www.yha.org.uk; Llaethdy; dm from £19, r with/without bathroom from £89/39; Apr-Sep; P) If you're an enthusiastic walker or you have your own transport, this former farmhouse tucked beneath Carn Llidi, 2 miles northwest of St Davids, is a wonderful option. The cow sheds now house snug dorms and twins, and an inviting communal kitchen. En suite rooms sleep four people.

Caerfai Bay Caravan & Tent Park CAMPGROUND $

(01437-720274; www.caerfaibay.co.uk; Caerfai Rd; 2-person sites from £16; Mar-Nov; P@) A 15-minute walk south of St Davids, this large campground has good facilities and exceptional views across St Brides Bay. It's set on the edge of a dairy farm, practically right on the coast path.

Eating & Drinking

St Davids Food & Wine DELI $

(01437-721948; www.stdavidsfoodandwine.co.uk; High St; mains £2.75-4.50; 9am-5pm Mon-Sat) Stock up on picnic supplies at this delicatessen, which specialises in local organic produce. Or you can grab a pastry or a made-to-order sandwich and enjoy it at the tables out the front.

Bishops PUB FOOD $$
(☎01437-720422; www.thebish.co.uk; 22-23 Cross Sq; mains £9-12; ⏲11am-midnight; 📶) A friendly, rambling pub full of locals, walkers and blow-ins, this place serves hearty pub grub with a smile. There's a roaring fire in winter, a decent pint on offer and great views of the cathedral from the beer garden.

Farmer's Arms PUB
(☎01437-721666; www.farmersstdavids.co.uk; 14 Goat St; ⏲4pm-midnight Mon-Fri, noon-midnight Sat & Sun; 📶🐾) Even though St Davids is a bit of a tourist trap, you'd be hard-pressed finding a more authentic country pub. There's real ale and Guinness on tap, and it's *the* place to be when the rugby's playing.

Information

National Park Visitor Centre & Tourist Office (☎01437-720392; www.orielyparc.co.uk; High St; ⏲9.30am-5pm) Located at Oriel y Parc.

National Trust Visitor Centre (☎01437-720385; High St; ⏲10am-4pm Mon-Sat Jan-Easter, 9am-5.30pm Mon-Sat, 10am-4pm Sun Easter-Dec) Sells gifts, local-interest books, Ordnance Survey maps and guides to NT properties in Pembrokeshire.

Getting There & Away

Public transport is limited, especially on Sundays and in winter.

The main Pembrokeshire Coastal Bus Services (p684) stopping here are the Strumble and Puffin shuttles. From 25 March to 25 September, there's also the Celtic Coaster, which circles between St Davids, St Non's Bay, St Justinian and Whitesands.

Other buses head to/from Haverfordwest (£3.30, 40 minutes, 10 daily), Newgale (£2.45, 21 minutes, nine daily), Solva (£1.50, 10 minutes, nine daily) and Fishguard (£3.70, 45 minutes, six daily).

Getting Around

The Celtic Trail (National Cycle Network Route 4) passes through St Davids. There's pleasant cycling on minor roads around the peninsula but no off-road action (the coast path is for walkers only).

St Davids and the surrounding area suffer from parking problems and congestion in summer.

Tony's Taxis (☎01437-720931; www.tonystaxis.net) provides a luggage-transfer service for Pembrokeshire Coast Path walkers, covering the area from Little Haven to Fishguard.

Porthgain & Around

For centuries the tiny harbour of Porthgain consisted of little more than a few sturdy cottages wedged into a rocky cove. From 1851 it began to prosper as the port for shipping out slate quarried just down the coast at Abereiddi, and by 1889 its own deposits of granite and fine clay had put it on the map as a source of building stone and brick. The post-WWI slump burst the bubble, and the sturdy stone quays and overgrown brick storage 'bins' are all that remain.

Despite having been an industrial harbour, Porthgain is surprisingly picturesque and today it is home to a couple of art galleries and eateries.

Sights & Activities

Blue Lagoon BAY
(Abereiddi) Slate was quarried at this site on the water's edge in Abereiddi right up until 1910 and then transported by tramway to the harbour at Porthgain. After the mining stopped, a channel was blasted through to the sea, flooding the pit and creating a brilliantly blue-green pool surrounded by a bowl of sheer stone walls. You can certainly swim here but be aware that the water is very deep and commensurately cold.

From Porthgain, the Blue Lagoon is best reached via a spectacular 30-minute walk west along the coast path.

Celtic Quest ADVENTURE SPORTS
(☎01348-881530; www.celticquestcoasteering.com; coasteering £44) Coasteering specialists, taking to the cliffs at Abereiddi all year round.

Preseli Venture ADVENTURE
(☎01348-837709; www.preseliventure.co.uk; Parcynole Fach, Mathry; 👪) 🍃 Has its own excellent backpackers' lodge near Abermawr, 6 miles east of Porthgain. Activities include coasteering, sea kayaking, surfing and coastal hiking.

Sleeping

★ **Old School Hostel** HOSTEL $
(☎01348-831800; www.theoldschoolhostel.co.uk; Ffordd-yr-Afon, Trefin; s/d £25/40; 🅿📶) 🍃 Set in a rambling old school building, this is one of the new breed of independent, brightly painted, personably run backpackers. The six rooms have en suite showers but share communal toilets. A good-quality

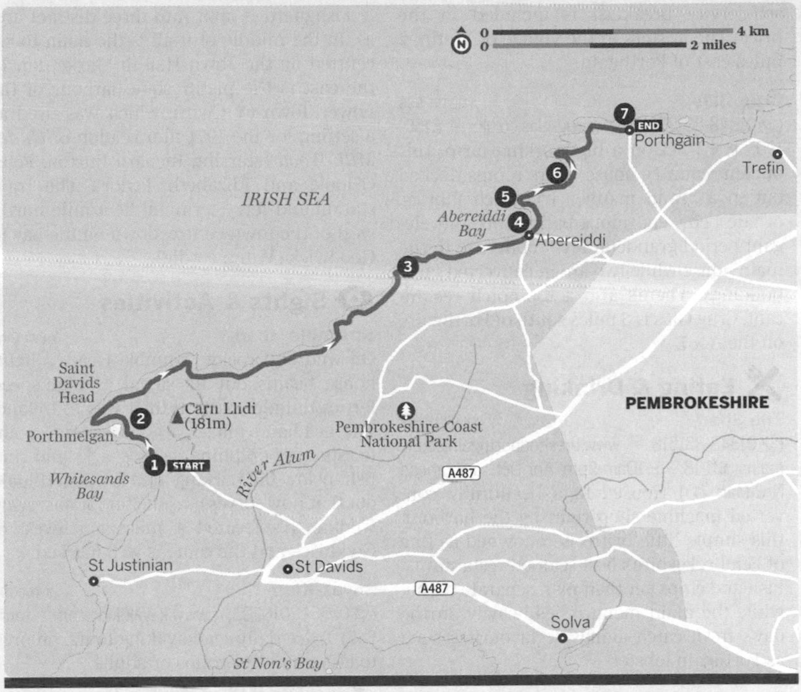

Coastal Walk
Whitesands to Porthgain

START WHITESANDS
END PORTHGAIN
LENGTH 10 MILES; FOUR TO SIX HOURS

Covering a beautiful but remote stretch of coast from popular Whitesands Bay near St Davids to the historic port of Porthgain, this rewarding walk takes you over rugged headlands and past dramatic cliffs, pretty coves and flooded quarries. It's a taxing route with several steep descents and ascents but it's well worth the effort. Bring provisions, as it's a long way between villages.

Start out at busy **1 Whitesands Bay** (p688) and head west onto wild and rocky St Davids Head. The start of the route is fairly easy with a good path, wide open views and craggy volcanic outcrops to admire. The only signs of human habitation here are ancient, with the simple **2 neolithic burial chamber** on the headline predating the surrounding remnants of Celtic forts.

The path soon becomes more rugged, with a rock scramble down to and up from the lovely little cove at **3 Aberpwll**. Continue on past crumbling cliffs to **4 Abereiddi**, looking out for seals in the coves, gannets and possibly porpoises diving for fish out at sea. The beach at Abereiddi is famous for its black sand full of tiny fossils. Ruined quarry buildings and slate workers' cottages flank the path beyond the beach that leads to the **5 Blue Lagoon**, a deep turquoise flooded slate quarry now popular with coasteerers and, in early September, cliff divers from all over the world who compete here, diving 27m into the icy water below.

The 45-minute walk from Abereiddi to Porthgain is one of the best stretches along the entire coast path, following a clifftop plateau past the often deserted beach at **6 Traeth Llyfn**. A flight of steep stairs leads down to the golden sand, but beware of strong undercurrents and the tide, which can cut off parts of the beach from the steps.

Continue on for the last descent into the tiny harbour of **7 Porthgain**, where you can reward yourself with some superb seafood at the Shed or a cold beverage at the welcoming Sloop Inn.

self-service breakfast is included in the price. The hostel's in the village of Trefin, 2 miles east of Porthgain.

Crug Glâs HOTEL $$$
(☎01348-831302; www.crug-glas.co.uk; r £150-190; P 📶) Set on a big working farm, this opulent country house offers rooms decked out in a grand manner with rich fabrics, ornate beds, enormous bathrooms and elegant period grandeur. Five rooms are in the main house while two are in converted farm buildings. There's also a top-notch restaurant. Crug Glâs is 3 miles south of Porthgain, off the A487.

Eating & Drinking

The Shed SEAFOOD $$
(☎01348-831518; www.theshedporthgain.co.uk; mains £11-18; ⏰10am-9pm Apr-Oct, call ahead Nov-Mar; 📶) Housed in a beautifully converted machine shop right by the harbour, this simple little bistro is renowned as one of Pembrokeshire's best seafood restaurants. Fish and chips get their own separate menu, while the main menu relies heavily on the day's fresh catch alongside favourites such as Porthgain lobster.

Farmers Arms PUB
(☎01348-831284; www.farmersarmsmathry.co.uk; Mathry; ⏰noon-11pm; 📶🐾) If you're a lover of village pubs, this ivy-clad tavern in the hilltop village of Mathry, 5 miles east of Porthgain, is well worth seeking out. There's nothing fancy about it, just rugby memorabilia on the walls, hard rock on the jukebox, good honest food and a rotating selection of hand-pulled guest ales.

Getting There & Away

The only bus heading here is the Strumble Shuttle, one of the Pembrokeshire Coastal Bus Services (p684).

Fishguard (Abergwaun)

POP 5400

Perched on a headland between its modern ferry port and former fishing harbour, Fishguard is often overlooked by travellers, many of them rushing through on the ferries to and from Ireland. It doesn't have any sights as such, but it's an appealing little town and it holds the quirky distinction of being the setting for the last foreign invasion of Britain (see box opposite).

Fishguard is split into three distinct areas. In the middle of it all is the main town, centred on the Town Hall in Market Sq. To the east is the picturesque harbour of the Lower Town (Y Cwm), which was used as a setting for the 1971 film version of *Under Milk Wood* (starring Richard Burton, Peter O'Toole and Elizabeth Taylor). The train station and ferry terminal lie a mile northwest of the town centre, down on the bay in Goodwick (Wdig; *oo*-dig).

Sights & Activities

Strumble Head VIEWPOINT
On wild and rocky Strumble Head, a lighthouse beams out its signal as high-speed ferries thunder past on their way to Ireland. The headland makes a good vantage point for spotting dolphins, seals, sharks and sunfish; below the parking area is a WWII lookout that now serves as a shelter for observing wildlife. It's located 4 miles northwest of Goodwick and the route is well marked.

Kayak-King KAYAKING
(☎07967 010203; www.kayak-king.com; tours £45) Twice-daily sea-kayaking tours, tailored to either family groups or adults.

Festivals & Events

Fishguard Folk Festival MUSIC
(www.pembrokeshire-folk-music.co.uk; ⏰late May) A four-day festival of music and dance held over the holiday weekend at the end of May, this is a wonderful way to experience Welsh musical traditions as well as modern-day interpretations of this ancient craft. Most performances are free and they include pub sessions, dance displays, open-mic events, workshops and a rip-roaring festival *twmpath* (traditional community dance).

Sleeping

Fishguard has some excellent B&Bs, and staying in the main part of town will give you easy access to the better bars and eateries. Goodwick is full of budget hotels and B&Bs catering to passengers catching the Irish ferries. There are also some memorable camping options in the surrounding countryside.

Fishguard

★Pentower B&B $$
(☎01348-874462; www.pentower.co.uk; Tower Hill; s/d from £55/85; P 📶) Built by Sir Evan Jones,

the architect who designed the harbour, this rambling turreted home is perched on a hill at the edge of town, overlooking his creation. The house is pretty and unassuming, apart from the grand tiled atrium. The three en suite guest rooms are spacious and romantic.

Manor Town House B&B **$$**
(☎01348-873260; www.manortownhouse.com; 11 Main St; s/d from £75/85; 📶) This graceful Georgian house has a lovely garden terrace where you can sit and gaze over the harbour. The young owners are charm personified and the house has been very tastefully renovated, with continual improvements being made to the six smart en-suite rooms.

Fern Villa B&B **$$**
(☎01348-874148; www.fernvillafishguard.co.uk; Church Rd, Goodwick; s/d from £45/70; 🅿) Situated on the slopes in Goodwick (head towards the church), this large Victorian house offers clean en suite rooms, some with exposed stone walls and sea views. It's a great option if you want to be close to the train station and ferry port.

Surrounds

Pwll Deri YHA HOSTEL **$**
(☎0845-371 9536; www.yha.org.uk; Castell Mawr, Trefasser; dm/r from £18/45; 🅿) Perched atop a 120m-high cliff overlooking the sea, this hostel has one of the finest locations in Britain. The views from the dining room would rival those from any top hotel and the sunsets are spectacular. The private rooms all have their own bathrooms.

Fishguard Bay Resort CAMPGROUND **$**
(☎01348-811415; www.fishguardbay.com; site for 2 incl car £20, pod £65, caravan/house per week from £435/695; 🐾) Dramatically positioned on a clifftop overlooking Fishguard Bay, this large complex offers a wide range of accommodation including tent sites, static caravans, self-contained cottages, luxury lodges and barrel-shaped 'glamping pods'. There's also a shop, a small playground and a 'pamper pod' used for massage. It's located 2.5 miles east of Fishguard, signposted from the A487.

Eating

Gourmet Pig DELI, CAFE **$**
(☎01348-874404; www.gourmetpig.co.uk; 32 West St; mains £4-8; ⏲9.30am-5.30pm Mon-Sat, 11am-3pm Sun; 📶) Delicious sandwiches, samosas, deli platters, pies and pastries are the main attractions at this relaxed deli-cafe, along with barista-made Coaltown coffee (roasted in Ammanford). Grab a window seat and watch Fishguard go about its business.

Number 3 ITALIAN **$$**
(☎01348-871845; www.number3restaurant.co.uk; 3 Main St; mains £12-18; ⏲6-9.30pm Wed-Sat; 📶) This simple restaurant with bare wooden floors, leather chairs and a mellow vibe turns out excellent pasta, pizza and risotto, but the fare's not all Italian by any means. A range of gourmet burgers rubs shoulders with rustic mains such as beef cheeks, pork belly and roast chicken.

THE LAST INVASION OF BRITAIN

While Hastings in 1066 may get all the press, the last invasion of Britain was actually at Carregwastad Point, northwest of Fishguard, on 22 February 1797. A ragtag collection of 1400 French mercenaries and bailed convicts, led by an Irish-American named Colonel Tate, had intended to land at Bristol and march to Liverpool, keeping English troops occupied while France mounted an invasion of Ireland. Bad weather blew them ashore at Carregwastad where, after scrambling up a steep cliff, they set about looting for food and drink.

The invaders had hoped that the Welsh peasants would rise up to join them in revolutionary fervour but, not surprisingly, their drunken pillaging didn't endear them to the locals. The French were quickly seen off by volunteer 'yeoman' soldiers, with help from the people of Fishguard, including, most famously, one Jemima Nicholas who single-handedly captured 12 mercenaries armed with nothing more than a pitchfork.

The beleaguered Tate surrendered and a mere two days after their arrival the invaders laid down their weapons at Goodwick and were sent off to the jail at Haverfordwest.

Drinking & Nightlife

Peppers BAR
(☎01348-874540; www.peppers-hub.co.uk; 16 West St; ⏲10am-10pm Fri & Sat, daily summer) This hip hub includes an interesting art gallery and an excellent restaurant, but what we really love about Peppers is its little burgundy-walled bar. There's a good selection of Welsh craft beer and cider, a decent choice of wine, and the staff know their way around a cocktail shaker. There are regular live gigs as well, particularly jazz.

Ship Inn PUB
(☎01348-874033; Old Newport Rd, Lower Town; ⏲6pm-midnight Wed-Fri, noon-midnight Sat & Sun) This lovely little 250-year-old pub has an open fire in winter and walls covered in memorabilia, including photos of Richard Burton filming *Under Milk Wood* outside (the street and nearby quay have not changed a bit).

Information

Tourist Office (☎01437-776636; www.visitpembrokeshire.com; Town Hall, Market Sq; ⏲9am-5pm Mon-Fri) As well as this helpful tourist office, the Town Hall contains the library (handy for free internet access) and the market hall, which hosts a general market on Thursday and a farmers market on Saturday mornings.

Getting There & Away

BOAT

Stena Line (☎08447 707 070; www.stenaline.co.uk; car & driver from £79, foot passenger £34; 📶) has two ferries a day, year-round between Rosslare in the southeast of Ireland and Fishguard Harbour.

BUS

Direct services to/from Fishguard include Haverfordwest (£3.40, 31 minutes, hourly), St Davids (£3.70, 45 minutes, six daily), Newport (£2.45, 15 minutes, hourly), Cardigan (£3.75, 37 minutes, hourly) and Aberystwyth (£6, 2½ hours, nine daily). The Pembrokeshire Coastal Bus Services (p684) are also useful.

TRAIN

There are direct trains to both Fishguard & Goodwick Station and Fishguard Harbour (both of which are actually in Goodwick) from destinations including Carmarthen (£9.30, 56 minutes, four daily), Swansea (£16, two hours, daily), Cardiff (from £10, three hours, two daily), Newport (£12, three hours, daily) and Manchester (£30, 6½ hours, daily).

Newport (Trefdraeth)

POP 1160

In stark contrast to the industrial city of Newport near the English border, the Pembrokeshire Newport is a pretty cluster of flower-bedecked cottages huddled beneath a small Norman castle (now a private residence). It sits at the foot of Mynydd Carningli, a large bump on the seaward side of the Preseli Hills, and in recent years it has gained a reputation for the quality of its restaurants and guesthouses.

Newport makes a pleasant base for walks along the coastal path or south into the Preseli Hills, but it does get crowded in summer. At the northwest corner of the town is little **Parrog Beach**, dwarfed by **Newport Sands** (Traeth Mawr) across the river.

History

Newport Castle was founded by a Norman nobleman called William FitzMartin – who was married to a daughter of Lord Rhys ap Gruffydd – after his father-in-law drove him out of nearby Nevern in 1191. Newport grew up around the castle, initially as a garrison town.

Sights

Carreg Coetan TOMB
(Pen-y-Bont) FREE It's now surrounded by houses but this little dolmen has been here for 6000 years. At first glance it looks like the capstone is securely supported by the four standing stones. A closer inspection suggests that some old magic has held it together all these thousands of years as it's balanced on only two of them. Archaeological investigations have uncovered the remains of cremated bones and urns. It's well signposted down a side road on the town's eastern edge.

St Brynach's Church CHURCH
(Nevern) With its overgrown castle and atmospheric church, the little village of Nevern, 2 miles east of Newport, makes a good objective for an easy walk or ride. St Brynach's beautifully melancholic churchyard dates from around the 6th century, predating the church itself. Its supremely gloomy alley of yew trees is estimated to be upwards of six centuries old. The second yew on the right is the so-called **bleeding yew**, named after the curious reddish-brown sap that oozes from it.

★Pentre Ifan TOMB

The largest dolmen in Wales, Pentre Ifan is a 5500-year-old neolithic burial chamber set on a remote hillside with superb views across the Preseli Hills and out to sea. The huge, 5m-long capstone, weighing more than 16 tonnes, is delicately poised on three tall, pointed, upright stones, made of the same bluestone that was used for the menhirs at Stonehenge. The site is about 3 miles southeast of Newport, on a minor road south of the A487; it's signposted.

Preseli Hills AREA

(Mynydd Preseli) The only upland area in Pembrokeshire Coast National Park, these hills rise to a height of 536m at Foel Cwmcerwyn. They encompass a fascinating prehistoric landscape, scattered with hill forts, standing stones and burial chambers, and are famous as the source of the mysterious bluestones of Stonehenge. The ancient **Golden Road** track, once part of a 5000-year-old trade route between Wessex and Ireland, runs along the crest of the hills, passing prehistoric cairns and the stone circle of Bedd Arthur.

★Castell Henllys HISTORIC SITE

(☎01239-891319; www.castellhenllys.com; Meline; adult/child £5/3.50; ⏰10am-5pm Apr-Oct, reduced hours Nov-Mar) If you've ever wondered what a Celtic village looked, felt and smelt like, take a trip back in time to this Iron Age fort, 4 miles east of Newport. From about 600 BC and right through the Roman occupation there was a thriving Celtic settlement here, and the whole thing has been reconstructed on its original foundations. Costumed staff bring the site to life, stoking the fires and performing traditional crafts.

Sleeping & Eating

Cnapan B&B $$

(☎01239-820575; www.cnapan.co.uk; East St; s/d £65/95; ⏰Easter–mid-Dec; P 📶) This listed Georgian town house has a flower-filled garden and five light-filled rooms above a popular **restaurant** (2-/3-course dinner £27/33; ⏰6.30-8.45pm Wed-Sun Easter–mid-Dec). A recent renovation has freshened up the decor and left brand new bathrooms in its wake. Ask for room 4 – it's a little bigger than the others.

★Canteen PIZZA, BURGERS $

(☎01239-820131; www.thecanteennewport.com; cnr Market & East Sts; mains £6-11; ⏰9.30am-2.30pm & 6-9pm Wed-Mon;) With names like *The Red Dragon*, *Land of my Fathers* and *Costa del Newport*, the Canteen's lip-smacking range of thin, crispy, stone-baked pizza has been suitably Welshified with the addition of quality, locally sourced toppings. It also serves burgers, salads and sandwiches, better-than-average coffee and a range of Welsh craft beer.

Information

National Park Information Centre & Tourist Office (☎01239-820912; Long St; ⏰10am-5.30pm Mon-Sat Easter-Oct, 10am-3.30pm Mon, Wed, Fri & Sat Nov-Easter) As well as friendly staff and stacks of information, there are interesting displays on Pembrokeshire Coast National Park.

Getting There & Away

BUS

Direct services to/from Newport include Haverfordwest (£4.45, 50 minutes, 10 daily), Fishguard (£2.45, 15 minutes, hourly), Dinas Cross (£1.50, six minutes, hourly), Cardigan (£3.35, 23 minutes, 12 daily) and Aberystwyth (£6, 2¼ hours, nine daily). The Pembrokeshire Coastal Bus Services (p684) are also useful.

CAR

Most visitors arrive by car. Expect to pay for, and possibly fight over, parking from April to September.

Brecon Beacons & Mid-Wales

Includes ➡

Best Places to Eat

- Ynyshir Hall (p715)
- Carlton Riverside (p708)
- Checkers (p711)
- St John's Place (p700)
- Tomatitos Tapas Bar (p698)

Best Places to Sleep

- Harbour Master (p719)
- The Bear (p698)
- Celyn Farm (p701)
- Beudy Banc (p714)
- Peterstone Court (p704)

Why Go?

The big draw here is the magnificent upland scenery of Brecon Beacons National Park, where high mountain roads dip down to remote hamlets and whitewashed ancient churches. The hiking and mountain-biking terrain here is superb, while the book-loving town of Hay-on-Wye caters to those with more cerebral interests.

By contrast the Powys countryside is Wales at its most rural – a landscape of lustrous green fields, wooded river valleys and small market towns; it's the part that the Industrial Revolution missed. Isolated, sea-battered Ceredigion is home to some of country's most unspoiled beaches, as well as the exuberant hot spot of Aberystwyth. Thrills can be found outside urban areas along lonely trails in the hills and valleys, and on two wheels down narrow country lanes.

Central Wales is thoroughly Welsh, with around 40% of people speaking the mother tongue – and more than 50% in Ceredigion.

When to Go

- If you're planning on walking, you'll get the most rain-free days between April and July; July and August are generally the warmest months.
- In May and June, the world's intelligentsia heads to Hay for its literary festival and for philosophy and music at HowTheLightGetsIn.
- In August, cap off the Green Man and Brecon Fringe Festival with a spot of bog snorkelling.
- Face the chill to earn your laurel wreath in Llanwrtyd Wells' mountain-bike chariot race in January.

Brecon Beacons & Mid-Wales Highlights

1 Black Mountains (p701) Taking a spectacular drive through the Vale of Ewyas.

2 Hay-on-Wye (p698) Soaking up the literary vibe of an elegant rural town.

3 Pen-y-Fan (p706) Avoiding the crowds on the tracks to the top of the region's highest mountain.

4 Powis Castle (p712) Discovering the magnificent gardens and ornate interiors of this castle near Welshpool.

5 Carreg Cennen (p706) Gazing up at Wales' most dramatically positioned ruined fortress.

6 Aberystwyth (p715) Experiencing a collision of high culture and student high-jinks.

7 Cardigan Bay (p721) Kayaking with dolphins and seals along this gloriously rugged stretch of coast.

8 Cambrian Mountains (p711) Enjoying the splendid isolation of the deserted Cambrian moorlands.

BRECON BEACONS NATIONAL PARK

Rippling dramatically for 45 miles from near Llandeilo in the west all the way to the English border, Brecon Beacons National Park (Parc Cenedlaethol Bannau Brycheiniog) encompasses some of the finest scenery in southern Wales. High mountain plateaus of grass and heather, their northern rims scalloped with glacier-scoured hollows, rise above wooded, waterfall-splashed valleys and green, rural landscapes.

There are four distinct regions within the park: the wild, lonely **Black Mountain** (Mynydd Du) in the west, with its high moors and glacial lakes; **Fforest Fawr** (Great Forest), whose rushing streams and spectacular waterfalls form the headwaters of the Rivers Tawe and Neath; the **Brecon Beacons** (Bannau Brycheiniog) proper, a group of very distinctive, flat-topped hills that includes Pen-y-Fan (886m), the park's highest peak; and the rolling heathland ridges of the **Black Mountains** (Y Mynyddoedd Duon) – not to be confused with the Black Mountain (singular) in the west.

Hay-on-Wye (Y Gelli Gandryll)

POP 1600

Hay-on-Wye, a pretty little town on the banks of the River Wye, just inside the Welsh border, has developed a reputation disproportionate to its size. First came the explosion in secondhand bookshops, a charge led by the charismatic and forthright local maverick Richard Booth.

With Hay established as the world's secondhand-book capital, a festival of literature and culture was founded in 1988, growing in stature each year to take in all aspects of the creative arts. Today the Hay Festival is a major attraction in its own right, famously endorsed by former US president Bill Clinton, a high-profile guest in 2001, as 'the Woodstock of the mind'.

The small town centre is made up of narrow sloping lanes, peppered by interesting shops and peopled by the differing types that such individuality and so many books tend to attract. Even outside of festival time, Hay-on-Wye has a vaguely alternative ambience.

History

Hay has had a tempestuous history, due to its borderlands position. In fact, at the time of the Norman Conquest it was administered separately as English Hay (the town proper) and Welsh Hay (the countryside to the south and west). For the next three and a half centuries Hay changed hands many times. Following the Tudor Acts of Union it settled down as a market town, and by the 18th century it had become a centre of the flannel trade.

Festivals & Events

Hay Festival LITERATURE
(01497-822629; www.hayfestival.com; May-Jun) The 10-day Hay Festival has become Britain's leading festival of literature and the arts – a kind of bookworms' Glastonbury or, according to Bill Clinton, 'the Woodstock of the mind'. Like those legendary music festivals, it pulls more than its fair share of the leading exponents of its genre.

HowtheLightGetsIn MUSIC, PHILOSOPHY
(www.howthelightgetsin.org; May-Jun) A low-key but appealing week-long philosophy and music event held at the same time as the Hay Festival.

Sleeping

★**The Bear** B&B $$
(01497-821302; www.thebearhay.com; 2 Bear St; s/d from £55/80; P) This friendly and well-run 1590 coaching inn retains its historic ambience and combines it with interesting art, sisal floors and bathrooms with tubs – bliss for tired hikers. One of the three chic bedrooms has a four-poster bed, and the excellent breakfasts include imaginative vegetarian options. Curl up with a book by the immense fireplace.

Hay Stables B&B $$
(01497-820008; www.haystables.co.uk; Oxford Rd; s/d from £45/70; P) Three modern en suite rooms decked out in neutral tones await you at this friendly guesthouse. There's a common area for guests and a large, fully equipped kitchen. Breakfast is a self-serve affair for your own fry-up.

Eating

★**Tomatitos Tapas Bar** SPANISH $
(01497-820770; www.haytomatitos.co.uk; 38 Lion St; tapas £2.25-5.95; 11am-11pm Mon-Sat, to 4pm Sun;) Friendly, bustling Tomatitos

Brecon Beacons National Park

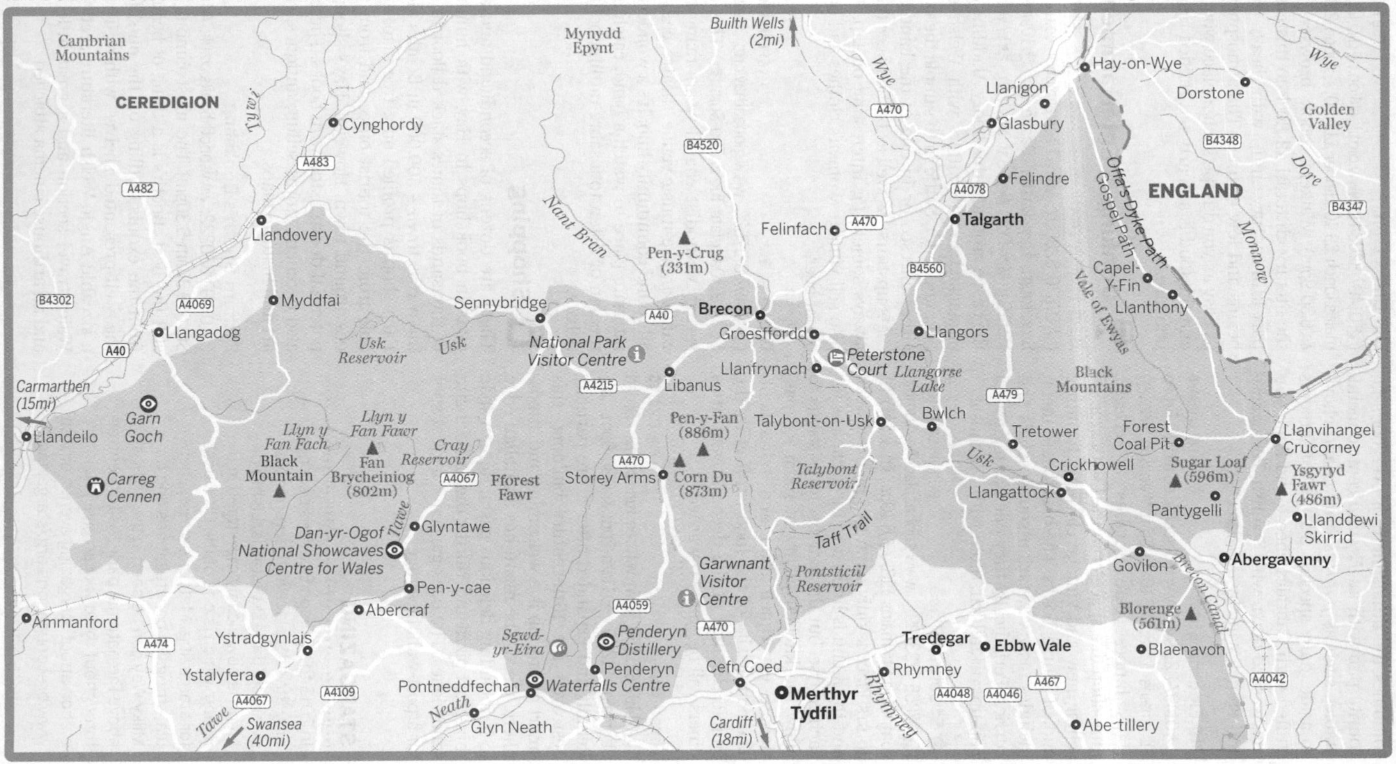

combines the atmosphere of everyone's favourite pub with an *España*-centric menu. Staples such as *patatas bravas* and chorizo aside, daily specials feature mushrooms stuffed with Cabrales cheese and lamb tagine, washed down with Spanish, Portuguese and French wine by the glass.

Old Electric Shop VEGETARIAN $

(☎01497-821194; www.oldelectric.co.uk; 10 Broad St; mains £5-8; ⏱10am-5pm Wed-Sun; Wi-Fi; vegetarian) Hay's hippest cafe inhabits an eclectic junk-shop-like space crammed with studios selling new and vintage clothing, furniture and, of course, books. The blackboard menu includes tasty vegetarian soups, salads and curries. Periodically they open at night as a pop-up cocktail bar, often with live music.

★**St John's Place** MODERN BRITISH $$

(☎07855 783799; www.stjohnsplacehay.tumblr.com; Lion St; mains £18; ⏱6-10pm Fri & Sat) St John's Place is only open two nights a week and the menu is limited to three choices for each course, but this narrow focus seems to allow the kitchen plenty of room for passionate experimentation and refinement. The complexity of the food is offset by the simple elegance of the decor. Adventurous diners will be amply rewarded.

Three Tuns PUB FOOD $$

(☎01497-821855; www.three-tuns.com; Broad St; mains £12-19; ⏱11am-2pm & 6.30-9pm; family-friendly) Rebuilt and expanded after a fire partially destroyed the 16th-century building, this smart gastropub is a welcoming and atmospheric place. The menu has an Italian edge to it, including delicious pasta, Roman-style thin-crust pizza and, during the day, ciabatta sandwiches. The back garden is a great spot for a post-walk beverage.

STARGAZING

In 2013 the Brecon Beacons became only the fifth place in the world to be awarded 'dark-sky' status. Light pollution is now closely monitored in the region, which is one of the UK's best for stargazing. Meteor showers, nebula, strings of constellations and the Milky Way can be seen in the night sky above the national park. Visitor centres throughout the park can give you information about stargazing events, or visit www.breconbeacons.org/stargazing.

Old Black Lion PUB FOOD $$

(☎01497-820841; www.oldblacklion.co.uk; Lion St; mains lunch £9-10, dinner £13-20; ⏱noon-2.30pm & 6.30-9pm) Walkers, book browsers and the literary glitterati all flock to this creaky, part-13th-century inn, with heavy black beams and low ceilings. The atmosphere is as cosy as you'd hope such a place would be and the food is a hearty but refined take on pub fare.

Drinking & Entertainment

Beer Revolution BEER HALL

(☎07870 628097; www.beerrevolution.co.uk; Old Storeroom, Hay Castle, Castle St; ⏱10am-5pm Mon-Sat Mar-Oct, Wed-Sat Nov-Feb; Wi-Fi) Within the castle grounds, this boozy Aladdin's cave is stacked to the rafters with Welsh craft beer and cider. Settle in to sample the range, either alfresco or in one of the handful of seats upstairs. As well as bottled beer there's always something interesting on tap. They also sell vintage women's clothes and books about beer.

Globe at Hay LIVE PERFORMANCE

(☎01497-821762; www.globeathay.org; Newport St; ⏱9.30am-late Tue & Thu-Sun; Wi-Fi) This converted Methodist chapel wears many hats: cafe, bar, live-music venue, theatre, club and all-round community hub. It's a wonderfully intimate place to watch a band, catch a comedian or listen to a sabre-rattling political debate.

Shopping

There are dozens of secondhand and antiquarian bookshops in Hay, with hundreds of thousands of tomes stacked floor to ceiling across town – 500,000 in Booth's alone. Each shop is profiled on a free map, available from the tourist office and from venues around town. However, Hay's shopping potential doesn't stop with books. There are also excellent stores selling antiques, craft, art and historic maps.

Richard Booth's Bookshop BOOKS

(☎01497-820322; www.boothbooks.co.uk; 44 Lion St; ⏱9.30am-5.30pm) The most famous and still the best, Booth's is a thing of beauty – from the exquisite tiling on the outside to the well-presented shelves within. There's a sizeable Anglo-Welsh literature section, a Wales travel section and a great little cafe and an arthouse cinema attached.

Mostly Maps MAPS
(☎01497-820539; www.mostlymaps.com; 2 Castle St; ⏰10.30am-5.30pm Tue-Sat) Exquisite antiquarian maps and illustrative plates, many hand-coloured.

Rose's Books BOOKS
(☎01497-820013; www.rosesbooks.com; 14 Broad St; ⏰10am-5pm) Rare children's and illustrated books.

Murder & Mayhem BOOKS
(☎01497-821613; www.hay-on-wycbooks.com; 5 Lion St; ⏰10am-5.30pm) This specialist branch of Addyman Books has a body outline on the floor, monsters on the ceiling and stacks of detective fiction, true crime and horror.

Information

Police Station (☎101; www.dyfed-powys.police.uk; Heol-y-Dwr)
Tourist Office (☎01497-820144; www.hay-on-wye.co.uk; Oxford Rd; ⏰noon-4pm Mar-Nov, 10am-1pm Dec-Jan) Stocks a map showing all of Hay's bookshops.

Getting There & Away

There are six buses per day (except on Sunday) to/from **Brecon** (£6.40, 37 minutes), Talgarth (£5.10, 18 minutes) and Felinfach (£5.90, 30 minutes); and three a day to/from **Hereford** (£8.40, 50 minutes).

Black Mountains (Y Mynyddoedd Duon)

The hills that stretch northward from Abergavenny to Hay-on-Wye are untamed and largely uninhabited, reaching a height of 811m at windswept Waun Fach.

The scenic and secluded Vale of Ewyas traces the path of the River Honddu through the heart of the Black Mountains, from the village of **Llanvihangel Crucorney** to the exposed Gospel Pass (542m), where a single-track road winds its way through a magically bleak landscape down to Hay-on-Wye. Along the way it passes the picturesque ruins of Llanthony Priory and the hamlet of **Capel-y-Ffin**, where there are more monastic ruins and the 18th-century Church of St Mary the Virgin.

Sights

Ysgyryd Fawr MOUNTAIN
(Skirrid) Of the glacially sculpted hills that surround Abergavenny, Skirrid (486m) is the most dramatic looking and has a history to match. A cleft in the rock near the top was once believed to have split open at the exact time of Christ's death and a chapel was built here on what was considered a particularly holy place (a couple of upright stones remain). During the Reformation, as many as 100 people would attend illegal Catholic Masses at this remote spot.

You can trek here from Llanvihangel Crucorney (5.5 miles) or take the B4521 from Abergavenny to the lay-by at the base of the hill (4 miles). It's a steep climb from here through the woods on a track that can be muddy; wear sensible shoes. Once you clear the tree line the walk is less steep, with a final climb right at the end to the summit where you'll be rewarded with extravagant views.

St Issui's Church CHURCH
(Patrishow) Halfway up a hillside on a narrow country lane, 5 miles northwest of Llanvihangel Crucorney, this tiny 11th-century church contains a remarkable, finely carved wooden rood screen and loft, dating from around 1500. On the walls are medieval frescoes of biblical texts, coats of arms and a red-ochre skeleton (once believed to have been painted with human blood) bearing an hourglass and scythe – the figure of Death. The church is usually open; leave a donation in the box.

Llanthony Priory RUINS
(Cadw; www.cadw.gov.wales; ⏰10am-4pm) FREE Halfway along the Vale of Ewyas lie the atmospheric ruins of this Augustinian priory, set among grasslands and wooded hills by the River Honddu. The buildings were completed in 1230 but were abandoned after Henry VIII dissolved Britain's monasteries in 1538. Though not as grand as Tintern Abbey, the setting is even more romantic. JMW Turner painted the scene in 1794.

Sleeping & Eating

★**Celyn Farm** B&B $$
(☎01873-890894; www.celynfarm.co.uk; Forest Coal Pit; s/d from £60/75) Set in 120 hectares of farmland reached by narrow lanes from either Llanvihangel Crucorney or Crickhowell (make sure you print out the directions), this remote country house offers four handsome rooms, excellent breakfasts and idyllic views over Sugar Loaf.

Skirrid Inn PUB FOOD $$
(☎01873-890258; www.skirridmountaininn.co.uk; Hereford Rd, Llanvihangel Crucorney; lunch £4-7, dinner £8-13; ⏰5.30-11pm Mon, 11am-2.30pm & 5.30-11pm Tue-Fri, 11.30am-11pm Sat, noon-5pm Sun; P) Those with a taste for the macabre and ghostly will love this place. Wales' oldest inn (pre 1110) once doubled as a court and over 180 people were hanged here. Just so you don't forget, a noose dangles from the well-worn hanging beam, outside the doors to three old-fashioned bedrooms (r £90). Downstairs they serve hearty food in front of roaring fires.

Getting There & Away

Bus X4 between Abergavenny (£4.60, 16 minutes) and Hereford (£5.30, 40 minutes) stops in Llanvihangel Crucorney seven times a day; no Sunday services.

Crickhowell (Crughywel)

POP 2070

This prosperous, picturesque, flower-bedecked village grew up around a Norman motte-and-bailey castle and a ford on the River Usk. All that remains of the **castle** are a few tumbledown towers, and the ford was superseded in the 17th century by the elegant **stone bridge** leading to the neighbouring village of Llangattock. The bridge is famous for having 12 arches on one side and 13 on the other.

There's not a lot to see in Crickhowell itself, but it's a pleasant place for an overnight stop and there's a good clutch of independent shops to peruse. The town's fiercely protective of its locally owned stores, banding together to prevent a supermarket chain opening a branch here in 2015. That rebellious spirit continued with a highly publicised tax revolt, protesting against the ability of large companies to make use of offshore tax havens by grouping together and setting up one of their own.

WORTH A TRIP

TRETOWER

Originally the home of the Vaughan family, **Tretower Court & Castle** (Cadw; www.cadw.gov.wales; Tretower; adult/child £6/4.20; ⏰10am-5pm Apr-Oct, to 4pm Wed-Fri Nov-Mar) gives you two historic buildings for the price of one – the sturdy circular tower of a Norman motte-and-bailey castle, and a 15th-century manor house with a fine medieval garden. Together they illustrate the transition from military stronghold to country house that took place in late medieval times. It's situated 3 miles northwest of Crickhowell on the A479.

Sights & Activities

Crug Hywel MOUNTAIN
(Table Mountain) Distinctive flat-topped Crug Hywel (Hywel's Rock; 451m), better known as Table Mountain, rises to the north of Crickhowell and gave the town its name. You can make a steep but satisfying hike to the impressive remains of an Iron Age fort at the top (3 miles round trip). The tourist office has a leaflet detailing the route.

Festivals & Events

Crickhowell Walking Festival SPORTS
(www.crickhowellfestival.com; ⏰Mar) Held in the week wrapped around St David's Day (1 March), this nine-day festival features guided treks, workshops on outdoorsy themes and music.

Green Man Festival MUSIC
(www.greenman.net; Glanusk Park; adult/child £175/20; ⏰mid-Aug) This four-day music festival has a sterling reputation for its mellow vibe, green ethos and for catering well to children and people with disabilities. It consistently attracts the current 'it' bands of the indie, alternative and folk music firmament, along with the occasional dead-set rock legend. Tickets include onsite camping. It's held 2 miles west of Crickhowell via the B4558.

Sleeping & Eating

Gwyn Deri B&B $$
(☎01873-812494; www.gwynderibedandbreakfast.co.uk; Mill St; s/d/f £40/70/100; P) The friendly couple who run this homely B&B keep its three modern guest bedrooms immaculately clean, and are more than happy to share their knowledge of the area. Bonuses include fresh fruit in the rooms and an excellent breakfast selection. Connecting rooms are available for family groups.

Number Eighteen CAFE $
(☎01873-810337; www.number-eighteen.com; 18 High St; mains £4-8; ⏰9am-6pm) The best of Crickhowell's cafes, this bright, contemporary eatery serves better-than-average

coffee, freshly made sandwiches, burgers and bistro-style lunches. There's always a tempting array of cakes in the counter cabinet, too.

Information

Tourist Office (☎01873-811970; www.visitcrickhowell.co.uk; Beaufort St; ⏰10am-5pm Mon-Sat, to 1.30pm Sun; 📶) Shares a building with an art gallery and stocks leaflets for local walks.

Getting There & Away

Direct bus services to/from Crickhowell include Abergavenny (£1.85, 11 minutes, 12 daily), Llanfrynach (£2.40, 35 minutes, seven daily), Brecon (£2.60, 25 minutes, 12 daily), Talgarth (£2.40, 27 minutes, weekdays) and Builth Wells (£4.65, 56 minutes, weekdays). No Sunday services.

Brecon (Aberhonddu)

POP 8250

The handsome market town of Brecon stands at the junction of the River Usk and the River Honddu. For centuries the town thrived as a centre of wool production and weaving. Today you'll find Brecon Beacons hikers rubbing shoulders with soldiers from the town's large military base in the bars, eateries and outdoor shops that dominate the old stone streets.

History

An Iron Age hill fort on Pen-y-Crug (331m), northwest of town, and the remains of a Roman camp at Y Gaer, to the west, testify to Brecon's antiquity. After the Romans, the area was ruled by the Irish-born king Brychan, who married into a Welsh royal house in the 5th century. The town takes its name from him, and his kingdom, Brycheiniog (anglicised to Brecknock), gave its name to the old county of Brecknockshire. The town of Merthyr Tydfil was named for Brychan's daughter, St Tudful.

It was not until Norman times that Brecon began to burgeon. The local Welsh prince, Rhys ap Tewdwr, was defeated in 1093 by Bernard de Neufmarché, a Norman lord, who then built the town's castle and monastery (which is now the cathedral).

Sights

★Brecon Cathedral CHURCH
(☎01874-623857; www.breconcathedral.org.uk; Cathedral Close; ⏰8.30am-6pm) Perched on a hill above the River Honddu, Brecon Cathedral was founded in 1093 as part of a Benedictine monastery, though little remains from the original Norman church except the vividly carved font. Most of the Gothic structure standing today dates from the early 13th century. Modern additions include an ornate 1937 altarpiece and a cross that seems to hover in mid-air at the end of the nave.

Activities

Dragonfly Cruises BOATING
(☎07831-685222; www.dragonfly-cruises.co.uk; Canal Basin, Canal Rd; adult/child £7.80/4.50, hire per 1/2/3 hours £15/25/40; ⏰Mar-Oct) Runs 2½-hour narrowboat cruises on the Monmouthshire & Brecon Canal. There are two to three departures on Wednesday, Saturday and Sunday, and on additional days from June to August. They also hire small boats.

Beacon Park Day Boats BOATING, CANOEING
(☎0800 612 2890; www.beaconparkdayboats.co.uk; Toll House, Canalside; per hour/half-day/day boats from £20/45/70, canoes from £15/25/40; ⏰10am-5pm Easter-Oct) Rents six- to eight-seater electric-powered boats and three-seater Canadian canoes. In a day, you can cruise southeast to Llangattock and back. It also has a fleet of luxury narrowboats for longer live-in voyages.

Bikes + Hikes OUTDOORS
(☎01874-610071; www.bikesandhikes.co.uk; Lion Yard; bikes per half/full day £18/25, canoes per 2hr £20) Hires canoes, mountain bikes and trail bikes (child seats available) and provides free delivery locally. Also offers guided rides, paddle and pedal packages, caving, gorge walking, rock climbing and more.

Festivals & Events

Brecon Fringe Festival MUSIC
(www.breconfringe.co.uk; ⏰Aug) Started as an alternative to the famous Brecon Jazz Festival (which sadly blew its last note in 2015), Brecon Fringe brings a wide range of musical styles to pubs in and around town over four days in August.

Brecon Beast SPORTS
(www.breconbeast.co.uk; ⏰Sep) A gruelling mountain-bike challenge over 44 or 68 miles, held in mid-September. The entry fee (£35) covers camping, refreshments on the route, a 'pasta party' and a T-shirt.

Brecon

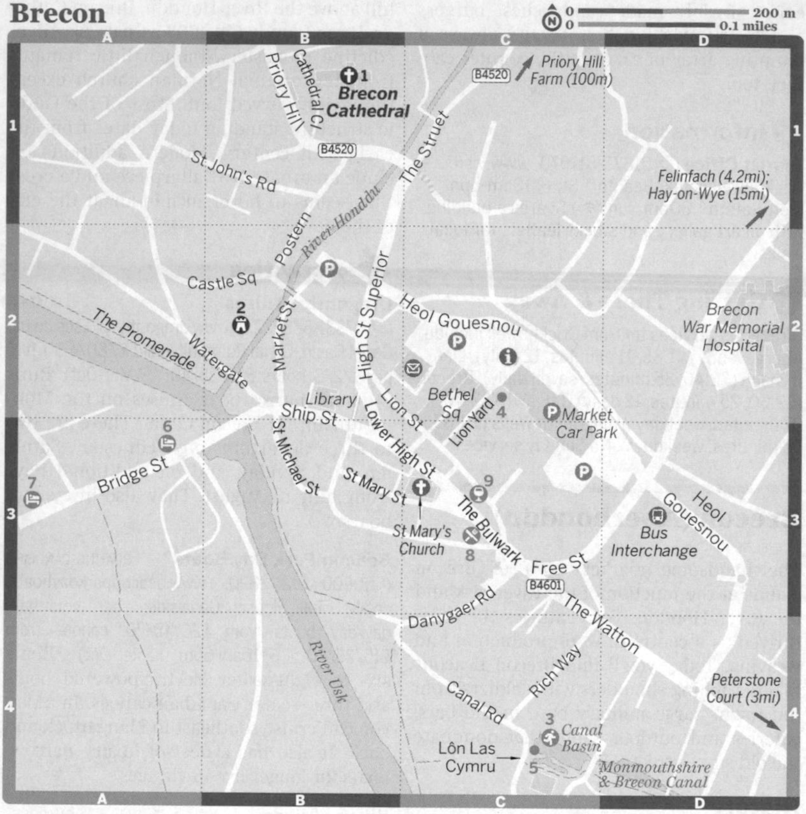

Sleeping

Town Centre

Coach House B&B $$

(☎07974 328437; www.coachhousebrecon.com; 12 Orchard St; r £83-104, ste £142;) This hospitable 19th-century coaching inn is well-attuned to the needs of walkers, with a drying room for hiking gear, generous breakfasts (including good vegetarian options) and packed lunches put together by the hosts. The six stylish, modern rooms, decorated in soothing creams, have ultra-comfy beds and good showers.

Bridge Cafe B&B $$

(☎01874-622024; www.bridgecafe.co.uk; 7 Bridge St; s/d with bathroom £60/70, without £45/55;) Owned by keen mountain bikers and hill walkers who can advise on local activities, the Bridge has three plain but attractive and comfortable bedrooms, with down-filled duvets and crisp cotton sheets. Only one has an en suite; the other two share a bathroom.

Surrounds

Priory Mill Farm CAMPGROUND $

(www.priorymillfarm.co.uk; Hay Rd; sites per adult £8; Easter-Oct; P) With a cobbled courtyard, ancient mill building, free-range chickens and a lush camping meadow, this small campground is pretty much camping heaven, and it's just a five-minute riverside walk from Brecon. It supplies local wood and charcoal so you can have your very own campfire.

★**Peterstone Court** HOTEL $$$

(☎01874-665387; www.peterstone-court.com; Llanhamlach; r from £150; P) At this elegant Georgian manor house, the rooms are large and comfortable, and the views across

Brecon

the valley to the Beacons are superb. The boutique spa centre is a big drawcard, pampering guests with organic beauty products. They also have an excellent restaurant. Llanhamlach is 3 miles southeast of Brecon, just off the A40.

Felin Fach Griffin PUB **$$$**
(01874-620111; www.felinfachgriffin.co.uk; Felinfach; s/d from £110/130;) Set above an acclaimed gastropub in Felinfach village 5 miles northeast of Brecon (just off the A470), the Griffin's quietly elegant rooms offer comfortable beds, fancy toiletries and homeimade biscuits. Old-fashioned radios take the place of TVs and there are plenty of books to read. A dinner-inclusive rate is available.

Eating & Drinking

Gurkha Corner NEPALESE **$**
(01874-610871; www.gurkhacorner.co.uk; 12 Glamorgan St; mains £6-10; noon-2.30pm & 5.30-11pm Tue-Sun;) Rustic scenes of the Himalayas brighten the windowless dining room of this friendly Nepalese restaurant. The food – curries, fried rice, lentils and rich veg side dishes – is delicious.

Brecon Tap BAR
(01874-620800; www.breconinns.co.uk; 4 The Bulwark) Crowdfunded into being by the lads at Brecon Brewing, the Brecon Tap is a treasure trove of craft beer, traditional cider, estate wines and locally baked meat pies.

Information

Breconshire War Memorial Hospital (01874-622443; www.powysthb.wales.nhs.uk/brecon-hospital; Cerrigcochion Rd; 24hr)

Tourist Office (01874-622485; www.midwalesmyway.com; Market car park; 9.30am-5pm Mon-Sat, 10am-4pm Sun)

Getting There & Away

Direct bus services run to/from Brecon's **bus interchange** (Heol Gouesnou). Destinations include Cardiff (£8.30, 1¾ hours, eight daily), Abergavenny (£3.40, 45 minutes, 12 daily), Crickhowell (£2.60, 25 minutes, 12 daily), Hay-on-Wye (£6.40, 37 minutes, six daily) and Llandrindod Wells (£4.65, one hour, seven daily). No Sunday services.

The Market car park offers short-stay pay-and-display parking. There are long-stay lots on Hoel Gouesnou and near the canal basin.

Regular taxi services as well as a walkers shuttle are offered by **Ride & Hike** (07989-242550; www.rideandhike.co.uk). Indicative fares for the six-seater shuttle: National Park Visitor Centre (£20), Merthyr Tydfil (£45), Cardiff (£100).

Fforest Fawr & Black Mountain

The western half of Brecon Beacons National Park is sparsely inhabited and devoid of any towns of note. **Fforest Fawr** (Great Forest) was once a Norman hunting ground and is now a Unesco geopark (www.fforestfawrgeopark.org.uk), famed for its varied landscapes ranging from bleak moorland to flower-flecked limestone pavement and lush wooded ravines choked with moss and greenery. Further west is the **Black Mountain** (Y Mynydd Du), a lonely expanse of barren peaks that throws down an irresistible gauntlet to intrepid hikers.

Sights

Penderyn Distillery DISTILLERY
(01685-810651; www.welsh-whisky.co.uk; Penderyn; tours £8.50; 9.30am-5pm) Though Wales has a long history of spirit distillation, this boutique distillery released its first malt whisky only in 2004, marking the resurgence of Welsh whisky-making after an absence of more than 100 years due to the popularity of the temperance movement in the late 19th century. Visitors can witness the creation of the liquid fire that's distilled with fresh spring water in a single copper

WORTH A TRIP

HIT YOUR PEAK

Ascending **Pen-y-Fan** (886m), the tallest peak in the Brecon Beacons, is one of the most popular hikes in the national park (around 120,000 people each year make the climb, giving it the nickname 'the motorway'). The shortest route begins at the Pont ar Daf car park on the A470, 10 miles southwest of Brecon. It's a steep but straightforward slog up to the summit of Corn Du (873m), followed by a short dip and final ascent to Pen-y-Fan (4.5 miles round trip; allow three hours).

A slightly longer (5.5 miles round trip) but just as crowded path starts at the Storey Arms outdoor centre, 1 mile to the north. The T4 bus stops here; note, the Storey Arms is not a pub! You can avoid the crowds by choosing one of the longer routes on the north side of the mountain, which also have the advantage of more interesting views on the way up. The best starting point is the Cwm Gwdi car park, at the end of a minor road 3.5 miles southwest of Brecon. From here, you follow a path along the crest of the Cefn Cwm Llwch ridge, with great views of the neighbouring peaks, with a final steep scramble up to the summit. The round trip from the car park is 7 miles; allow three to four hours. Starting and finishing in Brecon, the total distance is 14 miles.

still, then matured in bourbon casks and finished in rich Madeira wine casks. Tours include tastings.

Waterfall Country WATERFALL

A series of dramatic waterfalls lies between the villages of Pontneddfechan and Ystradfellte, where the Rivers Mellte, Hepste and Pyrddin pass through steep forested gorges. The finest is **Sgwd-yr-Eira** (Waterfall of the Snow), where you can actually walk behind the torrent. At one point the River Mellte disappears into **Porth-yr-Ogof** (Door to the Cave), the biggest cave entrance in Britain (3m high and 20m wide), only to reappear 100m further south.

Red Kite Feeding Centre BIRD SANCTUARY

(☎01550-740617; www.redkiteswales.co.uk; Llanddeusant; adult/child £4/2; ⏰3pm Apr-Oct, 2pm Nov-Mar) A multitude of majestic birds of prey swoop in daily for their afternoon meal at this remote feeding centre. You're likely to see upwards of 50 red kites, alongside buzzards and ravens.

Garn Goch RUINS

FREE You're likely to have the remains of Garn Goch to yourself, despite their impressiveness. It's one of the largest Iron Age hill forts in Wales. Two distinct, immense, circular, stone ramparts can be discerned as you wander the hilltop, which offers endless views of the surrounding countryside. To get here, follow the signs from Llangadog through Bethlehem village and into the hills beyond.

★**Carreg Cennen** CASTLE

(Cadw; ☎01558-822291; www.carregcennencastle.com; Trapp; adult/child £4/3.50; ⏰9.30am-6.30pm Apr-Oct, to 4pm Nov-Mar) Dramatically perched atop a steep limestone crag, high above the River Cennen, are the brooding ruins of Wales' ultimate romantic castle, visible for miles in every direction. Originally a Welsh castle, the current structure dates back to Edward I's conquest of Wales in the late 13th century. It was partially dismantled in 1462 during the War of the Roses. It's well signposted from the A483, heading south from Llandeilo.

Sleeping & Eating

There are some good hostels and campgrounds scattered about this section of the national park. Alternatively you could base yourself in Llandovery, Llandeilo or Merthyr Tydfil.

★**Coed Owen Bunkhouse** HOSTEL $

(☎01685-722628; www.breconbeaconsbunkhouse.co.uk; Cwmtaff; dm/r £30/60; P) Set on a working sheep farm just up the road from the Garwnant Visitor Centre, this excellent custom conversion of an old barn offers smart six- and 10-bed bunkrooms and one small, private double. There's also an excellent kitchen. On the weekends it's usually booked up by groups, but solo travellers shouldn't have trouble midweek.

Mandinam CABIN $$

(☎01550-777368; www.mandinam.com; Llangadog; cabin £100; ⏰Easter-Oct; P) This wonderfully remote estate on the northwestern fringe of the national park offers a bohemian back-to-nature experience in little wagon-like huts, complete with kitchens and wood-fired hot tubs for a spot of romantic stargazing. You needn't worry about privacy as the huts are positioned well apart from each other within the vast property.

Carreg Cennen Tearoom WELSH $
(☎01558-822291; www.carregcennencastle.com; Trapp; mains £4-8; ⏰9.30am-5.30pm) Possibly the best castle tearoom anywhere. The farmer/owner's longhorn beef is on the menu in the form of cottage pie and beef salad, plus they serve warming *cawl* (traditional Welsh stew) and excellent home-made cakes. The location is an impressive converted barn, which sits just below the castle.

Information

Garwnant Visitor Centre (☎01685-722481; www.naturalresourceswales.gov.uk/garwnant; parking £2; ⏰9am-5pm; 👪) Natural Resources Wales' visitor centre sits at the head of the Llwyn-on Reservoir, 5 miles north of Merthyr Tydfil on the A470. It's the starting point for a couple of easy forest walks. It also has a cafe, a mini mountain-bike course, an adventure play area and a rope course for kids.

Getting There & Away

The only useful bus routes through this region are bus 63 between Brecon and Ystradgynlais, which stops at the Dan-yr-Ogof National Showcaves Centre when it's open; and bus T3 between Cardiff and Newtown (via Merthyr Tydfil, Brecon and Llandrindod Wells), which stops near the Garwnant Visitor Centre.

POWYS

Small villages, quiet market towns and an abundance of sheep litter the undulating hills and moorland of rural Powys, by far Wales' biggest county. Named after an ancient Welsh kingdom, this modern entity was formed in 1974 from the historic counties of Montgomeryshire, Radnorshire and Brecknockshire. It's an overwhelmingly rural place, ideal for walking and cycling, but this county isn't just green in a literal sense – Machynlleth has become a focal point for the nation's environmentally friendly aspirations, and all over the county efforts to restore the threatened red kite have been met with outstanding success. The bird is now the very symbol of Powys, the county at Wales' green heart.

Llanwrtyd Wells (Llanwrtyd)

POP 630

Llanwrtyd (khlan-*oor*-tid) Wells is an odd little town – mostly deserted except during one of its unconventional festivals, when it's packed to the rafters with crazy contestants and their merrymaking supporters.

Apart from this recent status as the capital of wacky Wales, Llanwrtyd Wells has long been surrounded by beautiful walking, cycling and riding country, with the Cambrian Mountains to the northwest and the Mynydd Epynt to the southeast.

Theophilus Evans, the local vicar, first discovered the healing properties of the Ffynon Drocllwyd (Stinking Well) in 1732 when he found it cured his scurvy. The popularity of the waters grew and Llanwrtyd became a spa town. Nowadays, however, its wells have been capped and, outside of the festivals, it's hard to find much by way of vital signs.

Festivals & Events

While mulling over how to encourage tourism in Llanwrtyd in the dark winter months, some citizens started an inspired roll call of unconventionality. There's something on every month (see www.green-events.co.uk).

Saturnalia Real Ale Ramble & Chariot Racing Championship SPORTS
(www.green-events.co.uk; ramble/chariot race £11/20; ⏰Jan) Roman-themed festival in mid-January including a 'best dressed Roman' competition, the devouring of stuffed bulls' testicles, rambling the course of old Roman roads and a race between bike-drawn chariots. And plenty of ale, of course.

Man vs Horse Marathon SPORTS
(www.green-events.co.uk; ⏰mid-Jun) The event that kicked off all the craziness in Llanwrtyd Wells, the Man vs Horse Marathon has been held every year since 1980 and has resulted in some tense finishes. Two-legged runners have won only twice, most recently in 2007. Held mid-June, the prize money jackpots each year a biped fails to win.

World Bog Snorkelling Championships SPORTS
(www.green-events.co.uk; Llanwrtyd Wells; adult/child £15/12; ⏰bank holiday Aug) The most famous of all Llanwrtyd's wacky events. Competitors are allowed wetsuits, snorkels and flippers to traverse a trench cut out of a peat

bog, using no recognisable swimming stroke and surfacing only to navigate. Spin-off events include Mountain Bike Bog Snorkelling ('like trying to ride through treacle') and the Bog Snorkelling Triathlon, both in July.

Real Ale Wobble & Ramble SPORTS
(www.green-events.co.uk; 1-/2-day ride £18/25; Nov) In conjunction with the Mid-Wales Beer Festival, every November cyclists and walkers follow waymarked routes (10, 15 or 25 miles for ramblers; 15 or 28 miles for the wobblers), supping real ales at the 'pint stops' along the way.

Mari Llwyd NEW YEAR
(New Year Walk In; www.green-events.co.uk; New Year's Eve) A revival of the ancient practice of parading a horse's skull from house to house on New Year's Eve while reciting Welsh poetry. The procession leaves from the centre of Llanwrtyd Wells at 10.30pm.

Sleeping & Eating

Plasnewydd B&B B&B $
(01591-610293; www.plasnewydd90.co.uk; Irfon Tce; s/d £35/60; P) Located in the heart of town, this spick-and-span B&B has won numerous fans thanks to its warm, cosy, individually styled rooms, an extensive breakfast spread (including Glamorgan – leek and cheese – sausages for vegetarians) and the accommodating attitude of its owners. Wet biker gear is given a place to dry, and nice touches include delicious homemade cakes.

Lasswade Country House B&B $$
(01591-610515; www.lasswadehotel.co.uk; Station Rd; s/d from £65/90; P) This excellent restaurant-with-rooms makes great use of a handsome, three-storey Edwardian house looking over the Irfon Valley towards the Brecon Beacons. Committed to green tourism (it's won a slew of awards, sources hydroelectric power and even offers electric vehicle recharging), it's also big on gastronomy: the chef/owner's three-course menu (£35) features Cambrian lamb, venison, Towy salmon and other delights.

Ardwyn House B&B $$
(01591-610768; www.ardwynhouse.co.uk; Station Rd; s/d £60/80; P) The young owners have been busy restoring the Arts-and-Crafts grandeur of this once derelict house. Some rooms have claw-foot baths and rural views, and there is period wallpaper and furnishings. There's also an oak-panelled guest lounge with a pool table and bar.

★**Carlton Riverside** WELSH $$
(01591-610248; www.carltonriverside.com; Irfon Cres; mains £15-21; 7-10.30pm Tue-Sat; P) This upscale restaurant has a boutique feel and a mantelpiece groaning under its many awards. There's a basement bar (open Tuesday to Sunday evenings) but the real star here is the restaurant and its superb menu featuring plenty of local produce. Lunch can be organised with at least a day's notice, from Tuesday to Saturday.

Drovers Rest WELSH $$
(01591-610264; www.food-food-food.co.uk; Y Sgwar; 3 courses £30; 10.30am-3.30pm & 7-9.30pm Tue & Thu-Sat, 12.30-2.30pm Sun;) Increasingly recognised as one of Mid-Wales' best dining venues, this charming restaurant does fantastic things with local produce. Snugly perched by the Irfon, it has a new riverside terrace and a few simple-but-cosy rooms (single/double £40/80, some en suite). The owners also run regular one-day cooking courses (£165 to £195) featuring Welsh cuisine, game and other delights.

Drinking & Nightlife

★**Neuadd Arms Hotel** PUB
(01591-610236; www.neuaddarmshotel.co.uk; Y Sgwar; 8.30am-midnight Sun-Thu, 8.30am-1am Fri & Sat) Like any good village pub, the Neuadd Arms is a focal point for the community. There's an interesting menu (mains £7 to £11), half- and full-board rooms (single/double £58/106 and £65/130) and excellent beers brewed in the stables out back. It's also Llanwrtyd's tourist information point, with everything you'll need to know about mountain biking, pony trekking or hiking in the area.

Getting There & Away

Bus 48 heads to Builth Wells (30 minutes).

Llanwrtyd is on the Heart of Wales Line (www.heart-of-wales.co.uk), with direct services to Swansea (£11.10, two hours), Llandeilo (£5.20, 45 minutes), Llandrindod Wells (£4.20, 31 minutes) and Shrewsbury (£13.90, 2¼ hours).

Builth Wells (Llanfair-Ym-Muallt)

POP 2829

Builth (pronounced 'bilth') Wells is by far the liveliest of the former spa towns, with a bustling, workaday feel. Once the playground of the Welsh working classes, it has a pretty location on the River Wye and prominence as a local farming centre. While there are no attractions per se, it's a handy base for walkers or cyclists tackling any of the long-distance paths that pass through.

Festivals & Events

Royal Welsh Show FAIR
(www.rwas.co.uk; Llanelwedd; adult/child per day £26/5; Jul;) Over 200,000 people descend on Builth for four days every July for the Royal Welsh Show (founded in Aberystwyth in 1904) to see everything from gussied-up livestock to lumberjack competitions and a food hall bursting with farm produce. The showgrounds – actually just over the Wye in Llanelwedd – host numerous other events throughout the year, from antiques fairs and garden shows to equestrian events.

Sleeping & Eating

Bronwye B&B $
(01982-553587; www.bronwye.co.uk; Church St; s/d from £40/60; P) Overlooking the River Wye, this imposing 19th-century house has five comfortable, modern rooms with good beds and bathrooms. It's cosily modern, rather than rich with period character, but there's a warm welcome and excellent breakfasts, which, at these rates, make it a bargain.

Caer Beris Manor HOTEL $$$
(01982-552601; www.caerberis.com; A483; s/d from £74/143) Once home to Lord Swansea, this half-timbered country manor lies at the end of a long driveway, winding through 11 hectares of parkland on the River Irfon. Classic styling, log fires and spacious rooms with swag curtains, heavy fabrics and tassled lamps await. The oak-panelled Restaurant 1896 serves a fine seasonal menu featuring plenty of local produce (mains £19 to £25).

The hotel is on the west side of Builth Wells, on the A483.

★ **Drawing Room** MODERN WELSH $$$
(01982-552493; www.the-drawing-room.co.uk; 3 courses £40; from 7pm, last orders 8.30pm;) Set in a Georgian country house, this two-rosette restaurant-with-rooms is one of the region's finest. Prime Welsh black beef, Brecon Mountain lamb and Cardigan Bay crab feature on the locally sourced menu, while the beautifully refurbished rooms are well worth considering (£125 to £150, including breakfast). It's 3 miles north of Builth, on the A470.

Information

Builth Wells Library (20 High St; 10am-1pm & 2-5pm Mon & Tue, 10am-1pm & 2-6pm Thu, 10am-1pm Fri, 10am-12.30pm Sat) There's no tourist office in Builth any more, but the library acts as a local information point.

Getting There & Away

Buses stopping here include the T4 to Llandrindod Wells (20 minutes), Brecon (45 minutes) and Newtown (70 minutes); the X16 and X17 to Rhayader (25 to 40 minutes, one daily schooldays and Saturdays); and the 48 to Llanwrtyd Wells (30 minutes, Monday to Saturday).

Rhayader (Rhaeadr Gwy)

POP 1824

Rhayader is a handsome, small and fairly uneventful livestock-market town revolving around a central crossroads marked by a war-memorial clock. It's a place that appeals to walkers visiting the nearby Elan Valley and tackling the 136-mile Wye Valley Walk. Distinguished by several extremely venerable timber buildings, it's largely deserted on Thursdays (when businesses trade for only half a day) but fills out on Wednesday – market day.

Sights & Activities

Rhayader Museum & Gallery MUSEUM
(01597-810561; www.carad.org.uk; East St; adult/child £4/free; 10am-4pm Tue-Sat) Focusing on local history and life in and around Rhayader, this small museum uses artefacts, film and more than 50 oral histories to explore everything from folk tales to sheep farming. The attached shop sells local craft, toys and books, and has plenty of information for visitors to the area, while the theatre houses dance, drama and music.

Gigrin Farm Red-Kite Feeding Station BIRDWATCHING
(01597-810243; www.gigrin.co.uk; South St (A470); adult/child £5/3; 12.30-5pm daily Jan-Oct, to 4pm Sat & Sun Nov & Dec) There's been a dramatic Mid-Wales resurgence in the UK's threatened population of red kites, and hundreds arrive at Gigrin Farm every day at 2pm (3pm during British Summer Time) to gorge on meat scraps. First come crows, then ravens, then the super-agile kites – often mugging the crows to get the meat – and lastly the buzzards.

Clive Powell Mountain Bike Centre
MOUNTAIN BIKING

(☎01597-811343; www.clivepowell-mtb.co.uk; West St; ⏰9am-1pm & 2-5.30pm) This centre is run by a former cycling champion and coach. You can hire a mountain/off-road bike here (£24/16 per day, including helmet and puncture kit), or take it easier with an electric bike (£30 per day).

Sleeping

Wyeside Caravan & Camping Park
CAMPGROUND $

(☎01597-810183; www.wyesidecamping.co.uk; Llangurig Rd; site/adult/child £3/8/3.50; ⏰Feb-Nov) A short walk from the centre of Rhayader, this relaxed, grassy campsite has river views, lots of trees, two shower blocks and a shop.

Horseshoe Guesthouse
B&B $$

(☎01597-810982; www.rhayader-horseshoe.co.uk; Church St; s/d £44/68; P 📶) This 18th-century former inn, once the Butcher's Arms, now offers comfortable modern rooms (five of seven are en suite) and plenty of communal space in the large dining room, garden, conservatory and walled courtyard. There's also a 20-seater restaurant (three courses for £16) and packed lunches for £6 per person.

Eating & Drinking

Old Swan Tearooms
CAFE $

(☎01597-811060; www.oldswantearooms.co.uk; West St; mains £5-6; ⏰10am-5pm) Using every cranny of a low-ceilinged, half-timbered, crooked-chimneyed 17th-century former inn in the dead centre of Rhayader, the Old Swan is great for breakfast, afternoon tea or something more substantial.

Triangle Inn
PUB

(☎01597-810537; www.triangleinn.co.uk; Cwmdauddwr; mains £8-12; ⏰6.30-11pm daily year-round, noon-3pm Tue-Sat May-Aug, noon-3pm Thu-Sat Sep-Apr; 📶) This tiny 16th-century inn, just over the bridge to Cwmdauddwr (the village adjoining Rhayader), is the pick of the local places to drink. It's so small that its toilets are across the road and there's a trapdoor in the floor for darts players (so they don't bang their heads on the extremely low ceiling). A very welcoming place, it serves real ales and hearty pub classics.

Getting There & Away

Bus X16 goes to Builth Wells (25 to 40 minutes, one daily schooldays and Saturdays) and the X47 to Llandrindod Wells (25 minutes).

Elan Valley

The Elan Valley is filled with strikingly beautiful countryside, split by imposing Victorian and Edwardian feats of civil engineering. In the late 19th century, dams were built on the River Elan (pronounced 'ellen'), west of Rhayader, mainly to provide a reliable water supply for Birmingham. Around 100 people had to move, but only landowners received compensation. During WWII, the earliest of the dams was used to perfect the 'bouncing bomb' used in the storied Dambusters raid on targets in Germany's Ruhr Valley. In 1952 a fourth, large dam was inaugurated on the tributary River Claerwen. Together their reservoirs now provide over 70 million gallons of water daily for Birmingham and parts of South and Mid-Wales.

The need to protect the 70-sq-mile watershed (called the Elan Valley Estate) has turned it and adjacent areas into an important wildlife conservation area. The dams and associated projects also produce some 4.2 megawatts of hydroelectric power.

Unless you have your own transport, the only way into the Elan Valley is a taxi from Rhayader.

Sleeping & Eating

Elan Valley Hotel
HOTEL $$

(☎01597-810448; www.elanvalleyhotel.co.uk; B4518; s/d £57/75; P 📶) This pleasant little hotel, with 11 bedrooms and a decent restaurant (mains £13 to £15) makes a good base for walking, cycling and birdwatching in the valley. It's on the B4518, 2.5 miles southwest of Rhayader.

Penbont House
TEAHOUSE

(☎01597-811515; ⏰11am-5pm Fri-Mon Mar-Jul, Sep & Oct, daily Aug; 👪) Delightfully situated on a verdant hillside below the Pen y Garreg dam, these traditional Welsh tearooms are definitely worth a stop when driving in the Elan Valley. *Bara brith* (a rich, fruit tea-loaf), Welsh cakes, properly brewed tea and light lunches can be taken on the lawn, or in the charming house itself.

The B&B accommodation (£70 for a quad or double) is outstanding value.

Information

Elan Valley Visitor Centre (☎01597-810880; www.elanvalley.org.uk; B4518; ⏰10am-5pm Easter-Oct) The visitor centre houses a new exhibit on the Water Scheme (complete with photos of houses being inundated), native wildlife and local history. It also provides leaflets on the estate's 80 miles of nature trails and footpaths, rents bicycles (£6/24 per hour/day) and offers activities such as birdwatching safaris and helicopter tours over the lakes and moorland.

The centre is just downstream of the lowest dam, 3 miles from Rhayader on the B4518. Parking is £2.

Montgomery

POP 986

Set around a market square lined with handsome stone and brick houses, and overlooked by the ruins of a Norman **castle** FREE, genteel Montgomery is one of the prettiest small towns in the country. A charming mixture of Georgian, Victorian and timber-framed houses (many marked by helpful historical plaques) lines the streets and there are a number of excellent places to eat.

A curiosity, for travellers, is **Bunners** (01686-668308; www.bunners.co.uk; Arthur St; 9am-5pm Mon-Sat), an old-fashioned ironmongers that seems to sell everything under the sun and which attracts customers from miles away. A mile east of town is one of the best-preserved sections of Offa's Dyke, with 6m-high ditches flanking the B4386.

Sights

St Nicholas' Church CHURCH
(Church Bank; 9am-dusk) Evocative Norman St Nicholas' Church dates from 1226 and boasts a vaulted ceiling decorated with intricate coloured bosses, a beautifully carved pre-Reformation rood screen and striking mid-19th-century stained-glass windows. Look out for the elaborate canopied tomb of local landowner Sir Richard Herbert and his wife Magdalen, parents of Elizabethan poet George Herbert.

Cloverlands Model Car Museum MUSEUM
(www.montgomeryinstitute.co.uk; Montgomery Institute, Arthur St; adult/child £2.50/75p; 2.15-5pm Fri & Sun, 10.30am-12.45pm Sat) With over 3000 exhibits, Cloverlands is a must for model-car lovers. Around half the cars are on loan from one collector, Gillian Rogers, including quarter-scale, working models of a Fiat 1936 Topolino and a 1935 Singer Le Mans, built especially for the collector and her sister. Appointments can be made for out-of-hours openings.

OFF THE BEATEN TRACK

CAMBRIAN MOUNTAINS

The Cambrian Mountains are a rather desolate but starkly beautiful area of uplands covering the region roughly between Snowdonia and the Brecon Beacons. Largely unpopulated and undeveloped, this wild, empty plateau of high moorland is the source of both the Rivers Severn and Wye. Hidden in the folds of the hills are lakes, waterfalls and deserted valleys as well as hill farms home to thousands of sheep. The region sees relatively few visitors except for around the Elan Valley; if you wish to get away from it all there is no finer place in Wales in which to hike or bike in solitude. Many tracks criss-cross the area, including the 83-mile Cambrian Way; you can find details of routes at www.walkingbritain.co.uk or more information about the region at www.cambrian-mountains.co.uk.

Sleeping & Eating

Dragon Hotel INN $$
(01686-668359; www.dragonhotel.com; Market Sq; s/d from £56/79;) Popular with walkers, this 17th-century half-timbered coaching inn has 20 en-suite rooms, a common snug (the Den), a pool and a restaurant run by Bistro 7, formerly of Welshpool (mains £13 to £18). The bar is as good a place as any to try ales brewed at Monty's, just down the road.

Castle Kitchen CAFE $
(01686-668795; www.castlekitchen.org; 8 Broad St; mains £4-8; 9am-4.30pm Mon-Sat, 11am-4.30pm Sun) This lovely little deli-cafe overlooking Monty's picturesque heart is perfect for stocking up on bottles, butter, charcuterie and other supplies for a picnic on Offa's Dyke or in the surrounding hills. Or you can just relax in-house, enjoying a wonderful selection of soups, breads, sandwiches, daily specials and, of course, luscious cakes.

★**Checkers** MODERN BRITISH $$$
(01686-669822; www.thecheckersmontgomery.co.uk; Broad St; 5/8 courses £55/75; dinner Tue-Sat;) It's no exaggeration to say that one of the main drawcards of Montgomery is this truly excellent restaurant-with-rooms. The modern French menu, put together from fresh, locally sourced ingredients, and

first-rate service have earned it a Michelin star and a loyal fan base. Upstairs, the five contemporary rooms are stylish, with extra-comfy beds, iPod docks and blissful bathrooms. Bed and dinner packages are available from £245.

Information

Library (☎01686-668937; Montgomery Institute, Arthur St; ⏰10am-noon & 3-5pm Mon, Wed & Fri, 10am-5pm Tue & Thu, 9.30am-noon Sat) Has a tourist information point.

Getting There & Away

Bus X71 runs to Welshpool (18 minutes) and Newtown (21 minutes).

Welshpool (Y Trallwng)

POP 5948

The English originally called this place Pool, after the 'pills' – boggy, marshy ground (long since drained) along the nearby River Severn. It was changed in 1835 to Welshpool, so nobody would get confused with Poole in Dorset. Set below a steeply wooded hill, it's a handsome market town with a mixture of Tudor, Georgian and Victorian buildings along its main streets but few other distractions in the town centre and a dearth of places to stay or eat. More compelling are the peripheral sights such as glorious Powis Castle and the narrow-gauge Welshpool & Llanfair Light Railway.

Sights & Activities

★Powis Castle CASTLE

(NT; ☎01938-551944; www.nationaltrust.org.uk; adult/child castle & gardens £12/6, gardens only £9.90/4.95; ⏰gardens 10am-6pm, castle 11-5pm) Surrounded by magnificent gardens, the redbrick Powis Castle was originally constructed in the 13th century by Gruffydd ap Gwenwynwyn, prince of Powys, and subsequently enriched by generations of the Herbert and Clive families. The castle's highlight, the **Clive Museum**, houses exquisite treasures brought back from India and the Far East by Clive of India (British conqueror of Bengal at the Battle of Plassey in 1757) and his son Edward, who married the daughter of the 1st Earl of Powys.

Powysland Museum & Montgomery Canal MUSEUM

(☎01938-554656; www.powys.gov.uk; Canal Wharf; adult/child £1/free; ⏰11am-1pm & 2-5pm Mon-Fri, 11am-1pm Sat, closed Wed Sep-May) The Montgomery Canal originally ran for 35 miles, starting at Newtown and ending at Frankton Junction in Shropshire, where it joined the Llangollen Canal. Beside the canal wharf in Welshpool is the Powysland Museum, marked outside by a big blue handbag (an Andy Hancock sculpture to commemorate the Queen's jubilee). Inside, the museum tells the story of the county, with fascinating details such as beautifully painted narrow-boat gear and the Roman recipe for stuffed dormouse.

Welshpool & Llanfair Light Railway TOURS

(☎01938-810441; www.wllr.org.uk; Raven Sq; adult/child £12.80/4; ⏰Mar-Oct, check times online) This sturdy narrow-gauge railway, completed in 1902 to bring livestock to market, runs through the pretty Banwy Valley. It's an 8-mile, 50-minute journey up steep inclines from Raven Square Station to Llanfair Caereinion. Closed in 1956, the line was reopened seven years later by enthusiastic volunteers and now even offers courses in steam-engine driving (£395).

Festivals & Events

Welshpool Country Music Festival MUSIC

(www.countrywestern.org.uk; weekend ticket £25; ⏰Jul) In mid-July, the county showground near Powis Castle becomes the unlikely venue for a weekend hoedown. Proceeds benefit children with disabilities, through the Heulwen Trust. There's free camping and caravanning sites, food stalls, beer tents and lots of knee-slapping.

Sleeping & Eating

Royal Oak HISTORIC HOTEL $$

(☎01938-552217; www.royaloakwelshpool.co.uk; The Cross; s/d £80/100; P 📶) Occupying a lovely Georgian coaching inn and known by the honorific 'Royal' ever since Queen Victoria visited, the Oak is easily the grandest hotel-restaurant in Welshpool. Adorned in bright patterns, the rooms are comfortably modern, while the public bar and restaurant serve the town both for casual trysts and destination dining (mains around £15).

Long Mountain B&B $$

(☎01938-553456; www.longmountainbandb.co.uk; Hope Rd, Little Hope; s/d £64/86; P 📶) A purpose-built B&B located 2 miles from Welshpool, Long Mountain is a modern extension to a 400-year-old timber-frame house. The three guest rooms have top-quality fittings with solid oak furniture, king-sized beds with Egyptian cotton bed linen and marble bathrooms. Offa's Dyke Path runs almost past the guesthouse and there are wonderful views. No children under 16.

Corn Store INTERNATIONAL **$$**
(☎01938-554614; 4 Church St; mains £12-16, 2-course menu £15; ⏰noon-3pm & 6-11pm Tue-Sun) If Welshpool has a dining institution, this is it. Run by chef-proprietor Rebecca for over 25 years, its avocado walls and cheery, round, rainbow mirrors overlook families of regulars tucking into Euro-Med-Asian dishes such as hake with leeks and rarebit or goat's-cheese tart with roasted red pepper and pesto. The best and friendliest place in town.

Information

Tourist Office (☎01938-552043; www.welshpool.org/tic.html; 1 Vicarage Gardens, Church St; ⏰9.30am-5pm Mon-Sat, 10am-4pm Sun) Has a bed-booking service and plenty of information on sights, activities and the rest in Welshpool.

Victoria Memorial Hospital (☎01938-558900; Salop Rd) Has a 24/7 Minor Injuries Department.

Getting There & Away

Bus X75 runs to Newtown (40 minutes) and Shrewsbury (48 minutes).

The daily National Express (www.nationalexpress.com) coach through Welshpool runs from Aberystwyth (£12, 1¾ hours) to London (£31.50, 5½ hours), via Shrewsbury (£4.80, 35 minutes) and Birmingham (£9.90, 2¼ hours).

Welshpool is on the Cambrian Line, which heads east from Aberystwyth (£15, 1½ hours) to Birmingham (£17.70, 1½ hours) and Shrewsbury (£6.10, 22 minutes) every hour or two and, in the other direction, Machynlleth (£12.70, 52 minutes) and Newtown (£5.20, 15 minutes).

Machynlleth

POP 2235

Little Machynlleth (ma-*hun*-khleth) punches well above its weight. Saturated in historical significance, it was here that nationalist hero Owain Glyndŵr established the country's first parliament in 1404. But even that legacy is close to being trumped by Machynlleth's reinvention as the green capital of Wales – thanks primarily to the Centre for Alternative Technology (CAT), 3 miles north of town.

OFF THE BEATEN TRACK

GLYNDŴR'S WAY

Named for the last native Prince of Wales, **Glyndŵr's Way** (http://nationaltrail.co.uk/glyndwrs-way) meanders some 135 miles from Welshpool, near the English border, to Machynlleth on the southern cusp of Snowdonia National Park. It then returns cross-country to Knighton, just below the dreamy Shropshire Hills.

The centre has given Machynlleth an eco-magneticism that attracts alternative lifestylers from far and wide. If you want to get your runes read, take up yoga or explore holistic dancing, Machynlleth is the ideal place for you. Unfortunately, it hasn't been enough to protect the town from failing fortunes, with some much-loved shops and cafes succumbing to economic pressures in recent years. Still a surprisingly cosmopolitan local town, Machynlleth is surrounded by serene countryside, particularly suited to mountain biking.

Sights

★Centre for Alternative Technology LANDMARK
(CAT; Canolfan y Dechnoleg Amgen; ☎01654-705950; www.cat.org.uk; Pantperthog; adult/child £8.50/4; ⏰10am-5pm; P 👪) 🌿 A small but dedicated band of enthusiasts have spent 40 years practising sustainability at the thought-provoking CAT, set in a beautiful wooded valley 3 miles north of Machynlleth. Founded in 1974 (well ahead of its time), CAT is an education and visitor centre that demonstrates practical solutions for sustainability. There are 3 hectares of displays dealing with topics such as composting, organic gardening, environmentally friendly construction, renewable energy sources and sewage treatment and recycling.

★MOMA Machynlleth GALLERY
(☎01654-703355; www.moma.machynlleth.org.uk; Penrallt St; ⏰10am-4pm Mon-Sat) FREE Housed partly in the **Tabernacle**, a neoclassical former Wesleyan chapel (1880), the Museum of Modern Art exhibits work by contemporary Welsh artists as well as an annual international competition (mid-July to late August). The small permanent collection is supplemented by a continuous roster of temporary exhibitions. The chapel itself has the feel of

a courtroom, but the acoustics are superb – it's used for concerts, theatre and talks.

Owain Glyndŵr Centre MUSEUM
(Canolfan Owain Glyndŵr; 01654-702932; www.canolfanglyndwr.org; Maengwyn St; 10am-4pm Easter-Sep) FREE Housed in a rare example of a late-medieval Welsh townhouse, the Owain Glyndŵr Centre houses a new exhibition telling the rip-roaring story of the Welsh hero's fight for independence. Although it's called the Old Parliament Building, it was probably built around 1460, some 50 years after Glyndŵr instituted his parliament on this site, but it's believed to closely resemble the former venue.

Activities

The rolling wooded hills that surround Machynlleth shelter some of the best mountain biking in the country, with numerous tracks and bridleways criss-crossing the hills and four excellent trails to follow. See Dyfi Mountain Biking for information and maps.

There's also Sustrans National Cycle Network Route 8, leading off the A487 just north of the train station, following a countryside path, crossing the Millennium Bridge and leading you towards the Centre for Alternative Technology by the greenest possible form of transport.

Dyfi Mountain Biking MOUNTAIN BIKING
(www.dyfimountainbiking.org.uk) This local collective has waymarked four mountain-bike routes from Machynlleth: the Mach 1, 2, 3 and 4, each longer and more challenging than the last. In the Dyfi Forest, near Corris, is the custom-built, 9-mile, ClimachX loop trail. In May the same crew runs the **Dyfi Enduro**, a 37-mile mountain-bike challenge attracting over 1000 riders.

Sleeping

★**Beudy Banc** CAMPGROUND $
(01650-511495; www.beudybanc.co.uk; Abercegir; sites/d from £20/75) Set on a working sheep farm nestled in the folds of the Dyfi Valley, this wonderful place offers back-to-basics camping in grassy meadows with glorious views. There are hot showers and composting toilets, campfires are allowed and, with a limited number of pitches, it never feels too crowded.

★**Glandyfi Castle** BOUTIQUE HOTEL $$
(01654-781238; www.glandyficastle.co.uk; A487, Glandyfi; r £90-250; P) Built in 1820 as a fashionable statement of wealth, this quirky Regency Gothic castle has been brought back to life as a gloriously indulgent hotel. The eight excellent-value rooms blend classical styling with modern sensibilities, while the turrets, towers, octagonal rooms and superb views over the vast grounds make it feel like an incredibly special place to stay.

Sunny View B&B $$
(01654-700387; www.sunnyviewbandb.weebly.com; Forge; s/d £50/70) Set in a quiet village 1 mile from Machynlleth, this bungalow has two immaculate en-suite rooms decorated in an unfussy modern style. The breakfasts are good, there's a very warm welcome and it's a great option for cyclists as the trails of Dyfi Mountain Biking pass through the village.

Wynnstay Wales HOTEL $$
(01654-702941; www.wynnstay.wales; Maengwyn St; s/d from £59/90; P) This erstwhile Georgian coaching inn (1780) remains the best all-rounder in town, with 22 charming older-style rooms, one with a four-poster bed, and creaky, uneven floors. Downstairs there's a good restaurant and, in the courtyard, a wood-fired pizzeria (pizzas £8).

★**Living Room Treehouses** CABIN $$$
(01172-047830; www.living-room.co; 3-day, 2-night double/family £349/379; P) Wonderfully designed, these six, cosy, rustic-glam tree houses blend organically into an enchanted forest off the A470. You're as close to nature as can be (up a tree!), yet the beds are luxurious, insulation and wood-burning stoves keep you warm all year and the seclusion is glorious. Arrival days are Sundays, Wednesdays and Fridays.

Eating

Market MARKET $
(www.machynllethmarket.co.uk; Maengwyn St; Wed) Chartered by Edward I himself, in 1291, the Wednesday street market has been going ever since and remains a lively affair.

Number Twenty One WELSH $$
(01654-703382; www.numbertwentyone.co.uk; 21 Maengwyn St; mains £13-17; noon-10pm Wed-Sun;) Run by a passionate young foodie couple with ambitions that exceed the usual small-town bistro, Number Twenty One has been popular since the day it opened. The food is imaginative without being fussy, the service is friendly but professional, children

are welcome and nothing seems too much trouble. Space is limited so book ahead.

★Ynyshir Hall GASTRONOMY **$$$**
(☎01654-781209; www.ynyshirhall.co.uk; Eglwysfach; 5-course lunch/dinner menu £39.50/55, tasting menus £89/120; ⏲noon-2pm & 7-9pm) Foraged wild foods, the best local meat and seafood and its own kitchen garden produce give the kitchen at Ynyshir Hall the foundations to concoct some of Wales' most fancied fare. A Michelin starred restaurant within a luxurious country retreat that once belonged to Queen Victoria, it offers set menus studded with delights such as scampi with black garlic and rhubarb.

Ynyshir Hall is off the A487, 6 miles southwest of Machynlleth.

ℹ Getting There & Away

If you're on a bike, Lôn Las Cymru (Sustrans National Cycling Network Route 8) passes through Machynlleth, heading north to Corris and southeast to Rhayader.

Bus routes include X28 to Aberystwyth (45 minutes); T2 to Dolgellau (30 minutes), Porthmadog (90 minutes), Caernarfon (2¼ hours) and Bangor (2¾ hours); X85 to Newtown (55 minutes); and 34 to the Centre for Alternative Technology (p713; seven minutes) and Corris (15 minutes).

The bus stops for Newtown (Maengwyn St) and other destinations (Pentrerhedyn St) are either side of the market cross in the centre of town.

By train, Machynlleth is on the Cambrian and Cambrian Coast Lines. Destinations include Aberystwyth (£6.50, 35 minutes), Porthmadog (£13.20, 1¾ hours), Pwllheli (£15.30, 2½ hours), Newtown (£9.10, 38 minutes) and Birmingham (£20.90, 2¼ hours).

CEREDIGION

Bordered by Cardigan Bay on one side and the Cambrian Mountains on the other, Ceredigion (pronounced with a 'dig' not a 'didge') is an ancient Welsh kingdom founded by the 5th-century chieftain Ceredig. The rural communities here escaped the population influxes of the south's coal-mining valleys and the north's slate-mining towns, and, consequently, the Welsh language is stronger here than in any other part of the country except Gwynedd and Anglesea.

The lack of heavy industry also left Ceredigion with some of Britain's cleanest beaches and, with no train access south of Aberystwyth, they tend to be less crowded. Adding to the isolation is the natural barrier known as the 'Green Desert of Wales' (the barren uplands of the Cambrian Mountains). Despite recent interest fuelled by the locally made bilingual detective series *Hinterland/Y Gwyll*, Ceredigion's sandy coves, sea cliffs, river valleys and arid mountains are as off-the-beaten-track as Wales gets.

Aberystwyth

POP 13,040

Sweeping around the curving shore of Cardigan Bay, the lively university town of Aberystwyth (aber-*ist*-with) has a stunning location but a bit of an identity crisis. Student bars and cheap restaurants line the streets, the flashing lights of traditional amusements twinkle from the pier, and tucked away in the side streets are a handful of chichi boutiques and organic, wholefood cafes. During term time the bars are buzzing and students play football on the promenade, while in summer the bucket-and-spade brigade invades and enjoys the beach. Meanwhile the trappings of this once-stately seaside resort remain in the terrace of grand Georgian houses painted in subtle pastel hues that line the promenade.

Welsh is widely spoken here and locals are proud of their heritage. Catching a show at the Arts Centre (p718), hearing the **male voice choir** (☎01970-623800; www.aberchoir.co.uk; Plascrug Ave; ⏲7-8.30pm Thu) perform or simply soaking up the sunset over Cardigan Bay are quintessential local experiences.

History

Aberystwyth's now mainly ruined castle (p716) was erected in 1277; like many other castles in Wales it was captured by Owain Glyndŵr at the start of the 15th century and slighted by Oliver Cromwell in the 17th. By the beginning of the 19th century, the town's walls and gates had completely disappeared and much of the stone was repurposed by locals.

The town developed a fishing industry, and silver and lead mining were also important here. With the arrival of the railway in 1864, the town reinvented itself as a fashionable seaside destination. In 1872 Aberystwyth was chosen as the site of the first college of the University of Wales (Aberystwyth University now has over 9000 students) and in 1907 it became home to the National Library of Wales (p716).

Sights

Marine Tce, with its impressive sweep of imposing pastel-hued houses overlooking North Beach, harks back to the town's halcyon days as a fashionable resort. When you reach the bottom of the 1.5-mile prom, it's customary to kick the white bar, although the locals can't seem to explain the rationale behind this ritual.

North Beach is lined by somewhat shabby Georgian hotels, albeit with a couple of notable exceptions. **Royal Pier** (www.royalpier.co.uk; Marine Tce; ⏲10am-9pm), the grand **Old College** (King St) and the enigmatic, sparse ruins of **Aberystwyth Castle** FREE are the major sights here.

The prom pivots before leading along **South Beach** – a more desolate but still attractive seafront. Many locals prefer the stony but emptier **Tanybwlch Beach**, just south of the harbour where the Rivers Rheidol and Ystwyth meet. Pen Dinas, the upland rising behind Tanybwlch, is the site of the important Iron Age hill fort **Dinas Maelor**. While the outline of the fort is still visible, the peak is now dominated by a monument to Wellington.

Ceredigion Museum MUSEUM
(☎01970-633088; www.ceredigion.gov.uk; Terrace Rd; ⏲10.30am-4pm Tue-Sat, noon-4pm Sun Apr-Sep) FREE This museum is in the Coliseum, which opened in 1905 as a theatre, then served as a cinema promising 'amusement without vulgarity' from 1932 onwards. The elegant interior retains its stage, around which are entertaining exhibitions on Aberystwyth's history – everything from old chemist furnishings and hand-knitted woollen knickers to a mini puppet theatre and re-creation of an 1850s cottage.

National Library of Wales LIBRARY
(☎01970-632800; www.llgc.org.uk; A487; ⏲9.30am-6pm Mon-Fri, to 5pm Sat) FREE Sitting proudly on a hilltop half a mile east of town, the National Library is a cultural powerhouse. Founded in 1911, it holds millions of books in many languages – as a copyright library it has copies of every book published in the UK. The **Hengwrt Room** holds gems such as the 12th-century Black Book of Carmarthen (the oldest existing Welsh text), a text of Chaucer penned by his scribe Adam Pinkhurst and a first edition of Milton's *Paradise Lost*.

Other galleries display an ever-stimulating set of changing exhibitions. The entrance to the library is off Penglais Rd (the A487); take a right just past the hospital.

Activities

Vale of Rheidol Railway RAIL
(Rheilffordd Cwm Rheidol; ☎01970-625819; www.rheidolrailway.co.uk; Park Ave; adult/child return £20/8; ⏲up to 5 daily late Mar-Oct, Sat & Sun Nov, closed late Dec–mid-Feb) This scenic narrow-gauge railway is one of Aberystwyth's most popular attractions. Steam locomotives built between 1923 and 1938 have been lovingly restored by volunteers and chug for almost 12 miles up the beautiful wooded valley of the River Rheidol to Devil's Bridge. The line opened in 1902 to bring lead and timber out of the valley.

Rheidol Cycle Trail CYCLING
Sticking mainly to designated cycle paths and quiet country lanes, the 17-mile Rheidol Cycle Trail heads from Aberystwyth Harbour to Devil's Bridge through the beautiful Rheidol Valley. Along the way it passes the Woodland Trust's Coed Geufron, and side routes lead to Bwlch Nant yr Arian (p718), Rheidol Power Station and Rheidol Mines. The last section is very steep.

Ystwyth Trail CYCLING
Suitable for cyclists and walkers, this 21-mile waymarked route mainly follows an old rail line from Aberystwyth southeast to Tregaron, shadowing the River Ystwyth for the first 12 miles and ending in the Teifi Valley. Pick up the trail from the footbridge on Riverside Tce in Aberystwyth or start from Tregaron if you prefer heading downhill.

Sleeping

Maes-y-Môr GUESTHOUSE $
(☎01970-639270; www.maesymor.co.uk; 25 Bath St; s/d £35/55; P 📶) Yes, that is a laundrette. But don't be fooled: venture upstairs from the drying machine and you will find nine clean, bright rooms and a warm welcome. Breakfast is not included but there's a kitchen for guest use and a locked shed for bicycles.

★**Gwesty Cymru** HOTEL $$
(☎01970-612252; www.gwestycymru.com; 19 Marine Tce; s/d from £70/95; ⏲restaurant noon-2.30pm & 6-9pm Tue-Sun; 📶) A real gem, the 'Wales Hotel' is a charismatic boutique property right on the waterfront with a strong sense of Welsh identity. Local slate features throughout, paired with rich aubergine car-

Aberystwyth

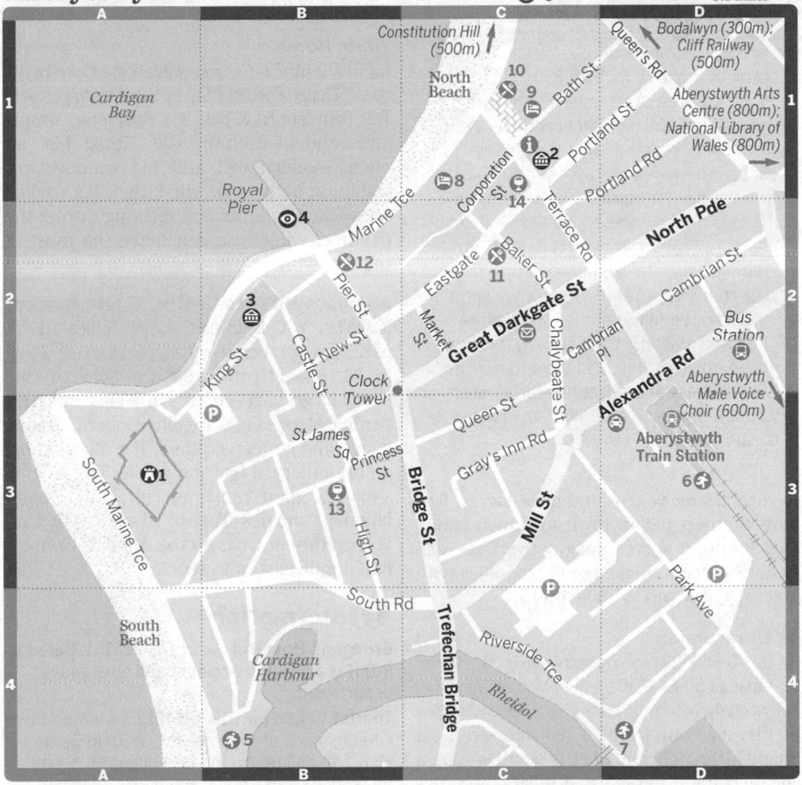

pets and contemporary styling. Of the eight en-suite rooms, those on the top floor offer baths with sea views.

Bodalwyn B&B **$$**
(☎01970-612578; www.bodalwyn.co.uk; Queen's Ave; s/d £55/80; 📶) Simultaneously upmarket and homely, this handsome Edwardian B&B offers tasteful rooms with sparkling new bathrooms and a hearty cooked breakfast (with vegetarian options). Five of the rooms have sea views, but ask for room 3, with the bay window.

Eating

Treehouse CAFE **$**
(☎01970-615791; www.treehousewales.co.uk; 14 Baker St; mains £8-10; ⏰10am-5pm Mon-Fri, from 9am Sat; 🌶) Spread over two floors of a Victorian house above an organic grocer, this excellent cafe uses local produce in a wide range of tempting dishes catering equally

Aberystwyth

Sights
1 Aberystwyth Castle A3
2 Ceredigion Museum C1
3 Old College B2
4 Royal Pier B2

Activities, Courses & Tours
5 Rheidol Cycle Trail B4
6 Vale of Rheidol Railway D3
7 Ystwyth Trail D4

Sleeping
8 Gwesty Cymru C1
9 Maes-y-Môr C1

Eating
10 Baravin C1
11 Treehouse C2
12 Ultracomida B2

Drinking & Nightlife
13 Ship & Castle B3
14 White Horse C1

WORTH A TRIP

BWLCH NANT YR ARIAN

Part of Natural Resources Wales, **Bwlch Nant yr Arian** (☎01970-890453; www.naturalresources.wales; Ponterwyd; parking 2hr £1.50; ⏲visitor centre & cafe 10am-5pm), pronouced *bull*-kheh nant ear *arr*-ee-en, is a picturesque piece of woodland set around a lake, ringed with mountain-bike and walking tracks. The main drawcard, however, is the red kite feeding, which takes place at 2pm daily year-round (3pm British Summer Time).

Even outside mealtimes you'll quite often see majestic birds of prey circling above. You can watch all the action from the terrace of the attractive turf-roofed visitor centre and cafe. It's 9 miles east of Aberystwyth on the A44.

to vegetarians, vegans and meat lovers. Perhaps the best bet in town for lunch (noon to 3.30pm), it serves imaginative fare such as harissa roast chicken or rice noodles with greens, gyoza and shiitake broth.

★Ultracomida TAPAS $$
(☎01970-630686; www.ultracomida.co.uk; 31 Pier St; tapas £1.50-6; ⏲10am-5pm Mon, to 9pm Tue-Sat, noon-4pm Sun; 🖉) This is a foodie's idea of nirvana: out front, a delicatessen with Spanish, French and Welsh goodies and a cheese counter to die for; out back, communal tables to sample the produce with an appropriate glass of wine. Favourite tapas can be eaten as mains (£10), while the *pintxos* plate – including two glasses of wine (£14) – is excellent value.

Baravin ITALIAN $$
(☎01970-611189; www.baravin.co.uk; Terrace Rd, Llys y Brenin; mains £10-15; ⏲10am-late Mon-Sat; 📶) If you've ever wondered how Italian food tastes when made with Welsh ingredients – think pizzas and calzones with Welsh pork sausage or Perl Wen cheese – this stylish bistro by the bay can help satisfy your curiosity.

Drinking & Entertainment

Ship & Castle PUB
(☎07773-778785; 1 High St; ⏲2pm-midnight Mon-Thu & Sun, 2pm-1am Fri, noon-1am Sat; 📶) A sympathetic renovation has left this 1830 pub as cosy and welcoming as ever, while adding big screens to watch the rugby on. It is the place to come for real ales, with a large, constantly revolving selection on tap, plus a few ciders.

White Horse PUB
(☎01970-615234; www.whitehorseaberystwyth.co.uk; Upper Portland St; ⏲10am-midnight Sun-Thu, 9am-1am Fri & Sat; 📶) Spacious, simple and student-friendly, the Horse has an open, modern feel and big windows for watching activity on the street. It's packed on weekend nights and relaxing during the daytime, when you can make the most of the free wi-fi.

Aberystwyth Arts Centre PERFORMING ARTS
(Canolfan Y Celfyddydau; ☎box office 01970-623232; www.aberystwythartscentre.co.uk; Penglais Rd; ⏲8am-11pm Mon-Sat, noon-8pm Sun) One of the largest arts centres in Wales, this happening place stages excellent opera, drama, dance and concerts, plus it has a bookshop, an art gallery, a bar and a cafe. The cinema shows a good range of cult and foreign-language movies. Part of Aberystwyth University, the centre is on the Penglais campus, half a mile east of town.

Information

Bronglais Hospital (☎01970-623131; Caradoc Rd) Has a 24-hour accident and emergency department.

Tourist Office (☎01970-612125; www.discoverceredigion.co.uk; Terrace Rd; ⏲10am-5pm Mon-Sat; 📶) Below the Ceredigion Museum, this office stocks maps and books on local history, has free wi-fi and the helpful staff can arrange accommodation. It's due for an upgrade, as part of the museum's 2017 expansion.

Getting There & Away

BUS

Routes include the X28 to Machynlleth (45 minutes); T2 to Dolgellau (1¼ hours), Porthmadog (2¼ hours), Caernarfon (three hours) and Bangor (3½ hours); 701 to Carmarthen (two hours), Swansea (2¾ hours) and Cardiff (4¼ hours); Thursday-only X18 to Rhayader (one hour), Llandrindod Wells (1½ hours) and Llanwrtyd Wells (2½ hours); and X50 to Aberaeron (45 minutes) and Cardigan (1½ hours).

A daily National Express coach heads to/from Newtown (£10, 80 minutes), Welshpool (£12, 1¾ hours), Shrewsbury (£15, 2¼ hours), Birmingham (£28, four hours) and London (£38, seven hours).

TRAIN

Aberystwyth is the terminus of the Arriva Trains Wales Cambrian Line, which crosses Mid-Wales every two hours en route to Birmingham (£30, three hours) via Machynlleth (£6.50, 35 minutes), Newtown (£13, 1¼ hours), Welshpool (£15, 1½ hours) and Shrewsbury (£20, two hours).

Getting Around

The **bus station** (Alexandra Rd) and **taxi stand** are immediately in front of the train station, while the Cliff Railway leaves from the northern end of Marine Tce.

Cliff Railway (Rheilffordd y Graig; 01970-617642; www.aberystwythcliffrailway.co.uk; Cliff Tce; adult/child one way £3/2, return £4/2.50; 10am-5pm Apr-Oct, shorter hours Nov-Mar) If your legs aren't up to the climb of Constitution Hill (130m), you can catch a lift on the trundling little Cliff Railway, the UK's longest electric funicular and possibly its slowest too, at a breakneck 4mph. It must have been glacial when first built, in 1896, when it was powered by a water-balance system.

Aberaeron

POP 1422

The elegant port of Aberaeron with its brightly painted Georgian houses was once a busy port and ship-building centre, its genteel architecture the result of planned expansion in the early 19th century. With heavy industry long gone, today Aberaeron is quietly bucking the trends of economic decline; its stylish streets and much-admired harbour are lined with independent shops and cafes, chic B&Bs and boutique hotels, and a number of excellent restaurants.

Sights & Activities

Llanerchaeron HISTORIC BUILDING

(NT; 01545-570200; www.nationaltrust.org.uk/llanerchaeron; Ciliau Aeron; adult/child £7.60/3.80; 10.30am-5.30pm, villa 11.30am-4pm) This beautifully maintained Georgian country estate offers a fascinating insight into the life of the Welsh gentry and their staff 200 years ago. The villa itself was designed by John Nash and is one of his most complete early works, featuring curved walls, false windows and ornate cornices.

SeaMôr Boat Trips BOATING

(07795-242445; www.seamor.org; Pen Cei; adult/child £20/10; May-Sep) New Quay-based SeaMôr also runs one-hour boat trips from Aberaeron's Quay Promenade past the dolphin-feeding sites of Llanina Reef and New Quay Bay. Grey seals, bottlenose dolphins and harbour porpoises are commonly seen and there are occasional sightings of sunfish, basking sharks, minke whales and even humpback whales. Departures are tide-dependent: enquire at the tourist office or call SeaMôr directly.

Sleeping

3 Pen Cei B&B $$

(01545-571147; www.pen-cei-guest-house.co.uk; 3 Pen Cei; d £105-160;) The affable owners John and Lesley have refurbished this grand Georgian shipping office beautifully, with crisp linens, bold colour schemes and fresh flowers. The larger rooms have super-king beds (one also has a free-standing bath) and the hosts go out of their way to make guests feel welcome.

★ **Harbour Master** BOUTIQUE HOTEL $$$

(01545-570755; www.harbour-master.com; Pen Cei; s/d from £75/145;) Commanding Aberaeron's harbour entrance, this small, hip hotel offers food and accommodation worthy of any chic city bolthole. The striking, violet-painted Georgian buildings hold 13 quirky rooms featuring Frette linens, vintage Welsh blankets, bold colour schemes and high-tech bathrooms. Those in the newly restored grain warehouse have excellent harbour views.

Downstairs its renowned restaurant (two-/three-course dinner £27.50/35) champions local ingredients with lobster and crab, and Welsh beef, lamb and cheeses whisked into imaginative and extremely satisfying dishes. The lively bar offers the same outstanding food in a more casual setting (mains from £10.50).

Getting There & Away

Between Monday and Saturday, buses T5 and X50 go regularly to Aberystwyth (45 minutes) and Cardigan (55 minutes).

Cardigan (Aberteifi)

POP 4184

Cardigan has the feel of a town waking from its slumber. An important entrepôt and herring fishery in Elizabethan times, it declined with the coming of the railway and the silting up of the River Teifi in the 19th century. Now its surrounding natural beauty, hip craft shops, home-grown fashion labels, gourmet food stores and homely B&Bs are bringing it back to life. Its alternative arts scene is growing and the jumble of historical architecture that lines its streets and lanes has been given a new lease of life. Most importantly, Cardigan Castle has been restored and now serves as a hub of Welsh language, culture and performance.

'Cardigan' is an Anglicisation of Ceredigion, the place of Ceredig, but the Welsh name, Aberteifi, refers to its location at the mouth of the River Teifi.

Sights

★Cardigan Castle CASTLE
(Castell Aberteifi; ☎01239-615131; www.cardigancastle.com; 2 Green St) Cardigan Castle holds an important place in Welsh culture, having been the venue for the first competitive National Eisteddfod, held in 1176 under the aegis of Lord Rhys ap Gruffydd. Neglected for years, it's sprung from the ashes via a multimillion-pound refurbishment and now stands as a major centre of local Welsh culture, with live performances, language classes, eisteddfods and more taking place within its hollowed-out walls.

Mwnt Church CHURCH
(www.friendsofmwntchurch.co.uk) Five miles of winding country lanes lead to tiny, whitewashed Mwnt Church, overlooking Cardigan Bay. It's the oldest church in Ceredigion, dating back to the 14th century. Signposted just north of town.

Activities

Set between the Pembrokeshire Coast Path (PCP) and the Ceredigion Coast Path (CCP), Cardigan offers plenty of options for walkers as well as anyone keen to try out some adventure sports.

> **WORTH A TRIP**
>
> **Y FFARMERS**
>
> Outstanding pub **Y Ffarmers** (☎01974-261275; www.yffarmers.co.uk; Llanfihangel y Creuddyn; mains £15-18; ⏱6-11pm Tue-Fri, noon-11pm Sat, noon-3pm Sun, extended hours in high season) is the main reason to visit the pretty hamlet 7 miles southeast of Aber. Ostensibly another snug, white-brick house of assembly, it does fantastic Welsh pub food: cockle cakes with laverbread sauce, guinea fowl with tarragon and shallots, and other lip-smacking creations. Take the A4340 to the village of New Cross and follow the signs.

Walking

For a challenging but spectacular day's walk, head to **St Dogmaels Abbey** (☎01239-615389; www.stdogmaelsabbey.org.uk; ⏱10am-4pm) FREE and tackle the last leg of the PCP in reverse, catching the bus back from Newport. In the other direction, the first day of the CCP is shorter, ending up in Aberporth where you can catch the 552 bus back.

If you don't fancy a full day's trek, you can walk or cycle from Cardigan through the **Teifi Marshes** to the **Welsh Wildlife Centre** (☎01239-621600; www.welshwildlife.org; Cilgerran; parking £3; ⏱10am-4pm) FREE (WWC). From the High St head downhill to the river, cross over the footbridge to Castle St and then cross the road. Take the pedestrian walkway leading onto the riverbank and follow it out of town past the reed beds and to the wildlife centre. The walk is about 1 mile long, but it's 4 miles by road.

The tourist office stocks the *Walking the Teifi Estuary* brochure, outlining five other graded walks in the area, including a 10-mile circular walk to the gorgeous hidden cove at **Mwnt**. Here a small arc of golden sand sits between folds of the cliffs, and a simple whitewashed church overlooks the sea where you'll often spot dolphins, seals and porpoises.

Other Activities

A Bay to Remember WILDLIFE WATCHING
(☎01239-623558; www.baytoremember.co.uk; Prince Charles Quay; 1hr trip adult/child £25/12; ⏱Mar-Oct) Running one- and two-hour trips into Cardigan Bay from St Dogmaels, Gwbert and Poppit Sands, this operation takes groups out in rigid-hulled inflatable boats to spot bottlenose dolphins, harbour porpoises, grey seals and seabirds. The booking office is at Prince Charles Quay, on the Teifi.

Cardigan Bay Active ADVENTURE SPORTS
(☎01239-612133; www.cardiganbayactive.co.uk; Granary Warehouse, Teifi Wharf, Castle St; ⏱9.30am-5pm Mon-Sat) CBA offers guided canoe or kayak trips through Cilgerran Gorge as well as climbing, coasteering, surfing, white-water rafting and bushcraft trips. Sea kayaking in Cardigan Bay, always a great spot to encounter bottlenose dolphins and Atlantic grey seals, is £40 per person.

Sleeping

Caernant B&B $
(☎01239-612932; www.caernant.co.uk; Gwbert Rd; s/d £40/60; P ᯤ) Big, bright, spacious

CARDIGAN BAY'S DOLPHINS

Cardigan Bay is home to an amazingly rich variety of marine animals and plants, but the star attraction is Europe's largest pod of bottlenose dolphins. With reliable sightings from May to September, there are few places where these sociable creatures are more easily seen in the wild. Along with the dolphins, harbour porpoises, Atlantic grey seals and a variety of bird life are regularly seen, as well as seasonal visitors such as sunfish, basking sharks and leatherback turtles.

Some of the best places to spot bottlenose dolphins from the shore are the beaches around New Quay: New Quay North, Little Quay, Cwmtydu and Llanina are good bets, as are the beautiful sandy beaches at Penbryn and Tresaith north of Cardigan. Aberystwyth, Aberporth and Mwnt also have regular sightings. You can learn more about Cardigan Bay's marine life at the **Cardigan Bay Marine Wildlife Centre** (01545-560032; http://cbmwc.org; Glanmore Tce; 9am-5pm Easter-Oct) FREE, in New Quay.

rooms are on offer at Caernant, a delightful modern B&B just outside Cardigan. With tea and scones on arrival, incredible breakfasts (including smoked salmon and buttered kippers) and heartfelt hospitality, it's well worth the short trip from town (less than a mile from the centre of Cardigan on the B4548).

Ty-Parc B&B B&B $$
(01239-615452; www.ty-parc.com; Park Ave; s/d £50/65; P) This appealing Edwardian house north of downtown Cardigan offers five bright en-suite rooms decked out in cream shades and blond-wood furnishings. Extra thoughtful touches include radios in the shower, fresh flowers and packed lunches on request.

Llety Teifi B&B $$
(01239-615566; www.lletyteifi-guesthouse.co.uk; Pendre; s/d from £45/75; P) Well-appointed and stylish, this large Victorian guesthouse has plenty of period character, despite the lurid pink exterior. Expect bold patterned fabrics and wallpapers, giant windows and spacious bathrooms. Breakfast is served next door and altogether it's a very good deal.

Eating

Fforest Pizzatipi PIZZA $
(01239-612259; www.pizzatipi.co.uk; Cambrian Quay; pizza £7-9; 4-10pm daily Jul & Aug, Sat & Sun late Jun & Sep) Brought to you by the hip folks at Cardigan's Fforest empire, this seasonal pop-up venue is the hottest ticket in town on summer nights. Pizzas pumping from two wood-fired ovens, craft beer, music and a buzzing atmosphere all set under a candlelit tepee in a hidden riverside courtyard: what more could you ask for?

1176 BISTRO $$
(01239-562002; www.cardigancastle.com/dining; Cardigan Castle; mains £15-18; 10am-4pm daily, 6.30-9.30pm Fri & Sat) Named for the year of Wales' first National Eisteddfod, held at Cardigan Castle, this gleaming new bistro is an integral part of the monument's 2015 rebirth. Popular for lunch and afternoon tea (£12 per person), it also opens for dinner on Fridays and Saturdays, when the produce of the castle's kitchen garden stars.

Entertainment

Theatr Mwldan THEATRE
(01239-621200; www.mwldan.co.uk; Bath House Rd; from 5pm Mon, from 10am Tue-Sat, from noon Sun until last performance) Located in the former slaughterhouse, Theatr Mwldan stages comedy, drama, dance, music and films, and has an art gallery and a good cafe. In summer there are open-air productions.

Information

Cardigan & District Memorial Hospital (01239-612214; Pont-y-Cleifion) Has no accident and emergency department.

Tourist Office (01239-613230; www.discoverceredigion.co.uk; Theatr Mwldan, Bath House Rd; 10am-4pm Tue, Wed, Fri & Sat) In the lobby of the Theatr Mwldan.

Getting There & Away

Bus routes include X50 to Aberystwyth (1½ hours); 407 to St Dogmaels (eight minutes) and Poppit Sands (15 minutes); 460 to Carmarthen (90 minutes); and the Poppit Rocket (405) to Fishguard (90 minutes). The **bus station** (Finch Sq) is on Finch Sq.

Bikes can be hired from **New Image Bicycles** (01239-621275; www.bikebikebike.co.uk; 29-30 Pendre; per half day/day £15/20; 10am-5pm Mon-Sat) for cycling around Cardigan Bay and the Teifi Valley.

Snowdonia & North Wales

Includes ➡

Best Places to Eat

- ➡ Blas (p748)
- ➡ Soul Food (p734)
- ➡ Osteria (p748)
- ➡ Coconut Kitchen (p745)
- ➡ Tyddyn Llan (p728)

Best Places to Sleep

- ➡ Ffynnon (p729)
- ➡ Victoria House (p747)
- ➡ Cleifiog (p756)
- ➡ Totters (p747)
- ➡ Bodysgallen Hall (p754)

Why Go?

Rugged mountain trails, historic train lines, World Heritage castles and rejuvenated seaside towns ensure North Wales holds its own against attractions down south. The region is dominated by Snowdonia National Park, where mighty peaks scrape moody skies.

Protected by such a formidable mountain shield, it's little wonder that the less-visited Llŷn Peninsula and the ancient island enclave of Anglesey have retained their traditional language and culture.

In fact, the whole region feels properly Welsh: you'll hear the language on the street, see the Celtic legacy in the landscape, and soak up the cultural pride in galleries, museums and attractions, all the way from the beaches of the North Coast to the river- threaded heartland of northeast Wales. In many ways, North Wales distills the very essence of Welshness – just don't mention that to the folks in Cardiff.

When to Go

- ➡ May is the driest month and Llandudno celebrates the warming weather with its Victorian Extravaganza festival.
- ➡ May to September arguably gives you the best hiking weather, but the warmest months – July and August – bring crowds.
- ➡ The Snowdon train runs to the summit between Easter and November.
- ➡ In July you can shuttle between the beaches and Llangollen's International Musical Eisteddfod and Fringe Festival.
- ➡ Late autumn and early winter bring the heaviest rains, while late winter and early spring are particularly raw and bracing.

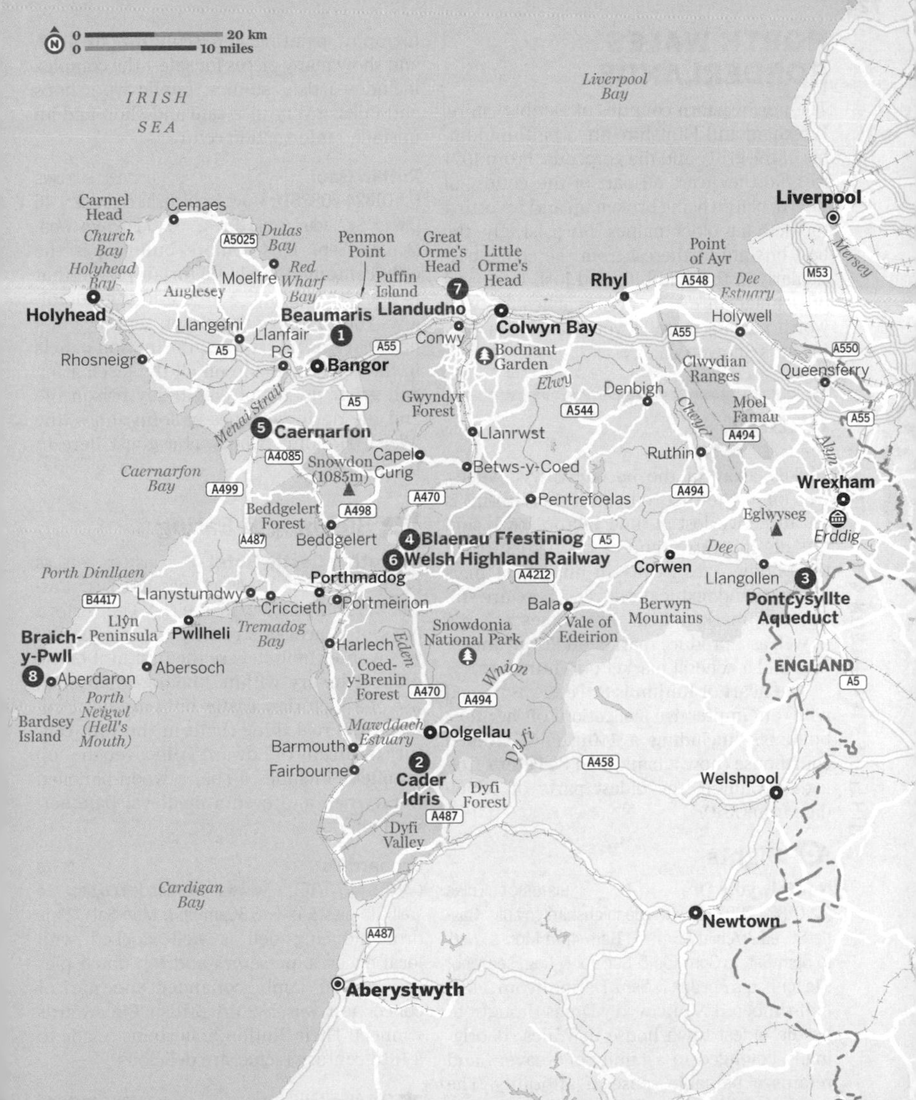

Snowdonia & North Wales Highlights

❶ **Beaumaris** (p756) Falling for the Georgian charms of Anglesey's finest town.

❷ **Cader Idris** (p728) Climbing Snowdonia's second most-famous peak.

❸ **Pontcysyllte Aqueduct** (p725) Floating through the air across this World Heritage Site.

❹ **Blaenau Ffestiniog** (p735) Testing claustrophobia in gloomy caverns.

❺ **Caernarfon Castle** (p747) Witnessing the Byzantine beauty of North Wales' mightiest fortress.

❻ **Welsh Highland Railway** (p744) Taking a coast-to-coast journey on a narrow-gauge railway.

❼ **Llandudno** (p752) Discovering vast Bronze Age mines alongside the Victoriana at this popular seaside resort.

❽ **Braich-y-Pwll** (p746) Gazing towards the magical 'Pilgrims' Island of Bardsey.

NORTH WALES BORDERLANDS

The northeastern counties of Denbighshire, Wrexham and Flintshire are a baffling jumble of the gritty and the gorgeous. From 1974 to 1996 they were all part of the county of Clwyd, before being broken up and reverting to their far older names. Surprisingly, the best bits are furtherest from the coast, particularly in the wild hills and lush farmland of Denbighshire's southern reaches. It's well worth pausing here as you make your way towards Snowdonia.

Ruthin

POP 5461

Tucked away in the bucolic Clwyd valley, well off any tourist route, Ruthin (rith-in) is an attractive lost-in-time hilltop town and the administrative hub of Denbighshire. In the Middle Ages it was an important market town and textile producer. There are still livestock markets held three times a week, as well as a produce market on Friday mornings and a general market on Thursdays.

The heart of Ruthin is St Peter's Sq, lined with an impressive collection of heritage buildings, including a 1401 half-timbered courthouse (now a bank) and St Peter's Collegiate Church, the oldest parts of which date from 1310.

Sights

Nantclwyd y Dre HISTORIC BUILDING
(☎01824-709822; www.denbighshire.gov.uk; Castle St; adult/child £5/4; ⏰11am-4pm Mon & Wed, to 5pm Sat, to 3pm Tue & Sun Jul & Aug, see website for hours Apr-Jun & Sep) Dating from 1435, half-timbered Nantclwyd y Dre is thought to be the oldest town house in Wales. It originally belonged to a family of weavers and retains a palpable sense of antiquity. The rooms have been restored and furnished to reflect the era of each addition, offering a window into the world of the various families that lived in them. The 13th-century Lord's Garden, behind the house, has been restored and is once again a green and pleasant place.

Ruthin Craft Centre ARTS CENTRE
(☎01824-704774; www.ruthincraftcentre.org.uk; Park Rd; ⏰10am-5.30pm; P) FREE Ruthin is lucky to have this excellent gallery and arts hub. Aside from the galleries – which do great work bringing the best of local photography, painting and sculpture to light, and show many pieces for sale – the complex includes artists' studios, public workshops and talks, a very nice cafe and shop and an unstaffed information centre.

Ruthin Gaol HISTORIC BUILDING
(☎01824-708281; www.denbighshire.gov.uk; 46 Clwyd St; adult/child £5/4; ⏰10am-5pm Wed-Mon Apr-Sep) This sombre building is the only Pentonville-style Victorian prison that is open to visitors. A free audio guide allows you to follow the prison sentence of a mystical prisoner, while information panels in the cells fill you in on all the fascinating and grisly details of day-to-day prison life and the daring escapes of John Jones, the 'Welsh Houdini', who was a guest here in the 1870s.

Sleeping & Eating

★**Ruthin Castle Hotel** HISTORIC HOTEL $$
(☎01824-702664; www.ruthincastle.co.uk; Castle St; r/ste from £129/189; P) The forlorn cries of peacocks strutting the gardens of this wonderful hotel are the first hint of the off-beat luxury within. Making unabashed use of a Victorian 'castle' built amid the ruins of the real thing (built in the 13th century by an ally of Edward I), its over-the-top grandeur includes a spa, a wood-panelled library/bar, and even a medieval banqueting hall.

Leonardo's DELI $
(☎01824-707161; www.leonardosdeli.co.uk; 4 Well St; pies £4; ⏰8.30am-5pm Mon-Sat) This drool-inducing deli is well stocked with local cheeses, preserves and top-notch pies (its Persian lamb, coriander and apricot concoction was a 2016 British Pie Awards winner). Their 'Ruthin honeybuns', made to a 16th-century recipe, are delicious.

★**On the Hill** MODERN BRITISH $$
(☎01824-707736; www.onthehillrestaurant.co.uk; 1 Upper Clwyd St; mains £14-17, 1-/2-/3-course lunch £13/16/19; ⏰noon-2pm Mon-Sat, 6.30-9pm nightly) The low ceilings and exposed beams of this 16th-century house near the square make a memorable setting for sophisticated country cooking. Classics such as duck breast with celeriac and redcurrant or sole stuffed with prawns and lobster and blanketed in sherry and cream sauce, sit alongside more contemporary creations, but all hit the mark. The lunch menu is fantastic value.

Getting There & Away

Bus X50 heads to/from Denbigh (20 minutes) and Wrexham (50 minutes).

Llangollen

POP 3466

Huddled around the banks of the tumbling River Dee (Afon Dyfrdwy) and with the mysterious hilltop ruins of Castell Dinas Brân as a backdrop, picturesque little Llangollen (khlan-goth-len) has long been recognised as a scenic gem. The riverside walk, heading west from the 14th-century bridge, has been a popular promenading spot since Victorian times.

In summer, Llangollen has a burgeoning walking and white-water-rafting scene, while in winter, under a thick blanket of snow, it just sits there and looks pretty. Two major arts festivals boost tourism, as do railway and engineering enthusiasts interested in the area's industrial legacy. That legacy accounts for the town's present layout: much of the original housing was relocated to make way for locomotives.

Llangollen takes its name from St Collen, a 7th-century monk who founded a religious community *(llan)* here. Centuries later it became an important stop on the London-to-Holyhead stagecoach route, linking the British capital to Ireland.

Sights

Plas Newydd HISTORIC BUILDING

(☎01978-862834; www.denbighshire.gov.uk/heritage; Hill St; adult/child £6/5; ⏲10am-5pm Wed-Mon Mar-Oct, plus Tue Jun-Aug) The 18th-century home of the Ladies of Llangollen, Plas Newydd is an atmospheric step back in time. The celebrated couple transformed the house into a hybrid of Gothic and Tudor styles, complete with stained-glass windows, carved-oak panels and the romantic, picturesque formal gardens. Admission to the house includes a good self-guided audio tour of the house, and the tranquil gardens are free to explore.

★**Pontcysyllte Aqueduct & Canal World Heritage Site** CANAL

(☎01978-292015; www.pontcysyllte-aqueduct.co.uk; guided tours £3; ⏲visitor centre 10am-4pm daily Easter-Oct, plus long weekends in Nov, Dec & late Feb–Easter) FREE The preeminent Georgian engineer, Thomas Telford (1757–1834) built the Pontcysyllte Aqueduct in 1805 to carry the canal over the River Dee. At 307m long, 3.6m wide, 1.7m deep and 38m high, it is the most spectacular piece of engineering on the entire UK canal system and the highest canal aqueduct ever built. In recognition of this, the aqueduct and an 11-mile stretch of the canal have been declared a Unesco World Heritage Site.

In the 18th century the horse-drawn canal barge was the most efficient way of hauling goods over long distances but, with the advent of the railway, most of them fell into disrepair. The Llangollen Canal fared better than most because it was used for many more years to carry drinking water from the River Dee to the Hurleston Reservoir in Cheshire. Today it's again in use, carrying visitors up and down the Vale of Llangollen. In addition, the old towpaths offer miles of peaceful, traffic-free walking.

Telford's goal was to connect up the haulage routes between the Rivers Dee, Severn and Mersey. To collect water for the canal from the River Dee, he also designed an elegant curving weir called Horseshoe Falls. The adjacent riverbank is a tranquil picnic spot.

Blue-badge guides run guided tours from near the aqueduct visitor centre, while canal boats offer trips along the 'stream in the sky' from the nearby quay and from Llangollen wharf. Otherwise you can simply stroll across, free of charge. Whichever way you choose, you'll need a head for heights.

DON'T MISS

'YOU RANG, M'LORD?'

For a glimpse into the life of the British upper class in the 18th and 19th centuries, and the 'upstairs-downstairs' social hierarchy of their bygone world, this stately house and gardens **Erddig** (NT; ☎01978-355314; www.nationaltrust.org.uk/erddig; adult/child £11.25/5.60, grounds only £7.20/3.60; ⏲house 12.30-3.30pm, grounds 10am-5pm; P), are highly recommended. The house, the earliest parts of which date from 1680, has hardly been altered since the early 20th century; there's no electricity and it still has extensive outbuildings.

Erddig is about 12 miles northeast of Llangollen in the village of Rhostyllen, signposted off the A483.

Horseshoe Falls is about 2 miles west of Llangollen (take the A5 west and after about 1.5 miles turn right across the river), while the aqueduct is 4 miles east, near the village of Trevor (on the A539 Ruabon road). Both are easily reached by the canal towpath, if you're in no hurry.

Castell Dinas Brân CASTLE

FREE The ever-visible ragged arches and tumbledown walls of Dinas Brân (Crow Castle) mark the remnants of a short-lived 13th-century castle of which it was said 'there was not a mightier in Wales nor a better in England'. It was burnt by Edward I after it was surrendered to him in advance of his invasion. Its fabulous 360-degree views over the Dee and surrounding countryside are well worth the 1½-hour return walk up the steep track from town.

Valle Crucis Abbey RUINS

(Abaty Glyn y Groes; Cadw; www.cadw.wales.gov.uk; A542; adult/child £3.50/2.50 Apr-Oct, free Nov-Mar; 10am-5pm, to 4pm Nov-Mar) The dignified ruins of this Cistercian abbey are a 2-mile walk north of Llangollen. Founded in 1201 by Madog ap Gruffydd, ruler of northern Powys, its largely Gothic form predates its more famous sibling at Tintern (which, on the eve of Valle Crucis's 1537 dissolution, was its only rival as the richest Cistercian abbey in the land). A small interpretation centre brings the monks' daily routines to life, and plays and other events sometimes animate the peaceful grounds.

Activities

Welsh Canal Holiday Craft BOATING

(01978-860702; www.horsedrawnboats.co.uk; Llangollen Wharf; mid-Mar–Oct) Peaceful horse-drawn narrowboats depart on 45-minute trips (adult/child £13/8) from Llangollen Wharf every half hour during the school holidays, and hourly otherwise (adult/child £7/3.50). Two-hour journeys head to the Horseshoe Falls and back, and motorised boats take you up to Pontcysyllte Aqueduct (p725) with the return journey by coach (adult/child £14/12). Self-drive boats are £130/180 per day/weekend.

Llangollen Railway TOUR

(01978-860979; www.llangollen-railway.co.uk; Abbey Rd; adult/child return £15/8; daily Apr-Sep, reduced services rest of year) Now extended, the 10-mile jaunt through the Dee Valley via Berwyn (near Horseshoe Falls) and Corwen on the former Ruabon to Barmouth Line is a superb day out for rail fans, families and heritage lovers alike. There are regular *Thomas the Tank Engine* theme days for children, and murder-mystery excursions are also popular.

Llangollen Outdoors OUTDOORS

(01978-897220; www.llangollenoutdoors.co.uk; Parade St, Fringe Shed; tubing & rafting £55; 8.30am-5pm) Catering to the recreational and the serious alike, this outfit runs rafting, tubing, canyoning, canoeing, rock climbing and bushcraft tasters and trips, starting from £45 per person. Offered year-round, their program even contains such recherché activities as axe-throwing.

Safe & Sound Outdoors ADVENTURE SPORTS

(01978-860471; www.sasoutdoors.co.uk; Chapel St; bike hire half/full day £20/22) This all-purpose adventure company is the only place in Llangollen that hires mountain and road bikes. It also does rafting, gorge walking, rock climbing, paintball and…err…stag dos.

Festivals & Events

International Musical Eisteddfod PERFORMING ARTS

(01978-862000; www.international-eisteddfod.co.uk; events from £5, full season ticket £210; Jul) The International Musical Eisteddfod was established after WWII to promote international harmony. Every July it attracts 4000 participants and 50,000 spectators from around 50 countries, transforming lovely Llangollen into a global village. In addition to folk music and dancing competitions, gala concerts at the Royal International Pavilion feature international stars. It was nominated for the Nobel Peace Prize in 2004.

Llangollen Fringe Festival PERFORMING ARTS

(08001-455779; www.llangollenfringe.co.uk; festival ticket £85; Jul) This small-town, volunteer-run arts festival, held over 11 days from mid-July, manages to attract some surprisingly big names: 2016's line-up included The Selecter and Gang of Four. There are also poetry readings, a jazz narrowboat cruise, special musical train services and a final concert in the ruins of Valle Crucis Abbey.

Sleeping & Eating

Llangollen Hostel HOSTEL $

(01978-861773; www.llangollenhostel.co.uk; Berwyn St, Isallt; dm/d from £20/45; P) This excellent independent hostel, based in a former family home, has friendly owners and a cared-for feel. It offers various rooms, from private en suite doubles to a six-bed dorm, as well as an orderly kitchen and cosy lounge. It actively welcomes cyclists, walkers and canoeists, offering laundry facilities and bike/boat storage. Prices include a self-service cereal-and-toast breakfast.

★mh Townhaus B&B **$$**

(☎01978-860775; www.manorhaus.com; Hill St; s/d £76/111;) A sister to the well-established Ruthin Manorhaus, this ultra-stylish guesthouse boasts six clean-cut rooms, a lounge and bar, and even a rooftop hot tub. Originally opened in 2012 as a restaurant with rooms, it now focuses more on accommodation (including a new six-bed room) but can still do wonderful three-course meals for groups (by arrangement).

Cornerstones Guesthouse B&B **$$**

(☎01978-861569; www.cornerstones-guesthouse.co.uk; 19 Bridge St; r £90-140;) All stripped floorboards and oak beams, this converted 16th-century house has charm and history in spades. It's now a five-star gold B&B with fires in winter, fantastic breakfasts and three beautifully appointed rooms.

Abbey Farm FARMSTAY **$$**

(☎01978-861297; www.theabbeyfarm.co.uk; cottage per week £240-490; ⊙Feb-Dec;) With three sweet stone self-catering cottages (the largest sleeping up to 14), a campsite in the lee of the impressive ruins of Valle Crucis Abbey, a farm shop and tearoom-cum-bistro, Abbey Farm covers many bases. If setting up your own tent seems like just too much trouble, their semifixed camping 'pods' make life a little easier.

Corn Mill PUB FOOD **$**

(☎01978-869555; www.brunningandprice.co.uk/cornmill; Dee Lane; light meals £7-11, mains £10-18; ⊙kitchen noon-9.30pm;) The water wheel still turns at the heart of this converted mill, now a cheerful, bustling pub and eatery. The deck is the best spot in town for an unfussy al fresco lunch, with views over the River Dee to the steam railway. The bar stays open for an hour or two longer than the kitchen.

Information

Tourist Office (☎01978-860828; www.northeastwales.co.uk; Castle St, The Chapel; ⊙9.30am-5pm) Helpful tourist office, well-stocked with maps, books and gifts. It doubles as an art gallery. Pick up the *Llangollen History Trail* brochure, which details a 9.5km walking circuit taking in Valle Crucis and Dinas Brân.

Getting There & Away

Bus T3 heads to Wrexham (30 minutes), Llandrillo (35 minutes), Bala (55 minutes), Dolgellau (1½ hours) and Barmouth (1¾ hours). National Express coaches head to Wrexham (£3.60, 25 minutes), Shrewsbury (£9.40, one change, 2½ hours) and Birmingham (£17, one change, four hours). Buses leave from Parade St near the museum.

Parking is at a premium in Llangollen. If your accommodation doesn't have its own, check whether it can provide a pass for the council car parks.

THE LADIES OF LLANGOLLEN

Lady Eleanor Butler and Miss Sarah Ponsonby, the 'Ladies of Llangollen', lived in **Plas Newydd** (New Home; p725) from 1780 to 1829 with their maid, Mary Carryl. They had fallen in love in Ireland but their aristocratic Anglo-Irish families discouraged the relationship. In a desperate bid to be allowed to live together, the women eloped to Wales, disguised as men, and set up home in Llangollen to devote themselves to 'friendship, celibacy and the knitting of stockings'.

Their romantic friendship became well known yet respected and they were visited by many national figures of the day, including the Duke of Wellington, William Wordsworth and Sir Walter Scott. Wordsworth was even suitably moved to pen the following words: 'Sisters in love, a love allowed to climb, even on this earth above the reach of time'.

The ladies' relationship with their maid, Mary, was also close. Mary managed to buy the freehold of Plas Newydd and left it to the 'sisters' when she died. They erected a large monument to her in the graveyard at St Collen's Parish Church in Llangollen, where they are also buried. Lady Eleanor died in 1829; Sarah Ponsonby was reunited with her soulmate just two years later.

SNOWDONIA NATIONAL PARK (PARC CENEDLAETHOL ERYRI)

Wales' best-known and most visited slice of nature became the country's first national park in 1951. Every year more than 350,000 people walk, climb or take the train to the 1085m summit of Snowdon. Yet the park is more than just Snowdon – its 823 sq miles embraces stunning coastline, forests, valleys, rivers, bird-filled estuaries and Wales' biggest natural lake.

Like Wales' other national parks, this one is lived-in, with sizeable towns at Bala, Dolgellau, Harlech and Betws-y-Coed, and a population in excess of 26,000. Two-thirds of the park is privately owned, with more than three-quarters used for raising sheep and cattle.

The Welsh name for Snowdonia, is Eryri (eh-*ruh*-ree) meaning highlands.

The park is the only home to two endangered species, an alpine plant called the Snowdon lily and the rainbow-coloured Snowdon beetle. The *gwyniad* is a species of whitefish found only in Llyn Tegid (Bala Lake), which incidentally also has probably the UK's only colony of glutinous snails.

DON'T MISS

TYDDYN LLAN

The glowing reputation of the Michelin-starred country restaurant **Tyddyn Llan Restaurant** (☎01490-440264; www.tyddynllan.co.uk; Llandrillo; 2-/3-course dinner £50/60; ⏰lunch Fri-Sun, dinner daily; P) is well deserved. We are still salivating at the memory of our last visit – some dishes went beyond merely good and approached extraordinary. The pairings of ingredients are classical rather than off-the-wall – spring asparagus, for example, with morels and duck egg. It's set among gardens near the pretty Georgian village of Llandrillo (located on the secondary B4401 route between Llangollen and Bala).

Cader Idris (Cadair Idris)

Cader Idris (893m), or the 'Seat of Idris' (a legendary giant), is a hulking, menacing-looking mountain with an appropriate mythology attached. It's said that hounds of the underworld fly around its peaks, and that strange light effects are often sighted in the area. It's also said that anyone who spends the night on the summit will awake either mad or a poet – although perhaps you'd have to be a little mad or romantic to attempt it in the first place. Regardless of its repute, it's popular with walkers and it's the park's favourite locale for rock climbers.

Activities

The usual route to the summit of Cader Idris is the 'Tŷ Nant' or **Pony Path** (6 miles return, five hours), which begins from the Tŷ Nant car park, 3 miles southwest of Dolgellau. It's a rocky but safe, straightforward route.

The easiest but longest route is the 'Tywyn' or **Llanfihangel y Pennant Path** (10 miles return, six hours), a gentle pony track that heads northeast from the hamlet of Llanfihangel y Pennant, joining the Tŷ Nant Path at the latter's midpoint. Llanfihangel is 1.5 miles from the terminus of the Talyllyn Railway at Abergynolwyn.

The shortest but steepest route is the **Minffordd Path** (6 miles return, five hours), which begins from the Dol Idris car park (four hours/day £2/4), 6 miles south of Dolgellau at the junction of the A487 and the B4405. This route requires the most caution, especially on the way back down, but there's the added incentive of a hot beverage awaiting at the tearoom, near the car park.

Whichever route you choose, wear stout shoes, carry protective clothing and check the weather conditions on the Met's website (www.metoffice.gov.uk). Printable maps can be downloaded from the Snowdonia National Park website (www.eryri-npa.gov.uk).

Near the Minffordd trailhead is **Tal-y-llyn**, a tranquil lake hemmed in by the encroaching mountains. It's stocked with trout and popular with both anglers and otters.

Sleeping

★**Old Rectory on the Lake** B&B **$$**
(☎01654-782225; www.rectoryonthelake.co.uk; Tal-y-Llyn; s/d from £45/90, 4-course meal £40; P 📶) If you think you might need a little pampering after your Cader Idris ascent – perhaps a gourmet meal, a complimentary glass of sherry or a soak in a hot tub – this wonderful adults-only B&B could be just the ticket. It's located on the shores of Tal-y-llyn, less than 2 miles from the Minffordd trailhead.

Getting There & Away

Bus 30 connects Dolgellau with Minffordd (15 minutes), Tal-y-llyn (20 minutes) and Abergynolwyn (27 minutes) once daily from Monday to Saturday. The easiest way to reach the trailheads is with your own wheels.

Dolgellau

POP 2688

Dolgellau (dol-*geth*-lye) is a charming little market town, steeped in history and boasting the highest concentration of heritage-listed buildings in Wales (more than 200). Once the county town of bygone Merionethshire, it was a regional centre for Wales' prosperous wool industry in the 18th and early 19th centuries and many of its finest buildings, sturdy and unadorned, were built at that time. Local mills failed to keep pace with mass mechanisation, however, and decline set in – preserving the town centre much as it was then.

The region bounced back when the Romantic Revival made Wales' wild landscapes popular with genteel travellers. There was also a minor gold rush in the 19th century. Famous for its pink tinge, Dolgellau gold became associated with royalty and the gold for the wedding rings of the current crop of senior royals was mined here. Today Dolgellau relies heavily on tourism.

Sights & Activities

Mawddach Estuary NATURE RESERVE

(www.mawddachestuary.co.uk) The Mawddach Estuary is a striking sight, flanked by woodlands, wetlands and the mountains of southern Snowdonia. There are two Royal Society for the Protection of Birds (RSPB) nature reserves in the valley, both easily reached on foot or by bike from Dolgellau or Barmouth via the Mawddach Trail. Arthog Bog is 8 miles west of Dolgellau on the access road to Morfa Mawddach station, off the A493, while Coed Garth Gell is 2 miles west, on the A496.

Mawddach Trail HIKING

(www.mawddachtrail.co.uk) The 9.5-mile Mawddach Trail is a flat (and in places wheelchair-accessible) walking and cycling path that follows an old train line through woods and past wetlands on the southern side of the beautiful Mawddach Estuary, before crossing over the train viaduct to Barmouth (where you can catch the bus back). The trail starts in the car park beside the bridge.

Precipice Walk HIKING

If you're not up to scaling Cader Idris, this 3.5-mile circular walk through the private Nannau estate is surprisingly varied and offers plenty of beautiful scenery. It leads you through woodland, along the side of a steeply sloped mountain and beside a lake (Llyn Cynwch). The walk starts from Saith Groesffordd car park, Llanfachreth, around 2.5 miles from Dolgellau.

Sleeping

HYB Bunkhouse HOSTEL $

(01341-421755; www.medi-gifts.com; 2-3 Bridge St; dm/r £21/84; P Wi-Fi) Attached to the ground-floor Medi Gift Shop, this bunkhouse has a series of oak-beamed rooms, each sleeping four people (in bunk beds, each group separated where possible), with handy kitchenettes. On the downside, there's no lounge, only one room is en suite and, during busy periods it's charged by the room rather than by the bed.

Bryn Mair House B&B $$

(01341-422640; www.brynmairbedandbreakfast.co.uk; Love Lane; s/d from £95/105; P Wi-Fi) This impressive stone house – a former Georgian rectory – sits among gardens on wistfully monikered Love Lane. Its three luxurious B&B rooms are all kitted out with Egyptian cotton sheets, DVD players and iPod docks; room 1 has sublime mountain views.

★ **Ffynnon** B&B $$$

(01341-421774; www.ffynnontownhouse.com; Love Lane; s/d from £100/150; P Wi-Fi) With a keen eye for contemporary design and a super-friendly welcome, this award-winning boutique B&B manages to be homey and stylish. French antiques are mixed in with modern chandeliers, claw-foot tubs and electronic gadgets, and each room has a seating area for admiring the stunning views in comfort. There's a bar, library and even an outdoor hot tub.

Penmaenuchaf Hall HOTEL $$$

(01341-422129; www.penhall.co.uk; Penmaenpool; s/d £130/180; P Wi-Fi pets) With grand furnishings, sculpted gardens and superb views, this upscale country hotel is the former pile of Bolton cotton magnate, James Leigh. The 14 rooms have a lavish old-world air with all the 21st-century conveniences.

1

2

STUNNEDMULLET / SHUTTERSTOCK ©

1. Keswick (p604), England **2.** Cape Cornwall (p346), England
3. Hiking Llanberis Path (p739), Snowdonia, Wales

Breathtaking Britain

Britain is best known for the historic capitals of London and Edinburgh, the university towns of Cambridge and Oxford, and the well-preserved Roman remains in Bath. However, beyond the urban sprawl lies another Britain: a landscape of high mountain vistas, dramatic valleys lined with lakes, and – as befitting an island – thousands of miles of spectacular coastline.

Lake District

The Lake District (p584) is home to the highest mountains in England, as well as some of the longest and most beautiful lakes. With summits snow-capped in winter, and spectacular at any time of year, this landscape inspired the poet William Wordsworth, and is a major magnet for hikers today.

Snowdonia

Wales is crowned with Snowdonia (p728) – a range of rocky peaks and glacier-hewn valleys stretching across the north of the country. Snowdon itself is accessible by Swiss-style cog railway, while Tryfan and Glyder Fawr offer equally challenging hikes and spectacular views, as well as more chance of solitude.

Cornwall's Coast

In Britain, you're spoilt for choice when it comes to beautiful coastline, but in the far southwest, the coast of Cornwall (p332) is hard to beat, with its stunning combination of sandy beaches, tranquil coves, picture-postcard fishing ports, adrenaline-pumping surf spots and rugged cliffs carved by Atlantic waves.

Scotland's Northwest Highlands

The long journey to the far northwest corner of the Scottish Highlands (p918) is repaid with some of the finest scenery anywhere in Britain. In this wild and remote region, the sheer mountainsides drop to the sea, while narrow sea lochs cut deep inland, creating a landscape that is almost other-worldly in its beauty.

WORTH A TRIP

COED Y BRENIN FOREST PARK

Covering 16 sq miles, this woodland park (8 miles north of Dolgellau off the A470) is the premier location for mountain biking in Wales. Ever-expanding, it's laced with more than 70 miles of purpose-built cycle trails, divided into eight graded routes to suit everyone from beginners to guns. Guidance is at hand in the form of old-fashioned waterproof trail cards or downloadable geocaches and MP3 audio files. Some of the more gung-ho trails – such as the Dragon's Back and the Beast of Brenin – are used for major mountain-biking events.

Wildlife here includes fallow deer; they're hard to spot but you're most likely to see them early in the morning.

The **Coed y Brenin Forest Park Visitor Centre** (01341-440747; www.naturalresources.wales/coedybrenin; car park per hour/day £1/5; 9.30am-5pm) has a cafe (offering a 10% discount to anyone arriving by public transport), toilets, showers and a children's play area, as well as trail and forest information. It's also the hub for foraging and survival-skills walks, craft workshops, races and other events.

Standards are similarly high in Llygad yr Haul, the hotel's garden restaurant. It's located 2 miles west of Dolgellau, off the A493.

Eating & Drinking

TH Roberts CAFE $

(01341-423552; Glyndŵr St, Parliament House; light mains £4-5; 9am-5.30pm Mon-Sat;) Occupying a Grade-II-listed building fitted with its original counter, glass cabinets and wooden drawers, this charismatic cafe still looks a lot like the ironmonger's it once was. The coffee and tea are proudly the best in Dolgellau, there's a reading room with books and papers, and the soup, sandwiches and rarebit (and Nan's scones) are all first rate.

Mawddach Restaurant EUROPEAN $$

(Bwyty Mawddach; 01341-421752; www.mawddach.com; Llanelltyd; mains £16-22; noon-2.30pm Thu-Sun, 6.30-9pm Thu-Sat) Occupying a smartly renovated former barn with views of Cader Idris and the estuary valley, Mawddach sits 2 miles west of Dolgellau on the A496. Tasteful slate floors and leather seats are matched by excellent food: slow-cooked local pork belly with confit fennel, or roasted hake with greens, garlic and anchovies. The Sunday lunch menu (two/three courses £21/24) is great value.

Y Sospan BISTRO $$

(01341-423174; www.ysospan.co.uk; Queen's Sq; breakfast & lunch £5-9, dinner £13-17; 8.30am-9.30pm;) In a book-lined, flag-stoned and rough-beamed 1606 building that once served as a prison, this relaxed local serves fry-up breakfasts, sandwiches, jacket potatoes and light meals during the day. Lamb and beef play a starring role on the more ambitious bistro menu available in the evenings, and most of the desserts have been on the booze.

Dylanwad Da WINE BAR

(01341-422870; www.dylanwad.co.uk; Finsbury Sq; snacks £5-7; 10am-6pm Tue-Thu, to 11pm Fri & Sat) Relocation to a slickly renovated new premises (one of Dolgellau's oldest) has seen this local institution shift emphasis from food to owner Dylan Rowlands' main interest – wine. Cheeses, serrano ham and other small plates are still available but – as the title of Dylan's book, *Rarebit and Rioja*, suggests – they're there as supporting cast to a star-studded list of wines.

Getting There & Away

Buses stop on the western side of Eldon Sq in the heart of town. Destinations include Machynlleth (route T2, 30 minutes), Betws-y-Coed (route X1, 1¼ hours, one daily Monday to Saturday), Llangollen (route T3, 1½ hours), Porthmadog (route T2, 50 minutes) and Caernarfon (route T2, 1½ hours). Note that some services, such as the 28 to Tywyn (55 minutes), stop on the southern side of the square.

Barmouth (Abermaw)

POP 2315

With a Blue Flag beach and the beautiful Mawddach Estuary on its doorstep, the seaside resort of Barmouth has been a popular tourist destination since the coming of the railway in 1867. In summer it becomes a typical seaside resort – chip shops, dodgem cars, donkey rides and crabbing – catering to thousands from England's West Midlands. Outside of the brash neon of high summer it's considerably mellower, allowing space to appreciate its Georgian and Victorian architecture, beautiful setting and superb walking trails.

The main commercial strip is spread out along the A496; as it passes through town it's known as Church St, High St and King Edward's St.

Sights

The oldest part of Barmouth is around the quay. The unusual round building, **Tŷ Crwn** (The Quay; 10.30am-5pm) FREE, was once a jail where drunk and disorderly sailors could cool off until morning. In the 15th century, supporters of Henry Tudor met in nearby **Tŷ Gwyn** to plot his ascension to the throne (the building now houses a bar and restaurant).

Barmouth Bridge BRIDGE
You're unlikely to miss Barmouth's foremost landmark: in fact, you'll probably arrive on it, either by train, on foot or on two wheels. Curving scenically into town, spanning 700 metres of the Mawddach Estuary mouth, it was built in 1867 for the new railway and is one of the longest wooden viaducts in Britain. Originally incorporating a drawbridge, it now has a swing bridge to allow tall shipping into the estuary.

Festivals & Events

Three Peaks Yacht Race SPORTS
(www.threepeaksyachtrace.co.uk; late Jun) The arduous Three Peaks Yacht Race runs from Barmouth to Fort William, with crew members running up Snowdon, Scafell Pike and Ben Nevis – the highest peaks of Wales, England and Scotland – en route. In all, that's 389 nautical miles of sailing, 29 miles of cycling and 59 miles of fell running.

The record time for the race thus far is two days, 14 hours and four minutes, achieved in 2002.

Sleeping

Hendre Mynach Caravan Park CAMPGROUND $
(01341-280262; www.hendremynach.co.uk; sites from £19; P) Right by the beach, this well-kept park has caravan sites marked out between manicured hedges and a couple of flat camping fields protected by windbreaks. It's just off the A496, immediately north of Barmouth.

Richmond House B&B $$
(01341-281366; www.barmouthbedandbreakfast.co.uk; High St; s/d £65/80; P) Undergoing renovation at the time of research, this handsome town house has big, contemporary rooms (two with sea views) and an attractive garden area for summer lounging on chunky wooden furniture. It's very handy for both the town centre and the beach.

Eating & Drinking

★**Bistro Bermo** EUROPEAN $$
(01341-281284; www.bistrobarmouth.co.uk; 6 Church St; mains £15-19; 6.30-10pm Tue-Sat, plus noon-2pm Wed-Sat Apr-Oct) Discreetly hidden behind an aqua-green shopfront, this intimate restaurant delivers a sophisticated menu chock-full of Welsh farm produce and fresh fish. Featuring dishes such as red bream with scallops and seafood bisque, the cooking is classical, rather than experimental, and generally excellent. There are only half a dozen tables, so book ahead.

Last Inn PUB
(01341-280530; www.lastinn-barmouth.co.uk; Church St; noon-11pm;) In a 15th-century cobbler's home now lives Barmouth's most characterful pub, full of old ship timber and other eclectic nautical memorabilia. Most unusually, the hillside forms the rear wall, with a spring emerging to form a gaudily decorated pond inside the building itself. Kids are welcome, the menu's full of crowd-pleasers and there's live music on Tuesday and Friday nights.

Getting There & Away

Train Barmouth is on the Cambrian Coast Line, with direct trains to Machynlleth (£9.30, one hour), Fairbourne (£2.80, seven minutes), Harlech (£4.90, 24 minutes), Porthmadog (£7.30, 50 minutes) and Pwllheli (£12, 1¼ hours).

Bus Buses stop on Jubilee Rd, across Beach Rd from the train station. Destinations include Harlech (route 38, 30 minutes), Dolgellau (route 38/T3, 20 minutes), Bala (route T3, one hour), Llandrillo (route T3, 1½ hours) and Llangollen (route T3, two hours).

Bicycle Cycle path Lôn Las Cymru passes through Barmouth, heading north to Harlech and east to Dolgellau.

Harlech

POP 1762

Hilly Harlech is best known for the mighty, grey stone towers of its castle, framed by gleaming Tremadog Bay and with the mountains of Snowdonia as a backdrop. Some sort of fortified structure has probably surmounted the rock since Iron Age times, but Edward I removed all traces when he commissioned the construction of his castle. Finished in 1289, Harlech Castle is the southernmost of four fortifications included in the 'Castles and Town Walls of King Edward in Gwynedd' Unesco World Heritage Site.

Harlech is such a thoroughly pleasant place that it has become one of the more gentrified destinations in Snowdonia – every other shop seems to sell antiques or tea. While it's bustling in summer, it can be deliciously sleepy otherwise. It makes a great base for a beach holiday or for day trips into the national park – and those views never get boring.

Sights & Activities

★Harlech Castle CASTLE

(Cadw; www.cadw.wales.gov.uk; Castle St; adult/child £6/4.20; 9.30am-5pm Mar-Jun & Sep-Oct, to 6pm Jul & Aug, to 4pm Nov-Feb) Edward I finished this intimidating yet spectacular building in 1289, the southernmost of his 'iron ring' of fortresses designed to keep the Welsh firmly beneath his boot. The grey sandstone castle's massive, twin-towered gatehouse and outer walls are still intact and give the illusion of impregnability even now. A new visitor centre, with interactive displays, kids' activities and films, was opened in 2015, where the Castle Hotel once stood.

Snowdonia Adventure Activities OUTDOORS

(01341-241511; www.snowdoniaadventureactivities.co.uk; 2 Sarn Hir, Llanbedr; adult/child £70/40) This young couple offers customised adventures within the national park, including rock climbing, abseiling, canyoning, gorge scrambling, canoeing, kayaking, mountain biking and guided hiking: a full day's program combines two activities. You'll find Llanbedr 3 miles south of Harlech, on the A496.

Sleeping & Eating

★Maelgwyn House B&B $$

(01766-780087; www.maelgwynharlech.co.uk; Ffordd Isaf; r £70-95; P wi-fi) A model B&B in an art-bedecked former boarding school, Maelgwyn has interesting hosts, delicious breakfasts and a small set of elegant rooms with tremendous views across the bay, and stocked with DVD players and tea-making facilities. Bridget and Derek can also help arrange birdwatching trips and fungus forays. Full marks.

Castle Cottage HOTEL $$$

(01766-780479; www.castlecottageharlech.co.uk; Ffordd Pen Llech; r from £135; P wi-fi) Within arrow's reach of the castle, this 16th-century cottage has spacious bedrooms in a contemporary style, with exposed beams, in-room DVD players and a bowl of fresh fruit for each guest. The award-winning fine-dining restaurant (two-/three-/five-course dinner £35/40/45) is a great showcase for Welsh produce: bacon from the Llŷn Peninsula, Rhydlewis salmon, Brecon venison and other delights.

★Soul Food CARIBBEAN $$

(01766-780416; www.soulfoodcaribbeanrestaurant.co.uk; High St; mains £13-15; 5.30-9pm Tue-Sat) Slaty Harlech is an unlikely locale for an authentic Tobagan joint, let alone the best Caribbean restaurant in Wales. But the locals – hungrily snapping up Trinidadian roti with goat and potato curry, caramelised lime chicken, jerk lamb, vegetarian pepper pot and other spicy delights – don't seem to notice anything incongruous.

Getting There & Away

Train Harlech is on the Cambrian Coast Line, with direct trains to Machynlleth (£12.60, 1½ hours), Fairbourne (£6, 34 minutes), Barmouth (£4.90, 25 minutes), Porthmadog (£4, 24 minutes) and Pwllheli (£8.40, 47 minutes). The station is at the base of the rocks below the castle; it's a strenuous 20-minute climb on one of several stepped tracks up to High St or about half a mile by road.

Bus Bus 38 to Barmouth (30 minutes) stops on High St; some buses continue on to Dolgellau (one hour).

Bicycle National Cycle Network path 8 (Lôn Las Cymru North) passes through Harlech, heading north to Porthmadog and south to Barmouth.

Blaenau Ffestiniog

POP 3662

Most of the slate used to roof 19th-century Britain came from Wales, and much of that came from the mines of Blaenau Ffestiniog. However, only about 10% of mined slate is usable, so for every tonne that goes to the factory, 9 tonnes remain as rubble. Despite being in the centre of Snowdonia National Park, the grey mountains of mine waste that surround Blaenau (*blay*-nye) prevented it from being officially included in the park – a slap in the face for this close-knit but impoverished town in the days before Wales' industrial sites were recognised as part of its heritage.

Although slate mining continues on a small scale, it's the abandoned workings of this once-mighty industry that are now Blaenau's attraction. By no means a 'pretty' town, opportunities to explore the slate caverns or tickle your adrenal gland with extreme sports make it a great day trip from Porthmadog, via the historic Ffestiniog Railway.

Sights

★Llechwedd Slate Caverns MINE

(☎01766-830306; www.llechwedd-slate-caverns.co.uk; tours £20; ⊙9.30am-5.30pm) Blaenau's main attraction takes you down into the bowels of a Victorian slate mine. You descend the UK's steepest mining cable railway into the 1846 network of tunnels and caverns, while 'enhanced-reality technology' brings to life the harsh working conditions of the 19th-century miners – be prepared to duck and scramble around dark tunnels. There's also a tour of the quarry in a military truck (an extra £20 per person). Check the website for tour times and prebooking.

Cellb ARTS CENTRE

(☎01766-832001; www.cellb.org; Park Sq; ⊙cafe/bar 10am-3pm Tue-Sat, 7-11pm Wed-Sat) Recently opened in the Edwardian-era police station (hence 'Cell B'), this multifunction centre hosts everything from yoga and Welsh-language classes to live bands and film screenings. It's also the town's most appealing dining and drinking space, with a cafe-bar and a cocktail bar. At the time of writing, they were putting the finishing touches to a new, 50-seat digital cinema and hostel accommodation.

Activities

Zip World Blaenau Ffestiniog ADVENTURE SPORTS

(☎01248-601444; www.zipworld.co.uk; Llechwedd Slate Caverns; ⊙booking office 8am-6.30pm; 👪) If you've ever wanted to practise trampoline tricks in a slate mine (and who hasn't?) then Bounce Below – a 'cathedral-sized' cavern with bouncy nets, walkways, tunnels and slides – is your chance (one hour, £25). There's also Titan – 8000m of zip wires over deep open pits (£50 per two hours) – and zip wires through the caverns (£60 for two hours).

Antur Stiniog MOUNTAIN BIKING

(☎01766-832214; www.anturstiniog.com; 1 uplift £17-19, day pass £29-33; ⊙10am-4pm Thu-Mon) If you're a serious mountain biker and don't know the meaning of fear, check out these six new blue and black runs down the mountainside near the slate caverns. There's a minibus uplift service, a cafe (9am to 4.30pm) and plans to introduce a 'velorail' (a pedal-powered vehicle running on the abandoned train line leading to Llan Festiniog).

Getting There & Away

Train Both the Conwy Valley Line from Betws y-Coed (£5.20, 34 minutes) and Llandudno (£8.70, 1¼ hours), and the steam-powered Ffestiniog Railway (p744) from Porthmadog terminate here.

Bus Buses head to/from Porthmadog (route 1B, 30 minutes); Dolgellau (route 35, 47 minutes); Betws-y-Coed (route X1, 25 minutes); and Llandudno (route X1, 1¼ hours).

Betws-y-Coed

POP 2253

Betws-y-Coed *(bet-*us-ee-*koyd)* sits at the junction of three river valleys (the Llugwy, the Conwy and the Lledr) and on the verge of the Gwydyr Forest. With around seven outdoor shops for every pub, walking trails leaving right from the centre and guesthouses occupying a fair proportion of its slate Victorian buildings, it's the perfect base for exploring Snowdonia.

The town has been Wales' most popular inland resort since Victorian times, when a group of countryside painters founded an artistic community to record the diversity of the landscape. The arrival of the railway in 1868 cemented its popularity, and today

WORTH A TRIP

MOUNTAIN SURFING

Lying just outside the national park's eastern border, in the lush Conwy Valley, is this unexpected little slice of Maui: **Surf Snowdonia** (☎01492-353123; www.surfsnowdonia.co.uk; Conway Rd, Dolgarrog; free; ⏰8am-11pm; 👪), an adventure park centred on a vast artificial wave pool (open 10am until sunset). If learning to surf (adult/child £50/35) doesn't excite, there are lagoon 'crash and splash' sessions (£25 per hour), kayaking, walking and a soft-play centre for kids.

Betws-y-Coed is as busy with families and coach parties as it is with walkers.

Sights

One of the joys of Betws is wandering its riverbanks and criss-crossing its historic bridges. The main road crosses the Conwy at the 32m-wide **Waterloo Bridge**: known locally as the 'iron bridge', it bears a large inscription celebrating its construction in the year of Wellington's victory over Boney (1815). Behind the information centre a pleasant path leads around the tongue of land framed by the convergence of the Rivers Conwy and Llugwy, and back past St Michael's Church. Nearby, **Sapper's Bridge** is a white suspension footbridge (1930) that crosses the Conwy and leads through the fields up to the A470.

At the other end of the village, the 15th-century stone **Pont-y-Pair** (Bridge of the Cauldron) crosses a set of rapids on the Llugwy. A riverside path leads about a mile downstream to the **Miners' Bridge**, named for the route miners took on their way to work in nearby lead mines. This was the oldest crossing of the Llugwy, but the original bridge is long gone.

The Rivers Conwy and Llugwy are rich with salmon in autumn. Outdoors shops are strung out along Holyhead Rd, selling equipment and specialist references for walkers, climbers and cyclists.

Swallow Falls WATERFALL

(Rhaeadr Ewynnol; £1.50) Betws-y-Coed's main natural tourist trap is located 2 miles west of town alongside the A5. It's a beautiful spot, with the torrent, Wales's highest, weaving through the rocks into a green pool below. Outside seasonal opening hours, bring a £1 coin for the turnstile.

★**Gwydyr Forest** FOREST

The 28-sq-mile Gwydyr Forest, planted since the 1920s with oak, beech and larch, encircles Betws-y-Coed and is scattered with the remnants of lead and zinc mine workings. Named for a more ancient forest in the same location, it's ideal for a day's walking, though it gets very muddy in wet weather. *Walks Around Betws-y-Coed* (£5), available from the National Park Information Centre, details several circular forest walks.

Activities

Go Below Underground Adventures ADVENTURE SPORTS

(☎01690-710108; www.go-below.co.uk; adult/child from £49/39) Head into the depths of an old slate mine and try your hand ziplining across lakes and abseiling down shafts. You don't have to have caving experience, or squeeze through tiny spaces, but claustrophobes may demur. The booking office is based at Conwy Falls, on the A5 south of Betws at the turn-off to Penmachno.

Zip World Fforest ADVENTURE SPORTS

(☎01248-601444; www.zipworld.co.uk; A470; 2hr 'Safari' £40; ⏰9am-4pm) Tree-top fun in the Fforest includes the 'Safari' – a network of rope ladders and zip-lines high in the tree tops – the 'Plummet' – which uses a 'powerfan' to simulate a parachute drop – and Skyride – a giant, five-person swing that reaches jaw-clenching velocity. There's a cafe for a soothing hot chocolate afterwards.

Sleeping

★**Coed-y-Celyn Hall** APARTMENT $

(☎07821-099595; www.snowdonia-self-catering.co.uk; A470, Coed-y-Celyn; apt per week from £300; P 📶) Built in the 1850s for a mining magnate, this grand pile on the banks of the Conwy was auctioned off in the 1950s and half of it has been converted into apartments. They're all different, but they're all huge – and terrifically good value. We particularly love apartment 4 for its moulded ceilings, grand windows and views over the front lawns.

Vagabond HOSTEL $

(☎01690-710850; www.thevagabond.co.uk; Craiglan Rd; dm from £19; P 📶 🐾) Sitting on the slopes below a forested crag, from which spills its own 'private' waterfall, the Vagabond is Betws's best hostel – and the only one within the town. It's a simple set-up, with freshly decorated dorm rooms, shared bathrooms and an appealing bar (4.30pm to 11pm), kitchen and common room downstairs. The obligatory £24 weekend rate includes a cooked breakfast.

Tyn-y-Fron B&B $$

(01690-710449; www.snowdoniabedandbreakfast.co.uk; Lon Muriau, off A470; s £70, d £78-110; P) The best of a clump of B&Bs over the fields from the town, this gracious old stone house has five guest rooms, all of which have been given a plush, modern makeover, and some of which have divine valley views. Mike and Lesley, the friendly, rugby-mad owners, serve an excellent breakfast, including award-winning sausages and bacon from the local butcher.

Maes-y-Garth B&B $$

(01690-710441; www.maes-y-garth.co.uk; Lon Muriau, off A470; r £75-130; P) Accessible from Betws by a footpath across the river and the fields (starting behind St Michael's Church), this newly built home has earned itself a legion of fans. Inside you'll find a warm welcome and five quietly stylish guest rooms with gorgeous views – perhaps the nicest is room 4, which has its own balcony and views of the valley.

Bod Gwynedd B&B $$

(01690-710717; www.bodgwynedd.com; Holyhead Rd; s/d from £60/75; P) On the western edge of town, this friendly B&B offers tastefully furnished bedrooms in a mid-Victorian slate house. The friendly owners keep everything spick-and-span and have plenty of local knowledge to impart.

Eating

Cwmni Cacen Gri CAFE $

(01690-710006; www.cwmnicacengri.co.uk; Station Approach; Welsh cakes 50p; 9am-4.30pm Tue-Sun;) At this pint-sized spot, local ladies Jen and Jo serve Welsh cakes straight from the griddle – from traditional fare to unusually flavoured sweet and savoury ones; all are made with organic Welsh eggs and butter. Pies, homemade cakes and good coffee are also available: all ideal picnic fodder.

★ **Bistro Betws-y-Coed** WELSH $$

(01690-710328; www.bistrobetws-y-coed.com; Holyhead Rd; lunch £6-9, dinner £13-20; noon-3pm & 6.30-9.30pm daily Jun-Sep, Wed-Sun Mar-May, 6.30-9.30pm Wed-Sun Dec-Feb) This cottage-style eatery's statement of intent is 'Traditional and Modern Welsh' and the menu features some interesting adaptations of Welsh recipes from the 18th and 19th centuries. Watch out for possible shot pellets in the sautéed breast of wild wood pigeon with blueberry pancakes and crispy bacon! And book in summer as it gets absolutely packed.

Tŷ Gwyn Hotel EUROPEAN $$

(01690-710383; www.tygwynhotel.co.uk; A5; mains £15-19; noon-2pm & 6-9pm;) This 400-year-old coaching inn oozes character from every one of its numerous exposed beams. The menu is full of intriguing modern takes on age-old local ingredients (locally reared suckling pig, whole lake trout from Llyn Brenig) and a decent number of veggie options (the wild mushroom and pine-nut stroganoff is as good as it sounds). Book ahead.

Information

Snowdonia National Park Information Centre (01690-710426; www.eryri-npa.gov.uk; Royal Oak Stables; 9.30am-5.30pm Easter-Oct, to 4pm rest of year) More than just a repository of books, maps and local craft, this office is an invaluable source of information about walking trails, mountain conditions and more.

Getting There & Away

Betws-y-Coed is on the Conwy Valley Line (www.conwyvalleyrailway.co.uk), with trains every day but Sunday to Llandudno (£6.30, 54 minutes) and Blaenau Ffestiniog (£5.20, 34 minutes).

Snowdon Sherpa bus services head to Swallow Falls (route S2, seven minutes), Capel Curig (route S2, 12 minutes), Pen-y-Pass (route S2, 25 minutes), Llanberis (route S2, 35 minutes) and Bangor (route S6, in summer, one hour); all trips are £1.50.

Other buses head to Llandudno (route X1/19, one hour), Conwy (route 19, 45 minutes), Blaenau Ffestiniog (route X1, 25 minutes) and Dolgellau (route X1, one daily Monday to Saturday, 1¼ hours).

Llanberis

POP 1844

Llanberis is a mecca for walkers and climbers, attracting a steady flow of rugged, polar-fleece wearers year-round but especially in July and August (when accommodation is at a premium). It's positioned just outside the national park but functions as a hub, partly because the Snowdon Mountain Railway leaves from here. While not the most attractive town in the area, its offbeat charm complements the appeal of its glorious surrounds.

Llanberis originally housed workers from the Dinorwig slate quarry; the massive waste tips are hard to miss. While tourism is the cornerstone of life these days, the town proudly wears its industrial heritage on its sleeve. Dinorwig, which once boasted the largest artificial cavern in the world, is now part of Europe's biggest pumped-storage power station. Some of the old quarry workshops have been reincarnated as a slate-industry museum, and the narrow-gauge railway that once hauled slate to the coast now transports excited toddlers along Llyn Padarn.

Sights & Activities

★National Slate Museum MUSEUM
(03001-112333; www.museumwales.ac.uk/en/slate; 10am-5pm Easter-Oct, to 4pm Sun-Fri Nov-Easter) FREE A slate museum sounds dull; it isn't. Even if you're not enraptured by industrial museums, this one's well worth checking out. At Llanberis much of the slate was carved out of the open mountainside – leaving behind a jagged, sculptural cliff-face that's fascinating if not quite beautiful. The museum occupies the Victorian workshops beside Llyn Padarn. It features video clips, a huge working water wheel, workers' cottages (each furnished in a progression from 1861 until 1969, when the quarries closed) and demonstrations.

Electric Mountain MUSEUM
(01286-870636; www.electricmountain.co.uk; tour adult/child £8.50/4.35; 10am-4.30pm Jan-May & Sep-Dec, 9.30am-5.30pm Jun-Aug) More than just Dinorwig Power Station's public interface, Electric Mountain is a tourist hub incorporating a gallery, cafe, children's playground, climbing wall and souvenir shop. It also has interactive exhibits on hydropower and is the starting point for a fascinating guided tour into the power station's guts, 750m under Elidir mountain.

The centre is by the lakeside on the A4086, near the south end of High St.

Llanberis Lake Railway TOURS
(01286-870549; www.lake-railway.co.uk; adult/child £8.20/4.50; Feb-Nov) If you need something to placate the kids on days that the Snowdonia Mountain Railway isn't operating, this little steam train might be just the ticket. It departs on a 5-mile return jaunt along the route used from 1843 to 1961 to haul slate to the port on the Menai Strait.

The gentle, scenic one-hour return trip heads alongside Llyn Padarn, past the National Slate Museum and through Padarn Country Park to the terminus at Penllyn. The starting point is either Llanberis Station (across the A4086 from the Snowdon Mountain Railway station) or Gilfach Ddu Station (in Padarn Country Park).

Sleeping

YHA Snowdon Llanberis HOSTEL $
(0845 371 9645; www.yha.org.uk; Capel Goch Rd; dm/r from £15/39; reception 8-10am & 5-10pm; P) Originally a quarry manager's house, this no-frills hostel offers great views (from an admittedly scrappy hillside locale), a self-catering kitchen and a drying room. It's about a 10-minute walk above the town, signposted from the High St.

★Beech Bank B&B $$
(01286-871085; www.beech-bank.co.uk; 2 High St; s/d £60/80; P) First impressions of this double-gabled, wrought iron–trimmed stone house are great, but step inside and it just gets better. A stylish renovation has left beautiful bathrooms and exuberant decor, which matches the gregarious nature of the host. Highly recommended, although not set up for children.

Plas Coch Guest House HOTEL $$
(01286-872122; www.plascochsnowdonia.co.uk; High St; s £60, d £80-90; P) More like a little hotel than a B&B, this large ivy-draped 1865 house is operated by a friendly couple with lots of local knowledge to impart. The rooms are stylishly renovated, very comfortable and, in some cases, large enough to qualify as suites.

Eating

Y Pantri CAFE $
(High St; mains £4-6; 10am-5pm) Good coffee! After that, everything else this cruisy, pastel-hued little cafe does is a bonus. But those extras – homemade cakes, sandwich-

es, soups and the like – are also from the top drawer.

Pete's Eats CAFE $

(01286-870117; www.petes-eats.co.uk; 40 High St; mains £3-7; 8am-8pm;) Pete's Eats is a local institution – a busy, primary-coloured cafe where hikers and climbers swap tips over monster breakfasts and under photos of their knee-trembling forebears. There's bunkhouse accommodation upstairs, a huge noticeboard full of travellers' information, a book exchange, a map and guidebook room, and computers for internet access.

★**Gallt-y-Glyn** PUB FOOD $$

(01286-870370; www.gallt-y-glyn.co.uk; A4086; mains £8-15; 6-9pm Wed-Sat;) Sure, it serves pasta, pies, steaks and salads too, but almost everyone comes for the pizza and the free-pint-with-every-main deal. Simply tick what you want on the paper menu and hand it over at the bar. You'll find Gallt-y-Glyn on the A4086, half a mile towards Caernarfon. It's a bit shabby, slightly eccentric, very family riendly and utterly brilliant.

Peak Restaurant INTERNATIONAL $$

(Bwyty'r Copa; 01286-872777; www.peakrestaurant.co.uk; 86 High St; mains £13-17; 7-10pm Wed-Sat;) A chef-patron who once clattered the pans at the legendary Chez Panisse in California is behind this restaurant's popularity and longevity. The open kitchen allows you to see her at work, turning good Welsh produce into internationally inspired dishes such as Anglesey sea bass with coriander butter and Welsh lamb shanks with white-onion puree.

Information

Joe Brown (01286-870327; 63 High St; 9am-5.30pm) A climbing shop that sells all things outdoors; its noticeboard includes weather forecasts and lots of information and advice for walkers.

Getting There & Away

Snowdon Sherpa buses stop by Joe Brown's on the High St. S1 heads to Pen-y-Pass (15 minutes), while S2 continues on to Capel Curig (35 minutes) and Betws-y-Coed (47 minutes).

Other buses head to Caernarfon (route 88, 25 minutes) and Bangor (route 85/86, 50 minutes).

Snowdon (Yr Wyddfa)

No Snowdonia experience is complete without coming face-to-face with Snowdon (1085m), one of Britain's most awe-inspiring mountains and the highest summit in Wales (it's actually the 61st highest in Britain, with the higher 60 all in Scotland). 'Yr Wyddfa' in Welsh (pronounced uhr-*with*-vuh, meaning 'the Tomb'), it's the mythical resting place of the giant Rhita Gawr, who demanded King Arthur's beard for his cloak and was killed for his temerity. On a clear day the views stretch to Ireland and the Isle of Man over Snowdon's fine jagged ridges, which drop away in great swoops to sheltered *cwms* (valleys) and deep lakes. Even on a gloomy day you could find yourself above the clouds. Thanks to the Snowdon Mountain Railway it's extremely accessible when the weather is clement. In fact, the summit and some of the tracks can get frustratingly crowded.

Sights & Activities

Just below the cairn that marks Snowdon's summit is Hafod Eryri (p740), a striking piece of architecture that opened in 2009 to replace the dilapidated 1930s visitor centre that Prince Charles famously labelled 'the highest slum in Europe'.

★**Snowdon Trails** HIKING

Six paths of varying length and difficulty lead to the summit, all taking around six hours return. Just because Snowdon has a train station and a cafe on its summit, doesn't mean you should underestimate it. No route is completely safe, especially in winter. People regularly come unstuck here and many have died over the years, including experienced climbers.

The most straightforward route to the summit is the **Llanberis Path** (9 miles return) running beside the train line. The two paths starting from Pen-y-Pass require the least amount of ascent but are nevertheless tougher walks: the **Miner's Track** (8 miles return) starts off wide and gentle but gets steep beyond Llyn Llydaw and the more interesting **Pyg Track** (7 miles return) is more rugged still.

Two tracks start from the Caernarfon–Beddgelert road (A4085): the **Snowdon Ranger Path** (8 miles return) is the safest route in winter, while the **Rhyd Ddu Path** (8 miles return) is the least-used route and boasts spectacular views. The most challenging route is the **Watkin Path** (8 miles return), involving an ascent of more than 1000m on its southerly approach from Nantgwynant and finishing with a scramble across a steep-sided, scree-covered slope.

The classic **Snowdon Horseshoe** (7.5 miles return) branches off from the Pyg Track to follow the precipitous ridge of **Crib Goch** (one of the most dangerous routes on the mountains and only recommended for the very experienced) with a descent over the peak of Y Lliwedd and a final section down the Miner's Track.

Allow six or seven hours for any of these trails.

★**Snowdon Mountain Railway** RAIL
(01286-870223; www.snowdonrailway.co.uk; Llanberis; adult/child return diesel £29/20, steam £37/27; 9am-5pm mid-Mar–Nov) If you're not physically able to climb a mountain, short on time or just plain lazy, those industrious, railway-obsessed Victorians have gifted you an alternative. Opened in 1896, the Snowdon Mountain Railway is the UK's highest – and its only public – rack-and-pinion railway. Vintage steam and modern diesel locomotives haul carriages from Llanberis up to Snowdon's summit in an hour.

Return trips involve a scant half-hour at the top before heading back down again. Single tickets can only be booked for the journey up (adult/child £22/17); if you want to walk up and ride down, you'll have to hope there's space. Tens of thousands of people take the train to the summit each season: make sure you book well in advance or you may miss out. Departures depend on customer demand and are weather dependent. From March to May (or during high winds) the trains can only head as far Clogwyn Station (adult/child £19/13) – an altitude of 779m.

Sleeping

YHA Snowdon Pen-y-Pass HOSTEL $
(08453-719534; www.yha.org.uk; A4086; dm/tw £29/55) This superbly situated hostel has three of Snowdon's trails literally on its doorstep. Comprehensively refurbished in 2014, it has a new kitchen, Mallory's Cafe/Bar (named for a past patron who perished on Everest) and some of the best rooms of any of the park's YHAs (half of which are en suite). It's 5.5 miles up the A4086 from Llanberis.

Pen-y-Gwryd HOTEL $$
(01286-870211; www.pyg.co.uk; Nant Gwynant; s/d from £45/90; P) Eccentric but full of atmosphere, this Georgian coaching inn was used as a training base by the 1953 Everest team, and memorabilia from their stay includes signatures on the restaurant ceiling. TV, wi-fi and mobile-phone signals don't penetrate here; instead, there's a comfy games room, sauna and a lake for those hardy enough to swim. You'll find the hotel below Pen-y-Pass, at the junction of the A498 and A4086.

Information

Hafod Eryri (10am–20min before last train departure;) Clad in granite and curved to blend into the mountain, Hafod Eryri houses a cafe, toilets and ambient interpretative elements built into the structure itself. A wall of picture windows gazes down towards the west, while a small row faces the cairn. Closed in winter or if the weather's terrible, it's open whenever the train is running.

Getting There & Away

It's worth considering public transport: car parks can fill up quickly and Pen-y-Pass car park costs £10 per day.

Before you decide which route you'll take to the summit, study the bus and train timetables. If you're based in Llanberis, you'll find it easiest to get to and from the Llanberis, Pyg and Miner's paths. The Snowdon Ranger and Rhyd Ddu paths are better connected to Beddgelert and Caernarfon.

The Welsh Highland Railway stops at the trailhead of the Rhyd Ddu Path and there is a request stop (Snowdon Ranger Halt) where you can alight for the Snowdon Ranger Path.

All the trailheads are accessible by Snowdon Sherpa bus services S1, S2, S4 or S97 (single/day ticket £1.50/5).

Another option is to take the Snowdon Mountain Railway from Llanberis to the top and walk back down. It's more difficult to do this the other way around as the train will only take on new passengers at the top if there is space.

Beddgelert

POP 453

Charming Beddgelert is a conservation village of dark stone cottages overlooking the River Colwyn and its ivy-covered bridge, just upstream from where it meets the River Glaslyn. Flowers festoon the village in spring and the surrounding hills are

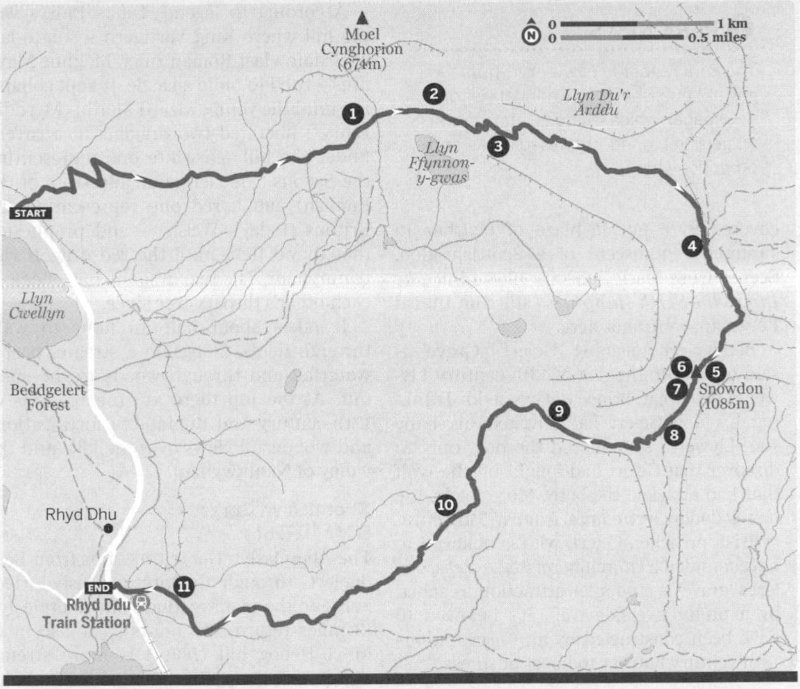

Mountain Walk
Up Snowdon Ranger, Down Rhyd Ddu

START SNOWDON RANGER YHA
END RHYD DDU TRAIN STATION
LENGTH 8 MILES, SIX HOURS

This particular Snowdon route is reasonably straightforward, quiet and doesn't involve difficult scrambles (that said, in snowy and icy conditions, the descent on the Rhyd Ddu Path should only be undertaken by experienced mountaineers equipped with crampons and ice picks; everyone else should double back on the Snowdon Ranger Path). Both trailheads are connected by buses and trains to accommodation in Caernarfon, Beddgelert and Porthmadog.

The original 'Snowdon Ranger' was John Morton, an English mountain guide who built an inn on the site of the current YHA in the early 1800s and led guests to the summit along this track. The path climbs gently along the lower slopes of ❶ **Moel Cynghorion** to ❷ **Bwlch Cwm Brwynog**, before it steepens and heads above ❸ **Clogwyn Du'r Arddu**. Eventually it draws parallel with the Snowdon Mountain Railway. The path crosses the tracks at a ❹ **standing stone**, turns right and merges with the Llanberis Path for the final approach to the ❺ **summit**.

When you're ready to descend, pick up the Rhyd Ddu Path below the ❻ **Hafod Eryri** visitor centre. After 200m a ❼ **standing stone** marks the point where the Watkin Path veers off; continue straight ahead. The next section, along ❽ **Bwlch Main** (meaning 'Slender Path'), is a narrow track with steep slopes on either side: if there's ice, snow or wind, this can be genuinely dangerous and is only for properly equipped and experienced walkers. Near the end of this stretch the path splits into two; keep on the right-hand track. From here the path broadens as it zigzags down and then edges along the ❾ **Llechog ridge**. It starts to flatten out after it passes the ❿ **ruins** of an old refreshment hut. The final stretch continues alongside the abandoned ⓫ **Ffridd Slate Quarry** before terminating near the Rhyd Ddu train station.

PARK NEWS

The Park Authority (www.eryri-npa.gov.uk) publishes a free annual visitor newspaper, which includes information on getting around, organised walks and other activities.

covered in a purple blaze of heather in summer, reminiscent of a Scottish glen. Scenes from Mark Robson's 1958 film, *The Inn of the Sixth Happiness* starring Ingrid Bergman, were shot here.

Beddgelert, meaning 'Gelert's Grave', is said to refer to the dog of 13th-century Llywelyn the Great, Prince of Gwynedd. Thinking his dog Gelert had savaged his baby son, Llywelyn slaughtered the dog, only to discover that Gelert had fought off the wolf that had attacked the baby. More likely, the name Beddgelert comes from a 5th-century Irish preacher, Celert, who is believed to have founded a church here. Regardless, Gelert's 'grave' is a popular attraction, reached by a pretty riverside trail. It's believed to have been constructed by an unscrupulous 18th-century hotelier to boost business.

Sights & Activities

Sygun Copper Mine MINE

(www.syguncoppermine.co.uk; A498; adult/child under 15 £8.95/6.95; 9.30am-5pm in British Summer Time, 10am-4pm Nov-Feb) This mine dates from Roman times, although extraction was stepped up in the 19th century. Abandoned in 1903, it has since been converted into a museum, with a half-hour self-guided underground tour containing dioramas that evoke the life of Victorian miners. You can also try your hand at metal detecting (£2.50) or panning for gold (£2). It's located a mile northeast of Beddgelert, along the A498.

Craflwyn & Dinas Emrys WALKING

(NT; 01766-510120; www.nationaltrust.org.uk/craflwyn-and-beddgelert) A mile northeast of Beddgelert, near Llyn Dinas, National Trust–owned Craflwyn Farm is the starting point for several short walks, including a path to Dinas Emrys, one of the most significant yet largely unheralded sites in Welsh mythology. To stay at Pretty Craflwyn Hall contact HF Holidays (www.hfholidays.co.uk), which leases it on behalf of the Trust.

According to legend, Dinas Emrys was the hill where King Vortigern – son-in-law of Britain's last Roman ruler, Magnus Maximus – tried to build a castle. It kept collapsing until the young wizard Merlin (Myrddin Emrys) liberated two dragons in a cavern under the hill – a white one representing the Saxons (the Germanic ancestors of the English) and a red one representing the Britons (today's Welsh) – and prophesied that they'd fight until the red dragon was triumphant. The two dragons have been at each other's throats ever since.

It takes about half an hour to walk through fields, alongside a stream, past a waterfall and through woods to the summit. At the top there are the remains of 12th-century and Roman-era fortifications and wonderful views over the lake and the valley of Nantgwynant.

Aberglaslyn Gorge & Moel Hebog WALKING

The Aberglaslyn Gorge trail runs from Beddgelert, through the pretty Glaslyn river gorge to the main road at Pont Aberglaslyn (3 miles return, two hours). The ascent of Moel Hebog hill (783m) is more strenuous (8-mile loop, five hours), and includes a lovely scenic ridge walk over two more peaks. Beddgelert's tourist office has leaflets on both hikes.

Sleeping & Eating

Sygun Fawr Country House HOTEL $$

(01766-890258; www.sygunfawr.co.uk; s/d from £43/86; P) A warm welcome awaits at this sturdy stone manor house, tucked away at the end of a narrow lane. Bits have been grafted on to the 1660s core over the centuries (including a conservatory), so each of the 12 comfortable bedrooms are quite different; some have spectacular mountain views. It's well signposted from the A498, immediately northeast of the village.

★**Hebog Beddgelert** BISTRO $$

(01766-890400; www.hebog-beddgelert.co.uk; Fford Caernarfon; mains £18-20;) A welcome addition to Beddgelert's dining (and sleeping) scene, Hebog is an upmarket cafe that morphs into a sleek bistro by night, serving the likes of monkfish tails in parma ham with prawns and lobster velouté. A self-catering apartment and summer terrace overlooking the babbling Glaslyn seal the deal.

Information

National Trust Shop (01766-890545; Stryd Yr Eglwys; 11am-5pm, shorter hours winter weekdays) Tŷ Isaf, a Grade II–listed 17th-century cottage on the south side of the central bridge, contains Beddgelert's National Trust shop. Along with crafts made from local materials, regional produce and literature, there are kids' activity packs and walking guides to the local area.

Tourist Office (01766-890615; www.eryri-npa.gov.uk; Canolfan Hebog; 9.30am-5pm Easter-Oct) Great for information on walks, cycling and accommodation in the area.

Getting There & Away

Snowdon Sherpa bus S4 heads to/from Caernarfon (30 minutes), Snowdon Ranger (10 minutes), Rhyd Ddu (six minutes) and Pen-y-Pass (20 minutes).

Bus S97 heads to Porthmadog (21 minutes), Tremadog (13 minutes) and Pen-y-Pass (18 minutes).

Beddgelert is a stop on the historic Welsh Highland Railway, which runs between Caernarfon (£29.10 return, 1½ hours) and Porthmadog (£20.90, 40 minutes) from Easter to October, with limited winter service, and stops at the Rhyd Ddu and Snowdon Ranger trailheads.

LLŶN PENINSULA

Jutting into the Irish Sea from the Snowdonia mountains, the Llŷn (pronounced 'khleen' and sometimes spelt 'Lleyn') is a green finger of land some 30 miles long and averaging 8 miles wide. This peaceful and largely undeveloped region has isolated walking and cycling routes, Iron-Age forts, beaches, a scattering of small fishing villages and 70 miles of wildlife-rich coastline (much of it in the hands of the National Trust, with almost 80% designated an Area of Outstanding Natural Beauty). Over the centuries the heaviest footfalls have been those of pilgrims heading to Bardsey Island.

Welsh is the everyday language. Indeed, this is about as Welsh as it gets. The Llŷn Peninsula and Anglesey were the last stops for the Romans and Normans, and both have maintained a separate identity.

This isolated place has been an incubator of Welsh activism. It was the birthplace of David Lloyd George, the first Welsh prime minister of the UK, and of Plaid Cymru (the Party of Wales), which was founded in Pwllheli in 1925 and now holds 18% of the seats in the Welsh Assembly.

Porthmadog

POP 4185

Despite a few rough edges, busy little Porthmadog (port-*mad*-uk) has an attractive estuarine setting and a conspicuously friendly, mainly Welsh-speaking populace. It straddles both the Llŷn Peninsula and Snowdonia National Park, and has the fantastical village of Portmeirion at its doorstep. Throw in abundant transport connections and you have a handy place to base yourself for a couple of days.

Porthmadog is a mecca for railway buffs. There are 'little trains' all over Wales, a legacy of Victorian industry, but Porthmadog is triply blessed. It forms the southern terminus for two of Wales' finest narrow-gauge train journeys and has a third steam-train line connected to a rail heritage centre.

Mullet abound in the shallow Traeth Bach estuary, which in turn attract ospreys. Keep an eye out for these large birds of prey as you walk around the cliffs of Borth-y-Gest and Porthmeirion.

History

Both Porthmadog and the neighbouring village of Tremadog (the latter now virtually a suburb of the former) were founded by and named after reforming landowner William Alexander Madocks. In the early 19th century he laid down the mile-long Cob causeway, drained the 400 hectares of wetlands that lay behind it and created a brand-new harbour. After his death, the Cob became the route for the Ffestiniog Railway: at its 1873 peak, it transported more than 116,000 tonnes of slate from the mines of Blaenau Ffestiniog to the harbour. In 1888 TE Lawrence (Lawrence of Arabia) was born in Tremadog, although the Lawrence family moved to Oxford 12 years later; look for his family home (marked with a plaque) near the church.

Sights & Activities

★**Portmeirion Village** VILLAGE
(01766-770000; www.portmeirion-village.com; adult/child £11/8; 9.30am-7.30pm; P) Set on its own tranquil peninsula reaching into the estuary, Portmeirion Village is a fantastical

collection of colourful buildings with a heavy Italian influence, masterminded by the Welsh architect Sir Clough Williams-Ellis. Starting in 1925, Clough collected bits and pieces from disintegrating stately mansions and set them alongside his own creations to create this weird and wonderful seaside utopia. Today the buildings are all heritage-listed and the site is a conservation area.

★**Welsh Highland Railway** TOUR
(☎01766-516000; www.festrail.co.uk; adult/child return £38/34.20; ⊙Easter-Oct, limited winter service) Leaving from the Porthmadog Harbour Station, as does the Blaenau-Ffestiniog Railway, the Welsh Highland runs to Caernarfon (£38 return, 2½ hours) via Rhd Ddu (£25.10 return) and Beddgelert (£20.90 return).

★**Ffestiniog Railway** RAIL
(Rheilffordd Ffestiniog; ☎01766-516024; www.festrail.co.uk; adult/child return £23/21; ⊙daily Easter-Oct, reduced service rest of year;) The world's oldest surviving narrow-gauge railway, the Ffestiniog wends its way from the slate-mining town of Blaenau Ffestiniog to Porthmadog. Long past its industrial heyday, its 150-year-old steam locomotives and monogrammed wooden carriages now ferry sightseers through oak woodlands, under towering peaks and by flashing rivers. Both the Ffestiniog and Welsh Highland lines terminate at Porthmadog Harbour Station.

Festivals & Events

PortmeiriCon CULTURAL
(Prisoner Convention; www.portmeiricon.com; Portmeirion; ⊙Apr) One to either pencil in or avoid, fans of the cult TV show *The Prisoner* converge on Portmeirion in April for a weekend of dress ups and human chess. Indoor events are only open to members of the Six of One (the *Prisoner* Appreciation Society) but anyone can catch outdoor shows or glimpses of celebrities bussed in for the occasion.

★**Festival No 6** PERFORMING ARTS
(☎08449-670002; www.festivalnumber6.com; ⊙Sep) Started in 2012, this rock and dance-music festival with arts, culture and comedy components has topped many best-festival lists and makes imaginative use of Portmeirion's varied and dreamlike environment. Headliners have included New Order, Fleetwood Mac and Cassius. It's held over a long weekend in September.

Sleeping & Eating

★**Yr Hen Fecws** B&B $$
(☎01766-514625; www.henfecws.com; 16 Lombard St; s/d from £65/80; P) Probably Porthmadog's nicest digs, this stylishly restored stone cottage has seven simply decorated en suite rooms with exposed-slate walls and fireplaces. Breakfast is served within the marigold walls and exposed beams of the cosy cafe downstairs (mains £6 to £10; open 8am to 4pm Monday to Saturday).

Hotel Portmeirion & Castell Deudraeth HOTEL $$$
(☎01766-770000; www.portmeirion-village.com; Portmeirion; hotel s/d £204/219, castle & village s/d from £139/169; P) You can live the fantasy and stay within the famous fairy-tale village itself in one of 17 whimsical cottages. Over-the-top Hotel Portmeirion, dating to 1850 but extended by Clough Ellis, has a plum spot by the water, with a terraced bar for afternoon tippling. Fanciful Castell Deudraeth is a more modern alternative, despite also dating to Victoria's reign.

★**Y Sgwâr** BISTRO $$$
(☎01766-515451; www.ysgwar-restaurant.co.uk; 12-16 Market Sq; mains £15-25; ⊙noon-2pm & 6-9pm) On the edge of Tremadog's main square, this French-accented Welsh restaurant has the best food in Porthmadog or Tremadog. The service is super-attentive and friendly, and dishes such as scallops with crispy belly pork, cauliflower puree and black pudding are a delight. There's value in the set menu (two/three courses £18/22) offered at lunch or between 6pm and 7pm.

Information

Ysbyty Alltwen (☎01766-510010; A487, Tremadog) The local hospital treats minor injuries but doesn't have a full emergency department.

Getting There & Away

Train Porthmadog is on the Cambrian Coast Line, with direct trains to Machynlleth (£14, two hours), Barmouth (£7.30, 50 minutes), Harlech (£4, 24 minutes), Criccieth (£2.80, seven minutes) and Pwllheli (£5.10, 25 minutes). See also the **Ffestiniog & Welsh Highland Railways** (www.festrail.co.uk) for steamy services to Blaenau Ffestiniog, the Snowdon trailheads and Caernarfon.

Bus Buses stop on High St and most services pass through Tremadog. Routes head to/from

Machynlleth (route T2; 1½ hours), Dolgellau (route T2; 50 minutes), Beddgelert (route S97; 25 minutes), Pwllheli (route 3; 40 minutes) and Caernarfon (route 1/1A, 45 minutes).

Bicycle The Lôn Las Cymru (National Cycle Route 8) passes through Porthmadog, heading west to Criccieth and south to Harlech.

Criccieth

POP 1753

This genteel slow-moving seaside town sits above two sand-and-stone Blue Flag beaches, 5 miles west of Porthmadog. Its main claim to fame is ruined Criccieth Castle, perched up on the clifftop and offering views stretching along the peninsula's southern coast and across Tremadog Bay to Harlech.

Sights

Criccieth Castle CASTLE

(Cadw; www.cadw.wales.gov.uk; Castle St; adult/child £3.50/2.50; 10am-5pm daily Mar-Oct, 9.30am-4pm Fri & Sat, from 11am Sun Nov-Mar) Ruined Criccieth Castle is perched on the clifftop and offers views stretching along the southern coast and across Tremadog Bay to Harlech. Constructed by Welsh prince Llywelyn the Great in 1239, it was overrun in 1283 by Edward I's forces and recaptured for the Welsh in 1404 by Owain Glyndŵr, whose forces promptly sacked it. Today there is a small but informative exhibition centre at the ticket office.

Sleeping & Eating

Bron Eifion HISTORIC HOTEL $$

(01766-522385; www.broneifion.co.uk; r £95-175; P) The former palace of a slate magnate, set in 2 hectares of fabulously formal gardens, grand old Bron Eifion has been refurbished with flat-screen TVs sitting alongside faux-Gothic carvings and wooden panels. The hotel is half a mile west of Criccieth, on the A497.

Dylan's INTERNATIONAL $$

(01766-522773; www.dylansrestaurant.co.uk; Maes y Mor; mains £12-17; noon-10pm; P) Making great use of Morannedd – a light-filled, 1950s deco-style beachside pavilion, designed by Portmeirion architect Sir Clough Williams-Ellis and once used by Butlin's for afternoon tea dances – Dylan's is the slickest place in Criccieth. Like its sibling in Menai Bridge, it offers fantastic sea views to complement a globe-trotting bistro menu including pizzas, curries and seafood.

Getting There & Away

Train Criccieth is on the Cambrian Coast Line, with direct trains to Machynlleth (£16, two hours), Barmouth (£8.10, one hour), Harlech (£6, 35 minutes), Porthmadog (£2.80, seven minutes) and Pwllheli (£3.60, 15 minutes).

Bus Buses head to/from Pwllheli (route 3; 24 minutes), Llanystumdwy (route 3; four minutes), Porthmadog (routes 1 and 3; 17 minutes) and Caernarfon (routes 1/1A, 45 minutes).

Bicycle The Lôn Las Cymru (National Cycle Route 8) passes through Criccieth, heading north to Caernarfon and east to Porthmadog.

Abersoch

POP 1990

Abersoch comes alive in summer with a 30,000-person influx of boatics, surfers and beach bums. Edged by gentle blue-green hills, the town's main attraction is its Blue Flag beach, one of the most popular on the peninsula. Surfers head further south for the Atlantic swell at **Porth Neigwl** (Hell's Mouth) and **Porth Ceiriad**.

Sleeping & Eating

★**Venetia** HOTEL $$

(01758-713354; www.venetiawales.com; Lôn Sarn Bach; r £108-148; P) No sinking old Venetian palazzo, just five luxurious rooms in a grand Victorian house decked out with designer lighting and modern art; room Cinque has a TV above its bathtub. The restaurant specialises in the traditional tastes of Venice (mains £12 to £24), particularly seafood and pasta dishes, and serves them under twinkling modern chandeliers.

★**Coconut Kitchen** THAI $$

(01758-712250; www.thecoconutkitchen.co.uk; Lôn Port Morgan; mains £13-16; 5.30-10pm daily,

LLŶN COASTAL BUS

Between March and October the **Llŷn Coastal Bus** (01758-721777) minibus runs between Nefyn and Abersoch, via Aberdaron, Porth Neigwl and Porthor, five times a day from Thursday to Sunday. At only £1 per trip, it's a boon for walkers on some of the more remote stretches of the Llŷn Coastal Path. Booking 24 hours ahead is advised.

closed Jan, Feb & Tue & Wed in low season; P) The Thai head chef and her Welsh partner started the Coconut Kitchen in a van and were quickly compelled to find a more substantial venue for their harmonious marriage of local ingredients and real Thai cuisine. Try Menai mussels in a lemongrass and chilli broth, five-spiced duck or any of the open kitchen's outstanding curries, salads and stir-fries. Book ahead.

Getting There & Away

Bus 18 stops on Stryd Fawr (High St), heading to/from Llanbedrog (15 minutes) and Pwllheli (25 minutes).

Aberdaron

POP 965

Aberdaron is an ends-of-the-earth kind of place with whitewashed, windswept houses contemplating the sands of Aberdaron Bay. It was traditionally the last resting spot before pilgrims made the treacherous crossing to Bardsey Island. The little Gwylan Islands, just offshore, are North Wales' most important puffin-breeding site, while choughs, peregrines, hares and grey seals all thrive in the wild splendour of the surrounding country.

Sights

St Hywyn's Church CHURCH
(www.st-hywyn.org.uk; 10am-6pm Apr-Oct, to 4pm Nov-Mar) Stoically positioned above the pebbly beach, the left half of St Hywyn's Church dates from 1100 while the right half was added 400 years later to accommodate the pilgrims. Inside there's information about local history, as well as two 6th-century memorial stones and a medieval font and holy-water stoup. Welsh poet RS Thomas was the minister here from 1967 to 1978 – an appropriate setting for his bleak, impassioned work.

Porth Oer BEACH
(Whistling Sands; NT; www.nationaltrust.org.uk; car park £1.50) This lovely remote scoop of beach, 2.5 miles north of Aberdaron, has sand which squeaks when you walk on it, giving it its English name, Whistling Sands. From here it's a 2-mile coastal walk southwest via the twin headlands of Dinas Bach and Dinas Fawr to the cove of Porth Orion.

★Braich-y-Pwll AREA
(NT; www.nationaltrust.org.uk) The rugged, ethereally beautiful extremity of the Llŷn Peninsula is where the medieval pilgrims set off to reach the holy island of Bardsey: one glimpse of their destination, rising out of the gunmetal-grey sea beyond the surf-pounded rocks hints at the drama of their final voyage. A path leads down past the remains of St Mary's Abbey to a Neolithic standing stone known as Maen Melyn, suggesting this was a holy place well before the Celts or their saints arrived.

Sleeping & Eating

★Tŷ Newydd HOTEL $$
(01758-760207; www.gwesty-tynewydd.co.uk; s/d from £60/90;) The location alone would make this a top pick, even if the digs weren't so cushy. Right on the beach, this friendly hotel has fully refurbished, light-drenched, spacious rooms and wonderful sea views. The tide comes in right under the terrace off the pub restaurant (mains £12 to £17), which seems designed with an afternoon gin and tonic in mind.

Y Gegin Fawr WELSH $
(The Big Kitchen; 01758-760359; mains from £7; 9am-6pm) With their spiritual needs sorted, the Bardsey-bound saints could claim a meal at Y Gegin Fawr, a little thick-walled building with tiny windows, just over the bridge in the centre of the village. Dating from 1300, it now dishes up locally caught crab and lobster, plus homemade cakes and scones. Even pilgrims need to pay these days, of course.

Getting There & Away

Buses head to/from Nefyn (route 8B, 30 minutes), Llanbedrog (17/17B, 30 minutes) and Pwllheli (17/17B, 40 minutes).

THE NORTH COAST

The North Wales coast has perennial natural charms, but seaside resorts of uneven appeal: some are outstanding examples of the genre, others more down at heel. The section west of Colwyn Bay includes glorious Unesco World Heritage–listed castles at Caernarfon and Conwy and the Victorian resort of Llandudno, a favourite family holiday hub. The sands stretch along a string of less appealing resort towns east of the bay, but there are greater attractions to be discovered by turning south into the delightful Conwy Valley.

Caernarfon

POP 9493

Wedged between the gleaming Menai Strait and the deep-purple hills, Caernarfon's main claim to fame is its fantastical castle. Given the town's crucial historical importance, its proximity to Snowdonia and reputation as a centre of Welsh culture (its percentage of native speakers is as high as anywhere), it's surprisingly down-at-heel in parts, with quite a few boarded-up buildings. Still, there's a lot of charm in its untouristy air and a tangible sense of history in the streets around the castle, especially Palace St, Castle Sq and Hole in the Wall St. Within the cobbled lanes of the old walled town are some fine Georgian buildings, and the waterfront is marching inevitably towards gentrification.

History

Caernarfon Castle was built by Edward I as the last link in his 'iron ring' and it's now part of the 'Castles and Town Walls of King Edward in Gwynedd' Unesco World Heritage Site. In an attempt by the then prime minister, David Lloyd George (himself a Welshman), to bring the royals closer to their Welsh constituency, the castle was designated as the venue for the 1911 investiture of the Prince of Wales. In retrospect, linking the modern royals to such a powerful symbol of Welsh subjugation may not have been the best idea. It incensed fervent nationalists and at the next crowning, that of Prince Charles in 1969, the sentiment climaxed with an attempt to blow up his train.

Sights & Activities

★Caernarfon Castle CASTLE

(Cadw; www.cadw.wales.gov.uk; adult/child £7.95/5.60; ⏲9.30am-5pm Mar-Jun, Sep & Oct, to 6pm Jul & Aug, to 4pm Nov-Feb) Majestic Caernarfon Castle was built between 1283 and 1330 as a military stronghold, seat of government and royal palace. Designed and mainly supervised by Master James of St George, from Savoy, its brief and scale were extraordinary. Today it remains one of the most complete and impressive castles in Britain – you can walk on and through the interconnected walls and towers gathered around the central green, most of which are well preserved but empty.

Dinas Dinlle BEACH

Dolphins and porpoises can sometimes be spotted from this long, sandy Blue Flag beach, 6 miles southwest of Caernarfon. The flatness of the surrounding land stands in contrast to the dramatically sculpted Llŷn Peninsula, visible in the distance. The exception is a solitary hill, with a path leading up to the remains of an Iron Age fort.

Plas Menai WATER SPORTS

(☎01248-670964; www.plasmenai.co.uk; half/full day £25/40; ⏲8.30am-7pm) The excellent National Watersports Centre offers year-round water-based courses for all interests (sailing, power boating, kayaking, windsurfing, stand-up paddleboarding) and abilities. Advance reservations are necessary. On-site accommodation includes B&B rooms (singles/doubles £45/70) and a bunkhouse (dorms £25).

It's located 3 miles along the A487 towards Bangor. Bus 1A (Caernarfon to Bangor) stops here.

Sleeping

★Totters HOSTEL $

(☎01286-672963; www.totters.co.uk; 2 High St; dm/d £18.50/50; 📶) Modern, clean and very welcoming, this excellent independent hostel is the best-value place to stay in town. The 14th-century arched basement gives a sense of history to guests' free breakfasts (cereal, toast and hot beverages are included in the price). In addition to dorms, there's a two-bed attic apartment, a TV room and book-swap library.

★Victoria House B&B $$

(☎01286-678263; 13 Church St; r £90-100; @📶) Victoria House is pretty much the perfect guesthouse – a delightful, solid Victorian building in the middle of Caernarfon's old town, run by exceptionally welcoming and attentive hosts. The four spacious, modern rooms include lovely touches – free toiletries, a DVD on the town's history, fresh milk and a welcoming drink in the bar fridge – and breakfast is a joy.

Plas Dinas Country House B&B $$

(☎01286-830214; www.plasdinas.co.uk; Bontnewydd; r from £109; P📶) Until the 1980s this large 17th-century house belonged to Lord Snowdon's family; his wife, Princess Margaret, often stayed here. Despite the ancestral photos in the hallway and the grand drawing room, the overall impression is surprisingly homey. The 10 bedrooms are filled with antiques and thoughtful touches, such as Molton Brown toiletries and fluffy bathrobes. Self-catering cottages are available, too.

It's set amid extensive grounds off the A487, 2 miles south of Caernarfon.

Eating

Y Gegin Fach CAFE **$**

(☎01286-672165; 5-9 Pool Hill; mains £5-7; ⌚9.30am-3pm) 'The Little Kitchen' is a proper old-fashioned Welsh-speaking *caffi*, right down to the net curtains and cheery red-polka-dot tablecloths. It's a great spot to tuck into traditional faves like rarebit, faggots, *lobscouse* (lamb stew) and Welsh cakes, and wish you had a Welsh granny. Opens later in summer.

★**Blas** WELSH **$$**

(☎01286-677707; www.blascaernarfon.co.uk; 23-25 Hole in the Wall St; mains £18-20; ⌚10.30am-3.30pm & 6-11pm Tue-Sat, 10am-3pm Sun) Blas (taste) abounds at this slick place in one of Caernarfon's most picturesque streets. Chef Daniel ap Geraint makes skilful use of Welsh produce in dishes such as ginger-and-lemongrass cured salmon with Aberdaron crab, and rib of Llanfair Hall beef with confit tomato. Local beers, ciders and spirits also feature, and tea is served in the afternoon.

★**Osteria** TUSCAN **$$**

(☎01286-238050; 26 Hole in the Wall St; mains £11; ⌚noon-3pm Thu-Sat, 6-9pm Tue-Sat) Two Florentine partners opened this excellent addition to Caernarfon's dining scene in a compact whitewashed-stone building hard up against the city walls. Specialising in interesting carpaccios and bruschette (think wild boar or poached turkey), they import many of their ingredients and wines from Tuscany and also prepare stuffed vegetables and more substantial daily specials.

Shopping

Iechyd Da! ALCOHOL

(☎01286-675373; www.iechyd-da.co; 19 Hole in the Wall St; ⌚10.30am-5pm Tue-Sun) Over 170 Welsh ales and ciders twinkle from the shelves of this Australian-owned hole-in-the-wall on Hole in the Wall St, alongside Welsh whisky, gin and vodka. Open longer hours in summer, it even manages to find room for that elusive beast, a Welsh wine. Oh, and the name (pronounced ya-*kee*-da) means 'good health!'

Palas Print BOOKS

(☎01286-674631; www.palasprint.com; 10 Palace St; ⌚9.30am-6pm Mon-Sat) Everything you'd want from a local, indie book shop, this little gem stocks English and Welsh books and CDs, with emphasis on local authors, Welsh folk and the history and landscape of the area. Crochet club meets every Wednesday evening.

Getting There & Away

Buses and coaches depart from the **bus station** (Pool Side). A daily National Express coach stops en route to Pwllheli (£8, 45 minutes) and London (£37, 10 hours) via Bangor (£7.10, 20 minutes), Llandudno (£8.40, one hour) and Birmingham (£32, 6½ hours). Other buses include 1/1A to Criccieth (45 minutes), Tremadog (45 minutes) and Porthmadog (50 minutes); 5/X5 to Bangor (30 minutes), Conwy (1¼ hours) and Llandudno (1½ hours); 12 to Parc Glynllifon (12 minutes) and Pwllheli (45 minutes); and 88 to Llanberis (30 minutes). Snowdon Sherpa bus S4 heads to Beddgelert (30 minutes) via the Snowdon Ranger (22 minutes) and Rhyd Ddu (24 minutes) trailheads.

Bicycle Beics Menai (☎01286-676804; www.beicsmenai.co.uk; 1 Slate Quay; half/full day £10/15; ⌚9.30am-5pm Mon-Sat) hires bikes and can advise on local cycle routes. A brochure on Gwynedd recreational cycle routes includes the 12.5-mile Lôn Eifion (starting near the Welsh Highland Railway station and running south to Bryncir) and the 4.5-mile Lôn Las Menai (following the Menai Strait to the village of Y Felinheli). Lôn Las Cymru passes through Caernarfon, heading northeast to Bangor and south to Criccieth.

Free street parking is at a premium but you might snatch a park in the walled town (try Church St) and there are highly contested free parks by the water on the south embankment of Victoria Dock.

Caernarfon is the northern terminus of the Welsh Highland Railway tourist train, which runs to Porthmadog (£38 return, 2½ hours) via Rhyd Ddu (£22.80 return, one hour) and Beddgelert (£29.10 return, 1½ hours) from Easter to October, with limited winter service. The station is near the river on St Helen's Rd.

Bangor

POP 17,988

While Bangor isn't the most attractive town in North Wales, it has a lively arts and cultural scene, boosted by the addition of two fantastic new venues: Pontio and Storiel. Dominated by its university and blessed with a multicultural population, it's the largest city in Gwynedd and a major transport hub for North Wales, with plenty of onward connections to Anglesey and Snowdonia.

St Deiniol established a monastery here in the 6th century, which grew up into Bangor's sweet little **cathedral** (http://bangor.churchinwales.org.uk; Glanrafon; ⏲9am-4.30pm Mon-Fri, 10.30am-1pm Sat). The main university building sits above it on a ridge, its contours aping those of the cathedral. Bangor University was founded in 1884 and it is now rated as the best university in Wales and one of the top 15 in the UK. During term time 10,000 students swell the city's population.

Sights & Activities

Storiel MUSEUM
(☎01248-353368; www.gwynedd.gov.uk/museums; Ffordd Gwynedd; ⏲11am-5pm Tue-Sat) FREE The former Gwynedd Museum & Art Gallery has moved into swankier premises and taken the portmanteau word 'Storiel' (a cross between the Welsh words for 'story' and 'gallery'). Essentially a folk museum for Gwynedd county, it makes great use of the former Bishop's Palace, with exhibitions of local artefacts (including the Roman 'Segontium sword'), photography, art and more. There's also a cafe and shop.

Penrhyn Castle CASTLE
(NT; www.nationaltrust.org.uk; off A5, Llandygai; adult/child £11.30/5.65; ⏲castle noon-5pm Mar–early Nov, grounds & museums year-round 11am-5pm; P) Funded by the vast profits from the slate mine of the Caribbean sugar-plantation owner and anti-abolitionist Baron Penrhyn, and extended and embellished by his great-great-nephew, this immense 19th-century neo-Norman folly is both tasteless and formidable. Flanked by a Victorian walled garden, the creeper-clad stone walls of the Norman 'fortress' embower the neo-Gothic hall with its darkly extravagant rooms, complete with intricately carved ceilings, stained-glass windows, opulent furniture and even early flushing toilets. There's also an on-site industrial **railway museum**.

Garth Pier LANDMARK
(adult/child 50/20p; ⏲8am-6pm Mon-Sat, 10am-5pm Sun) Given the large expanse of mudflats exposed at high tide (a paradise for all manner of wading birds), it's surprising that the Victorians chose to build one of Britain's longest pleasure piers here. Built in 1896, Garth Pier stretches 460m into the Menai Strait – most of the way to Anglesey. Ornate kiosks are scattered along its length and there's a tearoom at the very end. In the distance you can glimpse Thomas Telford's handsome Menai Suspension Bridge.

Zip World Bethesda ADVENTURE SPORTS
(☎01248-601444; www.zipworld.co.uk; Penrhyn Quarry, Bethesda; single ride £60; ⏲8am-6.30pm) The old Penrhyn slate quarry, nearly a mile long and 360m deep, is now home to Europe's longest (and the world's fastest) zip line – Zip World Velocity. Flying over the lake at the heart of the still-operational quarry, speeds of 100mph can be achieved. Bethesda is on the A5, about 4miles southeast of Bangor.

Festivals & Events

Bangor Music Festival MUSIC
(☎01248-382181; www.bangormusicfestival.org.uk; ⏲Mar) Trends in contemporary composition, avant-garde performances, masterclasses, talks and conferences all come together during this six-day festival, held in collaboration with Bangor University's Music School.

Sleeping & Eating

Management Centre HOTEL $$
(☎01248-365900; www.themanagementcentre.co.uk; Bangor Business School, College Rd; s £70-80, d £90; P 📶) Bangor isn't exactly blessed with accommodation options, but this university business centre has 57 modern en suite rooms and makes for a comfortable stay. There's an on-site restaurant and bar if you don't fancy the steep walk down into town and back.

Blue Sky CAFE $
(☎01248-355444; www.blueskybangor.co.uk; Ambassador Hall, rear 236 High St; mains £5-11; ⏲9.30am-5.30pm Mon-Sat, open evenings when gigs are held; 🖉) Blue Sky cafe hides down an alleyway in a former Jehovah's Witness Kingdom Hall, but the secret is out: it's hands down the best joint in town for breakfasts, soups, sandwiches, burgers and salads, with all ingredients sourced from local suppliers. Equally good for afternoon tea and homemade cakes or catching an evening gig.

★ Entertainment

Pontio PERFORMING ARTS
(☎01248-383838, box office 01248-382828; www.pontio.co.uk; Deiniol Rd; ⊙8.30am-11pm Mon-Sat, noon-8pm Sun) Pontio cements Bangor's place as the cultural capital of North Wales. Within the fluid, Guggenheim-esque interior of this ambitious new multimillion-pound arts and innovation centre are a 450-seat main theatre, a 120-seat studio theatre and a cinema. Run by Bangor University, it stages drama in English and Welsh, classical music and circus performances and other arts, film festivals and more.

ℹ Information

Ystyby Gwynedd (☎01248-384384; Penrhos Rd, Penrhosgarnedd) Located 2 miles southwest of the city centre, this is the regional hub for accident and emergency (A&E) treatment.

ℹ Getting There & Away

National Express coaches head to/from Caernarfon (£6.90, 25 minutes), Holyhead (£20, 50 minutes), Birmingham (£29.30, six hours) and London (£38.70, 9½ hours).

The bus station (Garth Rd) is located behind the Deiniol Shopping Centre. Bus routes include 5/X5 to Caernarfon (30 minutes), Conwy (40 minutes) and Llandudno (one hour); 53-58 to Menai Bridge (12 minutes) and Beaumaris (35 minutes); 85/86 to Llanberis (30 to 50 minutes); T2 to Caernarfon (30 minutes), Porthmadog (one hour), Dolgellau (two hours), Machynlleth (2½ hours) and Aberystwyth (3¼ hours); and X4 to Menai Bridge (12 minutes), Llanfair PG (18 minutes), Llangefni (36 minutes) and Holyhead (1½ hours).

Over summer Snowdon Sherpa S6 runs three times per day on weekends and public holidays to Capel Curig (50 minutes) and Betws-y-Coed (one hour).

Bangor's train station is on Holyhead Rd, just off the southwest end of the High St. Direct services head to/from Holyhead (£9.40, 35 minutes), Rhosneigr (£6.70, 25 minutes), Llanfair PG (£3.10, six minutes), Conwy (£6.90, 17 minutes) and London (£91, 3¼ hours).

Conwy

POP 3873

A visit to Britain's most complete walled town should be high on the itinerary for anyone with even a mild crush on things historic. The World Heritage–listed castle continues to dominate the town, as it's done ever since Edward I first planted it here in the late 13th century.

Approaching from the east, the scene is given another theatrical flourish by a tightly grouped trio of bridges crossing the River Conwy, including Thomas Telford's 1826 suspension bridge (one of the first of its kind in the world) and Robert Stephenson's 1848 wrought-iron railway bridge (the first ever tubular bridge).

👁 Sights

★Conwy Castle CASTLE
(Cadw; ☎01492-592358; www.cadw.wales.gov.uk; Castle Sq; adult/child £7.95/5.60; ⊙9.30am-5pm Mar-Jun, Sep & Oct, to 6pm Jul & Aug, to 4pm Nov-Feb; P) Caernarfon is more complete, Harlech more dramatically positioned and Beaumaris more technically perfect, yet out of the four castles that comprise the Unesco World Heritage Site, Conwy is the prettiest to gaze upon. Exploring the castle's nooks and crannies makes for a superb, living-history visit, but best of all, head to the battlements for panoramic views and an overview of Conwy's majestic complexity.

Town Wall HISTORIC BUILDING
FREE The survival of most of its 1300m-long town wall, built concurrently with the castle, makes Conwy one of the UK's prime medieval sites. It was erected to protect the English colonists from the Welsh, who were forbidden from living in the town and were even cleared from the surrounding countryside. You can enter the town walls at several points and walk along the battlements.

Plas Mawr HISTORIC BUILDING
(Cadw; www.cadw.wales.gov.uk; High St; adult/child £6/4.20; ⊙9.30am-5pm Easter-Sep) Completed in 1585 for the merchant and courtier Robert Wynn, Plas Mawr is one of Britain's finest surviving Elizabethan town houses. The tall, whitewashed exterior is an indication of the owner's status, but gives no clue to the vivid interior, with its colourful friezes and plasterwork ceilings. The admission price includes a helpful audioguide.

Royal Cambrian Academy GALLERY
(☎01492-593413; www.rcaconwy.org; Crown Lane; ⊙11am-5pm Tue-Sat) FREE Founded in 1881 and still going strong, the academy runs a full calendar of exhibitions by its members in its twin white-walled galleries, plus visiting shows from the National Museum Wales and elsewhere. Its excellent

Annual Summer Exhibition, featuring the cream of contemporary fine art in Wales under one roof each August and September, is now over 130 years old.

Sleeping

Conwy YHA HOSTEL $
(08453-719732; www.yha.org.uk; Sychnant Pass Rd, Larkhill; dm/r £22/47; P) Perched on a hill above the town, this former hotel has been converted into a top-notch hostel. Dorms have either two or four beds, and many of the private rooms have en suites. Head up to the large dining room for awesome views of the mountains and the sea. Wi-fi only works in the common areas.

To get here, continue from Upper Gate St onto Sychnant Pass Rd; the hostel's up a long drive to the left.

★ **Gwynfryn** B&B $$
(01492-576733; www.gwynfrynbandb.co.uk; 4 York Pl; r £65-90;) Although it seems in danger of being engulfed by butterfly ornaments and dangling mobiles, this very friendly five-bedroom B&B – set in a refurbished Victorian property just off the main square – is a great place to stay. The clean, bright rooms are filled with thoughtful extras such as small fridges, biscuits, chocolates and earplugs. Guests must be 15 and over.

Bryn B&B B&B $$
(01492-592449; www.bryn.org.uk; Sychnant Pass Rd; s/d £60/80; P) This sturdy Victorian house abutting the town walls has five sumptuous guest rooms decked out in soothing creams, three with king-size beds. Breakfast is a delight, with freshly baked bread and organic/fair-trade ingredients. Special diets are accommodated and nothing is too much trouble for the congenial proprietor.

Eating & Drinking

★ **Parisella's of Conwy Ice Cream** ICE CREAM $
(www.parisellasicecream.co.uk; Conwy Quay; per scoop £2; 10.30am-5.30pm) The kiosk on the quay sells a selection of what we consider to be the best ice cream in Wales. The best of Parisella's 50-plus flavours include mint choc chip, salted caramel, and amaretto and black cherry. It also has a parlour at 12 High St (open 10am to 5pm); seagulls gather outside both locations to mug unsuspecting lickers on busy days.

Edwards of Conwy DELI $
(01492-592443; www.edwardsofconwy.co.uk; 18 High St; pies £5; 7am-5.30pm Mon-Sat) While first and foremost a butchery with a great line in Welsh meat, Edwards also sells savoury pies, local cheeses and freshly filled baps and sandwiches. Awards are continually piled on the deli for everything from its sausages to its pork pies.

★ **Watson's Bistro** WELSH $$
(01492-596326; www.watsonsbistroconwy.co.uk; Bishop's Yard, Chapel St; 2-course lunch £13, mains £18-20; noon-2pm Wed-Sun, 5.30-8pm Tue-Sun) Hidden in a verdant garden setting in the lee of the town wall, Watson's marries French bistro cooking with quality local ingredients. Everything is homemade, from the chicken-liver pâté to the ox-cheek with 'dirty carrots' to the ice cream. Book to arrive before 6.30pm for the early-bird set menu (three courses £21).

Alfredo's ITALIAN $$
(01492-592381; 9-10 Lancaster Sq; mains £9-23; 6-9.30pm Mon-Sat;) There's something tremendously appealing about the stereotypical Italian-ness of Alfredo's (chequered tablecloths, fake ivy, fairy lights draped from the ceiling, shabby carpets and a giant menu of pasta, pizza and traditional grills) that could only be enhanced with comedy moustaches and loud exclamations of 'mamma mia'. Importantly, the food is very good.

★ **Albion Ale House** PUB
(01492-582484; www.albionalehouse.weebly.com; 1-4 Upper Gate St; noon-11pm;) Born out of a collaboration of four Welsh craft breweries (Purple Moose, Conwy, Nant and Great Orme), this heritage-listed 1920s boozer is a serious beer-drinker's nirvana. Of the 10 hand pulls, eight are loaded with real ale and two with cider. Winner of multiple Wales and North Wales pub-of-the-year awards, the Albion looks after wine and whisky drinkers, too.

There's no TV or background music – just the crackle of the fire, the gentle hum of conversation and the odd contented slurp. The good news for Conwy's Camra (Campaign for Real Ale) connoisseurs is that the collective looks set to create something similar in the Bridge Inn, opposite the castle.

DON'T MISS

BODNANT ESTATE

Whether you're a lover of gardens or fine food, the publicly accessible attractions on this privately owned agricultural estate (www.bodnant-estate.co.uk) should not be missed. While many large country estates fell on hard times in the 20th century, the McLaren family (holders of the title Baron Aberconway) managed to keep hold of theirs. The 2nd Baron Aberconway, a keen horticulturist, donated **Bodnant Garden** (NT; ☎01492-650460; www.bodnant-estate.co.uk/bodnant-garden; Bodnant Estate, Tal-y-Cafn; adult/child whole property £11.25/5.60, winter £5.60/2.80; ⊙10am-5pm Mar-Oct, to 4pm Nov-Feb, to 8pm Wed May-Aug; P 👪) to the National Trust in 1949, although the family continues to maintain it on the trust's behalf.

Should you get peckish from your perambulations, there's **Bodnant Welsh Food** (☎01492-651100; www.bodnant-welshfood.co.uk; Furnace Farm, Tal-y-Cafn; ⊙farm shop 10am-6pm Mon-Sat, 10am-4pm Sun; P), the **Furnace Tea Room** (☎01492-651100; www.bodnant-welshfood.co.uk/furnace-tea-room; Bodnant Welsh Food, Furnace Farm, Tal-y-Cafn; mains £5-7; ⊙9am-5pm Mon-Thu, 9am-5.30pm Fri & Sat, 10am-4.30pm Sun) and the **Hayloft Restaurant** (☎01492-651102; www.bodnant-welshfood.co.uk/hayloft-restaurant; Bodnant Welsh Food, Furnace Farm, Tal-y-Cafn; mains £17-20; ⊙noon-3pm Tue-Sun, 6-9pm Tue-Sat) to assuage your hunger.

The estate is also home to the **National Beekeeping Centre Wales** (☎01492-651106; www.beeswales.co.uk; Furnace Farm, Tal-y-Cafn; tours adult/child £7/3.50; ⊙10am-4pm Wed-Sun late-Mar–early Sep), the **Farmhouse** (☎01492-651100; www.bodnant-welshfood.co.uk/accommodation; Bodnant Welsh Food, Furnace Farm, Tal-y-Cafn; s/d from £65/100; P 📶) B&B and several self-contained cottages.

Getting There & Away

The estate is located east of the River Conwy, 4 miles south of Conwy. Bodnant Welsh Food is on the A470, while the garden is accessed by a well-signposted side road.

There's no public transport to the estate, so you'll need your own wheels.

ℹ Information

Tourist Office (☎01492-577566; www.visitllandudno.org.uk; Muriau Buildings, Rose Hill St; ⊙9am-5pm Mon-Fri, 10am-4pm Sat & Sun) Extremely busy office, well stocked with pamphlets and souvenirs and staffed by very helpful local experts. There's an interesting interactive exhibition on the princes of Gwynedd in the adjoining room.

ℹ Getting There & Away

BUS

Bus routes include 5/X5 to Caernarfon (1¼ hours), Bangor (40 minutes) and Llandudno (22 minutes); 14/15 to Llandudno (20 minutes); and 19 to Llandudno (22 minutes) and Betws-y-Coed (50 minutes).

Buses to Llandudno leave from the stop near Castle Sq, while those to **Bangor/Caernarfon** leave from outside the train station.

CAR

Through-traffic bypasses Conwy on the A55 via a tunnel under the river. The main road into town from Bangor skirts the outside of the town walls before cutting inside the walls, crawling along Berry and Castle Sts and heading across the road bridge. The rest of the narrow grid within the walls has a one-way system and restricted parking during the day.

There are pay-and-display car parks on Mt Pleasant and by the castle. If you're after a free park and don't mind a 10-minute walk, turn right off Bangor Rd on the second-to-last street before you reach the town walls, cross the narrow rail bridge and park on residential Cadnant Park.

TRAIN

Conwy's train station is just inside the town walls on Rosemary Lane. Direct services head to/from Holyhead (£14.70, one hour), Rhosneigr (£14.70, 44 minutes), Llanfair PG (£8.20, 26 minutes), Bangor (£6.90, 20 minutes) and Shrewsbury (£17.50, two hours).

Llandudno

POP 15,371

Wales' biggest seaside resort straddles a peninsula with long sandy beaches on either side. Developed as an upmarket holiday town for Victorian visitors, Llandudno still retains much of its 19th-century grandeur, with graceful Victorian wedding-cake architecture lining its sweeping waterfront promenade. Innumerable B&Bs and small private hotels cater to mainly mature-aged travellers in the low season, while young families descend with their buckets and spades in summer.

Alongside the lost-in-time charms of the British seaside (pier, promenade, Punch and Judy shows), Llandudno's main attraction is the near-wilderness of the Great Orme on its doorstep, a striking, rough-hewn headland where there are breathtaking views of the Snowdonia range and miles of trails to explore.

A very tenuous link to *Alice In Wonderland* (Alice Liddell, the real inspiration for Lewis Carroll's fictional Alice, used to holiday here with her family) has seen statues of the book's characters sprout around the town.

Sights

Llandudno Promenade WATERFRONT

Llandudno's iconic 2-mile promenade is one of its distinctive sights. It was here that Queen Victoria herself watched Professor Codman's Punch & Judy Show (p755), performed by the same family since 1860 – we hope she was amused. Mr Punch's iconic red-and-white-striped tent sits by the entrance to the Victorian pier.

Llandudno Pier LANDMARK

(9am-6pm;) A trip to Llandudno isn't complete until you've strolled along the Victorian pier, eating ice cream and shooing away seagulls. At 670m it's Wales' longest. When it opened in 1878 its main use was as a disembarkation point for passengers from the Isle of Man steamers. Those days are long gone, and candyfloss, slot machines and views of the offshore wind farm are now the order of the day. High art it ain't, but the kids will love it.

Great Orme Tramway CABLE CAR

(01492-577877; www.greatormetramway.co.uk; Victoria Station, Church Walks; adult/child return £7/5; 10am-6pm Easter-Oct) Head to the top of the Great Orme without breaking a sweat in an original 1902 tramcar. It's one of only three cable-operated trams in the world (the other two are in equally glamorous Lisbon and San Francisco). Trips head up the steep incline every 20 minutes, weather permitting; change to a second tram at the Halfway Station.

★Great Orme HILL

(Y Gogarth) From sea level it's difficult to gauge the sheer scale of the Great Orme (Y Gogarth), yet it stretches for around 2 miles and rises to a height of 207m. Named after a Norse word for 'worm' or 'sea serpent', this gentle giant looms benevolently over the town. Designated a Site of Special Scientific Interest (SSSI), the headland is home to a cornucopia of flowers, butterflies and sea birds and a herd of around 150 wild Kashmir mountain goats.

Three waymarked trails (of which the Haulfre Gardens Trail is the easiest to negotiate) lead to the summit and there's a neolithic burial chamber, a Bronze Age mine, the remains of an Iron Age fort, and an ancient church dedicated to Llandudno's namesake, St Tudno. At the summit there's a cafe, bar, gift shop, minigolf and other amusements, as well as the Great Orme Country Park Visitor Centre (p755), which has lots of fascinating displays including a 15-minute video. Views – across the Irish Sea and its fertile wind farms in one direction, overlooking Llandudno towards Snowdonia in the other – are stunning.

★Great Orme Mines MINE

(www.greatormemines.info; adult/child £6.75/4.75; 9.30am-5.30pm mid-Mar–Oct) Sitting unobtrusively near the top of the Great Orme is the largest prehistoric mine ever discovered. Nearly paved over for a car park, this site of tremendous historical importance has been developed as a must-see attraction, with a visitor centre and the chance to explore portions of the 5 miles of tunnels dug over centuries in search of copper. What is truly astounding is that 4000 years ago the tools used to excavate this maze were just stones and bones.

A 45-minute self-guided tour explains how the ancients turned rock into copper at the smelting site and then heads underground for about 200m into 3500-year-old tunnels. The site was worked again from the 17th to 19th centuries; its discovery moved Britain's metallurgic history back a cool 2000 years.

West Shore BEACH

When the main beach gets too frantic, go west to this considerably less built-up stretch on Conwy Bay. The views over Anglesey and the mountains of Snowdonia can be stunning, especially as the sun sets, and there's a model boating pool at the Orme end. It's just a shame that the water quality on this side is substandard.

Festivals & Events

Victorian Extravaganza PERFORMING ARTS
(www.victorian-extravaganza.com; Llandudno; May) Llandudno plays dress-up for this annual event, held over the early May bank holiday weekend. It's the social event of the year, with a daily parade, strolling Victorian characters, bands, funfairs – and grossly over-inflated accommodation prices.

Sleeping

★ **Escape B&B** B&B $$
(01492-877776; www.escapebandb.co.uk; 48 Church Walks; r £95-149; P) Escape brought a style revolution to Llandudno with its boutique-chic ambience and magazine-spread design. Its most recent, design-led makeover then added a host of energy-saving and trendsetting features. Even if you're not a *Wallpaper** subscriber, you'll love the honesty-bar lounge, Bose iPod docks, DVD library, tasty breakfasts and atmosphere of indulgence. Unique.

Clontarf Hotel HOTEL $$
(01492-877621; www.clontarfhotel.co.uk; 2 Great Ormes Rd; s £46, d £66-89; P) The nine individually styled rooms at this small, friendly hotel come with luxurious touches: sophisticated showers in three of the rooms and a four-poster bed and whirlpool bath in the Romantic room. All rooms look out either onto the sea or the Great Orme (p753), a small bar contributes to evening relaxation and the friendly proprietor cooks up delicious breakfasts.

Can-y-Bae HOTEL $$
(01492-874188; www.can-y-baehotel.com; 10 Mostyn Cres; s/d from £40/80;) Just down the road from Venue Cymru, this welcoming, gay-friendly hotel accommodates many a visiting thespian among its mainly older clientele. Signed memorabilia blankets the walls of the little residents' bar and there's a piano if anyone wants to start a sing along. It's even smarter, following a refurb in 2015.

★ **Bodysgallen Hall** HISTORIC HOTEL $$$
(NT; 01492-584466; www.bodysgallen.com; s/d/ste from £160/180/435; P) Managed by the National Trust, this magnificent pink-stone 1620 country house set in spectacular French-style formal gardens lets you lose yourself in the wood-panelled world of the Jacobean gentry. The rooms, split between the main hall and outlying cottages, are traditional with a nod to mod cons, and there's a well-regarded restaurant and spa centre in the grounds.

Bodysgallen is 3 miles south of Llandudno, on the A470.

Osborne House HOTEL $$$
(01492-860330; www.osbornehouse.co.uk; 17 North Pde; ste £175-200; P) All marble, antique furniture and fancy drapes, the lavish Osborne House takes a classical approach to aesthetics and the results are impressive. The best suites are on the 1st floor with Victorian-style sitting rooms and sea views. Guests have use of the spa and swimming pools at nearby sister property, the Empire Hotel.

Eating

Orient-Express CAFE $
(01492-879990; 8 Gloddaeth St; mains £5-10; 8am-5pm;) Brown leather, dark wood, chandeliers and tight confines conjure a faint impression of train travel's golden age, but above all this is simply a welcoming, child-friendly cafe. While it's possible to get standard British cafe food here, the best bets are the Turkish dishes that show the owner's origins – halloumi, grilled chicken, dolmas, baklava and the like.

Fish Tram Chips FISH & CHIPS $
(01492-872673; www.fish-tram-chips.co.uk; 22-24 Old Rd; mains £7-10; noon-7.30pm) Consistently serving up tasty, fresh fish and homemade side dishes with unaffected friendliness, this is where the locals head for good-value fish meals. Probably the best bargain in Llandudno, its opening hours are extended in summer.

★ **Characters** CAFE $$
(01492-872290; www.charactersllandudno.com; 11 Llewelyn Ave; lunch £5-7, dinner £15-21; 11am-4pm Mon-Thu, 11am-8.30pm Fri & Sat;) If you're wondering whether it's the place that's full of character or the people running it, it's both. Llandudno's hippest tearoom serves wonderful cream teas (£5) and three-tiered high teas (£10), along with light lunches of sandwiches, soup and jacket potatoes; avoid the coffee. Weekends sizzle with hot-stone dinners.

★ Cottage Loaf PUB FOOD $$
(☎ 01492-870762; www.the-cottageloaf.co.uk; Market St; mains £9-16; ⏲ kitchen noon-9pm; 📶) Tucked down an alleyway off Mostyn St, this charismatic pub has print-strewn walls, carpeted wooden floors and an atmosphere of genuine bonhomie. The excellent food ranges from the traditional – slow-roasted pork belly, beef-and-ale pie and their ilk – to the more exotic, and there are both plenty of good beers and a flower-strewn terrace to enhance it.

Seahorse SEAFOOD $$$
(☎ 01492-875315; www.the-seahorse.co.uk; 7 Church Walks; mains £15-23; ⏲ 4.30-10pm) The chef at this, Llandudno's only dedicated seafood restaurant, is a keen fisherman and the menu reflects his passion for the local catch: specials might be local mussels, or fresh anchovies in tempura batter. The restaurant is a split-level affair: upstairs is decorated with large Mediterranean murals, while the more intimate cellar room has a cosier feel.

☆ Entertainment

Professor Codman's Punch & Judy Show PERFORMING ARTS
(☎ 07900-555515; www.punchandjudy.com/codgal.htm; The Promenade; ⏲ 2pm & 4pm Sat & Sun year-round, daily school holidays Easter–mid-Sep) Queen Victoria herself watched this show, performed by the same family with the same puppets since 1860. Mr Punch's iconic red-and-white-striped tent sits near the entrance to the pier (p753). If you're not familiar with the Punch and Judy tradition, you might be surprised by the violence and puppet-spouse abuse – but the kids don't seem to mind.

Venue Cymru PERFORMING ARTS
(☎ 01472-872000; www.venuecymru.co.uk; The Promenade; ⏲ box office 10am-7pm Mon-Sat, plus 1hr before performances) Having undergone a major expansion, Venue Cymru is one of North Wales' leading event and performance venues. The line-up covers all bases from big rock gigs to high-brow classical performances, big-name stand-ups, musicals and shows for children.

ℹ Information

Great Orme Country Park Visitor Centre (www.conwy.gov.uk/greatorme; ⏲ 9.30am-5.30pm Easter-Oct) The visitor centre on the summit of the Great Orme (p753) has 3D and interactive displays on the geology and flora and fauna of the area. It organises two-hour guided walks of the headland every Sunday from May to September.

Llandudno General Hospital (☎ 01492-860066; Hospital Rd; ⏲ 8am-10pm) One mile south of the town centre, off the A546. The nearest accident and emergency (A & E) department is at Ystyby Gwynedd (p750) in Bangor.

Llandudno Tourist Office (☎ 01492-577577; www.visitllandudno.org.uk; Mostyn St; ⏲ 9.30am-4.30pm) In the library building, with helpful staff and an accommodation booking service.

ℹ Getting There & Away

Llandudno's train station is centrally located on Augusta St. Direct services head to/from Betws-y-Coed (£6.30, 50 minutes), Blaenau Ffestiniog (£8.70, 1¼ hours), Chester (£20, one hour) and Manchester Piccadilly (£33, 2¼ hours); for other destinations you'll need to change at Llandudno Junction (£2.90, eight minutes).

Buses **stop** on the corner of Upper Mostyn St and Gloddaeth St. National Express coaches head to/from Liverpool (£14.20, 2½ hours), Manchester (£18.20, four hours), Birmingham (£35, five hours) and London (£37.50, 8¾ hours). Other bus routes include 5/X5 to Caernarfon (1½ hours), Bangor (one hour) and Conwy (22 minutes); 14/15 to Conwy (21 minutes); and 19 to Conwy (22 minutes) and Betws-y-Coed (70 minutes).

Parking is metered during the day on the main part of the Promenade, but it's free once you get past the roundabout east of Venue Cymru.

ISLE OF ANGLESEY (YNYS MÔN)

At 276 sq miles, the Isle of Anglesey is Wales' largest island and bigger than any in England. It's a popular destination for visitors with miles of inspiring coastline, hidden beaches and Wales' greatest concentration of ancient sites. A brush with royalty has given Anglesey an added cachet in recent years, with the Duke and Duchess of Cambridge setting up home here for the three years Wills served at the Royal Air Force base in Valley.

Almost all of the Anglesey coast has been designated as an Area of Outstanding Natural Beauty. The handsome Georgian town of Beaumaris is its most obviously attractive, but there are hidden gems scattered all over the island. It's very much a living centre of Welsh culture, too, as you can see for yourself at **Oriel Ynys Môn** (☎ 01248-724444;

www.orielynysmon.info; Rhosmeirch, Llangefni; ⌚10.30am-5pm; P) FREE.

History

From prehistoric times, Anglesey's fertile land was settled by small communities of farmers. The island was holy to the Celts and, in AD 60, it was the last part of Wales to fall to the Romans. Given its outpost status and singular character, Anglesey has as fair a claim as any to being the Welsh heartland. One ancient name for the isle, bestowed by the prelate and historian Gerald of Wales in the 12th century, was Môn mam Cymru: 'Mother of Wales'.

Beaumaris (Biwmares)

POP 1370

Anglesey's prettiest town offers a winning combination of a waterfront location, ever-present views of the mountains, a romantic castle lording it over an elegant collection of mainly Georgian buildings and a burgeoning number of boutiques, galleries, smart hotels and chic eateries. Many of the houses are extremely old; the local real estate agent occupies a half-timbered house dating from 1400 – one of the oldest in Britain (look for it on Castle St near the bottom of Church St).

The town's romantic name dates back to the time of French-speaking Edward I, who built the castle. It's a corruption of *beau marais* (meaning 'beautiful marsh') rather than *beau maris* (meaning 'good husbands') – although, unlike in French, the final 's' is sounded. Today, it's an understandably popular place for retirees.

OFF THE BEATEN TRACK

HIGH-FLYING PUB

Tucked away in the southwest corner of Anglesey on Holy Island is **White Eagle** (☎01407-860267; www.white-eagle.co.uk; Rhoscolyn; mains £13-16; ⌚kitchen noon-9pm, bar to 11pm;) – a busy gastropub, with a huge decking area and gardens for kids to explore. The menu is surely more inventive than in its village-pub days, but the portions remain generously pub-sized and the service is friendly. There's also a good selection of beer.

Sights

★Beaumaris Castle CASTLE

(Cadw; www.cadw.wales.gov.uk; Castle St; adult/child £6/4.20; ⌚9.30am-5pm Mar-Oct, to 6pm Jul & Aug, 11am-4pm Nov-Feb) Started in 1295, Beaumaris was the last of Edward I's great castles of North Wales and today it's deservedly a World Heritage Site. With swans gliding on a water-filled moat and a perfect, symmetrical design, it's what every sandcastle maker unknowingly aspires to. The four successive lines of fortifications and concentric 'walls within walls' make it the most technically perfect castle in Great Britain, even though it was never fully completed.

Beaumaris Gaol HISTORIC BUILDING

(www.visitanglesey.co.uk; Steeple Lane; adult/child £5/4, incl Beaumaris Courthouse £7.90/6.50; ⌚10.30am-5pm Sat-Thu Apr-Oct) This fortress-like jail, built in the early 19th century, was modern for its time, with toilets in every cell and a treadmill water pump. However, that's not enough to dispel the gloom of the windowless punishment cell, the condemned cell where prisoners awaited their demise at the gibbet or the stone-breaking yard where inmates were subjected to hard labour.

Penmon Priory CHURCH

(Cadw; www.cadw.wales.gov.uk; Penmon; parking £2.50; ⌚10am-4pm; P) FREE Penmon, 4 miles north of Beaumaris, is Anglesey at its most numinous. An early Celtic monastery was established here in the 6th century by St Seiriol; burnt in AD 971, its last relic is the basin of the holy well, tucked behind the current simple stone church. The earliest extant parts of that church include two 10th-century Celtic crosses, a font from around the turn of the millennium and some wonderful 12th-century Romanesque arches.

Sleeping & Eating

★Cleifiog B&B $$

(☎01248-811507; www.cleifiogbandb.co.uk; Townsend; s £85, d £90-110;) A charming little gem, this art-filled townhouse oozes character and history and boasts superb views over the Menai Strait, particularly as the morning sun streams in. The front bedrooms have their original 18th-century wood panelling, while the rear room has a 16th-century barrel ceiling; all three are stylishly decorated.

DON'T MISS

PLAS NEWYDD

When you pull up into the car park, don't get too excited by the impressive building you can see in front of you – that's just the stables! The grand manor house of the Marquesses of Anglesey, **Plas Newydd** (NT; www.nationaltrust.org.uk; adult/child £9.80/4.90, garden only £7.70/3.85; ⏰house 11am-4.30pm Mar–early Nov, garden 10.30am-5.30pm Mar-Oct, 11am-3pm Nov-Feb; P), is set well back from the road, surrounded by tranquil gardens, gazing out across the Menai Strait to Snowdonia. The earliest parts date from the early 15th century, but most of the Gothic masterpiece that stands today took shape in the 1790s.

Inside, the walls are hung with gilt-framed portraits of worthy ancestors of the Paget family (William Paget was secretary of state to Henry VIII), who owned the house until 1976. A highlight is a giant painting by Rex Whistler filling an entire wall of the dining room, which magically changes perspective as you walk around the room. In the grounds there's a tearoom, a cafe, an adventure playground and a luxuriant rhododendron garden.

The house is 2 miles southwest of Llanfair PG, along the A4080.

★ **Tredici Italian Kitchen** ITALIAN $$
(☎01248-811230; www.tredicibeaumaris.com; 13 Castle St; ⏰6-9pm Sun-Thu, 5-10pm Fri & Sat, noon-3pm Sat & Sun) Occupying an intimate 1st-floor dining room above a quality butcher and grocer, Tredici has brought a touch of the Mediterranean to wind-blown Anglesey. While some Welsh produce is used (local lamb cutlets are pan-fried with mint and redcurrant, and the sea bass almost has the same postcode), the swordfish, figs and the like naturally come from sunnier climes.

ℹ Information

Tourist Office (www.visitbeaumaris.co.uk; Town Hall, Castle St; ⏰10am-2pm Mon-Fri) This information point is only staffed for limited hours; at other times, it's still accessible, and a handy spot to pick up brochures.

ℹ Getting There & Away

Buses stop on Church St. Routes include the 53-58 to Menai Bridge (18 minutes) and Bangor (35 minutes); buses 57 and 58 continue on to Penmon (11 minutes).

There's a large pay-and-display car park on the waterfront by the castle. If you're prepared to walk, there are often free parks on the Menai Bridge approach to town.

Holyhead (Caergybi)

POP 11,431

In the heyday of the mail coaches, Holyhead (confusingly pronounced 'holly head') was the vital terminus of the London road and the main hub for onward boats to Ireland. The coming of the railway only increased the flow of people through town, but the recent increase in cheap flights has reduced the demand for ferries and Holyhead has fallen on hard times. Regeneration funding allowed the impressive Celtic Gateway bridge to be built (linking the train station and ferry terminal to the main shopping street) and a radical waterfront redevelopment has been promised; but for now, the town centre remains a rather moribund affair.

Holyhead isn't actually on Anglesey at all. Holy Island is divided from the west coast of Anglesey by a narrow channel, although the various bridges obstruct the views these days, and you might not realise that you're crossing onto another island.

Sights

★ **South Stack Cliffs RSPB Reserve** WILDLIFE RESERVE
(Ynys Lawd; ☎01407-762100; www.rspb.org.uk/wales; South Stack Rd; ⏰visitor centre 10am-5pm; P) FREE Two miles west of Holyhead, the sea vents its fury against the cliffs of South Stack, an important RSPB reserve – home to thousands of seabirds. A steep, serpentine flight of steps leads down to the suspension bridge that crosses over to the **South Stack Lighthouse** (☎01407-763900; www.trinityhouse.co.uk; South Stack Rd; adult/child £5.80/3.15; ⏰10.30am-5pm Sat-Thu Easter–early Sep) for tremendous cliff views. Numerous paths lead into the bracken-covered, hilly interior, climbing the 219m Holyhead Mountain (Mynydd Twr) and skirting Neolithic stone circles. South Stack Kitchen, an interpretive-centre-cum-cafe providing maps and information, is open all year.

Holyhead Maritime Museum MUSEUM
(☎01407-769745; www.holyheadmaritimemuseum.co.uk; Newry Beach; adult/child £5/free; ⏲10am-4pm Tue-Sun Easter-Oct; 🚸) Small but lovingly restored, this little museum is housed in what is believed to be the oldest lifeboat house in Wales (c 1858). It's a family-friendly visit with model ships, photographs and exhibits on Holyhead's maritime history from Roman times onwards. The exhibition 'Holyhead at War' occupies an adjacent WWII air-raid shelter.

Sleeping & Eating

Yr-Hendre B&B $$
(☎01407-762929; www.yr-hendre.net; Porth-y-Felin Rd; r £65-75; P@📶) A former minister's house set in a large garden on the quiet edge of town, Yr-Hendre is perhaps the best place to stay in Holyhead. Professionally managed and homey, the three bedrooms have a feminine touch and one has sea views. Walkers are welcomed and safe bicycle storage is available.

Ucheldre Kitchen CAFE $
(www.ucheldre.org; Millbank; mains £5-7; ⏲10am-4.30pm Mon-Sat, 2-4.30pm Sun) Avoid the greasy spoons around the high street and head up to the cafe attached to the **arts centre** (Canolfan Ucheldre; ☎01407-763361; www.ucheldre.org; Millbank; ⏲10am-5pm Mon-Sat, 2-5pm Sun) instead. Lit by skylights and decked with art, it's a relaxed spot for light lunches (wraps, toasted sandwiches, paninis, soup) or tea and cake.

Information

Holyhead doesn't have a tourist information centre but some of the local stores stock brochures. The South Stack Cliffs RSPB Reserve (p757) visitor centre is a good source of advice about local walks.

Getting There & Away

When the weather's poor, it always pays to check with the ferry companies – **Irish Ferries** (☎08718 300 400; www.irishferries.com; foot passenger/motorcycle/car from £31/55/104) and **Stena Line** (☎08447 707 070; www.stenaline.co.uk; foot passenger/bicycle/car from £34/42/105) – before heading to the **ferry terminal** (www.holyheadport.com), as services are sometimes cancelled. Direct trains head to/from Rhosneigr (£4.50, 12 minutes), Llanfair PG (£8.30, 29 minutes), Bangor (£9.40, 30 minutes), Conwy (£1, 1¼ hours) and London Euston (£94.80, four to five hours).

National Express coaches stop at the ferry terminal, heading to/from Bangor (£20, 35 minutes), Liverpool (£31, 2¾ hours), Manchester (£36, 4¾ hours), Birmingham (£35, four hours) and London (£29, 7¼ hours). The main bus stops are on Summer Hill. Destinations include Trearddur (route 4; 13 minutes), Cemaes (61; 44 minutes), Llanfair PG (X4; one hour), Menai Bridge (X4; 1¼ hours) and Bangor (X4; 1½ hours).

Scotland

ISLE OF SKYE (P927); HELEN HOTSON / SHUTTERSTOCK ©

Scotland Highlights

❶ **Edinburgh** (p761) Exploring Scotland's capital, one of the world's most fascinating cities.

❷ **Glasgow** (p800) Enjoying Victorian architecture, great nightlife and friendly locals.

❸ **Northwest Highlands Coast** (p918) Getting permanent jawdrop.

❹ **Border Abbeys** (p821) Experiencing the romantic ruins.

❺ **Glen Coe** (p908) Uncovering scenic beauty and tragic history.

❻ **Cuillin Hills** (p931) Capturing the brooding splendour of Skye.

❼ **Ben Nevis** (p913) Climbing the highest point in Britain.

❽ **Highland Perthshire** (p904) Admiring the magnificent forests and lochs.

❾ **Orkney** (p941) Discovering 5000-year-old neolithic sites.

Edinburgh

POP 498,810

Includes ➡

Best Places to Eat

- ➡ Castle Terrace (p767)
- ➡ Gardener's Cottage (p789)
- ➡ The Dogs (p789)
- ➡ Ondine (p788)
- ➡ Fishers Bistro (p790)
- ➡ Timberyard (p788)

Best Places to Sleep

- ➡ Witchery by the Castle (p784)
- ➡ Knight Residence (p785)
- ➡ Sheridan Guest House (p785)
- ➡ Southside Guest House (p785)
- ➡ Millers 64 (p786)

Why Go?

Edinburgh is a city that begs to be explored. From the vaults and wynds (narrow lanes) that riddle the Old Town to the urban villages of Stockbridge and Cramond, it's filled with quirky, come-hither nooks that tempt you to walk just a little bit further. And every corner turned reveals sudden views and unexpected vistas – green sunlit hills, a glimpse of rust-red crags, a blue flash of distant sea.

But there's more to Edinburgh than sightseeing – there are top shops, world-class restaurants and a bacchanalia of bars to enjoy. This is a city of pub crawls and impromptu music sessions, late-night drinking, all-night parties and wandering home through cobbled streets at dawn.

All these superlatives come together at festival time in August, when it seems as if half the world descends on Edinburgh for one enormous party. If you can possibly manage it, join them.

When to Go

- ➡ May brings good weather (usually), flowers and cherry blossom everywhere, and (gasp!) no crowds.
- ➡ August is festival time! Crowded and mad but irresistible.
- ➡ Christmas decorations, cosy pubs with open fires and ice skating in Princes Street Gardens herald the festive season come December.

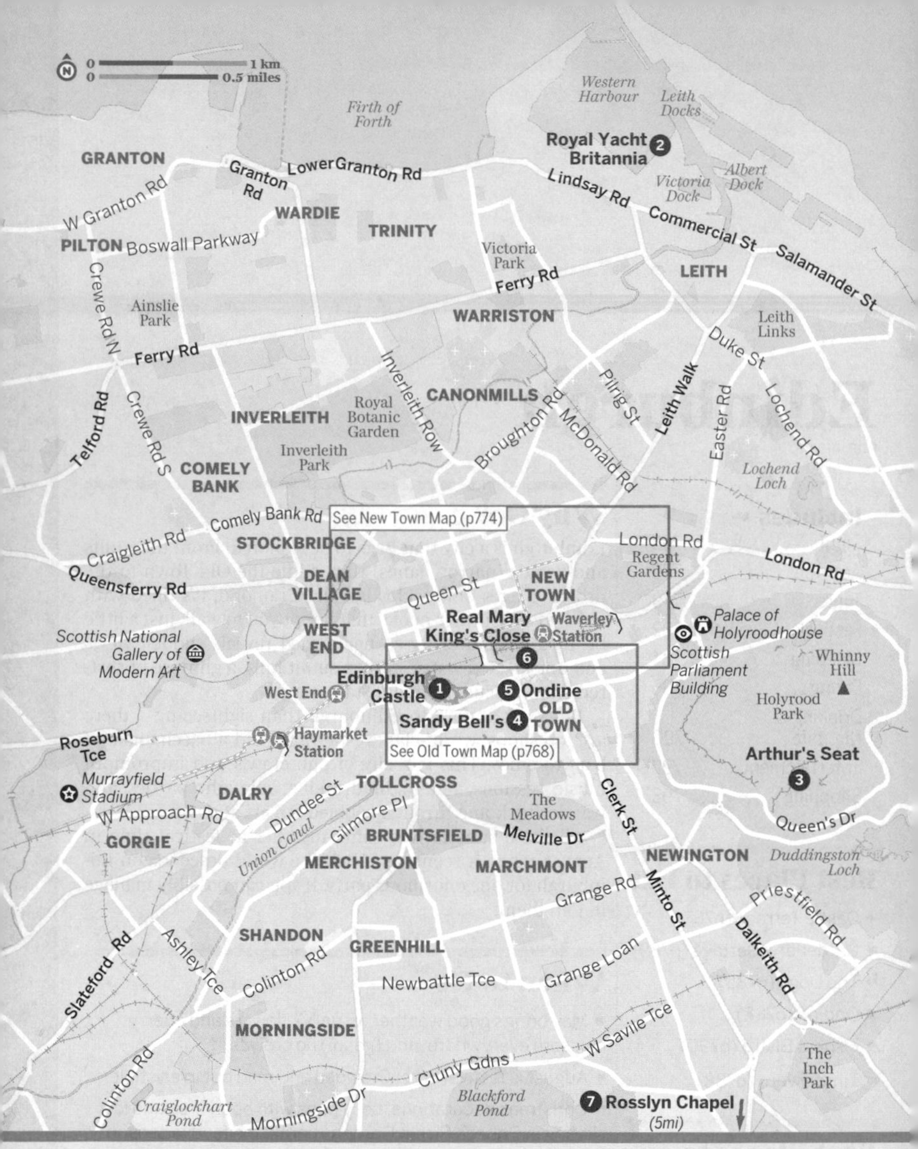

Edinburgh Highlights

1 **Edinburgh Castle** (p763) Taking in the views from the battlements.

2 **Royal Yacht Britannia** (p778) Nosing around the Queen's private quarters.

3 **Arthur's Seat** (p771) Climbing to the summit of the city's miniature mountain.

4 **Sandy Bell's** (p792) Listening to live folk music.

5 **Ondine** (p788) Enjoying the finest of Scottish seafood.

6 **Real Mary King's Close** (p768) Exploring Edinburgh's subterranean history in these haunted vaults.

7 **Rosslyn Chapel** (p779) Trying to decipher the Da Vinci Code at this mysterious chapel.

History

Edinburgh owes its existence to the Castle Rock, the glacier-worn stump of a long-extinct volcano that provided a near-perfect defensive position guarding the coastal route from northeast England into central Scotland.

In the 7th century the Castle Rock was called Dun Eiden (meaning 'Fort on the Hill Slope'). When it was captured by invaders from the kingdom of Northumbria in northeast England in 638, they took the existing Gaelic name 'Eiden' and tacked it onto their own Old English word for fort, 'burh', to create the name Edinburgh.

Originally a purely defensive site, Edinburgh began to expand in the 12th century when King David I held court at the castle and founded the abbey at Holyrood. The royal court came to prefer Edinburgh to Dunfermline and, because parliament followed the king, Edinburgh became Scotland's capital. The city's first effective town wall was constructed around 1450, enclosing the Old Town as far east as Netherbow and south to the Grassmarket. This overcrowded area – by then the most populous town in Scotland – became a medieval Manhattan, forcing its densely packed inhabitants to build upwards instead of outwards, creating tenements five and six storeys high.

The capital played an important role in the Reformation (1560–1690), led by the Calvinist firebrand John Knox. Mary, Queen of Scots held court in the Palace of Holyroodhouse for six brief years, but when her son James VI succeeded to the English throne in 1603 he moved his court to London. The Act of Union in 1707 further reduced Edinburgh's importance.

Nevertheless, cultural and intellectual life flourished during the Scottish Enlightenment (c 1740–1830), and Edinburgh became known as 'a hotbed of genius'. In the second half of the 18th century the New Town was built, and in the 19th century the population quadrupled to 400,000, as suburbs of Victorian tenements spread north and south.

In the 1920s the city's borders expanded again to encompass Leith in the north, Cramond in the west and the Pentland Hills in the south. Following WWII the city's cultural life blossomed, stimulated by the Edinburgh International Festival and its fellow traveller, the Fringe, both held for the first time in 1947 and now recognised as world-class arts festivals.

Edinburgh entered a new era following the 1997 referendum vote in favour of a devolved Scottish parliament, which first convened in 1999 in a controversial modern building at the foot of the Royal Mile. The 2014 independence referendum saw Scots vote to remain part of the United Kingdom.

Sights

Edinburgh's main attractions are concentrated in the city centre – on and around the Old Town's Royal Mile between the castle and Holyrood, and in the New Town. A major exception is the Royal Yacht Britannia, which is in the redeveloped docklands district of Leith, 2 miles northeast of the centre.

Old Town

Edinburgh's Old Town stretches along a ridge to the east of the castle, and tumbles down Victoria St to the broad expanse of the Grassmarket. It's a jagged and jumbled maze of masonry riddled with closes (alleys) and wynds, stairs and vaults, and cleft along its spine by the cobbled ravine of the Royal Mile.

Until the founding of the New Town in the 18th century, old Edinburgh was an overcrowded and insanitary hive of humanity squeezed between the boggy ground of the Nor' Loch (North Loch, now drained and occupied by Princes Street Gardens) to the north and the city walls to the south and east. The only way for the town to expand was upwards, and the five- and six-storey tenements that were raised along the Royal Mile in the 16th and 17th centuries were the skyscrapers of their day, remarked upon with wonder by visiting writers such as Daniel Defoe. All classes of society, from beggars to magistrates, lived cheek by jowl in these urban ant nests, the wealthy occupying the middle floors – high enough to be above the noise and stink of the streets, but not so high that climbing the stairs would be too tiring – while the poor squeezed into attics, basements, cellars and vaults amid rats, rubbish and raw sewage.

★ Edinburgh Castle CASTLE
(Map p768; www.edinburghcastle.gov.uk; Castle Esplanade; adult/child £16.50/9.90, audioguide additional £3.50; ⏲9.30am-6pm Apr-Sep, to 5pm Oct-Mar, last admission 1hr before closing; 🚌23, 27, 41, 42) Edinburgh Castle has played a pivotal role in Scottish history, both as a royal residence – King Malcolm Canmore (r 1058–93)

EDINBURGH SIGHTS

Royal Mile

A GRAND DAY OUT

Planning your own procession along the Royal Mile involves some tough decisions – it would be impossible to see everything in a single day, so it's wise to decide in advance what you don't want to miss and shape your visit around that. Remember to leave time for lunch, for exploring some of the Mile's countless side alleys and, during festival time, for enjoying the street theatre that is bound to be happening in High St.

The most pleasant way to reach the Castle Esplanade at the start of the Royal Mile is to hike up the zigzag path from the footbridge behind the Ross Bandstand in Princes Street Gardens (in springtime you'll be knee-deep in daffodils). Starting at **Edinburgh Castle** ❶ means that the rest of your walk is downhill. For a superb view up and down the length of the Mile, climb the **Camera Obscura's Outlook Tower** ❷ before visiting **Gladstone's Land** ❸ and **St Giles Cathedral** ❹.

CLAUDIO DIVIZIA / SHUTTERSTOCK ©

Edinburgh Castle
If you're pushed for time, visit the Great Hall, the Honours of Scotland and the Prisons of War exhibit. Head for the Half Moon Battery for a photo looking down the length of the Royal Mile.

ROYAL VISITS TO THE ROYAL MILE

1561: Mary, Queen of Scots arrives from France and holds an audience with John Knox.
1745: Bonnie Prince Charlie fails to capture Edinburgh Castle, and instead sets up court in Holyroodhouse.
2004: Queen Elizabeth II officially opens the Scottish Parliament building.

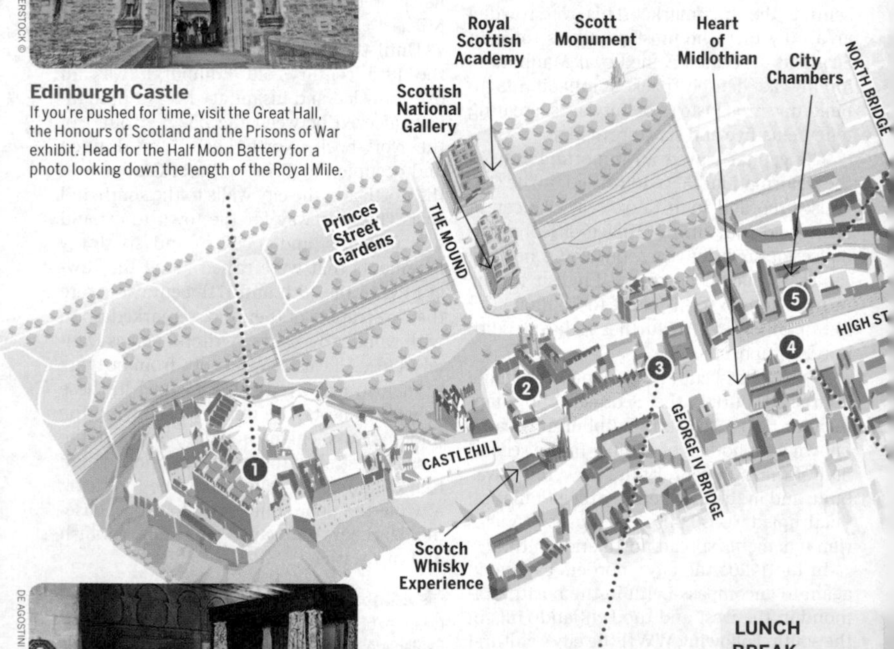

DE AGOSTINI / W. BUSS / GETTY IMAGES ©

Gladstone's Land
The 1st floor houses a faithful recreation of how a wealthy Edinburgh merchant lived in the 17th century. Check out the beautiful Painted Bedchamber, with its ornately decorated walls and wooden ceilings.

LUNCH BREAK

Burger and a beer at **Holyrood 9A**; steak and chips at **Maxie's Bistro**; slap-up seafood at **Ondine**.

If history's your thing, you'll want to add **Real Mary King's Close** ❺, **John Knox House** ❻ and the **Museum of Edinburgh** ❼ to your must-see list.

At the foot of the mile, choose between modern and ancient seats of power – the **Scottish Parliament** ❽ or the **Palace of Holyroodhouse** ❾. Round off the day with an evening ascent of Arthur's Seat or, slightly less strenuously, Calton Hill. Both make great sunset viewpoints.

TAKING YOUR TIME

Minimum time needed for each attraction:

» **Edinburgh Castle**: two hours
» **Gladstone's Land**: 45 minutes
» **St Giles Cathedral**: 30 minutes
» **Real Mary King's Close**: one hour (tour)
» **Scottish Parliament**: one hour (tour)
» **Palace of Holyroodhouse**: one hour

Real Mary King's Close

The guided tour is heavy on ghost stories, but a highlight is standing in an original 17th-century room with tufts of horsehair poking from the crumbling plaster, and breathing in the ancient scent of stone, dust and history.

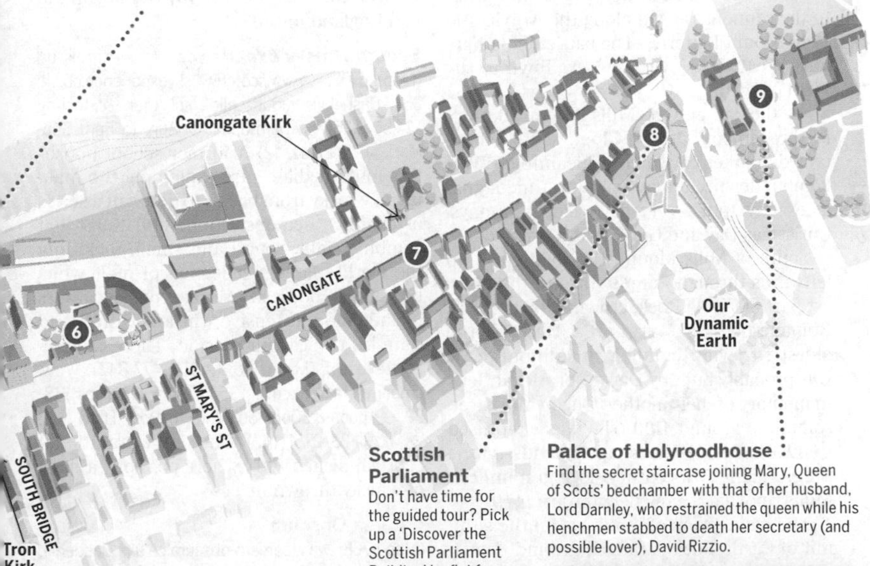

Scottish Parliament

Don't have time for the guided tour? Pick up a 'Discover the Scottish Parliament Building' leaflet from reception and take a self-guided tour of the exterior, then hike up to Salisbury Crags for a great view of the complex.

Palace of Holyroodhouse

Find the secret staircase joining Mary, Queen of Scots' bedchamber with that of her husband, Lord Darnley, who restrained the queen while his henchmen stabbed to death her secretary (and possible lover), David Rizzio.

DAVID IONUT / SHUTTERSTOCK ©

St Giles Cathedral

Look out for the Burne-Jones stained-glass window (1873) at the west end, showing the crossing of the River Jordan, and the bronze memorial to Robert Louis Stevenson in the Moray Aisle.

PHOTOPROFI30 / SHUTTERSTOCK ©

HEARTLAND ARTS / SHUTTERSTOCK ©

and Queen Margaret first made their home here in the 11th century – and as a military stronghold. The castle last saw military action in 1745; from then until the 1920s it served as the British army's main base in Scotland. Today it is one of Scotland's most atmospheric and popular tourist attractions.

The brooding, black crags of Castle Rock, rising above the western end of Princes St, are the very reason for Edinburgh's existence. This rocky hill was the most easily defended hilltop on the invasion route between England and central Scotland, a route followed by countless armies from the Roman legions of the 1st and 2nd centuries AD to the Jacobite troops of Bonnie Prince Charlie in 1745.

The **Entrance Gateway**, flanked by statues of Robert the Bruce and William Wallace, opens to a cobbled lane that leads up beneath the 16th-century **Portcullis Gate** to the cannons ranged along the Argyle and Mills Mount Batteries. The battlements here have great views over the New Town to the Firth of Forth.

At the far end of Mills Mount Battery is the famous **One O'Clock Gun**, where crowds gather to watch a gleaming WWII 25-pounder fire an ear-splitting time signal at exactly 1pm (every day except Sundays, Christmas Day and Good Friday).

South of Mills Mount, the road curls up leftwards through **Foog's Gate** to the highest part of Castle Rock, crowned by the tiny, Romanesque **St Margaret's Chapel**, the oldest surviving building in Edinburgh. It was probably built by David I or Alexander I in memory of their mother, Queen Margaret, sometime around 1130 (she was canonised in 1250). Beside the chapel stands **Mons Meg**, a giant 15th-century siege gun built at Mons (in what is now Belgium) in 1449.

The main group of buildings on the summit of Castle Rock is ranged around Crown Sq, dominated by the shrine of the **Scottish National War Memorial**. Opposite is the Great Hall, built for James IV (r 1488–1513) as a ceremonial hall and used as a meeting place for the Scottish parliament until 1639. Its most remarkable feature is the original, 16th-century hammer-beam roof.

The **Castle Vaults** beneath the Great Hall (entered via the **Prisons of War** exhibit) were used variously as storerooms, bakeries and a prison. The vaults have been renovated to resemble 18th- and early 19th-century prisons, where graffiti carved by French and American prisoners can be seen on the ancient wooden doors.

On the eastern side of the square is the **Royal Palace**, built during the 15th and 16th centuries, where a series of historical tableaux leads to the highlight of the castle – a strongroom housing the **Honours of Scotland** (the Scottish crown jewels), among the oldest surviving crown jewels in Europe. Locked away in a chest following the Act of Union in 1707, the crown (made in 1540 from the gold of Robert the Bruce's 14th-century coronet), sword and sceptre lay forgotten until they were unearthed at the instigation of the novelist Sir Walter Scott in 1818. Also on display here is the Stone of Destiny (p772).

Among the neighbouring **Royal Apartments** is the bedchamber where Mary, Queen of Scots gave birth to her son James VI, who was to unite the crowns of Scotland and England in 1603.

Scotch Whisky Experience MUSEUM

(Map p768; www.scotchwhiskyexperience.co.uk; 354 Castlehill; adult/child incl tour & tasting £14.50/7.25; ⏲10am-6pm Apr-Aug, to 5pm Sep-Mar; 🚌23, 27, 41, 42) A former school houses this multimedia centre explaining the making of whisky from barley to bottle in a series of exhibits, demonstrations and talks that combine sight, sound and smell, including the world's largest collection of malt whiskies (3384 bottles!). More expensive tours include more extensive whisky tastings and samples of Scottish cuisine. There's also a **restaurant** (Map p768; ☎0131-477 8477; www.amber-restaurant.co.uk; 354 Castlehill; mains £13-22; ⏲noon-8.30pm Sun-Thu, to 9pm Fri & Sat; 📶👪; 🚌23, 27, 41, 42) that serves traditional Scottish dishes with, where possible, a dash of whisky thrown in.

Camera Obscura MUSEUM

(Map p768; www.camera-obscura.co.uk; Castlehill; adult/child £14.50/10.50; ⏲9am-9pm Jul & Aug, 9.30am-7pm Apr-Jun & Sep-Oct, 10am-6pm Nov-Mar; 🚌23, 27, 41, 42) Edinburgh's camera obscura is a curious 19th-century device – in constant use since 1853 – that uses lenses and mirrors to throw a live image of the city onto a large horizontal screen. The accompanying commentary is entertaining and the whole experience has a quirky charm, complemented by an intriguing exhibition dedicated to illusions of all kinds. Stairs lead up through various displays to the **Outlook Tower**, which offers great views over the city.

Gladstone's Land HISTORIC BUILDING

(NTS; Map p768; www.nts.org.uk/Property/Gladstones-Land; 477 Lawnmarket; adult/child £6.50/5; ⏲10am-6.30pm Jul & Aug, to 5pm Apr-Jun & Sep-Oct; 🚌23, 27, 41, 42) One of Edinburgh's most prominent 17th-century merchants was Thomas Gledstanes, who in 1617 purchased the tenement later known as Gladstone's Land. It contains fine painted ceilings, walls and beams, and some splendid furniture from the 17th and 18th centuries. The volunteer guides provide a wealth of anecdotes and a detailed history.

St Giles Cathedral CHURCH

(Map p768; www.stgilescathedral.org.uk; High St; suggested donation £3; ⏲9am-7pm Mon-Fri, to 5pm Sat, 1-5pm Sun May-Sep, 9am-5pm Mon-Sat, 1-5pm Sun Oct-Apr; 🚌23, 27, 41, 42) The great grey bulk of St Giles Cathedral dates largely from the 15th century, but much of it was restored in the 19th century. One of the most interesting corners of the kirk is the **Thistle Chapel**, built in 1911 for the Knights of the Most Ancient & Most Noble Order of the Thistle. The elaborately carved Gothic-style stalls have canopies topped with the helms and arms of the 16 knights – look out for the bagpipe-playing angel amid the vaulting.

Properly called the High Kirk of Edinburgh (it was only a true cathedral – the seat of a bishop – from 1633 to 1638 and from 1661 to 1689), the church was named after the patron saint of cripples and beggars. The interior lacks grandeur but is rich in history: a Norman-style church was built here in 1126 but was destroyed by English invaders in 1385 (the only substantial remains are the central piers that support the tower). St Giles was at the heart of the Scottish Reformation, and John Knox served as minister here from 1559 to 1572.

There are several ornate monuments in the church, including the tombs of **James Graham, Marquis of Montrose**, who led Charles I's forces in Scotland and was hanged in 1650 at the Mercat Cross; and his Covenanter opponent **Archibald Campbell, Marquis of Argyll**, who was decapitated in 1661 after the Restoration of Charles II. There's also a bronze memorial to author **Robert Louis Stevenson**, and a copy of the National Covenant of 1638.

By the side of the street, outside the western door of St Giles, is the **Heart of Midlothian** (Map p768; High St; 🚌23, 27, 41, 42), set into the cobblestone paving. This marks the site of the Tolbooth. Built in the 15th century and demolished in the early 19th century, the Tolbooth served variously as a meeting place for parliament, the town council and the General Assembly of the Reformed Kirk, before becoming law courts and, finally, a notorious prison and place of execution. Passers-by traditionally spit on the heart for luck (don't stand downwind!).

EDINBURGH IN...

Two Days

A two-day trip to Edinburgh should start at **Edinburgh Castle** (p763), followed by a stroll down the Royal Mile to the **Scottish Parliament Building** (p769) and the **Palace of Holyroodhouse** (p770). You can work up an appetite by climbing **Arthur's Seat** (p771), then satisfy your hunger with dinner at **Ondine** (p788) or **Castle Terrace** (Map p768; ☎0131-229 1222; www.castleterracerestaurant.com; 33-35 Castle Tce; 3-course lunch/dinner £29.50/65; ⏲noon-2.15pm & 6.30-10pm Tue-Sat; 🚌2) 🌿. On day two spend the morning in the **National Museum of Scotland** (p771), then catch the bus to Leith for a visit to the **Royal Yacht Britannia** (p778). In the evening, have dinner at one of Leith's many excellent restaurants, or scare yourself silly on a guided ghost tour.

Four Days

Two more days will give you time for a morning stroll around the **Royal Botanic Garden** (p778), followed by a trip to the enigmatic and beautiful **Rosslyn Chapel** (p779), or a relaxing afternoon visit to the seaside village of **Cramond** (p779) – bring binoculars (for birdwatching and yacht-spotting) and a book (to read in the sun). Dinner at **Gardener's Cottage** (p789) could be before or after your sunset walk to the summit of **Calton Hill** (p776). On day four head out to the harbour village of **Queensferry** (p796), beneath the Forth Bridges, and take a cruise to Inchcolm island.

Old Town

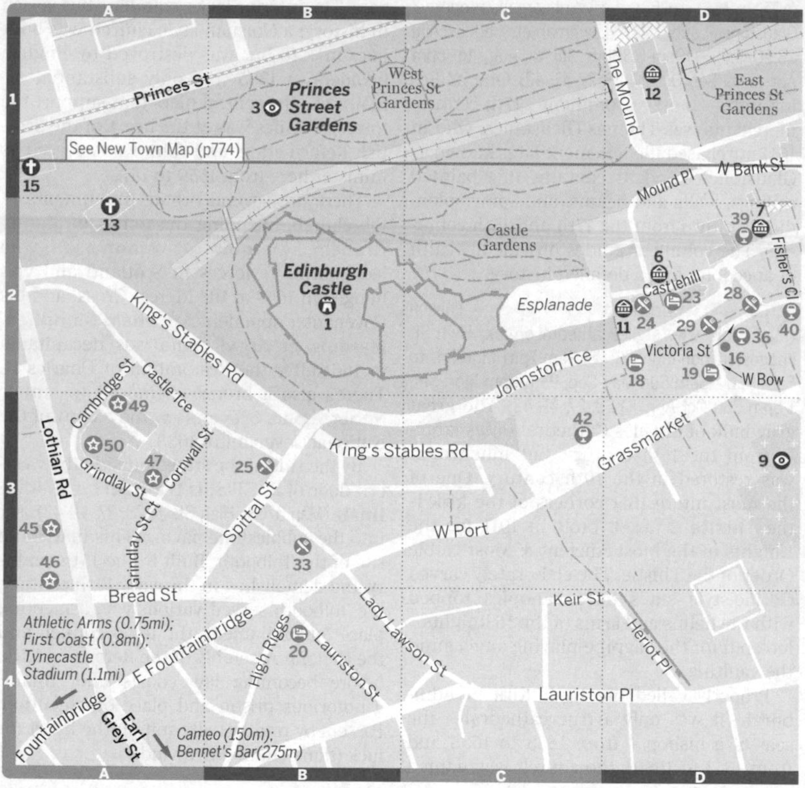

At the other end of St Giles is the **Mercat Cross** (🚍35), a 19th-century copy of the 1365 original, where merchants and traders met to transact business and royal proclamations were read.

★Real Mary King's Close HISTORIC BUILDING

(Map p768; ☎0845 070 6244; www.realmarykingsclose.com; 2 Warriston's Close, High St; adult/child £14.50/8.75; ⏲10am-9pm daily Apr-Oct, 10am-5pm Sun-Thu, 10am-9pm Fri & Sat Nov-Mar; 🚍23, 27, 41, 42) Edinburgh's 18th-century City Chambers were built over the sealed-off remains of Mary King's Close, and the lower levels of this medieval Old Town alley have survived almost unchanged amid the foundations for 250 years. Now open to the public, this spooky, subterranean labyrinth gives a fascinating insight into the everyday life of 17th-century Edinburgh. Costumed characters lead tours through a 16th-century town house and the plague-stricken home of a 17th-century gravedigger. Advance booking recommended.

The scripted tour, complete with ghostly tales and gruesome tableaux, can seem a little naff, milking the scary and scatological aspects of the close's history for all they're worth. But there are many things of genuine interest to see; there's something about the crumbling 17th-century **tenement room** that makes the hairs rise on the back of your neck, with tufts of horsehair poking from the collapsing lath-and-plaster, the ghost of a pattern on the walls, and the ancient smell of stone and dust thick in your nostrils.

In one of the former bedrooms off the close, a psychic once claimed to have been approached by the ghost of a little girl called Annie. It's hard to tell what's more frightening – the story of the ghostly child, or the bizarre heap of tiny dolls and teddies left in a corner by sympathetic visitors.

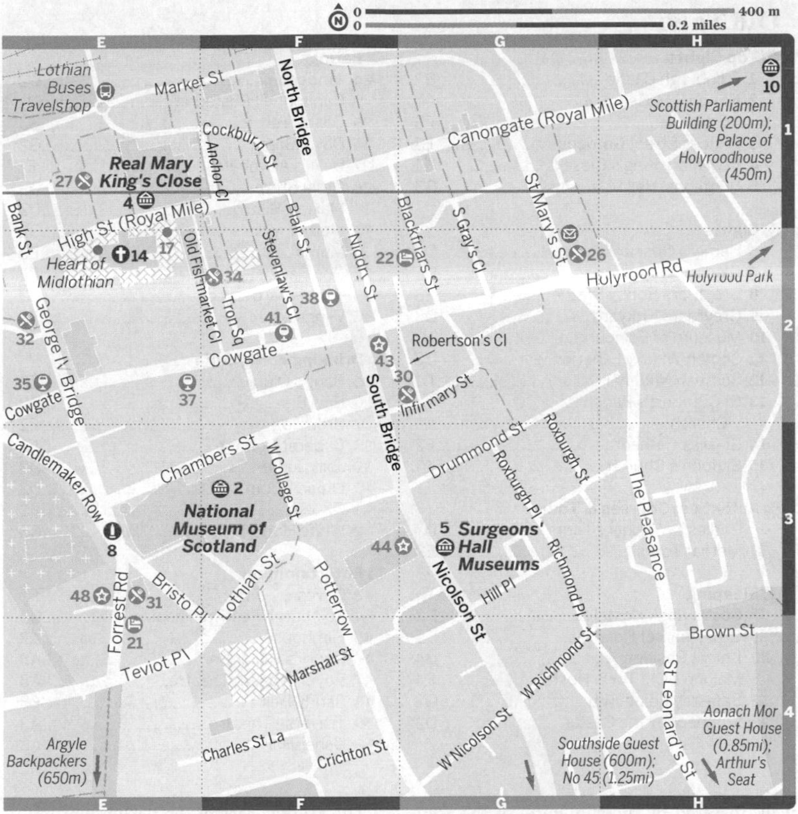

Museum of Edinburgh MUSEUM

(Map p768; ☎0131-529 4143; www.edinburghmuseums.org.uk; 142 Canongate; ⏲10am-5pm Mon-Sat year-round, noon-5pm Sun Aug; 🚌35) FREE You can't miss the colourful facade of Huntly House, brightly renovated in red and yellow ochre, opposite the Tolbooth clock on the Royal Mile. Built in 1570, it houses a museum covering Edinburgh from its prehistory to the present. Exhibits of national importance include an original copy of the National Covenant of 1638, but the big crowd-pleaser is the dog collar and feeding bowl that once belonged to Greyfriars Bobby (p772), the city's most famous canine citizen.

Holyrood & Arthur's Seat

★Scottish Parliament Building NOTABLE BUILDING

(☎0131-348 5200; www.scottish.parliament.uk; Horse Wynd; ⏲9am-6.30pm Tue-Thu & 10am-5pm Mon, Fri & Sat in session, 10am-5pm Mon-Sat in recess; 🚌6, 35) FREE The Scottish parliament building, on the site of a former brewery, was officially opened by HM the Queen in October 2005. Designed by Catalan architect Enric Miralles (1955–2000), the ground plan of the parliament complex is said to represent a 'flower of democracy rooted in Scottish soil' (best seen looking down from Salisbury Crags). Free, one-hour guided tours (advance booking recommended) include a visit to the Debating Chamber, a committee room, the Garden Lobby and an MSP's (Member of the Scottish Parliament) office.

Miralles believed that a building could be a work of art. However, this weird concrete confection at the foot of Salisbury Crags has left the good people of Edinburgh staring and scratching their heads in confusion. What does it all mean? The strange forms of the exterior are all symbolic in some way, from the oddly shaped windows on the west

Old Town

Top Sights
1 Edinburgh Castle ... B2
2 National Museum of Scotland ... F3
3 Princes Street Gardens ... B1
4 Real Mary King's Close ... E1
5 Surgeons' Hall Museums ... G3

Sights
6 Camera Obscura ... D2
7 Gladstone's Land ... D2
8 Greyfriars Bobby Statue ... E3
9 Greyfriars Kirkyard ... D3
10 Museum of Edinburgh ... H1
11 Scotch Whisky Experience ... D2
12 Scottish National Gallery ... D1
13 St Cuthbert's Parish Church ... A2
14 St Giles Cathedral ... E2
15 St John's Church ... A1

Activities, Courses & Tours
16 Cadies & Witchery Tours ... D2
17 Mercat Tours ... E2

Sleeping
18 Castle Rock Hostel ... D2
19 Grassmarket Hotel ... D2
20 Knight Residence ... B4
21 Malone's Old Town Hostel ... E4
22 Safestay Edinburgh ... G2
23 Witchery by the Castle ... D2

Eating
24 Amber ... D2
Cannonball Restaurant ... (see 11)
25 Castle Terrace ... B3
26 David Bann ... G2
27 Devil's Advocate ... E1
28 Grain Store ... D2
29 Maxie's Bistro ... D2
30 Mother India's Cafe ... G2
31 Mums ... E3
32 Ondine ... E2
33 Timberyard ... B3
34 Wings ... F2

Drinking & Nightlife
35 Bongo Club ... E2
36 Bow Bar ... D2
37 BrewDog ... E2
38 Cabaret Voltaire ... F2
39 Jolly Judge ... D2
40 Liquid Room ... D2
41 OX 184 ... F2
42 White Hart Inn ... C3

Entertainment
43 Caves ... F2
44 Edinburgh Festival Theatre ... G3
45 Filmhouse ... A3
46 Henry's Cellar Bar ... A3
47 Royal Lyceum Theatre ... A3
48 Sandy Bell's ... E3
49 Traverse Theatre ... A3
50 Usher Hall ... A3

wall (inspired by the silhouette of the *Reverend Robert Walker Skating on Duddingston Loch,* one of Scotland's most famous paintings), to the asymmetric panels on the main facade (representing a curtain being drawn aside, a symbol of open government).

The **Main Hall**, inside the public entrance, has a low, triple-arched ceiling of polished concrete, like a cave, or cellar, or castle vault. It is a dimly lit space, the starting point for a metaphorical journey from this relative darkness up to the **Debating Chamber** (sitting directly above the Main Hall), which is, in contrast, a palace of light – the light of democracy. This magnificent chamber is the centrepiece of the parliament, designed not to glorify but to humble the politicians who sit within it. The windows face Calton Hill, allowing MSPs to look up to its monuments (reminders of the Scottish Enlightenment), while the massive, pointed oak beams of the roof are suspended by steel threads above the MSPs' heads like so many Damoclean swords.

The public areas of the parliament building – the Main Hall, where there is an exhibition, a shop and cafe, and the public gallery in the Debating Chamber – are open to visitors (free tickets needed for public gallery – see website for details). If you want to see the parliament in session, check the website to see when it will be sitting – business days are normally Tuesday to Thursday year-round.

★**Palace of Holyroodhouse** PALACE
(www.royalcollection.org.uk; Horse Wynd; adult/child incl audioguide £12/7.20; ⏲9.30am-6pm Apr-Oct, to 4.30pm Nov-Mar; 🚌6, 35) This palace is the royal family's official residence in Scotland, but is more famous as the 16th-century home of the ill-fated Mary, Queen of Scots. The highlight of the tour is **Mary's Bed Chamber**, home to the unfortunate queen from 1561 to 1567. It was here that her jealous second husband, Lord Darnley, restrained the pregnant queen while his henchmen murdered her secretary Rizzio. A

plaque in the neighbouring room marks the spot where he bled to death.

The palace developed from a guesthouse, attached to Holyrood Abbey, which was extended by King James IV in 1501. The oldest surviving part of the building, the northwestern tower, was built in 1529 as a royal apartment for James V and his wife, Mary of Guise. Mary, Queen of Scots spent six turbulent years here, during which time she debated with John Knox, married both her second and third husbands, and witnessed the murder of her secretary David Rizzio.

The self-guided audio tour leads you through a series of impressive royal apartments, culminating in the **Great Gallery**. The 89 portraits of Scottish kings were commissioned by Charles II and supposedly record his unbroken lineage from Scota, the Egyptian pharaoh's daughter who discovered the infant Moses in a reed basket on the banks of the Nile. The tour continues to the oldest part of the palace, which contains Mary's Bed Chamber, connected by a secret stairway to her husband's bedroom, and ends with the ruins of Holyrood Abbey.

★**Arthur's Seat** VIEWPOINT

(Holyrood Park; 🚌6, 35) The rocky peak of Arthur's Seat (251m), carved by ice sheets from the deeply eroded stump of a long-extinct volcano, is a distinctive feature of Edinburgh's skyline. The view from the summit is well worth the walk, extending from the Forth Bridges in the west to the distant conical hill of North Berwick Law in the east, with the Ochil Hills and the Highlands on the northwestern horizon. You can hike from Holyrood to the summit in around 45 minutes

South of the Royal Mile

★**National Museum of Scotland** MUSEUM

(Map p768; www.nms.ac.uk; Chambers St; fee for special exhibitions varies; 🕙10am-5pm; 👪; 🚌2, 23, 27, 35, 41, 42, 45) FREE Broad, elegant Chambers St is dominated by the long facade of the National Museum of Scotland. Its extensive collections are spread between two buildings, one modern, one Victorian – the golden stone and striking modern architecture of the new building, opened in 1998, is one of the city's most distinctive landmarks. The five floors of the museum trace the history of Scotland from its geological beginnings to the 1990s, with many imaginative and stimulating exhibits. Audioguides are available in several languages.

The new building connects with the original Victorian museum, dating from 1861, the stolid, grey exterior of which gives way to a beautifully bright and airy, glass-roofed exhibition hall. The old building houses an eclectic collection covering natural history, archaeology, scientific and industrial technology, and the decorative arts of ancient Egypt, Islam, China, Japan, Korea and the West.

THE ROYAL MILE

This mile-long street earned its regal nickname in the 16th century when it was used by the king to travel between the castle and the Palace of Holyroodhouse. There are five sections (the Castle Esplanade, Castlehill, Lawnmarket, High St and Canongate), the names of which reflect their historical origins.

Castle Esplanade Open area outside the castle gates; originally a parade ground, it forms the stage for the Military Tattoo (p783) during festival time.

Castlehill The short slope connecting the Castle Esplanade to the Lawnmarket.

Lawnmarket A corruption of 'Landmarket', a market selling goods from land outside the city; takes its name from the large cloth market that flourished here until the 18th century. This was the poshest part of the Old Town, where many of its most distinguished citizens made their homes.

High St Stretches from George IV Bridge down to the Netherbow at St Mary's St. It's the heart and soul of the Old Town, home to the city's main church, the law courts, the city council and – until 1707 – the Scottish parliament.

Canongate The stretch of the Royal Mile from Netherbow to Holyrood takes its name from the Augustinian canons (monks) of Holyrood Abbey. From the 16th century it was home to aristocrats attracted to the Palace of Holyroodhouse. Originally governed by the monks, Canongate was an independent burgh separate from Edinburgh until 1856.

★**Surgeons' Hall Museums** MUSEUM
(Map p768; www.museum.rcsed.ac.uk; Nicolson St; adult/child £6/3.50; ⏲10am-5pm daily Apr-Oct, noon-4pm Mon-Fri Nov-Mar; 🚌all South Bridge buses) Housed in a grand Ionic temple designed by William Playfair in 1832, these three fascinating museums were originally established as teaching collections. The **History of Surgery Museum** provides a look at surgery in Scotland from the 15th century – when barbers supplemented their income with bloodletting, amputations and other surgical procedures – to the present day. The highlight is the exhibit on **Burke and Hare**, which includes Burke's death mask and a pocketbook made from his skin.

The adjacent **Dental Collection**, with its wince-inducing collections of extraction tools, covers the history of dentistry, while the **Pathology Museum** houses a gruesome but compelling 19th-century collection of diseased organs and massive tumours pickled in formaldehyde.

Greyfriars Kirkyard CEMETERY
(Map p768; www.greyfriarskirk.com; Candlemaker Row; ⏲8am-dusk; 🚌2, 23, 27, 35, 41, 42, 45) Greyfriars Kirkyard is one of Edinburgh's most evocative cemeteries, a peaceful green oasis dotted with elaborate monuments. Many famous Edinburgh names are buried here, including the poet Allan Ramsay (1686–1758), architect William Adam (1689–1748) and William Smellie (1740–95), the editor of the first edition of the *Encyclopedia Britannica*. If you want to experience the graveyard at its scariest – inside a burial vault, in the dark, at night – go on one of the City of the Dead (p779) guided tours.

Greyfriars Bobby Statue MONUMENT
(Map p768; cnr George IV Bridge & Candlemaker Row; 🚌2, 23, 27, 35, 41, 42, 45) Probably the most popular photo opportunity in Edinburgh, the life-size statue of Greyfriars Bobby, a Skye terrier who captured the hearts of the British public in the late 19th century, stands outside Greyfriars Kirkyard. From 1858 to 1872, the wee dog maintained a vigil over the grave of his master, an Edinburgh police officer. The story was immortalised in a novel by Eleanor Atkinson in 1912, and in 1963 was made into a movie by – who else? – Walt Disney.

The statue is always surrounded by crowds of visitors taking photos of themselves posing beside the little dog. Bobby's own grave, marked by a small, pink granite

THE STONE OF DESTINY

On St Andrew's Day 1996 a block of sandstone – 26.5 inches by 16.5 inches by 11 inches in size, with rusted iron hoops at either end – was installed with much pomp and ceremony in Edinburgh Castle. For the previous 700 years it had lain in London, beneath the Coronation Chair in Westminster Abbey. Almost all English, and later British, monarchs from Edward II in 1307 to Elizabeth II in 1953 have parked their backsides firmly over this stone during their coronation ceremony.

The legendary Stone of Destiny – said to have originated in the Holy Land, and on which Scottish kings placed their feet during their coronation (not their bums; the English got that bit wrong) – was stolen from Scone Abbey near Perth by King Edward I of England in 1296. It was taken to London and there it remained for seven centuries – except for a brief removal to Gloucester during WWII air raids, and a three-month sojourn in Scotland after it was stolen by Scottish Nationalist students on Christmas in 1950 – as an enduring symbol of Scotland's subjugation by England.

The Stone of Destiny returned to the political limelight in 1996, when the then Scottish Secretary and Conservative Party MP Michael Forsyth arranged for the return of the sandstone block to Scotland. A blatant attempt to boost the flagging popularity of the Conservative Party in Scotland prior to a general election, Forsyth's publicity stunt failed miserably. The Scots said thanks very much for the stone and then, in May 1997, voted every Conservative MP in Scotland into oblivion.

Many people, however, believe Edward I was fobbed off with a shoddy imitation in 1296 and that the true Stone of Destiny remains safely hidden somewhere in Scotland. This is not impossible – some descriptions of the original stone state that it was made of black marble and decorated with elaborate carvings. Interested parties should read *Scotland's Stone of Destiny* by Nick Aitchinson, which details the history and cultural significance of Scotland's most famous lump of rock.

stone, is just inside the entrance to Greyfriars Kirkyard, behind the monument, and you can see his original collar and bowl in the Museum of Edinburgh (p769).

New Town & Around

Edinburgh's New Town lies north of the Old, on a ridge running parallel to the Royal Mile and separated from it by the valley of Princes Street Gardens. Its regular grid of elegant, Georgian terraces is a complete contrast to the chaotic tangle of tenements and wynds that characterises the Old Town, and is the world's most complete and unspoilt example of Georgian architecture and town planning.

Apart from the streetscape, the main sights are the art galleries and gardens on Princes St, and the Scottish National Portrait Gallery near St Andrew Sq, all within walking distance of each other.

Princes St is one of the world's most spectacular shopping streets. Built up on the north side only, it catches the sun in summer and allows expansive views across Princes Street Gardens to the castle and the crowded skyline of the Old Town.

The western end of Princes St is dominated by the red-sandstone edifice of the Caledonian Hilton Hotel and the tower of **St John's Church** (Map p768; Princes St; all Princes St buses), worth visiting for its fine Gothic Revival interior. It overlooks **St Cuthbert's Parish Church** (Map p768; Lothian Rd; all Lothian Rd buses), built in the 1890s on a site of great antiquity – there has been a church here since at least the 12th century, and perhaps since the 7th century. There is a circular **watchtower** in the graveyard – a reminder of the Burke and Hare days when graves had to be guarded against robbers.

At the eastern end is the prominent clock tower – traditionally three minutes fast so you don't miss your train – of the Balmoral Hotel (p790; originally the North British Hotel, built by the railway company of the same name in 1902) and the beautiful 1788 **Register House** (Map p774; Princes St; all Princes St buses), designed by Robert Adam, with a statue of the Duke of Wellington on horseback in front. It houses the National Archives of Scotland and the ScotlandsPeople genealogical research centre.

Princes Street Gardens (Map p768; Princes St; dawn-dusk; all Princes St buses) FREE lie in a valley that was once occupied by the Nor' Loch, a boggy depression that was drained in the early 19th century. The gardens are split in the middle by **The Mound**, which was created from around two million cartloads of earth excavated from the foundations of the New Town and dumped here to provide a road link across the valley to the Old Town. It was completed in 1830.

★ Scottish National Portrait Gallery
GALLERY

(Map p774; www.nationalgalleries.org; 1 Queen St; 10am-5pm; ; St Andrew Sq) FREE The Venetian Gothic palace of the Scottish National Portrait Gallery reopened its doors in 2011 after a two-year renovation, emerging as one of the city's top attractions. Its galleries illustrate Scottish history through paintings, photographs and sculptures, putting faces to famous names from Scotland's past and present, from Robert Burns, Mary, Queen of Scots and Bonnie Prince Charlie to Sean Connery, Billy Connolly and poet Jackie Kay.

The gallery's interior is decorated in Arts and Crafts style, and nowhere more splendidly than in the **Great Hall**. Above the Gothic colonnade a processional frieze painted by William Hole in 1898 serves as a 'visual encyclopedia' of famous Scots, shown in chronological order from Calgacus (the chieftain who led the Caledonian tribes into battle against the Romans) to writer and philosopher Thomas Carlyle (1795–1881). The murals on the 1st-floor balcony depict scenes from Scottish history, while the ceiling is painted with the constellations of the night sky.

The gallery's selection of 'trails' leaflets adds a bit of background information while leading you around the various exhibits; the Hidden Histories trail is particularly interesting.

Scott Monument
MONUMENT

(Map p774; www.edinburghmuseums.org.uk; East Princes Street Gardens; admission £5; 10am-7pm Apr-Sep, 10am-4pm Oct-Mar; Princes St) The eastern half of Princes Street Gardens is dominated by the massive Gothic spire of the Scott Monument, built by public subscription in memory of the novelist Sir Walter Scott after his death in 1832. The exterior is decorated with 64 carvings of characters from his novels; inside you can see an exhibition on Scott's life, and climb the 287 steps to the top for a superb view of the city.

New Town

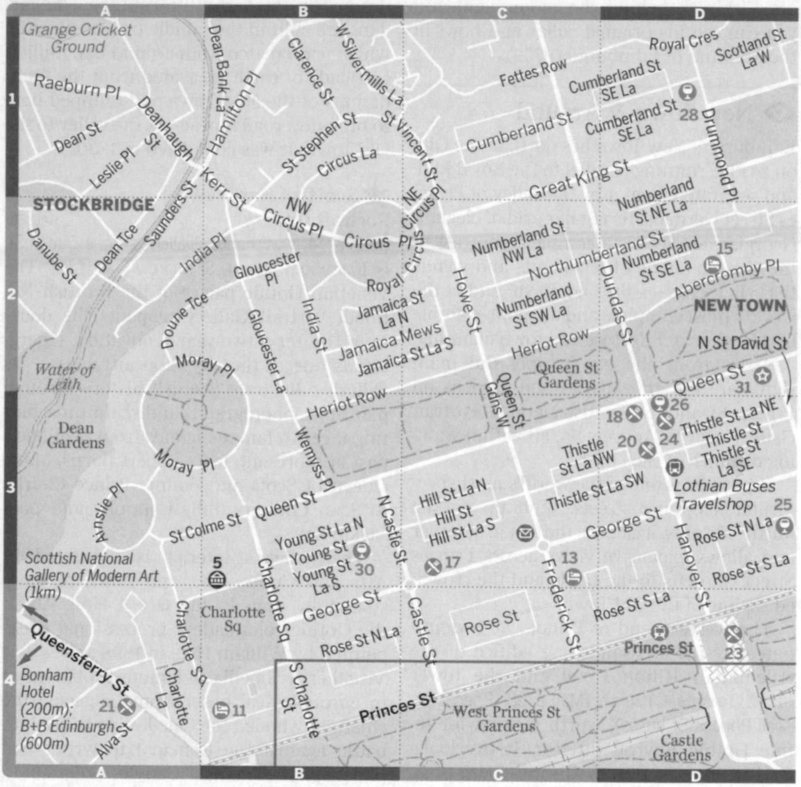

Scottish National Gallery GALLERY

(Map p768; www.nationalgalleries.org; The Mound; fee for special exhibitions varies; ⏲10am-5pm Fri-Wed, to 7pm Thu; 🚊Princes St) **FREE** Designed by William Playfair, this imposing classical building with its Ionic porticoes dates from the 1850s. Its octagonal rooms, lit by skylights, have been restored to their original Victorian decor of deep-green carpets and dark-red walls. The gallery houses an important collection of European art from the Renaissance to post-Impressionism, with works by Verrocchio (Leonardo da Vinci's teacher), Tintoretto, Titian, Holbein, Rubens, Van Dyck, Vermeer, El Greco, Poussin, Rembrandt, Gainsborough, Turner, Constable, Monet, Pissarro, Gauguin and Cézanne.

The upstairs galleries house portraits by Sir Joshua Reynolds and Sir Henry Raeburn, and a clutch of **Impressionist paintings**, including Monet's luminous *Haystacks*, Van Gogh's demonic *Olive Trees* and Gauguin's hallucinatory *Vision After the Sermon*. But the painting that really catches your eye is the gorgeous portrait of *Lady Agnew of Lochnaw* by John Singer Sargent.

The basement galleries dedicated to **Scottish art** include glowing portraits by Allan Ramsay and Sir Henry Raeburn, rural scenes by Sir David Wilkie and Impressionistic landscapes by William MacTaggart. Look out for Sir George Harvey's hugely entertaining *A Schule Skailin* (A School Emptying) – a stern dominie (teacher) looks on as the boys stampede for the classroom door, one reaching for a confiscated spinning top. Kids will love the fantasy paintings of Sir Joseph Noel Paton in room B5; the incredibly detailed canvases are crammed with hundreds of tiny fairies, goblins and elves.

Recent research has suggested that the iconic 1790s painting of *Reverend Robert Walker Skating on Duddingston Loch*, his-

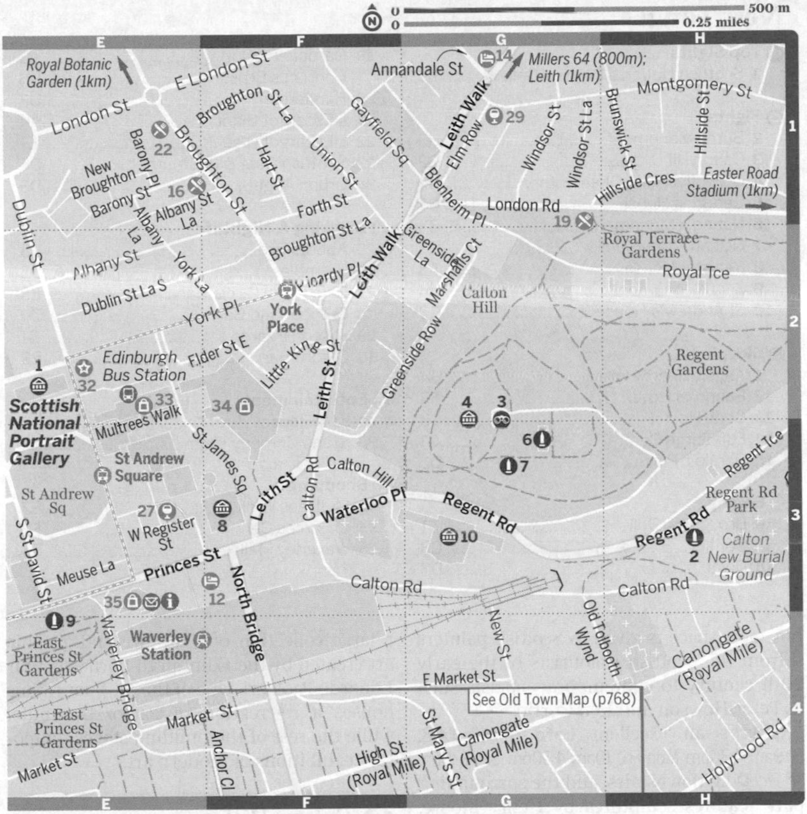

torically attributed to Sir Henry Raeburn, may in fact be the work of French artist Henri-Pierre Danloux.

Each January the gallery exhibits its **collection of Turner watercolours**, bequeathed by Henry Vaughan in 1900. Room X is graced by Antonio Canova's white marble sculpture, *The Three Graces;* it's owned jointly with London's Victoria & Albert Museum.

Georgian House HISTORIC BUILDING

(NTS; Map p774; www.nts.org.uk; 7 Charlotte Sq; adult/child £7/5.50; ⌚10am-6pm Jul & Aug, 10am-5pm Apr-Jun & Sep-Oct, 11am-4pm Mar & Nov; 🚌36, 47) The National Trust for Scotland's Georgian House has been beautifully restored and furnished to show how Edinburgh's wealthy elite lived at the end of the 18th century. The walls are decorated with paintings by Allan Ramsay, Sir Henry Raeburn and Sir Joshua Reynolds, and there's a fully equipped 18th-century kitchen complete with china closet and wine cellar.

★Scottish National Gallery of Modern Art GALLERY

(www.nationalgalleries.org; 75 Belford Rd; fee for special exhibitions varies; ⌚10am-5pm; 🚌13) **FREE** Edinburgh's gallery of modern art is split between two impressive neoclassical buildings surrounded by landscaped grounds some 500m west of Dean Village. As well as showcasing a stunning collection of paintings by the popular, post-Impressionist Scottish Colourists – in *Reflections, Balloch,* Leslie Hunter pulls off the improbable trick of making Scotland look like the South of France – the gallery is the starting point for a walk along the Water of Leith, following a trail of sculptures by Antony Gormley.

The main collection, known as **Modern One**, concentrates on 20th-century art, with various European movements represented by the likes of Matisse, Picasso, Kirchner, Magritte, Miró, Mondrian and Giacometti. American and English artists are also represented,

New Town

Top Sights
1 Scottish National Portrait Gallery E2

Sights
2 Burns Monument H3
3 Calton Hill G2
4 Collective/City Observatory G2
5 Georgian House B3
6 National Monument G3
7 Nelson Monument G3
8 Register House F3
9 Scott Monument E4
10 St Andrew's House G3

Sleeping
11 Angels Share Hotel B4
12 Balmoral Hotel F3
13 Code Hostel C3
14 Edinburgh Central SYHA G1
15 Gerald's Place D2

Eating
16 Broughton Deli E1
17 Contini C3
18 Dogs D3
19 Gardener's Cottage G1
Hadrian's Brasserie .... (see 12)
20 Henderson's D3
21 L'Escargot Blanc A4
22 L'Escargot Bleu E1
23 Scottish Cafe & Restaurant D4
24 Urban Angel D3

Drinking & Nightlife
25 Abbotsford D3
26 Bramble D3
27 Café Royal Circle Bar E3
28 Cumberland Bar D1
29 Joseph Pearce's G1
30 Oxford Bar B3

Entertainment
31 Jam House D2
32 Stand Comedy Club E2

Shopping
33 Multrees Walk E2
34 St James Centre F2
35 Waverley Mall E3

but most space is given to Scottish painters – from the Scottish Colourists of the early 20th century to contemporary artists such as Peter Howson and Ken Currie.

There's an excellent **cafe** (mains £4-8; 9am-4.30pm Mon-Fri, 10am-4.30pm Sat & Sun; ; 13) downstairs, and the surrounding park features sculptures by Henry Moore, Rachel Whiteread and Barbara Hepworth, among others, as well as a 'landform artwork' by Charles Jencks, and the **Pig Rock Bothy**, a rustic timber performance and exhibition space created in 2014 as part of the Bothy Project (www.thebothyproject.org).

A footpath and stairs at the rear of the gallery lead down to the **Water of Leith Walkway**, which you can follow along the river for 4 miles to Leith. This takes you past **6 Times**, a sculptural project by Antony Gormley consisting of six human figures standing at various points along the river. (The statues are designed to fall over in flood conditions, so some of them may not be visible after heavy rain.)

Scottish National Gallery of Modern Art – Modern Two

(www.nationalgalleries.org; Belford Rd; 10am-5pm; 13) FREE Directly across Belford Rd from Modern One, another neoclassical mansion (formerly an orphanage) houses its annexe, Modern Two, which is home to a large collection of sculpture and graphic art created by the Edinburgh-born artist Sir Eduardo Paolozzi. One of the 1st-floor rooms houses a re-creation of Paolozzi's studio, while the rest of the building stages temporary exhibitions of modern art.

Calton Hill

Calton Hill (Map p774; all Leith St buses) (100m), rising dramatically above the eastern end of Princes St, is Edinburgh's acropolis, its summit scattered with grandiose memorials dating mostly from the first half of the 19th century. It is also one of the best viewpoints in the city, with a panorama that takes in the castle, Holyrood, Arthur's Seat, the Firth of Forth, New Town and the full length of Princes St.

On the southern side of the hill, on Regent Rd, is the modernist facade of **St Andrew's House** (Map p774; Regent Rd; 15, 26, 44), built between 1936 and 1939 and housing the civil servants of the Westminster government's Scottish Office until they were moved to the new Scottish Executive building in Leith in 1996.

Just beyond St Andrew's House, and on the opposite side of the road, is the imposing **Royal High School** building, dating from 1829 and modelled on the Temple of Theseus in Athens. Former pupils include

Robert Adam, Alexander Graham Bell and Sir Walter Scott. It now stands empty. To its east, on the other side of Regent Rd, is the 1830 **Burns Monument** (Map p774; Regent Rd; 104, 113), a Greek-style memorial to Robert Burns.

You can reach the summit of Calton Hill via the road beside the Royal High School or by the stairs at the eastern end of Waterloo Pl. The largest structure on the summit is the **National Monument** (Map p774; Calton Hill; all Leith St buses), an over-ambitious attempt to replicate the Parthenon in Athens and intended to honour Scotland's dead in the Napoleonic Wars. Construction – paid for by public subscription – began in 1822, but funds ran dry when only 12 columns had been completed.

Looking a bit like an upturned telescope – the similarity is intentional – and offering superb views, the **Nelson Monument** (Map p774; www.edinburghmuseums.org.uk; Calton Hill; admission £5; 10am-7pm Mon-Sat, noon-5pm Sun Apr-Sep, 10am-3pm Mon-Sat Oct-Mar; all Leith St buses) was built to commemorate Admiral Lord Nelson's victory at Trafalgar in 1805.

The design of the **City Observatory** (Map p774; 0131-556 1264; www.collectivegallery.net; Calton Hill; 10am-5pm Tue-Sun Apr-Jul & Sep, to 4pm Oct-Mar, to 6pm daily Aug; all Leith St buses) FREE, built in 1818, was based on the ancient Greek Temple of the Winds in Athens. Its original function was to provide a precise, astronomical time-keeping service for marine navigators, but smoke from Waverley train station forced the astronomers to move

UNDERGROUND EDINBURGH

As Edinburgh expanded in the late 18th and early 19th centuries, many old tenements were demolished and new bridges were built to link the Old Town to the newly built areas to its north and south. South Bridge (built between 1785 and 1788) and George IV Bridge (built between 1829 and 1834) lead south from the Royal Mile over the deep valley of Cowgate, but so many buildings have been constructed around them you can hardly tell they are bridges – George IV Bridge has a total of nine arches but only two are visible; South Bridge has no fewer than 18 hidden arches.

These subterranean vaults were originally used as storerooms, workshops and drinking dens. But as Edinburgh's population swelled in the early 19th century with an influx of penniless Highlanders cleared from their lands, and Irish refugees from the potato famine, the dark, dripping chambers were given over to slum accommodation and abandoned to poverty, filth and crime.

The vaults were eventually cleared in the late 19th century, then lay forgotten until 1994 when the South Bridge vaults were opened to guided tours. Certain chambers are said to be haunted and one particular vault was investigated by paranormal researchers in 2001.

Nevertheless, the most ghoulish aspect of Edinburgh's hidden history dates from much earlier – from the plague that struck the city in 1645. Legend has it that the disease-ridden inhabitants of Mary King's Close (a lane on the northern side of the Royal Mile, on the site of the City Chambers – you can still see its blocked-off northern end from Cockburn St) were walled up in their houses and left to perish. When the lifeless bodies were eventually cleared from the houses, they were so stiff that workmen had to hack off limbs to get them through the small doorways and narrow, twisting stairs.

From that day on, the close was said to be haunted by the spirits of the plague victims. The few people who were prepared to live there reported seeing apparitions of severed heads and limbs, and the largely abandoned close fell into ruin. When the Royal Exchange (now the City Chambers) was constructed between 1753 and 1761, it was built over the lower levels of Mary King's Close, which were left intact and sealed off beneath the building.

Interest in the close revived in the 20th century when Edinburgh's city council began to allow occasional guided tours to enter. Visitors have reported many supernatural experiences – the most famous ghost is 'Annie', a little girl whose sad tale has prompted people to leave gifts of dolls in a corner of one of the rooms. In 2003 the close was opened to the public as the Real Mary King's Close (p768).

to Blackford Hill in the south of Edinburgh in 1895. It has been redeveloped as a stunning space for contemporary visual art, and opened to the public for the first time in its history.

Leith

Two miles northeast of the city centre, Leith has been Edinburgh's seaport since the 14th century and remained an independent burgh with its own town council until it was incorporated by the city in the 1920s. Like many of Britain's dockland areas, it fell into decay in the decades following WWII but has been undergoing a revival since the late 1980s.

★Royal Yacht Britannia SHIP

(www.royalyachtbritannia.co.uk; adult/child £15/8.50; 9.30am-6pm Jul-Sep, to 5.30pm Apr-Jun & Oct, 10am-5pm Nov-Mar, last admission 90min before closing; 11, 22, 34, 35, 36) Built on Clydeside, the former Royal Yacht *Britannia* was the British royal family's floating holiday home during their foreign travels from the time of her launch in 1953 until her decommissioning in 1997, and is now moored permanently in front of **Ocean Terminal** (0131-555 8888; www.oceanterminal.com; Ocean Dr; 10am-8pm Mon-Fri, to 7pm Sat, 11am-6pm Sun; ; 11, 22, 34, 35, 36). The tour, which you take at your own pace with an audioguide (included in the admission fee and available in 20 languages), lifts the curtain on the everyday lives of the royals, and gives an intriguing insight into the Queen's private tastes.

Britannia is a monument to 1950s decor, and the accommodation reveals Her Majesty's preference for simple, unfussy surroundings. There was nothing simple or unfussy, however, about the running of the ship. When the Queen travelled, with her went 45 members of the royal household, five tons of luggage and a Rolls-Royce that was carefully squeezed into a specially built garage on the deck. The ship's company consisted of an admiral, 20 officers and 220 yachtsmen.

The decks (of Burmese teak) were scrubbed daily, but all work near the royal accommodation was carried out in complete silence and had to be finished by 8am. A thermometer was kept in the Queen's bathroom to make sure the water was the correct temperature, and when in harbour one yachtsman was charged with ensuring that the angle of the gangway never exceeded 12 degrees. Note the mahogany windbreak that was added to the balcony deck in front of the bridge. It was put there to stop wayward breezes from blowing up skirts and inadvertently revealing the royal undies.

Britannia was joined in 2010 by the 1930s racing yacht *Bloodhound,* which was owned by the Queen in the 1960s. She is moored alongside *Britannia* (except in July and August, when she is away cruising) as part of an exhibition about the royal family's love of all things nautical.

The Majestic Tour (p782) bus runs from Waverley Bridge to *Britannia* during opening times.

Greater Edinburgh

★Royal Botanic Garden GARDENS

(0131-248 2909; www.rbge.org.uk; Arboretum Pl; 10am-6pm Mar-Sep, to 5pm Feb & Oct, to 4pm Nov-Jan; 8, 23, 27) FREE Edinburgh's Royal Botanic Garden is the second oldest institution of its kind in Britain (after Oxford), and one of the most respected in the world. Founded near Holyrood in 1670 and moved to its present location in 1823, its 70 beautifully landscaped acres include splendid **Victorian glasshouses** (admission £5.50), colourful swaths of rhododendron and azalea, and a world-famous rock garden.

The **John Hope Gateway** visitor centre is housed in a striking, environmentally friendly building overlooking the main entrance on Arboretum Pl, and has exhibitions on biodiversity, climate change and sustainable development, as well as displays of rare plants from the institution's collection and a specially created biodiversity garden.

Edinburgh Zoo ZOO

(www.edinburghzoo.org.uk; 134 Corstorphine Rd; adult/child £19/14.55; 9am-6pm Apr-Sep, to 5pm Oct & Mar, to 4.30pm Nov-Feb;) Opened in 1913, Edinburgh Zoo is one of the world's leading conservation zoos. Edinburgh's captive breeding program has helped save many endangered species, including Siberian tigers, pygmy hippos and red pandas. The main attractions are the two **giant pandas**, Tian Tian and Yang Guang, who arrived in December 2011, and the **penguin parade** (the zoo's penguins go for a walk every day at 2.15pm).

The zoo is 2.5 miles west of the city centre; take Lothian Bus 12, 26 or 31, First Bus 16, 18, 80 or 86, or the Airlink Bus 100 westbound from Princes St.

Activities

Edinburgh is lucky to have several good walking areas within the city boundary, including Arthur's Seat (p771), Calton Hill (p776), **Blackford Hill** (Charterhall Rd; 🚌24, 38, 41), **Hermitage of Braid** (www.fohb.org; 🚌5, 11, 15, 16), Corstorphine Hill and the coast and river at **Cramond**. The **Pentland Hills** (www.pentlandhills.org) FREE, which rise to over 500m, stretch southwest from the city for over 15 miles, offering excellent high- and low-level walking.

You can follow the Water of Leith Walkway (p775) from the city centre to Balerno (8 miles), and continue across the Pentlands to Silverburn (6.5 miles) or Carlops (8 miles), and return to Edinburgh by bus. Another good walk is along the **Union Canal towpath**, which begins in Fountainbridge and runs all the way to Falkirk (31 miles). You can return to Edinburgh by bus at Ratho (8.5 miles) or Broxburn (12 miles), and by bus or train from Linlithgow (21 miles).

Scottish Rights of Way & Access Society (☎0131-558 1222; www.scotways.com; 24 Annandale St) provides information and advice on trails and rights of way in Scotland.

Tours

Walking Tours

There are plenty of organised walks around Edinburgh, many of them related to ghosts, murders and witches.

City of the Dead Tours WALKING
(www.cityofthedeadtours.com; adult/concession £10/8) This tour of Greyfriars Kirkyard is probably the scariest of Edinburgh's 'ghost' tours. Many people have reported encounters with the 'Mackenzie Poltergeist', the ghost of a 17th-century judge who persecuted the Covenanters, and now haunts their former prison in a corner of the kirkyard. Not suitable for young children.

Cadies & Witchery Tours WALKING
(Map p768; ☎0131-225 6745; www.witcherytours.com; adult/child £10/7.50; 🚌2) The becloaked and pasty-faced Adam Lyal (deceased) leads a 'Murder & Mystery' tour of the Old Town's darker corners. These tours are famous for their 'jumper-ooters' – costumed actors who 'jump oot' when you least expect it.

Edinburgh Literary Pub Tour WALKING
(www.edinburghliterarypubtour.co.uk; adult/student £14/10; ⏲7.30pm daily May-Sep, limited days Oct-Apr) An enlightening two-hour trawl through Edinburgh's literary history – and its associated howffs (pubs) – in the entertaining company of Messrs Clart and McBrain. One of the city's best walking tours.

Mercat Tours WALKING
(Map p768; ☎0131-225 5445; www.mercattours.com; Mercat Cross; adult/child £12/7) Mercat offers a wide range of fascinating history

WORTH A TRIP

ROSSLYN CHAPEL

The success of Dan Brown's novel *The Da Vinci Code* and the subsequent Hollywood film has seen a flood of visitors descend on Scotland's most beautiful and enigmatic church – **Rosslyn Chapel** (Collegiate Church of St Matthew; www.rosslynchapel.org.uk; Chapel Loan, Roslin; adult/child £9/free; ⏲9.30am-6pm Mon-Sat Apr-Sep, to 5.30pm Oct-Mar, noon-4.45pm Sun year-round; P). The chapel was built in the mid-15th century for William St Clair, third earl of Orkney, and the ornately carved interior – at odds with the architectural fashion of its time – is a monument to the mason's art, rich in symbolic imagery. Hourly talks by qualified guides are included in the admission price.

As well as flowers, vines, angels and biblical figures, the carved stones include many examples of the pagan 'Green Man'; other figures are associated with Freemasonry and the Knights Templar. Intriguingly, there are also carvings of plants from the Americas that predate Columbus' voyage of discovery. The symbolism of these images has led some researchers to conclude that Rosslyn is some kind of secret Templar repository, and it has been claimed that hidden vaults beneath the chapel conceal anything from the Holy Grail or the head of John the Baptist to the body of Christ himself. The chapel is owned by the Episcopal Church of Scotland and services are held on Sunday mornings.

The chapel is on the eastern edge of the village of Roslin, 7 miles south of Edinburgh's centre. Lothian Bus 15 (not 15A) runs from the west end of Princes St in Edinburgh to Roslin (£1.60, 30 minutes, every 30 minutes).

Rosslyn Chapel

DECIPHERING ROSSLYN

Rosslyn Chapel is a small building, but the density of decoration inside can be overwhelming. It's well worth buying the official guidebook by the Earl of Rosslyn first; find a bench in the gardens and have a skim through before going into the chapel – the background information will make your visit all the more interesting. The book also offers a useful self-guided tour of the chapel, and explains the legend of the Master Mason and the Apprentice.

Entrance is through the **north door** ❶. Take a pew and sit for a while to allow your eyes to adjust to the dim interior; then look up at the ceiling vault, decorated with engraved roses, lilies and stars, (Can you spot the sun and the moon?). Walk left along the north aisle to reach the Lady Chapel, separated from the rest of the church by the **Mason's Pillar** ❷ and the **Apprentice Pillar** ❸. Here you'll find carvings of **Lucifer** ❹, the Fallen Angel, and the **Green Man** ❺. Nearby are **carvings** ❻ that appear to resemble Indian corn (maize). Finally, go to the western end and look up at the wall – in the left corner is the head of the **Apprentice** ❼; to the right is the (rather worn) head of the **Master Mason** ❽.

E&E IMAGE LIBRARY / AGE FOTOSTOCK ©

Lucifer, the Fallen Angel
At head height, to the left of the second window from the left, is an upside-down angel bound with rope, a symbol often associated with Freemasonry. The arch above is decorated with the Dance of Death.

EXPLORE SOME MORE

After visiting the chapel, head downhill to see the spectacularly sited ruins of Roslin Castle, then take a walk along leafy Roslin Glen.

The Apprentice
High in the corner, beneath an empty statue niche, is the head of the murdered Apprentice, with a deep wound in his forehead above the right eye. Legend says the Apprentice was murdered in a jealous rage by the Master Mason. The worn head on the side wall to the left of the Apprentice is that of his mother.

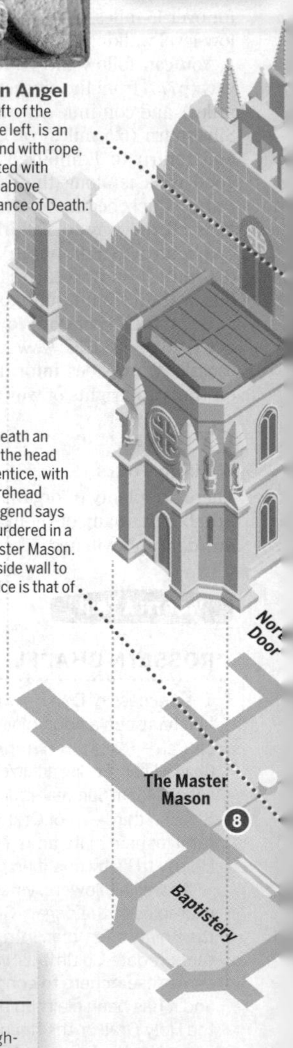

ROSSLYN CHAPEL & THE DA VINCI CODE

Dan Brown was referencing Rosslyn Chapel's alleged links to the Knights Templar and the Freemasons – unusual symbols found among the carvings, and the fact that a descendant of its founder, William St Clair, was a Grand Master Mason – when he chose it as the setting for his novel's denouement. Rosslyn is indeed a coded work, written in stone, but its meaning depends on your point of view. See The Rosslyn Hoax? by Robert LD Cooper for an alternative interpretation of the chapel's symbolism.

PRACTICAL TIPS

Local guides give hourly talks throughout the day, which are included in the admission price. No photography is allowed inside the chapel.

Green Man

On a boss at the base of the arch between the second and third windows from the left is the finest example of more than a hundred 'green man' carvings in the chapel, pagan symbols of spring, fertility and rebirth.

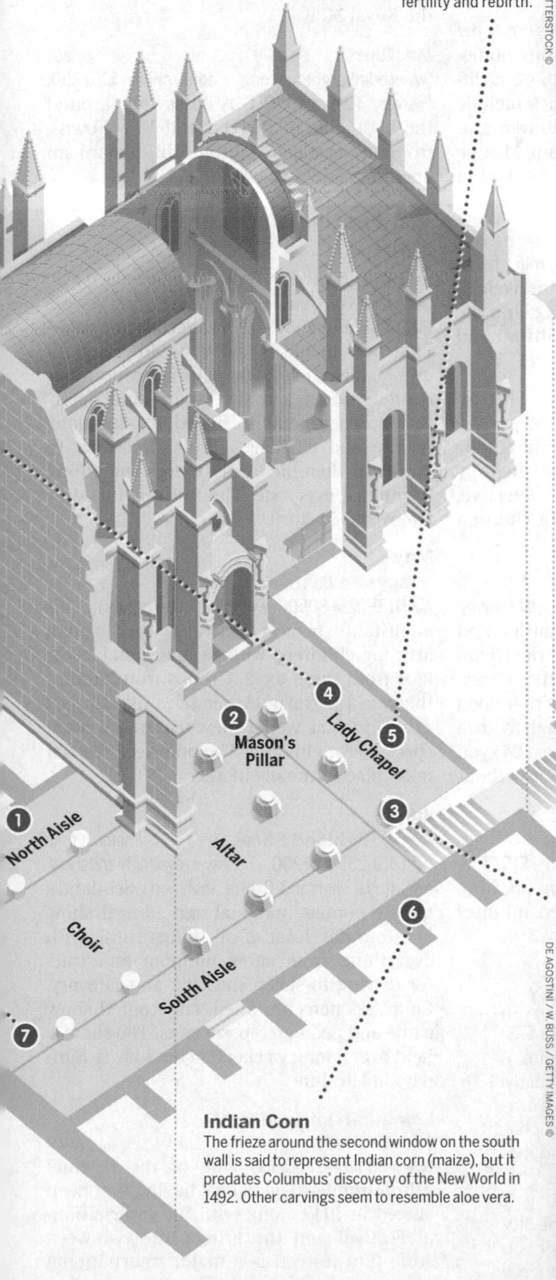

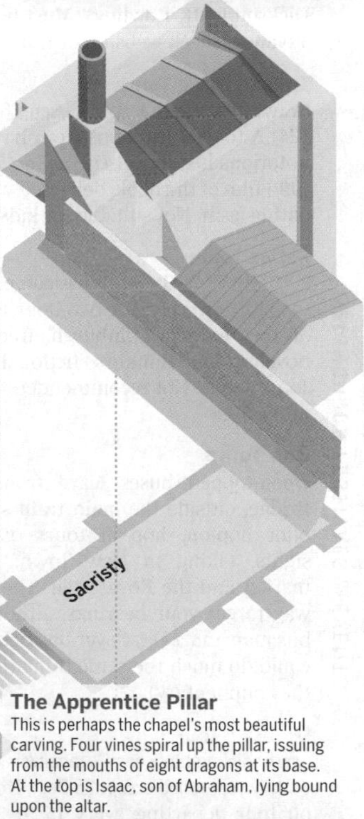

The Apprentice Pillar

This is perhaps the chapel's most beautiful carving. Four vines spiral up the pillar, issuing from the mouths of eight dragons at its base. At the top is Isaac, son of Abraham, lying bound upon the altar.

Indian Corn

The frieze around the second window on the south wall is said to represent Indian corn (maize), but it predates Columbus' discovery of the New World in 1492. Other carvings seem to resemble aloe vera.

walks and 'Ghosts & Ghouls' tours, but its most famous is a visit to the haunted, underground vaults beneath South Bridge.

Invisible (Edinburgh) WALKING
(☎07500-773709; www.invisible-cities.org; per person £8) A new venture that trains homeless people as tour guides to explore a different side of the city. Tour themes include Crime & Punishment (includes Burke and Hare) and Powerful Women (from Maggie Dickson to JK Rowling). Must be booked in advance; check website for times.

Trainspotting Tours WALKING
(www.leithwalks.co.uk; per person £6, min charge £24) A tour of locations from Irvine Welsh's notorious 1993 novel *Trainspotting,* and the 1996 film of the book, delivered with wit and enthusiasm. Not suitable for kids.

Rebus Tours WALKING
(☎0131-553 7473; www.rebustours.com; per person £10; ⊙noon Sat) A two-hour guided tour of the 'hidden Edinburgh' frequented by novelist Ian Rankin's fictional detective, John Rebus. Not recommended for children under 10.

Bus Tours

Open-topped buses leave from Waverley Bridge, outside the main train station, and offer hop-on, hop-off tours of the main sights, taking in New Town, the Grassmarket and the Royal Mile. They're a good way to get your bearings, although with a bus map and a Day Saver bus ticket (£4) you could do much the same thing (but without the commentary).

Majestic Tour BUS
(www.edinburghtour.com; adult/child £15/7.50; ⊙daily year-round except 25 Dec) Hop-on, hop-off tour departing every 15 to 20 minutes from Waverley Bridge to the Royal Yacht *Britannia* at Ocean Terminal via the New Town, Royal Botanic Garden and Newhaven, returning via Leith Walk, Holyrood and the Royal Mile.

MacTours BUS
(www.edinburghtour.com; adult/child £15/7.50; ⊙every 30 min Apr-Oct) A quick tour around the highlights of the Old and New Towns, from the castle to Calton Hill, aboard an open-topped vintage bus.

Festivals & Events

April

Edinburgh International Science Festival FESTIVAL
(☎0844-557 2686; www.sciencefestival.co.uk) First held in 1987, it hosts a wide range of events, including talks, lectures, exhibitions, demonstrations, guided tours and interactive experiments designed to stimulate, inspire and challenge. From dinosaurs to ghosts to alien life forms, there's something to interest everyone. The festival runs over two weeks in April.

May

Imaginate Festival ART
(☎0131-225 8050; www.imaginate.org.uk) This is Britain's biggest festival of performing arts for children, with events suitable for kids from three to 12. Groups from around the world perform classic tales like *Hansel and Gretel,* as well as new material written specially for children. The one-week festival takes place annually in May.

June

Royal Highland Show AGRICULTURE
(☎0131-335 6200; www.royalhighlandshow.org; Royal Highland Centre, Ingliston) Scotland's hugely popular national agricultural show is a four-day feast of all things rural, with everything from show jumping and tractor driving to sheep shearing and falconry. Countless pens are filled with coiffed show cattle and pedicured prize ewes. The show is held over a long weekend (Thursday to Sunday) in late June.

Edinburgh International Film Festival FILM
(www.edfilmfest.org.uk) One of the original Edinburgh Festival trinity, having first been staged in 1947 along with the International Festival and the Fringe, the two-week June film festival is a major international event, serving as a showcase for new Brit-

EDINBURGH'S HOGMANAY

Edinburgh's **Hogmanay** (☎0844 573 8455; www.edinburghshogmanay.com; tickets £20) is the biggest winter festival in Europe. Events run from 27 December to 1 January, and include a torchlight procession, huge street party and the famous 'Loony Dook', a chilly sea-swimming event on New Year's Day. To get into the main party area in the city centre after 8pm on 31 December you'll need a ticket – book well in advance.

ish and European films, and staging the European premieres of one or two Hollywood blockbusters.

July

Scottish Real Ale Festival BEER
(www.sraf.camra.org.uk; Corn Exchange, Chesser Ave) A celebration of all things fermented and yeasty, Scotland's biggest beer-fest gives you the opportunity to sample a wide range of traditionally brewed beers from Scotland and around the world. Froth-topped bliss. The festival is held over a long weekend in June or July.

Edinburgh International Jazz & Blues Festival MUSIC
(www.edinburghjazzfestival.com) Held annually since 1978, the Jazz & Blues Festival pulls in top talent from all over the world. It runs for nine days, beginning on a Friday, a week before the Fringe and Tattoo begin. The first weekend sees a carnival parade on Princes St and an afternoon of free, open-air music in Princes Street Gardens.

August

The Edinburgh International Festival, the Edinburgh Festival Fringe, the Edinburgh International Book Festival and the Military Tattoo are all held around the same time in August. See the Festival City box (below) for details.

Edinburgh Food Festival FOOD & DRINK
(www.edfoodfest.com) This four-day festival, in George Square Gardens, precedes the opening of the Edinburgh Fringe with a program of talks, cookery demonstrations, tastings, street food stalls and entertainment.

December

Edinburgh's Hogmanay (box opposite) is the biggest winter festival in Europe.

Edinburgh's Christmas CHRISTMAS
(☎0844 545 8252; www.edinburghschristmas.com) First held in 2000, the Christmas bash runs from late November to early January and includes a big street parade, a Christmas market, a fairground and Ferris wheel, and an ice rink in Princes Street Gardens.

FESTIVAL CITY

August in Edinburgh sees a frenzy of festivals, with several world-class events running at the same time. The Fringe takes place over 3½ weeks in August, the last two weeks overlapping with the first two of the three-week International Festival, which ends on the first Saturday in September.

Edinburgh Military Tattoo (☎0131-225 1188; www.edintattoo.co.uk) August kicks off with the Edinburgh Military Tattoo, a spectacular display of military marching bands, massed pipes and drums, acrobats, cheerleaders and motorcycle display teams, all played out in front of the magnificent backdrop of the floodlit castle. Each show traditionally finishes with a lone piper, dramatically lit, playing a lament on the battlements. The Tattoo takes place during the first three weeks of August.

Edinburgh Festival Fringe (☎0131-226 0026; www.edfringe.com) When the first Edinburgh Festival was held in 1947, there were eight theatre companies who didn't make it onto the main program. Undeterred, they grouped together and held their own mini-festival, on the fringe, and an Edinburgh institution was born. Today the Edinburgh Festival Fringe is the biggest festival of the performing arts anywhere in the world.

Edinburgh International Festival (☎0131-473 2000; www.eif.co.uk) First held in 1947 to mark a return to peace after the ordeal of WWII, the Edinburgh International Festival is festooned with superlatives – the oldest, the biggest, the most famous, the best in the world. The original was a modest affair, but today hundreds of the world's top musicians and performers congregate in Edinburgh for three weeks of diverse and inspirational music, opera, theatre and dance.

Edinburgh International Book Festival (☎0845 373 5888; www.edbookfest.co.uk) Held in a little village of marquees in the middle of Charlotte Sq, the Edinburgh International Book Festival is a fun fortnight of talks, readings, debates, lectures, book signings and meet-the-author events, with cafes and tented bookshops thrown in. The festival lasts for two weeks in August (usually the first two weeks of the Edinburgh International Festival).

Sleeping

Edinburgh offers a wide range of accommodation options, from moderately priced guesthouses set in lovely Victorian villas and Georgian town houses to expensive and stylish boutique hotels. There are also plenty of international chain hotels, and a few truly exceptional hotels housed in magnificent historic buildings. At the budget end of the range, there is no shortage of youth hostels and independent backpacker hostels, which often have inexpensive double and twin rooms available.

Old Town

★Malone's Old Town Hostel HOSTEL $

(Map p768; ☎0131-226 7648; www.maloneshostel.com; 14 Forrest Rd; dm £12-20; @ 📶; 🚌2, 23, 27, 41, 42, 45) No fancy decor or style credentials here, but they've got the basics right: it's clean, comfortable and friendly, and set upstairs from an Irish pub where guests get discounts on food and drink. The cherry on the cake is its superbly central location, an easy walk from the Royal Mile, the castle, the Grassmarket and Princes St.

Castle Rock Hostel HOSTEL $

(Map p768; ☎0131-225 9666; www.scotlands-top-hostels.com; 15 Johnston Tce; dm £14-17, d £55; @ 📶; 🚌2) With its bright, spacious, mixed or female-only dorms, superb views and friendly staff, the 200-bed Castle Rock has lots to like. It has a great location, a games room, reading lounge and big-screen video nights. No under-18s.

Safestay Edinburgh HOSTEL $

(Map p768; ☎0131-524 1989; www.smartcityhostels.com; 50 Blackfriars St; dm £13-20; @ 📶) A big, modern hostel, with a convivial cafe where you can buy breakfast, and mod cons such as keycard access and charging stations for mobile phones, MP3 players and laptops. Lockers in every room, a huge bar and a central location just off the Royal Mile make this a favourite among the young, party-mad crowd – don't expect a quiet night!

★Witchery by the Castle B&B $$$

(Map p768; ☎0131-225 5613; www.thewitchery.com; Castlehill; ste £325-395; 🚌23, 27, 41, 42) Set in a 16th-century Old Town house in the shadow of Edinburgh Castle, the Witchery's nine lavish Gothic suites are extravagantly furnished with antiques, oak panelling, tapestries, open fires, four-poster beds and roll-top baths, and supplied with flowers, chocolates and complimentary champagne. Overwhelmingly popular – book several months in advance to be sure of getting a room.

Grassmarket Hotel HOTEL $$$

(Map p768; ☎0131-220 2299; www.grassmarkethotel.co.uk; 94-96 Grassmarket; s/d from £120/140; 📶; 🚌2) An endearingly quirky hotel set in a historic Grassmarket tenement in the heart of the Old Town, this place has bedroom walls plastered with front pages from the *Dandy* (a DC Thomson comic published in Dundee) and coffee stations supplied with iconically Scottish Tunnock's teacakes and Irn Bru. Some bargain rates available direct through the website.

New Town & Around

Code Hostel HOSTEL $

(Map p774; ☎0131-659 9883; www.codehostel.com; 50 Rose St N Lane; dm from £25, d £99; 📶; 🚊Princes St) This upmarket hostel, bang in the middle of the New Town, combines cute designer decor with innovative sleeping cubicles that offer more privacy than bunks (four to six people per dorm, each with en suite shower room). There's also a luxurious double apartment called the Penthouse, complete with kitchenette and roof terrace.

Gerald's Place B&B $$

(Map p774; ☎0131-558 7017; www.geraldsplace.com; 21b Abercromby Pl; d £89-149; @ 📶; 🚌23, 27) Gerald is an unfailingly charming and helpful host, and his lovely Georgian garden flat (just two guest bedrooms, each with a private bathroom) has a great location across from a peaceful park, an easy stroll from the city centre. There may be a minimum three-night stay in peak season.

Angels Share Hotel HOTEL $$

(Map p774; ☎0131-247 7000; http://angelssharehotel.com/; 9-11 Hope St; r from £115; 📶; 🚌all Princes St buses) You'll be right in the middle of the New Town action at this small but buzzing hotel, with Princes St shops and George St cocktail bars just a short stagger away. Rooms are understated but stylish, each decorated with a huge image of a Scottish celeb – fine if you don't mind Lulu or Rod Stewart looming over your bed!

★B+B Edinburgh HOTEL $$$

(☎0131-225 5084; www.bb-edinburgh.com; 3 Rothesay Tce; d/ste from £138/190; 📶; 🚊West End) Built in 1883 as a grand home for the proprietor of the *Scotsman* newspaper, this Victorian extravaganza of carved oak, parquet floors, stained glass and elaborate fireplaces was given a designer makeover to create a striking contemporary hotel. Rooms on the 2nd floor are the most spacious, but the top-floor rooms enjoy the finest views.

Bonham Hotel BOUTIQUE HOTEL **$$$**
(0131-226 6050; www.townhousecompany.com/thebonham; 35 Drumsheugh Gardens; r from £160; P ; 19, 36, 37, 41) The Bonham manages a successful fusion of Victorian interiors with bold modern colours and contemporary design. Cool, crisp bed linen, luxury bathrooms and friendly but unobtrusive service make for a memorable stay. Though set in a quiet, West End backstreet, the Bonham is only five minutes' walk from Princes St.

South Edinburgh

Argyle Backpackers HOSTEL **$**
(0131-667 9991; www.argyle-backpackers.co.uk; 14 Argyle Pl; dm £16-18, s/tw from £54/60; @ ; 41) The Argyle, spread across three adjacent terrace houses, is a quiet and relaxed hostel offering single, double and twin rooms as well as four- to six-bed dorms (mixed or female-only). There is a comfortable TV lounge, an attractive little conservatory and a pleasant walled garden at the back where you can sit outside in summer.

★ **Southside Guest House** B&B **$$**
(0131-668 4422; www.southsideguesthouse.co.uk; 8 Newington Rd; s/d from £80/105; ; all Newington buses) Though set in a typical Victorian terrace, the Southside transcends the traditional guesthouse category and feels more like a modern boutique hotel. Its eight stylish rooms ooze interior design, standing out from other Newington B&Bs through the clever use of bold colours and modern furniture. Breakfast is an event, with Bucks Fizz (cava mixed with orange juice) on offer to ease the hangover!

No 45 B&B **$$**
(0131-667 3536; www.edinburghbedbreakfast.com; 45 Gilmour Rd; s/d £70/120; ; all Newington buses) A peaceful setting, large garden and friendly owners contribute to the appeal of this Victorian terraced house, which overlooks the local bowling green. The decor is a blend of 19th and 20th century, with bold Victorian reds, pine floors and a period fireplace in the lounge, and a 1930s vibe in the three spacious bedrooms.

Aonach Mor Guest House B&B **$$**
(0131-667 8694; www.aonachmor.com; 14 Kilmaurs Tce; r per person £33-65; @ ; 2, 14, 30, 33) This elegant Victorian terrace house is located on a quiet backstreet and has seven bedrooms, beautifully decorated, with many original period features. Our favourite is the four-poster bedroom with polished mahogany furniture and period fireplace. Located 1 mile southeast of the city centre.

Knight Residence APARTMENT **$$$**
(Map p768; 0131-622 8120; www.theknightresidence.co.uk; 12 Lauriston St; 1-/2-bedroom apt from £180/270; P ; 2) Works by contemporary artists adorn these modern studio, one- and two-bedroom apartments (available by the night; the latter sleep up to four adults and one child), each with fully equipped kitchen and comfortable lounge with cable TV, video and stereo. It has a good central location in a quiet street only a few minutes' walk from the Grassmarket.

Leith & Around

Edinburgh Central SYHA HOSTEL **$**
(SYHA; Map p774; 0131-524 2090; www.syha.org.uk; 9 Haddington Pl, Leith Walk; dm/s/tw £22/46/74; @ ; all Leith Walk buses) This modern, purpose-built hostel, about a half-mile north of Waverley train station, is a big (300 beds), flashy, five-star establishment with its own cafe-bistro as well as self-catering kitchen, smart and comfortable eight-bed dorms and private rooms, and mod cons including keycard entry and plasma-screen TVs.

★ **Wallace's Arthouse** B&B **$$**
(07941 343714; www.wallacesarthousescotland.com; 41/4 Constitution St; s/d £99/120; ; 12, 16) This Georgian apartment, housed in the neoclassical Leith Assembly Rooms (a Grade A listed building), offers two beautifully nostalgic bedrooms styled by former fashion designer Wallace, who comes as part of the package – your charming host and breakfast chef is an unfailing source of colourful anecdotes and local knowledge.

★ **Sheridan Guest House** B&B **$$**
(0131-554 4107; www.sheridanedinburgh.com; 1 Bonnington Tce, Newhaven Rd; r from £95; P ; 7, 11, 14) Flowerpots filled with colourful blooms line the steps of this little haven hidden away to the north of the New Town. The eight bedrooms (all en suite) blend crisp colours with contemporary furniture,

stylish lighting and colourful paintings, which complement the house's clean-cut Georgian lines, while the breakfast menu adds omelettes, pancakes with maple syrup, and scrambled eggs with smoked salmon to the usual offerings.

Take bus 11 from the city centre.

Millers 64 B&B **$$**
(☎0131-454 3666; www.millers64.com; 64 Pilrig St; s from £80, d £90-150; Wi-Fi; bus 11) Luxury textiles, colourful cushions, stylish bathrooms and fresh flowers added to a warm Edinburgh welcome make this Victorian town house a highly desirable address. There are just two bedrooms (and a minimum three-night stay during festival periods), so book well in advance.

Eating

Eating out in Edinburgh has changed beyond all recognition in the last 20 years. Two decades ago, sophisticated dining meant a visit to the Aberdeen Angus Steak House for a prawn cocktail, steak (well done) and chips, and Black Forest gateau. Today, eating out has become a commonplace event and the city has more restaurants per head of population than any other city in the UK, including a handful with Michelin stars.

Old Town

★Mums CAFE **$**
(Map p768; ☎0131-260 9806; www.monstermashcafe.co.uk; 4a Forrest Rd; mains £8-11; 9am-10pm Mon-Sat, 10am-10pm Sun; Wi-Fi, child-friendly; bus 23, 27, 41, 42) This nostalgia-fuelled cafe serves up classic British comfort food that wouldn't look out of place on a 1950s menu – bacon and eggs, bangers and mash, shepherd's pie, fish and chips. But there's a twist – the food is all top-quality nosh freshly prepared from local produce. There's also a good selection of craft beers and Scottish-brewed cider.

Wings FAST FOOD **$**
(Map p768; ☎0131-629 1234; http://wingsedinburgh.com; 5/7 Old Fishmarket Close; per portion £3.50; 4-11pm Mon, noon-11pm Tue-Sun; bus 23, 27, 41, 42) Eateries don't come much simpler. Order some bowls of barbecued chicken wings (six wings per portion) with the sauce of your choice (a couple of dozen to choose from, whether soused in tequila and lime juice or slathered with hot chilli) and a drink. If you're still hungry, order more. Genius. Great sci-fi/comic-book decor too.

Walking Tour
Old Town Alleys

START CASTLE ESPLANADE
END COCKBURN ST
LENGTH 1 MILE; ONE TO TWO HOURS

This walk explores the alleys and side streets around the Royal Mile, and involves a bit of climbing up and down steep stairs.

Begin on the **1 Castle Esplanade**, which provides a grandstand view south over Grassmarket; the prominent quadrangular building with all the turrets is George Heriot's School, which you'll be passing later on. Head towards Castlehill and the start of the Royal Mile.

The 17th-century house on the right is known as **2 Cannonball House** because of the iron ball lodged in the wall (look between, and slightly below, the two largest windows on the wall facing the castle). It was not fired in anger, but marks the gravitation height to which water would flow naturally from the city's first piped water supply.

The low, rectangular building across the street (now a touristy tartan-weaving mill) was originally the reservoir that held the Old Town's water supply. On its west wall is the **3 Witches Well**, where a bronze fountain commemorates around 4000 people (mostly women) who were executed between 1479 and 1722 on suspicion of witchcraft.

Go past the reservoir and turn left down Ramsay Lane. Take a look at **4 Ramsay Garden** – one of Edinburgh's most desirable addresses – where late-19th-century apartments were built around the octagonal Ramsay Lodge, once home to poet Allan Ramsay. The cobbled street continues around to the right below student residences to the towers of the **5 New College**, home to Edinburgh University's Faculty of Divinity. Nip into the courtyard to see the statue of John Knox (a firebrand preacher who led the Protestant Reformation in Scotland, and was instrumental in the creation of the Church of Scotland in 1560).

Just past New College turn right and climb the stairs into Milne's Court, a student residence belonging to Edinburgh University. Exit into Lawnmarket, cross the street (bearing slightly left) and duck into

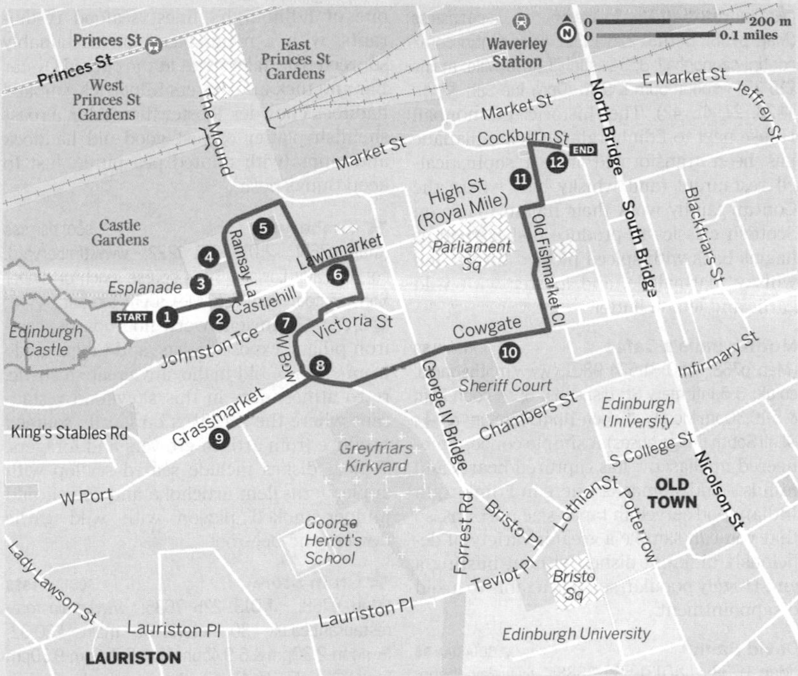

6 **Riddell's Court**, a typical Old Town close at No 322–8. You'll find yourself in a small courtyard, but the house in front of you (built in 1590) was originally the edge of the street (the building you just walked under was added in 1726 – look for the inscription in the doorway). The arch with the inscription *Vivendo discimus* (We live and learn) leads into the original 16th-century courtyard.

Go back into the street, turn right and right again down Fisher's Close, which leads to the delightful Victoria Terrace, strung above the cobbled curve of shop-lined Victoria St. Wander right, enjoying the view – 7 **Maxie's Bistro** (p789), at the far end of the terrace, is a great place to stop for a drink – then descend the stairs at the foot of Upper Bow and continue downhill to the Grassmarket. At the east end, outside Maggie Dickson's pub, is the 8 **Covenanters Monument**, which marks the site of the gallows where more than 100 Covenanters were martyred in the 17th century.

If you're feeling peckish, the Grassmarket has several good places to eat and a couple of good pubs – Robert Burns once stayed at the 9 **White Hart Inn** (34 Grassmarket). Head east along the gloomy defile of the Cowgate, passing under the arch of George IV Bridge – the buildings to your right are the new law courts, while high up to the left you can see the complex of buildings behind Parliament Sq. Past the courts, on the right, is 10 **Tailors Hall** (built 1621, extended 1757), now a hotel and bar but formerly the meeting place of the Companie of Tailzeours (Tailors' Guild).

Turn left and climb steeply up Old Fishmarket Close, a typical cobbled Old Town wynd, and emerge once more onto the Royal Mile. Across the street and slightly downhill is 11 **Anchor Close**, named for a tavern that once stood there. It hosted the Crochallan Fencibles, an 18th-century drinking club that provided its patrons with an agreeable blend of intellectual debate and intoxicating liquor. The club was founded by William Smellie, editor of the first edition of the *Encyclopedia Brittanica;* its best-known member was the poet Robert Burns.

Go down Anchor Close, to finish the walk on 12 **Cockburn St**, one of the city's coolest shopping streets, lined with record shops and clothing boutiques. The street was cut through Old Town tenements in the 1850s to provide an easy route between Waverley Station and the Royal Mile.

★Cannonball Restaurant SCOTTISH $$

(Map p768; 0131-225 1550; www.contini.com/contini-cannonball; 356 Castlehill, Royal Mile; mains £15-25; noon-5pm & 5.30-10pm Tue-Sat; 23, 27, 41, 42) The historic Cannonball House next to Edinburgh Castle's esplanade has been transformed into a sophisticated restaurant (and whisky bar) where the Contini family work their Italian magic on Scottish classics to produce dishes such as haggis balls with spiced pickled turnip and whisky marmalade, and lobster with wild garlic and lemon butter.

Mother India's Cafe INDIAN $$

(Map p768; 0131-524 9801; www.motherindia.co.uk; 3-5 Infirmary St; dishes £4-6; noon-2pm & 5-10.30pm Mon-Wed, noon-11pm Thu-Sun; all South Bridge buses) A simple concept pioneered in Glasgow has captured hearts and minds – and stomachs – here in Edinburgh: Indian food served in tapas-size portions, so that you can sample a greater variety of deliciously different dishes without busting a gut. Hugely popular, so book a table to avoid disappointment.

David Bann VEGETARIAN $$

(Map p768; 0131-556 5888; www.davidbann.com; 56-58 St Mary's St; mains £11-13; noon-10pm Mon-Fri, 11am-10pm Sat & Sun; 35) If you want to convince a carnivorous friend that cuisine à la veg can be as tasty and inventive as a meat-muncher's menu, take them to David Bann's stylish restaurant – dishes such as Thai fritter of broccoli and smoked tofu, and aubergine, chickpea and cashew kofta are guaranteed to win converts.

Devil's Advocate PUB FOOD $$

(Map p768; 0131-225 4465; http://devilsadvocateedinburgh.co.uk; 9 Advocates Close; mains £14-24; food served noon-4pm & 5-10pm; 6, 23, 27, 41, 42) No trip to Edinburgh is complete without exploring the narrow closes (alleys) that lead off the Royal Mile. Lucky you if your explorations lead to this cosy split-level pub-restaurant set in a converted Victorian pump house, with a menu of top-quality pub grub – the burgers are among the best in town. It gets rammed on weekends, so book a table.

★Ondine SEAFOOD $$$

(Map p768; 0131-226 1888; www.ondinerestaurant.co.uk; 2 George IV Bridge; mains £17-40, 2-/3-course lunch £25/30; noon-3pm & 5.30-10pm Mon-Sat; 23, 27, 41, 42) Ondine is one of Edinburgh's finest seafood restaurants, with a menu based on sustainably sourced fish. Take a seat at the curved Oyster Bar and tuck into oysters Kilpatrick, smoked haddock chowder, lobster thermidor, a roast shellfish platter or just good old haddock and chips (with minted pea purée, just to keep things posh).

★Timberyard SCOTTISH $$$

(Map p768; 0131-221 1222; www.timberyard.co; 10 Lady Lawson St; 4-course lunch or dinner £55; noon-2pm & 5.30-9.30pm Tue-Sat; 2, 35) Ancient worn floorboards, cast-iron pillars, exposed joists, and tables made from slabs of old mahogany create a rustic, retro atmosphere in this slow-food restaurant where the accent is on locally sourced produce from artisan growers and foragers. Typical dishes include seared scallop with apple, Jerusalem artichoke and sorrel; and juniper-smoked pigeon with wild garlic flowers and beetroot.

★Grain Store SCOTTISH $$$

(Map p768; 0131-225 7635; www.grainstore-restaurant.co.uk; 30 Victoria St; mains £20-32; noon-2.30pm & 6-9.45pm Mon-Sat, 6pm-9.30pm Sun; 2, 23, 27, 41, 42) An atmospheric upstairs dining room on picturesque Victoria St, the Grain Store has a well-earned reputation for serving the finest Scottish produce, perfectly prepared – from wood pigeon with leek and hickory risotto to seared monkfish with scallop ravioli and mustard beurre blanc. The three-course lunch for £16 is good value.

New Town

Broughton Deli CAFE $

(Map p774; 0131-558 7111; www.broughton-deli.co.uk; 7 Barony St; mains £6-10; 8am-7pm Mon-Fri, 9am-6pm Sat, 10am-5pm Sun; 8) Mismatched cafe tables and chairs in a bright back room behind the deli counter provide an attractive setting for brunch just off the main drag of the New Town's bohemian Broughton St. Brunch is served till 2pm weekdays or 3pm on weekends; choose from American-style pancakes, veggie fry-ups, and poached eggs on toast with organic smoked salmon.

Henderson's VEGETARIAN $

(Map p774; 0131-225 2131; www.hendersonsofedinburgh.co.uk; 94 Hanover St; mains £6-12; 8am-9pm Mon-Sat, 10.30am-4pm Sun; 23, 27) Established in 1962, Henderson's is the grandmother of Edinburgh's vegetarian restaurants. The food is mostly organic and guaranteed GM-free, and special dietary requirements can be catered for. The place still has something of a 1970s canteen feel to it (in a good, nostalgic way), and the daily salads and hot dishes are as popular as ever.

Around the corner on Thistle St is Henderson's Vegan, a 100% vegan branch.

★ **Gardener's Cottage** SCOTTISH $$

(Map p774; 0131-558 1221; www.thegardenerscottage.co; 1 Royal Terrace Gardens, London Rd; lunch mains £16-17, dinner set menu £40; noon-2pm & 5-10pm Mon & Wed-Fri, 10am-2pm & 5-10pm Sat & Sun; all London Rd buses) This country cottage in the heart of the city, bedecked with flowers and fairy lights, offers one of Edinburgh's most interesting dining experiences – two tiny rooms with communal tables made of salvaged timber, and a menu based on fresh local produce (most grown in a local organic garden). Bookings essential; brunch served at weekends.

★ **Dogs** BRITISH $$

(Map p774; 0131-220 1208; www.thedogsonline.co.uk; 110 Hanover St; mains lunch £6, dinner £9-22; noon-2.30pm & 6-10pm Mon-Fri, noon-4pm & 6-10pm Sat & Sun; ; 23, 27) One of the coolest tables in town, this bistro-style place uses cheaper cuts of meat and less well-known, more sustainable species of fish to create hearty, no-nonsense dishes such as devilled kidneys on toast; shredded lamb with skirlie (fried oatmeal and onion), pomegranate seeds and almonds; and beetroot and horseradish spelt risotto.

★ **Contini** ITALIAN $$

(Map p774; 0131-225 1550; www.contini.com/contini-ristorante; 103 George St; mains £11-30; 7.30am-11pm Mon-Fri, 9am-midnight Sat, 9am-11pm Sun; ; all Princes St buses) A palatial Georgian banking hall enlivened by fuchsia-pink banners and lampshades is home to this lively, child-friendly Italian bar and restaurant, where the emphasis is on fresh, authentic ingredients (produce

BEST VALUE BISTROS

Many restaurants in Edinburgh offer good-value lunches. Here are a few suggestions from various parts of the city.

Urban Angel (Map p774; 0131-225 6215; www.urban-angel.co.uk; 121 Hanover St; mains £6-13; 8am-5pm Mon-Fri, 9am-5pm Sat & Sun; ; 23, 27) A wholesome deli that puts the emphasis on fair-trade, organic and locally sourced produce, Urban Angel is also a delightfully informal cafe-bistro that serves all-day brunch (porridge with honey, French toast, eggs Benedict), tapas and a wide range of light, snacky meals.

L'Escargot Bleu (Map p774; 0131-557 1600; www.lescargotbleu.co.uk; 56 Broughton St; mains £13-19; noon-2.30pm & 5.30-10pm Mon-Thu, noon-3pm & 5.30-10.30pm Fri & Sat; ; 8) As with its sister restaurant, **L'Escargot Blanc** (Map p774; 0131-226 1890; www.lescargotblanc.co.uk; 17 Queensferry St; 3-course lunch/dinner £13.90/25; noon-2.30pm & 5.30-10pm Mon-Thu, noon-3pm & 5.30-10.30pm Fri & Sat; ; 19, 36, 37, 41, 47) on Queensferry St, this cute little bistro is as Gallic as garlic but makes fine use of quality Scottish produce – the French-speaking staff will lead you knowledgeably through a menu that includes authentic Savoyard *tartiflette, quenelle* of pike with lobster sauce, and pigs' cheeks braised in red wine. Two-course lunch/early-bird menu £12.90.

First Coast (0131-313 4404; www.first-coast.co.uk; 97-101 Dalry Rd; mains £12-20; noon-2pm & 5-11pm Mon-Sat; ; 2, 3, 4, 25, 33, 44) This popular neighbourhood bistro has a striking main dining area with sea-blue wood panelling and stripped stonework, and a short and simple menu offering hearty comfort food such as fish with creamy mash, brown shrimp and garlic butter, or leek and bread pudding, creamed leeks and braised fennel. Lunchtime and early evening there's an excellent two-course meal for £12.50.

Maxie's Bistro (Map p768; 0131-226 7770; www.maxiesbistro.com; 5b Johnston Tce; mains £9-22; 11am-11pm; ; 23, 27, 41, 42) This candlelit bistro, with its cushion-lined nooks set amid stone walls and wooden beams, is a pleasant setting for a cosy dinner, but at summer lunchtimes people queue for the outdoor tables on the terrace overlooking Victoria St. The food is dependable, ranging from pasta, steaks and stir-fries to seafood platters and daily specials. Best to book, especially in summer.

imported weekly from Milan; homemade bread and pasta) and uncomplicated enjoyment of food.

Hadrian's Brasserie SCOTTISH, FRENCH $$
(Map p774; ☎0131-557 5000; www.roccofortehotels.com; Balmoral Hotel, 1 Princes St; mains £15-22; ⏲7-10.30am, noon-2.30pm & 5.30-10pm Mon-Fri, 7.30-11am & 12.30-10.30pm Sat & Sun; 🚼; 🚌all Princes St buses) The brasserie at the **Balmoral Hotel** (Map p774; ☎0131-556 2414; s/d from £277/299; P📶🏊; 🚌all Princes St buses) has a 1930s art-deco feel, with pale-green walls, dark-wood furniture, and waiters dressed in white aprons and black waistcoats. The menu includes posh versions of fish and chips, haggis with whisky sauce, and rump steak with Café de Paris sauce.

Scottish Cafe & Restaurant SCOTTISH $$
(Map p774; ☎0131-226 6524; www.thescottishcafeandrestaurant.com; The Mound; mains £13-15; ⏲9am-5.30pm Fri-Wed, to 7pm Thu; 📶🚼; 🚌Princes St) 🍃 This appealing modern restaurant (part of the Scottish National Gallery complex) has picture windows providing a view along Princes Street Gardens. Try traditional Scottish dishes such as Cullen skink (smoked haddock soup) and leek and potato soup, or seasonal, sustainably sourced produce including smoked salmon and trout, free-range chicken and pork.

Leith

★Fishers Bistro SEAFOOD $$
(☎0131-554 5666; www.fishersbistros.co.uk; 1 The Shore; mains £12-25; ⏲noon-10.30pm Mon-Sat, 12.30-10.30pm Sun; 📶🍷🚼; 🚌16, 22, 35, 36) This cosy little restaurant, tucked beneath a 17th-century signal tower, is one of the city's best seafood places. The menu ranges widely in price, from cheaper dishes such as classic fish cakes with lemon and chive mayonnaise to more expensive delights such as North Berwick lobster thermidor.

Leith Chop House STEAK $$
(☎0131-629 1919; www.chophousesteak.co.uk; 102 Constitution St; mains £10-26; ⏲noon-3pm & 5-10pm Mon-Fri, 10am-11pm Sat & Sun; 📶; 🚌12, 16) A modern take on the old-fashioned steakhouse, this 'bar and butchery' combines slick designer decor (the ceramic brick tiles are a nod to traditional butcher shops) with a meaty menu of the best Scottish beef, dry-aged for at least 35 days and char-grilled to perfection.

★Kitchin SCOTTISH $$$
(☎0131-555 1755; http://thekitchin.com; 78 Commercial Quay; 3-course lunch/dinner £30/70; ⏲12.15-2.30pm & 6.30-10pm Tue-Thu, to 10.30pm Fri & Sat; 🍷; 🚌16, 22, 35, 36) Fresh, seasonal, locally sourced Scottish produce is the philosophy that has won a Michelin star for this elegant but unpretentious restaurant. The menu moves with the seasons, of course, so expect fresh salads in summer and game in winter, and shellfish dishes such as baked scallops with white wine, vermouth and herb sauce when there's an 'r' in the month.

Drinking & Nightlife

Edinburgh has always been a drinker's city. It has more than 700 pubs – more per square mile than any other UK city – and they are as varied and full of character as the people who drink in them, from Victorian palaces to stylish pre-club bars, and from real-ale howffs to trendy cocktail lounges.

Old Town

The pubs in the Grassmarket have outdoor tables on sunny summer afternoons, but in the evenings are favoured by boozed-up lads on the pull, so steer clear if that's not your thing. The Cowgate – the Grassmarket's extension to the east – is Edinburgh's clubland.

★Bow Bar PUB
(Map p768; www.thebowbar.co.uk; 80 West Bow; ⏲noon-midnight Mon-Sat, to 11.30pm Sun; 🐾; 🚌2, 23, 27, 41, 42) One of the city's best traditional-style pubs (it's not as old as it looks), serving a range of excellent real ales, Scottish craft gins and a vast selection of malt whiskies, the Bow Bar often has standing-room only on Friday and Saturday evenings.

★Cabaret Voltaire CLUB
(Map p768; www.thecabaretvoltaire.com; 36-38 Blair St; ⏲5pm-3am Mon-Thu, noon-3am Fri-Sun; 📶; 🚌all South Bridge buses) An atmospheric warren of stone-lined vaults houses this self-consciously 'alternative' club, which eschews huge dance floors and egotistical DJ worship in favour of a 'creative crucible' hosting an eclectic mix of DJs, live acts, comedy, theatre, visual arts and the spoken word. Well worth a look.

Bongo Club CLUB
(Map p768; www.thebongoclub.co.uk; 66 Cowgate; admission free-£6; ⏲11pm-3am Tue & Thu, 7pm-3am Fri-Sun; 📶; 🚌2) Owned by a local

arts charity, the weird and wonderful Bongo Club boasts a long history of hosting everything from wild club nights and local bands to performance art and kids' comedy shows, and is open as a cafe and exhibition space during the day.

OX 184 BAR

(Map p768; ☎0131-226 1645; www.ox184.co.uk; 184-186 Cowgate; ⏰11am-3am; 📶; 🚌35, 45) A big, booming industrial-chic bar with more than 100 whiskies on offer (Scotch, Irish, American and Japanese), as well as a fine selection of real ales and craft beers, the OX's standout feature is a huge wood-fired grill on which burgers, ribs and steaks are constantly sizzling. DJs and live bands.

Jolly Judge PUB

(Map p768; www.jollyjudge.co.uk; 7a James Ct; ⏰noon-11pm Mon-Thu, to midnight Fri & Sat, 12.30-11pm Sun; 📶; 🚌23, 27, 41, 42) A snug little howff tucked away down a close, the Judge exudes a cosy 17th-century atmosphere (low, timber-beamed painted ceilings) and has the added attraction of a cheering open fire in cold weather. No music or gaming machines, just the buzz of conversation.

BrewDog BAR

(Map p768; www.brewdog.com; 143 Cowgate; ⏰noon-1am Mon-Sat, 12.30pm-1am Sun; 📶; 🚌35, 45) The Edinburgh outpost of Scotland's self-styled 'punk brewery', BrewDog stands out among the sticky-floored dives that line the Cowgate, with its polished concrete bar and cool, industrial-chic decor. As well as its own highly rated beers, there's a choice of guest real ales, and – a sign of a great trad pub – coat hooks under the edge of the bar.

Liquid Room CLUB

(Map p768; www.liquidroom.com; 9c Victoria St; admission free-£20; ⏰live music from 7pm, club 10.30pm-3am Wed, Fri & Sat; 🚌23, 27, 41, 42) Set in a subterranean vault deep beneath Victoria St, the Liquid Room is a superb club venue with a thundering sound system. There are regular club nights on Wednesday, Friday and Saturday, as well as live bands.

TOP FIVE TRADITONAL PUBS

Bennet's Bar (☎0131-229 5143; www.bennetsbaredinburgh.co.uk; 8 Leven St; ⏰11am-1am; 🚌all Tollcross buses) Situated beside the King's Theatre, Bennet's has managed to hang on to almost all of its beautiful Victorian fittings, from the leaded stained-glass windows and ornate mirrors to the wooden gantry and the brass water taps on the bar (for your whisky – there are over 100 malts from which to choose).

Café Royal Circle Bar (Map p774; www.caferoyaledinburgh.co.uk; 17 West Register St; ⏰11am-11pm Mon-Wed, to midnight Thu, to 1am Fri & Sat, 12.30-11pm Sun; 📶; 🚊Princes St) Perhaps *the* classic Edinburgh pub, the Café Royal's main claims to fame are its magnificent oval bar and its Doulton tile portraits of famous Victorian inventors. Sit at the bar or claim one of the cosy leather booths beneath the stained-glass windows, and choose from the seven real ales on tap.

Athletic Arms (Diggers; ☎0131-337 3822; 1-3 Angle Park Tce; ⏰11am-1am Mon-Sat, 12.30pm-1am Sun; 🚌1, 34, 35) Nicknamed for the cemetery across the street – gravediggers used to nip in and slake their thirst here – the Diggers dates from the 1890s. It's still staunchly traditional – the decor has barely changed in 100 years – and is a real-ale drinker's mecca, serving locally brewed 80-shilling ale. Packed to the gills with football and rugby fans on match days.

Abbotsford (Map p774; ☎0131-225 5276; www.theabbotsford.com; 3 Rose St; ⏰11am-11pm Mon-Thu, to midnight Fri & Sat, 12.30-11pm Sun; 📶; 🚌all Princes St buses) One of the few pubs in Rose St that has retained its Edwardian splendour, the Abbotsford has long been a hang-out for writers, actors, journalists and media people, and has many loyal regulars. Dating from 1902, and named after Sir Walter Scott's country house, the pub's centrepiece is a splendid mahogany island bar. Good selection of real ales.

Sheep Heid Inn (www.thesheepheidedinburgh.co.uk; 43-45 The Causeway; ⏰11am-11pm Mon-Thu, to midnight Fri & Sat, noon-11pm Sun; 👪; 🚌42) Possibly the oldest inn in Edinburgh (with a licence dating back to 1360) the Sheep Heid feels more like a country pub than an Edinburgh bar. Set in the semirural shadow of Arthur's Seat, it's famous for its 19th-century skittles alley and the lovely little beer garden.

New Town

Oxford Bar PUB
(Map p774; ☎0131-539 7119; www.oxfordbar.co.uk; 8 Young St; ⊙11am-midnight Mon-Sat, 12.30-11pm Sun; ; 19, 36, 37, 41, 47) The Oxford is that rarest of things: a real pub for real people, with no 'theme', no music, no frills and no pretensions. 'The Ox' has been immortalised by Ian Rankin, author of the Inspector Rebus novels, whose fictional detective is a regular here. Occasional live folk music.

Joseph Pearce's PUB
(Map p774; ☎0131-556 4140; www.bodabar.com/joseph-pearces; 23 Elm Row; ⊙11am-midnight Sun-Thu, to 1am Fri & Sat; ; all Leith Walk buses) This traditional Victorian pub has been remodelled and given a new lease of life by the Swedish owners. It's a real hub of the local community with good food (very family friendly before 5pm), a relaxed atmosphere, and events like Monday night Scrabble games and August crayfish parties.

Cumberland Bar PUB
(Map p774; ☎0131-558 3134; www.cumberlandbar.co.uk; 1-3 Cumberland St; ⊙noon-midnight Mon-Wed, to 1am Thu-Sat, 11am-midnight Sun; ; 23, 27) Immortalised as the stereotypical New Town pub in Alexander McCall Smith's serialised novel *44 Scotland Street*, the Cumberland has an authentic, traditional wood-brass-and-mirrors look (despite being relatively new) and serves well-looked-after, cask-conditioned ales and a wide range of malt whiskies. There's also a pleasant little beer garden outside.

Bramble COCKTAIL BAR
(Map p774; ☎0131-226 6343; www.bramblebar.co.uk; 16a Queen St; ⊙4pm-1am; 23, 27) One of those places that easily earns the sobriquet 'best-kept secret', Bramble is an unmarked cellar bar where a maze of stone and brick hideaways conceals what is arguably the city's best cocktail venue. No beer taps, no fuss, just expertly mixed drinks.

Leith

★Roseleaf BAR
(☎0131-476 5268; www.roseleaf.co.uk; 23-24 Sandport Pl; ⊙10am-1am; ; 16, 22, 35, 36) Cute, quaint and verging on chintzy, the Roseleaf could hardly be further from the average Leith bar. Decked out in flowered wallpaper, old furniture and rose-patterned china (cocktails are served in teapots), the real ales and bottled beers are complemented by a range of speciality teas, coffees and fruit drinks (including rose lemonade), and well-above-average pub grub.

Lioness of Leith BAR
(☎0131-629 0580; www.facebook.com/Thelionessofleith; 21-25 Duke St; ⊙noon-midnight Mon-Thu, 11am-1am Fri & Sat, 12.30pm-midnight Sun; ; 21, 25, 34, 35, 49) Duke St was always one of the rougher corners of Leith, but the emergence of pubs like the Lioness is a sure sign of creeping gentrification. Distressed timber and battered leather benches are surrounded by vintage *objets trouvés* from chandeliers and glitterballs to mounted animal heads, a pinball machine and a pop-art print of Allen Ginsberg. Good beers and cocktails.

☆ Entertainment

The comprehensive source for what's-on info is *The List* (www.list.co.uk), an excellent listings magazine covering both Edinburgh and Glasgow. It's available from most newsagents, and is published fortnightly on a Thursday.

Live Music

★Sandy Bell's TRADITIONAL MUSIC
(Map p768; www.sandybellsedinburgh.co.uk; 25 Forrest Rd; ⊙noon-1am Mon-Sat, 12.30pm-midnight Sun; 2, 23, 27, 41, 42, 45) This unassuming pub is a stalwart of the traditional music scene (the founder's wife sang with the Corries). There's music almost every evening at 9pm, and from 3pm Saturday and Sunday, plus lots of impromptu sessions.

Jam House LIVE MUSIC
(Map p774; ☎0131-220 2321; www.thejamhouse.com; 5 Queen St; admission from £4; ⊙6pm-3am Fri & Sat; 10, 11, 12, 16, 26, 44) The brainchild of rhythm-and-blues pianist and TV personality Jools Holland, the Jam House is set in a former BBC TV studio and offers a combination of fine dining and live jazz and blues performances. Admission is for over-21s only, and there's a smart-casual dress code.

Caves LIVE MUSIC
(Map p768; ☎0131-557 8989; www.thecavesedinburgh.com; 8-12 Niddry St South; 35) A spectacular subterranean club venue set in the ancient stone vaults beneath the South Bridge, the Caves stages a series of one-off club nights and live-music gigs, as well as *ceilidh* nights during the festival – check the What's On link on the website for events.

Henry's Cellar Bar LIVE MUSIC
(Map p768; 0131-629 2992; www.henryscellarbar.co.uk; 16 Morrison St; admission free-£6; 5pm-1am Sun-Thu, to 3am Fri & Sat; all Lothian Rd buses) One of Edinburgh's most eclectic live-music venues, Henry's has something going on most nights of the week, from rock and indie to 'Balkan-inspired folk' and from funk to hip-hop to hardcore, staging both local bands and acts from around the world.

Cinemas

Cameo CINEMA
(0871 902 5723; www.picturehouses.co.uk; 38 Home St; ; all Tollcross buses) The three-screen, independently owned Cameo is a good, old-fashioned cinema showing an imaginative mix of mainstream and art-house movies. There is a good program of late-night films and Sunday matinees, and the seats in screen 1 are big enough to get lost in.

Filmhouse CINEMA
(Map p768; 0131-228 2688; www.filmhousecinema.com; 88 Lothian Rd; ; all Lothian Rd buses) The Filmhouse is the main venue for the annual Edinburgh International Film Festival (p782) and screens a full program of art-house, classic, foreign and second-run films, with lots of themes, retrospectives and 70mm screenings. It has wheelchair access.

Classical Music, Opera & Ballet

Edinburgh Festival Theatre THEATRE
(Map p768; 0131-529 6000; www.edtheatres.com/festival; 13-29 Nicolson St; box office 10am-6pm Mon-Sat, to 8pm show nights, 4pm-showtime Sun; all South Bridge buses) A beautifully restored art-deco theatre with a modern frontage, the Festival is the city's main venue for opera, dance and ballet, but also stages musicals, concerts, drama and children's shows.

Usher Hall CLASSICAL MUSIC
(Map p768; 0131-228 1155; www.usherhall.co.uk; Lothian Rd; box office 10.30am-5.30pm, to 8pm show nights; all Lothian Rd buses) The architecturally impressive Usher Hall hosts concerts by the Royal Scottish National Orchestra (RSNO) and performances of popular music.

Theatre, Musicals & Comedy

★**Summerhall** THEATRE
(0131-560 1580; www.summerhall.co.uk; 1 Summerhall; 41, 42, 67) Formerly Edinburgh University's veterinary school, the Summerhall complex is a major cultural centre and entertainment venue, with old halls and lecture theatres (including an original anatomy lecture theatre) now serving as venues for drama, dance, cinema and comedy performances. It's also one of the main venues for Edinburgh Festival events.

Royal Lyceum Theatre THEATRE
(Map p768; 0131-248 4848; www.lyceum.org.uk; 30b Grindlay St; box office 10am-6pm Mon-Sat, to 8pm show nights; ; all Lothian Rd buses) A grand Victorian theatre located beside the Usher Hall, the Lyceum stages drama, concerts, musicals and ballet.

Traverse Theatre THEATRE
(Map p768; 0131-228 1404; www.traverse.co.uk; 10 Cambridge St; box office 10am-6pm Mon-Sat, to 8pm show nights; ; all Lothian Rd buses) The Traverse is the main focus for new Scottish writing and stages an adventurous program of contemporary drama and dance. The box office is only open on Sunday (from 4pm) when there's a show on.

Stand Comedy Club COMEDY
(Map p774; 0131-558 7272; www.thestand.co.uk; 5 York Pl; tickets £2-15; from 7.30pm Mon-Sat, from 12.30pm Sun; St Andrew Sq) The Stand, founded in 1995, is Edinburgh's main independent comedy venue. It's an intimate cabaret bar with performances every night and a free Sunday lunchtime show.

Sport

Edinburgh has two rival football (soccer) teams playing in the Scottish Premier League – **Heart of Midlothian** (aka Hearts, nicknamed the Jam Tarts or Jambos), founded in 1874, and **Hibernian** (aka Hibs, Hibbies or Hi-bees), founded in 1875.

From January to March, Scotland's national rugby team takes part in the **Six Nations Rugby Union Championship** (www.rbs6nations.com). The most important fixture is the clash against England for the Calcutta Cup, which takes place in Edinburgh in even-numbered years (and at Twickenham in London in odd-numbered years). At club level, the season runs from September to May. **Murrayfield Stadium** (www.scottishrugby.org; 112 Roseburn St; Murrayfield Stadium), about 1.5 miles west of the city centre, is the venue for international matches.

Shopping

Princes St is Edinburgh's principal shopping street, lined with all the big high-street stores, with many smaller shops along pedestrianised Rose St, and more expensive designer boutiques on George St and Thistle St. For more off-beat shopping – including fashion, music, crafts, gifts and jewellery – head for the cobbled lanes of Cockburn, Victoria and St Mary's Sts, all near the Royal Mile in the Old Town; William St in the western part of the New Town; and the Stockbridge district, immediately north of the New Town.

There are two big shopping centres in the New Town – **Waverley Mall** (Map p774; ☎0131-557 3759; www.waverleymall.com; Waverley Bridge; ⏰9am-6pm Mon-Wed & Fri-Sat, to 7pm Thu 11am-5pm Sun; 🚌all Princes St buses), at the eastern end of Princes St, and the nearby **St James Centre** (Map p774; ☎0131-558 1200; www.stjamesshopping.com; 1 Leith St; ⏰9am-6pm Mon-Wed & Fri-Sat, to 8pm Thu, 10am-6pm Sun; 🚊York Pl) at the top of Leith St, plus **Multrees Walk** (Map p774; www.multreeswalk.co.uk; St Andrew Sq; 🚊St Andrew Sq), a designer shopping complex with a flagship Harvey Nichols store on the eastern side of St Andrew Sq.

The Ocean Terminal (p778) in Leith is the biggest shopping centre in the city.

Information

EMERGENCY

Police Scotland New Town (☎non-emergency 101; www.scotland.police.uk; Gayfield Sq; ⏰24hr; 🚌all Leith Walk buses)

Police Scotland West End (☎non-emergency 101; www.scotland.police.uk; 3-5 Torphichen Pl; ⏰9am-5pm Mon-Fri)

INTERNET ACCESS

There are internet-enabled telephone boxes scattered around the city centre, and countless wi-fi hot spots. Internet cafes, such as **Coffee Home** (☎0131-477 8336; www.coffeehome.co.uk; 28 Crighton Pl, Leith Walk; per 20min 60p; ⏰10am-9pm Mon-Fri, 10am-8pm Sat, noon-8pm Sun; 📶🐾; 🚌all Leith Walk buses) in Leith, are spread around the city and most cafes and bars offer free wi-fi for customers.

MEDICAL SERVICES

For urgent medical advice you can call the **NHS 24 Helpline** (☎111; www.nhs24.com). Chemists (pharmacists) can advise you on minor ailments. At least one local chemist remains open round the clock – its location will be displayed in the windows of other chemists.

For urgent dental treatment, you can visit the walk-in **Chalmers Street Dental Clinic** (☎0131-536 4800; 3 Chalmers St; ⏰9am-4.45pm Mon-Thu, to 4.15pm Fri; 🚌23, 27, 35, 45, 47). In the case of a dental emergency in the evenings or at weekends, call **Lothian Dental Advice Line** (☎0131-536 4800; ⏰5-10pm Mon-Fri, 9am-10pm Sat & Sun).

Boots (☎0131-225 6757; 48 Shandwick Pl; ⏰7.30am-8pm Mon-Fri, 9am-6pm Sat, 10.30am-5pm Sun; 🚊West End) Chemist open longer hours than most.

Edinburgh Royal Infirmary (☎0131-536 1000; www.nhslothian.scot.nhs.uk; 51 Little France Cres, Old Dalkeith Rd; ⏰24hr) Edinburgh's main general hospital; has 24-hour accident and emergency department.

Edinburgh Rape Crisis Centre (☎08088-01 03 02; www.rapecrisisscotland.org.uk)

Royal Hospital for Sick Children (☎0131-536 0000; www.nhslothian.scot.nhs.uk; 9 Sciennes Rd; ⏰24hr) Casualty department for children aged under 13 years; located in Marchmont (moving to a new location near the Edinburgh Royal Infirmary in autumn or winter of 2017).

Western General Hospital (☎0131-537 1000; www.nhslothian.scot.nhs.uk; Crewe Rd South; ⏰8am-9pm) For non-life-threatening injuries and ailments, you can attend the Minor Injuries Clinic without having to make an appointment.

POST

The UK postal system is generally reliable. You can find up-to-date rates at www.royalmail.com.

Frederick St Post Office (Map p774; 40 Frederick St; ⏰9am-5.30pm Mon & Wed-Fri, 9.30am-5.30pm Tue, 9.30am-12.30pm Sat)

St Mary's St Post Office (Map p768; 46 St Mary's St; ⏰9am-5.30pm Mon-Fri, to 12.30pm Sat)

Waverley Mall Post Office (Map p774; Waverley Mall; ⏰9am-5.30pm Mon & Wed-Sat, 9.30am-5.30pm Tue)

TOURIST INFORMATION

Edinburgh Airport Information Centre (☎0131-473 3690; www.edinburghairport.com; Edinburgh Airport; ⏰7.30am-7.30pm Mon-Fri, to 8pm Sat & Sun) VisitScotland Information Centre in the airport's terminal extension.

Edinburgh Festival Guide (www.edinburghfestivals.co.uk) Everything you need to know about Edinburgh's many festivals.

Edinburgh Information Centre (Map p774; ☎0131-473 3868; www.edinburgh.org; Waverley Mall, 3 Princes St; ⏰9am-7pm Mon-Sat, 10am-7pm Sun Jul & Aug, to 6pm Jun, to 5pm Sep-May; 📶; 🚊St Andrew Sq) Has an accommodation booking service, currency exchange, gift and bookshop, internet access and counters selling tickets for Edinburgh city tours and Scottish Citylink bus services.

USEFUL WEBSITES

Edinburgh Festival Guide (www.edinburghfestivals.co.uk) Everything you need to know about Edinburgh's many festivals.

Lonely Planet (www.lonelyplanet.com/edinburgh) Destination information, hotel bookings, great for planning.
The List (www.list.co.uk) Local listings and reviews for restaurants, bars, clubs and theatres
VisitScotland Edinburgh (www.edinburgh.org) Official Scottish tourist board site.

Getting There & Away

AIR

Edinburgh Airport (EDI; ☎0844 448 8833; www.edinburghairport.com), 8 miles west of the city, has numerous flights to other parts of Scotland and the UK, Ireland and mainland Europe. There's a **VisitScotland Information Centre** (p794) in the airport's extension.

FlyBe/Loganair (☎0371 700 2000; www.loganair.co.uk) operates daily flights to Inverness, Wick, Orkney, Shetland and Stornoway.

BUS

Edinburgh Bus Station (Map p774; entrances on Elder St & St Andrew Sq; left luggage lockers per 12hr £5-8; ⏰4.30am-midnight Sun-Thu, 4.30am-12.30am Fri & Sat) At the northeast corner of St Andrew Sq, with pedestrian entrances from the square and from Elder St. For timetable information, contact **Traveline** (☎0871 200 22 33; www.travelinescotland.com).

Scottish Citylink (☎0871 266 3333; www.citylink.co.uk) Buses connect Edinburgh with all of Scotland's cities and major towns. The following are sample one-way fares departing from Edinburgh.

DESTINATION	FARE (£)
Aberdeen	31
Dundee	16.60
Fort William	35
Glasgow	7.50
Inverness	31
Portree	56
Stirling	8.20

It's also worth checking with **Megabus** (☎0141-352 4444; www.megabus.com) for cheap intercity bus fares (from as little as £5) from Edinburgh to Aberdeen, Dundee, Glasgow, Inverness and Perth.

There are various buses to Edinburgh from London and the rest of the UK.

TRAIN

The main train terminus in Edinburgh is **Waverley train station**, located in the heart of the city. Trains arriving from, and departing for, the west also stop at Haymarket station, which is more convenient for the West End.

> **BUS INFO ON YOUR PHONE**
>
> Lothian Buses has created free smartphone apps that provide route maps, timetables and live waiting times for city buses. Search for EdinBus (iPhone), My Bus Edinburgh (Android) or BusTracker Edinburgh (Windows Phone).

You can buy tickets, make reservations and get travel information at the **Edinburgh Rail Travel Centre** (Waverley Station; ⏰5am-midnight Mon-Sat, 7am-midnight Sun) in Waverley station. For fare and timetable information, phone the **National Rail Enquiry Service** (☎08457-48 49 50; www.nationalrail.co.uk) or use the journey planner on the website.

If you're travelling as a pair, consider purchasing a **Two Together Railcard** (www.twotogether-railcard.co.uk; per year £30), which offers you up to 30% off your combined fares on train rides taken throughout Great Britain.

ScotRail (☎0344-811 0141; www.scotrail.co.uk) operates regular train services to the following:

Aberdeen (£35, 2½ hours)
Dundee (£17.90, 1¼ hours)
Glasgow (£12.50, 50 minutes, every 15 minutes)
Inverness (£42, 3½ hours)

Getting Around

TO/FROM THE AIRPORT

Bus Lothian Buses' **Airlink** (www.flybybus.com) service 100 runs from Waverley Bridge, outside the train station, to the airport (one way/return £4.50/7.50, 30 minutes, every 10 minutes from 4am to midnight) via the West End and Haymarket.

Tram Edinburgh Trams (www.edinburghtrams.com) run from the airport to the city centre (one way/return £5.50/8.50, 33 minutes, every six to eight minutes from 6am to midnight).

Taxi An airport taxi to the city centre costs around £20 and takes about 20 to 30 minutes. Trams, buses and taxis all depart from outside the arrivals hall; go out through the main doors and turn left.

BUS

Bus timetables, route maps and fare guides are posted at all main bus and tram stops, and you can pick up a copy of the free *Lothian Buses Route Map* from Lothian Buses Travelshops on **Waverley Bridge** (Map p768; 31 Waverley Bridge; ⏰9am-6pm Mon-Wed & Fri, to 7pm Thu, to 5.30pm Sat, 10am-5.30pm Sun) and **Hanover St** (Map p774; 27 Hanover St; ⏰9am-6pm Mon-Fri, 9am-5.30pm Sat).

Adult fares within the city are £1.60; purchase from the bus driver. Children aged under five travel free and those aged five to 15 pay a flat fare of 80p.

On Lothian Buses you must pay the driver the exact fare, but First buses will give change. Lothian Bus drivers also sell a day ticket (£4) that gives unlimited travel on Lothian buses and trams for a day; a family day ticket (up to two adults and three children) costs £8.50.

Night-service buses, which run hourly between midnight and 5am, charge a flat fare of £3.50.

You can also buy a Ridacard (from Travelshops; not available from bus drivers) that gives unlimited travel for one week for £18.

The Lothian Buses lost-property office is in the Hanover St Travelshop.

CAR & MOTORCYCLE

Though useful for day trips beyond the city, a car in central Edinburgh is more of a liability than a convenience. There is restricted access on Princes St, George St and Charlotte Sq, many streets are one-way, and finding a parking place in the city centre is like striking gold. Queen's Dr around Holyrood Park is closed to motorised traffic on Sunday.

Car Rental

All the big, international car-rental agencies have offices in Edinburgh, including **Avis** (☎ 0844 544 6059; www.avis.co.uk; 24 East London St; ⏰ 8am-6pm Mon-Fri, 8am-2pm Sat, 10am-2pm Sun) and **Europcar** (☎ 0871 384 3453; www.europcar.co.uk; Platform 2, Waverley Train Station, Waverley Bridge; ⏰ 7am-8pm Mon-Fri, 7am-5pm Sat & Sun).

There are many smaller, local agencies that offer better rates. **Arnold Clark** (☎ 0141-237 4374; www.arnoldclarkrental.co.uk) charges from £32 a day, or £185 a week for a small car, including VAT and insurance.

Parking

There's no parking on main roads into the city from 7.30am to 6.30pm Monday to Saturday. Also, parking in the city centre can be a nightmare.

On-street parking is controlled by self-service ticket machines from 8.30am to 6.30pm Monday to Saturday, and costs £1.80 to £3.60 per hour, with a 30-minute to four-hour maximum.

If you break the rules, you'll get a fine, often within minutes of your ticket expiring – Edinburgh's parking wardens are both numerous and notorious. The fine is £60, reduced to £30 if you pay up within 14 days. Cars parked illegally will be towed away. There are large, long-stay car parks at the St James Centre, Greenside Pl, New St, Castle Tce and Morrison St. Motorcycles can be parked free at designated areas in the city centre.

TAXI

Edinburgh's black taxis can be hailed in the street, ordered by phone (extra 80p charge) or picked up at one of the many central ranks. The minimum charge is £2.10 (£3.10 at night) for the first 450m, then 25p for every subsequent 188m – a typical 2-mile trip across the city centre will cost around £6 to £7. Tipping is up to you – because of the high fares local people rarely tip on short journeys, but occasionally round up to the nearest 50p on longer ones.

Central Taxis (☎ 0131-229 2468; www.taxis-edinburgh.co.uk)

City Cabs (☎ 0131-228 1211; www.citycabs.co.uk)

ComCab (☎ 0131-272 8001; www.comcab-edinburgh.co.uk)

TRAM

Edinburgh's tram system (www.edinburghtrams.com) began service in 2014. The line runs from Edinburgh Airport to York Pl, at the top of Leith Walk, via Haymarket, the West End and Princes St.

Tickets are integrated with the city's Lothian Buses, costing £1.60 for a single journey within the city boundary, or £5.50 to the airport. Trams run every eight to 10 minutes Monday to Saturday and every 12 to 15 minutes on a Sunday, from 5.30am to 11pm.

QUEENSFERRY & THE FORTH BRIDGES

Queensferry is at the narrowest part of the Firth of Forth, where ferries have crossed to Fife from the earliest times. The village takes its name from Queen Margaret (1046–93), who gave pilgrims free passage across the firth on their way to St Andrews. Ferries continued to operate until 1964 when the graceful **Forth Road Bridge** was opened; this was followed by a second road bridge, the **Queensferry Crossing** (2017).

Predating the first road bridge by 74 years, the magnificent **Forth Bridge** – only outsiders ever call it the Forth Rail Bridge – is one of the finest engineering achievements of the 19th century. Completed in 1890 after seven years' work, its three huge cantilevers span 1447m and took 59,000 tonnes of steel, eight million rivets and the lives of 58 men to build.

Glasgow & Southern Scotland

POP 596,500

Includes ➡

Best Places to Eat

- Ubiquitous Chip (p814)
- Mother India (p814)
- Ox & Finch (p811)
- Coltman's (p821)
- Auld Alliance (p830)

Best Places to Sleep

- Malmaison (p810)
- 15Glasgow (p810)
- Corsewall Lighthouse Hotel (p831)
- Old Bank House (p822)

Why Go?

For many, southern Scotland is what you drive through on the way further north. Big mistake. It means there are plenty of peaceful corners here. The south's proximity to England brought strife, but the ruins of Borders castles and the abbeys they protected make wonderfully atmospheric historic sites. The hillier west enjoys extensive forest cover; hills cascade down to sandy coasts blessed with Scotland's sunniest weather.

The region's premier urban attraction is marvellous Glasgow, Scotland's biggest city and a fascinatingly vital place. Glaswegians are proud of their working-class background, black humour and leftist traditions, and their city combines art, architecture, great food and nightlife, style, edgy urbanity and the people's legendary friendliness in a captivating blend that will leave you wanting more.

When to Go

- February's drizzle won't lift? Maroon yourself in one of Glasgow's fabulous pubs or clubs.
- The West End Festival and the Jazz Festival make Glasgow music heaven in June, while spectacular gardens bloom around southern Scotland's numerous stately homes.
- Glasgow is super-friendly at any time, but in summertime, when the sun is shining, there's no happier city in Britain.

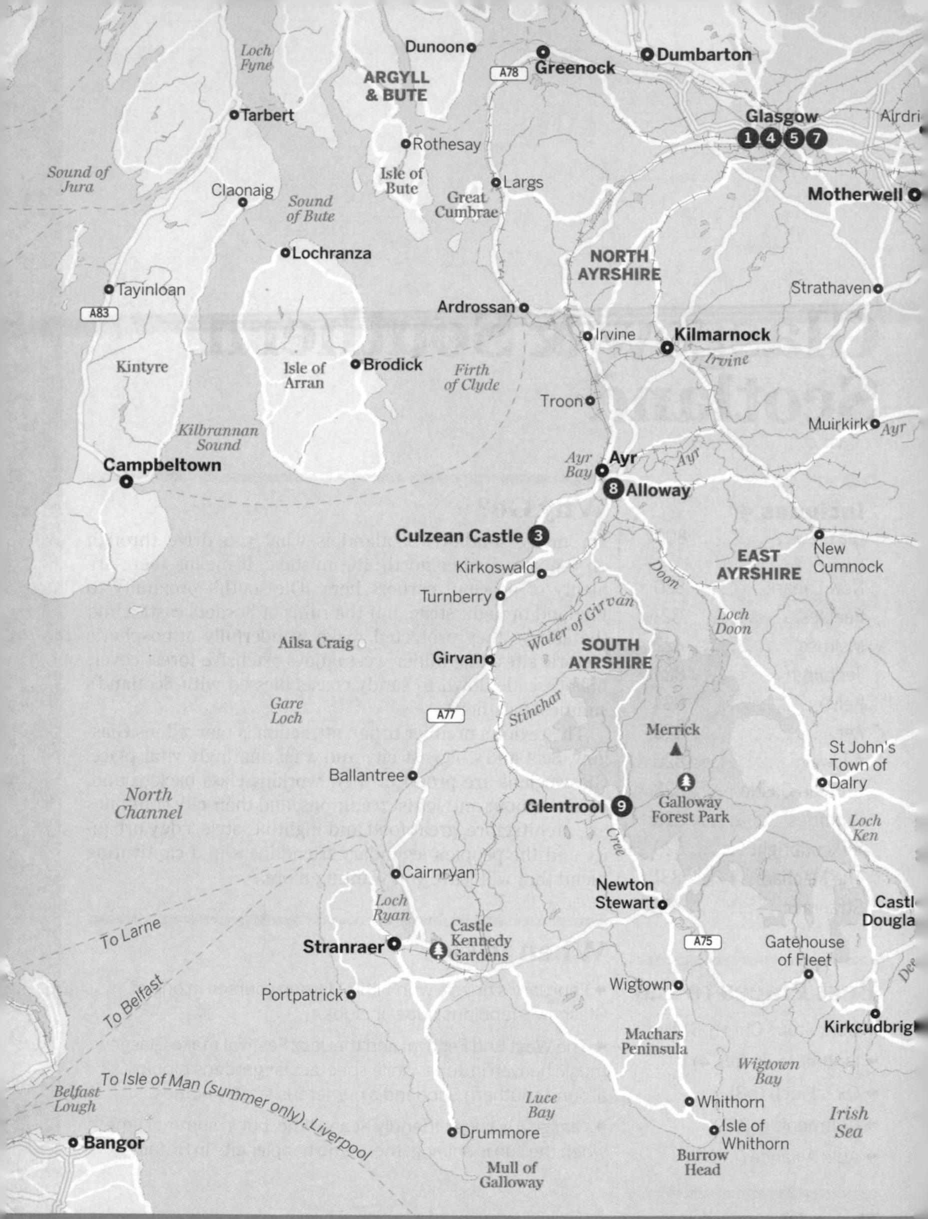

Glasgow & Southern Scotland Highlights

❶ **Art** (p805) Exploring Glasgow's wealth of paintings, beginning at the Kelvingrove Art Gallery & Museum.

❷ **Border Abbeys** (p821) Exploring the noble, evocative ruins of these abbeys and the area's other historic sights.

❸ **Culzean Castle** (p828) Admiring the 18th-century architectural genius of a castle perched on wild sea cliffs.

❹ **Ubiquitous Chip** (p814) Dining in the Glasgow restaurant that set the scene for the West End's culinary excellence.

5 Architecture (p800) Discovering the work of Charles Rennie Mackintosh, such as Glasgow School of Art.

6 New Lanark (p820) Admiring the radical social reform instituted in this handsome mill community.

7 Live Music (p816) Seeing a band at King Tut's Wah Wah Hut or at any other venue in Glasgow's legendary, diverse live-music scene.

8 Robert Burns Birthplace Museum (p827) Learning Lallans words from the Scottish Bard's verses.

9 Glentrool (p829) Biking down forest trails at Glentrool and other hubs.

GLASGOW

History

Glasgow grew around the cathedral founded by St Kertigan, later to become St Mungo, in the 6th century. Unfortunately, with the exception of the cathedral, virtually nothing of the medieval city remains. It was swept away by the energies of a new age – the age of capitalism, the Industrial Revolution and the British Empire.

In the 18th century, much of the tobacco trade between Europe and the USA was routed through Glasgow, providing a great source of wealth. Even after the tobacco trade declined in the 19th century, the city continued to prosper as a centre of textile manufacturing, shipbuilding and the coal and steel industries. The outward appearance of prosperity, however, was tempered by the dire working conditions in the factories.

In the first half of the 20th century Glasgow was the centre of Britain's munitions industry, supplying arms and ships for the two world wars, in the second of which the city was carpet-bombed. Post-war, however, the port and heavy industries began to dwindle, and by the early 1970s, the city looked doomed. Glasgow became synonymous with unemployment, economic depression and urban violence, centred around high-rise housing schemes such as the infamous Gorbals. More recently, urban development and a booming cultural sector have injected style and confidence into the city; though the standard of living remains low for Britain and life continues to be tough for many, the ongoing regeneration process gives grounds for optimism. The successful hosting of the 2014 Commonwealth Games highlighted this regeneration to a wide global audience.

Sights

City Centre

★Glasgow School of Art HISTORIC BUILDING

(Map p802; ☎0141-353 4526; www.gsa.ac.uk/tours; 167 Renfrew St; tours adult/child £9.75/4.75; ⊙10am-4.30pm) Charles Rennie Mackintosh's greatest building – extensively damaged by fire in 2014, and due to re-open in 2018 – still fulfils its original function, so just follow the steady stream of eclectically dressed students up the hill to find it. It's one of Glasgow's architectural showpieces and has now been joined by Steven Holl's spectacular glacial, green School of Design right opposite. A risqué combination, but it works. Tours leave from the new building, which also holds a free design exhibition.

Visits to the Mackintosh building are by excellent hour-long guided tours (11am and 3pm, plus 1pm May to September, multilingual translations available) run by architecture students. While reconstruction is ongoing, they visit the building's exterior only. Book online or by phone at busy times. Once the building is reopened, tour frequency will likely increase.

Particularly impressive is the thoroughness of the design; the architect's pencil seems to have shaped everything down to the smallest detail. The interior is strikingly austere, with simple colour combinations (often just black and cream) and the uncomfortable-looking high-backed chairs for which Mackintosh is famous. The library, designed as an addition in 1907, is a masterpiece.

There's a Mackintosh shop at the end of the tour. If you liked the visit, the same folk run recommended architecturally minded **walking tours** of central Glasgow; see the website for details.

★City Chambers HISTORIC BUILDING

(Map p802; www.glasgow.gov.uk; George Sq; ⊙9am-5pm Mon-Fri) FREE The grand seat of local government was built in the 1880s at the high point of Glasgow's wealth. The interior is even more extravagant than the exterior, and the chambers have sometimes been used as a movie location to represent the Kremlin or the Vatican. You can have a look at the opulent ground floor during opening hours. To see more, free guided tours are held at 10.30am and 2.30pm Monday to Friday; it's worth popping in earlier that day to prebook.

Gallery of Modern Art GALLERY

(GoMA; Map p802; ☎0141-287 3050; www.glasgowmuseums.com; Royal Exchange Sq; ⊙10am-5pm Mon-Thu & Sat, until 8pm Thu, 11am-5pm Fri & Sun) FREE Scotland's most popular contemporary-art gallery features modern works from international artists, housed in a graceful neoclassical building. The original interior is an ornate contrast to the daring, inventive art often on display. There's also a big effort made to keep the kids entertained. Usually

GLASGOW IN...

Two Days

On your first day, hit the East End for **Glasgow Cathedral** (below), **St Mungo's Museum** (below) and a wander through the hillside **necropolis** (p809). Later, take in the **Kelvingrove** (p805), one of the city's top museums. As evening falls, head to trendy Merchant City for a stroll and dinner; try **Café Gandolfi** (p811). Check out **Artà** (p815) for a pre- or post-meal drink. The next day, visit whichever museum you missed yesterday, and then it's Mackintosh time. **Glasgow School of Art** (opposite) is his finest work: if you like his style, head to the West End for **Mackintosh House** (p807). Hungry? Thirsty? Some of the city's best restaurants and bars are up this end of town, so you could make a night of it. Make sure to check out one of the numerous excellent **music venues** around the city.

Four Days

A four-day stay gives better scope to get to grips with Glasgow. Spend a day along the Clyde – the **Riverside Museum** (p804) and the **Glasgow Science Centre** (p805). Plan your weekend around a night out at the **Cathouse** (p815) or the legendary **Sub Club** (p815), and a day strolling the stylish city-centre clothing emporia or attending a football game. Don't miss at least one of the city's classic curry houses.

the horseback statue of the Duke of Wellington outside is cheekily crowned with a traffic cone; the authorities grumble, but it keeps happening and is now an icon.

The Lighthouse HISTORIC BUILDING
(Map p802; ☎0141-276 5365; www.thelighthouse.co.uk; 11 Mitchell Lane; ⏱10.30am-5pm Mon-Sat, noon-5pm Sun) FREE Mackintosh's first building, designed in 1893, was a striking new headquarters for the *Glasgow Herald*. Tucked up a narrow lane off Buchanan St, it now serves as Scotland's Centre for Architecture & Design, with fairly technical temporary exhibitions (sometimes admission is payable for these), as well as the Mackintosh Interpretation Centre, a detailed (if slightly dry) overview of his life and work. On the top floor of the 'lighthouse', drink in great views over the rooftops and spires of the city centre.

★**Sharmanka Kinetic Theatre** THEATRE
(Map p802; ☎0141-552 7080; www.sharmanka.com; 103 Trongate; adult/child short show £6/5, long show £8/6; ⏱45min shows 3pm Wed-Sun plus 4.15pm Sat, 70min shows 7pm Thu & Sun) This extraordinary mechanical theatre is located at the Trongate 103 arts centre. The amazing creativity of Eduard Bersudsky, a Russian sculptor and mechanic, now resident in Scotland, has created a series of large, wondrous figures sculpted from bits of scrap and elaborate carvings. Set to haunting music, these perform humorous and tragic stories of the human spirit. It's great for kids and very moving for adults: inspirational one moment and macabre the next, but always colourful, clever and thought-provoking.

The gallery is open just before performances Wednesday to Sunday – the sculptures and their stories are fascinating even when not in motion.

East End

The oldest part of the city is concentrated around Glasgow Cathedral, to the east of the modern centre. It's a 15-minute walk from George Sq, but numerous buses pass nearby, including buses 11, 12, 36, 37, 38 and 42.

★**Glasgow Cathedral** CATHEDRAL
(HES; Map p802; ☎0141-552 8198; www.historicenvironment.scot; Cathedral Sq; ⏱9.30am-5.30pm Mon-Sat & 1-5pm Sun Apr-Sep, 10am-4pm Mon-Sat & 1-4pm Sun Oct-Mar) FREE Glasgow Cathedral has a rare timelessness. The dark, imposing interior conjures up medieval might and can send a shiver down the spine. It's a shining example of Gothic architecture, and unlike nearly all of Scotland's cathedrals, survived the turmoil of the Reformation mobs almost intact. Most of the current building dates from the 15th century.

★**St Mungo's Museum of Religious Life & Art** MUSEUM
(Map p802; ☎0141-276 1625; www.glasgowmuseums.com; 2 Castle St; ⏱10am-5pm Tue-Thu

Central Glasgow

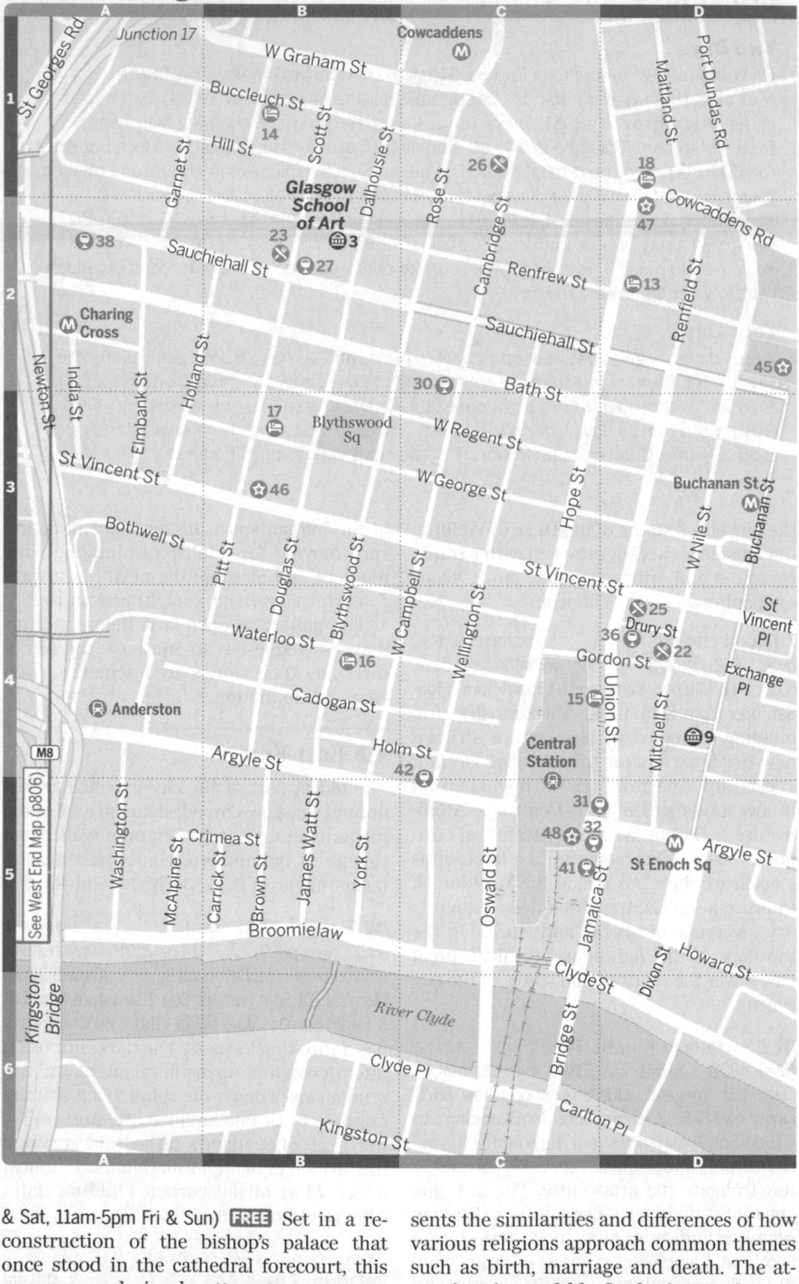

& Sat, 11am-5pm Fri & Sun) FREE Set in a reconstruction of the bishop's palace that once stood in the cathedral forecourt, this museum audaciously attempts to capture the world's major religions in an artistic nutshell. A startling achievement, it presents the similarities and differences of how various religions approach common themes such as birth, marriage and death. The attraction is twofold: firstly, impressive art that blurs the lines between religion and culture; and secondly, the opportunity to delve

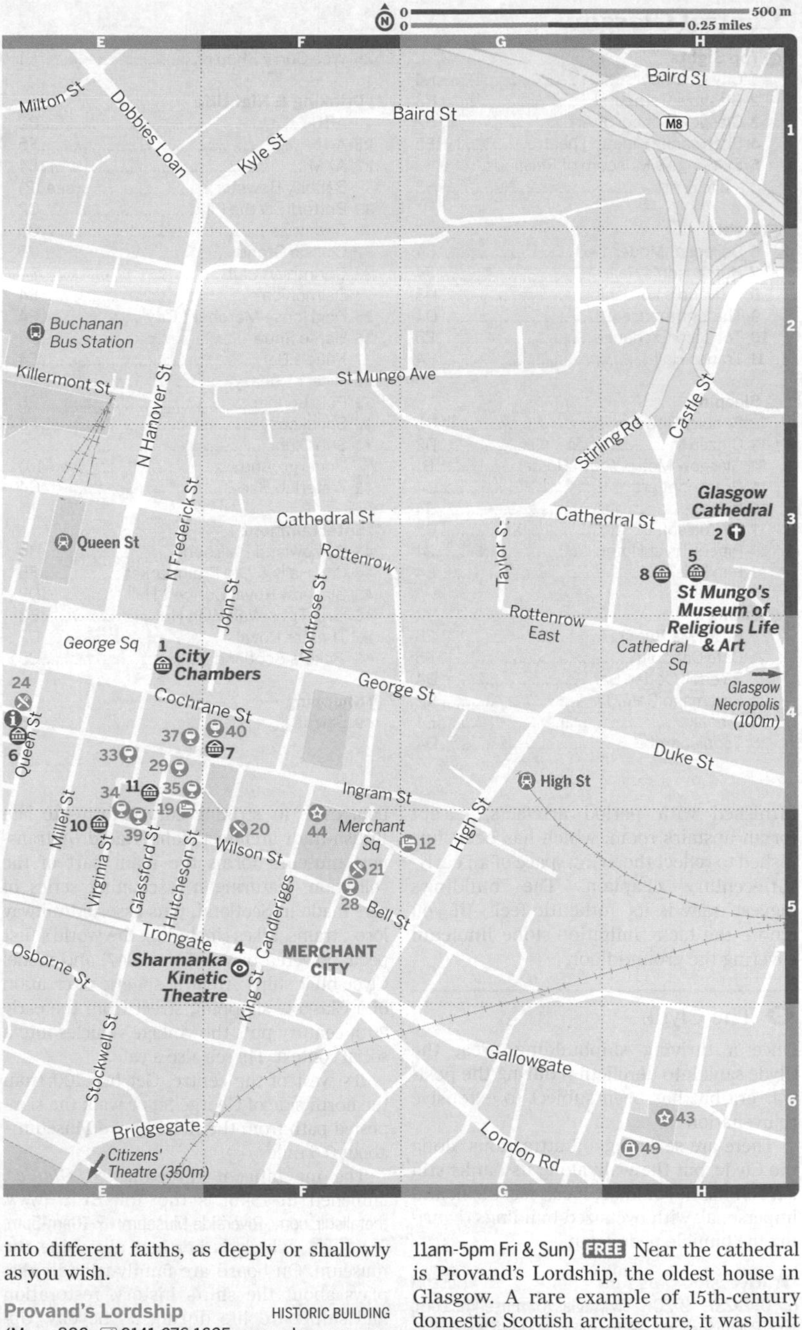

into different faiths, as deeply or shallowly as you wish.

Provand's Lordship HISTORIC BUILDING

(Map p802; 0141-276 1625; www.glasgowmuseums.com; 3 Castle St; 10am-5pm Tue-Thu & Sat, 11am-5pm Fri & Sun) FREE Near the cathedral is Provand's Lordship, the oldest house in Glasgow. A rare example of 15th-century domestic Scottish architecture, it was built in 1471 as a manse. The ceilings and doorways are low, and the rooms are sparsely

Central Glasgow

Top Sights
1 City Chambers ... E4
2 Glasgow Cathedral ... H3
3 Glasgow School of Art ... B2
4 Sharmanka Kinetic Theatre ... F5
5 St Mungo's Museum of Religious Life & Art ... H3

Sights
6 Gallery of Modern Art ... E4
7 Hutcheson's Hall ... F4
8 Provand's Lordship ... H3
9 The Lighthouse ... D4
10 Tobacco Exchange ... E5
11 Trades Hall ... E4

Sleeping
12 Babbity Bowster ... G5
13 Citizen M ... D2
14 Glasgow Metro Youth Hostel ... B1
15 Grasshoppers ... C4
16 Indigo ... B4
17 Malmaison ... B3
18 Pipers Tryst Hotel ... D1
19 Rab Ha's ... E4

Eating
20 Brutti Ma Buoni ... F5
21 Café Gandolfi ... F5
22 Riverhill Coffee Bar ... D4
23 Saramago Café Bar ... B2
24 Smoak ... E4
25 Topolabamba ... D4
26 Wee Curry Shop ... C1

Drinking & Nightlife
27 ABC ... B2
28 Artà ... F5
29 AXM ... E4
Babbity Bowster ... (see 12)
30 Butterfly & the Pig ... C2
31 Cathouse ... C5
32 Classic Grand ... C5
33 Corinthian Club ... E4
34 Delmonica's ... E4
35 DogHouse Merchant City ... E4
36 Horse Shoe ... D4
37 Katie's Bar ... E4
38 Nice 'n' Sleazy ... A2
39 Polo Lounge ... E5
40 Speakeasy ... F4
41 Sub Club ... C5
Underground ... (see 40)
42 Waterloo Bar ... C4

Entertainment
43 Barrowland Ballroom ... H6
44 City Halls & Old Fruitmarket ... F5
45 Glasgow Royal Concert Hall ... D2
46 King Tut's Wah Wah Hut ... B3
47 Theatre Royal ... D2
48 Tickets Scotland ... C5

Shopping
49 Barras ... H6

furnished with period artefacts, except for an upstairs room, which has been furnished to reflect the living space of an early-16th-century chaplain. The building's biggest draw is its authentic feel – if you ignore the tacky imitation-stone linoleum covering the ground floor.

The Clyde

Once a thriving shipbuilding area, the Clyde sank into dereliction during the post-war era but has been subject to extensive rejuvenation.

There are several good attractions along the Clyde, but the walk along its banks still isn't all that it could be; it can feel bleak and impersonal, with oversized buildings dwarfing the humble pedestrian.

★ **Riverside Museum** MUSEUM
(0141-287 2720; www.glasgowmuseums.com; 100 Pointhouse Pl; 10am-5pm Mon-Thu & Sat, 11am-5pm Fri & Sun;) FREE This visually impressive modern museum at Glasgow Harbour owes its striking curved forms to late British-Iraqi architect Zaha Hadid. A transport museum forms the main part of the collection, featuring a fascinating series of cars made in Scotland, plus assorted railway locos, trams, bikes (including the world's first pedal-powered bicycle from 1847) and model Clyde-built ships. An atmospheric re-creation of a Glasgow shopping street from the early 20th century puts the vintage vehicles into a social context. There's also a cafe.

It's west of the centre. Get bus 100 from the north side of George Sq or walk the signposted path from the Kelvingrove Museum – about 0.6 miles.

The magnificent three-masted *Glenlee*, launched in 1896, is the **Tall Ship** (www.thetallship.com; Riverside Museum; 10am-5pm;) FREE, which is berthed alongside the museum. On board are family-friendly displays about the ship's history, restoration and shipboard life during its heyday. Upkeep costs are high, so do donate something or have a coffee below decks.

★Glasgow Science Centre MUSEUM
(Map p806; ☎0141-420 5000; www.glasgowsciencecentre.org; 50 Pacific Quay; adult/child £11/9, IMAX, tower or planetarium extra £2.50-3.50; ⏰10am-5pm Wed-Sun Nov-Mar, 10am-5pm daily Apr-Oct; 👪) This ultramodern science museum will keep the kids entertained for hours (that's middle-aged kids, too!). It brings science and technology alive through hundreds of interactive exhibits on four floors: a bounty of discovery for inquisitive minds. There's also an **IMAX theatre** (see www.cineworld.com for current screenings), a rotating 127m-high **observation tower**; a **planetarium**, and a **Science Theatre**, with live science demonstrations. To get here, take bus 89 or 90 from Union St.

West End

With its appealing studenty buzz, trendy bars and cafes and nonchalant swagger, the West End is probably the most engaging area of Glasgow – it's great for people-watching, and is as close as Glasgow gets to bohemian. From the centre, buses 9, 16 and 23 run towards Kelvingrove; buses 8, 11, and 16 to the university; and buses 20, 44 and 66 to Byres Rd

★Kelvingrove Art Gallery & Museum GALLERY, MUSEUM
(Map p806; www.glasgowmuseums.com; Argyle St; ⏰10am-5pm Mon-Thu & Sat, 11am-5pm Fri & Sun) FREE A magnificent stone building, this grand Victorian cathedral of culture is a fascinating and unusual museum, with a bewildering variety of exhibits. You'll find fine art alongside stuffed animals, and Micronesian shark-tooth swords alongside a Spitfire plane, but it's not mix 'n' match: rooms are carefully and thoughtfully themed, and the collection is a manageable size. It has an excellent room of Scottish art, a room of fine French Impressionist works, and quality Renaissance paintings from Italy and Flanders.

Salvador Dalí's superb *Christ of St John of the Cross* is also here. Best of all, nearly

THE GENIUS OF CHARLES RENNIE MACKINTOSH

Great cities have great artists, designers and architects contributing to their urban environment while expressing their soul and individuality. Charles Rennie Mackintosh was all of these and his quirky, linear and geometric designs have had an enormous influence on Glasgow. Many of the buildings Mackintosh designed are open to the public, and you'll see his tall, thin, art-nouveau typeface repeatedly reproduced.

Born in 1868, Mackintosh studied at the Glasgow School of Art. It was there that he met the influential artist and designer Margaret Macdonald, whom he married; they collaborated on many projects and were major influences on each other's work. In 1896, aged only 27, he won a competition for his design of the School of Art's new building, Mackintosh's supreme architectural achievement. The first section was opened in 1899 and is considered to be the earliest example of art nouveau in Britain. This building demonstrates his skill in combining function and style.

Although Mackintosh's genius was quickly recognised on the Continent, he did not receive the same encouragement in Scotland. His architectural career here lasted only until 1914, when he moved to England to concentrate on furniture design. He died in 1928, and it is only since the last decades of the 20th century that Mackintosh's genius has been widely recognised. For more about the man and his work, contact the **Charles Rennie Mackintosh Society** (Map p806; ☎0141-946 6600; www.crmsociety.com; Mackintosh Church, 870 Garscube Rd). Check its website for special events.

Another of Mackintosh's finest works is **Hill House** (NTS; ☎01436-673900; www.nts.org.uk; Upper Colquhoun St; adult/child £10.50/7.50; ⏰11.30am-5.30pm Apr-Oct), in Helensburgh. If you're planning to visit some of the farther-flung attractions, the **Mackintosh Trail ticket** (£10), available at the **tourist office** (Map p802; www.visitscotland.com; Gallery of Modern Art, Royal Exchange Sq; ⏰10am-4.45pm, till 7.45pm Thu, from 11am Fri & Sun; 📶) or any Mackintosh building, gives you a day's admission to Hill House, the **Mackintosh Church** (Queen's Cross Church; Map p806; ☎0141-946 6600; www.mackintoshchurch.com; 870 Garscube Rd; adult/child £4/free; ⏰10am-5pm Mon-Fri Apr-Oct, 10am-4pm Mon, Wed & Fri Nov-Dec & Feb-Mar, closed Jan) and **House for an Art Lover** (☎0141-353 4770; www.houseforanartlover.co.uk; Bellahouston Park, Dumbreck Rd; adult/child £4.50/3; ⏰10am-4pm Mon-Wed, to 12.30pm Thu-Sun) as well as unlimited bus and subway travel.

West End

everything, including the paintings, has an easy-reading paragraph of interpretation. You can learn a lot about art here, and it's excellent for children, with plenty to do and displays aimed at a variety of ages. Free hour-long guided tours begin at 11am and 2.30pm. Bus 17, among many others, runs here from Renfield St.

Hunterian Museum MUSEUM

(Map p806; www.hunterian.gla.ac.uk; University Ave; ⏰10am-5pm Tue-Sat, 11am-4pm Sun) **FREE**

West End

Top Sights

1	Glasgow Science Centre	A6
2	Kelvingrove Art Gallery & Museum	B4
3	Mackintosh House	B2

Sights

4	Hunterian Art Gallery	B2
5	Hunterian Museum	B3
6	Kelvin Hall	A3
7	Mackintosh Church	D1

Sleeping

8	15Glasgow	D4
9	Alamo Guest House	B4
10	Amadeus Guest House	D2
11	Glasgow SYHA	C3
12	Heritage Hotel	B2

Eating

13	Bay Tree Café	C2
14	Finnieston	C5
15	Gannet	B4
16	Mother India	C4
17	Ox & Finch	C4
18	Stravaigin	C3
19	Ubiquitous Chip	B2

Drinking & Nightlife

20	Brel	B2
21	Brewdog Glasgow	B4
22	Hillhead Bookclub	B2
23	Jinty McGuinty's	B2
24	Òran Mór	B1

Entertainment

25	Clyde Auditorium	B6
26	Hydro	C6

Housed in the glorious sandstone university building, which is in itself reason enough to pay a visit, this quirky museum contains the collection of renowned one-time student of the university, William Hunter (1718–83). Hunter was primarily an anatomist and physician, but as one of those wonderfully well-rounded Enlightenment figures, he interested himself in everything the world had to offer. This collection is scheduled to become part of the new museum at Kelvin Hall but probably not until 2020.

Pickled organs in glass jars take their place alongside geological phenomena, potsherds gleaned from ancient brochs, dinosaur skeletons and a creepy case of deformed animals. The main halls of the exhibition, with their high vaulted roofs, are magnificent in themselves. A highlight is the 1674 Chinese *Map of the Whole World* in the World Culture section.

Hunterian Art Gallery GALLERY
(Map p806; www.hunterian.gla.ac.uk; 82 Hillhead St; 10am-5pm Tue-Sat, 11am-4pm Sun) FREE Across the road from the Hunterian Museum, and part of the same bequest, the bold tones of the Scottish Colourists (Samuel Peploe, Francis Cadell, JD Fergusson and Leslie Hunter) are well represented in this gallery. There are William MacTaggart's Impressionistic Scottish landscapes and a gem by Thomas Millie Dow. There's also a special collection of James McNeill Whistler's limpid prints, drawings and paintings. Upstairs, in a section devoted to late-19th-century Scottish art, you can see works by several of the Glasgow Boys.

★ **Mackintosh House** HISTORIC BUILDING
(Map p806; www.hunterian.gla.ac.uk; 82 Hillhead St; adult/child £5/3; 10am-5pm Tue-Sat, 11am-4pm Sun) Attached to the Hunterian Art Gallery (p807), this is a reconstruction of the first home that Charles Rennie Mackintosh bought with his wife, noted designer/artist Margaret Macdonald. It's fair to say that interior decoration was one of their strong points; Mackintosh House is startling even today. The house is scheduled to become part of the new museum at **Kelvin Hall** (Map p806; www.glasgowlife.org.uk; 1445 Argyle St), but probably not until 2020.

Activities

The **Clyde Walkway** stretches from Glasgow upriver to the Falls of Clyde near New Lanark, about 40 miles away. The tourist office has information outlining different sections of this walk. The 10-mile section through Glasgow has interesting parts, though most of the old shipyards are no longer there.

The well-trodden, long-distance footpath the **West Highland Way** begins in Milngavie, 8 miles north of Glasgow (you can walk to Milngavie from Glasgow along the River Kelvin), and runs for 95 spectacular miles to Fort William. There are several long-distance pedestrian/cycle routes that begin in Glasgow and follow off-road routes for most of the way. Check www.sustrans.org.uk for more details.

Festivals & Events

Celtic Connections MUSIC
(0141-353 8000; www.celticconnections.com; Jan) This two-week music festival focuses on roots music and folk from Scotland and around the world.

Glasgow Jazz Festival MUSIC
(www.jazzfest.co.uk; Jun) Excellent festival sees big-name international acts come to town, with stages set up in George Sq and Merchant City.

West End Festival PERFORMING ARTS
(0141-341 0844; www.westendfestival.co.uk; Jun) This music and arts event is Glasgow's biggest festival. Runs for three weeks.

Sleeping

The city centre can get very rowdy at weekends, and accommodation options fill up fast, mostly with groups who will probably roll home boisterously some time after 3am. If you prefer an earlier appointment with your bed, you'll be better off in a smaller, quieter lodging, or in the West End. Booking ahead is essential at weekends and in July and August. Most accommodation providers set prices according to demand, so if there's a big-name concert on a Saturday, expect to pay a premium, even for mediocre places.

City Centre

Glasgow Metro Youth Hostel HOSTEL $
(SYHA; Map p802; 0345-293 7373; www.syha.org.uk; 89 Buccleuch St; s £34, without bathroom £27; late Jun-Aug;) Student accommodation belonging to the nearby Glasgow School of Art provides the venue for this summer hostel. All rooms are comfortable singles, many with en suite, there are kitchen facilities and it's a very good deal for solo travellers or groups. It's slightly cheaper midweek.

★ **Citizen M** HOTEL $$
(Map p802; 0141-404 9485; www.citizenm.com; 60 Renfrew St; r £72-130;) This modern chain does away with some normal hotel accoutrements in favour of self-check-in terminals and minimalist, plasticky modern rooms with just two features: a big, comfortable king-sized bed and a decent shower with mood lighting. The idea is that guests make liberal use of the public areas, and why wouldn't you, with upbeat, super-comfortable designer furniture, 24-hour cafe, and iMacs.

★ **Grasshoppers** HOTEL $$
(Map p802; 0141-222 2666; www.grasshoppersglasgow.com; 87 Union St; r £100-120;) Discreetly hidden atop a timeworn railway administration building right alongside Glasgow Central, this small, well-priced hotel is a modern, upbeat surprise. Rooms are compact (a few are larger) but well-appointed, with unusual views over the station roof's glass sea. Numerous nice touches: friendly staff, interesting art, proper in-room coffee, free cupcakes, and weeknight suppers make this among the centre's homiest choices.

There's a very good deal available (£6 per day) at a car park a block away.

Indigo HOTEL $$
(Map p802; 0141-226 7700; www.hotelindigoglasgow.com; 75 Waterloo St; r £110-190;) Once the power station for early trams, this boutique-chain conversion of an elegant building has resulted in a satisfying, surprisingly quiet option in the heart of things. Rooms have mural-style artwork, great beds and free minibar (the contents improve as you go up the room grades). Space is good, and bathrooms have rainfall showers. Prices vary; there are usually good online deals.

Rab Ha's INN $$
(Map p802; 0141-572 0400; www.rabhas.com; 83 Hutcheson St; r £69-89;) This Merchant City favourite is an atmospheric pub-restaurant with four stylish rooms upstairs. They are all quite distinct and colourful. Room 1 is the best and largest, but all are comfortable, and the location is great. The personal touches like fresh flowers, iPod docks, a big welcome and any-time breakfast make you feel special.

Pipers Tryst Hotel HOTEL $$
(Map p802; 0141-353 5551; www.thepipingcentre.co.uk; 30-34 McPhater St; s/d £89/99;) The name is no tartan tourist trap; rather this intimate, cosy hotel in a noble building is actually run by the adjacent bagpiping centre, and profits go towards maintaining it. Cheery staff, great value and a prime city-centre location make this a wise choice. You won't have far to migrate after a night of Celtic music and fine single malts in the snug bar-restaurant downstairs.

Babbity Bowster INN $$
(Map p802; 0141-552 5055; www.babbitybowster.com; 16-18 Blackfriars St; s/d £55/75; P)

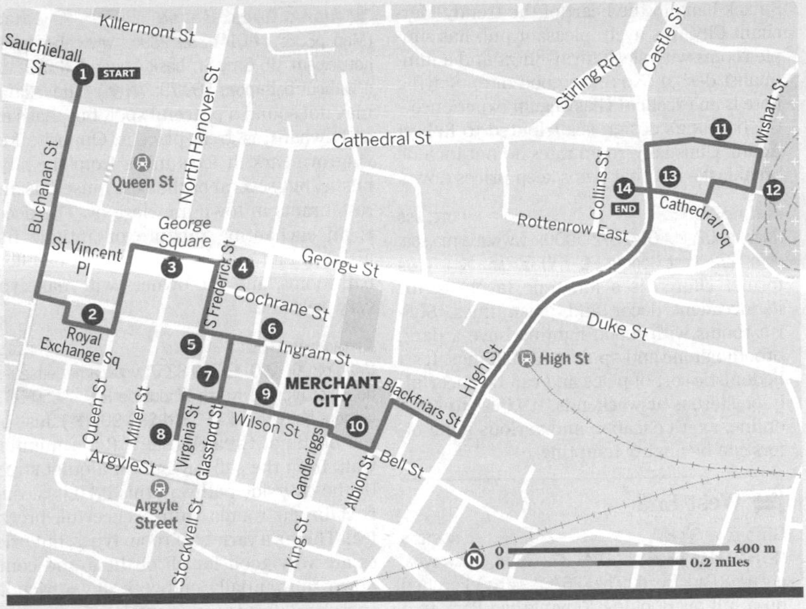

City Walk Glasgow

START BUCHANAN ST
END GLASGOW CATHEDRAL
LENGTH 1¾ MILES; 1½ HOURS

This stroll takes you to Glasgow Cathedral through trendy Merchant City.

Start at the junction of two major shopping thoroughfares, Sauchiehall and Buchanan Sts, overseen by a bronze **1 statue of Donald Dewar**, Scotland's inaugural First Minister. Stroll down pedestrian Buchanan St, then left through one of the handsome gateways into Merchant City. Here, the strikingly colonnaded **2 Gallery of Modern Art** (p800) was once the Royal Exchange and now hosts some of the country's best contemporary art displays. Turn left up Queen St to **3 George Square**, surrounded by imposing Victorian architecture, including the grandiose **4 City Chambers** (p800). Statues include Robert Burns, James Watt and Sir Walter Scott.

Walk down South Frederick St. Ahead of you, the former Court House cells now house the **5 Corinthian Club** (p815); drop into the bar for a glimpse of the extravagant interior, then continue to **6 Hutcheson's Hall**. This was built in 1805 as a hospital and school for the poor with a bequest from the brothers whose statues stand in the facade. Retrace your steps one block and continue south down Glassford St past **7 Trades Hall**, designed by Robert Adam in 1791 to house the trades guild. Turn right into Wilson St and left along Virginia St, lined with the old warehouses of the Tobacco Lords; many of these have been converted into posh flats. The **8 Tobacco Exchange** is flanked by pretty Virginia Court. Sugar and tobacco were traded here in the 18th and 19th centuries.

Back on Wilson St, the **9 Old Sheriff Court** fills a whole block and has been both Glasgow's town hall and main law court. Continue east on Wilson St past Ingram Sq to **10 Merchant Square**, a covered courtyard that was once the city's fruit market but now bustles with cafes and bars.

Head up Albion St, then right into Blackfriars St. Emerging onto High St, turn left and follow it up to **11 Glasgow Cathedral** (p801). Behind the cathedral wind your way up through the **12 necropolis**, which offers great city views. Lastly, check out **St 13 Mungo's Museum of Religious Life & Art** (p801) and **14 Provand's Lordship** (p803).

Smack bang in the heart of the trendy Merchant City, this lively, pleasant pub has simple rooms with sleek furnishings and a minimalist design (No 3 is a good one). Staying here is an excellent Glaswegian experience – the building's design is attributed to Robert Adam. Unusually, room rates do not include breakfast – but that helps keep prices down.

Malmaison HOTEL $$$
(Map p802; ☎0141-572 1000; www.malmaison.com; 278 West George St; r £135-215;) This former church is a longtime favourite for its decadent decor and plush lines. Stylish rooms with mood lighting have a dark, brooding tone and opulent furnishings. It's a hedonistic sort of place and can be cheerfully boisterous at weekends. It's best to book online, as it's cheaper, and various suite offers can be mighty tempting.

West End

Glasgow SYHA HOSTEL $
(SYHA; Map p806; ☎0141-332 3004; www.syha.org.uk; 8 Park Tce; dm/tw £26/62; @) Perched on a hill overlooking Kelvingrove Park in a charming townhouse, this place is one of Scotland's best official hostels. Dorms are mostly four to six beds with padlock lockers, and all have their own en suite. The common rooms are spacious, plush and good for lounging about. There's no curfew, it has a good kitchen, and meals are available.

Heritage Hotel HOTEL $
(Map p806; ☎0141-339 6955; www.theheritagehotel.net; 4 Alfred Tce, Great Western Rd; s/d £40/60; P) A stone's throw from all the action of the West End, this friendly hotel has an open, airy feel despite the rather dilapidated raised terrace it's located on. Generally, rooms on the 1st and 2nd floors are a bit more spacious (No 21 is best of the doubles) and have a better outlook. Good location, parking and fair prices.

★**15Glasgow** B&B $$
(Map p806; ☎0141-332 1263; www.15glasgow.com; 15 Woodside Pl; d/ste £125/155; P) Glasgow's 19th-century merchants certainly knew how to build a beautiful house, and this 1840s terrace is a sumptuous example. Huge rooms with lofty ceilings have exquisite period detail complemented by attractive modern greys, striking bathrooms and well-chosen quality furniture. Your welcoming host makes everything easy for you: an in-room breakfast, overlooking the park, is a real treat. The host prefers no under-5s.

★**Alamo Guest House** B&B $$
(Map p806; ☎0141-339 2395; www.alamoguesthouse.com; 46 Gray St; basic/superior d £99/149, d without bathroom £69-79; @) The Alamo may not sound a peaceful spot, but that's exactly what this great place is. Opposite Kelvingrove Park, it feels miles from the city's hustle, but several of the best museums and restaurants in town are close by. The decor is an enchanting mixture of antique furnishings and modern design, with excellent bathrooms, and the owners will make you very welcome.

Amadeus Guest House B&B $$
(Map p806; ☎0141-339 8257; www.amadeusguesthouse.co.uk; 411 North Woodside Rd; s £50-55, s without bathroom £35-38, d £80-90;) Just off the bustle of Great Western Rd, a minute's walk from the subway but on a quiet street by the riverside pathway, this B&B has compact bright rooms with a cheerful, breezy feel. There's a variety of room types, but prices are very good for all of them and come down substantially midweek. It's a friendly spot; breakfast is continental.

Hotel du Vin HOTEL $$$
(One Devonshire Gardens; ☎0141-378 0385; www.hotelduvin.com; 1 Devonshire Gardens; r £169-279; P@) This is traditionally Glasgow's favoured hotel of the rich and famous, and the patriarch of sophistication and comfort. A study in elegance, it's sumptuously decorated and occupies three classical sandstone terrace houses. There's a bewildering array of room types, all different in style and size. The hospitality is old-school courteous, and there's an excellent restaurant on site with a vast wine selection.

Eating

Glasgow is the best place to eat in Scotland, with an excellent range of eateries. The West End is the culinary centre, with Merchant City also boasting a high concentration of quality restaurants and cafes. Many Glasgow restaurants post offers on the internet (changing daily) at 5pm.co.uk. Pubs and bars (p814) are often good mealtime options too.

City Centre

★**Saramago Café Bar** CAFE $
(Map p802; ☎0141-352 4920; www.facebook.com/saramagocafebar; 350 Sauchiehall St; light meals £3-9; ⏲food noon-10pm Sun-Wed, noon-11.30pm

Thu-Sat;) In the airy atrium of the Centre for Contemporary Arts, this place does a great line in eclectic vegan fusion food, with a range of top flavour combinations from around the globe. The upstairs bar has a great deck on steep Scott St and packs out inside with a friendly hipstery crowd enjoying the DJ sets and quality tap beers.

★ Riverhill Coffee Bar CAFE $

(Map p802; 0141-204 4762; www.riverhillcafe.com; 24 Gordon St; rolls £4-5; 7am-5pm Mon-Fri, 8am-5pm Sat, 10am-5pm Sun;) Chain cafes plaster Glasgow's centre, so it's a joy to come across this tiny place, which offers great coffee and hot chocolate as well as delicious filled rolls and tempting pastries. Ingredients are sustainably sourced and seriously tasty. It's extremely friendly; you'd come every day if you lived nearby.

★ Ox & Finch FUSION $

(Map p806; 0141-339 8627; www.oxandfinch.com; 920 Sauchiehall St; portions £4-8; noon-10pm;) This fashionable place could almost sum up the thriving modern Glasgow eating scene, with a faux-pub name, sleek but comfortable contemporary decor, tapas-sized dishes and an open kitchen. Grab a cosy booth and be prepared to have your tastebuds wowed with innovative, delicious creations aimed at sharing, drawing on French and Mediterreanean influences but focusing on quality Scottish produce.

Brutti Ma Buoni MEDITERRANEAN $

(Map p802; 0141-552 0001; www.brunswickhotel.co.uk; 106 Brunswick St; mains £7-11; 11am-10pm Sun-Thu, to 11pm Fri & Sat;) If you like dining in a place that has a sense of fun, Brutti delivers – it's the antithesis of some of the pretentious places around the Merchant City and offers decent food at happily low prices. Italian and Spanish influences give rise to tapas-like servings or full-blown meals, which are imaginative, fresh and frankly delicious. The £5 mini-dishes make a more-than-decent lunch.

Wee Curry Shop INDIAN $

(Map p802; 0141-353 0777; www.weecurryshop.co.uk; 7 Buccleuch St; 2-course lunch £5.50, dinner mains £6-8; noon-2pm & 5.30-10.30pm Mon-Thu, noon-11pm Fri, noon-2pm & 5.30-11pm Sat, 5-10pm Sun;) This tiny place has great home-cooked curries. It's wise to book – it's a snug place with a big reputation.

★ Topolabamba MEXICAN $$

(Map p802; 0141-248 9359; www.topolabamba.com; 89 St Vincent St; portions £5-10; food noon-10pm Sun-Thu, noon-10.30pm Fri & Sat;) Lots of fun and attractively kitted-out in hipster Mexican decor – all skulls, figurines and tequila crates – this brings a real slice of authentic cuisine to Glasgow, with zingy tacos, tasty tostadas and not a plate of nachos in sight. The stuffed calamari are especially good, but it's all refreshingly flavoursome. Portions are tapa-sized, so order a few. An interesting list of mescal, *raicilla* and other distillates make out-of-the-ordinary accompaniments.

Café Gandolfi CAFE, BISTRO $$

(Map p802; 0141-552 6813; www.cafegandolfi.com; 64 Albion St; mains £10-16; 8am-11.30pm Mon-Sat, 9am-11.30pm Sun;) In Merchant City, this cafe was once part of the old cheese market. It's been pulling in the punters for years and attracts an interesting mix of die-hard Gandolfers, the upwardly mobile and tourists. It covers all the bases with excellent breakfasts and coffee, an enticing upstairs bar, and top-notch bistro food, including Scottish and Continental options, in an atmospheric medieval-like setting. There's an expansion, specialising in fish, a couple of doors up, with a takeaway outlet.

Smoak AMERICAN $$

(Map p802; 0141-228 4721; www.smoakbbq.co.uk; 6 Royal Exchange Sq; dishes £6-16; 10am-9.30pm;) This simple, cosy wood-lined eatery is among the best of the many barbecue-type restaurants that have popped up in Glasgow in recent years. The menu is short and focuses on burgers, ribs and pulled pork. The slow-cooking works wonders with the melt-in-your-mouth meat, and the rich sauces make even a simple burger into a sinful, sticky experience. BYO alcohol.

West End

There are excellent restaurants in the West End. They cluster along Byres Rd and just off it, on Ashton Lane and Ruthven Lane. Gibson St and Great Western Rd also have plenty to offer, while the Argyle Rd strip in Finnieston has interesting new options.

Bay Tree Café CAFE $

(Map p806; 0141-334 5898; www.thebaytreewestend.co.uk; 403 Great Western Rd; mains £7-11; 9am-10.30pm Mon-Sat, 9am-9.30pm Sun;

1. Scottish haggis, neeps and tatties **2.** Roast beef and Yorkshire pudding **3.** Fried sausage **4.** English breakfast

PHOTOED / SHUTTERSTOCK ©

Flavours of Britain

Food fans know that Britain has finally shaken off its reputation for bland meals. Wherever you go it's easy to find quality dishes, celebrating tradition – often with a modern twist – with local ingredients.

For many visitors, the culinary day begins in a hotel or B&B with the 'Full English Breakfast' – also available as the Full Welsh, Full Scottish, Full Yorkshire etc – a plate full of mainly fried meat that might shock, but there's enough fuel here for several hours of energetic sightseeing.

Lunch or dinner is the time to try regional specialities such as haggis or salmon in Scotland, lamb or laver bread in Wales, Cumberland sausage in northern England, Stilton cheese in the Midlands,curry in Birmingham's Balti Triangle or London's Brick Lane, and seafood just about anywhere on the coast.

And if you're feeling peckish in between meals, look out for country cafes serving cream teas: scones, jam and cream, with that other British classic, a hot cup of tea.

BRITISH CLASSICS

Fish and Chips Longstanding favourite, best sampled in coastal towns.

Haggis Scottish icon, mainly offal and oatmeal, traditionally served with 'tatties and neeps' (potatoes and turnips).

Sandwich Global snack today, but an English 'invention' from the 18th century.

Laverbread Laver is a type of seaweed, mixed with oatmeal and fried to create this traditional Welsh speciality.

Ploughman's lunch Bread and cheese – pub menu regular, perfect with a pint.

Roast beef & Yorkshire pudding Traditional lunch on Sunday for the English.

Cornish pasty Savoury pastry, southwest speciality, now available country-wide.

) There are many good cafes in the two or three blocks around here, but the Bay Tree is still a solid choice. It has lots of vegan and vegetarian options, smiling staff, filling mains (mostly Middle Eastern and Greek), generous salads and a good range of hot drinks. The cafe is famous for its all-day breakfasts.

★Stravaigin SCOTTISH, FUSION **$$**

(Map p806; 0141-334 2665; www.stravaigin.co.uk; 28 Gibson St; bar dishes £6-12, restaurant mains £15-19; food 9am-11pm Mon-Fri, 11am-11pm Sat & Sun;) Stravaigin is a serious foodie's delight, with a menu constantly pushing the boundaries of originality and offering creative culinary excellence. The cool contemporary dining space in the basement has booth seating and helpful, laid-back waitstaff. Entry level has a buzzing two-level bar with a different menu. Scottish classics like haggis take their place alongside a range of Asian-influenced dishes. It's all delicious.

★Mother India INDIAN **$$**

(Map p806; 0141-221 1663; www.motherindia.co.uk; 28 Westminster Tce, Sauchiehall St; mains £8-16; 5.30-10.30pm Mon-Thu, noon-11pm Fri, 1-11pm Sat, 1-10pm Sun;) Glasgow curry buffs forever debate the merits of the city's numerous excellent South Asian restaurants, and this features in every discussion. It may lack the trendiness of some of the up-and-comers, but it's been a stalwart for years, and the quality and innovation on show are superb. The three dining areas are all attractive and it makes an effort for kids, with a separate menu.

There are various other innovative, distinct sister restaurants around town.

Finnieston SEAFOOD **$$**

(Map p806; 0141-222 2884; www.thefinniestonbar.com; 1125 Argyle St; mains £13-19; food noon-10pm Mon-Sat, noon-9pm Sun;) A flagship of this increasingly vibrant strip, this gastropub recalls the area's sailing heritage with a cosily romantic below-decks atmosphere and artfully placed nautical motifs. It's been well thought through, with excellent mixed drinks and cocktails accompanying a short menu of high-quality upmarket pub fare focusing on sustainable Scottish seafood.

Gannet SCOTTISH **$$**

(Map p806; 0141-204 2081; www.thegannetgla.com; 1155 Argyle St; mains £16-22; noon-2.30pm & 5-9.30pm Tue-Sat, 1-7.30pm Sun;) Trendy but comfortably so, this jewel of the Finnieston strip offers a cosy wood-panelled ambience and gourmet food that excels on presentation and taste without venturing towards cutting edge. The short, polished daily menu features quality produce sourced mostly from southern Scotland and the interesting wine list backs it up very well indeed. Solicitous, professional service is another plus point.

★Ubiquitous Chip SCOTTISH **$$$**

(Map p806; 0141-334 5007; www.ubiquitouschip.co.uk; 12 Ashton Lane; 2-/3-course lunch £17/21, mains £22-35, brasserie mains £10-15; noon-2.30pm & 5-11pm Mon-Sat, 12.30-3pm & 5-11pm Sun;) The original champion of Scottish produce, this is legendary for its unparalleled Scottish cuisine and lengthy wine list. Named to poke fun at Scotland's culinary reputation, it offers a French touch but resolutely Scottish ingredients, carefully selected and following sustainable principles. The elegant courtyard space offers some of Glasgow's best dining, while, above, the cheaper brasserie offers exceptional value for money.

Drinking & Nightlife

Some of Britain's best nightlife is found in the din and sometimes roar of Glasgow's pubs and bars. There are as many different styles of bar as there are punters to guzzle in them. Some pubs and, especially, clubs have begun to enforce a 21-year-old minimum age.

Glasgow's clubbing scene has been hit by recent closures, but it's still lively. Glaswegians usually hit clubs after the pubs have closed, so many clubs offer discounted admission and cheaper drinks if you go early. Entry costs £5 to £10 (up to £25 for big events), although bars often hand out free passes. Clubs shut comparatively early, so keep your ear to the ground to find out where the after parties are at.

City Centre

★DogHouse Merchant City BAR

(Map p802; 0141-552 6363; www.brewdog.com; 99 Hutcheson St; 11am-midnight Mon-Fri, 10am-midnight Sat & Sun;) Brewdog's zingy beers are matched by its upbeat attitude, so this recent opening in Merchant City was always going to be a fun place. An open kitchen doles out slidery, burgery smoked-meat fare while 25 taps run quality craft beer from morning till night.

Sub Club CLUB
(Map p802; www.subclub.co.uk; 22 Jamaica St; ⏲typically 10pm-4am Tue-Sun) Saturdays at the Sub Club are one of Glasgow's legendary nights, offering serious clubbing with a sound system that aficionados usually rate as the city's best. The claustrophobic, last-one-in vibe is not for those faint of heart. Check the website for other nights. Closes one of Sunday or Monday.

Babbity Bowster PUB
(Map p802; ☎0141-552 5055; www.babbitybowster.com; 16-18 Blackfriars St; ⏲11am-midnight Mon-Sat, 12.30pm-midnight Sun; 📶) In a quiet corner of Merchant City, this handsome spot is perfect for a tranquil daytime drink, particularly in the adjoining beer garden. Service is attentive, and the smell of sausages may tempt you to lunch; it also offers accommodation. This is one of the city centre's most charming pubs, in one of its noblest buildings. There's a regular folk-music scene here.

Corinthian Club BAR
(Map p802; ☎0141-552 1101; www.thecorinthianclub.co.uk; 191 Ingram St; ⏲10am-2am Sun-Thu, 10am-3am Fri & Sat; 📶) A breathtaking domed ceiling and majestic chandeliers make this casino a special space. Originally a bank and later Glasgow's High Court, this regal building's main bar, Teller's, has to be seen to be believed. Cosy wraparound seating and space to spare are complemented by a snug wine bar and a plush club downstairs in old court cells.

Butterfly & the Pig PUB
(Map p802; ☎0141-221 7711; www.thebutterflyandthepig.com; 153 Bath St; ⏲11am-1am Mon-Thu, 11am-3am Fri & Sat, 12.30pm-midnight Sun; 📶) A breath of fresh air, this offbeat spot makes you feel comfortable as soon as you plunge into its basement depths. The decor is eclectic with a cosy retro feel. There's regular live jazz or similar and a sizeable menu – if you can decipher it – of pub grub, plus a rather wonderful tearoom upstairs, great for breakfast before the pub opens.

Artà BAR, CLUB
(Map p802; www.arta.co.uk; 62 Albion St; ⏲5pm-1am Thu, 5pm-3am Sat; 📶) This place is so baroque that when you hear a Mozart concerto over the sound system, it wouldn't surprise you to see the man himself at the other end of the bar. Set in a former cheese market, it really does have to be seen to be believed. Despite the luxury, it's got a relaxed, chilled vibe and does a decent cocktail.

It also does Spanish-influenced food but is better as a bar in our opinion.

Horse Shoe PUB
(Map p802; www.horseshoebar.co.uk; 17 Drury St; ⏲10am-midnight Sun-Fri, 9am-midnight Sat) This legendary city pub and popular meeting place dates from the late 19th century and is largely unchanged. It's a picturesque spot, with the longest continuous bar in the UK, but its main attraction is what's served over it – real ale and good cheer. Upstairs in the lounge is some of the best-value pub food (three-course lunch £4.50) in town.

Nice 'n' Sleazy BAR, CLUB
(Map p802; ☎0141-333 0900; www.nicensleazy.com; 421 Sauchiehall St; ⏲noon-3am Mon-Sat, 1pm-3am Sun; 📶) On the rowdy Sauchiehall strip, students from the nearby School of Art make the buzz here reliably friendly. If you're over 35, you'll feel like a professor not a punter, but retro decor, a big selection of tap and bottled beers, 3am closing, and nightly alternative live music downstairs followed by a club at weekends make this a winner.

Classic Grand CLUB
(Map p802; ☎0141-847 0820; www.classicgrand.com; 18 Jamaica St; ⏲variable; 📶) Rock, industrial, electronic and powerpop grace the stage and the turntables at this unpretentious central venue. It doesn't take itself too seriously, drinks are cheap and the locals are welcoming. Hours vary according to events, but core opening is 11pm to 3am Thursday to Saturday.

Cathouse CLUB
(Map p802; www.cathouse.co.uk; 15 Union St; ⏲10.30pm-3am Wed-Sun; 📶) It's mostly rock, alternative and metal with a touch of goth and post-punk at this long-standing indie venue. There are two dance floors: upstairs is pretty intense with lots of metal and hard rock; downstairs is a little more tranquil.

ABC CLUB
(O_2ABC; Map p802; ☎0141-332 2232; www.o2abcglasgow.co.uk; 300 Sauchiehall St; ⏲club 11pm-3am Thu-Sat; 📶) Both nightclub and venue, this reference point on Sauchiehall

has two large concert spaces with big-name gigs, plus several attractive bars. It's a good all-rounder, with a variety of DJs playing every Thursday to Saturday.

West End

Brewdog Glasgow PUB
(Map p806; ☎0141-334 7175; www.brewdog.com; 1397 Argyle St; ⊙noon-midnight; 📶) Perfect for a pint after the Kelvingrove Museum, this great little spot offers the delicious range of artisanal beers from the brewery of the same name. Punk IPA is refreshingly hoppy, more so than formidable WattDickie, which comes in at a whisky-like 35%. Tasting flights mean you can try several, while burgers and dogs are on hand to soak it up.

Hillhead Bookclub BAR
(Map p806; ☎0141-576 1700; www.hillheadbookclub.co.uk; 17 Vinicombe St; ⊙11am-midnight Mon-Fri, 10am-midnight Sat & Sun; 📶) Atmosphere in spades is the call sign of this easygoing West End bar. An ornate wooden ceiling overlooks two levels of well-mixed cocktails, seriously cheap drinks, comfort food and numerous intriguing decorative touches. There's even a ping-pong table in a cage.

Òran Mór BAR, CLUB
(Map p806; ☎0141-357 6200; www.oran-mor.co.uk; cnr Byres & Great Western Rds; ⊙9am-2am Mon-Wed, 9am-3am Thu-Sat, 10am-3am Sun; 📶) Now some may be a little uncomfortable with the thought of drinking in a church. But we say: the Lord giveth. This sizeable converted church is now a bar, restaurant, club and theatre venue. Look out for the 'A Play, a Pie and a Pint' deals. There's an excellent array of whiskies. The only thing missing is holy water on your way in.

Brel BAR
(Map p806; ☎0141-342 4966; www.brelbar.com; 39 Ashton Lane; ⊙11am-midnight Mon-Sat, noon-midnight Sun; 📶) Perhaps the best bar on Ashton Lane, this can seem tightly packed, but there's a conservatory for eating out the back so you can pretend you're sitting outside when it's raining, and when the sun does peek through, there's a beer garden. Its got a huge range of Belgian beers, and also does mussels and langoustines among other tasty fare.

Jinty McGuinty's PUB
(Map p806; ☎0141-339 0747; 23 Ashton Lane; ⊙11am-midnight Mon-Sat, 12.30pm-midnight Sun; 📶) Unlike many, there's actually something rather authentically Irish about this place, which has an aged wooden floor, unusual booth seating, a literary hall of fame and a beer garden alongside. There's live music most nights.

☆ Entertainment

Glasgow is Scotland's entertainment city, from classical music, fine theatres and ballet to an amazing range of live-music venues. To tap into the scene, check out *The List* (www.list.co.uk), an invaluable events guide released every four weeks and available at newsagents and bookshops.

For theatre tickets, book directly with the venue. For concerts, a useful booking centre is **Tickets Scotland** (Map p802; ☎0141-204 5151; www.tickets-scotland.com; 237 Argyle St; ⊙9am-6pm Mon-Wed & Fri- Sat, 9am-7pm Thu, 11.30am-5.30pm Sun).

Live Music

Glasgow is the king of Scotland's live-music scene. Year after year, touring musicians and travellers alike name Glasgow one of their favourite cities in the world to enjoy live music. Much of Glasgow's character is encapsulated in the soul and humour of its inhabitants, and the main reason for the city's musical success lies within its audience and the musical community it has bred and nurtured for years.

There are so many venues it's impossible to keep track of them all. For the latest listings, pick up a copy of the *Gig Guide* or check its website (www.gigguide.co.uk). It's available free in most pubs and venues.

One of the city's premier live-music pub venues, the excellent King Tut's Wah Wah Hu hosts bands every night of the week; Oasis were signed after playing here. Classic Grand (p815) and Nice 'n' Sleazy (p815) are also great for live music, and the ABC (p815) is a popular venue.

★ **King Tut's Wah Wah Hut** LIVE MUSIC
(Map p802; ☎0141-221 5279; www.kingtuts.co.uk; 272a St Vincent St; ⊙noon-midnight) One of the city's premier live-music pub venues, hosting bands every night of the week. A staple of the local scene, and a real Glasgow highlight.

Hydro LIVE PERFORMANCE
(Map p806; ☎0141-248 3000; www.thessehydro.com; Finnieston Quay; 📶) Another spectacular modern building to keep the adjacent 'Arma-

dillo' company, the Hydro amphitheatre is a phenomenally popular venue for big-name concerts and shows.

Barrowland Ballroom CONCERT VENUE

(The Barrowlands; Map p802; www.glasgow-barrowland.com; 244 Gallowgate) A down-at-heel but exceptional old dancehall catering for some of the larger acts that visit the city. It's one of Scotland's most atmospheric venues.

Clyde Auditorium LIVE PERFORMANCE

(Map p806; 0844 395 4000; www.secc.co.uk; Finnieston Quay) Also known as the Armadillo because of its bizarre shape, the Clyde adjoins the SECC auditorium, and caters for big national and international acts.

Theatres & Concert Halls

Theatre Royal CONCERT VENUE

(Map p802; 0844 871 7647; www.glasgowtheatreroyal.org.uk; 282 Hope St) Proudly sporting an eyecatching modern facelift, Glasgow's oldest theatre is the home of Scottish Opera and Scottish Ballet.

City Halls & Old Fruitmarket CONCERT VENUE

(Map p802; 0141-353 8000; www.glasgowconcerthalls.com; Candleriggs) In the heart of Merchant City, there are regular performances here by the Scottish Chamber Orchestra and the Scottish Symphony Orchestra. The adjacent Old Fruitmarket venue, a spectacular vaulted space, also has concerts, both classical and rock.

GAY & LESBIAN GLASGOW

Glasgow has a vibrant LGBTIQ scene, with the gay quarter found in and around the Merchant City (particularly Virginia, Wilson and Glassford Sts). The city's gay community has a reputation for being very friendly.

To tap into the scene, check out *The List* (www.list.co.uk) and the free *Scots Gay* (www.scotsgay.co.uk) magazine and website.

Many straight clubs and bars have gay and lesbian nights.

AXM (Map p802; 0141-552 5761; www.axmgroup.co.uk; 80 Glassford St; 11pm-4.30am Sun-Thu, 10am-5.30am Fri & Sat) This popular Manchester club's Glasgow branch is a cheery spot, not too scene-y, with all welcome. It makes for a fun place to finish off a night out.

Delmonica's (Map p802; 0141-552 4803; www.delmonicas.co.uk; 68 Virginia St; noon-1am) In the heart of the Pink Triangle, this is a popular bar with a good mix of ages and orientations. It's packed on weekday evenings, but is a pleasant spot for a quiet drink during the day. Drop in here before heading to the adjacent Polo Lounge, as it often gives out free or cheaper passes.

Underground (Map p802; 0141-553 2456; www.underground-glasgow.com; 6a John St; noon-midnight;) Downstairs on cosmopolitan John St, Underground sports a relaxed crowd and, crucially, a free jukebox. You'll be listening to indie rather than Abba here.

Speakeasy (Map p802; www.speakeasyglasgow.co.uk; 10 John St; 5pm-3am Wed-Sat) Relaxed and friendly bar that starts out pub-like and gets louder with gay anthem DJs as the night progresses. Serves food too, so it's a good all-rounder.

Katie's Bar (Map p802; 0141-237 3030; www.katiesbar.co.uk; 17 John St; noon-midnight;) With an easily missed entrance between a Spanish and an Italian restaurant, this basement space is a friendly LGBT pub with a pool table and regular gigs at weekends. It's a pleasant, low-key space to start off the night and especially popular with women.

Waterloo Bar (Map p802; www.facebook.com/waterloobar1; 306 Argyle St; noon-midnight Fri & Sat, noon-11pm Sun-Thu) This traditional pub is Scotland's oldest gay bar. It attracts punters of all ages. It's very friendly and, with a large group of regulars, a good place to meet people away from the scene.

Polo Lounge (Map p802; www.pologlasgow.co.uk; 84 Wilson St; 11pm-3am Sun-Thu, 10pm-3am Fri, 9pm-3am Sat) This doesn't have the friendliest staff, but it still attracts talent. It's an attractive spot, with opulent furnishings. The downstairs Polo Club and Club X areas still pack out on weekends; just the main bars open on other nights. One of them, the Riding Room, has cabaret shows.

Glasgow Royal Concert Hall CONCERT VENUE
(Map p802; ☎0141-353 8000; www.glasgowconcerthalls.com; 2 Sauchiehall St;) A feast of classical music is showcased at this concert hall, the modern home of the Royal Scottish National Orchestra. There are also regular pop, folk and jazz performances, typically by big-name solo artists.

Citizens' Theatre THEATRE
(☎0141-429 0022; www.citz.co.uk; 119 Gorbals St) South of the Clyde, this is one of the top theatres in Scotland. It's well worth trying to catch a performance here.

Sport

Two football clubs – **Rangers** (☎0871 702 1972; www.rangers.co.uk; Ibrox Stadium, 150 Edmiston Dr) and **Celtic** (☎0871 226 1888; www.celticfc.net; Celtic Park, Parkhead) – dominate the sporting scene in Scotland, having vastly more resources than other clubs and a long history (and rivalry). This runs along partisan lines, with Rangers representing Protestant supporters, and Celtic, Catholic. It's worth going to a game; both play in magnificent arenas with great atmosphere. Games between the two (normally four a year) are fiercely contested, but tickets aren't sold to the general public; you'll need to know a season-ticket holder. In recent years, Rangers have had to work their way back up the divisions after a financial meltdown, arriving back in the top flight in 2016.

Shopping

Boasting the UK's largest retail phalanx outside London, Glasgow is a shopaholic's paradise. The 'Style Mile' around Buchanan St, Argyle St and Merchant City (particularly upmarket Ingram St) is a fashion hub, while the West End has quirkier, more bohemian shopping options: Byres Rd is great for vintage clothing.

Barras MARKET
(Map p802; www.glasgow-barrowland.com; btwn Gallowgate & London Rd; ⏲10am-5pm Sat & Sun) At Glasgow's legendary weekend flea market, the Barras on Gallowgate, cheap tat rules the roost these days. But it's still an intriguing stroll, as much for the assortment of local characters as what's on offer. People come here just for a wander, and it's got a real feel of a nearly vanished Britain of whelk stalls and rag-and-bone merchants. Watch your wallet.

Information

The List (www.list.co.uk) Available from newsagents, this is Glasgow and Edinburgh's invaluable guide to films, theatre, cabaret, music and clubs, released every four weeks. The excellent *Eating & Drinking Guide*, published by the *List* every second April, covers both Glasgow and Edinburgh.

INTERNET ACCESS

There's a free wi-fi zone across the city centre (network: GlasgowCC Wifi). You can get a local SIM card for about a pound and data packages are cheap.

Gallery of Modern Art (☎0141-229 1996; Royal Exchange Sq; ⏲10am-5pm Mon-Thu & Sat, 11am-5pm Fri & Sun;) Basement library; free internet access. Bookings recommended.

Hillhead Library (☎0141-276 1617; www.glasgowlife.org.uk; 348 Byres Rd; ⏲10am-8pm Mon-Thu, 10am-5pm Fri & Sat, noon-5pm Sun;) Free internet terminals.

iCafe (www.icafe.uk.com; 250 Woodlands Rd; per hr £2.50; ⏲8.30am-9.30pm;) Sip a coffee and munch on a pastry while you check your emails on super-fast connections. Wi-fi too. It's actually a very good cafe in its own right. There are other branches, including one on **Sauchiehall St** (www.icafe.uk.com; 315 Sauchiehall St; ⏲7am-10pm Mon-Fri, 8am-10pm Sat & Sun;).

Mitchell Library (☎0141-287 2999; www.glasgowlife.org.uk; North St; ⏲9am-8pm Mon-Thu, 9am-5pm Fri & Sat) Free internet access; bookings recommended.

Yeeha Internet Cafe (www.yeeha-internet-cafe.co.uk; 48 West George St; per hr £2.50; ⏲9.30am-6pm Mon-Fri, 10am-6pm Sat) Upstairs location in the heart of the city.

MEDICAL SERVICES

Glasgow Dental Hospital (☎0141-211 9600; www.nhsggc.org.uk; 378 Sauchiehall St)

Glasgow Royal Infirmary (☎0141-211 4000; www.nhsggc.org.uk; 84 Castle St) Medical emergencies and outpatient facilities.

Queen Elizabeth University Hospital (☎0141-201 1100; www.nhsggc.org.uk; 1345 Govan Rd) Modern; south of the river.

TOURIST INFORMATION

Glasgow Information Centre (p805) In the Gallery of Modern Art.

Glasgow Airport Information Centre (☎0141-566 4089; www.visitscotland.com; Glasgow International Airport; ⏲7.30am-5pm Mon-Sat, 8am-3.30pm Sun)

Getting There & Away

AIR

Glasgow International Airport (GLA; 0844 481 5555; www.glasgowairport.com;) Ten miles west of the city. Handles international and domestic flights.

Glasgow Prestwick Airport (PIK; 0871 223 0700; www.glasgowprestwick.com) Thirty miles southwest of Glasgow. Used by Ryanair and some other budget airlines, with connections mostly to southern Europe.

BUS

All long-distance buses arrive at and depart from **Buchanan bus station** (Map p802; 0141-333 3708; www.spt.co.uk; Killermont St;), which has pricey lockers, ATMs and wi-fi.

Megabus (0141-352 4444; www.megabus.com) Your first port of call if you're looking for the cheapest fare. Megabus offers very cheap demand-dependent prices on many major bus routes, including to Edinburgh and London.

National Express (0871 781 8181; www.nationalexpress.com) Also runs daily to several English cities.

Scottish Citylink (0871 266 3333; www.citylink.co.uk) Has buses to Edinburgh (£7.50, 1¼ hours, every 15 minutes) and most major towns in Scotland.

TRAIN

As a general rule, Glasgow Central station serves southern Scotland, England and Wales, and Queen Street station serves the north and east. Buses run between the two stations every 10 minutes. There are direct trains to London's Euston station; they're much quicker (advance purchase single £62, full fare off-peak/peak £134/183, 4½ hours, more than hourly) and more comfortable than the bus.

Scotrail (p795) runs Scottish trains. Destinations include the following:

Aberdeen £39.60, 2½ to 3½ hours, hourly

Dundee £22, 1½ hours, hourly

Edinburgh £13.60, 50 minutes, every 15 minutes

Fort William £29.20, 3¾ hours, four to five daily

Inverness £87.70, 3½ to four hours, 10 daily (four on Sunday)

Oban £23.90, three hours, three to six daily

Getting Around

TO/FROM THE AIRPORT

There are buses every 10 or 15 minutes from Glasgow International Airport to Buchanan bus station via Central and Queen Street train stations (single/return £7/9.50, 25 minutes). This is a 24-hour service. You can include a day ticket on the bus network for £9 total.

Another bus, the 747, covers the same route via Finnieston and Kelvingrove, taking longer (£5).

A taxi costs around £25.

There are also buses from Buchanan bus station direct to/from Edinburgh Airport (£11.40, one hour, half-hourly).

BICYCLE

The **Nextbike** (www.nextbike.co.uk, per 30min £1) citybike scheme is easy; download the app for the most convenient use.

There are several places to hire a bike; the **tourist office** (p805) has a full list.

Bike Station (0141-248 5409; www.thebikestation.org.uk; 65 Haugh Rd; half-day/day/wk £15/20/70; 9am-5pm Mon-Sat, to 8pm Wed)

Gear Bikes (0141-339 1179; www.gearbikes.com; 19 Gibson St; half-day/1 day/3 days/wk £15/20/40/70; 10am-6pm Mon-Sat, noon-5pm Sun)

CAR & MOTORCYCLE

The most difficult thing about driving in Glasgow is the sometimes-confusing one-way system. For short-term parking (up to two hours), you've got a decent chance of finding something on the street, paying at the meters, which cost up to £4 per hour. Otherwise, multistorey car parks are probably your best bet and are not so expensive. Ask your hotel in advance if they offer parking discounts.

There are numerous car-rental companies; both big names and discount operators have airport offices.

Arnold Clark (0141-423 9559; www.arnoldclarkrental.com; 43 Allison St; 8am-5.30pm Mon-Fri, 8am-4pm Sat, 11am-4pm Sun)

Avis (0844 544 6064; www.avis.co.uk; 70 Lancefield St; 8am-6pm Mon-Fri, 8am-1pm Sat, 10am-2pm Sun)

Europcar (0141-204 1280; www.europcar.co.uk; 76 Lancefield Quay; 8am-6pm Mon-Fri, 8am-4pm Sat)

Enterprise (0141-221 2124; www.enterprise.co.uk; 40 Oswald St; 7am-9pm Mon-Fri, 8am-4pm Sat, 10am-3pm Sun)

Hertz (0849 309 3032; www.hertz.co.uk; 138 Hydepark St; 8am-6pm Mon-Fri, 8am-1pm Sat)

PUBLIC TRANSPORT

Public transport in and around Glasgow is co-ordinated by SPT (www.spt.co.uk).

Bus City bus services, mostly run by **First Glasgow** (0141-420 7600; www.firstglasgow.com), are frequent. You can buy tickets when you board buses, but on most you must have the exact change. Short journeys in town cost £1.40 or £2.15; a day ticket (£4.50) is good value and is valid until 1am, when a night network starts. A weekly ticket is £15.50. Check route maps online at www.spt.co.uk.

Train & Underground There's an extensive suburban network of trains in and around Glasgow; tickets should be bought before travel if the station is staffed, or from the conductor if it isn't. There's also an underground line, the Subway, that serves 15 stations in the centre, west and south of the city (single £1.60). The train network connects with the Subway at Buchanan St underground station, next to Queen St overground station, and St Enoch underground station, near Central railway station. The All Day Ticket (£4) gives unlimited travel on the Subway for a day, while the Roundabout ticket gives a day's unlimited train and Subway travel for £6.60. The subway annoyingly shuts down at around 6pm on a Sunday.

Combined Ticket The Daytripper ticket gives you a day's unlimited travel on buses, the Subway, rail and some ferries in the Glasgow region, including Loch Lomond, Ayrshire and Lanarkshire. It costs £11.60 for one adult or £20.50 for two. Two kids per adult are included free.

TAXI

There's no shortage of taxis, and if you want to know anything about Glasgow, striking up a conversation with a cabbie is a good place to start. Fares are very reasonable – you can get across the centre for around £6, and there's no surcharge for calling a taxi. You can pay by credit card with **Glasgow Taxis** (☎ 0141-429 7070; www.glasgowtaxis.co.uk) if you order by phone; most of its taxis are wheelchair accessible. Download its app to make booking easy.

LANARK & NEW LANARK

POP 8900

Below the market town of Lanark, in an attractive gorge by the River Clyde, is the World Heritage Site of New Lanark – an intriguing collection of restored mill buildings and warehouses.

Once Britain's largest cotton-spinning complex, it is better known for the pioneering social experiments of Robert Owen, who managed the mill from 1800. New Lanark is really a memorial to this enlightened capitalist. He provided his workers with housing, a cooperative store, the world's first nursery school, adult-education classes, a sick-pay fund for workers and a social centre he called the New Institute for the Formation of Character. Devote half a day to exploring this site as there's plenty to see and do, including appealing walks along the riverside. What must once have been a thriving, noisy, industrial village is now a peaceful oasis with only the swishing of trees and the rushing of the River Clyde to be heard.

Sights & Activities

★New Lanark Visitor Centre MUSEUM
(☎ 01555-661345; www.newlanark.org; adult/child/family £9.50/7/30; ⏰ 10am-5pm Apr-Oct, 10am-4pm Nov-Mar) The main attractions of this World Heritage mill town are accessed via a single ticket. These include a huge working spinning mule, producing woollen yarn, and the **Historic Schoolhouse**, which contains an innovative, high-tech journey to New Lanark's past via a 3D hologram of the spirit of Annie McLeod, a 10-year-old mill girl who describes life here in 1820. The kids will love it as it's very realistic, although the 'do good for all mankind' theme is a little overbearing.

★Falls of Clyde WALKING
From New Lanark, you can walk through the beautiful nature reserve up to **Corra Linn** (0.75 miles) and **Bonnington Linn** (1½ miles), two of the Falls of Clyde that inspired Turner and Wordsworth. You could return via the muddier path on the opposite bank, pass New Lanark and cross the river further downstream to make a circular walk of it (3 miles).

Sleeping

Wee Row Hostel HOSTEL $
(☎ 01555-666710; www.newlanarkhostel.co.uk; Rosedale St, New Lanark; s/tw £49/59; P @ 🛜) This hostel has a great location in an old mill building in the heart of the New Lanark complex. It has comfortable en suite rooms with both beds and bunks and a really good downstairs common area. Prices come down substantially outside high season. Dorm rates (£16 to £18) may be offered subject to availability. Closed between 11am and 3pm.

New Lanark Mill Hotel HOTEL $$
(☎ 01555-667200; www.newlanarkmillhotel.co.uk; New Lanark; r £107-125; P @ 🛜 ≋ 🐾) Cleverly converted from an 18th-century mill, this hotel is full of character and is a stone's throw from the major attractions. It has luxury rooms (only a little extra for a spacious superior room), with contemporary art on the walls and views of the churning Clyde

below. It also has self-catering accommodation in charming cottages.

Information

Lanark Tourist Office (01555-668249; www.visitscotland.com; 18 Ladyacre Rd; 10am-5pm Mon-Fri year-round, plus 10am-5pm Sat & Sun Apr-Oct) Close to the bus and train stations.

Getting There & Around

Lanark is 25 miles southeast of Glasgow. Express bus 240X runs hourly Monday to Saturday (£6.20, one hour); trains from Glasgow Central also run (£6.90, 55 minutes, every 30 minutes, hourly on Sundays).

It's a pleasant walk to New Lanark, but there's also a half-hourly bus service from the train station (daily). If you need a taxi, call **Clydewide** (0800-050 9264; www.clydewidetaxis.co.uk).

BORDERS REGION

The Borders has had a rough history: centuries of war and plunder have left a battle-scarred landscape, encapsulated by the magnificent ruins of the Border abbeys. Their wealth was an irresistible magnet during cross-frontier wars, and they were destroyed and rebuilt numerous times. Today these massive stone shells are the region's finest attraction.

But the Borders is also genteel. Welcoming villages with ancient traditions pepper the countryside and grandiose mansions await exploration. It's fine walking and cycling country too.

Peebles

POP 8600

With a picturesque main street set on a ridge between the River Tweed and the Eddleston Water, Peebles is one of the most handsome of the Border towns. Though it lacks a major sight, the agreeable atmosphere and good walking options in the rolling, wooded hills thereabouts will entice you to linger for a couple of days.

Activities

The riverside walk along the River Tweed has plenty of grassed areas ideal for a picnic, and there's a children's playground (near the main road bridge).

Nearby in Glentress forest is the busiest of the 7stanes mountain-biking **hubs** (www.7stanesmountainbiking.com) FREE, as well as osprey viewing and marked walking trails. There are also swing and zip-line **forest routes** (www.goape.co.uk; Glentress Forest; adult/child £33/25; Feb-Nov), not to mention **camping huts** (www.glentressforestlodges.co.uk). In town, you can hire bikes to explore the region from **Bspoke Cycles** (01721-723423; www.bspokepeebles.co.uk; Old Tweeddale Garage, Innerleithen Rd; bikes per day from £25; 9am-5.30pm Mon-Sat).

There are further mountain-biking trails at Innerleithen, 7 miles east of Peebles.

Sleeping & Eating

Tontine Hotel HOTEL $$
(01721-720892; www.tontinehotel.com; High St; s £60, d £110-120; P) Right in the heart of things, this is a bastion of Borders hospitality. Refurbished rooms have high comfort levels, modish colours and top-notch bathrooms, while service couldn't be more helpful. There's a small supplement for rooms with four-poster beds and/or river views. There are also a good restaurant and bar here. It's in the heart of town.

Rowanbrae B&B $$
(01721-721630; www.aboutscotland.co.uk/peebles/rowanbrae.html; 103 Northgate; s/d £45/68;) In a quiet cul-de-sac but not far from the main street, this hospitable spot treats its guests like family friends. The traditional old building has modern comforts but retains a pleasant, comfortably old-fashioned feel; there are three upstairs bedrooms, two of them en suite, and a commodious guest lounge for relaxation.

Cocoa Black CAFE $
(01721-721662; www.cocoablack.com; 1 Cuddy Bridge; sweets £1.50-3; 9.30am-5pm Mon-Fri, 9am-5pm Sat, 10.30am-4pm Sun;) Chocaholics should make a beeline for this friendly cafe, where exquisite cakes and other patisserie offerings will satisfy any cacao-focused cravings. It also runs a school where you can learn to make them yourself.

★**Coltman's** BISTRO, DELI $$
(01721-720405; www.coltmans.co.uk; 71 High St; mains £11-19; 10am-5pm Sun-Wed, 10am-10pm Thu-Sat;) This main street deli has numerous temptations, such as excellent cheeses and Italian smallgoods, as well as perhaps Scotland's tastiest sausage roll – buy two to avoid the walk back for another one. Behind the shop, the good-looking dining

area serves up confident bistro fare and light snacks with a variety of culinary influences, using top-notch local ingredients.

Information

Peebles Tourist Office (01721-728095; www.visitscottishborders.com; 23 High St; 9am-5pm Mon-Sat, 11am-4pm Sun) Closed Sundays from January to March. Open until 5.30pm mid-June to August.

Getting There & Away

The bus stop is beside the post office on Eastgate. Bus 62A/X62 runs half-hourly (hourly on Sundays) to Edinburgh (£5.20, 1¼ hours). In the other direction it heads for Galashiels, where you can change for Melrose (£6, some through services).

Melrose

POP 2500

Tiny, charming Melrose is a polished village running on the well-greased wheels of tourism. Sitting at the feet of the three heather-covered Eildon Hills, Melrose has a classic market square and one of the great abbey ruins. Just outside town is Abbotsford (opposite), the home of Sir Walter Scott, which makes another superb visit.

Sights

★**Melrose Abbey** RUINS
(HES; 01896-822562; www.historicenvironment.scot; adult/child £5.50/3.30; 9.30am-5.30pm Apr-Sep, 10am-4pm Oct-Mar) Perhaps the most interesting of the Border abbeys, red-sandstone Melrose was repeatedly destroyed by the English in the 14th century. The remaining broken shell is pure Gothic and the ruins are famous for their decorative stonework – look out for the pig gargoyle playing the bagpipes. Though Melrose had a monastery way back in the 7th century, this abbey was founded by David I in 1136 for Cistercian monks, and later rebuilt by Robert the Bruce, whose heart is buried here.

Festivals & Events

Melrose Rugby Sevens SPORTS
(www.melrose7s.com; mid-Apr) Rugby followers fill the town to see this famous one-day sevens competition.

Sleeping & Eating

★**Old Bank House** B&B $$
(01896-823712; www.oldbankhousemelrose.co.uk; 27 Buccleuch St; s/d £50/75;) Right in the centre, this is a superb B&B in a charming old building. The owner's artistic touch is evident throughout, from walls covered with paintings, some his own, to a house full of curios and tasteful art nouveau features, and a sumptuous breakfast room. Rooms are spacious with comfortable furniture and top modern bathrooms; they are complemented by a generous can-do attitude. It goes the extra mile, and that makes it a great Borders base.

★**The Townhouse** HOTEL $$$
(01896-822645; www.thetownhousemelrose.co.uk; Market Sq; s/d/superior d £95/132/149;) The classy Townhouse exudes warmth and professionalism, and has some of the best rooms in town, tastefully furnished with attention to detail. The superior rooms are enormous in size with lavish furnishings and excellent en suites, some with Jacuzzi. Standard rooms are a fair bit smaller but recently refurbished and very comfortable. It's well worth the price.

Russell's CAFE $
(28 Market Sq; light meals £6-10; 9.30am-5pm Tue-Sat) Solid wooden furniture and big windows looking out over the centre of Melrose make this stylish little tearoom a popular option. It has a large range of snacks and some more substantial lunch offerings, with daily specials. It's famous throughout the Borders for its excellent scones. New owners were refurbishing at time of last research.

The Townhouse SCOTTISH $$
(01896-822645; www.thetownhousemelrose.co.uk; Market Sq; mains £13-19; noon-2pm & 6-9pm Sun-Thu, noon-2pm & 6-9.30pm Fri & Sat;) The brasserie and restaurant here turn out just about the best gourmet cuisine in town and offer decent value. There's some rich, elaborate, beautifully presented fare here, with plenty of venison and other game choices, but for a lighter feed you can always opt for the range of lunchtime sandwiches.

Information

Melrose Tourist Office (01896-820178; www.visitscottishborders.com; Abbey St; 10am-5pm Mon-Sat, 1-5pm Sun Apr-Oct) Located by the abbey.

Getting There & Away

The reopened Borders Railway runs from Edinburgh to Tweedbank (£10.10, one hour, half-hourly), which is 1½ miles from Melrose. Some buses run from here to Melrose, but check

DON'T MISS

TRAQUAIR HOUSE

One of Scotland's great country houses, **Traquair House** (☎01896-830323; www.traquair.co.uk; adult/child/family £8.70/4.40/24; ⏲11am-5pm Easter-Sep, 11am-4pm Oct, 11am-3pm Sat & Sun Nov) has a powerful, ethereal beauty, and exploring it is like time travel. Odd, sloping floors and a musty odour bestow a genuine feel, and parts of the building are believed to have been constructed long before the first official record of its existence in 1107. The massive tower house was gradually expanded but has remained virtually unchanged since the 17th century. Traquair is 1.5 miles south of Innerleithen, about 6 miles southeast of Peebles.

Since the 15th century, the house has belonged to various branches of the Stuart family, and the family's unwavering Catholicism and loyalty to the Stuart cause led to famous visitors like Mary, Queen of Scots and Bonnie Prince Charlie, but also to numerous problems after the deposal of James II of England in 1688. The family's estate, wealth and influence were gradually whittled away, as life as a Jacobite became a furtive, clandestine affair.

One of Traquair's most interesting places is the concealed room where priests secretly lived and performed Mass – up until 1829 when the Catholic Emancipation Act was finally passed. Other beautiful, time-worn rooms hold fascinating relics, including the cradle used by Mary for her son, James VI of Scotland (who also became James I of England), and fascinating letters from the Jacobite Earls of Traquair and their families, including one particularly moving one written from death row in the Tower of London.

The main gates to the house were locked by one earl in the 18th century until the day a Stuart king reclaimed the throne in London, so meanwhile you'll have to enter by a side gate. In addition to the house, there's a garden **maze**, a small **brewery** producing the tasty Bear Ale, and a series of **craft workshops**.

Bus 62 runs from Edinburgh via Peebles to Innerleithen and on to Galashiels and Melrose.

with Traveline Scotland (www.travelinescotland.com) first, as there may be a faster connection if you get off the train in nearby Galashiels. Otherwise a taxi into Melrose is inexpensive.

Buses run to/from Galashiels, which has bus connections to Edinburgh (£7.20, 1½ to two hours, hourly) and other Borders destinations.

Around Melrose

In the vicinity of Melrose are a couple of excellent attractions intimately connected with Sir Walter Scott.

★Abbotsford HISTORIC BUILDING
(☎01896-752043; www.scottsabbotsford.com; visitor centre free, house adult/child £8.95/4.50; ⏲10am-5pm Apr-Oct, 10am-4pm Nov-Mar, house closed Dec-Feb) Just outside Melrose, this is where to discover the life and works of Sir Walter Scott, to whom we arguably owe both the modern novel and our mind's-eye view of Scotland. This whimsical, fabulous house where he lived – and which ruined him when his publishers went bust – really brings this 19th-century writer to life. The grounds on the banks of the Tweed are lovely, and Scott drew much inspiration from rambles in the surrounding countryside.

★Dryburgh Abbey RUINS
(HES; ☎01835-822381; www.historicenvironment.scot; adult/child £5.50/3.30; ⏲9.30am-5.30pm Apr-Sep, 10am-4pm Oct-Mar) This is the most beautiful and complete of the Border abbeys, partly because the neighbouring town of Dryburgh no longer exists (a victim of the wars) and partly because of its lovely site by the Tweed in a sheltered valley. Dating from about 1150, the abbey belonged to the Premonstratensians, a religious order founded in France, and evokes 12th-century monastic life more successfully than its nearby counterparts. The pink-hued stone ruins are the burial place of Sir Walter Scott.

Jedburgh

POP 4000

Attractive Jedburgh, where many old buildings and wynds (narrow alleys) have been intelligently restored, invites exploration by foot. It's centred on the noble skeleton of its ruined abbey.

WORTH A TRIP

HERMITAGE CASTLE

The 'guardhouse of the bloodiest valley in Britain', **Hermitage Castle** (HES; www.historicenvironment.scot; adult/child £4.50/2.70; ⌚9.30am-5.30pm Apr-Sep) embodies the brutal history of the Scottish Borders. Desolate but proud with its massive squared stone walls, it looks more like a lair for orc raiding parties than a home for Scottish nobility, and is one of the bleakest and most stirring of Scottish ruins. The castle is about 12 miles south of Hawick on the B6357.

Sights

★Jedburgh Abbey RUINS
(HES; www.historicenvironment.scot; Abbey Rd; adult/child £5.50/3.30; ⌚9.30am-5.30pm Apr-Sep, 10am-4pm Oct-Mar) Dominating the town skyline, this was the first of the great Border abbeys to be passed into state care, and it shows – audio and visual presentations telling the abbey's story are scattered throughout the carefully preserved ruins (good for the kids). The red-sandstone ruins are roofless but relatively intact, and the ingenuity of the master mason can be seen in some of the rich (if somewhat faded) stone carvings in the nave.

Mary, Queen of Scots' Visitor Centre HISTORIC BUILDING
(Queen St; ⌚9.30am-4.30pm Mon-Sat, 10.30am-4pm Sun Mar-Nov) FREE Mary stayed at this beautiful 16th-century tower house in 1566 after her famous ride to visit the injured earl of Bothwell, her future husband, at Hermitage Castle. The interesting exhibition evokes the sad saga of Mary's life and death. Various objects associated with her – including a lock of her hair – are on display.

Sleeping & Eating

Maplebank B&B $
(☎01835-862051; maplebank3@btinternet.com; 3 Smiths Wynd; s/d £30/50; P 📶 🐾) It's very pleasing to come across places like this, where it really feels like you're staying in someone's home. Here, that someone is like your favourite aunt: friendly, chaotic and generous. There's lots of clutter and it's very informal. Rooms are comfortable and large, sharing a good bathroom. Breakfast (including fruit, yoghurts and homemade jams) is brilliant – better than at most posher places.

Willow Court B&B $$
(☎01835-863702; www.willowcourtjedburgh.co.uk; the Friars; s/d £75/86; P 📶) It seems inadequate to call this impressive option a B&B; it's more like a boutique hotel. Impeccable rooms with elegant wallpaper, showroom bathrooms and great beds are complemented by a courteous, professional welcome. Every time we visit it's been improved in some way: the sign of a standout establishment. The conservatory lounge is great for admiring the views over garden and town.

Capon Tree SCOTTISH $$
(☎01835-869596; www.thecapontree.com; 61 High St; mains £13-19; ⌚noon-2.30pm & 6-9pm Tue-Sat year-round, daily Jun-Aug; 📶) Attractively combining smart and casual, this welcoming bistro and bar does modern Scottish cuisine. Plates are beautifully, though not fussily, presented and ingredients are of high quality. A couple of flavour combinations don't work so well, but the overall package is appealing, the service good and the ambience romantic. There are handsome rooms available too.

Information

There's a free wi-fi zone around the centre, which is strongest around the tourist office.

Jedburgh Library (☎01835-863592; www.scotborders.gov.uk; Castlegate; ⌚10am-1pm & 2-5pm Mon & Thu, 2-7pm Tue, 10am-3pm Fri, 9.30am-12.30pm Sat) Free internet.

Jedburgh Tourist Office (☎01835-863170; www.visitscotland.com; Murray's Green; ⌚9am-5.30pm Mon-Sat, 10am-5pm Sun Apr-Oct, 10am-4pm Mon-Sat Nov-Mar; 📶) Head tourist office for the Borders region. Very helpful.

Getting There & Away

Jedburgh has good bus connections to Hawick, Melrose and Kelso (all around 25 minutes, roughly hourly, two-hourly on Sunday). Buses also run to Edinburgh (£7.30, two hours, three to six daily).

Kelso

POP 5600

Kelso, a prosperous market town with a broad, cobbled square flanked by Georgian buildings, has a cheery feel and historic appeal. During the day it's a busy little place, but after 8pm you'll have the streets to yourself. The town has a lovely site at the junction of the Tweed and Teviot, and is one of the most enjoyable places in the Borders.

Sights

Floors Castle HISTORIC BUILDING
(01573-223333; www.floorscastle.com; adult/child castle & grounds £8.50/4.50, incl gardens £12.50/6.50; 10.30am-5pm mid-Apr–mid-Oct) Grandiose Floors Castle is Scotland's largest inhabited mansion, home to the Duke of Roxburghe, and overlooks the Tweed about a mile west of Kelso. Built by William Adam in the 1720s, the original Georgian simplicity was 'improved' in the 1840s with the addition of rather ridiculous battlements and turrets. Inside, view the vivid colours of the 17th-century Brussels tapestries in the drawing room and the intricate oak carvings in the ornate ballroom. The impressive walled garden is entered by a separate ticket.

Kelso Abbey RUINS
(HES; www.historicenvironment.scot; Bridge St; 9.30am-5.30pm Apr Sep, 9.30am-4.30pm Sat-Wed Oct-Mar) FREE Once one of the richest abbeys in southern Scotland, Kelso Abbey was built by the Tironensians, an order founded in Picardy and brought to the Borders around 1113 by David I. English raids in the 16th century reduced it to ruins, though what little remains today is some of the finest Romanesque architecture in Scotland.

Sleeping

★ **Edenbank House** B&B $$
(01573-226734; www.edenbank.co.uk; Stichill Rd; s/d £50/80; P) Half-a-mile down the Stichill road, this grand Victorian house sits in spacious grounds where only bleating lambs in the green fields and birds in the garden break the silence. It's a fabulous place, with huge opulent rooms, lovely views over the fields, and incredibly warm, generous hospitality. Breakfast features homemade produce, and a laissez-faire attitude makes for an utterly relaxing stay.

Don't just show up: call ahead.

★ **Old Priory** B&B $$
(01573-223030; www.theoldpriorykelso.com; 33 Woodmarket; s/d £55/85; P) Fantastic rooms here are allied with numerous personal details – the operators turn down the beds at night and make you feel very welcome. Doubles are top-notch and the family room really excellent. The good news extends to the garden – perfect for a coffee in the morning – and a comfortable conservatory lounge. The huge windows flood the rooms with natural light. Top-class B&B.

Inglestone House B&B $$
(01573-225800; www.inglestonehouse.co.uk; Abbey Row; s/d/f £55/80/120;) The Northumbrian owners here are welcoming and very cordial but also leave you space for yourself, giving this spot behind the main street an appealing blend of hotel and guesthouse. Rooms are a good size with firm mattresses and – unusually for the Borders – the wi-fi is fast.

Eating & Drinking

★ **Cobbles** BISTRO $$
(01573-223548; www.thecobbleskelso.co.uk; 7 Bowmont St; mains £10-17; food noon-2.30pm & 5.45-9pm Mon-Fri, noon-9pm Sat, noon-8pm Sun;) This inn off the main square is so popular you will need to book a table at weekends. It's cheery, very welcoming and warm, and serves excellent upmarket pub food in generous portions. Pick and mix from bar menu, steaks and gourmet options. Leave room for cheese and/or dessert. The bar's own microbrewed ales are excellent. A cracking place.

★ **Rutherfords** PUB
(07803-208460; www.rutherfordsmicropub.co.uk; 38 The Square; 4-9pm Mon, noon-9pm Tue-Thu & Sun, noon-10pm Fri & Sat) This enchanting small bar prioritises conversation and has no TV or music. It's a charming place with gin on tap poured through a microscope, carefully selected craft beers and spirits, and a warm, convivial atmosphere.

WORTH A TRIP

SMAILHOLM TOWER

Perched on a rocky knoll above a small lake, **Smailholm Tower** (HES; www.historicenvironment.scot; adult/child £4.50/2.70; 9.30am-5.30pm Sat & Sun Apr-Sep), a narrow stone tower, provides one of the most evocative sights in the Borders and keeps its bloody history alive. Although displays inside are sparse, the panoramic view from the top is worth the climb. The tower is 6 miles west of Kelso, a mile south of Smailholm village on the B6397.

Information

Kelso Tourist Office (☎01573-221119; www.visitscottishborders.com; The Square; ⊙10am-3.30pm Mon-Sat Apr-Oct, to 5pm plus 10am-2pm Sun mid-Jun–Aug) In the town hall building.

Getting There & Away

There are six daily direct bus services to Edinburgh (£7.30, two hours, one to two on Sunday) and regular routes to other Borders towns and Berwick-upon-Tweed.

AYRSHIRE

Ayrshire is synonymous with golf and Robert Burns – and there's plenty on offer here to satisfy both of these pursuits. Troon and Turnberry have world-famous courses, and there's enough Burns memorabilia in the region to satisfy even his most fanatical admirers.

The best way to appreciate the Ayrshire coastline is on foot: the **Ayrshire Coastal Path** (www.ayrshirecoastalpath.org;) offers 100 miles of spectacular waterside walking.

Ayr

POP 46,710

Ayr's long sandy beach has made it a popular family seaside resort since Victorian times, but it has struggled in the recent economic climate. Parts of the centre have a neglected air, though there are many fine Georgian and Victorian buildings, and it makes a convenient base for exploring this section of coast. The huge drawcard is Alloway, 3 miles south, with its Robert Burns heritage. Most things to see in Ayr are also Robert Burns–related.

Sights

Auld Brig BRIDGE

(Old Bridge) Several of Burns' poems are set here in Ayr; in *Twa Brigs,* Ayr's old and new bridges argue with one another. The Auld Brig was built in 1491 and spans the river just north of the church.

Auld Kirk CHURCH

(Old Church; www.auldkirk.org; Blackfriars Walk; ⊙1-2pm Tue Mar-Jun & Sep-Nov, 10.30am-12.30pm Sat Jul & Aug) FREE Robert Burns was baptised in the Auld Kirk (Old Church). The atmospheric cemetery here overlooks the river and is good for a stroll, offering an escape from the bustle of High St.

Sleeping & Eating

26 The Crescent B&B $$

(☎01292-287329; www.26crescent.co.uk; 26 Bellevue Cres; d £70-97;) When the blossoms are out, this is Ayr's prettiest street, and it boasts an excellent place to stay. The rooms are impeccable – an upgrade to the spacious four-poster room is a sound investment. Bathrooms are excellent. Though there's more space on the 1st floor, we like the top-floor chambers with sloping roof. The welcome is genuinely friendly.

XXII BISTRO $$

(No 22 Bar & Grill; ☎01292-280820; www.22ayr.com; 22 Beresford Tce; mains £9-16; ⊙food 9am-9.30pm;) Buzzy and attractive, this serves a wide-ranging fusion menu as well as cocktails, breakfasts and more. Mediterranean and, particularly, Italian influences take pride of place, backed up by things like tempura and steaks. It's very hit-and-miss but outranks the local competition: not a tough task. There's a wide choice of wines by the glass.

Information

Ayr Tourist Office (☎01292-290300; www.ayrshire-arran.com; 22 Sandgate; ⊙9am-5pm Mon-Sat year-round, plus 10am-5pm Sun Apr-Sep;) In the centre.

Getting There & Away

BUS

Ayr is 33 miles from Glasgow and is Ayrshire's major transport hub. There are frequent express services to Glasgow (£6.20, 50 minutes to one hour) via Prestwick Airport, as well as services to Stranraer (£8.60, two hours, four to eight per day) and several Ayrshire towns. The bus station sits at the corner of Fullarton St and Sandgate.

TRAIN

There are at least two trains an hour that run between Ayr and Glasgow Central station (£8.30, 55 minutes), and some trains continue south from Ayr to Stranraer (£10.90, 1½ hours).

Alloway

POP 6100

The pretty, lush village of Alloway (3 miles south of Ayr) should be on the itinerary of every Robert Burns fan – he was born here on 25 January 1759. Even if you haven't been seduced by Burnsmania, it's still well worth a visit, as the Burns-related exhibitions give a good impression of life in Ayrshire in the late 18th century.

Bus 361 runs hourly between Alloway and Ayr (£1.85, six minutes). The X77 runs direct here from Glasgow via Prestwick airport and Ayr. Otherwise walk or cycle here from Ayr.

★ Robert Burns Birthplace Museum MUSEUM

(NTS; ☎0844-493 2601; www.burnsmuseum.org.uk; Murdoch's Lone; adult/child £9/7; ⏲10am-5pm Oct-Mar, to 5.30pm Apr-Sep, closed Christmas-early Jan) This impressive museum has collected a solid range of Burns memorabilia, including manuscripts and possessions of the poet, like the pistols he packed for his daily work as a taxman. There's good biographical information, and a series of displays that bring to life individual poems via background snippets, translations and recitations. Appropriately, the museum doesn't take itself too seriously: there's plenty of humour that the poet surely would have approved of, and entertaining audio and visual performances will keep the kids amused.

The admission ticket also covers the atmospheric **Burns Cottage**, connected via a walkway to the Birthplace Museum. Born in the little box-bed in this cramped thatched dwelling, the poet spent the first seven years of his life here. It's an attractive display that gives you a context for reading plenty of his verse. Much-needed translation of some of the more obscure Scots farming terms he loved to use decorate the walls.

Alloway Auld Kirk RUIN, CHURCH

(Monument Rd; ⏲24hr) FREE Near the Robert Burns Birthplace Museum are the ruins of the kirk, the setting for part of Burns' verse tale 'Tam o' Shanter'. Burns' father, William, is buried in the kirkyard; read the poem on the back of the gravestone.

Burns Monument & Memorial Gardens GARDENS

(⏲24hr) FREE Within these gardens near the Robert Burns Birthplace Museum is a striking neo-Grecian monument to the poet, completed in 1823. It affords a view of the nearby 13th-century Brig o' Doon, another Burns landmark.

THE SCOTTISH BARD

Best remembered for penning the words of 'Auld Lang Syne', Robert Burns (1759–96) is Scotland's most famous poet and a popular hero; his birthday (25 January) is celebrated as Burns Night by Scots around the world.

Burns was born in Alloway to a poor family, who scraped a living gardening and farming. At school he soon showed an aptitude for literature and a fondness for the folk song. He later began writing his own songs and satires. When the problems of his arduous farming life were compounded by the threat of prosecution from the father of Jean Armour, with whom he'd had an affair, he decided to emigrate to Jamaica. He gave up his share of the family farm and published his poems to raise money for the journey.

The poems were so well reviewed in Edinburgh that Burns decided to remain in Scotland and devote himself to writing. He went to Edinburgh in 1787 to publish a 2nd edition, but the financial rewards were not enough to live on and he had to take a job as an excise officer in Dumfriesshire. Though he worked well, he wasn't a taxman by nature, and described his job as 'the execrable office of whip-person to the blood-hounds of justice'. He contributed many songs to collections, and a 3rd edition of his poems was published in 1793. A prodigious writer, Burns composed more than 28,000 lines of verse over 22 years. He died (probably of heart disease) in Dumfries in 1796, aged 37, having fathered more than a dozen children to several different women. Generous-spirited Jean bore nine of them and took in another, remarking 'Oor Robbie should hae had twa wives'.

Many of the local landmarks mentioned in the verse tale 'Tam o' Shanter' can still be visited. Farmer Tam, riding home after a hard night's drinking in a pub in Ayr, sees witches dancing in Alloway churchyard. He calls out to the one pretty witch, but is pursued by them, and has to reach the other side of the River Doon to be safe. He just manages to cross the Brig o' Doon, but his mare loses her tail to the witches.

The Burns connection in southern Scotland is milked for all it's worth and tourist offices have a Burns Heritage Trail leaflet leading you to every place that can claim some link with the bard. Burns fans should have a look at www.robertburns.org.

Culzean Castle

★Culzean Castle & Country Park PALACE

(NTS; ☎01655-884400; www.culzeanexperience.org; castle adult/child/family £15.50/11.50/38; ⏰castle 10.30am-5pm Apr-Oct, last entry 4pm, park 9.30am-sunset year-round;) The Scottish National Trust's flagship property, magnificent Culzean (kull-*ane*) is one of the most impressive of Scotland's great stately homes. On approach the castle floats into view like a mirage. Designed by Robert Adam, who was encouraged to exercise his romantic genius, this 18th-century mansion is perched dramatically on a clifftop.

There's a great play area for kids, which re-creates the castle on a smaller scale, as well as a re-creation of a Victorian vinery, an orangery, a deer park and an aviary. Stagecoach buses running between Ayr and Girvan stop outside the gates, from where it's a 1-mile walk to the castle itself.

DUMFRIES & GALLOWAY

Some of Southern Scotland's finest attractions lie in the gentle hills and lush valleys of Dumfries and Galloway. It's an ideal destination for families, as there's plenty on offer for the kids. Galloway Forest – with its sublime views, mountain-biking and walking trails, red deer, kites and other wildlife – is a highlight, as are the dream-like ruins of Caerlaverock Castle. Adding to the appeal of this enticing region is a string of southern Scotland's most idyllic towns, which are charming when the sun shines. And shine it does. Warmed by the Gulf Stream, this is the mildest region in Scotland, allowing the development of some famous gardens.

Dumfries

POP 32,900

Lovely, red-hued sandstone bridges crisscross the wide, grassy-banked River Nith, which runs through the centre of pleasant Dumfries. Historically the town held a strategic position in the path of vengeful English armies; consequently, although it has existed since Roman times, the oldest standing building dates from the 17th century. Plenty of famous names have passed through: Robert Burns lived here and worked as a tax collector, Peter Pan creator JM Barrie was schooled here and DJ Calvin Harris hails from the town.

Sights

★Burns House MUSEUM

(☎01387-255297; www.dumgal.gov.uk/museums; Burns St; ⏰10am-5pm Mon-Sat & 2-5pm Sun Apr-Sep, 10am-1pm & 2-5pm Tue-Sat Oct-Mar) FREE This is a place of pilgrimage for Burns enthusiasts. It's here that the poet spent the last years of his life, and there are various possessions of his in glass cases, as well as manuscripts and, entertainingly, letters: make sure you have a read.

Robert Burns Centre MUSEUM

(☎01387-253374; www.dumgal.gov.uk/museums; Mill Rd; audiovisual presentation £2.30; ⏰10am-5pm Mon-Sat & 2-5pm Sun Apr-Sep, 10am-1pm & 2-5pm Tue-Sat Oct-Mar) FREE A worthwhile Burns exhibition in an old mill on the banks of the River Nith; it tells the story of the poet and Dumfries in the 1790s. The optional audiovisual presentations give more background on Dumfries, and explain the exhibition's contents. The centre functions as a cinema in the evenings.

Sleeping & Eating

★Merlin B&B $

(☎01387-261002; www.themerlin.webeden.co.uk; 2 Kenmure Tce; s/d without bathroom £35/56;) Beautifully located on the riverbank across a pedestrian bridge from the centre, this is a top place to hole up. So much work goes on behind the scenes here that it seems effortless. Numerous small details and a friendly welcome make this a very impressive setup. Rooms share a bathroom, and have super-comfy beds.

Ferintosh Guest House B&B $$

(☎01387-252262; www.ferintosh.net; 30 Lovers Walk; s £35-40, d £64-68;) A Victorian villa opposite the train station, Ferintosh is a good-humoured place with excellent rooms and a warm welcome. These people have the right attitude towards hospitality, with comfortable plush beds, a free dram on arrival, and plenty of good chat on distilleries. The showers sound like aircraft taking off but deliver impressive results. The owner's original artwork complements the decor.

Cyclists are welcomed with a shed and bike-washing facilities.

Cavens Arms PUB FOOD $

(☎01387-252896; 20 Buccleuch St; mains £8-12; ⏰food 11.30am-9pm Tue-Sat, noon-8.30pm Sun;) Engaging staff, 10 real ales on tap and a warm, contented buzz make this a legendary

Dumfries pub. Generous portions of typical pub nosh backed up by a long list of more adventurous daily specials make it one of the town's most enjoyable places to eat too. It gets packed at weekends, but staff still try to find a table for all. If you were going to move to Dumfries, you'd make sure you were within a block or two of this place.

Information

Dumfries Tourist Office (☎ 01387-253862; www.visitdumfriesandgalloway.co.uk; 64 Whitesands; 9.30am-4.30pm Mon-Sat Nov-Mar, 9.30am-5pm or 5.30pm Mon-Sat, 11am-4pm Sun Apr-Oct) By the river. Offers plenty of information on the region.

Getting There & Away

BUS

Buses run via towns along the A75 to Stranraer (£7.40, 2¼ hours, seven daily Monday to Saturday, three on Sunday) as well as to Castle Douglas and Kirkcudbright. Bus 102 runs to/from Edinburgh (£9.20, 2¾ to three hours, four to seven daily), via Moffat and Biggar.

TRAIN

There are trains between Carlisle and Dumfries (£10.80, 40 minutes, every hour or two), and direct trains between Dumfries and Glasgow (£16.20, 1¾ hours, nine daily Monday to Saturday). Services are reduced on Sundays.

South of Dumfries

Caerlaverock

★Caerlaverock Castle CASTLE

(HES; ☎ 01387-770244; www.historicenvironment.scot; Glencaple; adult/child £5.50/3.30; 9.30am-5.30pm Apr-Sep, 10am-4pm Oct-Mar) The ruins of Caerlaverock Castle, by Glencaple on a beautiful stretch of the Solway coast, are among the loveliest in Britain. Surrounded by a moat, lawns and stands of trees, the unusual pink-stoned triangular castle looks impregnable. In fact, it fell several times, most famously when it was attacked in 1300 by Edward I: the siege became the subject of an epic poem, 'The Siege of Caerlaverock'.

New Abbey

The small, picturesque whitewashed village of New Abbey lies 7 miles south of Dumfries and has several worthwhile things to see and do in and around it.

Sweetheart Abbey RUINS

(HES; www.historicenvironment.scot; adult/child £4.50/2.70; 9.30am-5.30pm Apr-Sep, 10am-4pm Sat-Wed Oct-Mar) The shattered red-sandstone remnants of this 13th-century Cistercian abbey stand in stark contrast to the manicured lawns surrounding them. The abbey, last of Scotland's major monasteries to be established, was founded by Devorgilla of Galloway in 1273 in honour of her dead husband John Balliol (the couple founded Balliol College, Oxford). On his death, she had his heart embalmed and carried it with her until she died 22 years later. She and the heart were buried by the altar: hence the name.

Kirkcudbright

POP 3400

Kirkcudbright (kirk-*coo*-bree), with its dignified streets of 17th- and 18th-century merchants' houses and appealing harbour, is the ideal base from which to explore the south coast. Look out for the nook-and-cranny

MOUNTAIN-BIKING HEAVEN

A brilliant way to experience southern Scotland's forests is by pedal power. The 7stanes (stones) are seven mountain-biking centres around southern Scotland, featuring trails through some of the finest forest scenery you'll find in the country.

Glentrool (www.7stanesmountainbiking.com; Glentrool Tourist Office) FREE is one of these centres; the **Blue Route** here is 5.6 miles in length and is a lovely ride climbing up to Green Torr Ridge overlooking Loch Trool. If you've more serious intentions, the **Big Country Route** is 36 miles of challenging ascents and descents that afford magnificent views of the Galloway Forest. It takes a full day and is not for wimps.

Another of the trailheads is at **Kirroughtree Visitor Centre** (☎ 01671-402165; www.gallowayforestpark.com; Palnure, off A75; 10am-5pm), 3 miles southeast of Newton Stewart. This centre offers plenty of singletrack at four skill levels. You can hire also bikes here (www.thebreakpad.com). For route information see www.7stanesmountainbiking.com.

closes and wynds in the elbow of beautifully restored High St. With its architecture and setting, it's easy to see why Kirkcudbright has been an artists' colony since the late 19th century.

Sights

Broughton House GALLERY

(NTS; 01557-330437; www.nts.org.uk; 12 High St; adult/child £6.50/5; noon-5pm Apr-Oct, 11am-4pm Thu-Sat Nov–mid-Dec) The 18th-century Broughton House displays paintings by EA Hornel (he lived and worked here), one of the Glasgow Boys. The library, with its wood panelling and stone carvings, is probably the most impressive room. Behind the house is a lovely Japanese-style garden.

MacLellan's Castle CASTLE

(HES; 01557-331856; www.historicenvironment.scot; Castle St; adult/child £4.50/2.70; 9.30am-1pm & 2-5.30pm Apr-Sep) Near the harbour, this is a large, atmospheric ruin built in 1577 by Thomas MacLellan, then provost of Kirkcudbright, as his town residence. Inside look for the 'lairds' lug', a 16th-century hidey-hole designed for the laird to eavesdrop on his guests.

Sleeping & Eating

★ **Greengate** B&B $$

(01557-331895; www.thegreengate.co.uk; 46 High St; s/d £60/80;) The artistically inclined should snap up the one double room in this lovely place, which has both historic and current painterly connections. The chamber is a comfortable front room with large bathroom and your own lounge alongside. The artistic, good-humoured hosts are a delight.

While staying, make sure you head down the side laneway – with cottages that were used by students of artist Jessie M King and her husband EA Taylor – to the huge, extraordinary and offbeat garden, complete with houseboat and piano, down the back.

★ **Selkirk Arms Hotel** HOTEL $$

(01557-330402; www.selkirkarmshotel.co.uk; High St; s/d £84/110, budget d £96;) What a haven of hospitality this is. All the rooms have been recently refurbished, and are looking good with a stylish purply finish and slate-floored bathrooms. Wood furnishings and views over the back garden give some of them an extra rustic appeal. Staff are happy to be there, and you will be too.

★ **Auld Alliance** SCOTTISH, FRENCH $$

(01557-330888; www.auldalliancekirkcudbright.co.uk; 29 St Cuthbert St; mains £14-21; 6-9pm Thu-Sat, plus Wed Jul-Sep;) Overlooking the heart of town, this restaurant's cuisine is true to its name, which refers to the historic bond between Scotland and France. Local produce is given a Gallic and Mediterranean twist, with dishes like Galloway lamb tagine or local haddock encrusted with oatmeal and black olive tapenade.

Information

Check out www.kirkcudbright.co.uk and www.artiststown.org.uk for heaps of information on the town.

Kirkcudbright Tourist Office (01557-330494; www.visitdumfriesandgalloway.co.uk; Harbour Sq; 11am-3pm Mon-Sat, 11am-5pm Sun Apr–mid-Jun, 9.30am-6pm Mon-Sat & 10am-5pm Sun mid-Jun–Aug, 10am-5pm Mon-Sat & 11am-3pm Sun Sep-Oct, 11am-4pm Mon-Sat Nov-Mar) Handy office with useful brochures detailing walks and road tours.

Getting There & Away

Kirkcudbright is 28 miles southwest of Dumfries. Buses run to Dumfries (£4.40, 1¼ hours) via/changing in Castle Douglas (£1.35, 15 minutes). Change at Ringford or Gatehouse of Fleet for Stranraer.

Galloway Forest Park

South and northwest of the small town of New Galloway is 300-sq-mile Galloway Forest Park, with numerous lochs and great whale-backed mountains covered in heather and pine. The highest point is **Merrick** (843m). The park is criss-crossed by off-road bike routes (p829) and some superb signposted walking trails, from gentle strolls to long-distance paths, including the **Southern Upland Way** (www.southernuplandway.gov.uk).

Walkers and cyclists should head for **Glentrool** in the park's west, accessed by the forest road east from Bargrennan off the A714, north of Newton Stewart. Located just over a mile from Bargrennan is the **Glentrool Visitor Centre** (01671-840302; www.gallowayforestpark.com; 10am-4.30pm mid-Mar–Oct, to 5.30pm Jul & Aug). The road then winds and climbs up to Loch Trool, where there are magnificent views.

The park is family focused; look out for the booklet of annual events in tourist offices. It's also great for **stargazing**; it has been named a Dark Sky Park by the International Dark-Sky Association (www.darksky.org).

The scenic 19-mile A712 (Queen's Way) between New Galloway and Newton Stewart slices through the southern section of the park. It's the only road through the park, but no buses run along it. The nearest public transport point for the western part of this road is Newton Stewart, for the east New Galloway. There's bike hire available in Newton Stewart.

Clatteringshaws Visitor Centre (☎01644-420285; www.gallowayforestpark.com; A712; ⏲10am-4.30pm mid-Mar–Oct, to 5.30pm Jul & Aug) is on the shore of Clatteringshaws Loch, 6 miles west of New Galloway. Pick up a copy of the Galloway Red Kite Trail leaflet here, which details a circular route through impressive scenery that offers a good chance to spot one of these majestic reintroduced birds.

The Machars

South of Newton Stewart, the Galloway Hills give way to the softly rolling pastures of the triangular peninsula known as the Machars. The south has many early Christian sites and the 25-mile Pilgrims Way walk.

Bus 415 runs every hour or so (only twice on Sundays) between Newton Stewart and Isle of Whithorn (£3, one hour) via Wigtown (15 minutes) and Whithorn. There are some intermediate services also.

Wigtown

POP 900

Little Wigtown, officially Scotland's National Book Town, has more than a dozen bookshops offering an astonishingly wide selection of volumes, giving book enthusiasts the opportunity to get lost here for days. A major **book festival** (www.wigtownbookfestival.com; ⏲late Sep) is also held here.

Hillcrest House B&B $$

(☎01988-402018; www.hillcrest-wigtown.co.uk; Station Rd; s/d £50/75; P 📶 🐾) A noble stone building in a quiet part of town, this offers a genuine welcome and a lovely interior featuring high ceilings and huge windows. Spend the extra for one of the superior rooms, which have stupendous views overlooking rolling green hills and the sea beyond. This is all complemented by a ripper breakfast involving fresh local produce. Dinners also often available.

ReadingLasses Bookshop Café CAFE $

(☎01988-403266; www.facebook.com/readinglasses; 17 South Main St; mains £7-8; ⏲10am-4pm Mon-Wed & 10am-4.30pm Thu-Sat year-round, plus 10.30am-4pm Sun May-Oct; 📶 ✍) 🌿 This bookshop is set around a brilliantly welcoming cafe serving decent coffee to prolong your reading time. It also offers a toothsome range of home cooking prepared with care, including several vegetarian/vegan options. It specialises in books on the social sciences and women's studies.

The Bookshop BOOKS

(☎01988-402499; www.the-bookshop.com; 17 North Main St; ⏲9am-5pm Mon-Sat) This claims to be Scotland's largest secondhand bookshop, and has a great collection of Scottish and regional titles.

Whithorn

POP 800

Whithorn has a broad, attractive High St that is virtually closed at both ends (it was designed to enclose a medieval market). There are few facilities in town, but it's worth visiting for its fascinating history.

In 397, while the Romans were still in Britain, St Ninian established the first Christian mission beyond Hadrian's Wall in Whithorn (pre-dating St Columba on Iona by 166 years). After his death, **Whithorn Priory**, the earliest recorded church in Scotland, was built to house his remains, and

WORTH A TRIP

CORSEWALL LIGHTHOUSE HOTEL

It's just you and the cruel sea out here at the fabulously romantic 200-year-old **Corsewall Lighthouse Hotel** (☎01776-853220; www.lighthousehotel.co.uk; Kirkcolm; d £140-250; P 📶). On a sunny day, the water shimmers with light, and you can see Ireland, Kintyre, Arran and Ailsa Craig. But when wind and rain beat in, it's just great to be cosily holed up in the bar-restaurant or snuggling under the covers in your room. It's right at the northwest tip of the peninsula, 13 miles northwest of Stranraer. Rooms in the lighthouse building itself are attractive if necessarily compact; chalets are also available. Dinner, bed and breakfast rates are available for an extra £20 per person.

Whithorn became the focus of an important medieval pilgrimage.

The ruined priory is part of the excellent **Whithorn Trust Discovery Centre** (☎01988-500508; www.whithorn.com; 45 George St; adult/child £4.50/2.25; ⏰10.30am-5pm Apr-Oct).

Isle of Whithorn

POP 300

The Isle of Whithorn, once an island but now linked to the mainland by a causeway, is a curious place with an attractive natural harbour and colourful houses. The roofless 13th-century **St Ninian's Chapel**, probably built for pilgrims who landed nearby, sits evocatively on the windswept rocky headland. Around Burrow Head, to the southwest but accessed off the A747 before you enter the Isle of Whithorn, is **St Ninian's Cave**, where the saint went to pray.

Stranraer

POP 10,400

The friendly but somewhat ramshackle port of Stranraer has seen its tourist mainstay, the ferry traffic to Northern Ireland, move up the road to Cairnryan. The town's still wondering what to do with itself, but there's lots to explore in the surrounding area.

Sights

Castle Kennedy Gardens GARDENS, CASTLE

(☎01776-702024; www.castlekennedygardens.com; Sheuchan; adult/child £5.50/2; ⏰10am-5pm daily Apr-Oct, Sat & Sun only Feb-Mar) Three miles east of Stranraer, these magnificent gardens are among Scotland's most renowned. They cover 30 hectares and are set on an isthmus between two lochs and two castles. The landscaping was undertaken in 1730 by the Earl of Stair, who used unoccupied soldiers. Buses heading east from Stranraer stop at the gate on the main road; it's a pleasant 20-minute stroll from here to the entrance.

Sleeping & Eating

Purgatory must look something like Stranraer at dinnertime. Several pubs and cafes do mediocre standards in big portions, so you won't go hungry at least.

Ivy House B&B $

(☎01776-704176; www.ivyhouse-ferrylink.co.uk; 3 Ivy Pl; s/d £35/55, s without bathroom £30; 📶) This is a great guesthouse that does Scottish hospitality proud, with excellent facilities, tidy en suite rooms and a smashing breakfast. Nothing is too much trouble for the genial host, who always has a smile for her guests. The room at the back overlooking the churchyard is particularly light.

Cairnryan B&B B&B $$

(☎07759-498130; www.cairnryan-bb.co.uk; Cairnryan Rd; s/d £55/70; P 📶) Overlooking the water in the centre of little Cairnryan, this is a modern bungalow with comfortable en suite rooms, but it's the genuinely welcoming hosts – old hands at excellent B&B – who make this a special experience. Breakfast features the odd homegrown treat.

Information

Stranraer Tourist Office (☎01776-702595; www.visitscotland.com; 28 Harbour St; ⏰10am-3pm Mon-Sat, plus 11am-3pm Sun mid-Jun–early Sep) Efficient and friendly.

Getting There & Away

Stranraer is 6 miles south of Cairnryan, which is on the eastern side of Loch Ryan. A service coinciding with Stena Line ferries runs between Stranraer and Cairnryan. Buses running frequently between Stranraer and Ayr also stop in Cairnryan. For a taxi, call **McLean's Taxis** (☎01776-703343; www.mcleanstaxis.com; 21 North Strand St; ⏰24hr): about £8.

BOAT

P&O (☎0800 130 0030; www.poferries.com) Runs six to eight fast ferries a day from Cairnryan to Larne (Northern Ireland). The crossing takes two hours.

Stena Line (☎08447 70 70 70; www.stenaline.co.uk) Runs five to six daily fast ferries from Cairnryan to Belfast (2¼ hours).

Prices for crossings vary but in high season are around £30/99 per person/car.

BUS

Scottish Citylink (www.citylink.co.uk) buses run to Glasgow (£18.50, 2½ hours, three daily) and Edinburgh (£21.50, four hours, three daily).

There are also several daily local buses to Kirkcudbright and the towns along the A75, such as Newton Stewart (£3.90, 40 minutes, at least hourly) and Dumfries (£7.40, 2¼ hours, seven daily Monday to Saturday, three on Sunday).

TRAIN

First Scotrail runs to/from Glasgow (£12.80, 2¼ hours). There are four direct services Monday to Saturday and none on Sunday; with more frequent daily connections changing in Ayr.

Stirling & Central Scotland

Includes ➡

Best Places to Eat

- ➡ Cellar Restaurant (p848)
- ➡ Adamson (p846)
- ➡ Café Fish (p873)
- ➡ Ee-usk (p870)
- ➡ Castlehill (p854)
- ➡ Café 52 (p858)

Best Places to Sleep

- ➡ Old Fishergate House (p845)
- ➡ Victoria Square Guesthouse (p840)
- ➡ Iona Hostel (p875)
- ➡ Globe Inn (p857)
- ➡ Malmaison (p854)

Why Go?

Covering everything from the green pastures of the northeast to the ferry port of Oban, from urban Dundee to the far Mull of Kintyre, this chapter's title is less a geographical region than a catch-all term for everything between the Lowlands and the northern Highlands. Anything you ever dreamed about Scotland can be found here: lochs aplenty, from romantic Lomond to the picturesque Trossachs; castles, ranging from royal Glamis to noble Stirling; whiskies, from the honeyed lotharios of Speyside to the peaty clan chiefs of Islay; and islands, from brooding, deer-studded Jura to emerald Iona, birthplace of Scottish Christianity.

The active are well catered for, with a welter of hills to climb and some of Britain's best long-distance trails to hike. Cyclists and walkers are spoiled for choice, with scenery ranging from the plains of Stirling to the rugged Argyll hills; from the fishing hamlets of Fife to the epic landscapes of Mull.

When to Go

➡ May is a magical time to explore Loch Lomond and the Trossachs before summer crowds arrive.

➡ The best month of the year for whale-watching off the west coast is August.

➡ Revellers gather for September's whisky and music festival in Dufftown.

Stirling & Central Scotland Highlights

1 Loch Lomond & the Trossachs (p863) Exploring the lovely lochscapes and accessible walking and cycling routes of this spectacular region.

2 St Andrews (p842) Pacing through the historic birthplace of golf to play the famous Old Course.

3 Stirling Castle (p836) Admiring the views across ancient independence battlefields from this magnificent castle.

4 Seafood restaurants (p870) Tucking into a platter of fresh local langoustines at Ee-Usk or one of Oban's other eateries.

5 Distillery tour (p864) Being initiated into the mysteries of malt whisky on a Speyside distillery tour.

6 Iona (p874) Journeying through wildlife-rich Mull to reach this holy emerald isle.

7 Islay (p879) Visiting the smoky heavyweights of the whisky world on their peaty home turf.

8 Scone Palace (p850) Strutting with the peacocks at this noble palace where Scottish kings were once crowned.

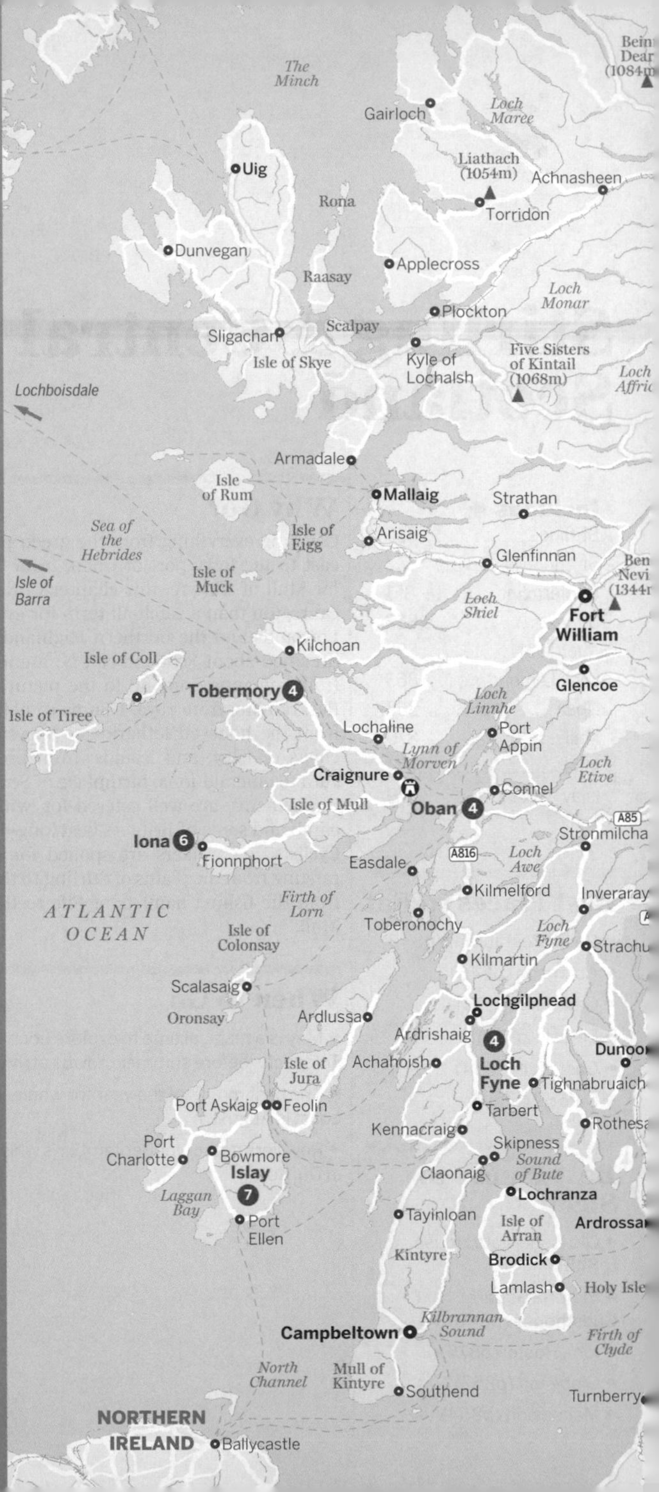

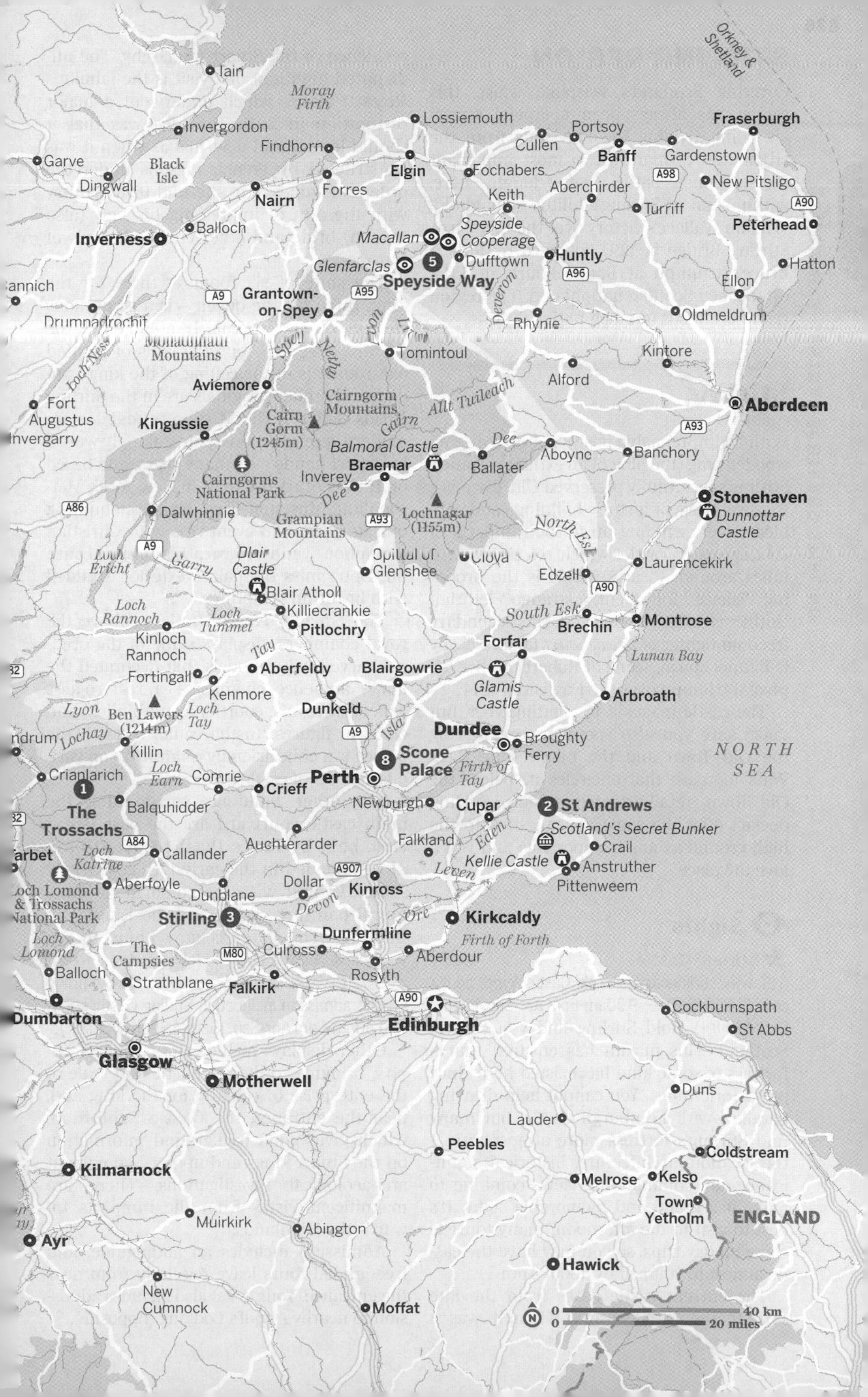

Orkney & Shetland
Iain
Moray Firth
Lossiemouth
Invergordon
Findhorn
Portsoy
Fraserburgh
Cullen
Banff
Gardenstown
Garve
Black Isle
Elgin
Fochabers
A98
New Pitsligo
Dingwall
Forres
Nairn
Keith
Aberchirder
A90
Turriff
Balloch
Speyside Cooperage
Peterhead
Inverness
Macallan
Huntly
Glenfarclas
5
Dufftown
Hatton
A96
Speyside Way
Deveron
Ellon
annich
A9
Grantown-on-Spey
A95
Rhynie
Oldmeldrum
Drumnadrochit
Monadhliath Mountains
Spey
Nethy
Avon
Livet
Tomintoul
Kintore
Loch Ness
Aviemore
Alford
Allt Tuileach
Fort Augustus
Cairngorm Mountains
Aberdeen
Cairn Gorm (1245m)
Kingussie
Gairn
Invergarry
A93
Balmoral Castle
Dee
Aboyne
Banchory
Braemar
Ballater
Cairngorms National Park
Inverey
Stonehaven
Dee
Lochnagar (1155m)
Dunnottar Castle
A86
Dalwhinnie
Grampian Mountains
A93
North Esk
A9
Loch Ericht
Garry
Blair Castle
Spittal of Glenshee
Clova
Laurencekirk
Edzell
A90
Blair Atholl
Loch Rannoch
Loch Tummel
Killiecrankie
South Esk
Brechin
Montrose
Pitlochry
Kinloch Rannoch
Forfar
Tay
Lunan Bay
Fortingall
Aberfeldy
Blairgowrie
Glamis Castle
Kenmore
Arbroath
Lyon
Ben Lawers (1214m)
Loch Tay
Dunkeld
Lochay
Isla
A9
Dundee
Broughty Ferry
NORTH SEA
ndrum
Killin
Scone Palace
8
Firth of Tay
Crianlarich
Loch Earn
Comrie
Perth
1
Crieff
The Trossachs
Balquhidder
Newburgh
Cupar
2
St Andrews
Scotland's Secret Bunker
Auchterarder
Falkland
Eden
Crail
A84
Loch Katrine
Callander
Kellie Castle
Anstruther
arbet
A907
Leven
Pittenweem
Aberfoyle
Dollar
Kinross
Loch Lomond & Trossachs National Park
Dunblane
Devon
Ore
Stirling
3
Kirkcaldy
Dunfermline
Firth of Forth
Loch Lomond
The Campsies
M80
Culross
Aberdour
Balloch
Strathblane
Rosyth
Falkirk
A90
Cockburnspath
Dumbarton
Edinburgh
St Abbs
Glasgow
Motherwell
Duns
Lauder
Coldstream
Peebles
Kilmarnock
Melrose
Kelso
Town Yetholm
ENGLAND
Muirkirk
Abington
Ayr
Hawick
New Cumnock
Moffat
0
40 km
0
20 miles

STIRLING REGION

Covering Scotland's wasplike waist, this region has always been a crucial strategic point dividing the Lowlands from the Highlands. Scotland's two most important independence battles were fought here, within sight of Stirling's hilltop stronghold. William Wallace's victory over the English at Stirling Bridge in 1297, followed by Robert Bruce's triumph at Bannockburn in 1314, established Scottish nationhood. The region remains a focus of much national pride.

Stirling

POP 36,150

With an impregnable position atop a mighty wooded crag (the plug of an extinct volcano), Stirling's beautifully preserved Old Town is a treasure trove of historic buildings and cobbled streets winding up to the ramparts of its impressive castle, which offer views for miles around. Clearly visible is the brooding Wallace Monument, a strange Victorian Gothic creation honouring the legendary freedom fighter of *Braveheart* fame. Nearby is Bannockburn, scene of Robert the Bruce's pivotal triumph over the English in 1314.

The castle makes a fascinating visit, but make sure you also spend time exploring the Old Town and the picturesque Back Walk footpath that encircles it. Below the Old Town, retail-oriented modern Stirling doesn't offer the same appeal; stick to the high ground as much as possible and you'll love the place.

Sights

★ **Stirling Castle** CASTLE

(HS; www.stirlingcastle.gov.uk; Castle Wynd; adult/child £14.50/8.70; 9.30am-6pm Apr-Sep, to 5pm Oct-Mar; P) Hold Stirling and you control Scotland. This maxim has ensured that a fortress of some kind has existed here since prehistoric times. You cannot help drawing parallels with Edinburgh Castle, but many find Stirling's fortress more atmospheric – the location, architecture, historical significance and commanding views combine to make it a grand and memorable sight. It's best to visit in the afternoon; many tourists come on day trips, so you may have the castle almost to yourself by about 4pm.

The current castle dates from the late 14th to the 16th century, when it was a residence of the Stuart monarchs. The undisputed highlight of a visit is the fabulous **Royal Palace**, which underwent a major restoration in 2011. The idea was that it should look brand new, just as when it was constructed by French masons under the orders of James V in the mid-16th century with the aim of impressing his new (also French) bride and other crowned heads of Europe.

The suite of six rooms – three for the king, three for the queen – is a sumptuous riot of colour. Particularly notable are the **Stirling Heads** – reproductions of painted oak roundels in the ceiling of the king's audience chamber (originals are in the Stirling Heads Gallery). The **Stirling tapestries** are modern reproductions, painstakingly woven by expert hands over many years, and based on 16th-century originals in New York's Metropolitan Museum. They depict the hunting of a unicorn – an event ripe with Christian metaphor – and are breathtakingly beautiful. Don't miss the palace exterior, studded with beautiful sculptures.

The **Stirling Heads Gallery**, above the royal chambers, displays some of the original carved oak roundels that decorated the king's audience chamber – a real rogue's gallery of royals, courtiers, and biblical and classical figures. In the vaults beneath the palace is a child-friendly **exhibition** on various aspects of castle life.

The other buildings surrounding the main castle courtyard are the vast **Great Hall**, built by James IV; the **Royal Chapel**, remodelled in the early 17th century by James VI and with the colourful original mural painting intact; and the King's Old Building. The latter is now home to the **Argyll & Sutherland Highlanders Regimental Museum** (www.argylls.co.uk; Stirling Castle; admisson included in Stirling Castle entry; 9.30am-5pm Apr-Sep, 10am-4.35pm Oct-Mar).

Other displays include the **Great Kitchens**, bringing to life the bustle and scale of the enterprise of cooking for the king and, near the entrance, the **Castle Exhibition**, which gives good background information on the Stuart kings and updates on current archaeological investigations. There are magnificent vistas from the ramparts towards the Highlands.

Admission includes an audioguide, and free guided tours leave regularly from near the entrance. Your ticket also includes admission to nearby Argyll's Lodging (opposite).

Stirling

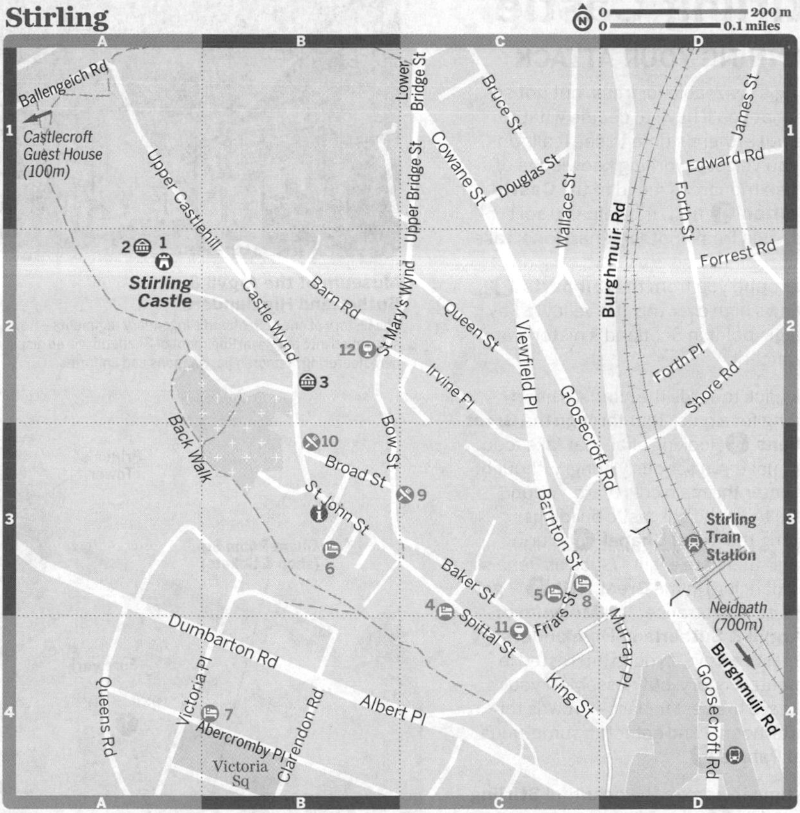

Stirling

Top Sights
1 Stirling Castle A2

Sights
2 Argyll & Sutherland Highlanders Regimental Museum A2
3 Argyll's Lodging B2

Sleeping
4 Colessio Hotel C3
5 Friars Wynd C3
6 Stirling SYHA B3
7 Victoria Square Guesthouse B4
8 Willy Wallace Backpackers Hostel C3

Eating
Breá .... (see 11)
9 Darnley Coffee House C3
10 Hermann's B3

Drinking & Nightlife
11 Brewdog C4
12 Settle Inn B2

Argyll's Lodging HISTORIC BUILDING
(www.stirlingcastle.gov.uk; Castle Wynd; admission included in Stirling Castle entry; 12.45-4pm) This elegant building is Scotland's most impressive 17th-century town house, built for a wealthy local merchant and later acquired by the Earl of Argyll when he thought that King Charles II might use Stirling Castle as a royal residence. It has been tastefully restored and gives an insight into the lavish lifestyle of 17th-century aristocrats. You can join a 20-minute guided tour (included in the Stirling Castle admission fee) or wander through the house at your leisure.

Stirling Castle

PLANNING YOUR ATTACK

Stirling's a sizeable fortress, but not so huge that you'll have to decide what to leave out – there's time to see it all. Unless you've got a working knowledge of Scottish monarchs, head to the **Castle Exhibition** ❶ first: it'll help you sort one James from another. That done, take on the sights at leisure. First, stop and look around you from the **ramparts** ❷; the views high over this flat valley, a key strategic point in Scotland's history, are magnificent.

Track back towards the citadel's heart, stopping for a quick tour through the **Great Kitchens** ❸; looking at all that fake food might make you seriously hungry, though. Then enter the main courtyard. Around you are the principal castle buildings, including the **Royal Chapel** ❹. During summer there are events (such as Renaissance dancing) in the **Great Hall** ❺ – get details at the entrance. The **Museum of the Argyll & Sutherland Highlanders** ❻ is a treasure trove if you're interested in regimental history, but missable if you're not. Leave the best for last – crowds thin in the afternoon – and enter the sumptuous **Royal Palace** ❼.

Take time to admire the beautiful **Stirling Tapestries** ❽, skillfully woven by hand on-site between 2001-2014.

THE WAY UP & DOWN

If you have time, take the atmospheric Back Walk, a peaceful, shady stroll around the Old Town's fortifications and up to the castle's imposing crag-top position. Afterwards, wander down through the Old Town to admire its facades.

TOP TIPS

» **Admission** Entrance is free for Historic Scotland members. If you'll be visiting several Historic Scotland sites a membership will save you plenty.

» **Vital Statistics** First constructed: before 1110; number of sieges: at least nine; last besieger: Bonnie Prince Charlie (unsuccessful); money spent refurbishing the Royal Palace: £12 million.

BRIAN JANNSEN / GEFOTOSTOCK ©

Museum of the Argyll & Sutherland Highlanders
The history of one of Scotland's legendary regiments – now subsumed into the Royal Regiment of Scotland – is on display here, featuring memorabilia, weapons and uniforms.

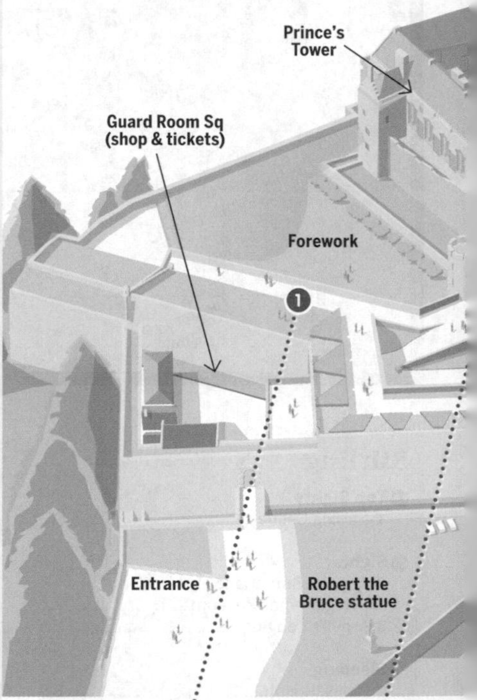

Castle Exhibition
A great overview of the Stewart dynasty here will get your facts straight, and also offers the latest archaeological titbits from the ongoing excavations under the citadel. Analysis of skeletons has revealed surprising amounts of biographical data.

Royal Palace
The impressive highlight of a visit to the castle is this recreation of the royal lodgings originally built by James V. The finely worked ceiling, ornate furniture and sumptuous unicorn tapestries dazzle.

Great Hall & Royal Chapel

Creations of James IV and VI, respectively, these elegant spaces around the central courtyard have been faithfully restored. The vast Great Hall, with its imposing beamed roof, was the largest medieval hall in Scotland.

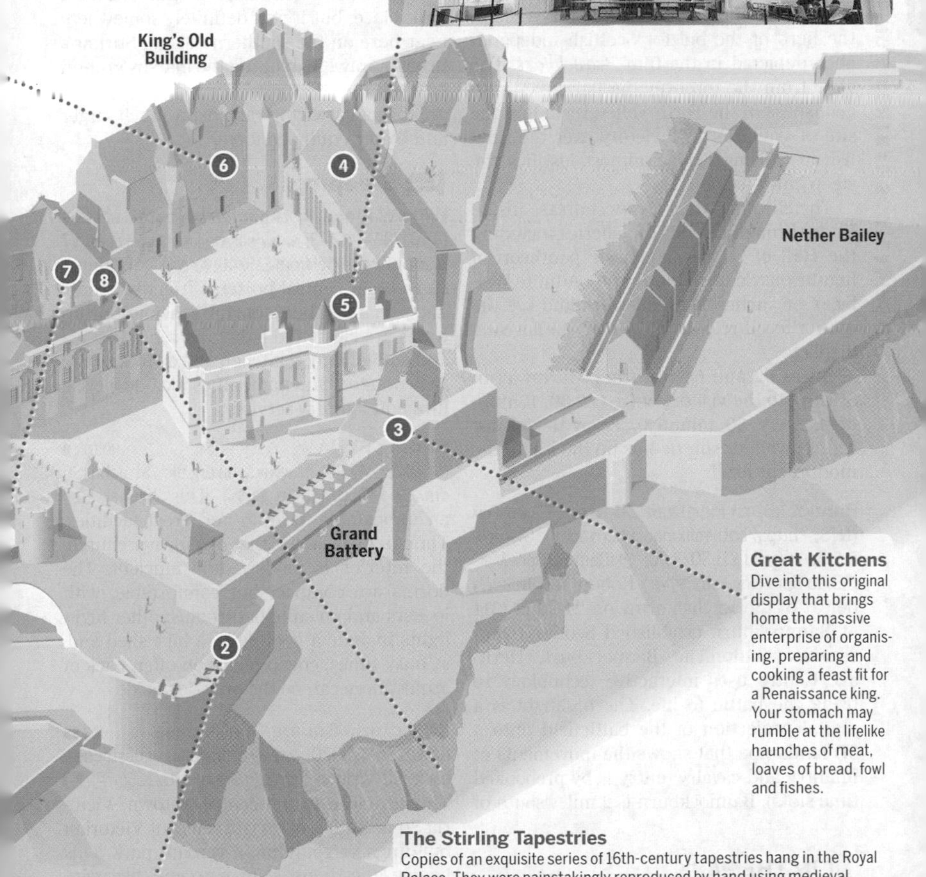

Great Kitchens

Dive into this original display that brings home the massive enterprise of organising, preparing and cooking a feast fit for a Renaissance king. Your stomach may rumble at the lifelike haunches of meat, loaves of bread, fowl and fishes.

The Stirling Tapestries

Copies of an exquisite series of 16th-century tapestries hang in the Royal Palace. They were painstakingly reproduced by hand using medieval techniques – each one took four years to make – and depict a unicorn hunt rich with Christian symbolism.

Ramparts

Perched on the wall you can appreciate the utter dominance of the castle's position atop this lofty volcanic crag. From its vantage points, you can see the site of Robert the Bruce's victory at Bannockburn and the monument to William Wallace.

National Wallace Monument MONUMENT
(☎01786-472140; www.nationalwallacemonument.com; Abbey Craig; adult/child £9.99/6.25; ⊙9.30am-5pm Apr-Jun, Sep & Oct, to 6pm Jul & Aug, 10.30am-4pm Nov-Feb, 10am-5pm Mar; P ♿) Perched high on a crag above the floodplain of the River Forth, this Victorian monument is so Gothic it deserves circling bats and croaking ravens. In the shape of a medieval tower, it commemorates William Wallace, the hero of the bid for Scottish independence depicted in the film *Braveheart*. The view from the top over the flat, green gorgeousness of the Forth Valley, including the site of Wallace's 1297 victory over the English at Stirling Bridge, almost justifies the steep entry fee.

The climb up the narrow staircase inside leads through a series of galleries including the Hall of Heroes, a marble pantheon of lugubrious Scottish luminaries. Admire Wallace's 66 inches of broadsword and see the man himself re-created in a 3D audiovisual display.

Buses 62 and 63 run from Murray Pl in Stirling to the visitor centre (£2.30, 10 minutes, every 30 minutes). From the visitor centre, walk or shuttle-bus up the hill to the monument itself.

Bannockburn Heritage Centre MUSEUM
(NTS; http://battleofbannockburn.com; Glasgow Rd; adult/child £11.50/8.50; ⊙10am-5.30pm Mar-Oct, to 5pm Nov-Feb; P ♿) Robert the Bruce's defeat of the English army on 24 June 1314 at Bannockburn established Scotland as a separate nation.The Bannockburn Heritage Centre uses interactive technology to bring the battle to life. The highlight is a digital projection of the battlefield onto a 3D landscape that shows the movements of infantry and cavalry (entry is by prebooked time slots). Bannockburn is 2 miles south of Stirling; First bus 24 or 54 run from Stirling (£1.80, 10 minutes, three per hour).

Outside the centre, the 'battlefield' itself is no more than an expanse of neatly trimmed grass, crowned with a circular monument inscribed with a poem by Kathleen Jamie, and a Victorian statue of the victor astride his horse. There has been much debate over exactly where the Battle of Bannockburn took place, but it was definitely somewhere near here on the southern edge of Stirling's urban sprawl. Exploiting the marshy ground around the Bannock Burn, Bruce won a great tactical victory against a much larger and better-equipped force.

T IN THE PARK

Scotland's biggest music festival, **T in the Park** (www.tinthepark.com), rocks this corner of the country over the second weekend in July. A major event, with six stages and top-name acts, it takes places in the grounds of Strathallan Castle near Auchterarder. It's a three-day affair, with camping available from the night before the kick-off. The site is 2.5 miles north of the A9, about halfway between Perth and Stirling.

Sleeping

Willy Wallace Backpackers Hostel HOSTEL $
(☎01786-446773; www.willywallacehostel.com; 77 Murray Pl; dm/tw from £15/46; @ 📶) This highly convenient central hostel is friendly, roomy and sociable. The colourful, spacious dormitories are clean and light, and it has free tea and coffee, a good kitchen and a laissez-faire atmosphere. Other amenities include bicycle hire and laundry service.

Stirling SYHA HOSTEL $
(☎01786-473442; www.syha.org.uk; St John St; dm/tw £17.50/44; P @ 📶) This hostel has an unbeatable location and great facilities. Though its facade is that of a former church, the interior is modern and efficient. The dorms are compact but comfortable, with lockers and en suite bathrooms; other highlights include a pool table, a bike shed and, at busy times, cheap meals on offer. Lack of atmosphere can be the only downside.

★**Victoria Square Guesthouse** B&B $$
(☎01786-473920; www.victoriasquareguesthouse.com; 12 Victoria Sq; s/d from £70/105; P 📶) Though close to the centre of town, Victoria Sq is a quiet oasis with elegant Victorian buildings surrounding a verdant park. This luxury guesthouse's huge rooms, bay windows and period features make it a winner – there's a great four-poster room (from £110) for romantic getaways, and some bedrooms have views to the castle towering above. No children.

Castlecroft Guest House B&B $$
(☎01786-474933; www.castlecroft-uk.com; Ballengeich Rd; s/d £75/85; P 📶) Nestling into the hillside under the back of the castle, this great hideaway feels like a rural retreat but is a short, spectacular walk from the heart

of Stirling. The lounge and deck area enjoy views over green fields to the nearby hills, the rooms have excellent modern bathrooms and the welcome couldn't be more hospitable. Breakfast features homemade bread, among other delights.

Neidpath B&B B&B $$
(01786-469017; www.accommodationinstirling.co.uk; 24 Linden Ave; s/d/f £55/70/95;) Offering excellent value and a genuine welcome, this fine choice is easily accessed by car. A particularly appealing front room is one of three excellent modernised bedrooms with fridges and good bathrooms. The owners also run various self-catering apartments around town; details via the website. Two-night minimum stay most nights in July and August.

★ **Friars Wynd** HOTEL $$$
(01786-473390; www.friarswynd.co.uk; 17 Friars St; r from £129;) Set in a lovingly restored 19th-century town house just a short walk from the train station, Friars Wynd offers eight bedrooms of varying sizes, many with period features such as Victorian cast-iron fire surrounds or exposed patches of original red-brick walls. Be aware that the 1st-floor rooms are directly above the bar and restaurant, so can be a little noisy at weekends.

Colessio Hotel BOUTIQUE HOTEL $$$
(01786-448880; www.hotelcolessio.com; 33 Spittal St; r from £129;) This new luxury hotel and spa occupies a landmark neoclassical building (a former hospital) in the heart of the Old Town. The luxury conversion includes sumptuous rooms and suites with a touch of designer decadence, and a sophisticated cocktail bar and restaurant.

Eating & Drinking

Darnley Coffee House CAFE $
(01786-474468; www.facebook.com/DarnleyCoffeeHouse; 18 Bow St; mains £3-5; 11am-4pm Mon-Sat, noon-4pm Sun;) Just down the hill from Stirling Castle, this is a good pit stop for home baking, soup and speciality coffees during a walk around the Old Town. The cafe is in the vaulted cellars of a 16th-century house where Darnley, the lover and later husband of Mary, Queen of Scots once stayed while visiting her.

Birds & Bees PUB FOOD $$
(01786-473663; www.thebirdsandthebees-stirling.com; Easter Cornton Rd, Causewayhead; mains £9-14; food served noon-2.30pm & 5-10pm;) A bit of a local secret this – a country pub in a converted barn, hidden away on a back road on the northern fringes of the city. There's faux-rustic decor and a crowd-pleasing pub-grub menu that runs from nachos and tempura king prawns to steaks, burgers, ribs and fish and chips. Outdoor seating and plenty of space for kids to run around.

Breá BISTRO $$
(www.brea-stirling.co.uk; 5 Baker St; mains £9-17; noon-9pm Sun-Thu, to 10pm Fri-Sat;) Bringing a bohemian touch to central Stirling, this busy bistro has pared-back contemporary decor and a short menu showcasing carefully sourced Scottish produce, including beef, venison, seafood, haggis and Brewdog beers, as well as gourmet burgers, pizza and a handful of vegetarian dishes.

Hermann's AUSTRIAN, SCOTTISH $$
(01786-450632; www.hermanns.co.uk; 58 Broad St; mains £11-20, 2-/3-course lunch £12/15; noon-3pm & 6-10pm;) This elegant Scottish-Austrian restaurant is a reliable and popular choice, with conservative decor oddly offset by magazine-spread skiing photos, but the food doesn't miss a beat and ranges from Scottish favourites such as Cullen skink to Austrian schnitzel and *spätzle* noodles. Vegetarian options are good, and quality Austrian wines provide an out-of-the-ordinary accompaniment.

Brewdog BAR
(01786-440043; www.brewdog.com/bars/uk/stirling; 7 Baker St; noon-midnight Sun-Thu, to 1am Fri-Sat;) The burgeoning Brewdog empire has come to Stirling, with a cool bar done out in designer-distressed timber offering no fewer than 16 taps dispensing craft beers from all over the world, including several from their own famously crowdfunded brewery near Fraserburgh in Aberdeenshire.

Settle Inn PUB
(01786-474609; 91 St Mary's Wynd; 11am-11pm Mon-Sat, 12.30-11pm Sun;) A warm welcome is guaranteed at Stirling's oldest pub (1733), a spot redolent with atmosphere, with its log fire, vaulted back room, low-slung ceilings and Friday night folk-music sessions. Guest ales, atmospheric nooks where you can settle in for the night, and a blend of local characters make it a classic of its kind.

Information

Stirling Community Hospital (☎01786-434000; www.nhsforthvalley.com; Livilands Rd) is south of the town centre. The nearest emergency department is Forth Valley Royal Hospital in Larbert, 9 miles southeast of Stirling.

Information can be found and accommodation booked at **Stirling Tourist Office** (☎01786-475019; www.destinationstirling.com; Old Town Jail, St John St; ⊙10am-5pm).

Getting There & Away

BUS

The **bus station** (Goosecroft Rd) is on Goosecroft Rd. **Citylink** (☎0871-266-3333; www.citylink.co.uk) offers a number of services to/from Stirling including the following:

Dundee £14.40, 1¾ hours, hourly
Edinburgh £8.20, 1¼ hours, hourly
Glasgow £7.70, 45 minutes, hourly
Perth £9.20, 50 minutes, at least hourly

Some buses continue to Aberdeen, Inverness and Fort William; more frequently a change will be required.

TRAIN

ScotRail (www.scotrail.co.uk) has services to/from a number of destinations, including the following:

Aberdeen £30, 2¼ hours, hourly weekdays, every two hours Sunday
Dundee £12, one hour, hourly weekdays, every two hours Sunday
Edinburgh £8.60, one hour, twice hourly Monday to Saturday, hourly Sunday
Glasgow £8.90, 50 minutes, twice hourly Monday to Saturday, hourly Sunday
Perth £13, 30 minutes, hourly weekdays, every two hours Sunday

FIFE

The Kingdom of Fife (www.visitfife.com) as it calls itself – it was home to Scottish kings for 500 years – is a tongue of land protruding between the Firths of Forth and Tay that has managed to maintain an individual Lowland identity quite separate from the rest of the country. Though southern Fife is part of Edinburgh's commuter-belt territory, eastern Fife's rolling green farmland and quaint fishing villages are prime turf for exploration, and the fresh sea air feels like it's doing you a power of good. Fife's biggest attraction, St Andrews, has Scotland's most venerable university and a wealth of historic buildings. It's also, of course, the headquarters of golf and draws professionals and keen slashers alike to take on the Old Course – the classic links experience.

Fife Coastal Path WALKING

(www.fifecoastalpath.co.uk) The Fife Coastal Path runs more than 80 miles, following the entire Fife coastline from the Forth Road Bridge to the Tay Bridge and beyond. It's well waymarked, picturesque and not too rigorous, though winds can buffet. It's easily accessed for shorter sections or day walks, and long stretches of it can also be tackled on a mountain bike.

Getting Around

The main bus operator here is **Stagecoach East Scotland** (www.stagecoachbus.com). You can buy a Fife Dayrider ticket (£8.40), which gives one day's unlimited travel around Fife on Stagecoach buses.

Fife Council produces a useful transport map, *Getting Around Fife*, available from tourist offices. Good public transport information can be found at www.fifedirect.org.uk.

If you are driving from the Forth bridges to St Andrews, a slower but much more scenic route than the M90/A91 is along the signposted Fife Coastal Tourist Route.

St Andrews

POP 16,900

For a small town, St Andrews has made a big name for itself: firstly as a religious centre and place of pilgrimage, then as Scotland's oldest (and Britain's third-oldest) university town. But it is its status as the home of golf that has propelled it to even greater fame, and today's pilgrims mostly arrive with a set of clubs in hand. Nevertheless, it's a lovely place to visit even if you've no interest in the game, with impressive medieval ruins, stately university buildings, idyllic white sands and excellent guesthouses and restaurants.

The Old Course, the world's most famous golf links, has a striking seaside location at the western end of town – it's a thrilling experience to stroll the hallowed turf. Nearby is magnificent West Sands beach, made famous by the film *Chariots of Fire*.

History

St Andrews is said to have been founded by St Regulus (also known as St Rule), who arrived from Greece in the 4th century bringing with him the bones of St Andrew, Scotland's patron saint. The town soon grew into a major pilgrimage centre and later developed into the ecclesiastical capital of Scotland. The university, the oldest in Scotland, was founded in 1410. Golf has been played at St Andrews for more than 600 years; the game's governing body, the Royal & Ancient Golf Club, was founded here in 1754 and the imposing Royal & Ancient Clubhouse was built 100 years later.

Sights

St Andrews Cathedral RUINS

(HS; www.historicenvironment.scot; The Pends; adult/child £4.50/2.70, incl castle £8/4.80; 9.30am-5.30pm Apr-Sep, 10am-4pm Oct-Mar) All that's left of one of Britain's most magnificent medieval buildings are ruined fragments of wall and arch, and a single towering gable, but you can still appreciate the scale and majesty of the edifice from these scant remains. There's also a **museum** with a collection of superb 17th- and 18th-century grave slabs, 9th- and 10th-century Celtic crosses, and the late 8th-century **St Andrews Sarcophagus**, Europe's finest example of early medieval stone carving.

Founded in 1160 and consecrated in 1318, the cathedral stood as the focus of this important pilgrimage centre until 1559, when it was pillaged during the Reformation. The bones of St Andrew himself lie beneath the altar; until the cathedral was built, they had been enshrined in the nearby **Church of St Regulus** (or Rule). All that remains of this church is **St Rule's Tower**, worth the claustrophobic climb for the view across St Andrews. The admission fee only applies for the museum and tower; you can wander freely around the atmospheric ruins.

St Andrews Castle CASTLE

(HS; www.historicenvironment.scot; The Scores; adult/child £5.50/3.30, incl cathedral £8/4.80; 9.30am-5.30pm Apr-Sep, 10am-4pm Oct-Mar) The castle is mainly in ruins, but the site itself is evocative and has dramatic coastline views. It was founded around 1200 as a fortified home for the bishop of St Andrews. After the execution of Protestant reformers in 1545, other reformers retaliated by murdering Cardinal Beaton and taking over the castle.

PLAYING THE OLD COURSE

The **St Andrews Old Course** (Reservations Department 01334-466718; www.standrews.com; Golf Pl) is the oldest and most famous golf course in the world. Golf has been played here since the 15th century, and by 1457 it was apparently so popular that James II had to ban it because it was interfering with his troops' archery practice. Although it lies beside the exclusive Royal & Ancient Golf Club, the Old Course is a public course and is not owned by the club.

To play the Old Course, you'll need to book in advance via the website, or by contacting the Reservations Department. Reservations open on the last Wednesday in August the year before you wish to play. No bookings are taken for weekends or the month of September (check the latest guidelines on the website).

Unless you've booked months in advance, getting a tee-off time is literally a lottery; enter the ballot at the **caddie office** (01334-466666; West Sands Rd), or by phone, before 2pm two days before you wish to play (there's no Sunday play). Be warned that applications by ballot are normally heavily oversubscribed, and green fees are £175 in summer.

Singles are not accepted in the ballot and should start queuing as early as possible on the day – 5am is good – in the hope of joining a group. You'll need a handicap certificate (24/36 for men/women). If your number doesn't come up, there are six other public courses in the area (book up to seven days in advance on 01334-466718, no handicap required), including the prestigious Castle Course (£120). Other summer green fees: New £75, Jubilee £75, Eden £45, Strathtyrum £30 and Balgove (nine-holer for beginners and kids) £15. There are various multiple-day tickets available. A caddie for your round costs £50 plus tip. If you play on a windy day, expect those scores to balloon: Nick Faldo famously stated, 'When it blows here, even the seagulls walk'.

There are **guided walks** (www.standrews.com; per person £10; 11am & 2pm daily Apr-Sep) of the Old Course, and you are free to walk over the course on Sunday, or follow the footpaths around the edge at any time.

St Andrews

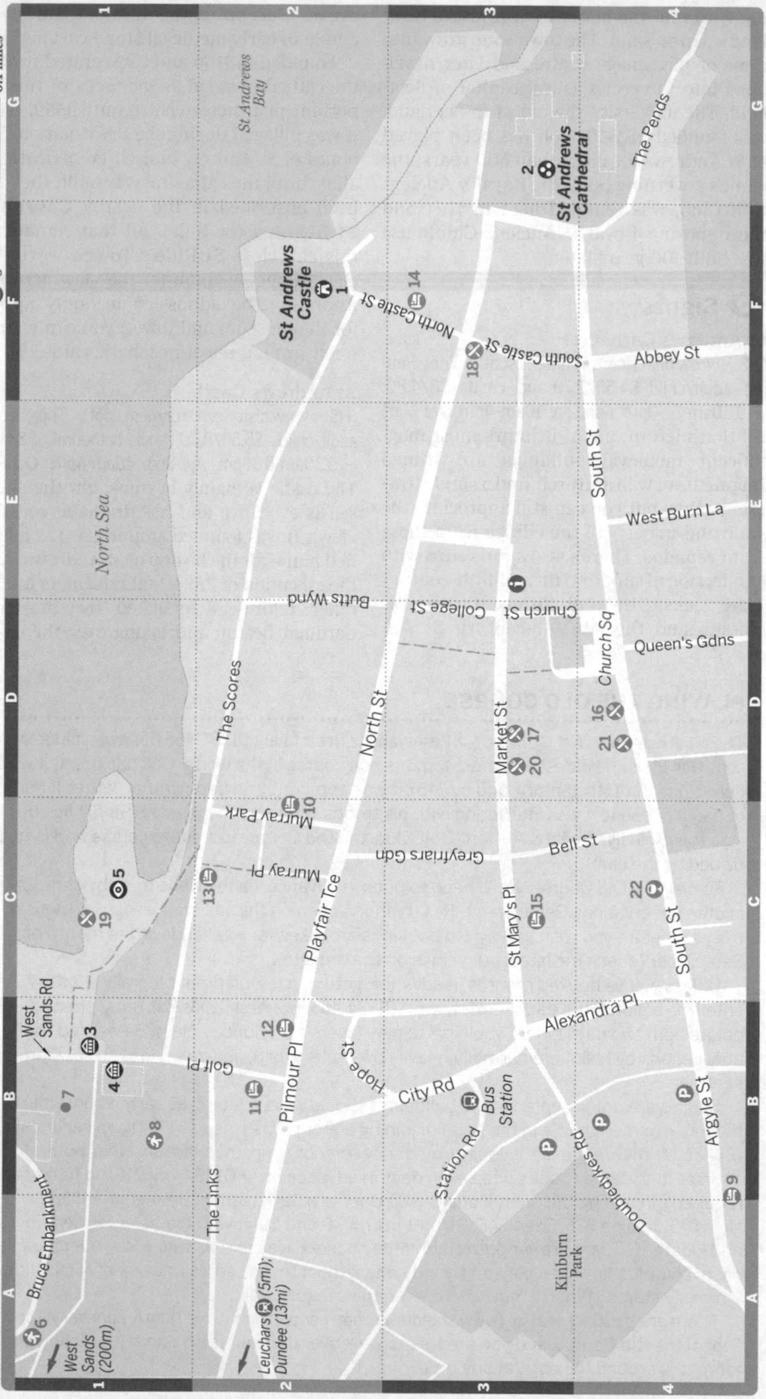

St Andrews Bay
North Sea
St Andrews Castle
St Andrews Cathedral
The Pends
North Castle St
South Castle St
Abbey St
South St
West Burn La
Butts Wynd
College St
Church St
Queen's Gdns
Church Sq
The Scores
North St
Market St
Murray Park
Murray Pl
Greyfriars Gdn
Bell St
Playfair Tce
St Mary's Pl
Alexandra Pl
Pilmour Pl
Hope St
City Rd
Bus Station
Golf Pl
West Sands Rd
Station Rd
Doubledykes Rd
Argyle St
The Links
Bruce Embankment
Kinburn Park
West Sands (200m)
Leuchars (5mi); Dundee (13mi)
0 200 m
0 0.1 miles

St Andrews

Top Sights
1 St Andrews Castle ... F2
2 St Andrews Cathedral ... G3

Sights
3 British Golf Museum ... B1
4 Royal & Ancient Clubhouse ... B1
5 St Andrews Aquarium ... C1

Activities, Courses & Tours
6 Caddie Pavilion ... A1
7 Old Course Guided walks ... B1
8 St Andrews Old Course ... B1

Sleeping
9 34 Argyle St ... B4
10 Cameron House ... C2
11 Fairways of St Andrews ... B2
12 Five Pilmour Place ... B2
13 Hazelbank Hotel ... C2
14 Old Fishergate House ... F3
15 St Andrews Tourist Hostel ... C3

Eating
16 Adamson ... D4
17 Mitchell's Deli ... D3
18 Northpoint Cafe ... F3
19 Seafood Restaurant ... C1
20 Tailend ... D3
21 Vine Leaf ... D4

Drinking & Nightlife
22 St Andrews Brewing Co ... C4

They spent almost a year holed up, during which they and their attackers dug a complex of **siege tunnels**; you can walk (or stoop) along their damp mossy lengths.

The visitor centre gives a good audio-visual introduction and has a small collection of Pictish stones.

British Golf Museum MUSEUM
(www.britishgolfmuseum.co.uk; Bruce Embankment; adult/child £7/3; 9.30am-5pm Mon-Sat, 10am-5pm Sun Apr-Oct, 10am-4pm daily Nov-Mar) This museum provides a comprehensive overview of the history and development of the game and the role of St Andrews in it. Favourite fact: bad players were formerly known as 'foozlers'. The huge collection ranges from the world's oldest set of clubs (late 17th century, used with feather-stuffed golf balls) to modern equipment, clothing and trophies, and there's a large collection of memorabilia from Open winners both male and female.

St Andrews Aquarium AQUARIUM
(01334-474786; www.standrewsaquarium.co.uk; The Scores; adult/child £10.50/8; 10am-5pm Mon-Fri, to 6pm Sat & Sun;) As well as a seal sanctuary, rays and sharks from Scottish waters and exotic tropical favourites, St Andrews Aquarium has penguins, alligators and a cute family of meerkats.

Sleeping

St Andrews' accommodation is expensive and often heavily booked, especially in summer, at weekends and during university events like graduation, so reserve well in advance. Almost every house on super-central Murray Park and Murray Pl is a guesthouse.

St Andrews Tourist Hostel HOSTEL $
(01334-479911; St Marys Pl; dm £13-15;) Laid-back and central, this hostel is the only backpacker accommodation in town. Occupying a stately old building, it has high corniced ceilings, especially in the huge lounge. There's a laissez-faire approach, which can verge on chaotic at times, but the staff and location can't be beaten. Reception closed between 2pm and 5pm.

Cairnsmill Caravan Park CAMPGROUND $
(01334-473604; www.cairnsmill.co.uk; Largo Rd; tent without/with car £10/18, bunkhouse per person £20; Apr-Oct;) About a mile west of St Andrews on the A915, this campsite has brilliant views over the town. Facilities are good, though it's very caravan-heavy. There's also a simple bunkhouse.

★ **Fairways of St Andrews** B&B $$
(01334-479513; www.fairwaysofstandrews.co.uk; 8a Golf Pl; d £98-130;) Just a few paces from golf's most famous 18th green, this is more like a boutique hotel than a B&B, despite its small size. There are just three super-stylish rooms; the best on the top floor is huge and has its own balcony with views over the Old Course.

★ **Old Fishergate House** B&B $$
(01334-470874; www.oldfishergatehouse.co.uk; North Castle St; s/d £85/115;) This historic 17th-century town house, furnished with period pieces, is in a great location – the oldest part of town, close to the cathedral and

castle. The two twin rooms are very spacious and even have their own sitting room. On a scale of one to 10 for quaintness, we'd rate it about a 9½. Cracking breakfast menu features fresh fish and pancakes.

34 Argyle St B&B $$
(☎07712 863139; www.34argylestreet.com; 34 Argyle St; r from £120; 📶) A new guesthouse set in a fine old terrace just west of the town centre, the Argyle has spacious, hotel-quality bedrooms with huge modern bathrooms of dark tile, chrome and glass (two of the four have free-standing bath tubs). Little touches like drinks offered on arrival, fresh flowers and sweets add to the atmosphere of hospitality.

Five Pilmour Place B&B $$
(☎01334-478665; www.5pilmourplace.com; 5 Pilmour Pl; s/d from £75/110; 📶) Just around the corner from the Old Course, this luxurious and intimate spot offers stylish, compact rooms with plenty of designer touches. The king-size beds are especially comfortable, and the lounge area is an Edwardian-style retreat of leather armchairs, polished wood and swagged curtains.

Cameron House B&B $$
(☎01334-472306; www.cameronhouse-sta.co.uk; 11 Murray Park; s/d £50/90; 📶) Beautifully decorated rooms and warm, cheerful hosts make this a real home away from home on this guesthouse-filled street. The two single rooms share a bathroom. Prices drop £10 per person outside peak season.

Old Course Hotel HOTEL $$$
(☎01334-474371; www.oldcoursehotel.co.uk; Old Station Rd; r from £275; P📶🏊) A byword for golfing luxury, this hotel is right alongside the famous 17th green (Road Hold) on the Old Course and has huge rooms, excellent service and a raft of facilities, including a spa complex. Fork out the extra £50 or so for a view over the Old Course. You can usually find good deals online.

Hazelbank Hotel HOTEL $$$
(☎01334-472466; www.hazelbank.com; 28 The Scores; d £129-189; 📶) Offering a genuine welcome, the family-run Hazelbank is the most likeable of the pleasingly old-fashioned hotels along The Scores. The more expensive front rooms have marvellous views along the beach and out to sea; prices drop significantly outside the height of summer. There's good karma if you are playing golf – Bobby Locke won the Open in 1957 while a guest here.

Eating & Drinking

Tailend FISH & CHIPS $
(www.thetailend.co.uk; 130 Market St; takeaway £4-9; ⊙11.30am-10pm) 🍃 Delicious fresh fish sourced from Arbroath, just up the coast, puts this a class above most chippies. It fries to order and it's worth the wait. The array of exquisite smoked delicacies at the counter will have you planning a picnic or fighting for a table in the licensed cafe out the back.

Northpoint Cafe CAFE $
(☎01334-473997; northpoint@dr.com; 24 North St; mains £3-7; ⊙8.30am-5pm Mon-Fri, 9am-5pm Sat, 10am-4pm Sun; 📶) The cafe where Prince William famously met his future wife Kate Middleton while they were both students at St Andrews serves good coffee and a broad range of breakfast fare, from porridge topped with banana to toasted bagels, pancake stacks and classic fry-ups. It's bit too busy for its own good these days, so get in early for lunch.

★**Adamson** BRASSERIE $$
(☎01334-479191; http://theadamson.com; 127 South St; mains £13-27; ⊙noon-3pm & 5-10pm Mon-Fri, noon-10pm Sat-Sun; 📶👪) Housed in the former post-office building, this loud and bustling brasserie panders to a youngish clientele of local families, well-heeled students and tourists with a crowd-pleasing menu of steaks and seafood, including local lobster with chips. Service can be over-eager or occasionally chaotic, but it all adds to the hectic buzz.

Mitchell's Deli DELI, SCOTTISH $$
(☎01334-441396; www.mitchellsdeli.co.uk; 110-112 Market St; ⊙8am-11pm Mon-Thu, 8am-midnight Fri-Sat, 9am-11pm Sun; 📶👪) 🍃 Railway sleeper floors, cut-down workbench tables and seats upholstered with old tweed jackets lend a utilitarian air to this excellent deli-cafe-restaurant where local produce is king. Breakfast (served till noon) includes free-range eggs Benedict, organic porridge and Arbroath smokies, while the evening menu runs to mussels and chips, steak and ale pie, and pork chop with black pudding.

★**Vine Leaf** SCOTTISH $$$
(☎01334-477497; www.vineleafstandrews.co.uk; 131 South St; 2-/3-course dinner £28/30; ⊙6-10pm Tue-Sat; 🖋) 🍃 Classy, comfortable and well established, the friendly Vine Leaf of-

fers a changing menu of sumptuous Scottish seafood, game and vegetarian dishes. There's a huge selection within the set-price menu, all well presented, and an interesting, mostly old-world wine list. It's down a close off South St. Reservations recommended.

Seafood Restaurant SEAFOOD **$$$**
(☎01334-479475; www.theseafoodrestaurant.com; The Scores; lunch mains £15-17, 3-course dinner £50; ⏲10am-10pm) The Seafood Restaurant occupies a stylish glass-walled room, built out over the sea, with polished wooden floors, crisp white linen, an open kitchen and panoramic views of St Andrews Bay. It offers top-notch seafood and an excellent wine list; look out for its special winter deals.

St Andrews Brewing Co MICROBREWERY
(www.standrewsbrewingcompany.com; 177 South St; ⏲noon-midnight;) Good beer, good food and good company are the order of the day in this friendly modern brewpub, with 16 beers on tap (inlcuding several of their own brews), more than 170 varieties in bottles, and around 30 craft gins.

Information

Free internet access is offered at the **library** (Church Sq; ⏲9.30am-5pm Mon, Fri & Sat, to 7pm Tue-Thu).

Services are available at **St Andrews Community Hospital** (☎01334-465656; www.nhsfife.org; Largo Rd).

The helpful staff at **St Andrews Tourist Office** (☎01334-472021; www.visitstandrews.com; 70 Market St; ⏲9.15am-6pm Mon-Sat, 10am-5pm Sun Jul & Aug, shorter hrs rest of yr) have a good knowledge of the city and Fife.

Getting There & Away

BUS

All buses leave from the **bus station** (Station Rd).

Anstruther £4.20, 25 minutes, hourly
Crail £4.20, 25 minutes, hourly
Dundee £4.80, 30 minutes, at least half-hourly
Edinburgh £11.70, two hours, hourly
Glasgow £11.70, 2½ hours, hourly
Stirling £8.20, two hours, every two hours Monday to Saturday

TRAIN

There is no train station in St Andrews itself, but you can take a train from Edinburgh (grab a seat on the right-hand side of the carriage for great sea views) to Leuchars (£13.90, one hour, half-hourly), 5 miles to the northwest. From here, buses leave regularly for St Andrews (£2.90, 10 minutes, every 10 minutes) or a taxi costs around £13.

Getting Around

To order a cab, call **Golf City Taxis** (☎01334-477788; www.golfcitytaxis.co.uk).

Spokes (☎01334-477835; www.spokescycles.com; 37 South St; per day/week £20/95; ⏲8.45am-5.30pm Mon-Sat) hires out mountain bikes.

East Neuk

This charming stretch of coast runs south from St Andrews to the headland at Fife Ness, then as far west as Earlsferry. Neuk is an old Scots word for 'corner', and it's certainly an appealing nook of the country to investigate, with picturesque fishing villages whose distinctive red pantiled roofs and crowstep gables are a legacy of centuries-old trading links with the Low Countries.

The Fife Coastal Path's most scenic stretches are in this area. It's easily visited from St Andrews, or even as a day trip from Edinburgh, but also offers many pleasant places to stay.

Crail

POP 1640

Pretty and peaceful, little Crail has a much-photographed stone-built harbour surrounded by quaint cottages with red-tiled roofs. The village's history is outlined in the **Crail Museum** (www.crailmuseum.org.uk; 62 Marketgate; ⏲11am-4pm Mon-Sat, 1-4pm Sun Jun-Sep, Sat & Sun only May & Oct) FREE, but the main attraction is just wandering the winding streets and hanging out by the harbour. There are views across to the Isle of May.

Crail is 10 miles southeast of St Andrews. Stagecoach (www.stagecoachbus.com) bus 95 between Leven, Anstruther, Crail and St Andrews passes through Crail hourly every day (£4.20, 25 minutes to St Andrews).

Hazelton Guest House B&B **$$**
(☎01333-450250; www.thehazelton.co.uk; 29 Marketgate North; r £55-85;) Hazelton is a welcoming, walker-friendly B&B in the centre of the village. The Victorian house is filled with period features, and the two top-floor rooms have great views across the rooftops to the Firth of Forth and the Isle of May.

Lobster Store SEAFOOD $
(☎01333-450476; 34 Shoregate; mains £4-11; ⊙noon-4pm Tue-Sun Jun-Sep, Sat-Sun only Oct-Apr) This quaint little shack overlooking Crail harbour serves dressed crab and freshly boiled lobster that has been caught locally. You can have a whole lobster (split) or lobster rolls. This is no-fuss takeaway – there's a single table out front, but you can find a place to sit and eat your catch anywhere around the harbour.

Anstruther

POP 3450

Once among Scotland's busiest fishing ports, cheery Anstruther (pronounced *en*-ster by locals) has ridden the tribulations of the declining fishing industry better than some, and now offers a pleasant mixture of bobbing boats, historic streets and visitors ambling around the harbour grazing on fish and chips, or contemplating a boat trip to the Isle of May.

Sights & Activities

Scottish Fisheries Museum MUSEUM
(www.scotfishmuseum.org; East Shore; adult/child £8/free; ⊙10am-5.30pm Mon-Sat, 11am-5pm Sun Apr-Sep, 10am-4.30pm Mon-Sat, noon-4.30pm Sun Oct-Mar) This excellent museum covers the history of the Scottish fishing industry in fascinating detail, including plenty of hands-on exhibits for kids. Displays include the **Zulu Gallery**, which houses the huge, partly restored hull of a traditional 19th-century Zulu-class fishing boat, redolent with the scents of tar and timber; and afloat in the harbour outside the museum lies the **Reaper**, a fully restored Fifie-class fishing boat built in 1902.

Isle of May NATURE RESERVE
The mile-long Isle of May, 6 miles southeast of Anstruther, is a spectacular nature reserve. Between April and July the island's cliffs are packed with breeding kittiwakes, razorbills, guillemots, shags and around 40,000 puffins. Inland are the remains of the 12th-century St Adrian's Chapel, dedicated to a monk who was murdered on the island by the Danes in 875. Several boats operating out of Anstruther harbour offer trips to the island.

May Princess BOATING
(☎07957 585200; www.isleofmayferry.com; adult/child £25/11; ⊙Apr-Sep) A five-hour boat trip to the Isle of May, including two to three hours ashore, sails from three to seven times weekly (weather permitting) from April to September (daily July to September). You can make reservations and buy tickets at the harbour kiosk at least an hour before departure. Departure times vary depending on the tide – check times for the coming week or so by calling, or check the website.

Sleeping & Eating

★**Murray Library Hostel** HOSTEL $
(☎01333-311123; http://murraylibraryhostel.com; 7 Shore St; dm/d £20/56; 📶) Set in a handsome, red-sandstone, waterfront building that once housed the local library, this brand-new hostel is beautifully furnished and equipped. There are four- to six-bed dorms, many with sea views, plus private twins and doubles, a gorgeous modern kitchen and a comfortable lounge.

★**Spindrift** B&B $$
(☎01333-310573; www.thespindrift.co.uk; Pittenweem Rd; d/f £92/120; P📶🐾) Arriving from the west, there's no need to go further than Anstruther's first house on the left, a redoubt of Scottish cheer and warm hospitality. The rooms are elegant, classy and extremely comfortable – some have views across to Edinburgh and one is a wood-panelled re-creation of a ship's cabin, courtesy of the sea captain who once owned the house.

There are DVD players and teddies for company, an honesty bar with characterful ales and malts, and fine company from your hosts. Breakfast includes porridge once voted the best in the kingdom. Dinner (£25 per person) is also available, but must be booked in advance.

Anstruther Fish Bar FISH & CHIPS $
(☎01333-310518; www.anstrutherfishbar.co.uk; 42-44 Shore St; mains £5-8; ⊙11.30am-10pm) An award-winning chippie famous for its deep-fried haddock and chips, this place also offers classy takes on traditional takeaway dishes, including dressed crab and battered prawns (both locally caught).

★**Cellar Restaurant** SCOTTISH $$$
(☎01333-310378; www.thecellaranstruther.co.uk; 24 East Green; 3-course lunch/dinner £28/48; ⊙12.30-1.45pm Thu-Sun, 6.30-9pm Wed-Sun, no lunch Thu Oct-Mar) 🍃 Tucked away in an alley behind the Scottish Fisheries Museum, the elegant and upmarket Cellar has been

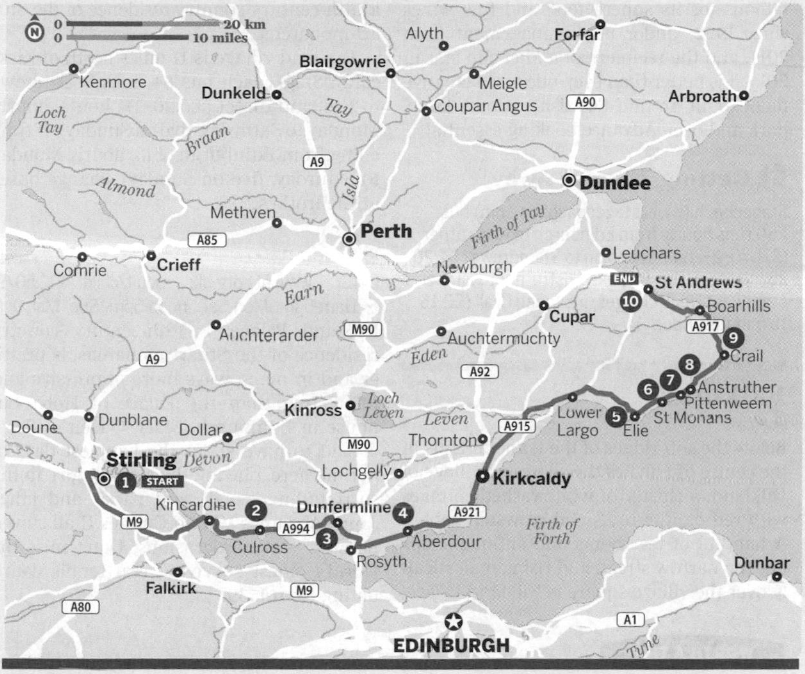

Driving Tour
The Fife Coast

START STIRLING
END ST ANDREWS
LENGTH 76 MILES; ONE DAY

This tour links two of the most popular tourist towns in Central Scotland via the scenic delights of the Fife coast.

Head south from **1 Stirling** (p836) on the M9 and at Junction 7 turn east towards Kincardine Bridge. As you approach the bridge, follow signs for Kincardine and Kirkcaldy; then once across the Firth of Forth, follow the Fife Coastal Tourist Route signposts to the historic village of **2 Culross** (p851). Spend an hour or so exploring the medieval buildings of Culross before continuing via the A994 to **3 Dunfermline** (p851), for a look at its fine abbey and palace ruins.

From Dunfermline take the M90 towards the Forth Road Bridge, but leave at Junction 1 (signposted A921 Dalgety Bay) and continue to the attractive seaside village of **4 Aberdour** for lunch at the Aberdour Hotel or the Room with a View restaurant. Stay on the A921 as far as Kirkcaldy, then take the faster A915 (signposted St Andrews) as far as Upper Largo where you follow the A917 towards Elie; from here, you will be following the brown Fife Coastal Tourist Route signs.

5 Elie, with its sandy beaches and coastal footpaths, is a great place to stretch your legs and take in some bracing sea air before driving just a couple of miles further on to explore the neighbouring fishing villages of **6 St Monans** and **7 Pittenweem**. Just 1 mile beyond Pittenweem, **8 Anstruther** (opposite) deserves a slightly longer stop for a visit to the Scottish Fisheries Museum, a stroll by the harbour and an ice cream. You may want to detour inland a couple of miles to visit Kellie Castle or Scotland's Secret Bunker.

The final stop before St Andrews is the pretty fishing village of **9 Crail** (p847), where the late afternoon or early evening light will provide ideal conditions for capturing one of Scotland's most photographed harbours. A hike along the coastal path towards Fife Ness, keeping an eye out for seals and seabirds, will round off the day before the last 10 miles into **10 St Andrews** (p842).

famous for its superb food and fine wines since 1982; under new management from 2014, and the recipient of a Michelin star in 2015, it is better than ever, offering a creative menu built around Scottish seafood, lamb, pork and beef. Advance booking essential.

Getting There & Away

Stagecoach (www.stagecoachbus.com) bus X60 runs hourly from Edinburgh to Anstruther (£11.70, 2¼ hours) and on to St Andrews (£4.20, 25 minutes). Bus 95 links Anstruther to all the other East Neuk villages, including Crail (£2.15, 15 minutes, hourly).

Falkland

POP 1100

Below the soft ridges of the Lomond Hills in the centre of Fife lies the charming village of Falkland, a cluster of whitewashed cottages with red pantile roofs and crowstep gables. A handful of tea rooms and antique shops dot the narrow street, and rising majestically over the village square is Falkland Palace, a 16th-century country residence of the Stuart monarchs.

Falkland village is 11 miles north of Kirkcaldy. Stagecoach bus 64 links St Andrews to Falkland direct (£6.20, 1¾ hours, hourly Monday to Saturday, five on Sunday). If travelling from Edinburgh (£13, hourly Monday to Saturday, five on Sunday), change buses at Glenrothes.

Falkland Palace PALACE

(NTS; www.nts.org.uk; adult/child £12.50/9; 11am-5pm Mon-Sat, noon-5pm Sun Mar-Oct) Falkland Palace, a 16th-century country residence of the Stuart monarchs, is prettier and in many ways more impressive and interesting than the Palace of Holyroodhouse in Edinburgh. Mary, Queen of Scots is said to have spent the happiest days of her life here 'playing the country girl' in the surrounding woods and parks, and kings James V, James VI and Charles II all stayed here on various occasions. Don't miss the world's oldest surviving real tennis court, dating from 1539.

WORTH A TRIP

SCONE PALACE

'So thanks to all at once and to each one, whom we invite to see us crowned at Scone.' This line from *Macbeth* indicates the importance of **Scone Palace** (01738-552300; www.scone-palace.co.uk; Scone Estate; adult/child £11/8; 9.30am-6pm May-Sep, 10am-5pm Easter-Apr & Oct, last admission 1hr before closing; P), pronounced 'skoon', as the coronation place of Scottish monarchs. The original palace of 1580, laying claim to this historic site, was rebuilt in the early 19th century as a Georgian mansion of extreme elegance and luxury. The self-guided tour takes you through a succession of sumptuous rooms filled with fine French furniture and noble portraits.

Scone has belonged for centuries to the Murray family, Earls of Mansfield, and many of the objects have a fascinating history attached to them (friendly guides are on hand to explain). Each room has comprehensive multilingual information; there are also panels relating histories of some of the Scottish kings crowned at Scone over the centuries. Outside, peacocks – each named after a monarch – shriek and strut around the magnificent grounds, which incorporate woods, a butterfly garden and a maze.

Ancient kings were crowned on **Moot Hill**, now topped by a chapel next to the palace. It's said that the hill was created by bootfuls of earth, brought by nobles attending the coronations as an acknowledgement of the king's rights over their lands, although it's more likely the site of an ancient motte-and-bailey castle. Here in 838, Kenneth MacAlpin became the first king of a united Scotland and brought to Scone the **Stone of Destiny**, on which Scottish kings were ceremonially invested. In 1296 Edward I of England carted this talisman off to Westminster Abbey, where it remained for 700 years before being returned to Scotland in 1997 (it now sits in Edinburgh Castle, but there are plans afoot to return it to Perth).

Scone Palace is 2 miles north of Perth; from the town centre, cross the bridge, turn left, and keep bearing left until you reach the gates of the estate. From here, it's a another half-mile to the palace (about 45 minutes' walk). Various buses from town stop here; the tourist office can advise.

Dunfermline

POP 49,700

Dunfermline is a large and unlovely town, but rich in history, boasting the evocative Dunfermline Abbey, its neighbouring palace and the attractive grounds of Pittencrieff Park, the latter gifted to the city by local boy made good, Andrew Carnegie (1835–1919), of US steel industry fame.

There are frequent buses between Dunfermline and Edinburgh (£6, 50 minutes), Stirling (£4.80, 1¼ hours) and St Andrews (£11.10, 1¼ hours), plus trains to/from Edinburgh (£5.30, 40 minutes).

Dunfermline Abbey & Palace RUINS

(HS; www.historicenvironment.scot; St Margaret St; adult/child £4.50/2.70; ⏲9.30am-5.30pm Apr-Sep, 9.30am-4.30pm Sat-Wed Oct-Mar) Dunfermline Abbey was founded by David I in the 12th century as a Benedictine monastery. The abbey and its neighbouring palace was already favoured by religious royals: Malcolm III married the exiled Saxon princess Margaret here in the 11th century, and both chose to be interred here. More royal burials followed, none more notable than Robert the Bruce, whose remains were interred here in 1329.

What remains of the abbey are the ruins of the impressive three-tiered refectory building, and the atmosphere-laden nave of the old church, endowed with geometrically patterned columns and fine Romanesque and Gothic windows. It adjoins the 19th-century **abbey church** (⏲10am-4.30pm Mon-Sat, 2-4.30pm Sun Apr-Oct) where Robert the Bruce lies entombed beneath the ornate pulpit.

Next to the refectory (and included in your abbey admission) is **Dunfermline Palace**. Once the abbey guesthouse, it was converted for James VI, whose son, the ill-fated Charles I, was born here in 1600. Below stretches the leafy, strollable **Pittencrieff Park**.

Culross

POP 400

Instantly familiar to fans of the TV series *Outlander*, in which it appears as the fictional village of Cranesmuir, Culross (*koo-*ross) is Scotland's best-preserved example of a 17th-century town. Limewashed white and yellow-ochre houses with red-tiled roofs stand amid a maze of cobbled streets, and the winding Back Causeway to the abbey is lined with whimsical cottages. The National Trust for Scotland (NTS) owns no fewer than 20 of the town's buildings.

As the birthplace of St Mungo, Glasgow's patron saint, Culross was an important religious centre from the 6th century. The burgh developed under local laird Sir George Bruce by extracting coal through ingenious tunnels extending under the seabed. When mining was ended by flooding of the tunnels, the town switched to making linen and shoes.

Culross is 16 miles east of Stirling, and 12 miles west of the Forth bridges. Buses run from Dunfermline (£2.90, 30 minutes, hourly) via Culross to Stirling (£4.80, 50 minutes, hourly Monday to Saturday).

Culross Palace HISTORIC SITE

(NTS; www.nts.org.uk; Low Causewayside; adult/child £10.50/7.50; ⏲noon-5pm daily Jun-Aug, Wed-Sun only Apr-May & Sep, noon-4pm Wed-Sun Oct) More large house than palace, the 17th-century residence of local laird Sir George Bruce features an interior largely unchanged since his time. The decorative wood panelling and painted timber ceilings are of national importance, particularly the allegorical scenes in the Painted Chamber, which survive from the early 1600s. Don't miss the re-creation of a 17th-century garden at the back, with gorgeous views from the top terrace.

The Town House (with ticket and information desk downstairs) and the Study, both dating from the early 17th century, can be visited on a 45-minute guided tour of the town (£2 per person, available between 1pm and 3pm).

DUNDEE & ANGUS

Angus is a fertile farming region stretching north from Dundee – Scotland's fourth-largest city – to the Highland border. It's an attractive area of broad straths (valleys) and low, green hills contrasting with the rich, red-brown soil of freshly ploughed fields. The romantic Angus Glens finger their way into the foothills of the Grampian Mountains, while the scenic coastline ranges from the red-sandstone cliffs of Arbroath to the long, sandy beaches around Montrose. This was the Pictish heartland of the 7th and 8th centuries, and many interesting Pictish symbol stones survive here.

Apart from the crowds visiting newly confident Dundee and the coach parties shuffling through Glamis Castle, Angus is a bit of a tourism backwater and a good place to escape the crowds.

Dundee

POP 147,300

London's Trafalgar Sq has Nelson on his column, Edinburgh's Princes St has its monument to Sir Walter Scott and Belfast has a statue of Queen Victoria outside City Hall. Dundee's City Sq, on the other hand, is graced – rather endearingly – by the bronze figure of Desperate Dan. Familiar to generations of British school children, Dan is one of the best-loved cartoon characters from the children's comic the *Dandy,* published by Dundee firm DC Thomson since 1937.

Dundee enjoys perhaps the finest location of any Scottish city, spreading along the northern shore of the Firth of Tay, and boasts tourist attractions of national importance in Discovery Point and the Verdant Works museum. Add in the attractive seaside town of Broughty Ferry and the Dundonians themselves – among the friendliest, most welcoming and most entertaining people you'll meet – and Dundee is definitely worth a stopover.

The waterfront around Discovery Point was undergoing a massive redevelopment at time of research, centred around the construction of the V&A Museum of Design. In the meantime, be prepared for construction sites, temporary street layouts and traffic diversions on the approach to the Tay Bridge.

History

During the 19th century Dundee grew from its trading port origins to become a major player in the shipbuilding, whaling, textile and railway engineering industries. Dundonian firms owned and operated most of the jute mills in India (jute is a natural fibre used to make ropes and sacking), and the city's textile industry employed as many as 43,000 people – little wonder Dundee earned the nickname 'Juteopolis'.

Dundee is often called the city of the 'Three Js' – jute, jam and journalism. According to legend, it was a Dundee woman, Janet Keillor, who invented marmalade in the late 18th century; her son founded the city's famous Keillor jam factory. Jute is no longer produced, and when the Keillor factory was taken over in 1988, production was transferred to England. Journalism still thrives, however, led by the family firm of DC Thomson. Best known for children's comics such as the *Beano* and the *Dandy,* and regional newspapers including the *Press and Journal,* Thomson is now the city's largest employer.

In the late 19th and early 20th centuries Dundee was one of the richest cities in the country – there were more millionaires per head of population here than anywhere else in Britain – but the textile and engineering industries declined in the second half of the 20th century, leading to high unemployment and urban decay.

In the 1960s and '70s Dundee's cityscape was scarred by ugly blocks of flats, office buildings and shopping centres linked by unsightly concrete walkways and most visitors passed it by. Since the mid-1990s, however, Dundee has reinvented itself as a tourist destination, and a centre for banking, insurance and high-tech industries, while its waterfront is undergoing a major redevelopment. It also has more university students – one in seven of the population – than any other town in Europe, except Heidelberg.

Sights

★V&A Museum of Design MUSEUM

(☎01382-305665; www.vandadundee.org; Riverside Esplanade) FREE The centrepiece of Dundee's revitalised waterfront is this stunning new building designed by Japanese architect Kengo Kuma. When it opens (scheduled in summer 2018) it will house an outpost of London's V&A museum of art and design. Exhibitions will showcase the work of Scottish designers past and present, from famous names such as Charles Rennie Mackintosh to modern creatives such as fashion designer Holly Fulton, alongside the best of art and design from around the world.

★Discovery Point MUSEUM

(www.rrsdiscovery.com; Discovery Quay; adult/child/family £9.25/5.50/27; ⊙10am-6pm Mon-Sat, 11am-6pm Sun Apr-Oct, to 5pm Nov-Mar; P ♿) The three masts of Captain Robert Falcon Scott's famous polar expedition vessel the RRS *Discovery* provide a historic counterpoint to the modern architecture of the V&A Design Museum. Exhibitions and audiovisual displays in the neighbouring visitor centre provide a fascinating history of both the ship and Antarctic exploration, but *Discovery* herself is the star attraction. You can visit the bridge, the galley and the mahogany-panelled officers' wardroom, and poke your nose into the cabins used by Scott and his crew.

The ship was built in Dundee in 1900, with a wooden hull at least half a metre thick to survive the pack ice, and sailed for the Antarctic in 1901 where it spent two winters trapped in the ice. From 1931 it was laid up in London where its condition steadily deteriorated, until it was rescued by the efforts of Peter Scott (Robert's son) and the Maritime Trust, and restored to its 1925 condition. In 1986 the ship was given a berth in its home port of Dundee, where it became a symbol of the city's regeneration.

A joint ticket that gives entry to both Discovery Point and the Verdant Works costs £16/9/43 per adult/child/family.

★Verdant Works MUSEUM

(www.verdantworks.com; West Henderson's Wynd; adult/child/family £9.25/5.50/27; ⏲10am-6pm Mon-Sat, 11am-6pm Sun Apr-Oct, shorter hours Nov-Mar; 👪) One of the finest industrial museums in Europe, the Verdant Works explores the history of Dundee's jute industry. Housed in a restored jute mill, complete with original machinery still in working condition, the museum's interactive exhibits and computer displays follow the raw material from its origins in India through to the manufacture of a wide range of finished products, from sacking to rope to wagon covers for the pioneers of the American West. The museum is 250m west of the city centre.

McManus Galleries MUSEUM

(www.mcmanus.co.uk; Albert Sq; ⏲10am-5pm Mon-Sat, 12.30-4.30pm Sun) FREE Housed in a solid Victorian Gothic building designed by Gilbert Scott in 1867, the McManus Galleries are a city museum on a human scale – you can see everything there is to see in a single visit, without feeling rushed or overwhelmed. The exhibits cover the history of the city from the Iron Age to the present day, including relics of the Tay Bridge Disaster and the Dundee whaling industry.

Computer geeks will enjoy the Sinclair ZX81 and Spectrum (pioneering personal computers with a whole 16K of memory!) which were made in Dundee in the early 1980s.

Dundee Contemporary Arts ARTS CENTRE

(www.dca.org.uk; Nethergate; ⏲11am-6pm Tue, Wed & Fri-Sun, 11am-8pm Thu) FREE Pioneering the development of the city's Cultural Quarter from its opening in 1999, Dundee Contemporary Arts is a centre for modern art, design and cinema. The galleries here

WORTH A TRIP

GLAMIS CASTLE

Looking every inch the Scottish Baronial castle, with its roofline sprouting a forest of pointed turrets and battlements, **Glamis Castle** (www.glamis-castle.co.uk; adult/child £11/8; ⏲10am-5.30pm Apr-Oct, last entry 4.30pm; 🅿👪) claims to be the legendary setting for Shakespeare's Macbeth. A royal residence since 1372, it is the family home of the earls of Strathmore and Kinghorne – the Queen Mother (born Elizabeth Bowes-Lyon; 1900–2002) spent her childhood at Glamis (pronounced 'glams') and Princess Margaret (the Queen's sister; 1930–2002) was born here.

The five-storey, L-shaped castle was given to the Lyon family in 1372, but was significantly altered in the 17th century. Inside, the most impressive room is the **drawing room**, with its vaulted plasterwork ceiling. There's a display of armour and weaponry in the haunted crypt and frescoes in the chapel (also haunted). **Duncan's Hall** is named for the murdered King Duncan from Macbeth (though the scene actually takes place in Macbeth's castle in Inverness). As with Cawdor Castle, the claimed Shakespeare connection is fictitious – the real Macbeth had nothing to do with either castle, and died long before either was built.

You can also look around the **royal apartments**, including the Queen Mother's bedroom. Hour-long guided tours (included in admission) depart every 15 minutes; the last tour is at 4.30pm.

Glamis Castle is 12 miles north of Dundee. There are two to four buses a day from Dundee (£6.45, 1½ hour) to Glamis; change at Forfar.

exhibit work by contemporary UK and international artists, and there are printmakers' studios where you can watch artists at work, or even take part in craft demonstrations and workshops. There's also the **Jute Cafe-Bar** (01382-909246; www.jutecafebar.co.uk; 152 Nethergate; mains £9-16; 10am-9.30pm;).

Sleeping

Dundee Backpackers HOSTEL $
(01382-224646; www.hoppo.com/dundee; 71 High St; dm £17, s/tw from £25/45;) Set in a beautifully converted historic building, with clean, modern kitchen, pool room, and an ideal location right in the city centre. Can get a bit noisy at night, but that's because it's close to pubs and nightlife.

Athollbank B&B $
(01382-801118; www.athollbank.com; 19 Thomson St; s/d £27/46;) A great-value B&B set on a quiet side street in the city's West End, Athollbank has smart, good-sized bedrooms (none are en suite, though) and is close to local pubs and restaurants.

Aabalree B&B $
(01382-223867; www.aabalree.com; 20 Union St; s/d £30/50;) This is a pretty basic B&B – there are no en suites, and no lift to the three floors – but the owners are welcoming (don't be put off by the dark entrance) and it couldn't be more central, close to both the train and bus stations. This makes it popular, so book ahead.

★**Malmaison** BOUTIQUE HOTEL $$
(01382-339715; www.malmaison.com; 44 Whitehall Cres; r from £75;) Housed in a Victorian hotel building, this place has been refurbished in typical Malmaison style with period features such as intricate wrought-iron balustrades complemented by delightfully over-the-top modern decor. The rooms on the south side overlook the new waterfront development and, when that's complete, will have gorgeous views. Room rates are excellent value; check website for special offers.

Apex City Quay Hotel HOTEL $$
(0845-365 0000; www.apexhotels.co.uk; 1 West Victoria Dock Rd; r from £89;) Though it looks plain and boxy from the outside, the Apex sports the sort of stylish, spacious, sofa-equipped rooms that make you want to lounge around all evening munching chocolate in front of the TV. If you can drag yourself away from your room, there are spa treatments, saunas and Japanese hot tubs to enjoy.

The hotel is just east of the city centre, overlooking the city's redeveloping waterfront and close to the HM Frigate *Unicorn*.

Eating

★**Parlour Cafe** CAFE $
(01382-203588; theparlourcafe.co.uk; 58 West Port; mains £6-8; 8am-6pm Mon-Fri, to 4pm Sat, 10am-3pm Sun;) Tiny but terrific, this friendly neighbourhood cafe is bursting with good things to eat including filled tortillas, savoury tarts, bean burgers, bagels and home-made soup, all freshly prepared using seasonal produce. Great coffee and cakes too, but be prepared to wait for a table or squeeze in among the locals.

Bridgeview Station SCOTTISH $
(01382-660066; www.bridgeviewstation.com; Riverside Dr; lunch mains £7-10, 3-course dinner £22; 8am-6pm Sun-Tue, to 10pm Wed-Sat;) Bridgeview enjoys a lovely setting in a red-brick Victorian railway station building on the western fringes of Dundee, with a view across the Firth of Tay. Covering everything from breakfast to dinner, the menu majors on fresh local produce with the lunch platters (seafood, vegetarian, or cheese and charcuterie) offering unbeatable value.

Playwright BISTRO $$$
(01382-223113; www.theplaywright.co.uk; 11 Tay Sq; mains £25-27; noon-2.30pm & 5-9.30pm Mon-Sat) Next door to the **Dundee Rep Theatre** (01382-223530; www.dundeereptheatre.co.uk; Tay Sq; box office 10am-6pm or start of performance), and decorated with photos of Scottish actors, this innovative bistro serves a set lunch (two courses £13), pre-theatre menu (two/three courses £17/20, 5pm to 6.30pm) and a gourmet à la carte menu that concentrates on fine Scottish produce.

★**Castlehill** MODERN SCOTTISH $$$
(01382-220008; www.castlehillrestaurant.co.uk; 22 Exchange St; 3-course lunch/dinner £19/36; noon-2.30pm & 5.30-10pm Tue-Sat) Thought by many to be on its way to earning Dundee's first Michelin star, the Castlehill is passionate about Scottish produce (the chef is a keen forager for wild herbs and fungi) and invests a lot of imagination into turning out beautifully presented dishes made with Angus lamb, Perthshire pork and Shetland scallops – art on a plate.

Information

Dundee Tourist Office (☎01382-527527; www.angusanddundee.co.uk; 16 City Sq; ⊙9.30am-5pm Mon-Sat)

Ninewells Hospital (☎01382-660111; www.nhstayside.scot.nhs.uk) At Menzieshill, west of the city centre.

Getting There & Away

AIR

Two and a half miles west of the city centre, **Dundee Airport** (www.hial.co.uk/dundee-airport) has daily scheduled services to London Stansted airport, Jersey and Amsterdam. A taxi from the city centre to the airport takes 10 minutes and costs around £5.

BUS

The bus station is northeast of the city centre. Some Aberdeen buses travel via Arbroath, others via Forfar.

Aberdeen £17.40, 1½ hours, hourly

Edinburgh £16.60, 1½ hours, hourly, some change at Perth

Glasgow £16.60, 1¾ hours, hourly

London £40, 11 hours; National Express, daily

Perth £7.70, 35 minutes, hourly

Oban £36.50, 5½ hours, three daily

TRAIN

Trains from Dundee to Aberdeen travel via Arbroath and Stonehaven.

Aberdeen £19.80, 1¼ hours, twice an hour

Edinburgh £17.90, 1¼ hours, at least hourly

Glasgow £22, 1½ hours, hourly

Perth £7.90, 25 minutes

Arbroath

POP 23,900

Arbroath is an old-fashioned seaside resort and fishing harbour, home of the famous Arbroath smokie (a form of smoked haddock). The humble smokie achieved European Union 'Protected Geographical Indication' status in 2004 – the term 'Arbroath smokie' can only be used legally to describe haddock smoked in the traditional manner within an 8km radius of Arbroath.

Arbroath Abbey HISTORIC BUILDING
(HS; www.historicenvironment.scot; Abbey St; adult/child £5.50/3.30; ⊙9.30am-5.30pm Apr-Sep, 10am-4pm Oct-Mar) The picturesque, red-sandstone ruins of Arbroath Abbey, founded in 1178 by King William the Lion, dominate the town of Arbroath. It is thought that Bernard of Linton, the abbot here in the early 14th century, wrote the famous Declaration of Arbroath in 1320, asserting Scotland's right to independence; an exhibition in the beautifully preserved Abbot's House includes a replica of the declaration. You can climb part way up one of the towers for a grand view over the ruins.

Harbour Nights Guest House B&B $$
(☎01241-434343; www.harbournights-scotland.com; 4 The Shore; r from £75; 📶) With a superb location overlooking the harbour, four stylishly decorated bedrooms and a gourmet breakfast menu, Harbour Nights is our favourite place to stay in Arbroath. Rooms 2 and 3, with harbour views, are a bit more expensive (from £80), but well worth asking for when booking.

But'n'Ben Restaurant SCOTTISH $$
(☎01241-877223; www.thebutnben.com; 1 Auchmithie; mains £8-26; ⊙noon-2pm Wed-Mon, 6-9pm Mon & Wed-Sat, 4-5.30pm Sun; 👪) Above the harbour in Auchmithie, this cosy cottage restaurant with open fireplace, rustic furniture and sea-themed art serves the best of local seafood – the Arbroath smokie pancakes are recommended – plus great home-made cakes and desserts, and high teas on Sunday (£16). Best to book.

Information

Visitor Centre & Tourist Office (☎01241-872609; Fishmarket Quay; ⊙10am-6pm Mon-Sat, noon-4pm Sun Apr-Oct, shorter hours Nov-Mar) Beside the harbour.

Getting There & Away

BUS

Bus 140 runs from Arbroath to Auchmithie (£2, 15 minutes, six daily Monday to Friday, three daily on Saturday and Sunday).

TRAIN

Trains from Dundee to Arbroath (£5.60, 20 minutes, two per hour) continue to Aberdeen (£19.40, 55 minutes) via Montrose and Stonehaven.

ABERDEENSHIRE

Since medieval times Aberdeenshire and its northwestern neighbour Moray have been the richest and most fertile regions of the Highlands. Aberdeenshire is famed for its Aberdeen Angus beef cattle, its many fine castles and the prosperous 'granite city' of Aberdeen.

North of Aberdeen, the Grampian Mountains fall away to rolling agricultural plains pocked with small, craggy volcanic hills. This fertile lowland corner of northeastern Scotland is known as Buchan; the old Scots dialect called the Doric lives on in everyday use here (if you think the Glaswegian accent is difficult to understand, just try listening in on a conversation in Fraserburgh).

The Buchan coast alternates between rugged cliffs and long, long stretches of sand, dotted with picturesque little fishing villages such as Pennan, where parts of the film *Local Hero* were shot.

Aberdeen

POP 195,000

Aberdeen is the powerhouse of northeast Scotland, fuelled by the North Sea petroleum industry. Oil money has made the city as expensive as London and Edinburgh, and there are hotels, restaurants and clubs with prices to match the depth of oil-wealthy pockets. Fortunately, most of the cultural attractions, such as the excellent Maritime Museum and the Aberdeen Art Gallery, are free.

Known throughout Scotland as the granite city, much of the town was built using silvery-grey granite hewn from the now abandoned Rubislaw Quarry, at one time the biggest artificial hole in the ground in Europe. On a sunny day the granite lends an attractive glitter to the city, but when low, grey rain clouds scud in off the North Sea it can be hard to tell where the buildings stop and the sky begins.

Royal Deeside is easily accessible to the west, Dunnottar Castle to the south, sandy beaches to the north and whisky country to the northwest.

Sights & Activities

Aberdeen Maritime Museum MUSEUM

(☎01224-337700; www.aagm.co.uk; Shiprow; ⏲10am-5pm Mon-Sat, noon-3pm Sun) FREE Overlooking the nautical bustle of Aberdeen harbour is the Maritime Museum, centred on a three-storey replica of a North Sea oil production platform, which explains all you ever wanted to know about the petroleum industry. Other galleries, some situated in **Provost Ross's House**, the oldest building in the city and part of the museum, cover the shipbuilding, whaling and fishing industries.

Sleek and speedy Aberdeen clippers were a 19th-century shipyard speciality, used by British merchants for the importation of tea, wool and exotic goods (opium, for instance) to Britain, and, on the return journey, the transportation of emigrants to Australia.

Aberdeen Art Gallery GALLERY

(☎01224-523700; www.aagm.co.uk; Schoolhill; ⏲10am-5pm Tue-Sat, 2-5pm Sun) FREE Behind the grand facade of Aberdeen Art Gallery (at time of writing closed for refurbishment until winter 2017) is a cool, marble-lined space exhibiting the work of contemporary Scottish and English painters, such as Gwen Hardie, Stephen Conroy, Trevor Sutton and Tim Ollivier. There are also several landscapes by Joan Eardley, who lived in a cottage on the cliffs near Stonehaven in the 1950s and '60s and painted tempestuous oils of the North Sea and poignant portraits of slum children.

Among the Pre-Raphaelite works upstairs, look out for the paintings by Aberdeen artist William Dyce (1806–64), ranging from religious works to rural scenes.

Marischal College HISTORIC BUILDING

(Broad St) Marischal College, founded in 1593 by the 5th Earl Marischal, merged with King's College (founded 1495) in 1860 to create the modern University of Aberdeen. The college's huge and impressive facade overlooking Broad St, in Perpendicular Gothic style – unusual in having such elaborate masonry hewn from notoriously hard-to-work granite – dates from 1906 and is the world's second-largest granite structure (after L'Escorial near Madrid).

A recent renovation project saw the facade returned to its original silvery grey glory, and the building now houses Aberdeen City Council's headquarters; outside, Marischal Sq is undergoing redevelopment as a pedestrian plaza, creating controversy over plans for modern architecture juxtaposed with the college's neogothic facade.

Clyde Cruises WILDLIFE WATCHING

(☎01475-721281; www.clydecruises.com; Aberdeen Harbour; adult/child from £16/8; ⏲daily Jul-late Aug, Thu-Sun late Aug–mid Sep) Operates 45-minute cruises around Aberdeen's bustling commercial harbour, and 1¼-hours trips (adult/child £25/12) outside the harbour to look for dolphins and other marine wildlife. If you're driving, park in Union Sq car park (two hours £3) and walk across Market St to the harbour.

Sleeping

There are clusters of B&Bs on Bon Accord St and Springbank Tce (both 400m southwest of the train station) and along Great Western Rd (the A93, a 25-minute walk southwest of the city centre). They're usually more expensive than the Scottish average and, with so many oil industry workers staying the night before flying offshore, single rooms are at a premium. Another side-effect of the industry is that rates tend to be significantly lower at weekends.

Aberdeen SYHA HOSTEL $

(SYHA; ☎01224-646988; www.syha.org.uk; 8 Queen's Rd; dm/d £20/50; @) This unexceptional but good-value hostel, set in a granite Victorian villa, is a mile west of the train station. Walk west along Union St and take the right fork along Albyn Pl until you reach a roundabout; Queen's Rd continues on the western side of the roundabout.

★ **Globe Inn** B&B $$

(☎01224-624258; www.the-globe-inn.co.uk; 13-15 North Silver St; s/d £70/75) This popular pub has seven appealing, comfortable guest bedrooms upstairs, done out in dark wood with burgundy bedspreads. There's live music in the pub on weekends so it's not a place for early-to-bed types, but the price vs location factor can't be beaten. No dining room, so breakfast is continental, served on a tray in your room. Cheaper at weekends.

★ **The Jays** B&B $$

(☎01224-638295; www.jaysguesthouse.co.uk; 422 King St; s/d from £50/100; P) Located halfway between the city centre (15 minutes walk) and Old Aberdeen (10 minutes walk), this elegantly decorated Edwardian villa is a cosy nest of hospitality, with welcoming owners who seemingly can't do enough to help their guests enjoy their stay. Popular, so book well in advance.

★ **Dutch Mill Hotel** HOTEL $$

(☎01224-322555; www.dutchmill.co.uk; 7 Queens Rd; s/d £105/125; P) The grand, granite-hewn, Victorian-era mansions that line Queens Rd house financial offices, private schools, medical practices and the occasional hotel – this one has nine bedrooms with beautifully understated modern decor, a popular bar and a conservatory restaurant. Rates are almost halved at weekends.

Bauhaus Hotel BOUTIQUE HOTEL $$

(☎01224-212122; www.thebauhaus.co.uk; 52-60 Langstane Pl; d/suite from £85/185;) Decor of exposed brick and leather wall panels, slate-lined bathrooms, and Corbusier armchairs in the more expensive suites, add a designer-ish touch to this centrally located, good-value hotel. Rates vary hugely, so check the website for special offers.

Butler's Guest House B&B $$

(☎01224-212411; www.butlersguesthouse.com; 122 Crown St; s/d from £55/65;) Butler's is a cosy place with a big breakfast menu that includes fresh fruit salad, kippers and kedgeree as alternatives to the traditional fry-up (rates include a continental breakfast – cooked breakfast is £6.50 extra per person). There are cheaper rooms with shared bathrooms.

Brentwood Hotel HOTEL $$

(☎01224-595440; www.brentwood-hotel.co.uk; 101 Crown St; s £45-85, d £59-95; P) The friendly and flower-bedecked Brentwood, set in a granite town house, is one of the most attractive hotels in the city centre. It's comfortable and conveniently located, but often busy during the week – weekend rates (Friday to Sunday) are much cheaper.

Eating

Ashvale Fish Restaurant FISH & CHIPS $

(www.theashvale.co.uk; 42-48 Great Western Rd; takeaway £5-10, sit-in £9-15; ⌚11.45am-10pm;) This is the flagship, 200-seat branch of the Ashvale, an award-winning fish-and-chip restaurant famed for its quality haddock. The Ashvale Whale – a 1lb fish fillet in batter (£12.45) – is a speciality; finish it off and you get a second one free (as if you'd want one by then!). It's 300m southwest of the west end of Union St.

★ **Adelphi Kitchen** MODERN SCOTTISH $$

(☎01224-211414; www.theadelphikitchen.co.uk; 28 Adelphi Ln, Union St; mains £10-28; ⌚noon-2.30pm & 5-10pm Tue-Sat;) Cool and clever flavour combinations are the hallmark of this little gem hidden down an alley off Union St, a small but sophisticated space decorated with weathered timber and muted natural colours. Charcoal grilling is a speciality, with aged Aberdeen Angus beef and pulled pork given the barbecue treatment alongside seafood treats such as west coast scallops and Shetland mussels.

Aberdeen

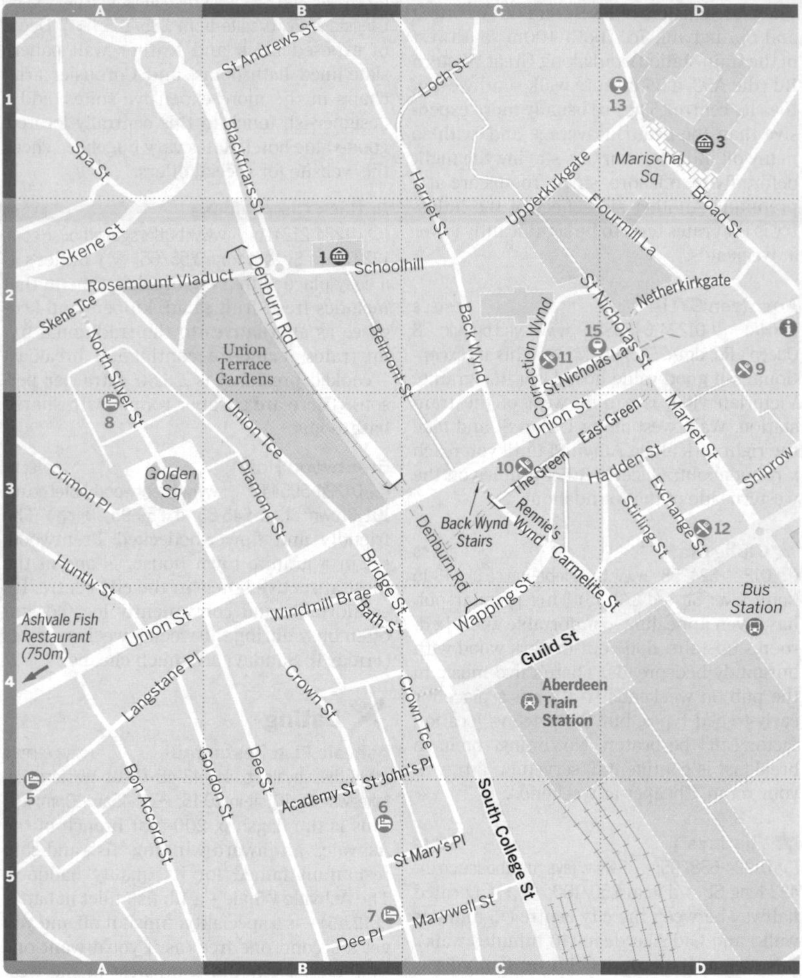

★Café 52

BISTRO $$

(☎01224-590094; www.cafe52.co.uk; 52 The Green; mains lunch £5, dinner £13; ⏰noon-midnight Mon-Sat, to 4pm Sun; 📶✍) This little haven of laid-back industrial chic – a high, narrow space lined with bare stonework, rough plaster and exposed ventilation ducts – serves some of the finest and most inventive cuisine in the northeast (black pudding with wine-poached pear, smoked haddock with fennel, basil and lemon crayfish sauce), and at incredible prices considering the quality on offer.

Sand Dollar Café

CAFE $$

(☎01224-572288; www.sanddollarcafe.com; 2 Beach Esplanade; mains £8-22; ⏰7.30am-9pm Mon-Wed, to 4pm Thu-Sat, to 6pm Sun, also 6-9pm Thu-Sat; 👪) A cut above your usual seaside cafe – on sunny days you can sit at the wooden tables on the prom and share a bottle of chilled white wine, or choose from a menu that includes pancakes with maple syrup, home-made burgers and chocolate brownie with Orkney ice cream.

An evening bistro menu (mains £16 to £27) offers steak and seafood dishes; best to

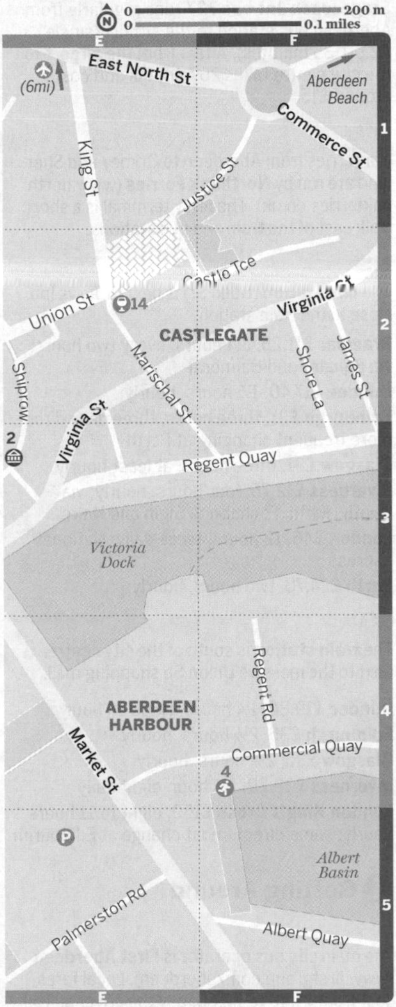

Aberdeen

Sights
1 Aberdeen Art Gallery B2
2 Aberdeen Maritime Museum E3
3 Marischal College D1

Activities, Courses & Tours
4 Clyde Cruises F4

Sleeping
5 Bauhaus Hotel A5
6 Brentwood Hotel B5
7 Butler's Guest House B5
8 Globe Inn A3

Eating
9 Adelphi Kitchen D2
10 Café 52 .... C3
11 Moonfish Café C2
12 Musa Art Cafe D3

Drinking & Nightlife
13 BrewDog D1
14 Old Blackfriars E2
15 Prince of Wales C2

book for this. The cafe is on the esplanade, 800m northeast of the city centre.

Musa Art Cafe MODERN SCOTTISH **$$**
(☎01224-571771; www.musaaberdeen.com; 33 Exchange St; mains lunch £9-14, dinner £13-25; ⏰noon-11pm Tue-Sat; 📶📝) 🌿 The bright paintings on the walls match the vibrant furnishings and smart gastronomic creations at this great cafe-restaurant, set in a former church. As well as a menu that focuses on quality local produce cooked in a quirky way – think haggis spring rolls with chilli and red-pepper jam – there are Brewdog beers from Fraserburgh, and interesting music, sometimes live.

Moonfish Café MODERN SCOTTISH **$$$**
(☎01224-644166; www.moonfishcafe.co.uk; 9 Correction Wynd; 2-/3-course dinner £33/38; ⏰noon-2pm & 6-9.30pm Tue-Sat) 🌿 The menu of this funky little eatery tucked away on a back street concentrates on good-quality Scottish produce but draws its influences from cuisines all around the world, from simple smoked haddock with charred leeks and toasted rice, to mussels with saffron, chorizo and orange. Two-course lunch £14.

Silver Darling SEAFOOD **$$$**
(☎01224-576229; www.thesilverdarling.co.uk; Pocra Quay, North Pier; 2-/3-course lunch £19.50/25.50, dinner mains £17-26; ⏰noon-4pm & 6.30-9.30pm Mon-Sat) 🌿 The Silver Darling (an old Scottish nickname for herring) is the place for a special meal, housed in a former Customs office at the entrance to Aberdeen harbour with picture windows overlooking the sea. Here you can enjoy fresh Scottish seafood prepared by a top French chef while you watch the porpoises playing in the harbour mouth. Bookings are recommended.

🍷 Drinking & Nightlife

BrewDog BAR
(www.brewdog.com/bars/aberdeen; 17 Gallowgate; ⏰noon-midnight Mon-Thu, to 1am Fri & Sat,

12.30pm-midnight Sun;) The original flagship bar of northeast Scotland's most innovative craft brewery brings a bit of industrial chic to Aberdeen's pub scene along with a vast range of guest beers from around the world.

Prince of Wales PUB

(www.princeofwales-aberdeen.co.uk; 7 St Nicholas Lane; 10am-midnight Mon-Thu, to 1am Fri & Sat, 11am-midnight Sun;) Tucked down an alley off Union St, Aberdeen's best-known pub boasts the longest bar in the city, a great range of real ales and good-value pub grub. Quiet in the afternoons, but standing-room only in the evenings.

Blue Lamp PUB

(www.jazzatthebluelamp.com; 121 Gallowgate; 11am-midnight Mon-Thu, to 1am Fri & Sat, 12.30-11pm Sun) A long-standing feature of the Aberdeen pub scene, the Blue Lamp is a favourite student hang-out – a cosy drinking den with good beer, good *craic* (lively conversation) and regular sessions of live jazz and stand-up comedy. The pub is 150m north of the city centre, along Broad St.

Old Blackfriars PUB

(www.oldblackfriars-aberdeen.co.uk; 52 Castlegate; 11am-midnight Mon-Thu, 11am-1am Fri, 10am-1am Sat, 10am-11pm Sun;) One of the most attractive traditional pubs in the city, with a lovely stone and timber interior, stained-glass windows and a relaxed atmosphere – a great place for an afternoon pint. Live folk music on Thursday from 9pm.

Information

Aberdeen Royal Infirmary (0345-456 6000; www.nhsgrampian.org; Foresterhill) Medical services. About a mile northwest of the western end of Union St.

Aberdeen Tourist Office (01224-269180; www.aberdeen-grampian.com; 23 Union St; 9am-6.30pm Mon-Sat, 10am-4pm Sun Jul & Aug, 9.30am-5pm Mon-Sat Sep-Jun;) Handy for general information; has internet access (£1 per 20 minutes).

Getting There & Away

AIR

Aberdeen Airport (ABZ; 0844-481 6666; www.aberdeenairport.com) is at Dyce, 6 miles northwest of the city centre. There are regular flights to numerous Scottish and UK destinations, including Orkney and Shetland, and international flights to the Netherlands, Norway, Denmark, Germany and France.

Stagecoach Jet bus 727 runs regularly from Aberdeen bus station to the airport (single £2.90, 35 minutes). A taxi from the airport to the city centre takes 25 minutes and costs around £15.

BOAT

Car ferries from Aberdeen to Orkney and Shetland are run by **Northlink Ferries** (www.northlinkferries.co.uk). The ferry terminal is a short walk east of the train and bus stations.

BUS

The **bus station** (Guild St) is next to Jurys Inn, close to the train station.

Braemar £11.25, 2¼ hours, every two hours; via Ballater and Balmoral
Dundee £17.40, 1½ hours, hourly
Edinburgh £31, three hours, three daily direct, more frequent changing at Perth
Glasgow £31, three hours, at least hourly
Inverness £12.75, four hours, hourly; via Huntly, Keith, Fochabers, Elgin and Nairn
London £46, 12 hours, twice daily; National Express
Perth £24.70, two hours, hourly

TRAIN

The **train station** is south of the city centre, next to the massive Union Sq shopping mall.

Dundee £19.80, 1¼ hours, twice an hour
Edinburgh £35, 2½ hours, hourly
Glasgow £35, 2¾ hours, hourly
Inverness £28.20, 2¼ hour, eight daily
London King's Cross £150, eight to 11 hours, hourly; some direct, most change at Edinburgh

Getting Around

BUS

The main city bus operator is **First Aberdeen** (www.firstgroup.com/aberdeen). Local fares cost from £1.40 to £2.60; pay the driver as you board the bus. A FirstDay ticket (£4) allows unlimited travel from the time of purchase until midnight on all First Aberdeen buses. Information, route maps and tickets are available from the **First Travel Centre** (47 Union St; 9am-5.30pm Mon-Fri, to 4.30pm Sat).

The most useful services for visitors are buses 15 and 19 from Union St to Great Western Rd (for B&Bs); bus 11 from Union St to Aberdeen SYHA and the airport; and bus 20 from Marischal College to Old Aberdeen.

CAR

Car rental companies include:

Arnold Clark (01224-622714; www.arnoldclarkrental.com; Canal Rd; 8am-7pm Mon-Fri, 8am-4.30pm Sat, 9am-4.30pm Sun)

WORTH A TRIP

OLD ABERDEEN

Just over a mile north of the city centre is the district called Old Aberdeen. The name is misleading – although Old Aberdeen is certainly old, the area around Castlegate in the city centre is older still. This part of the city was originally called Aulton, from the Gaelic for 'village by the stream', and this was Anglicised in the 17th century to Old Town.

Bus 20 from Littlejohn St (just north of Marischal College) runs to Old Aberdeen every 15 to 20 minutes.

St Machar's Cathedral (www.stmachar.com; The Chanonry; ⌚9.30am-4.30pm) The 15th-century St Machar's, with its massive twin towers, is a rare example of a fortified cathedral. According to legend, St Machar was ordered to establish a church where the river takes the shape of a bishop's crook, which it does just here. The cathedral is best known for its impressive **heraldic ceiling**, dating from 1520, which has 48 shields of kings, nobles, archbishops and bishops. Sunday services are held at 11am and 6pm.

King's College Chapel (College Bounds; ⌚10am 3.30pm Mon-Fri) It was here that Bishop Elphinstone established King's College, Aberdeen's first university (and Scotland's third), in 1495. The 16th-century college chapel is easily recognised by its crown spire; the interior is largely unchanged since it was first built, with impressive stained-glass windows and choir stalls.

Enterprise Car Hire (☎01224-642642; www.enterprise.co.uk; 80 Skene Sq; ⌚7am-7pm Mon-Fri, 8am-4pm Sat, 10am-3pm Sun).

TAXI

The main city-centre taxi ranks are at the train station and on Back Wynd, off Union St. To order a taxi, phone **ComCab** (☎01224-353535; www.comcab-aberdeen.co.uk) or **Rainbow City Taxis** (☎01224-878787; www.rainbowcitytaxis.com).

Around Aberdeen

Dunnottar Castle CASTLE

(☎01569-762173; www.dunnottarcastle.co.uk; adult/child £7/3; ⌚9am-6pm Apr-Sep, 10am-5pm or dusk Oct-Mar; P) A pleasant, 20-minute walk along the clifftops south of Stonehaven harbour leads to the spectacular ruins of Dunnottar Castle, spread out across a grassy promontory 50m above the sea. As dramatic a film set as any director could wish for, it provided the backdrop for Franco Zeffirelli's *Hamlet* (1990), starring Mel Gibson. The original fortress was built in the 9th century; the keep is the most substantial remnant, but the drawing room (restored in 1926) is more interesting.

Crathes Castle CASTLE

(NTS; ☎01330-844525; www.nts.org.uk; adult/child £12.50/9; ⌚10.30am-5pm daily Apr-Oct, 11am-3.45pm Sat & Sun Nov-Mar; P) The atmospheric, 16th-century Crathes Castle is famous for its Jacobean painted ceilings, magnificently carved canopied beds, and the 'Horn of Leys', reputedly presented to the Burnett family by Robert the Bruce in the 14th century. The beautiful formal gardens include 300-year-old yew hedges and colourful herbaceous borders. The castle is signposted off the A93; Stagecoach buses 201 and 202 from Aberdeen stop at the castle entrance (£4.90, 45 minutes, every 30 minutes).

MORAY

The old county of Moray (*murr*-ay), centred on the county town of Elgin, lies at the heart of an ancient Celtic earldom and is famed for its mild climate and rich farmland – the barley fields of the 19th century once provided the raw material for the Speyside whisky distilleries, one of the region's main attractions for present-day visitors.

Elgin

POP 23,130

Elgin has been the provincial capital of Moray for over eight centuries and was an important town in medieval times. Dominated by a hilltop monument to the 5th Duke of Gordon, Elgin's main attraction is its impressive ruined cathedral, where the tombs of the duke's ancestors lie.

Sights

Elgin Cathedral CATHEDRAL

(HS; www.historicenvironment.scot; King St; adult/child £5.50/3.30; 9.30am-5.30pm Apr-Sep, 10am-4pm Sat-Wed Oct-Mar) Many people think that the ruins of Elgin Cathedral, known as the 'lantern of the north', are the most beautiful and evocative in Scotland; its octagonal chapter house is the finest in the country. Consecrated in 1224, the cathedral was burned down in 1390 by the infamous Wolf of Badenoch, the illegitimate son of Robert II, following his excommunication by the Bishop of Moray. Guided tours are available on weekdays.

Elgin Museum MUSEUM

(www.elginmuseum.org.uk; 1 High St; donations accepted; 10am-5pm Mon-Fri, 11am-4pm Sat Apr-Oct) FREE Scotland's oldest independent museum is an old-fashioned cabinet of curiosities, a captivating collection artfully displayed in a beautiful, purpose-built Victorian building. Exhibits range from Ecuadorian shrunken heads to Peruvian mummies, and include internationally important fish and reptile fossils discovered in local rocks, and mysterious Pictish carved stones.

Johnstons of Elgin FASHION & ACCESSORIES

(01343-554009; www.johnstonscashmere.com; Newmill; 9am-5.30pm Mon-Sat, 11am-5pm Sun) Founded in 1797, Johnstons is famous for its cashmere woollen clothing, and is the only UK woollen mill that still sees the manufacturing process through from raw fibre to finished garment. There's a retail outlet and coffee shop, and free guided tours of the works.

Sleeping & Eating

Moraydale B&B $$

(01343-546381; www.moraydaleguesthouse.com; 276 High St; s/d/f from £55/75/85; P) The Moraydale is a spacious Victorian mansion filled with period features – check out the stained glass and the cast-iron and tile fireplaces. The bedrooms are all en suite and equipped with modern bathrooms – the three large family rooms are particularly good value.

Southbank Guest House B&B $$

(01343-547132; www.southbankguesthouse.co.uk; 36 Academy St; s/d/f from £55/90/140; P) The family-run, 15-room Southbank is set in a large Georgian town house in a quiet street south of Elgin's centre, just five minutes' walk from the cathedral and other sights.

★ **Drouthy Cobbler** CAFE, BAR $$

(01343-596000; thedrouthycobbler.co.uk; 48a High St; mains £11-15; food served 8am-10pm;) This brand new cafe-bar is an all-day venue serving everything from breakfast to dinner, with a bistro-style menu that changes regularly but includes dishes such as carpaccio of beef, Caesar salad, scallops and pancetta, and home-made burgers. It's tucked away up a side alley, and also hosts live music and comedy gigs in the evenings.

Getting There & Away

The **bus station** is a block north of High St, and the train station is 900m south of the town centre.

BUS

Aberdeen £12.75, 2½ hours, hourly

Banff & Macduff £10.40, 1¾ hours, hourly

Dufftown £5.80, 50 minutes, hourly Monday to Saturday

Inverness £10.40, 1½ hours, hourly

TRAIN

Aberdeen £18.90, 1¾ hours, five daily

Inverness £12.30, 40 minutes, five daily

Dufftown & Aberlour

Rome may be built on seven hills, but Dufftown's built on seven stills, say the locals. Founded in 1817 by James Duff, 4th Earl of Fife, Dufftown is 17 miles south of Elgin and lies at the heart of the Speyside whisky-distilling region. With seven working distilleries nearby, Dufftown has been dubbed Scotland's malt-whisky capital and is host to the biannual Spirit of Speyside (p864) whisky festival. Ask at the whisky museum about the **Malt Whisky Trail** (www.maltwhiskytrail.com), a self-guided tour around the local distilleries.

Aberlour (www.aboutaberlour.co.uk) – or Charlestown of Aberlour, to give it its full name – is prettier than Dufftown, straggling along the banks of the River Spey. It is famous as the home of Walkers Shortbread, and has Aberlour Distillery right on the main street. Attractions include salmon fishing on the Spey, nearby Knockando Woolmill, and some lovely walks along the Speyside Way.

Buses link Elgin to Dufftown (£5.80, 50 minutes) and Aberlour (£5.50, 40 minutes) hourly Monday to Saturday, continuing to Huntly and Aberdeen.

LOCH LOMOND & THE TROSSACHS

The 'bonnie banks' and 'bonnie braes' of Loch Lomond, and the scenic Trossachs region to its east have long been Glasgow's rural retreat – a landscape of craggy hills, romantic lochs and healthy fresh air within easy reach of Scotland's largest city.

Loch Lomond became the heart of **Loch Lomond & the Trossachs National Park** (www.lochlomond-trossachs.org) – Scotland's first national park, created in 2002. The park extends over a huge area, from Balloch north to Tyndrum and Killin, and from Callander west to the forests of Cowal. The length of Loch Lomond means that access between the western part of the park and the Trossachs is either in the far north of the region via Crianlarich or the far south via Drymen.

Loch Lomond

Loch Lomond is mainland Britain's largest lake and, after Loch Ness, the most famous of Scotland's lochs. Its proximity to Glasgow (20 miles away) means that the tourist honeypots of Balloch, Loch Lomond Shores and Luss get pretty crowded in summer. The eastern shore, which is followed by the West Highland Way long-distance footpath, is quieter and offers a better chance to appreciate the loch away from the busy main road.

Loch Lomond straddles the Highland border. The southern part is broad and island-studded, fringed by woods and Lowland meadows. However, north of Luss the loch narrows, occupying a deep trench gouged out by glaciers during the Ice Age, with 900m mountains crowding either side

Activities

The **West Highland Way** (www.west-highland-way.co.uk) runs along the loch's eastern shore, while the **Rob Roy Way** (www.robroyway.com) heads from Drymen to Pitlochry via the Trossachs. The **Three Lochs Way** (www.threelochsway.co.uk) loops west from Balloch through Helensburgh and Arrochar before returning to Loch Lomond at Inveruglas. There are numerous shorter walks around: get further information from tourist offices.

Rowardennan is the starting point for ascents of **Ben Lomond** (974m), a popular and relatively straightforward (if strenuous) climb.

The mostly traffic-free **Clyde and Loch Lomond Cycle Way** links Glasgow to Balloch (20 miles), where it joins the **West Loch Lomond Cycle Path**, which continues along the loch shore to Tarbet (10 miles). The park website (www.lochlomond-trossachs.org) details some other local routes.

Cruise Loch Lomond BOATING
(☎01301-702356; www.cruiselochlomond.co.uk; Tarbet/Luss; ⏰8.30am-5.30pm early Apr-late Oct) With departures from Tarbet and Luss, this operator offers short cruises and two-hour trips to Arklet Falls and Rob Roy's Cave (adult/child £15/8). There are several options. You can also be dropped off at Rowardennan to climb Ben Lomond (£15/9), getting picked up in the afternoon, or get

ROB ROY

Nicknamed Red (*'ruadh'* in Gaelic, anglicised to 'roy') for his ginger locks, Robert MacGregor (1671–1734) was the wild leader of the wildest of Scotland's clans, outlawed by powerful neighbours, hence their sobriquet, Children of the Mist. Incognito, Rob became a prosperous livestock trader, before a dodgy deal led to a warrant for his arrest.

A legendary swordsman, the fugitive from justice then became notorious for daring raids into the Lowlands to carry off cattle and sheep. Forever hiding from potential captors, he was twice imprisoned, but escaped dramatically on both occasions. He finally turned himself in and received his liberty and a pardon from the king. He lies buried – perhaps – in the churchyard at Balquhidder; his uncompromising later epitaph reads 'MacGregor despite them'. His life has been glorified over the years due to Walter Scott's novel and the 1995 film. Many Scots see his life as a symbol of the struggle of the common folk against the inequitable ownership of vast tracts of the country by landed aristocrats.

picked up at Inversnaid after a 9-mile hike along the West Highland Way (£15/9).

From its Tarbet office, it also rents out boats (half/full day £95/150) and bikes (£13/17).

CanYou Experience OUTDOOR
(☎01389-756251; www.canyouexperience.com; Loch Lomond Shores; ⏲10am-5.30pm Easter-Oct) Offers a huge range of activities on water and land from various bases around Loch Lomond. Hire mountain bikes (£13/17 per half-/full day), canoes and kayaks, or go abseiling, canoeing, paddleboarding or more. The six-hour canoe safari (£50) explores the loch's islands. The website gives a full rundown.

Sleeping & Eating

Rowardennan SYHA HOSTEL $
(☎01360-870259; www.syha.org.uk; Rowardennan; dm/tw/q £21/52/96; ⏲late Mar-late Oct; P 📶) Where the road ends on the eastern side of the loch, this is a postcard-quality retreat in an elegant ex-hunting lodge with lawns stretching right down to the water's edge. Whether you're walking the West Highland Way, climbing Ben Lomond or just putting your feet up, it's a great choice with a huge lounge whose windows overlook Loch Lomond.

Meals are available but the food is better in the nearby hotel.

Cashel Campsite CAMPGROUND $
(☎01360-870234; www.campingintheforest.co.uk; Rowardennan; tent site for 2 £24.15; ⏲Mar-late Oct; P 🐾) The most attractive campsite in the area is 3 miles north of Balmaha, on the loch shore.

Oak Tree Inn INN $$
(☎01360-870357; www.theoaktreeinn.co.uk; Balmaha; dm/s/d £30/70/90; P 📶) An attractive traditional inn built in slate and timber, this offers bright modern guest bedrooms for pampered hikers, plus super-spacious superior chambers, self-catering cottages and two four-bed bunkrooms for hardier souls. The rustic restaurant brings locals, tourists and walkers together and dishes up hearty meals that cover lots of bases (mains £9 to

BLAZE YOUR OWN WHISKY TRAIL

Visiting a distillery can be memorable, but only hardcore malthounds will want to go to more than one or two. Some are great to visit; others are depressingly corporate.

Aberlour (☎01340-881249; www.aberlour.com; tours from £14; ⏲tours 10am & 2pm daily Apr-Oct, by appointment Mon-Fri Nov-Mar; P) Has an excellent, detailed tour with a proper tasting session. It's on the main street in Aberlour.

Glenfarclas (☎01807-500257; www.glenfarclas.co.uk; admission £7.50; ⏲10am-4pm Mon-Fri Oct-Mar, to 5pm Mon-Fri Apr-Sep, 10am-4pm Sat Jul-Sep; P) Small, friendly and independent, Glenfarclas is 5 miles south of Aberlour on the Grantown road; the last tour leaves 90 minutes before closing. The in-depth Connoisseur's Tour (Fridays only, July to September) is £40.

Glenfiddich (☎01340-820373; www.glenfiddich.co.uk; admission free, tours from £10; ⏲9.30am-4.30pm Apr-Oct, 11am-3pm Nov-Mar; P) It's big and busy, but handiest for Dufftown and foreign languages are available. The standard tour (£10) starts with an overblown video, but it's fun and informative. An in-depth half-day Pioneer's Tour (£50) must be prebooked.

Macallan (☎01340-872280; www.themacallan.com; Easter Elchies, Craigellachie; tours £15; ⏲9.30am-6pm Mon-Sat Easter-Oct, to 5pm Mon-Fri Nov-Mar; P) Macallan makes an excellent sherry-casked malt. The 1¾-hour tours (maximum group of 10) should be prebooked. Lovely location 1 mile west of Craigellachie.

Speyside Cooperage (☎01340-871108; www.speysidecooperage.co.uk; adult/child £3.50/2; ⏲9am-5pm Mon-Fri, closed late Dec-early Jan) Here you can see the fascinating art of barrel-making in action. It's a mile from Craigellachie on the Dufftown road.

The biannual **Spirit of Speyside** (www.spiritofspeyside.com) whisky festival in Dufftown has a number of great events. It takes place in early May and late September; both accommodation and events should be booked well ahead.

£12; food noon to 9pm). There's lots of outdoor seating.

But it doesn't end there; the Oak Tree is an impressive set-up that brews its own beers, makes its own ice cream (and sells it in an adjacent cafe), and smokes its own fish.

Drover's Inn PUB FOOD $$

(☎01301-704234; www.thedroversinn.co.uk; Ardlui; bar meals £9-14; ⏲11.30am-10pm Mon-Sat, 11.30am-9.30pm or 10pm Sun; P 📶) Don't miss this low-ceilinged howff (drinking den) just north of Ardlui with its smoke-blackened stone, kilted bartenders, and walls festooned with moth-eaten stags' heads and stuffed birds. The bar, where Rob Roy allegedly dropped by for pints, serves hearty hill-walking fuel and hosts live folk music at weekends. Recommended more as an atmospheric place to eat and drink than somewhere to stay.

Rooms could do with an upgrade. Singles cost £35 to £55, doubles £75 to £90.

ℹ Information

Balloch Tourist Office (☎01389-753533; www.visitscotland.com; Balloch Rd; ⏲9.30am-6pm Jul & Aug, 9.30am-5.30pm Jun & Sep, 10am-5pm Oct-May) Opposite Balloch train station.

Balmaha National Park Centre (☎01389-722100; www.lochlomond-trossachs.org; Balmaha; ⏲9.30am-4pm Apr-Jun & Sep-Oct, 9.30am-6pm Jul & Aug, 9.30am-4pm Sat & Sun Nov-Mar) Has maps showing local walking routes.

National Park Gateway Centre (☎01389-751035; www.lochlomondshores.com; Loch Lomond Shores, Balloch; ⏲10am-6pm Apr-Sep, 10am-5pm Oct-Mar; 📶) At Loch Lomond Shores by Balloch, with a shop and cafe. Being refurbished at last visit and due to reopen in 2017.

ℹ Getting There & Away

BUS

First Glasgow (www.firstglasgow.com) Bus 1/1A runs from Argyle St in central Glasgow to Balloch (£5, 1½ hours, at least two per hour) and bus C8 runs to Drymen (£5.20, 1¼ hours, two daily).

Scottish Citylink (www.citylink.co.uk) Coaches from Glasgow stop at Luss (£8.80, 55 minutes, 17 daily), Tarbet (£8.80, 65 minutes, 17 daily) and Ardlui (£16, 1¼ hours, nine daily).

TRAIN

Glasgow–Balloch £5.30, 45 minutes, every 30 minutes

Glasgow–Arrochar & Tarbet £11.80, 1¼ hours, seven daily, four Sunday

Glasgow–Ardlui £15.50, 1½ hours, seven daily, four Sunday, continuing to Oban or Fort William

Callander

POP 3100

Callander, the principal Trossachs town, has been pulling in tourists for over 150 years, and has a laid-back ambience along its main thoroughfare that quickly lulls visitors into lazy pottering. There's an excellent array of accommodation options here, and some intriguing places to eat.

Wheels Cycling Centre CYCLING

(☎01877-331100; http://scottish-cycliing.com; bike per hour/day/week from £8/20/90, ⏲10am-6pm Mar-Oct) The Trossachs is a lovely area to cycle around. On a cycle route, excellent Wheels Cycling Centre has a wide range of hire bikes. To get there, take Bridge St off Main St, turn right onto Invertrossachs Rd and continue for a mile.

Sleeping

★**Callander Hostel** HOSTEL $

(☎01877-331465; www.callanderhostel.co.uk; 6 Bridgend; dm £18.50-23.50, d £60-70; P @ 📶) This hostel in a mock-Tudor building has been a major labour of love by a local youth project and is now a top-class facility. Well-furnished dorms offer bunks with individual light and USB charge ports, while en suite doubles have super views. Staff are welcoming and friendly, and it has a spacious common area and share kitchen as well as a cafe and garden.

White Shutters B&B $

(☎01877-330442; www.incallander.co.uk/directory/white-shutters-bb; 6 South Church St; s/d £26/46; 📶) A cute little house just off the main street, White Shutters offers pleasing rooms with shared bathroom and a friendly welcome. The large double is particularly appealing, but it's all clean and comfortable and offers exceptional value.

Roslin Cottage B&B $$

(☎01877-339787; www.roslincottage.com; Stirling Rd; s £45, d £55-80; P 📶) A cottage that's a haven of good hospitality holds three snug en suite rooms that make an enticing

TROSSACHS TRANSPORT

In a bid to cut public transport costs, **Demand Responsive Transport** (DRT; 01786-404040; www.stirling.gov.uk)) now covers the Trossachs area. It sounds complex, but basically it means you get a taxi to where you want to go, for the price of a bus. There are various zones. Taxis should preferably be booked 24 hours in advance; call 01786-404040.

Trossachs base. They all have charm: we love the Kirtle room with the original 17th-century wall exposed. Other delights include a lovely big back garden, a log fire in the lounge and sociable chef-cooked breakfasts.

It's on the right as you enter Callander from the east, before the petrol station. It was up for sale at time of research so may change.

Abbotsford Lodge HOTEL $$

(01877-330066; www.abbotsfordlodge.com; Stirling Rd; s/d £65/80; Mar-Nov; P) This friendly Victorian house offers something different from the norm, with tartan and florals consigned to the bonfire, replaced by stylish, comfortable contemporary design that enhances the building's original features. There are fabulous, spacious superiors (from £125) with modish grey fabrics as well as cheaper top-floor rooms – shared bathroom – with lovably offbeat under-roof shapes. Room-only and continental breakfast rates are available.

Arden House B&B $$

(01877-339405; www.ardenhouse.org.uk; Bracklinn Rd; s from £75, d £80-100; Mar-Oct; P) This elegant home has a fabulous hillside location with verdant garden and lovely vistas; close to the centre but far from the crowds. The commodious rooms are impeccable, with lots of natural light. They include large upstairs doubles with great views. Welcoming owners, noble architectural features – super bay windows – and a self-catering studio make this a top option.

There's a two-night minimum stay in summer.

★**Roman Camp Hotel** HOTEL $$$

(01877-330003; www.romancamphotel.co.uk; off Main St; s/d/superior £110/160/220; P) Callander's best hotel is centrally located but feels rural, set by the river in beautiful grounds. Endearing features include a lounge with blazing fire and a library with a tiny secret chapel. It's an old-fashioned warren of a place with four grades of room; standards are certainly luxurious, but superiors are even more appealing, with period furniture, excellent bathrooms, armchairs and fireplace.

The upmarket restaurant is open to the public. Reassuringly, the name refers not to toga parties but to a ruin in the adjacent fields.

Eating & Drinking

★**Venachar Lochside** SEAFOOD $$

(Harbour Cafe; 01877-330011; www.venachar-lochside.com; Loch Venachar; mains £9-15; lunch noon-4pm Jan-Nov, plus dinner 5.30-8.30pm Fri & Sat Jun-Sep;) On lovely Loch Venachar, 4½ miles west of Callander, this cafe-restaurant has a stunning waterside setting and does a nice line in delicious fresh seafood. It opens from 10am to 5pm daily for coffees, teas and baked goods. You can also hire boats and tackle to go fishing for trout on the loch here.

★**Callander Meadows** SCOTTISH $$

(01877-330181; www.callandermeadows.co.uk; 24 Main St; 2-/3-course lunch £12/17, mains £13-17; 10am-9pm Thu-Mon;) Informal and cosy, this well-loved restaurant in the centre of Callander occupies the front rooms of a main street house. It's truly excellent; there's a contemporary flair for presentation and unusual flavour combinations, but a solidly British base underpins the cuisine. There's a great beer/coffee garden out the back, where you can also eat. Opens daily from June to September.

Lunch is offered from noon to 2.30pm, and dinner from 6pm to 9pm. At other times, it does teas, light meals, breakfasts and the like.

Lade Inn PUB

(www.theladeinn.com; Kilmahog; noon-11pm Mon-Thu, noon-1am Fri & Sat, 12.30-10.30pm Sun;) Callander's best pub isn't in Callander – it's a mile west of town. It pulls a good pint (with its own real ales), and next door it has a shop with a dazzling selection of Scottish beers. There's low-key live music here at weekends. The food (noon to 9pm, from 12.30pm Sunday; mains £9 to £14) is solid rather than spectacular.

Information

Callander Tourist Office (☎01877-330342; www.lochlomond-trossachs.org; 52 Main St; ⊙9.30am-5pm Apr-Oct, to 4pm Nov-Mar; 📶) Very helpful for information on the region and national park.

Getting There & Away

First (www.firstgroup.com) operates buses from Stirling (£5.20, 45 minutes, hourly Monday to Saturday, every two hours Sunday).

Kingshouse (☎01877-384768; www.kingshousetravel.com) buses run from Killin (£5.70, 40 minutes, six Monday to Saturday).

For Aberfoyle, use **DRT** (opposite) or get off a Stirling-bound bus at Blair Drummond safari park and cross the road.

Lochs Katrine & Achray

This rugged area, 7 miles north of Aberfoyle and 10 miles west of Callander, is the heart of the Trossachs. **Boats** (☎01877-376315; www.lochkatrine.com; Trossachs Pier; 1hr cruise adult £11-13, child £5.50-6.50; ⊙Easter-Oct) run cruises from Trossachs Pier at the eastern tip of Loch Katrine. One of these is the fabulous centenarian steamship *Sir Walter Scott;* check the website departures, as it's worth coinciding with this veteran if you can. There are various one-hour afternoon sailings, and at 10.30am (plus additional summer departures) there's a departure to Stronachlachar at the other end of the loch (single/return adult £13/16, child £6.50/8, two hours return). From Stronachlachar (accessible by car via a 12-mile road from Aberfoyle), you can reach the eastern shore of Loch Lomond at isolated Inversnaid. A tarmac path links Trossachs Pier with Stronachlachar, so you can take the boat out and walk/cycle back (14 miles). At Trossachs Pier, **Katrinewheelz** (☎01877-376366; www.katrinewheelz.co.uk; Trossachs Pier, Loch Katrine; hire per half/full day from £15/20; ⊙9am-5pm Apr-Oct, 11am-3pm Sat & Sun Nov-Dec & Feb-Mar) hires out good bikes and even electric buggies. Bring a picnic; the cafe is mediocre.

Killin

POP 800

A fine base for the Trossachs or Perthshire, this lovely village sits at the western end of Loch Tay and has a spread-out, relaxed feel, particularly around the scenic **Falls of Dochart**, which tumble through the centre. On a sunny day people sprawl over the rocks by the bridge, pint or picnic in hand. Killin offers fine walking around the town, and mighty mountains and glens close at hand.

Activities

Five miles northeast of Killin, **Ben Lawers** (1214m) rises above Loch Tay. Walking routes abound; one rewarding **circular walk** heads up into the Acharn forest south of town, emerging above the treeline to great views of Loch Tay and Ben Lawers. Killin Outdoor Centre offers walking advice.

Glen Lochay runs westwards from Killin into the hills of Mamlorn. You can take a **mountain bike** up the glen; the scenery is impressive and the hills aren't too difficult. It's possible, on a nice summer day, to climb over the top of **Ben Challum** (1025m) and descend to Crianlarich, but it's hard work. A potholed road, not maintained and no longer suitable for cars, also connects Glen Lochay with Glen Lyon.

Killin is on the **Lochs & Glens Cycle Way** from Glasgow to Inverness. Hire bikes from helpful **Killin Outdoor Centre** (☎01567-820652; www.killinoutdoor.co.uk; Main St; bike £25 per 24hr, kayak/canoe £25/30 per 2hr; ⊙9am-5.30pm), which also has canoes and kayaks or, in winter, crampons and snowshoes.

Sleeping & Eating

Old Bank B&B **$$**

(☎01567-829317; www.theoldbankkillin.co.uk; Manse Rd; s/d £55/80; P📶) This solid four-square building with a pretty garden stands proud above the main street. It's a genuinely welcoming place, with a host who does everything in her power to make you feel welcome. Breakfast is abundant and the rooms are super-comfortable, with contemporary colours, hill views and thoughtful extras. Two share a bathroom.

Falls of Dochart Inn PUB FOOD **$$**

(☎01567-820270; www.falls-of-dochart-inn.co.uk; mains £10-16; ⊙noon-3pm & 6-9pm Mon-Thu, to 9.30pm Fri, noon-9.30pm Sat, noon-8.30pm Sun; P📶) In a prime position overlooking the falls, this is a terrific pub: a snug, atmospheric space with a roaring fire, real ales, personable service and decent pub grub, with fresh seafood and Asian flavours adding a dimension to tasty staples and daily specials. The outside tables are great spots on a sunny day.

The rooms (single/double from £60/80) are handsome, but a few glitches like poor heating let some of them down.

Getting There & Away

Kingshouse (p867) Runs six buses Monday to Saturday to Callander (£5.70, 40 minutes), where you can change for Stirling.

Ring of Breadalbane Explorer (www.breadalbane.org; Tue, Wed & Sun Jul-Sep) A summer bus service does a hop-on hop-off Breadalbane circuit around Crieff, Comrie, St Fillans, Lochearnhead, Killin, Kenmore, Acharn and Aberfeldy.

ARGYLLSHIRE

Oban

POP 8600

Oban, the main gateway to many of the Hebridean islands, is a peaceful waterfront town on a delightful bay, with sweeping views to Kerrera and Mull. OK, that first bit about peaceful is true only in winter; in summer the town centre is jammed with traffic and crowded with holidaymakers and travellers headed for the archipelago. But the setting is still lovely, and Oban's brilliant seafood restaurants are marvellous places to be as the sun sets over the bay.

Sights

Dunollie Castle CASTLE
(01631-570550; www.dunollie.org; Dunollie Rd; adult/child £5.50/2.80; 10am-4pm Mon-Sat & 1-4pm Sun Apr-Oct) A pleasant 1-mile stroll along the coast road leads to Dunollie Castle, built by the MacDougalls of Lorn in the 13th century and unsuccessfully besieged for a year during the 1715 Jacobite rebellion. It's ruined, but you can enter the ground floor, and work is underway to restore the staircase. The nearby 1745 House – seat of Clan MacDougall – is an intriguing museum of local and clan history, and there are pleasant wooded grounds and a cafe. Free tours run twice daily.

Oban Distillery DISTILLERY
(01631-572004; www.discovering-distilleries.com; Stafford St; tour £8; noon-4.30pm Dec-Feb, 9.30am-5pm Mar-Jun & Oct-Nov, 9.30am-7.30pm Mon-Fri & 9.30am-5pm Sat & Sun Jul-Sep) This handsome distillery has been producing since 1794. The standard guided tour leaves regularly (worth booking) and includes a dram, a take-home glass and a taste straight from the cask. Specialist tours (£40) run once Mondays to Fridays in summer. Even without a tour, it's still worth a look at the small exhibition in the foyer.

McCaig's Tower HISTORIC BUILDING
(cnr Laurel & Duncraggan Rds; 24hr) Crowning the hill above town is this Colosseum-like Victorian folly, commissioned in 1890 by local worthy John Stuart McCaig, with the philanthropic intention of providing work for unemployed stonemasons. To reach it on foot, make the steep climb up Jacob's Ladder (a flight of stairs) from Argyll St; the bay views are worth the effort.

Activities

Hire a **bike** (01631-566033; www.obancyclescotland.com; 87 George St; per day/week £25/125; 10am-5pm Tue-Sat) and pedal one of the local bike rides listed in a leaflet at the tourist office, including a 16-mile route to the Isle of Seil. Various operators offer **boat trips** (adult/child £10/5) to spot seals and other marine wildlife, departing from North Pier.

Sea Kayak Oban KAYAKING
(01631-565310; www.seakayakoban.com; Argyll St; 10am-5pm Mon-Fri, 9am-5pm Sat, 10am-4pm Sun) Has a well-stocked shop, great route advice and sea-kayaking courses, including an all-inclusive two-day intro for beginners (£170 per person). Also full equipment rental for experienced paddlers – trolley your kayak from the shop to the ferry (kayaks carried free) to visit the islands. Three-hour excursions (adult/child £60/35) leave regularly in season.

Basking Shark Scotland BOATING
(07975-723140; www.baskingsharkscotland.co.uk; Apr-Oct) Runs entertaining boat trips with optional snorkelling, focused on finding and observing basking sharks – the world's second largest fish – and other notable marine species.

Sleeping

Despite having lots of B&B accommodation, Oban's beds can still fill up quickly in July and August, so try to book ahead. Avoid the B&Bs south of the roundabout on Dunollie Road. If you can't find a bed in Oban, consider Connel, 4 miles north.

Backpackers Plus HOSTEL $
(☎01631-567189; www.backpackersplus.com; Breadalbane St; dm/s/tw with breakfast £20/29/52; @📶) This is a friendly place with a good vibe and a large and attractive communal lounge with lots of sofas and armchairs. Buffet breakfast is included in the price, plus there's free tea and coffee, a laundry service and powerful showers. Private rooms are available in a separate building (also with kitchen) just up the road: they are a very good deal.

Oban Backpackers HOSTEL $
(☎01631-562107; www.obanbackpackers.com; Breadalbane St; dm £17.50-19.50; @📶) Simple, colourful, relaxed and casual, this has plenty of atmosphere. Dorms are simple, with high ceilings and plenty of space; price varies according to size. Top bunks are wall-mounted. There's a sociable downstairs lounge with big windows and zebrapard couches, plus a sizeable kitchen. Breakfast is available for £2 and a safe is on hand (no lockers).

Oban SYHA HOSTEL $
(☎01631-562025; www.syha.org.uk; Corran Esplanade; dm/tw £24/54; P@📶) Set in a grand Victorian villa on the Esplanade, 0.75 miles north of the train station, this is modernised to a high standard with comfy wooden bunks, lockers, good showers and a lounge with great views across Oban Bay. All dorms are en suite; the neighbouring lodge has three- and four-bedded rooms. Breakfast available.

Oban Caravan & Camping Park CAMPGROUND $
(☎01631-562425; www.obancaravanpark.com; Gallanachmore Farm; tent/campervan site £16/20; ⏱Apr-Oct; P📶🐾) This spacious campsite has a superb location overlooking the Sound of Kerrera, 2.5 miles south of Oban (two buses on school days). A one-person tent with no car is £8. No prebooking – it's first-come, first-served. There are also bungalows and camping pods that sleep up to four (for two/four £40/50).

★**Old Manse Guest House** B&B $$
(☎01631-564886; www.obanguesthouse.co.uk; Dalriach Rd; s/d £75/88; P📶) Set on the hillside above town, this commands magnificent views over to Kerrera and Mull. It's run with genuine enthusiasm, and the owners are constantly adding thoughtful new features to the bright, cheerful rooms – think binoculars, DVDs, poetry, corkscrews and tartan hot-water bottles. There are breakfast menus, with special diets catered for.

★**Elderslie Guest House** B&B $$
(☎01631-570651; www.obanbandb.com; Soroba Rd; s £50-55, d £72-85; P📶) B&B is a difficult balancing act: making things modern without losing cosiness; being friendly and approachable without sacrificing privacy. At this spot a mile south of town the balance is absolutely right, with a big variety of commodious rooms with big showers, large towels and lovely outlooks over greenery. Breakfast is great, there's outdoor lounging space and the hosts are really excellent.

Sandvilla Guesthouse B&B $$
(☎01631-564483; www.holidayoban.co.uk; Breadalbane St; d £75-90; P📶) Upbeat, colourful and modern, the rooms in this welcoming spot are lovely, bright and very well kept. Enthusiastic owners guarantee a personal welcome and service with a smile. It's our favourite of several options on this street.

Kilchrenan House B&B $$
(☎01631-562663; www.kilchrenanhouse.co.uk; Corran Esplanade; s £50, d £70-110; P📶) You'll get a warm welcome at the Kilchrenan, an elegant Victorian villa built for a textile magnate in 1883. Most of the rooms have views across Oban Bay, but rooms 5 and 9 are the best: the former has a huge freestanding bath tub, perfect for soaking weary bones.

Manor House HOTEL $$$
(☎01631-562087; www.manorhouseoban.com; Gallanach Rd; r £180-250; P📶🐾) Built in 1780 for the Duke of Argyll, the old-fashioned Manor House is now one of Oban's finest hotels. It has small but elegant Georgian-style rooms – some with sea views – a posh bar frequented by yachties, and a fine restaurant serving Scottish and French cuisine (table d'hôte dinner £42). Rates include gym access and free golf at a nearby course. No under-12s.

Eating

Oban Seafood Hut SEAFOOD $
(www.obanseafoodhut.co.uk; Railway Pier; mains £3-13; ⏱10am-6pm Mar-Oct) If you want to savour superb Scottish seafood without the expense of an upmarket restaurant, head for Oban's famous seafood stall – it's the green shack on the quayside near the ferry terminal. Here you can buy fresh and cooked seafood to take away – excellent

prawn sandwiches, dressed crab and fresh oysters for a pittance.

Kitchen Garden DELI, CAFE $
(☎01631-566332; www.kitchengardenoban.co.uk; 14 George St; light meals £3-8; ⏰9am-5pm Mon-Sat, 10.30am-4.30pm Sun; 📶) A deli packed with delicious picnic food, including some great cheeses. Also has a great little cafe – good coffee, scones, cakes, homemade soups and sandwiches.

Oban Chocolate Company SWEETS $
(☎01631-566099; www.obanchocolate.co.uk; 34 Corran Esplanade; hot chocolate £3; ⏰10am-5pm Feb-Dec; 📶👪) Specialises in hand-crafted chocolates (you can watch them being made) and also has a cafe serving excellent coffee and hot chocolate (try the chilli chocolate for a kick in the tastebuds), with big leather sofas in a window with a view of the bay. Open to 9pm Thursday to Saturday in July and August, when there's sometimes live music.

Waterfront Fishouse Restaurant SEAFOOD $$
(☎01631-563110; www.waterfrontfishouse.co.uk; 1 Railway Pier; mains £12-20; ⏰noon-2pm & 5.30-9pm, extended hours Jun-Aug; 📶👪) Housed on the top floor of a converted seamen's mission, the Waterfront's stylish, unfussy decor, bathed by the summer evening sun, does little to distract from the seafood freshly landed at the quay just a few metres away. The menu ranges from classic haddock and chips to fresh oysters, scallops and langoustines. Best to book for dinner.

★ **Ee-Usk** SEAFOOD $$$
(☎01631-565666; www.eeusk.com; North Pier; mains £14-24; ⏰noon-3pm & 5.45-9.30pm; 📶) Bright and modern Ee-Usk (how you pronounce *iasg*, Gaelic for fish) occupies a prime pier location. Floor-to-ceiling windows allow diners on two levels to enjoy sweeping views while sampling local sustainable seafood ranging from fragrant fish cakes to langoustines and succulent fresh fish. A bevy of serving staff make it swift and efficient, and they'll try to give you the best view available.

Both food and location are first class. Closes 2.30pm and 9pm in winter.

Information

Lorn & Islands District General Hospital (☎01631-567500; www.obanhospital.com; Glengallan Rd) At the southern end of town.

Oban Tourist Office (☎01631-563122; www.oban.org.uk; 3 North Pier; ⏰10am-5pm Mon-Sat, 11am-4pm Nov-Mar Sun, 9am-6pm Mon-Sat, 10am-5pm Sun Apr-May & Sep-Oct, 9am-6pm Jun, 9am-7pm Jul & Aug) Helpful; on the waterfront.

Getting There & Away

AIR

Hebridean Air Services (☎0845 805 7465; www.hebrideanair.co.uk) Flies from Connel airfield to the islands of Coll, Tiree, Colonsay and Islay.

BOAT

Oban is a major gateway to the Hebrides. CalMac ferries run from here to Mull, Islay, Colonsay, Coll, Tiree, Barra and Lismore. The **ferry terminal** (☎01631-562244; www.calmac.co.uk; Railway Pier) is in the centre, close to the train station.

BUS

Four to five Citylink (www.citylink.co.uk) buses connect Glasgow (£19.40, three hours) with Oban. Most of these travel via Tarbet and Inveraray; in summer, one goes via Crianlarich. Three daily buses head north to Fort William (£9.40, 1½ hours).

TRAIN

Scotrail trains run to Oban from Glasgow (£23.90, three hours, five to six daily). Change at Crianlarich for Fort William.

Mull

POP 2800

From the rugged ridges of Ben More and the black basalt crags of Burg to the blinding white sand, rose-pink granite and emerald waters that fringe the Ross, Mull can lay claim to some of the finest and most varied scenery in the Inner Hebrides. Noble birds of prey soar over mountain and coast, while the western waters provide good whale-watching. Add a lovely waterfront 'capital', an impressive castle, the sacred island of Iona and easy access from Oban, and you can see why it's sometimes impossible to find a spare bed on the island.

Tours

Mull Eagle Watch BIRDWATCHING
(☎01680-812556; www.mulleaglewatch.com; adult/child £8/4; ⏰Apr-Sep) Britain's largest bird of prey, the white-tailed eagle, or sea eagle, has been successfully reintroduced to Mull, and the island is crowded with bird-

Mull, Coll & Tiree

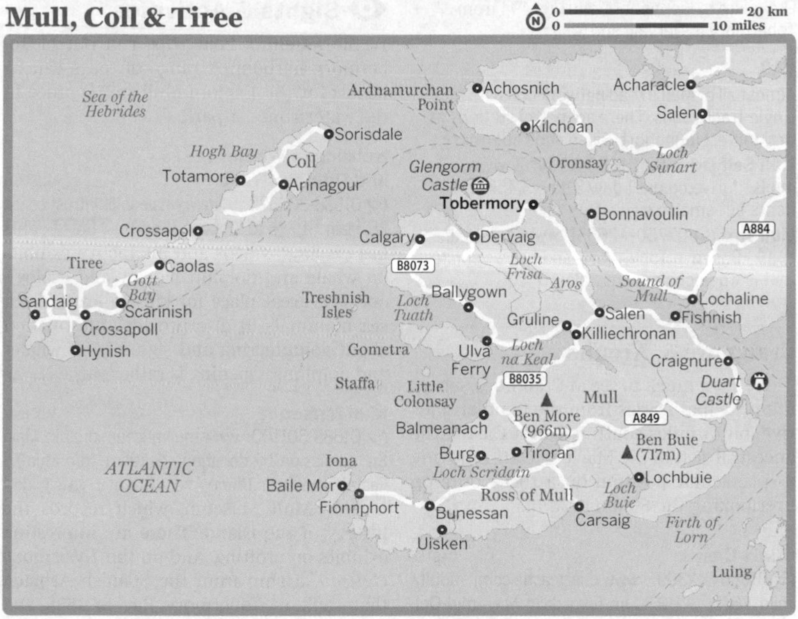

watchers raptly observing the raptor. Two-hour tours to observe this bird are held in the mornings and afternoon, and must be prebooked.

Staffa Tours BOATING
(☎07831-885985; www.staffatours.com) Runs boat trips from Fionnphort & Iona to Staffa (adult/child £30/15, three hours, daily April to October), or Staffa plus the Treshnish Isles (£60/30, five hours, Sunday to Friday May to July). The latter tour is also available from Tobermory and Ardnamurchan; there are also connection-plus-tour options leaving from Oban.

ℹ Information

There's a bank with ATM in Tobermory; otherwise you can get cashback with a purchase from Co-op food stores.

Craignure Tourist Office (☎01680-812377; www.visitscotland.com; Craignure; ⏲9am-6pm Mon-Sat, 10am-6pm Sun Apr-Jun & Sep-Oct, 9am-7.30pm Mon-Sat, 10am-7.30pm Sun Jul & Aug) Opposite the ferry slip.

Explore Mull (☎01688-302875; www.isle-of-mull.net; Ledaig; ⏲9am-5pm Easter-Oct, to 7pm Jul-Aug; 📶) In Tobermory car park. Local information, books all manner of island tours and hires bikes.

ℹ Getting There & Away

Three **CalMac** (☎0800 066 5000; www.calmac.co.uk) (www.calmac.co.uk) car ferries link Mull with the mainland:

Lochaline to Fishnish (adult/car £2.30/6.90, 15 minutes, at least hourly) On the east coast of Mull.

Oban to Craignure (adult/car £3.45/13, 40 minutes, every two hours) The busiest route – booking advised for cars.

Tobermory to Kilchoan (adult/car £2.65/8.40, 35 minutes, seven daily Monday to Saturday, plus five Sunday May to August) Links to the Ardnamurchan peninsula.

ℹ Getting Around

BICYCLE

You can hire bikes for around £20 per day from various places around the island, including Explore Mull in Tobermory.

BUS

West Coast Motors (☎01680-812313; www.westcoastmotors.co.uk) connects ferry ports and main villages. Its Discovery Day Pass (adult/child £15/7.50) is available from April to October and grants a day's unlimited bus travel.

The routes useful for visitors are bus 495 from Craignure to Tobermory, bus 496 from

Craignure to Fionnphort, and bus 494 from Tobermory to Dervaig and Calgary.

CAR

Almost all of Mull's road network consists of single-track roads. There are petrol stations at Craignure, Fionnphort, Salen and Tobermory.

Mull Self Drive (01680-300402; www.mullselfdrive.co.uk; 1 day/3 days £45/117) Rents out small cars.

Mull Taxi (07760-426351; www.mulltaxi.co.uk) Based in Tobermory, and has a vehicle that is wheelchair accessible.

Craignure & Around

There's not much to see at Craignure, where the principal ferries from the mainland arrive, but 3 miles south is Duart Castle, the ancestral seat of the Maclean clan, enjoying a spectacular position on a rocky outcrop overlooking the Sound of Mull.

Duart Castle CASTLE
(01680-812309; www.duartcastle.com; adult/child £6/3; 10.30am-5pm daily May–mid-Oct, 11am-4pm Sun-Thu Apr) The ancestral seat of the Maclean clan enjoys a spectacular position on a rocky outcrop overlooking the Sound of Mull. Originally built in the 13th century, it was abandoned for 160 years before a 1912 restoration. As well as the dungeons, courtyard and battlements with memorable views, there's a lot of clan history – pantomime boos go to Lachlan Cattanach, who took his wife on an outing to an island in the strait, then left her there to drown when the tide came in.

A bus to the castle meets some of the incoming ferries at Craignure, but it's a pretty walk too.

Tobermory

POP 1000

Mull's main town is a very picturesque little fishing and yachting port with brightly painted houses arranged around a sheltered harbour. The children's TV program *Balamory* was set here, and while the series stopped filming in 2004, regular repeats mean that the town still swarms in summer with toddlers (and nostalgic teenagers) towing parents around (you can get a *Balamory* info sheet from tourist offices).

Sights & Activities

Whale-watching boat trips run out of Tobermory harbour. A range of tours can be booked at the Explore Mull (p871) office in the waterfront car park.

Hebridean Whale and Dolphin Trust MUSEUM
(01688-302620; www.whaledolphintrust.co.uk; 28 Main St; 10.30am-4.30pm) FREE This has displays, videos and interactive exhibits on whale and dolphin biology and ecology, and is a great place for kids to learn about sea mammals. It also provides information about volunteering and sightings of whales and dolphins. Opening is rather variable.

Mull Museum MUSEUM
(01688-301100; www.mullmuseum.org.uk; Main St; admission by donation; 10am-4pm Mon-Fri Easter–mid-Oct) Places to go on a rainy day include Mull Museum, which records the history of the island. There are interesting exhibits on crofting, and on the *Tobermory Galleon*, a ship from the Spanish Armada that sank in Tobermory Bay in 1588 and has been the object of treasure seekers ever since.

Sea Life Surveys WILDLIFE
(01688-302916; www.sealifesurveys.com; Ledaig) Whale-watching trips head from Tobermory harbour to the waters north and west of Mull. An all-day whale-watch gives up to seven hours at sea (£80), and has a 95% success rate for sightings. The five-hour Family Whalewatch cruise (adult/child £50/40) is better for young kids. Shorter seal-spotting excursions are also available (adult/child £30/20, two hours).

Sleeping

Tobermory has dozens of B&Bs, but the place can still be booked solid any time from May through to August, especially at weekends.

Tobermory SYHA HOSTEL $
(01688-302481; www.syha.org.uk; Main St; dm/q £20/92; Mar-Oct; @) This hostel has a great location in a Victorian house right on the waterfront. It's got an excellent kitchen and spotless, if somewhat austere dorms, as well as good triples and quads for families. It books out fast in summer.

Tobermory Campsite CAMPGROUND $
(01688-302624; www.tobermory-campsite.co.uk; Newdale, Dervaig Rd; tent site per adult/

child £7.50/3; Mar-Oct;) A quiet, family-friendly campsite 1 mile west of town on the road to Dervaig. It also has a self-catering house, cute little glamping huts and static caravans available. Credit/debit cards not accepted.

Harbour View B&B $$
(01688-301111; www.tobermorybandb.com; 1 Argyll Tce; s £80-90, d £90-100;) This beautifully renovated fisherman's cottage is perched on the edge of Tobermory's 'upper town'. Exposed patches of original stone walls add a touch of character, while an extension provides the family suite (two adjoining rooms with shared bathroom, sleeps four) with an outdoor terrace that enjoys breathtaking views across the harbour.

Sonas House B&B $$
(01688-302304; www.sonashouse.co.uk; the Fairways, Erray Rd; apt & s/d £90/125;) Here's a first – a B&B with a heated, indoor 10m swimming pool! Sonas is a large, modern house – follow signs to the golf course – offering luxury B&B in a beautiful setting with superb views over Tobermory Bay; ask for the 'Blue Poppy' bedroom, which has its own balcony. There's also a self-contained studio apartment with double bed.

★**Highland Cottage** HOTEL $$$
(01688-302030; www.highlandcottage.co.uk; Breadalbane St; d £155-170; Apr–mid-Oct;) Antique furniture, four-poster beds, embroidered bedspreads, fresh flowers and candlelight lend this small hotel (only six rooms) an appealingly old-fashioned cottage atmosphere, but with all mod cons, including cable TV, full-size baths and room service. There's also an excellent restaurant here (dinner £42.50), and the personable owners are experts in guest comfort.

Eating & Drinking

Fish & Chip Van FISH & CHIPS $
(01688-301109; www.tobermoryfishandchipvan.co.uk; Main St; fish & chips £6-10; 12.30-9pm Mon-Sat Apr-May, 12.30-9pm daily Jun-Sep, 12.30-7pm Mon-Sat Oct-Mar) If it's takeaway you're after, you can tuck into some of Scotland's best gourmet fish and chips down on the waterfront. And where else will you find a chip van selling freshly cooked scallops?

★**Café Fish** SEAFOOD $$
(01688-301253; www.thecafefish.com; the Pier; mains £13-24; noon-3pm & 5.30-11.30pm Mar–Oct;) Seafood doesn't come much fresher than the stuff served at this warm and welcoming little restaurant overlooking Tobermory harbour – as its motto says, 'The only thing frozen here is the fisherman'! Crustaceans go straight from boat to kitchen to join rich seafood stew, fat scallops, fish pie and catch-of-the-day on the daily-changing menu, where confident use of Asian ingredients adds an extra dimension. Book ahead.

★**Mishnish Hotel** PUB
(01688-302009; www.mishnish.co.uk; Main St;) 'The Mish', near the pier on the harbourfront, is a favourite hang-out for visiting yachties and a great place for a pint, with a very convivial atmosphere. Wood-panelled and flag-draped, this is a good old traditional pub where you can listen to live folk music, toast your toes by the open fire, or challenge the locals to a game of pool.

North Mull

The road from Tobermory west to Calgary cuts inland, leaving most of Mull's north coast wild and inaccessible. It continues through the settlement of Dervaig to the glorious beach at Calgary. From here onwards you are treated to spectacular coastal views; it's worth doing the route in reverse from Grunart for the best vistas.

Sights

Glengorm Castle GALLERY, PARK
(01688-302321; www.glengormcastle.co.uk; Glengorm; 10am-5pm Easter-Oct) FREE A long, single-track road leads north for 4 miles from Tobermory to majestic Glengorm Castle, with views across the sea to Ardnamurchan, Rum and the Outer Hebrides. The castle outbuildings house an **art gallery** featuring local artists, a **farm shop** and an excellent cafe (p874). The castle, which offers upmarket **B&B** (r £135-250; mid-Feb–mid-Dec;), is not open to the public, but you're free to explore the beautiful grounds, where several good walks are signposted. Guided nature walks also run from here; check the website for times.

Calgary Beach BEACH
Mull's best (and busiest) silver-sand beach, flanked by cliffs and with views out to Coll and Tiree, is about 12 miles west of Tobermory. And yes – this is the place from which Canada's more famous Calgary takes its name.

Sleeping & Eating

Calgary Bay Campsite CAMPGROUND
(Calgary) FREE You can camp for free in a lovely setting at the southern end of the beach at Calgary Bay. There are no facilities other than the public toilets across the road; water comes from the stream.

Dervaig Hostel HOSTEL $
(01688-400491; www.mull-hostel-dervaig.co.uk; Dervaig; dm/q £18/60;) Basic but very comfortable bunkhouse accommodation in Dervaig's village hall, with self-catering kitchen and sitting room.

★ **Calgary Farmhouse** SELF-CATERING $$
(01688-400256; www.calgary.co.uk; Calgary; apt & cottages per week summer £480-1750, studios & cabin 3 days £180;) This brilliant complex near Calgary Beach offers a number of fantastic apartments, cottages and houses, beautifully designed and fitted out with timber furniture and wood-burning stoves. The Hayloft is spectacular, with noble oak and local art, while the wood-clad longhall-like Beach House offers luxury and dreamy views. Romantic Kittiwake, a beautiful wooden camping cabin among trees, has bay views and a boat ceiling.

There are options sleeping from two to 10. The larger ones go by the week in summer, but smaller ones are available for shorter stays. There's a good on-site cafe that sells some foodstuffs too. Bikes available for hire.

Glengorm Coffee Shop CAFE $
(01688-302321; www.glengormcastle.co.uk; Glengorm; light meals £3-9; 10am-5pm Easter-Oct;) Set in a cottage courtyard in the grounds of Glengorm Castle, this licensed cafe serves superb lunches (from noon to 4.30pm) – the menu changes daily, but includes sandwiches and salads (much of the salad veg is grown on the Glengorm estate), soups and tasty specials.

Am Birlinn SCOTTISH $$
(01688-400619; www.ambirlinn.com; Penmore, Dervaig; mains £13-23; noon-2.30pm & 5-9pm Wed-Sun;) Occupying a spacious modern wooden building between Dervaig and Calgary, this is an interesting dining option. Locally caught crustaceans and molluscs are the way to go here, though there are burgers, venison and other meat dishes available. Free pick-up and drop-off from Tobermory or other nearby spots is offered.

South Mull

The road from Craignure to Fionnphort climbs through wild and desolate scenery before reaching the southwestern part of the island, which consists of a long peninsula called the **Ross of Mull**. The Ross has a spectacular south coast lined with black basalt cliffs that give way further west to white-sand beaches and pink granite crags. The cliffs are highest at Malcolm's Point, near the superb **Carsaig Arches**.

The village of **Bunessan** is home to a cottage museum; a minor road leads south from here to the beautiful white-sand bay of **Uisken**, with views of the Paps of Jura.

At the western end of the Ross, 35 miles from Craignure, is **Fionnphort** (*finn*-a-fort) and the Iona ferry. The coast here is a beautiful blend of pink granite rocks, white sandy beaches and vivid turquoise sea.

★ **Seaview** B&B $$
(01681-700235; www.iona-bed-breakfast-mull.com; Fionnphort; s 59, d £80-95;) Just up from the ferry, this has beautifully decorated bedrooms and a breakfast conservatory with grand views across to Iona. The owners are incredibly helpful and also offer tasty three-course dinners (not in summer), often based around local seafood. Breakfasts include locally sourced produce and the rooms are compact and charming, with gleaming modern bathrooms. Bikes available for guests to hire.

★ **Ninth Wave** SCOTTISH $$$
(01681-700757; www.ninthwaverestaurant.co.uk; Bruach Mhor, Fionnphort; 3-/4-course dinner £46/54; from 7pm Wed-Sun May-Oct) This croft restaurant is owned and operated by a lobster fisherman and his Canadian wife. The daily menu makes use of locally landed shellfish and crustaceans, vegetables and salad grown in the garden, and quality local meats with a nose-to-tail ethos, all served in a stylishly converted bothy. It's excellent. Advance booking (think a couple of weeks at least) essential. No under-12s.

Iona

POP 200

Like an emerald teardrop off Mull's western shore, enchanting, idyllic Iona, holy island and burial ground of kings, is a magical place that lives up to its lofty reputation. From the moment you embark on the ferry towards its sandy shores and green fields, you'll notice something different about it. To appreciate its charms, spend the night: there are some excellent places to do it. Iona has declared itself a fair-trade island and actively promotes ecotourism.

History

St Columba sailed from Ireland and landed on Iona in 563, establishing a monastic community with the aim of Christianising Scotland. It was here that the *Book of Kells* – the prize attraction of Dublin's Trinity College – is believed to have been transcribed. It was taken to Ireland for safekeeping from 9th-century Viking raids.

The community was re-founded as a Benedictine monastery in the early 13th century and prospered until its destruction during the Reformation. The ruins were given to the Church of Scotland in 1899, and by 1910 a group of enthusiasts called the Iona Community Council had reconstructed the abbey. It's still a flourishing spiritual community offering regular courses and retreats.

Sights & Activities

Past the abbey, look for a footpath on the left signposted **Dun I** (dun-ee). An easy 15-minute walk leads to Iona's highest point, with fantastic 360-degree views.

★**Iona Abbey** HISTORIC BUILDING
(HES; 01681-700512; www.historicenvironment.scot; adult/child £7.10/4.30; 9.30am-5.30pm Apr-Sep, 10am-4.30pm Oct-Mar) Iona's ancient but heavily reconstructed abbey is the spiritual heart of the island. The spectacular **nave**, dominated by Romanesque and early Gothic vaults and columns is a powerful space; a door on the left leads to the beautiful **cloister**, where medieval grave slabs sit alongside modern religious sculptures. Out the back, the **museum** displays fabulous carved high crosses and other inscribed stones, along with lots of background information. A replica of the intricately carved St John's Cross stands outside the abbey

Next to the abbey is an ancient **graveyard** where there's an evocative Romanesque chapel as well as a mound that marks the burial place of 48 of Scotland's early kings, including Macbeth. Former Labour party leader John Smith is also buried in this cemetery. The ruined **nunnery** nearby was established at the same time as the Benedictine abbey.

Iona Heritage Centre MUSEUM
(01681-700576; www.ionaheritage.co.uk; adult/child £3.40/1.70; 10am-5.15pm Mon-Sat Easter-Oct) Covers the history of Iona, crofting and lighthouses; there's a craft shop and a cafe serves delicious home baking.

Sleeping & Eating

There are B&B options, camping, a hostel and a pair of hotels on the island. It's imperative to book accommodation well ahead in spring and summer.

★**Iona Hostel** HOSTEL $
(01681-700781; www.ionahostel.co.uk; dm adult/child £21/17.50; P) This working ecological croft and environmentally sensitive hostel is one of Scotland's most rewarding and tranquil places to stay. Lovable black Hebridean sheep surround the building, which features pretty, practical, and comfy dorms

THAR SHE BLOWS!

The North Atlantic Drift – a swirling tendril of the Gulf Stream – carries warm water into the cold, nutrient-rich seas off the Scottish coast, resulting in huge plankton blooms. Small fish feed on the plankton, and bigger fish feed on the smaller fish; this huge seafood smorgasbord attracts large numbers of marine mammals, from harbour porpoises and dolphins to minke whales and even – though sightings are rare – humpback and sperm whales.

There are dozens of operators around the coast offering whale-watching boat trips lasting from a couple of hours to all day; some have sighting success rates of 95% in summer.

While seals, porpoises and dolphins can be seen year-round, minke whales are migratory. The best time to see them is from June to August, with August being the peak month for sightings. The website of the **Hebridean Whale & Dolphin Trust** (www.whaledolphintrust.co.uk) has lots of information on the species you are likely to see, and how to identify them.

WORTH A TRIP

STAFFA

Felix Mendelssohn, who visited the uninhabited island of Staffa, off Mull, in 1829, was inspired to compose his 'Hebrides Overture' after hearing waves echoing in the impressive and cathedral-like Fingal's Cave. The cave walls and surrounding cliffs are composed of vertical, hexagonal basalt columns that look like pillars (Staffa is Norse for 'Pillar Island'). You can land on the island and walk into the cave via a causeway. Nearby Boat Cave can be seen from the causeway, but you can't reach it on foot. Staffa also has a sizable puffin colony, north of the landing place.

Unless you have your own boat, the only way to reach Staffa and the Treshnish Isles is on an organised boat trip.

and an excellent kitchen-lounge. There's a fabulous beach nearby, and a hill to climb for views. It's just over a mile from the ferry, past the abbey.

Iona Campsite CAMPGROUND $
(☎07747-721275; www.ionacampsite.co.uk; tent site per adult/child £7.50/4; ⏲Apr-Oct; 🐾) This basic, welcoming grassy campsite is about 1 mile west of the ferry. Sleeping bags and mats are available for hire.

★**Argyll Hotel** HOTEL $$
(☎01681-700334; www.argyllhoteliona.co.uk; s £76, d £95-114; ⏲Mar-Oct; 📶🐾) 🍃 This loveable, higgledy-piggledy warren of a hotel has great service and appealing snug rooms (a sea view costs more – £167 for a double), including good-value family options. The rooms offers simple comfort and relaxation rather than luxury. Most look out to the rear, where a huge organic garden supplies the restaurant. This is a relaxing and amiably run Iona haven.

Getting There & Around

The ferry from Fionnphort to Iona (£3.30 adult return, five minutes, hourly) runs daily. Cars can only be taken with a permit. There are also various day trips available to Iona from Tobermory and Oban.

Iona Taxi (☎07810-325990) Useful for lugging bags in the rain.

Inveraray

POP 600

There's no fifty shades of grey around here: this historic planned village is all black and white – even logos of high street chain shops conform. Spectacularly set on the shores of Loch Fyne, Inveraray was built by the Duke of Argyll in Georgian style when he revamped his nearby castle in the 18th century.

Sights & Activities

Inveraray Castle CASTLE
(☎01499-302203; www.inveraray-castle.com; adult/child/family £10/7/29; ⏲10am-5.45pm Apr-Oct) This visually stunning castle on the north side of town has been the seat of the Dukes of Argyll – chiefs of Clan Campbell – since the 15th century. The 18th-century building, with its fairytale turrets and fake battlements, houses an impressive armoury hall, its walls patterned with more than 1000 pole-arms, dirks, muskets and Lochaber axes.

Inveraray Jail MUSEUM
(☎01499-302381; www.inverarayjail.co.uk; Church Sq; adult/child £10.95/6.50; ⏲9.30am-6pm Apr-Oct, 10am-5pm Nov-Mar; 👪) At this entertaining interactive tourist attraction you can sit in on a trial, try out a cell and discover the harsh tortures that were meted out to unfortunate prisoners. The attention to detail – including a life-sized model of an inmate squatting on a 19th-century toilet – more than makes up for the sometimes tedious commentary.

Sleeping & Eating

Claonairigh House B&B $
(☎01499-302160; www.inveraraybandb.co.uk; A83, Bridge of Douglas; s/tw/d £45/55/60; P@📶) This attractive 18th-century house, built for the Duke of Argyll in 1745, is set in 3 hectares of grounds on a riverbank complete with waterfall and salmon fishing. There are three homely en suite rooms, one with a four-poster bed, others compact and cute with exposed stone and sloping ceiling. It's a cheerful country home with a resident menagerie, 4 miles south of town.

George Hotel INN $$
(☎01499-302111; www.thegeorgehotel.co.uk; Main St E; d £85-115; P📶🐾) The George boasts a magnificent choice of opulent, individual rooms complete with four-poster beds, pe-

riod furniture, Victorian roll-top baths and private Jacuzzis (superior rooms cost £135 to £180 per double). Some are in an annexe opposite. The cosy wood-panelled bar, with rough stone walls, flagstone floor and peat fires, is a delightful place for all-day bar meals and has a beer garden.

Samphire SEAFOOD $$
(01499-302321; www.samphireseafood.com; 6a Arkland; dinner mains £12-23; noon-2.30pm & 5-8.45pm;) There's lots to like about this compact restaurant that makes an effort to source sustainable local seafood. There's a fairly light touch from the kitchen, which tends to let the natural flavours shine through, with very pleasing results.

Getting There & Away

Scottish Citylink (www.citylink.co.uk) buses run from Glasgow to Inveraray (£12.40, 1¾ hours, nine daily). Five continue to Campbeltown (£13.40, 2½ hours); the others to Oban (£10.20, 1¼ hours, four daily). There are also buses to Dunoon (£3.90, 1¼ hours, three daily Monday to Saturday)

Kilmartin Glen

This magical glen is the focus of one of the biggest concentrations of prehistoric sites in Scotland. Burial cairns, standing stones, stone circles, hill forts and cup-and-ring-marked rocks litter the countryside. Within a 6-mile radius of Kilmartin village there are 25 sites with standing stones and over 100 rock carvings.

In the 6th century, Irish settlers arrived in this part of Argyll and founded the kingdom of Dál Riata (Dalriada), which eventually united with the Picts in 843 to create the first Scottish kingdom. Their capital was the hill fort of Dunadd, on the plain to the south of Kilmartin.

Kilmartin House Museum MUSEUM
(01546-510278; www.kilmartin.org; Kilmartin; adult/child £6/2; 10am-5.30pm Mar-Oct, 11am-4pm Nov-23 Dec) This museum, in Kilmartin village, is a fascinating interpretive centre that provides a context for the ancient monuments you can go on to explore, alongside displays of artefacts recovered from various sites. Funding is being sought to further develop the museum and seek World Heritage status for Kilmartin. It also has a cafe and a good shop with handicrafts and books on Scotland.

Dunadd Fort ARCHAEOLOGICAL SITE
(24hr) FREE This hill fort, 3.5 miles south of Kilmartin village, was the seat of power of the first kings of Dál Riata, and may have been where the Stone of Destiny was originally located. Faint rock carvings of a boar and two footprints with an Ogham inscription may have been used in inauguration ceremonies. The prominent little hill rises straight out of the boggy plain of Moine Mhor Nature Reserve.

A slippery path leads to the summit where you can gaze out on much the same view that the kings of Dál Riata enjoyed 1300 years ago.

Kintyre

The 40-mile long Kintyre peninsula is almost an island, with only a narrow isthmus at Tarbert connecting it to Knapdale. During the Norse occupation of the Western Isles, the Scottish king decreed that the Vikings could claim as their own any island they circumnavigated in a longship. So in 1098 the wily Magnus Barefoot stood at the helm while his men dragged their boat across this neck of land, validating his claim to Kintyre.

The coastline is spectacular on both sides, with stirring views of Arran, Islay, Jura and Northern Ireland. On a sunny day the water shimmers beyond the stony shore. Hiking the Kintyre Way is a nice means of experiencing the peninsula, which has a couple of cracking golf courses at Machrihanish near Campbeltown.

WORTH A TRIP

MULL OF KINTYRE

A narrow winding road, 15 miles long, leads south from Campbeltown to the Mull of Kintyre, passing some good sandy beaches near Southend. This remote headland was immortalised in Paul McCartney's famous song – the former Beatle owns a farmhouse in the area. From where the road ends, a 30-minute steep downhill walk leads to a clifftop lighthouse, with Northern Ireland, only 12 miles away, visible across the channel. Don't leave the road when the frequent mists roll in as it's easy to become disoriented.

Tarbert

POP 1100

The attractive fishing village and yachting centre of Tarbert is the gateway to Kintyre, and is most scenic, with buildings strung around its excellent natural harbour. A crossroads for nearby ferry routes, it's a handy stepping stone to Arran or Islay, but is well worth a stopover on any itinerary.

The picturesque harbour is overlooked by the crumbling, ivy-covered ruins of **Tarbert Castle** (24hr) FREE, rebuilt by Robert the Bruce in the 14th century. You can hike up via a signposted footpath beside **Loch Fyne Gallery** (www.lochfynegallery.com; Harbour St; 10am-5pm Mon-Sat, 10.30am-5pm Sun) FREE, which showcases the work of local artists.

Knap Guest House B&B $$
(01880-820015; www.knapguesthouse.co.uk; Campbeltown Rd; d £75-99;) A flight of stairs lit by Edwardian stained glass leads to this 1st-floor flat with three spacious en suite bedrooms sporting an attractive blend of Scottish and Far Eastern decor. The welcome is warm, and there are great harbour views from the lounge (leather sofas, log fire and a small library) and breakfast room.

★ **Starfish** SEAFOOD $$
(01880-820733; www.starfishtarbert.com; Castle St; mains £11-19; 6-9pm Sun-Thu, noon-2pm & 6-9pm Fri & Sat;) Simple but stylish describes not only the decor in this friendly restaurant but the seafood too. A great variety of specials – anything from classic French fish dishes to Thai curries – are prepared with whatever's fresh off the Tarbert boats that day. Best to book. It may open for lunch daily in summer. Sweet rooms too.

Campbeltown

POP 4800

Blue-collar Campbeltown, set around a beautiful harbour, still suffers from the decline of its fishing and whisky industries and the closure of the nearby air-force base, but is rebounding on the back of golf tourism and a ferry link to Ayrshire. The spruced-up seafront backed by green hills lends the town a distinctly optimistic air.

Sights & Activities

Springbank DISTILLERY
(01586-552009; www.springbankwhisky.com; 85 Longrow; tours from £7; tours 10am & 1.30pm Mon-Sat) There were once no fewer than 32 distilleries around Campbeltown, but most closed in the 1920s. Today this is one of only three operational. It is also one of the few around that distills, matures and bottles all its whisky on the one site, making for an interesting tour. It's a quality malt, one of Scotland's finest.

Davaar Cave CAVE
(24hr) FREE A very unusual sight awaits in this cave on the southern side of Davaar island, at the mouth of Campbeltown Loch. On the wall of the cave is an eerie painting of the Crucifixion by local artist Archibald MacKinnon, dating from 1887. You can walk to the island at low tide: check tide times with the tourist office.

Machrihanish Golf Club GOLF
(01586-810277; www.machgolf.com; Machrihanish; green fee £65) Machrihanish Golf Club is a classic links course, designed by Old Tom Morris. It's remarkably good value compared to courses of a similar standard in Scotland. The famous first hole requires a very decent drive across the bay, or you'll literally end up on the beach. Nearby is an upmarket hotel and restaurant, as well as self-catering villas.

Mull of Kintyre Seatours BOATING
(07785-542811; www.mull-of-kintyre.co.uk; Apr-Sep) Operates high-speed boat trips out of Campbeltown harbour to the spectacular sea cliffs of the Mull of Kintyre, Arran, Ailsa Craig (£35; gannet colony and puffins), or Sanda Island (£30; seals, puffins and other seabirds) as well as whalewatching (£35, best late July to early September). Book in advance by phone or at the tourist office. Operates from the pontoon next to the pier.

Sleeping & Eating

★ **Campbeltown Backpackers** HOSTEL $
(01586-551188; www.campbeltownbackpackers.co.uk; Big Kiln St; dm £20;) This beautiful hostel occupies a central former school building: it's great, with a modern kitchen, disabled access and state-of-the-art wooden bunks. Profits go to maintain the Heritage Centre that runs it. Rates are £2 cheaper if you prebook.

Royal Hotel HOTEL $$$
(01586-810000; www.machrihanishdunes.com; Main St; r £142-172; food noon-9pm Sun-Thu, noon-10pm Fri & Sat;) Historically Campbeltown's best address, this reddish sandstone hotel opposite the harbour is looking swish again. It caters mostly to yachties and

golfers; though rack rates feel overpriced, there are often online specials and rooms are very spacious and attractive. There are some excellent midweek specials that include golf at Machrihanish Dunes and a couple of extras.

Getting There & Away

AIR

Loganair/FlyBe (www.loganair.co.uk) Flies six days a week between Glasgow and Campbeltown's mighty runway at Machrihanish.

BOAT

CalMac (www.calmac.co.uk) Runs thrice weekly May to September between Ardrossan in Ayrshire and Campbeltown (adult/car £7.65/40.50, 2¾ hours); the Saturday return service stops at Brodick on Arran.

Kintyre Express (☎01586-555895; www.kintyreexpress.com) Operates a small, high-speed passenger ferry from Campbeltown to Ballycastle in Northern Ireland (£45/80 one way/return, 1½ hours, daily June to August, four weekly April and September). You must book in advance.

BUS

Scottish Citylink (www.citylink.co.uk) Runs from Campbeltown to Glasgow (£20.50, four to 4¼ hours, five daily) via Tarbert, Inveraray and Loch Lomond. Change at Inveraray for Oban.

Islay

POP 3200

The home of some of the world's greatest and peatiest whiskies, whose names reverberate on the tongue like a pantheon of Celtic deities, Islay (*eye*-lah) is a wonderfully friendly place whose welcoming inhabitants offset its lack of scenic splendour compared to Mull or Skye. The distilleries are well geared-up for visits; even if you're not a fan of single malt, the birdlife, fine seafood, turquoise bays and basking seals are ample reason to visit. Locals are among Britain's most genial: a wave or cheerio to passersby is mandatory, and you'll soon find yourself unwinding to relaxing island pace. The only drawback is that the waves of well-heeled whisky tourists have induced many sleeping and eating options to raise prices to eye-watering levels.

Festivals & Events

★ Fèis Ìle MUSIC, WHISKY

(Islay Festival; www.islayfestival.com; ⌚late May) A week-long celebration of traditional Scottish music and whisky. Events include *ceilidhs* (evenings of traditional Scottish entertainment), pipe-band performances, distillery tours, barbecues and whisky tastings.

Islay, Jura & Colonsay

0 — 20 km
0 — 10 miles

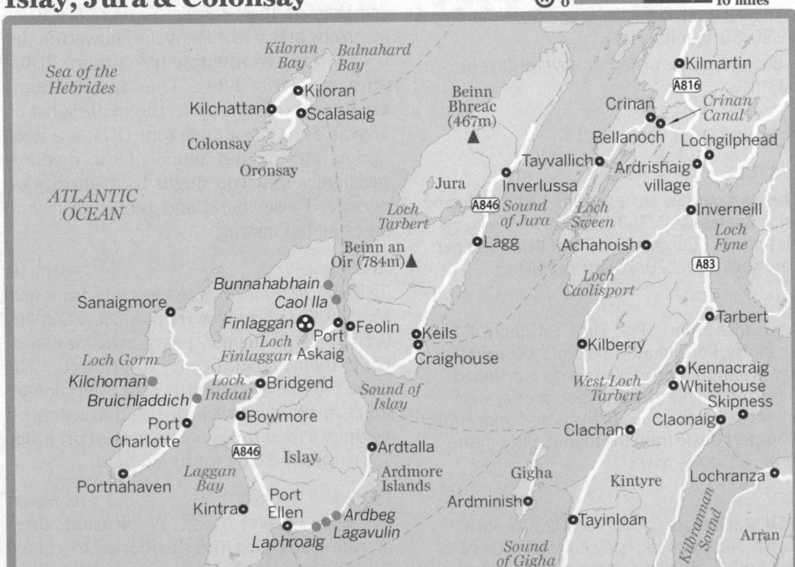

Islay Jazz Festival MUSIC
(www.islayjazzfestival.co.uk; 2nd weekend Sep) This three-day festival features a varied line-up of international talent playing at various venues across the island.

Information

Bowmore Tourist Office (01496-305165; www.islayinfo.com; the Square, Bowmore; 10am-5pm Mon-Sat, noon-3pm Sun Apr-Jun, 9.30am-5.30pm Mon-Sat, noon-3pm Sun Jul & Aug, 10am-5pm Mon-Sat Sep-Oct, 10am-3pm Mon-Fri Nov-Mar) One of the nation's best tourist offices. Staff bend over backwards to find you a bed if things are full up.

Getting There & Away

AIR

Loganair/FlyBe (www.loganair.co.uk) flies up to three times daily from Glasgow to Islay, while **Hebridean Air Services** (p870) operates twice daily Tuesday and Thursday from Oban to Colonsay and Islay.

BOAT

There are two ferry terminals: Port Askaig on the east coast, and Port Ellen in the south. Islay airport lies midway between Port Ellen and Bowmore.

CalMac (www.calmac.co.uk) runs ferries from Kennacraig to Port Ellen or Port Askaig (adult/car £6.50/32.50, two to 2¼ hours, three to five daily). On Wednesdays and Saturdays in summer you can travel to Colonsay (adult/car £4/16.80, 1¼ hours, day trip possible) and Oban (adult/car £9.30/50, four hours).

Book car space on ferries several days in advance.

Getting Around

BICYCLE

There are various places to hire bikes, including **Islay Cycles** (07760-196592; www.islaycycles.co.uk; 2 Corrsgeir Pl, Port Ellen; bikes per day/week from £20/70) in Port Ellen.

BUS

A bus links Ardbeg, Port Ellen, Bowmore, Port Charlotte, Portnahaven and Port Askaig (Monday to Saturday only). You can get unlimited travel for 24 hours for £10, but fares are low anyway. Pick up a copy of the *Islay & Jura Public Transport Guide* from the tourist office or the ferry on the way over.

CAR

D&N MacKenzie (01496-302300; www.carhireonislay.co.uk; Islay Airport) offers car hire from £35 a day and can meet ferries.

TAXI

There are various taxi services on Islay; **Carol's Cabs** (07775-782155, 01496-302155; www.carols-cabs.co.uk) is one that can take bikes.

Port Ellen & Around

Port Ellen is Islay's principal entry point. The coast stretching northeast is one of the loveliest parts of the island, where within 3 miles you'll find three of whisky's biggest names: Laphroaig, Lagavulin and Ardbeg.

The kelp-fringed skerries (small rocky islands or reefs) of the **Ardmore Islands**, near Kildalton, are a wildlife haven and home to Europe's second-largest colony of common seals.

Laphroaig DISTILLERY
(01496-302418; www.laphroaig.com; tours from £6; 9.45am-5pm daily Mar-Oct, 9.45am-4.30pm daily Nov & Dec, 9.45am-4.30pm Mon-Fri Jan-Feb) Laphroaig produces famously peaty whiskies just outside Port Ellen. Of the various premium tastings that it offers, the 'Water to Whisky' tour (£90) is recommended – you see the water source, dig peat, have a picnic and try plenty of drams.

Lagavulin DISTILLERY
(01496-302749; www.discovering-distilleries.com; tours from £6; 9am-6pm Mon-Fri & 9am-5pm Sat-Sun Jun-Aug, 9am-5pm daily Apr & Sep, 9am-6pm Mon-Fri & 9am-5pm Sat-Sun May, 9am-5pm Mon-Fri & 10am-4pm Sat-Sun Oct & Mar, 10am-4pm Mon-Sat Nov-Feb) Peaty and powerful, this is one of the triumvirate of southern distilleries near Port Ellen. The standard tours are free if you sign up to the mailing list on arrival. The Core Range tour (£15) is a good option, cutting out much of the distillery mechanics that you might have already experienced elsewhere, and replacing it with an extended tasting.

Ardbeg DISTILLERY
(01496-302244; www.ardbeg.com; tours from £5; 9.30am-5pm Mon-Fri, plus Sat & Sun Apr-Oct) Ardbeg's iconic peaty whiskies start with their magnificent 10-year-old. The basic tour is good, and it also offers longer tours involving walks, stories and extended tastings. Three miles northeast of Port Ellen. There's a good cafe for lunch here.

Kildalton Cross MONUMENT
(Kildalton; 24hr) FREE A pleasant drive or ride leads past the distilleries to ruined **Kildalton Chapel**, 8 miles from Port Ellen.

In the kirkyard is the exceptional late-8th-century Kildalton Cross. There are carvings of biblical scenes on one side and animals on the other.

Kintra Farm CAMPGROUND, B&B $

(01496-302051; www.kintrafarm.co.uk; tent site £6-8, plus adult/child £4/2, s/d £50/80; May-Sep;) At the southern end of Laggan Bay, 3.5 miles northwest of Port Ellen, Kintra is a basic but beautiful campsite on buttercup-sprinkled turf amid the dunes, with a sunset view across the beach. There's also B&B available.

Old Kiln Café CAFE $

(01496-302244; www.ardbeg.com; Ardbeg; mains £8-15; 10.30am-4pm;) Housed in the former malting kiln at Ardbeg distillery, this serves homemade soups, tasty light meals, heartier daily specials and a range of desserts, including traditional clootie dumpling (a rich steamed pudding filled with currants and raisins).

Bowmore

POP 700

Islay's attractive Georgian capital was built in 1768 to replace the village of Kilarrow, which just had to go – it was spoiling the view from the laird's house. Its centrepieces are the Bowmore distillery and distinctive **Round Church** at the top of Main St, built in circular form to ensure that the devil had no corners to hide in. He was last seen in one of the island's distilleries.

Bowmore DISTILLERY

(01496-810441; www.bowmore.com; School St; tours from £7; 9am-5pm Mon-Fri & 9am-12.30pm Sat Oct-Mar, 9am-5pm Mon-Sat & noon-4pm Sun Apr-Sep) In the centre of Bowmore, this distillery malts its own barley. The tour begins with an overblown marketing video, but is redeemed by a look at (and taste of) the germinating grain laid out in golden billows on the floor of the malting shed. Various premium tours are available.

★**Lambeth House** B&B $$

(01496-810597; lambethguesthouse@tiscali.co.uk; Jamieson St; s/d £65/96;) Cheerily welcoming, and with smart modern rooms with top-notch en suite bathrooms, this is a sound option in the centre of town. The host is a longtime expert in making guests feel welcome, and her breakfasts are reliably good. Rooms vary substantially in size, so ask for a larger one when booking, as the price is the same.

★**Harbour Inn** BRITISH $$

(01496-810330; www.harbour-inn.com; the Square; mains £15-20; noon-2.30pm & 6-9.30pm;) Owned by the Bowmore distillery, this restaurant has changed in philosophy a few times in recent years. We enjoyed our last visit, with plates strong on presentation, with just a whiff of molecular and forage trends but based on solid mostly Scottish produce. Local oysters are an obvious choice. The conservatory-style dining area offers wonderful sunset views over the water.

Port Charlotte & Around

Eleven miles from Bowmore, on the opposite shore of Loch Indaal, is attractive Port Charlotte, a former distillery town that appeals as a base. Museums in town and distilleries close by mean there's plenty to do.

Six miles southwest of Port Charlotte the road ends at **Portnahaven**, a picturesque fishing village. For seal-spotting, you can't do better; there are frequently dozens of the portly beasts basking in the small harbour.

Sights

Bruichladdich DISTILLERY

(01496-850190; www.bruichladdich.com; Bruichladdich; tours £5; 9am-6pm Mon-Fri, 9.30am-4pm Sat, 12.30-3pm Sun Apr-Sep, 9am-5pm Mon-Fri, 9.30am-4pm Sat Oct-Mar) A couple of miles from Port Charlotte, Bruichladdich (brook-*lad*dy) is an infectiously fun place to visit and produces a mind-boggling range of bottlings; there's always some new experiment cooking. One of the peaty cognac-finished Port Charlotte bottlings particularly impressed us at last visit. They also make a gin here, the Botanist, infused with local herbs.

Museum of Islay Life MUSEUM

(01496-850358; www.islaymuseum.org; Port Charlotte; adult/child £3.50/1; 10.30am-4.30pm Mon-Fri Apr-Oct) Islay's long history is lovingly recorded in this museum, housed in the former Free Church. Prize exhibits include an illicit still, 19th-century crofters' furniture, and a set of leather boots once worn by the horse that pulled the lawnmower at Islay House (so it wouldn't leave hoof prints on the lawn!).

Sleeping & Eating

Islay SYHA HOSTEL $

(☎01496-850385; www.syha.org.uk; Main St, Port Charlotte; dm/tw/q £19/45/85; ⊙Apr-Oct; @ 📶) This clean and modern brick hostel has spotless dorms with washbasin and a large kitchen and living room. It's housed in a former distillery building with views over the loch. The bus stops nearby. Breakfast and heatable dinners are available.

Port Mòr Campsite CAMPGROUND $

(☎01496-850441; www.islandofislay.co.uk; tent sites per adult/child £8/4; P @ 📶) The sports field in Port Charlotte has a campsite – there are toilets, showers, laundry and a children's play area in the main building, which also has a licensed cafe-bistro. Open all year.

Port Charlotte Hotel HOTEL $$$

(☎01496-850360; www.portcharlottehotel.co.uk; Main St, Port Charlotte; s/d £135/210; P 📶 🐾) This lovely old Victorian hotel has stylish, individually decorated bedrooms with sea views. It's a friendly, old-style place with a plush lounge, cosy bar and quality restaurant. Rooms are in modern classic style with tartan throws, crisp white sheets and quality toiletries.

Finlaggan

Three miles southwest of Port Askaig, lush meadows swathed in buttercups and daisies slope down to reed-fringed Loch Finlaggan. This bucolic setting was once the most important settlement in the Hebrides, the central seat of power of the Lords of the Isles from the 12th to the 16th centuries.

Buses between Bowmore and Port Askaig stop at the road junction, from where it's a 15-minute walk to the loch.

★Finlaggan RUINS, MUSEUM

(☎01496-840644; www.finlaggan.org; adult/child £4/2; ⊙ruins 24hr, museum 10.30am-4.15pm Mon-Sat Apr-Oct) Three miles from Port Askaig, tumbledown ruins of houses and a chapel on an islet in a shallow loch mark what remains of the stronghold of the Lords of the Isles. A wooden walkway leads over the reeds and water lilies to the island, where information boards describe the remains. Start your exploration at the visitor centre, which has some good explanation of the site's history and archaeology and a video featuring Tony Robinson. The island itself is open at all times.

Jura

POP 200

Jura lies long, dark and low off the coast like a vast Viking longship, its billowing sail the distinctive triple peaks of the Paps of Jura. A magnificently wild and lonely island, it's the perfect place to get away from it all – as George Orwell did in 1948. Orwell wrote his masterpiece *1984* while living at the remote farmhouse of Barnhill in the north of the island, describing it in a letter as 'a very un-get-at-able place'.

Jura takes its name from the Old Norse *dyr-a* (deer island) – an apt appellation, as the island supports a population of around 6000 red deer, outnumbering their human cohabitants by about 30 to one.

Sights

Jura Distillery DISTILLERY

(☎01496-820385; www.jurawhisky.com; Craighouse; tours from £6; ⊙10am-4.30pm Mon-Sat Mar-Oct, 10am-4pm Mon-Fri Nov-Feb) Apart from the superb wilderness walking and wildlife-watching, there's not a whole lot to do on the island of Jura except for visiting the Isle of Jura Distillery. The standard tour runs twice a day, while specialist tours (£15 to £25) take you deeper into the production process and should be prebooked.

Activities

There are few proper footpaths, and off-path exploration often involves rough going through giant bracken, knee-deep bogs and thigh-high tussocks. Most of the island is occupied by deer-stalking estates, and hill access may be restricted during the stalking season (July to February); the Jura Hotel can provide details.

Look out for adders – the island is infested with them, but they're shy snakes and will move away as you approach.

Sleeping & Eating

Places to stay are very limited, so book ahead – don't rely on just turning up. As well as the hotel, there's a handful of B&B options and several self-catering cottages that are let by the week (see www.juradevelopment.co.uk). One of these is **Barnhill** (☎01786-850274; www.escapetojura.com; from £1000 per week; P 🐾), where Orwell stayed, at the far north of the island.

You can camp (£5 per person) in the field below the Jura Hotel; there's a toilet and shower block (small charge) that walkers, yachties and cyclists can also use. From July to February, check on the deer-stalking situation before wild camping.

Jura Hotel HOTEL $$
(☎ 01496-820243; www.jurahotel.co.uk; Craighouse; s £50-60, d £94-125; P 📶) The heart of Jura's community is this hotel, which is warmly welcoming and efficiently run. Rooms vary in size and shape, but all are renovated and feel inviting. The premier rooms – all of which have sea view – are just lovely, with understated elegance and polished modern bathrooms. Eat in the elegant restaurant or the convivial pub.

Antlers CAFE $
(☎ 01496-820496; www.juradevelopment.co.uk; Craighouse; light meals £4-8; ⏲ 10am-4pm Easter-Oct, plus 6.30-8.30pm Fri) 🍃 This community-owned cafe has a craft shop and displays on Jura heritage. It does tasty home baking, sandwiches and the like, and is also open for more elaborate dinners on Fridays. Not licensed – £3 corkage.

ℹ Getting There & Around

A **car ferry** (☎ 01496-840681) shuttles between Port Askaig on Islay and Feolin on Jura (adult/car/bicycle £1.70/9.05/free, five minutes, hourly Monday to Saturday, every two hours Sunday). There is no direct car-ferry connection to the mainland.

From April to September, **Jura Passenger Ferry** (☎ 07768-450000; www.jurapassengerferry.com; one way £20; ⏲ Apr-Sep) runs from Tayvallich on the mainland to Craighouse on Jura (one hour, one or two daily except Wednesday). Booking recommended.

The island's only **bus service** (☎ 01436-810200; www.garelochheadcoaches.co.uk) runs between the ferry slip at Feolin and Craighouse (20 minutes, six to seven Monday to Saturday), timed to coincide with ferry arrivals and departures. Some of the runs continue north as far as Inverlussa.

ARRAN

POP 4600

Enchanting Arran is a jewel in Scotland's scenic crown. The island is a visual feast, and boasts culinary delights, its own brewery and distillery, and stacks of accommodation options. The variations in Scotland's dramatic landscape can all be experienced on this one island, best explored by pulling on the hiking boots or jumping on a bicycle.

Isle of Arran

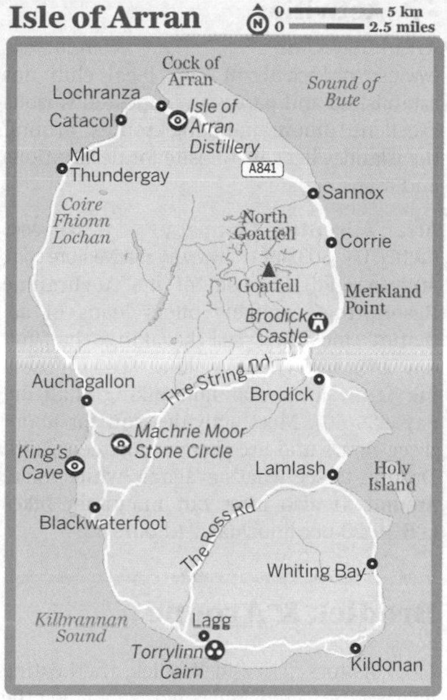

Arran offers some challenging walks in the mountainous north, while the island's circular coastal road is very popular with cyclists.

ℹ Information

The main **tourist office** (☎ 01770-303774; www.visitarran.com; ⏲ 9am-5pm Mon-Sat Mar-Oct, plus 10am-5pm Sun Apr-Sep, 10am-4pm Mon-Sat Nov-Feb) is in Brodick; the ferry from Ardrossan also has an information counter. Useful websites include www.visitarran.com.

ℹ Getting There & Away

Calmac ferries (www.calmac.co.uk) run between Ardrossan and Brodick (adult/car £3.75/15.10, 55 minutes, four to nine daily). From April to late October services also run between Claonaig on the Kintyre peninsula and Lochranza (adult/car £2.80/9.40, 30 minutes, seven to nine daily). In winter this service runs to Tarbert (1¼ hours) once daily and must be reserved.

ℹ Getting Around

Four to seven buses daily go from Brodick pier to Lochranza (£3, 45 minutes), and many head the other way to Lamlash (£2.10) and Whiting Bay (£3, 30 minutes), then on to Kildonan and Blackwaterfoot. Pick up a timetable from the tourist office. An Arran Dayrider costs £5.60 from the driver, giving a day's travel. Download a bus timetable from www.spt.co.uk.

Activities

Arran Bike Club MOUNTAIN BIKING
(www.arranbikeclub.com) This local club has established and partially signposted various excellent mountain-biking routes around the island. Check its website for descriptions and maps.

Arran Adventure Company OUTDOORS
(01770 303349; www.arranadventure.com; Auchrannie Rd) Run out of the Auchrannie Resort, this company offers loads of activities, including sea kayaking (half/full day £49/90), gorge walking (£49), abseiling (£49) and mountain biking (half/full day £35/60). Most activities run for about three hours and are cheaper for teens/kids. Drop in to see what's available while you're around. It also hires out mountain bikes (£6/15/20 per hour/day/24 hours).

Brodick & Around

POP 800

Most visitors arrive in Brodick, the beating heart of the island, and congregate along the coastal road to admire the town's long curving bay. On a clear day it's a spectacular vista, with Goatfell looming over the forested shore. Several of Brodick's main attractions are just out of town, off the Lochranza road.

Sights & Activities

The 55-mile coastal circuit is popular with cyclists and has few serious hills – more in the south than the north. There are plenty of walking booklets and maps available and trails are clearly signposted around the island. Several leave from Lochranza, including the spectacular walk to the island's northeast tip, the **Cock of Arran**, finishing in the village of Sannox (8 miles one way).

Goatfell HIKING
The walk up and down Goatfell (874m), the island's highest point, is 8 miles return (up to eight hours), with trailheads at Brodick and Brodick Castle among others. In fine weather there are superb views to Ben Lomond and Northern Ireland. It can, however, be very cold and windy up there; take the appropriate maps (available at the tourist office), waterproofing and a compass.

Brodick Castle CASTLE
(NTS; 01770-302202; www.nts.org.uk; castle & park adult/child £12.50/9, park only £6.50/5.50; castle 11am-4pm May-Aug, 11am-3pm Apr & Sep, park 9.30am-sunset year-round) This elegant castle 2 miles north of Brodick evolved from 13th-century origins into a stately home and hunting lodge for the Dukes of Hamilton and was used until the 1950s. You enter via the hunting gallery, wallpapered with deer heads. The rest of the interior is characterised by fabulous 19th-century wooden furniture and an array of horses 'n' hounds paintings. Helpful guides and laminated sheets – the kids' ones are more entertaining – add info.

The extensive grounds, now a country park with various trails among the rhododendrons, justify the steep entry fee.

Sleeping & Eating

Brodick Bunkhouse HOSTEL $
(01770-302897; www.brodickbunkhouse.co.uk; Alma Rd; dm £25; P) A short stroll from the ferry, behind the Douglas Hotel, this recently opened hostel has attractive, comfortable triple-decker bunks with individual plugs and USB ports. It's generally unstaffed, with keycode access. It has a simple kitchen and disabled access. No under-18s are admitted.

Glenartney B&B $$
(01770-302220; www.glenartney-arran.co.uk; Mayish Rd; d £86-94; Easter-Sep; P) Uplifting bay views and genuine, helpful hosts make this a cracking option. Airy, stylish rooms make the most of the natural light available at the top of the town. Cyclists will appreciate bike wash, repair and storage facilities, while hikers can benefit from drying rooms and expert trail advice. It makes big efforts to be sustainable.

★Kilmichael Country House Hotel HOTEL $$$
(01770-302219; www.kilmichael.com; Glen Cloy; s £98, d £163-205; Apr-Oct; P) The island's best hotel is also the oldest building – one bit dates from 1650. Luxurious and tastefully decorated, it's a mile outside Brodick but seems a world away in deep countryside. With just eight spacious, very individual rooms and excellent four-course dinners (£45, open to nonguests), it's an ideal, utterly relaxing hideaway that feels very classy without being overly formal.

★Brodick Bar & Brasserie BRASSERIE $$
(01770-302169; www.brodickbar.co.uk; Alma Rd; mains £13-26; noon-2.30pm & 5.30-9pm Mon-Sat;) Though prices have soared in recent years, this is still one of Arran's most

enjoyable eating experiences. The regularly changing blackboard menu brings modern French flair to this Brodick pub, with great presentation, efficient service and delicious flavour combinations. You'll have a hard time choosing, as it's all brilliant. It's very buzzy on weekend evenings.

Lochranza

The village of Lochranza has a stunning location in a small bay on the island's north coast. It's characterised by the ruined 13th-century **Lochranza Castle** (HES; www.historicenvironment.scot; ⌚24hr) FREE, a ruin standing proud on a little promontory. The nearby distillery produces a light, aromatic single malt. The Lochranza area bristles with red deer, who wander insouciantly into the village to crop the grass.

Isle of Arran Distillery DISTILLERY
(☎01770-830264; www.arranwhisky.com; tours adult/child £7.50/free; ⌚10am-5.30pm Mar-Oct, 10.30am-4pm Nov-Feb) The Isle of Arran Distillery produces a light, aromatic single malt. The tour is a good one; it's a small distillery and the whisky-making process is thoroughly explained. There are three to five tours daily. You can opt for just a tutored tasting of several malts (£15) or a film and a dram (£3.50). There are also tours of the warehouse available.

★ **Lochranza SYHA** HOSTEL $
(☎01770-830631; www.syha.org.uk; dm/d/q £22/58/96; ⌚mid-Mar–Oct plus Sat & Sun year-round; P@☎🐾) An excellent hostel in a charming place, with lovely views. Rooms sport chunky wooden furniture, keycards and lockers. Rainwater toilets, energy-saving heating solutions and a wheelchair-accessible room show thoughtful design, while plush lounging areas, a kitchen you could run a restaurant out of, a laundry, a drying room, red deer in the garden and welcoming management combine for a top option.

Castlekirk B&B $$
(☎01770-830202; www.castlekirkarran.co.uk; s/d £45/75; ⌚Mar-Oct; P☎🐾) This unusual and warmly welcoming place is a converted church chock-full of excellent artworks; there's a gallery downstairs, and paintings decorate the passageways and rooms. The breakfast area is dignified by a rose window, and there are great views of the castle. Rooms are cosy under the sloping ceiling.

West Coast

Blackwaterfoot is the west coast's largest village, with a shop and hotel. It's pleasant enough, though not the most scenic of Arran's settlements. You can walk to **King's Cave** (⌚24hr) FREE from here (6 miles); this walk can easily be extended to the Machrie Moor Stone Circle, the highlight of the area.

Machrie Moor Stone Circle ARCHAEOLOGICAL SITE
(⌚24hr) FREE On the western side of the island is Machrie Moor Stone Circle, a pleasant 1.2-mile stroll from the parking area on the coastal road. There are actually several separate groups of stones of varying sizes, erected around 4000 years ago. You pass a Bronze Age burial cairn along the path.

South Coast

The landscape in the south of Arran is gentler than in the north; the road drops into little wooded valleys, and it's particularly lovely around **Lagg**, where a 10-minute walk goes to **Torrylinn Cairn**, a chambered tomb over 4000 years old. **Kildonan** has pleasant sandy beaches, a gorgeous water outlook, a hotel, a campsite and an ivy-clad ruined castle.

In genteel **Whiting Bay**, strung out along the water, you'll find small sandy beaches and easy one-hour walks through the forest to the **Giant's Graves** and **Glenashdale Falls** – keep an eye out for golden eagles and other birds of prey.

★ **Sealshore Campsite** CAMPGROUND $
(☎01770-820320; www.campingarran.com; Kildonan; 1-/2-person tent £8/16, pods for 2 people £35; ⌚Apr-Oct; P☎🐾) Living up to its name, this excellent small campsite is right by the sea (and the Kildonan Hotel) with one of Arran's finest views from its grassy camping area. There's a good washroom area with heaps of showers, kitchen facilities and the breeze keeps the midges away. Cosy camping pods or a fabulously refurbished Roma caravan offer non-tent choices.

Kildonan Hotel HOTEL $$
(☎01770-820207; www.kildonanhotel.com; Kildonan; s/d/ste £75/99/125; P@☎🐾) Appealing rooms and a grounded attitude – dogs and kids are made very welcome – combine at one of Arran's better options. Oh, and it's

right by the water, with seals basking on the rocks. Standard rooms are decent; the suites – with private terrace or small balcony – are just great. Nearly all rooms have sea views; other attractions include friendly staff, a bar and a restaurant.

Coast BISTRO **$$**
(01770-700308; www.coastarran.co.uk; Shore Rd, Whiting Bay; mains £10-19; 10am-4pm & 5-9pm Wed-Sun, hours vary by season;) Offering a sun-drenched conservatory on the water's edge, this serves grills, seafood and salads in the evening, with lighter offerings during the day. There are several appealing vegetarian choices. It closes Wednesday and Sunday evenings outside of summer.

Lamlash

POP 1000

Lamlash, just 3 miles south of Brodick, is in a dazzling setting, strung along the beachfront. The bay was used as a safe anchorage by the navy during WWI and WWII.

Holy Island ISLAND
Just off Lamlash, this island is owned by the Samye Ling Tibetan Centre and used as a retreat, but day visits are allowed. A tide-dependent passenger **ferry** (01770-600998; tomin10@btinternet.com; adult/child return £12/6; daily May-Sep; by arrangement Tue & Fri winter) zips across from Lamlash. No dogs, bikes, alcohol or fires are allowed on Holy Island. A good walk to the top of the hill (314m), takes two or three hours return. You can stay at the **Holy Island Centre for World Peace & Health** (01770-601100; www.holyisle.org; dm/s/d £29/49/74; Apr-Oct). Prices include full (vegetarian) board.

★**Glenisle Hotel** HOTEL **$$$**
(01770-600559; www.glenislehotel.com; Shore Rd; s/d/superior d £90/139/172;) This stylish hotel offers great service and high comfort levels. Rooms are decorated with contemporary fabrics; 'cosy' rooms under the sloping roof are a little cheaper. All feel fresh and include binoculars for scouring the seashore; upgrade to a superior for the best water views. Downstairs is excellent pub food (mains £10 to £15) with Scottish classics and a good wine list.

★**Drift Inn** PUB FOOD **$$**
(01770-600608; www.driftinnarran.com; Shore Rd; mains £10-18; food noon-9pm;) In our more-or-less humble opinion, this is the island's best pub, offering a plush interior with leather chairs and a fireplace, as well as a fabulous beer garden – enjoy magnificent views from both across to Holy Island. Great bar food is on offer – upmarket, inventive fare with thoughtful vegetarian options – plus Arran ales on tap and blues on the stereo.

Inverness & the Northern Highlands & Islands

Includes ➡

Best Places to Eat

- Café 1 (p891)
- Lime Tree (p911)
- The Albannach (p922)
- Three Chimneys (p933)
- Foveran (p946)

Best Places to Sleep

- Grange (p911)
- The Torridon (p925)
- Milton Eonan (p909)
- Hillstone Lodge (p933)
- Albert Hotel (p945)

Why Go?

Scotland's vast and melancholy soul is here, in an epic landscape whose stark beauty imprints the hearts of those who journey through it. Mist, peat, rock, heather...and long, sun-blessed summer evenings that repay the occasional days of horizontal rain.

The hills and glens of Highland Perthshire offer a memorable first taste. The region's capital, Inverness, is backed by the craggy Cairngorms, which draw hikers and skiers to their slopes. Further north, ancient stones stand testament to prehistoric builders on the magical islands of Orkney and Shetland, where squadrons of seabirds wheel above huge nesting colonies.

The most epic mountain scenery – you really need an orchestra to do it justice – is in the northwest Highlands, and it continues into Skye, where the mighty Cuillin Hills tower jaggedly in the setting sun. Beyond, on the Atlantic fringe, the Outer Hebrides offer the nation's most beautiful beaches and a glimpse of traditional island life.

When to Go

- Hit the Cairngorms for skiing or the Shetland Islands for Up Helly Aa, a fiery Viking festival in January.
- June's long evenings see the Highlands at their most romantic, while Fort William hosts the Mountain Bike World Cup.
- September is the ideal time for hiking and hill walking – midges are dying off, and the weather is still reasonably good.

Inverness & the Northern Highlands & Islands

❶ **Glen Lyon** (p909) Exploring the woods and mountains around this gorgeous glen.

❷ **South Harris** (p938) Dipping your toes in the water at the beautiful beaches in the Western Isles.

❸ **Cuillin Hills** (p931) Shouldering the challenge of these hills, brooding over the skyscape of Skye.

❹ **Far northwest** (p920) Picking your jaw up off the floor as you marvel at the epic Highland scenery.

❺ **Skye** (p929) Launching yourself in a sea kayak to explore the otter-rich waters of the Isle of Skye.

❻ **Skara Brae** (p949) Shaking your head in astonishment at prehistoric perfection that predates the pyramids.

❼ **Royal Deeside** (p903) Exploring the villages, hills and forests around Balmoral Castle.

❽ **Bird-watching** (p960) Capering with puffins and dodging skuas at Hermaness nature reserve.

❾ **Glen Coe** (p908) Soaking up the moody but magnificent scenery.

❿ **Ben Nevis** (p913) Making it to the summit of the UK's highest mountain.

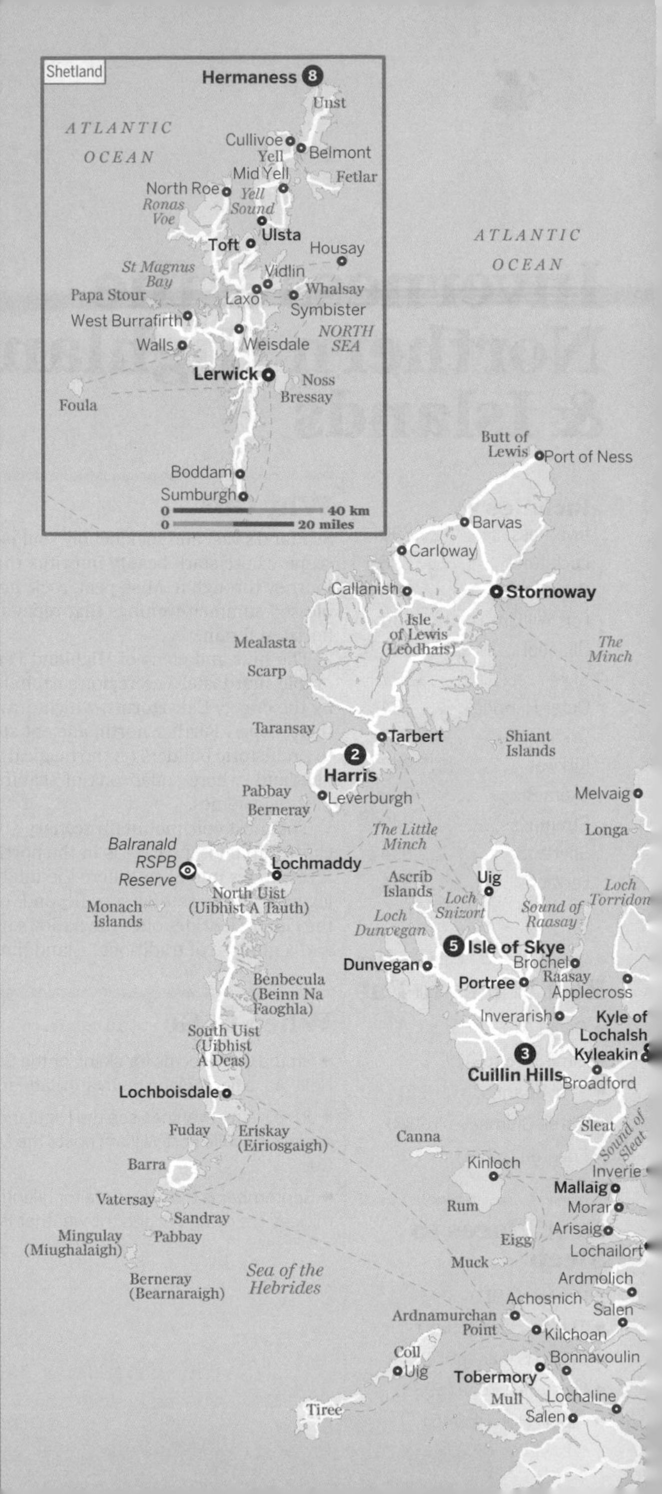

0 40 km
0 20 miles
N
Westray
Papa Westray
North Ronaldsay
Pierowall
Beltane
Northwall
Rapness
Sanday
Kettletoft
Eday
Rousay
Papa Stronsay
Orkney
Birsay
Backaland
Whitehall
Evie
Stronsay
To Shetland Islands
Skara Brae 6
Auskerry
NORTH SEA
Stromness
Kirkwall
Mainland
Moaness
Deerness
Copinsay
Hoy
Lyness
St Margaret's Hope
South Ronaldsay
Pentland Firth
Burwick
Dunnet Head
Scrabster
Duncansby Head
Sandwood Bay
Durness
Melvich
Thurso
Castle of Mey
John O'Groats
Coldbackie
Bettyhill
Sinclair's Bay
Kinlochbervie
Tongue
Strathy
Halladale
Watten
Wick
Wick
Tarbet
Ben Loyal (764m)
Naver
Handa
Laxford Bridge
Scourie
Thurso
Achavanich
4 Durness & Ullapool
NORTH SEA
Eddrachillis Bay
Point of Stoer
Ben Klibreck (961m)
Lybster
Kylesku
Kinbrace
Dunbeath
Ben More Assynt (998m)
Clachtoll
Achmelvich
Lochinver
SUTHERLAND
Helmsdale
Loch Shin
Helmsdale
Stac Pollaidh (612m)
Brora
To Orkney & S
Knockan
Tirry
Achiltibuie
Runie
Oykel
Lairg
Dunrobin Castle
Golspie
Invercassley
Gruinard Bay
Dornoch Firth
Bonar Bridge
Ullapool
Drumchork
Croick
Dornoch
Ardgay
Dundonnell
Portmahomack
Midtown
Beinn Dearg (1084m)
Tain
Moray Firth
Gairloch
Ben Wyvis (1046m)
Loch Maree
ROSS
Invergordon
Banff
Liathach (1054m)
Kinlochewe
Garve
Cromarty
Elgin
Dingwall
Fort George
Nairn
Brodie Castle
Torridon
Achnasheen
Fortrose
Shieldaig
Carron
Orrin
Cawdor Castle
Keith
Inverness
Spey
Kishorn
Culloden
Isla
Huntly
Lochcarron
Struy
Glass
Findhorn
ABERDEENSHIRE
Plockton
Grantown-on-Spey
Eilean Donan Castle
Cannich
Drumnadrochit
Affric
Urquhart Castle
Loch Ness
Carrbridge
Glenelg
Five Sisters of Kintail (1068m)
Invermoriston
Foyers
Monadhliath Mountains
Cairngorm Mountains
Alford
Don
Arnisdale
Aviemore
Fort Augustus
Kincraig
Royal Deeside
Loch Quoich
Tarff
Killin
Cairn Gorm (1245m)
Balmoral Castle
Invergarry
Kingussie
Newtonmore
7
Dee
Strathan
Loch Lochy
Cairngorms National Park
Braemar
Ballater
Tarbet
Loch Arkaig
Spey
Lochnagar (1155m)
Achnacarry
Glenfinnan
Dalwhinnie
Grampian Mountains
Roy Bridge
South Esk
Loch Eil
Fort William
Loch Ericht
Blair Castle
10 Ben Nevis (1344m)
Garry
Blair Atholl
Ardle
Strontian
Loch Rannoch
Glencoe
Kinlochleven
Kinloch Rannoch
ANGUS
Pitlochry
Montrose
9
Loch Linnhe
Glen Lyon 1
Forfar
Glen Coe
Tay
Aberfeldy
Dunkeld
Blairgowrie
Ben Lawers (1214m)
Kenmore
Loch Tay
PERTHSHIRE & KINROSS
ARGYLL & BUTE
Killin
Dundee

INVERNESS & THE GREAT GLEN

Inverness, one of the fastest growing towns in Britain, is the capital of the Highlands. It's a transport hub and jumping-off point for the central, western and northern Highlands, the Moray Firth coast and the Great Glen.

The Great Glen is a geological fault running in an arrow-straight line across Scotland from Fort William to Inverness. The glaciers of the last ice age eroded a deep trough along the fault line, which is now filled by a series of lochs – Linnhe, Lochy, Oich and Ness. The glen has always been an important communication route – General George Wade built a military road along the southern side of Loch Ness in the early 18th century, and in 1822 the various lochs were linked by the Caledonian Canal to create a cross-country waterway. The modern A82 road along the glen was completed in 1933 – a date that coincides neatly with the first modern sightings of the Loch Ness Monster.

Inverness

POP 61,235

Inverness has a great location astride the River Ness at the northern end of the Great Glen. In summer it overflows with visitors intent on monster hunting at nearby Loch Ness, but it's worth a visit in its own right for a stroll along the picturesque River Ness, a cruise on Loch Ness, and a meal in one of the city's excellent restaurants.

Inverness was probably founded by King David in the 12th century, but thanks to its often violent history few buildings of real age or historical significance have survived – much of the older part of the city dates from the period following the completion of the Caledonian Canal in 1822. The broad and shallow River Ness, famed for its salmon fishing, runs through the heart of the city.

Sights & Activities

★Ness Islands PARK

The main attraction in Inverness is a leisurely stroll along the river to the Ness Islands. Planted with mature Scots pine, fir, beech and sycamore, and linked to the river banks and each other by elegant Victorian footbridges, the islands make an appealing picnic spot. They're a 20-minute walk south of the castle – head upstream on either side of the river (the start of the Great Glen Way), and return on the opposite bank.

On the way you'll pass the red-sandstone towers of **St Andrew's Cathedral** (11 Ardross St), dating from 1869, and the modern **Eden Court Theatre** (☎01463-234234; www.eden-court.co.uk; Bishop's Rd; wi-fi), which hosts regular art exhibits, both on the west bank.

Loch Ness by Jacobite BOATING

(☎01463-233999; www.jacobite.co.uk; Glenurquhart Rd; adult/child £33/26) From June to September, boats depart from Tomnahurich Bridge twice daily for a three-hour cruise along the Caledonian Canal to Loch Ness and back, with a live commentary on local history and wildlife. You can buy tickets at the tourist office and catch a free minibus to the boat. Other cruises and combined cruise/coach tours, from one to 6½ hours, are also available, some year-round.

Dolphin Spirit WILDLIFE WATCHING

(☎07544-800620; www.dolphinspirit.co.uk; Inverness Marina, Longman Dr; adult/child £16/10; ⏲Easter-Oct) Four times a day in season, this outfit runs cruises from Inverness into the Moray Firth to spot the UK's largest pod of bottlenose dolphins – around 130 animals. The dolphins feed on salmon heading for the rivers at the head of the firth, and can often be seen leaping and bow-surfing.

Sleeping

Inverness has a good range of backpacker accommodation, and also has some excellent boutique hotels. There are lots of guesthouses and B&Bs along Old Edinburgh Rd and Ardconnel St on the east side of the river, and on Kenneth St and Fairfield Rd on the west bank; all are within 10 minutes' walk of the city centre.

The city fills up quickly in July and August, so you should either prebook your accommodation or get an early start looking for somewhere to stay.

Bazpackers Backpackers Hotel HOSTEL $

(☎01463-717663; www.bazpackershostel.co.uk; 4 Culduthel Rd; dm/tw £18/50; @wi-fi) This may be Inverness' smallest hostel (34 beds), but it's hugely popular. It's a friendly, quiet place – the main building has a convivial lounge centred on a wood-burning stove, and a small garden and great views (some rooms are in a separate building with no garden). The dorms and kitchen can be a bit cramped, but the showers are great.

Inverness Millburn SYHA HOSTEL $
(SYHA; ☎01463-231771; www.syha.org.uk; Victoria Dr; dm/tw £22/55; P@) Inverness' modern 166-bed hostel is 10 minutes' walk northeast of the city centre. With its comfy beds and flashy stainless-steel kitchen, some reckon it's the best SYHA hostel in the country. Booking is essential, especially at Easter and in July and August.

★**Trafford Bank** B&B $$
(☎01463-241414; www.traffordbankguesthouse.co.uk; 96 Fairfield Rd; d £120-140; P) Lots of word-of-mouth rave reviews for this elegant Victorian villa, which was once home to a bishop, just a mitre-toss from the Caledonian Canal and 10 minutes' walk west from the city centre. The luxurious rooms include fresh flowers and fruit, bathrobes and fluffy towels – ask for the Tartan Room, which has a wrought-iron king-size bed and Victorian roll-top bath.

Ardconnel House B&B $$
(☎01463-240455; www.ardconnel-inverness.co.uk; 21 Ardconnel St; r per person £36-45;) The six-room Ardconnel is one of our favourites (advance booking is essential, especially in July and August) – a terraced Victorian house with comfortable en suite rooms, a dining room with crisp white table linen, and a breakfast menu that includes Vegemite for homesick Antipodeans. Kids under 10 not allowed.

Ach Aluinn B&B $$
(☎01463-230127; www.achaluinn.com; 27 Fairfield Rd; r per person £40-45; P) This large, detached Victorian house is bright and homely, and offers all you might want from a B&B – private bathroom, TV, reading lights, comfy beds with two pillows each, and an excellent breakfast. Less than 10 minutes' walk west from the city centre.

Heathmount Hotel BOUTIQUE HOTEL $$
(☎01463-235877; www.heathmounthotel.com; Kingsmills Rd; s/d from £75/105; P) Small and friendly, the Heathmount combines a popular local bar and restaurant with eight designer hotel rooms, each one different, ranging from a boldly coloured family room in purple and gold to a slinky black velvet four-poster double. Five minutes' walk east of the city centre.

★**Rocpool Reserve** BOUTIQUE HOTEL $$$
(☎01463-240089; www.rocpool.com; Culduthel Rd; s/d from £195/230; P) Boutique chic meets the Highlands in this slick and sophisticated little hotel, where an elegant Georgian exterior conceals an oasis of contemporary cool. A gleaming white entrance hall lined with red carpet and contemporary art leads to designer rooms in shades of chocolate, cream and gold; a restaurant by Albert Roux completes the luxury package.

Expect lots of decadent extras in the more expensive rooms, ranging from two-person showers to balcony hot tubs with aqua-vision TV.

Eating

Velocity Cafe CAFE $
(☎01463-419956; http://velocitylove.co.uk; 1 Crown Ave; mains £4-7; ⊙9am-5pm Mon, Wed, Fri & Sat, 9am-9pm Thu, 11am-5pm Sun;) This cyclists' cafe serves soups, sandwiches and salads prepared with organic, locally sourced produce, as well as yummy cakes and coffee. There's also a workshop where you can repair your bike or book a session with a mechanic.

★**Café 1** BISTRO $$
(☎01463-226200; www.cafe1.net; 75 Castle St; mains £13-25; ⊙noon-2.30pm & 5-9.30pm Mon-Fri, noon-2.30pm & 6-9.30pm Sat;) Café 1 is a friendly, appealing bistro with candle-lit tables amid elegant blonde-wood and wrought-iron decor. There is an international menu based on quality Scottish produce, from Aberdeen Angus steaks to crisp pan-fried sea bass and meltingly tender pork belly. The set lunch menu (two courses for £12) is served noon to 2.30pm Monday to Saturday.

Contrast Brasserie BRASSERIE $$
(☎01463-223777; www.glenmoristontownhouse.com; 20 Ness Bank; mains £14-21; ⊙noon-2.30pm & 5-10pm) Book early for what we think is one of the best-value restaurants in Inverness – a dining room that drips designer style, with smiling professional staff and truly delicious food prepared using fresh Scottish produce. The two-/three-course lunch menu (£11/14) and three-course early-bird menu (£16, 5pm to 6.30pm) are bargains.

Mustard Seed BISTRO $$
(☎01463-220220; www.mustardseedrestaurant.co.uk; 16 Fraser St; mains £13-21; ⊙noon-3pm & 5.30-10pm) The menu at this bright and bustling bistro changes weekly, but focuses on Scottish and French cuisine with a modern twist. Grab a table on the upstairs

Inverness

0 200 m
0 0.1 miles

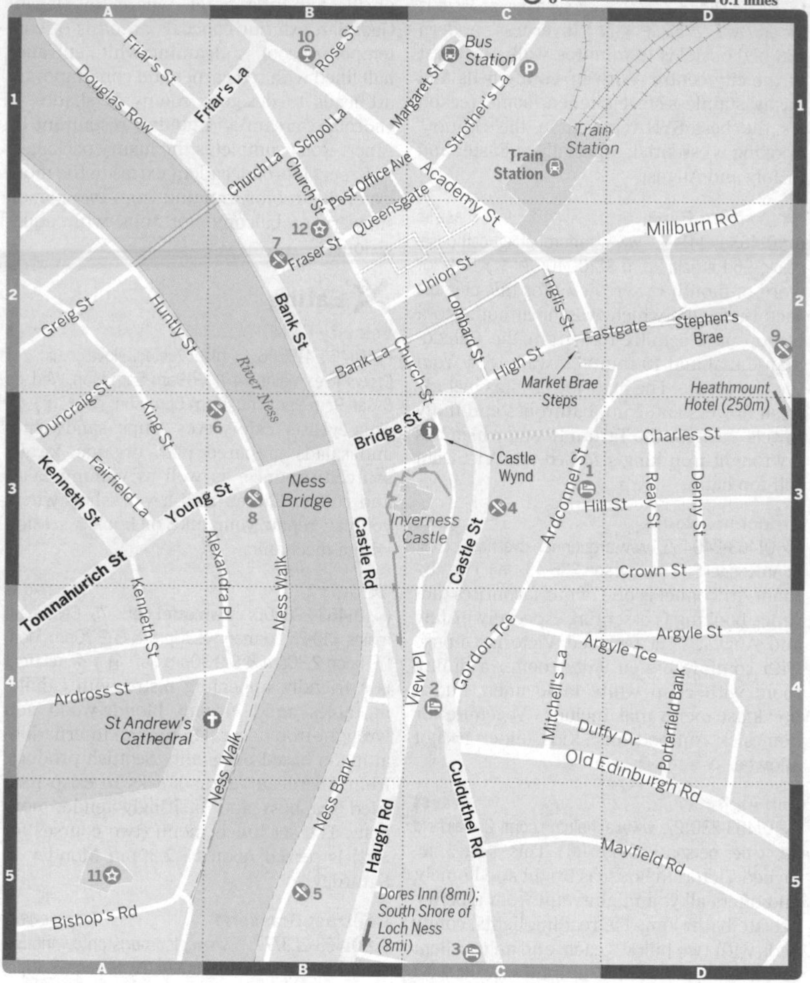

balcony if you can – it's the best outdoor lunch spot in Inverness, with a great view across the river. And a two-course lunch for £9 – yes, that's right – is hard to beat.

Kitchen Brasserie MODERN SCOTTISH **$$**

(☎01463-259119; www.kitchenrestaurant.co.uk; 15 Huntly St; mains £9-20; ⊙noon-3pm & 5-10pm;) This spectacular glass-fronted restaurant offers a great menu of top Scottish produce with a Mediterranean or Asian touch, and a view over the River Ness – try to get a table upstairs. Great value two-course lunch (£9, noon to 3pm) and early-bird menu (£13, 5pm to 7pm).

Rocpool MEDITERRANEAN **$$$**

(☎01463-717274; www.rocpoolrestaurant.com; 1 Ness Walk; mains £13-23; ⊙noon-2.30pm & 5.45-10pm Mon-Sat) Lots of polished wood, crisp white linen and leather booths and banquettes lend a nautical air to this relaxing bistro, which offers a Mediterranean-influenced menu that makes the most of quality Scottish produce, especially seafood. The two-course lunch is £16.

Inverness

Sleeping

1 Ardconnel House C3
2 Bazpackers Backpackers Hotel C4
3 Rocpool Reserve C5

Eating

4 Café 1 .... C3
5 Contrast Brasserie B5
6 Kitchen Brasserie B3
7 Mustard Seed B2
8 Rocpool B3
9 Velocity Cafe D2

Drinking & Nightlife

10 Phoenix B1

Entertainment

11 Eden Court Theatre A5
12 Hootananny B2

Drinking & Entertainment

Clachnaharry Inn PUB
(01463-239806; www.clachnaharryinn.co.uk; 17-19 High St, Clachnaharry; 11am-11pm Mon-Thu, 11am-1am Fri & Sat, noon-11pm Sun;) Just over a mile northwest of the city centre, on the bank of the Caledonian Canal just off the A862, this is a delightful old coaching inn (with beer garden out the back) serving an excellent range of real ales and good pub grub.

Phoenix PUB
(01463-233685; 108 Academy St; 11am-1am Mon-Sat, noon-midnight Sun) Beautifully refurbished, this is the most traditional of the pubs in the city centre, with a mahogany horseshoe bar and several real ales on tap, including beers from the Cairngorm, Cromarty and Isle of Skye breweries.

Hootananny LIVE MUSIC
(01463-233651; www.hootanannyinverness.co.uk; 67 Church St) Hootananny is the city's best live-music venue, with traditional folk- and/or rock-music sessions nightly, including big-name bands from all over Scotland (and, indeed, the world). The bar is well stocked with a range of beers from the local Black Isle Brewery.

Information

Inverness Tourist Office (01463-252401; www.visithighlands.com; Castle Wynd; internet access per 20min £1; 9am-5pm Mon-Sat, 10am-3pm Sun, longer hours Mar-Oct) Bureau de change and accommodation booking service; also sells tickets for tours and cruises. Opening hours limited November to March.

Getting There & Away

AIR

Inverness Airport (INV; 01667-464000; www.hial.co.uk/inverness-airport) At Dalcross, 10 miles east of the city, off the A96 towards Aberdeen. There are scheduled flights to Amsterdam, London, Manchester, Dublin, Orkney, Shetland and the Outer Hebrides, as well as other places in the UK

BUS

Services depart from **Inverness bus station** (Margaret St). Most intercity routes are served by **Scottish Citylink** (0871-266 3333; www.citylink.co.uk).

Aberdeen (Stagecoach; 01463-233371; www.stagecoachbus.com) £12.75, 3¾ hours, hourly

Aviemore £10.20, 45 minutes, eight daily

Edinburgh £31, 3½ to 4½ hours, hourly

Fort William £11.60, two hours, five daily

Glasgow £31, 3½ to 4½ hours, hourly

London (National Express; 08717-818181; www.nationalexpress.com) £45, 13 hours, one daily; more frequent services requiring a change at Glasgow.

Portree £25, 3¼ hours, three daily

Thurso (Stagecoach) £19.80, three hours, three to five daily

Ullapool £13.20, 1½ hours, two daily except Sunday

If you book far enough in advance, **Megabus** (0141-352 4444; www.megabus.com) offers fares from as little as £1 for buses from Inverness to Glasgow and Edinburgh, and £10 to London.

TRAIN

Aberdeen £21, 2¼ hours, eight daily

Edinburgh £38, 3½ hours, eight daily

Glasgow £38, 3½ hours, eight daily

Kyle of Lochalsh £18, 2½ hours, four daily Monday to Saturday, two Sunday; one of Britain's great scenic train journeys

London £120, eight to nine hours, one daily direct; others require a change at Edinburgh

Wick £16, 4½ hours, four daily Monday to Saturday, one or two on Sunday; via Thurso

Getting Around

TO/FROM THE AIRPORT

Stagecoach bus 11/11A runs from the airport to Inverness bus station (£4, 20 minutes, every 30 minutes).

BICYCLE

Ticket to Ride (☎01463-419160; www.ticketoridehighlands.co.uk; Bellfield Park; per day from £25; ⏰9am-6pm Apr-Oct) Hires out mountain bikes, hybrids and tandems; can be dropped off in Fort William. Will deliver bikes free to local hotels and B&Bs.

BUS

City services and buses to places around Inverness, including Nairn, Forres, the Culloden battlefield, Beauly, Dingwall and Lairg, are operated by Stagecoach (p893). An Inverness City Dayrider ticket costs £3.50 and gives unlimited travel for a day on buses throughout the city.

CAR

Focus Vehicle Rental (☎01463-709517; www.focusvehiclerental.co.uk; 6 Harbour Rd) The big boys charge from around £50 to £65 per day, but Focus has cheaper rates starting at £40 per day.

Around Inverness

Culloden Battlefield

The Battle of Culloden in 1746 – the last pitched battle ever fought on British soil – saw the defeat of Bonnie Prince Charlie and the end of the Jacobite dream when 1200 Highlanders were slaughtered by government forces in a 68-minute rout. The Duke of Cumberland, son of the reigning King George II and leader of the Hanoverian army, earned the nickname 'Butcher' for his brutal treatment of the defeated Jacobite forces. The battle sounded the death knell for the old clan system, and the horrors of the Clearances soon followed. The sombre moor where the conflict took place has scarcely changed in the ensuing 260 years.

Culloden is 6 miles east of Inverness. Bus 5A runs from Eastgate shopping centre in Inverness to Culloden battlefield (£2.45, 30 minutes, hourly except Sunday).

Culloden Visitor Centre MUSEUM
(NTS; www.nts.org.uk/culloden; adult/child £11/8.50; ⏰9am-6pm Jun-Aug, to 5.30pm Apr, May, Sep & Oct, 10am-4pm Nov-Mar; Ⓟ) This impressive visitor centre has everything you need to know about the Battle of Culloden in 1746, including the lead-up and the aftermath, with perspectives from both sides. An innovative film puts you on the battlefield in the middle of the mayhem, and a wealth of other audio presentations must have kept Inverness' entire acting community in business for weeks. The admission fee includes an audioguide for a self-guided tour of the battlefield itself.

Fort George

The headland guarding the narrows in the Moray Firth opposite Fortrose is occupied by the magnificent and virtually unaltered 18th-century artillery fortification of Fort George.

Fort George FORTRESS
(HS; ☎01667-462777; adult/child £8.50/5.10; ⏰9.30am-5.30pm Apr-Sep, 10am-4pm Oct-Mar; Ⓟ) One of the finest artillery fortifications in Europe, Fort George was established in 1748 in the aftermath of the Battle of Culloden, as a base for George II's army of occupation in the Highlands. By the time of its completion in 1769 it had cost the equivalent of around £1 billion in today's money. It still functions as a military barracks; public areas have exhibitions on 18th-century soldiery, and the mile-plus walk around the ramparts offers fine views out to sea and back to the Great Glen.

Given its size, you'll need at least two hours to do the place justice. The fort is off the A96 about 11 miles northeast of Inverness; there is no public transport.

Cawdor Castle

Cawdor Castle CASTLE
(☎01667-404615; www.cawdorcastle.com; Cawdor; adult/child £10.70/6.70; ⏰10am-5.30pm May-Sep; Ⓟ) This castle, 5 miles southwest of Nairn, was once the seat of the Thane of Cawdor, one of the titles bestowed on Shakespeare's *Macbeth*. The real Macbeth – an ancient Scottish king – couldn't have lived here though, since he died in 1057, 300 years before the castle was begun. Nevertheless the tour gives a fascinating insight into the lives of the Scottish aristocracy.

Glen Affric

The broad valley of Strathglass extends about 18 miles inland from Beauly, followed by the A831 to Cannich (the only village in the area), where there's a grocery store and a post office.

Glen Affric (www.glenaffric.org), one of the most beautiful glens in Scotland, extends deep into the hills beyond Cannich.

The upper reaches of the glen, now designated as **Glen Affric Nature Reserve** (www.nnr-scotland.org.uk/glen-affric), is a scenic wonderland of shimmering lochs, rugged mountains and native Scots pine forest, home to pine marten, wildcat, otter, red squirrel and golden eagle.

About 4 miles southwest of Cannich is **Dog Falls**, a scenic spot where the River Affric squeezes through a narrow, rocky gorge. A circular walking trail (red waymarks) leads from Dog Falls car park to a footbridge below the falls and back on the far side of the river (2 miles, allow one hour).

Stagecoach (www.stagecoachbus.com) Buses 17 and 117 run from Inverness to Cannich (£5.30, one hour, three a day Monday to Saturday) via Drumnadrochit, and continue from Cannich to Tomich (10 minutes).

Ross's Minibuses (www.ross-minibuses.co.uk) From the first Monday in July to the 2nd Friday in September, a minibus runs from Inverness bus station to the Glen Affric car park via Drumnadrochit and Cannich (£8.50, 1½ hours, once daily Monday, Wednesday and Friday). It shuttles between Cannich and Glen Affric (30 minutes) twice more on the same days. Check the website for the latest timetables.

★ Struy Inn HOTEL **$$**
(☎ 01463-761308; www.thestruy.co.uk; Struy village; d £95; ⏲ Wed-Sun; P 📶) Set in the heart of lovely Strathglass, on the road between Cannich and Beauly, this fine old Victorian inn is a haven of old-fashioned charm. It has just two guest bedrooms and a top-quality restaurant (mains £17 to £27, served from

MONSTERS, MYTHS & LOCH NESS

Highland folklore is filled with tales of strange creatures living in lochs and rivers, notably the kelpie (water horse) that lures unwary travellers to their doom. The use of the term 'monster', however, is a relatively recent phenomenon, whose origins lie in an article published in the *Inverness Courier* on 2 May 1933, entitled 'Strange Spectacle on Loch Ness'.

The article recounted the sighting of a disturbance in the loch by Mrs Aldie Mackay and her husband: 'There the creature disported itself, rolling and plunging for fully a minute, its body resembling that of a whale, and the water cascading and churning like a simmering cauldron.'

The story was taken up by the London press and sparked a flurry of sightings that year, including a notorious on-land encounter with London tourists Mr and Mrs Spicer on 22 July 1933, again reported in the *Inverness Courier*:

'It was horrible, an abomination. About 50 yards ahead, we saw an undulating sort of neck, and quickly followed by a large, ponderous body. I estimated the length to be 25 to 30 feet, its colour was dark elephant grey. It crossed the road in a series of jerks, but because of the slope we could not see its limbs. Although I accelerated quickly towards it, it had disappeared into the loch by the time I reached the spot. There was no sign of it in the water. I am a temperate man, but I am willing to take any oath that we saw this Loch Ness beast. I am certain that this creature was of a prehistoric species.'

The London newspapers couldn't resist. In December 1933 the *Daily Mail* sent Marmaduke Wetherall, a film director and big-game hunter, to Loch Ness to track down the beast. Within days he found 'reptilian' footprints in the shoreline mud (soon revealed to have been made with a stuffed hippopotamus foot). Then in April 1934 came the famous 'long-necked monster' photograph taken by the seemingly reputable Harley St surgeon Colonel Kenneth Wilson. The press went mad and the rest, as they say, is history.

In 1994, however, Christian Spurling – Wetherall's stepson, by then 90 years old – revealed that the most famous photo of Nessie ever taken was in fact a hoax, perpetrated by his stepfather with Wilson's help. Today, of course, there are those who claim that Spurling's confession is itself a hoax. And, ironically, the researcher who exposed the surgeon's photo as a fake still believes wholeheartedly in the monster's existence.

There have been regular sightings of the monster through the years (see www.lochnesssightings.com), with a peak in 1996–97 (the Hollywood movie *Loch Ness* was released in 1996), but reports have tailed off in recent years.

Hoax or not, the bizarre mini-industry that has grown up around Loch Ness and its mysterious monster since that eventful summer last century is a spectacle in itself.

5.30pm) serving the finest Scottish cuisine. Booking essential.

★ Kerrow House B&B $$
(☎01456-415243; www.kerrow-house.co.uk; Cannich; per person £40-45; P) This wonderful Georgian hunting lodge has bags of old-fashioned character – it was once the home of Highland author Neil M Gunn – and has spacious grounds with 3.5 miles of private trout fishing. It's a mile south of Cannich on the minor road along the east side of the River Glass.

Loch Ness

Deep, dark and narrow, Loch Ness stretches for 23 miles between Inverness and Fort Augustus. Its bitterly cold waters have been extensively explored in search of Nessie, the elusive Loch Ness monster, but most visitors see her only in the form of a cardboard cut-out at Drumnadrochit's monster exhibitions. The busy A82 road runs along the northwestern shore, while the more tranquil and picturesque B862 follows the southeastern shore. A complete circuit of the loch is about 70 miles – travel anticlockwise for the better views.

Drumnadrochit

POP 1100

Seized by monster madness, its gift shops bulging with Nessie cuddly toys, Drumnadrochit is a hotbed of beastie fever, with two monster exhibitions battling it out for the tourist dollar.

Sights & Activities

Urquhart Castle CASTLE
(HS; ☎01456-450551; adult/child £8.50/5.10; ⊙9.30am-6pm Apr-Sep, to 5pm Oct, to 4.30pm Nov-Mar; P) Commanding a superb location 1.5 miles east of Drumnadrochit, with outstanding views (on a clear day), Urquhart Castle is a popular Nessie-hunting hot spot. A huge visitor centre (most of which is beneath ground level) includes a video theatre (with a dramatic 'reveal' of the castle at the end of the film) and displays of medieval items discovered in the castle. The site includes a huge gift shop and a restaurant, and is often very crowded in summer.

The castle was repeatedly sacked and rebuilt (and sacked and rebuilt) over the centuries; in 1692 it was blown up to prevent the Jacobites from using it. The five-storey tower house at the northern point is the most impressive remaining fragment and offers wonderful views across the water.

Loch Ness Centre & Exhibition MUSEUM
(☎01456-450573; www.lochness.com; adult/child £7.95/4.95; ⊙9.30am-6pm Jul & Aug, to 5pm Easter-Jun, Sep & Oct, 10am-3.30pm Nov-Easter; P) This Nessie-themed attraction adopts a scientific approach that allows you to weigh the evidence for yourself. Exhibits include the original equipment – sonar survey vessels, miniature submarines, cameras and sediment coring tools – used in various monster hunts, as well as original photographs and film footage of sightings. You'll find out about hoaxes and optical illusions, as well as learning a lot about the ecology of Loch Ness – is there enough food in the loch to support even one 'monster', let alone a breeding population?

Nessie Hunter BOATING
(☎01456-450395; www.lochness-cruises.com; adult/child £15/10; ⊙Easter-Oct) One-hour monster-hunting cruises, complete with sonar and underwater cameras. Cruises depart from Drumnadrochit hourly (except 1pm) from 9am to 6pm daily.

Sleeping & Eating

BCC Loch Ness Hostel HOSTEL $
(☎07780-603045; www.bcclochnesshostel.co.uk; Glen Urquhart; tr/q £75/90, tent site per person £5, 2-person pod £70; P) Clean, modern, high-quality budget accommodation located halfway between Cannich and Loch Ness; advance booking recommended. There's also a good campsite with the option of luxury glamping pods.

Loch Ness Inn INN $$
(☎01456-450991; www.staylochness.co.uk; Lewiston; s/d/f £89/112/145; P) The Loch Ness Inn ticks all the weary traveller's boxes, with comfortable bedrooms (the family suite sleeps two adults and two children), a cosy bar pouring real ales from the Cairngorm and Isle of Skye breweries, and a rustic restaurant (mains £10 to £20) serving hearty, wholesome fare.

It's conveniently located in the quiet hamlet of Lewiston, between Drumnadrochit and Urquhart Castle.

Benleva Hotel MICROBREWERY
(☎01456-450080; www.benleva.co.uk; Kilmore Rd; ⊙noon-midnight Mon-Thu, to 1am Fri, to 12.45am

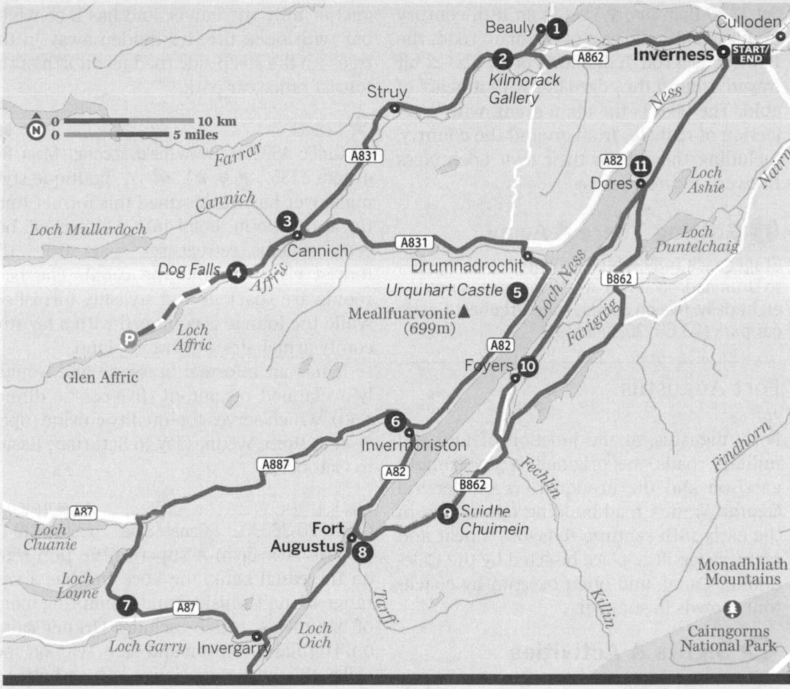

Driving Tour
A Loch Ness Circuit

START INVERNESS
END INVERNESS
LENGTH 130 MILES; SIX TO SEVEN HOURS

Head out of Inverness on the A862 to ❶ **Beauly**, arriving in time for breakfast at Corner on the Square. Backtrack a mile and turn right on the A831 to Cannich, passing ❷ **Kilmorack Gallery**, which exhibits contemporary art in a converted church. The scenery gets wilder as you approach ❸ **Cannich**; turn right and follow the single-track road to the car park at ❹ **Dog Falls**. Take a stroll along the rushing river, or hike to the viewpoint (about one-hour round trip; 2.5 miles) for a glimpse of remote Glen Affric.

Return to Cannich and turn right on the A831 to Drumnadrochit, then right on the A82 past picturesque ❺ **Urquhart Castle** (opposite) and along the shores of Loch Ness. At ❻ **Invermoriston**, pause to look at the old bridge, built by Telford in 1813, then head west on the A887 towards Kyle of Lochalsh; after 16 miles go left on the A87 towards Invergarry. You are now among some of the finest mountain scenery in the Highlands; as the road turns east above Loch Garry, stop at the famous ❼ **viewpoint** (layby on right, signposted Glengarry Viewpoint). Through a quirk of perspective, the lochs to the west appear to form the map outline of Scotland.

At Invergarry, turn left on the A82 to reach ❽ **Fort Augustus** and a late lunch at the Lovat (p898) or Lock Inn (p898). Take the B862 out of town, following the line of General Wade's 18th-century military road, to another viewpoint at ❾ **Suidhe Chuimein**. A short (800m) walk up the well-worn path to the summit affords an even better panorama.

Ahead, you can choose the low road via the impressive ❿ **Falls of Foyers**, or stay on the the high road (B862) for more views; both converge on Loch Ness at ⓫ **Dores**, at the Dores Inn, where you can sip a pint with a view along Loch Ness, and even stay for dinner before returning to Inverness.

Sat, 12.30-11pm Sun;) Set in an 18th-century manse a half-mile east of the main road, the Benleva is a rough diamond of a pub – a bit frayed around the edges but with a heart of gold. The beer is the main event, with a selection of real ales from around the country, including those from their own Loch Ness Brewery, located nearby.

Getting There & Away

Stagecoach (p893) buses run from Inverness to Drumnadrochit (£3.30, 30 minutes, six to eight daily, five on Sunday) and Urquhart Castle car park (£3.60, 35 minutes).

Fort Augustus

POP 620

Fort Augustus, at the junction of four old military roads, was originally a government garrison and the headquarters of General George Wade's road-building operations in the early 18th century. Today it's a neat and picturesque little place bisected by the Caledonian Canal, and often overrun by coach-tour crowds in summer.

Sights & Activities

Caledonian Canal CANAL

(www.scottishcanals.co.uk) At Fort Augustus, boats using the Caledonian Canal are raised and lowered 13m by a 'ladder' of five consecutive locks. It's fun to watch, and the neatly landscaped canal banks are a great place to soak up the sun or compare accents with fellow tourists. The **Caledonian Canal Centre** (01320-366493; Ardchattan House, Canalside; 10am-4pm) FREE, beside the lowest lock, has information on the history of the canal.

Cruise Loch Ness BOATING

(01320-366277; www.cruiselochness.com; adult/child £14/8; hourly 10am-4pm Apr-Oct, 1 & 2pm only Nov-Mar) One-hour cruises on Loch Ness are accompanied by the latest high-tech sonar equipment so you can keep an underwater eye open for Nessie. There are also one-hour evening cruises, departing 8pm daily (except Friday) April to August, and 90-minute speedboat tours.

Sleeping & Eating

Morag's Lodge HOSTEL $

(01320-366289; www.moragslodge.com; Bunoich Brae; dm/tw/f from £23/54/76;) This large, well-run hostel is based in a big Victorian house with great views of Fort Augustus' hilly surrounds, and has a convivial bar with open fire. It's hidden away in the trees up the steep side road just north of the tourist office car park.

★ **Lovat** HOTEL $$$

(01456-459250; www.thelovat.com; Main Rd; d from £135;) A boutique-style makeover has transformed this former huntin'-and-shootin' hotel into a luxurious but eco-conscious retreat set apart from the tourist crush around the canal. The bedrooms are spacious and stylishly furnished, while the lounge is equipped with a log fire, comfy armchairs and grand piano.

It has an informal brasserie and a highly acclaimed restaurant (five-course dinner £50), which serves top-quality cuisine (open 7pm to 9pm, Wednesday to Saturday, Easter to October).

Lock Inn PUB FOOD $$

(01320-366302; Canal Side; mains £10-14; meals noon-8pm) A superb little pub right on the canal bank, the Lock Inn has a vast range of malt whiskies and a tempting menu of bar meals, which includes Orkney salmon, Highland venison and daily seafood specials; the house speciality is beer-battered haddock and chips.

Information

There's an ATM and bureau de change in the post office beside the canal.

Fort Augustus Tourist Office (01320-345156; Main Car Park; 9.30am-5pm Mon-Sat & 10am-4pm Sun Apr-Sep, shorter hours Oct-Mar)

Getting There & Away

Scottish Citylink (www.citylink.co.uk) and **Stagecoach** (www.stagecoachbus.com) buses from Inverness to Fort William stop at Fort Augustus (£7 to £10.60, one hour, five to eight daily Monday to Saturday, five on Sunday).

THE CAIRNGORMS

The Cairngorms National Park (www.cairngorms.co.uk) is the largest national park in the UK, more than twice the size of the Lake District. It stretches from Aviemore in the north to the Angus Glens in the south, and from Dalwhinnie in the west to Ballater and Royal Deeside in the east.

The park encompasses the highest landmass in Britain – a broad mountain plateau,

The Cairngorms

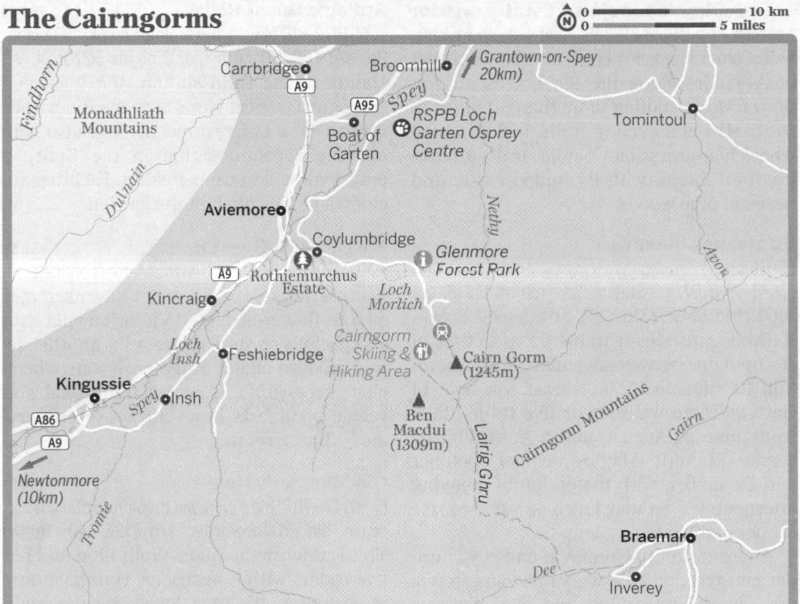

riven only by the deep valleys of the Lairig Ghru and Loch Avon, with an average altitude of over 1000m and including five of the six highest summits in the UK. This wild mountain landscape of granite and heather has a sub-Arctic climate and supports rare alpine tundra vegetation and high-altitude bird species, such as snow bunting, ptarmigan and dotterel.

The harsh mountain environment gives way lower down to scenic glens softened by beautiful open forests of native Scots pine, home to rare animals and birds such as pine martens, wildcats, red squirrels, ospreys, capercaillies and crossbills.

This is prime hill-walking territory, but even couch potatoes can enjoy a taste of the high life by taking the Cairngorm Mountain Railway up to the edge of the Cairngorm plateau.

Aviemore

POP 3150

The gateway to the Cairngorms, Aviemore is the region's main centre for transport, accommodation, restaurants and shops. It's not the prettiest town in Scotland by a long stretch – the main attractions are in the surrounding area – but when bad weather puts the hills off-limits, Aviemore fills up with hikers, cyclists and climbers (plus skiers and snowboarders in winter) cruising the outdoor-equipment shops or recounting their latest adventures in the cafes and bars. Add in tourists and locals and the eclectic mix makes for a lively little town.

Aviemore is on a loop off the A9 Perth–Inverness road; almost everything of note is to be found along the main drag, Grampian Rd; the train station and bus stop are towards its southern end.

The Cairngorm Mountain funicular railway and ski area lie 10 miles southeast of Aviemore along the B970 (Ski Rd) and its continuation, past Coylumbridge and Glenmore.

Sights

★Rothiemurchus Estate FOREST

(www.rothiemurchus.net) The Rothiemurchus Estate, which extends from the River Spey at Aviemore to the Cairngorm summit plateau, is famous for having one of Scotland's largest remnants of **Caledonian forest**, the ancient forest of Scots pine that once covered most of the country. The forest is home to a large population of red squirrels, and is one of the last bastions of the capercaillie and the Scottish wildcat.

The **Rothiemurchus Estate visitor centre** (☎01479-812345; Ski Rd, Inverdruie; ⊙9.30am-5.30pm; P) FREE, a mile southeast of Aviemore along the B970, sells an *Explorer Map* detailing more than 50 miles of **footpaths** and **cycling trails**, including the wheelchair-accessible 4-mile trail around **Loch an Eilein**, with its ruined castle and peaceful pine woods.

Strathspey Steam Railway HERITAGE RAILWAY
(☎01479-810725; Station Sq; return ticket per adult/child £14.25/7.15; P) Strathspey Steam Railway runs steam trains on a section of restored line between Aviemore and Broomhill, 10 miles to the northeast, via Boat of Garten. There are four or five trains daily from June to August, and a more limited service in April, May, September, October and December, with the option of enjoying afternoon tea, Sunday lunch or a five-course dinner on board.

An extension to Grantown-on-Spey is under construction (see www.railstograntown.org); in the meantime, you can continue from Broomhill to Grantown-on-Spey by bus.

Sleeping

Aviemore SYHA HOSTEL $
(SYHA; ☎01479-810345; www.syha.org.uk; 25 Grampian Rd; dm £21; P@) Upmarket hostelling in a spacious, well-equipped modern building, five minutes' walk south of the village centre. There are four- and six-bed rooms, and a comfortable lounge with views of the mountains.

Rothiemurchus Camp & Caravan Park CAMPGROUND $
(☎01479-812800; www.rothiemurchus.net; Coylumbridge; sites per adult/child £11/3) The nearest campsite to Aviemore is this year-round park, beautifully sited among Scots pines at Coylumbridge, 1.5 miles along the B970.

Aviemore Bunkhouse HOSTEL $
(☎01479-811181; www.aviemore-bunkhouse.com; Dalfaber Rd; dm/d/f from £19/50/65; P@) This independent hostel provides accommodation in bright, modern six- or eight-bed dorms, each with private bathroom, and one twin/family room. It has a drying room, secure bike storage and wheelchair-accessible dorms. From the train station, cross the pedestrian bridge over the tracks, turn right and walk south on Dalfaber Rd.

Ardlogie Guest House B&B $$
(☎01479-810747; www.ardlogie.co.uk; Dalfaber Rd; s/d £60/80, bothy per 3 nights £270; P) Handy to the train station, the five-room Ardlogie has great views over the River Spey towards the Cairngorms. There's also self-catering accommodation in the Bothy, a cosy, two-person timber cabin. Facilities include a boules pitch in the garden.

Ravenscraig Guest House B&B $$
(☎01479-810278; www.aviemoreonline.com; Grampian Rd; s/d £55/88; P) Ravenscraig is a large, flower-bedecked Victorian villa with six spacious en suite rooms, plus another six in a modern chalet at the back (one wheelchair accessible). It serves traditional and veggie breakfasts in an attractive conservatory dining room.

Old Minister's House B&B $$$
(☎01479-812181; www.theoldministershouse.co.uk; Ski Rd, Inverdruie; s/d £125/140; P) This former manse dates from 1906 and has five rooms with a luxurious, country-house atmosphere. It's in a lovely setting amid Scots pines on the banks of the River Druie, southeast of Aviemore.

Eating & Drinking

★**Mountain Cafe** CAFE $
(www.mountaincafe-aviemore.co.uk; 111 Grampian Rd; mains £7-12; ⊙8.30am-5pm Tue-Thu, to 5.30pm Fri-Mon; P) The Mountain Cafe offers freshly prepared local produce with a Kiwi twist (the owner is from New Zealand) – healthy breakfasts of muesli, porridge and fresh fruit (till 11.30am); hearty lunches of seafood chowder, burgers and imaginative salads; and home-baked breads, cakes and biscuits. Vegan, coeliac and nut-allergic diets catered for.

Roo's Leap AMERICAN $$
(☎01479-811161; www.roosleap.com; Station Sq; mains £7-14, steaks £20-30; ⊙noon-2.30pm & 5-9pm Mon-Fri, noon-9pm Sat & Sun;) Friendly service, cold bottled beer and great barbecue contribute to the antipodean atmosphere at this lively restaurant set in the old railway station building. However, the menu is more like classic American and Tex Mex – sizzling steaks, juicy burgers, buffalo wings and nachos.

Information

There are ATMs outside the Tesco supermarket, and currency exchange at the post office and the tourist office, all located on Grampian Rd.

Aviemore Tourist Office (☎ 01479-810930; www.visitaviemore.com; The Mall, Grampian Rd; ⏲ 9am-5pm Mon-Sat, 10am-4pm Sun year-round, longer hours Jul & Aug)

Getting There & Away

BUS

Buses stop on Grampian Rd opposite the train station; buy tickets at the tourist office. Services include the following:

Edinburgh £27, four hours, five daily

Glasgow £27, 2¾ hours, five daily

Grantown-on-Spey £3.60, 35 minutes, five daily weekdays, two Saturday

Inverness £10.20, 45 minutes, eight daily

Perth £19.80, 2¼ hours, five daily

TRAIN

The train station is on Grampian Rd.

Edinburgh £40, three hours, six daily

Glasgow £40, three hours, six daily

Inverness £12.10, 40 minutes, 12 daily

Getting Around

BICYCLE

Several places in Aviemore, Rothiemurchus Estate and Glenmore have mountain bikes for hire. An off-road cycle track links Aviemore with Glenmore and Loch Morlich.

Bothy Bikes (☎ 01479-810111; www.bothybikes.co.uk; 5 Granish Way, Dalfaber; per half-/full day from £16/20; ⏲ 9am-5.30pm) Charges £20 a day for a quality bike with front suspension and disc brakes.

BUS

Bus 31 links Aviemore to Cairngorm Mountain car park (£2.55, 30 minutes, hourly) via Coylumbridge and Glenmore. A Strathspey Dayrider/Megarider ticket (£6.70/17) gives one/seven days unlimited bus travel from Aviemore as far as Cairngorm, Carrbridge and Kingussie; buy them from the bus driver.

Around Aviemore

Cairngorm Mountain

Cairngorm Mountain Railway FUNICULAR
(☎ 01479-861261; www.cairngormmountain.org; adult/child return £11.50/7.50; ⏲ every 20min 10am-4pm May-Nov, 9am-4.30pm Dec-Apr; P) The national park's most popular attraction is this funicular railway that will whisk you to the edge of the Cairngorm plateau (altitude 1085m) in just eight minutes. The bottom station is at the Coire Cas car park at the end of Ski Rd; at the top is an exhibition, a shop (of course) and a restaurant. Unfortunately, for environmental and safety reasons, you're not allowed out of the top station in summer unless you book a guided walk or mountain-bike descent.

Cairngorm Mountain Ski Area SNOW SPORTS
(www.cairngormmountain.org; 1-day ski pass per adult/child £35/21) Aspen or Val d'Isère it ain't, but with 19 runs and 23 miles of piste Cairngorm is Scotland's biggest ski area. When the snow is at its best and the sun is shining you can close your eyes and imagine you're in the Alps; sadly, low cloud, high winds and horizontal sleet are more likely. Ski or snowboard hire is around £25/19 per adult/child per day; there are lots of hire outlets at Coire Cas, Glenmore and Aviemore.

Loch Morlich

Six miles east of Aviemore, Loch Morlich is surrounded by some 8 sq miles of pine and spruce forest that make up the Glenmore Forest Park. Its attractions include a sandy beach (at the east end) and a water-sports centre.

Bus 31 links Aviemore with Loch Morlich and Glenmore (£2.55, 20 minutes, hourly).

The visitor centre at Glenmore has a small exhibition on the Caledonian forest and sells the *Glenmore Forest Park Map,* detailing local walks. The **circuit of Loch Morlich** (one hour) makes a pleasant outing; the trail is pram- and wheelchair-friendly.

★ **Glenmore Lodge** ADVENTURE SPORTS
(☎ 01479-861256; www.glenmorelodge.org.uk; Glenmore; one-day courses from £75) One of Britain's leading adventure-sports training centres, offering courses in hill walking, rock climbing, ice climbing, canoeing, mountain biking and mountaineering. The centre's comfortable **B&B accommodation** (s/tw £60/80; P ☎) is available to all, even if you're not taking a course, as is the indoor climbing wall, gym and sauna.

Cairngorm Reindeer Centre TOURS
(www.cairngormreindeer.co.uk; Glenmore; adult/child £14/8; ⏲ closed early Jan–mid-Feb; 👪) The warden here will take you on a guided walk to see and feed Britain's only herd of

reindeer, who are very tame and will even eat out of your hand. Walks take place at 11am daily year-round (weather-dependent), plus another at 2.30pm from May to September, and a third at 3.30pm Monday to Friday in July and August.

Cairngorm Lodge SYHA HOSTEL $
(☎01479-861238; www.syha.org.uk; Glenmore; dm/tw £17/45; ⊙closed Nov & Dec; P@) Set in a former shooting lodge that enjoys a great location at the east end of Loch Morlich; prebooking is essential.

Glenmore Campsite CAMPGROUND $
(☎01479-861271; www.campingintheforest.co.uk; tent & campervan sites £27; ⊙year-round) Campers can set up base at this attractive lochside site with pitches amid the Scots pines; rates include up to four people per tent/campervan.

Boat of Garten

Boat of Garten is known as the Osprey Village because these rare and beautiful birds of prey nest nearby at the **RSPB Loch Garten Osprey Centre** (☎01479-831694; www.rspb.org.uk/lochgarten; Tulloch; osprey hide adult/child £5/2; ⊙osprey hide 10am-6pm Apr-Aug). The ospreys migrate here each spring from Africa and nest in a tall pine tree.

Boat of Garten is 6 miles northeast of Aviemore. The most interesting way to get here is on the Strathspey Steam Railway (p900) from Aviemore.

Kingussie & Newtonmore

The old Speyside towns of Kingussie (kin-*yew*-see) and Newtonmore sit at the foot of the great heather-clad humps known as the Monadhliath Mountains. Newtonmore is best known as the home of the excellent Highland Folk Museum; Kingussie for one of the Highlands' best restaurants.

The road west from Newtonmore to Spean Bridge passes Ardverikie Estate and Loch Laggan, famous as the setting for the BBC TV series *Monarch of the Glen*.

Sights & Activities

Highland Folk Museum MUSEUM
(☎01540-673551; www.highlandfolk.museum; Kingussie Rd, Newtonmore; ⊙10.30am-5.30pm Apr-Aug, 11am-4.30pm Sep & Oct; P) FREE This open-air museum comprises a collection of historical buildings and artefacts revealing many aspects of Highland culture and lifestyle. Laid out like a farming township, it has a community of traditional thatch-roofed cottages, a sawmill, a schoolhouse, a shepherd's bothy (hut) and a rural post office. Actors in period costume give demonstrations of woodcarving, wool-spinning and peat-fire baking. You'll need at least two to three hours to make the most of a visit here.

Laggan Wolftrax MOUNTAIN BIKING
(http://scotland.forestry.gov.uk/visit/laggan-wolftrax; Strathmashie Forest; trails free, parking £3; ⊙10am-6pm Mon, 9.30am-5pm Tue, Thu & Fri, 9.30am-6pm Sat & Sun) Ten miles southwest of Newtonmore, on the A86 road towards Spean Bridge, this is one of Scotland's top mountain-biking centres with purpose-built trails ranging from open-country riding to black-diamond downhills with rock slabs and drop-offs. Includes bike hire outlet and a good cafe (open 11am to 4pm Friday to Sunday).

Sleeping & Eating

★**Eagleview Guest House** B&B $$
(☎01540-673675; Perth Rd, Newtonmore; r per person from £39; P) Welcoming Eagleview is one of the best places to stay in the area, with beautifully decorated bedrooms, super-king-size beds, spacious bathrooms with power showers (except room 4, which has a Victorian slipper bath!), and nice little touches such as cafetières (coffee plungers) with real coffee – and fresh milk – on your hospitality tray, and Scottish kippers on the breakfast menu.

Hermitage B&B $$
(☎01540-662137; www.thehermitage-scotland.com; Spey St, Kingussie; s/d from £72/82; P) The five-bedroom Hermitage is a lovely old house with plenty of character, filled with Victorian period features – ask for room 5 (Feshie), with double bed, Chesterfield sofa, and a view of the hills. The lounge has deep sofas ranged by a log fire, and there are good views of the Cairngorms from the breakfast room and garden.

★**Cross** SCOTTISH $$$
(☎01540-661166; www.thecross.co.uk; Tweed Mill Brae, off Ardbroilach Rd, Kingussie; 3-course lunch/dinner £25/55; ⊙noon-2pm & 7-8.30pm; P) Housed in a converted watermill, the Cross is one of the finest restaurants in the Highlands. The intimate, low-raftered

dining room has an open fire and a patio overlooking the stream, and serves a daily-changing menu of fresh Scottish produce accompanied by a superb wine list (booking essential).

If you want to stay the night, there are eight stylish rooms (double or twin £110 to £180) to choose from.

Getting There & Away

BUS

Kingussie and Newtonmore are served by **Scottish Citylink** (☎0871-266 3333; www.citylink.co.uk) buses:

Aviemore £7.90, 25 minutes, twice daily
Inverness £13.80, one hour, twice daily
Perth £16.50, 1¾ hours, twice daily

TRAIN

Kingussie and Newtonmore are on the Edinburgh/Glasgow to Inverness railway line.

Edinburgh £36, 2½ hours, seven a day Monday to Saturday, two Sunday
Inverness £12.10, one hour, eight a day Monday to Saturday, four Sunday

Royal Deeside

The upper valley of the River Dee stretches west from Aboyne and Ballater to Braemar, closely paralleled by the A93 road. Made famous by its long association with the monarchy – today's royal family still holiday at Balmoral Castle, built for Queen Victoria in 1855 – the region is often called Royal Deeside.

The River Dee, renowned world-over for its salmon fishing, has its source in the Cairngorm Mountains west of Braemar, the starting point for long walks into the hills. The FishDee website (www.fishdee.co.uk) has all you need to know about fishing on the river.

Ballater

POP 1530

The attractive little village of Ballater owes its 18th-century origins to the curative waters of nearby Pannanich Springs (now bottled commercially as Deeside Natural Mineral Water), and its prosperity to nearby Balmoral Castle.

The village recently received a double dose of misfortune when the Old Royal Station (its main tourist attraction) burned down in May 2015, followed by the worst flooding in living memory in January 2016. The station may remain closed until 2018.

As you approach Ballater from the east the hills start to close in, and there are many pleasant walks in the surrounding area. The steep woodland walk up **Craigendarroch** (400m) takes just over one hour. **Morven** (871m) is a more serious prospect, taking about six hours, but offers good views from the top; ask at the tourist office for more info.

You can hire bikes from **CycleHighlands** (☎01339-755864; www.cyclehighlands.com; The Pavilion, Victoria Rd; bicycle hire per half-day/day £12/18; ⏲9am-6pm) and **Bike Station** (☎01339-754004; www.bikestationballater.co.uk; Station Sq; bicycle hire per 3hr/day £12/18; ⏲9am-6pm), which also offer guided bike rides and advice on local trails.

Balmoral Castle

Balmoral Castle CASTLE
(☎01339-742534; www.balmoralcastle.com; Crathie; adult/child £11.50/5; ⏲10am-5pm Apr-Jul, last admission 4.30pm; P) Built for Queen Victoria in 1855 as a private residence for the royal family, Balmoral kicked off the revival of the Scottish Baronial style of architecture that characterises so many of Scotland's 19th-century country houses. The admission fee includes an interesting and well thought-out audioguide, but the tour is very much an outdoor one through garden and grounds.

Braemar

POP 450

Braemar is a pretty little village with a grand location on a broad plain ringed by mountains where the Dee valley and Glen Clunie meet. In winter this is one of the coldest places in the country – temperatures as low as -29°C have been recorded – and during spells of severe cold, hungry deer wander the streets looking for a bite to eat. Braemar is an excellent base for hill walking, and there's also skiing at nearby Glenshee.

The **tourist office** (☎01399-741600; The Mews, Mar Rd; ⏲9am-6pm Aug, 9am-5pm Jun, Jul, Sep & Oct, shorter hours Nov-May), opposite the Fife Arms Hotel, has lots of useful info on walks in the area.

Sights & Activities

Braemar Castle CASTLE
(www.braemarcastle.co.uk; adult/child £8/4; 10am-4pm daily Jul & Aug, Wed-Sun Apr-Jun, Sep & Oct; P) Just north of Braemar village, turreted Braemar Castle dates from 1628 and served as a government garrison after the 1745 Jacobite rebellion. It was taken over by the local community in 2007, which now offers guided tours of the historic castle apartments. There's a short walk from the car park to the castle.

Braemar Mountain Sports CYCLING
(01339-741242; www.braemarmountainsports.com; 5 Invercauld Rd; bike hire per day £18; 9am-6pm) You can hire bikes from Braemar Mountain Sports. They also rent skiing and mountaineering equipment.

Braemar Gathering HIGHLAND GAMES
(01339-755377; www.braemargathering.org; adult/child from £12/2) There are Highland games in many towns and villages throughout the summer, but the best known is the Braemar Gathering which takes place on the first Saturday in September. It's a major occasion, organised every year since 1817 by the Braemar Royal Highland Society

Sleeping & Eating

Rucksacks Bunkhouse HOSTEL $
(01339-741517; 15 Mar Rd; bothy £7, dm £12-15, tw £36; P) This appealing cottage has a comfy dorm, and cheaper beds in an alpine-style bothy (shared sleeping platform for 10 people; bring your own sleeping bag). Extras include a drying room (for wet-weather gear), a laundry and even a sauna (£10 an hour). The friendly owner is a fount of knowledge about the local area.

Braemar SYHA HOSTEL $
(01339-741659; www.syha.org.uk; 21 Glenshee Rd; dm/tw £21/48; Feb-Oct; P @) This hostel is housed in a grand former shooting lodge just south of Braemar village centre on the A93 to Perth. It has a comfy lounge with pool table, and a barbecue in the garden.

Craiglea B&B $$
(01339-741641; www.craigleabraemar.com; Hillside Dr; d/f from £76/105; P) Craiglea is a homely B&B set in a pretty stone cottage with three en suite bedrooms. Vegetarian breakfasts are available and the owners can rent you a bike and give advice on local walks.

Braemar Lodge Hotel HOTEL, BUNKHOUSE $$
(01339-741627; www.braemarlodge.co.uk; Glenshee Rd; dm/s/d from £15/80/120; P) This Victorian shooting lodge on the southern outskirts of Braemar has bags of character, not least in the wood-panelled Malt Room bar, which is as well stocked with mounted deer heads as it is with single malt whiskies. There's a good restaurant with views of the hills, plus a 12-berth hikers' bunkhouse (book in advance) in the hotel grounds.

Taste CAFE $
(01339-741425; www.taste-braemar.co.uk; Airlie House, Mar Rd; mains £4-8; 10am-5pm Tue-Sat;) Taste is a relaxed little cafe with armchairs in the window bays, serving homemade soups, sandwiches, coffee and cakes.

Getting There & Away

Bus 201 runs from Aberdeen to Braemar (£11.50, 2¼ hours, every two hours Monday to Saturday, five on Sunday). The 50-mile drive from Perth to Braemar is beautiful, but there's no public transport on this route.

HIGHLAND PERTHSHIRE

The Highland border cuts diagonally across Scotland from Dumbarton to Stonehaven, dividing the county of Perthshire into two distinctive regions. Highland Perthshire, spreading north of a line from Comrie to Blairgowrie, is a land of mountains, forest and lochs, with some of the finest scenery in the UK. The ancient city of Dunkeld, on the main A9 road from Perth to Inverness, is the main gateway to the region.

DUNKELD WALKS: THE HERMITAGE

One of the most popular walks is The Hermitage, just outside Dunkeld, where a well-marked trail follows the River Braan to Ossian's Hall, a quaint folly built by the Duke of Atholl in 1758 overlooking the spectacular Falls of Braan (salmon can be seen leaping here, especially in September and October).

Dunkeld & Birnam

POP 1005

The Tay runs like a storybook river through the heart of Perthshire's Big Tree Country, where the twin towns of Dunkeld and Birnam are linked by Thomas Telford's graceful bridge of 1808. As well as Dunkeld's ancient cathedral, there's much walking to be done in this area of magnificent forested hills. These same walks were one of the inspirations for Beatrix Potter to create her children's tales.

There's less to see in Birnam, a name made famous by Macbeth. There's not much left of Birnam Wood, but a riverside path leads to the Birnam Oak, a venerable 500-year-old survivor from Shakespeare's time, its ageing boughs propped up with timber supports. Nearby is the 300-year-old Birnam Sycamore.

Sights & Activities

Dunkeld Cathedral CHURCH

(HS; www.dunkeldcathedral.org.uk; High St; ⏲10am-6.30pm Apr-Sep, to 4pm Oct-Mar) FREE Situated on the grassy banks of the River Tay, Dunkeld Cathedral is one of the most beautifully sited churches in Scotland; don't miss it on a sunny day, when there are few lovelier places to be. Half the cathedral is still in use as a church; the rest is a romantic ruin. It partly dates from the 14th century, having suffered damage during the Reformation and the battle of Dunkeld (Jacobites vs government) in 1689.

Loch of the Lowes Wildlife Centre WILDLIFE RESERVE

(☎01350-727337; www.swt.org.uk; adult/child £4/50p; ⏲10am-5pm Mar-Oct, 10.30am-4pm Fri-Sun Nov-Feb; P) Loch of the Lowes, 2 miles east of Dunkeld off the A923, has a visitor centre devoted to red squirrels and the majestic osprey. There's a birdwatching hide (with binoculars provided), where you can see the birds nesting during breeding season (late April to August), complete with a live video link to the nest.

Sleeping & Eating

★**Jessie Mac's** HOSTEL, B&B $

(☎01350-727324; www.jessiemacs.co.uk; Murthly Tce, Birnam; dm/d £18/70;) Set in a Victorian manse complete with baronial turret, Jessie Mac's is a glorious cross between B&B and luxury hostel, with three gorgeous doubles and four shared or family rooms with bunks. Guests make good use of the country-style lounge, sunny dining room and well-equipped kitchen, and breakfasts are composed of local produce, from organic eggs to Dunkeld smoked salmon.

★**Taybank** PUB FOOD $$

(☎01350-727340; www.thetaybank.co.uk; Tay Tce; mains £9-12; ⏲food served noon-9pm; P) Top choice for a sun-kissed pub lunch by the river is the Taybank, a regular meeting place and performance space for folk musicians and a wonderfully welcoming bar serving ales from the local Strathbraan Brewery. There's live music several nights per week, and the menu features local produce with dishes such as smoked venison or grilled sea trout.

Information

Dunkeld Tourist Office (☎01350-727688; www.dunkeldandbirnam.org.uk; The Cross; ⏲10.30am-4.30pm Mon-Sat, 11am-4pm Sun Apr-Oct, longer hours Jul & Aug, Fri-Sun only Nov-Mar) Has information on local hiking and biking trails.

Getting There & Away

Citylink (p893) buses running between Glasgow/Edinburgh and Inverness stop at the Birnam Hotel (£17, two hours, two daily). **Stagecoach** (www.stagecoachbus.com) runs hourly buses (only five on Sunday) between Perth and Dunkeld (£2.50, 40 minutes), continuing to Aberfeldy.

There are also buses from Dunkeld to Blairgowrie (£2.60, 40 minutes, twice daily except Sunday).

Pitlochry

POP 2780

Pitlochry, with the scent of the Highlands already in the air, is a popular stop on the way north. In summer the main street can be a conga line of tour groups, but linger a while and it can still charm – on a quiet spring evening it's a pretty place with salmon leaping in the Tummel and good things brewing at the Moulin Hotel.

Sights

One of Pitlochry's attractions is its beautiful **riverside**; the River Tummel is dammed here, and if you're lucky you might see salmon swimming up the **fish ladder** to Loch Faskally above (May to November; best month is October).

★Edradour Distillery DISTILLERY
(☎01796-472095; www.edradour.co.uk; Moulin Rd; tour adult/child £7.50/2.50; ⊙10am-5pm Mon-Sat late Apr-late Oct; P) This is proudly Scotland's smallest and most picturesque distillery and one of the best to visit: you can see the whole process, easily explained, in one building. It's 2.5 miles east of Pitlochry by car, along the Moulin road, or a pleasant 1-mile walk.

Explorers Garden GARDENS
(☎01796-484600; www.explorersgarden.com; Foss Rd; adult/child £4/1; ⊙10am-5pm Apr-Oct; P) This gem of a garden is based around plants brought to Scotland by 18th- and 19th-century Scottish botanists and explorers such as David Douglas (after whom the Douglas fir is named), and celebrates 300 years of collecting and the 'plant hunters' who tracked down these exotic species.

Sleeping

Ashleigh B&B $
(☎01796-470316; www.ashleighbedandbreakfast.com; 120 Atholl Rd; s/d £30/57;) Genuine welcomes don't come much better than Nancy's, and her place on the main street makes a top Pitlochry pit stop. Two comfortable doubles share an excellent bathroom, and there's an open kitchen stocked with goodies where you make your own breakfast in the morning. A home away from home and a standout budget choice. Cash only; no kids.

She also has a good self-catering apartment with great views, available by the night.

Pitlochry Backpackers Hotel HOSTEL $
(☎01796-470044; www.scotlands-top-hostels.com; 134 Atholl Rd; dm/tw £20/53; ⊙Apr–mid-Nov; P@) Friendly, laid-back and very comfortable, this is a cracking hostel smack bang in the middle of town, with three- to eight-bed dorms that are in mint condition. There are also good-value en suite twins and doubles, with beds, not bunks. Cheap breakfast and a pool table add to the convivial party atmosphere. No extra charge for linen.

Pitlochry SYHA HOSTEL $
(☎01796-472308; www.syha.org.uk; Knockard Rd; dm/tw £18/48; ⊙Mar-Oct; P@) Great location overlooking the town centre. Popular with families and walkers.

★Craigatin House B&B $$
(☎01796-472478; www.craigatinhouse.co.uk; 165 Atholl Rd; d £98-108, ste £125; P@) Several times more tasteful than the average Scottish B&B, this elegant house and garden is set back from the main road. Chic contemporary fabrics covering expansive beds offer a standard of comfort above and beyond the reasonable price; the rooms in the converted stable block are particularly inviting. A fabulous breakfast and lounge area gives views over the lush garden.

★Fonab Castle Hotel HISTORIC HOTEL $$$
(☎01796-470140; www.fonabcastlehotel.com; Foss Rd; r from £195; P) This Scottish Baronial fantasy in red sandstone was built in 1892 as the country house of Lt Col George Sandeman, a scion of the famous port and sherry merchants. Opened as a luxury hotel and spa in 2013, it has a tasteful modern extension with commanding views over Loch Faskally, and a superb restaurant serving the finest Scottish venison, beef and seafood.

Eating & Drinking

★Moulin Hotel PUB FOOD $$
(☎01796-472196; www.moulinhotel.co.uk; Kirkmichael Rd; mains £9-16; P) A mile away from town but a world apart, this atmospheric inn has low ceilings, ageing wood and snug booths. It's a wonderfully romantic spot for a home-brewed ale (there's a microbrewery out back) and a portion of Highland comfort food: try the mince and tatties, or venison stew. It's a pleasant uphill stroll from Pitlochry, and an easy roll down afterwards.

Port-na-Craig Inn BAR, BISTRO $$
(☎01796-472777; www.portnacraig.com; Port-na-Craig; mains £13-22, 2-/3-course lunch £13/15; ⊙11am-8.30pm; P) Across the river from the town centre, this cute little cottage sits in what was once a separate hamlet. Top-quality main meals are prepared with confidence and panache; there are also simpler sandwiches, kids' meals and light lunches. Or you could just sit outdoors by the river with a pint and watch the anglers.

Entertainment

★Pitlochry Festival Theatre THEATRE
(☎01796-484626; www.pitlochryfestivaltheatre.com; Port-na-Craig; tickets £26-35) Founded in 1951 (in a tent!), this famous and much-loved theatre is the focus of Highland Perthshire's

cultural life. The summer season, from May to mid-October, stages a different play each night of the week except Sunday.

Information

Pitlochry Tourist Office (01796-472215; www.perthshire.co.uk; 22 Atholl Rd; 9.30am-5.30pm Mon-Sat, 10am-4pm Sun Mar-Oct, longer hours Jul & Aug, shorter hours Nov-Feb) Good information on local walks.

Getting There & Away

BUS

Citylink (www.citylink.co.uk) Buses run two to four times daily to Inverness (£17.20, 1¾ hours), Perth (£11.10, 50 minutes), Edinburgh (£17, two to 2½ hours) and Glasgow (£17, 2¼ hours).

Megabus (0871-266 3333; www.megabus.com) Offers discounted fares to Inverness, Perth, Edinburgh and Glasgow.

Stagecoach (www.stagecoachbus.com) Buses run to Aberfeldy (£3.50, 40 minutes, hourly Monday to Saturday, three Sunday), Dunkeld (£2.50, 40 minutes, hourly Monday to Saturday) and Perth (£3.70, 1¼ hours, hourly Monday to Saturday).

TRAIN

Pitlochry is on the main railway line from Perth (£13.60, 30 minutes, nine daily Monday to Saturday, five on Sunday) to Inverness (£22, 1½ hours, same frequency).

Blair Castle

★Blair Castle CASTLE
(01796-481207; www.blair-castle.co.uk; Family/adult/child £28.90/10.70/6.40; 9.30am-5.30pm Easter-Oct, 10am-4pm Sat & Sun Nov-Mar; P)
One of the most popular tourist attractions in Scotland, magnificent Blair Castle – and its surrounding estates – is the seat of the Duke of Atholl, head of the Murray clan. (The current duke visits the castle every May to review the **Atholl Highlanders**, Britain's only private army.) It's an impressive white heap set beneath forested slopes above the River Garry. Thirty rooms are open to the public and they present a wonderful picture of upper-class Highland life from the 16th century on.

The original tower was built in 1269, but the castle underwent significant remodelling in the 18th and 19th centuries. Highlights include the second-floor **Drawing Room** with its ornate Georgian plasterwork and Zoffany portrait of the 4th duke's family, complete with a pet lemur (yes, you read that correctly) called Tommy; and the **Tapestry Room** draped with 17th-century wall hangings created for Charles I. The **dining room** is sumptuous – check out the 9-pint wine glasses – and the **ballroom** is a vast oak-panelled chamber hung with hundreds of stag antlers.

Local buses run between Pitlochry and Blair Atholl (£2.25, 25 minutes, three to seven daily). Three buses a day (Monday to Saturday) go directly to the castle, which is nearly a mile from the village.

There are trains from Perth (£13.60, 40 minutes, nine daily Monday to Saturday, five on Sunday).

Lochs Tummel & Rannoch

The scenic route along Lochs Tummel and Rannoch (www.rannochandtummel.co.uk) is worth doing any way you can – by foot, bicycle or car. Hillsides shrouded with ancient birchwoods and forests of spruce, pine and larch make up the fabulous **Tay Forest Park**, whose wooded hills roll into the glittering waters of the lochs; a visit in autumn is recommended, when the birch leaves are at their finest.

The **Queen's View** at the eastern end of Loch Tummel is a magnificent viewpoint with a vista along the loch to the prominent mountain of Schiehallion. The nearby visitor centre provides parking and houses a cafe and gift shop.

Eighteen miles west of Kinloch Rannoch the road ends at romantic and isolated **Rannoch Station**, which lies on the Glasgow–Fort William railway line. Beyond sprawls the desolate expanse of Rannoch Moor. There's an excellent tearoom on the station platform, and a welcoming small hotel alongside.

Loch Tay

Loch Tay is the heart of the ancient region known as Breadalbane (from the Gaelic Bràghad Albainn, 'the heights of Scotland') – mighty **Ben Lawers** (1214m), looming over the loch, is the highest peak outside the Ben Nevis and Cairngorms regions. Much of the land to the north of Loch Tay falls within the **Ben Lawers National Nature Reserve** (www.nnr-scotland.org.uk/ben-lawers), known for its rare alpine flora.

SALMON FISHING ON THE TAY

The Tay is Scotland's longest river (117 miles) and the most powerful in Britain, discharging more water into the sea each year than the Thames and Severn combined. It is also Europe's most famous salmon river, attracting anglers from all over the world (the season runs from 15 January to 15 October). The British record rod-caught salmon, weighing in at 64lb (29kg), was hooked in the Tay near Dunkeld in 1922, by local girl Georgina Ballantine.

Salmon fishing has an air of exclusivity, and can be expensive, but anyone, even complete beginners, can have a go. There is lots of information on **FishTay** (www.fishtay.co.uk), but novices will do best to hire a guide – check out **Fishinguide** (www.fishinguide.co.uk).

Loch Tay is famous for its **fishing** – salmon, trout and pike are all caught here. **Fish'n'Trips** (☎07967 567347; www.lochtayfishntrips.co.uk) can kit you out for a day's fishing with boat, tackle and guide for £95 per person, or rent you a boat for £60 a day.

The picturesque village of Kenmore lies at Loch Tay's eastern end, 6 miles west of Aberfeldy. Dominated by a striking archway leading to Taymouth Castle (not open to the public), it was built by the 3rd Earl of Breadalbane in 1760 to house his estate workers.

★Scottish Crannog Centre MUSEUM
(☎01887-830583; www.crannog.co.uk; tours adult/child £8.75/6.50; ⏲10am-5.30pm Apr-Oct; P 🚸) Less than a mile south of Kenmore on the banks of Loch Tay is the fascinating Scottish Crannog Centre, perched on stilts above the loch. Crannogs – effectively artificial islands – were a favoured form of defensive dwelling from the 3rd millennium BC onwards. This superb re-creation (based on studies of Oakbank crannog, one of 18 discovered in Loch Tay) offers a guided tour that includes an impressive demonstration of fire making and Iron Age crafts.

WEST HIGHLANDS

This region extends from the bleak blanket-bog of the Moor of Rannoch to the west coast beyond Glen Coe and Fort William, and includes the southern reaches of the Great Glen. The scenery is grand throughout, with high, rocky mountains rising above wild glens. Great expanses of moor alternate with lochs and patches of commercial forest. Fort William, at the inner end of Loch Linnhe, is the only sizeable town in the area.

Since 2007 the region has been promoted as Lochaber Geopark (www.lochabergeopark.org.uk), an area of outstanding geology and scenery.

Glen Coe

Scotland's most famous glen is also one of its grandest and – in bad weather – its grimmest. The approach to the glen from the east is guarded by the rocky pyramid of **Buachaille Etive Mor** – the Great Shepherd of Etive – and the lonely **Kings House Hotel** (☎01855-851259; www.kingshousehotel.co.uk; Kingshouse; s/d £45/100; P), on the old military road from Stirling to Fort William (now followed by the West Highland Way). After the Battle of Culloden in 1745 it was used as a Hanoverian garrison – hence the name.

The modern road leads over the Pass of Glencoe and into the narrow upper glen. The southern side is dominated by three massive, brooding spurs, known as the **Three Sisters**, while the northern side is enclosed by the continuous steep wall of the knife-edged **Aonach Eagach** ridge, a classic mountaineering challenge. The road threads its way past deep gorges and crashing waterfalls to the more pastoral lower reaches of the glen around Loch Achtriochtan and the only settlement here, **Glencoe village**.

A few miles east of Glen Coe, on the south side of the A82, is **Glencoe Mountain Resort** (☎01855-851226; www.glencoemountain.com; Kingshouse; chairlift adult/child £10/5; ⏲9am-4.30pm), where commercial skiing in Scotland first began back in 1956. Two miles west of the ski centre, a minor road leads along peaceful and beautiful **Glen Etive**, which runs southwest for 12 miles to the head of Loch Etive. On a hot summer's day the River Etive contains many tempting pools for swimming in, and there are lots of good picnic sites.

Glen Coe was written into the history books in 1692 when the resident MacDonalds were murdered by Campbell soldiers in what became known as the Glencoe Massacre.

Steven Fallon Mountain Guides OUTDOORS
(☎0131-466 8152; www.stevenfallon.co.uk; per person from £50) If you lack the experience or confidence to tackle Glen Coe's challenging mountains alone, then you can join a guided hill walk or hire a private guide from this outfit.

Glencoe Village

The little village of Glencoe stands on the south shore of Loch Leven at the western end of the glen, 16 miles south of Fort William.

Sights & Activities

Glencoe Folk Museum MUSEUM
(☎01855-811664; www.glencoemuseum.com; adult/child £3/free; ⏲10am-4.30pm Mon-Sat Easter-Oct) This small, thatched cottage houses a varied collection of farm equipment, tools of the woodworking, blacksmithing and slate-quarrying trades, and military memorabilia, including a riding boot that once belonged to Robert Campbell of Glenlyon (who took part in the Massacre of Glencoe).

Glencoe Visitor Centre MUSEUM
(NTS; ☎01855-811307; www.glencoe-nts.org.uk; adult/child £6.50/5; ⏲9.30am-5.30pm Easter-Oct, 10am-4pm Thu-Sun Nov-Easter; P) The centre provides comprehensive information on the geological, environmental and cultural history of Glen Coe via high-tech interactive and audiovisual displays, charts the history of mountaineering in the glen, and tells the story of the Glencoe Massacre in all its gory detail. It's 1.5 miles east of Glencoe village.

Sleeping & Eating

Glencoe Independent Hostel HOSTEL $
(☎01855-811906; www.glencoehostel.co.uk; dm/bunkhouse £17/15; P @) This handily located hostel, just 1.5 miles southeast of Glencoe village, is set in an old farmhouse with six- and eight-bed dorms, and a bunkhouse with another 16 bed spaces in communal, alpine-style bunks. There's also a cute little wooden cabin that sleeps up to three (£80 per night).

Clachaig Inn HOTEL $$
(☎01855-811252; www.clachaig.com; s/d £53/106; P) The Clachaig, 2 miles east of Glencoe village, has long been a favourite haunt of hill walkers and climbers. As well as comfortable en suite accommodation, there's a smart, modern lounge bar with snug booths and high refectory tables, mountaineering

WORTH A TRIP

GLEN LYON

The 'longest, loneliest and loveliest glen in Scotland', according to Sir Walter Scott, stretches for 32 unforgettable miles of rickety stone bridges, native woodland and heather-clad hills, becoming wilder and more uninhabited as it snakes its way west. The ancients believed it to be a gateway to Faerieland, and even the most sceptical of visitors will be entranced by the valley's magic.

From Fortingall, a narrow road winds up the glen, while another steep and spectacular route from Loch Tay crosses the hills to meet it at Bridge of Balgie. The road continues west as far as the dam on Loch Lyon, passing a memorial to Robert Campbell (1808–94; a Canadian explorer and fur trader, who was born in the glen).

There are no villages in the glen – the majestic scenery is the main reason to be here – just a cluster of houses at Bridge of Balgie and the **Bridge of Balgie Tearoom** (☎01887-866221; Bridge of Balgie; snacks £3-5; ⏲10am-5pm Apr-Oct; P).

Milton Eonan (☎01887-866337; www.miltoneonan.com; Bridge of Balgie; per person £39-43; P) is a must for those seeking tranquillity. On a bubbling stream where a watermill once stood, it's a working rare-breed croft with a romantic one-bedroom cottage at the bottom of the garden (available as B&B or self-catering). It can sleep three at a pinch.

The helpful owners offer packed lunches and evening meals using local and homegrown produce. After crossing the bridge at Bridge of Balgie, you'll see Milton Eonan signposted to the right.

photos and bric-a-brac, and climbing magazines to leaf through.

Climbers usually head for the lively **Boots Bar** on the other side of the hotel – it has log fires, serves real ale and good pub grub (mains £9 to £18, served noon to 9pm), and has live Scottish music on Saturday nights.

★Glencoe Café CAFE $
(☎01855-811168; www.glencoecafe.co.uk; Glencoe village; mains £4-8; ⏲10am-4pm daily, to 5pm May-Sep, closed Nov; P 📶) This friendly cafe is the social hub of Glencoe village, serving breakfast fry-ups till 11.30am (including vegetarian versions), light lunches based around local produce (think Cullen skink, smoked salmon quiche, venison burgers), and the best cappuccino in the glen.

ℹ Getting There & Away

Scottish Citylink (☎0871-266 3333; www.citylink.co.uk) buses run between Fort William and Glencoe (£8, 30 minutes, four to eight daily) and from Glencoe to Glasgow (£22, 2½ hours, four to eight daily). Buses stop at Glencoe village, Glencoe Visitor Centre and Glencoe Mountain Resort.

Stagecoach (www.stagecoachbus.com) bus 44 links Glencoe village with Fort William (£3.80, 35 minutes, hourly Monday to Saturday, three on Sunday) and Kinlochleven (£2, 15 minutes).

Fort William

POP 9910

Basking on the shores of Loch Linnhe amid magnificent mountain scenery, Fort William has one of the most enviable settings in the whole of Scotland. If it weren't for the busy dual carriageway crammed between the less-than-attractive town centre and the loch, and one of the highest rainfall records in the country, it would be almost idyllic. Even so, the Fort has carved out a reputation as 'Outdoor Capital of the UK' (www.outdoorcapital.co.uk), and easy access by rail and bus makes it a good place to base yourself for exploring the surrounding mountains and glens.

Magical Glen Nevis begins near the northern end of the town and wraps itself around the southern flanks of Ben Nevis (1345m) – Britain's highest mountain and a magnet for hikers and climbers. The glen is also popular with movie makers – parts of *Braveheart*, *Rob Roy* and the Harry Potter movies were filmed there.

Sights

★Jacobite Steam Train HERITAGE RAILWAY
(☎0844 850 4685; www.westcoastrailways.co.uk; day return adult/child £34/19; ⏲daily Jul & Aug, Mon-Fri mid-May–Jun, Sep & Oct) The Jacobite Steam Train, hauled by a former LNER K1 or LMS Class 5MT locomotive, travels the scenic two-hour run between Fort William and Mallaig. Classed as one of the great railway journeys of the world, the route crosses the historic Glenfinnan Viaduct, made famous in the Harry Potter films – the Jacobite's owners supplied the steam locomotive and rolling stock used in the film.

Trains depart from Fort William train station in the morning and return from Mallaig in the afternoon. There's a brief stop at Glenfinnan station, and you get 1½ hours in Mallaig.

West Highland Museum MUSEUM
(☎01397-702169; www.westhighlandmuseum.org.uk; Cameron Sq; ⏲10am-5pm Mon-Sat Apr-Oct, to 4pm Mar & Nov-Dec, closed Jan & Feb) FREE This small but fascinating museum is packed with all manner of Highland memorabilia. Look out for the secret portrait of Bonnie Prince Charlie – after the Jacobite rebellions, all things Highland were banned, including pictures of the exiled leader, and this tiny painting looks like nothing more than a smear of paint until viewed in a cylindrical mirror, which reflects a credible likeness of the prince.

Sleeping

It's best to book well ahead in summer, especially for hostels.

Calluna APARTMENT $
(☎01397-700451; www.fortwilliamholiday.co.uk; Heathercroft, Connochie Rd; dm/tw £17/40, 6- to 8-person apt per week £575; P 📶) Run by well-known mountain guide Alan Kimber and wife Sue, the Calluna offers self-catering apartments geared to groups of hikers and climbers, but also takes individual travellers prepared to share; there's a fully equipped kitchen and an excellent drying room for your soggy hiking gear.

Fort William Backpackers HOSTEL $
(☎01397-700711; www.scotlands-top-hostels.com; Alma Rd; dm/tw £18.50/47; P @ 📶) A 10-minute walk from the bus and train stations, this lively and welcoming hostel is set in a grand Victorian villa, perched on a hillside with great views over Loch Linnhe.

Ashburn House B&B $$
(☎01397-706000; www.ashburnhouse.co.uk; Achintore Rd; r per person £55; ⊙Mar-Oct; P 📶) Gorgeously bright and spacious bedrooms – some with views over Loch Linnhe – are the norm at this grand Victorian villa south of the centre. The leather sofas in the residents lounge and the breakfast tables in the dining room enjoy sea views. No children under 12.

Lime Tree HOTEL $$
(☎01397-701806; www.limetreefortwilliam.co.uk; Achintore Rd; s/d from £110/120; P 📶 🐾) Much more interesting than your average guesthouse, this former Victorian manse overlooking Loch Linnhe is an 'art gallery with rooms', decorated throughout with the artist-owner's atmospheric Highland landscapes. Foodies rave about the restaurant, and the gallery space – a triumph of sensitive design – stages everything from serious exhibitions (works by David Hockney and Andy Goldsworthy have appeared) to folk concerts.

No 6 Caberfeidh B&B $$
(☎01397-703756; www.6caberfeidh.com; 6 Caberfeidh, Fassifern Rd; d/f £75/120; 📶) Friendly owners and comfortable accommodation make a great combination; add a good central location and you're all set. Choose from one of two family rooms (one double and one single bed) or a romantic double with four-poster. Freshly prepared breakfasts include scrambled eggs with smoked salmon.

St Andrew's Guest House B&B $$
(☎01397-703038; www.standrewsguesthouse.co.uk; Fassifern Rd; s/d £57/70; P 📶) Set in a lovely 19th-century building that was once a rectory and choir school, St Andrew's retains period features such as carved masonry, wood panelling and stained-glass windows. It has six spacious bedrooms; those at the front have stunning views.

★Grange B&B $$$
(☎01397-705516; www.grangefortwilliam.com; Grange Rd; d £145; P 📶) An exceptional 19th-century villa set in its own landscaped grounds, the Grange is crammed with antiques and fitted with log fires, chaise lounges and Victorian roll-top baths. The Turret Room, with its window seat in the turret overlooking Loch Linnhe, is our favourite. It's 500m southwest of the town centre. No children.

Eating & Drinking

★Lime Tree SCOTTISH $$
(☎01397-701806; www.limetreefortwilliam.co.uk; Achintore Rd; mains £16-20; ⊙6.30-9.30pm; P 📶) Fort William is not over-endowed with great places to eat, but the restaurant at this small hotel and art gallery has put the UK's Outdoor Capital on the gastronomic map. The chef turns out delicious dishes built around fresh Scottish produce, ranging from Loch Fyne oysters to Loch Awe trout and Ardnamurchan venison.

Bayleaf SCOTTISH $$
(Cameron Sq; mains lunch £5-11, dinner £13-20; 👪) A great new addition to the town's restaurant scene, this place combines crisp, modern decor, friendly service (the chef often comes out to chat with customers), and the best of Scottish beef, lamb and seafood freshly and simply prepared. If Scotland's national dish hasn't appealed, try a haggis fritter with Drambuie mayonnaise!

Crannog Seafood Restaurant SEAFOOD $$
(☎01397-705589; www.crannog.net; Town Pier; mains £15-23; ⊙noon-2.30pm & 6-9pm) The Crannog wins the prize for the best location in town – perched on the Town Pier, giving window-table diners an uninterrupted view down Loch Linnhe. Informal and unfussy, it specialises in fresh local fish – there are three or four daily fish specials plus the main menu – though there are lamb, venison and vegetarian dishes, too. Two/three-course lunch £15/19.

Grog & Gruel PUB
(☎01397-705078; www.grogandgruel.co.uk; 66 High St; ⊙noon-midnight; 📶) The Grog & Gruel is a traditional-style, wood-panelled pub with an excellent range of cask ales from regional Scottish and English microbreweries.

Information

Fort William Tourist Office (☎01397-701801; www.visithighlands.com; 15 High St; internet per 20min £1; ⊙9am-5pm Mon-Sat, 10am-3pm Sun, longer hrs Jun-Aug) Has internet access.

Getting There & Away

The bus and train stations are next to the huge Morrisons supermarket, reached from the town centre via an underpass next to the Nevisport shop.

BUS

Scottish Citylink (☎ 0871-266 3333; www.citylink.co.uk) buses link Fort William with other major towns and cities.

Edinburgh £35, five hours, seven daily with a change at Glasgow; via Glencoe and Crianlarich

Glasgow £24, three hours, eight daily

Inverness £11.60, two hours, six daily

Oban £9.40, 1½ hours, two daily

Portree £311, three hours, three daily

Shiel Buses (☎ 01397-700700; www.shielbuses.co.uk) service 500 runs to Mallaig (£6.10, 1½ hours, three daily Monday to Friday, plus one daily weekends April to September) via Glenfinnan (£3.30, 30 minutes) and Arisaig (£5.60, one hour).

TRAIN

The spectacular West Highland line runs from Glasgow to Mallaig via Fort William. The overnight **Caledonian Sleeper** (www.sleeper.scot) service connects Fort William and London Euston (from £125 sharing a twin-berth cabin, 13 hours).

There's no direct rail connection between Oban and Fort William – you have to change at Crianlarich, so it's faster to use the bus.

Edinburgh £35, five hours; change at Glasgow's Queen St station, three daily, two on Sunday

Glasgow £26, 3¾ hours, three daily, two on Sunday

Mallaig £12.20, 1½ hours, four daily, three on Sunday

Getting Around

BICYCLE

Nevis Cycles (☎ 01397-705555; www.neviscycles.com; cnr Montrose Ave & Locheil Rd, Inverlochy; per day from £25; ⏲ 9am-5.30pm) Located a half-mile northeast of the town centre, this place rents everything from hybrid bikes and mountain bikes to full-suspension downhill racers. Bikes can be hired here and dropped off in Inverness.

BUS

A Zone 2 Dayrider ticket (£8.60) gives unlimited travel for one day on Stagecoach bus services in the Fort William area, as far as Glencoe and Fort Augustus. Buy from the bus driver.

CAR

Fort William is 146 miles from Edinburgh, 104 miles from Glasgow and 66 miles from Inverness. The tourist office has listings of car-hire companies.

Easydrive Car Hire (☎ 01397-701616; www.easydrivescotland.co.uk; North Rd) Hires out small cars from £36/165 a day/week, including tax and unlimited mileage, but not Collision Damage Waiver (CDW).

TAXI

There's a taxi rank on the corner of High St and the Parade.

Around Fort William

Glen Nevis

Scenic Glen Nevis – used as a filming location for *Braveheart* and the Harry Potter movies – lies just an hour's walk from Fort William town centre. The **Glen Nevis Visitor Centre** (☎ 01397-705922; www.bennevisweather.co.uk; ⏲ 8.30am-6pm Jul & Aug, 9am-5pm Apr-Jun, Sep & Oct, 9am-3pm Nov-Mar; P) is situated 1.5 miles up the glen, and provides information on hiking, weather forecasts, and specific advice on climbing Ben Nevis.

From the car park at the far end of the road along Glen Nevis, there is an excellent 1.5-mile walk through the spectacular Nevis Gorge to Steall Meadows, a verdant valley dominated by a 100m-high bridal-veil waterfall. You can reach the foot of the falls by crossing the river on a wobbly, three-cable wire bridge – one cable for your feet and one for each hand – a real test of balance!

Bus 41 runs from Fort William bus station to the Glen Nevis SYHA Hostel (£2, 15 or 20 minutes, two daily year-round, five daily Monday to Saturday June to September). Check at the tourist office for the latest timetable, which is liable to alteration.

Glen Nevis Caravan & Camping Park CAMPGROUND **$**
(☎ 01397-702191; www.glen-nevis.co.uk; tent sites £9, incl car £11, campervan £13 plus per person £3.50; ⏲ mid-Mar–early Nov; 📶) This big, well-equipped site is a popular base camp for Ben Nevis and the surrounding mountains. The site is 2.5 miles from Fort William, along the Glen Nevis road.

Achintee Farm B&B, HOSTEL **$$**
(☎ 01397-702240; www.achinteefarm.com; Achintee; B&B d £90-100, hostel tw/tr £50/75; ⏲ B&B May-Sep, hostel year-round; P 📶) This attractive farmhouse offers excellent B&B accommodation and also has a small hostel attached. It's at the start of the path up Ben Nevis.

★Ben Nevis Inn SCOTTISH $$

(☎01397-701227; www.ben-nevis-inn.co.uk; Achintee; mains £9-16; ⏲noon-11pm daily Apr-Oct, Thu-Sun only Nov-Mar; P) This great barn of a pub serves real ale and tasty bar meals, and has a comfy 24-bed bunkhouse downstairs (beds £16.50 per person). It's at the start of the path from Achintee up Ben Nevis, and only a mile from the end of the West Highland Way.

Nevis Range

Six miles to the north of Fort William lies Nevis Range ski area, where a gondola gives access to the upper part of Aonach Mor mountain. The facility operates year-round, allowing visitors to access mountain paths and downhill mountain-biking trails outside of the ski season.

Nevis Range Downhill & Witch's Trails MOUNTAIN BIKING

(☎01397-705825; http://bike.nevisrange.co.uk; single/multitrip ticket £14/32; ⏲downhill course 10.15am-3.45pm mid-May–mid-Sep, forest trails 24hr year-round) A world championship downhill mountain-bike trail – for experienced riders only – runs from the Snowgoose restaurant at the Nevis Range ski area to the base station; bikes are carried up on a rack on the gondola cabin. A multi-trip ticket gives unlimited uplift for a day; full-suspension bike hire costs from £40/70 per single run/full day.

Nevis Range OUTDOORS

(☎01397-705825; www.nevisrange.co.uk; gondola return trip per adult/child £12.50/7.25; ⏲10am-5pm summer, 9.30am-dusk winter, closed mid-Nov–mid-Dec) The Nevis Range ski area, 6 miles north of Fort William, spreads across the northern slopes of Aonach Mor (1221m). The

CLIMBING BEN NEVIS

As the highest peak in the British Isles, Ben Nevis (1345m) attracts many would-be ascensionists who would not normally think of climbing a Scottish mountain – a staggering (often literally) 100,000 people reach the summit each year.

Although anyone who is reasonably fit should have no problem climbing Ben Nevis on a fine summer's day, an ascent should not be undertaken lightly; every year people have to be rescued from the mountain. You will need proper walking boots (the path is rough and stony, and there may be snow on the summit), warm clothing, waterproofs, a map and compass, and plenty of food and water. And don't forget to check the weather forecast (www.bennevisweather.co.uk).

Here are a few facts to mull over before you go racing up the tourist track: the summit plateau is bounded by 700m-high cliffs and has a sub-Arctic climate; at the summit it can snow on any day of the year; the summit is wrapped in cloud nine days out of 10; in thick cloud, visibility at the summit can be 10m or less; and in such conditions the only safe way off the mountain requires careful use of a map and compass to avoid walking over those 700m cliffs.

The tourist track (the easiest route to the top) was originally called the Pony Track. It was built in the 19th century for the pack ponies that carried supplies to a meteorological observatory on the summit (now in ruins), which was in use continuously from 1883 to 1904.

There are three possible starting points for the tourist track ascent – Achintee Farm; the footbridge at Glen Nevis SYHA Hostel; and, if you have a car, the car park at Glen Nevis Visitor Centre. The path climbs gradually to the shoulder at Lochan Meall an t-Suidhe (known as the Halfway Lochan), then zigzags steeply up beside the Red Burn to the summit plateau. The highest point is marked by a trig point on top of a huge cairn beside the ruins of the old observatory; the plateau is scattered with countless smaller cairns, stones arranged in the shape of people's names and, sadly, a fair bit of litter.

The total distance to the summit and back is 8 miles; allow at least four or five hours to reach the top, and another 2½ to three hours for the descent. Afterwards, as you celebrate in the pub with a pint, consider the fact that the record time for the annual Ben Nevis Hill Race is just under 1½ hours – up *and* down. Then have another pint.

gondola that gives access to the bottom of the ski area at 655m operates year-round (15 minutes each way). At the top there's a restaurant and a couple of hiking trails through nearby Leanachan Forest, as well as excellent mountain-biking trails.

Road to the Isles

The 46-mile A830 road from Fort William to Mallaig is traditionally known as the Road to the Isles, as it leads to the jumping-off point for ferries to the Small Isles and Skye, itself a stepping stone to the Outer Hebrides. This is a region steeped in Jacobite history, having witnessed both the beginning and the end of Bonnie Prince Charlie's doomed attempt to regain the British throne in 1745–46.

The final section of this scenic route, between Arisaig and Mallaig, has been upgraded to a fast straight road. Unless you're in a hurry, opt instead for the more scenic old road (signposted Alternative Coastal Route).

Between the A830 and the A87 far to the north lie Knoydart and Glenelg – Scotland's 'Empty Quarter'.

Glenfinnan

POP 100

Glenfinnan is hallowed ground for fans of Bonnie Prince Charlie; the monument here marks where he raised his Highland army. It is also a place of pilgrimage for steam train enthusiasts and Harry Potter fans – the famous railway viaduct features in the Potter films, and is regularly traversed by the Jacobite Steam Train (p910).

Glenfinnan Visitor Centre MUSEUM

(NTS; adult/child £3.50/2.50; 9.30am-5pm Jul & Aug, 10am-5pm Easter-Jun, Sep & Oct; P) This centre recounts the story of the '45, as the Jacobite rebellion of 1745 is known, when Bonnie Prince Charlie's loyal clansmen marched and fought their way from Glenfinnan south via Edinburgh to Derby, then back north to final defeat at Culloden.

Glenfinnan Station Museum MUSEUM

(www.glenfinnanstationmuseum.co.uk; admission by donation, suggested £1; 9am-5pm Easter-Oct; P) This fascinating little museum records the epic tale of building the West Highland railway line. The famous 21-arch **Glenfinnan viaduct**, just east of the station, was built in 1901, and featured in several Harry Potter movies. A pleasant walk of around 0.75 miles east from the station (signposted) leads to a viewpoint for the viaduct and for Loch Shiel.

Arisaig & Morar

The 5 miles of coast between Arisaig and Morar is a fretwork of rocky islets, inlets and gorgeous silver-sand beaches backed by dunes and machair, with stunning sunset views across the sea to the silhouetted peaks of Eigg and Rum. The **Silver Sands of Morar**, as they are known, draw crowds of bucket-and-spade holidaymakers in July and August, when the many campsites scattered along the coast are filled to overflowing.

Old Library Lodge & Restaurant SCOTTISH **$$**

(01687-450651; www.oldlibrary.co.uk; Arisaig; mains £10-19; P) The Old Library is a charming restaurant with rooms (single/double £75/120) set in converted 200-year-old stables overlooking the waterfront in Arisaig village. The lunch menu concentrates on soups, burgers and smoked fish or meat platters, while dinner is a more sophisticated affair offering local seafood, beef and lamb.

Mallaig

POP 800

If you're travelling between Fort William and Skye, you may find yourself overnighting in the bustling fishing and ferry port of Mallaig (*mahl*-ig). Indeed, it makes a good base for a series of day trips by ferry to the Small Isles and Knoydart.

Seaview Guest House B&B **$$**

(01687-462059; www.seaviewguesthousemallaig.com; Main St; r per person £35-40, cottage per week £400-495; Mar–mid-Nov; P) This comfortable B&B has grand views over the harbour, not only from the upstairs bedrooms but also from the breakfast room. There's also a cute little cottage next door that offers self-catering accommodation (www.selfcateringmallaig.com; one double and one twin room).

Fish Market Restaurant SEAFOOD **$$**

(01687-462299; www.thefishmarketrestaurant.co.uk; Station Rd; mains £10-22; noon-3pm & 6-9pm) At least half-a-dozen signs in Mallaig advertise 'seafood restaurant', but this bright, modern, bistro-style place next to the harbour is our favourite, serving simply prepared scallops, smoked salmon, mussels, and fresh Mallaig haddock fried in breadcrumbs, as well as the tastiest Cullen skink on the west coast.

Getting There & Away

BOAT

A passenger ferry operated by **Western Isles Cruises** (01687-462233; westernislescruises.co.uk; one-way/day return £10/18, bike £2) links Mallaig to Inverie on the Knoydart Peninsula (25 to 40 minutes) four times daily Monday to Saturday from April to October.

CalMac (0800 066 5000; www.calmac.co.uk) operates the passenger-only ferry from Mallaig to the following destinations in the Small Isles:

Canna £10.50 return, two hours, six a week

Eigg £7.70 return, 1¼ hours, five a week

Muck £8.90 return, 1½ hours, five a week

Rum £8.30 return, 1¼ hours, five a week

There are Calmac car ferry services to Armadale in Skye (car/passenger £9.40/2.80, 30 minutes, eight daily Monday to Saturday, five to seven on Sunday), and Lochboisdale in South Uist (car/passenger £56/10.15, 3½ hours, one a day).

BUS

Shiel Buses (p912) Bus 500 runs from Fort William to Mallaig (£6.10, 1½ hours, three daily Monday to Friday, plus one daily weekends April to September) via Glenfinnan (£3.30, 30 minutes) and Arisaig (£5.60, one hour).

TRAIN

The West Highland line runs between Fort William and Mallaig (£12.20, 1½ hours, four daily, three on Sunday).

EAST COAST

In both landscape and character, the east coast is where the real barrenness of the Highlands begins to unfold. A gentle splendour and a sense of escapism mark the route along the twisting A9, as it heads north for the last of Scotland's far-flung, mainland population outposts. With only a few exceptions the tourism frenzy is left behind once the road traverses Cromarty Firth and snakes its way along wild and pristine coastline.

While the interior is dominated by the vast and mournful Sutherland mountain range, along the coast great heather-covered hills heave themselves out of the wild North Sea. Rolling farmland drops suddenly into the icy waters, and small, historic towns are moored precariously on the coast's edge.

Dornoch

POP 1200

On the northern shore of Dornoch Firth, 2 miles off the A9, this attractive old market town, all elegant sandstone, is one of the east coast's most pleasant settlements. Dornoch is best known for its championship golf course, but there's a fine cathedral among other noble buildings. Other historical oddities: the last witch to be executed in Scotland was boiled alive in hot tar here in 1722 and Madonna married Guy Ritchie here in 2000.

Have a walk along Dornoch's golden-sand **beach**, which stretches for miles. South of Dornoch, **seals** are often visible on the sandbars of Dornoch Firth

There are buses roughly hourly from Inverness (£10.40, 1¼ hours), with some services continuing north to Wick or Thurso.

Dornoch Cathedral CHURCH

(www.dornoch-cathedral.com; St Gilbert St; 9am-7pm or later) FREE Consecrated in the 13th century, Dornoch Cathedral is an elegant Gothic edifice with an interior softly illuminated through modern stained-glass windows. The controversial first Duke of Sutherland, whose wife restored the church in the 1830s, lies in a sealed burial vault beneath the chancel.

Royal Dornoch GOLF

(01862-810219; www.royaldornoch.com; Golf Rd, Dornoch; summer green fee £130) One of Scotland's most famous links, described by Tom Watson as 'the most fun I have ever had on a golf course'. It's public, and you can book a slot online. Twilight rates are the most economical. A golf pass (www.dornochfirthgolf.co.uk) lets you play several courses in the area at a good discount.

★2 Quail B&B $$

(01862-811811; www.2quail.com; Castle St; r £105-115;) Intimate and upmarket, 2 Quail offers a warm main street welcome. Tasteful, spacious chambers are full of old-world comfort, with sturdy metal bed frames, plenty of books and plump duvets. The downstairs guest lounge is an absolute delight, while the guest dinners (2-/3-courses £18/22) are a treat as one of the owners is a noted chef. It's best to book ahead.

Dunrobin Castle

★Dunrobin Castle CASTLE
(☎01408-633177; www.dunrobincastle.co.uk; A9, Golspie; adult/child £11/6.50; ⏲10.30am-4.30pm Mon-Sat, noon-4.30pm Sun Apr, May & Sep–mid-Oct, 10am-5pm daily Jun-Aug) Magnificent Dunrobin Castle, a mile past Golspie, is the Highlands' largest house. Although it dates to 1275, most of what you see was built in French style between 1845 and 1850. A home of the dukes of Sutherland, it's richly furnished and offers an intriguing insight into the aristocratic lifestyle. The beautiful castle inspires mixed feelings locally; it was once the seat of the first Duke of Sutherland, notorious for some of the cruellest episodes of the Highland Clearances.

CAITHNESS

Once you pass Helmsdale, you are entering Caithness, a place of jagged gorse-and-grass-topped cliffs hiding tiny fishing harbours. Scotland's top corner was once Viking territory, historically more connected to Orkney and Shetland than the rest of the mainland. It's a mystical, ancient land dotted with ancient monuments and peopled by folk who are proud of their Norse heritage.

THE RIGHT SIDE OF THE TRACKS

Scotland has some unusual hostels and **Sleeperzzz** (☎01408-641343; www.sleeperzzz.com; dm £18-20, tw £50; ⏲Mar-Sep; P) is one of them. Set in three caringly converted railway carriages, an old bus and a beautiful wooden caravan parked in a siding by Rogart station, Sleeperzzz has cute two-person bedrooms, kitchenettes and tiny lounges. The owners make an effort to run the hostel on sustainable lines.

It's on the A839, 10 miles east of Lairg, but is also easily reached by train on the Inverness–Wick line (10% discount if you arrive this way or by bike). There's a local pub that does food, as well as beautifully lonely Highland scenery in the vicinity.

Lybster & Around

This spectacular stretch of coast follows the folds of the undulating landscape through villages established on the shoreline when communities were evicted from the interior in the Highland Clearances in the early 19th century.

Seven miles north of Helmsdale is Badbea, an abandoned crofting village established at this time. The village of Dunbeath is spectacularly set in a deep glen. Lybster is a purpose-built fishing village dating from 1810, with a stunning harbour area surrounded by grassy cliffs. In its heyday, it was Scotland's third-busiest port. Things have changed – now there are only a couple of boats – but there are several interesting prehistoric sites in the area.

Whaligoe Steps HISTORIC SITE
(Ulbster; ⏲24hr) FREE At Ulbster, 5 miles north of Lybster, this staircase cut into the cliff provides access to a tiny natural harbour, with ideal grassy picnic spot, ringed by vertical cliffs and echoing with the cackle of nesting fulmars. The path begins at the end of the minor road opposite the road signposted 'Cairn of Get'. There's a cafe at the top, open Thursday to Sunday (10.30am to 5.30pm).

Grey Cairns of Camster ARCHAEOLOGICAL SITE
(⏲24hr) FREE Dating from between 4000BC and 2500BC, these burial chambers are hidden in long, low mounds rising from an evocatively lonely moor. The Long Cairn measures 60m by 21m. You can enter the main chamber, but must first crawl into the well-preserved Round Cairn, which has a corbelled ceiling. From a turn-off a mile east of Lybster on the A99, the cairns are 4 miles north. You can continue 7 further miles to approach Wick on the A882.

Wick

POP 7100

More gritty than pretty, Wick has been down on its luck since the collapse of the herring industry. It was once the world's largest fishing port for the 'silver darlings', but when the market dropped off after WWII, job losses were huge and the town hasn't ever totally recovered. It's worth a visit though, particularly for its excellent museum and attractive, spruced-up harbour area.

★ **Wick Heritage Centre** MUSEUM
(☎01955-605393; www.wickheritage.org; 20 Bank Row; adult/child £4/50p; ⏲10am-5pm Apr-Oct, last entry 3.45pm) Tracking the rise and fall of the herring industry, this great town museum displays everything from fishing equipment to complete herring boats. It's absolutely huge inside, and is crammed with memorabilia and extensive displays describing Wick's heyday in the mid-19th century. The Johnston collection is the star exhibit. From 1863 to 1977, three generations photographed everything that happened around Wick and the 70,000 photographs are an amazing record.

Mackays Hotel HOTEL $$
(☎01955-602323; www.mackayshotel.co.uk; Union St; s/d £90/119; 📶) Hospitable Mackays is Wick's best hotel by a long stretch. Attractive, mostly refurbished rooms vary in layout and size, so ask to see a few; prices are usually lower than the rack rates. On-site **No 1 Bistro** (☎01955-602323; www.mackayshotel.co.uk; Union St; mains £13-22; ⏲noon-2pm & 5-9pm; 📶) is a fine option for lunch or dinner. The world's shortest street, 2.06m-long Ebenezer Place, is one side of the hotel.

Bord de l'Eau FRENCH $$
(☎01955-604400; 2 Market St; mains £16-24; ⏲6-9pm Tue-Fri, noon-2pm & 6-9pm Sun & Sat) This serene, relaxed French restaurant is Wick's best place to eat. It overlooks the river and serves a changing menu of mostly meat and game French classics, backed up by daily fish specials. Starters are great value, and mains include a huge assortment of vegetables, so you won't go hungry. The conservatory dining room with water views is lovely on a sunny evening.

ℹ Information

Wick Information Centre (☎01955-602547; 66 High St; ⏲9am-5.30pm Mon-Sat) Upstairs in McAllans Clothing Store. Has a good selection of information.

ℹ Getting There & Away

AIR

Wick is a Caithness transport gateway. Flybe/Loganair flies to Edinburgh and **Eastern Airways** (☎0870 366 9100; www.easternairways.com) to Aberdeen (three daily, Monday to Friday).

BUS

Stagecoach and Citylink operate to/from Inverness (£19.80, three hours, six daily) and Stagecoach to Thurso (£3.80, 40 minutes, hourly). There's also connecting service to John O'Groats and Gills Bay (£3.40, 30 minutes, four to five Monday to Saturday) for the passenger and car ferries to Orkney.

TRAIN

Trains service Wick from Inverness (£20, 4¼ hours, four daily Monday to Saturday, one on Sunday).

John O'Groats

POP 300

Though not the northernmost point of the British mainland (that's Dunnet Head), John O'Groats still serves as the end point of the 874-mile trek from Land's End in Cornwall, a popular if arduous route for cyclists and walkers, many of whom raise money for charitable causes. Most of the settlement is taken up by a stylish modern self-catering complex. There's a passenger ferry from here to Orkney. **John O'Groats Information Centre** (☎01955-611373; www.visitjohnogroats.com; ⏲10am-4pm Apr, to 5pm May & Sep-Oct, 9am-6pm Jun-Aug) has souvenirs plus a fine selection of local novels and nonfiction.

Duncansby Head VIEWPOINT
Two miles east of John O'Groats, Duncansby Head has a small lighthouse and 60m-high cliffs sheltering nesting fulmars. A 15-minute walk through a sheep paddock yields spectacular views of the sea-surrounded monoliths known as Duncansby Stacks.

Dunnet Head

Eight miles east of Thurso a minor road leads to dramatic Dunnet Head, the most northerly point on the British mainland. There are majestic cliffs dropping into the turbulent Pentland Firth, inspiring views of Orkney, basking seals and nesting seabirds below, and a lighthouse built by Robert Louis Stevenson's grandad. Just west, the excellent curving strand of Dunnet Bay is one of Scotland's finest beaches.

Thurso & Scrabster

POP 7600

Britain's most northerly mainland town, Thurso makes a handy overnight stop if you're heading west or across to Orkney. There's a pretty town beach, riverside strolls and a good museum. Ferries for Orkney leave from Scrabster, 2.5 miles away.

Sleeping & Eating

Sandra's Backpackers HOSTEL $
(01847-894575; www.sandras-backpackers.co.uk; 24 Princes St; dm/d/f £18/42/65; P @) In the heart of town above a chip shop, this budget backpacker option offers en suite dorms, mostly four-berthers with aged mattresses, a spacious kitchen and traveller-friendly facilities such as help-yourself cereals and toast. It's not luxurious but it's a reliable cheap sleep.

★ **Pennyland House** B&B $$
(01847-891194; www.pennylandhouse.co.uk; Thurso; s/d £78/98; P) A super conversion of a historic house, this is a standout B&B choice. It offers phenomenal value for this level of accommodation, with huge oak-furnished rooms named after golf courses: we especially loved St Andrews – super-spacious, with a great chessboard-tiled bathroom. Hospitality is enthusiastic and helpful, and there's an inviting breakfast space, garden and terraced area with views across to Hoy.

Two-night minimum stay in summer.

Marine B&B $$
(01847-890676; www.themarinethurso.co.uk; 38 Shore St, Thurso; s £80, d £90-105; P) Tucked away in Thurso's most appealing corner you'll find a top spot right by the pretty town beach, offering spectacular vistas over it and across to Orkney. Rooms are just fabulous, with a designer's touch and a subtle maritime feel, and surfers can study the breakers from the stunning conservatory-lounge. Two rooms in the adjacent house make a great family option.

Holborn Hotel BISTRO $$
(01847-892771; www.holbornhotel.co.uk; 16 Princes St; bar meals £8-11, restaurant mains £13-20; noon-2pm & 6-8pm Mon-Thu, noon-2pm & 6-9pm Fri, noon-2.30pm & 6-9pm Sat & Sun;) A trendy, comfortable place decked out in light wood, the Holborn contrasts starkly with more traditional Thurso watering holes. Uncomplicated but decent meals are available in the bar, while quality seafood – including delicious home-smoked salmon – is the mainstay of a short menu fleshed out by specials at the evening-only Red Pepper restaurant, where desserts are excellent too. Service can be slow when busy.

It also has decent accommodation (single/double £65/90).

★ **Captain's Galley** SEAFOOD $$$
(01847-894999; www.captainsgalley.co.uk; Scrabster; 5-course dinner £53.50, with wine flight £77; 6.30-11pm Tue-Sat, last orders 9pm) Classy but friendly Captain's Galley, just by the Scrabster ferry, offers a short, seafood-based menu featuring local and sustainably sourced produce prepared in delicious ways that let the natural flavours shine through. The chef picks the best fish off the local boats, and the menu describes exactly which fishing grounds your morsel came from. It's worth scheduling a night in Thurso to eat here.

Information

Thurso Information Centre (01847-893155; www.visitscotland.com; High St; 10am-6pm Mon-Fri, to 5pm Sat, plus noon-5pm Sun May-Aug) Located in the Caithness Horizons museum.

Getting There & Away

BUS

Stagecoach/Citylink buses link Thurso/Scrabster with Inverness (£19.80, three hours, five daily). There are also buses roughly every hour to Wick (£3.80, 40 minutes), as well as every couple of hours to John O'Groats (£4.40 to £7.50, 40 minutes to one hour, five to eight Monday to Saturday).

TRAIN

There are four daily trains (one on Sunday) from Inverness (£20, 3¾ hours), with a connecting bus to Scrabster.

It's a 2-mile walk from Thurso train station to the ferry at Scrabster; there are buses from Olrig St.

NORTH & WEST COAST

Carving its way from Thurso to Kyle of Lochalsh, Scotland's north and northwest coastline is a feast of deep inlets, forgotten beaches and surging peninsulas. Within the rugged confines of the deep interior are vast, empty spaces, enormous lochs and some of Scotland's highest peaks.

Thurso to Durness

It's 80 winding – and utterly spectacular – coastal miles from Thurso to Durness.

Bettyhill

POP 500

Bettyhill is a crofting community of resettled tenant farmers kicked off their land during the Clearances. The spectacular panorama of a sweeping, sandy beach backed by velvety green hills with rocky outcrops makes a sharp contrast to that sad history.

Strathnaver Museum MUSEUM
(☎01641-521418; www.strathnavermuseum.org.uk; adult/child £2/1; ⏲10am-5pm Mon-Sat Apr-Oct) Housed in an old church, this museum tells the sad story of the Strathnaver Clearances through posters written by local kids. The museum contains memorabilia of Clan Mackay, various items of crofting equipment and a 'St Kilda mailboat', a small wooden boat-shaped container bearing a letter that was used by St Kildans to send messages to the mainland.

Outside the back door of the church is the **Farr Stone**, a fine carved Pictish cross-slab.

★**Farr Cottage** B&B $
(☎01641-521755; www.bettyhillbedandbreakfast.co.uk; Farr; s/d £50/70; P 📶) A good B&B option is this welcoming white bungalow amid the bleating of sheep and beautiful scenery and vistas a mile off the main road. There are two rooms, modern and compact, with sparkling bathrooms. The delightful owner is a seafood chef, so excellent dinners are a bargain at £15 for two courses. Packed lunches are also available. Follow signs to Farr.

★**Côte du Nord** MODERN SCOTTISH $$$
(☎01641-521773; www.cotedunord.co.uk; The School House, Kirtomy; degustation £39, with wine flight £75; ⏲7-9pm Wed, Fri & Sat Apr-Sep) Brilliantly innovative cuisine, wonderfully whimsical presentation and an emphasis on local ingredients are the highlights of the excellent gastronomic degustation menu here. It's an unlikely spot to find such a gourmet experience; the chef is none other than the local GP who forages for wild herbs and flavours in between surgery hours. Top value. It's tiny, so reserve well ahead.

Kirtomy is signposted off the main road about 2½ miles east of Bettyhill; the restaurant is about a mile down this road.

Coldbackie & Tongue

POP 500

Coldbackie has outstanding views over sandy beaches, turquoise waters and offshore islands. Two miles further is Tongue, with the evocative 14th-century ruins of Castle Varrich, once a Mackay stronghold. To get to the castle, take the trail next to the Royal Bank of Scotland – it's an easy stroll.

★**Cloisters** B&B $$
(☎01847-601286; www.cloistersbandb.co.uk; Talmine; s/d £40/70; P 📶 🐾) Superbly located Cloisters has three en suite twin rooms and absolutely brilliant views over the Kyle of Tongue and offshore islands. Breakfast is in the artistically converted church alongside, and it can do evening meals at weekends. From Tongue, cross the causeway and take the right-hand turn to Melness; Cloisters is a couple of miles down this road.

Durness

POP 400

Scattered Durness (www.durness.org) is wonderfully located, strung out along cliffs rising from a series of pristine beaches. When the sun shines, the effects of blinding white sand, the cry of seabirds and the spring-green-coloured seas combine in a magical way.

Sights & Activities

Walking around the sensational sandy coastline is a highlight, as is a visit to **Cape Wrath**. Durness's beautiful beaches include **Rispond** to the east, **Sango Sands** below town and **Balnakeil** to the west. At Balnakeil, under a mile beyond Durness, a craft village occupies a onetime early-warning radar station. A walk along the beach to the north leads to **Faraid Head**, where you can see puffin colonies in early summer. You can hire bikes from a shed on the square.

Smoo Cave CAVE
(www.smoocave.org) FREE A mile east of the centre is a path down to Smoo Cave. From the vast main chamber, you can head through to a smaller flooded cavern where a waterfall sometimes cascades from the roof. There's evidence the cave was inhabited about 6000 years ago. You can take a **boat trip** (☎01971-511704; adult/child £4/2; ⏲11am-4pm Apr-May & Sep, 10am-5pm Jun-Aug) to explore a little further into the interior.

Sleeping & Eating

Lazy Crofter Bunkhouse HOSTEL $
(01971-511202; www.durnesshostel.com; dm £19;) Durness' best budget accommodation is here, opposite the supermarket. A bothy vibe gives it a very Highland feel. Inviting dorms have plenty of room and lockers, and there's also a sociable shared table for meals and board games, and a great wooden deck with sea views, perfect for midge-free evenings.

Sango Sands Oasis CAMPGROUND $
(07838 381065; www.sangosands.com; sites per adult/child £8/6, 2nd child £3, others free;) You couldn't imagine a better location for a campsite: great grassy areas on the edge of cliffs, descending to two lovely sandy beaches. Facilities are good and very clean and there's a pub next door. Electric hookup is an extra £4. You can camp free from November to March but don't complain about the cold.

★ **Mackays Rooms** HOTEL $$
(01971-511202; www.visitdurness.com; d standard £129, deluxe £139-149; May–mid-Oct;) You really feel you're at the furthest corner of Scotland here, where the road turns through 90 degrees. But whether heading south or east, you'll go far before you find a better place to stay than this haven of Highland hospitality. With big beds, contemporary colours and soft fabrics, it's a romantic spot with top service and numerous boutique details. There's also a new self-contained cabin here, which can be rented on a self-catering or B&B basis. With two rooms, it sleeps up to four.

★ **Cocoa Mountain** CAFE $
(01971-511233; www.cocoamountain.co.uk; Balnakeil; hot chocolate £3.95, 10 truffles £9.90; 9am-6pm Easter-Oct) At the Balnakeil craft village, this upbeat cafe and chocolate maker offers handmade treats including a chilli, lemongrass and coconut white-chocolate truffle, plus many more unique flavours. Tasty espresso and hot chocolate warm the cockles on those blowy horizontal-drizzle days. It offers light lunches and home-baking too, plus chocolate-making workshops.

Information

Durness Information Centre (01971-511368; www.visithighlands.com; 10am-5pm Mon-Sat, to 3pm Sun Easter-Oct, shorter hours in winter) Very helpful, with good info on local walks and transport.

Getting There & Away

From mid-May to mid-September, one **D & E Coaches** (01463-222444; www.decoaches.co.uk; mid-May–mid-Sep) service runs four to six times weekly from Durness to Inverness (£17, four hours) via Ullapool (£12.70, 1½ hours). You can take bikes (£6) but they must be prebooked (during office hours).

A year-round **Far North Bus** (07782 110007; www.thedurnessbus.com) heads daily to Lairg (£8.10, 2½ hours, Monday to Friday), where there is a train station. On Saturday buses head to Inverness (£11.80, three hours) or Thurso (£9.40, 2½ hours). All these services should be prebooked; you can do the Inverness and Thurso ones online.

There are also two Tuesday **services** (01847-601238; http://transportfortongue.co.uk) between Tongue and Durness.

Durness to Ullapool

Perhaps Scotland's most spectacular road, the 69 miles connecting Durness to Ullapool is a smorgasbord of dramatic scenery, almost too much to take in. From Durness you pass through a broad heathered valley with the looming grey bulk of Foinaven and Arkle to the southeast. Heather gives way to a rockier landscape of Lewisian gneiss pockmarked with hundreds of small lochans. This is the most interesting zone geologically in the UK, with Britain's oldest rock. Next come gorse-covered hills prefacing the magnificent Torridonian sandstone mountains of Assynt and Coigach, including Suilven's distinctive sugarloaf, ziggurat-like Quinag and pinnacled Stac Pollaidh. The area has been named as the **Northwest Highlands Geopark** (www.nwhgeopark.com).

Kylesku & Loch Glencoul

Hidden away on the shores of Loch Glencoul, tiny Kylesku served as a ferry crossing on the route north until it was made redundant by beautiful Kylesku Bridge in 1984. It's a good base for walks; you can hire bikes too.

Eas a'Chuil Aluinn WATERFALL
Five miles southeast of Kylesku, in wild, remote country, lies 213m-high Eas a'Chuil Aluinn, Britain's highest waterfall. You can hike to the top of the falls from a parking area at a sharp bend in the main road 3 miles south of Kylesku; allow five hours for the 6 miles return trip. It can also be seen on **boat trips** (01971-502231; www.kyleskuboat

WORTH A TRIP

CAPE WRATH

Though its name actually comes from the Norse word for 'turning point', there is something daunting and primal about Cape Wrath, the remote north-western point of the British mainland, crowned by a lighthouse built by the famous Stevenson family of engineers and close to the seabird colonies of **Clo Mor**, Britain's highest coastal cliffs. A cafe at the lighthouse serves soup and sandwiches.

Getting to Cape Wrath involves taking a **ferry** (07719 678729; www.capewrathferry.co.uk; single/return £4.50/6.50; Easter-Oct) – passengers and bikes only – across the Kyle of Durness (10 minutes). It connects with the **Cape Wrath Minibus** (01971-511284; www.visitcapewrath.com; single/return £7/12; Easter-Oct), which runs the 11 miles to the cape (40 minutes).

This combination is a friendly but eccentric and sometimes shambolic service with limited capacity, so plan on waiting in high season, and call ahead to make sure the ferry is running. The ferry leaves from 2 miles southwest of Durness, and runs twice or more daily from April to September. If you eschew the minibus, it's a spectacular 11-mile ride or hike from boat to cape over bleak scenery.

South of Cape Wrath, Sandwood Bay boasts one of Scotland's best and most isolated beaches, guarded at one end by the spectacular rock pinnacle Am Buachaille. Sandwood Bay is about 2 miles north of the end of a track from Blairmore (approach from Kinlochbervie), or you could walk south from the cape (allow eight hours) and on to Blairmore. Sandwood House is a creepy ruin reputedly haunted by the ghost of a 16th-century shipwrecked sailor from the Spanish Armada.

tours.com; Kylesku; adult/child £25/18; Apr-Sep) from Kylesku.

★ **Kylesku Hotel** SEAFOOD $$
(01971-502231; www.kyleskuhotel.co.uk; Kylesku; mains £11-22; noon-2.30pm & 5.30-8.30pm mid-Feb–Apr & Oct-Nov, noon-9pm May-Sep;) In this remote loch-side location, it's a real pleasure to gorge yourself on delicious sustainable seafood in this convivial restaurant, with a new extension offering extra water-view seating. Local langoustines, squat lobsters and mussels are the specialities. There's still a good atmosphere of mingling locals and visitors at the bar.

Lochinver & Assynt

With its otherworldly scenery of isolated peaks rising above a sea of crumpled, lochan-spattered gneiss, Assynt epitomises the northwest's wild magnificence. Glaciers have sculpted the hills of Suilven (731m), Canisp (846m), Quinag (808m) and Ben More Assynt (998m) into strange, wonderful silhouettes.

Lochinver is the main settlement, a busy little fishing port that's a popular port of call with its laid-back atmosphere, good facilities and striking scenery. Just north of Lochinver (or if coming from the north, not far south of Kylesku), a 23-mile detour on the narrow B869 rewards with spectacular views and fine beaches. From the lighthouse at Point of Stoer, a one-hour cliff walk leads to the Old Man of Stoer, a spectacular sea stack.

The limestone hills around Inchnadamph are famous for their caves. The **Assynt Visitor Centre** (01571-844194; www.discoverassynt.co.uk; Main St, Lochin; 10am-4.30pm Mon-Sat, 11am-3pm Sun Easter-Jun, Sep & Oct, 9.30am-5pm Mon-Sat, 10am-4pm Sun Jul & Aug) in Lochinver has plenty of information on walking and other activities.

Sleeping & Eating

An Cala Bunkhouse HOSTEL $
(Lochinver Bunkhouse; 01571-844598; http://ancalacafeandbunkhouse.co.uk; Culag Park, Lochinver; s/d bunk £22/40; P) Housed near the harbour in the former fishermen's mission, this is an appealing modern hostel with three functional dorms and a good kitchen and lounge. Call ahead on Sunday when the cafe downstairs is closed and there's nobody on the premises.

Clachtoll Beach Campsite CAMPGROUND $
(01571-855377; www.clachtollbeachcampsite.co.uk; B869, Clachtoll; site £6-14, plus per adult/child £4/1; Apr-Sep; P) Set among the machair beside a lovely white-sand beach and emerald seas, Clachtoll is a divine

coastal camping spot, though somewhat overwhelmed by the adjacent self-catering development. It's 6 miles north of Lochinver by road.

Achmelvich Beach SYHA HOSTEL $

(☎01571-844480; www.syha.org.uk; dm/tw £20/50; ⏲Apr-Sep) Off the B869, this whitewashed cottage is set beside a great beach at the end of a side road. Dorms are simple, and there's a sociable common kitchen and eating area. Heat-up meals are available as well as a basic shop in summer; otherwise, there's a chip van at the adjacent campsite or take the 4-mile walk to Lochinver.

★ Albannach HOTEL $$$

(☎01571-844407; www.thealbannach.co.uk; Baddidarroch, Lochinver; s/d/ste incl dinner £240/320/385; ⏲Tue-Sun Mar-Dec; P 📶) One of the Highlands' top places to stay and eat, this hotel combines old-fashioned country-house elements – steep creaky stairs, stuffed animals, fireplaces and noble antique furniture – with strikingly handsome rooms that range from a sumptuous four-poster to more modern spaces with things like underfloor heating and, in one case, a private deck with outdoor spa.

The restaurant serves a table d'hôte (tailored to your needs) that's famed throughout Scotland (£70 for non-residents); the welcoming owners grow lots of their own produce and focus on organic and local ingredients. Glorious views, spacious grounds and great walks in easy striking distance make this a perfect place to base yourself.

Lochinver Larder & Riverside Bistro CAFE, BISTRO $$

(☎01571-844356; www.lochinverlarder.co.uk; 3 Main St, Lochinver; pies £5, mains £11-15; ⏲10am-7.45pm Mon-Sat, to 5.30pm Sun; 📶) An outstanding menu of inventive food made with local produce is on offer here. The bistro turns out delicious seafood dishes in the evening, while the takeaway counter sells tasty pies with a wide range of gourmet fillings (try the wild boar and apricot). It also does quality meals to take away and heat up: great for hostellers and campers.

Getting There & Away

There are buses from Ullapool to Lochinver (£5, one hour, two to three Monday to Saturday) and a summer bus that goes on to Durness.

Coigach

The region south of Assynt, west of the main A835 road from Ullapool to Ledmore Junction, is known as Coigach (www.coigach.com). A lone, single-track road penetrates this wilderness, leading through gloriously wild scenery to remote settlements. At the western end of Loch Lurgainn, a branch leads north to Lochinver, a scenic backroad so narrow and twisting that it's nicknamed the Wee Mad Road.

Coigach is a wonderland for walkers and wildlife enthusiasts, with a patchwork of sinuous silver lochs dominated by the isolated peaks of Cul Mor (849m), Cul Beag (769m), Ben More Coigach (743m) and Stac Pollaidh (613m). The main settlement is the straggling township of **Achiltibuie**, 15 miles from the main road, with the gorgeous Summer Isles moored just off the coast, and silhouettes of mountains skirting the bay.

Summer Isles Seatours CRUISE

(☎07927 920592; www.summerisles-seatours.co.uk; adult/child £30/15; ⏲Mon-Sat May-Sep) Cruises to the Summer Isles from Old Dornie pier, northwest of Achiltibuie. You get to spend some time ashore on Tanera Mòr.

Ullapool

POP 1500

This pretty port on the shores of Loch Broom is the largest settlement in Wester Ross and one of the most alluring spots in the Highlands, a wonderful destination in itself as well as a gateway to the Western Isles. Offering a row of whitewashed cottages arrayed along the harbour and special views of the loch and its flanking hills, the town has a very distinctive appeal. The harbour served as an emigration point during the Clearances, with thousands of Scots watching Ullapool recede behind.

Sights & Activities

Ullapool Museum MUSEUM

(www.ullapoolmuseum.co.uk; 7 West Argyle St; adult/child £3.50/free; ⏲10am-5pm Mon-Fri, 11am-4pm Sat Apr-Oct) Housed in a converted Telford church, this museum relates the prehistoric, natural and social history of the town and Lochbroom area, with a particular focus on the emigration to Nova Scotia and other places. There's also a genealogy section if you want to trace your Scottish roots.

Shearwater Cruises BOATING
(☎01854-612472; www.summerqueen.co.uk; ⊙Mon-Sat May-Sep) Weather permitting, the catamaran *Shearwater* takes you out to the Summer Isles for a three-hour cruise (adult/child £35/25) or a shorter 1½-hour jaunt (£25/20).

Sleeping

There's a good selection of B&Bs, with some standout options. Note that during summer Ullapool is very busy and finding accommodation can be tricky – book ahead.

Broomfield Holiday Park CAMPGROUND $
(☎01854-612020; www.broomfieldhp.com; West Lane; 1-/2-person tent £8/15, car £2; ⊙Apr-Sep; P) This campsite has a great grassy headland location, very close to the centre. Kids stay free, and there are midge-busting machines in action.

Ullapool SYHA HOSTEL $
(☎01854-612254; www.syha.org.uk; Shore St; dm/tw/q £20/46/90; ⊙Apr-Oct;) You've got to hand it to the SYHA – it's chosen some very sweet locations for its hostels. This is right in the heart of town on the pretty waterfront; some rooms have harbour views and the busy dining area and little lounge are also good spots for contemplating the water.

★**Tamarin Lodge** B&B $$
(☎01854-612667; www.tamarinullapool.com; 9 The Braes; s/d £43/86; P) Effortlessly elegant modern architecture in this hilltop house is noteworthy in its own right, but the glorious vistas over the hills opposite and water far below are unforgettable. All rooms face the view; some have a balcony, and all are very spacious, quiet and utterly relaxing, with unexpected features and gadgets. The great lounge and benevolent hosts are a delight.

Follow signs for Braes from the Inverness road.

★**West House** B&B $$
(☎01854-613126; www.westhousebandb.co.uk; West Argyle St; s £70, d £80-90; ⊙May-Oct; P) Slap bang in the centre, this solid white house, once a manse, offers excellent rooms with contemporary style and great bathrooms. Breakfast is continental: you've got a fridge stocked with fresh fruit, cheeses, yoghurts, homemade bread, proper coffee and juice so you can eat at your leisure in your own chamber. Most rooms have great views, as well as lots of conveniences.

There's a minimum two-night stay. The genial owners also have tempting self-catering options in the Ullapool area.

House on the Point B&B $$
(☎01854-613454; www.ullapoolpoint.com; 27 West Shore St; r £85-90; ⊙Easter–mid-Oct; P) At the end of the shorefront road, this has a prime position with wraparound water vistas. The large double has views both ways but there's a great outlook whichever room you pick. A good continental breakfast, including fruit compote and fresh croissants, is taken in your room, and Angus is a solicitous host.

★**Ceilidh Place** HOTEL $$$
(☎01854-612103; www.theceilidhplace.com; 14 West Argyle St; s £66-92, d £140-172; ⊙Feb-Dec; P) This hotel is a celebration of Scottish culture: we're talking literature and traditional music, not tartan and Nessie dolls. Rooms go for character over modernity; instead of a TV they come with a selection of books chosen by Scottish literati, eclectic artwork and cosy touches. The sumptuous lounge has sofas, chaises longues and an honesty bar. There's a bookshop here too.

It's one of the Highlands' more unusual and delightful places to stay.

Eating

West Coast Delicatessen CAFE $
(☎01854-613450; www.westcoastdeli.co.uk; 5 Argyle St; light meals £3-7; ⊙9am-5pm Mon-Sat;) A likeable venue for coffee or a snack,

NORTH COAST 500

The drive along Scotland's far northern coastline is one of Europe's finest road trips. Words fail to describe the sheer variety of the scenic splendour that unfolds as you cross this awe-inspiring landscape of desolate moorlands, brooding mountains, fertile coastal meadows and stunning white-sand beaches.

In a clever piece of marketing it's been dubbed the **North Coast 500** (www.northcoast500.com), because the round-trip from Inverness is roughly that many miles, though you'll surely clock up a few more if you follow your heart down narrow byroads and seek perfect coastal vistas at the end of dead-end tracks.

this upbeat modern place has tasty sub rolls, decent coffee and a variety of deli produce, including some very tasty cheeses. It also does a good soup, perfect for the windier Ullapool days.

Arch Inn PUB FOOD $$

(☎01854-612454; www.thearchinn.co.uk; West Shore St; mains £10-18; ⏲kitchen noon-2.30pm & 5-9pm Mon-Sat, 12.30-2.30pm & 5-9pm Sun; 📶) There's pleasing pub food to be had at this shorefront establishment, where the cosy bar and restaurant area dishes up generously proportioned, well-presented mains that range from tender chicken and fish dishes to more advanced blackboard specials with local seafood a highlight. Service is helpful and efficient. The outdoor tables right beside the lapping water are a top spot for a pint.

ℹ Information

Ullapool Information Centre (☎01854-612486; ullapool@visitscotland.com; 6 Argyle St; ⏲9am-6pm Mon-Sat, 9.30am-4.30pm Sun Jul & Aug, 9.30am-5pm Mon-Sat, 10am-3pm Sun Jun & Sep, 9.30am-4.30pm Mon-Sat, 10am-3pm Sun Easter-May & Oct) Can book ferries and buses.

ℹ Getting There & Away

Citylink has buses from Inverness to Ullapool (£13.20, 1½ hours, one to three daily), connecting with the Lewis ferry.

Ullapool to Kyle of Lochalsh

Although it's less than 50 miles as the crow flies from Ullapool to Kyle of Lochalsh, it's more like 150 miles along the circuitous coastal road – but don't let that put you off. It's a deliciously remote region and there are fine views of beaches and bays backed by mountains all the way along.

Twelve miles southeast of Ullapool at Braemore, the A832 doubles back towards the coast as it heads for Gairloch (the A835 continues southeast across the wild, sometimes snowbound, Dirrie More pass to Garve and Inverness). If you're hurrying to Skye, use the A835 and catch up with the A832 further south, near Garve.

Falls of Measach WATERFALL

(Corrieshalloch Gorge) Just west of the junction of the A835 and A832, 2 miles south of Braemore, a car park gives access to the Falls of Measach, which spill 45m into spectacularly deep and narrow Corrieshalloch Gorge. You can cross the gorge on a swaying suspension bridge, and walk west for 250m to a viewing platform that juts out dizzyingly above a sheer drop. The thundering falls and misty vapours rising from the gorge are very impressive.

Gairloch & Around

POP 1000

Gairloch is a group of villages (comprising Achtercairn, Strath and Charlestown) around the inner end of a loch of the same name. Gairloch is a good base for whale- and dolphin-watching excursions and the surrounding area has beautiful sandy beaches, good trout fishing and birdwatching. Hill walkers also use Gairloch as a base for the Torridon hills and An Teallach.

Sights & Activities

★ **Inverewe Garden** GARDENS

(NTS; www.nts.org.uk; adult/concession £10.50/7.50; ⏲9.30am-6pm Jun-Aug, 10am-5.30pm Sep, 10am-5pm Apr, May & Oct, 10am-3pm Nov-Mar) Six miles north of Gairloch, this splendid place is a welcome splash of colour on this otherwise bleak coast. The climate here is warmed by the Gulf Stream, which allowed Osgood MacKenzie to create this exotic woodland garden in 1862. There are free guided tours on weekdays at 1.30pm (March to October). There's a licensed cafe-restaurant here which serves great cakes.

Gairloch Marine Wildlife Centre & Cruises WILDLIFE

(☎01445-712636; www.porpoise-gairloch.co.uk; Pier Rd; cruises adult/child £20/15; ⏲10am-4pm Easter-Oct) FREE This small visitor centre has audiovisual and interactive displays, lots of charts, photos and knowledgeable staff. From here, cruises run three times daily (weather permitting); during the two-hour trips you may see basking sharks, porpoises and minke whales. The crew collects data on water temperature and conditions, and monitors cetacean populations, so you are subsidising important research.

Sleeping & Eating

Rua Reidh Lighthouse LODGE $$

(☎01445-771263; www.stayatalighthouse.co.uk; d £85-95; ⏲Easter-Oct; P🐾) Three miles down a private road beyond Melvaig (11 miles north of Gairloch), this simple yet excellent lodge gives a taste of a lighthouse keeper's life. It's a wild, lonely location great for walking and birdwatching. Breakfast is included and tasty evening meals are available. There's no mobile signal or wi-fi and there's usually a two-night minimum stay: book well ahead. There's a separate self-catering apartment that's available year-round.

Gairloch View Guest House B&B **$$**
(01445-712[illegible], [illegible]; Auchtercairn; s/d £55/80; P wi-fi) The unique selling point of this unassuming modern house is a patio with a stunning view over the sea to Skye – a view you can also enjoy from your breakfast table. The three bedrooms, with plenty of natural light, are comfortably furnished in classic country style, and the lounge has satellite TV and a small library of books and games.

Mountain Coffee Company CAFE **$**
(01445-712316; Strath Sq, Strath; light meals £4-7; 9am-5.30pm, shorter hours low season) More the sort of place you'd expect to find on the gringo trail in the Andes, this offbeat and cosy (if occasionally a touch brusque) spot is a shrine to mountaineering and travelling. It serves tasty savoury bagels, home baking and sustainably sourced coffees. The conservatory is the place to lap up the sun, while the attached Hillbillies Bookshop is worth a browse.There are rather sweet rooms available too.

Loch Maree & Around

Stretching 12 miles between Poolewe and Kinlochewe, Loch Maree is considered one of Scotland's prettiest lochs. At its southern end, tiny Kinlochewe makes a good base for outdoor activities.

Beinn Eighe Mountain Trail WALKING
This waymarked 4-mile return walk to a plateau and cairn on the side of Beinn Eighe offers magnificent views over Loch Maree. It's quite exposed up here, so take some warm clothing. It starts from a car park on the A832 about a mile and a half northwest of the Beinn Eighe visitor centre.

★ **Whistle Stop Cafe** CAFE, BISTRO **$$**
(01445-760423; Kinlochewe; meals £8-16; 9am-6pm Mar-Nov, check for evening opening hours) A colourful presence in the former village hall, this is a tempting place to drop by for anything from a coffee to enticing bistro fare. There are great daily specials and delicious home baking, juices and smoothies. It's very friendly, and used to pumping life back into chilled walkers and cyclists. It's unlicensed, but you can take your own wine (£1 corkage).

Torridon & Around

The road southwest from Kinlochewe passes through Glen Torridon, amid some of Britain's most beautiful scenery. Carved by ice from massive layers of ancient sandstone that takes its name from the region, the mountains here are steep, shapely and imposing, whether flirting with autumn mists, draped in dazzling winter snows, or reflected in the calm blue waters of Loch Torridon on a summer day.

The road reaches the sea at spectacularly sited Torridon village, then continues westwards to lovely Shieldaig, which boasts an attractive main street of whitewashed houses right on the water.

Torridon Sea Tours BOATING
(01520-755353; www.torridonseatours.com; Shieldaig) Runs various trips from Shieldaig, including 1½-hour morning or evening cruises on Loch Torridon (adult/child £30/20) and half-day (£50/30) or full-day (£100/50) cruises around offshore islands. You're a good chance of seeing wildlife including sea eagles and porpoises.

★ **The Torridon** HOTEL **$$$**
(01445-791242; www.thetorridon.com; Torridon; r standard/superior/master £245/370/450; closed Jan, plus Mon & Tue Nov, Dec, Feb & Mar; P @ wi-fi pets) If you prefer the lap of luxury to the sound of rain beating on your tent, head for this lavish Victorian shooting lodge with a romantic lochside location. Sumptuous contemporary rooms with awe-inspiring views and top bathrooms and a cheery Highland cow atop the counterpane couldn't be more inviting. This is one of Scotland's top country hotels, always luxurious but never pretentious.

Master suites are lavish in size and comfort, with a more classic decor and bay windows making the most of the panoramas. Service is excellent, with muddy boots positively welcomed, and dinners are sumptuous affairs, open to nonguests (£60). Friendly staff can organise any number of activities on land or water.

Shieldaig Bar & Coastal Kitchen SEAFOOD $$

(☎01520-755251; www.shieldaigbarandcoastalkitchen.co.uk; Shieldaig; mains £9-17; ⏰noon-2.30pm & 6-8.30pm Sep-Jun, noon-8.30pm Jul & Aug; 📶) This attractive pub has real ales and waterside tables plus a great upstairs dining room and outdoor deck for more casual dining, with an emphasis on local seafood and bistro-style meat dishes like steak-frites or sausages and mash. Blackboard specials feature the daily catch.

Applecross

POP 200

The delightfully remote seaside village of Applecross feels like an island retreat due to its isolation and the magnificent views of Raasay and the hills of Skye that set the pulse racing, particularly at sunset. On a clear day it's an unforgettable place. The campsite and pub fill to the brim in school holidays.

A road leads here 25 winding miles from Shieldaig, but more spectacular (accessed from further south on the A896) is the magnificent Bealach na Ba (626m; Pass of the Cattle), the third-highest motor road in the UK, and the longest continuous climb. Originally built in 1822, it climbs steeply and hair-raisingly via hairpin bends perched over sheer drops, with gradients up to 25%, then drops dramatically to the village with views of Skye.

Applecross Campsite CAMPGROUND $

(☎01520-744268; www.applecross.uk.com; sites per adult/child £9/4.50, 2-person hut £45; ⏰Mar-Oct; P📶🐾) Just above and behind the waterfront and inn, this offers green grassy plots, cute little wooden cabins and a good greenhouse-like cafe.

★Applecross Inn INN $$

(☎01520-744262; www.applecross.uk.com; Shore St; mains £9-18; ⏰noon-9pm; P📶) 🍃 The perfect shoreside location for a sunset pint, with its spectacular vistas of Skye, Raasay and the sea, this remote inn is deservedly famous for its food. Most of what's on offer are daily blackboard specials concentrating on local seafood and venison. It's all delicious but you should book your table ahead. Priority is given to room guests.

Plockton

POP 400

Idyllic little Plockton, with its perfect cottages lining a perfect bay, looks like it was designed as a film set. And it has indeed served as just that – scenes from *The Wicker Man* (1973) were filmed here, and the village became famous as the location for the 1990s TV series *Hamish Macbeth*.

With all this picture-postcard perfection, it's hardly surprising that Plockton is a tourist hot spot, crammed with day trippers and holidaymakers in summer. But there's no denying its appeal, with 'palm trees' (actually hardy New Zealand cabbage palms) lining the waterfront, a thriving small-boat sailing scene and several good places to stay, eat and drink. The big event of the year is the Plockton Regatta.

Calum's Seal Trips BOATING

(☎01599-544306; www.calums-sealtrips.com; adult/child £11.50/6; ⏰Apr-Oct) Seal-watching cruises visit swarms of the slippery fellas just outside the harbour. There's an excellent commentary and you may even spot otters too. Trips leave several times daily. There's also a longer dolphin-watching trip available.

🛏 Sleeping & Eating

Plockton Station Bunkhouse HOSTEL $

(☎01599-544235; mickcoe@btInternet.com; dm £16; P📶) Airily set in the former train station (the new one is opposite), this hostel has cosy four-bed dorms, a garden and kitchen-lounge with plenty of light and good perspectives over the frenetic comings-and-goings (OK, that last bit's a lie) of the platforms below. The owners also do good-value B&B accommodation (single/double £35/54) next door in the inaccurately named 'Nessun Dorma'.

★Tigh Arran B&B $$

(☎01599-544307; www.plocktonbedandbreakfast.com; Duirinish; s/d £60/70; P📶🐾) It's hard to decide which is better at this sweet spot 2 miles from the Plockton shorefront – the warm personal welcome or the absolutely stunning views across to Skye. All three of the en suite rooms – with appealing family options – enjoy the views, as does the comfy lounge. A top spot, far from stress and noise; great value too.

Plockton Hotel INN $$
(☎01599-544274; www.plocktonhotel.co.uk; 41 Harbour St; s/d £95/140, cottage s/d £60/90;) Black-painted Plockton Hotel is one of those classic Highland spots that manages to make everyone happy, whether it's thirst, hunger or fatigue that brings you knocking. Assiduously tended rooms are a delight, with excellent facilities and thoughtful touches. Those without a water view are consoled with more space and a balcony with rock-garden perspectives. The cottage nearby offers simpler comfort.

★ **Plockton Shores** SEAFOOD $$
(☎01599-544263; www.plocktonshoresrestaurant.com; 30 Harbour St; mains £11-19; noon-2.15pm & 6-9pm Tue-Sat, noon-2.30pm & 6-9pm Sun;) This welcoming restaurant attached to a shop sports a tempting menu of local seafood, including good-value platters with langoustines, mussels, crab, squat lobster and more, or succulent hand-dived tempura scallops. There's also a very tasty line in venison, steaks and a small selection of tasty vegetarian dishes that are more than an afterthought. Breakfast, teas and snacks are served from morning until night.

Getting There & Away

Trains running between Kyle of Lochalsh (£2.70, 15 minutes) and Inverness (£21.90, 2½ hours) stop in Plockton up to four times daily each way.

Kyle of Lochalsh

POP 700

Before the bridge was opened in 1995, this was Skye's principal mainland ferry port. Visitors now tend to buzz through town, but Kyle has some good boat trips if you're interested in marine life and there's some great seafood eating to be done here.

There's a string of B&Bs just outside of town on the road to Plockton.

Citylink runs two to three daily buses from Inverness (£20.50, two hours) and three from Glasgow (£39, five to six hours).

The train route between Kyle of Lochalsh and Inverness (£22.80, 2½ hours, up to four daily) is marvellously scenic.

Eilean Donan Castle

Eilean Donan Castle CASTLE
(☎01599-555202; www.eileandonancastle.com; A87, Dornie; adult/child/family £7/6/17; 10am-6pm Apr-Oct, to 4pm Nov-Jan, to 5pm Feb-Mar) Photogenically sited at the entrance to Loch Duich, Eilean Donan is one of Scotland's most evocative castles and must now be represented in millions of photo albums. It's on an offshore islet, elegantly linked to the mainland by a stone-arched bridge. It's very much a re-creation inside, with an excellent introductory exhibition. Citylink buses from Fort William and Inverness to Portree stop opposite the castle.

SKYE

POP 10,000

The Isle of Skye (an t-Eilean Sgiathanach in Gaelic) takes its name from the old Norse *sky-a*, meaning 'cloud island', a Viking reference to the often-mist-enshrouded Cuillin Hills. It's the second-largest of Scotland's islands, a 50-mile-long patchwork of velvet moors, jagged mountains, sparkling lochs and towering sea cliffs.

The stunning scenery is the main attraction, but when the mist closes in there are plenty of castles, crofting museums and cosy pubs and restaurants; there are also dozens of art galleries and craft studios.

Along with Edinburgh and Loch Ness, Skye is one of Scotland's top-three tourist destinations. However, the crowds tend to stick to Portree, Dunvegan and Trotternish – it's almost always possible to find peace and quiet in the island's further-flung corners. Come prepared for changeable weather: when it's fine it's very fine indeed, but all too often it isn't.

Activities

Walking

Skye offers some of the finest – and in places, the roughest and most difficult – walking in Scotland. There are many detailed guidebooks available, including a series of four walking guides by Charles Rhodes, available from the **Aros Centre** (☎01478-613750; www.aros.co.uk; Viewfield Rd, Portree; exhibition £5; 9am-5pm; P) FREE and the tourist office in Portree. You'll need Ordnance Survey (OS) 1:50,000 maps 23 and 32, or Harvey's 1:25,000 *Superwalker – The Cuillin*. Don't attempt the longer walks in bad weather or in winter.

Skye Wilderness Safaris (☎01470-552292; www.skye-wilderness-safaris.com; per person £95-120; May-Sep) runs one-day

Skye & Outer Hebrides

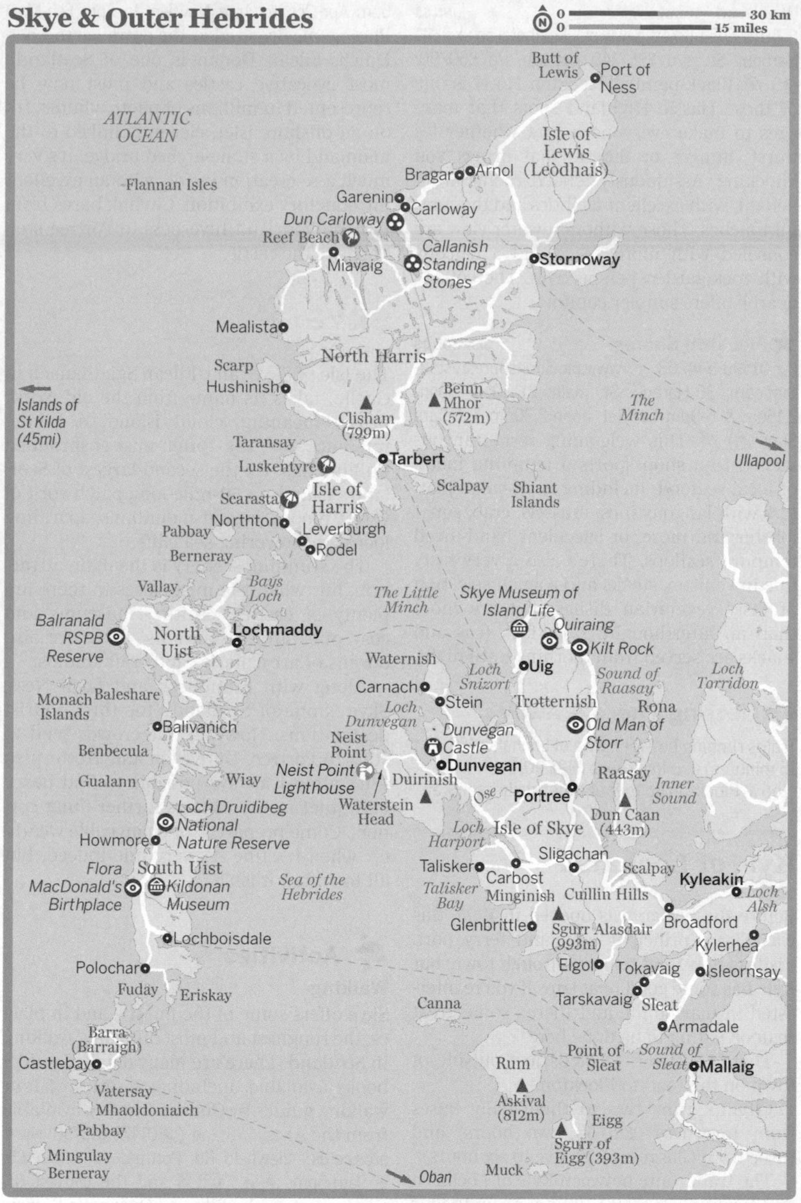

guided hiking trips for small groups (four to six people) through the Cuillin Hills, into the Quiraing or along the Trotternish ridge; transport to/from Portree included.

Climbing

The Cuillin Hills is a playground for rock climbers, and the two-day traverse of the **Cuillin Ridge** is the finest mountaineering expedition in the British Isles. There are several mountain guides in the area who can provide instruction and safely introduce inexperienced climbers to the more difficult routes.

Skye Guides (☎01471-822116; www.skyeguides.co.uk) offers a two-day introduction to rock climbing course for around £420; a private mountain guide can be hired for £260 a day (both rates are for two clients).

Sea Kayaking

The sheltered coves and sea lochs around the coast of Skye provide enthusiasts with magnificent sea-kayaking opportunities.

Skyak Adventures KAYAKING
(☎01471-820002; www.skyakadventures.com; 29 Lower Breakish, Breakish; 1-day course per person from £100) Expeditions and courses for both beginners and experienced paddlers to otherwise inaccessible places. Specialist courses include photography and tidal race paddling.

Whitewave Outdoor Centre KAYAKING
(☎01470-542414; www.white-wave.co.uk; 19 Linicro, Kilmuir; half-day kayak session per person £40-50; ⏲Mar-Oct) Provides sea kayaking instruction and guiding for both beginners and experts; prices include equipment hire. Other activities include mountain-boarding, bushcraft and rock climbing.

Tours

There are several operators who offer guided minibus tours of Skye, covering history, culture and wildlife. Rates are from £150 to £200 for a six-hour tour for up to six people.

SkyeBus BUS
(☎01470-532428; www.realscottishjourneys.com; adult/child £43/38) Runs full-day minibus tours from Portree to remote parts of the island, including the Quiraing, Neist Point, and the Fairy Pools in Glenbrittle.

Skye Tours BUS
(☎01471-822716; www.skye-tours.co.uk; adult/child £35/30; ⏲Mon-Sat) Five-hour sightseeing tours of Skye in a minibus, taking in the Old Man of Storr, Kilt Rock and Dunvegan Castle. Depart from Kyle of Lochalsh train station at 11.30am (connects with 8.55am train from Inverness, returns to Kyle by 4.45pm in time to catch the return train at 5.13pm).

Information

Only Portree and Broadford have banks and ATMs. Portree's tourist office has a currency exchange desk.

Portree Tourist Office (☎01478-612992; www.visitscotland.com; Bayfield Rd; ⏲9am-6pm Mon-Sat, 10am-4pm Sun Jun-Aug, shorter hours Sep-May;) The only tourist office on the island; provides internet access and currency exchange. Ask for the free *Art Skye – Gallery & Studio Trails* booklet.

Getting There & Away

BOAT

Despite the bridge, there are still a couple of ferry links between Skye and the mainland. Ferries also operate from Uig on Skye to the Outer Hebrides.

The **CalMac** (☎0800 066 5000; www.calmac.co.uk; per person/car £2.80/9.40) ferry between Mallaig and Armadale (30 minutes, eight daily Monday to Saturday, five to seven on Sunday) is very popular on weekends and in July and August. Book ahead if you're travelling by car.

Skye Ferry (www.skyeferry.co.uk; car with up to 4 passengers £15; ⏲Easter–mid Oct) runs a tiny vessel (six cars only) on the short Kylerhea to Glenelg crossing (five minutes, every 20

MADDENING MIDGES

Forget Nessie; the Highlands have a real monster. A voracious bloodsucking female fully 3mm long named the Highland midge *(culicoides impunctatus)*. The bane of campers and as much a symbol of Scotland as the kilt or dram, they drive sane folk to distraction, descending in biting clouds.

Though normally vegetarian, the female midge needs a dose of blood in order to lay her eggs. And, like it or not, if you're in the Highlands between June and August, you just volunteered as a donor. Midges especially congregate near water, and are most active in the early morning, though squadrons also patrol in the late evening.

Repellents and creams are reasonably effective, though some walkers favour midge veils. Light-coloured clothing also helps. Many pubs and campsites have midge-zappers. Check www.midgeforecast.co.uk for activity levels by area, but don't blame us: we've been eaten alive when the forecast said moderate too.

minutes). The ferry operates from 10am to 6pm daily (till 7pm June to August).

BUS

There are buses from Glasgow to Portree (£42, seven hours, three daily), and Uig (£42, 7½ hours, two daily) via Crianlarich, Fort William and Kyle of Lochalsh, plus a service from Inverness to Portree (£25, 3¼ hours, three daily).

CAR & MOTORCYCLE

The Isle of Skye became permanently tethered to the Scottish mainland when the Skye Bridge opened in 1995. The controversial bridge tolls were abolished in 2004 and the crossing is now free.

Much of the driving is on single-track roads – remember to use passing places to allow any traffic behind you to overtake. There are petrol stations at Broadford (open 24 hours), Armadale, Portree, Dunvegan and Uig.

Getting Around

BUS

Getting around the island by public transport can be a pain, especially if you want to explore away from the main Kyleakin–Portree–Uig road. Here, as in much of the Highlands, there are fewer buses on Saturday and only a handful of Sunday services.

Stagecoach (www.stagecoachbus.com) operates the main bus routes on the island, linking all the main villages and towns. Its Skye Dayrider/Megarider ticket gives unlimited bus travel for one day/seven days for £8.50/32. For timetable info, call Traveline (p795).

TAXI

You can order a taxi or hire a car (arrange for the car to be waiting at Kyle of Lochalsh train station) from **Kyle Taxi Company** (☎01599-534323; www.skyecarhire.co.uk; car hire day/week from around £40/240).

Broadford (An T-Ath Leathann)

POP 750

The long, straggling village of Broadford is a service centre for the scattered communities of southern Skye.

Broadford has a 24-hour petrol station, a bank and a large **Co-op supermarket** (⏲8am-10pm Mon-Sat, 9am-6pm Sun) with an ATM.

There are lots of B&Bs in and around Broadford and the village is well placed for exploring southern Skye by car.

★Tigh an Dochais B&B $$

(☎01471-820022; www.skyebedbreakfast.co.uk; 13 Harrapool; d £105; P ᯤ) A cleverly designed modern building, Tigh an Dochais is one of Skye's best B&Bs – a little footbridge leads to the front door, which is on the 1st floor. Here you'll find the dining room (gorgeous breakfasts) and lounge offering a stunning view of sea and hills; the bedrooms (downstairs) open onto an outdoor deck with that same wonderful view.

★Creelers SEAFOOD $$

(☎01471-822281; www.skye-seafood-restaurant.co.uk; Lower Harrapool; mains £14-19; ⏲noon-8.30pm Tue-Sat Mar-Oct;) Broadford has several places to eat but one really stands out: Creelers is a small, bustling, no-frills restaurant that serves some of the best seafood on Skye. The house speciality is traditional Marseille *bouillabaisse* (a rich, spicy seafood stew). Best to book ahead.

Armadale & Sleat

If you cross over the sea to Skye on the ferry from Mallaig you arrive in Armadale, at the southern end of the long, low-lying peninsula known as Sleat (pronounced 'slate'). The landscape of Sleat itself is not exceptional, but it provides a grandstand for ogling the magnificent scenery on either side – take the steep and twisting minor road that loops through Tarskavaig and Tokavaig for stunning views of the Isle of Rum, the Cuillin Hills and Bla Bheinn.

Armadale, where the ferry from Mallaig arrives, is little more than a store, a post office, a cluster of craft shops and a scattering of houses.

The northern part of Sleat, around Isleornsay, has a cluster of fine-dining restaurants attached to luxury hotels. Most famous is Kinloch Lodge, where you can attend **cookery courses** (☎01471-833333; www.kinloch-lodge.co.uk; Kinloch, Sleat) run by Lady Claire Macdonald.

There are six or seven buses a day Monday to Saturday (three on Sunday) from Armadale to Broadford (£3.60, 30 minutes) and Portree (£7, 1¼ hours).

Museum of the Isles MUSEUM

(☎01471-844305; www.clandonald.com; adult/child £8.50/6.95; ⏲9.30am-5.30pm Apr-Oct, occasionally shorter hours Oct; P) Just along the road from Armadale pier is the part-ruined

Armadale Castle, former seat of Lord MacDonald of Sleat. The neighbouring museum will tell you all you ever wanted to know about Clan Donald, and also provides an easily digestible history of the Lordship of the Isles. Prize exhibits include rare portraits of clan chiefs, and a wine glass that was once used by Bonnie Prince Charlie. The ticket also gives admission to the lovely castle gardens.

★Toravaig House Hotel HOTEL $$
(☎01471-820200; www.toravaig.com; Toravaig; d £110-149; P 📶) This hotel, 3 miles south of Isleornsay, is one of those places where the owners know a thing or two about hospitality – as soon as you arrive you'll feel right at home, whether relaxing on the sofas by the log fire in the lounge or admiring the view across the Sound of Sleat from the lawn chairs in the garden.

The spacious bedrooms – ask for room 1 (Eriskay), with its enormous sleigh bed – are luxuriously equipped, from the crisp bed linen to the huge, high-pressure shower heads. The elegant restaurant serves the best of local fish, game and lamb. After dinner you can retire to the lounge with a single malt and flick through the yachting magazines – you can even arrange a day trip aboard the hotel's 50ft sailing yacht.

Cuillin Hills

The Cuillin Hills are Britain's most spectacular mountain range (the name comes from the Old Norse *kjöllen*, meaning 'keel-shaped'). Though small in stature – Sgurr Alasdair, the highest summit, is only 993m – the peaks are near-alpine in character, with knife-edge ridges, jagged pinnacles, scree-filled gullies and hectares of naked rock. While they are a paradise for experienced mountaineers, the higher reaches of the Cuillin are off limits to the majority of walkers.

The good news is that there are also plenty of good low-level hikes within the ability of most walkers. One of the best (on a fine day) is the steep climb from Glenbrittle campsite to **Coire Lagan** (6 miles round-trip; allow at least three hours). The impressive upper corrie contains a lochan for bathing (for the hardy!), and the surrounding cliffs are a playground for rock climbers – bring your binoculars.

Even more spectacular, but much harder to reach on foot, is **Loch Coruisk** (from the Gaelic Coir'Uisg, the Water Corrie), a remote loch ringed by the highest peaks of the Cuillin. Accessible by **boat trip** (☎0800 731 3089; www.bellajane.co.uk; Elgol Pier; adult/child £26/14; ⏲Apr-Oct) from Elgol, or via an arduous 5.5-mile hike from Kilmarie, Coruisk was popularised by Sir Walter Scott in his 1815 poem *Lord of the Isles*. Crowds of Victorian tourists and landscape artists followed in Scott's footsteps, including JMW Turner, whose watercolours were used to illustrate Scott's work.

There are two main bases for exploring the Cuillin – **Sligachan** to the north (on the Kyle of Lochalsh–Portree bus route), and **Glenbrittle** to the south (no public transport).

Sligachan Hotel HOTEL $$$
(☎01478-650204; www.sligachan.co.uk; Sligachan; per person from £70; P 📶) The Slig, as it has been known to generations of climbers, is a near village in itself, encompassing a comfortable hotel, a microbrewery, self-catering cottages, a small mountaineering museum, a big barn of a pub – **Seamus Bar** (mains £10-15; ⏲food served 11am-9.30pm; 📶 👪) – and an adventure playground.

Portree (Port Righ)

POP 2300

Portree is Skye's largest and liveliest town. It has a pretty harbour lined with brightly painted houses, and there are great views of the surrounding hills. Its name (from the Gaelic for King's Harbour) commemorates James V, who came here in 1540 to pacify the local clans.

🛏 Sleeping

Portree is well supplied with B&Bs, but accommodation fills up fast in July and August, so be sure to book ahead.

Portree Youth Hostel HOSTEL $
(SYHA; ☎01478-612231; www.syha.org.uk; Bayfield Rd; dm/tw £24/66; P 📶) This brand new SYHA hostel (formerly Bayfield Backpackers) has been completely renovated and offers brightly decorated dorms and private rooms, a stylish lounge with views over the bay, and outdoor seating areas, with an ideal location in the town centre just 100m from the bus stop.

Torvaig Campsite CAMPGROUND $
(☎01478-611849; www.portreecampsite.co.uk; Torvaig; sites per adult/child £8/3; ⏱Apr-Oct; 📶) An attractive, family-run campsite located 1.5 miles north of Portree, on the road to Staffin.

Ben Tianavaig B&B B&B $$
(☎01478-612152; www.ben-tianavaig.co.uk; 5 Bosville Tce; r £78-90; P📶) 🍃 A warm welcome awaits from the Irish-Welsh couple who run this appealing B&B bang in the centre of town. All four bedrooms have a view across the harbour to the hill that gives the house its name and breakfasts include free-range eggs and vegetables grown in the garden. Two-night minimum stay April to October; no credit cards.

Woodlands B&B $$
(☎01478-612980; www.woodlands-portree.co.uk; Viewfield Rd; r £70; ⏱Mar-Oct; P📶) A great location, with views across the bay, and unstinting hospitality make this modern B&B, a half-mile south of the town centre, a good choice.

Cuillin Hills Hotel HOTEL $$$
(☎01478-612003; www.cuillinhills-hotel-skye.co.uk; Scorrybreac Rd; r from £240; P📶) Located on the eastern fringes of Portree, this luxury hotel enjoys a superb outlook across the harbour towards the Cuillin mountains. The more expensive rooms cosset guests with four-poster beds and panoramic views, but everyone can enjoy the scenery from the glass-fronted restaurant and well-stocked whisky bar.

Eating

Café Arriba CAFE $
(☎01478-611830; www.cafearriba.co.uk; Quay Brae; mains £6-12; ⏱7am-6pm daily May-Sep, 8am-5pm Thu-Sat Oct-Apr; ✎) 🍃 Arriba is a funky little cafe, brightly decked out in primary colours and offering delicious flatbread melts (bacon, leek and cheese is a favourite), as well as the best choice of vegetarian grub on the island, ranging from a veggie breakfast fry-up to falafel wraps with hummus and chilli sauce. Also serves excellent coffee.

★**Scorrybreac** MODERN SCOTTISH $$
(☎01478-612069; www.scorrybreac.com; 7 Bosville Tce; 2-/3-course dinner £27.50/32.50; ⏱5-9.30pm Tue-Sat) 🍃 Set in the front rooms of what was once a private house, and with just eight tables, Scorrybreac is snug and intimate, offering fine dining without the faff. Chef Calum Munro (son of Donnie Munro, of Gaelic rock band Runrig fame) sources as much produce as possible from Skye, including foraged herbs and mushrooms, and creates the most exquisite concoctions.

Dulse & Brose MODERN SCOTTISH $$
(☎01478-612846; www.bosvillehotel.co.uk; Bosville Hotel, 7 Bosville Tce; mains £15-22; ⏱noon-3pm & 6-10pm; 📶) 🍃 This hotel restaurant sports a relaxed atmosphere, an award-winning chef and a menu that makes the most of Skye produce – including lamb, game, seafood, cheese, organic vegetables and berries – and adds a French twist to traditional dishes. The neighbouring **Merchant Bar** serves tapas-style bar snacks through the afternoon.

Getting There & Around

BUS

The main bus stop is at Somerled Sq. There are six Scottish Citylink buses every day from Kyle of Lochalsh to Portree (£6.70, one hour) continuing to Uig.

Local buses (mostly six to eight Monday to Saturday, three on Sunday) run from Portree to:

Armadale (£7, 1¼ hours) Connecting with the ferry to Mallaig.

Broadford (£5.30, 40 minutes)

Dunvegan Castle (£4.80, 40 minutes, one daily)

There are also three buses a day on a circular route around Trotternish (in both directions), taking in Flodigarry (£4.10, 35 minutes), Kilmuir (£4.80, 45 minutes) and Uig (£3.60, 30 minutes).

BICYCLE

Island Cycles (☎01478-613121; www.islandcycles-skye.co.uk; The Green; hire bike per half-/full day £8.50/17.50; ⏱9am-5pm Mon-Sat) You can hire bikes here.

Dunvegan (Dun Bheagain) & Around

Dunvegan, an unremarkable village on the western side of Skye, is famous for its historic namesake castle which has links to Sir Walter Scott and Bonnie Prince Charlie.

The Duirinish peninsula to the west of Dunvegan, and Waternish to the north, boast some of Skye's most atmospheric hotels and restaurants, plus an eclectic range of artists studios and crafts workshops.

Dunvegan Castle CASTLE

(☎01470-521206; www.dunvegancastle.com; adult/child £12/9; ⏲10am-5.30pm Apr–mid-Oct; P) Skye's most famous historic building, and one of its most popular tourist attractions, Dunvegan Castle is the seat of the chief of Clan MacLeod. In addition to the usual castle stuff – swords, silver and family portraits – there are some interesting artefacts, including the Fairy Flag, a diaphanous silk banner that dates from some time between the 4th and 7th centuries, and Bonnie Prince Charlie's waistcoat and a lock of his hair, donated by Flora MacDonald's granddaughter.

★Hillstone Lodge B&B $$

(☎01470-511434; www.hillstonelodge.com; 12 Colbost; s/d £110/120; P 📶) You can't help notice the many new houses on Skye that bear the hallmarks of award-winning local architects Rural Design – weathered timber walls and modern materials used with traditional shapes and forms. Hillstone is one of the best, with tasteful modern styling and stunning views across Loch Dunvegan. It's about 1km north of the Three Chimneys, above the pier.

★Red Roof Café CAFE $$

(☎01470-511766; www.redroofskye.co.uk; Glendale, Duirinish; mains £9-13; ⏲11am-5pm Sun-Thu Easter-Oct; P 📶) Tucked away up a glen, a mile off the main road, this restored 250-year-old byre is a wee haven of home-grown grub. As well as great coffee and cake, there are lunch platters (noon to 3pm) of Skye seafood, game or cheese served with salad leaves and edible flowers grown just along the road.

★Three Chimneys MODERN SCOTTISH $$$

(☎01470-511258; www.threechimneys.co.uk; Colbost; 3-course lunch/dinner £38/65; ⏲12.15-1.45pm Mon-Sat mid-Mar–Oct, plus Sun Easter-Sep, 6.15-9pm daily year-round; P 📶) Halfway between Dunvegan and Waterstein, the Three Chimneys is a superb romantic retreat combining a gourmet restaurant in a candlelit crofter's cottage with sumptuous five-star rooms (double £345) in the modern house next door. Book well in advance, and note that children are not welcome in the restaurant in the evenings.

DINOSAUR FOOTPRINTS ON SKYE

The occasional dinosaur bone has been turning up in the Jurassic rocks of the Trotternish peninsula since 1982 – intriguing, but nothing very exciting. Then, following a storm in 2002, a set of fossilised dinosaur footprints was exposed at An Corran in Staffin Bay. Their interest piqued, geologists began taking a closer interest in the Trotternish rocks and, in 2015, a major discovery was made near Duntulm Castle – a 170-million-year-old trackway of footprints left by a group of sauropods. Skye is now a major focus for research into dinosaur evolution.

A collection of Jurassic fossils and further information on dinosaur sites in Skye can be found at the **Staffin Dinosaur Museum** (www.facebook.com/StaffinDinosaurMuseum; 3 Ellishadder, Staffin; adult/child £2/1; ⏲10.30am-1pm Mon, Tue, Thu & Fri Easter-Sep; P).

Trotternish

The Trotternish Peninsula to the north of Portree has some of Skye's most beautiful – and bizarre – scenery. A loop road allows a circular driving tour of the peninsula from Portree, passing through the village of Uig, where the ferry to the Outer Hebrides departs.

★Quiraing ROCK FORMATION

Staffin Bay is dominated by the dramatic basalt escarpment of the Quiraing: its impressive land-slipped cliffs and pinnacles constitute one of Skye's most remarkable landscapes. From a parking area at the highest point of the minor road between Staffin and Uig you can walk north to the Quiraing in half an hour.

Old Man of Storr ROCK FORMATION

(P) The 50m-high, pot-bellied pinnacle of crumbling basalt known as the Old Man of Storr is prominent above the road 6 miles north of Portree. Walk up to its foot from the car park at the northern end of Loch Leathan (2-mile round-trip). This seemingly unclimbable pinnacle was first scaled in 1955 by English mountaineer Don Whillans, a feat that has been repeated only a handful of times since.

Skye Museum of Island Life MUSEUM
(☎01470-552206; www.skyemuseum.co.uk; Kilmuir; adult/child £2.50/50p; ⊙9.30am-5pm Mon-Sat Easter-late Sep; P) The peat-reek of crofting life in the 18th and 19th centuries is preserved in the thatched cottages, croft houses, barns and farm implements of the Skye Museum of Island Life. Behind the museum is Kilmuir Cemetery, where a tall Celtic cross marks the grave of Flora MacDonald; the cross was erected in 1955 to replace the original monument, of which 'every fragment was removed by tourists'.

★**Cowshed Boutique Bunkhouse** HOSTEL $
(☎07917 536820; www.skyecowshed.co.uk; Uig; dm/tw £20/80, pod £70; P) This new hostel enjoys a glorious setting overlooking Uig Bay, with superb views from its ultra-stylish lounge. The dorms have custom-built wooden bunks that offer comfort and privacy, while the camping pods (sleeping up to four, but more comfortable with two) have heating and en suite shower rooms; there are even mini 'dog pods' for your canine companions.

OUTER HEBRIDES

The Western Isles, or Na h-Eileanan an Iar in Gaelic – also known as the Outer Hebrides – are a 130-mile-long string of islands lying off the northwest coast of Scotland. There are 119 islands in total, of which the five main inhabited islands are Lewis and Harris (two parts of a single island, although often described as if they are separate islands), North Uist, Benbecula, South Uist and Barra. The middle three (often referred to simply as 'the Uists') are connected by road-bearing causeways.

The ferry crossing from Ullapool or Uig to the Western Isles marks an important cultural divide – more than a third of Scotland's registered crofts are in the Outer Hebrides, and no less than 60% of the population are Gaelic speakers. The rigours of life in the old island blackhouses are still within living memory.

Religion still plays a prominent part in public and private life, especially in the Protestant north, where shops and pubs close their doors on Sunday and some accommodation providers prefer guests not to arrive or depart on the Sabbath. The Roman Catholic south is a little more relaxed about these things.

If your time is limited, head straight for the west coast of Lewis with its prehistoric sites, preserved blackhouses and beautiful beaches. As with Skye, the islands are dotted with arts and crafts studios – the tourist offices can provide a list.

Information

Castlebay Tourist Office (☎01871-810336; www.visithebrides.com; Main St, Castlebay; ⊙9.15am-1pm & 2-4.45pm Mon-Sat, noon-4pm Sun Jul & Aug, shorter hours Apr-May & Sep)
Stornoway Tourist Office (☎01851-703088; www.visithebrides.com; 26 Cromwell St, Stornoway; ⊙9am-6pm Mon-Sat year-round)
Tarbert Tourist Office (☎01859-502011; www.visithebrides.com; Pier Rd; ⊙9am-5pm Mon-Sat Apr-Oct)

Getting There & Away

AIR

There are airports at Stornoway (Lewis), Benbecula and Barra. Flights operate to Stornoway from Edinburgh, Inverness, Glasgow and Aberdeen. There are also two flights a day (Tuesday to Thursday only) between Stornoway and Benbecula.

There are daily flights from Glasgow to Barra, and from Tuesday to Thursday to Benbecula. At Barra, the planes land on the hard-sand beach at low tide, so the schedule depends on the tides.

Eastern Airways (☎0870 366 9100; www.easternairways.com)
FlyBe/Loganair (☎01857-873457; www.loganair.co.uk)

BOAT

Standard one-way fares on **CalMac** (☎0800 066 5000; www.calmac.co.uk) ferries:

CROSSING	DURATION (HRS)	CAR (£)	DRIVER/PASSENGER (£)
Ullapool–Stornoway	2¾	49.50	9.20
Uig–Lochmaddy	1¾	30	6.10
Uig–Tarbert	1½	30	6.10
Oban–Castlebay	4¾	66	14.30
Mallaig–Lochboisdale	3½	56	10.15

There are two or three ferries a day to Stornoway, one or two a day to Tarbert and Lochmaddy, and one a day to Castlebay and Lochboisdale.

Advance booking for cars is recommended (essential in July and August); foot and bicycle passengers should have no problems. Bicycles are carried free.

Getting Around

Despite their separate names, Lewis and Harris are actually one island. Berneray, North Uist, Benbecula, South Uist and Eriskay are all linked by road bridges and causeways. There are car ferries between Leverburgh (Harris) and Berneray and between Eriskay and Castlebay (Barra).

The local council publishes timetables of all bus and ferry services within the Outer Hebrides, which is available at tourist offices. Timetables can also be found online at www.cne-siar.gov.uk/travel.

BICYCLE

Bikes can be hired for around £12 to £15 a day or £60 to £80 a week in Stornoway (Lewis), Uig (Lewis), Leverburgh (Harris), Howmore (South Uist) and Castlebay (Barra).

BUS

The bus network covers almost every village in the islands, with around four to six buses a day on all the main routes; however, there are no buses at all on Sunday. You can pick up timetables from tourist offices, or call **Stornoway bus station** (01851-704327) for information.

CAR & MOTORCYCLE

Apart from the fast, two-lane road between Tarbert and Stornoway, most roads are single track. The main hazard is posed by sheep wandering about or sleeping on the road. Petrol stations are far apart (almost all of those on Lewis and Harris are closed on Sunday), and fuel is about 10% more expensive than on the mainland.

There are petrol stations at Stornoway, Barvas, Borve, Uig, Breacleit (Great Bernera), Ness, Tarbert and Leverburgh on Lewis and Harris; Lochmaddy and Cladach on North Uist; Balivanich on Benbecula; Howmore, Lochboisdale and Daliburgh on South Uist; and Castlebay on Barra.

Cars can be hired from around £35 per day.

Arnol Motors (018510-710548; www.arnolmotors.com; Arnol, Lewis; per day from £40; 8am-5pm Mon-Sat)

Lewis Car Rentals (01851-703760; www.lewis-car-rental.co.uk; 52 Bayhead St; per day from £40; 8am-5pm Mon-Sat)

Lewis (Leodhais)

POP 21,000 (INCLUDING HARRIS)

The northern part of Lewis is dominated by the desolate expanse of the Black Moor, a vast, undulating peat bog dimpled with glittering lochans, seen clearly from the Stornoway–Barvas road. But Lewis' finest scenery is on the west coast, from Barvas southwest to Mealista, where the rugged landscape of hill, loch and sandy strand is reminiscent of the northwestern Highlands. The Outer Hebrides' most evocative historic sites – Callanish Standing Stones, Dun Carloway and Arnol Blackhouse Museum – are also to be found here.

Stornoway (Steornabhagh)

POP 5715

Stornoway is the bustling 'capital' of the Outer Hebrides and the only real town in the whole archipelago. It's a surprisingly busy little place, with cars and people swamping the centre on weekdays. Though set on a beautiful natural harbour, the town isn't going to win any prizes for beauty or atmosphere, but it's a pleasant enough introduction to this remote corner of the country.

Sights

Lews Castle CASTLE

(01851-822750; www.lews-castle.co.uk; 10am-5pm Mon-sat May-Sep, shorter hours Oct-Apr; P) FREE The Baronial mansion across the harbour from Stornoway town centre was built in the 1840s for the Matheson family, then owners of Lewis; it was gifted to the community by Lord Leverhulme in 1923. A major redevelopment sees the new **Museum nan Eilean** (Museum of the Isles) opening here from late 2016, covering the history of the Outer Hebrides and exploring traditional island life. It's hoped that some of the famous Lewis chessmen will be on display.

The beautiful wooded grounds, crisscrossed with walking trails, are open to the public and host the Hebridean Celtic Festival (p936) in July.

An Lanntair Arts Centre ARTS CENTRE

(01851-708480; www.lanntair.com; Kenneth St; 10am-9pm Mon-Wed, to 10pm Thu, to midnight Fri & Sat) FREE The modern, purpose-built An Lanntair (Gaelic for 'lighthouse'), complete with art gallery, theatre, cinema and restaurant, is the centre of the town's cultural life.

It hosts changing exhibitions of contemporary art and is a good source of information on cultural events.

Festivals & Events

Hebridean Celtic Festival MUSIC
(www.hebceltfest.com; Jul) A four-day extravaganza of folk, rock and Celtic music held in the second half of July.

Sleeping

Heb Hostel HOSTEL $
(01851-709889; www.hebhostel.com; 25 Kenneth St; dm £18;) The Heb is a friendly, easy-going hostel close to the ferry, with comfy wooden bunks, a convivial living room with peat fire and a welcoming owner who can provide all kinds of advice on what to do and where to go.

Laxdale Holiday Park CAMPGROUND $
(01851-703234; www.laxdaleholidaypark.com; 6 Laxdale Lane; tent sites £9-11, plus per person £3.50; Mar-Oct;) This campsite, 1.5 miles north of town off the A857, has a sheltered woodland setting, though the tent area is mostly on a slope – get there early for a level pitch. There are also wooden camping pods (per night £36 to £42), and a bunkhouse (£18 per person) that stays open year-round.

Hal o' the Wynd B&B $$
(01851-706073; www.halothewynd.com; 2 Newton St; s/d from £60/80;) Touches of tartan and Harris Tweed lend a traditional air to this welcoming B&B, conveniently located directly opposite the ferry pier. Most rooms have views over the harbour to Lews Castle. There's also a cafe on the premises.

Park Guest House B&B $$
(01851-702485; www.the-parkguesthouse.com; 30 James St; s/d from £79/110;) A charming Victorian villa with a conservatory and six luxurious rooms (mostly en suite), the Park Guest House is comfortable and central and has the advantage of an excellent restaurant specialising in Scottish seafood, beef and game plus one or two vegetarian dishes (three-course dinner around £35). Rooms overlooking the main road can be noisy on weekday mornings.

Braighe House B&B $$$
(01851-705287; www.braighehouse.co.uk; 20 Braighe Rd; s/d from £95/130; P) This spacious and luxurious guesthouse, 3 miles east of the town centre on the A866, has stylish, modern bedrooms and a great seafront location. Good bathrooms with powerful showers, hearty breakfasts and genuinely hospitable owners round off the perfect package.

Eating

Artizan Cafe CAFE $
(01851-706538; www.facebook.com/artizanstornoway; 12-14 Church St; 10am-6pm Mon-Fri, 9am-11pm Sat;) Recycled timber and cool colours mark out this cafe-gallery as one of Stornoway's hip hangouts, serving great coffee and cake and tapas-style lunches (noon to 2.30pm). Hosts cultural events, including poetry nights on Saturday.

★ **Digby Chick** BISTRO $$
(01851-700026; www.digbychick.co.uk; 5 Bank St; mains £18-25, 2-course lunch £14.50; noon-2pm & 5.30-9pm Mon-Sat;) A modern restaurant that dishes up bistro cuisine such as haddock and chips, slow-roast pork belly or roast vegetable panini at lunchtime, the Digby Chick metamorphoses into a candlelit gourmet restaurant in the evening, serving dishes such as grilled langoustines, seared scallops, venison and steak. Three-course early-bird menu (5.30pm to 6.30pm) for £22.

Information

Sandwick Rd Petrol Station (Engebret Ltd; 01851-702304; www.engebret.co.uk; Sandwick Rd; 6am-11pm Mon-Sat, 10am-4pm Sun) The only shop in town that's open on a Sunday, selling groceries, alcohol, hardware, fishing tackle and outdoor kit. The Sunday papers arrive around 2pm.

Getting There & Away

The bus station (p935) is on the waterfront next to the ferry terminal (left luggage 25p to £1.30 per piece). Bus W10 runs from Stornoway to Tarbert (£4.80, one hour, four or five daily Monday to Saturday) and Leverburgh (£6.80, two hours).

The Westside Circular bus W2 runs a circular route from Stornoway through Callanish (£2.70, 30 minutes), Carloway, Garenin and Arnol; the timetable allows you to visit one or two of the sites in a day.

Arnol

Arnol Blackhouse HISTORIC BUILDING
(HS; 01851-710395; www.historicenvironment.scot; Arnol; adult/child £4.50/2.70; 9.30am-5.30pm Mon-Sat Apr-Sep, 10am-4pm Mon, Tue &

Thu-Sat Oct-Mar; P) One of Scotland's most evocative historic buildings, the Arnol Blackhouse is not so much a museum as a perfectly preserved fragment of a lost world. Built in 1885, this traditional blackhouse – a combined byre, barn and home – was inhabited until 1964 and has not been changed since the last inhabitant moved out. The museum is about 3 miles west of Barvas.

Garenin (Na Gearrannan)

The picturesque and fascinating Gearrannan Blackhouse Village is a cluster of nine restored thatch-roofed blackhouses perched above the exposed Atlantic coast. One of the cottages is home to the **Blackhouse Museum** (01851-643416; www.gearrannan.com; adult/child £3/1; 9.30am-5.30pm Mon-Sat Apr-Sep; P), a traditional 1955 blackhouse with displays on the village's history, while another houses the **Taigh an Chocair Cafe** (mains £3-6; 9.30am-5.30pm Mon-Sat).

Carloway (Carlabagh)

Dun Carloway HISTORIC SITE

(Dun Charlabhaigh; P) Dun Carloway is a 2000-year-old, dry-stone broch, perched defiantly above a beautiful loch with views to the mountains of North Harris. The site is clearly signposted along a minor road off the A858, a mile southwest of Carloway village. One of the best-preserved brochs in Scotland, its double walls (with internal staircase) still stand to a height of 9m and testify to the engineering skills of its Iron Age architects.

Callanish (Calanais)

Callanish, on the western side of Lewis, is famous for its prehistoric standing stones. One of the most atmospheric prehistoric sites in the whole of Scotland, its ageless mystery, impressive scale and undeniable beauty leave a lasting impression.

Callanish Standing Stones HISTORIC SITE

(01851-621422; 24hr) FREE The Callanish Standing Stones, 15 miles west of Stornoway on the A858 road, form one of the most complete stone circles in Britain. It is one of the most atmospheric prehistoric sites anywhere. Sited on a wild and secluded promontory overlooking Loch Roag, 13 large stones of beautifully banded gneiss are arranged, as if in worship, around a 4.5m-tall central monolith.

Some 40 smaller stones radiate from the circle in the shape of a cross, with the remains of a chambered tomb at the centre. Dating from 3800 to 5000 years ago, the stones are roughly contemporary with the pyramids of Egypt.

Calanais Visitor Centre MUSEUM

(01851-621422; www.callanishvisitorcentre.co.uk; admission free, exhibition £2.50; 9.30am-8pm Mon-Sat Jun-Aug, 10am-6pm Mon-Sat Apr, May, Sep & Oct, 10am-4pm Tue-Sat Nov-Mar; P) This visitor centre near the Callanish Standing Stones is a tour de force of discreet design. Inside is a small exhibition that speculates on the origins and purpose of the stones, and an excellent **cafe** (mains £4-7).

Harris (Na Hearadh)

POP 2000

Harris, to the south of Lewis, is the scenic jewel in the necklace of islands that comprise the Outer Hebrides. It has a spectacular blend of rugged mountains, pristine beaches, flower-speckled machair and barren rocky landscapes. The isthmus at Tarbert splits Harris neatly in two: North Harris is dominated by mountains that rise forbiddingly above the peat moors to the south of Stornoway – Clisham (799m) is the highest point. South Harris is lower-lying, fringed by beautiful white-sand beaches in the west and a convoluted rocky coastline to the east.

Harris is famous for Harris Tweed, a high-quality woollen cloth still hand-woven in islanders' homes. The industry employs around 400 weavers; staff at Tarbert tourist office can tell you about weavers and workshops you can visit.

Tarbert (An Tairbeart)

POP 480

Tarbert is a harbour village with a spectacular location, tucked into the narrow neck of land that links North and South Harris. It is one of the main ferry ports for the Outer Hebrides, and home to the new Isle of Harris Distillery.

Isle of Harris Distillery DISTILLERY

(01859-502212; www.harrisdistillery.com; Main St; tours £10; 10am-5pm Mon-Sat; P) This brand new distillery started production in 2015, so its first batch of single malt whisky won't be ready till 2019; meanwhile, they're producing Isle of Harris gin too. The modern building is very stylish – the lobby feels like a luxury hotel – and 75-minute tours depart two or three times daily in summer (they're popular, so book in advance). There's a **cafe** here too.

Tigh na Mara B&B $
(☎01859-502270; East Tarbert; per person £25-30; P) Excellent-value B&B (though the single room is a bit cramped) just five minutes from the ferry – head up the hill above the tourist office and turn right. The owner bakes fresh cakes every day, which you can enjoy in the conservatory with a view over the bay.

Hotel Hebrides HOTEL $$$
(☎01859-502364; www.hotel-hebrides.com; Pier Rd; s/d/f £75/150/180;) The location and setting don't look promising – a nondescript building squeezed between the ferry pier and car park – but this modern establishment brings a dash of urban glamour to Harris, with flashy fabrics and wall coverings, luxurious towels and toiletries, and a stylish restaurant and lounge bar.

Hebscape CAFE $
(www.hebscapegallery.co.uk; Ardhasaig; mains £3-7; 10.30am-4.30pm Tue-Sat Apr-Oct; P) This stylish cafe-cum-art-gallery, a couple of miles outside Tarbert on the road north towards Stornoway, occupies a hilltop site with breathtaking views over Loch A Siar. Enjoy home-baked cakes or scones with Suki tea or freshly brewed espresso, or a hearty bowl of homemade soup, while admiring the gorgeous landscape photography of co-owner Darren Cole.

South Harris

The west coast of South Harris has some of the most beautiful beaches in Scotland. The blinding white sands and turquoise waters of Luskentyre and Scarasta would be major holiday resorts if they were transported to somewhere with a warm climate; as it is, they're usually deserted.

The east coast is a complete contrast to the west – a strange, rocky moonscape of naked gneiss pocked with tiny lochans, the bleakness lightened by the occasional splash of green around the few crofting communities. Film buffs will know that the psychedelic sequences depicting an alien landscape in *2001: A Space Odyssey* were shot from an aircraft flying low over the east coast of Harris.

The narrow, twisting road that winds its way along this coast is known locally as the **Golden Road** because of the vast amount of money it cost per mile. It was built in the 1930s to link all the tiny communities known as 'The Bays'.

Sights

Clò Mòr MUSEUM
(☎01859-502040; Old School, Drinishader; 9am-5.30pm Mon-Sat Mar-Oct; P) FREE The Campbell family has been making Harris tweed for 90 years, and this exhibition (behind the family shop) celebrates the history of the fabric known in Gaelic as *clò mòr* (the 'big cloth'); ask about live demonstrations of tweed weaving on the 70-year-old Hattersley loom. Drinishader is 5 miles south of Tarbert on the east coast road.

St Clement's Church HISTORIC BUILDING
(Rodel; 9am-5pm Mon-Sat) At the southernmost tip of the east coast of Harris stands the impressive 16th-century St Clement's Church, built by Alexander MacLeod of Dunvegan between the 1520s and 1550s, only to be abandoned after the Reformation. There are several fine tombs inside, including the cenotaph of Alexander MacLeod, finely carved with hunting scenes, a castle, a *birlinn* (the traditional longboat of the islands) and various saints, including St Clement clutching a skull.

Sleeping & Eating

Am Bothan HOSTEL $
(☎01859-520251; www.ambothan.com; Ferry Rd, Leverburgh; dm £22.50; P) An attractive, chalet-style hostel, Am Bothan has small, neat dorms and a great porch where you can enjoy morning coffee with views over the bay. The hostel offers bike hire and can arrange wildlife-watching boat trips.

Sorrel Cottage B&B $$
(☎01859-520319; www.sorrelcottage.co.uk; 2 Glen, Leverburgh; s/d from £65/85;) Sorrel Cottage is a pretty crofter's house with beautifully modernised rooms, about 1.5 miles west of the ferry at Leverburgh. Vegetarians and vegans are happily catered for. Bike hire available.

★Skoon Art Café CAFE $

(☎01859-530268; www.skoon.com; Geocrab; mains £4-7; ⏰10am-4.30pm Tue-Sat Apr-Sep, shorter hours Oct-Mar; P) Set halfway along the Golden Road, this neat little art gallery doubles as an excellent cafe serving delicious homemade soups, sandwiches, cakes and desserts (try the marmalade and ginger cake).

Getting There & Away

A CalMac (p934) car ferry zigzags through the reefs of the Sound of Harris from Leverburgh to Berneray (pedestrian/car £3.45/13.15, one hour, three or four daily Monday to Saturday, two or three Sunday).

There are two to four buses a day (except Sunday) from Tarbert to Leverburgh; W10 takes the main road along the west coast (£3.20, 40 minutes), while W13 winds along the Golden Road on the east (£3.20, one hour).

Berneray (Bearnaraigh)

POP 138

Berneray was linked to North Uist by a causeway in October 1998, and that hasn't altered the peace and beauty of the island. The beaches on its west coast are some of the most beautiful and unspoilt in Britain, and seals and otters can be seen in Bays Loch on the east coast.

Accommodation on the island is limited to the **Gatliff Hostel** (www.gatliff.org.uk; dm adult/child £14/8, camping per person £9), one B&B, and half a dozen self-catering cottages (see the full listing at www.isleofberneray.com), so be sure to book ahead.

North Uist (Uibhist A Tuath)

POP 1255

North Uist, an island half-drowned by lochs, is famed for its trout fishing (www.nuac.co.uk) but also has some magnificent beaches on its north and west coasts. For birdwatchers this is an earthly paradise, with regular sightings of waders and wildfowl ranging from redshank to red-throated diver to red-necked phalarope. The landscape is less wild and mountainous than Harris but it has a sleepy, subtle appeal.

Little Lochmaddy is the first village you hit after arriving on the ferry from Skye.

Balranald RSPB Reserve WILDLIFE RESERVE

(P) FREE Birdwatchers flock to this Royal Society for the Protection of Birds (RSPB) nature reserve, 18 miles west of Lochmaddy, in the hope of spotting the rare red-necked phalarope or hearing the distinctive call of the corncrake. There's a visitor centre with a resident warden who offers 1½-hour guided walks (£5), departing at 10am Tuesday from May to September.

★Langass Lodge HOTEL $$

(☎01876-580285; www.langasslodge.co.uk; Locheport; s/d £95/115; P 📶) The delightful Langass Lodge Hotel is a former shooting lodge set in splendid isolation overlooking Loch Langais. Refurbished and extended, it now offers a dozen appealing rooms, many with sea views, as well as one of the Hebrides' best **restaurants** (mains £15-21, 3-course dinner £34; ⏰6-8.30pm), noted for its fine seafood and game.

Rushlee House B&B $$

(☎01876-500274; www.rushleehouse.co.uk; Lochmaddy; s/d £50/75; P) A lovely modern bungalow with three luxuriously appointed bedrooms and great views of the hills to the south. No evening meals, but it's just a short walk to the restaurant at Hamersay House. The B&B is 0.75 miles from the ferry pier; take the first road on the right, then first left.

South Uist (Uibhist A Deas)

POP 1755

South Uist is the second-largest island in the Outer Hebrides and saves its choicest corners for those who explore away from the main north–south road. The low-lying west coast is an almost unbroken stretch of white-sand beach and flower-flecked machair – a waymarked hiking trail, the **Machair Way**, follows the coast – while the multitude of inland lochs provide excellent trout fishing (www.southuistfishing.com). The east coast, riven by four large sea lochs, is hilly and remote, with spectacular **Beinn Mhor** (620m) the highest point.

Driving south from Benbecula you cross from the predominantly Protestant northern half of the Outer Hebrides into the mostly Roman Catholic south, a religious transition marked by the granite statue of **Our Lady of the Isles** on the slopes of Rueval (the hill with the military radomes on its summit) and the presence of many roadside shrines.

The ferry port of **Lochboisdale** is the island's largest settlement.

Sights & Activities

Kildonan Museum MUSEUM
(01878-710343; www.kildonanmuseum.co.uk; Kildonan; adult/child £2.50/free; 10am-5pm Apr-Oct; P) Six miles north of Lochboisdale, Kildonan Museum explores the lives of local crofters through its collection of artefacts, an absorbing exhibition of B&W photography and first-hand accounts of harsh Hebridean conditions. There's also an excellent tearoom (mains £4 to £8, open 11am to 4pm) and craft shop.

Amid Milton's ruined blackhouses, half a mile south of the museum, a cairn marks the site of Flora MacDonald's birthplace.

Loch Druidibeg National Nature Reserve WILDLIFE RESERVE
FREE The northern part of North Uist is mostly occupied by the watery expanses of Loch Bee and Loch Druidibeg. Loch Druidibeg National Nature Reserve is an important breeding ground for birds such as dunlin, redshank, ringed plover, greylag goose and corncrake; you can take a 5-mile self-guided walk through the reserve. Ask for details at the Scottish Natural Heritage office on the main road beside the loch.

Sleeping & Eating

Uist Storm Pods CAMPGROUND $
(01878-700845; www.uiststormpods.co.uk; Lochboisdale; per pod per night £60; P) This place has two Scandinavian-style timber camping pods set on a hillside on a working farm. Each has an outdoor deck and barbecue overlooking the sea; a mini-kitchen, fridge and chemical toilet; and can sleep up to four people. They are a short walk from the ferry; take the second road on the left, immediately before the RBS bank.

Wireless Cottage B&B $
(01878-700660; www.wirelesscottage.co.uk; Lochboisdale; per person from £25;) This pretty little cottage, which once housed the local telephone exchange, is now a welcoming and good-value B&B with just two bedrooms (one double, one family). It's a short (300m) walk from the ferry.

★ **Polochar Inn** INN $$
(01878-700215; www.polocharinn.com; Polochar; s/d from £75/95; P) This 18th-century inn has been transformed into a stylish, welcoming hotel with a stunning location looking out across the sea to Barra. The excellent restaurant and bar menu (mains £11 to £20; booking recommended) includes seafood chowder, venison casserole, local salmon and scallops, and Uist lamb. Polochar is 7 miles southwest of Lochboisdale, on the way to Eriskay.

Getting There & Around

Bus W17 runs about four times a day (except Sunday) between Berneray and Eriskay via Lochmaddy, Balivanich and Lochboisdale. The trip from Lochboisdale to Lochmaddy (£5.20) takes 1¾ hours.

Rothan Cycles (07740 364093; www.rothan.com; Howmore; 9am-5pm) offers a delivery and pick-up service at various points between Eriskay and Stornoway.

Barra (Barraigh)

POP 1175

With its beautiful beaches, wildflower-clad dunes, rugged little hills and strong sense of community, diminutive Barra – just 14 miles in circumference – is the Outer Hebrides in miniature. For a great view of the island, walk up to the top of Heaval (383m), a mile northeast of Castlebay (Bagh a'Chaisteil), the largest village.

Accommodation on Barra is limited, so make a reservation before committing to a night on the island. Wild camping (on foot or by bike) is allowed almost anywhere; campervans and car campers are restricted to official sites – check www.isleofbarra.com for details.

Kisimul Castle CASTLE
(HS; 01871-810313; www.historicenvironment.scot; Castlebay; adult/child incl ferry £5.50/3.30; 9.30am-5.30pm Apr-Sep) Castlebay takes its name from the island fortress of Kisimul Castle, first built by the MacNeil clan in the 11th century. A short boat trip (weather permitting) takes you out to the island, where you can explore the fortifications and soak up the view from the battlements.

The castle was restored in the 20th century by American architect Robert MacNeil, who became the 45th clan chief; he gifted the castle to Historic Scotland in 2000 for an annual rent of £1 and a bottle of whisky (Talisker single malt, if you're interested).

Dunard Hostel HOSTEL $
(☎01871-810443; www.dunardhostel.co.uk; Castlebay; dm/tw from £18/40; P 📶) Dunard is a friendly, family-run hostel just a five-minute walk from the ferry terminal. The owners can help to organise sea-kayaking trips.

Castlebay Hotel HOTEL $$
(☎01871-810223; www.castlebayhotel.com; Castlebay; s/d from £69/115; P 📶) The Castlebay Hotel offers spacious bedrooms decorated with a subtle tartan motif – it's worth paying a bit extra for a sea view – and there's a comfy lounge and conservatory with grand views across the harbour to the islands south of Barra. The hotel bar is the hub of island social life, with regular sessions of traditional music.

The restaurant specialises in local seafood and game (often rabbit)

Getting There & Around

AIR
There are two daily flights from Glasgow to Barra airport.

BOAT
CalMac (p934) ferries link Eriskay with Ardmhor (pedestrian/car £2.95/10.25, 40 minutes, three to five daily) at the northern end of Barra. Ferries also run from Castlebay to Oban.

BICYCLE
You can hire bikes from **Barra Cycle Hire** (☎01871-810846; Paduls's Island Store, Castlebay; per day/week £15/50; ⏰9am-5pm Mon-Sat), at the western end of Castlebay.

BUS
A bus service links ferry arrivals and departures at Ardmhor with Castlebay (£1.80, 20 minutes). Bus W32 makes a circuit of the island up to five times daily (except Sunday), and also connects with flights at the airport.

ORKNEY

POP 21,670

There's a magic to Orkney that you begin to feel as soon as the Scottish mainland slips astern. Only a few short miles of ocean separate the chain of islands from Scotland's north coast, but the Pentland Firth is one of Europe's most dangerous waterways, a graveyard of ships that adds an extra mystique to these islands shimmering in the sea mists.

An archipelago of mostly flat, green-topped islands stripped bare of trees and ringed with red sandstone cliffs, its heritage dates back to the Vikings whose influence is still strong today. Famed for ancient standing stones and prehistoric villages, for sublime sandy beaches and spectacular coastal scenery, it's a region whose ports tell of lives shared with the blessings and rough moods of the sea, and a destination where seekers can find melancholy wrecks of warships and the salty clamour of remote seabird colonies.

Tours

Orkney Archaeology Tours TOURS
(☎01856-721450; www.orkneyarchaeologytours.co.uk) Specialises in all-inclusive multiday tours focusing on Orkney's ancient sites with an archaeologist guide. Also run customisable private tours.

Wildabout Orkney BUS
(☎01856-877737; www.wildaboutorkney.com) Operates tours covering Orkney's history, ecology, folklore and wildlife. Day trips operate year-round and cost £59, with pick-ups in Stromness (to meet the morning ferry) and Kirkwall.

Getting There & Away

AIR
Flybe (☎0371-700 2000; www.flybe.com) Flies daily from Kirkwall to Aberdeen, Edinburgh, Glasgow, Inverness and Sumburgh (Shetland). Most summers it also serves Bergen (Norway).

BOAT
During summer, book car spaces ahead. Peak-season fares are quoted here.

Northlink Ferries (☎0845 6000 449; www.northlinkferries.co.uk) Operates ferries from Scrabster to Stromness (passenger/car £19.40/59, 1½ hours, two to three daily), from Aberdeen to Kirkwall (passenger/car £31.50/111, six hours, three or four weekly) and from Kirkwall to Lerwick (passenger/car £24.65/103, six to eight hours, three or four weekly) on Shetland. Fares are up to 35% lower off-season.

Pentland Ferries (☎0800 688 8998; www.pentlandferries.co.uk; adult/child/car/bike £16/8/38/free) Leave from Gills Bay, 3 miles west of John O'Groats, and head to St Margaret's Hope on South Ronaldsay three to four times daily. The crossing takes an hour.

Orkney

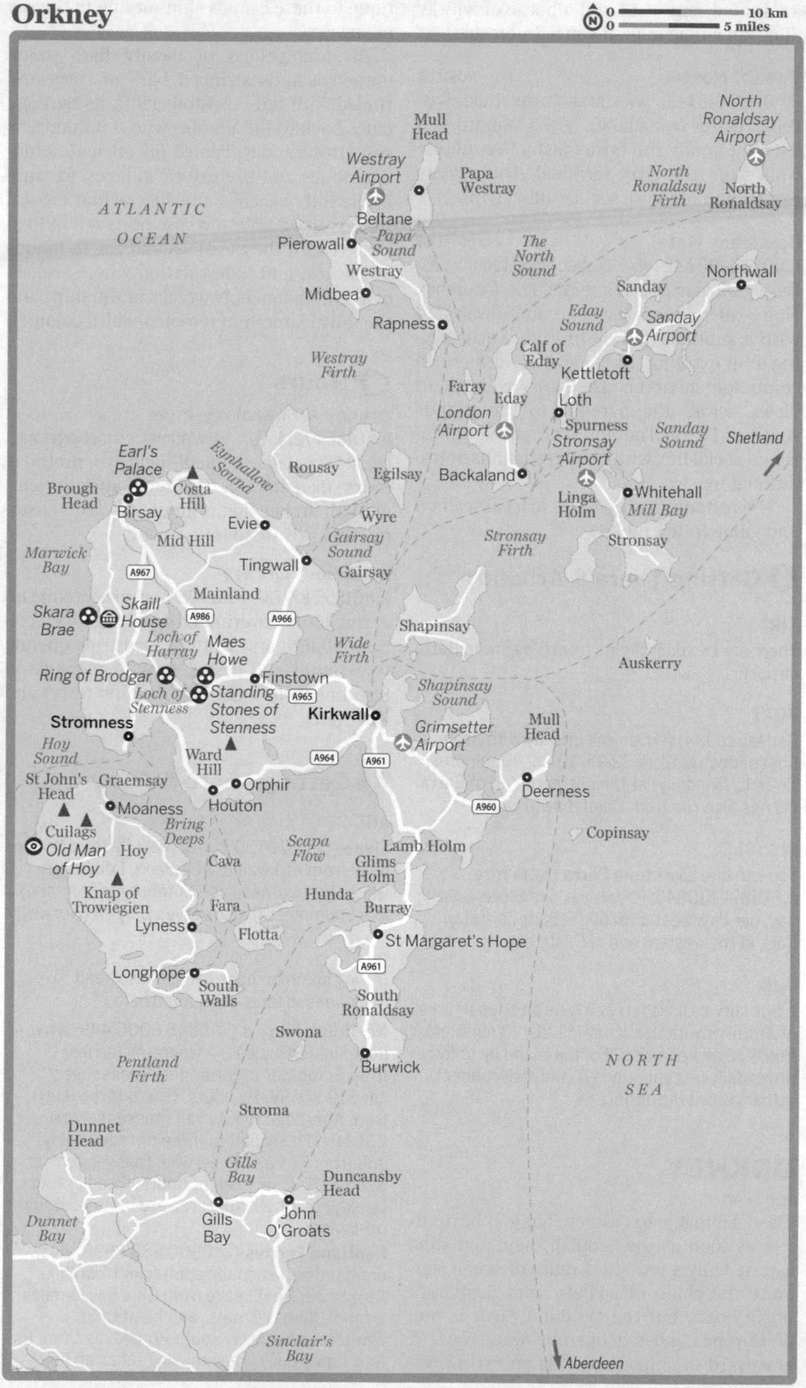
0 10 km
0 5 miles
North Ronaldsay Airport
North Ronaldsay
North Ronaldsay Firth
Mull Head
Westray Airport
Papa Westray
ATLANTIC OCEAN
Beltane
Papa Sound
Pierowall
Westray
Midbea
Rapness
The North Sound
Northwall
Sanday
Eday Sound
Sanday Airport
Calf of Eday
Kettletoft
Westray Firth
Faray
Eday
Loth
London Airport
Spurness
Sanday Sound
Stronsay Airport
Shetland
Earl's Palace
Eynhallow Sound
Rousay
Egilsay
Backaland
Brough Head
Costa Hill
Birsay
Linga Holm
Whitehall
Mill Bay
Wyre
Evie
Mid Hill
Gairsay Sound
Stronsay Firth
Stronsay
Marwick Bay
A967
Tingwall
Gairsay
Mainland
Skaill House
Skara Brae
A986
A966
Shapinsay
Loch of Harray
Maes Howe
Wide Firth
Auskerry
Ring of Brodgar
Finstown
Loch of Stenness
Standing Stones of Stenness
A965
Shapinsay Sound
Stromness
Kirkwall
Grimsetter Airport
Mull Head
Hoy Sound
Ward Hill
A964
A961
St John's Head
Graemsay
Orphir
Deerness
Moaness
Houton
A960
Cuilags
Bring Deeps
Copinsay
Old Man of Hoy
Hoy
Scapa Flow
Lamb Holm
Cava
Glims Holm
Knap of Trowiegien
Hunda
Fara
Burray
Lyness
Flotta
St Margaret's Hope
A961
Longhope
South Walls
South Ronaldsay
Swona
Burwick
Pentland Firth
NORTH SEA
Stroma
Dunnet Head
Gills Bay
Duncansby Head
Gills Bay
John O'Groats
Dunnet Bay
Sinclair's Bay
Aberdeen

John O'Groats Ferries (☎01955-611353; www.jogferry.co.uk; single £17, incl bus to Kirkwall £18; ⏰May-Sep) Passenger-only service from John O'Groats to Burwick, on the southern tip of South Ronaldsay, with connecting bus to Kirkwall. Two to three departures daily. Forty-minute crossing.

BUS

Citylink (www.citylink.co.uk) Runs daily from Inverness to Scrabster, connecting with the Stromness ferries.

John O'Groats Ferries (☎01955-611353; www.jogferry.co.uk; ⏰May-Sep) Has summer-only 'Orkney bus' services from Inverness to Kirkwall. Tickets (one way £25, five hours) include bus-ferry-bus travel from Inverness to Kirkwall. There are two daily from June to August.

Getting Around

The *Orkney Transport Guide* details all island transport and is free from tourist offices.

The largest island, Mainland, is linked by causeways to four southern islands; others are reached by air and ferry.

AIR

Loganair (☎01856-873457; www.loganair.co.uk) operates interisland flights from Kirkwall to Eday, Stronsay, Sanday, Westray, Papa Westray and North Ronaldsay. Fares are reasonable, with some special discounted tickets if you stay a night on the outer islands.

BICYCLE

Various locations on Mainland hire out bikes, including **Cycle Orkney** (☎01856-875777; www.cycleorkney.com; Tankerness Lane, Kirkwall; per day/3 days/week £15/30/60; ⏰9am-5.30pm Mon-Sat) and **Orkney Cycle Hire** (☎01856-850255; www.orkneycyclehire.co.uk; 54 Dundas St, Stromness; per day £10-15). Both offer out-of-hours pick-ups and options for kids.

BOAT

Orkney Ferries (☎01856-872044; www.orkneyferries.co.uk) Operates car ferries from Mainland to the islands. See individual islands for details. An Island Explorer pass costs £42 for a week's passenger travel in summer. Bikes are carried free.

BUS

Stagecoach (☎01856-870555; www.stagecoachbus.com) Runs buses on Mainland and connecting islands. Most don't operate on Sunday. Dayrider (£8.30) and 7-Day Megarider (£18.50) tickets allow unlimited travel.

CAR

Small-car rates are around £40/200 per day/week, although there are specials for as low as £30 per day.

Orkney Car Hire (☎01856-872866; www.orkneycarhire.co.uk; Junction Rd, Kirkwall; per day/week £40/210) Recommended. Close to Kirkwall bus station.

WR Tullock (☎01856-875500; www.orkneycarrental.co.uk; Castle St, Kirkwall; per day/week £36/196) Opposite Kirkwall bus station.

Kirkwall

POP 7000

Orkney's main town is the islands' commercial centre and there's a comparatively busy feel to its main shopping street and ferry dock. It's set back from a wide bay, and its vigour, combined with the atmospheric paved streets and twisting wynds (lanes), gives Orkney's capital a distinctive character. Magnificent St Magnus Cathedral takes pride of place in the centre of town, and the nearby Earl's and Bishop's Palaces are also worth a ramble. Founded in the early 11th century, the original part of Kirkwall is one of the best examples of an ancient Norse town.

Sights

★St Magnus Cathedral CATHEDRAL
(☎01856-874894; www.stmagnus.org; Broad St; ⏰9am-6pm Mon-Sat, 1-6pm Sun Apr-Sep, 9am-1pm & 2-5pm Mon-Sat Oct-Mar) FREE Constructed from local red sandstone, Kirkwall's centrepiece, dating from the early 12th century, is among Scotland's most interesting cathedrals. The powerful atmosphere of an ancient faith pervades the impressive interior. Lyrical and melodramatic epitaphs of the dead line the walls and emphasise the serious business of 17th- and 18th-century bereavement. Tours of the upper level (£7.75) run on Tuesdays and Thursdays; phone to book.

★Highland Park Distillery DISTILLERY
(☎01856-874619; www.highlandpark.co.uk; Holm Rd; tour adult/child £7.50/free; ⏰10am-5pm Mon-Sat & noon-5pm Sun May-Aug, 10am-5pm Mon-Fri Apr & Sep, 1-5pm Mon-Fri Oct-Mar) South of the centre, this distillery is great to visit. They malt their own barley; you can see it and the peat kiln used to dry it on the excellent, well-informed hour-long tour. The standard

Kirkwall

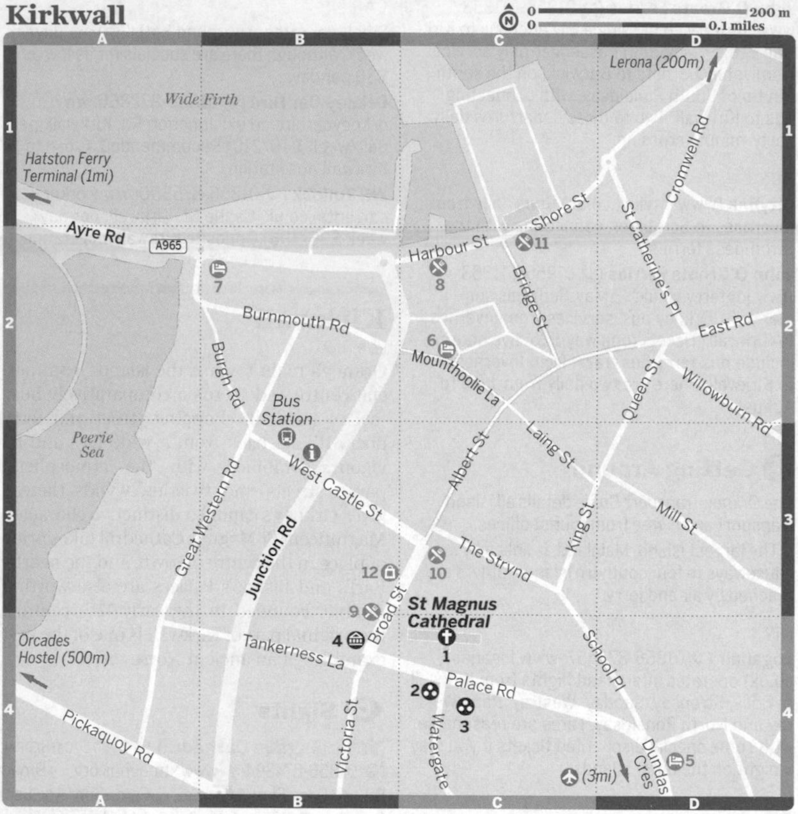

Kirkwall

Top Sights

Sights

Sleeping

Eating

Shopping

12-year-old is a soft, balanced malt, great for novices and aficionados alike; the 18-year-old is among the world's finest drams. This and older whiskies can be tasted on more specialised tours (£20 to £75), which you can prearrange.

Earl's Palace RUINS

(HES; ☎01856-871918; www.historicenvironment.scot; Watergate; adult/child £4.50/2.70; ⊙9.30am-5.30pm Apr-Sep) The intriguing Earl's Palace was once known as the finest example of French Renaissance architecture in Scotland. One room features an interesting history of its builder, Earl Patrick Stewart, executed in Edinburgh for treason. He started construction in about 1600, but ran out of money and never completed it. Admission includes the adjacent **Bishop's Palace** (HES; ☎01856-871918; www.historicenvironment.scot; Watergate; admission incl in Earl's Palace; ⊙9.30am-5.30pm Apr-Sep).

Orkney Museum MUSEUM
(☎01856-873191; www.orkney.gov.uk; Broad St; ⏱10.30am-5pm Mon-Sat year-round, closed 12.30-1.30pm Nov-Apr) FREE This labyrinthine display is housed in a former merchant's house. It has an overview of Orcadian history and prehistory, including Pictish carvings and a display on the Ba' (p947). Most engaging are the last rooms, covering 19th- and 20th-century social history.

Festivals & Events

St Magnus Festival ARTS, MUSIC
(☎01856-871445; www.stmagnusfestival.com; ⏱late Jun) Running for a week over midsummer, this is a colourful celebration of music and the arts.

Sleeping

Orcades Hostel HOSTEL $
(☎01856-873745; www.orcadeshostel.com; Muddisdale Rd; dm/s/d £20/40/52; P@) Book ahead to get a bed in this cracking hostel on the western edge of town. It's a guesthouse conversion, so there's a very smart kitchen and lounge, and great-value doubles. Comfortable dorms with space and just four bunks make for sound sleeping; enthusiastic owners give the place spark. There are lockers for valuables at reception.

Kirkwall Peedie Hostel HOSTEL $
(☎01856-875477; www.kirkwallpeediehostel.com; Ayre Rd; dm/s/d £15/20/30; P) Nestling into a corner at the end of the Kirkwall waterfront, this cute hostel set in former fisherfolk's cottages squeezes in all the necessary features for a comfortable stay. Despite the compact appearance, the dorms actually have plenty of room – and there are three tiny kitchens, so you should find some elbow room. A separate bothy (hut) sleeps four.

Lerona B&B $$
(☎01856-874538; Cromwell Cres; s/d £35/70; P) Guests come first here, but the wee folk – a battalion of garden gnomes and clans of dolls with lifelike stares – are close behind. The rooms, some en suite, are a good size, and friendly owners give an easygoing welcome. It's cheaper if you stay more than one night. Cromwell Crescent comes off the waterfront road just east of the centre. No wi-fi.

2 Dundas Crescent B&B $$
(☎01856-874805; www.twodundas.co.uk; 2 Dundas Cres; s/d £45/80; P) This former manse is a magnificent building with four enormous rooms blessed with large windows and sizeable beds. There are plenty of period features, but the en suite bathrooms are not among them: they're sparklingly new, and one has a free-standing bathtub. Both the welcome and the breakfast will leave you most content. The location just up from the cathedral is great.

★ **Albert Hotel** HOTEL $$$
(☎01856-876000; www.alberthotel.co.uk; Mounthoolie Lane; s £96, d £142-158;) Stylishly refurbished in plum and grey, this central but peaceful hotel is Kirkwall's finest address. Comfortable contemporary rooms in a variety of categories sport super-inviting beds and smart bathrooms. Staff are helpful, and will pack you a breakfast box if you've got an early ferry. A great Orkney base, with the more-than-decent **Bothy Bar** (mains £7-12; ⏱noon-2pm & 5-9pm;) downstairs. Walk-in prices are often cheaper.

Eating & Drinking

Judith Glue Real Food Cafe CAFE $
(☎01856-874225; www.judithglue.com; 25 Broad St; light meals £7-14; ⏱9.30am-5.30pm Mon-Sat, 11am-5pm Sun Jan-Mar, 9am-6pm Mon-Sat, 11am-5pm Sun Apr-May & Oct-Dec, 9am-10pm Mon-Sat, 10am-6pm Sun Jun-Sep;) At the back of a lively craft shop opposite the cathedral, this licensed cafe-bistro serves toothsome sandwiches and salads, as well as daily specials and succulent seafood platters. There's a strong emphasis on sustainable and organic ingredients, but put the feel-good factor aside for a moment and fight for a table at lunchtime. Check Facebook for regular events.

Reel CAFE $
(www.facebook.com/thereelkirkwall; Albert St; sandwiches £3-6; ⏱9am-6pm Mon-Sat, 10am-5pm Sun;) Part music shop and part cafe, Kirkwall's best coffee-stop sits alongside the cathedral, and bravely puts tables outside at the slightest threat of sunshine. It's a relaxed spot, good for a morning-after debriefing, a quiet Orkney ale, or lunchtime panini and musically named sandwiches (plus the cheese-and-mushroom Skara Brie). It's a local folk-musicians' centre, with regular evening sessions.

★ **Foveran** SCOTTISH $$
(☎01856-872389; www.thefoveran.com; St Ola; mains £15-26; ⏲6.30-8.30pm mid-Apr–mid-Oct, Fri & Sat only plus other days by arrangement off-season; 📶) Three miles down the Orphir road, one of Orkney's best dining options is surprisingly affordable for the quality. Tranquilly located, with a cosy eating area overlooking the sea, it shines presenting classic Orcadian ingredients – the steak with haggis and whisky sauce is feted throughout, while North Ronaldsay lamb comes in four different, deliciously tender cuts.

Shore GASTROPUB $$
(☎01856-872200; www.theshore.co.uk; 6 Shore St; bar meals £9-10, restaurant mains £10-15; ⏲food noon-2pm & 6-8.30pm Mon-Fri, 10am-5pm & 6-8.30pm Sat & Sun; 📶) This popular harbourside eatery offers high-standard bar meals with a bit of local seafood added into the mix in the evening fare in the restaurant section. It's run with a customer-comes-first attitude and is a convivial spot.

Helgi's PUB FOOD $$
(www.helgis.co.uk; 14 Harbour St; mains £10-13; ⏲food noon-9pm, from 12.30pm Sun; 📶) There's a traditional cosiness about this place, but the decor has moved beyond the time-honoured beer-soaked carpet to a comfortable contemporary slate floor and quotes from the *Orkneyinga Saga* plastering the walls. It's more find-a-table than jostle-at-the-bar and serves cheerful, well-priced comfort food – light bites only between 2pm and 5pm. Take your pint upstairs for quiet harbour contemplation.

Shopping

Kirkwall has some gorgeous jewellery and crafts along Albert St, as well as shops selling quality Orcadian food and drink.

Longship JEWELLERY, CRAFT
(☎01856-888790; www.thelongship.co.uk; 7 Broad St; ⏲9am-5.30pm daily Jun-Aug, 10am-5pm Mon-Sat Sep-May) The Longship, established in 1859, has Orkney-made crafts, food, gifts and exquisite designer jewellery across adjacent shops.

Information

Kirkwall Information Centre (☎01856-872856; www.visitorkney.com; West Castle St; ⏲9am-5pm Mon-Sat Oct-Mar, 9am-5pm daily Apr-Sep) Has a good range of Orkney info. Shares a building with the bus station.

Getting There & Away

AIR

Kirkwall Airport (www.hial.co.uk) is located a few miles east of town and served regularly by bus 4 (15 minutes).

BOAT

Ferries to the Northern Islands depart from the town harbour; however, ferries to Aberdeen and Shetland use the Hatston terminal, 1 mile northwest. Bus X10 shuttles out there regularly.

BUS

All services leave from the **bus station** (West Castle St):

Bus X1 Stromness (£3.10, 30 minutes, hourly, seven Sunday); in the other direction to St Margaret's Hope (£2.90).

Bus 2 Orphir and Houton (£2.55, 20 minutes, four or five daily Monday to Saturday, five on Sunday from mid-June to mid-August).

Bus 6 Evie (£3.40, 30 minutes, three to five daily Monday to Saturday) and Tingwall (Rousay ferry). Runs Sunday in summer to Tingwall only.

East Mainland to South Ronaldsay

After a German U-boat sank battleship HMS *Royal Oak* in 1939, Winston Churchill had causeways of concrete blocks erected across the channels on the eastern side of Scapa Flow, linking Mainland to the islands of Lamb Holm, Glims Holm, Burray and South Ronaldsay. The Churchill Barriers, flanked by rusting wrecks of blockships, now support the main road from Kirkwall to Burwick.

Lamb Holm & Burray

Italian Chapel CHURCH
(☎01865-781268; Lamb Holm; adult/child £3/free; ⏲9am-6.30pm Jun-Aug, 9am-5pm Mon-Sat, noon-5pm Sun May & Sep, 10am-4pm Mon-Sat, noon-3pm Sun mid-Mar–Apr & Oct, 11am-2pm Mon-Sat Nov–mid-Mar) The Italian Chapel is all that remains of a POW camp that housed the Italian soldiers who worked on the Churchill Barriers. They built the chapel in their spare time, using two Nissen huts, scrap metal and their considerable artistic skills. One of the artists returned in 1960 to restore the paintwork. It's quite extraordinary inside and definitely worth seeing.

★**Fossil & Heritage Centre** MUSEUM
(☎01865-731255; www.orkneyfossilcentre.co.uk; adult/child £4.50/3; ⏲10am-5pm Apr-Oct) This eclectic museum is a great visit, combining some excellent 360-million-year-old Devonian fish fossils found locally with a well-designed exhibition on the world wars and Churchill Barriers. Upstairs is a selection of household and farming implements. There's a good little gift shop and an enjoyable coffee shop here. It's on the left half a mile after crossing to Burray, coming from Kirkwall.

South Ronaldsay

POP 900

South Ronaldsay's main village, pristine **St Margaret's Hope**, was named after the Maid of Norway, who died here in 1290 on her way to marry Edward II of England (strictly a political affair: Margaret was only seven years old). The island has some intriguing prehistoric tombs and fine places to stay and eat, and is also the docking point of two of the three mainland ferries.

Sights

★**Tomb of the Eagles** ARCHAEOLOGICAL SITE
(☎01856-831339; www.tomboftheeagles.co.uk; Cleat; adult/child £7.50/3.50; ⏲9.30am-5.30pm Apr-Sep, 10am-noon Mar, 9.30am-12.30pm Oct) Two significant archaeological sites were found here by a farmer on his land. The first is a Bronze Age stone building with a firepit, indoor well and plenty of seating: a communal cooking site or the original Orkney pub? Beyond, in a spectacular clifftop position, the neolithic tomb (wheel yourself in prone on a trolley) is an elaborate stone construction that held the remains of up to 340 people who died some five millennia ago.

An excellent personal explanation is given to you at the **visitor centre**; you meet a few spooky skulls and can handle some of the artefacts found, plus absorb information on the mesolithic period. It's about a mile's airy walk to the tomb from the centre, which is near Burwick.

Banks Chambered Tomb ARCHAEOLOGICAL SITE
(Tomb of the Otters; ☎01856-831605; www.bankschamberedtomb.co.uk; Cleat; adult/child £6/2.50; ⏲10.30am-5pm Apr-Sep) Discovered while digging a car park, this 5000-year-old chambered tomb has yielded a vast quantity of human bones, well preserved thanks to the saturation of the earth. The tomb is dug into bedrock and makes for an atmospheric if claustrophobic visit. The guided tour mixes homespun archaeological theories with astute observations. Within the adjacent bistro, you can handle finds of stones and bones, including the remains of otters, who presumably used this as a den. Follow signs for Tomb of the Eagles.

Sleeping & Eating

★**Eastward Guest House** B&B $$
(The Missing Bell; ☎01956-831551; www.eastwardhouse.com; A961; d £90-105, dinner £40-60; P@≋) Not a bed-and-breakfast in any sense that the phrase is usually understood, this utterly captivating haven is a converted church that offers a foodie experience like few others. Patrick and Keiko aren't just passionate about food – they've taken it several steps beyond, to the realms of philosophy, of religion, of a messianic determination to cook the way they believe in.

★**Bankburn House** B&B $$
(☎01856-831310; www.bankburnhouse.co.uk; A961, St Margaret's Hope; s/d £48.75/72.50, without bathroom £42.50/65; P@≋🐾) This large rustic house does everything right, with smashing good-sized rooms and engaging owners who put on quality breakfasts and take pride in constantly innovating to improve guests' comfort levels. The huge lawn overlooks St Margaret's Hope and the bay – perfect for sunbathing on shimmering Orkney summer days. Prices drop substantially for multinight stays.

THE BA'

Every Christmas Day and New Year's Day, Kirkwall holds a staggering spectacle: a crazy ball game known as the ba'. Two enormous teams, the Uppies and the Doonies, fight their way, no holds barred, through the streets, trying to get a leather ball to the other end of town. The ball is thrown from the Market Cross to the waiting teams; the Uppies have to get the ba' to the corner of Main St and Junction Rd, the Doonies must get it to the water. Violence, skulduggery and other stunts are common, and the event, fuelled by plenty of strong drink, can last hours.

Skerries Bistro SEAFOOD $$
(☎01856-831605; www.skerriesbistro.co.uk; Cleat; lunches £5-9, dinner mains £10-18; ⊙11am-5pm & 6-9pm Wed-Mon, 11am-4pm Tue Mar-Oct) This cafe-bistro occupies a spectacular setting at the southern end of South Ronaldsay; it's a smart, modern glass-walled building with a deck and great clifftop views. Meals range from soups and sandwiches to daily fish and shellfish specials. Dinner should be booked ahead. A romantic little separate pod is available for private dining.

Maes Howe & Around

★Maeshowe ARCHAEOLOGICAL SITE
(HES; ☎01856-761606; www.historicenvironment.scot; adult/child £5.50/3.30; ⊙9.30am-5pm Apr-Sep, 10am-4pm Oct-Mar, tours hourly 10am-4pm, plus 6pm and 7pm Jul & Aug.) Egypt has pyramids, Scotland has Maeshowe. Constructed about 5000 years ago, it's an extraordinary place, a Stone Age tomb built from enormous sandstone blocks, some of which weighed many tons and were brought from several miles away. Creeping down the long stone passageway to the central chamber, you feel the indescribable gulf of years that separate us from the architects of this mysterious place.

Entry is by 45-minute guided tours on the hour: you must reserve your tour slot ahead by phone.

Though nothing is known about who and what was interred here, the scope of the project suggests it was a structure of great significance.

In the 12th century, the tomb was broken into by Vikings searching for treasure. A couple of years later, another group sought shelter in the chamber from a three-day blizzard. Waiting out the storm, they carved runic graffiti on the walls. As well as the some-things-never-change 'Olaf was 'ere' and 'Thorni bedded Helga', there are also more intricate carvings, including a particularly fine dragon and a knotted serpent.

Buy tickets in Tormiston Mill across the road. Oversized groups mean guides tend to only show a couple of the Viking inscriptions, but they'll happily show more if asked.

By chance or design, for a few weeks around the winter solstice the setting sun shafts up the entrance passage, and strikes the back wall of the tomb in spooky alignment. If you can't be there, check the webcams on www.maeshowe.co.uk.

NESS OF BRODGAR

Ongoing excavations on the **Ness of Brodgar** (www.nessofbrodgar.co.uk; ⊙tours 2-3 times daily early Jul-late Aug) FREE, between the Stenness standing stones and the Ring of Brodgar, are rapidly revealing that this was a neolithic site of huge importance. Probably a major power and religious centre and used for over a millennium, the settlement had a mighty wall, a large building (a temple or palace?) and as many as 100 other structures, some painted. Each dig season reveals new, intriguing finds.

Standing Stones of Stenness ARCHAEOLOGICAL SITE
(HES; www.historicenvironment.scot; ⊙24hr) FREE Within sight of Maeshowe, four mighty stones remain of what was once a circle of 12. Recent research suggests they were perhaps erected as long ago as 3300 BC, and they impose by their sheer size; the tallest measures 5.7m in height. The narrow strip of land they're on, the Ness of Brodgar, separates the Harray and Stenness lochs and was the site of a large settlement inhabited throughout the neolithic period (3500–1800 BC).

Barnhouse Neolithic Village ARCHAEOLOGICAL SITE
(HES; www.historicenvironment.scot; ⊙24hr) FREE Alongside the Standing Stones of Stenness are the excavated remains of a village thought to have been inhabited by the builders of Maeshowe. Don't skip this: it brings the area to life. The houses are well preserved and similar to Skara Brae with their stone furnishings. One of the buildings was entered by crossing a fireplace: possibly an act of ritual significance.

Ring of Brodgar ARCHAEOLOGICAL SITE
(HES; www.historicenvironment.scot; ⊙24hr) FREE A mile northwest of Stenness is this wide circle of standing stones, some over 5m tall. The last of the three Stenness monuments to be built (2500–2000 BC), it remains a most atmospheric location. Twenty-one of the original 60 stones still stand among the heather. On a grey day with dark clouds thudding low across the sky, the stones are a spine-tingling sight.

Skara Brae

★Skara Brae ARCHAEOLOGICAL SITE

(HES; www.historicenvironment.scot; adult/child £6.10/3.70, incl Skaill House adult/child £7.10/4.30; ⌚9.30am-5.30pm Apr-Sep, 10am-4pm Oct-Mar) Idyllically situated by a sandy bay 8 miles north of Stromness, and predating Stonehenge and the pyramids of Giza, extraordinary Skara Brae, one of the world's most evocative prehistoric sites, is northern Europe's best-preserved prehistoric village. Even the stone furniture – beds, boxes and dressers – has survived the 5000 years since a community lived and breathed here. It was hidden until 1850, when waves whipped up by a severe storm eroded the sand and grass above the beach, exposing the houses underneath.

There's an excellent interactive exhibit and short video, arming visitors with facts and theory, which will enhance the impact of the site. You then enter a reconstructed house, giving the excavation (which you head on to next) more meaning. The official guidebook, available from the visitor centre, includes a good self-guided tour.

The joint ticket also gets you into **Skaill House** (⌚Apr-Oct), a mansion built for the bishop in 1620. It's a bit anticlimactic catapulting straight from the neolithic to the 1950s decor, but you can see a smart hidden compartment in the library as well as the bishop's original 17th-century four-poster bed.

Buses run to Skara Brae from Kirkwall and Stromness a few times weekly in summer, but not all are useful to visit the site. It's possible to walk along the coast from Stromness to Skara Brae (9 miles), or it's an easy taxi (£15), hitch or cycle from Stromness.

Stromness

POP 1800

This appealing grey-stone port has a narrow, elongated, flagstone-paved main street and tiny alleys leading down to the waterfront between tall houses. It lacks Kirkwall's size but makes up for that with bucketloads of character, having changed little since its heyday in the 18th century, when it was a busy staging post for ships avoiding the troublesome English Channel during European wars. Stromness is ideally located for trips to Orkney's major prehistoric sites.

Sights

★Stromness Museum MUSEUM

(☎01856-850025; www.stromnessmuseum.co.uk; 52 Alfred St; adult/child £5/1; ⌚10am-5pm daily Apr-Sep, 10am-5pm Mon-Sat Oct, 11am-3.30pm Mon-Sat Nov) This superb museum, run with great passion, is full of knick-knacks from maritime and natural-history exhibitions covering whaling, the Hudsons Bay Company and the sunk German fleet. There's always an excellent summer exhibition too. You can happily nose around for a couple of hours. Across the street is the house where local poet and novelist George Mackay Brown lived.

Pier Arts Centre GALLERY

(☎01856-850209; www.pierartscentre.com; 30 Victoria St; ⌚10.30am-5pm Tue-Sat, plus Mon mid-Jun–Aug) FREE This gallery has really rejuvenated the Orkney modern-art scene with its sleek lines and upbeat attitude. It's worth a look as much for the architecture as for its high-quality collection of 20th-century British art and the changing exhibitions.

Festivals & Events

Orkney Folk Festival MUSIC

(www.orkneyfolkfestival.com) A four-day event in late May, with folk concerts, *ceilidhs* (evenings of traditional Scottish entertainment) and casual pub sessions. Stromness packs out, and late-night buses from Kirkwall are laid on. Book tickets and accommodation ahead.

Sleeping

Hamnavoe Hostel HOSTEL $

(☎01856-851202; www.hamnavoehostel.co.uk; 10a North End Rd; dm £20-22, s £22, tw £30-33;) This well-equipped hostel is efficiently run and boasts excellent facilities, including a fine kitchen and a lounge room with great perspectives over the water. The dorms are very commodious, with duvets, decent mattresses and reading lamps (bring a pound coin for the heating), and the showers are good. Ring ahead as the owner lives off-site.

Point of Ness Caravan & Camping Park CAMPGROUND $

(☎office hours 01856-873535, site 01856-850532; https://orkney.campstead.com; Ness Rd; tent sites 1/2 people £7.65/11.80; ⌚Apr-Sep; P) This breezy, fenced-in campsite has a super location overlooking the bay at the southern end of town and is as neat as a pin.

Brown's Hostel HOSTEL $

(01856-850661; www.brownsorkney.com; 45 Victoria St; s £22.50, d £40-50;) On the main street, this handy, sociable place has cosy private rooms – no dorms, no bunks – at a good price. There's an inviting common area, where you can browse the free internet or swap pasta recipes in the open kitchen. There are en suite rooms in a house up the street, with self-catering options available.

★**Brinkies Guest House** B&B $$

(01856-851881; www.brinkiesguesthouse.co.uk; Brownstown Rd; s £50, d £80-90;) Just a short walk from the centre, but with a lonely, king-of-the-castle position overlooking the town and bay, this exceptional place offers five-star islander hospitality. Compact, modern rooms are handsome, stylish and comfortable, public areas are done out most attractively in wood, but above all it's the charming owner's flexibility and can-do attitude that makes this so special.

Breakfast is 'continental Orcadian' – a stupendous array of quality local cheese, smoked fish and homemade bere bannocks (a wheat-barley bread). Want a lie-in? No problem, saunter down at 10am. Don't want breakfast? How about packed lunch instead? Take Outertown Rd off Back Rd, turn right on to Brownstown Rd, and keep going.

Burnside Farm B&B $$

(01856-850723; www.burnside-farm.com; North End Rd/A965; s £60, d £85-90;) On a working dairy farm on the edge of Stromness, this offers lovely views over green fields, town and harbour. Rooms are elegant and maintain the style from when the house was built in the late forties, with elegant period furnishings. The top-notch bathrooms, however, are sparklingly contemporary. Breakfast comes with views, and the kindly owner couldn't be more welcoming.

Eating

Bayleaf Delicatessen DELI $

(01856-851605; www.bayleafdelicatessen.co.uk; 19 Graham Pl; snacks £2-5; 10am-5pm Mon-Sat, plus 10am-4pm Sun Jun-Aug) On one of the numerous little wynds off the main street through Stromness you'll find this very likeable little deli. Local cheeses and yoghurts are a highlight, alongside smoked fish, takeaway seafood salads and other tasty Orkney produce. There's good coffee too, though nowhere to sit down to sip it.

Hamnavoe Restaurant SEAFOOD $$

(01856-851226, 01856-850606; 35 Graham Pl; mains £15-22; 7-9pm Tue-Sun Jun-Aug) Tucked away off the main street, this Stromness favourite specialises in excellent local seafood in an intimate, cordial atmosphere. There's always something good off the boats, and the chef prides himself on his lobster. Booking is a must. It opens some weekends off-season; it's worth calling.

Information

Stromness Information Centre (01856-850716; www.visitorkney.com; Ferry Rd; 10am-3pm Mon-Sat Apr-Sep) In the ferry terminal.

Getting There & Around

Northlink Ferries (p941) Runs services from Stromness to Scrabster on the mainland (passenger/car £19.40/59, 1½ hours, two to three daily).

Bus X1 runs regularly to Kirkwall (£3.10, 30 minutes, hourly, seven Sunday), with some going on to St Margaret's Hope (£5.75, 1¼ hours).

Orkney Cycle Hire (p943) Family options include kids' bikes and child trailers.

Hoy

POP 400

Orkney's second-largest island, Hoy (meaning 'High Island'), got the lion's share of the archipelago's scenic beauty. Shallow turquoise bays lace the east coast and massive seacliffs guard the west, while peat and moorland cover Orkney's highest hills. Much of the north is a reserve for breeding seabirds.

Sights

Old Man of Hoy ROCK FORMATION

Hoy's best-known sight is this spectacular 137m-high rock stack jutting from the ocean off the tip of an eroded headland. It's a tough ascent and for experienced climbers only, but the walk to see it is a Hoy highlight, revealing much of the island's most spectacular scenery. You can also spot the Old Man from the Scrabster–Stromness ferry.

The easiest approach to the Old Man is from Rackwick Bay, a 5-mile walk by road from Moaness Pier (in Hoy village on the east coast, where the ferries dock) through the beautiful Rackwick Glen. You'll pass the 5000-year-old **Dwarfie Stane**, the only example of a rock-cut tomb in Scotland. On your return you can take the path via the Glens of Kinnaird and Berriedale Wood, Scotland's most northerly tuft of native forest.

From Rackwick Bay, where there's a hostel, the most popular path climbs steeply westwards then curves northwards, descending gradually to the edge of the cliffs opposite the Old Man of Hoy. Allow seven hours for the return trip from Moaness Pier, or three hours from Rackwick Bay.

Scapa Flow Visitor Centre & Museum MUSEUM

(01856-791300; www.orkney.gov.uk; Lyness; 10am-4.30pm Mon-Sat Mar-Apr & Oct, 9am-4.30pm Mon-Sat, 1st to last ferry Sun May-Sep) FREE Lyness was an important naval base during both world wars, when the British Grand Fleet was based in Scapa Flow. This fascinating museum and photographic display, located in an old pumphouse that once fed fuel to the ships, is a must-see for anyone interested in Orkney's military history. Take your time to browse the exhibits and have a look at the folders of supplementary information: letters home from a seaman lost when the *Royal Oak* was torpedoed are particularly moving.

It's just by the ferry slip at Lyness, so easily visited. There's a decent cafe here.

Sleeping & Eating

Hoy Centre HOSTEL $

(office hours 01856-873535, warden 01856-791315; https://orkney.campstead.com; dm/tw £19.20/53.50; P wifi) This clean, bright modern hostel has an enviable location, around 15 minutes' walk from Moaness Pier, at the base of the rugged Cuilags. Rooms are all en suite and include good-value family options; it also has a spacious kitchen and DVD lounge. Book via the website to avoid an admin fee.

Quoydale B&B $

(01856-791315; www.orkneyaccommodation.co.uk; s/d £35/60; P wifi pets) This welcoming B&B is nestled at the base of Ward Hill, on a working farm 1 mile south of the Moaness ferry terminal. It has spectacular views over Scapa Flow and offers tours and a taxi service. There's also a self-catering cottage available.

Getting There & Away

Orkney Ferries (p943) runs a passenger/bike ferry (adult £4.25, 30 minutes, two to six daily) between Stromness and Moaness at Hoy's northern end, and a car ferry to Lyness (with one service to/from Longhope) from Houton on Mainland (passenger/car £4.25/13.60, 40 minutes, up to seven daily Monday to Friday, two or three Saturday and Sunday); book cars well in advance. Sunday service is May to September only.

The Moaness ferry also stops at Graemsay. The Houton one also links to Flotta.

Northern Islands

The group of windswept islands north of Mainland is a haven for birds, rich in archaeological sites and blessed with wonderful white-sand beaches and azure seas. Though some are hillier than others, all offer a broadly similar landscape of flattish green farmland running down to scenic coastline. Some give a real sense of what Orkney was like before the modern world impinged upon island life.

Accessible by reasonably priced ferry or plane, the islands are well worth exploring. Though you can see 'the sights' in a matter of hours, the key is to stay a day or two and relax into the pace of island life.

Note that the 'ay' at the end of island names (from the Old Norse for 'island') is pronounced closer to 'ee'.

Orkney Ferries (p943) and Loganair (p943) enable you to make day trips to many of the islands from Kirkwall. That said, it's really best to stay and soak up the slow, easy pace of life.

Rousay

POP 200

Just off the north coast of Mainland, hilly Rousay merits exploration for its fine assembly of prehistoric sites, great views and relaxing away-from-it-all ambience. Connected by regular ferry from Tingwall, it makes a great little day trip, but you may well feel a pull to stay longer. A popular option is to hire a bike from Trumland Farm (p952) near the ferry and take on the 14-mile circuit of the island.

★ Midhowe Cairn & Broch ARCHAEOLOGICAL SITE

(HES; www.historicenvironment.scot; 24hr) FREE Six miles from the ferry, mighty Midhowe Cairn has been dubbed the 'Great Ship of Death'. Built around 3500 BC and enormous, it's divided into compartments, in which the remains of 25 people were found. Covered by a protective stone building, it's nevertheless memorable. Adjacent Midhowe Broch, whose sturdy stone lines echo the rocky shoreline's striations, is a muscular Iron Age fortified compound with a mezzanine floor. The sites are on the water, a 10-minute walk downhill from the main road.

Prehistoric Sites ARCHAEOLOGICAL SITE
(HES; www.historicenvironment.scot; ⏲24hr) FREE The major archaeological sites are clearly labelled from the road ringing the island. Heading west from the ferry, you soon come to **Taversoe Tuick**, an intriguing burial cairn constructed on two levels, with separate entrances – perhaps a joint tomb for different families; a semidetached solution in posthumous housing. Not far beyond are two other significant cairns; **Blackhammer**, then **Knowe of Yarso**, the latter a fair walk up the hill but with majestic views.

Trumland Farm HOSTEL $
(☎01856-821252; trumland@btopenworld.com; sites £6, dm £14-15; P 🐾) 🍃 An easy stroll from the ferry (turn left at the main road), this organic farm has a hostel with two dorms, a pretty little kitchen and common area. You can pitch tents and use the facilities; there's also well-equipped self-catering in a cottage and various farm buildings.

Taversoe INN $$
(☎01856-821325; www.taversoehotel.co.uk; s £40-55, d £80-95; P 📶) Two miles west from the ferry pier, the island's only hotel is an attractively low-key place, with renovated rooms offering excellent bathrooms – one a disabled-friendly wet room – and beautiful water views. The best views are from the dining room, which serves good-value meals. The friendly owners will collect you from the ferry.

Food is served from noon to 5pm Monday, noon to 9pm Tuesday to Saturday and noon to 7.30pm Sunday May to September, with shorter hours in winter.

ℹ Getting There & Around

BOAT

A small **ferry** (☎01856-751360; www.orkneyferries.co.uk) connects Tingwall on Mainland with Rousay (passenger/bicycle/car £4.25/free/13.60, 30 minutes, up to six daily) and the nearby islands of **Egilsay** and **Wyre**. Vehicle bookings are compulsory.

TAXI

Rousay Tours (☎01856-821234; www.rousaytours.co.uk; adult/child £32/10) offers taxi service and recommended guided tours of the island, including wildlife-spotting (seals and otters), visits to the prehistoric sites and optional tasty packed lunch.

Westray

POP 600

If you've time to visit only one of Orkney's Northern Islands, make Westray (www.westraypapawestray.co.uk) the one. The largest of the group, it has rolling farmland, handsome sandy beaches, great coastal walks and several appealing places to stay.

👁 Sights & Activities

★Noltland Castle CASTLE
(⏲8am-8pm) FREE A half-mile west of Pierowall stands this sturdy ruined towerhouse, built in the 16th century by Gilbert Balfour, aide to Mary, Queen of Scots. The castle is super-atmospheric and bristles with shot holes, part of the defences of the deceitful Balfour, who plotted to murder Cardinal Beaton and, after being exiled, the king of Sweden. Like a pantomime villain, he met a sticky end.

At the nearby Links of Noltland, archaeological investigation has resumed and interesting neolithic finds are being unearthed with regularity. Most intriguing has been a chamber built over a spring, which was possibly used as a sauna.

Noup Head NATURE RESERVE
FREE This bird reserve at Westray's northwestern tip is a dramatic area of sea cliffs with vast numbers of breeding seabirds from April to July. You can walk here along the clifftops from a car park, passing the impressive chasm of **Ramni Geo**, and return via the lighthouse access road (4 miles).

Westray Heritage Centre MUSEUM
(☎01857-677414; www.westrayheritage.co.uk; Pierowall; adult/child £3/50p; ⏲11.30am-5pm Mon, 9am-noon & 2-5pm Tue-Sat & 1.30-5pm Sun early May-late Sep) This has displays on local history, nature dioramas and archaeological finds, with some famous neolithic carvings (including the 5000-year-old 'Westray Wife'). These small sandstone figurines are the oldest known depictions of the human form so far found in the British Isles.

Westraak DRIVING
(☎01857-677777; www.westraak.co.uk; Quarry Rd, Pierowall; adult £59) This husband-and-wife outfit runs informative and engaging trips around the island, covering everything from Viking history to puffin mating habits. It also runs the island's taxi service.

Sleeping & Eating

★West Manse B&B $
(☎01857-677482; www.westmanse.co.uk; Westside; r per person £25; P 🛜 🐾) 🌿 No timetables reign at this imposing house with arcing coastal vistas; make your own breakfast when you feel like it. Your welcoming hosts have introduced a raft of green solutions for heating, fuel and more. Kids will love this unconventional place, with its play nooks and hobbit house, while art exhibitions, eclectic workshops, venerably comfortable furniture and clean air are drawcards for parents.

There's also a self-catering apartment, Brotchie (£300 per week), and soon a fabulous little waterside cottage in Pierowall totally designed for the needs of a disabled visitor accompanied by a carer.

Chalmersquoy & The Barn B&B, HOSTEL $
(☎01857-677214; http://chalmersquoywestray.co.uk; Pierowall; dm/s/q £22/29/65, apt for 4/6 £60/100, tent sites £7-10 plus per adult/child £2/1; P 🛜) This excellent, intimate, modern hostel is an Orcadian gem. It's heated throughout and has pristine kitchen facilities and an inviting lounge; rooms sleep two or three in comfort. Out the front, the lovely owners have top self-catering apartments with great views, and spacious en suite B&B rooms. It also has a campsite and a fabulous byre that hosts atmospheric concerts. A recommended all-round choice.

Pierowall Hotel PUB FOOD $
(☎01857-677472; www.pierowallhotel.co.uk; Pierowall; mains £8-11; ⊙food noon-2pm & 5-8.30pm Mon-Thu, 6-9pm Fri & Sat, 1-2.30pm & 6-8pm Sun; 🛜) The heart of this island community, the refurbished local pub is famous throughout Orkney for its popular fish and chips – whatever has turned up in the day's catch by the hotel's boats is displayed on the blackboard. There are also some curries available, but the sea is the way to go here. It also has rooms and hires bikes (£10 per day).

Getting There & Away

AIR

There are daily Loganair (p943) flights from Kirkwall to Westray (one way £37, 20 minutes).

BOAT

Orkney Ferries (p943) links Kirkwall with Rapness (passenger/car £8.35/19.70, 1½ hours, daily). A bus to the main town, Pierowall, meets the ferry.

Papa Westray

Known locally as Papay, this exquisitely peaceful, tiny island (4 miles by 1 mile) is home to possibly Europe's oldest domestic building, the 5500-year-old **Knap of Howar** (⊙24hr) FREE, and largest Arctic tern colony. Plus the two-minute hop from Westray is the world's shortest scheduled air service. It's a charming island with seals easily spotted while walking its coast.

Beltane House GUESTHOUSE, HOSTEL $
(☎01857-644224; www.papawestray.co.uk; Beltane; dm/s/d £20/28/44; P 🛜 🐾) Owned by the local community, this is the island's hub, with the only shop, and functions as a makeshift pub on a Saturday night. One wing is a hostel with bunks, the other a guesthouse with immaculate rooms with en suite. There are two kitchens, zippy wi-fi (when it works), a big lounge/eating area and views over grassy fields to the sea beyond.

It's just over a mile north of the ferry. You can also camp here (£8/4 per adult/child).

Getting There & Away

AIR

There are two or three daily **Loganair** (p943) flights to North Ronaldsay (£18, 20 minutes) from Kirkwall. The £21 return offer (you must stay overnight) is great value. Some of the Kirkwall flights go via Westray (£17, two minutes, the world's shortest scheduled flight) or North Ronaldsay (£17, 10 minutes).

BOAT

A passenger-only Orkney Ferries (p943) ferry runs from Pierowall on Westray to Papa Westray (£4.15, 25 minutes, three to six daily in summer); the crossing is free if you've come straight from the Kirkwall–Westray ferry. From October to April the boat sails by arrangement (01857-677216). On Fridays a car ferry from Kirkwall makes the journey to Papa Westray.

SHETLAND

Close enough to Norway geographically and historically to make nationality an ambiguous concept, the Shetland Islands are Britain's most northerly outpost. There's a Scandinavian lilt to the local accent, and streets named King Haakon or St Olaf remind that Shetland was under Norse rule until 1469, when it was gifted to Scotland in lieu of the dowry of a Danish princess.

The stirringly bleak setting – it's a Unesco geopark – still feels uniquely Scottish, though, with deep, naked glens flanked by steep hills, twinkling, sky-blue lochs and, of course, sheep on the roads.

Despite the famous ponies and woollens, it's no agricultural backwater. Offshore oil makes it quite a busy, well-heeled place, with hotels frequently block-booked for workers. Nevertheless nature still rules the seas and islands, and the birdlife is spectacular: pack binoculars.

ℹ Information

Lerwick Information Centre (p958) In the centre of the main town, this has comprehensive information on the islands.

Sumburgh Airport Information Centre (☎01950-460905; www.shetland.org; Sumburgh Airport; ⏲8.45am-4.45pm Mon-Fri, 10.15am-4pm Sat, 10.30am-5.30pm Sun, closed Sat Nov-Mar) Brochures are available when the office is shut.

www.shetland.org An excellent website with good info on accommodation, activities and more.

ℹ Getting There & Away

AIR

The main **airport** (LSI; ☎01950-461000; www.hial.co.uk) is at Sumburgh, 25 miles south of Lerwick. **Flybe** (☎0371 700 2000; www.flybe.com) runs daily services to Aberdeen, Kirkwall, Inverness, Edinburgh and Glasgow, and summer services to Bergen (Norway).

BOAT

Northlink Ferries (☎0845 600 0449; www.northlinkferries.co.uk; 📶) runs daily overnight car ferries between Aberdeen and Lerwick (high-season one way passenger/car £41/146, 12 to 15 hours), some stopping at Kirkwall, Orkney. With a basic ticket you can sleep in recliner chairs or the bar area. It's £36.50 for a berth in a shared cabin and £84 up to £137 for a comparatively luxurious double cabin. Sleeping pods (£18) are comfortable, reclinable seats. Ferries have a cafe, bar, paid lounge and cinema on board, plus slow wi-fi.

ℹ Getting Around

Public transport within and between the islands of Shetland is managed by ZetTrans (www.zettrans.org.uk). Timetable information for all air, bus and ferry services can be obtained at www.travel.shetland.org, from the ZetTrans website and from Lerwick's Viking bus station (p958).

AIR

Interisland flights are operated by **DirectFlight** (☎01595-840246; www.directflight.co.uk) from Tingwall airport, 6.5 miles northwest of Lerwick. There are big discounts for under-25s.

BOAT

Ferry services run by Shetland Islands Council (www.shetland.gov.uk/ferries) link Mainland to other islands from various points.

BICYCLE

If it's fine, cycling on the islands' excellent roads can be an exhilarating way to experience the stark beauty of Shetland. It can, however, be very windy and there are few spots to shelter. You can hire bikes from several places, including Grantfield Garage in Lerwick.

BUS

An extensive bus network, coordinated by ZetTrans (www.zettrans.org.uk), radiates from Lerwick to all corners of Mainland, and on (via ferry) to the islands of Yell and Unst. Schedules aren't great for day tripping from Lerwick.

CAR & MOTORCYCLE

Shetland has broad, well-made roads (think 'oil money'). Car hire is fuss-free, and vehicles can be delivered to transport terminals. Prices are usually around £40/200 for a day/week.

Bolts Car Hire (☎01595-693636; www.boltscarhire.co.uk; 26 North Rd, Lerwick) Office in Lerwick and does airport and ferry terminal rentals.

Grantfield Garage (☎01595-692709; www.grantfieldgarage.co.uk; North Rd, Lerwick; ⏲9am-5.30pm Mon-Sat) The cheapest. A short walk towards town from the Northlink ferry terminal.

Star Rent-a-Car (☎01595-692075; www.starrentacar.co.uk; 22 Commercial Rd, Lerwick) Opposite the bus station. Has an office at Sumburgh airport.

Lerwick

POP 6800

Built on the herring trade and modernised by the oil trade, Lerwick is Shetland's only real town, home to a third of the islands' population. It has a solidly maritime feel, with aquiline oilboats competing for space

Shetland

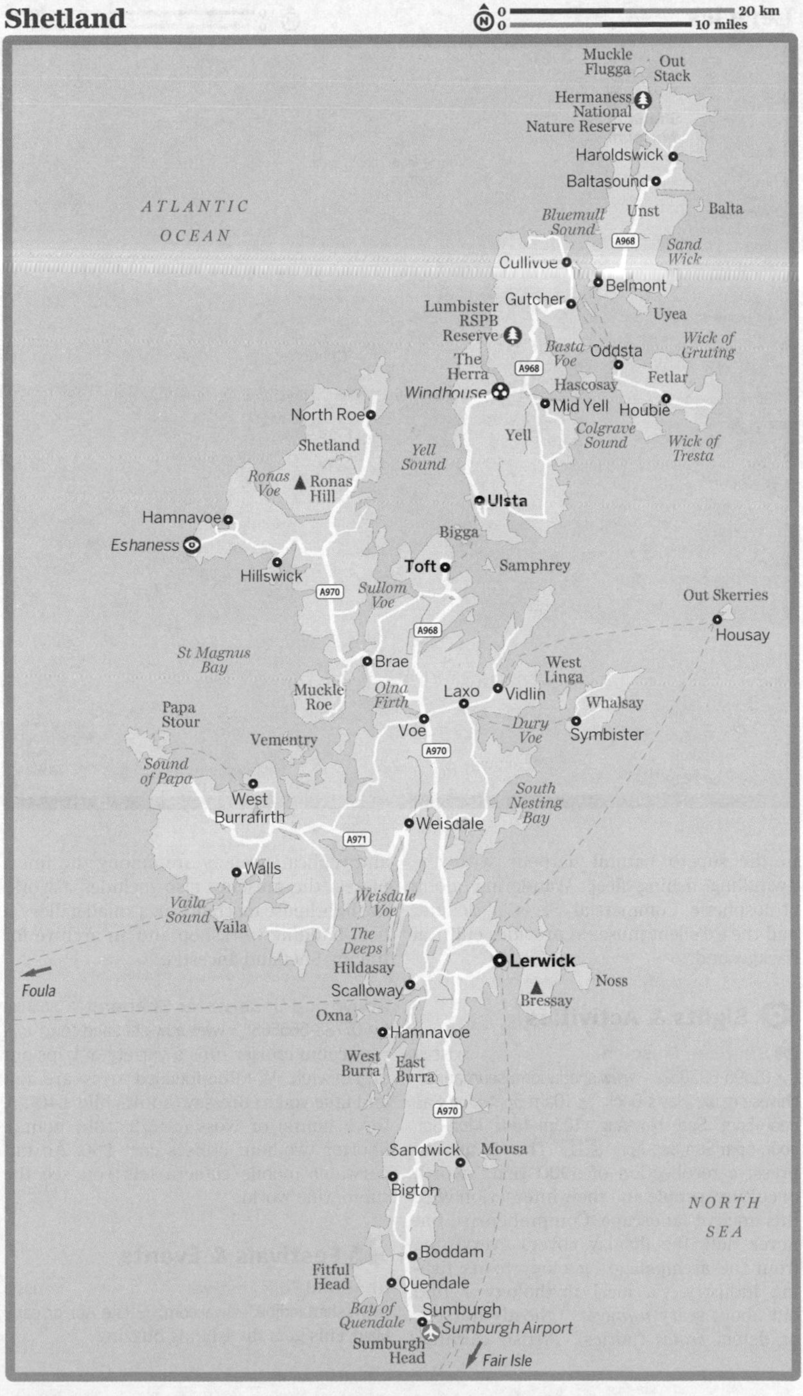
0 20 km
0 10 miles
Muckle Flugga
Out Stack
Hermaness National Nature Reserve
Haroldswick
Baltasound
ATLANTIC OCEAN
Bluemull Sound
Unst
Balta
A968
Sand Wick
Cullivoe
Belmont
Gutcher
Lumbister RSPB Reserve
Uyea
Basta Voe
Oddsta
Wick of Gruting
The Herra
A968
Fetlar
Windhouse
Hascosay
Mid Yell
Houbie
North Roe
Yell
Colgrave Sound
Wick of Tresta
Shetland
Yell Sound
Ronas Voe
Ronas Hill
Ulsta
Hamnavoe
Bigga
Eshaness
Toft
Samphrey
Hillswick
A970
Sullom Voe
Out Skerries
A968
Housay
St Magnus Bay
Brae
West Linga
Muckle Roe
Olna Firth
Laxo
Vidlin
Whalsay
Papa Stour
Voe
Dury Voe
Symbister
Vementry
A970
Sound of Papa
West Burrafirth
South Nesting Bay
Weisdale
A971
Walls
Weisdale Voe
Vaila Sound
Vaila
The Deeps
Hildasay
Lerwick
Foula
Noss
Scalloway
Bressay
Oxna
Hamnavoe
West Burra
East Burra
A970
Sandwick
Mousa
Bigton
NORTH SEA
Boddam
Fitful Head
Quendale
Sumburgh
Bay of Quendale
Sumburgh Airport
Sumburgh Head
Fair Isle

Lerwick

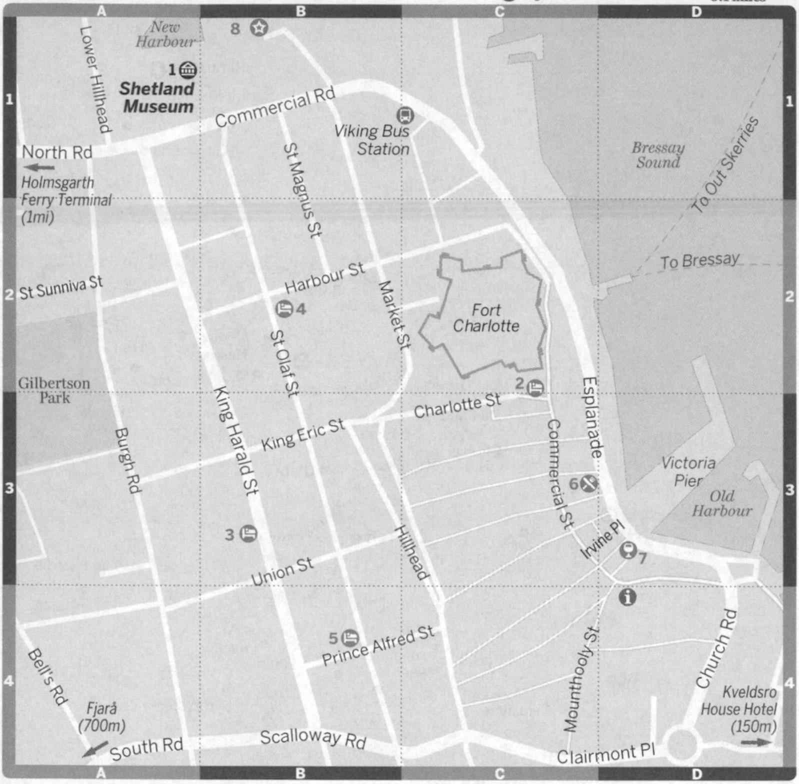

in the superb natural harbour with the dwindling fishing fleet. Wandering along atmospheric Commercial St is a delight, and the excellent museum provides cultural background.

Sights & Activities

★**Shetland Museum** MUSEUM
(☎01595-695057; www.shetlandmuseumandarchives.org.uk; Hay's Dock; ⏲10am-5pm Mon-Sat, noon-5pm Sun May-Aug, 10am-4pm Mon-Sat, noon-5pm Sun Sep-Apr) FREE This is an impressive recollection of 5000 years' worth of culture, people and their interaction with this ancient landscape. Comprehensive but never dull, the display covers everything from the archipelago's geology to its fishing industry, via local mythology – find out about scary *nyuggles* (ghostly horses), or detect *trows* (fairies). Pictish carvings and replica jewellery are among the finest pieces; the museum also includes a working lighthouse mechanism, a small gallery, a boat-building workshop and an archive for tracing Shetland ancestry.

Above and Underwater Shetland BOATING
(☎07788-665565; www.auw-shetland.com) A cosy cabin cruiser runs a variety of trips out of Lerwick. Wildlife-focused trips are fun and take you to Bressay (adult/child £40/25, three hours) or Noss (£45/25, 3½ hours). Shorter two-hour cruises cost £30. An underwater mobile camera lets you see the submarine world.

Festivals & Events

Shetland Folk Festival MUSIC
(www.shetlandfolkfestival.com; ⏲late Apr or early May) This gets the islands buzzing.

Lerwick

Sleeping

Lerwick has very average hotels but excellent B&Bs. It fills year-round; book ahead. There's no campsite within 15 miles.

Islesburgh House Hostel HOSTEL $
(01595-745100; www.islesburgh.org.uk; King Harald St; dm/tw/q £21/42/60; P @) This typically grand Lerwick mansion houses an excellent hostel, with comfortable dorms, a shop, a laundry, a cafe and an industrial kitchen. Electronic keys offer reliable security and no curfew. It's wise to book ahead in summer.

Woosung B&B $
(01595-693687; conroywoosung@hotmail.com; 43 St Olaf St; d £65, s/d without bathroom £35/60;) A budget gem in the heart of Lerwick B&B-land, this has a wise and welcoming host, and comfortable, clean, good-value rooms with fridge and microwave. Two of them share a compact but spotless bathroom. The solid stone house dates from the 19th century, built by a clipper captain who traded tea out of the Chinese port it's named after.

★ **Fort Charlotte Guesthouse** B&B $$
(01595-692140; www.fortcharlotte.co.uk; 1 Charlotte St; s/d £40/80;) Sheltering under the fortress walls, this friendly place offers summery en suite rooms, including great singles. Views down the pedestrian street are on offer in some; sloping ceilings and oriental touches add charm to others. It has local salmon for breakfast and a bike shed. Very popular; book ahead.

Rockvilla Guest House B&B $$
(01595-695804; www.rockvillaguesthouse.com; 88 St Olaf St; s/d £65/90;) Some of Shetland's B&Bs are aimed more at oilworkers than visitors, but this is quite the reverse: a relaxing, welcoming spot in a fine house behind a pretty garden. The three rooms are colour themed: Blue is bright, with a front-and-back outlook, Red is sultry with a sofa in the window, and smaller Green is shyer under the eaves.

Your hosts are friendly, and Jeff runs day tours to Sumburgh, Eshaness or Unst, among other places.

Kveldsro House Hotel HOTEL $$$
(01595-692195; www.shetlandhotels.com; Greenfield Pl; s/d £115/145; P) Lerwick's best hotel overlooks the harbour and has a quiet but central setting. It's a dignified small set-up that will appeal to older visitors or couples. All doubles cost the same, but some are markedly better than others, with four-poster beds or water views. All boast new stylish bathrooms and iPod docks. The bar area is elegant and has fine perspectives.

Eating

Mareel Cafe CAFE $
(01595-745500; www.mareel.org; Hay's Dock; light meals £3-5; 10am-11pm Sun-Thu, 10am-1am Fri & Sat, food to 9pm;) Buzzy, arty and colourful, this cheery venue in Mareel overlooks the water and does sandwiches and baked potatoes by day, and some cute Shetland tapas in the evenings. The coffee is decent, too, and it's a nice place for a cocktail.

Peerie Shop Cafe CAFE $
(01595-692816; www.peerieshop.co.uk; Esplanade; light meals £3-8; 9am-6pm Mon-Sat;) If you've been craving proper espresso since leaving the mainland, head to this gem, with art exhibitions, wire-mounted halogens and industrial-gantry chic. Newspapers, scrumptious cakes and sandwiches, hot chocolate that you deserve after that blasting wind outside, and – more rarely – outdoor seating give everyone a reason to be here.

★ **Hay's Dock** CAFE $$
(01595-741569; www.haysdock.co.uk; Hay's Dock, Shetland Museum; mains lunch £8-12, dinner £16-23; 10am-5pm Mon-Sat, noon-5pm Sun, plus 5.30-9pm Fri & Sat year-round & Tue-Thu Jun-Aug;

Upstairs in the Shetland Museum, this sports a wall of picture windows and a fairweather balcony that overlooks the harbour. Clean lines and pale wood recall Scandinavia, but the menu relies on carefully selected local and Scottish produce, with a substantial dash of international influence. Lunch ranges from delicious fish and chips to chowder, while evening menus concentrate on seafood and steak.

Fjarå CAFE **$$**
(01595-697388; www.fjaracoffee.com; Sea Rd; mains £8-18; 8am-10pm, food to 8pm;) A cute wooden building in a super location, Fjarå is perched above a rocky shore and takes full advantage of its vistas, with big picture windows looking out over the water and perhaps some basking seals. It does a bit of everything, with breakfasts, sandwiches, salads and bagels at lunch, beers, cocktails and some decent seafood dinner plates.

It's across the road from the Tesco supermarket at the southern entrance to town.

Drinking & Entertainment

Captain Flint's PUB
(01595-692249; 2 Commercial St; 11am-1am;) This port-side bar – Lerwick's liveliest – throbs with happy conversation and loud music, and has a distinctly nautical, creaky-wooden feel. There's a cross-section of young 'uns, tourists, boat folk and older locals. It has live music some nights and a pool table upstairs. Try a G&T with the seaweed-infused version of the local Reel gin.

Mareel ARTS VENUE
(01595-745500; www.mareel.org; Hay's Dock) Modern Mareel is a thriving arts centre, with a cinema, concert hall and cafe in a great waterside location.

Information

Lerwick Information Centre (01595-693434; www.shetland.org; cnr Commercial & Mounthooly Sts; 9am-5pm Mon-Sat & 10am-4pm Sun Apr-Sep, 10am-4pm Mon-Sat Oct-Mar) Helpful, with a good range of books and maps.

Getting There & Away

BOAT

Northlink Ferries (p954) from Aberdeen and Kirkwall dock at **Holmsgarth terminal** (Holmsgarth Rd), a 15-minute walk northwest from the town centre.

BUS

From **Viking bus station** (01595-694100; Commercial Rd), buses service various corners of the archipelago, including regular services to/from Sumburgh Airport.

Sumburgh

From Lerwick, it's 25 miles down a narrow, hilly tail of land to Sumburgh Head. Important prehistoric sights, fabulous bird-watching and glorious white-sand beaches make it one of Shetland's most interesting areas. The lapping waters are an inviting turquoise – if it weren't for the raging Arctic gales, you'd be tempted to have a dip.

Sights & Activities

★Sumburgh Head Visitor Centre LIGHTHOUSE, MUSEUM
(01595-694688; www.sumburghhead.com; adult/child £6/2; 11am-5.30pm Apr-Sep) High on the cliffs at Sumburgh Head, this excellent attraction is set across several buildings. Displays explain about the lighthouse, foghorn and radar station that operated here, and there's a good exhibition on the local marine creatures and birds. You can visit the lighthouse itself on a guided tour for an extra charge.

Jarlshof ARCHAEOLOGICAL SITE
(HES; 01950-460112; www.historicenvironment.scot; adult/child £5.50/3.30; 9.30am-5.30pm Apr-Sep, 9.30am-dusk Oct-Mar) Old and new collide here, with Sumburgh airport right by this picturesque, instructive archaeological site. Various periods of occupation from 2500 BC to AD1500 can be seen; the complete change upon the Vikings' arrival is obvious: their rectangular longhouses present a marked contrast to the preceding brochs, roundhouses and wheelhouses. Atop the site is 16th-century Old House, named 'Jarlshof' in a novel by Sir Walter Scott. There's an informative audio tour included with admission.

Old Scatness ARCHAEOLOGICAL SITE
(01595-694688; www.shetland-heritage.co.uk/old-scatness; adult/child £5/4; 10.15am-4.30pm Fri mid-May–Aug;) This dig brings Shetland's prehistory vividly to life; it's a must-see for archaeology buffs, but fun for kids, too. Clued-up guides in Iron Age clothes show you the site, which has provided important clues on the Viking takeover and dating of Shetland material. It has an im-

pressive broch from around 300 BC, roundhouses and later wheelhouses. Best of all is the reconstruction with peat fire and working loom. At time of research, lack of funding had badly restricted the opening hours.

★ Sumburgh Head BIRDWATCHING
(www.rspb.org.uk) At Mainland's southern tip, these spectacular cliffs offer a good chance to get up close to puffins, and huge nesting colonies of fulmars, guillemots and razorbills. If you're lucky, you might spot dolphins, minke whales or orcas. Also here is an excellent visitor centre, in the lighthouse buildings.

Getting There & Away

Bus 6 runs to Sumburgh and Sumburgh Airport from Lerwick (£2.70 to Sumburgh, £3.10 to the airport; one hour, eight Monday to Saturday, five Sunday).

The North Isles

Yell, Unst and Fetlar make up the North Isles, which are connected to each other by ferry, as is Yell to Mainland. All are great for nature-watching; Unst has the most to offer overall. If you're going to spend a night on both Yell and Fetlar or Unst, visit Yell on the way back, as the ferry to Unst is free if you are coming from Mainland that same day.

Yell

POP 1000

Yell if you like but nobody will hear; the desolate peat moors here are typical Shetland scenery. Still, the bleak landscape has an undeniable appeal.

Lots of excellent self-catering cottages are dotted around the island; check www.welcometoyell.com for options.

Old Haa Museum MUSEUM
(☎01957-722339; www.shetlandheritageassociation.com; Burravoe; ⏰10am-4pm Mon-Thu & Sat & 2-5pm Sun May-Sep) FREE This has a medley of curious objects (pipes, piano, doll-in-cradle, tiny bibles, ships in bottles and a sperm-whale jaw) as well as an archive of local history and a tearoom. It's in Burravoe, 4 miles east of the southern ferry terminal in Ulsta. Monday opening varies.

Lumbister RSPB Reserve BIRDWATCHING
(www.rspb.org.uk) At this nature reserve red-throated divers, merlins, skuas and other bird species breed. The area is home to a large otter population, too, best viewed around Whale Firth, where you may also spot common and grey seals.

Windhouse Lodge HUT $
(☎office 01595-694688, warden 01957-702350; www.camping-bods.com; Mid-Yell; dm £10; ⏰Mar-Oct) Below the haunted ruins of Windhouse, and on the A968, you'll find this well-kept, clean, snug camping *böd* (hut) with power and a pot-belly stove to warm your toes. It's one of the cosiest, with a modern interior. Mattresses are thin. Book via phone or the website.

Quam B&B B&B $$
(☎01957-766256; www.quambandbyellshetland.co.uk; Westsandwick; d £70; P 📶) Just off the main road through the island, this farm B&B has friendly owners and three good rooms. Breakfast features eggs from the farm, which also has cute ponies that you can meet. Dinners (£15 per person) can be arranged.

Getting There & Away

BOAT

Yell is connected with Mainland by **ferries** (☎01595-745804; www.shetland.gov.uk/ferries) between Toft and Ulsta (passenger/car return £5.30/7.70, 20 minutes, frequent). It's wise to book car space in summer.

BUS

One bus runs Monday to Saturday from Lerwick to Yell (£4.20), connecting with ferries to Fetlar and Unst; connecting services cover other parts of the island.

UP HELLY AA!

Shetland's long Viking history has rubbed off in more ways than just street names and square-shouldered locals. Most villages have a fire festival, a continuation of Viking midwinter celebrations of the rebirth of the sun. The most spectacular happens in Lerwick.

Up Helly Aa (www.uphellyaa.org; ⏰Jan) takes place on the last Tuesday in January. Squads of *guizers* dress in Viking costume and march through the streets with blazing torches, dragging a replica longship, which they then surround and burn, bellowing out Viking songs from behind bushy beards.

Unst

POP 600

You're fast running out of Scotland once you cross to rugged Unst (www.unst.org). Scotland's most northerly inhabited island is prettier than Yell, with bare, velvety-smooth hills and settlements clinging to waterside locations, fiercely resisting the buffeting winds.

Sights

★Hermaness Nature Reserve NATURE RESERVE
(www.nnr-scotland.org.uk) At marvellous Hermaness headland, a 4.5-mile round walk takes you to cliffs where gannets, fulmars and guillemots nest, and numerous puffins frolic. You can see Scotland's most northerly point, the rocks of **Out Stack**, and **Muckle Flugga**, with its lighthouse built by Robert Louis Stevenson's uncle. Duck into the **visitor centre** (☎01595-711278; ⏲9am-5pm May-early Sep) FREE, with its poignant story about long-time resident Albert Ross.

The path to the cliffs is guarded by a squadron of great skuas who nest in the nearby heather, and dive-bomb at will if they feel threatened. They're damn solid birds too, but don't usually make contact.

★Unst Bus Shelter LANDMARK
(www.unstbusshelter.shetland.co.uk; Baltasound) At the turnoff to Littlehamar, just past Baltasound, is Britain's most impressive bus stop. Enterprising locals, tired of waiting in discomfort, decided to do a job on it, and it now boasts posh seating, novels, numerous decorative features and a visitors' book to sign. The theme and colour scheme changes yearly.

Sleeping & Eating

★Gardiesfauld Hostel HOSTEL, CAMPGROUND $
(☎01957-755279; www.gardiesfauld.shetland.co.uk; 2 East Rd, Uyeasound; tent sites per adult/child £6/2, dm adult/child £15/8; ⏲Apr-Sep; P 📶) This spotless hostel has very spacious dorms with lockers, family rooms, a garden, an elegant lounge and a wee conservatory dining area with great bay views. You can camp here too, with separate areas for tents and vans. The bus stops right outside. Bring 20p pieces for the showers.

Baltasound Hotel HOTEL $$
(☎01957-711334; www.baltasoundhotel.co.uk; Baltasound; d £98-110; ⏲May–mid-Oct; P 📶) Brightly decorated, commodious rooms – some bigger than others – are complemented by wooden chalets arrayed around the lawn. It's worth the upgrade to the 'large doubles', which sport good modern bathrooms. There's a lovely country outlook, and evening bar meals (mains £8 to £13; food served 6pm to 8pm) in a dining room dappled by the setting sun. 'Unserviced' rooms offer a cheaper deal.

Getting There & Around

BICYCLE

Hire **bikes** (☎01957-711393; www.unstcyclehire.co.uk; Haroldswick; per day/week £10/50; ⏲11.30am-5pm Mon-Sat, 1-4pm Sun, can hire out of hours) in the chocolate shop at the Saxa Vord complex in Haroldswick.

BOAT

Unst is connected with Yell and Fetlar by a **ferry** (p959) between Gutcher and Belmont (free if coming from Mainland that day, otherwise passenger/car £5.30/7.70 return, 10 minutes, frequent).

BUS

One bus runs Monday to Saturday from Lerwick to the Unst ferry (£4.20, two hours). There are connecting services around Unst itself.

Understand Great Britain

Great Britain Today

For Britain and the British, the first decade and a half of the 21st century has been a time of change, controversy and national soul-searching. As Scottish and Welsh nationalism have gained ground, the English seemed to become less certain about their own identity. In 2016 a referendum vote on whether to remain part of the European Union revealed a nation divided over its future, and the long-term consequences remain uncertain.

Best on Film

Brief Encounter (1945) Classic tale of buttoned-up English love affair.
My Beautiful Laundrette (1985) Touching and comic study of racism and homophobia in Thatcher-era London.
Trainspotting (1996) The gritty underbelly of life among Edinburgh drug addicts.
Under Milk Wood (1972) Film of Dylan Thomas' play about life in a fictional Welsh fishing village.
Suffragette (2015) Compelling account of the pre-WWI fight to secure votes for women.

Best in Print

Notes from a Small Island (Bill Bryson; 1995) An American's fond and astute take on Britain.
Raw Spirit (Iain Banks; 2003) An enjoyable jaunt around Scotland in search of the perfect whisky.
Slow Coast Home (Josie Drew; 2003) The chatty tale of a 5000-mile cycle tour through England and Wales.
On the Black Hill (Bruce Chatwin; 1982) Traces 20th-century Welsh rural life through the lens of an oddball pair of twins.
On the Slow Train (Michael Williams; 2011) A paean to the pleasure of British rail travel.

Goodbye to Europe?

On June 24 2016, Britain awoke to monumental news. By a slim referendum vote the UK had opted to leave the European Union, cutting ties stretching back 43 years. Within hours of the so-called 'Brexit' (British exit) result the Prime Minister, David Cameron, who'd campaigned to remain within the EU, announced his resignation. The pound fell to its worst level for 31 years; the FTSE 100 share index fell to an eight-year low.

The result mattered so much because British and EU laws had become intertwined, from migration to trade, from fishing to human rights, from weights and measures to the environment. The closeness of that relationship was a comfort to some but anathema to others. Remain supporters felt protected by Europe-wide civil rights; Leave supporters felt Britain's right to shape its own destiny was under threat. These divisions were brought sharply into focus by a fierce, often acrimonious, referendum campaign.

The referendum result was very close: 52% voted to leave the EU against 48% for remain, revealing a country polarised by different views. Some argued the country would be freed from the shackles of an ailing EU, while others saw a country cast dangerously adrift. The economy and health service were central issues, but – against the backdrop of a Europe-wide refugee crisis – the real flashpoint was immigration, an issue that has bubbled uncomfortably under the surface of British politics for decades.

This time the debate revolved around whether Britain should have the right to set limits on immigration from within the EU. Some argued Britain didn't have enough resources to cope with more migrants, others pointed to the ranks of EU workers fulfilling important roles, notably in the health service. There were bitter arguments over whether high levels of migration meant 'Britishness' itself was under threat. For some it was a debate about latent racism, for others it was about sovereignty.

The State of the Union

Perhaps those divisions have something to do with the differences between Great Britain, the United Kingdom and the four nations that comprise the UK. They're confusing but crucial. Great Britain is the collective name for England, Scotland and Wales. The UK is the political union between Great Britain and Northern Ireland, not to be confused with the British Isles – a purely geographical term for a bunch of islands including Great Britain and Ireland. And if you can find a British person who can nail the finer points of those distinctions, bravo. It tends to mean people in Britain are increasingly unsure how to identify themselves – English, Scottish, Welsh, Irish, British or European?

These distinctions might have major political consequences because the EU referendum results were divided by nation: England and Wales voted to leave the EU (both around 53% in favour), but Scotland (62% against) and Northern Ireland (56% against) voted to remain.

In a 2014 referendum Scotland had voted 55% to 45% to remain within the UK. Within hours of the EU referendum result, Scotland's First Minister, Nicola Sturgeon, said that to prevent Scotland being taken out of the EU against its will, a second Scottish Independence referendum was now 'highly likely'. Meanwhile, there were calls in Northern Ireland for a broader poll on whether it should now unite with the Republic of Ireland. The state of this centuries-old union has become very uncertain.

Keep Calm and Carry On

One thing the British are united about is the monarchy. It consistently enjoys popular support; a 2015 YouGov poll found that 68% of Britons thought the royal family was good for the country. Many put the monarchy's success down to Queen Elizabeth II, Britain's longest-serving monarch, who celebrated, amid much fanfare, her 90th birthday in 2016.

One slogan you'll see repeated time and again is 'Keep Calm and Carry On'. The phrase comes from a WWII government motivational poster, which was rediscovered in 2000. Merchandisers seized on it, stamping the distinctive text, often with 'witty' modifications, on everything from T-shirts and tea towels to knickers and coffee mugs. It's hugely popular, largely because it evokes a very British attitude towards adversity – to keep your chin up and get on with things amid chaos. In the immediate Brexit aftermath, many wits argued the slogan would come in very handy. But the wheels of government grind slowly, and it's unlikely that visitors will notice anything different – except perhaps for the exchange rate – for at least the next few years.

POPULATION: **61.4 MILLION**

AREA: **88,500 SQ MILES**

GDP PER CAPITA: **£29,807**

GDP GROWTH: **2.3%**

INFLATION: **0.3%**

UNEMPLOYMENT: **4.9%**

if Great Britain were 100 people

87 would be white
7 would be Asian
3 would be black
3 would be mixed/other

belief systems

(% of population)

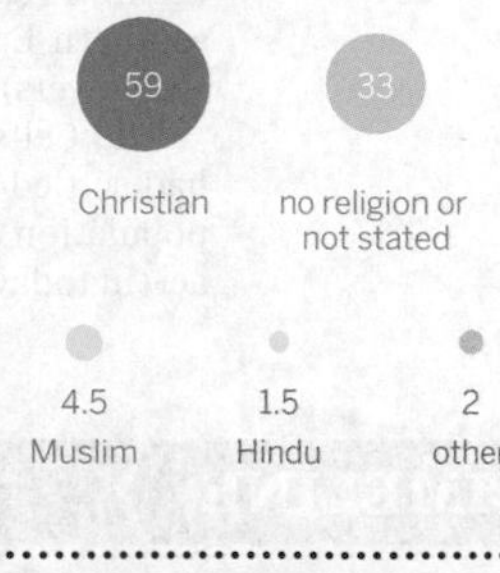

population per sq km

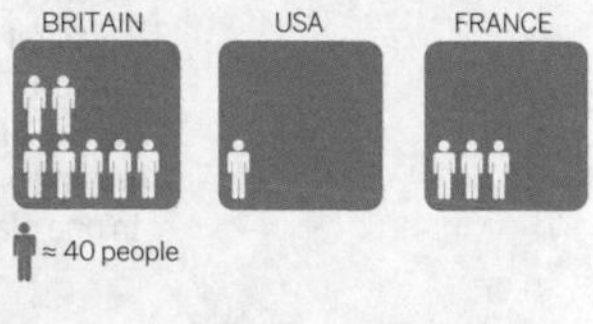

History

Britain may be a small country on the edge of Europe, but it has rarely been on the sidelines of history. For thousands of years, invaders and immigrants have arrived, settled and made their mark. The result is Britain's fascinating mix of landscape, culture and language. That rich historic legacy – everything from Stonehenge to Culloden, via Hadrian's Wall, Canterbury Cathedral, Caernarfon Castle and the Tower of London – is one of the country's most absorbing aspects.

Great Britain consists of the countries of England, Wales and Scotland. The United Kingdom (UK) is Great Britain plus Northern Ireland. The British Isles is a *geographical* term for the islands that make up the UK and the Republic of Ireland, plus others such as the Channel Islands.

First Arrivals

Around 4000 BC, as glaciers retreated in the wake of the Ice Age, a group of migrants arrived from Europe, but instead of hunting and moving on, they settled in one place and started farming. Alongside their fields, Britain's Stone Age people used rocks and turf to build massive burial mounds; the remains of many of these can still be seen, including West Kennet Long Barrow in Wiltshire, Pentre Ifan in Pembrokeshire and Maeshowe in Orkney. But the most impressive legacies left by these nascent Britons were the enigmatic stone circles of Callanish, Avebury and Stonehenge.

Iron & Celts

During the Iron Age (from 800 BC to AD 100) the population expanded and began to divide into specific tribes. Forests were cleared as more land was used for farming. This led to a patchwork pattern of fields, woods and small villages that still exists today in many parts of rural Britain. As the population grew, territorial defence became an issue, so the Iron Age people left another legacy: the great 'earthwork' castles of southern England, stone forts in northern England and brochs (defensive towers) in Wales and Scotland.

The Celts, a people who originally migrated from Central Europe, had settled across much of Britain by around 500 BC. A Celtic-British population developed, comprising about 20 tribes, including the Cantiaci (in today's county of Kent), the Iceni (Norfolk), the Brigantes (north-

TIMELINE

4000 BC

Neolithic peoples migrate from continental Europe. They differ significantly from previous arrivals: instead of hunting and moving on, they settle in one place and start farming.

c 500 BC

The Celts, a group originally from Central Europe, arrive in Britain, and by the middle of the 1st millennium BC have settled across much of the island, absorbing the indigenous people.

c 55 BC

Relatively small groups of Roman invaders under the command of Julius Caesar make forays into southern England from the northern coast of Gaul (today's France).

west England), the Picts and Caledonii (Scotland), the Ordivices (parts of Wales) and the Scotti (Ireland).

You noticed the Latin-sounding names? That's because the tribal tags were first handed out by the next arrivals on Britain's shores...

Probably built around 3000 BC, Stonehenge has stood on Salisbury Plain for more than 5000 years and is older than the famous Great Pyramids of Egypt.

Enter the Romans

Julius Caesar, the Roman ruler everyone remembers, made forays to the island of Britain in 55 BC. But the real Roman invasion happened a century later, when Emperor Claudius led a ruthless campaign resulting in the Romans controlling pretty much everywhere in southern England by AD 50.

Much of the occupation was straightforward: several Celtic-British tribal kings realised collaboration was more profitable than battle. It wasn't all plain sailing, though, and some locals fought back. The most famous freedom fighter was warrior-queen Boudica, who led an army as far as Londinium, the Roman port on the present site of London.

However, opposition was mostly sporadic and no real threat to the legions' military might. By around AD 80 the new province of Britannia (much of today's England and Wales) was firmly under Roman rule.

Exit the Romans

Settlement by the Romans in Britain lasted almost four centuries. Intermarriage was common between locals and incomers (many from other parts of the empire, including today's Belgium, Spain and Syria), and a Romano-British population evolved, particularly in the towns, while indigenous Celtic-British culture remained in rural areas.

Along with stability and wealth, the Romans introduced a new religion called Christianity, officially recognised by Emperor Constantine in AD 313. Although Romano-British culture was thriving by this time, back in its Mediterranean heartland the empire was already in decline.

It was an untidy finale. Britannia was simply dumped by Rome, and the colony slowly fizzled out of existence. But historians are tidy folk, and the end of Roman power in Britain is generally dated at AD 410.

Historical Websites

- www.royal.uk
- www.bbc.co.uk/history
- www.englishmonarchs.co.uk
- www.victorianweb.org

The Emergence of England

Britain's post-Roman power vacuum didn't go unnoticed and once again invaders arrived from the European mainland. Angles and Saxons (Teutonic tribes from the land we now call Germany) advanced across the former Roman turf.

Historians disagree on exactly what happened next. Either the Anglo-Saxons largely replaced or absorbed the Romano-British and Celtic population, or the indigenous tribes simply adopted Anglo-Saxon language

AD 43 Emperor Claudius leads the first proper Roman invasion of England. His army wages a ruthless campaign, and the Romans control most of southern England by AD 50.

60 Warrior-queen Boudica leads an army against the Romans, destroys the Roman town of Colchester and gets as far as Londinium, the Roman port on the present site of London.

60 In Wales the Celts, led by their mystic faith-healers, the druids, fight a last stand on Anglesey against the Roman army; they are beaten but not totally conquered.

122 Rather than conquer wild north British tribes, Emperor Hadrian settles for building a coast-to-coast barricade. For nearly 300 years, Hadrian's Wall marks the northernmost limit of the Roman Empire.

Boudica was queen of the Iceni, a Celtic-British tribe whose territory was invaded by the Romans around AD 60. A year later, she led an army against the Roman settlements of Camulodunum (now Colchester) and Londinium (London), but was eventually defeated at the Battle of Watling Street (in today's Shropshire).

and culture. Either way, by the late 6th century much of the area we now call England was dominated by the Anglo-Saxons and divided into three kingdoms: Wessex (in today's southern England), Mercia (the Midlands) and Northumbria (northern England).

In many areas the original inhabitants lived alongside the Anglo-Saxons and remained unaffected by the incomers (the Celtic language was still being spoken in parts of southern England when the Normans invaded 500 years later), but the overall impact was immense: the core of the modern English language is Anglo-Saxon, many place names have Anglo-Saxon roots, and the very term 'Anglo-Saxon' has become a (much-abused and factually incorrect) byword for 'pure English'.

The Waking of Wales

The Celts on the western fringes of the British Isles (particularly in Ireland) kept alive their own distinct yet Roman-influenced culture. And while the Anglo-Saxons occupied eastern Britain, towards the end of the 5th century the Scotti (from today's Ireland) invaded what is today Wales and western Scotland.

In response to the invasion, people from the kingdom of Gododdin (near today's Edinburgh) moved to northwest Wales to drive out the invaders, then stayed and settled in the area, which became the kingdom of Gwynedd. (The modern county in northern Wales still proudly bears this name.) More settlers came to Wales from Cornwall and western France, and Christian missionaries arrived from Ireland in the 6th and 7th centuries.

Christianity was introduced to Britain by the Romans and adopted by the Celts, but the Anglo-Saxons were pagans, and their invasion of Britain forced the Christian religion, along with other aspects of Celtic culture, to the edges of the British Isles – today's Wales, Scotland and Ireland.

The people of Wales were also under pressure to the east, harassed by the Anglo-Saxons. In response, by the 8th century the disparate tribes of Wales had started to band together and sow the seeds of nationhood. They called themselves *cymry* (fellow countrymen), and today Cymru is the Welsh word for Wales.

The Stirring of Scotland

While Wales was becoming established in the west of Britain, similar events were taking place to the north. The Picts were the region's dominant indigenous tribe (in the north and east) and named their kingdom Alba, which remains to this day the Gaelic word for Scotland. Ancient Britons inhabited the southwest.

Following the end of Roman rule in Britannia, Alba was invaded from two sides: first, towards the end of the 5th century, the Scotti crossed the sea from Ireland and established the kingdom of Dalriada (in what is now Argyll); then in the 7th century Anglo-Saxons from the expanding English kingdom of Northumbria moved in to colonise the southeast.

200

The Romans build a defensive wall around the city of London with four main entrance gates, still remembered today by the districts of Aldgate, Ludgate, Newgate and Bishopsgate.

c 410

As the classical world's greatest empire finally declines after more than three centuries of relative peace and prosperity, Roman rule ends in Britain with more of a whimper than a bang.

5th century

Teutonic tribes (known today as the Anglo-Saxons) from the area now called Germany migrate to England and quickly spread across much of the country.

Late 5th century

The Scotti people (from today's Ireland) invade the land of the Picts (today's Scotland). In today's Argyll they establish the kingdom of Dalriada.

But by this time the Scotti were well dug in alongside the Picts, foreshadowing the time when yet another name – Scotland – would be applied to northern Britain.

A History of Britain by historian and TV star Simon Schama is a highly accessible set of three books, examining events from 3000 BC to AD 2000.

The Viking Era

In the 9th century, just as the new territories of England, Wales and Scotland were becoming established, Britain was yet again invaded by a bunch of pesky continentals. This time, it was the Vikings – Nordic people from today's Scandinavia.

It's another classic historical image: blonde hair, horned helmets, big swords, square-sailed longboats, rape and pillage. Tradition has it that Vikings turned up, killed everyone, took everything and left. There's *some* truth in that, but in reality many Vikings settled in Britain, and their legacy is especially evident in today's northern England, Orkney and Shetland.

After conquering northern and eastern areas, the Vikings started to expand into central England. Blocking their route were the Anglo-Saxon armies led by Alfred the Great, the king of Wessex and one of English history's best-known characters.

The battles that followed were seminal to the foundation of the nation-state of England, but the fighting didn't all go Alfred's way. For a few months he was on the run, wading through swamps, hiding in peasant hovels and famously burning cakes. It was the stuff of legend, and by 886 Alfred had gathered his strength and pushed the Vikings back to the north.

United England?

Thus England was divided in two: north and east was the Viking 'Danelaw', while south and west was Anglo-Saxon territory. Alfred was hailed as king of the English – the first time the Anglo-Saxons regarded themselves as a truly united people.

Alfred's son and successor was Edward the Elder. After more battles, he gained control of the Danelaw, and thus became the first king to rule the whole of England. His son, Athelstan, took the process a stage further and was specifically crowned King of England in 927. But it was hardly cause for celebration: the Vikings were still around, and later in the 10th century more raids from Scandinavia threatened this fledgling English unity. Over the following decades, control swung from Saxon (King Edgar) to Dane (King Knut) and back to Saxon again (King Edward the Confessor). As England came to the end of the 1st millennium AD, the future was anything but certain.

Myths and Legends of the British Isles by Richard Barber is an ideal read if you want a break from firm historical facts. Learn about King Arthur and the Knights of the Round Table, plus much more from the mists of time.

Early 6th century

St Columba establishes a Christian mission on the Scottish island of Iona. By the late 8th century the mission is responsible for the conversion of most of Scotland.

597

Pope Gregory sends missionary St Augustine to southern England to revive interest in Christianity among the southern Anglo-Saxons. His colleague St Aidan similarly converts many people in northern England.

7th century

Anglo-Saxons from the expanding English kingdom of Northumbria attempt to colonise southeast Alba (today's southern Scotland) and are met by the Scotti.

685

The Pictish king Bridei defeats the Northumbrians at Nechtansmere in Angus, an against-the-odds victory that sets the foundations for Scotland as a separate entity.

Highs & Lows in Wales

Meanwhile, as England fought off the Viking threat, Wales was also dealing with the Nordic intruders. Building on the initial cooperation forced upon them by Anglo-Saxon oppression, in the 9th and 10th centuries the small kingdoms of Wales began cooperating, through necessity, to repel the Vikings.

King Rhodri Mawr (who died in 878) defeated a Viking force off the Isle of Anglesey and began the unification process. His grandson Hywel the Good is thought to have been responsible for drawing up a set of laws to bind the disparate Welsh tribes. But just as Wales was becoming a recognisable entity, the fledgling country was faced with more destructive onslaughts than it could handle and in 927 the Welsh kings recognised the Anglo-Saxon King Athelstan as their overlord, in exchange for an anti-Viking alliance.

Scotland Becomes a Kingdom

In the 9th century, the king of the Scotti of Dalriada was one Kenneth MacAlpin. His father was a Scot, but his mother was a Pictish princess, so MacAlpin took advantage of the Pictish custom of matrilineal succession to declare himself ruler of both the Scots *and* the Picts, and therefore king of all Alba.

In a surprisingly short time, the Scots gained cultural and political ascendancy. The Picts were absorbed, and their culture disappeared; from the union of Alba and Pictland came the beginnings of a Scottish kingdom.

In the 11th century, Scottish nation-building was further consolidated by King Malcolm III (whose most famous act was the 1057 murder of Macbeth, immortalised by William Shakespeare). With his English queen, Margaret, he founded the Canmore dynasty that would rule Scotland for the next two centuries.

1066 & All That

Back in England things were unsettled, as the royal pendulum swung between Saxon and Viking monarchs. When King Edward the Confessor died, the crown passed to Harold, his brother-in-law. That should've settled things, but Edward had a cousin in Normandy (the northern part of today's France) called William, who thought that *he* had a right to the throne of England.

The result was the Battle of Hastings in 1066, the most memorable of dates for anyone who's studied English history – or for anyone who hasn't. William sailed from Normandy with an army of Norman soldiers, the Saxons were defeated and Harold was killed (according to tradition, by an arrow in the eye).

The Year 1000 by Robert Lacey and Danny Danziger looks long and hard at English life a millennium ago. Apparently it was cold and damp then, too.

8th century

King Offa of Mercia orders the construction of a clear border between his kingdom and Wales – a defensive ditch called Offa's Dyke, still visible today.

850

Vikings come from today's Denmark and conquer east and northeast England. They establish their capital at Jorvik, today's city of York.

872

The King of Norway creates an earldom in Orkney; Shetland is also governed from here. These island groups become a Viking base for raids and colonisation into Scotland and northern England.

9th century

Kenneth MacAlpin, the king of the Scotti, declares himself ruler of both the Scots *and* the Picts, thus uniting Scotland north of the Firth of Forth into a single kingdom.

Norman Wisdom

William became king of England, earning the title William the Conqueror. It was no idle nickname – to control the Anglo-Saxons, the Norman invaders wisely built castles across their newly won territory, and by 1086 the Domesday Book provided a census of England's current stock and future potential.

In the years after the invasion, the French-speaking Normans and the English-speaking Anglo-Saxons kept pretty much to themselves. A strict hierarchy of class developed, known as the feudal system.

Intermarriage was not completely unknown; William's son, Henry I, married a Saxon princess. Nonetheless, such unifying moves stood for nothing after Henry's death: a bitter struggle for succession followed, finally won by Henry II, who took the throne as the first king of the Plantagenet dynasty.

At the top of the feudal system came the monarch, followed by nobles (barons, dukes and bishops), then earls, knights, lords and ladies. At the bottom were peasants or 'serfs'. This strict hierarchy became the basis of a class system that still exists in Britain today.

Post-Invasion Wales & Scotland

To secure his new kingdom, and keep the Welsh in theirs, William the Conqueror built castles and appointed feudal barons along the border. The Lords Marcher, as they were known, became massively rich and powerful, and the parts of western England along the Welsh border are still called the Marches today.

In Scotland, King Malcolm III and Queen Margaret were more accommodating to Norman ways. Malcolm's successor, David I (1124–53), adopted the Norman feudal system, as well as granting land to great Norman families. By 1212 a courtier called Walter of Coventry remarked that the Scottish court was 'French in race and manner of life, in speech and in culture'.

But while the French-Norman effect changed England and lowland Scotland over the following centuries, further north the Highland clans remained inaccessible in their glens, and were a law unto themselves for another 600 years.

MAGNA CARTA

In 1215 the barons found King John's erratic rule increasingly hard to swallow and forced him to sign a document called Magna Carta (the Great Charter), limiting the monarch's power for the first time in British history. Although originally intended as a set of handy ground rules, the Magna Carta was a fledgling bill of human rights that eventually led to the creation of parliament – a body to rule the country, independent of the throne. The signing took place at Runnymede, near Windsor, and you can still visit the site today.

927

Athelstan, grandson of Alfred the Great, son of Edward the Elder, is the first monarch to be specifically crowned King of England, building on his ancestors' success in regaining Viking territory.

1066

Battle of Hastings – a crucial date in English history. Incumbent King Harold is defeated by an invading Norman army, and England has a new monarch: William the Conqueror.

1095

The start of the First Crusade – a campaign of Christian European armies against the Muslim occupation of Jerusalem and the 'Holy Land'. A series of crusades continues until 1272.

1124–53

The rule of David I of Scotland – the Scottish aristocracy adopts the Norman feudal system, and the king grants land to great Norman families.

Royal & Holy Squabbling

When the reign of England's Henry I came to an end, the enduring British habit of competition for the throne introduced an equally enduring tendency for bickering between royalty and the church. Things came to a head in 1170 when Henry II had the 'turbulent priest' Thomas Becket murdered in Canterbury Cathedral, where a memorial to Becket can still be seen today.

Perhaps the next king, Richard I, wanted to make amends for his forebears' unholy sentiments by leading a crusade (a Christian 'holy war') to liberate Jerusalem and the Holy Land from occupation by Muslim 'heathens' under their leader Saladin. The campaign became known as the Third Crusade, and although the Christian armies captured the cities of Acre and Jaffa, they did not take Jerusalem.

Unfortunately, Richard's overseas activities meant he was too busy crusading to bother about governing England and in his absence the country fell into disarray, although his bravery and ruthlessness earned him the sobriquet Richard the Lionheart.

Richard was succeeded by his brother John, but under his harsh rule things got even worse for the general population. According to legend, during this time a nobleman called Robert of Loxley, better known as Robin Hood, hid in Sherwood Forest and engaged in a spot of wealth redistribution.

Expansionist Edward

Edward I of England (1272–1307) was a skilled ruler and ambitious general. During a busy 35-year reign he was unashamedly expansionist in his outlook, leading campaigns into Wales and Scotland.

Some decades earlier, the Welsh king Llywelyn the Great (d 1240) had attempted to set up a state in Wales, and his grandson Llywelyn the Last

HELL OF A JOB

Despite immense power and privilege, the position of monarch (or, perhaps worse, *potential* monarch) probably ranks as one of history's most dangerous occupations. English kings have been killed in battle (Harold), beheaded (Charles I), assassinated (William II), murdered by a wicked uncle (allegedly; Edward V) and bumped off by their queen and her lover (Edward II). Life was just as uncertain for the rulers of Wales and Scotland: some murdered by a wicked uncle (really; James I of Scotland), others killed in battle (Llewelyn the Last of Wales, and James IV of Scotland, last British monarch to die on the battlefield).

12th century
Oxford University is founded. There's evidence of teaching in the area since 1096, but King Henry II's 1167 ban on students attending the University of Paris solidified Oxford's importance.

1215
King John signs the Magna Carta, limiting the monarch's power for the first time in English history in an early step along the path towards constitutional rule.

13th century
Wales is invaded by English King Edward I, bringing to an end the rule of Welsh leader 'Llywelyn the Last'. Edward builds a ring of castles to suppress further Welsh uprisings.

1296
King Edward I marches on Scotland with an army of 30,000 men and in a brutal invasion captures the castles of Berwick, Edinburgh, Roxburgh and Stirling.

was recognised by Henry III as the first Prince (but not King) of Wales. But Edward I had no time for such niceties, and descended on Wales in a bloody invasion that lasted much of the 1270s. In the end, Wales became a dependent principality, owing allegiance to England. There were no more Welsh kings, and Edward made his own son Prince of Wales. Ever since, the British sovereign's eldest son has automatically been given the title. (Most recently, Prince Charles was formally proclaimed Prince of Wales at Caernarfon Castle in 1969, much to the displeasure of Welsh nationalists.)

Edward I then looked north. For 200 years, Scotland had been ruled by the Canmores, but the dynasty effectively ended in 1286 with the death of Alexander III. He was succeeded by his four-year-old granddaughter Margaret ('the Maid of Norway'), who was engaged to the son of Edward I, but she died in 1290 before the wedding could take place.

The story of William Wallace is told in the Mel Gibson epic *Braveheart*. In devolution debates of the 1990s, the patriotic pride engendered by this movie did more for Scottish nationalism than any politician's speech.

Scotland Wins Independence

There followed a dispute for the Scottish throne between John Balliol and Robert Bruce of Annandale. Arbitration was needed and Edward I chose Balliol. But Edward then sought to formalise his feudal overlordship and travelled through Scotland forcing local leaders to swear allegiance. In a final blow to Scottish pride, Edward removed the Stone of Destiny, on which the kings of Scotland had been crowned for centuries, and sent it to London.

That was too much. In response, Balliol got in touch with Edward's old enemy, France, and arranged a treaty of cooperation, the start of an anti-English partnership 'the Auld Alliance', which was to last for many centuries (and to the present day when it comes to rugby or football).

Edward wasn't the sort of bloke to brook opposition, though. In 1296 the English army defeated Balliol, forcing the Scottish barons to accept Edward's rule, and his ruthless retaliation earned him the title 'Hammer of the Scots'. But still the Scottish people refused to lie down; in 1297, at the Battle of Stirling Bridge, the English were defeated by a Scots army under the leadership of William Wallace. Over 700 years later, Wallace is still remembered as a Scottish hero.

By this time, Robert the Bruce (grandson of Bruce of Annandale) had crowned himself king of Scotland (1290), been beaten in battle, gone on the run and, while hiding in a cave, been famously inspired to renew his efforts by a spider persistently spinning its web. Bruce's army went on to defeat Edward II's superior English forces at the Battle of Bannockburn in 1314, a famous victory which led to the official recognition of Scotland as an independent nation, with Bruce as its king, in 1328.

1298–1305

William Wallace is proclaimed Guardian of Scotland in 1298. After Edward's army defeats the Scots at the Battle of Falkirk, Wallace goes into hiding but is betrayed and executed in 1305.

1314

An army under Robert the Bruce wins against the English at the Battle of Bannockburn – a victory that consolidated Scottish independence for the next 400 years.

1328

Continuing raids by the Scots into northern England force the English to sue for peace; the Treaty of Northampton gives Scotland its independence, with Robert I, the Bruce, as king.

1337–1453

England battles France in a long conflict known as the Hundred Years' War. It was actually a series of small conflicts. And it lasted for more than a century, too...

Shakespeare's *Henry V* (1989) was filmed as a superb epic starring Kenneth Branagh as the eponymous king. Also worth catching is the earlier movie of the same name starring Laurence Olivier, made in 1944 as a patriotic rallying cry.

Stewarts Enter the Scene

While the Hundred Years' War (1337–1453) rumbled on between England and France, things weren't much better in Scotland. After the death of Robert the Bruce in 1329, the country was ravaged by endless internal conflicts and plague epidemics.

Bruce's son became David II of Scotland, but he was soon caught up in battles against fellow Scots disaffected by his father and aided by England's Edward III. So when David died in 1371, the Scots quickly crowned Robert Stewart (Robert the Bruce's grandson) as king, marking the start of the House of Stewart, which was to crop up again in England a bit further down the line.

Houses of York & Lancaster

In 1399 the ineffectual Richard II of England was ousted by a powerful baron called Henry Bolingbroke, who became Henry IV, the first monarch of the House of Lancaster. Less than a year later, his rule was disrupted by a final cry of resistance from the downtrodden Welsh, led by royal descendant Owain Glyndŵr (Owen Glendower). But the rebellion was crushed, Glyndŵr died an outlaw and the Welsh elite were barred from public life for many years.

Henry IV was followed by Henry V, who stirred up the dormant Hundred Years' War and defeated France at the Battle of Agincourt. The patriotic speech penned for him by Shakespeare in *Henry V* ('Cry "God for Harry, England, and St George!"') has ensured his position among the most famous English kings of all time.

When the Hundred Years' War finally ground to a halt in 1453, you'd have thought things would be calm for a while, but no. The English forces returning from France threw their energies into a civil war dubbed the Wars of the Roses.

Briefly it went like this: Henry VI of the House of Lancaster (emblem, a red rose) was challenged by Richard, Duke of York (emblem, a white rose). Henry was weak and it was almost a walkover for Richard. But Henry's wife, Margaret of Anjou, was made of sterner stuff and her forces defeated the challenger. It didn't rest there. Richard's son Edward entered the scene with an army, turned the tables and finally drove out Henry. He became King Edward IV, first monarch of the House of York.

Dark Deeds in the Tower

Edward IV hardly had time to catch his breath before Richard Neville, Earl of Warwick, and Margaret of Anjou teamed up in 1471 to force him into exile and bring Henry VI back to the throne. But a year later Edward

1348
The bubonic plague (called the Black Death) arrives, ultimately killing more than a third of the population. For peasant labourers who survived, an upside was a rise in wages.

1400
Welsh nationalist hero Owain Glyndŵr leads the Welsh in rebellion, declaring a parliament in Machynlleth, but his rebellion is short-lived and victory fleeting.

1459–71
The Wars of the Roses takes place – an ongoing conflict between two competing dynasties, the Houses of Lancaster and York. The Yorkists are eventually successful, enabling King Edward IV to gain the throne.

1485
Henry Tudor defeats Richard III at the Battle of Bosworth to become King Henry VII, establishing the Tudor dynasty and ending York–Lancaster rivalry for the throne.

IV came bouncing back: he killed Warwick, captured Margaret and had Henry snuffed out in the Tower of London.

Although Edward IV's position seemed secure, he ruled for only a decade before being succeeded by his 12-year-old son, Edward V. But the boy-king's reign was even shorter than his dad's. In 1483 he was mysteriously murdered, along with his brother, and once again the Tower of London was the scene of the crime.

With the 'princes in the Tower' dispatched, this left the throne open for their dear old Uncle Richard. Whether he was the princes' killer is still the subject of debate, but his rule as Richard III was short-lived. Despite being given another famous Shakespearean sound bite ('A horse, a horse! My kingdom for a horse!'), few tears were shed in 1485 when he was tumbled from the top job by a nobleman from Wales called Henry Tudor, who became Henry VII.

Moves Towards Unity

After the Wars of the Roses, Henry VII's Tudor neutrality was important. He mended fences with his northern neighbours by marrying his daughter to James IV of Scotland, linking the Tudor and Stewart lines, though this didn't stop James IV invading England in 1513, only to be killed at the Battle of Flodden. Henry VII married Edward IV's daughter, Elizabeth of York (daughter of Edward IV and niece of Richard III), further cementing his claim to the throne.

Matrimony may have been more useful than warfare for Henry VII, but the multiple marriages of his successor, Henry VIII, were a very different story. Fathering a male heir was his problem, hence the famous six wives, but the pope's disapproval of divorce and remarriage led to a split with the Roman Catholic Church. Parliament made Henry the head of the Protestant Church of England – the beginning of a pivotal division between Catholics and Protestants that still exists in some areas of Britain.

In 1536 Henry followed this up by 'dissolving' many monasteries in Britain and Ireland, a blatant takeover of their land and wealth rather than a symptom of the struggle between church and state. Nonetheless, the general populace felt little sympathy for the wealthy (and often corrupt) abbeys, and in 1539–40 another monastic land grab swallowed the larger ones as well.

At the same time, Henry signed the Acts of Union (1536 and 1543), formally uniting England and Wales for the first time. Meanwhile, in Scotland, James IV had been succeeded by James V, who died in 1542. His baby daughter Mary became queen, and Scotland was ruled by regents.

Six Wives: The Queens of Henry VIII, by historian David Starkey, is an accessible modern study of the multi-marrying monarch.

1509–47
The reign of King Henry VIII. The Pope's disapproval of Henry's serial marriage and divorce results in the English Reformation – the founding of the Church of England.

1536 & 1543
English authority is exerted over Wales; the Laws in Wales Acts, also known as the Acts of Union, formally tie the two countries as a single political entity.

1560
The Scottish Parliament creates a Protestant Church that is independent of Rome and the monarchy, as a result of the Reformation. The Latin Mass is abolished and the pope's authority denied.

1588
The first complete translation of the Bible into Welsh helps the cause of Protestantism and also helps the survival of the neglected Welsh language.

The 1998 film *Elizabeth*, directed by Shekhar Kapur and starring Cate Blanchett, covers the early years of the Virgin Queen's rule, as she graduates from princess to commanding monarch – a time of forbidden love, unwanted suitors, intrigue and death.

The Elizabethan Age

Henry VIII died in 1547, succeeded by his son Edward VI, then by his daughter Mary I, but their reigns were short. So, unexpectedly, Elizabeth, third in line, came to the throne.

As Elizabeth I, she inherited a nasty mess of religious strife and divided loyalties, but after an uncertain start she gained confidence and turned the country around. Refusing marriage, she borrowed biblical imagery and became known as the Virgin Queen, making her perhaps the first British monarch to create a cult image.

It paid off. Her 45-year reign was a period of boundless optimism, characterised by the naval defeat of the Spanish Armada, the expansion of trade due to the global explorations of seafarers such as Walter Raleigh and Francis Drake, not to mention a cultural flourishing thanks to writers such as William Shakespeare and Christopher Marlowe.

United & Disunited Britain

Elizabeth I died in 1603 without an heir, and was succeeded by her closest relative, James, the safely Protestant son of the executed Mary. He became James I of England and James VI of Scotland, the first English monarch of the House of Stuart (Mary's time in France had Gallicised the Stewart name). Most importantly, James united England, Wales and Scotland into one kingdom for the first time in history – another step towards British unity.

James' attempts to smooth religious relations were set back by the anti-Catholic outcry that followed the infamous Guy Fawkes Gunpowder Plot, a terrorist attempt to blow up parliament in 1605. The event is still

MARY, QUEEN OF SCOTS

During Elizabeth I's reign, her cousin Mary (the Catholic daughter of Scottish King James V) had become known as Mary, Queen of Scots. She'd spent her childhood in France and had married the French *dauphin* (crown prince), thereby becoming queen of France as well. Why stop at two? After her husband's death, Mary returned to Scotland, where she claimed the English throne as well, on the grounds that Elizabeth I was illegitimate.

However, Mary's plans failed. She was imprisoned and forced to abdicate in favour of her son (a Protestant, who became James VI of Scotland), but she escaped to England and appealed to Elizabeth for help. This was a bad move; Mary was seen, not surprisingly, as a security risk and imprisoned once again. In an uncharacteristic display of indecision, Elizabeth held Mary under arrest for nearly 19 years before finally ordering her execution. As a prisoner, Mary was frequently moved from house to house, so that today Britain has many stately homes (and even a few pubs) claiming 'Mary, Queen of Scots slept here'.

1558–1603

The reign of Queen Elizabeth I, a period of boundless English optimism. Enter stage right playwright William Shakespeare. Exit due west navigators Walter Raleigh and Francis Drake.

1603

James VI of Scotland inherits the English throne in the so-called Union of the Crowns, becoming James I of England and James VI of Scotland.

1642–49

English Civil War between the king's Cavaliers and Oliver Cromwell's Roundheads establishes the Commonwealth of England.

1688

William of Orange and his wife, Mary, daughter of King James II, jointly ascend the throne after William defeats his father-in-law in the Glorious Revolution.

celebrated every 5 November with fireworks, bonfires and burning effigies of Guy himself.

Alongside the Catholic–Protestant rift, the divide between king and parliament continued to smoulder. The power struggle worsened during the reign of the next king, Charles I, and eventually degenerated into the Civil War of 1642–49. The antiroyalist (or 'parliamentarian') forces were led by Oliver Cromwell, a Puritan who preached against the excesses of the monarchy and established Church. His army (known as the Roundheads) was pitched against the king's forces (the Cavaliers) in a conflict that tore England apart. It ended with victory for the Roundheads, with the king executed, England declared a republic and Cromwell hailed as 'Protector'.

The Civil War extended into Scotland where the main struggle was between royalists and radical 'Covenanters', who sought freedom from state interference in church government.

The Return of the King

By 1653 Cromwell was finding parliament too restrictive and he assumed dictatorial powers, much to his supporters' dismay. On his death in 1658, he was followed half-heartedly by his son, but in 1660 parliament decided to re-establish the monarchy, as republican alternatives were proving far worse.

Charles II (the exiled son of Charles I) came to the throne, and his rule, known as 'the Restoration', saw scientific and cultural activity bursting forth. Exploration and expansion were also on the agenda. Backed by the army and navy (modernised, ironically, by Cromwell), British colonies stretched down the American coast, while the East India Company set up headquarters in Bombay (now Mumbai), laying foundations for what was to become the British Empire.

The next king, James II, had a harder time. Attempts to ease restrictive laws on Catholics ended with his defeat at the Battle of the Boyne by William III, the Protestant king of Holland, better known as William of Orange. William was married to James' own daughter Mary, but it didn't stop him having a bash at his father-in-law.

William and Mary came to the throne as King and Queen, each in their own right (Mary had more of a claim, but William would not agree to be a mere consort), and their joint accession in 1688 was known as the Glorious Revolution.

On the chilly day of his execution, dethroned King Charles I reputedly wore two shirts to avoid shivering and being regarded as a coward.

Act of Union

In 1694 Mary died, leaving William as sole monarch. He died a few years later and was succeeded by his sister-in-law Anne (the second daughter of James II). In 1707, during Anne's reign, the Act of Union was passed,

1692

The Massacre of Glencoe causes further rifts between those clans loyal to the British crown and those loyal to the old ways.

1707

The Act of Union brings England and Scotland under one parliament, one sovereign and one flag.

1745–46

The culmination of the Jacobite uprisings sees Bonnie Prince Charlie land in Scotland, gather an army and march southwards, to be eventually defeated at the Battle of Culloden.

1749

Author and magistrate Henry Fielding founds the Bow Street Runners, cited as London's first professional police force. A 1792 Act of Parliament allows the Bow Street model to spread across England.

Walks Through Britain's History (published by the Automobile Association) guides you on foot to castles, battlefields and hundreds of other sites with a link to the past. Take the air. Breathe in history!

bringing an end to the independent Scottish Parliament and linking the countries of England, Wales and Scotland under one parliament (based in London) for the first time. The nation of Great Britain was now established as a single state, with a bigger, better and more powerful parliament, and a constitutional monarchy with clear limits on the power of the king or queen.

The new-look parliament didn't wait long to flex its muscles. The Act of Union banned any Catholic, or anyone married to a Catholic, from ascending the throne – a rule still in force today. In 1714 Anne died without leaving an heir, marking the end of the Stuart line. The throne was then passed to distant (but still safely Protestant) German relatives: the House of Hanover.

The Jacobite Rebellions

Despite, or perhaps because of, the 1707 Act of Union, anti-English feeling in Scotland refused to disappear. The Jacobite rebellions, most notably those of 1715 and 1745, were attempts to overthrow the Hanoverian monarchy and bring back the Stuarts. Although these are iconic events in Scottish history, in reality there was never much support for the Jacobite cause outside the Highlands: the people of the lowlands were mainly Protestant and feared a return to the Catholicism that the Stuarts represented.

The 1715 rebellion was led by James Edward Stuart (the Old Pretender), the son of the exiled James II of England (James VII of Scotland), but when the attempt failed he fled to France. To impose control on the Highlands, General George Wade was commissioned to build a network of military roads through many previously inaccessible glens.

In 1745 James' son Charles Edward Stuart (Bonnie Prince Charlie, the Young Pretender) landed in Scotland to claim the crown for his father. He was initially successful, moving south into England as far as Derby, but the prince and his Highland army suffered a catastrophic defeat at the Battle of Culloden in 1746; his legendary escape to the western isles is remembered in 'The Skye Boat Song'. General Wade is remembered too, as many of the roads his troops built are still in use today.

The Empire Strikes Out

By the mid-18th century, struggles for the British throne seemed a thing of the past, and the Hanoverian kings increasingly relied on parliament to govern the country. As part of the process, from 1721 to 1742 a senior parliamentarian called Sir Robert Walpole effectively became Britain's first prime minister.

1776–83

The American War of Independence is the British Empire's first major reverse, a fact not missed by French ruler Napoleon.

1799–1815

In the Napoleonic Wars, Napoleon threatens invasion on a weakened Britain, but his ambitions are curtailed by Nelson and Wellington at the famous battles of Trafalgar (1805) and Waterloo (1815).

1858 & 1860

The first modern national Eisteddfods are held in Llangollen and Denbigh – although earlier ones had been organised from the end of the 18th century as part of a Welsh cultural revival.

1837–1901

The reign of Queen Victoria, during which the British Empire – 'on which the sun never sets' – expands from Canada through Africa and India to Australia and New Zealand.

Meanwhile, the British Empire continued to grow in America, Canada and India. The first claims were made on Australia after Captain James Cook's epic voyage of exploration in 1768.

The empire's first major reverse came when the American colonies won the War of Independence (1776–83). This setback forced Britain to withdraw from the world stage for a while, a gap not missed by French ruler Napoleon. He threatened to invade Britain and hinder the power of the British overseas, before his ambitions were curtailed by naval hero Admiral Nelson and military hero the Duke of Wellington at the famous battles of Trafalgar (1805) and Waterloo (1815).

Captain Cook's voyage to the southern hemisphere was primarily a scientific expedition. His objectives included monitoring the transit of Venus, an astronomical event that happens only twice every 180 years or so (most recently in 2004 and 2012). 'Discovering' Australia was just a sideline.

The Industrial Age

While the empire expanded abroad, at home Britain became the crucible of the Industrial Revolution. Steam power (patented by James Watt in 1781) and steam trains (launched by George Stephenson in 1830) transformed methods of production and transport, and the towns of the English Midlands became the first industrial cities.

From about 1750, much of the Scottish Highlands was emptied of people, as landowners casually expelled entire farms and villages to make way for more profitable sheep, a seminal event in Scotland's history known as the Clearances. Although many of the dispossessed left for the New World, others headed to the burgeoning cotton mills of Lanarkshire and the shipyards of Glasgow.

By the early 19th century, copper, iron and slate were being extracted in the Merthyr Tydfil and Monmouth areas of Wales. The 1860s saw the Rhondda valleys opened up for coal mining, and Wales soon became a major exporter of coal, as well as the world's leading producer of tin plate.

Across Britain, industrialisation meant people were on the move as never before, leaving the farms and villages their families had occupied for generations. The rapid change from rural to urban society caused great dislocation, and although knowledge of science and medicine also improved alongside industrial advances, for many people the adverse side effects of Britain's economic blossoming were poverty and deprivation.

At its height, the British Empire covered 20% of the land area of the earth and contained a quarter of the world's population.

Age of Empire

Despite the social turmoil of the early 19th century, by the time Queen Victoria took the throne in 1837 Britain's factories dominated world trade and British fleets dominated the oceans. The rest of the 19th century was seen as Britain's Golden Age, a period of confidence not enjoyed since the days of the last great queen, Elizabeth I.

1847

Publication of a government report, dubbed the 'Treason of the Blue Books', suggests the Welsh language is detrimental to education in Wales, and fuels the Welsh-language struggle.

1900

James Keir Hardie (usually known as just Keir Hardie) becomes the first Labour MP, winning a seat in the Welsh mining town of Merthyr Tydfil.

1914

Archduke Franz Ferdinand of Austria is assassinated in the Balkan city of Sarajevo – the final spark in a decade-long crisis that starts the Great War, now called WWI.

1916

The Welsh Liberal MP David Lloyd George becomes the British prime minister in an alliance with the Conservative Party, having built a reputation for championing the poor and needy.

Victoria ruled a proud nation at home and great swaths of territories abroad, from Canada through much of Africa and India to Australia and New Zealand, trumpeted as 'the empire on which the sun never sets'.

The times were optimistic, but it wasn't all tub-thumping jingoism. Prime Minister Disraeli, who rose to office in 1868, and his successor William Gladstone, also introduced social reforms to address the worst excesses of the Industrial Revolution. Education became universal, trade unions were legalised and the right to vote was extended in a series of reform acts, finally being granted to all men over the age of 21 in 1918, and to all women in 1928.

World War I

When Queen Victoria died in 1901, it seemed Britain's energy fizzled out too. The new king, Edward VII, ushered in the relaxed Edwardian era – and a long period of decline.

Meanwhile, in continental Europe, other states were more active: four restless military powers (Russia, Austria-Hungary, Turkey and Germany) focused their sabre-rattling on the Balkan states, and the assassination of Archduke Ferdinand at Sarajevo in 1914 finally sparked a clash that became the 'Great War' we now call WWI. Soldiers from Britain and Allied countries were drawn into a conflict of horrendous slaughter, most infamously on the killing fields of Flanders and the beaches of Gallipoli.

By the war's weary end in 1918, over a million Britons had died (plus millions more from many other countries) and there was hardly a street or village untouched by death, as the sobering lists of names on war memorials all over Britain still show.

Disillusion & Depression

For the soldiers that did return from WWI, the war had created disillusion and a questioning of the social order. Many supported the ideals of a new political force, the Labour Party, to represent the working class.

Meanwhile, the bitter Anglo-Irish War (1919–21) saw most of Ireland achieving full independence from Britain. Six counties in the north remained British, creating a new political entity called the United Kingdom of Great Britain and Northern Ireland. But the decision to partition the island of Ireland was to have long-term repercussions that still dominate political agendas in both the UK and the Republic of Ireland today.

The Labour Party won for the first time in the 1923 election, in coalition with the Liberals. James Ramsay MacDonald was the first Labour prime minister, but by the mid-1920s the Conservatives were back. The world economy was now in decline and in the 1930s the Great Depression meant another decade of misery and political upheaval.

One of the finest novels about WWI is *Birdsong* by Sebastian Faulks. Understated, perfectly paced and intensely moving, it tells of passion, fear, waste, incompetent generals and the poor bloody infantry.

1926

Increasing mistrust of the government, fuelled by soaring unemployment, leads to the General Strike. Millions of workers – train drivers, miners, ship builders – down tools and bring the country to a halt.

1939–45

WWII rages across Europe, and much of Africa and Asia. Britain and Allies, including America, Russia, Australia, India and New Zealand, eventually defeat the armies of Germany, Japan and Italy.

1948

Aneurin Bevan, the health minister in the Labour government, launches the National Health Service – the core of Britain as a 'welfare state'.

1952

Princess Elizabeth becomes Queen Elizabeth II when her father, George VI, dies. Her coronation takes place in Westminster Abbey in June 1953.

World War II

In 1933 Adolf Hitler came to power in Germany and in 1939 Germany invaded Poland, once again drawing Britain into war. The German army swept through Europe and pushed back British forces to the beaches of Dunkirk (northern France) in June 1940. An extraordinary flotilla of rescue vessels turned total disaster into a brave defeat, and an event that is still remembered with pride and sadness every year in Britain.

By mid-1940 most of Europe was controlled by Germany. In Russia, Stalin had negotiated a peace agreement. The USA was neutral, leaving Britain virtually isolated. Into this arena came a new prime minister, Winston Churchill.

Between September 1940 and May 1941, the German air force launched the Blitz, a series of (mainly night-time) bombing raids on London and other cities. Despite this, morale in Britain remained strong, thanks partly to Churchill's regular radio broadcasts. In late 1941 the USA entered the war, and the tide began to turn.

By 1944 Germany was in retreat. Russia pushed back from the east, and Britain, the USA and other Allies were again on the beaches of France. The Normandy landings (or D-Day, as they are better remembered) marked the start of the liberation of Europe's western side. By 1945 Hitler was dead and the war was finally over.

Normandy Landings Statistics

Largest military armada in history

More than 5000 ships

Approximately 150,000 Allied troops landed

Campaign time: four days

WINSTON CHURCHILL

Born in 1874 to an aristocratic family, Winston Churchill is Britain's most famous prime minister. As a young man he joined the British Army and saw action in India and Africa. He was first elected to parliament as a Conservative MP (Member of Parliament) in 1900, and held various ministerial positions through the 1920s.

In 1939 Britain entered WWII, and by 1940 Churchill was prime minister, taking additional responsibility as minister of defence. Hitler had expected an easy victory, but Churchill's extraordinary dedication, not to mention his radio speeches (most famously offering nothing but 'blood, toil, tears and sweat' and promising to 'fight on the beaches'), inspired the British people to resist.

Between July and October 1940 the Royal Air Force withstood Germany's aerial raids to win what became known as the Battle of Britain, a major turning point in the war – in Churchilll's words of praise for the RAF, 'never was so much owed by so many to so few'. It was an audacious strategy, but it paid off and Churchill was lauded as a national hero – praise that continued to the end of the war, and well beyond his death in 1965.

1955 & 1959

Cardiff is declared the Welsh capital in 1955, and Wales gets its own official flag (the red dragon on a green and white field) in 1959.

1971

Britain adopts the 'decimal' currency (one pound equals 100 pence) and drops the ancient system of one pound equals 20 shillings or 240 pennies, the centuries-old bane of school maths lessons.

1979

A Conservative government led by Margaret Thatcher wins the national election, a major milestone of Britain's 20th-century history, ushering in a decade of dramatic political and social change.

1982

Britain is victorious in a war against Argentina over the invasion of the Falkland Islands, leading to a rise in patriotic sentiment.

Swinging & Sliding

Despite victory in WWII, there was an unexpected swing on the political front in 1945. An electorate tired of war and hungry for change tumbled Churchill's Conservatives in favour of the Labour Party.

In 1952 George VI was succeeded by his daughter Elizabeth II and, following the trend set by earlier queens Elizabeth I and Victoria, she has remained on the throne for over six decades, overseeing a period of massive social and economic change.

By the late 1950s, recovery was strong enough for Prime Minister Harold Macmillan to famously remind the British people they had 'never had it so good'. By the time the 1960s had started, grey old Britain was suddenly more fun and lively than it had been for generations.

Although the 1960s were swinging, the 1970s saw an economic slide thanks to a grim combination of inflation, the oil crisis and international competition. The rest of the decade was marked by strikes, disputes and all-round gloom.

Neither the Conservatives (also known as the Tories), under Edward Heath, nor Labour, under Harold Wilson and Jim Callaghan, proved capable of controlling the strife. The British public had had enough, and in the elections of 1979 the Conservatives won a landslide victory, led by a little-known politician named Margaret Thatcher.

The Thatcher Years

Soon everyone had heard of Margaret Thatcher. Love her or hate her, no one could argue that her methods weren't dramatic. Looking back from a 21st-century vantage point, most commentators agree that by economic measures the Thatcher government's policies were largely successful, but by social measures they were a failure and created a polarised Britain: on one side were the people who gained from the prosperous wave of opportunities in the 'new' industries, while on the other side were those left unemployed and dispossessed by the decline of the 'old' industries such as coal-mining and steel production.

Despite, or perhaps thanks to, policies that were frequently described as uncompromising, Margaret Thatcher was, by 1988, the longest-serving British prime minister of the 20th century.

The six decades since the end of WWII are neatly covered in *A History of Modern Britain*, a handy overview focusing on political events, by TV presenter and commentator Andrew Marr.

New Labour, New Millennium, New Start

The political pendulum started to swing again in the early 1990s. The turning point came in 1997, when 'New' Labour swept to power, with leader Tony Blair declared the new prime minister.

The Labour Party enjoyed an extended honeymoon period, and the next election (in 2001) was another walkover. The Conservative Party

1990

Mrs Thatcher is ousted as leader and the Conservative Party enters a period of decline but remains in power thanks to inept Labour opposition.

1997

The general election sees Tony Blair lead 'New' Labour to victory in the polls, with a record-breaking parliamentary majority, ending more than 20 years of Tory rule.

1999

The first National Assembly is elected for Wales, with the members sitting in a new building in Cardiff; Rhodri Morgan becomes First Minister.

1999–2004

Scottish Parliament is convened for the first time on 12 May 1999. Five years later, after plenty of scandal and huge sums of money, a new parliament building is opened at Holyrood in Edinburgh.

continued to struggle, allowing Labour to win a historic third term in 2005, and a year later Tony Blair became the longest-serving Labour prime minister in British history.

In May 2010 a record 13 years of Labour rule came to an end, and a coalition government (the first in the UK since WWII) was formed between the Conservative and the Liberal Democrats.

It was an experiment that ended disastrously for the Lib Dems at the 2015 general election: they lost 49 seats, and were left with just eight MPs. The same vote left the defeated Labour Party divided and in turmoil, and the Conservatives back in sole charge.

Just over a year later a referendum saw the people of the UK vote, by 52% to 48%, to leave the EU in defiance of the main parties which had wanted the country to remain.

For detail on the 1980s, read *No Such Thing as Society* by Andy McSmith. Drawing on Margaret Thatcher's famous proclamation, this book studies the era dominated by the Iron Lady.

2001 Tony Blair and Labour continue to enjoy a honeymoon period and another victory at the 2001 general election, although their majority is reduced.

2003 Britain joins America and other countries in the invasion of Iraq, initially with some support from parliament and public, despite large anti-war street demonstrations in London and other cities.

2007 The Government of Wales Bill heralds the largest transfer of power from Westminster to Cardiff since the founding of the National Assembly.

2016 A referendum is held asking the question 'Should the UK remain a member of the EU or leave the EU?' The result was: 52% voted Leave, 48% voted Remain.

The British Table

The idea of British cuisine was once a bit of a joke. But a culinary landmark came in 2005, when food bible *Gourmet* magazine famously singled out London as having the best collection of restaurants in the world. In the years since then the choice for food lovers – whatever their budget – has continued to improve. London is now regarded as a global gastronomic capital, and it's increasingly easy to find great food all over Britain.

Britain's most popular restaurant dish is chicken tikka masala, an 'Indian' curry dish created specifically for the British palate and unheard of in India itself.

Eating in Britain

The infamous outbreaks of 'mad cow' disease in the 1990s are ancient history now, and British beef is once again exported to the world, but an upside of the bad press at the time was a massive surge in demand for good-quality food. That means wherever you go in Britain today, you'll find a plethora of organic, natural, unadulterated, chemical-free, free-range, hand-reared, locally farmed, non-intensive foods available in shops, markets, cafes and restaurants.

Alongside this greater awareness of quality and provenance, there have been other changes to British food thanks to outside influences. For decades most towns have boasted Italian, Chinese and Indian restaurants, so spaghetti carbonara, chow mein and vindaloo are no longer considered exotic, but in more recent times dishes from Japan, Korea, Thailand and other Asian countries have also become widely available.

The overall effect of these foreign influences has been the introduction to 'traditional' British cuisine of new techniques, new ingredients and new herbs and spices. So now we have 'modern British cuisine', where even humble bangers and mash (sausage with mashed potato) are raised to new heights when handmade pork, apple and thyme-scented sausages are paired with lightly chopped fennel and red wine gravy.

But beware the domination of style over substance: you're often better spending £10 or less on a top-notch curry in Birmingham or a home-made steak-and-ale pie in a country pub than forking out £30 or more in a city restaurant for a 'modern European' concoction that tastes like it came from a can.

The Full British

Although grazing on a steady supply of snacks is increasingly commonplace in Britain, as it is in many other industrialised nations, the British culinary day is still punctuated by the three traditional meals of breakfast, lunch and dinner. And just to keep you on your toes, lunch and dinner are also called dinner and tea or lunch and supper – depending on social class and geographical location.

Breakfast

Many people in Britain make do with toast or a bowl of cereal before dashing to work, but visitors staying in hotels and B&Bs will undoubtedly encounter a phenomenon called the 'full English Breakfast' – or one of its regional equivalents. This usually consists of bacon, sausages, eggs, tomatoes, mushrooms, baked beans and fried bread. In Scotland the 'full Scottish breakfast' might include tattie scones (potato bread) instead of fried bread. In Wales you may be offered laver bread, which is not a bread at all but seaweed – a tasty speciality often served with oatmeal and bacon on toast. In northern England you may get black pudding. And just in case you thought this insufficient, it's still preceded by cereal, and followed by toast and marmalade.

If you don't feel like eating half a farmyard first thing in the morning, most places offer a lighter alternative or local speciality such as kippers (smoked fish) or a 'continental breakfast', which completely omits the cooked stuff and may even add something exotic such as croissants.

According to the Soil Association (www.soilassociation.org), the leading organic-food campaign group, more than 85% of people in Britain want pesticide-free food.

Lunch

One of the many great inventions that Britain gave the world is the sandwich, often eaten as a midday meal. Slapping a slice of cheese or ham between two bits of bread may seem a simple concept, but no one apparently thought of it until the 18th century, when the Earl of Sandwich (his title comes from the southeast England town of Sandwich that originally got its name from the Viking word for sandy beach) ordered his servants to bring cold meat between bread so he could keep working at his desk, or, as some historians claim, continue playing cards late at night.

Another lunch classic that perhaps epitomises British food more than any other – especially in pubs – is the ploughman's lunch. Basically it's bread and cheese, and although hearty yokels probably did carry such food to the fields (no doubt wrapped in a red-spotted handkerchief) in days of yore, the meal is actually a modern phenomenon. It was invented in the 1960s by the marketing chief of the national cheese-makers' organisation as a way to boost consumption, neatly cashing in on public nostalgia and fondness for tradition.

You can still find a basic ploughman's lunch offered in some pubs – and it undeniably goes well with a pint or two of local ale at lunchtime – but these days the meal has usually been smartened up to include butter, salad, pickle, pickled onion and dressings. At some pubs you get a selection of cheeses. You'll also find other variations, such as a farmer's lunch (bread and chicken), stockman's lunch (bread and ham), Frenchman's lunch (brie and baguette) and fisherman's lunch (you guessed it, with fish).

For cheese and bread in a different combination, try Welsh rarebit – a sophisticated variation on cheese on toast, seasoned and flavoured with butter, milk and sometimes a little beer. For a takeaway lunch in Scotland, look out for Forfar bridies (pastry turnovers filled with minced beef and onion).

Sherry trifle was considered the height of sophistication at dinner parties during the 1970s, but then fell out of fashion. A few decades later this combination of custard, fruit, sponge cake, whipped cream, and – of course – sherry is back in style, and enjoying a renaissance in many British restaurants.

Dinner

For generations, a typical British dinner has been 'meat and two veg'. The meat is pork, beef or lamb, one of the vegetables is potatoes and the other inevitably carrots, cabbage or cauliflower – and just as inevitably cooked long and hard. Although tastes and diets are changing, this classic combination still graces the tables of many British families several times a week.

And when the British say beef, they usually mean roast beef – a dish that's become a symbol of the nation, and the reason why the French call

EATING PRICE RANGES

In reviews, the following price ranges refer to a main dish.

£ less than £10 (London less than £12)

££ £10–20 (London £12–25)

£££ more than £20 (London more than £25)

NAME THAT PASTY

A favourite speciality in southwest England is the Cornish pasty. Originally a mix of cooked vegetables wrapped in pastry, it's often available in meat varieties (much to the scorn of the Cornish people) and now sold everywhere in Britain. The pasty was originally an all-in-one-lunch pack that tin miners carried underground and left on a ledge ready for mealtime. So that pasties weren't mixed up, they were marked with their owner's initials – always at one end, so the miner could eat half and safely leave the rest to snack on later without it mistakenly disappearing into the mouth of a workmate. Before going back to the surface, the miners traditionally left the last few crumbs of the pasty as a gift for the spirits of the mine, known as 'knockers', to ensure a safe shift the next day.

the British *les rosbifs*. Perhaps the most famous beef comes from Scotland's Aberdeen Angus cattle, while the best-known meat from Wales is lamb. Venison – usually from red deer – is readily available in Scotland, as well as in parts of Wales and England, most notably in the New Forest.

With beef – especially at Sunday lunches – comes another British classic: Yorkshire pudding. It's simply roast batter, but very tasty when cooked properly. Yet another classic British dish brings together Yorkshire pudding and sausages to create the delightfully named 'toad-in-the-hole'.

Perhaps the best-known British meal is fish and chips, often bought from the 'chippie' wrapped in paper to carry home – it's especially popular with families on Friday evenings. Late at night, epicures may order their fish and chips 'open' to eat immediately while walking back from the pub. It has to be said that quality varies outrageously across the country; sometimes the chips are limp and soggy, and the fish greasy and tasteless, especially once you get away from the sea, but in towns with salt in the air, this classic deep-fried delight is always worth trying.

Puddings & Desserts

In British English, 'pudding' has two meanings: the course that comes after the main course (ie dessert); and a type of food that might be sweet (such as Bakewell pudding) or savoury (such as Yorkshire pudding).

A classic British dessert is rhubarb crumble: the juicy stem of a large-leafed garden plant, stewed and sweetened, then topped with a crunchy mix of flour, butter and more sugar, and served with custard or ice cream.

Scotland's classic pudding is 'clootie dumpling' (a rich fruit pudding that is wrapped in a cotton cloth, or *cloot* in Scots dialect, while being steamed). Other sweet temptations include cranachan, whipped cream flavoured with whisky and mixed with toasted oatmeal and raspberries, and Atholl brose, a mixture of cream, whisky and honey, flavoured with oatmeal.

Other favourite British puddings include treacle sponge, bread-and-butter pudding and plum pudding, a dome-shaped cake with fruit, nuts and brandy or rum, traditionally eaten at Christmas, when it's called – surprise, surprise – Christmas pudding. This pudding is steamed (rather than baked), cut into slices and served with brandy butter.

In Yorkshire, the eponymous pudding is traditionally a *starter*, a reminder of days when food was scarce and the pudding was a pre-meal stomach-filler.

While key ingredients of most puddings are self-explanatory, they are perhaps not so obvious for another well-loved favourite: spotted dick. The origin of 'dick' in this context is unclear (it may be a corruption of 'dough' or derived from the German *dicht,* meaning 'thick', or even from 'spotted dog') but the ingredients are easy: it's just a white suet pudding dotted with black currants. Plus sugar, of course. Most British puddings have loads of butter or loads of sugar, preferably both. Light, subtle and healthy? No chance!

Top Paella in Covent Garden (p81), London
Bottom Rhubarb crumble

LUCKY_ELEPHANT / SHUTTERSTOCK ©

Drinking in Britain

To help you find the best of ales and a fine pub to drink them in, check out the *Good Beer Guide to Great Britain*, by the Campaign for Real Ale, and *Good Pub Guide*, by Fiona Stapley.

The drinks most associated with Britain are tea, beer and whisky. The first two are unlike drinks of the same name found elsewhere in the world, and all three are well worth sampling on your travels around the country.

Tea & Coffee

In Britain, if a local asks 'Would you like a drink?', don't automatically expect a gin and tonic. They may well mean a 'cuppa' – a cup of tea – Britain's best-known beverage. It's usually made with dark tea leaves to produce a strong, brown drink, more bitter in taste than tea served in some other Western countries, which is partly why it's usually served with a dash of milk.

Although tea is sometimes billed as the national drink, coffee is equally popular these days; the Brits consume 165 million cups a day and the British coffee market is worth almost £700 million a year – but with the prices some coffee shops charge, maybe that's not surprising.

A final word of warning: when you're ordering a coffee and the server says 'white or black', don't panic. It simply means 'Do you want milk in it?'

Beer & Cider

British beer typically ranges from dark brown to amber in colour, and is often served at room temperature. Technically it's called ale and is more commonly called 'bitter' (or 'heavy' in Scotland). This is to distinguish it from lager – the drink that most of the rest of the word calls 'beer', which is generally yellow and served cold.

Bitter that's brewed and served traditionally is called 'real ale' to distinguish it from mass-produced brands, and there are many regional varieties. But be ready! If you're used to the 'amber nectar' or 'king of beers', a traditional British brew may be served warmer and less carbonated than you might expect. This is partly to do with Britain's climate, and partly to do with the beer being served by hand pump rather than gas pressure. Most important, though, is the integral flavour: traditional British beer doesn't need to be chilled or fizzed to make it palatable.

The increasing popularity of real ales and a backlash against the bland conformity of globalised multinational brewing conglomerates has seen a huge rise in the number of artisan brewers and microbreweries springing up all over Britain – by 2016 there were around 1500 in operation, with around 75 in London alone. They take pride in using only natural ingredients, and many try to revive ancient recipes, such as heather- and seaweed-flavoured ales.

Another key feature is that real ale must be looked after, which usually means a willingness on the part of the pub manager or landlord to put in extra effort. This often translates into extra effort on food, atmosphere, cleanliness and so on, too. But the extra effort is why many pubs don't serve real ale.

If beer doesn't tickle your palate, try cider – available in sweet and dry varieties and, increasingly, as craft cider, often with various fruit or herb-

WHERE THERE'S SMOKE...

All restaurants and cafes in Britain are nonsmoking throughout. Virtually all pubs have the same rule, which is why there's often a small crowd of smokers standing on the pavement outside, though some places provide specific outdoor smoking areas. Smoking is permitted in pub gardens, so nonsmokers sometimes need to go *inside* to escape the fumes.

al flavours added. In western parts of England, notably Herefordshire and the southwestern counties of Devon and Somerset, you could try 'scrumpy', a very strong dry cider traditionally made from local apples. Many pubs serve it straight from the barrel.

On hot summer days, you could go for shandy – beer and lemonade mixed in equal quantities. You'll usually need to specify 'lager shandy' or 'bitter shandy'.

Many towns and cities in England hold regular farmers markets – a chance for food producers large and small to sell direct to the public. For more info and a database, see www.localfoods.org.uk.

Wine

Many visitors are surprised to learn that wine is produced in Britain, and has been since the time of the Romans. Today, more than 400 vineyards produce between three and four million bottles a year – many highly regarded and frequently winning major awards. English sparkling wines have been a particular success story, especially those produced in south-east England where the chalky soil and climatic conditions are similar to those of the Champagne region in France.

Whisky

The spirit most visitors associate with Britain – and especially Scotland – is whisky (note the spelling – it's Irish whiskey that has an 'e'). There's a big difference between single malt whisky, made purely from malted barley in a single distillery, and blended whisky, made from a blend of cheaper grain whisky and malt whiskies from several distilleries.

A single malt, like a fine wine, somehow captures the terroir or essence of the place where it was made and matured – a combination of the water, the barley, the peat smoke, the oak barrels in which it was aged and (in the case of certain coastal distilleries) the sea air and salt spray. Each distillation varies from the one before, like different vintages from the same vineyard.

Bars & Pubs

In Britain the difference between a bar and a pub is sometimes vague, but generally bars are smarter, larger and louder than pubs, possibly with a younger crowd. Drinks are more expensive, too, unless there's a gallon-of-vodka-and-Red-Bull-for-a-fiver promotion – which there often is.

As well as beer, cider and wine, pubs and bars offer the usual choice of spirits, often served with a 'mixer', producing British favourites such as gin and tonic, rum and coke, and vodka and lime. These drinks are served in measures called 'singles' and 'doubles'. A single can be either 25mL or 35mL (depending on the bar) – just over one US fluid ounce. A double is, of course, 50mL or 70mL – still disappointingly small when compared with measures in other countries. To add further to your disappointment, the vast array of cocktail options, as found in America, is generally restricted to more upmarket city bars in Britain.

And while we're serving up warnings, here are two more: first, if you see a pub calling itself a 'free house', it's simply a place that doesn't belong to a brewery or pub company, and thus is 'free' to sell any brand of beer. Unfortunately, it doesn't mean the booze is free of charge; second, remember that drinks in British pubs are ordered and paid for at the bar. You can always spot the freshly arrived tourists – they're the ones sitting forlornly at an empty table hoping to spot a waiter.

When it comes to gratuities, it's not usual to tip pub and bar staff. However, if you're ordering a large round, or the service has been good all evening, you can say to the person behind the bar '...and one for yourself'. They may not have a drink, but they'll add the monetary equivalent to the total you pay and keep it as a tip.

The Campaign for Real Ale promotes the understanding of traditional British beer. Look for endorsement stickers on pub windows, and for more info, see www.camra.org.uk.

Architecture in Britain

The history of British architecture spans more than three millennia, from the mysterious stone circles of Stonehenge and Callanish to the glittering skyscrapers of modern London. The country's built heritage includes Roman baths and parish churches, mighty castles and magnificent cathedrals, humble cottages and grand stately homes, and exploring it all is one of the great joys of a visit to Britain.

Above London's modern skyline

Early Foundations

The oldest surviving structures in Britain are the grass-covered mounds of earth called 'tumuli' or 'barrows', used as burial sites by the country's prehistoric residents. These mounds, measuring anything from a rough hemisphere just 2m high to oval domes around 5m high and 10m long, are dotted across the countryside and are especially common in areas of chalk such as Salisbury Plain and the Wiltshire Downs in southern England.

Perhaps the most famous mound, and certainly the largest and most mysterious, is Silbury Hill near Marlborough. Historians are not sure exactly why this huge conical mound was built – there's no evidence of it actually being used for burials. Theories include the possibility it was used at cultural ceremonies or in the worship of deities in the style of South American pyramids. Whatever its original purpose, it's still awe inspiring today.

Even more impressive than the giant tumuli are the most prominent legacy of the neolithic era – the iconic stone circles of Stonehenge and Avebury, both in Wiltshire. Again, their original purpose is a mystery, providing fertile ground for hypothesis and speculation. The most recent theories suggest that Stonehenge may have been a place of pilgrimage for the sick, like modern-day Lourdes, though it was also used as a burial ground and a place of ancestor worship.

Bronze Age & Iron Age

After the neolithic era's great stone circles, the Bronze Age architecture we can see today is more domestic in scale. Hut circles from this period can still be seen in parts of Britain, most notably on Dartmoor in Devon. The Scottish islands hold many of Europe's best surviving Bronze and Iron Age remains, in places like the stone villages of Skara Brae in Orkney and Jarlshof in Shetland.

During the Iron Age, the early peoples of Britain began organising themselves into clans or tribes. Their legacy includes forts built to defend territory and protect from rival tribes or other invaders. Most forts consisted of a steep mound of earth behind a large circular or oval ditch; a famous example is Maiden Castle in Dorset.

The Roman Era

Remains of the Roman Empire are found in many towns and cities (mostly in England and Wales, as the Romans didn't colonise Scotland). There are impressive remains in Chester, Exeter and St Albans, as well as in the lavish Roman spa and bath house complex in Bath. Britain's largest and most impressive Roman relic is the 73-mile-long sweep of Hadrian's Wall, built in the 2nd century as a defensive line stretching from coast to coast across the island. Originally intended to defend the Empire's territories in the south from the marauding tribes further north, it became as much a symbol of Roman power as a fortification.

Medieval Masterpieces

In the centuries following the Norman Conquest of 1066, the perfection of the mason's art saw an explosion of architecture in stone, inspired by the two most pressing concerns of the day: religion and defence. Early structures of timber and rubble were replaced with churches, abbeys and

Britain's Best Castles

- *Alnwick*
- *Balmoral*
- *Beaumaris*
- *Berkeley*
- *Carlisle*
- *Caernarfon*
- *Caerphilly*
- *Chepstow*
- *Conwy*
- *Edinburgh*
- *Eilean Donan*
- *Glamis*
- *Harlech*
- *Ludlow*
- *Pembroke*
- *Raglan*
- *Richmond*
- *Skipton*
- *Stirling*
- *Tintagel*

DOMINATING THE LANDSCAPE

If you're travelling through Wales, it won't take you long to notice the country's most striking architectural asset: castles. There are about 600 in all, giving Wales the dubious honour of being Europe's most densely fortified country. Most were built in medieval times, first by William the Conqueror and then by other Anglo-Norman kings, to keep the Welsh in check. In the late 13th century Edward I built spectacular castles at Caernarfon, Harlech, Conwy and Beaumaris, now jointly listed as a Unesco World Heritage Site. Other castles to see include Rhuddlan, Denbigh, Criccieth, Raglan, Pembroke, Kidwelly, Chepstow and Caerphilly. While undeniably great for visitors, the castles are a sore point for patriotic Welsh; the writer Thomas Pennant called them 'the magnificent badge of our subjection'.

Salisbury Cathedral (p267), England

The Callanish Standing Stones on Scotland's Isle of Lewis, dating from 3800 to 5000 years ago, are even older than those at Stonehenge and Avebury.

monasteries built in dressed stone. The round arches, squat towers and chevron decoration of the Norman or Romanesque style (11th to 12th centuries) slowly evolved into the tall pointed arches, ribbed vaults and soaring spires of the Gothic (13th to 16th centuries), a history that can often be seen all in the one church – construction often took a couple of hundred years to complete. Many cathedrals remain modern landmarks, such as Salisbury, Winchester, Canterbury and York.

Stone was also put to good use in the building of elaborate defensive structures. Castles range from the atmospheric ruins of Tintagel and Dunstanburgh, and the sturdy ramparts of Conwy and Beaumaris, to the stunning crag-top fortresses of Stirling and Edinburgh. And then there's the most impressive of them all: the Tower of London, guarding the capital for more than 900 years.

Stately Homes

The medieval period was tumultuous, but by the start of the 17th century life had become more settled and the nobility had less need for fortifications. While they were excellent for keeping out the riff-raff, castles were often too cold and draughty for comfortable aristocratic living.

HOUSE & HOME

In Britain, it's not all about big houses. Alongside the stately homes, ordinary domestic architecture can still be seen in rural areas. Black-and-white 'half-timbered' houses characterise counties such as Worcestershire, brick-and-flint buildings pepper Suffolk and Sussex, and hardy, centuries-old cottages and farm buildings of slate and local stone are a feature of North Wales. In northern Scotland, the blackhouse is a classic basic dwelling, with walls of dry, unmortared stone packed with earth and a roof of straw and turf.

Big Ben (p71), London

Many castles underwent the home improvements of the day, with larger windows, wider staircases and better drainage installed. Others were simply abandoned for a brand-new dwelling next door, as at Hardwick Hall in Derbyshire.

Following the Civil War, the trend away from castles gathered pace, and throughout the 17th century the landed gentry developed a taste for fine 'country houses' designed by famous architects of the day. Many became the stately homes that are a major feature of the British landscape and a major attraction for visitors. Among the most extravagant are Chatsworth House and Blenheim Palace in England, Powis Castle in Wales and Floors Castle in Scotland.

The great stately homes all display the proportion, symmetry and architectural harmony that was in vogue during the 17th and 18th centuries. These styles were later reflected in the fashionable town houses of the Georgian era, most notably in the city of Bath, where the stunning Royal Crescent is the ultimate example of the genre.

Victoriana

The Victorian era was a time of great building activity. A style called Victorian Gothic developed, imitating the tall, narrow windows and ornamented spires featured in the original Gothic cathedrals. The most famous example is London's Houses of Parliament and the clock tower that everyone knows as Big Ben, which was officially renamed Elizabeth Tower in 2012 to celebrate the Queen's diamond jubilee. Other Victorian Gothic highlights in England's capital include the Natural History Museum and St Pancras train station. The style was copied all around the country, especially for civic buildings, with the finest examples including Manchester Town Hall and Glasgow City Chambers.

As well as many grand cathedrals, Britain has thousands of parish churches, many with historical or architectural significance, especially in rural areas.

Founded by German immigrant Nikolaus Pevsner after WWII, Pevsner Architectural Guides are the classic travellers' handbooks of British architecture. Around 80 volumes, published between 1951 and the present day, lovingly document the significant buildings of England, Scotland and Wales.

Industrialisation

Through the late 19th and early 20th centuries, as Britain's cities grew in size and stature, the newly moneyed middle classes built smart town houses in streets and squares. Elsewhere, the first town planners oversaw the construction of endless terraces of 'back-to-back' and 'two-up-two-down' houses to accommodate the massive influx of workers required for the country's factories. In South Wales, similar, though often single-storeyed houses were built for the burgeoning numbers of coal miners. The industrial areas of Scotland saw the construction of tenements, usually three or four storeys high, with a central communal staircase and two dwellings on each floor. In many cases the terraced houses and basic tenements are not especially scenic, but they are perhaps the most enduring mark on the British architectural landscape.

Postwar Pains & Pride

WWII bombing damaged many of Britain's cities and the rebuilding that followed showed little regard for the overall appearance of the cities or for the lives of people who lived in them. Rows of terraces were swept away in favour of high-rise tower blocks, while the brutalist architecture of the 1950s and '60s embraced the modern and efficient building materials of steel and concrete.

Perhaps this is why the British are largely conservative in their architectural tastes. They often resent ambitious or experimental designs, especially applied to public buildings or when a building's form appears more important than its function. However, a familiar pattern unfolds: after a few years of resentment, the building is given a nickname, then it gains grudging acceptance, and finally it becomes a source of pride and affection. The British just don't like to be rushed, that's all.

The 21st Century

During the first decade of this century, many areas of Britain placed new importance on having progressive, popular architecture as part of a wider regeneration. Top examples include Manchester's Imperial War Museum North, Birmingham's Bullring shopping centre, Edinburgh's Scottish Parliament Building, the Welsh National Assembly building and the Wales Millennium Centre (both on the Cardiff waterfront), the overlapping arches of Glasgow's Scottish Exhibition and Conference Centre (affectionately called 'the Armadillo') and the Sage concert hall in Gateshead in northeast England.

Britain's largest and highest-profile architectural project of recent times was the Olympic Park, the centrepiece of the 2012 Olympic Games. Situated in the London suburb of Stratford, it was renamed the Queen Elizabeth Olympic Park after the games. The main Olympic Stadium – now home to West Ham United football club – and other arenas, including the much-admired Velodrome and Aquatics Centre, were built using cutting-edge techniques and are all dramatic structures in their own right.

Perhaps the best-known example of 1950/60s brutalist architecture is London's Southbank Centre. A building of its time, it was applauded when finished, then reviled for its ugliness, and is now regarded by Londoners with something close to pride and affection.

Meanwhile, in the centre of the capital, the Shard – a giant, pointed glass skyscraper – dominates the South Bank; at 306m, it's one of Europe's tallest buildings. On the other side of the River Thames, two more giant skyscrapers were completed in 2014: 20 Fenchurch St (thanks to its shape, nicknamed 'the Walkie-Talkie') and the slanting-walled Leadenhall Building (dubbed, inevitably, 'the Cheese Grater').

London continues to grow upwards and British architecture continues to push new boundaries of style and technology. The buildings may look a little different, but they're still iconic and impressive.

The Arts

Britain's contributions to the worlds of literature, drama, cinema and music are celebrated around the world, thanks in no small part to the global dominance of the English language. As you travel around Britain today you can explore artists' childhood homes and the landscapes and locations made famous in lyrics, movie backdrops and literary settings – from the centuries-old birthplace of Shakespeare in Stratford-upon-Avon to Abbey Road of The Beatles fame.

Literature

First Stars

The first big name in Britain's literary history is Geoffrey Chaucer, best known for *The Canterbury Tales*. This mammoth collection of fables, stories and morality tales, using travelling pilgrims (the Knight, the Wife of Bath, the Nun's Priest and so on) as a narrative hook, is considered an essential of the canon.

After Chaucer, two centuries passed before Britain's next major literary figure rose to prominence: enter stage left William Shakespeare. Best known for his plays, he was also a prolific and influential poet. 'Shall I compare thee to a summer's day?' is just one of his famous lines still widely quoted today.

A collection of folk tales discovered in medieval Welsh manuscripts of the 14th century, *The Mabinogion* was translated into English in the mid-19th century. Drawing on pre-Christian Celtic myths, several stories deal with the legendary feats of King Arthur and the knights of the round table.

The *Oxford Guide to Literary Britain & Ireland*, edited by Daniel Hahn and Nicholas Robins, gives details of towns, villages and the countryside immortalised by writers, from Chaucer's Canterbury and Austen's Bath to Scott's Highlands.

The 17th & 18th Centuries

The 17th century saw the publication of John Milton's epic blank verse poem *Paradise Lost,* a literary landmark inspired by the biblical tale of Adam and Eve's expulsion from the Garden of Eden. This was followed a few years later by the equally seminal *Pilgrim's Progress* by John Bunyan, an allegorical tale of the everyday Christian struggle. For mere mortals, reading these books in their entirety can be hard going, but they're worth dipping into for a taste of the rich language.

More familiar to most British people are the words of *Auld Lang Syne,* penned by Scotland's national poet Robert Burns, and traditionally sung at New Year. His more unusual *Address to a Haggis* is also still recited annually on Burns Night, a Scottish celebration held on 25 January (the poet's birthday).

Another milestone work of this period is Daniel Defoe's *Robinson Crusoe.* On one level it's an adventure story about a man shipwrecked on an uninhabited island, but it's also a discussion on civilisation, colonialism and faith, and is regarded by many scholars as the first English-language novel. It's also been an armchair travellers' favourite since its publication in 1719.

Graham Greene's novel *Brighton Rock* (1938) is a classic account of wayward English youth. For an even more shocking take, try *A Clockwork Orange* by Anthony Burgess, later infamously filmed by Stanley Kubrick in 1971.

The Romantic Era

As industrialisation began to take hold in Britain during the late 18th and early 19th century, a new generation of writers, including William Blake, John Keats, Percy Bysshe Shelley, Lord Byron and Samuel Taylor

For a taste of surreal humour, try two of Britain's funniest (and most successful) writers: Douglas Adams (*The Hitchhiker's Guide to the Galaxy* plus sequels) and Terry Pratchett (the *Discworld* series).

Coleridge, drew inspiration from human imagination and the natural world (in some cases aided by a healthy dose of laudanum). Known as the 'Romantics', the best known of all was William Wordsworth; his famous line from the poem commonly known as 'Daffodils' – 'I wandered lonely as a cloud' – was inspired by a walk along the shores of Ullswater in the Lake District.

Victoriana

During the reign of Queen Victoria (1837–1901), key novels of the time explored social themes. Charles Dickens is the best-known writer of the period: *Oliver Twist* is a tale of child pickpockets surviving in the London slums, while *Hard Times* is a critique of the excesses of capitalism.

At around the same time, but in a rural setting, George Eliot (the pen name of Mary Anne Evans) wrote *The Mill on the Floss*, whose central character, Maggie Tulliver, searches for true love and struggles against society's expectations.

Meanwhile, Thomas Hardy's classic *Tess of the D'Urbervilles* deals with the peasantry's decline, and *The Trumpet Major* paints a picture of idyllic English country life interrupted by war and encroaching modernity. Many of Hardy's works are in the fictionalised county of Wessex, largely based on today's Dorset and surrounding counties, where towns such as Dorchester are popular stops on tourist itineraries today.

Displaying similarly close links to the landscape is *Waverley* by Scotland's greatest historical novelist, Sir Walter Scott. Written in the early 19th century and set in the mountains and glens of Scotland during the time of the Jacobite rebellion, it is usually regarded as the first historical novel in the English language. Scott's bestselling works, which include the narrative poem 'The Lady of the Lake' and the novel *Rob Roy*, are often credited with kick-starting the Scottish tourist industry.

The Modern World

Britain – and its literature – changed forever following WWI and the social disruption of the period. This fed into the modernist movement, with DH Lawrence perhaps its finest exponent. *Sons and Lovers* follows the lives and loves of generations in the English Midlands as the country changes from rural idyll to industrial landscape, while his controversial exploration of sexuality in *Lady Chatterley's Lover* was banned until 1960 because of its 'obscenity'.

Other highlights of this period included Daphne du Maurier's romantic suspense novel *Rebecca*, with close connections to Cornwall; Evelyn Waugh's *Brideshead Revisited*, an exploration of moral and social disintegration among the English aristocracy in the 1920s and '30s; and Richard Llewellyn's Welsh classic *How Green Was My Valley*. A decade

LITERARY LOCATIONS

Bath Grandeur that never tired Jane Austen's heroines.

Canterbury Synonymous with Chaucer's *Canterbury Tales*.

Haworth Home of the Brontë sisters, surrounded by wuthering moors.

Lake District Source of inspiration for William Wordsworth.

Laugharne Dylan Thomas' home, with a 'heron-priested shore' and a 'castle as brown as owls'.

Edinburgh Unesco's first City of Literature, with links to Burns, Scott and Stevenson (and even JK Rowling).

Stratford-upon-Avon Birthplace of William Shakespeare.

CHILDREN'S FAVOURITES

Britain's greatest literary phenomenon of the 21st century is JK Rowling's *Harry Potter* series, a set of other-worldly adventures that have entertained millions of children (and many grown-ups too) from the publication of the first book in 1996 to the stage play, *Harry Potter and the Cursed Child*, in 2016. The magical tales, brought vividly to life in the Harry Potter movies, are the latest in a long line of British children's classics that are also enjoyed by adults. The pedigree stretches back to the works of Lewis Carroll (*Alice's Adventures in Wonderland*), E Nesbit (*The Railway Children*), AA Milne (*Winnie-the-Pooh*), CS Lewis (*The Chronicles of Narnia*) and Roald Dahl (*Charlie and the Chocolate Factory*, *Matilda*). Newcastle's Seven Stories – The Centre for Children's Books is a wonderful place to get acquainted, or reacquainted, with favourites old and new.

or so later, after WWII, Compton Mackenzie lifted postwar spirits with *Whisky Galore,* a comic novel about a cargo of booze shipwrecked on a Scottish island.

In the 1950s, the poet Dylan Thomas found fame with his *Portrait of The Artist As A Young Dog,* although his most celebrated work is a radio play *Under Milk Wood* (1954), exposing the social tensions of small-town Wales.

Then came the swinging '60s. Liverpool poet Roger McGough and friends determined to make art relevant to daily life produced *The Mersey Sound* – landmark pop poetry for the streets. Other new writers included Muriel Spark, who introduced the world to a highly unusual Edinburgh school mistress in *The Prime of Miss Jean Brodie.*

The 1970s saw the arrival of two novelists who went on to become prolific through the rest of the century and beyond. Martin Amis produced a string of novels whose common themes include the absurdity and unappealing nature of modern life, such as *London Fields* (1989). Ian McEwan made his debut with *The Cement Garden* (1978), and earned critical acclaim for finely observed studies of the English character in works such as *Atonement* (2001) and *On Chesil Beach* (2007).

Kate Roberts explored the experiences of working men and women in rural Wales, often evoking qualities of a time since past with *Feet in Chains* (1977). The elegant *On the Black Hill* (1982), by Bruce Chatwin, also evokes the joys and hardships of small-town life, exploring Welsh spirit and cross-border antipathy through the lives of torpid twin-brother farmers.

Modern novels in a different vein include 1993's *Trainspotting* by Irvine Welsh, a dark look at Edinburgh's drug culture, while the grim realities of modern Glasgow are vividly conjured in the 1983 short story collection *Not Not While the Giro* by James Kelman, whose controversial novel *How Late It Was, How Late* won the 1994 Booker Prize.

Other well known Scots writers of this period include Janice Galloway *(The Trick Is To Keep Breathing)* and Liz Lochhead *(Mary Queen of Scots Got Her Head Chopped Off).*

> The painter, writer, poet and visionary William Blake (1757–1827) mixed fantastical landscapes and mythological scenes with motifs drawn from classical art, religious iconography and legend. For more, see www.blakearchive.org.

The New Millennium

As the 20th century came to a close, and the new millennium dawned, Britain's multicultural landscape proved a rich inspiration for contemporary novelists. Hanif Kureishi sowed the seeds with his ground-breaking 1990 novel *The Buddha of Suburbia,* followed by Zadie Smith's acclaimed debut *White Teeth* (2000) and a string of subsequent bestsellers. Andrea Levy found acclaim with *Small Island* (2004), and Monica Ali's *Brick Lane* was shortlisted for the 2003 Man Booker Prize, a high-profile literary award.

Also popular is Julian Barnes, whose book *England, England* is a darkly ironic study of nationalism and tourism, while *The Sense of an*

> Helen Fielding's *Bridget Jones's Diary* is a fond look at the heartache of a modern single woman's blundering search for love and epitomised the late-1990s 'chick lit' genre.

The British Film Institute (BFI) is dedicated to promoting film and cinema in Britain, and publishes the monthly academic journal *Sight & Sound*. See www.bfi.org.uk and www.screenonline.org.uk for complete coverage of Britain's film and TV industry.

Ending won the 2011 Man Booker Prize. Hilary Mantel, author of many novels on an astoundingly wide range of subjects, won the Man Booker Prize twice, first in 2009 for historical blockbuster *Wolf Hall* (about Henry VIII and his ruthless advisor Thomas Cromwell), and then 2012 for its sequel *Bring Up the Bodies*; the third and final instalment, *The Mirror and the Light,* is expected by 2017.

Meanwhile, the genre known as 'Tartan Noir' – crime fiction set in Scotland – continues to grow. Ian Rankin, best known for his Edinburgh-set Inspector Rebus novels, is a master of the form, but Val McDermid, Louise Welsh and Christopher Brookmyre are right up there with him.

Cinema

British cinema has a long history, with many early directors cutting their teeth in the silent-film industry. Perhaps the best-known of these was Alfred Hitchcock, who directed *Blackmail,* one of the first British 'talkies' in 1929, and who went on to direct a string of films during the 1930s, before migrating to Hollywood in the early 1940s.

Early Days

During WWII, British films were dominated by patriotic stories designed to raise morale: *Went the Day Well?* (1942), *In Which We Serve* (1942) and *We Dive at Dawn* (1943) are prime examples of the genre. During this period David Lean directed the classic tale of repressed passion, *Brief Encounter* (1945), before graduating to Hollywood epics, including *Lawrence of Arabia* and *Doctor Zhivago*.

Another great film of the 1940s is *How Green Was My Valley,* a tale of everyday life in the coal-mining villages of Wales. Perhaps the best-known movie about Wales, it manages to annoy more Welsh people than any other with its stereotyped characters, absence of Welsh actors, and the fact that it was shot in a Hollywood studio. It's worth seeing, though, for its period flavour.

After the War

Following the hardships of the war, British audiences were in the mood for escape and entertainment. During the late 1940s and early '50s, the domestic film industry specialised in eccentric British comedies epitomised by the output of Ealing Studios: notable titles include *Passport to Pimlico* (1949), *Kind Hearts and Coronets* (1949) and *The Titfield Thunderbolt* (1953).

Dramatic box-office hits of the time included *Hamlet* (1948; the first British film to win an Oscar in the Best Picture category), starring Laurence Olivier, and Carol Reed's *The Third Man* (1949). In a post-

HAMMER HORROR

The British company Hammer Film Productions produced low-budget horror films in the 1950s and '60s, still revered by fans around the globe. Early flicks included *The Quatermass Xperiment* (1955) and *The Curse of Frankenstein* (1957). The stars of the latter – Peter Cushing as Dr Frankenstein and Christopher Lee as the Monster – would feature in many of Hammer's best films over the next 20 years, including a string of nine *Dracula* films (most of which star Lee as Dracula and Cushing as Van Helsing or his descendants) and six *Frankenstein* sequels.

The studio also launched the careers of several other notable actors (including Oliver Reed, who made his debut in *The Curse of the Werewolf;* 1961) and even spawned its very own spoof, *Carry On Screaming* (1966) – the ultimate British seal of approval. From 1979 the company went into hibernation, but its fortunes revived in 2012 with the release of *The Woman in Black,* starring Harry Potter lead Daniel Radcliffe.

war Britain still struggling with rationing and food shortages, tales of heroic derring-do such as *The Dam Busters* (1955) and comedies like *Whisky Galore!* (1949; a remake was filmed in 2016) helped lighten the national mood.

Swinging Sixties

In the late 1950s, 'British New Wave' and 'Free Cinema' explored the gritty realities of life in an intimate, semidocumentary style, with Lindsay Anderson and Tony Richardson crystallising the movement with films such as *This Sporting Life* (1963) and *A Taste of Honey* (1961).

At the other end of the spectrum were the *Carry On* films, packed with bawdy gags and double entendres, and starring a troupe of 'national treasures' including Barbara Windsor, Sid James and Kenneth Williams.

The 1960s saw the birth of another classic British icon: super-spy James Bond, adapted from the Ian Fleming novels and first played by Sean Connery in *Dr No* (1962). Since then over 20 Bond movies have been made, with Bond played by a series of actors from Roger Moore and George Lazenby to Pierce Brosnan and Daniel Craig.

Withnail and I (1987) is one of the great British cult comedies. Directed by Bruce Robinson, it stars Paul McGann and Richard E Grant as a pair of hapless out-of-work actors on a disastrous holiday to the Lake District.

Burning Gold

After the boom of the 1960s, British cinema entered troubled waters for a decade or so, but was revived in the 1980s thanks partly to David Puttnam's *Chariots of Fire*, the Oscar-winning tale of two British athletes competing at the 1924 Olympics.

The newly established (1982) Channel 4 invested in edgy films such as *My Beautiful Laundrette* (1985), while the British producing duo of Ismail Merchant and James Ivory played Hollywood at its own game with period epics such as *Heat and Dust* (1983) and *A Room With A View* (1985), capitalising on the success of Richard Attenborough's big-budget *Gandhi* (1982), which bagged eight Academy Awards.

Brit Flicks

In the 1990s, the massively successful *Four Weddings and a Funeral* (1994), which introduced Hugh Grant in his trademark role as the likeable, self-deprecating Englishman (an archetype he reprised in subsequent hits *Notting Hill*, 1999, and *Love, Actually*, 2003) spearheaded the 'Brit-flick' genre. *The Full Monty* (1997), about a troupe of laid-off steel workers turned male strippers, was Britain's most successful film ever (until overtaken by the Harry Potter franchise in 2001), while *The Englishman Who Went Up a Hill and Came Down a Mountain* (1995), is an affectionate story about a hill in North Wales.

Grittier films of the 1990s included *Trainspotting* (1996), a visually innovative, hard-hitting film about Edinburgh's drugged-out underworld, which launched the careers of Scottish actors Ewan McGregor and Robert Carlyle, while Mike Leigh's *Secrets and Lies* (1996), a Palme d'Or winner at Cannes, tells the story of an adopted black woman who seeks out her white mother.

Other landmark films of the decade included: gangster movie *Lock, Stock and Two Smoking Barrels* (1998), which spawned a host of copycats; *Breaking the Waves* (1996), a perfect study of culture clash in 1970s Scotland; *Human Traffic* (1999), an edgy romp through Cardiff's clubland; and the Oscar-winning Austen adaptation *Sense and Sensibility* (1995) starring English doyennes Emma Thompson and Kate Winslet as the Dashwood sisters, with Hugh Grant as (you guessed it) a likeable and self-deprecating Englishman.

Award-winning Welsh-language films of the time include *Hedd Wynn* (1992), a heartbreaking story of a poet killed in WWI, and *Solomon and Gaenor* (1999), a passionate tale of forbidden love at the turn of the

The Ladykillers (1955) is a classic Ealing comedy about a band of hapless bank robbers holed up in a London guest house, and features Alec Guinness sporting quite possibly the most outrageous set of false teeth ever captured on celluloid.

20th century, starring Ioan Gruffudd and filmed twice; once in the Welsh language and once in English.

The decade ended with films such as *East Is East* (1999), a beautifully understated study of the clash between first- and second-generation immigrant Pakistanis in Britain, and *Billy Elliott* (2000), about a boy's quest to learn ballet and escape the slag-heaps of post-industrial northern England.

The 21st Century

In the early part of the 21st century, literature continued to provide the richest seam mined by the British film industry. Hits include the blockbuster Harry Potter franchise (based on the books of JK Rowling, and the most financially successful film series of all time) starring Daniel Radcliffe, as well as 2005's *The Constant Gardener* (based on a John Le Carré novel), 2007's *Atonement* (based on Ian McEwan's novel), 2011's *War Horse* (directed by Stephen Spielberg and based on Michael Morpurgo's novel), and 2012's *Anna Karenina*, directed by Joe Wright and starring Keira Knightley. *T2* (2017), the much anticipated sequel to *Trainspotting*, is based on Irvine Welsh's novel *Porno*.

Meanwhile, the oldest of British film franchise rolls on, with James Bond played as a tough, toned and occasionally fallible character by Daniel Craig in *Casino Royale* (2006), *Quantum of Solace* (2008), *Skyfall* (2012) and *Spectre* (2015); in 2016 Craig hinted he may pass on the baton to another actor.

Britain's main broadcasters are known for their long-running 'soaps' (soap operas) such as *EastEnders* (BBC), *Emmerdale* and *Coronation Street* (both ITV), which have collectively been running on British screens for well over a century.

Pop & Rock Music

Britain's been putting the world through its musical paces ever since a mop-haired four-piece from Liverpool tuned up their Rickenbackers and created The Beatles. And while some may claim that Elvis invented rock 'n' roll, it was the Fab Four who transformed it into a global phenomenon, backed by the other bands of the 1960s 'British Invasion' – The Rolling Stones, The Who, Cream, The Kinks and soul man Tom Jones.

Glam to Punk

Glam rock swaggered onto the stage at the start of the 1970s, led by the likes of Marc Bolan and David Bowie in their tight-fitting jumpsuits and chameleon guises, and succeeded by early boy-band Bay City Rollers, art-rockers Roxy Music, outrageously costumed Elton John and anthemic popsters Queen. In the same era, Led Zeppelin, Deep Purple and Black Sabbath laid down the blueprint for heavy metal, while the psychedelia of the previous decade morphed into the spacey noodlings of prog rock, epitomised by Pink Floyd, Genesis and Yes.

By the late '70s, glam and prog bands were looking out of touch in a Britain wracked by rampant unemployment and industrial unrest, and punk rock exploded onto the scene, summing up the air of doom with nihilistic lyrics and three-chord tunes. The Sex Pistols remain the best-known band of the era, while other punk pioneers included The Clash, The Damned, The Buzzcocks and The Stranglers.

Punk begat New Wave, with acts such as The Jam and Elvis Costello blending spiky tunes and sharp lyrics into a more radio-friendly sound. A little later, along came bands like The Specials and baggy-trousered rude boys Madness, mixing punk, reggae and ska sounds. Meanwhile, another punk-and-reggae-influenced band called The Police – fronted by bassist Sting – became one of the biggest names of the decade.

The BBC is a public-service broadcaster, financed by the licence fee of £145.50, paid annually by every house in Britain with a TV set, rather than by advertising. This means shows are not interrupted by commercial breaks.

Mode, Metal & Miserabilism

The conspicuous consumption of Britain in the early 1980s was reflected in the decade's pop scene. Big hair and shoulder pads became the

ROCK 'N' ROLL LOCATIONS

Fans buy the music, then the T-shirt. However, true fans visit the locations featured on album covers. Here are some favourites, many in London, plus a few others around the country:

Abbey Rd, St John's Wood, London – *Abbey Road*, The Beatles

Battersea Power Station, London – *Animals*, Pink Floyd

Berwick St, Soho, London – *(What's the Story) Morning Glory*, Oasis

Big Ben, London – *My Generation* (US version), The Who.

Camden Market, London – *The Clash*, The Clash

Heddon St, off Regent St, London – *The Rise and Fall of Ziggy Stardust & the Spiders from Mars*, David Bowie

Porthmadog (Black Rock Sands) – *This is My Truth Tell Me Yours*, Manic Street Preachers

Salford Lads Club, Manchester – *The Queen is Dead*, The Smiths

Thor's Cave, Manifold Valley, near Ashbourne, Peak District National Park – *A Storm In Heaven*, The Verve

Yes Tor, Dartmoor, Devon – *Tomato*, Yes

uniform of New Romantics such as Spandau Ballet, Duran Duran and Culture Club, while the increased use of synthesizers led to the development of a new electronic sound in the music of Depeche Mode and The Human League. More hits and highlights were supplied by Texas, Eurythmics and Wham! – a boyish duo headed by a bright young fellow named George Michael.

Away from the glitz, fans enjoyed the doom-laden lyrics of The Cure, Bauhaus and Siouxsie & the Banshees, while Britain's heavy rock heritage inspired acts such as Iron Maiden. In a different tone entirely, the disaffection of mid-1980s Britain was summed up by the arch-priests of 'miserabilism', The Smiths, fronted by quiffed wordsmith Morrissey.

The Spice Girls were one of the most famous pop creations of the 1990s, and they became the world's best-selling all-female group. Sporty, Scary, Baby, Ginger and Posh famously reunited in 2012 to perform at the London Olympics closing ceremony.

Raves, Indie & Britpop

The beats and bleeps of 1980s electronica fuelled the burgeoning dance-music scene of the early '90s. An eruption of ecstasy-saturated rave culture, centred on famous clubs like Manchester's Haçienda and London's Ministry of Sound, overflowed into the mainstream through chart-topping artists such as The Prodigy and Fatboy Slim. Manchester was also a focus for the burgeoning British 'indie' scene, driven by guitar-based bands such as The Charlatans, The Stone Roses, James and Happy Mondays.

Indie grew up in the mid- to late-1990s, and the term 'Britpop' was coined, with Oasis at the forefront but covering a wide range of bands including Blur, Elastica, Suede, Supergrass, Ocean Colour Scene, The Verve, Pulp, Travis, Feeder, Super Furry Animals, Stereophonics, Catatonia and the Manic Street Preachers.

Pop Today, Gone Tomorrow

The new millennium saw no let-up in the British music scene's shape-shifting and reinvention. Jazz, soul, R&B and hip-hop have fused into an 'urban' sound epitomised by artists like Dizzee Rascal, Tinie Tempah and Plan B.

In a totally different genre, British folk and roots music, and folk-influenced acoustic music, is enjoying its biggest revival since the

POP ON FILM

If you want to combine British pop music with British cinema, try some of these films:

Backbeat (1994) A look at the early days of The Beatles.

Sid and Nancy (1986) The demise of Sex Pistols bassist Sid Vicious and his American girlfriend.

Velvet Goldmine (1998) A tawdry glimpse of the 1970s glam-rock scene.

24 Hour Party People (2002) A totally irreverent and suitably chaotic film about the 1990s Manchester music scene.

Control (2007) Biopic about Joy Division's lead singer Ian Curtis.

Nowhere Boy (2009) About John Lennon in his pre-Beatles days.

1960s, with major names including Eliza Carthy, Mumford & Sons and Welsh band Allan Yn Y Fan.

Meanwhile, the singer-songwriter, exemplified by Katie Melua, Ed Sheeran, the late Amy Winehouse, James Bay and the all-conquering Adele, has made a comeback, and the spirit of British punk and indie stays alive thanks to the likes of Florence & the Machine, Muse, Kasabian, Radiohead, The Horrors and breakthrough grunge-pop band Wolf Alice.

But the biggest commercial success of all has been boy-band One Direction, becoming the first artists ever to have each of their four albums debut at number one in the US charts, having the biggest grossing concert tour ever in 2014, and being named Billboard Artist of the Year in 2014.

Painting & Sculpture

For many centuries, continental Europe – especially Holland, Spain, France and Italy – set the artistic agenda. The first artist with a truly British style and sensibility was arguably William Hogarth, whose riotous canvases exposed the vice and corruption of 18th-century London. His most celebrated work is *A Rake's Progress*, which kick-started a long tradition of British caricatures that can be traced right through to the work of modern-day cartoonists such as Gerald Scarfe and Steve Bell. It's displayed at Sir John Soane's Museum in London.

Portraits & Landscapes

While Hogarth was busy satirising society, other artists were hard at work showing it in its best light. The leading figures of 18th-century British portraiture were Sir Joshua Reynolds, Thomas Gainsborough and George Romney, while George Stubbs is best known for his intricate studies of animals (particularly horses). Works by these artists are displayed at Tate Britain and the National Gallery in London.

The works of Henry Moore and Barbara Hepworth can be seen at the Yorkshire Sculpture Park, between Sheffield and Leeds, in northern England. Hepworth is also forever associated with St Ives in Cornwall, while the Hepworth Wakefield gallery is dedicated to her life and work.

In the 19th century, leading painters favoured the landscape. John Constable's best-known works include *Salisbury Cathedral* and *The Hay Wain*, depicting a mill in Suffolk (and now on show in the National Gallery, London), while JMW Turner was fascinated by the effects of light and colour, with his works becoming almost entirely abstract by the 1840s – vilified at the time but prefiguring the Impressionist movement that was to follow 50 years later.

Fables & Flowers

In the mid- to late-19th century, the Pre-Raphaelite movement harked back to the figurative style of classical Italian and Flemish art, tying in with the prevailing Victorian taste for fables, myths and fairy tales. Key members of the movement included Sir John Everett Millais and William Holman Hunt. Millais' *Ophelia*, showing the damsel picturesquely drowned in a river, is an excellent example of their style, and can be seen at the Tate Britain. However, one of the best collections of Pre-Raphaelite art is in the Birmingham Museum and Art Gallery.

A good friend of the Pre-Raphaelites was William Morris; he saw late-19th-century furniture and interior design as increasingly vulgar, and with Dante Gabriel Rossetti and Edward Burne-Jones founded the Arts and Crafts movement to encourage the revival of a decorative approach to features such as wallpaper, tapestries and windows. Many of his designs are still used today.

North of the border, Charles Rennie Mackintosh, fresh from the Glasgow School of Art, fast became a renowned artist, designer and architect. He is still Scotland's great art nouveau exponent, and much of his work remains in Glasgow. He also influenced a group of artists from the 1890s that became known as the Glasgow School (often divided into two groups: the Glasgow Boys and the Glasgow Girls), among them Margaret and Frances MacDonald, James Guthrie and EA Walton. Much of their work can be seen in the Kelvingrove Art Gallery in Glasgow.

Around Britain, buildings associated with notable people are marked with a (usually blue) plaque. In early 2012, a plaque was placed at 23 Heddon St in London to commemorate David Bowie's fictional pop character Ziggy Stardust.

Stone & Sticks

In the tumultuous 20th century, British art became increasingly experimental, with key painters including Francis Bacon, whose work was influenced by Freudian psychoanalysis, and the group known as the Scottish Colourists – Francis Cadell, SJ Peploe, Leslie Hunter and JD Fergusson. Meanwhile, pioneering sculptors such as Henry Moore and Barbara Hepworth experimented with natural forms in stone and new materials.

At around the same time, Welsh artist Gwen John painted introspective portraits of women friends, cats and nuns (and famously became the model and lover of French artist Rodin), while her brother Augustus John became Britain's leading portrait painter, with famous sitters such as Thomas Hardy and George Bernard Shaw. One place to admire the Johnses' works is at the Glynn Vivian Art Gallery in Swansea.

Pop Art

The mid-1950s and early '60s saw an explosion of British artists plundering TV, music, advertising and popular culture for inspiration. Leaders of this new 'pop art' movement included David Hockney, who used bold colours and simple lines to depict his dachshunds and swimming pools, and Peter Blake, who designed the collage cover for The Beatles' landmark *Sgt. Pepper's Lonely Hearts Club Band* album.

The '60s also saw the rise of sculptor Anthony Caro, who held his first groundbreaking exhibition at the Whitechapel Art Gallery in 1963. Creating large abstract works in steel and bronze, he remains one of Britain's most influential sculptors.

Britart & Beyond

Thanks partly to the support (and money) of advertising tycoon Charles Saatchi, a new wave of British artists came to the fore in the 1990s. The movement was dubbed, inevitably, 'Britart'; its leading members included Damien Hirst, initially famous (or infamous) for works involving pickled sharks, semi-dissected human figures and a diamond-encrusted skull entitled For the Love of God. His pregnant, naked and half-flayed *Verity* towers 20m high beside the harbour mouth at Ilfracombe in north Devon.

A contemporary is Tracey Emin. Once considered an enfant terrible, she incurred the wrath of the tabloids for works such as *My Bed*, a messed-up bedroom scene which sold for £2.2 million in 2014, but is

Antony Gormley's *Angel of the North* is one of the most viewed works of art in the world. Standing beside the busy A1 London to Edinburgh road, millions of drivers each year can't help but see it.

now a respected figure and patron of the new Turner Gallery in Margate, named for the famous English artist JMW Turner.

Theatre

Theatre in Britain has its roots in medieval morality plays, court jesters and travelling storytellers. Its origins can possibly be traced all the way back to dramas during Roman times in amphitheatres, a few of which still remain at places such as Chester and Cirencester. Most scholars agree that the key milestone in the story is the opening of England's first theatre, called simply The Theatre, in London in 1576. A few years later, two more theatres appeared, the Rose and the Globe, and the stage was set for the entrance of Britain's best-known playwright.

Shakespeare

For most visitors to Britain (and for many locals) drama means just one name: Shakespeare. Born in 1564 in the Midlands town of Stratford-upon-Avon, William Shakespeare made his name in London, where most of his plays were performed at the Globe Theatre.

He started writing plays around 1585, and his early theatrical works are grouped together as 'comedies' and 'histories', many of which are household names today – such as *All's Well that Ends Well, The Taming of the Shrew, A Midsummer Night's Dream, Richard III* and *Henry V*. Later in his career Shakespeare wrote the plays known collectively as the 'tragedies', including *Romeo and Juliet, Macbeth, Julius Caesar, Hamlet* and *King Lear*. His brilliant plots and spectacular use of language, plus the sheer size of his body of work, have turned him into a national – and international – icon.

Today, almost 400 years after he shuffled off his mortal coil, the Bard's plays still pull in big crowds, and can be enjoyed at the rebuilt Globe on London's South Bank and at the Royal Shakespeare Company's own theatre in his original hometown of Stratford-upon-Avon.

British Theatre Today

However you budget your time and money during your visit to Britain, be sure to see some theatre. It easily lives up to its reputation as the finest in the world, especially in London (whatever New Yorkers may say), while other big cities around the country boast their own top-class venues, such as the Birmingham Repertory Theatre, the Bristol Old Vic, the Chichester Festival Theatre, the Playhouse in Nottingham, the New Theatre in Cardiff and the Royal Lyceum in Edinburgh.

For big names, most people head for London's West End, where famous spots include the Shaftsbury, the Adelphi, and the Theatre Royal, Drury Lane. Such venues are mostly the preserve of classic plays, including *The Mousetrap,* the legendary whodunnit and world's longest-running play, showing continuously since 1952.

In 2012, the massively successful musical *Matilda*, based on the novel by Roald Dahl, broke records by winning seven Olivier Awards, the most prestigious prize in British theatre, going on to take four US Tony Awards in 2013.

West End Musicals

As well as drama, London's West End means big musicals, with a long history of crowd-pullers such as *Cats*, *The Wizard of Oz*, *Les Misérables*, *Sweeney Todd*, *The Phantom of the Opera* and *The Lion King*, with many of today's shows raiding the pop world for material, such as *We Will Rock You,* inspired by the music of Queen, and Abba-based *Mamma Mia!*

The British Landscape

When it comes to landscapes, Britain is not a place of extremes; there are no Alps or Himalaya here, no Amazon or Sahara. But there's plenty to keep you enthralled. The country may be small, but even a relatively short journey takes you through a surprising mix of scenery. Seeing the change as you travel – subtle in some areas, dramatic in others – is one of this country's great attractions.

Location, Location, Location

Geologically at least, Britain is part of Europe. It's on the edge of the Eurasian landmass, separated from the mother continent by the shallow English Channel. (The French are not so proprietorial, and call it La Manche – 'the sleeve'.) Until about 10,000 years ago, Britain was connected to Europe by land, but then sea levels rose and created the island we know today. Only in more recent times has there been a reconnection, in the form of the Channel Tunnel.

Wildlife of Britain by George McGavin et al is subtitled 'the definitive visual guide'. Although too heavy to carry around, this beautiful photographic book is great for pre-trip inspiration or post-trip memories.

Southern England is covered in a mix of cities, towns and gently undulating countryside. Eastern England (especially the area called East Anglia) is almost entirely low and flat, while southwest England has wild moors, granite outcrops and rich pastures (Devon's cream is world famous), plus a rugged coast with sheltered beaches, making it a favourite holiday destination.

In the north of England, farmland is interspersed with towns and cities, but the landscape is noticeably more rugged. A spine of large hills called the Pennines (fondly tagged 'the backbone of England') runs from Derbyshire to the Scottish border, and includes the peaty plateau of the Peak District, the wild moors around Haworth (immortalised in Brontë novels), the delightful valleys of the Yorkshire Dales and the frequently windswept but starkly beautiful hills of Northumberland.

Perhaps England's best-known landscape is the Lake District, a small but spectacular cluster of mountains and lakes in the northwest, where Scafell Pike (a towering 978m) is England's highest peak.

The landscape of Wales is also defined by hills: notably the rounded Black Mountains and Brecon Beacons in the south, and the spiky peaks of Snowdonia in the north, with Snowdon (1085m) the highest Welsh summit. In between lie the wild Cambrian Mountains of central Wales, rolling to the west coast of spectacular cliffs and shimmering river estuaries.

BRITAIN'S BEST BEACHES

Other great beaches can be found in Suffolk, Norfolk, Lancashire, Yorkshire and Northumberland in England, and pretty much anywhere on the Welsh coast between the Gower Peninsula and Llandudno. Scotland offers even more choice, from the rocky bays of the west coast to the gorgeous white-sand beaches of the Outer Hebrides.

Britain's best resort beaches earn the coveted international Blue Flag (www.blueflag.global) award, meaning sand and water are clean and unpolluted. Other parameters include the presence of lifeguards, litter bins and recycling facilities – meaning some wild beaches may not earn the award, but are still stunning nonetheless.

For real mountains, you need to head to Scotland, especially the wild, remote and thinly populated northwest Highlands – separated from the rest of the country by a diagonal gash in the earth's crust called the Great Glen Fault. Ben Nevis (1345m) is Scotland's – and Britain's – highest summit, but there are many more to choose from. The Highlands are further enhanced by the vast cluster of beautiful islands that lie off the loch-indented west coast.

South of the Scottish Highlands is the relatively flat central Lowlands, home to the bulk of Scotland's population. Further south, down to the border with England, things get hillier again; this is the southern Uplands, an area of rounded heather-clad hills and fertile farms.

National Parks

Back in 1810, English poet and outdoor fan William Wordsworth suggested that the wild landscape of the Lake District in Cumbria, northwest England, should be 'a sort of national property, in which every man has a right'. More than a century later, in 1951, the Lake District did indeed become a national park along with the Peak District, Dartmoor and Snowdonia, followed in later years by the Brecon Beacons, Cairngorms, Exmoor, Loch Lomond and The Trossachs, New Forest, Norfolk and Suffolk Broads, Northumberland, North York Moors, Pembrokeshire Coast, South Downs, and Yorkshire Dales.

Britain's national parks combined cover over 10% of its area, but the term 'national park' can cause confusion. First, these areas are not state owned: nearly all land in Britain is privately owned, belonging mostly to aristocratic families, private trusts and conservation organisations. Second, they are not areas of wilderness as in many other countries. In Britain's national parks you'll see cropfields in lower areas and grazing sheep on the uplands, as well as roads, railways and villages. Some national parks even contain towns, quarries and factories. It's a reminder of the balance that needs to be struck in this crowded country between protecting the natural environment and catering for the people who live in it.

But don't be put off. Despite these apparent anomalies, Britain's national parks still contain mountains, hills, downs, moors, woods, river valleys and other areas of quiet countryside, all ideal for long walks, easy rambles, cycle rides, sightseeing or just lounging around. To help you get the best from the parks, they all have information centres, and all provide various recreational facilities (trails, car parks, campsites etc) for visitors.

Finally, it's worth noting that there are many beautiful parts of Britain that are *not* national parks (such as central Wales, the North Pennines in England, and many parts of Scotland). These can be just as good for outdoor activities or simply exploring by car or foot, and are often less crowded than the popular national parks.

Wildlife

For a small country, Britain has a very diverse range of plants and animals. Many native species are hidden away, but there are some undoubted gems, from lowland woods carpeted in shimmering bluebells to stately herds of deer on the high moors. Taking the time to have a closer look will enhance your trip enormously, especially if you have the time and inclination to enjoy some walking or cycling through the British landscape.

Farmland

In farmland areas, rabbits are everywhere, but if you're hiking through the countryside be on the lookout for brown hares, an increasingly rare species. They're related to rabbits, but much larger. Males who battle for territory by boxing on their hind legs in early spring are, of course, as 'mad as a March hare'.

BRITAIN'S NATIONAL PARKS

NATIONAL PARK	FEATURES	ACTIVITIES	BEST TIME TO VISIT
Brecon Beacons	great green ridgelines, waterfalls; Welsh mountain ponies, otters, red kites, buzzards, peregrine falcons, kingfishers	horse riding, cycling, caving, canoeing, hang-gliding	Mar & Apr (spring lambs on the hills)
Cairngorms	snowy mountains, pine forests; ospreys, pine martens, wildcats, grouse, capercaillies	skiing, climbing, birdwatching, walking	Feb (for the snow)
Dartmoor	rolling hills, rocky outcrops, serene valleys; wild ponies, deer, peregrine falcons	walking, mountain biking, horse riding	May & Jun (wildflowers in bloom)
Exmoor	sweeping moors, craggy sea cliffs; red deer, wild ponies, horned sheep	horse riding, walking	Sep (heather in bloom)
Lake District	majestic fells, rugged mountains, shimmering lakes; red squirrels, osprey, golden eagles	water sports, walking, mountaineering, climbing	Sep & Oct (summer crowds depart, autumn colours abound)
Loch Lomond & the Trossachs	sparkling lochs, brooding mountains; deer, squirrels, badgers, foxes, otters, buzzards	climbing, walking, cycling, canoeing	May (bluebell woods; before the summer rush)
New Forest	woods, heathland; wild ponies, otters, Dartford warblers, southern damselflies	walking, cycling, horse riding	Apr-Sep (lush vegetation)
Norfolk & Suffolk Broads	shallow lakes, rivers, marshlands, water lilies; otters, wildfowl	walking, cycling, boating	Apr & May (birds most active)
North York Moors	heather-clad hills, deep-green valleys; merlins, curlews, golden plovers	walking, mountain biking	Aug & Sep (heather flowering)
Northumberland	wild rolling moors, heather, gorse; red squirrels, black grouse; Hadrian's Wall	walking, cycling, climbing	Apr & May (lambs), Sep (heather flowering)
Peak District	high moors, tranquil dales, limestone caves; badgers, kestrels, grouse	walking, cycling, mountain biking, hang-gliding, climbing	Apr & May (even more lambs)
Pembrokeshire Coast	wave-ravaged shorelines, cliffs, beaches; puffins, fulmars, shearwaters, grey seals, dolphins, porpoises	walking, kayaking, coasteering, mountain biking, horse riding	Apr & May (lambs again)
Snowdonia	major mountain ranges, lakes, estuaries, Snowdon lilies; wild goats, polecats, curlews, choughs, red kites, buzzards	walking, kayaking, climbing, mountain biking, horse riding	May-Sep (better weather)
South Downs	rolling chalky hills, tranquil farmland, sheer white sea-cliffs, bastard toadflax; Adonis Blue butterflies, buzzards, red kites, peregrine falcons	walking, mountain biking, cycling, horse riding	any time of year (thanks to mild climate)
Yorkshire Dales	rugged hills, lush valleys, limestone pavements; red squirrels, hares, curlews, lapwings, buzzards	walking, cycling, mountain-biking, climbing	Apr & May (you guessed it, lambs)

WILDLIFE IN YOUR POCKET

Is it a rabbit or a hare? A gull or a tern? Buttercup or cowslip? If you need to know a bit more about Britain's plant and animal kingdoms the following field guides are ideal for entry-level naturalists:

➡ *Complete Guide to British Wildlife* by Paul Sterry is portable and highly recommended, covering mammals, birds, fish, plants, snakes, insects and even fungi, with brief descriptions and excellent photos.

➡ If feathered friends are enough, the *Complete Guide to British Birds* by Paul Sterry combines clear photos and descriptions, plus when and where each species may be seen.

➡ *Wildlife of the North Atlantic* by world-famous film-maker Tony Soper beautifully covers the animals seen from beach, boat and clifftop in the British Isles and beyond.

➡ Collins Gem series includes handy little books on wildlife topics such as *Birds*, *Trees*, *Fish* and *Wild Flowers*.

Although hare numbers are on the decline, otters are making a comeback. In southern Britain they inhabit the banks of rivers and lakes, and in Scotland they frequently live on the coast where they are easier to spot. Although their numbers are growing, they are mainly nocturnal, but keep your eyes peeled in the daytime and you might be lucky.

You're much more likely to see a red fox. This classic British mammal was once seen only in the countryside, but these wily beasts adapt well to any situation, so these days you're just as likely to see them scavenging in towns and even in city suburbs.

Elsewhere, another British classic, the badger, is under threat from farmers who believe they transmit bovine tuberculosis to cattle, although conservationists say the case is far from proven.

Common birds of farmland and similar landscapes (and urban gardens) include: the robin, with its instantly recognisable red breast and cheerful whistle; the wren, whose loud trilling song belies its tiny size; and the yellowhammer, with a song that sounds like (if you use your imagination) 'a-little-bit-of-bread-and-no-cheese'. In open fields, the warbling cry of a skylark is another classic, but now threatened, sound of the British outdoors. You're more likely to see a pheasant, a large bird originally introduced from Russia to the nobility's shooting estates, but now considered naturalised.

Between the fields, hedges provide cover for flocks of finches, but these seed-eaters must watch out for sparrowhawks – birds of prey that come from nowhere at tremendous speed. Other predators include barn owls, a wonderful sight as they fly silently along hedgerows listening for the faint rustle of a vole or shrew. In rural Wales or Scotland you will see plenty of buzzards, Britain's most common large raptor.

Woodland

In woodland areas, mammals include the small white-spotted fallow deer and the even smaller roe deer. Woodlands are full of birds too, but you'll hear them more than see them. Listen out for willow warblers (which, as the name suggests, have a warbling song with a descending cadence) and chiffchaffs (they make a repetitive 'chiff chaff' noise).

If you hear rustling among the fallen leaves it might be a hedgehog – a cute-looking, spiny-backed insect eater – but it's an increasingly rare sound these days; conservationists say they'll be extinct in Britain by 2025, due to insecticides in farming, increased building in rural areas and hedgehogs' notoriously poor ability to cross roads safely.

In no such danger are grey squirrels, originally introduced from North America. They have proved very adaptable, to the extent that native red

Herds of 'wild' ponies roam the New Forest, Exmoor and Dartmoor; these animals certainly roam free, but in reality they are privately owned and managed.

squirrels are severely endangered because the greys eat all the food. Pockets of red squirrels survive in the English Lake District and in many parts of Scotland, especially north of the central Lowlands.

Much larger than squirrels are pine martens, which are seen in some forested regions, especially in Scotland. With beautiful brown coats, they were once hunted for their fur, but are now fully protected.

Britain's most wooded county is Surrey, despite its proximity to London. The soil is too poor for agriculture, so Surrey's trees were spared. But almost half of all Britain's forested areas are in Scotland.

Mountain & Moorland

On mountains and high moors – including Exmoor, Dartmoor, the Lake District, Northumberland and much of Scotland – the most visible mammal is the red deer. Males of the species grow their famous large antlers between April and July, and shed them again in February.

Also on the high ground, well known and easily recognised birds include the red grouse, which often hides in the heather until almost stepped on then flies away with a loud warning call. On the high peaks of Scotland you may see the grouse's northern cousin, the ptarmigan, dappled brown in summer but white in winter.

Look out, too, for the curlew, with its stately long legs and elegant curved bill. With luck you may see beautifully camouflaged golden plovers, while the spectacular aerial displays of lapwings are impossible to miss.

Other mountain birds include red kites (there have been various successful projects around the country to reintroduce these spectacular fork-tailed raptors). Also in the Scottish mountains, keep an eye peeled for golden eagles, Britain's second-largest birds of prey, as they glide and soar along ridges.

Rivers & Coasts

If you're near inland water, you have a chance of spotting an osprey; the best places in Britain to see this magnificent bird include Rutland Water in the English Midlands and the Cairngorms in Scotland. You could also look along the riverbanks for signs of water voles, endearing rodents that were once very common but have been all but wiped out by wild mink (fur farm escapees first introduced from America).

On the coasts of Britain, particularly in Cornwall, Pembrokeshire and northwest Scotland, the dramatic cliffs are a marvellous sight in early summer (around May), when they are home to hundreds of thousands of breeding seabirds. Guillemots, razorbills and kittiwakes, among others, fight for space on impossibly crowded rock ledges. The cliffs become white with droppings and the air is filled with their shrill calls. Even if you're not into bird spotting, this is one of Britain's finest wildlife spectacles.

Another bird to look out for in coastal areas is the comical puffin (especially common in Shetland), with its distinctive rainbow beak and 'nests' burrowed in sandy soil. In total contrast, gannets are one of the largest seabirds and make dramatic dives for fish, often from a great height. The biggest tick in coastal birdwatching, though, is the white-tailed eagle, Britain's largest bird of prey, which can be seen in the west of Scotland, notably on Mull and Skye.

Estuaries and mudflats are feeding grounds for numerous migrant wading birds; easily spotted are black-and-white oystercatchers with their long red bills, while flocks of small ringed plovers skitter along the sand.

And finally, the sea mammals. There are two species of seal that frequent British waters; the larger grey seal is more often seen than the (misnamed) common (or harbour) seal. Boat trips to see their offshore colonies are available at various points around the coast, and are especially popular when the seal pups are born.

Dolphins, porpoises and minke whales can all be seen off the west coast of Britain, particularly off Scotland, and especially from May to September when viewing conditions are better. Whale-watching trips

Would-be twitchers can easily spot majestic red kites in the mountains and moors of the Brecon Beacons, particularly at feeding stations such as Gigrin Farm in Rhyader, Wales.

Britain is home to herds of wild goats who've gambolled on the moorland in Devon for almost 1000 years. The Great Orme peninsula in North Wales and many parts of Scotland also feature wild goats, but these are new kids on the block, having been introduced barely a century ago.

(also good for seeing other marine wildlife such as basking sharks) are available from harbour towns, especially in Scotland.

Plants

In any part of Britain, the best places to see wildflowers are areas that have escaped large-scale farming. In the chalky downs of southern England and in limestone areas such as the Peak District and Yorkshire Dales, for example, many fields erupt with great profusions of cowslips and primroses in April and May.

Some flowers prefer woodland and the best time to visit is also April and May. This is because the leaf canopy of the woods is not yet fully developed, allowing sunlight to break through to encourage plants such as bluebells (a beautiful and internationally rare species). Another classic British plant is gorse – you can't miss the swaths of this spiky bush in heath areas, most notably in the New Forest in southern England, and all over Scotland.

In contrast, the blooming season for heather is quite short. On the Scottish mountains, the Pennine moors of northern England, and Dartmoor in the south, the landscape is covered in purple in August and September.

Britain's natural deciduous trees include oak, ash, beech, birch, hazel and rowan, with seeds and leaves supporting a vast range of insects and birds. The New Forest in southern England and the Forest of Dean on the Wales–England border are good examples of this type of habitat. In some parts of Scotland, most notably Glen Affric, remnants of indigenous Caledonian pine forest can still be seen. As you travel through Britain you're also likely to see non-native conifers, often in vast plantations empty of wildlife, although an increasing number of deciduous trees are also planted these days.

Environmental Issues

With Britain's long history, it's not surprising that the country's appearance is almost totally the result of human interaction with the environment. Since the earliest times, people have been chopping down trees and creating fields for crops or animals, but the most dramatic changes in rural areas came in the late 1940s, continuing into the '50s and '60s, when a postwar drive to be self-reliant in food meant new and intensive large-scale farming methods. The result was lowland Britain's ancient patchwork of small meadows becoming a landscape of vast fields, as walls were demolished, woodlands felled, ponds filled, wetlands drained and, most notably, hedgerows ripped out.

In most cases the hedgerows were lines of dense bushes, shrubs and trees forming a network that stretched across the countryside, protecting fields from erosion, supporting a varied range of flowers, and providing shelter for numerous insects, birds and small mammals. But in the rush to improve farm yields, thousands of miles of hedgerows were destroyed in the postwar decades, and between the mid-1980s and the early 2000s another 25% disappeared.

In addition to hedgerow clearance, other farming techniques remain hot environmental issues. Studies have shown that the use of pesticides and intensive irrigation results in rivers running dry or being poisoned by run-off. In 2014 scientists announced that neonicotinoid pesticides – introduced in the 1990s to replace harmful chemicals such as DDT – may actually be even more dangerous, and are implicated in the collapse of the bee population.

Meanwhile, monocropping means vast fields with one type of grass, dubbed 'green deserts' by conservationists as they support no insects, are causing wild bird populations to plummet. This is not a case of wizened old peasants recalling the idyllic days of their forebears; you only have to be over about 40 in Britain to remember a countryside where birds such as skylarks or lapwings were visibly much more numerous.

Britain's new 'hedgerows' are the long strips of grass and bushes alongside motorways and major roads. Rarely trod by humans, they support rare flowers and thousands of insect species, plus mice, shrews and other small mammals – hence kestrels are often seen hovering nearby.

Sporting Britain

If you want a shortcut into the heart of British culture, then watch the British at play. They're passionate about their sport – as participants and spectators. Every weekend thousands of people turn out to cheer their favourite team, and sporting highlights such as Wimbledon keep the entire nation enthralled.

Playing the Game

The British invented many of the world's favourite team sports – or at least codified their modern rules – including cricket, tennis, rugby, golf and football (soccer), although, it has to be said, the national teams in the high-profile sports aren't always that successful internationally. This applies mainly to the male teams – the women's national teams have a better record of success, with the England women's football team taking third place in the FIFA Women's World Cup in 2015, and the England women's cricket team winning the World Cup in 2009.

But whether the British 'home teams' are winning or losing – be they the individual teams of England, Wales and Scotland, or national teams representing Great Britain or the whole of the UK – nothing dulls the enthusiasm of the fans.

The word 'soccer', often used outside Britain, derives from the sport's official name Association Football (as opposed to rugby football), or possibly from 'sock' – a leather foot-cover worn in medieval times, ideal for kicking a pig's bladder around the park on a Saturday afternoon.

Football (Soccer)

Despite what the football fans may say in Madrid or Sao Paulo, the English Premier League has some of the finest teams in the world, dominated in recent years by the four top teams – Arsenal, Liverpool, Chelsea and Manchester United – joined in 2012 by a fifth big player in the shape of Manchester City. Their big pockets weren't enough in 2016, however, when unfancied Leicester City stunned the pundits and delighted neutrals by winning the league title.

Down from the Premier League, 72 other teams play in the English divisions called the Championship, League One and League Two.

THE FA CUP

The Football Association (FA) held its first interclub knockout tournament in 1871. Fifteen clubs took part, playing for a nice piece of silverware called the FA Cup – then worth about £20.

Nowadays, around 600 clubs compete for this legendary and priceless trophy. It differs from many other competitions in that every team – from the lowest-ranking part-timers to the stars of the Premier League – is in with a chance. The preliminary rounds begin in August, and the world-famous Cup Final is held in May at the iconic Wembley Stadium in London.

Manchester United are the team with the most cup victories, but public attention, and affection, is invariably focused on the 'giant-killers' – minor clubs that claw their way up through the rounds, unexpectedly beating higher-ranked competitors. The best-known giant-killing event occurred in 1992, when Wrexham, then ranked 24th in Division 3, famously beat league champions Arsenal.

For the dates and details of major football and cricket matches, horse racing and other sporting fixtures across Britain, a great place to start is the sports pages of www.britevents.com.

The Scottish football scene has a similar pattern: best teams in the Scottish Premiership, the rest in the Scottish Football League. The top flight has long been dominated by Glasgow teams Celtic and Rangers, although the latter were forced into liquidation in 2012 over a tax dispute and kicked out of the premier league. Celtic had an easy run while their traditional rivals clawed their way back to the top, eventually gaining readmittance to the premiership in 2016.

In Wales football is less popular (rugby is the national sport) and the main Welsh football teams, such as Wrexham, Cardiff and Swansea, play in the lower English leagues.

The football season is the same for all divisions (August to May), so seeing a match can easily be tied into most visitors' itineraries. However, tickets for Premier League matches are like gold dust – your chances of bagging one are pretty much zilch unless you're a club member or know someone who is – you're better off buying tickets for a lower-division game, which are cheaper. You can often buy tickets on the spot at stadiums, or go to club websites or online agencies such as www.ticketmaster.co.uk and www.myticketmarket.com.

Golf

Golf is a very popular sport in Britain, with millions taking to the fairways every week. The main tournament for spectators is the Open Championship, often referred to simply as The Open (or the 'British Open' outside the UK). It's the oldest of professional golf's major championships (dating back to 1860) and the only one held outside the USA, and is watched by many thousands of golf fans. It is usually played over the third weekend in July and the location changes each year, using nine courses around the country – check www.theopen.com for details of past, present and future championships.

Perhaps Great Britain's most famous golfing destination is the Old Course at St Andrews, often dubbed the 'home of golf' as it was one of the first places the sport was played, all the way back in the early 1400s. Playing here is almost a spiritual experience for golf enthusiasts, but you'll need to plan well ahead to get a game. If you fancy a round as part of your visit to Britain, there are around 2000 private and public golf courses to choose from, with 500 in Scotland alone. (There are more golf courses per capita in Scotland than in any other country in the world.) Some private clubs admit members or golfers with a handicap certificate, but most welcome visitors. Public golf courses are open to anyone. A round costs around £10 to £30 on public courses, and up to £200 on famous championship courses.

Rugby

A wit once said that football was a gentlemen's game played by hooligans, while rugby was a hooligans' game played by gentlemen. That may be true, but rugby is very popular, especially since England became world champions in 2003 (and nearly did it again in 2007). It's worth catching a game for the display of skill (OK, and brawn), and the fun atmosphere in the grounds. Tickets for games cost around £15 to £50 depending on the club's status and fortunes.

There are two versions of the game in Britain: Rugby Union (www.englandrugby.com) is played more in southern England, Wales and Scotland, and is traditionally the game of the middle and upper classes, while Rugby League (www.rugby-league.com) is played predominantly in northern England, traditionally by the working classes – although these days there's a lot of crossover.

Both rugby codes trace their roots back to a football match in 1823 at Rugby School, in Warwickshire. A player called William Webb Ellis, frustrated at the limitations of mere kicking, reputedly picked up the ball and ran with it towards the opponents' goal. True to the British tradition of fair play, rather than Ellis being dismissed from the game, a whole new sport was developed around his tactic, and the Rugby Football Union was formally inaugurated in 1871. Today, the Rugby World Cup is named the Webb Ellis trophy after this enterprising young tearaway.

The highlight of rugby union's international calendar is the annual Six Nations Championship (www.rbs6nations.com), between teams from England, Wales, Scotland, Ireland, France and Italy. A simple points system sees teams compete to win the Grand Slam or Triple Crown, or at least avoid the Wooden Spoon award for coming last.

The Rugby League World Cup is dominated by Australia and New Zealand (the 2017 tournament will be held in Australia); the next Rugby Union World Cup will be hosted by Japan in 2019. For details, see www.rugbyworldcup.com.

Cricket

Although it is played in Wales and Scotland too, cricket is a quintessentially English sport. Dating from the 18th century – although its roots are much older – the sport spread throughout the Commonwealth during Britain's colonial era. Australia, the Caribbean and the Indian subcontinent took to the game with gusto, and today the former colonies delight in giving the old country a good spanking on the cricket pitch.

While many English people follow cricket like a religion, to the uninitiated it's an impenetrable spectacle. Spread over one-day games or five-day test matches, progress seems so *slow* (surely, say the unbelievers, this is the game for which TV highlights were invented) and dominated by arcane terminology such as innings, over, googlie, out-swinger, leg-bye and silly-mid-off. Nonetheless, at least one cricket match should feature in your travels. If you're patient and learn the intricacies, you could find cricket as absorbing and enriching as all the fans who remain glued to their radio or computer all summer, 'just to see how England are getting on'.

One-day games and international tests are played at grounds including Lord's in London, Edgbaston in Birmingham and Headingley in

Causing ructions in the cricket world, the fast-paced Twenty20 format emphasises big-batting scores, rather than slow and careful run-building. Traditionalists say it's changing the character of the game, but there's no doubting its popularity – many Twenty20 matches are quickly sold out.

THE ASHES

The historic test cricket series between England and Australia known as the Ashes has been played every other year since 1882, bar a few interruptions during wartime (women's cricket has its own Ashes series, played intermittently since the 1930s). It is played alternately in England and Australia with each of the five matches in the series held at a different cricket ground, always in the summer in the host location.

The contest's name dates back to the landmark test match of 1882, won (for the very first time) by the Australians. Defeat of the mother country by the colonial upstarts was a source of profound national shock: a mock obituary in the *Sporting Times* lamented the death of English cricket and referred to the game's ashes being taken to Australia.

Later the name was given to a terracotta urn presented the following year to the English captain Ivo Bligh, purportedly containing the cremated ashes of a stump or bail used in this landmark match. Since 1953 this hallowed relic has resided at the Marylebone Cricket Club (MCC) Museum at Lord's Cricket Ground. Despite the vast importance given to winning the series, the urn itself is a diminutive 15cm high.

The recent history of the Ashes has not been without drama. In the 2010–11 series England thrashed Australia, winning on Australian turf for the first time in 24 years. Then in 2013 Australia thrashed England 5-0, the third time in Ashes history that the Aussies have had a clean sweep. And in 2015 England won again 3-2. The next series takes place in Australia in 2017–18.

SPORTING COVERAGE

Mainstream sports are also covered by all the major British TV channels, as well as specialist channels such as BT Sport (sport.bt.com) and Sky Sports (www.skysports.com), but pride of place goes to the BBC's weekly *Match of the Day*, which features football highlights and has been running since 1964 (screened on Saturdays during the soccer season).

Leeds. Tickets cost from £30 to well over £200. The County Championship pits the best teams from around the country against each other; tickets cost £5 to £25, and only the most crucial games tend to sell out. Details are on the website of the English Cricket Board (www.ecb.co.uk).

The easiest way to watch cricket – and often the most enjoyable – is stumbling across a local game on a village green as you travel around the country. There's no charge for spectators, and no one will mind if you nip into the pub during a quiet period.

Horse Racing

The tradition of horse racing in Britain stretches back centuries, and there's a 'race meeting' somewhere pretty much every day. For all but the major events you should be able to get a ticket on the day, or buy in advance from the British Horse Racing Authority's website (www.greatbritishracing.com), which also has lots of information about social events such as music festivals that coincide with the races.

The top event in the calendar is Royal Ascot at Ascot Racecourse in mid-June, where the rich and famous come to see and be seen, and the fashion is almost as important as the nags. Even the Queen turns up to put a fiver each way on Lucky Boy in the 3.15.

Other highlights include the Grand National steeplechase at Aintree in early April and the Derby at Epsom on the first Saturday in June. The latter is especially popular with the masses so, unlike at Ascot, you won't see many morning suits or outrageous hats.

Tennis

Tennis is widely played in Britain, but the best known tournament for spectators is the All England Championships – known to everyone as Wimbledon – when tennis fever sweeps through Britain in the last week of June and first week of July. Although there's something more English than British about the combination of grass courts, polite applause and umpires in straw hats, it was a Scotsman, Andy Murray, who in 2013 became the first British men's singles champion since 1936, winning again in 2016.

Over 27 tonnes of strawberries and 7000L of cream are consumed during the two weeks of the annual Wimbledon Tennis Championships.

Demand for seats at Wimbledon always outstrips supply, but to give everyone an equal chance tickets are sold through a public ballot. You can also take your chance on the spot; about 6000 tickets are sold each day (excluding the final four days), but you'll need to be an early riser: dedicated fans start queuing before dawn. For more information, see www.wimbledon.com.

Survival Guide

Directory A–Z

Accommodation

Accommodation in Britain is as varied as the sights you visit. From hip hotels to basic barns, the wide choice is all part of the attraction.

B&Bs

The B&B (bed and breakfast) is a great British institution. At smaller places it's pretty much a room in somebody's house; larger places may be called a 'guesthouse' (halfway between a B&B and a full hotel). Prices start from around £30 per person for a simple bedroom and shared bathroom; for around £35 to £45 per person you get a private bathroom – either down the hall or en suite.

In country areas, most B&Bs cater for walkers and cyclists, but some don't, so let them know if you'll be turning up with dirty boots or wheels.

When booking, check where your B&B actually is. In country areas, postal addresses include the nearest town, which may be 20 miles away – important if you're walking! Some B&B owners will pick you up by car for a small charge.

➡ **Prices** Usually quoted per person, based on two people sharing a room. Single rooms for solo travellers are harder to find, and attract a 20% to 50% premium. Some B&Bs simply won't take single people (unless you pay the full double-room price), especially in summer.

➡ **Booking** Advance reservations are preferred at B&Bs and are essential during popular periods. You can book many B&Bs via online agencies, but rates may be cheaper if you book direct. If you haven't booked in advance, most towns have a main drag of B&Bs; those with spare rooms hang up a 'Vacancies' sign. Many B&Bs require a minimum two-night stay at weekends. Some places reduce rates for longer stays (two or three nights) mid-week. If a B&B is full, owners may recommend another place nearby (possibly a private house taking occasional guests, not in tourist listings).

➡ **Food** Most B&Bs serve enormous breakfasts; some offer packed lunches (around £6) and evening meals (around £15 to £20).

➡ **Bed & Breakfast Nationwide** (www.bedandbreakfastnationwide.com)

SLEEPING PRICE RANGES

Reviews of places to stay use the following price ranges, all based on double room with private bathroom in high season. Hotels in London are more expensive than the rest of the country, so have different price ranges.

CATEGORY	LONDON	ELSEWHERE
£	less than £100	less than £65
££	£100–200	£65–130
£££	more than £200	more than £130

Bunkhouses

A bunkhouse in Britain is a simple place to stay, usually in country areas, with a communal sleeping area and bathroom, plus stoves for self-catering. You provide a sleeping bag and possibly cooking gear. Most charge around £12 to £15 per person per night.

Some basic places are called 'camping barns' – usually converted farm buildings. Take everything you'd need to camp except the tent. Charges are from around £6 to £10 per person.

Camping

Campsites range from farmers' fields with a tap and basic toilet, costing from £5 per person per night, to smarter affairs with hot showers and many other facilities, charging up to £15. You usually need all your own kit.

A few campsites also offer self-catering accommodation in chalets, caravans, tepees, yurts and stylish wooden camping 'pods', often dubbed 'glamping'.

If you're touring Britain with a tent or campervan (motorhome), consider joining the **Camping & Caravanning Club** (www.campingandcaravanningclub.co.uk), which provides up to 30% discount on its sites for an annual membership fee of £37. The club owns almost 100 campsites and lists thousands more in the invaluable *Big Sites Book* (free to members).

Hostels

There are two types of hostel in Britain: those run by the **Youth Hostels Association** (www.yha.org.uk) and **Scottish Youth Hostels Association** (www.syha.org.uk); and independent hostels, most listed in the **Independent Hostel Guide** (www.independenthostelguide.co.uk).

Hostels can be found in rural areas, towns and cities, and are aimed at all types of traveller, young and old. Some hostels are converted cottages, country houses and even castles – often in wonderful locations. Sleeping is usually in dormitories; most hostels also have twin- or four-bed rooms.

YHA & SYHA HOSTELS

The simplest YHA and SYHA hostels cost around £13 to £17 per person per night. Larger hostels with more facilities are £18 to £30. London's YHA hostels cost from £32. Advance bookings and payments with credit card are usually possible.

You don't have to be a member of the YHA or SYHA (or another Hostelling International organisation) to stay, but most hostels charge extra if you're not a member (£3 at YHA hostels; £1 at SYHA hostels), so it's usually worth joining. Annual YHA membership costs £20; annual SYHA membership costs £10; younger people and families get discounts.

Most hostel prices vary according to demand and season. Book early for a Tuesday night in May and you'll get the best rate. Book late for a weekend in August and you'll pay top price – if there's space at all. We have generally quoted the cheaper rates (in line with those listed on the YHA's website); you may find yourself paying more.

YHA hostels tend to have complicated opening times and days, especially in remote locations or out of tourist season, so check before turning up.

INDEPENDENT HOSTELS

In rural areas some independent hostels are little more than simple bunkhouses (charging around £13), or almost up to B&B standard (£20 or more). In cities, independent backpacker hostels are usually aimed at young budget travellers. Most are open 24 hours, with a lively atmosphere, a range of rooms (doubles or dorms), bar, cafe, wi-fi and laundry. Prices go from around £20 for a dorm bed to £40 for a bed in a private room.

Hotels

There's a massive choice of hotels in Britain, from small town houses to grand country mansions, from no-frills locations to boutique hideaways. At the bargain end, single/double rooms cost from £45/60. Move up the scale and you'll pay £100/150 or beyond.

PRACTICALITIES

Newspapers Tabloids include the *Sun* and *Mirror*, and *Daily Record* (in Scotland); quality 'broadsheets' include (from right to left, politically) the *Telegraph*, *Times*, *Independent* and *Guardian*.

TV All TV in the UK is digital. Leading broadcasters include BBC, ITV and Channel 4. Satellite and cable TV providers include Sky and Virgin Media.

Radio Main BBC stations and wavelengths are Radio 1 (98–99.6MHz FM), Radio 2 (88–92MHz FM), Radio 3 (90–92.2 MHz FM), Radio 4 (92–94.4MHz FM) and Radio 5 Live (909 or 693 AM). National commercial stations include Virgin Radio (1215Hz MW) and non-highbrow classical specialist Classic FM (100–102MHz FM). All are available on digital.

DVD PAL format (incompatible with NTSC and Secam).

Weights & Measures Britain uses a mix of metric and imperial measures (eg petrol is sold by the litre but beer by the pint; mountain heights are in metres but road distances are in miles).

BOOK YOUR STAY ONLINE

For more accommodation reviews by Lonely Planet authors, check out http://lonelyplanet.com/hotels/. You'll find independent reviews, as well as recommendations on the best places to stay. Best of all, you can book online.

SOMETHING DIFFERENT?

For some more unusual accommodation options, the **Landmark Trust** (www.landmarktrust.org.uk) rents historic buildings; your options include ancient cottages, medieval castles, Napoleonic forts and 18th-century follies. Or try **Distinctly Different** (www.distinctlydifferent.co.uk), specialising in unusual and bizarre places to stay.

If all you want is a place to put your head down, budget chain hotels can be a good option. Most are lacking in ambience, but who cares? You'll only be there for 12 hours, and eight of them you'll be asleep. Prices vary on demand: at quiet times twin-bed rooms start from £30; at the height of the tourist season you'll pay £60 or more. Some options:

Ibis Hotels (www.ibis.com)

Premier Inn (www.premierinn.com)

Travelodge (www.travelodge.co.uk)

RATES

There's no such thing as a 'standard' hotel rate in Britain. Many hotels, especially larger places or chains, vary prices according to demand – or have different rates for online, phone or walk-in bookings – just like airlines and train operators. So if you book early for a night when the hotel is likely to be quiet, rates are cheap. If you book late, or aim for a public holiday weekend, you'll pay a lot. But wait until the very last minute, and you can *sometimes* get a bargain as rates drop again. The end result: you can pay anything from £25 to £200 for the very same hotel room. With that in mind, the hotel rates we quote are often guide prices only. (In contrast, B&B prices tend to be much more consistent.)

Houseboats

A popular English holiday option is renting a houseboat on one of England's picturesque waterways, combining accommodation and transport for a few days or a week.

ABC Boat Hire (www.abcboathire.com)

Hoseasons (www.hoseasons.co.uk)

Wandering Duck (www.wanderingduck.co.uk) 'Floating hostels' for budget travellers.

Pubs & Inns

As well as selling drinks, many pubs and inns offer lodging, particularly in country areas. For bed and breakfast, you'll pay around £30 per person for a basic room, around £45 for something better. An advantage for solo tourists: pubs often have single rooms.

Rental Accommodation

If you want to stay in one place, renting for a week can be ideal. Choose from neat apartments in cities or quaint old houses (always called 'cottages', whatever the size) in country areas. Cottages for four people cost between £275 and £700 in high season. Rates fall at quieter

Climate

London

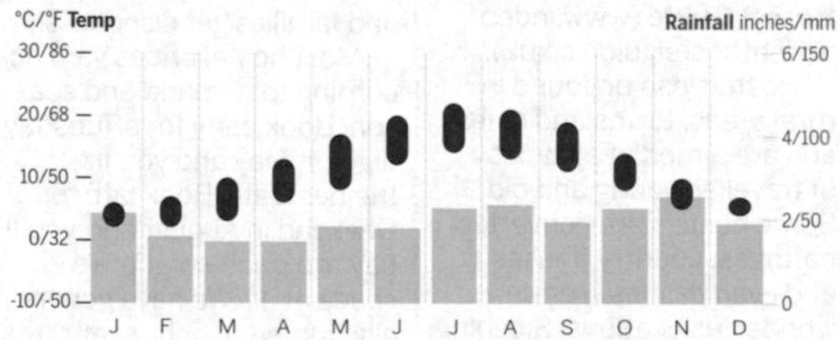

Newquay

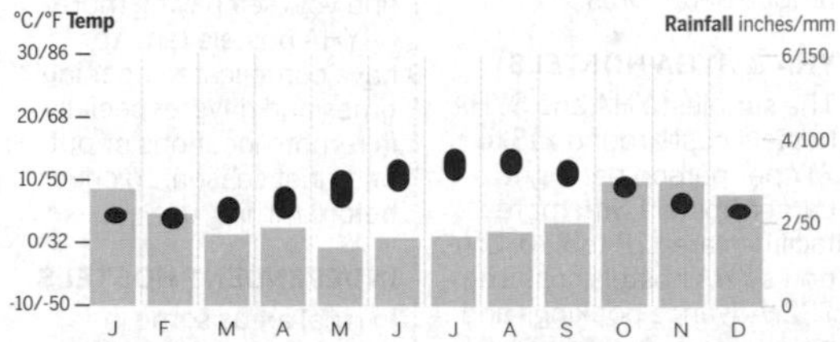

York

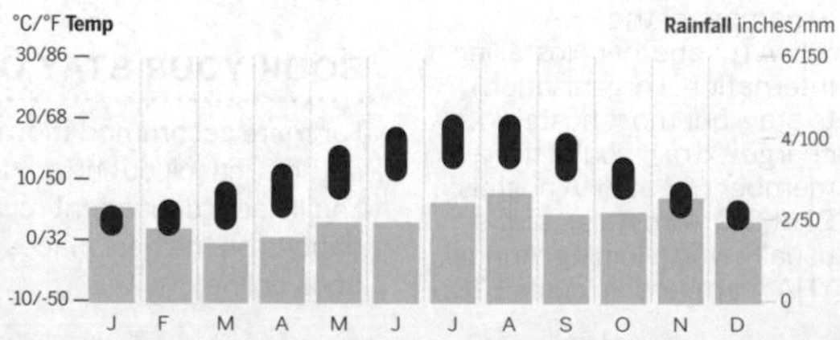

times and you may be able to rent for a long weekend. Some handy websites:

Cottages & Castles (www.cottages-and-castles.co.uk)

Cottages4you (www.cottages4you.co.uk)

Hoseasons (www.hoseasons.co.uk)

National Trust (www.nationaltrust.org.uk/holidays)

Stilwell's (www.stilwell.co.uk)

University Accommodation

During vacations, many universities offer accommodation to visitors. You usually get a functional single bedroom, and self-catering flats are also available. Prices range from £25 to £60 per person. A handy portal is www.universityrooms.co.uk.

Customs Regulations

Travellers arriving in the UK from EU countries don't have to pay tax or duty on goods for personal use, and can bring in as much EU duty-paid alcohol and tobacco as they like. However, if you bring in more than the following, you'll probably be asked some questions:

- 800 cigarettes
- 1kg of tobacco
- 10L of spirits
- 90L of wine
- 110L of beer.

Travellers from outside the EU can bring in, duty-free:

- 200 cigarettes *or* 100 cigarillos *or* 50 cigars *or* 250g of tobacco
- 16L of beer
- 4L of non-sparkling wine
- 1L of spirits *or* 2L of fortified wine or sparkling wine
- £390 worth of all other goods, including perfume, gifts and souvenirs.

Anything over this limit must be declared to customs officers on arrival. For further details, and for information on reclaiming VAT on items purchased in the UK by non-EU residents, go to www.gov.uk and search for 'Bringing goods into the UK'.

Discount Cards

There's no specific discount card for visitors to Britain, although travel cards are discounted for younger and older people.

Electricity

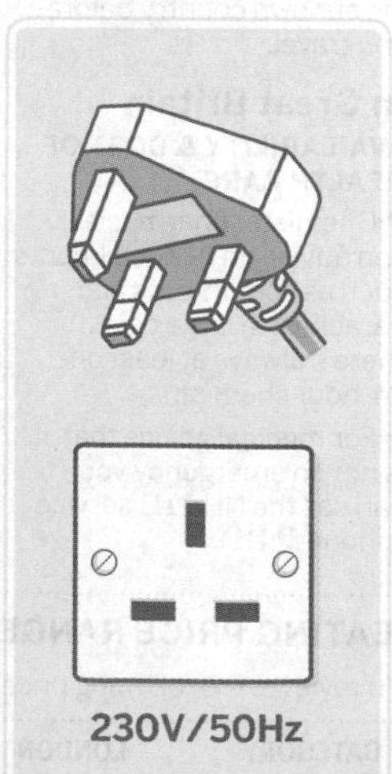

Cardiff

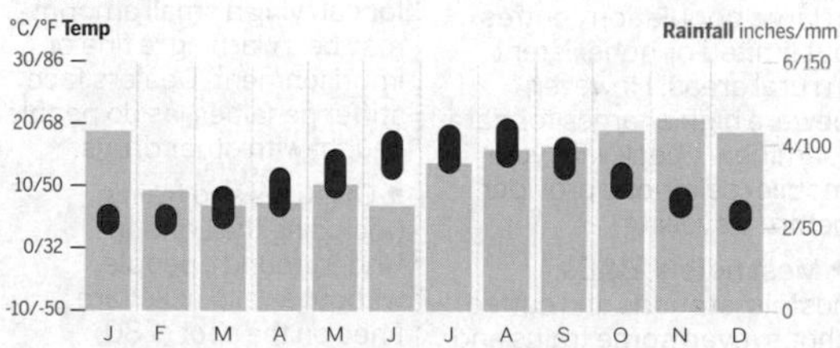

Inverness

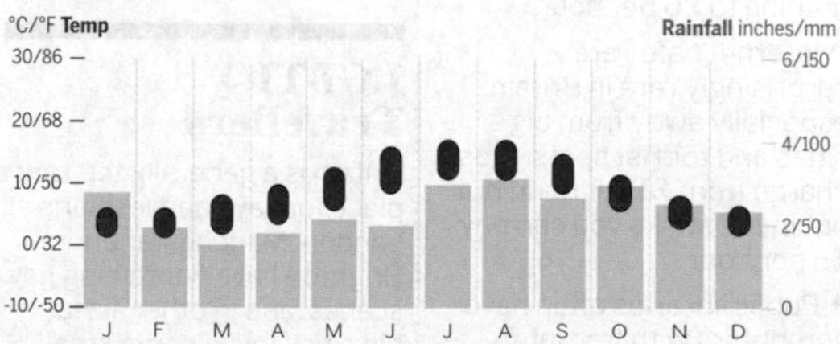

Edinburgh

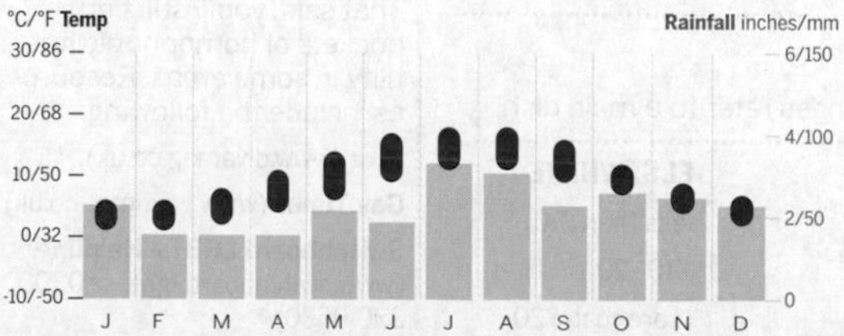

Health

Before You Go

HEALTH INSURANCE

➡ If you're an EU citizen, a European Health Insurance Card (EHIC) – available from health centres or, in the UK, post offices – covers you for most medical care. An EHIC will not cover you for non-urgent cases, or emergency repatriation. This arrangment could change once Britain exits the EU; check the latest situation with your own national health service before travelling.

➡ Citizens from non-EU countries should find out if there is a reciprocal arrangement for free medical care between their country and the UK.

➡ If you do need health insurance, make sure you get a policy that covers you for the worst possible scenarios, including emergency flights home.

VACCINATIONS

➡ No jabs (vaccinations) are required to travel to Britain. For more information, check with your medical provider in your own country before you travel.

In Great Britain

AVAILABILITY & COST OF HEALTH CARE

➡ Chemists (pharmacies) can advise on minor ailments such as sore throats and earaches. In large cities, there's always at least one 24-hour chemist.

➡ For medical advice that is not an emergency you can call the NHS 111 service (phone ☎111).

TAP WATER

The tap water is safe to drink.

Insurance

Although everyone receives free emergency treatment, regardless of nationality, travel insurance is still highly recommended. It will usually cover medical and dental consultation and treatment at private clinics, which can be quicker than NHS places – as well as the cost of any emergency flights – plus all the usual stuff like loss of baggage.

Worldwide travel insurance is available at www.lonelyplanet.com/travel-insurance. You can buy, extend and claim online anytime, even if you're already on the road.

Internet Access

➡ 3G and 4G mobile broadband coverage is good in large population centres, but limited or nonexistent in rural areas. However, beware high charges for data roaming – check with your mobile/cellphone provider before travelling.

➡ Most hotels, B&Bs, hostels, stations and coffee shops (even some trains and buses) have wi-fi access, charging anything from nothing to £6 per hour.

➡ Internet cafes are surprisingly rare in Britain, especially away from big cities and tourist spots. Most charge from £1 per hour, but out in the sticks you can pay £5 per hour.

➡ Public libraries often have computers with free internet access, but only for 30-minute slots, and demand is high. All the usual warnings apply about keystroke-capturing software and other security risks.

EATING PRICE RANGES

In reviews, the following price ranges refer to a main dish.

CATEGORY	LONDON	ELSEWHERE
£	less than £12	less than £10
££	£100–200	£10–20
£££	£12–25	more than £20

Legal Matters

➡ Police have the power to detain, for up to six hours, anyone suspected of having committed an offence punishable by imprisonment (including drugs offences). Police have the right to search anyone they suspect of possessing drugs.

➡ You must be over 18 to buy alcohol and cigarettes. You usually have to be 18 to enter a pub or bar, although rules are different for under-18s if eating. Some bars and clubs are over-21 only.

➡ Illegal drugs are widely available, especially in clubs. Cannabis possession is a criminal offence; punishment for carrying a small amount may be a warning, a fine or imprisonment. Dealers face stiffer penalties, as do people caught with other drugs.

➡ On buses and trains (including the London Underground), people without a valid ticket are fined on the spot (£80, reduced to £40 if you pay within 21 days).

LGBTIQ Travellers

Britain is a generally tolerant place for gays and lesbians. London, Manchester and Brighton have flourishing gay scenes, and in other sizeable cities (even some small towns), you'll find communities not entirely in the closet. That said, you'll still find pockets of homophobic hostility in some areas. Resources include the following:

Diva (www.divamag.co.uk)

Gay Times (www.gaytimes.co.uk)

Switchboard LGBT+ Helpline (www.switchboard.lgbt; ☎0300 330 0630)

Money

ATMs

ATMs (usually called 'cash machines' in Britain) are common in cities and even small towns. Cash withdrawals from some ATMs may be subject to a small charge, but most are free. If you're not from the UK, your home bank will likely charge you for withdrawing money overseas. Watch out for tampered ATMs; a common ruse is to attach a card reader or mini camera.

Credit & Debit Cards

Visa and MasterCard credit and debit cards are widely accepted in Britain. Other credit cards, including Amex, are not so widely accepted. Most businesses will assume your card is 'Chip and PIN' enabled (using a PIN instead of signing). If it isn't, you should be able to sign instead, but some places may not accept your card. Some smaller country B&Bs don't take cards, so you'll need to pay with cash.

Currency

The currency of Britain is the pound sterling (£). Paper money ('notes') comes in £5, £10, £20 and £50 denominations. Some shops don't accept £50 notes because fakes circulate.

Other currencies are rarely accepted, except at some gift shops in London, which may take euros, US dollars, yen and other major currencies.

Money Changers

Cities and larger towns have banks and exchange bureaux for changing your money into pounds. Check rates first; some bureaux offer poor rates or levy outrageous commissions. You can also change money at some post offices – very handy in country areas, and exchange rates are fair.

SCOTTISH BANKNOTES

Scottish banks issue their own sterling banknotes. They are interchangeable with Bank of England notes, but you'll sometimes run into problems outside Scotland – shops in the south of England may refuse to accept them. They are also harder to exchange once you get outside the UK, though British banks will always exchange them.

Taxes & Refunds

Value-added tax (VAT) is a 20% sales tax levied on most goods and services. Restaurants must always include VAT in their prices, but it is not always included in hotel-room prices, so be sure to ask when booking. It's sometimes possible for visitors to claim a refund of VAT paid on goods; see www.gov.uk/tax-on-shopping/taxfree-shopping for eligibility criteria.

Tipping

Restaurants Around 10% in restaurants and teashops with table service. Nearer 15% at smarter restaurants. Tips may be added to your bill as a 'service charge'. Paying a tip or a service charge is not obligatory.

Pubs & Bars Not expected unless table service for your meal and drinks is provided, then 10% is usual.

Taxis Around 10%, or rounded up to the nearest pound, especially in London.

Opening Hours

Opening hours may vary throughout the year, especially in rural areas where many places have shorter hours, or close completely, from October or November to March or April.

Banks 9.30am to 4pm or 5pm Monday to Friday; some are open 9.30am to 1pm Saturday.

Pubs & Bars 11am to 11pm Monday to Thursday, 11am to 1am Friday and Saturday, 12.30pm to 11pm Sunday.

Shops 9am to 5.30pm (or 6pm in cities) Monday to Saturday, and often 11am to 5pm Sunday. Big city convenience stores open 24/7.

Restaurants Lunch is noon to 3pm, dinner 6pm to 9pm/10pm (or later in cities).

Post Offices 9am to 5pm (5.30pm or 6pm in cities) Monday to Friday; 9am to 12.30pm Saturday (main branches to 5pm).

Museums & Sights

➡ Large museums and sights usually open daily.

➡ Some smaller places open Saturday and Sunday but close Monday and/or Tuesday.

➡ Smaller places open daily in high season but operate weekends only or completely close in low season.

Public Holidays

Holidays for the whole of Britain:

New Year's Day 1 January (plus 2 January in Scotland)

Easter March/April (Good Friday to Easter Monday inclusive)

May Day First Monday in May

Spring Bank Holiday Last Monday in May

Summer Bank Holiday Last Monday in August

Christmas Day 25 December

Boxing Day 26 December

If a public holiday falls on a weekend, the nearest Monday is usually taken instead. In England and Wales most businesses and banks close on official public holidays

SCHOOL HOLIDAYS

Roads get busy and hotel prices go up during school holidays. Exact dates vary from year to year and region to region, but are roughly as follows:

Easter Holiday Week before and week after Easter

Summer Holiday Third week of July to first week of September in England and Wales, end of June to mid-August in Scotland

Christmas Holiday Mid-December to first week of January

There are also three week-long 'half-term' school holidays – usually late February (or early March), late May and late October. These vary among Scotland, England and Wales.

(hence the quaint term 'bank holiday'). In Scotland, bank holidays are just for the banks, and many businesses stay open. Many Scottish towns normally have a spring and autumn holiday, but the dates vary.

On public holidays, some small museums and places of interest close, but larger attractions have their busiest times. If a place closes on Sunday, it'll probably be shut on bank holidays as well.

Virtually everything – attractions, shops, banks, offices – closes on Christmas Day, although pubs are open at lunchtime. There's usually no public transport on Christmas Day, and a very minimal service on Boxing Day.

Safe Travel

Britain is a remarkably safe country, but crime is not unknown – especially in London and other cities.

➡ Watch out for pickpockets and hustlers in crowded areas popular with tourists, such as around Westminster Bridge in London.

➡ When travelling by tube, tram or urban train services at night, choose a carriage containing other people.

➡ Many town centres can be rowdy on Friday and Saturday nights when the pubs and clubs are emptying.

➡ Unlicensed minicabs – a bloke with a car earning money on the side – operate in large cities, and are worth avoiding unless you know what you're doing.

Telephone

Mobile Phones

The UK uses the GSM 900/1800 network, which covers the rest of Europe, Australia and New Zealand, but isn't compatible with the North American GSM 1900.

Though roaming charges within the EU are due to be entirely eliminated by June 2017, other international roaming charges can be prohibitively high, and you'll probably find it cheaper to get a UK number. This is easily done by buying a SIM card (from £5 including calling credit) and sticking it in your phone. Your phone may be locked to your home network, however, so you'll have to either get it unlocked, or buy a cheap pay-as-you-go phone along with your SIM card (from £10 including calling credit).

Pay-as-you-go phones can be recharged by buying vouchers from any post office or at supermarkets and convenience stores where you see the green 'top-up' sign.

Phone Codes

Dialling into the UK Dial your country's international access code then ☎44 (the UK country code), then the area code (dropping the first ☎0) followed by the telephone number.

Dialling out of the UK The international access code is ☎00; dial this, then add the code of the country you wish to dial.

Making a reverse-charge (collect) international call Dial ☎155 for the operator. It's an expensive option, but not for the caller.

Area codes in the UK Do not have a standard format or length, eg Edinburgh ☎0131, London ☎020, Ambleside ☎015394.

Directory Assistance A host of agencies offer this service – numbers include ☎118 118, ☎118 500 and ☎118 811 – but fees are extortionate (around £6 for a 45-second call); search online for free at www.thephonebook.bt.com.

Mobile phones Codes usually begin with ☎07.

Free calls Numbers starting with ☎0800 or ☎0808 are free.

National operator ☎100

International operator ☎155

Time

Britain is on GMT/UTC. The clocks go forward one hour for 'summer time' at the end of March, and go back at the end of October. The 24-hour clock is used for transport timetables.

Time Differences

Paris, Berlin, Rome One hour ahead of Britain

New York Five hours behind

Sydney Nine hours ahead Apr-Sep, 10 hours Oct, 11 hours Nov-Mar

Los Angeles Eight hours behind

Mumbai 5½hr ahead, 4½hr Mar-Oct

Tokyo Nine hours ahead, Eight hours Mar-Oct

Toilets

➡ Public toilets in Britain are generally clean and modern, but cutbacks in public spending mean that many facilities have been closed down.

➡ Your best bet is to use the toilets in free-to-enter museums; those in railway and bus stations often charge a fee (from 20p to 50p).

➡ Most pubs and restaurants stipulate that their toilets are for customers only.

Tourist Information

Most British cities and towns, and some villages, have a tourist information centre or visitor information centre – for ease we've called all these places 'tourist offices'.

Such places have helpful staff, books and maps for sale, leaflets to give away, and advice on things to see or do. Some can also assist with booking accommodation. Some are run by national parks and often have small exhibits about the area.

Most tourist offices keep regular business hours; in quiet areas they close from October to March, while in popular areas they open daily year-round. In recent years, cost-cutting has seen many smaller tourist offices close down; some have been replaced with 'tourist information points' – racks of leaflets and maps in locations such as public libraries and town halls.

Before leaving home, check the comprehensive website of Britain's official tourist board, Visit Britain (www.visitbritain.com), covering all the angles of national tourism, with links to numerous other sites.

Travellers with Disabilities

All new buildings have wheelchair access, and even hotels in grand old country houses often have lifts, ramps and other facilities. Hotels and B&Bs in historic buildings are often harder to adapt, so you'll have less choice here.

Modern city buses and trams have low floors for easy access, but few have conductors who can lend a hand when you're getting on or off. Many taxis take wheelchairs, or just have more room in the back.

For long-distance travel, coaches may present problems but the main operator, **National Express** (www.nationalexpress.com) has wheelchair-friendly coaches on many routes. For details, see the website or ring the dedicated Disabled Passenger Travel Helpline (☎0371 781 8181).

On most intercity trains there's more room and better facilities, compared with travel by coach, and usually station staff around; just have a word and they'll be happy to help. A **Disabled Person's Railcard** (www.disabled-persons-railcard.co.uk) costs £20 and gets you 33% off most train fares.

Useful organisations:

Disability Rights UK (www.disabilityrightsuk.org) Published titles include a holiday guide. Other services include a key for 7000 public disabled toilets across the UK.

Good Access Guide (www.goodaccessguide.co.uk)

Tourism for All (www.tourismforall.org.uk)

To download Lonely Planet's free Accessible Travel guides, visit http://lptravel.to/AccessibleTravel.

HERITAGE ORGANISATIONS

A highlight of a journey through Britain is visiting the numerous castles and historic sites that pepper the country. Membership of a heritage organisation gets you free admission (usually a good saving) as well as information handbooks and so on.

National Trust (www.nationaltrust.org.uk) A charity protecting historic buildings and land with scenic importance across England and Wales. Annual membership is £63 (discounts for under-26s and families). A Touring Pass allows free entry to NT properties for one/two weeks (£26/31 per person); families and couples get cheaper rates. The **National Trust for Scotland** (www.nts.org.uk) is a similar organisation in Scotland; annual membership is £54.

English Heritage (www.english-heritage.org.uk) State-funded organisation responsible for numerous historic sites. Annual membership is £52 (couples and seniors get discounts). An Overseas Visitors Pass allows free entry to most sites for nine/16 days for £30/36 (cheaper rates for couples and families). In Wales and Scotland the equivalent organisations are **Cadw** (www.cadw.wales.gov.uk) and **Historic Environment Scotland** (www.historicenvironment.scot).

You can join at the first site you visit. If you join an English heritage organisation, it covers you for Wales and Scotland, and vice versa.

Visas

➡ If you're a citizen of the EEA (European Economic Area) nations or Switzerland, you don't need a visa to enter or work in Britain – you can enter using your national identity card.

➡ Visa regulations are always subject to change, and immigration restriction is currently big news in Britain, so it's essential to check with your local British embassy, high commission or consulate before leaving home.

➡ Currently, if you're a citizen of Australia, Canada, New Zealand, Japan, Israel, the USA and several other countries, you can stay for up to six months (no visa required), but are not allowed to work.

➡ Nationals of many countries, including South Africa, will need to obtain a visa: for more info, see www.gov.uk/check-uk-visa.

➡ The Youth Mobility Scheme, for Australian, Canadian, Japanese, Hong Kong, Monegasque, New Zealand, South Korean and Taiwanese citizens aged 18 to 31, allows working visits of up to two years, but must be applied for in advance.

➡ Commonwealth citizens with a UK-born parent may be eligible for a Certificate of Entitlement to the Right of Abode, which entitles them to live and work in the UK.

➡ Commonwealth citizens with a UK-born grandparent could qualify for a UK Ancestry Employment Certificate, allowing them to work full time for up to five years in the UK.

➡ British immigration authorities have always been tough; dress neatly and carry proof that you have sufficient funds with which to support yourself. A credit card and/or an onward ticket will help.

Transport

GETTING THERE & AWAY

Most visitors reach Britain by air. As London is a global transport hub, it's easy to fly to Britain from just about anywhere. In recent years, the massive growth of budget ('no-frills') airlines has increased the number of routes – and reduced the fares – between Britain and other countries in Europe.

The other main option for travel between Britain and mainland Europe is ferry, either port-to-port or combined with a long-distance bus trip, although journeys can be long and financial savings not huge compared with budget airfares.

International trains are much more comfortable and a 'green' option; the Channel Tunnel allows direct rail services between Britain, France and Belgium, with onward connections to many other European destinations.

Flights, cars and rail tickets can be booked online at lonelyplanet.com/bookings.

Air

Departure tax is included in the price of a ticket.

London Airports

Heathrow (LHR; www.heathrowairport.com) Britain's main airport for international flights; often chaotic and crowded. About 15 miles west of central London.

Gatwick (LGW; www.gatwickairport.com) Britain's number-two airport, mainly for international flights, 30 miles south of central London.

Stansted (STN; www.stanstedairport.com) About 35 miles northeast of central London, mainly handling charter and budget European flights.

Luton (LTN; www.london-luton.co.uk) Some 35 miles north of central London, well known as a holiday-flight airport.

London City (LCY; www.londoncityairport.com) A few miles east of central London, specialising in flights to/from European and other UK airports.

Regional Airports

Some planes on European and long-haul routes avoid London and use major regional airports including Manchester and Glasgow. Smaller regional airports such as Southampton, Cardiff and Birmingham are served by flights to and from continental Europe and Ireland.

Land

Bus & Coach

You can easily get between Britain and other European countries via long-distance bus or coach. The international network **Eurolines** (www.eurolines.com) connects a huge number of destinations; you can buy tickets online via one of the national operators.

Services to/from Britain are operated by **National Express** (www.nationalexpress.com). Sample

CLIMATE CHANGE & TRAVEL

Every form of transport that relies on carbon-based fuel generates CO_2, the main cause of human-induced climate change. Modern travel is dependent on aeroplanes, which might use less fuel per mile per person than most cars but travel much greater distances. The altitude at which aircraft emit gases (including CO_2) and particles also contributes to their climate change impact. Many websites offer 'carbon calculators' that allow people to estimate the carbon emissions generated by their journey and, for those who wish to do so, to offset the impact of the greenhouse gases emitted with contributions to portfolios of climate-friendly initiatives throughout the world. Lonely Planet offsets the carbon footprint of all staff and author travel.

journey times to/from London include: Amsterdam 12 hours; Barcelona 24 hours; Dublin 12 hours; and Paris eight hours.

If you book early, and can be flexible with timings (ie travel when few other people want to), you can get some very good deals. For example, between London and Paris or Amsterdam from about £25 one-way (although paying £35 to £45 is more usual).

Train

CHANNEL TUNNEL PASSENGER SERVICE

High-speed **Eurostar** (www.eurostar.com) passenger services shuttle at least 10 times daily between London and Paris (2½ hours) or Brussels (two hours). Buy tickets from travel agencies, major train stations or the Eurostar website.

The normal one-way fare between London and Paris/Brussels costs around £145; advance booking and off-peak travel gets cheaper fares as low as £29 one-way.

CHANNEL TUNNEL CAR SERVICE

Drivers use **Eurotunnel** (www.eurotunnel.com). At Folkestone in England or Calais in France, you drive onto a train, get carried through the tunnel and drive off at the other end.

Trains run about four times an hour from 6am to 10pm, then hourly through the night. Loading and unloading takes an hour; the journey lasts 35 minutes.

Book in advance online or pay on the spot. The standard one-way fare for a car and up to nine passengers is between £75 and £100 depending on time of day; promotional fares often bring it down to £59 or less.

Sea

Ferry Routes

The main ferry routes between Great Britain and other European countries include the following:

- Hull–Zeebrugge (Belgium)
- Dover–Calais (France)
- Dover–Boulogne (France)
- Newhaven–Dieppe (France)
- Liverpool–Dublin (Ireland)
- Holyhead–Dublin (Ireland)
- Fishguard–Rosslare (Ireland)
- Pembroke Dock–Rosslare (Ireland)
- Newcastle–Amsterdam (Netherlands)
- Harwich–Hook of Holland (Netherlands)
- Hull–Rotterdam (Netherlands)
- Cairnryan–Larne (Northern Ireland)
- Portsmouth–Santander (Spain)
- Portsmouth–Bilbao (Spain)

Ferry Fares

Most ferry operators offer flexible fares, meaning great bargains at quiet times of day or year. For example, short crosschannel routes such as Dover to Calais or Boulogne can be as low as £45 for a car plus two passengers, although around £75 to £105 is more likely. If you're a foot passenger, or cycling, there's less need to book ahead; fares on short crossings cost about £30 to £50 each way.

Ferry Bookings

Book direct with one of the operators listed following, or use the very handy www.directferries.co.uk – a single site covering all sea-ferry routes, plus **Eurotunnel** (www.eurotunnel.com).

Brittany Ferries (www.brittany-ferries.com)

DFDS Seaways (www.dfdsseaways.co.uk)

Irish Ferries (www.irishferries.com)

P&O Ferries (www.poferries.com)

Stena Line (www.stenaline.com)

TRAIN & FERRY CONNECTIONS

As well as Eurostar, many 'normal' trains run between Britain and mainland Europe. You buy one ticket, but get off the train at the port, walk onto a ferry, then get another train on the other side. Routes include Amsterdam–London (via Hook of Holland and Harwich). Travelling between Ireland and Britain, the main train-ferry-train route is Dublin to London, via Dun Laoghaire and Holyhead. Ferries also run between Rosslare and Fishguard or Pembroke (Wales), with train connections on either side.

GETTING AROUND

Transport in Britain can be expensive compared to Continental Europe; bus and rail services are sparse in the more remote parts of the country. For timetables, check out www.traveline.info. Tourist offices can provide maps and information.

Car Useful for travelling at your own pace, or for visiting regions with minimal public transport. Cars can be hired in every town or city.

Train Relatively expensive, with extensive coverage and frequent departures throughout most of the country.

Bus Cheaper and slower than trains, but useful in more remote regions that aren't serviced by rail.

Air

If you're really pushed for time, flights on longer routes across Britain (eg Exeter or Southampton to Newcastle, Edinburgh or Inverness), or to the Scottish islands, are handy, although you miss the glorious scenery in between. On some shorter routes (eg London to Newcastle, or Manchester to Newquay) trains compare favourably with planes on time, once airport downtime is factored in. On costs, you might get a bargain airfare, but trains can be cheaper if you buy tickets in advance.

Some of Britain's domestic airline companies:

British Airways (www.britishairways.com)

EasyJet (www.easyjet.com)

FlyBe (www.flybe.com)

Loganair (www.loganair.co.uk)

Ryanair (www.ryanair.com)

Bicycle

Britain is a compact country, and hiring a bike – for an hour or two, or a week or longer – is a great way to really see the country if you've got time to spare.

Hire in London

London is famous for its **Santander Cycles** (☎0343 222 6666; www.tfl.gov.uk/modes/cycling/santander-cycles), known as 'Boris bikes' after the mayor that introduced them to the city. Bikes can be hired on the spot from automatic docking stations. For more information visit the website. Other rental options in the capital are listed at www.lcc.org.uk (under Advice/Bike Shops).

Hire Elsewhere

The **nextbike** (www.nextbike.co.uk) bike-sharing scheme currently has stations in Exeter, Oxford, Coventry, Glasgow, Stirling and Bath, while tourist towns such as York and Cambridge have plentiful bike-rental options. Bikes can also be hired in national parks and forestry sites now primarily used for leisure activities, such as Kielder Water in Northumberland, Grizedale Forest in the Lake District and the Elan Valley in Mid-Wales. In some areas, disused railway lines are now bike routes, notably the Peak District in Derbyshire. Rental rates start at about £12 per day, or £20 and up for a quality machine.

Bikes on Trains

Bicycles can be taken free of charge on most local urban trains (although they may not be allowed at peak times when the trains are crowded) and on shorter trips in rural areas, on a first-come, first-served basis – though there may be space limits.

Bikes can be carried on long-distance train journeys free of charge, but advance booking is required for most conventional bikes. (Folding bikes can be carried on pretty much any train at any time.) In theory, this shouldn't be too much trouble as most long-distance rail trips are best bought in advance anyway, but you have to go a long way down the path of booking your seat before you start booking your bike – only to find space isn't available. A better course of action is to buy in advance at a major rail station, where the booking clerk can help you through the options.

A final warning: when railways are repaired, cancelled trains are replaced by buses – and they won't take bikes.

The **PlusBike** scheme provides all the information you need for travelling by train with a bike. Leaflets are available at major stations, or downloadable from www.nationalrail.co.uk/118390.aspx.

Boat

There are around 90 inhabited islands off the western and northern coasts of Scotland, which are linked to the mainland by a network of car and passenger ferries. There are two main ferry operators.

Caledonian MacBrayne (CalMac; ☎0800 066 5000; www.calmac.co.uk) Operates car ferry services to the Inner and Outer Hebrides and the islands in the Firth of Clyde.

Northlink Ferries (☎0845 600 0449; www.northlinkferries.co.uk) Operates car ferry services from Aberdeen and Scrabster to the Orkney and Shetland islands.

> **PASSPORT CHECK**
>
> Travelling between Britain's three nations of England, Scotland and Wales is easy. The bus and train systems are fully integrated and in most cases you won't even know you've crossed the border; passports are not required.

Bus & Coach

If you're on a tight budget, long-distance buses (called coaches in Britain) are nearly always the cheapest way to get around, although they're also the slowest – sometimes by a considerable margin. Many towns have separate stations for local buses and long-distance coaches; make sure you go to the right one!

Long-Distance Buses

National Express (www.nationalexpress.com) is the main coach operator, with a wide network and frequent services between main centres. North of the border, services tie in with those of **Scottish Citylink** (www.citylink.co.uk), Scotland's leading coach company. Fares vary: they're cheaper if you book in advance and travel at quieter times, and more expensive if you buy your ticket on the spot and it's Friday afternoon. As a guide, a 200-mile trip (eg London to York) will cost £15 to £25 if you book a few days in advance.

Megabus (www.megabus.com) operates a budget coach service between about 30 destinations around the country. Go at a quiet time, book early and your ticket will be very cheap. Book later, for a busy time and... You get the picture.

INFORMATION SERVICE

Traveline (www.traveline.info) is a very useful information service covering bus, coach, taxi and train services nationwide. The website offers access to online timetables, a journey planner, route maps and limited fares information.

Bus Passes

National Express offers discount passes, called Young Persons Coachcards, to full-time students and under-26s. These cost £10 and give you 30% off standard adult fares. Also available are coachcards for people over 60, families and disabled travellers.

For touring the country, National Express offers Brit Xplorer passes, allowing unlimited travel for seven/14/28 days (£79/139/219). You don't need to book journeys in advance: if the coach has a spare seat, you can take it.

Car & Motorcycle

Travelling by car or motorbike around Britain means you can be independent and flexible, and reach remote places. Downsides for drivers include traffic jams, the high price of fuel and high parking costs in cities.

Hire

CAMPERVAN

Hiring a motorhome or campervan (£650 to £1100 a week) is more expensive than hiring a car, but saves on accommodation costs and gives almost unlimited freedom. Sites to check:

Just Go (www.justgo.uk.com)

Wicked Campers (www.wickedcampers.co.uk)

Wild Horizon (www.wildhorizon.co.uk)

CAR

Compared with many countries (especially the USA), hire rates are expensive in Britain; the smallest cars start from about £130 per week, and it's around £190 and upwards per week for a medium car. All rates include insurance and unlimited mileage, and can rise at busy times (or drop at quiet times). Some main players:

Avis (www.avis.co.uk)

Budget (www.budget.co.uk)

Europcar (www.europcar.co.uk)

Sixt (www.sixt.co.uk)

Thrifty (www.thrifty.co.uk)

Another option is to look online for small local car-hire companies in Britain that can undercut the international franchises. Generally those in cities are cheaper than in rural areas. Using a rental-broker or comparison site such as **UK Car Hire** (www.ukcarhire.net) or **Kayak** (www.kayak.com) can also help find bargains.

Insurance

It's illegal to drive a car or motorbike in Britain without (at least) third-party insurance. This will be included with all rental cars. If you're bringing a car from Europe, you'll need to arrange it.

Motoring Organisations

Motoring organisations in Britain include the **Automobile Association** (www.theaa.com) and the **RAC** (www.rac.co.uk). For both, annual membership starts at around £40, including 24-hour roadside breakdown assistance.

Britannia (www.lv.com/breakdown-cover) offers better value at £30 a year, while a greener alternative is the **Environmental Transport Association** (www.eta.co.uk); it provides breakdown assistance but doesn't campaign for more roads.

Parking

Many cities have short-stay and long-stay car parks; the latter are cheaper though may be less convenient. 'Park & Ride' systems allow you to park on the edge of the city then ride to the centre on frequent nonstop buses for an all-in-one price.

Yellow lines (single or double) along the edge of the road indicate restrictions. Nearby signs spell out when you can and can't park. In London and other big cities, traffic wardens operate with efficiency; if you park on the yellow lines at the wrong time, your car will be clamped or towed away, and it'll cost you £130 or more to get driving again. In some cities there are also red lines, which mean no stopping at all. Ever.

Roads

Motorways and main A-roads deliver you quickly from one end of the country to another. Lesser A-roads, B-roads and minor roads are much more scenic – ideal for car or motorcycle touring. You can't travel fast, but you won't care.

Speed limits are usually 30mph (48km/h) in built-up areas, 60mph (96km/h) on main roads and 70mph (112km/h) on motorways and most (but not all) dual carriageways.

Road Rules

A foreign driving licence is valid in Britain for up to 12 months.

Drink driving is taken very seriously; you're allowed a maximum blood-alcohol level of 80mg/100mL (0.08%) in England and Wales, and 50mg/100mL (0.05%) in Scotland.

Some other important rules:

- drive on the left (!)
- wear fitted seat belts in cars
- wear helmets on motorcycles
- give way to your right at junctions and roundabouts
- always use the left lane on motorways and dual carriageways unless overtaking (although so many people ignore this rule, you'd think it didn't exist)

➡ don't use a mobile phone while driving unless it's fully hands-free.

Hitching

Hitching is not as common as it used to be in Britain: maybe because more people have cars and maybe because few drivers give lifts any more. It's perfectly possible, however, if you don't mind long waits. Nevertheless, hitching is never entirely safe, and we don't recommend it. Travellers who hitch should understand that they are taking a small but potentially serious risk. If you decide to do so, note that it's illegal to hitch on motorways; you must use approach roads or service stations.

However, it's all different in remote rural areas such as Mid-Wales or northwest Scotland, where hitching is a part of getting around – especially if you're a walker heading back to base after a hike on the hills. On some Scottish islands, local drivers may stop and offer a lift without you even asking.

Local Transport

Local Buses

There are good local bus networks year-round in cities and towns. Buses also run in some rural areas year-round, although timetables are designed to serve schools and businesses, so there aren't many midday and weekend services (and they may stop running during school holidays), or buses may link local villages to a market town on only one day each week.

In tourist areas (especially national parks), there are frequent services from Easter to September. However, it's always worth double-checking at a tourist office before planning your day's activities around a bus that may not actually be running.

If you're taking a few local bus rides in one area, day passes (with names like Day Rover, Wayfarer or Explorer) are cheaper than buying several single tickets. Often they can be bought on your first bus, and may include local rail services. It's always worth asking ticket clerks or bus drivers about your options.

Taxi

There are two sorts of taxi in Britain: those with meters that can be hailed in the street; and minicabs, which are cheaper but can only be called by phone. Unlicensed minicabs operate in some cities.

In London, most taxis are the famous 'black cabs' (some with advertising livery in other colours) which charge by distance and time. Depending on the time of day, a 1-mile journey takes five to 10 minutes and costs £6 to £9. Longer journeys are proportionally cheaper.

Black cabs also operate in some other large cities around Britain, with rates usually lower than in London.

In London, taxis are best flagged down in the street; a 'for hire' light on the roof indicates availability. In other cities, you can flag down a cab if you see one, but it's usually easier to go to a taxi rank.

Apps such as **Uber** (www.uber.com) and **Kabbee** (www.kabbee.com) allow you to book a minicab in double-quick time.

In rural areas, taxis need to be called by phone; the best place to find the local taxi's phone number is the local pub. Fares are £3 to £5 per mile.

Train-Taxi (www.traintaxi.co.uk) is a portal site that helps 'bridge the final gap' between the train station and your hotel or other final destination.

Train

Information

Your first stop should be **National Rail Enquiries** (www.nationalrail.co.uk), the nationwide timetable and fare information service. Its website advertises special offers and has real-time links to station departure boards and downloadable maps of the rail network.

Train Operators

About 20 different companies operate train services in Britain, while Network Rail operates track and stations. For some passengers this system can be confusing at first, but information and ticket-buying services are mostly centralised. If you have to change trains, or use two or more train operators, you still buy one ticket – valid for the whole journey. The main railcards and passes are also accepted by all train operators.

Where more than one train operator services the same route, eg York to Edinburgh, a ticket purchased from one company may not be valid on trains run by another. So if you miss the train you originally booked, it's worth checking which later services your ticket will be valid for.

HOW MUCH TO...?

When travelling by long-distance bus, coach or train in Britain, it's important to realise that there's no such thing as a standard fare. Prices vary according to demand and when you buy your ticket. Book long in advance and travel on Tuesday mid-morning and it's cheap. Buy your ticket on the spot late Friday afternoon and it'll be a lot more expensive. Ferries use similar systems. We have generally quoted sample fares somewhere in between the very cheapest and most expensive options. The price you pay will almost certainly be different.

Tickets & Reservations

BUYING TICKETS

Once you've found the journey you need on the National Rail Enquiries website, links take you to the relevant train operator to buy the ticket. This can be mailed to you (UK addresses only) or collected at the station on the day of travel from automatic machines. There's usually no booking fee on top of the ticket price.

You can also use a centralised ticketing service to buy your train ticket. These cover all train services in a single site, and make a small booking fee on top of every ticket price. The main players include:

QJump (www.qjump.co.uk)

Rail Easy (www.raileasy.co.uk)

Train Line (www.thetrainline.com)

To use operator or centralised ticketing websites, you always have to state a preferred time and day of travel, even if you don't mind when you go, but you can change it as you go through the process, and with a little delving around you can find some real bargains.

You can also buy train tickets on the spot at stations, which is fine for short journeys (under about 50 miles), but discount tickets for longer trips are usually not available and must be bought in advance by phone or online.

COSTS

For longer journeys, on-the-spot fares are always available, but tickets are much cheaper if bought in advance. The earlier you book, the cheaper it gets. You can also save if you travel off-peak. Advance purchase usually gets a reserved seat, too.

Whichever operator you travel with and wherever you buy tickets, these are the three main fare types:

Anytime Buy anytime, travel anytime – usually the most expensive option.

Off-peak Buy ticket any time, travel off-peak (what is off-peak depends on the journey).

Advance Buy ticket in advance, travel only on specific trains – usually the cheapest option.

For an idea of the price difference, an Anytime single ticket from London to York will cost £112 or more, an Off-peak around £56, with an Advance around £36 to £46, and possibly less if you book early enough or don't mind arriving at midnight.

The cheapest fares are nonrefundable, so if you miss your train you'll have to buy a new ticket.

ONWARD TRAVEL

If the train doesn't get you all the way to your destination, you can add a **PlusBus** (www.plusbus.info) supplement when making your reservation to validate your train ticket for onward travel by bus. This is more convenient, and usually cheaper, than buying a separate bus ticket.

Train Classes

There are two classes of rail travel: first and standard. First class costs around 50% more than standard fare (up to double at busy periods) and gets you bigger seats, more leg-room, and usually a more peaceful business-like atmosphere, plus extras such as complimentary drinks and newspapers. At weekends some train operators offer 'upgrades' to first class for an extra £5 to £25 on top of your standard class fare, payable on the spot.

Train Passes

DISCOUNT PASSES

If you're staying in Britain for a while, passes known as Railcards (www.railcard.co.uk) are worth considering:

16-25 Railcard For those aged 16 to 25, or a full-time UK student.

Senior Railcard For anyone over 60.

Family & Friends Railcard Covers up to four adults and four children travelling together.

Railcards cost £30 (valid for one year, available from major stations or online) and get 33% discount on most train fares, except those already heavily discounted. With the Family card, adults get 33% and children get 60% discounts, so the fee is easily repaid in a couple of journeys.

LOCAL & REGIONAL PASSES

Local train passes usually cover rail networks around a city (many include bus travel too) and are detailed in those relevant regional sections.

If you're concentrating your travels on southeast England (eg London to Dover, Weymouth, Cambridge or Oxford), a **Network Railcard** (per year £30) covers up to four adults and up to four children travelling together outside peak times.

NATIONAL PASSES

For country-wide travel, **BritRail** (www.britrail.net) passes are available for visitors from overseas. They must be bought in your country of origin (not in Britain) from a specialist travel agency. Available in seven different versions (eg England only; Scotland only; all Britain; UK and Ireland) for periods from four to 30 days.

STATION NAMES

London has several mainline train stations positioned in a rough circle around the city's central area (and mostly linked by the Circle underground line). The stations' proper names are London Victoria, London Paddington, London King's Cross and so on, and this is how you'll see them on official timetables, information boards and booking websites – although the British never say the 'London' part in everyday speech.

Glossary

almshouse – accommodation for the aged or needy
ap – prefix in a Welsh name meaning 'son of'

bag – originally to 'catch' – a shooting term – now used to mean 'reach the top of' (as in to 'bag a couple of peaks' or *'Munro bagging'*)
bailey – outermost wall of a castle
bar – gate (York, and some other northern cities)
beck – stream (northern England)
bill – the total you need to pay after eating in a restaurant ('check' to Americans)
billion – the British billion is a million million (unlike the American billion – a thousand million)
blackhouse – traditional low-walled stone cottage with thatch or turf roof and earth floors; shared by both humans and cattle and typical of the Outer Hebrides until the early 20th century (Scotland)
bloke – man (colloquial)
Blue Flag – an award given to beaches for their unpolluted sand and water
böd – once a simple trading booth used by fishing communities, today it refers to basic accommodation for walkers etc (used only in Shetland)
bothy – very simple hut or shelter, usually in mountain or wilderness area, used by walkers and hikers
brae – hill (Scotland)
bridleway – track for horse riders that can also be used by walkers and cyclists
broch – ancient defensive tower
burgh – town
burn – stream
bus – local bus; see also *coach*

Cadw – the Welsh historic monuments agency
cairn – pile of stones marking path, junction of paths or the summit of a mountain
CalMac – Caledonian MacBrayne, the main Scottish island ferry operator
canny – good, great, wise (northern England)
castell – castle (Welsh)
ceilidh – (*kay*-lee) a session of traditional music, song and dance; originally Scottish, now more widely used across Britain
Celtic high cross – a large, elaborately carved stone cross decorated with biblical scenes and Celtic interlace designs dating from the 8th to 10th centuries
cheers – goodbye; thanks (colloquial); also a drinking toast
chemist – pharmacist
chine – valley-like fissure leading to the sea (southern England)
chippy – fish-and-chip shop
circus – junction of several city streets, usually circular, and usually with a green or other feature at the centre
Clearances – eviction of Highland farmers from their land by *lairds* wanting to use it for grazing sheep
close – entrance to an alley
coach – long-distance bus
coasteering – adventurous activity that involves making your way around a rocky coastline by climbing, scrambling, jumping or swimming
cob – mixture of mud and straw for building
corrie – circular hollow on a hillside
cot – small bed for a baby ('crib' to Americans)
court – courtyard
craic – lively conversation; pronounced, and sometimes spelt, 'crack'
craig – exposed rock
crannog – an artificial island in a loch built for defensive purposes
croft – smallholding, usually in marginal agricultural area (Scotland); the activity is known as 'smallholding'
Cymraeg – Welsh language (Welsh); also Gymraeg
Cymru – Welsh word for Wales

dene – valley
dirk – dagger
DIY – do-it-yourself, ie home improvements
dram – a measure of whisky
dodgy – suspect, bad, dangerous (colloquial)
dolmen – chambered tomb (Wales)
dough – money (colloquial)
downs – rolling upland, characterised by lack of trees
duvet – quilt replacing sheets and blankets ('doona' to Australians)

EH – English Heritage; state-funded organisation responsible for historic sites

en suite room – hotel room with private attached bathroom (ie shower, basin and toilet)

eisteddfod – literally a gathering or session; festival in which competitions are held in music, poetry, drama and the fine arts; plural eisteddfodau (Welsh)

Evensong – daily evening service (Church of England)

fell race – tough running race through hills or moors

fen – drained or marshy low-lying flat land

firth – estuary

fiver – £5 note (colloquial)

flat – single dwelling in a larger building ('apartment' to Americans)

flip-flops – plastic sandals with a single strap over toes ('thongs' to Australians)

footpath – path through countryside and between houses, not beside a road (that's called a 'pavement')

gate – street (York, and some other northern cities)

graft – work (not corruption, as in American English; colloquial)

grand – 1000 (colloquial)

gutted – very disappointed (colloquial)

guv, guvner – from governor, a respectful term of address for owner or boss; can sometimes be used ironically

hart – deer

HI – Hostelling International (organisation)

hire – rent

Hogmanay – Scottish celebration of New Year's Eve

howff – pub or shelter (Scotland)

HS – Historic Scotland; organisation that manages historic sites in Scotland

inn – pub with accommodation

jumper – woollen item of clothing worn on torso ('sweater' to Americans)

ken – Scottish term for 'understand' or 'know', as in 'do you ken' = 'do you know'

kirk – church (northern England and Scotland)

knowe – burial mound (Scotland)

kyle – strait or channel (Scotland)

laird – estate owner (Scotland)

lass – young woman (northern England and Scotland)

lift – machine for carrying people up and down in large buildings ('elevator' to Americans)

linn – waterfall (Scotland)

loch – lake (Scotland)

lochan – small *loch*

lock – part of a canal or river that can be closed off and the water levels changed to raise or lower boats

lolly – money (colloquial); candy on a stick (possibly frozen)

lorry (s), lorries (pl) – truck

Mabinogion – key source of Welsh folk legends

machair – grass- and wildflower-covered sand dunes

mad – insane (not angry, as in American English)

Marches – borderlands between England and Wales or Scotland

menhir – standing stone

Mercat Cross – a symbol of the trading rights of a market town or village, usually found in the centre of town and usually a focal point for the community

mere – a body of water, usually shallow; technically a lake that has a large surface area relative to its depth

merthyr – burial place of a saint (Welsh)

midge – mosquito-like insect

motorway – major road linking cities (equivalent to 'interstate' or 'freeway')

motte – early Norman fortification consisting of a raised, flattened mound with a keep on top; when attached to a *bailey* it is known as a motte-and-bailey

Munro – hill or mountain 3000ft (914m) or higher, especially in Scotland; those over 2500ft are called Corbetts

Munro bagger – a hill walker who tries to climb all the *Munros* in Scotland

naff – inferior, in poor taste (colloquial)

NCN – National Cycle Network

newydd – new (Welsh)

NNR – National Nature Reserve, managed by the Scottish Natural Heritage (SNH)

NT – National Trust; organisation that protects historic buildings and land with scenic importance in England and Wales

NTS – National Trust for Scotland; organisation dedicated to the preservation of historic sites and the environment in Scotland

oast house – building containing a kiln for drying hops

ogham – ancient Celtic script

oriel – gallery (Welsh)

OS – Ordnance Survey

p – (pronounced pee) pence; ie 2p is 'two p' not 'two pence' or 'tuppence'

pele – fortified house

Picts – early inhabitants of north and east Scotland (from Latin pictus, or 'painted', after their body-paint decorations)

pile – large imposing building (colloquial)

pissed – slang for drunk (not angry)

pissed off – angry (slang)

pitch – playing field

postbus – minibus delivering the mail, also carrying passengers in remote areas

provost – mayor

punter – customer (colloquial)

quid – pound (colloquial)

ramble – short easy walk

reiver – warrior or raider (historic term; northern England)

return ticket – round-trip ticket

RIB – rigid inflatable boat

rood – an old Scots word for a cross

RSPB – Royal Society for the Protection of Birds

RSPCA – Royal Society for the Prevention of Cruelty to Animals

sarsen – boulder, a geological remnant usually found in chalky areas (sometimes used in neolithic constructions, eg Stonehenge and Avebury)

Sassenach – from Gaelic 'Sasannach': anyone who is not a Highlander (including Lowland Scots)

sheila-na-gig – Celtic fertility symbol of a woman with exaggerated genitalia, often carved in stone on churches and castles; rare in England, found mainly in the *Marches*, along the border with Wales

single ticket – one-way ticket

SMC – Scottish Mountaineering Club

SNH – Scottish Natural Heritage, a government organisation directly responsible for safeguarding and improving Scotland's natural heritage

snickelway – narrow alley (York)

snug – usually a small separate room in a pub

sporran – purse worn around waist with the kilt (Scotland)

SSSI – Site of Special Scientific Interest

Sustrans – sustainable transport charity encouraging people to walk, cycle and use public transport; also responsible for instigating and developing the NCN (National Cycle Network)

SYHA – Scottish Youth Hostel Association

tarn – a small lake or pool, usually in mountain areas in England, often in a depression caused by glacial erosion

tenner – £10 note (colloquial)

TIC – Tourist Information Centre

ton – 100 (colloquial)

tor – pointed hill

torch – flashlight

Tory – Conservative (political party)

towpath – path running beside a river or canal, where horses once towed barges

twitcher – obsessive birdwatcher

Tube, the – London's underground railway system (colloquial)

Underground, the – London's underground railway system

wolds – open, rolling countryside

wynd – lane or narrow street (northern England and Scotland)

YHA – Youth Hostels Association

Behind the Scenes

SEND US YOUR FEEDBACK

We love to hear from travellers – your comments keep us on our toes and help make our books better. Our well-travelled team reads every word on what you loved or loathed about this book. Although we cannot reply individually to your submissions, we always guarantee that your feedback goes straight to the appropriate authors, in time for the next edition. Each person who sends us information is thanked in the next edition – the most useful submissions are rewarded with a selection of digital PDF chapters.

Visit **lonelyplanet.com/contact** to submit your updates and suggestions or to ask for help. Our award-winning website also features inspirational travel stories, news and discussions.

Note: We may edit, reproduce and incorporate your comments in Lonely Planet products such as guidebooks, websites and digital products, so let us know if you don't want your comments reproduced or your name acknowledged. For a copy of our privacy policy visit lonelyplanet.com/privacy.

OUR READERS

Many thanks to the travellers who used the last edition and wrote to us with helpful hints, useful advice and interesting anecdotes:

Charlie Morgan, Ilse Adema, Jade Lao, Jenn Nelson, Jill Edwards, Lynn Chong, Mayhew Lester, Robert Durenkamp, Rolf Wrelf

WRITER THANKS

Oliver Berry

Thanks to James Smart for giving me the gig and for guidance and support along the way; to Kate Ardron, Justin Foulkes, Dave Jones, Kate Whinney, Grace Hickock and Sarah Fox for their tips and suggestions; to the team at Wild Card PR and Watergate Bay for north coast adventures; and to Susie and Gracie Berry as always for keeping the home fires burning. Special thanks to Rosie Hillier for accompanying me on my southwest adventures and for never failing to make me smile.

Fionn Davenport

A big thanks to all my new friends in Manchester for their sterling efforts in getting up to speed with an ever-changing city. Thanks to Laura for accompanying me on my research trips and to the editors at Lonely Planet who helped put shape on my scratchings.

Marc Di Duca

Big thanks to all who helped me throughout the Southeast, especially staff at the tourist offices in Sandwich, Eastbourne and Rye. Thanks also to my wife, Tanya, and sons Taras and Kirill for accompanying me on some long days of research.

Belinda Dixon

Researching a place is a real joint effort. It's the result of B&B, bar and hotel staff who share their recommendations; tourist office workers who share their knowledge; random strangers who share their time and countless kindnesses. Huge thanks to all. And again to James Smart for the gig, LP's behind the scenes teams, and fellow authors for humour, wisdom and travellers' tales.

Peter Dragicevich

It's always a joy to meet up with friends on the road, so many thanks to Tim Benzie, Rob Carpenter, Catherine Cole, Matt Swaine, and Kerri and Finn Tyler for your company and good cheer.

Damian Harper

Gratitude to all those people who offered assistance along the way and came up with tips and ideas: Fiona Jenkins, James Munroe, Jon Tyler, Daisy Harper, Amy Williams, Arlene Fraser, Sarah Andrews, Timothy Benjamin and Emma

Rosalind. Thanks (and apologies) to anyone I may have overlooked.

Catherine Le Nevez

Cheers first and foremost to Julian, and to all of the locals, fellow travellers and tourism professionals who provided insights, inspiration and good times, especially to Ade Andrews. Huge thanks too to Destination Editor James Smart, Senior Cartographer Mark Griffiths and everyone at LP. As ever, *merci encore* to my parents, brother, *belle-sœur* and *neveu*.

Hugh McNaughtan

All possible thanks to Peter Dragicevich for his guidance on this project, to my editor James Smart, to the kind people I met in Wales and, most importantly, to Tasmin, Maise and Willa.

Isabella Noble

Cheers to everyone who helped out on the road. Big thanks to my talented co-authors, especially fellow Oxbridger Belinda Dixon for the 'healthy' competition. Thanks also to Ellie, Cathy, Rose and David in the Cotswolds; Becky, Doug, Ali and Christine in Oxford; and Elly for perfect Michelin-starred dining company. Extra special thanks to my favourite research assistants Sarah, Jack, Dan, Andrew and Paps.

Andy Symington

I owe thanks to many, but first to Jenny Neil and Brendan Bolland for being great friends and superb hosts, to Juliette and David Paton for their perpetual generosity and warm welcome and to my father for the whisky and much more. Gratitude goes also to Morwynne Carlow, Riika Åkerlind and numerous helpful folk met along the way. Big thanks also go to co-author Neil Wilson, editor James Smart and the LP team.

ACKNOWLEDGEMENTS

Climate map data adapted from Peel MC, Finlayson BL & McMahon TA (2007) 'Updated World Map of the Köppen-Geiger Climate Classification', *Hydrology and Earth System Sciences*, 11, 1633–44.

Cover photograph: Walker on the South West Coast Path, Zennor Head, Cornwall, England. Justin Foulkes/4Corners ©

Illustrations: pp88-9 (Tower of London), pp636-7 (Hadrian's Wall), pp764-5 (Royal Mile), pp780-1 (Rosslyn Chapel), pp838-9 (Stirling Castle) by Javier Zarracina; pp110-11 (River Thames) by Javier Zarracina and Michael Weldon.

THIS BOOK

This 12th edition of Lonely Planet's *Great Britain* guidebook was researched and written by Neil Wilson, Oliver Berry, Fionn Davenport, Marc Di Duca, Belinda Dixon, Peter Dragicevich, Damian Harper, Catherine Le Nevez, Hugh McNaughtan, Isabella Noble and Andy Symington. They, and Anna Kaminski, also worked on the previous edition.

This guidebook was produced by the following:

Destination Editor James Smart

Product Editors Kate Chapman, Elizabeth Jones, Anne Mason, Amanda Williamson

Senior Cartographer Mark Griffiths

Book Designer Virginia Moreno

Assisting Editors Judith Bamber, Imogen Bannister, Michelle Bennett, Melanie Dankel, Andrea Dobbin, Paul Harding, Victoria Harrison, Gabby Innes, Kate James, Kellie Langdon, Kristin Odijk, Lauren O'Connell, Rosie Nicholson, Fionnuala Twomey, Simon Williamson

Assisting Cartographers Valentina Kremenchutskaya

Assisting Book Designer Wibowo Rusli

Cover Researcher Naomi Parker

Thanks to Cheree Broughton, Joel Cotterell, Liz Heynes, Kate Mathews, Clara Monitto, Jenna Myers, Susan Paterson, Kirsten Rawlings, Victoria Smith, Tony Wheeler

Index

Map Pages **000**
Photo Pages **000**

D

Map Pages **000**
Photo Pages **000**

Map Pages **000**
Photo Pages **000**

M

Map Pages **000**
Photo Pages **000**

N

Map Pages **000**
Photo Pages **000**

Map Pages **000**
Photo Pages **000**

Y

Z

Map Legend

Sights
- Beach
- Bird Sanctuary
- Buddhist
- Castle/Palace
- Christian
- Confucian
- Hindu
- Islamic
- Jain
- Jewish
- Monument
- Museum/Gallery/Historic Building
- Ruin
- Shinto
- Sikh
- Taoist
- Winery/Vineyard
- Zoo/Wildlife Sanctuary
- Other Sight

Activities, Courses & Tours
- Bodysurfing
- Diving
- Canoeing/Kayaking
- Course/Tour
- Sento Hot Baths/Onsen
- Skiing
- Snorkelling
- Surfing
- Swimming/Pool
- Walking
- Windsurfing
- Other Activity

Sleeping
- Sleeping
- Camping

Eating
- Eating

Drinking & Nightlife
- Drinking & Nightlife
- Cafe

Entertainment
- Entertainment

Shopping
- Shopping

Information
- Bank
- Embassy/Consulate
- Hospital/Medical
- Internet
- Police
- Post Office
- Telephone
- Toilet
- Tourist Information
- Other Information

Geographic
- Beach
- Gate
- Hut/Shelter
- Lighthouse
- Lookout
- Mountain/Volcano
- Oasis
- Park
- Pass
- Picnic Area
- Waterfall

Population
- Capital (National)
- Capital (State/Province)
- City/Large Town
- Town/Village

Transport
- Airport
- Border crossing
- Bus
- Cable car/Funicular
- Cycling
- Ferry
- Metro station
- Monorail
- Parking
- Petrol station
- S-Bahn/Subway station
- Taxi
- T-bane/Tunnelbana station
- Train station/Railway
- Tram
- Tube station
- U-Bahn/Underground station
- Other Transport

Note: Not all symbols displayed above appear on the maps in this book

Routes
- Tollway
- Freeway
- Primary
- Secondary
- Tertiary
- Lane
- Unsealed road
- Road under construction
- Plaza/Mall
- Steps
- Tunnel
- Pedestrian overpass
- Walking Tour
- Walking Tour detour
- Path/Walking Trail

Boundaries
- International
- State/Province
- Disputed
- Regional/Suburb
- Marine Park
- Cliff
- Wall

Hydrography
- River, Creek
- Intermittent River
- Canal
- Water
- Dry/Salt/Intermittent Lake
- Reef

Areas
- Airport/Runway
- Beach/Desert
- Cemetery (Christian)
- Cemetery (Other)
- Glacier
- Mudflat
- Park/Forest
- Sight (Building)
- Sportsground
- Swamp/Mangrove

Belinda Dixon
Cambridge & East Anglia, Bath & Southwest England Only happy when her feet are suitably sandy, Belinda has been (gleefully) travelling, researching and writing for Lonely Planet since 2006. See her VideoBlog posts at https://belindadixon.com

Peter Dragicevich
Cardiff, Pembrokeshire & South Wales; Brecon Beacons & Mid-Wales; Snowdonia & North Wales After a successful career in niche newspaper and magazine publishing, both in his native New Zealand and in Australia, Peter finally gave in to Kiwi wanderlust, giving up staff jobs to chase his diverse roots around much of Europe. During the past decade he's written literally dozens of guidebooks for Lonely Planet on an oddly disparate collection of countries, all of which he's come to love. He once again calls Auckland, New Zealand his home – although his current nomadic existence means he's hardly ever there.

Damian Harper
London Damian has been working largely full time as a travel writer (and translator) since 1997 and has also written for National Geographic Traveler, Dorling Kindersley (*Where To Go When: Great Britain & Ireland*; *The Road Less Travelled*), Fodor's (*London*), *The Guardian*, *The Daily Telegraph*, Abbeville Press (*Celestial Realm: The Yellow Mountains of China*), Lexean, Frequent Traveller, China Ethos and various other magazines and newspapers.

Catherine Le Nevez
Birmingham, the Midlands & the Marches; Newcastle & Northeast England Catherine's wanderlust kicked in when she roadtripped across Europe from her Parisian base aged four, and she's been hitting the road at every opportunity since, travelling to around 60 countries. She recommends travelling without any expectations.

Hugh McNaughtan
Brecon Beacons & Mid-Wales; Snowdonia & North Wales A former English lecturer, Hugh swapped grant applications for visa applications, and turned his love of travel intro a full-time thing. A long-time castle tragic with an abiding love of Britain's Celtic extremities, he jumped at the chance to explore Wales, from the Cambrian Mountains to the tip of Anglesey. He's never happier than when on the road with his two daughters. Except perhaps on the cricket field....

Isabella Noble
Oxford, Cotswolds & Around Isabella's travels have taken her across India, Southeast Asia, Australia, North America and Europe. She has lived in southern Spain and Melbourne, though she's now (loosely) based in London.

Andy Symington
Glasgow & Southern Scotland; Inverness & the Northern Highlands & Islands Andy has written or worked on more than a hundred books and other updates for Lonely Planet (especially in Europe and Latin America) and other publishing companies, and has published articles on numerous subjects for a variety of newspapers, magazines and websites. He part-owns and operates a rock bar, has written a novel and is currently working on several fiction and non-fiction writing projects. Andy, from Australia, moved to northern Spain many years ago. When he's not off with a backpack in some far-flung corner of the world, he can probably be found watching the tragically poor local football side or tasting local wines after a long walk in the nearby mountains.

OUR STORY

A beat-up old car, a few dollars in the pocket and a sense of adventure. In 1972 that's all Tony and Maureen Wheeler needed for the trip of a lifetime – across Europe and Asia overland to Australia. It took several months, and at the end – broke but inspired – they sat at their kitchen table writing and stapling together their first travel guide, *Across Asia on the Cheap*. Within a week they'd sold 1500 copies. Lonely Planet was born.

Today, Lonely Planet has offices in Franklin, London, Melbourne, Oakland, Dublin, Beijing and Delhi, with more than 600 staff and writers. We share Tony's belief that 'a great guidebook should do three things: inform, educate and amuse'.

OUR WRITERS

Neil Wilson

Yorkshire; Edinburgh; Glasgow & Southern Scotland; Stirling & Central Scotland; Inverness & the Northern Highlands & Islands Neil was born in Scotland and has lived there most of his life. Based in Perthshire, he has been a full-time writer since 1988, working on more than 80 guidebooks for various publishers, including the Lonely Planet guides to Scotland, England, Ireland and Prague. An outdoors enthusiast since childhood, Neil is an active hill-walker, mountain-biker, sailor, snowboarder, fly-fisher and rock-climber, and has climbed and tramped in four continents, including ascents of Jebel Toubkal in Morocco, Mount Kinabalu in Borneo, the Old Man of Hoy in Scotland's Orkney Islands and the Northwest Face of Half Dome in California's Yosemite Valley. Neil also wrote Plan, Understand and Survival guide.

Oliver Berry

Bath & Southwest England; the Lake District & Cumbria Oliver is a writer and photographer based in Cornwall. His first trip abroad was to the south of France, aged two. Since then he's travelled to Corsica, New Zealand, the South Pacific and midwestern USA.

Fionn Davenport

Manchester, Liverpool & Northwest England Irish by birth and conviction, Fionn has been writing about his native country for more than two decades. He was pushed to travel in order to escape Dublin's comfortable stasis and by the promise of adventure, and this has cemented his belief that Ireland remains his favourite place to visit, if not always live in. These days, he has a weekly commute home to Dublin, from Manchester, where he lives with his partner, Laura, and their car, Trevor. In Dublin he presents *Inside Culture* on RTE Radio 1 and writes travel features for a host of publications, including the *Irish Times*.

Marc Di Duca

Canterbury & Southeast England A travel author for the past decade, Marc has worked for Lonely Planet in Siberia, Slovakia, Bavaria, England, Ukraine, Austria, Poland, Croatia, Portugal, Madeira and on the Trans-Siberian Railway.

OVER PAGE MORE WRITERS

Published by Lonely Planet Global Limited
CRN 554153
12th edition – May 2017
ISBN 978 1 78657 416 9

10 9 8 7 6 5 4 3 2 1
Printed in China